Boyer's The American Nation

Paul Boyer

HOLT, RINEHART AND WINSTON

A Harcourt Classroom Education Company

Austin • New York • Orlando • Atlanta • San Francisco • Boston • Dallas • Toronto • London

Editorial

Sue Miller, *Director*
Steven L. Hayes, *Executive Editor*
Robert Wehnke, *Managing Editor*
Rhonda Haynes, *Senior Editor*

PUPIL'S EDITION

Dr. Melissa Langley Biegert, *Project Editor*
Ed Connolly, *Associate Editor*
Marc Segers, *Associate Editor*

TEACHER'S EDITION

Suzanne Hurley, *Project Editor*
Lakshmi Bollini, *Associate Editor*

ANCILLARIES

Matt Herring, *Associate Editor*

TECHNOLOGY RESOURCES

Patricia Platt, *Associate Editor*

FACT CHECKING

Bob Fullilove, *Editor*
Vaishali Jhaveri, *Assistant Editor*
Annette Saunders, *Assistant Editor*

COPY EDITING

Merillat Frost, *Copy Editor*
Julie Beckman, *Copy Editor*

Editorial Permissions

Amy E. Minor, *Permissions Editor*

Art, Design, and Photo

BOOK DESIGN

Diane Motz, *Senior Design Director*
Marta Kimball, *Design Manager*
Jason Wilson, *Designer*
Ed Diaz, *Design Associate*

IMAGE ACQUISITIONS

Joe London, *Director*
Michelle Rumpf, *Art Buyer Supervisor*
Sean Moynihan, *Art Buyer*
Bob McClellan, *Photo Researcher*
Elinor Strot, *Photo Coordinator*
Elisabeth McCoy, *Photo Coordinator*
Photo Research by Picture Research
   Consultants, Inc.

BOOK DESIGN AND PRODUCTION

DECODE, Inc.

COVER DESIGN

Jason Wilson

New Media

Kate Bennett, *Associate Director*
Ken Whiteside, *Senior Project Manager II*
Armin Gutzmer, *Manager Technical and
   Training Support*
Cathy Kuhles, *Technical Assistant*
Nina Degollado, *Technical Assistant*

Pre-Press Production

Gene Rumann, *Production Manager*
Leanna Ford, *Production Coordinator*

Media Production

Susan Mussey, *Production Supervisor*
Kadonna Knape, *Production Coordinator*
Kim A. Scott, *Sr. Production Manager*

Manufacturing

Jevara Jackson, *Manufacturing
   Coodinator*

**Cover: *Fireworks over the U.S. Capitol in
Washington D.C. celebrate the American spirit.***

Cover Photo: © CORBIS/Bill Ross

Copyright © 2001 by Holt, Rinehart and Winston

For acknowledgements, see page 1157, which is an extension of the copyright page.

Printed in the United States of America

ISBN 0-03-054928-0

1 2 3 4 5 6 7 8 9   032   03 02 01 00 99

CONTRIBUTORS

DR. THOMAS CLARKIN
University of Texas at San Antonio
San Antonio, Texas

DR. PAUL HUTTON
Western History Association
University of New Mexico
Albuquerque, New Mexico

DR. RAYMOND HYSER
James Madison University
Harrisonburg, Virginia

DR. MARY CARROLL JOHANSEN
The Ranney School
Tinton Falls, New Jersey

DR. CAROL KARLSEN
University of Michigan
Ann Arbor, Michigan

DR. RICHARD SALVUCCI
Trinity University
San Antonio, Texas

DR. OTEY SCRUGGS
Syracuse University
Syracuse, New York

CONTENT REVIEWERS

DR. MARY C. BRENNAN
Southwest Texas State
post–World War II, U.S. political

DR. MAUREEN FLANAGAN
Michigan State University
20th century, urban, political, women

DR. PAUL GILJE
University of Oklahoma
U.S., 1492–1865

DR. JULIE GREENE
University of Colorado at Boulder
U.S. labor, political

DR. CHRISTOPHER HENDRICKS
Armstrong Atlantic State University
historic preservation, colonial

DR. MELVIN HOLLI
University of Illinois at Chicago
urban and ethnic

DR. RAYMOND HYSER
James Madison University
Gilded Age and Progressive Era

DR. ANYA JABOUR
University of Montana
antebellum reform, women, southern

DR. F. DANIEL LARKIN
SUNY-Oneonta
late 19th, early 20th century

DR. MARVIN LUNENFELD
State University of New York
Renaissance, Spain

DR. CARL H. MONEYHON
University of Arkansas at Little Rock
southern, Civil War, Reconstruction

DR. DAVID SWITZER
Plymouth State College of the University
System of New Hampshire
American Revolution, U.S. Maritime

EDUCATIONAL REVIEWERS

PEGGY ALTOFF, SUPERVISOR
Carroll County Public Schools
Westminster, Maryland

DEAN BRINK
Roosevelt High School
Seattle, Washington

BARBARA HARBOUR
Lewis Cass Technical High School
Detroit, Michigan

JAY HARMON
Catholic High School
Baton Rouge, Louisiana

DR. KAREN HOPPES
Lakeridge High School
Lake Oswego, Oregon

PAUL HORNE
A.C. Flora High School
Columbia, South Carolina

STEPHEN MARLOWE
Hunter High School
Gastonia, North Carolina

DOUG ODOM
El Dorado High School
El Dorado, Kansas

SUE REEDER
Winter Springs High School
Winter Springs, Florida

JACK ROUSSO
Roosevelt High School
Seattle, Washington

JENIFER ROWRAY
SE Polk High School
Runnells, Iowa

MADELEINE SCHMITT
St. Louis Public Schools
St. Louis, Missouri

DEANNA SPRING
Cincinnati Public Schools
Cincinnati, Ohio

ANDREW TURAY
Bronx High School
Bronx, New York

DIANE URICK
McCallum High School
Austin, Texas

FIELD TEST TEACHERS

MATT BERGLES
Rangeview High School
Aurora, Colorado

VINCE CASTELLANO
Arvada Senior High
Arvada, Colorado

MARIAN HALEY
Aqua Fria Union High School
Avondale, Arizona

KEVIN MCNAMARA
Horizon High School
Thornton, Colorado

GREGORY K. MILLER
Douglas High School
Oklahoma City, Oklahoma

GARY MINOR
Canyon de Oro High School
Tucson, Arizona

ROBERTA MYRICKS
Clifford J. Scott High School
East Orange, New Jersey

ANNA PRONI
Miami Senior High School
Miami, Florida

TOM WORKMAN
Hobart High School
Hobart, Indiana

Contents

An astrolabe

U·N·I·T 1

Beginnings
Prehistory – 1800 . . . . **xxiv**

CHAPTER 1

The World by 1500
Prehistory – 1500 2

CHAPTER 2

Empires of the Americas
1492 – 1800 . . . . **32**

CHAPTER 3

The English Colonies
1620 – 1763 . . . . **64**

U·N·I·T 2

George Washington accepts the U.S. Constitution

Early U.S. coins

U·N·I·T 3

Growth and Change

CHAPTER 7

Nationalism and Economic Growth

CHAPTER 8

Regional Societies

Circuit rider

Richmond, Virginia, in the 1830s

A cotton gin

CHAPTER 9

Working for Reform

The burning of Atlanta

A cowboy's spur

Fan from
the 1800s

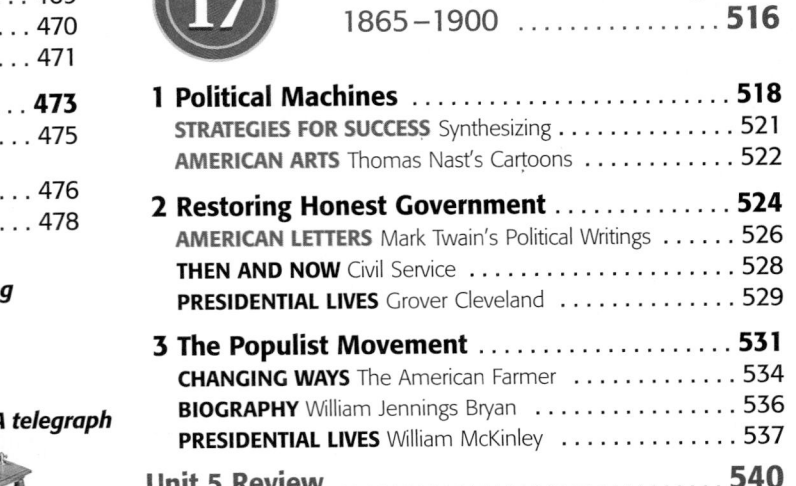

*Edison inventing
the light bulb*

A telegraph

THE GRANGER COLLECTION, NEW YORK

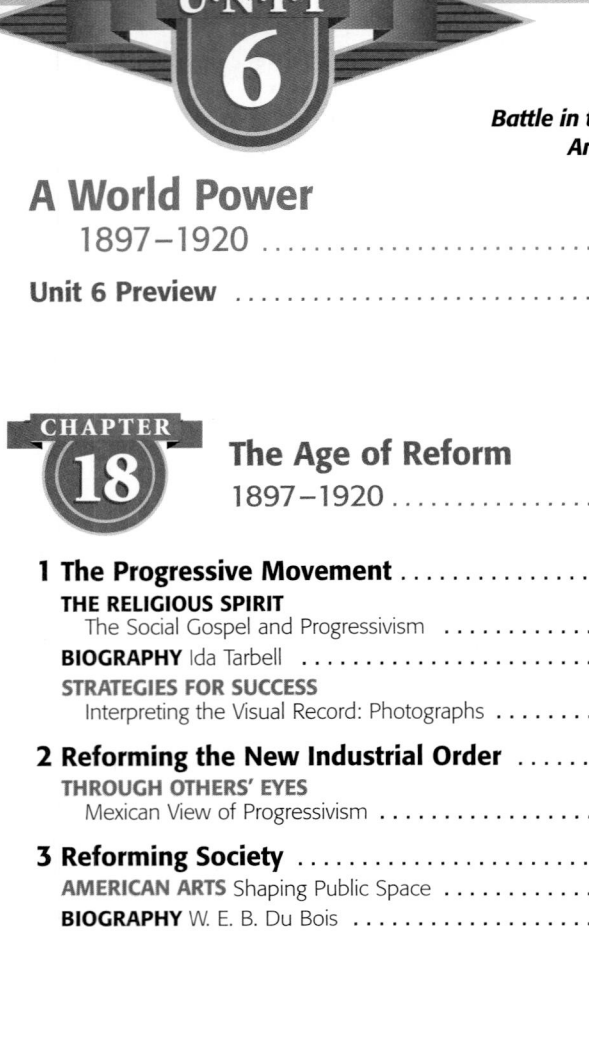

Battle in the Spanish-American War

A World Power

Results of 1929 stock market crash

THE GRANGER COLLECTION, NEW YORK

King Oliver's Creole Jazz Band

U·N·I·T 8

World Conflicts
1921–1960

*Eisenhower
campaign button*

U·N·I·T 9

A Changing Home Front

Women's rights march and civil rights button

U·N·I·T 10

Modern Times

CHAPTER 34
From Nixon to Carter

CHAPTER 35
The Republican Revolution

John Glenn (waving) and fellow astronauts, 1998

CHAPTER 36
Life in the 1990s and Beyond

Features

Changing Ways

Great Debates

HISTORICAL DOCUMENTS

HISTORY IN THE MAKING

Science & Technology

Model T

Strategies for Success

Maps

A Diverse Nation, c. 1990

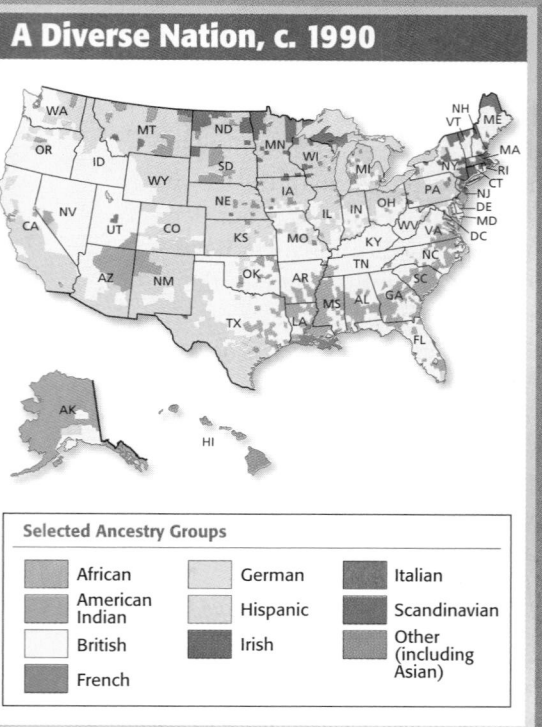

Selected Ancestry Groups

- African
- American Indian
- British
- French
- German
- Hispanic
- Irish
- Italian
- Scandinavian
- Other (including Asian)

Themes in American History

The American Nation begins every chapter with a set of theme statements. These statements are drawn from seven broad themes central to American history: Global Relations, our Constitutional Heritage, Democratic Values, Technology and Society, Cultural Diversity, Geographic Diversity, and Economic Development. They provide a context for the historical events in each chapter. This context will help you understand the connections between historical events and see how past events are relevant to today's social, political, and economic concerns.

As you begin each chapter, examine the theme statements and agree or disagree with them based on your own experiences or prior knowledge. Keep a record of your answers in a themes journal. As you read the chapter, explore how the theme statements relate to its history. When you finish reading the chapter, look back at your answers to the theme statements and note whether you would now answer them differently. By using your themes journal to trace the themes through the book, you will be able to see how each theme has developed over time.

Global Relations

This theme asks you to explore the global context in which the United States exists. From its settlement by Asian immigrants tens of thousand of years ago to the first arrival of European, African, and later Asian immigrants to today, America has influenced and been influenced by other parts of the world. Your exploration of the Global Relations theme will help you understand how the relations the United States has maintained with other countries over time have affected our nation's political, social, and economic development. It will also help you appreciate the problems and possibilities of living in an interdependent world community.

English medal c. 1600

Constitutional Heritage

The study of American history would not be complete without an exploration of the Constitution, the legal framework that structures our democratic government. The Constitutional Heritage theme asks you to think about the origin of the Constitution and the ways in which the Constitution has been interpreted and amended over time. You will explore how the laws and government institutions have evolved through amendments, Supreme Court rulings, and congressional actions. Your examination of this theme will encourage you to understand the part individuals play in promoting the goals—such as justice and democratic rights—enshrined in the Constitution's preamble.

Democratic Values

This theme concerns the continuing struggle to define and protect such democratic values as individual liberty, political representation, freedom of religion, and freedom of speech. The Democratic Values theme asks you to consider the impact of changing social, economic, and political conditions on these values. For example, in the years before the Civil War, enslavement of African Americans—a violation of the democratic value of individual liberty—was practiced in the South. Some slaveholders justified this practice by arguing that the democratic value of right to property should be the overriding concern. It took a bloody civil war to settle the issue. Conflicts over democratic values recur throughout American history, and this theme explores the attempts at resolution.

African American school, late 1800s

Technology and Society

From computers in your homes and class-rooms to communications satellites orbiting the Earth, technology influences many aspects of society. The Technology and Society theme asks you to trace technological developments and explore their influence on the economy and our lives.

Cultural Diversity

Different ethnic, racial, and religious groups have all contributed to America's rich and unique culture. The Cultural Diversity theme asks you to explore how the United States has dealt with diversity from the days of the first encounters between American Indians and Spanish and English settlers to its status today as a haven for immigrants from all over the world.

Geographic Diversity

The majestic old-growth forests of the Pacific Northwest, the rich coal deposits of the Appalachian and Rocky Mountains, the oil fields of Texas and Alaska, and the tropical plantations on the volcanic islands of Hawaii have all enriched the U.S.

The Sojourner rover on Mars

economy. The Geographic Diversity theme asks you to consider how the development of the nation's diverse natural resources has shaped U.S. society, politics, and the economy. The theme also explores how government and public awareness of the effects of natural resource development has changed over time.

Economic Development

The United States has developed one of the world's strongest economies. The Economic Development theme explores the influence of the nation's economy on domestic politics and social life and on international relations. The theme asks you to explore the implications of such economic issues as trade, depression and expansion, poverty, taxation, government regulation, and the status of workers.

Geography Themes

History and geography share many common elements. Geography describes how physical environments affect human events and how people influence the environment. Geographers have developed five themes:—location, place, region, movement, and human-environment interaction—to organize information.

Location describes a site's position. It is the spot on the earth where something is found, often expressed in terms of its position in relation to other places.

Place refers to the physical features and human influences that define a site and make it different from other sites. Physical features include landscape, climate, and vegetation. Human influences include land use, architecture, and population size.

Region is the common cultural or physical features of an area that distinguish it from other areas. One region may be different from another area because of physical characteristics, such as landforms or climate, or because of cultural features, such as dominant languages or religions.

Movement describes the way people interact as they travel, communicate, and trade goods and services. Movement includes human migration as well as the exchange of goods and ideas.

Human-Environment Interaction deals with the ways in which people interact with their natural environments, such as clearing forests, irrigating the land, and building cities. This theme is particularly important to the study of history in that it shows how people shape and are shaped by their surroundings.

Critical Thinking
and the Study of History

hroughout *Boyer's The American Nation,* you are asked to think critically about the events and issues that have shaped U.S. history. Critical thinking is the reasoned judgment of information and ideas. The development of critical thinking skills is essential to effective citizenship. Such skills empower you to exercise your civic rights and responsibilities. Helping you develop critical thinking skills is an important goal of *Boyer's The American Nation.* The following 14 critical thinking skills appear in the sections reviews and chapter reviews.

1 Using Historical Imagination involves mentally stepping into the past to consider an event or situation as people at the time would have considered it. In putting yourself in their place, you might note whether they lived before or after historical turning points such as advances in medicine or technology. Keep in mind what the people of the time knew and did not know. For example, to grasp the experience of a soldier wounded in the Civil War, you need to understand that little was known then about the causes of disease and infection.

2 Understanding Geography involves using the five themes of geography to analyze and understand the relationship between geography and historical events. In the United States, geography has greatly shaped the nation's economy, society, and political developments. The critical thinking skill allows students to explore how this has occurred.

3 Recognizing Point of View means identifying the factors that influence the outlook of an individual or group. A person's point of view includes belief and attitudes that are shaped by factors such as age, gender, religion, race, and economic status. This critical thinking skill helps us examine why people see things as they do and reinforces the realization that people's views may change over time or with a change in circumstances.

4 Comparing and Contrasting examines events, situations, or points of view for their similarities and differences. *Comparing* focuses on both the similarities and the differences. *Contrasting* focuses only on the differences. For example, a comparison of early Irish and Chinese immigrants to the United States would point out that both groups were recruited to help build railroads and that both groups faced discrimination and experienced difficulties in finding well-paying jobs. In contrast, language and racial barriers generally proved more of a problem for Chinese immigrants.

5 Identifying Cause and Effect is part of interpreting the relationships between historical events. A cause is any action that leads to an event. The outcome of that action is an effect. To explain historical events, historians often point out multiple causes and effects. For example, economic and political differences between the North and South, as well as the issue of slavery, brought about the Civil War— which in turn had many far-reaching effects.

6 Analyzing is the process of breaking something down into its parts and examining the relationships between them. Analyzing enables you to better understand the whole. To analyze the outcome of the 1912 presidential election, for example,

The Trail of Tears

The USS Constitution *battles the HMS* Guerriére

you might study the results state by state to show how Woodrow Wilson won a majority in the electoral college without winning a majority of the popular vote.

7 **Assessing Consequences** means studying an action, an event, or a trend to predict its long-term effects—and to judge the desirability of those effects. *Consequences* often are effects that are indirect and unintended. They may appear long after the event that led to them.

8 **Distinguishing Fact from Opinion** means separating the facts about something from what people say about it. A fact can be proved or observed; an opinion, on the other hand, is a personal belief or conclusion. We often hear facts and opinions mixed in everyday conversation—as well as in advertising, in political debate, and in historical sources. Although some opinions can be supported by facts, in an argument, opinions do not carry as much weight as facts.

9 **Identifying Values** involves recognizing the core beliefs that a person or group holds. Values are more deeply held than opinions and are less likely to change. Values commonly concern matters of right and wrong and may be viewed as desirable in and of themselves. The values of freedom and justice, for example, motivated the struggle to abolish slavery, just as the value of equality has been a foundation of the civil rights and women's movements.

10 **Hypothesizing** means forming a possible explanation for an event, a situation, or a problem. A hypothesis is not a proven fact. Rather, it

is a theory based on available evidence and tested against new evidence. A historian, for example, might hypothesize that the Civil War was primarily the result of a power struggle between the ruling classes of the North and South over control of the United States' western frontier. The historian would then organize the evidence to support this hypothesis and challenge other explanations of the war's causes.

11 **Synthesizing** is combining information and ideas from several sources or points in time to gain a new understanding of a topic or event. Much of the narrative writing in this book is a synthesis. It pulls together historical data from many sources and perspectives from many people into a chronological story of our nation.

12 **Problem Solving** is the process of reviewing a situation and then making decisions and recommendations for improving or correcting it. Before beginning, however, the problem must be identified and stated. For instance, in considering a solution to the nation's drug-abuse crisis, you might state the problem in terms of the relationship of drug addiction to violent crime. You would then propose and evaluate possible solutions or courses of action, selecting the one you think is best and giving reasons for your choice.

13 **Evaluating** assesses the significance or overall importance of something, such as the success of a reform movement or the legacy of a president. You should base your judgment on standards that others will understand and are likely to share. An evaluation of the early women's movement, for example, might assess the short- and long-term effects of its focus on women's suffrage.

Early U.S. money

14 **Taking a Stand** is identifying an issue, deciding what you think about it, and persuasively expressing your position. Your stand should be based on specific information. In taking a stand, even on controversial or emotional issues, state your position clearly and give reasons to support it.

Beginnings
Prehistory–1800

English settler John White created this drawing of the Algonkin Indians in the Virginia Colony in 1585.

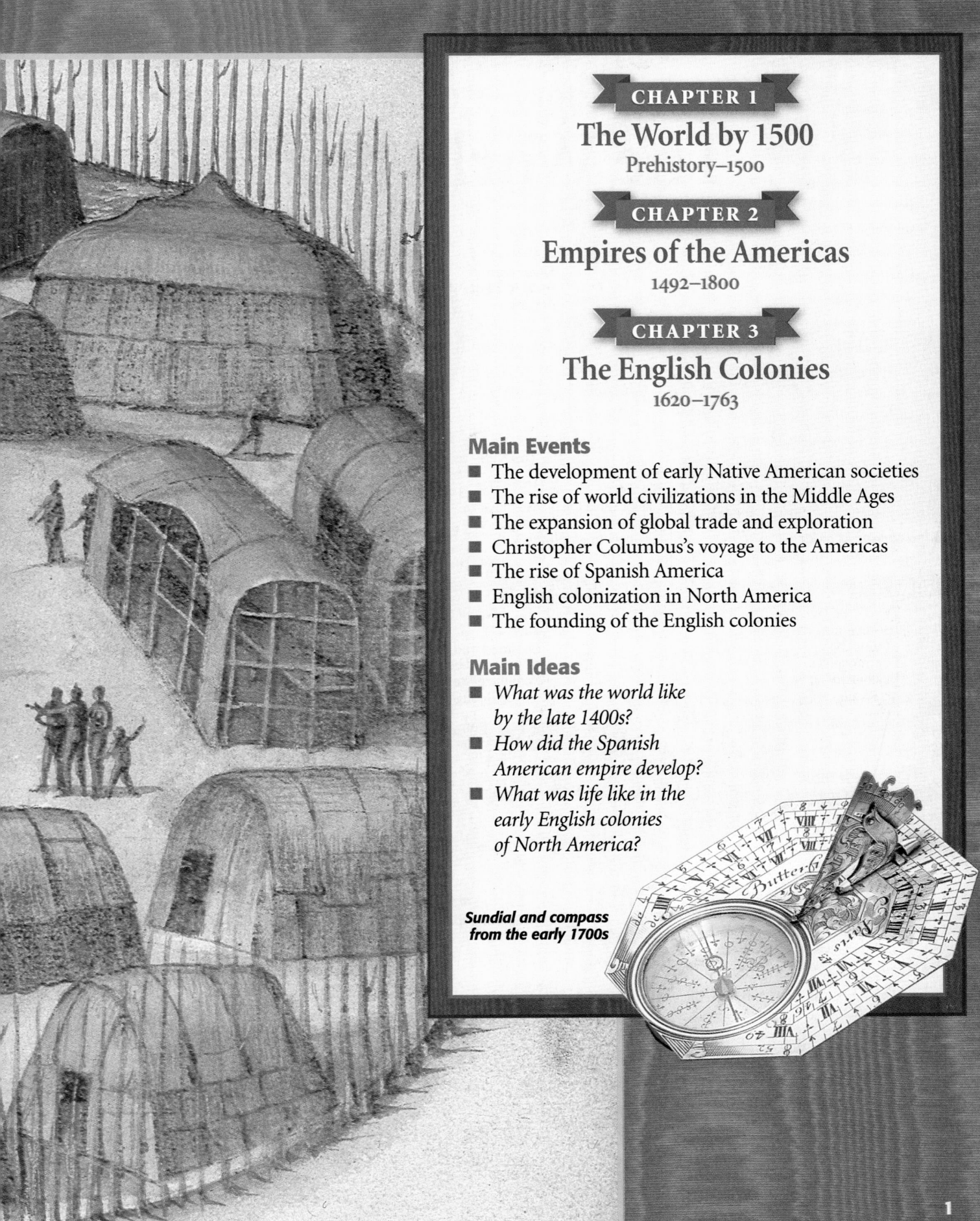

UNIT 1

CHAPTER 1
The World by 1500
Prehistory–1500

CHAPTER 2
Empires of the Americas
1492–1800

CHAPTER 3
The English Colonies
1620–1763

Main Events
- The development of early Native American societies
- The rise of world civilizations in the Middle Ages
- The expansion of global trade and exploration
- Christopher Columbus's voyage to the Americas
- The rise of Spanish America
- English colonization in North America
- The founding of the English colonies

Main Ideas
- *What was the world like by the late 1400s?*
- *How did the Spanish American empire develop?*
- *What was life like in the early English colonies of North America?*

Sundial and compass from the early 1700s

1

Prehistory–1500
The World by 1500

Silver coin from ancient Athens

560 B.C.
Business and Finance
Greeks begin to use coins as legal tender.

214 B.C.
The Arts
Chinese begin building the Great Wall of China.

Viking carving of skier

2500–2000 B.C.
The Arts
Vikings carve the oldest-known picture of a person skiing on a rock near Rodoy, Norway.

1200–100 B.C.
World Events
Olmec civilization flourishes in Mesoamerica.

5000 B.C.	2000 B.C.	1000 B.C.	1 B.C.

5000 B.C.
Daily Life
Communities in Mexico cultivate corn.

2000 B.C.
Business and Finance
Trade routes begin to spread from the eastern Mediterranean throughout Europe.

509 B.C.
Politics
The Roman Republic is established.

221 B.C.
Politics
The Qin dynasty comes to power in China.

Stone tools used to grind corn

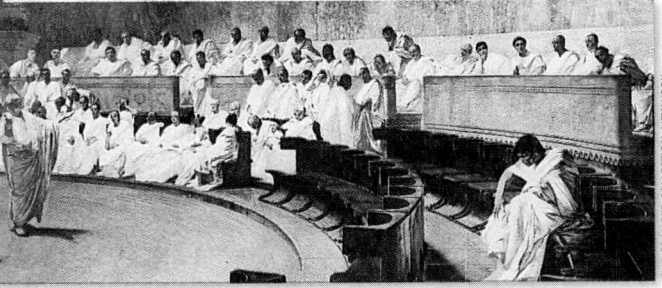

THE GRANGER COLLECTION, NEW YORK

Mural depicting a meeting of the Roman Senate

Before You Read

Build on What You Know

I t may seem odd to begin a book on U.S. history with a discussion of the world's earliest peoples. Why discuss Ice Age hunters who crossed a land bridge from Asia to America tens of thousands of years ago? Why examine Asia, Africa, and Europe in the Middle Ages? What do they have to do with our United States? We begin with the story of these early peoples because their histories laid the foundation for the creation of the United States. Today's American society draws on their histories, laws, and cultures.

Anasazi cliff dwellings

Isabella and Ferdinand are married.

c. 700
Daily Life
The Anasazi civilization begins to develop in the North American desert.

Viking carving honoring warriors

C. A.D. 40
Daily Life
One of the earliest Christian churches is established in the Greek city of Corinth.

610
Daily Life
Muhammad receives a vision that leads to the establishment of Islam.

800s
World Events
Vikings invade England, Ireland, France, and Iceland.

1469
Politics
Isabella of Castile and Ferdinand II of Aragon marry.

A.D. 1	250	500	750	1000	1250	1500

271
Science and Technology
The first form of a compass is most likely used in China.

553
Business and Finance
The Byzantine Empire establishes a monopoly on the silk trade.

c. 850
Science and Technology
Arabs develop an improved astrolabe.

c. 1450
Science and Technology
German printer Johannes Gutenberg invents a printing press that uses movable type.

1498
The Arts
Renaissance artist Michelangelo completes the sculpture *Pietà*.

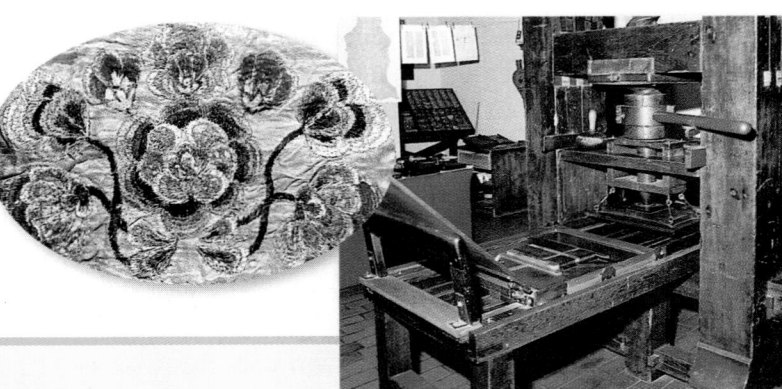

Silk embroidery from a trading center on the Silk Road

The printing press invented by Johannes Gutenberg

Think About Themes

Themes Journal

*Decide whether you **agree** or **disagree** with the following statements. Note why in your journal.*

Cultural Diversity When groups of people meet, the culture of one group will always be transformed by the other.

Economic Development Extensive contact with other societies will both benefit and harm a society's economic development.

Technology and Society Technological advances will expand international trade, cultural exchange, and exploration.

Early Peoples of the Americas

OBJECTIVES

Read to understand:

1. how the first people arrived in the Americas
2. how the Agricultural Revolution affected Native Americans
3. what the major characteristics of the Olmec, Maya, Aztec, and Inca societies were
4. what the major characteristics of the Native American cultures of North America were

KEY TERMS

Paleo-Indians
hunter-gatherers
Agricultural Revolution
Olmec
Maya
Toltec
city-state
Aztec
Inca
Anasazi
Mound Builders

KEY PEOPLE

Pachacutec Inca Yupanqui

KEY PLACES

Mesoamerica
Tikal
Tenochtitlán
Cuzco
Cahokia

Read More About It

Free Find:
  Creation Myths
  After reading the Tuskegee and Caddo myths on the **Holt Researcher** CD–ROM, create your own myth about the origins of America.

EYEWITNESSES TO History

❝ *Giant Tortoise continued to stretch himself. And so the world became larger and larger. . . . After many, many years had passed by, the Sky Holder . . . decided to create some people. He wanted them to surpass all others in beauty, strength, and bravery. So . . . the Sky Holder brought forth six pairs of people. . . . He taught these people and their descendants many useful arts and crafts.* ❞
—Native American legend

Native American religious artifact

This story has been passed down for generations by Native Americans living in what is now the northeastern United States. According to the story, Earth was once a large tortoise, ruled over by a divine being called the Sky Holder. Native American myths offer many such explanations of the origins of the first inhabitants of the Americas.

The First Americans

Scientists offer other theories about the origins of Native Americans. They believe that long after human populations were well established in Europe, Africa, and Asia, the American continents remained empty of human life. From the frozen lands of the Arctic to the southernmost tip of South America, no human voice had ever echoed through the wilderness. No human foot had ever left a print in the soil.

Life in a new land. Most archaeologists agree that the first people to enter the vast American wilderness came from Asia. They disagree about the date, however. Estimates range from 12,000 to 40,000 years ago. Scientists believe that during this period of the last Ice Age, glaciers—thick sheets of ice—formed, covering much of northern Asia, North America, and Europe. The glaciers locked up so much of the world's water that the sea level dropped by several hundred feet. This exposed a wide land bridge—Beringia—between Siberia and what is now Alaska.

The first Americans, called **Paleo-Indians**, probably followed the animal herds they depended on for food across Beringia to their new home in North America. The Paleo-Indians brought with them skills that were well suited to the environment of their new homeland. They knew how to make fire and how to find food and shelter in a harsh environment. The Paleo-Indians were **hunter-gatherers** who stalked whatever game their stone-tipped weapons could kill. Such game included caribou, bison, mammoths, and other mammals. The animals provided them with food as well as with furs and skins for clothing. In the short spring and summer, when the vegetation of the tundra—an often barren, arctic region—briefly flourished, the Paleo-Indians gathered roots, berries, and other edible plants. As hunter-gatherers, they lived as nomads, moving from place to place in search of food.

The changing environment. Sometime between 10,000 and 5,000 B.C., the climate of the Americas grew warmer and drier. This climatic change dramatically transformed the landscape. Continents were left much as they would later appear to the first European explorers. Scientists believe that as the climate changed, some Paleo-Indians moved south. In a migration that took thousands of years, they spread throughout the Americas and established distinct cultures in various regions.

Because none of the Native American tribes of that era kept written records, much of their history is lost to us. One way we can learn about early Native Americans, however, is through the work of archaeologists. These scientists study ancient artifacts and ruins in order to learn about the people who made them. Other scientists piece together early American history by studying modern-day Native Americans, including the myths and legends that had been handed down by previous generations. After all, most Native American cultures preserved their histories through the telling of stories. Scholars gain important clues to understanding the Paleo-Indians with their study of these oral records.

Most Native American myths reveal something about their past. For example, a popular myth offers an explanation of what happened to the Paleo-Indians after some time on the American continent.

> 66 For a long time everyone spoke the same language, but suddenly people began to speak in different tongues. Kulsu [the Creator], however, could speak all languages, so he called the people together and told them the names of the animals in their own language, taught them to get food, and gave them their laws and rituals. Then he sent each tribe to a different place to live. 99

The earliest inhabitants of the Americas did indeed develop different languages, laws, rituals, and ways of gathering food. Many of these cultural variations resulted from differences in their environments. The first Americans found a varied land rich in wildlife and plants. Water from the melting glaciers had formed fast-flowing rivers and huge lakes teeming with fish. Musk-oxen, reindeer, mammoths, and giant bison roamed the vast lowland regions. The hills and mountains were full of saber-toothed tigers, mountain lions, and bears.

Many of the Paleo-Indians living in North America hunted with spears tied to stone tips called Clovis points. Named for Clovis, New Mexico, where archaeologists first found them, these stone tips were more effective against large game than earlier spear tips. Abundant wildlife and an effective method of hunting gave the Paleo-Indians a plentiful and reliable food supply.

As the mammoths and other large game died out—perhaps hunted to extinction—the Paleo-Indians were forced to develop new skills in order to survive. Paleo-Indians experimented with new types of hunting and trapping. The men and women of the Eastern Woodlands, for example, learned to burn large areas of forest to make it easier to spot and track smaller game such as rabbit and deer. They also began to trap fish and birds and to collect a wider variety of plants to eat.

✔ **READING CHECK:** How did the first people arrive in the Americas?

INTERPRETING THE VISUAL RECORD
Hunter-gatherers. Skeletal remains of the large North American mammoth have been discovered in the Great Plains region of the present-day United States. *How would the mammoth's size affect the hunting practices of Native Americans?*

These Clovis points were found in the southwestern part of the present-day United States.

AMERICAN *Letters*

Native American Myths

Native Americans have preserved a rich and historic tradition of oral literature. In the following creation myths, the Tewa of present-day New Mexico recount a story about the origins of their tribe, and the Abenaki of present-day Maine describe the origins of corn.

"The Origins of Our People"
by the Tewa tribe

North American mountain lion

The Tewa were living in "Sipofene," beneath Sandy Place Lake far to the north. The world under the lake was like this one, but it was dark. Supernaturals, men, and animals lived together at this time, and death was unknown. Among the supernaturals were the first mothers of all Tewa, known as "Blue Corn Woman, Near to Summer," or the Summer mother, and "White Corn Maiden, Near to Ice," the Winter mother.

These mothers asked one of the men present to go forth and explore the way by which the people might leave the lake. . . . On his way he came upon an open place and saw all the "tsiwi" [predatory mammals and carrion-eating birds] gathered there. . . . The animals gave him a bow and arrows and a quiver, dressed him in buckskin . . . and told him, "You have been accepted. These things we have given you are what you shall use henceforth. . . . " . . . When he returned to the people he came as Mountain Lion, or Hunt chief. This is how the first made person came into being.

"The Origins of Corn"
by the Abenaki tribe

A long time ago, when the Indians were first made, one man lived alone, far from any others. He did not know fire, and so he lived on roots, bark, and nuts. This man became very lonely for companionship. . . . [One day] he saw a beautiful woman with long *light* hair! . . . He sang to her about his loneliness, and begged her not to leave him.

At last she replied, "If you will do exactly what I tell you to do, I will also be with you." He promised that he would try his very best. . . . "Now get two dry sticks," she told him, "and rub them together fast while you hold them in the grass."

Soon a spark flew out. The grass caught fire, and as swiftly as an arrow takes flight, the ground was burned over. Then the beautiful woman spoke again: "When the sun sets, take me by the hair and drag me over the burned ground."

"Oh, I don't want to do that!" the man exclaimed.

"You must do what I tell you to do," said she. "Wherever you drag me, something like grass will spring up, and you will see something like hair coming from between the leaves. Soon seeds will be ready for your use."

The man followed the beautiful woman's orders. And when the Indians see silk on the cornstalk, they know that the beautiful woman has not forgotten them.

Harvested corn

UNDERSTANDING LITERATURE

1. According to the first myth, who are the Tewa mothers and how did they help to create human beings?
2. How does the Abenaki legend account for the existence of corn silk?
3. What do the two myths reveal about Native American oral literature?

The Agricultural Revolution

The most dramatic change made by Paleo-Indians was to shift from hunting and gathering to the domestication, or adapting and controlling, of plants. Called the **Agricultural Revolution**, this shift occurred worldwide as the biggest game died out, first in Africa, Asia, and Europe, and finally in the Americas.

Archaeological evidence indicates that by 5000 B.C. communities in Mexico were growing maize (corn) and by 2000 B.C. people living in the Andes were growing potatoes. By 1500 B.C. farming was well established throughout much of the Andes, Central America, and Mexico. The people living in what is now the southwestern United States began farming about 3500 B.C. Scholars believe that these desert people learned farming techniques from their southern neighbors.

The cultivation of crops increased food supplies and made them more reliable. Human populations began to increase. Small villages formed where people settled down to grow their food. At first, most people practiced subsistence farming—growing just enough crops for survival. Over time, though, new techniques emerged—such as using animals to pull plows—that increased food production.

As populations grew, villages gave way to cities. The first cities appeared in southwestern Asia about 3500 B.C. Over the next few thousand years, this "urban revolution" took place in other parts of Asia as well as in northern Africa, the Americas, and southern Europe.

With the rise of cities came a more elaborate division of labor. Some Native American men specialized in farming. Other men became artisans, government officials, laborers, merchants, physicians, priests, scholars, and soldiers. Women took on essential tasks such as cooking, raising children, spinning, and weaving. As a result, the basic equality that characterized hunter-gatherer and simple farming societies gave way to the development of social classes. In most societies, for example, men became more powerful than women. Likewise, the small number of government officials, successful merchants, and priests often became more powerful than the masses of artisans, farmers, and laborers.

✔ **READING CHECK:** How did the Agricultural Revolution affect Native American societies?

INTERPRETING THE VISUAL RECORD
Agricultural society. Crops such as maize provided a reliable food source for Paleo-Indians. They used these stones for grinding maize. *How did the shape, size, and durability of these tools help Paleo-Indians provide food for their community?*

Native American Cultures

By the A.D. 1400s more than 650 distinct groups were living in the Americas. Each group had its own culture and language. Some of the earliest large civilizations arose in an area called Mesoamerica or Middle America—what is now known as southern Mexico and Central America. Estimates suggest that at its height the region boasted a population of some 25 million.

The Olmec. The first great Mesoamerican culture was the **Olmec**. The Olmec people lived on the fertile coastal lowlands along the Gulf of Mexico. Historians call the Olmec the mother culture of Mesoamerica because the culture so strongly influenced later societies.

Olmec culture flourished from approximately 1200 to 100 B.C. One of the first Olmec settlements, San Lorenzo, may have emerged as early as 1500 B.C.

Sacred or Scientific Sites?

Over the years, many Native American burial sites have been unearthed and destroyed when bones and artifacts have been removed from graves for research. This practice has led to a bitter conflict between some Native Americans and the anthropologists and archaeologists doing the digging. Researchers argue that studying skeletal remains and the objects buried with them reveals much about Native American cultures that might otherwise remain unknown. Skeletal remains also provide a physical record. They can trace the development and spread of many diseases.

Native American pot found at a burial site

They show the effects of diet, pollution, and other factors on health. This information can be useful in preventing and treating diseases. "Indians living today," argues one anthropologist, "stand to benefit from our conclusions."

To many Native Americans, however, the burial sites are sacred places that should not be disturbed. They believe that excavation of the sites shows a disregard for their cultural traditions. An attorney for a tribe in New Mexico recently asked: "Why single out Indians? Why not dig up everybody's ancestors?" Through recent lawsuits, some Native Americans have succeeded in obtaining the return of their ancestors' remains for reburial. Native Americans have been assisted in their efforts by the Native American Grave Protection and Repatriation Act, passed by Congress in 1990.

Archaeologists studying the San Lorenzo site have found small pyramids, clusters of earthen mounds, and a rectangular courtyard believed to be the earliest ball court in Mesoamerica.

The sacred ball game played in such courts remained popular for centuries and spread to groups as far away as present-day Honduras and Arizona. This game had similarities to the modern-day sports of basketball and soccer. One later Spanish observer described the game, in which padded players bounced a rubber ball off their legs, hips, and elbows.

> 66 The ball court . . . consisted of two walls, twenty or thirty feet apart, . . . about eight and a half feet high, and . . . in the middle of the walls, in the center of the court, were two stones, like millstones hollowed out, opposite each other, and each one had a hole wide enough to contain the ball. . . . The one who put the ball in it [the hole] won the game. 99

The Olmec also placed huge heads carved of stone—believed to be portraits of Olmec rulers—around the San Lorenzo site. Scholars such as Miguel Covarrubias marvel at the Olmec's "masterfully carved colossal monuments of basalt, splendid statuettes of precious jade, and sensitively modeled figures of clay." In addition, the Olmec developed the beginnings of a calendar and writing.

The Olmec were farmers who practiced slash-and-burn agriculture. Toward the end of the dry season, they cut down and burned sections of the jungle. Then, before the arrival of the rainy season, they planted beans, chili peppers, maize, and squash in the ash-enriched soil.

The Maya. The **Maya**, who inherited much from the Olmec culture, rose to prominence about A.D. 300. Their civilization flourished for more than 500 years, primarily in what is now southern Mexico and Guatemala. The Maya refined the Olmec calendar, developing a more accurate system than the one being used at the same time in Europe. Maya mathematicians devised a number system that included zero long before Europeans adopted the concept from the Arabs. Maya scholars also developed a complex system of writing with glyphs, or pictures—the only complete writing system in early America. This enabled the Maya to express their spoken language non-verbally.

The glyphs reveal important information about Maya culture. Some tell how three settlements—Tikal in present-day Guatemala, Palenque in what is now Mexico, and Copan in present-day Honduras—emerged as the principal cities in the Maya Empire. Most of the population lived in cities. Many worked as farmers. Some Maya traded with other cultures. For example, the feathers of the quetzal (ket-SAHL), a bird associated with royalty, were traded for black obsidian from the north.

The Maya civilization began to decline after A.D. 800. As with the Olmec, archaeologists are unsure why this decline occurred. The Maya culture has persisted, however, with a small number of Maya still living in Central America. More significantly though, Maya culture endured by blending with the cultures of other Mesoamerican people, influencing the beliefs and practices of Paleo-Indians throughout the Americas.

✔ **READING CHECK:** What were the major characteristics and accomplishments of the Olmec and Maya cultures?

The Toltec and the Aztec. In the century before the Maya's decline, invading groups from the north descended upon a region in central Mexico. About A.D. 900, one of these groups, the **Toltec** (TOHL-tek), came to dominate the area. The Toltec built Tula, a great **city-state**—independent city. The Toltec empire became the center of a great trading network. Pottery from as far away as present-day Costa Rica has been found at Toltec sites. Maya religion and architecture reveal the influence of Toltec culture. For example, the Maya city of Chichén Itzá displays examples of Toltec architecture. During the 1100s, however, internal conflicts weakened Toltec society. As a result, the empire soon fell to new invading groups from the north. A later poet described the destruction of the city of Tula: "Everywhere can be seen the remains of clay vessels. . . . Everywhere are their ruins, truly the Toltecs once lived there."

The conquerors of the Toltec fought among themselves until one group, the **Aztec,** emerged victorious. Although they were a fierce warrior society, the Aztec, or Mexica, as they called themselves, settled down and adopted the ways of the Toltec people. They built their capital, Tenochtitlán (tay-nawch-teet-LAHN)—the site of present-day Mexico City—on an island in Lake Texcoco (tays-KOH-koh). Over time, Tenochtitlán grew into an impressive city with hundreds of buildings, an elaborate system of canals, and more than 300,000 residents.

Over a period of 200 years, the Aztec gained control of an empire of 5 million people. Eventually, a class system developed in Aztec society. Some members grew wealthy from the gold, silver, and precious stones they demanded as tribute—a forced payment from conquered peoples. Men and women from the noble class served as priests and government officials. Ordinary citizens worked as farm laborers, porters, servants, and slaves.

The Aztec viewed warfare as a sacred duty. They believed that the sun god, Huitzilopochtli (wee-tsee-loh-POHCH-tlee), had to battle the forces of darkness each night in order for a new day to dawn. The Aztec believed that human sacrifices gave Huitzilopochtli the strength to fight the Moon and stars and therefore return the next day. To satisfy their god, the Aztec sacrificed thousands of war prisoners on Tenochtitlán's sacred altars.

The Inca. As the cultures of Mesoamerica developed, similar advances took place in South America. Farming cultures developed on the Pacific coastal plains, in the high valleys of the Andes, and along the upper Amazon River. The most powerful group—the **Inca**—gained control of this region by the mid-1400s.

Science. The Maya used observatories like this one to expand their knowledge of astronomy and to establish the Maya calendar. *What other types of technical know-how are revealed by the existence of these ruins?*

Infrastructure. The capital of the Aztec Empire, Tenochtitlán, was built on an island and contained an extensive system of canals. *What does this image reveal about the organization of the Aztec Empire?*

Native American Culture Areas

Learning from Maps By 1500 Native Americans lived in vastly different geographic settings: frozen tundra, mountains, dry grasslands, deserts, lush woodlands, and tropical forests.

? HUMAN–ENVIRONMENT INTERACTION How might the geography and climate of an area influence the culture that develops there?

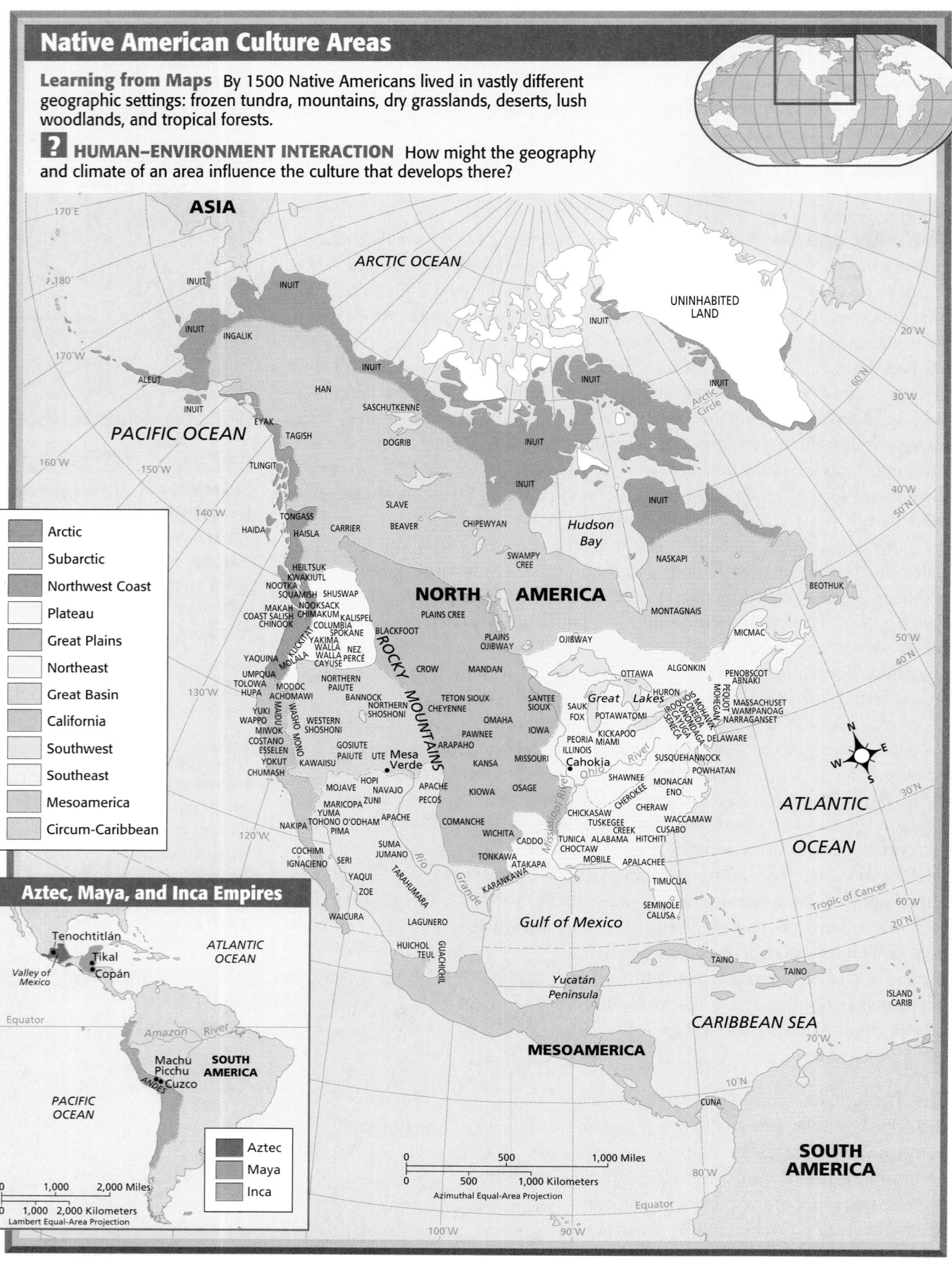

Legend:
- Arctic
- Subarctic
- Northwest Coast
- Plateau
- Great Plains
- Northeast
- Great Basin
- California
- Southwest
- Southeast
- Mesoamerica
- Circum-Caribbean

Aztec, Maya, and Inca Empires
- Aztec
- Maya
- Inca

Tenochtitlán
Valley of Mexico
Tikal
Copán
ATLANTIC OCEAN
Equator
Amazon River
Machu Picchu
Cuzco
SOUTH AMERICA
ANDES
PACIFIC OCEAN
0   1,000   2,000 Miles
0   1,000   2,000 Kilometers
Lambert Equal-Area Projection

ASIA
ARCTIC OCEAN
UNINHABITED LAND
INUIT
INGALIK
ALEUT
HAN
SASCHUTKENNE
EYAK
TAGISH
DOGRIB
SLAVE
Arctic Circle
PACIFIC OCEAN
TLINGIT
TONGASS
HAIDA
HAISLA
CARRIER
BEAVER
CHIPEWYAN
Hudson Bay
SWAMPY CREE
NASKAPI
BEOTHUK
HEILTSUK
KWAKIUTL
NOOTKA
SQUAMISH SHUSWAP
MAKAH NOOKSACK
COAST SALISH CHIMAKUM
CHINOOK COLUMBIA
KALISPEL
SPOKANE
YAKIMA
WALLA WALLA
CAYUSE
NEZ PERCÉ
BLACKFOOT
PLAINS CREE
MONTAGNAIS
MICMAC
NORTH   AMERICA
OJIBWAY
PLAINS OJIBWAY
OTTAWA
ALGONKIN
HURON
PENOBSCOT
ABNAKI
KLICKITAT
MOALA
YAQUINA
UMPQUA
TOLOWA
HUPA
ACHOMAWI
MODOC
NORTHERN PAIUTE
BANNOCK
NORTHERN SHOSHONI
CROW
MANDAN
TETON SIOUX
CHEYENNE
SANTEE SIOUX
SAUK
FOX
POTAWATOMI
IROQUOIS
MOHAWK
ONEIDA
ONONDAGA
CAYUGA
SENECA
MOHEGAN
PEQUOT
MASSACHUSET
WAMPANOAG
NARRAGANSET
YUKI
WAPPO
MAIDU
WASHO
MONO
WESTERN SHOSHONI
GOSIUTE
PAIUTE
UTE
Mesa Verde
ARAPAHO
OMAHA
PAWNEE
IOWA
MISSOURI
KANSA
PEORIA
ILLINOIS
KICKAPOO
MIAMI
DELAWARE
SUSQUEHANNOCK
POWHATAN
Great Lakes
Cahokia
Ohio River
SHAWNEE
MONACAN
ENO
CHEROKEE
ATLANTIC OCEAN
MIWOK
COSTANO
ESSELEN
YOKUT
CHUMASH
KAWAIISU
HOPI
MOJAVE
NAVAJO
MARICOPA
YUMA
TOHONO O'ODHAM
PIMA
ZUNI
APACHE
PECOS
KIOWA
OSAGE
COMANCHE
WICHITA
CADDO
CHICKASAW
TUSKEGEE
CREEK
TUNICA ALABAMA HITCHITI
CHOCTAW
MOBILE
APALACHEE
CHERAW
WACCAMAW
CUSABO
NAKIPA
COCHIMI
IGNACIENO
SERI
SUMA
JUMANO
YAQUI
ZOE
TARAHUMARA
Rio Grande
KARANKAWA
TONKAWA
ATAKAPA
TIMUCUA
SEMINOLE
CALUSA
Gulf of Mexico
TAINO
TAINO
ISLAND CARIB
CARIBBEAN SEA
WAICURA
LAGUNERO
HUICHOL
TEUL
GUACHICHIL
Yucatán Peninsula
MESOAMERICA
CUNA
SOUTH AMERICA
ROCKY MOUNTAINS
Mississippi River
Tropic of Cancer
Equator

0   500   1,000 Miles
0   500   1,000 Kilometers
Azimuthal Equal-Area Projection

The Inca established their capital high in the Andes, in the city of Cuzco (KOO-skoh), during the A.D. 1000s. About 1440, they launched a great campaign of expansion and conquest that gave them control of an immense region covering much of present-day Bolivia, Chile, Ecuador, and Peru. This was the largest empire in the Americas at the time—with some 12 million people who spoke more than 20 languages.

Unlike the Aztec, the Inca did not force their newly conquered subjects to pay tribute. However, they did require their labor. The first major Inca ruler, Pachacutec (pah-chah-KOO-tek) Inca Yupanqui (yooh-PAHNG-kee), ordered 20,000 men to rebuild Cuzco, the capital city, after the Inca had conquered it. "Four thousand of them quarried and cut the stones; six thousand hauled them with great cables of leather and hemp," a later historian explained. "The others dug the ditch and laid the foundations, while still others cut poles and beams for the timbers." Inca laborers built massive buildings as well as thousands of miles of roads that linked the vast empire.

✔ **READING CHECK:** What were the main characteristics of the Aztec and Inca cultures?

Early Cultures of North America

The cultures of the Mesoamerican civilizations reached as far as North America. The farming methods, pottery styles, and social practices of Native Americans living in what is now the southwestern United States show very strong Mesoamerican influences. The population of North America, however, was too small and spread out to support societies of the size found in Mesoamerica and South America. As a result, Native Americans living in North America developed distinct regional cultures.

The Southwest. The **Anasazi** (ah-nuh-SAH-zee) were one of several groups who settled in the barren hills and deserts of the Southwest. Sometime between A.D. 700 and 1300 the Anasazi constructed multistory rock and adobe dwellings—many nestled against cliffs and some with as many as 800 rooms. Anasazi families built their rooms around plazas, and each extended family had its own kiva, a round room that served as a sacred and ceremonial space. Archaeologists believe that a crisis of some kind—probably drought—caused the Anasazi to abandon their communities about 1300. By the mid-1400s they had ceased to exist as a distinct people. Researchers believe, however, that the Anasazi were probably the ancestors of the Pueblo Indians, whom Spanish explorers encountered in the 1500s.

The East and Southeast. The Adena and Hopewell cultures of the Eastern Woodlands combined hunting and gathering with farming to support relatively large populations. The two cultures, often called the **Mound Builders**, dominated the eastern region for about 1,700 years. Both cultures created distinctive earthworks that served as elaborate burial mounds. Originating in the Ohio River valley about 1000 B.C., the Adena eventually occupied an area extending from

INTERPRETING THE VISUAL RECORD

Inca artistry. The Inca highly valued artistic achievement, as can be seen in the architecture of the Inca city of Machu Picchu and this vessel in the shape of a human figure. *What other aspects of Inca life can you infer from this image of the ancient ruins of Machu Picchu and this vessel?*

Characteristics of North American Culture Areas

Culture Area	Characteristics
Northwest Coast	• Coastal dwellers • Fishers • Developed complex culture
Plateau	• River dwellers • Primarily fishers • Relatively low population
Great Plains	• Grassland dwellers • Nomadic buffalo hunters after introduction of horse
Northeast	• Forest dwellers • Mostly hunter-gatherers; also farmers and fishers
Great Basin	• Desert basin dwellers • Mostly gatherers, due to barren surroundings • Low population
California	• Desert, mountain, river, or coastal dwellers • Farmers, nomadic hunters
Southwest	• Canyon, mountain, and desert dwellers • Farmers, nomadic hunters
Southeast	• River valley dwellers • Mostly farmers; also hunter-gatherers, fishers

Learning from Charts Native Americans who lived in North America before the arrival of Europeans developed significantly different cultures.

? Building Chart Skills How might the availability of food affect a society's way of life?

present-day Kentucky to New York. About 300 B.C., however, the Hopewell began to push the Adena out of the region. The Hopewell's cultural influence extended into present-day Louisiana, New York, and Wisconsin.

The more advanced Mississippian culture of the Southeast later replaced the Hopewell culture, which declined about A.D. 400. Beginning about A.D. 800 in the lower Mississippi River valley, the Mississippian culture spread to occupy much of the Southeast and Midwest. Huge temple mounds, resembling Mesoamerican pyramids, dominated their villages. The largest Mississippian settlement was located at Cahokia (kuh-HOH-kee-uh), near present-day St. Louis. It extended six miles and contained 85 burial and temple mounds. The largest covered 16 acres and stood about 100 feet high.

At its peak, Cahokia's population may have numbered about 40,000. The chiefs of Cahokia controlled a network of trade routes that stretched from the Great Lakes to the Gulf of Mexico and into Mesoamerica. Perhaps because of climate changes or crop failures, Cahokia was abandoned during the 1200s. However, the Mississipian culture continued to flourish elsewhere for several centuries.

✔ **READING CHECK:** What were the major characteristics of the Native American cultures of North America?

SECTION REVIEW

Define and explain the significance of the following terms:
Paleo-Indians
hunter-gatherers
Agricultural Revolution
Olmec
Maya
Toltec
city-state
Aztec
Inca
Anasazi
Mound Builders

Identify and explain the significance of the following individual:
Pachacutec Inca Yupanqui

Locate and explain the importance of the following places:
Mesoamerica   Cuzco
Tikal   Cahokia
Tenochtitlán

1. **Using Graphic Organizers** Copy the table below. Use the table to list the major societies of Mesoamerica, South America, and North America and their cultural traits.

Mesoamerican Groups	Cultural Traits
1.	1.
2.	2.
3.	3.
4.	4.
South American Groups	**Cultural Traits**
1.	1.
North American Groups	**Cultural Traits**
1.	1.
2.	2.
3.	3.

2. **Analyzing** Where did the first people to arrive in the Americas come from? How did they get to the Americas?

3. **Synthesizing** Why was there great variety among early Native American cultures? In what ways did Native American cultures share traditions and knowledge?

4. **Evaluating** How do the Mound Builder societies provide evidence of the spread of Mesoamerican culture into the area of the present-day United States?

Critical Thinking

5. What might have happened to the early Native Americans had it not been for the Agricultural Revolution?
Consider:
• what the Agricultural Revolution was
• what effect the Agricultural Revolution had on Native Americans
• agriculture's effect on later Native American civilizations

Early World-Trading Kingdoms

EYEWITNESSES TO History

❝ No town is more densely populated than al-Fustat, with its numerous sheiks and notables, its wonderful specialties and merchandise, its good souks [markets] and its good crafts, its [public] baths which are the height of excellence, its enclosed markets. . . . I have been told that a single building can house as many as two hundred souls. ❞

—al-Muqaddasi

Egyptian marketplace

Arab geographer al-Muqaddasi (al-muh-kahd-duh-SEE) wrote these words in 985 to describe the Egyptian trading center of al-Fustat—present-day Cairo—where many merchants and travelers met together. While Native Americans were living in relative isolation, large trading cultures were flourishing in Asia and Africa. Al-Muqaddasi's description provides evidence of this bustling commercial life.

China

The Chinese Empire controlled vast areas of ancient Asia. By the time China began to trade extensively with other kingdoms, it had many technological and cultural developments to share.

Under the rule of the Qin and Han dynasties—between 221 B.C. and A.D. 220—the Chinese made significant advances in science and technology. Chinese astronomers calculated the length of the year with great precision and observed sunspots. Chinese scientists also invented a simple yet highly sensitive seismograph to register earthquakes. Another important Chinese invention was paper, developed in A.D. 105. The use of paper later spread to other areas in Asia and eventually to Europe. The Chinese invented a system of printing with carved blocks of wood. They also made the world's first-known printed book, the *Diamond Sutra*, in 868.

Chinese society changed in the 1200s, when Mongol invaders from Central Asia overran the country. The Mongol leader, Kublai Khan (koo-bluh KAHN), was the grandson of Genghis Khan, who had established a powerful empire. In 1264 Kublai Khan set up his capital in what is now Beijing. The city was a great achievement in planning and architecture. European visitor Marco Polo described Kublai Khan's capital.

The imperial palace, called the Forbidden City, enclosed by a moat and a high wall occupied the center of Beijing.

❝ This new city is a perfect square, with each side six miles long. The wall of the city has 12 gates, 3 on each side of the square. The whole city was laid out by line. The streets are so straight that if you stand above one of the gates, you can see the gate on the opposite side of the city. ❞

Mongol leader Kublai Khan, shown on the left, conquered China.

Under Kublai Khan's rule, China became the largest empire in the world and became more open to trade with the Western world. After Kublai Khan's death in 1294, the Mongols' power declined, and the Chinese eventually regained control. The new leaders sought to protect their culture from foreign influences by isolating their society from the non-Asian world. They limited the entry of foreigners into the empire, although trade continued as Chinese merchants carried goods to and from other countries across a network of land paths.

Beginning in 1405, the Chinese became more open to the world, launching a series of seven sailing expeditions to trade and to explore new lands. These expeditions sailed to present-day Vietnam, Indonesia, Sri Lanka, India, the Arabian Peninsula, and East Africa. After these explorations, however, China once again returned to its relative isolation.

✔ **READING CHECK:** What advances did Chinese civilization make in science and technology?

Asia in the Middle Ages

Learning from Maps The Muslims and Mongols conquered vast areas of land from the Mediterranean Sea to the eastern reaches of Asia.

❓ MOVEMENT What natural feature barred the southern expansion of Kublai Khan's empire?

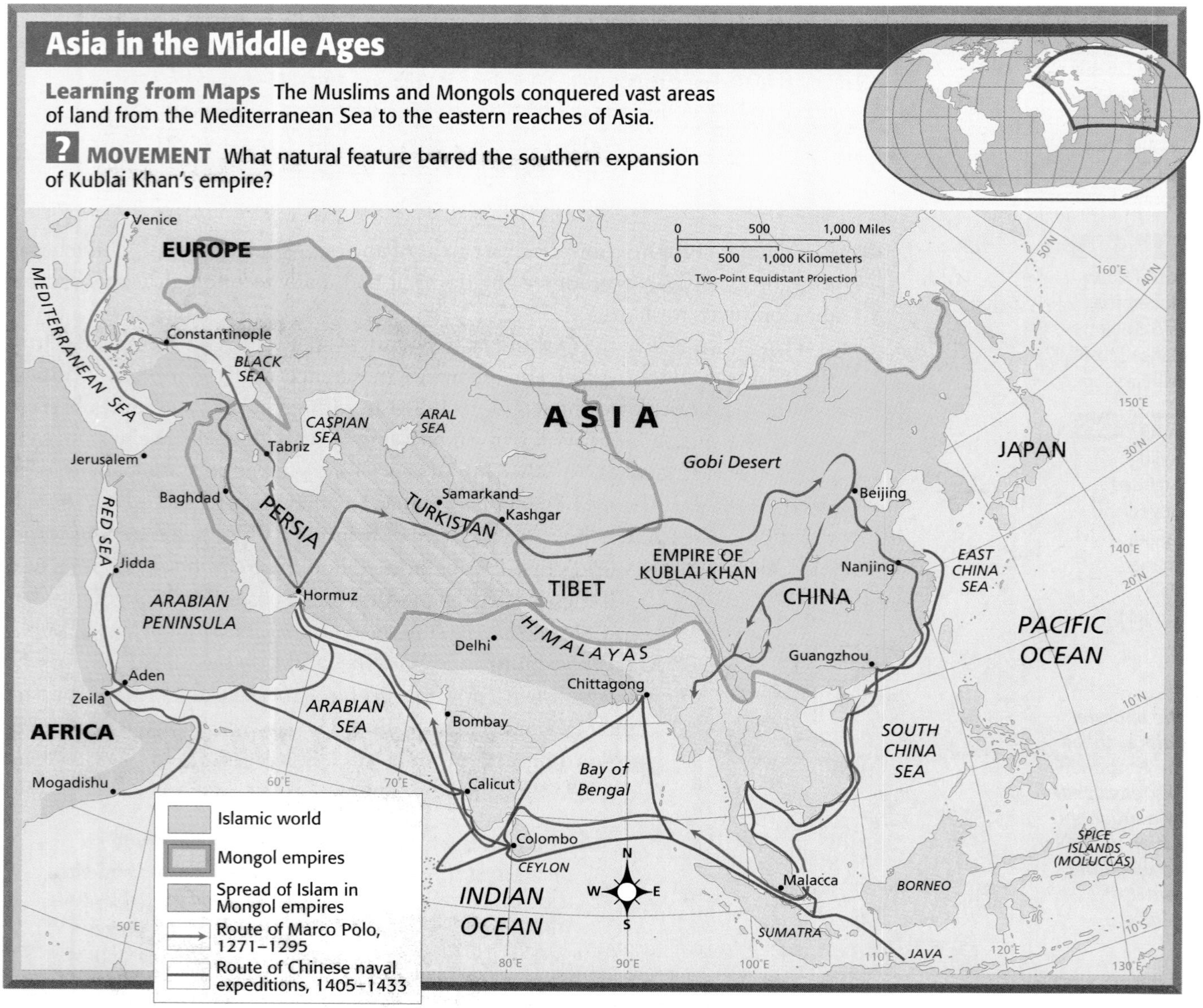

0   500   1,000 Miles
0   500   1,000 Kilometers
Two-Point Equidistant Projection

EUROPE
Venice
Constantinople
BLACK SEA
MEDITERRANEAN SEA
Jerusalem
CASPIAN SEA
ARAL SEA
Tabriz
ASIA
Gobi Desert
JAPAN
Baghdad
PERSIA
Samarkand
TURKISTAN
Kashgar
Beijing
RED SEA
Jidda
Hormuz
EMPIRE OF KUBLAI KHAN
Nanjing
EAST CHINA SEA
ARABIAN PENINSULA
TIBET
CHINA
PACIFIC OCEAN
Delhi
HIMALAYAS
Guangzhou
Aden
Chittagong
Zeila
ARABIAN SEA
Bombay
SOUTH CHINA SEA
AFRICA
Mogadishu
Calicut
Bay of Bengal
Colombo
CEYLON
Malacca
BORNEO
SPICE ISLANDS (MOLUCCAS)
INDIAN OCEAN
N
W   E
S
SUMATRA
JAVA

Legend:
- Islamic world
- Mongol empires
- Spread of Islam in Mongol empires
- Route of Marco Polo, 1271–1295
- Route of Chinese naval expeditions, 1405–1433

Strategies for Success — Reading a Time Line

Chronology is often called the skeleton of history. Knowledge of the chronological order of historical events—that is, the sequence in which they occurred—is essential to understanding them. A time line is a visual aid that provides a framework for the chronology of a specific historical period. Studying a time line involves learning the dates of particular historical events and knowing the possible relationships between these events.

How to Read a Time Line

1. **Determine the framework.** Note the years that the time line covers and the intervals of time into which it is divided.
2. **Study the sequence of events.** Study the dates and the order of events on the time line, noting particularly the amount of time between events.
3. **Supply additional information.** Think about people, places, and other events that are associated with each item on the time line. Use this information to "flesh out" the time line's coverage of the historical period.
4. **Identify relationships.** Consider how each event on the time line relates to earlier and later events. Look for cause-and-effect relationships and long-term historical developments.

Applying the Strategy

Study the time line below, which covers Chinese history between 1200 and 1300. Note that when more than one event is listed for the same year, they are stacked with the earliest event on top. The entries for 1264 illustrate the establishment of Kublai Khan as leader of the Mongol Empire.

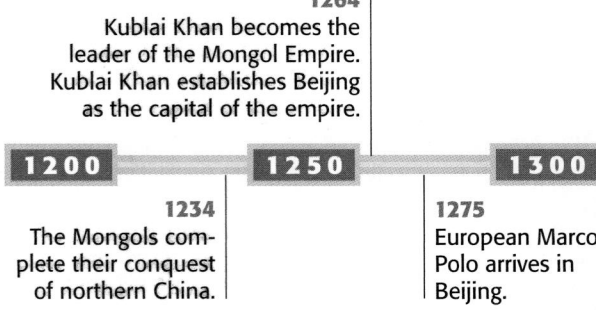

1264
Kublai Khan becomes the leader of the Mongol Empire.
Kublai Khan establishes Beijing as the capital of the empire.

| 1200 | 1250 | 1300 |

1234
The Mongols complete their conquest of northern China.

1275
European Marco Polo arrives in Beijing.

Practicing the Strategy

Using the time line above, answer the following questions.
1. What other events might belong on the time line?
2. What long-term historical development is suggested by the entry for 1275?

The Islamic World

Using the trade routes established between Asia and Africa, traders brought Chinese as well as other Asian goods such as cloth and horses to exchange them for African goods, including gold, ivory, and slaves. Trade played an instrumental role in Africa's early history by connecting its peoples to those of Asia. After 900, much of this trade was controlled by Muslim merchants.

Muslims are followers of the religion known as Islam. An Arab merchant named Muhammad founded Islam after experiencing a vision in the year 610. The teachings of Muhammad emphasized devotion to one God, Allah. The Muslim leader commanded his followers to convert nonbelievers. Although Muslim armies helped spread the faith by conquering new lands, many people were introduced to Islam through trade. Carrying the **Qur'an** (kuh-RAN)—the holy book of Muhammad's teachings—Muslim merchants tirelessly preached their religion wherever they went. By the year 750, vast areas of Asia, Africa, and Europe had become part of the Muslim Empire.

As in the Chinese Empire, intellectual life flourished in the Islamic world. Muslim scholars excelled at mathematics and improved algebra. Using knowledge

Copies of the Qur'an were carried by Muslim traders to introduce the Islamic faith to fellow travelers and traders.

gained from the mathematicians of India, they refined the Arabic numeral system and the concept of zero. Muslim geographers advanced the art of cartography, or mapmaking. Through trade, many of these advances found their way to cultures outside the Islamic world.

✔ **READING CHECK:** What role did trade play in the Islamic world?

The African Trading Kingdoms

Muslim merchants were aided in their efforts to spread their faith to Africa by an extensive network of trading kingdoms that had existed on the continent for centuries. Early African kingdoms established a pattern of trading practices that most later African empires adopted.

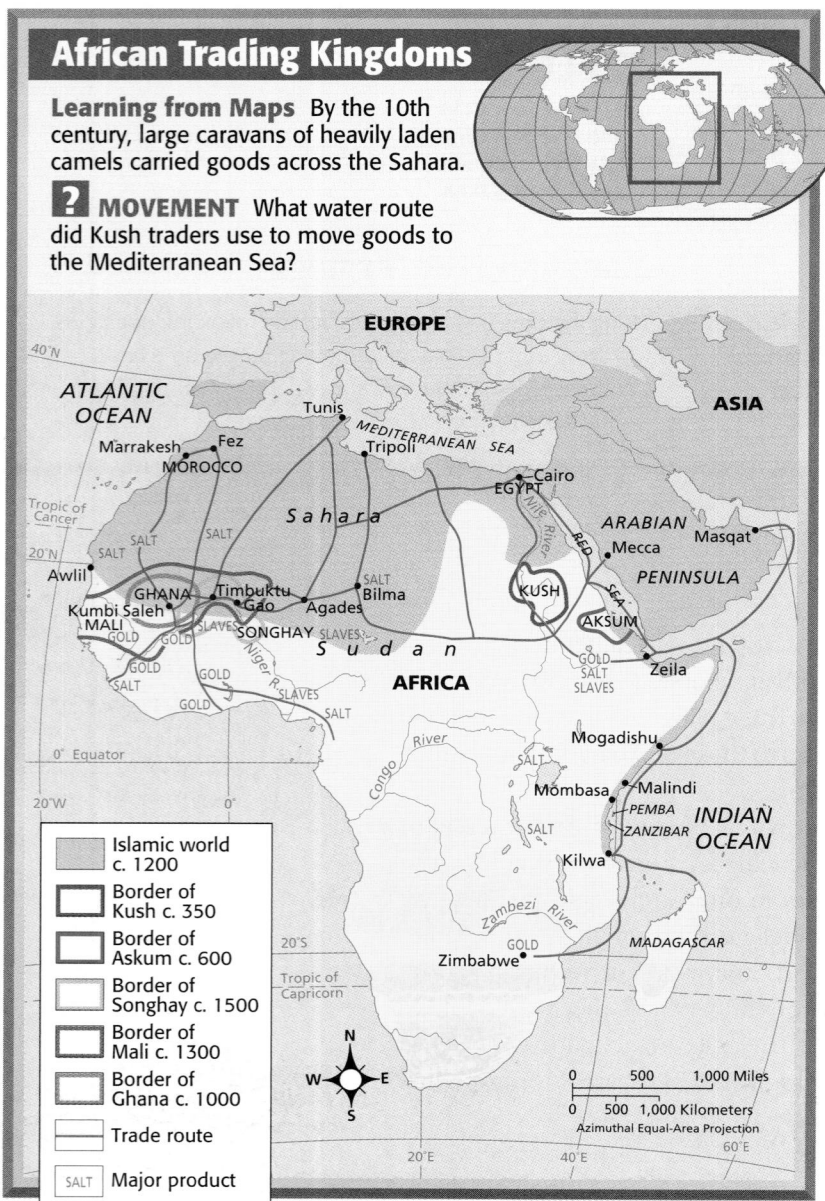

African Trading Kingdoms

Learning from Maps By the 10th century, large caravans of heavily laden camels carried goods across the Sahara.

? MOVEMENT What water route did Kush traders use to move goods to the Mediterranean Sea?

Islamic world c. 1200
Border of Kush c. 350
Border of Askum c. 600
Border of Songhay c. 1500
Border of Mali c. 1300
Border of Ghana c. 1000
Trade route
SALT Major product

East African city-states. During the 700s many African people moved to the coast and became involved in trade with Asia. Some traders shipped goods to the Arabian Peninsula, where they were traded to Asian merchants.

Many of these traders were Arabs who had fled to East Africa to escape upheaval in their homelands. Over time, the mix of newcomers and locals created a unique East African coastal culture. For example, **Swahili** (swah-HEE-lee), the language spoken in East Africa, is a form of Bantu with strong Arabic influences.

Over time, many East African trading villages grew into powerful and wealthy city-states. At first, northern city-states such as Mogadishu (mahg-uh-DEE-shoo) were the most prosperous. Eventually, however, commercial activity moved southward.

West African kingdoms. Trade was also important to the early history of West Africa. The earliest of the West African kingdoms, Ghana (GAH-nuh), developed from a trading post founded about A.D. 300 at the southern end of a caravan route from Morocco (muh-RAH-koh). In the 770s an Arab geographer, al-Fazari, described Ghana as "the land of gold." Abundant reserves of this precious metal resulted in great wealth and power for Ghana's kings. Arab geographer al-Bakri described Tenkaminen, Ghana's leader in about 1065, as "the master of a large empire and a formidable power." Ghana's prosperous empire began to crumble when Muslims overran the kingdom in 1076. Ghana was eventually overtaken by its neighbors, the Malinke people, who established a new kingdom called Mali.

Mali's best-known leader was Mansa Musa, who ruled from 1307 to around 1332. A devout Muslim, he undertook a **hajj**, or pilgrimage, to the Islamic holy city of Mecca in 1324. Mansa Musa saw this journey as an opportunity to display Mali's wealth. After Mansa Musa's death in the 1330s, Mali gradually lost its powerful position in the region. A succession of powerful leaders from various West African kingdoms controlled the major north-south trade routes.

In the mid-1300s the relatively weak state of Songhay (SAWNG-hy)—once under Mali's rule—won its independence. Songhay eventually became the dominant power in West Africa, flourishing as a center of Islamic learning. The city of Timbuktu, for example, was home to three universities and 180 Islamic schools.

Read More About It

Free Find:
Two Views of Africa
After reading al-Mas'udi's and Ibn Battuta's accounts of traveling in Africa on the **Holt Researcher** CD–ROM, create a travel guide to these areas during the times the authors were there.

✔ **READING CHECK:** What role did trade play in the development of African kingdoms?

Science & Technology

Archaeology

Asia and Africa are important locations for the study of archaeology because these areas have produced some of the oldest civilizations on Earth. The archaeologist's task of locating sites where human beings once lived is often difficult. Scientists use several methods to decide where to excavate, or dig, for clues to humankind's past. First, they consult written records that may give hints about location. Once they have narrowed down the location, archaeologists use a technique called a resistivity survey to find exactly where to dig. The resistivity survey measures the ability of soil to conduct electricity. If ruins lie buried beneath the ground, the soil in that location exhibits resistance by conducting electricity poorly. In contrast, "empty" soil conducts electricity very well.

Scientific dating techniques developed after 1900 allow archaeologists to determine the age of the ancient artifacts that they uncover. Because carbon 14 in artifacts or fossils breaks down at a constant rate over time, scientists can estimate the age of an object by measuring how much carbon 14 is left in it. Carbon-dating the wood from an African spear handle, for instance, indicates when the trees used to carve the handle were cut. This gives an approximate time that the spear would have been used.

In recent years, archaeologists have used carbon-dating to try to verify the location of Viking Leif Eriksson's settlement of Vinland, at a site now called L'Anse aux Meadows (The Creek of the Meadows) in Newfoundland.

Understanding Science and History

1. What types of scientific techniques are used in archaeology? Why are they used?
2. How does science contribute to the study of history?

❶ **Grid system for keeping track of location of artifacts**

❷ **Brushing dirt from the artifact**

❸ **Screen for sifting soil samples**

Architecture. This photograph shows the Colosseum in modern-day Rome. *Based on this photo, what arguments could be made about the importance of ancient Roman architecture in modern-day Europe?*

Europe During the Rise of Trading Kingdoms

European involvement in trade over the centuries was somewhat uneven. While European trade with Africa and Asia during the era of large trading kingdoms was limited, Europeans had been involved in trade centuries before as a part of the Roman Empire. In 509 B.C. the city-state of Rome established a **republic**—a system of government run by elected officials rather than monarchs alone.

By 27 B.C., the Roman Republic had grown into an empire, eventually ruling over most of Europe and some of what would become the Islamic world. Until the collapse of the empire in the late A.D. 400s, arts and sciences flourished. The Romans created elaborate buildings and vast road networks for travel and trade.

By A.D. 500 the western part of the Roman Empire lay in ruins. It was the victim of political strife and repeated attacks by migrating tribes from northern Europe and western Asia. In its place arose many small warring kingdoms, marking the beginning of Europe's Middle Ages—roughly A.D. 500–1500. Among the most feared of the migrating tribes were the Vikings of northern Europe. These skilled Scandinavian seafarers sailed thousands of miles to raid, trade with, and colonize new territory. The Vikings began to move into England and Ireland around 800. By the early 900s many Vikings had settled in northern France. Others had ventured west to Iceland and later to Greenland.

In about the year 1000, Viking leader Leif Eriksson established what is believed to be the first European settlement in North America. Eriksson called his settlement Vinland. There he and his followers encountered numerous Native Americans. The settlement did not last, however. Because of Europe's isolation, few non-Vikings even knew that the voyage had taken place.

✔ **READING CHECK:** Why was Europe slow to become involved in world trade?

SECTION 2 REVIEW

Define and explain the significance of the following terms:

Diamond Sutra   hajj
Qur'an   republic
Swahili

Identify and explain the significance of the following individuals:

Kublai Khan   Mansa Musa
Muhammad   Leif Eriksson
Tenkaminen

Locate and explain the importance of the following places:

Beijing   Ghana
Baghdad   Mali
Mogadishu   Timbuktu
Sahara

1. **Using Graphic Organizers** Copy the graphic organizer below. Using the organizer, list elements of African and Asian cultures, including inventions, that were unique to each continent and elements that were shared by both cultures.

Asia

Africa

2. **Understanding Geography: Location** How did the location of East and West African kingdoms prove important to their development as trading centers?
3. **Assessing Consequences** How did trade contribute to the spread of cultures and ideas in Asia and Africa before 1500?
4. **Identifying Cause and Effect** What prevented Europe from joining the Asia-Africa trade system?

Critical Thinking

5. What relationship does trade have to a region's scientific advancement?
   Consider:
   • what advances were made in China
   • what advances were made in Africa
   • how trade assisted in the spread of knowledge

Europe in the Middle Ages

OBJECTIVES

Read to understand:

1. what led to the rise and fall of feudalism
2. how the Crusades affected Europe
3. how the Renaissance arose, and what effect it had on Europe
4. what factors led to the rise of nation-states

KEY TERMS

feudalism
manors
Crusades
bourgeoisie
Magna Carta
Renaissance
Reconquista

KEY PEOPLE

King John
Roger Bacon
Johannes Gutenberg
Isabella of Castile
Ferdinand II of Aragon

KEY PLACES

Jerusalem
England
France
Spain

Peasants regularly worked the fields, raising food for the entire manor.

EYEWITNESSES TO *History*

66 *Renovatio, imperi, romani! (Renewal of the Roman Empire)* 99
—European slogan

So shouted the European people, using the slogan of a great king named Charlemagne, ruler of the Frankish kingdom. This was one of many small European kingdoms. In the 770s Charlemagne attempted to rebuild the great Roman Empire. With the help of powerful armies, he succeeded in gaining control over much of continental Europe. Once the land was under his control, Charlemagne divided the territory into small sections to be ruled by nobles. After Charlemagne's death in 814, his empire fell apart as a result of fighting among his heirs and invasions from outside forces such as the Vikings. Once again Europe lacked political unity.

Sculpted bust of Charlemagne

The Early Middle Ages

The nobility system established by Charlemagne played an important role in Europe during the Middle Ages. Kings relied on the nobles to protect their territory and to conduct the business of government.

To combat the Vikings and other invaders, many European rulers enlisted the aid of nobles under a system later known as **feudalism**. In return for land and protection from invasion, the nobles pledged their loyalty and military assistance to the rulers. Feudal society operated under a rigid class system. At the top of society was the noble class. The nobles managed estates called **manors**. Each manor was almost completely self-sufficient and included a house, fields, and a village. Peasants, known as serfs, provided most of the labor required to keep the manor functioning.

Noblemen spent their days managing their estates, hunting, or engaging in battle. Most noblewomen spent their days directing the servants in such duties as caring for livestock, cleaning, cooking, spinning, weaving, and working in the fields. When the noblemen were away fighting, the women were often left in charge of running the estates.

Most serfs spent their days in unending physical labor. Both men and women worked in the fields, and women performed the household tasks as well. The lords received a large portion of the crops grown by the serfs. Many nobles also required their workers to pay them fees, such as taxes on marriage or inheritances. Few people in feudal Europe ever traveled more than 25 miles from their homes. Life centered around the manor and the Roman Catholic Church.

Virtually all the important events in people's lives took place at their village church. Parish priests led mass, conducted baptisms, weddings, and funerals, and performed many acts of charity. In monasteries and

Growing Up in the Middle Ages

Painting of young Europeans in the 1300s

Teen life, that period when children make the transition to adulthood, is generally thought of today as taking place from age 13 to 19. During the Middle Ages, this period of transition often began much earlier. Most children were expected to provide manual labor for their families starting at a very young age. When they were about 14 years old, many of these children entered apprenticeships or became servants.

Children born into nobility usually found their lives determined by birth order and gender. Following a system of inheritance called primogeniture, aristocratic families left their estates to the eldest son and expected him to marry a noble woman and carry on the family name. Younger sons often remained unmarried, and many went into service for the church or the military. The eldest daughter in a noble family almost always entered a convent to become a nun. Wealthy younger daughters born into nobility tended to get married before age 18.

Medieval merchants often sold luxury items like this porcelain vase from China.

convents, the monks and the nuns worshipped, studied the scriptures, and preserved the writings of the ancient Greeks and Romans. The medieval church promoted art and culture and left behind a rich heritage of religious music, tapestries, illuminated manuscripts, and grand cathedrals. Most important, the Roman Catholic Church, led by the pope, played a leading role in guiding the politics of Europe. It often stepped in to settle disputes between warring Christian kingdoms. Church leaders also sometimes negotiated political alliances and suggested various courses of action to political leaders.

Beginning about 1100, a series of changes brought about a gradual end to feudal society. New farm equipment such as heavy plows increased the amount of land that could be farmed. Laborers could produce enough food to sustain large armies and a growing number of townspeople.

As the military strength of the kingdoms grew, invaders were less likely to attempt to take by force what they could get by trade. Trading towns and cities gradually replaced manors as the center of economic activity. As a result, many serfs moved from manors to towns, where they could either work for wages or farm rented plots of land surrounding the town.

✔ **READING CHECK:** What led to the rise and fall of feudalism?

The Crusades and Trade

The series of military and religious expeditions known as the **Crusades** also prompted a shift away from feudalism. Between 1096 and the late 1200s, waves of Christian crusaders fought Muslims for control of Palestine. This was an area of the eastern Mediterranean sacred to Christians, Jews, and Muslims.

Various groups of Muslims had controlled the Holy Land since the 600s. In 1071 the sacred city of Jerusalem fell to Muslims from Central Asia. This development made it increasingly difficult for Christians to visit the holy city. The First Crusade began in 1096 as an effort to retake Jerusalem. Christian invaders from Europe captured the city and established several kingdoms in the area. Muslims retook Jerusalem in the late 1100s, however, resulting in additional Crusades.

The Crusades had important consequences for trade. Merchants in the Italian city-states of Genoa (JE-noh-uh), Pisa, and Venice funded the Crusades in return for trading privileges. Italian traders brought back rare spices, fine silks, and other exotic Asian goods from the Muslim lands.

The impact of trade changed Europe's political and social order. The merchants who organized trading voyages helped lead to the formation of a new social class—the **bourgeoisie** (boohzh-wah-ZEE), or urban middle class. The bourgeoisie supported monarchs, who could provide better political stability and allow trade to flourish.

In return, the bourgeoisie demanded a greater degree of economic and political freedom for themselves and their cities. Kings and lords reluctantly granted self-government to towns, and some of them even organized assemblies, the forerunners of modern legislatures, to help the monarchs decide on taxes and government policies. In 1215 English nobles who were angered by new taxes forced King John to sign **Magna Carta**, a charter limiting the powers of the monarchy. In addition to guaranteeing basic liberties for nobles, the charter protected their trading rights.

✔ **READING CHECK:** How did the Crusades affect European society?

The Renaissance

In addition to spurring trade and political reform, the Crusades contributed to a rebirth of European learning and artistic creativity later known as the **Renaissance**. During the early Middle Ages, much of Europe had been closed off intellectually from the rest of the world. Crusaders and traders brought back classical Greek and Roman texts and new ideas in science, technology, art, and philosophy.

Magna Carta

In 1215 a group of English nobles forced King John to sign Magna Carta, a document that limited the powers of the monarchy. Since its signing, Magna Carta has provided a foundation for the protection of individual rights and constitutional government.

Know that we . . . have confirmed, by this our present charter that . . . a widow, after the death of her husband, shall straightway, and without difficulty, have her marriage portion and her inheritance . . . .

No widow shall be forced to marry when she prefers to live without a husband. . . .

No bailiff, on his own simple assertion, shall henceforth put any one to his law, without producing faithful witness in evidence.

No freeman shall be taken, or imprisoned, or disseized [deprived of his land], or outlawed, or exiled, or in any way harmed—nor will we go upon or send upon him—save by the lawful judgment of his peers [equals] or by the law of the land.

To none will we sell, to none deny or delay, right or justice. . . .

It has been sworn, on our part as well as on the part of the barons, that all these above mentioned provisions shall be observed with good faith and without evil intent.

After coming into contact with the works of classical and Muslim thinkers, European scholars were inspired to learn more about science. Roger Bacon, an English monk and scientist, speculated about the future.

> **❝ Machines may be made by which the largest ships, with only one man steering them, will move faster than if they were filled with rowers; wagons may be built which will move with unbelievable speed and without the aid of beasts. ❞**

The Renaissance began in Italy in the 1300s and soon spread to the rest of Europe. A major factor in this cultural diffusion was the work of a German printer, Johannes Gutenberg. About 1450 he invented a printing press that used movable type. His printing press made it possible to print a large number of books quickly—and thus to spread ideas far and wide.

✔ **READING CHECK:** What led to the Renaissance and what effect did it have on Europe?

The Rise of Nation-States

The other great transformation of the Middle Ages was the rise of nation-states. Feudal kingdoms, independent city-states, and church-controlled lands slowly gave way to national monarchies in most of western Europe. Among the first to achieve national unity during this period were England, France, Portugal, and Spain. Most

Roger Bacon, an English monk who lived during the 1200s, studied science, mathematics, and philosophy.

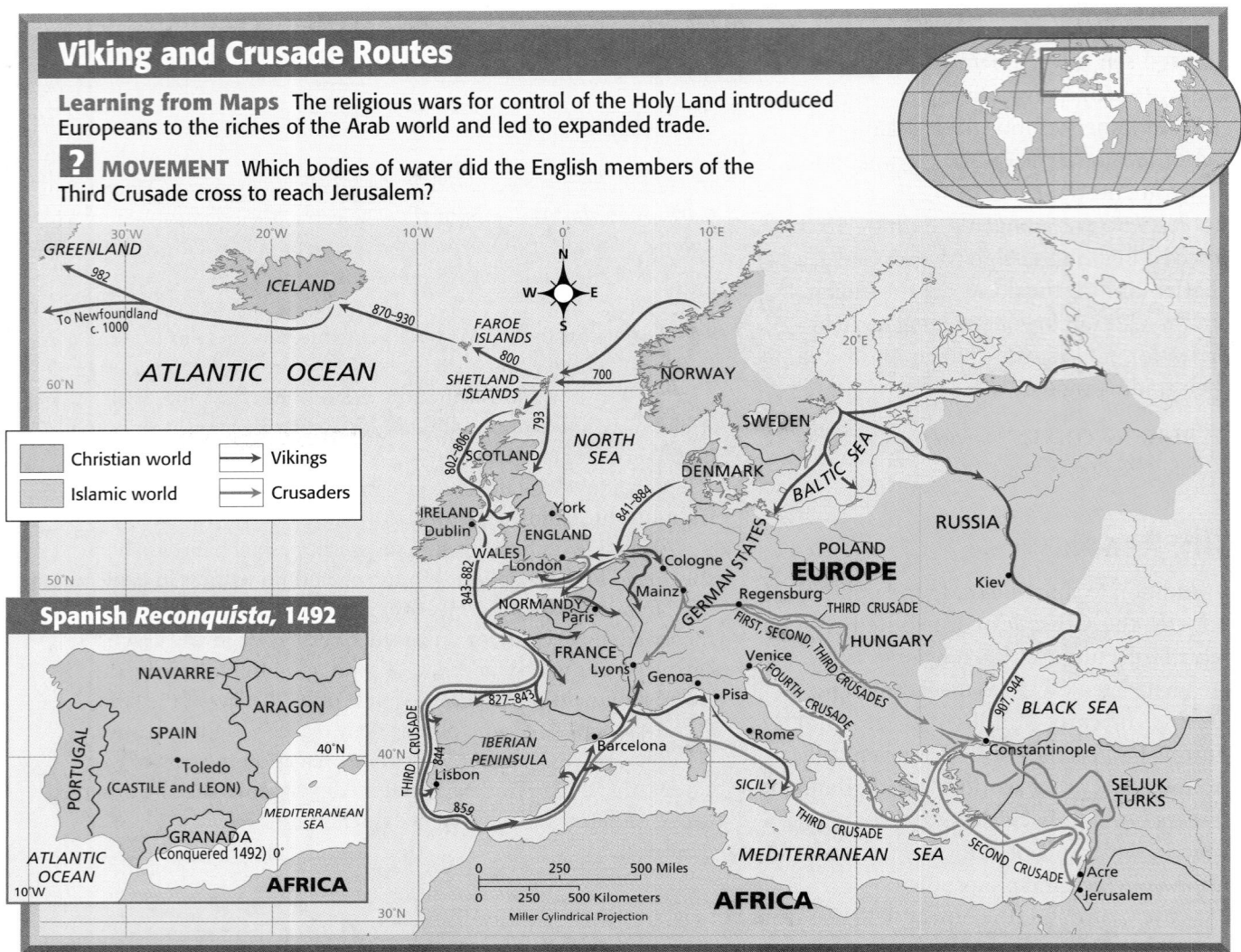

Viking and Crusade Routes

Learning from Maps The religious wars for control of the Holy Land introduced Europeans to the riches of the Arab world and led to expanded trade.

? MOVEMENT Which bodies of water did the English members of the Third Crusade cross to reach Jerusalem?

Legend:
- Christian world
- Islamic world
- → Vikings
- → Crusaders

Spanish *Reconquista*, 1492

NAVARRE
ARAGON
PORTUGAL
SPAIN (CASTILE and LEON)
Toledo
GRANADA (Conquered 1492)
IBERIAN PENINSULA
Lisbon
Barcelona
ATLANTIC OCEAN
MEDITERRANEAN SEA
AFRICA

0 250 500 Miles
0 250 500 Kilometers
Miller Cylindrical Projection

Read More About It

Free Find: Isabella

After reading the biography of Queen Isabella on the **Holt Researcher** CD–ROM, imagine that you are Isabella and write a fictional letter to the pope explaining what you, as Isabella, have done during your reign to spread Catholicism.

often these changes came as a result of warfare, but sometimes they were the result of marriage between royal families. Portugal won its independence from the kingdom of Castile (ka-STEEL) in the 1100s and was unified under King John I in the early 1400s. Louis XI unified the various French provinces by the time his reign ended in 1483. After 30 years of bloody fighting, Henry VII unified England in 1485.

The unification of Spain. The unification of Spain was more complicated. Four Christian kingdoms—Aragon, Castile, Navarre (nuh-VAHR), and Portugal—controlled most of the Iberian Peninsula. Muslims held the southernmost kingdom of Granada. The first step toward the unification of Spain occurred when Isabella of Castile and Ferdinand II of Aragon married in 1469. They did not unite their kingdoms until 1479. They did quickly join forces in the *Reconquista* (re-kawng-KEE-stah)—the ongoing battle to recapture Spanish lands from the Muslims. The *Reconquista* ended in 1492, when Spain defeated the Muslims in Granada. Isabella and Ferdinand believed that the best way to unify their kingdom was to make Spain a completely Catholic nation. Having already expelled the Muslims, in March 1492 they ordered all Jews to convert to the Catholic faith or leave Spain.

BIOGRAPHY

Queen Isabella

La Católica. Isabella's efforts to promote Catholicism in Spain earned her the title *la Católica*—or the Catholic—granted by Pope Alexander VI. The daughter of John II, Isabella lived from 1451 to 1504. While her older half-brother, King Enrique IV, ruled Castile, Isabella lived with her grandmother. From an early age Isabella developed strong beliefs about the purpose of the monarchy. In 1474, five years after marrying Ferdinand, she became queen of Castile following the death of her brother. In a speech designed to motivate her subjects for battle in 1475, Isabella made a passionate proclamation.

> 66 What greater honor, what greater benefit, what greater service to God, could there be than joining battle? . . . If you say to me that women, since they do not face such dangers, ought not to speak of them . . . to this I say that I do not know who risks more than I do, for I risked my King and Lord [Ferdinand], whom I love above all else in the world. 99

Isabella was considered a powerful monarch by her contemporaries. Ambassador Pedro Mártir, on his return from Egypt in 1502, described her as "stronger than a strong man, more constant than any human soul, a marvelous example of honesty and virtue; Nature has made no other woman like her."

Isabella and Ferdinand's aggressive rule did much to achieve their goal of an all-Catholic Spain. However, their religious intolerance carried a price for the country. Among the nearly 150,000 expelled Jews were some of the nation's leading bankers, government officials, merchants, and scholars.

INTERPRETING THE VISUAL RECORD

Nation-states. Isabella and Ferdinand accept the surrender of Muslim forces at Granada. *How does this painting suggest the birth of a new nation-state?*

✔ **READING CHECK:** What factors led to the rise of the nation-state of Spain?

SECTION REVIEW

Define and explain the significance of the following terms:

feudalism
manors
Crusades
bourgeoisie
Magna Carta
Renaissance
Reconquista

Identify and explain the significance of the following individuals:

King John
Roger Bacon
Johannes Gutenberg
Isabella of Castile
Ferdinand II of Aragon

Locate and explain the importance of the following places:

Jerusalem
England
France
Spain

1. **Using Graphic Organizers** Copy the flowchart below. Use it to list the factors that led to the rise of feudalism, the elements of feudalism, and the factors that contributed to its decline.

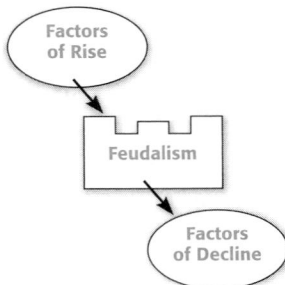

Factors of Rise

Feudalism

Factors of Decline

2. **Comparing and Contrasting** How was political and social life in Europe different before and after the Crusades?
3. **Identifying Cause and Effect** What caused the rise of the Spanish nation-state?
4. **Taking a Stand** Were the national monarchies that developed in the Middle Ages better for Europe than the old systems? Why or why not?

Critical Thinking

5. Considering the many changes during the time of the Renaissance, how did the Renaissance define European society of that era?
Consider:
• what the Renaissance was
• what effect it had on Europe
• what it means to define a society

The Lure of Trade and Exploration

EYEWITNESSES TO History

66 In one [land], there is a race of great stature, like giants, foul and horrible to look at; they have one eye only, in the middle of their foreheads. . . . [In another were] ugly folk without heads, who have eyes in each shoulder; their mouths are round, like a horseshoe, in the middle of their chest. 99

—Sir John Mandeville

Detail of a sea monster from a medieval map

This fanciful account by Sir John Mandeville described strange new worlds that were believed to exist beyond Europe. Books like Mandeville's became popular in Europe as life there grew more stable and some inhabitants ventured beyond the continent. Although Mandeville's tale was largely fictional, other books provided a more accurate description of life beyond Europe. Between 1271 and 1295, a merchant from Venice named Marco Polo visited China and served in the Chinese court under the Mongols. In the *Travels of Marco Polo,* a popular chronicle of his real-life adventures, Polo described the magnificence of the Mongol Empire. Polo's dramatic tales inspired Europeans to explore new lands. The lure of trade with the East, however, became the most compelling reason for adventurers to risk their lives in this new era of exploration.

Sailing in Search of Trade

Wealthy Europeans wanted African gold and grain, Chinese silk to make fine clothes, and Persian rugs, Chinese glass, and porcelain to decorate their homes. They also wanted cloves, cinnamon, and nutmeg from the Spice Islands of the Indies, and pepper from India to flavor and preserve their foods. Demand for these costly goods motivated Europeans to seek the most economical trade route possible.

Trade monopolies. Muslim trading empires and Italian city-states controlled the trade from Asia and Africa. Prices for goods were often high because these goods usually changed hands a number of times, with traders marking up the prices each time. Some of the profit went to the Muslim traders who controlled the Asian trade routes. Much more, however, went to the Italian merchants from Genoa and Venice. They bought the goods from Muslim traders in North Africa or in Black Sea ports and shipped them across the Mediterranean Sea to be sold to customers in Europe.

The newly emerging nation-states of Europe wanted to share in this wealth. Envious of Genoa and Venice's near monopoly, or exclusive control, of East-West trade, other European merchants began looking for cheaper ways to get Asian goods. An all-sea route to the East seemed the most promising answer.

The port of Genoa was one of the busiest trading ports during the Renaissance era.

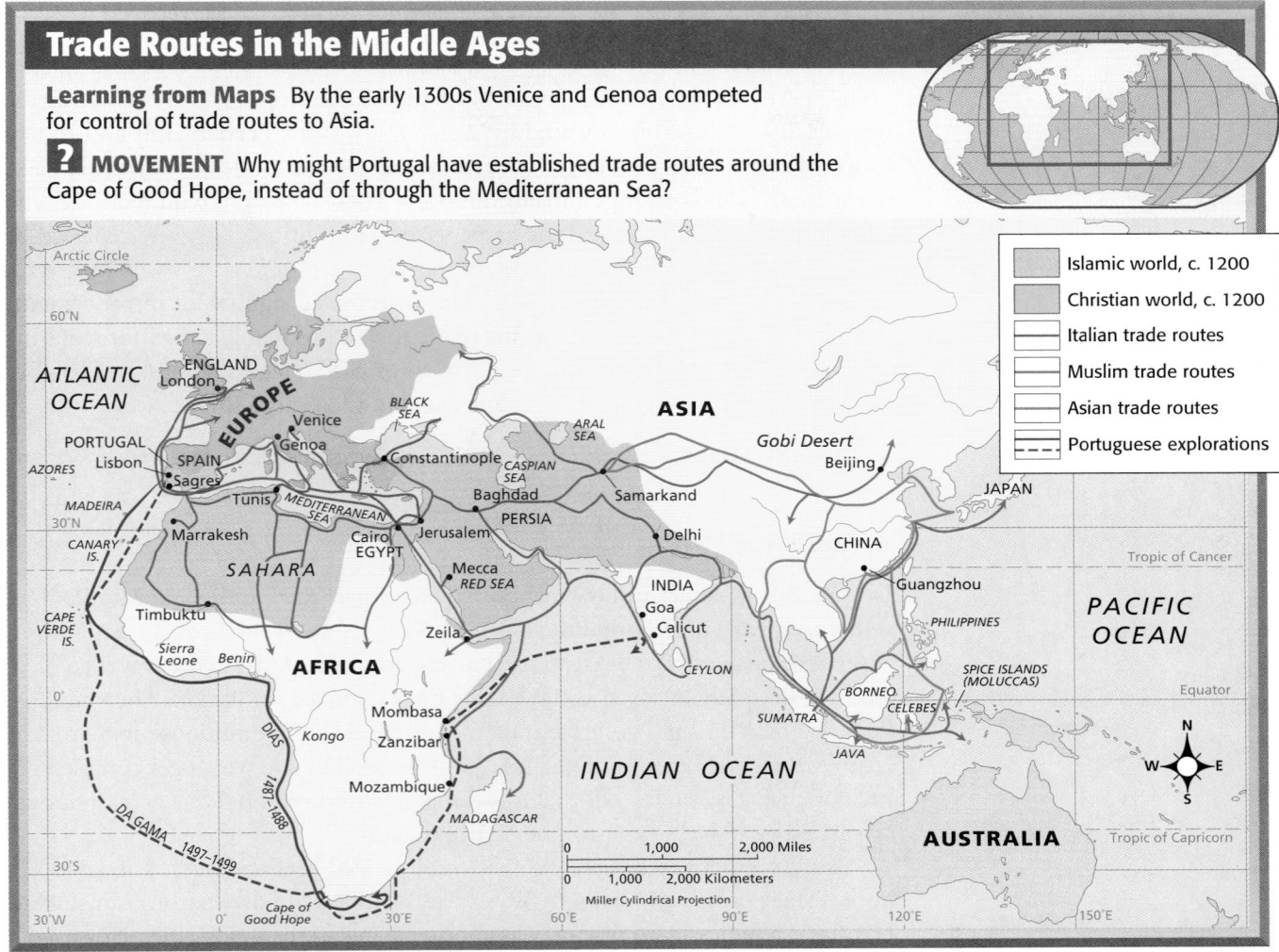

Trade Routes in the Middle Ages

Learning from Maps By the early 1300s Venice and Genoa competed for control of trade routes to Asia.

? MOVEMENT Why might Portugal have established trade routes around the Cape of Good Hope, instead of through the Mediterranean Sea?

Legend:
- Islamic world, c. 1200
- Christian world, c. 1200
- Italian trade routes
- Muslim trade routes
- Asian trade routes
- Portuguese explorations

New technology. Europeans could never have pursued their dreams of reaching the East without new technological advances. Poor navigational tools and the Catholic Church's control over scientific inquiry limited mapmakers' ability to chart Europe and the surrounding areas accurately.

By the Middle Ages, most educated Europeans believed that God had created Earth as a sphere. Nevertheless, geographers were bound by the church to follow its biblical scholars' interpretations. Mapmakers continued until the 1400s to draw Earth as a flat disk surrounded by water. In addition, medieval scholars mistakenly believed Earth to be at the center of the universe, with the Moon, Sun, and heavens rotating around it. Most Renaissance Europeans overcame these misconceptions.

European navigators developed the skills necessary to travel the world's oceans, learned from Muslims how to use astrolabes to calculate latitude—the distance north or south of the equator. Astrolabes measured the distance of the Sun and stars above the horizon. With this device, Europeans could figure the latitudes for important ports and islands. They recorded the information in tables that could be consulted by other seafarers. By the 1200s Europeans had started to use a Chinese invention called a compass—a magnetized needle that pointed north-south. The compass allowed them to determine their direction even when the stars were hidden by clouds.

European sailors learned of tools like this astrolabe from Muslim traders.

Shipbuilding advanced as Europeans designed larger ships that could better withstand the rough Atlantic Ocean. Since the 800s, Europeans had been using the lateen sail—probably introduced by seafarers from the Persian Gulf and Indian Ocean. These sails formed large triangles that could be trimmed or adjusted to take advantage of wind coming from any direction. These new ships required wider and deeper hulls, which increased the cargo space. In addition, oars were replaced by rudders attached to the rear, or stern, of the ship.

Portuguese shipbuilders in particular introduced significant improvements during the 1400s. The improvements made their ships highly suited for seafaring explorations. Called **caravels**, Portuguese ships used lateen sails and rudders but were smaller, and therefore more maneuverable, than cargo ships.

✔ **READING CHECK:** How did new technological developments improve sea exploration?

A Sailor's Life

Despite the advances in new technology, sea travel during the late Middle Ages remained extremely dangerous. One witness of the return of an expedition described the hardships the seafarers had experienced. "Most of the crew had died. And those which survived could hardly be recognized as human. They had lost flesh and hair, the nails gone from their hands and feet." Conditions on board seafaring vessels were often filthy. These "foul stinkes," as one passenger complained, became such a haven for rats that most ships' charters required that at least one cat be carried on board to control the rat population.

A sailor's diet at sea usually consisted of pickled beef and pork, known as salt horse. Their only fresh drinking water was collected in barrels from rainstorms. Hardtack, a saltless hard biscuit, was another staple in the sailors' diet. However, it typically became soggy, moldy, and infested with bugs on long journeys. One sailor reported that "what with the heat and dampness, our ship biscuit had become so wormy that . . . I saw many who waited for darkness to eat the porridge made of it, that they might not see the maggots."

The hardships of life at sea affected a sailor's habits and temperament. An English writer named Richard Braithwait described a typical sailor.

> 66 He makes small or no choice of his pallet [bed]; he can sleep as well on a sack of pumice [rocks] as a pillow of down . . . . He has been so long acquainted with the surges of the sea, as too long a calm distempers [upsets] him. . . . He can spin up a rope like a Spider, and down again like lightning. . . . Death he has seen in so many shapes, as it cannot amaze him. 99

In exchange for their hazardous labor and difficult living conditions, sailors earned wages, received clothing, and were granted occasional bonuses. Some sailors also belonged to Shipmen's Guilds—organizations similar to unions—to help protect them from exploitation by shipowners.

Known as gromets during their first year at sea, young boys also experienced the rigors of the sailor's life at sea. Despite its hardships, a sailor's

INTERPRETING THE VISUAL RECORD
Life of the sailor. Early sailors such as this one lived a rough life at sea. *What does their activities and appearance tell us about their daily lives?*

life offered unequaled opportunity for excitement and adventure. Sailors encountered new lands and cultures of which those who never left the shore could only dream.

✔ **READING CHECK:** What difficulties did sailors endure on their voyages?

Portugal Leads the Way

The small country of Portugal led the way in exploration. A strong desire to seize a share of the East-West trade drove the Portuguese to seek a new all-water route to Asia. Their country's geographic location on the west coast of the Iberian Peninsula determined the route the Portuguese took—southward into the Atlantic Ocean and around Africa. The Portuguese government actively encouraged and sponsored several overseas explorations.

BIOGRAPHY
Prince Henry

Prince Henry's school. Prince Henry of Portugal led the Crown's efforts to promote the study of geography and exploration. Born in 1394, he was the third son of King John I and Philippa of Lancaster. Prince Henry's strong commitment to exploration originated from his belief in God. He believed that through exploration Christianity could triumph over Islam and that this would lead to the recovery of Jerusalem. His burning desire was to find the rich African "gold kingdoms" he had heard described while fighting in Morocco. He also yearned to find an all-sea route to Asia.

Prince Henry established a center for the study of navigation around 1420. The center brought together the country's best navigators, mapmakers, and ship designers. The prince oversaw all their work. He encouraged them to experiment with new navigation methods, to draw more accurate maps, and to build ships capable of withstanding the stormy Atlantic. Prince Henry put the results to practical use by sponsoring a number of voyages of exploration southward down the African coast. Although he never sailed on any of these voyages, Prince Henry's immense contribution to Portugal's seafaring efforts earned him the nickname the Navigator.

African explorations. By the 1430s Portuguese adventurers had explored and colonized the Madeira (mah-DAYR-uh) and the Azores, groups of islands off Africa's northwest coast. The islands became important ports for resupplying ships heading to settlements on the North African coast. The Azores also served as a port of refuge for Atlantic navigators. In the 1450s the Portuguese reached the Cape Verde Islands off the coast of Senegal.

The Lives of Sailors

Modern sailor on the USS Hercules

Thanks to modern technology, the lives of sailors today are much improved over the lives of those in the 1400s. Sea travel today is much safer than ever before, and sailors enjoy fresher food than did their earlier counterparts. Some large shipping companies provide their employees with comfortable sleeping quarters, hold barbecues on board, and allow sailors' families to accompany them on voyages to ease the loneliness of life at sea. Despite such improvements on large ships, however, life for many seafarers remains difficult. Many merchant ships operate with crews of fewer than 15 people, most of whom are young men. Many crewmembers receive low wages, experience prolonged isolation during long voyages, and sometimes face abuse by their supervisors.

Sailors who make their living aboard military ships lead lives quite different from those on merchant vessels. U.S. Navy ships, for example, carry hundreds of crewmembers on board. In recent years, women have also joined naval crews in increasing numbers. Life aboard a naval ship is often extremely busy. Sailors perform a wide variety of administrative, technological, and service jobs to keep the ship ready for combat.

HOLT RESEARCHER
Read More About It

Free Find:
Henry the Navigator
After reading information about Prince Henry on the **Holt Researcher** CD–ROM, create a list of classes that students wanting to be explorers would need to take.

The exploration of Africa's west coast began primarily as a quest for scientific knowledge. It eventually gave rise to a profitable trade system for the Portuguese. One of Prince Henry's navigators, Gil Eanes (YAH-neesh), led the first expedition, bravely sailing beyond Cape Bojador—near the tip of the great bulge of western Africa. Although Prince Henry died in 1460, the work he had begun continued. Successive expeditions attempted to sail farther south down the coast. In 1474, when Portuguese king Alfonso V granted the monopoly on trading with Africa to his heir, exploration increased even more. Eight years later the Crown built the fort of São João da Mina. This was a trading base for an extensive area that included most of West Africa. By the late 1400s, trade with Africa brought the Portuguese monarchs more than 1,500 pounds of gold per year, surpassing the value of all the rest of their income combined.

✔ **READING CHECK:** How did Portugal become a leader in world exploration?

The African Slave Trade

When the Portuguese first arrived on Africa's Atlantic coast, trading consisted mostly of African spices and gold. In time, however, another business—the trade in human beings—came to dominate their dealings with Africa. Slavery was not unknown to Africans, but its form differed from what it would become under European control. Traditionally, most slaves in West African society were either criminals or captives taken in war. Their rights were restricted, but they did have some protection under the law. Most could marry, and their children did not necessarily become slaves. Moreover, slavery was usually temporary, and individuals could obtain their freedom. In time, Europeans took most of these rights away from slaves and created a system of permanent bondage from birth.

In the late 1400s, Portugal's role in the slave trade was relatively small. By the end of the following century, however, the slave trade had become a major source of income, replacing gold in economic value. The Portuguese sent many enslaved Africans to other Portuguese colonies. There they endured terrible living conditions. Eventually, the slave trade led to the **African Diaspora** (dy-AS-pruh)—the displacement of Africans from their native lands. Millions of African people were forcibly resettled on other continents. Estimates suggest that during the approximately 400 years that the slave trade operated, more than 10 million Africans were removed from their homeland as slaves. Countless more died as a result of capture or on the horrible voyage to the Americas.

The slave trade devastated African society. Villages began targeting their enemies for capture because of the enormous profits that could be made. The result was an increase in warfare among the various West African nations.

With the strong emphasis placed on family ties in African cultures, the experience of having a family member or friend captured was particularly devastating. In 1444 Gomes Eanes de Zurara (GOH-mish YAH-neesh duh zoo-RAH-ruh), the official chronicler for the Portuguese king, described the horrors brought about by the traffic in slaves:

> 66 Mothers would clasp their infants in their arms, and throw themselves on the ground to cover them with their bodies, disregarding any injury to their own persons, so that they could prevent their children from being separated from them. 99

Because of the enormous profits to be gained, however, Portugal ignored the slave trade's human costs.

✔ **READING CHECK:** How did Portugal begin its involvement in the slave trade?

A Route to the Indies

The realization by Europeans of the profits to be made from trading Asian goods prompted further searches for new routes around Africa to Asia. During the mid-1480s, Portuguese sailors came upon the mouth of the Congo River and charted the southwest coast of Africa. In 1488 Bartolomeu Dias rounded the Cape of Good Hope, Africa's southernmost tip, and established a route to the Indian Ocean. Dias went no farther, however. His crew, fearing the great expanse of unknown ocean that lay ahead of them, panicked and forced the ship to turn back.

In 1497 a fleet of four ships outfitted by Dias and commanded by Vasco da Gama set out from Portugal to complete the African voyage. By early 1498 da Gama rounded the Cape of Good Hope. In time, he made landfall on the west coast of India, finally completing a sea route to the East. Over the next 50 years, the Portuguese established trading forts in West and East Africa, India, the Spice Islands, and southern China, thereby gaining control of East-West sea trade. Other powerful nation-states of Europe, envious of Portugal's success, soon began to sponsor voyages of their own.

✔ **READING CHECK:** How did Portugal gain control of East-West trade?

INTERPRETING THE VISUAL RECORD

New trade routes. After his long voyage, Vasco da Gama and his crew met with representatives of India. *What does this image express about the economic importance of his arrival for Portugal?*

SECTION 4 REVIEW

Define and explain the significance of the following terms:
caravels
African Diaspora

Identify and explain the significance of the following individuals:
Prince Henry
King Alfonso V
Bartolomeu Dias
Vasco da Gama

Locate and explain the importance of the following places:
Spice Islands
Genoa
Venice
Portugal
Madeira Islands
Cape Verde Islands
Cape of Good Hope

1. **Using Graphic Organizers** Copy the chart below. Use it to list the steps by which Portugal came to dominate East-West trade.

   1. Technological advances occur.

   2. _____

   3. _____

   4. _____

   5. Vasco da Gama establishes an all-water East-West trade route.

2. **Hypothesizing** How might Europe's history have been different without technological advances in sailing and navigation?

3. **Using Historical Imagination** Imagine that you are a young sailor in the Middle Ages. Write a short paragraph describing your life at sea.

4. **Assessing Consequences** How did the trading practices of Portugal affect Africa?

Critical Thinking

5. How did Asian trading practices change the course of European and African history?
   Consider:
   • how Asian countries carried out trade
   • how this led to a desire for an all-sea route to the East
   • the effect this desire had on European and African history

Review

Creating a Time Line

Copy the time line below onto a sheet of paper. Complete the time line by filling in the events and dates from the chapter that you think were most significant. Pick three events and explain why you think they were significant.

5000 B.C.   1 A.D.   1500

Writing a Summary

Using the Reading Checks as a guide, write an overview of the events in the chapter.

Identifying People and Ideas

Identify the following terms or individuals and explain their significance.

1. Paleo-Indians
2. Agricultural Revolution
3. Muhammad
4. Qur'an
5. feudalism
6. Crusades
7. Isabella of Castile
8. caravels
9. Prince Henry
10. African Diaspora

Understanding Main Ideas

SECTION 1

1. What were some characteristics of the major early Native American civilizations?

SECTION 2

2. How did technology shape China?
3. What role did trade play in the development of kingdoms in Asia and Africa?

SECTION 3

4. What were the major European economic and political systems that developed in the Middle Ages?
5. How did the Renaissance emerge, and how did it change Europe?

SECTION 4

6. What advances in sailing were achieved in Europe?

Reviewing Themes

1. **Cultural Diversity** What evidence suggests that cultural exchange occurred between Native American cultures in Mesoamerica and in North America?
2. **Economic Development** How did the Crusades affect European economies?
3. **Technology and Society** How did technological advances influence cultural development in medieval Europe?

Thinking Critically

1. **Evaluating** How did the isolation of the Americas shape the history of Native American cultures?
2. **Comparing and Contrasting** Write a brief paragraph comparing daily life for people in Europe and in the Americas in the year 1200.
3. **Analyzing** How did religion influence cultural exchange among Africa, Asia, and Europe?
4. **Understanding Geography: Human-Environment Interaction** How did geography and the changing environment of the Americas affect Paleo-Indian culture?
5. **Synthesizing** What factors led to the development of nation-states? How did nation-states like Portugal affect East-West trade?

Writing About History

Writing to Create Copy the chart below. Use it to list the major characteristics of life in the 1200s in Africa, the Americas, Asia, or Europe. Then choose one of these places and write a poem or short skit about life there at the time.

Africa	Americas	Asia	Europe

Strategies **for Success** Review the **Strategies for Success** on *Reading a Time Line.* Then study the time line below and answer the questions that follow.

1419
Prince Henry of Portugal establishes a center for the study of navigation.

1488
Bartolomeu Dias rounds the Cape of Good Hope.

1400 ——— **1450** ——— **1500**

c. 1430
Portugal establishes colonies on the Madeira and Azores Islands.

c. 1462
Portuguese sailors reach Sierra Leone.

1498
Vasco da Gama travels around Africa to India.

1. What is the subject of the time line?
2. What historical developments does it illustrate?

Linking History and Geography

Study the map below. What geographic feature aided Paleo-Indians in their journey to the Americas?

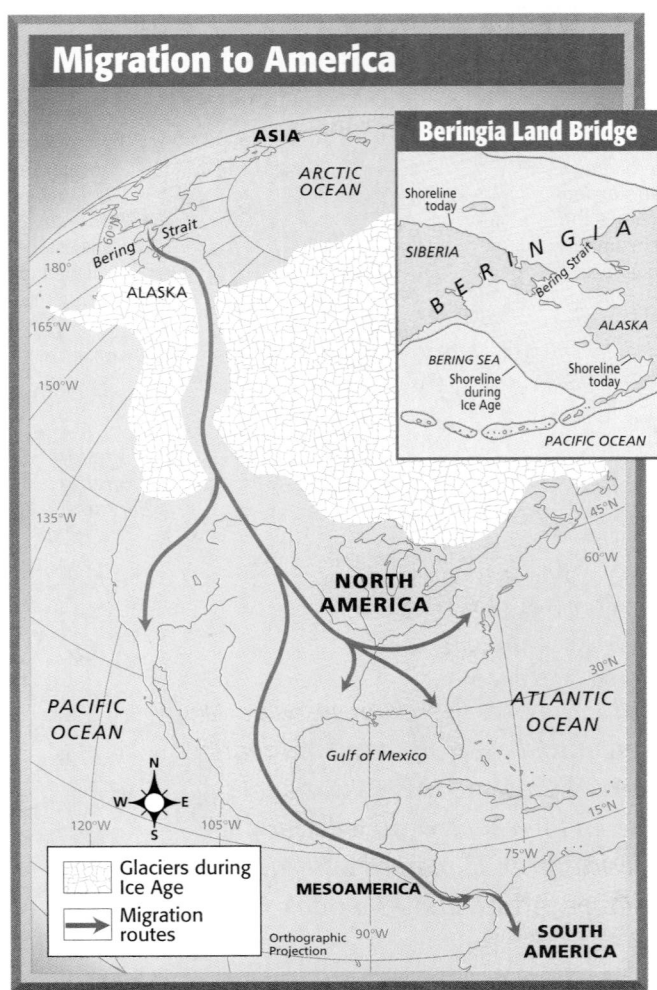

Migration to America

Beringia Land Bridge

Glaciers during Ice Age

Migration routes

internet connect

TOPIC: The Olmec Empire
GO TO: go.hrw.com
KEYWORD: SD1 Olmec

Accessing the Internet through the HRW Web site, research information about one or more of the following: the history of the Olmec, their society, why they declined, their art, and their architecture. Then create a mural or collage that displays what you have found.

BUILDING YOUR PORTFOLIO

Complete one or all of the following projects independently or cooperatively.

Caravels developed by Portuguese ship builders and navigators

1 Economic Development
Imagine that you are a trader in the late 1400s. **Prepare a map** that shows trade routes between Europe, Africa, and Asia. Draw symbols on the map to indicate major items of trade.

2 Global Relations
Imagine that you are a museum researcher preparing an exhibit on cultural exchanges in North and South America. Select two groups who appear to have had cultural contact prior to 1500. **Create a wall chart** that illustrates the nature of the contact.

3 Technology and Society
From among the compass, astrolabe, printing press, and caravel, choose the invention you think most affected the world. Then **draw a diagram or build a model** of what the invention might have looked like when it was created.

1492–1800
Empires of the Americas

Ornamented silver from the Inca Empire

English medal commemorating the defeat of the Spanish Armada

1492 World Events
Christopher Columbus lands in the Caribbean.

1494 Politics
The Treaty of Tordesillas divides the world's unexplored lands between Spain and Portugal.

1544 Business and Finance
Spanish explorers discover profitable silver mines in Potosí, Peru.

1565 World Events
Europeans establish the first permanent settlement in the present-day United States at St. Augustine, Florida.

1588 World Events
The English navy defeats the Spanish Armada.

1594 The Arts
William Shakespeare writes *Romeo and Juliet.*

1450   1500   1550   1600

1495 The Arts
Leonardo da Vinci begins his masterpiece fresco, *The Last Supper,* in Milan, Italy.

1521 Politics
Hernán Cortés captures the Aztec capital of Tenochtitlán.

1519–1522 Science and Technology
Sailor Ferdinand Magellan's expedition becomes the first to circumnavigate the globe.

1619 Politics
The first representative assembly in North America is established in Virginia.

The Last Supper by Leonardo da Vinci

Magellan planning his route

Before You Read

Build on What You Know

*I*n the 1400s a desire for trade motivated Europeans to seek an eastward sea route to Asia that would replace dangerous and expensive overland routes. Scientific and technological advances gave Europeans the navigational skills to explore greater distances than ever before. In this chapter you will learn how Christopher Columbus's arrival in the Americas in 1492 marked a turning point in world history, bringing the cultures of Europe, Africa, and Asia into contact with the Americas.

Pueblo Indians rebelling against Spanish settlers

Coffee plant

Mission Concepción

1639
Science and Technology
The first printing press in North America is used.

1680
Politics
The Pueblo Revolt drives the Spanish out of Santa Fe.

1698
Science and Technology
Paper manufacturing begins in North America.

1727
Daily Life
Coffee is first planted in Brazil.

1755
The Arts
Mission Concepción is completed in San Antonio.

1650　　　　**1700**　　　　**1750**　　　　**1800**

1670
Business and Finance
The Hudson Bay Company is formed to trade in the Hudson Bay region of North America.

1689
The Arts
Juana Inés de la Cruz publishes her first book of poetry.

1721
Daily Life
Regular postal service is established between London and New England.

c. 1765
Daily Life
The potato, originally from the Americas, is one of the most popular foods in Europe.

Title page of an early edition of de la Cruz's book of poems

Potatoes

Think About Themes

Decide whether you agree or disagree with the following statements. Note why in your journal.

Global Relations Disputes between two countries involving armed conflict usually harm other nations.

Economic Development Pouring money and energy into overseas expansion and conquest will hurt a nation's economy in the long run.

Cultural Diversity People's values and past experiences will determine how they react to new cultures they encounter.

SECTION 1

First Contact

OBJECTIVES

Read to understand:

1. why Columbus sailed west
2. how Native Americans reacted to Columbus
3. why the *encomienda* system developed, and how it affected American Indians
4. what reforms Bartolomé de Las Casas urged the Spanish Crown to undertake

KEY TERMS

viceroy
Taino
encomienda

KEY PEOPLE

Christopher Columbus
Guacanagarí
Bartolomé de Las Casas

KEY PLACES

Bahama Islands
San Salvador
Hispaniola
La Navidad

 EYEWITNESSES TO History

66 *[The islands were] full of trees of a thousand kinds, so lofty that they seem to reach the sky. . . . Some of them were in flower, some in fruit. . . . And the nightingale was singing, and other birds of a thousand sorts, in the month of November.* 99
—Christopher Columbus

Colored woodcut from 1572 of the fruit trees on the island of Hispaniola

So wrote an adventurous mariner named Christopher Columbus, who, on Friday, October 12, 1492, landed on an island in the Bahamas. The landscape and vegetation were like nothing Columbus had seen before. At once, he "broke out the royal banner, and the captain's two flags with the green cross," he later recalled, staking Spain's first claim to land in the Americas. The Spanish and other Europeans who followed them believed that these beautiful lands were theirs for the taking. As a result, European contact initiated profound changes in the Americas, Europe, and Africa. Columbus's daring voyage introduced the Americas to the rest of the world, thus beginning a new era of trade, colonization, and cultural exchange.

Christopher Columbus

By the 1400s, Europeans desired a cheaper, faster trade route to the East without going through the Mediterranean. Portugal took the lead, concentrating on finding a sea passage around the southernmost tip of Africa. Spain, however, largely because of the boldness and imagination of one man—Christopher Columbus—looked westward. In 1492 Columbus set sail from Spain on the first in a series of historic Atlantic crossings. Like most sailors of his time, Columbus believed that Earth was round. He concluded that if he sailed far enough west, he could establish a more direct trade route to Asia.

BIOGRAPHY

Christopher Columbus

THE METROPOLITAN MUSEUM OF ART

Columbus grew up in Genoa, a bustling port city on Italy's northwestern coast. Fascinated by the sea, the adventurous youth sailed on Genoese trading vessels. He quickly became an excellent navigator. A former shipmate recalled Columbus's skill: "By a simple look at the night sky, he would know what route to follow or what weather to expect."

Eventually, Columbus made his way to Lisbon, Portugal, the center of European knowledge about sea travel. While in Lisbon, he studied charts of contemporary geographers and astronomers. He also read summaries of ancient Greek and Roman texts, the Bible, and Marco Polo's exciting account of his travels in Asia. As a result of his studies, Columbus developed a theory about a westward route to Asia. Breaking with the scientific theories of the time, Columbus concluded that the western sea could not be very large. He believed that the great trading cities of Asia lay only about 2,400 miles west of Portugal. Some scholars thought it was more than 10,000 miles westward from Europe to the Indies (Asia). The actual distance to Asia did prove to be about 12,000 miles—almost five times greater than Columbus had calculated.

In the 1480s Columbus tried in vain to persuade various European monarchs to sponsor a westward voyage across the Atlantic Ocean. In 1484 he asked John II of Portugal to "give him some vessels to go and discover the Isle of Cypango [Japan, as described by Marco Polo] by this Western Ocean." King John rejected the plan because he doubted the accuracy of Columbus's calculation of the distance to Asia.

Initially, Columbus had no better luck with the Spanish monarchs, Ferdinand and Isabella. Columbus persisted, however. He described to them the golden palaces and temples of Asia mentioned in Marco Polo's tales and tempted them with visions of the riches that could belong to Spain. Columbus also vowed to take the Catholic faith to the peoples of foreign lands. This idea impressed the deeply religious Ferdinand and Isabella. Nevertheless, only after the monarchs had defeated the Muslims at Granada in January 1492 were they willing to back an expedition. On April 17, 1492, the king and queen authorized the necessary funding for Columbus's journey.

To reward Columbus for his future discoveries, Ferdinand and Isabella agreed that the mariner would be knighted, appointed an admiral, and made **viceroy**, or governor, over all the lands he might discover. In addition, he would receive at least 10 percent of the riches he obtained on Spain's behalf.

✔ **READING CHECK:** Why did Columbus sail west from Europe?

THE GRANGER COLLECTION, NEW YORK

Marco Polo's adventures were translated into many languages, inspiring many young explorers. This edition was published in Germany in the late 1400s.

The Fateful First Voyage

Columbus outfitted three ships—the *Santa María*, the *Niña*, and the *Pinta*—and recruited a crew of some 90 sailors, most of whom were Spaniards. At dawn on August 3, 1492, Columbus and his crew departed from Palos, Spain. The small fleet first journeyed approximately 820 miles southwest to the Canary Islands, Spain's westernmost possession. Going so far south allowed Columbus's ships to catch the fast-moving trade winds of the Atlantic. Then, in September, the three vessels set out for a long journey across the uncharted sea.

After a month at sea, the men aboard the three small ships had not sighted land since leaving the Canaries. The crew's patience was wearing thin. Many sailors hoped that the ships would turn back. In the early morning hours of October 12, as the lookout on the lead ship scanned the horizon, he shouted out the long-awaited cry: "*Tierra!*" Land!

The people of the Indies.
The October 12 entry in Columbus's *Journal*, his diary of the voyage, reads: "[At] daylight Friday . . . they

INTERPRETING THE VISUAL RECORD

Columbus's voyage. After a month at sea, Columbus's crew kept constant watch for any sign of land such as birds, cloudbanks, or green weeds. *Based on this image, where would be the best place to keep a lookout for signs of land?*

reached an islet . . . which was called Guanahani [gwahn-uh-HAHN-ee]." Columbus and his men struck land on a tiny coral island in the central Bahama Islands, about 400 miles southeast of present-day Florida. Columbus named the island San Salvador, meaning Holy Savior. Confident that he had reached Asia—the so-called Indies—the admiral called the island dwellers *Indios*, the Spanish word for inhabitants of the Indies.

The Native Americans Columbus encountered called themselves **Taino** (TY-noh), the word for "good" or "noble" in their Arawak language. The Taino were farmers and fishers who lived in small settlements. Some groups traded salt, shells, and other goods peacefully with their neighbors. Other groups participated in raids against neighboring islands. On the larger islands of the Caribbean, for example present-day Cuba, Hispaniola (his-puhn-YOH-luh), Jamaica, and Puerto Rico—lived groups with more complex social and political organizations.

The Spanish praised the Taino's generosity. "They invite you to share anything that they possess, and show as much love as if their hearts went with it," noted Columbus. He believed that it would be easy to convert them to Catholicism. He also took the Taino's generosity to mean that they "could all be subjugated [conquered] and compelled to do anything one wishes."

INTERPRETING THE VISUAL RECORD

Columbus's arrival. This painting, completed during the 1800s, depicts Columbus's landing on a Caribbean island. *What clues does this painting provide about the purposes behind Columbus's voyage?*

The search for gold. Because some of the Taino wore small gold ornaments, Columbus concluded that gold mines must be close at hand. Over the next month, the explorers sailed from island to island—naming and claiming each for Spain—in search of gold. Then, on Christmas Eve, 1492, the *Santa María* either landed or was shipwrecked off the island that Columbus had named Hispaniola—the site of present-day Haiti and the Dominican Republic. Columbus decided to establish the first Spanish colony there. He named the settlement La Navidad, meaning the nativity, in honor of the day of its founding.

Like the inhabitants of Guanahani, the American Indians of Hispaniola were generous to the Spanish. Their chief, Guacanagarí (gwah-kahn-uh-gah-REE), showered Columbus with gold nuggets and ornaments—even promising "a statue of pure gold" the size of Columbus himself. This impressive display convinced some of Columbus's men to remain in the settlement.

Columbus sailed back to Spain in January 1493, taking with him two dozen Taino captives and evidence of the riches of the Indies. Ferdinand and Isabella gave him a hero's welcome. They greeted Columbus with the titles they had promised: "Admiral of the Ocean Sea, Viceroy and Governor of the Islands that he hath discovered in the Indies." The monarchs speedily approved a second voyage.

The captive islanders became the objects of both sympathy and curiosity in Spain. The queen ordered that the Indians on Hispaniola and elsewhere in the Americas be treated humanely and converted to the Roman Catholic faith. However, she left open the possibility that anyone who resisted the authority of the Spanish Crown could be enslaved.

✔ **READING CHECK:** How did the Native Americans react to Columbus?

HOLT RESEARCHER

Read More About It

Free Find: Columbus and the Taino

After reading the letter in which Columbus describes his contact with the Taino on the **Holt Researcher** CD–ROM, imagine that you are a Taino Indian. In that role, write your own letter to a friend describing your experience and thoughts when you saw Columbus for the first time.

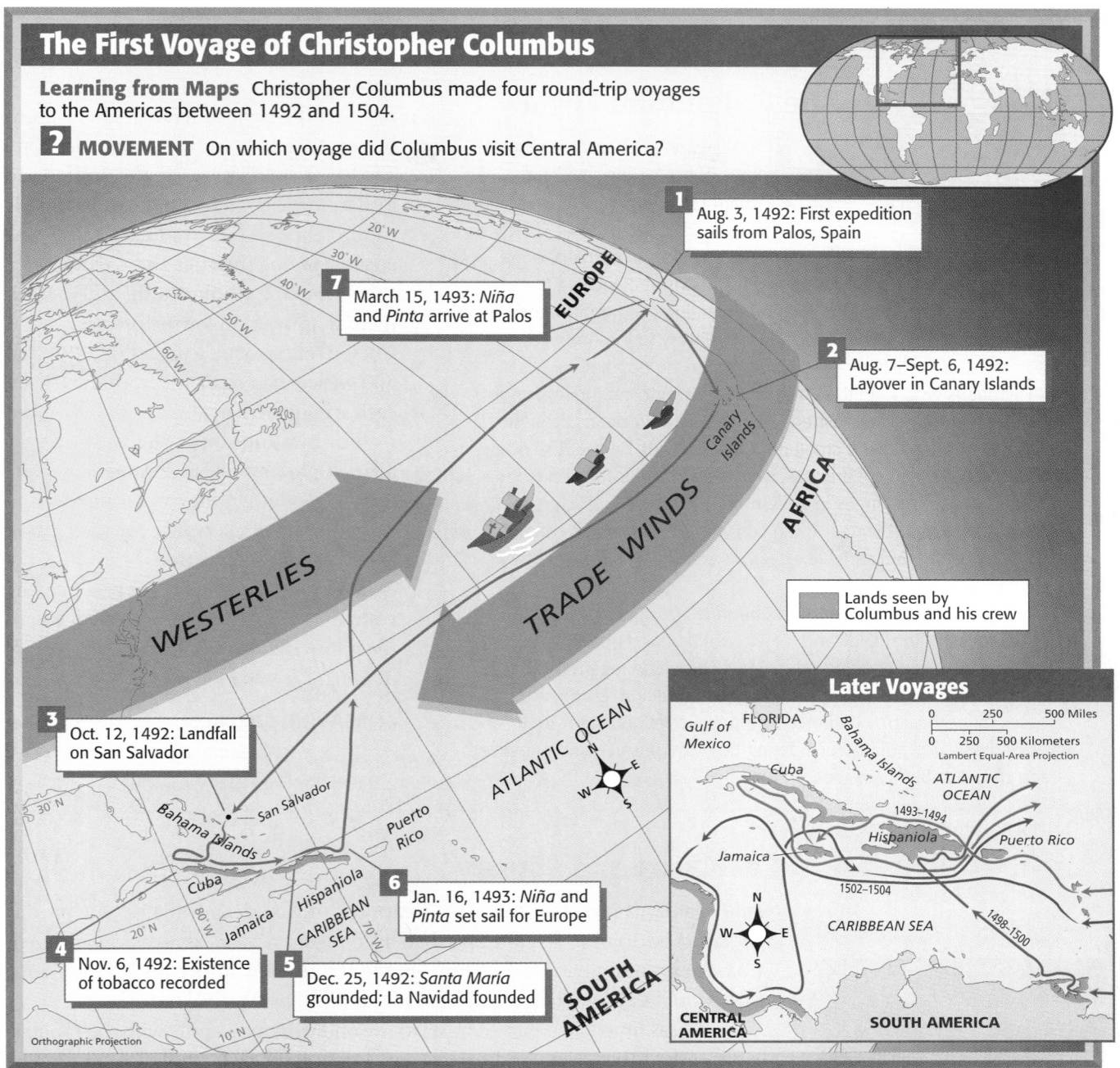

The First Voyage of Christopher Columbus

Learning from Maps Christopher Columbus made four round-trip voyages to the Americas between 1492 and 1504.

? MOVEMENT On which voyage did Columbus visit Central America?

1 Aug. 3, 1492: First expedition sails from Palos, Spain

2 Aug. 7–Sept. 6, 1492: Layover in Canary Islands

7 March 15, 1493: *Niña* and *Pinta* arrive at Palos

3 Oct. 12, 1492: Landfall on San Salvador

4 Nov. 6, 1492: Existence of tobacco recorded

5 Dec. 25, 1492: *Santa María* grounded; La Navidad founded

6 Jan. 16, 1493: *Niña* and *Pinta* set sail for Europe

Lands seen by Columbus and his crew

WESTERLIES

TRADE WINDS

ATLANTIC OCEAN

EUROPE

AFRICA

Canary Islands

Bahama Islands

San Salvador

Puerto Rico

Cuba

Jamaica

Hispaniola

CARIBBEAN SEA

SOUTH AMERICA

Orthographic Projection

Later Voyages

FLORIDA

Gulf of Mexico

Bahama Islands

Cuba

ATLANTIC OCEAN

1493–1494

Hispaniola

Jamaica

Puerto Rico

1502–1504

1498–1500

CARIBBEAN SEA

CENTRAL AMERICA

SOUTH AMERICA

0   250   500 Miles
0   250   500 Kilometers
Lambert Equal-Area Projection

Columbus the colonizer. When Columbus returned to La Navidad 11 months later, he found the colony destroyed. All the Spaniards were dead or gone. Some probably had left to find gold, but most had either fallen victim to illness or died in disputes with one another or with the Taino. Columbus ordered the construction of another settlement, Isabela. He then left the settlement under the care of his brother Bartolomé and spent the next three years sailing the Caribbean searching for gold. While Columbus was away, the pressure the colonists put on the Taino to provide food and gold provoked the Indians to revolt. Columbus's failure to maintain order eventually led the monarchs to replace him as viceroy.

Before his replacement, Columbus granted the colonists control over Indian labor, introducing what would become the *encomienda* (en-koh-mee-EN-duh).

Great Debates

The Columbian Legacy

Historians offer different interpretations of the lasting significance of Columbus's voyages to the Americas. In 1992 the 500th anniversary of Columbus's first voyage brought these differences of opinion to the height of historical debate. Traditional historians applauded Columbus for expanding Western civilization and enlarging geographic knowledge. Others blamed him for introducing slavery to the Americas and for the massive reduction of the Native American population.

Historians who hold the traditional viewpoint see the legacy of Columbus's voyage as almost entirely positive: Europeans brought civilization to the relatively small populations living on the American continents. European culture, they argue, was significantly enriched as contact brought changes in government, religion, and science. Eventually the United States—often considered the world's champion of democracy and individual liberty—was created as a result of this contact between hemispheres.

Other historians believe that Columbus's voyage had fatal consequences for both the "Old" and "New" worlds. They note that the Europeans enslaved people and generally had little regard for the cultural heritage of the peoples they met. In addition, European diseases helped destroy entire civilizations. Some historians try to balance these viewpoints, considering both the positive and negative effects of Columbus's voyages.

Under this system the colonists, or *encomenderos* (en-koh-muhn-DE-rohs), received the right to have a certain number of American Indians work for them. The *encomenderos* used the Indians to build houses, mine gold, and provide food. The system required that the *encomenderos* instruct their workers in the Roman Catholic faith and permit them to grow food for themselves.

Queen Isabella learned in 1499 that 300 settlers had returned from the Indies, each with an American Indian slave given to him by Columbus. She became very angry. In her eyes, Native Americans were not slaves. Rather, they were supposed to be paid a small allowance for their labor. Over Isabella's objections, however, the *encomienda* continued. In practice the system amounted to group enslavement for many Indians because they were seldom paid.

✔ **READING CHECK:** What was the purpose of the *encomienda* system? How did it affect Native Americans?

Las Casas and Slavery

Some Spaniards protested the harsh treatment of American Indians. One prominent critic, Bartolomé de Las Casas, had lived for some years as an *encomendero* in Cuba. He spent a great deal of time giving the Indians under his care religious instruction. Las Casas, however, began to question the system.

Las Casas urged Spanish colonists to live and work peacefully with the Indians. He also asked that friars and priests convert Indians to Catholicism gradually, through "love, gentleness, and kindness." In his *Apologetic History of the Indies,* published in 1566, he argued that the Indians' humanity equaled that of Europeans.

Bartolomé de Las Casas urged the Spanish government and settlers to treat the Indians with more humanity.

66 Not only have [the Indians] shown themselves to be very wise peoples and possessed of lively and marked understanding, . . . but they have equaled many diverse nations of the . . . past and present . . . and exceed by no small measure the wisest of all these. 99

Few Spaniards shared the views of Las Casas. Within a century, however, the *encomienda* had largely ended as a consequence of the enormous decline of the American Indian population, rather than of humanitarian concerns. Overwork and malnutrition contributed to the decline, but disease took by far the greatest toll.

European diseases proved particularly deadly because the American Indians had no immunity to them. The Western Hemisphere's isolation from the rest of the world meant that American Indians had never been exposed to common illnesses in Europe and Africa such as chickenpox, measles, smallpox, and typhus. When Europeans and Africans arrived in the Americas, they unknowingly introduced the organisms that caused these diseases.

In some remote areas the epidemics preceded the appearance of the Europeans, since the diseases spread easily from Indian to Indian. No doubt the resulting devastation made it much easier for the Spanish to conquer the Indians. One Maya chronicle records the effects of an epidemic.

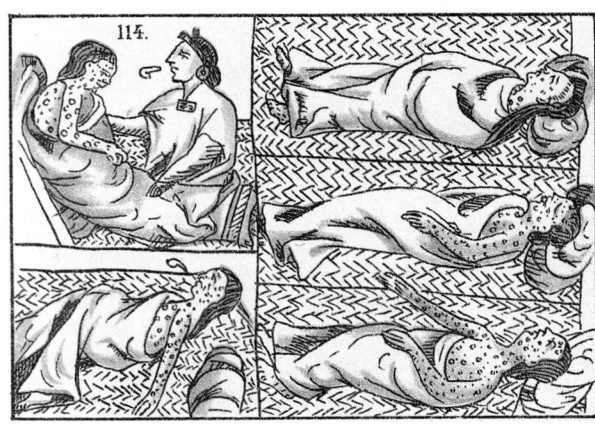

66 Great was the stench of the dead. After our fathers and grandfathers succumbed [died], half of the people fled to the fields. . . . The mortality was terrible. Your grandfathers died, and with them died the son of the king and his brothers and kinsmen. So it was that we became orphans, oh, my sons! So we became when we were young. All of us were thus. 99

Although the death rate for American Indians varied, in some areas their numbers had declined by more than 90 percent by the mid-1500s. To replace the Indian laborers, the Spanish began importing African slaves. The first slaves reached the West Indies in the early 1500s. By 1540 at least 10,000 enslaved Africans were arriving annually in the Spanish colonies. Many enslaved Africans performed hard labor on sugar plantations or other large farms. This is a tragic example of how European exploration in the Americas affected people's lives throughout the world.

✔ **READING CHECK:** What reforms did Bartolomé de Las Casas urge the Spanish Crown to undertake?

SECTION 1 REVIEW

Define and explain the significance of the following terms:
viceroy
Taino
encomienda

Identify and explain the significance of the following individuals:
Christopher Columbus
Guacanagarí
Bartolomé de Las Casas

Locate and explain the importance of the following places:
Bahama Islands
San Salvador
Hispaniola
La Navidad

1. **Using Graphic Organizers** Copy the chart below. Compare the goals that various people had for American Indians and the methods they proposed for achieving those goals.

	Goals for American Indians	Methods
Columbus		
Isabella		
Las Casas		

2. **Analyzing** How did the *encomienda* system benefit the Spanish settlers? What effect did it have on American Indians?

3. **Assessing Consequences** Why did the reforms that Bartolomé de Las Casas proposed for American Indians achieve only limited success?

4. **Using Historical Imagination** Imagine that you are a Taino living on San Salvador. Draw or describe a plan for a mural that portrays your interactions with the Spanish explorers.

Critical Thinking

5. How did European trading goals change the course of the history of the Americas?
   Consider:
   • how trade led to the search for new trade routes
   • how this search affected Columbus's route
   • how Columbus's landing in the Americas shaped its history

Conquest of the Mainland

OBJECTIVES

Read to understand:

1. who the early European explorers of America were
2. how Hernán Cortés conquered the Aztec
3. what methods Francisco Pizarro used to conquer the Inca
4. how American Indians responded to the conquistadores

KEY TERMS

Treaty of Tordesillas
circumnavigate
conquistadores

KEY PEOPLE

Vasco Núñez de Balboa
Ferdinand Magellan
Álvar Núñez Cabeza de Vaca
Hernán Cortés
Malintzin
Moctezuma II
Francisco Pizarro

KEY PLACES

Isthmus of Panama
Cajamarca

EYEWITNESSES TO History

66 *Since our Redeemer has given this victory to our most illustrious King and Queen ... for this all Christendom ought to feel joyful and make celebrations ... with many ... prayers for the great exaltation which it will have, in the turning of so many peoples to our holy faith, and afterwards for material benefits, since not only Spain but all Christians will hence have refreshments and profit.* 99
—Christopher Columbus

King John II of Portugal

Christopher Columbus prepared this letter to Ferdinand and Isabella as he made his triumphant voyage back to Europe in 1493 to inform them of his discovery. Before arriving in Spain, however, he stopped at Lisbon, Portugal, to repair his ship. While there, he proudly announced his success in finding what he believed was a shorter sea route to the Indies to King John II. Earlier the king had dismissed Columbus's ideas and had declined to finance his voyage. The king surprised Columbus by immediately claiming Columbus's new lands for Portugal. Columbus was unaware that a previous treaty with Spain had awarded lands discovered south of the latitude of the Canary Islands to Portugal.

Exploring the Americas

The Portuguese viewed Christopher Columbus's Spanish voyages as a serious threat to their control of the Atlantic. To avoid further boundary disputes, the two Catholic countries agreed to divide control over any newly encountered lands. In 1494 they signed the **Treaty of Tordesillas** (tawr-day-SEEL-yahs). This treaty shifted the earlier north-south Line of Demarcation, or separation, established by Pope Alexander VI. It drew a new Line of Demarcation around the world. Territory explored west of the line would belong to Spain; east of the line, to Portugal.

Maps like this one helped Portuguese navigators explore South America during the 1500s.

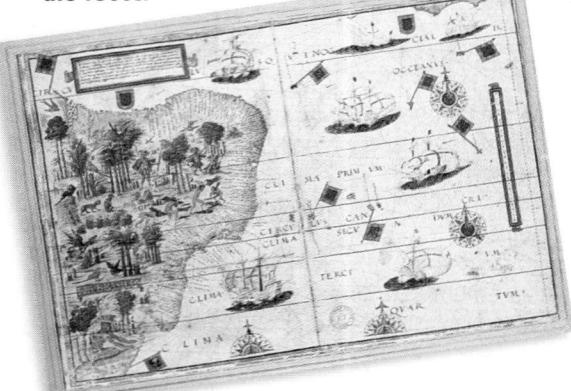

The Pacific. Some explorers traveled to the lands of North America and South America, claiming them for Spain. In 1513 Vasco Núñez de Balboa (NOON-yays day bahl-BOH-uh) explored the area now known as Panama. Balboa crossed the Isthmus of Panama and came upon a great body of water, which he called the South Sea. Balboa was probably the first European to glimpse this body of water—later named the Pacific, or "peaceful," Ocean—from the Americas.

Ferdinand Magellan was a Portuguese mariner sponsored by the Spanish Crown. He believed that by sailing west of the Line of Demarcation he could find a water passageway around the Americas leading to the Indies. As with Columbus, the Portuguese king rejected Magellan's plan to find a westward route to Asia. Magellan took his proposal to the king of Spain. He reasoned that the treasured Spice Islands would fall west of the Line of Demarcation—and therefore belong to Spain if discovered. Bartolomé de Las Casas described the sailor's interview with the king.

> 66 Magellan brought with him a well-painted globe showing the entire world, and thereon traced the course he proposed to take, save that the Strait was purposely left blank so that nobody could anticipate him. . . . This [Ferdinand Magellan] must have been a brave man, valiant in thought and for undertaking great things. 99

Although at least one Portuguese historian considered him a traitor, Magellan exhibited remarkable ability, courage, and skill. The Spanish king granted his request.

In 1519 Magellan set out to find a way to pass the Americas and continue on to Asia. He found the passageway he sought at the southern tip of South America. After threading through the turbulent, narrow waterway, Magellan triumphantly sailed into the Pacific Ocean. Although he had succeeded in finding a westward route to Asia, Magellan died before he could return to Spain. He lost his life in a battle with the natives of the Philippine Islands. In September 1522 the *Victoria*—the only ship remaining of Magellan's five-vessel fleet—sailed into the harbor near Cádiz (KAH-dees), Spain. Captain Juan Sebastián de Elcano (el-KAHN-oh) and his 17 shipmates. Among only 35 survivors of the original 250 or so people on the expedition, they became the first people to successfully **circumnavigate**, or sail completely around, the world.

Magellan. Attempting to find a westward route to Asia, Magellan used tools like this sundial with a compass inside. *How would these tools aid Magellan in his voyage around the world?*

The South and Southwest. Not every explorer was successful in reaching his goals. In the 1520s Pánfilo de Narváez (PAHN-fee-loh day nahr-BAH-ays) led a failed attempt to colonize North America's coastline along the Gulf of Mexico for Spain. One by one, the ships in Narváez's fleet disappeared or were shipwrecked. After his ship capsized near Galveston Island, Álvar Núñez Cabeza de Vaca (kah-BAY-sah day BAH-kah) swam ashore with some 80 other survivors. The men "escaped [as] naked as we were born," Cabeza de Vaca wrote, "and our bodies were so emaciated . . . that we looked like pictures of death." Within a few months, just 15 men were still alive. Cabeza de Vaca and three other men began walking from village to village. Eventually they traveled through present-day Texas, New Mexico, and Arizona.

In 1539 Estevanico, an African who was one of the original explorers traveling with Cabeza de Vaca, became the first non-Indian to visit the Pueblo Indians in present-day New Mexico. In the 1540s Spanish explorer Hernando de Soto explored southeastern North America and the Mississippi River. Around the same time, Francisco Vásquez de Coronado marched through the present-day southwestern United States. His group was looking for the "Seven Cities of Gold," believed to be further in the interior. Although his group never found the mythical cities of wealth, their explorations paved the way for many later explorers.

✔ **READING CHECK:** Who were the early Spanish and Portuguese explorers of the Americas?

Building Vocabulary

In your study of history, you will regularly come across new and unfamiliar words. Learning the meaning of these words will enlarge your vocabulary and help you understand new information and ideas.

How to Build Vocabulary

1. **Identify new words.** As you read your textbook or supplemental assignments, create a list of words that you cannot pronounce or define. When reading *Boyer's The American Nation*, make sure to review the key terms at the beginning of each section.
2. **Study the context of new words.** Study the paragraph and the sentence where you find a new word. This context, or setting, may provide clues to the word's meaning through examples or a definition using more familiar words.
3. **Use a dictionary.** Use a dictionary to learn the pronunciation and the precise meaning of each word on your list.

4. **Review new vocabulary words.** Look for ways to use new words—in homework assignments, classroom discussions, or even everyday conversation. The best way to master a new word is to use it.

Applying the Strategy

As you read Section 2, create a list of the new words that you encounter in the text. Write down what you think each word means, then check your definitions against those in a dictionary.

Practicing the Strategy

Answer the following questions.
1. What does the word *circumnavigate* mean? How did its use in the section help you arrive at this definition?
2. What does the word *conquistador* mean? How did its use in the section help you arrive at this definition?
3. What does the word *encomienda* mean? How did its use in the section help you arrive at this definition?

The Spanish Encounter the Aztec

Spanish conquerors, known as **conquistadores** (kahn-kees-tuh-DAWR-eez), soon followed in the footsteps of the early explorers. By the early 1500s, Spanish soldiers set out to conquer the Americas, to gain riches for themselves, and to spread the Catholic religion throughout the world.

Hernán Cortés. One of the most able and adventurous of the conquistadores was Hernán Cortés. A professional soldier, Cortés settled in Cuba as an *encomendero*. Intrigued by stories of gold on the Mexican mainland, Cortés gathered a force of some 600 Spaniards and enslaved Africans and set sail in February 1519. On the Mexican coast Cortés's army battled American Indians. They defeated the Indians, and through them he learned much about the wealthy Aztec Empire.

Living among these coastal Indians was a young Aztec princess known as Malintzin (mah-LINT-suhn), or Malinche (mah-LEEN-chay), and also called Doña Marina by the Spanish. Malintzin became a valuable interpreter and adviser to Cortés. She revealed Aztec weaknesses to the ambitious soldier, explaining that many Indian groups hated the Aztec. Indians conquered by the Aztec were occasionally sacrificed to appease the Aztec war god, while others bore heavy tax burdens imposed by the empire. Armed with this knowledge, Cortés set off to confront the Aztec ruler, Moctezuma (MAWK-tay-SOO-mah) II.

Moctezuma learned of Cortés's arrival almost immediately. A scout who witnessed the Spanish defeat of the coastal Indians raced on foot to the capital city of

Aztec princess Malintzin provided crucial information to Hernán Cortés that helped him conquer the Aztec Empire.

Tenochtitlán. He told Moctezuma of the pale-skinned men who rode horses—which they thought were deer. The scout reported that these bearded strangers were taller than a house and had cannons powerful enough to crack a hole in the side of a mountain.

The deeply religious Aztec ruler contemplated this amazing news. According to an ancient prophecy, a light-skinned god called Quetzalcoatl (kwet-suhl-kuh-WAH-tuhl) would one day return to rule over the Aztec. Moctezuma feared that the prophecy was now coming true.

Moctezuma believed that the god's arrival would mean the end of his reign. He sent gold and other gifts to Cortés to persuade him not to come to Tenochtitlán. Instead, the gifts made Cortés even more determined to conquer the Aztec.

Cortés conquers the Aztec. To defeat the Aztec, Cortés, with Malintzin's help, persuaded American Indians who had been defeated by the Aztec to join his forces. Cortés's army of Indian recruits grew to several thousand as he led them closer and closer to the Aztec capital.

Moctezuma welcomed Cortés as an honored guest. The determined conquistador, however, imprisoned Moctezuma. Cortés let the ruler retain his title—though not his power—as emperor of the Aztec.

This fragile arrangement collapsed when Cortés left Tenochtitlán. In his absence his lieutenant, Pedro de Alvarado, ordered the killing of scores of men, women, and children attending an Aztec religious ceremony. The Aztec fought back. When Cortés returned, he found the Aztec capital in chaos. In desperation, he urged Moctezuma to try to calm his angry subjects. Many Aztec no longer trusted their ruler, however. When Moctezuma attempted to intervene, he was killed. Spanish and Aztec sources dispute which side murdered the emperor.

With Moctezuma dead and the Aztec in full revolt, the Spanish knew they had no choice but to leave the capital. They tried to flee during the night by crossing the main causeway over Lake Texcoco, but a woman drawing water sounded an alarm. Thousands of Aztec attacked the Spanish. The Spanish managed to leave the city, but heavy casualties resulted on both sides.

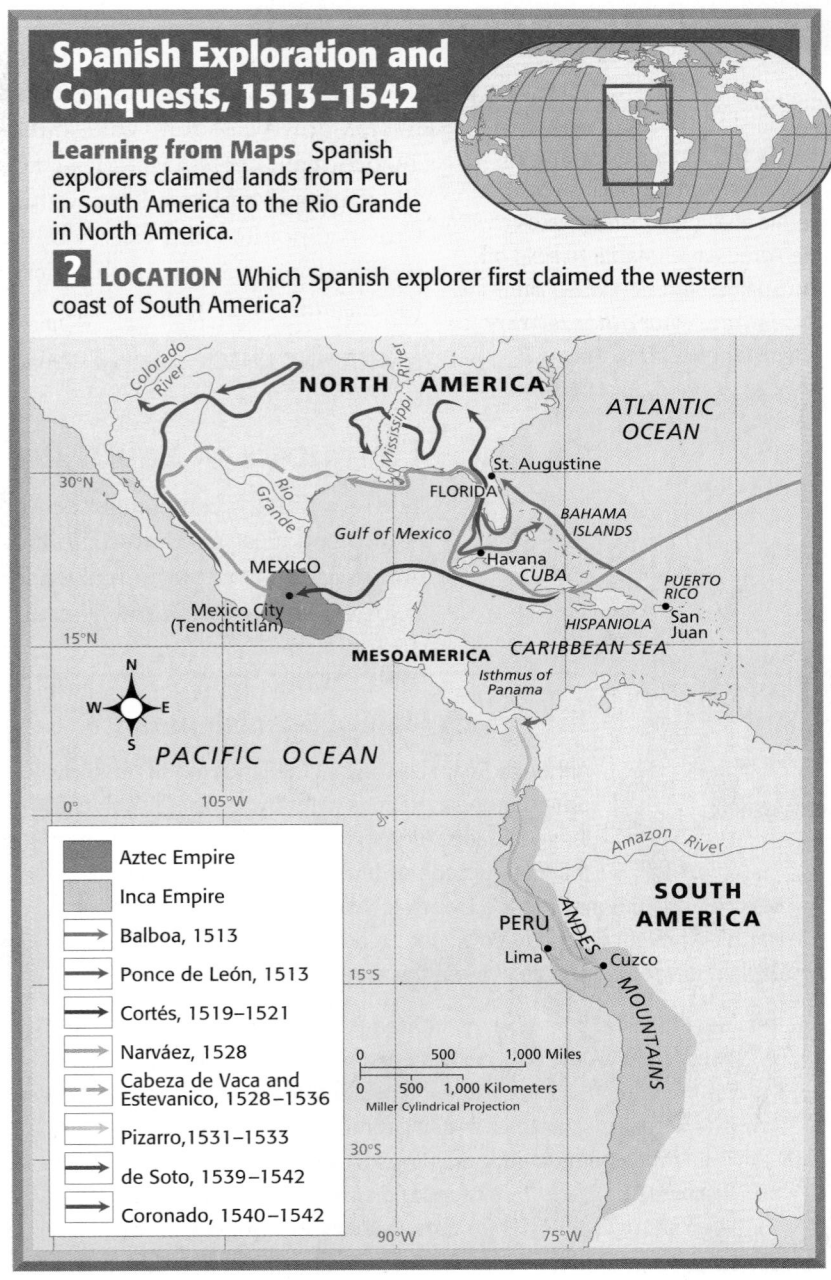

Spanish Exploration and Conquests, 1513–1542

Learning from Maps Spanish explorers claimed lands from Peru in South America to the Rio Grande in North America.

? LOCATION Which Spanish explorer first claimed the western coast of South America?

Aztec Empire
Inca Empire
Balboa, 1513
Ponce de León, 1513
Cortés, 1519–1521
Narváez, 1528
Cabeza de Vaca and Estevanico, 1528–1536
Pizarro, 1531–1533
de Soto, 1539–1542
Coronado, 1540–1542

In the following months Cortés regrouped his forces and obtained reinforcements. In May 1521 he attacked the capital city of Tenochtitlán. A four-month siege by the Spaniards left the Aztec worn-out and starving. A smallpox epidemic that swept through the city further weakened the native population. On August 13 Cortés attacked again, and the great city fell. Soon he controlled all of central Mexico. An Aztec poet expressed his people's sadness at defeat.

> 66 Broken spears lie in the roads;
> we have torn our hair in our grief.
> The houses are roofless now, and their walls
> are red with blood. 99

After the conquest the Spanish leveled Aztec temples and other buildings and destroyed Aztec works of art. They also melted down elaborate gold jewelry and shipped it to Spain. Over the ruins of Tenochtitlán, Cortés built Mexico City, the present-day capital of Mexico.

Cortés lived like a king within the conquered region. In 1522 the Spanish Crown appointed him viceroy of the region. As Cortés quickly became one of the wealthiest people in Spanish America, the proud Aztec people were absorbed into the *encomienda* system.

✔ **READING CHECK:** How did Hernán Cortés conquer the Aztec?

INTERPRETING THE VISUAL RECORD

Battle for Tenochtitlán.
Suffering from a smallpox epidemic and a lack of resources, the Aztec were unable to hold off the Spanish forces. *Based on this image, what other military advantages did the Spanish have over the Aztec warriors?*

Conquests in South America

The Inca Empire, centered in the Andes of South America, became Spain's next target for conquest. In 1531–32 Francisco Pizarro (pee-SAHR-roh), a Spanish soldier and treasure hunter who had explored with Balboa, led a small army to the very heart of the empire. Traveling cautiously along steep, narrow passes, they reached the town of Cajamarca (kah-hah-MAHR-kah) in present-day northern Peru.

Pizarro conquers the Inca. After Pizarro lured the Inca ruler, Atahualpa (ah-tah-WAHL-pah), to his camp, a Spanish priest told Atahualpa that the Inca must convert to Catholicism. Atahualpa asked to see the book—the Bible—that "spoke" their god's words. According to an Inca account:

> 66 [Atahualpa] took the book and began to leaf through its pages. And the Inca said, 'Why does it not speak to me? This book tells me nothing!' And . . . [Atahualpa] threw the book from his hands. 99

THROUGH OTHERS' EYES

The French View of Spanish America

Although Spain claimed all the lands in the Americas, other European nations with strong navies soon challenged Spanish dominance in the region. The riches that conquistadores brought back to Spain from Mexico and Peru inspired the French to search for other lands farther north that might be rich in gold. One French scholar of the period explained why his people entered the race for empires:

> 66 The French above all were spurred [motivated] by a desire to do likewise in areas that had not been reached by [the Spaniards], for the French did not esteem [consider] themselves less than [the Spaniards], neither in navigation . . . nor in any other calling. The French persuaded themselves that [the Spaniards] had not discovered all, and that the world was large enough to reveal even stranger things than those already known. 99

Atahualpa's actions outraged the Spaniards, who attacked the Inca and captured the emperor. To gain his freedom, Atahualpa promised to fill his large prison quarters with gold and silver. Desperate to save their emperor-god, the Inca delivered a large ransom in gold and silver. Pizarro accepted the ransom but ordered Atahualpa killed, not freed.

After Pizarro's arrival in Cajamarca, an internal dispute divided the Inca people. One group allied with Pizarro, and the other group retreated to a remote area of the Andes where they resisted the Spanish for many years. Control of the vast South American empire eventually passed into Spanish hands, however.

✔ **READING CHECK:** How did Pizarro conquer the Inca?

Postconquest American Indian society.
To maintain control over the conquered American Indians, Spanish military forces often went to desperate lengths to wipe out American Indian cultures. They tore down Indian temples, destroyed Indian art, and reorganized Indian settlements. American Indian cultures were not completely destroyed, however. They live on in the people and customs of most modern Latin American nations today.

Some American Indians resisted the influence of Spanish culture. Others realized that survival of their heritage meant the mixing of Spanish and American Indian culture. Some Indian tribes eagerly adopted European trading goods such as cattle, horses, and tools. Many Indians created a new religion by mixing their practices with Catholic rituals. Over time, both American Indians and Spaniards adopted elements of the other's language and customs. Eventually, a new culture emerged that blended ingredients of American Indian and Spanish ways of life.

✔ **READING CHECK:** How did American Indians respond to the conquistadores?

INTERPRETING THE VISUAL RECORD

Catholicism. Father Valverde discussed his Catholic faith with Atahualpa and the Inca. *How does Father Valverde use religious symbols to explain his faith?*

SECTION 2 REVIEW

Define and explain the significance of the following terms:
Treaty of Tordesillas
circumnavigate
conquistadores

Identify and explain the significance of the following individuals:
Vasco Núñez de Balboa
Ferdinand Magellan
Álvar Núñez Cabeza de Vaca
Hernán Cortés
Malintzin
Moctezuma II
Francisco Pizarro

Locate and explain the importance of the following places:
Isthmus of Panama
Cajamarca

1. **Using Graphic Organizers** Copy the flow chart below. List the explorers who came to the Americas, the peoples they encountered (if any), and the outcome of their explorations.

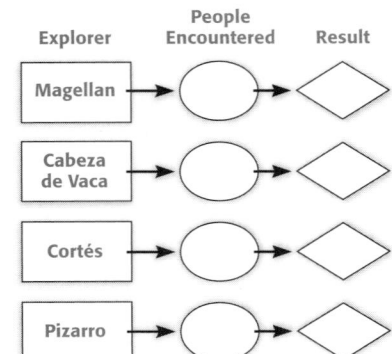

2. **Identifying Cause and Effect** Why did the Spanish explorers come to the Americas? How did their motives shape their actions?
3. **Hypothesizing** Why do you think the Spaniards tore down Aztec temples? What impact do you think this had on Aztec religion?
4. **Recognizing Point of View** How could the actions of some American Indians be seen as an attempt to preserve their culture?

Critical Thinking

5. How did Cortés use various aspects of Aztec culture and society to help him conquer the Aztec Empire?
   Consider:
   • how the Aztec ruled their subjects
   • what role the Aztec religion played in Cortés's conquest
   • how Malintzen helped Cortés to defeat the Aztec

The Spanish Settle the Americas

OBJECTIVES

Read to understand:

1. where the Spanish established settlements in North America
2. how missions, haciendas, and ranchos aided Spanish rule
3. which elements of Spanish culture affected the Americas

KEY TERMS

Pueblo Revolt
viceroyalties
peons

KEY PEOPLE

Pedro Menéndez de Avilés
Juan de Oñate
Popé
Juan Rodríguez Cabrillo
Junípero Serra
Juana Inés de la Cruz

KEY PLACES

Florida
St. Augustine
Santa Fe
San Diego
San Francisco

66 *Believing [the] land to be an island, they named it* La Florida . . . *because they discovered it at the season, which the Spaniards call* Pascua Florida *[the Floral Passover]. . . . Ponce . . . went ashore to discover and take possession.* 99

—Antonio de Herrera

The search for the "Fountain of Youth"

Antonio de Herrera, Spain's official historian at the time, described the European claim of Florida by the crew of a red-haired conquistador named Juan Ponce de León. In the spring of 1513 the crew set sail northward from the islands of the Caribbean. The goal of this voyage was to find the legendary "Fountain of Youth"—rumored to be on an island north of Cuba. After sighting land, the fleet sailed along the coastline seeking a safe harbor and finally anchored near shore on April 2. Florida quickly became an important base for the Spanish, who used the newly discovered strong current of the Gulf Stream to give their ships a powerful boost on their way back to Europe. However, Ponce de León never found his Fountain of Youth.

Spanish Settlements in North America

The explorations and conquests of Hernán Cortés, Francisco Pizarro, and others enabled Spain to claim vast portions of the Americas. Over the next two centuries, the Spanish fanned out from Mexico City—the center of their North American empire called New Spain—and from their island colonies in the Caribbean. Armed with the soldier's sword and the priest's cross, they went to gain riches and to spread the Roman Catholic faith.

Florida. By the early 1500s the Spanish already had turned their attention to La Florida. This was a territory encompassing the entire eastern seaboard from present-day Florida to Newfoundland. Because Spanish ships from the Caribbean often sailed up the Atlantic coast on their way back to Europe, Spain wanted to establish settlements to provide safe harbors.

One early attempt to establish a permanent settlement in Florida took place in 1526. Lucas Vázquez de Ayllón (yl-YAWN) led some 500 colonists from Hispaniola to a site believed to be on the coast of either present-day Georgia or South Carolina. The expedition, which included families, missionaries, and African slaves, built San Miguel de Gualdape (gwahl-DAHP-ay). The colony did not survive the first winter, however. Sick and too weak to farm or to catch fish, nearly two thirds of the settlers perished. The others straggled back to Hispaniola in early 1527.

Spanish settlers built sturdy defenses such as this one in St. Augustine, Florida, to protect their harbors from raiding forces.

Attempts to establish a colony farther south along the Florida coast met with other difficulties. American Indian groups living in the area—such as the Apalachee, Calusa, and Timucua (tim-uh-KOOUH)—fought the Spanish to prevent them from settling in the area. In 1565, however, an expedition led by Pedro Menéndez de Avilés (may-NAYN-days day ah-bee-LAYS) at last succeeded in planting a permanent settlement in Florida. This settlement was St. Augustine, the oldest city established by Europeans within the boundaries of the present-day United States.

New Mexico and Arizona.
Some 1,500 miles west of St. Augustine, Juan de Oñate established the first Spanish settlement in New Mexico in 1598. Under Oñate's leadership, Spanish forces set out to explore and conquer all the lands and Indians in the area. Oñate resigned as governor in 1607 and seven years later was convicted of cruelty, immorality, and lying while he had been in office.

In 1609, the newly appointed governor of New Mexico, Pedro de Peralta (pay-RAHL-tah), established New Mexico's capital at Santa Fe. From this outpost, the Spanish maintained a fragile hold on the northernmost borderland of New Spain for more than 200 years. The Pueblo Indians and the Spanish struggled bitterly for control of this territory. The Pueblo resented Spanish demands that they pay taxes and convert to Catholicism. In 1680 the Pueblo drove the Spanish out of Santa Fe. Under the leadership of Popé (poh-PAY), a Pueblo prophet, the Pueblo launched a series of attacks against Spanish settlers. By the time the **Pueblo Revolt** had ended, some 400 Spaniards lay dead, and some 2,000 settlers had fled south. After the American Indians drove the Spanish out, Pueblo witnesses recalled:

> 66 Popé . . . ordered . . . that they instantly break up and burn . . . everything pertaining to Christianity. . . . They were ordered likewise not to teach the Castilian [Spanish] language in any pueblo and to burn the seeds which the Spaniards sowed and to plant only maize and beans, which were the crops of their ancestors. 99

Popé hoped that the destruction of all traces of Spanish culture would help the Pueblo recover their way of life. The Pueblo regained control of their territory only temporarily, however. In the 1690s New Mexico's new governor, Diego de Vargas, re-established Spanish rule. At the same time, the Spanish began moving into present-day Arizona. Father Eusebio Kino (yoo-sayb-yoh KEE-noh) built missions near present-day Nogales (noh-GAHL-es) in 1687 and Tucson in 1700. Kino also explored the southern reaches of the Colorado River.

During the 1700s fears of French and British expansion prompted the Spanish to intensify their colonization of the southwestern United States. They established forts called presidios and religious communities called missions in addition to large ranches, villages, and towns. The Spanish influences on the Southwest can still be seen in the many Spanish place names and in the culture of the region.

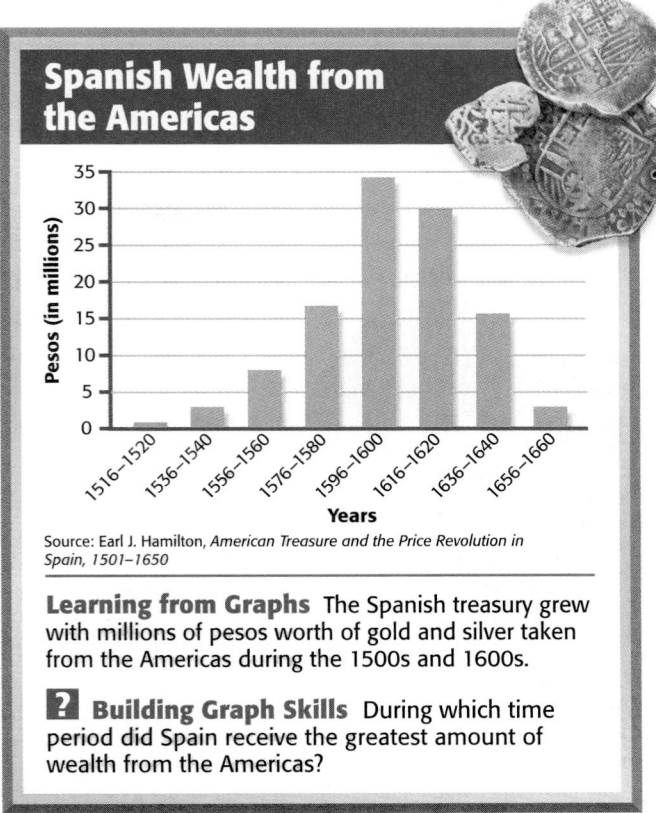

Spanish Wealth from the Americas

Pesos (in millions) vs. Years

Source: Earl J. Hamilton, *American Treasure and the Price Revolution in Spain, 1501–1650*

Learning from Graphs The Spanish treasury grew with millions of pesos worth of gold and silver taken from the Americas during the 1500s and 1600s.

? Building Graph Skills During which time period did Spain receive the greatest amount of wealth from the Americas?

Pueblo Revolt. To halt the growing influence of Spanish settlers, Pueblo Indians turned to violence to drive the Spanish settlers from Sante Fe. *What kinds of cultural differences between the Spanish and the Pueblo can you find in this illustration of the revolt?*

Friar Junípero Serra helped to spread Christianity to American Indians by establishing missions throughout California.

Texas. Despite the early explorations of Álvar Núñez Cabeza de Vaca and others, Spanish settlement in present-day Texas proceeded slowly. The first permanent Spanish colony was founded at Ysleta (ees-LE-tuh) in 1682 by settlers driven from New Mexico by the Pueblo Revolt.

By 1690 France's colonizing activity in North America spurred Spain to strengthen its hold on Texas. Spanish missionaries established the San Francisco de los Tejas mission near the Neches (NE-chuhz) River in 1690. They built the San Antonio de Valero mission in 1718. Several other settlements emerged along the lower Rio Grande. However, lack of mineral resources and constant raids by the Apache and the Comanche Indians slowed settlement.

California. California was the last of Spain's territories in North America to be colonized. Juan Rodríguez Cabrillo (kah-BREE-yoh) explored much of the California coastline for Spain as early as 1542. Spanish leaders did not attempt to set up permanent settlements in the region, however, until the late 1700s, when they became alarmed by Russian explorations in northern California. In 1769 Gaspar de Portolá (pawr-toh-LAH) founded San Diego. Seven years later Juan Bautista de Anza (bow-TEE-stah day AHN-sah) founded San Francisco.

Friar Junípero Serra (hoo-NEE-pay-roh SER-rah), a scholarly Franciscan missionary, came to California with de Portolá's expedition. Serra founded a mission at San Diego and established eight more missions along the Pacific coast before his death in 1784.

✔ **READING CHECK:** Where in North America did Spain establish most of its settlements?

Changing Ways   Hispanics in America

■ **Understanding Change** Since the 1500s, when the first Spanish colonist arrived to settle in what is now known as the United States, Spanish-speaking immigrants have maintained a significant presence. Today, the Hispanic population continues to grow, influencing American culture. *Approximately how large is the Hispanic population in the United States today? What differences do you see in these two images of Hispanic families?*

Hispanic America

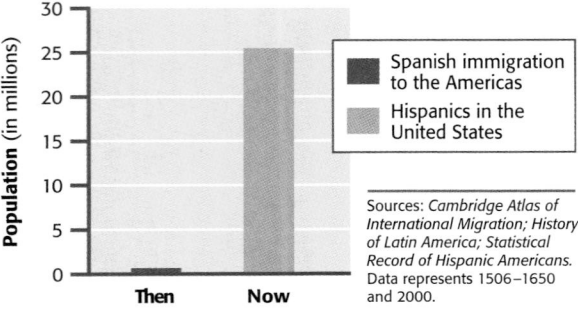

Population (in millions)

■ Spanish immigration to the Americas
■ Hispanics in the United States

Sources: *Cambridge Atlas of International Migration; History of Latin America; Statistical Record of Hispanic Americans.* Data represents 1506–1650 and 2000.

THEN

Now

The Spanish Empire

By 1780 Spanish America comprised one of the largest colonial empires the world had ever known. Within its vast borders were lands of rich diversity.

Colonial government. To oversee this empire, Spain organized its territory into large provinces called **viceroyalties**. New Spain and Peru were the first viceroyalties formed. Then, in the mid-1700s, two more viceroyalties were added. These were New Granada, which stretched from Panama to Ecuador and Venezuela, and La Plata, which comprised Argentina, Bolivia, Chile, Paraguay, and Uruguay. The king appointed a viceroy to oversee each viceroyalty and to supervise lesser officials. Viceroys ruled as the king's personal representatives, but they also were advised by a council—the *audencia*—whose members reported directly and privately to the king of Spain. The king's Council of the Indies, a group of government officials based in Spain, oversaw the entire American empire.

Colonial government worked better in theory than in practice, however. Orders issued by the Crown or the Catholic Church in Spain had to be carried thousands of miles by messenger—first by ship and then by horseback or on foot—to the distant outposts of the empire. Although government officials in Spanish America often became impatient with the delays and made their own decisions, they were rarely penalized. *Encomenderos* also frequently exercised independence and ignored the orders of the viceroy. In the 1540s Francisco Pizarro's brother Gonzalo murdered Peru's first viceroy. Later viceroys learned to ignore unpopular orders from the king, following the practice "I obey but I do not execute." Colonists, particularly those in the remote corners of the empire, usually organized their own settlements and established independent local governments.

Missions. The Catholic Church played a central role in the Spanish exploration and settlement of the Americas. Priests usually accompanied the conquistadores, and missions became a common form of Spanish settlement. Spain's King Philip II issued the Royal Orders for New Discoveries in 1573. He declared that "preaching the gospel . . . is the principal purpose for which we order new . . . settlements to be made." The Royal Orders commanded priests to teach Catholicism as well as "the use of . . . bread, silk, linen, horses, cattle, tools, and weapons."

More than 150 of these Spanish missions were established in the present-day United States. At the center of each mission stood a simple church, surrounded by living quarters and workshops where American Indians worked at blacksmithing, weaving, and other crafts. In fields nearby, missionaries and Indians raised cattle and grew grain, grapes, and other crops.

The missionaries labored to convert American Indians to Catholicism, to teach them Spanish ways, and to make them loyal Spanish subjects. In their zeal, however, they often pushed Indian culture aside and enforced a harsh labor system resembling the *encomienda*. Some American Indians adapted to this new way of life by combining European customs with their own cultural practices. Many Indians, however, resented the forced labor and harsh discipline and fled from the missions. Many others died from European diseases against which they had no immunity.

Catholicism. One of the principal goals of Spanish settlers in North America was the conversion of American Indians to Catholicism. *In this image of the baptism of Indians, why do you think that Spanish settlers would carry weapons during the ceremony?*

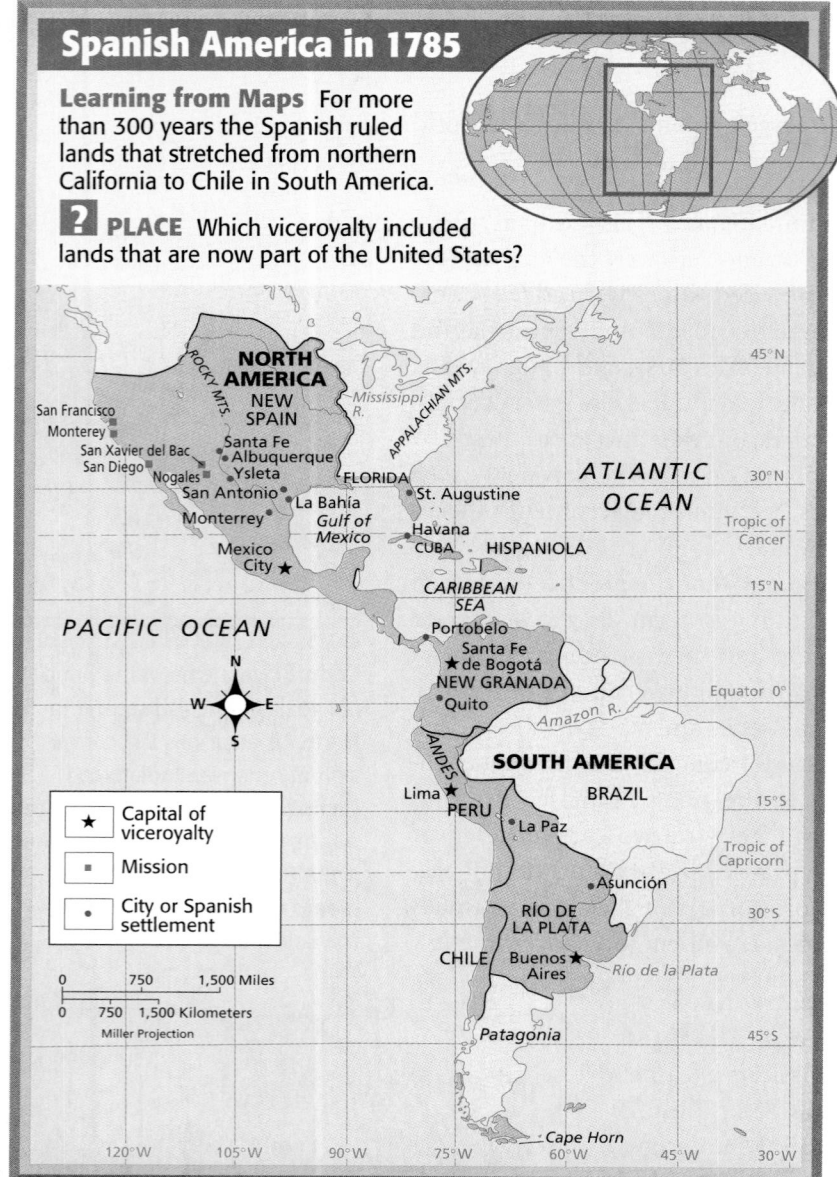

Spanish America in 1785

Learning from Maps For more than 300 years the Spanish ruled lands that stretched from northern California to Chile in South America.

? PLACE Which viceroyalty included lands that are now part of the United States?

Capital of viceroyalty

Mission

City or Spanish settlement

0   750   1,500 Miles
0   750   1,500 Kilometers
Miller Projection

Haciendas and ranchos. Outside the missions, the Spanish government divided the land into farming and ranching estates. Haciendas, some consisting of hundreds of thousands of acres, were the largest. Smaller farms and ranches were called ranchos.

Peons, or landless laborers—most of whom were American Indians—worked on the haciendas. In theory, hacienda owners paid the peons, who were free to come and go as they wished. In reality, however, many landowners controlled the workers through debt. Hacienda owners required the peons to purchase daily necessities from the hacienda store, usually at inflated prices. Before they could seek employment elsewhere, workers had to pay off their debts—an impossible task for many. In addition, children often had to assume the debts of their deceased parents.

Most rancho owners lived on their land and worked alongside their laborers. Skilled Spanish horsemen called vaqueros (vah-KER-ohs) drove the cattle on haciendas and ranchos. Developing the lasso and the rodeo, their lifestyle became a model for later North American cowboys.

✔ **READING CHECK:** How did missions, haciendas, and ranchos help establish Spanish rule in the Americas?

Daily Life in Spanish America

Spanish America maintained a unique social structure. *Peninsulares* (pay-nin-soo-LAHR-ays), Spaniards born in Spain, and *criollos* (kree-OH-yohs), Spaniards born in the colonies, held the most privileged positions in the Americas. Many lived in huge houses with servants and owned businesses and haciendas. Spaniards held high government positions and studied law, medicine, or theology.

Beneath the Spaniards in social status were mestizos (me-STEE-zohs), men and women born of European-Indian parents. Some mestizos had the opportunity to acquire high-level positions in Spanish American society. Most mestizos, however, lived modestly as artisans, estate supervisors, shopkeepers, or traders. Mulattoes—people of African-European ancestry—held a status roughly equal to that of the mestizos.

At the bottom of the social structure were American Indians, Africans, and *zambos*—people of Indian-African ancestry. These groups were legally prevented

In this early-1800s watercolor, a hacienda owner meets a vaquero.

THE GRANGER COLLECTION, NEW YORK

from holding public office and certain jobs. Most Indians became farmers or farm laborers, although some made a living as sailors, tavern keepers, or wagon drivers. Most enslaved Africans worked as hacienda supervisors or as artisans.

Women's roles were also determined by ethnic or family background. Spanish women—who made up just some 10 percent of colonists in the early 1500s—maintained a degree of economic independence because they could own property. In addition, many managed family businesses, ranchos, and haciendas, either with their husbands or, if widowed, by themselves.

BIOGRAPHY

Juana Inés de la Cruz

Many wealthy Spanish women learned to cook, read, sew, and write either at home or in boarding schools called house-homes. There were few opportunities for women to pursue higher education. One Spanish American woman, Juana Inés de la Cruz, did become well educated. Born near Mexico City in 1651 as Juana Inés de Asbaje, she learned to read by the age of seven. Dreaming of furthering her education, she pleaded with her mother that she "might study and take courses at the university" located in Mexico City. Her mother refused, but Asbaje nevertheless decided to educate herself. She "found a way to read many different books my grandfather owned," as she later wrote.

HOLT RESEARCHER

Read More About It

Free Find:
Juana Inés de la Cruz
After reading the biography on Juana Inés de la Cruz on the **Holt Researcher** CD–ROM, write a short essay describing the freedoms and restrictions women faced in the new Spanish colonies.

AMERICAN ARTS

Spanish Architecture in the Southwest

Spanish colonization left a lasting mark on the architecture of the Americas, particularly in the present-day southwestern United States. The Spanish influence on architecture stems from missionaries who oversaw the construction of impressive structures designed to help convert the local American Indians to Catholicism. The Spanish built dozens of missions in Arizona, California, New Mexico, and Texas during the 1600s and 1700s. They reflected many European styles.

The architecture of some Spanish missions has its roots in the baroque style popular in Europe during the late 1500s and beyond. Baroque architecture often uses strong contrasts of light and shadow that create dramatic effects. Elaborate detail, individualism, and spirituality also are important characteristics of the baroque style. The church at Mission Concepción (kawn-sep-SYAWN)—one of several missions established near San Antonio, Texas, in the early 1700s—is an excellent example of Spanish colonial architecture. Its Romanesque forms and gothic arches are typical of other Spanish missions built in the Americas.

Mission Concepción

Understanding the Arts

1. What aspects of the baroque style did the Spanish missions incorporate?
2. Describe some of the unique architectural features of Mission Concepción.

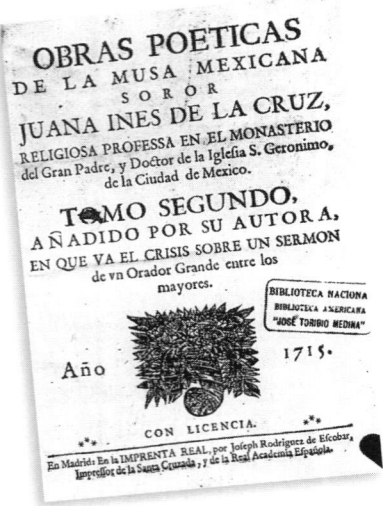

Published 20 years after her death, this title page to a second edition of a volume of poetry by Juana Inés de la Cruz describes her as the muse, or poet, of Mexico.

In 1669, Asbaje decided to enter the San Jerónimo convent, taking the name Sor (Sister) Juana Inés de la Cruz. Convents in Mexico during the 1600s did not require the same isolated living conditions as convents in Europe. Nuns at San Jerónimo worked in a pleasant and relaxed atmosphere where they entertained visitors, cooked extraordinary feasts, and enjoyed playing music. The convent also offered women the freedom to study. For 25 years de la Cruz read extensively in the humanities and sciences, accumulating a large library. During this time she also became a popular poet in Mexico, publishing two volumes of poetry during her lifetime. Her works gained great admiration among Spanish officials and even royalty. Her plays were performed for many wealthy nobles.

"Of all my country," de la Cruz wrote, "I was the venerated [honored] figure, one of those idols that inspire the general applause." One of de la Cruz's poems explains her choice of scholarly pursuits.

66 World, in hounding me, what do you gain? How can it harm you if I choose, astutely [wisely], rather to stock my mind with things of beauty, than waste its stock on every beauty's claim? . . .
   Mine is the better and the truer way: to leave the vanities of life aside, not throw my life away on vanity. 99

In 1695 de la Cruz died after contracting a disease from sick nuns whom she was helping. Many scholars consider her the greatest American poet of the 1600s.

Few women obtained an education equal to the status of nuns like de la Cruz. Most African, Indian, and mestizo women learned useful traditional skills at home such as cooking, pottery making, and weaving.

✔ **READING CHECK:** How did Spanish culture affect the Americas?

SECTION 3 REVIEW

Define and explain the significance of the following terms:
Pueblo Revolt
viceroyalties
peons

Identify and explain the significance of the following individuals:
Pedro Menéndez de Avilés
Juan de Oñate
Popé
Juan Rodríguez Cabrillo
Junípero Serra
Juana Inés de la Cruz

Locate and explain the importance of the following places:
Florida
St. Augustine
Santa Fe
San Diego
San Francisco

1. **Using Graphic Organizers** Copy the pyramid below. List the different classes in Spanish American society and explain what role each class played in daily life.

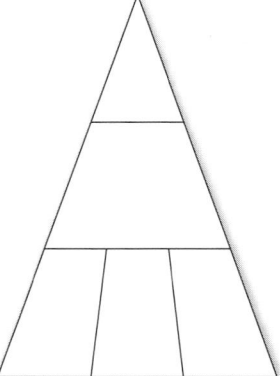

2. **Identifying Cause and Effect** What led to the Pueblo Revolt? How successful was it?
3. **Understanding Geography: Location** Where and when did Spanish colonists found settlements in North America?
4. **Synthesizing** How did the Spanish use missions, haciendas, and ranchos to administer their empire in the Americas?

Critical Thinking

5. Can it be said that American Indian cultures in the Spanish Empire soon became Spanish American Indian cultures? Explain your answer.
Consider:
• what aspects of Spanish culture were adopted by American Indians
• how well American Indians were integrated into Spanish society
• to what extent American Indians continued their traditional cultural practices

The English in North America

Read to understand:

1. how the Protestant Reformation affected colonization
2. why the defeat of the Spanish Armada was significant
3. how the English attempted colonization
4. how the growth of Jamestown affected relations between American Indians and settlers

KEY TERMS

Northwest Passage
Protestant Reformation
Spanish Armada
inflation
Charter of 1606
Powhatan
indentured servant

KEY PEOPLE

John Cabot
Martin Luther
Francis Drake
Walter Raleigh
John Smith
Wahunsonacock
Pocahontas
John Rolfe

KEY PLACES

Newfoundland
St. Lawrence River
Virginia
Roanoke Island
Jamestown

EYEWITNESSES TO History

66 *[John Cabot is given the right] to subdue, occupy and possess . . . Isles, countries, regions or provinces of the [American Indians] . . . unknown to all Christians. . . . [And to share] their fruits, profits, [and] gains.* 99

—King Henry VII

John Cabot sets sail from England

In 1497 King Henry VII of England commissioned Italian seafarer Giovanni Caboto, also known as John Cabot, to seek out and claim land in North America for England. In the dark hours of the morning of June 24, 1497, Cabot's crew made landfall on the shores of what is now known as Newfoundland. After carefully guiding his small ship, *Mathew,* through treacherous fog and ice, the experienced mariner went ashore and claimed the area for England. Cabot and his crew chose not to land again on this voyage, however. Fearing hostility from American Indians, Cabot believed his small crew should not explore inland any farther than the range of a crossbow from his ship. A more fierce enemy, perhaps, may have been the swarms of huge, disease-carrying mosquitoes that bred in the melting snow waters on Newfoundland's rocky shores. In 1498 Cabot returned to sail along the coasts of present-day Nova Scotia and New England in exchange for a small amount of money and trading privileges from the king.

Early Claims

Shortly after Christopher Columbus's first voyage, other mariners such as John Cabot joined the search for a route to Asia. As a result, geographic knowledge of the Americas slowly grew. Vasco Núñez de Balboa's sighting of the Pacific Ocean and Ferdinand Magellan's voyage around the tip of South America motivated non-Spanish explorers to seek a northern route to the Pacific and thus to Asia. The explorers hoped the discovery of a **Northwest Passage** would break the Spanish monopoly. Such a passage does not exist, though many European claims in North America resulted from failed attempts to find the passage.

The voyages of Giovanni da Verrazano (vayr-raht-SAHN-oh) and Jacques Cartier (kahr-tyay) formed the basis for later French claims in North America. Verrazano, an Italian, failed in 1524 to find a westward water route to Asia. He did, however, claim for France lands along North America's east coast. Ten years later, Cartier explored the Gulf of St. Lawrence and the St. Lawrence River as far west as present-day Montreal. Cartier's attempts to start a settlement were unsuccessful, but his efforts strengthened French claims to what is now Canada.

While Spain began settlement in Central and South America as well as parts of North America during the 1500s, other European powers laid claim to trading posts in North America. They chose, however, not to establish permanent colonies.

The Religious Spirit

THE PROTESTANT REFORMATION

Martin Luther, a German Catholic priest, launched the Protestant Reformation in 1517 when he published his Ninety-five Theses, challenging many practices of the Catholic Church. This included the sale of indulgences. Catholics who paid money to the church were granted indulgences, or promises that loved ones who had died would move more quickly into heaven. Luther wrote in his 94th and 95th theses that "Christians must be exhorted [urged] to follow Christ their head with utter devotion through punishment, through death, through hell." Said Luther, "In this way let them have confidence that they will enter heaven through many tribulations [challenges], rather than through a false assurance of peace."

Martin Luther preaching

Luther's refusal to take back his teachings led to his excommunication, or formal expulsion, from the Catholic Church and condemnation by Holy Roman Emperor Charles V. As a result, he fled into hiding, where he wrote pamphlets on religious reform and translated the New Testament into German. He devoted the rest of his life to religious writing and the organization of the alternative church he founded. Luther's ideas spread throughout northern and eastern Europe and eventually led to dramatic political and cultural transformations. Supporters of the Reformation called for increased literacy and encouraged people to read the Bible themselves. Some new congregations also rejected the assigned leadership of the Catholic Church and began electing their own clergy.

At that time, most European countries were still more concerned with reaching Asia than with organizing settlements. Since the French and the English were more concerned with domestic issues and events in Europe, nearly a century passed before these nations successfully colonized North America.

The delay in colonization efforts can also be attributed to the religious upheaval known as the **Protestant Reformation**. The Reformation began in the German city of Wittenberg in 1517, when a monk named Martin Luther protested against corruption in the Roman Catholic Church. Protests quickly spread to other areas of Europe. Reformers established a number of Protestant churches as alternatives to Catholicism.

This conflict between Protestants and Catholics became not only a religious struggle but also a territorial and political one. For a time, the Reformation commanded Europe's attention. France, for example, was too involved with a civil war between Catholics and Protestants (1562–98) to follow up on its claims in North America until the 1600s.

During the Reformation, Spain, the most powerful nation in Europe, clung to the Catholic faith. Other countries, such as England, officially became Protestant states. This division led to a drawn-out conflict between the two nations as each tried to achieve religious and political dominance in Europe.

✔ **READING CHECK:** How did the Protestant Reformation affect colonization efforts in the Americas?

England Challenges Spain

The earliest challenges to Spain's American empire came in the late 1500s. European pirates—particularly the English "sea dogs"—began attacking Spanish galleons and seizing their cargoes of treasure as they left the Americas.

One highly successful sea dog was Francis Drake. In 1577 Drake ventured from England with a fleet of swift, heavily armed vessels on a voyage of exploration and piracy against Spanish ships in the Americas.

Queen Elizabeth I embraced Drake as a hero, knighting him on the deck of his pirate ship, the *Golden Hind.* The queen's action naturally angered King Philip II of Spain, who viewed Drake's actions as a challenge to Spanish power.

Determined to strike back, King Philip assembled a massive fleet of some 130 ships and some 27,000 men, known as the **Spanish Armada**, to invade England. In 1588 most of the Armada sailed to the port of Calais, France, just across the Strait of Dover from England. There they waited for additional troops.

The Spanish had a fearsome reputation in Europe for their well-armed military. However, England's sea captains skillfully used the speed of their smaller, newly constructed ships to great advantage. They propelled burning ships toward the Armada, whose ships quickly became separated and more vulnerable to attack. As the Spanish ships attempted to flee, a furious storm developed, damaging the battered fleet. Only about half of the original Spanish Armada returned to Spain.

The failure of the Armada in 1588 revealed Spanish naval weaknesses. By the 1600s, Spanish economic weaknesses became apparent as well. With tons of colonial silver flowing into its treasury, Spain seemed quite prosperous. The prosperity was deceptive, however because the Spanish used most of the silver to buy goods from other countries. John Campbell, an English writer, explained:

> 66 [Spanish] galleons bring the silver into Spain, but . . . it runs out as fast as it comes in. . . . The silver . . . and very little of the goods or manufactures . . . belong to the subjects of the crown of Spain. It is evident, therefore, . . . that the greatest part of the returns from the West Indies belong to . . . [foreigners]. 99

Some historians believe that the steady flow of resources and silver from the Americas caused **inflation**, or an increase in prices, throughout Europe. When the flow of silver and resources slowed in the 1600s, Spain found itself with little currency to buy imported goods.

In addition, the Spanish government had taken out loans from other countries to fight its endless wars. These debts and the weak Spanish economy prevented Spain from carrying out new plans for further North American colonization. As a result, Spain's weaknesses opened the way for the Dutch, English, and French to begin colonization.

✔ **READING CHECK:** Why was the defeat of the Spanish Armada important?

England's First Attempts at Colonization

Even before the shattering defeat of the Spanish Armada, English adventurers had planned to colonize the lands claimed by John Cabot and others. They were eager to develop profitable commerce with the Americas, as Spain had done.

Sir Humphrey Gilbert sailed to Newfoundland in 1583 to start an English colony, but on the return voyage he and his ship were lost in a storm. The following year Gilbert's half-brother, Sir Walter Raleigh, explored the Atlantic seaboard for a suitable site to colonize. He named the area that he chose Virginia, in honor of Elizabeth, the "Virgin Queen."

In 1585 Raleigh sent a small group of colonists to Virginia. They settled on Roanoke Island, off the coast of present-day North Carolina. After almost a year of hardship, the colonists returned to England. In 1587 Raleigh tried again, sending about 100 people, including women and children, under the command of John White. After establishing a new Roanoke colony, White headed back to England for supplies.

Events in Europe delayed White's return. When he finally reached Roanoke in 1590, all he found were the words CRO and CROTOAN carved near the settlement. *Crotoan* was the American Indian name for an island off the coast. Searchers found no other trace of the colonists. The fate of the "Lost Colony" remains a mystery. After that, English

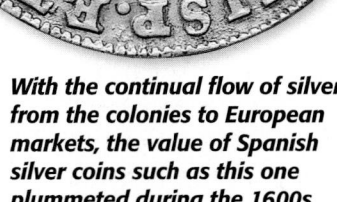

With the continual flow of silver from the colonies to European markets, the value of Spanish silver coins such as this one plummeted during the 1600s.

INTERPRETING THE VISUAL RECORD

Colonial life. This watercolor of American Indians fishing from a dugout canoe was painted by John White between 1585 and 1587. *What is White suggesting about the availability of food and the ingenuity of Indians in this illustration?*

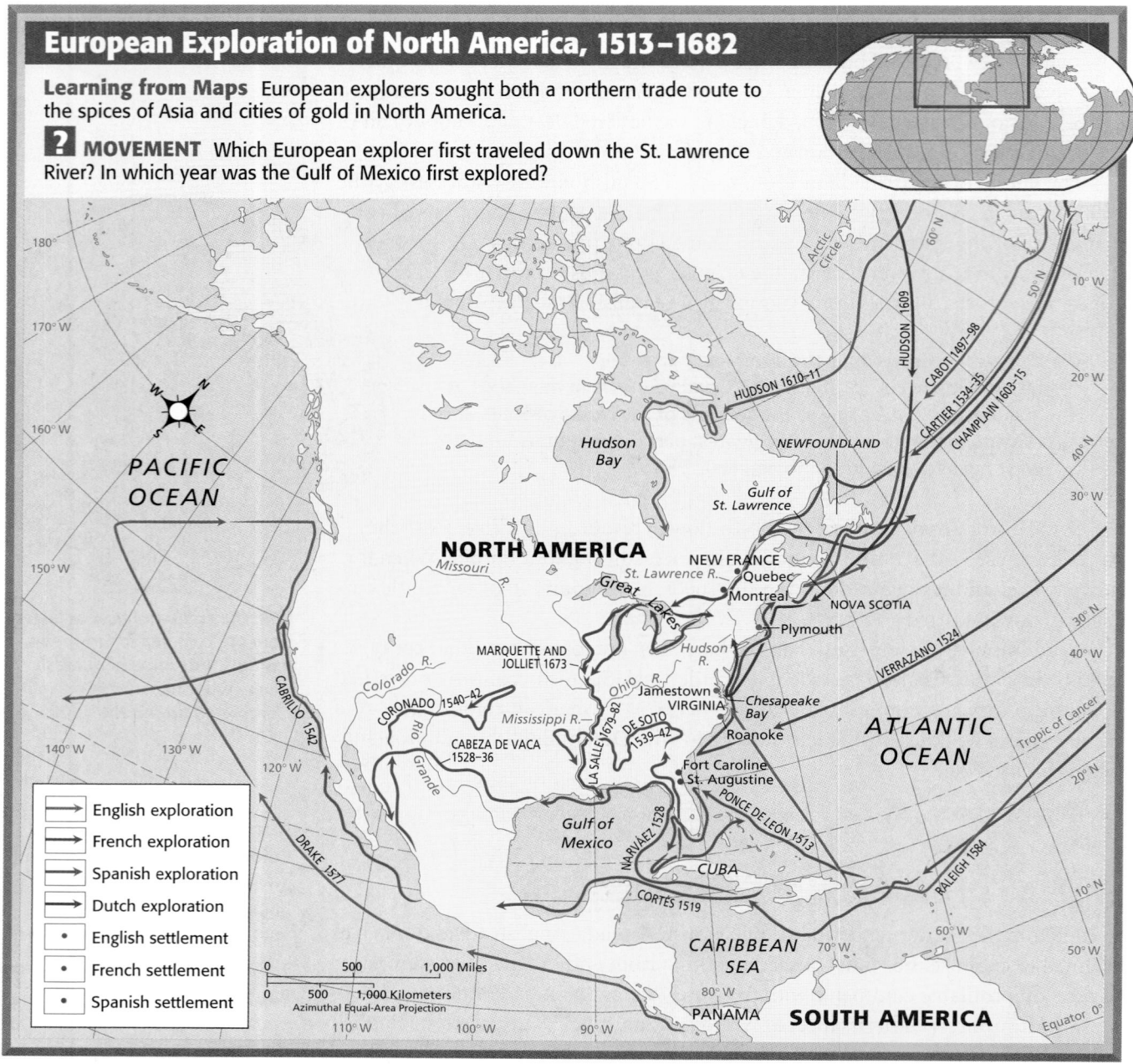

European Exploration of North America, 1513–1682

Learning from Maps European explorers sought both a northern trade route to the spices of Asia and cities of gold in North America.

? MOVEMENT Which European explorer first traveled down the St. Lawrence River? In which year was the Gulf of Mexico first explored?

Legend:
- English exploration
- French exploration
- Spanish exploration
- Dutch exploration
- English settlement
- French settlement
- Spanish settlement

0   500   1,000 Miles
0   500   1,000 Kilometers
Azimuthal Equal-Area Projection

officials began to focus more on issues and problems existing in England. More than 25 years would pass before the next English colonization effort.

King James I issued the **Charter of 1606**, which licensed the Plymouth Company and the London Company to organize settlements in Virginia. The two groups were joint-stock companies, in which investors shared operating costs as well as any profits or losses. The charter gave the companies the right to establish settlements and "to dig, mine, and search for all manner of mines of gold, silver, and copper." The Plymouth Company was given the right to settle anywhere between the 38th and 45th parallels—from present-day Virginia to Maine. The London Company could settle anywhere between the 34th and 41st parallels, from present-day South Carolina to New York.

✔ **READING CHECK:** How did the English try to colonize North America?

The Experiment at Jamestown

The first permanent English settlers—some 100 men recruited by the London Company—reached Virginia in the spring of 1607. They chose a location near one of the rivers along Chesapeake Bay for their settlement, naming it Jamestown in honor of their king.

THE GRANGER COLLECTION, NEW YORK

The early years. Unfortunately, Jamestown was located on a low, wooded peninsula near a marsh infested with disease-carrying mosquitoes. Disease, exposure to the elements, and starvation killed many people the first year.

The settlers elected Captain John Smith—an adventurous explorer, mapmaker, and soldier—as president of the council of settlers in 1608. Smith quickly made plans for strengthening the colony.

The help of the local American Indians, called **Powhatan** by the English, prevented total disaster. The Powhatan actually consisted of a large confederation of some 30 small tribes under the leadership of Wahunsonacock (wah-hoohn-SUH-nuh-kahk). They were skilled in agriculture and fishing. The Powhatan gave the settlers food and taught them how to cultivate corn—a crop new to the English.

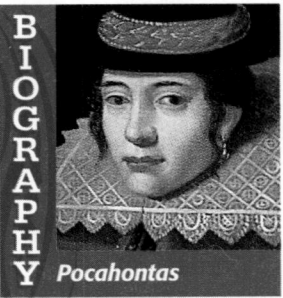
BIOGRAPHY
Pocahontas

An Indian ally. Pocahontas, the favorite daughter of Wahunsonacock, gave invaluable help to the English colonists. Although she was young—10 or 12 years old—when the colonists arrived, Pocahontas became an indispensable intermediary between the English and the Powhatan. She frequently visited Jamestown, bringing food and gifts and establishing trade between the two groups.

Pocahontas charmed and fascinated the colonists. In 1608 Captain Smith wrote that in personality Pocahontas "much exceedeth any of the rest" of the local Indians. Smith once described his capture by the Powhatan and subsequent rescue by Pocahontas when she "hazarded the beating out of her own brains" by throwing herself over his body to prevent his execution.

Despite historians' doubts about this romantic legend, Pocahontas did play a vital role in maintaining peace between the Powhatan and the English. As a mutually trusted intermediary, she negotiated the release of Powhatan prisoners and protected the colonists from her father's anger during disputes.

Nevertheless, relations with the Powhatan grew more strained after Smith returned to England, and Pocahontas no longer voluntarily visited the settlement. Desperate for food in the harsh winter of 1609–10, the English raided local American Indian villages—stealing food, burning shelters, and killing many of the Indians.

Captured by colonists in 1613, Pocahontas spent the following year as a well-treated hostage in Jamestown. During this time, she converted to Christianity and was baptized as "the Lady Rebecca." Her marriage in 1614 to a colonist named John Rolfe temporarily brought an end to the fighting between the colonists and the Powhatan. In June 1616 the Indian princess traveled to England with her husband and infant son, Thomas. She died suddenly in England in March 1617.

INTERPRETING THE VISUAL RECORD

Pocahontas. Pocahontas assisted the English colonists of Jamestown, bringing them corn and other goods as well as mediating the relationship between the colonists and the Powhatan. *How does this image reflect Pocahontas's role in helping the colonists?*

HOLT RESEARCHER

Read More About It

Free Find:
Pocahontas
After reading the biography on Pocahontas on the **Holt Researcher** CD–ROM, write a short essay describing the way the Powhatan treated the English settlers of Jamestown.

AMERICAN *Letters*

The Early Colonial Experience

Life as an early settler in the English colonies proved extremely difficult for most people. Individuals had significantly different experiences, however, depending on their social standing. In the first of the following two letters written by colonists, John Pory, the secretary of the Jamestown colony, notes the beginnings of the cultivation of tobacco. The second letter, written by indentured servant Richard Frethorne, reveals the harsh reality of early colonial life for many people.

A Letter to "The Right Honorable and My Singular Good Lord" September 30, 1619
by John Pory

As touching the quality of this country, three things there be, which in few years may bring this Colony to perfection; the English plough, Vineyards, & Cattle. . . . We have had this year a plentiful crop of English wheat. . . . In July last so soon as we had reaped this self-sown wheat, we set Indian corn upon the same ground, which is come up in great abundance; and so by this means we are to enjoy two crops in one year from off one & the same field. . . . All our riches for the present do consist in Tobacco, wherein one man by his own labor hath in one year, raised to himself to the value of 200 £ sterling; and another by the means of six servants hath cleared [earned] at one crop a thousand pound english. These be true, yet indeed rare examples, yet possible to be done by others. Our principal wealth (I should have said) consisteth in servants. . . .

Tobacco leaves

We are not the veriest [greatest] beggars in the world, our Cow-keeper here of James city on Sundays goes acowtered [dressed] all in fresh flaming silks and a wife of one . . . wears her rough beaver hat with a fair pearl hat-band, and a silken suit.

Letter to his Father and Mother: March 20, April 2 and 3, 1623
by Richard Frethorne

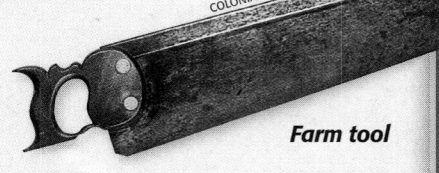

COLONIAL WILLIAMSBURG FOUNDATION

Farm tool

Loving and kind father and mother my most humble duty remembered. . . . This is to let you understand that I your child am in a most heavy case by reasons of the nature of the country is such that it causeth much sickness . . . and when we are sick there is nothing to comfort us; for since I came out of the ship, I never had any thing but peas, and loblollie (that is water gruell) as for deer or venison I never saw any since I came into this land, there is indeed some foul, but we are not allowed to go, and get it, but must work hard both early, and late for a mess of water gruel, and a mouthful of bread, and beef. . . . We live in fear of the enemy [Indians] every hour. . . . We are in great danger, for our Plantation is very weak, by reason of the death, and sickness, of our Company.

[A friend] much marveled that you would send me [as] a servant to the Company, he saith I had been better knocked on the head, and indeed so I find it now to my great grief and misery, and saith, that if you love me you will redeem [free] me suddenly, for which I do intreat and beg.

UNDERSTANDING LITERATURE

1. What crops did the earliest English colonists grow?
2. What was life in the colonies like for Richard Frethorne?
3. How did the experiences of John Pory and Richard Frethorne differ?

Tobacco and prosperity. A major source of conflict between the American Indians and colonists arose over tobacco, a plant native to the Americas. Spanish and Portuguese sailors introduced tobacco to Europe around 1550. By the early 1600s the smoking of tobacco in pipes had become increasingly popular, suggesting a new enterprise for the struggling Virginia colonists. John Rolfe successfully introduced the desirable Caribbean tobacco to Virginia in 1612. Soon the Jamestown colonists were shipping large quantities of tobacco to England.

To provide laborers for tobacco cultivation, Jamestown's backers introduced the headright system. In this system sponsors received 50 acres of land for each worker, or "head," they paid to bring to Jamestown. The backers also set up a new arrangement for bringing settlers to Jamestown known as indentured servitude. An **indentured servant** was bound for a period of years to the person who paid his or her way to America. At first, most of those who survived their term of service—far from a certainty in Jamestown—acquired land to work for themselves.

As Jamestown's population grew, the colonists' tobacco farms expanded onto American Indian hunting grounds. The Indians viewed the taking of their lands as an act of war. In the spring of 1622, Indians attacked Jamestown's outlying farmhouses, killing some 350 settlers—including John Rolfe—and burning most of the buildings. The English struck back fiercely. They even concluded one "peace conference" by murdering some 200 American Indians with poisoned wine. These actions brought an end to peace between the settlers and the Indians.

✔ **READING CHECK:** How did the growth of Jamestown affect American Indians' relationships with the settlers?

INTERPRETING THE VISUAL RECORD

Indentured servants. Hoping to gain land of their own, many debtors and poor workers from England traveled to the North American colonies as indentured servants. *What type of work do you think this indentured servant is doing?*

SECTION **4** REVIEW

Define and explain the significance of the following terms:
Northwest Passage
Protestant Reformation
Spanish Armada
inflation
Charter of 1606
Powhatan
indentured servant

Identify and explain the significance of the following individuals:

John Cabot	John Smith
Martin Luther	Wahunsonacock
Francis Drake	Pocahontas
Walter Raleigh	John Rolfe

Locate and explain the importance of the following places:

Newfoundland	Roanoke Island
St. Lawrence River	Jamestown
Virginia	

1. Using Graphic Organizers Copy the problem/solution chart below. List the problems that colonists encountered in Virginia and the solutions they and their allies devised to those problems.

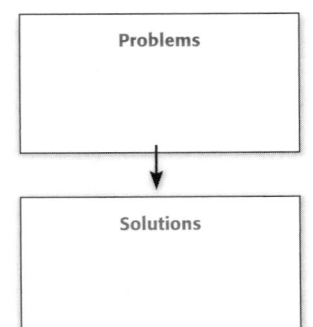

2. Assessing Consequences How did the Protestant Reformation affect colonization?

3. Synthesizing What did the defeat of the Spanish Armada mean to Europe and to the settlement of North America?

4. Taking a Stand Do you think that Pocahontas was an effective intermediary between the colonists and the American Indians? Provide examples from the text that support your position.

Critical Thinking

5. Was the English or Spanish method more effective in achieving the country's goals of colonization? Explain your answer.
   Consider:
   • what the Spanish colonization goals and methods were
   • what the English colonization goals and methods were
   • how well each country achieved its goals

CHAPTER 2

Review

Creating a Time Line

Copy the time line below onto a sheet of paper. Complete the time line by filling in the events and dates from the chapter that you think were most significant. Pick three events and explain why you think they were significant.

| 1492 | 1600 | 1700 | 1800 |

Writing a Summary

Using the Reading Checks as a guide, write an overview of the events in the chapter.

Identifying People and Ideas

Identify the following terms or individuals and explain their significance.

1. Christopher Columbus
2. Treaty of Tordesillas
3. *encomienda*
4. conquistadores
5. Hernán Cortés
6. Pueblo Revolt
7. Juana Inés de la Cruz
8. Protestant Reformation
9. Spanish Armada
10. indentured servant

Understanding Main Ideas

SECTION 1
1. What instructions did Spain give Christopher Columbus and early settlers to guide them in their relationships with Native Americans?
2. What reforms did Bartolomé de Las Casas recommend to Spain?

SECTION 2
3. How were the Aztec defeated?

SECTION 3
4. How did Spain manage its American empire?
5. What were women's roles in Spanish America?

SECTION 4
6. How did tobacco affect the history of Jamestown?

Reviewing Themes

1. **Global Relations** How did the outcome of the conflict between England and Spain affect colonization in the Americas?
2. **Economic Development** How did the Spanish and English colonization of the Americas affect the economies of Spain and England?
3. **Cultural Diversity** How did differences in beliefs and values affect relations between Europeans and American Indians?

Thinking Critically

1. **Evaluating** How successful was the Catholic Church in protecting American Indians and improving their lives?
2. **Hypothesizing** Suppose the Spanish Armada had defeated the English in 1588. Do you think Spain would have continued to dominate the Americas? Explain your answer.
3. **Comparing and Contrasting** How did American Indians' behavior toward European colonists both resemble and differ from the colonists' behavior toward the American Indians?
4. **Identifying Cause and Effect** What were the differences between Spanish and English methods of colonization? How did these differences affect their colonies?

Writing About History

Writing to Evaluate Write an essay explaining why Columbus's first voyage was a turning point in history. Use the following graphic to organize your thoughts.

Columbus's Voyage → Short-Term Effects → Long-Term Effects

Spanish mission of San Jose near San Antonio de Bexar

Strategies for Success Review the **Strategies for Success** on *Building Vocabulary*. Then create a list of at least 10 new words that you came across in this chapter. Write a definition for each word, check it against that in a dictionary, and compose a sentence that uses the word in a completely new context.

Linking History and Geography

Study the map below. Explain how geography and trade with local American Indian villages appears to have affected the location of settlements in the Chesapeake.

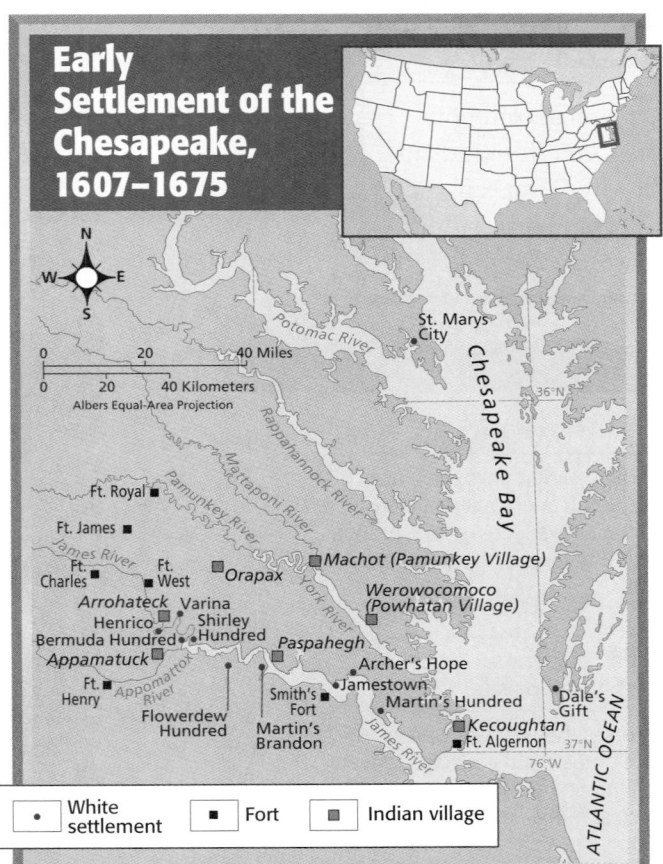

Early Settlement of the Chesapeake, 1607–1675

N
W E
S

0   20   40 Miles
0   20   40 Kilometers
Albers Equal-Area Projection

Potomac River
St. Marys City
Chesapeake Bay
36°N
Rappahannock River
Mattaponi River
Pamunkey River
Ft. Royal
Ft. James
James River
Ft. Charles
Ft. West
Orapax
Machot (Pamunkey Village)
Arrohateck
Varina
Werowocomoco (Powhatan Village)
Henrico
Shirley Hundred
Bermuda Hundred
Paspahegh
Appamatuck
Archer's Hope
Ft. Henry
Appomattox River
Jamestown
Smith's Fort
Martin's Hundred
Dale's Gift
Flowerdew Hundred
Martin's Brandon
Kecoughtan
Ft. Algernon
37°N
York River
James River
76°W
ATLANTIC OCEAN

• White settlement   ■ Fort   ▪ Indian village

internet**connect**

TOPIC: Columbus and the Spanish Empire
GO TO: go.hrw.com
KEYWORD: SD1 Columbus

Accessing the Internet through the HRW Web site, research and write journal entries on one or both of the following:
1. Imagine that you are Columbus and describe your journey, your crew, and what factors led to the success of your first voyage to America.
2. As an American Indian in the *encomienda* system, describe the impact of Columbus's arrival on your people and your interactions with the Spaniards.

BUILDING YOUR PORTFOLIO

Complete one or all of the following projects independently or cooperatively.

1 Economic Development
Imagine that you are an Italian merchant in the 1500s. ***Create a map*** *that details trade routes between Europe, Africa, Asia, and the Americas during this period. Include symbols to represent major items of trade.*

2 Democratic Values
Imagine that you are a Spanish priest opposed to slavery in the Americas. ***Plan a mural*** *that conveys your concerns about the* encomienda *system and about the introduction of African slavery to the Americas.*

3 Cultural Diversity
Imagine that you are a theater writer and actor. ***Write and perform dramatic readings*** *of first-person accounts of exchanges between Africans or American Indians and colonists, mission priests, or Spanish conquistadores.*

The Columbian Exchange

Columbus began an exchange of goods across the Atlantic Ocean that would transform the world. Europeans introduced familiar food crops and livestock to the Americas, hoping to transform the region into another Europe. American food plants were also quickly introduced into Africa, Asia, and Europe. Many of these plants were particularly useful because they produced high yields and could tolerate a wide range of climates.

The Movement of Plants and Animals

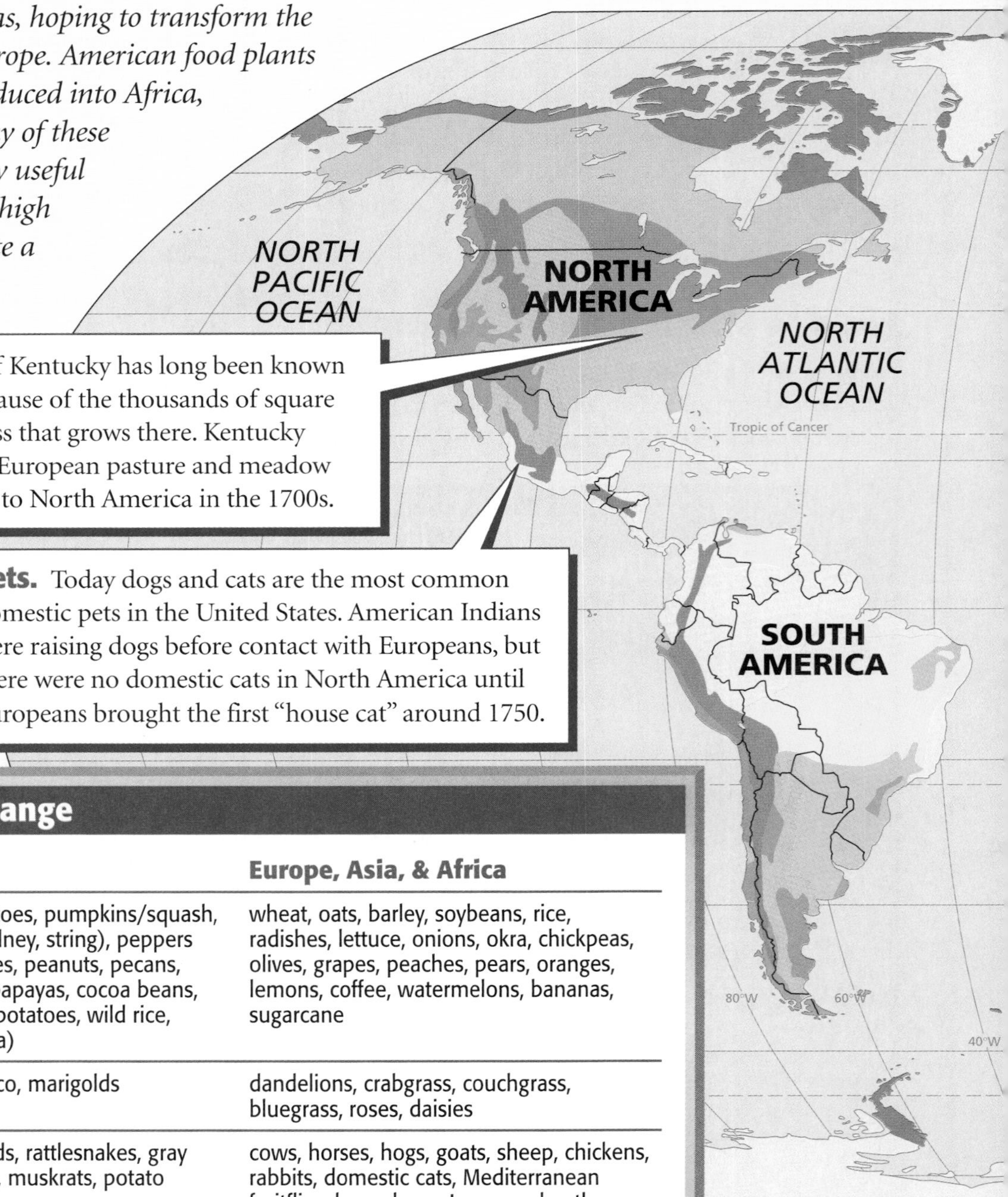

NORTH PACIFIC OCEAN

NORTH AMERICA

NORTH ATLANTIC OCEAN

Tropic of Cancer

SOUTH AMERICA

80°W   60°W

40°W

Bluegrass. The state of Kentucky has long been known as the Bluegrass State because of the thousands of square miles of bluish-green grass that grows there. Kentucky Bluegrass originated as a European pasture and meadow grass. It was transplanted to North America in the 1700s.

Pets. Today dogs and cats are the most common domestic pets in the United States. American Indians were raising dogs before contact with Europeans, but there were no domestic cats in North America until Europeans brought the first "house cat" around 1750.

The Columbian Exchange

	The Americas	Europe, Asia, & Africa
Food Plants	corn, potatoes, tomatoes, pumpkins/squash, beans (navy, lima, kidney, string), peppers (bell, chili), pineapples, peanuts, pecans, cashews, avocados, papayas, cocoa beans, vanilla beans, sweet potatoes, wild rice, cassava roots (tapioca)	wheat, oats, barley, soybeans, rice, radishes, lettuce, onions, okra, chickpeas, olives, grapes, peaches, pears, oranges, lemons, coffee, watermelons, bananas, sugarcane
Other Plants	cotton, rubber, tobacco, marigolds	dandelions, crabgrass, couchgrass, bluegrass, roses, daisies
Animals and Insects	turkeys, hummingbirds, rattlesnakes, gray squirrels, guinea pigs, muskrats, potato beetles	cows, horses, hogs, goats, sheep, chickens, rabbits, domestic cats, Mediterranean fruitflies, honeybees, Japanese beetles, sparrows, starlings, mice, rats

Tomatoes and peppers. Many of today's popular dishes in Italy and India are made with tomatoes and peppers, products that originated in the Americas. Although tomatoes were brought to Europe in the 1500s, few Europeans ate them at first. Some people thought tomatoes were poisonous and grew them only for decoration. In India, vitamin-rich chili peppers became an important ingredient in curries and improved the diet of the poor.

Rice. Asiatic rice is believed to have originated in China as a grass plant, while African rice was developed independently from a similar plant in West Africa. Rice eventually became a popular dietary staple in the Americas. Rice grows particularly well in both East Asia and southeastern North America.

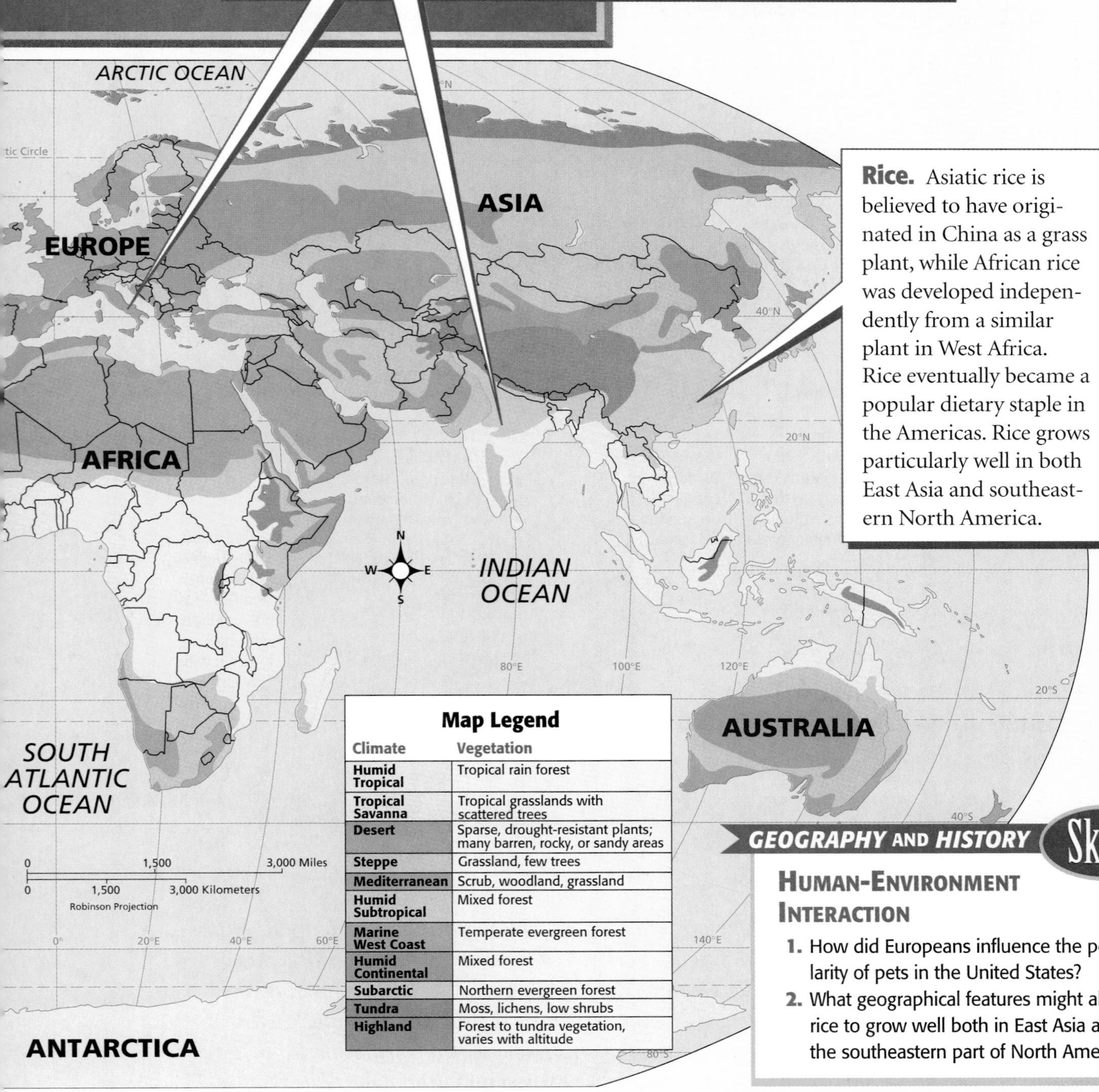

ARCTIC OCEAN

EUROPE

ASIA

AFRICA

INDIAN OCEAN

SOUTH ATLANTIC OCEAN

AUSTRALIA

ANTARCTICA

Map Legend	
Climate	**Vegetation**
Humid Tropical	Tropical rain forest
Tropical Savanna	Tropical grasslands with scattered trees
Desert	Sparse, drought-resistant plants; many barren, rocky, or sandy areas
Steppe	Grassland, few trees
Mediterranean	Scrub, woodland, grassland
Humid Subtropical	Mixed forest
Marine West Coast	Temperate evergreen forest
Humid Continental	Mixed forest
Subarctic	Northern evergreen forest
Tundra	Moss, lichens, low shrubs
Highland	Forest to tundra vegetation, varies with altitude

0   1,500   3,000 Miles
0   1,500   3,000 Kilometers
Robinson Projection

GEOGRAPHY AND HISTORY Skills

HUMAN-ENVIRONMENT INTERACTION

1. How did Europeans influence the popularity of pets in the United States?
2. What geographical features might allow rice to grow well both in East Asia and in the southeastern part of North America?

1620–1763
The English Colonies

A meeting of the Virginia House of Burgesses

Engraving of a sawmill

1630
Politics
The first General Court meets in the Massachusetts Bay Colony.

1640
The Arts
The *Bay Psalm Book* is the first book published in the English colonies.

1650
The Arts
Anne Bradstreet publishes *The Tenth Muse Lately Sprung Up in America*.

1661
Politics
Virginia passes an act recognizing African slavery.

1670
The Arts The first engraving, of Reverend Richard Mather, is produced in America.

| 1620 | 1630 | 1640 | 1650 | 1660 | 1670 | 1680 | 1690 |

1627
Business and Finance
Virginia exports half a million pounds of tobacco.

1639
Daily Life
Massachusetts sets up the first colonial printing press.

1648
World Events
Work is completed on India's Taj Mahal.

1665
Daily Life
The English introduce sports such as horse racing to New Netherland.

1688
World Events
The English people launch the Glorious Revolution, replacing King James II with William and Mary.

An early tobacco plantation

The Taj Mahal

Before You Read

Build on What You Know

Europeans began to explore and conquer the Americas in the late 1400s. Within a few decades, Spanish settlers arrived in these lands, determined to change the course of America's future. The English were soon at their heels. By the early 1600s, the English were also eager to colonize these American lands. In this chapter you will learn that the English colonists who settled North America in the 1600s and 1700s came for many reasons. These various factors contributed to the development of distinct cultures within England's North American colonies.

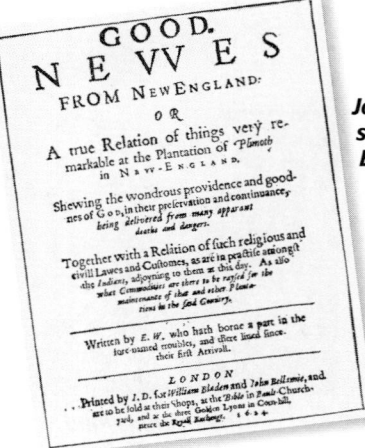

Journal promoting settlement in New England

Benjamin Franklin

1704
Daily Life
The colonies' first continuous newspaper, the weekly *Boston News-Letter,* is founded.

1721
The Arts
Gustavus Hesselius paints the Last Supper to decorate the inside of a Maryland church.

1730
Business and Finance New York undergoes a business recession, which lasts for several years.

1742
Science and Technology
Benjamin Franklin invents the Franklin stove.

1751
Business and Finance
Parliament passes an act forbidding the printing of paper money in New England.

1763
World Events
The Treaty of Paris is signed.

1700	1710	1720	1730	1740	1750	1760	1770

1711
Science and Technology
The patent medicine Tuscarora Rice becomes a common treatment for tuberculosis.

1714
Politics
Samuel Mulford, speaking before the New York assembly, demands that colonists' rights be protected against customs officials.

1731
Daily Life
The first colonial subscription library opens in Philadelphia.

1741
Daily Life
Jonathan Edwards preaches his "Sinners in the Hands of an Angry God" sermon.

1748
World Events
The Treaty of Aix-la-Chapelle ends the War of the Austrian Succession.

1757
The Arts
Colonial painters exhibit their work in New York.

Silver spoon and cups from the 1700s

Preacher George Whitefield

Think About Themes

Themes Journal *Decide whether you **agree** or **disagree** with the following statements. Note why in your journal.*

Cultural Diversity The cultural backgrounds of settlers will influence the development of a region.

Economic Development The economic needs of one nation can have a dramatic effect on the population of another nation.

Global Relations A sponsoring country has an obligation to maintain tight control over its colonies.

The New England Colonies

Adam van Breen painted this scene of the Puritans leaving Delft's harbor.

EYEWITNESSES TO History

66 *They fell upon their knees and blessed the God of heaven, who had brought them over the vast and furious ocean, and delivered them from all the perils and miseries thereof, again to set their feet on the firm and stable earth.* **99**

—**William Bradford**

The Pilgrims land at Plymouth Rock.

William Bradford described the feelings of the 101 passengers and some 25 crewmembers aboard the *Mayflower* when they arrived on the shore of present-day Massachusetts in November 1620. They had been at sea for almost nine weeks, much of that time enduring violent storms. Originally bound for the Hudson River near Manhattan, they decided to stay where they were, on the land they called New Plymouth. According to Bradford, it was a "hideous and desolate wilderness . . . and the whole country, full of woods and thickets, represented a wild and savage hue." Despite their inhospitable surroundings, on December 25, 1620, the Pilgrims began building their first homes in North America.

The Pilgrims

In 1620 the men and women aboard the *Mayflower* reached Cape Cod Bay, near what is now Provincetown, Massachusetts. There they founded the colony of Plymouth. Known as **Pilgrims**, they had left England because of religious conflict. They saw themselves as wanderers who, like the pilgrims and exiles portrayed in the Bible, traveled in search of a place to worship God in their own way.

The Pilgrim faith. Conflicts over religious doctrine had raged in England since 1534, when King Henry VIII broke with the Roman Catholic Church to form the Church of England, or Anglican Church. Henry's motives had been primarily personal—the pope had refused to grant him a divorce from his first wife. At heart still a Roman Catholic, he had created a church that remained largely Catholic in form. This deeply troubled many English Christians, who longed for a truly Protestant church.

The Pilgrims were **Separatists**, so called because they had broken with the Anglican Church. The Pilgrims were the most radical of the **Puritans**, Protestants who wished to "purify" the Anglican Church of all Catholic rituals and traditions. The Puritans objected, for example, to the clergy's elaborate robes. They insisted that church leaders should be known for "their purity of mind, not their adornment of person."

Some Separatists, including the Pilgrims, left England for the more religiously tolerant Netherlands after King James I threatened to "harry them out of the land, or else do worse." There they were forced into low-paid, unskilled work and confronted with what one Pilgrim called the "grim & grisly face of poverty." Equally alarming was the prospect of their children being led away from the faith by Dutch customs. Puritan minister John Robinson summed up the Pilgrims' experience in the Netherlands as "exiled from country, spoiled of goods, destitute of friends, few in number, and mean in condition." Seeking "some place of better advantage and less danger," William Bradford and others obtained permission from the Virginia Company to settle on lands it owned near the mouth of the Hudson River.

Plymouth colony. The Pilgrims did not reach their original destination. Their ship was blown off course, and they landed farther north, in Massachusetts's Cape Cod Bay. Rather than risk additional travel, they decided to stay. To maintain order in the new settlement, Pilgrim leaders had drawn up an agreement for the men to sign. This document, the **Mayflower Compact**, established a self-governing colony based on the majority rule of male church members. Once the Compact was signed, the colonists elected John Carver as their governor and turned to the challenge of surviving the winter. They then set out to establish what one colonist called "the most glorious edifice [building] of Mount Zion [a holy place] in a Wilderness." Disease and hunger, however, soon took their toll. The colony's record for March 24, 1621, notes, "In three months past dies half our company. . . . The living [are] scarce able to bury the dead."

Like Jamestown, the colony owed its survival in part to American Indians. Soon after the first encounter between the Wampanoag (wahm-puh-NOH-ag) and the Pilgrims, the two groups signed a peace treaty. As one colonist wrote, "by friendly usage, love, peace, . . . [and] good counsel," the Pilgrims and the Wampanoag strove to "live in peace in that land." The settlers were particularly indebted to Squanto, a member of the Patuxet band of the Wampanoag who taught them how to grow crops. Squanto also spoke English. Kidnapped in about 1614, he had lived in Spain and England before returning home in 1619 to find his village wiped out by disease. With Squanto's aid, the Pilgrims enjoyed a bountiful harvest in the fall. The Pilgrims then joined the Wampanoag in a harvest celebration. "For three days we entertained and feasted," wrote one colonist. This celebration later became the basis for the Thanksgiving holiday tradition.

The Great Migration. In contrast to the Pilgrims, most Puritans remained in England and did not leave the Anglican Church. These religious dissenters hoped to reform the church from within.

COURTESY OF THE PILGRIM SOCIETY, PLYMOUTH, MASSACHUSETTS

The Mayflower Compact

★ HISTORICAL DOCUMENTS ★

The Mayflower Compact

On November 21, 1620, while still aboard the Mayflower, *41 of the male passengers signed an agreement designed to help them govern their new colony. Although it did not set forth the organization of the government in detail, the Mayflower Compact did establish a precedent for governments based on written agreements and the consent of the governed.*

We, whose names are underwritten, . . . Having undertaken for the Glory of God, and Advancement of the Christian Faith, and the Honour of our King and Country, a Voyage to plant the first colony in the northern Parts of Virginia; Do by these Presents [this document], solemnly and mutually in the Presence of God and one another, covenant and combine ourselves together into a civil Body Politick, for our better Ordering and Preservation, and Furtherance of the Ends aforesaid; And by Virtue hereof do enact, constitute, and frame, such just and equal Laws, Ordinances, Acts, Constitutions, and Offices, from time to time, as shall be thought most meet and convenient for the general Good of the Colony; unto which we promise all due Submission and Obedience.

The Crown, however, opposed reform. James I feared that Puritan demands would lead to political unrest. Religious dissent, or disagreement, he declared, "as well agreth with a Monarchy as God and the Devil." James's son Charles, who inherited the throne in 1625, was even more determined to stop dissent. Charles also wished to stop Puritan ministers and practices.

The English Puritans faced economic difficulties as well. In recent years England's population had dramatically increased, but employment had not. The growing profitability of wool production encouraged large landowners to turn from farming to raising sheep. They fenced their lands and drove off the tenant farmers, many of whom were Puritans. Land was scarce, and the money needed to purchase an acre or two in England would purchase several hundred acres in America. Then in the 1620s crop failures and an economic depression in the wool industry hit Puritan farmers and weavers.

To escape both religious persecution and economic ruin, many Puritans decided to risk a move to the colonies. Beginning in 1630, in what is known as the **Great Migration**, some 60,000 people left England for the Americas. While most of them went to the West Indies, 10,000 to 20,000 settled in Massachusetts.

Most Puritans, however, did not leave England. In 1642 the conflict between the Puritans and the Royalists—the supporters of King Charles I—erupted in civil war. Led by Oliver Cromwell, the Puritans won. During the civil war and Cromwell's rule between 1653 and 1658, Puritan emigration almost ceased.

✔ **READING CHECK:** What problems did the Pilgrims and other Puritans face in England?

Massachusetts Bay Colony

By the late 1620s a group of English Puritan leaders had become interested in settling in North America. The year before the Puritan migration began, a group of wealthy Puritans obtained a royal charter for the Massachusetts Bay Company that allowed them to establish a colony there. In 1630 the company's fleet of 11 ships carried some 1,000 settlers to Massachusetts. These Puritans did not wish to cut all ties with England or with the Anglican Church. Rather, inspired by a sense of mission, they hoped to provide other Christians with an example of a model community. While still aboard ship, John Winthrop, their leader, expressed their vision and warned against failure.

66 We must consider that we shall be as a city upon a hill. The eyes of all people are upon us. So that if we shall deal falsely with our God in this work we have undertaken, and so cause Him to withdraw His present help from us, we shall be made a story and a byword through the world. 99

Most colonists, wrote Winthrop, expected to find in their new home more of God's "wisdom, power, goodness and truth than formerly we have been acquainted with." Their expectations arose from their belief that they had a covenant, or sacred contract, with God to build a society based on the Bible and a covenant with one another "to walk together in all His ways."

INTERPRETING THE VISUAL RECORD

Cultures meet. John Winthrop, governor of the Massachusetts Bay Colony, meets with a Narraganset Indian. *What do the clothes the two men are wearing suggest about their respective cultures?*

The charter of the Massachusetts Bay Company allowed Winthrop and the other stockholders to govern the colony however they wished. They could not, however, violate English law. They established their colony as a place where everyone, guided by English law and the Bible, was expected to work together for the common good. The stockholders granted voting rights to all freemen, that is, adult men who were church members and property owners. The freemen in each town then elected representatives to the General Court, or governing body, to make laws for the colony. Only about half of the men in the colony—and none of the women—had the right to vote.

The Puritan commonwealth was based on cooperation between church and state—a relationship the colonists referred to as the **New England Way**. The meetinghouse, in which Puritans held both town meetings and church services, symbolized this cooperation. The outside walls of the plain, unpainted clapboard building served as a public notice board. Sermons delivered within on Sundays and on important occasions instructed the congregation in the New England Way. Such lessons were important because the Puritans believed that everyone in the community had to live a moral life. Otherwise, the entire community would suffer God's anger. When catastrophe struck, the faithful often blamed the occurrence on New England's sinfulness.

The Puritans also believed in predestination—that an all-knowing God had already determined who would be saved, but that strict self-examination could reveal clues as to who was among the chosen. The church granted full membership to those who convinced the congregation that they were among the chosen. In 1662 partial membership was offered to those who could not offer such testimony.

The New England Way depended on educated people who could understand the Bible. The General Court thus required parents to make sure that their children learned to read. In 1636 the General Court founded Harvard College, the first college in North America. The college's primary purpose was the training of young men for the ministry. A law passed in 1647 required individual towns to maintain schools. The "Old Deluder Law," as it was known, was designed to defeat the "chief project of that old deluder, Satan, to keep men from the knowledge of the Scriptures." Other colonies were slower to establish schools. In 1701 a second college, Yale, was founded in Connecticut as a response to Harvard's perceived departure from church doctrine.

✔ **READING CHECK:** Why did the Puritans emphasize the importance of education?

Harvard College was founded in 1636.

COURTESY OF THE PILGRIM SOCIETY, PLYMOUTH, MASSACHUSETTS

INTERPRETING THE VISUAL RECORD
The meetinghouse. In 1683 the Puritans built a new meetinghouse. *How does the building's design reflect the Puritans' beliefs?*

New England Life

By the time Massachusetts Bay Colony passed its school law, it had more than 20,000 inhabitants. The men who immigrated there were primarily educated artisans or farmers. According to Deputy Governor Thomas Dudley, they were "godly men . . . endowed with grace and furnished with means." Three out of four had paid their own way to the colony.

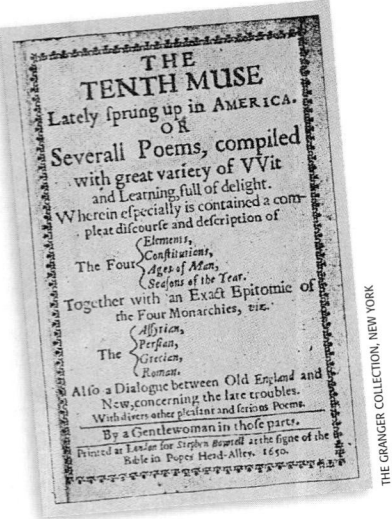

Anne Bradstreet's collection was the first book of poetry published in the colonies.

INTERPRETING THE VISUAL RECORD

Colonial homes. A woman works a spinning wheel in her kitchen. Puritan women made the family's clothing, often including shoes, like the ones pictured below. *What can you determine from the image about the design of colonial homes?*

Women and families. In contrast to the Jamestown colonists, Puritan men brought along their wives and children. Puritans considered orderly families to be essential to a stable society. Women were expected to obey their fathers or husbands. Most Puritan women accepted their role. As Lucy Winthrop Downing wrote to her brother John Winthrop: "I am but a wife and therefore it is sufficient for me to follow my husband." Poet Anne Bradstreet, who came to Massachusetts in 1630, also expressed acceptance of the inequality of the sexes.

> 66 Let Greeks be Greeks, and women what they are,
> Men have precedency and still excel,
> It is but vain, unjustly to wage war;
> Men can do best, and women know it well. 99

Court records from the era show, however, that some Puritan women rejected the authority of their husbands. A few even successfully brought suit against their husbands for not fulfilling their role as providers for the family.

Following English custom, New England women usually did not work in the fields, although they did help at harvest time. Instead, they took on many other tasks required to run a farm. They made many of the things their families needed: soap, candles, yarn, clothes, butter, and cheese. Women might sell their occasional surplus in town to help support their families. In her husband's absence, wrote one minister, a woman might also act as "wife and deputy-husband."

Families in New England tended to be large. Most had at least six children, and families with nine or more children were common. Food was plentiful, and the diseases that had plagued Jamestown were unable to survive in New England's cold climate. As a result, in one town 85 percent of all children lived to adulthood. Colonist Mary Buell's tombstone shows just how large these families could be—it records that she died at age 90 leaving behind 336 living descendants.

✔ **READING CHECK:** What duties and responsibilities did women in New England have?

Commerce. Although there were indentured servants and slaves in New England, most large families had relatively little need for extra laborers. Fathers and sons could supply all the labor needed to transform the "remote, rocky, barren, bushy, wild-woody wilderness," as Edward Johnson described it in 1653, into "a second England." Because of long winters and the poor soil found in much of New England, however, farmers did not raise a large surplus of crops to sell.

To pay for supplies and luxury items from England, some residents of the New England colonies turned to fishing, trade, and business. New Englanders distilled rum and built ships. They sold fish, grain, meat, lumber, and naval stores (turpentine, pitch, tar, and rosin) to England, Spain, Portugal, and the West Indies. They also traded with England's other American colonies. Merchants earned substantial profits by selling their shipping services. Johnson remarked that it could not have been "imagined, that this wilderness should turn [into] a mart for merchants in so short a space."

Conflicts in the Colony

Despite the prosperous times, Massachusetts was not without its difficulties. Some people, rejecting the Puritan laws and ways, eventually left the colony.

Religious dissent. Minister Thomas Hooker and his congregation left Massachusetts partly because of religious differences with Puritan leaders and partly because the commonwealth's "towns were set so near to each other." To get more farmland, they moved southwest, establishing a colony in the Connecticut Valley. In 1639 Hooker's settlers adopted the **Fundamental Orders of Connecticut**, widely considered to be the first written constitution in the world.

Other colonists were forced to leave Massachusetts Bay Colony because they questioned Puritan ways. One such person was Roger Williams, a minister who, unlike most other Puritans, believed in strict separation of church and state. His beliefs so angered Puritan leaders that they banished Williams. He purchased land from the Narraganset Indians and in 1636 founded a settlement that later became known as Providence, Rhode Island. Williams obtained a royal charter for the colony in 1644 that gave religious freedom to its inhabitants.

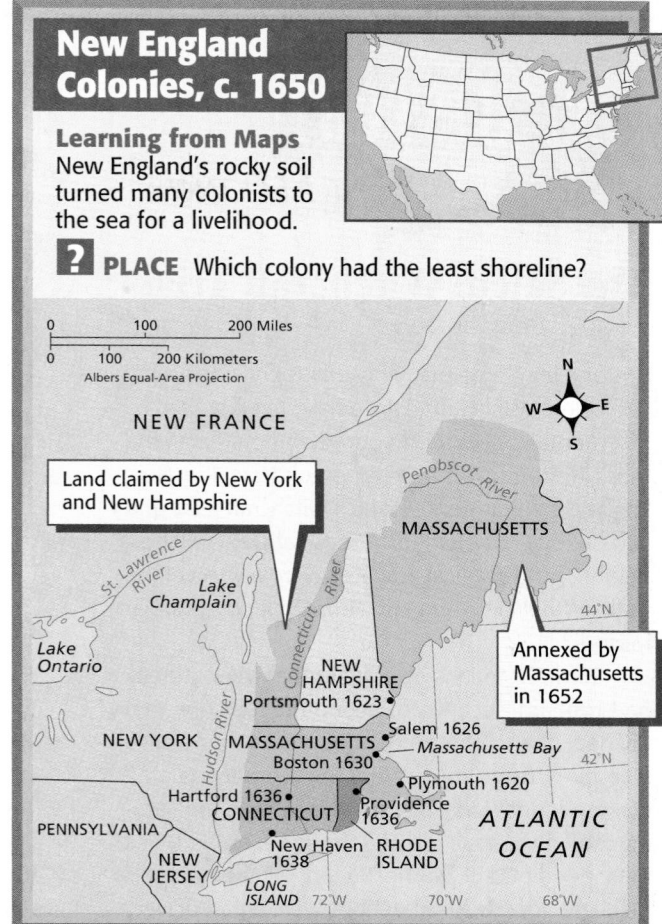

New England Colonies, c. 1650

Learning from Maps
New England's rocky soil turned many colonists to the sea for a livelihood.

? PLACE Which colony had the least shoreline?

Land claimed by New York and New Hampshire

Annexed by Massachusetts in 1652

BIOGRAPHY
Anne Hutchinson

Challenging authority. Anne Hutchinson was another Puritan who found refuge in Rhode Island after refusing to follow the New England Way. Born in England in 1591, Hutchinson came to Boston, the capital of Massachusetts Bay Colony, in 1634 with her family. Governor Winthrop called her "a woman of a ready wit and bold spirit." Hutchinson worked as a nurse and midwife and devoted herself to Bible study and teaching. She hosted meetings in her home, where she discussed the sermons of Boston's leading ministers. She attracted a following of women as well as wealthy merchants, many of whom resented the Puritan ministers' authority.

Increasingly, Hutchinson expressed ideas that opposed the established clergy's teachings. In 1636 her followers included the governor and many prominent citizens. Fearing a growing rebellion, officials arrested Hutchinson in 1637 and charged her with weakening the authority of the church. The fact that she was a woman added to the authorities' displeasure. Her meetings, Governor Winthrop told her, were "not tolerable . . . in the sight of God nor fitting for your sex." The clergy found particularly dangerous Hutchinson's claim that she received her religious insights directly from God. To the leaders of the colony, Hutchinson's claim threatened the authority of both the community and the church. Banished in 1638, she moved to Rhode Island and later to Long Island. When Hutchinson was killed

Read More About It

Free Find:
Anne Hutchinson
After reading about Anne Hutchinson on the **Holt Researcher** CD–ROM, create a news report that explains both sides of her conflict with the clergy.

HISTORY
IN THE MAKING

The Salem Witchcraft Trials
BY CAROL F. KARLSEN

For a long time many historians considered the Salem witchcraft trials to have been started by mentally disturbed young women, liars, and mass hysteria. Today most emphasize the New England environment in which witchcraft fears and accusations flourished. Ideas about witches, demons, and magical practices were all part of the Puritans' belief system and New England's popular folklore.

Some historians also argue that the outbreak had roots in decades of economic tensions that divided the community. The accusations also stemmed from men's fear of women gaining economic and social independence—and threatening the power structure and the social order. These new perceptions of the Salem witchcraft trials highlight how such accusations were a part of New England culture and society. Such greater awareness makes the Salem outbreak appear less bizarre but no less fascinating.

in an American Indian attack in 1643, Massachusetts ministers declared it "the just vengeance of God."

The Salem witchcraft trials. Other conflicts were confined within the colony. By 1690 some two dozen people had been accused of witchcraft in Massachusetts. Early in 1692 several girls in Salem Village, a farming community near bustling Salem Town, were stricken with seizures. The girls had become fascinated with stories of magic told to them by an enslaved West Indian woman named Tituba. The local minister and other villagers attributed the girls' seizures to witchcraft. As the girls named those supposedly responsible for their afflictions, other residents of Salem Village and nearby towns testified that they, too, were victims of witchcraft. They claimed other villagers had used demonic powers to kill their children, sicken their farm animals, and otherwise harm their families and property.

By June hundreds of people, mainly older women but also some men, had been accused of witchcraft. Dozens were tried, and 19 were hanged. Several years later Samuel Sewall, a judge in the witch trials, stood in his church pew with his head bowed while his minister read his confession. "[Sewall] desires to take the Blame and Shame of it [the witch-hunt], Asking pardon of Men, And especially desiring prayers that God . . . would pardon that Sin and all his other Sins." Many of the colony's inhabitants, however, probably continued to believe that the witches were a punishment for their sins.

✔ **READING CHECK:** What incidents threatened the unity of society in Massachusetts?

SECTION 1 REVIEW

Define and explain the significance of the following terms:
Pilgrims
Separatists
Puritans
Mayflower Compact
Great Migration
New England Way
Fundamental Orders of Connecticut

Identify and explain the significance of the following individuals:
William Bradford
Squanto
John Winthrop
Thomas Hooker
Roger Williams
Anne Hutchinson

Locate and explain the importance of the following places:
Massachusetts
Plymouth
Connecticut
Rhode Island
Salem

1. **Using Graphic Organizers** Copy the following graphic organizer. Use it to explain the factors that led the Pilgrims and Puritans to settle in New England.

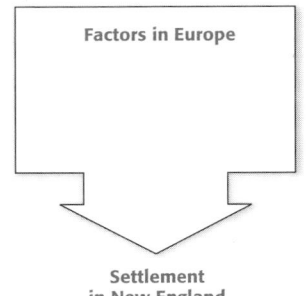

Factors in Europe

Settlement
in New England

2. **Identifying Values** Why was education important to the Puritan community?
3. **Recognizing Point of View** Write a paragraph describing English settlement in New England from the perspective of a female colonist.
4. **Analyzing** How did the Massachusetts Bay Colony's leaders react to colonists whose ideas threatened their authority?

Critical Thinking

5. How well did the Puritan form of government work?
   Consider:
   • the main characteristics of the Puritan government
   • the goals of the government
   • weaknesses in the system

The Southern Colonies and Slavery

OBJECTIVES

Read to understand:

1. how and why the Chesapeake differed from New England
2. why the Chesapeake was slow to develop towns and how that affected the region
3. what led to Bacon's Rebellion
4. why Chesapeake planters came to favor slavery over indentured servitude

KEY TERMS

Toleration Act
Bacon's Rebellion
House of Burgesses
Middle Passage
Quakers
abolitionists

KEY PEOPLE

Cecilius Calvert
Nathaniel Bacon
Olaudah Equiano

KEY PLACE

Chesapeake Bay

These female settlers are arriving in Jamestown, Virginia.

THE GRANGER COLLECTION, NEW YORK

EYEWITNESSES TO History

66 *The use of negroes . . . would both occasion great numbers of white people to come here, and also would render us capable to subsist [survive] ourselves, by raising provisions upon our lands, until we could make some produce fit for export.* 99

—Southern Colonists

A group of southern colonists argued for the increased use of slaves, even though the founder of their new colony opposed slavery there. By the end of the 1600s, many southern planters had come to rely on the labor of enslaved Africans. The Royal African Company had a monopoly on the slave trade in Virginia at this time, but it was not always able to meet the planters' demands. Illegal slave ships, known as interlopers, sometimes tried to land on Virginia's shore. One such ship, the *Society*, was captured in 1687, and about 100 Africans aboard were seized. According to colonial records, 90 of the Africans, including several children, brought in a collective price of more than £1,500.

Landing a group of slaves at Jamestown

Settling the Chesapeake

By 1640, several decades before slavery became firmly established, Virginia was a thriving colony with a population of some 10,000. Tobacco fueled the economy and remained the most valuable export of the colony for many years. The promise of huge profits led more than one wealthy Englishman to dream of establishing a colony in the Chesapeake—the land surrounding Chesapeake Bay. The first to do so was George Calvert, the first Lord Baltimore.

After Calvert's death in 1632, King Charles I made Calvert's son Cecilius proprietor, or owner, of millions of acres in the upper Chesapeake. The colony was named Maryland, after Charles's French wife, Henrietta Maria. As proprietor, Calvert was free to use the land and to govern—within loose guidelines—as he wished.

Calvert wanted to create a haven for fellow Roman Catholics who faced persecution in Protestant England. He also hoped to make money. Because there were not enough Catholic immigrants to make his venture profitable, Calvert opened his colony to Protestants. Soon Protestant colonists greatly outnumbered Catholics. To protect the Catholic minority's legal rights, the Maryland Assembly passed the **Toleration Act** in 1649, which granted a degree of religious freedom. That year Maryland governor William Stone promised immigrants to Maryland "liberty in religion and privileges of English subjects."

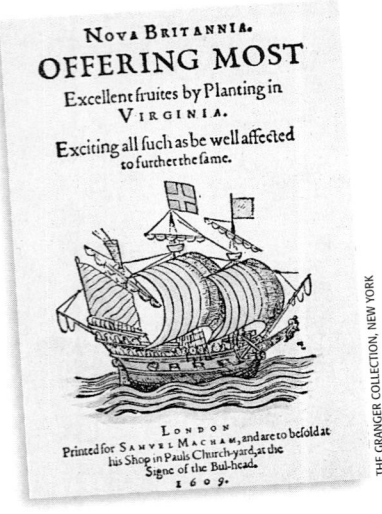

NOVA BRITANNIA.
OFFERING MOST
Excellent fruites by Planting in
VIRGINIA.
Exciting all such as be well affected
to further the same.

LONDON
Printed for SAMVEL MACHAM, and are to be sold at
his Shop in Pauls Church-yard, at the
Signe of the Bul-head.
1609.

THE GRANGER COLLECTION, NEW YORK

INTERPRETING THE VISUAL RECORD

Advertising. This pamphlet was published to attract settlers to Virginia. *How does the image of Virginia suggested by the pamphlet compare to what life was like in the colony?*

Chesapeake Society

Catholic and Protestant settlers in Maryland soon followed Virginia's lead and devoted much of their land to tobacco production. As a result, both colonies developed a distinct culture that shaped life in the Chesapeake.

Population. Most white colonists came to the Chesapeake as indentured servants. One indentured servant, John Harrower, described how some servants were bought and sold once they arrived in Virginia.

> 66 Soul drivers . . . are men who make it their business to go on board all ships who have in either Servants or Convicts and buy sometimes the whole and sometimes a parcell of them. . . . Then they drive them through the Country like a parcell of Sheep until they can sell them to advantage. 99

Of the colonists who came to Virginia as indentured servants, some 75 percent were men or boys between the ages of 15 and 24. They were likely attracted by pamphlets such as George Alsop's *Character of the Province in Maryland,* published in 1666. This pamphlet presented a favorable but often misleading account of the bright future awaiting Maryland servants. Alsop also tried to recruit some women, declaring "they are no sooner on shoar, but they are courted into . . . Matrimony." Indeed, Maryland suffered from a lack of women. Even into the early 1700s, more than three times as many white men as white women were living in the colony. With this gender imbalance, many men never married.

High death rates also affected the Chesapeake population. Throughout the 1600s typhoid, malaria, and other diseases affected the colonists. Some 40 percent of immigrants to the Chesapeake region died within two years of their arrival. Only immigration assured Virginia's survival in its early days. Life expectancy slowly improved by about 1700 as native-born colonists—who had better immunity to the region's diseases—increased in number.

The high death rates gave rise to family patterns that differed from those of New England. There, low death rates meant that most people married only once. In one Maryland county, half of all marriages in the late 1600s ended within seven years because of the death of a partner. In most cases the surviving partner remarried. As a result of this trend, most families included stepparents, stepsiblings, half siblings, and sometimes the children of deceased relatives or friends.

✔ **READING CHECK:** How and why did the population of the Chesapeake differ from that of New England?

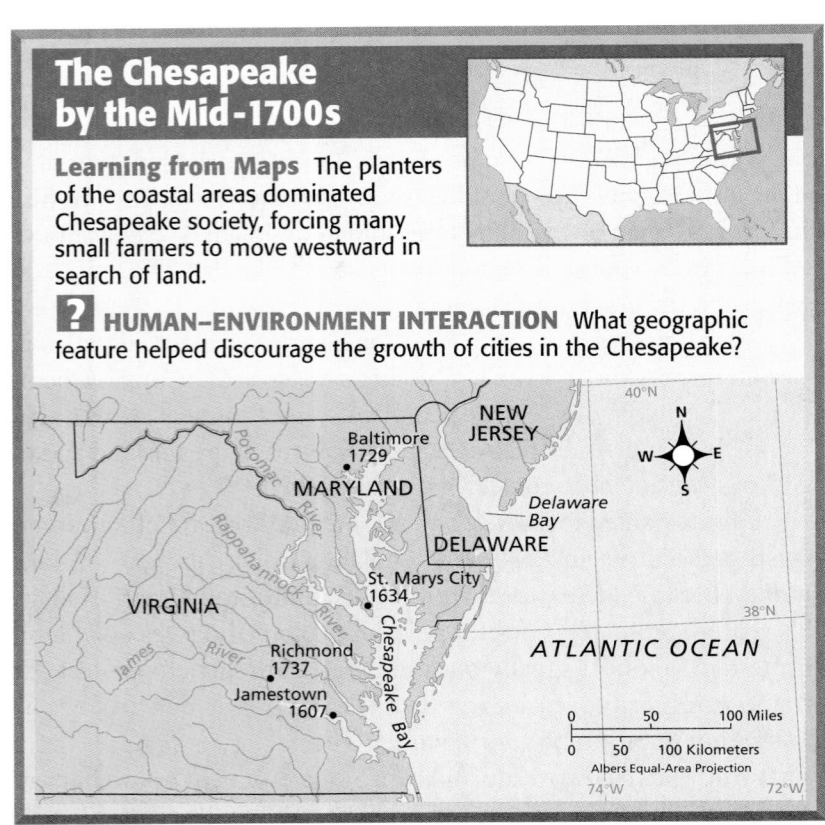

The Chesapeake by the Mid-1700s

Learning from Maps The planters of the coastal areas dominated Chesapeake society, forcing many small farmers to move westward in search of land.

❓ **HUMAN-ENVIRONMENT INTERACTION** What geographic feature helped discourage the growth of cities in the Chesapeake?

NEW JERSEY
Baltimore 1729
MARYLAND
Delaware Bay
DELAWARE
St. Marys City 1634
VIRGINIA
Richmond 1737
Jamestown 1607
Potomac River
Rappahannock River
James River
Chesapeake Bay
ATLANTIC OCEAN
40°N
38°N
74°W   72°W
0   50   100 Miles
0   50   100 Kilometers
Albers Equal-Area Projection

The Chesapeake Region

Understanding Change During the 1600s large numbers of people migrated from England to the Chesapeake region. Nearly all of these people brought some professional skills with them. Over time, however, the region's economy changed and its residents adapted by learning new skills. *What differences do you observe between the images of Chesapeake area workers in the 1600s and in the 1990s? Which statistics in the graph have changed the most? the least?*

Occupations

Gentry	Agriculture and fishing
Professions	Craftswork
Merchants	Government
Trade/sales	Semiskilled and unskilled labor

Data represents occupational status of free male emigrants from England to the Chesapeake, 1607–99, and all residents of the Chesapeake, c. 2000.

Sources: *Adapting to a New World: English Society in the Seventeenth-Century Chesapeake; Demographics USA.*
Due to rounding, graph may not add up to 100 percent.

THEN

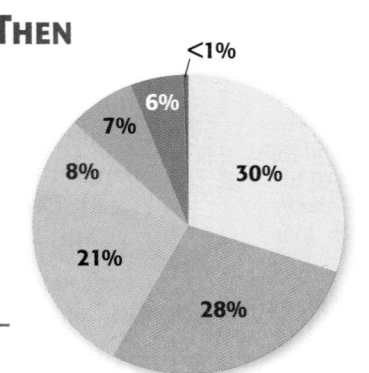

<1%
6%
7%
8%
30%
21%
28%

Now

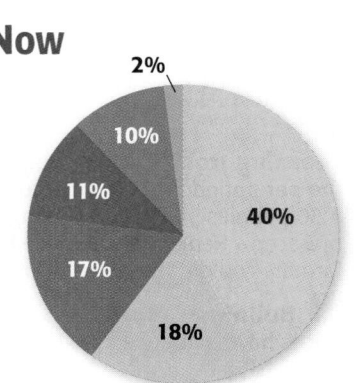

2%
10%
11%
40%
17%
18%

A rural society.

The vast majority of colonists in the Chesapeake lived on widely scattered farms and plantations. They produced tobacco for export and grew or made many of the things they needed. Most of the large plantations were located on one of the many navigable rivers that flowed into Chesapeake Bay.

The fact that planters did not bring their crops to a central market hindered the growth of towns. Without large towns to provide customers, the region was slow to develop a substantial class of independent artisans and shopkeepers. The slow growth of towns also hindered the development of schools. Many areas did not have enough children to make up a school. Education was thus left to individual families. Wealthy families made sure that their own children—both boys and girls—were educated by hiring tutors. They did not, however, support schooling for others. As a result, literacy rates were low compared to New England.

✔ **READING CHECK:** Why was the Chesapeake slow to develop towns, and what effect did this have on the region?

Bacon's Rebellion

As life expectancy and immigration increased, Virginia became home to a growing number of freed indentured servants. About 1660 tobacco prices tumbled, making it difficult for these people to earn enough money to start their own farms. Landless laborers and small landowners grew increasingly discontented.

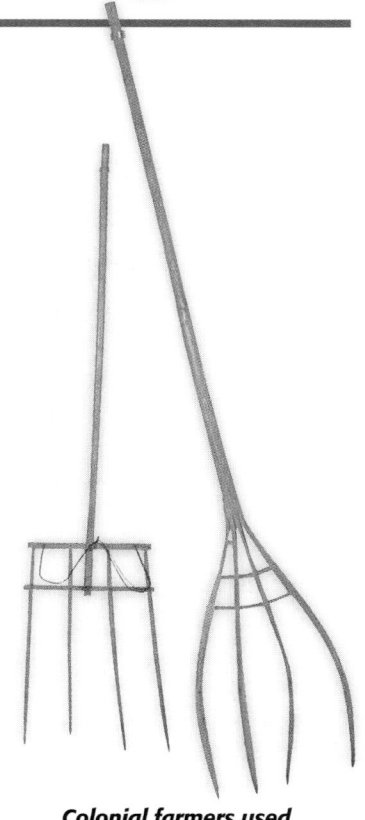

Colonial farmers used handmade tools such as these.

Tobacco Prices, 1618–1700

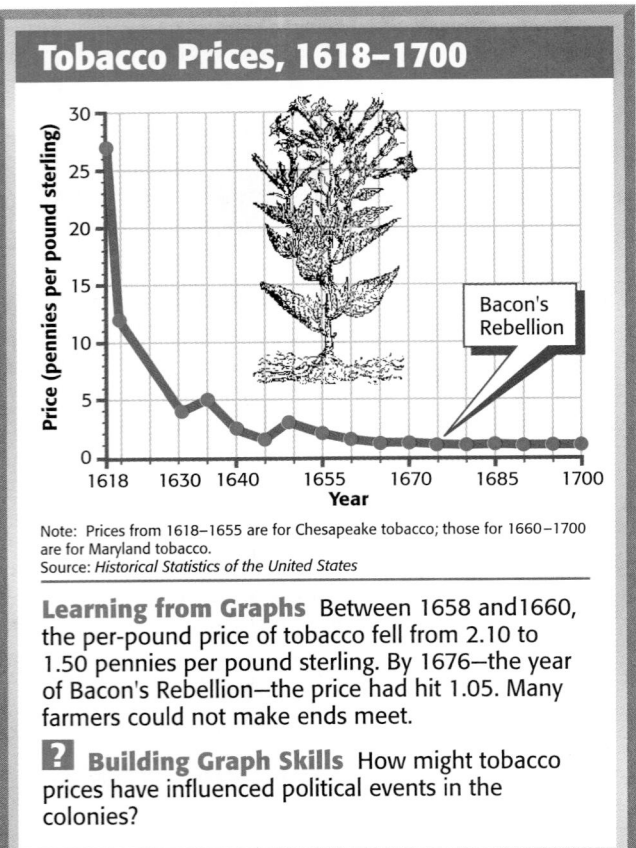

Price (pennies per pound sterling)

30
25
20
15
10
5
0

1618 1630 1640 1655 1670 1685 1700
Year

Bacon's Rebellion

Note: Prices from 1618–1655 are for Chesapeake tobacco; those for 1660–1700 are for Maryland tobacco.
Source: *Historical Statistics of the United States*

Learning from Graphs Between 1658 and 1660, the per-pound price of tobacco fell from 2.10 to 1.50 pennies per pound sterling. By 1676—the year of Bacon's Rebellion—the price had hit 1.05. Many farmers could not make ends meet.

? **Building Graph Skills** How might tobacco prices have influenced political events in the colonies?

(CHART ILLUSTRATION) THE GRANGER COLLECTION, NEW YORK

This discontent erupted in violence in western Virginia in 1675. Many poor farmers and laborers wanted to settle the area in western Virginia guaranteed to the Powhatan in a 1646 treaty. Ignoring the treaty, white settlers began to move onto Indian lands. After some settlers killed a group of friendly Susquehannock (suhs-kwuh-HA-nuhk) and no compensation was made to the tribe, the Indians attacked outlying farms. The colonists then demanded war against all Indians in the Chesapeake.

Governor William Berkeley refused, but Nathaniel Bacon pushed ahead anyway. Described by his enemies as "ambitious and arrogant" with a "dangerous hidden pride of heart," this well-connected young planter raised an army of western settlers in 1676 and attacked American Indians on the frontier. Bacon's followers, joined by indentured servants and enslaved Africans, looted wealthy plantations. The rebels also seized and burned Jamestown, then briefly took over the government.

Bacon's Rebellion ended with its leader's sudden death from illness. King Charles II ordered Governor Berkeley to return to Great Britain. The large planters in the **House of Burgesses**—Virginia's assembly—quieted opposition by limiting the governor's power over land and by opening American Indian lands to colonists.

✔ **READING CHECK:** What factors led to Bacon's Rebellion?

Slavery

Bacon's Rebellion was short-lived, but it did have one far-reaching effect: it strengthened the move already under way among planters to switch from indentured to slave labor. Indentured servants would eventually be released. This ultimately meant more discontented freed servants. Slaves did not pose this problem.

Surviving court records suggest that the institution of slavery developed gradually in the Chesapeake. The first Africans arrived in the Chesapeake in 1619 and were probably treated as indentured servants. Virginia court records for 1640, however, include the first reference to lifelong servitude. When three servants were recaptured after running away, the two white servants had their terms lengthened. The African man, however, was sentenced to serve "for the time of his natural life."

INTERPRETING THE VISUAL RECORD

African art. This bronze statue of a Portuguese soldier was made in Benin in the 1500s. *What does the statue tell you about the people of West Africa and how they viewed Europeans?*

The slave trade. The expansion of slavery in North America gave new life to the slave trade. Slave traders destroyed African families and villages. Once captured, Africans were inspected, branded, and held in prisons until there were enough slaves to fill a ship. Once on the ships, they were packed in, one captain wrote, until "they had not so much room *as a man in his coffin.*" As a result, many Africans died from disease, suffocation, or violence during the dreaded **Middle Passage**—the voyage across the Atlantic Ocean. Some captives killed themselves rather than face further horrors. Another captain reported that they "often leap'd . . . into the sea, and kept under water till they were drowned."

Crop Cultivation and Processing

Some observers criticized southern farmers for relying too much on tobacco rather than experimenting with other crops. A few early colonial farmers did experiment with crop cultivation, successfully growing apples, blackberries, blueberries, peaches, and perhaps most importantly, the indigo plant, which is used to produce a dye for cloth.

Colonists had tried to cultivate indigo as early as 1650, but it was many years before Eliza Lucas—later Eliza Lucas Pinckney—produced American indigo dye. She began to experiment on her family's plantation in the Chesapeake with seeds her father sent from the West Indies. She had "greater hopes" for indigo than for the other plants she tried, but she still struggled for several years to produce her first healthy crop.

Lucas also developed a reliable method for processing indigo plants. Slaves packed the fresh indigo into outdoor vats where it was weighted down with heavy timbers. After the plants soaked in water for at least half a day, the slaves drained the liquid into a smaller vat. There they whipped the liquid with wooden paddles for several hours, causing the "indigo mud" to sink to the bottom of the vat. Several cycles of boiling and cooling followed, then the mud was pumped into another vat and strained. Slaves scraped off the indigo that remained on the strainer and dried it into small dye cakes the size of soap bars.

In 1744 Lucas sent the indigo to Great Britain, where merchants were highly pleased with its quality. Soon other colonists were also growing indigo. In 1747 more than 135,000 pounds were produced for export, thus ensuring its agricultural success.

THE GRANGER COLLECTION, NEW YORK

Understanding Science and History

1. How did Eliza Lucas come to cultivate indigo?
2. What do you think the letters marked on the diagram of indigo processing indicate?

BIOGRAPHY

Olaudah Equiano

The experience of slavery. Olaudah Equiano (oh-LOW-duh ek-wee-AHN-oh), a member of the Ibo people who lived in present-day Nigeria, was kidnapped and sold into slavery in the mid-1700s, when he was 11 or 12. He later described the ordeal of the Middle Passage in his autobiography. At first he was terrified that he and the other captives were "to be eaten by those white men with horrible looks, red faces, and long hair." He was eventually reassured that he would not be eaten, but new horrors confronted him when he was put below deck.

> ❝ There I received such a salutation in my nostrils as I had never experienced in my life: so that with the loathsomeness [disgust] of the stench, and crying together, I became so sick and low that I was not able to eat, nor had I the least desire to taste any thing. I now wished for the last friend, death, to relieve me; but soon, to my grief, two of the white men offered me eatables; and, on my refusing to eat, one of them held me fast by the hands . . . and tied my feet, while the other flogged me severely. ❞

Read More About It

Free Find:
Olaudah Equiano
After reading about Olaudah Equiano on the **Holt Researcher** CD–ROM, create a brochure for a museum exhibition on Equiano that shows the different stages of his life, from his kidnapping as a young boy to his later years as a lecturer living in England.

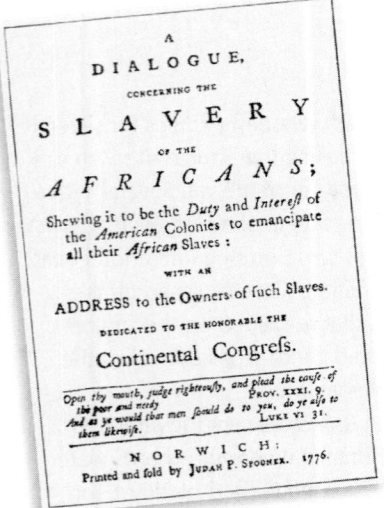

This 1776 pamphlet called for the freeing of all African slaves.

Soon after Equiano arrived in the colonies, a Virginia planter purchased him and then sold him to a British naval officer, Michael Pascal, who renamed him Gustavus Vassa. Later he was sold to an English merchant, for whom he worked as a sailor. By 1766 Equiano had earned enough money to buy his freedom. He continued to work as a sailor and even accompanied an expedition to the Arctic.

In 1777 Equiano settled in England and later devoted himself to the antislavery movement. He lectured widely on the evils of slavery. Published in 1789, his popular autobiography convinced many people of the need to stop the slave trade.

Reactions to slavery. Equiano was not the only person to speak out against the institution of slavery. A group of **Quakers**—members of a Protestant sect that rejected wealth and even clergy— also took a public stand against slavery as early as 1688. Although **abolitionists**, or those who wanted slavery abolished, did not become a strong force in the United States until the early 1800s, some colonists did denounce the institution.

Despite such protests, slavery was practiced in all the English colonies. As Africans became more numerous after 1660, they were—by law and by custom— treated as inferior to whites. In 1705 Virginia consolidated its various laws and customs into one "slave code." Other colonies did the same. The slave codes were designed to prevent escape and discourage revolt. The codes forbade slaves to meet together in large numbers, to leave the plantation without permission, to learn to read or write, or to own weapons. The codes even declared that a master who killed a slave while "correcting" him or her could not be tried for murder.

Harsh rules did not prevent rebellion, however. Newly arrived Africans often ran away. There were also several uprisings. The largest occurred in 1739 in Stono, South Carolina. Slaves killed some 30 white colonists before the uprising was put down. The slaves who survived the rebellion were "put to the most cruel Death."

✔ **READING CHECK:** Why did Chesapeake planters prefer slaves to indentured servants?

SECTION  REVIEW

Define and explain the significance of the following terms:
Toleration Act
Bacon's Rebellion
House of Burgesses
Middle Passage
Quakers
abolitionists

Identify and explain the significance of the following individuals:
Cecilius Calvert
Nathaniel Bacon
Olaudah Equiano

Locate and explain the importance of the following place:
Chesapeake Bay

1. **Using Graphic Organizers** Copy the flowchart below. Use it to describe aspects of life in the Chesapeake and what caused those traits.

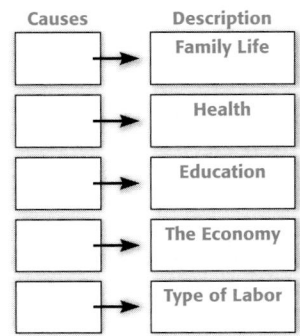

Causes	Description
→	Family Life
→	Health
→	Education
→	The Economy
→	Type of Labor

2. **Understanding Geography: Place** How did the late development of towns in the Chesapeake affect the region?
3. **Recognizing Point of View** Why did many farmers support Bacon's Rebellion?
4. **Hypothesizing** Without Bacon's Rebellion, would planters have begun to favor slavery over indentured servitude? Explain your answer.

Critical Thinking

5. To what extent was the early history of the Chesapeake shaped by economics?
   Consider:
   • economic factors that motivated colonization
   • economic effects on the political structure
   • economic effects on political conflicts and their outcomes

The Colonies After the Restoration

OBJECTIVES

Read to understand:

1. how the English came to settle the Carolinas and possess New York and New Jersey
2. what social ideals guided the founding of Pennsylvania and Georgia
3. how the Navigation Acts both helped and hurt the colonies
4. how the colonists reacted to the Glorious Revolution
5. what beliefs the Great Awakening promoted

KEY TERMS

Restoration
task system
mercantilism
balance of trade
Navigation Acts
Glorious Revolution
Enlightenment
Great Awakening

KEY PEOPLE

Charles II
Peter Stuyvesant
William Penn
James Oglethorpe
James II
Edmund Andros
Jonathan Edwards
George Whitefield

KEY PLACES

North Carolina
South Carolina
New York
New Jersey
Pennsylvania
Delaware
Georgia

EYEWITNESSES TO History

66 *We . . . found as good tracts of land, dry, well-wooded, pleasant, and delightful as we have seen anywhere in the world. . . . The woods [are] stored with abundance of deer and turkeys everywhere. . . . Oaks . . . also a very tall large tree of great bigness which some do call cypress . . . growing in swamps. Likewise walnut, birch, beech, maple, ash, bay willow, alder, and holly.* 99
—**William Hilton**

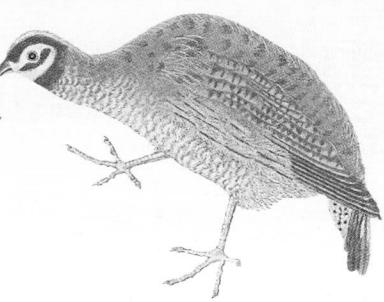

Colonists were amazed by the amount of wild game they found in North America.

In 1663 Carolina's proprietors sent Captain William Hilton of Massachusetts to locate a good spot for new settlement. Hilton explored the region along the Cape Fear River in present-day North Carolina, which he had visited the year before. His report, *A Relation of a Discovery,* was published in London the following year. In it, he praised the quality of this land, declaring it could "accommodate thousands of our English nation." As a reward for his work, the Carolina promoters granted him 1,000 acres of land adjoining the river.

The Carolinas

After the death of Puritan leader Oliver Cromwell, Charles II restored the monarchy's power in England. During this era, called the **Restoration**, another wave of colonization began when the king rewarded his supporters with grants of land. In 1663 he gave eight supporters a charter for a colony located between Virginia and Spanish Florida. The colony was named Carolina—a Latin form of the name Charles. Later the colony was divided into North and South Carolina. The proprietors proved to be poor governors, and in the 1720s the Crown officially took over both colonies.

King Charles II of England

Many settlers from the Chesapeake established small farms in North Carolina. South Carolina's first colonists came primarily from Barbados. They raised cattle, cut timber, and traded with American Indians. Some settlers tried to grow rice but failed. However, enslaved Africans who came from rice-growing regions of West Africa knew the proper cultivation techniques. Settlers used the Africans' knowledge and labor to transform the swampy coastal region into very profitable rice plantations.

The Carolinas and the thriving port of Charles Town—present-day Charleston—attracted Scots, Scotch-Irish, Germans, European Jews, West Indians, and, after 1685, French Huguenots, or Protestants, fleeing religious persecution. In

INTERPRETING THE VISUAL RECORD

Charleston. This painting shows a view of colonial Charleston, South Carolina, as seen from the harbor. *What does this image tell you about the economy of Charleston in the 1700s?*

South Carolina, however, the demand for plantation workers was so great that by 1720, slaves made up nearly two thirds of the population.

On the large rice plantations, slaves had relatively little contact with white colonists. As a result, they retained more of their African traditions than did slaves in other areas. Slaves on the rice plantations worked under the **task system**. Each day the slaves were assigned particular duties. Once they had completed their assigned tasks, the slaves could tend their own small plots and raise their own livestock. Some sold their chickens, hogs, and produce or worked for wages on their own time. A few slaves earned enough to buy their freedom if the slaveholders permitted it. Over time, though, slaveholders began to worry that their slaves—who outnumbered them—were becoming too independent. Fearful of slave revolts, they successfully pressed the colony to adopt a harsh slave code.

New York and New Jersey

Attracted by the profitable fur trade, the Dutch West India Company established a colony in North America in 1613. New Netherland extended inland along the Hudson River valley and included the town of New Amsterdam, founded in 1626 on Manhattan Island. The Dutch West India Company had little luck attracting Dutch settlers. The company did attract a variety of other inhabitants. As early as 1644 the colony's director general reported that the settlers spoke some 18 different languages.

Most settlers in New Netherland believed that their leaders were poor. As a result, they refused to defend the colony when an English fleet sailed into the harbor of New Amsterdam, the colony's capital, in 1664 and demanded that the Dutch surrender. Without a shot being fired, the colony's governor, Peter Stuyvesant, surrendered to the English. The new governor, Richard Nicolls, promised to treat all colonists "with all humanity and gentleness consistent with safety and honor."

Charles II made his brother, James, the Duke of York, proprietor of New Netherland. James kept part of the colony—renamed New York—and gave the rest—New Jersey—to two friends. New Amsterdam's leaders renamed their town New York City in James's honor. People from other colonies soon settled New Jersey.

✔ **READING CHECK:** How did England settle the Carolinas and come to possess the New York and New Jersey colonies?

INTERPRETING THE VISUAL RECORD

New Amsterdam. Peter Stuyvesant surrendered the colony of New Amsterdam to the English on September 8, 1664. *How does the architecture of the buildings shown compare to those in other colonies?*

Colonial Experiments

The colonies of Pennsylvania, Delaware, and Georgia were founded between 1681 and 1732. Each colony was established for a different reason and therefore developed unique characteristics.

Pennsylvania and Delaware. In 1681 King Charles II repaid a £16,000 debt he owed Sir William Penn by making Penn's son William proprietor of a large tract of land near New York. Penn's holdings increased the following year when the Duke of York gave him Delaware.

Penn wanted to make his colony, which the king named Pennsylvania, a haven for his fellow Quakers. Persecuted by Anglicans and Puritans alike as "violators of order," the Quakers had no formal clergy, opposed warfare, and ignored class privileges. Penn also wanted Pennsylvania to be a "Holy Experiment," where people of different nationalities and religious beliefs "could shape their own lives" and live peacefully together. He extended his tolerance to American Indians, paying them for their lands and treating them fairly.

Often referred to as the "best poor man's country," Pennsylvania attracted thousands of poor immigrants who made the crossing on cramped ships. One German immigrant, Gottlieb Mittelberger, described how they were packed "like herrings" and endured "stench, fumes, horror, . . . scurvy, . . . mouthrot." He added:

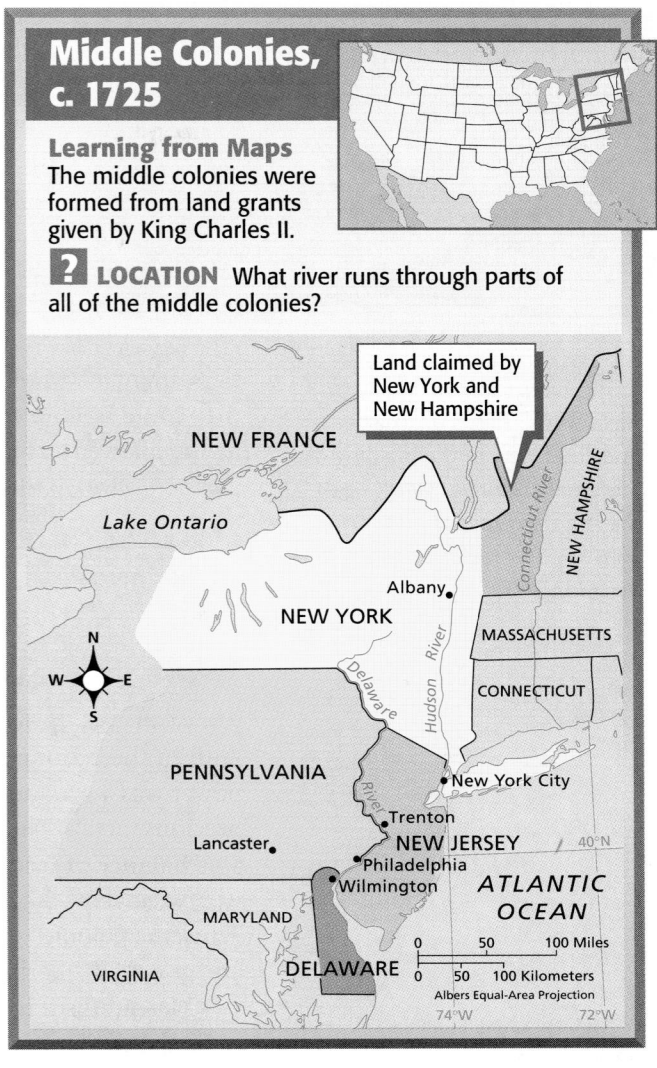

Middle Colonies, c. 1725

Learning from Maps The middle colonies were formed from land grants given by King Charles II.

? LOCATION What river runs through parts of all of the middle colonies?

> 66 Children from 1 to 7 years rarely survive the voyage; and many a time parents are compelled to see their children miserably suffer and die from hunger, thirst and sickness, and then to see them cast into the water. I witnessed such misery in no less than 32 children in our ship, all of whom were thrown into the sea. 99

Despite these hardships, "people were coming in fast," according to colonist James Claypole in 1683. Those who survived the voyage found cheap, fertile land and a mild climate. Pennsylvania farmers produced a surplus of grain. They milled much of it into flour and exported it to other colonies and the West Indies. Butchers bought livestock and exported salted meat. Philadelphia, the colony's capital, had a waterfront that boasted a large number of shops and a market. The colonists spent their profits on English manufactured goods and luxuries. Some also bought slaves.

Georgia. While Pennsylvania began as a "Holy Experiment," Georgia was a social experiment. This last British colony was established on the southern frontier of British North America in 1732, more than a century after Jamestown's founding. James Oglethorpe and a group of trustees planned the colony in order to provide a fresh start for the English poor. Parliament supported the project in the hope that, as one member explained, it would "carry off the . . . poor that pester the streets of

Savannah. This is an artist's imagined view of the building of Savannah, Georgia. *What does the painting reveal about the construction techniques used by colonists?*

London." Parliament also intended the colony to provide a buffer between South Carolina's prosperous plantations and Spanish Florida.

As a social experiment, the colony failed. Oglethorpe and his partners wanted to aid only the most "virtuous and industrious" poor. However, very few debtors qualified, and the colony attracted few other settlers because of its rigid rules, which included prohibitions against rum and slavery. The settlers, many of whom were from South Carolina, complained that without slaves they could not build prosperous plantations. In 1750 the founders reluctantly gave in and allowed slavery. Still the colony did not prosper. In 1752 Oglethorpe and his partners gave up their experiment and let Georgia become a royal colony.

✔ **READING CHECK:** How did social ideals influence the founding of Pennsylvania and Georgia?

Trade

Above all else, the founding of the Restoration colonies was driven by the Crown's faith in the economic policy of **mercantilism**. Mercantilists held that a nation's power was a product of wealth, and a nation's wealth was measured by its stock of precious metals. The best way for a nation to obtain wealth was to maintain a favorable **balance of trade**, that is, to export more than it imported. Only nations that were relatively self-sufficient could maintain a favorable balance of trade, however. Thus, the colonies were vitally important to England as a source of raw materials and as a ready market for goods from the homeland.

Mercantilism had the support of many merchants, who voiced their opinion to England's Parliament. In 1650 Parliament began passing a series of mercantilist laws—the **Navigation Acts**—to promote the "wealth, safety, and strength of this kingdom." The acts required European goods destined for the colonies to be routed through England.

In addition, all colonial products had to be carried on ships built and owned by British subjects in England, Ireland, and the colonies. The acts also regulated which colonial products could be exported only to England or to other destinations within the empire. The list was expanded over the years and eventually included cotton, naval stores, sugar, and tobacco. In New England, colonists did not always obey these acts.

Southern colonists produced most of the goods covered by the Navigation Acts. Although the restrictions cut into profits, the acts protected the colonies' monopoly on tobacco by prohibiting its cultivation in England. The acts also did not hurt northern shipbuilders and merchants. As English subjects they could build and sail their own ships. Colonial shipbuilders thrived because timber and naval stores were much cheaper in America than in Europe. By 1760 the colonists had built about one third of all merchant ships flying the British flag.

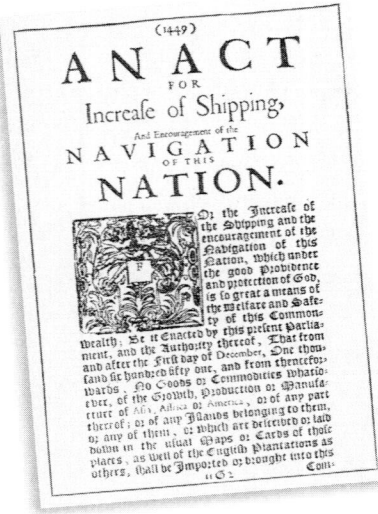

Title page of a proposed Navigation Act

✔ **READING CHECK:** In what ways did the Navigation Acts both help and hurt the colonial economies?

AMERICAN *Letters*

Benjamin Franklin on Colonial Life

Well known throughout his lifetime as a statesman, printer, scientist, and inventor, Benjamin Franklin is equally remembered for his writings about colonial life. Poor Richard's Almanack, which began to be published annually in 1732, contained advice for colonists on a variety of topics. In the following passage, Franklin advises thrift rather than spending and debt. In his Autobiography, published in pieces starting in 1771, he looked back on the lessons he had learned during the colonial era. In the following excerpt he offers his summary of the ideal human values.

from *Poor Richard Improved*

Now to save . . . observe these few Directions.

Benjamin Franklin

THE GRANGER COLLECTION, NEW YORK

1. When you incline to have new Cloaths, look first well over the old Ones, and see if you cannot shift with them another Year, either by Scouring, Mending or even Patching if necessary. Remember a Patch on your Coat, and Money in your Pocket, is better and more creditable than a Writ on your Back [debt], and no money to take it off [pay it].

2. When you incline to buy China Ware, Chinces [fabric], *India* Silks, or any other of their flimsey slight Manufactures; I would not be so hard with you, as to insist on your absolutely *resolving against it*; all I advise is, to *put it off* (as you do your Repentance) *till another Year*; and this, in some Respects, may prevent an Occasion of Repentance. . . .

Thus at the Year's End, there will be *An Hundred Thousand Pounds* more Money in your country.

If Paper Money in ever so great a Quantity could be made, no Man could get any of it without giving something for it. But all he saves in this Way, will be *his own for nothing*; and his Country actually so much richer.

from *The Autobiography*

1. TEMPERANCE. Eat not to Dulness. Drink not to Elevation.
2. SILENCE. Speak not but what may benefit others or yourself. Avoid trifling Conversation.
3. ORDER. Let all Things have their Places. Let each Part of your Business have its Time.
4. RESOLUTION. Resolve to perform what you ought. Perform without fail what you resolve.
5. FRUGALITY. Make no Expense but to do good to others or yourself: i.e. Waste nothing.
6. INDUSTRY. Lose no Time. Be always emply'd in something useful. Cut off all Unnecessary Actions.
7. SINCERITY. Use no hurtful Deceit. Think innocently and justly; and, if you speak, speak accordingly.
8. JUSTICE. Wrong none, by doing Injuries or omitting the Benefits that are your Duty.
9. MODERATION. Avoid Extremes. Forbear resenting Injuries so much as you think they deserve.
10. CLEANLINESS. Tolerate no Uncleanliness in Body, Clothes or Habitation.

UNDERSTANDING LITERATURE

1. What advice does Benjamin Franklin give to colonists on saving money?
2. What do Franklin's virtues emphasize?
3. Based on Franklin's writings, what were the main concerns of many colonists?

Edmund Andros angered the people of Boston.

James II and the Glorious Revolution

The Lords of Trade, a committee established in 1675 to oversee the colonies for the Crown, sent customs agents to the colonies to enforce the Navigation Acts. After an English official reported that the Massachusetts colonists "violate all acts of trade and navigation," the English government revoked the colony's charter in 1684. The following year James, Duke of York, became King James II. To increase royal authority over the colonies, the new king authorized the Lords of Trade to organize the northern colonies into the Dominion of New England. In 1686 the committee placed the Dominion under the control of former colonial governor Edmund Andros. The colonists quickly became angry when Andros abolished the Massachusetts General Court and imposed taxes without their consent.

James II was no more popular in England than Andros was in New England. James's Catholicism upset English Protestants, and his practice of ruling by decree angered Parliament. In 1688 the Protestant opposition staged a bloodless rebellion called the **Glorious Revolution**. They invited the king's Protestant daughter, Mary, and her Dutch husband, William, Prince of Orange, to take the throne. James fled to France in 1688. To prevent future abuses of power, Parliament enacted a bill of rights in 1689.

Colonists used the Glorious Revolution to rid themselves of hated officials. Colonists in Boston threw Andros in jail and then sent him back to England. An unofficial meeting of the General Court soon voted to "reestablish the government as it was before . . . until there shall be a legal establishment." William and Mary broke up the Dominion of New England and restored the representative assemblies.

✔ **READING CHECK:** How did the colonists react to the Glorious Revolution?

The Great Awakening

The Glorious Revolution established that royal power flowed from the consent of Parliament, not from the will of God through the monarch. Changing views of divine power were not confined to politics. In the 1700s Europe experienced the **Enlightenment**, a revolution in ideas. Enlightenment thinkers emphasized human reason as the key to improving society.

Some people longed for more than reason. They found it in a series of religious revivals—known as the **Great Awakening**— that swept through the British colonies in the mid-1700s.

Jonathan Edwards is often credited with launching New England's Great Awakening. A native of Connecticut, Edwards felt a religious calling while still a child. When he was 17, Edwards wrote, he had "not only a conviction, but

Jonathan Edwards

The Religious Spirit

POLITICS AND THE GREAT AWAKENING

The Great Awakening, with its emphasis on individual free will over predestination and the absolute power of God, had political as well as spiritual aspects. For some believers, the freedom to choose one's religion led to a greater desire to choose whether to follow certain political leaders. In Connecticut, some believers even formed their own political organization and succeeded in gaining control of the legislature.

Some believers in religious free will emphasized the free will of citizens. To them, a democratic political system fit more closely with God's will for the universe than did a system without representation for the people. As tensions with Great Britain grew, many colonists began to see a connection between their quest for greater religious freedom and their desire for greater political independence. One minister warned, "The life of every sincere Christian is a warfare against a great number of Enemies, some of them very potent, others very politik." As the number of converts to the churches of the Great Awakening increased, so did support for greater political freedom. ▪

a *delightful* conviction" of God's power after facing a serious illness. His pastorship at a church in Northampton, Massachusetts, began in 1729, where he appealed to people's emotions as a way to open their hearts to God. In the 1730s a religious revival began in Edwards's church and spread to surrounding churches.

In 1741, during the height of the Great Awakening, Edwards delivered his famous sermon, "Sinners in the Hands of an Angry God," to a congregation in Connecticut. Edwards warned, "There is nothing that keeps wicked men at any moment out of hell, but the mere pleasure of God." Edwards added, however, that God was merciful and offered love to anyone who freely accepted it and repented of their sins. This idea contrasted with many Protestants' belief that God predetermined people's futures even before they were born.

By the end of the decade, Edwards began to fall out of favor with church leaders, who believed that he was overstepping the bounds of his appointed office. In 1750 he was dismissed from his church duties. He died eight years later, shortly after becoming president of the College of New Jersey, now known as Princeton.

British minister George Whitefield also spread the message of the Great Awakening throughout the colonies, beginning in 1738. During his several tours of the colonies, Whitefield inspired crowds of thousands. "Hearing him preach," wrote Nathan Cole, a farmer, "gave me a heart wound." One woman, Fanny Lewis, wrote that at a Baltimore revival "there was such a gust of the power of God, that it appeared to me the very gates of hell would give way."

The Great Awakening sparked the growth of many new Protestant churches, particularly Baptist and Methodist ones. Their emotional services appealed to many people, particularly to the poor and the enslaved, whom established churches often neglected.

 **Read More About It**

Free Find:
Jonathan Edwards
After reading about Jonathan Edwards on the **Holt Researcher** CD–ROM, imagine that you had attended one of his sermons. Write a letter to a friend explaining how Edward's teachings differ from what many Protestants of the time believed.

✔ **READING CHECK:** What religious beliefs did preachers of the Great Awakening hold?

SECTION 3 REVIEW

Define and explain the significance of the following terms:
Restoration
task system
mercantilism
balance of trade
Navigation Acts
Glorious Revolution
Enlightenment
Great Awakening

Identify and explain the significance of the following individuals:
Charles II
Peter Stuyvesant
William Penn
James Oglethorpe
James II
Edmund Andros
Jonathan Edwards
George Whitefield

Locate and explain the importance of the following places:
North Carolina
South Carolina
New York
New Jersey
Pennsylvania
Delaware
Georgia

1. **Using Graphic Organizers** Copy the web diagram below. Use it to list the colonies that were created during the Restoration. Then explain when and why each colony was formed.

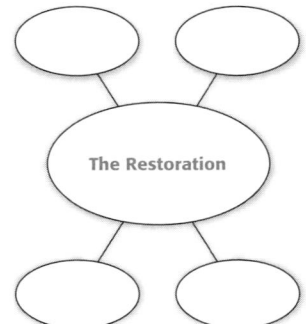

The Restoration

2. **Assessing Consequences** How did the large number of enslaved Africans in South Carolina affect slave life in the colony?
3. **Comparing And Contrasting** How and why did the colonists and the English government view the Navigation Acts differently?
4. **Synthesizing** How did the Glorious Revolution and the Great Awakening lead to broader changes in colonial society?

Critical Thinking

5. How and why did the experimental colonies of Pennsylvania and Georgia differ in their success?
   Consider:
   • the goals for Pennsylvania
   • the goals for Georgia
   • who came to these colonies and why
   • how well each colony accomplished these goals

The Struggle for Land

OBJECTIVES

Read to understand:
1. which North American lands were claimed by France
2. how American Indians responded to colonists' desires for land and fur
3. how the British won the French and Indian War

KEY TERMS

Iroquois League
Albany Plan of Union
French and Indian War
land speculators

KEY PEOPLE

René-Robert de La Salle
Metacomet
William Pitt
James Wolfe
Louis-Joseph de Montcalm

KEY PLACES

St. Lawrence River
Fort Duquesne
Oswego
Fort William Henry
Quebec

EYEWITNESSES TO History

❝ *Our land forces laid siege to the town of Louisburg. This they did with such effect that one day I saw some of the ships set on fire by the shells from the batteries. . . . At last Louisburg was taken.* ❞

—Olaudah Equiano

The French surrender to the British at Louisburg.

Enslaved African Olaudah Equiano, then serving under a British naval officer, described the 1758 British victory in the midst of a colonial war with France. The French fortress at Louisburg on Cape Breton Island in Nova Scotia had been of major concern to the British since its construction in the 1720s. Louis Antoine de Bougainville, a French military official, also witnessed the fall of Louisburg from the opposing side. "The night of seventeenth to eighteenth the enemy opened the trenches," he recalled. "The landing made, the capture of the city was inevitable. . . . The place surrendered July 26."

The French in North America

The conflict between the French and the British erupted as Britain's North American colonial empire was growing and expanding. As British frontiersmen and traders crossed the Appalachian Mountains into the Ohio Valley, they moved into territory claimed by both France and Britain. French land claims were based on the early voyages of Giovanni da Verrazano and Jacques Cartier, among others. Only after René-Robert de La Salle's explorations of the Mississippi River in the late 1600s did the French begin to build a series of forts along the river.

The founding of New Orleans in 1718 gave the French command of the Mississippi River. Four years later, according to one observer, New Orleans was still a "wild, lovely place" with only about 100 homes and a store that doubled as a church. Control of the Mississippi—combined with their thriving colonies along the St. Lawrence River and their knowledge of a water route through the Great Lakes—put the French in a position to dominate the North American interior.

New France—France's North American empire—never reached its potential strength. France claimed a huge area but settled very little of it. Most French colonists were either single men in search of riches and adventure or Jesuit priests seeking to convert American Indians.

✔ **READING CHECK:** What land did France claim in North America?

Map of New France

THE GRANGER COLLECTION, NEW YORK

Cultures Clash

The French colonial economy was tied to that of the American Indians. Indians included French fur traders in their trade networks early in the 1600s. American Indians desired European trade goods such as firearms, horses, and metal tools. To pay for those goods, they traded beaver pelts and other furs. "The beaver does everything perfectly well," one American Indian explained. "It makes kettles, hatchets, swords, knives, bread . . . in short, it makes everything."

The fur trade. The European desire for furs altered the way of life of many American Indians. Increasingly they became dependent on the fur trade for survival. Some villages devoted so much time to trapping and preparing furs that they were forced to buy food that they had once produced for themselves.

The fur trade also disrupted relations among tribes. As they killed off fur-bearing animals in one area, Indian trappers moved their settlements to areas where the animals were still plentiful. Previously distant tribes came into contact and competition with each other.

These Dutch settlers trade with American Indians.

Strategies for Success — Reading Effectively

Reading historical literature can be quite demanding. Textbook and supplemental reading assignments often cover large amounts of complex information. A well-planned reading strategy can help you organize and learn this information efficiently. It can also help you take note of questions and ideas that you should study further when preparing for a test.

How to Read Effectively

1. **Preview the assignment.** Before you begin reading the text of an assignment, carefully read the title, introduction, and any conclusions or summaries. Then look over any headings, subheadings, illustrations, and study questions. This process of previewing the text should give you a general idea of what you are about to learn.
2. **Read actively.** Rather than trying to read the whole assignment nonstop, divide it into small, manageable sections. As you read each section, keep an active lookout for key people, events, ideas, and relationships. If you have time, create notes about particularly important information on a separate sheet of paper.

3. **Review regularly.** When you reach the end of a small section, pause and recall the highlights of what you have just read. Then answer any study questions that are addressed in the section. When you finish reading the assignment, make sure that you can formulate answers to any review questions. Then decide which questions are most likely to appear on a future test.

Applying the Strategy

Before you read the segment of Section 4 on the French and Indian War, spend a minute previewing it. Then write a short paragraph that explains what you expect to learn from the section. Read the section.

Practicing the Strategy

Answer the following questions.
1. What is the general topic of this section?
2. Who took part in the events described in this section? Where did these events take place?
3. What are three questions that you expect this section to answer?

Conflicts over land. The European desire for land had even more disastrous consequences for American Indians than did the European demand for furs. Europeans believed that land not registered by deed, cleared, or built upon was not owned. Since most Indian land appeared wild and unused, Europeans believed that it was there for the taking or even that it was going to waste. As one settler told a land agent, "It was against the laws of God and nature that so much land should be idle while so many Christians wanted it to work on."

American Indians viewed land differently. They recognized territorial boundaries, but not individual ownership. The loss of the land had serious consequences because it meant losing sources of food and sacred sites. English agricultural practices also destroyed many animal habitats. Miantonomo (my-an-tuh-NOH-moh), a Narraganset, observed as early as 1642:

> 66 Our plains were full of deer, as also our woods, and of turkies, and our coves full of fish and fowl. But these English having gotten our land, they with scythes cut down the grass, and with axes fell the trees; their cows and horses eat the grass, and their hogs spoil our clam banks, and we shall be starved. 99

War in New England. Less than 20 years after Plymouth Colony was founded, the Pequot and the English went to war over land. Beginning in 1636, the Pequot War pitted the English and their Narraganset and Mohegan allies against the Pequot, who were allied in the fur trade with the Dutch of New Netherland. The war ended in 1637, when the English burned a Pequot village and killed hundreds of people, virtually destroying the Pequot. Seeing what had happened to the Pequot, other tribes soon signed a formal treaty with the English. War broke out again in 1675, when the Wampanoag chief Metacomet—called King Philip by the English—led the American Indians against the colonists. An estimated 3,000 Indians—including Metacomet—died in the fighting. The Puritans sold most of the surviving Wampanoag as slaves. Ten years later a Frenchman observed that Indians in New England posed little threat: "The last Wars . . . have reduced them to a small Number, and consequently they are incapable of defending themselves."

The Iroquois League. In part, New Englanders owed their victory over the Wampanoag to the Mohawk. At the urging of the governor of New York, the Mohawk had driven Metacomet's forces out of New York, dealing them a crippling blow.

The Mohawk belonged to the powerful **Iroquois League**. The Cayuga, Mohawk, Oneida, Onondaga, and Seneca of New York and Pennsylvania had formed the confederation in the 1400s or 1500s. After 1712 the Tuscarora, who had been forced out of North Carolina by settlers, joined them, and the confederation became known as the Six Nations.

The union allowed the Iroquois League to dominate the fur trade, to extend its influence over American Indians to the west, and to protect its members' independence. The Iroquois also acted as middlemen by obtaining furs from other American Indians and selling the furs to the English. They skillfully played the English and the French against each other, as needed to help the League.

✔ **READING CHECK:** How did American Indians respond to the colonists' desires for fur and land?

This peace treaty ended Queen Anne's War.

HOLT RESEARCHER
Read More About It

Free Find: Iroquois Great Law of Peace
After reading about the Iroquois Great Law of Peace on the **Holt Researcher** CD–ROM, create a version of the Great Law of Peace for the students in your class.

The French and Indian War

While the Iroquois League was building its trading community, England, France, and Spain were engaged in a worldwide struggle for empire. The fighting often spilled over into North America. Between 1689 and 1748, English colonists were dragged into three wars: King William's War (1689–97), Queen Anne's War (1702–13), and King George's War (1744–48).

To plan for defense and to recruit the Iroquois as allies, representatives from seven colonies and the Iroquois League met in Albany, New York, in 1754. Benjamin Franklin had earlier supported the idea of uniting the colonies. It "would be a very strange thing," Franklin wrote in 1751, if the Iroquois League could form such a confederation "yet a like Union should be impracticable for ten or a dozen English colonies to whom it is more necessary and must be more advantageous." At the Albany Congress Franklin had a chance to present these views. The colonial delegates adopted his **Albany Plan of Union**, which called for a loose confederation to promote defense. Parliament rejected the plan, however, fearing that it would weaken Britain's power over the colonies.

Benjamin Franklin created this illustration of the Albany Plan of Union.

French and Indian War, 1754–1763

Learning from Maps At the end of the French and Indian War, France gave up most of its claims in North America to the victorious British.

? LOCATION Where did French victories take place?

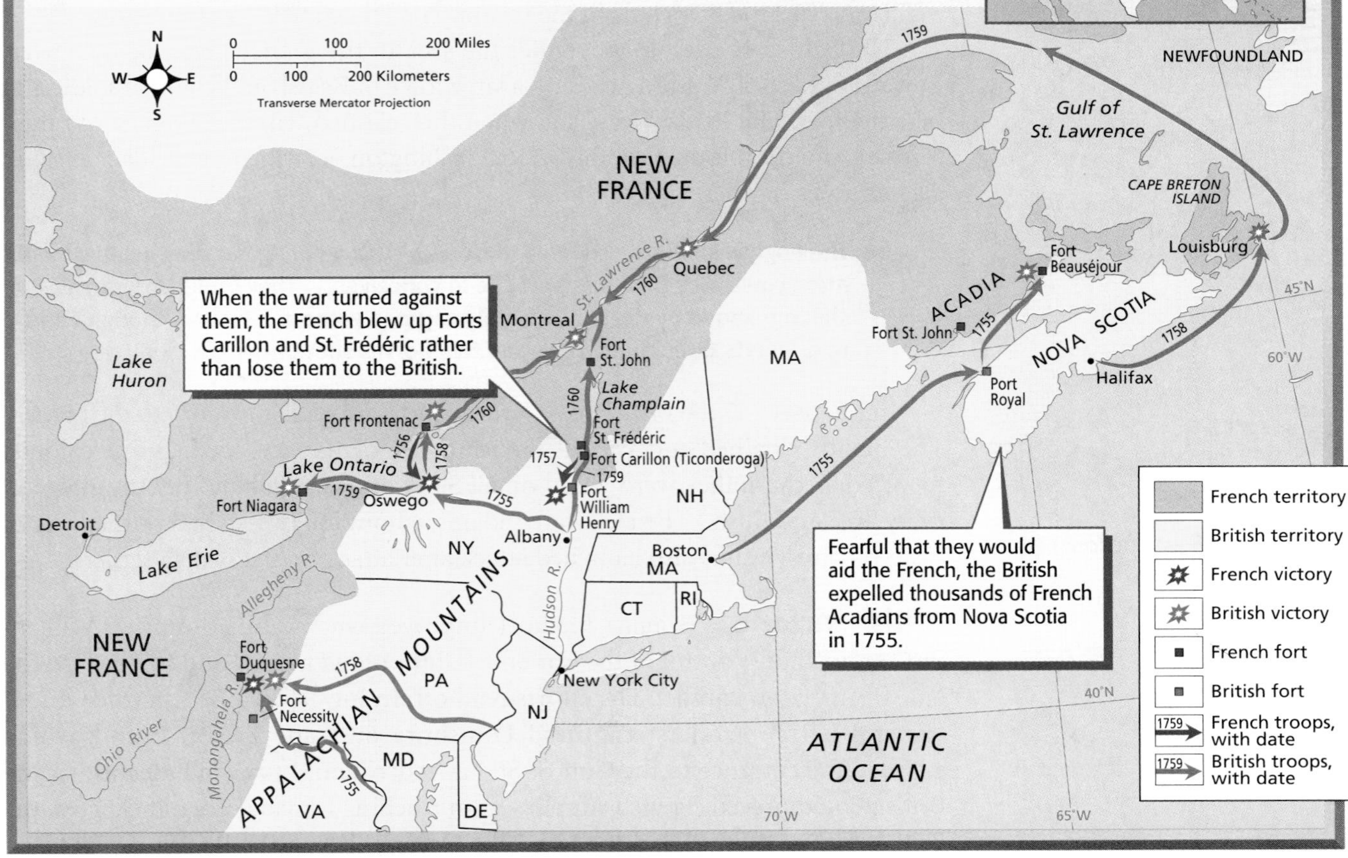

When the war turned against them, the French blew up Forts Carillon and St. Frédéric rather than lose them to the British.

Fearful that they would aid the French, the British expelled thousands of French Acadians from Nova Scotia in 1755.

NEWFOUNDLAND

Gulf of St. Lawrence

CAPE BRETON ISLAND

NEW FRANCE

Louisburg

Fort Beauséjour

ACADIA

NOVA SCOTIA

Fort St. John

1755

1758

Halifax

Port Royal

1755

Quebec

Montreal

Fort St. John

Lake Champlain

Fort St. Frédéric

Fort Carillon (Ticonderoga)

Fort William Henry

MA

NH

Lake Huron

Fort Frontenac

Lake Ontario

Fort Niagara

Oswego

Detroit

Lake Erie

NY

Albany

Boston MA

CT RI

Allegheny R.

Hudson R.

NEW FRANCE

Fort Duquesne

Fort Necessity

APPALACHIAN MOUNTAINS

PA

New York City

NJ

MD

DE

VA

Monongahela R.

Ohio River

ATLANTIC OCEAN

70°W

65°W

40°N

45°N

60°W

0   100   200 Miles
0   100   200 Kilometers
Transverse Mercator Projection

N W E S

	French territory
	British territory
✹	French victory
✹	British victory
■	French fort
■	British fort
1759 →	French troops, with date
1759 →	British troops, with date

Spain and the Seven Years' War

Spain's role in the Seven Years' War reflected the country's growing resentment of British power. Just a few years before Spain entered the war as an ally of France, the Spanish queen had said, "London needs to feel a telling blow; otherwise she will be insupportable [unbearable] deeming herself mistress of the world." Although her husband, Carlos III, attempted to negotiate a truce that would end the war, the Spanish ambassador to Britain believed that Spain would inevitably have to fight in order to prevent British domination. In January 1761 he wrote the king, "We shall be forced either to take up arms or to submit to any conditions the English care to impose upon us." A few months later Carlos signed the first Family Pact with France, which declared "Who attacks one, attacks the other." This aid came at a time when France badly needed help.

As the fighting spread, Spain achieved some successes against British forces in South America, but suffered severe defeats in Cuba and the Philippines. Then, less than a year after Spain entered the war, France ignored its alliance and began peace talks with Britain. At the Treaty of Paris, Spain's representatives ceded territory to Britain. As a result, Britain's control over North America was stronger than ever.

Competition for the Ohio Valley.

Unlike previous hostilities, the next major colonial conflict—the **French and Indian War** (1754–63)—began in the colonies. The conflict then spread to Europe in 1756, where it was known as the Seven Years' War. The war had first broken out in the Ohio River valley. Both the French and the British considered this region highly valuable.

Virginia **land speculators**—people who bought land expecting a quick profit from its resale—had acquired a large land grant in the Ohio Valley in 1749. To protect their investments, the Virginians began building a fort at the junction of the Ohio, Allegheny (al-uh-GAY-nee), and Monongahela (muh-nahn-guh-HEE-luh) Rivers. The French, who considered the land theirs, drove the Virginians off, completed the fort, and named it Fort Duquesne (doo-KAYN). Outraged, Lieutenant Governor Robert Dinwiddie of Virginia sent young George Washington and a company of militia to expel the French from the region. The French held firm, however.

The British refused to surrender the area to the French. They sent General Edward Braddock, Washington, and a large force of British and colonial soldiers to take the fort. The British panicked when they clashed with the French and their force of American Indians in July 1755. Washington described the British defeat in a letter to his mother.

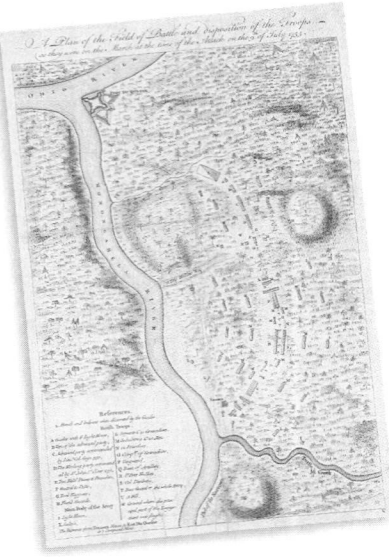

This map shows the location of Fort Duquesne.

> 66 The English soldiers . . . were struck with such a panic that they behaved with more cowardice than it is possible to conceive. . . . They broke and ran as sheep pursued by dogs. . . . I luckily escaped without a wound, though I had four bullets through my coat, and two horses shot under me. 99

In August 1757 the British lost Oswego and Fort William Henry to the French. The "lightly cloathed and armed" French and Indians succeeded, as one colonist reported, because they were "often on all Sides of us, . . . taking the Advantage of every Tree and Bush." The Delaware Indians, whom the British had pushed out of eastern Pennsylvania, also launched attack after attack on the British settlers.

British victories. Britain's fortunes improved when cabinet minister William Pitt assumed full control of the war effort. Pitt poured money and troops into the North American conflict. His efforts paid off. In July 1758 a British force under General Jeffrey Amherst captured Louisburg on Cape Breton Island, which guarded the entrance to the Gulf of St. Lawrence. Louisburg's fall meant that the British could prevent French supplies from reaching Canada. Then in August, the British captured Fort Frontenac on Lake Ontario. When the British marched on

Fort Duquesne in November, the French blew up the fort rather than surrender. The British then built a new fort near the same site, calling it Fort Pitt. It later became the site of present-day Pittsburgh.

After these British military successes, the Iroquois decided to support the British. As the tide turned against the French, they lost their Indian allies in the Ohio Valley. The French soon withdrew to Canada.

The British pursued the French, determined to take Quebec. General James Wolfe was unable to lure the French commander, General Louis-Joseph de Montcalm, into battle. This changed once the British discovered a path that led from the St. Lawrence River up the cliff to Quebec. Under cover of night on September 13, 1759, the British army climbed up and assumed battle formation outside the city. One British officer described the coming battle as a "total rout [defeat] of the enemy." Injuries sustained during the battle took the lives of both Wolfe and Montcalm. Quebec soon surrendered to the British. When Montreal fell a year later, France lost the last of its Canadian holdings.

The spoils of war. The war in North America essentially ended in 1761, but fighting continued elsewhere for two more years. In 1763 the Treaty of Paris ended hostilities in North America and awarded territories. The victorious British claimed Canada and all French holdings east of the Mississippi River except New Orleans. Spain, which had joined the French war effort in 1762, surrendered Florida to the British. In anticipation of this loss, Spain had received France's vast Louisiana territory west of the Mississippi in the 1762 Treaty of Fontainebleau.

INTERPRETING THE VISUAL RECORD

Fort Duquesne. General Braddock's forces march toward Fort Duquesne. *How might the position of the British forces in the forest have put them at a disadvantage against American Indian forces?*

✔ **READING CHECK:** What led to a British victory in the French and Indian War?

SECTION 4 REVIEW

Define and explain the significance of the following terms:
Iroquois League
Albany Plan of Union
French and Indian War
land speculators

Identify and explain the significance of the following individuals:
René-Robert de La Salle
Metacomet
William Pitt
James Wolfe
Louis-Joseph de Montcalm

Locate and explain the importance of the following places:
St. Lawrence River
Fort Duquesne
Oswego
Fort William Henry
Quebec

1. **Using Graphic Organizers** Copy the tree chart below. Use it to trace the outcome of France's experience in North America from early exploration to the French and Indian War.

1. French North America
2. Early Exploration
3. Relationship with Indians
4. Struggle for Land
5. French and Indian War

2. **Assessing Consequences** How did the Europeans' desire for furs and land affect American Indians?

3. **Identifying Cause and Effect** Why did American Indians become involved in conflicts between the French and the British? How did this affect the tribes?

4. **Using Historical Imagination** Imagine that you are a British general in the French and Indian War. Describe how you plan to defeat the French.

Critical Thinking

5. Did the growth of the British colonial population make the French and Indian War inevitable? Why or why not?
   Consider:
   • the effect of British population growth on relations with American Indians
   • the effect of British population growth on relations with France
   • specific conflicts that led to the French and Indian War

CHAPTER 3

Review

Creating a Time Line

Copy the time line below onto a sheet of paper. Complete the time line by filling in the events and dates from the chapter that you think were most significant. Pick three events and explain why you think they were significant.

Writing a Summary

Using the Reading Checks as a guide, write an overview of the events in the chapter.

Identifying People and Ideas

Identify the following terms or individuals and explain their significance.

1. Squanto
2. John Winthrop
3. Anne Hutchinson
4. Toleration Act
5. Olaudah Equiano
6. Glorious Revolution
7. Great Awakening
8. Jonathan Edwards
9. Albany Plan of Union
10. James Wolfe

Understanding Main Ideas

SECTION 1
1. What led the Pilgrims and Puritans to settle in North America?
2. What issues threatened New England's stability?

SECTION 2
3. What was Chesapeake society like?
4. What led to Bacon's Rebellion?

SECTION 3
5. How did the colonies founded after the Restoration differ from the New England colonies?
6. How did the Glorious Revolution and the Great Awakening shape the colonies?

SECTION 4
7. How did the British win the French and Indian War?

Reviewing Themes

1. **Cultural Diversity** How did the cultural backgrounds of the colonists affect the development of the colonies in which they settled?
2. **Economic Development** How did the French and British desire for land and trade goods affect one another?
3. **Global Relations** Why did England regulate colonial trade?

Thinking Critically

1. **Evaluating** How effective was the English government in maintaining political authority in the colonies? Support your answer with examples.
2. **Hypothesizing** Would Massachusetts Bay Colony's Bible commonwealth have worked in the Chesapeake? Why or why not?
3. **Comparing and Contrasting** How did family life in New England and the southern colonies reflect larger differences between the regions?
4. **Identifying Cause and Effect** How did the organization of labor in the Chesapeake contribute to Bacon's Rebellion? How did the rebellion change the organization of labor?

Writing About History

Writing to Evaluate Write an essay explaining how slavery grew in the English colonies. Include a discussion of how changes in indentured servitude contributed to the rise of slavery. Use the following diagram to organize your thoughts.

Strategies **for Success** Review the **Strategies for Success** on *Reading Effectively.* Then look over each of this chapter's four section reviews and select the short-answer question that you think is most likely to appear on a test. Write five new questions that might appear on a chapter test. Save your notes for future study.

Linking History And Geography

Study the map below. Which were New England colonies? middle colonies? southern colonies? Which region's colonies covered the most landmass?

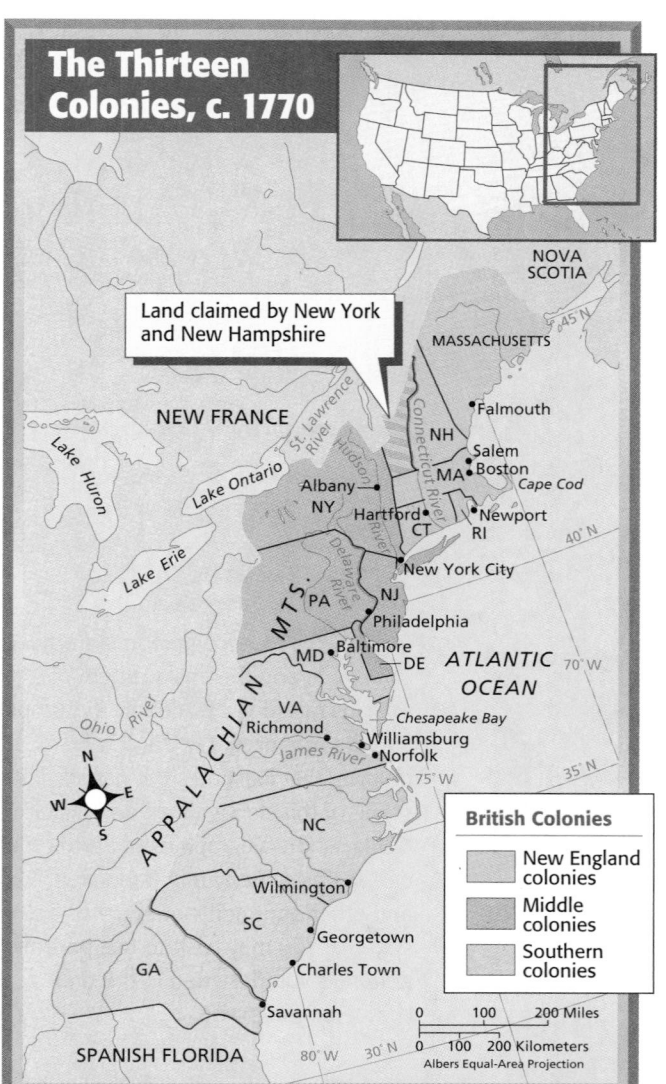

The Thirteen Colonies, c. 1770

Land claimed by New York and New Hampshire

NEW FRANCE

NOVA SCOTIA

MASSACHUSETTS

Falmouth
NH
Salem
Boston
MA
Albany
NY
Hartford
CT
Newport
RI
Cape Cod

Lake Huron
Lake Ontario
Lake Erie

New York City
NJ
PA
Philadelphia
MD
Baltimore
DE
VA
Richmond
Williamsburg
Norfolk
Chesapeake Bay

ATLANTIC OCEAN

70° W
75° W
35° N
40° N

Ohio River
James River

APPALACHIAN MTS.

NC

Wilmington
SC
Georgetown
GA
Charles Town
Savannah

SPANISH FLORIDA

80° W   30° N

British Colonies
- New England colonies
- Middle colonies
- Southern colonies

0   100   200 Miles
0   100   200 Kilometers
Albers Equal-Area Projection

internet**connect**

TOPIC: French colonialism
GO TO: go.hrw.com
KEYWORD: SD1 French

Accessing the Internet through the HRW Web site, research the North American empire of the French in the 1600s and 1700s. Then write a pamphlet to encourage people to come to New France. Your pamphlet, written in the style of the times, should describe: the benefits of coming to New France, life in the new settlements, and some aspects of French culture that immigrants will find in North America.

BUILDING YOUR PORTFOLIO

Complete one or all of the following projects independently or cooperatively.

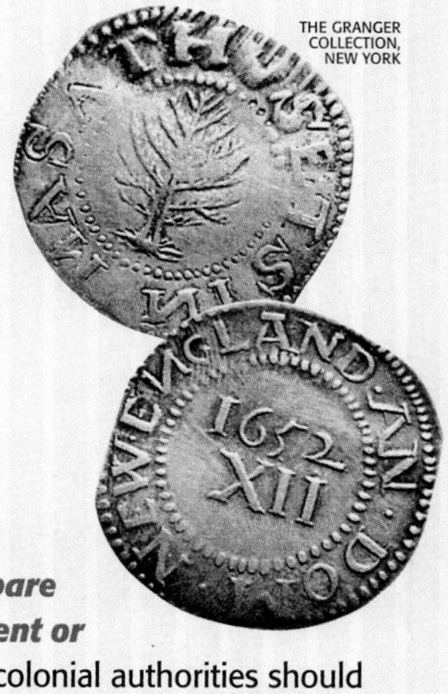

THE GRANGER COLLECTION, NEW YORK

1 Economic Development
Create a map that reflects French and English trading patterns with North America during the 1600s.

2 Democratic Values
Imagine you are a religious leader in the colonies. **Prepare a newspaper advertisement or a handbill** explaining why colonial authorities should allow colonists the freedom to practice their religion as they see fit.

3 Cultural Diversity
Imagine you are a colonial artist. **Develop a series of drawings and captions** that illustrate some of the ways in which contact between British and French colonists, American Indians, and African slaves affected each culture.

Review

BUILDING YOUR PORTFOLIO

Outlined below are three projects. Independently or cooperatively, complete one and use the products to demonstrate your mastery of the historical concepts involved.

1 Economic Development

Trade expanded worldwide from the time of the Crusades through the mid-1700s, bringing diverse cultures into contact with one another. *Write a proposal* for a trade agreement to be presented at an international trade conference in the mid-1700s. Your trade proposal should take into account the interests of delegates from each participating nation. You may wish to use portfolio materials you designed in the unit chapters to help you.

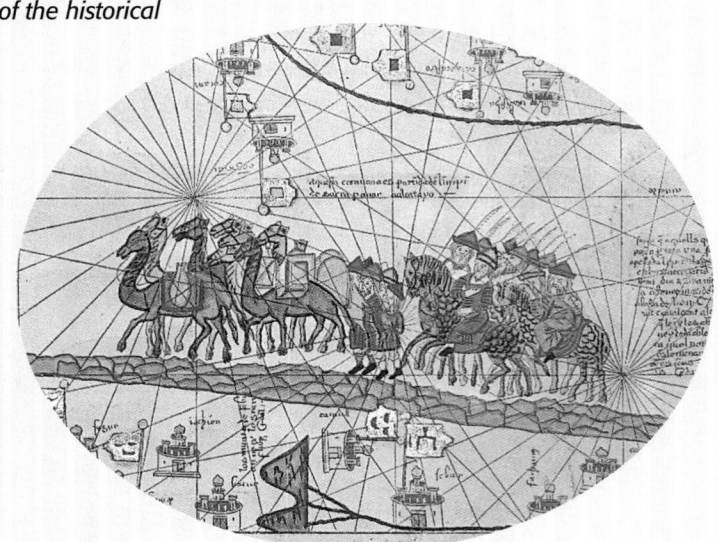

Camel caravan from 1375

Aztec drawing of the encomienda system

2 Democratic Values

The *encomienda* system and the enslavement of Africans raised public debate in Europe and the Americas. *Create a wall display* that illustrates the nature and scope of this debate. Include in your display short biographies of Bartolomé de Las Casas, Benjamin Banneker, and other opponents of either or both systems. You may wish to use portfolio materials you designed in the unit chapters to help you.

THE GRANGER COLLECTION, NEW YORK

3 Global Relations

People from many different nations and cultures exchanged technology, food, religion, and ideas in the Americas. *Prepare a brochure* that explains the variety of exchanges covered by a museum exhibit on exchanges in the Americas. Then present your brochure and exhibit to the class. Be sure you include the following in your brochure: the origin of foods such as the potato, the tomato, corn, and rice; the introduction of cattle and horses to the Americas; and the spread of Catholicism. You may wish to use portfolio materials you designed in the unit chapters to help you.

The First Thanksgiving 1621
by J. L. G. Ferris

Further Reading

Applebaum, Herbert. *Colonial Americans at Work.* University Press of America, 1996. Overview of the daily lives and work habits of the English colonists.

Clendinnen, Inga. *Aztecs.* Cambridge University Press, 1991. Explores life in the Aztec capital in the period immediately before the arrival of the first Spanish explorers and conquistadores.

Hawke, David F. *Everyday Life in Early America.* Harper & Row, 1988. Portrait of life in early New England.

Josephy, Alvin M. Jr., ed. *America in 1492: The World of the Indian Peoples Before the Arrival of Columbus.* Vintage, 1993. Panorama of North and South American life from prehistoric times to the early 1400s.

Nash, Gary B. *Red, White, and Black: The Peoples of Early North America.* Prentice Hall, 1992. Account of interaction among American Indians, Africans, and whites during colonial times.

Weber, David J. *The Spanish Frontier in North America.* Yale University Press, 1992. Overview of Spanish exploration and colonization.

Internet Connect and Holt Researcher CD-ROM Review

In assigned groups, develop a multimedia presentation about the Americas from prehistory through 1763. Choose information from the chapter Internet Connect activities and from the **Holt Researcher** CD-ROM that best reflect the major topics of the period. Write an outline and a script for your presentation, which may be shown to the class.

Creating a Nation
1763–1815

More than 50 delegates met in Philadelphia during the summer of 1787 to draft a new Constitution.

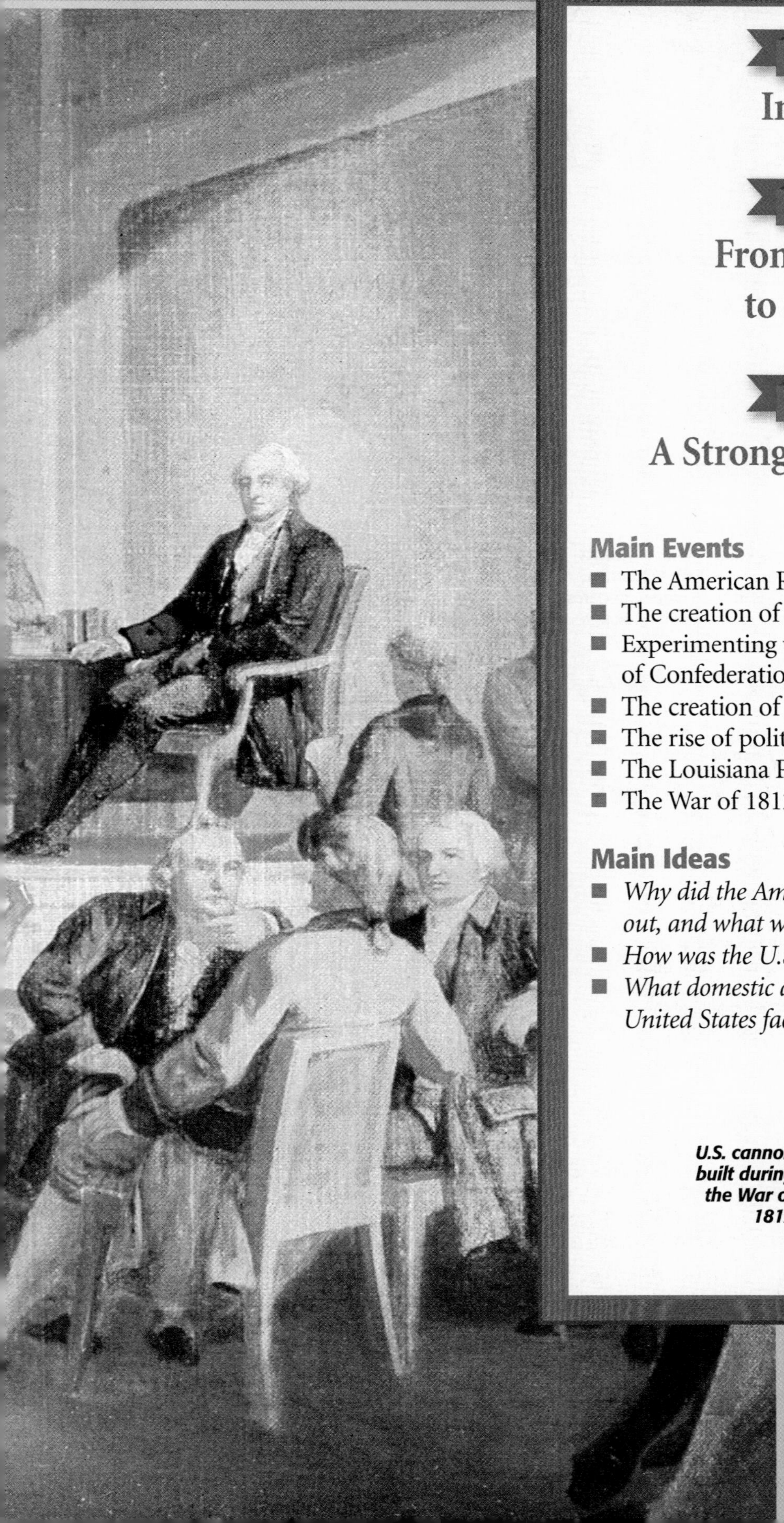

CHAPTER 4

Independence!

1763–1783

CHAPTER 5

From Confederation to Federal Union

1776–1789

CHAPTER 6

A Strong Start for the Nation

1789–1815

Main Events

- The American Revolution
- The creation of the Declaration of Independence
- Experimenting with government under the Articles of Confederation
- The creation of the U.S. Constitution
- The rise of political parties
- The Louisiana Purchase
- The War of 1812

Main Ideas

- *Why did the American Revolution break out, and what was unique about it?*
- *How was the U.S. Constitution formed?*
- *What domestic and foreign-policy conflicts did the United States face in its early years?*

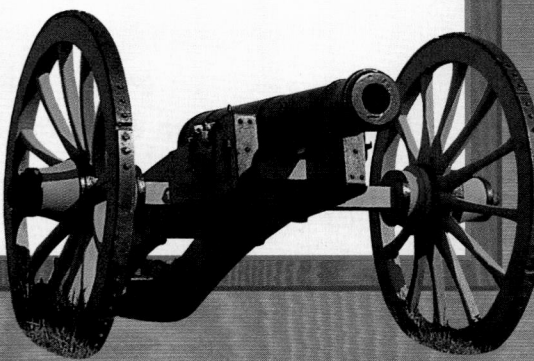

U.S. cannon built during the War of 1812

1763–1783
Independence!

Southwark Theater

1763
The Arts
James Bremner opens a music school in Philadelphia.

1763
Politics
The Proclamation of 1763 is issued.

1763
World Events
The Seven Years' War ends in Europe.

1766
The Arts
Southwark Theater, the first permanent theater in the colonies, opens in Philadelphia.

1768
World Events
The Ottoman Empire declares war on Russia.

1770
Daily Life
Britain's North American colonies reach an estimated population of 2.2 million.

| 1763 | 1765 | 1767 | 1769 | 1771 | 1773 |

THE GRANGER COLLECTION, NEW YORK

The Boy with the Squirrel
by John Singleton Copley

1765
Daily Life
Philadelphia's population reaches 25,000.

1765
Politics
Parliament passes the Stamp Act.

1765
The Arts
American artist John Singleton Copley paints *The Boy with the Squirrel.*

1767
Business and Finance
The Townshend Acts place import duties on a variety of widely used items.

1767
Science and Technology
David Rittenhouse builds the colonies' first model of the solar system.

1773
The Arts
African American poet Phillis Wheatley publishes her first book of poetry.

1773
Politics
Patriots stage the Boston Tea Party.

Boston Tea Party

Before You Read

Build on What You Know

The settlers who came to North America in the 1600s and 1700s established a variety of distinctive societies in Great Britain's territory. They also carried on a continuing struggle for land and resources against American Indians. After its victory in the French and Indian War, the British government faced the difficulty of governing and financing an even larger empire. In this chapter you will learn how this issue led to conflict between Britain and its colonies along the Atlantic seaboard.

The battle at Lexington

Continental currency

1774
World Events
Louis XVI becomes king of France.

1776
Business and Finance
Congress issues paper money.

1776
Politics
The Declaration of Independence is issued.

1781
World Events
Serfdom is abolished in Austria.

1781
World Events
British forces surrender to American Troops at Yorktown, Virginia.

1775 **1777** **1779** **1781** **1783** **1785**

King Louis XVI of France

1775
Politics
The Revolutionary War begins at Lexington and Concord.

1775
The Arts
Mercy Otis Warren publishes *The Group.*

1775
Science and Technology
David Bushnell builds the first practical submarine, the *American Turtle.*

1778
The Arts
Jonathan Carver publishes *Travels Through the Interior Parts of North America.*

1778
World Events
France signs a formal alliance with the United States.

1780
Science and Technology
The American Academy of Arts and Sciences is founded in Boston.

1783
Science and Technology
Benjamin Franklin invents bifocals.

1783
Politics
John Adams helps negotiate the Treaty of Paris, ending the Revolutionary War.

Patriot John Adams

Think About Themes

Themes Journal

*Decide whether you **agree** or **disagree** with the following statements. Note why in your journal.*

Economic Development Economic issues are usually the most important factors in shaping a country's relationship with its colonies.

Democratic Values In a democracy, individuals and groups have the right to use any means to protest taxes and laws that they think are unfair.

Global Relations The foreign-policy decisions of powerful nations are shaped by events in less-powerful nations.

The Seeds of Unrest

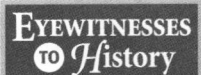

66 *The American colonies stand no longer in need of England's protection. England will call on them to help contribute toward supporting the burden they have helped to bring on her, and they will answer by striking off all dependence.* 99
—Charles Gravier

COLONIAL WILLIAMSBURG FOUNDATION

Teapot bearing an anti-British slogan

OBJECTIVES

Read to understand:

1. how the British Crown responded to Pontiac's Rebellion
2. why the British government passed the Sugar Act and the Stamp Act
3. how the colonists responded to the Stamp Act
4. what events led to the Boston Massacre

KEY TERMS

Pontiac's Rebellion
Proclamation of 1763
Sugar Act
duty
Stamp Act
nonimportation agreements
Sons of Liberty
Stamp Act Congress
Declaratory Act
Townshend Acts
writs of assistance
Quartering Act
Boston Massacre

KEY PEOPLE

Neolin
Samuel Adams
John Adams

Charles Gravier (grawv-yay), Comte de Vergennes (ver-zhen), a French government official, was very clear about how he thought a conflict between Great Britain and her colonies would be resolved. Victory in the French and Indian War had left Britain with a huge debt and large amounts of territory to govern and defend. British officials expected the American colonists to help pay for administering this expanded empire. The colonists, however, believed that they had the right to determine their own financial affairs. These differing opinions set the stage for a major conflict.

Governing the New Territories

The Treaty of Paris of 1763 forced France to give up its North American empire. Spain also surrendered some of its territory. With the stroke of a pen, the British gained control of Canada, Spanish Florida—except New Orleans—and the rich land between the Appalachian Mountains and the Mississippi River. Trader and American Indian agent George Croghan traveled through this western territory in 1765. He noted in his diary that a "good hunter, without much fatigue to himself, could here daily supply one hundred men with meat." Croghan described the amazing variety of terrain he encountered.

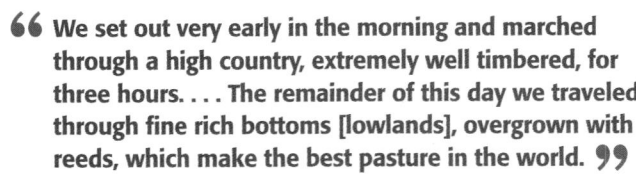

66 We set out very early in the morning and marched through a high country, extremely well timbered, for three hours. . . . The remainder of this day we traveled through fine rich bottoms [lowlands], overgrown with reeds, which make the best pasture in the world. 99

Such glowing reports drew many farmers and speculators to the region. Ignoring American Indian claims to the land, they demanded that the territory be opened for settlement. British officials opposed these demands because they feared that conflicts between settlers and American Indians would result.

American Indian resistance. The British authorities had good reason to be concerned. Following the French and Indian War, the British had limited the amount of ammunition and rum available for trade with American Indians.

INTERPRETING THE VISUAL RECORD

Plants. Ohio Valley settlers and traders saw many colorful species of plants, such as this wild honeysuckle. *How might settlers and traders have been influenced by this painting?*

They had also abandoned the French practice of presenting annual gifts to the Indians. These changes angered many American Indians who considered the trade goods and presents fair payment for allowing colonists to use their lands. George Croghan warned that the Indians who "had great expectations of being very generally supplied by us" might wage war.

American Indians grew increasingly upset by the large number of settlers that poured into the western lands. Many tribes had already seen their traditional ways of life disrupted by European trade. Now they faced losing their lands as well.

Neolin, an American Indian also known as the Delaware Prophet, traveled among these troubled western tribes. He appealed to them to return to their ancient practices. Neolin denounced the use of European goods and customs and urged his audiences to drive out the settlers. "They are my enemies," he said of the British. "They are your brothers' enemies."

Pontiac, an Ottawa chief, heard Neolin's message and acted upon it. Pontiac called on the Delaware, Ojibway, Seneca, Shawnee, Wyandot, and other American Indians to unite and "exterminate from our lands this nation which seeks only to destroy us." For most of 1763, war raged all along the frontier. Pontiac's forces killed some 2,000 settlers and destroyed many British forts.

Pontiac's Rebellion ended, however, when the Indians failed to take Fort Detroit and Fort Pitt. Pontiac's men attacked the forts for months without success. With winter approaching and ammunition in short supply, the Indian forces began to doubt that victory was possible. Faced with disheartened warriors and no hope of French aid, Pontiac called off the siege. Instead of being driven off by the rebellion, the British now possessed military control of Indian lands in the West.

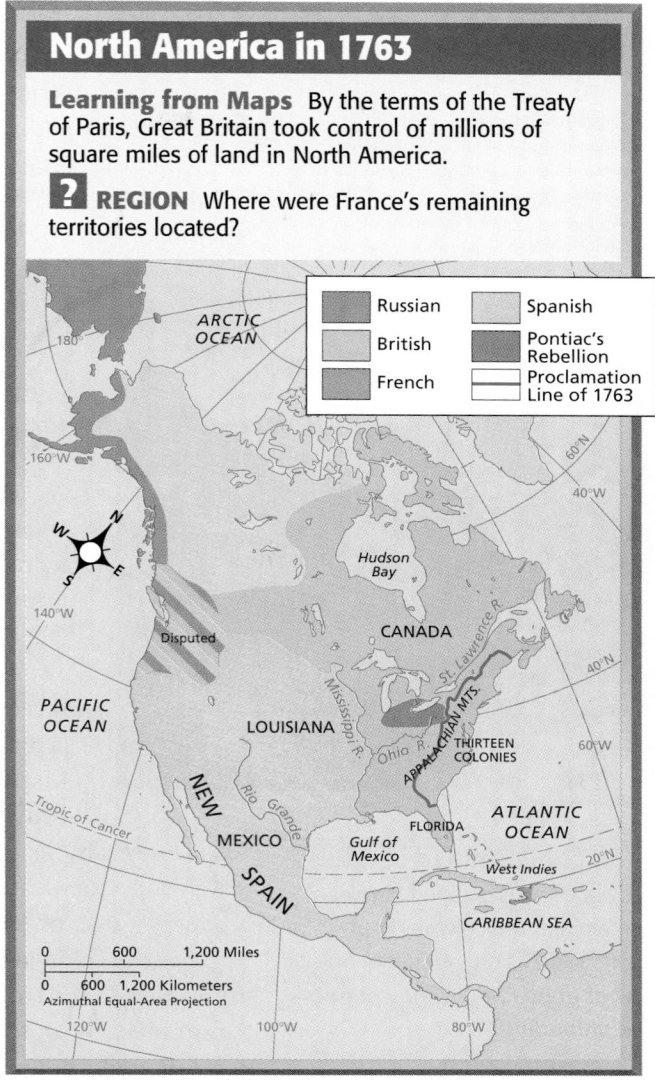

North America in 1763

Learning from Maps By the terms of the Treaty of Paris, Great Britain took control of millions of square miles of land in North America.

? REGION Where were France's remaining territories located?

Legend:
- Russian
- British
- French
- Spanish
- Pontiac's Rebellion
- Proclamation Line of 1763

The Proclamation of 1763. Pontiac's Rebellion and other American Indian uprisings convinced British authorities that although they had gained military control of the frontier, they could not effectively protect British settlers there. As a result, Britain issued the **Proclamation of 1763**, barring settlement west of the Appalachian Mountains. The law also required fur traders to obtain royal permission before entering the territory.

British officials hoped that separating settlers and American Indians would end fighting on the frontier. However, the proclamation was difficult to enforce. Land-hungry colonists resented the measure. Moreover, colonial governors, often land speculators themselves, did little to enforce it. As a result, settlers continued to pour into the territory.

After his defeat in the rebellion, Pontiac formed friendly relations with the British.

✔ **READING CHECK:** How did the British Crown respond to Pontiac's Rebellion?

Financing the Empire

The Proclamation of 1763 was not the only British policy that colonists resented. They were also angered by Parliament's efforts to make them pay part of the costs of "protecting and securing" the frontier. The British government was deeply in debt after the French and Indian War and needed assistance from its colonies. Englishman Thomas Whately stated the Crown's position on this issue in his pamphlet *Considerations on the Trade and Finances of This Kingdom.*

Trade. Goods shipped between Britain and the colonies kept ports like this one in Britain busy. *What goods might the workers be unloading?*

66 **We are not yet recovered from a War undertaken . . . for their Protection. No Time was ever so seasonable [appropriate] for claiming their Assistance. The Distribution is too unequal, of Benefits only to the Colonies, and of all the Burdens upon the Mother Country.** 99

For British officials, the question of how to raise this needed revenue always came back to one solution—taxes. As a first step to increase revenue, Parliament passed the **Sugar Act** of 1764. This act imposed a **duty**, or import tax, on foreign sugar, molasses, and several other items entering Britain's American colonies.

This was not the first time the British had imposed a duty on foreign molasses and sugar in the colonies. In fact, the new law actually lowered the existing duty on molasses. It was, however, the first time officials seriously enforced such a law. Until this time, British officials had been quite lenient in enforcing colonial trade laws. For example, they had often ignored obvious smuggling by colonists. Now royal inspectors searched homes, ships, and warehouses for smuggled goods. The Crown's judges presided over courts without juries to hear smuggling cases.

For the colonial merchants, rum distillers, and shipowners who profited from foreign trade and smuggling, the Sugar Act meant decreased business. They formed committees to protest the law and refused to cooperate with Royal Navy officers who entered colonial ports. Some merchants in Newport, Rhode Island, even persuaded the local sheriff to arrest an inspector who was particularly strict about enforcing the Sugar Act.

As this controversy raged, Parliament slapped another revenue law on the American colonies, the **Stamp Act** of 1765. Far more sweeping than the Sugar Act, the Stamp Act placed a tax on printed matter of all kinds: advertisements, diplomas, legal documents, newspapers, and playing cards. These materials had to be printed on stamped paper or have special stamps attached to show that the tax had been paid.

✔ **READING CHECK:** Why did the British government pass the Sugar Act and the Stamp Act?

Colonial Protests

British officials had expected the colonists to oppose the Stamp Act, but they were unprepared for the intensity of colonial resistance. In the past, the colonists had accepted taxes passed by the colonial assemblies. In the colonists' eyes, however, this tax was different. It had been passed by Parliament, where the colonists had no direct representation.

Colonial assemblies met in protest. In May 1765 the Virginia House of Burgesses passed a series of resolutions that condemned the Stamp Act. The resolutions declared:

> 66 The taxation of the people by themselves, or by persons chosen by themselves to represent them . . . is the only security against a burdensome taxation, and [is] the distinguishing characteristic of British freedom. 99

British officials responded by claiming that the colonists enjoyed "virtual representation," since Parliament represented all British subjects. Many colonists rejected this argument and decided it was time to express their discontent.

A call to action. Colonial merchants signed **nonimportation agreements**, promising not to buy or import British goods. Workers and artisans who opposed the Stamp Act took to the streets in demonstrations. Though most of these protests were peaceful, some turned violent, such as one that occurred in Boston on a hot August night in 1765. A mob led by shoemaker Ebenezer MacIntosh wrecked a building belonging to Andrew Oliver, a stamp agent, and then hung an effigy—a crude likeness—of Oliver. Within two weeks, the mob struck again. They destroyed court records and wrecked the house of the chief customs officer. They then looted and vandalized the elegant mansion of Oliver's brother-in-law, Thomas Hutchinson. Hutchinson was the lieutenant governor of the colony and the judge who had upheld the Stamp Act. Throughout the colonies, terrified stamp agents resigned their posts—making the Stamp Act almost impossible to enforce.

British officials singled out MacIntosh as the mob's leader, but they also suspected that the members of the Boston **Sons of Liberty** were involved. The Sons of Liberty were committees of artisans, lawyers, merchants, and politicians formed to protest the Stamp Act. The Sons of Liberty generally relied on pamphlets, petitions, and public meetings to rally support. Sometimes, though, they resorted to violence.

THE GRANGER COLLECTION, NEW YORK

The Stamp Act. The Stamp Act required colonists to display tax stamps such as these on all printed documents. *What do the symbols on the stamps represent?*

B I O G R A P H Y *Samuel Adams*
THE GRANGER COLLECTION, NEW YORK

Repeal of the Stamp Act. Samuel Adams was a leader of the Boston Sons of Liberty. The son of a local merchant and brewer, Adams was born in 1722. He graduated from Harvard College while he was still in his teens. After graduation, he worked for his father in the family brewing business, which he later inherited but lost to creditors. He also became involved in Boston politics and served in a series of local offices, including tax collector. In 1765 he was elected to the Massachusetts House of Representatives. The Stamp Act crisis turned him into a key political activist. Adams became a leader in the fight for the colonists' rights. He explained, "If we suffer tamely a lawless attack upon our liberty, we encourage it."

A peer of Adams described him as a man who "eats little, drinks little, sleeps little, thinks much, and is most decisive and indefatigable [tireless] in the pursuit of his objects." A master of propaganda, Adams proved particularly skillful at staging demonstrations and writing articles that influenced the public's perception of events. His elegant writings both expressed and heightened the colonists' anger at the British government:

Read More About It

Free Find:
Samuel Adams
After reading about Samuel Adams on the **Holt Researcher** CD–ROM, imagine that you are a reporter for a Boston newspaper interviewing Adams about colonial opposition to British taxes. Write a series of questions about specific acts of Parliament and the answers you think Samuel Adams would give.

Scotch-Irish in the Backcountry

teen Life

Some of the strongest opposition to the acts of the British government came from young Scotch-Irish colonists. In the half century before the Revolutionary War, more than 250,000 people of Scottish descent immigrated to North America from Ulster, a province in northern Ireland. Their ancestors had come to Ulster in the early 1600s. In the early 1700s, facing economic depression, drought, and religious discrimination, the Scotch-Irish began crossing the Atlantic to start a new life in America.

An anvil used by Scotch-Irish in Tennessee

Many of the Scotch-Irish moved to the western backcountry, where they worked small farms and faced the danger of conflict with local American Indians. Despite the hardships of frontier life, however, they placed a strong emphasis on the institutions of church and school. Scotch-Irish youngsters were taught by Presbyterian ministers who doubled as schoolmasters.

A strong distaste for the British government caused many Scotch-Irish teens to enthusiastically support American independence. Andrew Jackson, for example, fought against the British when he was 14 years old. He and his brother Robert were captured and thrown in prison, where they contracted smallpox. Robert died from the illness, but Andrew survived and went on to become the seventh president of the United States.

INTERPRETING THE VISUAL RECORD

Protests. In this 1766 British cartoon celebrating the repeal of the Stamp Act, members of Parliament carry the "dead" act in a small coffin. *What do the tall ships in the background signify?*

---

66 When the people are oppressed, when their Rights are infringed [violated], when their property is invaded, when taskmasters are set over them . . . in such circumstances the people will be discontented, and they are not to be blamed. 99

Led by Samuel Adams and others, the colonists decided to inform the king of their dissatisfaction. In October 1765, delegates from nine colonies gathered in New York City for the **Stamp Act Congress**. The delegates expressed the "warmest sentiments of affection and duty to His Majesty's Person and Government." They pledged "all due subordination [obedience]" to Parliament. Yet they also voiced their objections to the Stamp Act and denied that Parliament had the right to tax the colonies. The congress marked an important step toward more unified resistance.

British merchants who relied on colonial trade joined in the protest against the Stamp Act. The nonimportation agreements were hurting their businesses. Fearing financial ruin and wanting to keep the colonies "firmly attached to their mother country," they pressured Parliament to repeal the Stamp Act. Thus, people on both sides of the Atlantic rejoiced when Parliament repealed the hated measure in March 1766.

Pleased with the end of the Stamp Act, most colonists took little notice of another law that Parliament passed at the same time. The **Declaratory Act** of 1766 asserted the "full power and authority" of Parliament "to make laws . . . to bind the colonies and people of *America*" in "all cases whatsoever." Clearly, the fight over whether Parliament had the right to tax the colonists remained unresolved.

✔ **READING CHECK:** How did the colonists respond to the Stamp Act?

THE LIBRARY COMPANY OF PHILADELPHIA

THE REPEAL
OR THE FUNERAL OF MISS AME-STAMP

The Townshend Acts

The colonists had objected to the Stamp Act because they did not believe that Parliament had the right to tax them. They argued that the Stamp Act was a clear example of Britain's meddling in their colonial affairs. Charles Townshend, Britain's finance minister, never grasped this point. Townshend believed that the colonists had opposed the stamp tax because it was collected within the colonies. They would, he reasoned, be willing to accept taxes that were collected at colonial ports.

Parliament agreed, passing the **Townshend Acts** in 1767. These laws placed import duties on such common items as tea, lead, glass, and dyes for paint. British customs officials revived the use of special search warrants called **writs of assistance** to enforce the Townshend Acts. Unlike modern search warrants, which must state the exact articles sought and the specific places to be searched, writs of assistance were general warrants. Armed with a writ, a customs officer could search any vessel, warehouse, or home on the mere suspicion that it contained smuggled goods.

Colonial opposition to the Townshend Acts.
The Townshend Acts aroused powerful opposition in the colonies. Although the colonists accepted Britain's right to regulate colonial trade, they strongly objected to these new duties that were intended strictly to raise money. Many colonial courts resisted the law by simply refusing to issue writs of assistance.

Troubled by these renewed protests, the Crown decided to station additional soldiers in the colonies. New York's colonial assembly responded by refusing to provide money to quarter, or house and supply, these troops as the **Quartering Act** of 1765 required. The British government promptly suspended the assembly.

The most active center of protest, however, was Boston. In February 1768 the Massachusetts legislature drafted a protest letter attacking taxation without representation. The legislature then sent the letter to the other colonial assemblies for endorsement. The British government reacted by dissolving the Massachusetts assembly. This only served to further fuel protests and trigger a new round of nonimportation agreements. One Massachusetts woman boasted that her friends would not touch "a Drop of Tea" that was imported from Britain. Many women held spinning parties to make their own cloth so that they would not have to buy textiles from Britain. Women in Middletown, Massachusetts, for example, wove more than 20,000 yards of cloth in 1769. Not all the protests were peaceful boycotts. Angry demonstrators boarded and smashed British ships, attacked customs officials, and tarred and feathered people who informed on smugglers.

The Boston Massacre.
In 1768 General Thomas Gage dispatched British troops to Boston to silence the protests and enforce the writs of assistance. Their presence, however, created even worse tensions that eventually exploded into violence. On the evening of March 5, 1770, an angry crowd gathered outside a customs house. Some 50 or 60 colonists faced a small group of British soldiers. The crowd yelled insults and began throwing snowballs, rocks, oyster shells, and pieces of coal at the soldiers. Then, according to John Adams, "the motley [mixed] mob of saucy [disrespectful] boys, negroes, . . . and outlandish jacktars [sailors]" pressed so hard

THE GRANGER COLLECTION, NEW YORK

INTERPRETING THE VISUAL RECORD

Conflict. British troops stream into Boston in this 1768 image. *How are the colonists in the image reacting to the British troops?*

The Boston Massacre. Boston silversmith Paul Revere engraved and printed this image of the Boston Massacre. *Which side does Revere depict as the aggressor? How can you tell?*

against the soldiers that there was no room to move. One soldier either slipped or was knocked down. His gun went off, and the other soldiers opened fire on the crowd. Three colonists lay dead. Two others died later.

News of the clash stunned the colonists. Lieutenant Governor Thomas Hutchinson claimed that "the people of Boston are run mad." Samuel Adams and the Sons of Liberty labeled the incident the **Boston Massacre** and promptly denounced British aggression. Poems and songs of patriotic resistance were written in honor of the victims. Some even noted with amazement that a sailor killed in the Boston Massacre and thought to have been a runaway slave had given his life for the cause of colonial liberty when most African Americans were still enslaved.

Months later the British soldiers were tried for murder. Josiah Quincy and John Adams—Samuel's cousin—agreed to defend them. Neither man sympathized with the British, but both insisted that the soldiers deserved a fair trial. As John Adams later wrote:

 [Legal] counsel ought to be the very last thing that an accused person should want [lack] in a free country; . . . and . . . persons whose lives were at stake ought to have the counsel they prefer. 99

In the end, two soldiers were convicted of manslaughter. As punishment, they were branded on the hands and released.

✔ **READING CHECK:** What events led to the Boston Massacre?

SECTION 1 REVIEW

Define and explain the significance of the following terms:
Pontiac's Rebellion
Proclamation of 1763
Sugar Act
duty
Stamp Act
nonimportation agreements
Sons of Liberty
Stamp Act Congress
Declaratory Act
Townshend Acts
writs of assistance
Quartering Act
Boston Massacre

Identify and explain the significance of the following individuals:
Neolin
Samuel Adams
John Adams

1. **Using Graphic Organizers** Copy the chart below. Fill in the objections that colonists had to each of the acts passed by Parliament, how colonists expressed their discontent, and the outcome in the case of each act.

	Sugar Act	Stamp Act
Objections		
Colonists' Actions		
Outcome		

2. **Analyzing** How did the British Crown attempt to bring peace to the western frontier after Pontiac's Rebellion?

3. **Using Historical Imagination** Imagine that you are an American Indian living west of the Appalachian Mountains in the early 1760s. Explain why you will or will not join Pontiac's Rebellion.

4. **Recognizing Points of View** How did Parliament justify its taxes on the colonies? From the colonists' point of view, was this a valid argument?

Critical Thinking

5. Could the Boston Massacre have been avoided? Explain your answer.
   Consider:
   • what led to the confrontation between colonists and soldiers
   • what events sparked the Boston Massacre
   • at what points the events could have been halted before blood was shed

SECTION 2

The Shot Heard Round the World

OBJECTIVES

Read to understand:

1. why the colonists in Massachusetts staged the Boston Tea Party
2. why Parliament passed the Intolerable Acts
3. what events led to the battles at Lexington and Concord
4. what actions the Second Continental Congress took

KEY TERMS

Committee of
   Correspondence
Tea Act
Boston Tea Party
Intolerable Acts
Quebec Act
First Continental Congress
Patriots
minutemen
Second Continental Congress
Battle of Bunker Hill
Olive Branch Petition

KEY PEOPLE

George III
Paul Revere
George Washington
William Howe

KEY PLACES

Lexington
Concord

The battle on the Lexington green

EYEWITNESSES TO History 66 It seems we have troublesome times a coming, for there is great disturbance abroad in the earth and they say it is tea that caused it. So then if they will quarrel about such a trifling thing as that, what must we expect but war. I think or at least fear it will be so. 99
—Jemima Condict Harrison

Jemima Condict Harrison, a young woman from New Jersey, noted these concerns in her diary in October 1774. During the early 1770s relations between Great Britain and the colonies worsened. A new tea act in 1773 provoked a dramatic protest in Boston. Less than one year later, Parliament passed a series of laws that angered many colonists as never before. Despite the growing crisis, some colonists still hoped for a peaceful resolution. Many, however, became convinced that war was inevitable.

Continuing Unrest

When Frederick, Lord North, became Britain's prime minister in 1770, he hoped to pacify the colonies with a partial repeal of the Townshend Acts. Parliament agreed and also allowed the Quartering Act to expire. The British kept a small duty on tea, however. As King George III explained, there must "always be one tax to keep up the right"—that is, to show that the British government still had the right to tax the colonists.

The repeal quieted the general unrest, but the calm was short-lived. In 1772 the Crown announced that it—not the colonial legislature—would pay the salaries of the governor and judges in Massachusetts. Colonists feared that if these officials did not depend on the legislature for their pay, they might more readily ignore colonial demands.

Led by Samuel Adams, Bostonians responded quickly to this latest threat. They created a 21-member **Committee of Correspondence** charged with keeping the rest of the colony—and "the World"—informed about "the Infringements [trespasses] and Violations" that Britain had made on colonial rights. For the next several years, similar

INTERPRETING THE VISUAL RECORD

British royalty. George III models his coronation robes in this 1760 oil painting. *How might King George's clothing in the portrait have furthered colonists' resentment of the king?*

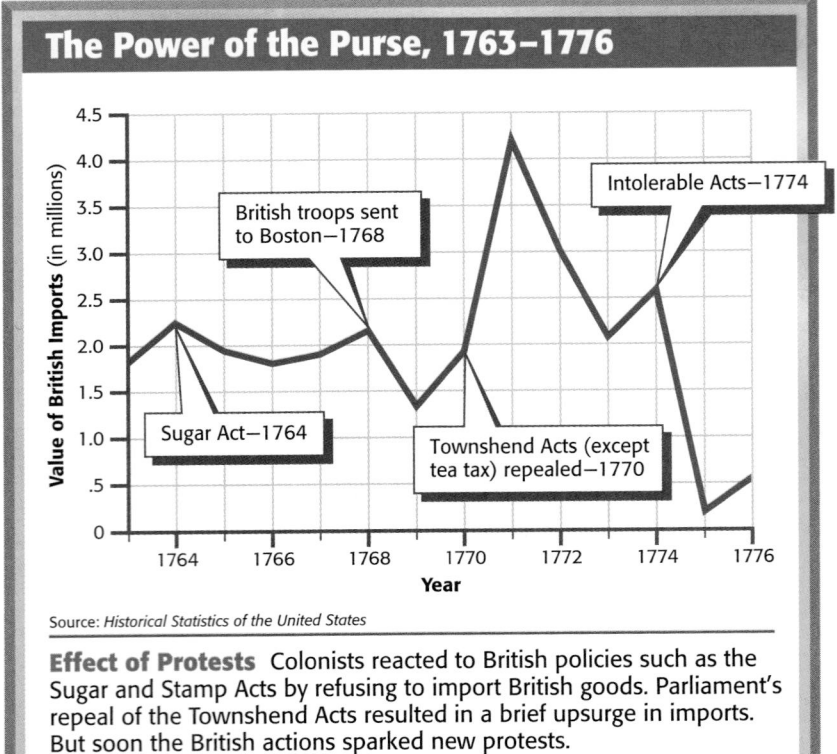

The Power of the Purse, 1763–1776

Value of British Imports (in millions) — y-axis: 0, .5, 1.0, 1.5, 2.0, 2.5, 3.0, 3.5, 4.0, 4.5

Year — x-axis: 1764, 1766, 1768, 1770, 1772, 1774, 1776

- Sugar Act—1764
- British troops sent to Boston—1768
- Townshend Acts (except tea tax) repealed—1770
- Intolerable Acts—1774

Source: *Historical Statistics of the United States*

Effect of Protests Colonists reacted to British policies such as the Sugar and Stamp Acts by refusing to import British goods. Parliament's repeal of the Townshend Acts resulted in a brief upsurge in imports. But soon the British actions sparked new protests.

? Building Graph Skills Between which two years did British imports experience the greatest drop?

committees in Massachusetts and other colonies helped shape public opinion.

The Tea Act of 1773. Even the business of selling tea provoked a crisis. By 1773 the British East India Company was almost bankrupt. To save the ailing company, Parliament passed the **Tea Act** of 1773. This law excused the company from paying certain duties and permitted it to bypass wholesalers and sell tea directly to American agents. As a result, the price of tea in the colonies soon fell lower than ever before.

Most of the colonists, however, opposed the Tea Act and refused to buy tea. The colonists were concerned that the East India Company would develop a monopoly of the tea trade. American wholesalers and merchants feared that other British companies would secure similar privileges from Parliament and force them out of business.

The Sons of Liberty in Philadelphia and New York threatened anyone who imported tea. Once again, the most heated protests occurred in Massachusetts. On December 16, 1773, after the governor refused colonists' demands that he send three shiploads of tea back to Britain, colonists held a mass meeting at Boston's Old South Church. Later that night, a well-organized group of colonists "dressed in an Indian manner" boarded the tea ships anchored in Boston Harbor. The colonists dumped 342 chests of tea into the water. One of the participants later remembered the incident.

66 In about three hours from the time we went on board, we had thus broken and thrown overboard every tea chest to be found. . . . We were surrounded by British armed ships, but no attempt was made to resist us. 99

News of the **Boston Tea Party** spread like wildfire at home and abroad. Many colonists cheered the tea's destruction. Others were shocked by such disregard for property rights.

✔ **READING CHECK:** Why did colonists in Massachusetts stage the Boston Tea Party?

This package of tea celebrates the Boston Tea Party.

The Intolerable Acts of 1774. The Boston Tea Party infuriated British officials. Parliament responded by passing the Coercive Acts—four laws designed to punish Boston and the rest of Massachusetts and to strengthen British control over all of the colonies. The colonists called these laws the **Intolerable Acts**.

The first act closed the port of Boston until the colonists paid for the destroyed tea. The second act revoked the Massachusetts charter of 1691 and forbade colonists in the region to hold town meetings without the governor's permission.

The third act allowed royal officials who were charged with crimes in Massachusetts to be tried in other colonies or in Britain so as to avoid hostile juries. Many colonists assumed that soldiers tried under this law would be punished lightly or would escape punishment entirely. The fourth law, a new Quartering Act, ordered local officials to provide food and housing, in private homes if necessary, for British soldiers stationed in the colonies.

The Intolerable Acts deepened colonial hostility toward Britain. Colonists everywhere responded with sympathy for Massachusetts. They sent food and money to Boston to help offset the effects of the port closing. At the same time, they denounced the actions of George III and Parliament for the threats they posed to colonial liberty.

The **Quebec Act**, also passed in 1774, further angered colonists. This law extended Quebec's boundary south to the Ohio River. Thus it overrode the claims of Connecticut, Massachusetts, and Virginia to the disputed western lands. It also granted full religious freedom to French Roman Catholics, upsetting many Protestant colonists.

The Intolerable Acts and the Quebec Act quickened the movement toward colonial unity. Colonists began to focus less on specific British policies. Instead, they concentrated their anger on what they saw as a growing pattern of oppression. Among those who questioned their loyalty to the Crown and Parliament, a new identity—not yet fully American, but no longer British—was developing.

✔ **READING CHECK:** Why did Parliament pass the Intolerable Acts?

The Revolutionary War Begins

Between September 5 and October 26, 1774, representatives from every colony except Georgia attended the **First Continental Congress** in Philadelphia. The Congress was not a lawmaking body but a convention where delegates could discuss their grievances and consider their options. Some delegates wanted the colonies to remain part of the British Empire. Others favored independence.

Both of these positions found their way into the Congress's final resolution—the Declaration of Resolves. Although the declaration expressed loyalty to the British Crown, it also stated that the colonists had rights as British subjects. In particular, the declaration maintained that the colonists had a right to the "free and exclusive power of legislation in their several provincial legislatures." To back up their demands, the delegates called for a ban on all trade with Great Britain. They pledged to meet again in May 1775 if their demands were not met.

The Continental Congresses produced many papers, such as the ones pictured here.

For King George III, the Continental Congress was the last straw. In November 1774 he wrote to Lord North: "The New England Governments are in a State of Rebellion, blows must decide whether they are to be subject to this Country or independent." Acting on the king's wishes, Parliament ordered General Thomas Gage to put down the rebellion.

AMERICAN *Letters*

Mercy Otis Warren's Revolutionary Writings

BEQUEST OF WINSLOW WARREN, COURTESY MUSEUM OF FINE ARTS, BOSTON, MA

The American Revolution inspired many talented writers. One of the best of these writers was Mercy Otis Warren, a poet and dramatist who was well acquainted with some of the Revolution's leaders. Warren wrote many of her poems and plays to increase public support for the cause of independence. In a number of these works, she used fictional characters and situations to represent real people and events. Warren paints an unattractive picture of British colonial officials in a stage direction from her play The Group, *in which a group of evil leaders from the country of Blunderland represent corrupt British officials. She employs similar techniques in her poem about the Boston Tea Party, "The Squabble of the Sea Nymphs; or the Sacrifice of the Tuscararoes." The fictional Tuscararoes represent the Patriots and Amphytrite represents people loyal to Britain.*

Mercy Otis Warren

Stage direction from *The Group*

The Group enter attended by a swarm of court sycophants [flatterers], hungry harpies [monsters], and unprincipled danglers . . . hovering over the stage in the shape of locusts, led by Massachusettensis in the form of a basilisk [lizard]; the rear brought up by Proteus [someone who allies with a side in a conflict for money], bearing a torch in one hand and a powder flask in the other, the whole supported by a mighty army and navy from Blunderland, for the laudable purpose of enslaving its best friends.

The first page of Mercy Otis Warren's The Group *lists the* dramatis personae, *or the characters, in the work.*

THE LIBRARY COMPANY OF PHILADELPHIA

from "The Squabble of the Sea Nymphs; or the Sacrifice of the Tuscararoes"

The champions of the Tuscararan race,
(Who neither hold, nor even wish a place,
While faction reigns, and tyrany presides,
And base oppression o'er the virtues rides; . . .
And avarice [greed] o'er the earth and sea prevails; . . .);
Lent their strong arm in pity to the fair, . . .
Pour'd a profusion of delicious teas,
Which, wafted by a soft favonian breeze,
Supply'd the wat'ry deities, in spite
Of all the rage of jealous Amphytrite.

UNDERSTANDING LITERATURE

1. What does the imagery used to describe the creatures surrounding the Group reveal about Warren's view of British officials?
2. How do the feelings of the Tuscararoes represent the Patriots' views of Great Britain?
3. How does Warren use language in these two pieces to try to win public support for the Patriot cause?

Lexington and Concord. Determined to reassert royal authority, General Gage decided to seize rebel military supplies stored in Concord, Massachusetts. On April 18, 1775, under cover of night, some 750 British troops left Boston and rowed across the Charles River. However, the **Patriots**, or colonists who supported independence, had stationed watchmen on the far shore. As soon as Gage's force emerged from the darkness, Patriots Paul Revere and William Dawes—later joined by Samuel Prescott—galloped off to alert sleeping households, shouting the alarm: "The British are coming!" Patriots throughout the countryside hurriedly gathered to confront the British.

On April 19, Captain John Parker and about 70 **minutemen** —members of the militia who promised to be ready at a minute's notice—waited for the British soldiers on the Lexington village green. When the British patrol arrived, its commander shouted, "Lay down your arms, you . . . rebels, and disperse!" The colonists began to leave, still holding their guns. Suddenly someone—each side later accused the other—fired "the shot heard round the world." A barrage of British gunfire followed. When the smoke cleared, 8 colonists lay dead, and 10 others were wounded.

The British troops, called Redcoats because of their bright red uniforms, marched on to Concord. They destroyed some of the Patriot supplies, then started back toward Boston. From behind stone walls along the route, hundreds of minutemen fired steadily at the retreating troops. The red uniforms and orderly marching formations used by the British made them easy targets. The Patriots were quite successful, suffering fewer than 100 casualties in the day's fighting, while killing or wounding 273 British soldiers. The Patriots' success earned them the respect of their enemy. A humbled British officer wrote: "Whoever looks upon them [the Patriots] as an irregular mob will find himself much mistaken."

✔ **READING CHECK:** What events led to the battles at Lexington and Concord?

The Second Continental Congress. The news of Lexington and Concord had spread through the colonies when the **Second Continental Congress** opened in Philadelphia on May 10. Radicals such as Samuel Adams pushed for the colonies to immediately declare their independence from Britain. Others, led by John Dickinson of Pennsylvania, successfully urged restraint. Nonetheless, by the middle of June the delegates had agreed to establish the Continental Army "for the defense of American liberty."

The delegates unanimously chose Virginian George Washington of Virginia to command this new army. Though not a fiery speaker or a profound political thinker, Washington inspired confidence. He had acquired military experience and a reputation for bravery while fighting for the British in the French and Indian War. After meeting him, Abigail Adams wrote to her husband: "The gentleman and soldier look agreeably blended in him. Modesty marks every line and feature of his

After his service in the French and Indian War, George Washington retired to his estate, Mount Vernon, to live as a gentleman farmer. The Revolutionary War brought him back into military service.

Revolutions

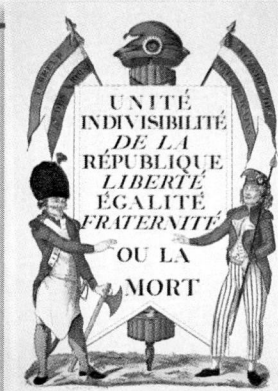

A poster from the French Revolution

Two aspects of the American Revolution have influenced many revolutionary movements over the last 225 years. First, it was an anticolonial war waged by colonists who demanded independence. During the 1800s and 1900s, revolutionary leaders in Africa, Asia, and Latin America looked to the United States for inspiration as they fought for independence from colonial powers. South American Simón Bolívar, a revolutionary, helped several colonies win independence from Spain in the early 1800s. He referred to his North American neighbor as a "land of freedom and home of civic virtue." Second, the American Revolution replaced a royal system of government with one based on a written constitution. Later revolutions in France, Mexico, and other nations followed similar patterns.

In another way, however, a number of revolutions in the 1900s differed from the American Revolution. Although the American Revolution made fundamental changes in how Americans were governed, it did not involve a rearrangement of the country's basic social and economic structure. In contrast, communist revolutions in China, Cuba, and Russia rejected capitalism and instituted economic systems that involved tight government control.

INTERPRETING THE VISUAL RECORD

Battle of Bunker Hill. Flames erupt on Bunker Hill in this British engraving. *What obstacles did the hills pose for the British soldiers?*

face." With war at hand, Washington devoted himself to the "glorious cause" of American rights.

The Battle for Boston.

On June 17, 1775, Patriot forces were again put to the test. Atop two hills overlooking Boston Harbor—Bunker Hill and Breed's Hill—New England militiamen dug in, awaiting an attack by British troops. To save ammunition, an American commander ordered his men: "Don't one of you fire until you see the whites of their eyes."

British troops commanded by General William Howe advanced in three bold assaults. Corporal Amos Farnsworth of the Massachusetts militia later recalled the **Battle of Bunker Hill**.

> 66 We . . . sustained the enemy's attacks with great bravery . . . and after bearing, for about 2 hours, as severe and heavy a fire as perhaps ever was known, and many having fired away all their ammunition . . . we were overpowered by numbers and obliged to leave. 99

The British took both hills but suffered 1,054 casualties. Fewer than 450 Americans were killed or injured. The Battle of Bunker Hill did not resolve anything. The British had captured the hills, but at a terrible cost. British general Gage wrote that "the number of killed and wounded is greater than our forces can afford to lose." The Patriots, despite losing control of Charlestown, Massachusetts, were encouraged by the results of Bunker Hill. General Nathanael Greene of Rhode Island wrote that "upon the whole, I think we have little reason to complain. . . . I wish we could sell them another hill at the same price."

Even after the battle, some colonists worked to avoid a permanent break with Britain. They persuaded the Continental

THE GRANGER COLLECTION, NEW YORK

Congress to send a final plea to George III. The **Olive Branch Petition** stated the colonists' loyalty to the king and asked for his help in ending the conflict.

The king rejected the petition and ordered the Royal Navy to blockade all shipping to the colonies. He also sent Hessian (HE-shuhn) mercenaries—hired soldiers primarily from the German state of Hesse—to help defeat the Americans.

Meanwhile, General Washington planned new military maneuvers. In a surprise move on March 4, 1776, he positioned troops and cannons on Dorchester Heights, which overlooked Boston. From there, the Patriots could easily fire on British forces in the city. Washington hoped to force Howe and his men to take the hill or flee Boston. Howe chose to flee. On March 26, the British, joined by some 1,000 colonists loyal to the Crown, sailed for Nova Scotia. They left, according to Washington, "in so much . . . confusion as ever troops did."

✔ **READING CHECK:** What actions did the Second Continental Congress take?

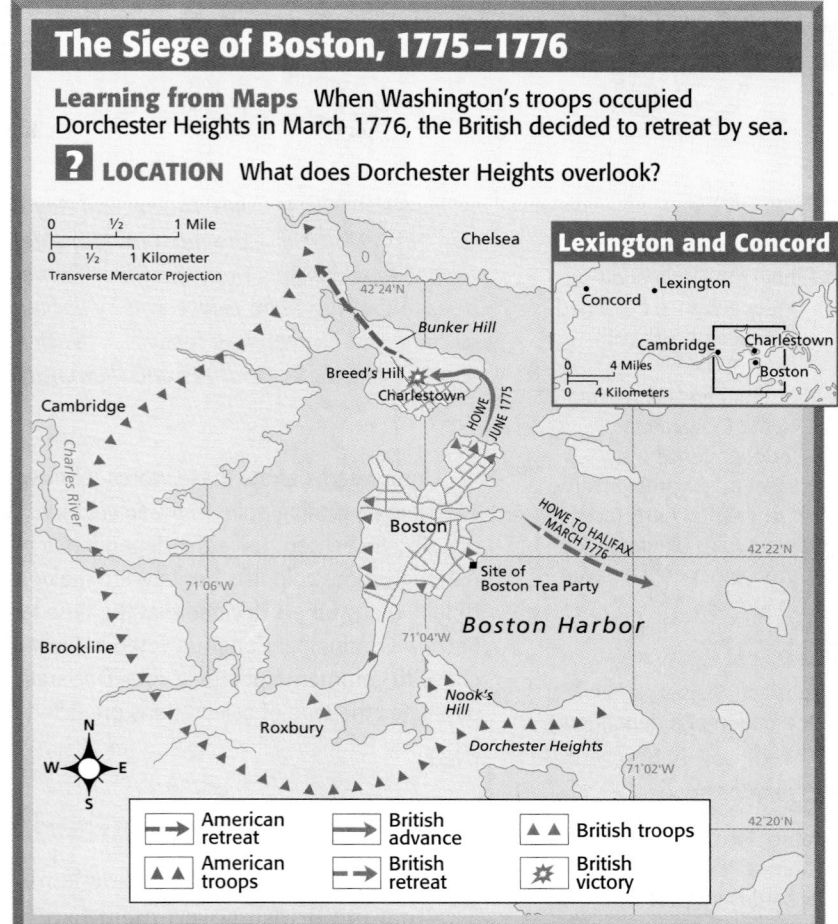

The Siege of Boston, 1775–1776

Learning from Maps When Washington's troops occupied Dorchester Heights in March 1776, the British decided to retreat by sea.

? LOCATION What does Dorchester Heights overlook?

Legend:
- → American retreat
- ▲▲ American troops
- → British advance
- → British retreat
- ▲▲ British troops
- ☼ British victory

SECTION REVIEW

Define and explain the significance of the following terms:

Committee of Correspondence
Tea Act
Boston Tea Party
Intolerable Acts
Quebec Act
First Continental Congress

Patriots
minutemen
Second Continental Congress
Battle of Bunker Hill
Olive Branch Petition

Identify and explain the significance of the following individuals:

George III
Paul Revere

George Washington
William Howe

Locate and explain the importance of the following places:

Lexington
Concord

1. **Using Graphic Organizers** Copy the following web. Use it to list the factors that contributed to the outbreak of fighting at Lexington and Concord.

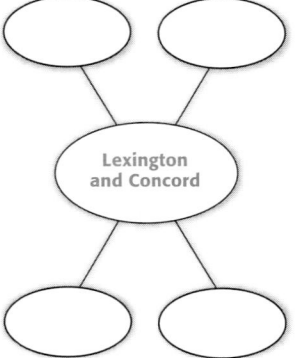

Lexington and Concord

2. **Synthesizing** How did colonists respond to the passage of the Tea Act and the Intolerable Acts?
3. **Understanding Geography: Location** How did the Patriots attempt to use geography to their advantage at Bunker Hill and at Dorchester Heights?
4. **Hypothesizing** What arguments might some members of the Second Continental Congress have used to persuade the other delegates to send the Olive Branch Petition to King George III?

Critical Thinking

5. How did the British government justify its actions in the colonies?
   Consider:
   - why Parliament passed some of the laws colonists opposed
   - how the British government viewed the colonies
   - how the British government reacted to the fighting at Lexington and Concord

Independence Declared

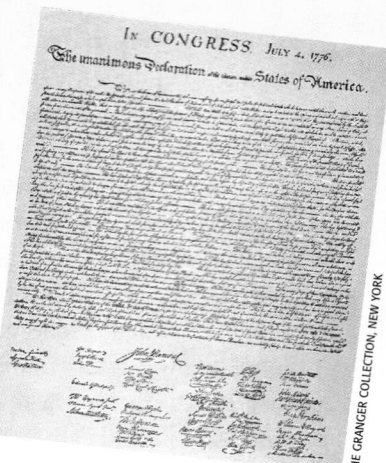

THE GRANGER COLLECTION, NEW YORK

The Declaration of Independence

Read to understand:
1. how the Declaration of Independence explained America's break with Great Britain
2. how Americans reacted to the Declaration of Independence
3. what major problems the Continental Army faced
4. what roles different groups of people played in the war

KEY TERMS

Common Sense
Declaration of Independence
Loyalists

KEY PEOPLE

Patrick Henry
Thomas Paine
Richard Henry Lee
Thomas Jefferson
Abigail Adams
Thayendanegea

EYEWITNESSES TO History

❝ *The second day of July, 1776, will be the most memorable epoch [time period] in the history of America. I am apt to believe that it will be celebrated by succeeding generations as the great anniversary festival . . . with shows, games, sports, guns, bells, bonfires and illuminations.* ❞
—John Adams

John Adams wrote these words to his wife, Abigail, describing a turning point in the Revolution. With fighting under way, the movement toward independence became irreversible. Although some colonists hesitated to make a final break with Britain, many others decided that the time for such action had come. On July 2, 1776, the Second Continental Congress voted in favor of independence. Although his fellow citizens chose to commemorate the formal Declaration of Independence that was adopted two days later, the type of celebrations predicted by Adams do continue even today.

Reasons for Independence

Many colonists favored independence for two basic reasons. First, they believed that the British government had violated their rights as British subjects. Second, some of their fellow colonists had already died defending these rights.

Patrick Henry and Thomas Paine emerged as powerful supporters of independence. Henry, a member of Virginia's Committee of Correspondence and a delegate to both Continental Congresses, argued that the dispute between the colonies and the Crown could not be resolved. In 1775 he reportedly delivered a speech that made his point in dramatic terms.

Before becoming a member of Virginia's Committee of Correspondence, Patrick Henry worked as a storekeeper and an attorney.

THE GRANGER COLLECTION, NEW YORK

❝ Gentlemen may cry peace, peace—but there is no peace. The war is actually begun! . . . Is life so dear, or peace so sweet, as to be purchased at the price of chains and slavery? Forbid it, Almighty God!—I know not what course others may take; but as for me, give me liberty, or give me death! ❞

Thomas Paine, a recent immigrant from Britain living in Philadelphia, also promoted the Patriot cause. Published in January 1776, Paine's pamphlet **Common Sense** stirred up public support for the Revolution and called for the end of Britain's rule of the colonies. Paine argued, "Government, even in its best state, is but a necessary evil; in its worst state, an intolerable one." The passionate words of Henry and Paine inspired many colonists to support the Revolution. *Common Sense* sold some 120,000 copies in three months and helped transform a disorganized colonial rebellion into a focused movement for independence.

The Declaration of Independence

On June 7, 1776, Richard Henry Lee of Virginia introduced a resolution in the Second Continental Congress declaring "that these United Colonies are, and of right ought to be, free and independent States . . . and that all political connection between them and the State of Great Britain is . . . totally dissolved." The resolution also called for the establishment of a confederation, or loose pact, of the states.

Before voting on Lee's proposal, the Congress appointed a five-person committee to draft a formal **Declaration of Independence**. Thomas Jefferson, a Virginia lawyer, planter, and slaveholder—and at 33 one of the youngest delegates—became chair of the committee and did most of the actual writing. On June 28 the committee presented the Declaration to the Congress.

Before turning their attention to the Declaration, the Congress debated—and quickly adopted—Lee's resolution for independence. The Congress officially declared on July 2 the new United States of America to be independent of Britain. Two days later, on July 4, the Congress formally adopted the Declaration of Independence.

The Declaration's immediate purpose was to win support for independence, both at home and abroad. To weaken the public's lingering loyalty to King George III, the Declaration detailed his misdeeds. It also outlined the basic principles of representative government and listed these "self-evident" truths.

> 66 We hold these truths to be self-evident, that all men are created equal, that they are endowed by their Creator with certain unalienable Rights, that among these are Life, Liberty, and the pursuit of Happiness. 99

The document also proclaimed the right of people "to alter or abolish" a government that deprives them of these "unalienable Rights." The men who signed the Declaration of Independence knew they were now traitors in the eyes of the Crown. The price for failing to win independence might well be imprisonment—or death.

✔ **READING CHECK:** How did the Declaration of Independence explain America's break with Great Britain?

★ HISTORICAL DOCUMENTS ★

THOMAS PAINE
Common Sense

Published almost nine months after the battles at Lexington and Concord, Thomas Paine's Common Sense *offered an impassioned argument for the cause of independence. In this widely read pamphlet, Paine attacked the British monarchy and contended that a Continental government was a "natural right" of the colonists.*

*L*et a crown be placed thereon, by which the world may know that, so far as we approve of monarchy, that in America *the law is king.* For as in absolute governments the king is law, so in free countries the law *ought* to be king; and there ought to be no other. But lest any ill use should afterward arise, let the crown at the conclusion of the ceremony be demolished and scattered among the people, whose right it is.

A government of our own is our natural right; and when a man seriously reflects on the precariousness of human affairs, he will become convinced that it is infinitely wiser and safer to form a Constitution of our own in a cool, deliberate manner while we have it in our power than to trust such an interesting event to time and chance.

THE GRANGER COLLECTION, NEW YORK

Carpenter's Hall was the meeting place of the First and Second Continental Congresses.

Reactions to Independence

The Declaration of Independence inspired mixed reactions throughout the colonies. Many Patriots rejoiced wildly—ringing "liberty bells," singing and dancing around bonfires, and celebrating at banquets. In New York City, Patriots even pulled down a huge statue of King George III. According to one independence-loving newspaper reporter, this small act of rebellion was "the just dessert of an ungrateful tyrant!" On July 13 Patriot Ezra Stiles noted in his diary that "the CONGRESS have tied a . . . knot, which the Parliament will find they can neither cut nor untie. The *thirteen united Colonies* now rise into an *Independent Republic* among the kingdoms, states and empires on earth."

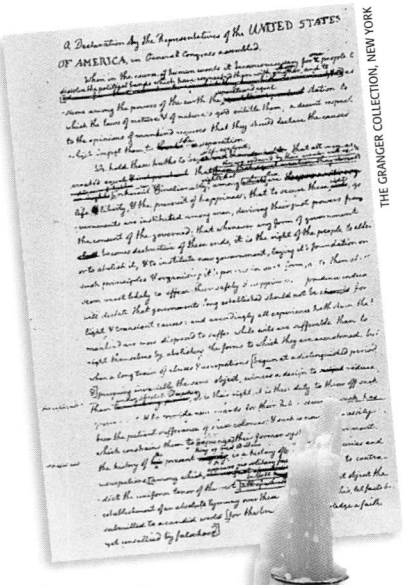

Thomas Jefferson wrote this draft of the Declaration of Independence.

BIOGRAPHY

Abigail Adams

Some people, such as Abigail Adams, had a more complex reaction to the news of independence. The daughter of a Congregational minister, Adams was born Abigail Smith in 1744 and grew up in rural Massachusetts with little formal education. Nevertheless, she was a constant reader and during her teenage years she taught herself French and developed remarkable letter-writing skills. In 1764 she married John Adams, with whom she raised four children.

During the Revolutionary War, John Adams spent much of his time attending to government matters in Philadelphia. Back in Massachusetts, Abigail Adams cared for their young children and managed the family's farm and business interests. She also wrote a series of letters to her husband that frequently commented on political issues. Abigail Adams strongly supported independence, championed the cause of women's rights, and forcefully opposed slavery. A few months before her husband was chosen to serve on the committee that would draft the Declaration of Independence, she wrote to him.

❝ I long to hear that you have declared an independancy—and by the way in the new Code of Laws which I suppose it will be necessary for you to make I desire you would Remember the Ladies, and be more generous and favorable to them than your ancestors. Do not put such unlimited power into the hands of the Husbands. Remember all Men would be tyrants if they could. ❞

Adams was disappointed by the response this suggestion received from her husband. He claimed "I cannot but laugh" at the idea of including women in official political business. She became an enthusiastic citizen of the new American nation, however, and continued to remark on political affairs until her death in 1818.

Other Americans opposed or simply ignored the Declaration of Independence. Among its opponents were the **Loyalists**, also known as Tories. Some Loyalists based their loyalty to Britain on the long-held belief that to resist the king was to rebel against God. "It is our duty not to disturb and destroy the peace of the community by becoming . . . rebellious subjects and resisting the ordinances of God," explained one Anglican minister. Other Loyalists stood to lose power and wealth if royal authority ended. Still others considered loyalty to the king as important as dedication to one's family.

As support for independence mounted, Loyalists began to fear for their safety. To many Patriots, a Loyalist was "a thing whose head is in England, and its body is

HOLT RESEARCHER

Read More About It

Free Find:

Abigail Adams

After reading about Abigail Adams on the **Holt Researcher** CD–ROM, write a fictional letter from her to her husband that explains the contributions women made to the success of the American Revolution.

in America, and its neck ought to be stretched [hanged]." More troubling than such words were the threats of violence to the Loyalists and their families. Many wealthy and influential Loyalists escaped to Canada, the British West Indies, or England. Those who remained either tried to stay out of the conflict or openly aided the British forces.

✔ **READING CHECK:** How did Americans react to the Declaration of Independence?

Fighting the War

To declare independence was one thing; to fight for it and win was another. The lack of a powerful central government made the American war effort particularly difficult. The Second Continental Congress had no real authority. It could ask the states for help, but it could not force them to comply. Some colonial merchants charged high prices for shoddy goods. Many farmers sold their produce to the highest bidder, whether American or British.

Because of these problems, George Washington's troops suffered. They endured bitter winters at Morristown, New Jersey, in 1777 and at Valley Forge, Pennsylvania, in 1777–78. James Thacher, a young doctor from Massachusetts, described the hardships at Valley Forge.

> ❝ At one time nearly three thousand men were [listed] unfit for duty from the want [lack] of clothing; and it was not uncommon to track the march of the men over ice and frozen ground by the blood from their naked feet. Several times . . . they experienced little less than a famine in camp; and more than once our general officers were alarmed by the fear of a total dissolution [breaking up] of the army from the want of provisions. ❞

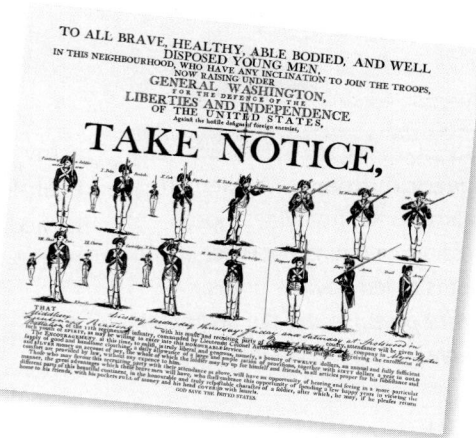

Recruitment posters like this one encouraged colonial men to join the Continental Army.

Disease also battered the Continental Army. Although Washington issued orders about cleanliness and hygiene, illness plagued the camps. Poorly prepared food spread germs, and camp toilets contaminated water supplies. Dysentery caused by these unsanitary conditions killed thousands. Making matters even worse, Washington faced constant troop shortages. He never had more than 26,000 Continentals available nationwide at any one time, although some 231,000 soldiers served in the Continental Army over the course of the war. Much of the problem stemmed from short-term enlistments. Most men signed on for one year—some for just three months—and the soldier-farmers in the ranks often deserted at planting or harvesting time. Such limitations made it impossible to maintain a large, well-trained fighting force.

✔ **READING CHECK:** What major problems did the Continental Army face?

Those Who Served

Despite their troubles, Patriot forces enjoyed two key advantages over the British: they often fought on familiar ground and they were motivated by revolutionary zeal. Many soldiers in the Continental Army served in units recruited from their home colonies, often with men they knew. State militias, which also fought in the war, were usually composed of enlistees from the same region. Many of these soldiers drew inspiration from their belief that they were defending their homes.

Continentals and Redcoats.
Most Continental soldiers and state militiamen firmly embraced the goal of independence. Fighting against the British was difficult, dangerous, and low-paying work. While the men who performed this work came from a variety of backgrounds, most were under 23 years old, owned little or no property, and had grown up on farms. Some of these soldiers were drafted into the Continental Army. Others served as paid replacements for draftees. Still others enlisted in order to receive small cash bonuses and promises of free land after the war. A great many fought, however, because they believed they were serving a "glorious cause." Joseph Hodgkins, a company officer from Massachusetts, explained this feeling in a letter to his wife.

> 66 I am willing to serve my Country in the Best way & manner that I am Capable of and as our Enemy are gone from us I Expect we must follow them. . . . I would not Be understood that I should Choose to March But as I am engaged in this glorious Cause I am willing to go where I am Called. 99

American troops. Minutemen march to the front lines. Some soldiers carried gunpowder in horns called powder horns. *What purpose did the drummer serve?*

Much like those who served in the Continental Army, the soldiers in the British army were mostly young men from poor rural backgrounds. Unlike their Patriot enemies, however, Britain's Redcoats were highly trained, well supplied, and accustomed to strict military discipline. Their professionalism helped distinguish the British army as one of the world's most reliable fighting forces.

African Americans and American Indians.
George Washington initially ordered that no black soldiers could serve in the Continental Army. Some colonial leaders feared that slaves would revolt if given weapons. Others believed that black men would not make good soldiers. In late 1775, however, the royal governor of Virginia offered freedom to slaves who would leave their owners to fight for the British cause. In a single week some 300 African Americans took up his offer.

In response, the Continental Army began to enlist free African Americans. Some were former slaves who had been freed by their owners in exchange for entering the army. Some 5,000 African American Patriots fought in the war. One Hessian soldier noted that "no regiment is to be seen in which there are not Negroes in abundance." Numerous black soldiers—such as Salem Poor and Peter Salem, both of whom fought at Bunker Hill—received official recognition for their courage.

American Indians also played an important role in the war. Their knowledge of the land in key locations between British and American forces could greatly aid either side. Initially, both the British and the Patriots tried to respect the tribes' neutrality. Soon, however, the urgent need for skilled fighters led both sides to recruit

Indian soldiers. This led to a split in the Iroquois League. In 1777 the League held a council to discuss the war. Thayendanegea (thah-yuhn-dah-ne-GAY-uh), an important Mohawk chief known to colonists as Joseph Brant, had received assurances from the British that they would protect Iroquois land rights. He was, therefore, strongly pro-British. The Cayuga, Mohawk, Onondaga, and Seneca agreed to follow Brant and fight for Great Britain. The Oneida and Tuscarora, however, did not share Brant's confidence in the British and fought for the Patriots.

Women. Patriot women served the revolutionary cause in important ways. A few even fought in the war, while others undertook dangerous missions as spies or messengers. Deborah Sampson Gannett of Massachusetts, for example, disguised herself as a man and became the "faithful and gallant soldier" Robert Shurtleff. She was said to be as "fleet as a gazelle, bounding through swamps . . . ahead of her companions." After she died in 1827, Congress granted her husband a pension as the "widow" of a Revolutionary War veteran.

Many other women accompanied the troops and worked as cooks, laundresses, and nurses. After one bloody South Carolina battle, women nursed injured American soldiers even as "men dared not come to minister to their wants," according to one observer. Most Patriot women served in their communities. They supported the war effort by distributing medical supplies, making uniforms, and helping manufacture bullets. With the men off to war, women managed businesses and farms, helping to keep the colonial economy going.

Loyalist women were also involved in the war effort. Although many fled their homes or were exiled, others spied for the British army, aided British prisoners, or hid British soldiers in their homes.

COLLECTION OF THE NEW-YORK HISTORICAL SOCIETY

INTERPRETING THE VISUAL RECORD

Uniforms. Despite their often common backgrounds, Continental and British soldiers dressed quite differently. *How might the British soldiers' uniforms have helped and hurt them in battle?*

✔ **READING CHECK:** What roles did African Americans, American Indians, common soldiers, and women play in the Revolutionary War?

SECTION 3 REVIEW

Define and explain the significance of the following terms:
Common Sense
Declaration of Independence
Loyalists

Identify and explain the significance of the following individuals:
Patrick Henry
Thomas Paine
Richard Henry Lee
Thomas Jefferson
Abigail Adams
Thayendanegea

1. **Using Graphic Organizers** Copy the chart below. Use it to explain the arguments that the Declaration of Independence offered in support of independence and how different groups of Americans reacted to the document.

Reasons for Independence	Reactions to Independence
1.	1.
2.	2.
3.	3.

2. **Identifying Values** What did the colonists' support for the Revolution reflect about their values?
3. **Problem Solving** If you had been an adviser to General Washington, what solutions would you have proposed to resolve the Continental Army's problems?
4. **Comparing and Contrasting** Compare the experiences of common soldiers, African Americans, American Indians, and women in the war.

Critical Thinking

5. Historians have noted that the Declaration of Independence was intended, in part, to convince the colonists to support the fight for independence. Explain why you agree or disagree.
Consider:
• the content of the Declaration of Independence
• how the Declaration of Independence affected colonists

The Declaration of Independence

In Congress, July 4, 1776
The unanimous Declaration of the thirteen
united States of America,

Thomas Jefferson wrote the first draft of the Declaration in a little more than two weeks.

Democratic Values

According to the first paragraph, why is it important for the signers to justify their political break with Great Britain?

impel: force
endowed: provided

"Laws of Nature" and "Nature's God" refer to the belief common in the Scientific Revolution that certain patterns are constant and predictable and that they come from a supreme being. Natural or "unalienable" rights (the rights to life, liberty, and the pursuit of happiness) cannot be taken away.

usurpations: wrongful seizures of power
evinces: clearly displays
despotism: unlimited power

When in the Course of human events, it becomes necessary for one people to dissolve the political bands which have connected them with another, and to assume among the Powers of the earth, the separate and equal station to which the Laws of Nature and of Nature's God entitle them, a decent respect to the opinions of mankind requires that they should declare the causes which impel them to the separation.

We hold these truths to be self-evident, that all men are created equal, that they are endowed by their Creator with certain unalienable Rights, that among these are Life, Liberty, and the pursuit of Happiness. That to secure these rights, Governments are instituted among Men, deriving their just powers from the consent of the governed, That whenever any Form of Government becomes destructive of these ends, it is the Right of the People to alter or to abolish it, and to institute new Government, laying its foundation on such principles and organizing its powers in such form, as to them shall seem most likely to effect their Safety and Happiness. Prudence, indeed, will dictate that Governments long established should not be changed for light and transient causes; and accordingly all experience hath shown, that mankind are more disposed to suffer, while evils are sufferable, than to right themselves by abolishing the forms to which they are accustomed. But when a long train of abuses and usurpations, pursuing invariably the same Object evinces a design to reduce them under absolute Despotism, it is their right, it is their duty, to throw off such Government, and to provide new Guards for their future security.— Such has been the patient sufferance of these Colonies; and such is now the necessity which constrains them to alter their former Systems of Government. The history

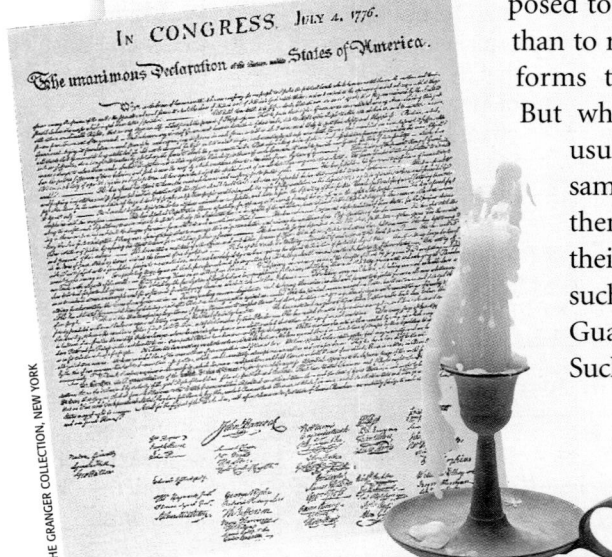

THE GRANGER COLLECTION, NEW YORK

The Declaration of Independence

of the present King of Great Britain is a history of repeated injuries and usurpations, all having in direct object the establishment of an absolute Tyranny over these States. To prove this, let Facts be submitted to a candid world.

He has refused his Assent to Laws, the most wholesome and necessary for the public good.

He has forbidden his Governors to pass Laws of immediate and pressing importance, unless suspended in their operation till his Assent should be obtained; and when so suspended, he has utterly neglected to attend to them.

He has refused to pass other Laws for the accommodation of large districts of people, unless those people would relinquish the right of Representation in the Legislature, a right inestimable to them and formidable to tyrants only.

He has called together legislative bodies at places unusual, uncomfortable, and distant from the depository of their Public Records, for the sole purpose of fatiguing them into compliance with his measures.

He has dissolved Representative Houses repeatedly, for opposing with manly firmness his invasions on the rights of the people.

He has refused for a long time, after such dissolutions, to cause others to be elected; whereby the Legislative Powers, incapable of Annihilation, have returned to the People at large for their exercise; the State remaining in the mean time exposed to all the dangers of invasion from without, and convulsions within.

He has endeavored to prevent the population of these States; for that purpose obstructing the Laws of Naturalization of Foreigners; refusing to pass others to encourage their migration hither, and raising the conditions of new Appropriations of Lands.

He has obstructed the Administration of Justice, by refusing his Assent to Laws for establishing Judiciary Powers.

He has made Judges dependent on his Will alone, for the tenure of their offices, and the amount and payment of their salaries.

He has erected a multitude of New Offices, and sent hither swarms of Officers to harass our people, and eat out their substance.

He has kept among us, in times of peace, Standing Armies without the Consent of our legislature.

He has affected to render the Military independent of and superior to the Civil Power.

He has combined with others to subject us to a jurisdiction foreign to our constitution, and unacknowledged by our laws; giving his Assent to their Acts of pretended legislation:

For quartering large bodies of armed troops among us:

For protecting them, by a mock Trial, from Punishment for any Murders which they should commit on the Inhabitants of these States:

For cutting off our Trade with all parts of the world:

tyranny: oppressive power exerted by a government or ruler
candid: fair

Beginning here the Declaration lists the charges that the colonists had against King George III.

relinquish: release, yield
inestimable: priceless
formidable: causing dread

annihilation: destruction

convulsions: violent disturbances

naturalization of foreigners: the process by which foreign-born persons become citizens
appropriations of land: setting aside land for settlement

tenure: term

a multitude of: many

 Democratic Values

What wrongful acts stated in the Declaration have been committed by the king and the British Parliament?

quartering: lodging, housing

Why were the colonists protesting British tax policies?

The "neighboring Province" referred to here is Quebec.
arbitrary: not based on law
render: make

abdicated: given up

foreign mercenaries: soldiers hired to fight for a country not their own
perfidy: violation of trust

insurrections: rebellions

petitioned for redress: asked formally for a correction of wrongs

For imposing taxes on us without our Consent:

For depriving us in many cases, of the benefits of Trial by Jury:

For transporting us beyond Seas to be tried for pretended offences:

For abolishing the free System of English Laws in a neighboring Province, establishing therein an Arbitrary government, and enlarging its Boundaries so as to render it at once an example and fit instrument for introducing the same absolute rule into these Colonies:

For taking away our Charters, abolishing our most valuable Laws, and altering fundamentally the Forms of our Governments:

For suspending our own Legislature, and declaring themselves invested with Power to legislate for us in all cases whatsoever.

He has abdicated Government here, by declaring us out of his Protection and waging War against us.

He has plundered our seas, ravaged our Coasts, burnt our towns, and destroyed the lives of our people.

He is at this time transporting large armies of foreign mercenaries to complete the works of death, desolation and tyranny, already begun with circumstances of Cruelty & perfidy scarcely paralleled in the most barbarous ages, and totally unworthy the Head of a civilized nation.

He has constrained our fellow Citizens taken Captive on the high Seas to bear Arms against their Country, to become the executioners of their friends and Brethren, or to fall themselves by their Hands.

He has excited domestic insurrections amongst us, and has endeavored to bring on the inhabitants of our frontiers, the merciless Indian Savages, whose known rule of warfare, is an undistinguished destruction of all ages, sexes and conditions.

In every stage of these Oppressions We have Petitioned for Redress in the most humble terms: Our repeated Petitions have been answered only by repeated injury. A Prince, whose character is thus marked by every act which may define a Tyrant, is unfit to be the ruler of a free People.

This painting by Robert Pine and Edward Savage depicts the Continental Congress voting for independence.

Nor have We been wanting in attention to our British brethren. We have warned them from time to time of attempts by their legislature to extend an **unwarrantable jurisdiction** over us. We have reminded them of the circumstances of our emigration and settlement here. We have appealed to their native justice and **magnanimity**, and we have **conjured** them by the ties of our common kindred to disavow these usurpations, which, would inevitably interrupt our connections and correspondence. They too have been deaf to the voice of justice and of **consanguinity**. We must, therefore, **acquiesce** in the necessity, which denounces our Separation, and hold them, as we hold the rest of mankind, Enemies in War, in Peace Friends.

We, therefore, the Representatives of the united States of America, in General Congress, Assembled, appealing to the Supreme Judge of the world for the **rectitude** of our intentions, do, in the Name, and by Authority of the good People of these Colonies, solemnly publish and declare, That these United Colonies are, and of Right ought to be Free and Independent States; that they are Absolved from all Allegiance to the British Crown, and that all political connection between them and the State of Great Britain, is and ought to be totally dissolved; and that as Free and Independent States, they have full Power to levy War, conclude Peace, contract Alliances, establish Commerce, and to do all other Acts and Things which Independent States may of right do. And for the support of this Declaration, with a firm reliance on the Protection of Divine Providence, we mutually pledge to each other our Lives, our Fortunes and our sacred Honor.

John Hancock	Benjamin Harrison	Lewis Morris
Button Gwinnett	Thomas Nelson Jr.	Richard Stockton
Lyman Hall	Francis Lightfoot Lee	John Witherspoon
George Walton	Carter Braxton	Francis Hopkinson
William Hooper	Robert Morris	John Hart
Joseph Hewes	Benjamin Rush	Abraham Clark
John Penn	Benjamin Franklin	Josiah Bartlett
Edward Rutledge	John Morton	William Whipple
Thomas Heyward Jr.	George Clymer	Samuel Adams
Thomas Lynch Jr.	James Smith	John Adams
Arthur Middleton	George Taylor	Robert Treat Paine
Samuel Chase	James Wilson	Elbridge Gerry
William Paca	George Ross	Stephen Hopkins
Thomas Stone	Caesar Rodney	William Ellery
Charles Carroll of Carrollton	George Read	Roger Sherman
George Wythe	Thomas McKean	Samuel Huntington
Richard Henry Lee	William Floyd	William Williams
Thomas Jefferson	Phillip Livingston	Oliver Wolcott
	Francis Lewis	Matthew Thornton

unwarrantable jurisdiction: unjustified authority

magnanimity: generous spirit

conjured: urgently called upon

consanguinity: common ancestry

acquiesce: consent to

rectitude: rightness

Congress adopted the final draft of the Declaration of Independence on July 4, 1776. A formal copy, written on parchment paper, was signed on August 2, 1776.

 Democratic Values

From whom did the signers of the Declaration receive their authority to declare independence?

The following is part of a passage that the Congress took out of Jefferson's original draft: "He has waged cruel war against human nature itself, violating its most sacred rights of life and liberty in the persons of a distant people who never offended him, captivating and carrying them into slavery in another hemisphere, or to incur miserable death in their transportation thither." *Why do you think the Congress deleted this passage?*

SECTION 4

An American Victory

OBJECTIVES

Read to understand:

1. the importance of the Battles of Trenton and Saratoga
2. how the Patriots defeated the British in the West and the South
3. what the terms of the Treaty of Paris were

KEY TERMS

Battle of Trenton
Battle of Saratoga
guerrilla warfare
Battle of Yorktown
Treaty of Paris

KEY PEOPLE

"Gentleman Johnny" Burgoyne
Charles Cornwallis
Bernardo de Gálvez
Marquis de Lafayette
George Rogers Clark
Francis Marion

KEY PLACES

Vincennes
Camden
Kings Mountain

EYEWITNESSES TO History

❝ *It invigorated the national spirit . . . and encouraged the public councils to resist the insidious [treacherous] plans of the British cabinet to disunite the American people and disarm opposition.* **❞**

—James Wilkinson

James Wilkinson, a Continental Army officer who took part in one of the most important battles of the war, said these words about a Patriot victory in October 1777. Counting on Loyalist support and the fighting skills of their well-trained troops, confident British generals had planned a quick end to the war. British plans that looked good on paper failed on the battlefield, however. Patriot forces scored their first major victory at Trenton, New Jersey, in December 1776. Just 10 months later, Continental troops, including Wilkinson, forced British general "Gentleman Johnny" Burgoyne to surrender his forces in the New York wilderness.

Rifle from the Revolutionary War era

The War Heats Up

With General Howe's evacuation of Boston in March 1776, General Washington knew the British would soon strike elsewhere. The most likely target was New York City, a Loyalist stronghold. On July 2 Howe sailed into New York Harbor, landing his troops on Staten Island. The British won an easy victory at Brooklyn Heights in late August and continued to hit the Patriots hard. After New York City fell to the British forces, Washington tried to regroup. Thomas Paine expressed the somber mood in his pamphlet *The Crisis.*

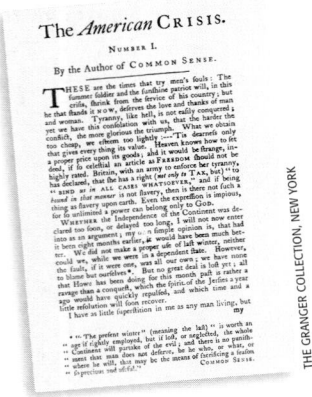

THE GRANGER COLLECTION, NEW YORK

Continental officers sometimes read excerpts from **The Crisis** *aloud to inspire their troops to remember the Patriot cause.*

❝ These are the times that try men's souls. The summer soldier and the sunshine patriot will, in this crisis, shrink from the service of their country; but he that stands it *now* deserves the love and thanks of man and woman. Tyranny, like hell, is not easily conquered. **❞**

The Battle of Trenton. Thinking the war was almost won, General Howe prepared to celebrate Christmas in New York. As a precaution he stationed some 1,400 Hessians at Trenton, New Jersey, to keep a close eye on the Patriots across the Delaware River. Rather than build fortifications against a possible Patriot attack, the Hessian commander Colonel Johann Rall boasted, "Let them come. We want no trenches. We will go at them with the bayonet."

Washington took advantage of the Hessian overconfidence. Ignoring the customary holiday halt in fighting, Washington and his troops boldly ferried across the ice-choked Delaware River on Christmas night. As Thomas Rodney, one of General Washington's officers, vividly recalled:

> 66 It was as severe a night as ever I saw, and after two battalions were landed, the storm increased so much, and the river was so full of ice, that it was impossible to get the artillery over. 99

Although Washington's troops had, in Rodney's words, "then been on duty four nights and days . . . without six hours sleep in the whole time," they surprised the Hessian camp at daybreak. In the **Battle of Trenton**, the Hessians quickly surrendered. Of the 1,400 Hessian soldiers at Trenton, about 120 were killed or wounded, and 918 were taken prisoner. The Americans suffered just five wounded and no dead in the battle.

General Charles Cornwallis, the British field commander, prepared to counterattack. However, the American troops slipped away by night, leaving their campfires burning to fool the British. Washington then struck inland, ambushing British regiments at Princeton. This hit-and-run campaign did not result in a clear-cut victory for the Patriots. However, their strong showing in this, their first major offensive attack, greatly raised American morale. British plans to end the war quickly were, as British official George Germain wrote, "blasted by the unhappy affair at Trenton."

INTERPRETING THE VISUAL RECORD

Washington's crossing.
E. G. Leutze's painting of George Washington crossing the Delaware has become one of the best-known depictions of the event. *How does Leutze's painting portray Washington?*

Strategies for Success   Identifying the Main Idea

When studying history, the ability to identify main ideas is key to understanding complex issues and events. *Boyer's The American Nation* is designed to help you develop this skill. Applying the following guidelines will help you identify the main ideas of any reading assignment.

How to Identify the Main Idea

1. **Observe study clues.** Read the title, introduction, and any other study clues that the assignment provides. These clues often point to the main ideas that will be covered.
2. **Develop study questions.** If the assignment does not provide study questions, formulate your own. Keeping these questions in mind will help focus your reading.
3. **Note the outline and arrangement of ideas.** As you read, pay particular attention to headings, subheadings, and opening paragraphs. Major ideas are often introduced in such material.
4. **Distinguish supporting details.** As you read, distinguish sentences that furnish supporting details

from the general statements they support. A string of sentences providing detailed information often leads to a conclusion that expresses a main idea.

Applying the Strategy

Read the Section 4 subsection entitled European powers provide aid. Compose a four-sentence paragraph that summarizes the subsection. Then condense your paragraph into a single sentence that states the main idea of the subsection.

Practicing the Strategy

Answer the following questions.
1. What is the main idea of each paragraph in the subsection?
2. What is the main idea of the entire subsection?
3. What study clues are helpful in identifying the subsection's main idea?
4. What supporting details does the author provide for the subsection's main idea?

Trenton. A surprise Patriot attack the day after Christmas led to the defeat of the Hessian garrison at Trenton. It was one of only a few American victories during 1776–77. *Who is the figure on the white horse?*

Read More About It

Free Find:

Battle of Saratoga

After reading about the Battle of Saratoga on the **Holt Researcher** CD–ROM, create a fictional account of how the British might have won the battle.

USA
15c

Gen. Bernardo de Gálvez
Battle of Mobile 1780

THE GRANGER COLLECTION, NEW YORK

Bernardo de Gálvez defeated the British in battles at Baton Rouge and Natchez, among others.

British disaster at Saratoga. The setbacks at Trenton and Princeton roused the British to redouble their efforts. In control of Canada to the north and New York City to the south, they decided to cut off New England, the hotbed of the rebellion, from the other British colonies.

British general "Gentleman Johnny" Burgoyne devised a plan: three separate British forces would converge at Albany, New York. The plan seemed simple enough. What the British did not realize—or ignored—was that their proposed lines of attack crossed many lakes, swamps, hills, and forests in areas teeming with Patriots.

Burgoyne's strategy failed miserably. Two of the British forces—those under Colonel Barry St. Leger and General Howe—never met up with Burgoyne's troops. Burgoyne's men left Canada in early June and began marching southward. His long caravan of supplies and artillery moved at a crawl. They were hampered by trails and bridges that had been blocked or destroyed by the American militia. In September Burgoyne and his men finally crossed the Hudson River, where they soon clashed with Patriot forces under General Horatio Gates in the **Battle of Saratoga**. Outfoxed and outnumbered, Burgoyne formally surrendered his troops on October 17, 1777.

European powers provide aid. Saratoga stands out as a turning point in the war for the Americans. Encouraged by the victory, France—which had been secretly aiding the Patriots—signed a formal alliance with the United States and recognized its independence in February 1778. French aid provided Americans with gold, naval support, supplies, and troops.

France also declared war on Great Britain. A year later Spain joined the war as an ally of France, followed in 1780 by the Netherlands. Bernardo de Gálvez, Spain's governor of Louisiana, gave the Patriots much-needed supplies. Gálvez also helped defeat the British in several key battles along the Gulf Coast and the Mississippi River.

New volunteers from Europe brought many useful military skills. Even before France and Spain entered the war, an impressive group of experienced Europeans had aided the Patriots. France's German-born officer Baron Johann Kalb, Minorca's George Farragut, Poland's Kazimierz Pulaski (kah-ZEEM-yesh pool-AHS-kee) and Tadeusz Kosciuszko (tah-DE-oosh kawsh-CHOOSH-kaw) all played important roles in the Continental Army.

In 1777 France's Marquis de Lafayette (lah-fah-yet), a 19-year-old nobleman, came to North America with Kalb to fight against the British. He so impressed George Washington when they met that he soon became an important member of the general's staff. A short time later, Prussia's Baron von Steuben took charge of training and drilling the Continental Army.

For the Americans, the alliance with France came just in time. During the severe winter of 1777–78, Washington's army was again reduced to a sick and hungry handful of soldiers. The news that powerful allies had joined them gave the Patriots new hope.

✔ **READING CHECK:** How did Trenton and Saratoga influence the war?

The Fight for Independence, 1776–1781

Learning from Maps The Revolutionary War was fought over a vast and varied landscape. Both sides faced the challenges of moving men and supplies across rivers and mountains and through dense forests and swamps.

? MOVEMENT George Rogers Clark moved his men and supplies from Fort Pitt to the western frontier by way of the Ohio River. Why do you think he chose this route? If he had taken a direct overland route from Fort Pitt to Kaskaskia, about how far would he have had to travel?

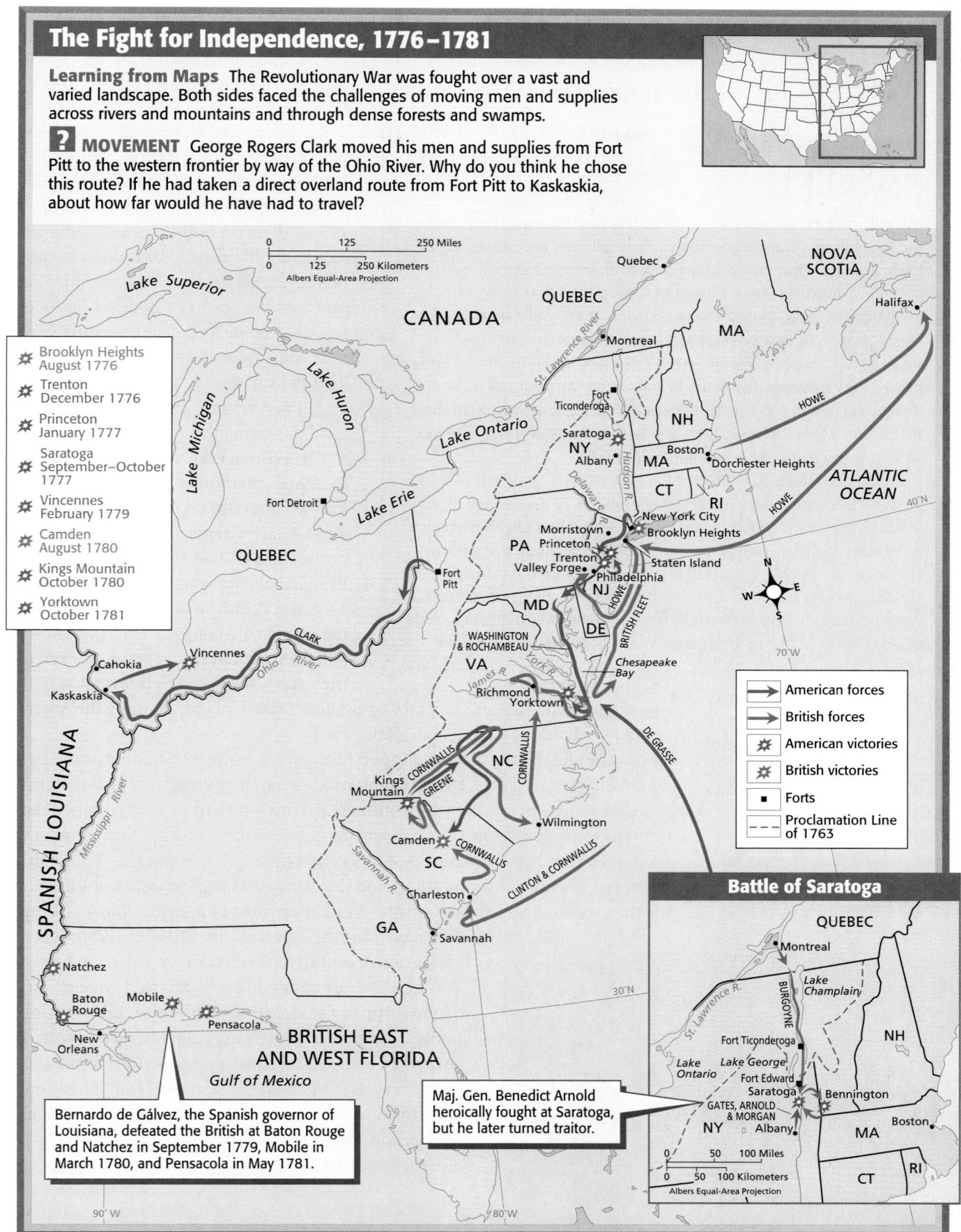

Battle legend:

- ✹ Brooklyn Heights August 1776
- ✹ Trenton December 1776
- ✹ Princeton January 1777
- ✹ Saratoga September–October 1777
- ✹ Vincennes February 1779
- ✹ Camden August 1780
- ✹ Kings Mountain October 1780
- ✹ Yorktown October 1781

0 125 250 Miles
0 125 250 Kilometers
Albers Equal-Area Projection

Map legend:
- → American forces
- → British forces
- ✹ American victories
- ✹ British victories
- ■ Forts
- - - - Proclamation Line of 1763

Bernardo de Gálvez, the Spanish governor of Louisiana, defeated the British at Baton Rouge and Natchez in September 1779, Mobile in March 1780, and Pensacola in May 1781.

Maj. Gen. Benedict Arnold heroically fought at Saratoga, but he later turned traitor.

Battle of Saratoga

0 50 100 Miles
0 50 100 Kilometers
Albers Equal-Area Projection

Great Debates

Independence

Perhaps more than any other topic, the meaning of the American Revolution has provoked heated and ongoing debates among historians. While the political fact of independence was one obvious consequence of the Revolution, Thomas Jefferson's words "all men are created equal" have, from the time they were written, been a source of controversy.

Some historians have chosen to focus on the limitations of revolutionary ideas. Clearly, the Declaration of Independence did not create political liberty for everyone. American women continued to be excluded from political life after 1776. Many slaves fought for and gained their freedom during the Revolutionary War, but slavery as a system did not end. American Indians also failed to benefit from the Revolution. Many lost their lands and homes during the war, and few were recognized by either side for their service.

Other historians have viewed the Revolution as an event of great social consequence. While America in the 1700s was full of inequalities, these scholars argue that the Revolution began to change Americans' ideas about how power should be distributed in society. No longer did people assume that a few "well-born" individuals should rule over everyone else. This fundamental change in attitude would eventually lead to the expansion of democratic rights to include all Americans, whatever their gender, race, or economic condition.

Fighting in the West and South

The Patriots had better luck in the West, where most of the fighting took place between small detachments of troops. In 1778 George Rogers Clark led a group of 175 soldiers on a military expedition to secure the Illinois country. With the help of local French settlers, Clark and his force captured the posts of Kaskaskia (ka-SKAS-kee-uh), Cahokia (kuh-HOH-kee-uh), and Vincennes (vin-SENZ) over the summer. The British retook Vincennes by year's end, however, and decided to camp there until the spring thaw.

In February 1779 Clark and his men marched 180 miles and crossed four flooded rivers to take the British by surprise. Clark's army recaptured the Vincennes post and went on to neutralize the British in the war's western theater. Late in 1778 the British focused their attacks on the southern colonies, where they anticipated strong Loyalist support. Backed by their navy, they occupied several seaport towns. From Charleston, General Cornwallis attacked inland, crushing the Americans in the Battle of Camden in 1780.

Cornwallis did not find the support he expected, however. Although some Loyalist militia patrolled the Carolina countryside, so did small groups of Patriot soldiers. Francis Marion, an officer in the Continental Army who had narrowly escaped capture at Camden, led one of the most aggressive of these outfits. Nicknamed the Swamp Fox for his elusive tactics, Marion and his band of South Carolina militia disrupted British communications and discouraged many Loyalists from fighting for the Crown. Britain's hold on the South also suffered a serious blow at Kings Mountain, South Carolina, in October 1780. There Patriot troops captured or killed an entire British force.

A new Patriot commander, Nathanael Greene, ultimately stopped the British in the South. Like Marion, Greene was a master of **guerrilla warfare**—wearing down the enemy in hit-and-run battles. Even in defeat Greene bragged, "We fight, get beat, rise, and fight again." Using forest cover and the element of surprise, Greene, Marion, and the Patriots eventually forced Cornwallis to leave the southern interior and retreat to the coastline.

✔ **READING CHECK:** How did Patriot forces defeat the British in the West and the South?

INTERPRETING THE VISUAL RECORD

Clark's troops. George Rogers Clark's soldiers make their way through a forest on their way to Vincennes. *In what condition are his troops?*

The Patriots Emerge Victorious

During the summer of 1781, General Cornwallis moved his army to Yorktown, Virginia, located on the peninsula between the York and James Rivers. There he had access to the British fleet and supplies.

On August 14 a dispatch reached General Washington's New York headquarters. Admiral François de Grasse, the French naval commander in the West Indies, was moving his fleet north to block Chesapeake Bay. Washington's army, along with a French force, rushed south to complete the trap. Boxed in by the French fleet, the British troops at Yorktown soon found themselves vastly outnumbered by American and French forces. Cornwallis soon admitted defeat. On October 19, 1781, as a band reportedly played the old English folk tune "The World Turned Upside Down," the British surrendered their weapons at the **Battle of Yorktown**.

Although some fighting continued in the South and on the frontier, Cornwallis's surrender effectively marked the end of the war. The **Treaty of Paris** was signed on September 3, 1783. It granted the United States independence, the land from the Atlantic coast westward to the Mississippi River and from the Great Lakes south to Florida, and fishing rights in the Gulf of St. Lawrence and off the coast of Newfoundland. The treaty also declared that Americans should pay any debts owed to the British.

The American delegates negotiated only with Britain. If they had been forced to sit at a peace table with delegates from Spain and France as well, the United States probably would have won its independence, but little else. Spain wanted to confine the United States to the land east of the Appalachian Mountains. Having regained Florida during the war, Spain hoped to expand northward to the Ohio Valley. The treaty gave the United States more room to grow as it faced the challenge of forging a new country.

Surrender at Yorktown. John Trumbull painted this scene of General Cornwallis surrendering to George Washington. *Do the troops in this painting look like they had fought a difficult battle? Explain.*

✔ **READING CHECK:** What were the terms of the Treaty of Paris?

SECTION 4 REVIEW

Define and explain the significance of the following terms:

Battle of Trenton   Battle of Yorktown
Battle of Saratoga   Treaty of Paris
guerrilla warfare

Identify and explain the significance of the following individuals:

"Gentleman Johnny" Burgoyne
Charles Cornwallis
Bernardo de Gálvez
Marquis de Lafayette
George Rogers Clark
Francis Marion

Locate and explain the importance of the following places:

Vincennes   Kings Mountain
Camden

1. **Using Graphic Organizers** Copy the chart below. Use it to summarize the battles that took place in the North, the West, and the South. Include the outcome of each battle.

North:
West:
South:

2. **Assessing Consequences** Why was Saratoga a turning point in the war?
3. **Comparing and Contrasting** How did the Patriot fighting tactics differ from those of the British in the West and the South?
4. **Hypothesizing** How did victory at Yorktown and the support of France and Spain affect the terms of the Treaty of Paris?

Critical Thinking

5. In your opinion, what was the most important consequence of the American Revolution? Explain your answer.
   Consider:
   • the immediate and long-term consequences of the war
   • which consequence was the most significant

Review

Creating a Time Line

Copy the time line below onto a sheet of paper. Complete the time line by filling in the events and dates from the chapter that you think were most significant. Pick three events and explain why you think they were significant.

1763	1773	1783

Writing a Summary

Using the Reading Checks as a guide, write an overview of the events in the chapter.

Identifying People and Ideas

Identify the following terms or individuals and explain their significance.

1. Neolin
2. Stamp Act
3. writs of assistance
4. Committee of Correspondence
5. George Washington
6. Declaration of Independence
7. Abigail Adams
8. Loyalists
9. George Rogers Clark
10. guerrilla warfare

Understanding Main Ideas

SECTION 1

1. How and why did British colonial policies change after 1763?
2. What led to the Boston Massacre?

SECTION 2

3. How did the colonists protest the Tea Act?
4. Why did Parliament pass the Intolerable Acts?

SECTION 3

5. Why did the Second Continental Congress issue the Declaration of Independence?

SECTION 4

6. What were the terms of the Treaty of Paris?

Reviewing Themes

1. **Economic Development** How did British attempts to raise revenue in the colonies conflict with colonial interests?
2. **Democratic Values** What role did democratic values play in the independence movement?
3. **Global Relations** How was the Revolutionary War affected by European nations other than Britain?

Thinking Critically

1. **Hypothesizing** Could the differences between Britain and the colonies have been resolved peacefully before 1775? Why or why not?
2. **Evaluating** What effect do you think Loyalists had on the outcome of the war? Explain your answer.
3. **Comparing and Contrasting** In what ways were the soldiers in the Continental Army and the British army similar? How were they different?
4. **Synthesizing** How did the Patriots defeat the British forces?
5. **Assessing Consequences** What effect did the participation of European powers have on the Revolutionary War?

Writing About History

Using Historical Imagination Imagine that you are a Loyalist or a Patriot. Write a letter to a friend explaining your position and how you are participating in the war effort. Use the following graphic to organize your thoughts.

Reasons for position	Actions in war

Strategies for Success Review the **Strategies for Success** on *Identifying the Main Idea*. Then reread the Section 2 subsection entitled The Intolerable Acts of 1774 and answer the following questions.

1. What is the main idea of the subsection? Where is this main idea stated most clearly?
2. What study clues are helpful in identifying the subsection's main idea?
3. How do the descriptions of specific laws in the second and fourth paragraphs help support the subsection's main idea?

Linking History and Geography

Study the map below. The Quebec Act extended Quebec's boundary southward. Which colonies were most directly affected by this boundary change? What alternative boundaries can you suggest? Why do you think the colonists were upset by the new boundary?

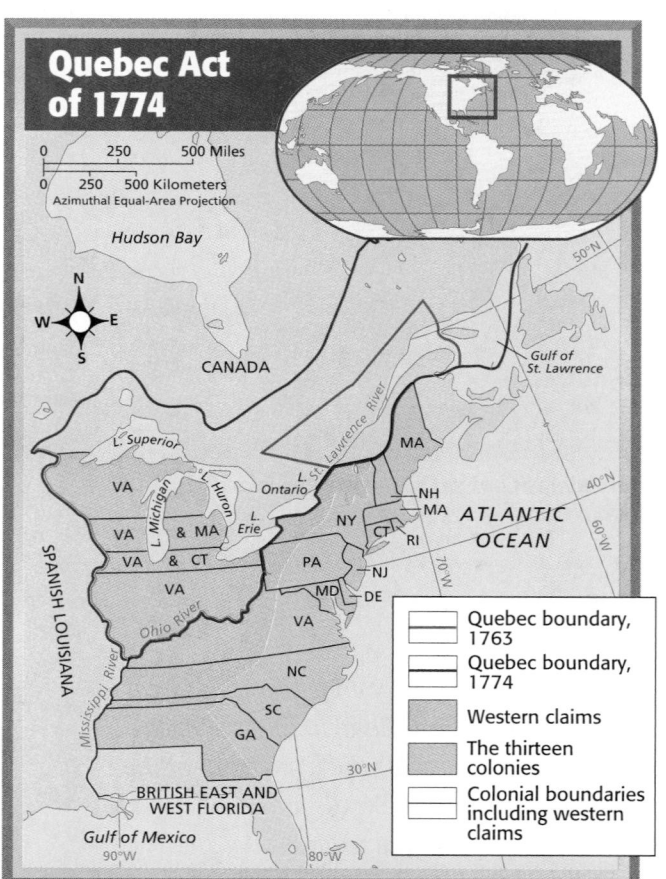

internet connect

TOPIC: Revolutionary War battles
GO TO: go.hrw.com
KEYWORD: SD1 Revolution

Accessing the Internet through the HRW Web site, research one of the following events: (a) Battle of Bunker Hill; (b) battles of Lexington and Concord; (c) Battle of Saratoga; or (d) Battle of Trenton. Then write a news report about the battle you selected. Be sure to include information about the battle's location, its major participants, and its importance in the war.

BUILDING YOUR PORTFOLIO

Complete one or more of the following projects independently or cooperatively.

1 Democratic Values

Imagine that you are the editor of a colonial newspaper. Select a specific tax, such as the tax imposed by the Sugar Act, and **create a list of interview questions** to ask a British official who is responsible for collecting that tax.

THE GRANGER COLLECTION, NEW YORK

Fighting at Boston

2 Cultural Diversity

Imagine that you are helping to publicize the Patriot war effort. **Create a poster** aimed at recruiting new soldiers for the Continental Army.

3 Global Relations

Imagine that you are the chief of an Iroquois tribe in 1777. **Prepare a short statement** that explains why you favor or oppose Thayendanegea's decision to join the British.

From Confederation to Federal Union

Benjamin West's painting Saul and the Witch of Endor

1776
Business and Finance
Adam Smith publishes *The Wealth of Nations,* a study of global economies.

1777
The Arts
American-born artist Benjamin West paints *Saul and the Witch of Endor.*

1778
The Arts
American portrait artist John Singleton Copley paints *Watson and the Shark.*

1782
World Events
A severe five-year famine begins in Japan.

1781
Business and Finance
The Bank of North America is chartered in Philadelphia.

1776	1777	1778	1779	1780	1781	1782

1776
Politics
Congress urges states to draft new constitutions.

1777
Science and Technology
American engineer David Bushnell invents the torpedo.

1777
Politics
Congress adopts the Articles of Confederation.

1778
Science and Technology
James Cook becomes the first European sailor to chart the Hawaiian Islands.

Cover of the Articles of Confederation

Captain James Cook's discovery of the island of Kauai, Hawaii

Before You Read

Build on What You Know

As colonists' grievances mounted and the desire for independence from Great Britain intensified, the American Revolution began. Recognizing the need for unity in their fight, the colonies joined forces under the leadership of the Continental Congress. In this chapter you will learn about the goals and challenges faced by the Patriot leaders as they attempted to forge national unity under the guidelines of the Articles of Confederation. Political problems soon arose that led to the drafting of the Constitution of the United States.

American historian Hannah Adams

The Game of Golf, *by an unknown artist*

A 1795 Liberty coin

1784
The Arts
American historian Hannah Adams publishes a study of American religion, *An Alphabetical Compendium of the Various Sects.*

1785
Business and Finance
The dollar currency is introduced in the United States.

1786
Daily Life
The South Carolina Golf Club is founded in Charleston.

1787
Daily Life
The Young Ladies Academy of Philadelphia opens, offering educational opportunities to women.

1788
Politics
The U.S. Constitution is ratified.

1788
World Events
The British Parliament considers a motion to abolish the slave trade.

1783 **1784** **1785** **1786** **1787** **1788** **1789**

1786
Politics
Shays's Rebellion erupts in western Massachusetts.

1787
Science and Technology
John Fitch launches one of the first steamboats on the Delaware River.

1787
Politics
The Constitutional Convention is held in Philadelphia.

1789
The Arts
Benjamin Franklin completes his autobiography.

1789
World Events
The French Revolution begins.

George Washington accepts the signed Constitution.

A steamboat on the Delaware River in 1787

THE GRANGER COLLECTION, NEW YORK

Think About Themes

Themes Journal

Decide whether you agree or disagree with the following statements. Note why in your journal.

Constitutional Heritage The organization of government will affect the way in which power is distributed and exercised in society.

Economic Development National economic policies can lead to political unrest in different sections of a country.

Democratic Values Giving every citizen a voice in government should be the highest priority of any political system.

The Articles of Confederation

KEY TERMS

Virginia Statute for Religious Freedom
Republican Motherhood
Articles of Confederation
Land Ordinance of 1785
Northwest Ordinance
depression
Shays's Rebellion

KEY PEOPLE

John Locke
Judith Sargent Murray
Benjamin Franklin
Daniel Shays

KEY PLACE

Northwest Territory

In 1690 John Locke published An Essay Concerning Human Understanding and Two Treatises on Government.

EYEWITNESSES TO History

66 *You and I have been sent into life at a time when the greatest lawgivers of antiquity would have wished to live. . . . How few of the human race have ever enjoyed an opportunity of making . . . government . . . for themselves or their children!* 99

—John Adams

The Continental Congress

John Adams expressed to a friend the optimism felt by many early American leaders as they faced the challenge of inventing a new nation. The American Revolution brought an end to the rule of the British monarchy in America and forced the royal governors from office. To fill this void, the Second Continental Congress advised the colonies "under the authority of the people" to form new state governments.

Republican Ideals and the State Constitutions

American experiments in self-government started even before the writing of the Declaration of Independence. In May 1776 the Second Continental Congress began urging the colonies to draft new constitutions to replace their British royal charters. Between 1776 and 1780 all of the states except Connecticut and Rhode Island drafted and ratified new constitutions. Connecticut and Rhode Island simply revised their royal charters. Despite the differences in their economies, geography, and population, the states adopted remarkably similar constitutions.

To form the new governments, the state legislatures relied on republicanism. According to this theory, political leaders receive from the citizens their authority to make and enforce laws. The Mayflower Compact of 1620 had incorporated this idea. Americans were also influenced by the works of Enlightenment thinkers such as John Locke, the English philosopher who developed the theory of "natural rights." Locke believed that all people were born with the rights of life, liberty, and property and that the role of the government was to protect these rights. Supporters of American republicanism embraced Locke's argument. They used it to challenge older forms of political and social organization.

For example, many Americans had resented the powerful royal governors, who had often overturned laws the elected assemblies had passed. In a declaration of independence issued by the town council of Malden, Massachusetts, local Patriots condemned the British colonial governor's denial of the rights of the colonists.

66 We long entertained hope that the spirit of the British nation would . . . bring to . . . punishment the elevated villains who have trampled upon the sacred rights of men. . . . We therefore . . . bid a final adieu [good-bye] to Britain. 99

Most of the new state constitutions restricted the powers of governors. This reflected their resentment of the influence of British colonial governors. A number of states limited governors to one-year terms and denied them the power to overturn laws. New York and Massachusetts had the most powerful governors. In both states, however, governors were elected by property owners rather than appointed by a legislature.

Many state constitutions also reduced the influence of the church on government. Before the Revolution, several colonies used tax money to support a particular church. Colonists were required to pay these taxes even if they did not belong to the church. Baptist and Presbyterian dissenters and some political thinkers such as Thomas Jefferson opposed this relationship between the government and one particular religious affiliation. Such a bond, they argued, often led to abuses of political power and to religious wars.

In 1779 Jefferson, who was then governor of Virginia, drafted the **Virginia Statute for Religious Freedom**. The statute stated that the human mind was created free and that government control over religious beliefs or worship was tyrannical. Jefferson also argued that every man has the right to act upon his own religious beliefs. In his argument for the adoption of the statute in 1785, James Madison declared, "Religion . . . must be left to the conviction [belief] and conscience of every man." Virginia adopted the statute in 1786. By 1833 every state had forbidden the establishment of official state churches supported by tax dollars.

✔ **READING CHECK:** What political ideas were reflected in the state constitutions?

Republicanism and Women

Although the republican state constitutions created governments that were more democratic than any others in the Western world up to that time, they did not grant full citizenship to women. Most men as well as many women opposed women's participation in politics. As a result, many state constitutions limited the right to vote and the right to hold office to white male property owners. Abigail Adams complained to her husband, John Adams. "I can not say that I think you very generous to the Ladies, for whilst you are proclaiming peace and good will to Men, Emancipating all Nations, you insist upon retaining an absolute power over Wives."

FROM THE COLLECTION OF HENRY FORD MUSEUM & GREENFIELD VILLAGE

Liberty and the American eagle exchange the cup of freedom in this patriotic painting.

★ HISTORICAL DOCUMENTS ★

THOMAS JEFFERSON

The Virginia Statute for Religious Freedom

Attempting to create a government that protected individual rights, Thomas Jefferson introduced a proposal for religious freedom. After much debate, Virginia adopted the proposal as the Statute for Religious Freedom in 1786. Jefferson hoped that by separating church and state, this law would allow Virginians to practice their religion—whatever it might be—freely.

JANUARY 16, 1786

1. *Whereas* Almighty God has created the mind free, that all attempts to influence it by temporal [civil] punishments or burdens . . . tend only to . . . beget [produce] habits of hypocrisy and meanness . . . [and] that to compel a man to furnish contributions of money for the propagation of opinions which he disbelieves is sinful and tyrannical; that even . . . forcing him to support this or that teacher of his own religious persuasion [belief] is depriving him of the comfortable liberty. . . .

2. *Be it enacted by the General Assembly* that no man shall be compelled to frequent or support any religious worship, place, or ministry whatsoever. . . . All men shall be free to profess [speak] . . . their opinion in matters of religion.

Republican Motherhood. This engraving advised women that their rightful place was within the home. *How does the image above reinforce this message?*

Republican Motherhood.

At the time, many people believed that women should not participate in politics directly. Some Americans, however, did conclude that women had an essential part to play in the creation of a new republican nation. Influential female writers such as Mercy Otis Warren and Judith Sargent Murray began to redefine the ideal of motherhood. They related it to the birth of the new nation.

This new concept of **Republican Motherhood** proposed that American women could influence politics and society through their work in the home. The Republican Mothers would offer moral guidance to their husbands and educate their children in the principles of liberty, democratic values, and civic responsibility. Supporters of the Republican Motherhood ideal emphasized its importance to the new nation. Women could instruct young American men to be good citizens and thereby ensure the healthy future of the new republic.

New opportunities for education.

The Republican Mother's responsibility for the civic education of her family created both limitations and possibilities for women. By stressing that women's primary duty was in the home, the idea of Republican Motherhood weakened women's chances of gaining greater political rights. Because women were responsible for their children's education, however, support grew for expanding women's educational opportunities. Even some men supported this idea. In a speech at the newly opened Young Ladies Academy of Philadelphia in 1787, physician and Patriot leader Benjamin Rush proclaimed, "Let the ladies of a country be educated properly, and they will not only make and administer its laws, but form its manners and character."

During the late 1700s, the number of young women attending private high schools rose steadily.

Supporters of Republican Motherhood actively challenged the traditional barriers that had limited women's education. Judith Sargent Murray of Massachusetts, one of the first female playwrights in the United States, argued that women and men had equal intelligence.

> **66** While we are pursuing the needle, or the superintendency [management] of the family, I repeat, that our minds are at full liberty for reflection; that imagination may exert itself in full vigor; and that if a just foundation [be] early laid, our ideas will then be worthy of rational beings. **99**

Arguments like Murray's led to the founding of several women's academies, or private high schools.

✔ **READING CHECK:** How did the idea of Republican Motherhood affect women's roles and opportunities?

A Plan for Confederation

The spirit of republicanism was sweeping through the colonies, increasing calls for a national framework of republican government. Although most states had created new constitutions by 1780, no such framework existed at the national level. The Second Continental Congress had performed some of the duties of a national government since 1775, but it lacked legal authority over the states.

Adoption of the Articles.

The states were willing to join in a loose union but were reluctant to hand over control to a national government. In 1776 a congressional committee led by John Dickinson began the difficult task of drafting a plan for a central government. An early supporter of the plan and an influential member of the committee was American's elder statesman Benjamin Franklin.

BIOGRAPHY

Benjamin Franklin

Benjamin Franklin was born in Boston in 1706. As one of the younger children of a candlemaker, Franklin received little formal education. At the age of 12 he became an apprentice at his brother's print shop. When he was 17 years old, Franklin left his family for a new life in Philadelphia.

He established a printing company and founded the newspaper the *Pennsylvania Gazette.* In 1732 Franklin began publishing his witty and widely read *Poor Richard's Almanac,* in which he coined such proverbs as "Early to bed, and early to rise, makes a man healthy, wealthy and wise." Franklin excelled as a scientist and inventor, developing bifocal eyeglasses, the Franklin stove, and the lightning rod. As an active contributor to his community, Franklin founded the American Philosophical Society, the first American circulation library, the first post office, and the first fire department.

Franklin began his political career in 1751 when he was elected to the Pennsylvania Assembly. Franklin proposed the Albany Plan of Union in 1754 and helped draft the Declaration of Independence. He also served as an ambassador and participated in negotiating the Treaty of Paris in 1783, which ended the Revolutionary War. Franklin continued to play an important role in shaping the U.S. government until his death in 1790.

On July 12, 1776, the congressional committee on which Franklin served presented its plan—called the **Articles of Confederation**—to the other delegates. Off and on for about 16 months the delegates debated this proposed plan for a "Perpetual Union," finally adopting it on November 15, 1777.

The Articles created a confederation, or association, of states while guaranteeing each state its "sovereignty, freedom, and independence." A sovereign nation or state has supreme power over its own affairs. All governmental powers not

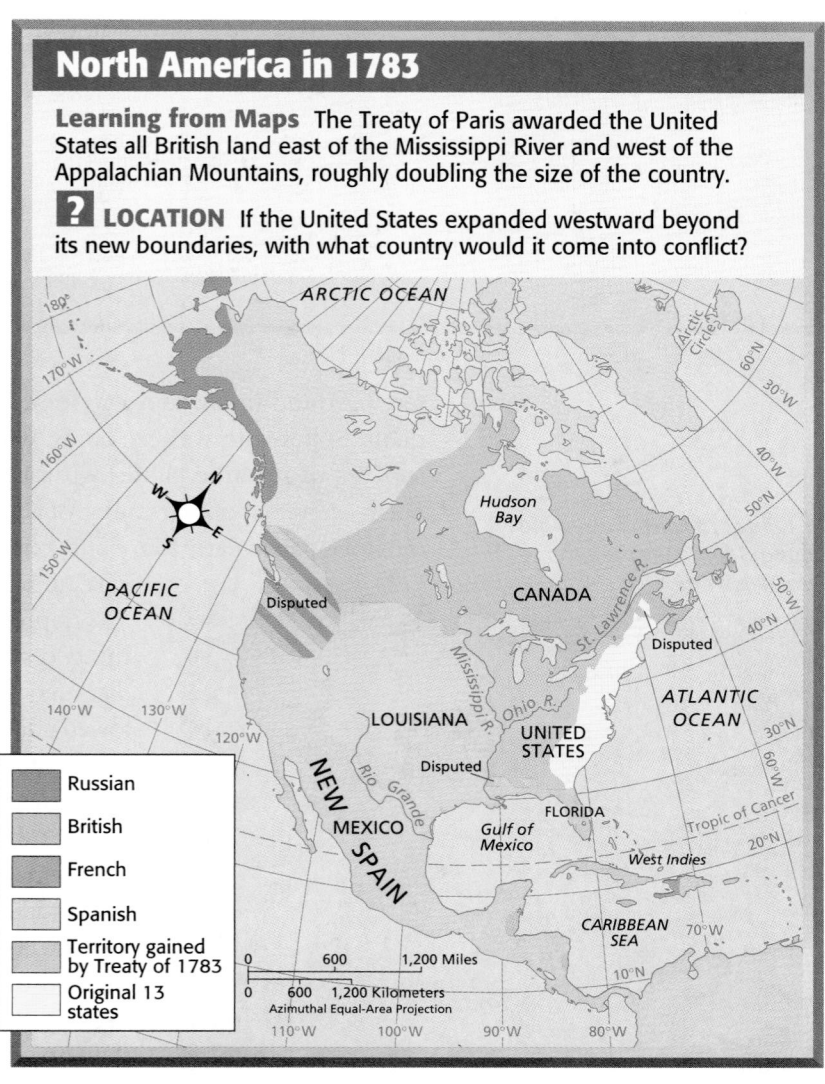

North America in 1783

Learning from Maps The Treaty of Paris awarded the United States all British land east of the Mississippi River and west of the Appalachian Mountains, roughly doubling the size of the country.

? LOCATION If the United States expanded westward beyond its new boundaries, with what country would it come into conflict?

ARCTIC OCEAN

PACIFIC OCEAN

Hudson Bay

CANADA

LOUISIANA

Disputed

UNITED STATES

ATLANTIC OCEAN

Disputed

NEW SPAIN

MEXICO

Gulf of Mexico

FLORIDA

West Indies

Tropic of Cancer

CARIBBEAN SEA

- Russian
- British
- French
- Spanish
- Territory gained by Treaty of 1783
- Original 13 states

0   600   1,200 Miles
0   600   1,200 Kilometers
Azimuthal Equal-Area Projection

Western Land Claims, 1781–1802

Learning from Maps Many of the original 13 states had claims to western lands that dated back to their colonial charters. Between 1784 and 1802 individual states ceded these lands to the United States.

? LOCATION Which states had no claims to western lands?

Disputed with Britain

CANADA

Boundary uncertain

Lake Superior

Lake Michigan

Lake Huron

Lake Erie

L. Ontario

VA 1784

MA claim ceded to NY in 1786

MI 1784

VA & MA 1784–85

VA & MA 1784–85

VA & CT 1784–86

NY & NH 1790

MA

NH

MA

NY

CT

RI

PA

NJ

MD

DE

VA

Ohio River

Mississippi River

ATLANTIC OCEAN

CT 1800

VA 1784

VA 1792

LOUISIANA

NC 1790

NC

VA

SC 1787

SC

GA 1802

GA

Disputed with Spain until 1795

GA 1802

FLORIDA

Gulf of Mexico

	Original 13 states by 1781
	Western lands claimed by states
1784	Date claims finally ceded to United States
	Boundary of Northwest Territory

0   200   400 Miles
0   200   400 Kilometers
Albers Equal-Area Projection

45°N   40°N   65°W   30°N   70°W   75°W   80°W   85°W   90°W   95°W

In 1748 Lord Fairfax hired the young George Washington to survey his property.

"expressly delegated" to Congress were to be retained by the states.

The Articles authorized Congress to borrow and coin money, conduct foreign affairs, set policy toward American Indians, and settle disputes between the states. Congress could ask, but not require, states to contribute money to the central government and to provide recruits for the military. The Articles allowed each state one vote in Congress, regardless of its population or number of representatives.

✔ **READING CHECK:** What powers did the Articles of Confederation grant the national government?

The problem of land. For the Articles of Confederation to take effect, all 13 states had to ratify, or approve, it. One major issue blocked ratification: control of the Allegheny Mountains and the land beyond, just east of the Mississippi River. On the basis of their old royal charters, several states claimed vast tracts of western land. States without land claims wanted the other states to surrender their holdings to the new national government.

This conflict among the states centered around the need for money. Congress expected each state to help pay war debts. States with western lands, which they could sell to settlers, had additional sources of revenue. States without surplus land faced the prospect of raising taxes—never a popular course of action. Leaders from some states without western territory, particularly Maryland, refused to ratify the Articles unless the larger states gave up some of their western landholdings.

To promote national unity, New York and Virginia— the two states with the largest landholdings—gave the disputed land to Congress. Other states eventually followed suit. By 1781 all of the states had agreed to enter the Confederation. The 13 former British colonies were now officially the "United States of America."

Members of Congress knew, however, that western land remained a problem. To regulate the distribution of the land, Congress passed the **Land Ordinance of 1785**. This ordinance marked off the land into townships and divided each township into 640-acre tracts. The ordinance permitted the cash sale of these tracts for not less than one dollar per acre and reserved one section of each township for the establishment of a school. This provision in the ordinance marked the first national government aid given to public education. Four sections in each township were to be reserved for veterans of the Revolutionary War.

Two years later, Congress passed the Land Ordinance of 1787. More commonly called the **Northwest Ordinance**, this act established a system for governing the Northwest Territory. This vast area extended north of the Ohio River to the Great Lakes and west of Pennsylvania to the Mississippi River. Anticipating that the Northwest Territory would eventually be divided into states, Congress also outlined in the 1787 ordinance the necessary steps to achieve statehood for areas within the territory. The present-day states of Illinois, Indiana, Michigan, Ohio, and Wisconsin eventually were carved out of the territory. The ordinance set a precedent that would also be used for settling territories farther west.

In addition to creating a system of government for the territory and a process for the establishment of states, the Northwest Ordinance guaranteed settlers' civil rights and banned slavery in the territory. The ban reflected a growing antislavery sentiment in the northern states. This was only a partial victory for slavery opponents, however. The ordinance also required that escaped slaves seeking freedom in the territory be returned to their owners.

✔ **READING CHECK:** How did the Northwest Ordinance try to resolve future conflicts over western lands?

Read More About It

Free Find: Schooling
After reading about public schools on the **Holt Researcher** CD–ROM, imagine that you are attending a public school in the late 1780s. Write a short account of your experiences.

The Northwest Territory

Learning from Maps The Land Ordinance of 1785 divided the Northwest Territory into townships. Each township was 6 miles square and was divided into 36 sections of 640 acres each.

? **PLACE** Which state in the Northwest Territory was the first to be admitted to the Union? Which was the last?

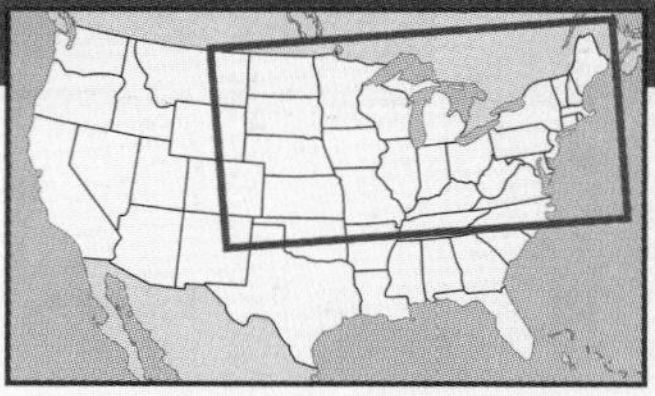

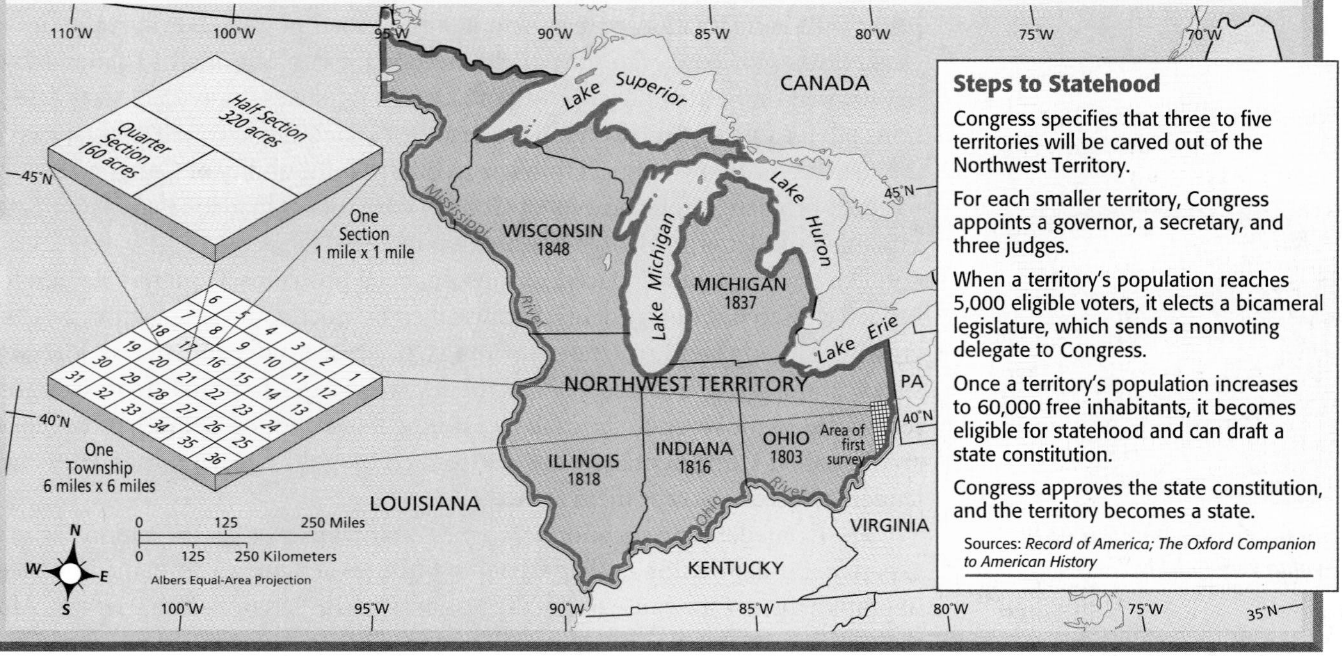

Quarter Section 160 acres

Half Section 320 acres

One Section 1 mile x 1 mile

One Township 6 miles x 6 miles

CANADA

Lake Superior

WISCONSIN 1848

Lake Michigan

Lake Huron

MICHIGAN 1837

Lake Erie

NORTHWEST TERRITORY

PA

ILLINOIS 1818

INDIANA 1816

OHIO 1803

Area of first survey

LOUISIANA

VIRGINIA

KENTUCKY

0   125   250 Miles
0   125   250 Kilometers
Albers Equal-Area Projection

Steps to Statehood

Congress specifies that three to five territories will be carved out of the Northwest Territory.

For each smaller territory, Congress appoints a governor, a secretary, and three judges.

When a territory's population reaches 5,000 eligible voters, it elects a bicameral legislature, which sends a nonvoting delegate to Congress.

Once a territory's population increases to 60,000 free inhabitants, it becomes eligible for statehood and can draft a state constitution.

Congress approves the state constitution, and the territory becomes a state.

Sources: *Record of America; The Oxford Companion to American History*

Cause-and-effect relationships are crucial to the study of history. To determine why an event took place, and what happened as a result of that event, historians ask questions such as: What was the background, or context, of the event? Who were the people involved in the event? What was the immediate activity that triggered the event?

How to Identify Cause and Effect

1. **Look for clues.** Certain words and phrases are immediate clues to the existence of a cause-and-effect relationship. *Because, led to, provoked,* and *inspired,* for example, are often indicators of a cause. *As a result, originating from, as a consequence, created by,* and *outcome* are often used to denote an effect.
2. **Identify the relationship.** Read carefully to determine the relationship between events. Writers of history do not always state the link between cause and effect; sometimes the reader has to infer the relationship on his or her own.
3. **Check for complex connections.** Beyond the immediate cause-and-effect relationship, check for

other, more complex connections. Note, for example, whether there were additional causes of a given effect, whether a cause had multiple effects, and if the effects themselves caused further events.

Applying the Strategy

The Articles of Confederation established a relatively weak national government over the United States of America. Using information from Section 1, create a flowchart that traces some of the effects of this problem.

Practicing the Strategy

Answer the following questions.
1. How did the Articles of Confederation affect Congress's ability to pay debts from the Revolutionary War?
2. How did Congress respond to the problem of paying these debts?
3. How did this response from Congress generate further effects?

Weaknesses in the Confederation

These Continentals lost their value very quickly.

The land ordinances established a pattern of land settlement for the next 75 years. Congress could point to few other noteworthy accomplishments, however. On paper the Confederation government enjoyed broad powers, but in reality it was weak. Proposed changes to the Articles needed the consent of all 13 states. Major new legislation needed the approval of at least nine states. Individual state delegations often could not agree on how to cast their state's single vote. The weakness of the Articles led many political thinkers to question the ability of Congress to solve national problems. "The powers of Congress are totally inadequate," Henry Knox explained in a letter to George Washington in 1786.

The government also faced serious financial problems. Congress desperately needed cash to pay its war debts. Because it could not tax the people directly, Congress had to appeal to the states for funds. Claiming independence as sovereign states, some states avoided paying their share of the national debt. Congress responded to the revenue shortfall by printing paper money. Because these bills of credit, called Continentals, were not backed by gold or silver, merchants and lenders refused to accept them at face value.

The Confederation's economic worries multiplied. In 1784 the nation began to experience a **depression**, a sharp drop in business activity accompanied by rising unemployment. One cause of the depression was the loss of British markets. After the war Britain closed some of its colonial markets to American commerce. Then the British flooded the United States with inexpensive goods. Struggling American merchants and artisans could not match the low prices. Congress was powerless to help, since the Articles did not give it authority to regulate international trade.

Shays's Rebellion

The depression and money shortage left farmers with fewer markets for their goods and little money to pay their debts. Instead of extending credit, merchants demanded payment in gold or silver, which farmers seldom possessed.

In Massachusetts the merchant-controlled legislature passed a law that imposed heavy taxes on land to help pay the state's war debt. If a landowner did not pay the tax, the courts would seize and sell the property. Outraged farmers in western Massachusetts sent petitions to the legislature, complaining of "taxation without representation." After the legislature adjourned in the summer of 1786 without addressing the tax or debt issues, farmers rebelled. Under the leadership of such men as Daniel Shays, a former Revolutionary War captain, angry farmers took up arms against the government. In what became known as **Shays's Rebellion**, farmers shut down debtor courts and stopped property auctions.

On December 26, 1786, Shays and some 1,200 farmers set out for Springfield, Massachusetts, intent on seizing the federal arsenal. Worried that Shays's forces would overrun the militia guarding the arsenal, the governor quickly called for more than 4,000 additional recruits. Shays and his men launched their attack in late January. However, when artillery fire killed four of the farmers, Shays's men fled. By the end of February the Massachusetts militia had crushed the rebellion.

The rebellion raised doubts about the central government's ability to deal with civil unrest. As a result, many people who had previously objected to a strong central government began calling for the Confederation to have additional powers.

✔ **READING CHECK:** What were some weaknesses of the Articles?

THE GRANGER COLLECTION, NEW YORK

INTERPRETING THE VISUAL RECORD

Shays's Rebellion. Daniel Shays's rebels occupy a western Massachusetts courthouse in this illustration. *How does their style of dress help you identify Shays's followers in the illustration?*

SECTION 1 **REVIEW**

Define and explain the significance of the following terms:
Virginia Statute for Religious Freedom
Republican Motherhood
Articles of Confederation
Land Ordinance of 1785
Northwest Ordinance
depression
Shays's Rebellion

Identify and explain the significance of the following individuals:
John Locke   Benjamin Franklin
Judith Sargent Murray   Daniel Shays

Locate and explain the importance of the following place:
Northwest Territory

1. **Using Graphic Organizers** Copy the graphic organizer below. Use it to explain the steps to statehood established by the Northwest Ordinance.

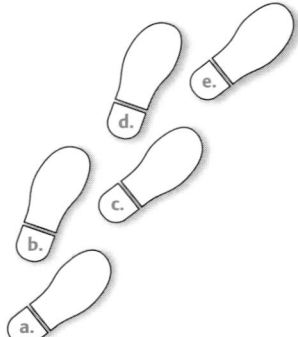

2. **Evaluating** What provisions did the states write into their new constitutions?
3. **Problem Solving** What solutions would you have proposed to address the problems with the Articles of Confederation?
4. **Identifying Cause and Effect** What powers did the Articles of Confederation grant to Congress? How did weaknesses in the Articles of Confederation contribute to Shays's Rebellion?

Critical Thinking

5. Overall, was Republican Motherhood an advance or a setback for women?
   Consider:
   • the definition of Republican Motherhood
   • the opportunities it created for women
   • the limitations it placed on women

Drafting and Ratifying the Constitution

OBJECTIVES

Read to understand:

1. how the Virginia Plan called for a stronger federal government
2. what major compromises were reflected in the Constitution
3. how the Antifederalists opposed the Constitution, and how the Federalists responded
4. why all 13 states ratified the Constitution

KEY TERMS

Constitutional Convention
Virginia Plan
federalism
bicameral
Great Compromise
Three-Fifths Compromise
tariffs
Federalists
Antifederalists
electors
The Federalist

KEY PEOPLE

James Madison
Patrick Henry
Roger Sherman

This engraving depicts Independence Hall during the Revolutionary era.

THE GRANGER COLLECTION, NEW YORK

EYEWITNESSES TO History

66 *I have often, and often in the course of the session, . . . looked at that [sun] behind the President without being able to tell whether it was rising or setting. But now at length I have the happiness to know that it is a rising and not a setting sun.* 99
—Benjamin Franklin

The "rising sun" chair

Benjamin Franklin made this observation on September 17, 1787, as a new national constitution was being signed to replace the Articles of Confederation. Franklin explained that over the past three and a half months of heated debates and delicate compromises he had often focused his concentration on the image of a sun on the back of the convention president's chair. Franklin had been worried about the problems of disunity under the Articles of Confederation. The rising sun that Franklin now saw, however, symbolized the birth of a new unified nation with a strong constitutional foundation.

The Call to Philadelphia

In the year preceding the convention, more and more American leaders concluded that the Articles needed improvements if the national unity of the former colonies was to be preserved. Striking evidence of the disunity of the Confederation came in September 1786. A meeting held in Annapolis, Maryland, to work out a cooperative trade agreement failed because only five states sent delegates. This disappointment, followed soon after by Shays's Rebellion, led Congress to consider the weaknesses of the Articles of Confederation. Congressional leaders issued a call for a **Constitutional Convention** to strengthen the government. The Convention was scheduled to begin in Philadelphia on May 14, 1787.

By the appointed day, only the delegates from Pennsylvania and Virginia had arrived. Others straggled in, delayed by muddy roads. By May 25 enough delegates were on hand for the proceedings to begin.

The Convention met in the Pennsylvania State House—now Independence Hall. The delegates agreed to keep the proceedings secret. They believed that it would be easier to debate and resolve their differences behind closed doors. Despite the sweltering heat, even the windows were kept tightly closed.

The delegates took their vow of secrecy seriously. When someone accidentally dropped some notes on the floor outside the meeting room, George Washington, the presiding officer, erupted in anger.

66 Gentlemen, I am sorry to find that some member of the body has been so neglectful to the secrets of the Convention as to drop in the State House a copy of their proceedings. . . . I know not whose paper it is, but here it is, let him who owns it take it. 99

Throwing the notes on the desk, Washington stalked from the room. Not surprisingly, none of the convention delegates made a move to claim the document.

George Washington and the 54 other convention delegates were a remarkable collection of politicians. Many had helped write their state constitutions. Almost all had held public office, many as delegates to the Continental Congress. They were a young group: James Madison of Virginia was 36; Alexander Hamilton of New York, 32. The youngest delegate, Jonathan Dayton of New Jersey, was 26. At 81, Benjamin Franklin was the elder statesman of the Convention. The delegates were generally wealthy and well educated. Many were bankers, merchants, and planters; more than half had studied law.

Several prominent Americans missed the Convention. Thomas Jefferson and John Adams were in Europe on diplomatic missions. Patrick Henry refused to attend. Saying he "smelled a rat," Henry claimed that the delegates were plotting to take away states' rights. He feared that "the tyranny of Philadelphia may be like the tyranny of [King] George III."

Federal Power Versus States' Rights

Congress had simply charged the delegates to revise the Articles of Confederation. Some delegates, however, believed that the Articles should be replaced with an entirely new plan of government. At issue were relations among the states and between the states and the central government.

On May 29, Governor Edmund Randolph of Virginia triggered a heated debate when he presented the **Virginia Plan**, drafted by James Madison. This proposal to restructure the government was a bold departure from the Articles of Confederation. The plan shifted political power away from the states and toward the central government, which would coordinate the states' activities for the benefit of the entire nation. The plan reflected the belief shared by Madison that the nation's survival depended on **federalism**, or the division of powers between a strong central government and the state governments.

James Madison

James Madison was born in 1751 to a prominent Virginia family. He was weak in childhood and prone to strange illnesses. Poor health prompted Madison to concentrate on strengthening his mind rather than his body. A contemporary described Madison as "no bigger than half a piece of soap." He was so quiet and reserved that an acquaintance called him "a gloomy, stiff creature."

Nevertheless, Madison enjoyed a distinguished political career, in which he helped draft Virginia's state constitution and served as a member of the Continental Congress. Madison's notes from the Constitutional Convention provide the most complete account of the creation of the Constitution. He later recalled:

❝ I chose a seat in front of the presiding member, with the other members, on my right and left hand. In this favorable position for hearing all that passed I noted in terms legible . . . what was read from the Chair or spoken by the members; and losing not a moment . . . I was enabled to write out my daily notes during the session or within a few finishing days after its close. ❞

Read More About It

Free Find:
  Road to Philadelphia
  After reading the selection on the political conferences held prior to the Constitutional Convention on the **Holt Researcher** CD–ROM, imagine that you are a political correspondent. Write a brief report on the significance of these early meetings.

A French View of the American Experiment

Anne-Robert-Jacques Turgot (toor-goh), a retired French government official, was among the many Europeans watching America's experiment in democracy. In 1778 Turgot described his thoughts in a letter to Richard Price, a British philosopher and writer who championed the United States. "The fate of America is already decided," Turgot wrote. "Behold her independent beyond recovery. But will she be free and happy?" Turgot wondered whether the 13 separate states would be able to work together. He also wondered whether people could be governed "only by nature, reason and justice" without falling prey to the greed and self-interest of individuals. Despite his doubts, Turgot wished the experiment well. Of the Americans he wrote, "They are the hope of the world."

Madison's leadership at the Constitutional Convention earned him the name "father of the Constitution."

The Virginia Plan gave Congress the right to overturn state laws, tax the states, and "bring the force of the Union against any [state] . . . failing to fulfill its duty." Such a drastic move away from states' sovereignty alarmed some delegates.

The Virginia Plan called for the federal government to be made up of three branches: executive, judicial, and legislative. Under this proposed plan the legislature would be **bicameral**—made up of two houses. Voters would elect representatives to the lower house, who would then choose members of the upper house. State populations would determine the number of representatives in each house.

A dispute quickly arose over the number of representatives each state could send to the legislature. States with large populations, such as Virginia and Pennsylvania, naturally favored representation based on population. States with small populations insisted on an equal number of representatives for each state. Said a delegate from Delaware: "We would sooner submit to a foreign power than . . . be thrown under the domination of the large states."

William Paterson of New Jersey offered an alternative to the Virginia Plan. Paterson's New Jersey Plan provided for a strong unicameral, or one-house, legislature in which each state would have one vote. It also proposed giving the federal government the power to tax and to regulate commerce. Madison and others objected to Paterson's plan because they believed that it did not correct the weaknesses of the Articles. On June 19, the Convention rejected the New Jersey Plan and resumed consideration of the Virginia Plan.

Delegates to the Constitutional Convention crowded into this room, sharing space at tables such as these.

✔ **READING CHECK:** In what ways did the Virginia Plan allow for a stronger federal government?

Compromise at the Convention

To balance the interests of large and small states, Roger Sherman of Connecticut proposed a two-house legislature that would allow for both equal representation and representation based on population. This **Great Compromise** granted each state, regardless of size, an equal voice in the upper house. In the lower house, representation would be according to population. The delegates narrowly approved this proposal, ending what Madison later described as "the most serious and threatening excitement" of the Convention.

The Three-Fifths Compromise.

The delegates resolved one dispute only to see another emerge. They now debated whether slaves should be counted as part of a state's population to determine representation. Southern delegates insisted that the slave population be included. Northern delegates strongly objected to this demand. Some deeply opposed slavery on moral grounds and argued that it violated the republican ideal of liberty. Others objected to including slaves for political reasons. Southern states' representation in the lower house would be greater if slaves were included in population counts.

In the end, northern and southern delegates accepted a compromise. The final agreement, known as the **Three-Fifths Compromise**, established that only three fifths of a state's slave population would count in determining its representation.

Compromises over commerce.

The states also clashed over control of commerce. Northern delegates favored giving the national government the power to regulate all trade with foreign nations and among the states. Southern delegates opposed such broad powers.

The southern economy depended on exports of rice, tobacco, and other products to Europe and to northern states. Southerners feared that if the national government imposed **tariffs**, or taxes on imports and exports, overseas buyers would have to pay more for southern agricultural products. If buyers refused to pay higher prices, sales would be hurt. Delegates finally agreed that Congress could levy tariffs on imports but not on exports.

Once again, however, problems arose. Planters now worried that Congress might use its power to tax imports to restrict the slave trade. Bowing to southern pressure, Convention delegates voted to permit the importation of slaves until the end of 1807. They also gave slaveholders the right to pursue runaway slaves across state lines. Some northern delegates agreed to the compromises because they feared the South would withdraw from the Union if planters thought their property and livelihood were threatened. James Madison argued that great as the evils of the slave trade were, "dismemberment of the union would be worse." Others agreed to the compromises because they mistakenly believed that slavery was a dying institution.

Completing the Constitution.

On July 26, 1787, a committee of five delegates began drafting the Constitution. They presented it to the full Convention on August 6. Between August 6 and September 10, the delegates debated the draft, hammering out such specifics as the terms of office for the president and for the members of both houses. Another committee prepared the finished document.

On September 17, 1787, the committee presented to the other delegates the final version of the Constitution, neatly handwritten by Gouverneur Morris of Pennsylvania. Some of the 55 delegates had already left Philadelphia, but of the 42 remaining, 39 signed it. With the Convention over, the Constitution went to Congress and then to the states for ratification.

✔ **READING CHECK:** What major compromises are reflected in the Constitution, and what do they reveal about the different interests of various groups of Americans?

INTERPRETING THE VISUAL RECORD

Slavery. Benjamin Henry Latrobe's watercolor *An Overseer Doing His Duty* shows slaves at work in the field. *How do the positions of the people in this watercolor represent their different levels of power and authority in late 1700s America?*

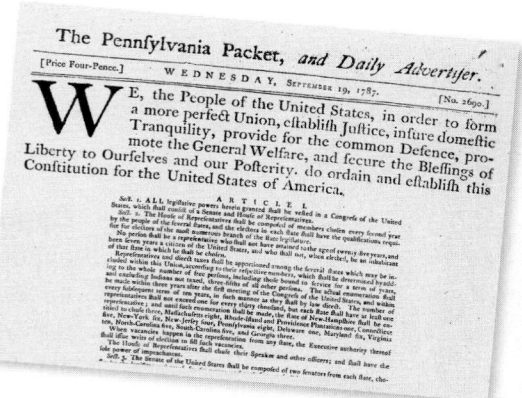

Many newspapers, like the **Pennsylvania Packet, and Daily Advertiser,** *printed the full text of the Constitution for their curious readers.*

★ HISTORICAL DOCUMENTS ★

JAMES MADISON
The *Federalist Papers*

Two of the most significant essays from the Federalist Papers *arguing for the ratification of the Constitution were papers No. 10 and No. 51. Both were written by James Madison. In essay No. 10, Madison argues that a strong national government is necessary to reduce conflict among opposing groups in society. In essay No. 51, Madison contends that the balance of power among different branches of government as outlined in the Constitution would prevent any one branch from gaining too much power.*

Federalist Paper "No. 10" (1787)

*A*mong the numerous advantages promised by a well-constructed Union, none deserves to be more accurately developed than its tendency to break and control the violence of faction [splinter group]. . . . The influence of factious [rebellious] leaders may kindle a flame within their particular states but will be unable to spread a general conflagration [larger fire] through the other states.

Federalist Paper "No. 51" (1788)

*T*he great security against a gradual concentration of the several powers in the same department consists in giving to those who administer each department the necessary constitutional means and personal motives to resist encroachments [advances] of the others. The provision for defense must . . . be made commensurate [equal] to the danger of attack.

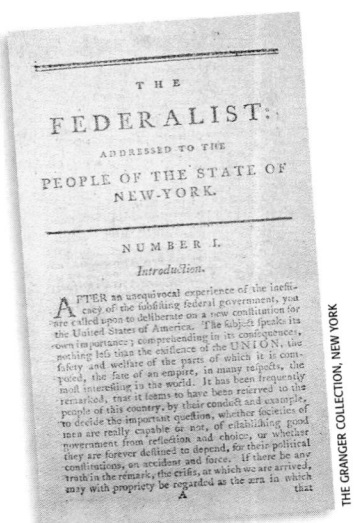

Federalists published pro-ratification essays hoping to build support for the new Constitution.

The Federalists and Antifederalists

To win ratification, the Constitution required the approval of 9 of the 13 states. Although many convention delegates hoped for unanimous approval as a show of national unity, citizens soon divided over the issue of ratification.

Support for ratification. One group, who called themselves **Federalists**, favored ratification of the Constitution. Wealthy merchants, planters, and lawyers typically were Federalists. They supported a strong national government that would be able to ensure a strong currency and protect property rights.

Many Americans who were not among the wealthy also supported the Constitution. They believed that a strong national government would provide stability and security against violent political unrest like Shays's Rebellion. Speaking before the Massachusetts ratifying convention, a farmer explained his reason for supporting the Constitution.

> 66 I have lived in a part of the country where I have learned the worth of good government by the lack of it. There was a black cloud of rebellion that rose in the east last winter and spread over the west. . . . Our distress was so great that we should have been glad to grab at anything that looked like a government. . . . Now when I saw this Constitution, I found it was a cure for these disorders. 99

Opposition to ratification. The other group, called **Antifederalists** by their opponents, feared a powerful national government. The Antifederalists offered three objections to the Constitution as written. First, they argued that delegates to the Constitutional Convention had conspired under a "veil of mystery" to create a new form of government and had gone beyond what they had been charged to do. Second, the Antifederalists claimed that a strong national government would destroy states' rights. Third, they argued that the new system of government resembled a monarchy because of its concentration of power. Thus it violated the principle of liberty that had guided the American Revolution.

The Antifederalists pointed to the election procedures outlined in the Constitution as proof that the new national government was undemocratic. Under the Constitution, voters did not directly elect the president and the vice president—**electors**, delegates selected by state governments, chose them. Ordinary voters would directly elect only the members of the lower house of Congress, the House of Representatives.

The anonymous "Cato"—believed by many to have been Governor George Clinton of New York—challenged citizens to consider the dangers of such a system.

> 66 For what did you throw off the yoke of Britain and call yourselves independent? Was it from a disposition fond of change, or to procure [get] new masters? . . . This new form of national government . . . will be dangerous to your liberty and happiness. 99

The Federalists answered their critics in a series of 85 essays written by John Jay, Alexander Hamilton, and James Madison. Between the fall of 1787 and the spring of 1788, 77 of the essays appeared in newspapers throughout the states. The essays were later published in a book, entitled *The Federalist*, which was also known as the *Federalist Papers*.

✔ **READING CHECK:** What were the main Antifederalist arguments against the new Constitution? How did the Federalists respond?

The Ratification Struggle

The question of a strong central government versus states' rights was at the heart of the ratification struggle. Another issue was individual rights. Unlike many state constitutions, the U.S. Constitution did not contain a bill of rights. This omission outraged the Antifederalists, some of whom refused to support ratification.

Ordinary citizens joined the debate over ratification. Amos Singletary, a Massachusetts farmer, argued that the Constitution would take away individual rights, just as Britain had done in the past.

> 66 We contended [fought] with Great Britain . . . because they claimed a right to tax us and bind us in all cases whatever. And does not this Constitution do the same? Does it not take away all we have—all our property? Does it not lay *all* taxes, duties, imposts [import fees], and excises? . . . These lawyers, and men of learning, and moneyed men . . . get all the power and all the money into their own hands, and then they will swallow up all us little folks. 99

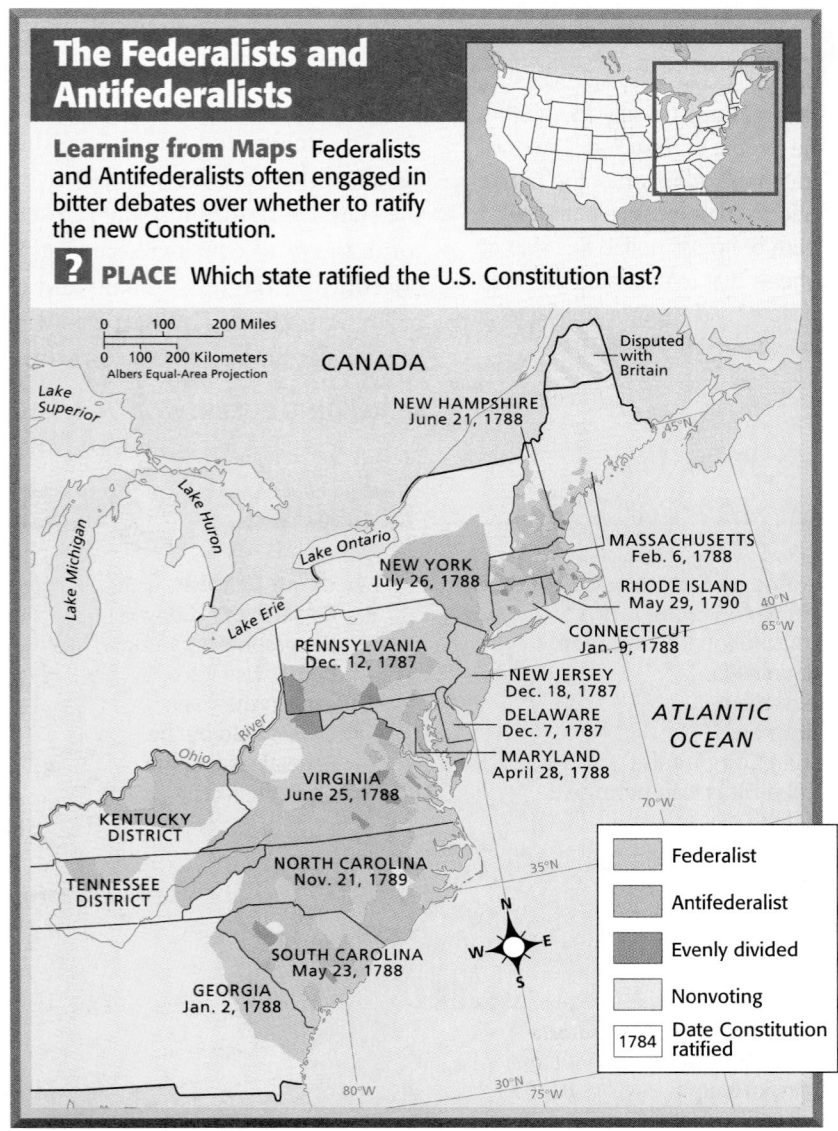

The Federalists and Antifederalists

Learning from Maps Federalists and Antifederalists often engaged in bitter debates over whether to ratify the new Constitution.

? **PLACE** Which state ratified the U.S. Constitution last?

CANADA

NEW HAMPSHIRE
June 21, 1788

Disputed with Britain

Lake Superior

MASSACHUSETTS
Feb. 6, 1788

RHODE ISLAND
May 29, 1790

NEW YORK
July 26, 1788

CONNECTICUT
Jan. 9, 1788

PENNSYLVANIA
Dec. 12, 1787

NEW JERSEY
Dec. 18, 1787

DELAWARE
Dec. 7, 1787

ATLANTIC OCEAN

MARYLAND
April 28, 1788

VIRGINIA
June 25, 1788

KENTUCKY DISTRICT

TENNESSEE DISTRICT

NORTH CAROLINA
Nov. 21, 1789

SOUTH CAROLINA
May 23, 1788

GEORGIA
Jan. 2, 1788

0   100   200 Miles
0   100   200 Kilometers
Albers Equal-Area Projection

Federalist
Antifederalist
Evenly divided
Nonvoting
1784 Date Constitution ratified

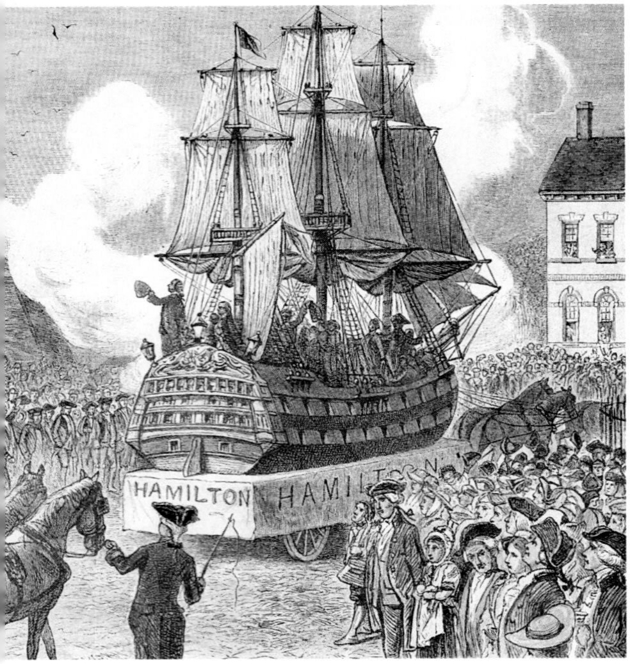

THE GRANGER COLLECTION, NEW YORK

INTERPRETING THE VISUAL RECORD

Ratification. On July 23, 1788, the people of New York City celebrated the adoption of the Constitution with a massive parade. A team of horses pulled this ship on wheels that represented the "ship of state." ***Why might the base of the ship read "HAMILTON?"***

Federalists claimed that the state constitutions adequately protected the rights of U.S. citizens. However, several states, including Virginia and New York, agreed to ratify the Constitution only if individual rights were guaranteed in a bill of rights. Although by June 21, 1788, enough states had ratified the Constitution for it to take effect, a union without the support of these two large states was viewed by many as too fragile.

The debates were bitter in both states' ratifying conventions. In Virginia, Patrick Henry eloquently argued against the proposed Constitution. "What right had they to say, 'We, the people'?" Henry inquired. "Who authorized them to speak the language of 'We, the people,' instead of, 'We, the states'?" James Madison and George Washington, however, strongly urged the Virginia delegates to vote for ratification. "We have seen the necessity of the Union," Madison argued in *The Federalist,* "as our bulwark [protection] against foreign danger, as the conservator [keeper] of peace among ourselves."

Making a bold statement, New York Federalists threatened to withdraw New York City from the state if the state did not ratify the Constitution. In the end both states ratified the Constitution, but only by very narrow margins.

The final state to ratify was Rhode Island, which had even refused to send delegates to the Constitutional Convention. After the Constitution had been drafted, the state legislature initially refused to call for a ratifying convention, prompting some towns to consider seceding. When the state—threatened with an economic boycott by Congress—finally did call a convention in 1790, ratification was narrowly approved. The battle had been long and the final vote close, but most Americans supported the Constitution once it was ratified.

✔ **READING CHECK:** What finally led all 13 states to ratify the Constitution?

SECTION 2 REVIEW

Define and explain the significance of the following terms:
Constitutional Convention
Virginia Plan
federalism
bicameral
Great Compromise
Three-Fifths Compromise
tariffs
Federalists
Antifederalists
electors
The Federalist

Identify and explain the significance of the following individuals:
James Madison
Patrick Henry
Roger Sherman

1. **Using Graphic Organizers** Copy the graphic organizer below. Use it to explain the main beliefs held by the Federalists and the Antifederalists.

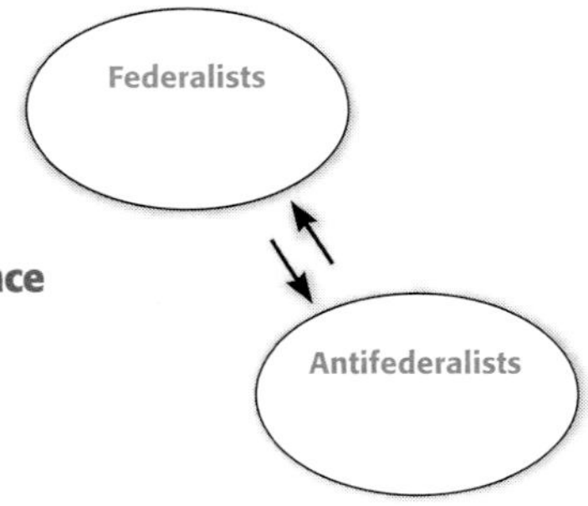

2. **Analyzing** Why did delegates to the Constitutional Convention believe it was best to keep the convention proceedings secret?
3. **Using Historical Imagination** Imagine that you are a legislator voting on the ratification of the Constitution. Will you vote for or against it? Why?
4. **Comparing and Contrasting** What were the advantages and disadvantages of the New Jersey Plan and the Virginia Plan?

Critical Thinking

5. Were the compromises in the Constitution the best solutions to the issues they addressed?
Consider:
   - what the main issues were
   - the purpose and results of the compromises
   - other possible solutions

The Constitution: A Living Document

OBJECTIVES

Read to understand:

1. how the Constitution divides power between the federal and state governments
2. how the separation of powers prevents each branch of government from becoming too strong
3. what potential drawbacks the system of checks and balances might have
4. what provisions in the Constitution allow for its flexibility

KEY TERMS

delegated powers
reserved powers
concurrent powers
supremacy clause
separation of powers
checks and balances
impeachment
veto
override
elastic clause

EYEWITNESSES TO History

66 *The Constitution has enough proven flexibility in it so that it can be stretched to accommodate the problems we face.* **99**
—Barbara Jordan

In 1987 Barbara Jordan, a former U.S. representative from Texas, reflected on the flexibility of the Constitution. Born out of great debate, the usefulness of the Constitution as a living, flexible document has been sustained through much discussion. Even today, the Constitution remains the subject of active debate, just as the signers intended. "I think they intended to draw up a document that would last, that would be adequate for all times and circumstances, one that succeeding generations would adapt and interpret as necessary," said Jordan. Also writing in 1987, legal scholar Charles Wiggins observed, "The Constitution celebrated today is the product of two hundred years of evolving and enlightened political, moral, and economic standards. That process continues."

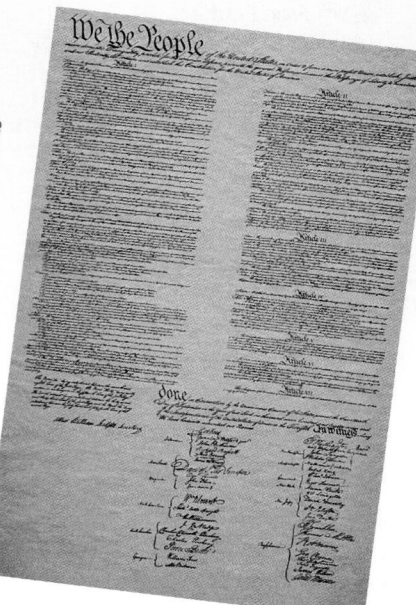

The Constitution of the United States

Federalism

The men who met in Philadelphia in 1787 are often referred to as the framers of the Constitution. They framed, or built, a new structure of national government. Drawing on their experiences with British rule and with the American government under the Articles of Confederation, the delegates to the Constitutional Convention struggled to form a stronger federal government. James Madison spoke of the need for the new government.

66 If men were angels, no government would be necessary. If angels were to govern men, neither external nor internal controls on government would be necessary. In framing a government which is to be administered by men over men, the great difficulty is this: You must first enable the government to control the governed; and in the next place, oblige it to control itself. **99**

The delegates worked to frame a constitution that would provide for a strong central government while protecting states' rights. To avoid possible abuses of power by the national government, the delegates divided and limited the powers of the federal government. Attempting to prevent conflict between the national government and the state governments, the framers identified powers to be held by each.

This 1788 print shows George Washington encircled by the seals of the 13 states and the seal of the United States.

Read More About It

Free Find:
Federal Powers
After reading about the
McCulloch v. *Maryland*
Supreme Court case on
the **Holt Researcher**
CD–ROM, write a short
essay that explains what
impact this case had on
the powers of the federal
government.

Delegated, reserved, and concurrent powers. Once the delegates settled on a federal system of government, they had to decide which powers would fall to the federal government and which powers the states would retain. They decided to give the federal government authority in most matters of concern to all the people. These **delegated powers**, which are listed in the Constitution, include the rights to coin money, to regulate trade with foreign nations and among the states, and to raise and support an army and a navy.

All powers not specifically granted to the federal government or denied to the states are kept, or reserved, by the states. These **reserved powers** are guaranteed by the Tenth Amendment, which was adopted in 1791. Examples of the states' reserved powers include establishing local governments and overseeing schools.

The powers that are held jointly by the federal government and state governments are called **concurrent powers**. Examples of concurrent powers include levying and collecting taxes, borrowing money, providing for the public welfare, and establishing courts to apply and enforce laws.

National supremacy. The delegates to the Constitutional Convention recognized that having two levels of government—state and national—exercising power at the same time would lead to some conflicts. Which laws would have ultimate authority?

Delegated, Reserved, and Concurrent Powers

Powers Delegated to National Government
- Declare war
- Raise and support armed forces
- Regulate interstate and foreign trade
- Admit new states
- Establish post offices
- Set standard weights and measures
- Coin money
- Establish foreign policy
- Create all laws necessary for carrying out delegated powers

Powers Reserved to States
- Establish and maintain schools
- Establish local governments
- Conduct elections
- Create corporate laws
- Regulate business within the state
- Create marriage laws
- Provide for public safety
- Assume other powers not delegated to the national government or prohibited to the states

Powers Shared (Concurrent Powers)
- Maintain law and order
- Levy taxes
- Borrow money
- Charter banks
- Establish courts
- Provide for public welfare

Learning from Charts The Constitution delegates certain powers to the national government, reserves other powers for the states, and allows some powers to be shared jointly.

? Building Chart Skills Why might the delegates to the Constitutional Convention have supported a division of power?

To answer this question, the delegates added a clause to the Constitution that clearly ranks the U.S. Constitution and all federal laws above state constitutions and state laws: "This Constitution, and the laws . . . and all treaties . . . of the United States, shall be the supreme law of the land." This statement, found in Article VI of the Constitution, is called the **supremacy clause**.

✔ **READING CHECK:** How does the Constitution divide power between the federal and state governments?

The first Congress under the Constitution met in Federal Hall, which was completed in 1789.

Separation of Powers

To prevent the federal government from abusing its powers, the framers of the Constitution separated the government into three branches: executive, legislative, and judicial. Each branch enjoys specific powers the other branches cannot claim. The legislative branch makes laws, the executive branch sees that they are carried out, and the judicial branch interprets and applies the laws. This **separation of powers** prevents any one branch of the federal government from becoming too powerful.

The executive and legislative branches.
The separation of powers is upheld by a system of **checks and balances** that gives each branch the means to restrain the powers of the other two. Congress, for example, has a responsibility to check presidential power. The Constitution's many checks on executive power reflect the framers' bitter experience with British royal governors. The president has the power to make treaties, but a two-thirds vote of the Senate is necessary to ratify them. Similarly, the president can appoint ambassadors, federal judges, and other important officials, but only with the "advice and consent" of the Senate. Congress can also check the president indirectly through "the power of the purse." Because it has the authority to appropriate government monies and approve the federal budget, Congress can slow or stop a presidential action that requires funding.

The most powerful restriction on presidential authority is the legal process of **impeachment**. The House of Representatives may impeach, or charge, a president who is thought to be guilty of "treason, bribery, or other high crimes and misdemeanors." An impeached president is then tried by the Senate and, if found guilty, removed from office. The legislative branch has rarely used the impeachment process to check presidential power. In 1867, members of Congress attempted to remove President Andrew Johnson for violating a law concerning the removal of cabinet members. Although the House of Representatives

THE GRANGER COLLECTION, NEW YORK

In his 1993 State of the Union address President Bill Clinton urged Congress to consider certain upcoming legislation.

voted for impeachment, the Senate fell one vote short of the two-thirds majority necessary for removal from office. In December 1998 the House voted to impeach President Bill Clinton for perjury and obstruction of justice stemming from a statement he had given to a grand jury. The Senate vote fell far short of conviction.

The president, in turn, can check the powers of Congress. The president can **veto**, or reject, bills passed by Congress. Although Congress possesses the power to **override**, or overrule, a presidential veto, the two-thirds majority necessary to do so is often difficult to obtain.

The president can also curb congressional power through influence and pressure. The Constitution grants the president the authority to call Congress into special session to deal with a national crisis. For example, President Abraham Lincoln called Congress into a special session at the outset of the Civil War. The president can also adjourn Congress if its members cannot agree when to end a session. In addition, the president can exert pressure on Congress by recommending measures judged to be "necessary and expedient [advantageous]" to maintaining effective government or by lobbying for specific legislation. The president can also

★ Changing Ways   The Federal Government

■ **Understanding Change** As a new, lasting government was being established in the early 1800s, hundreds of Americans were employed by the federal government. They delivered mail, surveyed land, and provided essential services to allow the new government to operate efficiently. Today there are millions of workers fulfilling a wide variety of services for the federal government—including law enforcement, industry and labor regulation, and mail delivery. *Which branch of the federal government has experienced the most growth in employees? What differences do you see between the image of the federal employee from the early 1800s and the image from the 1990s?*

Then

Now

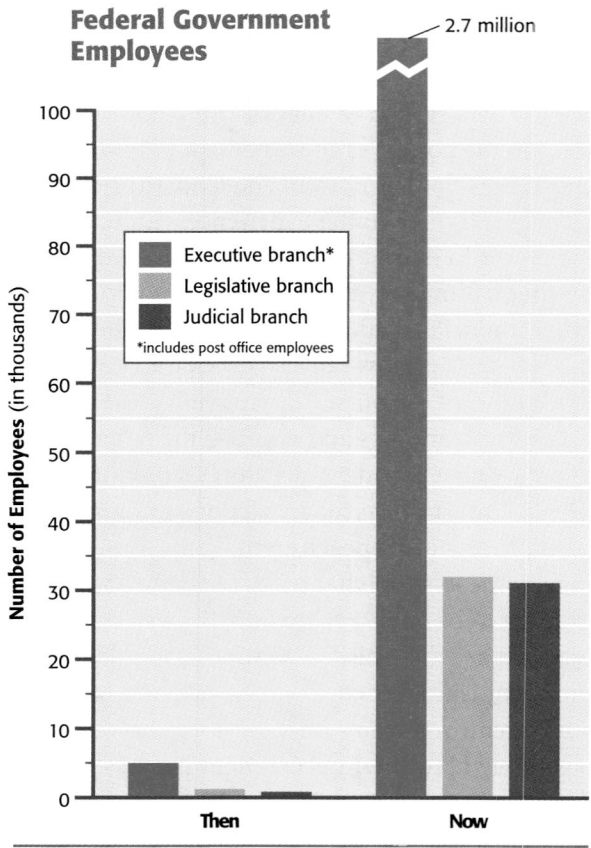

Federal Government Employees

2.7 million

Number of Employees (in thousands)

- Executive branch*
- Legislative branch
- Judicial branch

*includes post office employees

Then   Now

Sources: *Historical Statistics of the United States; Statistical Abstract of the United States: 1998.* Data represents 1816 and 1997.

influence Congress through annual State of the Union messages and through press conferences and public speeches.

The judicial branch. The judicial branch can check legislative power. The Supreme Court has the power to judge laws unconstitutional. This power helps ensure the Constitution's continued effectiveness. The framers did not include this power in the Constitution. Many legal scholars, however, believe that the framers intended the Supreme Court to exercise such a power. James Madison often argued that the Supreme Court could declare any law void if the justices found that the law violated the Constitution. Madison noted, however, that the Court would still be expected to uphold all laws, "however unjust."

The first two sessions of the Supreme Court were held in the Water Street Exchange, a building in New York City. Judges used gavels like the one above when court was in session.

While arguing for an independent judiciary, Alexander Hamilton warned in *Federalist Paper* "No. 78" that problems may arise from a judiciary capable of reviewing legislation:

66 **The interpretation of the laws is the proper and peculiar province of the courts. . . . It therefore belongs to them to ascertain . . . the meaning of any particular act. . . . It can be of no weight to say that the courts . . . may substitute their own pleasure to the constitutional intentions of the legislature. This might as well happen in the case of two contradictory statutes; or . . . in every [judicial decision] upon any single statute. The courts must declare the sense of the law; and if they should be disposed to exercise WILL instead of JUDGMENT, the consequence would equally be . . . the substitution of their pleasure to that of the legislative body.** 99

The executive and legislative branches can both check judicial powers as well. The judicial selection process provides the most basic check. Although the president appoints all federal judges, the Senate must approve them. Just as Congress has the power to impeach the president, it also has the power to impeach judges for "high crimes and misdemeanors." In addition, Congress can propose constitutional amendments to overturn earlier Court rulings. For example, the Supreme Court ruled unconstitutional a provision in the Voting Rights Act of 1970 that would have lowered the voting age. Congress reacted by passing the Twenty-sixth Amendment in March 1971, which lowered the voting age from 21 to 18. The amendment was ratified by the states less than four months later.

As a further curb on judicial power, the president can pardon or delay the punishment of persons convicted of federal crimes. However, neither the president nor Congress can remove judges from their position simply because they or their decisions may be unpopular. Unless impeached and found guilty of serious crimes, federal judges may hold their offices for life.

✔ **READING CHECK:** How does the separation of powers prevent each branch of government from becoming too strong?

The Balance of Powers

In a 1936 speech to the American public, President Franklin D. Roosevelt declared, "The American form of Government [is] a three horse team. . . . The three horses, are, of course, the three branches of government." Over the years, the balance of powers between the three branches of govern-

President Bill Clinton signs the line-item veto bill into law.

ment has shifted—sometimes causing great controversy among the nation's leaders and the public.

Recently, Americans debated the constitutionality of the line-item veto. The Line-Item Veto Act, which gave the president the authority to veto specific items in a spending bill without vetoing the entire bill, became law in 1996. Supporters of the line-item veto argued that it would help curb government spending, but legal challenges were immediately brought against it. Opponents believed it disrupted the balance of power between the legislative and executive branches. In 1998 the Supreme Court agreed with the opponents and declared the line-item veto unconstitutional because it altered the balance of power between the legislative and executive branches of government.

Critics of the system. The framers built the system of separation of powers and checks and balances into the structure of government to prevent any government branch from exercising too much power. The system, however, has always had its critics.

Some argue that the system permits political disputes to hold up the workings of government. For example, a president who belongs to one political party and a Congress dominated by another party may not agree on necessary legislation. One branch may continually block the actions of the other. In 1995 the Republican-led Congress and President Bill Clinton, a Democrat, were unable to agree on the national budget, resulting in a partial government shutdown. Nevertheless, the system of checks and balances has prevented what the framers of the Constitution feared most: unrestricted governmental power.

✔ **READING CHECK:** What is a potential drawback to the system of checks and balances in government?

Flexibility and Change

The Constitution has remained effective for more than 200 years because it is a living document that can adapt to changes in our society. The Constitution works as well today for an industrialized nation of 50 states and a population of more than 270 million as it did in 1790 for an agricultural nation of 13 states and fewer than 4 million inhabitants.

The continued effectiveness of the Constitution owes much to its flexibility. James Madison urged his colleagues to consider "the changes which ages will produce." To allow for needed amendments, the framers specified a procedure by which the Constitution may be changed—through passing amendments. Exercising one of the methods of amendment in 1919, Congress,

INTERPRETING THE VISUAL RECORD

The Nineteenth Amendment. Suffragists parade down a Washington, D.C., street in 1913. *How did the suffragists, pictured here, use patriotic symbols to advance their cause?*

THE GRANGER COLLECTION, NEW YORK

by more than a two-thirds majority, passed the Nineteenth Amendment guaranteeing women's right to vote. The necessary three fourths of the states soon ratified the amendment. The framers deliberately made the amendment process difficult, intending it to be used only when a change is critical. Only 27 amendments have been added to the Constitution since 1789, although many amendments have been proposed.

The Constitution's "necessary and proper" clause, also known as the **elastic clause**, has increased the document's flexibility. To the specific powers granted to Congress, this clause adds the power "to make all Laws which shall be necessary and proper for carrying into Execution the foregoing Powers." The elastic clause allows Congress to exert its powers in ways not specifically outlined in the Constitution. For example, the framers of the Constitution could not have anticipated the development of computers and the Internet. Congress, however, has the power to pass laws relating to new technology that may affect other items covered in the Constitution, such as commerce. In this way, the government can stretch the Constitution to fit changing times.

✔ **READING CHECK:** What provisions in the Constitution allow for its flexibility?

Great Debates

The Constitution

For more than 200 years, historians have debated the revolutionary implications of the Constitution. Writing in the 1800s, historian George Bancroft celebrated the U.S. Constitution as a flawless revolutionary document that created a system of government based on democracy and equality. "The Constitution establishes nothing that interferes with equality and individuality," Bancroft noted. "It knows nothing of differences by descent [ancestry], or opinions, of favored classes, or legalized religion, or the political power of property."

This view of the Constitution has been challenged by many historians. Writing in the early 1900s, Charles Beard argued that the framers of the Constitution were acting in their own economic interest. "The dominant classes," he observed, "must . . . obtain from government such rules as are consonant [in agreement] with . . . their economic processes."

Other scholars noted that many Americans such as women, slaves, and men without property were initially left out of the Constitution. Recent scholars have tried to acknowledge both the revolutionary aspects and the limitations of the document. They note that one of the great achievements of the framers was in providing a flexible constitution whose democratic nature could be expanded.

SECTION REVIEW

Define and explain the significance of the following terms:
delegated powers
reserved powers
concurrent powers
supremacy clause
separation of powers
checks and balances
impeachment
veto
override
elastic clause

1. **Using Graphic Organizers** Copy the graphic organizer below. Use it to list the powers held by the federal government, state governments, and the powers shared by both.

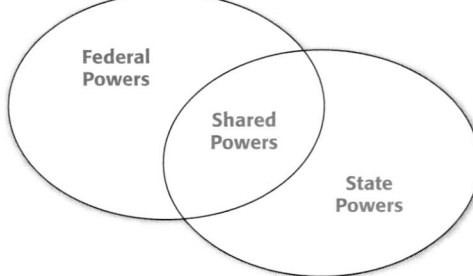

2. **Identifying Values** How did the checks and balances and the separation of powers reflect the concerns of U.S. citizens in the late 1700s?

3. **Assessing Consequences** How might the system of checks and balances both increase and reduce the government's ability to function efficiently in different situations?

4. **Synthesizing** Why can the Constitution be considered a flexible, living document?

Critical Thinking

5. What, in your opinion, is the most significant provision of the Constitution? Explain your answer.
   Consider:
   • the provisions of the Constitution
   • the uniqueness of the provisions
   • the effects of the provisions

CHAPTER 5

Review

Creating a Time Line

Copy the time line below onto a sheet of paper. Complete the time line by filling in the events and dates from the chapter that you think were most significant. Pick three events and explain why you think they were significant.

1776   1783   1790

Writing a Summary

Using the Reading Checks as a guide, write an overview of the events in the chapter.

Identifying People and Ideas

Identify the following terms or individuals and explain their significance.

1. John Locke
2. Virginia Statute for Religious Freedom
3. Articles of Confederation
4. Daniel Shays
5. James Madison
6. Virginia Plan
7. Three-Fifths Compromise
8. *The Federalist*
9. supremacy clause
10. checks and balances

Understanding Main Ideas

SECTION 1

1. How did the weak national government created by the Articles of Confederation cause problems for the new nation?
2. What were the provisions of the ordinances to organize and govern the Northwest Territory?

SECTION 2

3. What were the main compromises reached during the Constitutional Convention?

SECTION 3

4. How does the Constitution balance power between the state and federal governments?
5. In what ways is the Constitution a flexible and unique political document?

Reviewing Themes

1. **Constitutional Heritage** How does the organization of the federal government reflect concern about a powerful national government?
2. **Economic Development** How did the government's economic policies lead to Shays's Rebellion?
3. **Democratic Values** How might the framers of the Constitution have helped to ensure that more citizens had a voice in government?

Thinking Critically

1. **Analyzing** What factors shaped the republican ideals at the heart of American governments?
2. **Hypothesizing** What might have happened if the framers of the Constitution had outlawed slavery?
3. **Taking a Stand** Under what conditions, if any, is a government justified in concealing its activities from the public?
4. **Identifying Cause and Effect** How did colonial experiences influence the way the state constitutions were written?
5. **Distinguishing Fact from Opinion** Some Antifederalists argued that the Constitution would inevitably destroy liberty. Is this argument based on fact or opinion? Explain your answer.

Writing About History

Writing to Persuade Imagine that you are an American in 1787 who supports the ratification of the Constitution. Write a speech explaining why you support the new plan of government over the Articles of Confederation. Use the following chart to organize your thoughts.

Weaknesses of the Articles	Improvements in the Constitution

Strategies for Success Review the **Strategies for Success** on *Identifying Cause and Effect.* Then reread the Section 2 subsection entitled Compromise at the Convention and answer the following questions.

1. What major issues did delegates from the northern and southern states disagree over at the Constitutional Convention?
2. How did the delegates resolve these disagreements?
3. What, in turn, were some further effects of these resolutions?

Linking History and Geography

Study the map below, noting the numbers on it. The map shows the order in which the states ratified the Constitution. Number your paper 1 to 13. Identify each state on the map and write the correct name of each state next to the corresponding number on your paper. Add the date each state ratified the Constitution.

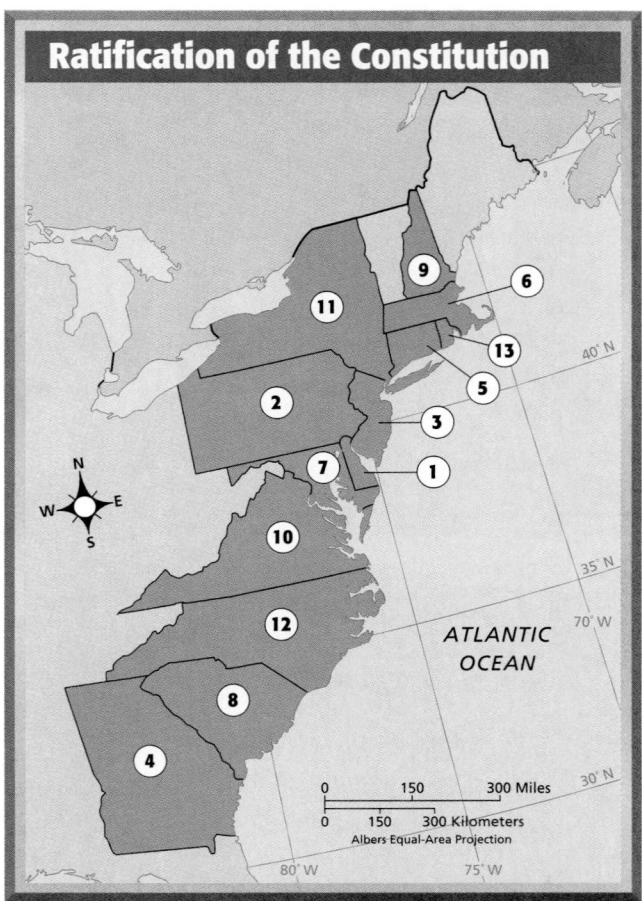

Ratification of the Constitution

internetconnect

TOPIC: The Federalist/Antifederalist Debate
GO TO: go.hrw.com
KEYWORD: SD1 Federalists

Accessing the Internet through the HRW Web site, research the Federalists and the Antifederalists. Make a list of three or four topics that the two groups might debate. Then select one side to "join" and hold a debate with another classmate. If you are working by yourself, write a script for a short debate that presents both sides.

BUILDING YOUR PORTFOLIO

Complete one or all of the following projects independently or cooperatively.

1 Democratic Values
Imagine that you are one of Shays's rebels. **Create a poster** *that reveals your position on taxes.*

2 Constitutional Heritage
Imagine that you are interested in including women's rights in the new Constitution. **Write a letter** *to the Constitutional Convention suggesting ways to represent women in the Constitution.*

3 Geographic Diversity
Imagine that you are attending a governors' conference in 1790. Choose one of the 13 original states to represent. **Prepare a speech or pamphlet** *outlining the issues of concern to your state.*

Delegates to the Constitutional Convention in 1787 signed the document that established the democratic government of the United States.

CONSTITUTION HANDBOOK

> 66 We the People of the United States, in Order to form a more perfect Union, establish Justice, insure domestic Tranquility, provide for the common defense, promote the general Welfare, and secure the Blessings of Liberty to ourselves and our Posterity, do ordain and establish this Constitution for the United States of America. 99
>
> —Preamble to the Constitution

*T*he delegates who met in the spring of 1787 to revise the Articles of Confederation included many of the ablest leaders of the United States. Convinced that the Confederation was not strong enough to bring order and prosperity to the nation, they abandoned all thought of revising the Articles. Instead, they proceeded to draw up a completely new Constitution. Patrick Henry called this action "a revolution as radical as that which separated us from Great Britain." Out of their long political experience, their keen intelligence, and their great learning, the framers of the Constitution fashioned a blueprint for a truly united nation—the United States of America.

Delegates met in Independence Hall in Philadelphia to draft the Constitution.

An unknown observer once referred to the U.S. Constitution as "the most wonderful work ever struck off at a given time by the brain and purpose of man." Revised, modified, and amended, the Constitution has served the American people for more than 200 years, becoming a model for representative government around the world. The Constitution has successfully survived the years for two reasons. First, it lays down rules of procedure and guarantees of rights and liberties that must be observed even in times of crisis. Second, it is a "living" document, capable of being amended to meet changing times and circumstances.

The U.S. Constitution

To Form a More Perfect Union

The framers of the Constitution wished to establish a strong central government, one that could unite the country and help it meet the challenges of the future. At the same time, however, they feared a government that was too strong. The memories of the troubled years before the Revolution were still fresh. They knew that unchecked power in the hands of individuals, groups, or branches of government could lead to tyranny.

The framers' response was to devise a system of government in which power is divided between, in the words of James Madison, "two distinct governments"—the states and the federal government—and then within each government. In *Federalist Paper* "No. 51," Madison described the advantages of such a system.

> ❝ In the compound republic of America, the power surrendered by the people is first divided between two distinct governments, and then the portion allotted to each subdivided among distinct and separate departments. Hence a double security arises to the rights of the people. The different governments will control each other, at the same time that each will be controlled by itself. ❞

U.S. Constitution commemorative stamps

The seven Articles that make up the first part of the Constitution provide the blueprint for this system. To help guard against tyranny and to keep any one part of the federal government from becoming too strong, the framers divided the government into three branches—the legislative branch (Congress), the executive branch (the president and vice president), and the judicial branch (the federal courts)—each with specific powers. As a further safeguard, the framers wrote a system of checks and balances into the Constitution. Articles I, II, and III outline the powers of each branch of government and the checks and balances.

Article IV outlines the relations among the states and between the states and the federal government. Among the issues addressed are each state's recognition of other states' public records and citizens' rights, the admission of new states, and the rights and responsibilities of the federal government in relation to the states.

Article V specifies the process by which the Constitution can be amended. The framers purposely made the process slow and difficult. They feared that if the process was too easy, the Constitution—the fundamental law of the land—would soon carry no more weight than the most minor law passed by Congress.

Article VI includes one provision that addressed the immediate concerns of the framers and two that have lasting significance. The short-term provision promises that the United States under the Constitution will honor all public debts entered into under the Confederation. The two long-term provisions declare the Constitution the supreme law of the land and prohibit religion being used as a qualification for holding public office.

Article VII is the framers' attempt to ensure ratification of the Constitution. The Constitutional Convention was summoned by the Congress to amend the Articles of Confederation. Under the Articles of Confederation, amendments had to be approved by all 13 states. Realizing that it would be difficult to get the approval of all the states—Rhode Island, for example, had not even sent delegates to Philadelphia—the framers specified that the Constitution would go into effect after ratification by only 9 states, not all 13. (This provision led some opponents of the Constitution to claim that it had been adopted by unfair means.)

Quill pen belonging to constitutional delegate James Madison

Protecting Individual Liberty

Opposition to a strong central government was in part a concern over states' rights. But it was also rooted in the desire to protect individual liberties. American colonists had always insisted on the protection of their civil liberties—their rights as individuals against the power of the government. The Constitution contains many important guarantees of civil liberties. On a broad level, the separation of powers and the system of checks and balances help safeguard citizens against the abuse of government power. But the Constitution also contains provisions that speak directly to an individual's right to due process of law. For example, Section 9 of Article I prohibits both *ex post facto* laws and bills of attainder.

An *ex post facto* law is a law passed "after the deed." Such a law sets a penalty for an act that was not illegal when it was committed. A bill of attainder is a law that punishes a person by fine, imprisonment, or seizure of property without a court

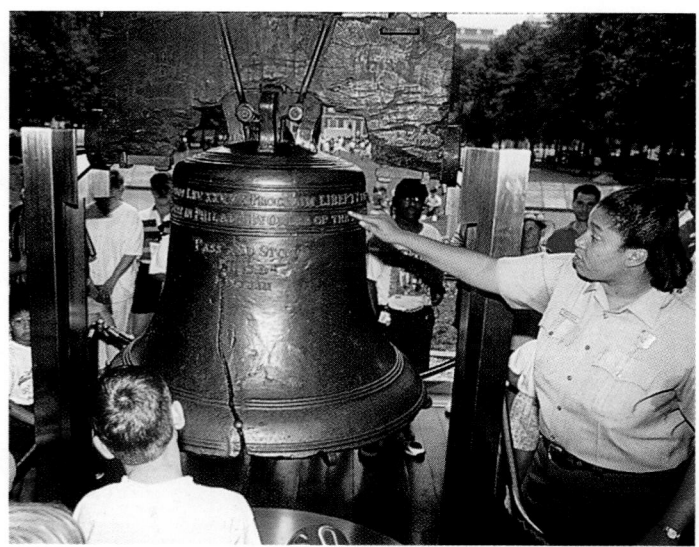

The Liberty Bell has become a symbol of the ideas of individual liberty protected in the Constitution.

trial. If Congress had the power to adopt bills of attainder, lawmakers could punish any American at will, and that person could do nothing to appeal the sentence. Instead, the Constitution provides that only the courts can impose punishment for unlawful acts, and then only by following the duly established law.

Section 9 of Article I also protects citizens by guaranteeing the privilege of the writ of *habeas corpus*. The writ of *habeas corpus* is a legal document that forces a jailer to release a person from prison unless the person has been formally charged with, or convicted of, a crime. The Constitution states that "the privilege of the writ of *habeas corpus* shall not be suspended, unless when in cases of rebellion or invasion the public safety may require it."

The Constitution also gives special protection to people accused of treason. The framers of the Constitution knew that the charge of treason was an old device used by tyrants to get rid of persons they did not like. Such rulers might bring the charge of treason against persons who merely criticized the government. To prevent such use of this charge, Section 3 of Article III carefully defines treason.

> 66 Treason against the United States, shall consist only in levying War against them, or in adhering to their Enemies, giving them Aid and Comfort. No Person shall be convicted of Treason unless on the Testimony of two Witnesses to the same overt Act, or on Confession in open Court. 99

Article III also protects the innocent relatives of a person accused of treason. Only the convicted person can be punished. No penalty can be imposed on the person's family.

The signing of the Constitution

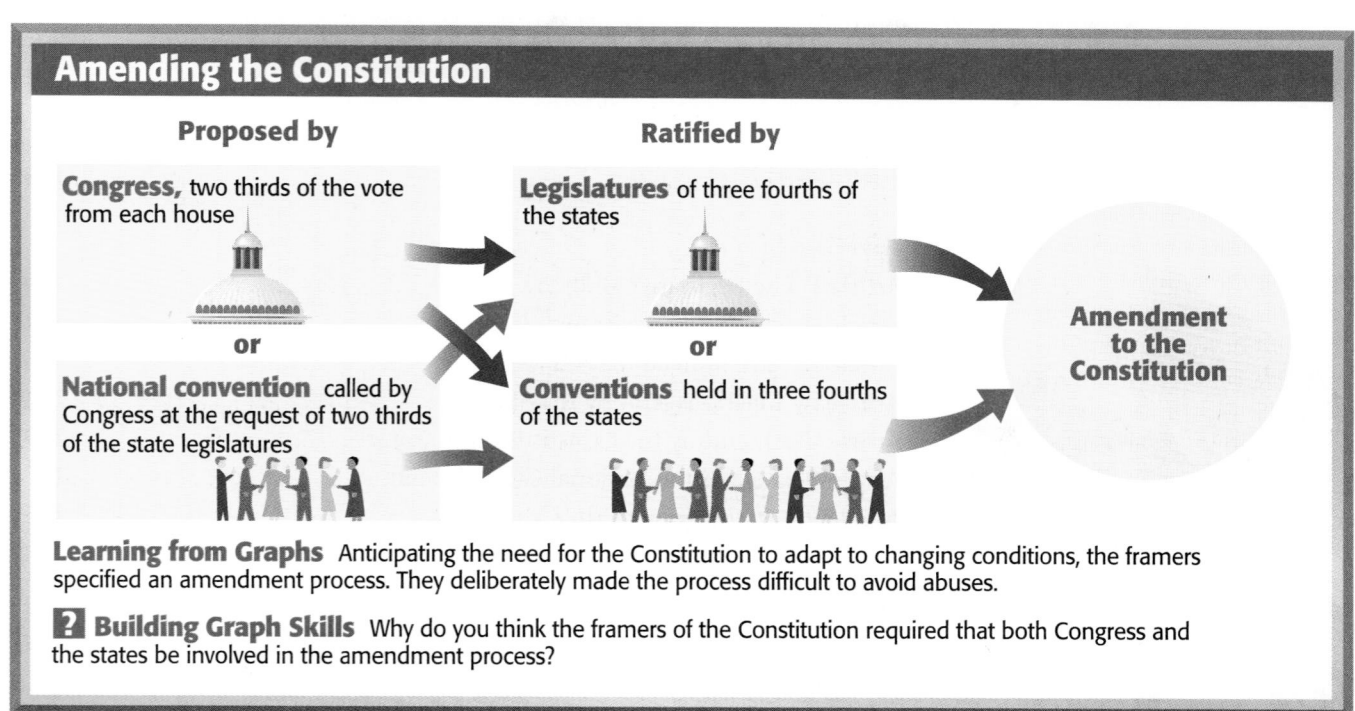

Amending the Constitution

Proposed by

Congress, two thirds of the vote from each house

or

National convention called by Congress at the request of two thirds of the state legislatures

Ratified by

Legislatures of three fourths of the states

or

Conventions held in three fourths of the states

Amendment to the Constitution

Learning from Graphs Anticipating the need for the Constitution to adapt to changing conditions, the framers specified an amendment process. They deliberately made the process difficult to avoid abuses.

? Building Graph Skills Why do you think the framers of the Constitution required that both Congress and the states be involved in the amendment process?

The Bill of Rights

Despite the safeguards written into the Articles of the Constitution, some states at first refused to ratify the framework because it did not offer greater protection to the rights of individuals. They finally agreed to ratification after they had been promised that a bill of rights would be added to the Constitution by amendment when Congress was called into session following ratification.

In 1789 the first Congress of the United States wrote some of the ideals of the Declaration of Independence into the Bill of Rights, the first 10 amendments to the Constitution. The Bill of Rights includes a protection for individuals against any action by the federal government that may deprive them of life, liberty, or property without "due process of law."

Among the guarantees of liberty in the Bill of Rights, several are especially important. The First Amendment guarantees freedom of religion, speech, press, assembly, and petition. The Fourth Amendment forbids unreasonable searches and seizures of any person's home. The Fifth, Sixth, and Eighth Amendments protect individuals from arbitrary arrest and punishment by the federal government.

The Bill of Rights was ratified by the states in 1791. It has remained one of the best-known features of the Constitution. The American people have turned to it for support whenever their rights as individuals have seemed to be in danger. No document in American history—except, perhaps, the Declaration of Independence—has been cherished more deeply.

Contents of the Constitution

Raising the new American flag, 1783

THE GRANGER COLLECTION, NEW YORK

President George Washington (left) and his advisers

State seals of North Carolina, Massachusetts, and New York

The bald eagle, a symbol of the United States

The Constitution of the United States of America

Preamble
The short and dignified Preamble explains the goals of the new government under the Constitution.

 Constitutional Heritage

According to the Preamble, what did the delegates hope the Constitution would provide for the nation?

Legislative Branch
Article I explains how the legislative branch, called Congress, is organized. The chief purpose of the legislative branch is to make the laws. Congress is made up of the Senate and the House of Representatives. The decision to have two bodies of government solved a difficult problem during the Constitutional Convention. The large states wanted membership in Congress to be based entirely on population. The small states wanted every state to have an equal vote. The solution to the problem of how the states were to be represented in Congress was known as the Great Compromise.

The number of members of the House is based on the population of the individual states. Each state has at least one representative. The current size of the House is 435 members, set by Congress in 1929.

PREAMBLE

We the People of the United States, in Order to form a more perfect Union, establish Justice, insure domestic Tranquility, provide for the common defense, promote the general Welfare, and secure the Blessings of Liberty to ourselves and our Posterity, do ordain and establish this Constitution for the United States of America.*

ARTICLE I

Section 1. All legislative Powers herein granted shall be vested in a Congress of the United States, which shall consist of a Senate and House of Representatives.

Section 2. The House of Representatives shall be composed of Members chosen every second Year by the People of the several States, and the Electors in each State shall have the Qualifications requisite for Electors of the most numerous Branch of the State Legislature.

No Person shall be a Representative who shall not have attained to the Age of twenty-five Years, and been seven Years a Citizen of the United States, and who shall not, when elected, be an inhabitant of that State in which he shall be chosen.

Representatives and direct Taxes shall be apportioned among the several States which may be included within this Union, according to their respective Numbers, ~~which shall be determined by adding to the whole Number of free Persons, including those bound to Service for a Term of Years, and excluding Indians not taxed, three fifths of all other Persons.~~ The actual Enumeration shall be made within three Years after the first Meeting of the Congress of the United States, and within every subsequent Term of ten Years, in such Manner as they shall by Law direct. The Number of Representatives shall not exceed one for every thirty Thousand, but

* Parts of the Constitution that have been ruled through are no longer in force or no longer apply.

each State shall have at Least one Representative; and until such enumeration shall be made, the State of New Hampshire shall be entitled to choose three; Massachusetts eight; Rhode Island and Providence Plantations one; Connecticut five; New-York six; New Jersey four; Pennsylvania eight; Delaware one; Maryland six; Virginia ten; North Carolina five; South Carolina five; and Georgia three.

When vacancies happen in the Representation from any State, the Executive Authority thereof shall issue Writs of Election to fill such Vacancies.

The House of Representatives shall choose their Speaker and other Officers; and shall have the sole Power of Impeachment.

Section 3. The Senate of the United States shall be composed of two Senators from each State, chosen by the Legislature thereof, for six Years; and each Senator shall have one Vote.

Immediately after they shall be assembled in Consequence of the first Election, they shall be divided as equally as may be into three Classes. The Seats of the Senators of the first Class shall be vacated at the Expiration of the second Year, of the second Class at the Expiration of the fourth Year, and of the third Class at the Expiration of the sixth Year, so that one third may be chosen every second Year; and if Vacancies happen by Resignation, or otherwise, during the Recess of the Legislature of any State, the Executive thereof may make temporary Appointments until the next Meeting of the Legislature, which shall then fill such Vacancies.

No Person shall be a Senator who shall not have attained to the Age of thirty Years, and been nine Years a Citizen of the United States, and who shall not, when elected, be an Inhabitant of that State for which he shall be chosen.

The Vice President of the United States shall be President of the Senate, but shall have no Vote, unless they be equally divided.

The Senate shall choose their other Officers, and also a President pro tempore, in the Absence of the Vice President, or when he shall exercise the Office of President of the United States.

The Senate shall have the sole Power to try all Impeachments. When sitting for that Purpose, they shall be on Oath or Affirmation. When the President of the United States is tried, the Chief Justice shall preside: And no Person shall be convicted without the Concurrence of two thirds of the Members present.

Judgment in Cases of Impeachment shall not extend further than to removal from Office, and disqualification to hold and enjoy any Office of honor, Trust or Profit under the United States: but the Party convicted shall nevertheless be liable and subject to Indictment, Trial, Judgment and Punishment, according to Law.

Section 4. The Times, Places and Manner of holding Elections for Senators and Representatives, shall be prescribed in each State by the Legislature thereof; but the Congress may at any time by Law make or alter such Regulations, except as to the Places of choosing Senators.

 Constitutional Heritage

According to the Constitution, who has the authority to fill a vacancy in the House of Representatives?

Every state has two senators. Senators serve a six-year term, but only one third of the senators reach the end of their terms every two years. In any election, at least two thirds of the senators stay in office. This system ensures that there are experienced senators in office at all times.

The only duty that the Constitution assigns to the vice president is to preside over meetings of the Senate. Modern presidents have given their vice presidents more and varied responsibilities.

In an impeachment, the House charges a government official of wrongdoing, and the Senate acts as a court to decide if the official is guilty.

Congress has decided that elections will be held on the Tuesday following the first Monday in November of even-numbered years. The Twentieth Amendment states that Congress shall meet in regular session on January 3 of each year. The president may call a special session of Congress whenever necessary.

According to the Constitution, who has the authority to judge elections, returns, and the behavior of congressmembers?

Congress makes most of its own rules of conduct. The Senate and the House each have a code of ethics that members must follow. It is the task of each house of Congress to discipline its own members. Each house keeps a journal, and a publication called the *Congressional Record* keeps records of what happens in congressional sessions. The general public can learn how their representatives voted on bills by reading the *Congressional Record.*

The framers of the Constitution wanted to protect members of Congress from being arrested on false charges by political enemies who did not want them to attend important meetings. The framers also wanted to protect members of Congress from being taken to court for something they said in a speech or in a debate.

The power to tax is the responsibility of the House of Representatives. Because members of the House are elected every two years, the framers felt that representatives would listen to the public and seek its approval before passing taxes.

The veto power of the president and the ability of Congress to override a presidential veto are two of the important checks and balances in the Constitution.

The Congress shall assemble at least once in every Year, and such Meeting shall be on the first Monday in December, unless they shall by Law appoint a different Day.

Section 5. Each House shall be the Judge of the Elections, Returns and Qualifications of its own Members, and a Majority of each shall constitute a Quorum to do Business; but a smaller Number may adjourn from day to day, and may be authorized to compel the Attendance of absent Members, in such Manner, and under such Penalties as each House may provide.

Each House may determine the Rules of its Proceedings, punish its Members for disorderly Behavior, and, with the Concurrence of two thirds, expel a Member.

Each House shall keep a Journal of its Proceedings, and from time to time publish the same, excepting such Parts as may in their Judgment require Secrecy; and the Yeas and Nays of the Members of either House on any question shall, at the Desire of one fifth of those Present, be entered on the Journal.

Neither House, during the Session of Congress, shall, without the Consent of the other, adjourn for more than three days, nor to any other Place than that in which the two Houses shall be sitting.

Section 6. The Senators and Representatives shall receive a Compensation for their Services, to be ascertained by Law, and paid out of the Treasury of the United States. They shall in all Cases, except Treason, Felony and Breach of the Peace, be privileged from Arrest during their Attendance at the Session of their respective Houses, and in going to and returning from the same; and for any Speech or Debate in either House, they shall not be questioned in any other Place.

No Senator or Representative shall, during the Time for which he was elected, be appointed to any civil Office under the Authority of the United States, which shall have been created, or the Emoluments whereof shall have been increased during such time; and no Person holding any Office under the United States, shall be a Member of either House during his Continuance in Office.

Section 7. All Bills for raising Revenue shall originate in the House of Representatives; but the Senate may propose or concur with Amendments as on other Bills.

Every Bill which shall have passed the House of Representatives and the Senate, shall, before it become a Law, be presented to the President of the United States; If he approve he shall sign it, but if not he shall return it, with his Objections to that House in which it shall have originated, who shall enter the Objections at large on their Journal, and proceed to reconsider it. If after such Reconsideration two thirds of that House shall agree to pass the Bill, it shall be sent, together with the Objections, to the other House, by which it shall likewise be reconsidered, and if approved by two thirds of that House, it shall become a Law. But in all such Cases the Votes of both Houses shall be determined by Yeas and Nays, and the Names of

the Persons voting for and against the Bill shall be entered on the Journal of each House respectively. If any Bill shall not be returned by the President within ten Days (Sundays excepted) after it shall have been presented to him, the Same shall be a Law, in like Manner as if he had signed it, unless the Congress by their Adjournment prevent its Return, in which Case it shall not be a Law.

Every Order, Resolution, or Vote to which the Concurrence of the Senate and House of Representatives may be necessary (except on a question of Adjournment) shall be presented to the President of the United States; and before the Same shall take Effect, shall be approved by him, or being disapproved by him, shall be repassed by two thirds of the Senate and House of Representatives, according to the Rules and Limitations prescribed in the Case of a Bill.

Section 8. The Congress shall have Power To lay and collect Taxes, Duties, Imposts and Excises, to pay the Debts and provide for the common Defense and general Welfare of the United States; but all Duties, Imposts and Excises shall be uniform throughout the United States;

To borrow Money on the credit of the United States;

To regulate Commerce with foreign Nations, and among the several States, and with the Indian Tribes;

To establish an uniform Rule of Naturalization, and uniform Laws on the subject of Bankruptcies throughout the United States;

To coin Money, regulate the Value thereof, and of foreign Coin, and fix the Standard of Weights and Measures;

To provide for the Punishment of counterfeiting the Securities and current Coin of the United States;

To establish Post Offices and post Roads;

To promote the Progress of Science and useful Arts, by securing for limited Times to Authors and Inventors the exclusive Right to their respective Writings and Discoveries;

To constitute Tribunals inferior to the supreme Court;

To define and punish Piracies and Felonies committed on the high Seas, and Offenses against the Law of Nations;

To declare War, grant Letters of Marque and Reprisal, and make Rules concerning Captures on Land and Water;

To raise and support Armies, but no Appropriation of Money to that Use shall be for a longer Term than two Years;

To provide and maintain a Navy;

To make Rules for the Government and Regulation of the land and naval Forces;

To provide for calling forth the Militia to execute the Laws of the Union, suppress Insurrections and repel Invasions;

To provide for organizing, arming, and disciplining, the Militia, and for governing such Part of them as may be employed in the Service of the United States, reserving to the States respectively, the Appointment of the

 Constitutional Heritage

What must Congress do with a bill to make it a law once both houses have approved it?

The framers of the Constitution wanted a national government that was strong enough to be effective. Section 8 lists the powers given to Congress. The last sentence in the section contains the so-called elastic clause, which has been stretched—like elastic—to fit many different circumstances. The clause was first disputed when Alexander Hamilton proposed a national bank. Thomas Jefferson said that the Constitution did not give Congress the power to establish a bank. Hamilton argued that the bank was "necessary and proper" in order to carry out other powers of Congress, such as borrowing money and regulating currency. This argument was tested in the court system in 1819 in the case of *McCulloch* v. *Maryland,* when Chief Justice John Marshall ruled in favor of the federal government. Powers exercised by the government using the "elastic clause" are called implied powers.

The delegates debated the articles of the Constitution in the Assembly Room of Independence Hall.

If Congress has implied powers, then there also must be limits to its powers. Section 9 lists powers that are denied to the federal government. Several of the clauses protect the people of the United States from unjust treatment. For instance, Section 9 guarantees the right of the writ of *habeas corpus* and prohibits bills of attainder and *ex post facto* laws.

Constitutional Heritage

What prohibitions does the Constitution make against nobility and titles from monarchies?

Officers, and the Authority of training the Militia according to the discipline prescribed by Congress.

To exercise exclusive Legislation in all Cases whatsoever, over such District (not exceeding ten Miles square) as may, by Cession of particular States, and the Acceptance of Congress, become the Seat of the Government of the United States, and to exercise like Authority over all Places purchased by the Consent of the Legislature of the State in which the Same shall be, for the Erection of Forts, Magazines, Arsenals, dock-Yards, and other needful Buildings;—And

To make all Laws which shall be necessary and proper for carrying into Execution the foregoing Powers, and all other Powers vested by this Constitution in the Government of the United States, or in any Department or Officer thereof.

Section 9. ~~The Migration or Importation of such Persons as any of the States now existing shall think proper to admit, shall not be prohibited by the Congress prior to the Year one thousand eight hundred and eight, but a Tax or duty may be imposed on such Importation, not exceeding ten dollars for each Person.~~

The Privilege of the Writ of Habeas Corpus shall not be suspended, unless when in Cases of Rebellion or Invasion the public Safety may require it.

No Bill of Attainder or ex post facto Law shall be passed.

No Capitation, or other direct, Tax shall be laid, unless in Proportion to the Census or Enumeration herein before directed to be taken.

No Tax or Duty shall be laid on Articles exported from any State.

No Preference shall be given by any Regulation of Commerce or Revenue to the Ports of one State over those of another: nor shall Vessels bound to, or from, one State, be obliged to enter, clear, or pay Duties in another.

No Money shall be drawn from the Treasury, but in Consequence of Appropriations made by Law; and a regular Statement and Account of the Receipts and Expenditures of all public Money shall be published from time to time.

No Title of Nobility shall be granted by the United States: And no Person holding any Office of Profit or Trust under them, shall, without the Consent of the Congress, accept of any present, Emolument, Office, or Title, of any kind whatever, from any King, Prince, or foreign State.

Section 10. No State shall enter into any Treaty, Alliance, or Confederation; grant Letters of Marque and Reprisal; coin Money; emit Bills of Credit; make any Thing but gold and silver Coin a Tender in Payment of Debts; pass any Bill of Attainder, ex post facto Law, or law impairing the Obligation of Contracts, or grant any Title of Nobility.

No State shall, without the Consent of the Congress, lay any Imposts or Duties on Imports or Exports, except what may be absolutely necessary for executing its inspection Laws: and the net Produce of all Duties and Imposts, laid by any State on Imports or Exports, shall be for the Use of the Treasury of the United States; and all such Laws shall be subject to the Revision and Control of the Congress.

No State shall, without the Consent of Congress, lay any Duty of Tonnage, keep Troops, or Ships of War in time of Peace, enter into any Agreement or Compact with another State, or with a foreign Power, or engage in War, unless actually invaded, or in such imminent Danger as will not admit of delay.

ARTICLE II

Section 1. The executive Power shall be vested in a President of the United States of America. He shall hold his Office during the Term of four Years, and, together with the Vice President, chosen for the same Term, be elected, as follows.

Each State shall appoint, in such Manner as the Legislature thereof may direct, a Number of Electors, equal to the whole Number of Senators and Representatives to which the State may be entitled in the Congress: but no Senator or Representative, or Person holding an Office of Trust or Profit under the United States, shall be appointed an Elector.

~~The Electors shall meet in their respective States, and vote by Ballot for two Persons, of whom one at least shall not be an Inhabitant of the same State with themselves. And they shall make a List of all the Persons voted for, and of the Number of Votes for each; which List they shall sign and certify, and transmit sealed to the Seat of the Government of the United States, directed to the President of the Senate. The President of the Senate shall, in the Presence of the Senate and House of Representatives, open all the Certificates, and the Votes shall then be counted. The Person having the greatest Number of Votes shall be the President, if such Number be a Majority of the whole Number of Electors appointed; and if there be more than one who have such majority, and have an equal Number of Votes, then the House of Representatives shall immediately choose by Ballot one of them for President; and if no Person have a Majority, then from the five highest on the List the said House shall in like Manner choose the President. But in choosing the President, the Votes shall be taken by States, the Representation from each State having one Vote; A quorum for this Purpose shall consist of a Member or Members from two thirds of the States, and a Majority of all the States shall be necessary to a Choice. In every Case, after~~

Section 10 lists the powers that are denied to the states. In our system of federalism, the state and federal governments have separate powers, share some powers, and are denied other powers. The states may not exercise any of the powers that belong solely to Congress.

 Constitutional Heritage

According to the Constitution, under what circumstances could a state engage in war?

Executive Branch
The president is the chief of the executive branch. It is the job of the president to enforce the laws. The framers wanted the president and vice president's terms of office and manner of selection to be different from those of members of Congress. They decided on four-year terms, but they had a difficult time agreeing on how to select the president and vice president. The framers finally set up an electoral system, which varies greatly from our electoral process today. The Twelfth Amendment changed the process by requiring that separate ballots be cast for president and vice president. The rise of political parties has since changed the process even more.

In 1845 Congress set the Tuesday following the first Monday in November of every fourth year as the general election date for selecting presidential electors.

Emolument means "salary, or payment." In 1999 Congress voted to set future presidents' salaries at $400,000 per year. The president also receives an annual expense account. The president must pay taxes only on the salary.

The oath of office is administered to the president by the chief justice of the United States. George Washington added "So help me, God." All succeeding presidents have followed this practice.

 Constitutional Heritage

According to the Constitution, who is in charge of the nation's military forces?

According to this section the president can form a cabinet of advisers. Every president, starting with George Washington, has appointed a cabinet.

Most of the president's appointments to office must be approved by the Senate.

~~the Choice of the President, the Person having the greatest Number of Votes of the Electors shall be the Vice President. But if there should remain two or more who have equal Votes, the Senate shall choose from them by Ballot the Vice President.~~

The Congress may determine the Time of choosing the Electors, and the Day on which they shall give their Votes; which Day shall be the same throughout the United States.

No Person except a natural born Citizen~~, or a Citizen of the United States, at the time of the Adoption of this Constitution,~~ shall be eligible to the Office of President; neither shall any Person be eligible to that Office who shall not have attained to the Age of thirty-five Years, and been fourteen Years a Resident within the United States.

In Case of the Removal of the President from Office, or of his Death, Resignation, or Inability to discharge the Powers and Duties of the said Office, the Same shall devolve on the Vice President, and the Congress may by Law provide for the Case of Removal, Death, Resignation or Inability, both of the President and Vice President, declaring what Officer shall then act as President, and such Officer shall act accordingly, until the Disability be removed, or a President shall be elected.

The President shall, at stated Times, receive for his Services, a Compensation, which shall neither be increased nor diminished during the Period for which he shall have been elected, and he shall not receive within that Period any other Emolument from the United States, or any of them.

Before he enter on the Execution of his Office, he shall take the following Oath or Affirmation:—"I do solemnly swear (or affirm) that I will faithfully execute the Office of President of the United States, and will to the best of my Ability, preserve, protect and defend the Constitution of the United States."

Section 2. The President shall be Commander in Chief of the Army and Navy of the United States, and of the Militia of the several States, when called into the actual Service of the United States; he may require the Opinion, in writing, of the principal Officer in each of the executive Departments, upon any Subject relating to the Duties of their respective Offices, and he shall have Power to grant Reprieves and Pardons for Offenses against the United States, except in Cases of Impeachment.

He shall have Power, by and with the Advice and Consent of the Senate, to make Treaties, provided two thirds of the Senators present concur; and he shall nominate, and by and with the Advice and Consent of the Senate, shall appoint Ambassadors, other public Ministers and Consuls, Judges of the supreme Court, and all other Officers of the United States, whose Appointments are not herein otherwise provided for, and which shall be established by Law: but the Congress may by Law vest the Appointment of such inferior Officers, as they think proper, in the President alone, in the Courts of Law, or in the Heads of Departments.

The President shall have Power to fill up all Vacancies that may happen during the Recess of the Senate, by granting Commissions which shall expire at the End of their next Session.

Section 3. He shall from time to time give to the Congress Information of the State of the Union, and recommend to their Consideration such Measures as he shall judge necessary and expedient; he may, on extraordinary Occasions, convene both Houses, or either of them, and in Case of Disagreement between them, with Respect to the Time of Adjournment, he may adjourn them to such Time as he shall think proper; he shall receive Ambassadors and other public Ministers; he shall take Care that the Laws be faithfully executed, and shall Commission all the Officers of the United States.

Section 4. The President, Vice President and all civil Officers of the United States, shall be removed from Office on Impeachment for, and Conviction of, Treason, Bribery, or other high Crimes and Misdemeanors.

ARTICLE III

Section 1. The judicial Power of the United States, shall be vested in one supreme Court, and in such inferior Courts as the Congress may from time to time ordain and establish. The Judges, both of the supreme and inferior Courts, shall hold their Offices during good Behavior, and shall, at stated Times, receive for their Services, a Compensation, which shall not be diminished during their Continuance in Office.

Section 2. The judicial Power shall extend to all Cases, in Law and Equity, arising under this Constitution, the Laws of the United States, and

The U.S. Supreme Court in the late 1990s

Every year the president presents to Congress a State of the Union message. In this message, the president explains the executive branch's legislative plans for the coming year.

This clause states that one of the president's duties is to enforce the laws.

 Constitutional Heritage

What actions might lead to the impeachment of a president, vice president, or other civil officer?

Judicial Branch
The Articles of Confederation did not make any provisions for a federal court system. One of the first things that the framers of the Constitution agreed upon was to set up a national judiciary. With all the laws that Congress would be enacting, there would be a great need for a branch of government to interpret the laws. In the Judiciary Act of 1789, Congress provided for the establishment of lower courts, such as district courts, circuit courts of appeals, and various other federal courts. The judicial system provides a check on the legislative branch; it can declare a law unconstitutional.

Treaties made, or which shall be made, under their Authority;—to all Cases affecting Ambassadors, other public Ministers and Consuls;—to all Cases of admiralty and maritime Jurisdiction;—to Controversies to which the United States shall be a Party;—to Controversies between two or more States;—between a State and Citizens of another State;—between Citizens of different States;—between Citizens of the same State claiming Lands under Grants of different States, and between a State, or the Citizens thereof, and foreign States, Citizens or Subjects.

In all Cases affecting Ambassadors, other public Ministers and Consuls, and those in which a State shall be Party, the supreme Court shall have original Jurisdiction. In all the other Cases before mentioned, the supreme Court shall have appellate Jurisdiction, both as to Law and fact, with such Exceptions, and under such Regulations as the Congress shall make.

The Trial of all Crimes, except in Cases of Impeachment, shall be by Jury; and such Trial shall be held in the State where the said Crimes shall have been committed; but when not committed within any State, the Trial shall be at such Place or Places as the Congress may by Law have directed.

Section 3. Treason against the United States, shall consist only in levying War against them, or in adhering to their Enemies, giving them Aid and Comfort. No Person shall be convicted of Treason unless on the Testimony of two Witnesses to the same overt Act, or on Confession in open Court.

The Congress shall have Power to declare the Punishment of Treason, but no Attainder of Treason shall work Corruption of Blood, or Forfeiture except during the Life of the Person attainted.

ARTICLE IV

Section 1. Full Faith and Credit shall be given in each State to the public Acts, Records, and judicial Proceedings of every other State. And the Congress may by general Laws prescribe the Manner in which such Acts, Records and Proceedings shall be proved, and the Effect thereof.

Section 2. The Citizens of each State shall be entitled to all Privileges and Immunities of Citizens in the several States.

A Person charged in any State with Treason, Felony, or other Crime, who shall flee from Justice, and be found in another State, shall on Demand of the executive Authority of the State from which he fled, be delivered up, to be removed to the State having Jurisdiction of the Crime.

No Person held to Service of Labor in one State, under the Laws thereof, escaping into another, shall, in Consequence of any Law or Regulation therein, be discharged from such Service or Labor, but shall be delivered up on Claim of the Party to whom such Service or Labor may be due.

Constitutional Heritage

What guidelines does the Constitution establish for criminal trials?

Congress has the power to decide the punishment for treason, but it can punish only the guilty person. Corruption of blood refers to punishing the family of a person who has committed treason. It is expressly forbidden by the Constitution.

The States
States must honor the laws, records, and court decisions of other states. A person cannot escape a legal obligation by moving from one state to another.

174 CONSTITUTION HANDBOOK

Section 3. New States may be admitted by the Congress into this Union; but no new State shall be formed or erected within the Jurisdiction of any other State; nor any State be formed by the Junction of two or more States, or Parts of States, without the Consent of the Legislatures of the States concerned as well as of the Congress.

The Congress shall have Power to dispose of and make all needful Rules and Regulations respecting the Territory or other Property belonging to the United States; and nothing in this Constitution shall be so construed as to Prejudice any Claims of the United States, or of any particular State.

Section 4. The United States shall guarantee to every State in this Union a Republican Form of Government, and shall protect each of them against Invasion; and on Application of the Legislature, or of the Executive (when the Legislature cannot be convened) against domestic Violence.

ARTICLE V

The Congress, whenever two thirds of both Houses shall deem it necessary, shall propose Amendments to this Constitution, or, on the Application of the Legislatures of two thirds of the several States, shall call a Convention for proposing Amendments, which, in either Case, shall be valid to all Intents and Purposes, as Part of this Constitution, when ratified by the Legislatures of three fourths of the several States, or by Conventions in three fourths thereof, as the one or the other Mode of Ratification may be proposed by the Congress; Provided that ~~no Amendment which may be made prior to the Year One thousand eight hundred and eight shall in any Manner affect the first and fourth Clauses in the Ninth Section of the first Article; and that~~ no State, without its Consent, shall be deprived of its equal Suffrage in the Senate.

ARTICLE VI

All Debts contracted and Engagements entered into, before the Adoption of this Constitution, shall be as valid against the United States under this Constitution, as under the Confederation.

This Constitution, and the Laws of the United States which shall be made in Pursuance thereof; and all Treaties made, or which shall be made, under the Authority of the United States, shall be the supreme Law of the Land; and the Judges in every State shall be bound thereby, any Thing in the Constitution or Laws of any State to the Contrary notwithstanding.

The Senators and Representatives before mentioned, and the Members of the several State Legislatures, and all executive and judicial Officers, both of the United States and of the several States, shall be bound by Oath or Affirmation, to support this Constitution; but no religious Test shall ever be required as a Qualification to any Office or public Trust under the United States.

Section 3 permits Congress to admit new states to the Union. When a group of people living in an area that is not part of an existing state wishes to form a new state, it asks Congress for permission to do so. The people then write a state constitution and offer it to Congress for approval. The state constitution must set up a representative form of government and must not in any way contradict the federal Constitution. If a majority of Congress approves the state constitution, the state is admitted as a member of the United States of America.

The Amendment Process
America's founders may not have realized just how enduring the Constitution would be, but they did make provisions for changing or adding to the Constitution. They did not want to make it easy to change the Constitution. There are two different ways in which changes can be proposed to the states and two different ways in which states can approve the changes and make them part of the Constitution.

National Supremacy
One of the biggest problems facing the delegates to the Constitutional Convention was the question of what would happen if a state law and a national law conflicted. Which law would be followed? Who decided? The second clause of Article VI answers those questions. When a national and state law are in conflict, the national law overrides the state law. The Constitution is the supreme law of the land. This clause is often called the "supremacy clause."

Ratification

The Articles of Confederation called for all 13 states to approve any revision to the Articles. The Constitution required that the vote of 9 out of the 13 states would be needed to ratify the Constitution. The first state to ratify was Delaware, on December 7, 1787. The last state to ratify the Constitution was Rhode Island, which finally did so on May 29, 1790, almost two and a half years later.

ARTICLE VII

The Ratification of the Conventions of nine States, shall be sufficient for the Establishment of this Constitution between the States so ratifying the Same.

Done in Convention by the Unanimous Consent of the States present the Seventeenth Day of September in the Year of our Lord one thousand seven hundred and Eighty seven and of the Independence of the United States of America the Twelfth. In witness whereof We have hereunto subscribed our Names.

George Washington—
President and deputy from Virginia

New Hampshire
John Langdon
Nicholas Gilman

Massachusetts
Nathaniel Gorham
Rufus King

Connecticut
William Samuel Johnson
Roger Sherman

New York
Alexander Hamilton

New Jersey
William Livingston
David Brearley
William Paterson
Jonathan Dayton

Pennsylvania
Benjamin Franklin
Thomas Mifflin
Robert Morris
George Clymer
Thomas FitzSimons
Jared Ingersoll
James Wilson
Gouverneur Morris

Delaware
George Read
Gunning Bedford Jr.
John Dickinson
Richard Bassett
Jacob Broom

Maryland
James McHenry
Daniel of St. Thomas Jenifer
Daniel Carroll

Virginia
John Blair
James Madison Jr.

North Carolina
William Blount
Richard Dobbs Spaight
Hugh Williamson

South Carolina
John Rutledge
Charles Cotesworth Pinckney
Charles Pinckney
Pierce Butler

Georgia
William Few
Abraham Baldwin

Attest: *William Jackson*, Secretary

THE AMENDMENTS

Articles in addition to, and Amendment of the Constitution of the United States of America, proposed by Congress, and ratified by the Legislatures of the several states, pursuant to the fifth Article of the original Constitution.

[The First through Tenth Amendments, now known as the Bill of Rights, were proposed on September 25, 1789, and declared in force on December 15, 1791.]

First Amendment

Congress shall make no law respecting an establishment of religion, or prohibiting the free exercise thereof; or abridging the freedom of speech, or of the press; or the right of the people peaceably to assemble, and to petition the Government for a redress of grievances.

Members of the Students Against Drunk Driving exercise their First Amendment right to expression by gathering in Washington, D.C., to speak out against drinking and driving.

Second Amendment

A well regulated Militia, being necessary to the security of a free State, the right of the people to keep and bear Arms, shall not be infringed.

The National Guard, which has replaced state militias, helps local citizens prevent a river from flooding.

Bill of Rights

One of the conditions set by several states for ratifying the Constitution was the inclusion of a bill of rights. Many people feared that a stronger central government might take away basic rights of the people that had been guaranteed in state constitutions. If the three words that begin the Preamble—"We the people"—were truly meant, then the rights of the people needed to be protected.

The First Amendment protects freedom of speech and expression, and forbids Congress to make any law "respecting an establishment of religion" or restraining the freedom to practice religion as one chooses.

 Constitutional Heritage

What rights do the First and Second Amendments guarantee?

Judges issue search warrants like this one to allow law enforcement officials to legally search a suspected criminal's property.

A police officer may enter a person's home with a search warrant, which allows the law officer to look for evidence that could convict someone of committing a crime.

The Fifth, Sixth, and Seventh Amendments describe the procedures that courts must follow when trying people accused of crimes. The Fifth Amendment guarantees that no one can be put on trial for a serious crime unless a grand jury agrees that the evidence justifies doing so. It also says that a person cannot be tried twice for the same crime.

The Sixth Amendment makes several promises, including a prompt trial and a trial by a jury chosen from the state and district in which the crime was committed. The Sixth Amendment also states that an accused person must be told why he or she is being tried and promises that an accused person has the right to be defended by a lawyer.

Third Amendment

No Soldier shall, in time of peace, be quartered in any house, without the consent of the Owner, nor in time of war, but in a manner to be prescribed by law.

Fourth Amendment

The right of the people to be secure in their persons, houses, papers, and effects, against unreasonable searches and seizures, shall not be violated, and no Warrants shall issue, but upon probable cause, supported by Oath or affirmation, and particularly describing the place to be searched, and the persons or things to be seized.

Fifth Amendment

No person shall be held to answer for a capital, or otherwise infamous crime, unless on a presentment or indictment of a Grand Jury, except in cases arising in the land or naval forces, or in the Militia, when in actual service in time of War or public danger; nor shall any person be subject for the same offense to be twice put in jeopardy of life or limb; nor shall be compelled in any criminal case to be a witness against himself, nor be deprived of life, liberty, or property, without due process of law; nor shall private property be taken for public use, without just compensation.

Sixth Amendment

In all criminal prosecutions, the accused shall enjoy the right to a speedy and public trial, by an impartial jury of the State and district wherein the crime shall have been committed, which district shall have been previously ascertained by law, and to be informed of the nature and

cause of the accusation; to be confronted with the witnesses against him; to have compulsory process for obtaining witnesses in his favor, and to have the Assistance of Counsel for his defense.

Seventh Amendment

In Suits at common law, where the value in controversy shall exceed twenty dollars, the right of trial by jury shall be preserved, and no fact tried by a jury shall be otherwise reexamined in any Court of the United States, than according to the rules of the common law.

Eighth Amendment

Excessive bail shall not be required, nor excessive fines imposed, nor cruel and unusual punishments inflicted.

Ninth Amendment

The enumeration in the Constitution, of certain rights, shall not be construed to deny or disparage others retained by the people.

Tenth Amendment

The powers not delegated to the United States by the Constitution, nor prohibited by it to the States, are reserved to the States respectively, or to the people.

Eleventh Amendment

[Proposed March 4, 1794; declared ratified January 8, 1798]

The Judicial power of the United States shall not be construed to extend to any suit in law or equity, commenced or prosecuted against one of the United States by Citizens of another State, or by Citizens or Subjects of any Foreign State.

Many Americans consider attendance in free public schools a right of citizenship.

The Seventh Amendment guarantees a trial by jury in cases that involve more than $20, but in modern times, usually much more money is at stake before a case is heard in federal court.

The Ninth and Tenth Amendments were added because not every right of the people or of the states could be listed in the Constitution.

 Constitutional Heritage

How does the Tenth Amendment limit the powers of the federal government?

The Twelfth Amendment changed the election procedure for president and vice president. Before this amendment, electors voted without distinguishing between president and vice president. Whoever received the most votes became president, and whoever received the next highest number of votes became vice president.

 Constitutional Heritage

According to the Twelfth Amendment, who chooses the president if no candidate has received a majority of the electoral votes?

Poster commemorating President Abraham Lincoln's Emancipation Proclamation, which freed slaves in the Confederacy

Twelfth Amendment

[Proposed December 9, 1803; declared ratified September 25, 1804]

The Electors shall meet in their respective states and vote by ballot for President and Vice President, one of whom, at least, shall not be an inhabitant of the same state with themselves; they shall name in their ballots the person voted for as President, and in distinct ballots the person voted for as Vice President, and they shall make distinct lists of all persons voted for as President, and of all persons voted for as Vice President, and of the number of votes for each, which lists they shall sign and certify, and transmit sealed to the seat of the government of the United States, directed to the President of the Senate;—The President of the Senate shall, in the presence of the Senate and House of Representatives, open all the certificates and the votes shall then be counted;—The person having the greatest number of votes for President, shall be the President, if such number be a majority of the whole number of Electors appointed; and if no person have such majority, then from the persons having the highest numbers not exceeding three on the list of those voted for as President, the House of Representatives shall choose immediately, by ballot, the President. But in choosing the President, the votes shall be taken by states, the representation from each state having one vote; a quorum for this purpose shall consist of a member or members from two thirds of the states, and a majority of all the states shall be necessary to a choice. ~~And if the House of Representatives shall not choose a President whenever the right of choice shall devolve upon them, before the fourth day of March next following, then the Vice-President shall act as President, as in the case of the death or other constitutional disability of the President;~~—The person having the greatest number of votes as Vice President, shall be the Vice President, if such number be a majority of the whole number of Electors appointed, and if no person have a majority, then from the two highest numbers on the list, the Senate shall choose the Vice President; a quorum for the purpose shall consist of two thirds of the whole number of Senators, and a majority of the whole number shall be necessary to a choice. But no person constitutionally ineligible to the office of President shall be eligible to that of Vice President of the United States.

Thirteenth Amendment

[Proposed January 31, 1865; declared ratified December 18, 1865]

Section 1. Neither slavery nor involuntary servitude, except as a punishment for crime whereof the party shall have been duly convicted, shall exist within the United States, or any place subject to their jurisdiction.

Section 2. Congress shall have power to enforce this article by appropriate legislation.

Fourteenth Amendment

[Proposed June 13, 1866; declared ratified July 28, 1868]

Section 1. All persons born or naturalized in the United States and subject to the jurisdiction thereof, are citizens of the United States and of the State wherein they reside. No State shall make or enforce any law which shall abridge the privileges or immunities of citizens of the United States; nor shall any State deprive any person of life, liberty, or property, without due process of law; nor deny to any person within its jurisdiction the equal protection of the laws.

Section 2. Representatives shall be apportioned among the several States according to their respective numbers, counting the whole number of persons in each State, excluding Indians not taxed. But when the right to vote at any election for the choice of electors for President and Vice President of the United States, Representatives in Congress, the Executive and Judicial officers of a State, or the members of the Legislature thereof, is denied to any of the male inhabitants of such State, being twenty-one years of age, and citizens of the United States, or in any way abridged, except for participation in rebellion, or other crime, the basis of representation therein shall be reduced in the proportion which the number of such male citizens shall bear to the whole number of male citizens twenty-one years of age in such State.

Section 3. No person shall be a Senator or Representative in Congress, or elector of President and Vice President, or hold any office, civil or military, under the United States, or under any State, who, having previously taken an oath, as a member of Congress, or as an officer of the United States, or as a member of any State legislature, or as an executive or judicial officer of any State, to support the Constitution of the United States, shall have engaged in insurrection or rebellion against the same, or given aid or comfort to the enemies thereof. But Congress may by a vote of two thirds of each House, remove such disability.

Section 4. The validity of the public debt of the United States, authorized by law, including debts incurred for payment of pensions and bounties for services in suppressing insurrection or rebellion, shall not be questioned. But neither the United States nor any State shall assume or pay any debt or obligation incurred in aid of insurrection or rebellion against the United States, or any claim for the loss or emancipation of any slave; but all such debts, obligations and claims shall be held illegal and void.

Section 5. The Congress shall have power to enforce, by appropriate legislation, the provisions of this article.

Fifteenth Amendment

[Proposed February 26, 1869; declared ratified March 30, 1870]

Section 1. The right of citizens of the United States to vote shall not be denied or abridged by the United States or by any State on account of race, color, or previous condition of servitude.

Section 2. The Congress shall have power to enforce this article by appropriate legislation.

Constitutional Heritage

According to the Fourteenth Amendment, who is a citizen of the United States, and what rights do citizens have?

In 1833 Chief Justice John Marshall ruled that the Bill of Rights limited the national government but not the state governments. The later effect of this ruling was that states were able to keep African Americans from becoming state citizens. If African Americans were not citizens, they were not protected by the Bill of Rights. The Fourteenth Amendment defines citizenship and prevents states from interfering in the rights of citizens of the United States.

The Fifteenth Amendment extended the right to vote to African American men.

Expanding on the federal government's right to levy taxes, outlined in Article I of the Constitution, the Sixteenth Amendment gave Congress the power to issue the income tax.

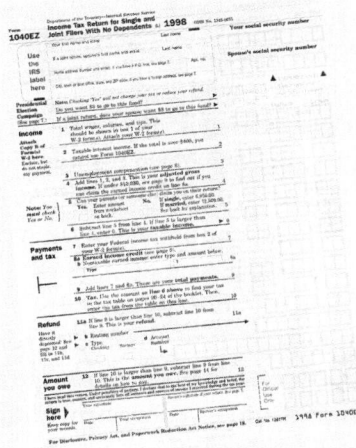

Federal income tax form

 Constitutional Heritage

What new provisions does the Seventeenth Amendment establish for the election of senators?

Sixteenth Amendment

[Proposed July 12, 1909; declared ratified February 25, 1913]

The Congress shall have power to lay and collect taxes on incomes, from whatever source derived, without apportionment among the several States, and without regard to any census or enumeration.

Seventeenth Amendment

[Proposed May 13, 1912; declared ratified May 31, 1913]

The Senate of the United States shall be composed of two Senators from each State, elected by the people thereof, for six years; and each Senator shall have one vote. The electors in each State shall have the qualifications requisite for electors of the most numerous branch of the State legislatures.

When vacancies happen in the representation of any State in the Senate, the executive authority of such State shall issue writs of election to fill such vacancies: Provided, That the legislature of any State may empower the executive thereof to make temporary appointments until the people fill the vacancies by election as the legislature may direct.

This amendment shall not be so construed as to affect the election or term of any Senator chosen before it becomes valid as part of the Constitution.

Although many people believed that prohibition was good for the health and welfare of the American people, the Eighteenth Amendment was repealed 14 years later.

Eighteenth Amendment

[Proposed December 18, 1917; declared ratified January 29, 1919; repealed by the Twenty-first Amendment December 5, 1933]

Section 1. After one year from the ratification of this article the manufacture, sale, or transportation of intoxicating liquors within, the importation thereof into, or the exportation thereof from the United States and all territory subject to the jurisdiction thereof for beverage purposes is hereby prohibited.

Section 2. The Congress and the several States shall have concurrent power to enforce this article by appropriate legislation.

Section 3. This article shall be inoperative unless it shall have been ratified as an amendment to the Constitution by the legislatures of the several States, as provided in the Constitution, within seven years from the date of the submission hereof to the States by the Congress.

Federal agents dispose of alcohol after the passage of the Eighteenth Amendment.

Nineteenth Amendment

[Proposed June 4, 1919; declared ratified August 26, 1920]

The right of citizens of the United States to vote shall not be denied or abridged by the United States or by any State on account of sex.

Congress shall have power to enforce this article by appropriate legislation.

Twentieth Amendment

[Proposed March 2, 1932; declared ratified February 6, 1933]

Women's suffrage button

Section 1. The terms of the President and Vice President shall end at noon on the 20th day of January, and the terms of Senators and Representatives at noon on the 3rd day of January, of the years in which such terms would have ended if this article had not been ratified; and the terms of their successors shall then begin.

Section 2. The Congress shall assemble at least once in every year, and such meeting shall begin at noon on the 3rd day of January, unless they shall by law appoint a different day.

Section 3. If, at the time fixed for the beginning of the term of the President, the President elect shall have died, the Vice President elect shall become President. If a President shall not have been chosen before the time fixed for the beginning of his term, or if the President elect shall have failed to qualify, then the Vice President elect shall act as President until a President shall have qualified; and the Congress may by law provide for the case wherein neither a President elect nor a Vice President elect shall have qualified, declaring who shall then act as President, or the manner in which one who is to act shall be selected, and such persons shall act accordingly until a President or Vice President shall have qualified.

Section 4. The Congress may by law provide for the case of the death of any of the persons from whom the House of Representatives may choose a President whenever the right of choice shall have devolved upon them, and for the case of the death of any of the persons from whom the Senate may choose a Vice President whenever the right of choice shall have devolved upon them.

~~**Section 5.** Sections 1 and 2 shall take effect on the 15th day of October following the ratification of this article.~~

~~**Section 6.** This article shall be inoperative unless it shall have been ratified as an amendment to the Constitution by the legislatures of three fourths of the several States within seven years from the date of its submission.~~

Abigail Adams was disappointed that the Declaration of Independence and the Constitution did not specifically include women. It took almost 150 years and much campaigning by women's suffrage groups for women to finally achieve voting privileges.

In the original Constitution, a newly elected president and Congress did not take office until March 4, which was four months after the November election. The officials who were leaving office were called "lame ducks" because they had little influence during those four months. The Twentieth Amendment changed the date that the new president and Congress take office. Members of Congress now take office on January 3, and the president takes office on January 20.

 Constitutional Heritage

According to the Twentieth Amendment, who becomes president if a president-elect dies before taking office?

The Twenty-first Amendment is the only amendment that has been ratified by state conventions rather than by state legislatures.

From the time of President Washington's administration, it was a custom for presidents to serve no more than two terms of office. Franklin D. Roosevelt, however, was elected to four consecutive terms. The Twenty-second Amendment made into law the custom of a two-term limit for each president.

 Constitutional Heritage

How does the Twenty-second Amendment limit the years a president can remain in office?

Until the Twenty-third Amendment, the residents of Washington, D.C., could not vote in presidential elections.

Aerial view of Washington, D.C.

Twenty-first Amendment

[Proposed February 20, 1933; declared ratified December 5, 1933]

Section 1. The eighteenth article of amendment to the Constitution of the United States is hereby repealed.

Section 2. The transportation or importation into any State, Territory, or possession of the United States for delivery or use therein of intoxicating liquors, in violation of the laws thereof, is hereby prohibited.

~~Section 3. This article shall be inoperative unless it shall have been ratified as an amendment to the Constitution by conventions in the several States, as provided in the Constitution, within seven years from the date of the submission hereof to the States by the Congress.~~

Twenty-second Amendment

[Proposed March 24, 1947; declared ratified March 1, 1951]

Section 1. No person shall be elected to the office of the President more than twice, and no person who has held the office of President, or acted as President, for more than two years of a term to which some other person was elected President shall be elected to the office of the President more than once. ~~But this Article shall not apply to any person holding the office of President when this Article was proposed by the Congress, and shall not prevent any person who may be holding the office of President, or acting as President, during the term within which this Article becomes operative from holding the office of President or acting as President during the remainder of such term.~~

~~Section 2. This Article shall be inoperative unless it shall have been ratified as an amendment to the Constitution by the legislatures of three fourths of the several States within seven years from the date of its submission to the States by the Congress.~~

Twenty-third Amendment

[Proposed June 16, 1960; declared ratified April 3, 1961]

Section 1. The District constituting the seat of Government of the United States shall appoint in such manner as the Congress may direct:

A number of electors of President and Vice President equal to the whole number of Senators and Representatives in Congress to which the District would be entitled if it were a State, but in no event more than the least populous State; they shall be in addition to those appointed by the States, but they shall be considered, for the purposes of the election of President and Vice President, to be electors appointed by a State; and they shall meet in the District and perform such duties as provided by the twelfth article of amendment.

Section 2. The Congress shall have power to enforce this article by appropriate legislation.

Twenty-fourth Amendment

[Proposed August 27, 1962; declared ratified February 4, 1964]

Section 1. The right of citizens of the United States to vote in any primary or other election for President or Vice President, for electors for President or Vice President, or for Senator or Representative in Congress, shall not be denied or abridged by the United States or any State by reason of failure to pay any poll tax or other tax.

Section 2. The Congress shall have power to enforce this article by appropriate legislation.

Twenty-fifth Amendment

[Proposed July 6, 1965; declared ratified February 23, 1967]

Section 1. In case of removal of the President from office or of his death or resignation, the Vice President shall become President.

Section 2. Whenever there is a vacancy in the office of the Vice President, the President shall nominate a Vice President who shall take office upon confirmation by a majority vote of both Houses of Congress.

Vice President Lyndon Johnson was sworn in as president after John F. Kennedy's assassination.

Section 3. Whenever the President transmits to the President pro tempore of the Senate and the Speaker of the House of Representatives his written declaration that he is unable to discharge the powers and duties of his office, and until he transmits to them a written declaration to the contrary, such powers and duties shall be discharged by the Vice President as Acting President.

Section 4. Whenever the Vice President and a majority of either the principal officers of the executive departments or of such other body as Congress may by law provide, transmit to the President pro tempore of the Senate and the Speaker of the House of Representatives their written declaration that the President is unable to discharge the powers and duties of his office, the Vice President shall immediately assume the powers and duties of the office as Acting President.

Thereafter, when the President transmits to the President pro tempore of the Senate and the Speaker of the House of Representatives his written declaration that no inability exists, he shall resume the powers and duties of his office unless the Vice President and a majority of either the principal officers of the executive department or of such other body as Congress may by law provide, transmit within four days to the President pro tempore of

Constitutional Heritage

What practices does the Twenty-fourth Amendment outlaw?

The illness of President Eisenhower in the 1950s and the assassination of President Kennedy in 1963 were the events behind the Twenty-fifth Amendment. The Constitution did not provide a clear-cut method for a vice president to take over for a disabled president or in the event of the death of a president. This amendment provides for filling the office of the vice president if a vacancy occurs. It also provides a way for the vice president to take over if the president is unable to perform the duties of that office.

According to the Twenty-seventh Amendment, if senators or representatives were to vote for a pay raise for themselves, when would it take effect?

The Voting Act of 1970 tried to set the voting age at 18 years old. However, the Supreme Court ruled that the act set the voting age for national elections only, not state or local elections. This ruling would make necessary several different ballots at elections. The Twenty-sixth Amendment gave 18-year-old citizens the right to vote in all elections.

the Senate and the Speaker of the House of Representatives their written declaration that the President is unable to discharge the powers and duties of his office. Thereupon Congress shall decide the issue, assembling within forty-eight hours for that purpose if not in session. If the Congress, within twenty-one days after receipt of the latter written declaration, or, if Congress is not in session, within twenty-one days after Congress is required to assemble, determines by two-thirds vote of both Houses that the President is unable to discharge the powers and duties of his office, the Vice President shall continue to discharge the same as Acting President; otherwise, the President shall resume the powers and duties of his office.

Twenty-sixth Amendment
[Proposed March 23, 1971; declared ratified July 5, 1971]

Section 1. The right of citizens of the United States, who are eighteen years of age or older, to vote shall not be denied or abridged by the United States or by any State on account of age.

Section 2. The Congress shall have power to enforce this article by appropriate legislation.

Twenty-seventh Amendment
[Proposed September 25, 1789; declared ratified May 7, 1992]

No law, varying the compensation for the services of the Senators and Representatives, shall take effect, until an election of Representatives shall have intervened.

These students are helping a local candidate campaign for office.

Amendments to the Constitution

Amendment	Year Enacted	Subject
1st	1791	Personal and political freedoms
2nd	1791	Right to keep weapons
3rd	1791	Quartering of troops
4th	1791	Search and seizure; search warrants
5th	1791	Rights of accused persons
6th	1791	Speedy trial
7th	1791	Jury trial
8th	1791	Bails, fines, punishments
9th	1791	Rights of the people
10th	1791	Powers of the states
11th	1798	Suits against the states
12th	1804	Election of president and vice president
13th	1865	Abolition of slavery
14th	1868	Rights of citizens; privileges and immunities, due process, and equal protection
15th	1870	Extension of suffrage to African American men
16th	1913	Income tax
17th	1913	Direct election of senators
18th	1919	Prohibition of liquor
19th	1920	Women's suffrage
20th	1933	Change in dates for presidential and congressional terms of office
21st	1933	Repeal of prohibition
22nd	1951	Two-term limit on presidential tenure
23rd	1961	Right to vote in presidential elections for residents of the District of Columbia
24th	1964	Poll tax banned in federal elections
25th	1967	Presidential disability and succession
26th	1971	Lowering of voting age to 18
27th	1992	Legislative salaries

THE GRANGER COLLECTION, NEW YORK

The Bill of Rights

Slave chains

Women's suffrage button

VOTES FOR WOMEN

Voter registration form

VOTER REGISTRATION CARD

1789–1815
A Strong Start for the Nation

New York zoological garden

COLLECTION OF THE NEW-YORK HISTORICAL SOCIETY

1798
Science and Technology
The first steamboat west of the Allegheny Mountains is built in Kentucky.

1798
Business and Finance
The pay of U.S. Army privates is raised from $4 to $6 a month.

1801
Daily Life
Some 200 different newspapers are published throughout the United States.

1789
Daily Life
The first zoological garden is advertised in New York.

1791
The Arts
Susanna H. Rowson publishes the novel *Charlotte, a Tale of Truth*, which sells 50,000 copies over the next two decades.

U.S. Army officer and private

1789 **1791** **1793** **1795** **1797** **1799** **1801**

1790
The Arts
George Washington sits 12 times to have his portrait painted by John Trumbull.

1794
Science and Technology
Construction begins on the USS *Constitution* in Boston, Massachusetts.

1798
Politics
A Federalist majority in Congress passes the Alien and Sedition Acts.

1800
Business and Finance
The financial holdings of all Americans total some $1.8 billion.

1789
World Events
French revolutionaries storm the Bastille in Paris.

The Storming of the Bastille

USS Constitution

1800
Daily Life
Charles Willson Peale presents a lecture series, "The Science of Nature," in his natural history museum in Philadelphia.

Before You Read

Build on What You Know

Victory in the Revolutionary War brought new challenges to the American people. Revolutionary leaders struggled to form a new, unified nation. After the failures of the Articles of Confederation, a new plan of government was developed at the Constitutional Convention. Newly elected government officials—the president and the members of Congress—set out to put the Constitution into action. In this chapter you will learn how the new federal government successfully addressed some of the problems at home and abroad.

Napoleon Bonaparte

The signing of the Treaty of Ghent

THE GRANGER COLLECTION, NEW YORK

1803
The Arts
Benjamin Latrobe takes over the construction of the U.S. Capitol Building.

1807
World Events
Great Britain's Parliament abolishes the slave trade in the British Empire.

1808
World Events
Napoleon I places his brother, Joseph, on Spain's throne.

1811
World Events
Paraguay becomes the first former Spanish colony in South America to gain independence.

1814
Politics
The United States and Britain sign the Treaty of Ghent, ending the War of 1812.

1814
The Arts
Francis Scott Key writes the poem "The Star-Spangled Banner" after viewing the British bombardment of Fort McHenry.

| **1803** | **1805** | **1807** | **1809** | **1811** | **1813** | **1815** |

1807
Science and Technology
The College of Physicians and Surgeons is established in New York City.

1810
The Arts
The first troupe of professional actors arrives in Kentucky.

1812
Politics
New York passes a law authorizing the state to pay for elementary school for children.

1815
Business and Finance
Daily wages for laborers range from 80 cents in rural areas to $1.50 in towns.

The U.S. Capitol Building in 1810

Elementary school reading textbook

Think About Themes

Themes Journal

Decide whether you agree or disgree with the following statements. Note why in your journal.

Constitutional Heritage Guaranteed protection of individual rights is needed even under a democratic government.

Economic Development The federal government should regulate economic development and everyday business practices.

Democratic Values The existence of competing political parties will always serve to strengthen a democracy.

A Federal Government is Established

OBJECTIVES

Read to understand:

1. what key decisions the first Congress made, and how they affected the nation
2. what the arguments for and against Hamilton's debt proposal were
3. why some Americans opposed a national bank
4. what conflicts occurred on the frontier in the 1790s

KEY TERMS

Bill of Rights
Judiciary Act of 1789
cabinet
capitalism
Bank of the United States
strict construction
loose construction
Whiskey Rebellion
Battle of Fallen Timbers
Treaty of Greenville

KEY PEOPLE

Alexander Hamilton
Little Turtle
Anthony Wayne

EYEWITNESSES TO History

66 *[For nearly] half a mile, you could see little else along the shore, in the street, and on board every vessel, but heads standing as thick as ears of corn before a harvest.* 99

—Elias Boudinot

Cup celebrating Washington's presidency

This observer described the scene on April 23, 1789. Crowds of people gathered to welcome President-elect George Washington. Tens of thousands of Americans flocked to New York City, the nation's temporary capital, to witness the event. Celebrations had been staged along the route that Washington followed from Mount Vernon, Virginia. Washington had been greeted by official delegations, military escorts, fireworks, bells, cannon fire, and triumphal arches. As he neared his destination, the crowds gathered in the streets and along the New York shore to welcome the boat carrying him. A parade accompanied Washington to the presidential mansion. One week later, Washington took his oath of office on the balcony of Federal Hall on Wall Street. As his last words echoed in the air, the crowd burst into wild cheers.

The First President

When Congress opened the ballots from the states on April 6, 1789, the unanimous choice for U.S. president was George Washington. This choice was not surprising. Washington's popularity had soared since the Continental Army's victory at Yorktown. Some Antifederalists who had hesitated to ratify the Constitution did so with the expectation that Washington would serve as the first president. Pierce Butler, a member of Congress, believed that the powers granted to the president in the Constitution would not have been so great "had not many of the members cast their eyes toward General Washington as President; and shaped their Ideas of the Powers to be given to a President, by their opinions of his Virtue."

Washington said he was reluctant to accept this honor, however. He doubted his abilities and feared that people would think that he wanted to be a king. Leaving his beloved Mount Vernon for his inauguration, he said he felt like "a culprit who is going to the place of his execution."

Washington and the other elected officials knew that each step they took would set a precedent, or guide, for future leaders. Although the spotlight was focused on Washington, the task of molding the new government belonged to the first Congress. The people's representatives needed to make critical decisions about policies and procedures. They faced a challenging agenda.

The first order of business was to add a protection of individual liberties to the Constitution to limit the power of the central government. Supporters of the Constitution had promised this during the struggle for ratification. From the 210 proposed amendments, 12 were recommended by Congress for adoption. Ten were ratified by the states in 1791. These amendments became known as the

THE GRANGER COLLECTION, NEW YORK

George Washington rides to his inauguration.

Bill of Rights. The Bill of Rights guarantees U.S. citizens specific rights, such as freedom of speech, religion, and the press. It sets out some rules for criminal and trial procedures. It also recognizes that states or the people retain the powers not specifically delegated to the federal government or prohibited by the Constitution.

Congress then created a federal court system. After much debate, Congress passed the **Judiciary Act of 1789**, which established a federal district court for each state. It specified that there would be five associate justices of the Supreme Court to be nominated by the president and approved by the Senate. The act also defined the courts' powers. Washington wrote to the justices about the importance of their positions. He said, "The happiness of the people of the United States depend[s] in a considerable degree on the interpretation and execution of its laws."

During its first session Congress also created three departments to assist the president. These were the State Department, to handle foreign affairs; the War Department, to manage military affairs; and the Treasury Department, to oversee the nation's finances. The president appointed the secretaries, or heads, of these departments to serve as his advisers. Over time, these advisers became known as the president's **cabinet**. Washington's first cabinet included Thomas Jefferson as secretary of state, Henry Knox as secretary of war, and Alexander Hamilton as secretary of the treasury. The president also appointed an attorney general, Edmund Randolph, to advise him on legal matters.

✔ **READING CHECK:** What key decisions did the first Congress make, and how did these actions strengthen the new nation?

Restoring the Nation's Credit

After years of war and deficit spending, the U.S. government had inherited serious financial problems. The treasury had neither the funds to pay off war debts nor the money to run the government. Congress therefore tackled the nation's finances.

BIOGRAPHY
Alexander Hamilton

The secretary of the treasury. Lawmakers turned to Secretary of the Treasury Alexander Hamilton, President Washington's most trusted adviser, for help. In doing so, they set an important precedent. Though Congress is responsible for passing laws, from its beginning it has sought guidance from the executive branch.

The slight, fair-haired Hamilton was one of the most brilliant—and often controversial—of the nation's founders. He was born in the British West Indies in 1755, the son of a failed Scottish merchant. At an early age he went to work in an accounting office, where his skills at business became evident. In 1773 Hamilton

---

The Religious Spirit

SEPARATION OF CHURCH AND STATE

The principle of the separation of church and state, as set forth in the Bill of Rights, was uniquely American. While French and Spanish governments were influenced by the Catholic Church and the British government was influenced by the Anglican Church, the U.S. government was not directly tied to any one church.

New England church bell

Although colonial America was settled by people of various religious beliefs, most colonists were Christian. Despite the numerous religious groups in the colonies, most colonies used tax revenue to support specific churches. These include the Congregational Church in New England and the Anglican Church in the middle and southern colonies. Eager to promote national unity, the framers of the U.S. Constitution followed the lead of the state constitutions and established a separation of church and state. This policy prevented possible divisions among delegates holding different religious beliefs.

Even with this separation of church and state, American life remained deeply influenced by religious beliefs. After visiting the new nation in the 1830s, Frenchman Alexis de Tocqueville observed, "In the United States religion exercises but little influence upon the laws and upon the details of public opinion, but it directs the manners of the community." ▪

Bill of Rights

First Amendment
guarantees freedom of religion, speech, and the press and the right to assemble peacefully and to petition the government.

Second Amendment
recognizes the necessity of state militias and thus the right to bear arms.

Third Amendment
prohibits quartering of troops without consent as regulated by law.

Fourth Amendment
prohibits searches and seizures without warrants, which can be issued only upon probable cause.

Fifth Amendment
requires a grand jury indictment before persons can be tried for serious criminal charges; prohibits persons from being tried twice for the same offense; prohibits forcing the accused to testify against themselves; guarantees that no one may be deprived of life, liberty, or property without due process of law.

Sixth Amendment
guarantees the right to a speedy trial in criminal cases, the right to know all charges, the right to question and obtain witnesses, and the right to have counsel.

Seventh Amendment
guarantees a jury trial in most civil cases.

Eighth Amendment
prohibits excessive fines and bail; prohibits cruel and unusual punishment.

Ninth Amendment
protects individual rights not specifically mentioned in the Constitution.

Tenth Amendment
reserves for the states and the people those powers not delegated to the national government or prohibited by the Constitution.

THE GRANGER COLLECTION, NEW YORK

Adam Smith's **Wealth of Nations** *called for limited government influence in the economy. It greatly influenced Alexander Hamilton.*

went to New York City, where he attended King's College, now Columbia University. Ambitious for public service, he read widely about political processes and even produced an influential revolutionary paper while still a teenager. He served as an aid to General Washington during the Revolutionary War. He was also a delegate to the Constitutional Convention and helped write the *Federalist Papers*. Through his writings and economic and political involvements, he exerted almost as great an influence on the young republic as the early presidents did.

Hamilton believed that the nation's future depended on a strong federal government controlled by the wealthy. Although his own wealth was self-made, he had little faith in the ability of common people to govern. They were, he said, "turbulent and changing" and made decisions based on their immediate needs. As he wrote in the *Federalist Papers,* "The people commonly *intend* the PUBLIC GOOD," but they do not "always *reason right* about the *means* of promoting it."

Hamilton's strong belief in federalism shaped his economic policy. He believed that one of the best ways to strengthen the government, both financially and politically, was to establish economic policies that helped business and industry. If businesspeople believed that the federal government had their best interests at heart, they would support its policies.

Scottish economist Adam Smith influenced Hamilton's views. In his 1776 book *Wealth of Nations*, Smith stated that industry and commerce—not just farming— were the most important sources of wealth. Smith supported **capitalism**—an economic system based on a free market and private ownership of property.

Hamilton's proposals. As a first step toward convincing the merchant class to support the new federal government, Hamilton advised Congress to strengthen the nation's credit by beginning to pay off the national debt. This was the money that the federal government owed to its creditors. Hamilton knew that a nation that did not pay its debts would have trouble borrowing additional money.

The total national and state debt was estimated to be a staggering $77 million, reflecting the heavy costs of the Revolutionary War. Included in this amount was about $40 million the Continental Congress still owed to individuals from whom it had borrowed money during the war. Most of this money had been obtained by selling government bonds. These are certificates issued by a government in exchange for loans. Each bond represented the government's promise to repay the loan plus interest. The government's credit had fallen so low, however, that its bonds were almost worthless. Many bondholders had panicked and sold their bonds to speculators, who bought them at a fraction of the original cost.

Hamilton's proposal to eventually pay the bonds in full caused an uproar. His critics rightly charged that speculators stood to make a fortune. Many of the original investors, though, would receive no compensation for their support of the government during the war. One farmer complained in the *Pennsylvania Gazette*.

PRESIDENTIAL *Lives*

1732–1799
In Office 1789–1797

George Washington

As president, George Washington refused to isolate himself from the general public, saying he did not want to be shut away "like an eastern Lama [holy man]." He set up a schedule for greeting citizens in his official residence. On Tuesday afternoons he met with men. On Friday evenings he and his wife, Martha, served refreshments to men and women.

Washington also had government officials to dinner every Thursday, rotating the invitations to avoid any appearance of playing favorites. The dinners were not formal functions as much as they were festive occasions. Washington loved social gatherings of all kinds, from intimate tea parties to fox hunts and lavish balls. He enjoyed playing games, attending the theater, and sharing good food and conversation.

> 66 [The] proposed funding system is grossly oppressive upon the poor soldiers and officers of the American army. They must all pay taxes, to raise their certificates to their full value in the hands of the purchasers of them. . . . For then, instead of being paid by the United States for their services, or for their limbs, they are brought in debt to them. 99

Government bonds such as this one were used by the U.S. government during the Revolutionary War to raise money.

In the end, however, Congress agreed with Hamilton that restoring the nation's credit depended on honoring these bonds. Hamilton's next proposal—that the federal government take over about $21.5 million of the $25 million in state debts—roused even stronger opposition. Many of the southern states had already paid most of their debts. They saw no reason why they should help pay the debts of other states. Only a last-minute compromise saved the plan. In return for southern votes, Hamilton's supporters pledged that the national capital would be moved from Philadelphia to a site across the Potomac River from Virginia. Virginians believed this new location, later named Washington, D.C. (District of Columbia), would give them more influence in the federal government.

✔ **READING CHECK:** What were the arguments for and against Alexander Hamilton's debt proposal?

Hamilton's Bank Proposal

Establishing good credit was not the only answer to the nation's financial woes. Alexander Hamilton asked Congress to create the **Bank of the United States**, or National Bank, consisting of a central bank with branches in major U.S. cities. Hamilton believed that such a bank would provide a safe place to deposit government funds; a sound, uniform currency issued in the form of banknotes, or paper money; and a source of loans to assist the government.

Hamilton argued that the nation had much to gain from the creation of the National Bank. Many Americans, particularly southern planters who depended on credit, did not share his enthusiasm. They feared that the Bank would be controlled by wealthy northeastern merchants. Others were suspicious of all banks. A Maryland representative stated, "This bank will raise in this country a moneyed interest at the devotion of Government; it may bribe both States and individuals."

Secretary of State Thomas Jefferson raised a more serious objection. He said that the proposed Bank was illegal. Nowhere in the Constitution had the federal government been given the power to set up a bank. Jefferson believed that the government could do only what the Constitution specifically allows. This philosophy of narrow constitutional interpretation is called **strict construction**.

Hamilton, on the other hand, supported the philosophy of constitutional interpretation called **loose construction**. That is, he believed that within broad limits the government can do anything the Constitution does not specifically forbid. In support of this view, he pointed to the clause in the Constitution that grants Congress the power "to make all laws . . . necessary and proper" for carrying out its constitutional powers. The government's power to collect taxes and borrow money could only be properly exercised, he argued, with the aid of a national bank.

In the end, President Washington sided with Hamilton. Congress chartered the Bank of the United States in 1791. The charter granted the Bank the right to operate for 20 years. The charter also provided that the Bank be jointly owned by the government and private investors.

✔ **READING CHECK:** Why did some Americans oppose a national bank?

Domestic Difficulties

Alexander Hamilton's next task was to raise the money to pay the government's debts. He did not believe it was necessary or possible to pay off the entire amount right away. He was more concerned with getting the nation on a secure financial footing with enough income to keep it running. Hamilton knew that the tariffs alone could not raise as much money as the nation needed. He asked Congress to impose a tax on certain domestically produced items, most notably whiskey. The tax was to be paid by whiskey producers.

The Whiskey Rebellion. The new tax on whiskey hit western farmers the hardest. Many farmers turned their surplus grain—their most important crop—into whiskey. The beverage was easy to transport to eastern markets, where it was used to barter for supplies. News of the tax infuriated the farmers. An anonymous poet described their reaction, "Their liberty they will maintain, They fought for't, and they'll fight again."

INTERPRETING THE VISUAL RECORD

U.S. currency. The U.S. Mint began to produce coins in 1792, providing a stable currency in the early years of the nation. *How do the decorative features on these coins represent the founding values of the United States?*

Read More About It

Free Find:

Alexander Hamilton
After reading the selection on Alexander Hamilton on the **Holt Researcher** CD–ROM, write a short essay explaining his contribution to the new government of the United States.

In June 1794 Congress passed a bill authorizing collection of the tax. When a federal marshal served notices to 75 men in western Pennsylvania ordering them to appear in court, a group of farmers gathered to spread the word that "the Federal Sheriff is taking away men." Some 500 men attacked federal officials, tarring and feathering some. They also burned the home of the head revenue agent.

The protesters then organized a larger militia that included residents of Pittsburgh. The newly formed units included some 6,000 men as well as a number of women. These discontented people intended to march on Philadelphia, then the nation's capital.

The **Whiskey Rebellion** challenged federal authority. President Washington called out the militias from Maryland, New Jersey, Pennsylvania, and Virginia, but many men resisted these orders. Still, Washington assembled a force of some 13,000 men, larger than any he had personally led during the Revolutionary War.

When faced with the threat of this force, the "Whiskey Boys" quickly melted away into the backwoods. Washington's troops captured only about 20 rebels.

Conflict on the frontier.
Even more serious trouble brewed in the Northwest Territory. American settlers continued to enter into the territory that American Indians believed they had a right to use. Peaceful efforts to work out terms of land ownership failed, partially from the lack of trust on both sides. A Shawnee spokesperson noted, "From all quarters we receive speeches from the Americans, and not one is alike. We suppose that they intend to deceive us."

Some 1,500 members of various tribes joined together in a loose confederation to defend their homes. Miami chief Michikinikwa (mi-chee-ken-EEK-wah), known as Little Turtle, commanded the group. A gifted strategist, Little Turtle led his warriors against U.S. forces. In 1791 Little Turtle's warriors soundly defeated U.S. troops in a battle along the Wabash River in present-day Indiana.

The defeat stunned the government. In response, President Washington ordered some 3,000 soldiers to protect the frontier. Revolutionary War hero Anthony "Mad Anthony" Wayne—so called because of his daring feats during

THE GRANGER COLLECTION, NEW YORK

During the Whiskey Rebellion, tax collectors and federal marshals were tarred and feathered by mobs of angry farmers.

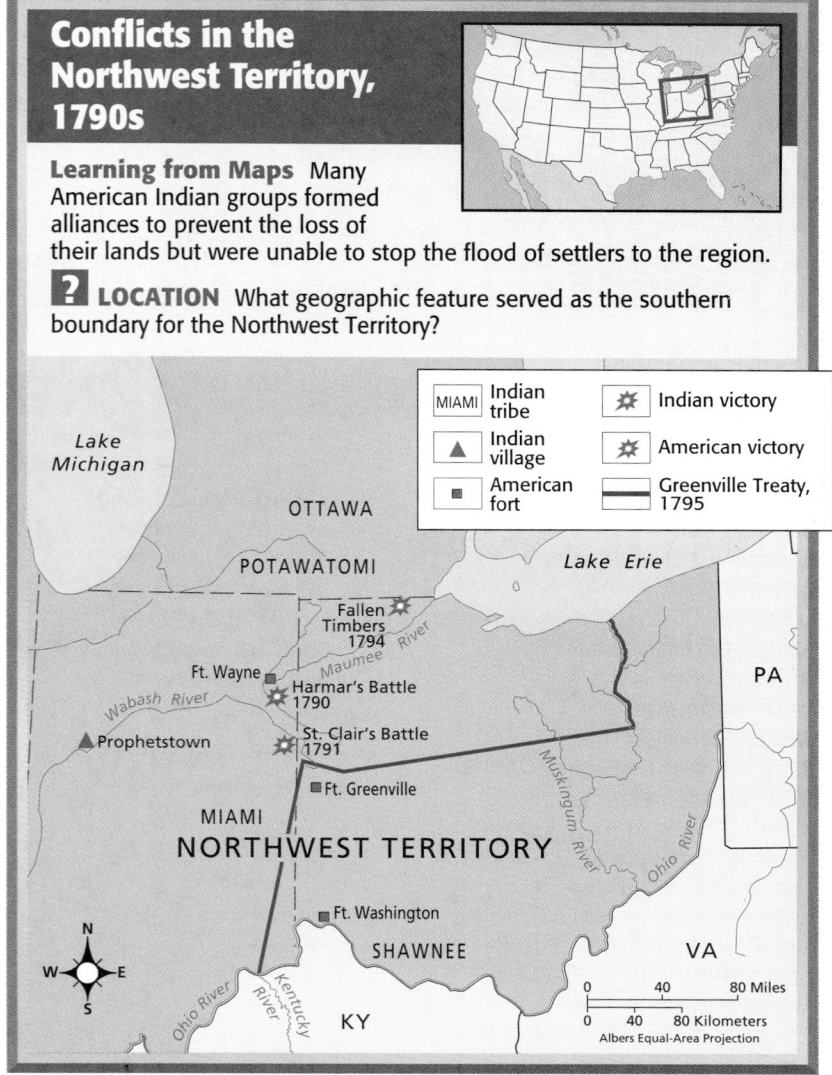

Conflicts in the Northwest Territory, 1790s

Learning from Maps Many American Indian groups formed alliances to prevent the loss of their lands but were unable to stop the flood of settlers to the region.

? LOCATION What geographic feature served as the southern boundary for the Northwest Territory?

MIAMI	Indian tribe		Indian victory
▲	Indian village		American victory
■	American fort		Greenville Treaty, 1795

Lake Michigan

OTTAWA

POTAWATOMI

Lake Erie

Fallen Timbers 1794

Ft. Wayne

Maumee River

Harmar's Battle 1790

Wabash River

St. Clair's Battle 1791

▲ Prophetstown

■ Ft. Greenville

MIAMI

NORTHWEST TERRITORY

Muskingum River

Ohio River

PA

■ Ft. Washington

SHAWNEE

VA

Ohio River

Kentucky River

KY

0   40   80 Miles
0   40   80 Kilometers
Albers Equal-Area Projection

that war—organized and led these forces. Although Little Turtle asked his British allies for help against Wayne, they agreed only to provide arms, not soldiers. Little Turtle recognized that the Indian forces faced heavy odds against well-trained soldiers who outnumbered them. He gave his allies advice.

Fallen Timbers. U.S. forces overwhelmed the confederation of American Indians in present-day Toledo, Ohio. *How did the supplies of the U.S. forces compare to the American Indians?*

66 **We have beaten the enemy twice under different commanders. We cannot expect the same good fortune to attend us always. The Americans are now led by a chief who never sleeps. Like the blacksnake, the day and the night are alike to him for during all the time he has been marching on our villages. . . . It would be prudent to listen to his offers of peace. 99**

When the other chiefs in the confederation rejected his advice, Little Turtle stepped down from command. In the summer of 1794 the confederation clashed with Wayne's army in the **Battle of Fallen Timbers**, near present-day Toledo, Ohio. As Little Turtle had predicted, the fighting ended in defeat for the confederation.

The Battle of Fallen Timbers dealt a severe blow to Indian resistance in the territory. In 1795 more than 1,000 tribal leaders, including Little Turtle, entered into negotiations with the U.S. government. The result was the **Treaty of Greenville**, which gave the United States title to American Indian lands making up much of present-day Ohio and part of Indiana. In exchange, Indians received $20,000 worth of goods and a formal acknowledgment of their claim to the lands they still held.

✔ **READING CHECK:** What conflicts occurred on the frontier in the 1790s?

SECTION 1 REVIEW

Define and explain the significance of the following terms:
Bill of Rights
Judiciary Act of 1789
cabinet
capitalism
Bank of the United States
strict construction
loose construction
Whiskey Rebellion
Battle of Fallen Timbers
Treaty of Greenville

Identify and explain the significance of the following individuals:
Alexander Hamilton
Little Turtle
Anthony Wayne

1. **Using Graphic Organizers** Copy the chart below. Explain the major challenges the new government faced in the 1790s and what solutions it proposed for these problems.

Problems
1.
2.
3.
Solutions
1.
2.
3.

2. **Evaluating** How did the first Congress help establish the new federal government?
3. **Problem Solving** Explain what policies you would have proposed to deal with the economic problems and objections to the National Bank in the 1790s?
4. **Comparing and Contrasting** Explain the similarities and differences in Thomas Jefferson's and Alexander Hamilton's views of the Constitution.

Critical Thinking

5. How did the government's reaction to problems on the frontier illustrate the differences between the new government and the government under the Articles of Confederation?
Consider:
• what conflicts arose on the frontier
• how the new government was different from that under the Articles
• how each government dealt with conflicts

Dealing with a Dangerous World

OBJECTIVES

Read to understand:

1. how Americans responded to political events in France
2. how political parties affected the election of 1796
3. how conflicts with France increased tensions between Republicans and Federalists

KEY TERMS

French Revolution
impressment
Jay's Treaty
Pinckney's Treaty
right of deposit
sectionalism
XYZ affair
Alien and Sedition Acts
Kentucky and Virginia Resolutions

KEY PEOPLE

Edmond Genet
John Jay
Thomas Pinckney
Charles-Maurice de Talleyrand

EYEWITNESSES TO History

" A system of finance has issued from the Treasury of the United States and has given rise to scenes of speculation calculated to aggrandize [increase] the few and the wealthy, by oppressing the great body of the people. "
—Philip Freneau

A 1791 edition of the **National Gazette**

Philip Freneau, editor of the *National Gazette,* spoke out against Alexander Hamilton's financial measures in 1792. Hamilton counterattacked in the *Gazette of the United States.* A newspaper war soon broke out in Philadelphia between the two papers. The *Gazette of the United States* generally supported Hamilton's ideas, while the *National Gazette,* which had been established with the help of Thomas Jefferson, opposed Hamilton's system. This newspaper war reflected the often hostile political climate in the United States. The new nation was increasingly divided by such domestic political differences as well as political events in Europe.

The French Revolution

A revolution in France had major consequences for American politics as well. France had been experiencing economic difficulties throughout the 1700s. Ordinary French people had suffered the most from these hard times through greater taxes. By the 1780s unemployment ran high, and a terrible crop failure in 1788 resulted in food shortages. Many French people felt that their king, Louis XVI, and his frivolous queen, Marie-Antoinette, did not care about their problems. For example, rumor had it that when a desperate mob had demanded bread Marie-Antoinette had sneered, "Let them eat cake."

French revolutionaries invented the guillotine, a mechanism that allowed for efficient means of execution.

The course of the revolution. In May 1789, as a grave financial crisis loomed, Louis XVI met with representatives of France's three major estates, or social classes. These estates consisted of the nobility, the clergy, and the commoners. Louis wanted to gain approval for his plan to raise taxes. However, the nobility and the clergy refused to give up certain privileges. In response, the delegates representing the third estate, the commoners, formed a National Assembly and prepared to write a constitution for France. Then, on July 14, 1789, French revolutionaries stormed the Bastille (ba-STEEL), a royal prison that was a hated symbol of oppression. This attack proved a key turning point in the **French Revolution**.

The French revolutionaries proclaimed their goals in the ringing cry "Liberty, Equality, Fraternity," but soon the rebellion turned into a bloodbath. During the period known as the Reign of Terror (1793–94), revolutionaries beheaded thousands of men and women, including Louis XVI and Marie-Antoinette. The revolutionaries saw themselves as champions fighting against the old

The French Revolution. This French engraving portrays Parisian women marching to the royal palace at Versailles. *What evidence does this engraving offer to support the argument that women played a significant role in the French Revolution?*

order. European monarchs feared that this revolutionary spirit would spread beyond France's borders. This fear led Austria, Great Britain, the Netherlands, Prussia, and Spain to join forces and declare war on France in 1792.

Americans and the French Revolution. Americans' reactions to these events in Europe were mixed. Some welcomed the news, pleased that France had followed the example of the United States. From Paris, Thomas Jefferson wrote excitedly to his friend James Monroe, "All the old spirit of 1776 is rekindling." Catharine Macaulay Graham, a British historian and friend of George Washington, commented in a letter to the president:

66 **All the friends of freedom on this side of the Atlantic are now rejoicing for an event which, in all probability has been accelerated by the American Revolution. You . . . have been the means of raising that spirit in Europe, which I sincerely hope will, in a short time, extinguish every remain of that barbarous servitude under which all the European nations . . . have so long been subject.** 99

Some Americans, however, did not share this enthusiasm. Many found it shocking that French liberty depended on beheading large numbers of people.

The European conflict disrupted American trade and threatened to draw the United States into war. Both France and Britain ignored the U.S. declaration of neutrality and seized American vessels bound for enemy ports. In addition, Britain's policy of **impressment**, or kidnapping, of American sailors to force them to serve in the British navy aroused American hostility. Between 1790 and 1812, while claiming to be capturing deserters from British naval vessels, Britain impressed some 10,000 American sailors.

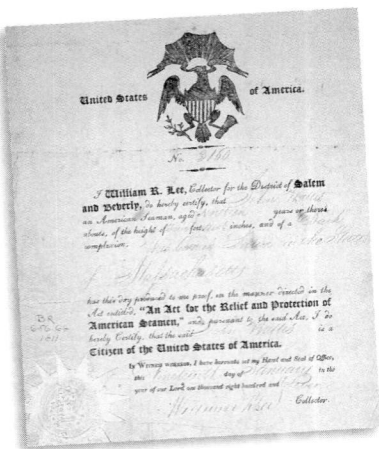

American sailors carried papers such as this one proving their citizenship in order to guard against impressment by the British navy.

Citizen Genet. The actions of French officials also caused resentment. In early 1793 Edmond Genet (zhuh-ne), a young French diplomat, arrived in the United States. Citizen Genet, as he was known, toured the nation. He hoped to organize "revolutionary clubs" and persuade Americans to honor their 1778 military alliance treaty with France.

President Washington, knowing that the United States was unprepared for war, refused to give in to pressure. On April 22, 1793, he issued a proclamation forbidding U.S. support for any nation at war. The French defied this neutrality policy. They armed a captured British merchant ship in Philadelphia's port and sent it out to attack British shipping. The newly christened ship, *La Petite Démocrate* (The Little Democrat), went on to become one of the most successful of the privateers, or private ships authorized by a nation to attack its enemies, operating off the U.S. coast. In response, Washington demanded that France recall its hotheaded diplomat. Genet was replaced in 1794, but the divisions he helped create remained.

✔ **READING CHECK:** How did Americans respond to the political events in France?

Negotiating Peace

Although supporters of the French Revolution accused the United States of favoring Britain, in reality the two countries' relations were strained. By March 1794, British naval officers ordered the seizure of more than 250 American ships in the West Indies. Although these ships were officially neutral, the British accused them of intending to trade with the French.

Jay's Treaty. Meanwhile, in the Northwest Territory the British had been providing American Indians, including Little Turtle's confederation, with weapons from their forts. The existence of these British forts, as well as the hundreds of British troops stationed there, violated the Treaty of Paris.

This situation further strained the tense relations between the United States and Britain. Hoping to avoid a war, President Washington sent Chief Justice John Jay to Britain in 1794 to negotiate a settlement. Among the terms of the resulting agreement, known as **Jay's Treaty**, the British agreed to abandon their northwestern forts. In return, the U.S. government agreed to pay debts owed to the British.

Britain, however, did not stop arming American Indians, impressing American sailors, or seizing American ships. Many Americans accused Jay of selling out to the British. One editor called him an "arch traitor," and declared that "he kissed the [British] Queen's hand . . . and with this kiss betrayed away the rights of man and the liberty of America." Mobs burned effigies, or images, of Jay.

Washington complained in a letter to Alexander Hamilton that the "cry against the Treaty is like that against a mad-dog." Despite the frenzied opposition to the treaty, the Senate ratified it. Washington had prevented war with Britain. The treaty also led to an increase in American shipping and trade.

Pinckney's Treaty. Jay's Treaty came just as Spain shifted alliances, joining France against Britain. Spain feared that a U.S. alliance with Britain could threaten Spanish territory in North America. Thus, Spain moved quickly to settle its disputes with the United States. The result was **Pinckney's Treaty**, negotiated in 1795 by Thomas Pinckney of South Carolina. Pinckney's Treaty recognized the southern boundary of the United States with Spanish Florida as the 31st parallel.

Pinckney's Treaty also guaranteed U.S. navigation rights on the Mississippi River. Frontier farmers and merchants used the Mississippi River and its westward-flowing tributaries, such as the Ohio River, to move their produce to the port of New Orleans. From there, goods were shipped to markets around the world. Pinckney's Treaty gave Americans the **right of deposit**—the right to temporarily unload goods at New Orleans without paying a duty to Spain.

The Election of 1796

In 1796 President Washington, who was re-elected easily in 1792, announced that he would not seek a third term. This set an informal precedent that was not broken until 1940. The president urged Americans to maintain neutrality abroad and unity at home. "The great rule of conduct for us," Washington declared, "is . . . to steer clear of permanent alliances with any portion of the foreign world." He also warned of the dangers posed by political groups and regional interests.

THE GRANGER COLLECTION, NEW YORK

INTERPRETING THE VISUAL RECORD

Jay's Treaty. As opponents of Jay's Treaty and supporters of Thomas Jefferson burned effigies of Chief Justice John Jay in reaction to the weak treaty, the nation's political divisions deepened. *How would actions like those portrayed in this engraving lead to increasing political tension and division in the United States?*

The most important step in taking a test is preparing beforehand. Keeping up with daily reading assignments and observing study clues as you read will allow you to spend your time reviewing on the days preceding a test. Going over material that you have already learned takes less time—and creates much less stress—than trying to "cram" right before a test.

Knowing what types of questions will be on a test can also help you prepare efficiently. Most history tests include several basic types of questions: matching, multiple choice, short answer, and essay. Matching, multiple-choice, and short-answer questions test your basic knowledge of important people, terms, and events. Essay questions require you to explain your understanding of more complex historical issues. When reviewing for a test, it is helpful to think about how the information you are studying might be posed to you in question form.

How to Take a Test

1. **Prepare beforehand.** Read carefully and consistently, observe study clues as you read, and review the material before the day of the test.
2. **Follow directions.** When you receive the test, read all of its instructions first. Listen carefully to any additional instructions that your teacher may provide.
3. **Preview the test.** Skim through the test and determine how much time you have for each section. Anticipate which areas of the test will be most difficult, and then begin work on the easier sections first.

4. **Work steadily and deliberately.** If you cannot determine the answer to a matching, multiple-choice, or short-answer question, make an intelligent guess and move on to the next question. When responding to an essay question, make sure that you know exactly what you are being asked to write about. Then, if time permits, sketch a brief outline of the main ideas and supporting details that you plan to use in your answer.
5. **Review your answers.** If time permits, return to questions that you skipped or were unsure of and work on them further. Then read over your essays and make any necessary additions or corrections.

Applying the Strategy

As you read Section 2, create a list of at least six terms and/or names that could serve as answers to matching or multiple-choice questions. Then create an essay question that would require you to use at least two of these terms and/or names in your answer.

Practicing the Strategy

Answer the following questions.
1. How could the term *French Revolution* be used in a matching question?
2. How could the term *XYZ affair* be used in a multiple-choice question?
3. What is an essay question that would require you to discuss the French Revolution and the XYZ affair?

Read More About It

Free Find:

Election of 1796
After reading the biographies of John Adams and Thomas Jefferson on the **Holt Researcher** CD–ROM, imagine that you are a political reporter from the era. Write an article covering the political candidates in the election.

The rise of political parties. Washington's warning went unheeded. By the mid-1790s heated debates over whether to stay neutral or to side with Britain or France had already deepened political divisions. Such debates had also helped give rise to the first American political parties. Washington had underestimated the depth of regional and economic differences within the United States. In the mid-1790s **sectionalism**, or loyalty to a particular part of the country, further contributed to the emergence of two parties. The Federalist Party was led by Alexander Hamilton and John Adams. The Democratic-Republican Party was led by Thomas Jefferson and James Madison. As Americans sided with one party or the other, the nation's two-party system took shape.

Merchants, manufacturers, lawyers, and church leaders from New England and the Atlantic seaboard tended to support the Federalist Party. John Adams called these Americans "the rich, the well-born, and the able." Federalists expected the rich to provide national leadership, because, as one leading Federalist put it, "those who own the country ought to govern it." Besides favoring a strong national government, Federalists wanted to promote the development of commerce, particularly with Britain.

The Democratic-Republican Party was later shortened to the Republican Party. It has no direct connection to today's Republican Party. The party included planters, small farmers, wage earners, artisans, workers, and tradespeople. It was particularly strong on the frontier and in the South, where its supporters believed that farmers deserved the greatest voice in government. The party also found support in the North, particularly in the middle states, or what became known as the Midwest. There the party was seen as a way to challenge established leadership and achieve political equality.

Both northern and southern Republicans shared certain common beliefs. Their main goal was to protect states' rights and individual liberties by limiting the power of the federal government. Republicans feared a strong national government and the financial and political powers that could create such a system. Because they distrusted the aristocratic British, they tended to be supportive of the French.

★ HISTORICAL DOCUMENTS ★

PRESIDENT GEORGE WASHINGTON
Washington's Farewell Address

Near the end of his second term, President George Washington prepared a Farewell Address to the country. His Farewell Address was not a speech, but rather an essay that was printed in newspapers for the nation to examine. Washington raised many issues that concerned him about current conditions in the United States, including his thoughts about political parties.

All combinations and associations, under whatever plausible character, with the real design to direct, control, counteract, or awe the regular deliberation and action of the constituted authorities, are destructive to this fundamental principle [obeying the established government].... They serve to organize faction; to give it an artificial and extraordinary force; to put in the place of the delegated will of the nation the will of a party, often a small but artful and enterprising minority of the community, and, according to the alternate triumphs of different parties, to make the public administration the mirror of ill-concerted and incongruous [inappropriate] projects of faction rather than the organ of consistent and wholesome plans, digested by common counsels and modified by mutual interests.

Federalists versus Republicans. President Washington's decision not to seek re-election in 1796 set in motion the first real competition for the presidency. In that election, Federalists John Adams and Thomas Pinckney faced off against Republicans Thomas Jefferson and Aaron Burr. The antagonism between the parties was evident from the beginning. Many Republicans agreed with Mercy Otis Warren's assessment that Adams had "a partiality for monarchy." Some Federalists accused Jefferson of plotting a reign of terror like that in revolutionary France.

Alexander Hamilton tried to prevent Adams, a rival within his own party, from winning. He secretly persuaded a few southern Federalist electors to vote only for Pinckney. According to the Constitution, whoever received the most electoral votes became president. The runner-up became vice president. Hamilton's strategy backfired when northern Federalists discovered the plan and responded by not voting for Pinckney, a southerner. When the votes were counted, Adams was president, and Jefferson—his Republican opponent—was vice president.

✔ **READING CHECK:** How did political parties affect the election of 1796?

The Federalist and Republican Parties used campaign banners like this one, portraying Thomas Jefferson, to build popular support for their candidates.

THE GRANGER COLLECTION, NEW YORK

Building a Navy

By the 1790s military preparations were under way in the United States. This included the increasing enlistment of men to form the U.S. Navy.

Congress authorized the construction of six medium-sized ships known as frigates. The USS *Constitution*, designed by Joshua Humphreys and constructed by George Claghorn in a Boston shipyard, was part of the navy's first fleet. More than 1,500 trees were used in the ship's beams, masts, planking, frame, and almost two-foot-thick hull. Skilled carpenters fitted each piece individually, and Paul Revere formed the copper bolts, spikes, and fastenings. Crushed rock salt packed against the ship's frame helped preserve the wood. When it was finished, the *Constitution* carried 20 cannons, 32 long guns, more than 40 sails, and a crew of 450.

In the late 1790s the newly launched *Constitution* fought pirates in the Caribbean and later in the Mediterranean. The ship received its nickname, "Old Ironsides," after a battle in the War of 1812. Despite severe bombardment, a British ship was unable even to dent the *Constitution*'s oak sides. The story goes that one of the sailors cried out, "Her sides are made of iron!" After almost 85 years of service, the *Constitution* was retired from active duty in 1882.

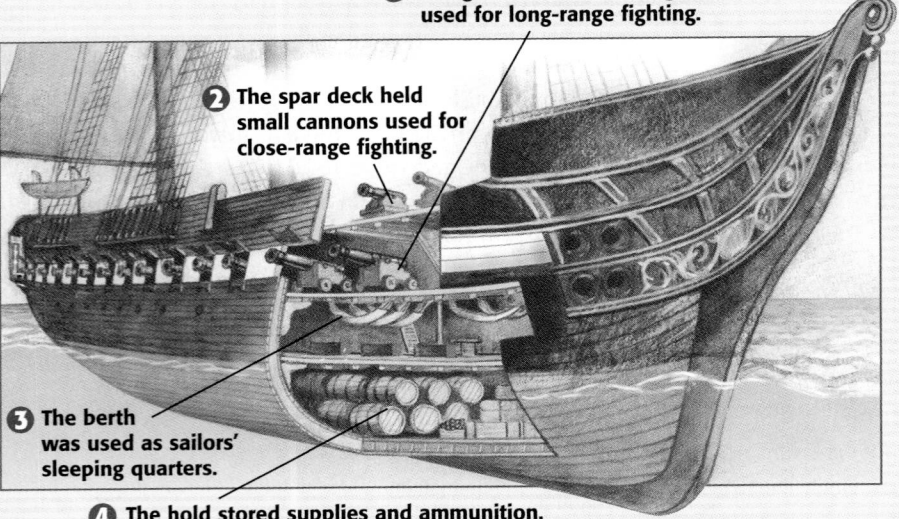

❶ The gun deck held main guns used for long-range fighting.

❷ The spar deck held small cannons used for close-range fighting.

❸ The berth was used as sailors' sleeping quarters.

❹ The hold stored supplies and ammunition.

Understanding Science and History

1. What made the USS *Constitution* so strong?
2. What were the different levels of the ship used for?

Foreign and Domestic Conflicts

President Adams faced many foreign-policy challenges. The French viewed Jay's Treaty and U.S. neutrality as evidence of pro-British leanings. In response, French privateers had begun to seize American ships bound for British ports.

In 1797 Adams sent diplomats to France to negotiate a new treaty. Three agents representing Charles-Maurice de Talleyrand, France's foreign minister, presented his demands. He wanted the United States to apologize publicly for anti-French remarks made by Adams, grant France a multimillion-dollar loan, and pay him a bribe of $240,000.

President Adams published these demands—with X, Y, and Z substituted for the names of Talleyrand's agents. Americans responded with fury, rallying around the slogan, "Millions for Defense, but Not One Cent for Tribute [bribery]." President Adams and Congress responded to this **XYZ affair** with a flurry of war preparations. They created the Navy Department, built warships, fortified harbors, and strengthened the army. Although the United States and France did fight an unofficial war mostly in the Caribbean, no formal declaration of war was ever passed.

In 1798, as the conflict with France was brewing, the Federalist majority in Congress passed the **Alien and Sedition Acts**. This series of laws was intended not only to protect the nation but also to weaken the Republicans. The Alien Act and the Alien Enemies Act authorized the president to imprison or expel "all such aliens [foreigners] as he shall judge dangerous to the peace and safety of the United States." The Sedition Act targeted U.S. citizens. Under the Sedition Act, anyone who wrote, said, or printed anything "false, scandalous, and malicious [with ill will]" about the government, the Congress, or the president "with intent to defame" could be fined and jailed. Congress also passed an act that required immigrants—who often voted Republican—to live in the United States for 14 years, instead of 5, before becoming a citizen.

Throughout the country, Republican newspaper editors and politicians were arrested for sedition; 25 were indicted, and 10 were convicted. The best known of these editors was Matthew Lyon, a Republican representative from Vermont, who was jailed for four months and fined $1,000 for denouncing the Sedition Act and President Adams.

Many Americans saw the Alien and Sedition Acts as attempts to curb the rights of individuals. The Sedition Act threatened freedom of the press and freedom of speech, two rights guaranteed by the First Amendment. Furious Republicans voiced their protests in the Kentucky Resolutions and the Virginia Resolutions, which were passed in 1798 and 1799 by those states' legislatures.

The **Kentucky and Virginia Resolutions** denounced the Alien and Sedition Acts as unconstitutional. Because the Federalists controlled most state governments, the Kentucky and Virginia Resolutions failed to win wide support.

THE GRANGER COLLECTION, NEW YORK

INTERPRETING THE VISUAL RECORD

Conflict. During a heated congressional debate over the Alien and Sedition Acts, Federalist Roger Griswald attacked Republican Matthew Lyon. *How does this engraving reflect the political divisions in the United States?*

✔ **READING CHECK:** How did the conflicts with France increase tensions between U.S. political parties?

SECTION 2 REVIEW

Define and explain the significance of the following terms:
French Revolution
impressment
Jay's Treaty
Pinckney's Treaty
right of deposit
sectionalism
XYZ affair
Alien and Sedition Acts
Kentucky and Virginia Resolutions

Identify and explain the significance of the following individuals:
Edmond Genet
John Jay
Thomas Pinckney
Charles-Maurice de Talleyrand

1. **Using Graphic Organizers** Copy the chart below. Compare and contrast the characteristics of the Republicans and the Federalists.

	Republicans	Federalists
Occupation of Members		
Geographic Strength		
Common Beliefs		
Differing Beliefs		

2. **Identifying Cause and Effect** What were the causes of the French Revolution? Why did American support for the revolutionary forces change?

3. **Distinguishing Fact from Opinion** Republicans argued that the Sedition Act was a ploy to silence them. What facts might help to assess this opinion?

4. **Assessing Consequences** How did French actions strain relations between political parties in the United States?

Critical Thinking

5. Was the development of political parties in 1796 good for the United States?
   Consider:
   • what were the positive results of political parties
   • what were the negative results of political parties
   • what alternatives were available

The Nation Expands

OBJECTIVES

Read to understand:

1. how judicial decisions affected the balance of power among the three branches of government
2. why Thomas Jefferson wanted to purchase Louisiana, and why Napoleon wanted to give it up
3. what the national and international significance of the Louisiana Purchase was

KEY TERMS

Twelfth Amendment
judicial review
Marbury v. Madison
Louisiana Purchase

KEY PEOPLE

Aaron Burr
John Marshall
Toussaint-Louverture
Meriwether Lewis
William Clark
Sacagawea
Zebulon Pike

KEY PLACES

Louisiana Territory
New Orleans

Bitterness between Aaron Burr and Alexander Hamilton resulted in a duel that left Hamilton fatally wounded.

66 *[Thomas Jefferson was] so meek and mild, yet dignified in his manners, with a voice so soft and low, with a [bearing] so benignant [agreeable] and intelligent.* **99**
—Margaret Bayard Smith

Thomas Jefferson entertaining guests at Monticello

Margaret Bayard Smith noted her surprise upon discovering Thomas Jefferson's quiet disposition. An architect, philosopher, writer, naturalist, and statesman, the Republican leader had many different aspects to his personality. After the Federalists' harsh enforcement of the Alien and Sedition Acts, Republicans became even more determined to win the presidency in 1800. They looked to Jefferson for leadership.

The Election of 1800

By the election of 1800, the power of the Federalist Party was slipping. The Republicans pitted Thomas Jefferson and Aaron Burr against Federalists John Adams and Charles Pinckney for the presidency. The Republicans took advantage of the Antifederalist sentiment and won control of Congress. However, neither the Republicans nor the Federalists had a formal ticket that specified who was the party's preferred candidate for president, as parties routinely do today. As a result, another electoral crisis arose. Jefferson and Burr received the same number of electoral votes for president.

The Constitution made clear that in the event of a tie, the president would be chosen by the House of Representatives. Thirty-five attempts to select a president failed. With Inauguration Day just weeks away, the United States was still without a president-elect. The electoral crisis might have worsened had help not come from an unexpected source. Preferring Jefferson over Burr, whom he considered "unprincipled and dangerous," Alexander Hamilton persuaded several Federalists to vote for Jefferson. Thus, with the help of his former rival, Jefferson became the third president of the United States.

To prevent future electoral crises, Congress proposed the **Twelfth Amendment** to the Constitution. With broad support the amendment was ratified in 1804. This amendment requires electors to vote for presidential and vice presidential candidates on separate ballots.

Hostility between Hamilton and Burr continued to grow over the years. In 1804 Hamilton publicly criticized Burr, who was then running for governor of New York. Burr's demand for an apology led to a duel in which Burr fatally wounded Hamilton.

THE GRANGER COLLECTION, NEW YORK

The Federalists and the Judiciary

The defeated Federalists feared that their programs would be abandoned. To help protect their programs, they pushed through the Judiciary Act of 1801. This act created a number of new circuit courts and federal judgeships. President Adams worked late into the night of his last day in office, appointing Federalists to these posts. These last-minute appointees were nicknamed "midnight judges."

Adams's most significant appointment, though not one of the "midnight judges," was his selection of John Marshall of Virginia as Chief Justice of the United States. During his more than 30 years on the bench, Marshall established many basic principles of U.S. constitutional law. Among these was the principle of **judicial review**—the power of the courts to declare an act of Congress unconstitutional. The Court first exercised this right in 1803 with the case of *Marbury* v. *Madison*.

For political reasons, Jefferson and Secretary of State James Madison refused to allow William Marbury, one of the "midnight judges," to take office as the District of Columbia's justice of the peace. Marbury appealed to the Supreme Court to force the Jefferson administration to allow him to serve his appointment. Although the Court agreed that Marbury had a right to his appointment, it ruled that it could hear the case only on appeal after it had gone through the lower courts. By denying that the case could go straight to the Supreme Court, Marshall declared a part of the Judiciary Act of 1789 unconstitutional. With this decision, Marshall initiated the Court's most important role—that of final interpreter of the Constitution.

Marshall also believed in the loose construction of the Constitution, a position that put him at odds with Jefferson. He expressed this view in *McCulloch* v. *Maryland,* an 1819 case in which the Supreme Court determined that the federal government had a right to legally establish a national bank.

✔ **READING CHECK:** How did judicial decisions affect the balance of power among the three branches of government?

PRESIDENTIAL *Lives*

1743–1826
In Office 1801–1809

Thomas Jefferson

Thomas Jefferson had a good-humored nature. A brilliant conversationalist, he could talk just as easily about chemistry or horse racing as politics or philosophy. He loved art, geography, and architecture. He not only knew French, Italian, Spanish, Greek, and Latin but also studied some 40 American Indian languages.

Though charming in person, Jefferson often recorded in his diary the petty gossip he heard about his rivals. Jefferson also struggled with a deep sense of loneliness. The death of his wife, Martha Wayles Skelton, and five of his six children caused him to mourn, "My evening prospects now hang on the thread of a single life."

INTERPRETING THE VISUAL RECORD

Westward movement. As the U.S. population grew larger, Americans moved west to clear land and establish new farms. *Based on this engraving, how did the American migration west alter the landscape?*

The Louisiana Purchase

Though Thomas Jefferson later declared the Republican victory in the 1800 election the "Revolution of 1800," the transition of power was peaceful. To fulfill his promise of moderation, Jefferson left some Federalist programs untouched. These included the National Bank and the debt payment plan, both of which he had once opposed. He also tried to maintain a neutral course in foreign affairs. Jefferson also supported a move that appealed strongly to Republican farmers by significantly expanding U.S. landholdings.

THE GRANGER COLLECTION, NEW YORK

AMERICAN Letters

Uniquely American Literature

By the early 1800s the United States had begun to develop a truly American literature. James Fenimore Cooper and Catharine Maria Sedgwick emerged as two of the leading authors of historical fiction who focused on the early American experience. Cooper explored the significance of the frontier, while Sedgwick's novels focused on the history and culture of early New England settlements.

from *The Deerslayer* (1841)
by James Fenimore Cooper

As Deerslayer [Natty Bumppo] drew nearer and nearer to the land, the stroke of his paddle grew slower, his eye became more watchful, and his ears and nostrils almost dilated with the effort to detect any lurking danger. . . . He was

The Deerslayer

entirely alone, thrown on his own resources, and . . . emboldened by no encouraging voice. Notwithstanding all these circumstances, the most experienced veteran in forest warfare could not have behaved better. . . .

When about a hundred yards from the shore, Deerslayer rose in the canoe, gave three or four vigorous strokes with the paddle, sufficient of themselves to impel the bark to land, and then quickly laying aside the instrument of labor, he seized that of war. He was in the very act of raising the rifle, when a sharp report, was followed by the buzz of a bullet that passed so near his body, as to cause him involuntarily to start. The next instant Deerslayer staggered, and fell his whole length in the bottom of the canoe. A yell—it came from a single voice—followed, and an Indian leaped from the bushes, upon the open area of the point, bounding towards the canoe. This was the moment the young man desired. He rose on the instant, and leveled his own rifle, at his uncovered foe; but his finger hesitated about pulling the trigger on one whom he held at such a disadvantage. This little delay, probably saved the life of the Indian, who bounded back into the cover.

from *Hope Leslie* (1827)
by Catharine Maria Sedgwick

Springfield [Massachusetts] assumed, . . . the aspect of a village. The first settlers followed the course of the Indians, and planted themselves on the borders of rivers. . . . The wigwams which constituted the village . . . the 'smoke' of the natives

Catharine Maria Sedgwick

gave place to the clumsy, but more convenient dwellings of the pilgrims.

Where there are now contiguous [ongoing] rows of shops, filled with the merchandise of the east, the manufactures of Europe, the rival fabrics of our own country, and the fruits of the tropics; where now stands the stately hall of justice—the academy—the bank—churches, orthodox and heretic, and all the symbols of a rich and populous community—were, at the early period of our history, a few log-houses, planted around a fort, defended by a slight embankment. . . .

The beautiful hill that is now the residence of the gentry . . . was then the border of a dense forest.

UNDERSTANDING LITERATURE

1. What type of relationship between frontierspeople and American Indians is depicted in *The Deerslayer?*
2. According to Sedgwick's *Hope Leslie,* how had Springfield, Massachusetts, changed?
3. How do these two excerpts represent American experiences?

The Louisiana Territory. Spain had held the region of Louisiana since 1762. President Jefferson had privately expressed hopes that Spain could hold on to Louisiana until the United States could take over its possession "piece by piece." In a secret treaty, however, French ruler Napoleon regained Louisiana from Spain.

In 1803 Jefferson sent James Monroe to Paris to assist with negotiations for a U.S. port at the mouth of the Mississippi or for access to New Orleans. Jefferson had instructed Monroe to offer Napoleon as much as $10 million for New Orleans and west Florida. No sooner had Monroe arrived, however, than Napoleon's representative asked how much the United States would pay for all of Louisiana. The astonished U.S. diplomat quickly agreed to pay about $15 million. Thus, for roughly four cents an acre, the United States completed the **Louisiana Purchase**. It has been called the largest land deal in history.

Napoleon Bonaparte chose to sell this valuable territory because of his failure to build an empire in the Western Hemisphere. To defend an empire in Louisiana, Napoleon needed a strong naval base in the West Indies. The most likely place was Saint Domingue—present-day Haiti—on the island of Hispaniola. However, France had lost control of the colony after its African slaves had revolted in 1791. Under the leadership of Toussaint-Louverture (too-san loo-ver-toohr), African slaves eventually took control of the whole colony. Toussaint-Louverture was a gifted military strategist, former slave, and grandson of an African chief.

In 1802 a French attempt to regain Saint Domingue ended in disaster. Although Napoleon's troops captured Toussaint-Louverture, who later died in prison, the Haitians and the effects of yellow fever combined to drive the French from the island. With no foothold in the West Indies from which to protect Louisiana, Napoleon decided to sell the territory. He also gained $15 million to fund his army. The events in Haiti thus led indirectly to the expansion of the size of the United States. They also led to a large migration of French Haitian immigrants to the United States, particularly to the new Louisiana Territory.

✔ **READING CHECK:** Why did Jefferson want to purchase Louisiana? Why did Napoleon sell it?

INTERPRETING THE VISUAL RECORD

The Louisiana Purchase. During a ceremony following the purchase of Louisiana, the French flag is lowered and the American flag is raised in its place. *How does this painting reflect the sense of pride that many Americans felt after the purchase?*

Read More About It

Free Find:
From Lewis's Journal
After reading the selection from Lewis's journal on the **Holt Researcher** CD–ROM, imagine that you are traveling with Lewis and Clark. Write your own journal entry for a typical day on the expedition.

Lewis and Clark. Neither buyer nor seller knew the exact size or boundaries of the Louisiana Territory. President Jefferson assigned the task of mapping the new territory to two skilled frontiersmen, Meriwether Lewis and William Clark. With a crew of 45 explorers, the Lewis and Clark expedition left St. Louis in May 1804. In response to the president's instructions to record all observations "with great care and accuracy," Lewis and Clark kept detailed journals of their travels. Their attention to detail is shown in an entry from May 23, 1805.

66 The river has become more rapid, the country much the same as yesterday, except that there is rather more rocks on the face of the hills, and some small spruce pine appears among the pitch. The wild roses are very abundant and now in bloom; they differ from those of the United States only in having the leaves and the bush itself of a somewhat smaller size. We find the mosquitoes troublesome, notwithstanding the coolness of the morning. The buffalo is scarce to-day, but the elk, deer, and antelope, are very numerous. 99

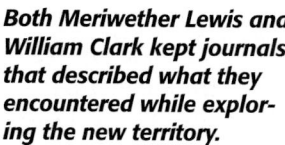

Both Meriwether Lewis and William Clark kept journals that described what they encountered while exploring the new territory.

The Louisiana Purchase

Learning from Maps The Louisiana Purchase added some 828,000 square miles of rich land to the United States, roughly doubling the nation's size.

❓ MOVEMENT What rivers did Lewis and Clark follow from St. Louis on their way to the Pacific Ocean?

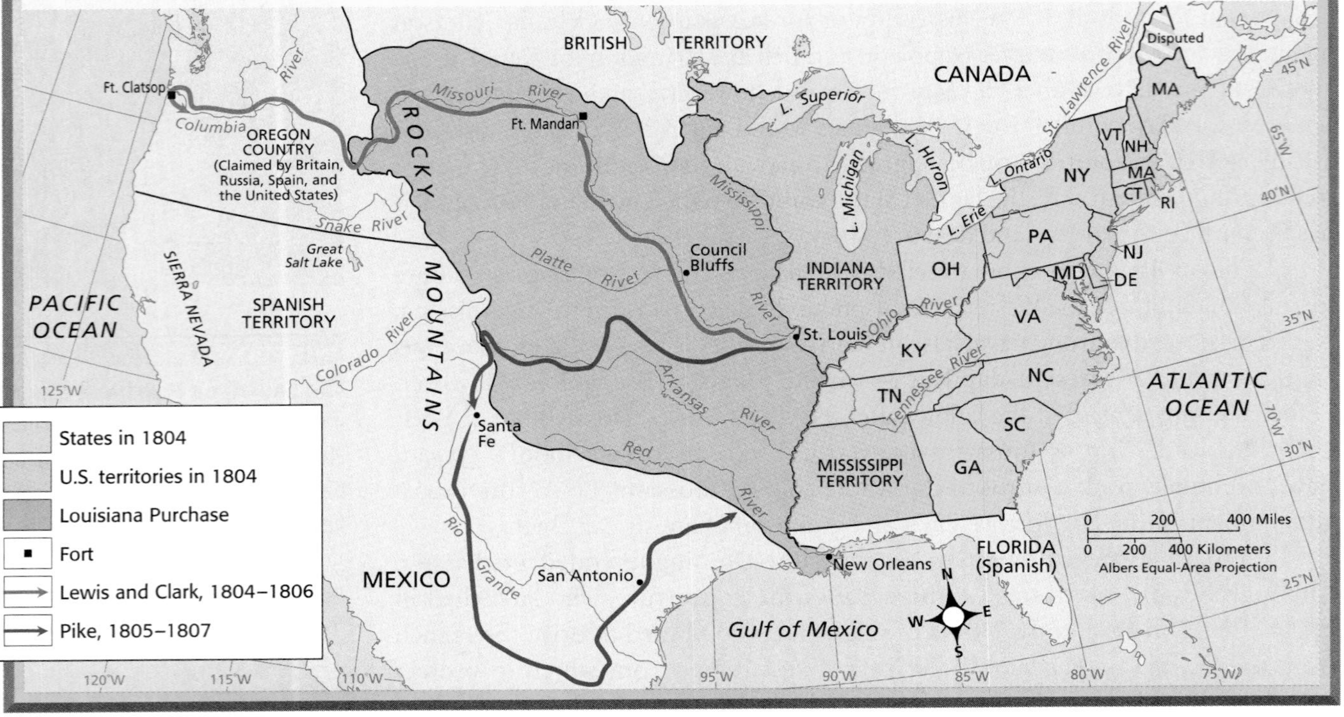

Legend:
- States in 1804
- U.S. territories in 1804
- Louisiana Purchase
- ■ Fort
- → Lewis and Clark, 1804–1806
- → Pike, 1805–1807

American Indians—particularly the Mandan and Shoshoni (shuh-SHOH-nee)—aided the expedition. After their first winter, Lewis and Clark hired a French-Canadian fur trader and his Shoshoni wife, Sacagawea (sak-uh-juh-WEE-uh), as guides and interpreters. Sacagawea proved invaluable to the expedition. She showed members of the expedition the best places to fish, to hunt game, and to find wild vegetables. As an interpreter, she helped the expedition obtain needed supplies at critical moments.

The expedition's relations with American Indians were further enhanced by the presence of a slave named York. In his journal, Clark observed that the Indians were "much astonished" by York, "who did not lose the opportunity of [displaying] his powers of Strength etc." Apparently, the Indians "never Saw a black man before," Clark wrote.

The Lewis and Clark expedition traveled up the Missouri River, crossed the Rocky Mountains, and canoed down the Snake and Columbia Rivers to the Pacific Ocean. After nearly two and a half years, the expedition returned. The travelers brought with them plant and animal specimens, animal bones and pelts, and various soil and mineral samples.

Zebulon Pike.
Before Lewis and Clark could publish the chronicles of their expedition, the reports of another explorer, Zebulon Pike, appeared in print. Pike visited the upper Mississippi Valley in 1805. He eventually traveled as far west as present-day Colorado, where he discovered the lofty mountain later named Pikes

As a guide and interpreter, Sacagawea greatly assisted Lewis and Clark during their exploration.

Peak in his honor. He returned home through Spanish territory, where he was arrested for trespassing and later released in the town of Santa Fe. Pike's descriptions gave Americans their first news of the lands beyond the Mississippi and helped spur expansion into Texas and the Southwest. His depiction of the Great Plains as a huge desert, however, led many people to view that region as unsuitable for settlement.

THE GRANGER COLLECTION, NEW YORK

The importance of the Louisiana Purchase.

The Louisiana Purchase added all or part of 13 future states to the nation. This vastly increased size made the United States more important in the eyes of other countries. As Robert R. Livingston, the U.S. ambassador to France who began the negotiations for the purchase, noted at the time of the purchase, "From this day the United States take their place among the powers of the first rank."

The purchase had important domestic consequences as well. In addition to removing the French threat from North America, it opened the interior of the continent to American settlement. As Americans devoted more energy to developing the frontier, they increasingly looked west, rather than east across the Atlantic. This shift promoted a greater sense of national identity.

INTERPRETING THE VISUAL RECORD

Zebulon Pike. This engraving shows the broken lands Zebulon Pike encountered in 1806. *How does this engraving portray the vastness of the Louisiana Territory?*

✔ **READING CHECK:** What was the international and national significance of the Louisiana Purchase?

SECTION 3 REVIEW

Define and explain the significance of the following terms:
Twelfth Amendment
judicial review
Marbury v. *Madison*
Louisiana Purchase

Identify and explain the significance of the following individuals:
Aaron Burr
John Marshall
Toussaint-Louverture
Meriwether Lewis
William Clark
Sacagawea
Zebulon Pike

Locate and explain the importance of the following places:
Louisiana Territory
New Orleans

1. **Using Graphic Organizers** Copy the graphic organizer below. Explain how Thomas Jefferson's and John Marshall's opinions differed on the power of judicial review, and how their interpretation of the Constitution differed.

Judicial Review

Jefferson   Marshall

Constitutional Interpretation

2. **Analyzing** What did the United States hope to gain by purchasing Louisiana from France? What did France hope to gain by selling it?

3. **Understanding Geography: Place** What did explorers learn about U.S. territory west of the Mississippi, and how was the U.S. acquisition of the territory significant?

4. **Using Historical Imagination** Imagine you have been asked to join the Lewis and Clark expedition. Will you go? Why or why not?

Critical Thinking

5. How did early judicial decisions help define the balance of power between the three branches of government?
Consider:
• what the significance of judicial review was
• how loose construction influenced the Supreme Court
• why *McCulloch* v. *Maryland* was important

The War of 1812

OBJECTIVES

Read to understand:

1. how Tecumseh hoped to hold American Indian lands

2. why the United States declared war on Great Britain in 1812

3. how the War of 1812 affected the United States and Great Britain

KEY TERMS

Orders in Council
Embargo Act
Non-Intercourse Act
Battle of Tippecanoe
Battle of the Thames
Battle of New Orleans
Treaty of Ghent
Hartford Convention

KEY PEOPLE

Tecumseh
William Henry Harrison
Dolley Madison
Andrew Jackson

KEY PLACE

Lake Erie

 **EYEWITNESSES TO History**

❝ *[John] Paul Jones with half a dozen frigates would totally destroy their [the pirate's] commerce . . . cutting them to pieces.* ❞
—Thomas Jefferson

The burning of the Philadelphia in Tripoli's harbor

President Thomas Jefferson was furious at the pirates of the Barbary States of North Africa, including Algiers (al-JIRZ), Morocco, Tunis, and Tripoli. Since 1783 the pirates had demanded protection money from American ships that sailed through the Mediterranean Sea. During Jefferson's administration, Congress authorized a bill allowing the government to take any steps necessary to safeguard American merchant ships in the Mediterranean. Jefferson's plan included sending a squadron of warships to the region. In 1803 one of these ships, the USS *Philadelphia,* ran ashore in Tripoli, and pirates captured the captain and his crew. The commander of the U.S. squadron decided to burn the ship rather than let it fall into the pirates' hands. While the ship was anchored in the harbor of Tripoli, Lieutenant Stephen Decatur and a raiding party slipped on board and set the ship on fire. The famous British admiral Horatio Nelson called this "the most daring act of the age."

The Perils of World Trade

The harassment by the pirates of the Barbary States convinced many Americans of the urgent need for a powerful navy. That conviction grew stronger as Napoleon's wars in Europe spilled over into the Atlantic Ocean. In 1807 Great Britain passed the **Orders in Council**, which forbade neutral vessels from trading with France or entering ports under French control. Napoleon reacted by threatening to seize all foreign ships that cooperated with the British Royal Navy. The United States was again caught in the deadly crossfire between France and Britain.

In the summer of 1807, events took an ugly turn. Facing a shortage of sailors in its navy, Britain stepped up its long-standing practice of impressment. On June 22 the captain of the British ship HMS *Leopard* demanded the right to board the USS *Chesapeake.* He wanted to search for four supposed British deserters. When the *Chesapeake*'s captain refused permission, the British opened fire, killing three U.S. sailors and wounding 18 others. The British then seized four sailors as deserters, three of whom were native-born Americans.

The *Chesapeake* incident outraged Americans. President Jefferson shared this outrage but wanted to maintain U.S. neutrality. In an effort at "peaceable coercion [use of force]," Jefferson urged Congress to pass the **Embargo Act** of 1807. This act stopped shipments of food and other American products to all foreign ports.

Not surprisingly, New England merchants angrily opposed this measure, as did many others who lost business because of it. John Lane Jones, an unemployed Boston laborer, complained directly to Jefferson:

 **Read More About It**

Free Find:

Embargo Act

After reading the selections on the Embargo Act on the **Holt Researcher** CD–ROM, write a short essay explaining the purpose and impact of the Embargo Act.

> 66 You infernal villain. How much longer are you going to keep this . . . Embargo on to starve us poor people. . . . You must . . . afford us some kind of relief. . . . I wish you could feel as bad as I do. 99

From 1807 to 1808, the value of U.S. exports fell from $108 million to $22 million. While American farmers and merchants suffered from the embargo, the American minister in Paris reported, "Here [the effects] are not felt, and in England . . . it is forgotten." Public pressure finally led Congress to repeal the embargo in March 1809. Congress then passed the **Non-Intercourse Act**, which prohibited U.S. trade with Britain and France. Like the embargo, the Non-Intercourse Act was unpopular and did little to resolve the conflicts with European powers.

Confrontation in the West

Problems abroad were compounded by events at home. Hunters, trappers, and farmers sought new lands in British Canada and Spanish Florida. They also pushed westward into lands occupied by American Indians. This rapid westward expansion fueled tensions between settlers and American Indians.

Westerners were particularly alarmed by the activities of Shawnee leader Tecumseh (tuh-KUHM-suh). Tecumseh had become convinced that American Indians' best hope for survival rested in a military alliance among the Indian nations. In the early 1800s he rallied Indian tribes east of the Mississippi River. From the Great Lakes to the Gulf of Mexico, he urged American Indians not to sell land to the settlers: "Sell a country! Why not sell the air, the clouds, and the great sea? . . . Did not the Great Spirit make them all for the use of his children?"

As Tecumseh gained support, settlers pressured the government to take action. In the fall of 1811, Tecumseh was away in the South seeking support from the Cherokee, Choctaw, and Creek. General William Henry Harrison marshalled his troops for an attack along the Tippecanoe River in Indiana Territory. At dawn on November 7, the Indians initiated an attack on the army camp. Although General Harrison's forces sustained heavy losses, the **Battle of Tippecanoe** ended in defeat for the Indians. When Tecumseh returned from the South in early 1812, he saw his dream of a united confederation shattered.

✔ **READING CHECK:** How did Tecumseh hope to hold American Indian lands?

Congress Declares War

The British had supplied Tecumseh's forces with weapons. As a result, most Americans blamed the American Indian uprisings on Britain. The cry for war against Britain again arose in Congress. New members of Congress, such as Henry Clay of Kentucky and John C. Calhoun of South Carolina, exhibited such war fever that others nicknamed them War Hawks. They called for an attack on Canada to seize land and end the British–American Indian alliance once and for all. Their cries, said John Randolph of Virginia, became "like the whip-poor-will, but one eternal monotonous tone—Canada! Canada! Canada!"

To reduce tensions, the British repealed the Orders in Council in June 1812. Before the news could reach the United States, however, President Madison, who had succeeded Jefferson in 1809, asked for a declaration of war. His message

INTERPRETING THE VISUAL RECORD

Tecumseh. Shawnee leader Tecumseh alarmed many Americans with his attempt to build a confederation of American Indian tribes. *How did the creator of this engraving try to portray Tecumseh? Explain.*

Reasons for the War of 1812

BY THOMAS CLARKIN

During the 1800s most historians maintained that the failure of economic sanctions to stop the British violations of American neutrality forced the United States to protect its national honor by declaring war. Known as the maritime interpretation because it involved events on the high seas, this theory did not explain why northeasterners, who suffered most from the British actions, offered the least support for the war.

Historians who rejected the maritime interpretation claimed that westerners and southerners sought war in an effort to acquire Canada and Florida. Americans in those regions may have also viewed war as a means to end British aid to the American Indians. Defenders of the maritime interpretation responded with the claim that interference with American trade created economic difficulties in the South and West.

More recently, historians have offered a new explanation for the war. They noted that the Republicans who controlled the government feared that their failure to resolve the ongoing crisis with Britain would return the Federalists to power. Thus, they feared an end to the nation's experiment with republicanism. Thus, economic concerns, national honor, desire for land, and party politics all played a role in causing the War of 1812.

was taken up by members of Congress who produced a report supporting war.

> 66 The mad ambition, the lust of power, and commercial avarice [greed] of Great Britain have left to neutral nations an alternative only between the base surrender of their rights, and a manly vindication [defense] of them. 99

After some debate, both houses of Congress voted to support the declaration of war. The vote was split almost exactly along sectional lines. Southerners and westerners—suffering from an agricultural depression and American Indian troubles that they blamed on Britain—overwhelmingly supported the declaration. Many people from the Middle Atlantic and the Northeast, fearing a British blockade of their coasts, were opposed to the declaration.

✔ **READING CHECK:** Why did the United States declare war on Great Britain in 1812?

The War of 1812

The United States was ill prepared for war. The Republicans' reluctance to levy taxes and their reduction of the military had left the army poorly equipped. The navy, however, enjoyed the advantages of well-trained sailors and officers and a high morale.

The war's first phase. U.S. war strategy focused on the conquest of Canada. With the British preoccupied by their struggle to stop Napoleon, Americans anticipated a quick victory. President Madison adopted a plan that called for a three-pronged attack on Montreal, the Niagara frontier, and the Detroit frontier. The campaign ended in failure. One Vermont newspaper declared that the campaign had produced nothing but "an unbroken series of disaster, defeat, disgrace, and ruin and death."

The United States enjoyed more success in the war at sea. In the first eight months of the war, U.S. frigates won many victories against British warships. The firepower of the nation's best frigate, the USS *Constitution,* destroyed several British ships. Meanwhile, American privateers seriously disrupted British commerce by raiding British ships both in the Caribbean and around the British Isles.

The U.S. Navy achieved even greater success on the Great Lakes. In 1813 a small, ragtag naval force commanded by Captain Oliver Hazard Perry won control of Lake Erie. After his victory, Perry notified General William Henry Harrison: "We have met the enemy and they are ours."

Encouraged by these naval victories, General Harrison and his forces crossed into Canada. With some 3,000 troops, Harrison defeated the British and their American Indian allies at the **Battle of the Thames**. The British hold on the Northwest Territory was finally broken.

With a small number of weapons like this cannon, the U.S. forces suffered bitter defeats in their land battles.

The war's second phase.

Soon after ending its war against France early in 1814, Britain sent 13,000 reinforcements to Canada. British strategists planned to invade the United States from the north through Canada and from the south through New Orleans. British forces would also continue to raid points along the Atlantic coast to disrupt American commerce.

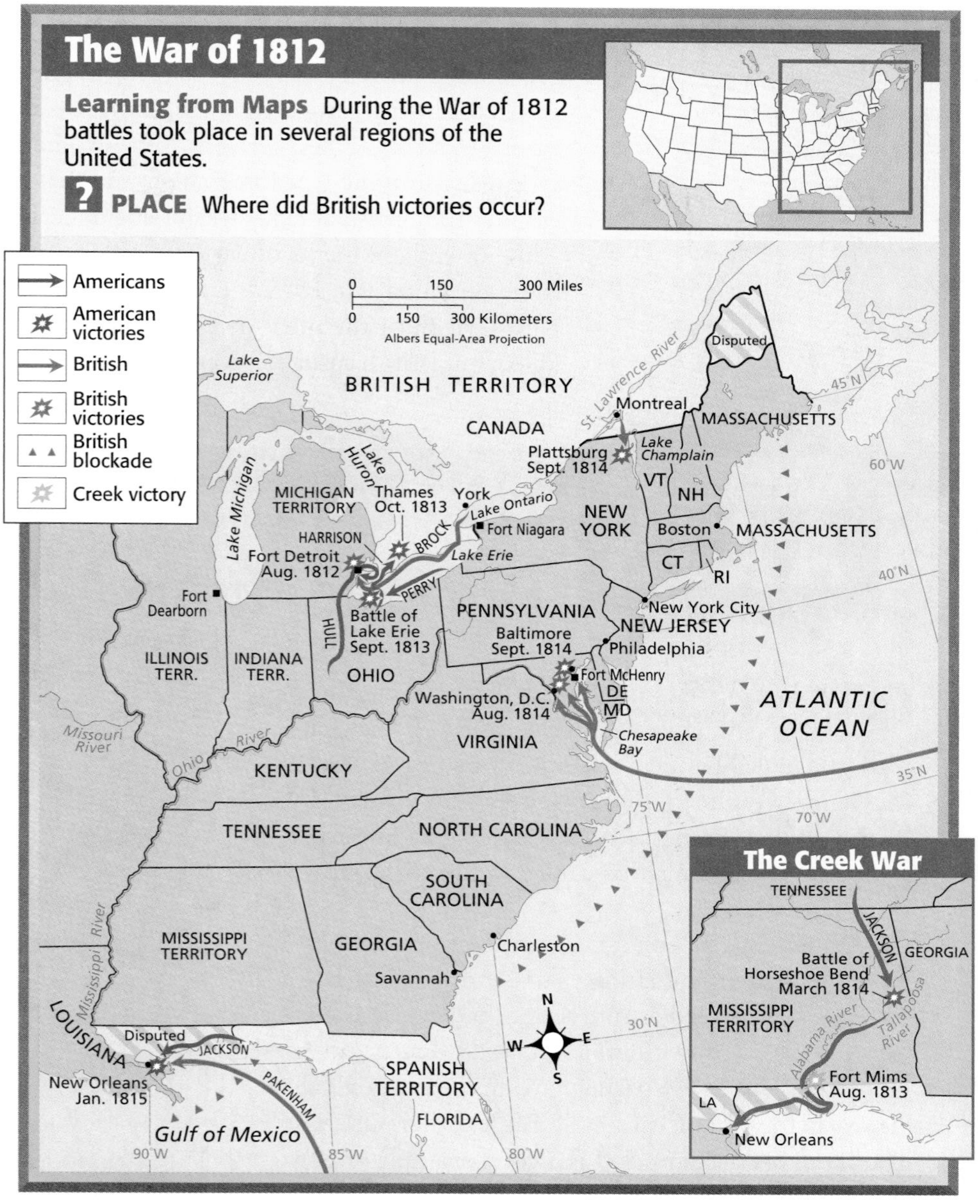

On the night of August 24, 1814, British forces struck Washington. Within a day they had captured the city, burning major public buildings. First Lady Dolley Madison escaped the executive mansion just hours before enemy forces crashed through the doors.

Dolley Payne Madison was born to a Quaker family in North Carolina in 1768. She moved with her family to Philadelphia, where she met and married lawyer John Todd. Todd died when a yellow fever epidemic broke out in 1793.

By the following spring, Dolley Todd had become acquainted with James Madison. The two were married in September 1794. During Madison's presidency, the White House sparkled as the center of Washington society. The Wednesday evening receptions hosted by the first lady became well known as gatherings for politicians, diplomats, and the general public.

In August 1814, as British troops prepared to raid the capital, Dolley Madison packed some of the nation's most precious belongings, including Gilbert Stuart's portrait of George Washington. After James Madison's presidency ended, the couple moved to Virginia. When he died in 1836, Dolley Madison returned to Washington, where her home once again became a social center until her death in 1849.

British soldiers, emboldened by their success, moved along the coast to the port city of Baltimore. There British vessels bombarded Fort McHenry, but the fort's

BIOGRAPHY

Dolley Madison

The War of 1812

Learning from Maps During the War of 1812 battles took place in several regions of the United States.

❓ PLACE Where did British victories occur?

Legend:
- → Americans
- ✦ American victories
- → British
- ✦ British victories
- ▲▲ British blockade
- ✦ Creek victory

0   150   300 Miles
0   150   300 Kilometers
Albers Equal-Area Projection

BRITISH TERRITORY

Lake Superior

CANADA

St. Lawrence River

Montreal

Disputed   45°N

MASSACHUSETTS

Plattsburg Sept. 1814

Lake Champlain

VT   NH   60°W

Lake Huron

Lake Michigan

MICHIGAN TERRITORY

Thames Oct. 1813

York

Lake Ontario

Fort Niagara

BROCK

NEW YORK

Boston   MASSACHUSETTS

Fort Detroit Aug. 1812

HARRISON

PERRY

Lake Erie

CT   RI   40°N

Fort Dearborn

HULL

Battle of Lake Erie Sept. 1813

PENNSYLVANIA

Baltimore Sept. 1814

New York City

NEW JERSEY

Philadelphia

ILLINOIS TERR.

INDIANA TERR.

OHIO

Fort McHenry

Washington, D.C. Aug. 1814

DE
MD

ATLANTIC OCEAN

Missouri River

Ohio River

VIRGINIA

Chesapeake Bay   35°N

KENTUCKY

TENNESSEE

NORTH CAROLINA

75°W   70°W

Mississippi River

MISSISSIPPI TERRITORY

SOUTH CAROLINA

GEORGIA

Charleston

Savannah

LOUISIANA

Disputed

JACKSON

PAKENHAM

New Orleans Jan. 1815

N   W   E   S   30°N

SPANISH TERRITORY

FLORIDA

Gulf of Mexico

90°W   85°W   80°W

The Creek War

TENNESSEE

JACKSON

Battle of Horseshoe Bend March 1814

GEORGIA

Tallapoosa River

MISSISSIPPI TERRITORY

Alabama River

Fort Mims Aug. 1813

LA

New Orleans

brave stand proved a major setback for the British. The failed attack on Baltimore ended the British campaign in the Chesapeake. Britain then assembled about 7,500 troops to strike at New Orleans. When General Andrew Jackson arrived in New Orleans to lead the U.S. forces, he found that few preparations had been made to counter the British attack. Jackson energetically organized his troops to construct a line of embankments of earth, fortified by cannons. When the invasion finally came on January 8, 1815, the well-protected U.S. troops easily won the **Battle of New Orleans**—the most decisive U.S. victory in the war. Few Americans were killed, but British casualties topped 2,000.

AMERICAN ARTS

Patriotic Music

The War of 1812 provided a dramatic backdrop for a new era of patriotic music. "The Star-Spangled Banner" celebrates the survival of Fort McHenry despite a night-long bombardment by British artillery. Francis Scott Key had the unique experience of witnessing this attack while on board a British warship.

A different wartime experience led Samuel Woodworth to write "The Hunters of Kentucky." In 1814 Andrew Jackson led a militia that had carried Kentucky rifles from Tennessee and Kentucky to Louisiana. There they participated in the greatest U.S. victory in the War of 1812—the Battle of New Orleans. The "Hunters of Kentucky" is a good example of how American patriotic music reflected the mood of the times and how Americans perceived their past.

THE GRANGER COLLECTION, NEW YORK (BOTH)

Lyrics and sheet music from the early 1800s

from "The Star-Spangled Banner"

O say can you see by the dawn's early light,
   What so proudly we hailed at the twilight's last
      gleaming;
Whose broad stripes and bright stars, through the
      perilous fight,
   O'er the ramparts we watched were so gallantly
      streaming?
And the rocket's red glare, the bombs bursting in air,
   Gave proof through the night that our flag was still
      there;
     O say does that Star-spangled Banner yet wave
     O'er the land of the free and the home of the
      brave?

from "The Hunters of Kentucky"

We are a hardy, free-born race,
   Each man to fear a stranger;
Whate'er the game we join in chase,
   Despising toil and danger,
And if a daring foe annoys,
   Whate'er his strength and forces,
We'll show him that Kentucky boys
   Are alligator horses.
Oh Kentucky, the hunters of Kentucky!
Oh Kentucky, the hunters of Kentucky!

Understanding the Arts

1. What emotions are described in "The Star-Spangled Banner"?
2. In what ways are "The Star-Spangled Banner" and "The Hunters of Kentucky" alike? In what ways are they different?

The End of the War

The fighting at New Orleans came after months of peace negotiations had already produced the **Treaty of Ghent**. The treaty was signed by U.S. and British representatives in Belgium on December 24, 1814. It officially ended the war and restored all conquered territory. Reports of the U.S. victory at New Orleans reached Washington at about the same time as news of the peace treaty, leading many to assume that the victory had affected the settlement.

Neither side gained much by the Treaty of Ghent. It also failed to solve the problems of impressment and trade embargoes. Nevertheless, the war was a turning point for the United States. It strengthened U.S. control over the Northwest Territory through the defeat of American Indians and the removal of their British allies. In addition, it ultimately resulted in a peace between the United States and Britain that marked the beginning of a long partnership.

At the same time, however, the war further divided the nation. New England Federalists had bitterly opposed the war. So great was their discontent that some of them met in December 1814 at Hartford, Connecticut, to discuss negotiating a separate peace with Britain. Some even suggested seceding from the Union. The majority at the **Hartford Convention** voted against secession, suggesting instead that the Federalists push for a constitutional amendment that would limit the powers of Congress and the southern states. The proposal arrived in Washington about the same time the city learned of the peace treaty.

In the wake of the Treaty of Ghent, the Hartford Convention appeared treasonous. The Federalist Party never recovered from the charge of disloyalty. It collapsed a few years after the war's end.

✔ **READING CHECK:** How did the War of 1812 affect the United States and Britain?

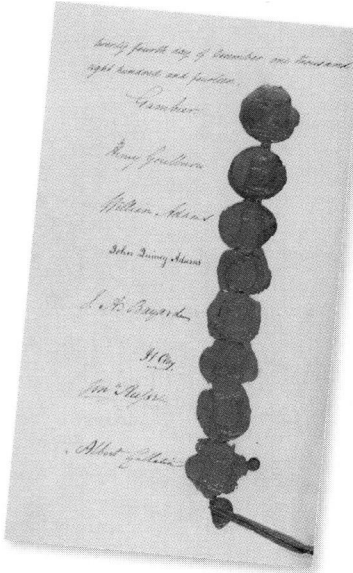

The Treaty of Ghent was signed on December 24, 1814, two weeks before the last battle of the war was fought in New Orleans.

SECTION 4 REVIEW

Define and explain the significance of the following terms:
Orders in Council
Embargo Act
Non-Intercourse Act
Battle of Tippecanoe
Battle of the Thames
Battle of New Orleans
Treaty of Ghent
Hartford Convention

Identify and explain the significance of the following individuals:
Tecumseh
William Henry Harrison
Dolley Madison
Andrew Jackson

Locate and explain the importance of the following places:
Lake Erie

1. **Using Graphic Organizers** Copy the diagram below. List the path of events that led to the outbreak of the War of 1812.

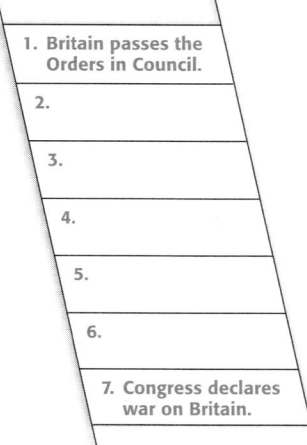

1. Britain passes the Orders in Council.
2.
3.
4.
5.
6.
7. Congress declares war on Britain.

2. **Problem Solving** What actions do you think the United States could have taken against the pirates in the Barbary States?
3. **Identifying Cause and Effect** Why did Tecumseh try to create an American Indian confederation? Why did the confederation fail to achieve its goals?
4. **Assessing Consequences** What was the significance of the War of 1812 for the United States and Great Britain?

Critical Thinking

5. How did U.S. forces prove in the War of 1812 that their victory in the Revolutionary War was not pure luck?
   Consider:
   • the major U.S. victories
   • the major U.S. defeats
   • how experiences of U.S. forces during the War of 1812 compared to experiences of U.S. forces in the Revolutionary War

Review

Creating a Time Line

Copy the time line below onto a sheet of paper. Complete the time line by filling in the events and dates from the chapter that you think were most significant. Pick three events and explain why you think they were significant.

1789   **1802**   **1815**

Writing a Summary

Using the Reading Checks as a guide, write an overview of the events in the chapter.

Identifying People and Ideas

Identify the following terms or individuals and explain their significance.

1. Bill of Rights
2. Alexander Hamilton
3. Whiskey Rebellion
4. right of deposit
5. John Marshall
6. Louisiana Purchase
7. Toussaint-Louverture
8. Sacagawea
9. Tecumseh
10. Dolley Madison

Understanding Main Ideas

SECTION 1
1. How did the creation of the Bill of Rights, the Judiciary Act of 1789, and the executive departments help to organize the new federal government?

SECTION 2
2. How did U.S. conflicts with France cause problems between members of U.S. political parties?

SECTION 3
3. How was the purchase of Louisiana beneficial for both France and the United States?

SECTION 4
4. How did the War of 1812 affect the United States and Great Britain?

Reviewing Themes

1. **Constitutional Heritage** How does the U.S. Constitution balance individual rights and the need to uphold the authority of government?
2. **Economic Development** Describe how Alexander Hamilton's financial program affected the economy.
3. **Democratic Values** How does a democracy encourage the formation of political parties?

Thinking Critically

1. **Using Historical Imagination** Imagine that you are an American Indian in the Louisiana Territory. Will you aid or oppose the Lewis and Clark expedition? Explain your answer.
2. **Hypothesizing** What effect do you think a sedition act might have on today's press?
3. **Problem Solving** What solutions would you, as a government official, have proposed in order to avoid war with Britain in 1812?
4. **Comparing and Contrasting** What were the differences between Thomas Jefferson's and Alexander Hamilton's views of the U.S. Constitution?
5. **Evaluating** Why did the purchase of Louisiana seem to be a contradiction to Thomas Jefferson's interpretation of the Constitution?

Writing About History

Writing to Express Imagine that you are a newspaper editor in the early 1800s. Write an editorial expressing your opinion about the declaration of war in 1812. Use the following graphic to organize your thoughts.

PRO — Declaration of War — CON

Americans fleeing Washington during the British attack in August 1814

 internet connect

TOPIC: War of 1812
GO TO: go.hrw.com
KEYWORD: SD1 War of 1812

Accessing the Internet through the HRW Web site, read about the War of 1812. Imagine that you are an American who has a friend in Great Britain. Since the restrictions against Britain have been lifted for the first time in years, you can now write a letter to your friend. Tell your friend about some of your experiences in the war and explain why you supported it.

Strategies for Success Review the **Strategies for Success** on *Taking a Test*. Then review this chapter and list four essay questions that you think may appear on a future test. Make an outline of the main ideas and supporting details that you would use to answer each question, and save your notes to study.

Linking History and Geography

Number your paper from 1 to 13. Study the map below, which shows the states, either in full or in part, that were formed from the Louisiana Purchase. Write the name of the state next to the corresponding number.

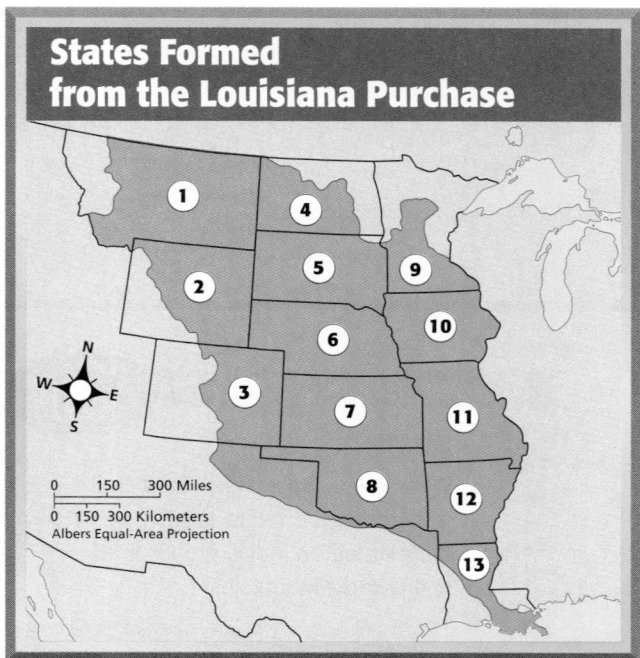

States Formed from the Louisiana Purchase

BUILDING YOUR PORTFOLIO

Complete one or all of the following projects independently or cooperatively.

1 Geographic Diversity
*Imagine that you are a resident of either the Northeast, the South, or the Midwest in the late 1700s. **Write a letter to a politician friend** in Washington explaining the ways in which the federal government is or is not meeting the political and economic interests of your region.*

2 Constitutional Heritage
*Imagine that you are a member of a group that thinks the Bill of Rights is inadequate. **Create a banner** showing two individual rights you want Congress to add to the Bill of Rights.*

3 Global Relations
*Imagine that you are a member of the U.S. War Department. **Create a chart** showing how you will supply the army and the navy during the War of 1812. Use icons or pictures to represent supplies.*

The American West

Popular views of the American West have changed greatly over time. As the United States expanded its borders from east to west, the area that most Americans once thought of as an uninviting wilderness became an exciting new land of opportunity. Yet many people—from American Indians to Spanish missionaries and French soldiers—were drawn to the West long before U.S. citizens began to settle there. Today the West continues to be one of the most culturally and ethnically diverse regions of the nation, attracting visitors and new settlers from throughout the world.

▢	U.S. territory
▢	Spanish territory
▢	British territory
▢	Northwest Territory
▪	Spanish settlements and missions
▪	French forts and settlements
YAKIMA	American Indian tribes

The West in 1790

MAKAH
CHINOOK SPOKANE
YAKIMA NEZ PERCÉ
CAYUSE WALLA WALLA
KLIKITAT WALLA WALLA

GREAT LAKES

Disputed

MA
VT NH MA CT
NY
IROQUOIS
PA RI NJ
DE MD

MODOC
BANNOCK
NORTHERN SHOSHONI
CROW
SIOUX SIOUX
SAUK FOX
CHEYENNE ARAPAHO

ROCKY

MIWOK
WESTERN SHOSHONI
PAIUTE
YOKUT
UTE
MTS.
PAWNEE
THE TRANS-APPALACHIAN WEST

NAVAJO
KIOWA
OSAGE
CHEROKEE NC
CHICKASAW
SC

YUMA
APACHE
COMANCHE
CHOCTAW
CREEK GA

SEMINOLE

APPALACHIAN MTS.
VA

0   250   500 Miles
0   250   500 Kilometers
Albers Equal-Area Projection

This sod house was made from bricks of soil.

The Trans-Appalachian West. In 1790 most Americans considered the Trans-Appalachian West—the area between the Appalachian Mountains and the Mississippi River—to be "the West." Few dared move beyond the Mississippi River. Spain claimed most of the territory west of the Mississippi. With the exception of a few small Spanish and French settlements, this territory remained the free domain of American Indians.

GEOGRAPHY AND HISTORY Skills

MOVEMENT
1. Where were most French forts and settlements located in 1790?
2. What American Indian groups lived in the Rocky Mountains?

The West Today

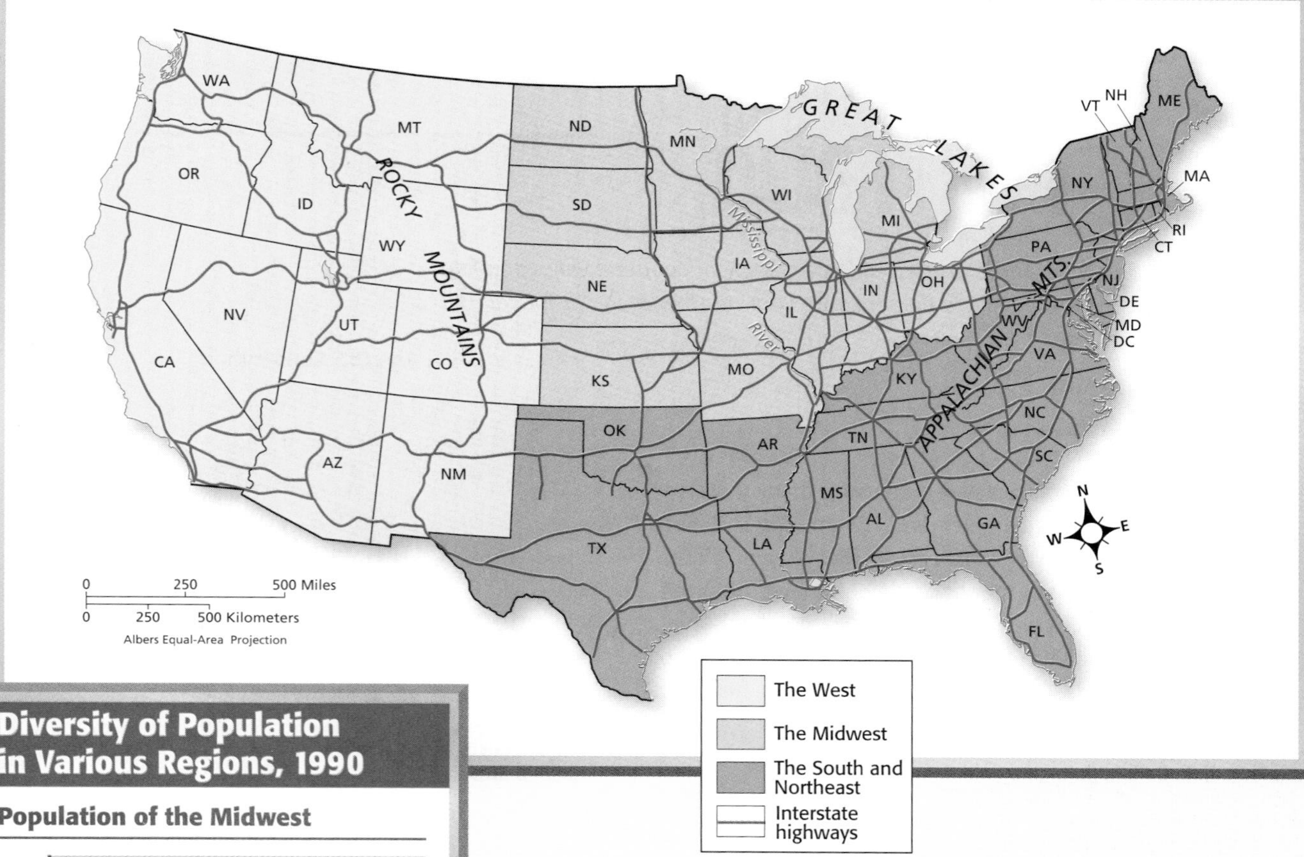

AMERICA'S Geography

The West

The Midwest

The South and Northeast

Interstate highways

0 250 500 Miles
0 250 500 Kilometers
Albers Equal-Area Projection

Diversity of Population in Various Regions, 1990

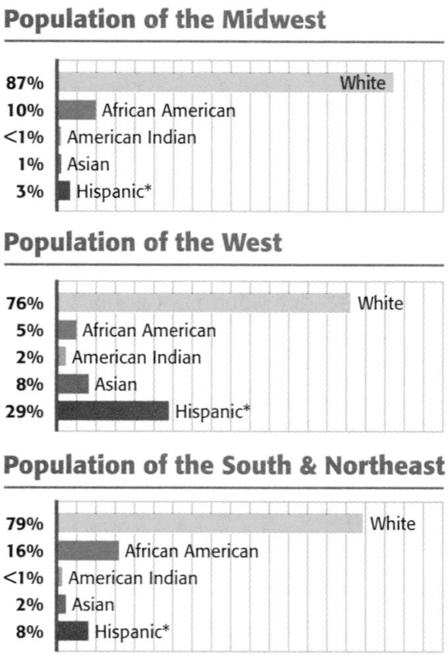

Population of the Midwest

- 87% White
- 10% African American
- <1% American Indian
- 1% Asian
- 3% Hispanic*

Population of the West

- 76% White
- 5% African American
- 2% American Indian
- 8% Asian
- 29% Hispanic*

Population of the South & Northeast

- 79% White
- 16% African American
- <1% American Indian
- 2% Asian
- 8% Hispanic*

*Hispanic may include persons of any race; thus charts represent more than 100 percent.

Source: Statistical Abstract of the United States: 1998

Defining the West. Although some people associate the West with images of cattle drives or American Indians, others see it as a place of great diversity. There is confusion as to the physical boundaries of the West. For example, although the U.S. Census considers Texas and Oklahoma to be southern states, many people consider them part of the West. The culture and ethnic composition of both states resembles that of the western states.

GEOGRAPHY AND HISTORY Skills

REGION

1. What ethnic groups have greater representation in the West than in any other region?
2. Which western state has the fewest miles of interstate highways?

219

U·N·I·T 2

Review

Outlined below are three projects. Independently or cooperatively, complete one and use the products to demonstrate your mastery of the historical concepts involved.

The USS Constitution

1 Global Relations

The United States experienced many threats to its security between 1775 and 1815. *Create an organizational chart* that illustrates how the War Department should have coordinated both the recruitment of troops and the provision of necessary supplies during this period. You may wish to use portfolio materials you designed in the unit chapters to help you.

Bostonians reading the Stamp Act of 1765

2 Constitutional Heritage

The right to protest is one of many rights that colonists defended during the Revolution. *Write a script for a debate* between government officials and protesting citizens that focuses on the government's right to tax versus the citizens' right to oppose unfair taxes. You may wish to use portfolio materials you designed in the unit chapters to help you.

Buttons commemorating George Washington's presidency

3 **Democratic Values**

Although George Washington hoped that the new nation would be spared from disunity, sectionalism encouraged the rise of political parties. *Write a political party platform* that addresses the concerns and interests of the states in your region. Your platform should outline the philosophy of the party, discuss specific issues affecting your region, and demonstrate how your party proposes to deal with those issues. You may wish to use portfolio materials you designed in the unit chapters to help you.

Further Reading

Ambrose, Stephen F. *Undaunted Courage.* Touchstone, 1997. Narrative of the Lewis and Clark expedition.

Faber, Doris, and Harold Faber. *The Birth of a Nation.* Scribner, 1989. Examination of the significant events in the early development of the U.S. federal government.

Hibbert, Christopher. *Redcoats & Rebels: The American Revolution through British Eyes.* Avon Books, 1991. The war for independence as seen by the British.

Hickey, Donald R. *The War of 1812: A Short History.* University of Illinois Press, 1989. A brief overview of the key events of the War of 1812.

Rutland, Robert. *The Ordeal of the Constitution: The Antifederalists and the Ratification Struggle of 1787–1788.* Northeastern University Press, 1983. Account of Antifederalists' attempts to prevent the ratification of the Constitution.

Wheeler, Richard. *Voices of 1776.* Meridian, 1991. Firsthand accounts of the American Revolution from both the British and American sides.

Internet Connect and Holt Researcher CD–ROM *Review*

In assigned groups, develop a multi-media presentation about America in the years between 1763 and 1815. Choose information from the chapter Internet Connect activities and from the **Holt Researcher** CD–ROM that best reflect the major topics of the period. Write an outline and a script for your presentation, which may be shown to the class.

Growth and Change

1790–1860

Samuel Waugh's 1847 painting, **The Bay and Harbor of New York,** *depicts the arrival of immigrants in a bustling New York port.*

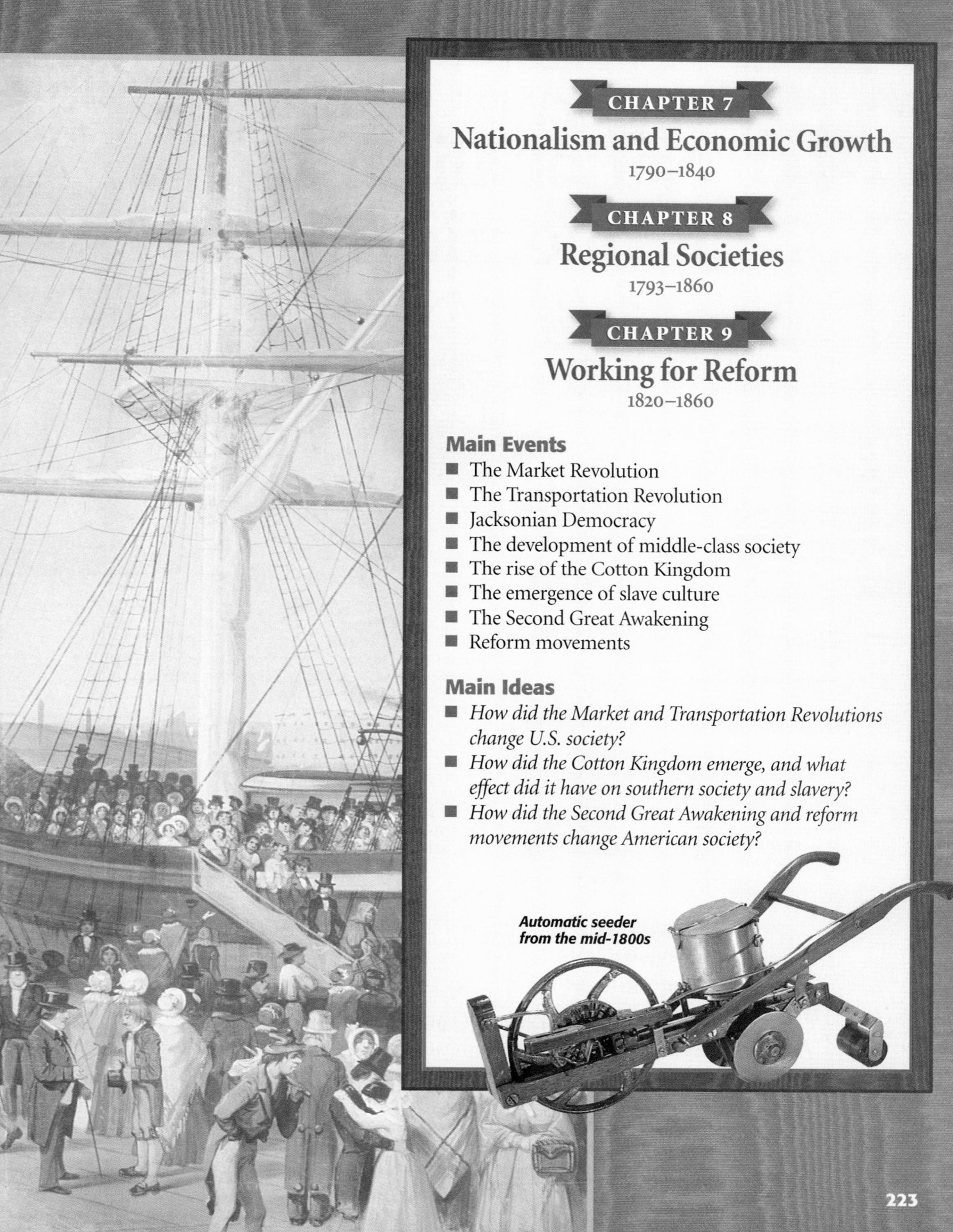

Main Events

- The Market Revolution
- The Transportation Revolution
- Jacksonian Democracy
- The development of middle-class society
- The rise of the Cotton Kingdom
- The emergence of slave culture
- The Second Great Awakening
- Reform movements

Main Ideas

- *How did the Market and Transportation Revolutions change U.S. society?*
- *How did the Cotton Kingdom emerge, and what effect did it have on southern society and slavery?*
- *How did the Second Great Awakening and reform movements change American society?*

Automatic seeder from the mid-1800s

CHAPTER 7

1790–1840

Nationalism and Economic Growth

One of Eli Whitney's machines for making musket parts

Clock made by Seth Thomas about 1855

1790
The Arts
The first musical competition in the United States is held.

1793
Daily Life
A yellow fever epidemic hits Philadelphia.

1798
Science and Technology
Eli Whitney develops interchangeable parts for gun manufacturing.

c. 1808
Daily Life
Men's ponytails go out of style.

1812
Business and Finance
Seth Thomas opens his factory for mass-producing wooden clocks.

1790

1800

1810

1791
Business and Finance
Samuel Slater's textile mill produces its first yarn.

1807
Science and Technology
Robert Fulton completes his improved steamboat, *Clermont.*

1814
Science and Technology
Deborah Skinner tests the first power-driven spinning loom.

Robert Fulton's steamboat, Clermont

Power loom in a textile mill

THE GRANGER COLLECTION, NEW YORK

Before You Read

Build on What You Know

The War of 1812 did not produce a clear-cut victory for the United States. It did, however, prove that the new nation could stand up to a major European power. Americans began to believe that the United States could become a power in its own right, free from Europe's influence and control. In this chapter you will learn how, after the War of 1812, Americans were filled with national pride and confidence in the future. U.S. officials asserted a stronger foreign policy as a new spirit of democracy and optimism swept the nation.

Embroidered Seminole bandolier bag

1817
World Events
U.S. invasion of Spanish Florida leads to the First Seminole War.

1817
Business and Finance
John C. Calhoun calls for the creation of a Second Bank of the United States.

1820
Politics
The Missouri Compromise settles the dispute over slavery in that state.

1827
The Arts
Several steamboats are named after Clara Fisher, the nation's most popular actress.

Woman dressed in 1820s evening wear

1830
Daily Life
Women's fashions include puffy sleeves and large hats adorned with flowers and ribbon.

1830
Science and Technology
The speed of the locomotive *Tom Thumb* is tested against a race horse.

1820

1830

1840

1819
Business and Finance
A financial panic leads to an economic depression.

1825
Science and Technology
Construction of the Erie Canal is finished.

1830
Politics
Congress passes the Indian Removal Act.

1836
Business and Finance
President Jackson issues a new money policy that leads to numerous bank failures.

1818
World Events
The Convention of 1818 establishes the border between the United States and Canada.

1830
World Events
Simón Bolívar, the "Liberator" of South America, dies.

1828
Politics
Andrew Jackson is elected president.

Andrew Jackson campaign item

Painting of Simón Bolívar

Think About Themes

Themes Journal

Decide whether you agree or disagree with the following statements. Note why in your journal.

Technology and Society The development of new technologies generally results in social progress and a better life for most citizens.

Economic Development Different geographic regions within a country will develop different economic systems.

Democratic Values Economic change can lead to greater political participation among all groups of people.

The Rise of Nationalism

OBJECTIVES

Read to understand:

1. how the War of 1812 helped increase nationalism in the United States
2. what steps U.S. officials took to try to prevent conflict with Great Britain
3. what led Spain to give up Florida to the United States
4. how the Monroe Doctrine reflected growing U.S. power

KEY TERMS

nationalism
Rush-Bagot Agreement
Convention of 1818
First Seminole War
Adams-Onís Treaty
Monroe Doctrine

KEY PEOPLE

James Monroe
Luis de Onís
Simón Bolívar

KEY PLACES

Oregon Country

 **EYEWITNESSES TO History**

66 *[American pride] blazes out everywhere and on all occasions.* 99
—British visitor to the United States

Frances Wright

This unknown British observer sounded a common sentiment about American patriotism after the War of 1812. This pride was exhibited in the way that Americans of the early 1800s celebrated Independence Day with great zest. Parades, picnics, and joyous parties marked the event. Even some foreign citizens saluted the country on this occasion. In the 1820s Frances Wright, a Scottish travel writer, gave a Fourth of July speech at New Harmony, Indiana. She praised the United States as the protector of "human liberty [and] the favored scene of human improvement." Soon, she predicted, "all mankind" would celebrate "the Jubilee of Independence."

Nationalism Takes Root

Much of the new national pride in the United States sprang from the country's success in the War of 1812. The nation did not gain any new territory. To most Americans, however, confirmation of the young republic's independence from Europe was far more important than any new lands. The war stirred a new sense of **nationalism**, or national pride and loyalty. Baltimore newspaper editor Hezekiah Niles captured the growing vitality of the United States in an 1815 editorial in his *Niles' Weekly Register.*

66 *The republic, reposing [resting] on the laurels of a glorious war, gathers the rich harvest of an honorable peace.* Everywhere the sound of the axe is heard, opening the forest to the sun and claiming for agriculture the range of the buffalo. Our cities grow and towns rise up as by magic. . . . The busy hum of 10,000 wheels fills our seaports. . . . The *republic lives,* and in honor! 99

The Niles' Weekly Register *was founded in 1811.*

One key to this prosperity was the continued avoidance of war. The presidents who followed James Madison promised to help the United States stay strong and safe. In 1816, Republicans in Congress nominated Madison's secretary of state, James Monroe of Virginia, for president. Monroe easily defeated the Federalist candidate, Senator Rufus King of New York.

The Federalist Party had angered many Americans by opposing the War of 1812. Even in New England, a longtime Federalist stronghold, the party was losing political power. The collapse of the Federalist Party began a period of political harmony in the United States known as the Era of Good Feelings. President Monroe moved quickly to bring that same harmony to foreign relations.

✔ **READING CHECK:** How did the War of 1812 help increase American nationalism?

Relations with Great Britain

One of the first foreign-policy issues facing President Monroe was the future of U.S. relations with Great Britain. Even after the War of 1812, the two countries continued to sail warships on the Great Lakes. Fearing further conflict, Monroe ordered acting Secretary of State Richard Rush to negotiate a disarmament plan with British foreign minister Charles Bagot. Bagot disliked Americans, but he knew that peace in the Great Lakes region would benefit Britain. Peace would allow Britain to move warships to other parts of its empire. In the **Rush-Bagot Agreement** of 1817, each nation pledged to limit its naval presence on the Great Lakes to a few armed ships.

James Monroe

1758–1831
In Office 1817–1825

James Monroe was the last president to have fought in the Revolutionary War. He also was the last of the Founding Fathers to occupy the White House. Indeed, Monroe looked very much the colonial statesman. He wore a powdered wig and dressed in the fashion of an earlier age. He wore a cutaway coat, waistcoat, knee britches, long stockings, and buckled shoes.

Monroe's generally quiet personality matched his elegant appearance. Thomas Jefferson was a longtime friend of Monroe. Jefferson remarked that Monroe was "a man whose soul might be turned wrong side outward, without discovering a blemish to the world."

Next, Monroe moved to settle a dispute over fishing rights in the waters between Canada and the United States. He also wanted to define the northern boundary of the Louisiana Purchase. In the **Convention of 1818**, Britain and the United States agreed to allow both countries to fish in the disputed waters. The agreement set the U.S.-Canada border at the 49th parallel west to the Rocky Mountains. The two nations also reached an agreement on the Oregon Country—a disputed area of the Pacific Northwest. They would jointly occupy it for 10 years and set a boundary later.

✔ **READING CHECK:** What steps did U.S. officials take to prevent further conflict with Great Britain?

Relations with Spain

Settling border disputes with U.S. neighbors to the south proved much trickier. As early as Thomas Jefferson's presidency, U.S. officials had tried to purchase Spanish-owned West Florida. This strip of land on the Gulf of Mexico stretched across what is now southern Mississippi, Alabama, and eastern Louisiana. In 1810 a group of American settlers in the area sparked a revolt by occupying a Spanish fort in Baton Rouge. These settlers tore down the Spanish flag and replaced it with one representing the "Republic of West Florida."

President Madison sensed that the residents of West Florida supported the revolt. He declared that the area should have been included in the Louisiana Purchase. It therefore rightfully belonged to the United States. Madison sent U.S. troops into the area to enforce this claim. By the end of the War of 1812 the United States controlled most of West Florida.

This flag flew over the short-lived Republic of West Florida.

The First Seminole War.
Spain was too busy with its own problems to resist the U.S. takeover of West Florida. One by one Spain's colonies in Central and South America—present-day Latin America—had declared their independence. To stop these revolts, Spain reassigned many of its soldiers from Florida to Latin

U.S. Boundaries in 1820

Learning from Maps The Convention of 1818 and the Adams-Onís Treaty settled major U.S. boundary disputes with Great Britain and Spain.

? LOCATION About how many miles of the permanent boundary were agreed upon by the Convention of 1818? What was the boundary's location?

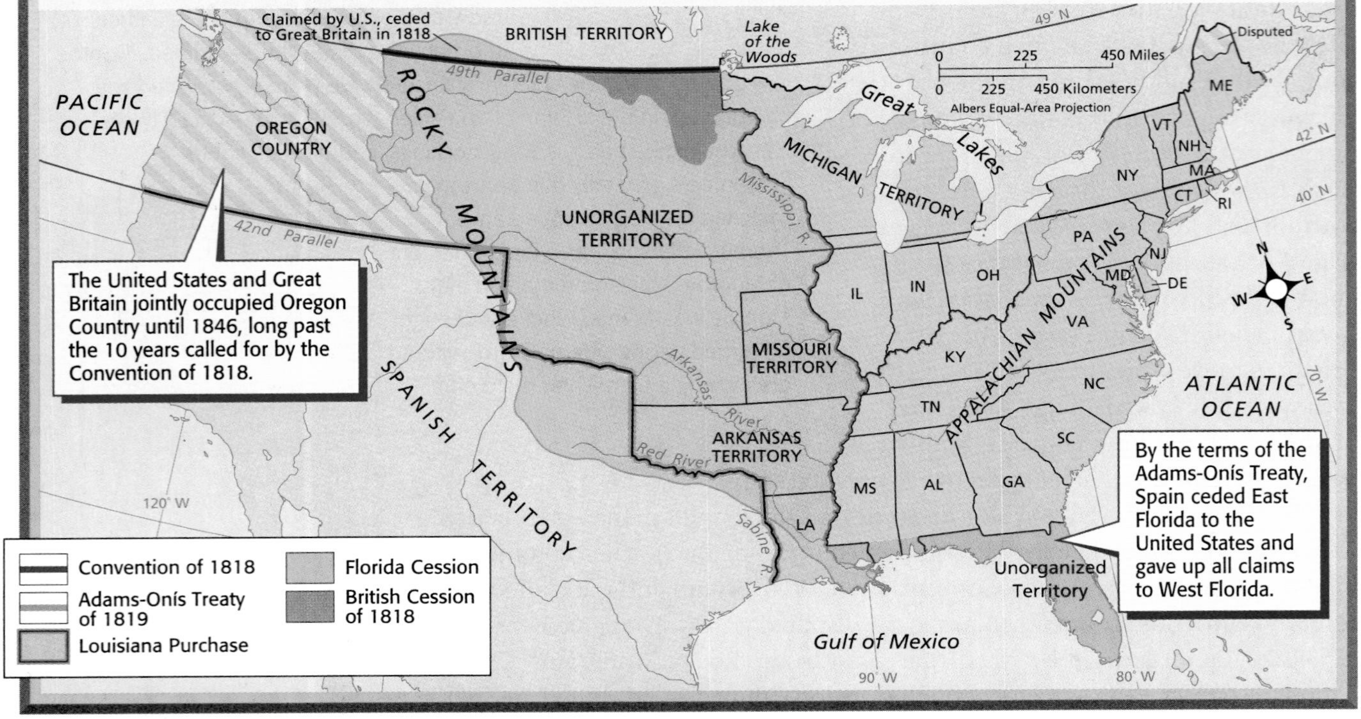

Claimed by U.S., ceded to Great Britain in 1818

BRITISH TERRITORY

Lake of the Woods

49° N

Disputed

PACIFIC OCEAN

49th Parallel

ROCKY MOUNTAINS

Great Lakes

MICHIGAN TERRITORY

ME

VT
NH
MA
NY
CT RI

42° N

40° N

OREGON COUNTRY

42nd Parallel

Mississippi R.

0   225   450 Miles
0   225   450 Kilometers
Albers Equal-Area Projection

The United States and Great Britain jointly occupied Oregon Country until 1846, long past the 10 years called for by the Convention of 1818.

UNORGANIZED TERRITORY

IL   IN   OH

PA
NJ
MD DE

VA

SPANISH TERRITORY

Arkansas River

MISSOURI TERRITORY

KY

APPALACHIAN MOUNTAINS

NC

ATLANTIC OCEAN

70° W

Red River

ARKANSAS TERRITORY

TN

SC

120° W

MS   AL   GA

LA

Sabine R.

Unorganized Territory

By the terms of the Adams-Onís Treaty, Spain ceded East Florida to the United States and gave up all claims to West Florida.

Gulf of Mexico

90° W   80° W

Convention of 1818
Adams-Onís Treaty of 1819
Louisiana Purchase
Florida Cession
British Cession of 1818

A Seminole chief

America. President Monroe saw this reduction of Spanish forces as a chance for the United States to gain control over the rest of Florida. Secretary of State John Quincy Adams began secret negotiations with Spanish minister Luis de Onís for the United States to buy the land.

Violence in East Florida soon threatened these negotiations. Georgia residents complained that the Seminole Indians were crossing the border to raid U.S. towns. The Seminole also harbored many runaway slaves from the South. In December 1817 President Monroe gave General Andrew Jackson command of a force to stop the Indian raids. The conflict that followed became known as the **First Seminole War.** Jackson's troops not only crossed over into East Florida but also began seizing Spanish forts in the area. The U.S. troops soon controlled virtually every Spanish fort in East Florida. Jackson even executed two British officials whom he claimed were aiding the Seminole.

European leaders expressed outrage over Jackson's attack. One British newspaper reacted angrily to the news of the executions. "We can hardly believe that any thing so offensive to public decorum [proper behavior] could be admitted, *even in America!*" The reaction within the United States differed sharply. Most Americans supported both Jackson and the invasion.

Spain decides to deal. Jackson's attack on Florida put President Monroe in an awkward position. He wanted to control Florida but feared triggering a war between the United States and Spain. Publicly, Monroe declared that Jackson had acted on his own, without presidential authority. Although he refused to punish the popular military leader, Monroe returned the captured forts to Spain. Meanwhile, Secretary of State Adams continued to negotiate with Luis de Onís. Noting that the attack had been sparked by concerns over the Seminole, Adams issued a forceful ultimatum. Spain must either guarantee that it could control the Seminole or else it must cede East Florida to the United States. Needing their military forces in Europe and South America, Spanish officials decided they had no choice. They gave up Florida. In the **Adams-Onís Treaty** of 1819, Spain transferred East Florida to the United States.

✔ **READING CHECK:** What led Spain to give up Florida to the United States?

Read More About It

Free Find:
Adams-Onís Treaty
After reading about the Adams-Onís Treaty on the **Holt Researcher** CD–ROM, imagine that you are a reporter for a Spanish newspaper. Write a short article supporting or opposing the treaty.

The Monroe Doctrine

Spain had little option but to give up Florida. By 1819 most of its Latin American colonies had launched revolutions. People in the United States tended to support these rebellions, many of which were inspired by the American Revolution. After the negotiations with Spain regarding Florida had concluded, the U.S. government issued an official policy recognizing the new Latin American republics.

Revolutions. One of the greatest of these Latin American revolutionaries was Simón Bolívar of Venezuela. He helped win independence for his own country in 1821. Bolívar fought in revolutions throughout Latin America, earning him the nickname the Liberator. His dream was that someday all the countries of South America would come together to form one large confederated country, similar to the United States. Bolívar and his followers won many admirers in the United States. Some people even compared him to George Washington.

However, President Monroe and other U.S. officials realized that the independence of these new Latin American nations was far from secure. Monroe knew that other European powers hoped to seize control of the unstable new republics. He was also alarmed by reports that France was prepared to supply troops to help Spain retake its former colonies. In October 1823 Monroe sent a letter to Thomas Jefferson. President Monroe wrote, "We would view an interference [in Latin America] on the part of the European powers as an attack on ourselves."

Adding to the unease was a dispute with Russia over the Pacific Northwest. In 1821 Russia had extended its land claims southward to the 51st parallel and had closed the surrounding coastal waters to foreign ships. In July 1823 Secretary of State John Quincy Adams warned the Russian foreign minister that the United States would not tolerate any new colonies on the American continents.

A warning. President Monroe reaffirmed this view in his annual message to Congress on December 2, 1823. In what came to be called the **Monroe Doctrine**, the president vowed that the United States would not interfere with any existing European colonies in Latin America. However, the United States would consider any European attempt to regain former colonies or establish new ones in the Western Hemisphere "as dangerous to our peace and safety."

Reaction to the doctrine was mixed. A newspaper in Maine proclaimed that the doctrine had been "received throughout the country with a warm and universal

INTERPRETING THE VISUAL RECORD
Portrait of Simón Bolívar.
Paulin Guerin painted this portrait of Simón Bolívar. *What type of leader does the painting suggest Bolívar was?*

★ HISTORICAL DOCUMENTS ★

PRESIDENT JAMES MONROE
The Monroe Doctrine

The Monroe Doctrine marked an important stage in the growth of the United States as a world power. With it, the United States declared its determination to defend not only its own liberty but also the freedom of other nations. Since it was first proclaimed in 1823, many U.S. presidents have cited the doctrine as a guide to foreign policy in Latin America.

With the existing colonies or dependencies of any European power we have not interfered and shall not interfere. But with the governments who have declared their independence and maintained it, and whose independence we have . . . acknowledged, we could not view any interposition [intervention] for the purpose of oppressing them, or controlling in any other manner their destiny, by any European power in any other light than as the manifestation of an unfriendly disposition toward the United States. . . .

Our policy in regard to Europe . . . remains the same, which is, not to interfere in the internal concerns of any of its powers. . . . But in regard to those continents [North and South America] circumstances are . . . different. It is impossible that the allied powers should extend their political system to any portion of either continent without endangering our peace and happiness. . . . It is equally impossible, therefore, that we should behold such interposition in any form with indifference [a lack of concern].

burst of applause." Yet some members of Congress worried that Monroe's statement would drag the nation into foreign wars. One representative called the doctrine "rash and inconsiderate." As the *Boston Advertiser* asked:

> **❝ Is there anything in the Constitution which makes our Government the Guarantors of the Liberties of the World? of . . . the Peruvians? the Chilese [Chileans]? the Mexicans or Colombians? ❞**

The self-proclaimed role of the United States as the "guarantor of liberties" in Latin America would not be challenged for many years. Eager to maintain free trade with the new republics, Britain helped protect their independence. Most other European powers were too busy with their own conflicts to pursue colonization in Latin America. In addition, Russia abandoned its land claims in the Pacific Northwest.

✔ **READING CHECK:** How did the Monroe Doctrine reflect growing U.S. power?

SECTION 1 REVIEW

Define and explain the significance of the following terms:
nationalism
Rush-Bagot Agreement
Convention of 1818
First Seminole War
Adams-Onís Treaty
Monroe Doctrine

Identify and explain the significance of the following individuals:
James Monroe
Luis de Onís
Simón Bolívar

Locate and explain the importance of the following place:
Oregon Country

1. **Using Graphic Organizers** Copy the chart below. Use it to explain the effects the War of 1812 had on the United States.

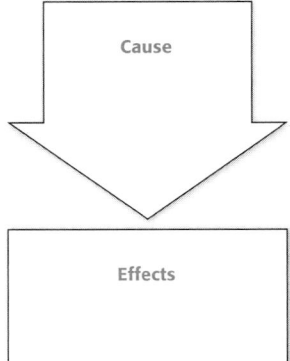

Cause

Effects

2. **Understanding Geography: Human-Environment Interaction** How did conflicts with Great Britain and Spain affect the borders of the United States?
3. **Taking a Stand** Write a brief statement either supporting or opposing President Monroe's major actions regarding foreign policy. Use specific examples from the chapter to explain your answer.
4. **Synthesizing** What did the Monroe Doctrine reveal about U.S. power and regional interests?

Critical Thinking

5. Did U.S. officials adopt the best strategy in its dealings with Great Britain?
   Consider:
   • the steps U.S. officials took to resolve differences with Great Britain
   • the British response to these steps
   • what alternate policies could have been pursued

SECTION 2
The Challenges of Growth

OBJECTIVES

Read to understand:

1. what the American System attempted to accomplish
2. how the Transportation and Market Revolutions affected the U.S. economy
3. how the Industrial Revolution changed the way goods were made in the United States

KEY TERMS

specie
American System
Tariff Act of 1816
National Road
Erie Canal
Market Revolution
Industrial Revolution
mass production
interchangeable parts
Panic of 1819

KEY PEOPLE

Henry Clay
Samuel Slater
Eli Whitney

EYEWITNESSES TO History

66 *We perambulated [walked about] the grounds, and scanned the capabilities of the place. . . . The remark was made that some of us might live to see the place contain twenty thousand inhabitants.* 99

—Nathan Appleton

Nathan Appleton

Boston business leader Nathan Appleton recalled how, a few years after the War of 1812, he joined a group of investors to find a location to build a new textile plant. He and his partners examined a spot that would take advantage of the power from a large waterfall off the Merrimack River in Massachusetts. The area contained few inhabitants and only a handful of houses surrounded the site. The settlement that he and his partners chose soon grew to be one of the most important manufacturing centers in the Northeast, beginning a new era of economic growth.

The Economy

During the War of 1812 the flow of European products to the United States was all but stopped by embargoes and naval blockades. Americans had been forced to produce goods themselves. This gave U.S. manufacturing a big boost. By 1815, during the Era of Good Feelings, many Republicans who had formerly opposed a strong central government were calling for national measures to promote manufacturing and to strengthen the country's financial system.

Many people began to agree with the Federalist view that to remain strong the United States needed to balance the needs of agriculture, manufacturing, and commerce. Even Thomas Jefferson, a promoter of agriculture, experienced a change of heart. "To be independent for the comforts of life," he wrote a colleague, "we must fabricate [make] them ourselves. We must now place the manufacturer by the side of the agriculturist."

The war also revealed weaknesses in the nation's financial system. By mid-1814 the war had drained the U.S. Treasury. Without the Bank of the United States, which Congress had refused to recharter in 1811, the Treasury had to rely on state banks for loans. Instead of borrowing from one central bank, the government had to negotiate with many banks. Securing loans was only part of the problem. Each bank printed its own notes, often in amounts far exceeding the **specie**—gold or silver coins—that the bank held to back up the notes. As a result, banks often refused to accept one another's notes.

Wartime also highlighted the nation's transportation problems. With sea trade blocked by British ships, merchants had to transport goods overland. This slowed delivery and increased the cost of goods. Many members of Congress came to believe that the solution to these problems required a combined effort between businesses and the federal government.

Notes issued by private banks

The American System

The War of 1812 had convinced many older Republicans to support a stronger federal government. Many younger party members, though, had already been thinking in these national terms. Chief among these "nationalists" was Representative Henry Clay of Kentucky.

Henry Clay

Read More About It

Free Find: Henry Clay
After reading about Henry Clay on the **Holt Researcher** CD–ROM, create a poster in support of Clay for president that shows the politician's many accomplishments.

Clay's idea. Henry Clay was born in Virginia in 1777. By the age of 15 he was working as a legal clerk, where he began to study the court system. In 1797 he passed the bar examination and became an attorney.

Clay greatly admired Thomas Jefferson and loved politics. After moving to Kentucky, he quickly established himself as a leader in the young state, winning a spot in the state legislature in 1803.

Clay served Kentucky in numerous roles. He was a U.S. senator and a member of the House of Representatives. A skilled politician, Clay was appointed Speaker of the House in 1811. He developed the office of Speaker into a powerful position. Clay also developed a strong desire to become president, a goal he never achieved before his death in 1852. Nonetheless, many historians consider him one of the most important politicians of the 1800s.

One of the programs for which Clay is most noted is his proposal to increase federal involvement in the economy. Known as the **American System**, Clay's plan had three main features. It called for a national bank to provide sound currency and free the government from having to borrow from many different banks. The plan also called for a protective tariff to encourage industrial development; and a national transportation system to unite northern manufacturers, western farmers, and southern planters. Clay explained that closer federal supervision of the economy would benefit all Americans.

66 On a general survey, we behold . . . the arts flourishing, the face of the country improved; our people fully and profitably employed, and the public countenance [bearing] exhibiting tranquillity, contentment and happiness. 99

Clay received support for much of his plan. By 1816 the public demand for a sound national currency was growing. Even President James Madison, a Republican who had opposed the Bank of the United States, declared in his annual message to Congress that a national bank was worth considering.

Clay and other nationalists in Congress took this message as a sign that Republicans would no longer oppose the creation of a national bank. On January 8, 1816, South Carolina representative John C. Calhoun introduced a bill to charter the Second Bank of the United States. President Madison signed the bill into law on April 10 of that year.

This handkerchief was created to show support for Henry Clay.

The Tariff of 1816. Clay's call for a protective tariff also won broad support. After the Treaty of Ghent was signed, British-made goods had again flooded U.S. ports. Unable to sell their goods as cheaply as the much larger British companies, American manufacturers demanded protective measures. Congress passed the **Tariff Act of 1816**. This act placed a 25 percent duty on most imported factory goods.

The tariff enjoyed wide support among northern manufacturers. However, New England importers and southern planters who relied on British trade opposed the tariff. Representative John Randolph of Virginia saw the fight over the tariff as a conflict between southern planters and northern manufacturers. Even Calhoun became a champion of the southern position by the 1820s.

Strategies for Success   Reviewing Map Basics

A map is a representation of a geographic area that is drawn to scale. Many maps share one or more of several common features. The *legend,* or key, explains any special symbols, colors, or shadings used on a map. The *directional indicator* marks the four cardinal points: *N* for north, *S* for south, *E* for east, and *W* for west. The *scale,* which is usually labeled in both miles and kilometers, relates distances on a map to actual distances on Earth's surface. *Grid lines* provide a frame of reference for a map in terms of *latitude* and *longitude.*

How to Read a Map

1. **Determine the focus of the map.** Read the map's title and labels to determine its subject and the geographic area it covers.
2. **Study the legend.** Read the legend to become familiar with the map's symbols, colors, or shadings.
3. **Check directions and distances.** Consult the directional indicator and the scale to determine the map's directions and distances.
4. **Analyze the information.** Examine the map's features and details, referring to the legend when necessary.
5. **Put the data to use.** Use your analysis of the data to form generalizations and draw conclusions.

Applying the Strategy

Study the map to the right. Note how it incorporates a variety of information in one map.

Practicing the Strategy

Using the map shown below, answer the following questions.
1. What parts of the United States were connected by canals and railroads in 1840?
2. What cities served as hubs for more than one type of transportation system?

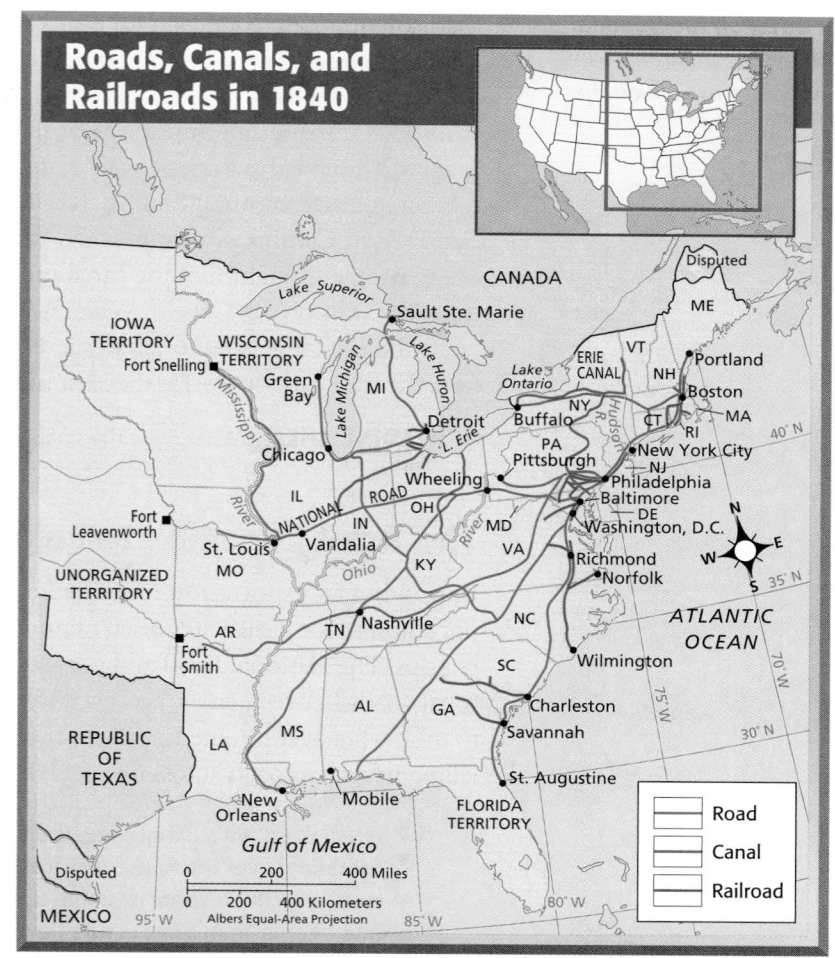

Roads, Canals, and Railroads in 1840

Legend:
- Road
- Canal
- Railroad

(DETAIL) MARYLAND HISTORICAL SOCIETY

The National Road. This painting by Thomas Ruckle shows the Fairview Inn, a rest stop on the National Road. *What can you tell about travel on the National Road from the painting? Who do you think traveled on the road?*

Transportation. In February 1817, however, Calhoun angered many southerners by introducing a bill to fund a national system of roads and canals, using money from tariffs. "Let us . . . bind the republic together with a perfect system of roads and canals," Calhoun told Congress. Congress welcomed the challenge. Most roads in the United States were little more than old trails. Moving goods and troops over such roads during the War of 1812 had been difficult. Many Americans recognized the urgent need for such internal improvements.

Some progress had already been made on a national transportation system. During Thomas Jefferson's presidency, Congress had authorized construction of a roadway from Cumberland, Maryland, across the mountains into the western territories. In 1811 construction of the Cumberland Road, later called the **National Road**, began. By 1818 it reached as far as present-day Wheeling, West Virginia, and was later extended to Vandalia, Illinois.

Although most roads and canals were built by the states or by private companies, Calhoun argued that the great scale of such undertakings required federal assistance. Many members of Congress agreed, and Calhoun's bill passed. President Madison opposed federal aid for roads and canals, however. As his last act in office, Madison vetoed the bill, claiming that it overstepped federal powers.

Despite the lack of federal support, in 1817 New York began one of the most ambitious transportation projects of the era—the **Erie Canal**. The 363-mile-long canal was intended as a cheaper and faster route to and from the interior of the country than roads. It eventually linked the Hudson River with Lake Erie. New York politician DeWitt Clinton worked tirelessly to persuade state officials to fund the project. Many people thought that the canal project was a waste of time. Some mockingly called it "Clinton's big ditch." When it was completed in 1825, however, one supporter boasted that New York had succeeded in building the canal "in the least time, with the least experience, for the least money, and to the greatest public benefit."

✔ **READING CHECK:** What were the goals of the American System?

The Transportation Revolution

Improving transportation remained a major concern. Before 1820 poor transportation made it difficult to sell manufactured goods and farm products between regions. The National Road and a few other major routes connected eastern cities. Most roads between cities, however, were little more than crude trails that turned to mud whenever it rained. British actress Fanny Kemble recalled the experience of riding in a stagecoach across one such road in New York in the 1830s.

66 Away went we . . . bumping, thumping, jumping, jolting, shaking, tossing and tumbling, over the wickedest road, I do think, the cruelest, hard-heartedest road, that ever wheel rumbled upon. Through bog and marsh, and ruts, wider and deeper than any . . . ruts I ever saw, with the roots of trees protruding across our path, . . . and, more than once, a half-demolished tree or stump lying in the middle of the road. 99

Canals and steamboats. Midwestern farmers faced the most severe transportation problems. Although flatboats floated farm products downriver, they were useless in moving goods upriver. Most goods from the East were shipped to the interior by wagon over mountain roads. This was a slow and costly process.

Canals offered one solution to the transportation problem. However, they were expensive and time-consuming to build. By 1816 only about 100 miles of canals had been dug. Canal construction soared, though, after the Erie Canal opened. The canal reduced the cost of moving goods between Buffalo, New York, and New York City by more than 90 percent. Impressed by this cost reduction, other states launched massive canal projects. By 1840, rivers and canals combined to provide a web of waterways stretching from Illinois to the Atlantic Ocean.

Improvements in steamboat construction also aided transportation to the interior. The first American steam-powered riverboat began operating in 1787. However, inventor Robert Fulton's *Clermont*, completed in 1807, was the first steamboat capable of carrying heavy loads upstream. Within just 10 years, steamboats were moving goods up and down the Mississippi River.

The junction of the Erie and Northern Canals was a busy commercial waterway.

Science & Technology

The Canal System

The technology to build canals has existed for more than 2,000 years. The Chinese were using canals as early as 300 B.C. To build a canal, workers dug a level, artificial waterway connecting two other waterways.

Canals served many different purposes. In some areas canals were used to shorten sea routes, such as the canals built across peninsulas to connect large bodies of water. In other areas canals served as an extended "highway" connecting towns and people to one another.

The invention of canal locks in China in the 900s greatly improved canal systems. Locks were closed-off sections of canals that contained little or no water. Working with a system of barrier gates, the canal operators raise the level of water in the lock to allow a boat to enter and float to the other end, where it either enters a new lock or a new waterway. This process allows canals to be built between waterways of differing levels. It even allows for the creation of canals that are not attached to a major waterway.

When industrialization began, some business leaders built canals to connect businesses. This created better transportation routes than the existing roads, which were poorly constructed. Although the use of canals declined in the late 1800s, some, including the Erie Canal, are still in use today.

① Towpaths were used by horses and mules as they pulled barges through the canal.

② The cement used in the Erie Canal was a special mixture of limestone and sand that hardened underwater.

Understanding Science and History

1. How does the lock system work on a canal?
2. How did canals affect business growth?

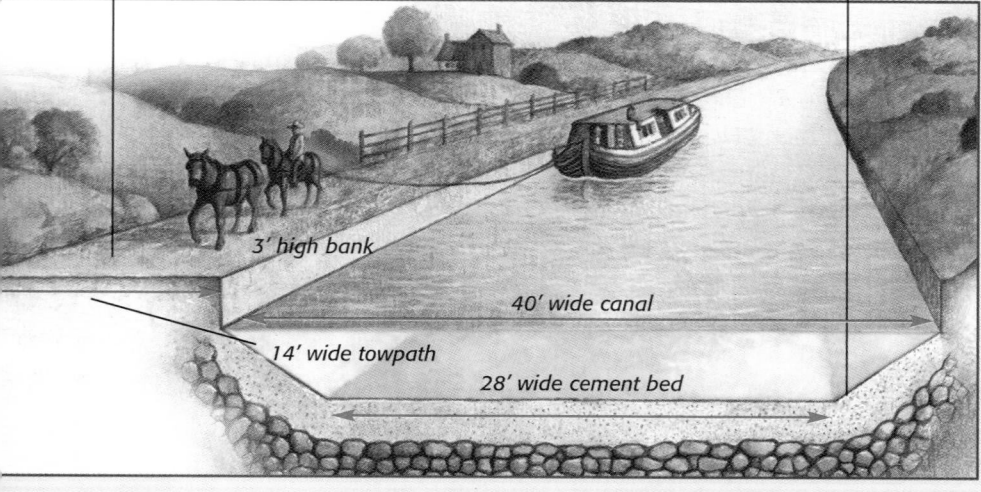

3' high bank

40' wide canal

14' wide towpath

28' wide cement bed

THE GRANGER COLLECTION, NEW YORK

Locomotives. Another steam-powered invention, the locomotive, originated in Europe and came into commercial use in the United States in the 1830s. Trains had one big advantage over steamboats—they could go anywhere that tracks could be laid. However, early locomotives were plagued by mechanical troubles. As a result, few people were surprised when the *Tom Thumb*, the first commercially successful steam locomotive in the United States, lost a race against a horse-drawn train. "The race was neck and neck, nose and nose," a witness recalled, until a part on the locomotive engine broke. Then he said, "The safety valve ceased to scream, and the engine for want of breath began to wheeze and pant." Engineers soon solved most of the trains' early mechanical problems. Over the next decade, American companies spent more than $200 million laying nearly 9,000 miles of track.

The Market Revolution. By making it easier and cheaper to move farm products, raw materials, and manufactured goods long distances, road and canal systems created national markets for the first time. Because regions no longer had to be self-sufficient, people could import needed goods and concentrate on producing what was most profitable. This creation of national markets has since come to be known as the **Market Revolution**. It increased farmers' and manufacturers' profits and changed the way they worked and did business. Linking small towns to larger markets increased the size of many towns, particularly in the Midwest. "The western country continues to rise in population and importance with unabated [nonstop] rapidity," reported one newspaper in 1816. The article cited the example of Mount Pleasant, Ohio. This area grew from a small settlement of just seven families in 1806 to a town of almost 100 families 10 years later.

✔ **READING CHECK:** How did the Transportation and Market Revolutions affect the U.S. economy?

The Industrial Revolution

Before the Market Revolution, skilled artisans provided most local manufactured goods. As markets grew, however, artisans could no longer keep up with demand. To produce enough goods, manufacturers reorganized the production process.

Early industrialization. A shift to machine production was part of the **Industrial Revolution**, a period of dynamic changes in manufacturing. The Industrial Revolution began in Britain in the mid-1700s with the invention of new spinning machines. The machines revolutionized the textile industry by allowing for **mass production**—the manufacture of large quantities of goods.

Fearing foreign competition, British officials tried to keep their new technology a secret. They outlawed the sale of textile machines abroad. They also prevented skilled textile workers from leaving the country. Some workers, though, posed as ordinary laborers or farmers and managed to slip out of the country. At least one of these textile workers had memorized machine plans down to the last detail.

THE GRANGER COLLECTION, NEW YORK

One such worker was Samuel Slater, who came to the United States in 1789 with hopes of making a fortune. He quickly convinced Moses Brown, a Rhode Island manufacturer, to finance the construction of a British-style spinning mill. "If I don't make as good yarn as they do in England," Slater promised Brown, "I will have nothing for my services, but will throw the whole of what I have attempted over the bridge." Slater's gamble paid off. Brown and Slater soon had mills all over Rhode Island and Massachusetts.

Inventors also contributed to the rise of U.S. industry. Chief among them was Eli Whitney, who employed **interchangeable parts** in the manufacture of firearms. He reasoned that various musket parts could be machine-produced in mass quantities and used interchangeably in making individual weapons. In 1812 Seth Thomas applied the technique to the manufacture of wooden clocks. Within three years workers in Thomas's factory were making some 500 clocks at a time.

Economic reversal. By 1818 all sections of the country were enjoying prosperity. However, trouble loomed on the horizon. Many manufacturers borrowed money from state banks to finance new enterprises. These banks tended to lend money freely, regardless of a borrower's credit history.

Late in 1818 the Second Bank of the United States attempted to bring this risky practice under control. The Bank ordered state banks to demand repayment of all loans. It also required state banks to exchange their notes for gold and silver. Few banks, however, could do this. The result was the **Panic of 1819**—a chain reaction of bank failures, falling land prices, and foreclosures. The nation quickly sank into an economic depression that lasted several years. The panic and depression ended the prosperity and weakened the optimism of the Era of Good Feelings.

✔ **READING CHECK:** How did the Industrial Revolution change U.S. manufacturing?

INTERPRETING THE VISUAL RECORD
Slater's factory. Samuel Slater's Pawtucket, Rhode Island, mill introduced modern textile manufacturing to the United States. *What is significant about the mill's location? Why is this important?*

 SECTION **2** REVIEW

Define and explain the significance of the following terms:
specie
American System
Tariff Act of 1816
National Road
Erie Canal
Market Revolution
Industrial Revolution
mass production
interchangeable parts
Panic of 1819

Identify and explain the significance of the following individuals:
Henry Clay
Samuel Slater
Eli Whitney

1. **Using Graphic Organizers** Copy the following flowchart. Use it to explain how tariffs, internal improvements, and manufacturing worked together under the American System.

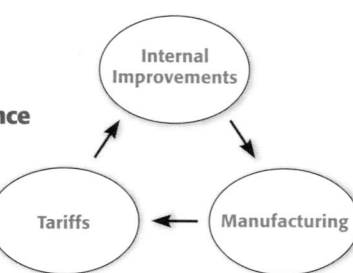

2. **Identifying Cause and Effect** What events shaped the Transportation Revolution? What effect did the Transportation and Market Revolutions have on the United States?

3. **Analyzing** How did the Industrial Revolution affect the U.S. economy?

4. **Distinguishing Fact from Opinion** Was the period after the War of 1812 really an "Era of Good Feelings"? Explain your answer.

Critical Thinking

5. What was Great Britain's role in shaping the U.S. economy in the early 1800s?
   Consider:
   • the effect of the War of 1812 on the U.S. economy
   • Britain's role in the Industrial Revolution
   • the role of trade with Britain

The Rise of Jacksonian Democracy

OBJECTIVES

Read to understand:
1. what role the Missouri Compromise played in the dispute over slavery
2. how the election of 1824 gave rise to charges of a "corrupt bargain," and what characterized John Quincy Adams's presidency
3. how Andrew Jackson's election broke with the politics of the past

KEY TERMS

Missouri Compromise
Democratic Party
spoils system
rotation in office

KEY PEOPLE

John Quincy Adams
Andrew Jackson

KEY PLACES

Missouri

66 *The existence of slavery impairs the industry and power of a nation. If her laborers are slaves, Missouri . . . will be unable to raise soldiers or to recruit seamen; and experience seems to have proved that manufactures do not prosper where the [workers] are slaves.* **99**
—Rufus King

Rufus King

Rufus King of New York was one of the many northern members of Congress who argued that slavery weakened the U.S. economy. King's point arose as slavery became an issue in the Missouri Territory. After the War of 1812, migration west of the Mississippi River increased tremendously. The Missouri Territory experienced some of the nation's fastest population growth between 1815 and 1819. At one point, between 30 and 50 wagonloads of settlers were crossing into the territory each day. Some of these settlers brought slaves with them, leading to a debate over whether slavery should be allowed in Missouri.

The Missouri Compromise

The debate over both slavery and Missouri's economy increased in 1819, when the territory applied for statehood. At that time the Missouri Territory counted some 10,000 enslaved African Americans among its population. Because the nation was then equally divided between slave states and free states (11 to 11), Missouri's admission as a slave state would tip the balance in the Senate in favor of the South.

Congressmember James Tallmadge of New York tried to amend the Missouri statehood bill to require the gradual elimination of slavery in the state. He argued that Congress had already exercised its power to ban slavery in the territories when it passed the Northwest Ordinance in 1787. Slaveholders saw this new proposal as part of a larger attempt to end slavery everywhere. They reacted with alarm and anger. A Georgia representative pointed a shaking finger at Tallmadge and cried, "You have kindled a fire which all the waters of the ocean cannot put out, which seas of blood can only extinguish."

To end the bitter debate, Henry Clay led Congress in working out the **Missouri Compromise** in 1820. The agreement admitted Missouri as a slave state and Maine as a free state, thus keeping the balance in the Senate. The agreement also banned slavery in the rest of the Louisiana Purchase north of latitude 36°30′—Missouri's southern boundary.

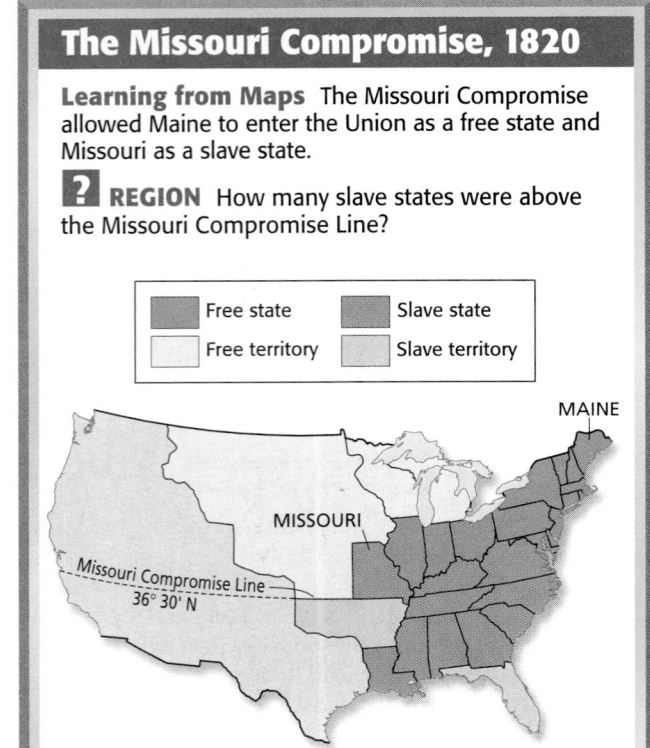

The Missouri Compromise, 1820

Learning from Maps The Missouri Compromise allowed Maine to enter the Union as a free state and Missouri as a slave state.

? **REGION** How many slave states were above the Missouri Compromise Line?

- Free state
- Free territory
- Slave state
- Slave territory

MAINE

MISSOURI

Missouri Compromise Line
36° 30′ N

The Missouri Compromise eased the sectional crisis. However, the debate left many Americans worried that the slavery issue would return. Former president Thomas Jefferson later wrote:

66 **This momentous question, like a fire-bell in the night, awakened and filled me with terror. I considered it at once as the knell of [sound of death for] the Union. It is hushed, indeed, for the moment. But . . . every new irritation will mark it deeper and deeper.** 99

✔ **READING CHECK:** What role did the Missouri Compromise play in the dispute over slavery?

The Election of 1824

Westward expansion played an important role in the presidential election of 1824. By the 1820s, voting laws had become more democratic. This was particularly true in the frontier states, where most white adult males could vote. The expansion of voting rights was accompanied by growing opposition to the nomination of presidential candidates by Congress. Thus, in the 1824 election, numerous state nominating conventions produced lists of candidates. The result was a crowded field of regional favorites.

Five candidates—all Republicans—competed for the presidency: William Crawford of Georgia, John C. Calhoun of South Carolina, John Quincy Adams of Massachusetts, Henry Clay of Kentucky, and Andrew Jackson of Tennessee. A serious illness soon derailed Crawford's candidacy. Calhoun was popular in the Lower South, but failed to build a national following. He eventually dropped out of the race. Adams, an economic nationalist with antislavery views, appealed mostly to northeastern voters. Clay, the architect of the Missouri Compromise and the American System, drew most of his support from the Midwest. Jackson, the famous military hero, represented the rural South.

John Quincy Adams

Jackson received the most popular votes, but no candidate won a majority of the electoral votes. In such situations the House of Representatives chose a president from the top three candidates. Having finished fourth, Clay was out of the race. He could help determine the winner, however, by recommending that his supporters back a particular candidate. Clay, who considered Jackson unqualified for the presidency, threw his support behind Adams. After Adams won the election and took office, he named Clay his secretary of state. Jackson and his followers angrily accused the two men of making a "corrupt bargain." Adams and Clay denied any wrongdoing, but the suspicions remained.

In contrast to lively "Andy" Jackson, Adams had a stern and reserved personality. One observer complained that Adams seemed "hard as a piece of granite and cold as a lump of ice." Adams had been a successful and diplomatic secretary of state, but his personality contributed to a frustrating and largely unsuccessful presidency. He supported a wide variety of federal government projects, from canals and roads to a national university and a standardized system of weights and measures. However, he was

Campaigning

Andrew Jackson campaign button

In many ways the presidential race of 1828 was the first modern election campaign. Unlike earlier candidates who relied on party supporters to campaign for them, Andrew Jackson and John Quincy Adams pursued votes themselves. They used mass-produced trinkets such as buttons, metal coins, and flags to sway the voters. Jackson in particular appealed directly to voters for support and began campaigning three years before the election.

Presidential candidates still focus on reaching out to the public by blanketing the country with bumper stickers, buttons, and signs. Today's office-seekers also appeal directly to voters, occasionally by traveling the country by plane, bus, or train. More often, however, candidates air television and radio commercials.

Jackson's 1828 campaign set another precedent by using county and state campaign committees. These committees held parades, cookouts, and rallies to attract voters. Jackson also created a campaign organization of friends and advisers in Nashville to help him plan his campaign strategy. His correspondence committee was an early version of today's Democratic and Republican National Committees. An organization that was unusual in 1828 has become necessary in modern presidential races.

Louisa Catherine Strobe painted this portrait of Rachel Jackson.

unwilling to "play politics" and to compromise with Congress, and thus failed to achieve most of his goals.

✔ **READING CHECK:** Why were Adams and Clay accused of striking a "corrupt bargain"? What characterized Adams's presidency?

The Election of 1828

Andrew Jackson, a sharp critic throughout John Quincy Adams's presidency, resigned from the Senate in 1825 to campaign for president in the 1828 election. Opponents of President Adams rallied around the tall war hero from Tennessee. One observer described Andrew Jackson as a "roaring, rollicking, . . . horse-racing, card-playing, mischievous fellow." His soldiers had nicknamed Jackson "Old Hickory" because he seemed as tough as the strong hardwood. Although he was a rich lawyer and planter, Jackson stressed his military skills and frontier roots to portray himself as a "man of the people." Jackson's image as a "common man" won the support of farmers, workers, and frontier settlers. His supporters, who had no official name at first, later became known as the **Democratic Party**.

Jacksonian Democracy. Like many modern political campaigns, the 1828 presidential race focused more on the candidates' personalities than on the issues. Each side used personal attacks to win votes. Adams's purchase of a chess set and billiard table for the White House raised charges that he was a snob who wasted money on "gambling devices."

Supporters of Adams labeled Jackson a murderer because of his involvement in a duel that had left a man dead. They also spread rumors about Jackson's beloved wife, Rachel Donelson Robards, who had been separated from her first husband when she met Jackson. Some Adams supporters even spread rumors about Jackson's mother!

Despite the nasty rumors about his personal life, Jackson swept the popular and electoral votes. "The virtuous portion of the people have well sustained me," Jackson rejoiced. "I am filled with gratitude." Jackson's political success reflected changes in American society caused in part by the Market Revolution. The old social structure led by well-born individuals gradually gave way to a society based more on economic success than on one's social class at birth. Jackson's image as a "self-made" man reflected this new sense of economic opportunity. He also held out this appealing promise for other Americans: "I believe man can be elevated," he said in a speech, to be "capable of governing himself."

Voting rolls swelled as states dropped property requirements for voting and holding office. By 1828, voters, rather than state legislatures, chose presidential electors and most public officials in almost every state. The expansion of voting rights paved the way for Jackson's re-election in 1832. This democratizing trend continued even after he left office. In 1836, for example, some 1.5 million people voted. Just four years later, roughly 2.4 million citizens cast their ballots. Only white men enjoyed full political rights at this time. However, the dramatic expansion of political participation regardless of class was a break from trends in the rest of the world. This expansion was known as Jacksonian Democracy.

PRESIDENTIAL Lives

Andrew Jackson

1767–1845
In Office 1829–1837

Andrew Jackson was born in 1767 to Scotch-Irish immigrants in a log cabin on the South Carolina frontier. Jackson, a poor speller who had little formal schooling, was orphaned at age 14. Jackson later moved to the Tennessee frontier and became a successful lawyer, land speculator, and planter, living on his estate, The Hermitage.

When Jackson's presidency ended in 1837, well-wishers streamed into Washington to say good-bye to "Old Hickory." Jackson received thousands of letters and many gifts as well. He received hats, pipes, canes, and a wagon made of hickory. On his last morning in office, Jackson rode with President-elect Martin Van Buren to the inauguration. The crowds along the road did not cheer for the incoming president, but removed their hats in respectful silence for the departing Jackson instead. "For once," an observer noted, "the rising sun was eclipsed by the setting sun."

A new government. The election of Andrew Jackson in 1828 marked a clear break with the politics of the past. On Inauguration Day the people celebrated this change. Jackson's supporters—thousands of ordinary Americans—lined the streets of Washington to see their hero go by. "It was a proud day for the people," declared one newspaper. "General Jackson is *their* own president." To emphasize this point, Jackson allowed his followers to join in a celebration party at the White House. The party soon got out of control when as many as 20,000 visitors joined the festivities. The crowd caused extensive damage to the presidential home. Margaret Bayard Smith recalled the event.

INTERPRETING THE VISUAL RECORD

Celebration. Guests at a party for President Andrew Jackson carve up a giant wheel of cheese. *What can you determine about the types of people who supported Jackson?*

66 What a scene did we witness! . . . Cut glass and china to the amount of several thousand dollars had been broken in the struggle to get the refreshments. Punch and other articles had been carried out in tubs and buckets. . . . Ladies fainted, men were seen with bloody noses, and such a scene of confusion took place as is impossible to describe. . . . But it was the people's day, and the people's President, and the people would rule. 99

Jackson continued to change the tone of politics. Once in office, he rewarded his supporters by giving some of them government jobs. This practice became known as the **spoils system**, from the expression "to the victor belong the spoils." By

THE GRANGER COLLECTION, NEW YORK

Campaign items like this souvenir image of Andrew Jackson
reflected a change in the way
people ran for office.

rewarding political supporters with government appointments, politicians could ensure future support from the state branches of their party.

Jackson also took steps to reform government bureaucracy by replacing public servants whom he judged "unfaithful or incompetent." He believed that those officials who stayed in public office too long often forgot that they were servants of the people. Thus, he favored **rotation in office**—the periodic replacement of officeholders. Yet Jackson's changes fell far short of complete rotation. During his presidency he never replaced more than 20 percent of government workers for political reasons.

During the campaign Jackson had promised major reforms. This led many people to expect that he would replace nearly all government employees who had been appointed by previous administrations. However, Jackson's goal was not simply to replace his opponents' supporters with his own. He believed that the government was supposed to be the servant of the people. Jackson therefore appointed to office those people whom he considered qualified. He kept competent workers regardless of their political party.

Perhaps the biggest change Jackson brought to politics was his willingness to select people from all walks of life. Previously, most politicians had believed that only the wealthy were qualified to serve in government. Jackson believed that every American—regardless of social or economic class—was potentially as competent as any other. This faith in the ability of the American people to govern themselves is a major reason why Jackson was considered the people's president.

 **READING CHECK:** How did Andrew Jackson's election to the presidency mark a break with the politics of the past?

SECTION 3 REVIEW

Define and explain the significance of the following terms:
Missouri Compromise   spoils system
Democratic Party   rotation in office

Identify and explain the significance of the following individuals:
John Quincy Adams
Andrew Jackson

Locate and explain the importance of the following places:
Missouri

1. **Using Graphic Organizers** Copy the chart below. Use it to explain the steps by which increased migration to Missouri eventually led to the passage of the Missouri Compromise, who the main people and groups involved in each step were, and what the terms of the agreement were.

2. **Recognizing Point of View** Why did Andrew Jackson charge that John Quincy Adams and Henry Clay had made a "corrupt bargain" in the election of 1824?

3. **Comparing and Contrasting** How were John Quincy Adams and Andrew Jackson both different and similar to each other? How were their differences reflected in their approach to the presidency?

4. **Identifying Values** How did President Jackson's inauguration and initial actions once in office reflect his image as the people's president?

Critical Thinking

5. How did the election of 1828 signal a broadening of democratic rights?
   Consider:
   • who was excluded from the political system before 1828
   • how participation in elections opened up in the 1820s
   • how the results of the election of 1828 reflected broader democratic participation

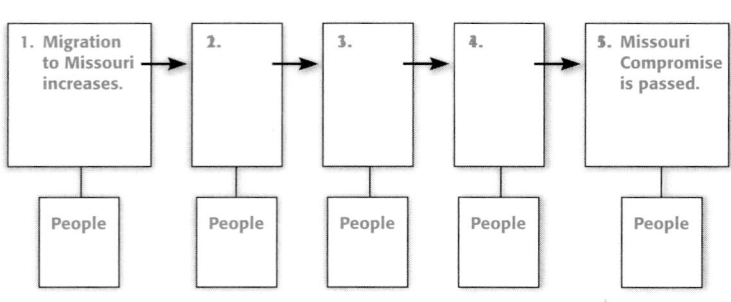

| 1. Migration to Missouri increases. | → | 2. | → | 3. | → | 4. | → | 5. Missouri Compromise is passed. |

| People | People | People | People | People |

SECTION 4

Jackson's Policies Define an Era

OBJECTIVES

Read to understand:

1. why U.S. officials wanted to move eastern American Indians westward, and how Indians resisted removal
2. what sparked the nullification crisis
3. what political divisions arose over the National Bank
4. how the Whigs came to power in 1840

KEY TERMS

Indian Removal Act
Second Seminole War
Worcester v. *Georgia*
Trail of Tears
doctrine of nullification
pet banks
Specie Circular
Panic of 1837

KEY PEOPLE

Sequoya
John C. Calhoun
Martin Van Buren
William Henry Harrison
John Tyler

KEY PLACES

Indian Territory

EYEWITNESSES TO History

66 *Brothers! I have listened to many talks from our great father [the white man]. When he first came over the wide waters, he was but a little man. . . . His legs were cramped by sitting long in his big boat, and he begged for a little land to light his fire on. . . . But when the white man had warmed himself before the Indians' fire and filled himself with their hominy, he became very large. . . . Brothers, I have listened to a great many talks from our great father. But they always began and ended in this— 'Get a little further; you are too near me.'* 99
—Speckled Snake

Cherokee stone ax

Creek leader Speckled Snake offered this warning when tribe members asked him how they should respond to President Jackson's order to move from their land. Speckled Snake was among the many American Indians who did not trust or admire Jackson.

A Question of Land

The issue of eastern Indians "getting a little further" from white settlers arose during Andrew Jackson's presidency. Before 1810 some U.S. officials, including Thomas Jefferson, had hoped that eastern Indians would eventually become farmers and blend in to American society. However, white Americans' hunger for land and the American Indians' support for the British during the War of 1812 led to a change in government policy. By the early 1820s many government officials had begun to call for the removal of all American Indians to lands beyond the U.S. borders.

This change in attitude profoundly affected many Indian groups, particularly the Cherokee, Chickasaw, Choctaw, Creek, and Seminole in the Southeast. Believing that their best hope for survival lay in adapting to white culture, many had given up hunting and had become farmers. The Cherokee, for example, had shifted to farming in the late 1700s. Over the next several decades, they built towns with thriving agricultural economies. They wrote a constitution modeled on that of the United States, created a judicial system, supported schools, and formed a militia.

Read More About It

Free Find: Sequoya
After reading about Sequoya on the **Holt Researcher** CD–ROM, create a plan for a memorial that honors Sequoya's efforts on behalf of the Cherokee people.

BIOGRAPHY

Sequoya

THE GRANGER COLLECTION, NEW YORK

The Cherokee were greatly assisted in their efforts by the work of one man—Sequoya (si-KWOY-uh), or Sikwayi. Sequoya was born in Tennessee sometime between 1760 and 1770. In 1813 he fought against the Creek as a member of a Cherokee regiment in the U.S. Army.

Although Sequoya neither spoke nor read English, he recognized the value of a written language. He saw that literacy benefited white settlers by enabling them to spread ideas, keep records, and communicate over long distances. He hoped that literacy would do the same for the Cherokee. Fascinated by the alphabet system that he observed Americans using, he decided to

The **Cherokee Phoenix** *was first published on February 21, 1828.*

develop a similar writing system for the Cherokee language. "I thought that would be like catching a wild animal and taming it," he said. For 12 years he worked to create a Cherokee writing system, finishing it in 1821. In 1828 Sequoya went to Washington to serve as a representative for his tribe. He died in Mexico about 1843. The language he created is still used by the Cherokee today.

The system that Sequoya developed contained 86 symbols based on the syllables of spoken Cherokee. Once the symbols were memorized, a person could read or write anything in Cherokee. Soon most of the tribe was literate in the language. White missionaries adopted the language to help them educate Cherokee children in mission schools. With the aid of missionary Samuel Worcester, the Cherokee secured a printing press. By 1828 the tribe was publishing its own newspaper, the *Cherokee Phoenix,* written in both English and Cherokee. In addition, numerous books, including editions of the Bible, were published in the Cherokee language.

Jackson's Indian Policy

American Indians' efforts to adopt practices similar to those of white Americans failed to ease the pressures against them. In fact, those who switched to farming soon found themselves viewed as competitors for valuable land. Indians in the Southeast occupied millions of acres of fertile land suitable for growing cotton. White farmers and land speculators pressured the government to open that land to white settlement. They soon found a friend in Andrew Jackson. The president denounced the continued presence of Indians in the East as a barrier to "the waves of population and civilization . . . rolling westward."

Jackson phrased his calls for removal in humanitarian terms. For their own protection, he suggested, Indians should be moved westward, where "their white brothers will not trouble them." In 1830 Congress passed the **Indian Removal Act**, providing for the relocation of Indian tribes living east of the Mississippi River to Indian Territory in present-day Oklahoma. Jackson promised eastern Indians that for "as long as grass grows and water runs. . . , [the land] *will be yours forever.*"

INTERPRETING THE VISUAL RECORD

Seminole. Osceola was a leader of the Seminole tribe. *What indications are there in the painting that Osceola adapted to changes caused by white settlement in Florida?*

Violent resistance. By the end of the decade, most American Indians had been removed from the Southeast. Few went willingly. Many doubted Jackson's promise of a permanent homeland. Some wrote appeals to Congress. "Our cause is your own," began one such letter. "It is the cause of liberty and of justice. It is based upon your own principles." Osceola (ahs-ee-OH-luh), a Seminole leader, was more defiant.

> 66 My Brothers! . . . the white man says I shall go, and he will send people to make me go; but I have a rifle, and I have some powder and some lead. I say, we must not leave our homes and lands. If any of our people want to go west we won't let them. 99

In Florida, resistance to removal led to the **Second Seminole War** (1835–42), which cost more money and lives than any other Indian war in U.S. history. The Seminole were aided by runaway slaves and fought bravely, but most were eventually killed or removed to Indian Territory. Only a few escaped by hiding in the Florida Everglades.

Resistance in court. The Cherokee fought for their rights through the courts. Arguing that they were a sovereign nation, similar to a foreign country, the tribe appealed to the Supreme Court. In 1831 the Court ruled that Indian tribes were not like foreign countries, but rather "domestic dependent nations," with neither the freedom of a foreign country nor the rights of U.S. citizens. This meant that while tribes were subject to federal laws, they did not have the right to sue in federal court.

To test whether this ruling applied to state as well as federal authority, Cherokee ally Samuel Worcester disobeyed an order from the Georgia militia to leave Indian lands. After he was arrested he appealed his case to the Supreme Court, arguing that the state of Georgia had no power over Indian lands. In the case of *Worcester v. Georgia*, Chief Justice John Marshall ruled in favor of Worcester and the Cherokee, limiting state power over them. The Court also indicated that the federal government had an obligation to protect the Cherokee from state governments that were trying to take their lands.

The victory was short-lived, however. Georgia officials—with Jackson's support—ignored the Court's ruling and continued to seize Cherokee lands. "John Marshall has made his decision," Jackson is said to have declared, "now let him enforce it." Without federal protection, the Cherokee could not hold out. In 1835 a group representing a minority of the tribe signed a treaty that granted Cherokee land to the United States. In return the Cherokee would receive money and land in Indian Territory. The tribe was ordered to move west within three years.

The Trail of Tears. By the 1838 deadline, few of the some 18,000 Cherokee had moved west. Federal troops began forcing the remaining Cherokee to make the journey to Indian Territory. An estimated 4,000 Cherokee died on the 800-mile journey that came to be known as the **Trail of Tears**. "Many fell by the wayside, too faint with hunger or too weak to keep up with the rest," remembered one of the survivors:

Indian Removal from the Southeast, 1830s

Learning from Maps The Indian Removal Act resulted in thousands of Choctaw, Creek, Chickasaw, Seminole, and Cherokee being driven from their lands and relocated to Indian Territory.

? MOVEMENT Which two groups completed part of the journey to Indian Territory via the Gulf of Mexico?

Map labels: IOWA TERRITORY · UNORGANIZED TERRITORY · IL · IN · OH · MO · KY · VA · NC · Mississippi R. · Ohio River · Arkansas R. · Springfield · TRAIL OF TEARS · Nashville · Tennessee River · Fort Gibson · INDIAN TERRITORY · AR · TN · Fort Smith · Memphis · Little Rock · Fort Towson · CHICKASAW 1832 · CHEROKEE 1835 · New Echota · SC · CHOCTAW 1830 · AL · CREEK 1832 · Fort Mitchell · GA · MS · Vicksburg · REPUBLIC OF TEXAS · LA · ATLANTIC OCEAN · 80° W · 30° N · 35° N · Disputed · Rio Grande · MEXICO · 95° W · 90° W · 85° W · New Orleans · Mobile · FLORIDA TERRITORY · Fort Mellon 1837 · 1836 · 1835 Fort Dade 1835 · Fort Armstrong 1836 · SEMINOLE 1832 · Okeechobee 1837 · Fort Jupiter 1838 · Lake Okeechobee · Fort Lauderdale 1842 · Gulf of Mexico · 0 200 400 Miles · 0 200 400 Kilometers · Albers Equal-Area Projection

Legend: Routes of removal · 1832 Ceded lands and cession dates · Battles of the Second Seminole War

Thousands of Cherokee from the southeastern United States were forced to move west on a journey known as the Trail of Tears.

■ **Understanding Change** European colonization of the Americas had a negative effect on the native people of the continents. American Indian population declined throughout the 1700s and 1800s. Since then, however, the American Indian population in what was Indian Territory has increased steadily. What is the approximate American Indian population in the former Indian Territory today?

THEN

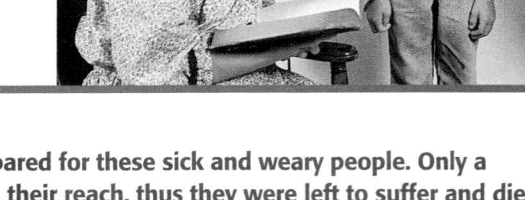
Now

American Indians in Indian Territory

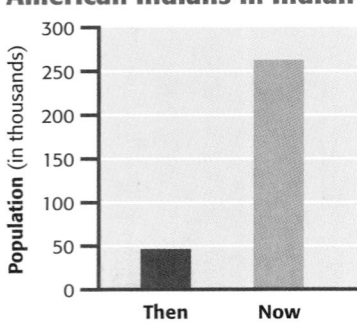

Sources: *Report of the Commissioner of Native American Affairs for 1866; Statistical Abstract of the United States: 1997.* Data represents Indian Territory in 1865 and Oklahoma in 2000 (projected).

❝ A crude bed was quickly prepared for these sick and weary people. Only a bowl of water was left within their reach, thus they were left to suffer and die alone. The little children piteously cried day after day. . . . They were once happy children. ❞

✔ **READING CHECK:** Why did U.S. officials want eastern Indians to move westward? How did Indians resist removal?

INTERPRETING THE VISUAL RECORD

Nullification. South Carolina's attempt to nullify federal laws inspired this political cartoon. *Do you think the cartoonist considered South Carolina's actions good for the nation? Explain your answer.*

The Nullification Crisis

Indian removal remains one of Andrew Jackson's most controversial legacies. Yet for many Americans at the time, the issue of states' rights seemed of more immediate concern. In 1828 Congress passed a new tariff that doubled the rates set in 1816 for certain imports. Outraged southern planters accused Congress of promoting the interests of the industrial North at the expense of southern agriculture. Southerners argued that the tariff would make British goods, on which southerners relied heavily, more expensive. They called it the Tariff of Abominations.

By 1828 Vice President John C. Calhoun had abandoned his earlier nationalist views. He no longer believed that the national government represented the best interests of his native region, the South. Responding to this tariff, Calhoun wrote an anonymous essay outlining the southern position. The essay argued that as creators of the federal Union, the states had the right to nullify, or refuse to obey, any act of Congress they considered unconstitutional. This view became known as the **doctrine of nullification**.

The tariff debate raged for the next few years. In 1832 Henry Clay attempted to create a compromise by pushing a slight tariff reduction through Congress. However, the reduction was too small to satisfy South Carolina. In November the state declared the 1828 and 1832 tariffs null and void. South Carolina threatened to secede if the federal government tried to collect tariffs within the state. Siding with his home state, Calhoun resigned as vice president.

A furious President Jackson privately warned that "if one drop of blood be shed there in defiance of the laws of the United States, I will hang the first man of them I can get my hands on to the first tree I can find." To calm tensions in South Carolina, Clay convinced Congress to pass a compromise tariff in 1833 that lowered rates over a 10-year period. At Calhoun's urging, South Carolina accepted the new tariff. The immediate crisis subsided. Regional tensions, though, continued to worsen.

✔ **READING CHECK:** What sparked the nullification crisis?

Opposing the Bank

For all the emotion that swirled around the issue of states' rights in the 1830s, the Second Bank of the United States may have caused even more controversy. President Jackson attacked the Bank as a dangerous monopoly that benefited rich investors at the expense of the poor, the honest, and the industrious. He insisted that such a privileged group should not be allowed to control the nation's money.

The Bank became a campaign issue when Jackson ran for re-election in 1832. Opposing Jackson was Henry Clay, nominee of the National Republicans. Clay, who supported the Bank, decided to force an election-year showdown over it. Although its charter was not due to expire until 1836, Clay pushed a bill through Congress in the summer of 1832 to recharter the Bank. Jackson vetoed the measure, sparking a fierce debate. Although Clay vigorously attacked the veto during the campaign, voters sided with Jackson. He and his running mate, Martin Van Buren of New York, won by a large margin. Jackson then moved to shut down the Bank.

The fight had become bitterly personal. "The Bank is trying to kill me, but I will kill it," Jackson grimly vowed. He stopped depositing federal funds in the National Bank. New deposits went to selected state banks chosen for their officers' loyalty to the Democratic Party—**pet banks**, as Jackson's enemies called them.

Nicholas Biddle, who had been president of the National Bank since 1823, made one final effort to save the institution. From the Bank's headquarters in Philadelphia, Biddle tightened credit to force a financial crisis. He hoped to show Jackson and the American public the folly of attacking such a stabilizing institution. Instead, this desperate power play by Biddle only reinforced Jackson's argument that the Bank had powers that could be used against the public good. The Bank's charter expired in March 1836.

✔ **READING CHECK:** What political divisions arose over the National Bank?

National Bank. This political cartoon represents the controversy that surrounded the National Bank. *Does the cartoon show President Jackson supporting or opposing the Bank? What elements of the cartoon indicate that?*

The Panic of 1837

President Jackson had won the Bank war. By weakening federal control over the banking system, however, he also opened the door to financial crisis. Jackson's pet banks issued their own banknotes, often in amounts far exceeding what they could

Great Debates

Jackson's Legacy

In his own day, Andrew Jackson was a very popular president. Since his death, however, scholars and politicians have disagreed over the meaning of his legacy. On the one hand, Jackson clearly helped widen democracy by pushing for the expansion of voting rights to all adult white males. On the other hand, he did little to increase equality for women or African Americans. He also openly violated American Indians' treaty rights and legal claims.

To many scholars, the most controversial part of Jackson's presidency was the way he challenged the balance of powers set forth by the Constitution. He believed that as the elected head of state, the president should be the most powerful person in the government. Many of his most controversial actions stemmed from his attempts to challenge Congress or the Supreme Court. Jackson vetoed more bills than all presidents before him combined. He insisted that Congress consult him before even considering any legislation. He rejected the principle established by Chief Justice John Marshall that the Supreme Court should be the final interpreter of the laws. This rejection influenced Jackson's refusal to enforce the Court's decision in *Worcester v. Georgia.* Most scholars agree that Jackson set a precedent that threatened the balance of powers. This mixed view of Jackson is shown by the fact that while many politicians today praise Thomas Jefferson and George Washington as role models, few point to the once very popular Andrew Jackson.

back up with gold or silver. Furthermore, the amount of money in circulation more than doubled between 1830 and 1837, as many banks eased their loan requirements.

The climate of easy credit fueled land speculation. Speculators bought millions of acres of public land in the Midwest, hoping to make quick profits by reselling it to settlers at higher prices. As land prices increased, so did the price of everything else. To curb this inflation, President Jackson issued the **Specie Circular** in July 1836. This executive order instructed the Treasury to accept only specie as payment for public land. Because few people had gold or silver, land sales plunged. Many people began demanding that their banks exchange banknotes for specie. As in 1819, banks that could not do so failed. Hundreds of banks had gone under by June 1837.

Contributing to the **Panic of 1837** was an economic crisis in Great Britain. Faced with financial problems at home, the British bought less southern cotton. British investors also pulled their money out of the United States, further decreasing the supply of specie. Factories closed, and construction projects stood idle. Thousands of workers lost their jobs. What had begun as a panic soon deepened into a full-scale depression that lasted until 1843.

THE GRANGER COLLECTION, NEW YORK

U.S. gold half eagle coins were scarce items when President Jackson issued the Specie Circular.

The Rise of the Whigs

President Jackson left office before the inflationary bubble burst. Vice President Martin Van Buren, who was Jackson's handpicked successor, was elected president in 1836. He suffered a wave of public criticism over the nation's mounting economic problems, threatening his re-election bid in 1840.

Jackson's opponents had created the Whig Party in 1834. They took their name from the old Whig Party in Britain that had opposed the power of the king. The Whigs, who referred to President Jackson as "King Andrew," initially attracted people who disliked Jackson's policies and use of federal power. Van Buren managed to defeat a divided Whig Party in 1836, but the Whigs' support grew over the next four years as the nation's economic problems deepened.

Rather than run party leader Henry Clay in the 1840 election, the Whigs nominated war hero General William Henry Harrison. Clay's nomination was opposed by such influential Whigs as John C. Calhoun and Daniel Webster. The Whigs wanted a candidate who could win broad support. Harrison enjoyed the advantage of having few political or regional enemies. "I am the most unfortunate man in the history of parties," Clay bitterly said upon hearing the news of Harrison's nomination, "always run by my friends when sure to be defeated, and now betrayed of a nomination when I, or any one, would be sure of election."

Clay's claim that any Whig candidate would win was probably correct. The economic crisis that battered the Van Buren administration practically guaranteed the election of a Whig president. The Whigs presented their candidate as a "man of the people," similar to Andrew Jackson. They portrayed Harrison, a rich landowner, as a simple, hardworking farmer who lived in a log cabin. The Whigs' favorite chant, "Tippecanoe and Tyler too," referred to the general's 1811 battle against American Indians at the Tippecanoe River and to his running mate, John Tyler of Virginia. Ridiculing Van Buren, they added: "Van, Van is a used up man!"

The Whigs' reliance on slogans during the campaign echoed the election of 1828 and continued the precedent that the election had set for U.S. politics. The "packaging" of candidates—emphasizing their image as much as or more than their ideas or abilities—had become standard practice.

Such techniques became the rule because they seemed to work. Harrison won an impressive 234 electoral votes to Van Buren's 60. Harrison did not enjoy his triumph for long, however. The president died of pneumonia four weeks after his inauguration, making his the shortest presidential term in U.S. history. Vice President Tyler, a states'-rights Virginian and strong opponent of Andrew Jackson, became president and inherited the ongoing economic crises.

✔ **READING CHECK:** How did the Whigs come to power in 1840?

THE GRANGER COLLECTION, NEW YORK

INTERPRETING THE VISUAL RECORD

Campaigning. This image was used to promote William Henry Harrison's 1840 presidential campaign. *What image of Harrison do you think this painting was trying to show? Explain your answer.*

SECTION **REVIEW**

Define and explain the significance of the following terms:
Indian Removal Act
Second Seminole War
Worcester v. *Georgia*
Trail of Tears
doctrine of nullification
pet banks
Specie Circular
Panic of 1837

Identify and explain the significance of the following individuals:
Sequoya
John C. Calhoun
Martin Van Buren
William Henry Harrison
John Tyler

Locate and explain the importance of the following place:
Indian Territory

1. **Using Graphic Organizers** Copy the flowchart below. Use it to evaluate the strength of the evidence for and against the argument that President Jackson's actions challenged the balance of powers. Indicate whether you agree or disagree.

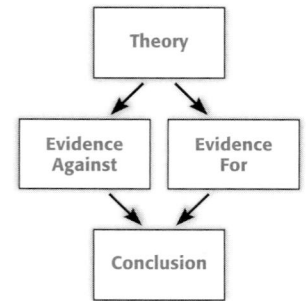

2. **Identifying Cause and Effect** Describe the relationship between the tariff of 1828, the doctrine of nullification, and South Carolina's threat to secede.
3. **Identifying Cause and Effect** How did the debate over the National Bank lead to political divisions?
4. **Problem Solving** Imagine that you are Martin Van Buren's campaign manager in the election of 1840. How will you advise him to counter the Whig campaign?

Critical Thinking

5. How did Indian removal reflect the lack of power afforded to American Indians by the U.S. government?
   Consider:
   • the government's reasons for removal
   • the Indians' attempts to resist removal
   • how the courts and the government addressed the rights of American Indians

Review

Creating a Time Line

Copy the time line below onto a sheet of paper. Complete the time line by filling in the events and dates from the chapter that you think were most significant. Pick three events and explain why you think they were significant.

1790   1815   1840

Writing a Summary

Using the Reading Checks as a guide, write an overview of the events in the chapter.

Identifying People and Ideas

Identify the following terms or individuals and explain their significance.

1. Rush-Bagot Agreement
2. James Monroe
3. American System
4. National Road
5. Industrial Revolution
6. Sequoya
7. Indian Removal Act
8. Trail of Tears
9. John C. Calhoun
10. doctrine of nullification

Understanding Main Ideas

SECTION 1

1. How did the United States obtain Florida?
2. What did the Monroe Doctrine reveal about U.S. diplomatic policy?

SECTION 2

3. How did the War of 1812 help prepare Americans to accept Henry Clay's American System?
4. How did the Transportation and Market Revolutions change the United States?

SECTION 3

5. What led to the passage of the Missouri Compromise?

SECTION 4

6. How did American Indians in the Southeast resist their forced removal to Indian Territory?
7. Why did South Carolina threaten to secede?

Reviewing Themes

1. **Economic Development** How did the Transportation and Market Revolutions lead to regional differences in economic development?
2. **Technology and Society** What were some of the ways in which 1800s America was changed by the Industrial Revolution?
3. **Democratic Values** Why can it be said that the Market and Industrial Revolutions aided the rise of Jacksonian Democracy?

Thinking Critically

1. **Evaluating** What was the most significant effect of the War of 1812 on the United States? Explain your answer.
2. **Identifying Values** What did the Monroe Doctrine reveal about American values?
3. **Analyzing** Could industrialization and the Transportation Revolution have occurred without each other? Why or why not?
4. **Comparing and Contrasting** How were the crises of Missouri statehood and tariffs similar? How were they different?
5. **Using Historical Imagination** If you had been a voter in 1828 and 1832, would you have supported Andrew Jackson? Why or why not?

Writing About History

Writing to Describe Imagine that you are a reporter in 1828. Write a short article tracing Andrew Jackson's political career from the election of 1824 through the election of 1828. Use the following graphic to organize your thoughts.

Election of 1824 → Jackson's activities, 1824–1828 → Election of 1828

Strategies for Success Review the **Strategies for Success** on *Reviewing Map Basics*. Then study the map in Section 4 entitled Indian Removal from the Southeast, 1830s, and answer the following questions.

1. What major southeastern tribes were relocated to Indian Territory during the 1830s?
2. What two tribes endured the longest overland journey to Indian Territory?
3. How did the Mississippi and Arkansas Rivers affect the routes taken by many Indians to Indian Territory?

Linking History and Geography

Study the map below. Note the number of Latin American countries that gained independence in the early 1800s. Which Latin American colonies were still under European control in 1830?

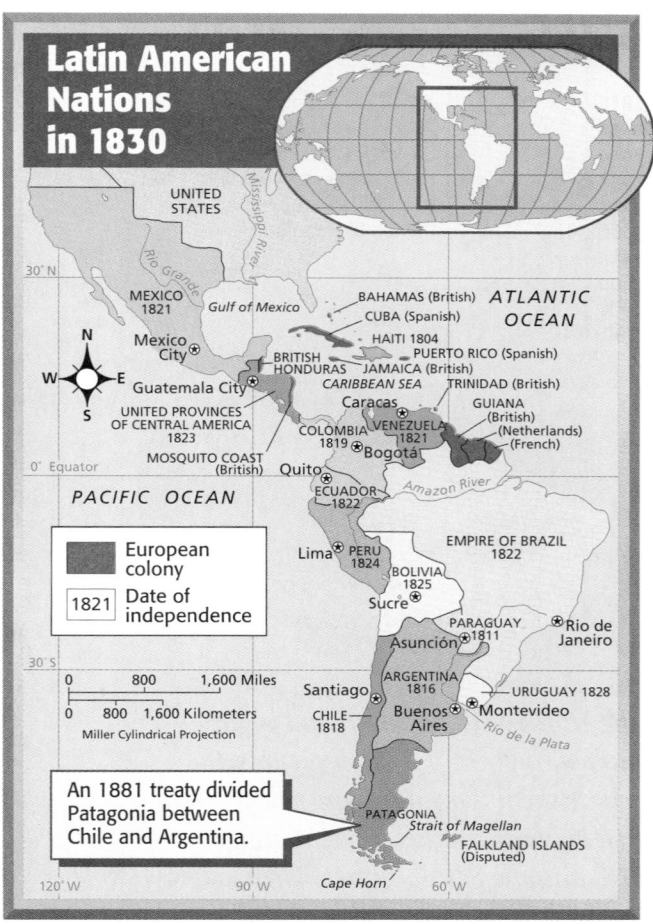

Latin American Nations in 1830

UNITED STATES

Rio Grande
Mississippi River

30° N

MEXICO 1821   Gulf of Mexico   BAHAMAS (British)   ATLANTIC OCEAN
                                CUBA (Spanish)
Mexico City ⊛   HAITI 1804   PUERTO RICO (Spanish)
            BRITISH HONDURAS   JAMAICA (British)
Guatemala City ⊛ CARIBBEAN SEA   TRINIDAD (British)
                Caracas   GUIANA (British)
UNITED PROVINCES   (Netherlands)
OF CENTRAL AMERICA COLOMBIA VENEZUELA   (French)
1823   1819 ⊛ 1821
MOSQUITO COAST   ⊛Bogotá
0° Equator (British) Quito ⊛
                ECUADOR
PACIFIC OCEAN   1822   Amazon River

            Lima ⊛ PERU   EMPIRE OF BRAZIL
                    1824   1822
                        BOLIVIA
                        1825
                    Sucre ⊛

                PARAGUAY   ⊛Rio de
0   800   1,600 Miles Asunción⊛1811   Janeiro
                ARGENTINA
0   800 1,600 Kilometers Santiago ⊛ 1816   URUGUAY 1828
Miller Cylindrical Projection CHILE   Buenos⊛ Montevideo
30° S   1818   Aires   Rio de la Plata

European colony

1821 Date of independence

An 1881 treaty divided Patagonia between Chile and Argentina.

PATAGONIA   Strait of Magellan
            FALKLAND ISLANDS (Disputed)
120° W   90° W   Cape Horn   60° W

internet connect

TOPIC: Indians of Oklahoma
GO TO: go.hrw.com
KEYWORD: SD1 Removal

Accessing the Internet through the HRW Web site, research one of these tribes: Choctaw, Cherokee, Chickasaw, Creek, or Seminole. Then prepare an oral report that describes the status of the tribe today and examines the historical events that brought them to their present situation.

BUILDING YOUR PORTFOLIO

Complete one or all of the following projects independently or cooperatively.

1 Economic Development
Imagine that you are a northern textile manufacturer. **Create an illustrated chart** for a new factory that shows what new technologies you will use to produce cloth from cotton and where you plan to build your factory. Keep in mind the need for a power source and for easy access to markets.

2 Global Relations
Imagine that you are a reporter for the Cherokee Phoenix. **Write a newspaper article** in English that traces U.S. policy toward the Cherokee nation from 1789 to 1835. In your article include the tribe's reactions to this policy.

3 Democratic Values
Imagine that you are a western farmer who supports Andrew Jackson in the 1832 presidential election. **Create a political poster** that illustrates why Jackson is a "man of the people." The poster should draw on events from Jackson's first term in office.

CHAPTER 8

1793–1860

Regional Societies

Francis Cabot Lowell's mill

1814
Business and Finance
Production begins at Francis Cabot Lowell's textile mill in Waltham, Massachusetts.

1822
Daily Life
Boston gets gas-powered streetlights.

1822
World Events
Brazil declares its independence from Portugal.

1790

1800

1810

1820

1793
Science and Technology
Eli Whitney develops a much-improved cotton gin.

Cotton gin

1810
Business and Finance
The South produces 178,000 bales of cotton, up from 3,000 in 1790.

Bales of cotton

1814
World Events
European nations meet at the Congress of Vienna to reorganize Europe after the fall of Napoleon.

Before You Read

Build on What You Know

By the mid-1700s the economies of the North and the South had begun to grow apart. Although farming remained important to both regions, the North diversified its economy to include the importation and sale of manufactured goods. In this chapter you will learn how the Market Revolution in the early 1800s affected society in both the North and the South. In the North, cities grew and the number of factories increased, while cotton and a slave-based social order dominated life in the South.

Irish potato famine of 1840

Castle Garden in New York City

The Lowell Offering

1842
World Events
At least 50,000 immigrants flee to the United States from Ireland to escape a potato famine.

1840
The Arts
The *Lowell Offering* begins publication.

1844
Daily Life
Castle Garden in New York City is converted into an open-air theater seating 8,000 people.

1845
Business and Finance
William Gregg publishes "Essays on Domestic Industry," urging industrialization in the South.

1859
Politics
Arkansas passes a law that requires all freed African Americans in the state to leave or be hired out as slaves.

1830	1840	1850	1860

1834
Business and Finance
The National Trades Union is founded.

1835
The Arts
William Gilmore Simms publishes the novels *The Yemassee* and *The Partisan*, which trace the early history of the Carolina region.

1837
Daily Life
The popular song "Woodman, Spare the Tree" mourns the destruction of American wilderness.

1846
Science and Technology
Elias Howe patents his sewing machine.

Miniature portrait by Charles Fraser

1857
The Arts
Charles Fraser exhibits more than 400 of his miniature paintings in Charleston.

Early sewing machine

Think About Themes

Themes Journal *Decide whether you agree or disagree with the following statements. Note why in your journal.*

Economic Development Economic changes always have a positive effect on society.

Cultural Diversity It would be impossible for enslaved people to develop a rich culture of their own.

Technology and Society New technology generally does more harm than good.

253

The North and the Midwest

OBJECTIVES

Read to understand:
1. what the differences were between the lifestyles of wealthy, poor, and middle-class families
2. what innovations transformed industrial and farm production and domestic life in the early 1800s
3. what the major issues concerning trade unions were, and what actions unions took in the early to mid-1800s
4. what groups immigrated to the United States in the mid-1800s, and how some Americans responded to this immigration
5. how life in the Midwest changed in the early 1800s

KEY TERMS

middle class
factory system
Lowell girls
strike
nativism
Know-Nothings

KEY PEOPLE

Francis Cabot Lowell
John Deere
Cyrus McCormick
Elias Howe
Sarah G. Bagley

EYEWITNESSES TO History

❝ *Town and country rival with each other in the eagerness of industrious pursuits. Machines are invented, new lines of communication established. . . . It is as if all America were but one gigantic workshop, over the entrance of which there is the blazing inscription* 'No admission here except on business.' ❞

—**Anonymous foreign visitor**

Business at Boston Harbor

Thus commented an 1830 visitor to the United States about the country's growing interest in business. In the early 1800s manufacturing had been of little importance to the United States. Secretary of the Treasury Albert Gallatin suggested that the lack of factories resulted from "the superior attractions of agricultural pursuits, . . . the high price of labor, and the want [lack] of sufficient capital." Within just a few decades, however, the economy's emphasis had changed.

Northern Society

From its earliest days, American society had its rich and poor citizens. The Market Revolution, however, widened the gap between these two groups.

The wealthy. Prosperous bankers, manufacturers, merchants, and their families made up a small elite: the wealthy upper class. They lived in lavish homes with running water, elegant furnishings, and many household conveniences. They attended expensive parties and balls and were concerned with maintaining their status.

In New York, leaders of the upper class formed a committee "to take charge of polite society, regulate its interests, keep it pure, and decide who shall be admitted hereafter to . . . annual entertainments," as one member put it. By deciding who would be admitted to social events, the committee determined everyone's "social grade." They voted using a secret system of white balls for "yes" votes and black balls for "no" votes. One black ball could exclude a person from important social gatherings.

Blackball voting box

The poor. The urban poor, by contrast, lived crowded into small apartments, attics, or damp cellars. They had few conveniences and no sewers. Poor neighborhoods were plagued by crime, disease, and filth. Disease took a terrible toll on children, particularly those living, as one doctor put it, "in confined, narrow, ill-ventilated rooms and cellars, among the poorest of the poor." For example, a cholera epidemic that swept New York City in 1849 apparently started in the slums.

In the mid-1800s a committee reported that the poor residents of Boston were "huddled together like brutes without regard to sex, age or a sense of decency." Most poor people, however, held on to their hope for a better future. Many believed that the new market economy would provide them with opportunities to improve their situation.

The middle class. Many poor people did improve their economic status. During the early 1800s a new social class arose between the wealthy and the poor. This **middle class** included prosperous artisans, farmers, lawyers, ministers, shopkeepers, and their families. Middle-class families lived in simple but comfortable homes with conveniences such as bathing stands and bowls, iron cookstoves, lamps, and rugs. Middle-class families had enough money to buy food, clothing, and other products made available by the Market Revolution. This meant that they no longer had to work together at home to produce these necessities.

The rise of the middle class led to a greater specialization of male and female roles. In middle-class society, work and family life began to be viewed as two very different spheres. Men and women were supposed to have very different roles. Men were expected to work outside the home and earn the money to support their families. More and more men shifted from farming to work in factories, mills, offices, and shops. In contrast, women were expected to stay at home and care for the children and do the housework, for which they received no pay. This process of emphasizing women as the moral center of the middle-class family has been called the "cult of true womanhood" by historians. These new roles became the ideal for the middle class, though not all middle-class families lived up to this standard.

Middle-class children typically did not have to work to help support their families. Instead, middle-class families sent their children—boys more often than girls—to school to learn the skills necessary for adulthood. Children also lived at home with their parents longer before venturing out to start independent lives. Older children came to be viewed as needing parental support and supervision. "Early departure from the homestead is a moral crisis that many of our youth do not show themselves able to meet," one social writer of the period said. "It comes at a tender age, when judgment is weakest and passion and impulse strongest."

The rapid growth of the middle class was noted both by Americans and visitors from other countries. French aristocrat Alexis de Tocqueville wrote: "The passion for physical comforts is essentially a passion of the middle classes. . . . From them it mounts to the higher orders of society and descends into the mass of the people. " The "comforts" of the middle class, particularly those who lived in cities, included entertainment such as concerts, museums, and plays.

This middle-class home uses a modern heater instead of a fireplace to provide warmth.

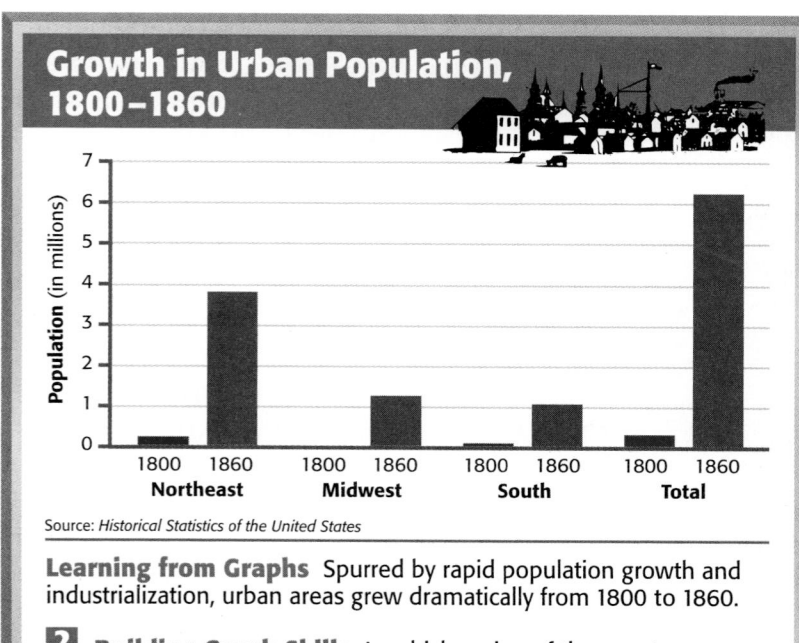

Growth in Urban Population, 1800–1860

Population (in millions)

Northeast   Midwest   South   Total
1800 1860   1800 1860   1800 1860   1800 1860

Source: *Historical Statistics of the United States*

Learning from Graphs Spurred by rapid population growth and industrialization, urban areas grew dramatically from 1800 to 1860.

? **Building Graph Skills** In which region of the country was urban growth most dramatic?

✔ **READING CHECK:** How did the lives of middle-class families differ from those of wealthy or poor families?

Changing Industrial and Farm Production

The Market Revolution was made possible by a dramatic change in the means of production. For centuries, skilled craftspeople had made goods by hand in small shops. In the early 1800s, however, Francis Cabot Lowell and others introduced a new way of manufacturing goods.

Read More About It

Free Find:

Francis Cabot Lowell

After reading about Francis Cabot Lowell on the **Holt Researcher** CD–ROM, create a poster advertising for workers for Lowell's factory. Include descriptions of the work and the benefits that are offered.

BIOGRAPHY

Francis Cabot Lowell

The factory system. Lowell was born in Massachusetts in 1775 to a prosperous merchant family. Early in his career, he tried his hand at real estate and commerce. Then, in 1810, he sailed to Lancashire, Scotland, where he toured many factories and cotton mills. Upon his return to the United States, Lowell and fellow Bostonian Nathan Appleton began to discuss building a waterpowered loom to produce cotton textiles like those Lowell had seen in Britain.

With some help, Lowell designed and constructed a power loom that he set up in a factory in Waltham, Massachusetts. Lowell and his partners were nearly ready to begin production by the end of 1813. "I well recollect the state of admiration and satisfaction with which I sat by the hour, watching the beautiful movement of this new and wonderful machine," Appleton wrote years later, "destined as it evidently was, to change the character of all textile industry." Lowell died in 1817, but his mills survived. His brother-in-law carried out Lowell's dream of building a city based on textile mills. That Massachusetts town north of Boston became known as Lowell in 1826.

Francis Cabot Lowell had originally hired young women to work in his mills. By 1826 the Waltham mills employed some 500 workers. To cut costs and increase output, machines did everything under one roof—from spinning the thread to weaving the cloth. This system of manufacturing came to be called the **factory system**.

Mill owners in Waltham and Lowell usually hired young, single women from New England farms. This was because most women had the necessary skills for textile mills since they had experience making cloth at home. They were also cheaper to hire than male workers. Women were paid less because they were presumed not to be the primary support for their families. These single women— known as **Lowell girls**—lived in company-owned boardinghouses where older women acted as chaperones. Despite this strict supervision, finding new employees proved easy in the early years. "The stage-coach and canal boat came every day, always filled with new recruits," remembered former Lowell girl Harriet Robinson.

At first Lowell's system won widespread praise. After a visit to Lowell's factory, Tennessee frontier settler and politician Davy Crockett wrote, "Here were thousands [of females], . . . with the prospect before them of future comfort and respectability." Unfortunately, these favorable conditions changed by the 1830s. Wanting larger profits, owners cut wages, increased working hours, and sped up production. The high level of unemployment meant that factory owners could easily replace any workers who complained.

INTERPRETING THE VISUAL RECORD

The Lowell mills. This table shows the scheduled working hours for the Lowell mills. *Why do you think the schedule changed during the course of the year?*

TIME TABLE OF THE LOWELL MILLS,

Arranged to make the working time throughout the year average 11 hours per day.

TO TAKE EFFECT SEPTEMBER 21st, 1853.

The Standard time being that of the meridian of Lowell, as shown by the Regulator Clock of AMOS SANBORN, Post Office Corner, Central Street.

From March 20th to September 19th, inclusive.

COMMENCE WORK, at 6.30 A. M. LEAVE OFF WORK, at 6.30 P. M., except on Saturday Evenings.
BREAKFAST at 6 A. M. DINNER, at 12 M. Commence Work, after dinner, 12.45 P. M.

From September 20th to March 19th, inclusive.

COMMENCE WORK at 7.00 A. M. LEAVE OFF WORK, at 7.00 P. M., except on Saturday Evenings.
BREAKFAST at 6.30 A. M. DINNER, at 12.30 P. M. Commence Work, after dinner, 1.15 P. M.

BELLS.

From March 20th to September 19th, inclusive.

Morning Bells.	Dinner Bells.	Evening Bells.
First bell.............4.30 A. M.	Ring out,...............12.00 M.	Ring out,............6.30 P. M.
Second, 5.30 A. M.; Third, 6.20.	Ring in,................12.35 P. M.	Except on Saturday Evenings.

From September 20th to March 19th, inclusive.

Morning Bells.	Dinner Bells.	Evening Bells.
First bell.............5.00 A. M.	Ring out,...............12.30 P. M.	Ring out at...........7.00 P. M.
Second, 6.00 A. M.;	Ring in,................1.05 P. M.	Except on Saturday Evenings.

SATURDAY EVENING BELLS.

During APRIL, MAY, JUNE, JULY, and AUGUST, Ring Out, at 6.00 P. M.

The remaining Saturday Evenings in the year, ring out as follows:

SEPTEMBER.	NOVEMBER.	JANUARY.
First Saturday, ring out 6.00 P. M.	Third Saturday ring out 4.00 P. M.	Third Saturday, ring out 4.25 P. M.
Second " 5.45 "	Fourth " 3.55 "	Fourth " 4.35 "
Third " 5.30 "		
Fourth " 5.20 "	DECEMBER.	FEBRUARY.
	First Saturday, ring out 3.50 P. M.	First Saturday, ring out 4.45 P. M.
OCTOBER.	Second " 3.55 "	Second " 4.55 "
First Saturday, ring out 5.05 P. M.	Third " 3.55 "	Third " 5.00 "
Second " 4.55 "	Fourth " 4.00 "	Fourth " 5.10 "
Third " 4.45 "	Fifth " 4.00 "	
Fourth " 4.35 "		MARCH.
Fifth " 4.25 "	JANUARY.	First Saturday, ring out 5.25 P. M.
	First Saturday, ring out 4.10 P. M.	Second " 5.30 "
NOVEMBER.	Second " 4.15 "	Third " 5.35 "
First Saturday, ring out 4.15 P. M.		Fourth " 5.45 "
Second " 4.05 "		

YARD GATES will be opened at the first stroke of the bells for entering or leaving the Mills.

SPEED GATES commence hoisting three minutes before commencing work.

Technological developments. Lowell's power looms transformed the factory system, as did new tools that allowed more precise cutting, stamping, and shaping of materials. Technological innovation was not limited to the textile industry. In fact, Englishman Joseph Whitworth noted in an 1854 report on U.S. manufacturing that Americans "call in the aid of machinery in almost every department of industry."

New technology also had a far-reaching impact on American farms and homes. New farming technology included improvements to the plow and the development of the mechanical reaper. John Deere, a blacksmith from Illinois, designed a light but strong steel plow that, according to one man, did not require "much physical strength to press and keep . . . in the ground." Cyrus McCormick developed a mechanical reaper that harvested six acres of grain in a day on its first trial practice. By 1857 McCormick had sold more than 23,000 reapers.

For the home, Elias Howe's invention of the sewing machine helped homemakers such as Bet Fisher. Her husband, George, wrote that Bet "has a sewing machine which is a great pleasure to her now that she is able to work it with skill." He further remarked:

This is an advertisement for an early sewing machine.

66 **How these inventions come, one after another, to facilitate labor & multiply & cheapen the comforts & accommodations of life! This ingenious little machine performs in an hour as much work as could be done with a needle in a day, and it is a very pleasant employment to use it—many ladies become very fond of the occupation and prefer it to a piano.** 99

Other household inventions and improvements included cooking utensils, butter churns, and better stoves, pots and pans, and water pumps.

✔ **READING CHECK:** What innovations transformed industrial and farm production and domestic life in the early 1800s?

The Rise of Trade Unions

Despite the general prosperity of the U.S. economy, many workers lived in poverty. In New York City's garment-making district, entire families worked through the night, earning barely enough money to survive. "It's awful," lamented a mother of four. "I must work, else we get nothing to eat. . . . Cooking? Oh, I cook nothing, for I haven't the time."

Lowell Girls

Although mill working conditions worsened in the 1830s, young women—many of them teenagers—continued to seek opportunities in the mills. Many of the Lowell girls decided for themselves to come to work at the mills, hoping to improve their lives. Mary Paul, a teenager employed as a farm servant, wrote to her father, "I want you to consent to let me go to Lowell if you can. I think it would be much better for me than to stay about here."

Life for the Lowell girls was difficult, and mill work was hard. However, many of the girls welcomed their independence and the opportunity to earn money. They used their salaries to help support their families, get married, purchase clothes and other personal items, and even pay for an education. Most girls saw mill work as a stepping-stone in their lives. This was a way of "bettering the condition of themselves and those they loved," wrote Lucy Larcom, who came to Lowell at the age of 11 and went on to become a well-known poet.

Although labor in the mills was demanding, some teenagers coming from rural farms found that factory work opened up new paths and opportunities for them. Larcom wrote years later about her time at the mills: "I was every day making discoveries about life, and about myself. . . . I know that I was glad to be alive, and to be just where I was." Some Lowell girls took evening classes, formed literary societies, listened to lectures, attended plays and concerts, and also published a magazine, the *Lowell Offering*.

The textile industry provided new opportunities for young women.

Scottish View of American Industry

Between 1820 and 1860, more than 5 million Europeans came to the United States in search of jobs. Although most arrived in the "promised land" with high hopes, many quickly realized that their dreams would not come true. Competition for good jobs was stiff, and skilled work was often hard to find. One Scottish immigrant expressed both despair and disappointment at his new home:

66 America is no place for lawyers, weavers, or shoemakers, for everyone is a pettifoger [corrupt lawyer], a weaver or a shoe-maker. For masons there is little use, for slaters [stone roofers] none. The houses are chiefly built with wood, and the roofs are shingled. Watch and clockmakers may stay at home [in Europe], for the Americans are regulated by the sun. It is no place for printers, there are but few readers. . . . The houses being very simply furnished, cabinet-makers are consequently not much in request. . . . In short, to gain a decent livelihood, the tradesman and labourer, must be a 'Jack of all trades.' 99

This union banner was created by the New York chapter of the United Brotherhood of Carpenters and Joiners.

Children living on farms had always worked, so manufacturers took for granted the availability of child labor for factory work as well. By 1832 in New England, two out of every five factory workers were children. These children faced very grim working conditions. Worsening conditions for all factory workers prompted some to organize unions. These were groups that fought for the interests of laborers.

Labor leaders held a national convention in 1834 and founded the National Trades Union, which sought work reforms such as a shorter workday. President Andrew Jackson responded in 1836 by giving some federal workers a 10-hour workday. Although President Martin Van Buren extended this law in 1840 to cover most government workers, working hours for most other occupations remained longer.

Labor unions used many methods to press for reforms. One tactic was the **strike**—the refusal to work until employers met union demands. During the 1830s workers organized more than 100 strikes, mostly to protest low wages and wage reductions. The wealth of the factory owners and the poverty of the factory workers caused tensions to grow between the two groups. A writer for the *Philadelphia Public Ledger* reacted to this increased tension by remembering idealistically the time "not far distant, when he [the average American] heard nothing from American presses about classes [of people] and *distinctions of rank.*"

Such issues erupted in 1836 in New York City when 20 members of a local tailors' union were found guilty of conspiracy after striking for higher wages. Supporters passed out handbills in working-class neighborhoods that exclaimed, "The *Rich* Against the *Poor!*" The handbill declared that the judge was "the tool of aristocracy, against the people!" It also argued that the jury had "established the precedent that working men have no right to regulate the price of labor."

Union activity forced politicians to pay attention to these problems. For example, after the textile mills cut wages by 15 percent in 1834, the Lowell girls went on strike. They marched in the streets and shouted, "Union is power." Massachusetts legislators responded to the strike by establishing a committee to investigate conditions in the textile mills. Lowell girl Sarah G. Bagley urged her co-workers to form a union after mill owners sped up production without raising wages. In 1844 she organized the Lowell Female Labor Reform Association. As its first president, Bagley collected more than 2,000 signatures on a petition that urged the Massachusetts legislature to limit the workday to 10 hours. Although the movement had little success in Massachusetts, several other states did pass 10-hour workday laws.

✔ **READING CHECK:** What issues concerned trade unions in the early to mid-1800s? What actions did they take in response?

Growth in Immigration

The labor force grew considerably in the 1830s as more than 500,000 newcomers poured into the country. In 1860 more than 4.1 million Americans—about 13 percent of the population—were foreign born. These immigrants were eager for equality, land, and work.

Irish immigrants. The largest group of immigrants—more than 1.9 million by 1860—came from Ireland. Hunger, discrimination, and poverty had driven them from their homeland. Most of Ireland's Roman Catholic population rented land. As the population grew rapidly, there was not enough land to go around. The situation worsened in the mid-1840s, when disease wiped out the potato crop, Ireland's major food source. More than 1 million people in Ireland—or one out of every eight —died from starvation or disease.

Many Irish people who could gather the money for a steamship ticket came to the United States. Able to afford only the cheapest accommodations, these immigrants made the journey crammed below deck in makeshift quarters. Passenger Robert Smith described the conditions.

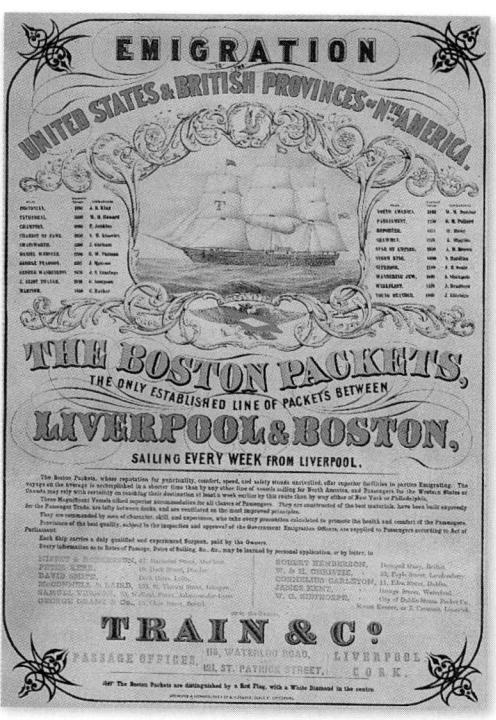

Advertisements like this one encouraged people to immigrate to the United States.

> 66 Hundreds of poor people, men, women and children of all ages, . . . huddled together without light, without air, . . . sick in body, dispirited in heart, . . . living without food or medicine, except as administered by the hand of casual charity. 99

Although most Irish immigrants had been farmers, few could afford to purchase land in the United States. The majority settled in crowded city slums, where they found they had to compete for even the lowest-paying or most-dangerous jobs. "You seldom see a gray-haired Irishman" became a common saying in the 1800s because the average life expectancy of Irish Americans was so short. Irish men helped build the nation's canals and railroads, mined coal, and unloaded freight. Irish women cared for children, cleaned houses, washed and mended clothes, and worked in factories. Irish immigrants also struggled against prejudice. Job listings in city newspapers often specified that employers would not hire Irish workers.

The Irish frequently faced difficult living conditions. Many lived in dark, poorly ventilated tenements in Boston, New York, and other eastern cities. Entire families crowded into single rooms, cellars, or attics. Diseases spread rapidly through poor Irish neighborhoods plagued by garbage and sewage. Ironically, Americans proved more willing to extend charity to the Irish overseas than to the Irish Americans. New Yorkers raised $9,000 in just a few days to buy wheat and other food to send to "the suffering people of Ireland." They neglected, however, to offer assistance to their Irish American neighbors.

Isolated by prejudice, many Irish living in eastern cities created their own communities. They established Catholic churches that served as centers of community life. The Irish also actively participated in local politics. By the 1880s Irish Americans ran the local governments of several cities. In return for votes, Irish politicians helped poor and working-class Irish immigrants by providing them with emergency food and money, jobs, and legal aid.

Strong anti-Irish feelings were expressed in popular songs.

German immigrants.

In the mid-1800s the second-largest group of immigrants to the United States came from what is now Germany. From 1831 to 1860, more than 1.5 million Germans came to the United States, peaking at 215,000 in 1854. Although most of the German immigrants were Protestant, about a third were Roman Catholic and some 250,000 were Jewish. Some came for political or religious reasons. Most, however, came in search of economic opportunity. German industrialization had left many traditional artisans without jobs. Farmland in Germany was growing scarce. Lacking economic opportunity at home, both farmers and urban artisans immigrated to the United States.

Many German immigrants went into skilled occupations, becoming bakers, brewers, butchers, cabinetmakers, cigar makers, machinists, or tailors. Most German-born women worked at home or on the farm. Women who sought outside employment tended to work in family shops or businesses that served the German immigrant community. Some of these immigrants enjoyed remarkable success, such as one young indentured servant couple who obtained their freedom. The wife spun and knitted, while the husband made shoes and hired himself out as a laborer. Within two years they paid off their debt and bought some land. Eventually, the couple became the wealthiest in their county.

Most German Jews remained on the East Coast, but other German immigrants settled in small towns and rural areas in Illinois, Missouri, Ohio, Pennsylvania, Texas, Wisconsin, and elsewhere. Those in larger cities usually lived in tightly knit communities where they read German newspapers and even attended public

INTERPRETING THE VISUAL RECORD

German immigants. This Pennsylvania birth certificate from the early 1800s was written in German. *What does this document demonstrate about German American culture?*

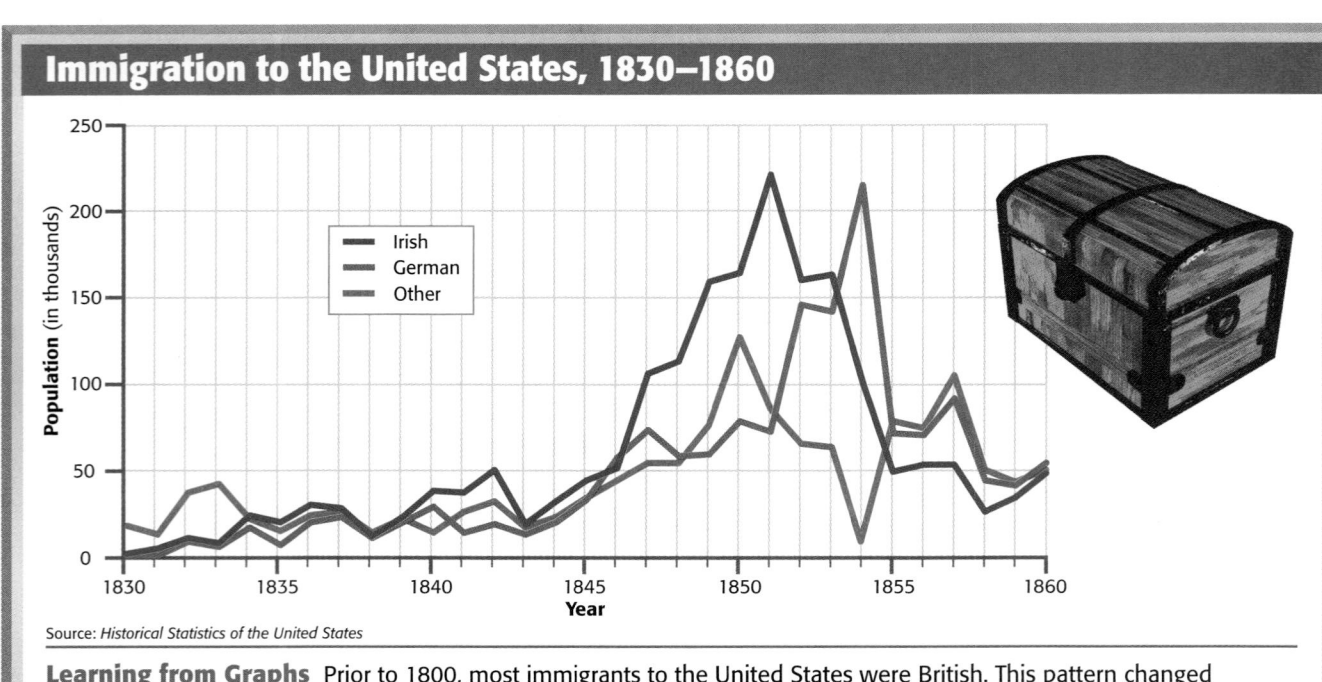

Immigration to the United States, 1830–1860

Population (in thousands) — Year (1830–1860)

Legend:
- Irish
- German
- Other

Source: *Historical Statistics of the United States*

Learning from Graphs Prior to 1800, most immigrants to the United States were British. This pattern changed in the 1800s as millions of Irish, German, and other non-British immigrants settled in the United States.

? **Building Graph Skills** In which year did Irish immigration reach its peak? In which year did German immigration reach its peak?

schools that conducted classes in the German language. "Supplied with newspapers in their own language, . . . and associating mainly with each other . . .," observed Swedish immigrant Gustaf Unonius, "many [German immigrants] do not even trouble to learn the language [English] or teach it to their children."

The Nativist Response

Some native-born Americans protested the arrival of these immigrants. Philip Hone, a wealthy New Yorker, wrote that "all Europe is coming across the ocean; all that part at least who cannot make a living at home; and what shall we do with them?" He claimed that of the immigrants, "not one in twenty is competent to keep [provide for] himself." Other native-born Americans disapproved of the immigrants' customs, such as the beer gardens and the isolation of the Germans. They also feared the growing political power of the Roman Catholic Irish.

Such feelings gave rise to **nativism**, or favoring native-born Americans over the foreign-born. Nativists viewed the immigrants, particularly the Irish, as politically corrupt and socially inferior. Nativists blamed the newcomers for slum conditions that were actually rooted in joblessness and low wages.

From the 1830s through the 1850s, anti-Catholic riots erupted in eastern cities. Vandalism against Catholic institutions grew so common that some insurance companies refused to cover Catholic schools and churches. A priest wrote in 1854 that he feared "to walk the streets after sunset." He reported that in the last month he had been stoned by young men, the windows and door of the church had been broken, and "a large rock entered my chamber unceremoniously [rudely] about 11 o'clock at night."

Some nativists urged restricting immigrants' rights to vote and hold public office. Nativists wanted to limit Irish Catholics' access to political power because they believed that the pope directed decisions for Irish Catholics. In 1849 a secret society of nativists known as the Order of the Star-Spangled Banner emerged. Members swore to support only native-born Protestants for public office. They also agreed to lobby for a 21-year waiting period for naturalization, and to fight the political power of the Roman Catholic Church. The group soon reorganized to form the American Party. When asked about their nativist activities, party members would answer "I know nothing." They were thus called the **Know-Nothings**. Their organization was nicknamed the Know-Nothing Party. The American Party gained widespread popularity and won numerous city and state elections with its nativist platform.

✔ **READING CHECK:** What groups immigrated to the United States in the mid-1800s, and how did some Americans respond to increasing immigration?

A FULL AND COMPLETE ACCOUNT OF THE LATE AWFUL RIOTS IN PHILADELPHIA.

EMBELLISHED WITH TEN ENGRAVINGS.

PHILADELPHIA:
JOHN B. PERRY, No. 198 MARKET STREET.
HENRY JORDAN, Third and Dock Street.
NEW YORK:—NAFIS & CORNISH.

THE LIBRARY COMPANY OF PHILADELPHIA

INTERPRETING THE VISUAL RECORD

Religious conflict. Violent anti-Catholic riots rocked the United States in the mid-1800s. *What do you think was the author's opinion of the rioters? Explain your answer.*

The Midwest

Many immigrants, particularly Dutch, Germans, Scandinavians, and Swiss, were looking for opportunity in the newly prosperous Midwest. Alexis de Tocqueville wrote of this migration, "No power on earth can shut out the immigrants from that fertile wilderness which offers resources to all industry and a refuge from all want." Many native-born Americans sought new land as well. In 1815 a committee of the

Frenchman Alexis de Tocqueville wrote about his 1831–32 tour of the United States.

This wooden stamp was used to indicate the butter maker's identity.

North Carolina legislature complained, "It is mortifying [very embarrassing] to witness the fact that thousands of our wealthy citizens . . . are annually moving to the West."

The food needs of northeastern city-dwellers and factory workers created a surge in demand for the crops grown by midwestern farmers. Many people who set out for new lives in the Midwest found prosperity. One newcomer owned "2 cows, 2 calves, 9 pigs, and one calf expected" within two years of his arrival empty-handed in Indiana. He added, "So good is the prospect for a man who must live by industry, that I wish all my friends and acquaintances were here with me." Some inhabitants of midwestern areas took part in the lumber or mining industries, but commercial farming dominated most of the region.

The Market Revolution reduced the cost of manufactured products. Farm families began purchasing from newly settled merchants items that they had previously made at home, such as cloth. Farm families also bought new mechanized farm machines, such as the reaper, that increased crop yields and allowed them to cultivate more land with less work. As a result, they moved past subsistence farming and began to specialize in growing cash crops such as wheat or corn, or raising livestock to sell at market.

Midwestern farm women, who had long made butter and cheese for their families, began making such items for sale. Women also continued to perform other home and farm chores. An 1862 Department of Agriculture report noted that "on three farms out of four the wife works harder [and] endures more than any other [person] on the place." Many women took pride in their ability to contribute directly to the growing family income.

✔ **READING CHECK:** How did life for many Americans in the Midwest change in the early to mid-1800s?

SECTION 1 REVIEW

Define and explain the significance of the following terms:
middle class
factory system
Lowell girls
strike
nativism
Know-Nothings

Identify and explain the significance of the following individuals:
Francis Cabot Lowell
John Deere
Cyrus McCormick
Elias Howe
Sarah G. Bagley

1. **Using Graphic Organizers** Copy the chart below. Use it to explain what caused working conditions to change in the early 1800s and how workers responded to these changes.

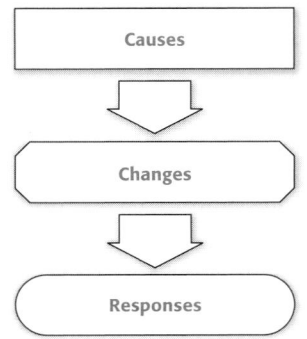

Causes

Changes

Responses

2. **Analyzing** What kinds of restrictions did nativists try to impose on immigrants?
3. **Identifying Cause and Effect** How did the Market Revolution and new technology affect families and workers in the North and the Midwest?
4. **Comparing and Contrasting** How did life in the United States differ for most Irish and German immigrants?

Critical Thinking

5. How did class differences in the 1800s reflect changes in the economy?
   Consider:
   • the lifestyles of wealthy, poor, and middle-class families
   • how economics shaped the development of these lifestyles
   • how these lifestyles had changed since the late 1700s

The Cotton Kingdom

EYEWITNESSES TO History

66 She has a faithful [slave] nurse . . . to whose care she abandons her babies entirely. . . . She is equally fortunate in having a housekeeper who gives out [work duties], [and] regulates [the household]. 99
—Mrs. Isaac H. Hilliard

A Louisiana plantation

Mrs. Isaac H. Hilliard of Arkansas commented enviously on what she perceived as a plantation mistress's seemingly carefree existence. In 1850 Mrs. Hilliard visited Leighton, a sugar plantation in Louisiana. On the surface, Leighton presented a romantic picture of southern plantation life. A minister preached to and baptized some 370 slaves, the plantation library was full of rare books as well as Italian art, orange trees and rose bushes bloomed in the garden, and the daughters were taught by their own governess. Yet plantation life was not as peaceful and prosperous as it appeared. Just four years later Leighton had to be sold to pay off debts. As with much of southern life, Leighton promoted an image that was very different from reality.

The Southern Economy

The South had long relied on agricultural products and slave labor to drive its economy. When tobacco prices fell in the early 1800s, many Americans thought that slavery and plantation-based agriculture would soon vanish. The invention of a new machine to remove the seeds from cotton, however, led to the emergence of the South as the Cotton Kingdom.

Whitney and the cotton boom. Southern farmers had grown cotton since the late 1600s, but they could not keep up with the demands of the world market. Mill owners preferred long-staple cotton to short-staple cotton because it took less time to remove the seeds from the long-staple variety. However, long-staple cotton only grew successfully in a very small region.

All this changed in 1793 when Eli Whitney developed a **cotton gin** that made it easier to gin, or separate, the seeds from short-staple cotton bolls. A person operating the gin could clean 50 times as much cotton in a day as a person working by hand. Whitney had previously declared that such a machine would be "a great thing both to the Country and to the inventor." Soon, farmers across the South planted cotton in order to reap its profits.

Cotton production in the South soared from about 730,000 bales harvested in 1830 to a peak of some 5,387,000 bales in 1859. From 1815 to 1860, cotton represented more than half of all American exports. In 1858 South Carolina senator James Hammond predicted that damage to cotton could shatter the world's economy.

66 What would happen if no cotton was furnished for three years[?] . . . England would topple headlong and carry the whole civilized world with her save the South. . . . No power on earth dares to make war on it. Cotton is king. 99

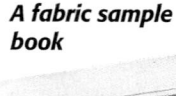

A fabric sample book

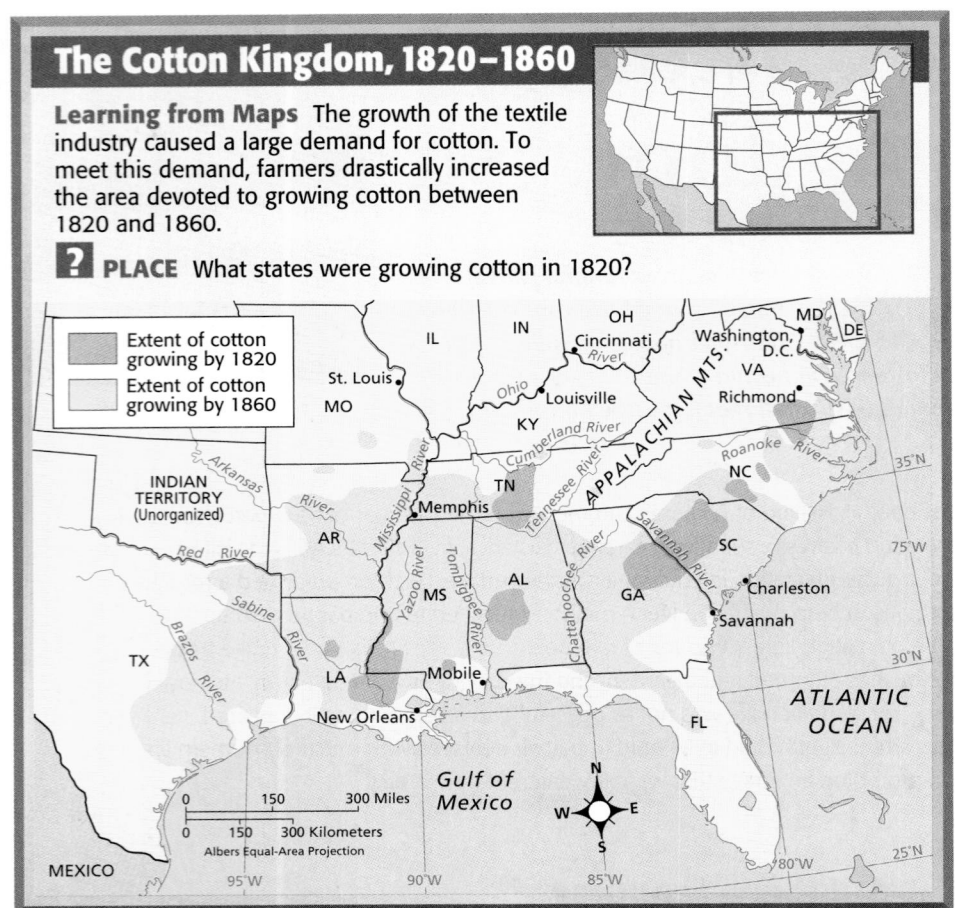

The Cotton Kingdom, 1820–1860

Learning from Maps The growth of the textile industry caused a large demand for cotton. To meet this demand, farmers drastically increased the area devoted to growing cotton between 1820 and 1860.

❓ PLACE What states were growing cotton in 1820?

Extent of cotton growing by 1820
Extent of cotton growing by 1860

Read More About It

Free Find:
Agriculture and Slavery
After learning about agriculture and slavery on the **Holt Researcher** CD–ROM, imagine that you are Eli Whitney and that you are trying to get financial backing to produce your cotton gin. Write a brief proposal explaining why you think your invention will sell and who your best customers for it will be.

Agricultural production.

Farmers in the Upper South had difficulty growing cotton because it required a lengthy warm-weather season. Instead, these farmers grew crops such as corn, hemp, tobacco, and wheat. In some parts of the Lower South, farmers also grew rice and sugarcane.

Because of its different climate and agricultural practices, the Upper South did not rely as heavily on slave labor as the Lower South. After the United States banned the importation of slaves from Africa in 1808, some planters in the Upper South sold slaves for a profit to the cotton-producing states of the Lower South.

Southern manufacturing.

Manufacturing also played a role in the economy of the Upper South. Brickyards, ironworks, sawmills, textile mills, and tobacco factories, as well as mills for processing corn, rice, sugar, and wheat, dotted the region. Southern goods competed with those from the North. Nathan Appleton of the Lowell textile mills complained to his agent in New Orleans that "many small factories in the Southern states send their goods to N.O. [New Orleans] calling them 'Lowell goods.'"

The South was home to the **Tredegar Iron Works** of Richmond, Virginia. One of the nation's largest and best-equipped ironworks, the company operated its rolling mills in the 1850s mainly with slave labor. Railroad construction and mining also strengthened the southern economy. The Mississippi River and other inland waterways and port cities such as Baltimore, Charleston, Mobile, and New Orleans bustled with trade. By 1860 New Orleans had become the nation's most prosperous export center and the fifth-largest U.S. city.

Despite the encouragement of some factory owners, industrialization developed more slowly in the South than in the North. This was true for several reasons. First, most southern investors put their money in land and slaves rather than in new factories. Second, planters used their influence to discourage states from imposing taxes to fund improvements that might have promoted manufacturing. Third, factory workers were in short supply because the region's reliance on slave labor discouraged immigrants from coming to the South. Finally, the market for manufactured goods suffered from the fact that slaves and poor whites—the bulk of the rural population—had little or no purchasing power.

✔ **READING CHECK:** What were the major elements of the southern economy?

Science & Technology

The Cotton Gin

As early as the 1740s, southerners used machines called cotton gins to remove the seeds from cotton. These early gins resembled the *churkha*, one of the first cotton gins, developed in India centuries earlier. These gins consisted of a frame and a pair of rollers that extended horizontally across the frame. A cotton farmer turned the rollers using a hand crank, and the rollers squeezed the seeds from the cotton as the cotton passed between them.

Although these early gins worked, their main disadvantage was their inability to remove the seeds from the type of cotton grown by farmers in Georgia and the Carolinas. Eli Whitney invented a completely new cotton gin that worked for all kinds of cotton. His gin consisted of rollers with wire teeth set against a box.

As the rollers turned they pulled the cotton from the box but left the seeds behind. Another cylinder equipped with brushes revolved in the opposite direction to sweep the cotton lint from the rollers to keep them from becoming clogged. Whitney predicted, "One man will clean ten times as much cotton as he can in any other way before known and also clean it much better than in the usual mode." Whitney patented his cotton gin. However, many southerners simply built their own versions of his cotton gin. Soon other inventors had improved upon Whitney's groundbreaking device.

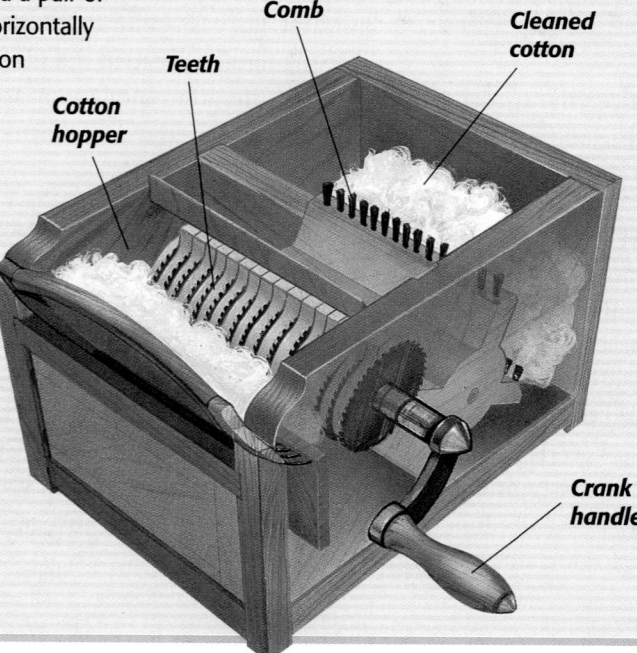

Comb • Cleaned cotton • Teeth • Cotton hopper • Crank handle

Understanding Science and History

1. How did Eli Whitney's cotton gin differ from earlier gins?
2. What was the advantage of the dual-cylinder system?

The Southern Class Structure

The class structure of the **antebellum**, or pre-Civil War, South reflected the importance of land and slaves to the region's economy. Just one in four southern whites owned slaves, but this group of slaveholders dominated southern society and politics.

Wealthy planters. Few slaveholders held 20 slaves or more. Those who did, however, often had extremely large holdings. Some of these richest planters lived elegantly in beautiful mansions. One Mississippi planter ordered furniture from France for one room of his mansion at the then-extremely high cost of $10,000. The majority of plantation owners—those holding fewer than 20 slaves—lived more modestly. Their homes were usually two-story, frame buildings with 8 to 10 rooms, deep porches, and comfortable but not luxurious furnishings.

The plantation owners' reputation for a life of ease was often more image than reality. They were kept busy managing the plantation. This involved assigning tasks to supervisors or slaves, keeping records of business transactions, writing to shipowners or bankers, and contracting with brokers. Bennet H. Barrow, a Louisiana cotton planter, kept a journal recording his daily concerns. Barrow described why he maintained a strict watch over his plantation:

THE COLONIAL WILLIAMSBURG FOUNDATION

This fan was used by a wealthy southerner.

INTERPRETING THE VISUAL RECORD

Plantation work. This illustration shows slaves working. *What different types of work can you identify?*

> 66 A plantation might be considered as a piece of machinery, to operate successfully, all of its parts should be uniform and exact, and the impelling [driving] force regular and steady; and the master, if he pretended at all to attend to his business, should be their impelling force. 99

Planters' wives supervised the food preparation, housecleaning, mending, spinning, and weaving. They also kept track of household finances, cared for the sick, supervised the house slaves, and often taught the children. Lucy Breckinridge, who grew up in a wealthy Virginia family, dreaded the idea of running a plantation after she married. "A woman's life after she is married . . . is nothing but suffering and hard work," she wrote. Compared to most farm wives, however, plantation mistresses' lives were free of hard physical work.

Small farmers. Beneath the planters on the social scale were the hundreds of thousands of **yeoman farmers** who made up the majority of southern white society. Southerner D. R. Hundley favorably compared them to the planters, declaring, "So far as hospitality goes, [they] are not a whit behind the Southern Gentleman, or any other class of gentlemen the world over." Although most of these small farmers lived on fertile lands, they often lacked easy access to markets. They built simple two-room log cabins filled with homemade furniture, raised cattle and pigs, and sold crops—typically grain or tobacco—for cash. They also grew their own food, usually in small plots near their homes. Although most small farmers owned no slaves, some managed to purchase a few.

The very poor. The poorest white people made up a small percentage of the South's population and farmed the least-productive soil. They lived in rough cabins, ate poorly, and sometimes suffered from medical problems such as malaria and hookworm. An observer told of one poor family of five adults and five children living in a log cabin not more than 15 feet square. These southerners owned no slaves. They often survived by hunting, fishing, farming, and raising pigs.

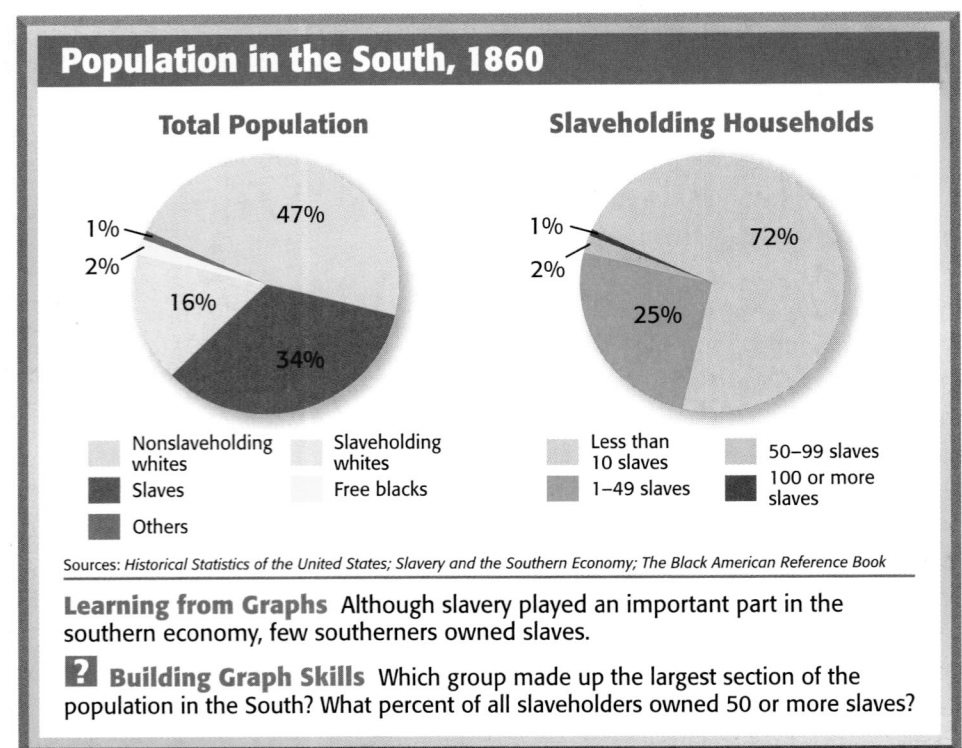

Population in the South, 1860

Total Population

47%
1%
2%
16%
34%

Nonslaveholding whites
Slaveholding whites
Slaves
Free blacks
Others

Slaveholding Households

1%
2%
72%
25%

Less than 10 slaves
1–49 slaves
50–99 slaves
100 or more slaves

Sources: *Historical Statistics of the United States; Slavery and the Southern Economy; The Black American Reference Book*

Learning from Graphs Although slavery played an important part in the southern economy, few southerners owned slaves.

❓ **Building Graph Skills** Which group made up the largest section of the population in the South? What percent of all slaveholders owned 50 or more slaves?

✔ **READING CHECK:** How did yeomen and poor white farmers differ from planters?

White Southern Culture

The difference between the social classes reflected the widely varying economic statuses and backgrounds of white southerners. In other respects, however, these classes shared a number of cultural characteristics.

Food and housing. Small southern farmers typically planted corn and raised pigs. Most southerners lived on corn—in the form of cornbread, cornmeal, and hominy—and pork, which many people ate almost daily. In the winter, when fresh fruits and vegetables were scarce, the typical southern diet was very plain, consisting of pork, hominy, and coffee. Likewise, many white southerners of various classes shared similar housing. Although some successful plantation owners built grand mansions to replace their log cabins, many others maintained simple homes even after gaining great wealth.

AMERICAN ARTS

Southern Folk Art

Around 1886 former slave Harriet Powers made this quilt showing Bible stories.

In the early 1800s, both white and African American southerners sewed heavy quilts to keep their families warm throughout the winter. Although the styles of the quilts varied greatly, all were remarkable for their usefulness and for the creativity they reflected. Plantation mistresses as well as slave women organized quilting parties. Here women helped each other with their work while enjoying the opportunity to socialize.

The quilts of African American women utilized patterns first developed in Africa more than 1,000 years ago. These quilts of pieced-together fabric were characterized by asymmetry, bright colors, large designs, and multiple patterns. They expressed complicated ideas, such as religious values and personal histories. Many of the features of the quilts derive from African cloth styles, where patterns could represent a person's occupation, status, and wealth.

Quilts made by white southern women were strongly influenced by European styles. These quilts had three layers: a top made of patchwork or appliquéd pieces, a cotton or wool layer, and a lining. Although cotton was plentiful in the South, extra fabric was often harder to come by and expensive. As a result, many quilters constructed only simple "everyday" quilts. Wealthier women, usually with the help of their slaves, also created fancier, more decorative quilts that often had elaborate color-coordinated patterns. Some of the most popular and complex patterns included the Double Wedding Ring and the Flower Garden.

Understanding the Arts

1. How did other cultures influence the style of southern quilts?
2. What does the quilt pictured here reveal about southern culture at the time it was made?

AMERICAN *Letters*

Southern Writers

Although both Edgar Allan Poe and Caroline Howard Gilman lived in the South, two more different writers would be hard to find. Poe grew up in the cities of Richmond, Virginia, and Baltimore, Maryland, but spent much of his adult life in New York. Poe's work shows his subtle, dark relationship with his southern heritage. The following excerpt from "The Fall of the House of Usher" (1839), one of Poe's most famous stories, demonstrates his skill at creating a mood of gloom and suspense. Gilman was a Boston native who moved to South Carolina in 1819. In Recollections of a Southern Matron *(1838), one of her most popular works, Gilman describes rural life in South Carolina. In this excerpt, the narrator of the story, a wealthy southerner, has recently seen her plantation home burn to the ground.*

---

from "The Fall of the House of Usher"
by Edgar Allan Poe

Edgar Allan Poe

During the whole of a dull, dark, and soundless day in the autumn of the year, when the clouds hung oppressively low in the heavens, I had been passing alone, on horseback, through a singularly dreary tract of country, and at length found myself, as the shades of the evening drew on, within view of the melancholy House of Usher. I know not how it was—but, with the first glimpse of the building, a sense of insufferable gloom pervaded my spirit. . . . I looked upon the scene before me—upon the mere house, and the simple landscape features of the domain—upon the bleak walls—upon the vacant eye-like windows—upon a few rank sedges [meadow plants]—and upon a few white trunks of decayed trees—with an utter depression of soul . . . the bitter lapse into every-day life—the hideous dropping off of the veil. There was an iciness, a sinking, a sickening of the heart—an unredeemed dreariness of thought which no goading of the imagination could torture into aught [anything] of the sublime. What was it—I paused to think—what was it that so unnerved me in the contemplation of the House of Usher?

from *Recollections of a Southern Matron*
by Caroline Howard Gilman

Caroline Howard Gilman

On the evening after the burning of Roseland, brother Ben and I visited the ruins. The sun had not set, and the [slave] laborers, retiring from their tasks, stopped to speak to me. . . . I must ask indulgence of general readers for mingling so much of the peculiarities of negroes with my details. Surrounded with them from infancy, they form a part of the landscape of a Southern woman's life; take them away, and the picture would lose half its reality. They watch our cradles; they are the companions of our sports; it is they who aid our bridal decorations, and they wrap us in our shrouds.

UNDERSTANDING LITERATURE

1. How does Edgar Allan Poe generate suspense in this selection?
2. How does Caroline Howard Gilman's narrator portray the relationship between white southerners and enslaved African Americans?
3. What different images of households do the two writers suggest? How might this reflect different perspectives of southerners?

Folkways. The folklife—music, tales, crafts, and folk art—of white southerners was influenced by the cultural contributions of the region's British and African heritage. Children in wealthy families were typically taught to play a musical instrument. Members of the yeomen class also sang and played traditional European music, such as English and Scottish ballads. In rural areas, many songs described the songwriter's surroundings or recounted heroic adventures. Frontier residents often attended parties where they danced to fiddle music.

Southerners prized handcrafted items—such as baskets and pottery—created by artisans for their usefulness. Such crafts also revealed much about the region's history. For instance, the techniques used to make baskets reflected the cultural influences of African Americans, American Indians, and European Americans. The South also had many painters. Folk artist John Toole traveled throughout Virginia in the early 1800s, recording the people and their daily lives in his paintings.

Religion. Religion may have united white southerners more than any other element of the region's culture. Churches functioned as a social center for many white southerners, particularly because so many people lived in isolated rural areas.

To justify slavery, many white southerners interpreted the Bible to mean that white people were superior to African Americans. Some white slaveholders saw themselves as spiritual guardians of their slaves. One minister in South Carolina expressed these sentiments. "We feel that the souls of our slaves are a solemn trust and we shall strive to present them faultless and complete before the presence of God." White Christian missionaries preached to slaves that their souls would only be saved if they remained loyal and obedient to their owners.

✔ **READING CHECK:** What cultural traits did white southerners of different classes share?

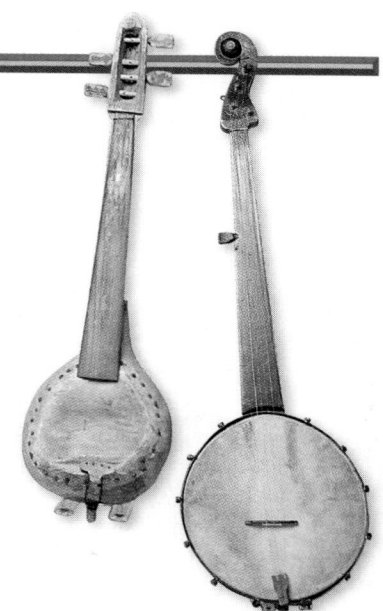

This handmade banjo and gourd fiddle date from the early 1800s.

The Urban South

Although myths of the Old South tend to focus on plantation life, thriving communities also existed in southern towns and cities. While southern cities differed in appearance and atmosphere from northern cities, they had similarities as well. City governments regulated economic affairs and provided public services such as city wells, free public schools, gas streetlights, and paved streets.

Southern cities were centers of change in this traditional society. With the emphasis of city-dwellers on business, the urban South came closest to resembling the North. Some urban southerners, however, still held slaves. Those who did not often "hired out" slaves. Urban slaves worked in bakeries, factories, markets, mills, and offices. Frederick Douglass, an escaped slave who became a prominent abolitionist, compared a city slave to a plantation slave. "He [the city slave] is much better fed and clothed, and enjoys privileges altogether unknown to the slave on the plantation." Some of these privileges including greater freedom of movement.

INTERPRETING THE VISUAL RECORD

The urban South. George Cooke painted this view of 1830s Richmond, Virginia. *What can you determine about life in Richmond at the time?*

Free African American Society

Some free African Americans were required to wear badges to prove they were not slaves.

Although most black southerners were enslaved, by 1860 some 260,000 free African Americans lived in the South. Nearly half of them made their homes in the Upper South. In Baltimore the number of free African Americans far exceeded the city's slave population. The pattern was reversed in the Lower South, where less than 2 percent of the African American population was free.

Some free African Americans worked as skilled craftspeople, such as mechanics or seamstresses. Others found domestic employment as cooks or servants. Some had never been slaves. Others had worked extra hours to earn money to purchase their freedom or were rewarded with freedom. William Ellison of South Carolina, for example, learned to repair cotton gins while a slave. After buying his freedom, he purchased the freedom of his wife and children. A small minority of free African Americans, including Ellison, became landowners, and some even purchased slaves themselves. Ellison became one of the wealthiest free African Americans in the antebellum South.

White southerners greatly restricted the rights of free African Americans. After 1830, southern legislatures required free African Americans to register with local authorities and to carry identification passes proving that they were not runaway slaves. They often had to post bonds—money or a pledge of property—as a guarantee of good behavior. Free African Americans in the South were not permitted to vote, hold public meetings, carry weapons, or testify in court against whites.

In many places, free African Americans were forbidden to attend all-black churches unless a white person was present. Nor could they go into business for themselves or learn how to read and write. Unemployed African Americans could be sold into servitude for months or even years. An editorial in an African American newspaper put it simply: "Though we are not slaves, we are not free."

✔ **READING CHECK:** What was life like for free African Americans in the South?

SECTION 2 REVIEW

Define and explain the significance of the following terms:
cotton gin
Tredegar Iron Works
antebellum
yeoman farmers

Identify and explain the significance of the following individuals:
Eli Whitney
William Ellison

1. **Using Graphic Organizers** Copy the graphic organizer below. Use it to describe the lifestyles of the different white southern classes, as well as the cultural elements they shared.

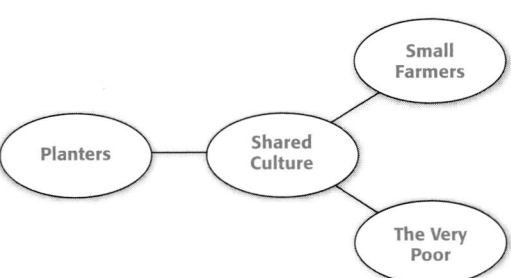

2. **Identifying Cause and Effect** What factors allowed for the development of the Cotton Kingdom? Why did industries grow more slowly in the South than in the North?

3. **Comparing and Contrasting** How were southern cities similar to and different from northern cities?

4. **Recognizing Point of View** Why might free African Americans have viewed the South differently from white southerners?

Critical Thinking

5. How did the reality of antebellum southern culture differ from idealized images of the Old South?
   Consider:
   • what life was like in the antebellum South
   • what some idealized images of the South were

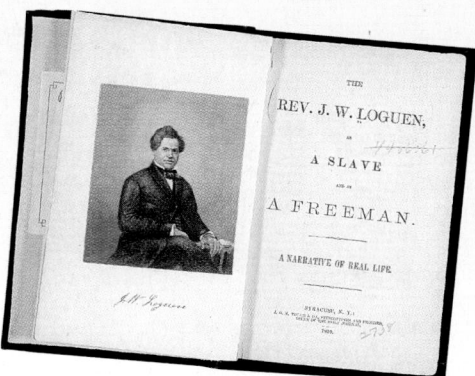
Reverend J. W. Loguen
and his memoir

Proslavery advocates argued that slaves like this nurse were very well-treated.

The Slave System

OBJECTIVES

Read to understand:

1. how critics and supporters of slavery explained their positions
2. what the living conditions of enslaved African Americans were like
3. what the cultural life of slaves was like
4. what types of resistance slaves practiced

KEY TERMS

overseers
drivers
gang labor
spirituals
Underground Railroad

KEY PEOPLE

Gabriel Prosser
Denmark Vesey
Nat Turner
Harriet Tubman

EYEWITNESSES TO History

66 *[The slave] was a thing for others' uses, and . . . he must bend his head, mind and body in conformity to that idea.* 99
—J. W. Loguen

J. W. Loguen escaped from slavery, attended college, and later became a minister. In 1859 he published his memoir of slave life, *The Rev. J. W. Loguen, as a Slave and as a Freeman.* After the publication of his memoir, Sarah Loguen, his former owner, discovered his whereabouts. She wrote him a letter asking him either to return or to send her $1,000 as compensation for the loss of his services. She stated, "You know we raised you as we did our own children." Loguen's reply was printed in an abolitionist newspaper. "Woman, did you raise your own children for the market?" he responded. "Did you raise them for the whipping post? Did you raise them to be driven off, bound . . . in chains?" Loguen's story demonstrates the degree to which slaveholders' view of slavery conflicted with the reality of life for enslaved African Americans.

Southerners and Slavery

As cotton plantations spread throughout the South, the number of slaves in the South also grew—from half a million in 1790 to nearly 4 million in 1860. Cotton cultivation required a great deal of labor. In the picking season alone, a slave might work each field five separate times. Though slave labor formed the foundation of the southern economy, some southerners, particularly those in the Upper South, criticized slavery. A few argued that an economy based on plantation agriculture and slavery was less profitable than one based on wage labor and industry. Some southerners criticized slavery as incompatible with liberty and freedom. Southern critics of slavery were drowned out by its supporters, however. Planters argued that slavery was the only way to ensure an adequate supply of field-workers for southern cash crops. Slavery's defenders also insisted that planters helped slaves by providing care in sickness and old age, as well as clothing, food, and shelter.

Virginia lawyer and writer George Fitzhugh contrasted the supposedly "secure" life of southern slaves with the sad plight of wage earners in northern U.S. and European factories and mines. Such workers, Fitzhugh argued, were at the mercy of employers. Factory owners paid them little, fired them at will, and heartlessly abandoned them when they became too old or sick to work. "Masters treat their sick, infant, helpless slaves well," Fitzhugh argued, "not only from feeling and affection, but from motives of self-interest. Good treatment renders them more valuable."

✔ **READING CHECK:** What were the various arguments presented by slavery's critics and supporters?

Slave labor. Haywood Dixon was a slave whose master often hired him out. *What skill do you think Dixon possessed?*

This 1860s image shows a slave family in front of their log cabin in the woods of Georgia.

COLLECTION OF THE NEW-YORK HISTORICAL SOCIETY

Slave Labor

More than 75 percent of enslaved African Americans lived and worked on plantations and farms. The lives of slaves in the cities were generally less grim than those of field hands. Frederick Douglass hired himself out for labor in Baltimore, Maryland. He later wrote:

> **❝ I was to be allowed all my time; to make all bargains for work; to find my own employment, and to collect my own wages; and, in return for this liberty, I was required, or obliged, to pay [to his owner] . . . three dollars at the end of each week. ❞**

In contrast, most field hands on plantations worked from dawn to dusk and beyond—as many as 18 to 20 hours per day during the harvest. Former slave Peter Clifton explained, "The rule on the place was: Wake up the slaves at daylight, begin work when they can see, and quit work when they can't see." Instead of working the fields, some slaves—particularly women—served the plantation household as cooks, maids, or nannies. Others did sewing or laundry. Some male slaves worked as blacksmiths, carpenters, coach drivers, or gardeners.

On small farms slaveholders usually supervised their slaves directly. On larger plantations **overseers**—who were usually small farmers, skilled workers, or planters' younger sons or other relatives—managed the slaves. To help supervise the slaves, overseers used **drivers**—assistants picked from among the slaves. Drivers occupied a difficult position between owner and slave. A driver might be praised by the owner for a job well done, but despised by slaves for working them too hard. Mississippi slave Henry Cheatam gave a typical slave's description of a driver when he called him "the meanest devil that ever lived."

On plantations, slaves were organized into work crews with drivers as foremen. This system of **gang labor** allowed overseers to assign groups of slaves to do specialized jobs, such as hoeing, picking, or plowing.

Slave Life

The lives of slaves varied depending on where they lived and what kind of owners they had. One thing unified all the slaves, however: they had little say in what happened to themselves or their families.

Housing and diet. Slave quarters were cramped and sparsely furnished. A family might live in a one-room log cabin with no comforts other than a fireplace. In winter, biting cold air penetrated through gaps between the logs and the uncovered openings used as doors and windows. In such homes, an observer noted, "the wind and rain will come in and the smoke will not go out."

Food was rationed on the plantation. Ben Horry, a former slave from South Carolina, recalled that on Saturdays, every slave on the plantation lined up at the smokehouse to draw his or her weekly share of grits, meal, meat, and rice.

These shares, however, were seldom enough to last the week. To supplement their diet, slaves hunted and fished at night or on Sundays and grew greens or sweet potatoes in small gardens. House slaves sometimes received food from the planter's kitchen. Many slaves also stole food when they did not get enough to eat.

Slaves' clothing was simple, usually made of linsey-woolsey—a coarse woolen and linen or cotton material similar to burlap. This cloth, said one former Virginia slave, "was just like needles when it was new. Never did have to scratch our back. Just wriggle your shoulders and your back was scratched."

John Burry, a slave on a plantation in Louisiana, made this woolen suit.

Treatment of slaves. Slaves' treatment varied from plantation to plantation. Some planters used rewards to gain their slaves' obedience. These included the promise of money, gifts of extra food or clothing, easier tasks, dances, days off, or shorter working hours. Those who obeyed orders might be granted small favors, given a garden plot, or moved from the fields to work in the house.

Other slaveholders relied on the use or threat of violence to control their slaves. As a planter wrote in the *Southern Patriot,* "The fear of punishment is the principle to which we must and do appeal, to keep them in awe and order." If slaves were late getting to the fields or did not work fast or hard enough, overseers could be brutal. Prince Smith, a former slave on a South Carolina plantation, recalled the use of the "sweat box" a particularly harsh form of solitary confinement. "[The box] was made the height of the person and no larger. . . . The box is nailed, and in summer is put in the hot sun; in winter it is put in the coldest, dampest place."

Whipping was the most common form of punishment. William Wells Brown was a former slave and the author of the first published novel by an African American. He wrote that the whip was used "very frequently and freely, and a small offence on the part of a slave furnished an occasion for its use." Many recipients of the lash resisted the owner's will as best they could, often by refusing to cry out. Occasionally, slaves would band together to protect fellow slaves who would not submit to a whipping. In these ways slaves could and did sometimes challenge their owners.

If such discipline failed, slaves could be sold "down river"—away from family and community ties. Slave children were often sold away from their parents. Slaveholders might even separate a married couple. Charles Ball, who had a wife and child in Maryland, was sold by his owner in 1805. He recalled, "[I] was told that I would be able to get another wife in Georgia."

✔ **READING CHECK:** What different living conditions did enslaved African Americans endure?

INTERPRETING THE VISUAL RECORD

Punishment. The woman in this picture has been forced to wear a metal collar as punishment. *How do you think the collar was intended to punish the woman?*

Slave Culture

Slaves' lives were controlled from sunrise to sunset. However, after dark and on Sundays and rare holidays, slaves could devote their time to family and community. Slaves created a unique African American culture. This culture blended customs drawn from the variety of African groups thrown together under slavery as well as from their new cultural experiences in America.

Family and kinship bonds. Preserving family ties was a challenge for enslaved African Americans, particularly because slave families constantly faced the risk of being split up by the sale of individual members. For example, Charles Ball lost nearly all his family to slave traders and was himself sold or hired out more than half a dozen times. Yet, in each of his new homes, he created strong, meaningful relationships within the slave community.

A slave family heads south after being sold at auction.

Many slaves made heroic efforts to stay in contact with family members. One slave told of how he ran away from his owner to seek his mother on a distant plantation years after their forced parting.

66 I asked [my mother] if she knew me? she said, no. . . . I then [described] . . . being sold into slavery, and how she grieved at my loss. . . . [Her] dire feelings . . . rushed to her mind; she saw her own son before her, for whom she had so often wept; and, in an instant, we were clasped in each other's arms. 99

Some literate slaves kept in contact with their separated family members through letters. One slave whose family was sold wrote a letter to his wife, begging her to "send me some of the children's hair in a separate paper."

Oral history, folktales, and humor. Most slaves were not allowed to learn to read, however. The spoken word was therefore very important, particularly for maintaining links to the past. Good storytellers used body language, sounds, and mimicking to help tell their stories. Slaves used tales to relate their family histories. Many slaves told their family members about Africa.

Slaves also told folktales to preserve and pass on their culture. These stories were based on African stories but incorporated local situations and personal experiences. Most of the tales concerned everyday human relationships, detailing the importance of friendship or a parent's love. Moral tales warned of the pitfalls of excessive pride or stressed the ideals of cooperation and love.

Storytelling, particularly the use of animal trickster tales, gave African Americans a way of talking about slaveholders and slavery in a guarded form. In these humorous tales, a strong animal attempts to trap a weaker animal but fails. Instead, the weaker animal, such as Anansi the spider or Brer Rabbit, tricks the stronger animal and gains power, success, and wealth. Such tales allowed African Americans to reverse, at least in their imaginations, the harsh reality of the owner-slave relationship. Humor helped slaves deal with painful situations. The ability to maintain hope in the face of overwhelming abuse was an important survival technique for slaves. However, white southerners often misinterpreted the laughter as a sign that slaves were happy with their situation.

Reading Charts

Charts are used to organize and present information visually. They categorize and display data in a variety of ways, depending on the subject matter of the data. Types of charts include flowcharts, organizational charts, and tables. A *flowchart* displays a sequence of related events or the steps in a process. Cause-and-effect relationships are often shown by flowcharts. An *organizational chart* exhibits the structure of an organization and the function, ranking, and relationships between its internal parts. A *table* is a chart that presents data in columns that are easy to understand and compare.

How to Read a Chart

1. **Read the title.** Read the title to identify the topic of the chart.
2. **Study the major components.** Read the chart's headings, subheadings, and labels to identify the categories it uses and the type of data it provides for each category.
3. **Analyze the details.** Read the chart's data carefully and systematically. When studying dates, take note of time intervals; when studying numerical information, take note of increases or decreases in amounts; when studying textual information, take note of special terms and definitions.
4. **Put the data to use.** Use your analysis of the data, along with your knowledge of the historical period, to form generalizations and draw conclusions.

Applying the Strategy

Study the following table, which presents similar-meaning words and phrases in English and Gullah, a language spoken by African American slaves and their descendants in parts of Georgia and South Carolina.

Practicing the Strategy

Using the table below, answer the following questions.
1. What Gullah words might likely be used as personal nicknames?
2. What Gullah words are still used regularly by English speakers in the United States?

Gullah Word Origins

Gullah word/phrase	English meaning	African origin
buckra	white man	Ibidio
da	mother, nurse, or elder woman	Ewe
eh	yes	Igbo
nana	elderly woman, grandmother	Twi
tote	to pick up	Kongo
yam	sweet potato	Mende
sweetmouth	flatter	Mende
hot the water	bring the water to boil	Mende
pakpakpak	knock	Mende

Sources: *Africanisms in the Gullah Dialect; The Water Brought Us; Bridges to Change*

Music and folk art. Music played an important role in the lives of slaves. The music's African heritage was reflected in its rhythmic structure, strong beat, and use of communal singing. In the evenings, the African American "musicianers," as their fellow slaves called them, would often bring out a banjo, drum, or fiddle to entertain the others and provide music for dancing. Slaves used music as a way to escape the pain of their lives as well as to express their feelings and thoughts. Slaves' songs also chronicled their daily experiences. They told of work, criticized white society, and protested bondage.

Slaves also expressed themselves through folk art such as woodcarvings and pottery. They wove baskets using the techniques of their African ancestors and

This doll is believed to have belonged to an enslaved African American child.

decorated gourds and clayware with patterns learned from previous generations. Other types of slave art blended both European and African techniques, demonstrating the close connection of the two cultures that influenced African American life.

Slave Religion

Religion played a vital role in the lives of enslaved African Americans. Most worship services included a rich blend of Christian elements and traditional African beliefs, dance, and music. Embracing the Christian belief in salvation helped some slaves endure the hardships they faced. Central to the slaves' religion was their belief that they were God's chosen people who, like the ancient Hebrew slaves in Egypt, would eventually reach a "promised land" free from their oppressors. The slaves' promised land was not just an afterlife in Heaven. It was also a world without slavery.

White southerners often censored African American ministers, most of whom were slaves. Consequently, the ministers had to preach obedience to owners. However, they took the opportunity to speak what was close to their hearts, particularly when they were alone with other slaves.

When slaveholders, fearful of rebellions, forbade slaves from congregating, even for religious meetings, enslaved African Americans continued to hold secret gatherings in the woods. To quiet the noise of these meetings, slaves devised several creative methods of muffling sound. With the noise muted, one former slave explained, that the gathered group "could shout and sing all they wanted to and the noise wouldn't go outside."

Of great importance to slave religion were haunting songs called **spirituals**. Rich in biblical lore, these songs of sorrow were sung during work, relaxation, and worship. Modeled partly on Christian hymns and partly on traditional African rituals and musical forms, spirituals differed significantly from the religious songs of white worshippers. Spirituals movingly expressed the slaves' deep longing for freedom. Favorites like "Go Down, Moses," "Blow Your Trumpet, Gabriel," and "Didn't My Lord Deliver Daniel?" tell of deliverance from slavery.

✔ **READING CHECK:** What kind of cultural life did slaves have?

INTERPRETING THE VISUAL RECORD

Religious worship. Religion played an important part in slaves' lives and helped them endure hardships. *Where is this religious meeting taking place? Why do you think the slaves chose to have their meeting there?*

Rebellion and Resistance

Although they lacked legal power, slaves used several strategies to improve their living and working conditions. African Americans found many ways to resist slavery.

Slave revolts. Several small uprisings involving slaves in the South occurred in the early 1800s. In 1800 Gabriel Prosser led a rebellion near Richmond, Virginia, involving hundreds of slaves. Another plot surfaced in 1822 in Charleston, South Carolina. Masterminded by Denmark Vesey, a free prosperous African American carpenter and preacher, the plan called for a massive slave uprising in Charleston and the surrounding areas.

The plan was discovered before it could be carried out. Vesey and the other leaders were tried and executed. It nevertheless struck terror into the hearts of white southerners, who destroyed the records of the trial, afraid that other slaves might see it. Most of the accused slaves had been liked, respected, and trusted by their owners.

White southerners' worst fears materialized in 1831, when Nat Turner led a violent slave uprising in Southampton County, Virginia. The deeply religious Turner believed that God had chosen him to free the slaves. On August 21, Turner and a small band of followers took action. They killed Turner's owner and about 60 other whites in the area. The state militia and terrified local whites organized a hunt for Turner. They killed at least 100 slaves during the two months that it took to track him down. After being captured at his hideout in a cave, the fugitive was brought to trial. Asked why he refused to plead guilty, Turner replied, "Because I don't feel guilty." He was hanged on November 11, 1831.

Following these slave uprisings, some southern states passed stricter slave codes. These laws made it illegal to teach slaves to read and placed increased restrictions on slaves' movements. Some white southerners took the law into their own hands, arresting, beating, and killing slaves at will.

Nat Turner's inspirational preaching ignited a violent uprising.

African Culture and Traditions

Modern dancers perform a ring shout.

When Africans were brought to North America as slaves, their traditions crossed the ocean with them. African ceremonial dances performed in a ring led to the ring shout in American slave culture. During the ring shout, slaves clapped their hands, sang, and shouted as they moved in a circle. Over time, the ring shout inspired new forms of dance, such as the Charleston.

New forms of music developed with the new dance. Some slaves adapted songs with Christian lyrics to the ring shout, resulting in the African American spiritual. Several leading concert artists of the 1900s, such as Paul Robeson, Marian Anderson, and Leontyne Price, helped popularize spirituals. The rhythms and emotional tones of the ring shout greatly influenced blues music as well, which, in turn, shaped much of today's popular music.

Other African traditions still survive in contemporary society. Gullah, the African American dialect spoken in the Sea Islands off the coast of Georgia and South Carolina, preserves elements of African languages that were brought to North America more than 300 years ago. Words such as *guy, jive,* and *hip* derived from African languages also remain in contemporary English.

The Underground Railroad

Learning from Maps Conductors on the Underground Railroad helped between 50,000 and 75,000 slaves find freedom.

? MOVEMENT Which water routes did slaves use to escape on the Underground Railroad?

Percentage of Slaves in Total Population in 1860

- Slave population 50% or more
- Slave population 10%–50%
- Slave population 10% or less
- Slave population 0% or no data
- → Escape route

CANADA

Lake Superior
Lake Michigan
Lake Huron
Lake Ontario
Lake Erie

Quebec
Montreal
MN
Unorganized Territory
St. Paul
WI
MI
Toronto
VT
ME
NH
Buffalo
Boston MA
NY
PA
CT
RI
NEBRASKA TERRITORY
IA
Des Moines
Chicago
Cleveland
OH
IN
New York City
Philadelphia
NJ
40°N
Mississippi River
IL
Cincinnati
MD
Washington
DE
Topeka
Missouri River
Evansville
Ohio River
Louisville
VA
Richmond
KANSAS TERRITORY
MO
Cairo
KY
Nashville
TN
NC
New Bern
35°N
INDIAN TERRITORY
AR
SC
Atlanta
TX
Austin
MS
AL
Montgomery
GA
Charleston
Savannah
30°N
LA
Baton Rouge
Tallahassee
Jacksonville
Houston
FL
ATLANTIC OCEAN
Gulf of Mexico
25°N
BAHAMAS
MEXICO
Tilted Perspective Projection
CUBA
95°W
90°W
85°W
80°W
75°W

N W E S

RAN AWAY!

Newspapers often published advertisements for the capture of runaway slaves.

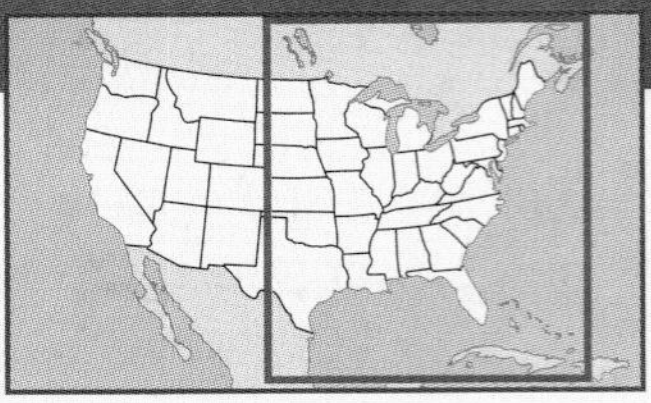

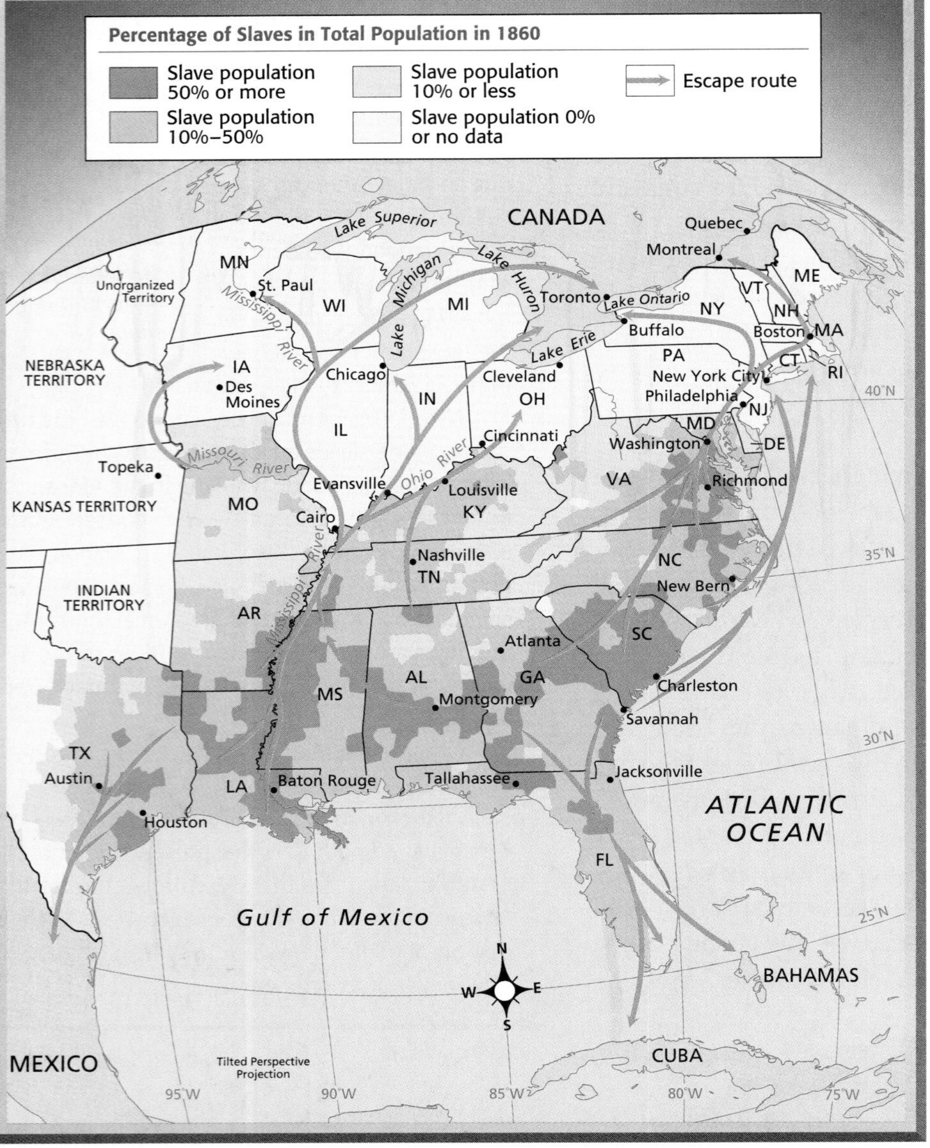

Slave resistance. Violent, organized rebellion was rare, but slaves constantly protested their bondage with individual actions. They might fake an illness, slow their work pace, steal property, or damage tools or other property in an effort to disrupt the plantation routine. In a few extreme cases, some slaves set fire to barns. These methods of resistance forced some owners to rule their slaves less strictly. In some cases, slaveholders simply hired out or sold the "difficult" slave.

The most tempting form of resistance to slavery was to run away. Often this was in response to an injustice on the part of the slaveholder. Many slaves stayed away for a short period—from a few days to several weeks—in order to deprive the planter of their work. Some slaves also escaped from the plantation to reunite with their families living on other farms.

Others ran away in hopes of securing their freedom in the North. Chances of success were slim, and punishment, if caught, could be brutal. Some assistance came from the **Underground Railroad**, a network of white and African American abolitionists who helped slaves escape to freedom in the North or in Canada. Escaping slaves made their way slowly out of the South. During the daytime they hid in attics and haylofts. At night, the escaping slaves were taken by "conductors" to the next safe house under the cover of darkness. Slaves were sometimes smuggled to safety in covered wagons and carriages and even hidden inside crates. The conductors on the Underground Railroad helped thousands of slaves gain their freedom. Harriet Tubman was the most famous and successful conductor.

BIOGRAPHY

Harriet Tubman

Tubman was born into slavery in Maryland about 1821. She first worked in the fields, but before long her owner hired her out to a family who wanted a maid. The family treated Tubman poorly and eventually returned her to the plantation. When she was just 15 years old, Tubman helped another slave escape. Trying to prevent the man from fleeing, the overseer threw a weight that struck Tubman in the head. From that point on, she was subject to sudden spells of dizziness and sleepiness.

This disability did not prevent Tubman from seeking her freedom. In 1849 she escaped to the North, leaving her parents and siblings behind. Two of her brothers accompanied her at first, but they returned, leaving Tubman to continue the journey alone. Tubman then risked her own freedom to help more slaves escape. She made at least 19 trips back to the South and led more than 300 slaves, including her parents, to safety. Despite a bounty of $40,000 placed on her, Tubman was never captured and she never lost a "passenger." She told the slaves she led, "You'll be free or die," and she always carried a pistol. Tubman believed, "There was one of two things I had a right to, liberty or death; if I could not have one, I would have the other; for no man should take me alive."

When not acting as a conductor, Tubman worked as a cook and spoke at antislavery meetings. Later in her life, she settled in Auburn, Massachusetts, where she founded a home for needy African Americans. She also told her story to a biographer, who published *Harriet Tubman: The Moses of Her People* in 1886. Tubman died in 1913 and was buried in Massachusetts with full military honors.

Despite the daring of the slaves and those who aided them, many fugitives were captured and returned to their masters. Still, the stream of runaways continued.

Read More About It

Free Find:
Harriet Tubman
After reading about Harriet Tubman on the **Holt Researcher** CD–ROM, imagine that you are a slave escaping the South with Harriet Tubman's aid. Write a fictional account of your journey.

✔ **READING CHECK:** In what ways did slaves resist their owners?

SECTION 3 REVIEW

Define and explain the significance of the following terms:
overseers
drivers
gang labor
spirituals
Underground Railroad

Identify and explain the significance of the following individuals:
Gabriel Prosser
Denmark Vesey
Nat Turner
Harriet Tubman

1. **Using Graphic Organizers** Copy the chart below. Use it to describe the different cultural forms enslaved African Americans used to help them survive slavery.

	Description
Family Ties	
Oral History	
Folktales & Humor	
Music & Folk Art	
Religion	

2. **Distinguishing Fact from Opinion** Some supporters of slavery argued that slaves could not survive on their own. What evidence might contradict that opinion?

3. **Using Historical Imagination** Write a brief journal entry describing the experiences of a slave on a plantation in the cotton belt.

4. **Comparing and Contrasting** How was life different for slaves on plantations and in urban areas?

Critical Thinking

5. To what extent can it be said that many slaves protested their condition every day and in every way possible?
Consider:
• how slave culture was a form of resistance
• what other forms of resistance slaves practiced
• the limitations of direct resistance

Review

Creating a Time Line

Copy the time line below onto a sheet of paper. Complete the time line by filling in the events and dates from the chapter that you think were most significant. Pick three events and explain why you think they were significant.

1800 — 1820 — 1840 — 1860

Writing a Summary

Using the Reading Checks as a guide, write an overview of the events in the chapter.

Identifying People and Ideas

Identify the following terms or individuals and explain their significance.

1. strike
2. Francis Cabot Lowell
3. nativism
4. Know-Nothings
5. Tredegar Iron Works
6. yeoman farmers
7. overseers
8. spirituals
9. Nat Turner
10. Harriet Tubman

Understanding Main Ideas

SECTION 1
1. How did increased immigration affect American society and politics?
2. How did the Market Revolution and industrialization change farming and farm life in the Midwest?

SECTION 2
3. What were the major elements of the southern economy?
4. How did free African Americans fit into southern society?

SECTION 3
5. How did slavery's critics and supporters justify their positions?
6. How did slaves respond to the working and living conditions on southern plantations?

Reviewing Themes

1. **Economic Development** What are some of the ways in which the growth of manufacturing affected northern society?
2. **Cultural Diversity** How did slavery influence African American culture in the 1800s?
3. **Technology and Society** What effect did Eli Whitney's cotton gin have on the economy of the South?

Thinking Critically

1. **Identifying Cause and Effect** In what ways did the new technology affect the lives of immigrants in northern society?
2. **Problem Solving** How might conflicts between labor and industry in the early 1800s have been resolved more easily?
3. **Synthesizing Information** How did economic factors affect the organization of southern society?
4. **Using Historical Imagination** Imagine that you are a European visitor to a southern plantation. Describe what life is like there and how it differs from what you expected.
5. **Hypothesizing** How might slavery have been affected if industrialization had advanced at the same pace in the South as it did in the North?

Writing About History

Writing to Describe Imagine that you are a "conductor" on the Underground Railroad. Write a diary entry describing your most recent efforts to help a slave family escape to freedom. Use the following graphic to organize your thoughts.

Description of Conductor and Slaves → Route to Freedom → Outcome

Strategies for Success Review the **Strategies for Success** on *Reading Charts.* Then study the following chart. How did the price of cotton change in relation to the increase in cotton production?

U.S. Cotton Production, 1800–1860

Year	Production (bales)	Average price (cents)
1800–01	210,526	44.00
1810–11	269,360	15.50
1820–21	647,482	14.32
1830–31	1,038,847	9.71
1840–41	1,634,954	9.50
1850–51	2,454,442	12.14
1859–60	4,861,492	11.00

Source: *Slavery and the Southern Economy*

Linking History and Geography

Many Irish immigrants and African American migrants moved to Boston before 1850. Study the map below. Where did African Americans live?

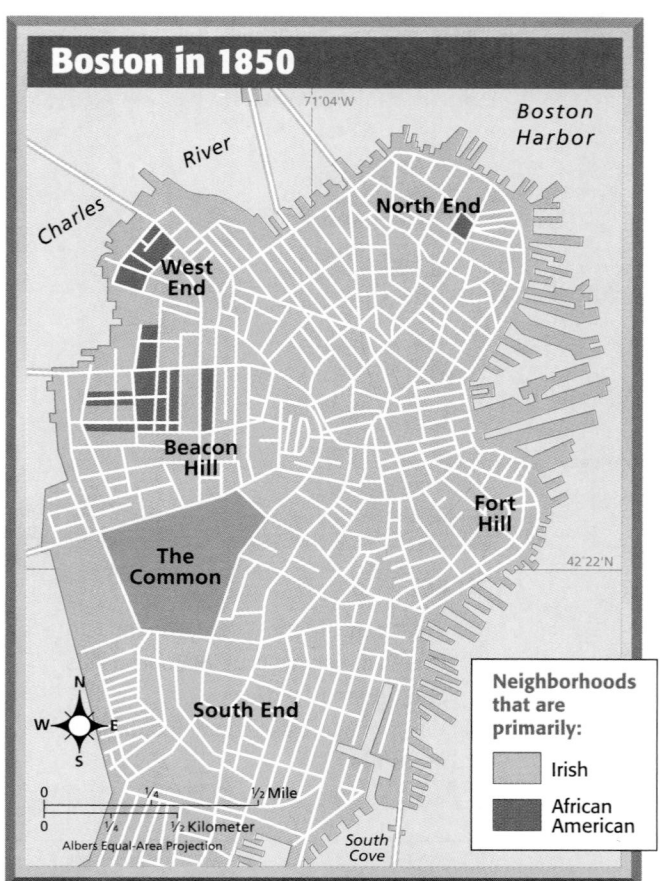

Boston in 1850

Charles River
Boston Harbor
North End
West End
Beacon Hill
Fort Hill
The Common
South End
South Cove

Neighborhoods that are primarily:
- Irish
- African American

0   ¼   ½ Mile
0   ¼   ½ Kilometer
Albers Equal-Area Projection

🖉 **internet connect**

TOPIC: Depicting Slave Life
GO TO: go.hrw.com
KEYWORD: SD1 Slavery

Accessing the Internet through the HRW Web site, research depictions of slave life in art and literature. Then write an explanation of how you think these depictions portray life under slavery.

BUILDING YOUR PORTFOLIO

Complete one or more of the following projects independently or cooperatively.

1 Economic Development
Imagine that you are a southern plantation owner. **Draw a map** that illustrates how the transportation revolution will make it easier for you to deliver your cotton to northern textile factories.

2 Cultural Diversity
Imagine that you are an immigrant who has recently arrived in New York City. **Present an oral account** of your trip to the United States, your passage through customs, and your current living and working conditions.

3 Democratic Values
Imagine that you are a factory worker on strike in the 1830s. **Write a speech** to be given to your co-workers inspiring them to join you in protesting unfair treatment.

Early labor union members

THE GRANGER COLLECTION, NEW YORK

Early Industrialization

Patterns of early industrialization in the United States were largely influenced by geography. Early factories relied heavily on waterpower. As rivers descend from the uplands to the lowlands, they often create waterfalls and rapids. The waterfalls and streams in New England contributed to its becoming the leading region of early industrialization.

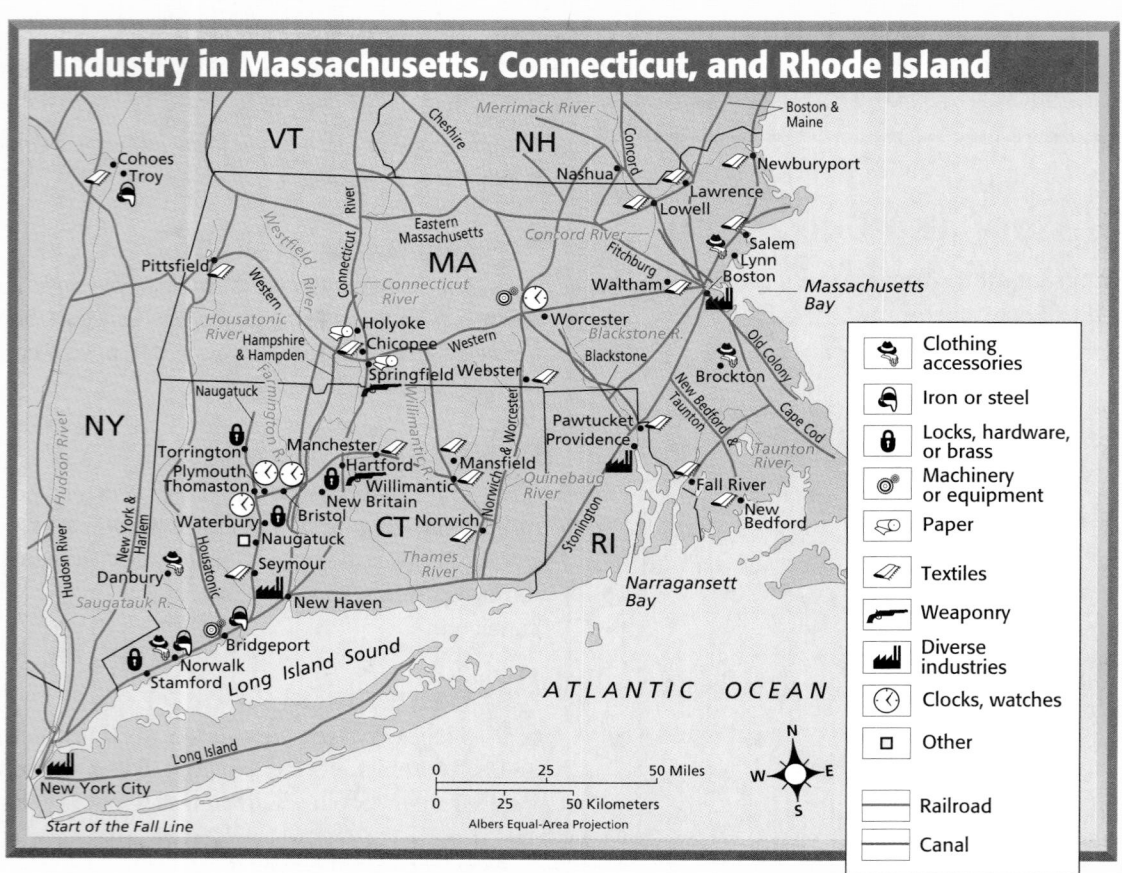

Industry in Massachusetts, Connecticut, and Rhode Island

Legend:
- Clothing accessories
- Iron or steel
- Locks, hardware, or brass
- Machinery or equipment
- Paper
- Textiles
- Weaponry
- Diverse industries
- Clocks, watches
- Other
- Railroad
- Canal

0   25   50 Miles
0   25   50 Kilometers
Albers Equal-Area Projection

Centers of industry. The boom in canal and railroad transportation had a tremendous impact on industry. Manufacturers could now ship materials and goods throughout the country. Connecticut, Massachusetts, and Rhode Island already contained a multitude of waterways that helped power numerous industries, particularly textiles. By the mid-1800s these three states were covered by webs of railroad lines connecting their major industrial centers.

GEOGRAPHY AND HISTORY Skills

PLACE

1. What was the most common industry overall in Connecticut, Massachusetts, and Rhode Island?
2. Which major cities contained diverse industries?

Industry in the North, c. 1860

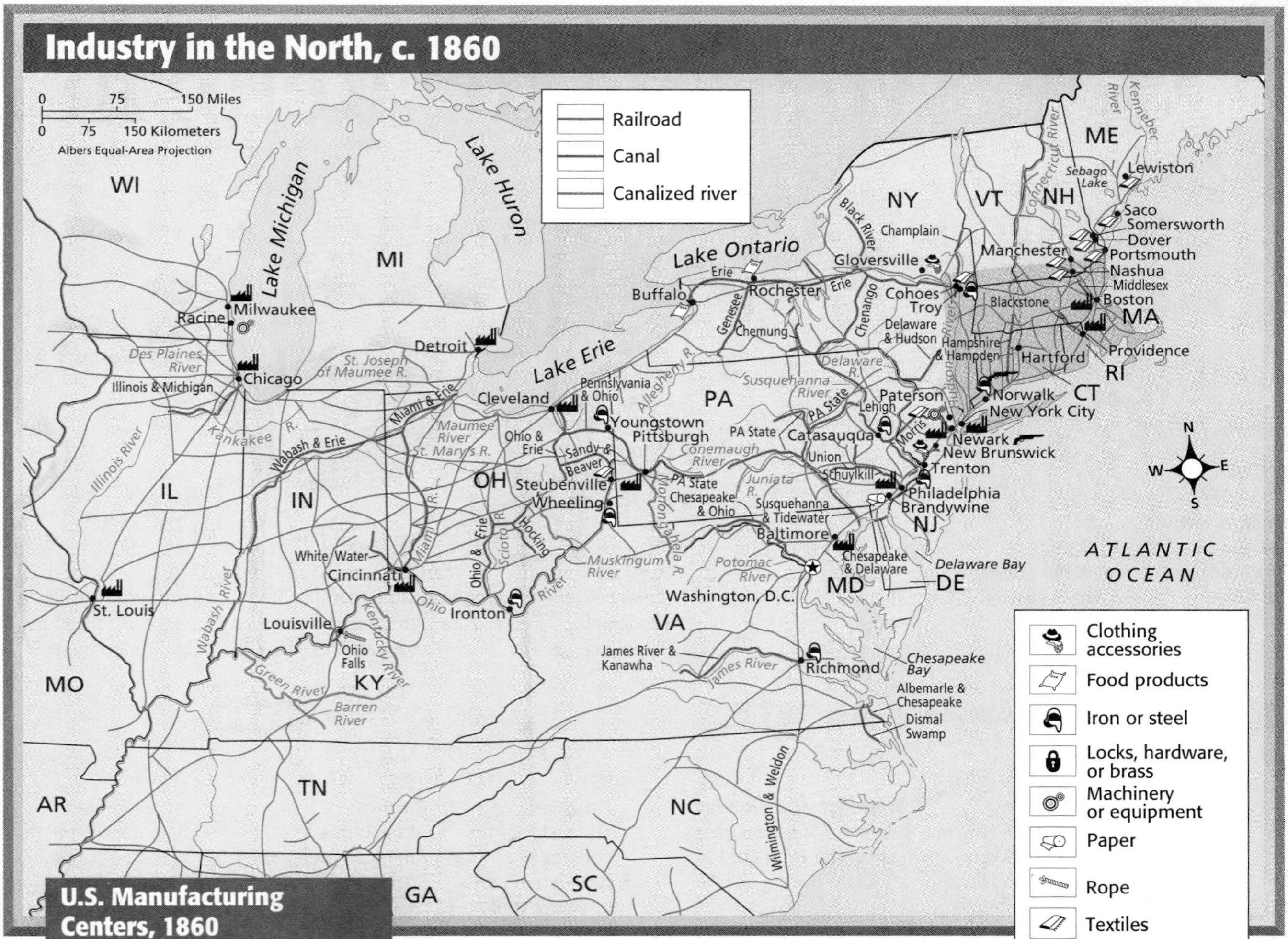

0   75   150 Miles
0   75   150 Kilometers
Albers Equal-Area Projection

Legend:
- Railroad
- Canal
- Canalized river

Map labels:
WI, MI, Lake Michigan, Lake Huron, Lake Ontario, Lake Erie, ME, NY, VT, NH, Kennebec River, Sebago Lake, Lewiston, Saco, Somersworth, Dover, Portsmouth, Nashua, Manchester, Middlesex, Boston, MA, Blackstone, Providence, RI, Hartford, Gloversville, Champlain, Black River, Rochester, Erie, Genesee, Buffalo, Chemung, Chenango, Cohoes, Troy, Delaware & Hudson, Hampshire & Hampden, Norwalk, CT, Paterson, New York City, Newark, New Brunswick, Trenton, Morris, Philadelphia, Brandywine, NJ, Racine, Milwaukee, Detroit, Des Plaines River, St. Joseph of Maumee R., Chicago, Illinois & Michigan, Cleveland, Pennsylvania & Ohio, PA, Susquehanna River, Delaware, PA State, Lehigh, Catasauqua, Union, Schuylkill, Kankakee R., Wabash & Erie, Maumee River, St. Marys R., Miami & Erie, Youngstown, Pittsburgh, Ohio & Erie, Sandy & Beaver, Conemaugh River, PA State, Juniata, Susquehanna & Tidewater, Baltimore, Chesapeake & Delaware, Delaware Bay, IL, IN, OH, Steubenville, Wheeling, Chesapeake & Ohio, Monongahela R., Potomac River, Chesapeake & Delaware, White Water, Cincinnati, Miami R., Scioto R., Hocking R., Muskingum River, Washington, D.C., MD, DE, ATLANTIC OCEAN, St. Louis, Wabash River, Louisville, Kentucky River, Ohio Falls, Ironton, Ohio River, VA, Chesapeake Bay, MO, KY, Green River, Barren River, James River & Kanawha, James River, Richmond, Albemarle & Chesapeake, Dismal Swamp, AR, TN, NC, SC, GA, Wilmington & Weldon

Compass rose: N, E, S, W

Industry legend:
- Clothing accessories
- Food products
- Iron or steel
- Locks, hardware, or brass
- Machinery or equipment
- Paper
- Rope
- Textiles
- Weaponry
- Diverse industries
- Clocks, watches
- Other

U.S. Manufacturing Centers, 1860

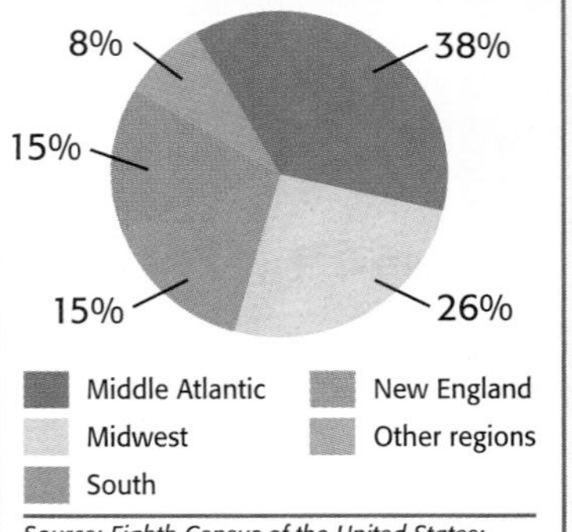

38%
8%
15%
15%
26%

- Middle Atlantic
- Midwest
- South
- New England
- Other regions

Source: *Eighth Census of the United States: Manufacturers, 1860.* Figures have been rounded and may not add up to 100 percent.

The canal boom. In the early 1800s canals created a revolution in transportation. In Ohio alone, some 1,000 miles of canals were constructed between 1825 and 1848. As railroads expanded, most canals fell into disrepair and were eventually shut down, as was the Ohio system in 1909.

Regional differences. By 1860 the small region of New England had as many manufacturing establishments as the entire South. The industrial imbalance between the North and the South added to the growing economic and political differences between the regions.

GEOGRAPHY AND HISTORY   Skills

MOVEMENT

1. How might canals have helped expand industry in New England?
2. If you had owned a business in Cleveland in 1860 and were trying to transport goods to Cincinnati, what form of transportation would you probably have used? Why?

283

1820–1860
Working for Reform

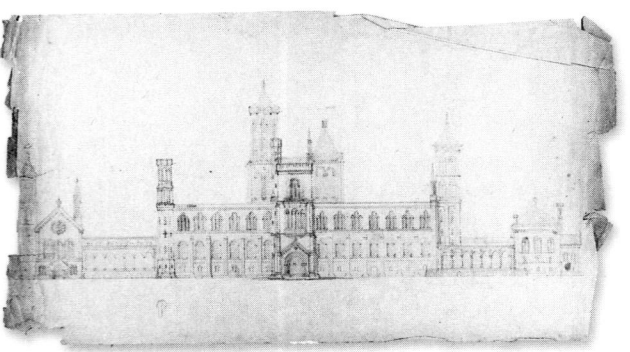

Design drawing for the Smithsonian Institute

1829
Science and Technology
British chemist James Smithson leaves £100,000 to found the Smithsonian Institution in Washington, D.C.

Showman P. T. Barnum

THE GRANGER COLLECTION, NEW YORK

1822
World Events
The American Colonization Society founds the city of Monrovia on Africa's west coast.

1829
World Events
Slavery is abolished in Mexico.

1835
Business and Finance
American showman P. T. Barnum begins his circus career.

1837
Daily Life
Horace Mann begins his work to reform public school education in Massachusetts.

1820

1828

1836

1821
Daily Life
The first free public high school in the United States, the English High School of Boston, opens.

1821
Politics
Ohio Quaker Benjamin Lundy begins to publish his antislavery newspaper *Genius of Universal Emancipation.*

1829
Business and Finance
The first U.S. patent on a typewriter is granted to William Burt of Detroit

1829
Daily Life
The Tremont House, the first modern hotel, opens in Boston.

1830
Daily Life
The first Mormon congregation is founded in western New York.

1833
Politics
Abolitionists form the American Anti-Slavery Society.

1837
World Events
Victoria is crowned queen of Great Britain.

The Queen Victoria *by Franz Winterhalter*

Before You Read

Build on What You Know

Industrialization and the Market Revolution transformed American society. Not all of these changes were positive, however. An increase in crime and poverty accompanied the rapid growth of cities. Other developments, including the mass migration to the West and the flood of new immigrants, altered the familiar social order. In this chapter you will learn how some people who were concerned about social changes came together in many different reform efforts with the hope of making the American vision of equality, justice, and opportunity possible for all citizens.

Dorothea Dix

Early snow-skiing equipment

1840
World Events
The World Anti-Slavery Convention is held in London.

1840
Business and Finance
2,816 miles of railway are in operation in the United States.

1843
Politics
Dorothea Dix reports the inhumane treatment of the mentally ill to the Massachusetts legislature.

1846
Business and Finance
Maine becomes the first state to prohibit the sale of alcohol.

1850
The Arts Nathaniel Hawthorne publishes *The Scarlet Letter.*

c. 1860
Daily Life
Snow-skiing becomes a competitive sport.

1844   **1852**   **1860**

1841
Daily Life
The first university degrees are granted to women.

1840
The Arts
French observer of American life Alexis de Tocqueville publishes *Democracy in America.*

1844
Science and Technology
Samuel Morse's telegraph is used for the first time, linking Washington, D.C., and Baltimore, Maryland.

1848
Politics
Women's rights activists hold the Seneca Falls Convention and sign the Declaration of Sentiments.

1855
The Arts
Walt Whitman publishes *Leaves of Grass.*

Alexis de Tocqueville's Democracy in America

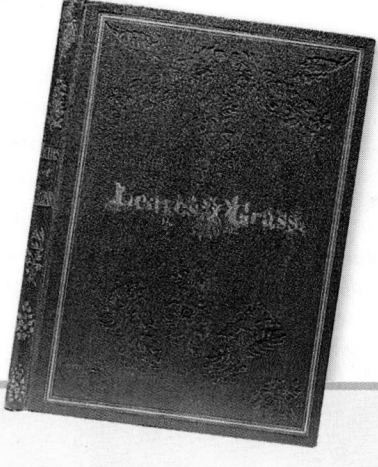

Walt Whitman's Leaves of Grass

Think About Themes

Decide whether you **agree** *or* **disagree** *with the following statements. Note why in your journal.*

Cultural Diversity Social changes will lead to a new interest in religion and to the creation of new forms of community.

Democratic Values Volunteer efforts by citizens' reform groups will alter public policy.

Constitutional Heritage Groups of people without constitutionally protected rights, such as the right to vote, have no influence on their political system.

Religious Zeal and New Communities

OBJECTIVES

Read to understand:

1. who participated in the Second Great Awakening
2. what the main characteristics of the Shakers and Mormons were
3. what ideas transcendentalism promoted

KEY TERMS

Second Great Awakening
revivals
denominations
utopias
Shakers
Mormons
transcendentalism
Unitarians

KEY PEOPLE

Charles Grandison Finney
Jarena Lee
Richard Allen
"Mother Ann" Lee
Joseph Smith
Brigham Young
Ralph Waldo Emerson
George Ripley

66 *I know of no country in the whole world in which the Christian religion retains a greater influence over the souls of men than in America.* **99**
—Alexis de Tocqueville

French visitor Alexis de Tocqueville wrote these words after visiting the United States in 1831. During the early 1800s, many Americans experienced a renewed interest in religious faith. One leader of this religious movement, which swept the urban Northeast as well as the western frontier, rejoiced that "God, in a remarkable manner, was pouring out his Spirit on the churches of New England." Americans established new religions and revitalized old ones. They founded communities where they could live according to their values and beliefs.

Religious artwork illustrating the paths of good and evil

The Second Great Awakening

Rapid social changes transformed the United States at the beginning of the 1800s. In response, many Americans turned to religious faith for direction. As early as the 1790s a renewed and passionate interest in religion, known as the **Second Great Awakening**, began to develop in towns in upstate New York. This evangelical movement quickly spread throughout New England, to Kentucky, Ohio, and beyond into the frontier regions farther south and west.

Huge crowds gathered during the Second Great Awakening. They listened to thunderous sermons, sang hymns, and sought God's help in reforming their lives. Many participants in these large religious gatherings known as **revivals** came away convinced of the possibility of attaining moral perfection, both for themselves and for society. Religious revivals swept the country in the early 1800s, drawing up to 20,000 people at a time to huge outdoor camp meetings. In 1801 James Finley, who later became a Methodist preacher, described the emotional intensity of one of the earliest revivals, held at Cane Ridge, Kentucky.

Religious revivals during the early 1800s attracted thousands of Americans.

THE GRANGER COLLECTION, NEW YORK

66 The vast sea of human beings seemed to be agitated as if by a storm. I counted seven ministers, all preaching at one time. . . . Some of the people were singing, others praying, some crying for mercy. A peculiarly strange sensation came over me. . . . I felt as though I must fall to the ground. **99**

Revival ministers expressed what many people felt at the time. This was a need for deep religious faith and an optimistic belief in an individual's ability to achieve eternal salvation and to improve his or her life. This optimism was fueled in part by changes in the United States such as economic growth and the expansion of democracy. Preachers traveled from town to town urging sinners to seek salvation. Charles Grandison Finney was a powerful and persuasive preacher with piercing eyes and a direct, forceful manner of speaking. He delivered hundreds of sermons in the 1820s and 1830s.

This religious enthusiasm sparked changes in Protestant congregations. The emotional, intensely personal sermons of evangelists during the Second Great Awakening appealed to many ordinary people. The revivalists' promise that salvation could be attained by everyone who repented of their sins also encouraged numerous religious converts. As a result, membership soared in various Protestant **denominations**, or religious groups.

African Americans and white women participated widely in the Second Great Awakening. In fact, female converts outnumbered males three to two. Women often led prayer groups, established and taught in Sunday schools, and supported missionary societies. One Methodist African American woman, Jarena Lee, traveled hundreds of miles to preach sermons to both black and white worshippers. Lee proclaimed that she had been called to preach by a heavenly voice. This voice told her, "Preach the Gospel; I will put words in your mouth, and will turn your enemies to become your friends."

African American men and women joined Baptist and Methodist churches in large numbers. They formed their own churches as well. In 1794 Richard Allen founded in Philadelphia one of the first African American churches, the Bethel African Methodist Episcopal Church. The African Methodist Episcopal (AME) Church soon expanded and developed into its own denomination.

In the South the spread of revivalism among enslaved African Americans met with a mixed reaction among slaveholders. Some slaveholders encouraged their slaves to convert to Christianity. Others, however, believed that Christianity might encourage the idea of equality and thus incite rebellion among slaves. Although Protestants stressed Bible reading, several southern states passed laws making it illegal to teach slaves to read. As a result, few Christian slaves could read the Bible for themselves.

✔ **READING CHECK:** Who participated in the revivals of the Second Great Awakening?

The Religious Spirit

CIRCUIT RIDERS

The circuit ridin' preacher used
   to ride across the land,
With a rifle on his
   saddle and a Bible
   in his hand;
He told the prairie
   people all about
   the promised land,
As he went riding,
   singing down the trail.

Traveling minister

I tinerant, or traveling, ministers—such as the one described in this hymn—were instrumental to the success of the Second Great Awakening. These emotional and often entertaining evangelists spread religious fervor throughout the country. They traveled to isolated frontier populations eager for religious leadership and connections to the outside world. Converts' shared faith linked them with other Americans across vast distances. In addition, itinerant ministers brought an array of religious choices to the frontier, as they represented new Protestant denominations.

Some new groups, such as the Wesleyan Methodists, turned the unorganized and unsupervised practice of itinerancy into an orderly yet mobile network called circuits. The founding bishop of the Methodist Church, Francis Asbury, argued that circuit riders—ministers who traveled the circuits—had become the very life of the church. "Next to the grace of God," Asbury exclaimed, "there is nothing *like this* for keeping the whole body alive from the center to the circumference." ▪

New Religions and Utopian Communities

The optimism that inspired revivals also led men and women to establish entirely new religious groups. Some founded **utopias**—communities designed to create a perfect society. More than 90 such communities sprang up in the United States between 1800 and 1850. Influenced by a wide range of religious beliefs and philosophies, these idealistic communities experimented with new ways of organizing family life, property ownership, and work.

METROPOLITAN MUSEUM OF NEW YORK

The Shakers. The United Society of Believers in Christ's Second Appearing—or **Shakers**, as the group came to be known from their tendency to shake their bodies during worship—founded communities in the eastern United States. They also inspired interest in utopian experiments. Shakers first arrived in America from Great Britain in 1774, led by "Mother Ann" Lee. She claimed to be the messiah who came to found a society free from sin. In the 1830s the sect's membership had reached a peak of between 5,000 and 6,000.

Shaker communities had separate but relatively equal roles for men and women, and community members jointly owned property. Shakers lived simply because they believed that the millennium—a time when some Christians believe Christ will return to rule over Earth—would soon begin. Shakerism declined after 1860 in part because members did not marry and have children and had difficulty recruiting new members.

Shakers. Shaker artisans became well known for the furniture they made. *What features of this Shaker desk reflect the lifestyle of many Shakers?*

The Mormons. Members of the Church of Jesus Christ of Latter-Day Saints, or **Mormons**, undertook one of the most enduring utopian ventures. Founder Joseph Smith claimed that divine assistance had enabled him to discover and translate buried golden plates that contained religious teachings. Smith published his translation of these teachings as the Book of Mormon and formed the first Mormon congregation in western New York in 1830.

Smith's religious teachings attracted many converts. Mormon principles also provoked strong opposition, however. Non-Mormons were particularly outraged by the Mormon practice of plural marriage, in which a man could be married to more than one woman at the same time.

This opposition to Mormon practices often led to violence. Many Mormons encountered violent resistance wherever they tried to establish a religious community. In 1844 a mob in Carthage, Illinois, killed Smith. Mormon Sarah Scott grieved over the leader's death as she wrote, "I can tell you it is a sorrowful time here at present."

Nevertheless, the Mormons endured. Under the leadership of Brigham Young, thousands of Smith's followers crossed the Rocky Mountains. They founded successful settlements in the Great Salt Lake valley, in territory that belonged to Mexico at the time.

✔ **READING CHECK:** What were the main characteristics of the Shaker and the Mormon communities?

Major Shaker Communities before 1860

Learning from Maps In 1776 the Shakers were the first group to try to form a utopian society in the United States.

❓ **REGION** In what region of the country were most Shaker communities founded?

0   200   400 Miles
0   200   400 Kilometers
Albers Equal-Area Projection

Lake Superior

CANADA

ME

Lake Huron

VT

NH

Sabbathday Lake 1794

Alfred 1793

Canterbury 1792

NY

Shirley 1793

Harvard 1791

Lake Ontario

Sodus 1826   Watervliet 1776

Hancock 1790

MA

WI

Lake Michigan

MI

Mount Lebanon 1787

CT   RI

Enfield 1790

Canaan 1787

40°N

Lake Erie

PA

NJ

ATLANTIC OCEAN

IL   IN   OH

MD   DE

Dayton 1806

West Union 1810

VA

Pleasant Hill 1809

KY

N

E

W

South Union 1809

S

35°N

NC

75°W

70°W

AMERICAN Letters

Transcendentalism and the Romantic Movement

During the early 1800s writers in the United States produced some of the first literature to be recognized as distinctively American. Much of this literature reflected the beliefs of the transcendentalists. It also reflected the romantic movement, which had its roots in Europe. Both movements emphasized the importance of the individual, natural simplicity, and spiritual renewal. Walt Whitman and Emily Dickinson were two of the most influential American romantic writers.

from *Leaves of Grass* (1855)
by *Walt Whitman*

Walt Whitman

The Americans of all nations at any time upon the earth have probably the fullest poetical nature. The United States themselves are essentially the greatest poem. . . . Here is not merely a nation but a teeming nation of nations. Here is action untied from strings necessarily blind to particulars and details magnificently moving in vast masses. . . . One sees it must indeed own the riches of the summer and winter, and need never be bankrupt while corn grows from the ground or the orchards drop apples or the bays contain fish. . . .

 . . . The genius of the United States is not best or most in its executives or legislatures, nor in its ambassadors or authors or colleges or churches or parlors, nor even in its newspapers or inventors . . . but always most in the common people. Their manners speech dress friendships . . . their deathless attachment to freedom . . . the air they have of persons who never knew how it felt to stand in the presence of superiors—the fluency of their speech—their delight in music, the sure symptom of manly tenderness and native elegance of soul . . . their good temper and openhandedness—the terrible significance of their elections—the President's taking off his hat to them not they to him—these too are unrhymed poetry.

untitled poem
by Emily Dickinson

Emily Dickinson

Some keep the Sabbath going
   to church;
I keep it staying at home,
With a bobolink* for a chorister,
And an orchard for a dome.

Some keep the Sabbath in surplice**;
I just wear my wings,
And instead of tolling the bell for church,
Our little sexton*** sings.

God preaches, —a noted clergyman, —
And the sermon is never long;
So instead of getting to heaven at last,
I'm going all along!

  *a songbird
 **priest's robes
***church caretaker

UNDERSTANDING LITERATURE

1. What role do arts play in Walt Whitman's view of the United States?
2. How does nature relate to Emily Dickinson's religious life?
3. What visual images does each work bring to mind?

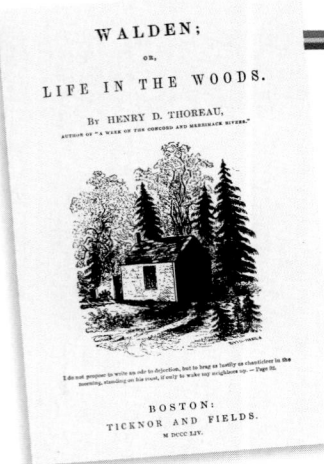

In his work entitled Walden, *Henry David Thoreau chronicled his experiences living near Walden Pond.*

HOLT RESEARCHER

Read More About It

Free Find:

Utopian Community

After reading the selection on utopian communities on the **Holt Researcher** CD–ROM, draw up an outline of beliefs for your own utopian community.

Transcendentalism

During this period of religious revival, some Americans embraced the philosophy of **transcendentalism**—the belief that people can transcend, or rise above, material things in life to reach a higher level of understanding. Influenced by German philosopher Immanuel Kant and British romantic poets, transcendentalists believed that human beings could approach perfection as they acquired knowledge about God, themselves, and the universe. Leading the transcendentalist movement was a small group of New England intellectuals, including writers Ralph Waldo Emerson, Henry David Thoreau, Margaret Fuller, and educator Bronson Alcott.

Many transcendentalists began as **Unitarians**—members of a religious reform movement that originally arose among New England Protestants in the late 1700s. In general, Unitarians rejected most Puritan beliefs such as predestination. They also believed people could become perfect.

Several young transcendentalists, including Emerson, became disenchanted with Unitarianism, however. Emerson had entered the ministry in 1826. He later came to believe that people should seek direct spiritual inspiration from God through a personal unification with nature.

Following Emerson's advice, Unitarian minister George Ripley founded one of the most famous utopian communities—Brook Farm—for a group of transcendentalists in 1841. In their community near Boston, Brook Farm residents withdrew from industrial society to live close to nature. They shared farm and household chores in order to allow time for study, discussion, and cultural pursuits. Dedicated to education and self-development, Brook Farm became a stimulating intellectual community. The experiment ended in 1846, however, after a fire destroyed part of the farm.

✔ **READING CHECK:** What ideas did transcendentalism promote?

SECTION 1 REVIEW

Define and explain the significance of the following terms:

Second Great Awakening
revivals
denominations
utopias
Shakers
Mormons
transcendentalism
Unitarians

Identify and explain the significance of the following individuals:

Charles Grandison Finney
Jarena Lee
Richard Allen
"Mother Ann" Lee
Joseph Smith
Brigham Young
Ralph Waldo Emerson
George Ripley

1. **Using Graphic Organizers** Copy the following graphic organizer. Use it to describe some of the new religious movements that grew out of the Second Great Awakening.

```
           Second
       Great Awakening
        /      |      \
   Shakers  Mormons  Unitarians
      |        |        |
```

Leaders: _____ _____ _____

Beliefs: _____ _____ _____
_____ _____ _____
_____ _____ _____
_____ _____ _____

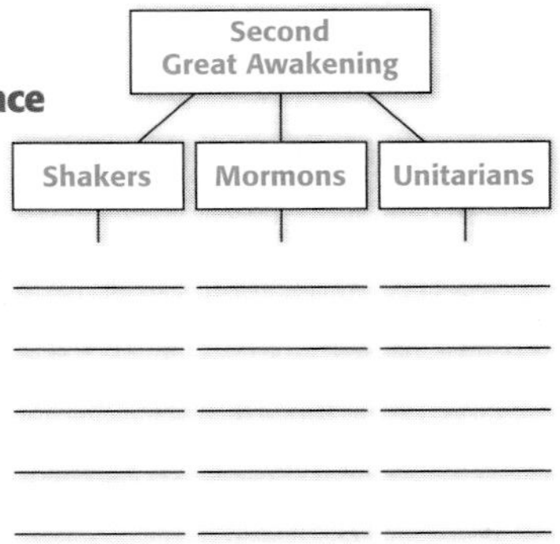

2. **Identifying Cause and Effect** Why did Protestant churches attract new members during the Second Great Awakening? What effect did this have on the churches' membership and structure?

3. **Assessing Consequences** Why can it be said that the Second Great Awakening had both positive and negative consequences for African Americans?

4. **Identifying Values** How did the philosophy of transcendentalism reflect democratic ideals?

Critical Thinking

5. How was transcendentalism both similar to and different from the religious movements that grew out of the Second Great Awakening?
Consider:
• what the beliefs and values of transcendentalism were
• what the beliefs and values of the Great Awakening religious groups were

Movements for Social Reform

OBJECTIVES

Read to understand:

1. what motivated temperance reformers
2. why some women believed it was important to become involved in reform movements
3. how educational opportunities changed in the early 1800s
4. how and why reformers worked to improve prisons and other institutions

KEY TERMS

temperance movement
prohibition
rehabilitation
penitentiary

KEY PEOPLE

Lyman Beecher
Catharine Beecher
Emma Willard
Mary Lyon
Horace Mann
Dorothea Dix

EYEWITNESSES TO History

66 *I was waked up for the war [for reform]! I was not headstrong, but I was heartstrong—oh, very, very!* 99
—Lyman Beecher

Lyman Beecher

Lyman Beecher, a leading minister of the Second Great Awakening, often described his commitment to reform as that of a warrior. The Second Great Awakening was accompanied by many similar cries for moral and social reform. In New England, Congregationalists established the Society for the Prevention of Vice and the Promotion of Good Morals. Also called the Moral Society, this group tried to uphold traditional standards of conduct and supervise behavior. Branches of the society were formed throughout Connecticut. Similar organizations soon developed in Massachusetts as well. Many reformers, like Lyman Beecher, were involved in a variety of movements.

The Crusade Against Alcohol

Many participants in the religious revivals of the Second Great Awakening firmly believed that it was possible for an individual to attain perfection. Their optimism soon led many to conclude that they could perfect society as well. Troubled by the effects of rapid industrialization, reformers in the Northeast began to direct their religious energy toward solving social problems.

Many reformers saw the abuse of alcohol as one of the most serious problems facing the nation in the early 1800s. In fact, in the 1830s Americans drank an average of seven gallons of alcohol per person each year. Lyman Beecher preached extensively about the evil effects of alcohol. People who drank alcohol, he thundered, were disobeying God's laws, "neglecting the education of their families—and corrupting their morals." With their emotional sermons, ministers such as Beecher won many converts. They persuaded many people to give up drinking completely. A woman described an 1842 revival meeting in Maryland that she attended.

66 **Upwards of 100 gallons of spirits were poured not down people's throats but on the sand and I believe there is now none in the place. Dean and Knotts [liquor sellers] have become members of the Temperance Society and are now earnestly seeking religion.** 99

Reformers organized the **temperance movement** to persuade others to limit alcohol consumption. These reformers argued that excessive drinking led to many other social problems such as criminal behavior, family violence, and poverty. A popular temperance novel later made into a play, *Ten Nights in a Bar-Room and What I Saw There* (1854), echoed this sentiment. As one character observed, he "never knew a man to go to the almshouse [poorhouse] that he hadn't rum to blame for his poverty."

Families were encouraged to sign temperance pledges such as this one.

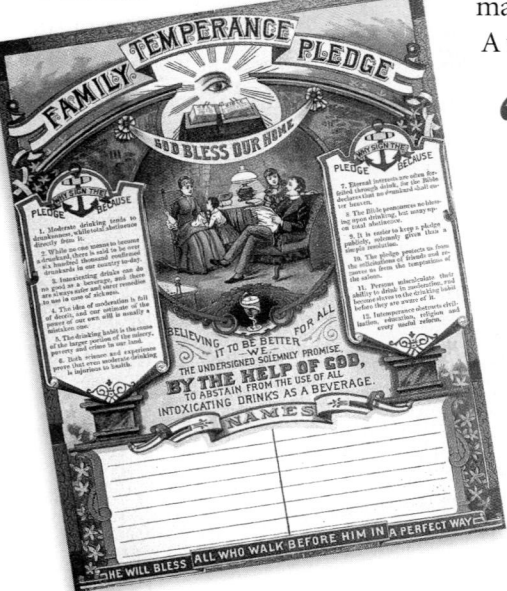

Temperance. Some members of the American Temperance Society smashed liquor containers to get their message across. *Why might the actions of these temperance supporters have been particularly shocking to the public?*

Beginning in the 1820s, temperance supporters—many of whom were women—established the American Temperance Society and later the American Temperance Union to spread their message. By the mid-1830s some 5,000 state and local temperance organizations had formed. Many women drawn to the temperance movement believed that avoiding alcohol could help preserve the family. Americans of many different backgrounds embraced temperance. Business leaders became enthusiastic supporters of the movement, in part because they saw how temperance contributed to a more disciplined workforce.

Many immigrants, on the other hand, viewed the temperance crusade as an attack on their customs, which often differed from those of native-born Protestant Americans. Most German and Irish immigrants did not view alcohol consumption as a social evil. For them, beer gardens and pubs were places where people came together to socialize. Both institutions helped German and Irish immigrants preserve their cultures in the United States, they argued.

Temperance supporters eventually called for legal reforms to limit alcohol consumption. Some reformers went so far as to demand **prohibition**—the complete ban on the manufacture, sale, and consumption of alcohol. In 1846 Maine became the first state to outlaw the sale of alcohol. A few other states followed, as did some communities. Many other states strictly licensed taverns and adopted heavy liquor taxes to discourage alcohol consumption. Temperance reform had a significant effect. By the mid-1800s the nationwide rate of alcohol consumption had declined substantially.

✔ **READING CHECK:** What motivated temperance reformers?

Women and Reform

Most women who joined reform efforts during the early 1800s were members of the new middle class that had emerged as a result of economic changes in the United States. The wives and daughters of this new class of merchants and professionals were at the forefront of efforts to improve social and moral conditions in the young nation. Middle- and upper-class women often hired domestic servants to maintain their households. This allowed them the leisure time to become involved in reform issues.

Many women of this period believed that, as females, they had a particular duty to become involved in social reform. The so-called cult of true womanhood that developed from the emphasis on women's responsibilities within the home actually led some middle-class women to expand their roles beyond the household. Women's growing sense of moral and civic responsibility led them to establish associations dedicated to improving society and uplifting its citizens. Women also argued that if they were to serve as the moral leaders of their families, then they must be allowed to acquire the education and training to do so.

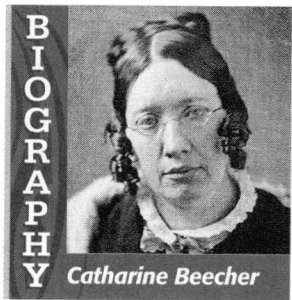

Catharine Beecher

Catharine Beecher was among those reformers who supported increased educational opportunities for women. She argued this would help them fulfill their roles as moral guides of the young. Born in 1800, Catharine Beecher became one of the best-known members of her socially active family. Other activists in her family included her father, Lyman Beecher, sister, Harriet Beecher Stowe, and brother, Henry Ward Beecher.

Like other unmarried middle-class women of her time, Beecher turned to teaching to support herself. She and her sister opened what became the Hartford Female Seminary in 1823. She became an influential educational reformer. Beecher wrote *An Essay on the Education of Female Teachers* in 1835 and *The Duty of American Women to Their Country* in 1845. Beecher believed that women had both the ability and the obligation to influence the men in their lives to become moral citizens. She argued:

> 66 Let every woman become so cultivated and refined in intellect . . . that every heart will repose [become calm] in her presence; then, the fathers, the husbands, and the sons, will find an influence thrown around them, to which they will yield not only willingly but proudly. 99

Beecher expanded her educational writings to include commentary on American families and society. Despite her own activism, Beecher opposed women's participation in public life. She believed that women's talents and influence were best used in the domestic sphere.

As a result of efforts by Beecher and other activists, women's educational opportunities slowly expanded in the early 1800s. Emma Willard founded the Troy Female Seminary, the first college-level school for women, in New York in 1821. During the 1830s other women's colleges opened, including Mount Holyoke Seminary, founded by Mary Lyon in South Hadley, Massachusetts. These schools allowed women to study subjects such as mathematics and philosophy that society had long believed only men could master.

✔ **READING CHECK:** Why did some women believe it was important that they become involved in reform movements?

Reforming Education

The expansion of women's education was part of a widespread effort to improve education in America. Prior to the 1840s most schools were private, and most families could not afford to send their children. The few public elementary schools that existed—most of them in the Northeast—had little money for books, supplies, or teachers' salaries. The curriculum was basic: reading, writing, arithmetic, and some history and geography. Furthermore, the quality of teaching in public schools was generally poor.

INTERPRETING THE VISUAL RECORD

Education. Some reformers argued that all children deserved the opportunity to gain an education. *What types of educational resources did this school have?*

THE METROPOLITAN MUSEUM OF ART, GIFT OF I.N. PHELPS STOKES, EDWARD S. HAWES, ALICE MARY HAWES, MARION AUGUSTA HAWES, 1937. [37.14.22]/PRC ARCHIVE

The public school movement. Reformers worried that the existing schools were inadequate to meet the needs of the growing nation. They argued that the nation needed public, tax-supported elementary schools to provide a free education to all children. Reformers insisted that schools were essential to educate citizens about democratic values, to heal social divisions, and to create a literate and disciplined workforce. The schools could achieve these goals, reformers hoped, by teaching a basic curriculum and instilling in students the middle-class values of hard work and respect for authority.

Horace Mann's reform efforts in Massachusetts established a model for free public elementary education. In 1837, as Massachusetts's first secretary of education, Mann united local school districts into a state system, raised teachers' salaries, and persuaded the legislature to increase spending on local schools. He also lengthened the school year, updated the curriculum, and established teacher training schools. Mann's school reforms soon spread throughout the United States. He convinced other educators that "the common [public] school, improved and energized, may become the most effective . . . of all the forces of civilization."

The public high school was another product of educational reform during this period. The nation's first, the English High School of Boston, opened in 1821. Free public high schools offered children who could not afford private schools a chance to pursue advanced courses that could prepare them for specialized careers.

Educational reform had little impact on the South, however. Many northern educational reformers also supported the abolition of slavery, making many southerners suspicious of northern educational reforms. As a result, the South was slow to adopt northern reforms. Planters hired private tutors or established private schools for their own children. They did not, however, support the establishment of public schools to educate all children.

College reform. Education beyond high school was accessible to few people in the United States before 1800. During the early 1800s opportunities for women and African Americans to receive a college education expanded.

Lincoln University was founded in 1854 to serve African American students.

House.   University.   Ashmun Institute.   Professor's House.

LINCOLN UNIVERSITY,
Oxford, Chester Co., Penna.

Oberlin College, established in Ohio in 1833, led the way in college reform. Oberlin was the first college in the United States to admit both men and women. Female graduates of Oberlin launched careers as doctors, journalists, reformers, teachers, and writers. Oberlin trustees voted to admit African Americans in 1835. Many African American graduates of Oberlin were escaped slaves and children of former slaves. Many graduates went on to become journalists, ministers, missionaries, and teachers. For many years the school's only African American students were men. In 1862, however, Oberlin College student Mary Jane Patterson became the first African American woman to receive a college degree in the United States.

✔ **READING CHECK:** How did educational opportunities change in the early 1800s?

Reforming Institutions

In addition to educational institutions, reformers turned their attention to creating and improving the facilities that cared for disadvantaged people. Reformers believed they could improve the lives of criminals, the mentally ill, and the poor by placing them in institutions that taught moral values. They would also provide a stable environment safe from the corrupting influences of city life. Middle-class women took the lead in many of these institutional reform efforts.

Dorothea Dix opposed the use of cages like this one to treat mentally ill people.

Dorothea Dix and the mentally ill. Dorothea Dix was one of the most effective female reformers. A deeply religious teacher, Dix became interested in the plight of the mentally ill in 1841 after seeing how they were treated in a Massachusetts prison. She was horrified to find mentally ill women confined in a damp dungeon with no attempt being made to treat them. While a few mental hospitals did exist, most mentally ill people were placed in prisons or poorhouses without any treatment for their conditions.

Outraged, Dix spent 18 months visiting jails and poorhouses throughout Massachusetts. In January 1843 she collected her observations into a detailed report and delivered it to Massachusetts legislators. In an impassioned speech, she told lawmakers that the mentally ill were kept "in *cages, closets, cellars, stalls, pens! Chained, naked, beaten with rods, and lashed* into obedience."

Dix emphasized the need to offer the mentally ill **rehabilitation**. This was treatment to restore them to a useful and productive place in society. The Massachusetts government responded by establishing institutions in which persons with mental illnesses could be treated humanely, apart from criminals. Eventually, Dix's efforts resulted in the founding of more than 100 hospitals across the nation where the mentally ill could receive professional treatment.

Prisons. The rehabilitation of criminals also stirred reformers' interest in the early 1800s. Up until that time, corporal, or physical, punishment and fines were the most common way of punishing criminals. Reformers argued that lawbreakers could be reformed and then returned to the community as productive citizens. Placing great faith in a new institution called the **penitentiary**, reformers had great hope that its isolated and structured environment would rid the country of crime. One supporter in Maryland praised the penitentiary as "a grand instrument of future reformation and happiness among mankind." The enthusiasm for this new type of reform persuaded lawmakers to provide money to build new prisons.

Prison reformers also worked to solve problems of overcrowding, to improve

THROUGH OTHERS' EYES

French Views of American Prisons

In 1831 Gustave de Beaumont (gooh-stahv duh boh-mohn) and Alexis de Tocqueville, two French aristocrats, visited the United States to observe American prisons firsthand. They were somewhat surprised to find that in a country where democratic liberties were so highly valued, prisoners often endured horrible conditions. They concluded:

66 To sum up the whole on this point it must be acknowledged that the penitentiary system in America is severe. Whilst society in the United States gives the example of the most extended liberty, the prisons of the same country offer the spectacle of the most complete despotism [oppression]. The citizens subject to the law are protected by it; they only cease to be free when they become wicked. 99

Poorhouses. Orphans and homeless children could find housing, education, and moral guidance in the poorhouses of large cities. *What services does this orphanage provide to homeless children?*

living conditions, and to remove children from institutions that housed adult offenders. During the early 1800s juvenile delinquents, orphans, and poor children were typically treated the same as adult criminals. New England prison reformer Josiah Quincy fought to establish different places of punishment for children and adults. Reformers built the first houses of correction and reform schools for young criminals during the 1820s. They sought to change offenders' behavior through education rather than through punishment alone. Children in these institutions attended classes, learned useful skills, and lived in a disciplined environment.

Poorhouses. Economic transformations, the growth of cities, and immigration during the early 1800s led to an increase in poverty. The ability of communities to take care of the poor grew strained. The mayor of Schenectady, New York, complained that cities had become "great resorts for the straggling and vagrant poor, who . . . call loudly for relief and assistance." Reformers worked to change laws that allowed the poor to be auctioned off for work to the lowest bidder. These workers might also be transferred from town to town regardless of their health or the weather.

Reformers sought to replace these practices with a new network of poorhouses, where the able-bodied poor would be required to work. They asserted that poorhouses would help control alcohol abuse—which many believed led to unemployment—and instill good work habits. Reformers also believed that almshouses could improve the lives of impoverished children. One poorhouse report claimed that children's "health and morals" were "improved and secured," and that they received "an education to fit them for future usefulness." Other reformers started Sunday schools to influence the behavior of poor children.

 READING CHECK: How and why did reformers work to improve prisons and other institutions?

SECTION 2 REVIEW

Define and explain the significance of the following terms:
temperance movement
prohibition
rehabilitation
penitentiary

Identify and explain the significance of the following individuals:
Lyman Beecher
Catharine Beecher
Emma Willard
Mary Lyon
Horace Mann
Dorothea Dix

1. **Using Graphic Organizers** Copy the web below. Use it to describe the reform movements that arose in the early 1800s. Include each movement's leaders, their motivations and goals, and your assessment of whether each movement succeeded.

2. **Analyzing** Why did reformers believe that the nation needed free public education?
3. **Using Historical Imagination** Imagine that you are a reporter in the early 1800s. Write a newspaper article describing the impact of the reform movements on either women or African Americans living in the North.
4. **Recognizing Point of View** How did Dorothea Dix view the mentally ill? How did this view influence her work?

Critical Thinking

5. Some people argued that reform was a natural outgrowth of women's domestic roles in the early 1800s. Do you agree or disagree? Explain.
Consider:
   • what women's domestic roles were
   • how reform affected domestic life
   • why women were interested in the reform movements

SECTION 3

The Crusade for Abolition

OBJECTIVES

Read to understand:
1. how African Americans changed the focus of anti-slavery efforts
2. what sparked the call for immediate abolition
3. how the Anti-Slavery Society spread its message
4. what obstacles the abolitionist movement faced

KEY TERMS

American Colonization Society
Liberator
American Anti-Slavery Society

KEY PEOPLE

Theodore Weld
David Walker
William Lloyd Garrison
Frederick Douglass
Sojourner Truth
Sarah Grimké
Angelina Grimké
Elijah Lovejoy

This currency was used in Liberia.

EYEWITNESSES TO History

" *We repeat it, every man knows that slavery is a curse. Whoever denies this, his lips libel his heart.* "
—Theodore Weld

Minister Theodore Weld's fiery words reflected a growing sentiment among the reformers who had begun to embrace the cause of abolition. Weld challenged northerners to oppose slavery and aid runaway slaves. A growing number of people began to take his advice. In 1804 Thomas Boude of Columbia, Pennsylvania, went south and bought a slave named Stephen Smith. Boude took Smith back to Columbia and freed him. Smith's mother, also a slave, soon escaped to find her son and join him in Columbia. When the owner of Smith's mother came to claim the slave, the Boudes refused to surrender her. Other residents of Columbia came to the Boudes' defense. Soon other northerners were taking similar actions. Despite strict laws that prohibited such activity, a network of people gradually developed who secretly transported and hid runaway slaves.

Henry "Box" Brown escaped from slavery in a box three feet long and two feet wide.

Early Opponents of Slavery

Many Americans involved in reform efforts such as the Second Great Awakening and the temperance movement believed that the institution of slavery should come to an end in the United States. During the 1830s abolitionists with diverse backgrounds and motivations came together in an intense campaign that called for the complete end of slavery.

During the colonial period, the Quakers were among the first Americans to speak out against slavery as a violation of religious principles. Ministers of the Second Great Awakening, such as Charles Finney, preached that each individual had a responsibility to end sinful practices and to uphold God's will in society. This message inspired many people to take up the cause of abolition. Other abolitionists argued that slavery contradicted the fundamental argument of the Declaration of Independence—that all people are created equal.

Colonization. Most northern states had abolished slavery by the early 1800s. After working for abolition in their own states, many antislavery northerners wanted to end slavery across the country. To achieve this goal, some northerners supported a plan by the **American Colonization Society** to send freed African Americans to Africa to found new settlements. In 1822 the society established Monrovia, the capital city of a settlement later called Liberia, on the west coast of Africa.

Some white southerners also supported colonization as a way to rid the South of free African Americans, whom they feared would incite slave rebellions. Unlike these southern supporters, most northern supporters of colonization genuinely wanted to end slavery in America. Most people in both groups, however, shared the prejudice that African Americans were inferior to whites and would never fit into American society.

African American reaction. Many northern free African Americans strongly objected to such negative characterizations. They opposed the American Colonization Society's plan to banish them from their country of birth. Henry Highland Garnet, a black abolitionist, declared:

> ❝ America is my home, my country, and I have no other. . . . I mourn because the accursed shade of slavery rests upon it. I love my country's flag, and I hope that soon it will be cleansed of its stains, and be hailed by all nations as the emblem of freedom and independence. ❞

At first, only free African Americans chose to resettle in Liberia. Later, however, a few southerners freed slaves solely to send them to Africa. Despite the discrimination that free African Americans faced, few wanted to leave the United States. By 1830 just some 1,400 African Americans had settled in Liberia. Since it was clear that colonization was not popular, many abolitionists who had once supported the colonization plan began to turn against it.

African Americans began organizing among themselves to end slavery. By 1826 they had formed more than 143 antislavery societies with the mission of freeing "their brothers in chains." In 1827 Samuel Cornish and John Russwurm started the first African American newspaper, *Freedom's Journal,* to proclaim opposition to slavery.

African American abolitionists such as Henry Highland Garnet strongly objected to the American Colonization Society's plan to send free African Americans to Liberia.

✔ **READING CHECK:** How did African Americans change the focus of antislavery efforts?

Abolitionists Call for Action

Over time, activists began shifting their focus from colonization to abolition, working to immediately end slavery. The appearance of two important publications, David Walker's *Appeal* and William Lloyd Garrison's *Liberator*, marked the start of a bold, energetic, and more organized attack on the institution of slavery.

In 1829 David Walker, a free African American businessman from Boston, published the *Appeal to the Colored Citizens of the World,* in which he demanded immediate, universal abolition. Walker called on free African Americans and slaves to take action—violent action if necessary—to gain freedom and equality. In a blistering attack, he criticized slaveholders' use of the Bible to justify slavery. He urged white Americans to condemn slavery and to recognize the rights and humanity of black Americans. Walker's *Appeal* reflected a new mood among abolitionists. Opponents of slavery, both African American and white, were becoming increasingly frustrated by the movement's lack of progress.

This impatience spurred William Lloyd Garrison, a white New England journalist, to action. With financial backing from wealthy African American and white abolitionists, Garrison launched the abolitionist newspaper the **Liberator** in 1831.

In the first issue, Garrison expressed his determination to work for the immediate abolition of slavery.

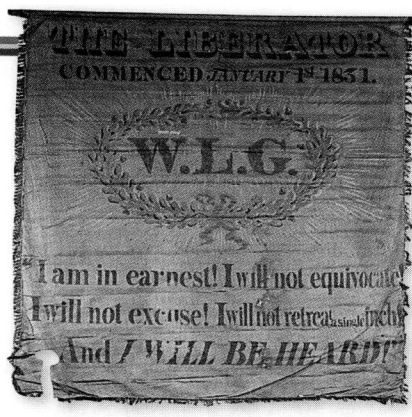

> 66 I *will* be as harsh as truth, and as uncompromising as justice. On this subject, I do not wish to think, to speak, or write, with moderation. . . . I am in earnest—I will not equivocate [avoid the truth]—I will not excuse—I will not retreat a single inch—AND I WILL BE HEARD! 99

Garrison soon became one of the most outspoken champions of immediate abolition. He insisted that slavery was a sin and a crime because it contradicted both the Bible and the Declaration of Independence. Garrison argued that the sin of slavery should be given up instantly in order to save the country. He fiercely attacked slavery and racial prejudice and argued that African Americans should enjoy equality with white Americans.

William Lloyd Garrison spread his abolitionist message on banners like this.

✔ **READING CHECK:** What helped spark the call for immediate abolition?

Strategies for Success Reading Graphs

Like charts, graphs are used to organize and present information visually. There are several types of graphs, each of which is particularly useful for displaying a certain kind of numerical data. A *line graph,* which has both a horizontal and a vertical axis, plots changes in quantities over time. A *bar graph* can also be used to show changes in quantities over time but is most often used to compare amounts within categories. A *pie graph,* or *circle graph,* displays proportions by dividing a circular whole into sections, with the whole equaling 100 percent.

How to Read a Graph

1. **Read the title.** Read the title to identify the topic of the graph.
2. **Study the labels.** Read the labels that define each axis, bar, or section of the graph to identify the type of information it presents.
3. **Analyze the details.** Study the information in the graph carefully and systematically. Take note of time intervals, increases or decreases in quantities, and proportions. Look for trends, relationships, disparities, and changes in the data.
4. **Put the data to use.** Use your analysis of the data, along with your knowledge of the historical period, to form generalizations and draw conclusions about how these trends affected history.

Applying the Strategy

Study the following line graph.

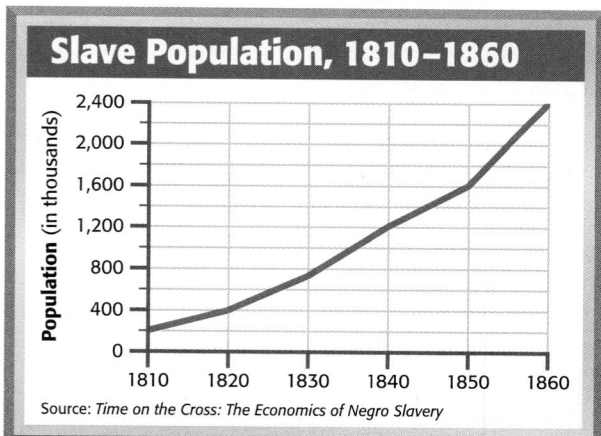

Source: *Time on the Cross: The Economics of Negro Slavery*

Practicing the Strategy

Using the graph above, answer the following questions.
1. How much did the slave population increase between 1810 and 1820?
2. During which two decades did the slave population increase most rapidly?
3. How might the trend depicted in this graph have affected northern attitudes toward abolition?

INTERPRETING THE VISUAL RECORD

Antislavery. The American Anti-Slavery Society published this almanac chronicling the antislavery efforts of Americans. *In what ways does the cover of this publication present its abolitionist viewpoint?*

Voices of the American Anti-Slavery Society

In 1833 prominent black and white abolitionists formed the **American Anti-Slavery Society**—first national antislavery organization to be devoted to immediate abolition and racial equality. The society soon boasted more than 200 branches across the North and the Midwest. Although the society excluded women from formal membership, many women assumed important roles in the society's efforts to abolish slavery. To spread its message, the organization flooded the country with antislavery publications and conducted petition drives to protest legislation supporting slavery. Most important, the society sponsored lecture tours of abolitionists who hoped to convince Americans that slavery was morally wrong.

Frederick Douglass. Among the best at winning members for the American Anti-Slavery Society was Frederick Douglass, a fugitive slave from Maryland. Douglass became the most prominent escaped slave to speak out publicly against slavery. His moving speeches about his life as a slave who "suffered under the lash without the power of resisting" convinced many people to support abolition.

Douglass also used his considerable skills as a writer to fight slavery. His autobiography, *Narrative of the Life of Frederick Douglass* (1845), became a classic critique of the institution of slavery. In addition, Douglass published an antislavery newspaper, the *North Star*, from 1847 to 1864. An editorial in the first issue urged those who had "*suffered the wrong* [of slavery]" to lead the abolitionist cause. "He who has *endured the cruel pangs of Slavery* is the man to *advocate* [support] *Liberty*," Douglass wrote.

Douglass's wife, Anna Murray Douglass, also actively supported the abolitionist cause. Using their home in Rochester, New York, as a depot for the Underground Railroad, she helped runaway slaves flee to Canada and freedom.

Sojourner Truth. Sojourner Truth was another former slave who worked tirelessly for the American Anti-Slavery Society. Truth was orginally named Isabella Baumfree. Born into slavery in 1797, she grew up working on the New York estate of a wealthy Dutch landowner. In 1827, the year before the abolition of slavery in New York, Baumfree managed to flee from her slaveholder. After her escape she joined religious reformers who preached on the streets of New York City. Six feet tall, extremely thin, and speaking with a Dutch accent, she made a powerful impression.

In 1843 Baumfree claimed to have had a religious vision in which God instructed her to find a new mission and a new identity. Adopting the name Sojourner Truth, she traveled throughout New England, preaching the gospel of abolition and women's rights.

The Grimké sisters. Two of the most effective antislavery activists, Sarah and Angelina Grimké (GRIM-kee), came from the South. After becoming Quakers, the sisters decided that they could no longer tolerate living in a society that endorsed slavery. They left their slaveholding family in South Carolina and moved to Philadelphia to join the abolitionist movement. In her 1836 pamphlet, *Appeal to the Christian Women of the South*, Angelina Grimké

As a former slave and fiery speaker, Sojourner Truth advanced the antislavery cause.

tried to convince other southern women to join her cause. "I know you do not make the laws," she wrote, "but . . . if you really suppose you can do nothing to overthrow slavery, you are greatly mistaken." She urged women to try to persuade all their acquaintances and family members "that slavery is a crime *against God and man.*"

As a result of this essay's popularity, the Grimkés were among the first women to speak on behalf of the American Anti-Slavery Society. They traveled throughout New England, delivering lectures and forming dozens of women's antislavery organizations. In 1839 they worked with Angelina's husband, Theodore Weld, to write and publish *American Slavery As It Is*—one of the most influential antislavery documents of the period.

✔ **READING CHECK:** How did members of the American Anti-Slavery Society spread the abolitionist message?

Problems for Abolitionists

By 1840, abolitionists had recruited some 200,000 northerners to their cause. Southern slaveholders felt increasingly threatened by the growing movement. Some northerners, however, also opposed abolition. William Lloyd Garrison once remarked that he found "contempt more bitter, opposition more active, . . . and apathy more frozen" in New England than in the South.

Violent resistance. As the antislavery movement gained strength in the 1830s, violence against abolitionists increased. An angry mob attacked and nearly killed Garrison in Boston in 1835. Elijah Lovejoy, an abolitionist editor in Alton, Illinois, was murdered in 1837 as he tried to prevent a mob from destroying his printing press.

Northern opposition to abolition arose from fear and prejudice against African Americans. Many northern wage earners feared competing with free African Americans for jobs. In addition, northern merchants and mill owners were afraid that abolition would disrupt cotton production. This would cut into the profits they earned selling cotton on the world market. One merchant warned abolitionists: "We mean, sir, to put you Abolitionists down—by fair means if we can, by foul means if we must."

The movement splinters. Abolitionists also faced divisions within their movement. Garrison, who frequently attacked churches and the government for accepting slavery, drew some criticism as his condemnations became more fierce. He also began to denounce the Constitution as a "covenant [sacred contract] with Death," warning abolitionists to rely on moral appeals alone to end slavery. Garrison's stubborn refusal to use less-offensive tactics angered moderate abolitionists, who supported slower change through the ballot box.

Then and Now

Human Rights

Just as it was for abolitionists during the 1800s, the issue of human rights continues to be important for social activists today. Basic human rights include freedom of expression, freedom of association, due process of law in legal matters, and equality before the law. One area of concern for human rights groups is China, the world's most populous country. Amnesty International, a leading watchdog of human rights abuses throughout the world, reported in 1998 that hundreds, if not thousands, of people who oppose China's communist government are held and imprisoned each year. Many of these protesters are sentenced after unfair trials or are held without charges or trials. In addition, torture and ill-treatment remain widespread, and the death penalty continues to be used extensively.

Modern activists working to end human rights abuses use many of the same techniques that antislavery activists did. These include organizing speaking tours, petition drives, and letter-writing campaigns. The Internet provides a powerful new tool for today's activists. Information about human rights abuses, speeches by refugees, and messages urging Internet users to join the fight by writing e-mail messages to legislative leaders are all easily accessible on the World Wide Web.

Modern Amnesty International logo

Read More About It

Free Find: African American Abolitionists After reading the selections on Frederick Douglass and Sojourner Truth on the **Holt Researcher** CD–ROM, write a short essay comparing their experiences.

Violence against abolitionists, like this attack in Illinois, became more common.

Just as troubling to many moderates was Garrison's call for equal rights for women. Many white male abolitionists believed that women should remain in the domestic sphere. They did not appreciate women's increased visibility and political activity within the movement. Many women, however, agreed with Sarah Grimké that "the sphere which her Creator has assigned her" included speaking out against the institution of slavery as well as other evils.

Reform-minded women such as the Grimké sisters played important roles in the abolitionist movement. African American journalist and teacher Maria W. Stewart won converts to abolition as early as 1832—the year before the formation of the American Anti-Slavery Society. She became the first American woman to speak to mixed-race audiences about abolition. Other women organized female abolitionist societies that sponsored petition drives and raised money.

When Garrison's supporters put a woman, Abby Kelley, on an important American Anti-Slavery Society committee in 1840, some moderates left the society and formed their own organization. The split did not seriously damage the cause, however. The number of local abolitionist organizations continued to grow. By the late 1840s more than 2,000 local societies—most of them in Massachusetts, New York, Ohio, and Pennsylvania—kept public attention focused on abolition.

✔ **READING CHECK:** What obstacles did the abolitionist movement face?

SECTION 3 REVIEW

Define and explain the significance of the following terms:
American Colonization Society
Liberator
American Anti-Slavery Society

Identify and explain the significance of the following individuals:
Theodore Weld
David Walker
William Lloyd Garrison
Frederick Douglass
Sojourner Truth
Sarah Grimké
Angelina Grimké
Elijah Lovejoy

1. **Using Graphic Organizers** Copy the graphic organizer below. Use it to explain the colonization movement's origins, aims, and actual effects.

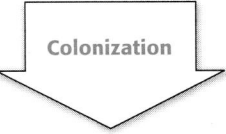

Origins

Colonization

Intended Effects

Actual Effects

2. **Distinguishing Fact from Opinion** Provide evidence to explain whether the following statement is fact or opinion: The active role African Americans took in antislavery efforts changed the focus of the abolitionist movement.
3. **Evaluating** How effective were the tactics of the American Anti-Slavery Society?
4. **Problem Solving** Identify conflicts that abolitionists faced, and discuss some steps that abolitionists could have taken to resolve these conflicts.

Critical Thinking

5. Was there any room for compromise between those people who supported immediate abolition and those who supported slavery? Explain your answer.
   Consider:
   • what the arguments for immediate abolition were
   • what the arguments against abolition were
   • how effective past compromises had been

The Cause of Women's Rights

OBJECTIVES

Read to understand:

1. how the women's rights movement grew out of the abolitionist movement, and what opposition it faced

2. what early women's rights activists demanded

3. what the early women's rights movement achieved, and what issues remained unresolved

KEY TERMS

Seneca Falls Convention
Declaration of Sentiments
Married Women's Property
  Act

KEY PEOPLE

Elizabeth Cady Stanton
Lucretia Mott
Lucy Stone
Susan B. Anthony

EYEWITNESSES TO History

" I never was so near fainting under the tremendous pressure. . . . My heart almost died within me. "

—Angelina Grimké

Abolitionist and women's rights supporter Angelina Grimké wrote her future husband, Theodore Weld, about her appearance before the Massachusetts legislature. In February 1838 Grimké had become the first woman to speak before a legislative body in the United States. As she stood before an audience of 1,500, Grimké spoke against slavery and for women's rights. Grimké presented Massachusetts lawmakers with 20,000 signatures on antislavery petitions that she and her sister Sarah had collected on their speaking tours. As public speakers in the antislavery movement, the Grimké sisters reflected the close relationship between abolition and women's rights.

Women's rights rally

Abolition and Women's Rights

Calls for women's rights began to be heard in the United States shortly after the Revolution. However, it was not until women became involved in religious and reform movements in the early 1800s that women's concerns became an important issue in the country. As they dedicated themselves to solving various social ills, female reformers mastered the skills of fund-raising, petitioning legislatures, and public speaking. They often met opposition to their roles as reformers, however. Resistance to female political activity made these women realize that they needed to secure economic and political rights if they were to participate fully in public life. As a result, some female reformers in the late 1840s expanded their work to include the struggle for their own rights. As Abby Kelley once explained, "In striving to strike [the slave's] irons off, we found most surely that *we* were manacled [chained] *ourselves*."

Sarah and Angelina Grimké were among the first activists to combine the fight for African Americans' rights with the fight for women's rights. Angelina Grimké argued for both groups.

Some female abolitionists carried purses with antislavery images on them.

" The discussion of the rights of the slave has opened the way for the discussion of other rights, and the ultimate result will most certainly be the breaking of *every* yoke . . . an emancipation far more glorious than any the world has ever yet seen. "

Activist Sojourner Truth also spoke on behalf of abolition and women's rights. At a women's rights convention in Akron, Ohio, in 1851, the former slave recounted her own experiences. Later-published accounts reported her remarks this way:

Truth. Sojourner Truth drew upon her personal experience to persuade Americans to support both abolition and women's rights. *What do you think the artist is trying to say about Truth's speaking style?*

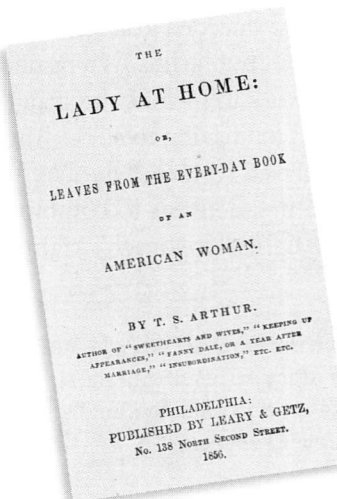

Publications like this one urged women to abandon the world of politics and business for domestic life.

66 **Look at my arm! I have ploughed and planted and gathered into barns . . . and ain't I a woman? I could work as much and eat as much as a man—when I could get it—and bear the lash as well! And ain't I a woman? I have born thirteen children, and seen most of 'em sold into slavery, and when I cried out with my mother's grief, none but Jesus heard me—and ain't I a woman?** 99

Female abolitionists met sharp opposition, however. As a supporter for women's traditional roles, Catharine Beecher criticized women for participating in abolitionist petition campaigns. "Petitions to Congress," she argued, "seem, IN ALL CASES, to fall entirely without [outside] the sphere of female duty. Men are the proper persons to make appeals to the rulers whom they appoint."

A group of Congregationalist ministers from Massachusetts echoed such sentiments. In 1837 they denounced the Grimkés for speaking before mixed audiences of men and women. The ministers said women's influence should be private, through quiet prayers and through their work at home and in church.

The Grimkés refused to back down, however. "Men and women were CREATED EQUAL," Sarah Grimké wrote. "They are both moral and accountable beings, and whatever is *right* for man to do, is *right* for woman." Her sister agreed that "it is a woman's right to have a voice in all the laws and regulations by which she is to be *governed*, whether in Church or State." Angelina added that society's "present arrangements" on these matters "are *a violation of human rights.*"

✔ **READING CHECK:** How did the women's rights movement grow out of the abolitionist movement? What opposition did the women's movement face?

Women Declare Their Rights

Issues of suffrage and property rights were of particular concern to female activists. Married women had few rights to own property—even property that they inherited—or to keep their own earnings. In addition, social prejudices limited women to a few professions. Women received lower wages than men. Most colleges still did not accept women. Laws also prevented women from obtaining custody of their children if they divorced their husbands.

Two noted abolitionists, Elizabeth Cady Stanton and Lucretia Mott, took the lead in organizing efforts to address these issues. Their experience at the World's Anti-Slavery Convention in London in 1840 sparked the two reformers to action. Convention leaders excluded female abolitionists from participating in the business of the convention. They were forced to watch the proceedings from behind a curtain that hid them from male participants' view. As a result, Stanton and Mott resolved "to hold a convention as soon as we returned home, and form a society to advance the rights of women," Stanton later wrote. In 1848 they finally held the first American meeting on women's rights in Seneca Falls, New York. More than 300 women and men attended the **Seneca Falls Convention**.

To voice the discontent that many women felt, nearly one third of the Seneca Falls participants signed a **Declaration of Sentiments** modeled on the democratic ideals set forth in the Declaration of Independence. The Declaration of Sentiments called for legal reforms that would grant married women the right to control property and earnings and to gain custody of their children in the event of a divorce. In addition, the document insisted that women be granted the right to vote.

Women's suffrage was the most fiercely debated issue at Seneca Falls. Stanton argued that attaining the vote was crucial to winning full equality because "the power to choose rulers and make laws, was the right by which all others could be secured." Opponents of women's suffrage believed that demanding the vote was too radical, however, and might jeopardize support for other women's rights.

✔ **READING CHECK:** What rights did the early women's rights activists demand?

Women's Rights Activism

Building on the foundation laid by early reformers, female activists pursued the difficult task of achieving the reforms called for at Seneca Falls. Three of these women— Susan B. Anthony, Elizabeth Cady Stanton, and Lucy Stone—made particularly significant contributions to the success of the movement.

Early leaders. As one of the first promoters of women's rights, Oberlin graduate Lucy Stone began her public career as a speaker for the American Anti-Slavery Society. She immediately took up the cause of women's rights, proclaiming: "I mean to plead not for the slave alone but for suffering humanity everywhere. Especially do I mean to labor for the elevation of my sex."

Stone became one of the most influential speakers in the women's movement. Stanton praised her powerful style, stating that Stone was "the first who really stirred the nation's heart on the subject of women's wrongs." Stone endured angry and sometimes violent heckling at her lectures on women's issues. She kept her composure, however. A man in one audience threw a prayer book at her, hitting her on the head. She skillfully noted that only a man without a good argument would stoop to such a low act.

Stone also challenged some of society's most traditional institutions, including marriage. At Stone's wedding to abolitionist Henry Blackwell in 1855, the couple rejected the "present laws of marriage." They proposed instead an "equal and permanent partnership." In addition, Stone decided to keep her maiden name. She continued to be known as Lucy Stone rather than as Mrs. Blackwell. For decades afterward, women who chose to keep their maiden names were known as Lucy Stoners.

Read More About It

Free Find: Declaration of Sentiments
After reading the selection on the Declaration of Sentiments on the **Holt Researcher** CD–ROM, imagine that you are a reporter at the Seneca Falls Convention. Write a short article on what the signers of the declaration hoped to achieve.

★ HISTORICAL DOCUMENTS ★

Seneca Falls Declaration of Sentiments

In 1848 women's rights activists met in Seneca Falls, New York, to demand equal rights for women. Modeled on the Declaration of Independence and signed by 100 people, their Declaration of Sentiments outlined women's grievances and laid the foundation for the future women's rights movement.

We hold these truths to be self-evident: that all men and women are created equal; that they are endowed by their Creator with certain inalienable rights; that among these are life, liberty, and the pursuit of happiness. . . .

The history of mankind is a history of repeated injuries and usurpations [wrongs] on the part of man toward woman, having in direct object the establishment of an absolute tyranny [unjust rule] over her. To prove this, let facts be submitted to a candid world:

He has never permitted her to exercise her inalienable right to the elective franchise [the vote]. . . .

He has taken from her all right in property, even to the wages she earns. . . .

He has denied her the facilities for obtaining a thorough education, all colleges being closed against her. . . .

He has endeavored, in every way that he could, to destroy her confidence in her own powers, to lessen her self-respect, and to make her willing to lead a dependent and abject [hopeless] life. . . .

Resolved, That woman is man's equal—was intended to be so by the Creator, and the highest good of the race demands that she should be recognized as such.

BIOGRAPHY

Elizabeth Cady Stanton

Like Lucy Stone, Elizabeth Cady Stanton began her career in the abolitionist movement. Born in 1815, Elizabeth Cady grew up in a wealthy and prominent family near Albany, New York. She enjoyed a carefree childhood and excelled in school. When she sought her father's approval for her accomplishments, however, his disappointed comment, "My daughter, you should have been a boy," left a lasting wound. At the age of 25, Elizabeth asserted her independence by marrying antislavery activist Henry Stanton against her father's wishes. The couple spent their honeymoon at the World Anti-Slavery Convention in London. There she met one of her future allies in the women's rights movement, Lucretia Mott.

Stanton developed a fruitful partnership on women's rights with Susan B. Anthony, another abolitionist and temperance worker. While Stanton managed her busy household and raised seven children, Anthony kept her informed and motivated to continue her work in the movement.

BIOGRAPHY

Susan B. Anthony

Unlike Stanton, Susan B. Anthony grew up in a family that supported the equality of men and women. They were members of the Hicksite Quakers—a progressive sect of orthodox Quakerism. Anthony's father, Daniel, worked as an abolitionist and temperance reformer. He also promoted the education of his daughters and encouraged their independence.

While working as a teacher in Canajoharie, New York, Anthony enjoyed an active social life and received several proposals of marriage. She remained single, however, and found fulfillment without what she perceived as the burdens of a husband and children. In 1851 Anthony met Elizabeth Cady Stanton while attending an antislavery conference in Seneca Falls. The two took an immediate liking to each other and became close friends. Eventually, Stanton convinced her younger friend to turn her efforts from temperance to women's rights.

From her involvement in the temperance and abolition movements, Anthony had already learned the limits society placed on women's roles in reform movements. In 1852 she was forbidden to speak at a temperance convention because of her gender. This event convinced her that women could not be effective in reform efforts until they won political rights. In addition, women's economic limitations were of particular interest to Anthony because she supported herself as a single woman. She argued that men and women should receive equal pay for equal work and that women should be allowed to enter traditionally male professions such as law, medicine, and the clergy.

Anthony's work became critically important to the campaign for women's rights, as she used her outstanding administrative abilities to expand the women's rights movement nationally. She gave speeches, organized petition campaigns and meetings, and raised money for the cause. To achieve their goals, activists created

INTERPRETING THE VISUAL RECORD

Women's rights. Elizabeth Cady Stanton and Susan B. Anthony presided over this women's rights meeting at a church. *Who might the men in attendance be?*

THE GRANGER COLLECTION, NEW YORK

a system of linked local organizations, held national women's rights conferences, and arranged a series of state conventions across the North and the Midwest.

Property rights. Although the Declaration of Sentiments called for women's right to vote, other goals were seen as more realistic. Anthony and Stanton campaigned for "full and total" property rights for women in New York State. Using a network of 60 women to cover every area of the state, Anthony collected more than 6,000 signatures to petition for a new property rights law. She believed that no woman could be free without "a purse of her own," as she wrote in her diary, "and how can this be so long as the Wife is denied the right to her individual and joint earnings."

In 1848 New York answered these calls by passing the **Married Women's Property Act**, which permitted married women to own property, file lawsuits, and retain their earnings. Although other states followed suit, political and legal equality on the national level, including the right to vote, would be slow in coming.

Great Debates

The Women's Rights Movement

Some historians have argued that the women's rights movement was slow to gain support because it represented only a narrow class of women. Northern white middle-class women—the primary leaders of the movement—were the greatest beneficiaries of victory on such issues as child custody, control over wages, and property rights. Few middle-class women's rights groups addressed the needs and concerns of African American women and white working-class women.

Most women's rights activists ignored workplace issues. As a result, most working-class women looked to other groups for support in their struggle for better wages and working conditions. For example, when women organized strikes, they allied themselves with working-class men who shared their concerns.

Some African American women participated in women's rights groups. Many more, however, devoted their energies to strengthening and aiding charitable and educational institutions in their own communities. In addition, they helped build organizations devoted to abolition and equality for all African Americans.

✔ **READING CHECK:** What reforms did the women's rights activists achieve? What issues remained unresolved?

SECTION 4 REVIEW

Define and explain the significance of the following terms:
Seneca Falls Convention
Declaration of Sentiments
Married Women's Property Act

Identify and explain the significance of the following individuals:
Elizabeth Cady Stanton
Lucretia Mott
Lucy Stone
Susan B. Anthony

1. **Using Graphic Organizers** Copy the graphic organizer below. Use it to explain the connections between the abolitionist and women's rights movements.

Abolitionist Movement — Women's Rights Movement

Connections
_____
_____
_____
_____
_____

2. **Identifying Values** How did the Declaration of Sentiments resemble the U.S. Declaration of Independence?

3. **Comparing and Contrasting** Compare and contrast Elizabeth Cady Stanton's and Susan B. Anthony's childhoods and their effects on each woman's career.

4. **Assessing Consequences** Explain how successful women's rights activists were in achieving their goals.

Critical Thinking

5. What obstacles hindered the success of the women's rights movement?
   Consider:
   • who supported the movement
   • why some people opposed the movement
   • how divisions might have weakened the movement

CHAPTER 9

Review

Creating a Time Line

Copy the time line below onto a sheet of paper. Complete the time line by filling in the events and dates from the chapter that you think were most significant. Pick three events and explain why you think they were significant.

1820   1840   1860

Writing a Summary

Using the Reading Checks as a guide, write an overview of the events in the chapter.

Identifying People and Ideas

Identify the following terms or individuals and explain their significance.

1. Second Great Awakening
2. Charles Grandison Finney
3. transcendentalists
4. Catharine Beecher
5. Dorothea Dix
6. David Walker
7. Sojourner Truth
8. Sarah and Angelina Grimké
9. Seneca Falls Convention
10. Susan B. Anthony

Understanding Main Ideas

SECTION 1
1. How did the Second Great Awakening affect religious life in America?

SECTION 2
2. How was education affected by the reform movements of the early 1800s?

SECTION 3
3. Why did support for abolition of slavery increase during the mid-1800s?
4. What tactics did abolitionists use?

SECTION 4
5. How did the abolition movement influence women's rights reformers?

Reviewing Themes

1. **Cultural Diversity** What social factors contributed to the rise of revivalism and the spread of utopian communities in the 1800s?
2. **Democratic Values** In what ways were reformers successful in changing laws?
3. **Constitutional Heritage** How did some African Americans and white women mobilize to change society in the early 1800s?

Thinking Critically

1. **Analyzing** How did reform movements reflect the diversity of American life?
2. **Synthesizing** How might the rise of an educated middle class have contributed to the rise of reform movements?
3. **Identifying Values** What factors may have motivated reformers to continue their efforts even under the threat of violence?
4. **Hypothesizing** How might reform movement have been different if women had not participated?
5. **Taking a Stand** Imagine that you are a reformer in the early 1800s. Choose an issue, explain why you support it, and what you would do to help increase public awareness of the cause.

Writing About History

Writing to Express Imagine that you are a politician running for office in the 1850s. Write a short speech that explains why you support one of the following: prohibition, public education, abolition, or women's rights. Use the following graphic to organize your thoughts.

Your Movement	
Your Goals	**Effects on Society**

Strategies for Success Review the **Strategies for Success** on *Reading Graphs*. Then study the graph below and answer the following questions.

1. What Protestant denomination claimed the most members in 1860?
2. Approximately how many members did all three denominations gain between 1845 and 1860?

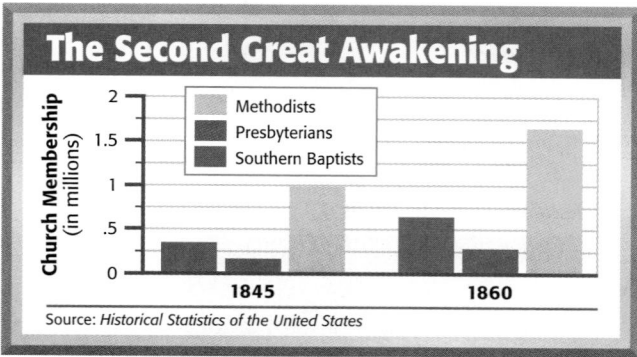

The Second Great Awakening

Church Membership (in millions)

☐ Methodists
■ Presbyterians
■ Southern Baptists

Source: *Historical Statistics of the United States*

Linking History and Geography

Study the map below. Each dot represents an organization associated with a reform movement. Where were reform movements most prominent? Why do you think reform movements were most active in these areas?

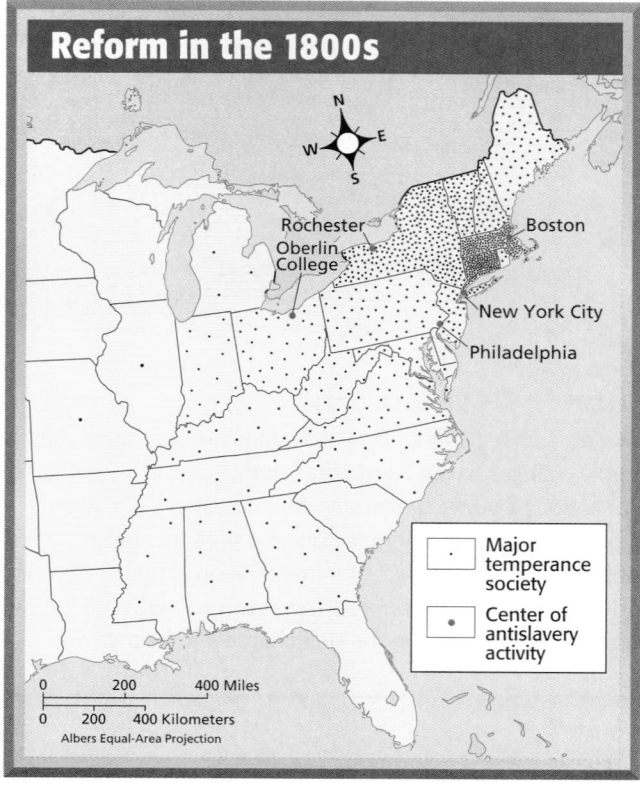

Reform in the 1800s

Rochester
Oberlin College
Boston
New York City
Philadelphia

· Major temperance society

⦿ Center of antislavery activity

0   200   400 Miles
0   200   400 Kilometers
Albers Equal-Area Projection

internetconnect

TOPIC: Women's Rights Activists
GO TO: go.hrw.com
KEYWORD: SD1 Rights

Accessing the Internet through the HRW Web site, research the lives and accomplishments of Susan B. Anthony, Elizabeth Cady Stanton, Sojourner Truth, Lucy Stone, and Lucretia Mott. Then create a political "talk show" in which you assume the identities of the women and debate the issues of their time.

BUILDING YOUR PORTFOLIO

Complete one or all of the following projects independently or cooperatively.

1 Constitutional Heritage
Imagine that you are a women's rights activist in the early 1800s. **Prepare a pamphlet** in support of women's rights. Anticipate possible criticisms of women's rights and respond to them.

2 Democratic Values
Imagine that you are establishing a new public school during the 1820s. Decide whether it should be an elementary school or high school and **develop a list of courses**, including their descriptions, for a typical student to take.

3 Cultural Diversity
Imagine that you are the founder of a new utopian community. **Develop a set of rules** that residents in the community should follow to create an ideal society. Include a drawing of your community.

Antislavery purses

Review

BUILDING YOUR PORTFOLIO

Outlined below are three projects. Independently or cooperatively, complete one and use the products to demonstrate your mastery of the historical concepts involved.

1 ### Technology and Society
The 1800s was a period of great technological innovation in North America. *Write a script for a panel discussion* about how technology affected daily life in American society during the early 1800s. Your panel should showcase the views of northern factory owners, southern cotton farmers, and middle-class consumers. You may wish to use portfolio materials you designed in the unit chapters to help you.

Textile mill in the 1830s

THE GRANGER COLLECTION, NEW YORK

St. Louis riverboat on the Mississippi River

2 ### Economic Development
The Market and Transportation Revolutions brought significant economic changes to the North, the South, and the Midwest. *Create a board game* that shows the movement of cotton from a southern plantation to a northern factory and then to various markets. Games should illustrate the impact of transportation systems, new technologies, and economic policies on new markets. You may wish to use the portfolio materials you designed in the unit chapters to help you.

3 Cultural Diversity

Poverty, hunger, and oppression drove many immigrants from their homelands during the 1800s. Many of these immigrants came to the United States seeking new opportunities and a better life. *Prepare a short one-scene play* about an immigrant's experiences in the United States. Plays might describe life in an ethnic community, encounters with nativists, workers' strikes, or tenement housing conditions. You may wish to use portfolio materials you designed in the unit chapters to help you.

Irish immigrants leaving for the United States

Further Reading

Ehle, John. *Trail of Tears: The Rise and Fall of the Cherokee Nation.* Anchor, 1989. History of the Cherokees' forced removal to Indian Territory.

Hirsch, Adam. *The Rise of the Penitentiary.* Yale University Press, 1992. The story of the early penitentiary reform movements.

Luchetti, Cathy. *Under God's Spell: Frontier Evangelists 1772–1915.* Harcourt, 1989. The lives and work of frontier evangelists told through primary sources.

Mellon, James, ed. *Bullwhip Days: The Slaves Remember.* Avon Books, 1988. Interviews with former slaves conducted in the 1930s.

Mintz, Steve, and Susan Kellogg. *Domestic Revolutions: A Social History of American Family Life.* Free Press, 1989. Overview of major changes in domestic life throughout the years.

Remini, Robert. *The Life of Andrew Jackson.* Penguin, 1990. Classic biography of one of our most complex presidents.

Selden, Bernice. *The Mill Girls.* Atheneum, 1983. Account of life for the early Lowell girls.

Internet Connect and Holt Researcher CD–ROM Review

In assigned groups, develop a multimedia presentation about America between 1815 and 1860. Choose information from the chapter Internet Connect activities and from the **Holt Researcher** CD–ROM that best reflect the major topics of the period. Write an outline and script for your presentation, which may be shown to the class.

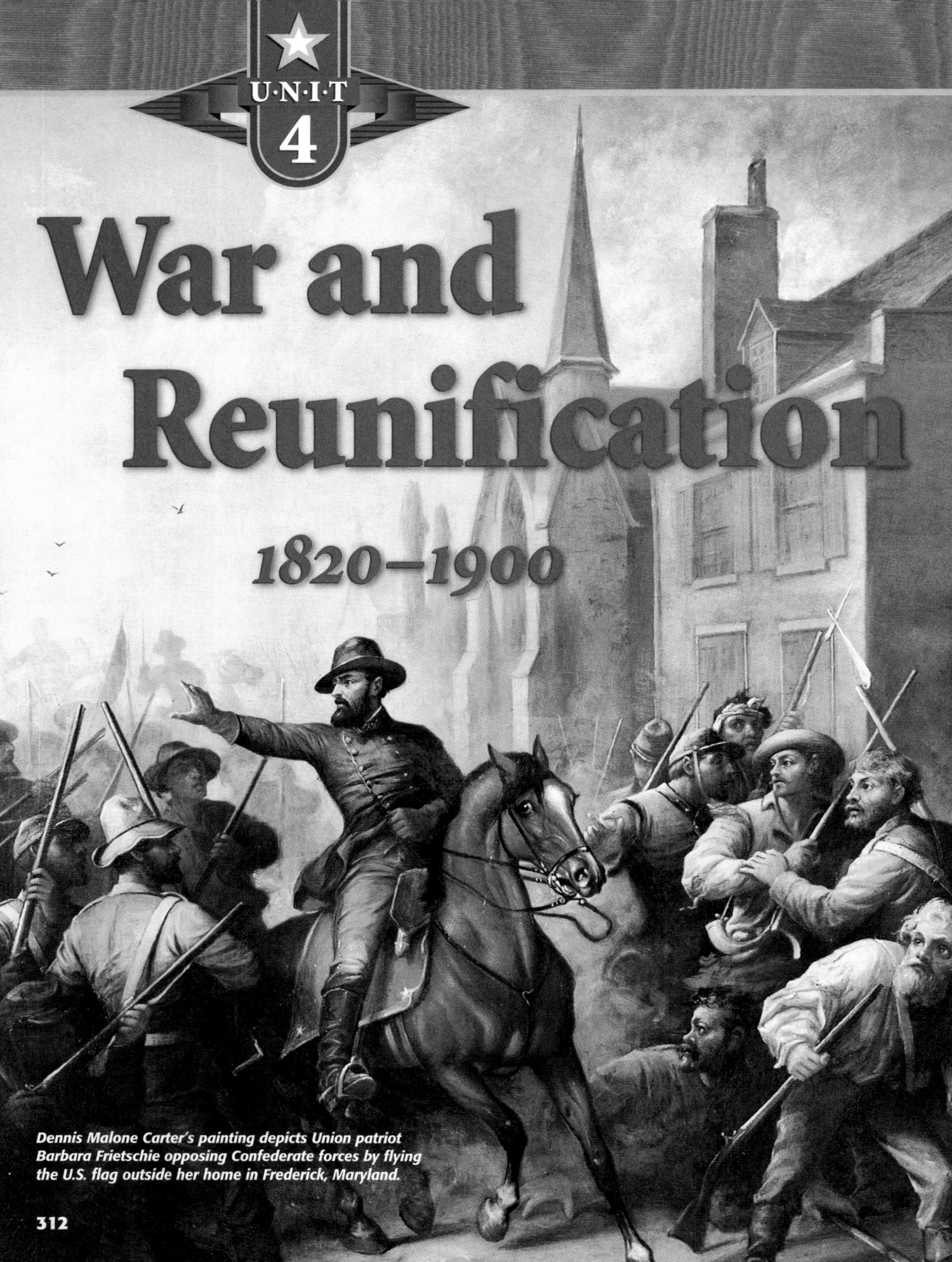

War and Reunification

1820–1900

Dennis Malone Carter's painting depicts Union patriot
Barbara Frietschie opposing Confederate forces by flying
the U.S. flag outside her home in Frederick, Maryland.

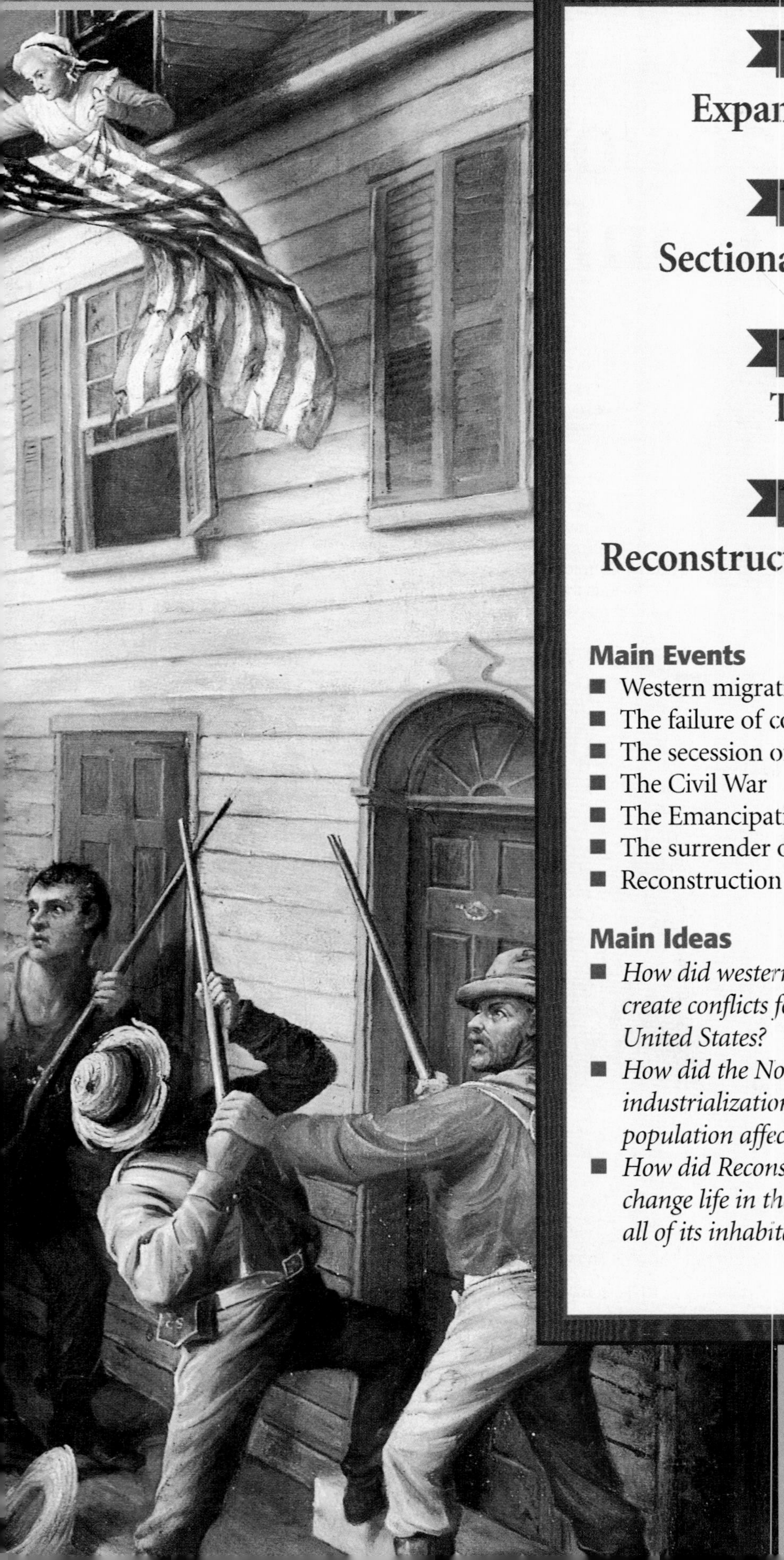

CHAPTER 10

Expansion and Conflict

1820–1860

CHAPTER 11

Sectional Conflict Increases

1845–1861

CHAPTER 12

The Civil War

1861–1865

CHAPTER 13

Reconstruction and the New South

1865–1900

Main Events

- Western migration and new conflicts
- The failure of compromises over slavery
- The secession of seven states from the Union
- The Civil War
- The Emancipation Proclamation
- The surrender of Confederate forces
- Reconstruction

Main Ideas

- *How did western expansion create conflicts for the United States?*
- *How did the North's superior industrialization and larger population affect the Civil War?*
- *How did Reconstruction change life in the South for all of its inhabitants?*

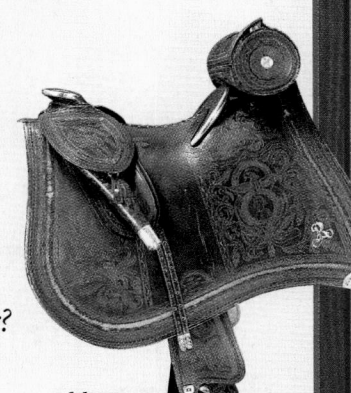

Old West saddle

1820–1860
Expansion and Conflict

The McCormick reaper

Moses Austin

1821
Business and Finance
Moses Austin becomes the first American to receive an *empresario* contract.

1831
Science and Technology
Cyrus McCormick invents the mechanical reaper.

1834
Daily Life
American missionaries arrive in Oregon Country.

1837
The Arts
Alfred Jacob Miller paints *Setting Traps for Beaver.*

1820

1828
1836

1821
World Events
Mexico wins independence from Spain.

1825
Business and Finance
Fur trappers in the Far West hold their first annual rendezvous.

1833
World Events
General Antonio López de Santa Anna establishes a dictatorship in Mexico.

1839
World Events
The Opium War breaks out between Great Britain and China.

1836
Politics
Texas declares its independence from Mexico.

Mexican flag

Fur trappers

Mexican general Antonio López de Santa Anna

THE GRANGER COLLECTION, NEW YORK

Before You Read

Build on What You Know

The boundaries of the United States expanded dramatically during the early 1800s. In 1803 the Louisiana Purchase added a vast area of land west of the Mississippi River to the nation. Then, in 1819, the United States acquired Florida from Spain. In this chapter you will learn how Americans—many of them drawn by the promise of economic opportunity—moved into the present-day states of California, New Mexico, Oregon, Texas, and Utah. This migration opened up new opportunities for some but created conflict for others.

Fan from James Polk's presidential campaign

The Treaty of Guadalupe Hidalgo

1844
Politics
James K. Polk is elected president.

1844
Science and Technology
The first American medical journal, the *American Journal of Psychiatry*, is published.

1846
Politics
The Mexican War begins.

1848
Politics
The Treaty of Guadalupe Hidalgo is signed.

1850
Daily Life
Mormon settlers begin publishing the *Deseret News* in Utah.

1853
Politics
The Gadsden Purchase is negotiated.

1857
The Arts
Herman Melville publishes *The Confidence-man*.

1844

1852

1860

1842
Science and Technology
Albert Gallatin founds the American Ethnological Society.

1845
Daily Life
John L. O'Sullivan coins the phrase "manifest destiny" to promote westward expansion.

1848
World Events
Revolutionary movements sweep across Europe.

1848
Business and Finance
Gold is discovered in California.

1851
Politics
The Treaty of Fort Laramie is signed.

1855
The Arts
John Mix Stanley paints *Chain of Spires Along the Gila River*.

Gold miner George W. Northrup

John Mix Stanley's Chain of Spires Along the Gila River

Think About Themes

Decide whether you agree or disagree with the following statements. Note why in your journal.

Cultural Diversity Nations with many cultures often experience short-term conflicts but emerge from such conflicts stronger.

Economic Development The economic choices made by individuals do not affect federal government policies.

Global Relations Territorial expansion by one nation always leads to international conflicts.

SECTION 1

The Lure of the West

OBJECTIVES

Read to understand:

1. how supporters and opponents of westward expansion defended their views
2. why the Mexican government encouraged American settlement in Texas
3. what events led to the Texas Revolution
4. what problems Texas faced after gaining its independence

KEY TERMS

manifest destiny
Tejanos
empresarios
Texas Revolution
Battle of San Jacinto

KEY PEOPLE

Stephen F. Austin
Antonio López de Santa Anna
Sam Houston
Juan Seguín

KEY PLACES

San Antonio
Goliad
San Jacinto

EYEWITNESSES TO History

66 *The North Americans have conquered whatever territory adjoins them. In less than half a century, they have become masters of extensive colonies which formerly belonged to Spain and France, and of even more spacious territories from which have disappeared the former owners, the Indian tribes.* 99
—General Manuel Mier y Terán

The Texas flag

General Manuel Mier y Terán was a hero of the Mexican struggle for independence from Spain. In 1829 he warned his fellow citizens about the growing American population in Mexican territory. During the early 1800s, few Americans had ventured into the Spanish territories of California, New Mexico, and Texas. After Mexico won its independence from Spain in 1821, however, American settlers began moving west in increasing numbers. Mier y Terán warned that people in the United States were already calling for the annexation of Texas. Soon, he argued, American settlers would begin to encourage "uprisings in the territory."

Manifest Destiny

In 1845 John L. O'Sullivan, a magazine editor, coined the phrase **manifest destiny**. He used these words to express a belief popular among Americans that God intended the United States to expand westward. O'Sullivan argued that the United States should extend its western boundary all the way to the Pacific Ocean:

66 Away, away with all these cobweb tissues of rights of discovery, exploration, settlement. . . . The American claim is by the right of our manifest destiny to overspread and to possess the whole of the continent which Providence [divine guidance] has given us for the development of the great experiment of liberty. 99

John Gast's 1879 painting shows the spirit of manifest destiny leading settlers and modern technology across the continent.

The idea of manifest destiny appealed to many Americans. Northerners troubled by economic problems and urban crowding hoped that western expansion would lessen population pressures and create new markets for industrial products. Southerners wanted western lands for increased cotton production.

Not all Americans supported manifest destiny. Some objected to expansion because many western lands were already claimed by other nations. Others feared that expansion would make the United States too large to govern effectively. Most Americans, however, found debates over manifest destiny of little practical concern. Land and opportunity interested them much more.

✔ **READING CHECK:** What arguments were made for and against westward expansion?

Distinguishing Fact from Opinion

Most historical sources contain a mixture of facts and opinions. A *fact* is a piece of information that can be proved or verified. An *opinion* is a statement that is based on the beliefs or judgment of an individual or group. The ability to distinguish between fact and opinion is essential for judging the soundness of an argument or the reliability of a historical account.

How to Distinguish Fact from Opinion

1. **Identify the facts.** As you study a historical source, determine whether the information it presents could be checked for accuracy in an encyclopedia, almanac, or some other historical reference work. If so, the information is probably factual; if not, it possibly contains an opinion.
2. **Identify the opinions.** When you encounter material that does not seem wholly factual, look for (1) phrases indicating a belief or conviction, such as *I think* or *in their view*, (2) comparative words like *greater, better, more,* or *less*, (3) words that imply a

judgment or evaluation, such as *useful, unfortunate,* or *admirable.* Such language usually signals a statement of opinion.

Applying the Strategy

Reconsider the following quotation by John L. O'Sullivan. As you study the quotation, look for signs that it is a statement of opinion.

66 The American claim is by the right of our manifest destiny to overspread and to possess the whole of the continent which Providence [divine guidance] has given us for the development of the great experiment of liberty. 99

Practicing the Strategy

Use the quotation above to answer the following questions.
1. What indicates that the statement is an opinion?
2. How does the text use facts and opinions to explain the popularity of O'Sullivan's statement?

Mexican Texas

The growing presence of American settlers in foreign territory was particularly visible in Texas. By 1815 several hundred Americans had already crossed the Sabine and Red Rivers and settled in northeastern Texas. This immigration increased significantly after Mexico won its independence from Spain in 1821. Mexican officials wanted to boost the non-American Indian population of Texas. To do this, they offered extremely cheap land and no taxes to U.S. citizens who agreed to settle in the territory. Officials hoped that the Americans who responded to their offer would serve as a barrier between communities in northern Mexico and Apache and Comanche raiders.

Spurs like this one were valuable horse-riding tools in the wide open spaces of the West.

The tactic served another purpose as well. Mexican officials feared that the United States, which had twice tried to purchase Texas, would one day take the territory by force. The few thousand **Tejanos** (tay-HAH-nohs)—native Mexicans who lived in Texas—stood little chance of blocking an invasion. If Mexico could recruit enough American settlers and turn them into loyal Mexican citizens, however, the country might be able to build a defensive force large enough to prevent a U.S. invasion.

To reduce the cultural influence of Americans in Mexico, the Mexican government also tried to recruit settlers from other foreign countries. It also did not offer land to every person who wanted it. Rather, it gave generous land grants to

Mary and John Rabb were two of the first settlers to receive land in Stephen F. Austin's colony.

empresarios (em-pruh-SAH-ree-ohs), people who agreed to recruit and take responsibility for new settlers. These *empresarios* attracted thousands of people to Texas during the 1820s.

Most *empresarios* came from the United States, but some were Tejanos. One such Tejano, named Martín de León, received a contract in 1824 to settle Mexican families in Texas. He founded the town of Victoria, Texas, as the capital of his colony. Moses Austin, a Missouri businessperson hoping to rebuild his fortunes after the Panic of 1819, was the first American to receive an *empresario* contract. In 1821 Austin obtained permission to start a colony in Texas, but he died before he could recruit any settlers. His son, Stephen F. Austin, assumed the grant and established a colony on the gulf coast of Texas in 1822.

Because Austin sold large lots for 12 cents an acre, he found it easy to recruit settlers. By contrast, public land in the United States sold for $1.25 an acre at that time. Many of the people who purchased land from Austin were southern cotton farmers who brought slaves with them. Although most were Protestant, settlers had to declare their loyalty to the Catholic Church, the only faith formally allowed in Mexico. By 1830 some 7,000 Americans had relocated to Texas.

✔ **READING CHECK:** Why did the Mexican government invite U.S. citizens to settle in Texas?

The Texas Revolution

By 1830 non-Mexicans in Texas outnumbered Tejanos by about two to one. Most of these new arrivals made little effort to learn Spanish or adapt to Mexican culture. Although required to become Catholics, most privately continued to practice their own faith. Fearing a rebellion in Texas as well as a U.S. invasion, in 1830 Mexico closed the Texas border to additional immigration from the United States. The Mexican government also prohibited the importation of slaves to Texas. These measures did little to slow immigration, however. By 1835 approximately 30,000 Americans, including some 3,000 slaves, lived in Texas. Many of them had entered illegally.

INTERPRETING THE VISUAL RECORD

The Alamo. Robert Onerdonk's painting shows the fall of the Alamo, where Jim Bowie, creator of the Bowie knife, died. *What does the painting suggest about the nature of the fighting at the Alamo?*

Trouble brews. American immigrants to Texas deeply resented the 1830 measures. Slaveholders feared that Mexican authorities would soon restrict the practice of slavery. Although the Mexican legislature had banned slavery in 1829, Texans had negotiated a special law that classified their slaves as indentured servants. Many Texans feared that the cotton industry would collapse if the government overturned the law.

Tensions grew even worse in 1833. After being elected president, General Antonio López de Santa Anna established dictatorial control over the Mexican government. This move angered the residents of many Mexican territories, including Texans. About that same time Mexican authorities jailed Stephen F. Austin, who had gone to Mexico City

FALL OF THE ALAMO BY ROBERT ONDERDONK, COURTESY OF FRIENDS OF THE GOVERNOR'S MANSION, AUSTIN, TEXAS/PRC ARCHIVE

hoping to peacefully resolve Texans' conflict with Mexican authorities. By the time Austin was released from jail in 1834, he had given up hope of a peaceful settlement. "War is our only recourse [option]," he advised fellow Texans. Outraged American settlers and Tejanos rose up in revolt the following year. Isolated clashes with the Mexican military quickly grew into a full-scale rebellion known as the **Texas Revolution**.

The Alamo and Goliad.
The Texas Revolution was relatively short but extremely hard-fought. In December 1835, Texas rebels captured the town of San Antonio, where additional volunteers soon joined them. Santa Anna, leading a force of several thousand Mexican troops, arrived at San Antonio in February 1836 to restore Mexican rule. At the Alamo, a mission-fort built by the Spanish, at least 189 Texas rebels led by William Travis and Jim Bowie fought off repeated attacks by Santa Anna's army. While under siege, Travis wrote a letter outlining the rebels' position. He declared:

> 66 I shall never surrender or retreat. . . . I call on you in the name of Liberty, of patriotism, and everything dear to the American character, to come to our aid with all dispatch [speed]. . . . If this call is neglected I am determined to sustain myself as long as possible and die like a soldier who never forgets what is due his honor and that of his country. VICTORY OR DEATH. 99

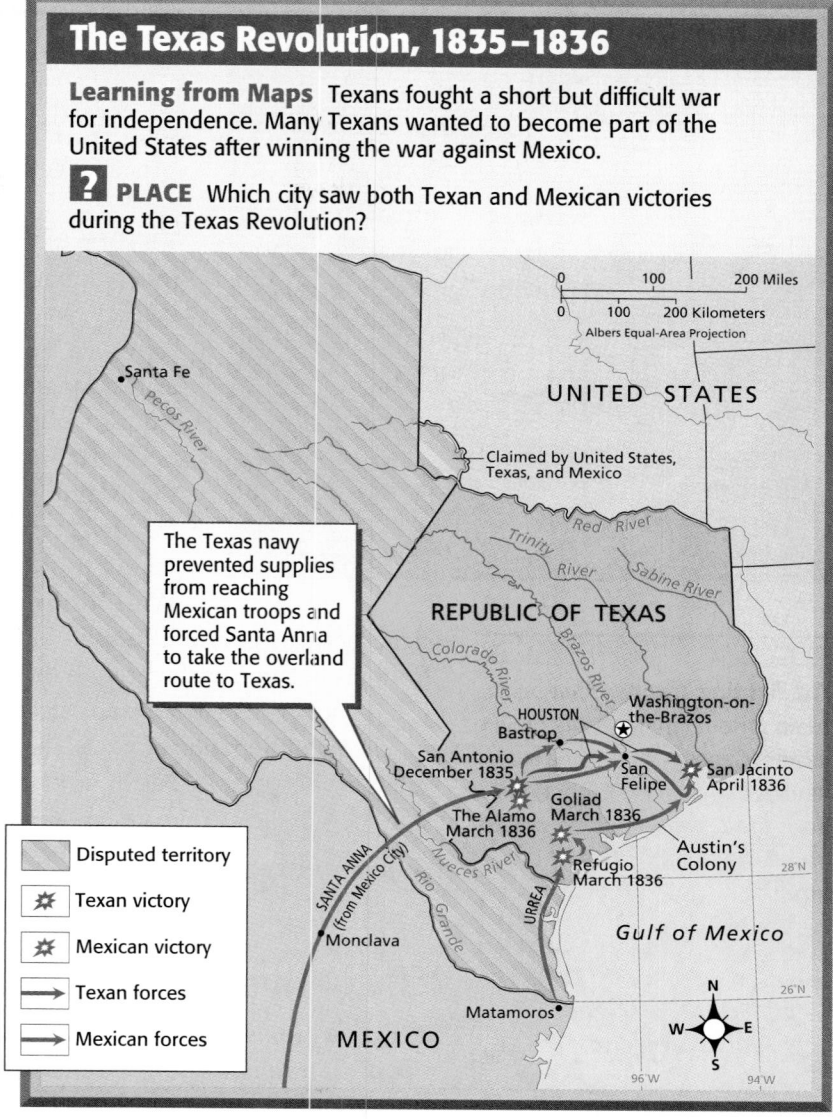

The Texas Revolution, 1835–1836

Learning from Maps Texans fought a short but difficult war for independence. Many Texans wanted to become part of the United States after winning the war against Mexico.

? PLACE Which city saw both Texan and Mexican victories during the Texas Revolution?

The Texas navy prevented supplies from reaching Mexican troops and forced Santa Anna to take the overland route to Texas.

Disputed territory
Texan victory
Mexican victory
Texan forces
Mexican forces

On March 6, Mexican troops finally overran the fort, killing all of the rebel fighters. The Mexicans suffered some 600 casualties. Santa Anna released a few civilians at the Alamo, such as Susanna Dickinson, whose husband had been killed in the fighting. Dickinson's account of the final days of the siege became widely known throughout Texas. She claimed that at one point William Travis had drawn a line in the sand with his sword, telling any defenders who crossed it that they could leave, while the rest would stand and defend the fort. According to legend, all stayed. The story added to the status of the Alamo defenders and spurred other Texans to support the cause of independence.

Several weeks later, another incident further fueled anti-Mexican feelings. After Mexican troops defeated a rebel army near Goliad (GOH-lee-ad), some 400 surviving Texans surrendered. General Santa Anna ordered that the prisoners be executed

The fighting Texans. After being taken prisoner in the Battle of San Jacinto, General Santa Anna surrendered to Sam Houston. *What does the Texans' clothing reveal about the organization of their army?*

for treason. The wife of a Mexican officer, Francita Alavez, saved some of the Texans by hiding them from the Mexican soldiers. Thereafter, Texans remembered Alavez as the "Angel of Goliad."

Victory at San Jacinto. The Texans, who had declared independence on March 2, were badly shaken by these defeats. On April 21, however, their luck changed dramatically. Led by Sam Houston, the commander of the Texas army, a force of approximately 900 rebels surprised Santa Anna's troops. The Mexican soldiers were taking an afternoon nap near the San Jacinto River. Shouting "Remember the Alamo!" and "Remember Goliad!" the Texans tore through Mexican lines, killing some 630 Mexican troops and taking Santa Anna prisoner in the **Battle of San Jacinto**. With his army weakened and supplies low, Santa Anna signed a treaty granting Texas its independence. Shortly thereafter he was removed from his position as the head of the Mexican government.

A short time later, Texans elected Sam Houston as the first president of the independent Republic of Texas. The Mexican government refused to recognize the republic, however. Mexican officials argued that Santa Anna had been forced to sign the San Jacinto agreement illegally.

✔ **READING CHECK:** What events and issues led to the Texas Revolution?

Life in the Republic of Texas

Texas petitioned the U.S. Congress for annexation in 1837. However, northern opposition to admitting another slave state as well as a cautious foreign policy toward Mexico prevented Texas from being accepted into the Union immediately. From 1836 to 1845, Texas existed as an independent republic. It was known as the Lone Star Republic because its flag had a single star.

French and German immigration. One of the republic's first tasks was to increase its population. In 1842 the Texas congress awarded Henri Castro, a French banker of Portuguese descent, an *empresario* grant in central Texas. Two years later, Castro brought 35 French colonists—many of them from the German-speaking region of Alsace—to found the town of Castroville just west of San Antonio. More than 2,000 settlers came during the colony's first year. They established farms, using seeds and supplies provided by Castro.

The Texas government also arranged for a German company to recruit settlers. In 1845 the company's agent, Prince Carl of Solms-Braunfels, and several German families founded the settlement of New Braunfels in central Texas. Over the next few years more than 7,000 German immigrants came to live in what they called the Paradise of North America.

Early living conditions in New Braunfels were less than ideal. Ferdinand Roemer, a German geologist and naturalist who traveled to Texas in the 1840s, described the new colony's homes:

> 66 Several families were packed into one house, no matter how small it was. The interior of such a house, where men, women, and children were cooped up with their unpacked chests and boxes, often looked like the steerage of an immigrant ship. 99

These crowded conditions were not permanent, however. Most families eventually moved out of town and settled on farms. Many kept their homes in town but used them only when they had business to conduct or community events to attend.

With New Braunfels serving as a social and cultural hub, German settlers spread their customs, farming practices, and language throughout the Hill Country of central Texas. German-language church services, newspapers, and local social clubs helped preserve the German language and customs for many generations.

Discrimination against Tejanos. Tejanos did not fare as well as German settlers in the Lone Star Republic. A number of Tejanos had fought beside other Texans during the revolution. After Texas achieved independence, however, Tejanos became victims of violence and discrimination. Many had their lands and property seized by white Texans. Some were even driven from the country. As one descendant of a Tejano family put it, "These men who had favored the independence, suffered from the very beginning. . . . Many lost their [land] grants, and all lost their ideal—The Republic of Texas."

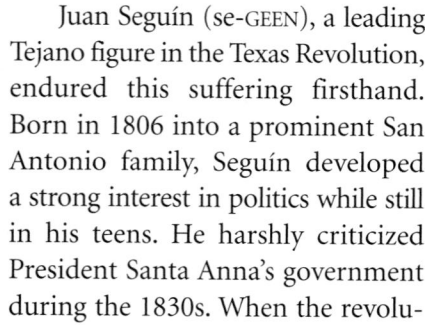

BIOGRAPHY
Juan Seguín

Juan Seguín (se-GEEN), a leading Tejano figure in the Texas Revolution, endured this suffering firsthand. Born in 1806 into a prominent San Antonio family, Seguín developed a strong interest in politics while still in his teens. He harshly criticized President Santa Anna's government during the 1830s. When the revolution began, he recruited a force of Tejano volunteers to fight Santa Anna and the Mexican army. After distinguishing himself in battle, he became a captain in the Texas cavalry.

Seguín escaped the slaughter at the Alamo because he had slipped through the Mexican lines in a desperate attempt to find reinforcements for the besieged rebels. He then joined Sam Houston's army and fought bravely in the Battle of San Jacinto. After the war ended, Seguín served as the mayor of San Antonio. He brought order to the town and attempted to protect its threatened Tejanos. Seguín later wrote about the conflict between white settlers and Tejanos.

> 66 The American straggling adventurers were . . . beginning to work their dark intrigues [plots] against the native families, whose only crime was, that they owned large tracts of land and desirable property. 99

Life for Teenage Immigrants

teen Life

Czech immigrants to Texas

Although the majority of settlers in Texas came from the United States and Mexico, a significant number emigrated from Europe. Between 1830 and 1860, thousands of people from Czechoslovakia, France, Germany, Ireland, Norway, Poland, and Sweden arrived in Texas. These immigrants formed new communities that reflected the unique cultural backgrounds of their founders.

During the 1850s, for example, Czech immigrants began forming small farming settlements in central Texas. These immigrants lived and worked in close-knit family units that emphasized the importance of Czech culture to their younger members. Jan Horák, who arrived in Texas with his family when he was 13 years old, described some of his early experiences:

> 66 Father bought a piece of land, and we farmed for two years. . . . There was no public school. The priests preached and taught in Czech. In spite of the oxen they had to use for transportation and their bare feet, the young people had a great time going to dances. 99

In 1842, white settlers in San Antonio falsely accused Seguín of retaining his loyalties to Mexico. "The necessity to defend myself for the loyal patriotism with which I had always served Texas, wounded me deeply," he later recalled. Fearful for the safety of his family, Seguín fled to Mexico. There he was forced to join the army. He later returned to Texas but lived out his last years in Mexico, where he died in 1890.

The economy and defense. Despite the flood of new migrants, Texas developed few towns and even fewer cities. With a population spread across such a large territory, travel and communication were often very difficult. The Texas economy relied heavily on its vast land resources, with farming and ranching the most common occupations. Texans had little cash, however, and tax revenues were quite small. The Republic of Texas quickly found itself millions of dollars in debt.

Finances and the spread-out population added to another problem for the nation—defense. Texas still faced hostility from Mexico as well as conflicts with local American Indian tribes. To protect the citizenry, Texas lawmakers organized a law-enforcement organization called the Texas Rangers. Texas's defense problems worsened when Mirabeau Lamar was elected president in 1838. Lamar boldly declared that Texans were ready to fight if necessary to defend their land. "If peace can only be obtained by the sword, let the sword do its work," he proclaimed. Lamar further fueled conflicts in 1841 by ordering an attack on the Mexican city of Santa Fe. The attack ended in defeat for the Texans and prompted counterattacks by Mexican forces. General Santa Anna, who had returned to power in 1839, occupied the city of San Antonio twice in the ensuing conflict. Sam Houston, who became president of Texas again in 1841, finally signed a peace treaty with Santa Anna in 1844. Tensions, though, continued to linger between the two nations.

✔ **READING CHECK:** What problems did the newly created Republic of Texas face?

Read More About It

Free Find: Juan Seguín
After reading about Juan Seguín on the **Holt Researcher** CD–ROM, imagine that you are a reporter interviewing Seguín for a Mexican newspaper. Write a series of questions and answers regarding Seguín's role in the Texas Revolution and what happened to him afterward.

SECTION 1 REVIEW

Define and explain the significance of the following terms:
manifest destiny
Tejanos
empresarios
Texas Revolution
Battle of San Jacinto

Identify and explain the significance of the following individuals:
Stephen F. Austin
Antonio López de Santa Anna
Sam Houston
Juan Seguín

Locate and explain the importance of the following places:
San Antonio
Goliad
San Jacinto

1. **Using Graphic Organizers** Copy the graphic organizer below. Use it to explain the causes and effects of the Texas Revolution.

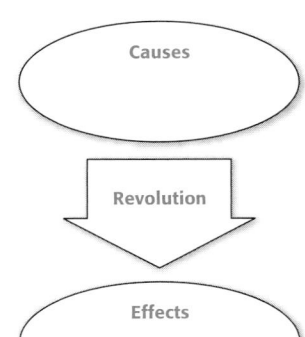

Causes

Revolution

Effects

2. **Identifying Values** What did arguments for and against western expansion reveal about American values in the early 1800s?
3. **Recognizing Point of View** What did the Mexican government hope to accomplish by encouraging people from the United States to settle in Texas? Was its goal accomplished? Explain your answer.
4. **Analyzing** What problems did Texas face after achieving independence?

Critical Thinking

5. How did the Mexican government's *empresario* policy contribute to cultural diversity in Texas?
   Consider:
   • how the *empresario* system worked
   • who came to Texas through the *empresario* system
   • how this migration affected the culture of Texas

SECTION 2

American Expansionism

OBJECTIVES

Read to understand:

1. how the annexation of Texas affected U.S.-Mexican relations
2. how the United States defeated Mexico in the Mexican War
3. what the terms of the Treaty of Guadalupe Hidalgo were
4. what problems confronted Mexican Americans after the Mexican War

KEY TERMS

Mexican War
Bear Flag Revolt
Treaty of Guadalupe Hidalgo
Mexican Cession
Gadsden Purchase

KEY PEOPLE

James K. Polk
Zachary Taylor
John Slidell
Stephen Kearny
John C. Frémont
Winfield Scott
Juan Cortina

KEY PLACES

Rio Grande
Nueces River
Monterey
Mexico City
Gila River

President James K. Polk and his wife, Sarah

EYEWITNESSES TO History

66 *Orders came last evening by express from Washington City directing General Taylor to move without any delay. . . . He is immediately to proceed with his whole command to the extreme western border of Texas and take up a position on the banks of or near the Rio Grande, and he is to expel any armed force of Mexicans who may cross that river. . . . Violence leads to violence, and if this movement of ours does not lead to others and to bloodshed, I am much mistaken.* 99
—Ethan Allen Hitchcock

Pistol from the Mexican War

Ethan Allen Hitchcock, a military officer serving under General Zachary Taylor in Louisiana, expressed a common view in this June 1845 diary entry. That spring, relations between the United States and Mexico had reached a new low. James K. Polk, a strong expansionist from Tennessee, had been elected president of the United States the previous fall, alarming many Mexicans. When the U.S. Congress voted to annex Texas in March 1845, many people in both countries concluded that it was simply a matter of time until war broke out.

Texas Annexation

After Texas declared its independence from Mexico in 1836, the question of its annexation drew considerable attention in the United States. Convinced that the United States was destined to expand westward, many Americans believed that Texas should be added to the Union as soon as possible. However, others opposed annexation because Texas allowed slavery. The issue quickly stirred heated debate in Congress.

The debate over annexation. Supporters of annexation worried that Texas might become an ally of Great Britain if it were not admitted to the United States. Britain wanted Texas to serve as a source of cotton and a market for British goods. Opponents of annexation, however, feared that the admission of Texas would increase the slave states' power in Congress.

The issue of western expansion dominated the 1844 presidential election. In this election, Whig Party candidate Henry Clay of Kentucky opposed Democrat James K. Polk, a former governor of Tennessee. Considered a dark-horse candidate—one who seems to have little chance of winning—Polk ran an effective campaign. He called for the annexation of Texas and the acquisition of more territory during his campaign. In contrast, Clay attempted to sidestep the annexation controversy. He ran on a campaign platform that did not even mention Texas.

Polk won by a narrow margin. He received 170 electoral votes to Clay's 105, but the popular vote was much closer. Despite the close vote, Polk interpreted his victory as a public cry for annexation.

James K. Polk

Most of James K. Polk's peers thought that he was unsociable—cold, formal, and closed-minded. He and his wife, Sarah, shunned the Washington social life and even banned dancing in the White House. Polk's work ethic left little time for recreation. "No President," he claimed, "who performs his duty faithfully and conscientiously can have any leisure."

Polk typically rose at dawn, took a walk, and ate breakfast before most of Washington was awake. He then put in a full day at the office and would often return to his desk after dinner and work late into the night. Polk confided in his diary that some of his duties as president puzzled him. After attending an elaborate diplomatic reception, he wrote, "Such ceremonies seem very ridiculous to an American."

Conflict with Mexico. Polk's victory increased tension between the United States and Mexico, which warned that it would consider U.S. annexation of Texas "equivalent to a declaration of war against the Mexican Republic." Congress ignored this warning and voted to admit Texas to the Union on March 3, 1845. Mexico responded by breaking diplomatic relations with the United States.

Polk increased tensions by demanding that Mexico recognize the Rio Grande as its northern border. The Rio Grande was about 100 miles south of the Nueces (noo-AY-suhs) River, which Mexico recognized as the dividing line between Texas and Mexico. To back up his demand, Polk ordered troops led by General Zachary Taylor to move into the disputed region.

After receiving word that Mexico was willing to negotiate, Polk sent John Slidell, a Louisiana lawyer and politician, to Mexico City in late 1845. Slidell's mission was to persuade Mexican officials to accept the Rio Grande boundary and to sell New Mexico and California to the United States. When Mexican citizens learned of this mission, they reacted angrily. Responding to the public outrage, the Mexican government changed its stance and refused to deal with Slidell. Polk immediately ordered General Taylor to move deeper into the disputed area. Although Polk publicly insisted that the troops were only defending U.S. territory, he hoped that Mexico would respond to their presence in a way that would justify war.

On May 9, 1846, Polk finally received the news he had been waiting for: Mexican troops had crossed the Rio Grande and attacked a U.S. patrol. The president quickly sent his war message to Congress. "Mexico," he said, "has invaded our territory and shed American blood upon American soil." Four days later Congress declared war on Mexico.

✔ **READING CHECK:** How did the annexation of Texas affect relations between the United States and Mexico?

INTERPRETING THE VISUAL RECORD

Taylor's crossing. The artwork on this cigar case shows General Taylor leading his troops across the Rio Grande. *What does this artifact suggest about the U.S. attitude toward the war with Mexico?*

The Mexican War

Some Americans, particularly Whigs and northerners, were critical of the **Mexican War**. Congressman Abraham Lincoln of Illinois, for example, introduced a series of "spot resolutions" in December 1847. Lincoln challenged the president to identify the exact spot on U.S. soil where American blood had been shed. If the site was indeed U.S. territory, Lincoln said, he would support the war; if not, he would oppose the war as unjustified. Some abolitionist opponents of "Mr. Polk's war" charged that its real goal was to acquire more slave territory. William Lloyd Garrison called the war an act "of aggression, of invasion, of conquest." In riveting public speeches, abolitionist Frederick Douglass demanded that the United States "leave off this horrid conflict, abandon [its] murderous plans, and forsake the way of blood."

Despite such opposition, most Americans—particularly southerners and westerners who wanted Mexican land—supported the war. Congress authorized the army to enlist 50,000 volunteers. Young men eager for adventure rushed to sign up.

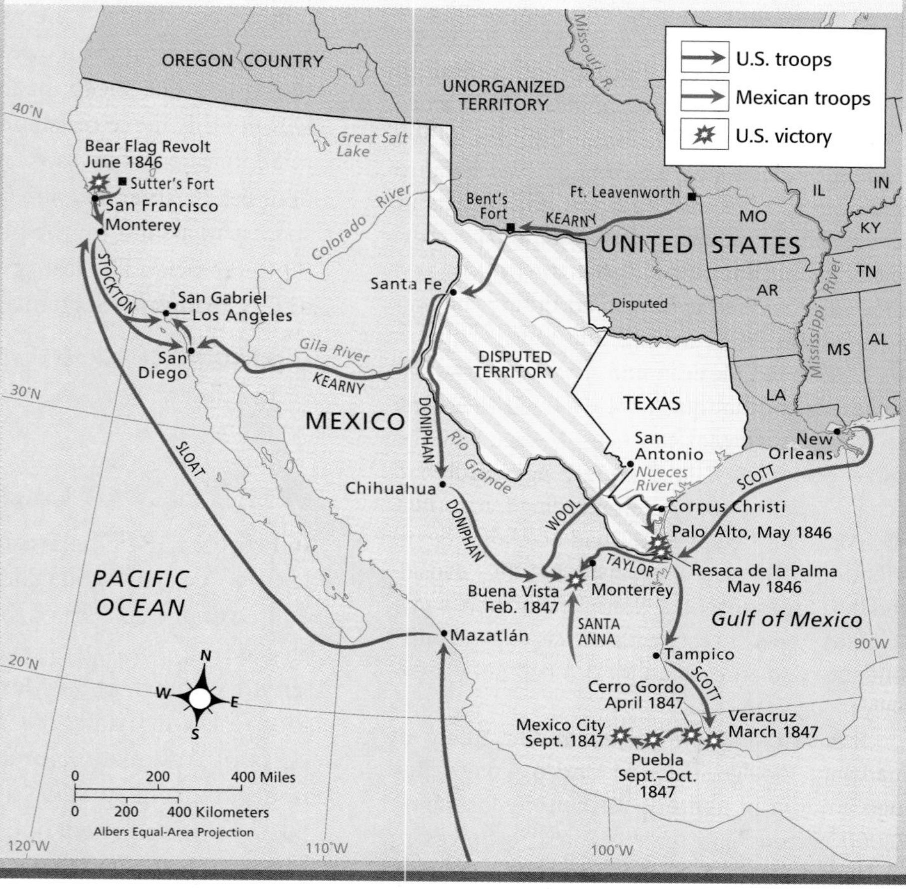

The two sides clash. While General Taylor led his troops into central Mexico, other U.S. forces seized New Mexico and California. In August 1846 an army led by Brigadier General Stephen Kearny (KAHR-nee) occupied Santa Fe and seized control of New Mexico. Kearny then advanced into California, where a group of American settlers had recently revolted against the Mexican government.

Captain John C. Frémont, a U.S. army officer and explorer who had headed an expedition

The Mexican War, 1846–1847

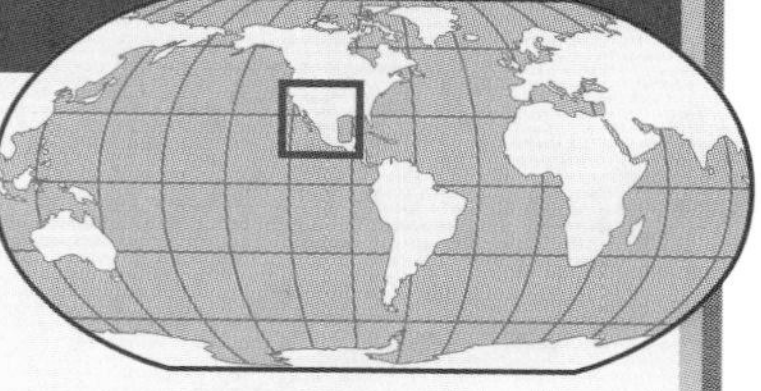

Learning from Maps Within months of declaring war, U.S. forces captured all the major cities and towns along the coast of California and controlled much of the territory north of Mexico City.

❓ MOVEMENT Which military commander led the U.S. forces from Fort Leavenworth to San Diego?

into California in 1845, led this revolt. After receiving a secret message from President Polk in May 1846, Frémont marched to the northern part of the province. Once there, he organized local settlers eager to throw off Mexican rule. On June 14 the settlers declared that California was an independent republic and raised a flag with the image of a grizzly bear painted on it. The flag gave the uprising its name—the **Bear Flag Revolt**.

Meanwhile, U.S. Marines under the command of Commodore John Sloat captured Monterey, the capital of California, in July 1846. The United States completed its conquest of California in January 1847. Troops led by Kearny and Commodore Robert F. Stockton won the final battle in California at San Gabriel.

A short time later, fierce fighting raged in Mexico near Buena Vista. In February 1847 Taylor led fewer than 5,000 troops against President Santa Anna and some 15,000 Mexican troops. Although Santa Anna was forced to withdraw, Taylor felt little joy at the victory. "The great loss on both sides," he wrote, "has deprived me of everything like pleasure."

California settlers raised this flag in 1846 to declare their independence from Mexico.

HISTORY
IN THE MAKING

The Mexican War
BY RICHARD SALVUCCI

Few modern Americans regard the Mexican War as a major turning point in U.S. history. Even in Brownsville, Texas—the site of two important battles—no great monuments stand to mark events. In contrast, Mexicans view the war as a critical historical event. A large memorial in Mexico City honors those who died in the fighting, and portraits of soldiers who served during the war appear on Mexican currency.

Why do the Mexican and American views differ? To answer that question, we need to look at the war through Mexican eyes. Mexico saw the United States as a land-hungry aggressor and Zachary Taylor's troops as an invading force. Thus, most Mexicans believed they had no choice but to defend their homeland against what they considered the "Colossus of the North." In addition, some Mexicans hoped to reconquer Texas, whose independence and annexation Mexico had not yet formally recognized.

The war and the terms of the Treaty of Guadalupe Hidalgo shattered Mexico. Along with a huge amount of territory, the country lost some 80,000 citizens and many natural resources to the United States. For many years after the war, Mexico struggled to stabilize its government and develop its economy. As the country and its economy grew stronger during the 1900s, some Mexican leaders used the war to criticize U.S. expansionism and foreign policy. Thus, even today, the Mexican War remains an important part of Mexican consciousness.

The siege of Mexico City. A bold siege of Mexico City marked the final campaign of the war in Mexico. Led by General Winfield Scott, some 10,000 U.S. soldiers captured a fortified castle in the city of Veracruz on the Gulf of Mexico in March 1847. Marching from this coastal base, Scott maneuvered his troops into position to attack the very heart of the Mexican nation.

Mexican soldiers valiantly defended the long, mountainous road to the capital. One wounded U.S. soldier wrote, "Nobody ever told us how [the Mexicans] . . . could fight. We thought they'd run like sheep; instead, they turned on us like bobcats." Despite this fierce resistance, Scott's forces reached Mexico City in September. They took over the National Palace, which President Santa Anna had already abandoned. They then launched a successful assault on the hilltop garrison of Chapultepec (chah-POOL-tay-pek). The last of Mexico City's defenders surrendered to U.S. troops on September 14, 1847.

✔ **READING CHECK:** How did U.S. forces defeat the Mexican army in the Mexican War?

The Treaty of Guadalupe Hidalgo

In February 1848 the **Treaty of Guadalupe Hidalgo** (gwah-dah-LOO-pay ee-DAHL-goh) ended the war on terms dictated by the United States. As part of the terms of the treaty, Mexico gave up all claims to Texas. It also surrendered to the United States a vast territory known as the **Mexican Cession**. This territory included the present-day states of California, Nevada, and Utah, as well as parts of Arizona, Colorado, New Mexico, and Wyoming. In return, the United States agreed to pay Mexico $15 million and take over the payment of damages claimed by Americans against Mexico. The United States also agreed to grant full citizenship to Mexicans who lived in the Mexican Cession.

The Treaty of Guadalupe Hidalgo transferred an enormous region from Mexico to the United States. Manuel Cresencio Rejón, a member of the Mexican congress, expressed the anger that many Mexican citizens felt about the treaty.

❝ I cannot see by what justification [the United States] comes to us giving us as a condition for the reestablishment of the peace . . . the renunciation [forfeit] of our northern frontier from sea to sea, and all for the measly sum of 18,250,000 pesos [$15 million]. ❞

In 1853 the United States grew even larger when James Gadsden, a U.S. diplomat, negotiated a deal with Mexico to secure an additional strip of land south of the Gila (HEE-luh) River for $10 million. With the **Gadsden Purchase** the United States acquired parts of the present-day states of Arizona and New Mexico.

✔ **READING CHECK:** What were the terms of the Treaty of Guadalupe Hidalgo?

Mexican Americans

As a result of the Treaty of Guadalupe Hidalgo, the United States gained some 80,000 Spanish-speaking citizens along with its new territory. Despite the treaty's guarantees, however, many Mexican Americans lost their lands. New American settlers challenged Spanish land titles, and Mexican Americans whose families had lived in parts of New Mexico and California for generations had to fight costly legal battles to defend their claims.

Many white Americans looked down on the culture of Mexican Americans, with its blend of Spanish and American Indian influences. The resulting atmosphere of prejudice and discrimination contributed to Mexican American rebellions in the Southwest. Juan Cortina, a member of a prominent Tejano family in South Texas, headed one such rebellion. In 1859 Cortina shot and wounded a Texas marshal who was beating a Tejano with his pistol. To avoid imprisonment, Cortina fled to Mexico. Over the next six months, he and his supporters attacked white settlers' ranches and businesses and engaged in skirmishes with Texas law enforcement officers. Cortina explained his actions:

Mariano Vallejo and his family owned more than 150,000 acres in California. During the revolt by American settlers in 1846, Vallejo was jailed for six weeks. After the war most of his land was taken.

66 Our object . . . has been to chastise [punish] the villainy [wrong doing] of our enemies. . . . These have connived with each other . . . to persecute and rob us, without any cause, and for no other crime on our part than that of being Mexican in origin. 99

U.S. troops eventually took control of the region, but Cortina continued his raids into the 1870s.

✔ **READING CHECK:** What problems did Mexican Americans face after the Mexican War?

SECTION 2 REVIEW

Define and explain the significance of the following terms:
Mexican War
Bear Flag Revolt
Treaty of Guadalupe Hidalgo
Mexican Cession
Gadsden Purchase

Identify and explain the significance of the following individuals:
James K. Polk
Zachary Taylor
John Slidell
Stephen Kearny
John C. Frémont
Winfield Scott
Juan Cortina

Locate and explain the importance of the following places:
Rio Grande   Mexico City
Nueces River   Gila River
Monterey

1. **Using Graphic Organizers** Copy the graphic organizer below. Use it to describe the major battles of the Mexican War of 1846 and their outcomes.

Battles	Outcomes
1.	
2.	
3.	

2. **Identifying Cause and Effect** What issues and events led to the Mexican War?
3. **Assessing Consequences** How did the treaty ending the Mexican War affect Mexican Americans living in the Mexican Cession?
4. **Understanding Geography: Location** What present-day states and parts of states did the United States acquire as a result of the Treaty of Guadalupe Hidalgo and the Gadsden Purchase?

Critical Thinking

5. Why might some people argue that Texas's independence led to the expansion of the southwestern United States?
   Consider:
   • how Texas's independence affected its relationship with the United States and Mexico
   • how the annexation of Texas was connected to the outbreak of the Mexican War
   • what the outcome of the Mexican War was

The Far West

EYEWITNESSES TO History

66 *The men had a great deal of anxiety and all the care of their families, but still the mothers had the families directly in their hands and were with them all the time, especially during sickness.*

Some of the women I saw on the road went through a great deal of suffering and trial. I remember distinctly one girl in particular about my own age that died and was buried on the road. Her mother had a great deal of trouble and suffering. It strikes me as I think of it now that mothers on the road had to undergo more trial and suffering than anybody else. 99

—Martha Ann Morrison

Conestoga wagon

Martha Ann Morrison, who traveled to Oregon Country at age 13, recalled the extreme hardships many settlers endured during the westward journey. During the early 1800s, American merchants and fur trappers established trails that brought a flood of new settlers like Morrison to the Far West in the 1840s and 1850s.

The Promise of Trade

U.S. contact with the Far West—territory west of the Mississippi River—began in the 1790s. At that time, New England mariners sailed around South America and up the Pacific coast to trade with the coastal communities of California. People in these communities were eager to exchange cattle hides, furs, and tallow—animal fat used in candles and soap—for American manufactured goods. American traders did not want to be arrested for violating the Spanish ban on foreign trade, however, so they seldom ventured far inland.

This situation changed with Mexico's independence from Spain in 1821. Eager to improve its economy, Mexico's new government encouraged trade with the United States. American merchants, in turn, looked to Mexico for new markets. One such merchant was William Becknell. In 1821 Becknell loaded a wagon train with tools, clothing, and other goods. He blazed a trail westward from Missouri to Santa Fe, in what is now New Mexico. Becknell made huge profits trading his merchandise for furs, livestock, and silver. His success encouraged other American merchants to follow the 780-mile-long **Santa Fe Trail**. By 1830 they controlled much of the trade that occurred in the Mexican borderlands.

Fur trappers, or **mountain men**, also came to the Far West for commercial reasons. Beaver pelts, used to make men's hats, were in great demand in the United States during the early 1800s. With the help of American Indians who served as guides, interpreters, and pelt processors, mountain men extended the fur trade to new areas in the West. Some made large amounts of money as well.

It was in the Rocky Mountains—along the Missouri River and its tributaries—that the fur trade proved most profitable. This success was partially attributable to the **rendezvous system**, a method of doing business developed by William Ashley. As the owner of a fur-trading company, Ashley recognized that transporting furs out of the Rockies was expensive. To cut costs, he persuaded the trappers who traded with his company to remain in the mountains full-time and gather once a year to sell their furs and purchase supplies. This system reduced expenses and therefore increased profits. Each year the group decided where they would meet the next year.

After each annual rendezvous, the mountain men fanned out across hundreds of miles in the Rockies to trap beavers. In the process, they explored the mountains thoroughly and pioneered the trails that settlers would later use to reach the Far West. Mountain men such as Jim Bridger, Kit Carson, and James Beckwourth became famous for their explorations.

Fur trappers often wore clothes like this coat.

✔ **READING CHECK:** How did mountain men extend the fur trade and contribute to western settlement?

U.S. Boundaries in 1853

Learning from Maps Many Americans supported westward expansion, believing that more territory would help ease social and economic problems.

❓ **PLACE** How many states were admitted to the Union between 1820 and 1853?

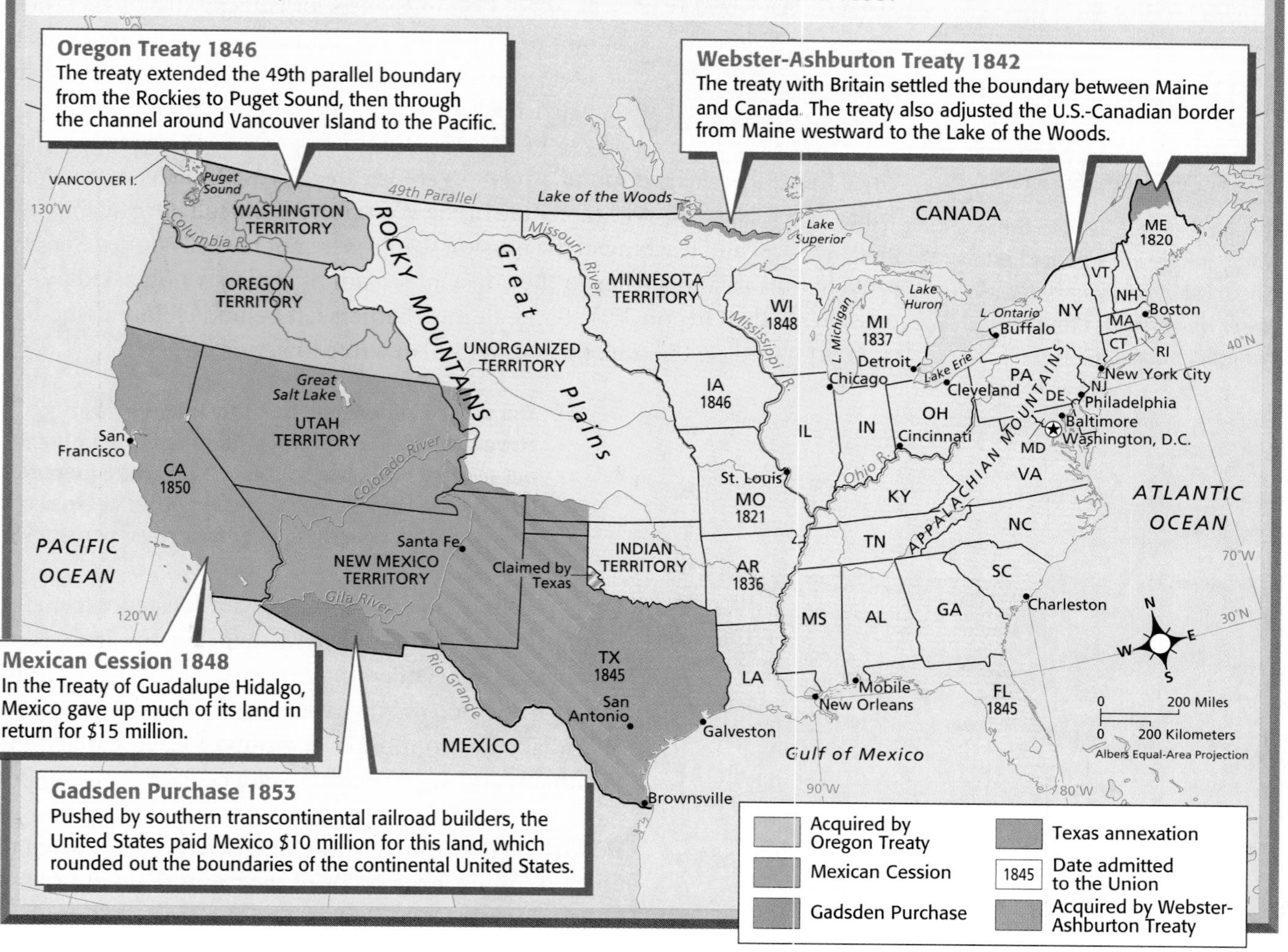

Oregon Treaty 1846
The treaty extended the 49th parallel boundary from the Rockies to Puget Sound, then through the channel around Vancouver Island to the Pacific.

Webster-Ashburton Treaty 1842
The treaty with Britain settled the boundary between Maine and Canada. The treaty also adjusted the U.S.-Canadian border from Maine westward to the Lake of the Woods.

Mexican Cession 1848
In the Treaty of Guadalupe Hidalgo, Mexico gave up much of its land in return for $15 million.

Gadsden Purchase 1853
Pushed by southern transcontinental railroad builders, the United States paid Mexico $10 million for this land, which rounded out the boundaries of the continental United States.

Map labels: VANCOUVER I., Puget Sound, 130°W, 49th Parallel, Lake of the Woods, CANADA, Columbia R., WASHINGTON TERRITORY, ROCKY MOUNTAINS, Missouri River, Lake Superior, ME 1820, OREGON TERRITORY, Great Plains, MINNESOTA TERRITORY, WI 1848, Lake Michigan, MI 1837, Lake Huron, L. Ontario, NY, VT, NH, Boston, Lake Erie, MA, CT, RI, UNORGANIZED TERRITORY, Detroit, Chicago, Cleveland, PA, Buffalo, 40°N, Great Salt Lake, UTAH TERRITORY, IA 1846, IL, IN, OH, Cincinnati, NJ, New York City, DE, Philadelphia, Baltimore, Washington, D.C., San Francisco, CA 1850, Colorado River, St. Louis, MO 1821, KY, Ohio R., MD, VA, ATLANTIC OCEAN, PACIFIC OCEAN, 120°W, Santa Fe, NEW MEXICO TERRITORY, Claimed by Texas, INDIAN TERRITORY, AR 1836, TN, NC, SC, 70°W, Gila River, MS, AL, GA, Charleston, 30°N, TX 1845, LA, San Antonio, Galveston, Mobile, New Orleans, FL 1845, Rio Grande, MEXICO, Brownsville, 90°W, 80°W, Gulf of Mexico, Albers Equal-Area Projection

Scale: 0 — 200 Miles; 0 — 200 Kilometers

Legend:
- Acquired by Oregon Treaty
- Mexican Cession
- Gadsden Purchase
- Texas annexation
- 1845 Date admitted to the Union
- Acquired by Webster-Ashburton Treaty

Settling Oregon Country

In 1811, American trappers founded a fur-trading post called Astoria near the mouth of the Columbia River in Oregon Country. Although the fur trade in the area proved disappointing, the Astoria trappers paved the way for more U.S. settlers. American newspapers publicized the trappers' route to Oregon Country in 1813. Known as the **Oregon Trail**, this route followed the Platte River across the Great Plains to the Rockies. It then descended into Oregon along the Snake and Columbia Rivers.

Farmers and missionaries. The Oregon Trail particularly interested farming families who wanted to settle in Oregon Country's Willamette Valley. Many missionaries were also attracted to Oregon Country, but not for farming. They saw the region as fertile ground for converting American Indians to Christianity. In 1833 a Methodist newspaper, the *Christian Advocate and Journal,* published a request for missionaries to teach the Christian faith to the American Indians of Oregon Country. The response to this request was swift.

BIOGRAPHY
Narcissa Whitman

Narcissa Prentiss Whitman was one of the early Protestant missionaries in Oregon Country. Born in 1806 in Prattsburg, New York, she grew up in a very religious household and became a primary school teacher. In 1835 she volunteered her services to the American Board of Commissioners for Foreign Missions, a Protestant organization that planned a series of missions to Oregon Country. Shortly before her journey west she married fellow missionary Marcus Whitman.

In 1836 the Whitmans arrived in Oregon Country. Once there, they helped found a mission among the Cayuse Indians in the Walla Walla Valley. Narcissa Whitman's life in the West proved difficult. Organizing religious services and teaching in the mission school were not her only duties. She also provided meals and shelter to the constant stream of settlers who passed by the mission on the Oregon Trail. Some of these settlers left behind children who had been orphaned on the trail. In 1846 Whitman wrote to her sister.

66 You will be astonished to know that we have eleven children in our family, and not one of them our own by birth, but so it is. . . . Destitute [penniless] and friendless, there was no other alternative—we must take them in or they must perish. 99

The Whitmans' mission met with resistance from the Cayuse. Many Cayuse blamed them for the increasing number of white settlers in the area. In late 1847 this resistance turned violent. After a measles epidemic killed some 30 Indians in two months, a group of Cayuse killed the Whitmans and 12 other white settlers.

Political impact. As more American settlers moved to Oregon Country, the status of the territory became a hot political issue. Great Britain and the United States had

HOLT RESEARCHER
Read More About It

Free Find:
Narcissa Whitman
After learning about Narcissa Whitman on the **Holt Researcher** CD–ROM, write a fictional journal entry describing her daily life as a missionary in the West.

INTERPRETING THE VISUAL RECORD

The Whitmans. In 1845 the Whitman mission was well established. *What can you determine about daily life at the mission from this painting?*

Changing Ways · Oregon

■ **Understanding Change** The states of Oregon, Washington, Idaho, and parts of Montana and Wyoming make up what was once Oregon Country. Although the region still possesses a lush environment, its population has changed greatly. *How has the ratio of men and women changed in Oregon? How has urbanization affected the population?*

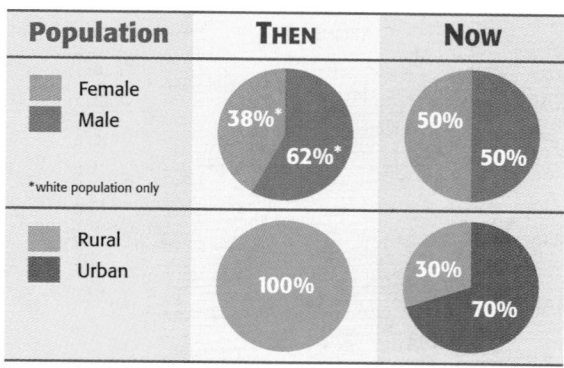

Population	THEN	NOW
Female / Male	38%* / 62%*	50% / 50%
Rural / Urban	100%	30% / 70%

*white population only

Sources: *Historical Statistics of the United States; Twenty-first Census of the United States; Statistical Abstract of the United States: 1997.* Data represents Oregon Territory in 1850 and Oregon state in 1990.

THEN

Now

jointly occupied Oregon Country since 1818. Several times the United States had suggested a division of Oregon at the 49th parallel, but Britain had always refused. During the 1844 presidential campaign, James K. Polk stunned and angered the British by proclaiming America's right to all of Oregon Country below the 54°40′ parallel. With "Fifty-four forty or fight" as his slogan, Polk declared that the United States would soon possess all of Oregon, up to the southern border of present-day Alaska.

After intense negotiations, the two sides reached an agreement in June 1846. They would extend the U.S. border to the 49th parallel. The agreement also allowed the British to keep Vancouver Island.

✔ **READING CHECK:** What were the effects of U.S. settlement in Oregon Country?

Traveling the Oregon Trail

Even before the United States and Great Britain settled their boundary dispute, American settlers poured into Oregon Country in ever-increasing numbers. During the 1840s and 1850s, thousands of families followed the overland trail to Oregon, which officially became a U.S. territory in 1848. Most organized themselves into large wagon trains to meet the challenges of the journey.

The difficult journey. The rugged nature of the trip required that travelers pool their resources. Traveling in large groups helped the pioneers deal with such obstacles as deep mud, heavy snow, rain-swollen rivers, and ravines. It also aided them in repairing broken equipment and defending themselves.

Despite such cooperation, some overland trips ended in tragedy. For example, the **Donner party** broke off from the Oregon Trail to head to California. The group

Frances Palmer's cartoon War! Or No War *shows two men discussing the conflict over Oregon.*

WAR! OR NO WAR

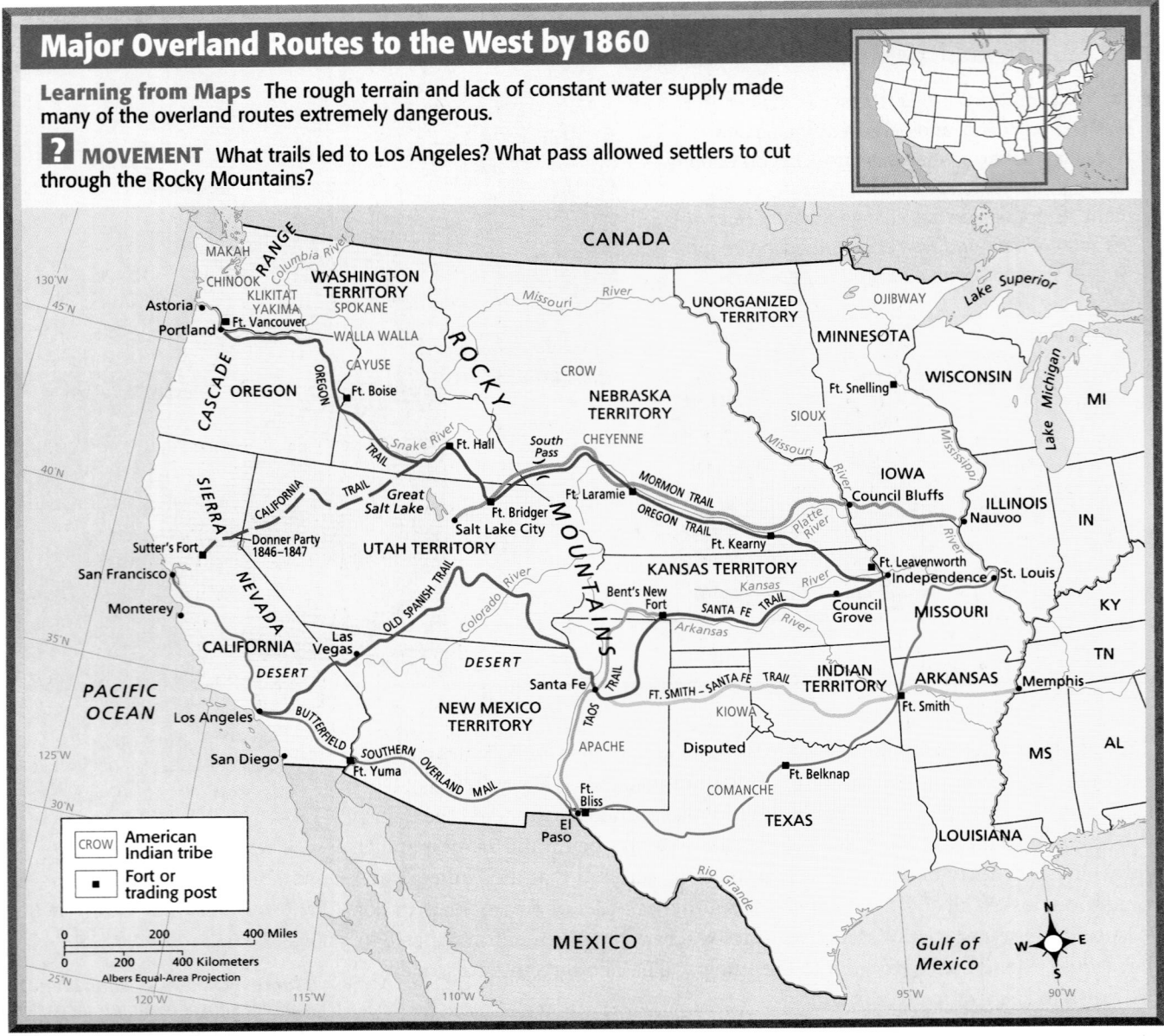

Major Overland Routes to the West by 1860

Learning from Maps The rough terrain and lack of constant water supply made many of the overland routes extremely dangerous.

? **MOVEMENT** What trails led to Los Angeles? What pass allowed settlers to cut through the Rocky Mountains?

CROW American Indian tribe

■ Fort or trading post

0   200   400 Miles
0   200   400 Kilometers
Albers Equal-Area Projection

became snowbound in the Sierra Nevada during the winter of 1846–47. Some 42 members of the Donner party died in the mountains.

Even under the best of circumstances, travelers on the Oregon Trail faced a long, difficult, and extremely dangerous journey. Wagon trains traveled slowly, the weather was unpredictable, and pioneers often fell prey to exhaustion and disease. Rivers and streams could take days to cross and sometimes took a toll in human and animal lives. Lucy Deady was 11 years old when her family traveled the Oregon Trail in 1846. She later described some of the hazards of the journey.

66 I remember how filled with terror I was when we experienced the violent thunderstorms. . . . Our oxen would try to stampede, our tents would be blown down, and everybody and everything would be soaked with the driving rains. . . . We had to cross a desert that took two days' and one night's travel. There was no water at all, so we filled every keg and dish with water so the cattle should have water as well as ourselves. 99

American Indians on the trail. American Indians often helped pioneers on the overland trails. They acted as guides, carried messages between wagon trains, and sold wild game to the travelers. Although eastern newspapers played up reports of American Indian "massacres," fewer than 400 pioneers lost their lives in Indian attacks between 1840 and 1860. Well-defended wagon trains were hard to attack, and most American Indians probably knew that the majority of settlers were only crossing Indian lands to locate somewhere farther west.

Still, settlers feared the possibility of attack. Responding to such fears, the U.S. government held a conference with the Great Plains tribes near present-day Laramie, Wyoming, in 1851. This meeting produced the **Treaty of Fort Laramie**. By the terms of the treaty, each tribe at the conference agreed to remain in a defined territory, pledged not to attack settlers moving west, and allowed the U.S. government to build roads and forts in its territory. In return, the United States promised to make annual payments to the American Indians and to honor each tribe's territorial boundaries.

✔ **READING CHECK:** What difficulties did American settlers encounter on the Oregon Trail?

Conflict in Oregon

After reaching Oregon Country, most American settlers moved into the Willamette Valley and established small farms. Although Oregon was not quite the paradise that some of them had expected, the majority stayed and prospered.

American settlers posed problems for American Indians in Oregon Country. During the 1830s and 1840s, contact between the two groups resulted in the spread of measles, smallpox, and other diseases that killed many American Indians. The settlers and their livestock also destroyed wildlife that the Indians depended on for survival.

As more and more people from the United States poured into American Indian lands, some tribes decided to fight back. The **Cayuse War**, for example, began after the killing of Narcissa and Marcus Whitman and 12 others in 1847. Fighting between the Cayuse and American settlers did not end until 1850, when U.S. officials executed five Cayuse leaders who had surrendered themselves in an attempt to avoid the destruction of the whole tribe. During the 1850s the Spokane, Walla Walla, Yakima (YA-kuh-maw), and other American Indian tribes in Oregon Country also tried to drive American settlers from their lands. They were unsuccessful, but for many years American Indians continued to fight people who moved onto their territory.

✔ **READING CHECK:** How did American Indians respond to American settlement of Oregon Country?

Westward Migration

L ike the millions of settlers who traveled west during the 1800s, Americans today have continued to move westward for a variety of reasons. New economic opportunities continue to motivate people to migrate. In recent decades, job opportunities in industries such as aerospace, banking, and defense have attracted northern and eastern migrants to western cities like Phoenix, Arizona.

During the 1990s the migration of people hoping to improve their quality of life helped produce rapid population increases in western states such as Colorado, Nevada, and Utah. These migrants also contributed to the tremendous growth of cities like San Francisco, California, and Seattle, Washington. Here people from across the United States and around the world moved to take advantage of career opportunities in the computer industry. By the late 1990s, Seattle was home to some 2,200 different technology companies. Yet, like the American Indians who encountered the first white migrants in the Far West, some longtime residents see problems resulting from new migrants. Rapid growth in Seattle has led to overburdened traffic systems and an increasing cost of living. Commented Seattle resident Ed Lazowska, "We have a long tradition of hoping it rains when people visit."

Seattle's skyline in the 1990s

The Mormons in Utah

As farmers and missionaries moved into Oregon Country, other white settlers migrated west to establish a new religious community. Led by Brigham Young, thousands of Mormons began to migrate to the Mexican territory of Utah in 1847. This migration increased after Utah became a U.S. possession in 1848. By 1860 some 40,000 Mormons had arrived in the territory. Most settled in the Great Salt Lake valley, but others continued to the Southwest where they founded smaller communities.

Mormon settlers constructed a system of canals to irrigate and farm the territory's arid desert soils. They also distributed land and built many schools, meetinghouses, and homes on a cooperative basis. Such efforts helped the Mormons attain a high level of economic, political, and religious independence.

This independence led to tension between the Mormons and the U.S. government. Many federal officials disliked Young's practice of appointing Mormon leaders to high offices in the territorial government. Officials also disapproved of the church's policy of allowing men to have more than one wife at a time. After a group of Mormons aided some American Indians in the attack of a wagon train of non-Mormon settlers in 1857, President James Buchanan sent U.S. troops to put down the "rebellion" in Utah. Very little violence occurred. However, disagreements between Mormon leaders and the federal government continued for decades.

✔ **READING CHECK:** What were some characteristics of Mormon communities in Utah? How did some of these characteristics lead to conflicts with the U.S. government?

INTERPRETING THE VISUAL RECORD

Fort Laramie. Alfred Jacob Miller painted this scene of American Indians camped at Fort Laramie. *What does the painting reveal about the relationship between the American Indians and the U.S. troops?*

SECTION 3 REVIEW

Define and explain the significance of the following terms:
Santa Fe Trail
mountain men
rendezvous system
Oregon Trail
Donner party
Treaty of Fort Laramie
Cayuse War

Identify and explain the significance of the following individuals:
William Becknell
William Ashley
Narcissa Prentiss Whitman
Marcus Whitman
Brigham Young

Locate and explain the importance of the following places:
Astoria
Willamette Valley

1. **Using Graphic Organizers** Copy the graphic organizer below. Use it to list examples of people who moved to the Far West, what their goals were, and how well they achieved those goals.

People	Goals	Result
mountain men:		
missionaries:		
Mormons:		

2. **Evaluating** How did the settlement of Oregon Country by Americans affect relations between the United States and Great Britain?
3. **Problem Solving** Imagine that you are a traveler making your way to Oregon Country. How would you have dealt with some of the problems that travelers faced on the Oregon Trail?
4. **Assessing Consequences** What were the consequences of the arrival of missionaries and other settlers in Oregon Country for American Indians?

Critical Thinking

5. Many Mormons moved to Utah to escape conflicts they had experienced back east. How successful were the Mormons in building their ideal community?
   Consider:
   • how Mormon communities reflected their religious beliefs
   • how Mormon practices led to conflicts with the U.S. government

The Rush to California

Wooden rocker used for mining gold

EYEWITNESSES TO History

❝ The news spreads that wonderful 'diggings' have been discovered. . . . [Men] rush vulture-like upon the scene and erect a round tent, where, in gambling, drinking, swearing and fighting, the many reproduce Pandemonium . . . while a few honestly and industriously commence digging for gold, and lo! as if a fairy's wand had been waved . . . a full-grown mining town hath sprung into existence. ❞

—Louise Smith Clappe

Louise Smith Clappe sailed to California with her husband in 1849. With the discovery of gold in 1848, thousands of prospectors from the United States and around the world poured into California. Seemingly overnight, miners constructed makeshift towns near the sites where they hoped to make their fortunes. As Clappe complained, however, the creation of these towns produced new problems.

Early Settlement

Long before the California Gold Rush came a long, slow process of European settlement. In 1769—the year Spain began to establish communities in California—approximately 300,000 American Indians lived in the territory. The number of Spaniards in California increased over the next several decades. This was because Catholic priests of the Franciscan order, aided by soldiers, founded 21 missions along the Pacific coast between San Diego and the San Francisco Bay. Since initially few single Spanish women migrated to California, many of the soldiers married American Indian women and settled permanently in the territory. Spanish officials promoted immigration to California by recruiting artisan families to teach the American Indians of the missions blacksmithing, carpentry, and herding. These first Spanish settlers and their descendants were known as **Californios**.

In 1834 the Mexican government began to transfer ownership of mission lands to Californios. It also issued the first of some 700 new land grants, mostly also along the Pacific coast between San Diego and San Francisco. Some of this land was supposed to be given to American Indians from the missions. Instead, most of it went to Californios and white settlers. As a result, many American Indians were landless, and some were forced to move inland. Meanwhile, California's non-Indian population continued to grow. By the 1840s some 8,000 to 12,000 Californios were dispersed among several major settlements, including San Diego, Los Angeles, Monterey, and Yerba Buena (yuhr-buh BWAY-nuh).

Many Californios became quite wealthy.

✔ **READING CHECK:** How did the Spanish settle California?

Gold in California

In 1830 only about 500 Americans—most of them merchants—lived in California. More non-Spanish settlers arrived during the 1830s and 1840s, drawn by cheap farmland and the territory's mild climate. Among these settlers was John Augustus Sutter, a Swiss adventurer who acquired a huge land grant from Mexico in 1839. Sutter's headquarters, an adobe fort and trading post near the Sacramento and American Rivers, was a major stopping point along the **California Trail**. This trail forked off the Oregon Trail near the southernmost point on the Snake River.

On January 24, 1848, one of Sutter's employees, James W. Marshall, detected flakes of heavy yellow metal at the bottom of a wooden canal used to divert water from the American River. Marshall later recalled, "I reached my hand down and picked it up; it made my heart thump, for I was certain it was gold." He was right, and word of his discovery spread quickly.

News of the gold strike fascinated people in California. Many of them rushed to the American River to try their luck. Soon one newspaper in San Francisco complained.

CALIFORNIAN.

SAN FRANCISCO, WEDNESDAY, MARCH 15, 1848.

GOLD MINE FOUND.—In the newly made raceway of the Saw Mill recently erected by Captain Sutter, on the American Fork, gold has been found in considerable quantities. One person brought thirty dollars worth to New Helvetia, gathered there in a short time. California, no doubt, is rich in mineral wealth; great chances here for scientific capitalists. Gold has been found in almost every part of the country.

This 1848 newspaper article announces the discovery of gold in California.

❝ **The whole country from San Francisco to Los Angeles, and from the shore to the base of the Sierra Nevada, resounds with the sordid [greedy] cry of *gold! Gold!! GOLD!!!* while the field is left half planted, the house half built, and everything neglected but the manufacture of shovels and pickaxes.** ❞

This was the newspaper's last issue. Left without any staff or advertisers, the editor suspended publication and rushed to the goldfields himself.

Americans on the East Coast first heard of the gold in California in September 1848. Breathless news dispatches told of former laborers collecting $50 of gold a day with nothing but shovels and dishpans. President Polk confirmed the accounts in a December message to Congress, and the great California Gold Rush was on.

By early 1849 hopeful gold seekers from as far away as Australia, China, and Europe were rushing to North America. They joined the thousands of Americans, Mexicans, and South Americans also trekking to the goldfields. Many of these migrants—called **forty-niners** because of the year, 1849—traveled to California through the mountain passes of the California Trail. By the end of May 1849 more than 40,000 people had risked the dangerous overland trip to California. Other forty-niners sailed down the eastern seaboard to Central America. They next crossed over by land to the Pacific Ocean and then sailed north to San Francisco.

THROUGH OTHERS' EYES

A Californio's View of Forty-niners

While some Californios took part in the early stages of the gold rush, most avoided the fate of the forty-niners. José Fernandez, a former captain in the Mexican army and mayor of San Jose, later recalled:

❝ The year '49 was the great epoch of California. During this year arrived hundreds of foreign ships loaded with passengers. All the nations of the earth vied [competed] with each other in sending us their quotas. . . .

But just as every day many set out full of hope and confidence in the future, so every day many returned, disgusted with the mines, where they had wasted their time and contracted diseases, coming to San Francisco to be cured of rheumatism and malignant [harmful] fevers which so often and so cruelly attacked the first miners who exploited [took advantage of] the placers. ❞

✔ **READING CHECK:** How and why did the forty-niners migrate to California?

Mining

During the initial phases of the California Gold Rush, many forty-niners worked mining claims with a minimum of equipment. Panning, the simplest and most labor-intensive mining technique, required miners to place loads of dirt into dishpans, submerge them in water, and shake them until any gold deposits had settled to the bottom. Some forty-niners also used sluice boxes—long, sloping wooden boxes that collected heavy minerals from flowing water.

By the mid-1850s, however, large mining companies with mechanized equipment had replaced most individual prospectors in the goldfields. Many of these companies engaged in hydraulic mining. This method used streams of high-pressure water to blast large amounts of mineral-rich earth through industrial sluices. At one mine in North Bloomfield, for example, workers removed massive amounts of dirt from the side of a cliff by spraying it with 60 million gallons of water a day. Such operations cut enormous gulches into the mountainous landscape of northern California.

Understanding Science and History

1. How did miners pan for gold?
2. What was the environmental impact of hydraulic mining?

Miners and Mining Camps

The great majority of gold seekers were young, unmarried men. The few women who migrated to California found a rough-and-tumble society very different from what they left behind. Mining camps—with names like Hangtown, Poker Flat, and Skunk Gulch—were dirty, disorderly, and dangerous. Drinking, gambling, fighting, and crime thrived in the uneasy atmosphere of these temporary communities. One observer of a mining camp described the scene.

> 66 Men without the restraint of law, indifferent to public opinion, and unburdened by families, drink whenever they feel like it, whenever they have the money to pay for it, and whenever there is nothing else to do. . . . Bad manners follow, profanity becomes a matter of course. . . . Excitability and nervousness brought on by rum help these tendencies along, and then to correct this state of things the pistol comes into play. 99

Some prospectors found immense riches in the mines. One man's claim reportedly yielded 52 pounds of gold in just eight days. Most prospectors, however, found only disappointment.

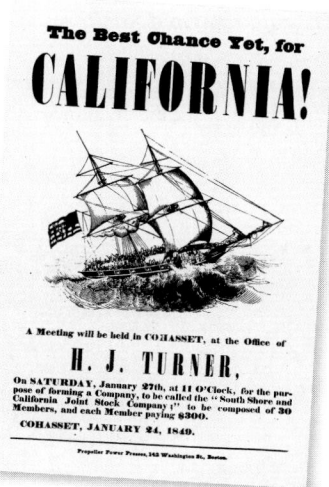

The Best Chance Yet, for
CALIFORNIA!

A Meeting will be held in COHASSET, at the Office of
H. J. TURNER,
On SATURDAY, January 27th, at 11 O'Clock, for the purpose of forming a Company, to be called the "South Shore and California Joint Stock Company!" to be composed of 30 Members, and each Member paying $300.
COHASSET, JANUARY 24, 1849.

Companies offering transportation to California aggressively advertised the prosperity to be found there.

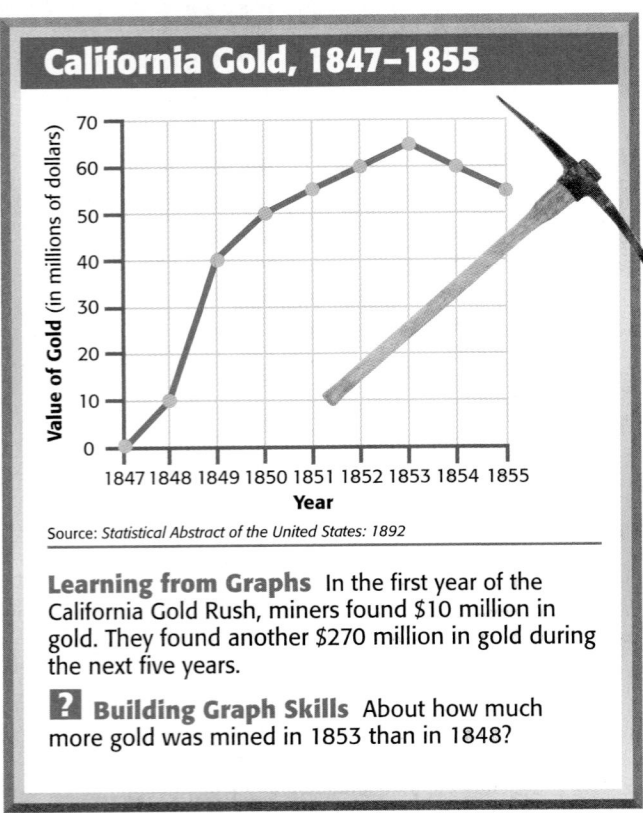

California Gold, 1847–1855

Value of Gold (in millions of dollars)

70
60
50
40
30
20
10
0

1847 1848 1849 1850 1851 1852 1853 1854 1855
Year

Source: *Statistical Abstract of the United States: 1892*

Learning from Graphs In the first year of the California Gold Rush, miners found $10 million in gold. They found another $270 million in gold during the next five years.

❓ **Building Graph Skills** About how much more gold was mined in 1853 than in 1848?

Whether they succeeded or failed, the forty-niners made California a much more diverse place. Nearly 80 percent were Americans—including some 4,000 African Americans—whereas about 8 percent came from Mexico. Others arrived from Australia, China, Europe, and South America. This international mix of gold seekers increased California's non–American Indian population from some 14,000 in 1848 to more than 220,000 in 1852.

The large migration also attracted people in search of other types of economic opportunities. The miners needed supplies and services, which many clever businesspeople were happy to provide. One such person was Levi Strauss, a tailor who had immigrated to the United States from Bavaria in 1847. During the gold rush, Strauss traveled to California to sew clothes for miners, who had a hard time finding trousers that stood up to the harshness of the mines. Strauss made a new style of sturdy work pants from tent canvas. The pants held up so well that soon Strauss was flooded with orders. The pants were soon made from denim instead of canvas. Dyed with indigo, they came to be nicknamed blue jeans.

✔ **READING CHECK:** What impact did the forty-niners have on California society?

The Gold Rush. Newly arrived gold miners camped on San Francisco's Telegraph Hill. *What can you determine about the rate of new arrivals to California during the Gold Rush?*

Conflict in the Mines

Because they were the first to reach the goldfields, Californios scored some of the first major gold strikes. By late 1849, however, white American miners outnumbered all other groups and began to drive Californios from their claims. They posted notices declaring that "foreigners" had no right to be in the mines and must leave immediately. These white American miners ignored the fact that under the terms of the Treaty of Guadalupe Hidalgo, Californios were U.S. citizens. Many Californios who refused to leave the mines were beaten and some were even killed.

Chinese and African American Miners.
Chinese prospectors fared little better than Californios. Shortly after word of the gold rush reached China, men from Guangdong (GWAHNG-DOOHNG) Province headed for California, which they called *Gam Saan,* or Gold Mountain. When they arrived at the mines, however, white prospectors prevented them from staking claims.

Frustrated by discrimination in the mining camps, many Chinese returned to China. Others became field-workers, joined railroad construction crews, or ran small farms. Still others settled in towns, where they worked as grocers, merchants, storekeepers, or unskilled laborers. By 1852 California's Chinese population numbered more than 11,000. Many of these immigrants continued to associate with each other in groups based on kinship, clan, and village ties that originated in China.

Fearing competition, white miners tried to ban African Americans from the mines and persuaded lawmakers to deny African Americans the right to vote. Despite these obstacles, some black miners made a living in California, and a handful even struck it rich.

American Indians in California. The Gold Rush led to disaster for many American Indians in California. White miners forced American Indians off gold-rich lands, and some were forced into service in the mines. Volunteer militia companies and regular army units in California also raided American Indian villages. In one incident, two miners returned to their camp to find the place ransacked and their five companions missing. Assuming that American Indians were responsible, the miners organized a posse and raided several Indian villages, killing more than 130 people.

Some California Indians took up arms against the forty-niners. For example, after their lands in the Sierra Nevada and the San Joaquin Valley had been taken over by miners, the Miwok (MEE-wahk) and Yokuts (YOH-kuhts) tribes began to raid the properties of white settlers in 1850. Lasting through 1851, these raids collectively became known as the **Mariposa War**. During the early 1850s, attacks by the Yuma and Mohave (moh-HAH-vee) tribes kept some prospectors from crossing the Colorado River into the Indians' territory. In response, the U.S. Army built Fort Yuma and attacked several Yuma villages. By 1860 such attacks, along with disease and starvation, had reduced California's American Indian population to about 35,000.

✔ **READING CHECK:** How were American Indians in California affected by the gold rush?

INTERPRETING THE VISUAL RECORD

Miners. Miners at Auburn Ravine posed for this photograph in 1852. *What does this image reveal about the variety of people who came to California in search of gold?*

HOLT RESEARCHER

Read More About It

Free Find: California
After reading about California on the **Holt Researcher** CD–ROM, imagine that you work for the state tourism board. Write a short pamphlet explaining the impact of the gold rush on California's history.

SECTION 4 REVIEW

Define and explain the significance of the following terms:
Californios
California Trail
forty-niners
Mariposa War

Identify and explain the significance of the following individuals:
John Augustus Sutter
James W. Marshall

1. **Using Graphic Organizers** Copy the graphic organizer below. Use it to summarize the Gold Rush's effect on each of the major population groups in California.

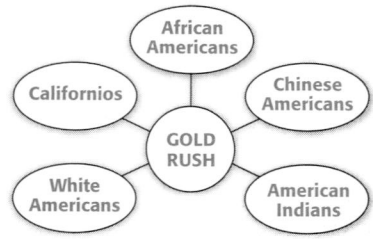

2. **Analyzing** How did the Spanish come to settle in California?
3. **Identifying Cause and Effect** What drew the forty-niners to California, and how did they get there?
4. **Using Historical Imagination** How might California have developed differently if gold had not been discovered there?

Critical Thinking

5. How did the forty-niners change California?
   Consider:
   • who the forty-niners were
   • how they affected California society
   • how they affected California's economy

Review

Creating a Time Line

Copy the time line below onto a sheet of paper. Complete the time line by filling in the events and dates from the chapter that you think were most significant. Pick three events and explain why you think they were significant.

1820   1840   1860

Writing a Summary

Using the Reading Checks as a guide, write an overview of the events in the chapter.

Identifying People and Ideas

Identify the following terms or individuals and explain their significance.

1. Tejanos
2. *empresarios*
3. Stephen Kearny
4. Gadsden Purchase
5. rendezvous system
6. Oregon Trail
7. Narcissa Whitman
8. Brigham Young
9. forty-niners
10. Mariposa War

Understanding Main Ideas

SECTION 1
1. What events led Texans to declare their independence from Mexico?
2. How did the Texas Revolution affect Tejanos?

SECTION 2
3. How did the United States win the Mexican War?

SECTION 3
4. Why did American missionaries journey to the Far West?
5. How did American Indians in the Far West respond to American settlement?

SECTION 4
6. What led to the migration of the forty-niners?

Reviewing Themes

1. **Economic Development** How did the U.S. government assist citizens who wanted to conduct trade and acquire land in the Far West?
2. **Cultural Diversity** What were some consequences of the mingling of cultures in California during the gold rush?
3. **Global Relations** How did territorial expansion affect U.S. relations with Mexico and Great Britain?

Thinking Critically

1. **Hypothesizing** Why do you think most American settlers in Texas did not become loyal to Mexico?
2. **Comparing and Contrasting** How and why did Mexico and the United States view the annexation of Texas differently?
3. **Synthesizing** What survival strategies did American settlers use on the Oregon Trail?
4. **Identifying Values** How did religious beliefs affect settlement in the West?
5. **Taking a Stand** Was the California Gold Rush a positive or negative development for the area? Explain your answer.

Writing About History

Writing to Persuade Imagine that you are Sam Houston. The year is 1836. Write a letter to the people of Texas asking them to support the revolution against Mexico. Use the following graphic to organize your thoughts.

1. Reasons for the revolt	2. Consequences of losing the war

Strategies for Success

Review the **Strategies for Success** on *Distinguishing Fact from Opinion*. Then reconsider Ethan Allen Hitchcock's quotation below and answer the questions that follow.

> 66 Orders came last evening by express from Washington City directing General Taylor to move without any delay. . . . He is to expel any armed force of Mexicans who may cross that river. . . . Violence leads to violence, and if this movement of ours does not lead to others and to bloodshed, I am much mistaken. 99

1. What facts does Hitchcock provide?
2. What opinion does Hitchcock express? Which words signal the presence of this opinion?

Linking History and Geography

Study the map below. In which town did all three major trails meet? What other route passed through this town? Why would the town's location have made it such an important point?

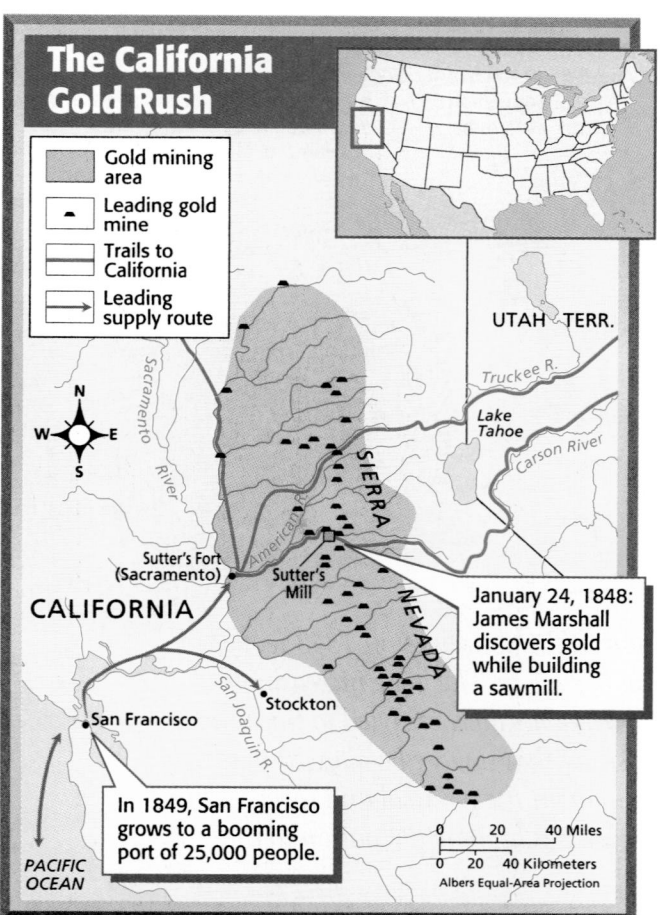

The California Gold Rush

Legend:
- Gold mining area
- Leading gold mine
- Trails to California
- Leading supply route

UTAH TERR.

Truckee R.

Lake Tahoe

Carson River

SIERRA NEVADA

Sacramento River

American

Sutter's Fort (Sacramento)

Sutter's Mill

CALIFORNIA

San Joaquin R.

Stockton

San Francisco

PACIFIC OCEAN

January 24, 1848: James Marshall discovers gold while building a sawmill.

In 1849, San Francisco grows to a booming port of 25,000 people.

0   20   40 Miles
0   20   40 Kilometers
Albers Equal-Area Projection

internet connect

TOPIC: The California Gold Rush
GO TO: go.hrw.com
KEYWORD: SD1 Gold

Accessing the Internet through the HRW Web site, learn what daily life and work was like for miners. Then imagine that you are a miner and write a series of "postcards" to your family on the East Coast. Tell them about your experiences.

BUILDING YOUR PORTFOLIO

Complete one or all of the following projects independently or cooperatively.

1 Geographic Diversity
Imagine that you are an American newspaper reporter in 1844. **Interview** *a Tejano, a Mexican government official, and a white Texas settler to obtain their views about the possible U.S. annexation of Texas.*

2 Global Relations
Imagine that you are a leader of the Cayuse Indians in 1850. **Write a short speech** *that explains why members of your tribe attacked the Whitman mission in 1847 and why you have now decided to surrender to U.S. officials.*

3 Cultural Diversity
Imagine that you are a Chinese immigrant during the California Gold Rush. **Write three diary entries** *that describe your reasons for coming to the United States, your experiences in the mining camps, and your plans for the future.*

1845–1861
Sectional Conflict Increases

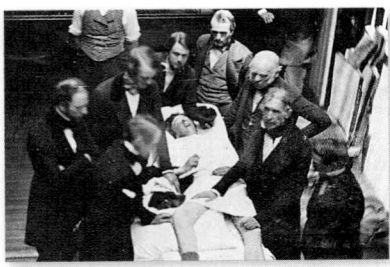

The first successful use of anesthesia in surgery

1847
The Arts
Benjamin Franklin White founds the Southern Musical Convention to promote multipart hymn singing, better known as sacred harp singing.

1849
World Events
Sponsored by wealthy U.S. southerners, Narciso López leads a force of volunteers in a failed revolution in Cuba.

Early locomotive

1846
Science and Technology
Ether is successfully used as anesthesia in surgery.

1850
Science and Technology
The Erie Railroad completes its 450-mile line running from the Hudson River to Lake Erie.

1844	1846	1848	1850	1852

1846
Daily Life
109 colleges are in operation throughout the United States.

1846
World Events
A severe year-long economic depression spreads across Europe.

1848
World Events
The Young Ireland Party turns to terrorism in an attempt to secure independence for Ireland.

1850
Business and Finance
About 65 percent of the U.S. population work as farmers.

1852
The Arts
Uncle Tom's Cabin As It Is, a play based on *Uncle Tom's Cabin,* opens in Baltimore, Maryland.

Poster for theatrical performance of Uncle Tom's Cabin

Weather vane depicting a farmer plowing

Before You Read

Build on What You Know

The U.S. acquisition of Mexican land in the Southwest in 1848 reopened the fierce debate over the extension of slavery. The issue increasingly divided the North and the South. While northerners tried to limit the expansion of slavery, white southerners insisted that slavery be allowed to spread into the West. In this chapter you will learn about the political and social battles that surrounded this issue and about the events that drew the nation to the brink of war.

British soldiers fighting in the Crimean War

Campaign pins for Stephen Douglas and Abraham Lincoln

1853
The Arts
The American Art Union closes its doors after operating for 13 years and distributing 2,400 works of art to its members.

1855
Politics
Pro-slavery Missouri residents cross into Kansas to cast votes for a pro-slavery legislature.

1856
World Events
The Crimean War ends as Russian forces yield to the British and French military forces.

1857
Politics
The U.S. Supreme Court rules that Dred Scott is not entitled to his freedom.

1858
Politics
The Lincoln-Douglas debates take place in Illinois.

1860
Business and Finance
U.S. imports total more than $3.5 million.

1861
Politics
The Confederate States of America is formed.

1854 **1856** **1858** **1860** **1862**

1853
Science and Technology
The Exhibition of the Industry of All Nations opens, showcasing American industrial technology.

1857
Business and Finance
An economic panic sets off a short depression in the United States.

1858
Science and Technology
The first transatlantic message is sent via cable.

1860
Daily Life
Godey's Lady's Book has approximately 150,000 subscribers.

Exhibition of the Industry of All Nations

Godey's Lady's Book

Think About Themes

Decide whether you agree or disagree with the following statements. Note why in your journal.

Constitutional Heritage Different groups interpret the Constitution differently to justify their own deeply held beliefs.

Democratic Values In a democratic system of government, groups or individuals who hold minority opinions must always give way to the majority.

Geographic Diversity People in different geographic regions have deeply conflicting political interests.

SECTION 1

An Uneasy Balance

OBJECTIVES

Read to understand:
1. how the slavery issue affected the debate over the acquisition of Texas and Mexican territory
2. what role the slavery issue played in elections and political debates of the late 1840s
3. what the provisions of Henry Clay's proposal to Congress were
4. why some people opposed the Compromise of 1850

KEY TERMS

popular sovereignty
Wilmot Proviso
Free-Soil Party
fire-eaters
Compromise of 1850

KEY PEOPLE

Lewis Cass
David Wilmot
Zachary Taylor
Henry Clay
Daniel Webster
John C. Calhoun
Millard Fillmore

EYEWITNESSES TO History

66 *This meeting, in which no member from a non-slaveholding State was admitted to participate, . . . prepared and adopted a gag-resolution. . . . It was accordingly presented to the House the next day, admitted by a suspension of the rules, debarred [shut off] from all deliberation . . . and carried by yeas and nays, 122 to 74.* 99

—John Quincy Adams

President John Quincy Adams

Former president John Quincy Adams was a Massachusetts representative when he recalled how the House came to adopt a so-called gag rule. The rule prohibited "all petitions, memorials, and papers, relating to the abolition of slavery or the slave trade" from being debated, printed, read, or even mentioned in Congress. On December 20, 1837, Representative William Slade of Vermont had presented a petition opposing slavery signed by 500 citizens of his state. He wanted the petition to be submitted to a committee considering the abolition of slavery and the slave trade in the District of Columbia. Southern members of Congress voted to adjourn the meeting. They met privately and drafted the gag resolution, which the House quickly passed. The gag rule prevented any similar petitions from even being discussed!

The Debate Reopens

The gag rule was a clear sign that tensions had mounted over the issue of slavery. The Missouri Compromise of 1820 had not ended the debate over the spread of slavery. Congress had admitted Arkansas and Michigan to the Union without dispute in 1836 and 1837, respectively. The balance of power in Congress remained the same, however, because Arkansas allowed slavery whereas Michigan did not. Slavery continued to trouble many citizens and politicians. Congressional debates dealing with the subject often ended in violence. Some representatives even carried Bowie knives into the House chamber. The tension erupted in February 1838, when two members of Congress—one from Maine and the other a slaveholder from Kentucky—fought a duel in which the northerner was fatally wounded.

Intense debates over slavery like this one took place on the floor of Congress.

The annexation of Texas. Further trouble arose when the Republic of Texas petitioned for annexation to the United States. The addition of Texas, which permitted slavery, would tip the balance of power in the Senate toward the slave states. Northerners responded with resolutions angrily opposing the annexation.

In 1845 Congress settled the issue on terms favorable to the South. Congress not only admitted Texas as a slave state but also added that the state legislature could divide Texas into as many as five states if it wished. At the same time, Congress extended westward the dividing line that had been set by the Missouri Compromise. The Missouri Compromise had banned slavery in the Louisiana Territory north of 36°30′—Missouri's southern boundary.

Popular sovereignty and the Wilmot Proviso.
The annexation of Texas did not resolve the issue of slavery. The prospect of victory in the Mexican War of 1846 revived the debate. The United States faced the question of whether slavery would be allowed in any territory acquired from Mexico. Pro-slavery and antislavery forces in Congress quickly took sides.

To quiet the debate, President James Polk and others suggested extending the Missouri Compromise line westward to the Pacific Ocean. Michigan senator Lewis Cass and Illinois senator Stephen Douglas proposed instead that the territories rely on **popular sovereignty**. This would allow the citizens of each new territory to vote on whether to permit slavery there.

Neither proposal satisfied the hard-liners. In August 1846, as the House began to consider a bill authorizing funds to buy territory from Mexico after the war, Representative David Wilmot of Pennsylvania introduced an amendment to the bill. His **Wilmot Proviso** banned slavery in all lands that would be acquired from Mexico. The House generally split along regional lines in its debates on the amendment. Eventually, all but one northern state rallied to its support. The southern states, however, threatened to secede if it became a law. Some southern politicians suggested cutting off all commercial relations with the North. Others proposed refusing to pay debts owed to northern banks and merchants. The Wilmot Proviso was cut from the final bill, much to Wilmot's dissatisfaction. "So dangerous do I believe the spirit and demands of the *Slave Power,* . . . if I saw the way open to strike an effectual [effective] and decisive blow against its domination at this time, I would do so."

✔ **READING CHECK:** Why did conflicts arise during the discussion of the annexation of Texas and Mexican territory?

CONGRESSIONAL SCALES,
A TRUE BALANCE

The 1848 Election

Victory in the Mexican War gave the United States much of Mexico's northern territory. However, as the national election of 1848 approached, Congress still had not settled the issue of whether slavery would be allowed in the Mexican Cession. As their presidential nominee, the Democrats chose Lewis Cass of Michigan. Cass favored popular sovereignty and had publicly denounced the Wilmot Proviso. The Whigs nominated a candidate whose political views were unknown—Mexican War hero General Zachary Taylor. His supporters organized political rallies under the banner "Independent" or "No Party" to present Taylor as a man above party politics. Taylor had made no public statement regarding the Wilmot Proviso, leading a Washington newspaper to call him the "candidate who can receive the support of the North and the South." The fact that Taylor held slaves, however, led both northerners and southerners to assume that he was sympathetic to pro-slavery views.

Angered by the reluctance of either party to address the slavery issue, antislavery Whigs and Democrats formed the **Free-Soil Party** in August 1848. The Free-Soilers demanded that Congress prohibit the expansion of slavery into the territories. Appealing to farmers, land reformers, and some industrial workers of the North and West, the Free-Soil platform supported free western homesteads as

Congressional scales. The proposal of the Wilmot Proviso to ban slavery in all lands acquired from Mexico outraged supporters of southern rights. *How does this cartoon depict the challenges that Zachary Taylor faces as he tries to work with pro-slavery and antislavery legislators?*

The Free-Soil Party drew support from a wide variety of Americans.

well as federal funding for internal improvements. Proclaiming "Free Soil, Free Speech, Free Labor, and Free Men," the party nominated former Democratic president Martin Van Buren.

The Free-Soil Party received just some 291,000 votes out of the nearly 2.9 million cast. However, it won enough Democratic votes in the key state of New York to enable the Whig candidate, Taylor, to win the election by a slim margin. Free-Soil candidates also won several seats in the House of Representatives. More important, the presence of the Free-Soil Party showed that politicians could not continue to ignore the slavery question.

The Slavery Issue in Congress

When Congress assembled in December 1849, tempers ran high over the slavery issue. Members of the House of Representatives voted 63 times and exchanged bitter threats before electing a Speaker. Congress was particularly divided over California and New Mexico—the territories of the Mexican Cession. California sought to enter the Union as a free state. Its voters supported a constitutional provision that "neither slavery nor involuntary servitude . . . shall ever be tolerated in this state." President Taylor urged Congress to admit California as a free state. Southern members of Congress, however, strongly opposed such action. The two sides clashed over New Mexico as well. Antislavery members of Congress pushed to ban slavery from the territory. Southern members, on the other hand, demanded a resolution affirming the right of settlers there to own slaves.

Arguments over other questions involving slavery also echoed through the halls of Congress. Texas became a source of conflict again, as it claimed that its boundary extended westward into an area the federal government considered part of the New Mexico territory. Antislavery members of Congress responded by declaring their intentions of limiting the slaveholding state's size. Pro-slavery forces also called for a tougher fugitive slave law. In 1842 the Supreme Court had ruled that state officials did not have to assist federal officials in capturing runaway slaves. Southerners now wanted a law that forced state officials to help with this task. Southern members of Congress also resisted a plan to abolish the slave trade in the District of Columbia and continued to block efforts to prohibit slavery in the territories.

✔ **READING CHECK:** What role did the slavery issue play in the elections and political debates of the late 1840s?

INTERPRETING THE VISUAL RECORD

The slavery debate. Elder statesman Henry Clay urged senators to reach a compromise on slavery. *How does this engraving show the urgency of the slavery debate and the need to find a compromise?*

Clay's Proposal

Early in 1850, a weary and ill Henry Clay returned to Congress after a long absence. He again urged northern and southern senators to compromise. "All society," he explained, "is formed upon the principle of mutual concession [compromise]." Meeting with his rival Daniel Webster, the veteran Whig leader, Clay presented a plan for satisfying both northern and southern interests. Encouraged by Webster's response, Clay presented his proposal to the Senate.

African American Population in 1850

Learning from Maps Just 5 percent of enslaved Africans were brought to British North America. Due to relatively low death rates, however, African Americans made up some 35 percent of all people of African descent living in the Western Hemisphere in 1825.

? PLACE In which states did African Americans make up a majority of the population?

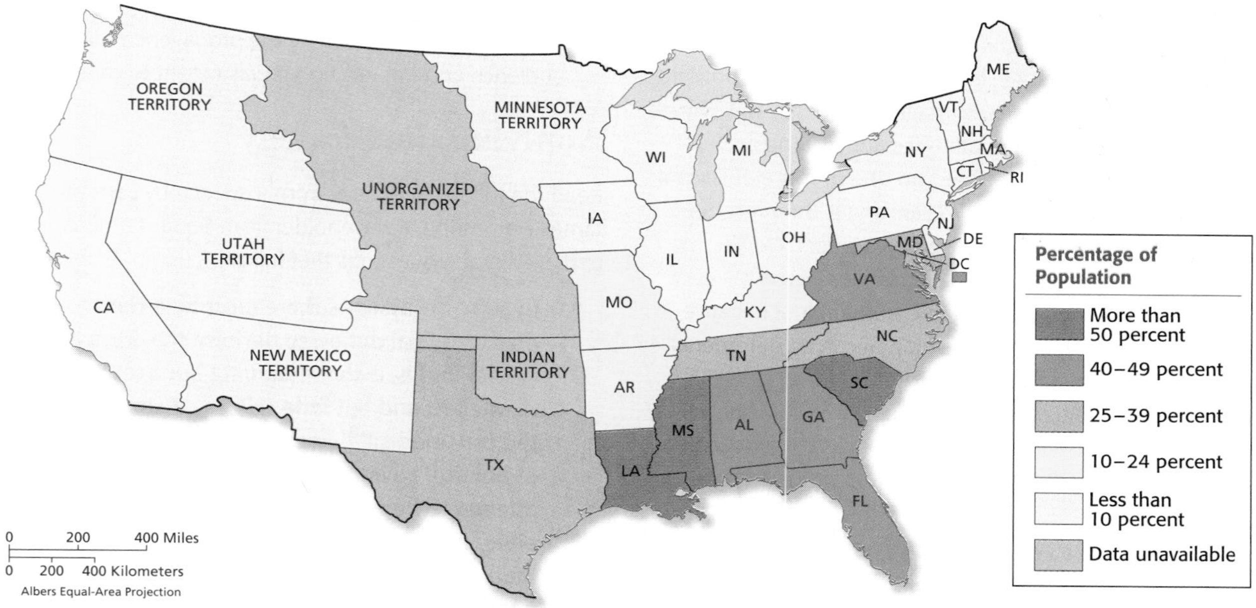

Percentage of Population

- More than 50 percent
- 40–49 percent
- 25–39 percent
- 10–24 percent
- Less than 10 percent
- Data unavailable

0   200   400 Miles
0   200   400 Kilometers
Albers Equal-Area Projection

To satisfy northern antislavery interests, Clay proposed admitting California as a free state and abolishing the slave trade—though not slavery itself—in the District of Columbia. He also advocated paying Texas $10 million to abandon its claim to the eastern part of the New Mexico Territory. To persuade southerners to accept these terms, Clay suggested that the New Mexico Territory be divided into two territories—New Mexico and Utah—on the basis of popular sovereignty. Finally, he added that Congress should pass a tougher fugitive slave law. This law would force state and local officials as well as private citizens to aid federal officials in the capture and return of escaped slaves.

Clay closed his speech by urging the lawmakers to put aside their sectional differences and prevent the breakup of the Union. Despite his pleas, angry calls from both northern and southern lawmakers supported the end of the Union.

Most of the northerners who supported the breakup of the Union were abolitionists. The southerners who did so were known as **fire-eaters**—a group of southern political leaders who held extreme pro-slavery views. Fire-eaters called for slavery to be protected by federal law or constitutional amendment and, even as early as the 1830s, for secession from the Union and the formation of a southern confederacy. Some of the fire-eaters, such as South Carolina's Robert Barnwell Rhett, represented the South in Congress. Rhett once said of his desire to protect the South: "Let it be, that I am a Traitor. The word has no terrors for me." He differed from most other southerners in that he had hoped the Wilmot Proviso would pass, for he believed it would provide the South with the motivation to secede.

✔ **READING CHECK:** What were the basic elements of Clay's proposal to Congress?

Edmund Ruffin of Virginia was one of the leading fire-eaters.

Recognizing Propaganda

Recognizing and interpreting propaganda are important aspects of the study of history. *Propaganda* is mass communication that is designed to win popular support for an issue, policy, or cause. It appeals primarily to emotion rather than reason and uses images, language, and symbols to influence people's attitudes and actions.

Most propaganda is based on one or more of several fundamental techniques. *Card-stacking* is the presentation of just one side of an issue or argument. *Name-calling* is the attachment of offensive—and usually misleading—labels to opponents to cast them in a negative light. *Sloganeering* is the repetition of catchy statements instead of well-reasoned arguments. *Bandwagoning* involves demanding support for a cause merely because it is popular. *Endorsements* are testimonials by famous people that propagandists use to gain support for a cause.

How to Recognize Propaganda

1. **Determine the context.** When you encounter a potential piece of propaganda, take note of its producers and the historical context in which it was produced. This information often makes it easier to understand the specific message being conveyed.
2. **Identify the message.** Read the item carefully and identify its central message. Pay particular attention to any emotionally charged language or visual imagery that the propaganda uses.
3. **Identify the techniques at work.** Identify the techniques that the item uses to convey its message.

4. **Determine the purpose.** Use your understanding of the propaganda, along with your knowledge of the historical period, to determine the propaganda's intended audience and the reaction it was meant to cause.

Applying the Strategy

Read the following excerpt from a speech by Senator James Hammond, a slaveholder from South Carolina, and answer the questions that follow.

66 In all social systems there must be a class to do the menial duties, to perform the drudgery of life. That is, a class requiring but a low order of intellect and but little skill. . . . It constitutes the very mud-sill [lowest level] of society and of political government; and you might as well attempt to build a house in the air, as to build either the one or the other, except on this mud-sill. Fortunately for the South, she found a race adapted to that purpose to her hand. . . . We use them for our purpose, and call them slaves. 99

Practicing the Strategy

1. What is the central message of the passage?
2. What propaganda techniques does Senator Hammond employ in his speech?
3. Who do you think Hammond was trying to persuade in the passage?

Read More About It

Free Find:

John C. Calhoun
After reading the biography on John C. Calhoun on the **Holt Researcher** CD–ROM, create a political profile of him. Be sure to give details of Calhoun's life and explain his position on important political issues of the era.

The Great Debate in Congress

For the next seven months Congress heatedly debated Clay's proposal. One of the most bitter attacks came from John C. Calhoun. Calhoun was the South's elder statesman and a leading fire-eater with pro-slavery views.

BIOGRAPHY

John C. Calhoun

THE GRANGER COLLECTION, NEW YORK

Calhoun was born in South Carolina in 1782 to parents of Scotch-Irish descent. His father, a prosperous slaveholding planter, had earlier served in the state legislature and opposed the ratification of the U.S. Constitution. Calhoun possessed a great love of learning and books. Reading southern newspapers reinforced for him a taste for politics. Calhoun graduated from Yale College in 1804 and spent the next year at a law school in Litchfield, Connecticut.

In 1810 Calhoun won election to the House of Representatives and began his long political career. Over the next 39 years, he also served as senator, secretary of war, secretary of state, and vice president. By the 1820s Calhoun was a strong supporter of southern rights. The debates over slavery in the Mexican Cession convinced him that the only adequate guarantee for the South's rights would be a dual presidency. One president would come from the North and another from the South.

Calhoun played a key role in the debates of 1850. Although he did not live to see the results of these debates, he remained a powerful supporter of the South until his death that year. Shortly before Calhoun's death, visitors to the U.S. Capitol watched intently as he was helped into the Senate chamber. Too ill to speak, he sat in silence as his speech was read. In it, Calhoun warned:

Daniel Webster spoke out in favor of Clay's compromise, outraging many northern anti-slavery members of Congress.

66 If something decisive is not now done . . . , the South will be forced to choose between abolition and secession. . . . The responsibility of saving the Union rests on the North, and not the South. 99

Daniel Webster of Massachusetts spoke out supporting Clay's proposal. Many northern members of Congress objected to Webster's speech and to Clay's compromise measures, arguing that compromise on slavery was wrong.

President Taylor did not live to see the outcome of the debate. He died suddenly in July 1850. Taylor, who had opposed Clay's compromise proposal, was succeeded by Vice President Millard Fillmore, who favored it. By September 20, Congress had passed Clay's measures, known as the **Compromise of 1850**.

✔ **READING CHECK:** Why did some people oppose the Compromise of 1850?

SECTION 1 REVIEW

Define and explain the significance of the following terms:
popular sovereignty
Wilmot Proviso
Free-Soil Party
fire-eaters
Compromise of 1850

Identify and explain the significance of the following individuals:
Lewis Cass
David Wilmot
Zachary Taylor
Henry Clay
Daniel Webster
John C. Calhoun
Millard Fillmore

1. **Using Graphic Organizers** Many northerners and southerners opposed the Compromise of 1850, but for different reasons. Copy the graphic organizer below. Use it to explain both views of the compromise.

2. **Understanding Geography: Place** How was the debate over slavery affected by the acquisition of Texas and the Mexican Cession?

3. **Identifying Cause and Effect** What led to the formation of the Free-Soil Party, and how did the party influence the outcome of the 1848 election?

4. **Taking a Stand** Imagine that you are a member of Congress participating in the debates about the terms of admitting California and the New Mexico territories into the Union. What stand would you take on the issue, and why?

Critical Thinking

5. Was the Compromise of 1850 a good solution to the conflict over slavery? Why or why not?
Consider:
• what the terms of the Compromise were and why it was proposed
• why some people objected to it
• what other solution might have achieved a peaceful resolution

Reasons for Northern Opposition

Compromise of 1850

Reasons for Southern Opposition

SECTION 2

Compromise Comes to an End

OBJECTIVES

Read to understand:

1. how northerners reacted to the enforcement of the Fugitive Slave Act
2. how people reacted to *Uncle Tom's Cabin*
3. what arguments were made against the Kansas-Nebraska Act, and why the Kansas elections led to escalating violence
4. what the goals of the Republican Party were, and why many Americans believed Douglas was siding with the party on the Kansas issue

KEY TERMS

Fugitive Slave Act
Kansas-Nebraska Act
Pottawatomie Massacre
Republican Party
Lecompton Constitution

KEY PEOPLE

Franklin Pierce
Winfield Scott
Harriet Beecher Stowe
John Brown
James Buchanan

KEY PLACES

Nebraska Territory
Kansas Territory

 EYEWITNESSES TO History

❝ *All the natural rights and claims and apologies are on the fugitive's side. He only did what any white man would be applauded for doing.* ❞
—Boston Newspaper

Boston poster protesting the capture of a suspected fugitive slave

The editors of a Boston newspaper were reacting to an incident that had stirred abolitionist sentiments in their city. Four slaves escaped from a Maryland plantation to a town in Pennsylvania in the 1850s, where an escaped slave named William Parker already lived. Parker had resolved to "assist in liberating everyone within my reach, at the risk of my own life." When he learned that the fugitives' owner was coming to capture them, he gathered the fugitives, along with other African Americans, in his house. Armed with pistols and muskets, they intended to protect the former Maryland slaves. In the ensuing conflict, the slaveowner and his son were beaten, and their posse was driven from the area. The episode drew widespread publicity throughout the South, with newspapers calling for the immediate punishment of the African Americans. Many northerners, however, supported the escaped slaves.

The Early 1850s

Although the Compromise of 1850 did not satisfy all Americans, most were hopeful that it had settled the slavery question. To tap into this optimistic mood, both major political parties adopted platforms supporting the compromise.

The election of 1852. At their 1852 convention the Democrats united behind Franklin Pierce of New Hampshire, a strong supporter of the Compromise of 1850. The Pierce managed to persuade people on both sides of the slavery issue that he shared their views. Some Free-Soilers, convinced that Pierce could hold the South in check, returned to the Democratic Party. Southerners in the meantime generally agreed that Pierce was "sound on all southern questions."

Having won the presidency in 1848 with General Zachary Taylor, the Whigs turned to another Mexican War hero, General Winfield Scott. However, southern Whigs did not believe Scott would enforce the Compromise of 1850. His campaign created little excitement among voters. The Free-Soil Party candidate, John P. Hale, also inspired little enthusiasm. Pierce won the election by a landslide. In his inaugural address, he called for national harmony and proceeded to appoint a cabinet that included both southerners and northerners. Pierce proved to be a weak leader, however, unable to control his diverse cabinet or to convince northerners that he was not caving in to southern pressure. Abolitionists labeled him a "northern man with southern principles."

The Democratic Party nominated Franklin Pierce for president in 1852.

The Fugitive Slave Act. The Compromise of 1850 began to fall apart even before Pierce's election, largely because of the inclusion of the **Fugitive Slave Act**. The law made it a federal crime to assist runaway slaves. It also authorized the arrest of escaped slaves even in states where slavery was illegal, and therefore met with vigorous opposition in the North.

Northerners came face to face with the inhumanity of the Fugitive Slave Act. After witnessing a slave catcher at work, Caroline Seabury wrote in her diary.

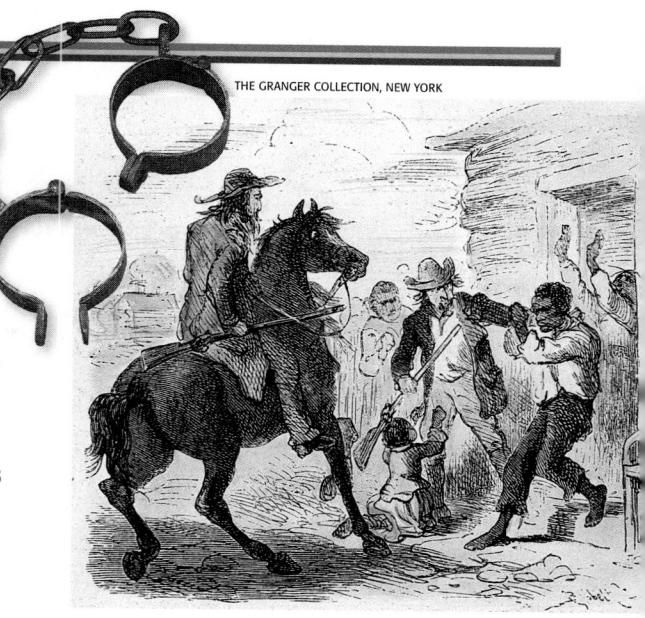

THE GRANGER COLLECTION, NEW YORK

66 We saw . . . a man on horseback riding at a quick pace, & by his side a tall negro coming steadily along. . . . We saw one chain going from his wrists to the saddle, another was around his ankles—giving him just room enough to walk—following them were two large thick-headed fierce-looking dogs. 99

As such scenes became more common, northerners reacted with horror. Abolitionist Frederick Douglass urged "forcible resistance." A former slave himself, Douglass protested that the Fugitive Slave Act made northerners "the mere *tools* and *body-guards* of the tyrants of Virginia and Carolina."

Even supporters of the Compromise of 1850 were shocked by the government's enforcement of the Fugitive Slave Act. Many northerners supported the passage of "personal liberty" laws that guaranteed legal assistance to captured runaway slaves. Amos A. Lawrence, a northern Democrat, voiced a common sentiment: "We have submitted to slavery long enough, and must not stand it any longer. . . . I am done catching [African Americans] for the South."

Some northerners took direct action. In New York and Massachusetts, angry mobs freed runaway slaves who had been taken into custody and helped them on their way to freedom in Canada. One observer wrote, "We went to bed one night old fashioned conservative Compromise Union Whigs and waked up stark mad Abolitionists."

✔ **READING CHECK:** In what ways did northerners react to the enforcement of the Fugitive Slave Act?

INTERPRETING THE VISUAL RECORD
Fugitive Slave Act. Many antislavery northerners opposed the Compromise of 1850, which authorized the forcible capture of runaway slaves in free states. *Does this engraving represent a northern or southern perspective? Explain your answer.*

Antislavery Literature

Abolitionists from the North and the Midwest used their pens to win people to their cause. These men and women hoped that their appeals, which were directed at the general public, would be more persuasive than political speeches and maneuverings. Their object, according to writer and abolitionist Lydia Maria Child, was "to change public opinion on the subject of slavery, by the persevering [continuing] utterance of truth."

Uncle Tom's Cabin. During the 1830s and 1840s, works by writers Ralph Waldo Emerson and Henry David Thoreau introduced antislavery ideas to an increasing number of Americans. The publication of Harriet Beecher Stowe's *Uncle Tom's Cabin* in the early 1850s proved particularly significant.

Read More About It

Free Find:
Harriet Beecher Stowe
After reading the biography on Harriet Beecher Stowe on the **Holt Researcher** CD–ROM, write a short book review of her novel *Uncle Tom's Cabin* that might have appeared when it was published.

BIOGRAPHY

Harriet Beecher Stowe

Harriet Beecher Stowe was born in 1811, the seventh child of fiery evangelical preacher Lyman Beecher and his wife, Roxana. Harriet turned to books at a young age and entered an academy for girls in 1819. At the age of 13, Harriet Beecher attended a female seminary run by her older sister Catharine. She remained at the school for eight years. She learned Latin, wrote poetry, shared her religious beliefs with other students, and served as editor of the school literary magazine. After finishing her studies, she remained at the academy as a full-time teacher.

By 1832 Harriet Beecher had begun to write textbooks for children. Her text *Primary Geography for Children* (1833) quickly went through five additional printings. Her first book for adults, *The Mayflower, or Sketches of Scenes and Characters Among the Descendants of the Pilgrims,* appeared in 1843.

In 1836 Harriet Beecher married Calvin Stowe, a teacher and minister who was interested in the British antislavery movement. By the end of the decade, Harriet Beecher Stowe had herself become involved in the abolitionist movement. In a letter, her sister suggested, "If I could use a pen as you can, I would write something that would make this whole nation feel what an accursed thing slavery is." Her sister's words inspired Harriet Beecher Stowe to make a decision. According to one of her children, she rose from her chair and declared, "I will write something. I will if I live." By March 1851 she had written the first parts of what would become *Uncle Tom's Cabin.* The work was serialized in an abolitionist newspaper before being published as a finished book in 1852.

The book brought Harriet Beecher Stowe immediate fame. In 1853 she followed it up with *A Key to Uncle Tom's Cabin,* a collection of documentary evidence that supported her attack on slavery. Stowe died in 1896.

Reactions to *Uncle Tom's Cabin.* *Uncle Tom's Cabin* showed how slavery broke up African American families and made a mockery of pro-slavery arguments. It depicted slavery in its many forms, from the harsh sugar plantations to the homes of slaveholders to the plight of runaway slaves. The book struck a chord with many northern readers. It helped to justify their feelings that slavery was morally wrong and should be abolished. After selling 300,000 copies within nine months, *Uncle Tom's Cabin* went on to sell more than 2 million copies by the end of the 1850s in the United States alone. Philadelphia lawyer and writer Sidney George Fisher called *Uncle Tom's Cabin* "the great book of the year," noting that it presented a "faithful picture of American slavery." Other readers were equally enthusiastic. "We have nothing like it in the previous history of books," declared one reviewer.

Although the book sold quickly in the North, southern audiences hated it. Southerner Margaret Johnson Erwin wrote to a friend, "*UTC* [*Uncle Tom's Cabin*] is the WORST piece of ENDLESS misrepresentation that I have ever read." The novel was banned in many parts of the South, where authors quickly wrote other novels that attempted to defend slavery. In the three years following its publication, at least 14 pro-slavery novels appeared.

Harriet Beecher Stowe's novel **Uncle Tom's Cabin** *sold hundreds of thousands of copies and helped convince many Americans of the moral wrongs of slavery.*

✔ **READING CHECK:** How did people react to *Uncle Tom's Cabin?*

AMERICAN Letters

Slave Narratives

In the 1840s and 1850s the narratives of slaves who had escaped from the South were very popular among northern readers. Frederick Douglass's Narrative of the Life of Frederick Douglass, *published in 1845, is the most famous of these works. In the excerpt below Douglass describes the harsh conditions on a Maryland farm. In* Incidents in the Life of a Slave Girl, *Harriet Jacobs describes how, to escape extremely cruel conditions, she sought refuge in the attic of her grandmother's home. She remained there for the next seven years until she and her children were able to flee to the North.*

from *Narrative of the Life of Frederick Douglass*
by Frederick Douglass

I was now, for the first time during a space of more than seven years, made to feel the painful gnawings of hunger. . . . I have said Master Thomas was a mean man. He was so. Not to give a slave enough to eat is regarded as

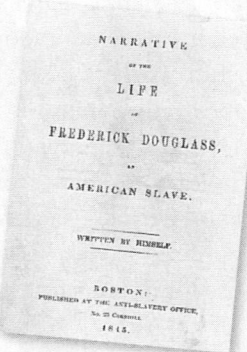

Title page of Frederick Douglass's autobiography

the most aggravated development of meanness even among slaveholders. The rule is, no matter how coarse the food, only let there be enough of it. This is the theory; and in the part of Maryland from which I came, it is the general practice,—though there were many exceptions. Master Thomas gave us of neither coarse nor fine food. . . . It was not enough for us to subsist upon. We were therefore reduced to the wretched necessity of living at the expense of our neighbors. This we did by begging and stealing, whichever came handy in the time of need. . . . A great many times have we poor creatures been nearly perishing with hunger, when food in abundance lay smouldering in the safe and smoke-house, and our pious mistress was aware of the fact; and yet that mistress and her husband would kneel every morning, and pray that God would bless them in basket and store!

from *Incidents in the Life of a Slave Girl*
by Harriet Jacobs

The garret [attic] was only nine feet long and seven wide. The highest part was three feet high, and sloped down abruptly to the loose board floor. There was no admission for either light or air. . . . To this hole I was conveyed as soon as I entered the house. The air was stifling; the darkness total. A bed had been

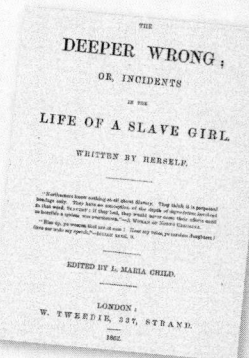

Title page of Harriet Jacobs's memoirs

spread on the floor. I could sleep quite comfortably on one side, but the slope was so sudden I could not turn on the other without hitting the room. The rats and mice ran over my bed; but I was weary, and I slept such sleep as the wretched may, when a tempest has passed over them. Morning came. I knew it only by the noises I heard; for in my small den day and night were all the same. I suffered for air even more than for light. But I was not comfortless. I heard the voices of my children. There was joy and there was sadness in the sound. It made my tears flow.

UNDERSTANDING LITERATURE

1. In the excerpt from Frederick Douglass's story, how does slaveholder treatment affect the slaves' behavior?
2. How would you describe the setting in the excerpt from Harriet Jacobs's story?
3. What different images of the hardships of slavery do the two writers convey?

Settling Kansas. With the extension of railroads and the organization of the Kansas Territory, many Americans headed west to settle the area. *What appeals does this poster make to settlers?*

The Kansas-Nebraska Act

The debate over the spread of slavery revived in early 1854. Illinois senator Stephen Douglas was an enthusiastic believer in westward expansion. He declared his support for settlement on the western prairies and construction of a railroad from Chicago, Illinois, to the Pacific Coast. Construction of the railroad, however, would require Congress to organize the western lands. This meant reopening the issue of whether slavery would be allowed in the West. Hoping to quiet congressional debate, Douglas introduced the **Kansas-Nebraska Act**, which organized the territories of Kansas and Nebraska on the basis of popular sovereignty.

The Kansas-Nebraska Act repealed the Missouri Compromise. It allowed the new states formed from the territories to "be received into the Union with or without slavery, as their constitution may prescribe at the time of their admission." Passage of the act in May 1854 renewed southern hopes of expanding slavery but outraged antislavery northerners. The *New York Times* denounced the Kansas-Nebraska Act as part of a "great scheme for extending and perpetuating the supremacy of the Slave Power."

Not everyone opposed the Kansas-Nebraska Act solely on abolitionist grounds. Some critics had economic motives. If slavery were allowed to spread to the territories, they argued, it would force out white workers. These critics reasoned that employers would choose to use slave labor rather than hire wage laborers. The *National Era,* a Washington antislavery newspaper, charged that the Kansas-Nebraska Act was part of "an atrocious [evil] plot to exclude from a vast unoccupied region, immigrants from the Old World and free laborers from our own States." A western newspaper editor wrote that he opposed slavery because "it blights [causes disease] and mildews the white man whose lot [fate] is toil, and whose capital is his labor."

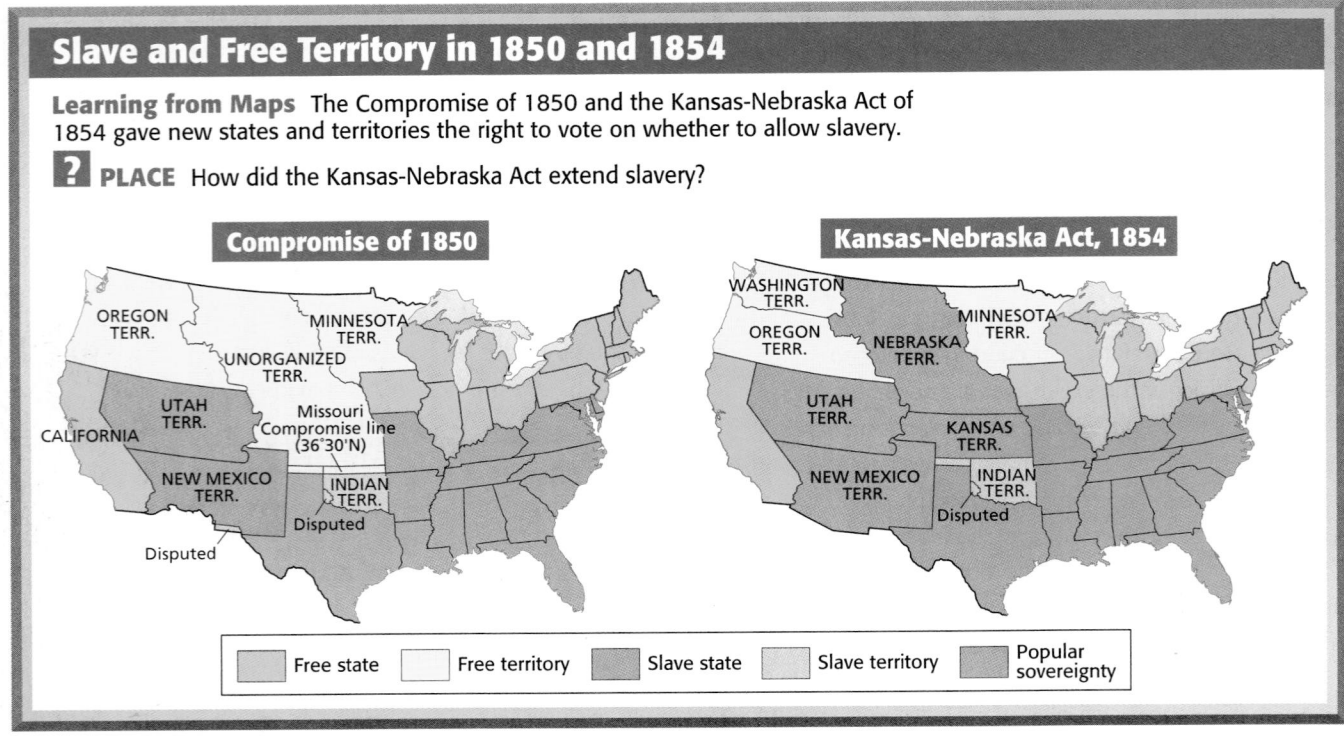

Slave and Free Territory in 1850 and 1854

Learning from Maps The Compromise of 1850 and the Kansas-Nebraska Act of 1854 gave new states and territories the right to vote on whether to allow slavery.

? PLACE How did the Kansas-Nebraska Act extend slavery?

Compromise of 1850

OREGON TERR.
MINNESOTA TERR.
UNORGANIZED TERR.
UTAH TERR.
CALIFORNIA
Missouri Compromise line (36°30'N)
NEW MEXICO TERR.
INDIAN TERR.
Disputed
Disputed

Kansas-Nebraska Act, 1854

WASHINGTON TERR.
OREGON TERR.
NEBRASKA TERR.
MINNESOTA TERR.
UTAH TERR.
KANSAS TERR.
NEW MEXICO TERR.
INDIAN TERR.
Disputed

Free state   Free territory   Slave state   Slave territory   Popular sovereignty

"Bleeding Kansas"

As tensions rose, William H. Seward of New York proclaimed to the Senate that the slave states had presented a challenge that he accepted "in behalf of the cause of freedom." The Kansas-Nebraska Act pitted antislavery and pro-slavery forces against one another for control of the new territories. To increase the number of antislavery settlers, New Englanders formed the Emigrant Aid Company to help antislavery families move to Kansas. Pro-slavery forces countered by urging southerners to migrate to the new territories. "We are playing for a mighty stake," warned Senator David Atchison of Missouri. "If we win, we carry slavery to the Pacific Ocean."

Kansas. As pro-slavery and anti-slavery settlers moved to Kansas, the threat of violence mounted. *How could photographs such as this one be seen as a warning to pro-slavery settlers?*

Elections in Kansas. Pro-slavery forces took action in March 1855. As Kansas settlers prepared to elect their first territorial legislature, some 5,000 pro-slavery Missouri residents crossed into the territory. In Douglas, a town with about 30 residents, more than 200 ballots were cast. Judges attempted to ensure that only permanent residents of the territory voted by making each voter swear a formal oath that they were citizens of the territory. Enforcement of this rule was difficult, however. One judge later recounted that some voters argued that the election should be open to all U.S. citizens. He also recalled open threats: "[Some people said] if I did not let them vote without swearing [taking the oath] that their men would get enraged and maybe hang me."

The illegal votes cast by the Missouri residents helped elect a pro-slavery legislature in Kansas. The new governing body immediately passed a code making it illegal to criticize slavery. It also banned newspapers that supported free states, abolitionist journals, and even the sermons of antislavery preachers. The pro-slavery press claimed victory, publishing articles that urged southerners to "bring your slaves and fill up the Territory." The antislavery settlers refused to recognize the legitimacy of this new government. They formed the Free State Party and elected their own legislature. As a result, Kansas had two territorial governments—one pro-slavery, the other antislavery—competing for control.

Pro-slavery settlers attack the antislavery settlement of Lawrence, Kansas.

Violence in Kansas. With two rival governments, conflict was inevitable. Pro-slavery raiders from Missouri attacked antislavery Kansas settlers. In May 1856 a pro-slavery mob of more than 700 invaded the town of Lawrence, Kansas, the headquarters of the Free State Party. They destroyed printing presses and the town library and set fire to the Free State Hotel.

In revenge, a group led by abolitionist John Brown attacked a pro-slavery settlement along Pottawatomie (pah-tuh-WAH-tuh-mee) Creek. The group dragged five men from their beds and brutally murdered them. The **Pottawatomie Massacre** enraged southerners, shocked northerners, and sparked more violence in what newspapers began calling "Bleeding Kansas." Even foreign journalists joined in the debate. A British journalist reported

THE GRANGER COLLECTION, NEW YORK

C.H.HAYES Sc

SOUTHERN CHIVALRY — ARGUMENT versus CLUB'S.

THE GRANGER COLLECTION, NEW YORK

Violence in the Senate.
Preston Brooks attacks Charles Sumner on the floor of the Senate. *Based on this image, what metaphor could be drawn from the object Sumner is using to defend himself?*

that the pro-slavery officials only used their power "that they might arrest, imprison, or hang Free-state men."

Brown and his followers went into hiding. Meanwhile, on Capitol Hill, the halls of Congress echoed the violence in Kansas. Among the most outspoken members of Congress was abolitionist senator Charles Sumner of Massachusetts. In his "Crime Against Kansas" speech, delivered on May 19–20, 1856, Sumner declared the Kansas-Nebraska Act "a swindle."

66 Slavery now stands erect, clanking its chains on the territory of Kansas, surrounded by a code of death, and trampling upon all cherished liberties. . . . It has been done for the sake of political power, in order to bring two new slaveholding senators upon this floor. 99

In addition, Sumner ridiculed pro-slavery senator Andrew Butler of South Carolina. Two days later, South Carolina representative Preston Brooks, a relative of Butler, struck back by savagely beating Sumner with a cane until it broke. The beating was so severe that Sumner did not recover from his injuries for several years. Admiring voters in Brooks's district showered him with presents of canes to replace the one he had broken in the assault. Whig leader David Davis wrote, however, that Brooks's shocking attack, coupled with the violence in Kansas, "made Abolitionists of those who never dreamed they were drifting into it."

✔ **READING CHECK:** What were the arguments made against the Kansas-Nebraska Act? Why did the Kansas elections lead to escalating violence?

The Republican Party

To carry their message to the nation, antislavery voters flocked to a new party gaining power in the North. In 1854 a group of antislavery Whigs and Democrats, together with some Free-Soilers, had organized a party firmly opposed to the expansion of slavery. Reviving the name of Thomas Jefferson's party, they called themselves the **Republican Party**.

Elections of 1854 and 1856. A number of state conventions drew up political platforms that opposed the extension of slavery and supported reform movements. The Republican Party worked together with the anti-immigrant, anti-Catholic American Party, or Know-Nothings, to defeat Democratic candidates in the congressional elections of 1854. By 1856 many of the antislavery Know-Nothings had joined the Republican Party. They nominated John C. Frémont for president. The party organized a campaign around the slogan "Free Soil, Free Speech, Free Men, Frémont, and Victory!"

The Democrats passed over incumbent Franklin Pierce, nominating James Buchanan of Pennsylvania for president instead. The party adopted a platform that supported the Kansas-Nebraska Act. The Know-Nothings and the remaining Whigs each nominated former president Millard Fillmore, who officially ran in the election as the American Party candidate.

The Democrats tried to paint the Republicans as the party of sectionalism. "The Union is in danger, and the people everywhere know it," stated Buchanan. Angry Republican speeches helped secure the Democratic victory. Republican

James Buchanan used campaign buttons such as this one during his 1856 bid for the presidency.

representative Joshua Giddings from Ohio, for example, declared that he looked forward to the day of "insurrection in the South, when the black man . . . shall assert his freedom and wage a war of extermination against his master." Election results revealed that Buchanan had won support in both slave and free states, receiving 174 electoral votes to Frémont's 114 and Fillmore's 8. Frémont, on the other hand, carried only free states, and Fillmore carried only Maryland. The election signaled the end of both the Whigs and the American Party.

The Lecompton Constitution. Meanwhile, tension remained high in Kansas. In 1857, voters elected delegates for the territory's upcoming constitutional convention. Suspecting that pro-slavery forces would rig the elections for delegates to the convention, the antislavery forces boycotted the elections. The constitutional convention, which was thus made up exclusively of pro-slavery delegates, met at Lecompton, Kansas. The delegates drafted a constitution that protected the rights of Kansas slaveholders. The **Lecompton Constitution** gave the voters of Kansas only the right to decide whether more slaves could enter the territory, not whether slavery should indeed exist in the territory.

Senator Stephen Douglas attacked the Lecompton Constitution, denouncing it as a fraud because it reflected only pro-slavery views. The constitution failed to meet Douglas's goal of popular sovereignty because it did not allow voters the right to outlaw slavery altogether. This stand cost Douglas much support among southerners. Many thought that Douglas was siding with the Republicans in order to prevent another slave state from entering the Union. Despite the eventual admission of Kansas as a free state in 1861, Douglas's principle of popular sovereignty had been largely discredited.

✔ **READING CHECK:** What were the goals of the Republican Party, and why did many Americans believe Douglas was siding with the new party on the Kansas issue?

The 1856 election. John C. Frémont, a well-known explorer who had scouted the Oregon Trail, ran for president opposing slavery. *How does this campaign poster capture Frémont's personal history and goals?*

SECTION  **REVIEW**

Define and explain the significance of the following terms:
Fugitive Slave Act
Kansas-Nebraska Act
Pottawatomie Massacre
Republican Party
Lecompton Constitution

Identify and explain the significance of the following individuals:
Franklin Pierce
Winfield Scott
Harriet Beecher Stowe
John Brown
James Buchanan

Locate and explain the importance of the following places:
Nebraska Territory
Kansas Territory

1. **Using Graphic Organizers** Copy the graphic organizer below. Use it to explain the different ways in which northerners and southerners reacted to *Uncle Tom's Cabin.*

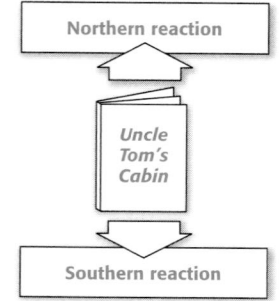

Northern reaction

Uncle Tom's Cabin

Southern reaction

2. **Assessing Consequences** How did enforcement of the Fugitive Slave Act affect northern public opinion of slavery?
3. **Analyzing** Why was the Kansas-Nebraska Act important? Why did it lead to so much controversy and violence?
4. **Identifying Values** How was the formation of the Republican Party a rejection of other parties' ideas?

Critical Thinking

5. Why did the policy of popular sovereignty fail to provide a solution to the slavery issue? How could it have succeeded?
Consider:
• the policy of popular sovereignty
• how the policy failed in the Lecompton Constitution
• how those factors could have been avoided

On the Brink of War

KEY TERMS

Dred Scott decision
Freeport Doctrine
Confederate States of America

KEY PEOPLE

Dred Scott
Roger B. Taney
Abraham Lincoln
Stephen Douglas
John Brown
John Bell
John Breckinridge
Jefferson Davis

EYEWITNESSES TO History

66 *When the people proclaimed their will the tempest at once subsided and all was calm. The voice of the majority, speaking in the manner prescribed by the Constitution, was heard, and instant submission followed. Our country alone could have exhibited so grand and striking a spectacle of the capacity of man for self-government.* 99

—James Buchanan

THE GRANGER COLLECTION, NEW YORK

James Buchanan's inaugural parade

On the day of his inauguration in March 1857, President James Buchanan presented an optimistic face to the people of the United States. The presidential election of 1856 reflected deep divisions within the country. In his inaugural address, however, Buchanan referred to the problems that had been dividing the American people as belonging to the past. Americans' belief in democracy and compromise had won, he argued. He also announced that the Supreme Court would soon decide a case that would clarify remaining questions about the future of slavery in the United States.

Dred Scott and the Supreme Court

The case that James Buchanan referred to in his inaugural address was that of Dred Scott, a slave held by John Emerson, an army surgeon from Missouri. Scott had accompanied Emerson when he served on army posts in the Midwest. Eventually, the two men returned to Missouri. In 1846, after Emerson's death, Scott sued for his freedom. He argued that his prior residence in the free state of Illinois and in the free Wisconsin Territory entitled him to freedom. The Missouri courts had already granted freedom to a number of slaves on similar grounds.

In 1856 the case reached the U.S. Supreme Court after moving through the lower courts. Chief Justice Roger B. Taney (TAW-nee), one of five southerners on the Court,

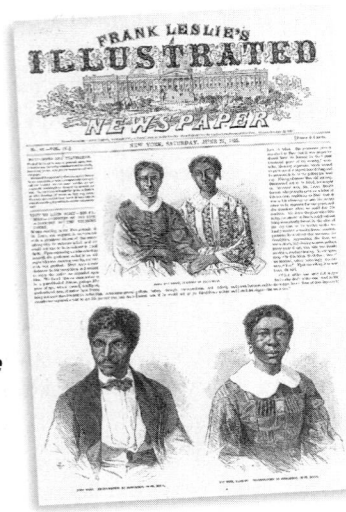

Newspapers such as this one described Dred Scott's life story and the Supreme Court decision against him.

wrote the majority opinion against Scott in March 1857. Taney declared that Scott was not a citizen and therefore could not bring suit in U.S. courts. The nation's founders, Taney asserted, had viewed African Americans as "beings of an inferior order" having "no rights which the white man was bound to respect." He concluded that no African American, slave or free, could ever enjoy the rights of a U.S. citizen.

In addition to rejecting Scott's claim, Taney denied that the federal government had any authority to limit the expansion of slavery. Taney based his decision on the view that the Missouri Compromise had violated the Fifth Amendment to the Constitution. This amendment forbids the government to deny anyone's right to property without "due process of law." Since slaves were legally classified as property, Taney asserted, Congress had acted unconstitutionally in barring slavery from the territory north of the 36°30′ latitude.

Although Dred Scott and his family were eventually freed by their owners, the ***Dred Scott* decision** outraged abolitionists and other opponents of the expansion of slavery. However, many antislavery leaders also saw the decision as an opportunity for action. The "fiercer the insult, the bitterer the blow, the better," exclaimed one abolitionist newspaper. African American leader Robert Purvis, speaking at a protest rally in the North, expressed the angry sentiments of the free African American community.

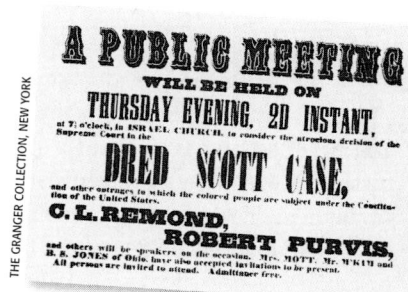

66 **This atrocious [very bad] decision furnishes final confirmation of the already well-known fact that, under the Constitution and government of the United States, the colored people are nothing and can be nothing but an alien, disfranchised [deprived of rights], and degraded class.** 99

After the passage of the Kansas-Nebraska Act and the Supreme Court's ruling in the *Dred Scott* case, there seemed no way to keep slavery from spreading into the territories. The struggle over slavery, declared Senator William Seward, had become an "irrepressible [uncontrollable] conflict."

✔ **READING CHECK:** Why did the Supreme Court rule as it did in the *Dred Scott* case?

Lincoln and Douglas

The debate over the *Dred Scott* decision continued to echo across the land. Many young politicians gained a reputation by taking a stand on these issues. The year after the *Dred Scott* decision, a political race in Illinois drew national attention as Republican Abraham Lincoln ran for a seat in the U.S. Senate. Lincoln had already served in the House of Representatives, but he had returned to practicing law in Springfield, Illinois, after just one term. The conflict over slavery and the Kansas-Nebraska Act prompted Lincoln's return to politics. In 1854, at the Illinois state fairgrounds in Springfield, he gave a speech attacking the act, which he said would raise slavery to a "sacred right." In the following few years, Lincoln continued to speak out against the expansion of slavery. In 1858 he ran against Senator Stephen Douglas, who was seeking a third term in the Senate.

Stephen Douglas

The Little Giant. Stephen Douglas was born in 1813 in Vermont. His father died when Douglas was just two months old, and he was raised by his mother on an uncle's farm. At the age of 15, Douglas left home to learn a trade. For eight months he served as an apprentice to a cabinetmaker. Douglas later traveled to New York to attend school.

Douglas eventually moved west, settling in Illinois, where he studied law. He became a lawyer at the age of 20 and enjoyed considerable success, winning a place on the Illinois Supreme Court seven years later. In 1843 Douglas was elected to the U.S. House of Representatives. Although small in stature, Douglas was a powerful public speaker and he soon became known as the Little Giant. In 1846 Douglas was elected to the Senate. As head of the Committee on Territories, Douglas helped draft the legislation by which several territories were admitted to the Union.

INTERPRETING THE VISUAL RECORD
Dred Scott. The Supreme Court's rejection of Dred Scott's claim to freedom and Chief Justice Roger B. Taney's denial of the federal government's right to limit slavery in newly acquired territories outraged many abolitionists. *How does this flier reveal the reaction many abolitionists had after the Dred Scott decision?*

Read More About It

Free Find:
Stephen Douglas
After reading the biography on Stephen Douglas on the **Holt Researcher** CD–ROM, imagine that you are hosting one of the Lincoln-Douglas debates. Compose a speech that introduces Stephen Douglas to the crowd of spectators.

Balancing Political Interests

In the 1850s the individual states held vastly different ideas concerning the issue of slavery. No question has so strongly divided the country since. Nevertheless, problems and concerns continue to arise, and states and regions often view them in a very different light. In the 1990s, pollution was one such issue, particularly as the northeastern region of the country experienced some of its worst smog problems ever.

Many of the country's industrial facilities, including power plants, are located in the Midwest. Because of prevailing wind patterns, air pollution produced by these factories often drifts to the Northeast. In 1997 eight northeastern states—including Connecticut, Massachusetts, and New York—turned to the Environmental Protection Agency (EPA) for help with this problem. The states petitioned the agency, demanding tougher laws on pollution-control. Other states in the region, however, felt that these states were asking for changes in pollution reduction too quickly. New Jersey, for instance, a major industrial state itself, parted from its neighbors and did not file a petition.

Not all states responded favorably to these demands for stricter pollution controls. Kentucky, Michigan, Missouri, and Ohio refused to lend their support to the measure. All of these states—with the exception of Michigan—would be forced under the new ruling to reduce pollution output by 40 percent or more. The problem of how to deal with the nation's pollution is just one example of issues that continue to divide the United States today.

Douglas strongly supported the policy of popular sovereignty. He opposed the Lecompton Constitution, which he believed had been adopted by pro-slavery forces through underhanded means. After President Buchanan spoke to Congress in 1857 to urge approval of the Lecompton Constitution, Douglas leaped to his feet to speak. "I have spent too much strength and breath, and health, too, to establish this great principle [of popular sovereignty] . . . now to see it frittered [wasted] away." Defying the president, a fellow Democrat, he continued: "If this constitution is to be forced down our throats, in violation of the fundamental principle of free government, . . . I will resist it to the last."

The Lincoln-Douglas debates. When selected to run against Douglas in the 1858 senatorial elections, Abraham Lincoln quoted from the Bible in his acceptance speech at the Republican Party's convention. He stated "A house divided against itself cannot stand." The nation, he argued, could not remain forever divided into slave and free states.

> 66 I believe this government cannot endure permanently half slave and half free. I do not expect the Union to be dissolved; I do not expect the house to fall; but I do expect it will cease to be divided. 99

Seeking statewide exposure, Lincoln challenged Douglas to a series of seven debates between August and October 1858. Douglas accepted the challenge but acknowledged that Lincoln was "the best stump speaker in the West." Throngs of people turned out at each event to hear the two men debate.

During the debates, Lincoln attacked the *Dred Scott* decision, which seemed to grant broad constitutional protection to slavery. "I do not believe it is a constitutional right to hold slaves in a territory of the United States," he declared. Like the Republican Party, Lincoln viewed slavery as "a moral, social, and political wrong." Although he was willing to tolerate slavery in the South, he firmly opposed its expansion in the territories.

In the heated debate at Freeport, Illinois, Lincoln challenged Douglas to explain how popular sovereignty was still workable in the wake of the *Dred Scott* decision. Douglas replied that the people of a territory could still keep slavery out simply by refusing to pass the local laws necessary to make a slave system work: "It matters not what way the Supreme Court may . . . decide. . . . The people have the lawful means to introduce [slavery] or exclude it as they please." This argument, which came to be called the **Freeport Doctrine**, helped Douglas narrowly defeat Lincoln in the U.S. Senate race.

✔ **READING CHECK:** What arguments did Lincoln and Douglas make about the slavery issue during their series of debates?

John Brown's Raid

The year after the Lincoln-Douglas debates, abolitionist John Brown, leader of the 1856 Pottawatomie Massacre, again captured the nation's attention. After fleeing Kansas, Brown made his way east. With money obtained from New England abolitionists, Brown armed a band of some 20 men, including five African Americans.

The attack on Harpers Ferry. On October 16, 1859, Brown's small force seized the federal arsenal at Harpers Ferry, Virginia. Brown planned to give the arsenal's guns to slaves living nearby and to establish an independent regime in the southern Appalachian Mountains. He hoped that runaway slaves and free African Americans would join him in his attempts to liberate slaves from their owners.

THE METROPOLITAN MUSEUM OF ART

Brown and his followers easily took possession of the armory and rifleworks. However, no slaves came to aid the group. In mid-October federal troops under the command of Colonel Robert E. Lee assaulted Brown's position, killing half of his men and capturing the rest.

Brown was convicted of "murder, criminal conspiracy, and treason against the Commonwealth of Virginia" and was hanged on December 2, 1859. Six of his followers were later executed as well. One of the condemned men, African American John Copeland, wrote his parents to assure them that he faced death with no regrets.

> 66 Remember that if I must die I die in trying to liberate a few of my poor and oppressed people from my condition of servitude. . . . I imagine that I hear you, and all of you, mother, father, sisters, and brothers, say—'No, there is not a cause for which we, with less sorrow, could see you die.' 99

Reactions to Brown. Though some people questioned Brown's sanity, many of his supporters remained convinced that he had acted justly and heroically. Sarah Everett, who supported his actions, demanded, "How is the great southern heart to be reached but by God's ministers of vengeance." Well-known abolitionists viewed Brown as a great moral figure. Writer Lydia Maria Child called him "a martyr [hero] to righteous principles" and offered to help Brown while he was in prison. Henry David Thoreau hailed him as "an angel of light."

In contrast, many southern whites, alarmed by the threat of slave revolts, viewed Brown as a bloodthirsty fanatic who deserved his punishment. Many southern secessionists, however, were actually pleased by the hysteria, believing that it helped their cause. The incident at Harpers Ferry, they believed, would result in the yeoman farmers and poor whites of the South supporting the planters' cause. The North "has sanctioned and applauded theft, murder, treason," exclaimed the pro-slavery *De Bow's Review,* "and . . . has shed Southern blood on Southern soil! There is—there can be no peace!" Tension also ran high in Congress. Senator James Hammond of South Carolina noted that "the only persons who do not have a revolver and a knife are those who have two revolvers."

INTERPRETING THE VISUAL RECORD

Harpers Ferry. John Brown and six others were executed for their seizure of a federal arsenal in Virginia. *How does this engraving portray Brown as a hero?*

✔ **READING CHECK:** How did northerners and southerners react to John Brown's raid?

The Election of 1860

Learning from Maps The election of 1860 clearly reflected the division between north and south. Lincoln's victory increased tensions between the regions, and secession soon followed.

? PLACE Which state had the most electoral votes? Which candidate won this state?

UNORGANIZED TERRITORY
WASHINGTON TERRITORY
OR 3
NEBRASKA TERRITORY
UTAH TERRITORY
CA 4
KANSAS TERR.
NEW MEXICO TERRITORY
Disputed
MN 4
WI 5
IA 4
MO 9
INDIAN TERR.
AR 4
TX 4
LA 6
MS 7
AL 9
GA 10
MI 6
IL 11
IN 13
OH 23
KY 12
TN 12
NC 10
SC 8
FL 3
VA 15
PA 27
NY 35
VT 5
NH 5
ME 8
MA 13
RI 4
CT 6
NJ 7*
DE 3
MD 8

CANDIDATE	PARTY	ELECTORAL VOTE	POPULAR VOTE	% OF POPULAR VOTE
Lincoln	Republican	180	1,865,593	39.8
Douglas	Northern Democrat	12	1,382,713	29.5
Breckinridge	Southern Democrat	72	848,356	18.1
Bell	Constitutional Union	39	592,906	12.6

*New Jersey cast four electoral votes for Lincoln and three for Douglas.

Source: *Historical Statistics of the United States*

The Election of 1860

Deeply divided, the nation approached the presidential election of 1860. Southern moderates formed the Constitutional Union Party. Nominating John Bell of Tennessee for president, they tried to play down sectional differences.

After two Democratic conventions, Stephen Douglas won the Democratic nomination for president. However, he lost the backing of southern Democrats. These southerners instead nominated Vice President John Breckinridge. Like many other southerners, Breckinridge interpreted the *Dred Scott* decision to mean that Congress had a duty to protect slavery in the territories.

The Republican Party nominated Abraham Lincoln, who seemed a more moderate choice than a strong abolitionist like William Seward. The Republicans designed their platform to attract northern industrialists and wage earners as well as midwestern farmers. The Republicans had little hope for success in the South and in the end did not even campaign in most southern states.

The election results mirrored the nation's sectional divisions. Breckinridge carried every state of the Lower South. Three states of the Upper South—Virginia, Kentucky, and Tennessee—favored Bell. Douglas, though second in the popular vote, won only Missouri and three of New Jersey's electoral votes. New Jersey's remaining votes went to Lincoln, along with those of the rest of the northern states and Oregon and California. Although Lincoln received only about 40 percent of the popular vote, his electoral victory was a landslide: 180 electoral votes to Breckinridge's 72, Bell's 39, and Douglas's 12.

✔ **READING CHECK:** What factors led to Lincoln's election in 1860?

Secession!

Despite Abraham Lincoln's moderate stance on slavery, many southerners viewed his victory as a victory for abolition. Lincoln's win particularly mobilized the Lower South. Within days of the election, the South Carolina legislature called a convention and unanimously voted to leave the Union. Alabama, Florida, Georgia, Louisiana, Mississippi, and Texas soon passed similar acts of secession. Early in 1861, delegates from six of the seven seceding states met in Montgomery, Alabama, and drafted a constitution for the **Confederate States of America**. This new constitution resembled the U.S. Constitution, with two key

Supporters displayed banners and medallions from Lincoln's 1860 presidential campaign.

exceptions: the Confederate constitution guaranteed the right to own slaves and it stressed that each state was "sovereign and independent." The delegates chose Mississippi planter and former U.S. senator and secretary of war Jefferson Davis as provisional president of the Confederacy.

As the Union dissolved, outgoing president James Buchanan announced that no state had the right to secede. However, he concluded that the federal government had no power to hold a state in the Union against its will. Caught in a dilemma, Buchanan let the incoming president deal with the problem.

The southern secessionists justified their position with the doctrine of states' rights. They asserted that since individual states had come together to form the Union, a state had the right to withdraw from the Union. Northerners countered with the argument that by ratifying the Constitution, the states had agreed to recognize it as the supreme law of the land. They argued that there could be no nation if a state was free to withdraw any time it did not like the actions of the federal government or of the majority of states.

The issue went beyond states' rights, however. Also at stake was the determination of the southerners to protect slavery. They feared that restricting slavery in the territories would ensure that the slave states remained a minority voting alliance. Then, eventually, the northern majority in Congress could not only prohibit slavery in the territories but also abolish it in the South.

Northern Republicans asserted that majority rule represented a fundamental principle of republican government. After taking office, President Lincoln spoke to a special session of Congress and argued that the South must accept the election results. "When ballots have [been] fairly, and constitutionally, decided," he said, "there can be no successful appeal back to bullets." Many in the South felt otherwise.

✔ **READING CHECK:** How did southerners and northerners differ in their opinions of secession?

THE SECEDING SOUTH CAROLINA DELEGATION.

INTERPRETING THE VISUAL RECORD

Secession. After Lincoln's election, delegates from South Carolina voted to secede from the Union. *Why do you think a major national publication like* Harper's Weekly *would put the delegates' portraits on its cover?*

SECTION 3 REVIEW

Define and explain the significance of the following terms:
Dred Scott decision
Freeport Doctrine
Confederate States of America

Identify and explain the significance of the following individuals:
Dred Scott
Roger B. Taney
Abraham Lincoln
Stephen Douglas
John Brown
John Bell
John Breckinridge
Jefferson Davis

1. **Using Graphic Organizers** Copy the graphic organizer below. Use it to explain the effect of John Brown's raid on public opinion in the North and the South and how it affected relations between the two regions.

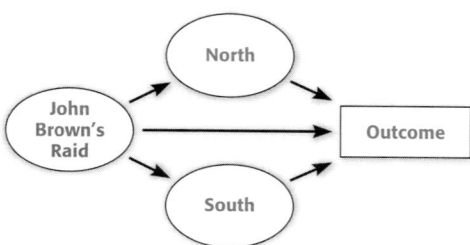

2. **Hypothesizing** Why did the Supreme Court rule as it did in the *Dred Scott* case? How would the conflict over slavery have been affected if the Court had ruled differently?

3. **Comparing and Contrasting** How did the views of Abraham Lincoln and Stephen Douglas regarding slavery and popular sovereignty differ? How were they similar?

4. **Distinguishing Fact from Opinion** Some secessionists argued that Lincoln's election proved that the slave states had lost their political power. Assess the validity of this argument.

Critical Thinking

5. Was secession justified? Why or why not?
   Consider:
   • arguments for secession
   • arguments against secession

CHAPTER 11

Review

Creating a Time Line

Copy the time line below onto a sheet of paper. Complete the time line by filling in the events and dates from the chapter that you think were most significant. Pick three events and explain why you think they were significant.

Writing a Summary

Using the Reading Checks as a guide, write an overview of the events in the chapter.

Identifying People and Ideas

Identify the following terms or individuals and explain their significance.

1. Stephen Douglas
2. popular sovereignty
3. Wilmot Proviso
4. Free-Soil Party
5. John C. Calhoun
6. Harriet Beecher Stowe
7. *Dred Scott* decision
8. Abraham Lincoln
9. Freeport Doctrine
10. John Brown

Understanding Main Ideas

SECTION 1

1. What proposals did Henry Clay and John C. Calhoun offer to end the disagreements between pro-slavery and antislavery forces?

SECTION 2

2. How did northern abolitionists use the written word to further their cause?
3. How did the actions of John Brown deepen the conflict over slavery?

SECTION 3

4. What were the goals of the Republican Party in 1860?
5. Why did the Lincoln-Douglas debates receive national attention?

Reviewing Themes

1. **Constitutional Heritage** How did the South use constitutional arguments to try to protect slavery?
2. **Democratic Values** How did Stephen Douglas try to use the principle of majority rule to end the debate over slavery in the territories?
3. **Geographic Diversity: Region** How did a region's geography contribute to people's support of or opposition to the expansion of slavery?

Thinking Critically

1. **Comparing and Contrasting** How do the terms of the Wilmot Proviso and the Compromise of 1850 compare to each other?
2. **Taking a Stand** Do you think antislavery northerners were justified in supporting John Brown's violent actions? Explain your answer.
3. **Using Historical Imagination** Imagine that you are an abolitionist writer. What style of literature would you use to convince your readers that slavery is morally wrong?
4. **Hypothesizing** How might the violence in Kansas have been avoided?
5. **Problem Solving** Once President Lincoln was elected, could he have done anything differently to stop secession? Explain your answer.

Writing About History

Writing to Explain Imagine that you are an aide to Senator Henry Clay in 1850. Write a proposal outlining some possible approaches to resolving the slavery issue. Use the following graphic to help organize your thoughts.

Conflicts over Slavery → Solutions

Strategies for Success

Review the **Strategies for Success** on *Recognizing Propaganda*. Then read the excerpt below from a speech by slavery opponent Carl Schurz.

> 66 Slaveholders of America, I appeal to you. Are you really in earnest when you speak of perpetuating slavery? Shall it never cease? Never? Stop and consider where you are and in what day you live. . . . This is the world of the nineteenth century. . . . You stand against a hopeful world, alone against a great century, fighting your hopeless fight . . . against the onward march of civilization. 99

Answer the following questions.
1. What is the central message of the passage?
2. What propaganda techniques does Schurz employ?
3. Whom, besides the "slaveholders of America," do you think Schurz was trying to reach in the passage?

Linking History and Geography

Study the map below. How soon after the pro-slavery attack on Lawrence did abolitionists strike back?

Bleeding Kansas in 1856

- ☀ Attack by abolitionists
- ☀ Attack by pro-slavery forces

Leavenworth

Missouri River

Kansas River

Kansas City

Topeka   Lecompton

Lawrence
May 21, 1856

MISSOURI

KANSAS TERRITORY

N W E S

Marais des Cygnes River

Osawatomie
Aug. 30, 1856

Pottawatomie Massacre ☀
May 24–25, 1856

Pottawatomie River

Osage River

0   15   30 Miles
0   15   30 Kilometers
Albers Equal-Area Projection

internet connect

TOPIC: Fugitive Slaves
GO TO: go.hrw.com
KEYWORD: SD1 Fugitive

Accessing the Internet through the HRW Web site, research information about attempts to aid runaway slaves. Then write four entries into a "diary" as if you were helping a slave travel to freedom. In each entry, describe your experiences. Include thumbnail maps to trace your trip.

BUILDING YOUR PORTFOLIO

Complete one or all of the following projects independently or cooperatively.

1 Democratic Values
Imagine that you are the organizer of one of the Lincoln-Douglas debates. **Create a poster** announcing the debate, listing highlights of the opponents' careers and summarizing their differing views on the extension of slavery into the western territories.

2 Constitutional Heritage
Imagine that you are a lawyer helping Dred Scott sue for his freedom. **Conduct an interview** with Scott. Your interview should include questions about the circumstances of Scott's case, his views on how his rights have been violated, and the reasons why he thinks he should be set free.

3 Geographic Diversity
Imagine that you are a settler in the Kansas Territory in 1860. **Write a letter** to a northern newspaper explaining what the southern states' secession might mean to your territory.

A MAN KIDNAPPED!

A PUBLIC MEETING AT

FANEUIL HALL!

WILL BE HELD

THIS FRIDAY EVEN'G,

May 26th, at 7 o'clock,

To secure Justice for A MAN CLAIMED AS A SLAVE by a

VIRGINIA KIDNAPPER!

THE GRANGER COLLECTION, NEW YORK

1861–1865
The Civil War

The bombardment of Fort Sumter

1864 camera

1861
Politics
Confederate forces open fire on Fort Sumter.

1861
World Events
Russian serfs gain their freedom.

1861
World Events
Great Britain and France purchase cotton from Egypt and India instead of from southern states.

1862
Politics
The Union captures New Orleans and wins the Battle of Antietam, while the Confederacy wins the Battle of Fredericksburg.

1862
The Arts
Mathew Brady presents "The Dead at Antietam," his first photographic exhibit of the Civil War.

1860 **1861** **1862**

Charles Dickens

THE GRANGER COLLECTION, NEW YORK

1861
The Arts
British author Charles Dickens writes *Great Expectations*.

1861
Science and Technology
Archaeopteryx—a prehistoric skeleton that indicates a possible evolutionary link between birds and reptiles—is discovered in Europe.

Red Cross medal

1862
World Events
Jean-Henri Dunant of Switzerland proposes the founding of a voluntary relief organization—the International Red Cross.

1862
The Arts
Julia Ward Howe publishes a poem that becomes the "Battle Hymn of the Republic."

Sheet music for the "Battle Hymn of the Republic"

Before You Read

Build on What You Know

Tensions between the North and the South continued to grow throughout the 1850s. The crisis came to a head when a Republican, Abraham Lincoln, was elected president in 1860. In this chapter you will learn how the large population and industrial power of the North gave the Union better resources to fight the long and bloody Civil War that ensued. Although the South's defensive strategy and superior military leadership enabled it to win many of the war's early battles, the Confederacy was unable to overcome the Union forces.

General Lee surrendering to General Grant

1865
Politics
General Robert E. Lee formally surrenders his Confederate army to General Grant's Union forces at Appomattox.

1865
Science and Technology
Thaddeus Lowe invents a machine that makes ice.

1863
Daily Life
Congress establishes free mail delivery to U.S. cities.

1863
Business and Finance
Tailor Ebenezer Butterick markets the first paper dress pattern.

1863
Politics
The Confederacy wins a victory at Chancellorsville; the Union wins at Gettysburg and Vicksburg.

1864
Business and Finance
"In God We Trust" first appears on U.S. coins.

1864
Science and Technology
Louis Pasteur invents the process of pasteurization.

1864 U.S. coin

1865
The Arts
Yale College opens the first Department of Fine Arts in the United States.

1863

1864

1865

1863
Daily Life
Food riots break out in several southern states.

THE MUSEUM OF THE CONFEDERACY–RICHMOND, VIRGINIA

Southern women rioting for bread in 1863

1864
World Events
The French capture Mexico City and proclaim Archduke Maximilian of Austria emperor of Mexico.

1864
Politics
General Ulysses S. Grant becomes commander of all Union armies.

1865
Daily Life
John MacGregor pioneers canoeing as a sport.

1865
Science and Technology
The federal armory at Springfield, Massachusetts, has produced 1.6 million rifled muskets since 1861.

Think About Themes

Themes Journal

Decide whether you agree or disagree with the following statements. Note why in your journal.

Geographic Diversity Geography has a significant impact on the way wars are fought.

Economic Development A nation's economy will be affected both positively and negatively by war.

Democratic Values Americans interpret the meaning of individual liberty in different ways.

SECTION 1

The Union Dissolves

President Lincoln hoped to keep the Union together.

EYEWITNESSES TO History

66 *This proclamation was like the first peal of a surcharged thunder-cloud, clearing the murky air. The . . . whole North arose as one man. . . .*

Hastily formed companies marched to camps of rendezvous. . . . Merchants and clerks rushed out from stores, bareheaded, saluting them as they passed. Windows were flung up; and women leaned out into the rain, waving flags and handkerchiefs.

I had never dreamed that New England . . . could be fired with so warlike a spirit. 99

—Mary Ashton Livermore

Mary Ashton Livermore

Mary Ashton Livermore wrote about the northern response to President Abraham Lincoln's call in April 1861 for volunteers to put down the southern rebellion. Such spirited enthusiasm swept the nation in early 1861. As war became inevitable, both sides prepared for what they believed would be a short conflict.

Last Attempts at Compromise

When President Abraham Lincoln took office in 1861, the nation stood on the brink of collapse. Seven southern states had already seceded from the Union—South Carolina, Mississippi, Florida, Alabama, Georgia, Louisiana, and Texas. Furthermore, the debate over secession continued to rage in the Upper South.

To preserve the Union, Senator John J. Crittenden of Kentucky had proposed the **Crittenden Compromise** in December 1860. Crittenden's plan called for the old Missouri Compromise line to be drawn west through the remaining territories. North of the line, slavery would be illegal; south of the line, slavery could expand. President-elect Lincoln quickly rejected the plan. Opposition to the spread of slavery united the Republican Party. Many Republicans might have turned against Lincoln if he had allowed slavery to expand. Lincoln did, however, support the part of Crittenden's plan that called for the protection of slavery where it already existed.

Lincoln's willingness to allow slavery to continue hardly affected the secessionists, who were caught up in the excitement of creating a new nation. "It is a revolution . . . of the most intense character," wrote one southern senator. "It can no more be checked by human effort, for the time, than a prairie fire by a gardener's watering pot."

The new president was determined to preserve the Union. In his inaugural address, Lincoln insisted to southerners that secession was unconstitutional: "No State upon its own mere motion can lawfully get out of the Union." As president, he was bound to enforce the Constitution in every state.

✔ **READING CHECK:** What attempts were made to compromise with the secessionists?

The Fall of Fort Sumter

The South did not respond to President Lincoln's pleas for unity. Instead, meeting little resistance, the Confederacy took over many federal forts, mints, and arsenals within its borders during the secession crisis. One fort that was very important to the South—Fort Sumter—remained under federal control.

Fort Sumter lay in a strategic location in the harbor of Charleston, South Carolina. The South needed the fort in order to control access to this major port city. In early March the fort's commander, Major Robert Anderson, sent word to Washington that he was nearly out of supplies. Without reinforcements, Sumter would soon fall to the Confederates.

The North did not want to lose the fort—it would be a sign that Lincoln would not protect federal property in the seceded states. The president hesitated, however, because the eight slave states that remained in the Union had threatened to secede if he used force against the Confederacy. Lincoln decided to resupply Fort Sumter, reasoning that if the Confederates fired on unarmed supply ships, then they, not the Union, would be the aggressors.

On April 6, 1861, Lincoln sent a messenger to alert South Carolina governor F. W. Pickens that supply ships were on their way, but that the ships carried only supplies, not troops or arms. Governor Pickens relayed the message to General P. G. T. Beauregard, the local Confederate military commander. Beauregard then ordered the federal troops to evacuate the fort. Major Anderson refused.

At 4:30 A.M. on April 12 the Confederate forces opened fire on Fort Sumter. Abner Doubleday, Anderson's second in command, described the scene within the fort.

> 66 Showers of balls . . . and shells . . . poured into the fort. . . . When the immense mortar shells, after sailing high in the air, came down in a vertical direction and buried themselves in the parade ground, their explosion shook the fort like an earthquake. 99

For 34 hours the Confederates bombarded Sumter. Finally, with much of the fort ablaze and their ammunition running low, Anderson and his men formally surrendered on April 13. Surprisingly, no one on either side was killed or seriously wounded during the fighting.

On April 15 Lincoln publicly announced the existence of a rebellion "too powerful to be suppressed by the ordinary course of judicial proceedings." He called

Fortifications. The Confederate attack on Fort Sumter marked the beginning of the Civil War. *What does the fort's location suggest about its importance?*

PRESIDENTIAL Lives

1809–1865
In Office 1861–1865

Abraham Lincoln

Superior leadership skills made Abraham Lincoln one of the nation's greatest presidents. The personal hardship of losing two children and the stresses of the Civil War took a toll, however. Lincoln endured periodic bouts of severe depression. He often used laughter to combat his depression. He believed laughter could "whistle down sadness," as a friend put it.

Throughout his life, Lincoln filled his everyday conversations with humor and homespun stories. "The Lord prefers common-looking people," he once said. "That is why he makes so many of them." On another occasion he commented about a book: "People who like this sort of thing will find this the sort of thing they like."

Even in personal defeat Lincoln put his famous dry wit to use. "I feel like the boy who stumped his toe," he said on losing the 1858 U.S. Senate race to Stephen Douglas. "I am too big to cry and too badly hurt to laugh."

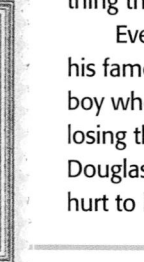

These women are filling cartridges at a federal arsenal in Watertown, Massachusetts.

for the states to provide 75,000 soldiers to put down the uprising. The recruits were to serve for just three months.

Choosing Sides

President Lincoln's fear of losing more states to the Confederacy quickly became a reality. Four more southern states—Arkansas, North Carolina, Tennessee, and Virginia—responded to the president's call for troops by seceding. The Confederates named Richmond, Virginia, as their capital.

Four other slave states—Delaware, Kentucky, Maryland, and Missouri—remained within the Union. Secession was never a serious threat in Delaware, where there were few slaves and most of the population sympathized more with the North than with the South. Kentucky, Maryland, and Missouri, on the other hand, were sharply divided over the issue of secession. The governors of both Missouri and Kentucky sympathized with the Confederacy, but neither state voted to secede. Lincoln kept Maryland in the Union by securing the state with federal troops. Maryland's secession would have meant losing the Union capital. Maryland surrounded Washington on three sides with already-seceded Virginia on the other side.

The mountainous counties of northwestern Virginia remained loyal to the Union as well. People living there held few slaves and had long resented the rich planter elite of the lowlands. They set up their own state government, and in 1863 the state was admitted to the Union as West Virginia. Although West Virginia had few slaves, slavery initially remained legal there.

The Upper South's white population remained divided over the issue of secession. Sections of several of these states raised Union regiments to fight the Confederacy. Some families were torn apart as members fought for opposing sides in the war.

One son of Kentucky senator John Crittenden became a Union general, and another became a Confederate general. President Lincoln's wife, Mary Todd, a southerner by birth, had four brothers and three brothers-in-law fighting in the Confederate army.

✔ **READING CHECK:** How did the fall of Fort Sumter affect the relationship between the Union and the Confederacy?

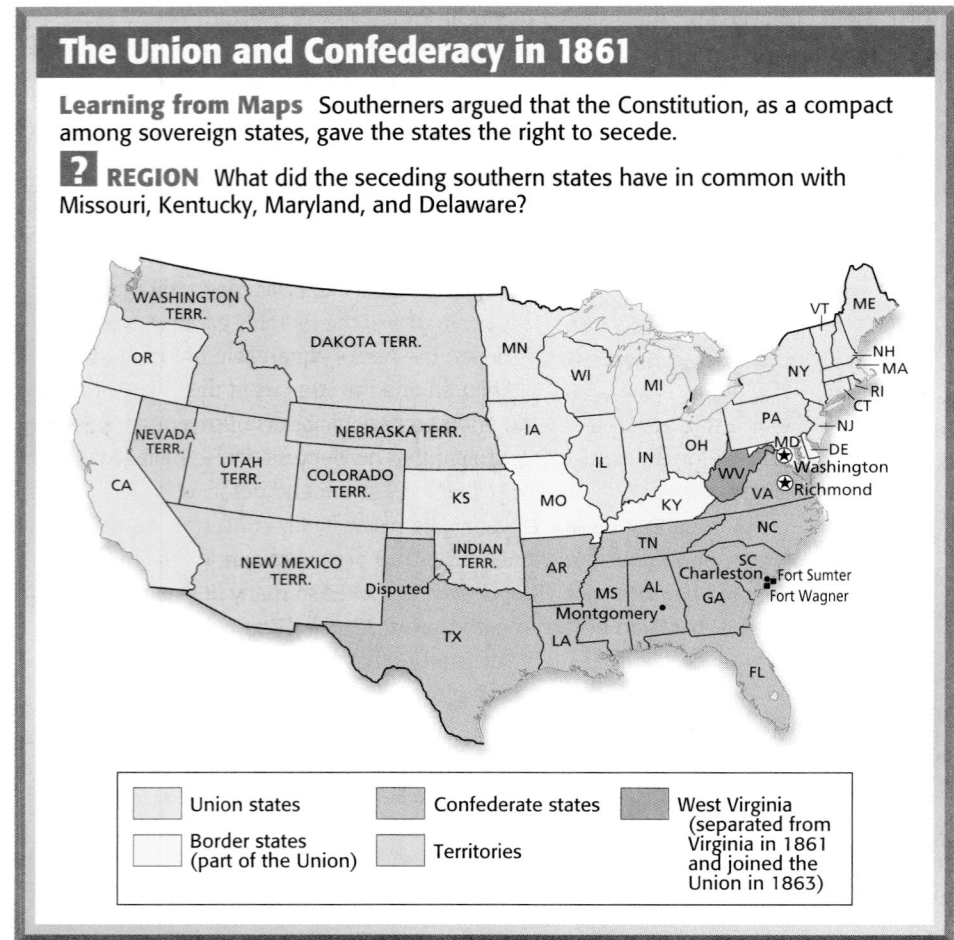

The Union and Confederacy in 1861

Learning from Maps Southerners argued that the Constitution, as a compact among sovereign states, gave the states the right to secede.

❓ REGION What did the seceding southern states have in common with Missouri, Kentucky, Maryland, and Delaware?

Union states
Border states (part of the Union)
Confederate states
Territories
West Virginia (separated from Virginia in 1861 and joined the Union in 1863)

Comparing North and South

The war that loomed after the fall of Fort Sumter appeared to be a mismatch. In many respects the North enjoyed military superiority over the South. The advantages held by the South were so important, however, that many objective observers expected a quick southern victory.

Northern advantages. With more than 22 million residents the North had a huge population advantage. The South's population totaled slightly more than 9 million, some 3.5 million of whom were slaves. As a result, the South had a much smaller pool of available soldiers.

The North also enjoyed an economic advantage. When the Civil War began, the North controlled more than 85 percent of the nation's industry and significant material resources. These advantages enabled the North to produce military supplies and replace lost or damaged equipment more rapidly than the Confederacy. Most southern wealth was in land and slaves.

In addition, since most of the nation's railroad lines were located in the Northeast and the Midwest, the Union could move troops and supplies with ease. Southern routes, in contrast, were short, with few connecting lines between major cities. Furthermore, because the North manufactured most of the nation's railroad equipment, the Confederacy found itself ill-prepared to replace broken or worn-out parts and equipment during the war.

Most of the U.S. Navy remained loyal to the Union, including such southern naval officers as David Farragut and Percival Drayton. With no ships and little naval expertise to draw upon, the South was forced to build its navy from scratch.

Resources of the North and South in 1861

Resources	North	South
Total population	22,000,000	9,000,000*
Bank deposits	$189,000,000	$47,000,000
Railroad mileage	20,000 miles	9,000 miles
Number of factories	100,500	20,600

*Southern population includes 3,500,000 slaves
Sources: *American Heritage Picture History of the Civil War;
Encyclopedia of American History*

Learning from Charts At the beginning of the Civil War, the North's abundant resources gave it a military advantage over the South.

? Building Chart Skills Which resource do you think had the greatest influence on the outcome of the Civil War?

Southern advantages. The South had two important advantages over the North. The Confederacy had only to fight a defensive war, protecting its territory until the Union tired of the struggle. In contrast, the Union needed to conquer an area of about 750,000 square miles. This was twice the size of the original thirteen colonies. The South also had excellent military leadership. In fact, most southern victories would result from the battle strategies of skillful Confederate officers.

B
I
O
G
R
A
P
H
Y

Robert E. Lee

Among the ablest of southern military leaders was Robert E. Lee, who was born into a prominent Virginia family in 1807. His father was Henry "Light-Horse Harry" Lee, a Revolutionary War hero. Robert excelled as a student at the U.S. Military Academy at West Point. After graduating in 1829, he served first in the Army Corps of Engineers and then in the cavalry. In 1831 Lee married Mary Custis, great-granddaughter of Martha Washington and the heir to Arlington Plantation in northern Virginia.

Lee first tested his military abilities during the Mexican War of 1846. He took part in the capture of Veracruz, serving as a captain under General Winfield Scott.

Read More About It

Free Find:
Robert E. Lee
After reading about Robert E. Lee on the **Holt Researcher** CD–ROM, write an obituary describing his accomplishments and his reasons for fighting for the Confederacy.

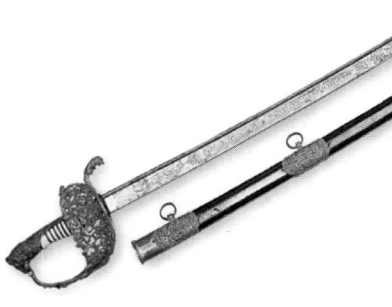
This sword belonged to General Robert E. Lee.

Lee's skill and bravery impressed his commander and earned him a promotion. After working as superintendent of West Point from 1852 to 1855, Lee served briefly in Texas and eventually moved to Arlington, Virginia. In 1859 he led the federal troops that captured abolitionist John Brown at Harpers Ferry.

As southern states began to secede from the Union, General Scott advised President Lincoln to ask his old friend, Robert E. Lee, to command the Union forces. Faced with a difficult choice between country and state, Lee regretfully declined, resigning his commission. Scott told him sadly, "You have made the greatest mistake of your life, but I feared it would be so." Lee opposed slavery and secession, but he refused to fight against Virginia. Lee wrote a letter to his sister.

66 With all my devotion to the Union and the feeling of loyalty and duty of an American citizen, I have not been able to make up my mind to raise my hand against my relatives, my children, my home. I have therefore resigned my commission in the Army, and save [except] in defense of my native State—with the sincere hope that my poor services may never be needed—I hope I may never be called on to draw my sword. 99

The armies. Lee was called upon not only to draw his sword, but eventually to lead the South's army. Both sides quickly built up their military strength. By the end of 1861 the Union had more than 527,000 soldiers and the Confederacy slightly more than 258,000. Most of these soldiers were between the ages of 18 and 29, with drummer boys as young as 9 years old.

Estimates of how many men fought in the war vary because many men reenlisted after their initial commissions expired. The U.S. government placed the official wartime enlistment in the Union army at 2,672,341, with another 105,963 men enlisted in the navy or marines. According to U.S. government statistics, some 3,530 American Indians and some 180,000 African Americans served in the Union army. Noncommissioned African American officers numbered nearly 7,000. About 100 African Americans were commissioned.

Historians estimate that some 750,000 men enlisted in the Confederate army. This figure included some 5,500 Cherokee, Creek, Chickasaw, and Choctaw. These American Indians included many slaveholders lured by the promise of an all-Indian state following the war. Some Mexican Americans from New Mexico and Texas fought on both sides during the war.

✔ **READING CHECK:** What advantages did each side possess at the beginning of the war?

THROUGH OTHERS' EYES

European Views of the Civil War

The nations of Europe had their own aims and expectations with respect to the U.S. Civil War. Judging that a divided United States would be less threatening to Europe, some officials in France and Britain hoped that the South would win. Sir Edward Bulwer-Lytton, a member of the British Parliament, remarked that a Confederate victory would "be attended with happy results to the safety of Europe." Believing that it was already too late to save the Union, Bulwer-Lytton noted that a united America "would have hung over Europe like a . . . thunder-cloud. No single kingdom in Europe could have been strong enough to maintain itself against a nation that had once consolidated the gigantic resources of a quarter of the globe."

Russia, on the other hand, supported the Union. Russia wanted to keep the United States united and strong. This would help hold Britain and France in check and thereby maintain a balance of power in the world. Russian foreign minister Prince Gorchakov remarked to a U.S. diplomat: "You know the sentiments of Russia! We desire, above all things, the maintenance of the American Union as one indivisible nation."

Recognizing Fallacies in Reasoning

In order to evaluate historical arguments and ideas, students must be able to recognize fallacies in reasoning. A *fallacy* is a false or mistaken idea. When included in a sequence of reasoning, a fallacy may result in an unsound argument or unsupported conclusion.

Most fallacies in reasoning fall into several basic categories. *Single cause* means identifying one cause for an event while ignoring other causes. History is complex, and very few historical events resulted from just one cause. *Coincidence as cause* means attributing the cause of one event to another event simply because they occurred at or near the same time. *Irrelevant evidence* means an argument or assertion is based on information that it is not related to logically.

How to Recognize Fallacies in Reasoning

1. **Identify the main ideas.** As you read a historical source, identify its main ideas and supporting details. Each time you identify a main idea, make a preliminary judgment of its soundness.
2. **Identify cause and effect.** Take note of cause-and-effect relationships that are mentioned explicitly and that you can infer from the source. Make sure to check for complex connections such as multiple causes and long-term effects.
3. **Evaluate the reasoning.** After you finish reading the source, assess the quality of its historical reasoning. Ask yourself the following questions: Are the arguments in this source logical? Are the cause-and-effect relationships fully proven? Do the conclusions follow from the information provided?

Applying the Strategy

Examine the following statement and identify the fallacy in its reasoning.

> The Civil War was fought over the issue of a state's right to make its own laws. If northerners had not wanted to make slavery illegal in the South, the war would not have occurred.

Practicing the Strategy

Answer the following questions.
1. What type of fallacy in reasoning does the statement contain?
2. What additional information might help correct this reasoning error?

The First Battle of Bull Run

General Winfield Scott believed the new Union troops still needed several months of training. Likewise, a Confederate officer reported his men to be so lacking in "discipline and instruction" that it would be "difficult to use them in the field." Despite these reservations, President Lincoln ordered General Irvin McDowell and some 35,000 barely trained troops to Richmond, Virginia, in mid-July 1861.

Fighting at Manassas. General McDowell's forces never reached Richmond. On July 21, 1861, some 35,000 Confederates met the Union troops near Manassas (muh-NAS-uhs) Junction, a railroad crossing about 30 miles outside Washington. Led by General Joseph E. Johnston, the Confederates dug in on high ground behind a creek called Bull Run. Northerners called the fighting that followed the **First Battle of Bull Run**. Southerners called it the Battle of Manassas.

At first the battle went in the Union's favor. The left flank of the Confederate line came close to cracking. Confederate general Thomas "Stonewall" Jackson and his men stopped the Union assault, however. Jackson's troops raced toward the Union line, filling the air with a terrifying scream: "Woh—who—ey! Who—ey!"

This Union drum bears the eagle symbol of the federal government.

The eerie sound, which came to be known as the Rebel Yell, sent chills through the northern troops.

The Union soldiers fell back and headed for Washington. Union colonel Andrew Porter wrote about the retreat.

66 Soon the slopes . . . were swarming with our retreating and disorganized forces, while riderless horses and artillery teams ran furiously through the flying crowd. All further efforts were futile. The words, gestures, and threats of our officers were thrown away upon men who had lost all presence of mind, and only longed for absence of body. 99

THE GRANGER COLLECTION, NEW YORK

INTERPRETING THE VISUAL RECORD

Bull Run. The fierce fighting and number of casualties at Bull Run surprised many Americans. *What do you think made the First Battle of Bull Run such a bloody fight?*

The aftermath of southern victory. The events at Bull Run caused most people to realize that the war would last longer than a few months. As a result, each side began to seriously train its forces for battle and to plan strategy. Confederate president Jefferson Davis named Joseph Johnston to command the Army of Northern Virginia and chose Robert E. Lee as his military adviser. President Lincoln named General George B. McClellan to head the Union forces.

The most important consequences of the First Battle of Bull Run may have been psychological. The defeat shamed and shocked the North. In the South, newspaper editorials proclaimed the superiority of the Confederacy. The victory lulled many Confederates into a false sense of security. Meanwhile, the Union army was becoming more determined.

✔ **READING CHECK:** What were the consequences of the First Battle of Bull Run?

SECTION 1 REVIEW

Define and explain the significance of the following terms:
Crittenden Compromise
First Battle of Bull Run

Identify and explain the significance of the following individuals:
Robert E. Lee
Joseph E. Johnston
Thomas "Stonewall" Jackson

Locate and explain the importance of the following places:
Fort Sumter
Richmond
West Virginia
Manassas Junction

1. **Using Graphic Organizers** Copy the graphic organizer below. Use it to list the military advantages of the North and the South at the beginning of the war.

Northern Advantages	Southern Advantages

2. **Identifying Cause and Effect** Why was Sumter an important fort, and how did its fall affect both the Union and the Confederacy?
3. **Analyzing** Why did efforts at compromise fail to prevent the Civil War?
4. **Assessing Consequences** How did soldiers' lack of training affect the First Battle of Bull Run?

Critical Thinking

5. How did northerners' and southerners' differing attitudes about the war affect reactions to the First Battle of Bull Run?
   Consider:
   • what northern and southern attitudes toward the war were before the battle
   • what northern and southern reactions were after the battle
   • how the attitudes and reactions related to one another

The North and South Face Off

EYEWITNESSES TO History

66 *We are going to kill the last Yankee before [spring] if there is any fight in them still. I believe that J. D. Walker's Brigade can whip 25,000 Yankees.* 99
—an Alabama soldier

This letter reveals the high spirits that marked the beginning of the war between the North and South. After joining the army, one volunteer from New York wrote his family, "I and the rest of the boys are in fine spirits . . . feeling like larks." People in both the North and the South had great confidence that their side would quickly win the war. In the North, author James Russell Lowell used a fictional character, Hosea Biglow, to describe this widespread optimism. Biglow recalled the days after Fort Sumter fell: "I hoped to see things settled 'fore this fall. The Rebbles licked, Jeff Davis hanged, an' all."

A Union soldier (top) and a Confederate soldier (bottom)

Strategies of War

From the beginning of the war, the North's primary goal was to restore the Union. To accomplish this goal, Lincoln and his military advisers adopted a three-part strategy. They sought first to capture Richmond, the Confederate capital; second, to gain control of the Mississippi River; and third, to institute a naval blockade of the South. The naval blockade was nicknamed the **Anaconda Plan** because it was designed to slowly squeeze the life out of the South like an anaconda snake. It was important because the South depended on foreign markets to sell its cotton and to buy supplies.

The North devised its battle strategy based on the region's geography. Since the Confederacy stretched from Virginia to Texas, the Appalachian Mountains divided most of the action in the Civil War into two arenas: the eastern theater and the western theater. The eastern theater lay east of the Appalachians. The western theater lay between these mountains and the Mississippi River. Control of the Mississippi River would enable the North to penetrate deep into the South. It would also prevent the Confederacy from using the waterway to resupply its forces.

While the North's strategy depended on dividing the South geographically, the South planned to capture Washington and invade the North. Southern leaders hoped for a successful offensive strike northward through the Shenandoah Valley into Maryland and Pennsylvania. They hoped this would shatter northern morale, disrupt Union communications, win European support, and bring the war to a speedy end.

Confederate leaders knew that winning the support of France or Great Britain was crucial to a victory for the South. Because the French and British economies depended heavily on cotton, the Confederacy had confidence that one of the nations would respond to the naval blockade by coming to the South's aid.

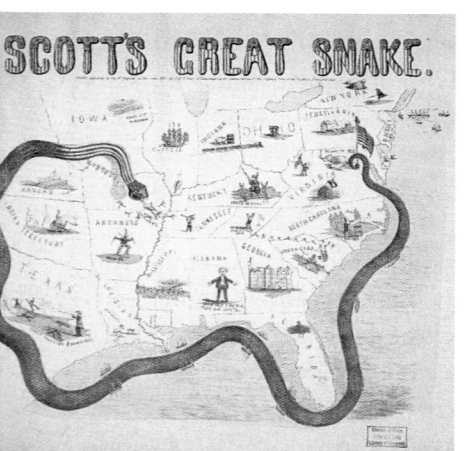

This cartoon illustrates General Scott's Anaconda Plan for a naval blockade of the Confederate states.

The South's strategy failed, however. Neither France nor Britain proved dependent on Confederate cotton. French and British mill owners had stockpiled cotton before Fort Sumter's fall. Once these reserves ran out, the mill owners turned to Egypt and India for new supplies. Additionally, French emperor Napoleon III's preoccupation with events in Mexico distracted him from the conflict between the Union and the Confederacy. With Napoleon's blessing, Mexico's ruling elite made the archduke of Austria, Maximilian, emperor in 1864. When widespread opposition to Maximilian broke out, Napoleon ordered French troops in Mexico to put down the resistance. In part because he did not want to fight two wars at the same time, Napoleon decided not to aid the Confederacy. The South's failure to secure French help meant that southerners had limited resources at their disposal.

✔ **READING CHECK:** How did the military strategies of the North and the South differ?

The Military Experience

While high-level leaders planned battle strategies, the officers under their command attempted to train troops to carry out these strategies. Young recruits in both the Union and Confederate ranks were generally enthusiastic when they first enlisted. Most of these newly recruited soldiers had little experience with military life, however.

Both sides faced shortages of clothing, food, and even rifles. At the beginning of the war, most troops did not even have standard uniforms. Some simply wore their own clothes from home. Eventually, each side adopted a distinguishing uniform. The Union chose blue and the Confederacy gray. However, many troops, particularly Confederates, lacked good shoes and warm coats throughout the war.

This persistent lack of provisions, coupled with unsanitary conditions in most field camps, led to deadly problems of disease. What little food existed in the camps often was spoiled. Describing the old meat served to his company, one Confederate soldier wrote, "A decent dog would have turned up his nose at it, but a hungry man will eat almost anything."

Thousands of soldiers died from illnesses such as influenza, pneumonia, and typhoid. Doctors and nurses could do little to help, since most hospitals had little in the way of medical provisions. As a result, some soldiers had to endure surgery without pain-killing anesthetics. Many with seemingly minor injuries died from infected wounds. In fact, disease, infection, and malnutrition took the lives of more than 65 percent of the soldiers who died during the war.

Nowhere were conditions worse than in the filthy, overcrowded prisoner-of-war camps in the North and South. One nun who worked as a nurse during the war commented, "It is hard to be sick, but to be a sick prisoner of war is indeed a

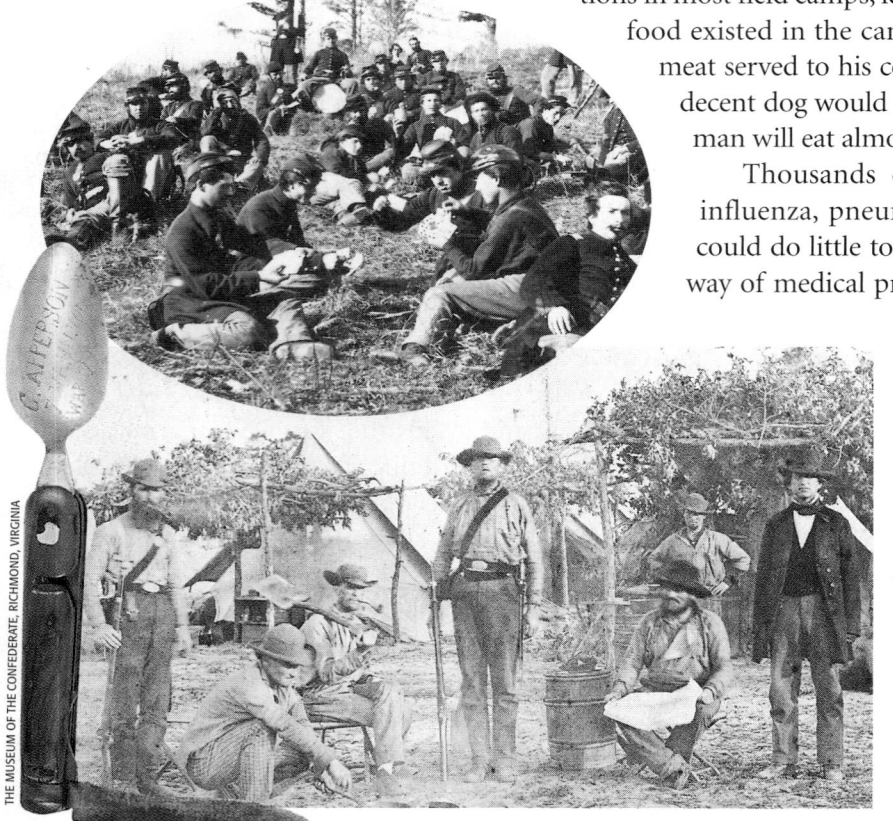

INTERPRETING THE VISUAL RECORD

Camp life. Union soldiers (top) and Confederate soldiers (bottom) relax in their camps. They used utensils like the folding knife and spoon shown to prepare their meals. *Based on these images, how would you describe camp life?*

heavy cross [burden]." Union prisoners held at Andersonville, a Confederate camp located in southwestern Georgia, endured the worst conditions, with no shelter and little food. At times, prisoners at Andersonville died at a rate of about 100 per day. In some camps more than 25 percent of the prisoners died before the end of the war.

In addition to their difficult living conditions, many soldiers suffered from extreme boredom, homesickness, and loneliness. Some men deserted, but most attempted to cope with their situation. Soldiers played cards, attended prayer meetings, sang, wrote letters home, or engaged in other recreational activities.

✔ **READING CHECK:** What were some of the daily hardships faced by soldiers?

AMERICAN ARTS

Mathew Brady's Photographs

The carving on Mathew Brady's tombstone reads "renowned photographer of the Civil War." Before the Civil War even began, Brady was already well known for his portraits of wealthy and famous Americans. When the war broke out in 1861, he set a goal of recording all the "prominent incidents of the conflict."

Because he had lost much of his eyesight, Brady took very few of the war photographs that were displayed in his galleries. Nonetheless, he was one of the first photographers to understand the dramatic impact that the art form could have on society. With this in mind, Brady financed, supervised, and organized groups of photographers to accompany Union troops. They created a pictorial history of the people and events of the war. Brady's photographers traveled to the battlefields in horse-drawn wagons that doubled as portable darkrooms, allowing photographs to be developed on location.

The long exposures required for these early photographs prevented photographers from recording any movement. While many photographers made portraits of soldiers and took pictures of equipment, fortifications, prisons, and hospitals, the most dramatic photographs are those of soldiers lying dead on battlefields. These images had a powerful effect on their audience. "If he has not brought bodies and laid them in our dooryards and along our streets, he has done something very like it," wrote the *New York Times* of one Brady exhibit.

Mathew Brady's Civil War photographs often shocked civilians by showing the horrors of the battlefield.

Understanding the Arts

1. What prevented Civil War photographers from recording movement in their photographs?
2. What is unusual about the bodies in the photograph above?

The Home Front

Mobilization for the war also had a profound effect on the Americans who stayed home during the conflict. Women and those men who were too young, too old, or physically unable to fight, fulfilled important responsibilities on the home front.

Read More About It

Free Find:

Mary Boykin Chesnut

After reading about Mary Boykin Chesnut on the **Holt Researcher** CD–ROM, create several fictional journal entries describing some of the events of the Civil War.

The North. In the North, women replaced the male factory workers and farmers who left for the battlefields. The Union's need for military supplies opened up more than 100,000 jobs for women in arsenals, factories, and sewing rooms. The nearly 450 women working as clerks in the Treasury Department served as the government's first female office workers. Other women worked as bankers, morticians, saloon keepers, and steamboat captains during the war. Women and boys took responsibility for growing food during the war, aided by new farm equipment such as the McCormick reaper that helped produce bumper crops. The Detroit *Free Press* reported in 1864 that women had grown much of the corn produced in Michigan that year.

Countless civilians also participated in volunteer groups that raised money for the Union cause or provided relief services for soldiers and their families. Ladies Aid Societies made bandages, bedclothes, and shirts for soldiers. The American Freedman's Aid Commission provided hundreds of female schoolteachers to educate former slaves. State and local governments established homes for injured soldiers and orphanages for the children of soldiers who died in the war.

The South. The diary of southerner Mary Boykin Chesnut provides a glimpse of life on the homefront during the war. The daughter of Mary and Stephen Miller, Mary Boykin was born in 1823 near Columbia, South Carolina. She grew up in a large and wealthy extended family that had lived in South Carolina since the 1750s. Mary followed her grandmother around like "her shadow." She learned how to manage the many different components of a plantation.

At the age of 17, after receiving a private education, Mary wed James Chesnut, heir to a nearby plantation. James Chesnut became an active politician. He served as a U.S. senator and later held several different positions in the Confederate and South Carolina governments. Mary Chesnut grew somewhat bored by plantation life. She found an outlet for her energetic personality in her passionate support of the Confederacy after war broke out. Living in Richmond, Virginia, during part of the war, she played an important role in political and military circles. She often wrote of her frustration, however, with what she saw as the incompetence of southern leaders. "Oh if I could put some of my reckless spirit into these . . . cautious lazy men!"

As the war progressed, Chesnut experienced pain and grief at the death of friends and family, as well as fear for the South's prospects. "With horror and amazement" she watched her world, "the only world we cared for, literally kicked to pieces." Chesnut eased the difficulty of her postwar life by preparing her diary for publication. Between 1881 and 1884 she rewrote her diary from the notes and entries she had made in the journal during the Civil War. Before the work was published, however, she died of heart failure in 1886 at the age of 63. Her diary was finally published in 1905.

BIOGRAPHY

Mary Boykin Chesnut

This writing desk belonged to Mary Chesnut.

Southerners like Chesnut supported the war effort with a series of patriotic events. At these parades and barbecues public figures urged young men to join the army, and wealthy members of society pledged money to buy arms and uniforms. Raffles and auctions raised much-needed funds for the Confederacy.

By 1862 the early romance with the war had faded, and the harsh effects of the blockade and providing for the war effort set in. The short supply of basic necessities such as shoes, clothing, and farm equipment caused inflation to skyrocket. In addition, the inability to obtain medicines caused untold suffering. City residents were hardest hit by the war. Many families lived in single rooms, using one fireplace for both heat and cooking. Food shortages forced people to live on beans, boiled potatoes, and corn fritters. Their social occasions became "starvation parties," with only water served for refreshment.

✔ **READING CHECK:** What was life like on the home front during the war?

Civilian Aid on the Battlefield

In addition to the vital roles they played on the homefront, many civilians, particularly women, actively aided the military. Some women even dressed like men so that they could fight. Cuban-born Loreta Janeta Velázquez (vay-LAHS-kays) disguised herself as a man and enlisted in the Confederate army. When she was found out and discharged, she became a spy for the South. Other women also served as spies. Rose O'Neal Greenhow was imprisoned for supplying information to the Confederacy. Mary Elizabeth Bowser, a maid who worked in Confederate president Jefferson Davis's home, and abolitionist Harriet Tubman both supplied information to the Union from behind enemy lines.

Many other women served the war effort in medical roles. Catholic nuns were among the most important female volunteers for medical duty. They sometimes transformed their convents into emergency hospitals throughout the North and the South. Many of these so-called nuns of the battlefield were Irish or German immigrants. They remained neutral and treated all victims of the war, becoming the only group allowed to move freely between Union and Confederate lines.

In the North, Elizabeth Blackwell, who was the first professionally licensed female doctor in the United States, helped run the **U.S. Sanitary Commission**. The commission worked to battle the diseases and infections that killed twice as many soldiers as bullets alone. Approximately 3,000 women served as nurses in the Union army. Some, like Clara Barton, ministered to the wounded on the battlefield. After the war, Barton founded the American Red Cross, which today serves disaster victims and others in need of assistance.

Growing Up During the Civil War

teen Life

Children experienced the impact of the Civil War both at home and on the battlefield. Many older boys and girls took on increased responsibilities in their households and on their farms when their fathers and older brothers left to fight in the war. Younger children also suffered from hardships such as malnutrition and a lack of clothing, particularly in the South.

Somewhere between 250,000 and 500,000 boys fought in the Civil War. Elisha Stockwell Jr., a 15-year-old living in Wisconsin, explained how he joined: "I told the recruiting officer I didn't know just how old I was but thought I was eighteen." Many boys served as company musicians, particularly drummers or buglers.

Like the other soldiers, boys quickly learned that most of their time would be spent not in battle, but marching mile after mile and performing boring tasks in camp. When the time for combat did arrive, many boys, including Elisha Stockwell, regretted their decision to leave home. "As we lay there and the shells were flying over us," Stockwell recalled, "my thoughts went back to my home, and I thought what a foolish boy I was to run away and get into such a mess as I was in. I would have been glad to have seen my father coming after me."

The young boys in this Mathew Brady photograph are members of a Union drum corps.

Hospitals. Wartime conditions led to the need for battlefield hospitals like this one. *What would be the advantages and disadvantages of such hospitals?*

Women in the South also provided medical aid to soldiers. Sally Louisa Tompkins was among the Confederate women who founded small hospitals and clinics. She was eventually commissioned as a captain in the Confederate army so that her Richmond, Virginia, hospital could qualify as a military hospital. This made Tompkins the only recognized female officer in the Confederate forces. Nurses experienced the horrors of war firsthand. Kate Cumming, a Confederate nurse from Alabama, wrote in her diary about her experiences at a makeshift hospital.

> 66 The men are lying all over the house on their blankets, just as they were brought from the battlefield. . . . The foul air from this mass of human beings at first made me giddy and sick, but I soon got over it. We have to walk and, when we give the men anything, kneel in blood and water; but we think nothing of it at all. 99

✔ **READING CHECK:** How did civilians contribute to the war effort?

Opposition to the War

Although many people on the home front worked to keep the war effort going and morale high, others voiced their displeasure with the war. Opposition grew as the bloody conflict dragged on longer than anyone had envisioned.

Southern opposition. Southern discontent intensified in the spring of 1862, when the Confederacy passed the first **conscription**, or draft, act in American history. Harsh living conditions in army camps as well as the difficulty of leaving families at home had caused a decrease in the number of southern volunteers. Southern military losses in the spring of 1862 convinced Jefferson Davis and southern generals of the draft's necessity.

The southern draft placed the major burden for fighting the war on poor farmers and working people. Draft exemptions for large plantation owners—who had led the Confederacy into war—created tension between wealthy southerners and nonslaveholding whites. Many white southerners openly criticized the policy. They claimed that it proved the conflict was a "rich man's war and a poor man's fight," as Confederate private Sam Watkins wrote in his memoirs. In response, plantation owners argued that some slaveholders had to remain at home to keep their slaves from running off. The Confederacy needed food and cloth, and few southerners believed that slaves would work without constant supervision.

Other southerners opposed the draft because they believed that it violated states' rights and freedom. These were the very principles that had led southern states to secede from the Union in the first place. Georgia governor Joseph E. Brown argued that "no act of the Government of the United States prior to the secession struck a blow at constitutional liberty so [fatal] as has been stricken by this conscription act."

As the war intensified, the Confederacy began to allow soldiers to pay farmers prices far below the market value for food, animals, and other property. This policy of impressment placed a heavy burden on food-producing families and led to serious food shortages. Many farmers called it robbery. Fear of starvation led to food riots in Alabama, Georgia, and North Carolina.

Confederate soldiers carried this flag into battle.

Northern opposition. Discontent also surfaced in the North. Some northerners sympathized with the South and urged peace. Others believed that the war was proving too costly in terms of money and human life.

Republican sponsorship of a Union draft law in 1863 caused violence to break out in New York City. Democratic newspapers stirred the fears and passions of their readers. They claimed that the draft was designed to force white working-class men to fight for the freedom of African Americans who would then come north and steal their jobs. Angry whites raged through African American neighborhoods. They attacked and killed people and looted and burned buildings. They also destroyed the property of wealthy Republicans. By the time Union troops brought the rioting under control, more than 100 people had been killed.

Most northern Democrats who sympathized with the South did not actively interfere with the war effort. Known as **Copperheads**—a type of poisonous snake—most southern sympathizers limited their antiwar activities to speeches and newspaper articles. In an attempt to quiet the Copperheads, President Lincoln suspended some civil liberties, including the constitutional right of *habeas corpus*—a protection against unlawful imprisonment. Thousands of Copperheads and other opponents of the war were arrested and held without trial.

THE GRANGER COLLECTION, NEW YORK

Copperheads. This cartoon shows the United States fighting the threat of the Copperheads. *Do you think the cartoonist had a favorable opinion of the Copperheads? Explain your answer.*

✔ **READING CHECK:** Why did some people oppose the war?

SECTION 2 REVIEW

Define and explain the significance of the following terms:
Anaconda Plan
U.S. Sanitary Commission
conscription
Copperheads
habeas corpus

Identify and explain the significance of the following individuals:
Mary Boykin Chesnut
Elizabeth Blackwell
Clara Barton
Sally Louisa Tompkins

1. **Using Graphic Organizers** Copy the graphic organizer below. Use it to explain how the North's military strategy differed from the South's at the beginning of the Civil War.

Northern Strategy	Southern Strategy
Main Goal:	Main Goal:
Plan of Action:	Plan of Action:

2. **Synthesizing** How were civilians on the home front affected by the war, and how did they aid the war efforts?
3. **Identifying Values** Why did some Americans on both sides, especially northern Democrats, oppose the war?
4. **Using Historical Imagination** Imagine that you are a young male soldier or a female civilian in either the North or the South during the Civil War. Write a diary entry describing your experiences during the war.

Critical Thinking

5. Was Sam Watkins correct in saying that the Civil War was "a rich man's war and a poor man's fight"? Explain your answer.
   Consider:
   • what Watkins meant by "a rich man's war and a poor man's fight"
   • who fought in the war
   • how the war affected the rich and the poor differently

SECTION 3
Fighting the War

Ulysses S. Grant

OBJECTIVES

Read to understand:

1. how Union forces gained control of the Mississippi River
2. how the northern and southern forces fared in the eastern campaigns
3. how the Union victory at Antietam changed the Union's war aims
4. how African American soldiers aided the Union
5. what the significance of the battles at Fredericksburg and Chancellorsville was

KEY TERMS

Battle of Shiloh
Emancipation Proclamation
Battle of Antietam
54th Massachusetts Infantry

KEY PEOPLE

Ulysses S. Grant
David Farragut
George B. McClellan
James E. B. "Jeb" Stuart
Martin Delany
Ambrose E. Burnside

KEY PLACES

Fredericksburg
Chancellorsville

The fighting at the Battle of Shiloh was very bloody.

EYEWITNESSES TO History

❝ My heart kept getting higher and higher until it felt to me as though it were in my throat. I would have given anything then to have been back in Illinois, but I had not the moral courage to know what to do; I kept right on. ❞
—Ulysses S. Grant

Ulysses S. Grant began his service in the Civil War as a colonel of the 21st Illinois Regiment. Leading an attack on a Confederate camp in Missouri, he pressed forward despite his fear. When he learned that the Confederates had fled, Grant realized that the enemy colonel "had been as much afraid of me as I had been of him. This was a view of the question I had never taken before; but it was one I never forgot. . . . The lesson was valuable." Many other Union military leaders never grasped this important lesson.

The War in the West

During 1862 the Confederacy won most of the major battles in the East. President Lincoln had little luck finding a general able to defeat Confederate generals Stonewall Jackson, Joseph E. Johnston, and Robert E. Lee in the eastern theater. As a result, the Union's eastern forces had four different commanders in just one year. In the West, however, the Union forces led by Ulysses S. Grant achieved great success.

General Grant had won a reputation as a determined military leader. President Lincoln found him invaluable, exclaiming *"I can't spare this man. He fights."* In February 1862 Grant captured Fort Henry and Fort Donelson in Tennessee. Command of these two forts plus the city of Nashville—captured by other Union forces—gave the North control over Kentucky and much of Tennessee.

Shiloh. Marching toward Mississippi in the spring of 1862, Grant rested his troops near a small log church named Shiloh and waited for reinforcements. Grant knew that Confederate generals Albert Johnston and P. G. T. Beauregard were nearby in Corinth, Mississippi. He did not expect them to attack. On April 6, 1862, thousands of Confederate troops surprised Grant's soldiers, beginning the **Battle of Shiloh**. By day's end the Confederate forces had pushed Grant's men back to the Tennessee River.

Confederate commanders believed that they could finish off Grant's army the next morning. After their long day of fighting at a level of intensity not yet seen in the war, some of Grant's officers advised him to retreat before the Confederates could renew their attack in the morning. "Retreat?" Grant replied. "No. I propose to attack at daylight and whip them." Grant's plan received more support after fresh Union troops arrived during the night.

Grant's April 7 surprise counterattack led to another day of fierce battle. By the middle of the afternoon, Grant's forces had subdued the Confederates. Southern general Beauregard gave the order to retreat. Both sides paid dearly, however. The Union suffered more than 13,000 casualties, and the Confederacy some 10,000—including General Johnston. Although Union forces were too badly hurt to pursue the Confederates, their victory at Shiloh gave the North a great advantage in the fight to control the Mississippi River valley.

Confederate forces fought desperately to stop the Union from controlling the Mississippi River.

New Orleans. Union control of the Mississippi River depended on its taking of New Orleans. It was the largest city in the South and a central port for supplying troops along and west of the river. Capturing New Orleans would allow the Union to cut off supplies to western Confederate forces and to move troops up the Mississippi River to join Grant's troops to the north. In late April 1862, Union ships commanded by David Farragut attacked the two forts guarding the approach to New Orleans from the Gulf of Mexico. After six days of unsuccessfully shelling the forts, Farragut decided to try to sail past them.

Seventeen Union warships advanced during the dark morning hours of April 24. The ensuing battle created a spectacular fireworks display. Confederate forces opened fire from gunboats, launched bombs from the shore, and pushed rafts set ablaze with towers of pine and pitch into the enemy ships. Despite the heavy pounding and nearly 200 casualties, all but four Union warships arrived in New Orleans. On April 29 the city was forced to surrender. Seventeen-year-old George Washington Cable witnessed the Union's capture of the city as "the crowds on the levee howled and screamed with rage."

By May 1862 the Union had achieved "a Deluge of Victories" in the West, as the New York *Tribune* reported. After the South's loss of 50,000 square miles of territory, 1,000 miles of navigable rivers, two state capitals, and its largest city, Confederate morale began to weaken. Mary Boykin Chesnut wrote after the capture of New Orleans, "Are we not cut in two? . . . I have nothing to chronicle but disasters. . . . The reality is hideous."

✔ **READING CHECK:** How did the Union win control of the Mississippi River?

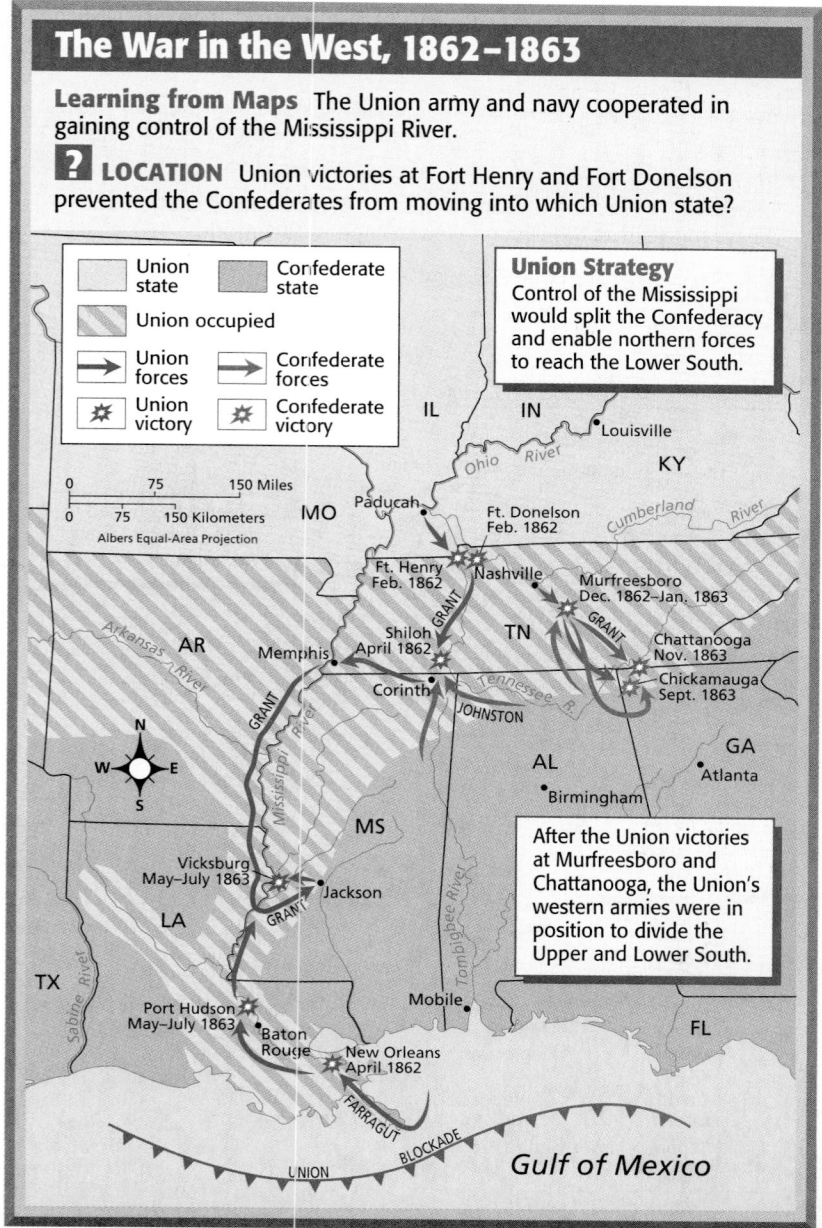

The War in the West, 1862–1863

Learning from Maps The Union army and navy cooperated in gaining control of the Mississippi River.

? LOCATION Union victories at Fort Henry and Fort Donelson prevented the Confederates from moving into which Union state?

Union state
Confederate state
Union occupied
Union forces
Confederate forces
Union victory
Confederate victory

0   75   150 Miles
0   75   150 Kilometers
Albers Equal-Area Projection

Union Strategy
Control of the Mississippi would split the Confederacy and enable northern forces to reach the Lower South.

After the Union victories at Murfreesboro and Chattanooga, the Union's western armies were in position to divide the Upper and Lower South.

IL   IN   Louisville
KY
Ohio River
MO   Paducah   Ft. Donelson Feb. 1862   Cumberland River
Ft. Henry Feb. 1862   Nashville   Murfreesboro Dec. 1862–Jan. 1863   GRANT
Shiloh April 1862   TN   GRANT   Chattanooga Nov. 1863
AR   Memphis   Corinth   Tennessee R.   Chickamauga Sept. 1863
JOHNSTON
GA
AL   Atlanta
Birmingham
MS
Vicksburg May–July 1863   Jackson   Tombigbee River
LA   GRANT
Arkansas River
TX   Sabine River   Mississippi River
Port Hudson May–July 1863   Mobile   FL
Baton Rouge   New Orleans April 1862
FARRAGUT
UNION BLOCKADE   *Gulf of Mexico*

Eastern Campaigns

While the Union racked up important victories in the West, President Lincoln remained committed to capturing Richmond. He ordered General George B. McClellan to return to Virginia in the spring of 1862.

The Peninsula Campaign. General McClellan trained his men well, teaching them both pride and discipline. His effectiveness as a military leader, however, suffered from his cautious nature. He often hesitated to commit his men to battle—much to the president's displeasure.

Lincoln reluctantly agreed to McClellan's strategy to take Richmond in what became known as the Peninsula Campaign. Rather than marching directly on the city, McClellan transported more than 100,000 men, 300 cannons, and 25,000 animals by water to the peninsula between the York and James Rivers. He planned to hit Richmond from the southeast, where the roads were better. This would put his army between Richmond and Confederate general Johnston's forces near Manassas, forcing the Confederates to move southward to defend Richmond. Once again, however, McClellan hesitated.

Yorktown and Seven Pines. In the first week of April 1862, General McClellan's forces met the Confederates at Yorktown, Virginia. Lincoln urged McClellan to attack but the general refused. He claimed that there were too many enemy troops. Actually, at first he faced only some 13,000 Confederates, led by General John B. Magruder. Lincoln sent a message warning that McClellan's "present hesitation . . . is but the story of Manassas repeated." He ordered, "*You must act.*" Instead, McClellan decided to lay siege to Yorktown. He wrote to his wife that if Lincoln wanted to defeat the rebels "he had better come & do it himself." Meanwhile, Confederate general Johnston moved his troops to the peninsula.

Johnston's and Magruder's forces held Yorktown until the beginning of May. Just as McClellan was about to overrun the Confederate defenses, Johnston began a month-long retreat toward Richmond. McClellan followed, and on May 31, 1862, the two sides clashed just east of Richmond in the Battle of Seven Pines. The South fared badly. Confederate colonel John B. Gordon wrote:

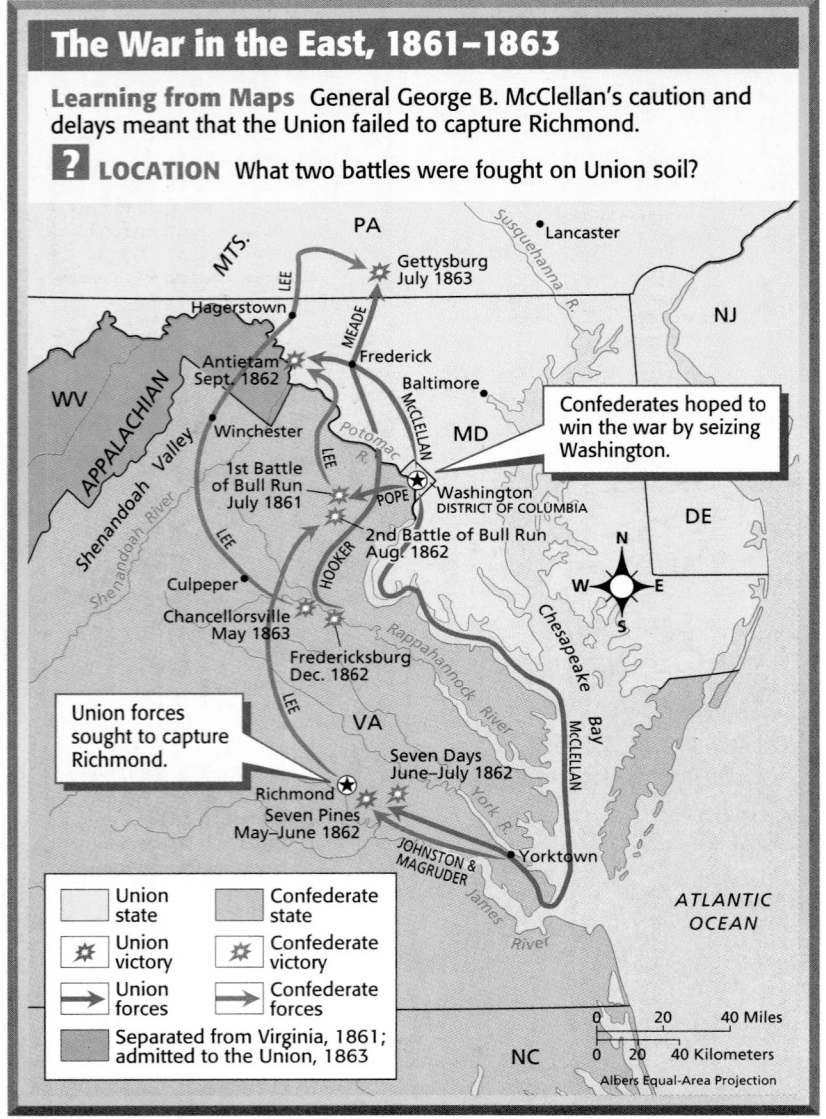

The War in the East, 1861–1863

Learning from Maps General George B. McClellan's caution and delays meant that the Union failed to capture Richmond.

? LOCATION What two battles were fought on Union soil?

Confederates hoped to win the war by seizing Washington.

Union forces sought to capture Richmond.

Legend:
- Union state
- Confederate state
- Union victory
- Confederate victory
- Union forces
- Confederate forces
- Separated from Virginia, 1861; admitted to the Union, 1863

0   20   40 Miles
0   20   40 Kilometers
Albers Equal-Area Projection

> 66 I was left alone on horseback, with my men dropping rapidly around me. . . . My field officers . . . were all dead. Every horse ridden into the fight, my own among them, was dead. Fully one half of my line officers and half my men were dead or wounded. 99

General Johnston was among the seriously wounded. When Jefferson Davis placed Robert E. Lee in command of the Confederate forces in Johnston's place, Lee promptly halted the fighting.

Seven Days Campaign. Even though the Confederates were badly weakened, McClellan again sat and waited. Lee did not. In a daring maneuver, Lee sent a cavalry unit commanded by 29-year-old James E. B. "Jeb" Stuart to gather information on enemy positions. Using Stuart's information, the combined forces of Lee and Stonewall Jackson attacked the Union army in the Seven Days Campaign. This fierce battle lasted from June 25 to July 1. Union casualties numbered nearly 16,000. Confederate casualties were even higher—more than 20,000—but the battle was considered a victory for the South because McClellan retreated.

President Lincoln soon removed McClellan and gave General John Pope command of the army in the field. In late August, while marching to Richmond, Pope and his men were defeated by Lee's forces at the Second Battle of Bull Run. Soon after, McClellan was back in command of the eastern forces.

✔ **READING CHECK:** What were the results of the eastern campaigns?

INTERPRETING THE VISUAL RECORD
Battles. Fighting in the Civil War was often fierce. *Whose perspective is the artist trying to portray? Explain your answer.*

A Shift in War Aims

As the months of warfare dragged on, many northerners began to question whether saving the Union without ending slavery was worth the price. Was it just or sensible, they asked, to sacrifice so much without the secessionist slaveholders who had caused the terrible bloodshed paying some price? "To fight against slaveholders, without fighting against slavery," charged abolitionist Frederick Douglass, "is but a half-hearted business."

Beginning to move against slavery. After fierce debate, Republicans pushed legislation through Congress in July 1862 that authorized African Americans to serve in the military. The legislation also freed slaves held by Confederate soldiers or by Confederate allies. President Lincoln signed the legislation. However, Horace Greeley, abolitionist editor of the New York *Tribune*, soon criticized Lincoln for not making slavery the central war issue. Lincoln replied by simply restating his original goal: "My paramount object in the struggle *is* to save the Union, and is *not* either to save or to destroy slavery."

Privately, however, the president had already concluded that slavery was too important to the southern war effort to be left alone. More slaves at work meant that more soldiers were available to fight against the Union. Lincoln hoped that if slaves learned that the North was fighting to free them, they would desert their masters, thereby weakening the South's economy.

This poster was made to commemorate Lincoln's decision to free southern slaves.

PRESIDENT ABRAHAM LINCOLN
The Emancipation Proclamation

After the Union victory at Antietam, President Lincoln believed he could take action toward freeing slaves in the South. The excerpts below are from the final Emancipation Proclamation that took effect on January 1, 1863.

On the first day of January, A.D. 1863, all persons held as slaves within any state or designated part of a state, the people whereof shall then be in rebellion against the United States, shall be then, thenceforward, and forever free. . . .

Now, therefore, I, Abraham Lincoln, President of the United States . . . do order and declare that all persons held as slaves within said designated states . . . are, and henceforward shall be, free. . . .

And I further declare and make known that such persons of suitable condition will be received into the armed service of the United States to garrison [defend] forts, positions, stations, and other places, and to man vessels of all sorts in said service.

And upon this act, sincerely believed to be an act of justice, warranted by the Constitution upon military necessity, I invoke [call upon] the considerate judgment of mankind and the gracious favor of Almighty God.

The Emancipation Proclamation.

President Lincoln lacked the constitutional authority to abolish slavery. As commander in chief of the armed forces, however, he did have the authority to institute military measures. Thus, in July 1862, Lincoln informed his cabinet that he planned to issue a new military order. As of a certain date, all slaves living in areas still rebelling against the United States would be free.

To quiet constitutional concerns about this order, Lincoln assured his cabinet that this **Emancipation Proclamation** would apply only to the Confederate states. This assurance also relieved concerns about the status of slaves in the border states.

President Lincoln decided to keep his plan secret until the Union won a major military victory. To issue the Proclamation when the war was going badly for the Union would look like an act of desperation. The needed victory came in September 1862.

Antietam

These soldiers are but a few of the thousands who died at Antietam.

General Robert E. Lee went on the offensive in September 1862. Confederate diplomats still believed that Britain might offer support to the Confederacy. Most British government officials were ready to formally recognize the Confederacy as an independent nation. They were waiting, though, to see if Lee could win a major victory on Union soil. On September 4, 1862, Lee began crossing the Potomac River into Maryland with some 55,000 men. Over the next few days, however, Lee lost about 5,000 soldiers as exhausted, hungry, and sick troops fell by the wayside. Union forces lost track of the Confederate troops for four days. Then, surprisingly, two Union soldiers happened upon a copy of Lee's battle plans wrapped around a discarded pack of cigars.

Armed with this information, General McClellan planned a counterattack. With some 75,000 troops, McClellan met Lee at Antietam (an-TEET-uhm) Creek in Maryland. The **Battle of Antietam** raged all day, becoming the bloodiest single-day battle in all of U.S. military history. The Confederates suffered more than 13,000 casualties; the Union more than 12,000.

Despite the Union army's good showing at Antietam, President Lincoln fired McClellan again after he allowed the Confederate troops to escape into Virginia. Although the Battle of Antietam was not a resounding Union victory, it raised confidence in the North. A major Confederate offensive had failed. This proved that General Lee could be defeated. Lee's loss also cost the South any hope of support from European countries.

The Union victory at Antietam gave Lincoln the necessary political support to move forward with his plans to free the slaves in the South. On September 22, the president issued a preliminary draft of the Emancipation Proclamation that would go into effect the first of the year. When January 1, 1863, found the Confederacy still in rebellion, Lincoln's Proclamation brought a decisive change in the war.

✔ **READING CHECK:** How did the Union victory at Antietam help shift the Union's war aims?

African Americans Take Up Arms

Both the July 1862 act allowing African Americans to serve in the military and the Emancipation Proclamation encouraged African Americans to enlist in the Union army. The first official black regiments were organized in August 1862 in the Union-controlled Sea Islands of coastal South Carolina. Frederick Douglass viewed military service as a step toward citizenship for African Americans.

66 **Let the black man get upon his person the brass letters, U.S.; let him get an eagle on his button, and a musket on his shoulder and bullets in his pocket, and there is no power on earth which can deny that he has earned the right to citizenship. 99**

Many of the first African American soldiers recruited by the Union army served in the **54th Massachusetts Infantry**. This regiment earned an honored place in U.S. military history. In July 1863, Union forces began attacking Confederate-held forts near Charleston, South Carolina. The Union could not break the Confederates' hold. As a result, Brigadier General Truman Seymour decided to send some 6,000 Union troops in a desperate frontal attack against Fort Wagner—which guarded the entrance to Charleston Harbor. The 54th Infantry would lead the charge.

The attack on Fort Wagner represented the first time that African American troops had been assigned a key role in a military campaign. However, the Union commander knew that the 54th would suffer great losses in their frontal assault on the Confederate lines. African American troops also faced a danger that white Union soldiers did not. Black soldiers captured by the Confederates were treated as outlaws. They could face execution or be sold into slavery.

On the night of July 18, in the middle of a storm of gunfire, commanding officer Colonel Robert Gould Shaw and the 54th clawed their way to the top of Fort Wagner's sloping walls. Both armies suffered staggering losses in the prolonged fight. The siege finally ended September 6, when Confederate forces, unable to hold out, evacuated the fort.

Despite the courageous performance of African American volunteers, the Union army did not offer them full equality. For much of the war, black soldiers earned less than half the pay of white soldiers. After much criticism by black soldiers and their commanding officers, Congress finally equalized the pay scale in June 1864. In addition, white officers commanded each black regiment. Only about 100 African Americans were commissioned as junior officers. In 1865 Martin Delany became the first African American promoted to the rank of major.

INTERPRETING THE VISUAL RECORD

Emancipation. This engraving celebrating the Emancipation Proclamation first appeared in 1863. *What do you think the various elements in the image symbolize?*

The Congressional Medal of Honor

Nearly 180,000 African American men served in the Union army, and more than 32,000 gave their lives. Some also served in the navy. More than 20 African American soldiers and sailors won the Congressional Medal of Honor.

✔ **READING CHECK:** How did African American soldiers help the Union cause?

New Union Commanders

The addition of African American soldiers came at a key time for the Union, which continued to suffer important defeats through the winter of 1862 and the spring of 1863. After Antietam, President Lincoln chose Ambrose E. Burnside to replace General McClellan.

Fredericksburg. On December 11 and 12, 1862, General Burnside sent some 114,000 Union soldiers across the Rappahannock (rap-uh-HAN-uhk) River near Fredericksburg, Virginia. General Lee and some 75,000 Confederate soldiers controlled the hills above the town. Reasoning that Lee would not expect a frontal attack, Burnside ordered his men across an open plain on the morning of December 13.

Lee took advantage of Burnside's positioning. From their high ground, the Confederates could easily pick off the Union soldiers as they crossed the open fields. The Union army suffered more than 12,000 casualties at Fredericksburg, and the

Science & Technology

Weapons and War

Technological developments changed the nature of warfare during the Civil War. Despite their great accuracy, rifles were seldom carried by the infantry before the 1850s. Rifles from this period had grooves carved inside the barrel that allowed a cone-shaped bullet to spin as it left the gun and travel four times farther than a bullet shot from a smoothbore barrel. Bullets large enough to spin, however, had to be rammed down the

barrel with a mallet—which was awkward and time-consuming.

In 1848 a French army captain named Claude E. Minié developed a smaller bullet that could be easily rammed down a rifle's barrel. These bullets were extremely expensive, however. James H.

Burton, an armorer at the Harpers Ferry Armory, created a less-expensive version of Minié's bullets. These "minié balls"—pronounced "minnie" by members of both armies—were used extensively during the Civil War.

Most soldiers on both sides of the conflict carried rifles by 1863. The primary effect of the change from smoothbores to rifles was an increase in the number of casualties.

rifling grooves

Understanding Science and History

1. What effect did the grooves in a rifle's barrel have?
2. What difficulties were involved in loading bullets that were large enough to spin inside a rifle barrel?

Confederates some 5,000. One northerner bitterly referred to the battle as a "great slaughter pen."

Chancellorsville. President Lincoln transferred Burnside and gave command of the eastern forces to General Joseph "Fighting Joe" Hooker. The new commander offered a daring plan to crush Lee's forces. He proposed dividing his large army into three parts in order to cut off supply lines and attack them from both flanks. The strategy seemed workable, particularly since Hooker's 134,000 troops were more than double the Confederate troops.

By April 30, 1863, Hooker had positioned his men in a deep forest known as the Wilderness, near Chancellorsville, Virginia. Lee divided his troops, sending Stonewall Jackson and some 30,000 men through the Wilderness to outflank Hooker. When Hooker discovered the troop movements, he assumed that the Confederates were retreating. Instead, Lee and Jackson attacked the Union forces from two sides. After several days of fighting, Hooker withdrew in defeat.

The South paid dearly for its victory at Chancellorsville, however. Riding back to Confederate lines after dark, Stonewall Jackson was mistaken for a Union cavalryman and shot by his own troops. The two bullets that hit his left arm required it to be amputated. As with countless other soldiers, Jackson's battle wounds led to serious infection. Eight days later, Lee's most valued general died.

General Stonewall Jackson is shot during the Battle of Chancellorsville.

✔ **READING CHECK:** What was the significance of the Battles of Fredericksburg and Chancellorsville?

SECTION 3 REVIEW

Define and explain the significance of the following terms:
Battle of Shiloh
Emancipation Proclamation
Battle of Antietam
54th Massachusetts Infantry

Identify and explain the significance of the following individuals:
Ulysses S. Grant
David Farragut
George B. McClellan
James E. B. "Jeb" Stuart
Martin Delany
Ambrose E. Burnside

Locate and explain the importance of the following places:
Fredericksburg
Chancellorsville

1. **Using Graphic Organizers** Copy the graphic organizer below. Use it to list each major battle of 1862 and early 1863, including its date and location, a brief description of each battle, and the battle's outcome.

	Date	Location	Outcome
Shiloh			
New Orleans			
Yorktown			
Seven Pines			
Seven Days			
Antietam			
Fredericksburg			
Chancellorsville			

2. **Comparing and Contrasting** Why did the Battle of Antietam have a positive effect on northern morale while the battles at Fredericksburg and Chancellorsville had negative effects?

3. **Distinguishing Fact from Opinion** Some white leaders argued that African Americans would not make good soldiers. What evidence from the Civil War would contradict this claim?

4. **Hypothesizing** What might have happened if President Lincoln had issued the Emancipation Proclamation before the Battle of Antietam?

Critical Thinking

5. Why did the shift in the Union's war aims increase support for the war among some northerners?
Consider:
 • why some northerners had wanted a shift in goals
 • what the shift in war goals was
 • how Lincoln's stated goals in 1863 satisfied some previous critics of the war

The Final Phase

OBJECTIVES

Read to understand:

1. what the outcomes were of the Battle of Gettysburg
2. why the Union victory at Vicksburg was significant
3. what General Grant's strategy was in the summer of 1864
4. what strategies General Sherman employed
5. what the terms were of the surrender at Appomattox

KEY TERMS

Battle of Gettysburg
Pickett's Charge
Gettysburg Address
Siege of Vicksburg
war of attrition
total war

KEY PEOPLE

George Meade
William Tecumseh Sherman

KEY PLACES

Gettysburg
Vicksburg
Atlanta
Savannah
Appomattox Courthouse

Thousands of Confederate and Union troops died in the Battle of Gettysburg.

EYEWITNESSES TO History

> 66 *There never were such men in an army before. They will go anywhere and do anything if properly led.* 99
> —Robert E. Lee

General Robert E. Lee praised his troops following their victory at Chancellorsville. The South received an enormous boost in confidence and morale from the victory, while northern morale plunged. When President Lincoln heard the news from the War Department on May 6, his face turned "ashen," a newspaper reporter recalled. "My God! my God! What will the country say?" Lincoln exclaimed. Republican Charles Sumner agreed. "Lost, lost, all is lost," he cried when he learned of the defeat. After achieving such an astounding victory with nearly half as many men as his enemy, Lee began to believe his men were invincible. Lee's confidence led him to devise his most ambitious plan to date—one that amazed and impressed other Confederate leaders.

General Robert E. Lee

Gettysburg

Following the victory at Chancellorsville, General Lee decided to invade the North again. This action would spare war-weary Virginia from further fighting. It also would allow Lee to resupply and feed his hungry troops by seizing provisions from the enemy.

In early June 1863 Lee crossed into Pennsylvania with some 75,000 troops. President Lincoln urged General Hooker to attack the Confederates before they could consolidate their troops. Hooker worried, however, that Lee's troops outnumbered his and hesitated to move. Fearing he had another General McClellan leading the army, Lincoln quickly replaced Hooker with General George Meade.

By the end of June, Confederate regiments had begun to assemble near the town of Gettysburg, Pennsylvania. When scouts reported a supply of shoes in the town, the Confederates organized a raiding party. The troops were unaware that two Union brigades had positioned themselves on high ground northwest of Gettysburg. As the Confederate raiding party approached the small town on July 1, it met a blaze of Union fire.

On the first day of the **Battle of Gettysburg**, the Confederates pushed the Union line back to Cemetery Hill and Cemetery Ridge. The Confederates held Seminary Ridge, a lower line of hills about a half mile away. Nevertheless, Lee knew that the danger to his forces would remain so long as the North held the higher ground. Expecting that Union reinforcements would

soon be arriving, he decided to attack quickly. On July 2 General Lee charged the Union's left flank, trying without success to capture a dome-shaped hill called Little Round Top. The next day he ordered some 15,000 men commanded by George Pickett to rush the Union center on Cemetery Ridge. Only half of the Confederate soldiers survived **Pickett's Charge**. Confederate lieutenant G. W. Finley later wrote, "Men were falling all around us, and cannon and muskets were raining death upon us." With few men left, Pickett could not organize a second attack. Bad weather prevented Meade from pursuing the Confederates, however, and Lee retreated to Virginia.

A staggering number of young men lost their lives at Gettysburg. After three days of fighting, Union casualties numbered more than 23,000 and Confederate casualties more than 20,000. In November 1863 President Lincoln helped dedicate a cemetery at the Gettysburg battlefield. Lincoln spoke for only a few minutes, but his **Gettysburg Address** remains a classic statement of democratic ideals.

Although the Union army emerged victorious at Gettysburg, it once again narrowly failed to end the war. A disappointed President Lincoln complained, "Our Army held the war in the hollow of their hand and they would not close it." The battle, however, marked a critical turning point. The Union army had proved that the Confederacy could be beaten.

✔ **READING CHECK:** What were the outcomes of the Battle of Gettysburg?

★ HISTORICAL DOCUMENTS ★

PRESIDENT ABRAHAM LINCOLN
The Gettysburg Address

On November, 19, 1863, Abraham Lincoln dedicated a national cemetery at the Gettysburg battlefield. His short but powerful speech became a lasting reminder to all Americans of the democratic ideals for which the Union soldiers at Gettysburg had died.

Four score and seven years ago our fathers brought forth on this continent, a new nation, conceived [created] in Liberty, and dedicated to the proposition that all men are created equal.

Now we are engaged in a great civil war, testing whether that nation, or any nation so conceived and so dedicated, can long endure. We are met on a great battlefield of that war. We have come to dedicate a portion of that field, as a final resting place for those who here gave their lives that that nation might live. . . .

But, in a larger sense, we can not dedicate—we can not consecrate [make holy]—we cannot hallow—this ground. The brave men, living and dead, who struggled here, have consecrated it, far above our poor power to add or detract. The world will little note nor long remember what we say here, but it can never forget what they did here. It is for us the living, rather, to be dedicated here to the unfinished work which they who fought here have thus far so nobly advanced. It is rather for us to . . . highly resolve that these dead shall not have died in vain—that this nation, under God, shall have a new birth of freedom—and that government of the people, by the people, for the people, shall not perish from the earth.

Lincoln Finds His General

The war continued in the West in 1863, with the Union attempting to control the Mississippi River valley. General Ulysses S. Grant won several significant victories for the North. President Lincoln soon recognized Grant's invaluable leadership.

Vicksburg. Grant knew that gaining full control of the Mississippi River required taking Vicksburg, Mississippi. Vicksburg's high river bluffs allowed the Confederate artillery to command an extensive area. In May 1863 Grant hatched a risky plan to take the city. Marching deep into enemy territory, he bottled up one Confederate force in nearby Jackson. Then he raced west to trap the other enemy force inside Vicksburg.

Confederate cannons at Vicksburg fire at Union gunboats along the Mississippi River.

For six weeks General Grant and his men laid siege to the town, preventing any Confederate reinforcements from arriving. During the **Siege of Vicksburg**, the city's defenders began eating mules and rats to keep from starving. One woman in the city wrote, "We are utterly cut off from the world, surrounded by a circle of fire." Finally, in late June the desperate Confederate soldiers sent a letter to their commander, urging him to surrender.

On July 3, 1863, General Grant and Confederate general John Pemberton met under an oak tree to discuss terms of surrender. The Confederates surrendered to Grant the next day. On July 8 the Confederate forces at Port Hudson, Louisiana, also fell. These victories gave the Union total control over the Mississippi River, thereby cutting off Arkansas, Louisiana, and Texas from the rest of the Confederacy.

✔ **READING CHECK:** Why was the Union victory at Vicksburg significant?

HOLT RESEARCHER

Read More About It

Free Find:
Southern Railroads
After reading about southern railroads on the Holt Researcher CD–ROM, create a map that shows how the railroads were vital to the Confederacy's war effort.

Summer of 1864. President Lincoln promoted General Grant to general in chief, commander of all Union forces, in the spring of 1864. Grant understood better than previous commanders how to take advantage of the North's soldiers and supplies. His strategy was to use these advantages against an enemy that was reeling from shortages. Grant informed Lincoln that he would march on Richmond, take his losses, and press on. He planned a **war of attrition**—that is, to continue fighting until the South ran out of men, supplies, and will.

In May 1864 Grant moved some 122,000 troops into the Wilderness near Chancellorsville, Virginia. For two days the northerners hurled themselves at some 66,000 Confederates, but the rebels held their ground. Grant's forces suffered nearly 18,000 casualties; the Confederates lost nearly 10,000.

Rather than rest, Grant pushed on, mile by bloody mile, just as he had promised Lincoln he would do. "I propose to fight it out on this line if it takes all summer," he wrote. Moving his forces a few miles to the south, Grant forced Lee to keep his weary men in the field. At Spotsylvania Court House, Virginia, Union and Confederate forces clashed several times between May 10 and May 19. Again, the Union forces suffered horrible losses. Shocked by the number of casualties, a southern soldier remarked of Grant: "We have met a man this time, who either does not know when he is whipped, or who cares not if he loses his whole army."

In mid-June Grant traveled south once more to attack Petersburg, Virginia. He hoped that capturing this railroad center would cut off Richmond's supplies. Lee held on, however. After three days even Grant was discouraged. Since May 12 his army had suffered some 60,000 casualties. He called off the direct assault and settled down to lay siege to Petersburg. Nevertheless, Grant's strategy was slowly succeeding. Lee's army steadily dwindled, and few reserves remained.

✔ **READING CHECK:** What was General Grant's strategy for winning the war in the summer of 1864?

Ulysses S. Grant and his staff posed for this photograph at their headquarters in Cold Harbor, Virginia, in June 1864.

The Final Campaigns, 1864–1865

Learning from Maps Although he suffered defeat after defeat, Grant kept attacking. When he failed to take Petersburg, Grant laid siege to the city for nine months. Defeated at Five Forks, Lee abandoned Petersburg and Richmond on April 2. A week later Lee surrendered to Grant.

? MOVEMENT Sherman's army took 17 days to march from Savannah to Columbia. On average, how many miles did his army need to cover each day?

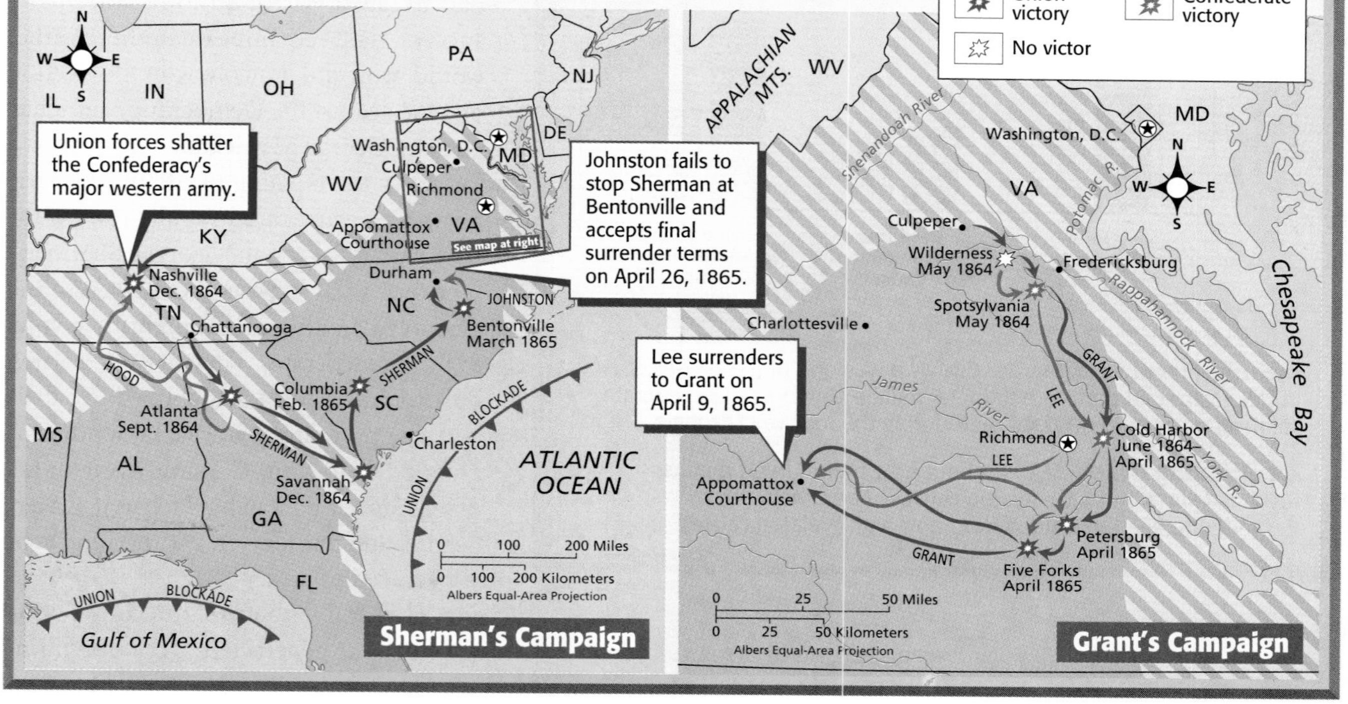

Union state	Confederate state
Union occupied	Union blockade
Union forces	Confederate forces
Union victory	Confederate victory
No victor	

Union forces shatter the Confederacy's major western army.

Johnston fails to stop Sherman at Bentonville and accepts final surrender terms on April 26, 1865.

Lee surrenders to Grant on April 9, 1865.

PA
NJ
DE
MD
Washington, D.C.
Culpeper
Richmond
WV
Appomattox Courthouse
VA
See map at right
KY
Nashville Dec. 1864
TN
Chattanooga
Durham
NC
JOHNSTON
Bentonville March 1865
Columbia Feb. 1865
SC
Charleston
HOOD
Atlanta Sept. 1864
SHERMAN
MS
AL
Savannah Dec. 1864
GA
FL
UNION BLOCKADE
Gulf of Mexico
ATLANTIC OCEAN
UNION BLOCKADE
IL IN OH

0 100 200 Miles
0 100 200 Kilometers
Albers Equal-Area Projection

Sherman's Campaign

APPALACHIAN MTS. WV
Washington, D.C. MD
Shenandoah River
Potomac R.
VA
Culpeper
Wilderness May 1864
Fredericksburg
Spotsylvania May 1864
Rappahannock River
Charlottesville
James River
Richmond
Cold Harbor June 1864– April 1865
York R.
LEE
GRANT
Chesapeake Bay
Appomattox Courthouse
GRANT
Five Forks April 1865
Petersburg April 1865

0 25 50 Miles
0 25 50 Kilometers
Albers Equal-Area Projection

Grant's Campaign

Sherman's March to the Sea

Union general William Tecumseh Sherman matched General Grant's determination. Moody, ambitious, and brilliant, Sherman had performed ably at Vicksburg and other battles. Grant rewarded Sherman by making him commander of the Tennessee army.

While Grant slowly pushed his way toward Richmond, Sherman undertook a campaign to destroy southern railroads and industries. In early May, he moved some 100,000 troops out of Tennessee toward Atlanta, Georgia. On his way, General Sherman repeatedly outmaneuvered Confederate general Johnston's forces. He then defeated General John Hood's attacks and pushed the Confederate forces back.

When Atlanta fell on September 2, 1864, the Confederates lost their last railroad link across the Appalachian Mountains. After ordering residents to evacuate, Sherman's men set fire to large portions of the city. Defending his tactics, he declared:

General Sherman's troops burned much of Atlanta.

66 If [southerners] raise a howl against my barbarity and cruelty, I will answer that war is war, and not popularity-seeking. If they want peace, they and their relatives must stop the war. 99

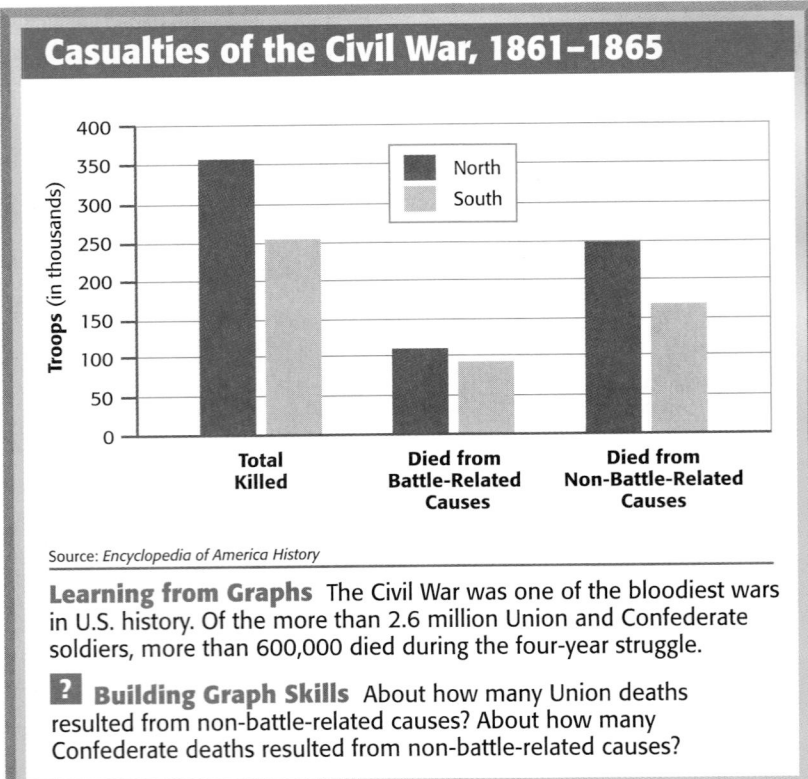

Casualties of the Civil War, 1861–1865

Troops (in thousands)

- North
- South

Categories:
- Total Killed
- Died from Battle-Related Causes
- Died from Non-Battle-Related Causes

Source: *Encyclopedia of America History*

Learning from Graphs The Civil War was one of the bloodiest wars in U.S. history. Of the more than 2.6 million Union and Confederate soldiers, more than 600,000 died during the four-year struggle.

② Building Graph Skills About how many Union deaths resulted from non-battle-related causes? About how many Confederate deaths resulted from non-battle-related causes?

Total war. General William Tecumseh Sherman led his troops on a destructive march to the sea. *What evidence of Sherman's total-war strategy can you identify in the photograph?*

The fall of Atlanta boosted President Lincoln's re-election campaign. The Union victory came at a critical moment when Lincoln appeared in danger of not even receiving his party's nomination. Many Republicans were upset that the war had dragged on for so long. Sherman's success renewed hope that the conflict would soon end. Lincoln won the election of 1864 against the Democratic candidate, General George McClellan.

After the burning of Atlanta, General Sherman's army raced rapidly toward the port city of Savannah, Georgia. Sherman's men took what supplies they could use and destroyed anything that might be helpful to the Confederates. They uprooted crops, burned farmhouses, slaughtered livestock, and tore up railroad tracks. In South Carolina, Mary Boykin Chesnut wrote in her diary, "Since Atlanta I have felt as if all were dead within me, forever. We are going to be wiped off the earth."

Although much of the destruction went beyond Sherman's orders, it stemmed from the general's strategy of fighting a **total war**. He believed that it was not enough to wage war against enemy troops. Rather, to win the war, the Union must strike at the enemy's economic resources. Sherman believed they "must make old and young, rich and poor, feel the hard hand of war. . . . We cannot change the hearts of those people of the South," he said, "but we can make war so terrible . . . that generations would pass away before they would again appeal to it." Although Sherman's tactics brought the Union's goals within reach, his actions left deep and bitter scars across the South.

In early December 1864, Sherman and his men reached Savannah, where they were resupplied by the Union navy. On December 22, the general sent President Lincoln a message: "I beg to present you, as a Christmas gift, the city of Savannah." One month later Sherman and his troops turned north in an effort to link up with General Grant's troops.

✔ **READING CHECK:** What strategies did General Sherman employ in his southern campaign?

Surrender at Appomattox

As General Sherman's army pushed northward through the Carolinas, General Grant's troops battered Richmond. On April 2, 1865, with Grant close on his heels, General Lee withdrew from Richmond. Within hours Union troops poured into the Confederate capital.

Lee's army was now only half the size of Grant's. Knowing his troops could not survive another summer like the one of 1864, Lee attempted to flee westward, hoping to join up with more troops. Grant cut off Lee's escape, however. With his once-proud army reduced to less than 30,000 men, many without food, Lee asked for terms of surrender.

On April 9, 1865, Grant and Lee met in a house in the tiny Virginia village of Appomattox Courthouse. Lee stood in full dress uniform with a jewel-studded sword at his side. Grant wore a private's shirt, unbuttoned at the neck. For a time the two men talked about their Mexican War days. Then they turned to the business at hand.

The terms of surrender were simple. Confederate officers could keep their side arms. All soldiers would be fed and allowed to keep their horses and mules. None would be tried for treason. "Let all the men who claim to own a horse or mule take the animals home with them to work their little farms," said Grant. "This will do much toward conciliating [uniting] our people," replied Lee.

As Lee rode off, Union troops started to celebrate the Union victory, but Grant silenced them. "The war is over," he said. "The rebels are our countrymen again." After the surrender, Lee returned to his men and quietly told them:

General Robert E. Lee signs the papers of surrender, ending the Civil War.

> 66 I have done for you all that it was in my power to do. You have done all your duty. Leave the result to God. Go to your homes and resume your occupations. Obey the laws and become as good citizens as you were soldiers. 99

The weary Confederates were then fed and allowed to depart for home. On April 26, 1865, General Joseph Johnston surrendered to General Sherman under similar terms at Durham Station, North Carolina. The war was over.

✔ **READING CHECK:** What were the terms of General Lee's surrender?

SECTION 4 REVIEW

Define and explain the significance of the following terms:
Battle of Gettysburg
Pickett's Charge
Gettysburg Address
Siege of Vicksburg
war of attrition
total war

Identify and explain the significance of the following individuals:
George Meade
William Tecumseh Sherman

Locate and explain the importance of the following places:
Gettysburg
Vicksburg
Atlanta
Savannah
Appomattox Courthouse

1. **Using Graphic Organizers** Copy the graphic organizer below. Use it to list the major events that occurred between General Grant's promotion and General Lee's surrender at Appomattox Courthouse.

1. Grant is promoted to lead the Union army
2. _____
3. _____
4. _____
5. _____
6. _____
7. _____
8. Lee surrenders at Appomattox Courthouse

2. **Assessing Consequences** How did the Battle of Gettysburg affect the course of the Civil War?
3. **Understanding Geography: Location** Why was the capture of Vicksburg necessary for the North to be in a position to win the war?
4. **Problem Solving** What were the strategies of Ulysses S. Grant and William Tecumseh Sherman? Was there another strategy that could have succeeded and led to less destruction in the South?

Critical Thinking

5. How did General Grant's terms of surrender promote reconciliation between the North and the South?
Consider:
• what the terms of the surrender were
• how both sides reacted to the terms
• what conditions he could have demanded

Review

Creating a Time Line

Copy the time line below onto a sheet of paper. Complete the time line by filling in the events and dates from the chapter that you think were most significant. Pick three events and explain why you think they were significant.

1861   1863   1865

Writing a Summary

Using the Reading Checks as a guide, write an overview of the events in the chapter.

Identifying People and Ideas

Identify the following terms or individuals and explain their significance.

1. Robert E. Lee
2. Thomas "Stonewall" Jackson
3. George B. McClellan
4. Elizabeth Blackwell
5. Ulysses S. Grant
6. Copperheads
7. Emancipation Proclamation
8. Martin Delany
9. war of attrition
10. William Tecumseh Sherman

Understanding Main Ideas

SECTION 1

1. What role did Fort Sumter play in the outbreak of the war?

SECTION 2

2. What contributions did civilians make during the war?

SECTION 3

3. What role did the Battle of Antietam play in the Emancipation Proclamation?

SECTION 4

4. What were the terms of Robert E. Lee's surrender at Appomattox Courthouse?

Reviewing Themes

1. **Geographic Diversity** What role did geography play in helping the North win the war?
2. **Economic Development** How did the economic resources of the North and the South affect the war?
3. **Democratic Values** How did the draft challenge ideas about individual liberty in the North and in the South?

Thinking Critically

1. **Hypothesizing** How might the outcome of the Civil War have been different if European powers had aided the South?
2. **Identifying Cause and Effect** How did fears of alienating the border states affect northern strategy during the war?
3. **Analyzing** How did the South, with fewer supplies and resources, manage to stall a northern victory for four years?
4. **Recognizing Point of View** Were those who opposed the draft correct in their assessment of its effects? Explain your answer.
5. **Comparing and Contrasting** How did people in the North and in the South experience the war in different ways?

Writing About History

Writing to Evaluate Write an essay evaluating whether total-war tactics were necessary for the Union to win the Civil War. Use the following chart to organize your thoughts.

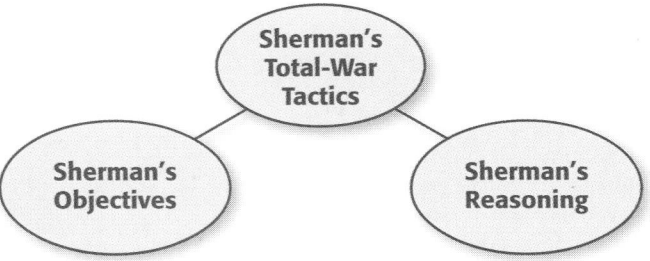

Sherman's Total-War Tactics

Sherman's Objectives

Sherman's Reasoning

Strategies for Success Review the **Strategies for Success** on *Recognizing Fallacies in Reasoning*. Then study the following statements and identify the reasoning error in each. Note additional information that would make each statement correct.

1. France and Britain did not support the Confederacy during the Civil War because it conscripted, or drafted, large numbers of young men into its army.
2. The Emancipation Proclamation was enacted on January 1, 1863, because the Confederacy had just scored a major victory at the Battle of Fredericksburg.
3. The North won the Civil War because it had a much more extensive railroad system than the South.
4. President Lincoln was dissatisfied with General McClellan because the military leader moved too quickly.
5. General Lee surrendered because Abraham Lincoln was elected for a second term as president.

Linking History and Geography

Study the map below and note how many slave and free states existed in 1860. Identify which slave states remained in the Union and explain why their location was significant.

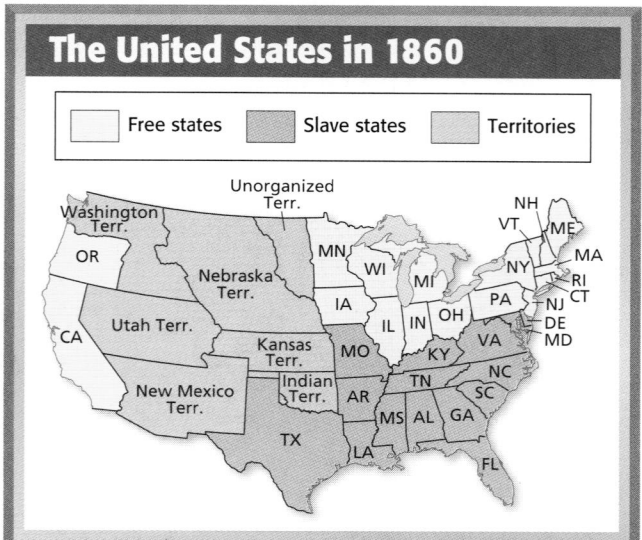

The United States in 1860

Free states | Slave states | Territories

Washington Terr.
OR
Unorganized Terr.
Nebraska Terr.
MN
WI
VT NH
ME
NY
MA
CA
Utah Terr.
IA
MI
PA
RI CT
NJ
Kansas Terr.
IL IN OH
DE
MD
New Mexico Terr.
Indian Terr.
MO
KY
VA
NC
AR
TN
SC
TX
MS AL GA
LA
FL

 internetconnect

TOPIC: War Photography
GO TO: go.hrw.com
KEYWORD: SD1 Photography

Accessing the Internet through the HRW Web site, research the Civil War photography of Mathew Brady. Then create original poetry that reflects the content of the images in the photographs, the emotional mood of the photographs, and the context in which the photographs were taken.

BUILDING YOUR PORTFOLIO

Complete one or all of the following projects independently or cooperatively.

1 Democratic Values

Imagine that you are an abolitionist in 1862. **Write a letter** to President Lincoln urging him to take a strong stand against slavery.

2 Geographic Diversity

Imagine that you are a member of a congressional committee attempting to formulate a compromise between the North and South to prevent a civil war. **Create a chart** that lists the economic, political, and social differences between the two sides that you think will be obstacles to an agreement and possible peaceful ways around these obstacles.

3 Cultural Diversity

Imagine that you are a reporter at Appomattox Courthouse. **Write an editorial** giving your impressions of General Lee's surrender and your evaluation of whether the war was worth the cost.

AMERICA'S Geography

Regionalism

By the mid-1800s the United States consisted of three distinct geographic regions, each with its own unique character and culture. Some people felt more loyalty to their region than to the nation as a whole. This concept of regionalism was particularly evident in the South. Unlike sectionalism, regionalism focuses more on cultural identity than political differences. Since regionalism primarily involves cultural identification, the regional identity of some states has shifted as the state's culture has changed. Many residents of Missouri, for instance, identified with the South before the Civil War. In the late 1800s, however, as industrialization, trade, and transportation increased in the state, its culture became closely identified with that of the Midwest.

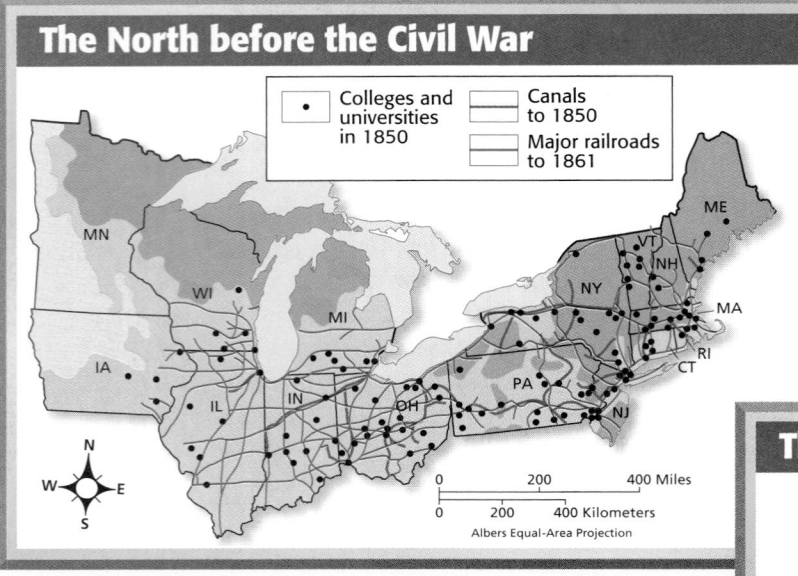

The North before the Civil War

Colleges and universities in 1850

Canals to 1850

Major railroads to 1861

ME
VT
NH
NY
MA
RI
CT
PA
NJ
OH
IN
IL
IA
MI
WI
MN

0   200   400 Miles
0   200   400 Kilometers
Albers Equal-Area Projection

Evergreen forest
Deciduous forest
Mixed forest
Tallgrass prairie
Shortgrass prairie
Shrub
Desert

The North. The smallest region—the North—was the center of industrialization in the United States. It was also the center of higher education. In 1850 most of the country's colleges and universities—63 percent—were located in the North.

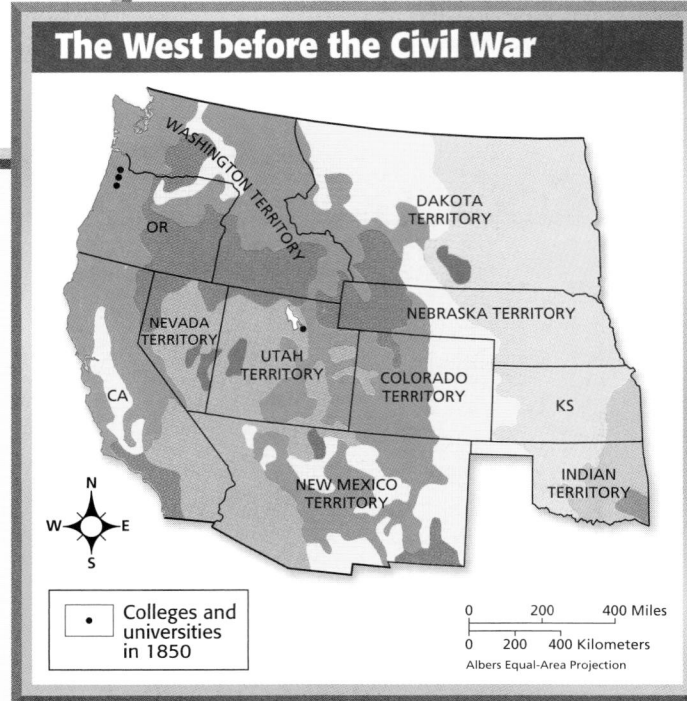

The West before the Civil War

WASHINGTON TERRITORY
OR
NEVADA TERRITORY
CA
UTAH TERRITORY
NEW MEXICO TERRITORY
DAKOTA TERRITORY
NEBRASKA TERRITORY
COLORADO TERRITORY
KS
INDIAN TERRITORY

Colleges and universities in 1850

0   200   400 Miles
0   200   400 Kilometers
Albers Equal-Area Projection

The West. Although the West was the largest region of the country in 1850, it had the smallest population. The first centers of education in the West were located on the frontier. The Mormons of Utah and followers of the Oregon Trail established the region's first universities.

The South before the Civil War

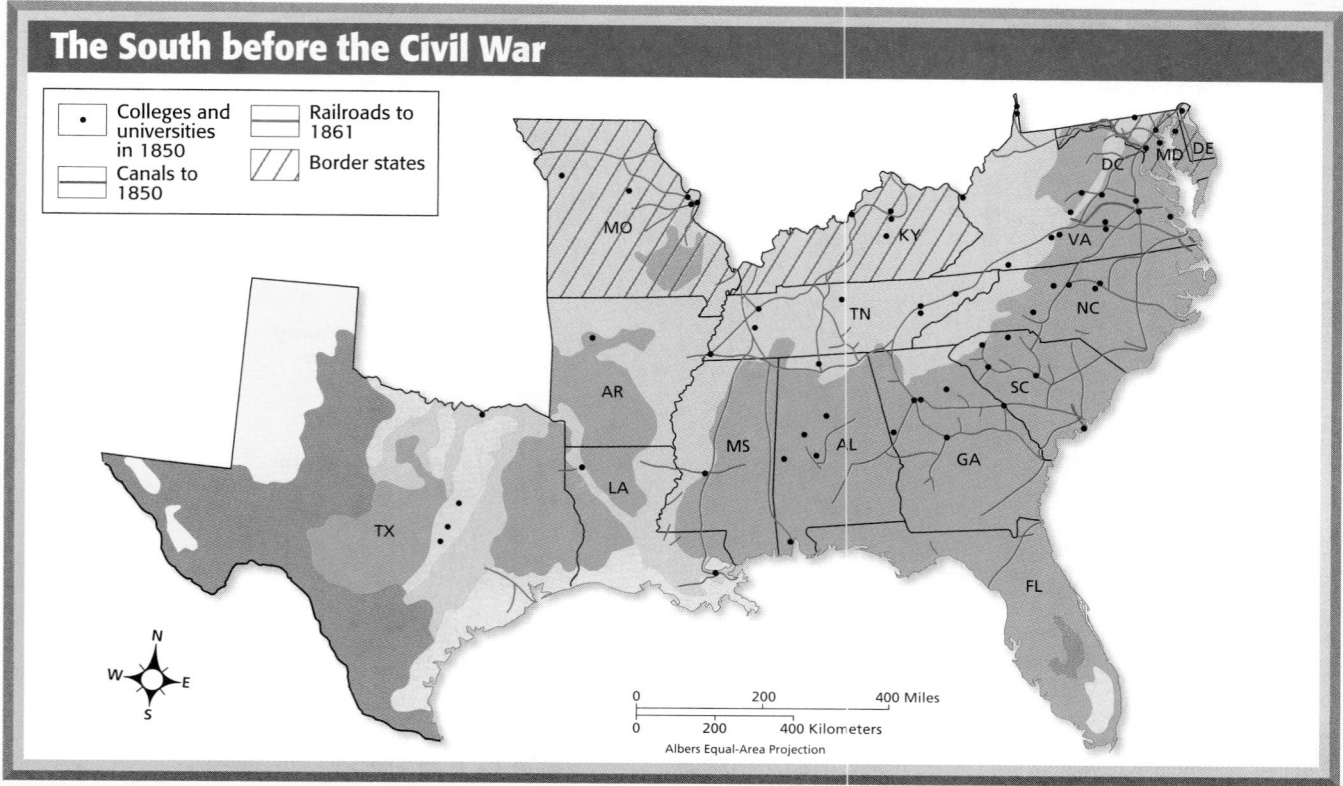

| Colleges and universities in 1850 | Railroads to 1861 |
| Canals to 1850 | Border states |

MO
KY
DC
MD
DE
VA
NC
TN
AR
SC
MS
AL
GA
LA
TX
FL

N
W E
S

0   200   400 Miles
0   200   400 Kilometers
Albers Equal-Area Projection

Diversity of Population, 1860

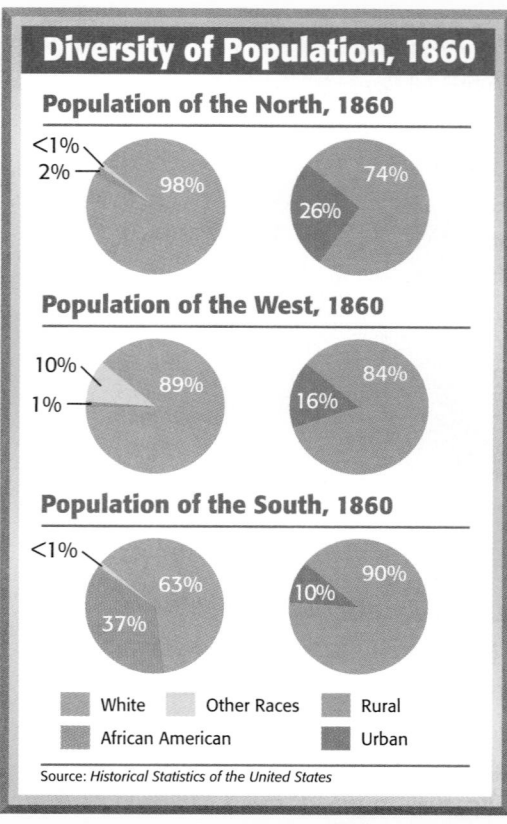

Population of the North, 1860

<1%
2%
98%
74%
26%

Population of the West, 1860

10%
1%
89%
84%
16%

Population of the South, 1860

<1%
63%
37%
90%
10%

White   Other Races   Rural
African American   Urban

Source: Historical Statistics of the United States

The South. Although the South had a larger population than the West, a smaller percentage of its population lived in urban areas. Many western settlers tended to move to booming cities such as San Francisco. Although the South had more colleges than the West, overall it lagged far behind the North in education. A majority of the country's residents who could not read lived in the South. Most were slaves who were not allowed to learn to read.

GEOGRAPHY AND HISTORY   Skills

REGION

1. How did the populations of the North, the South, and the West differ?
2. Which southern state had no colleges in 1850?

1865–1900

Reconstruction and the New South

Members of Congress cast votes on the impeachment of President Johnson

Harvesting cotton

THE GRANGER COLLECTION, NEW YORK

1866
Daily Life
Race riots erupt in Memphis and New Orleans.

1868
Politics
President Andrew Johnson is impeached.

1878
Business and Finance
Good land for growing cotton can be purchased in North Carolina for as low as $5 an acre.

1881
The Arts
The Southern Art Union is organized.

1881
World Events
Alexander II, czar of Russia, is assassinated.

| 1865 | 1870 | 1875 | 1880 |

1865
Politics
The passage of the Thirteenth Amendment abolishes slavery.

1867
Business and Finance
Southern crops bring in just half their expected price, ruining many planters.

1867
Daily Life
Howard University is established for African American students.

1867
Politics
Congress passes the first Reconstruction Act.

1871
The Arts
The Fisk Jubilee Singers tour the United States.

The Fisk Jubilee Singers

1881
Politics
The first Jim Crow law requires African Americans to ride in separate railway cars from whites.

Before You Read

Build on What You Know

Beginning with the framing of the Constitution and continuing through the Civil War, slavery caused political tension in the United States. Although many Americans agreed that slavery was incompatible with democratic ideals, it took a bloody civil war to finally bring an end to slavery. The war's end, however, raised a new challenge: how to bring emancipated slaves into a free society. In this chapter you will learn how the nation struggled to define the rights of freed African Americans, while also seeking to restore the southern states to the Union.

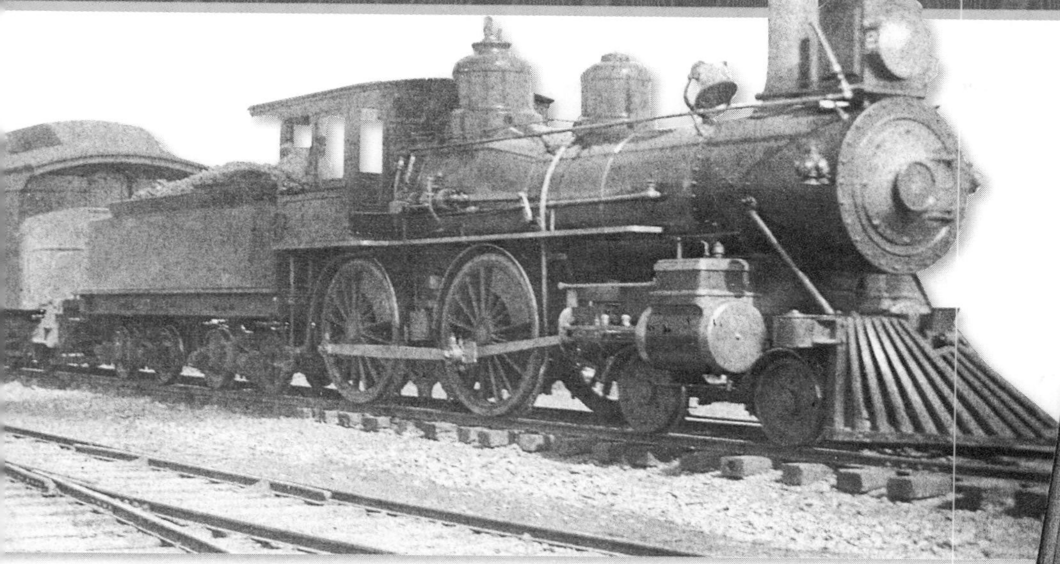

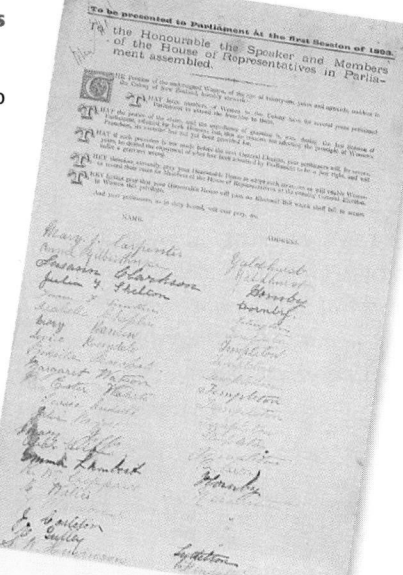

Southern railroad in the late 1800s

1890
Science and Technology
The mileage of railways in the South is double what it was in 1878.

1888
World Events
Brazil abolishes slavery.

1899
The Arts
Charles W. Chesnutt publishes his short-story collection, *The Wife of His Youth.*

The Wife of His Youth

1885

1890

1895

1900

1885
Daily Life
Riots against Chinese immigrants break out in the Washington Territory.

1886
Politics
The Georgia Supreme Court upholds the will of a former slaveholder who left much of his wealth to African American Amanda Eubanks, making her the wealthiest black woman in the United States.

1890
Business and Finance
The value of tobacco products in Kentucky, North Carolina, and Virginia is almost $31 million.

1893
World Events
New Zealand becomes the first country to give women the vote.

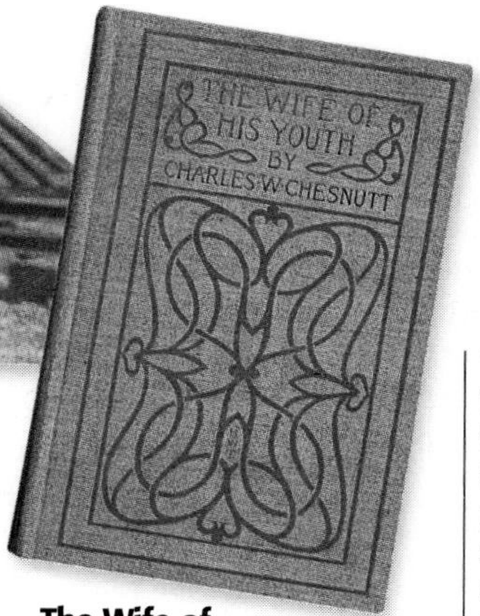

Petition for voting rights by New Zealand women

Think About Themes

Themes Journal

Decide whether you **agree** *or* **disagree** *with the following statements. Note why in your journal.*

Constitutional Heritage A government that cannot adapt to change poses a threat to the very society it has been created to govern.

Democratic Values A nation's definition of a democratic society changes over time in response to war and other significant events.

Economic Development A region's dependence on the sale of a single product ultimately serves to limit the region's economic development.

Presidential Reconstruction

OBJECTIVES

Read to understand:
1. what hopes and expectations African Americans had for their lives as freedpeople
2. how President Lincoln and Congress differed over plans for Reconstruction
3. how President Johnson's Reconstruction plan benefited former Confederates
4. how the Black Codes affected freedpeople

KEY TERMS
Reconstruction
amnesty
Thirteenth Amendment
Black Codes

KEY PEOPLE
John Wilkes Booth
Andrew Johnson

EYEWITNESSES TO History

❝ Let a great earthquake swallow us up first! Let us leave our land and emigrate to any desert spot of the earth, rather than return to the Union. ❞

—Sarah Morgan

Emancipation parade

Such feelings expressed by a white southern woman were common among many former Confederates after the Civil War. African Americans in the South reacted very differently. After Charleston, South Carolina, surrendered in February 1865, the city's African American residents hosted a parade they called a "jubilee of freedom." In April, after Union forces captured Richmond, Virginia, President Abraham Lincoln visited the city. African American T. Chester Morris wrote in the *Philadelphia Press,* "There is no describing the scene along the route. The colored population was wild with enthusiasm."

The Old South Destroyed

The Civil War inflicted mass devastation on the South, leaving many cities in ruins. A visitor to Columbia, South Carolina, described "a wilderness of crumbling walls, naked chimneys, and trees killed by flames." Illness swept the region, resulting in thousands of deaths in the South in the year after the war.

The Civil War also shattered the South's economy. Tens of thousands of Confederate veterans were left without jobs. Similarly, most of the approximately 4 million emancipated slaves found themselves homeless and penniless. "It came so sudden on 'em," recalled former slave Parke Johnston.

❝ Just think of whole droves of people, that had always been kept so close, and hardly ever left the plantation before, turned loose all at once, with nothing in the world, but what they had on their backs. ❞

Despite the obstacles, most freedpeople looked eagerly to the future. Like former slave Henry Turner, they yearned to enjoy their "rights in common with other men." They hoped to establish their own churches and schools and to legalize their marriages. Many freedpeople expected to choose their own livelihood. With freedom anything seemed possible, even finding family members who had been sold away. Former slave Hawkins Wilson sent a letter to his sister, address unknown, believing that it would somehow find its way to her. "Your little brother Hawkins is trying to find out where you are and where his poor old mother is," he wrote. "Let me know and I will come to see you."

INTERPRETING THE VISUAL RECORD

The South in ruins. Many southern cities lay in ruins after the Civil War. *What problems do you think damage like this caused for southern residents?*

Above all, African Americans hoped, like Garrison Frazier, "to have land . . . and till it by our own labor." Most wanted land to support themselves and to protect their independence. Many believed that it was their due. "Our wives, our children, our husbands, has been sold over and over again to purchase the lands we now locates upon," argued former slave Bayley Wyat. "We have a divine right to the land." General William T. Sherman had encouraged such hopes in January 1865, when he ordered part of South Carolina to be divided into 40-acre parcels and given to freedpeople. Rumors spread that the federal government would give each freedman "40 acres and a mule."

✔ **READING CHECK:** What hopes and expectations did African Americans in the South have for their lives as freedpeople?

President Lincoln and Reconstruction

President Abraham Lincoln wanted to bring the rebel states back into the Union quickly. He had not gone to war to destroy the South, but to preserve the Union. Even before the war's end, he had begun planning for **Reconstruction**—rebuilding the former Confederate states and reuniting the nation.

The beginning of Reconstruction.
To encourage southerners to abandon the Confederacy, Lincoln had issued the Proclamation of Amnesty and Reconstruction on December 8, 1863. The proclamation offered **amnesty**. This would give a full pardon to all southerners—except high-ranking Confederate leaders and a few others—who would swear allegiance to the U.S. Constitution and accept federal laws ending slavery. The proclamation also permitted a state to rejoin the Union when 10 percent of its residents who had voted in 1860 swore their loyalty to the nation.

Many members of Congress objected to this so-called Ten Percent Plan. They did not trust the Confederates to become loyal U.S. citizens or to protect the rights of former slaves. Congress laid out its own Reconstruction plan in the Wade-Davis Bill, passed in July 1864. The bill called for the Confederate states to abolish slavery and to delay Reconstruction until a majority of each state's white males took a loyalty oath. Lincoln vetoed the bill because he was not ready to "be inflexibly committed to any single plan of restoration," he said. In his second inaugural address, delivered on March 4, 1865, Lincoln clarified his goal for Reconstruction.

> 66 With malice toward none, with charity for all, with firmness in the right as God gives us to see the right, let us strive on . . . to bind up the nation's wounds . . . to do all which may achieve . . . a just and lasting peace. 99

✔ **READING CHECK:** How did President Lincoln and Congress disagree over the course Reconstruction should take?

★ Then and Now

Juneteenth

A recent Juneteenth parade in Texas

On June 19, 1865, Union soldiers arriving in Galveston, Texas, shared with the city's African Americans the contents of an important general order: "The people of Texas are informed that in accordance with a Proclamation from the Executive of the United States, all slaves are free." Since then, June 19 has been celebrated by African Americans in many areas of the South as Emancipation Day, or Juneteenth.

Complete with parades and marching bands, the earliest Juneteenth celebrations were usually held in rural areas. They often included rereadings of the proclamation, speeches, and songs. African Americans dressed up, cooked special food, danced, played baseball, and rejoiced in their freedom.

The celebration of Juneteenth declined in the early 1900s but regained its popularity in the 1960s. In 1980 Texas named Juneteenth an official state holiday. Today communities throughout the country still enthusiastically celebrate the holiday. Modern Juneteenth festivities include traditional elements, such as guest speakers, prayer services, and barbecues. Official Juneteenth festivals also offer a wide array of activities, such as pageants, lectures, art shows, and even a blues festival in Houston, Texas. Juneteenth celebrates African American freedom in addition to bringing people of all cultures together in harmony.

Comparing Points of View

Historians often encounter conflicting accounts of events because of differing points of view. Every person has a point of view, or personal frame of reference, from which he or she experiences and thinks about things. Factors such as age, sex, education, and family background, as well as social and historical circumstances, help to shape this point of view. Comparing points of view can lead to historical insights and a better understanding of the causes of historical conflicts.

How to Compare Points of View

1. **Identify the sources.** When you encounter conflicting historical accounts, verify the identity of each author or speaker. If possible, find out about the personal, social, and historical background of each source.
2. **Identify and compare the main ideas.** Identify the main idea expressed by each source. Then note the similarities and differences between these ideas.
3. **Examine the supporting details.** Determine whether each source supports its main idea with relevant facts, opinions, or a combination of both.
4. **Evaluate the points of view.** Use your analysis of the sources, main ideas, and supporting details, along with your knowledge of the historical period, to assess the reliability of each account and its accompanying point of view.

Applying the Strategy

Read and compare the following statements about how the Union should treat the South.

> These gentlemen of the South mean to win. They meant it in 1861 when they opened fire on Sumter. . . . They mean it now. The moment we remove the iron hand from the Rebels' throats they will rise and attempt the mastery.
> —*New York* Tribune *editor Horace Greeley*

> The war being at an end, the Southern states having laid down their arms and the questions at issue between them and the Northern states having been decided, I believe it to be the duty of everyone to unite in the restoration of the country and the reestablishment of peace and harmony.
> —*Confederate general Robert E. Lee*

Practicing the Strategy

Answer the following questions.
1. How do you think the background of each author affected his statement?
2. What is the main idea of each statement? Is this idea supported by facts, opinions, or both?
3. Whose point of view seems most reliable? Why?

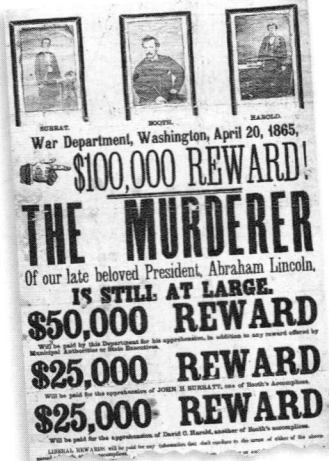

After President Lincoln's assassination, the War Department offered a reward for the capture of John Wilkes Booth.

Lincoln's assassination. How Reconstruction might have developed under Lincoln's direction will never be known. On April 14, 1865, just days after General Robert E. Lee's surrender, Confederate sympathizer John Wilkes Booth shot the president as he and his wife watched a play at the Ford Theatre in Washington. Lincoln died early the following morning.

Across the country, Americans remembered Lincoln by displaying bits of black cloth outside their homes. Thousands filed through the rotunda of the nation's Capitol to pay their respects before he was laid to rest. Hundreds of thousands more stood beside railroad tracks as the funeral train made its way from Washington to Lincoln's burial site in Illinois.

Many ordinary Americans feared the impact that Lincoln's death might have on the country. Sidney George Fisher believed that his death might be harder on the South than the North. He noted, "Mr. Lincoln's humanity & kindness of heart stood between them [southerners] and the party of the North who urge measures of vengeance & severity." The assassination also increased the distrust between the North and the South. Many northerners believed that Booth was part of a conspiracy organized or encouraged by Confederate leaders.

President Johnson and Reconstruction

After President Lincoln's death, Vice President Andrew Johnson assumed the presidency. Johnson was a Democrat, a one time slaveholder, and a former U.S. senator from Tennessee. He had been chosen as Lincoln's running mate in 1864 because of his pro-Union sympathies. Republican leaders had hoped he would appeal to northern Democrats and southern Unionists.

Despite his support for the Union and his wartime experience as Tennessee's military governor, Johnson proved ill-suited to the challenges of Reconstruction. Defining African Americans' new rights proved to be a challenge also. He favored a government controlled by white citizens. He also suffered, as one contemporary observer noted, from "almost unconquerable prejudices against the African race." Johnson also lacked Lincoln's political skill, often refusing to compromise.

In May 1865 Johnson issued a complete pardon to all rebels except former Confederate officeholders and the richest planters. These people he pardoned on an individual basis. Johnson's forgiveness extended to the rebel states as well. For readmission to the Union, his plan required only that they nullify their acts of secession, abolish slavery, and refuse to pay Confederate government debts. The last provision was intended to punish southerners who had financed the Confederacy.

Southerners, including General Robert E. Lee, enthusiastically supported President Johnson's plan. They liked it because it allowed Confederate leaders to take charge of Reconstruction. These men—some of whom continued to wear their army uniforms—dominated the new state legislatures. Even former Confederate vice president Alexander H. Stevens, who had been charged with treason, took office in the nation's capital as a representative.

These former Confederate lawmakers made sure that the new state constitutions did not grant voting rights to freedmen. When the lawmakers complained of the "painful humiliation" inflicted by the presence of African American soldiers in the South, President Johnson had the troops removed. By recognizing Mississippi's new government, Johnson even overlooked the state's refusal to ratify the **Thirteenth Amendment**—which Congress had passed in January 1865 to abolish slavery.

✔ **READING CHECK:** How did President Johnson's programs benefit former Confederates?

HOLT RESEARCHER

Read More About It

Free Find:
Andrew Johnson
After reading the biography on Andrew Johnson on the **Holt Researcher** CD–ROM, imagine that you are in Washington at the time of Lincoln's assassination. Write a report on what plans for Reconstruction you expect Johnson to propose.

INTERPRETING THE VISUAL RECORD
Ex-Confederates. Many southern legislators like these continued to wear their Confederate uniforms when conducting political business. *What message would the wearing of such uniforms convey?*

The Black Codes

President Johnson's actions encouraged former Confederates to adopt laws limiting the freedom of former slaves. These **Black Codes** closely resembled pre–Civil War slave codes. Mississippi, for example, simply recycled its old code, substituting the word "freedman" for "slave."

The Black Codes varied from state to state. However, they all aimed to prevent African Americans from achieving social, political, and economic equality with southern whites. African Americans could not hold meetings unless whites were present. The code also forbade them to travel without permits, own guns, attend schools with whites, or sit on juries. Most importantly the codes reestablished white control over African American labor.

Many laws in the South were passed to maintain an African American labor force to work the fields of white-owned plantations.

Without slaves to do the work, "our fields everywhere lie untilled," one white southerner said. To force former slaves to return to the fields, some local codes prohibited African Americans from living in towns unless they were servants and from renting land outside of towns or cities. Several states required freedpeople to sign long-term labor contracts. Those who refused could be arrested and have their labor put up for auction. Other codes required African Americans to obtain a special license to work in a skilled profession.

The codes also allowed judges to decide whether African American parents could support their children. Children without "adequate" support could be bound, or hired, out against their will. The former owner usually was given the first opportunity to bid. Judges' decisions were often arbitrary. In North Carolina an African American man who worked and supported a wife and child was still considered an "orphan" to be bound out. Some courts hired out children without even informing their parents.

Many African Americans realized that emancipation had not greatly improved their daily lives. Of the Black Codes, one African American veteran demanded, "If you call this Freedom, what do you call Slavery?" Although African Americans immediately denounced these laws as "a disgrace to civilization," they had little political power. Many felt they had to accept the codes in order to survive.

Northerners criticized the Black Codes as an attempt to re-establish slavery. The Chicago *Tribune* reprinted the Mississippi code and proclaimed,

66 **The men of the North will convert the State of Mississippi into a frog pond before they will allow such laws to disgrace one foot of soil in which the bones of our soldiers sleep and over which the flag of freedom waves.** 99

✔ **READING CHECK:** How did the Black Codes affect the lives of freedpeople?

SECTION 1 REVIEW

Define and explain the significance of the following terms:
Reconstruction
amnesty
Thirteenth Amendment
Black Codes

Identify and explain the significance of the following individuals:
John Wilkes Booth
Andrew Johnson

1. **Using Graphic Organizers** Copy the chart below. Use it to compare the Reconstruction plans of President Lincoln, Congress, and President Johnson.

Lincoln's Plan	Congress's Plan	Johnson's Plan

2. **Synthesizing** What was life like for southern African Americans immediately after the Civil War?
3. **Recognizing Point of View** Why might President Johnson's plan for Reconstruction have been considered unfair by many Americans, particularly southern African Americans?
4. **Analyzing** How did the Black Codes attempt to limit opportunities for African Americans?

Critical Thinking

5. How did disagreements over Reconstruction policy reflect different views about what the lasting effects of the Civil War should be?
   Consider:
   • Congress's views
   • President Lincoln's views
   • President Johnson's views

Congressional Reconstruction

EYEWITNESSES TO History

❝ *Reformation* must *be effected; the foundation of* [southern] *institutions, both political, municipal, and social* must *be broken up and relaid, or all our blood and treasure* have been spent in vain. *This can only be done by treating and holding them as a conquered people. . . . The whole fabric of southern society* must *be changed, and never can it be done if this opportunity is lost. Without this, this Government can never be, as it has never been, a true republic.* ❞
—Thaddeus Stevens

Thaddeus Stevens

Pennsylvania representative Thaddeus Stevens issued this challenge to Congress in 1865. Many southerners argued that such a harsh approach to Reconstruction would only lead to another civil war. "The day of reckoning cometh, and it will be terrible," warned one southern newspaper.

The Moderates Versus the Radicals

Even Republicans disagreed over the course Reconstruction should take. The issue of African American voting rights proved particularly divisive. Most Republicans were moderates who viewed Reconstruction as a practical matter of restoring the southern states to the Union. Their main concern was keeping former Confederates out of government. They favored giving African Americans some civil equality but not the vote.

Supporters of African American suffrage. In contrast, Radical Republicans like Thaddeus Stevens insisted that African Americans be given the right to vote. These Republicans believed that the proper aim of Reconstruction was to create a new South where all men would enjoy equal rights.

Few northerners, even abolitionists, supported giving African Americans in the South the right to vote. Some Republicans even supported giving the vote only to northern African American men. Although few Americans publicly supported voting rights for African Americans, Frederick Douglass did. Douglass demanded "the immediate, unconditional, and universal 'enfranchisement [right to vote] of the black man, in every State in the Union.'"

BIOGRAPHY
Frederick Douglass

Frederick Douglass was born into slavery in 1817 on a tobacco plantation in eastern Maryland. His mother was hired out when he was still an infant. He later recalled that he did not see his mother "more than four or five times in my life." When Douglass was about six years old, he was sent to a nearby plantation where he ran errands and performed simple chores. Douglass learned in 1825 that he was to be sent away from the plantation to Baltimore. He received this news with

+ FAMILY RECORD +

BEFORE THE WAR AND SINCE THE WAR

INTERPRETING THE VISUAL RECORD

Family records. After the Civil War, many former slaves tried to find lost relatives. *What ideals does this family record registry suggest about prosperity and family life for African Americans after the Civil War?*

"joy" and "ecstasy." Douglass spent most of the next seven years in the household of Hugh and Sophia Auld, looking after their young son. Sophia Auld also taught him to read and write.

Douglass was sent to a farm some 40 miles from Baltimore when he was about 15 years old. Longing for freedom, Douglass began planning his escape. One of the other slaves involved, however, betrayed the plan. Douglass was spared the common punishment of being sold. Instead, his captors returned him to Baltimore where he worked in the shipyards for the next two years. In 1838 he again decided to run away. Using borrowed papers that stated he was a free African American sailor, Douglass traveled north. Douglass arrived in New York on September 4, 1838. He became a leader in the antislavery cause and wrote his life story, the *Narrative of the Life of Frederick Douglass,* which was published in 1845.

After the war, Douglass embraced the policies of Reconstruction and Radical Republicanism. He remained active, editing a newspaper in Washington and serving as president of the Freedmen's Bank. Along with several other African Americans, Douglass attempted to advise President Johnson on how to keep "peace between races," hoping to bring an end to the ongoing violence in the South. He served as a U.S. marshal, a recorder of deeds, and as the U.S. minister to Haiti. Douglass died of heart failure on February 20, 1895.

Land reform. Some political leaders emphasized African American suffrage and civil equality. Others, though, saw land reform as the key to changing southern society. Representative Thaddeus Stevens agreed with Senator Charles Sumner of Massachusetts, who insisted that "the great plantations . . . must be broken up, and the freedmen must have the pieces." According to Stevens, economic independence for the former slaves would ensure their freedom. Such independence would also destroy the political power of the "proud, bloated, and defiant rebels."

Despite the efforts of Stevens and Sumner, land reform—particularly government seizure of land—never won wide support. The *New York Times* accused land reformers of starting "a war on property . . . to succeed the war on Slavery." Even many Radical Republicans were skeptical of land reform. They believed that African Americans could achieve social and economic independence if they were granted civil equality, the right to vote, and the right to labor freely.

✔ **READING CHECK:** What issues divided the Republican Party during the early years of the Reconstruction era?

THROUGH OTHERS' EYES

Latin American Views of Reconstruction

Having experienced civil war in their own countries, some wealthy Latin Americans traveled to the United States in the 1860s and 1870s, where they witnessed Reconstruction firsthand. Some Latin Americans saw the Reconstruction of the South as the triumph of a strong, centralized government.

Other Latin Americans praised Reconstruction's economic programs. Several Brazilian visitors felt that the U.S. government's programs effectively aided former slaves to become skilled workers and farmers, which, in turn, helped promote industrialization and cotton production in the South. Still others complained that Reconstruction eroded the small-town life of the South by turning the region over to the hands of big business. Not everyone saw this as a negative, however. Many Mexicans, Brazilians, and Colombians hoped that the U.S. system of business would serve as a model for Latin America.

Still other Latin Americans saw Reconstruction as a blueprint for the day when their countries would end slavery. As Camacho Roldán of Colombia said, when Abraham Lincoln freed the American slaves, he "prepared the way for freedom for the three millions more in the Spanish colonies and Brazil."

Congress Versus Johnson

The split between the moderate Republicans and Radical Republicans did not last long, however. In early 1866 Congress began hearings on conditions in the South. Witness after witness testified before the Joint Committee on Reconstruction presenting evidence of postwar violence. African Americans recounted stories of murder and of homes, schools, and churches reduced to "ashes and cinders." Southern Unionists told of death threats. These reports and others like them convinced moderate Republicans to join forces with the Radical Republicans.

The Freedmen's Bureau. One move made by the Republicans was to extend the life of the **Freedmen's Bureau**. Congress had created the bureau in March 1865 to aid the millions of southerners left homeless and hungry by the war. The bureau distributed food and clothing, served as an employment agency, set up hospitals, and operated schools.

The Freedmen's Bureau played a major role in providing education for African Americans, who had been denied this opportunity under slavery. By 1869 hundreds of schools for African Americans had been established in the South. Many of the teachers were women from the North. Northerners also helped establish colleges for black southerners, including Atlanta University in Georgia, Howard University in Washington, and Fisk University in Nashville, Tennessee. Union general Samuel Chapman Armstrong, who had led African American troops in the Civil War, founded the Hampton Institute in Virginia in 1868.

The Freedmen's Bureau also helped settle contract disputes between African American laborers and white planters. In most cases the bureau encouraged laborers to continue working on plantations, even under unfavorable conditions. Two freedmen who believed that their contracts were unfair sued Mary Jones, a plantation owner. The bureau agent forced the men to go back to work. Once they returned to the plantation, Jones expressed her feelings.

> 66 that in . . . doubting my word they [the African American men] had offered me the greatest insult I ever received in my life; that I had considered them friends and treated them as such . . . ; but that now they were only laborers under contract, and only the law would rule between us. 99

Congress had originally intended for the Freedmen's Bureau to remain in operation for one year. In light of the congressional hearings on postwar violence, however, most members of Congress supported legislation to extend the life of the agency. African Americans largely agreed. Many thought that the Freedmen's Bureau too often encouraged former slaves to remain on plantations and to sign labor contracts. However, they acknowledged that the bureau's presence forced white southerners to recognize the emancipation of slaves. One African American told a government official that "if the Freedman Bureau was removed, a colored man would have better sense than to speak a word in behalf of the colored man's rights, for fear of his life."

INTERPRETING THE VISUAL RECORD

Freedmen's Bureau. Established by Congress, the Freedmen's Bureau provided southerners with food, clothing, and other services. *What does this drawing reveal about the role of the Freedmen's Bureau?*

Southern African Americans struggled to improve their lives after the Civil War.

INTERPRETING THE VISUAL RECORD
Civil Rights Act of 1866.
Despite the passage of the Civil Rights Act of 1866, many African Americans continued to suffer much as they did under slavery. *How does this poster mock the effectiveness of the civil rights legislation?*

In an attempt to weaken the bureau, President Johnson sent two generals to tour the South in 1866. Johnson hoped that the generals would uncover complaints about the organization. Instead, they encountered widespread support among African Americans for the agency. In February 1866 Congress passed the Freedmen's Bureau Bill to extend the life of the agency. To the surprise of many, Johnson vetoed the bill, citing constitutional and financial reasons. "It was never intended that the Freedmen should be fed, clothed, educated and sheltered by the United States," he said.

The Civil Rights Act of 1866. Furious with the president, Congress promptly passed the **Civil Rights Act of 1866**, the first civil rights law in the nation's history. Although the act declared that everyone born in the United States was a citizen with full civil rights, it did not guarantee voting rights. Legislators designed the act to overturn discriminatory laws and the Supreme Court's 1857 *Dred Scott* ruling that African Americans were not citizens. "If the President vetoes the Civil Rights Bill," wrote one Ohio senator, "we shall be obliged to draw our swords."

Johnson did not heed the warning, however. He vetoed the bill, arguing that it would centralize power in the federal government. Johnson's veto eroded his support in Congress and united both moderate and Radical Republicans against him. Congress overrode Johnson's veto of the Civil Rights Act. Returning to the matter of the Freedmen's Bureau, Congress passed a new bill to extend it, and overrode yet another presidential veto.

The Fourteenth Amendment. Congressional Republicans feared that a future Congress controlled by Democrats might repeal the Civil Rights Act. They therefore wrote the act's provisions into the **Fourteenth Amendment**, passed in June 1866. The amendment required states to extend equal citizenship to African Americans and all people "born or naturalized in the United States." It also denied states the right to deprive anyone of "life, liberty, or property without due process of law." Further, it promised all citizens the "equal protection of the laws." The amendment's ratification in July 1868 granted the nation's citizens rights—enjoyed equally by all—that could be enforced by the federal government.

The Fourteenth Amendment did not guarantee African American voting rights. It did, however, reduce the number of representatives a state could send to Congress based on how many of the state's male citizens were denied the right to vote. The more African American men who were not allowed to vote, the fewer representatives that state could send to Congress. Republicans hoped that southern states would give African Americans the right to vote rather than lose their representation in Congress.

✔ **READING CHECK:** Why did moderate and Radical Republican lawmakers join forces, and what actions did they take to protect the rights of African Americans?

The Radicals Come to Power

President Johnson tried to make the Fourteenth Amendment an issue in the 1866 congressional elections. Calling the Radical Republicans traitors, he campaigned throughout the Midwest in support of candidates who opposed the amendment. Most voters were not receptive, however. Many people felt deeply troubled by the ongoing violence against African Americans in the South.

Race riots. Race riots were becoming increasingly common in the South. On May 1, 1866, two carriages collided on the streets of Memphis. When police officers arrested the African American driver but not the white one, a group of African American veterans protested. A white mob soon gathered. The resulting conflict led to a three-day spree of violence in which white rioters—consisting mainly of police officers and firefighters—killed 46 African Americans and burned 12 schools and four churches. "If anything could reveal . . . the demoniac spirit . . . toward the freedmen," one reporter noted, this violence would.

In July 1866 the Louisiana legislature called for new elections, which placed a Confederate mayor in power in New Orleans. In response, Louisiana governor James Madison Wells, a planter and former slaveholder, supported the Radical Republicans. He attempted to give African Americans the vote, to bar former Confederates from voting, and to form a new state government. His actions led to a white uprising. More than 30 African Americans and three white Republicans were killed in the resulting riot. General Philip H. Sheridan, President Johnson's military commander in Texas and Louisiana, referred to the event as "an absolute massacre."

The elections of 1866 and the Reconstruction Acts. Such violence made President Johnson's call for leniency toward the southern rebels seem particularly absurd. Johnson's campaign called for a stronger union between the North and the South. However, his speeches filled with angry protest displeased voters. While speaking in St. Louis, he even blamed Congress for the New Orleans riot. Wisconsin senator James R. Doolittle estimated that the president's campaign tour cost his candidates about 1 million votes. Fearing they might lose the fruits of their Civil War victory, northerners overwhelmingly voted Republican in 1866. Firmly in command of Congress, the Republicans, with the Radicals at the helm, seized control of the Reconstruction process.

Although the issue had previously divided their party, Republicans quickly decided that African Americans must have the vote. In January 1867 a bill granting African Americans the vote in the District of Columbia passed over Johnson's veto. Congress next extended this right to the country's territories. Despite Johnson's

PRESIDENTIAL Lives

1808–1875
In Office 1865–1869

Andrew Johnson

Born in North Carolina, Andrew Johnson was a self-made man who never attended school. Johnson was very young when his father died, and his mother apprenticed him to a tailor when he was 14. One person commented that the young Johnson "was very industrious and quiet, talked but little, and always had a book by his side." Later, Johnson's wife taught him to write and to do simple arithmetic.

After moving to Tennessee in 1826, Johnson did well as a tailor. Although he bought property, Johnson never identified with the planter class. His loyalties were to farmers and artisans, and he always saw himself as a political outsider. Johnson never forgot his early poverty. He continued to make all his own clothes until he went to Washington. Even after he became president, Johnson often stopped by tailor shops to chat.

INTERPRETING THE VISUAL RECORD

Race riots. In 1866 southern whites in Louisiana attacked African Americans and white Republicans. *How does this illustration reflect the event as "an absolute massacre?"*

declaration that "old southern leaders . . . must rule the South," Republicans passed the **Reconstruction Acts** of 1867. These acts divided the former Confederacy—with the exception of already-reconstructed Tennessee—into five military districts. Union army troops were stationed in each district to enforce order. To gain readmission to the Union, states were required to ratify the Fourteenth Amendment as well as submit to Congress new constitutions guaranteeing all men the vote. The act further required that African Americans be allowed to vote for delegates to the state constitutional conventions as well as to serve as delegates.

Presidential Impeachment

The Radical Republicans knew that the success of the Reconstruction Acts depended on their enforcement. They were equally sure that President Johnson would not cooperate. To protect Reconstruction policies and Republican officeholders, Congress passed the Tenure of Office Act in 1867. This act required Senate approval of a replacement before the president could remove an appointed official who had been confirmed by the Senate.

Believing the law unconstitutional, Johnson put it to the test. In February 1868 he removed Secretary of War Edwin Stanton, an ally of the Radical Republicans.

The House of Representatives responded by voting to impeach the president. The House charged Johnson with violating the Tenure of Office Act, making "scandalous" speeches, and bringing Congress "into disgrace."

Some senators argued that such flaws were not impeachable offenses. Senator Lyman Trumbull of Illinois, a Johnson critic, predicted, "No future President will be safe who happens to differ with a majority of the House and two-thirds of the Senate." Trumbull worried that an aggressive Congress threatened the checks and balances of the Constitution. Other senators shared his fear.

The case against Johnson was weak from the start. The impeachment articles did not really address the Radical Republicans' underlying grievances against Johnson: that he was unfair, governed poorly, and tried to halt Congress's plan for Reconstruction. Many members of Congress even feared that Johnson might lead the country into another civil war.

Johnson's Senate trial began in March 1868. Seven members of the House of Representatives stated the case for impeachment. These representatives were so critical in their attack, however, that public opinion began to turn against them. One representative even waved a blood-stained nightshirt that he asserted came from a white northerner who had been beaten by southerners. Within a month, some prominent people were calling for Johnson's acquittal. A writer for the *Nation* claimed that the House had made Johnson a villain without proving any charges.

The trial lasted eight weeks, unfolding in front of a gallery of eager spectators. On May 16, 1868, the Senate voted to acquit the president. The final tally fell one vote short of the two-thirds majority needed to convict Johnson and remove him

THE GRANGER COLLECTION, NEW YORK (BOTH)

INTERPRETING THE VISUAL RECORD

Impeachment. Admittance to President Johnson's impeachment was limited. Visitors and reporters were required to present a ticket to gain entry to the Senate gallery. *How do these images reflect the importance and drama of the event?*

from office. Risking the disapproval of their party and their constituents, seven Republican senators had joined 12 Democratic senators to vote for acquittal. The entire proceedings, concluded Republican senator Joseph Smith Fowler of Tennessee, had become "mere politics." The ordeal, however, took a toll on many of the legislators. Iowa senator James W. Grimes suffered a stroke after his constituents denounced him as a traitor for supporting the president. More importantly, with 35 senators from his own party against him, Johnson's power was broken.

✔ **READING CHECK:** Why was President Johnson impeached, and why did the Senate fail to remove him from office?

Ulysses S. Grant

1822–1885
In Office 1869–1877

Born in Ohio, Ulysses S. Grant graduated from the U.S. Military Academy at West Point in 1843 but had no intentions of making a career of military service. "A military life had no charms for me, and I had not the faintest idea of staying in the army even if I should be graduated, which I did not expect." Contrary to his expectations, Grant stayed in the army until 1854.

Grant was plagued by failure after resigning his commission. He drifted through a series of jobs, including peddling firewood and collecting rents. He tried his hand at farming without much success. His financial problems were such that in 1857 Grant was forced to pawn his gold watch for $22. When the Civil War broke out in 1861, Grant was almost 39 years old and clerking at his family's leather-goods store in Galena, Illinois. He returned to the army as a colonel and at last found success. His presidency followed in 1869.

After leaving office, Grant and his wife toured the world for more than two years. Back in New York, he unsuccessfully tried to make his fortune in business. He had just completed writing his memoirs when he died in 1885.

Further Political Difficulties

The Radical Republicans' attempt to force President Johnson from office as well as their emphasis on African American suffrage cost them some popular support. Many voters had grown tired of the problems posed by Reconstruction. Some northern legislatures even joined the voices opposing African American voting rights.

The election of 1868. As the 1868 election neared, the Radical Republicans sensed trouble. To retain voters, they nominated General Ulysses S. Grant for president. General Grant lacked political experience but was a popular war hero.

The Democrats chose former New York governor Horatio Seymour to run against Grant. Seymour had sharply criticized the Lincoln administration during the Civil War. Secretary of State William Henry Seward noted that the Democrats "could have nominated no candidate who would have taken away fewer Republican votes." Seymour's running mate, Francis Preston Blair, further diminished Seymour's chances when he pursued a campaign strategy based on white supremacy.

Southern Democrats relied on economic threats against African Americans to keep them from voting for the Republicans. One white Democrat addressed African Americans.

> 66 We have the capital and give employment. We own the lands and require labor to make them productive. . . . You desire to be employed. . . . We know we can do without you. We think you will find it very difficult to do without us. . . . We have the wealth. 99

Despite such tactics, new African American voters supported the Republican ticket. Grant defeated Seymour in a very close race, and Republicans realized that African American voters had given them their narrow win.

Southern Democrat officials such as the election judge shown in this engraving often prevented African Americans from voting for Republican candidates.

Celebration. This poster was created to celebrate the passage of the Fifteenth Amendment. *What might be the significance of the flags at the top of the poster?*

The Fifteenth Amendment. Eager to protect their power in the North as well as in the South, the Republicans drafted the **Fifteenth Amendment**. It stated, "The right of citizens of the United States to vote shall not be denied or abridged by the United States or by any state on account of race, color, or previous condition of servitude."

The passage of the Fifteenth Amendment in February 1869 and its subsequent ratification in 1870 brought triumph to African Americans and Radical Republicans. Abolitionist William Lloyd Garrison rejoiced in "this wonderful, quiet, sudden transformation of four millions of human beings from . . . the auction-block to the ballot-box." The amendment failed to guarantee African Americans the right to hold office, however. It also did not prevent states from limiting the voting rights of African Americans through discriminatory requirements.

Significantly, the Fifteenth Amendment failed to extend the vote to women. Women's rights leaders, most of them former abolitionists, had split over the amendment. Arguing that "this hour belongs to the negro," one group had urged women to postpone the more controversial women's suffrage issue so as not to endanger passage of the amendment. Elizabeth Cady Stanton replied: "My question is this: Do you believe the African race is composed entirely of males?" Stanton and others opposed ratification of the Fifteenth Amendment until all women were also given the vote. The bitter debate over the amendment alienated many African American women from the women's movement.

✔ **READING CHECK:** Why were African Americans crucial to the presidential election of 1868, and how did Republicans respond to their support?

SECTION 2 REVIEW

Define and explain the significance of the following terms:
Freedmen's Bureau
Civil Rights Act of 1866
Fourteenth Amendment
Reconstruction Acts
Fifteenth Amendment

Identify and explain the significance of the following individuals:
Thaddeus Stevens
Frederick Douglass
Ulysses S. Grant

1. **Using Graphic Organizers** Copy the graphic organizer below. Use it to describe the major legislation that Congress passed to implement its plan for Reconstruction.

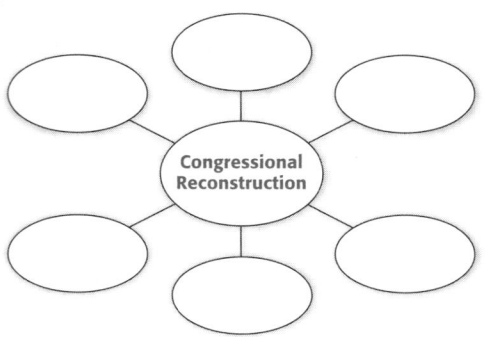

Congressional Reconstruction

2. **Identifying Cause and Effect** What issues divided the Republican Party in the 1860s? What actions of President Johnson served to unite the party?
3. **Evaluating** What rights did the Fourteenth and Fifteenth Amendments guarantee for African Americans?
4. **Recognizing Point of View** In what way was the passage of the Fifteenth Amendment a reaction by the Republican Party to the results of the election of 1868?

Critical Thinking

5. Was Congress justified in its effort to remove President Johnson from office? Explain your answer.
   Consider:
   • why Congress impeached President Johnson
   • what Johnson's defense was
   • if the conflict could have been resolved any other way

SECTION 3

Reconstruction in the South

OBJECTIVES

Read to understand:

1. how African Americans attempted to improve their lives during the Reconstruction era
2. what reforms the Republican governments enacted
3. how some African Americans responded to harassment by the Ku Klux Klan
4. what caused Reconstruction to end

KEY TERMS

carpetbaggers
scalawags
Ku Klux Klan
Enforcement Acts
Panic of 1873
Civil Rights Act of 1875
Redeemers
Compromise of 1877

KEY PEOPLE

Samuel J. Tilden
Rutherford B. Hayes

EYEWITNESSES TO History

❝ *The people of New Orleans witnessed last night one of the noblest scenes of which an American city can boast, . . . a phalanx [group] of freemen walking the streets with national colors flying and transparencies enunciating [spelling out] the principles of a free government.* **❞**
—*New Orleans Tribune*

African Americans enjoying the right to vote

The African American newspaper the *New Orleans Tribune* described the festivities that took place in May 1867 after the passage of the Reconstruction Acts. The evening ended with skyrockets and dancing in the streets. "This marks a new and glorious era in our history," the newspaper proudly declared.

African American Activism

With the passage of the Reconstruction Acts, African Americans saw a new era begin. The rise of Congressional Reconstruction gave the former slaves further hope for equal citizenship. Many registered to vote and began lobbying for the equality promised by the Civil Rights Act and the Fourteenth Amendment. Even the churches found that "politics got in our midst" and overtook "our revival or religious work," according to one African American minister.

African Americans joined political groups such as the Union League. Begun in the North as a patriotic club, the league spread the views of the Republican Party to freed slaves as well as to poor whites. In addition to sponsoring political activity, the Union League built schools and churches for African Americans and helped care for the sick. African American education and literacy expanded greatly during Reconstruction. White northerners founded many schools, but African Americans launched educational institutions as well. The league also provided African Americans with a place to develop their political skills. After literate members read newspapers aloud, everyone present debated the issues of the day. "We just went there," explained one Union League member, "and we talked a little; made speeches on one question and another."

As African Americans became more involved in politics, they served as delegates to all the state constitutional conventions. In Louisiana and South Carolina, African American delegates outnumbered whites. In other states they made up 10 to 40 percent of the delegates. Although many of these new delegates were black southerners, northern African Americans participated as well.

Desiring to create a better life for themselves, African Americans established schools and other institutions that served freed slaves.

✔ **READING CHECK:** How did African Americans attempt to improve their lives during the Reconstruction era?

Carpetbaggers. Many southerners believed that northerners had come to impose their ideas and way of life on the South. *How is this belief expressed in this cartoon?*

Reconstruction Governments

The arrival of northern Republicans—both whites and African Americans—eager to participate in the state conventions increased resentment among many white southerners. They called these northern Republicans **carpetbaggers**. The newcomers, they joked, were "needy adventurers" of "the lowest class" who could carry everything they owned in a carpet-bag—a type of cheap suitcase.

Former Confederates heaped even greater scorn on southern whites who had backed the Union cause and now supported Reconstruction. They called these whites **scalawags**, or scoundrels. They viewed them as "southern renegades, betrayers of their race and country."

Reconstruction supporters soon formed a Republican alliance. Although they disagreed on issues such as land reform, they saw themselves as the "party of progress, and civilization." They hoped to seize economic and political power from the planters and then rebuild the South, improving conditions for poor white farmers and African Americans alike.

The Republican alliance used its political leverage to draft new state constitutions. The Republican state governments abolished property qualifications for jurors and political candidates. They also guaranteed white and African American men the right to vote. Once Congress approved the new constitutions, state legislators raised taxes to finance new road, bridge, and railroad construction as well as to increase services, such as free public education.

✔ **READING CHECK:** What reforms did the Republican governments enact?

The Ku Klux Klan

The Reconstruction governments' reforms, the election of African Americans to office, and African Americans' growing political participation were soon met by a vicious response. Angry white southerners formed secret terrorist groups to prevent African Americans from voting. One such group, the **Ku Klux Klan**, was founded in 1866 by six former Confederates. The organization grew quickly, attracting planters, lawyers, and other professionals, as well as poor farmers and laborers.

Concealing their identity with hoods and robes, Klan members used threats and violence to prevent African Americans from voting.

Klan attacks. The head of the Klan—"Grand Wizard" Nathan Bedford Forrest, a former slave-trader and Confederate general—bluntly warned Republicans that he intended "to kill the radicals." This was no idle threat. The Klan and similar groups were determined to destroy the Republican Party, to keep African Americans from voting, and to frighten African American political leaders into submission. The Klan murdered or attacked many Republican legislators and leaders—both white and black. Klan members also attacked African Americans who voted for Republican candidates.

The Klan did not limit its attacks to politically active African American and white Republicans, however. Klansmen assaulted and killed thousands of African Americans whom they regarded as too successful. One North Carolina freedman recalled the words of the Klansmen who had beaten him:

> 66 [They] told me the law—their law, that whenever I met a white person, no matter who he was, whether he was poor or rich, I was to take off my hat. 99

Klansmen also burned homes, schools, and churches, and stole livestock in an effort to chase African Americans and pro-Reconstruction whites from the South.

Steps against the Klan. African Americans struck back at the Klan when possible. Often able to recognize their tormentors by voices and other physical characteristics—despite the members' hoods and long robes—some African Americans retaliated by burning barns of Klansmen. More often, African Americans gathered in defense of an intended victim. Residents of the African American town of Avery, Alabama, learned that Klan members planned to burn their schoolhouse. "Let them come," declared Miles Prior, who organized a group of armed men. "Fifty men couldn't burn that schoolhouse and let me live." The Klansmen backed down and left the schoolhouse intact.

As the violence mounted, African Americans demanded that Congress act to "enable us to exercise the rights of citizens." Congress responded to this call in 1870 and 1871 by passing legislation designed to stop violence against African Americans. Known as the **Enforcement Acts**, these three laws empowered the federal government to combat terrorism with military force and to prosecute guilty individuals. The Democrats called them the Force Acts and claimed that they threatened individual freedom.

✔ **READING CHECK:** How did some African Americans respond to intimidation by the Ku Klux Klan?

Changes in Reconstruction

For a time the federal government's intervention brought a dramatic decline in Ku Klux Klan violence. However, the attention of Republicans increasingly turned toward national economic issues and political corruption in the North. Gradually the interest of Republicans in Reconstruction faded.

Shifting Republican interests. A particularly severe economic depression, known as the **Panic of 1873**, hit the nation. Republican leaders came under pressure as workers threatened strikes and farmers demanded relief. The partnership between antilabor, northern businesspeople—who formed the core of the Republican Party—and the freed slaves had never been a stable one. Soon it dissolved altogether.

Republicans also abandoned universal voting rights as thousands of immigrants joined the Democratic Party. Some Republicans claimed that universal suffrage "cheapened the ballot." Their calls to restrict the voting rights of immigrants and the urban poor weakened public support for African Americans' rights as well.

HISTORY
IN THE MAKING

Interpretations of Reconstruction
BY OTEY SCRUGGS

For a century afterward, the standard interpretation of Reconstruction among historians was that northern "carpetbaggers," southern "scalawags," and uneducated African Americans combined to impose tyrannical rule over the defeated South. They forced southern whites to organize groups like the Ku Klux Klan in order to overturn corrupt Republican state governments. This view became permanently stamped on the popular mind through the 1915 film *Birth of a Nation.* African American historian W. E. B. Du Bois challenged this interpretation in his monumental 1935 study, *Black Reconstruction in America.* The civil rights movement of the 1950s and 1960s completely overturned the older historical view of Reconstruction.

More recent interpretations tend to analyze the intersection between economic forces—land, labor, and transportation—and the political process. Not only were the ex-slaves guaranteed political and civil rights, recent historians note, but some steps were also taken toward economic justice. Central in the new explanation is the assertive role played by African Americans themselves. Some historians argue that it was the fear that African Americans would leave their assigned place at the bottom of the sociopolitical structure that really ended Reconstruction.

Reconstruction in the South, 1868–1877

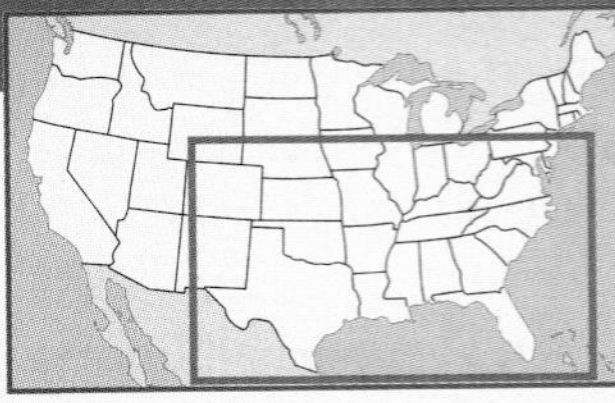

Learning from Maps The Reconstruction Acts established military districts in the South that would be removed when the southern states drafted new constitutions and adopted the Fourteenth Amendment.

❓ REGION During Reconstruction, which former Confederate state was not part of a military district?

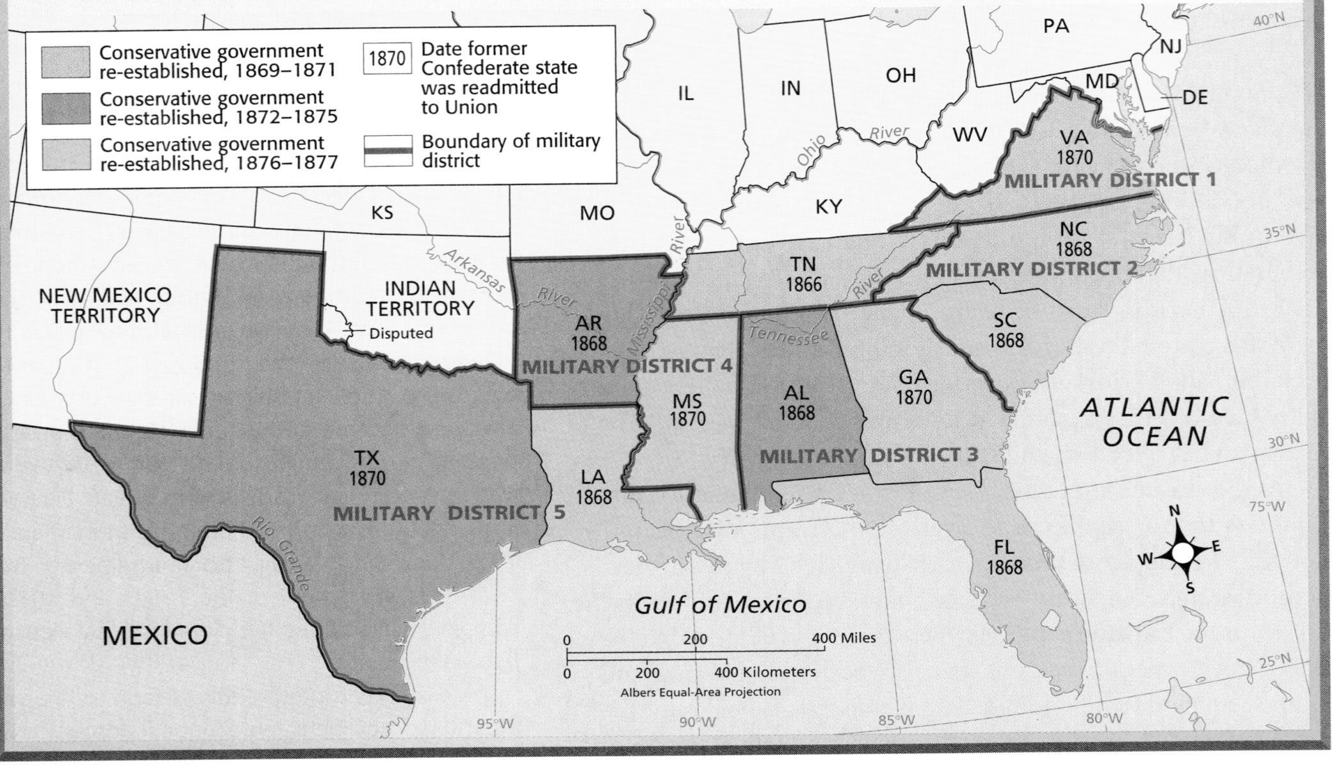

Legend:
- Conservative government re-established, 1869–1871
- Conservative government re-established, 1872–1875
- Conservative government re-established, 1876–1877
- 1870 Date former Confederate state was readmitted to Union
- Boundary of military district

PA
NJ
MD
DE
IL
IN
OH
WV
VA 1870 — MILITARY DISTRICT 1
Ohio River
KS
MO
KY
TN 1866
NC 1868 — MILITARY DISTRICT 2
NEW MEXICO TERRITORY
INDIAN TERRITORY — Disputed
Arkansas River
AR 1868
Tennessee River
SC 1868
MILITARY DISTRICT 4
Mississippi River
MS 1870
AL 1868
GA 1870
ATLANTIC OCEAN
TX 1870
MILITARY DISTRICT 5
LA 1868
MILITARY DISTRICT 3
FL 1868
Rio Grande
MEXICO
Gulf of Mexico

0   200   400 Miles
0   200   400 Kilometers
Albers Equal-Area Projection

The southern Redeemers.

The discontent caused by the Panic of 1873 turned voters against the Republican-controlled Congress. In the 1874 congressional elections Democrats gained dozens of seats in the House, giving them a 60-seat majority. In the South the Democrats attracted white voters with promises of lower taxes and through appeals to white supremacy.

When Congress reconvened, Republicans made one final effort to enforce Reconstruction by enacting the **Civil Rights Act of 1875**. This bill prohibited businesses that served the public—such as hotels and transportation facilities—from discriminating against African Americans. However, white Republican supporters of the bill had begun to see Reconstruction as a political burden.

Many southern white Democrats reached the same conclusion. Convinced that the federal government would not stop them, Mississippi Democrats used terrorism to win the 1875 state elections. In Clay County, against a backdrop of Confederate flags, white Democrats shot and killed several African Americans who declared their intention of voting Republican. The next year Democrats in Louisiana and South Carolina adopted similar tactics to "redeem," or win back, their states from the Republicans. These supporters of white-controlled governments called themselves the **Redeemers**.

In 1876 the Redeemers focused on the presidential election, which pitted Democrat Samuel J. Tilden of New York against Republican Rutherford B. Hayes

As Republican attention shifted away from Reconstruction, southern African Americans faced increasing violence.

of Ohio. Opponents of Reconstruction vowed to win the election even "if we have to wade in blood knee-deep." In the popular vote they succeeded: Tilden beat Hayes by some 250,000 votes. The electoral vote was another story.

The election results in four states were challenged by various parties. A commission set up to rule on the validity of the returns gave Hayes the presidency by one electoral vote. Democrats in the House protested. To defuse the crisis, leading Republicans and southern Democrats struck a deal—the **Compromise of 1877**. In return for the Democrats' acceptance of Hayes as president, the Republicans agreed to withdraw the remaining federal troops from the South.

Denied federal protection, the last of the Reconstruction governments fell. Once in power, the Redeemers rewrote state constitutions and overturned many of the Reconstruction governments' reforms. African American Charles Harris, a former legislator from Alabama, protested,

Great Debates

Reconstruction

The relative successes and failures of Reconstruction have long been debated by scholars. In many ways, Reconstruction did not accomplish its goals. The failure of land-reform efforts allowed white planters to maintain control over many southern institutions. Southern African Americans saw little economic improvement because the basic economic structure of the South remained intact. They also achieved few lasting civil and political rights.

The new state constitutions adopted in the South during the Reconstruction era, however, did help reform the states' judicial and legislative systems. African American leaders also created institutions—churches, schools, and strong family networks—that helped sustain black communities through the difficult post-Reconstruction years. The Reconstruction era also left a legal legacy. Although they were rarely enforced for almost a century, the Civil Rights Act of 1866 and the Fourteenth and Fifteenth Amendments provided an important legal framework that enabled later civil rights leaders to win back voting rights for African Americans and to end legal segregation.

66 We obey laws; others make them. We support state educational institutions, whose doors are virtually closed against us. . . . From these and many other oppressions . . . our people long to be free. **99**

✔ **READING CHECK:** What caused the Reconstruction era come to an end?

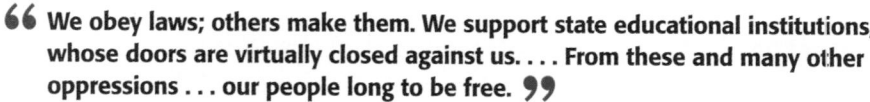

SECTION ③ REVIEW

Define and explain the significance of the following terms:
carpetbaggers
scalawags
Ku Klux Klan
Enforcement Acts
Panic of 1873
Civil Rights Act of 1875
Redeemers
Compromise of 1877

Identify and explain the significance of the following individuals:
Samuel J. Tilden
Rutherford B. Hayes

1. **Using Graphic Organizers** Copy the graphic organizer below. Use it to describe the similarities and differences between the tactics of the Ku Klux Klan and the Redeemers, and how African Americans responded to the groups.

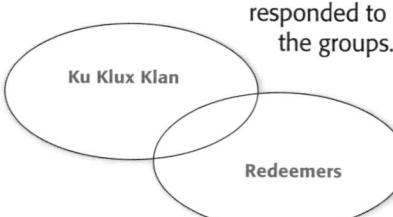

2. **Evaluating** What role did African Americans play in shaping Reconstruction?
3. **Assessing Consequences** How did the Republican governments change legislation in southern states?
4. **Hypothesizing** What special abilities and knowledge might African American legislators have been able to bring to the new southern governments?

Critical Thinking

5. How and why did Reconstruction fail to achieve its goals?
   Consider:
   • what the goals of Reconstruction were
   • what events and issues ended Reconstruction
   • what goals were left unmet

The New South

OBJECTIVES

Read to understand:

1. what the drawbacks were to the sharecropping system
2. how Jim Crow laws and the *Plessy* v. *Ferguson* decision changed life for southern African Americans
3. how African Americans attempted to improve their economic situation after Reconstruction
4. how Booker T. Washington and Ida B. Wells differed in their opinions of how African Americans should respond to Jim Crow laws

KEY TERMS

sharecropping
crop-lien system
poll taxes
literacy tests
segregation
Jim Crow laws
Plessy v. *Ferguson*

KEY PEOPLE

Madame C. J. Walker
Booker T. Washington
Ida B. Wells

EYEWITNESSES TO History

❝ *[Former slaves exhibit] a growing dislike to being controlled by or working for white men. They prefer to get a little patch where they can do as they choose.* ❞
—Anonymous white farmer

Former slave tending to the family garden

This Tennessee planter noted the increasing desire among freedpeople to own their own land. Frances Leigh, another planter, remarked that as soon as her field hands were paid, many of them purchased small plots of land, usually in the pine woods "where the land was so poor they could not raise a peck of corn to the acre." Although Leigh thought the field hands had been cheated in these land deals, she could not help but notice the enthusiasm the African American farmers brought to their new lives under freedom.

Changing Economies in the South

Some southern planters lost their lands after the Civil War because they could not pay their debts or their taxes. Most of their lands fell into the hands of other planters or northern investors.

Sharecropping. Whether planters were southerners or northerners, however, all were faced with labor shortages. Few whites or former slaves wanted to work for the low wages planters were willing—or, in many cases, able—to pay.

Some planters solved their labor problems with **sharecropping**. Under this system a farmer worked a parcel of land in return for a share of the crop, a cabin, seed, tools, and a mule. Sharecropping enabled planters to get their lands worked when they did not have enough cash to pay laborers. Sharecropping gave laborers a place to live and lands to work without close supervision. By the end of the 1870s many poor white southerners and the majority of African Americans in the South worked as sharecroppers.

The arrangement had a serious drawback, however. Sharecroppers had no income until harvest time. To obtain needed supplies each year, they had to promise their crops to local merchants who then sold them goods on credit. Any outstanding debts were added to their bills the following year. This arrangement was known as the **crop-lien system**. A lien is a creditor's legal claim on the debtor's property.

In effect, the system made it impossible for sharecroppers to work their way out of poverty or to gain independence. Former slave Thomas Hall judged the system to be "little better than slavery." The crop-lien system kept the southern economy tied primarily to one-crop agriculture. Merchants gave credit only to farmers who grew certain crops, most often cotton. As a result, cotton displaced other crops to such an extent that the South had to import food and animal feed from the North.

✔ **READING CHECK:** What were the drawbacks of the sharecropping system?

African American families like this one suffered under the sharecropping and crop-lien systems.

★ Changing Ways The South

■ **Understanding Change** Much has changed in the South since the late 1800s, yet much remains the same. Although the average income in the South is nearly that of the national average, it still lags behind in wealth. *How has the South's population changed? How has the average per capita income changed as compared to the rest of the country?*

THEN

Now

	THEN	Now
Population	36% Nonwhite / 64% White	23% Nonwhite / 77% White
	12% Urban / 88% Rural	31% Rural / 69% Urban
Ratio of Per Capita Income Compared to the U.S. Average	32%	90%

Nonwhite / White
Rural / Urban

Sources: *Historical Statistics of the United States; Statistical Abstract of the United States: 1997.* Data reflects 1870 and 1990.

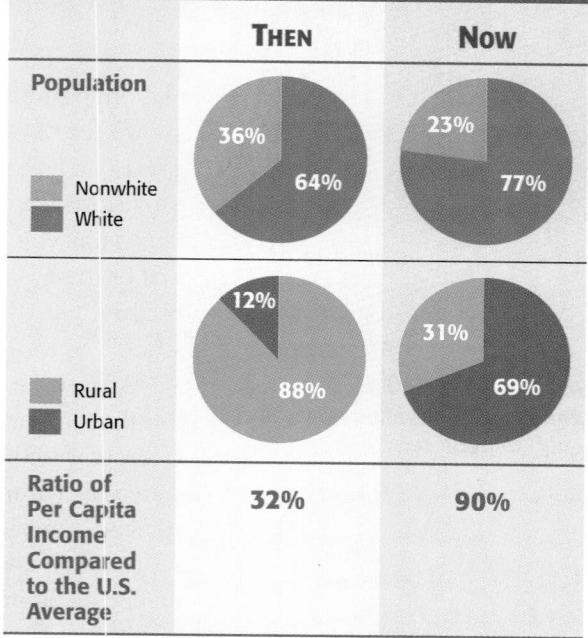

Industrial growth. Henry W. Grady, the editor of the Atlanta *Constitution,* believed that one-crop agriculture kept the South in poverty and economically dependent on the North. The New South, he argued, should manufacture its own goods. Supporters of this New South idea joined with northern and British investors to finance factories and ironworks, while southerners raised the capital to build textile mills and other enterprises. Southern railroads were rebuilt and integrated into northern rail systems.

Not everyone benefited equally from industrialization in the South, however. Factory owners and investors profited at the expense of poorly paid workers. White industrial workers in the South earned far lower wages than their northern counterparts. Most African Americans could not find any factory work at all. Many industrial workers were forced to buy goods on credit from the company store and to live in ramshackle company houses. Like sharecroppers, they soon found themselves locked in a cycle of debt.

The Rise of Jim Crow

For African Americans, the so-called New South closely resembled the Old South. They were tied to the land through sharecropping and by their exclusion from most factory jobs. Moreover, Democrats had taken control of the southern state legislatures and stepped up their attempts to strip African Americans of their rights.

To deprive African Americans of the right to vote, southern legislatures instituted **poll taxes**—fixed taxes imposed on every voter—and **literacy tests**—tests that barred those who could not read from voting. Because most African American southerners were poor and had been denied an education, these legal barriers

THE GRANGER COLLECTION, NEW YORK

INTERPRETING THE VISUAL RECORD

The New South. Many southerners supported the building of new industries and railroad systems in the late 1800s. *How does this painting express the goals of the New South movement?*

NEGRO EXPULSION FROM RAILWAY CAR, PHILADELPHIA.

THE GRANGER COLLECTION, NEW YORK

Jim Crow laws prohibited African Americans from riding on "whites only" railroad cars.

INTERPRETING THE VISUAL RECORD

Segregation. African Americans established many institutions to serve their community. *How does this image of an African American church service reflect the importance of community during the Jim Crow era?*

effectively disfranchised African Americans. Even literate African Americans often "failed" the test, since white officials decided who passed. These rules, however, were often waived for poor or illiterate whites. Whites also used violence and intimidation to prevent African Americans from voting.

To further deprive African Americans of their rights, state legislatures initiated a series of laws designed to enforce **segregation**, or separation, of the races. These provisions were called **Jim Crow laws**, so-named after a minstrel song that contained the refrain "Jump—jump—jump Jim Crow." Passed in Tennessee in 1881, the first of these laws required separate railway cars for African Americans and whites. By the 1890s all southern states had legally segregated public transportation and schools. Segregation soon extended to cemeteries, parks, and other public places.

African Americans sued for equal treatment under the Civil Rights Act of 1875, but the Supreme Court refused to overturn the Jim Crow laws. In the *Civil Rights Cases* of 1883 the Court ruled that the Fourteenth Amendment prohibited only state governments, not individuals or businesses, from discriminating against African Americans. The Supreme Court upheld segregation again in ***Plessy v. Ferguson***, a lawsuit brought in 1896 after African American Homer Plessy was denied a seat in a first-class railway car. The Court ruled that "separate but equal" facilities did not violate the Fourteenth Amendment. Justice John Marshall Harlan disagreed, declaring, "Our Constitution is color-blind, and neither knows nor tolerates classes among citizens."

✔ **READING CHECK:** How did the enactment of Jim Crow laws and the *Plessy* v. *Ferguson* decision change life for southern African Americans?

African American Life

Despite segregation, in some southern cities a growing African American middle class began to emerge, made up of doctors, government workers, teachers, and lawyers. African Americans formed mutual aid societies, started businesses, supported churches, and built schools. The African Methodist Episcopal (AME) Church, the AME Zion Church, and the African American Baptist Church grew rapidly.

Farmers and planters. Most African Americans had little opportunity to improve their economic status. Despite numerous obstacles, however, some did purchase farmland and in a few cases large plantations. According to writer Charles Nordhoff, African Americans in Georgia owned "nearly 400,000 acres of farming real estate, besides city property."

Some African Americans also formed cooperatives to buy farmland. In addition to producing crops and providing jobs, the cooperatives often provided for the care of sick members "if unable to care for themselves." Cooperatives sometimes imposed taxes "to provide for the education of the young and the comfortable maintenance of the aged and helpless."

AMERICAN Letters

Black Writers During the Late 1800s

Many African American writers of the post-Reconstruction period focused their attention on the difficulties faced by African Americans after their emancipation, as well as on the African American experience more generally. Charles W. Chesnutt's 1899 story "The Wife of His Youth" deals with the choice one man must make between the woman he married while still a slave and the young widow he is courting. Paul Laurence Dunbar's 1890s poem "Ode for Memorial Day" expresses the pain of the Civil War and its joyful outcome.

from "The Wife of His Youth"
by Charles W. Chesnutt

Suppose that this husband, soon after his escape, had learned that his wife had been sold away, and that such inquires as he could make brought no information of her whereabouts. Suppose that he was young, and she much older than he; that he was light, and she was black; that their marriage was a slave marriage, and legally binding only if they chose to make it so after the war. Suppose, too, that he made his way to the North, as some of us have done, and there, where he had larger opportunities, had improved them, and had in the course of all these years grown to be as different from the ignorant boy who ran away from fear of slavery as the day is from the night. Suppose, even, that he had qualified himself, by industry, by thrift, and by study, to win the friendship and be considered worthy. . . . And then suppose that accident should bring to his knowledge the fact that the wife of his youth, the wife he had left behind him, . . . was alive and seeking him, but that he was absolutely safe from recognition or discovery, unless he chose to reveal himself. My friends, what would the man do?"

Collection of poetry by Charles W. Chesnutt

from "Ode for Memorial Day"
by Paul Laurence Dunbar

Done are the toils and the
    wearisome marches. . . .
Out of the blood of a conflict
    fraternal,
    Out of the dust and the
      dimness of death,
Burst into blossoms of glory
    eternal
    Flowers that sweeten the world with their breath.
Flowers of charity, peace, and devotion
    Bloom in the hearts that are empty of strife;
Love that is boundless and broad as the ocean
    Leaps into beauty and fulness of life.
So, with the singing of paeans [praises] and chorals,
    And with the flag flashing high in the sun,
Place on the graves of our heroes the laurels
    Which their unfaltering valor has won!

Paul Laurence Dunbar

UNDERSTANDING LITERATURE

1. How does Chesnutt portray slave marriage in "The Wife of His Youth"?
2. How does Dunbar refer to the ideals behind the fighting of the Civil War?
3. What sentiments about life after the Civil War do these authors express?

Industry and business. African Americans also formed nonagricultural cooperatives. In cities such as Baltimore, Charleston, and Richmond, cooperatives bought large parcels of land. They then sold that land to members for building homes. After being excluded from dock work, African Americans in Baltimore organized the Chesapeake, Marine, and Dry Dock Company. This cooperative raised and borrowed thousands of dollars to buy a shipyard and a marine railway. It hired 1,000 African American caulkers and carpenters to do repair work, won a government contract, and paid off its entire debt within five years.

Some African Americans also owned small businesses such as barber shops, blacksmith shops, general stores, and restaurants. African American women could be found in open-air markets throughout southern cities, selling candy and vegetables. A leading African American entrepreneur, Madame C. J. Walker, became one of the first women in the United States to become a millionaire.

BIOGRAPHY

Madame C. J. Walker

Madame C. J. Walker was born Sarah Breedlove in 1867 in Louisiana. Her parents were poverty-stricken sharecroppers, and Walker worked in the cotton fields as a child. She married at age 14 and gave birth to her daughter, A'Leila, four years later. By the time Walker was 20, her first husband had died, apparently killed by a lynch mob. For the next 17 years she worked as a cook and laundress.

By 1905 Walker had developed a hair-conditioner treatment for African American women. With her life savings of $1.50, she opened a hair preparations company, which she operated out of the attic of her home. Six months later she married journalist C. J. Walker, who adopted her daughter. The couple traveled for the next year and a half to promote Walker's products, leaving A'Leila Walker behind to run the mail-order business.

After divorcing her husband, Walker and her daughter moved in 1908 to Pittsburgh, Pennsylvania, where they founded Leila College, a beauty school. Soon cosmetologists were practicing the Walker method for hair care. By 1910 Walker had established beauty parlors, production facilities, and laboratories throughout the country and in the Caribbean and South America. Within another nine years, 25,000 African American women were Walker "agents," selling her products.

By 1914 Walker's company was earning more than $1 million per year. Until her death in 1919, Walker was a generous contributor to African American causes, particularly schools and equal rights organizations. She relentlessly promoted the belief that African Americans could better themselves economically. During one public speech, Walker said:

> 66 The girls and women of our race must not be afraid to take hold of business endeavor. . . . I want to say to every Negro woman present, don't sit down and wait for the opportunities to come. . . . Get up and make them! 99

✔ **READING CHECK:** In what ways did African Americans attempt to better their economic situation after Reconstruction?

INTERPRETING THE VISUAL RECORD

Entrepreneurship. Madame C. J. Walker built a factory for the production of beauty products in Indianapolis, Indiana, in 1910. *How do you think this advertisement might have helped Walker sell her merchandise?*

Responses to the Jim Crow Era

Despite the success of some individuals, African Americans continued to encounter widespread discrimination in the late 1870s. Two influential African American leaders differed in their approaches to this discrimination.

Booker T. Washington believed that African Americans should concentrate on achieving economic independence, which he saw as the key to political and social equality. He urged African Americans to seek practical training in trades and professions. He discouraged them from protesting against discrimination, arguing that it merely increased whites' hostility. At the same time, however, Washington secretly provided support to groups fighting Jim Crow laws and racial violence.

Some African American leaders disagreed with Washington's public position calling for cooperation with southern whites. They argued instead that African Americans should protest unfair treatment. Civil rights activist, journalist, and teacher Ida B. Wells—later Wells-Barnett—focused her attention on stopping the lynching of African Americans. In fiery editorials she urged African Americans to leave the South. She herself moved from Memphis to Chicago. Wells uged others to follow her example.

Booker T. Washington founded the Tuskegee Institute in 1881.

> 66 There is therefore only one thing left that we can do; save our money and leave a town which will neither protect our lives [nor] property. 99

Although lynchings decreased only slightly in the early 1900s, Wells's tireless efforts kept the public's attention focused on the issue.

✔ **READING CHECK:** How do Booker T. Washington's and Ida B. Wells's beliefs represent differing approaches to how African Americans should have responded to Jim Crow laws?

Read More About It

Free Find: Ida B. Wells
After reading the biography on Ida B. Wells on the **Holt Researcher** CD–ROM, write a short biography that describes her political activities and accomplishments.

SECTION 4 REVIEW

Define and explain the significance of the following terms:
sharecropping
crop-lien system
poll taxes
literacy tests
segregation
Jim Crow laws
Plessy v. *Ferguson*

Identify and explain the significance of the following individuals:
Madame C. J. Walker
Booker T. Washington
Ida B. Wells

1. **Using Graphic Organizers** Copy the graphic organizer below. Use it to explain the advantages and disadvantages of the sharecropping system. Consider the effects of the sharecropping system on the landowner, the laborers, and the southern economy as a whole.

2. **Assessing Consequences** How did the Jim Crow laws affect African Americans?

3. **Using Historical Imagination** Imagine that you are a reporter for a national magazine after Reconstruction. Write a brief article summarizing how African Americans are working together to improve their social and economic situations.

4. **Comparing and Contrasting** Write a brief paragraph comparing and contrasting the views of Booker T. Washington and Ida B. Wells.

Critical Thinking

5. How did the New South compare to the antebellum South?
   Consider:
   • how the economy changed or stayed the same
   • how racial attitudes changed or stayed the same
   • how political power changed or stayed the same

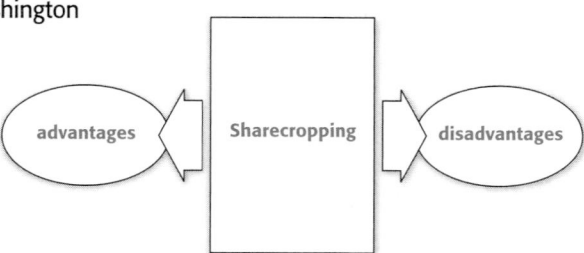

advantages ← Sharecropping → disadvantages

CHAPTER 13 Review

Creating a Time Line

Copy the time line below onto a sheet of paper. Complete the time line by filling in the events and dates from the chapter that you think were most significant. Pick three events and explain why you think they were significant.

1860   1875   1890   1905

Writing a Summary

Using the Reading Checks as a guide, write an overview of the events of the chapter.

Identifying People and Ideas

Identify the following terms or individuals and explain their significance.

1. amnesty
2. Andrew Johnson
3. Black Codes
4. Reconstruction Acts
5. carpetbaggers
6. Compromise of 1877
7. sharecropping
8. Jim Crow laws
9. Madame C. J. Walker
10. Booker T. Washington

Understanding Main Ideas

SECTION 1
1. How did the Reconstruction plans of President Lincoln and President Johnson differ?

SECTION 2
2. How did President Johnson's plans for Reconstruction differ from Radical Republican plans?
3. What laws did Congress pass to protect the rights of African Americans?

SECTION 3
4. Why did Reconstruction come to an end?

SECTION 4
5. How did conditions for southern farmers and laborers change from 1865 to 1900?
6. How did Jim Crow laws affect African Americans?

Reviewing Themes

1. **Constitutional Heritage** How did the Thirteenth, Fourteenth, and Fifteenth Amendments change the U.S. Constitution to reflect changing conditions after the Civil War?
2. **Democratic Values** How was democracy in the United States expanded during Reconstruction?
3. **Economic Development** What role did cotton play in the New South?

Thinking Critically

1. **Hypothesizing** How might conditions in the New South have been different if land had been distributed to African Americans after the war?
2. **Evaluating** Why did many southern whites react so strongly to gains made by African Americans during Reconstruction?
3. **Identifying Cause and Effect** What political gains did African Americans make during Reconstruction?
4. **Using Historical Imagination** Imagine that you are a senator during the impeachment trial of President Johnson. How would you vote? Why?
5. **Taking a Stand** Do you agree or disagree with the Compromise of 1877? Why or why not?

Writing About History

Writing to Express Imagine that you are an African American sharecropper in the postwar South. Write a letter to a local newspaper explaining how Reconstruction policies have affected your economic and social status and why you oppose the Compromise of 1877. Use the following graphic organizer to help organize your thoughts.

Reconstruction Policies → Effect on Economic Status → Reasons for Supporting Compromise

Review the **Strategies for Success** on *Comparing Points of View.* Then reconsider the excerpt below from President Lincoln's second inaugural address. Compare the excerpt to the quotation included in the Strategies for Success, and answer the questions that follow.

> 66 **With malice toward none, with charity for all, with firmness in the right as God gives us to see the right, let us strive on . . . to bind up the nation's wounds . . . to do all which may achieve and cherish a just and lasting peace.** 99

1. How do you think President Lincoln's personal background and political circumstances influenced what he said in his second inaugural address?
2. What is the main idea of the excerpt? Is this idea supported by facts, opinions, or both?
3. Does Lincoln's point of view more closely resemble that of Horace Greeley or Robert E. Lee? Why?

Linking History and Geography

Study the map below. Where were most African American colleges that were founded before 1900 located? Explain why you think this pattern was the case.

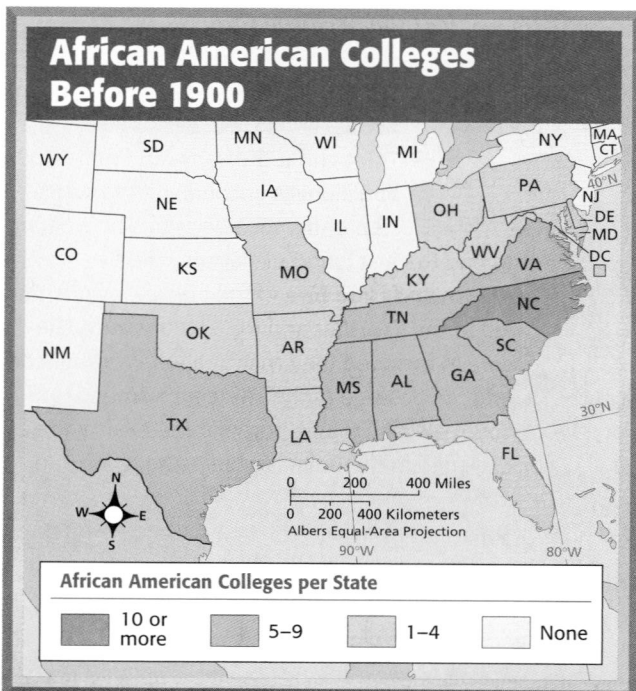

African American Colleges Before 1900

African American Colleges per State

| 10 or more | 5–9 | 1–4 | None |

internet connect

TOPIC: Impeachment of Andrew Johnson
GO TO: go.hrw.com
KEYWORD: SD1 Johnson

Accessing the Internet through the HRW Web site, research the impeachment trial of Andrew Johnson. Concentrate on the circumstances that led to the trial, the trial proceedings, and the results of the trial. For a group activity, assume the roles of the principal figures and dramatize a part of the trial in front of the class. For an individual activity, write a statement that explains why you would have voted to convict or acquit the president.

BUILDING YOUR PORTFOLIO

Complete one or all of the following projects independently or cooperatively.

THE PRESIDENT IS DEAD!

WAR DEPARTMENT,
Washington, April 15, 1865.

To MAJ. GEN. DIX.

Abraham Lincoln died this morning at 22 minutes after Seven o'clock.

E. M. STANTON. Sec. of War.

1 Geographic Diversity

Imagine that you are a newspaper editor. **Prepare a list of headlines, story ideas, and possible illustrations** to explain how people in different parts of the nation feel about the assassination of President Abraham Lincoln.

2 Democratic Values

Imagine that you are a southern governor opposed to northern politicians' plans for the South during Reconstruction. **Create an outline** for a Reconstruction plan that would address the interests of planters, former soldiers, and African Americans in your state.

3 Constitutional Heritage

Imagine that you are an attorney representing Homer Plessy. **Prepare a closing statement** arguing that segregation, as practiced in "separate but equal" facilities for African Americans and whites, violates the Fourteenth Amendment.

U·N·I·T 4

Review

BUILDING YOUR PORTFOLIO

Outlined below are four projects. Independently or cooperatively, complete one and use the products to demonstrate your mastery of the historical concepts involved.

1 Cultural Diversity

As Americans migrated west of the Mississippi, settlers came into contact with inhabitants who had various cultural traditions. Imagine that you are an anthropologist who studies the way people of different cultures meet and interact. *Create a journal entry* recording how two different groups interact and chronicling their cultural differences. Describe what advantages and disadvantages each group experienced as a result of the contact. You may wish to use portfolio materials you designed in the unit chapters to help you.

Mexican American cowboys

2 Democratic Values

Throughout the early- and mid-1800s abolitionists encouraged the extension of democratic values by working to end the institution of slavery. *Create an illustrated time line* of the political events that led to the Civil War and the end of slavery. Be sure to included the Emancipation Proclamation and the passage of the Thirteenth Amendment. You may wish to use portfolio materials you designed in the unit chapters to help you.

Georgia cotton plantation

3 Geographic Diversity

Differences between the North and the South created a rift that led to the Civil War and left deep scars that Reconstruction failed to erase. **Create an outline for an argument in a debate** that discusses whether Reconstruction served the political, economic, and social interests of the North more than the South. You may wish to use portfolio materials you designed in the unit chapters to help you.

Carpetbag carried by northerners traveling south during Reconstruction

4 Constitutional Heritage

The Thirteenth Amendment ended the institution of slavery. It did not, however, end legal discrimination against African Americans. **Create an outline and a visual aid for a press conference** to discuss these issues. Your questions at the conference should focus on how the lives of African Americans have changed with the adoption of the new amendment. You may wish to use portfolio materials you designed in the unit chapters to help you.

Segregated classroom from the early 1900s

Further Reading

Emilio, Luis F. *A Brave Black Regiment.* Bantam Books, 1992. Collection of documents written about the 54th Regiment of the Massachusetts Volunteer Infantry.

Foner, Eric. *A Short History of Reconstruction, 1863–1877.* HarperCollins, 1990. A well-balanced overview of the Reconstruction years.

Franklin, John Hope. *Reconstruction: After the Civil War.* University of Chicago Press, 1995. An account of the Radicals' efforts to legislate the South during Reconstruction.

Holliday, J. S. *The World Rushed In: The California Gold Rush Experience.* Simon and Schuster, 1983. Eyewitness accounts of the California Gold Rush.

Meltzer, Milton, ed. *Voices from the Civil War.* HarperCollins, 1989. Northern and southern views of the war and its effects from 1861 to 1865.

Schlissel, Lillian. *Women's Diaries of the Westward Journey.* Schocken Books, 1992. A collection of personal accounts of women who migrated west during the 1800s.

Internet Connect and Holt Researcher CD–ROM *Review*

In assigned groups, develop a multimedia presentation about America between 1820 and 1900. Choose information from the chapter Internet Connect activities and from the **Holt Researcher** CD–ROM that best reflect the major topics of the period. Write an outline and a script for your presentation, which may be shown to the class.

A Nation Transformed

1860–1910

Wason Railcar Works used this facility to manufacture railroad cars during the 1870s.

1845. – WASON – 1872.
CAR MANUFACTURING CO.

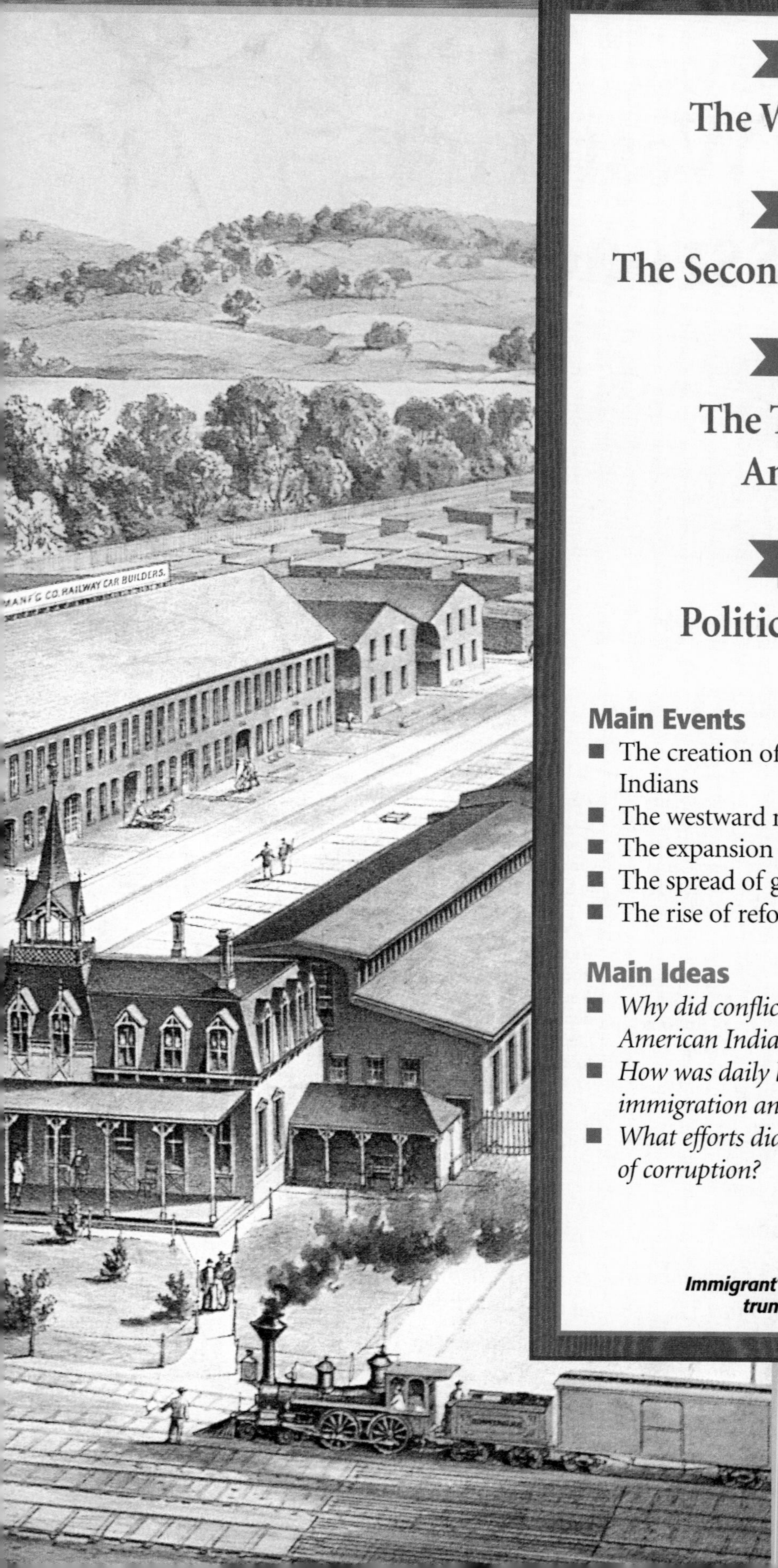

CHAPTER 14
The Western Crossroads
1860–1910

CHAPTER 15
The Second Industrial Revolution
1865–1905

CHAPTER 16
The Transformation of American Society
1865–1910

CHAPTER 17
Politics in the Gilded Age
1865–1900

Main Events
- The creation of a reservation system for American Indians
- The westward migration of American settlers
- The expansion of industrialization and immigration
- The spread of government corruption
- The rise of reform movements

Main Ideas
- *Why did conflicts erupt between western settlers and American Indians?*
- *How was daily life in U.S. cities transformed by immigration and industrialization?*
- *What efforts did Americans take to rid government of corruption?*

Immigrant's trunk

431

1860–1910
The Western Crossroads

Pony Express stamp

Signing of the Alaska treaty

Queen Victoria

1876
World Events
Queen Victoria of Great Britain becomes Empress of India.

1876
Politics
Colorado becomes the 38th state admitted to the Union.

1883
Business and Finance
Railroad companies create the time-zone system.

1860
Daily Life
The Pony Express begins delivering mail between Missouri and San Francisco.

1867
Politics
Congress approves the purchase of Alaska from Russia.

1860

1870

1880

1861
World Events
The Italian parliament declares Italy a kingdom.

1860
Science and Technology
Oliver Winchester introduces the repeating rifle.

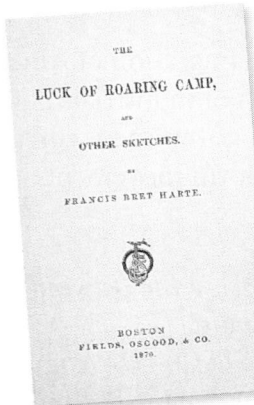

THE
LUCK OF ROARING CAMP,

OTHER SKETCHES.

FRANCIS BRET HARTE.

BOSTON
FIELDS, OSGOOD, & CO.
1870.

Bret Harte's **The Luck of Roaring Camp**

1870
The Arts
Bret Harte publishes *The Luck of Roaring Camp*, about life in California.

1873
Daily Life
Cable streetcars are introduced in San Francisco.

1873
Business and Finance
A severe economic depression slows the growth of railroad networks.

1879
Daily Life
Thousands of African Americans migrate from the South to Kansas.

1878
Politics
The Timber and Stone Act allows for the sale of western public land that cannot be used for farming.

Before You Read

Build on What You Know

The resolution of the Oregon boundary dispute in 1846 and the Treaty of Guadalupe Hidalgo in 1848 reshaped the United States. These treaties opened up more than 1 million square miles of western land for U.S. settlement. In this chapter you will learn that Americans who settled in the West came for many reasons. American Indians suffered the consequences of this settlement. They endured continued conflict and violence as non-Indians established farms and ranches in the lands of the American West.

A Sioux child's doll

U.S. troops posing with Hotchkiss guns

1885
World Events
King Leopold II of Belgium assumes sovereignty over the African Congo.

1890
Politics
Troops of the U.S. 7th Cavalry attack Sioux camped at Wounded Knee Creek in South Dakota.

1890
Business and Finance
The Midwest is the center of the meatpacking industry.

1896
World Events
Italy recognizes Abyssinia—modern-day Ethiopia—as an independent nation.

1896
Daily Life
Americans living in rural areas receive mail delivery for free.

1905
World Events
Czar Nicholas II of Russia institutes reforms after a series of strikes paralyzes the nation.

1890

1900

1910

1886–87
Daily Life
Devastating winter storms lash the Great Plains.

1889
Daily Life
President Harrison opens to settlers Oklahoma Territory lands that had been reserved for American Indians.

1898
The Arts
The Royal Italian Opera performs Puccini's *La Bohème* in San Francisco.

1906
Science and Technology
An astronomical observatory opens at Mt. Wilson, California.

Settlers racing to claim land in Oklahoma

Think About Themes

Themes Journal

*Decide whether you **agree** or **disagree** with the following statements. Note why in your journal.*

Cultural Diversity Cultural differences between groups can lead to misunderstandings and even violence.

Economic Development The impact that some economic activities have upon the environment may not be readily apparent.

Technology and Society Improvements in technology may actually worsen conditions for some laborers.

433

War in the West

OBJECTIVES

Read to understand:

1. why the U.S. government created the American Indian reservation system
2. what the sources of conflict between the Plains Indians and the U.S. government were
3. how Chief Joseph, Geronimo, and Sarah Winnemucca responded to white treatment of American Indians
4. how the U.S. government tried to assimilate American Indians

KEY TERMS

Bureau of Indian Affairs
Sand Creek Massacre
Battle of the Little Bighorn
Massacre at Wounded Knee
Dawes General Allotment Act

KEY PEOPLE

Cochise
John M. Chivington
Sitting Bull
George Armstrong Custer
Wovoka
Chief Joseph
Geronimo
Sarah Winnemucca

KEY PLACES

Standing Rock Reservation
Bosque Redondo Reservation

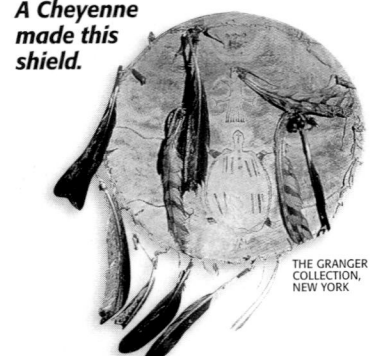

A Cheyenne made this shield.

THE GRANGER COLLECTION, NEW YORK

EYEWITNESSES TO History

❝ *When I was young, I walked all over this country, east and west, and saw no other people than the Apaches. After many summers I walked again and found another race of people had come to take it.* ❞
—Cochise

Chiricahua Apache

Cochise, a Chiricahua (chir-uh-KAH-wuh) Apache leader, mourned over the crisis faced by American Indians as white settlers poured into their homelands. The Chiricahua Apache resisted, however. During the 1850s the Chiricahua had permitted settlers traveling to California to pass through Apache lands in present-day Arizona. In 1861, however, a rancher accused the Chiricahua of stealing a child and cattle from his ranch. U.S. Army officials attempted to hold Cochise and his relatives hostage until the child and cattle were returned. The incident led to years of deadly warfare between the Chiricahua and the United States.

Indian Country

By 1850 most American Indians—some 360,000—lived west of the Mississippi River. The 1851 Treaty of Fort Laramie had guaranteed American Indian land rights on the Great Plains. However, as non-Indians moved west in search of farmland and gold, government officials sought to acquire additional American Indian lands. They negotiated new treaties in which American Indians agreed to move to reservations. In return, Indians received some money and guarantees that the reservation lands would be theirs forever. These treaties also promised yearly supplies for 30 years.

In addition to opening new lands to settlement, some government officials hoped that keeping American Indians on the reservations would force them to become farmers. This would also force some American Indians to abandon their traditional ways of life. The **Bureau of Indian Affairs** (BIA) was the government agency responsible for managing American Indian issues. BIA chief Luke Lea supported the reservation system. He declared in 1850 that American Indians should "be placed in positions where they can be controlled, and finally compelled by stern necessity to resort to agricultural labor or starve." Other officials recognized the harm this would do to American Indians. Thomas Fitzpatrick was an Indian agent who had helped to negotiate several treaties. In 1853 Fitzpatrick condemned the notion of a reservation system as "expensive, vicious, [and] inhumane."

American Indians who went willingly to the reservations discovered that the U.S. government often failed to honor its treaties. In addition, the government reduced the size of many reservations as settlers demanded more land. To make matters worse, in many cases the promised supplies never arrived. Government agents often diverted elsewhere the supplies intended for American Indians.

Anger over inadequate supplies and broken treaties exploded into violence on the Santee Sioux reservation in 1862. When a government agent refused to release food supplies even though people were starving, the Sioux attacked the Indian agency and nearby farms and towns. Army troops soon ended the uprising and executed 38 Sioux for their actions. The tribe was relocated, first to the Dakota Territory and then to Nebraska.

✔ **READING CHECK:** Why did the U.S. government create the American Indian reservation system?

Years of Struggle

Many Plains Indians, including independent groups of Arapaho, Cheyenne, Comanche, and Sioux, refused to live on the reservations. The importance of following the roaming buffalo herds to their cultures caused them to reject the restrictions of settled life.

The Plains Indians faced strong opposition. Some 20,000 U.S. Army troops, many of them Civil War veterans, were assigned to confine the tribes to the reservations. The army also enlisted some American Indians as scouts or as soldiers. Struggling to confine or relocate American Indians, U.S. troops occasionally became involved in violent conflicts with groups of American Indians.

Sand Creek. One early confrontation in the West between the military and American Indians occurred in Colorado Territory. Eager to open more land to U.S. settlers, territorial governor John Evans pressured the Cheyenne and Arapaho to sell their hunting grounds and move to reservations. In 1861 some Cheyenne and Arapaho leaders agreed to move their groups to a reservation south of the Arkansas River. Others, however, refused to leave.

Cheyenne and Arapaho forces clashed with the local militia throughout the summer of 1864. By fall, Cheyenne chief Black Kettle had tired of the fighting. On the way to Fort Lyon to surrender, his group camped along Sand Creek. While most of the Cheyenne men were away hunting, U.S. Army colonel John M. Chivington and some 700 Colorado volunteers arrived at the camp. Having raised a U.S. flag above his lodge as a sign of peace, Black Kettle reassured his people that they were safe. One eyewitness later recalled, "Suddenly the troops opened fire on this mass of men, women, and children, and all began to scatter and run." Some 200 of Black Kettle's group, most of them women and children, died in the **Sand Creek Massacre.**

Chivington defended his actions, declaring, "It is right and honorable to use any means under God's heaven to kill Indians." However, the slaughter horrified most Americans. A congressional committee investigating the incident called Sand Creek a "scene of murder and barbarity." Shock over the massacre led some members of Congress to call for reform of the government's Indian policy.

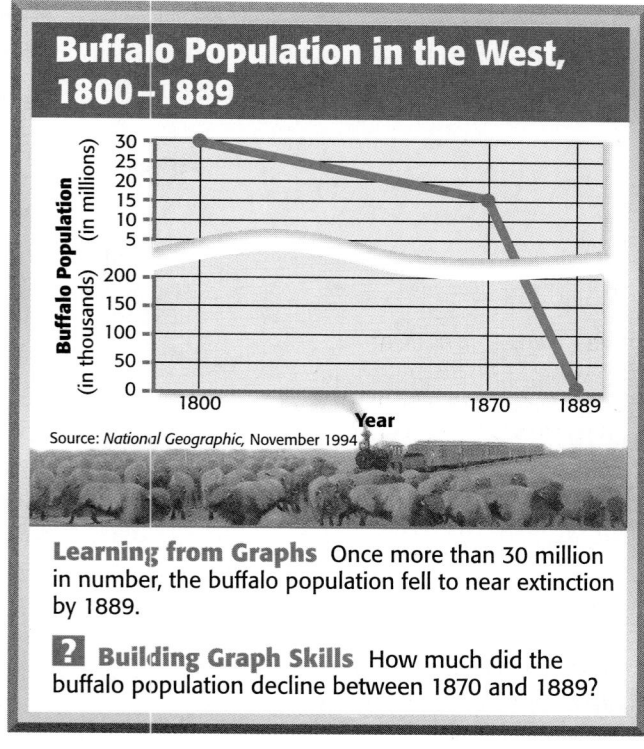

Buffalo Population in the West, 1800–1889

Source: *National Geographic,* November 1994

Learning from Graphs Once more than 30 million in number, the buffalo population fell to near extinction by 1889.

? **Building Graph Skills** How much did the buffalo population decline between 1870 and 1889?

INTERPRETING THE VISUAL RECORD

Buffalo. This painting by John Mix Stanley features a scene of the West. *What does the painting reveal about the techniques American Indians used to hunt buffalo?*

The Sand Creek Massacre shocked many Americans.

While government officials debated reform, news of the Sand Creek Massacre swept across the Plains, prompting raids by the Arapaho and Cheyenne. The Sioux also stepped up their attacks. Neither side emerged victorious, however. To end the fighting, the U.S. government created a peace commission to negotiate new treaties. Meeting with the southern Plains Indians in 1867, Senator John B. Henderson told them that the buffalo would soon be gone, so "the Indian must change the road his father trod." One Comanche replied, "I love the open prairie, and I wish you would not insist on putting us on a reservation." Despite such feelings, tribal leaders signed the Treaty of Medicine Lodge. Southern Plains Indians agreed to give up much of their lands in exchange for reservations in Indian Territory. The following year, in a second Treaty of Fort Laramie, the Sioux agreed to move to a reservation in the Black Hills region of South Dakota.

American Indian Reservations and Battles to 1890

Learning from Maps Fighting against overwhelming odds, American Indians were forced to give up their lands and move to reservations.

? LOCATION When was the last major American Indian battle fought?

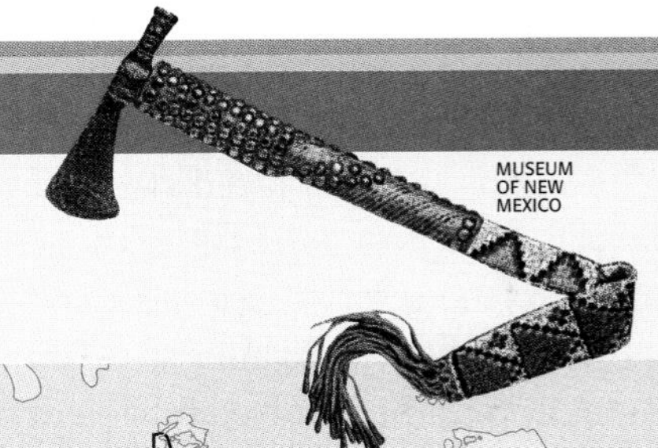

MUSEUM OF NEW MEXICO

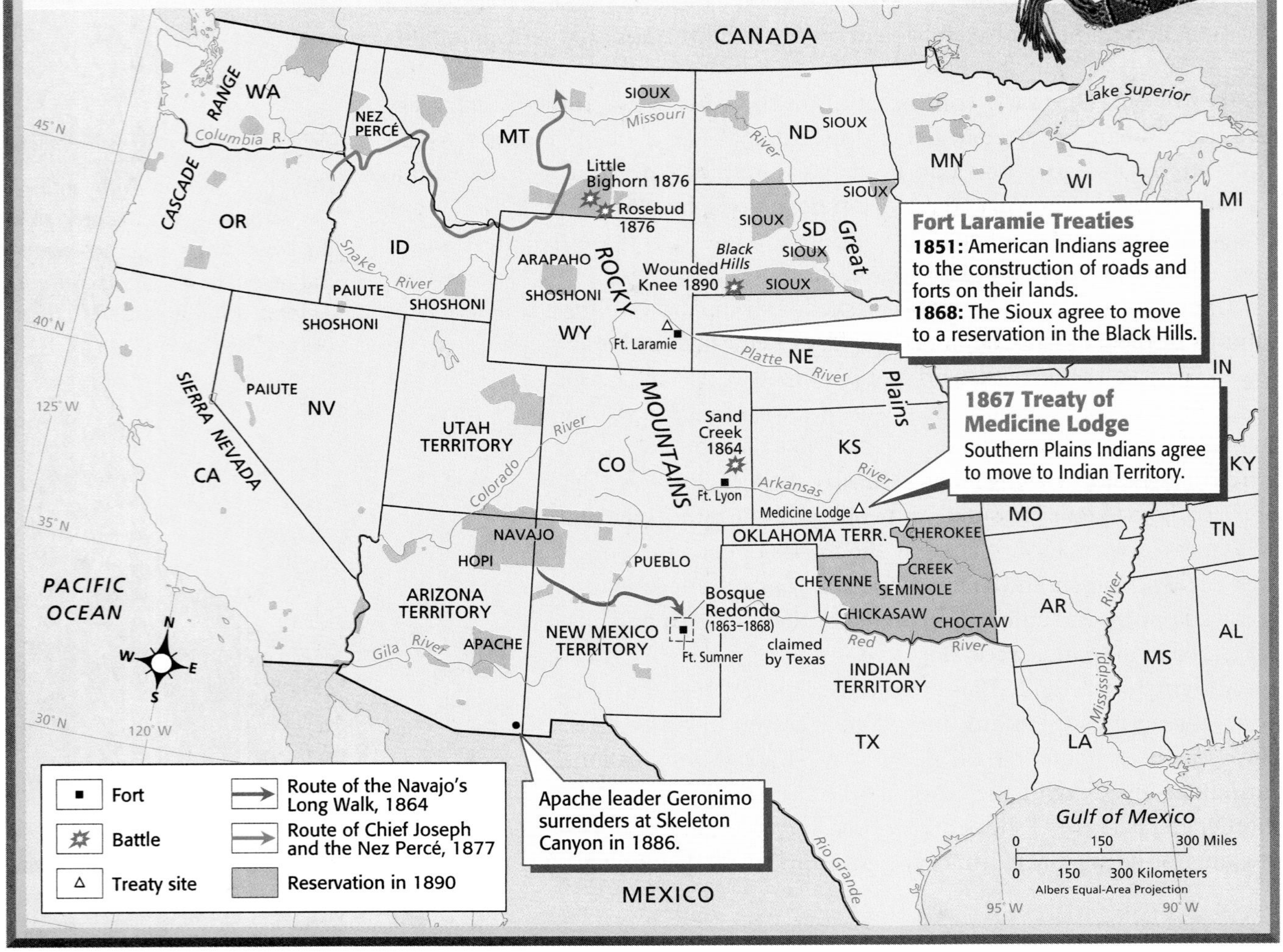

CANADA

Lake Superior

CASCADE RANGE
WA
NEZ PERCÉ
Columbia R.
45° N
MT
SIOUX
Missouri
ND SIOUX
MN
WI
MI

Little Bighorn 1876
Rosebud 1876

OR
ID
Snake River
ARAPAHO
ROCKY
Black Hills
SIOUX
SD SIOUX
Great

PAIUTE
SHOSHONI
SHOSHONI
Wounded Knee 1890
SIOUX

SHOSHONI
WY
40° N
Ft. Laramie
Platte NE
River
IN

Fort Laramie Treaties
1851: American Indians agree to the construction of roads and forts on their lands.
1868: The Sioux agree to move to a reservation in the Black Hills.

SIERRA NEVADA
125° W
PAIUTE
NV
River
MOUNTAINS
Plains
KY

UTAH TERRITORY
CO
Sand Creek 1864
KS

Colorado
Ft. Lyon
Arkansas River

1867 Treaty of Medicine Lodge
Southern Plains Indians agree to move to Indian Territory.

Medicine Lodge △
MO
TN

35° N
NAVAJO
HOPI
PUEBLO
OKLAHOMA TERR.
CHEROKEE
CREEK

PACIFIC OCEAN

ARIZONA TERRITORY
Bosque Redondo (1863–1868)
CHEYENNE
SEMINOLE
AR
AL

APACHE
NEW MEXICO TERRITORY
Ft. Sumner
CHICKASAW
CHOCTAW
MS

Gila River
claimed by Texas
Red River
INDIAN TERRITORY

30° N
120° W
TX
LA

Apache leader Geronimo surrenders at Skeleton Canyon in 1886.

Rio Grande

MEXICO

Gulf of Mexico

0   150   300 Miles
0 150 300 Kilometers
Albers Equal-Area Projection
95° W   90° W

Legend:
- ■ Fort
- ✳ Battle
- △ Treaty site
- → Route of the Navajo's Long Walk, 1864
- → Route of Chief Joseph and the Nez Percé, 1877
- Reservation in 1890

Little Bighorn. The peace was short-lived, however. In 1874 the government violated the terms of the 1868 Treaty of Fort Laramie by sending an army expedition into the Black Hills to search for gold. Gold was discovered, and the government tried to negotiate a new treaty with the Sioux. The Sioux refused. War clouds again gathered over the Plains.

BIOGRAPHY
Sitting Bull

Tatanka Iyotake, a Lakota Sioux also called Sitting Bull, emerged as an important leader of Sioux resistance. Born about 1831 along the banks of the Missouri River, Sitting Bull was nicknamed "Slow" as a child. At age 14 he fought in his first battle, a small skirmish with the Crow Indians. As a result, he earned the right to wear an eagle feather, a symbol of bravery, and was given the name Sitting Bull.

Over time, Sitting Bull gained the respect of his people for his courage, wisdom, generosity, and ability to endure pain without complaint. He became known as a spiritual leader and medicine man. Committed to the traditional Sioux way of life, Sitting Bull strongly opposed the intrusion of non-Indians onto Sioux lands. He mocked American Indians who willingly moved to reservations. "You are fools," he argued, "to make yourselves slaves to a piece of fat bacon, some hard-tack [biscuits], and a little sugar and coffee." Many agreed, and by the spring of 1876 thousands of Sioux and their Cheyenne allies were camped on Rosebud Creek in southern Montana.

During the summer of 1876, Sitting Bull had a vision in which he saw soldiers attacking an American Indian village. However, the soldiers and their horses were upside down, which Sitting Bull understood to mean that they would all die. Inspired by this vision, several hundred American Indians rode off to fight U.S. troops. During the Battle of the Rosebud in June 1876, the Indians battled an army twice the size of their own. Although they did not achieve an outright victory, their performance at Rosebud gave them confidence in their ability to fight the U.S. soldiers.

After the battle, the Indians proceeded west to camp near a stream known by the army as Little Bighorn River. They were joined by hundreds of American Indians fleeing the BIA-sponsored encampments, where food was in short supply. By late June the camp contained some 2,500 men prepared to fight.

On the morning of June 25, 1876, General George Armstrong Custer and about 600 members of the U.S. Army 7th Cavalry reached the American Indian camp. Although his troops had ridden through most of the night, Custer ordered an immediate attack. After dividing his men so that they could attack from three sides, Custer led a battalion of more than 200 men into the camp. Cheyenne warrior Two Moons described the battle. "We circled all round . . . swirling like water around a stone. We shoot, we ride fast, we shoot again. Soldiers drop, and horses fall on them." After the final attack, which lasted less than an hour, Custer and every soldier in his battalion lay dead.

The **Battle of the Little Bighorn** proved to be the last victory for the Sioux. The shock of Custer's

Read More About It

Free Find: Sitting Bull
After reading about Sitting Bull on the **Holt Researcher** CD–ROM, imagine that you are an author preparing a biography of Sitting Bull. Create an outline that shows the reasons why you think he was a good or bad leader for his people.

INTERPRETING THE VISUAL RECORD

The Little Bighorn. Kicking Bear created this painting of the Battle of the Little Bighorn. *What do you think Kicking Bear thought of the Battle of the Little Bighorn?*

History

IN THE MAKING

George Custer
BY PAUL F. HUTTON

Many Americans were shocked in 1876 to learn of George Armstrong Custer's death at the Battle of the Little Bighorn. A popular figure with the American people, Custer was the subject of magazine articles that celebrated his battles with Indians during the early 1870s. After his death, poets, novelists, and artists responded to the nation's sense of loss with works that portrayed Custer as a hero who gave his life to end the Indians' domination of the American West. The play *Custer's Last Charge* kept the image of the heroic Custer alive during the 1880s and 1890s. In the 1900s, filmmakers produced nearly 20 movies before 1941 that portrayed Custer as a defender of the settlers.

However, some people questioned Custer's reputation. Novels such as Frederic Van de Water's *Glory-Hunter* depicted Custer as a brutal man. Films such as *Sitting Bull* (1954) portrayed the American Indians as courageously defending their homelands against a cruel Custer. Histories that offered the Indian perspective of the wars on the Plains further eroded the Custer myth to such a degree that in 1991 Congress passed legislation removing Custer's name from the national monument at Little Bighorn.

Some Ghost Dancers believed that Ghost Shirts such as this one protected them from harm.

defeat prompted the army to increase its efforts to move the American Indians onto reservations. Over the next several months the American Indian forces broke into smaller groups to evade army troops. Group by group, they surrendered and settled near the BIA encampments. Sitting Bull fled to Canada but eventually returned and settled on the Standing Rock Reservation in Dakota Territory.

The Ghost Dance. The final chapter of the Plains Indian–U.S. Army wars took place on the Pine Ridge Reservation in South Dakota. Unhappy with life on the reservation, many Sioux took heart when they heard the message of Wovoka (woh-VOH-kuh). A Paiute, Wovoka began a religious movement known as the Ghost Dance. He claimed that the Ghost Dance could cause white settlers to vanish, dead Indian ancestors to return to life, the buffalo to return, and traditional Indian ways of life to revive.

Wovoka's message brought hope to discouraged American Indians throughout the West. The Sioux living on reservations in the Dakotas wore "Ghost Shirts," believing that the shirts' special symbols could stop bullets.

James McLaughlin, the BIA agent at the Standing Rock Reservation, dismissed the Ghost Dance as an "absurd craze." However, some government officials feared that the religious movement would inspire rebellion. When the Ghost Dance spread to Standing Rock Reservation, the military ordered the arrest of Sitting Bull, who had joined the movement. When reservation police surrounded Sitting Bull's cabin on December 15, 1890, a skirmish broke out and 14 Indians—including Sitting Bull—were killed.

Wounded Knee. Frightened and angry after Sitting Bull's death, many Sioux joined the Ghost Dancers farther west. Some traveled with Big Foot, a Sioux leader who had initially supported the Ghost Dance but had gradually turned away from it. Government officials wanted to arrest Big Foot because they feared he might cause trouble. Hoping to avoid conflict with army troops, Big Foot decided to lead his group to the Pine Ridge Reservation. On December 28, 1890, army troops found Big Foot and some 350 members of his group. The Sioux made camp for the night along Wounded Knee Creek.

The next morning, Colonel James Forsyth of the 7th Cavalry ordered the removal of Indian rifles. Reinforced by four Hotchkiss guns that fired exploding shells, some 500 mounted soldiers surrounded the camp. When the Sioux surrendered only a few guns, soldiers began to search the tepees. Tensions ran high. Nerves snapped, and the Sioux and U.S. soldiers began shooting. The Hotchkiss guns ripped into the camp. By day's end some 300 Sioux and about 30 U.S. soldiers had been killed. Some people declared that Custer and the 7th Cavalry had been "avenged," but the **Massacre at Wounded Knee** shocked many Americans. The incident marked the end of the bloody conflict between soldiers and American Indians on the Great Plains.

✔ **READING CHECK:** What were the sources of conflict between the Plains Indians and the U.S. government?

The End of Resistance

American Indians west of the Great Plains were also forced to resettle. The Nez Percé tried to remain in their homelands in northeastern Oregon. They surrendered much of their land in an 1855 treaty and agreed to remain on a reservation. When settlers moved onto reservation land, the Nez Percé did not turn to violence. When the government ordered the Nez Percé to relocate to a reservation in Idaho, their leader Chief Joseph, reluctantly agreed. However, some young Nez Percé killed 11 white settlers. Fearing war, the Nez Percé fled, with the army in close pursuit.

The Nez Percé journeyed east and north through Idaho, Wyoming, and Montana, picking up additional followers along the way. The group eventually numbered from 700 to 800. They hoped to escape to Canada, but winter weather made travel difficult. Chief Joseph surrendered to the U.S. Army just 30 miles from the Canadian border. An interpreter wept as he relayed the leader's surrender statement.

> ❝ I am tired of fighting. Our chiefs are killed. . . . It is cold and we have no blankets. The little children are freezing to death. . . . My heart is sick and sad. From where the sun now stands, I will fight no more forever. ❞

The Nez Percé were first sent to prison in Kansas, then to a reservation in Indian Territory. In 1885 the U.S. government permitted some to return to the reservation in Oregon, but sent Chief Joseph and some 150 others to a reservation in Washington State.

In the mid-1870s, the government forced the seminomadic Apache in New Mexico and Arizona to settle on the San Carlos Reservation, along Arizona's Gila River. When army troops moved into the territory in 1881, the Apache leader Geronimo fled the reservation with about 75 followers. Geronimo's group raided settlements throughout Arizona and Mexico. After the women and children following Geronimo were captured in 1884, Geronimo surrendered and briefly accepted reservation life. By 1885, however, Geronimo and 134 followers escaped from the reservation and resumed raids on settlements. On September 4, 1886, with his followers outnumbered, Geronimo gave up. "Once I moved about like the wind," he told his captors. "Now I surrender to you and that is all." After his final surrender, Geronimo and his followers were sent to Florida as prisoners of war. His surrender marked the end of armed resistance to the reservation system in the Southwest.

The Religious Spirit

THE GHOST DANCE

A Ghost Dance

The Ghost Dance combined elements from American Indian religions and Christianity. The son of a medicine man, Wovoka lived for a time with a white family that regularly read Bible passages aloud. Kicking Bear, who brought Wovoka's message to the Sioux, told them they would be "led by the Messiah who came once to live on earth with the white man." This reference to Jesus Christ revealed Christianity's influence on Wovoka's thought.

The Ghost Dance was similar to the Paiute round dance. Men and women formed a circle by holding hands and then stepped to the left. Dancers had their faces painted and wore Ghost Shirts—cotton garments decorated with pictures of animals and sacred symbols. The Sioux added features from their own Sun Dance, making the circle around a sacred pole and at times staring into the Sun as they performed the dance.

James Mooney was a social scientist who interviewed several Ghost Dancers in 1891. He interpreted the religion as the spiritual expression of a people whose societies had been devastated. "Hope becomes a faith and the faith becomes a creed [belief] of priests and prophets, until the hero is a god and the dream a religion, looking to some great miracle of nature for its culmination [climax] and accomplishment," he explained. The Ghost Dance movement faded away when the promised miracle never occurred. ▪

Helen Hunt Jackson's 1881 book chronicled the mistreatment of American Indians.

Voices of Protest

By the 1880s, American Indians had surrendered more than half a billion acres to the U.S. government. In addition to military conflicts with the army, Indians suffered as settlers killed most of the buffalo herds. With the loss of the buffalo, American Indians had little hope of maintaining an independent existence on the Plains. "All our people now were settling down in square gray houses, scattered here and there across this hungry land," recalled Black Elk of the Teton Sioux.

Troubled by the treatment of American Indians, reformers organized groups such as the Indian Rights Association and the Women's National Indian Association. These groups urged the federal government to craft a more humane Indian policy. Helen Hunt Jackson of Massachusetts supported this cause. In 1881 she wrote an influential book, *A Century of Dishonor*, that criticized the government for its years of broken promises and mistreatment of American Indians.

Thoc-me-tony, a Paiute reformer also known as Sarah Winnemucca, called attention to the problems of American Indians. Winnemucca noted that although the government had authorized the building of two mills on the Paiute reservation, they were never constructed. She wondered:

66 The [mills] were never seen or heard of by my people, though the printed report . . . says twenty-five thousand dollars was appropriated to build them. Where did [the money] go? . . . Is it that the government is cheated by its own agents who make these reports? 99

The forced removal of the Paiute to the Yakima Reservation in Washington Territory in 1878 so outraged Winnemucca that she began lecturing on the Paiute's behalf to non-Indian audiences. In 1880 she asked President Rutherford B. Hayes to allow the Paiute to return to their homelands. Hayes agreed, but the BIA's agents did not carry out the president's order.

✔ **READING CHECK:** How did Chief Joseph, Geronimo, and Sarah Winnemucca respond to white treatment of American Indians?

Assimilating American Indians

Many government officials and most reformers viewed assimilation, or the cultural absorption of American Indians into "white America," as the only long-term way to ensure Indian survival. To speed the process of assimilation, the U.S. government established a system of American Indian schools. Some Indian children attended reservation schools, but others were forced to leave their families to attend boarding schools. At the schools, students were forced to speak only English, to wear "proper" clothes, and to change their names to "American" ones. The schools were places of misery for most students. Luther Standing Bear later recalled, "How lonesome I felt for my father and mother!"

Government officials had hoped that life on reservations would force American Indians to become farmers and adopt the lifestyles of non-Indian settlers. In 1887 Congress passed the **Dawes General Allotment Act**, which required that Indian lands be surveyed and that American Indian families receive an allotment of 160 acres of reservation land for farming. Any land that remained

THE GRANGER COLLECTION, NEW YORK

Sarah Winnemucca demanded fair treatment for American Indians.

would be sold. The Indian Rights Association claimed that private ownership of land would lead to "the gradual breaking up of the reservations." This assessment proved correct. In less than 50 years, they lost two thirds of their land. Some of the land was sold to settlers and developers as surplus when allotments were made. In other cases, Indians sold or were cheated out of their allotments.

Despite the government's hopes, many American Indians rejected farming. Even before the Dawes Act, the government had tried to force the Navajo to abandon sheep raising and become settled farmers. To carry out this plan, the U.S. Army waged military campaigns against the Navajo in northwestern New Mexico and northeastern Arizona in 1863. Soldiers destroyed Navajo houses, herds of sheep, and corn crops. Without food or shelter, many Navajo surrendered in early 1864.

That same year, the U.S. Army led the Navajo on the Long Walk, a forced march to the Bosque Redondo Reservation in eastern New Mexico. Soldiers stationed at nearby Fort Sumner prevented the Navajo from leaving the reservation. The U.S. government gave the Navajo seeds and farming tools, but the land was not suitable for farming. Because the few trees were quickly cut down, the Navajo had to use roots for firewood. Many Navajo died from malnutrition and disease.

In 1868 the government admitted its failure and granted the Navajo a reservation in New Mexico and Arizona. They rebuilt their communities, concentrating on sheep raising, weaving, and silversmithing. By the 1880s their economy had stabilized and their population had begun to increase.

✔ **READING CHECK:** How did the U.S. government try to assimilate American Indians?

INTERPRETING THE VISUAL RECORD

Assimilation. These photographs show three American Indian boys before and after they attended an American Indian school. *What evidence of their assimilation can you see?*

SECTION 1 REVIEW

Define and explain the significance of the following terms:
Bureau of Indian Affairs
Sand Creek Massacre
Battle of the Little Bighorn
Massacre at Wounded Knee
Dawes General Allotment Act

Identify and explain the significance of the following individuals:
Cochise
John M. Chivington
Sitting Bull
George Armstrong Custer
Wovoka
Chief Joseph
Geronimo
Sarah Winnemucca

Locate and explain the importance of the following places:
Standing Rock Reservation
Bosque Redondo Reservation

1. **Using Graphic Organizers** Copy the chart below. Use it to describe the conflicts between the United States and various American Indian tribes.

Tribe & Leader	Conflict	Outcome
Cheyenne		
Sioux		
Nez Percé		
Apache		

2. **Analyzing** Why did the U.S. government attempt to resettle American Indians on reservations?
3. **Taking a Stand** How would you have responded to protests made by Chief Joseph, Geronimo, and Sarah Winnemucca against the treatment of American Indians?
4. **Distinguishing Fact from Opinion** How did the experience of the Navajo weaken the argument of some government officials that the best solution for American Indians was to assimilate into white culture?

Critical Thinking

5. Could conflict between American Indians and the U.S. government have been avoided as white settlement increased? If so, how?
   Consider:
   • what the root causes were of the conflict
   • how each side viewed the other
   • what mistakes each side made in dealing with the other side

Western Farmers

OBJECTIVES

Read to understand:

1. how the U.S. government aided economic development in the West
2. why people migrated west
3. how the environment influenced farming practices and daily life in the West
4. what difficulties farm families faced on the Great Plains

KEY TERMS

Homestead Act
Pacific Railway Act
Morrill Act
Exodusters
sod houses
U.S. Department of Agriculture
bonanza farm

KEY PEOPLE

Benjamin Singleton
Willa Cather

EYEWITNESSES TO History

66 *To say that I was homesick, discouraged, and lonely, is but a faint [poor] description of my feelings. . . . Not a tree, plant nor shrub on which to rest my weary eye, to break the monotony of the sand beds and cactus of the Great American Desert.* **99**
—Annie Green

A pioneer woman in southern California receives the deed to her homestead.

Annie Green moved to Colorado in 1870. She and her husband were among the thousands of American families who headed west to the Great Plains in the years following the Civil War. Green felt like "a stranger in a strange land" in her new home. In order to reassure her husband she "resolved . . . to cultivate [encourage] a cheerful disposition." Like many settlers, Green and her family discovered that hard work, determination, and a little luck were necessary to prosper.

Economic Development of the West

During the Civil War, Republicans sought to manage western development to ensure that the new western states and territories would be free of slavery. They also wanted them to be populated by independent farmers who would improve the land. After the southern states seceded from the Union, Republicans took the opportunity to pass a series of acts in 1862 to put public lands to productive use.

Land acts. Three government land acts increased non-Indian settlement of the Great Plains. The **Homestead Act** permitted "any citizen or intended citizen to select any surveyed land up to 160 acres and to gain title to it after five years' residence" if the person cultivated the land. The Civil War slowed the initial response to the act. Eventually, however, some 400,000 families took advantage of the offer. The **Pacific Railway Act** gave lands to railroad companies to develop a railroad line linking the East and West Coasts. The **Morrill Act** granted more than 17 million acres of federal land to the states. The act ordered the sale of this land to finance the construction of agricultural and engineering colleges. The Morrill Act led to the eventual founding of more than 70 state universities.

Competition for land was fierce. In October 1889, for example, a flood of prospective settlers responded to a government offer of free homesteads in Oklahoma. The acreage came from former Creek and Seminole lands. In March, President Benjamin Harrison had announced that the land would be available to the first takers beginning at noon on April 22. By the appointed day, about 50,000 people had gathered to race one another for the land. Some rode horses or bicycles. Others pushed wheelbarrows filled with supplies. Subsequent "runs" took place in other parts of Oklahoma. This occurred at the expense of American Indians, who lost nearly 12 million acres in Oklahoma to non-Indian settlers.

COLLECTION OF THE NEW-YORK HISTORICAL SOCIETY

Posters like this one persuaded many people that a better life waited for them out west.

The railroads. Railroad companies also lured settlers to the West. Between 1869 and 1883, four rail lines were built across the West. Within 10 years of the passage of the Pacific Railway Act, the U.S. government had given railroad companies more than 125 million acres of public land. State and local governments donated nearly 100 million acres of additional land. These grants limited the amount of land available to settlers under the Homestead Act. Government officials believed that railroad companies would promote western settlement and economic growth. Railroad companies sold any surplus land to homesteaders in an effort to offset the high cost of laying tracks. The homesteaders benefited from the nearby railroad lines, using them to ship their crops to distant markets.

Eager to encourage settlement along their rail routes, railroad companies advertised in the East and in Europe. The companies offered to pay the fares of potential land buyers and sell them land on credit. Some railroad companies gave free trips to newspaper reporters, who then wrote glowing reports of the land and towns along the rail line. One Indiana editor wrote:

66 I never saw finer country in the world than that part of Kansas passed over by the Atchison, Topeka & Santa Fe [rail]road. Corn waist high, wheat in the shock [stacked], oats in fine condition, and vegetables in abundance. 99

✔ **READING CHECK:** How did the U.S. government promote the economic development of the West?

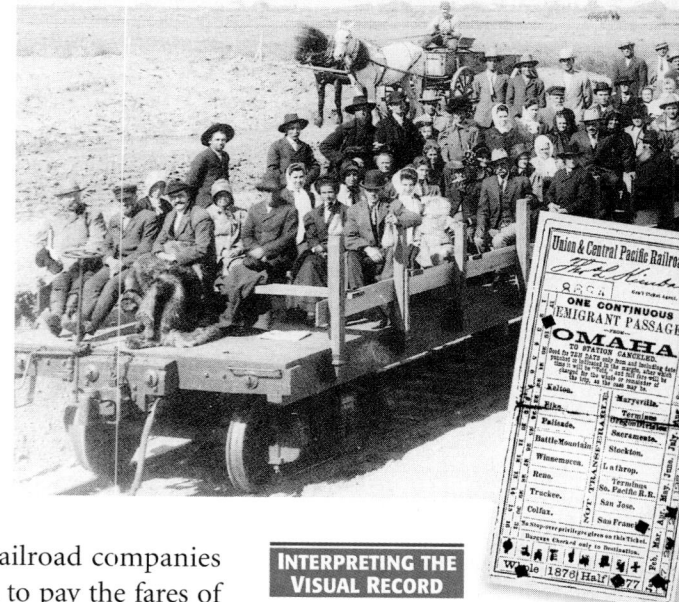

The road west. With tickets like this one, many migrants rode the rails to their new homes in the West, sometimes riding on flatcars to get there. *What do you think travel conditions were like for the migrants in this photograph?*

Moving West

The West lured migrants who hoped for a better life. Some sought economic opportunity. Others hoped to find racial tolerance. Three main groups traveled westward after the Civil War: white Americans from the East, African Americans from the South, and immigrants from foreign countries.

White newcomers came from more-settled areas of the eastern United States. Because of the high cost of transporting supplies, it was mainly middle-class farmers and businesspeople who could afford to move west. Some farmers came in search of more fertile soil. Civil War veterans, particularly those from the South, came to make a new start. The majority of white settlers moved from states in the Mississippi Valley, where land had grown expensive and difficult to obtain. A Nebraska settler explained simply, "I am well satisfied that I can do better here than I can in Illinois." Susan Lomax, who moved west with her family from Mississippi, offered a different reason: "We wanted to come to a new country so our children could grow up with the country."

For African Americans, moving west offered a chance to escape the violence and persecution they faced following the withdrawal of federal troops from the South in 1877. Kansas particularly appealed to African American settlers, as John Brown had fought against slavery there. The biggest rush of black settlers occurred during the so-called Kansas Fever Exodus of 1879. Some 20,000 to 40,000 African

This Schuttler Wagon Company advertisement offers a depiction of the migration of farmers to the West in search of fertile soil.

Exodusters. Many African Americans escaped persecution in the South by moving west. *What evidence can you see that this family is homesteading on the Great Plains?*

Americans fled the South, where violence had broken out during elections in 1878. Known as **Exodusters**, these African American settlers trekked west, following leaders such as Benjamin "Pap" Singleton, a 70-year-old former slave.

European immigrants also flocked to the western United States. "America Fever" infected thousands of Danes, Norwegians, and Swedes. In 1882 alone, more than 100,000 left their homes for the American West. In addition, many Irish who had helped build the railroads and a great number of Germans who had settled in the Mississippi Valley decided to move to the Plains. Russian Mennonites, members of a Protestant sect, also migrated to the Great Plains. After the Russian czar ended the Mennonites' special privileges, including exemption from military service, American railroad companies urged them to move to the United States. The Mennonites brought with them experience in farming wheat on the Russian steppes, or grasslands, including a hardy wheat variety that thrived on the Great Plains. They may have also brought the Russian thistle, a plant that became well known throughout the West as the tumbleweed.

Many of the Chinese immigrants who had come to the United States during the California Gold Rush had also turned to farming by 1880. In California alone, some 3,200 Chinese farmers raised crops in 1880. Throughout the West, Chinese immigrants worked as farm laborers, produce vendors, or sharecroppers. Some owned large farms. In 1870 one Chinese farmer in Sacramento County, California, earned $9,500 from farming. This was an enormous amount for the time.

✔ **READING CHECK:** For what reasons did various groups of people migrate to the West?

Western Environments and Farming

Although settlers homesteaded some 80 million acres of public land in the Great Plains between 1862 and 1900, the region did not immediately prosper. Even though the land was free, supplies and transportation were expensive. In addition, the environment posed problems for farmers.

This Chinese worker is tending an irrigation ditch in a California orchard.

Scarce resources. Water was in short supply throughout much of the West. In parts of the Southwest, Hispanic and American Indian farmers had developed effective irrigation systems that used canals, dams, and sloping fields to control water flow. They established farms that fanned out in thin strips from water sources so that all community members had access to water. New settlers adopted these methods to survive. The Great Plains also had few water sources. Many farmers had to travel several miles to a river or stream where they would fill large barrels and haul them back to the farm. Digging wells proved difficult and time-consuming. One Nebraska farmer spent two years digging with a pick and shovel before reaching water 300 feet below the surface. Many settlers hired professional drillers who used drilling equipment developed by petroleum companies. Farmers also used new models of windmills to draw the water from their wells. These were wind-powered water pumps designed to withstand the region's strong winds.

Trees were another scarce resource on the Great Plains. Settlers developed clever solutions to cope with the lack of wood for fuel or building materials. Some burned dried buffalo manure, an excellent source of fuel. Settlers built **sod houses**, buildings made from chunks cut from the heavy topsoil that were stacked like bricks. A layer of soil covered the roof, which was made of a few scarce pieces of wood. Building with sod was difficult, however. A Kansas settler wrote, "The sod is heavy and when you take 3 or 4 bricks on a litter or hand barrow, and carry it 50 to 150 feet, I tell you it is no easy work."

Created in 1862, the **U.S. Department of Agriculture** (USDA) helped farmers adapt to their new environment. USDA experts sought out and publicized new varieties of wheat suitable for the Great Plains, where the environment was too harsh for traditional winter wheat. These new wheat crops replaced the grasses that had once covered the Great Plains. USDA agents also began teaching dry farming—new planting and harvesting techniques that conserved moisture. For example, agents advised farmers to plow deep furrows to bring moisture to the surface and to break up the soil after a rainfall to prevent evaporation.

New farming equipment. The development of new farming equipment also helped the Plains farmers. James Oliver's plow factory in South Bend, Indiana, produced thousands of plows with sharp, durable blades that could slice through the tough sod of the Plains. "Self-binding" harvesters not only cut wheat but also tied it into bundles. The combine cut wheat, separated it from the plant, and cleaned the grain all in one operation. Many of the new farming devices used steam-powered engines. However, the new technology plunged many small farmers into debt when they bought the equipment necessary to compete with larger landholders.

Efficient new farm machinery and cheap, abundant land enabled some companies to create a new kind of large-scale operation, the **bonanza farm**. Most bonanza farms were owned by large companies and operated like factories, with machinery, professional managers, and specialized laborers for different tasks. These large farms required from 500 to 1,000 extra workers at planting and harvesting times. Most owners divided their vast enterprises into small units, with a foreman in charge of each. Migrant workers, who were often unemployed cowboys possessing "nothing but small bundles containing a clean shirt and a few socks," performed much of the seasonal labor.

The era of bonanza farming soon faded. When weather conditions were favorable, bonanza farms produced large profits because of lower production costs. Because bonanza farm owners bought seed and equipment in bulk, suppliers often gave them special deals. However, in times of severe drought or low wheat prices, bonanza farm profits fell. With fewer workers to pay and less money invested in equipment, family farmers could better handle boom-and-bust cycles. By the 1890s most bonanza farms had been broken up into smaller farms.

✔ **READING CHECK:** How did the environment influence farming practices in the West?

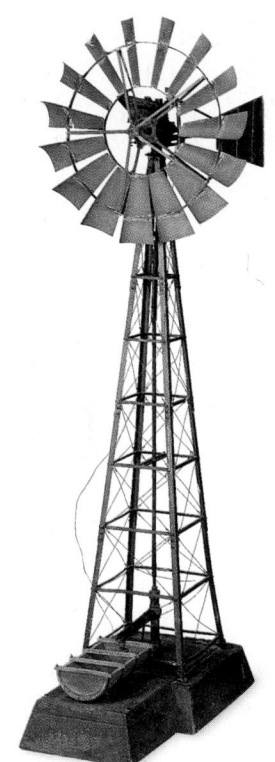

Windmills drew water from beneath the ground, allowing settlers to farm the Great Plains.

INTERPRETING THE VISUAL RECORD

Bonanza farms. As the Great Plains were opened to farming, some companies created large, factory-like farms. *What suggests that this was a bonanza farm and not a family-owned farm?*

AMERICAN Letters

The Western Novel

Several writers recognized the great beauty of the American West. Hamlin Garland, who as a boy hated farm life in Wisconsin, described the Great Plains in his 1899 novel, Boy Life on the Prairie. *Mary Hallock Foote, an artist and writer who lived in California, described the western landscape in her 1894 short story, "A Cloud on the Mountain."*

from *Boy Life on the Prairie*
by Hamlin Garland

Hamlin Garland

For a few days Lincoln and Owen had nothing to do but to keep the cattle from straying, and they seized the chance to become acquainted with the country round about. It burned deep into Lincoln's brain, this wide, sunny, windy country,—the sky was so big and the horizon line so low and so far away. The grasses and flowers were nearly all new to him. On the uplands the herbage [grasses] was short and dry and the plants stiff and woody, but in the swales the wild oat shook its quivers of barbed and twisted arrows, and the crow's-foot, tall and willowy, bowed softly under the feet of the wind, while everywhere in the lowlands, as well as on the sedges, the bleaching white antlers of monstrous elk lay scattered to testify of the swarming millions of wild cattle which once fed there.

To the south the settlement thickened, for in that direction lay the country town, but to the north and west the unclaimed prairie rolled, the feeding ground of the cattle, but the boys had little opportunity to explore that far. One day his father said:—

"Well, Lincoln, I guess you'll have to run the plough team this fall. I've got so much to do around the house, and we can't afford to hire."

This seemed a very fine and manly commission [task], and the boy drove his team out into the field one morning with vast pride.

from "A Cloud on the Mountain"
by Mary Hallock Foote

Mary Hallock Foote

Ruth Mary . . . paused often in her work and looked towards the high pastures with the pale brown lights and purple shadows on them, rolling away and rising towards the great timbered ridges, and these lifting here and there along their profiles a treeless peak or bare divide into the regions above vegetation.

She had no misgivings about her home. Fences would not have improved her father's vast lawn, to her mind, or white paint the low-browed front of his dwelling; nor did she feel the want of a stair-carpet and a parlor-organ. She was sure that they, the strangers, had never seen anything more lovely than her beloved river dancing down between the hills, tripping over rapids, wrinkling over sand-bars of its own spreading, and letting out its speed down the long reaches where the channel was deep.

UNDERSTANDING LITERATURE

1. Identify some of the words that each author uses to describe the landscape.
2. How did the geography described in the two excerpts differ?
3. Based on these passages, how did the two authors feel about the western landscape?

Farm Life on the Plains

Farm families on the Plains faced many problems for which inventors, manufacturers, and agricultural experts had no ready answers. Sod houses were well insulated, windproof, and fireproof. However, they were also damp and dirty. Many families hung a canopy inside the house to prevent dirt falling from the ceiling from landing on the dinner table. The roofs leaked and sometimes even collapsed in rainy weather. One woman described her efforts to keep herself and her baby dry in their sod house during a spring rainstorm.

66 The house leaked so badly that we rolled the bedding up and tied it with a rope, and put the oil cloth from the table over it to keep it dry. I put the baby on top of the roll and put the parasol over it to keep her dry. Soon the rain ran off the ribs of the parasol and soaked around the baby so I fixed a place for her in the cupboard shelf—the only dry place in the house. I walked around with a slicker, a man's hat and overshoes to keep dry. 99

Home on the plains. Sylvester Rawding and his family posed for this photograph outside their home in Custer County, Nebraska, in 1886. *What does the Rawding family's house appear to be made of?*

Harsh weather and hard work. The climate of the Great Plains caused hardships for farming families. Winter on the Plains often brought blizzards and bone-chilling cold. The summer heat on the Plains could be just as fierce. Settlers described droughts during which "the earth opened in great cracks several inches across and two feet deep." There was no relief as "the leaves on the trees shriveled and dried up, and every living thing was seeking shelter from the hot rays of the sun."

Insects also created problems on the Great Plains. In the 1870s farmers faced swarms of grasshoppers that devoured everything in their path, even the wooden handles of farming tools. Farmers killed thousands of the greedy insects to little effect. Moaned one homesteader: "Two new grasshoppers arrived to attend each dead one's funeral."

Settlers dreaded the raging fires that sometimes swept across the prairies. Most families sent someone onto the roof at night to search the horizon for signs of fire in the distance. Farmers soon learned to plow firebreaks—cleared areas with nothing to burn—around their houses and fields.

Even in good times, Plains farming demanded hard work from everyone in the family. Men did most of the heavy labor of building houses, fencing the land, and farming. In addition to household and child-rearing tasks, women often spent hours in the field. In 1878 a Kansas newspaper praised a local woman who "does her own plowing. . . . This year she has one hundred acres of fine wheat and will cut and bind it herself." Another woman wrote home to her family in the East, explaining that she had been her husband's "sole help in getting up and stacking at least 25 tons of hay and oats." Many farm wives also cared for garden plots, preserved fruits and vegetables, and tended farm animals.

Children had to do their share, too. Their chores included fetching water, tending gardens, and churning butter. One farmer described his two-year-old son, Baz, who could "run all over, fetch up cows out of the stock fields, or oxen, carry in stove wood and climb in the corn crib and feed the hogs and go on errands down to his grandma's."

Harsh winter weather added to the difficulties of life on the Great Plains.

Read More About It

Free Find: Willa Cather

After reading about Willa Cather on the **Holt Researcher** CD–ROM, draw a picture of what you think her home on the Great Plains looked like. Include captions explaining the various elements in your drawing.

My Antonia
portrays prairie life.

BIOGRAPHY

Willa Cather

Storytellers of the Plains. Western writers recorded stories about life on the Great Plains. Willa Cather, born in Virginia in 1873, was one such writer. As a young girl Cather traveled west with her family to a farm in Nebraska. Her grandparents had moved there eight years earlier.

Although she was homesick for Virginia, Cather soon found Nebraska fascinating. "I think the first thing that interested me after I got to the homestead was a heavy hickory cane . . . which my grandmother always carried with her when she went to the garden to kill rattlesnakes," Cather wrote. "She had killed a good many snakes with it, and that seemed to argue that life might not be so flat as it looked there."

The Cather family soon moved to the nearby town of Red Cloud, where Willa attended high school. After graduating from the University of Nebraska, she taught high school in Pittsburgh and then took a job as an associate editor for *McClure's* magazine in New York. She turned to writing full-time in 1912. Cather published her first novel about life on the Plains, *O Pioneers!,* in 1913. In a 1925 interview she explained, "I write only of the Mid-Western American life that I know thoroughly." Cather's other novels—including *My Ántonia,* published in 1918, and *Death Comes for the Archbishop,* published in 1927—also examined life in the American West.

Although some settlers such as Cather were inspired by the West, difficulties overwhelmed many Plains farmers. Many were forced to abandon their farms. However, thousands stayed. They formed communities with churches and schools, newspapers and clubs, and even theaters and concert halls. Although harvests might be poor one year, there was always hope for better luck to come.

✔ **READING CHECK:** What difficulties did families face as they farmed the Great Plains?

SECTION 2 REVIEW

Define and explain the significance of the following terms:
Homestead Act
Pacific Railway Act
Morrill Act
Exodusters
sod houses
U.S. Department of Agriculture
bonanza farm

Identify and explain the significance of the following individuals:
Benjamin Singleton
Willa Cather

1. **Using Graphic Organizers** Copy the flowchart below. Use it to describe environmental problems that western farmers faced and how they attempted to solve those problems.

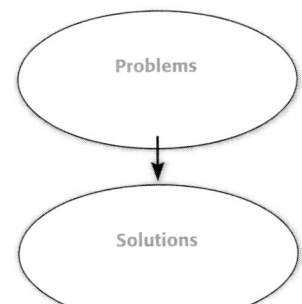

2. **Synthesizing** How did the U.S. government promote economic development and assist farmers in the West?

3. **Understanding Geography: Location** Why did large-scale farms fade more quickly than smaller farms during the late 1800s?

4. **Using Historical Imagination** Imagine that you are a migrant to the West in the late 1800s. Write a letter to relatives explaining why you came to the Great Plains and how your life has changed.

Critical Thinking

5. Do you think the hardships faced by settlers on the Plains caused most of them to regret their decision to move west? Why or why not?
   Consider:
   • why most people moved west
   • what their experiences were in the West
   • what they gained and lost from the experience

SECTION

3

The Cattle Boom

OBJECTIVES

Read to understand:

1. how cattle and sheep ranching developed in the West
2. what life was like for cowboys and residents of cattle towns
3. what ranches were like
4. why the cattle boom on the open range ended

KEY TERMS

Texas longhorn
long drives
railhead
open range
barbed wire

KEY PEOPLE

Joseph Glidden

KEY PLACES

Abilene
Dodge City
Cheyenne
Ogallala

Well suited to living on the Plains, Texas longhorns helped the cattle industry grow.

EYEWITNESSES TO History

❝ *[Abilene was] a very small, dead place, consisting of about one dozen log huts, low, small, rude affairs, four-fifths of which were covered with dirt for roofing; indeed, but one shingle roof could be seen in the whole city.* ❞
—Joseph McCoy

Joseph McCoy

Joseph McCoy, a young cattleman from Illinois, described the bleak town of Abilene, Kansas, which he visited in 1867. Despite the town's outward appearance, McCoy recognized opportunity when he saw it. He noted that Abilene was "the farthest point east at which a good depot for cattle business could be made" because it had a railroad line. McCoy purchased property and had stockyards constructed. Meanwhile, he instructed a friend to go to Texas to convince cattle owners to bring their herds to Abilene. From there they could be shipped east to packing plants. McCoy's vision transformed the West, sparking an economic boom that entered both American history and myth.

Ranching in the West

Spaniards who imported cattle from Spain in the 1500s were the earliest ranchers in the American West. By the 1850s, Texans had interbred English cattle with Spanish cattle to produce a new breed—the **Texas longhorn**. Although their meat was typically tough and stringy, longhorns were hardy, able to travel long distances on little water, and could live year-round on grass. Equally important, longhorns were immune to Texas fever, a cattle disease carried by ticks.

The growth of eastern cities ensured an increasing demand for beef. Texas cattle ranching grew rapidly after the Civil War, spreading across the Great Plains as the buffalo died out. In 1866 a steer that could bring about $4 in Texas could be sold for $40 or more in eastern markets.

Sheep ranching, also introduced by the Spanish, was an important economic activity in the West. American Indian groups, including the Pueblo and the Navajo, raised sheep in New Mexico and Arizona. During the California Gold Rush, thousands of sheep were herded to California to feed the hungry miners. Cowboys despised sheep, which they believed ate the roots of the grass and ruined it for cattle. Early environmentalist John Muir called them "hoofed locusts" for the damage they did to the prairie. Clashes between shepherds and cowboys at times became violent. Angry cowboys even drove herds of sheep off cliffs.

Despite such conflicts, sheep ranching remained a profitable enterprise. Basque shepherds, originally from a region in northern Spain, emigrated from South America and ranged their flocks of sheep in California. By 1900 some 10,000 Basques were living in the West.

✔ **READING CHECK:** How did cattle and sheep ranching develop in the West?

Ranching. In 1877 James Walker painted this scene, called *Vaqueros of California Roping Horses in a Corral. From their clothing, what can you tell about the men in the painting?*

Cattle drives were long journeys that required the supervision of an experienced trail boss.

The Cattle Industry

The workers who took care of a rancher's cattle were known as cowboys. Popular culture romanticized cowboy life, but it was difficult. Cowboys worked hard in all kinds of weather and made little money. Most worked the range for just seven years before settling down in towns or on farms.

The cowboys. Many of the cowboys were Confederate veterans of the Civil War. African American, Mexican, and Mexican American cowboys made up about one third of the some 35,000 cowboys in the West. African American cowboys managed to escape most of the discrimination of the postwar era. They worked, bunked, and ate alongside fellow cowboys. They also received the same wages.

Mexican ranch hands known as vaqueros had worked with cattle and horses since long before the days of the cattle boom. In the 1880s most Mexican and Mexican American cowboys worked on ranches in Texas. Mostly sons of ranchers or farmers, vaqueros sometimes owned their own ranches. Although they were paid higher wages and treated better than those who handled menial ranch jobs, Mexican cowboys often encountered discrimination.

Life on the trail. Moving the cattle from Texas to the rail lines in Missouri and Kansas posed a major problem for cattle ranchers. To reach the railroads, cowboys herded as many as 3,000 cattle on **long drives**. These overland treks covered hundreds of miles and lasted several months. The trail usually ended in Kansas because cattle herded to Missouri often contracted Texas fever. Over the years, cowboys drove some 4 million cattle from Texas to Kansas.

On a typical long drive, a trail boss managed a crew of about 10 cowboys. The cook rode in front of the herds in a chuck wagon that carried food and the cowboys' bedrolls. Managing the herd was a tough job. River crossings, where swift currents might drown hundreds of animals, proved particularly hazardous. George Duffield headed a long drive in 1866. He described one river crossing: "We worked all day in the river & at dusk got the last beefe over. . . . There was one of our party drowned today . . . & several narrow escapes."

The worst danger was a stampede. Almost any unexpected sound—a coyote's wail, a thunderclap, a sneeze—could panic the cattle. Cowboys learned to prevent stampedes by "circling around and around the terrified herd, singing loudly and steadily, . . . [with other cowboys] separating a bunch here and there."

Cattle Towns

Every long drive ended at a **railhead**, a town located along a railroad, where brokers bought cattle to ship east on railroad cars. The Kansas towns of Abilene, Dodge City, and Wichita were among the best-known railhead stops. They came to be known as cattle towns. Farther north and west, long drives ended in Cheyenne, Wyoming, and Ogallala, Nebraska.

Early cattle towns consisted of little more than a general store, a hotel or boardinghouse, a railroad depot, and a stockyard. Towns that attracted enough cattle business grew larger. They bustled with activity from spring to fall, when the long drives took place. Cowboys were paid at the end of the drive. They usually got a shave and a haircut upon arriving in town, then bought new clothes. After completing their purchases, many cowboys visited gambling halls and saloons, freely spending their hard-earned money.

Prosperous cattle towns attracted businesspeople, doctors, lawyers, and their families. Once families arrived, the cattle towns built schools, hired teachers, and established police forces to maintain order. Reformers, many of them women, set out to "civilize" the rough cowboy towns by organizing poor-relief and temperance societies. However, their calls to limit alcohol consumption met with little success so long as cattle town economies depended on saloons.

✔ **READING CHECK:** What was life like for cowboys and the residents of cattle towns?

THE GRANGER COLLECTION, NEW YORK

This engraving of Dodge City shows the arrival of cowboys driving a herd of cattle to market.

Frontier Artists

The American West captured the imagination of artists. They were eager to portray its natural beauty and the lives of its inhabitants. Perhaps the most influential artist was Frederic Remington. This New Yorker painted and sculpted a wide variety of subjects including American Indians, cowboys, and mountain men. Remington's work celebrated western settlement, as did paintings by Charles Wimar. Wimar saw the story of the West as an epic of heroic conquest. Not all artists glorified western settlement, however. Charles Russell lived in Montana for most of his life and worked for over a decade as a cowboy. Russell was more sensitive to the settlers' impact on the land and on American Indians.

American Indians were often portrayed as either savages or noble people. In both cases, frontier art gave the general impression that they were doomed to vanish from the West. Art historians have also noted that frontier artists concentrated on images of men at work or play. They usually neglected the role that women played in the settlement of the West. Eliza Barchus became known for her depictions of life in Oregon. However, she was one of the few female artists in the West whose work received significant attention.

Frederic Remington's **Defending the Waterhole**

Understanding the Arts

1. How did frontier art portray American Indians?
2. What elements of the West most interested frontier artists?
3. What image of the West does the painting by Remington above suggest?

Ranch Life

Teenagers often shared the burden of the hard work of ranching. One of 14 children in a Colorado ranching family, Jake Goss started working with horses when he was 13. Two years later he found work on a neighboring ranch, cutting hay and branding cat-

Raising cattle today

tle. By age 17, Goss owned 23 head of cattle. He knew the responsibilities that came with owner-ship. When he broke his arm so badly that "it was hangin' out my sleeve with splinters," he stayed with the calves until someone could take his place. A little over a year later, he bought his own ranch, which he worked for most of the rest of his life.

Young women also did their share of work on the ranches. Agnes Morley Cleveland grew up on the family ranch in New Mexico. Later she recalled, "Cattle became the circumference of our universe and their behavior absorbed our entire waking hours." Cleveland rode the range in search of lost calves, checked fences for damage, and branded cattle. Once she discovered that a sheriff had mistreated one of her favorite horses. When he refused to return it, Cleveland stam-peded a herd of 50 to 60 horses through his camp.

Ranching

As the U.S. government converted more American Indian terri-tory into public land, cattle ranching spread west into Colorado and New Mexico and north into the Dakotas, Kansas, Montana, Nebraska, and Wyoming. The government allowed cattle ranch-ers to use public land as **open range**, or free grazing land. This access to free pastureland helped make cattle ranching prof-itable. The introduction of higher-grade cattle breeds from the East Coast and from Europe led to even bigger profits.

Ranch profits. Although many families established ranches, mainly large investment companies took advantage of the govern-ment's offer of land. Financed by eastern and European investors, these companies created huge ranches. A group of Chicago investors owned the 3.5-million-acre XIT Ranch in the Texas Pan-handle. A Scottish enterprise called the Prairie Cattle Company owned an even more impressive spread: 5.5 million acres in Col-orado, New Mexico, and Texas, with 139,000 head of cattle.

Most ranches were smaller than these, but many still covered thousands of acres. Large ranches were necessary because cattle needed vast expanses of grazing land to get enough nourishment. Cattle also needed access to water. Streams, rivers, and lakes deter-mined the size and location of ranches. "Wherever there is any water, there is a ranch," noted one Colorado cattleman.

Ranch life. Both cattle and sheep ranches demanded hard labor from ranch families. Everyone had to work to ensure that the ranch prospered. On most ranches, women did housework, cooked for all the hired cowboys, and helped out with fence-mending, herding, and other chores. Some women organized their own ranch-related businesses. Because ranches were far apart, loneliness took its toll. Susan Newcomb, a Texas ranch wife, described the isolation of ranch life.

> 66 **A man that is cowhunting with a lively crowd has no idea how long and lonesome the time passes with his wife at home. . . . A man can see his friends, hear the news and pass the time . . . while his wife is at home and sees and hears nothing until he returns from a long trip tired and worn out.** 99

The roundup. During the spring and fall, ranch life centered on the roundup. With help from the cowboys, ranchers drove their cattle from the open range to a central location. Here cowboys from each ranch "cut out," or separated, the cattle, which were identified by each ranch's distinctive brand. The cattle would then be rounded up for the long drive to a railhead.

Cowboys generally lived together in a bunkhouse, although they often slept outdoors during the summer months. When not working a roundup, cowboys

The Cattle Boom and Western Railroads, late 1800s

Learning from Maps The development of railroads and cattle trails allowed for the transportation of livestock and goods between eastern and western states.

? MOVEMENT What geographic feature made travel to the Pacific coast particularly difficult?

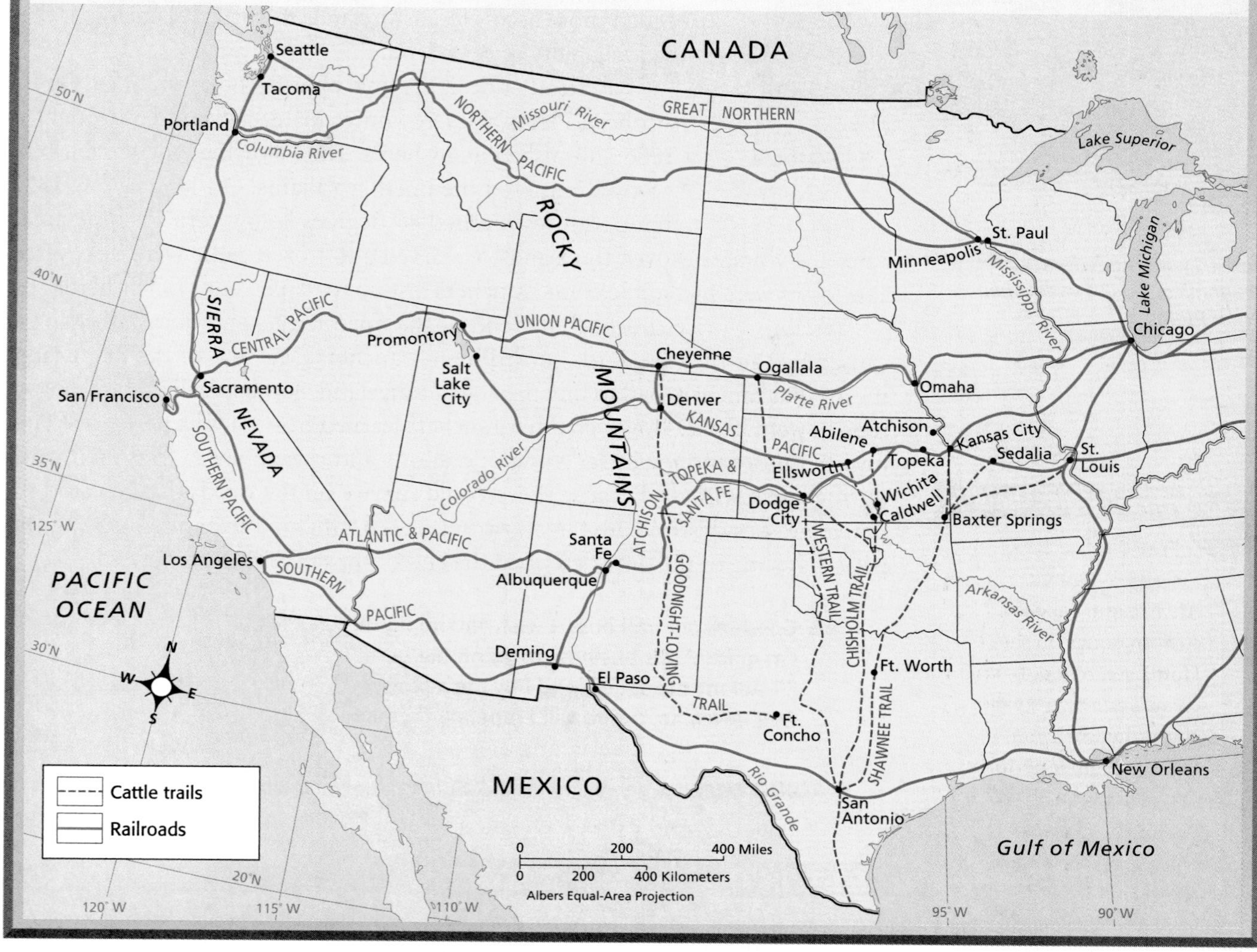

Legend:
- - - - Cattle trails
———— Railroads

0   200   400 Miles
0   200   400 Kilometers
Albers Equal-Area Projection

rode the range to check water sources and search for lost or injured cattle. As ranching became big business, ranch owners began to treat cowboys more like common laborers. In 1888 the XIT Ranch published a list of 23 rules for cowboys, including bans on pistols, card playing, and "intoxicating liquors."

✔ **READING CHECK:** What were ranches like?

The End of the Cattle Boom

The cattle boom lasted about 20 years. Several factors led to its early end. First, ranchers eager for large profits crowded the open range with too many cattle. Prices crashed in 1885, as supply far exceeded demand. In 1882 cattle had brought $35 a head in Chicago. They sold for only $8 in 1885. Second, open-range ranching declined after the invention of **barbed wire**. Illinois farmer Joseph Glidden

A Colt revolver

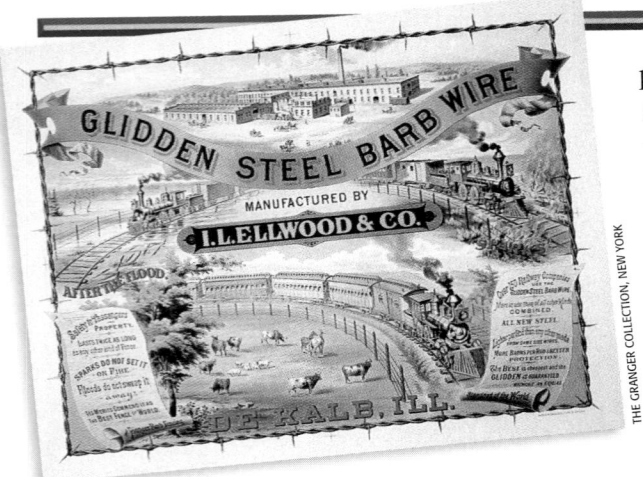

Barbed wire made fencing economical on the wide-open Great Plains.

patented this cheap fencing material in 1874. Ranchers initially refused to use barbed wire, fearing that it would injure their cattle. However, by the 1880s cattle ranchers and farmers had erected miles of barbed wire across the open range to control access to land and water. As overgrazing depleted the grass cover, cattle needed more access to pasturelands to survive. Fencing limited the availability of open land.

Bad weather dealt the final blow to the open range. On the southern Plains a severe winter in 1885–86 and a drought in 1886 diminished many herds. The following year, terrible blizzards hammered the northern Plains. On January 15, 1887, temperatures reached 46 degrees below zero in some areas. After the worst was over, thousands of starved and frozen cattle were discovered. The losses were incredible. Some ranchers lost up to 90 percent of their herds.

Declining prices for beef, the end of the open range, and devastating losses caused by the 1887 blizzards ruined many ranchers. The end of the open range meant that ranchers had to buy their own rangeland. Some large ranching corporations went broke. However, other ranchers learned from their experiences. They invested more money in ranching operations and raised hay to feed their cattle during harsh winters. Because sheep could survive on the weeds that replaced the native grasses destroyed by overgrazing, sheep ranching expanded during this period. A song of the time described the end of the era of the cowboy.

> 66 **Good-by, old trail boss, I wish you no harm;**
> **I'm quittin' this business to go on the farm.**
> **I'll sell my old saddle and buy me a plow;**
> **And never, no, never, will I rope another cow.** 99

✔ **READING CHECK:** Why did the cattle boom on the open range end?

Read More About It

Free Find:
Cowboy Songs
After reading about cowboy songs on the **Holt Researcher** CD–ROM, create your own song about the work you or a family member performs.

SECTION 3 REVIEW

Define and explain the significance of the following terms:
Texas longhorn
long drives
railhead
open range
barbed wire

Identify and explain the significance of the following individual:
Joseph Glidden

Locate and explain the importance of the following places:
Abilene, Kansas
Dodge City
Cheyenne
Ogallala

1. **Using Graphic Organizers** Copy the chart below. Use it to describe the factors that led to the growth of ranching and the factors that led to its decline.

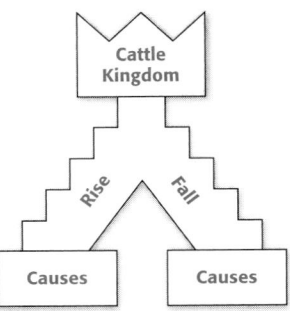

2. **Evaluating** Who were the cowboys? How did their lives on the long drives differ from their lives on the ranch?
3. **Assessing Consequences** How did the cattle drives affect the economy and growth of towns at railheads?
4. **Identifying Values** Why did officials in some towns want to banish cowboys? What values did these officials hold?

Critical Thinking

5. How did business needs shape the lives of those who lived on ranches?
   Consider:
   • what the business goals of the ranches were
   • how life was organized on the ranches
   • who lived and worked on ranches

The Mining Boom

Read to understand:

1. what role mining played in bringing more people west
2. how the arrival of families changed life in mining camps
3. why large companies took over most mining operations, and how this changed the lives of miners

KEY TERMS

Comstock Lode
patio process
hydraulic mining
hard-rock mining

KEY PEOPLE

William H. Seward

66 *The men who worked in the mines . . . were [a] happy-go-easy set of fellows, fond of good living, and not particularly interested in religious affairs. . . .*

Men quarreled at times and firearms were discharged with but slight provocation. Nevertheless they all had an acute instinct of right and wrong . . . [and] a high sense of honor. **99**

—J. N. Flint

This silver bar was minted in San Francisco.

Virginia City, Nevada, enjoyed an economic boom that began in 1859 when prospectors discovered silver in the region. Thirty years later, J. N. Flint recalled life in a prosperous mining town. Flint recalled that while working in the mines he longed for "the companionship of forest trees, green fields and running brooks," all of which were missing in the arid regions surrounding Virginia City. Flint's recollections capture the atmosphere of the towns where people hoped to make their fortunes by digging for gold and silver.

Western Mining

The economic impact of mining changed the face of the West. Farmers and ranchers slowly expanded across the Great Plains, establishing homesteads and ranches. Meanwhile, miners raced across the continent, hoping to be the first to strike it rich. Mining opened many new regions in the West to settlement.

Gold and silver. The first promising mining discoveries after the California Gold Rush took place in Colorado. Prospectors found gold near Pikes Peak in late 1858. By early 1859, thousands of people had flocked to Colorado. A popular tune captured their enthusiasm.

Miners search for precious metals using a sluice.

> **66** The gold is there, 'most anywhere.
> You can take it out rich, with an iron crowbar,
> And where it is thick, with a shovel and pick,
> You can pick it out in lumps as big as a brick. **99**

The song exaggerated the riches, however. Many prospectors left in disappointment by midsummer.

In 1859 the Carson River valley in present-day Nevada was another center of frantic activity. In addition to gold, the area contained the famous **Comstock Lode**, one of the world's richest silver veins. Over a period of 20 years its mines yielded more than $500 million worth of precious metals.

Some miners went south to Arizona, where Hispanics had been mining silver since the mid-1700s. Hispanic miners introduced mining methods that originated in Mexico and South America. These methods included a mill that separated gold

Individual prospectors often made the first discovery of precious metals, but it took large companies to extract the valuable ore.

from quartz and the *patio* process—which used mercury to extract silver from ore. The newer arrivals used these methods to mine the Comstock Lode and the region around Tucson, in present-day Arizona. Other miners headed north.

Northern ventures. During the late 1850s some miners pushed as far north as the Fraser River valley of British Columbia. This movement into Canada had important consequences for Russia and the United States. Russia, which at that time owned Alaska, offered to sell it to the United States. U.S. Secretary of State William H. Seward negotiated the purchase of Alaska in 1867. Seward believed the price, which came out to less than 2 cents an acre, was a good deal.

Many Americans, however, considered Alaska worthless, ridiculing the purchase as "Seward's Folly" or "Seward's Ice Box." However, Seward's confidence that Alaska "possesses treasures . . . equal to those of any other region of the continent" proved correct. In 1896, prospectors discovered gold in the Klondike district of Canada's Yukon Territory, which bordered Alaska. This discovery launched the Klondike Gold Rush. By the summer of 1897, Yukon miners had extracted gold worth more than $1 million. For the next two years, almost 100,000 people traveled through Alaska to seek their fortunes. Gold discoveries in Alaska in 1898 and 1902 attracted even more settlers.

✔ **READING CHECK:** What role did mining play in bringing more people to the West?

Strategies for Success — Comparing and Contrasting

Comparing and contrasting are fundamental aspects of historical study. To *compare* is to examine the similarities and the differences between two or more events, ideas, people, situations, social groups, or things. To *contrast* is to explore only the differences between two or more subjects. Comparing and contrasting are particularly effective techniques for organizing historical information, tracking change over time, and understanding the origins of different points of view.

How to Compare and Contrast

1. **Identify the similarities.** When you encounter subjects that require comparison, observe the ways in which they are alike. Each time you identify a similarity, assess its importance. Record your findings.
2. **Identify the differences.** When you have noted as many similarities as possible, examine the ways in which your subjects are different. Each time you identify a difference, assess its importance. Record your findings.
3. **Put the comparison to use.** Use the results of your comparison, along with your knowledge of the historical period, to form generalizations and draw conclusions about your subjects.

Applying the Strategy

Review the material on cattle ranches in Section 3 and mining companies in this section. Then create a list of similarities and differences between the two industries.

Practicing the Strategy

Answer the following questions.
1. Who invested in cattle ranches and mining companies?
2. What role did the U.S. government play in the ranching and mining industries?
3. Who supplied the labor in each industry?
4. How did each industry affect community formation in the West?
5. How did each industry affect the western environment?

Life in Mining Communities

Mining camps sprang up overnight wherever news of possible wealth brought prospectors together. Unlike ranching and farming, prospecting was typically not a family enterprise. Most camps initially consisted almost entirely of male residents. A visitor to one Colorado mining camp estimated the population to be about 4,000, with just 12 female inhabitants.

The settlers. Mining camps drew a wide range of settlers. One newspaper reporter wrote, "Here were congregated the most varied elements of humanity . . . belonging to almost every nationality and every status of life." In the mining regions of Southern California, many Californios, Chileans, Mexicans, and Peruvians maintained their own separate settlements. In other mining areas the mix of prospectors included U.S. citizens, Irish and Chinese men who had come to work on the railroads, and miners from the Cornwall region of England.

At first, life in the mining camps was crude, and comforts were few. Moreover, the atmosphere in most camps was one of intense competition. Prospector William Parsons remembered.

Mining. Mining camps were often little more than a hastily constructed group of tents or shacks. *What do you think miners ate while in camp?*

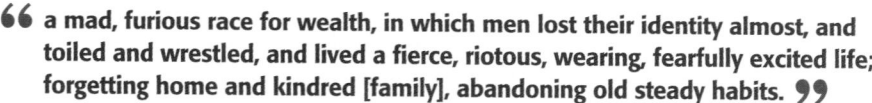

❝ a mad, furious race for wealth, in which men lost their identity almost, and toiled and wrestled, and lived a fierce, riotous, wearing, fearfully excited life; forgetting home and kindred [family], abandoning old steady habits. ❞

Such brutal competition led to discrimination in the mining camps. Miners in the Cripple Creek camp in Colorado forcibly excluded eastern and southern Europeans as well as Hispanics. In 1882 a mob of masked men drove the Chinese inhabitants of Rico, Colorado, out of town. The local newspaper called the incident "one of the most shameful affairs that ever disgraced any so-called civilized country and would have met the hearty approval of the most barbarous savage." Most Chinese miners left the Rocky Mountain camps because of the hostile treatment they received from other miners.

Instability. Western mining camps were some of the most violent places in the United States during the late 1800s. Tensions between ethnic groups often led to fighting. Gamblers and swindlers swarmed in, and conflicts over claims set off brawls. Deadwood, South Dakota, gained a reputation as a particularly rough town. An outlaw's haven, Deadwood became the final resting place of lawman Wild Bill Hickok, shot dead as he played cards. Legend has it that Hickok was holding a pair of aces and a pair of eights, which thereafter became known as the dead man's hand.

The absence of law enforcement sometimes led people in mining camps to form vigilante committees to combat theft and violence. Montana newspaper editor Thomas Dimsdale claimed that it was "an absolute necessity that good, law-loving, order-sustaining men should unite for mutual protection and salvation of the community." However, vigilante committees often used violence to resolve the community's problems, hanging the accused after a quick trial.

Read More About It

Free Find:
Mining Camps
After reading about mining camps on the **Holt Researcher** CD–ROM, imagine you are a reporter for an East Coast magazine. Write an article for your readers that describes a day in a mining town.

Great Debates

The Old West

Conflicting images of life in the West reflect the continuing debate over the meaning of western settlement. Books, movies, and television programs offer one side of the debate. Most Americans are familiar with images such as a solitary miner panning for gold in a remote mountain stream; a cowboy riding off alone into the sunset; and a farm or ranch family carving out a living on the empty Plains. These legendary western figures represent the American ideal of rugged individuals conquering a barren and uninhabited land. Seen this way, the history of western settlement is a powerful and deeply meaningful symbol of the American Dream.

However, many historians choose to focus on other aspects of western development. They argue that most westerners, including cowboys and miners, labored for others—often large companies—rather than for themselves. In addition, western settlers relied upon assistance from the federal government. It sold lands at low rates, subsidized railroad development, and used the military to remove American Indians. These historians view the West as a land shaped by technology, big business, and the federal government—a portrayal radically different from the "Wild West" of outlaws, lone cowboys, and isolated pioneers.

Stability came to the mining camps as they grew into towns. The camps attracted a host of businesses eager to feed and clothe the miners. James Morley of Montana noted, "I shouldn't have the patience to count the business places" in an area that "only eighteen months ago . . . was a 'howling desert.'" Owners of saloons and stores had a better chance of striking it rich than miners. Cooking, cleaning, and providing lodging were especially profitable. One industrious woman boasted that she earned "nine hundred dollars in nine weeks, clear of all expenses, by washing!" Later known as the Cattle Queen of Montana, Elizabeth Collins was offered a job as cook at a Montana mining camp. She recalled, "Prompted by kindness and a desire to see these hardworking men as comfortable as possible—also craving for the $75 per month—I promptly accepted the offer."

The few children living in the camps had unique opportunities to earn money. They hunted for gold dust under the raised, wooden sidewalks or panned and scavenged for gold dust after the miners had finished for the day. Much more profitable, however, was selling fresh food to miners, who quickly grew tired of eating canned food. One brother and sister made $800 one summer selling butter and bacon to the miners.

With the arrival of more families, many camps turned into permanent communities. Prosperity brought law and order and the establishment of churches, newspapers, schools, and even theaters and music groups. Denver and Boulder, Colorado; Carson City, Nevada; and Helena, Montana, all began as mining camps before evolving into major urban centers.

✔ **READING CHECK:** How did the arrival of families change life in the mining camps?

INTERPRETING THE VISUAL RECORD

A new town. Helena, Montana, is one mining camp that developed into a prosperous city. *What evidence indicates that Helena is no longer a temporary community?*

Mining as Big Business

Individual prospectors roaming the West with their packhorses and hand tools made the earliest strikes, or mining discoveries. However, the era of the lone miner did not last long. Within a few years after a strike, most of the easily accessible mineral deposits were "worked out." Mining ore deposits deep below Earth's surface required resources and technology far beyond the means of the average prospector. As a result, mining became dominated by large, well-financed companies.

Mining companies relied on technological know-how rather than on guesswork or luck. Corps of college-educated geologists and engineers located the ore and instructed the companies on how best to extract the minerals—copper, iron, lead, and zinc—in demand by factories in the East.

To reach the ore, companies used one of two methods. In **hydraulic mining**, water shot at high pressure ripped away gravel and dirt to expose the minerals beneath. This process devastated the environment. The displaced soil choked rivers and caused flooding. **Hard-rock mining** involved sinking deep shafts to obtain ore locked in veins of rocks.

New technology changed the working conditions in the mines. Laborers sank the shafts, built the tunnels, drilled, and processed the ore. The work was dirty and dangerous. Temperatures deep in the mines sometimes rose as high as 150°F. Poor ventilation contributed to respiratory illnesses. Cave-ins, rockfalls, and the use of explosives such as dynamite sometimes caused injury or death. Injured miners had little hope of receiving compensation for their suffering. After William Kelley was blinded in a mining accident, the Montana Supreme Court ruled that it was "an unforeseen and unavoidable accident incident to [part of] the risk of mining." The mining company did not have to pay Kelley any damages.

As the hope of sudden riches faded, miners grew dissatisfied with wages and working conditions. In some communities miners formed unions. Dues paid to the unions helped injured miners and the families of miners who had been killed on the job. Unions also negotiated with or battled against owners who tried to cut wages. Many also opposed Chinese miners, who were willing to work for lower pay. During the early 1900s, mining increasingly became the task of large companies. Mining companies greatly affected the landscape and the environment of the West.

INTERPRETING THE VISUAL RECORD

Hydraulic mining. These Colorado miners are using a water hose to sift through dirt in search of gold. *What impact did this type of mining have on the landscape and environment?*

✔ **READING CHECK:** Why did large companies take over most mining interests? How did this change affect the lives of miners?

SECTION  4 REVIEW

Define and explain the significance of the following terms:
Comstock Lode
patio process
hydraulic mining
hard-rock mining

Identify and explain the significance of the following individual:
William H. Seward

1. **Using Graphic Organizers** Copy the graphic organizer below. Use it to explain the ways in which mining affected the United States during the late 1800s.

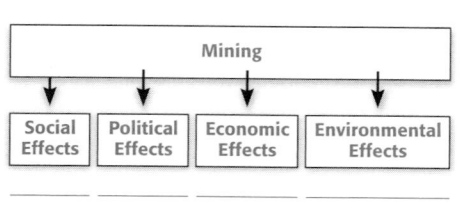

2. **Assessing Consequences** How did mining encourage the migration of people westward?
3. **Synthesizing** Why were the mining camps often violent places? How did they change over time?
4. **Recognizing Point of View** How did the methods of the early miners and those of mining company owners differ?

Critical Thinking

5. Overall, do you think the mining era benefited or harmed the West?
   Consider:
   • how the mining boom benefited the West
   • what harm the boom caused to the West
   • how the boom could have been handled differently

CHAPTER 14

Review

Creating a Time Line

Copy the time line below onto a sheet of paper. Complete the time line by filling in the events and dates from this chapter that you think were most significant. Pick three events and explain why you think they were significant.

1860   1885   1910

Writing a Summary

Using the Reading Checks as a guide, write an overview of the events in the chapter.

Identifying People and Ideas

Identify the following terms or individuals and explain their significance.

1. Sitting Bull
2. Massacre at Wounded Knee
3. Dawes General Allotment Act
4. Homestead Act
5. Exodusters
6. Willa Cather
7. Texas longhorn
8. Joseph Glidden
9. Comstock Lode
10. hydraulic mining

Understanding Main Ideas

SECTION 1
1. How and why did different American Indian tribes resist relocation to reservations?
2. How did the government fail to achieve its goal of assimilation?

SECTION 2
3. Why did many Americans choose to move to the West during the second half of the 1800s?

SECTION 3
4. What led to the rise and fall of the Cattle Kingdom?

SECTION 4
5. How did mining companies change the daily lives of miners in the West?

Reviewing Themes

1. **Cultural Diversity** How did differing views of white settlement in the West contribute to the Massacre at Wounded Knee?
2. **Economic Development** In what ways did farming, mining, and ranching alter the western landscape and environment?
3. **Technology and Society** How did new technology change the ways in which miners worked?

Thinking Critically

1. **Hypothesizing** How would western settlement have been different if the U.S. government had honored all the treaties it signed with American Indians?
2. **Evaluating** Did most settlers find what they were expecting in the West? Why or why not?
3. **Recognizing Point of View** In what ways did African Americans and Mexican Americans experience both expanded opportunities and limitations in the West?
4. **Comparing and Contrasting** How were the experiences of cowboys and miners similar and different?
5. **Analyzing** How does the history of the Old West differ from many images of it presented in popular culture?

Writing About History

Writing to Describe Copy the graphic organizer below. Use it to list the major aspects of life in Plains settlements, in cattle towns, and in mining towns. Then write an essay comparing and contrasting two of the types of communities.

Plains Settlements	Cattle Towns	Mining Towns

Strategies for Success

Review the **Strategies for Success** on *Comparing and Contrasting.* Then reread the subsection entitled Moving West in Section 2 and answer the following questions.

1. What similar motivations did migrants from the East, African Americans from the South, and immigrants from Europe and Asia have for moving to the American West?
2. What different motivations did each of these groups have for moving to the West?
3. What conclusions does this comparison help you draw about the pursuit of opportunity in the West?

Linking History and Geography

The mining boom shaped many areas in the West. Study the map below and identify which states or territories had both silver- and gold-mining regions. Which states or territories had major lodes?

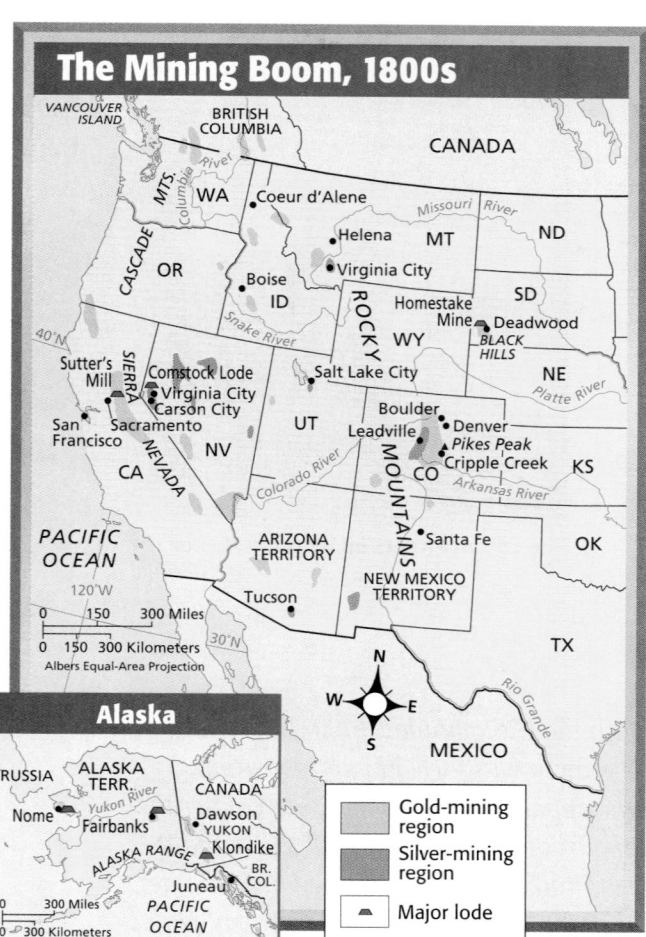

The Mining Boom, 1800s

---

internet**connect**

TOPIC: Western Writers
GO TO: go.hrw.com
KEYWORD: SD1 Writers

Accessing the Internet through the HRW Web site, research the work of Willa Cather, Bret Harte, and Laura Ingalls Wilder. Then create an annotated display that illustrates the differences among the writers as well as how their work helped shape the public's perception of the West.

BUILDING YOUR PORTFOLIO

Complete one or all of the following projects individually or cooperatively.

1 Global Relations

Imagine that you are a Sioux living on the Pine Ridge Reservation in South Dakota in 1895. **Compose an oral account** *for your grand-children that describes how conflict between the Sioux and non-Indian settlers has affected your life and the lives of other Sioux. Be sure to include details of the conflict.*

Ho for Kansas!

Brethren, Friends, & Fellow Citizens:
I feel thankful to inform you that the
REAL ESTATE
AND
Homestead Association,
Will Leave Here the
15th of April, 1878,
In pursuit of Homes in the Southwestern Lands of America, at Transportation Rates, cheaper than ever was known before.
For full information inquire of
Benj. Singleton, better known as old Pap,
NO. 5 NORTH FRONT STREET.
Beware of Speculators and Adventurers, as it is a dangerous thing to fall in their hands.
Nashville, Tenn., March 18, 1878.

2 Geographic Diversity

Prepare a pamphlet that advertises one region of the West in order to attract settlers.

3 Economic Development

Prepare a government report that discusses the working conditions in mines. Conclude your report with recommendations for improving the lives of the miners.

1865–1905
The Second Industrial Revolution

Pullman Sleeping Car

The First Real Pullman Sleeping Car – 1865

1865
Business and Finance
George Pullman patents a railway sleeping car.

1869
Politics
Uriah S. Stephens establishes the Knights of Labor, the first major national union.

The first telephone

1876
Science and Technology
Alexander Graham Bell receives a patent for the telephone.

1879
Science and Technology
Thomas Edison uses bamboo fiber in his design for the first long-lasting incandescent lightbulb.

1879
Business and Finance
Frank W. Woolworth establishes the first of a chain of Woolworth dime stores.

Edison's lightbulb

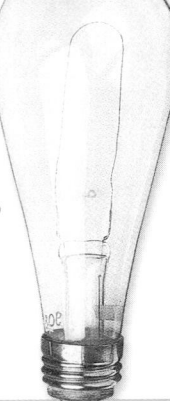

1865   **1873**   **1881**

1869
The Arts
Horatio Alger Jr. begins publishing the series *Luck and Pluck.*

1874
Daily Life
Mary Ewing Outerbridge establishes the first American tennis courts on Staten Island, New York.

1876
The Arts
American artist Winslow Homer paints *The Cotton Pickers.*

Advertisement picturing a Staten Island sports club

The Cotton Pickers by Winslow Homer

Before You Read

Build on What You Know

During the first half of the 1800s, both the U.S. population and westward settlement expanded rapidly. This growth was fueled by immigration, industrialization, and the economic opportunities of the frontier. After the Civil War these trends accelerated even more. In this chapter you will learn about the many inventions that began a new age of industrialization in the United States. Poor working conditions in the new industries, however, led many American workers to organize unions to improve their daily lives.

The public humiliation of French army captain Alfred Dreyfus

A steelworker in Andrew Carnegie's largest mill in Pittsburgh, Pennsylvania

1884
The Arts
Mark Twain publishes *The Adventures of Huckleberry Finn.*

1890
Politics
The Sherman Antitrust Act is passed, outlawing monopolies and trusts that restrain trade.

1894
World Events
Alfred Dreyfus is arrested on questionable treason charges, leading to political upheaval in France.

1901
Business and Finance
Andrew Carnegie sells his steel company to J. P. Morgan for nearly $500 million.

1889

1897

1905

1886
Politics
1,500 U.S. labor strikes erupt.

1893
World Events
Europe sinks into a major economic depression.

1893
Daily Life
The first motorcar to be built in the United States is completed by the Duryea brothers.

1903
Science and Technology
The Wright brothers test their airplane near Kitty Hawk, North Carolina.

A strike turns violent in Chicago, Illinois.

The Duryea brothers ride in their horseless carriage.

Think About Themes

Themes Journal

*Decide whether you **agree** or **disagree** with the following statements. Note why in your journal.*

Economic Development Technological innovations lead to economic growth by increasing production and industrialization.

Technology and Society Technology brings about social reform and improves people's daily lives.

Democratic Values The actions of both American business leaders and labor organizers lead to greater equality and an expansion of democracy.

463

The Age of Invention

OBJECTIVES

Read to understand:

1. how the development of steel and oil refining affected U.S. industry
2. what innovations were made in transportation
3. how the innovations in communications technology changed business practices and daily life in the United States
4. why Thomas Edison wanted to open a research laboratory, and how it changed American life

KEY TERMS

Bessemer process
patent
transcontinental railroad
trunk lines
telegraph

KEY PEOPLE

Edwin L. Drake
Elijah McCoy
George Westinghouse
Alexander Graham Bell
Thomas Alva Edison
Lewis Latimer

EYEWITNESSES TO History

66 *The telephone is a curious device that might fairly find place in the magic of Arabian Tales. Of what use is such an invention? Well, there may be occasions of state when it is necessary for officials who are far apart to talk with each other.* 99
—New York *Tribune* reporter

1876 Centennial Exposition

A reporter visiting the 1876 Centennial Exposition in Philadelphia discussed in the New York *Tribune* his amazement at the invention of the telephone. In the years following the Civil War, the United States experienced a wave of scientific discoveries and inventions. Americans celebrated this "age of invention" at the exposition in Philadelphia. Inventors presented new technologies such as the telephone to the public for the first time. The potential impact of these inventions on the future of American business and daily life was uncertain.

Industrial Innovations

From 1865 to 1900 the United States experienced a surge of industrial growth. These years marked the beginning of a Second Industrial Revolution. This new era of industrial transformation began with numerous discoveries and inventions that significantly altered manufacturing, transportation, and the everyday lives of Americans.

Coal and steam made possible the original Industrial Revolution in the United States. Coal-fed steam engines powered factories. These factories in turn produced the goods that generated economic growth. In the late 1800s an abundance of steel helped spur a second period of industrialization. Steel was used in the construction of heavy machinery that mass-produced goods. Steel was also used to build railroad tracks, bridges, and tall city buildings.

Steel. Metal workers and manufacturers had known of steel long before the Second Industrial Revolution. Until the mid-1800s, however, the process of converting iron ore into steel was too expensive to be used practically. In the 1850s, however, Henry Bessemer in Great Britain and William Kelly in the United States both developed a method of steelmaking that burned off the impurities in molten iron with a blast of hot air. Known as the **Bessemer process**, this method could produce more steel in a day than the older techniques could turn out in a week. American engineer Alexander Holley adapted and improved the Bessemer process. Largely because of this process, American steel production skyrocketed from about 15,000 tons in 1865 to more than 28 million tons by 1910.

The production of steel required iron ore. Barges and steamers carried unprocessed iron ore from the Midwest

John Ferguson Weir's painting **Forging the Shaft** *depicts steelmaking in the 1870s.*

THE METROPOLITAN MUSEUM OF ART

through the Great Lakes to the southern shores of Lake Michigan and Lake Erie. Cities such as Gary, Indiana; Cleveland, Ohio; and Pittsburgh, Pennsylvania, became major centers for steel manufacturing. Coal mined in Pennsylvania and West Virginia provided an inexpensive source of fuel for steel production.

The increased availability of steel in the late 1800s resulted in its widespread industrial use. A major consumer of steel was the railroad industry, which began replacing iron rails with stronger, longer-lasting steel ones. Recognizing its strength as a building material, builders began to use steel in the construction of bridges and buildings. Using steel to create a skeletal frame in buildings allowed architects to design larger, multistory buildings. Steel's resistance to rust also made it an ideal material for everyday items such as nails and wire.

Oil. Like the advances in steel production, the development of a process to refine oil also affected industrial practices. American Indians and settlers had known of the existence of crude oil for hundreds of years. Some Indians used this unprocessed dark thick ooze for medicinal purposes and to grease wagons and tools.

By the late 1850s, however, chemists and geologists from a number of countries had made significant progress in developing a process to refine crude oil. With this process, crude oil could be turned into kerosene, which could be burned in lamps to produce light or used as a fuel. Kerosene provided a cheap substitute for whale oil, which had become increasingly difficult to acquire.

Noting the growing demand for this inexpensive fuel, Edwin L. Drake used a steam engine to drill for oil near Titusville, Pennsylvania, in 1859. The venture seemed so impractical that curious onlookers questioned Drake's sanity, calling the project Drake's Folly. When the oil began to flow at a rate of some 20 barrels a day, however, other prospectors, or "wildcatters," hurried to dig their own wells. Like the California Gold Rush of 1849, the oil boom in western Pennsylvania created intense excitement and encouraged prospecting. Prospectors even referred to oil as "black gold." By the 1880s oil wells dotted Ohio, Pennsylvania, and West Virginia. Production topped 25 million barrels of oil in 1880 alone.

Although kerosene remained a primary product of oil refining, by 1880 refiners had developed other petroleum products that increased the industrial uses of oil. Refiners developed waxes and lubricating oil for use in new industrial machines. Elijah McCoy made a significant contribution to the industrial use of oil. The son of runaway slaves, McCoy invented a lubricating cup that fed oil to parts of a machine while it was running.

Like other inventors, McCoy received a **patent**—a guarantee to protect an inventor's rights to make, use, or sell the invention. McCoy's innovative breakthrough helped many kinds of machines operate more smoothly and quickly.

Black gold. Edwin Drake, wearing a top hat, visits his oil well drilled in 1859 near Titusville, Pennsylvania. *What materials did Drake use to construct his well?*

✔ **READING CHECK:** How did the development of steel and oil refining affect U.S. industry?

Transportation

Innovations in the steel and oil industries led to a surge of new advances in the transportation industry. Many of the discoveries during this "age of invention" contributed to the development of new, more technologically advanced forms of transportation.

New technology in the late 1800s resulted in a massive expansion of the American railroad network. Entirely new discoveries laid the groundwork for air flight and the automobile. These developments in transportation made travel much more efficient. This brought Americans into closer contact with each other. Railroads linked isolated regions of the country to the rest of the United States.

INTERPRETING THE VISUAL RECORD

Transcontinental railroad. The completion of the first transcontinental railroad in 1869 allowed trains to transport goods and people from coast to coast in a matter of days. *How does this photograph reveal the importance of this moment to U.S. history?*

Railroads. The availability of cheap steel provided by the Bessemer process had a significant impact on railroad expansion. As steel production soared, prices dropped dramatically. Steel that had sold for $100 a ton in 1873 went for $12 a ton by the late 1890s. The availability of cheaper steel encouraged railroad companies to lay thousands of miles of new track.

The rapid increase of railroad lines led to a more efficient network of rail transportation. Prior to the Civil War, most railroads in the United States were short. They averaged some 100 miles in length and primarily served local transportation needs. In 1860, passengers and freight traveling between New York and Chicago, for example, had to change lines 17 times over a period of two days. By the next decade, however, the rapid expansion of rail lines allowed passengers and freight to make the same trip in less than 24 hours without changing trains.

The country's first **transcontinental railroad** was completed in 1869. The project was completed when the Central Pacific and Union Pacific Railroads were joined to create a single rail line from Omaha, Nebraska, to the Pacific Ocean. To celebrate its completion, railroad tycoon Leland Stanford hammered in the last spike at Promontory, Utah. By 1900 almost a half-dozen **trunk lines**, or major railroads, crossed the Great Plains to the Pacific coast. Feeder, or branch, lines connected the trunk lines to outlying areas. This huge railroad grid joined every state and linked remote towns to urban centers.

Additional innovations further improved rail transportation. Bigger, more efficient locomotives made it possible to pull larger loads at faster speeds. George Westinghouse's compressed-air brake increased railroad safety by enabling the locomotive and all its cars to stop at the same time. Granville T. Woods improved on Westinghouse's air brake. He also developed a communications system that enabled trains and stations to send and receive messages.

Changes in track design also improved rail service. Double sets of tracks allowed train traveling in opposite directions to pass each other. Equally important, the adoption in the 1870s of a standard gauge, or width between the rails, made rail transportation faster and cheaper. Passengers and freight no longer had to be transferred from train to train each time they reached a different line.

The growth of railroads had far-reaching consequences. Railroads increased western settlement by making travel affordable and easy. They also stimulated urban growth. Wherever railroads were built, new towns sprang up, and existing towns grew into major cities.

The economic impact of the railroads was immeasurable. For much of the late 1800s railroad companies provided many of the country's jobs. They also spurred the growth of other industries. The railroad companies' demands for locomotives, rails, and railcars poured money into the steel and railroad-car construction industries. Innovations like refrigerated freight cars helped develop the meatpacking industry. In addition, the network of railroad lines allowed companies to sell their products nationally. A Pennsylvania steel foundry could obtain iron ore from the Great Lakes region, and a Philadelphia furniture company could sell its products in small midwestern towns.

Railroads also shaped American popular culture and folk music. One ballad immortalized Casey Jones, the Illinois Central engineer killed in a crash with a freight train in 1900. Other songs celebrated famous trains like the Wabash Cannonball.

Railroads. The Illinois Central Railroad connected rural Americans with the rest of the world. *What do the various images in this cartoon represent?*

The horseless carriage. The innovations in oil refining in the late 1800s led to advances in the development of motors and the creation of a new mode of transportation. The horseless carriage, a self-propelled vehicle and forerunner to the automobile, had originally been developed about 1770. A French artillery officer named Nicolas-Joseph Cugnot had mounted a steam engine to a three-wheeled carriage. The use of steam power for these early automobiles was expensive and inefficient for the small amount of power needed for these carriages.

Efforts to develop a gasoline-powered engine led to the creation of a more practical self-propelled vehicle. Innovations in oil refining led Nikolaus A. Otto to invent the first internal combustion engine powered by gasoline in 1876. In the 1880s ambitious designers in Europe and the United States attempted to use this gasoline engine to power horseless carriages. In 1893 Charles and J. Frank Duryea built the first practical motorcar in the United States.

The 1890s brought further innovations to the horseless carriage. By the turn of the century, more Americans had begun to use the carriages in their daily lives. The use of this new mode of transportation was limited, however, since only wealthy citizens could afford it. Nevertheless, automobile production rapidly became a substantial commercial industry.

Airplanes. The internal combustion engine also led to advances in flight. Using small gasoline engines, Orville and Wilbur Wright of Dayton, Ohio, developed one of the first working airplanes.

The Wright brothers had experimented with glider designs. They also experimented with engines based on European designs in the mid-1890s. On December

With experience gained from operating a bicycle shop and experimenting with small engines and gliders, the Wright brothers developed a plane and made the first piloted flight in 1903.

17, 1903, near Kitty Hawk, North Carolina, Orville Wright made the first piloted flight—12 seconds and 120 feet—in a powered plane. Orville Wright made a statement summing up the significance of the achievement.

66 This flight lasted only twelve seconds, but it was, nevertheless, the first in the history of the world in which a machine carrying a man had raised itself by its own power into the air in full flight, had sailed forward without reduction of speed, and had finally landed at a point as high as that from which it started. "

The Wright brothers' first flight received little public attention or press coverage. Some Americans even questioned its inappropriateness for human beings. However, as word of their achievement spread, a surge of related inventions and patents by other engineers dramatically demonstrated the importance of this new form of transportation.

✔ **READING CHECK:** What innovations were made in transportation in the late 1800s?

Communications

Just as developments in transportation made traveling easier and brought people into closer contact, innovations in communications technology also brought Americans closer together. These advances also furthered the growth of American industry.

Telegraph. One of the most significant advances in communications in the 1800s was the **telegraph**. The telegraph was developed by Samuel F. B. Morse as a means of communicating over wires with electricity. The telegraph attracted little attention when Morse filed for a patent on his version in 1837. In time, however, people recognized its business potential. Using Morse's dot-and-dash code, a telegraph operator could send a business order to a distant location in minutes.

By 1866 Western Union, the leading telegraph company, had more than 2,000 telegraph offices. The telegraph grew along with the railroad. Telegraph companies established offices in train stations and strung telegraph wire on poles alongside the railroad lines. Telegraphs sent information for businesses, the government, newspapers, and private citizens.

Gradually, Americans began to see the importance of the telegraph to the daily functioning of the nation and its businesses. A reporter for *Harper's Magazine* compared the telegraph to the nervous system of the human body.

66 Every phase of the mental activity of the country is more or less represented in this great system. . . . Almost instantaneously . . . [information] reaches the nearest ganglion [nerve center] of our great artificial nervous system, and it spreads simultaneously in every direction throughout the land. 99

■ **Understanding Change** The "age of invention" transformed American life. Much of the technology developed in the late 1800s remains important today. Examine the chart of items used for various purposes in the mid-1800s and today. *What items used in the mid-1800s are still in use by some people today? How has their use changed? How would life today be different without the items on the right?*

THEN

Now

Technology	THEN	Now
Energy	firewood	oil, natural gas, nuclear power
Transportation	horse and buggy	automobile
Communication	handwritten letters	Internet
Popular Entertainment	live theater	television, films
Household Appliances	washboard underground icehouse hammer fireplace livestock	washing machine refrigerator electric drill microwave oven lawnmower

Data reflects mid-1800s and 1999.

Telephone. Patented by Alexander Graham Bell in March 1876, the "talking telegraph," or telephone, had an even greater impact. Bell demonstrated his invention at the Philadelphia Centennial Exposition in June 1876. Judges there pronounced it "perhaps the greatest marvel hitherto [thus far] achieved by the electric telegraph." Businesses quickly found the telephone indispensable. By the end of the 1800s more than a million telephones had been installed in American offices and homes.

Early telephones required operators to connect callers, and many women rushed to fill these newly created jobs. A former telephone operator described the fast-paced work.

66 **On the second floor where the switchboards were located there arose a dull roar like that of locusts on a sunburnt prairie, a sense of many voices without any one being distinguishable. . . . I could see their hands working swiftly, pulling cords out of the holes, jabbing others in. Serving the Thing that signaled them with little flashing lights, making them hurry, hurry. 99**

INTERPRETING THE VISUAL RECORD

Telephone. Alexander Graham Bell's invention of the telephone created new employment opportunities for women. *What does the photograph above of telephone operators during the late 1800s reveal about the positive and negative aspects of the job?*

Typewriter. Christopher Sholes developed the typewriter in 1867. By allowing users to quickly produce easily legible documents, the typewriter revolutionized communications. Sholes sold his typewriter patent in 1873 to E. Remington & Sons. Although other typewriter designs had preceded Sholes's design, his was the first to be marketed. Sholes's keyboard design, with only a few changes, is still used today in typewriters and computers. Carbon paper, also introduced during this period, allowed users of typewriters to produce multiple copies of a document at the same time.

The invention of the typewriter soon gave rise to the use of typing pools. These business departments were made up of many clerical workers whose main task was to type. Women made up the majority of workers in the typing pools. The pools offered many working-class women the opportunity to move into a skilled profession for the first time. Lillian Sholes, Christopher Sholes's daughter, was probably the first professional female typist. Christopher Sholes was aware of the impact of the typewriter on communications and on the expansion of job opportunities for women. He later wrote, "I feel that I have done something for the women who have always had to work so hard."

Christopher Sholes's typewriter revolutionized business communication.

✔ **READING CHECK:** How did innovations in communications technology change business practices and the daily lives of Americans?

Science & Technology

Electricity

The late 1800s brought significant advances in the uses of electricity. One such advance was the lightbulb. In simple terms, the lightbulb produces light when electricity flows through a filament that resists that flow. This resistance gives off energy in the form of heat—so much heat that the filament glows, producing light. To prevent the filament from being consumed by the heat, inventors created a vacuum through the use of a glass bulb. This reduces the oxygen around the filament. The bulb was filled with inert gas.

While many inventors experimented with the incandescent lightbulb, Thomas Edison and his team at Menlo Park, New Jersey, made the most significant contributions by finding a filament that would light up without burning up. Edison and his associates discovered in 1880 that carbonized bamboo

fiber could last an average of 600 hours. Eventually filaments made of the element tungsten were used.

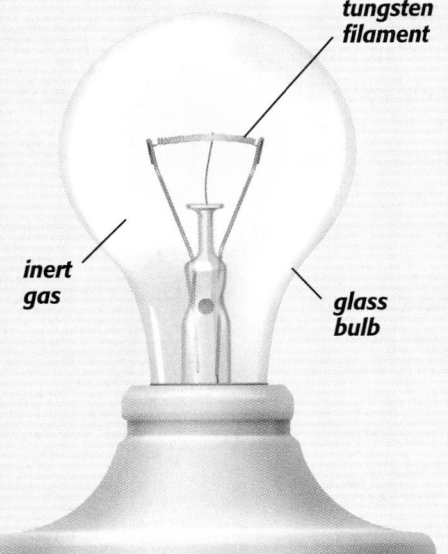

tungsten filament

inert gas

glass bulb

Power plants soon arose to supply electricity for lightbulbs in homes and industries. However, electricity could not be transmitted over long distances with direct current (DC) because too much energy was lost in transportation over power lines. Inventor Nikola Tesla patented an alternating current (AC) generator that could produce electricity for transmission over longer distance with less loss of energy. With this advance, the use of electricity spread rapidly.

Understanding Science and History

1. What advances did Edison's team make with the lightbulb and electricity?

2. What purposes does the glass bulb serve?

Edison and Menlo Park

Thomas Alva Edison was another pioneer of communications technology. His first major invention was a telegraph that could send up to four messages over the same wire simultaneously. Edison's early inventions had a significant impact on telegraphic communications. However, his influence on American life extends well beyond the history of the telegraph. An active innovator, Edison and his fellow researchers made significant discoveries and advances in electricity, lightbulbs, phonographs, and early motion-picture cameras.

Thomas Edison

Born in a small Ohio town in 1847, Edison received the majority of his schooling at home. He became a newsboy at age 12 and later worked as a telegraph operator. An eager amateur scientist, Edison conducted experiments and read widely in his spare time. In 1869 he patented an electric vote recorder. That year he also received his second patent, for a telegraphic stock ticker. Other inventions followed. In 1876 he went into the "invention business" full-time. He opened a workshop in Menlo Park, New Jersey, where he assembled a team of researchers. Excited about his new facility, Edison sent an invitation to a friend to come visit.

> 66 **Brand-new laboratory . . . at Menlo Park . . . the prettiest spot in New Jersey, on the [Pennsylvania] Railway, on a High Hill. Will show you around, go strawberrying.** 99

Edison promised that he and his fellow researchers would deliver "a minor invention every ten days and a big thing every six months or so." He kept his word. His researchers invented the phonograph in 1877 and the lightbulb in 1879. When he died in 1931, the "Wizard of Menlo Park" held more than 1,000 patents. Describing his process of invention to a colleague, Edison explained the secret to his success.

> 66 **I have the right principle and am on the right track, but time, hard work and some good luck are necessary too. It has been just so in all of my inventions. The first step is an intuition, and [it] comes with a burst, then difficulties arise. . . . Months of intense watching, study and labor are requisite [required] before commercial success or failure is certainly reached.** 99

Edison's work at Menlo Park was a team effort. Some of the most significant contributions to the development of the lightbulb were made not by Edison but by his assistant Lewis Latimer. Latimer was also a skilled draftsman. As an expert in patent law, Latimer testified in several court cases to support Edison's patents.

Read More About It

Free Find:
Thomas Edison
After reading the biography on Thomas Edison on the **Holt Researcher** CD–ROM, create a list of the most important of Edison's inventions and explain why each was significant.

INTERPRETING THE VISUAL RECORD
Menlo Park. Thomas Edison's team at Menlo Park developed more than 1,000 patented inventions. *What conclusions can be drawn from this image about the working environment at Menlo Park?*

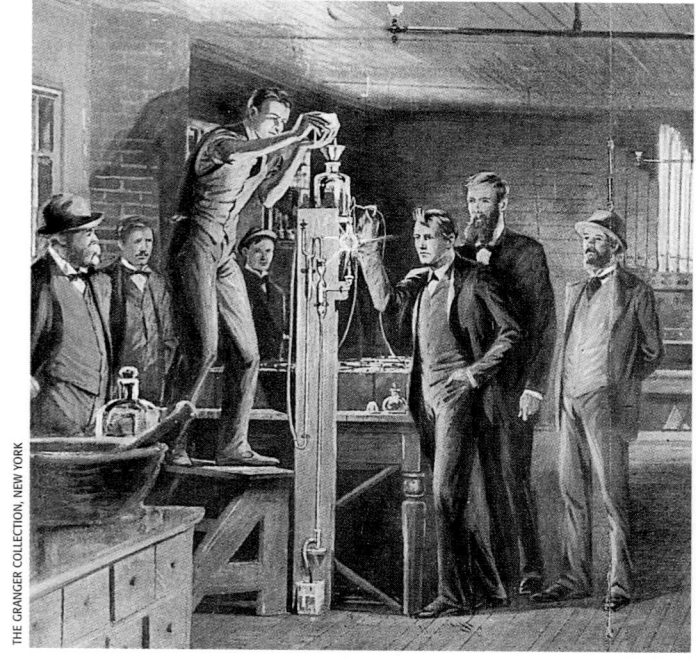

THE GRANGER COLLECTION, NEW YORK

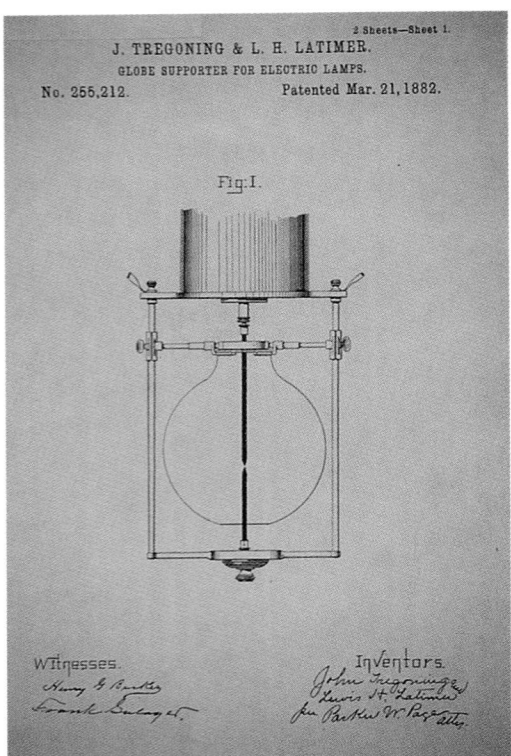

J. TREGONING & L. H. LATIMER.
GLOBE SUPPORTER FOR ELECTRIC LAMPS.
No. 255,212.   Patented Mar. 21, 1882.

2 Sheets—Sheet 1.

Fig.1.

Witnesses.

Inventors.

Lewis Latimer developed a globe supporter for the electric lightbulb in 1882.

In 1882 Edison opened one of the world's first electric power plants in New York City. Edison's New York plant served only a few buildings. Using direct current (DC) electricity the plant could only deliver electricity to the homes and offices in a very small area surrounding the plant. Despite the initial limitations, New Yorkers marveled at the new advances. One reporter from the *New York Times* explained that with electric lighting in the newspaper's offices, "it seemed almost like writing by daylight."

George Westinghouse and Nikola Tesla made additional advances beginning in the late 1880s. They developed a transformer that could transmit a high-voltage alternating current (AC) over long distances. The development of the alternating current allowed continued expansion of the use of electricity in urban households and industry.

At the 1893 World's Columbian Exposition in Chicago, Illinois, a Westinghouse-Tesla generator powered the twinkling lights outlining the major buildings at night. The electric lights enchanted visitors. They marveled at the "fairyland" and frequently referred to the illuminated exposition as the White City. To many witnesses, it symbolized a transformation of American life. Indeed, by the end of the century, electric lights had begun to replace gaslights. The availability of electrical power also made possible another major change. In many cities, horse-drawn vehicles gave way to electric streetcars.

✔ **READING CHECK:** Why did Thomas Edison open a research laboratory? How did it change American life?

SECTION 1 REVIEW

Define and explain the significance of the following terms:
Bessemer process
patent
transcontinental railroad
trunk lines
telegraph

Identify and explain the significance of the following individuals:
Edwin L. Drake
Elijah McCoy
George Westinghouse
Alexander Graham Bell
Thomas Alva Edison
Lewis Latimer

1. **Using Graphic Organizers** Copy the graphic organizer below. Use it to list and describe the various innovations that affected industry, transportation, and communications in the late 1800s.

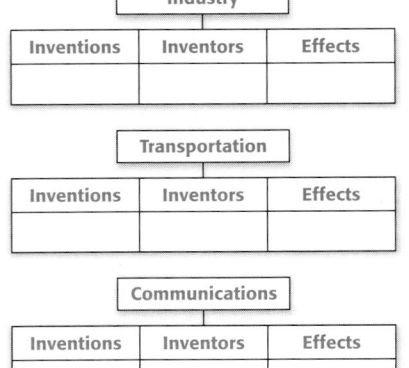

Industry		
Inventions	Inventors	Effects

Transportation		
Inventions	Inventors	Effects

Communications		
Inventions	Inventors	Effects

2. **Evaluating** How was American daily life transformed by the technological innovations of the late 1800s?

3. **Hypothesizing** Many technological advances such as the telegraph and the Wright brothers' flight attracted little public attention or respect at first. Why might these important breakthroughs not have been recognized at the time they occurred?

4. **Identifying Cause and Effect** Why did Thomas Edison establish a research laboratory, and how did it change society?

Critical Thinking

5. If you were an inventor, what would be the advantages and disadvantages of working in a laboratory like Edison's Menlo Park, rather than on your own?
   Consider:
   • aspects of working on your own
   • aspects of working in a group
   • the results that might come from both types of work

The Rise of Big Business

OBJECTIVES

Read to understand:

1. what various arguments business leaders and social critics made about the role of government in business
2. how business strategies changed during the Second Industrial Revolution
3. how entrepreneurs took advantage of changes in business organization
4. how new methods of marketing products changed American life

KEY TERMS

laissez-faire capitalism
free enterprise
communism
social Darwinism
corporation
trust
monopoly
vertical integration
horizontal integration

KEY PEOPLE

Andrew Carnegie
Horatio Alger Jr.
John D. Rockefeller
Cornelius Vanderbilt
George Pullman

Horatio Alger celebrated rugged individualism.

EYEWITNESSES TO History

66 *Eureka! We have found it. Here was something new to all of us, for none of us had ever received anything but from toil.* 99
—Andrew Carnegie

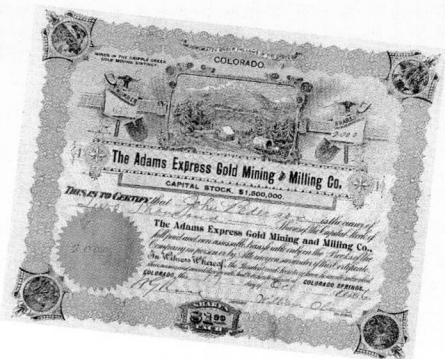

Certificate of business investment

Young Andrew Carnegie recalled his excitement after receiving his first payment of profits from investments. The rapid technological advances in industrial materials, transportation, and communications created new sources of wealth for some Americans. Foresighted business-people began to invest in these new industries, often earning large profits. Andrew Carnegie was a young man working as a private secretary to a railroad executive when he invested money he had borrowed in a company called Adams Express. Soon he began investing in the railroad and iron industries. Within a few years Carnegie's wise investments had made him a wealthy man.

A New Capitalist Spirit

Entrepreneurs, or risk-taking businesspeople, set out to gain economic wealth by building industries that took advantage of the era's new technological advances. Many of these industries made enormous profits. With the rapid increase in business ventures and wealth, new ideas began to emerge that would transform traditional business practices.

Motivated to gain wealth and better their lives, business leaders shared an American ideal of self-reliant individualism. During the Second Industrial Revolution, Horatio Alger Jr. published a popular series of stories that reflected the increasing importance placed on individualism. These novels, such as those in the 1869 *Luck and Pluck* series, were typically based on a rags-to-riches theme. In these stories poor children improve their social and financial status through hard work and self-motivation. Like the characters in Alger's stories, many American business leaders attributed their successes to their work ethic. A high regard for individualism and self-reliance led many business leaders to champion the ideal of **laissez-faire capitalism**. *Laissez-faire* means "to let people do as they choose." The theory of laissez-faire capitalism calls for no government intervention in the economy. Most business leaders believed that the economy would prosper if businesses were left free from government regulation and allowed to compete in a free market. This idea is sometimes called **free enterprise**. These entrepreneurs argued that any government regulation would reduce individuals' prosperity and their self-reliance.

Critics respond. Business leaders hoped to keep industry free of government regulation. However, some critics argued that the rapid industrialization of factory life was harmful and unjust to the working class. This view of capitalism was most forcefully argued in the mid-1800s by Karl Marx, a German philosopher. Marx proposed a political system that would remove the inequalities of wealth. He developed a political theory, later called marxism, that called for the overthrow of the capitalist economic system.

Marx argued that capitalism allowed the bourgeoisie—the people who own the means of production—to take advantage of the proletariat—the workers. From this argument, Marx suggested that a new society could be formed on principles of **communism**. This theory proposes that individual ownership of property should not be allowed. In a communist state, property and the means of production are owned by everyone in the community. The community in turn ideally provides for the needs of all the people equally without regard to social rank.

Social Darwinism. American businesspeople also responded to some of the same concerns about the working class raised by Marx. These business leaders began to embrace the newly emerging theory of **social Darwinism**. Originally proposed by English social philosopher Herbert Spencer, social Darwinism adopted the ideas of Charles Darwin's biological theory of natural selection and evolution. Social Darwinists argued that society progressed through natural competition. The "fittest" people, businesses, or nations should and would rise to positions of wealth and power. The "unfit" would fail. Following the law of the "survival of the fittest," social Darwinists believed that any attempts to help the poor or less capable actually slowed social progress. "Nature's cure for most social and political diseases is better than man's," wrote American educator and philosopher Nicholas Murray Butler.

Some religious leaders offered religious support for social Darwinism by suggesting that great wealth was a sign of Christian virtue. Baptist minister Russell H. Conwell declared, "You ought to get rich, and it is your duty to get rich. . . . To make money honestly is to preach the gospel."

✔ **READING CHECK:** What arguments did business leaders and social critics make about the role of government in business?

Charles Darwin never expected his scientific theories of biology to be applied to social issues.

The Corporation

In the late 1800s a series of changes took place in the way businesses were organized. At the close of the Civil War, businesses typically consisted of small companies owned by individuals, families, or two or more people in a partnership. These traditional business organizations proved unable to manage some of the giant new industries such as oil, railroads, or steel. Nor could these organizations raise the money needed to fund such industries. Business leaders therefore turned to another form of business organization—the **corporation**. Corporations had existed in one form or another since colonial times. In a corporation, organizers raise money by selling shares of stock, or certificates of ownership, in the company. Stockholders— those who buy the shares—receive a percentage of the corporation's profits, known as dividends.

Giving advice to a group of young men, steel baron Andrew Carnegie urged them to invest in stocks as he had. He suggested, "If any of you have saved as much as $50 or $100 I do not know any branch of business into which you cannot plunge at once." Although stockholders could earn large profits from the companies, they played little or no part in the corporation's daily operations. One corporate

Read More About It

Free Find:

Andrew Carnegie
After reading the biography of Andrew Carnegie on the **Holt Researcher** CD–ROM, write a short essay about Carnegie's values. Be sure to discuss his work ethic and philanthropy.

executive described owning shares of stock as simply representing "nothing more than good will and prospective [future] profits."

A corporation has several advantages over small businesses. First, a corporation's organizers can raise large sums of money by selling stock to many people. Second, unlike small-business owners, stockholders enjoy limited liability. In other words, they are not responsible for the corporation's debt. Finally, a corporation is a stable organization because it is not dependent on a specific owner or owners for its existence. A corporation continues to exist no matter who owns the stock. Moreover, the public ownership and trading of stock provides another source of income for entrepreneurs. For example, a former New York grocery clerk named Jay Gould later became a successful stock market manager. Gould earned an estimated $77 million just from trading railroad stock.

Corporations, however, needed more than organizational stability to deal with the economic climate of the late 1800s. Where competition was fierce, prices and profits tended to rise and fall wildly. Some corporations responded by forming trusts. In a **trust**, a group of companies turn control of their stock over to a common board of trustees. The trustees then run all of the companies as a single enterprise. This practice limits overproduction and other inefficient business practices by reducing competition in an industry. If a trust gains exclusive control of an industry, it holds a **monopoly**. With little or no competition, a company with a monopoly has almost complete control over the price and quality of a product.

✔ **READING CHECK:** How did business strategies change in the Second Industrial Revolution?

TRY YOUR STRENGTH, GENTS!

Carnegie and Steel

Steel leader Andrew Carnegie was a master at utilizing these new business strategies. Carnegie began life in humble surroundings. He was born in 1835 in the attic of a small one-story house in Dunfermline, Scotland. His father was a weaver in the textile industry. In 1848, at the age of 12, Carnegie immigrated to the United States. That same year, Carnegie began his first job, working at a cotton mill, winding thread onto bobbins, or spools, for $1.20 a week.

BIOGRAPHY
Andrew Carnegie

At age 17, Carnegie took a job as a private secretary to a railroad company superintendent. He quickly advanced to a management position. Saving money from his earnings and borrowing from others, Carnegie began to invest in stock in numerous ventures such as bridges, iron, oil, railroads, and telegraph lines. These early investments further inspired Carnegie's entrepreneurial interest and provided the capital that allowed him to invest in the steel industry.

The Religious Spirit

PHILANTHROPY AND THE GOSPEL OF WEALTH

During the late 1800s, many people began to see a relationship between religious values and earning great wealth. In fact, many supporters of free enterprise believed that accumulating great wealth was a sign of God's blessing, in spite of the sometimes ruthless business practices that might be used to gain that wealth. These supporters, nevertheless, were compelled by their religious values to believe that the power and wealth they accumulated must be used responsibly to better society. This philosophy became known as the Gospel of Wealth.

In his essay "The Gospel of Wealth," Andrew Carnegie insisted that the wealthy had a solemn obligation to use their riches for the advancement of society. In Carnegie's view the rich had been chosen to serve as "stewards of wealth."

"The man who dies . . . rich," Carnegie argued, "dies disgraced." He believed that the rich had a responsibility to give their wealth to society before their death. Like many social Darwinists, Carnegie believed that giving aid directly to the poor would increase the poor's dependency on others. The best way to help the poor, he said, was "to place within [their] reach the ladders upon which the aspiring can rise." Carnegie's "ladders" included universities and libraries. ■

Carnegie Library in Pittsburgh

Carnegie entered the iron and steel business in the early 1860s. He readily admitted that he understood little about making steel, but he did know how to run an iron business. Carnegie hired the best people in the steel industry and drove them relentlessly. He fitted his plants with the most modern machinery.

Carnegie's real success, however, lay in reducing production costs. Carnegie realized that by buying supplies in bulk and producing goods in large quantities he could lower production costs and increase profits. This principle is known as economies of scale. To control costs, Carnegie also used **vertical integration**— that is, he acquired companies that provided the materials and services upon which his enterprises depended. For example, Carnegie purchased iron and coal mines, which provided the raw materials necessary to run his steel mills. He also bought steamship lines and railroads to transport these materials. An admirer explained the great advantages of this approach.

> ❝ From the moment these crude stuffs were dug out of the earth until they flowed in a stream of liquid steel in the ladles, there was never a price, profit, or royalty paid to an outsider. ❞

Because Carnegie controlled businesses at each stage of production, he could sell steel at a much lower price than his competitors.

In 1899 Carnegie organized all of his companies into the Carnegie Steel Company. It dominated the steel industry. When Carnegie sold his company in 1901 to banker J. P. Morgan for nearly $500 million, he retired as the world's richest man. Although Carnegie gained great wealth, money was not his only motivation. Through hard work, simple living, and large philanthropic, or charitable, donations, Carnegie also sought to be viewed as a virtuous citizen. Describing his philosophy as "the Gospel of Wealth," Carnegie insisted that the rich were morally obligated to manage their wealth in a way that benefited their fellow citizens. He explained:

> ❝ This, then, is held to be the duty of the man of wealth: To set an example of modest, unostentatious [simple] living, shunning display or extravagance . . . the man of wealth thus becoming the mere trustee and agent for his poorer brethren. . . . In bestowing [giving] charity, the main consideration should be to help those who will help themselves; . . . to give those who desire to rise the aids by which they may rise. ❞

Carnegie donated more than $350 million to charity. Much of the funds were used to establish public libraries and other institutions that provide the tools for individuals to better their lives.

Rockefeller and Oil

The business career of tycoon John D. Rockefeller, one of the founders of the Standard Oil Company, followed a course similar to Andrew Carnegie's. After earning a small fortune in the wholesale food business, Rockefeller entered the growing oil-refining industry in 1863. During its early years, the oil-refining industry was composed of numerous small, fiercely competitive companies. Arguing that such competition was inefficient, Rockefeller set out to gain control of the industry.

Like Carnegie, Rockefeller used vertical integration to make his company more competitive. He acquired barrel factories, oil fields, oil-storage facilities, pipelines, and railroad tanker cars. By owning companies that contributed to each stage of oil refining, Rockefeller was able to sell his oil for a cheaper price than his competitors. His main method of expansion was called **horizontal integration**—one company's control of other companies producing the same product. Standard Oil tried to control the oil refineries it could not buy, establishing one of the nation's first trusts in the early 1880s.

To drive his competitors out of business, Rockefeller made deals with suppliers and transporters to receive cheaper supplies and freight rates. George Rice, a small oil refiner driven out of business by Rockefeller's practices, complained to the U.S. Industrial Commission in 1899.

Standard Oil. Oil towns like this one in Pennsylvania became more common as Standard Oil grew. *How did the expansion of the oil industry alter the landscape in this photograph?*

> 66 I have been driven from pillar to post, from one railway line to another, for twenty years, in the absolutely vain endeavor [wasted attempt] to get equal and just freight rates with the Standard Oil Trust, . . . but which I have been utterly unable to do. I have had to consequently shut down, with my business absolutely ruined. 99

Rice was not alone. Rockefeller forced most of his rivals to sell out. By 1880 the Standard Oil Company controlled some 90 percent of the country's petroleum-refining capacity. Despite his competitive business practices, Rockefeller, like Carnegie, gave generously to various charities. He also established a fund to support the arts, created a medical institute, and gave more than $80 million to the University of Chicago. During his lifetime, Rockefeller donated approximately $550 million to philanthropic causes.

The Railroad Giants

Andrew Carnegie and John D. Rockefeller profited hugely from technological innovations in the steel and oil-refining industries, respectively. Other entrepreneurs built large fortunes by capitalizing on the booming railroad industry.

Strategies for Success — Evaluating Historical Actions

Evaluating the actions of individuals and groups is a practice that students of history do routinely. To *evaluate* is to make a judgment about the significance, worth, or desirability of something. An evaluation of a historical action should be based on the range of choices available to the historical actor as well as on the effects the action had on an individual or society.

How to Evaluate a Historical Action

1. **Establish the context.** When you encounter an action that requires evaluation, identify the historical setting and the specific steps through which the action was completed. Make sure that you understand the assumptions and the goals of the individual or group that took the action.
2. **Determine the outcome.** Once you have established the context of the action, determine its results. Make sure that you recognize any unintended consequences or long-term effects of the action.
3. **Consider alternative courses of action.** Identify other courses of action that the individual or group could have taken. Then assess the potential advantages and disadvantages of these alternatives.

4. **Evaluate the action.** Use your analysis of the action, along with your consideration of possible alternatives, to make a judgment about its value and significance.

Applying the Strategy

Review the material in this section on John D. Rockefeller and the oil industry. As you do so, evaluate the business practices that Rockefeller and his Standard Oil Company employed.

Practicing the Strategy

Answer the following questions.
1. What were Rockefeller's assumptions and goals concerning the oil industry?
2. What business practices did Rockefeller employ through Standard Oil?
3. What were the results of Rockefeller's business practices?
4. What other courses of action could Rockefeller have taken? What do you think the results of these actions would have been?
5. What is your evaluation of Rockefeller's business practices?

Cornelius Vanderbilt's railroad investments brought him power and wealth.

THE GRANGER COLLECTION, NEW YORK

Vanderbilt. Cornelius Vanderbilt was a pioneer of the railroad industry. Prior to the Civil War, Vanderbilt operated a profitable shipping business. When the use of water traffic slowed during the war, however, he invested more in railroads. By 1869, just four years after the war's end, Vanderbilt had gained control over the New York Central Railroad and two other lines that connected the Central with New York City. He continued to add to his railroad holdings. Soon he controlled lines between Chicago, Cleveland, New York, and Toledo.

Vanderbilt extended his railroad system by purchasing smaller lines. He then combined them to make direct routes between urban centers. By providing more efficient service, Vanderbilt took advantage of the growing demand for rail transportation. At the time of his death in 1877, Vanderbilt controlled more than 4,500 miles of railroad track. His personal fortune was estimated at $100 million.

Westinghouse. George Westinghouse also made a large fortune in the railroad industry. At the age of 23, Westinghouse established the Westinghouse Air Brake Company. He hoped to capitalize on his invention, the compressed-air brake. The air brake was an important safety feature for the railroad industry. The brakes made it possible for trains to haul more cars and to travel at greater speeds.

Railroad investors were initially skeptical of the air brake. Vanderbilt condemned the invention as trying to "stop a train with wind." After several dramatic public demonstrations, however, Westinghouse's business grew. Within five years of his invention, more than 7,000 passenger cars were equipped with the compressed-air brake.

Pullman. One of the most successful railroad giants was George Pullman. He designed and manufactured railroad cars that made long-distance rail travel more comfortable. Pullman created a massive passenger-railroad-car industry. His factories built sleeping cars, dining cars, and luxurious cars for wealthy passengers. With an increasing demand for his sleeping cars, Pullman decided to build a new factory south of Chicago in 1880.

The company town of Pullman, Illinois, contained everything the company thought workers should need.

Disturbed by the poor conditions of city life, Pullman set out to create a company town. He hoped that it would encourage educated, healthy, peaceful, and virtuous workers. Pullman built a planned community next to his factory. The town offered Pullman's employees and their families clean, well-built homes, shops, a church, a library, a theater, medical and legal offices, and an athletic field. Pullman strictly controlled daily life in the company town, causing dissatisfaction to grow among many of the workers. Expressing a common feeling of the residents, economist Richard Ely proclaimed in 1884 that Pullman's town represented a "benevolent [kindly], well-wishing feudalism, which desires the happiness of the people, but in such a way as shall please the authorities."

✔ **READING CHECK:** How did entrepreneurs take advantage of changes in business organization?

Mass Marketing

Industrialists knew that using new inventions, cutting production costs, and reducing competition were not the only ways to increase profits. They also developed new methods of marketing to sell their products.

Marketing products. With the rapid growth of manufacturing, companies developed new ways of pursuading consumers to purchase their products. Brand names and packaging played important roles in promoting goods. For example, the name "Standard Oil" conveyed the idea that the company's product set the industry standard. Other companies used brightly colored packages or unique logos to set their products apart.

Companies also used advertising to promote their products. Magazines, newspapers, and roadside billboards carried advertisements urging people to buy "the Purest" soap or telephones "warranted to work *one mile*, unaffected by changes in the weather."

INTERPRETING THE VISUAL RECORD

Advertising. During the late 1800s manufacturers began to use advertisements like this one to entice customers to buy their products. *What images in the advertisement relate to the product?*

This increase in the use of advertising and brand names helped create a new, lively consumer culture in the United States. The expansion of manufacturing and mass marketing transformed the daily lives of many Americans, even those outside the large urban centers who gained access to new products.

Products such as Ruthstein steel-soled shoes and the Scotch Knocker horse collar were advertised to farmers through local newspapers, mail-order publications, and special catalogs that catered to the rural market. Mail-order companies like Montgomery Ward and Sears, Roebuck, and Co. offered a seemingly endless variety of goods. Customers selected goods from a catalog, then ordered, paid for, and received the merchandise by mail.

The department store. In cities, new types of stores that sold a variety of goods were created to cater to the demands of the urban market. Department stores carried a wide variety of products under one roof. Pioneered by business leaders such as John Wanamaker in Philadelphia, Marshall Field in Chicago, and R. H. Macy in New York City, department stores bought products in bulk and could therefore offer low prices to consumers.

Department stores became the special domain of women, both as places to work and as places to shop. Wanting to create a homelike and welcoming atmosphere in their stores, department-store owners hired young women to work as clerks. Department-store advertisements also targeted women as customers.

Like department stores, chain stores—stores with branches in many cities—bought goods in large quantities. They then passed on their savings to customers. Perhaps the most famous chain store was founded by Frank W. Woolworth in 1879. By 1900 Woolworth had a network of 59 stores.

INTERPRETING THE VISUAL RECORD

Marketing. Mail-order companies offered goods such as clothing, farm equipment, furniture, and musical instruments. *What ideas does this catalog convey?*

✔ **READING CHECK:** How did new methods of marketing products change American life?

SECTION 2 REVIEW

Define and explain the significance of the following terms:
laissez-faire capitalism
free enterprise
communism
social Darwinism
corporation
trust
monopoly
vertical integration
horizontal integration

Identify and explain the significance of the following individuals:
Andrew Carnegie
Horatio Alger Jr.
John D. Rockefeller
Cornelius Vanderbilt
George Pullman

1. **Using Graphic Organizers** Copy the web below. Use it to describe the major entrepreneurs of the late 1800s, what business each pursued, and how they revolutionized their industries.

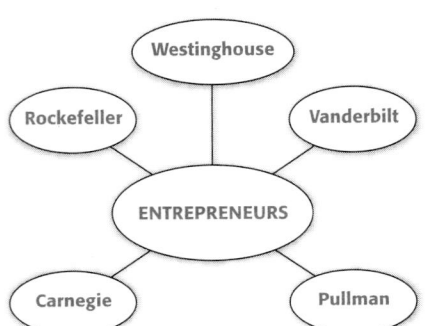

2. **Recognizing Point of View** How did business leaders and social critics view government's role in business differently?
3. **Hypothesizing** How do you think the theory of social Darwinism shaped the business practices of Andrew Carnegie and John D. Rockefeller?
4. **Assessing Consequences** In what ways did new marketing practices change life in the United States?

Critical Thinking

5. Did the business developments of the late 1800s create opportunities or limit them? Explain your answer.
   Consider:
   • how business opportunities were created
   • how business opportunities were limited
   • whether businesses more often created new opportunities or limited them

SECTION 3
Labor Strives to Organize

OBJECTIVES

Read to understand:

1. why some Americans wanted trusts to be banned, and how the government responded
2. what types of working conditions laborers faced in the new age of rapid industrialization
3. how the Knights of Labor attempted to address the needs of many workers
4. how businesses reacted to strikes in the late 1800s, and how this affected unions

KEY TERMS

Sherman Antitrust Act
Knights of Labor
Great Upheaval
Haymarket Riot
anarchists
American Federation of Labor

KEY PEOPLE

Terence V. Powderly
Mary Harris Jones
Eugene V. Debs

KEY PLACES

Haymarket Square
Homestead
Pullman

EYEWITNESSES TO History

66 *It is true that wealth has been greatly increased . . . but these gains are not general. In them the lowest class do not share. . . . This association of poverty with progress is the great enigma [mystery] of our times.* **99**

—Henry George

American economist Henry George

Henry George offered this critical look at American life during the 1870s in his book *Progress and Poverty*. Although a few entrepreneurs earned huge profits from rapid industrialization, many more Americans experienced severe poverty and poor working conditions. Indeed, industrial life was often terribly harsh for the men, women, and children who worked in the factories. Describing her first impression of Kansas City in 1888, Kate Richards O'Hare later recalled, "The poverty, the misery, the want, the wan-faced [pale] women and hunger pinched children, . . . the sordid [dirty], grinding, pinching poverty of the workless workers . . . will always stay with me."

Government and Business

The U.S. government's policies concerning business practices most often benefited the industrialists, not the workers. Supporters of laissez-faire capitalism claimed to oppose government interference in business activities. However these same business leaders welcomed government assistance when it helped them. By placing high tariffs on imports, the U.S. government allowed American businesses to dominate the domestic market. In 1875, for example, Congress raised tariff rates to make imported steel considerably more expensive than domestic steel.

At the same time, the government did little to regulate business practices, despite growing pressure from the general public. As Carnegie Steel, Standard Oil, and other large corporations grew in power, many Americans demanded that trusts be outlawed. These critics reasoned that without competition, these large monopolies would have no incentive to maintain the quality of their goods or keep prices low. Congress responded in 1890 by passing the **Sherman Antitrust Act**, which outlawed all monopolies and trusts that restrained trade. However, the law failed to define what constituted a monopoly or trust and thus proved difficult to enforce.

While serving the interests of corporations, the U.S. government offered little assistance to American industrial workers. Government leaders were often distracted by issues of political corruption and paid little attention to the widening gulf between the wealthy and the poor. By 1890 just 10 percent of the population controlled close to 75 percent of the nation's wealth. At the same time, nearly 50 percent of unskilled industrial workers in the United States earned less than

Some Americans saw the monopoly as a giant octopus.

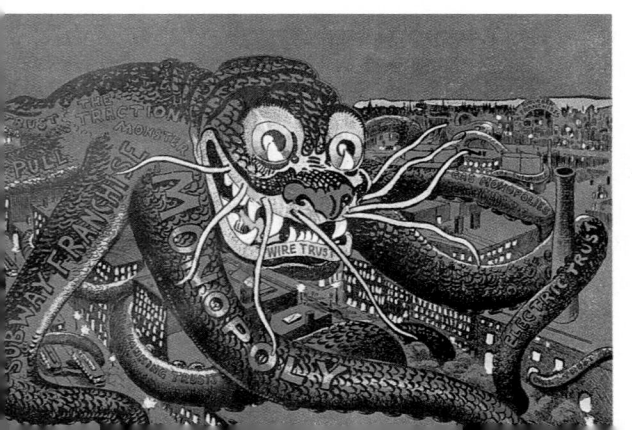

THE SECOND INDUSTRIAL REVOLUTION **481**

$500 per year. By providing a cheap source of labor, these workers were essential to the nation's industrialization.

✔ **READING CHECK:** Why did some Americans demand that trusts be made illegal? How did the federal government respond?

The New Working Class

The demand for labor soared under the new industrial order. These jobs were filled largely by the flood of immigrants who came to the United States during the late 1800s. A working-class newspaper, *Workingman's Advocate,* explained that immigrants "viewed a sojourn [temporary stay] in America as a means to acquire capital with which to purchase land, provide dowries for their daughters, and assist their sons to enter business." By 1900 about one third of the country's industrial workers were foreign-born.

African Americans. These immigrant workers were joined by hundreds of thousands of rural Americans who moved to the cities in search of jobs. Among this group were thousands of African Americans from the South who moved north to find work. In Chicago, for example, by 1900 more than 80 percent of the city's African American workers had been born in states south of Illinois.

Some northern and midwestern industries offered working opportunities to African Americans. The vast majority of southern industries, however, barred African Americans from holding factory jobs. Nearly all southern textile workers were native-born whites. Cigar factories did employ some African Americans—women cleaned and sorted tobacco leaves, men made the cigars—but their numbers were few. In 1891 just 7,400 black southerners held industrial jobs.

Many African Americans from the South hoped to find improved conditions in the North, but industrial employment remained out of reach for most. The best jobs still went to native-born white workers or to immigrants. Even skilled African American male laborers generally found themselves confined to the dirtiest or most dangerous work or to such service-related jobs as gardening.

Women and children. African American women in northern cities competed with poor immigrant women for domestic jobs and unskilled factory work. Most women worked because their families needed the income. As a state official in Massachusetts noted, "A family of workers can always live well, but the man with a family of small children to support, unless his wife works also, has a small chance of living properly." The number of female workers doubled between 1870 and 1890. By 1900 women accounted for about 18 percent of the labor force—with some 5 million workers.

The number of children in the workforce doubled during this period for the same reason. By 1890 close to 20 percent of American children between ages 10 and 15—some 1.5 million in all—worked for wages. In the textile mills of North Carolina, one

INTERPRETING THE VISUAL RECORD

Workers. While southern industries often barred African Americans from holding factory jobs, African American workers occasionally found employment opportunities in northern and midwestern industries. *In what type of industry do you think these African American women might be employed?*

in every four workers was younger than 16 years old. The ratio was much lower in Massachusetts mills—1 in 20.

Across the nation, countless boys and girls worked in garment factories or at home, making clothing or other items by the piece. Others labored in the nation's canneries, mines, and shoe factories. Pauline Newman began working at a garment factory in New York in 1901 while still a child. Describing her experiences, she recalled, "It wasn't heavy work, but it was monotonous, because you did the same thing from seven-thirty in the morning till nine at night."

Working Conditions

Children in the labor force often faced terrible conditions. In some textile mills, for instance, children worked 12-hour shifts—often at night—for pennies a day. Low wages and long hours affected all industrial workers, however, regardless of their age, sex, or race. Conditions were particularly difficult for unskilled workers. Most unskilled white male laborers worked at least 10 hours a day, six days a week, for less than $10 a week. Many African American, Asian American, and Mexican American men worked the same number of hours for even lower wages. Furthermore, employers made few allowances for women and children, expecting them to work the same number of hours as men for sometimes as little as half the pay.

Such long hours left workers exhausted at the end of the day. This fatigue made already unsafe working conditions even more dangerous. In 1881 alone, some 30,000 railroad workers were killed or injured on the job. Most employers felt no responsibility for work-related deaths and injuries. They made little effort to improve workplace safety.

Many workers endured hardships that extended beyond the factory. Some employers sought to increase their control over their workers. They built company towns, where the company owned the workers' housing and the retail businesses they used. Residents of company towns usually received their wages in scrip. This was paper money that could be used only to pay rent to the company or to buy goods at company stores. Prices at company stores were usually much higher than at regular stores. Workers often spent whole paychecks on necessities like food and clothing.

✔ **READING CHECK:** What types of working conditions did laborers face in the new age of industrialization?

INTERPRETING THE VISUAL RECORD

Working conditions. Many children working in factories worked long hours in unsafe working conditions. *What aspects of this child's working conditions might be dangerous?*

THROUGH OTHERS' EYES

Austrian View of U.S. Workers

In 1871 Austrian diplomat Joseph Alexander, Graf von Hübner, visited the United States. Von Hübner was impressed by the opportunities Americans enjoyed in their increasingly industrialized society. He noted, however, that fierce competition in business took its toll on working people.

❝ In the New World man is born to conquer. Life is a perpetual struggle, . . . a race in the open field across terrible obstacles, with the prospect of enormous rewards for reaching the goal. The American cannot keep his arms folded. He must embark on something, and once embarked he must go on and on forever; for if he stops, those who follow him would crush him under their feet. His life is one long campaign, a succession of never-ending fights, marches, and countermarches.

In such a militant existence, what place is left for the sweetness, the repose [rest], the intimacy of home or its joys? Is he happy? Judging by his tired, sad, exhausted, anxious, and often delicate and unhealthy appearance, one would be inclined to doubt it. Such an excess of uninterrupted labor cannot be good for any man. ❞

The Knights of Labor

As conditions grew worse, workers called for change. Alone they could do little. If they banded together, they reasoned, the factory owners and politicians might listen to their demands.

Led by Uriah Stephens, nine Philadelphia garment workers founded the **Knights of Labor**, one of the earliest national unions, in 1869. It remained largely a white male organization until 1879, when Terence V. Powderly, an Irish Catholic machinist and the mayor of Scranton, Pennsylvania, became its leader. Under his leadership the Knights' membership expanded rapidly.

Powderly wanted the Knights of Labor to attract workers who were often excluded from other unions. He therefore opened the union to both skilled and unskilled laborers. Powderly also welcomed thousands of women into the union's ranks. A number of women, including Mary Harris Jones, played prominent roles in the Knights of Labor.

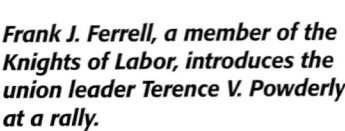
BIOGRAPHY
Mary Harris Jones

Born in Cork, Ireland, in 1830, Mary Harris came to the United States as a young child. She married George Jones, a union supporter, in 1861. Six years later, after her husband and four children died in a yellow fever epidemic, she began to devote herself to the labor movement. At the invitation of striking workers, Jones became an organizer for the Knights of Labor in the 1870s. Declaring that her place was "wherever there is a fight," she organized strikes, marches, and demonstrations. In 1912 Jones explained to a reporter the reasons behind her activism.

> 66 My life work has been to try to educate the worker to a sense of the wrongs he has had to suffer, and does suffer—and to stir up the oppressed to a point of getting off their knees and demanding that which I believe to be rightfully theirs. 99

Jones's ambitious drive to educate and organize laborers was so effective that some opponents called her "the most dangerous woman in America." Because she viewed her actions as more motherly than radical, most people called her Mother Jones. Jones was sentenced to 20 years in jail for her part in a 1912 West Virginia strike, but a public outcry caused the governor of the state to free her. Mother Jones continued fighting for the rights of America's working people until her death in 1930. She was 100 years old.

Although the Knights of Labor offered membership to female workers, Powderly did not encourage African Americans to join the union until 1883. By the mid-1880s the Knights claimed some 60,000 black members. African American delegate Frank Ferrell spoke at the Knights' 1886 national convention in Richmond, Virginia. He told the crowd, "One of the objects of our Order is the abolition of these distinctions which are maintained by creed or color."

Read More About It

Free Find:
Mother Jones
After reading the biography of Mary Harris Jones on the **Holt Researcher** CD–ROM, write a short speech that she might have given to workers that draws upon her life experiences.

Frank J. Ferrell, a member of the Knights of Labor, introduces the union leader Terence V. Powderly at a rally.

THE GRANGER COLLECTION, NEW YORK

Not all African American Knights, however, agreed with this assessment. "The white Knights of Labor prevent me from getting employment because I am a colored man," complained a North Carolina mason, "although I belong to the same organization." Still, the Knights did more than other early unions to try to meet the needs of African American workers. The Knights were not equality-minded when it came to everyone, however. Powderly, like many working-class Americans, actively opposed Chinese workers, claiming they stole jobs from white Americans.

Powderly led the Knights of Labor for 15 years. Under his leadership, the union fought for temperance, the eight-hour workday, equal pay for equal work, and an end to child labor. By 1886 the Knights boasted a membership of more than 700,000.

✔ **READING CHECK:** In what ways did the Knights of Labor attempt to address the needs of many workers?

The Great Upheaval

The Knights of Labor owed its phenomenal growth partly to the great railroad strike of 1877. The union also grew after a successful strike that the Knights had launched against railroad tycoon Jay Gould in 1884. Both strikes made workers more willing to press for the better working conditions being championed by the Knights. The union enjoyed immense popularity. However, in 1886 the nation experienced a year of intense strikes and violent labor confrontations that became known as the **Great Upheaval**.

By 1886, American workers were ready for action. An economic depression in the early 1880s had led to massive wage cuts. Workers demanded relief. When negotiations with management failed, many workers took direct action. By the end of 1886 some 1,500 strikes involving more than 400,000 workers had swept the nation. Many of these strikes turned violent, as angry strikers clashed head-on with aggressive employers and police officers. Perhaps the most notorious of these confrontations was the **Haymarket Riot**.

Then and Now

Labor Unions

Labor unions' membership and organization have changed over the years. Their goals today, however, are not so different from earlier groups. Despite a gradual decline in membership, unions are still involved in American life.

Teamsters picketing during the UPS strike

They continue to have an impact on working conditions. Several strikes in recent years have attracted much media attention.

In 1997 about 185,000 members of the Teamsters' union struck against United Parcel Service (UPS) over pensions and the increasing use of part-time laborers. The 15-day strike caused delays in shipping for many businesses. However, during the strike, the union received a great deal of support. One Gallup Poll reported that 55 percent of the public approved of the strike. Many Americans shared the concerns of the strikers. As one labor expert suggested, "What's on the bargaining table gets discussed at the dinner table, too." The strikers' efforts resulted in additional full-time jobs. In 1998 the United Auto Workers (UAW) union also received public support. That year it launched a strike against General Motors to protest both the loss of jobs to foreign factories and unsafe working conditions. However, the UAW strikers' gains were not as decisive as those of the Teamsters in the UPS strike.

The Haymarket Riot. The seeds for the Haymarket Riot were sown when some 40,000 Chicago workers joined a strike against the McCormick Harvesting Machine Company. On May 1, 1886, they struck to demand an eight-hour workday. Although local craft unions launched the strike, it soon fell under the leadership of a group of political radicals and **anarchists**. These anarchists were people who oppose all forms of government. On May 3 a confrontation between the police and the strikers left two strikers dead.

In protest, strikers called a meeting for the next day in Chicago's Haymarket Square. Peaceful and small, the rally was about to break up when nearly 200 police officers arrived. Suddenly, a bomb exploded in the midst of the police, who responded with gunfire. When the smoke cleared, some 70 officers lay wounded. Seven police

This poster encouraged workers to rally at Haymarket Square.

officers and one civilian were dead. The police arrested eight well-known anarchists—only one of whom had been present—charging them with conspiracy. All eight were found guilty of incitement to murder. Four were hanged.

Worker activism declines. Despite the early wave of protests and strikes, worker activism actually decreased by the close of the year. Encouraged by the Haymarket convictions, employers struck back at the unions. Employers drew up blacklists—lists of union supporters—that they shared with one another. Blacklisted workers found it almost impossible to get jobs. Many employers also forced job applicants to sign agreements—called yellow-dog contracts by the workers—promising not to join unions. When these measures failed and workers struck anyway, many companies instituted lockouts. They barred workers from their plants, and brought in nonunion strikebreakers. Many of these strikebreakers were African Americans or others who felt abandoned by the unions. As labor suffered repeated defeats, the tide of public sentiment turned against workers. Union membership shrank.

Alarmed by the violence of the Great Upheaval and by the response of the employers, many skilled workers broke ranks with the unskilled laborers. They joined the **American Federation of Labor** (AFL), a new union founded by Samuel Gompers in 1886. The AFL organized independent craft unions into a group that worked to advance the interests of skilled workers.

Major Labor Strikes, 1870–1900

Learning from Maps Workers went on strike to improve wages and working conditions. Many strikes cost lives and accomplished little for the workers.

? PLACE Which state had no strikes or riots from 1870 to 1900?

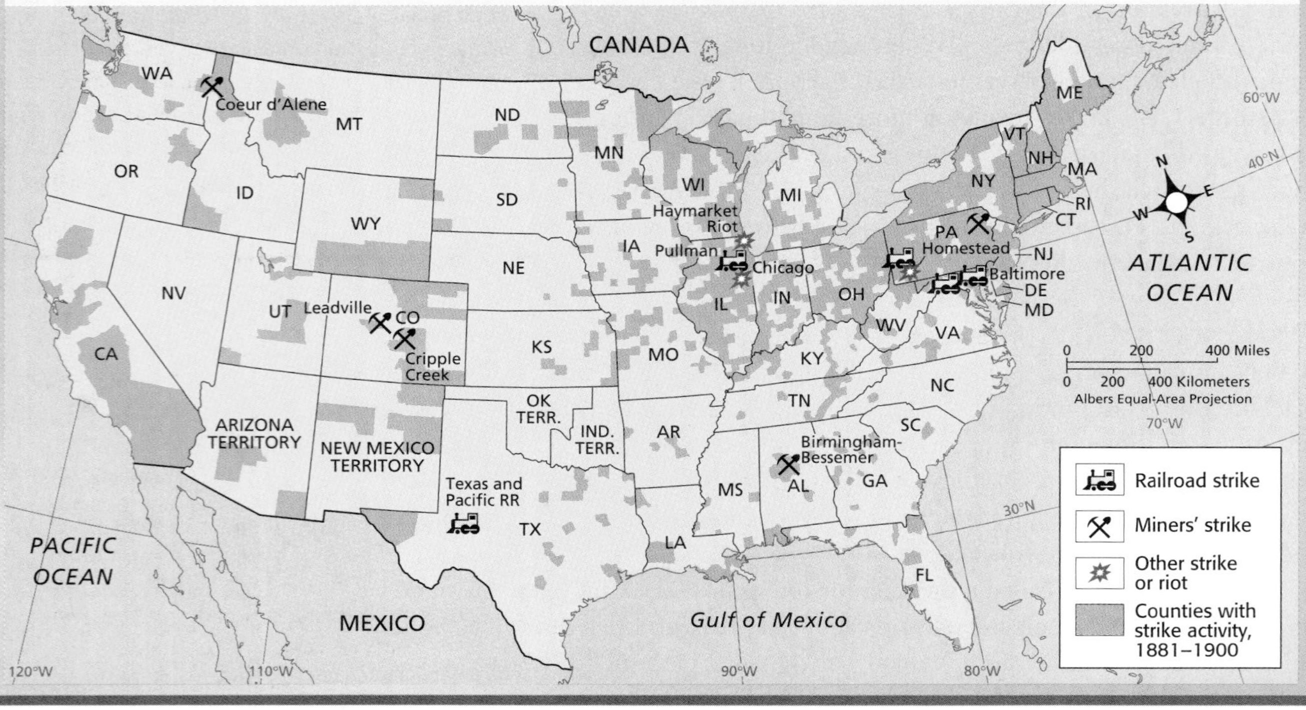

Railroad strike	
Miners' strike	
Other strike or riot	
Counties with strike activity, 1881–1900	

Map labels: CANADA; WA; Coeur d'Alene; MT; OR; ID; ND; MN; WI; MI; ME; VT; NH; MA; NY; RI; CT; PA; Homestead; NJ; Haymarket Riot; Pullman; Chicago; IA; IN; OH; WV; VA; DE; MD; ATLANTIC OCEAN; SD; WY; NV; UT; Leadville; CO; Cripple Creek; NE; KS; MO; KY; NC; TN; SC; CA; ARIZONA TERRITORY; NEW MEXICO TERRITORY; OK. TERR.; IND. TERR.; AR; MS; AL; Birmingham-Bessemer; GA; Texas and Pacific RR; TX; LA; FL; PACIFIC OCEAN; MEXICO; Gulf of Mexico; Baltimore; 200 400 Miles; 200 400 Kilometers; Albers Equal-Area Projection

The Homestead and Pullman Strikes

Industrial unrest broke out again in 1892 at Andrew Carnegie's Homestead Steel Works in Homestead, Pennsylvania. In June, workers went on strike to protest a wage cut. Managers responded by instituting a lockout and hiring some 300 guards to protect the plant. A violent clash between strikers and the guards in early July resulted in 16 deaths.

In June 1894, workers at the Pullman sleeping-car factory in Pullman, Illinois, went on strike. George Pullman had cut wages but refused to lower rents or prices at the stores in his company town. As head of the American Railway Union (ARU), Eugene V. Debs supported the Pullman strikers. They urged other union members to refuse to work or ride on all trains that included Pullman cars. Debs proclaimed:

> **66** The struggle . . . has developed into a contest between the producing classes and the money power of the country. . . . Workingmen are entitled to a just proportion of the proceeds of their labor. **99**

In support of the strikers, railroad workers brought rail traffic to a halt throughout the Midwest. The railroad companies quickly turned to the federal government for help. The government ordered an end to the ARU strike, claiming that the strikers were committing a federal offense by preventing the delivery of U.S. mail. When ARU officials ignored the order, they were jailed.

Meanwhile, President Grover Cleveland ordered federal troops into Pullman in July. The troops helped to restore normal factory operations. In the process, the Pullman strike had been broken and the ARU destroyed.

✔ **READING CHECK:** How did businesses react to the strikes in the late 1800s? How did this affect unions?

THE GRANGER COLLECTION, NEW YORK

INTERPRETING THE VISUAL RECORD
Homestead Strike. After the violent confrontation between strikers and some 300 hired guards at the Homestead Steel Works, violence spread to other plants. *How does this image convey the tension caused by these strikes?*

SECTION ③ REVIEW

Define and explain the significance of the following terms:
Sherman Antitrust Act
Knights of Labor
Great Upheaval
Haymarket Riot
anarchists
American Federation of Labor

Identify and explain the significance of the following individuals:
Terence V. Powderly
Mary Harris Jones
Eugene V. Debs

Locate and explain the importance of the following places:
Haymarket Square
Homestead
Pullman

1. **Using Graphic Organizers** Copy the graphic organizer below. Use it to explain what labor unions hoped to accomplish with strikes and what effects the strikes actually had.

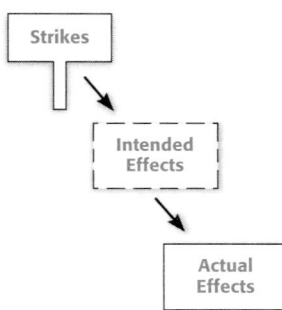

Strikes

Intended Effects

Actual Effects

2. **Recognizing Point of View** Why did some Americans oppose trusts? How did the government respond to their concerns?
3. **Using Historical Imagination** Imagine that you are an industrial laborer in the United States during the late 1800s. Describe your working conditions.
4. **Analyzing** How did union organizers such as Terence Powderly attempt to represent diverse groups of workers?

Critical Thinking

5. Why did some union workers participate in strikes despite the potential of danger?
   Consider:
   • the violence that occurred during some strikes
   • the grievances union workers had
   • what they hoped to gain by striking

CHAPTER 15

Review

Creating a Time Line

Copy the time line below onto a sheet of paper. Complete the time line by filling in the events and dates from the chapter that you think were most significant. Pick three events and explain why you think they were significant.

| 1865 | 1880 | 1895 | 1910 |

Writing a Summary

Using the Reading Checks as a guide, write an overview of the events in the chapter.

Identifying People and Ideas

Identify the following terms or individuals and explain their significance.

1. Bessemer process
2. Elijah McCoy
3. telegraph
4. Thomas Edison
5. Andrew Carnegie
6. social Darwinism
7. trust
8. monopoly
9. Mary Harris Jones
10. Great Upheaval

Understanding Main Ideas

SECTION 1
1. How did innovations in the transportation and communications industries affect business practices?

SECTION 2
2. How did laissez-faire capitalism and marxism interpret the role of government in business differently?

SECTION 3
3. Describe the working conditions laborers faced during the late 1800s.

Reviewing Themes

1. **Economic Development** What impact did new technology have on the nation's economy?

2. **Technology and Society** How did technological developments change Americans' daily lives in the late 1800s?
3. **Democratic Values** Why did unions only partially succeed in ensuring the rights of working people?

Thinking Critically

1. **Synthesizing** Describe how the steel, railroad, and telegraph industries were interconnected.
2. **Taking a Stand** What do you think was the single most important invention of the late 1800s? Why?
3. **Identifying Values** How did the business practices of some industrialists contradict their philanthropic values?
4. **Distinguishing Fact from Opinion** Read the following statement from an 1882 advertisement for an "electric corset." Then identify which words or phrases represent opinions. "A wonderful invention for ladies who desire vigorous health and a graceful figure. They always do good, cannot harm."
5. **Hypothesizing** What might have happened to unions if violence involving strikers had not occurred in the late 1800s?

Writing About History

Writing to Create Using a business leader or an industrial factory worker as a main character, create an outline for a short story. Use the graphic organizer below to help you organize your story.

Setting:
Main Character:
Secondary Characters:
Conflict:
Plot:
Resolution:

Strategies for Success

Review the **Strategies for Success** on *Evaluating Historical Actions.* Then reread the material in Section 3 on the Pullman strike and answer the following questions.

1. Why did workers at the Pullman sleeping-car factory in Chicago go on strike? How did the strike spread to other unionized railroad workers?
2. How did the railroad companies and federal government respond to the strike?
3. What were the ultimate results of each group's actions?
4. What other courses of action could each group have taken during the strike? What do you think the results of these actions would have been?
5. What is your evaluation of the actions that each group took during the strike?
6. What conclusions can you draw concerning the justifications each group had for its actions?

Linking History and Geography

Study the map below. Considering the location of most industries in the late 1800s, what generalizations can be made about the relationship between geography and industrialization? Explain why these trends might have occurred.

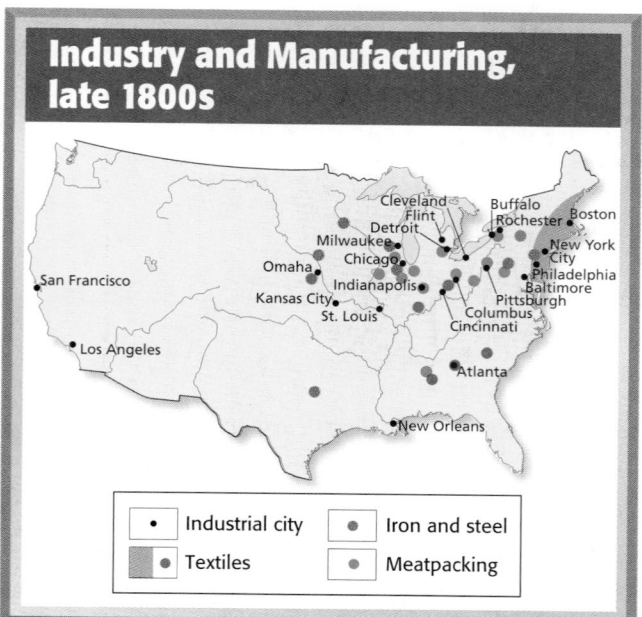

Industry and Manufacturing, late 1800s

Legend	
• Industrial city	Iron and steel
Textiles	Meatpacking

internet connect

TOPIC: Thomas Edison
GO TO: go.hrw.com
KEYWORD: SD1 Edison

Accessing the Internet through the HRW Web site, research the life of Thomas Alva Edison and the inventions he and his research team developed at the Menlo Park laboratory. Then choose an invention and write a description of its function and its social impact.

BUILDING YOUR PORTFOLIO

Complete one or all of the following projects independently or cooperatively.

1 Democratic Values

The First Real Pullman Sleeping Car – 1865

Imagine that you are an employee at Pullman's sleeping-car factory and live in his company town. **Create a list of grievances** that you and your fellow workers want addressed. In order to rally support for your cause, compose a slogan or song to encourage your fellow workers.

2 Technology and Society

Imagine that you are a land speculator attempting to develop a rural area. **Outline a plan** to use new technologies such as the telephone, electric lighting, and innovations in transportation to attract residents and businesses.

3 Economic Development

Imagine that you are the executive of a small but rapidly growing oil, steel, or railroad company. You are about to make a speech to your stockholders about the long-range plans of your company. **Make a visual chart** presenting your plans for helping the company grow. Include informative diagrams to illustrate your strategy.

1865–1910

The Transformation of American Society

Edwin Booth

The New York World

1868
Business and Finance
The first professional training schools for pharmacy and architecture are established.

1869
The Arts
Romeo and Juliet opens in New York, starring the popular actor Edwin Booth.

1876
The Arts
Mark Twain publishes *The Adventures of Tom Sawyer.*

1883
Business and Finance
Joseph Pulitzer purchases the *New York World,* a daily newspaper.

1865

1870

1875

1880

1885

1865
World Events
The Salvation Army is founded in London by religious revivalist William Booth.

1869
Daily Life
Aaron Champion organizes the first professional baseball team, the Cincinnati Red Stockings.

1876
Science and Technology
British inventors introduce the first bicycle to the United States at the Centennial Exposition in Philadelphia.

1885
Science and Technology
William Le Baron Jenney constructs the Home Insurance Co. Building in Chicago.

Cincinnati Red Stockings professional baseball team in 1869

Bicycle advertisement from the 1800s

Before You Read

Build on What You Know

During the late 1800s many innovative thinkers made significant scientific discoveries, inventions, and advances in technology. These breakthroughs, along with developments in American business practices, launched a new age of industrialization. In this chapter you will learn about the impact of new immigrants on these industries and on American life. Immigration and industrialization led to rapid growth in U.S. cities. This growth generated a series of broad transformations in the daily lives of nearly all Americans.

Ellis Island immigration station

Phoebus Theodore Levene

1909
Science and Technology
Discoveries by Russian American chemist Phoebus Theodore Levene lead to the identification of RNA and eventually DNA.

1892
Politics
The U.S. Bureau of Immigration opens a processing station on Ellis Island.

1899
Daily Life
Dankmar Adler and Louis Sullivan design the Carson Pirie Scott & Co. store in Chicago.

1903
Daily Life
The first World Series is played between the Pittsburgh Pirates and the Boston Red Sox.

| **1890** | **1895** | **1900** | **1905** | **1910** |

1896
The Arts
Charles M. Sheldon's best-selling novel, *In His Steps,* is published.

1899
The Arts
Scott Joplin's "Maple Leaf Rag" becomes an instant commercial success and a ragtime classic.

1905
The Arts
Edith Wharton publishes *The House of Mirth.*

1891
Daily Life
Dr. James Naismith invents the game of basketball.

1897
Daily Life
Steeplechase amusement park opens on Coney Island, New York.

1905
Daily Life
In one season of intercollegiate football, 18 student athletes die and 154 are seriously injured.

"Maple Leaf Rag" sheet music

Think About Themes

Themes Journal

Decide whether you agree or disagree with the following statements. Note why in your journal.

Cultural Diversity Mass immigration introduces new cultural values and ways of life to society.

Technology and Society New technological developments revolutionize life for Americans of all social and economic backgrounds.

Democratic Values Public institutions such as schools attempt to better the lives of all Americans.

The New Immigrants

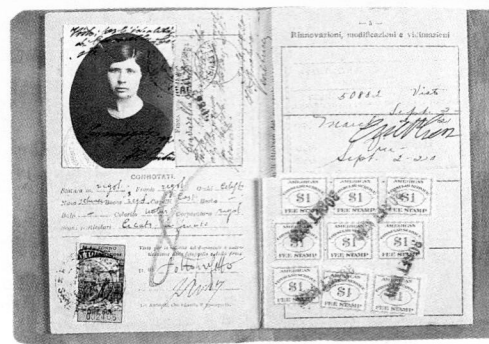

Immigrant passport

OBJECTIVES

Read to understand:

1. how immigration changed during the late 1800s
2. what challenges immigrants faced as they settled in the United States
3. where new immigrants found assistance
4. why nativists opposed new immigration

KEY TERMS

old immigrants
new immigrants
steerage
benevolent societies
Chinese Exclusion Act
Immigration Restriction League

KEY PEOPLE

Dennis Kearney
Grover Cleveland

EYEWITNESSES TO History

❝ *All of a sudden, we heard a big commotion and we came to America and everybody started yelling—they see the Statue of Liberty. . . . I remember my father putting his arms around my mother and the two of them standing and crying and my father said to my mother, 'You're in America now. You have nothing to be afraid of.'* ❞
—**Esther Gidiwicz**

Esther Gidiwicz and her mother immigrated to New York from Romania in 1905. Like many immigrants, Esther already had family members and friends in the United States, including her father. These friends provided a network of support for her. While urban life in New York for immigrants was frighteningly new and hectic, many immigrants settled in neighborhoods where residents often spoke their native language and provided a village-like community. Esther described her mother's first experience shopping in the United States. "The butcher was very nice to her, and she was so happy that they spoke to her. They spoke in her language."

The Lure of America

Esther Gidiwicz was just one of the millions of immigrants who came to the United States in search of opportunity and a better life. These hopes brought a new wave of immigrants to the United States during the late 1800s.

A new wave of immigrants. From 1800 to 1880, more than 10 million immigrants came to the United States. Often called the **old immigrants**, many of them were Protestants from northwestern Europe. Then, a new wave of immigration swept over the United States. Between 1891 and 1910, some 12 million immigrants arrived on U.S. shores. The increase was so great that by the early 1900s, about 60 percent of the people living in the nation's 12 largest cities were either foreign-born or had foreign-born parents.

About 70 percent of these **new immigrants** were from southern or eastern Europe. Among the many nationalities were Czech, Greek, Hungarian, Italian, Polish, Russian, and Slovak. Most were Catholic, Greek Orthodox, or Jewish. Arabs, Armenians, Chinese, French Canadians, and Japanese also arrived by the thousands.

Like the old immigrants, many new immigrants came to the United States to escape poverty or persecution. Most of the Armenian and Jewish families fled their homelands to escape religious or political persecution. Most of the Italian and Slavic immigrants were men seeking economic opportunities in the United States that were scarce in their home countries. Many made enough money in the United States to return home and buy land. Others, however, put down roots and stayed.

This family of immigrants arrived in New York in 1905.

Carla Martinelli's father left a poor northern Italian village for the United States. "My *papà mia* was a barber. He went to America twice, back and forth," she recalled. "I was young. He went to get work. Make money." Carla's reasons for immigrating were more complicated. She explained:

66 When I was sixteen, I was supposed to marry a man in Italy, but I didn't want him. My mama tell me, 'Either you marry this guy or you go to America.' But I told her, 'I don't like him.' She say, 'Then you go to America.' That's why I came to America. There was nothing in Italy, nothing in Italy. That's why we came. To find work, because Italy didn't have no work. Mama used to say, 'America is rich, America is rich.' 99

The journey. Many immigrants learned of the opportunities available in the United States from railroad and steamship company promoters. These companies painted a tempting—and often false—picture of the United States as a land of unlimited opportunity. Some railroad companies exaggerated the availability of employment opportunities. The steamship lines also charged low fares to attract passengers.

Most of the millions who yielded to these appeals found the journey difficult and dangerous. The ocean voyage was no pleasure trip for those traveling in the poorest accommodations, called **steerage**. Traveling in steerage, immigrants resided below deck on the ship's lower levels near the steering mechanisms. The quarters were cramped, with no privacy and little ventilation. Despite these harsh conditions, many immigrants clung to the hope for a better life in the United States.

✔ **READING CHECK:** How did immigration change during the late 1800s?

Read More About It

Free Find:
Immigrant Voices
After reading the selection of immigrant stories on the **Holt Researcher** CD–ROM, write your own story about what you might have experienced as an immigrant coming to the United States.

Arriving in America

Millions of newcomers in the late 1800s first set foot on U.S. soil on Ellis Island in New York Harbor or Angel Island in San Francisco Bay. Both islands served as immigration stations during this period.

Ellis Island opened in 1892 to receive record numbers of European immigrants. Upon their arrival, many immigrants caught their first glimpse of the Statue of Liberty, a symbol of hope for many. As one immigrant explained, "All of us [immigrants] . . . clustered on the foredeck . . . and looked with wonder on this miraculous land of our dreams."

All newcomers who passed through Ellis Island were subjected to a physical exam. Those with contagious diseases, mental disorders, or serious health problems like tuberculosis were deported. Those who passed the physicals entered a maze of crowded aisles where inspectors questioned them about their background, job skills, and relatives. Those with criminal records, or without the means to support themselves, were sent back. The vast majority were allowed to stay.

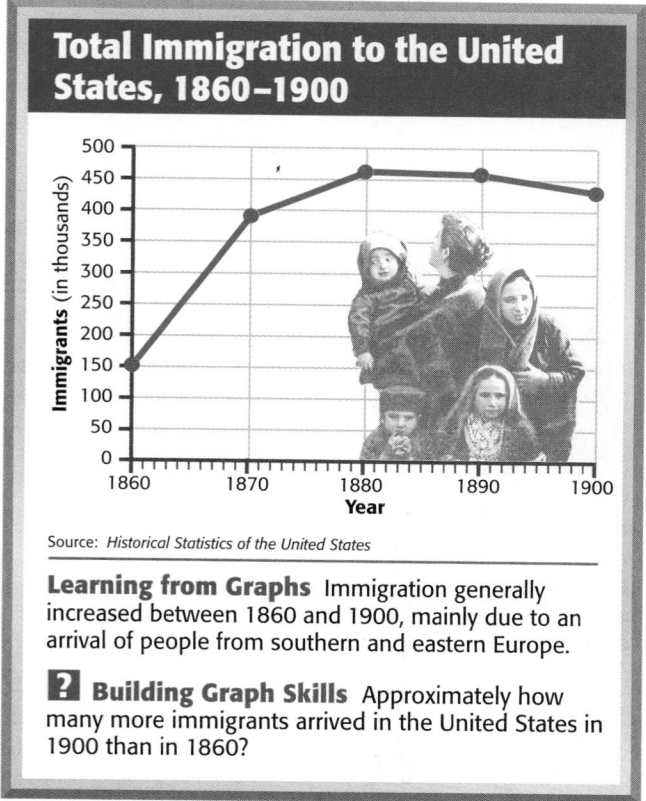

Total Immigration to the United States, 1860–1900

Source: *Historical Statistics of the United States*

Learning from Graphs Immigration generally increased between 1860 and 1900, mainly due to an arrival of people from southern and eastern Europe.

❓ **Building Graph Skills** Approximately how many more immigrants arrived in the United States in 1900 than in 1860?

Changing Ways | Immigration

■ **Understanding Change** In the late 1800s, immigration patterns changed dramatically as more immigrants came to the United States from eastern Europe. In recent years, immigration patterns have shifted again, as more immigrants come from other parts of North and South America and from Asia. *Where did the most immigrants come from then? now?*

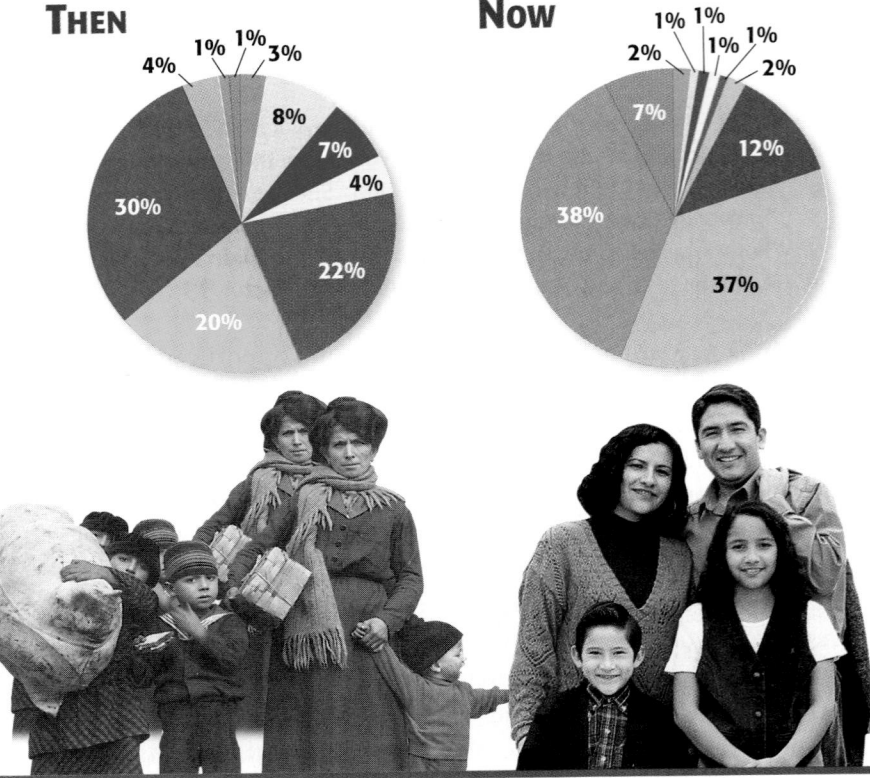

THEN

4% 1% 1% 3%
8%
7%
4%
30%
22%
20%

Now

1% 1%
2% 1% 1%
1% 2%
7%
12%
38%
37%

Immigration

- Great Britain
- Ireland
- Scandinavia
- Germany
- Italy
- Russia
- Other European Countries
- Asia
- North and South America
- Other

Sources: *Historical Statistics of the United States; Statistical Abstract of the United States: 1998.* Data reflect 1900 and 1995. Due to rounding, numbers may not add up to 100 percent.

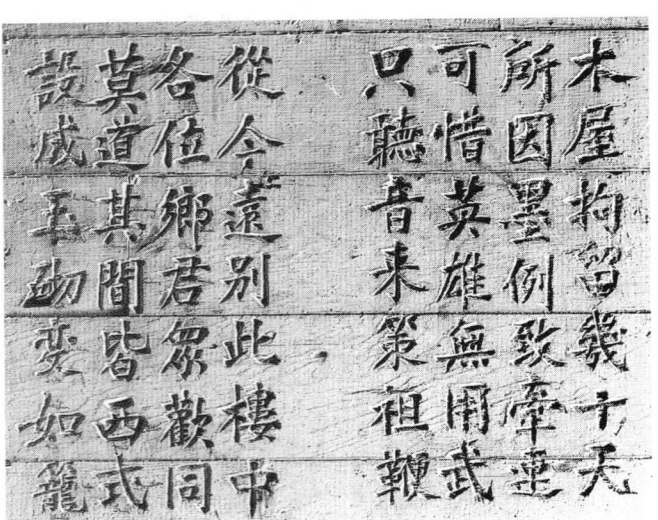

Imprisoned and waiting for rulings in their cases, Chinese immigrants often carved poems such as this one on their cell walls.

On Angel Island, thousands of Asian newcomers, mostly from China, underwent similar processing. Chinese applicants faced strict immigration laws. These laws limited entrance to certain skilled groups or to individuals who could show that their parents were born in the United States.

Some applicants who could not meet the restrictions were deported. Others were detained on the island as they awaited a ruling on their cases. For most immigrants, the anxiety they experienced during processing gave way to a renewed sense of hope once they finally set foot on their adopted homeland.

✔ **READING CHECK:** What challenges did immigrants face as they settled in the United States?

A New Life

Many immigrants found life in the United States an improvement on the conditions of their homeland. Nevertheless, the newcomers frequently endured hardships in their new home. Most immigrants settled in crowded cities where they could find only low-paying unskilled jobs. As a result, they were generally forced into poor housing located in crowded neighborhoods and slums.

Immigrant communities. Many industrial cities of the Northeast and Midwest became a patchwork of ethnic neighborhoods with numerous pockets of diverse immigrant communities. Social reformer Jacob Riis was himself a Danish immigrant. He noted that an 1890s map of New York City colored according to nationality, "would show . . . more colors than any rainbow." Settling in close-knit immigrant communities, newcomers found institutions and neighbors that made their transition more bearable both financially and culturally. In these neighborhoods, for example, residents often spoke the same languages and followed the customs of the old country.

Religious institutions. The neighborhood churches, synagogues, and temples provided community centers that helped immigrants maintain a sense of identity and belonging. In Chicago religious organizations such as the United Hebrew Relief Association, which served Jews, and the St. Vincent de Paul Society, which served mainly Irish Catholics, provided economic assistance to needy immigrants in their communities. Moreover, some churches, such as St. George's Episcopal Church in New York City and Russell H. Conwell's Baptist Temple in Philadelphia provided many services. They offered day care for children, gymnasiums, reading rooms, sewing classes, social clubs, and training courses for new immigrants.

Residents in many cities formed religious and non-religious aid organizations known as **benevolent societies** to help immigrants in cases of sickness, unemployment, and death. The size and number of charitable organizations grew rapidly along with the boom in immigration. They attempted to provide an important function by helping immigrants obtain education, health care, and jobs. Some benevolent societies offered loans to new immigrants to start businesses. Others set up insurance plans that provided money for families whose breadwinners were sick or had died. "We visit our sick and bury our dead" was one society's slogan.

Americanization. Immigrants were often urged by employers, public institutions, and sometimes even their own family members to join the American mainstream. Many older

The Religious Spirit

ORTHODOX RELIGIONS

Greek Orthodox icon

Many new immigrants were members of orthodox religious communities. Orthodox religions generally follow traditional practices that strictly conform to the faith's religious doctrines.

For example, Orthodox Judaism closely follows the Torah, the Jewish holy book, applying its principles to daily life. The Greek and Russian Orthodox faiths strictly follow ancient rites and teachings of the early Christian Church.

The Greek and Russian Orthodox Churches grew out of a split between the Roman Catholic Church and the Christian Church of the Byzantine Empire in 1054. The split resulted from the breakup of the Roman Empire and controversies including the use of icons, or sacred images, and the role of the pope. The Greek Orthodox Church is particularly known for its intricate mosaics and decorative icons. The Russian Orthodox Church has a long tradition of missionary work. Russian missionaries established Orthodox churches in Alaska during the late 1700s when Russians were settling in the region. In 1864 the first Orthodox church was established in the United States, in New Orleans. Orthodox churches, particularly in large cities, provided a community center and important services for immigrants. ■

MUSEUM OF THE CITY OF NEW YORK

Americanization. For some immigrant children the process of Americanization began as soon as they arrived in the United States. *How do the activities portrayed in this photo of immigrant children support this argument?*

This seamstress is using a sewing machine in a New York City sweatshop.

immigrants cherished their ties to the old country. By contrast, their children often adopted American cultural practices and tended to view their parents' old-world language and customs as old-fashioned. A second-generation Polish immigrant expressed bittersweet feelings about his parents' way of life. It was, he noted, "a slowly decaying world of aged folks living largely in a dream. One day it would pass and then there would remain only Americans whose forebears had once been Poles."

The immigrant worker. Whether they adopted American habits or remained tied to the traditions of their homeland, most new immigrants shared a common work experience. Many did the country's "dirty work."

Whether in construction, mines, or sweatshops, most immigrants found their work to be difficult. The labor was physically exhausting. Hours were long, and wages were low. At the age of 15, Sadie Frowne began working in a garment factory in Brooklyn, New York. In 1902, Frowne recalled:

> 66 **The machines go like mad all day, because the faster you work the more money you get. Sometimes in my haste I get my finger caught and the needle goes right through it. . . . At the end of the day one feels so weak that there is a great temptation to lie right down and sleep.** 99

Some immigrants worked as many as 15 hours a day to earn a living wage. Even the best-paid workers made little more than the minimum necessary to support themselves and their families.

✔ **READING CHECK:** Where did new immigrants find assistance?

Chinese immigrants. Barred from many occupations, Chinese immigrants often opened their own businesses. *What services does this Chinese American merchant provide to his community?*

The Nativist Response

Immigrant workers played an important role in running the factories that contributed to a strong U.S. economy. Nevertheless, many native-born Americans saw immigration as a threat. They agreed with poet Thomas Bailey Aldrich, who warned against a "wild motley [ragged] throng [crowd]." He argued that immigrants brought "unknown gods and rites" and spoke "accents of menace." Many saw these newcomers as too different to fit into American society. Others went further, blaming immigrants for social problems such as crime, poverty, and violence as well as for spreading radical political ideas.

Nativists also opposed immigration for economic reasons. Many charged that the immigrants' willingness to work cheaply robbed native-born Americans of jobs and lowered wages for all. Supported by nativist workers, labor unions began demanding restrictions on immigration. Nativists achieved the greatest success in the West.

Chinese exclusion. For years Chinese laborers had been tolerated—and taken advantage of—on the West Coast, particularly in California. However, as unemployment mounted following the Panic of 1873 workers grew less tolerant. The new Workingmen's Party of California angrily cried, "The Chinese must go." The party leader, Dennis Kearney, was himself an Irish immigrant. He addressed crowds across the state, exciting them with his vicious speeches. Mobs attacked the Chinese, killing some and burning the property of others.

Leaders of California's Chinese community appealed to the authorities for protection. Help, however, was not forthcoming. In fact, the state's political leaders responded by amending the state constitution to forbid Chinese residents to own property or work at certain jobs.

In 1882 Congress passed the **Chinese Exclusion Act**, which denied citizenship to people born in China and prohibited the immigration of Chinese laborers. The act made conditions worse for Chinese Americans. In 1885 a mob in Rock Springs, Wyoming Territory, murdered 28 Chinese and drove out hundreds more. Neither the Chinese Exclusion Act nor the violence completely stopped Chinese immigrants from coming to the United States. Many Chinese immigrants still came to the United States only to be held for months at immigration stations.

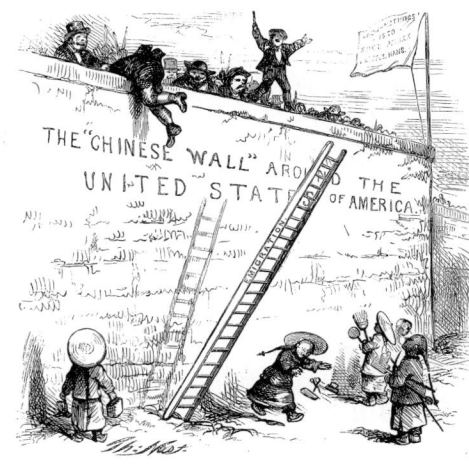

Immigration Restriction League. Immigrants endured additional discrimination as new organizations took up the anti-immigration cause. Founded in 1894 by wealthy Bostonians, the **Immigration Restriction League** sought to impose a literacy test on all immigrants. Congress passed such a measure, but President Grover Cleveland vetoed it, calling it "illiberal, narrow, and un-American." Over the next several years Congress tried several times—without success—to pass a similar measure. Despite efforts to impose restrictions, immigration continued. Contrary to nativists' arguments, the new immigrants made positive contributions to American society. The rapid industrialization of the United States in the late 1800s would have been impossible without immigrant workers. Their varied cultures also added new dimensions to American life.

✔ **READING CHECK:** Why did nativists oppose new immigration?

SECTION 1 REVIEW

Define and explain the significance of the following terms:
old immigrants
new immigrants
steerage
benevolent societies
Chinese Exclusion Act
Immigration Restriction League

Identify and explain the significance of the following individuals:
Dennis Kearney
Grover Cleveland

1. **Using Graphic Organizers** Copy the graphic organizer below. Use it to describe the differences and similarities of the old immigrants and the new immigrants.

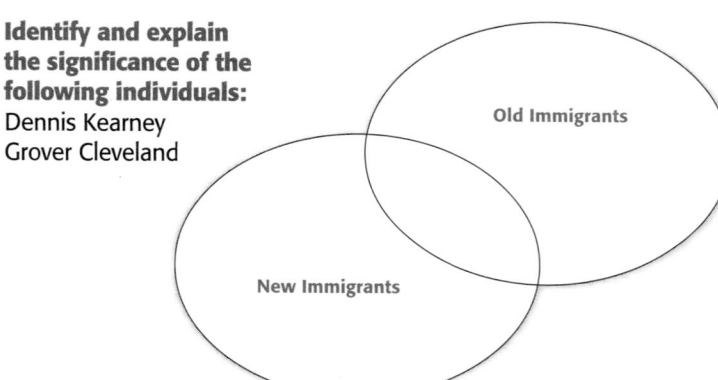

Old Immigrants

New Immigrants

2. **Using Historical Imagination** Imagine that you are a recent immigrant to the United States in 1900. What aspects of the journey to the United States and the adjustment to American life do you think were most difficult?

3. **Analyzing** Where did immigrants find assistance in adjusting to American life?

4. **Assessing Consequences** How did the new immigrants contribute to making American society more diverse?

Critical Thinking

5. Imagine that you are a member of Congress arguing against nativist legislation like the Chinese Exclusion Act. What arguments could be made to support your cause?
Consider:
• how immigrants have contributed to U.S. history
• why the Chinese were singled out for exclusion
• how the Chinese contributed to American life

The Urban World

OBJECTIVES

Read to understand:

1. how technological innovations altered the urban landscape
2. what social values the new class of wealthy city-dwellers expressed
3. how life changed for middle-class Americans during the late 1800s
4. what urban life was like for the poorest city-dwellers
5. how social reformers used settlement houses and churches to improve the lives of the poor

KEY TERMS

skyscrapers
mass transit
suburbs
nouveau riche
conspicuous consumption
tenements
settlement houses
Social Gospel

KEY PEOPLE

Elisha Otis
Jane Addams
Janie Porter Barrett
Caroline Bartlett

The Flatiron Building's internal steel skeleton is visible.

EYEWITNESSES TO History

66 *The rushing streams of commerce have worn many a deep and rugged chasm. Each of these canyons is closed in by a long frontage of towering cliffs, and these soaring walls of brick and limestone and granite rise higher and higher with each succeeding year.* 99
—Henry Blake Fuller

New York City in 1901

Henry Blake Fuller of Chicago described the emergence of the multistory buildings in his 1893 novel, *The Cliff-Dwellers.* During the late 1800s U.S. cities experienced "growing pains" as a result of a massive increase in population. Horace Greeley summed up the problem when he wrote, "We cannot all live in cities, yet nearly all seem determined to do so." New technological developments, such as multistory buildings, changed life for many residents in America's growing cities. The construction of tall buildings also greatly altered the urban landscape.

The Changing City

Before the Second Industrial Revolution, cities were compact. Few buildings were taller than three or four stories. Even in the largest cities, most people lived less than a 45-minute walk from the city center. By the late 1800s new technological innovations and a flood of immigrants began to transform the urban landscape. Between 1865 and 1900, the percentage of Americans living in cities doubled, from 20 percent to 40 percent. This population growth had a wide-ranging impact on urban life in the United States. Improvements in technology contributed to the increase of people living in cities.

In order for urban centers to accommodate the growing number of residents, architects needed to build **skyscrapers**, or large, multistory buildings. The height of buildings had previously been limited to some five stories, the number of flights of stairs that most people could comfortably climb. In 1853 Elisha Otis solved this problem with the development of the mechanized elevator. The elevator allowed architects to construct buildings well above the former five-story limit.

The use of masonry walls to support the entire weight of structures had also limited building height. Architects solved this problem by developing steel frames for buildings. The steel frame relieved the walls from the burden of carrying the weight of the building. It also allowed buildings to be built to new heights and with more windows and less wall space devoted to supporting the building. The introduction of the skyscraper transformed city life by accommodating a greater concentration of workers in the central business districts.

While skyscrapers extended cities upward, the development of **mass transit** extended U.S. cities outward. Mass transit included forms of public transportation such as electric commuter trains, subways, and trolley cars. Prior to the development of mass transit, a typical city covered about three square miles. Such a city extended as far as a person could travel walking in a few hours. With the development of mass transit, workers no longer had to live within walking distance of jobs or markets. With the growth of mass transit systems, some urban areas expanded to cover as much as 20 square miles.

Frank J. Sprague, an electrical engineer who had worked with Thomas Edison, designed one of the first mass transit systems. Sprague's electric trolley, or streetcar, began serving Richmond, Virginia, in 1887. Other cities quickly adopted the invention. By 1895 the nation boasted over 10,000 miles of electric railways.

The expansion of transportation to areas beyond the urban center led to the growth of **suburbs**—residential neighborhoods on the outskirts of a city. Commuter railroads offered the first chance for wealthy residents to settle outside the built-up city core. The daily fares of 15 to 25 cents had effectively excluded the working classes and poor from suburban life. The expansion of streetcar transportation made commuting and, in turn, suburban life more affordable. The five-cent flat-rate fares charged by some transit companies allowed middle-class office workers and some skilled laborers the opportunity to leave the city. Mass transit altered urban life by helping create suburbs. One Philadelphia resident argued that the streetcar encouraged the "spread of the city over a vast space, with all the advantages of compactness and also the advantages of pure air, gardens, and rural pleasure."

✔ **READING CHECK:** How did technological innovations alter the urban landscape?

INTERPRETING THE VISUAL RECORD

Electric streetcars. Streetcars such as this one in New York City provided transportation to areas previously outside the city limits. *What social background do you think the passengers of this streetcar were from?*

Growth of Cities, 1880–1900

Learning from Maps The population of urban centers grew significantly between 1880 and 1900.

❓ **REGION** Which region had the greatest number of large cities in both 1880 and 1900?

Urban Population

Symbol	Range	Symbol	Range
·	50,000–100,000	●	300,000–1,000,000
•	100,000–300,000	⬤	More than 1,000,000

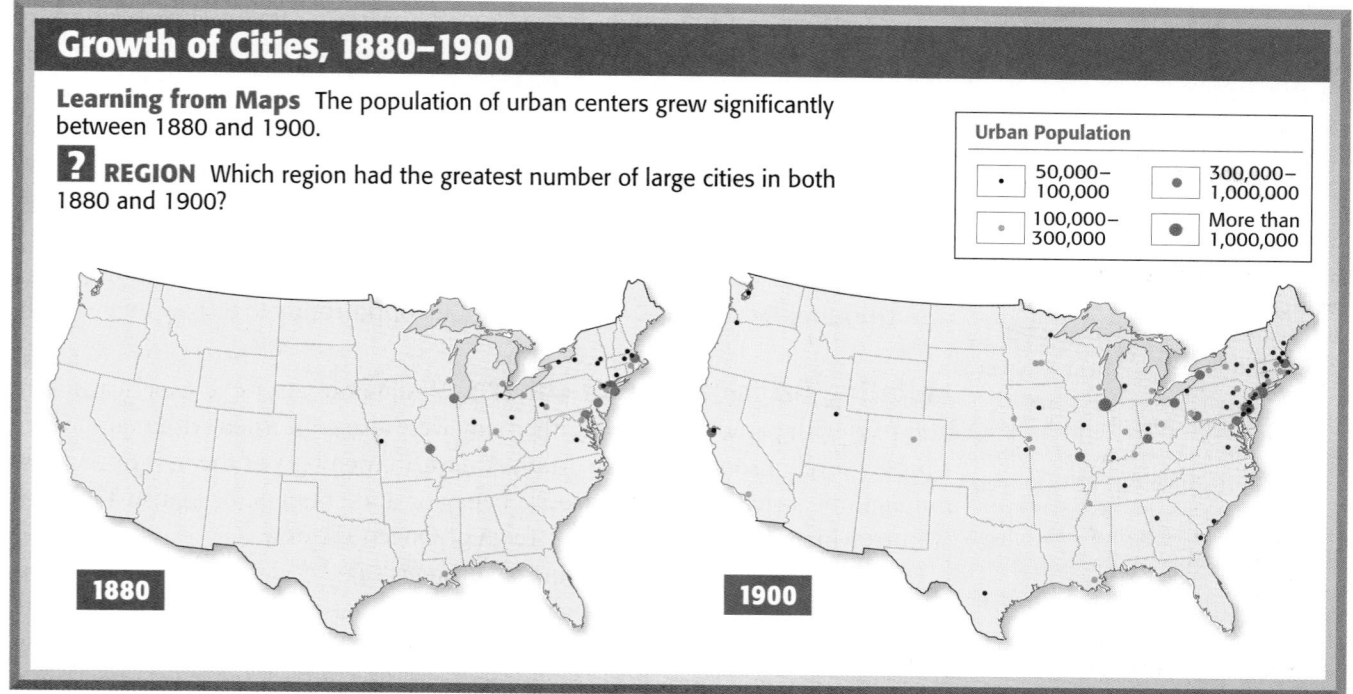

1880

1900

Upper-Class Life

As the landscape of U.S. cities evolved, the social habits of city-dwellers were also changing. During the late 1800s a new class of wealthy city-dwellers emerged. Distinguished by their social values, these Americans became known as the **nouveau riche** (noo-voh REESH), a French term meaning "newly rich." There had been wealthy people in America since colonial times. However, the urban upper class of the late 1800s was a new breed. The nouveau riche—individuals like Andrew Carnegie, John D. Rockefeller, and Cornelius Vanderbilt—made their money in new industries, such as steel, mining, or railroads. Their quickly earned fortunes usually dwarfed those of the old upper-class bankers, landowners, and merchants.

Some upper-class urban residents carried accessories such as this fan and pair of opera glasses when in public.

Conspicuous consumption. Many members of this nouveau riche class of city-dwellers made an effort to publicly display their wealth. For the newly rich, author William Dean Howells noted sarcastically, "The dollar is the measure of every value, the stamp of every success." Many of the nouveau riche spent their great wealth freely so that everyone would know how successful they were. Social scientist Thorstein Veblen labeled this behavior **conspicuous consumption**.

Elegant residential streets such as New York City's Fifth Avenue served as showcases for the wealth of the nouveau riche. They built large houses whose design imitated Gothic castles or Italian Renaissance palaces. Andrew Carnegie even purchased an actual Scottish castle. In the summer the urban wealthy class left their city homes for equally magnificent country estates. The nouveau riche thought nothing of paying thousands of dollars to stage one night's amusement. Mr. and Mrs. Bradley Martin of New York, for example, once hosted a fancy ball at the Waldorf-Astoria Hotel in 1897 that was estimated to cost $370,000.

Many Americans criticized such extravagances. Ward McAllister, a lawyer and member of the "Four Hundred"—the wealthiest group of New York's upper class—came to their defense. "The mistake made by the world at large is [in thinking] that fashionable people are selfish, frivolous, and indifferent to [do not care about] the welfare of their fellow creatures." Indeed, some wealthy people did support social causes. They gave money to art galleries, libraries, and museums; endowed universities; and established new opera companies, symphony orchestras, and theater groups. As critics quickly pointed out, however, not all rich men and women saw philanthropy as a way to do good. Some simply used it as another opportunity to display their wealth.

Imitating British Victorian culture. While nouveau riche Americans were occupied with parading their wealth, many were also concerned with maintaining a proper level of social behavior. Many American members of the new upper class imitated the strict standards of social behavior and etiquette of British Victorian culture, which developed under the reign of Queen Victoria.

During the late 1800s magazines like *Godey's Lady's Book, The Ladies' Home Journal,* and *The Modern Housewife* instructed upper class Americans on how to behave properly while visiting social peers and dining. These publications governed marriage and home life in addition to setting standards for social interaction.

Victorian literature and instructive guides held up an ideal of domestic life. This ideal glorified the role of the woman as a homemaker. According to this vision, the home was the sole domain of the Victorian woman. Her responsibilities included organizing and decorating the home as well as offering moral and social guidance to her family. Although the Victorian woman had a certain moral authority within the home, her influence was typically limited to private life.

✔ **READING CHECK:** What social values did the new class of wealthy city-dwellers express?

Middle-Class Life

During the late 1800s the growth of new industries brought about an increase in the number of middle-class city-dwellers. As with the upper class, a middle class of doctors, lawyers, small-business owners, and teachers had existed since colonial times. However, by the late 1800s the rise of modern corporations had swelled the ranks of the middle class with accountants, clerks, engineers, managers, and salespeople.

Professionalization. New industries and a growing urban population created a huge demand for educated workers with a mastery of specialized fields. These fields included education, engineering, law, and medicine. Prior to the late 1800s, however, few standards or organizations existed to certify the professional standing of doctors, lawyers, teachers, or technicians. City-dwellers had few means for choosing truly skilled professionals.

During the 1870s and 1880s professional schools and organizations were formed to set standards, issue licenses, and review practices within specialized occupations. The creation of these schools and professional organizations gave more respect to these professions and their middle-class practitioners.

Middle-class women. Despite the demand for middle-class professionals, few women were permitted in professional occupations. Nevertheless, rapid urban growth did increase the opportunities for women to work outside the home. The Victorian-era upper class and earlier generations of middle-class Americans had viewed work outside the home as a male activity. The rise of big business, however, created a variety of new jobs, such as salesclerks, secretaries, and stenographers. Business owners increasingly hired young, single women to fill these positions, paying them lower wages than men. By 1910 some 35 percent of the nearly 2 million clerical workers were women.

Most married middle-class women, however, worked in the home. Smaller families, increased reliance on purchased goods, and new household technologies such as running water changed middle-class women's domestic work. For example,

The Debutante Ball

teen Life

Debutante ball

Prior to the age of 17 or 18, teenagers from wealthy families were not usually included in social functions in the late 1800s, although they were trained in proper etiquette. Some upper class schools required students to take classes in "ball-room deportment," to prepare them to participate in formal dances as adults. Debutante balls, also called coming-out parties, marked the time when young women of upper-class Victorian social circles were formally presented and accepted as members of high society.

Before a young woman's debut into society, she would spend weeks training. She would practice gracefully climbing in and out of a carriage, walking elegantly, and acting according to proper etiquette when dining, greeting guests, and being courted. "There were so many of these little rules to remember," explained Katherine Chorley, reflecting upon her Victorian childhood, "but we were drilled (by Nanny) so that it was no effort to remember them."

One of the main functions of the debutante ball was for young women to meet prospective husbands. Most Victorian socialites viewed marriage as the most important event in a woman's life. Young women involved in high society during the Victorian Age usually married within two or three years after their coming-out parties.

Middle-class women. The rapid growth of industry during the late 1800s created new opportunities for middle-class women to work outside the home. *What type of work are these women employed in?*

the availability of ready-made clothing lightened the sewing loads of many middle-class women. The use of hot and cold running water meant that doing laundry no longer required pumping, hauling, and heating the water. Some middle-class families could afford to hire servants to handle many household chores. In such families, women had more free time to focus on their children and to take part in the growing number of cultural events in cities. Many women joined reading and social clubs. Others participated in and led reform movements.

✔ **READING CHECK:** How did life change for middle-class Americans during the late 1800s?

How the Poor Lived

Most city-dwellers lived worlds away from the comfort of the middle class or the luxury of the wealthy. Although industries and factories offered new opportunities to working-class men and women, the ever-growing population of laborers eager to work kept wages low. Living conditions for the working-class city-dwellers during the late 1800s were made worse by housing shortages and the rising cost of rent. To make ends meet, working-class families often had to rent out parts of their homes or apartments to boarders.

New York City served as a magnet for hundreds of thousands of immigrants and other migrants. Some 43,000 **tenements**—poorly built apartment buildings—housed more than 1.6 million poor New Yorkers in 1900—nearly half the city's population. These rundown buildings were usually clustered in poor neighborhoods. These neighborhoods were typically within walking distance of the factories, ports, and stockyards where many poor city-dwellers worked. The dark, airless tenements sometimes housed as many as 12 families per floor. Outside the crowded tenements, raw sewage and piles of garbage littered unpaved streets and alleys. Worse still, the slums usually adjoined industrial areas where factories belched pollution. "The stink is enough to knock you down," one New York resident complained. In such an environment, sickness and death were common.

Although all residents of poor neighborhoods faced grim conditions, African Americans typically experienced the greatest difficulties. Because of widespread discrimination, most could get only low-paying jobs. African Americans also had to pay outrageous rents for the most appalling apartments, and faced frequent police harassment. Yet many preferred living in the North to the South. As one African American journalist explained, "They sleep in peace at night; what they earn is paid them, if not they can appeal to the courts. They vote without fear of the shot-gun, and their children go to school."

✔ **READING CHECK:** What was urban life like for the poorest Americans?

Tenements. In his study of the urban working class, Jacob Riis explained that an entire immigrant family would frequently live in a single room that served as the bedroom, parlor, and dining room. *How does this photograph support Riis's description?*

The Drive for Reform

In the late 1800s few government programs existed to help the poor. What assistance the poor received was limited to charitable handouts of food and clothing. Some idealistic young Americans were certain that more must be done to assist poor city-dwellers.

The settlement houses.

To confront the problem of urban poverty head-on, some reformers established and lived in **settlement houses**—community service centers—in poor neighborhoods. Settlement houses offered educational opportunities, skills training, and cultural events to neighborhood residents. Jane Addams was at the forefront of the American settlement-house movement.

Jane Addams

Jane Addams was born in 1860 to a wealthy family in Cedarville, Illinois. There, she grew up in an atmosphere of politics and philanthropy. Her Quaker father was a strong abolitionist. As a state senator he had worked to pass social reform legislation. The young Addams set out to be a doctor. A back problem, however, ended her studies. She eventually decided to dedicate her life to helping the urban poor.

Addams began her settlement-house work in 1889. She and Ellen Gates Starr established Hull House, located in a run-down mansion in one of Chicago's immigrant neighborhoods. The early days of Hull House were busy. "Memory of the first years at Hull-House is more or less blurred with fatigue," Addams recalled.

Addams founded the settlement house with the ambition of providing social and cultural services to needy Americans. In her memoir, *Twenty Years at Hull-House*, she elaborated:

66 **The Settlement casts aside none of those things which cultivated men have come to consider reasonable and goodly, but it insists that those belong as well to that great body of people who, because of toilsome [hard-working] and underpaid labor, are unable to procure [obtain] them for themselves.** 99

Addams's central goals were to provide educational and cultural opportunities to the poor and to improve living conditions in the neighborhoods. She also hoped that Hull House would provide fulfilling careers for settlement-house volunteers, who were mostly young women. She expected that for "young women who had been given over too exclusively to study," Hull House "might restore a balance of activity" and help them "learn of life from life itself."

The volunteers who joined Addams were mostly young, college-educated women. They set up a day nursery and kindergarten for the children of working mothers and gave adult-education classes. The experience gained at settlement houses provided the women with the skills and knowledge to make important contributions to social reform and politics.

In time, Addams's work expanded to include other important causes. She tirelessly promoted women's suffrage and

Read More About It

Free Find:

Jane Addams

After reading the biography of Jane Addams on the **Holt Researcher** CD–ROM, create a list of community services you would provide if you worked in a settlement house.

INTERPRETING THE VISUAL RECORD

Hull House. Jane Addams recorded in her memoir how she and other volunteers at Hull House provided important services such as day care and education for immigrants. *How do you think these immigrant children benefited from the settlement house?*

Kindergarten. Acting in accordance with the Social Gospel, Caroline Bartlett organized kindergarten classes and other public services out of her People's Church in Kalamazoo, Michigan. *What public services does this kindergarten class provide to the community of Kalamazoo?*

served as president of the Women's International League for Peace and Freedom from 1919 until her death in 1935. Worldwide recognition for her efforts came in 1931, when she was awarded the Nobel Peace Prize.

Hull House served as a model for others hoping to aid the poor. In 1890 African American teacher Janie Porter Barrett founded one of the first African American settlement houses—the Locust Street Social Settlement—in Hampton, Virginia. Three years later, Lillian Wald started the Henry Street Settlement on New York's Lower East Side. By the end of the century, nearly 100 settlement houses had opened across the country.

The Social Gospel movement. At the same time that the settlement houses began their work, a number of Protestant ministers joined the battle against poverty. They developed the idea of the **Social Gospel**, which called for people to apply Christian principles to address social problems. Washington Gladden, a Congregational minister in Columbus, Ohio, was an early leader of the Social Gospel movement. Arguing that the church had a moral duty to confront social injustice, Gladden led crusades to improve conditions for industrial workers.

Many churches attempted to act according to the Social Gospel by providing classes, counseling, job training, libraries, and other social services. Caroline Bartlett's People's Church in Kalamazoo, Michigan, was one such church. Bartlett became a Unitarian minister in 1889, the same year she began her work at what became the People's Church. Drawing on Social Gospel ideals, Bartlett threw open the doors of her church seven days a week. She established a free public kindergarten and a gymnasium and offered classes in domestic and industrial skills. Bartlett also set up a meals program for workers and sponsored creative activities.

✔ **READING CHECK:** How did social reformers use settlement houses and churches to improve the lives of the urban poor?

SECTION 2 REVIEW

Define and explain the significance of the following terms:
skyscrapers
mass transit
suburbs
nouveau riche
conspicuous consumption
tenements
settlement houses
Social Gospel

Identify and explain the significance of the following individuals:
Elisha Otis
Jane Addams
Janie Porter Barrett
Caroline Bartlett

1. **Using Graphic Organizers** Copy the graphic organizer below. Use it to describe the class divisions that developed in the cities and what characteristics distinguished the different social groups.

2. **Understanding Geography: Human-Environment Interaction** In what ways did the physical landscape of U.S. cities change in the late 1800s?
3. **Assessing Consequences** How did new technological developments change city life?
4. **Comparing and Contrasting** How was the work of Jane Addams at Hull House and Caroline Bartlett at the People's Church similar? How was it different?

Critical Thinking

5. Did city life in the late 1800s offer more opportunities or more limitations for most residents? Explain your answer.
   Consider:
   • what opportunities the city offered
   • what limitations the city imposed
   • whether most city residents experienced more limits or more opportunities

Daily Life in the Cities

OBJECTIVES

Read to understand:

1. how public education and colleges changed in the late 1800s
2. how publishers appealed to readers
3. how outdoor activities and sports provided a source of leisure for Americans
4. what new forms of popular music and theater developed in the late 1800s

KEY TERMS

compulsory education laws
yellow journalism
City Beautiful movement
vaudeville
ragtime

KEY PEOPLE

John Dewey
Frederick Law Olmsted
Walter Camp
James Naismith
Edwin Booth
Scott Joplin

EYEWITNESSES TO History

❝ It must be admitted unhesitatingly that we are only just learning how to play. We steal away for our holidays ... determined to rest and take life at its easiest. We promise ourselves to forswear all thoughts of business and the outer world. ❞
—Caspar W. Whitney

Relaxing in a city park

Caspar W. Whitney thus described Americans' changing views of leisure in the late 1800s. The incredible pace of industrialization and urban growth greatly affected daily life in U.S. cities. The daily struggles of work and crowded living conditions prompted many city-dwellers to seek leisure activities. Many urban residents relaxed in new city parks. They enjoyed watching and playing sports, attended new musical and theater shows, and found leisure through reading daily newspapers and literature.

Education

U.S. cities grew rapidly during the late 1800s. Urban life became increasingly difficult for workers and those with little education. To aid the urban working class, social reformers worked to expand educational opportunities.

Few children had access to public education during the early 1800s. Noting the steady growth of U.S. cities, reformers urged the expansion of public schools to educate this new population of urban children. The movement gained momentum after 1860, as more and more states began to pass **compulsory education laws**— laws requiring parents to send children to school. From 1870 to 1900, the number of students in school grew from some 7 million to more than 15 million—from 57 percent of the school-age population to 72 percent. Expenditures for these schools rose from about $63 million in 1870 to some $215 million in 1900.

As enrollments grew, educational reformers proposed that schools do more than teach reading, writing, and arithmetic by rote memorization. One of the main reformers was philosopher John Dewey. His "Laboratory School" at the University of Chicago stressed cooperative "learning by doing." He also emphasized art, history, and science. Ella Flagg Young, superintendent of schools in Chicago, worked with Dewey to fulfill his ideas. Most urban schools, however, were slow to adopt the new teaching methods.

Other reformers like William Torrey Harris and Elwood Cubberley stressed different issues. They believed that one essential function of public education was to instruct students in matters beyond reading and writing. They hoped to instruct students—particularly immigrant children—in proper behavior, civic loyalty, and American cultural values. Reformers like Cubberley

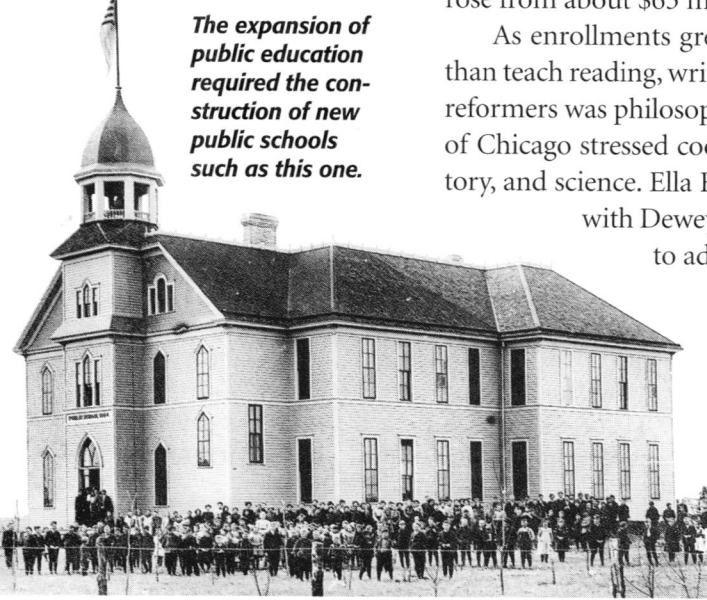

The expansion of public education required the construction of new public schools such as this one.

This teacher instructs her students in a Washington, D.C., public school classroom in the early 1900s.

and Harris feared the effects of mass immigration. They hoped that public education would help cities avoid social unrest by instilling a sense of order and discipline in the immigrant and working-class students.

Even with this drive to teach American values, children of many different cultures in most public schools during this era remained segregated by race. Most schools for African American, Asian American, and Hispanic students were poorly equipped. State and local governments spent little money on them. The expansion of public schools, however, did create more opportunities for young women. In 1900 about 60 percent of high school graduates were female.

The number of American colleges and their enrollments also rose during this period. At the close of the Civil War, the United States had approximately 500 colleges. By 1900 that number had grown to 1,000 institutions. Meanwhile, the enrollment in American colleges had expanded from 50,000 to 350,000 students. Although more students began to seek higher levels of education, colleges remained primarily accessible to wealthy and upper-middle-class students.

✔ **READING CHECK:** How did public education and colleges change in the late 1800s?

Strategies for Success — Analyzing

Much like comparing and contrasting, analyzing is a basic skill used in historical study. To *analyze* is to break a topic or issue down into its essential parts and examine the relationships between those parts. Analyzing enables one to gain a more complete understanding of a subject, particularly when the subject can be interpreted in varying ways. As a result, analyzing helps one to draw conclusions about the subject.

How to Analyze

1. **Identify the subject.** Identify the topic or issue that you wish to analyze. You may want to rephrase the topic or issue as a question to be answered.
2. **Examine the facts.** Examine each piece of information that your source material provides about the subject. Make sure to study any statistics or graphic information carefully.
3. **Examine different points of view.** If the subject can be interpreted in varying ways, identify the main idea expressed by each side. Then determine whether each idea is supported by facts, opinions, or a combination of both.
4. **Draw conclusions.** Use your examination of facts and ideas to draw conclusions and evaluate any different

points of view. If you rephrased the subject for analysis as a question, answer it.

Applying the Strategy

Formulate a question about U.S. public education during the late 1800s. Then analyze the material in the subsection above entitled Education and answer your question.

Practicing the Strategy

Answer the following questions.

1. What new education laws did some states begin to pass after 1860?
2. How did school attendance figures change between 1870 and 1900?
3. What activities did educational reformers engage in during the late 1800s?
4. How did women participate in the public education system during the late 1800s?

Use your responses to answer the following questions.

5. How did U.S. public education change during the late 1800s?
6. What were the strengths and weaknesses of the public education system during the late 1800s?

Publishing

The expansion of public education made newspapers and literature more important in the daily lives of many Americans. The growing number of students meant that by 1900 some 90 percent of Americans could read. This rise in literacy launched an age of publishing. Print media became the primary source of information for urban populations.

Popular journalism. Along with an increase in literacy, new developments in printing technology spurred a dramatic rise in the number of newspapers published during the late 1800s. During the 1870s and 1880s printers developed an inexpensive new type of paper that was durable enough to withstand high-speed printing. Using this paper allowed publishers to print a huge volume of newspapers. Between 1865 and 1910 the number of daily newspaper publications in the United States increased from about 500 to approximately 2,600. Circulation grew as these papers sold for just pennies each.

Daily newspapers in the same city often battled each other for a larger number of readers. The wildest circulation wars took place in New York between Joseph Pulitzer's *New York World* and William Randolph Hearst's *New York Journal.* To attract readers, publishers developed new journalistic practices. The *World* tried to win readers by running sensational news stories. It also used fancy illustrations and photographs. The *Journal* competed with even more sensational stories. Both papers attempted to appeal to a broad readership by including comic strips, advice columns, special women's sections, and separate sports sections.

The newspapers also competed for readers by publishing the popular comic series "The Yellow Kid," one of the first cartoons published in color. The lead character was a young tenement dweller who was dressed in a yellow gown and reflected stereotypes many Americans had about immigrants. The hugely popular cartoon inspired many critics to refer to the *World* and the *Journal's* style of sensational reporting as **yellow journalism.**

Literature. The publication of popular literature also experienced significant growth as a result of the increase of literacy among Americans. Dime and half-dime novels promoted by publishers like Erastus Beadle attempted to entice readers with adventure stories. Beadle wrote frontier novels such as *Deadly Eye* and *Spitfire Saul, the King of the Rustlers.* Martha Finley's stories about virtuous character Elsie Dinsmore gained a huge following among young girls.

Older readers favored realistic books about city life. For example, Edith Wharton's 1905 novel, *The House of Mirth,* describes the conflicts between New York City's nouveau riche and old upper class. Published in 1885, William Dean Howells's *Rise of Silas Lapham* weaves a tale of greed and social ambition.

INTERPRETING THE VISUAL RECORD

Yellow journalism. Earning the name yellow journalism, newspapers such as the *New York World* published sensational stories and color cartoons like this one featuring "The Yellow Kid" to attract readers. *What aspects of this cartoon might attract readers to the newspaper?*

Amusement Parks

Advertisement for an amusement park on Coney Island

The original amusement parks of the late 1800s provided places for middle- and working-class families to find inexpensive leisure activities just outside the city. Borrowing ideas from the hugely popular world fairs like the 1893 Chicago Exposition, parks like Dreamland, Luna, and Steeplechase on Coney Island offered grand architecture, mechanical rides, small replicas of exotic places and foreign villages, daily theatrical shows, and re-enactments of current events. One journalist described the amusement parks of Coney Island as an "enchanted, story book land of . . . domes, minarets [towers], lagoons, and lofty aerial flights. . . . It was a world removed—shut away from the sordid clatter and turmoil of the streets."

Today's theme parks offer a similarly fantastic escape. While the price has risen from the 10-cent admission to Coney Island to more than $35 for one day's admission to many amusement parks, parks continue to provide a way for many Americans to retreat from everyday life into a world of fantasy. Disneyland founder Walt Disney once explained, "I don't want the public to see the world they live in while they're in Disneyland, I want them to feel they're in another world."

Frederick Law Olmsted's design for Central Park created a rural setting in the heart of New York City.

THE GRANGER COLLECTION, NEW YORK

The most commercially successful novels during the late 1800s, however, were ones that focused on Christian principles. Charles M. Sheldon's 1896 novel, *In His Steps,* was the era's most popular book, selling millions of copies. Sheldon depicted characters who addressed their personal problems by asking the question, "What would Jesus do?"

✔ **READING CHECK:** How did publishers appeal to readers?

Leisure Time in Urban Parks

During the late 1800s Americans increasingly counted on leisure activities to provide relief from busy city life. City planners developed large urban parks to offer a natural refuge from the crowded, built-up city. Urban residents eagerly used these parks as a space for relaxation where they could participate in a variety of new leisure activities.

In 1857 landscape architect Frederick Law Olmsted designed Central Park in New York City. He sought to create a rural setting within New York's urban environment. The park included pedestrian paths, ponds, and trees. Olmsted designed the 2.5-mile-long park for people of all social classes to gather and enjoy the natural landscape. In 1871 more than 10 million people visited the park—roughly 30,000 visitors each day.

Olmsted's success helped spur an American planning movement known as the **City Beautiful movement**. The movement adopted a number of ideas from a British planning movement called Garden City. Supporters of the City Beautiful movement stressed the importance of including public parks and attractive boulevards in the design of cities. Those city planners claimed that such designs could be a civilizing influence for city-dwellers.

Americans took advantage of those new city parks to pursue a variety of outdoor activities during this period. Bicycling became immensely popular among both men and women during the late 1800s. By the turn of the century about 4 million Americans were riding bicycles. Playing croquet in city parks was also popular among Americans. In this simple game, a player uses a mallet to drive a ball through a series of wire wickets, or small arches. Played on lawns and park grounds, croquet was a sociable sport that became a fashionable pastime for many middle-class women.

Leisure and Sports

During the late 1800s many Americans spent their leisure time playing the era's new organized sports. Many urban residents found sports like baseball and football exciting to play as well as watch. Afternoon games and matches became a regular activity for many urban residents. During the late 1800s a number of spectator sports in the United States became increasingly more professional.

Baseball. Popular myth holds that Abner Doubleday invented the game of baseball. However, the basic organization and rules of the game actually evolved in the early and mid-1800s from the British game called rounders. Prior to the Civil War, young middle- and working-class city-dwellers organized neighborhood baseball teams. These teams like the New York Knickerbockers played teams in surrounding neighborhoods and cities. The outbreak of the Civil War interrupted the development of these clubs. However, the war greatly expanded the popularity of the sport. Troops from all over the United States grew familiar with the game.

In 1869 Aaron Champion organized the first professional baseball team, the Cincinnati Red Stockings. Talented players such as Harry Wright no longer had to balance a busy baseball schedule with work. The Red Stockings were a success, beating every team they played that year. Other clubs soon began to hire professional ball players as well.

Concerned about issues of gambling, players' contracts, and standardized rules, William Hulbert organized the National League in 1876. He created a governing body for the sport. Hulbert also established rules for play, strict guidelines for players' contracts, and rules limiting players' association with gamblers.

Baseball's popularity continued to rise. By 1890 professional teams were drawing an estimated 60,000 fans daily. A second professional league was founded in 1900. Three years later the first World Series was held between the Pittsburgh Pirates and the Boston Red Sox.

INTERPRETING THE VISUAL RECORD

Baseball. Fans used scorecards such as this one to keep track of their favorite teams' records and statistics. *How is the late-1800s baseball gear pictured here similar to the equipment used today?*

Baseball had become, in one sportswriter's words, "the national game of the United States." Not all Americans were allowed to play in the professional leagues, however. In 1887 team manager Adrian "Cap" Anson refused to let his team play against teams with African American players. Anson's action and the widespread discrimination in the baseball leagues resulted in African Americans being excluded from major league teams for 60 years. African Americans formed their own league, however, which produced many outstanding players.

Football. Like baseball, many Americans enjoyed watching football during their leisure time. Similar to soccer and the British game of rugby, football developed during the late 1800s on the college campuses of upper class New England schools. Walter Camp played football for Yale during the late 1870s. He made considerable contributions to the structure of the sport, establishing many of the rules and principles of the game. Discussing the spirit of the game, Camp stated, "There is no substitute for hard work and effort beyond the call of mere duty. That is what strengthens the soul and ennobles one's character."

Walter Camp poses in his Yale football uniform.

As football grew in popularity among college students in the late 1800s, many people objected to the violent nature of this sport. The *Chicago Tribune* documented the deaths of 18 college players and 46 high school players in the 1905 season. The sport's brutality led to discussions in Congress about outlawing it. Rule changes reduced the sport's danger. Football's popularity continues to grow.

Basketball. Like football, basketball was first played by students. James Naismith, a physical educator in Springfield, Massachusetts, invented the game of basketball in 1891. He was attempting to find a sport that could entertain a group of unruly students during the long, cold months of winter. Naismith claimed that basketball "demanded and fostered alert minds and supple [flexible] bodies. Decisions had to be made quickly. Play had to be neat and nimble [quick]." By the mid-1890s colleges in the East and Midwest had created both male and female teams. Basketball was one of the few sports during the late 1800s in which women's participation was encouraged.

✔ **READING CHECK:** How did outdoor activities and sports provide a source of leisure for Americans?

Basketball. Basketball served as a popular recreational activity for college students during the winter months. *How do these female college students benefit from playing basketball?*

Edwin Booth, the brother of President Lincoln's assassin, was one of the era's most popular actors. He drew critical praise for his performance in Hamlet.

Entertainment

While sports like baseball provided entertainment for many city-dwellers, others sought different sources of amusement. During the late 1800s people of every income level spent leisure time enjoying music and the theater.

Theater. Rapid urban growth brought many new entertainment seekers into U.S. cities. Many of these city-dwellers turned to the stage for entertainment. Portraying William Shakespeare's tragic heroes, Edwin Booth proved to be one of the most popular attractions of the 1860s and 1870s. Booth was considered one of the premier actors of his day. Due to public demand one season, Booth acted in 100 consecutive performances of *Hamlet*. Tickets for his opening performance in *Romeo and Juliet* in 1869 sold for as much as $125.

While the classic Shakespearean plays attracted a sophisticated audience, many Americans preferred more melodramatic shows. Because of their easily identifiable character types, these shows attracted a broad working-class audience. Often the villain was cast as a wealthy aristocrat, while the hero and heroine represented honest working-class people.

Attracting a similar audience, **vaudeville**—the French word for "light play"—was a type of variety show that featured a wide selection of short performances. Vaudeville shows often included animal acts, comics, famous impersonations, jugglers, magicians, singers, and skits. Some promoters of vaudeville became highly successful and went on to open chains of theaters.

Ragtime. Performed in vaudeville shows at the turn of the century, a new form of music known as **ragtime** proved popular with audiences. Created by African American musicians, ragtime emerged during the 1890s. It varied radically from the traditional Victorian waltzes and marches popular earlier that century. Copying the customary foot stomping of audiences listening to folk songs, ragtime pianists played a stomping or driving rhythm with the left hand and a syncopated or improvised melody with the right hand.

BIOGRAPHY

Scott Joplin

Known as the King of Ragtime, Scott Joplin was born into a family of musicians from East Texas in 1868. Joplin learned to play the piano before the age of seven. In his early teens, he began playing in bars and saloons throughout the Mississippi Valley. After playing briefly at the Chicago Exposition in 1893, Joplin settled in the St. Louis area and concentrated on composing new musical arrangements and experimenting with syncopated melodies.

As the ragtime craze spread across the United States, Joplin further refined his style. He found a growing audience for his music. Hearing Joplin play at the Maple Leaf Club in 1899, John Stillwell Stark immediately offered to publish Joplin's tune, the "Maple Leaf Rag." The tune became an instant hit. It sold hundreds of thousands of copies in the first decade of publication and made Joplin's name a household word.

After the success of the "Maple Leaf Rag" and several vaudeville tours, Joplin gave up playing for audiences. He began to concentrate on teaching music and composing. He spent much of the rest of his life working on an opera that had little success. Nevertheless, Joplin's ragtime songs remained popular among young city-dwellers even after his death in 1917.

Known as rags, ragtime songs inspired a host of new dances whose liveliness and self-expression contrasted sharply with the restraint of Victorian culture. Dances like the Cakewalk, the Grizzly Bear, and the Turkey Trot became popular in dance halls. Young middle- and working-class city-dwellers eagerly pursued these new forms of entertainment and leisure.

INTERPRETING THE VISUAL RECORD

Ragtime. The popularity of ragtime music grew with the emergence of lively dances. *How did the publisher of this ragtime tune incorporate the dance craze into the marketing of the sheet music?*

✔ **READING CHECK:** What new forms of popular music and theater developed in the late 1800s?

SECTION 3 REVIEW

Define and explain the significance of the following terms:
compulsory education laws
yellow journalism
City Beautiful movement
vaudeville
ragtime

Identify and explain the significance of the following individuals:
John Dewey
Frederick Law Olmsted
Walter Camp
James Naismith
Edwin Booth
Scott Joplin

1. **Using Graphic Organizers** Copy the graphic organizer below. Use it to describe the different leisure activities that were popular in the late 1800s.

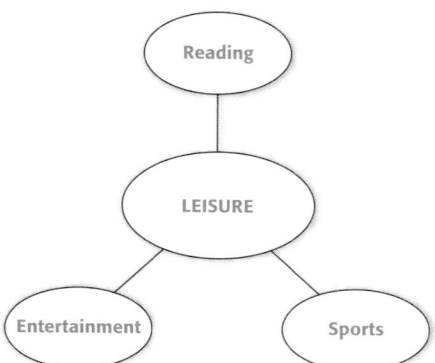

2. **Synthesizing** What impact do you think the expansion of public education had on the publishing industry of the late 1800s?
3. **Identifying Values** How did the development of public education and yellow journalism reflect democratic values?
4. **Evaluating** What leisure activities attracted working-class people? What did wealthy people do for leisure? What reasons can you give to explain why one economic class would take up different leisure practices than other classes?

Critical Thinking

5. Why is it important to set aside public "green space," such as parks, in cities?
   Consider:
   • what benefits green space offers to city-dwellers
   • what might happen if green space were not set aside

Review

Creating a Time Line

Copy the time line below onto a sheet of paper. Complete the time line by filling in the events and dates from the chapter that you think were most significant. Pick three events and explain why you think they were significant.

| 1865 | 1880 | 1895 | 1910 |

Writing a Summary

Using the Reading Checks as a guide, write an overview of the events in the chapter.

Identifying People and Ideas

Identify the following terms or individuals and explain their significance.

1. new immigrants
2. benevolent societies
3. Elisha Otis
4. mass transit
5. conspicuous consumption
6. Jane Addams
7. compulsory school laws
8. Frederick Law Olmsted
9. yellow journalism
10. Scott Joplin

Understanding Main Ideas

SECTION 1

1. What changes occurred in the pattern of immigration during the late 1800s?
2. Why did nativists argue against immigration?

SECTION 2

3. Why did cities grow in terms of population and size during the late 1800s?

SECTION 3

4. For what purpose did urban planners design large city parks?
5. How did popular literature, journalism, and other types of entertainment cater to a broad audience?

Reviewing Themes

1. **Cultural Diversity** What cultural practices did immigrants bring to the United States in the late 1800s?
2. **Technology and Society** How did technological developments alter U.S. cities and change the daily lives of city-dwellers?
3. **Democratic Values** In what ways did settlement houses, public schools, and newspapers assist all Americans equally?

Thinking Critically

1. **Evaluating** Why do you think President Grover Cleveland called a bill that would require all immigrants to take a literacy test "un-American?"
2. **Synthesizing** In what ways were new immigrants Americanized?
3. **Drawing Conclusions** How did class differences influence the way urban Americans enjoyed their leisure time?
4. **Identifying Cause and Effect** What factors led to a growth in the popularity of playing and watching sports during the late 1800s?
5. **Problem Solving** What do you think was the biggest problem facing U.S. cities in the late 1800s? How would you have solved this problem?

Writing About History

Writing to Persuade Imagine that you run a settlement house. Write a letter to a wealthy family persuading them to donate money to your settlement house. Be sure to explain the purpose of the settlement house, the specific programs it offers, and its effects on the city. Use the following chart to help organize your thoughts.

Settlement House		
Purpose	Programs and Services	Benefits

Strategies for Success

Review the **Strategies for Success** on *Analyzing*. Then reread the Section 1 subsection entitled The Nativist Response and answer the following questions.

1. What reasons did nativists have for opposing immigration to the United States?
2. How were economic concerns of working-class, native-born Americans a factor in the nativist response to immigration?
3. Explain the purpose of the Chinese Exclusion Act and the Immigration Restriction League.

Use your responses to answer the following questions.

4. Why and how did nativists respond to increased immigration during the late 1800s?
5. What political goals did the nativists hope to achieve? Were they successful?

Linking History and Geography

Settlement houses and benevolent societies often existed in cities with large immigrant populations. Study the map below. If the relationship between settlement houses, benevolent societies, and immigration holds true, what conclusions can you draw about patterns of immigrant population in the early 1900s?

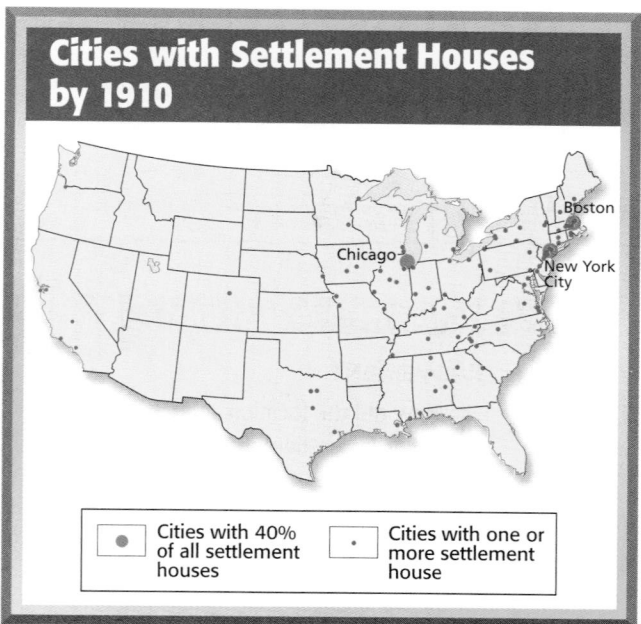

Cities with Settlement Houses by 1910

- ● Cities with 40% of all settlement houses
- · Cities with one or more settlement house

 internetconnect

TOPIC: Ellis Island and Angel Island
GO TO: go.hrw.com
KEYWORD: SD1 Ellis Island

Accessing the Internet through the HRW Web site, research Ellis Island or Angel Island. In addition to general information about these places, look for specific information about the process by which immigrants were admitted to the United States and the conditions under which they waited for permission to enter. Then, imagining that you are an immigrant, write a journal entry that contains specific references to information found in your research.

BUILDING YOUR PORTFOLIO

Complete one or all of the following projects independently or cooperatively.

Woman bicycling in the late 1800s

1 Cultural Diversity
Imagine that you are a new immigrant in the United States during the late 1800s and that you have a family member who is planning to immigrate as well. **Write a letter** *to your relative describing your experiences during the journey, what type of job you found, and who helped you adjust to American life.*

2 Technology and Society
Imagine that it is 1900 and you are a middle-class city office worker who is about to retire. **Create a comic strip** *to share with your grandchildren that describes the technological changes you have witnessed in the past 45 years and the impact of those changes on your daily life.*

3 Economic Development
Imagine that you are a member of a working-class family living in a tenement during the late 1800s. Keeping your small budget in mind, **plan an itinerary** *of leisure activities for an entire month.*

Conquering Distance

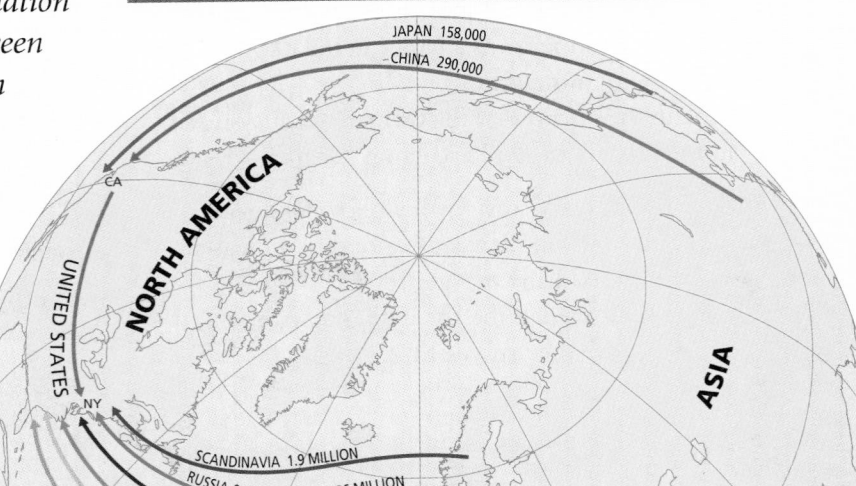

JAPAN 158,000
CHINA 290,000
CA
NORTH AMERICA
UNITED STATES
NY
ASIA
SCANDINAVIA 1.9 MILLION
RUSSIA & THE BALTICS 2.36 MILLION
IRELAND 2.3 MILLION
GREAT BRITAIN 2.79 MILLION
GERMANY 3.86 MILLION
ITALY 3.07 MILLION
EUROPE

The late 1800s saw massive population shifts in the United States. Between 1860 and 1910, some 23 million immigrants crossed the Atlantic and Pacific Oceans to reach America (see map at right). Many of these immigrants joined the millions of people making the cross-country trek to settle the American West. This westward migration was aided by railroad lines and improved systems of communication that linked numerous western cities together, forming the basis of a modern transcontinental economy.

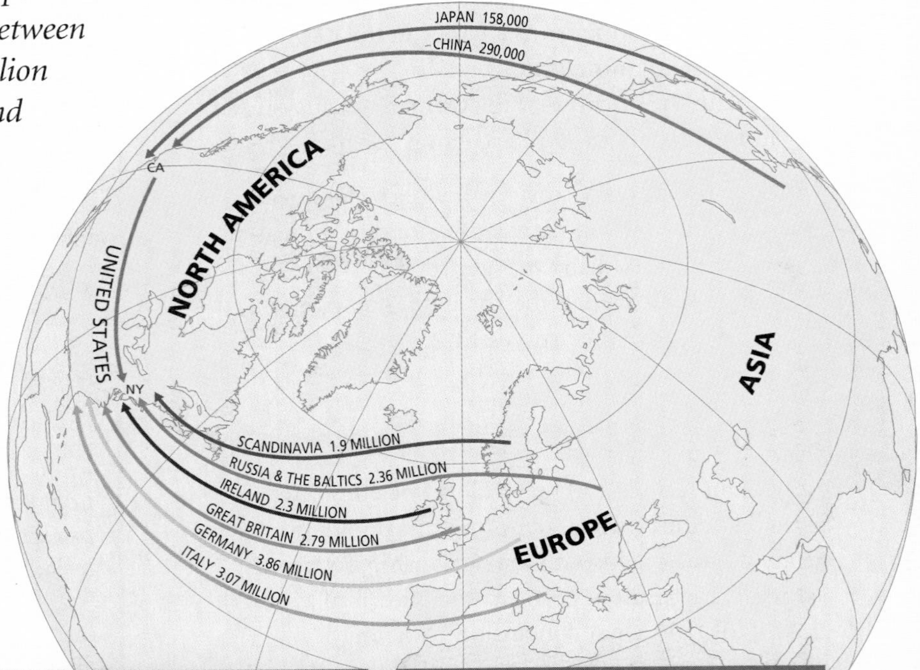

Asian immigration.

Immigrants from Asia had to travel twice as far as European immigrants to reach the United States. Although most Chinese immigrants initially settled along the West Coast, some eventually journeyed across the United States. In 1870 a Massachusetts factory owner began recruiting Chinese laborers from California to take the place of striking workers. As this practice caught on, more Chinese laborers made the trip to the East Coast. This migration led to the development of thriving Chinatowns in Boston and New York.

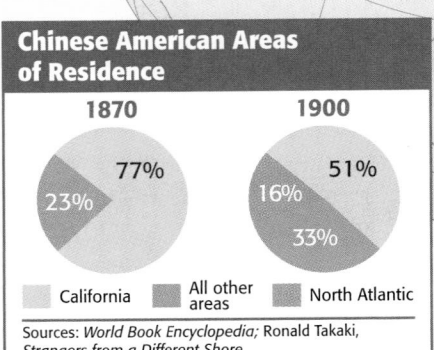

Chinese American Areas of Residence

1870
23%
77%

1900
16%
33%
51%

California | All other areas | North Atlantic

Sources: *World Book Encyclopedia*; Ronald Takaki, *Strangers from a Different Shore*

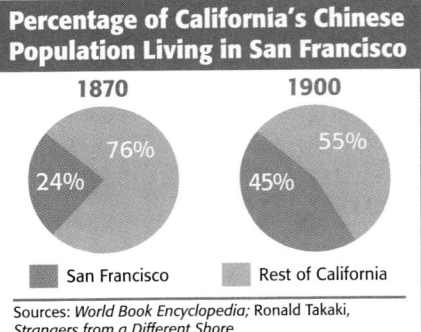

Percentage of California's Chinese Population Living in San Francisco

1870
24%
76%

1900
45%
55%

San Francisco | Rest of California

Sources: *World Book Encyclopedia*; Ronald Takaki, *Strangers from a Different Shore*

GEOGRAPHY AND HISTORY Skills

MOVEMENT

1. How did the location of Chinese American settlement shift between 1870 and 1900?
2. What country contributed the most immigrants to the United States between 1860 and 1910?

Conquering Distance across the West

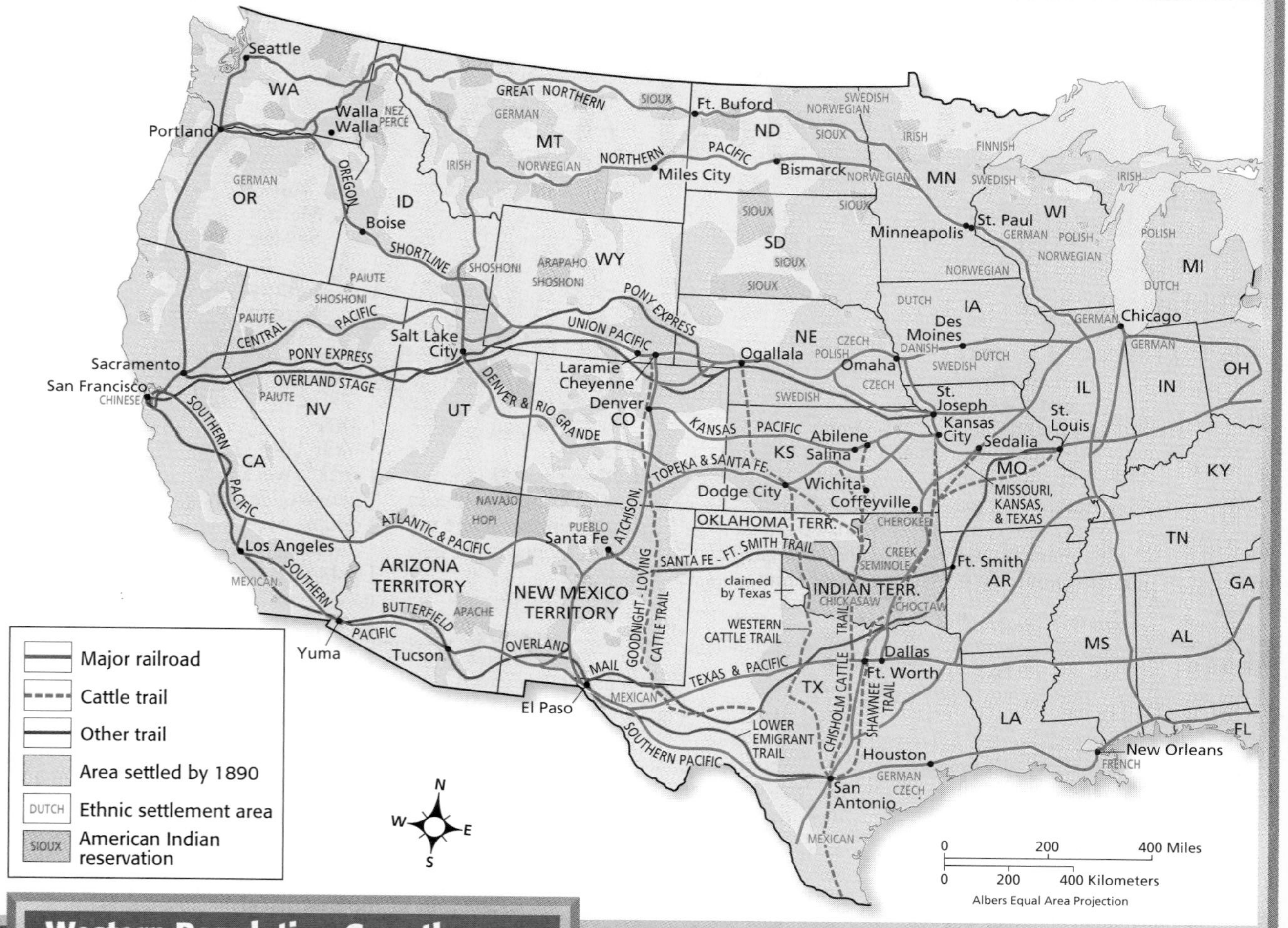

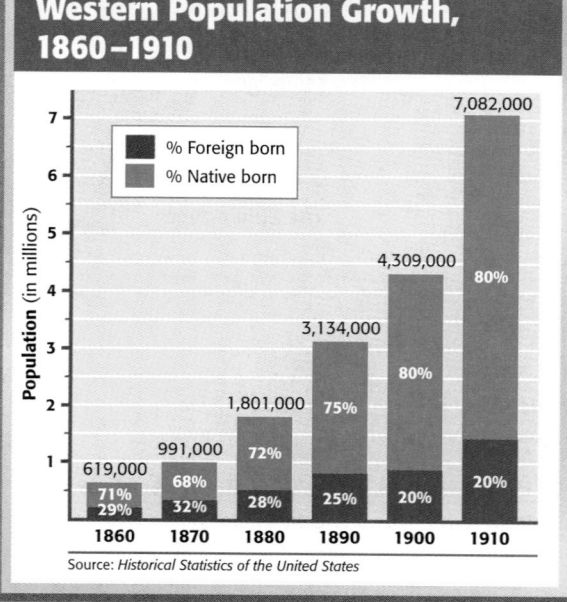

Legend:
- Major railroad
- Cattle trail
- Other trail
- Area settled by 1890
- DUTCH Ethnic settlement area
- SIOUX American Indian reservation

Scale: 0 — 200 — 400 Miles / 0 — 200 — 400 Kilometers
Albers Equal Area Projection

Western Population Growth, 1860–1910

Population (in millions)

Year	Total	% Native born	% Foreign born
1860	619,000	71%	29%
1870	991,000	68%	32%
1880	1,801,000	72%	28%
1890	3,134,000	75%	25%
1900	4,309,000	80%	20%
1910	7,082,000	80%	20%

Legend:
- % Foreign born
- % Native born

Source: *Historical Statistics of the United States*

Immigrant migration. As the network of railroads and western population increased, many immigrants began settling inland, rather than staying in cities on the East or West coast. This migration resulted in the presence of distinct ethnic traditions and cultures in many western cities.

GEOGRAPHY AND HISTORY Skills

LOCATION

1. In what year was the percentage of foreign-born residents living in the West the highest?
2. Identify the ethnic groups that established western settlements.

1865–1900
Politics in the Gilded Age

Young Mother Sewing by Mary Cassatt

U.S. gold dollar

1869
Business and Finance
Jay Gould's and Abel Rathbone Corbin's attempt to corner the gold market fails, causing a massive drop in the price of gold.

1870
World Events
The kingdom of Italy is unified under the leadership of Victor Emmanuel II.

1873
Business and Finance
The U.S. Congress votes to stop coining silver and to convert money to the gold standard.

1877
Daily Life
Puck, a weekly periodical featuring double-page cartoons, is published.

1880
The Arts
American impressionist artist Mary Cassatt paints *Young Mother Sewing.*

| 1865 | 1870 | 1875 | 1880 |

1866
Politics
Political boss William Marcy Tweed takes over the Tammany Hall political machine.

1871
The Arts
Thomas Nast begins his series of cartoons attacking the Tweed Ring.

1877
Politics
The Farmers' Alliance movement begins in Texas.

1879
World Events
The Zulu nation, founded in 1816, is dissolved by British forces after a violent military campaign.

A Thomas Nast cartoon of the Tweed Ring

THE GRANGER COLLECTION, NEW YORK

A leader of the Zulu nation

Before You Read

Build on What You Know

Life for many Americans changed dramatically during the late 1800s. Rapid industrialization and new opportunities drew increasing numbers of people to U.S. cities. In this chapter you will learn that politics in the United States during the late 1800s was frequently corrupt. These episodes of corruption inspired new efforts to restore honest government. Meanwhile, rural Americans grew more politically active, attempting to improve the conditions of their daily lives.

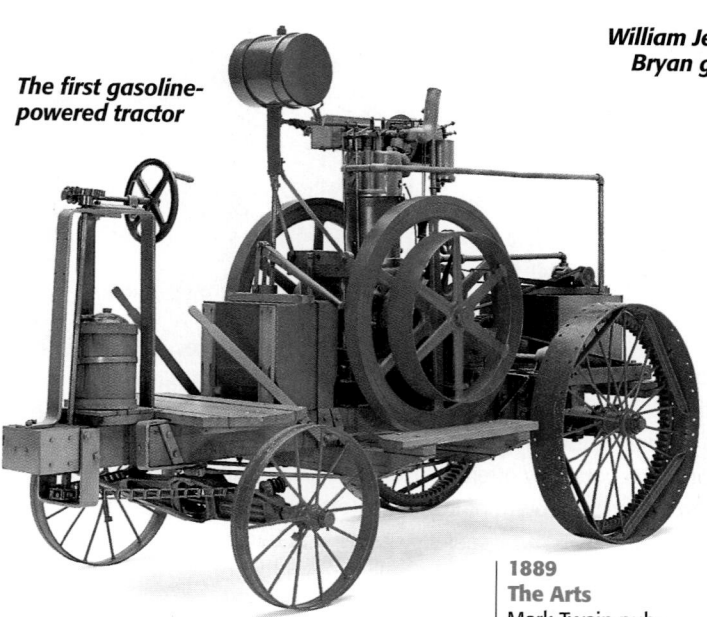

The first gasoline-powered tractor

William Jennings Bryan giving a speech

Eastman Kodak's Brownie box camera

1883
Politics
The U.S. Congress establishes the Civil Service Commission.

1889
The Arts
Mark Twain publishes the novel *A Connecticut Yankee in King Arthur's Court.*

1892
Science and Technology
The first gasoline-powered tractor is built in Iowa.

1892
Politics
The Populist Party is founded.

1896
Politics
William Jennings Bryan delivers his "Cross of Gold" speech.

1900
Daily Life
Eastman Kodak introduces a Brownie box camera that sells for $1, making photography accessible to nearly everyone.

1885   **1890**   **1895**   **1900**

1885
World Events
The Indian National Congress is formed in British-controlled India.

1888
Science and Technology
William S. Burroughs patents a machine that adds, subtracts, and prints.

1895
Daily Life
The Kellogg brothers patent peanut butter.

1897
Science and Technology
The world's largest refracting telescope, with a 40-inch lens, is installed at the Yerkes Observatory in Wisconsin.

An adding machine

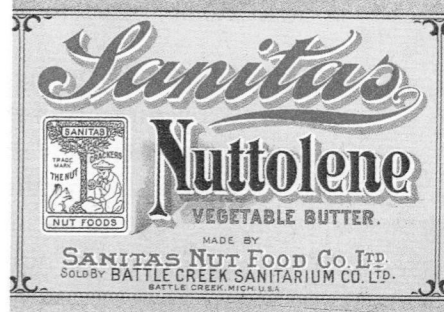

Peanut butter advertisement

Think About Themes

*Decide whether you **agree** or **disagree** with the following statements. Note why in your journal.*

Cultural Diversity In order to gain power, political parties in large U.S. cities must attract supporters from diverse groups of residents.

Democratic Values Testing is the best way to determine who should be hired to fill government jobs.

Geographic Diversity New political parties cannot win national power if they focus only on issues of concern to one geographic region.

Political Machines

OBJECTIVES

Read to understand:

1. how political machines emerged in U.S. cities
2. why immigrants were important to political machines
3. how corruption and illegal activities developed in many political machines
4. what events led to the collapse of public support for the Tweed Ring

KEY TERMS

political machines
political bosses
graft
kickbacks

KEY PEOPLE

Alexander Shepherd
James Pendergast
George Washington Plunkitt
William Marcy Tweed
Thomas Nast

EYEWITNESSES TO History

66 *I know what Parks is doing, but what do I care. He has raised my wages. Let him have his [illegal gains]!* 99
—Anonymous city worker

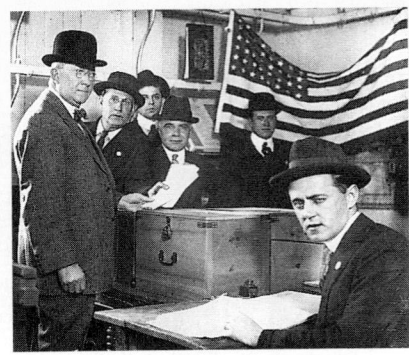

A New York official voting in the early 1900s

This city worker was responding to the charges of corruption of a New York politician. Despite the public awareness of corruption, local political leaders managed to gain broad support from their voters by offering favors and jobs. Many of these jobs came from public-works projects. The growth of urban centers during the late 1800s meant that cities required new streets, new sewer systems, and larger police and fire departments. Unfortunately, the need for these services also created an opportunity for political leaders to gain power and personal wealth.

The Rise of the Political Machine

The overwhelming growth of urban populations in the United States during the late 1800s created new challenges for city governments. New demands were placed on public services such as fire, police, and sanitation departments. Growing urban populations also required the expansion or new construction of bridges, parks, schools, streets, sewer systems, and utility systems. With the support of very well organized political parties, city council members and district representatives took charge of city governments. They oversaw new public services and, in many cases, pocketed money meant for the public good.

Political bosses. During the late 1800s well-organized political parties dominated city governments in the United States. Because of their success in getting their members elected to local political offices, these parties were called **political machines**. Powerful **political bosses** managed these machines. Bosses dictated party positions on city ordinances and made deals with business leaders. They also controlled the precinct captains, aldermen, and council members who kept the machine running smoothly.

Although bosses provided party leadership, the real strength of political machines lay in the relationship between precinct captains and potential voters living in the urban neighborhoods. By offering jobs, political favors, and services to local residents, precinct captains won support for the political machine. At election time, ward bosses and precinct captains instructed local residents to vote for their selected candidates. This practice ensured the continued power of the political machine.

Growing American cities struggled to meet increasing demands for public services such as sanitation services.

Public services. During the late 1800s political machines attempted to provide the public services required by growing U.S. cities. Political bosses such as Alexander Shepherd of Washington financed expanded sewer and water systems, paved streets, and provided other public services. Between 1871 and 1873 Shepherd's board of public works spent $20 million, creating significant civic improvements and new jobs in the nation's capital. This boom of public-works projects meant that bosses could distribute many jobs among loyal supporters.

By providing jobs, political favors, and services to local residents, political machines were able to win support from many poor and working-class city-dwellers. Political bosses and local precinct representatives often formed close relationships with local voters.

✔ **READING CHECK:** How did political machines emerge in American cities?

Immigrants and Political Machines

Because political machines helped the urban poor, new immigrants often became particularly loyal supporters of political machines. New immigrants in the largest cities commonly suffered from harsh living and working conditions.

Machine politicians often met immigrants as soon as they arrived in the United States. They helped the newcomers get settled in their new homeland. During the 1890s Tammany Hall, the powerful Democratic political machine in New York City, sent numerous party workers to Ellis Island to meet the new immigrants. The party workers assisted the immigrants by finding them temporary housing and jobs. Tammany Hall workers also helped immigrants become naturalized citizens and thus eligible to vote for Tammany Hall candidates. Tammany Hall gained considerable power during the 1860s and early 1870s. However, Tammany officials failed to offer any extensive programs to address poverty and poor housing conditions.

Political bosses ensured voter loyalty among immigrant groups by providing jobs in exchange for votes. James Pendergast was a particularly well-liked boss in Kansas City, Missouri. He began his political career while running a saloon in the industrial river-bottom district where many immigrants lived and worked. Pendergast gained considerable political support by providing jobs and special services to his African American, Irish American, and Italian American constituents. "There is no kinder hearted or more sympathetic man in Kansas City than Jim Pendergast," said one Kansas City resident. "He will go down in his pockets after his last cent to help a friend. No man is more easily moved to sympathy or good sense than Jim Pendergast." Another immigrant described the efforts of a local political boss.

66 To this one he lends a dollar; for another he obtains a railroad ticket without payment; he has coal distributed in the depth of winter; . . . he sometimes sends poultry at Christmas time; he buys medicine for a sick person; he helps bury the dead. 99

This "Tammany Bank" was inspired by political corruption in the 1870s. Place a coin in the Tammany politician's hand and he deposits it in his pocket.

James Pendergast ran a political machine in Kansas City, Missouri.

Most political machines maintained their political power with the support of immigrant voters. In some cities, however, immigrants became active members of political machines, serving as officeholders, organizers, and representatives. In Boston, for example, the Irish American population was highly influential in the local Democratic machine. During the mid-1800s Irish Americans in Boston accounted for more than one third of the city's voters.

Because Irish Americans spoke English as a first language, they had slightly easier access to American political processes than many other immigrant groups. Many Irish Americans who were loyal to the political machine in Boston were rewarded with jobs in the local police and fire departments. Ambitious Irish American politicians rose quickly through the ranks of Boston's political machine. Second-generation immigrants John F. Fitzgerald—President John F. Kennedy's grandfather—and James Michael Curley both rose from the ranks of local boss to become mayor of the city during the late 1800s.

✔ **READING CHECK:** Why were immigrants important to political machines?

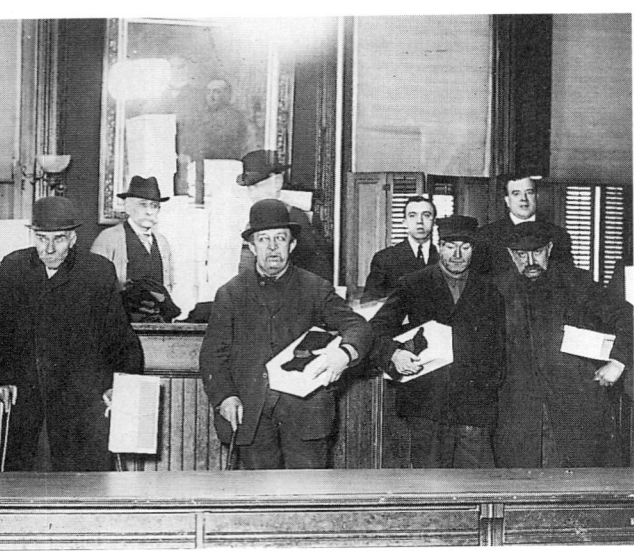

Graft and Corruption

Political machines often resorted to corruption in their attempt to take control of city governments. Although political machines successfully got party members re-elected, machine corruption often interfered with the important functions of city government.

Election fraud. For political machines to maintain their power, their candidates had to win elections. When jobs and political favors were not enough to build popular support during elections, some political machines turned to fraud. A New York resident testified before the U.S. House of Representatives on election fraud.

66 Gangs or bodies of men hired for the purpose, assembled at these headquarters where they were furnished with names and numbers, and under a leader or captain, they went out . . . in nearly every part of the city, registering many times each, and when the day of election came these repeaters, supplied abundantly with intoxicating drinks, and changing coats, hats, or caps, as occasion required to avoid recognition or detection, commenced the work of 'voting early and often.' 99

Voting fraud was widespread in many U.S. cities. For example, during one election in Philadelphia, a voting district with just 100 registered voters somehow returned 252 votes!

Graft. Once inside city government, political bosses often became even more corrupt. They looked for ways to increase their own political power and personal wealth. One way to get rich was to take advantage of the massive amounts of public funds involved in providing essential city services. Many city officials practiced graft—the acquisition of money or political power through illegal or dishonest methods. Graft was a common problem in almost every U.S. city with a powerful political machine.

Politicians often received bribes, payoffs, or **kickbacks**—payments of part of the earnings from a job or contract. Business leaders often paid kickbacks when lobbying for an opportunity to provide public services for a city. During the late 1890s a railway corporation paid Chicago aldermen as much as $25,000 to vote for local ordinances that would grant it special privileges. Also in Chicago, business leader Charles Tyson Yerkes built an empire of street railway lines by paying Alderman John Powers to support city ordinances favorable to his company. Yerkes was granted a virtual monopoly over Chicago's mass transit system. Explaining his loyalty to Yerkes, Powers once confessed, "You can't get elected to the [city] council unless Mr. Yerkes says so."

NEW-YORK HISTORICAL SOCIETY

This painting shows Tammany Hall.

Strategies for Success Synthesizing

Synthesizing is a key part of interpreting the past. To synthesize is to combine information and ideas from several different sources or points of view to obtain a new understanding of a topic or event. Most of the narrative writing in *The American Nation* is a synthesis. It pulls together data from a variety of sources to form an original account of our nation's history.

How to Synthesize

1. **Identify the subject and sources.** Identify the general topic or issue addressed by your sources. Then, if possible, find out about the personal, social, and historical background of the author of each source.

2. **Analyze the sources.** Examine carefully the information that each source provides about the subject. If your sources present different points of view, identify the main idea expressed by each source and determine whether it is supported by facts, opinions, or a combination of both.

3. **Compare and contrast the sources.** Examine the similarities and the differences between the information and ideas in your sources. As you do so, look for ways to link the sources together. Try to account for any different points of view.

4. **Form your own interpretation of the subject.** Use your analysis and comparison of the sources, along with your knowledge of the historical period, to form your own interpretation of the subject.

Applying the Strategy

Read George Washington Plunkitt's description of "honest graft" on the next page. Then synthesize this description with the following account of "honest graft" from a recent historical text.

66 George Washington Plunkitt, a Tammany ward 'heeler' or boss, liked to call [the practice of profiting from one's office] 'honest graft,' a fair exchange of cash, influence, liquor, and above all jobs for working-class votes. Plunkitt and his fellow Tammany bosses lined their own pockets, stealing millions of dollars from the public treasury while allowing important decisions on issues such as public transportation to be made by those private entrepreneurs willing to pay large bribes. 99

Practicing the Strategy

Answer the following questions.

1. Are the ideas expressed in each of these sources based on facts, opinions, or a combination of both?

2. How are these two accounts of "honest graft" similar? How are they different?

3. Based on these two sources and the knowledge you have gained from the text, what is your interpretation of "honest graft"?

When journalists and reformers began speaking out against the corruption of machine politics, some bosses attempted to defend their practices and personal economic gain. Political boss George Washington Plunkitt of Tammany Hall explained what he called "honest graft."

66 My party's in power in the city, and it's goin' to undertake a lot of public improvements. Well, I'm tipped off, say, that they're going to lay out a new park at a certain place. . . . I go to that place and I buy up all the land I can in the neighborhood. Then the board of this or that makes its plan public, and there is a rush to get my land. . . . Ain't it perfectly honest to charge a good price and make a profit on my investment and foresight? . . . Well, that's honest graft. 99

✔ **READING CHECK:** How did corruption and illegal activities develop in many political machines?

AMERICAN ARTS

Thomas Nast's Cartoons

One of the most influential political cartoonists of the late 1800s was Thomas Nast. Nast's cartoons increased the importance of cartoons in the American press. Nast drew cartoons with recognizable images and made creative use of standard cartoonist techniques such as caricatures—the portrayal of political figures with comically exaggerated features. Many of the common characters used in modern-day political cartoons, such as Uncle Sam, the Republican elephant, and the Democratic donkey, were first popularized by Nast. Editors for *Harper's Weekly* claimed that Nast's bold and witty cartoons increased the magazine's subscriptions by some 200,000.

The popularity of Nast's cartoons for *Harper's Weekly* inspired other journals to hire political cartoonists to boost circulation. Throughout the late 1800s publications such as *Puck, Judge,* and *Life* hired political cartoonists to offer witty and sharp commentary on political events. In doing so, political cartoonists perfected their use of analogies and literary allusions to refer to political events and characters. For example, many cartoonists portrayed politicians as Shakespearean characters such as Hamlet and Caesar, who engaged in political intrigue, to depict particular events of American political life. As in modern-day political cartoons, the cartoons of the late 1800s offered critical political commentary as well as humor.

Thomas Nast cartoon depicting U.S. political parties in the 1880s

Understanding the Arts

1. What do the donkey and the elephant represent in this cartoon?
2. What techniques do cartoonists use to depict political events?

The Tweed Ring. Plunkitt's bold admission of his own graft offers a clue as to the amount of corruption in Tammany Hall. Tammany Hall had a long history as a social and political organization dating back to 1789. However, it is best known for the period during the 1860s when William Marcy Tweed reigned as its boss.

Tweed had considerable control over the issuing of contracts for public projects and government jobs. Tweed and his ring of political supporters used this position of power to gain bribes and kickbacks. Historians have estimated that the Tweed Ring collected more than $200 million in graft between 1865 and 1871.

Tweed's political power and control over the Tammany machine collapsed abruptly when public opinion turned against him. The corruption of Tammany Hall and the Tweed Ring was mercilessly revealed in a series of political cartoons drawn by Thomas Nast. In 1871 Nast published some 50 cartoons in *Harper's Weekly* that sharply criticized Tweed and Tammany Hall. Aware of the power of Nast's cartoons to influence public opinion, Tweed demanded, "Stop them . . . pictures. I don't care so much what the papers write about me. My constituents can't read. But . . . they can see pictures."

Along with a series of articles published in the *New York Times,* Nast's cartoons exposed the corruption of Tammany Hall and contributed to Tweed's indictment for fraud and extortion in 1871. Tweed escaped from jail but was arrested in Spain. Officials there recognized him from one of Nast's drawings. While serving the remainder of his 12-year sentence, Tweed died in jail.

INTERPRETING THE VISUAL RECORD

Tweed Ring. Thomas Nast's cartoons helped expose Boss Tweed. *What characteristics of this cartoon suggest corruption?*

✔ **READING CHECK:** What events led to the collapse of public support for the Tweed Ring?

SECTION 1 REVIEW

Define and explain the significance of the following terms:
political machines
political bosses
graft
kickbacks

Identify and explain the significance of the following individuals:
Alexander Shepherd
James Pendergast
George Washington Plunkitt
William Marcy Tweed
Thomas Nast

1. Using Graphic Organizers Copy the graphic organizer below. Use it to explain how political machines built support for their candidates.

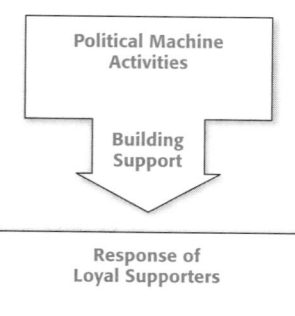

Political Machine Activities

Building Support

Response of Loyal Supporters

2. Synthesizing What kinds of corrupt activities did political bosses engage in once they gained power?

3. Analyzing How did political machines build support among immigrant groups?

4. Hypothesizing Despite the evidence of corruption, political machines retained strong public support. Why did people continue to support the machines?

Critical Thinking

5. Review the Thomas Nast cartoon at the top of this page. What effect did Nast's political cartoons have on public support for the Tweed Ring?
Consider:
• how William Marcy Tweed is portrayed in the cartoon
• what political statement a newspaper reader might be able to interpret from the drawing
• what the cartoon does that newspaper articles cannot do

SECTION 2
Restoring Honest Government

OBJECTIVES

Read to understand:

1. what scandals plagued the Grant administration
2. why Americans wanted political reform, and how this desire affected the Republican Party
3. why President Arthur's positions on civil service reform changed, and how this affected his political party
4. how President Harrison dealt with President Cleveland's reforms

KEY TERMS

Gilded Age
Stalwarts
Pendleton Civil Service Act
mugwumps

KEY PEOPLE

James A. Garfield
Chester A. Arthur
Grover Cleveland
Benjamin Harrison

EYEWITNESSES TO History

❝ Mr. Lincoln . . . held that ours is a government of the people, by the people, for the people. I maintain, on the contrary, that it is a government of politicians, by politicians, for politicians. ❞
—William McElroy

Political cartoon depicting corruption

William McElroy expressed a sentiment held by many Americans in this fictional letter of advice to a young politician that was printed in the *Atlantic Monthly* in 1880. Corruption and fraud affected politics at a national level as well as locally. During the late 1800s national scandals exposed illegal financial practices by high-ranking politicians. Many Americans began to question the character of some elected officials. Most observers of the time offered similar condemnations of national political life. "One might search the whole list of Congress, Judiciary, and Executive [branches] during the 25 years 1870 to 1895, and find little but damaged reputation," claimed historian Henry Adams. "The period was poor in purpose and barren in results."

Scandal in the White House

In 1869 political boss William Tweed and his gang looted the New York City treasury. That same year, Ulysses S. Grant began his turbulent service as president of the United States. Republican Party leaders seeking a moderate candidate had selected Grant to run for the presidency. His fame as a Union army general made him a popular candidate. With the slogan "Let us have peace," Grant won the election. He seemed to be the leader the country needed to get through the post–Civil War years.

Grant's first term. Grant's first term in office, however, was marred by several scandals. Grant's troubles began on Black Friday—September 24, 1869. On that day financier Jay Gould and James Fisk—the president's brother-in-law—made an attempt to corner the gold market. Many Wall Street investors and speculators were ruined financially. A congressional investigation into the event revealed that Gould and Abel Rathbone Corbin had tried to influence the government's financial policies to their own benefit. The president refused to follow Gould and Corbin's advice, but the two spread rumors anyway that Grant had agreed with them. These rumors had led to widespread speculation in the gold market. There was even some evidence that the president's wife, Julia Grant, had invested $500,000 in the gold market.

In 1872 an even greater scandal surfaced. This time Grant's vice president, Schuyler Colfax, was involved. In 1867, directors of the

These headlines report the economic troubles of 1869.

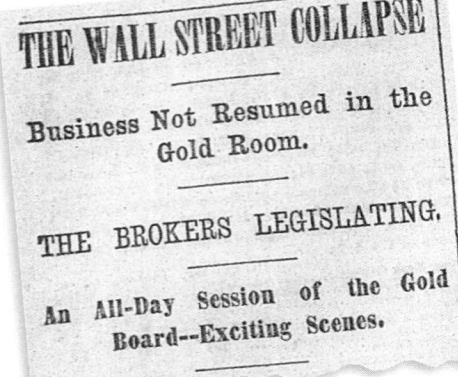

THE WALL STREET COLLAPSE

Business Not Resumed in the Gold Room.

THE BROKERS LEGISLATING.

An All-Day Session of the Gold Board--Exciting Scenes.

Union Pacific Railroad had formed the Crédit Mobilier corporation. They then awarded the company contracts to build a section of the transcontinental railroad. Union Pacific Railroad stockholders gave or sold shares of stock in the construction of the transcontinental railroad to congressmembers. The stockholders hoped to gain influence and favorable legislation.

The Crédit Mobilier stock proved to be a profitable deal for the members of Congress. Congress issued federal subsidies for the cost of the railroad construction. The U.S. government paid little attention to Crédit Mobilier's operations and was unaware of costs of the construction it had subsidized. Crédit Mobilier was able to overcharge Union Pacific by more than $20 million. These excess profits went straight into the pockets of Crédit Mobilier's stockholders. These stockholders included members of Congress such as Schuyler Colfax, who was then Speaker of the House. Although the schemes took place before Grant became president, the subsequent scandal tarnished his administration's image because of Colfax's position as vice president.

Newspaper editor Horace Greeley ran against President Grant in the 1872 election.

The election of 1872. The multiplying scandals encouraged political opponents to challenge Grant in the presidential election of 1872. Many critics saw the corruption in Grant's administration as a by-product of the spoils system. Rather than award civil service jobs as rewards, they wanted ability to be the deciding factor. Reformers proposed that applicants who earned the highest grades on competitive examinations should receive the jobs.

Civil service reform was the battle cry of *New York Tribune* editor Horace Greeley, Grant's Liberal Republican opponent in the 1872 presidential race. The Liberal Republican Party was formed by Republicans shocked by the Grant scandals and tired of Reconstruction. Hoping to benefit from the split in the Republican Party, Democrats also threw their support behind Greeley.

Liberal Republicans saw the Crédit Mobilier scandal as a nail in Grant's political coffin. However, Grant played on his image as a war hero and easily won re-election. Disheartened and exhausted, Greeley died just 24 days after the election. His party did not last much longer. It seemed that civil service reform was finished too.

✔ **READING CHECK:** What scandals plagued the Grant administration?

Grant's second term. The episodes of corruption continued during Grant's second term in office. In 1874 a new scandal erupted over the taxation of whiskey. Some officials at the Treasury Department who had received their positions as a result of the spoils system were charged with accepting bribes from distillers and distributors of whiskey. In return, treasury officials reduced the amount of taxes that the whiskey distributors had to pay. Public exposure of the so-called Whiskey Ring further encouraged reformers. Hoping to end the fraud under the spoils system, reformers pushed to end the practice of granting jobs as political rewards. The scandals also increased many Americans' distrust of politicians.

INTERPRETING THE VISUAL RECORD

Grant's administration. Public exposure of corruption in Grant's administration led to increasing opposition to the spoils system. *What does this cartoon suggest about Grant's administration?*

Mark Twain's Political Writings

Throughout his literary career, Mark Twain had a rare ability to present compelling and often humorous stories that dealt with important issues in American society. Twain used satire, a form of writing that uses humor to point out human faults. In the 1873 novel The Gilded Age, *Twain and co-author Charles Dudley Warner present a satirical conversation about Congress's inability to weed out corrupt politicians. Twain's 1889 novel,* A Connecticut Yankee in King Arthur's Court, *offers a commentary on American political ambition. In the tale a Connecticut man finds himself transported back in time to medieval England. The excerpt describes the man's thoughts as he begins to discover that he is in the 500s, not the 1800s.*

from *The Gilded Age*

"I think Congress always tries to do as near right as it can, according to its lights. A man can't ask any fairer than that. The first preliminary it always starts out on, is to clean itself, so to speak. It will arraign [put on trial] two or three dozen of its members, or maybe four or five dozen, for taking bribes to vote for this and that and the other bill last winter."

Mark Twain

"It goes up into the dozens, does it?"

"Well, yes; in a free country like ours, where any man can run for Congress and anybody can vote for him, you can't expect immortal purity all the time—it ain't in nature. . . . "

"So Congress always lies helpless in quarantine ten weeks of a session. That's encouraging. Colonel, poor Laura will never get any benefit from our bill. Her trial will be over before Congress has half purified itself.—And doesn't it occur to you that by the time it has expelled all its impure members there may not be enough members left to do business legally?"

"Why I did not say Congress would expel anybody. . . . But good God we *try* them, don't we!"

from *A Connecticut Yankee in King Arthur's Court*

Wherefore, being a practical Connecticut man, . . . I made up my mind to two things: if it was still the nineteenth century and I was among lunatics and couldn't get away, I would presently boss that asylum or know the reason why; and if, on the other hand, it was really the sixth century, all right, I didn't want any softer thing: I would boss the whole country inside of three months; for I judged I would have the start of the best-educated man in the kingdom by a matter of thirteen hundred years and upward.

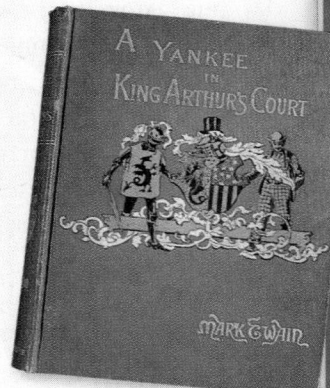

Cover of A Connecticut Yankee in King Arthur's Court

UNDERSTANDING LITERATURE

1. Why would Congress try its members for corruption but not expel them?
2. How does the Connecticut man resemble politicians in the late 1800s?
3. How does Twain use humor and exaggeration in these selections to portray American political life?

Politics of the Gilded Age. The politics of scandal and corruption shocked and troubled many voters. Citizens began to cast a more skeptical eye on the behavior and ethical standards of their political leaders. In 1873 Mark Twain and Charles Dudley Warner published a satirical novel. The book examined the values of wealthy Americans and the nature of national politics after the Civil War. Twain and Warner titled their novel *The Gilded Age.* They believed that politics was like the base material that hides beneath the glittering gold surface of a gilded object. In politics corruption and greed lurked below the polite and prosperous luster of American society during the late 1800s. The image struck a chord, and the era became known as the **Gilded Age**.

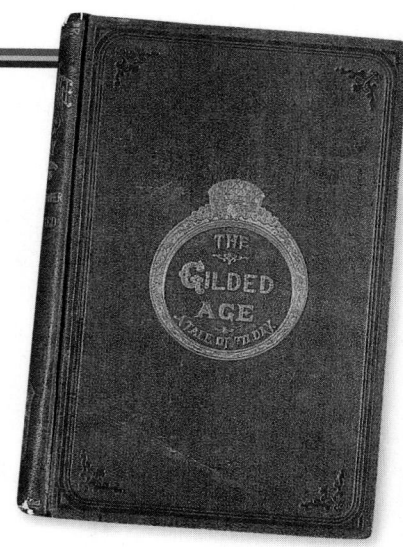

Mark Twain and Charles Dudley Warner's novel The Gilded Age *described American political life as a gilded surface with corruption and greed lying underneath.*

The authors had ample evidence to support their view—particularly in the area of politics. Despite the upper and middle classes' adoption of British Victorian culture, Twain argued that Americans were actually driven by "money lust." Twain accused Americans of holding the motto "Get rich; dishonestly if we can, honestly if we must." Politicians of both parties—and at every level of government—made speeches about the great honor of holding public office. However, they often showed more interest in taking advantage of their positions to steal from the public treasury than in serving the public good. "Unless you can get . . . a Senator, or a Congressman, . . . to use his 'influence' in your behalf, you cannot get an employment of the most trivial nature in Washington," wrote Twain. "Mere merit, fitness and capability, are useless baggage to you without 'influence.'" Motivated by a distrust of political leaders, many Americans began to push for political reforms during the Gilded Age.

The Struggle for Reform

Reforming the spoils system again became a major issue in the 1876 presidential campaign. Democrats hoped to make the corruption of the Grant administration a campaign issue. They nominated New York governor Samuel J. Tilden as their presidential candidate. Tilden had won national attention by helping break up the corrupt Tweed Ring. The Republicans also nominated a reform candidate, Ohio governor Rutherford B. Hayes, who was a well-known supporter of civil service reform. Hayes narrowly won the election.

A split in the Republican Party. President Hayes's reform efforts soon angered his party. The Republicans had split into two groups—nicknamed the **Stalwarts** and the Half-Breeds—over the issue of patronage, or rewarding political supporters with government jobs. Led by Senator Roscoe Conkling of New York, the Stalwarts strongly opposed reform. Conkling referred to the proposed merit system for government jobs as "snivel service."

Led by James G. Blaine of Maine, who claimed to support reform, the Half-Breeds did not completely oppose patronage jobs. Julius Bing was an early supporter of civil service reform. While still a young congressional aide, Bing published an article in the journal *The North American Review.* He argued in favor of the use of civil service exams to grant jobs on merit rather than by patronage.

Civil Service

Modern Americans taking a civil service exam

Although the Pendleton Civil Service Act transferred just 10 percent of federal jobs to a merit-based system of hiring, the act did create the Civil Service Commission (CSC). The CSC established policies for examination and hiring based on merit rather than political patronage. At the time, many officials were concerned that geographical biases of the testing would cause most jobs to go to well-educated New Englanders. To avoid this bias in testing, the CSC specified that the examinations should be "practical in character." The exam should test applicants on skills and knowledge closely related to the actual tasks of the job.

The use of civil service examinations has greatly expanded since 1883. The variety of government jobs requiring exams has also grown. The federal government disbanded the CSC in 1978 and assigned its tasks to other federal agencies. Many state and city civil service commissions still exist to oversee nonfederal government jobs. Today, examinations are given to applicants for positions in fields such as air-traffic control, foreign service, law enforcement, and postal service. Once employed, civil service employees have special protection against politically motivated dismissals. To ensure the strength of the merit system, civil service commissions review dismissals to verify that employees are dismissed only for reasons directly related to job performance.

> ❝ Argument against the reform of the present chaos is the fear of a permanent bureaucracy, and of the anti-republican tendencies of such permanent institutions. We entertain no such apprehensions [fears]. A permanent bureaucracy is only dangerous when it is *incompetent and practically irresponsible.* ❞

Civil service reform remained controversial within both political parties throughout the Gilded Age.

Hayes chose not to run for re-election in 1880, noting the political conflict between the Stalwarts and the Half-Breeds within his own party. He explained to his wife, "I am heartily tired of this life of bondage, responsibility, and toil." At the Republican convention, the Stalwarts and the Half-Breeds battled to control the party ticket. The Half-Breeds won. They named the relatively unknown senator James A. Garfield as the Republican Party's presidential candidate. To satisfy the Stalwarts, they placed Conkling's political ally Chester A. Arthur on the ticket as the vice presidential nominee.

✔ **READING CHECK:** Why did Americans want political reform? How did this desire affect the Republican Party?

Garfield's assassination. Garfield edged out his Democratic rival, Civil War veteran General Winfield Scott Hancock, by fewer than 10,000 votes. His presidency was short-lived, however. On July 2, 1881, Garfield was shot, less than four months after his inauguration. The assassin was Charles Guiteau (guh-TOH), a mentally unstable man who had unsuccessfully sought a government job. Ironically, in the days before the incident Garfield had refused to increase the security around the White House. He commented, "Assassination can no more be guarded against than death by lightning; and it is not best to worry about either."

President James A. Garfield was shot by Charles Guiteau in a Washington train station.

THE GRANGER COLLECTION, NEW YORK

Guiteau had believed that killing Garfield would further the Stalwart cause. The shooting had the opposite effect, however. After Garfield died in September, his successor, Arthur, responded sympathetically to the calls for reform and abandoned his opposition to it.

Reforms and reactions. In 1883 President Arthur helped secure passage of the **Pendleton Civil Service Act**. The bill established the Civil Service Commission to administer competitive examinations to those people seeking government jobs. The act proved to be an important step toward reform. It established as law the idea that federal jobs below the policy-making level should be filled based on merit. Critics charged, however, that the act was of limited value. They noted that it covered only about 10 percent of federal jobs.

PRESIDENTIAL Lives

1837–1908
In Office 1885–1889
and 1893–1897

Grover Cleveland

Grover Cleveland is the only U.S. president to serve two nonconsecutive terms. After completing his first term, Cleveland did not miss the busy life of the presidency. He wrote in 1889, "You cannot imagine the relief which has come to me with the termination of my official term." Enjoying his free time, Cleveland described his new interests, "I started the fishing branch of the firm business today. . . . I caught twenty-five fish with my own rod and line."

In 1892 the Democratic Party began searching for a candidate to run against Benjamin Harrison. They again called upon Cleveland. He was not eager to run again after his defeat four years earlier. "The office of President has not, to me personally, a single allurement [attraction]." Nevertheless, Cleveland felt compelled by a sense of duty to his party to run for the presidency.

Angered by Arthur's reform efforts, many Stalwarts refused to support his bid for the 1884 Republican presidential nomination. Instead, they cast their votes for James Blaine, the leader of the Half-Breeds. Blaine's nomination upset Republican reformers. They charged that the candidate "wallowed in spoils like a rhinoceros in an African pool." Called **mugwumps**—the Algonquian word for "big chiefs"—these reformers supported the Democratic candidate, Grover Cleveland. Like Samuel Tilden, Cleveland had gained national attention when he opposed Tammany Hall while governor of New York.

Instead of a discussion of the issues, mudslinging dominated the campaign. A bachelor, Cleveland was accused of fathering a child out of wedlock. He refused to participate in the mudslinging however, replying, "The other side can have a monopoly of all the dirt in this campaign." The New York *World* defended Cleveland, listing four reasons for supporting the candidate. "1. He is an honest man; 2. He is an honest man; 3. He is an honest man; 4. He is an honest man." Despite the charges against Cleveland's character and private life, he won the election.

✔ **READING CHECK:** How did Chester A. Arthur change his position on civil service reform after Garfield's assassination? How did this affect his political party?

Advances and Setbacks

Proclaiming that "a public office is a public trust," President Cleveland entered the White House determined to promote political reform. Cleveland hoped to end the days when government jobs were handed out in reward for political favors. Toward this end, he doubled the number of federal jobs requiring civil service exams.

James Blaine (left), leader of the Half-Breeds, won the Republican Party nomination for president in 1884. Grover Cleveland (right) received the Democratic nomination.

Read More About It

Free Find:

Grover Cleveland

After reading the biography on Grover Cleveland on the **Holt Researcher** CD–ROM, write a short essay summarizing the role of Cleveland in the history of civil service reform in the United States.

Cleveland's support of reform efforts outraged many Stalwarts and Democratic legislators. One Democratic member of Congress defended the spoils system by arguing that civil service reform was inconsistent with the U.S. republican electoral process.

66 **Take the President. On this theory, Cleveland should have said to Arthur on March 4th [inauguration day], 'Mr. Arthur, it's true the people have chosen me to fill your place. But I believe that when a man is in office and is doing well, he should not be disturbed. Everyone says you are a good President, so I'll just go back to my law practice in Buffalo and leave you in the White House.'** 99

Although Cleveland's stand on reform annoyed some party leaders, he won the Democratic presidential nomination in 1888. To oppose him, the Republicans chose Benjamin Harrison of Indiana, a grandson of the ninth president, William Henry Harrison. Cleveland won the popular election by some 100,000 votes. However, Harrison came out on top in electoral votes and won the race.

The new president and Congress quickly set out to reward their supporters, thereby weakening the reform efforts of Cleveland. The Republicans filled practically every job not on the civil service list with members of their own party. During 1890 Republican politicians controlled Congress and the presidency. They passed laws easily, spending considerable amounts of money on Civil War pensions for Union veterans—who mostly voted Republican—and other pet projects. Congress spent money so freely that it became known as the Billion Dollar Congress.

✔ **READING CHECK:** How did President Harrison deal with the reform efforts of President Cleveland?

SECTION 2 REVIEW

Define and explain the significance of the following terms:
Gilded Age
Stalwarts
Pendleton Civil Service Act
mugwumps

Identify and explain the significance of the following individuals:
James A. Garfield
Chester A. Arthur
Grover Cleveland
Benjamin Harrison

1. **Using Graphic Organizers** Copy the graphic organizer below. Use it to explain how the desire of voters for political reform influenced Republican Party politics.

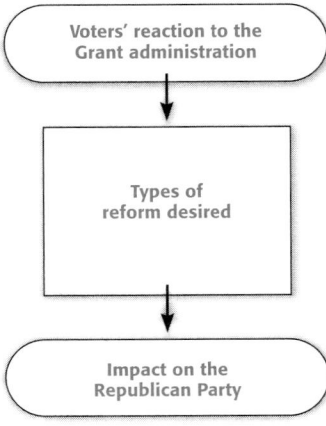

Voters' reaction to the Grant administration

↓

Types of reform desired

↓

Impact on the Republican Party

2. **Identifying Values** Why do you think many Stalwarts argued that ending the spoils system was antirepublican and contrary to the democratic heritage of the United States?
3. **Identifying Cause and Effect** What caused President Arthur to change his position on civil service reform? What effect did this have on his party?
4. **Comparing and Contrasting** How did President Harrison's position on civil service reform differ from his predecessor?

Critical Thinking

5. What were the long-term effects of President Grant's administration on U.S. politics? Be sure to discuss the public reaction to Grant's administration.
   Consider:
   • the degree of national political corruption
   • the public's opinion of politics and politicians
   • the efforts made by national politicians to rid government of corruption

The Populist Movement

OBJECTIVES

Read to understand:

1. what factors led to economic hardships for farmers
2. what the farmers' movements hoped to achieve, and what weakened their efforts
3. why farmers supported money backed by silver
4. what issues the Populist Party supported
5. how silver affected the economy and the 1896 presidential election

KEY TERMS

National Grange
cooperatives
Interstate Commerce Act
graduated income tax
gold standard
Bland-Allison Act
Sherman Silver Purchase Act
Populist Party

KEY PEOPLE

Mary Elizabeth Lease
James B. Weaver
William McKinley
William Jennings Bryan

> 66 *The farmers of the United States are up in arms. . . . The American farmer is steadily losing ground. His burdens are heavier every year and his gains are more meager [small].* 99
> —Washington Gladden

This Kansas family has been forced off their farm.

Washington Gladden, a Congregational minister in Columbus, Ohio, described the plight of the farmer during the late 1800s. Farmers had endured severe hardships and received little political support. Falling crop prices, rising railroad rates, and mounting expenses forced many farmers to default on their mortgages and loans. Foreclosures by banks forced many farmers off their land. Desperately attempting to preserve their way of life, many farmers began organizing, pressing for political solutions to their problems.

The Farmers' Plight

In addition to transforming urban life, the surge in industrialization during the late 1800s changed farmers' lives significantly. The rapidly growing population in the urban centers had to be fed. Farmers responded by raising more crops and animals each year. Unfortunately for Americans, farmers in other nations did the same. Prices soon tumbled as supply exceeded demand. At the same time, farm costs, such as railroad freight charges and the price of new machinery, continued to rise. As farm profits plunged, many farmers bought more land and increased production. This greater production pushed prices even lower.

To make matters worse, most farm families had borrowed money to pay for their land or to buy new equipment. They often put their farms up as security for loans. Those who could not repay the loans lost their farms. Many ended up as tenant farmers. Others were forced to become farm laborers. One Minnesota farmer expressed the bitterness felt by many farmers.

> 66 I settled on this land in good faith; built house and barn, broken up part of the land. Spent years of hard labor grubbing [digging], fencing, and improving. Are they going to drive us out like trespassers? 99

This tractor was powered by kerosene.

To farmers, the situation seemed terribly unfair. The merchants who sold farm equipment were making money. Also prospering were the bankers who lent farmers money and the railroads that hauled the farmers' grain and livestock to market. All that the farmers had to show for their long days of backbreaking labor were rising debts. One farmer wrote, "The railroads have never been so prosperous. . . . The banks have never done a better . . . business. . . . And yet agriculture languishes [declines]."

✔ **READING CHECK:** What factors led to economic hardships for farmers?

Farmers Organize

Farmers began organizing in an attempt to improve their situation. Many farmers joined local organizations that were committed to assisting them in their day-to-day struggles. These organizations soon merged to form a nationwide movement. Hoping to better their lives by provoking reforms in railroad and banking practices, many farmers supported these rapidly growing national organizations.

The Grange movement. The first major farmers' organization, the National Grange of the Patrons of Husbandry, or the **National Grange**, was founded by Oliver Hudson Kelley in 1867. Kelley created the Grange primarily as a social organization. As membership increased and farmers' financial problems grew, the Grange began tackling economic and political issues.

To lower costs, some Grange members formed **cooperatives**, or organizations in which groups of farmers pooled their resources to buy and sell goods. Cooperative members sold their products directly to big-city markets. They bought farm equipment and other goods in large quantities at wholesale prices—thereby cutting costs. The Grange's main focus, however, was on forcing states to regulate railroad freight and grain-storage rates. In the early 1870s state legislatures began to respond to pressure from farmers. Illinois, Iowa, Minnesota, and Wisconsin passed "Granger laws" that created state commissions to standardize such rates.

Many railroad companies challenged the Granger laws in the courts. In a victory for farmers in 1877, the Supreme Court declared in the case of *Munn* v. *Illinois* that state legislatures had the right to regulate businesses such as railroads that involved the public interest. However, the Court modified its decision nine years later, in *Wabash* v. *Illinois*, ruling that state governments had no power to regulate traffic that moved across state boundaries. Only the federal government had that right, the justices ruled.

The Court's decision led directly to the passage of the **Interstate Commerce Act** in 1887. The act prohibited railroads from giving secret rebates, or refunds, to large shippers or charging more for short hauls than for long hauls over the same line. It also stated that railroad rates had to be "reasonable and just." To monitor railroad activities, the act created the Interstate Commerce Commission (ICC). However, the ICC was given little power to enforce its rulings. When it charged railroads with violating the law, the courts almost always ruled in the railroads' favor.

The Alliance movement. While the National Grange lobbied on behalf of railroad regulation, a more powerful farm organization—the Farmers' Alliance—took shape. Beginning in Texas in the 1870s, the Alliance movement spread quickly. Debt-ridden farm families eagerly embraced the Alliance message of unity and hope. Like the Grange, the Alliance organized cooperatives to buy equipment and to market farm products. The Alliance offered farmers low-cost insurance. It also lobbied for tougher bank regulations, government ownership of the railroads, and a **graduated income tax** that taxed higher incomes at a higher rate.

The National Grange. The National Grange established cooperatives and pushed for legislation that would assist farmers. *How does this poster celebrate the lives of American farmers?*

THE GRANGER COLLECTION, NEW YORK

Agricultural Regions in 1900

Learning from Maps The diverse climates and soils of the United States enabled farmers to grow a wide variety of crops.

? LOCATION What types of agricultural products did people raise along the western coast of the United States in 1900?

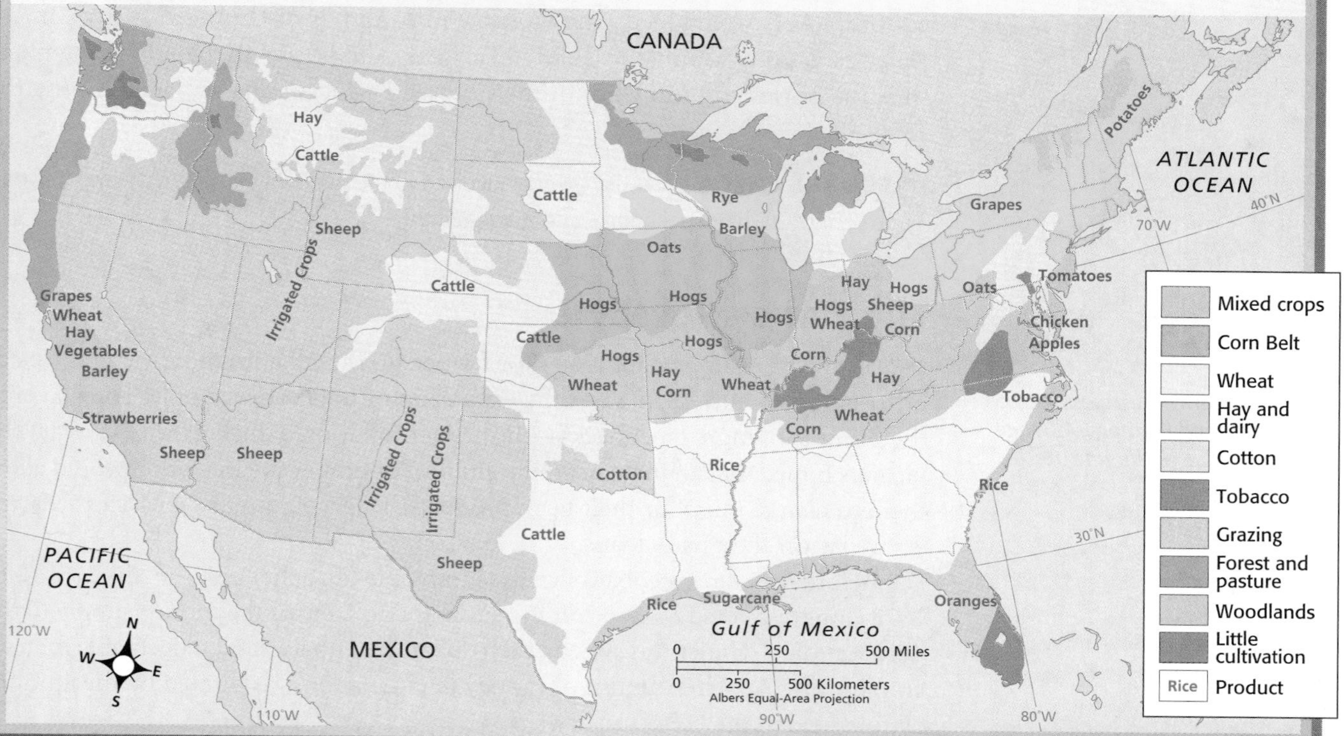

[Map of the United States showing agricultural regions in 1900, with labels including: CANADA, ATLANTIC OCEAN, PACIFIC OCEAN, Gulf of Mexico, MEXICO. Crop and product labels across the map include: Hay, Cattle, Sheep, Irrigated Crops, Grapes, Wheat, Hay, Vegetables, Barley, Strawberries, Rye, Barley, Oats, Hogs, Corn, Wheat, Cotton, Rice, Sugarcane, Tobacco, Tomatoes, Chicken, Apples, Grapes, Potatoes, Oranges.]

Map legend:
- Mixed crops
- Corn Belt
- Wheat
- Hay and dairy
- Cotton
- Tobacco
- Grazing
- Forest and pasture
- Woodlands
- Little cultivation
- Rice — Product

Scale: 0 250 500 Miles / 0 250 500 Kilometers — Albers Equal-Area Projection

By 1890 the Alliance movement claimed more than 1 million members. Alliance leaders traveled the country urging people to take action. Among the most effective speakers was Mary Elizabeth Lease from Kansas. She told her audiences:

> 66 The great common people of this country are slaves, and monopoly is the master. . . . The politicians said we suffered from overproduction. Overproduction, when 10,000 little children, so statistics tell us, starve to death every year in the United States. . . . We will stand by our homes and stay by our fireside by force if necessary, and we will not pay our debts to the loan-shark companies until the government pays its debts to us. 99

The Alliance movement consisted of three organizations: the National Farmers' Alliance, the all-white Southern Alliance, and the Colored Farmers' Alliance. Each organization pushed for the same legislative goals and helped their members in times of hardship. Nevertheless, a variety of reasons kept the Alliance organizations from consolidating their leadership into one single organization.

African American farmers.
Despite the common goals of the Southern and Colored Farmers' Alliances, they remained separate, segregated institutions. Racial divisions in southern society prevented a tight coalition of farmers that crossed color lines.

THE GRANGER COLLECTION, NEW YORK

Mary Elizabeth Lease spread the cause of the Alliance movement, speaking out against monopolies.

African American farmers looked to the Colored Farmers' Alliance for assistance in the late 1880s.

The racial divisions within the Alliance movement brought about the violent end of the Colored Farmers' Alliance. In 1891 Colored Farmers' Alliance leader R. M. Humphrey organized a strike of cotton pickers demanding to be paid $1 for every 100 pounds picked. The strike led to a series of violent confrontations in Arkansas between white farmers and African American cotton pickers. At least 15 cotton pickers were killed. The violence in Arkansas discouraged many African Americans from joining the Colored Farmers' Alliance. With dwindling membership, the power and influence of the Colored Farmers' Alliance faded during the 1890s.

✔ **READING CHECK:** What did farmers involved in the national farmers' movements hope to achieve? What weakened these movements?

The Money Question

One of the most important issues for farmers in the Alliance movement as well as other agrarian movements was the expansion of the money supply. They favored the printing of more greenbacks—the paper money used during the Civil War. The farmers hoped that an increase in the amount of money in circulation would allow them to charge more for their farm products. This would make it easier for farmers to pay off their bank loans.

Before the war, greenbacks were redeemable for either gold or silver coins. In 1873 Congress voted to stop coining silver and to convert the money supply to the **gold standard**. Under this system, each dollar was equal to and redeemable for a set amount of gold. The amount of money in circulation was limited by the amount of gold held in the U.S. Treasury.

★ Changing Ways   The American Farmer

■ **Understanding Change** Farming was once a primary occupation in the United States. *By how much has the percentage of workers engaged in farming changed? Calculate the average farm size then and now. How has it changed over time?*

	THEN	Now
Population Employed in Farming ▪ Farming ▪ Nonfarming	38% / 62%	3% / 97%
Number of farms	5.7 million	2 million
Total farmland	841 million acres	968 million acres

Sources: *Historical Statistics of the United States; Statistical Abstract of the United States: 1997.* Data reflect 1900 and 1996.

THEN

Now

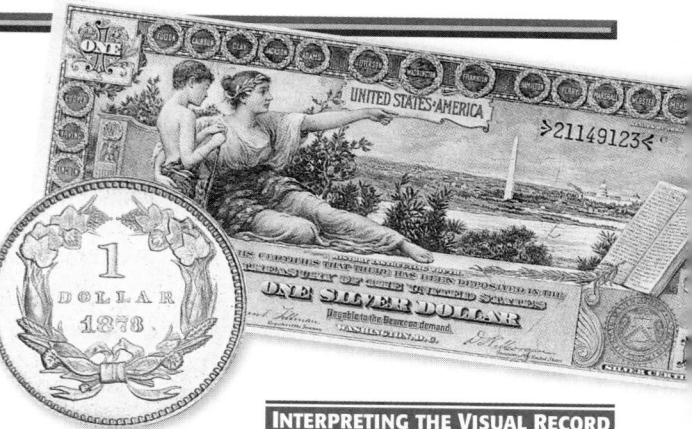

The conversion to the gold standard resulted in a decrease in the amount of money in circulation and a lowering of prices. Many farmers demanded that the government back the money supply with silver. This metal was plentiful in the West—as was gold. Bowing to pressure, Congress passed the **Bland-Allison Act** in 1878 and the **Sherman Silver Purchase Act** in 1890. Both acts required the government to buy silver each month and mint it into coins. Because the government bought so little silver, however, the money supply did not increase enough to satisfy silver supporters.

Disappointed Alliance members threw themselves into the 1890 elections, supporting any candidate who backed their pro-farmer platform. The results were remarkable. Alliance-backed candidates won more than 40 seats in Congress, four southern governorships, and numerous other political offices.

✔ **READING CHECK:** Why did farmers and Alliance members demand that paper money be backed by silver?

A Decade of Populist Politics

Pleased by their successes in the 1890 election, Alliance movement leaders sought to build on their popular support by forming a new political party. Throughout the 1890s Alliance leaders began a large grassroots campaign, gaining a considerable amount of influence on national politics.

The Populist Party. Between 1891 and 1892, Alliance members met with labor leaders and other reformers to draw up plans for a national political party. The People's Party was founded at a convention in St. Louis in February 1892. This coalition of Alliance members, farmers, labor leaders, and reformers became more commonly known as the **Populist Party**.

The party platform echoed National Grange and Alliance demands. It called for a graduated income tax, bank regulation, government ownership of railroad and telegraph companies, and the free, or unlimited, coinage of silver. The platform also called for restrictions on immigration, a shorter workday, and voting reforms.

The Populists nominated James B. Weaver to run in the 1892 presidential election against Republican incumbent Benjamin Harrison and Democrat Grover Cleveland. Cleveland was a former president who had lost to Harrison in the 1888 election. Although Cleveland won the 1892 election, the Populist Party elected more than 10 party members to Congress as well as numerous state leaders. Weaver pulled in a respectable 1 million popular votes, carrying four western states and 22 electoral votes.

✔ **READING CHECK:** What issues did the Populist Party support?

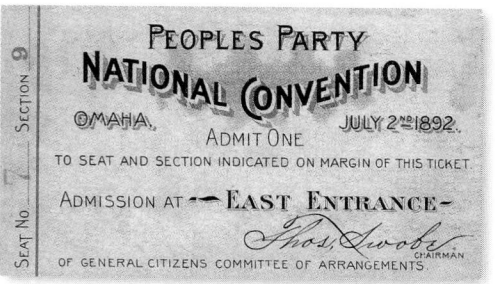

This ticket entitled its holder to attend the Populist Party convention in 1892.

Economic depression. In May 1893, just two months after Cleveland took office, one of the country's leading railroad companies failed. The failure triggered the Panic of 1893, a financial panic that sent stock prices plunging. The country quickly slid into an economic depression. By the end of 1893, some 3 million people were unemployed—100,000 in Chicago alone. In New York City some 20,000 homeless people desperately sought shelter in jails. Strikes and protests swept the country.

The depression had many causes, including a worldwide financial panic. President Cleveland chose to focus only on one cause—the Sherman Silver Purchase Act. This law required the government to pay for silver purchases with Treasury notes redeemable in either gold or silver. New discoveries of silver decreased the metal's value, and people rushed to exchange their notes for gold. The situation put a terrible strain on the Treasury's gold reserves. To protect the gold standard and to restore confidence in the economy, Cleveland called for Congress to repeal the Sherman Silver Purchase Act. Congress did so in October 1893.

The Election of 1896

President Cleveland's actions saved the gold standard, but this did not end the debate on the money supply. Silver became a central issue in the 1896 election.

The Republicans chose Ohio governor William McKinley as their presidential candidate and adopted a conservative platform upholding the gold standard. A deeply split Democratic Party rejected President Cleveland. Instead, they nominated free-silver supporter William Jennings Bryan, a two-term representative from Nebraska. Because its free-silver platform had been adopted by the Democratic Party, the Populist Party threw its support behind Bryan.

Bryan. William Jennings Bryan was born in 1860 into a very religious and Democratic family. Bryan's father served in the Illinois state senate and on the Illinois circuit court, guided by his religious beliefs and his Democratic ideals.

Bryan was greatly influenced by his father. At the age of 21 he left his childhood home in Salem, Illinois, to attend law school in Chicago. After receiving his law degree, Bryan eventually moved to Lincoln, Nebraska. He established a law firm and ran for political office as a Democratic candidate in Nebraska, a predominantly Republican state. At the age of 31, Bryan was elected to the U.S. House of Representatives.

Bryan's youth, charisma, and strong support of silver-backed currency gained him broad support among populists within the Democratic Party in the 1890s. During the Democratic convention where he received the nomination to run for president, Bryan gave his now famous "Cross of Gold" speech. He stressed the importance of the silver issue to farmers and less-fortunate people all over the United States.

> 66 If they [the Republicans] dare to come out in the open field and defend the gold standard as a good thing, we will fight them to the uttermost. Having behind us the producing masses of this nation and the world, supported by the commercial interests, the laboring interests, and the toilers everywhere, we will answer their demand for a gold standard by saying to them: You shall not press down upon the brow of labor this crown of thorns, you shall not crucify mankind upon a cross of gold. 99

Read More About It

Free Find: William Jennings Bryan

After reading the biography on William Jennings Bryan on the **Holt Researcher** CD–ROM, explain how his political views were influenced by his family and his experiences growing up in the midwestern United States.

Judge magazine published this cartoon on its cover after William Jennings Bryan gave his "Cross of Gold" speech.

William Jennings Bryan

Bryan remained politically active throughout his life. He published several papers on populism and ran for political office repeatedly during the early 1900s. He died in 1925.

The end of populism. Terrified of Bryan's populism, many business leaders contributed millions of dollars to the Republican campaign. When the popular votes were counted, McKinley had edged out Bryan by some 500,000 votes. The Populists were in shock. Free silver had proven too weak an issue for a national campaign, and urban workers and immigrants had found little that appealed to them in the Populists' agenda.

The election defeat and improvements in farmers' economic conditions brought an end to the power of the Populist Party. However, the party's platform laid the groundwork for future reform. As Populist leader Mary Elizabeth Lease noted in 1914, "The seeds we sowed out in Kansas did not fall on barren ground."

PRESIDENTIAL *Lives*

1843–1901
In Office 1897–1901

William McKinley

William McKinley used presidential power so effectively that a Republican newspaper concluded: "No executive in the history of the country . . . has given a greater exhibition of his influence over Congress." Even his political enemies respected his tact and persuasiveness. Speaker of the House Tom Reed said of him with envy, "My opponents in Congress go at me tooth and nail, but they always apologize to William when they are going to call him names."

A courteous manner characterized McKinley in private life as well. He was devoted to protecting and caring for his wife, Ida. She suffered headaches and seizures that often kept her from fulfilling her role as first lady. He stayed close to her during state dinners and receptions. If she fainted, he would tend to her, continuing with conversation so as not to embarrass her.

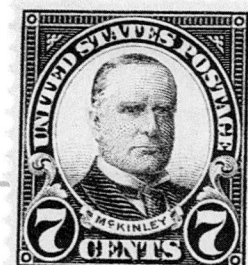

✔ **READING CHECK:** How did silver affect the economy and the 1896 presidential election?

SECTION 3 REVIEW

Define and explain the significance of the following terms:
National Grange
cooperatives
Interstate Commerce Act
graduated income tax
gold standard
Bland-Allison Act
Sherman Silver Purchase Act
Populist Party

Identify and explain the significance of the following individuals:
Mary Elizabeth Lease
James B. Weaver
William McKinley
William Jennings Bryan

1. **Using Graphic Organizers** Copy the chart below. List the political concerns and typical supporters of the National Grange, the Farmers' Alliance, and the Populist Party.

	Grange	Alliance	Populist
Political Issues			
Supporters			

2. **Hypothesizing** Considering the economic troubles that farmers faced, why do you think many of them supported the political agenda of the National Grange?
3. **Evaluating** What factors weakened the Alliance movement?
4. **Analyzing** Why did William Jennings Bryan lose the 1896 presidential election?

Critical Thinking

5. The currency issue was debated nationally for more than 40 years in the United States. Why do you think the debate over silver-backed currency lasted so long?
   Consider:
   • who wanted a gold standard and who wanted silver-backed money
   • what reasons each group had for supporting its view
   • how silver influenced the economy

Review

Creating a Time Line

Copy the time line below onto a sheet of paper. Complete the time line by filling in the events and dates from the chapter that you think were most significant. Pick three events and explain why you think they were significant.

| 1865 | 1875 | 1890 | 1900 |

Writing a Summary

Using the Reading Checks as a guide, write an overview of the events in the chapter.

Identifying People and Ideas

Identify the following terms or individuals and explain their significance.

1. political machines
2. graft
3. William Marcy Tweed
4. Stalwarts
5. Chester A. Arthur
6. Grover Cleveland
7. National Grange
8. Mary Elizabeth Lease
9. gold standard
10. William Jennings Bryan

Understanding Main Ideas

SECTION 1
1. What reforms did political machines do to build and maintain support for their party?
2. What caused the decline in public support for the Tweed Ring?

SECTION 2
3. What reforms did the Stalwarts want? What reforms did the Half-Breeds want?
4. What role did President Grant's administration play in the civil service reform movement?

SECTION 3
5. What issues did the Populist Party support?
6. Why did the Populists lose the 1896 election?

Reviewing Themes

1. **Cultural Diversity** How were political machines able to unite immigrant groups to support their candidates?
2. **Democratic Values** Why might many Stalwarts have considered civil service reform a violation of the democratic heritage of the United States?
3. **Geographic Diversity** Why did William Jennings Bryan win such strong support in some parts of the country but so little in other regions?

Thinking Critically

1. **Drawing Conclusions** Why do you think voters supported corrupt political machines?
2. **Identifying Cause and Effect** What motivated Charles Guiteau to assassinate President Garfield? Did he accomplish his political goal?
3. **Evaluating** Overall, were the National Grange and Farmers' Alliance movements a success or a failure? Explain your answer.
4. **Analyzing** Was "the Gilded Age" an appropriate nickname for the late 1800s? Why or why not?
5. **Hypothesizing** Would William Jennings Bryan have won the election of 1896 if he had not focused so much on the gold and silver issue? Why or why not?

Writing About History

Writing to Persuade Copy the following graphic organizer and use it to explain the give-and-take relationship between political machines and voters. Then write a letter to the editor of a newspaper to persuade the public to support civil service reform. Be sure to explain how civil service reform would change the relationship between political machines and voters.

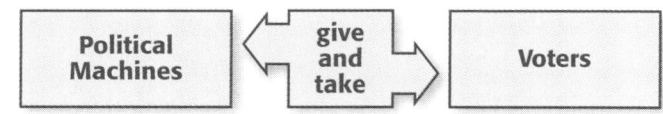

Strategies **for Success** Review the **Strategies for Success** on *Synthesizing.* Then review the Eyewitnesses to History feature that opens Section 3. Synthesize its content with the description below about the Alliance movement, and answer the question that follows.

> [The Alliance movement] was, first and most centrally, a movement that imparted [passed on] a sense of self-worth to individuals and provided them with the instruments of self-education about the world they lived in. The movement taught them to believe that they could perform specific political acts of self-determination.
>
> —*Lawrence Goodwyn,* The Populist Moment, *1978*

Based on these two sources and the knowledge you have gained from the text, why do you think farmers supported the Alliance movement during the late 1800s?

Linking History and Geography

Study the map below. Which candidate won the most states? What regions of the United States gave the most support to William Jennings Bryan? to William McKinley? Why might that be so?

The Election of 1896

CANDIDATE	PARTY	ELECTORAL VOTE	POPULAR VOTE	% OF POPULAR VOTE
McKinley	Republican	271	7,102,246	51.1
Bryan	Democratic	176*	6,492,559	46.7
Other		0	315,398	2.3

*One elector in California and one in Kentucky voted for Bryan.

Source: *Historical Statistics of the United States*

internet**connect**

TOPIC: Political Cartoons
GO TO: go.hrw.com
KEYWORD: SD1 Cartoons

Accessing the Internet through the HRW Web site, research the work of the political cartoonist Thomas Nast. Then create a political cartoon that addresses an issue of the Gilded Age.

BUILDING YOUR PORTFOLIO

Complete one or all of the following projects independently or cooperatively.

1 Democratic Values
Imagine that you are a political satirist, like Mark Twain, living in the Gilded Age. ***Write a short story*** about an episode of corruption during the period.

2 Economic Development
Imagine that you are a farmer who has just joined the National Grange movement. ***Draft a letter*** to a neighboring farmer that explains the hardships you have experienced and why you think joining the Grange movement will help solve your problems.

3 Constitutional Heritage
Imagine that you are living in a large city during the late 1800s and want a government job. In this particular city, a political machine runs the local government but there is a strong possibility that a merit-based civil service system will soon be used to hire people. ***Create a political cartoon*** that explains what you need to do to get a job in either the patronage system or a merit-based hiring system.

Review

BUILDING YOUR PORTFOLIO

Outlined below are four projects. Independently or cooperatively, complete one and use the products to demonstrate your mastery of the historical concepts involved.

1 Cultural Diversity

Westward expansion, immigration, and industrialization often created conflicts between different groups in American society. ***Develop a series of dramatic sketches*** and monologues that address these conflicts and explore the positive consequences of cultural diversity for society. You may wish to use portfolio materials you designed in the unit chapters to help you.

American Indian refusing to let a wagon train pass

Advertisement for union labels

2 Economic Development

In the late 1800s technological advances and the growth of industry dramatically changed the lifestyles and work habits of many Americans. Imagine that you own a factory. ***Prepare a presentation*** highlighting the technological developments being used in your factory. Be sure to describe how the changes in the factory affected the lives of workers and what problems you have encountered as workers have unionized. You may wish to use portfolio materials you designed in the unit chapters to help you.

Washington, D.C., streetcar

3 Technology and Society

With the increasing industrialization in the late 1800s, cities across the United States expanded in population and in size. *Create a map* of a major U.S. city in 1910 that illustrates the growth of the city. Be sure to include new forms of transportation, the growth of suburbs, and the development of immigrant neighborhoods. You may wish to use portfolio materials you designed in the unit chapters to help you.

4 Democratic Values

Corruption in various levels of government and problems in rural America led many citizens to work for political change. *Create a series of flip charts for a meeting* between politicians, farmers, and reform-minded citizens to discuss what political changes are needed and how these groups can work together to accomplish the reforms. You may wish to use portfolio materials you designed in the unit chapters to help you.

Cartoon depicting political corruption

Further Reading

Andrist, Ralph K. *The Long Death: The Last Days of the Plains Indians.* Macmillan, 1993. History of the struggle of the Plains Indians.

Coan, Peter Morton. *Ellis Island Interviews: In Their Own Words.* Facts on File, 1997. A broad collection of accounts recalling immigration experiences.

Katz, William L. *The Black West.* Open Hand, 1987. History of the African American pioneers who helped develop the West.

Luchetti, Cathy, and Carol Olwell. *Women of the West.* Orion, 1982. Firsthand accounts of women's lives in the West taken from photographs and diaries.

Mohl, Raymond A. *The New City: Urban America in the Industrial Age, 1860–1920.* Harlan Davidson, 1985. A thorough history of the changes in urban life during the late 1800s.

Schlereth, Thomas J. *Victorian America: Transformations in Everyday Life, 1876–1915.* HarperCollins, 1991. Detailed historical overview of the impact of immigration, expansion, and industrialization on American society.

Internet Connect and Holt Researcher CD–ROM Review

In assigned groups, develop a multimedia presentation about America between 1860 and 1910. Choose information from the chapter Internet Connect activities and from the **Holt Researcher** CD–ROM that best reflect the major topics of the period. Write an outline and a script for your presentation, which may be shown to the class.

A World Power

1897–1920

This 1898 painting by Fred Pansing depicts the Great White Fleet entering into New York Harbor.

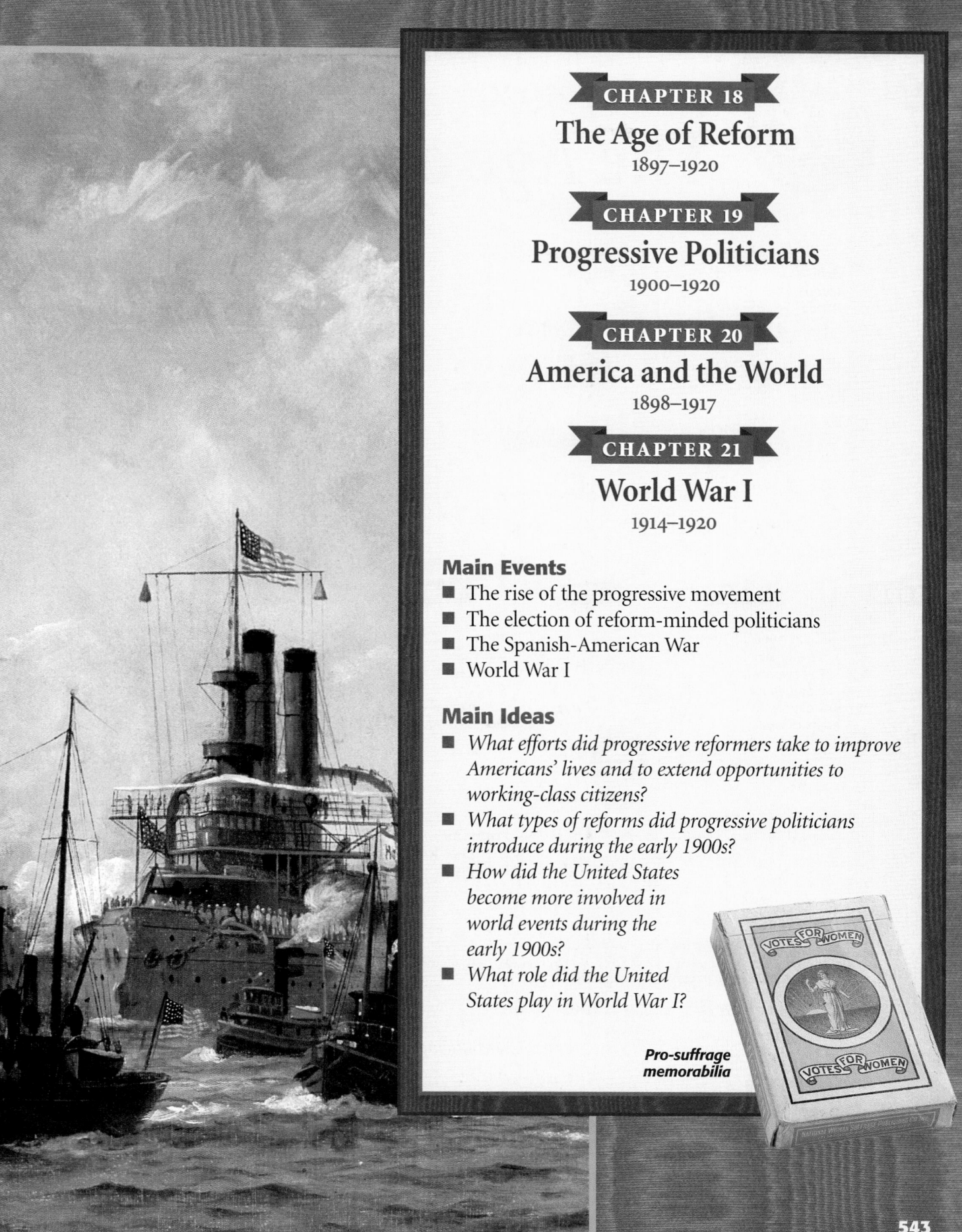

CHAPTER 18

The Age of Reform
1897–1920

CHAPTER 19

Progressive Politicians
1900–1920

CHAPTER 20

America and the World
1898–1917

CHAPTER 21

World War I
1914–1920

Main Events
- The rise of the progressive movement
- The election of reform-minded politicians
- The Spanish-American War
- World War I

Main Ideas
- *What efforts did progressive reformers take to improve Americans' lives and to extend opportunities to working-class citizens?*
- *What types of reforms did progressive politicians introduce during the early 1900s?*
- *How did the United States become more involved in world events during the early 1900s?*
- *What role did the United States play in World War I?*

Pro-suffrage memorabilia

1897–1920
The Age of Reform

British troops in Africa

1900
The Arts
Theodore Dreiser publishes the novel *Sister Carrie.*

1902
World Events
The British defeat the Dutch Boers in Africa.

1904
Science and Technology
The first completed section of the New York City subway system opens to the public.

Building the New York City subway

| 1898 | 1900 | 1902 | 1904 | 1906 | 1908 |

1900
Daily Life
The average laborer earns $1.50 a day for 10 hours of work.

No. 201
EDISON FILM
COPYRIGHTED 1903
THE GREAT TRAIN
ROBBERY

Poster for The Great Train Robbery

1903
Daily Life
The Great Train Robbery, the first movie to tell a story, is produced.

1905
The Arts
H. Siddons Mowbray begins work on a mural for the J. P. Morgan Library in New York.

1905
World Events
The Russian czar's troops fire on unarmed protesters, beginning the Russian Revolution of 1905.

1907
Science and Technology
Engineers develop suspension insulators, which soon allow power lines to carry up to 150,000 volts of electricity.

Before You Read

Build on What You Know

Although industrial development during the Gilded Age generated great profits for some Americans, it also created many problems. Moreover, politics became increasingly corrupt as leaders sought financial gains. Populists, ministers, and reformers such as Jane Addams tried to bring the nation's attention to those Americans left out of economic prosperity. In this chapter you will learn about the large-scale reform movements that swept the United States at the beginning of the 1900s and the effects that these movements had on American society.

The Whitney Museum of American Art

Busy New York City street

1914
Daily Life
Some 2 million skilled workers belong to the American Federation of Labor.

1914
Business and Finance
The total value of U.S. imports reaches nearly $2 billion.

1916
Business and Finance
Local canning companies merge to form California Packing, a nationwide organization to market their goods.

The American Federation of Labor logo

1920
Daily Life
More than half of all Americans live in urban areas.

1909
The Arts
Gertrude Vanderbilt Whitney opens a modern art gallery in New York.

1913
World Events
Norway grants women full political rights.

1910	1912	1914	1916	1918	1920

1910
Daily Life
About one third of American working men and women live in poverty.

1913
Business and Finance
The United States is the world's leading producer of coal.

1915
Science and Technology
Deaths from tuberculosis drop significantly thanks to the efforts of the National Tuberculosis Association.

1917
Politics
Congress proposes the Eighteenth Amendment, which prohibits the manufacture, sale, and distribution of alcoholic beverages.

1909
Politics
The National Association for the Advancement of Colored People is founded.

A young boy working in a coal mine

Temperance leader Carry Nation

Think About Themes

Themes Journal

Decide whether you agree or disagree with the following statements. Note why in your journal.

Economic Development State governments have a responsibility to regulate how businesses treat workers.

Democratic Values A democracy has a duty to protect and assist the poorest and weakest of its citizens.

Constitutional Heritage Reform movements are necessary in order to lay the groundwork for constitutional change.

SECTION 1

The Progressive Movement

OBJECTIVES

Read to understand:

1. what the backgrounds of the reformers were
2. what issues concerned progressives, and how they tried to make changes
3. what issues muckrakers addressed
4. how progressive writers and thinkers viewed American society

KEY TERMS

progressivism
McClure's Magazine
muckrakers

KEY PEOPLE

Ida Tarbell
Lincoln Steffens
Ray Stannard Baker
Theodore Dreiser
Edith Wharton
Herbert Croly

66 *The 'tramp' comes with the locomotive, and almshouses [poorhouses] and prisons are as surely the marks of 'material progress' as are costly dwellings, rich warehouses, and magnificent churches.* 99

—Henry George

Henry George wrote these words in his 1879 book, *Progress and Poverty.* In the book he discussed the problems facing the United States as both the number of poor people and the nation's wealth increased. George hoped for a time when the country's progress might be measured by its movement "toward equality, not toward inequality." *Progress and Poverty* soon became a best-seller. One economist noted that it was read by tens of thousands of members of the working and lower classes "who never before looked between the covers of an economics book." By the early 1900s a drive for economic and social reform had begun. Many Americans sought to make the country's laws and institutions more responsive to the conditions of the nation's poorest and most disadvantaged citizens.

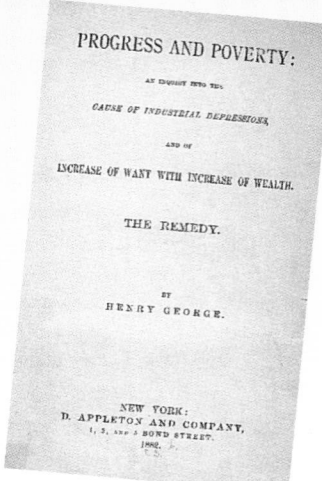

Henry George's **Progress and Poverty**

The Progressive Spirit

By the early 1900s industrialization had transformed the United States. Economic growth led to many new goods and services as well as an expanding middle class. However, growth also widened the gap between the rich and the poor and led to unsafe working conditions and crowded cities.

Such problems aroused a spirit of reform known as **progressivism**. In the late 1800s members of the Populist Party had protested what they saw as unfair business practices and had pressed for government action to stop them. Populism was mainly a rural movement. Progressivism, however, focused on urban problems, such as the plight of workers, poor sanitation, and corrupt political machines.

The progressives. People from all walks of life participated in reform efforts during the Progressive Era. However, most progressives were native born, middle or upper class, and college educated. Many Americans' first exposure to the social problems of the industrial United States came while taking college courses. "My life began at Johns Hopkins University," progressive Frederic Howe recalled. "I came alive. I felt a sense of responsibility. I wanted to change things."

Men and women of the urban middle class—doctors, engineers, ministers, small-business owners, social workers, teachers, and writers—found progressivism particularly attractive. This urban middle class had grown from some 750,000 in 1870 to about 10 million by 1910. Kansas editor William Allen White described this change. He said that by the 1900s populism had "shaved its whiskers, washed its shirt, put on a derby, and moved up into the middle class."

Women and progressivism. Previous generations of women had joined reform efforts because they were an acceptable way for women to influence politics and society. Many middle-class women were drawn to the progressive movement for the same reason. Women enrolled in colleges in increasing numbers during the early 1900s, but their career choices remained limited. Reform work offered college-educated women a way to use their knowledge of medicine, psychology, sociology, and other subjects.

In 1909 Ella Flagg Young became Chicago's superintendent of schools—the first woman to hold such a job in a major city. Young promoted public education by raising teachers' salaries. Published in 1910, Rheta Childe Dorr's widely read book *What Eight Million Women Want* noted the special role of women in the reform movement. "Women have ceased to exist as a subsidiary [lower] class in the community," she wrote. "The modern . . . educated woman came into a world which is losing faith in the commercial ideal and is endeavoring to substitute in its place a social ideal."

Some women made careers of reform work. Others volunteered their time through groups such as the General Federation of Women's Clubs and the National Association of Colored Women. Women also participated in the 1913 Progressive Party convention in Chicago. The party's platform supported women's suffrage and an end to child labor. Describing her experience as a delegate, Jane Addams wrote that it did not seem strange for women to take part. "It would have been much more unnatural if they had not been there, when such matters of social welfare were being considered."

✔ **READING CHECK:** What were the backgrounds of many of the reformers?

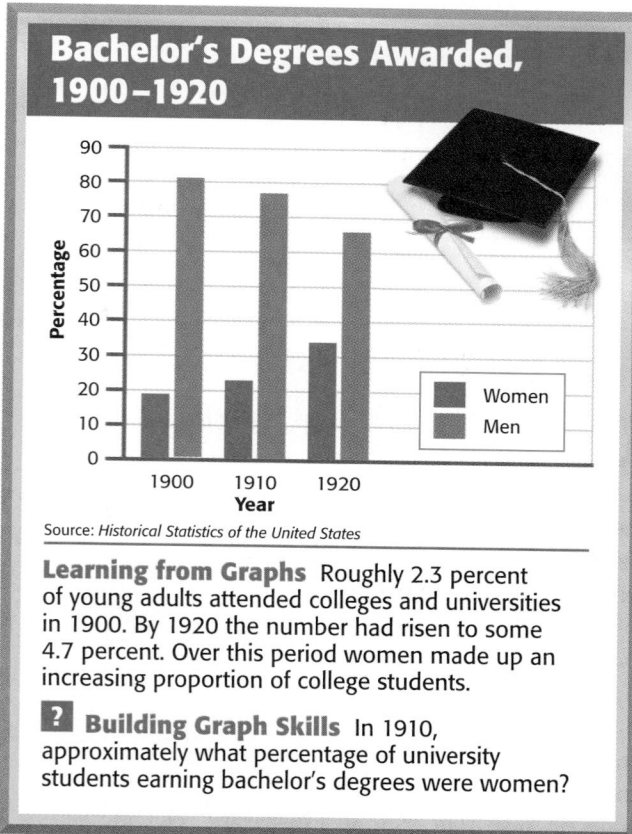

Bachelor's Degrees Awarded, 1900–1920

Source: *Historical Statistics of the United States*

Learning from Graphs Roughly 2.3 percent of young adults attended colleges and universities in 1900. By 1920 the number had risen to some 4.7 percent. Over this period women made up an increasing proportion of college students.

? **Building Graph Skills** In 1910, approximately what percentage of university students earning bachelor's degrees were women?

Progressive Issues

Progressives tried to reform American institutions while preserving ideals of the past, such as a sense of community. Progressive reformers took a leading role in promoting change in the United States.

A dangerous workplace. A major concern of the progressives was the way corporate America did business. Industrial workers often faced dangerous conditions and long hours. In 1910 some 70 percent of all American industrial laborers worked an average of 54 hours a week. As a result, American workers had higher accident rates than workers in other industrialized countries. In one Pittsburgh steel mill 3,723 laborers—25 percent of its workforce—were injured or killed on the job each year between 1907 and 1910.

Education for women. These women attended Vassar College in the 1920s. *What can you determine about their economic background?*

The Religious Spirit

THE SOCIAL GOSPEL AND PROGRESSIVISM

Charles M. Sheldon's 1896 Social Gospel novel, *In His Steps,* focused on characters in a typical midwestern city who based their behavior on the question, "What would Jesus do?" The results were remarkable. Manufacturers ran their businesses for the benefit of employees, and wealthy businesspeople bought slum property and improved it for the benefit of the tenants. While such dramatic results were not often seen in real life, Social Gospel thought had a profound effect on the progressive movement. Many progressives, including Jane Addams, were greatly influenced by the Social Gospel writers. Progressivism

Walter Rauschenbusch

promoted the same goals as Social Gospel thinkers, including the abolition of child labor as well as the support of higher wages, industrial regulations, and shorter workweeks.

Walter Rauschenbusch, a professor at Rochester Theological Seminary in New York, was one of the leading writers and thinkers of both the Social Gospel movement and the progressive movement. In *For God and the People: Prayers of the Social Awakening* (1910), he called for "a new type of Christian." He wanted Christians to become involved in social issues as an extension of their love for God. Rauschenbusch wrote prayers for specific groups of workers, such as his "For Children Who Work," "For Workingmen," and "For Women Who Toil." He participated actively in the Social Gospel movement, helping to popularize it. He also moved it more concretely toward the progressive movement's goal of addressing the social consequences of industrialization and rapid urban growth. ■

These conditions led progressives to demand limits on corporate power. They promoted laws to prohibit monopolies and to help smaller businesses compete in the economy. Progressives also called for an eight-hour workday, a minimum wage, safer working conditions, and an end to child labor. Not surprisingly, most business owners opposed such legislation.

Social problems. Like the Populists, progressives wanted the people to have greater control of the government. They called for new election reforms and proposed political measures to make government more responsive to the desires of the voters. Reformer Benjamin Parke De Witt wanted to give "the people direct and continuous control over all the branches of government." Like Populists and Social Gospel ministers, progressives were inspired by the spirit of social justice. Progressive Theodore Roosevelt wrote, "If we wish to do good work for our country, we must be unselfish."

Progressives firmly believed in the power of science and technology to solve social problems. Progressive philosopher John Dewey believed that public education should prepare students to function well and efficiently in society, not simply give them factual knowledge. To this end, Dewey promoted a curriculum closely tied to real-life activities.

With the help of universities, progressives began many social-research projects. Some progressives, however, worried that the university might become too involved. Jane Addams warned against turning settlement houses "into one more laboratory; another place in which to . . . observe and record."

✔ **READING CHECK:** With what issues did progressives concern themselves, and how did they try to make changes?

Built for the 1893 World's Columbian Exposition in Chicago, the "White City" showed what many progressives thought modern cities should be like.

THE GRANGER COLLECTION, NEW YORK

Inspiration for Reform

Progressive journalists helped spread the reform message. Popular magazines such as *Munsey's* and *Everybody's* published stories exploring corruption in politics and business as well as social problems such as slums and child labor. ***McClure's Magazine***, another national magazine, had been founded in 1893 by the reform-minded Scotch-Irish immigrant S. S. McClure.

The muckraking press.

In 1906 Theodore Roosevelt described in a speech a man with a muckrake who "fixes his eyes . . . only on that which is vile and debasing [harmful and corrupt]." The vivid image stuck, and investigative journalists became known as **muckrakers**—a name many accepted with much pride. Walter Lippmann, a young progressive, noted in 1914 that "muckraking was what the people wanted to hear."

    McClure's publication in October 1902 of "Tweed Days in St. Louis," by journalists Lincoln Steffens and Claude Wetmore, marked the real beginning of this style of journalism. The article exposed the corrupt political machine in St. Louis, comparing it to Boss Tweed's control of New York City.

Articles in **McClure's Magazine** informed the public about how corruption in business and politics affected their lives.

Ida Tarbell

Tarbell and Standard Oil.

In November 1902 *McClure's* ran the first installment of Ida Tarbell's "History of the Standard Oil Company." Tarbell, the daughter of an independent oil producer, was born in western Pennsylvania in 1857. Tarbell was deeply angered when John D. Rockefeller's Standard Oil Company began swallowing up independent oil companies. Her father's company went bankrupt.

    In 1876 Tarbell entered Allegheny College as the only female in an incoming class of 40 "hostile or indifferent" males, as she recalled. After graduation she began her career as a writer. By the 1890s she was writing a popular series for *McClure's*. In 1900 *McClure's* assigned her to investigate Standard Oil. Tarbell published her findings in a series of 19 articles on Standard Oil's business practices.

> 66 One of the most depressing features . . . is that instead of such methods arousing contempt, they are more or less openly admired. . . . There is no gaming table in the world where loaded dice are tolerated, no athletic field where men must not start fair. Yet Mr. Rockefeller has systematically played with loaded dice. . . . Business played in this way loses all its sportsmanlike qualities. It is fit only for tricksters. 99

McClure's readers hailed Tarbell as "the Terror of the Trusts." Unlike many other reporters, Tarbell was dismayed to find that she had been labeled a muckraker. Many of her readers continued to expect such exposés and seemed uninterested in more-balanced findings. "Was it not as much my business as a reporter to present this [the favorable] side of the picture as to present the other?" Tarbell wondered. Later in life she participated in numerous government conferences and committees dealing with such issues as defense, industry, and unemployment. Five years before her death in 1944, she wrote her autobiography, *All in the Day's Work*.

HOLT RESEARCHER ***Read More About It***

Free Find: Ida Tarbell
After reading about Ida Tarbell on the **Holt Researcher** CD–ROM, create a magazine cover for a muckraking story about a present-day issue that concerns you.

This cartoon shows Standard Oil as a giant octopus that crushes all opposition in its tentacles.

Muckraking books. Books by other muckraking writers poured off the presses. In 1904 Lincoln Steffens documented urban political corruption in *The Shame of the Cities.* Writer Ray Stannard Baker toured the nation in 1904 examining the plight of African Americans. Published in 1908, Baker's *Following the Color Line* described a lynching in Springfield, Ohio.

> 66 The worst feature of all in this Springfield lynching was the apathy of the public. No one really seemed to care. . . . If ever there was an example of good citizenship lying flat on its back . . . Springfield furnished an example of that condition. 99

✔ **READING CHECK:** What issues did muckrakers address?

Strategies for Success

Interpreting the Visual Record: Photographs

The visual record of an event, period, or place can help one understand its history in ways the written word sometimes cannot. Like other historical sources, however, photographs must be interpreted carefully. If a photograph includes people, their knowledge of the photographer's presence is important. Spontaneous snapshots usually look much different than ones that are posed. Furthermore, every photograph has a frame, or set of borders, that includes some details and excludes others. The manner in which a photographer selects this frame is another crucial issue. Finally, a photographer's choice of camera equipment, lighting, and developing technique all affect the appearance of a photograph. It is therefore important to analyze the manner in which a photograph is produced along with its actual content.

How to Interpret a Photograph

1. **Identify the subject.** Look at the photograph as a whole and identify its basic subject.
2. **Study the details.** Examine the details in the photograph for information about its historical context.
3. **Determine the photographer's point of view.** Look for information that suggests the photographer's purpose. Note how the photograph was framed and if anyone in the photograph knew it was being taken.

Applying the Strategy

The photograph below depicts an immigrant family in their New York City tenement. It was taken in 1910 by Jessie Tarbox Beals, a muckraking photographer who documented urban living conditions.

Practicing the Strategy

Study the photograph above to answer the following questions.

1. What information is provided by the photograph?
2. What message is Beals trying to communicate about the family in the photograph?
3. Does the photograph seem to represent accurately the urban living conditions of immigrant workers during the early 1900s? Explain your answer.

Writers and Social Problems

Novelists and intellectuals also explored the darker side of the new industrial society's effect on people's behavior and values. In their works, these writers presented stories of the harsh effects of industrial society on the poor.

In novels such as *Sister Carrie* (1900) and *The Financier* (1912), Theodore Dreiser depicted workers brutalized by greedy business owners. In Edith Wharton's 1905 work, *The House of Mirth*, the closed-mindedness of elite society leads the good-hearted heroine to social isolation and despair.

Progressive intellectuals proposed alternatives to the idea that fierce competition was the best formula for social progress. In *The Promise of American Life* (1909), political theorist Herbert Croly argued that the government should use its regulatory and tax powers to promote the welfare of all its citizens. He opposed the government's support of the interest of business owners over other Americans.

In 1902, in *Democracy and Social Ethics*, Jane Addams urged private citizens to show more social responsibility as well. "We are bound to move forward or [slip backward] together. None of us can stand aside; our feet are mired [stuck] in the same soil, and our lungs breathe the same air." Although progressives such as Addams and Croly wanted to transform U.S. society and its values, they remained committed to democracy. Most progressives sought reforms of local government, businesses, and city life to ensure that the full promise of democracy became available to all citizens.

These Progressive Era books explored the challenges of American life in the new industrial age.

✔ **READING CHECK:** How did progressive writers and thinkers view American society?

SECTION 1 REVIEW

Define and explain the significance of the following terms:
progressivism
McClure's Magazine
muckrakers

Identify and explain the significance of the following individuals:
Ida Tarbell
Lincoln Steffens
Ray Stannard Baker
Theodore Dreiser
Edith Wharton
Herbert Croly

1. **Using Graphic Organizers** Copy the graphic organizer below. Use it to explain what issues progressives addressed and how they hoped to bring about change.

Progressives

Big Business	Political Rights	Social Justice

2. **Analyzing** What characteristics describe the background of many of the progressive reformers?

3. **Evaluating** What issues did muckraking journalists concentrate on during the first decades of the 1900s? What effects did their articles have on politics and the lives of poor Americans?

4. **Using Historical Imagination** Imagine that you are a progressive novelist in the early 1900s. Create an outline for an article or short story that reflects an issue of concern to you.

Critical Thinking

5. In what ways were the goals of Populists and progressives similar and different?
   Consider
   • what the goals of the Populists were
   • what the goals of the progressives were

Reforming the New Industrial Order

OBJECTIVES

Read to understand:

1. what workplace problems progressives targeted
2. what the results of the Triangle Shirtwaist Fire were
3. what rulings the Supreme Court made on labor laws
4. what successes and failures unions saw in the early 1900s

KEY TERMS

Triangle Shirtwaist Fire
freedom of contract
Muller v. Oregon
closed shop
socialism
International Ladies' Garment Workers Union
open shop
Industrial Workers of the World

KEY PEOPLE

Samuel Gompers
Florence Kelley
Rose Schneiderman
Louis D. Brandeis
William "Big Bill" Haywood

EYEWITNESSES TO History

❝ *Miners' families . . . had to make their purchases of all the necessaries of life, meager [few] as they were, from the company stores at double the prices for which they could be had elsewhere. . . . It was a common saying that children were brought into the world by the company doctor, lived in a company house . . . were buried in a company coffin, and laid away in the company graveyard.* ❞
—Samuel Gompers

Samuel Gompers

Union leader Samuel Gompers explained in his *Autobiography* how mining companies controlled the lives of their workers. As one union official stated, the company owned "every single thing there is" in the entire town, from the miners' homes to the buildings in the community—even school and church buildings. Some mining companies paid little attention to safety conditions underground. Mines owned by John D. Rockefeller, for example, experienced cave-ins and serious explosions that took the lives of miners almost every year.

Reforming the Workplace

In 1900 the average laborer worked nearly 10 hours a day, six days a week, for about $1.50 a day. Women and children earned even less.

Female and child laborers. In the early 1910s almost half of the women who worked in such jobs as factory workers, store clerks, and laundresses earned less than $6 a week. The Commission on Industrial Relations reported in 1916 that this salary "means that every penny must be counted, every normal desire stifled, and each basic necessity of life barely satisfied."

Women often faced significant barriers when they tried to increase their income. For instance, pieceworkers could be penalized for working too fast. Rebecca August, a buttonhole maker in Chicago, recalled that she was paid 3.5 cents per buttonhole. When her supervisor realized how many buttonholes she was able to make—and thus how much money she could earn—he cut her pay. The supervisor said, "It was an *outrage* for a *girl* to make $25 a week." When August tried to organize a protest, her employer fired her.

The commission's report also attacked child labor practices. It declared "The Nation is paying a heavy toll in ignorance, deformity of body or mind, and premature old age [among children]." In *The Bitter Cry of the Children* (1906), John Spargo charged the textile industries with the "enslavement of children." He reported that children were employed to do work that he "could not do . . . and live."

This political cartoon shows child workers as the slaves of big business.

Spargo found that few child laborers had ever attended school or could read. Many mothers explained that they put their children to work in the mills because it was either that or starve. During an investigation of a miners' strike in 1903, a nine-year-old child reported that he was being forced to pay money that his father, who had died in the mine, owed to the company for rent.

Labor laws. Progressives and labor union activists campaigned for new laws that would prohibit or limit child labor and improve conditions for female workers. Reformer Florence Kelley worked tirelessly for this cause. She helped persuade the Illinois legislature in 1893 to prohibit child labor as well as to limit the number of hours women could work.

Although most children worked in agriculture, children in the factories—more than 2 million by 1910—faced the worst conditions. Reformers heard stories of supervisors splashing cold water on children's faces to keep them awake and of young girls working 16 or more hours a day in canning factories. Orphans also were sent to work in factories. "Capital has neither morals nor ideals," cried one critic.

Labor reform. This poster calls for a national eight-hour workday. *What symbols of work do you see in the picture?*

In 1904 Kelley helped organize the National Child Labor Committee to persuade state legislatures to pass laws against employing young children. By 1912, child-labor laws had been passed in 39 states. Some states even limited older children's employment to 8 or 10 hours a day and barred them from working at night or in dangerous occupations. Other states required that children be able to read and write before they were sent to work.

Enforcement of such laws was lax, however. Claiming that their business success depended on cheap child labor, many employers simply refused to obey the laws and continued to hire child workers. George Creel was a journalist and the author of *Children in Bondage* (1913). He estimated that "at least two million children were being fed annually into the steel hoppers of the modern industrial machine . . . all mangled in mind, body, and soul."

Progressives also campaigned for laws that would force factories to limit the long hours employers demanded of their adult workers. In 1903 Florence Kelley helped lobby the Oregon legislature to pass a law limiting female laundry workers to 10-hour days. Earlier, Utah had enacted a law limiting workdays in certain dangerous occupations to eight hours.

Progressive reformers also fought for higher wages. Some 30 million men and 7.5 million women were employed in 1910, and about one third of them lived in poverty. That year Catholic Church official Monsignor John Ryan called for "the establishment by law of minimum rates of wages that will equal or approximate the normal standards of living for the different groups of workers." Two years later Massachusetts responded to progressive lobbying by passing the nation's first minimum-wage law. This law set base wages for women and children. Other states gradually followed suit. Not until 1938, however, did Congress pass a national minimum-wage law.

✔ **READING CHECK:** What workplace problems did progressives target in the early 1900s?

"Omnia Vincit Labor"

SAMUEL GOMPERS

President American Federation of Labor

COURT HOUSE

Thursday, June 3

7:45 P. M.

SUBJECT

Shorter Work Day

Laboring men, business and professional men and the ladies are invited to hear this eloquent and able advocate of the 8-hour day—the head of the greatest labor organization in the world, with a membership of over a million.

Meeting under the auspices of the CENTRAL LABOR UNION

Press of O. H. Hebb, Terre Haute, Ind.

Labor leaders encourage workers to attend a speech by Samuel Gompers on the fight for a shorter workday.

Mexican View of Progressivism

Progressive reformers won shorter workdays, better working conditions, and other improvements for many U.S. workers. Such changes, however, were unknown to the immigrants who crossed the border from Mexico to work the fields, mines, and railroads of the southwestern United States. These immigrant workers experienced both harsh working conditions and bitter prejudice. In 1910 the Mexican newspaper *Diario del Hogar* wondered what drove "our workingmen, so attached to the land, to abandon the country [Mexico], even at the risk of the Yankee contempt with which they are treated on the other side of the Bravo [Rio Grande]." Some Mexican laborers were assaulted or lynched. Venustiano Carranza, Mexico's president from 1917 to 1920, claimed that 114 Mexicans had been murdered across the border.

The Triangle Shirtwaist Fire

Progressives also sought to improve workplace safety. A tragic event in 1911 catapulted the need for such reforms onto the front pages of the nation's newspapers. On Saturday, March 25, some 500 employees—most of them young Jewish or Italian immigrant women—were completing their six-day workweek at New York City's Triangle Shirtwaist Company. As they rose from their crowded work tables and started to leave, a fire erupted in a rag bin.

Within moments the entire eighth floor of the 10-story building was ablaze. Escape was impossible. There were only two stairways, and because managers were afraid workers would steal fabric, most of the fire doors were kept locked. Some women tried to take the freight elevators to safety, but the elevator jammed as women on higher floors jumped down the elevator shaft to flee the flames. Desperate for a way out, some 60 workers leaped from the windows to their death. "I looked upon the heap of dead bodies," wrote a journalist who witnessed the fire. "I remembered their great strike of last year in which these same girls demanded more sanitary conditions and more safety precautions in the shops. These dead bodies were the answer."

Through the night, weeping family members wandered among the crushed bodies on the sidewalk, looking for their loved ones. By the time firefighters gained control of the blaze, some 140 workers had perished in the **Triangle Shirtwaist Fire**. Rose Schneiderman, a Women's Trade Union League organizer, argued that only a strong working-class movement could bring real change to the workplace. She noted:

> 66 This is not the first time girls have been burned alive in the city. Each week I must learn of the untimely death of one of my sister workers. Every year thousands of us are maimed. The life of men and women is so cheap and property is so sacred. There are so many of us for one job it matters little if 143 of us are burned to death. 99

It did matter to the public, however. Popular outrage was so great that lawmakers soon passed protective legislation to help workers. As a result of the Triangle Shirtwaist Fire the New York legislature enacted the nation's strictest fire-safety code.

✔ **READING CHECK:** What were the results of the Triangle Shirtwaist Fire?

INTERPRETING THE VISUAL RECORD
Unsafe working conditions.
The Triangle Shirtwaist Fire was a terrible tragedy that horrified many Americans. *What can you determine about the extent of the damage caused by the fire and the tone of the public reaction to the fire?*

THE GRANGER COLLECTION, NEW YORK

THE BROOKLYN DAILY EAGLE

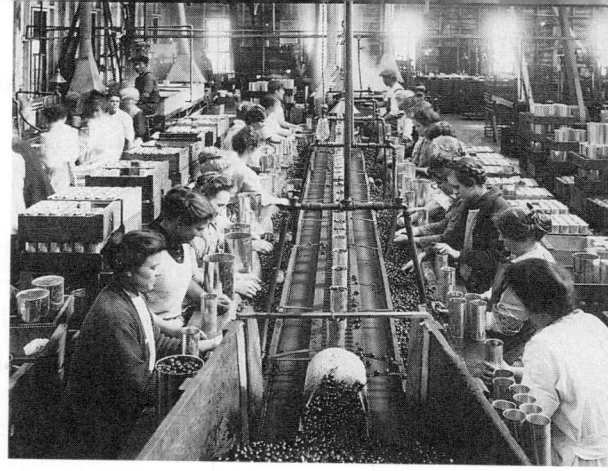

Progressivism and the Supreme Court

As more states passed protective legislation, business owners fought back through the courts. The Fourteenth Amendment to the Constitution prohibits states from depriving "any person of life, liberty, or property, without due process of law." Owners claimed that laws regulating their businesses deprived them of their property unfairly. The Supreme Court sided with business owners and declared much of the early social legislation unconstitutional.

The Court also ruled that some social legislation violated the Constitution by denying workers their **freedom of contract**, or the freedom to negotiate the terms of their employment. In the 1905 case *Lochner* v. *New York*, the Court overturned a New York law limiting bakers' workdays to 10 hours. Workers, the Court ruled, should be free to accept any conditions of employment that business owners required—even if that meant working 14 or 16 hours.

The Supreme Court did uphold some social legislation. In the 1908 case ***Muller v. Oregon***, an employer challenged the 10-hour-workday law that Florence Kelley had helped push through the Oregon legislature. Kelley and another woman, Josephine Goldmark, responded quickly. Goldmark gathered information for the brief, or legal argument, to defend the law. Kelley asked Goldmark's brother-in-law, a brilliant lawyer named Louis D. Brandeis, to argue the case.

The "Brandeis Brief" contained many examples of the harm that working long hours did to women's health and well-being. This research convinced the Court to uphold the Oregon law and became a model for the defense of other social legislation. Justice David Brewer noted that although the materials presented by Brandeis might not be authoritative, "they are significant of a widespread belief that woman's physical structure . . . [justifies] special legislation restricting or qualifying the conditions under which she should be permitted to toil."

✔ **READING CHECK:** What rulings did the Supreme Court make on labor laws?

INTERPRETING THE VISUAL RECORD

Factory work. These women are canning olives in a California factory. *What does the picture reveal about the conditions of factory work?*

Labor Unions

Progressive reformers were not the only ones fighting for workers' rights. Labor unions continued to fight for better working conditions and for the **closed shop**—a workplace where all the employees must belong to a union. Most union members favored "working within the system." They wanted to change how workers were treated, but they did not want to threaten capitalism's very existence. Some, however, wanted to replace capitalism with an economic system controlled by workers. Many in this group favored **socialism**, or the system under which the government or worker cooperatives own most factories, utilities, and transportation and communications systems.

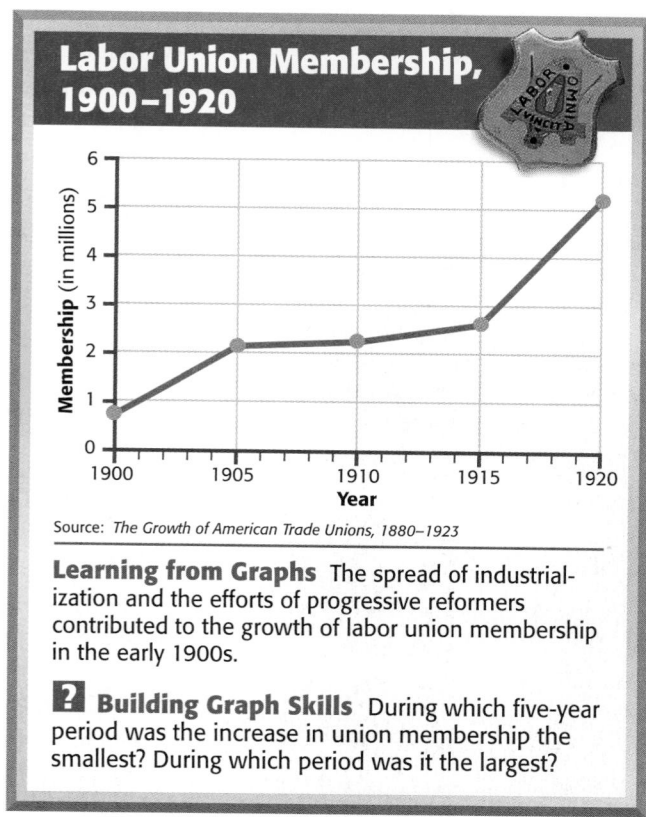

Labor Union Membership, 1900–1920

Source: *The Growth of American Trade Unions, 1880–1923*

Learning from Graphs The spread of industrialization and the efforts of progressive reformers contributed to the growth of labor union membership in the early 1900s.

? **Building Graph Skills** During which five-year period was the increase in union membership the smallest? During which period was it the largest?

The AFL. The major labor organization in these years remained the American Federation of Labor (AFL). The AFL favored working within the system. Led by Samuel Gompers, the AFL grew fourfold from 1900 to 1914. Gompers used the same organizational structure as trusts. "We welcome their organization," he said. "When they assume a right for themselves, they cannot deny that same right to us."

The AFL excluded unskilled workers—most of whom were eastern European immigrants or African Americans. AFL leaders believed that skilled workers had the greatest potential to cause change. However, this approach left most urban workers without organized support. By 1902 only about 3 percent of African American workers were union members.

The ILGWU. One AFL union that tried to organize unskilled workers was the **International Ladies' Garment Workers Union** (ILGWU). Established in 1900 in New York City, it sought to unionize workers—mainly Jewish and Italian immigrant women—employed in sewing shops. In 1909, workers at three different New York factories walked off their jobs. The workers then turned to the ILGWU to call a general strike. Union leaders hesitated, but the speech of Clara Lemlich, a young Jewish immigrant, changed their minds. "I am a working girl, one of those striking against intolerable conditions," she addressed a crowd of garment workers. "I am tired of listening to speakers who talk in generalities. What we are here for is to decide whether or not to strike. I offer a resolution that a general strike be declared—now." The frenzied crowd agreed with her.

This label identified clothes made by ILGWU members.

In November female garment workers staged the "Uprising of 20,000." Thousands of workers heeded the union's call and walked off their jobs to demand that their companies recognize the ILGWU as their union. The strike lasted through the bitter winter. Hard-pressed strikers received generous aid from progressive groups such as the Women's Trade Union League. This organization of wealthy women supported the efforts of working women to form unions. Many employers brought in African American women to take the place of their strikers, but several hundred of these workers went on strike also. One young African American woman wrote, "It's a good thing, this strike is. It makes you feel like a real grown-up person."

The strike's results were mixed. Most employers agreed to many of the ILGWU's demands, including wage increases and reduced working hours. However, they were determined to run an **open shop**, or nonunion workplace. Thus, they refused to recognize the union—the ILGWU's most basic demand. After this strike, ILGWU membership rose from 400 to 65,000.

Songbooks like this one for the IWW helped strengthen support for the union cause.

The IWW. While Gompers and the AFL unions negotiated with business owners for worker gains, a new union emerged with a different agenda. Founded in Chicago in 1905, the **Industrial Workers of the World** (IWW) opposed capitalism. Referring to the Continental Congress that had declared U.S. independence, IWW leader William "Big Bill" Haywood asserted:

❝ **Fellow workers, this is the continental congress of the working class. We are here to confederate the workers of this country into a working-class movement that shall have for its purpose the emancipation of the working class from the slave bondage of capitalism.** ❞

Haywood denounced the AFL's cooperation with business owners and its failure to include unskilled workers. He vowed to organize lumber workers, migrant farm-workers, miners, and textile workers to overthrow the capitalist system. The IWW enlisted African American, Asian American, and Hispanic American workers. An IWW-led union in Philadelphia succeeded in raising wages for its largely African American membership from $1.25 a day to $4 a day. The IWW also actively recruited female workers and the wives of male workers. An IWW newspaper expressed optimism that union women working "side by side with men in strikes will soon develop a fighting force that will end capitalism and its horrors in short order."

INTERPRETING THE VISUAL RECORD

IWW strike. The local militia was called in to break the IWW-led strike in Lawrence, Massachu-setts. *What does this picture reveal about the government's attitude toward strikers?*

The Wobblies, as the members of the IWW came to be called, pursued their goals through boycotts, general strikes, and indus-trial sabotage. Their greatest hour came in 1912. That year, they led 20,000 workers in a strike against the textile mills of Lawrence, Massachusetts, to protest large cut in wages. After a bitter and much publicized two-month strike, the mill owners gave in.

Success was short-lived, however. Several later IWW-led strikes failed miserably. Most Americans grew fearful of the IWW's revolutionary aims and methods. As member Frederick C. Mills put it, the IWW "is trying to teach them [poor or unem-ployed workers] how to get their share of the goods of this world." The government cracked down on the union with increasing force. The government believed, perhaps, that IWW members, as described by Mills, were "living, eating and breathing agitation, agitation that is really anarchy." Disagreements among IWW leaders also weakened the union's power. Within a few years the IWW collapsed and eventually faded from power.

✔ **READING CHECK:** What successes and failures did labor unions see in the early 1900s?

SECTION 2 REVIEW

Define and explain the significance of the following terms:
Triangle Shirtwaist Fire
freedom of contract
Muller v. *Oregon*
closed shop
socialism
International Ladies' Garment Workers Union
open shop
Industrial Workers of the World

Identify and explain the significance of the following individuals:
Samuel Gompers
Florence Kelley
Rose Schneiderman
Louis D. Brandeis
William "Big Bill" Haywood

1. **Using Graphic Organizers** Copy the chart below. Use it to describe the suc-cesses and failures unions experienced in the early 1900s.

Unions	
Successes	Failures

2. **Problem Solving** What solutions would you have proposed to improve working conditions for women and children?
3. **Assessing Consequences** How did the Triangle Shirtwaist Fire lead to improved workplace safety?
4. **Identifying Values** What concerns prompted the Supreme Court to strike down some progressive legislation?

Critical Thinking

5. Were the goals of employers and the goals of employees in the early 1900s really in conflict? Explain your answer.
   Consider:
   • what the goals of employers were
   • what the goals of employees were
   • how meeting the goals of one group might affect the other group

SECTION
③ Reforming Society

OBJECTIVES

Read to understand:
1. how reformers tried to improve life in U.S. cities
2. how reformers hoped to improve moral standards
3. how African Americans and American Indians organized to improve their lives
4. why immigrants were left out of some progressive reforms, and how they contributed to other reforms

KEY TERMS

prohibition
Woman's Christian Temperance Union
Eighteenth Amendment
National Association for the Advancement of Colored People
National Urban League
Society of American Indians

KEY PEOPLE

Lawrence Veiller
Daniel Burnham
Billy Sunday
Frances Willard
W. E. B. Du Bois

This little girl is collecting firewood on the city streets.

EYEWITNESSES TO History

❝ *The home is very unattractive for children and they are glad to get out to meet their friends. They want to supply a social need, and they go out and meet other friends and the home has no tie upon them. . . . The tenement house is not the only thing, but a very strong influence. I believe the entire economic conditions in this country are another influence.* ❞
—Henry Moscowitz

A subway porter

Tenement resident Henry Moscowitz described to a progressive journalist the negative effects on a family that accompanied the poverty and other ills of the cities. Reformers hoped that increasing wages would help bring many families out of poverty, but they knew that other factors affected the quality of people's lives. Progressives therefore set out to attack numerous ills that they believed weakened American society.

Reforming City Life

By 1920, for the first time in U.S. history, more than 50 percent of Americans lived in urban areas. As urban populations soared, cities struggled to provide garbage collection, safe and affordable housing, health care, police and fire protection, and adequate public education. "The challenge of the city," declared one progressive, "has become one of decent human existence."

Cleaning up the city. Some reformers called for a campaign to make the cities a more healthful and livable home for all residents. "The community is one great family," explained Louise DeKoven Bowen, the president of Chicago's Woman's City Club. "Each member of it is bound to help the other." Various women's clubs, men's clubs, and reform organizations enlisted the aid of local governments to clean up the cities. Some groups took the cleanup campaign literally, working to rid the cities of garbage. Other organizations worked for better housing or to improve public education.

Lawrence Veiller (VYL-uhr), a settlement-house worker, attacked irresponsible tenement owners "who for the sake of a large profit on their investments sacrifice the health and welfare of countless thousands." As the secretary to the New York State Tenement House Commission, Veiller campaigned tirelessly for improved housing. In 1900 he questioned Henry Moscowitz, who in 17 years had lived in 14 different tenements on New York's Lower East Side. Moscowitz described the stench, dirt, and noise, and the lack of light, fresh air, water, electricity, and bathing facilities.

The commission discovered that New York had "the most serious tenement house problem in the world." In 1901 Veiller succeeded in getting the New York

State Tenement House Bill passed. The law required that any new tenements be built around open courtyards that would let in light and air. New buildings also had to contain one bathroom for each apartment or for every three rooms. Previously, bathrooms in apartment buildings had been limited to one or two for an entire floor. Housing reformers in other states used the New York law as a model for their own legislative proposals.

To further improve urban living conditions, a group of physicians and reform-minded citizens formed the National Tuberculosis Association. The group focused on education and on lobbying the government to fund special hospitals to treat victims of tuberculosis. Thanks in part to this effort, by 1915 the death rate from "the white plague" had dropped significantly.

Other reformers campaigned for the creation of safe places for children to play. A 1908 Massachusetts law required all cities with a population greater than 10,000 to hold a referendum on whether that city should build at least one playground. Within the year, 41 out of 42 cities had shown their support for such actions. By 1920 cities had spent millions of dollars building playgrounds.

Some middle- and upper-class Americans objected to spending tax dollars on recreational facilities for the poor. One journalist in Lawrence, Massachusetts, reported that "pandemonium [disorder] reigned" when "bands of foreigners and trouble makers" used public space to celebrate the Fourth of July. Cleveland city council member Frederic Howe was shunned by his upper-class friends for supporting recreational facilities for the poor. However, Howe and his allies succeeded. "On Saturday and Sunday the whole population played baseball in the hundreds of parks laid out for that purpose," Howe reported.

City planning.

The city-planning movement grew out of progressives' belief that cleaned-up cities would produce better citizens. The first National Conference on City Planning was held in 1909. Its participants hoped that wise planning could halt the spread of slums and beautify cities. Beautiful cities and impressive public architecture, they argued, would instill patriotism among the immigrant population.

In 1909 Daniel Burnham, a leading architect and city planner, produced a magnificent plan for redesigning Chicago. It was the first comprehensive plan to redesign a U.S. city. The centerpiece of Burnham's vision for Chicago was a soaring city hall that would inspire all residents to be good citizens. "Make no little plans," said Burnham. "They have no magic to stir men's blood."

City-planning commissions in Cleveland, San Francisco, and Washington, D.C., also hired Burnham to develop grand schemes for their cities. His plans were never fully built, but some, such as those for Washington, D.C., were a success. Above all, his efforts helped people realize that city planning—developing parks, building codes, sanitation standards, and zoning—was a necessary function of municipal government.

✔ **READING CHECK:** How did reformers try to improve life in U.S. cities?

City planning. Daniel Burnham (left) created the plan for redesigning Chicago. *What are the unique characteristics shown in the design?*

Shaping Public Space

The City Beautiful movement in the early 1900s rose out of the success of several fairs that led architects and designers to create large open spaces in urban centers. For instance, Frederick Law Olmsted, a landscape architect for the World's Columbian Exposition of 1893, had created a series of lagoons surrounding Chicago's tall and shapely buildings. These pools of water, along with electric lights, reflected off the monumental buildings and led people to call Chicago the "Magic City."

Soon Daniel Burnham and other architects set to work to improve other U.S. cities. In Washington, D.C., the Senate Parks Commission assigned the task of completing Pierre Charles L'Enfant's original plans for the city to a team of architects, artists, and planners. They looked to the colonial cities of the United States as well as the great capitals of Europe for inspiration.

One of Burnham's first actions was to move the railroad station from the Mall. He located it on Capitol Hill, where it served as a gateway to the city. The surrounding landscaping accented the station's monumental proportions. Although work halted during World War I, in the 1920s the lands around the Potomac River were transformed into level ground. Builders created the Lincoln Memorial and a decorative canal known as the Reflecting Pool, which

The design of Washington, D.C., incorporates many of the ideas of city planning.

connects the Lincoln Memorial to the Washington Monument. During the 1920s many public buildings made of white stone were built, and sculptures were erected, transforming Washington, D.C., into an impressive national capital.

Understanding the Arts

1. What gave rise to the City Beautiful movement of the early 1900s?
2. What did Daniel Burnham do to the railroad station in Washington, D.C.?

This poster encouraged support for prohibition.

Moral Reform

Progressives also wanted to "clean up" what they considered to be immoral behavior. They called for **prohibition**—a ban on the manufacture, sale, and transportation of alcoholic beverages—and the closing of the nation's saloons. Reformers believed that prohibition would reduce crime and the breakup of families.

Journalists described alcohol as "the arch enemy of progress." Magazines published articles such as "The Story of an Alcohol Slave, as Told by Himself." Muckraker George Kibbe Turner wrote in *McClure's* in 1909 that to truly reform the rapidly growing U.S. cities, the saloons must be closed.

The drive for prohibition took many forms. During the Progressive Era, many colleges did not allow student athletes to drink. Some industrialists initiated programs intended to convince their workers to not drink alcohol. School textbooks included information on the dangers of alcohol.

The passage of prohibition. The Anti-Saloon League (ASL) and the **Woman's Christian Temperance Union** (WCTU) led the crusade against alcohol. By 1902 the ASL had branches in 39 states with 200 paid staff members.

Thousands of volunteer speakers, many of them Protestant ministers, spread the antisaloon message in the nation's churches. Billy Sunday, an ex-ballplayer turned Presbyterian evangelist, preached that saloons were "the parent of crimes and the mother of sins." Frances Willard headed the WCTU from 1879 to 1898. Willard eventually made the WCTU a powerful national force for temperance, moral purity, and the rights of women.

During World War I, prohibitionists drew on Americans' spirit of patriotic sacrifice. The U.S. Navy banned the consumption of alcohol in 1914. During the vote on prohibition in Congress, Senator William Kenyon of Iowa drew on this fact. He asked, "If liquor is a bad thing for the boys in the trenches, why is it a good thing for those at home?"

In 1917 Congress proposed the **Eighteenth Amendment**, which barred the manufacture, sale, and distribution of alcoholic beverages. The states ratified it in 1919. However, the amendment proved unpopular and difficult to enforce. It was repealed in 1933.

The coming of prohibition inspired this sheet music. This fan shows WCTU leader Frances Willard.

Moviegoing. The growing popularity of the newly invented motion picture worried some urban reformers who believed that movies were a threat to morality. The first movie to tell a story, *The Great Train Robbery*, was made in 1903. By 1910, millions of Americans were going to the movies each week. In 1916 the *New York Times* reported that films were the fifth-largest U.S. industry.

To the urban poor, a 5- or 10-cent movie ticket—bought at movie houses called nickelodeons—offered cheap, readily available entertainment. Many middle-class Americans, however, believed that movies—particularly the steamy romances—and movie houses were immoral and sources of temptation. Writer William Dean Howells described the situation.

> 66 The pictures thrown upon the luminous [lighted] curtain of the stage have been declared extremely corrupting to the idle young people lurking in the darkness before it. The darkness itself has been held a condition of inexpressible depravity [immorality] and a means of allurement [attraction] to evil. 99

Declaring that moviegoing promoted immoral values, reformers demanded that movies be censored. Several states and cities set up censorship boards to ban movies they considered immoral. In 1909 the movie industry began to censor itself.

✔ **READING CHECK:** How did reformers hope to improve Americans' moral standards?

INTERPRETING THE VISUAL RECORD
Movie theaters. The popularity of motion pictures led to the building of fancy theaters. *Why do you think the cost of admission varied by time of day?*

Progressivism and Racial Discrimination

For nonwhites the progressive movement had mixed results. Most progressives were concerned about the plight of the poor. However, few white progressives devoted very much energy to the problems of discrimination and prejudice against African Americans and American Indians. Some progressives expressed open prejudice against these groups. Many African Americans and American Indians, however, drew on progressive ideas to develop programs appropriate to their communities.

W. E. B. Du Bois

Views of Du Bois. One of the most influential African American leaders to emerge during this period was W. E. B. Du Bois (doo BOYS). Born in 1868 in Great Barrington, Massachusetts, Du Bois had a happy childhood. Du Bois attended Sunday school with African American and white children. Not until high school did he begin to realize that his skin color caused some people not to like him. He had many friends among the white students, however.

A bright student, Du Bois was encouraged by his school's principal to prepare for college. Great Barrington's residents and churches raised money to send Du Bois to Fisk University, an African American school in Nashville, Tennessee. After graduating, he studied history in Germany and at Harvard University. In 1895 he became the first African American to earn a doctorate from Harvard. Two years later he was appointed as a professor of history and economics at Atlanta University, a leading African American college, where he taught until 1910.

By the early 1900s Du Bois was recognized as a brilliant thinker and strong supporter of African American civil rights and culture. He believed that access to a college education and vocational training offered the best chance of progress for African Americans. He also believed that African Americans should be politically active in the struggle for racial equality. Du Bois's view contrasted sharply with that of African American leader Booker T. Washington. Washington argued that African Americans should not spend their time fighting discrimination. He urged African Americans to focus on improving their own education and economic prosperity. Du Bois believed that this focus would unfairly make African Americans responsible for correcting racial injustice.

Throughout his life Du Bois maintained a passionate interest in Africa, which he regarded as the spiritual homeland of all black people. In his influential 1903 book, *The Souls of Black Folk*, Du Bois eloquently expressed his dual identity as both African and American.

Read More About It

Free Find:
W. E. B. Du Bois
After learning about
W. E. B. Du Bois on the
Holt Researcher CD–ROM,
write a poem that
describes Du Bois's life.

66 One ever feels his two-ness—an American, a Negro; two souls, two thoughts, two un-reconciled strivings. He [the African American] simply wishes to make it possible for a man to be both a Negro and an American, without being cursed and spit upon by his fellows, without having the doors of Opportunity closed roughly in his face. 99

W. E. B. Du Bois's The Souls of Black Folk

In the 1920s Du Bois organized a series of Pan-African congresses that attracted black leaders from around the world. This was done to create greater unity among people of African descent. During the 1930s and 1940s Du Bois continued his career as a scholar and political activist. By the 1950s he, like many prominent American intellectuals, had embraced socialism for its promise of social justice. In 1961, at age 93, Du Bois joined the Communist Party and moved to Ghana. He died there two years later.

African Americans organize. In 1909 Du Bois and a group of African American and white progressives met in New York City. They discussed the lynching of two African American men in Springfield, Illinois, the previous year. Out of this meeting came the **National Association for the Advancement of Colored People** (NAACP), an organization dedicated to ending racial discrimination. Du Bois edited its monthly magazine, *The Crisis*, which publicized cases of racial inequality. The publication also called for social reforms that would ensure equal rights for African Americans. By 1918 the magazine's circulation had risen to 100,000.

The NAACP used the court system to fight restrictions on voting and on other civil rights. In 1915 it won its first major victory in *Guinn* v. *United States*. In this case the Supreme Court outlawed the "grandfather clause." Southern states had used the clause to ensure that suffrage requirements designed to keep African Americans from voting would not apply to whites. Two years later NAACP lawyers won *Buchanan* v. *Warley*, which overturned a Louisville, Kentucky, law requiring racially segregated housing. As a result, similar laws were struck down across the country.

The **National Urban League** also fought for racial equality. Founded in 1910 by concerned African Americans and white reformers, the league worked to improve job opportunities and housing for urban African Americans. One of its goals was to help African American migrants from the South adjust to their new lives in northern cities. The NAACP and the National Urban League made some important gains for African American citizens. Nevertheless, most African Americans still faced discrimination.

W. E. B. Du Bois wanted The Crisis *to honestly address important issues.*

Lynchings, 1889–1918

Learning from Maps Some 75 percent of lynching victims were African American men. Most of the other victims were white men. However, women, American Indians, Hispanics, and Asian Americans were also victims of lynch mobs.

❓ REGION In which region did most lynchings occur?

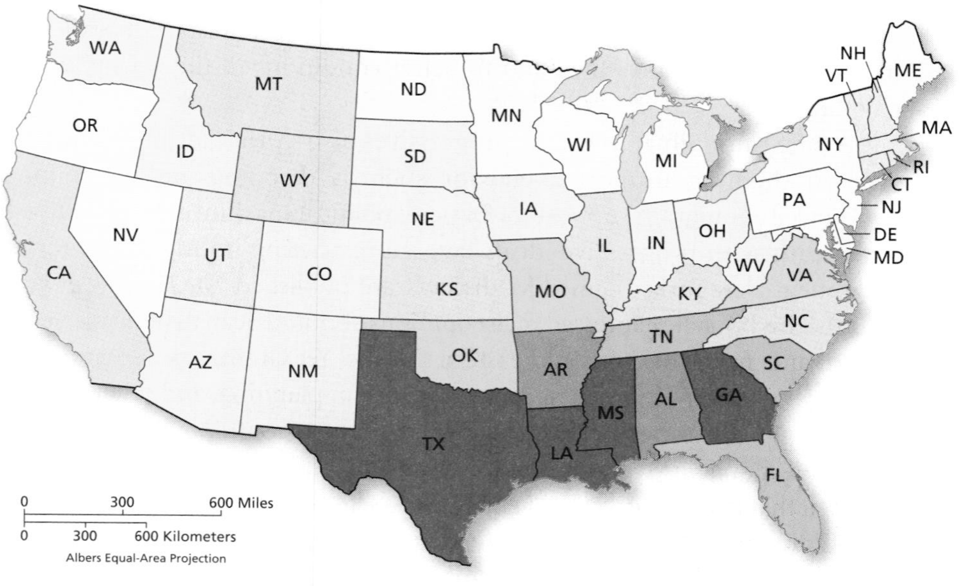

Lynchings of Whites and African Americans

Period	Whites	African Americans
1889–1893	261	571
1894–1898	223	549
1899–1903	77	465
1904–1908	25	342
1909–1913	32	308
1914–1918	27	253
TOTALS	645	2,488

Source: *Historical Statistics of the United States*

Number of Lynchings

None	51–100
1–5	101–200
6–20	201–300
21–50	301–386

0   300   600 Miles
0   300   600 Kilometers
Albers Equal-Area Projection

Jim Thorpe was one of the greatest athletes in U.S. history.

American Indians organize. Demands for equal rights and greater opportunities for American Indians also surfaced during this period. It had become clear that the Dawes Act of 1887 had caused many American Indians to lose their property to land speculators and fall deeper into poverty. Some progressives took up the American Indians' cause. They argued for a more gradual approach: slowing down land allotment and maintaining the reservation system for a time. In 1911 a group of 50 American Indians, most of them middle-class professionals, formed the **Society of American Indians** to address the problems facing Indians. One of its members, Seneca historian Arthur C. Parker, urged American Indians "to strike out into the duties of modern life and . . . find every right that had escaped them before."

Although some members supported strengthening tribal values, most favored complete assimilation. The organization publicized the accomplishments of famous American Indians such as Olympic gold medalist Jim Thorpe and lobbied against the use of insulting terms for Indians. Members also discussed ways to improve Indian civil rights, education, health, and local government. The organization's moderate positions on most issues, however, led to disputes with members who wanted more aggressive action. These disputes weakened the organization.

Dr. Carlos Montezuma, a Yavapai Apache member of the society, criticized the Bureau of Indian Affairs for mismanaging reservations. Other members refused to take such a strong antigovernment stand, and the group's influence declined. However, the Society of American Indians did provide a forum for American Indian leaders. It laid the groundwork for later attempts to improve conditions for American Indians.

✔ **READING CHECK:** What efforts did African Americans and American Indians make to improve their positions in American society during the Progressive Era?

Immigrants and Assimilation

The progressive movement had mixed results for immigrants as well. On one hand, many reformers sympathized with the plight of the newcomers who labored in factories and were crowded into slum tenements. These reformers lobbied for laws to improve immigrants' lives and to better conditions in the workplace and in city slums.

At the same time, however, progressives also criticized immigrants. They accused them of immoral behavior such as drinking and gambling and denounced immigrant support for big-city political machines. Some native-born Americans with progressive ideals favored restricting immigration. In 1916 a prominent New Yorker named Madison Grant published *The Passing of the Great Race*. In this book he expressed racist opinions about African Americans, Jews, and immigrants from southern and eastern Europe. Yet Grant was also a progressive who supported environmental protection, urban planning, and other reforms.

Many progressives believed that immigrants should be "Americanized" as quickly as possible. William Maxwell was a prominent New York educator. He declared that his goal was to make the public school "a melting pot which converts the children of the immigrants of all races and languages into sturdy, independent American citizens." Russian immigrant Eugene Lyons described the effects of this process on immigrants.

> 66 We sensed a disrespect for the alien traditions in our homes and came unconsciously to resent and despise those traditions . . . because they seemed [impossible] barriers between ourselves and the adopted land. 99

Chinese immigrant Victor Wong recalled that in school, teachers tried to "dissuade us . . . from everything Chinese. Their view of the Chinese ways was that they were evil, heathen, non-Christian." The lack of respect for their cultural backgrounds led some immigrants to reject the assistance of social reformers.

Some progressives welcomed the diversity that immigrant groups brought to the United States. In his 1924 book, *Culture and Democracy in the United States*, philosopher Horace Kallen supported pluralism. He envisioned a nation that would be home to a number of distinctive cultures. Some immigrants also supported a course of Americanization that could be achieved without giving up their ethnic identities.

Poor immigrants and the political bosses who represented them supported middle-class progressives when they fought for practical reforms such as worker protection and public-health programs. For example, a New York state legislative committee set up to investigate factory conditions after the Triangle Shirtwaist Fire won strong backing from New York City's immigrant-based Democratic machine. In his autobiography, Frederic Howe asserted that New York City owed its playgrounds, public baths, and public parks, among other services, to Irish immigrants and their political machines. "Unconsciously aiming to shape the state to human ends," he declared, "the Irish have made New York what it is."

INTERPRETING THE VISUAL RECORD

Americanizing immigrants.
This poster was created to encourage immigrants to learn English. *Do you think that the poster shows respect for immigrants' culture?*

✔ **READING CHECK:** Why were immigrants left out of some progressive reforms, and how did immigrants contribute to other reforms?

SECTION ③ REVIEW

Define and explain the significance of the following terms:
prohibition
Woman's Christian Temperance Union
Eighteenth Amendment
National Association for the Advancement of Colored People
National Urban League
Society of American Indians

Identify and explain the significance of the following individuals:
Lawrence Veiller
Daniel Burnham
Billy Sunday
Frances Willard
W. E. B. Du Bois

1. **Using Graphic Organizers** Copy the organizational web below. Use it to explain the different approaches that progressives took in cleaning up cities.

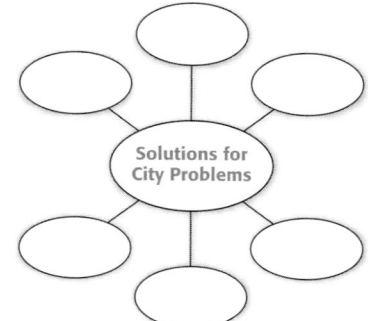

Solutions for City Problems

2. **Synthesizing** How did some reformers attempt to influence the personal behavior of Americans?
3. **Comparing and Contrasting** What methods did African Americans and American Indians use to fight racism and discrimination, and how successful were they?
4. **Identifying Values** Why did progressives support prohibition and the elimination of saloons?

Critical Thinking

5. If you had been an immigrant in 1910, would you have supported the progressive movement? Explain your answer.
   Consider:
   • how some progressives treated immigrants
   • how some immigrants contributed to reform
   • how the progressive movement affected immigrants overall

CHAPTER 18

Review

Creating a Time Line

Copy the time line below onto a sheet of paper. Complete the time line by filling in the events and dates from the chapter that you think were most significant. Pick three events and explain why you think they were significant.

1900   1910   1920

Writing a Summary

Using the Reading Checks as a guide, write an overview of the events in the chapter.

Identifying People and Ideas

Identify the following terms or individuals and explain their significance.

1. progressivism
2. muckrakers
3. Ray Stannard Baker
4. Samuel Gompers
5. Florence Kelley
6. freedom of contract
7. socialism
8. Lawrence Veiller
9. Frances Willard
10. Society of American Indians

Understanding Main Ideas

SECTION 1
1. How did women work for progressive goals?
2. What roles did intellectuals, muckrakers, and writers play in the progressive movement?

SECTION 2
3. Which labor issues did reformers hope to remedy through legislation?
4. How did the Supreme Court rule on labor issues?

SECTION 3
5. What actions did progressive reformers take to improve conditions in cities?
6. How did African Americans and American Indians address the problems facing their communities?

Reviewing Themes

1. **Economic Development** Why did states pass laws to protect workers' rights?
2. **Democratic Values** How did progressives propose to extend opportunities to all citizens? Were they successful in these efforts? Why or why not?
3. **Constitutional Heritage** How did progressives help win passage of the Eighteenth Amendment?

Thinking Critically

1. **Analyzing** How did industrialization influence progressive reform efforts?
2. **Hypothesizing** How might the course of reform have been different if the Supreme Court had been more supportive of early social legislation?
3. **Comparing and Contrasting** How did the American Federation of Labor and the Industrial Workers of the World differ in their views on the scope and nature of labor reform?
4. **Taking a Stand** Write a brief paragraph explaining your position on spending tax dollars on city improvements.
5. **Problem Solving** Imagine you are a progressive reformer. Outline a campaign to improve safety in the workplace.

Writing About History

Writing to Persuade Imagine that you are Louis D. Brandeis. Write a closing argument to convince the Supreme Court to uphold laws that guarantee workers' rights. Use the following graphic to organize your thoughts.

Strategies for Success

Review the **Strategies for Success** on *Interpreting the Visual Record: Photographs*. Then study Arnold Genthe's photograph of a Chinese immigrant family below and answer the following questions.

1. What information is provided by the details in this photograph?
2. What message is Genthe trying to convey about the family in the photograph?
3. How does the photograph contribute to your understanding of progressive attempts to "Americanize" immigrants to the United States?

THE GRANGER COLLECTION, NEW YORK

Linking History and Geography

Study the map below. Do any regional trends exist in the timing of different states' banning of alcohol? What might explain such differences?

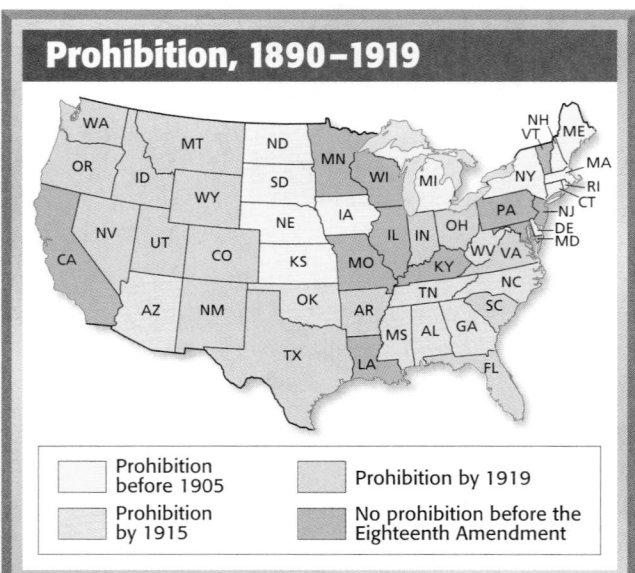

Prohibition, 1890–1919

Prohibition before 1905
Prohibition by 1915
Prohibition by 1919
No prohibition before the Eighteenth Amendment

BUILDING YOUR PORTFOLIO

Complete one or all of the following projects independently or cooperatively.

1 Economic Development
Imagine that you are a progressive reformer in the early 1900s. **Write an editorial** for *McClure's* or another progressive magazine. Editorials might examine corporate abuses, poor working conditions, or public-health concerns. Be sure to suggest a possible solution to the problem.

2 Democratic Values
Imagine that you are a progressive reformer working to promote women's rights. **Prepare a speech** on women's rights to deliver at an Independence Day celebration. Be sure to outline the various problems and concerns faced by women in the early 1900s.

3 Technology and Society
Imagine that it is the early 1900s and you are an architect interested in redesigning your town in order to make it more accessible and pleasant. **Sketch out your designs** and write a paragraph describing how these changes will improve the quality of life in your town.

1900–1920
Progressive Politicians

Oil gusher in
Spindletop oil
field

*African American
farmers in the
early 1900s*

1906
Politics
Congress passes the
Meat Inspection Act.

1906
**Science and
Technology**
Lee De Forest
invents the three-
element vacuum
repeater for tele-
phones, improving
voice quality in
long-distance calls.

1904
**Business
and Finance**
The U.S. Supreme
Court rules that the
Northern Securities
Company has violated
antitrust laws and
orders it dissolved.

1901
Science and Technology
Oil production increases with new
drilling practices that yield an estimated 100,000 barrels a day in a
nine-day period in one Texas well.

1908
Business and Finance
Thirty-five percent of
American workers are
employed in agriculture.

1900　　　　　　　　　　**1904**　　　　　　　　　　**1908**

1900
Daily Life
A hurricane strikes Galveston, Texas,
killing at least 6,000 people.

1904
Daily Life
The winning vehicle
in the Vanderbilt
Challenge Cup auto-
mobile race averages
52.2 miles per hour.

1906
The Arts
Upton Sinclair publishes
his novel *The Jungle*.

1908
Politics
A White House conference
on conservation leads to
the creation of a commis-
sion to study natural
resource issues.

*Hurricane
damage
in Galveston,
Texas, in 1900*

THE JUNGLE
BY
UPTON SINCLAIR

DOUBLEDAY, PAGE & Cº
NEW YORK

*Cover of Upton
Sinclair's novel
The Jungle*

Before You Read

Build on What You Know

During the early 1900s, many Americans took a new interest in reforming
society. Now known as the Progressive Era, this time period was marked by
great optimism and faith in scientific efficiency. Progressive reformers set
out to conquer such negative effects of industrialization and rapid urbanization as
unsafe working conditions, long hours, low wages, and slum housing. In this chapter
you will learn about the successes and failures of progressive politicians, including
Presidents Theodore Roosevelt, William Howard Taft, and Woodrow Wilson.

George Bellow's
Lone Tenement,
completed in 1909

THE GRANGER COLLECTION, NEW YORK

1917
The Arts
The era of the American Renaissance in art draws to a close.

1917
Daily Life
Americans spend $175 million on electrical appliances.

1917
World Events
Mexico adopts a new constitution.

1919
Business and Finance
Per capita income among southerners is 40 percent lower than the national average.

1910
World Events
A Chinese army tries to take direct control of Tibet's government by force.

1913
Business and Finance
The Federal Reserve Act reorganizes the national banking system.

1914
Politics
The Clayton Antitrust Act is passed.

1912

1916

1920

1912
Politics
Theodore Roosevelt and his supporters form the Progressive Party.

1914
Science and Technology
The amount of electric power used in manufacturing industries reaches 3.8 million horsepower.

1920
Politics
The Nineteenth Amendment gives American women the right to vote.

PROGRESSIVE PARTY FOR PRESIDENT

THEODORE ROOSEVELT

Theodore Roosevelt campaign banner

MR. PRESIDENT WHAT WILL YOU DO FOR WOMAN SUFFRAGE

Suffrage supporter

Think About Themes

Themes Journal

Decide whether you **agree** *or* **disagree** *with the following statements. Note why in your journal.*

Democratic Values The management of a business corporation provides a good model for city government.

Economic Development Government regulation of business should never limit or restrict the free-enterprise system.

Constitutional Heritage Each new generation should reinterpret the Constitution for itself, as social and economic realities change.

569

SECTION 1

Reforming Government

OBJECTIVES

Read to understand:

1. what reforms were enacted to make U.S. voting procedures more democratic
2. how reformers sought to improve city governments
3. what the goals of progressive state leaders were

KEY TERMS

direct primary
Seventeenth Amendment
initiative
referendum
recall
Wisconsin Idea

KEY PEOPLE

Samuel M. Jones
Tom Johnson
Robert M. La Follette

This 1889 cartoon criticizes the influence of trusts on the U.S. Senate.

THE GRANGER COLLECTION, NEW YORK

EYEWITNESSES TO History

❝ *The American reformer's story is a modern tragedy of defeat, humiliation, martyrdom. . . . [There is evidence] to show the regular, outrageous grafting . . . in all public business.* ❞
—Oliver McClintock

Author
Lincoln Steffens

Pittsburgh reformer Oliver McClintock "knew and could prove what was going on," progressive reformer Lincoln Steffens wrote. Steffens's eye-opening book *The Shame of the Cities* vividly depicted the workings of turn-of-the-century urban politics. In many cities, he said, a boss controlled municipal government. The boss had a strong opponent, however—the reformer.

Government Corruption

Progressive reformers such as Lincoln Steffens found corruption at all levels of government, from city hall to Washington, D.C. City political machines were often linked to the Democratic or Republican state machines. The state machines catered to special interests, making deals with railroads, lumber companies, or anyone else seeking tax breaks or other favors from state legislatures. In return, the machines expected generous gifts, often in the form of campaign contributions.

In the 1890s some people began referring to the U.S. Senate as the Millionaire's Club. Some said that Senator James McMillan of Michigan represented shipping and lumber interests instead of his constituents. Others argued that Senator Joseph Foraker of Ohio put Standard Oil's needs above all others. Often put into power by state machines, some U.S. senators accepted bribes to vote the way corporations wished. In 1906 progressive writer David Graham Phillips published "The Treason of the Senate," a series of articles documenting how special interests influenced U.S. politics.

❝ The greatest single hold of 'the interests' is the fact that they are the 'campaign contributors.' . . . Who pays the big election expenses of your congress man, of the men you send to the legislature to elect senators? Do you imagine those who foot those huge bills are fools? Don't you know that they make sure of getting their money back, with interest? ❞

Election Reforms

Reformers seeking a return to honest government rallied to the slogan, "Give the government back to the people!" Only when government listened to the public's voice, they believed, could the urgent problems facing Americans be fixed.

Progressives sought to break the power of the bosses by reforming the election process. First, they wanted to take the power of choosing political candidates away from political machines. Therefore, progressives pushed for the **direct primary**—

a nominating election in which voters choose the candidates who later run in a general election. Mississippi adopted the direct primary in 1902. Wisconsin followed in 1903. By 1916 most others states had done the same.

Next, progressives proposed to change the method of electing U.S. senators. The U.S. Constitution gave the power to elect senators to state legislatures. Progressives believed that this procedure made it easy for the political bosses and machines with influence over state officials to control government. By 1912 the progressive tide had grown strong enough that Congress proposed the **Seventeenth Amendment**, which gave voters the power to elect their senators directly. The amendment was ratified the next year.

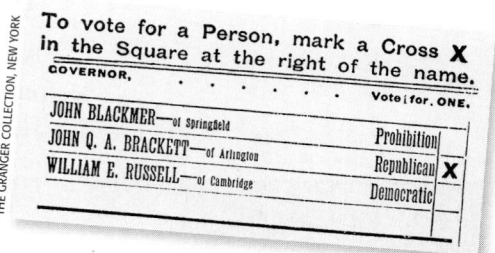

The Australian ballot lists all candidates on a single, uniform sheet of paper.

Progressives also sought to reform the voting process itself. At the time, each political party printed its own ballot in a distinctive color. At polling places, the colored ballots made it easy to see how people voted. Without secrecy, voters could be pressured to support certain candidates. To lessen this threat, progressives proposed using the secret ballot. Developed in Australia, the secret ballot lists all candidates on a single, uniform sheet of paper. The ballot is also printed at public expense. By 1910 most states had switched to the secret ballot.

Finally, progressives urged states to adopt three additional election-reform measures: the initiative, the referendum, and the recall. The **initiative** gives voters the power to initiate, or introduce, legislation. If a certain percentage of voters in a state—usually 5 to 15 percent—sign a petition, a proposed policy must be put on the ballot for public approval. The **referendum** is a companion to the initiative. By securing a specified number of signatures on a petition, citizens can force the legislature to place a recently passed law on the ballot, allowing voters to approve or veto the measure. The **recall** enables voters to remove an elected official from office by calling for a special election.

Many reformers believed they were making major changes. William Allen White referred to voting reforms as "a big moral movement in democracy." In 1910 White claimed victory for reformers.

> 66 Today in states having the primary under the state control the corporation [political machine] candidate for any public office is handicapped. 99

In practice, however, the effects of the voting reforms were mixed and business continued to influence elections.

✔ **READING CHECK:** What reforms were enacted to make U.S. voting procedures more democratic?

THROUGH OTHERS' EYES

The Australian Ballot

In 1855 William Nicholson of Victoria proposed a motion in Australia's legislature that "in the opinion of this House any new Electoral Act should provide for electors recording their vote by secret ballot." The following year the act passed. By 1887 the use of an official secret ballot had been established throughout Australia in national and local elections. The new law required that voters be provided with private voting booths where they could strike out the names of the candidates they did not select on a preprinted ballot. The ballots were then deposited in a locked box in the presence of voting officials.

The success of the ballot system in Australia encouraged ballot reform in Great Britain. Francis S. Dutton, a member of South Australia's legislature, described the effects of Australia's secret ballot reform to a specially appointed British parliamentary committee. "The very notion of exercising coercion [force] and improper influence absolutely died out of the country," he announced. Robert Torrens, former premier of South Australia, also testified. He described the voting situation before the ballot reform. "We had . . . bribery, a great deal of rioting, and broken heads, and broken panes of glass, and of smashing windows; exactly the same thing that goes on in this country." In 1872 a law enacting the "Australian" ballot passed the British House of Commons.

Reforming City Government

The drive to clean up city government typically owed its successes to enthusiastic local leaders and active reformers. Through such efforts, the "good-government" campaign put some reform mayors into office.

Two of the most successful reform mayors were elected in Ohio. Both Samuel M. Jones and Tom Johnson were self-made men who earned their fortunes early in life. Then in midlife they traded business for politics.

The mayors. Samuel M. "Golden Rule" Jones's nickname came from his belief in the biblical Golden Rule—"Do unto others as you would have them do unto you." Seeking to apply this principle to government, Jones successfully ran for mayor of Toledo in 1897. During the next seven years he overhauled the police force, improved municipal services, set a minimum wage for city workers, and opened kindergartens for children.

During this same period, Tom Johnson served as Cleveland's mayor. Johnson created new, more humane rules for the treatment of prisoners by Cleveland's police department. He also strongly supported a new, fairer single tax system. Frederic Howe described Johnson's desire for such a system as "a passion for freedom, for a world of equal opportunity for all." Johnson's success led Lincoln Steffens to call him "the best mayor of the best governed city in the United States."

A mixed record. A few popular mayors alone, however, could not conquer established patterns of corruption in city government. The reformers' attempts to achieve basic governmental changes had mixed results. Lincoln Steffens concluded that voters did not necessarily prefer democratic governments because machine-run politics was more predictable. Reformers were also disappointed by some of the results of their direct government movement that encouraged voters' input in government decisions. For instance, voters rejected some measures favored by progressives such as municipal ownership of public utilities, tax reform, and pensions for city employees.

Electoral reform was further hindered by the fact that many middle-class progressives feared that the lower classes might gain too much power. They wanted to curb the power of big business, but feared that urban masses would gain too great a voice in political decision making. One reform leader, F. E. Chadwick of Newport, Rhode Island, maintained that a voter who paid higher taxes "should be assured a representation in the committee which . . . spends the money which he contributes." Chadwick believed that a "truly democratic" government would "give the property owner a fair show."

City commissions and managers. A devastating hurricane that struck Galveston, Texas, in 1900 produced an alternative to the political machine. A tidal wave created by the storm killed at least 6,000 people and destroyed the city. Galveston's government was unable to cope with the emergency. The state legislature therefore named a five-person city commission to rebuild the area. The commissioners were experts in their fields rather than party loyalists. Citizens praised the commission as being more honest and efficient than the city's previous government. Galveston kept the system, and other cities in the United States soon established similar commissions.

The desire for increased government efficiency also gave rise to the hiring of city managers. These individuals are expert administrators employed to run cities as they might run a business.

✔ **READING CHECK:** How did reformers try to improve city government?

As one of the progressive movement's most energetic leaders, Robert M. La Follette supported a reform program in Wisconsin that became a model for other states.

Reforming State Government

The spirit of reform also stirred many politicians at the state level. In Wisconsin, Robert M. "Fighting Bob" La Follette began his political career as a loyal Republican. However, he soon found himself at odds with Wisconsin's Republican political machine, which was dominated by railroad and lumber interests. La Follette served as a county district attorney and as a member of Congress in the late 1800s. He then signaled his break with the party machine by refusing a bribe from a party boss.

Elected governor in 1900, La Follette vigorously backed a reform program—soon known as the **Wisconsin Idea**—that became a model for other states. First, La Follette called for a direct primary. Although he was opposed by the Republican machine for two years, La Follette refused to accept a compromise. He declared that "in legislation *no bread* is often better than *half a loaf*." He then urged the state legislature to increase taxes on railroads and public utilities—electric, gas, and streetcar companies—and to create commissions to regulate these companies in the public interest. La Follette helped pass laws that curbed excessive lobbying. He also backed labor reforms and worked to conserve Wisconsin's natural resources. In 1905 the Wisconsin legislature elected La Follette to the U.S. Senate. La Follette remained committed to "the struggle between labor and those who would control, through slavery in one form or another, the laborers."

La Follette influenced other state leaders. New York governor Charles Evans Hughes established stricter controls of insurance companies and utilities. Progressive Democrat James Vardaman of Mississippi and Hoke Smith of Georgia led white farmers in a fight against corporate power. As governor, Vardaman abolished the use of convict labor. He also regulated corporations and improved social services for poor whites. However, these southern progressives often supported racial segregation and tried to keep African Americans from voting.

✔ **READING CHECK:** What goals did progressive state leaders have?

SECTION  REVIEW

Define and explain the significance of the following terms:
direct primary
Seventeenth Amendment
initiative
referendum
recall
Wisconsin Idea

Identify and explain the significance of the following individuals:
Samuel M. Jones
Tom Johnson
Robert M. La Follette

1. **Using Graphic Organizers** Copy the diagram below. Use it to explain what reforms progressives proposed at the city and state levels and where those reforms overlapped.

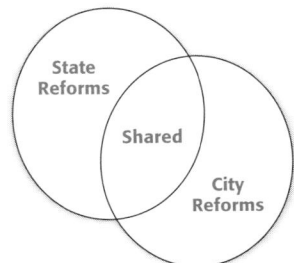

2. **Identifying Values** What did the widespread corruption in U.S. politics reveal about political values in the early 1900s?
3. **Evaluating** How did many U.S. cities try to increase government efficiency and lessen corruption?
4. **Assessing Consequences** How did changes in voting procedures enable government leaders to be elected more democratically?

Critical Thinking

5. Why can it be said that the Wisconsin Idea reforms were examples of the progressive spirit?
   Consider:
   • the reforms that made up the Wisconsin Idea
   • your definition of the progressive spirit
   • how well the Wisconsin Idea lived up to the ideals of the Progressive Era

SECTION
2

Roosevelt and the Square Deal

OBJECTIVES

Read to understand:

1. how the response to the miners' strike and Square Deal reflected President Roosevelt's governing style
2. why the government tried to regulate trusts and the food and drug industries
3. what stand Gifford Pinchot and Theodore Roosevelt took on the environment

KEY TERMS

arbitration
Square Deal
Elkins Act
Hepburn Act
Meat Inspection Act
Pure Food and Drug Act
reclamation

KEY PEOPLE

Theodore Roosevelt
Upton Sinclair
Gifford Pinchot

Theodore Roosevelt served as vice president to President William McKinley. After the assassination of McKinley in 1901, Roosevelt became president.

66 *[The tower] assumes a magical aspect, as if it had been summoned forth by the genius of our united people.* **99**
—*Cosmopolitan Magazine*

Pan-American Exposition button

A writer for *Cosmopolitan Magazine* described the Electric Tower at the Pan-American Exposition held in Buffalo, New York, in 1901. Standing 375 feet tall, the tower served as a powerful symbol of American success. Americans at the turn of the century saw this and the other exhibits at the Pan-American Exposition as commemorating their industrial progress, rising prosperity, and increasing world power. The visit of President William McKinley was intended to be the highlight of the exposition. He believed that such public festivities not only recorded American achievements and led to greater enthusiasm and energy for industrial pursuits, but also brought joy to the American people.

Roosevelt Becomes President

In 1900 President McKinley ran for re-election with Theodore Roosevelt as his running mate. The Democrats again nominated William Jennings Bryan and made free silver and the economy the focus of their campaign. However, in 1900 most Americans felt prosperous, and McKinley and Roosevelt sailed to victory.

As governor of New York, Roosevelt had worked to reform government and regulate big business. New York's conservative Republican Party leaders were angered by this progressive activism. They had tried to ease Roosevelt out of state office by persuading him to run as vice president. Senator Mark Hanna, a conservative from Ohio, was alarmed by this move. He warned that there would be "only one life between this madman and the Presidency."

Roosevelt takes office. The nation was shocked when, on September 6, 1901, anarchist Leon Czolgosz shot McKinley at the Pan-American Exposition. An unemployed laborer, Czolgosz claimed to act on behalf of the poor and the forgotten. A week later the president died, and Roosevelt became the nation's chief executive.

Roosevelt was just 42 years old when he took the presidential oath. He set about the task of reform with enthusiasm and energy. Roosevelt brought dynamic leadership to the progressive movement. He helped reshape the country as surely as he renamed the Executive Mansion the White House.

During the Gilded Age U.S. presidents generally took a hands-off approach to government. Roosevelt, however, believed that the president should use the office as a "bully pulpit" to speak out on vital issues. One of Roosevelt's goals as president was to fight against class distinctions. "No republic can permanently exist when it becomes a republic of classes," he warned.

PROGRESSIVE POLITICIANS **575**

Theodore Roosevelt

Theodore Roosevelt enjoyed the limelight. As one of his children remarked, Roosevelt always wanted to be "the bride at every wedding, the corpse at every funeral." This hero of the Rough Riders became a legend in his own time. Roosevelt always lived life to the fullest. "No President has ever enjoyed himself as much as I have enjoyed myself," he claimed. An old friend explained Roosevelt's great love of life: "You must always remember that the President is about six [years old]."

Roosevelt was an all-around athlete whose energy was legendary. For example, when the French ambassador once visited the White House, he and the president played tennis, jogged, and then worked out with weights. Roosevelt turned to his guest and asked, "What would you like to do now?" "If it's just the same with you, Mr. President," said the ambassador, "I'd like to lie down and die."

UNITED STATES POSTAGE

THEODORE ROOSEVELT 1901–1909

30 CENTS 30

The United Mine Workers strike.

Soon after Roosevelt became president, a labor dispute helped define his approach to the office. In the spring of 1902 some 150,000 coal miners struck for higher wages and recognition of their United Mine Workers union. The mine owners—mostly railroad companies—refused to negotiate. As the strike dragged on, Washington Gladden, a reform minister, petitioned Roosevelt for help. Speaking on behalf of working-class laborers, Gladden wrote, "You can speak as no one else can speak for the plain people of this country. Every workingman knows you are his friend; no capitalist of common sense can imagine that you are his enemy." Thousands signed this petition, which was sent to the White House.

Conservatives urged Roosevelt to send in the U.S. Army to force the strikers to return to work, while some progressives wanted him to place the mines under federal control. Instead, Roosevelt encouraged the two sides to accept **arbitration**. Arbitration is the process by which two opposing sides allow a third party to settle the dispute. As winter approached, Roosevelt threatened to take over the mines. This convinced the mine owners to agree to his plan of appointing a commission of arbitrators.

After a five-week investigation, the arbitrators announced their decision. They gave both the miners and the mine owners part of what they had wanted. The workers won a shorter workday and higher pay, but the mining companies did not have to recognize the union or bargain with it. It was a landmark compromise. For the first time, the federal government had intervened in a strike to protect the interests of the workers and the public. Satisfied, Roosevelt pronounced the compromise a "square deal."

The Square Deal.

The **Square Deal** became Roosevelt's 1904 campaign slogan. He promised to "see to it that every man has a square deal, no less and no more." This pledge summed up Roosevelt's belief in balancing the interests of business, consumers, and labor. Roosevelt's Square Deal called for limiting the power of trusts, promoting public health and safety, and improving working conditions.

The president was so popular with voters that no Republican dared challenge him for the 1904 nomination. Even the *New York Sun*, a pro–big business, antireform newspaper, supported Roosevelt. The paper preferred "the impulsive candidate of the party of conservatism to the conservative candidate of the party which the business interests regard as permanently and dangerously impulsive." Roosevelt won the election, easily defeating his Democratic opponent, Judge Alton Parker of New York.

✔ **READING CHECK:** How did the response to the miners' strike and the Square Deal reflect President Roosevelt's governing style?

INTERPRETING THE VISUAL RECORD

Labor. President Theodore Roosevelt met with these coal miners during the 1902 United Mine Workers strike. *What type of reaction do you think these strikers had to Roosevelt's efforts?*

Regulating Business

President Roosevelt sought to regulate large corporations during both of his terms in office. Although he considered big business essential to the nation's growth, he also believed companies should be forced to behave responsibly. "We don't wish to destroy corporations," he said, "but we do wish to make them subserve [serve] the public good." The public agreed with him. As journalist Walter Lippmann wrote, "The trusts made enemies right and left. . . . Labor was no match for them, state legislatures were impotent [powerless] before them."

Trustbusting. In 1902 the president took action, directing the U.S. attorney general to sue the Northern Securities Company. Controlled by J. P. Morgan and railroad barons James J. Hill and E. H. Harriman, the company monopolized railroad shipping from Chicago to the Northwest. In 1904 the Supreme Court ruled that the monopoly violated the Sherman Antitrust Act and ordered the corporation dissolved. Justice John Marshall Harlan wrote, "It is manifest [obvious] that if the Anti-Trust Act is held not to embrace a case such as is now before us, the plain intention of the legislative branch of the Government will be defeated."

Encouraged by this victory, the Roosevelt administration launched a "trustbusting" campaign. It filed 44 suits against business combinations believed not to be in the public interest. It was not size that mattered, Roosevelt declared, but whether a particular trust was good or bad for the public as a whole. "Bad" trusts did such things as forcing companies to give them discounts or rebates, selling inferior products, competing unfairly, and corrupting public officials. As Roosevelt put it, "We draw the line against misconduct, not against wealth."

The Roosevelt administration also promoted railroad regulation. At the president's urging, Congress passed two laws that turned the Interstate Commerce Commission (ICC) into a significant regulatory agency. The first, the 1903 **Elkins Act**, forbade shipping companies from accepting rebates, or money given back in return for business. Politicians as well as railroad owners supported this new law. The second, the 1906 **Hepburn Act**, authorized the ICC to set railroad rates and to regulate other companies engaged in interstate commerce, such as pipelines and ferries.

Trustbusting. Responding to public concerns, President Theodore Roosevelt made great efforts to break up trusts. *What roles are Roosevelt and the trust assigned in this 1904 cartoon entitled "Jack the Giant-Killer"? Why?*

Practices of food and drug companies.

Roosevelt also responded to growing public concern about practices of the food and drug industries. By the early 1900s clear evidence existed that some drug companies, food processors, and meat packers were selling dangerous products. Scientific developments had enabled industrial chemists to add substances to food to make it appear fresh. Chemists learned that churning spoiled butter with skim milk would make it look fresh. It was then sold as fresh butter. The chemical formaldehyde was added to old eggs to take away their odor. The eggs too were then sold as fresh. North Dakota's food commissioner Edward F. Ladd found that most foods he analyzed had chemical additives. "There was but one brand of catsup which was pure," he reported at a meeting in 1904. The other brands contained pulp and skins, unripe and overripe tomatoes, and preservatives.

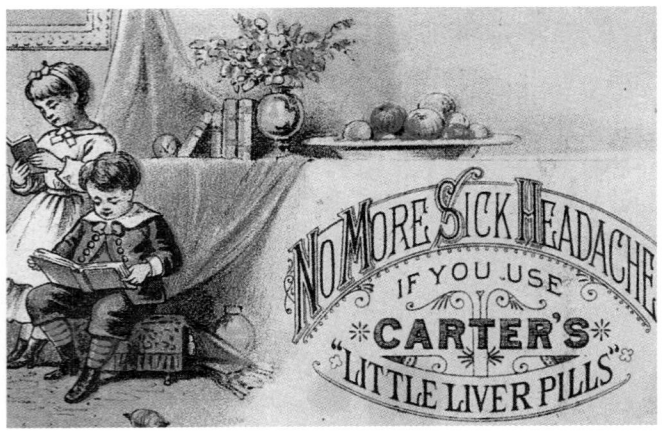

Some drug companies sold worthless over-the-counter medicines that contained dangerous drugs such as alcohol, cocaine, or morphine. Journalist Samuel Hopkins Adams wrote about drug industry abuses.

> 66 Gullible [easily fooled] America will spend this year some seventy-five millions of dollars in the purchase of patent [over-the-counter] medicines. . . . It will swallow huge quantities of alcohol, an appalling amount of opiates and narcotics. 99

Adams charged that the drug companies' claims that their "health tonics" could cure everything from baldness to cancer amounted to fraud. Edward Bok, another journalist, compared the label for Mrs. Winslow's Soothing Syrup, used to bring pain relief to teething babies, with a British label for the same medicine. The British label marked the tonic "Poison."

Protecting the consumer. Reformers worked to put pressure on the government to pass laws requiring manufacturers to use pure ingredients in their products. As the primary purchasers of foods and medicines, many women participated in this movement. For example, Alice Lakey set up a series of lectures to alert Americans to this danger. At the St. Louis Exposition of 1904 the groups working for food reform set up a booth where they displayed artificially colored foods. They extracted the dyes from the foods, and then demonstrated how that very dye could be used to color wool and silk fabric. The exhibit attracted attention from politicians, journalists, and consumers alike. Then, in 1906, Upton Sinclair published *The Jungle,* an explosive novel that depicted the wretched and unsanitary conditions at a meatpacking plant.

Responding to public pressures, Roosevelt ordered Secretary of Agriculture James Wilson to investigate the conditions in the packing houses. "We saw meat shovelled from filthy wooden floors, piled on tables rarely washed, pushed from room to room in rotten box carts," Wilson stated in his final report. "In all of which processes it [the meat] was in the way of gathering dirt, splinters, floor filth, and the expectoration [saliva] of tuberculous and other diseased workers." The report was so shocking that the *New York Post* composed a jingle based on it.

> 66 Mary had a little lamb,
> And when she saw it sicken,
> She shipped it off to Packingtown,
> And now it's labelled chicken. 99

In 1906 the U.S. Congress enacted two new consumer-protection laws. The **Meat Inspection Act** required federal government inspection of meat shipped across state lines. The **Pure Food and Drug Act** forbade the manufacture, sale, or transportation of food and patent medicine containing harmful ingredients. The law also required that containers of food and medicines carry ingredient labels.

✔ **READING CHECK:** Why did Roosevelt and other government officials want to regulate trusts and the food and drug industries?

INTERPRETING THE VISUAL RECORD

Protecting the consumer. The Pure Food and Drug Act established regulations to prevent drug companies from making false claims about their products. *What claims does this drug advertisement make?*

HOLT RESEARCHER

Read More About It

Free Find:

Reform Journalist

After reading the selection on muckraking journalists on the **Holt Researcher** CD–ROM, write a short essay that explains how these journalists were able to influence the politics of their era.

Stamps like this one from the early 1900s were used to label unsafe foods.

AMERICAN *Letters*

Progressive Literature

During the Progressive Era literature reflected the concerns and social ills of the time. It also influenced political reform. Frank Norris's 1901 novel The Octopus *portrays railroad financiers as villains in a story involving railroads and wheat growers in California. In the excerpt below, wheat farmers have formed a committee to try to secure the election of a commissioner who will crack down on the railroads. Upton Sinclair's* The Jungle *(1906) revealed to a horrified American public the conditions of Chicago's meatpacking industry. The excerpt below describes a typical scene at a meatpacking plant.*

from *The Octopus*
by Frank Norris

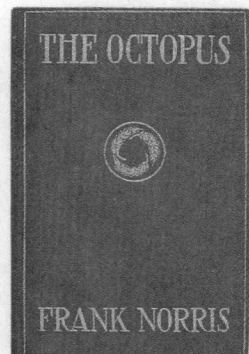

Frank Norris's
1901 novel

The campaign for Railroad Commissioner had been very interesting. At the very outset [beginning] Magnus's committee found itself involved in corrupt politics. The primaries had to be captured at all costs and by any means, and when the convention assembled it was found necessary to buy outright the votes of certain delegates. The campaign fund raised by contributions from Magnus, Annixter, Broderson, and Osterman was drawn upon to the extent of five thousand dollars.

Only the committee knew of this corruption. The League, ignoring ways and means, supposed as a matter of course that the campaign was honourably conducted.

For a whole week after the consummation [completion] of this part of the deal, Magnus had kept to his house, refusing to be seen, alleging [complaining] that he was ill, which was not far from the truth. The shame of the business, the loathing [disgust] of what he had done, were to him things unspeakable. . . . He was hopelessly caught in the mesh. Wrong seemed indissolubly [permanently] knitted into the texture of Right. He was blinded, dizzied, overwhelmed, caught in the current of events, and hurried along he knew not where. He resigned himself.

from *The Jungle*
by Upton Sinclair

Upton Sinclair's
1906 novel

There were the wool-pluckers, whose hands went to pieces even sooner than the hands of the pickle-men; for the pelts of the sheep had to be painted with acid to loosen the wool, and then the pluckers had to pull out this wool with their bare hands, till the acid had eaten their fingers off. . . . Some worked at the stamping-machines, and it was very seldom that one could work long there at the pace that was set, and not give out and forget himself, and have a part of his hand chopped off. . . . Worst of any, however, were . . . those who served in the cooking-rooms. . . . Their peculiar trouble was that they fell into the vats; and when they were fished out, there was never enough of them left to be worth exhibiting,—sometimes they would be overlooked for days, till all but the bones of them had gone out to the world as Durham's Pure Leaf Lard!

UNDERSTANDING LITERATURE

1. How did Magnus win the election in *The Octopus?*
2. According to *The Jungle,* what were working conditions like in the meatpacking plant?
3. How is corruption depicted by both writers?

Thomas Moran attempted to convey the beauty and grandeur of Yellowstone National Park in his painting The Grand Canyon of the Yellowstone.

Protecting the Environment

President Roosevelt's most enduring legacy may be his work in the conservation movement. He recognized that the natural resources of the United States were limited and that the needs of business had always taken priority over the environment. "In the past, we have admitted the right of the individual to injure the future of the Republic for his own present profit," he charged. "The time has come for a change."

At the end of the 1800s the country's public land was being lost to greed and mismanagement. Lumber companies acquired the rights to forestland and proceeded to cut down every tree. Ranchers grazed cattle and sheep in government-owned forests and left not even a blade of grass or a seedling behind. In 1891 fires destroyed 12 million acres of forests. Most had been started by cowhands, hunters, or sheepherders.

Gifford Pinchot (PIN-shoh) was a strong conservationist, forester, and a friend of Roosevelt. He first came up with the word *conservation* to describe the need to protect the country's natural environment. Pinchot wrote, "The conservation of

National Parks and Conservation, 1872–1984

Learning from Maps The National Park System includes parks, monuments, and historic parks. It protects the nation's cultural and historic sites as well as its natural wonders.

? LOCATION Which state has the greatest land area set aside in national parks?

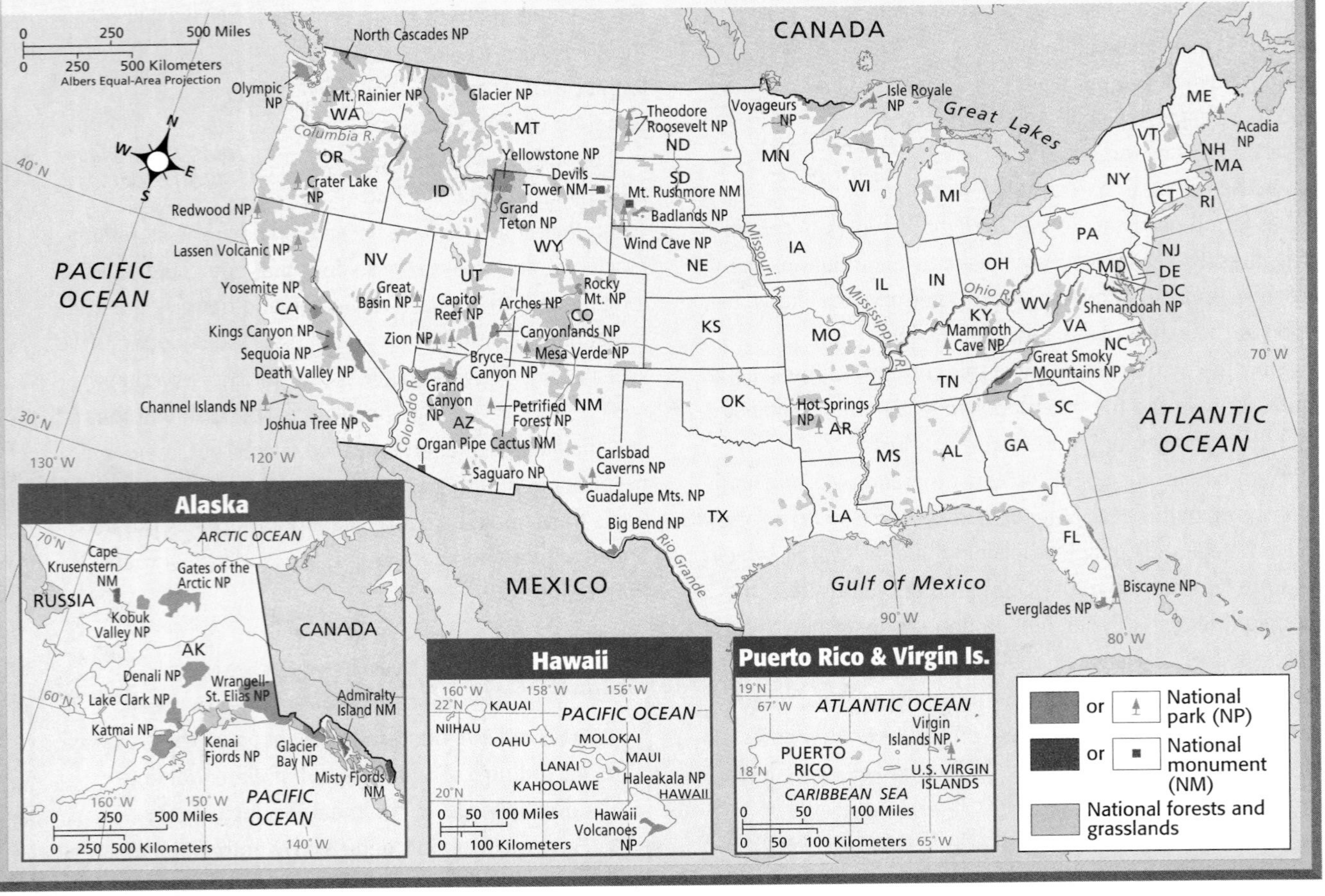

CANADA

North Cascades NP

Olympic NP
WA
Mt. Rainier NP
Columbia R.
OR
Crater Lake NP
Redwood NP
Lassen Volcanic NP
NV
Yosemite NP
CA
Kings Canyon NP
Sequoia NP
Death Valley NP
Channel Islands NP
Joshua Tree NP

Glacier NP
MT
Yellowstone NP
Devils Tower NM
Grand Teton NP
ID
WY
Great Basin NP
UT
Capitol Reef NP
Arches NP
Canyonlands NP
CO
Zion NP
Bryce Canyon NP
Mesa Verde NP
Grand Canyon NP
AZ
Petrified Forest NP
NM
Organ Pipe Cactus NM
Saguaro NP
Carlsbad Caverns NP
Guadalupe Mts. NP
Big Bend NP
TX

Theodore Roosevelt NP
ND
Mt. Rushmore NM
SD
Badlands NP
Wind Cave NP
NE
KS
OK
Hot Springs NP
AR

Voyageurs NP
MN
WI
IA
IL
MO
TN
MS
AL
LA

Isle Royale NP
Great Lakes
MI
IN
OH
KY
Mammoth Cave NP

ME
Acadia NP
VT
NH
MA
NY
CT RI
PA
NJ
MD DE
DC
WV
VA
Shenandoah NP
NC
Great Smoky Mountains NP
SC
GA
FL

PACIFIC OCEAN
ATLANTIC OCEAN
MEXICO
Gulf of Mexico
Everglades NP
Biscayne NP

40°N
30°N
130°W
120°W
90°W
80°W
70°W

Missouri R.
Mississippi R.
Ohio R.
Rio Grande
Colorado R.

0   250   500 Miles
0   250   500 Kilometers
Albers Equal-Area Projection

Alaska

ARCTIC OCEAN
Cape Krusenstern NM
Gates of the Arctic NP
RUSSIA
Kobuk Valley NP
AK
Denali NP
Lake Clark NP
Wrangell-St. Elias NP
Katmai NP
Kenai Fjords NP
Glacier Bay NP
Misty Fjords NM
CANADA
Admiralty Island NM
PACIFIC OCEAN
70°N
60°N
160°W
150°W
140°W
0   250   500 Miles
0   250   500 Kilometers

Hawaii

160°W   158°W   156°W
22°N   KAUAI
NIIHAU
OAHU   MOLOKAI
LANAI   MAUI
KAHOOLAWE   Haleakala NP
HAWAII
20°N
Hawaii Volcanoes NP
PACIFIC OCEAN
0   50   100 Miles
0   100 Kilometers

Puerto Rico & Virgin Is.

19°N
67°W
ATLANTIC OCEAN
Virgin Islands NP
PUERTO RICO
U.S. VIRGIN ISLANDS
18°N
CARIBBEAN SEA
0   50   100 Miles
0   50   100 Kilometers
65°W

or ▲ National park (NP)
or ■ National monument (NM)
National forests and grasslands

natural resources is the key to the future. It is the key to the safety and prosperity of the American people." The president proved receptive to Pinchot's ideas and made conservation a priority during his second term.

Roosevelt withdrew from sale millions of acres of public land and set aside nearly 150 million acres as forest reserves. At his urging, Congress created national parks and wildlife sanctuaries. In 1902 Congress passed the Newlands Reclamation Act. This law allowed money from the sale of public lands to be used for irrigation and **reclamation**—the process of making damaged land productive again. Roosevelt also organized a 1908 White House conference on conservation. This led to the creation of a National Conservation Commission to study natural resource issues. The conference also inspired the establishment of conservation agencies in 41 states.

Although conservation plans limited the amount of land in private hands, some businesspeople supported this new trend. Minnesota railroad business leader James J. Hill, for instance, listened to Pinchot's predictions. Hill acknowledged that using up all of the nation's mineral resources would endanger future generations—and future business. At times, the needs of the industrialists and the reformers were not so far apart. One of Pinchot's associates pointed out that conservation "was only a means to an end and the end was economic justice."

✔ **READING CHECK:** What stand did Gifford Pinchot and President Roosevelt take on the environment?

Then and Now

National Parks

National park guide

Today, the National Park Service manages some 380 sites on more than 80 million acres of land. As in previous years, the Park Service is caught between those who wish to preserve and expand park land and those who want to make use of the natural resources. Conservationists charge that businesses are destroying wildlife habitats and old-growth forests. Business leaders counter that the demand for wood and mineral products—not to mention the protection of thousands of jobs—requires the use of wilderness resources.

Lawmakers and Park Service officials also face the problem of maintaining the parks while containing costs. More than 280 million people visit the national parks annually. To counteract the strain on park resources, officials have proposed that visitation be limited.

SECTION 2 REVIEW

Define and explain the significance of the following terms:
arbitration
Square Deal
Elkins Act
Hepburn Act
Meat Inspection Act
Pure Food and Drug Act
reclamation

Identify and explain the significance of the following individuals:
Theodore Roosevelt
Upton Sinclair
Gifford Pinchot

1. **Using Graphic Organizers**
   President Roosevelt's Square Deal promised to balance the interests of business, labor, and consumers. Copy the graphic organizer below. Use it to describe Roosevelt's actions toward these groups.

Labor
Business
Consumers
Square Deal

2. **Identifying Values** How were President Roosevelt's values reflected in the Square Deal and in his handling of the miners' strike?

3. **Identifying Cause and Effect** Why did reformers support the Meat Inspection Act and the Pure Food and Drug Act? How did these acts help consumers?

4. **Taking a Stand** Take a stand on the side of either the conservationists or the industrialists and explain how that group might feel about Roosevelt's environmental policies.

Critical Thinking

5. How did Roosevelt's actions against trusts and railroads reflect a break with the past?
   Consider:
   • Roosevelt's policies against trusts and railroads
   • previous policies against trusts and railroads
   • how Roosevelt's policies compared to those of previous administrations

SECTION 3 Reform Under Taft

OBJECTIVES

Read to understand:

1. what progressive reforms were enacted during President Taft's administration
2. what divisions in the Republican Party led to the formation of the Progressive Party
3. what ensured Woodrow Wilson's victory in the 1912 presidential election

KEY TERMS

Mann-Elkins Act
Sixteenth Amendment
Payne-Aldrich Tariff
Ballinger-Pinchot affair
Progressive Party
New Freedom

KEY PEOPLE

William Howard Taft
Richard Ballinger
Joseph Cannon
George Norris
Woodrow Wilson
Eugene Debs

William Howard Taft received the Republican Party nomination for president in 1908.

EYEWITNESSES TO History

66 *He is not an American, you know, he is America.* 99
—John Morley

Theodore Roosevelt

Many people agreed with British diplomat John Morley's assessment of President Theodore Roosevelt. By the time Roosevelt neared the end of his second term in office, he was one of the most admired men in the world. Despite such international praise, Roosevelt decided not to run for president again. "The country needs a change," he declared. "We have had four years of uprooting and four years of crusading. The country has had enough of it and of me." To take himself out of the public eye, Roosevelt set out on a year-long safari to Africa as soon as the election of 1908 had ended.

Taft Takes Office

At the 1908 Republican convention President Roosevelt threw his support behind his secretary of war, William Howard Taft. Taft won the nomination on the first ballot. At the time, Roosevelt fully believed that Taft had the same reform tendencies as he did. He even told a friend that rarely had "two public men . . . ever been so much at one in all the essentials of their beliefs and practices." The Democrats again nominated William Jennings Bryan, whose pro-labor platform won the backing of the American Federation of Labor. However, the Democratic platform and Roosevelt's stances were actually quite similar. The Democrats lost the election by a wide margin in the electoral college, but by just 1.25 million popular votes.

It quickly became clear that Taft would be a different kind of president than Roosevelt. Roosevelt enjoyed being in the public eye. Taft did not. Although Taft had worked in government for years, most of his experience had come through appointed positions. He had avoided the often hostile realm of electoral politics. "I don't like politics," he once wrote. "I don't like the limelight."

An intelligent but cautious man, Taft was fearful of overstepping the bounds of his presidential authority. Nevertheless, he chalked up a long list of accomplishments. His administration filed 90 antitrust suits, more than twice the number begun under Roosevelt.

At Taft's urging, Congress passed the **Mann-Elkins Act** in 1910, extending the regulatory powers of the Interstate Commerce Commission to telephone and telegraph companies. Taft also promoted environmental conservation by adding vast areas to the nation's forest reserves. He supported reforms to aid working people, particularly child laborers.

With his approval, Congress created the Department of Labor to enforce labor laws. Congress also passed mine-safety laws and established an eight-hour workday for employees of companies holding contracts with the federal government.

The Taft administration was partly responsible for the adoption of the **Sixteenth Amendment**. Proposed in 1909 and ratified in 1913, the amendment permitted Congress to levy taxes based on an individual's income. Progressives had long supported such a graduated income tax as a way to fund needed government programs in a fair manner.

✔ **READING CHECK:** What progressive reforms were enacted during President Taft's administration?

Taft Angers the Progressives

Despite these reforms, President Taft lost the support of progressive Republicans. This split began in April 1909 with the passage of a tariff bill.

The Payne-Aldrich Tariff. Both Taft and the progressives favored tariff reductions to lower the prices of consumer goods. Some conservative members of Congress, however, wanted high tariffs to protect American industries. They won out when the House sent a low-tariff bill to the Senate, and Senator Nelson Aldrich of Rhode Island turned it into a high-tariff measure.

Taft could have vetoed the bill or pressured Aldrich to change the tariff rates. However, Taft lacked the political skill to oppose conservative Republicans in Congress. Despite his misgivings, he signed the **Payne-Aldrich Tariff**, as the bill was called. To make matters worse, he called it "the best tariff bill that the Republican party ever passed." Outraged progressives accused Taft of betraying the reform cause.

The Ballinger-Pinchot affair. Progressives also attacked Taft for sabotaging former president Roosevelt's conservation program. The dispute revolved around Taft's secretary of the interior, Richard Ballinger, who believed that the Roosevelt administration had exceeded its authority when it stopped the sale of public land. Ballinger approved the sale of a vast tract of coal-rich Alaska timberland. As head of the U.S. Forest Service, Gifford Pinchot attacked Ballinger for favoring private interests over conservation. Taft warned Pinchot to stop criticizing Ballinger. When Pinchot ignored this warning, Taft fired him.

Taft's administration later restored the Alaskan land to the federal forest reserve. However, for progressives, the **Ballinger-Pinchot affair** signaled Taft's weakness on conservation. Taft also made one particularly dangerous enemy— Theodore Roosevelt. While Taft sent letters to Roosevelt, then on safari in Africa, defending the actions of his administration, Pinchot visited his old friend. After

HISTORY IN THE MAKING

Views of Taft
BY RAYMOND HYSER

Many historians have compared William Howard Taft with Theodore Roosevelt. While Roosevelt expanded the power of the presidency and supported social-welfare legislation, Taft was reluctant to use the full powers of the presidency. He believed that judicial interpretation of the law was paramount. In a time when the American people demanded progressive change and presidential leadership, Taft moved slowly and narrowed presidential power.

Historians have offered critical assessments of Taft's presidency. Making the inevitable comparison with the Roosevelt presidency, they have emphasized Taft's political blunders and indecisiveness to explain his failings as president. One early biographer, however, argued that he was successful because he supported important legislation through a hostile Congress. In recent years, historians have provided a more balanced, objective view of Taft. Donald Anderson argues that Taft believed in the constitutional limits on the presidency and he held an almost religious commitment to the rule of law. This philosophy helps explain the conflict between Roosevelt's and Taft's leadership styles. Paola Coletta argues that Taft ranks as an "average" president who had a solid legislative record. He was a "constitutional conservator," whose term was bracketed by two powerful progressive presidents (Roosevelt and Wilson).

Theodore Roosevelt's The New Nationalism *outlined his view of government's role in American society.*

speaking with Pinchot, Roosevelt confided in Senator Henry Cabot Lodge, "I don't think that under the Taft . . . regime there has been a real appreciation of the needs of the country." Roosevelt soon broke with Taft over the Pinchot controversy.

Roosevelt and the elections of 1910.
In the congressional elections of 1910, Roosevelt campaigned on behalf of progressive Republicans who opposed Taft. Roosevelt proposed a program called New Nationalism—a series of tough laws to protect workers, ensure public health, and regulate business. He declared:

> 66 The true friend of property, the true conservative, is he who insists that property shall be the servant and not the master of the commonwealth. . . . The citizens of the United States must effectively control the mighty commercial forces which they have themselves called into being. 99

Government, Roosevelt said, must become the "steward [manager] of the public welfare." His call for a more activist federal government represented an even more progressive position than he had taken as president. Delighted, reformers hailed the New Nationalism as a revival of the progressive spirit.

Despite Roosevelt's help on the campaign trail, the Republicans lost control of the House of Representatives for the first time in 16 years. Nearly all the newly elected Democrats unseated conservative Republicans. Roosevelt, as well as Taft, was deeply disappointed by the election.

The Republican Party Divides

Not long before Theodore Roosevelt proposed New Nationalism, a bitter dispute in Congress had further deepened the gulf between President Taft and the progressives. In the spring of 1910, progressive Republicans in Congress launched a major attack on Speaker of the House Joseph "Uncle Joe" Cannon of Illinois, a conservative Republican. Cannon, a 73-year-old tobacco-chewing poker player, was one of Washington's most powerful politicians. He ruled the House with an iron hand, appointing all its committees and naming their chairpersons. As head of the powerful Rules Committee, which determined the order of business in the House, Cannon prevented bills he opposed from even reaching the House floor for debate.

Republican Party division. After the elections of 1910, president Taft and former president Theodore Roosevelt held increasingly opposing positions on progressive reforms. *How does this cartoon depict the opposition between Taft and Roosevelt?*

THE GRANGER COLLECTION, NEW YORK

The Cannon debate.
Progressives charged that Cannon used his power to block reform legislation. "Not one cent for scenery," he had growled in dismissing a call for environmental protection. In March 1910 Representative George Norris, a progressive from Nebraska, began an effort to break Cannon's power. Norris proposed that House members elect the Rules Committee and that the Speaker be excluded from membership on it.

After a heated debate, Norris's motion passed. A year later, the representatives also stripped the Speaker of the House of the power to appoint members to other committees—a major progressive victory. However, Taft's refusal to take their side throughout this bitter debate angered many progressives.

Roosevelt returns to politics. Completely at odds with President Taft, Theodore Roosevelt decided to run again for the presidency. Borrowing a prize-fighting term, he declared, "My hat is in the ring." Roosevelt won almost every Republican state primary, including the one in Taft's home state, Ohio.

Nevertheless, Taft's allies firmly held control of the party machinery. At the Republican Convention, they refused to seat many of Roosevelt's delegates. "Don't you realize you're wrecking the Republican Party?" shouted one progressive senator. When Taft won the nomination, Roosevelt's supporters walked out. Their leaders organized their own convention, asking those in the Roosevelt camp to oppose this "crime which represents treason to the people." They adopted a platform based on the New Nationalism and nominated Roosevelt as their presidential candidate. Thus was born the **Progressive Party**, also called the Bull Moose Party after Roosevelt declared that he felt "fit as a bull moose" to run.

✔ **READING CHECK:** What were the divisions within the Republican Party that led to the formation of the Progressive Party?

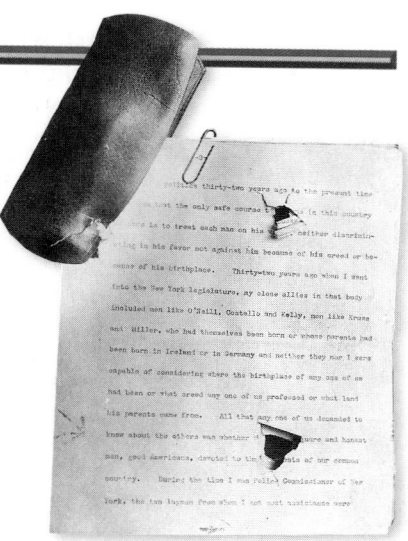

While giving a speech in 1912, Theodore Roosevelt was wounded in an assassination attempt. He finished the speech with a bullet lodged in his body.

A Democratic Victory

The division in the Republican Party practically assured a Democratic victory. The Democrats united behind one candidate, Governor Woodrow Wilson of New Jersey. He ran on a platform calling for tariff reduction, banking reform, laws benefiting wage earners and farmers, and stronger antitrust legislation.

The Wilson program. A native of Virginia and a political newcomer, Wilson had long nurtured dreams of high office. He eventually became a professor of political science at Princeton University in New Jersey. Wilson later served as its president. He was elected governor in 1910. In his short time as governor, he fought the state's Democratic Party bosses and pushed through laws regulating business. Wilson's status as an outspoken reformer and eloquent speaker made him the presidential choice of progressives in the Democratic Party.

In the 1912 campaign, Wilson's **New Freedom** program made proposals to help small businesses. He also called for a return to an America where people were free from the heavy hand of big business and government. Wilson asserted:

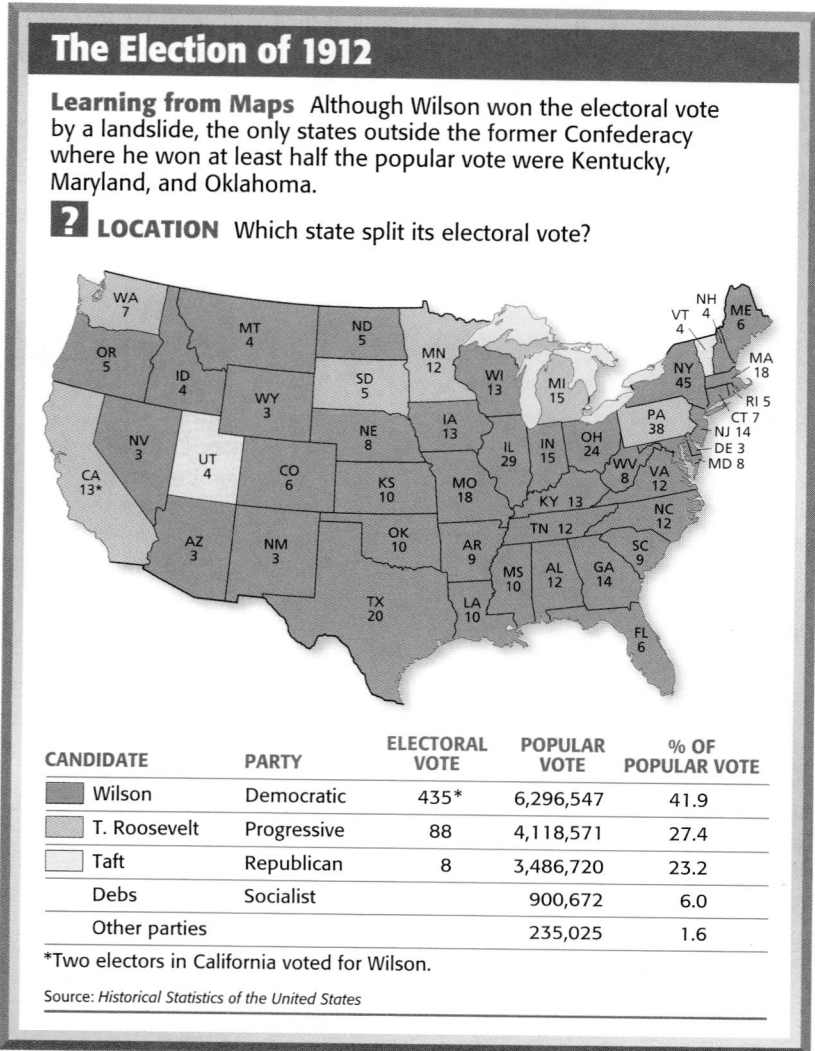

The Election of 1912

Learning from Maps Although Wilson won the electoral vote by a landslide, the only states outside the former Confederacy where he won at least half the popular vote were Kentucky, Maryland, and Oklahoma.

❓ **LOCATION** Which state split its electoral vote?

CANDIDATE	PARTY	ELECTORAL VOTE	POPULAR VOTE	% OF POPULAR VOTE
Wilson	Democratic	435*	6,296,547	41.9
T. Roosevelt	Progressive	88	4,118,571	27.4
Taft	Republican	8	3,486,720	23.2
Debs	Socialist		900,672	6.0
Other parties			235,025	1.6

*Two electors in California voted for Wilson.

Source: *Historical Statistics of the United States*

Read More About It

Free Find:

Woodrow Wilson

After reading the biography on Woodrow Wilson on the **Holt Researcher** CD–ROM, imagine that you are a political journalist. Write a short summary of the outcome of the election and what it says about the desires of American voters.

> **66** The only way that government is kept pure is by keeping . . . channels open, so that . . . there will constantly be coming new blood into the veins of the body politic. **99**

Although Wilson shared the progressive belief that government should be an agent of reform, he believed that if government became too strong it could limit individual freedom. He believed that reform efforts should seek to remove barriers to free competition but not significantly alter the free-enterprise system.

Wilson sweeps the election.

Wilson's reform goals differed from those of Roosevelt, who accepted the new corporate and industrial order even as he proposed to regulate and control it. Wilson's ideas also differed from another candidate for president, Eugene Debs of the Socialist Party. The Socialist Party had done very well in the 1910 elections. It supported a radically different economic order, including public ownership of all major industries. In Debs, Wilson, and Roosevelt, American voters had a choice of three strong, reform-minded candidates. Even Taft supported some reform programs, although he appeared to represent a more conservative viewpoint.

As expected, Wilson won the election. Some Republicans even voted for him, seeing it as a vote against Roosevelt. Wilson received 435 electoral votes to Roosevelt's 88 and Taft's 8. Debs won more than 900,000 popular votes but no electoral votes. Of the more than 15 million votes cast, the three reform-minded challengers received some 11 million. Although Wilson won just 6 million popular votes, he took office with a strong call for reform.

✔ **READING CHECK:** How did Woodrow Wilson win the 1912 presidential election?

Woodrow Wilson's moderate reform proposals attracted many voters during the 1912 election.

SECTION ③ REVIEW

Define and explain the significance of the following terms:
Mann-Elkins Act
Sixteenth Amendment
Payne-Aldrich Tariff
Ballinger-Pinchot affair
Progressive Party
New Freedom

Identify and explain the significance of the following individuals:
William Howard Taft
Richard Ballinger
Joseph Cannon
George Norris
Woodrow Wilson
Eugene Debs

1. **Using Graphic Organizers** Copy the diagram below. Use it to explain the steps that led from Taft's victory in 1908 to Wilson's victory in 1912.

2. **Synthesizing** What progressive reforms did President Taft institute?

3. **Hypothesizing** What might have happened if Taft had vetoed the Payne-Aldrich Tariff and not fired Gifford Pinchot?

4. **Distinguishing Fact from Opinion** Supporters of the Progressive Party believed that Taft betrayed the progressive ideals of the Roosevelt administration. Comparing Taft's reform record to Roosevelt's, was this a fair assessment? Why or why not?

Critical Thinking

5. What did the positions of the candidates in the 1912 election reveal about the range of progressive reform ideas?
   Consider:
   • what the positions of the candidates were in 1912
   • how well those positions reflected progressive ideals

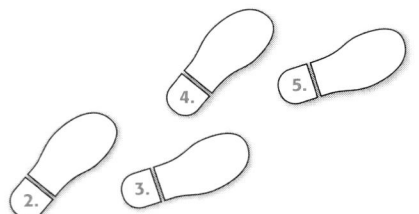

6. With the Republican Party divided, Wilson wins easily in 1912.

1. Taft wins in 1908 with Roosevelt's support.

SECTION 4

Wilson's "New Freedom"

OBJECTIVES

Read to understand:

1. how President Wilson's proposals affected big business and U.S. citizens
2. how Wilson attempted to help farmers and laborers, and how successful his efforts were
3. how American women gained the right to vote

KEY TERMS

Federal Reserve Act
Clayton Antitrust Act
Federal Trade Commission
Adamson Act
Keating-Owen Child Labor Act
National American Woman Suffrage Association
Nineteenth Amendment

KEY PEOPLE

Alice Paul
Carrie Chapman Catt

EYEWITNESSES TO History

66 *We have been proud of our industrial achievements, but we have not . . . stopped . . . to count the . . . fearful physical and spiritual cost to the men and women and children upon whom the . . . weight and burden of it all has fallen. . . . This is not a day of triumph; it is a day of dedication. Here muster [gather], not the forces of party, but the forces of humanity.* **99**
—Woodrow Wilson

President Wilson and friend Edward M. House

President Woodrow Wilson eloquently summed up the spirit of the progressive reform movement in his first inaugural address on March 4, 1913. In the months before his inauguration, Wilson prepared for the work ahead of him. Wilson turned to his friend, Edward M. House for help planning his cabinet and policies. Wilson considered House a man who "wants . . . to serve the common cause and to help me and others."

Reform on Many Fronts

President Wilson and Edward House settled on a cabinet that included the first-ever secretary of labor, a position that went to a labor leader. Its creation was in itself a progressive act. Wilson's appointments attempted to reflect and satisfy the divisions within the Democratic Party.

After settling on a cabinet, Wilson presented his legislative agenda. It included tariff and banking reforms and stronger antitrust laws. The program was opposed by business groups and lobbyists, but Wilson skillfully rallied support in Congress and among the American people.

In his inaugural address on March 4, 1913, President Woodrow Wilson explained that reform legislation would be a top priority.

Tariffs. Wilson's first priority was to lower tariffs. This had long been a goal of the Democratic Party's southern pro-agriculture wing. Wilson knew that supporters of big business had blocked tariff reduction during Taft's presidency. To plead his case, Wilson addressed both houses of Congress in person—something that had not been done since President John Adams's administration. The opponents of a lower tariff did not easily give way to presidential pressure. Describing the strength of the business lobby, Secretary of Agriculture David Houston wrote, "It was impossible to move around without bumping into [lobbyists]—at hotels, clubs, and even private houses." Wilson criticized the "money without limit" spent by the lobbyists and began a public campaign to combat their influence.

His strategy worked. Despite initial Senate opposition Congress passed the Underwood Tariff Act in 1913. It reduced tariffs to their lowest levels in more than 50 years. To make up for lost revenue, the bill introduced a graduated income tax. This would tax people with high incomes at a higher rate than those with low incomes. The new tax initially affected people earning $20,000—who paid

Woodrow Wilson

Woodrow Wilson had a reputation for being overly serious and inflexible. He often found it difficult to compromise. At times he opposed legislation that he himself had originally proposed if it had been amended by someone else. He once told a political associate, "I am sorry for those who disagree with me. . . . Because I know they are wrong."

Yet, despite his seriousness, Wilson was superstitious when it came to the number 13, which he believed was his lucky number. He pointed out that there were 13 letters in his name and often referred to the fact that the United States originally had 13 states. When he sailed to Europe

for the Paris Peace Conference following World War I, he even instructed the captain to delay docking for one day. He wanted to arrive on the 13th of December.

1 percent of their income in taxes—to people earning more than $50,000—who paid 6 percent. By 1916, individuals who made as little as $3,000 annually also had to pay income tax. People who supported an income tax boasted that it made major strides toward a fairer tax system.

Banking. Next on Wilson's agenda was banking reform. At the time, no central fund existed from which banks could borrow to prevent collapse during financial panics. As a result, banks commonly failed when many people withdrew their deposits at the same time. Reform was clearly necessary, but Americans disagreed on how to change the banking system. Conservative business groups wanted to give the nation's large private banks more control. In contrast, many Democrats and progressive Republicans wanted the government to run the system.

Wilson helped draft the **Federal Reserve Act** of 1913, which combined these two views. It created a three-tiered banking system. At the top was the Federal Reserve Board, a group appointed by the president and charged with running the system. At the second level were 12 Federal Reserve banks, under mixed public and private control. These "bankers' banks" served other banks rather than individuals. At the third level were private banks, which could borrow from the Federal Reserve banks at interest rates set by the Board. The bill particularly helped farmers by giving them access to lower interest rates. "It puts them on a footing with other business men and masters of enterprise, as it should," Wilson pointed out. "They will find themselves quit of many of the difficulties which now hamper them in the field of credit."

Big business. Having achieved important tariff and banking reforms, Wilson turned to business regulation. He wanted to limit the power of monopolies, which he viewed as a threat to small businesses. Toward this end, Wilson backed passage of the **Clayton Antitrust Act** in October 1914. This act clarified and extended the 1890 Sherman Antitrust Act by clearly stating what corporations could not do. For example, companies could not sell goods below cost to drive competitors out of business. Nor could they buy competing companies' stock to create a monopoly. The bill did not outlaw these actions in all cases. It was only illegal when the government could prove that a company was doing these things to intentionally create a monopoly. One senator concluded that the original Clayton bill "was a raging lion with a mouth full of teeth." The act as passed, however, had

This 1913 cartoon depicts President Wilson's antitrust legislation as a fence protecting small businesses.

"degenerated [been reduced] to a tabby cat with soft gums, a plaintive [sad] mew, and an anemic appearance." Despite its shortcomings, the American Federation of Labor (AFL) enthusiastically praised Wilson's support of the Clayton Act. AFL leader Samuel Gompers called it "the Magna Charter of American labor."

As part of the New Freedom program, the Wilson administration backed the creation of the **Federal Trade Commission** (FTC) by Congress in Sepember 1914. The FTC was authorized to investigate corporations. It could issue "cease and desist orders" to corporations engaged in unfair or fraudulent practices and use the courts to enforce its rulings. The FTC targeted abuses such as mislabeled products and false claims. Progressives were displeased, however, when Wilson appointed a number of people who were sympathetic to big business to the commission.

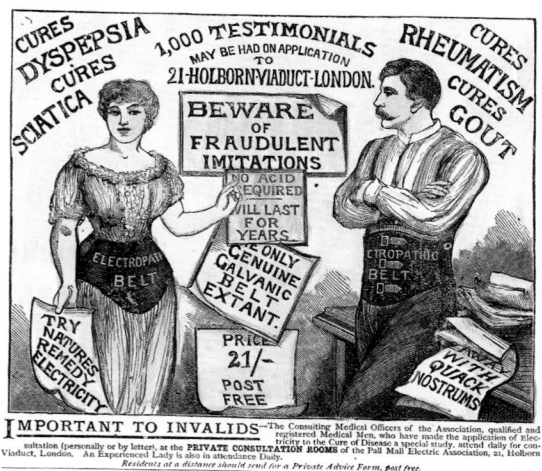

Advertisements like this one made unsupported claims about a product's benefits.

✔ **READING CHECK:** How did Wilson's proposals affect big business and U.S. citizens?

Wilson and Workers

In 1914 Walter Lippmann assessed President Wilson's New Freedom program. He wrote, "The New Freedom means the effort of small business men and farmers to use the government against the larger collective organization of industry." Throughout his first term, Wilson supported legislation to aid working people.

Farm and labor acts. Congress passed the Federal Farm Loan Act in 1916. This act provided low-interest loans to farmers by setting up 12 federal farm-loan banks, each with $750,000 capital to distribute to needy farmers. Some politicians complained that the act used "public resources to do for some what is not done for others." However, the law won strong support in rural areas of the United States.

Also in 1916, a railroad strike threatened to paralyze the nation's rail lines. Wilson invited labor leaders and railroad managers to the White House to work out an agreement. He reminded both sides about the disastrous effects such a strike could have on the nation's economy and citizens. When these efforts failed, he addressed Congress in support of a law that would reduce the workday for railroad workers from 10 to 8 hours without a cut in pay. The ensuing **Adamson Act** not only won applause from reformers but prevented the strike.

Congress also passed the Federal Workmen's Compensation Act with Wilson's support to provide benefits to federal workers injured on the job. Other Wilson labor initiatives included a provision in the Clayton Antitrust Act that affirmed labor's right to strike so long as property was not permanently damaged.

Child labor. The Wilson administration was less successful in its campaign against child labor. For years progressives had wanted to keep young children from working in factories, mills, and mines. Labor organizer Mother Jones later recalled the impact of such work.

> 66 Every day little children came into Union Headquarters, some with their hands off, some with the thumb missing, some with their fingers off at the knuckle. They were stooped little things, round shouldered and skinny. Many were not over ten years of age. 99

INTERPRETING THE VISUAL RECORD

Mother Jones. Mary Harris Jones fought for better working conditions and child labor laws throughout her life. At the age of 70, she marched in this 1910 protest march. *Why do you think Mother Jones continued to march in protests?*

Rising protests against child labor from the National Consumers' League and other groups prompted Congress to pass the **Keating-Owen Child Labor Act** in 1916. Backed by Wilson, the act outlawed the interstate sale of products produced by child labor. In 1918, however, the Supreme Court declared the law unconstitutional because it restricted commerce instead of directly outlawing child labor. Another law, passed in 1919, met the same fate.

✔ **READING CHECK:** How did President Wilson attempt to help farmers and laborers? How successful were these efforts?

The Armory Show

The progressive reform spirit influenced art as well as economic policies in the early 1900s. Just as reformers attacked business trusts, artists tackled the leading American museums' control over which paintings and sculptures the public saw. Determined to introduce the American public to modern art, a small group of artists formed the Association of American Painters and Sculptors (AAPS) in 1912. The group combed galleries and studios in Berlin, Munich, Paris, and The Hague in search of works to display. On February 17, 1913, the International Exhibition of Modern Art opened in the 69th Regiment Armory in New York City. The Armory Show, as it was called, presented some 1,600 works by both European and American artists.

Newspaper reporters raved about the show, calling it "an event not to be missed." Art critics were not so kind. They blasted Vincent Van Gogh as "unskilled" and Paul Cézanne as "absolutely without talent." As for Marcel Duchamp's *Nude Descending a Staircase,* one critic described it as "an explosion in a shingle factory." Ironically, the critics' hostility boosted attendance, which exceeded the organizers' wildest dreams.

Even if it failed to win over some critics to modern art, the Armory Show was a huge success in terms of attendance and publicity. Before the show moved to Chicago, the AAPS honored its "friends and enemies" in the press with a steak dinner. Speeches were made; diners sang and danced. One hostile critic offered grudging praise. "It was a good show," he said, "but don't do it again."

Marcel Duchamp's **Nude Descending a Staircase**

Understanding the Arts

1. What was the purpose of the Armory Show?
2. How did some critics react to modern art?

The Struggle for Women's Suffrage

Another part of the progressive agenda—the campaign for women's suffrage—faced strong opposition. Liquor interests feared that women would vote for prohibition. Businesses feared that the vote would empower women to demand better wages and working conditions. When one state senator expressed the belief that the vote would rob women of their beauty and charm, a suffragist reacted angrily.

66 We have women working in the foundries. . . . Women in the laundries . . . stand for 13 or 14 hours in the terrible steam and heat with their hands in hot starch. Surely these women won't lose any more of their beauty and charm by putting a ballot in a ballot box once a year than they are likely to lose standing in foundries or laundries all year. 99

Different approaches. One leading force in the suffrage movement was the **National American Woman Suffrage Association** (NAWSA), founded in 1890. Its first two presidents, Elizabeth Cady Stanton and Susan B. Anthony, distrusted party politics because of Republican leaders' failure after the Civil War to press for voting rights for women. As a result, they took a nonpartisan, local approach, trying to get state legislatures to grant women the vote. They achieved few successes in their first few years of lobbying, however. By 1901 just four states, all located in the western region of the country, had given women full voting rights.

In 1914 Alice Paul, a militant young Quaker suffragist, broke away from NAWSA. She formed a second organization, the Congressional Union for Woman Suffrage, which in 1916 became the National Woman's Party. The party adopted a national rather than a state-by-state strategy, focusing on passing a constitutional amendment guaranteeing women the right to vote.

Paul had studied in Britain and adopted the attention-getting protest tactics used by British suffragists. For example, in January 1917, after Wilson's re-election, the National Woman's Party began round-the-clock picketing of the White House in an effort to pressure Wilson to support a suffrage amendment. They held banners asking, "Mr. President, What Will You Do for Woman Suffrage?" and "How Long Must Women Wait for Liberty?" Some women chained themselves to railings. Many were arrested. Some went on hunger strikes in prison. Paul's efforts convinced thousands of women of the importance of the suffragists' cause.

Meanwhile, the suffrage movement picked up momentum. Massachusetts, New Jersey, New York, and Pennsylvania all held special referendums on women's suffrage in 1915. Although the motions were defeated in each state, support for women's suffrage ranged from 35 to 46 percent of the total votes. NAWSA saw its membership grow to nearly 2 million. Energized by the leadership of the highly skilled organizer Carrie Chapman Catt, the organization continued its use of traditional political strategies to attain voting rights.

INTERPRETING THE VISUAL RECORD
Women's suffrage. Suffragists struggled to convince both men and women that politics was a proper activity for women. *In what ways do you think these demonstrators were able to further the suffragist cause?*

Alice Paul gives a speech to members of the National Woman's Party.

Magazine covers from the 1920s celebrated the success of the suffrage movement.

Carrie Chapman Catt

A new NAWSA leader. Carrie Chapman Catt was born Carrie Clinton Lane in 1859 in Wisconsin. From childhood on, Catt was interested in women's rights. When she was 13, Catt was surprised that her mother was not going to vote in the presidential elections of 1872. "I think it's very unfair that women can't vote, don't you?" she asked a neighbor boy.

In 1877 Catt began attending Iowa State Agricultural College—now Iowa State University. While at school, Catt won for female students the right to speak at the school literary society. There she initiated a debate on women's suffrage. She argued: "How is it possible that a woman who is unfit to vote, should be the mother of, and bring up, a man who is?"

After graduating in 1880, Catt went to work as a teacher. She became superintendent of schools of Mason City, Iowa, in her second year. In 1885 she resigned her position after marrying Leo Chapman. Married women were not allowed to work in the schools. Catt began working as co-editor with her husband on the local newspaper. She also wrote a weekly feature called "Woman's World." After Chapman died of typhoid fever, Catt began a new career as a lecturer.

Catt soon became involved with the women's suffrage movement and served as a delegate at the NAWSA convention. About this time, she married George Catt, who enthusiastically supported her work. Over the next decade, Carrie Chapman Catt continued to travel and campaign on behalf of women's suffrage. In 1900 she became the president of NAWSA. She remained president until 1904, when she resigned to serve as president of the International Woman Suffrage Alliance (IWSA). As president of IWSA, Catt traveled around the world, seeking to win women to the cause of feminism. After returning to the United States, Catt again threw herself into the task of achieving women's suffrage. Catt remained a political and social activist until her death in 1947.

Success. Launching what came to be called Catt's Winning Plan in 1916, NAWSA won a string of successes for suffrage at the state level. After the United States entered World War I in 1917, leaders of the movement—along with millions of American women—lent strong support to the war effort. Their patriotism helped

The Progressive Legacy

Great Debates

Although progressivism made reforms in many areas, some of its reforms failed to bring about the anticipated changes. Although the government's ability to regulate the economy and pay for new programs improved, many business regulations fell short of remaking the capitalist system. Reforms such as the initiative, referendum, and recall were primarily used at the local level. Thus they had little impact on broad questions of national public policy.

One of progressivism's greatest successes, the settlement-house movement, improved opportunities for women, brought urban reform, and focused attention on the plight of immigrants. However, few settlement-house workers addressed the problems of African Americans. In general, the progressive presidents showed little interest in racial issues. Some critics argued that President Theodore Roosevelt set back the African American cause in 1906. White residents in Brownsville, Texas, had started violent protests against black soldiers at a nearby fort. Despite little evidence that the soldiers were involved in any violence, Roosevelt issued dishonorable discharges to the entire company to pacify the white community. Presidents Taft and Wilson both supported racial segregation.

Despite these shortcomings, some scholars note that progressives took real strides toward making the new industrial society more just, orderly, and humane. Their efforts to end child labor, protect workers and consumers, and promote conservation profoundly influenced the nation. Supporters argue that their greatest legacy was the demonstration that the U.S. democratic system could respond and adapt to changes in American life.

weaken opposition to women's suffrage. Even President Wilson came out in support of women's suffrage in a speech in 1918.

A 1918 Senate vote on a constitutional amendment to grant women the vote fell short by just two votes. Suffragists immediately targeted four senators up for election that November who had voted against women's suffrage. A strong message was sent to other politicians when three of the four lost their re-election bid. Finally, in 1919, Congress proposed the **Nineteenth Amendment**, granting women full voting rights. It was ratified in 1920.

Labor lawyer Crystal Eastman declared at the amendment's passage, "What we must do is to create conditions of outward freedom in which a free woman's soul can be born and grow." Carrie Chapman Catt declared, "Now that we have the vote let us remember we are . . . free and equal citizens. Let us do our part to keep it a true and triumphant democracy." She cautioned, however, that the vote was only an "entering wedge." Women still had to force their way through the "locked door" of political decision making.

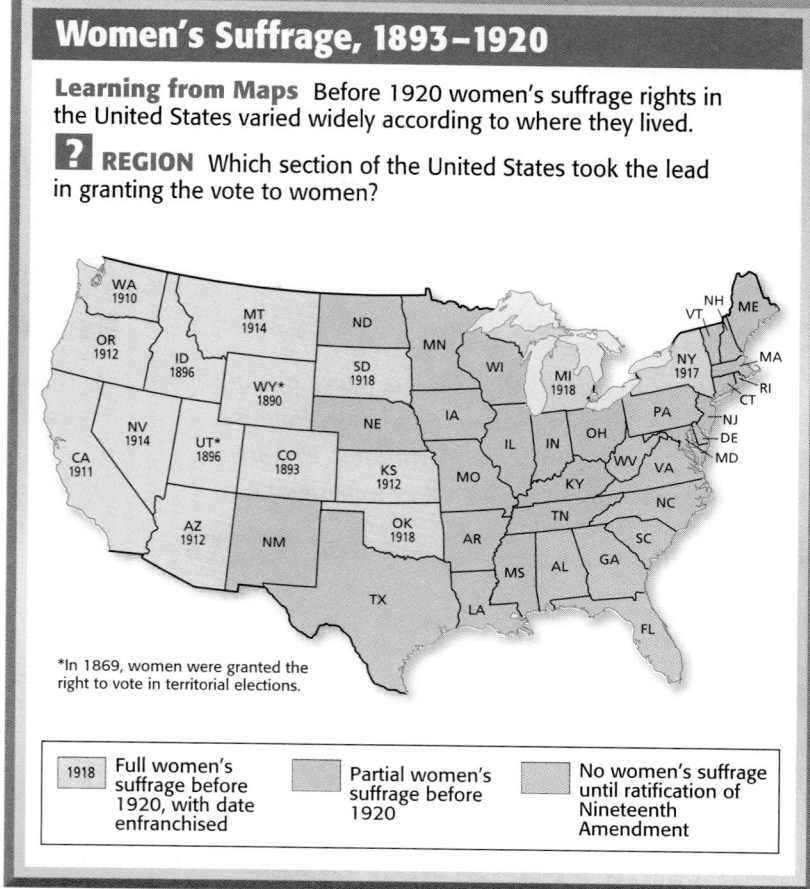

Women's Suffrage, 1893–1920

Learning from Maps Before 1920 women's suffrage rights in the United States varied widely according to where they lived.

? REGION Which section of the United States took the lead in granting the vote to women?

*In 1869, women were granted the right to vote in territorial elections.

| 1918 | Full women's suffrage before 1920, with date enfranchised | | Partial women's suffrage before 1920 | | No women's suffrage until ratification of Nineteenth Amendment |

✔ **READING CHECK:** How did American women gain the right to vote?

SECTION **4** REVIEW

Define and explain the significance of the following terms:
Federal Reserve Act
Clayton Antitrust Act
Federal Trade Commission
Adamson Act
Keating-Owen Child Labor Act
National American Woman Suffrage Association
Nineteenth Amendment

Identify and explain the significance of the following individuals:
Alice Paul
Carrie Chapman Catt

1. Using Graphic Organizers Copy the web below. Use it to describe the reforms passed during Woodrow Wilson's administration.

Big Business
Banking
Child Labor
WILSON'S ADMINISTRATION
Tariffs
Women's Rights
Farm & Labor

2. Analyzing How did the Wilson administration build on the work of previous presidents?

3. Recognizing Point of View Why did some suffragists argue that President Wilson was not doing enough for women's suffrage?

4. Evaluating How well did the progressive politicians accomplish the goals of progressive reformers?

Critical Thinking

5. How successful was Wilson in enlisting the "forces of humanity" to help child laborers, farmers, and railroad and federal workers?
Consider:
• what Wilson meant by "forces of humanity"
• Wilson's reforms for farmers, railroad and federal workers, and child laborers
• how these groups were helped by reforms

CHAPTER 19

Review

Creating a Time Line

Copy the time line below onto a sheet of paper. Complete the time line by filling in the events and dates from the chapter that you think were most significant. Pick three events and explain why you think they were significant.

1900   **1910**   **1920**

Writing a Summary

Using the Reading Checks as a guide, write an overview of the events in the chapter.

Identifying People and Ideas

Identify the following terms or individuals and explain their significance.

1. initiative
2. Samuel M. Jones
3. Hepburn Act
4. reclamation
5. Richard Ballinger
6. Woodrow Wilson
7. New Freedom
8. Federal Reserve Act
9. Adamson Act
10. Alice Paul

Understanding Main Ideas

SECTION 1

1. What were the strengths of the city-commission and city-manager forms of government?
2. How did the Wisconsin Idea lay the foundation for further reforms?

SECTION 2

3. How did the Square Deal reflect President Theodore Roosevelt's approach to government?

SECTION 3

4. What failures and successes did President Taft experience during his term in office?

SECTION 4

5. What were the basic points of President Wilson's New Freedom program?

Reviewing Themes

1. **Democratic Values** How did reformers seek to limit the power of big business and make government more democratic in the early 1900s?
2. **Economic Development** How did President Roosevelt attempt to regulate business without discouraging free enterprise?
3. **Constitutional Heritage** Why did some reformers view the Nineteenth Amendment as a means of accomplishing reform in politics and business?

Thinking Critically

1. **Evaluating** How did the controversy over tariffs contribute to Taft's defeat in the 1912 election?
2. **Analyzing** What interests worked against the campaign for women's suffrage in the early 1900s?
3. **Hypothesizing** How might the presidential election of 1912 have been different if the Progressive Party had not been formed?
4. **Comparing and Contrasting** Compare the successes of Presidents Roosevelt, Taft, and Wilson in enacting reform legislation.
5. **Using Historical Imagination** Imagine that you are a voter considering the new legislation enacted to reform voting procedures. Do you think these reforms will influence your voting practices? Why or why not?

Writing About History

Writing to Evaluate Write an essay evaluating the progressives' record. Use the following graphic to organize your thoughts.

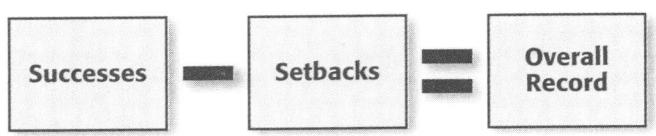

Successes — Setbacks = Overall Record

Strategies for Success

Review the **Strategies for Success** on *Interpreting the Visual Record: Political Cartoons.* Then study the cartoon below and answer the questions that follow.

1. What do the characters and the setting in this cartoon represent?
2. How do the captions and labels help clarify the meaning of the cartoon?
3. What message is the cartoonist trying to communicate through this cartoon?

THE LION-TAMER

4. How does the cartoon contribute to your understanding of business trusts and progressive "trustbusting" in the early 1900s?

Linking History and Geography

One method that progressives used to fight child labor was increased use of laws to require children to be in school. Study the map below. Which section of the country was the last to adopt compulsory education laws?

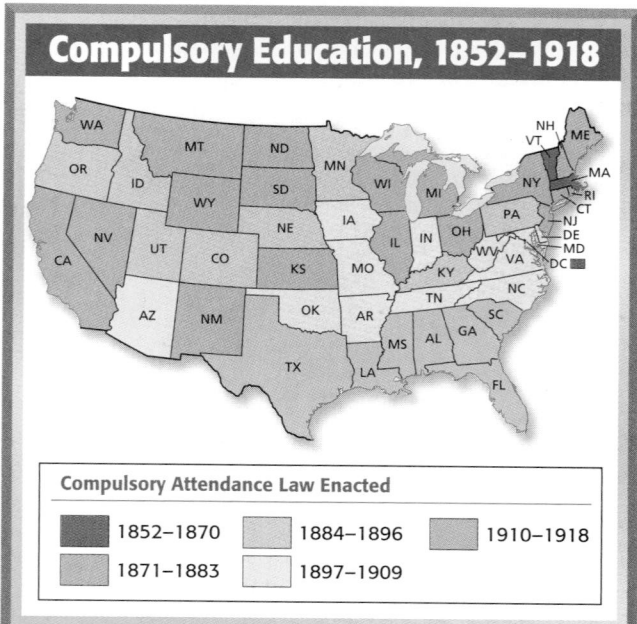

Compulsory Education, 1852–1918

Compulsory Attendance Law Enacted

- 1852–1870
- 1871–1883
- 1884–1896
- 1897–1909
- 1910–1918

internet connect

TOPIC: National Parks
GO TO: go.hrw.com
KEYWORD: SD1 Parks

Accessing the Internet through the HRW Web site, research information about the National Parks System established by President Theodore Roosevelt. Look for information on the history of the parks, their geographical features, and their locations. Then create postcards for at least three of the parks with illustrations on the front and descriptive information on the back.

BUILDING YOUR PORTFOLIO

Complete one or all of the following projects independently or cooperatively.

1 Constitutional Heritage

Imagine that you are a delegate at the 1912 Progressive Party convention. **Write a platform** for the party that translates the problems of political machines, women's suffrage, business regulation, and worker protection into specific reforms your party hopes to institute.

2 Democratic Values

Imagine that you are a supporter of women's suffrage during the 1910s. **Write an editorial** indicating why you believe that progressives are not adequately addressing the needs of working-class women.

3 Economic Development

Imagine that you are a campaign worker for either Roosevelt, Taft, or Wilson. **Create a campaign poster** that shows the reforms your candidate enacted and the reforms the others failed to get passed.

1898–1917
America and the World

Theodore Roosevelt as an international police officer

THE GRANGER COLLECTION, NEW YORK

1898
World Events
The Spanish-American War is fought.

1898
Science and Technology
Marie Curie discovers radium, the first known radioactive element.

1900
Daily Life
The hamburger is introduced in New Haven, Connecticut.

1900
The Arts
The Wizard of Oz by L. Frank Baum is published.

A hamburger

1904
Politics
Theodore Roosevelt states his corollary to the Monroe Doctrine.

1898 **1900** **1902** **1904** **1906**

1898
The Arts
H. G. Wells's *War of the Worlds* is published.

1899
Politics
The U.S. Senate votes to annex the Philippines.

1901
Business and Finance
J. P. Morgan creates the United States Steel Company, the world's first billion-dollar corporation.

1901
Science and Technology
The Nobel Prizes are awarded for the first time.

1904
World Events
The Russo-Japanese War begins.

H. G. Wells

The Nobel Prize

Before You Read

Build on What You Know

After recovering from the Civil War, the United States resumed its economic growth and westward expansion. Creating tremendous wealth for some and jobs for many, the Industrial Revolution transformed the nation. In this chapter you will learn how the United States established itself as a world power. After more than a century of following George Washington's advice and avoiding foreign entanglements, the United States became deeply involved in events abroad, from nearby Cuba and Mexico to distant China and Japan.

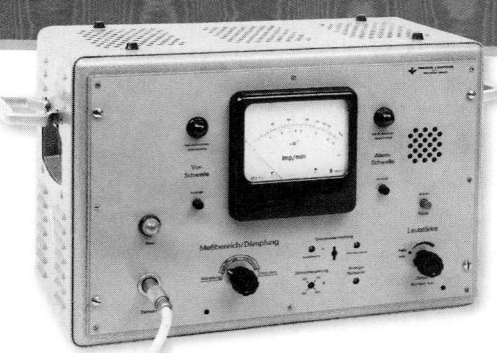

1907
Science and Technology
The Geiger counter, which detects radioactivity, is invented.

An early example of a Geiger counter

Albert Einstein

1916
Science and Technology
Albert Einstein publishes his general theory of relativity.

1907
Daily Life
Mother's Day is observed for the first time.

1910
World Events
The Mexican Revolution begins.

1908	**1910**	**1912**	**1914**	**1916**

1907
Science and Technology
Frenchman Paul Cornu constructs the first vertical flying helicopter that can hold a person.

1911
The Arts
W. C. Handy's song "Memphis Blues" gains great popularity.

1914
Politics
The United States occupies the city of Veracruz, Mexico.

1907
The Arts
Pablo Picasso paints *Les Demoiselles d'Auvignon,* a masterpiece in the cubist style of painting.

Sheet music of W. C. Handy's "Memphis Blues"

Think About Themes

Themes Journal *Decide whether you* **agree** *or* **disagree** *with the following statements. Note why in your journal.*

Global Relations Business interests often play a key role in the making of foreign policy.

Economic Development Investments by foreigners will greatly benefit a country's economy.

Democratic Values The acquisition of foreign colonies conflicts with democratic principles and the ideal of liberty.

Expansion in the Pacific

OBJECTIVES

Read to understand:

1. what major factors drove imperialism
2. how the United States acquired Hawaii
3. what the U.S. role in China was
4. how Japan became a world power

KEY TERMS

imperialism
subsidy
spheres of influence
Open Door Policy
Boxer Rebellion
Russo-Japanese War

KEY PEOPLE

Henry Cabot Lodge
Alfred Thayer Mahan
Kalakaua
Liliuokalani
John Hay
Matthew Perry

EYEWITNESSES TO History

❝ *A new consciousness seems to have come upon us—the consciousness of strength—and with it a new appetite, the yearning to show our strength. . . . Ambition, interest, land hunger, pride, the mere joy of fighting, whatever it may be, we are animated by a new sensation. We are face to face with a strange destiny. The taste of Empire is in the mouth of the people even as the taste of blood in the jungle. It means an Imperial policy, the Republic, renascent [reawakened], taking her place with the armed nations.* ❞
—*Washington Post*

This cartoon shows Uncle Sam gathering the fruits of imperialism.

This editorial appeared in a June 1896 edition of the *Washington Post.* It reflected the growing strength of the United States and Americans' willingness to use this strength. The United States was ready to join the other great powers of the world and compete in a global economy.

The Impulse for Imperialism

In March 1889 in the South Pacific harbor of Apia, in present-day Western Samoa, seven warships—one British, three German, and three U.S.—faced off. Before a shot could be fired, a typhoon struck, destroying all but the British ship and possibly preventing a war. **Imperialism**—the quest for colonial empires—had led these three nations to the brink of war. Between 1876 and 1915 a handful of industrialized nations seized control of vast areas of Africa, Asia, and Latin America.

Imperialism was driven by a need for markets and raw materials as well as the desire for power and prestige. Aided by efficient machines and abundant capital, workers in these industrial nations produced far more goods than could be consumed at home. In response, industrialists turned to Africa, Asia, and Latin America for new customers and new sources of raw materials. To protect these new markets from competition, industrialized nations tried to colonize these areas. Senator Henry Cabot Lodge of Massachusetts explained that the United States needed to join this competition to maintain its economic and military strength.

A modern navy helped the United States compete against other global powers.

❝ Small states are of the past and have no future. . . . The great nations are rapidly absorbing for their future expansion and their present defense all the waste places of the earth. It is a movement which makes for civilization and the advancement of the race. As one of the great nations of the world, the United States must not fall out of the line of march. ❞

American enthusiasm for overseas expansion never matched that of the European powers, but support did grow during the late 1800s. One particularly influential supporter was Alfred Thayer

Mahan of the U.S. Naval College. In his widely read book *The Influence of Sea Power upon History*, Mahan argued that the United States needed a strong navy to protect its economic interests in foreign markets. Mahan wrote that such a navy required overseas bases.

66 Having . . . no foreign establishments, either colonial or military, the ships of war of the United States, in war, will be like land birds, unable to fly far from their own shores. To provide resting-places for them, where they can coal and repair, would be one of the first duties of a government proposing to itself the development of the power of the nation at sea. 99

Other supporters of expansion claimed that the United States had a duty to spread its political system and the Christian religion throughout the world. Whatever the reason, many Americans supported expansion. The competition for territory and markets across the globe is what led the United States, Great Britain, and Germany to clash in Samoa in 1889. Ten years later, the United States won control over Eastern Samoa, and Germany gained control over Western Samoa. Today Western Samoa is independent, while Eastern (or American) Samoa remains a U.S. territory.

✔ **READING CHECK:** What major factors drove imperialism?

Acquiring Hawaii

Another Pacific island nation—Hawaii—also interested imperial powers. The Hawaiian Islands had a tropical climate and fertile, lava-enriched soil. In 1778 British explorer Captain James Cook visited the islands and renamed them the Sandwich Islands. About 1800 the Hawaiian chief Kamehameha united the eight major islands, creating a monarchy that held power until 1893.

The Hawaiian Islands lie some 2,000 miles west of California in the Pacific Ocean. They were the perfect place to build the naval bases and coaling stations that Alfred Thayer Mahan suggested the United States needed. To others the Hawaiians were an uncivilized people who needed to be introduced to modern industrial society and Christianity. One early visitor described Hawaiian culture.

66 The ease with which the Hawaiians on their own land can secure their food supply has undoubtedly interfered with their social and industrial advancement. . . . [It] relieves the native from any struggle and unfits him for sustained competition with men from other lands. The fact that food is supplied by nature takes from the native all desire for the acquisition of more land. Today's food can be had for the picking, and tomorrow's as well. Instead of grasping all he can get, he divides with his neighbor, and confidently expects his neighbor to divide with him. 99

The Religious Spirit

THE AMERICAN MISSIONARY MOVEMENT

During the early 1800s Christian missionary societies in the United States began sending missionaries to other parts of the world. The missionary movement grew steadily over the years and then expanded rapidly toward the end of the century. It grew from 16 American missionary societies in the 1860s to 90 in 1900. Tens of thousands of American Christians traveled abroad to spread their religious faith. Women played a major role in the missionary movement and made up many of the missionary groups in foreign countries.

Missionary Grace Roberts in Manchuria in 1903

Lottie Moon was one such woman. After teaching school in Kentucky and Georgia, she entered missionary service in 1873. For the next 40 years she worked at Southern Baptist stations in northeastern China. The missionary experience not only brought change to nations such as China, but also changed the missionaries themselves. As Lottie Moon wrote, her time in China changed her from "a timid self-distrustful girl into a brave self-reliant woman." In addition to teaching their religious beliefs, missionaries offered classes in mathematics, science, and English. ■

INTERPRETING THE VISUAL RECORD

Sugar. These workers are harvesting sugarcane. American settlers built a profitable sugar industry in Hawaii. *Does harvesting sugarcane appear to be difficult work? Explain your answer.*

Read More About It

Free Find:

Liliuokalani

After reading about Liliuokalani on the **Holt Researcher** CD–ROM, write a song that honors her work on behalf of the Hawaiian people.

During the 1800s ships began arriving in Hawaii more often. The ships brought missionaries, settlers, and traders. They also brought diseases that reduced the Hawaiian population from about 300,000 in 1778 to fewer than 150,000 by 1819.

American influence. The first U.S. contact with the Hawaiian Islands was made by Pacific trading and whaling ships that stopped at the islands for refreshments and supplies. In the 1820s Protestant missionaries from New England traveled to the islands to convert Hawaiians to Christianity. Missionaries and their families settled on the islands and began raising crops, particularly sugar.

American investors in the sugar industry gradually increased their control over the islands. As Hawaii's economy boomed, sugar planters grew rich. Hawaiian sugar production rose, and the influence of Americans increased. Expansion of the sugar industry meant that more laborers were needed. Since Hawaiians were dying off at a high rate, planters brought in thousands of Japanese and Chinese workers, who soon outnumbered Hawaiians. By the 1870s Americans controlled most of Hawaii's land and trade. They exercised growing influence over the Hawaiian king Kalakaua (kah-LAH-KAH-ooh-ah), who took the throne in 1874.

An 1875 treaty exempted Hawaiian sugar from U.S. tariffs. In exchange, Hawaii promised not to grant territory or special privileges in the islands to any other country. In 1886, U.S. officials demanded control of Pearl Harbor in exchange for renewing tax-free status for Hawaiian sugar. Kalakaua refused. Some 400 American businesspeople, planters, and traders in Hawaii then formed the secret Hawaiian League. Their goal was to overthrow the monarchy and persuade the United States to annex Hawaii.

In July 1887 the League forced Kalakaua at gunpoint to sign a new constitution that limited his role to that of a figurehead. It also limited native Hawaiians' right to hold office in their own country. Hawaiians resented what they called the Bayonet Constitution. Kalakaua had no choice but to renew the treaty and grant the United States exclusive rights to build a fortified naval base at Pearl Harbor.

In 1890 Congress enacted the McKinley Tariff, which created a crisis by ending Hawaii's favored position in the sugar trade. The law permitted all countries to ship sugar duty-free to the United States. It also gave sugar producers in the United States a **subsidy**—a government bonus payment—of two cents per pound. This caused sugar prices to drop, and the Hawaiian economy suffered.

Liliuokalani

A nationalist queen. In 1891 Kalakaua died and his sister Liliuokalani (li-lee-uh-woh-kuh-LAHN-ee) succeeded him. Liliuokalani was a champion of Hawaiian nationalism and pledged to regain "Hawaii for the Hawaiians." Liliuokalani was born into a Hawaiian ruling family in 1838. As a young girl she saw the monarchy reclaim Hawaiian independence after a brief British takeover. She never forgot the pride she felt as the Hawaiian flag was again raised over her native land.

Early in her reign, Queen Liliuokalani began working to overturn the Bayonet Constitution and replace it with one that would return power to native Hawaiians. In 1893 she announced her plan to publish a new constitution. In response, the supporters of annexation forcibly occupied government buildings, declared the end of the monarchy, and set up a provisional government of their own. Without authorization, the U.S. minister to Hawaii, John L. Stevens, ordered marines ashore from the cruiser *Boston*, supposedly to protect American lives and property. With Gatling guns and cannons in place, the marines took up positions facing Iolani Palace and Liliuokalani.

No shots were fired, and the revolutionaries established a new government with Sanford B. Dole as president. Again acting without authority, Stevens recognized the new government and proclaimed Hawaii to be under U.S. protection on February 1, 1893. "The Hawaiian pear is now fully ripe," proclaimed Stevens, "and this is the golden hour for the United States to pluck it." Not wanting to see Hawaiians killed, a deeply saddened Queen Liliuokalani reluctantly surrendered her throne.

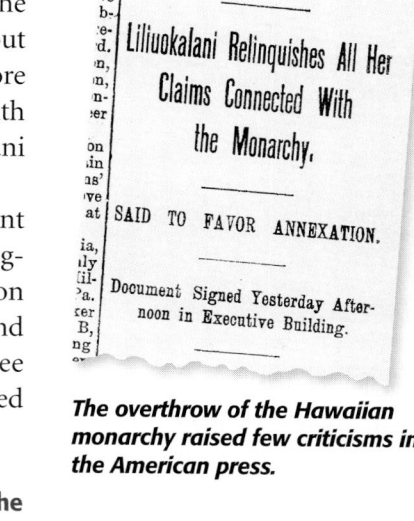

The overthrow of the Hawaiian monarchy raised few criticisms in the American press.

66 I, Liliuokalani, . . . protest against any and all acts done against myself and the constitutional government of the Hawaiian kingdom. . . . Now, to avoid any collision of armed forces and perhaps the loss of life, I do, under this protest, and impelled by said forces, yield my authority until such time as the government of the United States shall . . . undo the action of its representatives and reinstate me. 99

The new government petitioned the United States for annexation, but anti-imperialists and Democratic senators blocked the proposed treaty. Newly elected president Grover Cleveland withdrew the treaty and ordered an investigation. The investigator's report condemned the revolt and the U.S. role in it. The report also proposed putting Liliuokalani back on the throne. Cleveland supported the report and asked the provisional government to resign. Dole, however, refused to step down.

Unwilling to use military force to restore Liliuokalani, Cleveland reluctantly recognized the Dole government but refused to approve annexation. From 1894 to 1898 the independent Republic of Hawaii waited for a friendly Washington administration. It came with the election of President William McKinley. The United States annexed Hawaii on July 7, 1898, despite the opposition of most of Hawaii's population.

This postcard shows the tropical beauty of Hawaii.

Liliuokalani lived out the rest of her life in Honolulu, serving as a proud reminder of Hawaii's past. She died in 1917 and was buried in the Royal Mausoleum. Hawaii became a U.S. territory in 1900 and the 50th state in 1959. In 1993 Congress apologized for the U.S. role in Liliuokalani's overthrow.

✔ **READING CHECK:** How did the United States acquire Hawaii?

China trade. Merchant ships unloaded their goods at Whampoa Anchorage near Canton, China. *How many flags of different nations can you identify?*

U.S. Involvement in China

Hawaii was valuable to the United States in part because it was a convenient stopping point for American trading ships sailing to China. Trade between China and the United States began in 1784 when the American ship *Empress of China* sailed for the port of Guangzhou.

Spheres of influence. In 1843 China officially opened five ports to trade with the United States and Europe. For the next 50 years China's rulers struggled to keep foreign interests from overrunning the country. In 1895, however, the Chinese government faced a threat from another direction. Japan attacked and defeated China, seizing China's Liaotung Peninsula, the large island of Taiwan, and Korea. European powers quickly took advantage of China's weakened position. Britain, France, Germany, and Russia carved out **spheres of influence**—regions where a particular country has exclusive rights over mines, railroads, and trade.

The Open Door Policy. The United States was in danger of being squeezed out of the China trade. Senator Henry Cabot Lodge declared, "We ask no favors; we only ask that we shall be admitted to that great market upon the same terms with the rest of the world." In 1899 Secretary of State John Hay called for an **Open Door Policy**, which would give all nations equal access to trade and investment in China.

That September Hay sent a series of Open Door notes to the European powers and Japan that asked them to agree to three principles. First, he asked that they keep all ports in their spheres open to all nations. Second, he asked that Chinese officials be allowed to collect all tariffs and duties. Finally, he requested that they guarantee equal harbor, railroad, and tariff rates in their spheres to all nations trading in China. Since the European nations and Japan neither rejected nor accepted the principles, Hay announced that the Open Door Policy had been accepted.

This Chinese print shows the Boxers attacking westerners.

The Boxer Rebellion. Chinese resentment of foreigners continued to grow. A secret society called the Fists of Righteous Harmony—known as the Boxers by westerners—circulated handbills blaming foreigners and missionaries for China's troubles. One handbill claimed that because "the Catholic and Protestant religions are insolent [disrespectful] to the gods, . . . the rain clouds no longer visit us. But 8 million Spirit Soldiers will descend from Heaven and sweep the Empire clean of all foreigners!"

In the spring of 1900 the Boxers attacked Western missionaries and traders in northern China, killing about 300. Known as the **Boxer Rebellion**, this uprising was supported by some Chinese government officials. The Boxers laid siege to the large, walled-in foreign settlement in Beijing, China's capital. Foreign countries responded by sending troops to China. In August, after an eight-week siege, the international force rescued the foreigners.

John Hay feared that Japan and other nations would use the Boxer Rebellion as an excuse to seize control of additional Chinese territory. In a second series of Open Door notes, Hay pressured the foreign powers to observe open trade throughout China and to preserve China's right to rule its own territory. China retained its sovereignty as a nation but was forced to pay the European powers $333 million for damages.

✔ **READING CHECK:** What role did the United States play in China?

Strategies for Success

Interpreting Economic Data

The use of economic data can broaden one's understanding of many historical topics. Information about exports, imports, incomes, prices, and production rates, for instance, can provide one with valuable clues about everyday life in a nation or region or the interactions between different nations or regions.

Like other historical statistics, however, economic data must be interpreted carefully. The information in a given chart or graph serves as a snapshot that shows one specific part of an economy from one specific angle. When interpreting this information, it is important to consider what you already know about the historical period.

How to Interpret Economic Data

1. **Determine the nature of the data.** Read the title of the chart or graph to identify the type of economic data it presents. Then read all of its headings, subheadings, and labels to determine the categories, amounts, and time intervals in which it presents the data.

2. **Analyze the details.** Study the information in the chart or graph carefully and systematically. Take note of increases or decreases in quantities, and look for trends, relationships, and conflicts in the data.

3. **Put the data to use.** Use your analysis of the data, along with your knowledge of the historical period, to form generalizations and draw conclusions.

Applying the Strategy

Study the graph below, which shows the value of U.S. exports to China between 1898 and 1908.

Practicing the Strategy

Use the graph below to answer the following questions.
1. In which year was the value of U.S. exports to China at its lowest? In which year was it at its highest?
2. Why do you think the value of U.S. exports to China rose and fell several times between 1898 and 1908?

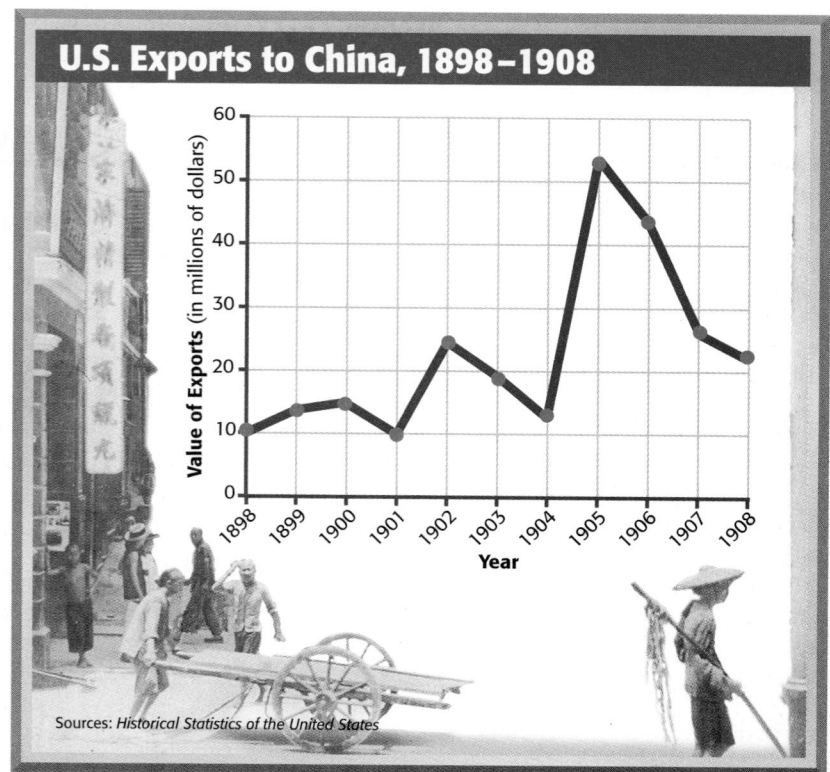

U.S. Exports to China, 1898–1908

Sources: *Historical Statistics of the United States*

Collectively known as the Great White Fleet because of the way they were painted, U.S. warships made stops in ports around the world as a show of U.S. military strength.

An Emerging Japan

Japan's 1894 invasion of China marked its emergence as an imperial power. Just 41 years earlier Japan had ended its almost complete isolation from the rest of the world. President Millard Fillmore had sent Commodore Matthew Perry to persuade Japan to open its doors to trade with the West. In 1854 Perry's fleet of seven warships sailed into Edo—present-day Tokyo—and presented Japan's rulers with gifts that included a telegraph transmitter and a model train.

The Japanese leaders agreed to the Western demands for trade. They reasoned that if they did not, foreigners might seize control of their nation. Japan rapidly transformed itself into an industrial power and built up its army and navy. Japan and Russia had long been rivals for Chinese territories. In February 1904, Japanese troops attacked Russian forces in Manchuria, starting the **Russo-Japanese War**.

The war worried President Theodore Roosevelt. He feared that if Russia won it might cut off U.S. trade with Manchuria, and if Japan won, it might threaten free trade in Asia. By May 1905, after winning a series of crucial battles, the Japanese asked Roosevelt to negotiate peace with Russia. In Portsmouth, New Hampshire, Roosevelt and representatives of the two countries hammered out a treaty that granted neither side all it wanted. Roosevelt was awarded the Nobel Peace Prize for his efforts.

Japan had become a modern world power and a rival to the United States for influence in China and the Pacific. Concerned by Japan's growing power, Roosevelt decided to remind the Japanese of America's military might. In late 1907 he sent a fleet of four destroyers and 16 battleships, painted a dazzling white, on a 46,000-mile world cruise that included a stop in the Japanese port of Yokohama.

✔ **READING CHECK:** How did Japan become a world power?

SECTION 1 REVIEW

Define and explain the significance of the following terms:
imperialism
subsidy
spheres of influence
Open Door Policy
Boxer Rebellion
Russo-Japanese War

Identify and explain the significance of the following individuals:
Henry Cabot Lodge
Alfred Thayer Mahan
Kalakaua
Liliuokalani
John Hay
Matthew Perry

1. **Using Graphic Organizers** Copy the chart below. Use it to list the events that led to the U.S. annexation of Hawaii.

   | 1. Kalakaua becomes king of Hawaii in 1874. |
   | 2. |
   | 3. |
   | 4. |
   | 5. |
   | 6. The United States annexes Hawaii on July 7, 1898. |

2. **Analyzing** Why did the United States and European nations begin to follow a policy of imperialism in the 1800s?
3. **Assessing Consequences** How did foreign expansion in Asia and the Boxer Rebellion affect U.S. policy toward China?
4. **Taking a Stand** Do you think any nation is ever justified in setting up a sphere of influence in a foreign country? Explain your answer.

Critical Thinking

5. Why did President Roosevelt decide to send a fleet of U.S. ships to Japan?
   Consider:
   • what the relationship had been between the United States and Japan
   • how Japan's power had grown
   • why Roosevelt saw Japan as a threat to U.S. interests

SECTION
(2)
War with Spain

OBJECTIVES

Read to understand:

1. how Spain responded to the revolt in Cuba
2. what the major causes of the Spanish-American War were
3. what the major battles of the Spanish-American War were
4. what happened to the Philippines after the Spanish-American War

KEY TERMS

USS *Maine*
Spanish-American War
Teller Amendment
Rough Riders
Philippine Government Act
Jones Act of 1916

KEY PEOPLE

José Martí
Valeriano Weyler
William Randolph Hearst
William McKinley
George Dewey
Emilio Aguinaldo

KEY PLACES

Cuba
Puerto Rico
Manila
Santiago
San Juan Hill

EYEWITNESSES TO History

" We know that they have formed a government; that they have held two elections. . . . They have risen against oppression, compared to which the oppression which led us to rebel against England is as dust in the balance. . . . No useful end is being served by the bloody struggle that is now in progress in Cuba, and in the name of humanity it should be stopped. . . . The responsibility is on us; we cannot escape it. We should . . . put a stop to that war which is now raging in Cuba and give to that island once more peace, liberty, and independence. "
—Henry Cabot Lodge

The United States protects Cuba from Spain.

In a speech delivered to the Senate on February 20, 1896, Senator Henry Cabot Lodge called for the United States to intervene in a rebellion in Cuba. Many Americans were eager to flex the nation's military muscle and put an end to a war so near its shores. Other people also wanted the United States to assert more authority and drive Spain out of the Western Hemisphere.

Conflict in Cuba

Supporters of U.S. expansion had long been interested in the Caribbean island of Cuba, located just 90 miles from the Florida Keys. In the late 1800s Cuba simmered with unrest. Cuba and its Caribbean neighbor Puerto Rico were the last of the Spanish colonies in the Americas. Since 1868, Cubans had launched a series of unsuccessful revolts against Spanish rule. To put down the rebellion, the Spanish government exiled many leaders of the independence movement.

BIOGRAPHY

José Martí

Foremost among these Cuban exiles was the poet José Martí. Born in Havana, Cuba, on January 28, 1853, Martí joined in a revolt against Cuba's Spanish rulers when he was just 15 years old. For his actions, Martí was banished to Spain, where he earned a university degree. He later worked in Mexico and in Guatemala. Martí returned to Cuba in 1878 but was banished again for his activism. He moved to New York City, where he worked for Cuban independence.

While in New York Martí wrote poems and newspaper articles promoting Cuban independence. He also urged Cuban exiles to mount an invasion of Cuba. "Let us rise up at once with a final burst of heartfelt energy . . . for the true republic, those of us who, with our passion for right and our habit of hard work, will know how to preserve it." When Cubans launched another revolt in February 1895, Martí and other exiles joined them. Martí became a martyr for Cuban independence when he was killed months later in a battle.

In 1896 Spain sent General Valeriano Weyler to put down the revolt. He forced thousands of farmers into concentration camps to prevent them from aiding the rebels. Some 200,000 Cubans died from starvation and disease in the camps.

✔ **READING CHECK:** How did Spain respond to the revolt in Cuba?

The United States Reacts

Many Americans saw similarities between the Cubans' struggle and the American Revolution and were therefore sympathetic to the Cuban rebels. The American press encouraged war with Spain and branded Weyler "the Butcher." Two New York City newspapers, William Randolph Hearst's *New York Journal* and Joseph Pulitzer's *New York World*, used sensational tales of Spanish atrocities to attract readers and sell more papers.

HOLT RESEARCHER

Read More About It

Free Find: William Randolph Hearst

After reading about William Randolph Hearst on the **Holt Researcher** CD–ROM, create a newspaper front page about current news stories that reflects Hearst's style of journalism.

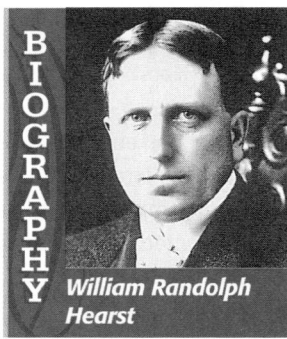

BIOGRAPHY

William Randolph Hearst

The influence of the media. Perhaps no American journalist was more interested in the Cuban situation than William Randolph Hearst. His father had made a fortune in the California gold fields and was a rich man when his only son was born in 1863. When Hearst was 10 he and his mother traveled to Europe.

Hearst was an undisciplined student prone to mischief—he was expelled from his high school and finished his studies at home with tutors. He then attended Harvard University where he displayed little interest in academics but great enthusiasm for business and publishing. Hearst left Harvard in his junior year and got a job in New York as a reporter for Pulitzer's *World*.

Hearst's father owned the *San Francisco Examiner*. In 1887 Hearst persuaded his father to let him run the newspaper. Using a sensational style of reporting, Hearst soon turned around the failing *Examiner*. After reviving that newspaper, Hearst returned to New York in 1895 to run the *Journal* and challenge Pulitzer. Hearst explained his view of the role of newspapers.

66 **The newspaper is the greatest force in civilization. . . . Newspapers form and express public opinion. They suggest and control legislation. They declare wars. They punish criminals, especially the powerful. They reward with approving publicity the good deeds of citizens everywhere. The newspapers control the nation because they REPRESENT THE PEOPLE.** 99

Hearst's growing newspaper empire made him a wealthy man. He built a mansion in San Simeon, California, and filled it with art and rare artifacts from around the globe. His lavish lifestyle continued until his death in 1951.

The *Maine* incident. Believing that newspapers should shape public opinion and policy, Hearst pressed for U.S. intervention in Cuba. In 1897 he sent artist Frederic Remington to Cuba to create drawings showing Spanish cruelty, which Hearst could use to increase U.S. support for war with Spain. President William McKinley, however, was a veteran of the

INTERPRETING THE VISUAL RECORD

Remember the *Maine*! The explosion of the battleship *Maine* led to the Spanish-American War. *What do you think the artist's purpose was in painting this scene?*

Civil War and resisted the calls for war. "I have been through one war. I have seen the dead piled up, and I do not want to see another," he explained.

Events soon changed McKinley's stance. On February 9, 1898, the *Journal* published a letter written by Spain's minister to the United States, Enrique Dupuy de Lôme, that had been intercepted by a Cuban spy and sold to Hearst. In this letter de Lôme ridiculed McKinley as "weak, and a bidder for the admiration of the crowd." Americans were outraged at the remarks, which the *Journal* called "the worst insult to the United States in its history."

The nation teetered on the brink of war until a tragedy in Cuba pushed it over the edge. The battleship **USS *Maine*** had been sent to Havana to protect U.S. lives and property. On February 15 the *Maine* blew up, killing 260 sailors. "DESTRUCTION OF THE WAR SHIP MAINE WAS THE WORK OF AN ENEMY!" screamed the *Journal's* headline, although there was no proof of this. Some historians believe that a fire in a coal bin caused the explosion. At the time, however, many Americans blamed Spain. "Remember the *Maine!*" became the rallying cry of war supporters.

Spanish officials agreed to a U.S.-proposed peace plan, but it was too late. On April 11 McKinley asked Congress to intervene in Cuba "in the name of humanity, in the name of civilization, and in behalf of endangered American interests." On April 25 Congress declared war on Spain. The **Spanish-American War** had begun.

✔ **READING CHECK:** What were the major causes of the Spanish-American War?

The media. The destruction of the *Maine* was front-page news throughout the United States. *How does the* **New York Journal** *explain the sinking?*

War with Spain

On April 20, 1898, Congress recognized Cuba's independence and voted to use U.S. military force to help Cuba attain it. Congress also adopted the **Teller Amendment**. This stated that once Cuba won its independence from Spain, the United States would "leave the government and control of the Island to its people."

Fighting in the Philippines.
The war's first battle was fought halfway around the world in the Spanish-held Philippine Islands. Weeks before war was declared, Assistant Secretary of the Navy Theodore Roosevelt had cabled secret orders to Commodore George Dewey in Hong Kong. In the event of war between the United States and Spain, Dewey was to attack the Philippines.

As dawn broke on May 1, 1898, Dewey's fleet steamed across Manila Bay, in the Philippines. Commodore Dewey stood on the bridge of his flagship, *Olympia.* He trained his eyes on the Spanish guns on the shore and the small Spanish fleet anchored in the harbor. The Spanish sighted the Americans and opened fire, but Dewey's ships were out of range. The U.S. ships slowly moved closer to shore. Shortly after 5:30 A.M., Dewey told the *Olympia*'s captain: "You may fire when you are ready, Gridley." The bay echoed with the roar of naval guns. As shells crashed into several Spanish vessels, they erupted into flames.

Led by George Dewey, U.S. forces destroyed the Spanish fleet in the Battle of Manila Bay.

U.S. troops in Cuba were poorly prepared for the tropical conditions they faced.

Dewey's fleet easily defeated the small Spanish fleet guarding the Philippine city of Manila. To capture the city, Dewey obtained the support of a rebel army of Filipino patriots led by Emilio Aguinaldo (ahg-ee-NAHL-doh). Filipinos had been fighting for independence from Spain for two years. Cut off by Dewey's warships and surrounded by Aguinaldo's rebels, Spanish forces in the Philippines surrendered on August 14, 1898.

Fighting in Cuba. Victory in Cuba proved more difficult than in the Philippines. With a regular army of just some 28,000 soldiers, the U.S. War Department was unprepared for land battles. U.S. troops had received little training and were outfitted in heavy wool uniforms—the only ones that army storehouses could supply—when they sailed for tropical Cuba in mid-June 1898. A soldier described life once the troops arrived in Cuba.

66 Heavy rains pouring down, no tents for cover, . . . standing in trenches in a foot of water and mud, day and night. . . . Ration issue consisting of a slice of sow belly, hardtack, and some grains of coffee. . . . Then came the issue of fleece-lined underwear in a 132 [degree] climate. . . . Then came on malaria. 99

On July 1, U.S. troops attacked the Spanish fort at Santiago. Their aim was to capture the territory above Santiago. This included El Caney and San Juan Hill, which would let them aim their guns down on Spanish troops. One U.S. division overcame Spanish forces at El Caney.

Lieutenant Colonel Theodore Roosevelt had resigned his naval post. In the war's most famous battle, he led a cavalry unit of about 1,000 soldiers toward the garrison on San Juan Hill. Composed largely of college athletes, cowboys, American Indians, and ranchers, the unit was known as the **Rough Riders**.

Because their horses had not been shipped to Cuba, the Rough Riders had to charge on foot under intense Spanish fire. The African American 9th and 10th Cavalries cleared the way for the final surge. By nightfall, U.S. troops controlled the ridge above Santiago. Then, on July 3, the U.S. Navy sank the Spanish fleet off the coast of Cuba as it tried to escape from a U.S. naval blockade. The battle resulted in more than 400 Spanish casualties. Two weeks later, Spanish troops in Cuba surrendered. Meanwhile, U.S. troops defeated Spanish forces in Puerto Rico.

The war proved costly for Spain. By the terms of the peace treaty, Spain gave up all claim to Cuba and ceded Puerto Rico and the Pacific island of Guam to the United States. Spain also gave up control of the Philippines in return for a U.S. payment of $20 million. By gaining control of overseas territories, the United States moved into the ranks of the imperialist world powers. Expansionists expressed delight, but the quest for empire troubled many Americans. Furthermore, the United States paid a heavy human toll for the war. Some 5,400 soldiers died, nearly 400 in battle and the rest from disease or food poisoning.

✔ **READING CHECK:** What were the major battles of the Spanish-American War?

San Juan Hill. Theodore Roosevelt led a cavalry unit known as the Rough Riders in the Spanish-American War. *What is unusual about the cavalry soldiers shown in the painting?*

AMERICAN Letters

Literature of the Spanish-American War

At the time of the Spanish-American War, the United States was still deeply divided by sectional tensions. Some of the literature that was inspired by the war tried to encourage a sense of unity among all Americans. Other writers, particularly journalists, tried to portray an accurate picture of the fighting. The two excerpts below illustrate these themes. In the first, Stephen Crane reports for the New York World *on the real-life experiences of soldiers. In the second excerpt, from* Crittenden, *a novel by John Fox Jr., a former Confederate soldier is rewarded for his services in the Spanish-American War.*

from "Night Attacks on the Marines and a Brave Rescue"
by *Stephen Crane*

Stephen Crane

GUANTANAMO, July 4.—The night attacks were heart-breaking affairs, from which the men emerged in the morning exhausted to a final degree, like people who had been swimming for miles. From colonel to smallest trumpeter went a great thrill when the dawn broke slowly in the eastern sky, and the weary band quite cheerfully ate breakfast. . . . Afterward the men slept, sunk upon the ground in an abandon [physical exhaustion] that was almost a stupor [daze].

Lieut. Neville, with his picket [forward group] of about twenty men, was entirely cut off from camp one night, and another night Neville's picket and the picket of Lieut. Shaw were cut off, fighting hard in the thickets [forests] for their lives. At the break of day the beleaguered [surrounded] camp could hear still the rifles of their lost pickets.

The guerrillas were still lurking [hiding] in the near woods, and it was unsafe enough in camp without venturing into the bush.

Volunteers from Company C . . . went out under Lieut. Lucas. They arrived in Neville's vicinity just as he and his men, together with Shaw and his men, were being finally surrounded at close range. Lucas and his seventeen men broke through the guerrillas and saved the pickets, and the whole body then fell back to Crest Hill. That is all there is to it.

from *Crittenden: A Kentucky Story of Love and War*
by *John Fox Jr.*

"You're a Sergeant, Crittenden," said the Captain.

He, Crittenden, in blood and sympathy the spirit of secession—bearer now of the Stars and Stripes! How his heart thumped, and how his head reeled when he caught the staff and looked dumbly up to the folds; and in spite of all his self-control, the tears came.

Right at that moment there was a great bustle in camp . . . and the victorious Stars and Stripes rose up. . . . On the very stroke of twelve, there came thunder—the thunder of two-score and one salutes. And the cheers—the cheers! . . . And on a little knoll not far away stood Sergeant Crittenden, swaying on his feet—colour-sergeant to the folds of the ever-victorious, ever-beloved Old Glory waving over him, with a strange new wave of feeling surging through him. For then and there, Crittenden, Southerner, died straightaway and through a travail of wounds, suffering, sickness, devotion, and love for that flag—Crittenden, American, was born.

UNDERSTANDING LITERATURE

1. What adjectives does Stephen Crane use to describe the soldiers' experiences?
2. How does the excerpt from *Crittenden* address the divisions in American society?
3. What similarities and differences do you notice in the two excerpts?

U.S. control brought modern developments like electricity, telephones, and streetcar service to the Philippines.

Uproar over the Philippines

In 1898 few Americans even knew where the Philippines were. Even President McKinley confessed that before he consulted a globe, he could not locate the islands "within two thousand miles." Now Americans faced an urgent question: Should Filipinos be forced to accept U.S. rule?

The debate over annexation. Some Americans questioned whether it was proper or wise for the United States to annex any foreign territory and rule its government and its people. Expansionists argued forcefully in favor of annexation. In addition to supporting annexation for commercial and security reasons, some believed that the United States would bring democracy to the Philippines. Others held that U.S. rule of the islands was necessary to keep out European powers. Charles Denby, a former U.S. minister to China, warned opponents of annexation that times had changed. "We have a great commerce to take care of. We have to compete with the commercial nations of the world in far-distant markets. Commerce, not politics, is king."

Opponents of annexation responded that by denying the Philippines independence, the United States would violate its own ideals expressed in the Declaration

Spanish-American War, 1898

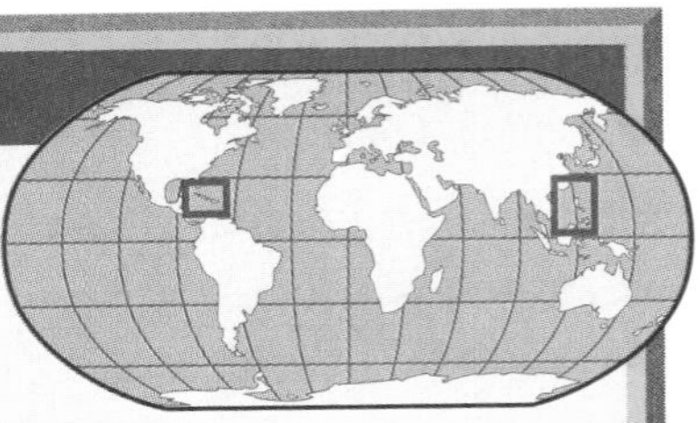

Learning from Maps The Spanish-American War was primarily decided at sea. The U.S. Navy easily conquered the Spanish fleets protecting Cuba and the Philippines. Both Spanish fleets were destroyed, while the Americans suffered few casualties.

? LOCATION Where did Commodore George Dewey destroy the Spanish fleet?

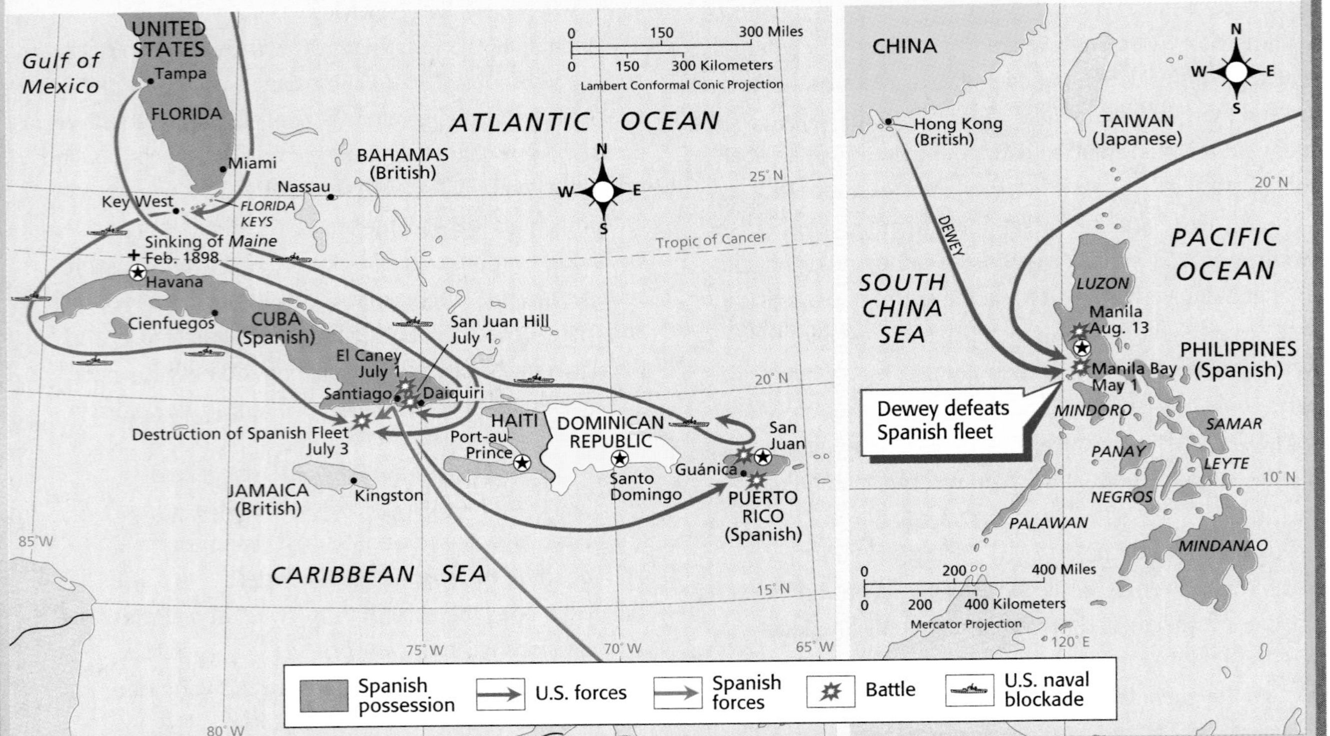

UNITED STATES
Gulf of Mexico
Tampa
FLORIDA
Miami
Key West
FLORIDA KEYS
Nassau
BAHAMAS (British)
ATLANTIC OCEAN
0   150   300 Miles
0   150   300 Kilometers
Lambert Conformal Conic Projection
25° N
Tropic of Cancer
Sinking of *Maine* Feb. 1898
Havana
Cienfuegos
CUBA (Spanish)
San Juan Hill July 1
El Caney July 1
Santiago Daiquiri
Destruction of Spanish Fleet July 3
JAMAICA (British)   Kingston
85° W
HAITI
Port-au-Prince
DOMINICAN REPUBLIC
Santo Domingo
Guánica
San Juan
PUERTO RICO (Spanish)
20° N
CARIBBEAN SEA
75° W   70° W   65° W
15° N
80° W

CHINA
Hong Kong (British)
TAIWAN (Japanese)
20° N
DEWEY
SOUTH CHINA SEA
LUZON
Manila Aug. 13
Manila Bay May 1
Dewey defeats Spanish fleet
MINDORO
PANAY
NEGROS
PALAWAN
SAMAR
LEYTE
PACIFIC OCEAN
PHILIPPINES (Spanish)
10° N
MINDANAO
0   200   400 Miles
0   200   400 Kilometers
Mercator Projection
120° E

Spanish possession | U.S. forces | Spanish forces | Battle | U.S. naval blockade

of Independence. In June 1898, opponents of U.S. imperialism formed the Anti-Imperialist League and announced their beliefs.

> 66 We regret that it has become necessary . . . to reaffirm that all men, of whatever race or color, are entitled to life, liberty, and the pursuit of happiness. . . . The subjugation of any people is 'criminal aggression' and open disloyalty to the . . . principles of our Government. 99

After a fierce debate, the Senate narrowly approved the treaty, annexing the Philippines on February 6, 1899.

Conquest and early rule. Emilio Aguinaldo had already set up a provisional government and proclaimed himself president of the new Philippine Republic. He warned that Filipinos would go to war if "American troops attempt to take forcible possession. Upon their heads will be all the blood which may be shed." For the next three years, Filipino independence fighters battled U.S. soldiers for control of the Philippines. By the time U.S. forces crushed the rebellion in 1902, hundreds of thousands of Filipinos and more than 4,000 U.S. soldiers had lost their lives.

In 1902 the U.S. Congress passed the **Philippine Government Act**, also known as the Organic Act, which established a governor and a two-house legislature to rule the Philippines. The United States would appoint the governor and the legislature's upper house, but Filipino voters would elect the lower house. The **Jones Act of 1916** granted Filipinos the right to elect both houses of their legislature. On July 4, 1946, the United States finally granted independence to the Philippines.

✔ **READING CHECK:** What happened to the Philippines after the Spanish-American War?

INTERPRETING THE VISUAL RECORD

Filipino opposition. This cartoon shows U.S. military power crushing Emilio Aguinaldo's government. *How does the cartoon justify U.S. actions in the Philippines?*

SECTION 2 REVIEW

Define and explain the significance of the following terms:
USS *Maine*
Spanish-American War
Teller Amendment
Rough Riders
Philippine Government Act
Jones Act of 1916

Identify and explain the significance of the following individuals:
José Martí
Valeriano Weyler
William Randolph Hearst
William McKinley
George Dewey
Emilio Aguinaldo

Locate and explain the importance of the following places:
Cuba
Puerto Rico
Manila
Santiago
San Juan Hill

1. **Using Graphic Organizers** Copy the chart below. Use it to list the actions taken by the United States and Spain leading up to and during the Spanish-American War.

United States

Spain

2. **Identifying Cause and Effect** How did Spain's reaction to the revolt in Cuba lead the United States to declare war against Spain in 1898?

3. **Understanding Geography: Human-Environment Interaction** What territories did the United States gain as a result of the Spanish-American War?

4. **Evaluating** How did publisher William Randolph Hearst influence the U.S. government to declare war on Spain?

Critical Thinking

5. Why did Filipinos rebel against the United States after the Spanish-American War?
Consider:
• the reasons the United States became involved in the Philippines
• the role of Filipino rebels in the war against Spain
• why the United States did not initially grant independence to the Philippines

Expansion in Latin America

U.S. soldiers questioning Filipino women

OBJECTIVES

Read to understand:
1. how the United States governed Cuba and Puerto Rico
2. what the major obstacles to building the Panama Canal were
3. what U.S. policy toward Latin America during the late 1800s and early 1900s was

KEY TERMS

Platt Amendment
protectorate
Foraker Act
Hay–Bunau-Varilla Treaty
Roosevelt Corollary
dollar diplomacy

KEY PEOPLE

Leonard Wood
Philippe Bunau-Varilla

KEY PLACES

Panama Canal

EYEWITNESSES TO History

❝ We believe that America had something better to offer to mankind than those aims she is now pursuing. . . . She has lost her unique position as a potential leader in the progress of civilization and has taken up her place simply as one of the grasping and selfish nations of the present day. ❞

—**Charles Elliot Norton**

In this 1899 letter, Charles Elliot Norton expressed his disappointment with the United States for seizing an empire by force and for annexing the Philippines. Many Americans shared Norton's concerns about the course the United States was following. Supporters of U.S. actions, however, argued that the territories would benefit from U.S. rule and protection.

General Leonard Wood posed for this photograph in the Governors Palace at Santiago, Cuba.

Governing Cuba and Puerto Rico

As the power of the United States grew in the Pacific, its role in Latin America expanded as well. Wanting to restore order in Cuba and Puerto Rico quickly and protect U.S. investments, President McKinley set up military governments to rule the islands. McKinley appointed General Leonard Wood as governor of Cuba in 1899. Wood authorized the construction of schools and a sanitation system. U.S. Army doctors Walter Reed and William Gorgas led sanitation efforts to reduce the mosquito population. Carlos Finlay (feen-LY), a Cuban doctor, had theorized that mosquitoes spread yellow fever. He was right. The sanitation system drained pools of standing water where mosquitoes bred. It all but eliminated yellow fever.

Wood also oversaw the drafting of a new constitution that limited Cuba's independence. Congress agreed to remove U.S. troops from the island only if Cuba made the **Platt Amendment** part of its constitution. The amendment limited Cuba's freedom to make treaties with other countries and authorized the United States to intervene in Cuban affairs as it saw necessary. It also required Cuba to sell or lease land to the United States for naval and fueling stations. This last clause led to the establishment of a U.S. naval base at Guantánamo Bay. In effect, the Platt Amendment made Cuba a U.S. **protectorate**. This meant that the United States promised to protect Cuba from other nations but reserved the right to intervene in Cuba's affairs. In 1902, after Cuba reluctantly accepted the Platt Amendment, U.S. troops withdrew. Over the next three decades, the United States intervened in Cuba several times. The Platt Amendment remained in force until 1934, when the United States renounced its right to intervene in Cuba.

U.S. policy in Puerto Rico followed a different course. The United States ruled the island as a territory like Samoa or the Philippines in the Pacific. The **Foraker Act** of 1900 established that Puerto Rico's governor and upper house of the legislature would be appointed by the United States. It also established that a lower house would be elected by Puerto Ricans. The **Jones Act of 1917** granted Puerto Ricans U.S. citizenship and gave them the right to elect both houses of their legislature. In 1952 Puerto Rico became a self-governing commonwealth of the United States, with continuing ties of citizenship and trade with the mainland.

✔ **READING CHECK:** How did the United States govern Cuba and Puerto Rico?

Read More About It

Free Find: Foraker Act
After learning about the Foraker Act on the **Holt Researcher** CD–ROM, write an encyclopedia entry describing the act's historical importance.

The Panama Canal

Having interests in both the Caribbean and the Pacific, the United States wanted to cut the travel time between the seas. Traveling around South America took several weeks. The United States proposed digging a canal across Central America.

Early steps toward a canal. In the 1880s, led by the man who had built the Suez Canal in Egypt, a French company began building a canal across the 50-mile-wide Isthmus of Panama. After less than 10 years and the loss of some 20,000 lives and more than $280 million, the French abandoned the effort.

In 1901 Secretary of State John Hay began negotiations with the Republic of Colombia—of which Panama was then a part. In 1903 a treaty was drafted. In return for a 99-year lease on a six-mile strip of land across the isthmus, the United States agreed to pay Colombia $10 million and a yearly rental of $250,000. However, Colombia's senate held out for better terms and adjourned without ratifying the treaty. President Roosevelt was furious. He vowed that the Colombians would not be allowed "to bar one of the future highways of civilization."

Revolution in Panama. Events in Panama soon turned in Roosevelt's favor. Key Panamanian leaders who wanted the canal built began plotting revolution against the Colombian government. Helping them was Philippe Bunau-Varilla (boo-noh-vah-ree-yah), the former chief engineer for the French canal-building attempt.

Bunau-Varilla traveled to Washington, D.C., to get American support for the revolution. On October 9, 1903, he met privately with President Roosevelt. On November 2 the U.S. gunboat *Nashville* arrived in Panama. The following day, Panamanians began their rebellion. U.S. Marines prevented Colombian forces from reaching the rebels.

The victorious rebels quickly set up a new government and declared Panama an independent nation. The United States recognized the Republic of Panama two days later, and Hay began negotiating a new canal treaty with Panama's special envoy, Bunau-Varilla. The **Hay–Bunau-Varilla Treaty** gave the United States complete and unending sovereignty over a 10-mile-wide Canal Zone. President Roosevelt later boasted, "I took the Canal Zone and let Congress debate."

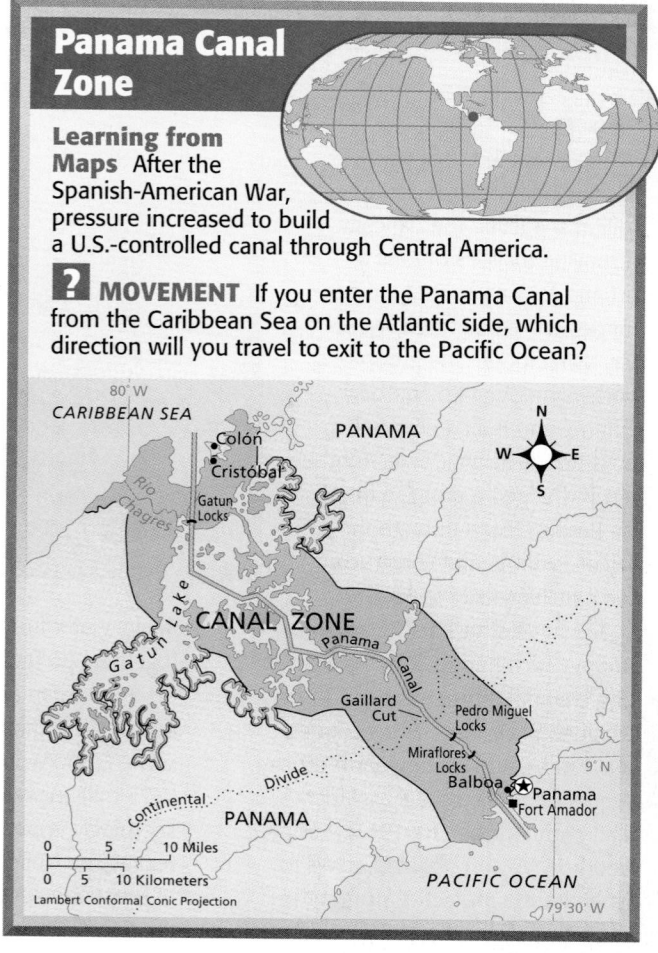

Panama Canal Zone

Learning from Maps After the Spanish-American War, pressure increased to build a U.S.-controlled canal through Central America.

? MOVEMENT If you enter the Panama Canal from the Caribbean Sea on the Atlantic side, which direction will you travel to exit to the Pacific Ocean?

This cartoon pokes fun at the many schemes that led to the building of the Panama Canal.

THE GRANGER COLLECTION, NEW YORK

Building the canal. Work on the canal began in 1904. However, harsh working conditions and shortages of labor and materials hampered U.S. efforts. The situation grew worse when a serious outbreak of yellow fever hit. By early 1905 the project had reached a near standstill.

To put the project back on track, Roosevelt appointed John F. Stevens as chief engineer and architect. Stevens tackled the technical problems and army colonel Dr. William C. Gorgas worked on improving living conditions. Gorgas applied to Panama the lessons he had learned in Cuba. By 1906 yellow fever had almost been eliminated. Malaria was under control by 1913.

Canal construction soon resumed. More than 60 giant steam shovels bit into the land, digging out nearly 160 trainloads of earth each day. More than 43,000 workers, many recruited from the British West Indies, built the canal. On August 15, 1914, the SS *Ancon* completed the first passage through the Panama Canal.

✔ **READING CHECK:** What were the major obstacles to building the Panama Canal?

Science & Technology

The Panama Canal

The Panama Canal was originally designed to be built at sea level. The difficulty of moving millions of tons of dirt and rock prompted a different design—an elevated waterway using locks. One group of workers dredged an approach channel and built a dam and locks on the Atlantic side. Another group dredged a passage from the Pacific Ocean through the Bay of Panama and constructed two smaller sets of locks.

The hardest task fell to another group, which had to blast an eight-mile-long channel through the mountainous Continental Divide. Geologic faults, heavy rains, and shifting earth caused frequent and often fatal avalanches. Finally, on October 10, 1913, President Woodrow Wilson signaled crews to dynamite the protective dike at the south end of the channel. In a dramatic

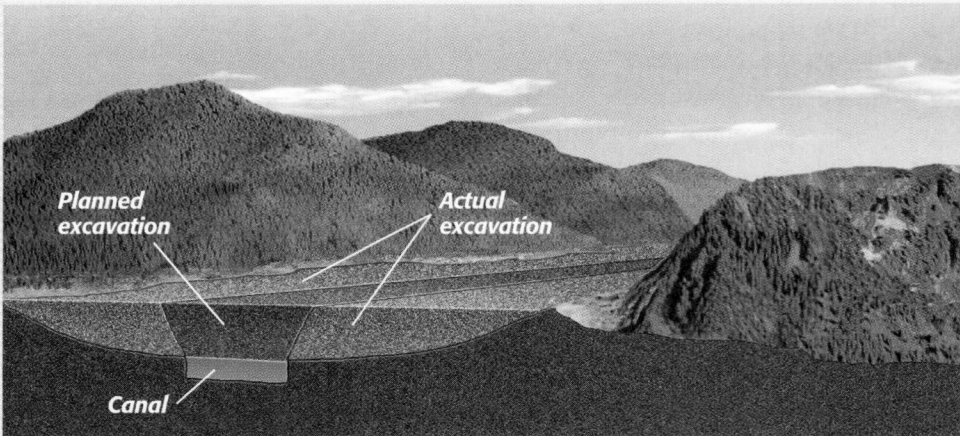

Planned excavation   Actual excavation

Canal

finale, water from the two sides rushed together—85 feet above sea level.

The human and economic costs of building the canal were staggering: some 6,000 workers died, and about $375 million was spent. However, the seemingly impossible had become a reality. The United States—and the rest of the world—now had a "Path Between the Seas."

Understanding Science and History

1. What was the most difficult obstacle that the builders of the Panama Canal had to overcome?
2. What was the cost of the canal in dollars and in lives?

Relations with Latin America

The United States has a long history of involvement in Latin America. Since the early 1800s it has sought to limit the influence of foreign nations there.

Applying the Monroe Doctrine.
Beginning in 1823 the Monroe Doctrine cast the United States as protector of the Western Hemisphere. For much of the century the doctrine served as little more than an idle threat. This changed following the Spanish-American War. Presidents Theodore Roosevelt, William H. Taft, and Woodrow Wilson actively enforced the Monroe Doctrine as a way to protect U.S. interests in Latin America.

Latin America's wealth of raw materials and its many potential laborers and consumers attracted a flood of European and American capital during the late 1800s. Much of this capital was in the form of high-interest bank loans. Many Latin American countries welcomed the loans, but the high interest rates made them difficult to repay. Foreign powers often intervened to collect the loans.

The Roosevelt Corollary.
President Roosevelt made it clear that he intended to enforce the Monroe Doctrine in 1904. The Dominican Republic was unable to repay its European lenders. Fearing that the Europeans would use force to collect the loans, he issued the **Roosevelt Corollary** to the Monroe Doctrine.

> 66 **If a nation . . . keeps order and pays its obligations, it need fear no interference from the United States. Chronic wrongdoing . . . in the Western Hemisphere . . . may force the United States, however reluctantly, . . . to the exercise of an international police power.** 99

Without seeking approval from any Latin American nation, Roosevelt had put into practice a West African proverb that he was fond of quoting. "Speak softly and carry a big stick; you will go far." The United States pledged to use armed forces to prevent any European country from seizing Dominican territory. To satisfy the Europeans' demand for repayment, the United States took control of collecting all Dominican customs duties. In 1916 civil unrest shook the Dominican Republic, and the U.S. government sent in marines. They remained until 1924. Some Latin American countries objected to Roosevelt's policy. Despite these protests, U.S. intervention in Latin America continued.

★ HISTORICAL DOCUMENTS ★

PRESIDENT THEODORE ROOSEVELT
The Roosevelt Corollary

Since it was first announced, the Monroe Doctrine had guided U.S. foreign policy in the Western Hemisphere. Events in the early 1900s led President Theodore Roosevelt to modify the Monroe Doctrine with the Roosevelt Corollary.

*I*t must be understood that under no circumstances will the United States use the Monroe Doctrine as a cloak for territorial aggression. We desire peace with all the world, but perhaps most of all with the other peoples of the American Continent. There are, of course, limits to the wrongs which any self-respecting nation can endure. It is always possible that wrong actions toward this Nation, or toward citizens of this Nation, in some State unable to keep order among its own people, unable to secure justice from outsiders, and unwilling to do justice to those outsiders who treat it well, may result in our having to take action to protect our rights; but such action will not be taken with a view to territorial aggression, and it will be taken at all only with extreme reluctance and when it has become evident that every other resource has been exhausted.

Intervention. These U.S. Marines were part of the force sent to Nicaragua by President Taft in 1912. *What does the photograph suggest about the type of fighting the marines did while in Nicaragua?*

Dollar diplomacy. Roosevelt's successor as president, William H. Taft, expanded U.S. influence in Latin America. Taft favored "substituting dollars for bullets"—economic influence for military force—as a means of protecting U.S. interests in Latin America. This policy came to be called **dollar diplomacy**. Taft suggested replacing European loans with American ones. He argued that increasing U.S. economic power would reduce the chances of European intervention. By 1914 American capital in Latin America had grown to over $1.6 billion, invested mainly in mines, railroads, and banana and sugar plantations.

Taft put dollar diplomacy to the test in Nicaragua. At the invitation of the Nicaraguan president, American bankers made loans totaling $1.5 million to Nicaragua in 1911. The following year, Taft sent more than 2,000 marines to crush a revolt and to protect the American investments.

Taft's successor, President Woodrow Wilson, believed that democratic governments, not U.S. dollars, would keep European powers out of Latin America. To keep Germany from taking control of strategic Caribbean territory, Wilson sent marines to several countries to put down rebellions and establish constitutional governments. In 1915, when revolution shook Haiti, Wilson sent in marines. Haiti was forced to accept a treaty that gave the United States powers in running the Haitian government, and the marines stayed until 1934. Some 1,500 Haitians died resisting U.S. control.

✔ **READING CHECK:** What was U.S. policy toward Latin America during the late 1800s and early 1900s?

SECTION 3 REVIEW

Define and explain the significance of the following terms:
Platt Amendment
protectorate
Foraker Act
Hay–Bunau-Varilla Treaty
Roosevelt Corollary
dollar diplomacy

Identify and explain the significance of the following individuals:
Leonard Wood
Philippe Bunau-Varilla

Locate and explain the significance of the following place:
Panama Canal

1. **Using Graphic Organizers** Copy the chart below. Use it to describe how Presidents Roosevelt, Taft, and Wilson interpreted the Monroe Doctrine. Then give an example of how each president applied the Monroe Doctrine in Latin America.

	Description	Example
Roosevelt		
Taft		
Wilson		

2. **Evaluating** How did the U.S. relationship with Cuba and Puerto Rico change after the Spanish-American War?
3. **Assessing Consequences** How did the growth in trade with Asia affect American public support for building a canal in Panama?
4. **Understanding Geography: Human-Environment Interaction** What obstacles did the environment of Panama present to building a canal, and how were they overcome?

Critical Thinking

5. Why did the United States support the Panamanian rebels and recognize the Republic of Panama?
   Consider:
   • U.S. interest in building a canal
   • the negotiations between the United States and Colombia
   • President Roosevelt's foreign policy

SECTION 4

Conflict with Mexico

OBJECTIVES

Read to understand:

1. what the major events of the Mexican Revolution were
2. what the causes of U.S. intervention in Mexico were
3. what the outcomes of the Mexican Revolution were

KEY TERMS

Mexican Revolution

KEY PEOPLE

Porfirio Díaz
Emiliano Zapata
Francisco Madero
Victoriano Huerta
Venustiano Carranza
Francisco "Pancho" Villa
John J. Pershing

KEY PLACES

Tampico
Veracruz
Columbus

Francisco Madero was a leader of the Mexican Revolution.

EYEWITNESSES TO History

❝ *A force of tyranny . . . oppresses us in such a manner that it has become intolerable. . . . The Mexican people . . . are thirsty for liberty, and . . . they reject with energy the Government of General Díaz. . . . Therefore, and in echo of the national will, I declare the late election illegal. . . . The people . . . anxiously call me from all parts of the country, to compel General Díaz by force of arms, to respect the national will.* ❞

—Francisco Madero

Francisco Madero ran for president of Mexico in the election of 1910. However, Porfirio Díaz—Mexico's longtime dictator—ordered Madero arrested and imprisoned. Madero fled to San Antonio, Texas, where on November 20, 1910, he issued the Plan of San Luis Potosi calling upon Mexicans to take up arms against the government. The war he began would last 10 years.

Mexico Under Díaz

Mexican president Porfirio Díaz had come to power in 1876 after Mexico had suffered almost 66 years of war and unrest. When Díaz took over, Mexico was in sad shape. The mines that had once been sources of great wealth were neglected or abandoned. Crime and violence was widespread. Díaz's first goal was to impose order, which he did by crushing or controlling his opponents.

Díaz's success in bringing order to Mexico attracted foreign investors. Confident that Díaz's government would protect their investments, foreigners poured millions of dollars into building Mexico's industries. Mexico had less than 500 miles of railroads when Díaz took office. By 1910 the country had 15,000 miles of railroads. Petroleum production began about the turn of the century and expanded rapidly. The mining industry, which had been largely inactive since colonial times, boomed again thanks to foreign capital. By 1908, American companies controlled three quarters of all Mexican mining operations.

By 1913 total foreign investments in Mexico amounted to some $2 billion, with more than half coming from the United States. However, although Díaz did improve Mexico's economy, foreign investors and Díaz's friends were the primary beneficiaries of this economic growth. Little trickled down to workers and peasants, and most Mexicans lived in poverty.

The Mexican Revolution

In 1910 Porfirio Díaz ran for re-election. Using force and fraud, he won his eighth term as president. However, opposition to Díaz's dictatorship had been growing. In the south, Emiliano Zapata led a rebel army that demanded land for the mostly American Indian peasant population. An American Indian himself, Zapata had

THE GRANGER COLLECTION, NEW YORK

Porfirio Díaz ruled Mexico for more than 25 years.

INTERPRETING THE VISUAL RECORD
The revolutionaries. Followers of Emiliano Zapata, known as *zapatistas,* march in August 1914. *What does the photograph reveal about the forces that fought the Mexican Revolution?*

been a tenant farmer on a sugar plantation. He is said to have been inspired to revolt because his master's horses lived in tiled stables while he and his family lived in dirt-floored shacks. Mexican intellectuals also organized against the Díaz government, reaching a high point with the 1909 publication of a book by Andrés Molina Enríquez. In his book Enríquez called for land redistribution and predicted that "it will come, whether in peace . . . or by revolution."

A wealthy landowner from northern Mexico, Francisco Madero was an unlikely candidate to unify the various opposition forces. He was considered a dreamer and an idealist, but his ideas sparked the **Mexican Revolution** that toppled the Díaz dictatorship. Rebel forces defeated Díaz's troops in key cities in northern and central Mexico. In May 1911, with mobs roaming the streets of Mexico City, Díaz resigned. He went into exile in Paris, where he died in 1915.

In Mexico's first democratic elections in 30 years, Madero easily won the presidency. The United States recognized Madero's government and placed an embargo on arms sales to his opponents. Madero tried to establish a democratic government but was soon overwhelmed by the very forces that he had unleashed in toppling Díaz.

Led by Díaz's nephew, supporters of the former dictator rebelled against Madero. For 10 days in February 1913 the roar of cannons echoed through the streets of Mexico City as rebels fought for control of the country. Many people died in the violence before Madero's commanding general, Victoriano Huerta (WER-tah), seized control of the government and restored calm. Huerta imprisoned Madero, who was then murdered when he allegedly attempted to escape. Four major revolu-

★ Changing Ways   Mexico and the United States

■ **Understanding Change** The economies of the United States and Mexico have been linked for many years. The United States used to ship more goods to Mexico than it received in return. In recent years that has changed. Fewer trade restrictions have boosted trade between the two countries. Mexico now produces many items for export to the United States. *Based on the information provided, how do you think the economic relationship between the United States and Mexico has changed?*

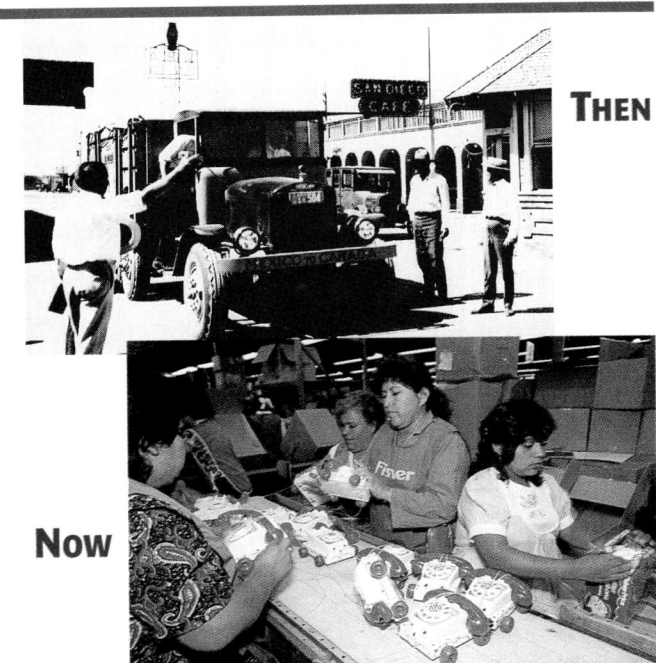

THEN

NOW

	THEN	NOW
Value of U.S. Exports to Mexico	$208 million	$71.4 billion
Value of Mexican Exports to the United States	$179 million	$85.9 billion

Sources: *Historical Statistics of the United States; Statistical Abstract of the United States: 1998.* Data reflect 1920 and 1997.

tionary armies continued to fight Huerta. However, their leaders—Venustiano Carranza (bay-noos-TYAHN-oh kahr-RAHN-sah), Francisco "Pancho" Villa, Emiliano Zapata, and Álvaro Obregón (oh-bray-GAWN)—were not united.

✔ **READING CHECK:** What were the major events of the Mexican Revolution?

U.S. Intervention

Victoriano Huerta soon gained recognition from most European countries. However, Francisco Madero's murder outraged Woodrow Wilson, the new U.S. president, who angrily refused to recognize Huerta. Wilson called Huerta's government a "government of butchers." In February 1914 Wilson lifted the embargo on arms sales to the revolutionary armies and adopted a policy of "watchful waiting." Wilson was looking for an opportunity to drive Huerta from power.

The USS **Dolphin** *was involved in an incident that gave President Wilson a reason to intervene in Mexico.*

Tampico. On April 9, 1914, an incident occurred that gave Wilson his opportunity. The USS *Dolphin* had been stationed in Mexican waters near the port of Tampico, which was under Huerta's control. Several crew members from the *Dolphin* went ashore for supplies and were arrested by soldiers loyal to Huerta. The Americans were quickly released unharmed, and the Mexicans' superior officer apologized for the incident. However, the U.S. admiral demanded a

66 **formal . . . apology for the act, together with your assurance that the officer responsible for it will receive severe punishment. Also that you publicly hoist the American flag in a prominent position on shore and salute it with twenty-one guns.** 99

President Wilson supported this unusual demand, which placed the United States in the ironic position of requesting an official apology from a government it did not recognize. On April 20 the president appeared before Congress asking for approval for the use of armed forces against Mexico. Congress moved swiftly, approving the use of force on April 22, but events in Mexico moved even faster.

The occupation of Veracruz. Before Congress could act, Wilson learned that a German ship transporting arms to Huerta was heading for Veracruz. He ordered the U.S. Navy to seize the port of Veracruz. On April 21, U.S. forces stopped the German ship. Under the cover of a naval bombardment, marines then landed at Veracruz. Huerta's forces had already withdrawn from the city, and only civilians and local authorities remained. During the brief struggle for control of the city, 19 marines were killed. Some 300 Mexicans died during the bombardment.

At this critical stage, Argentina, Brazil, and Chile—sometimes called the ABC powers—organized a conference to resolve the crisis. In June the conference proposed a plan that called for Huerta's resignation and the creation of a provisional government. Huerta refused, but his enemies were closing in. That July Huerta resigned and fled to Spain.

✔ **READING CHECK:** What factors led to the U.S. intervention in Mexico?

The Revolution Winds Down

By early 1915 Mexico was in chaos. Pancho Villa and Emiliano Zapata controlled nearly two thirds of the country. In March Venustiano Carranza re-entered Mexico City and assumed the title of "First Chief." He promised to protect American lives and property. The United States recognized his government in October 1915.

Pancho Villa's raid. In April 1915 Carranza's general, Álvaro Obregón, defeated Villa's troops in the central state of Guanajuato. After another major defeat, Villa disbanded his army. Villa was upset by the U.S. recognition of Carranza and decided to take revenge on the Americans. Villa explained his reasoning.

Pancho Villa (second from right) inspects his troops' rifles.

66 **We have decided not to fire a bullet more against Mexicans, our brothers, and to prepare and organize ourselves to attack the Americans in their own dens and make them know that Mexico is a land for the free and a tomb for thrones, crowns, and traitors.** 99

In March 1916 some of Villa's men crossed the border into New Mexico to raid Columbus, a small, isolated town. Striking at dawn, Villa's men burned and looted the town. In the battle 18 Americans—ten civilians and eight soldiers—and more than 100 of Villa's men were killed.

U.S. Interests in Latin America, Early 1900s

Learning from Maps U.S. policy in Latin America was aimed at protecting U.S. interests and keeping other European countries out of the area.

? **PLACE** Which countries were U.S. protectorates?

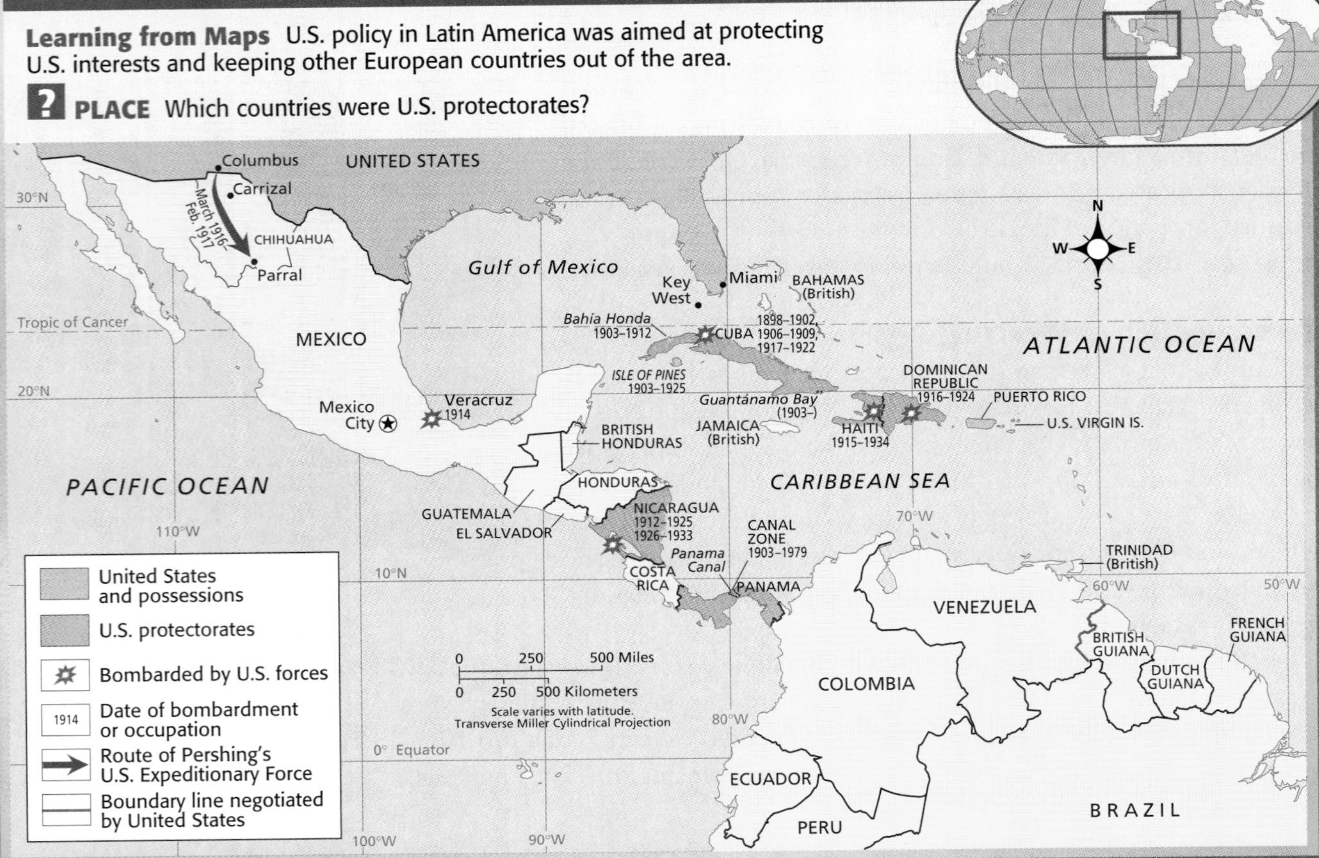

Columbus
Carrizal
March 1916–Feb. 1917
CHIHUAHUA
Parral
30°N
UNITED STATES
Gulf of Mexico
Key West
Miami
BAHAMAS (British)
Tropic of Cancer
Bahía Honda 1903–1912
1898–1902
CUBA 1906–1909, 1917–1922
ATLANTIC OCEAN
MEXICO
ISLE OF PINES 1903–1925
20°N
Mexico City
Veracruz 1914
Guantánamo Bay (1903–)
DOMINICAN REPUBLIC 1916–1924
PUERTO RICO
U.S. VIRGIN IS.
BRITISH HONDURAS
JAMAICA (British)
HAITI 1915–1934
PACIFIC OCEAN
110°W
HONDURAS
CARIBBEAN SEA
GUATEMALA
EL SALVADOR
NICARAGUA 1912–1925 1926–1933
Panama Canal
CANAL ZONE 1903–1979
70°W
TRINIDAD (British)
60°W
50°W
10°N
COSTA RICA
PANAMA
VENEZUELA
80°W
COLOMBIA
BRITISH GUIANA
DUTCH GUIANA
FRENCH GUIANA
0° Equator
ECUADOR
BRAZIL
100°W
90°W
PERU

Legend
- United States and possessions
- U.S. protectorates
- ☼ Bombarded by U.S. forces
- 1914 Date of bombardment or occupation
- → Route of Pershing's U.S. Expeditionary Force
- Boundary line negotiated by United States

0   250   500 Miles
0   250   500 Kilometers
Scale varies with latitude.
Transverse Miller Cylindrical Projection

Pursuing Pancho Villa. Without requesting approval from the Carranza government, President Wilson ordered a military expedition into Mexico to capture Villa "dead or alive." A week after Villa's raid on Columbus, General John J. Pershing led his forces into Chihuahua, Villa's home state. Although Pershing later increased his troop size to more than 10,000 men, Villa still eluded capture. The deeper Pershing pushed into Mexican territory, the more the Mexicans resented the Americans.

When one of Pershing's cavalry units attempted to pass through the town of Carrizal, the commander of the Mexican garrison refused passage. Pershing chose to enter Carrizal rather than bypass the town, and a battle followed.

By early September 1916 nearly 150,000 U.S. National Guardsmen were stationed along the Mexican border. Wilson realized that the threat of war increased with each day U.S. troops remained in Mexico. The president finally ordered U.S. troops withdrawn in January 1917.

THE GRANGER COLLECTION, NEW YORK

General John Pershing (center) led the unsuccessful expedition to capture Pancho Villa.

Carranza in power. With Pancho Villa in hiding and Emiliano Zapata contained in the south, Venustiano Carranza called a constitutional convention in December 1916. After two months of negotiations, a new constitution was completed and put into effect on February 5, 1917. This new constitution contained several revolutionary ideas. It placed the interests of common welfare above individual rights and provided protection for workers. This protection included an eight-hour workday, an end to child labor, and the right to form unions and bargain collectively.

Most significant to the United States was the constitution's declaration that the nation owned all mineral, oil, and water rights. This part of the constitution would have important effects on American oil companies operating in Mexico in the 1930s.

✔ **READING CHECK:** What were the outcomes of the Mexican Revolution?

SECTION 4 REVIEW

Define and explain the significance of the following term:
Mexican Revolution

Identify and explain the significance of the following individuals:
Porfirio Díaz   John J. Pershing
Emiliano Zapata
Francisco Madero
Victoriano Huerta
Venustiano Carranza
Francisco "Pancho" Villa

Locate and explain the significance of the following places:
Tampico   Columbus
Veracruz

1. **Using Graphic Organizers** Copy the chart below. Use it to list various leaders who fought for control of Mexico and what happened to them.

Leader		What Happened?
	→	
	→	
	→	
	→	
	→	

2. **Recognizing Point of View** How did the Mexican Revolution affect American views of Mexico?
3. **Taking a Stand** Did the United States have the right to stop a German ship from delivering its cargo to Mexico? Explain your answer.
4. **Synthesizing** How did U.S. intervention both help and hurt Mexico?

Critical Thinking

5. Do you think the Mexican Revolution resulted in a positive outcome for Mexico? Explain your answer.
   Consider:
   • the conditions under Porfirio Diaz
   • the goals of the revolutionary leaders
   • the government established by Venustiano Carranza

CHAPTER 20

Review

Creating a Time Line

Copy the time line below onto a sheet of paper. Complete the time line by filling in the events and dates from the chapter that you think were most significant. Pick three events and explain why you think they were significant.

1900   **1910**   **1920**

Writing a Summary

Using the Reading Checks as a guide, write an overview of the events in the chapter.

Identifying People and Ideas

Identify the following terms or individuals and explain their significance.

1. imperialism
2. Liliuokalani
3. spheres of influence
4. John Hay
5. José Martí
6. Emilio Aguinaldo
7. Leonard Wood
8. dollar diplomacy
9. Porfirio Díaz
10. Venustiano Carranza

Understanding Main Ideas

SECTION 1
1. What led industrialized nations to seek overseas colonies in the late 1800s and early 1900s?

SECTION 2
2. What were the major causes of the Spanish-American War?

SECTION 3
3. What steps did the United States take to build the Panama Canal?

SECTION 4
4. Who were the major leaders that participated in the Mexican Revolution?
5. How and why did the United States intervene in Mexico?

Reviewing Themes

1. **Global Relations** Why was the U.S. interested in controlling Cuba?
2. **Economic Development** How did foreign investors affect Mexico's economy?
3. **Democratic Values** Why might some people argue that U.S. actions in the Philippines conflicted with democratic principles?

Thinking Critically

1. **Evaluating** Why did the U.S. government oppose the revolution led by Emilio Aguinaldo in the Philippines but support the revolution led by Venustiano Carranza in Mexico?
2. **Analyzing** Why was Japan not divided into European spheres of influence like China?
3. **Hypothesizing** What might have been the effect on U.S. relations with Cuba, Puerto Rico, and the Philippines if the United States had adopted an Open Door Policy toward each of those countries?
4. **Using Historical Imagination** Imagine that President Cleveland had reinstated Liliuokalani as queen of Hawaii. Write a paragraph describing what might have happened to Hawaii.
5. **Assessing Consequences** How does the Spanish-American War continue to affect the United States today?

Writing About History

Writing to Explain Write an essay that traces the negotiations and events that helped the United States build and control the Panama Canal. Use the following graphic organizer to help you prepare your essay.

1. A canal across Panama is proposed.
2.
3.
4.
5. United States builds Panama Canal.

Strategies for Success

Review the **Strategies for Success** on *Interpreting Economic Data.* Then study the graph below and answer the following questions.

1. What was the value of U.S. exports in 1885? in 1915?
2. By how much did U.S. imports increase between 1895 and 1915?

U.S. Trade, 1885–1915

Value (in billions of dollars)

- Imports
- Exports

Source: *Historical Statistics of the United States*

Linking History and Geography

Study the map below. How many islands in the Pacific were under U.S. control by 1900?

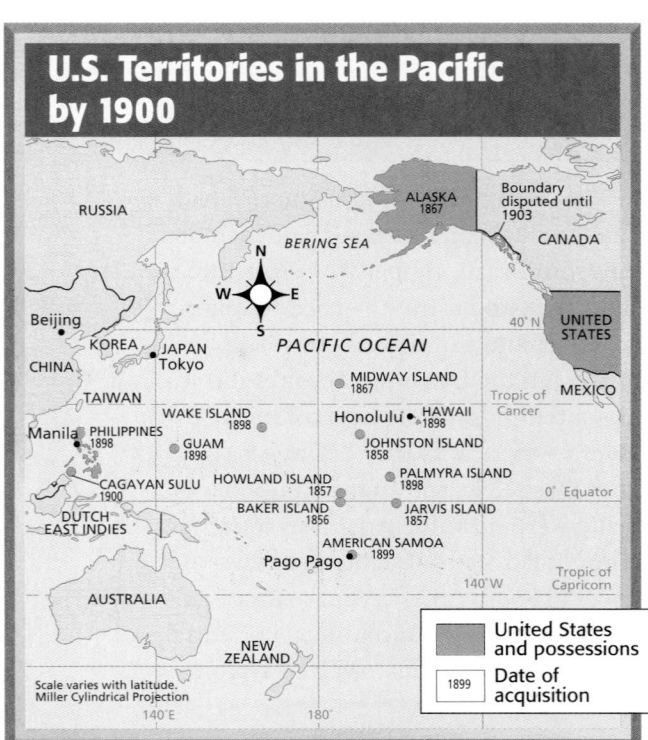

U.S. Territories in the Pacific by 1900

RUSSIA

ALASKA 1867 — Boundary disputed until 1903

BERING SEA

CANADA

Beijing

CHINA — KOREA — JAPAN Tokyo

PACIFIC OCEAN

40°N — UNITED STATES

TAIWAN

MIDWAY ISLAND 1867 — MEXICO — Tropic of Cancer

WAKE ISLAND 1898 — HAWAII 1898 — Honolulu

Manila — PHILIPPINES 1898 — GUAM 1898 — JOHNSTON ISLAND 1858

CAGAYAN SULU 1900 — HOWLAND ISLAND 1857 — PALMYRA ISLAND 1898 — 0° Equator

DUTCH EAST INDIES — BAKER ISLAND 1856 — JARVIS ISLAND 1857

AMERICAN SAMOA 1899 — Pago Pago — 140°W — Tropic of Capricorn

AUSTRALIA

NEW ZEALAND

Scale varies with latitude. Miller Cylindrical Projection

140°E — 180°

United States and possessions

1899 Date of acquisition

internet connect

TOPIC: Panama Canal
GO TO: go.hrw.com
KEYWORD: SD1 Panama

Accessing the Internet through the HRW Web site, research the construction of the Panama Canal. Then create a poster in which you outline the steps in the canal's construction. Your display should include illustrations, graphics, and a table with at least 10 statistics about the canal.

BUILDING YOUR PORTFOLIO

Complete one or more of the following projects independently or cooperatively.

1 Global Relations

Imagine that you are a member of the State Department in the early 1900s. **Write a memorandum** to the president that addresses concerns about U.S. relations with

China, Japan, South America, Mexico, or Spain. Your memorandum should mention specific issues dealing with each country or region.

2 Cultural Diversity

Imagine that you are a U.S. Army recruiting officer in 1898. **Create a series of recruiting posters** aimed at attracting a wide range of recruits—such as American Indians, college students, cowboys, and would-be adventurers—to serve in the Spanish-American War.

3 Democratic Values

Imagine that you are a descendant of Queen Liliuokalani living in Hawaii today. **Plan a campaign to raise awareness** about Hawaii's history as an independent nation.

The United States and the World

By 1914, on the eve of World War I, many nations were connected to one another in a complex web of economic trade and investment. The vast majority of this economic activity was controlled by European nations, particularly Great Britain. Compared to the European empires, the United States had relatively little financial investment in other countries. Yet even the United States expanded its economic and political involvement in foreign nations during this period.

The United States and the World, 1900–1914

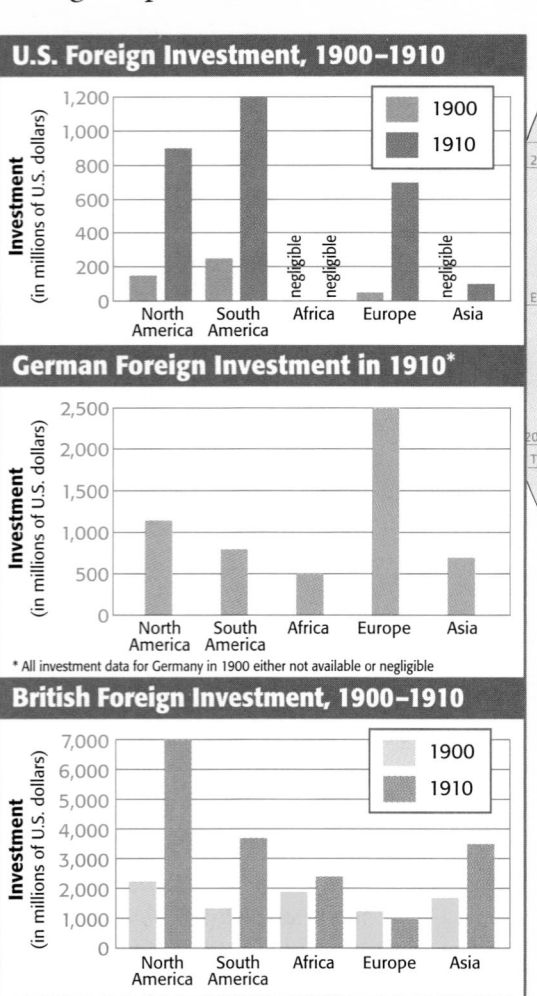

U.S. Foreign Investment, 1900–1910

Investment (in millions of U.S. dollars)

Legend: 1900, 1910

- North America: 1900 ≈ 150, 1910 ≈ 900
- South America: 1900 ≈ 250, 1910 ≈ 1,200
- Africa: negligible / negligible
- Europe: 1900 ≈ 50, 1910 ≈ 700
- Asia: negligible / 1910 ≈ 100

German Foreign Investment in 1910*

Investment (in millions of U.S. dollars)

- North America ≈ 1,150
- South America ≈ 800
- Africa ≈ 500
- Europe ≈ 2,500
- Asia ≈ 700

* All investment data for Germany in 1900 either not available or negligible

British Foreign Investment, 1900–1910

Investment (in millions of U.S. dollars)

Legend: 1900, 1910

- North America: 1900 ≈ 2,200, 1910 ≈ 7,000
- South America: 1900 ≈ 1,350, 1910 ≈ 3,700
- Africa: 1900 ≈ 1,900, 1910 ≈ 2,400
- Europe: 1900 ≈ 1,200, 1910 ≈ 1,100
- Asia: 1900 ≈ 1,650, 1910 ≈ 3,500

Source: *Rand McNally Atlas of World History*

South America. South America had many valuable resources. These included tin from Brazil, copper from Argentina and Peru, and nitrates—used to make fertilizer and explosives—from Chile. Although the European empires did not attempt to create new colonies in South America, as they did in Africa, they invested heavily in the economies of self-governing South American countries. The United States also increased investment in South America, but many of its investments were concentrated in Central America and the Panama Canal region.

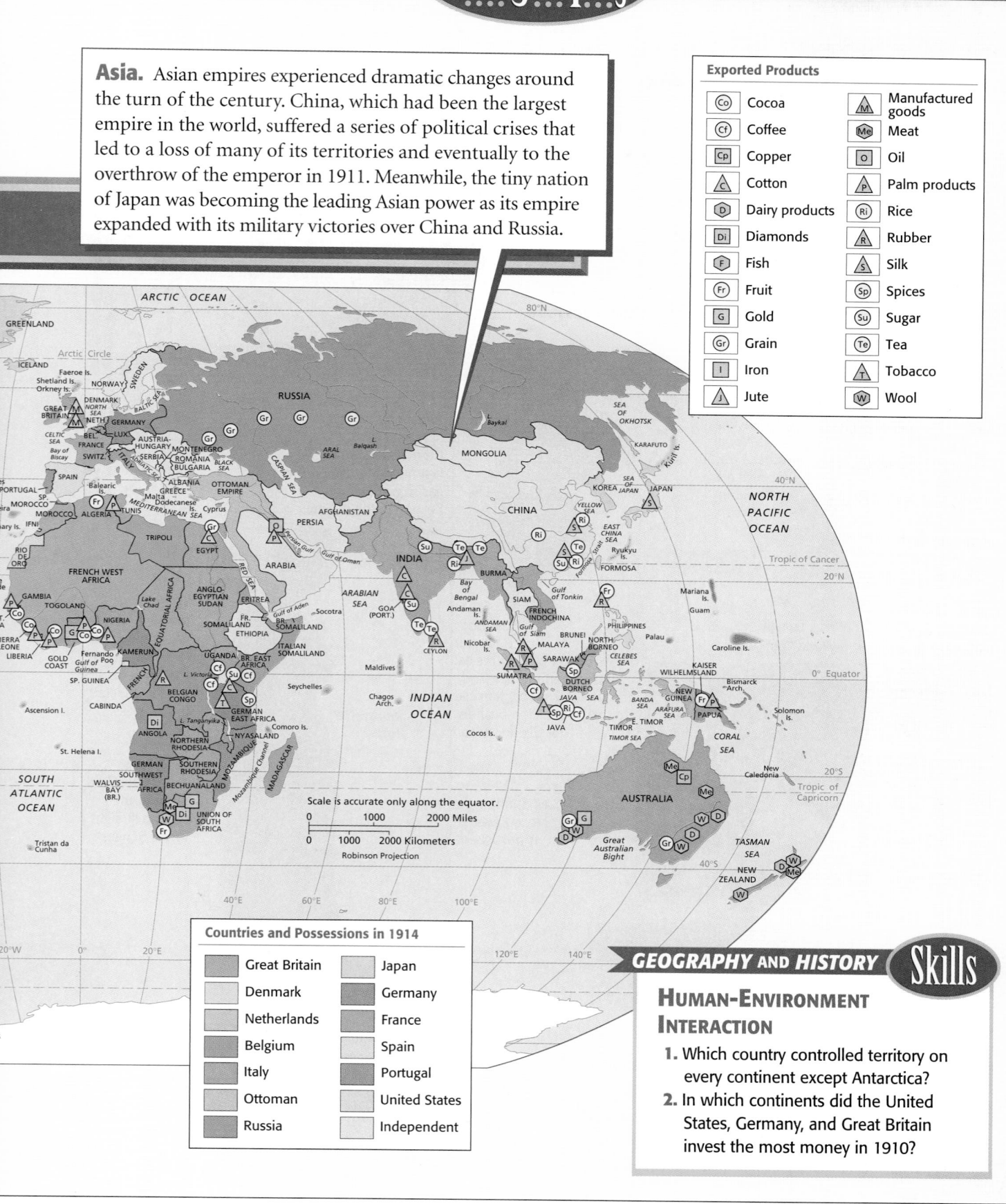

Asia. Asian empires experienced dramatic changes around the turn of the century. China, which had been the largest empire in the world, suffered a series of political crises that led to a loss of many of its territories and eventually to the overthrow of the emperor in 1911. Meanwhile, the tiny nation of Japan was becoming the leading Asian power as its empire expanded with its military victories over China and Russia.

Exported Products

Co	Cocoa	M	Manufactured goods
Cf	Coffee	Me	Meat
Cp	Copper	O	Oil
C	Cotton	P	Palm products
D	Dairy products	Ri	Rice
Di	Diamonds	R	Rubber
F	Fish	S	Silk
Fr	Fruit	Sp	Spices
G	Gold	Su	Sugar
Gr	Grain	Te	Tea
I	Iron	T	Tobacco
Ju	Jute	W	Wool

Countries and Possessions in 1914

Great Britain	Japan
Denmark	Germany
Netherlands	France
Belgium	Spain
Italy	Portugal
Ottoman	United States
Russia	Independent

GEOGRAPHY AND HISTORY Skills

HUMAN-ENVIRONMENT INTERACTION

1. Which country controlled territory on every continent except Antarctica?
2. In which continents did the United States, Germany, and Great Britain invest the most money in 1910?

1914–1920
World War I

Panama Canal brochure

World War I tanks

World War I gas mask

1914
Science and Technology
The Panama Canal opens to traffic.

1914
Daily Life
The first national Mother's Day is declared by President Wilson.

1915
Science and Technology
Germany becomes the first nation to use poison gas in warfare at the Second Battle of Ypres.

1916
Science and Technology
Tanks are used in battle for the first time at the Battle of the Somme.

1914

1915

1916

German troops traveling to war

THE GRANGER COLLECTION, NEW YORK

1914
World Events
World War I begins.

1915
Business and Finance
Driven by high prices and wartime demand, the U.S. wheat harvest tops 1 million bushels for the first time.

1915
The Arts
Carl Sandburg's *Chicago Poems* is published.

Jeannette Rankin

1916
Politics
Montana representative Jeannette Rankin is the first woman elected to Congress.

1916
Daily Life
The Boston Red Sox win their second straight World Series.

Before You Read

Build on What You Know

During the 1800s several empires dominated Europe and much of the world. Nations scrambled to gain control of colonies and their natural resources to fuel the Industrial Revolution. European nations built up strong rivalries, which ultimately helped lead to war. In this chapter you will learn how the United States tried to remain neutral when war swept Europe. Once the United States joined the Allied cause in 1917, the government quickly mobilized the economy and built public support for the war.

1917
Business and Finance
U.S. income tax revenue exceeds revenue from customs duties for the first time.

1917
Daily Life
The Selective Service Act is passed.

1917
Business and Finance
U.S. automakers produce 1,745,792 automobiles, more than three times as many as were made in 1914.

The U.S. secretary of war draws numbers for the draft lottery.

The Grand Canyon

1918
World Events
U.S. troops join the fighting in Europe.

1919
Daily Life
The Grand Canyon National Park is established.

1917   **1918**   **1919**   **1920**

1917
Business and Finance
Millionaires in the United States number more than 40,000—up from 4,000 in 1892.

1917
Politics
The U.S. Congress declares war on Germany.

1919
World Events
World leaders sign the Treaty of Versailles.

1919
Politics
The U.S. Senate rejects the Treaty of Versailles.

The Paris Peace Conference meeting in the Hall of Mirrors at Versailles

Think About Themes

Themes Journal

Decide whether you agree or disagree with the following statements. Note why in your journal.

Global Relations A country should consider only its own interests in deciding whether to go to war.

Economic Development Fighting in an overseas military conflict can help improve a nation's economy at home.

Democratic Values During wartime, a government has the right to limit the individual liberties of citizens.

SECTION 1

World War I Breaks Out

OBJECTIVES

Read to understand:

1. what the major causes of unrest in Europe were
2. what the results of the early fighting in the war were
3. why the war settled into a stalemate

KEY TERMS

militarism
Allied Powers
Central Powers
First Battle of the Marne
no-man's-land
trench warfare
Battle of the Somme

KEY PEOPLE

Franz Ferdinand
Gavrilo Princip
Manfred von Richthofen
Edward Rickenbacker

KEY PLACES

Balkans
Austria-Hungary
Bosnia and Herzegovina
Belgium

EYEWITNESSES TO History

❝ *As I write, Germany is reported to have declared war against Russia and France, and the participation of England on the one side and of Italy on the other seems imminent [close at hand]. Nothing like it has occurred since the great Napoleonic wars, and with modern armaments and larger populations nothing has occurred like it since the world began. . . . All of Europe is to be a battleground. . . . The future looks dark indeed.* ❞
—**William Howard Taft**

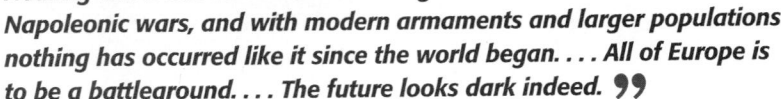

World War I artillery

Former president William Howard Taft published "A Message to the People of the United States" in August 1914. He expressed the surprise and fear many Americans felt at the news that Europe was at war. Few Americans had seen the war coming. Europe had appeared peaceful for more than 40 years. However, while the Wilson administration was wrestling with problems created by the Mexican Revolution, tensions in Europe exploded into global war.

The Causes of the War

One longterm cause of the war lay in the growth of nationalism throughout Europe. In the 1860s nationalism united Italians in their fight to free themselves from Austrian rule. Nationalism also helped Otto von Bismarck join the German states into a single nation in the 1870s.

Nationalism and territorial rivalries. Nationalism was particularly strong in the central European region of the Balkans. This region was so unstable that it was called the powder keg of Europe. The Ottoman Empire (Turkey) gained control of the Balkans in the 1400s and ruled the area until the 1800s. By then the region's four main ethnic groups—Albanians, Greeks, Romanians, and Slavs—were each struggling for independence. Greece began a successful revolt in the 1820s, and Romania followed in 1859. Following a war between Russia and the Ottoman Empire in 1878, the Bulgarians, Montenegrins, and Serbs each staked their claims to nationhood. Soon after, Austria-Hungary occupied the small Balkan kingdoms of Bosnia and Herzegovina (often just called Bosnia).

The newly independent Serbia saw Bosnia as part of its rightful territory. Austria-Hungary's 1908 annexation of the territories produced open hostility. Serbia's growing strength threatened Austria-Hungary's control of its territories in the Balkans. This encouraged the Slavs to push for independence. Austro-Hungarian chief of staff Baron Conrad von Hötzendorf foresaw a major conflict.

This 1912 British cartoon shows European leaders trying to keep a lid on trouble in the Balkans.

THE BOILING POINT

> **66** The unification of the South Slav[s] . . . is one of the powerful national movements which can neither be ignored nor kept down. The question can only be, whether that unification will take place within the boundaries of the Monarchy [the Austro-Hungarian Empire]—that is, at the expense of Serbia's independence—or under Serbia's leadership at the expense of the Monarchy. **99**

Militarism and alliances. Because large European countries frequently overpowered smaller ones, relations between nations were characterized by a strong spirit of **militarism**, or the glorification of military strength. Leaders of the major European powers believed that disputes would ultimately be settled on the battlefield. As a result, they engaged in an arms race in which they tried to develop larger armies and more powerful weapons than their rivals. In this dangerous atmosphere, leaders formed alliances with other nations, each promising to aid the other in case of attack by a third power.

Germany had a longtime ally in Austria. France's 1892 alliance with Russia threatened to surround Germany with enemies. Eventually Italy joined Austria-Hungary and Germany in one alliance, and Great Britain joined France and Russia in another. The alliances avoided war for a time, but created the risk that a minor incident could trigger a major war.

✔ **READING CHECK:** What were the major causes of unrest in Europe?

The Great War Begins

In June 1914 Archduke Franz Ferdinand, the heir to the Austro-Hungarian throne, visited the Bosnian capital, Sarajevo (sahr-uh-YAY-voh). As the archduke rode through the city streets, Serbian nationalist Gavrilo Princip (PREENT-seep) stepped out of the crowd. He fired two shots, killing the archduke and his wife, Sophie.

Austria-Hungary quickly declared war on Serbia. Germany immediately offered its support. Russia, with a large Slav population of its own, was compelled to honor its alliance with Serbia. The alliance system soon turned a local conflict into a global war. The **Allied Powers** of Britain, France, and Russia were pitted against the **Central Powers** of Germany, Austria-Hungary, the Ottoman Empire, and Bulgaria. Italy remained neutral until 1915, when it joined the Allies. Eventually some 30 nations took sides in what became known as the Great War.

Germany's military strategy called for a massive strike against France to defeat it quickly, leaving British forces stranded on the other side of the English Channel. With France and Britain out of

Bosnia and Herzegovina—a nation about the size of West Virginia—has been a place of unrest for many years. After being controlled by various kingdoms for several centuries, Bosnia fought for and gained its independence in about 1200. It remained independent until 1463, when it was conquered by the Ottoman Turks. Bosnia remained under Ottoman rule for the next 400 years. In 1878 Austria-Hungary took control of Bosnia from the Turks.

This man in Gorazde, Bosnia, is gathering supplies dropped from planes.

At the end of World War I, Serbia's ruler was crowned king of the newly created nation of Yugoslavia, which included Bosnia. After World War II, Yugoslavia was reorganized into six republics—Bosnia and Herzegovina, Croatia, Macedonia, Montenegro, Serbia, and Slovenia.

In the late 1980s Yugoslavia's government began to disintegrate. Serbian president Slobodan Milosevic sought to create a Greater Serbia, uniting all Serbs in a single state under his leadership. At that time Bosnia's population of about 4 million included three ethnic groups: Croats, Serbs, and Slavic Muslims. Early in 1992 some 70 percent of the country's voters—including many Bosnian Serbs—voted for independence from the rest of Yugoslavia. That March, Serbian forces began seizing territory in northern and eastern Bosnia. They drove out much of the non-Serbian population. The United States and most of the international community recognized Bosnia's independence in April 1992. On May 22, Bosnia was admitted as a full member of the United Nations. Fighting continued, however, until a 1994 treaty ended the civil war. The United Nations sent in a peacekeeping force to help the country maintain peace.

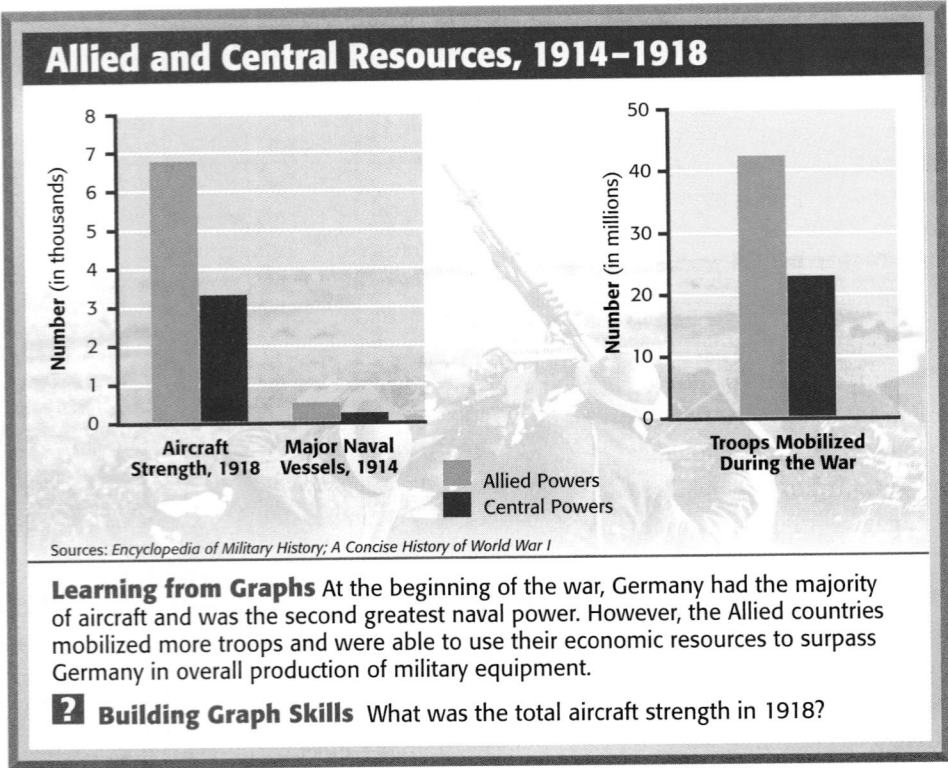

Allied and Central Resources, 1914–1918

Aircraft Strength, 1918 / **Major Naval Vessels, 1914** (Number in thousands, 0–8)

Troops Mobilized During the War (Number in millions, 0–50)

Allied Powers
Central Powers

Sources: *Encyclopedia of Military History; A Concise History of World War I*

Learning from Graphs At the beginning of the war, Germany had the majority of aircraft and was the second greatest naval power. However, the Allied countries mobilized more troops and were able to use their economic resources to surpass Germany in overall production of military equipment.

❓ **Building Graph Skills** What was the total aircraft strength in 1918?

HOLT RESEARCHER

Read More About It

Free Find:

Trench Warfare

After learning about trench warfare on the Holt Researcher CD–ROM, imagine that you are a soldier fighting on the western front. Write a letter home describing your experiences.

Soldiers faced horrible conditions in World War I trenches.

the war, Germany would then focus its attention on defeating Russia in the east. Known as the Schlieffen Plan, this strategy called for German forces to avoid the heavily defended French-German border by invading France through the neutral country of Belgium.

German troops poured into Belgium and France on August 3, 1914. The small Belgian army put up unexpectedly strong resistance, giving the French and British time to rush troops into the battle. The German invasion forced the Allies back to the Marne River in northeastern France. That September, during the **First Battle of the Marne**, the Allies pushed the German lines back some 40 miles. As 1914 drew to a close, leaders of both sides realized that there would be no quick victory.

✔ **READING CHECK:** What were the results of the early fighting in the war?

The War Reaches a Stalemate

Leaders had thought that this war would resemble earlier conflicts—with cavalry charges, decisive battles, and a quick victory. German kaiser Wilhelm II told troops they would be home "before the leaves have fallen from the trees." Both sides threw troops and arms into battle, expecting to achieve a clear victory. Instead, each side battered and bloodied the other in a brutal stalemate.

Trench warfare. By early 1915 both armies were holed up in trenches along a front running for hundreds of miles from the North Sea to the border of Switzerland. Separating the two sides was a thin strip of bombed-out territory—strewn with barbed wire and land mines—called **no-man's-land**. A new type of fighting, known as **trench warfare**, emerged on the western front. Battles began with massive artillery barrages. Then soldiers went "over the top" of the trenches and charged across the no-man's-land toward the enemy trenches. As they ran, thousands of soldiers were cut down by a hail of machine-gun fire.

The war remained locked in a stalemate throughout 1915. Determined to break out, each side prepared massive offensives for 1916. In February 1916 the Germans launched a huge offensive designed to "bleed the French army white" by causing unsustainable casualties. The Germans targeted the fortified French city of Verdun because they knew the French would feel compelled to defend it. The battle began with a staggering 21-hour artillery barrage in which more than 1 million shells were fired. Then the 1 million soldiers of the German Fifth Army advanced on some 200,000 French defenders. For months the battle raged back and forth.

In July the Allied Powers launched an offensive near the Somme River in northern France. They had the same goal as the German attack on Verdun—to exhaust the enemy's reserves. In the **Battle of the Somme**, British forces suffered some 60,000 casualties in a single day. This four-month-long battle left more than 1 million dead

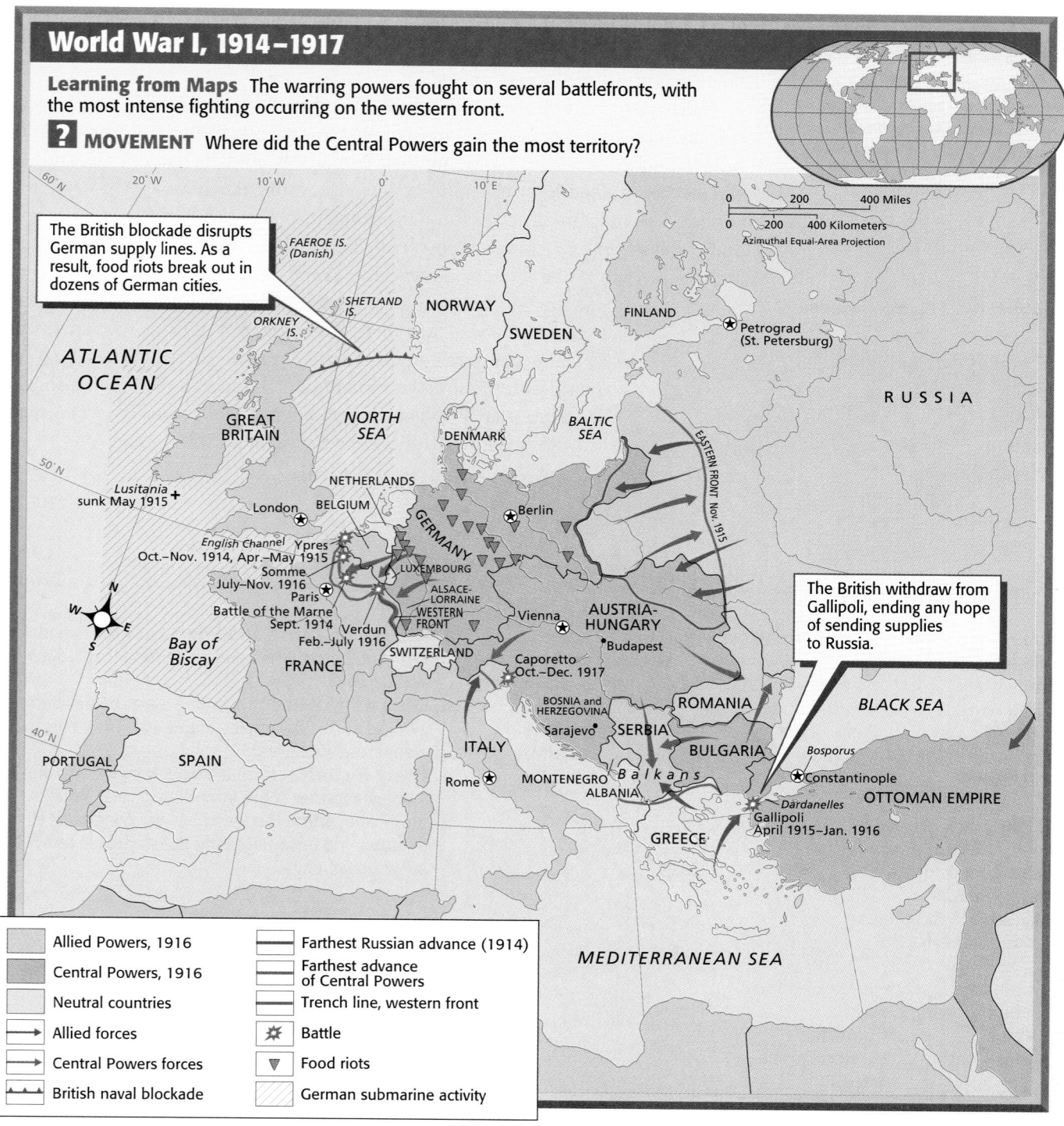

World War I, 1914–1917

Learning from Maps The warring powers fought on several battlefronts, with the most intense fighting occurring on the western front.

? MOVEMENT Where did the Central Powers gain the most territory?

The British blockade disrupts German supply lines. As a result, food riots break out in dozens of German cities.

The British withdraw from Gallipoli, ending any hope of sending supplies to Russia.

0 200 400 Miles
0 200 400 Kilometers
Azimuthal Equal-Area Projection

FAEROE IS. (Danish)
SHETLAND IS.
ORKNEY IS.
NORWAY
SWEDEN
FINLAND
Petrograd (St. Petersburg)
ATLANTIC OCEAN
GREAT BRITAIN
NORTH SEA
BALTIC SEA
RUSSIA
DENMARK
Lusitania sunk May 1915
London
NETHERLANDS
BELGIUM
GERMANY
Berlin
EASTERN FRONT Nov. 1915
English Channel
Ypres Oct.–Nov. 1914, Apr.–May 1915
Somme July–Nov. 1916
Paris
Battle of the Marne Sept. 1914
LUXEMBOURG
ALSACE-LORRAINE
WESTERN FRONT
Verdun Feb.–July 1916
SWITZERLAND
Vienna
AUSTRIA-HUNGARY
Budapest
Bay of Biscay
FRANCE
Caporetto Oct.–Dec. 1917
BOSNIA and HERZEGOVINA
Sarajevo
SERBIA
Balkans
ROMANIA
BLACK SEA
Bosporus
BULGARIA
Constantinople
PORTUGAL
SPAIN
ITALY
Rome
MONTENEGRO
ALBANIA
GREECE
Dardanelles
Gallipoli April 1915–Jan. 1916
OTTOMAN EMPIRE
MEDITERRANEAN SEA

Allied Powers, 1916
Central Powers, 1916
Neutral countries
Allied forces
Central Powers forces
British naval blockade
Farthest Russian advance (1914)
Farthest advance of Central Powers
Trench line, western front
Battle
Food riots
German submarine activity

Many Allied ships like this one were sunk by torpedoes fired from German submarines.

and wounded. At Verdun, the longest battle of the war, the two sides suffered nearly 1 million more casualties, half of them deaths.

Even for those who avoided death, the trenches were a living nightmare. Rats and lice plagued the soldiers. Rain flooded the trenches, drenching the soldiers in mud. The dead often lay unburied for days. Unsanitary conditions bred disease and sickness that claimed nearly as many lives as the fighting did.

New weapons. Deadly new weapons added to the horror of trench warfare. Machine guns fired hundreds of rounds per minute. Partly to counter the machine gun's deadly impact, the Allies introduced tanks at the Battle of the Somme. One British soldier reported that tanks scared the Germans "out of their wits" and made them "scuttle like frightened rabbits."

Perhaps the most feared new weapon introduced during World War I was poison gas. It could be released as a cloud of mist that silently drifted over the trenches or be launched inside an exploding shell. Either way, soldiers had only seconds to slip on their gas masks or else suffer a slow, suffocating death.

Modern machines such as submarines and airplanes brought terror to the seas and the skies. Submarines slipped silently beneath the waves to sink commercial and military ships with little or no warning. Some airplane pilots engaged enemy planes in aerobatic dogfights. Although these skirmishes did little to influence the

A World War I German airplane

course of the war, they made celebrities out of those who survived. Skilled pilots were known as aces. The most successful was the German Baron Manfred von Richthofen, known as the Red Baron. He had a reported 80 kills, or enemy aircraft shot down. The top American ace was Edward Rickenbacker, with 26 kills.

✔ **READING CHECK:** What led to the stalemate on the battlefields?

SECTION 1 REVIEW

Define and explain the significance of the following terms:
militarism
Allied Powers
Central Powers
First Battle of the Marne
no-man's-land
trench warfare
Battle of the Somme

Identify and explain the significance of the following individuals:
Franz Ferdinand
Gavrilo Princip
Manfred von Richthofen
Edward Rickenbacker

Locate and explain the importance of the following places:
Balkans
Austria-Hungary
Bosnia and Herzegovina
Belgium

1. **Using Graphic Organizers** Copy the diagram below. Use it to list the factors that contributed to the outbreak of World War I.

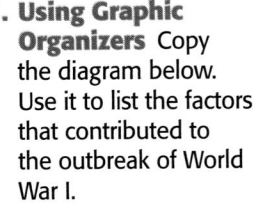

World War I begins

2. **Identifying Cause and Effect** How did nationalism contribute to the unrest in Europe that led to World War I?

3. **Comparing and Contrasting** What battle strategies did each side employ in the war? How effective were these strategies?

4. **Using Historical Imagination** Imagine you are a British reporter at the front during 1916. Write a newspaper article that describes the conditions at the front and encourages the British people to continue fighting.

Critical Thinking

5. What led to the stalemate on the western front?
   Consider:
   • new weapons used during the war
   • the tactics of trench warfare
   • the transportation available to the opposing sides

SECTION 2

The United States Goes to War

OBJECTIVES

Read to understand:

1. what challenges the United States faced while trying to remain neutral
2. what events led to U.S. entry into the war
3. how the United States prepared its military for World War I
4. what types of experiences Americans had while serving in Europe

KEY TERMS

Sussex pledge
National Defense Act
Zimmerman Note
Selective Service Act
convoy system

KEY PEOPLE

Robert Lansing
Jeannette Rankin
John J. Pershing

EYEWITNESSES TO History

❝ *In August, 1914, I was a cowboy on a ranch in the interior of British Columbia. . . . An early Saturday morning in August found me jogging slowly along the trail to Dog Creek . . . our post office and trading center. . . . We had heard rumors of a war in Europe. We all talked it over in the evening and decided it was another one of those fights that were always starting in the Balkans. One had just been finished a few months before and we thought it was about time another was underway so we gave the matter no particular thought. But when I got within sight of Dog Creek I knew something was up. The first thing I heard was that . . . the Germans were fighting. . . . Then a big Indian came up to me . . . and told me England's . . . going to war, or had gone. He wasn't certain which, but he was going too. Would I? I laughed at him. 'What do you mean, go to war?' I asked him. I wasn't English; I wasn't Canadian. I was from the good old U. S. A. And from all we could understand the States were neutral. So, I reasoned, I ought to be neutral too.* ❞

—Joseph Smith

World War I soldiers carried all the equipment they needed on their backs.

After some thought, Joseph Smith decided to join his Canadian friends and volunteered to fight. Like many people, Smith and his friends first "regarded the whole war . . . as more or less of a lark." Enthusiasm for the glory of war faded quickly when soldiers actually witnessed the horrors of the battlefields.

The National Woman's Peace Party organized a telegram campaign to show Americans' support for peace.

U.S. Neutrality

Most Americans were surprised by the outbreak of war. However, they tended to look on it as a strictly European matter. President Woodrow Wilson received strong support when he announced a policy of neutrality. He urged all Americans to be "neutral in fact as well as in name . . . impartial in thought as well as action." Wilson hoped that the United States would be able to negotiate a settlement to the conflict. He pursued this goal throughout 1915 and 1916, but without success.

The United States remained neutral in action, but few of its citizens were impartial in thought. Some 28 million Americans—nearly 30 percent of the population—were either immigrants or the children of immigrants. Some Americans of Austrian, German, Hungarian, or Turkish background sympathized with the Central Powers. Some Irish Americans hoped the war would help free Ireland from the rule of Great Britain.

Many more Americans, however, backed the Allies. A common language and culture bound many Americans to Great Britain. The British propaganda campaign, which painted the Germans as brutal killers, also increased American support for the Allied cause.

The sinking of the Lusitania, shown in this drawing by Charles Dixon, caused strong anti-German feelings in the United States.

Despite its policy of neutrality, the United States could not remain untouched by the war. When the war began, the British navy blockaded Germany and laid mines in the North Sea. The British even stopped U.S. ships bound for neutral countries and searched their cargoes—including the mail. They were looking for goods that might ultimately be destined for Germany. Wilson protested this violation of U.S. neutrality.

Early in 1915 Germany responded to the blockade by establishing a "war zone" around Britain. Any ships entering this zone—even those from neutral nations—were subject to attack by U-boats, or German submarines. Wilson warned that, in accordance with international laws of neutrality, the United States would hold Germany accountable for any injury to American lives or property on the high seas.

On March 28, 1915, a U-boat sank a British passenger liner in the Irish Sea, killing more than 100 people, including one American. While the White House considered its response, a far more serious incident occurred. On May 7, 1915, a U-boat patrolling off the Irish coast torpedoed another British passenger liner, the *Lusitania*. The dead included 128 Americans. The *New York Times* called the Germans "savages drunk with blood." Outraged Americans agreed. German leaders pointed out that they had placed advertisements in American newspapers warning Americans against sailing into the war zone. They also charged that the *Lusitania* was transporting armaments for Britain—an accusation that later proved true.

Nevertheless, President Wilson protested angrily to the German government. He demanded specific pledges against unrestricted submarine warfare against civilian ships. Secretary of State William Jennings Bryan charged that the president's protest amounted to an ultimatum and resigned. Bryan argued that the United States could not issue ultimatums to other nations and remain neutral.

THROUGH OTHERS' EYES

The Sinking of the *Lusitania*

Germany's Baron von Schwarzenstein offered the following response to the outrage over the sinking of the *Lusitania*.

66 It was only after England declared the whole North Sea a war zone . . . that Germany with precisely the same right declared the waters around England a war zone and announced her purpose of sinking all hostile commercial vessels found therein. . . . In the case of the *Lusitania* the German Ambassador even further warned Americans through the great American newspapers against taking passage thereon. Does a pirate act thus? Does he take pains to save human lives? . . . Nobody regrets more sincerely than we Germans the hard necessity of sending to their deaths hundreds of men. Yet the sinking was a justifiable act of war. . . . The scene of war is no golf links [course], the ships of belligerent powers no pleasure places. . . . We have sympathy with the victims and their relatives, of course, but did we hear anything about sympathy . . . when England adopted her diabolical [evil] plan of starving a great nation? 99

✔ **READING CHECK:** What challenges did the United States face while trying to remain neutral?

The Road to War

The sinking of the *Lusitania* brought the conflict in Europe closer to home for many Americans. Even so, most people still hoped the United States could stay out of the war. Further challenges to U.S. neutrality, however, were not long in coming.

Wilson's actions criticized. In August 1915 a German submarine sank the *Arabic*, another British liner, killing two Americans. Then, in March 1916, the French passenger vessel *Sussex* was attacked, injuring several Americans. In a sternly worded message to the German government, President Wilson threatened to cut diplomatic ties if Germany did not abandon its unrestricted submarine warfare. The German government responded with the ***Sussex* pledge**, a renewal of an earlier promise not to sink liners without warning or without ensuring the passengers' safety.

Most Americans supported the president's approach. A number of prominent politicians, however, criticized Wilson for not responding more strongly to German aggression. Former president Theodore Roosevelt accused Wilson of "cowardice and weakness."

Others accused Wilson of abandoning neutrality. Former secretary of state William Jennings Bryan argued that Wilson's commercial and trade policies helped the Allies and therefore the United States was no longer impartial in action. As secretary of state, Bryan had discouraged American bankers from making loans to either side, but this policy was soon abandoned. Large American banks lent millions of dollars to Britain and France. Bryan's successor, Robert Lansing, encouraged the trade of war materials with the Allies. By 1916 U.S. arms sales to the Allies had reached some $500 million, about 80 times the amount sold in 1914.

Preparedness and peace. In 1916 President Wilson launched a military "preparedness" program. This program was strongly supported by the banks and war industries that had a large economic interest in an Allied victory. Passed in June 1916, the **National Defense Act** increased the number of soldiers in the regular army from some 90,000 to about 175,000, with an ultimate goal of 223,000. Wilson established the National Guard's size at some 450,000 troops. Two months later, Congress passed another bill appropriating $313 million to build up the navy.

With the presidential election nearing, President Wilson assured Americans that he had not abandoned neutrality. Running on the slogan "He Kept Us Out of War," Wilson narrowly defeated Republican Charles Evans Hughes to win re-election.

Wilson still hoped to negotiate a settlement to the war. In a January 1917 speech, he called for "peace without victory." A lasting peace, he said, had to be one between equals, not between the victor and the defeated. Once again, the warring nations rejected Wilson's effort to mediate.

Diplomatic relations broken. On February 1, 1917, Germany resumed full-scale U-boat warfare. The Germans were gambling that their U-boat fleet could defeat the Allies before the United States joined the war. Wilson followed through on his threat to break off diplomatic relations. He also ordered the arming of American merchant ships sailing into the war zone. Nonetheless, German torpedoes sank five American ships.

INTERPRETING THE VISUAL RECORD

The *Lusitania*. The German government ran this warning in the announcement of the *Lusitania*'s 1915 voyage. *Does this notice provide enough warning to Americans traveling on the Lusitania? Explain your answer.*

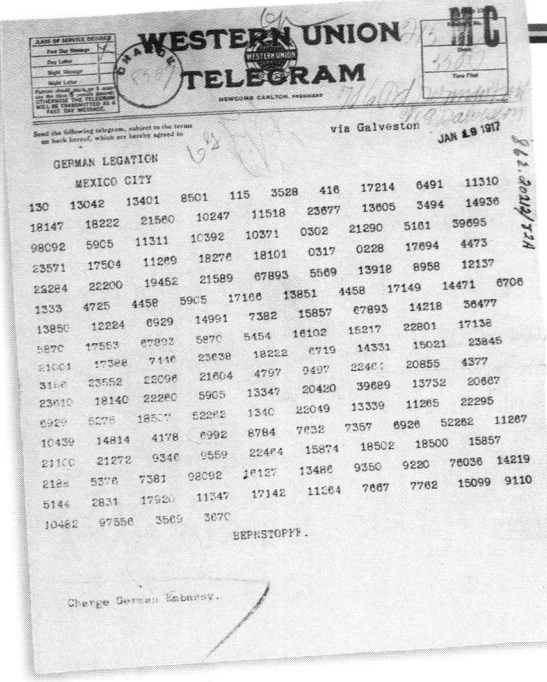

WESTERN UNION
TELEGRAM

The Zimmerman Note. This telegram sent to the German minister in Mexico proposed an alliance between Germany and Mexico. *Does this telegram look like an official document from the German government? Explain your answer.*

On March 1, 1917, American newspapers published an intercepted cable from German foreign secretary Arthur Zimmermann to the German minister in Mexico. Dubbed the **Zimmerman Note**, the cable proposed a Mexican alliance with Germany. The cable offered German support to help Mexico "reconquer the lost territory in New Mexico, Texas, and Arizona."

As the weeks passed, Wilson reluctantly concluded that the United States could no longer stay out of the conflict. On April 2, 1917, the president addressed Congress, asking for a declaration of war.

Congress declares war. A hushed Congress heard Wilson condemn Germany's submarine warfare for its "wanton [vicious] and wholesale destruction." Wilson, however, did not rest his case solely on the evils of U-boat warfare. He summoned Americans to a crusade for a better world.

> 66 We are glad . . . to fight thus for the ultimate peace of the world and for the liberation of its peoples, . . . for the rights of nations—great and small—and the privilege of men everywhere to choose their way of life. . . . The world must be made safe for democracy. 99

At these words, cheers and applause rang through the Capitol. Later, Wilson told an aide: "My message today was a message of death for our young men. How strange it seems to applaud that."

The Senate declared war on April 4, 1917. The House followed two days later. The vote was not unanimous—six senators and 50 representatives opposed the declaration. Representative Jeannette Rankin of Montana was among the opposition. "I want to stand by my country," she explained, "but I cannot vote for war."

✔ **READING CHECK:** What events led to U.S. entry into the war?

Mobilizing U.S. Military Power

In his war message on April 2, President Wilson pledged all the nation's material resources to the Allied war effort. What the Allies most urgently needed were fresh troops. Few Americans, however, rushed to volunteer for military service.

Recruiting an army. On May 18, 1917, Congress passed the **Selective Service Act**. It required men between the ages of 21 and 30 to register with local draft boards. This was later changed to men between the ages of 18 and 45. By the end of the war, some 24 million men had registered, and 2.8 million of them had been drafted. More than half of the almost 4.8 million Americans who served in the armed forces during World War I were draftees.

Supporters of the draft argued that it would help build a more democratic United States by bringing together soldiers from different backgrounds. In reality, African Americans, American Indians, Mexican Americans, and many foreign-born soldiers faced segregation and often discrimination. Most foreign-born soldiers, for example, were assigned to separate units where they were taught civics and English. Congress did eventually offer citizenship to the some 10,000 American Indians who served during the war.

The more than 370,000 African American recruits experienced particularly harsh discrimination. They were blocked from service in the marines and limited to kitchen duties in the navy. Most African Americans in the army served in all-black support units commanded by white officers. Furthermore, African American draftees who were sent to army training camps in the South often faced harassment from the local population.

Pressure from the National Association for the Advancement of Colored People (NAACP) and other African American organizations convinced the army to open up more opportunities for black soldiers. A school was established to train African American officers, and more African American soldiers were assigned combat duty. However, the army made no effort to integrate black and white soldiers in the same units.

Training the troops. Putting uniforms on young men did not make them soldiers. That required long and hard training, but the United States did not have the facilities to house such a large army. Massive training camps had to be hastily constructed. In the summer of 1917, workers began building barracks to house draftees at 16 separate locations. Completing the task in the planned 60 days seemed impossible. However, by using simple designs, a huge workforce, and mass-production techniques, thousands of buildings were ready by September. There were not enough uniforms and equipment for all the troops yet, but at least they had a place to live while training.

The military hoped to use a similar accelerated process for the troops' training as well. One of the recruits, Private Harry R. Richmond, wrote about his training camp in New Mexico.

> 66 The burden of creating an army at short notice, falls most heavily upon the recruit. The rookie is expected to learn now in three weeks, what his fellow soldiers acquired a year ago in three months. We are drilled nearly 7 or 8 hours per day. 99

Upon arrival at a training camp, recruits were herded like cattle through a series of medical examinations. Most of their days were spent learning military rules, drilling with their equipment, exercising, and preparing for inspections. "Every man is supposed to be slicked up, shoes shined, clothes clean, and he must be shaved," recalled one recruit. "This is one thing they insist on in the army—everything must be clean."

Soldiers also spent a lot of time learning how to fight the enemy. In addition to many hours on the rifle range, recruits practiced hand-to-hand combat using bayonets. Frank Sweeney wrote that recruits faced dummies "hanging from large cross beams" and were "taught the best method of approach and the

HISTORY
IN THE MAKING

The Doughboy's Pack
BY PAUL BOYER

History is much more than a study of dates, documents, or facts about famous people. Ordinary objects also leave a historical record about an event or an era. For example, common items provided to soldiers during a war tell a story about how that war was fought.

During World War I, U.S. infantry troops carried all their necessary equipment inside a canvas "field kit" strapped to their backs. The around-the-waist design with pockets was adopted during World War I because of automatic weapons. Rifles could now fire as many as five bullets per minute, and a soldier needed easy access to large amounts of ammunition during the heat of battle.

The gas mask filtered out poisonous fumes that could suffocate or blind a soldier. The soldier's steel helmet extended to the top of the ear line to help prevent head wounds. Soldiers also carried a tent, tent poles, a rain poncho, a bayonet, a blanket, a sewing kit, socks, identification tags, a compass, and a flashlight. Sturdy metal containers protected two days' worth of rations—hard biscuits called hardtack and dried meat—from rain, rats, and insects. On a long march, soldiers might have cursed their heavy packs, but they also knew that burden could mean the difference between life and death.

Read More About It

Free Find:
General Pershing
After reading about General John J. Pershing on the **Holt Researcher** CD–ROM, imagine that you are introducing General Pershing at a banquet being held in Pershing's honor. Write a short speech describing his accomplishments.

proper jabs to get him before he gets us." Sweeney noted that "sometimes the men enter into this game so heartily that they break their bayonets." The training left most soldiers in excellent physical health. At the end of his training one soldier felt that "if I am here another year I could outwalk a horse and carry a hundred pounds besides." This strength would be severely tested in France.

✔ **READING CHECK:** How did the United States prepare its military for war?

Over There

With mobilization well under way, U.S. troops began sailing to France as part of the American Expeditionary Force (AEF). Under the command of General John J. Pershing, the first U.S. troops reached France in late June 1917.

John J. Pershing

Born in Missouri in 1860, General Pershing was the U.S. Army's most experienced combat officer. He graduated from the U.S. Military Academy at West Point in 1886. Pershing then spent four years fighting with the cavalry against American Indians in the Southwest and in South Dakota. In 1891 Pershing became a military instructor at the University of Nebraska. He later moved on to teach military tactics at the U.S. Military Academy in 1897.

Pershing fought in the Spanish-American War and served a tour of duty in the Philippines from 1899 to 1903. After an assignment as an observer with Japanese forces during the Russo-Japanese War, Pershing was promoted from captain to brigadier general. He returned to the Philippines for a second tour of duty in 1906 before being named commander of the 8th Cavalry Brigade.

Early in 1917 Pershing was ordered to lead the expedition into Mexico that pursued Pancho Villa. Despite the failure to capture Villa, Pershing's appointment to head the AEF came as no surprise. A determined leader, Pershing refused to allow the Allies to dictate how his troops would be used. He insisted that U.S. forces fight as a separate unit, rather than be added to the Allied forces bit by bit.

On July 4, 1917, thousands of "Yanks"—U.S. soldiers—cheered on by huge crowds, marched through Paris, France. They stopped at the tomb of the Marquis de Lafayette, the French hero of the American Revolution. "Lafayette, we are here!" proclaimed one of Pershing's aides. By fighting for France's freedom the United States was repaying the French for their help during the Revolutionary War.

U.S. Army lieutenant Edward F. Graham wrote home about the sense of purpose that he and many other soldiers felt. "The desperate contest between justice and empire . . . is

INTERPRETING THE VISUAL RECORD
Medical care. Many women served as ambulance drivers during World War I. *Do these ambulances look equipped to provide medical care at the scene of a battle? Explain your answer.*

now on. You should be proud to have me . . . participate in the struggle as a part of the human wall against a second Dark Ages." As the weeks went by, U.S. troops arrived in France in ever-swelling numbers. Army engineers built docks and railroads and strung up networks of telephone and telegraph lines. The engineers also constructed ammunition depots, camps, hospitals, and storage sheds.

Some 10,000 American women worked in these hospitals. Emily Vuagniaux, an Army Medical Corps nurse, described life in a battlefield hospital.

> 66 We . . . have worked . . . sometimes 18 hours straight. I have the operating room and they run four tables day and night and have between 200 and 300 patients right off the field, so you . . . know we are quite close in. 99

Thousands more American women went to Europe as volunteers for the Red Cross, the YMCA, and other agencies.

Escorted by U.S. warships, merchant vessels transported troops, supplies, and volunteers through the submarine-infested North Atlantic. This **convoy system** proved quite effective. Of the more than 2 million U.S. soldiers who crossed the Atlantic Ocean, not one died as the result of an enemy attack on the high seas. U.S. warships also patrolled the waters of the western Atlantic, protecting the U.S. coastline. To contain the U-boats, U.S. ships laid some 70,000 mines in a lethal 240-mile necklace across the North Sea from Norway to the Orkney Islands off Britain. This barrier created hazards for German U-boats trying to return to their bases.

World War I soldiers faced both brutal hand-to-hand combat and deadly new weapons.

✔ **READING CHECK:** What types of experiences did Americans have in Europe?

SECTION 2 REVIEW

Define and explain the significance of the following terms:
Sussex pledge
National Defense Act
Zimmerman Note
Selective Service Act
convoy system

Identify and explain the significance of the following individuals:
Robert Lansing
Jeannette Rankin
John J. Pershing

1. **Using Graphic Organizers** Copy the graphic below. Use it to list the steps the U.S. government took to prepare the military for war.

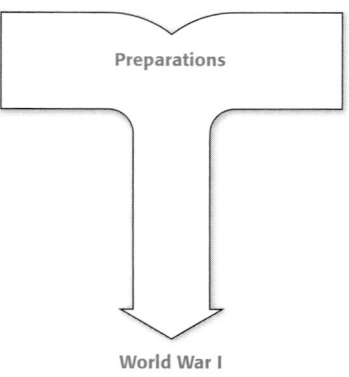

Preparations

World War I

2. **Hypothesizing** How might the United States have responded differently to the events that challenged its neutrality?
3. **Analyzing** Did the draft make the United States more democratic? Explain your answer.
4. **Using Historical Imagination** Imagine that you are a U.S. soldier. Write a letter to President Wilson describing your experiences in Europe.

Critical Thinking

5. Why did the United States declare war on Germany?
   Consider:
   • the war's economic impact on the United States
   • German U-boat attacks on American shipping
   • the effect a German victory might have on the United States

The War at Home

OBJECTIVES

Read to understand:

1. how the U.S. government prepared the nation for war
2. how organized labor and volunteers contributed to the war effort
3. why African Americans moved to the North
4. how the government created support for, and limited opposition to, the war

KEY TERMS

Food Administration
War Industries Board
National War Labor Board
Great Migration
Committee on Public Information
Espionage Act
Sedition Act

KEY PEOPLE

William McAdoo
Herbert Hoover
Bernard Baruch
Harriot Stanton Blatch
Juliette Gordon Low

EYEWITNESSES TO History

66 *Billy, my nephew, is twelve years old. . . . They call the suburb in which Billy lives one hundred per cent patriotic. Everybody is in war work. Even the children under five years have an organization known as the Khaki Babes. . . . Billy's crowd is indefatigable [tireless] in its labors. . . . The boys usher at meetings, assist in parades, deliver bundles and run errands. They are tireless collectors of nutshells, peach pits and tinsel paper. . . . One bit of voluntary war work was carried on through the periods of the gasoline-less Sundays when the four boys took positions on Commonwealth Avenue in such a way as to obstruct passing vehicles. If a car did not carry a doctor's or military sign, they threw pebbles and yelled 'O you Slacker!' It was exciting work because guilty drivers put on full speed ahead and Billy admitted that he was almost run over, but he added that the cause was worth it.* 99

—Florence Woolston

THE GRANGER COLLECTION, NEW YORK

The U.S. government encouraged all Americans to support the war.

Florence Woolston described her nephew's contribution to the war effort in the *New Republic* magazine. The efforts of Billy and millions of other Americans helped win the war.

Mobilizing the Nation

Once the United States entered the war, President Wilson quickly moved to mobilize the nation. The government set up programs to finance the war, conserve scarce resources, and redirect industry and labor toward wartime production. The president also launched a huge propaganda campaign to mobilize support for the war effort. As the government whipped up enthusiasm for the war, however, intolerance of antiwar opinions spread across the land.

Directing the economy. At the outset of the war, Wilson had noted that "there are no armies in this struggle; there are entire nations armed." Wilson realized that the U.S. economy had to be reorganized. The first step in this process was raising money to pay for the war, which eventually cost the United States about $35 billion, including loans to the Allies.

The government raised money through four issues of Liberty bonds during the war and one of Victory bonds after the end of the fighting. Posters, parades, and rallies promoted each bond issue. William McAdoo was secretary of the treasury and Wilson's son-in-law. He declared that "Every person who refuses to subscribe . . . is a friend of Germany," and "is not entitled to be an American citizen." These promotions were a huge success.

Movie stars Douglas Fairbanks, Mary Pickford, and Charlie Chaplin help sell Liberty bonds.

The government also sought to raise money by increasing taxes. This proved more difficult than selling bonds. Congress debated a new tax program for months before reaching an agreement in October 1917. The new taxes on business incomes and large personal incomes produced about $10 billion for the war.

Mobilizing the economy for war entailed more than raising money, however. It also involved coordinating the actions of government, business, and industry. This was done through a number of federal war boards. Although the federal government never took complete control of the economy, it exercised sweeping economic power through these various agencies. It set the prices and production levels of commodities and regulated businesses crucial to the war effort.

Conserving resources. Among the most successful of the federal war boards were the **Food Administration** and the Fuel Administration. They were charged with regulating the production and supply of these essential resources. To direct the Food Administration, Wilson chose Herbert Hoover, a prosperous mining engineer who had managed a food-relief campaign for war-stricken Belgium. Hoover saw his task as twofold: to encourage increased agricultural production and to conserve existing food supplies.

To stimulate wartime production, Hoover guaranteed farmers high prices. Farm production soared. For example, farmers increased their production of wheat, harvesting some 921 million bushels in 1919—a dramatic increase over the 1917 figure of some 637 million bushels.

Announcing that "food will win the war," Hoover called on Americans to reduce their food consumption by observing wheatless and meatless days. To supplement their diets, he suggested that they plant "victory gardens" filled with vegetables. The campaign proved very effective—without, as Hoover proudly noted, resorting to forced rationing.

Fuel Administration director Harry Garfield, son of former president James A. Garfield, took a similar course of action, encouraging people to observe heatless Mondays. Garfield was not unwilling to use force, however. When the nation ran short of coal in early 1918, he closed all factories east of the Mississippi River for several days.

Organizing industry. Hundreds of other federal boards and agencies were created to regulate industrial production and distribution. Led by William McAdoo, the Railroad Administration reorganized the railroad system by setting limits on transportation rates and workers' wages.

The work of all these boards was coordinated by the government's central war agency, the **War Industries Board** (WIB). Its director, Wall Street investor Bernard Baruch, had overall responsibility for allocating scarce materials, establishing production priorities, and setting prices. Baruch preferred to persuade business leaders to comply with his wishes. However, when steel owners refused to cut prices, the government threatened to take over their foundries and mills.

At first some business leaders were critical of Wilson's economic mobilization programs. They argued that government intervention would permanently damage the U.S. system of free enterprise. When profits soared, however, these business leaders stopped complaining.

✔ **READING CHECK:** How did the U.S. government prepare the nation for war?

HELPING HOOVER IN OUR U.S. SCHOOL GARDEN

INTERPRETING THE VISUAL RECORD
Victory gardens. Many Americans supported the war effort by growing food at home to make more available for troops overseas. *Does this poster make a persuasive argument for growing a victory garden? Why or why not?*

Working women. These women helped the war effort by working in a Detroit munitions factory. *What dangers do these women face in their workplace?*

Mobilizing Workers

Meeting the demands of the war required a massive, cooperative effort. Millions of people, paid employees and volunteers alike, pitched in as the nation mobilized for the military campaign.

Organized labor. Because of the war, hundreds of thousands of men were drafted into the army and European immigration slowed to a trickle. American industries found themselves desperately short of labor as they geared up for the war effort. Taking advantage of this situation, unionized workers across the country went on strike. They demanded higher wages and other benefits. Nearly 4,500 strikes involving more than 1 million workers erupted in 1917 alone. The tactic worked. Working conditions substantially improved throughout the war.

To ensure that the voice of labor was heard, President Wilson established the **National War Labor Board** (NWLB) in April 1918. Composed of representatives from business and labor, the NWLB arbitrated disputes between workers and employers. The board heard more than 1,200 cases, ruling in favor of labor more often than not. In this climate of official support, union membership grew rapidly. Membership in the American Federation of Labor (AFL) rose from some 2 million in 1916 to roughly 3.2 million by 1919. By the end of the decade, some 15 percent of the nation's nonagricultural workforce was unionized.

The labor shortage strengthened unions and also brought about changes in the workforce. The number of women working outside the home grew by about 6 percent during the war. Many of these women took traditionally male jobs. They worked as automobile mechanics, bricklayers, metalworkers, railroad engineers, or truck drivers. In all, some 1.5 million American women worked in industry during the war. Norma B. Kastl was an interviewer with a women's service bureau during World War I. She explained that many women considered it their patriotic duty to work.

> 66 The navy is taking on women as yeomen [clerks] to do shore duty. . . . Every girl that becomes a yeoman can have the satisfaction of knowing that she is releasing, as from prison, some sailor who had been fuming . . . because he had to spend his days in an office instead of on the deck of a destroyer. 99

Women also helped plan wartime mobilization. Carrie Chapman Catt, a women's suffrage leader, sat on the Women's Committee of the Council of National Defense. This was a civilian agency organized to support the war effort. Harriot Stanton Blatch, the daughter of suffragist Elizabeth Cady Stanton, headed the Food Administration's Speakers' Bureau.

Women's war efforts helped produce one very important political change—the passage of the Nineteenth Amendment. Wilson, who had previously wavered on women's suffrage, threw his support behind the amendment in recognition of women's wartime contributions. "The greatest thing that came out of the war," Catt later noted, "was the emancipation of women, for which no man fought."

This woman is assembling ammunition for rifles.

Volunteerism. Intense patriotism swept the country, motivating many Americans, from young children to senior citizens, to contribute to the war effort. Americans voluntarily conserved energy, recycled essential materials, and planted victory gardens, all to make more items available for the soldiers overseas. Americans also contributed directly to the war by purchasing Liberty bonds that provided the government with funds to pay for equipment and supplies.

BIOGRAPHY

Juliette Gordon Low

One of the most active American volunteers was Juliette Gordon Low, also known as Daisy. Born in 1860 to a wealthy family in Savannah, Georgia, Juliette Gordon received the finest private-school education. She was a serious student who was particularly gifted in the arts. After completing her education, she traveled extensively. On one trip to England she met wealthy William Low, whom she married in 1886.

The Lows divided their time between homes in the United States and Britain, living the leisurely life of the idle rich. Juliette's life was not a happy one, however. Marital troubles and the challenge of her increasing deafness, caused by two separate ear injuries, led her to suffer from frequent bouts of depression.

After her husband died in 1905, the financially independent widow traveled the world looking for a purpose in her life. She found this purpose in 1911, when she met the founder of the Boy Scouts, British war hero Sir Robert Baden-Powell. Low became actively involved in the Scouts' sister organization, the Girl Guides. She poured her energies into the movement, forming several troops in Britain before bringing the Girl Guides to the United States in 1912.

The organization grew quickly, and by 1915 the American Girl Guides were known as the Girl Scouts of America. Using mostly her own money and refusing to surrender to any obstacle, Low soon spread the Girl Scouts nationwide. The organization grew quickly during the war, and Low encouraged Girl Scouts to throw all their energies into helping the war effort. Many worked directly for the Food Administration. "A girl cannot die for her country, but she can live for it," Low declared. The Girl Scouts' role in the war effort helped boost membership from some 500 girls in 1915 to 50,000 by 1920. By the time of Juliette Low's death in 1927, total membership had reached almost 168,000.

✔ **READING CHECK:** How did organized labor and volunteers contribute to the war effort?

teen Life

Mobilizing for the War Effort

Wartime mobilization efforts targeted American children and teenagers as well as adults. Young people across the United States volunteered both money and labor to help win the war. Young Americans also contributed money from their own pockets, which they earned working at odd jobs such as painting barns, waiting tables, gathering nuts, and polishing shoes.

These Girl Scouts are collecting peach pits to be used in gas mask filters.

Helping to feed the soldiers overseas was a main task of American youth. "Do not permit your child to take a bite or two from an apple and throw the rest away," advised the February 21, 1918, edition of *Life* magazine. "Nowadays even children must be taught to be patriotic to the core." Many young people grew their own vegetable gardens. Some 2 million boys and girls eventually joined the U.S. Garden Army and grew $48 million worth of produce.

New York passed laws so that 12-year-old children could miss up to seven months of school in order to work on farms. In 1918, boys older than 16 were let out of high schools in the Northwest to help plant the spring wheat crop. They were rewarded with credit for the full school term. Founded in 1917, the U.S. Boy's Working Reserve formed a virtual army of agricultural labor. Some 200,000 young men between the ages of 16 and 20 were recruited to help harvest crops across the United States. In a time of desperate need, American youth performed the work of adults and helped win the war.

The Influenza Epidemic

In 1918 World War I was raging in Europe, claiming thousands of lives. Meanwhile, a silent killer was sweeping the globe—influenza, commonly known as the flu. Initially, people believed that the illness was nothing serious and that doctors would find a cure. "Everybody had a preconception of what the flu was: it's a miserable cold and, after a few days, you're up and around," explains historian Alfred Crosby. "This was a flu that put people into bed as if they'd been hit with a 2 x 4. That turned into pneumonia, that turned people blue and black and killed them."

Decades of major discoveries and advances had given Americans great faith in science and medicine. However, scientists knew almost nothing about viruses at the time. They thought that a type of bacteria caused the flu. Wild rumors regarding the origin of the pandemic, or worldwide epidemic, spread quickly. One common rumor was that German agents had planted the virus in the United States.

The flu claimed some 12,000 lives in September, but the worst was still to come. In October more than 11,000 people died in Philadelphia, Pennsylvania, and nearly 200,000 died nationwide. Then, like a fire burning itself out, the flu vanished.

The influenza epidemic left almost 600,000 dead in the United States alone, nearly as many Americans as were killed in the Civil War. At least 20 million people died worldwide.

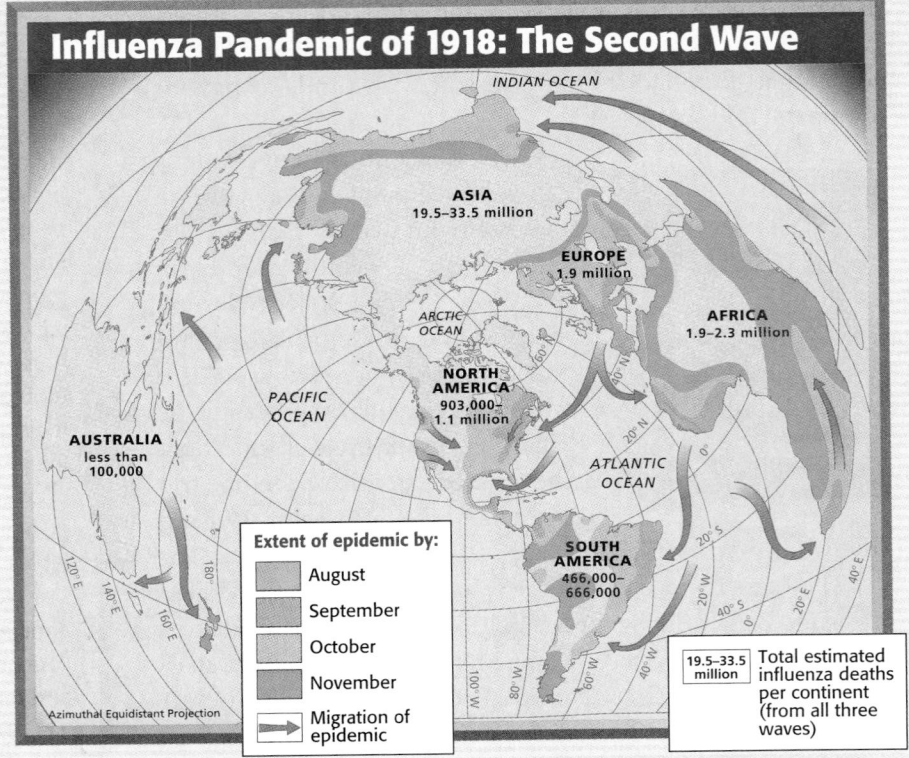

Influenza Pandemic of 1918: The Second Wave

INDIAN OCEAN

ASIA
19.5–33.5 million

EUROPE
1.9 million

ARCTIC OCEAN

AFRICA
1.9–2.3 million

PACIFIC OCEAN

NORTH AMERICA
903,000–1.1 million

ATLANTIC OCEAN

AUSTRALIA
less than 100,000

SOUTH AMERICA
466,000–666,000

Azimuthal Equidistant Projection

Extent of epidemic by:
- August
- September
- October
- November
- → Migration of epidemic

19.5–33.5 million | Total estimated influenza deaths per continent (from all three waves)

Understanding Science and History

1. What causes influenza?
2. Which continents experienced the greatest number of deaths from influenza?

The Great Trek North

The labor shortage that drew women into the workforce also spurred immigration from Mexico. Some were fleeing the Mexican Revolution. Others were lured by southwestern employers who depended on Mexican labor. Some 150,000 men and women migrated from Mexico to the United States during the war.

Job opportunities and the chance of higher wages brought about one of the most important population shifts in U.S. history. This was the **Great Migration** of African Americans from the South to northern cities between 1915 and 1930. Hundreds of thousands of African Americans moved northward to escape discrimination and difficult living and working conditions. African American newspapers strongly encouraged the migration: "Get out of the South," declared an editorial in the Chicago *Defender*. "The *Defender* says come."

Many African Americans moved to northern cities in search of wartime jobs.

African Americans went to the North with great hope. For many, however, life there proved harsh. Although they typically enjoyed a better standard of living than they had in the South, racial violence remained a serious problem. The most brutal wartime racial incident occurred in East St. Louis, Illinois, on July 2, 1917. White rioters rampaged through African American neighborhoods, leaving at least 39 dead. Shocked and angered, many African Americans asked themselves why they should fight for freedom in Europe when they enjoyed so little of it at home.

✔ **READING CHECK:** What were the reasons African Americans moved to the North?

Influencing Attitudes

Whether for religious, political, or personal reasons, many Americans believed that the United States should have stayed out of the war. President Wilson wanted all Americans to support the war effort. Therefore, he established the **Committee on Public Information** (CPI) in the spring of 1917. Headed by George Creel, the CPI led a propaganda campaign to encourage the American people to support the war.

The CPI initially put out fact-based material that was censored to present an upbeat picture of the war. Very quickly, however, the CPI began churning out raw propaganda that pictured the Germans as evil monsters. Hollywood joined in, producing movies such as *The Claws of the Hun,* and *The Kaiser, the Beast of Berlin.* CPI pamphlets warned citizens to be on the lookout for German spies. Dozens of "patriotic organizations" sprang up, with names like the American Protective League and the American Defense Society. These groups spied, tapped telephones, and opened other people's mail in an effort to identify "spies and traitors."

These groups targeted almost anyone who called for peace, questioned the Allies' progress, or criticized the government's policies. They were particularly hard on German Americans, many of whom lost their jobs. Sometimes this anti-German sentiment took absurd turns. German books vanished from library shelves, schools stopped teaching German language courses, and German music disappeared from concert programs. People even renamed German-sounding items: sauerkraut became liberty cabbage, dachshunds became liberty pups, and hamburger became Salisbury steak. Some Americans publicly humiliated people of German heritage by forcing them to kiss the flag, recite the Pledge of Allegiance, or buy war bonds. Sometimes these acts turned violent.

Suppressing Opposition

Despite the hysterical atmosphere, some Americans continued to oppose the war. Quakers and Mennonites, committed by their faith to pacifism—the refusal to use violence to settle disputes—were particularly outspoken. Considered traitors by many Americans, they experienced violence and abuse. Other opponents of the war included Representative Jeannette Rankin, Senator Robert La Follette, and settlement-house leader Jane Addams.

INTERPRETING THE VISUAL RECORD

Propaganda. The U.S. government directed most of its propaganda at Americans, encouraging them to work hard and make sacrifices to help win the war. *What elements in these posters reflect the behavior they are trying to inspire?*

CAN Vegetables Fruit AND the Kaiser too

Tomatoes   Peas

Kaiser Brand Unsweetened

Write for Free Book to NATIONAL WAR GARDEN COMMISSION WASHINGTON, D.C.

Charles Lathrop Pack, President   P.S. Ridsdale, Secretary

OVER THE TOP FOR YOU

Buy U.S. Gov't Bonds THIRD LIBERTY LOAN

Socialists. Many Socialists questioned the reasons for fighting World War I. *What does this button suggest about the goals of the Socialist Party?*

The Socialist Party also proclaimed its opposition to the war. To most party members, the warring nations were simply using working people as tools in a capitalist struggle for control of world markets. The Industrial Workers of the World (IWW) had a similar view of the war and led strikes in a number of war-related industries.

To silence opponents of the war, Congress passed the **Espionage Act** in June 1917 and the **Sedition Act** a year later. These measures outlawed acts of treason and made it a crime to "utter, print, write, or publish any disloyal . . . or abusive language" criticizing the government, the flag, or the military. Opposition to the draft, to war-bond drives, or to the arms industry also became a crime.

The CPI rallied support for the war, while the Espionage and Sedition Acts crushed opposition to the war. More than 1,000 people—including some 200 members of the IWW—were convicted of violating these laws. Socialist Party leader Eugene V. Debs was sentenced to 10 years in prison for making a speech against the war.

Many Americans, even some who supported the war, believed that the Espionage and Sedition Acts violated the First Amendment. The Supreme Court, however, disagreed. Justice Oliver Wendell Holmes wrote the opinion in the 1919 landmark case *Schenck* v. *United States*.

❝ The question . . . is whether the words used are used in such circumstances and are of such a nature as to create a clear and present danger. . . . When a nation is at war many things that might be said in time of peace . . . will not be endured [and] no Court could regard them as protected by any constitutional right. ❞

✔ **READING CHECK:** How did the government try to increase support for, and limit opposition to, the war?

SECTION  REVIEW

Define and explain the significance of the following terms:
Food Administration
War Industries Board
National War Labor Board
Great Migration
Committee on Public Information
Espionage Act
Sedition Act

Identify and explain the significance of the following individuals:
William McAdoo
Herbert Hoover
Bernard Baruch
Harriot Stanton Blatch
Juliette Gordon Low

1. **Using Graphic Organizers** Copy the diagram below. Use it to list the steps the U.S. government took to mobilize the economy for war.

Neutrality

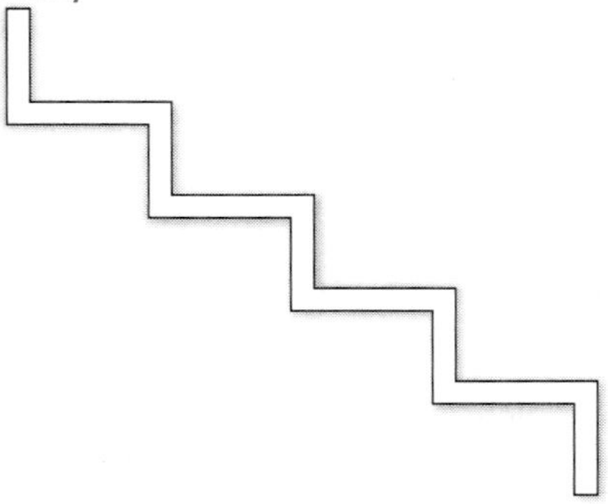

War

2. **Taking a Stand** Do you think the U.S. government was justified in taking control of the economy during the war? Why or why not?
3. **Evaluating** How did wartime labor shortages affect unions and volunteer organizations?
4. **Using Historical Imagination** Imagine that you are an African American who migrated to the North during the war. Write a letter to a northern newspaper that outlines why you moved and what experiences you have had in the North.

Critical Thinking

5. Were the steps the government took to shape and control public opinion during the war appropriate? Explain your answer.
   Consider:
   • the constitutional right to free speech
   • the danger of spying and sabotage
   • the need for cooperation on the homefront

SECTION 4

The War's End and Aftermath

OBJECTIVES

Read to understand:

1. what the final events of World War I were
2. what the goals of President Wilson's Fourteen Points were
3. what the terms of the Treaty of Versailles were
4. why the U.S. Senate rejected the Treaty of Versailles
5. what the global impact of World War I was

KEY TERMS

Bolsheviks
Battle of the Argonne Forest
Fourteen Points
League of Nations
Big Four
reparations
Treaty of Versailles

KEY PEOPLE

David Lloyd George
Georges Clemenceau
Vittorio Orlando
Henry Cabot Lodge

KEY PLACES

Czechoslovakia
Yugoslavia
Estonia
Finland
Latvia
Lithuania
Poland
Saar

EYEWITNESSES TO History

66 *Along all the roads of France, in all the trenches, in every gunpit you can hear one song being sung. They sing it while they load their guns, they whistle it as they march up the line, they hum it while they munch their bully-beef and hardtack. You hear it on the regimental bands and grinding out from gramophones in hidden dugouts.*

Over there. Over there.
Send the word, send the word over there,
That the Yanks are coming—

Men repeat that ragtime promise as tho' it were a prayer. . . . We could have won without the Yanks—we're sure of that. Still, we're glad they're coming and we walk jauntily. We may die before the promise is sufficiently fulfilled to tell. What does that matter? The Yanks are coming. We shall not have died in vain. They will reap the peace for the world which our blood has sown. 99

—Coningsby Dawson

THE GRANGER COLLECTION, NEW YORK

George M. Cohan's "Over There" celebrated the arrival of U.S. forces in Europe.

Anticipating the arrival of U.S. forces, Coningsby Dawson wrote this letter home from his trench on the western front. His mixed emotions reflected the fact that no victory could erase the horrible costs of World War I. U.S. help was welcomed by the Allied Powers, but it could not undo the damage that had already been done.

The End of the War

The entry of the United States into the war came none too soon for the Allies. In the summer of 1917 the Allies launched an offensive to break the deadlock on the western front. It failed, shattering the Allied troops' already shaky morale. That fall, mutinies broke out in French units all along the front.

Revolution in Russia. More bad news arrived from Russia, which had been hit hard by the war. In March 1917, workers in Petrograd who were unable to buy bread marched out of the factories and protested in the streets. Demanding a change in government and an end to the war, the Russian people overthrew the czar.

Political turmoil continued until November, when the **Bolsheviks**, a group of radical Russian socialists, seized power. The Bolshevik leader, Vladimir Lenin, opposed the war and moved quickly to withdraw Russia from it. The Bolsheviks signed a treaty with the Central Powers in March 1918 that left the Central Powers free to concentrate their forces on the western front.

Germany's last bid for victory. On March 21, 1918, some 1 million German soldiers launched a tremendous offensive against the Allies. The Germans were backed by some 6,000 artillery pieces, including "Big Bertha," heavy guns capable

of firing a 2,100-pound shell almost nine miles. By late May the Germans had pushed the Allies back to the Marne River, just 50 miles from Paris.

In light of the desperate situation, General Pershing agreed to place U.S. troops under the command of Marshal Ferdinand Foch of France. The introduction of U.S. forces made the difference. In a last-ditch defense of Paris, U.S. troops helped the French stop the Germans at Château-Thierry on June 3–4. Nearby, a division of U.S. Marines attacked the Germans and recaptured Belleau Wood and two other villages. After fierce fighting, the German advance was halted. Paris was saved.

On July 15 the Germans threw everything into a final assault around Reims. The Allied lines held, however, and Foch ordered a counterattack three days later. Led by U.S. troops, the charge pushed the Germans back. The tide had turned in favor of the Allies.

Over time, some trenches became little more than muddy holes.

Strategies for Success

Interpreting Literature as Historical Evidence

Literature—imaginative or creative writing in all of its various forms—can serve as an extraordinary source of historical knowledge. Poetry and prose contain a wealth of information about the beliefs, customs, ideas, and values that were important to people of different cultures during different historical periods. Because most literature is meant to be subjective, however, it is particularly important to interpret it carefully.

How to Interpret Literature as Historical Evidence

1. **Become familiar with the source.** Before you begin to read a literary work, look over its title, publication information, and table of contents, if it has one. If possible, find out about the personal, social, and historical background of the author.
2. **Read the material carefully.** Read the work carefully and thoroughly. As you do so, take note of any references to real historical settings or events.
3. **Identify the work's themes.** Once you have finished reading the work, identify and think about its central themes. Consider how these themes may reflect the point of view of the author.
4. **Put the information to use.** Compare the themes to information about the historical period that you have gained through other sources. Then determine how the work can help you broaden your understanding of the historical period.

Applying the Strategy

Erich Maria Remarque's novel *All Quiet on the Western Front* portrays fighting in World War I through the eyes of a German soldier. The following excerpt describes an encounter between German and French soldiers.

66 The moment we are about to retreat three faces rise up from the ground in front of us. Under one of the helmets [I see] a dark pointed beard and two eyes that are fastened on me. I raise my hand, but I cannot throw into those strange eyes; for one mad moment the whole slaughter whirls like a circus round me . . . then the head rises up . . . and my hand-grenade flies through the air and into him.

We make for the rear, pull wire cradles into the trench and leave bombs behind us with the strings pulled, which ensures us a fiery retreat. The machine-guns are already firing from the next position.

We have become wild beasts. We do not fight, we defend ourselves against annihilation. . . . No longer do we lie helpless, . . . we can destroy and kill, to save ourselves . . . and to be revenged. 99

Practicing the Strategy

Use the passage above to answer the following questions.
1. What point is made about trench warfare?
2. How does the passage affect your view of war?

Allied victory. In the late summer of 1918 Foch seized the initiative and ordered a major offensive along the entire western front. For three months the Allies pushed deep into German-held territory. Americans led the attack that pushed the Germans back at Saint-Mihiel, France, that September. The Americans next drove toward Sedan, a French rail center that the Germans had held since 1914. For more than a month the Americans pushed northward along the Meuse River and through the rugged Argonne Forest, facing artillery and machine-gun fire all the way. The Americans suffered some 120,000 casualties in the **Battle of the Argonne Forest**. By November, however, they had reached and occupied the hills around Sedan.

African American troops played a major role in the Argonne offensive. Members of the 369th Infantry, an African American regiment whose men hailed from New York, so distinguished themselves that the French awarded them the Croix de Guerre (krwah-di-GER), or "Cross of War," a French military honor.

Repeatedly hammered during the Allied offensive, the Central Powers' forces began to disintegrate. Morale in the German military sagged. One soldier expressed his hunger for peace in a letter home.

> 66 **In what way have we sinned, that we should be treated worse than animals? Hunted from place to place, cold, filthy . . . we are destroyed like vermin. Will they never make peace?** 99

Mutinies broke out in both the German army and navy. German civilians rioted in the streets, demanding food, not war. Realizing that the war was lost, the kaiser fled to the Netherlands in early November. Two days later, Germany's new government agreed to an armistice, or cease-fire. On November 8, 1918, representatives of the German government arrived at the Allied headquarters in Compiègne (kohmp-yehn) to hear the armistice terms. The Allies demanded that the Germans evacuate Alsace-Lorraine, Belgium, France and Luxembourg and surrender an enormous amount of military equipment.

Early on the morning of November 11, the warring parties signed the armistice. At 11 A.M. the cease-fire went into effect. The constant crashing of guns was replaced, according to one American, by a "silence [that] was nearly unbearable." At long last, the war had ended. A peace conference was set for January 1919 in Paris.

✔ **READING CHECK:** What were the final events of World War I?

Wilson's Fourteen Points

News of the November 11 armistice set off a joyful celebration in the United States. President Wilson shared the people's great happiness at the Allied victory, but he knew that the difficult task of forging a just peace lay ahead.

© DORLING KINDERSLEY LTD./COURTESY OF SPINK & SON LTD. LONDON

The French government rewarded these African American soldiers with the Croix de Guerre (left) for their bravery during the war.

Americans in Washington, D.C., celebrate the news that the war is over.

PRESIDENT WOODROW WILSON
The Fourteen Points

On January 8, 1918, President Woodrow Wilson presented to Congress his plan for building peace in the postwar world.

The program of the world's peace . . . is our program; and that program, the only possible program, as we see it, is this:
. . . no private international understandings of any kind. . . . Absolute freedom of navigation upon the seas. . . . The removal . . . of all economic barriers and . . . equality of trade conditions among all the nations . . . guarantees . . . that national armaments will be reduced. . . . A free, open-minded, and absolutely impartial adjustment of all colonial claims, . . . the evacuation of all Russian territory. . . . Belgium . . . must be evacuated and restored. . . . All French territory should be freed and the invaded portions restored. . . . A readjustment of the frontiers of Italy . . . along clearly recognizable lines of nationality. . . . The peoples of Austria-Hungary . . . should be accorded the freest opportunity of autonomous development. . . . Rumania, Serbia, and Montenegro should be evacuated, occupied territories restored. . . . The Turkish portions of the present Ottoman Empire should be assured a secure sovereignty, but the other nationalities . . . under Turkish rule should be assured an . . . opportunity of autonomous development. . . . An independent Polish state should be erected. . . . A general association of nations must be formed . . . for the purpose of affording mutual guarantees of political independence and territorial integrity to great and small states alike.

This challenge had long been on Wilson's mind. Late in 1917 he had invited a group of scholars to advise him on peace terms. Drawing from their work, Wilson had developed the **Fourteen Points**, a program for world peace. He presented a summary of his principles and Allied war aims to Congress on January 8, 1918.

Nine of the points dealt with the issue of self-determination—the right of people to govern themselves—and with the various territorial disputes created by the war. Other points focused on what Wilson considered the causes of modern war: secret diplomacy, the arms race, violations of freedom of the seas, and trade barriers. The final point—the establishment of the **League of Nations**—was the heart of the program. The League would be an international body designed to prevent offensive wars.

Congress and the American public warmly received the Fourteen Points. The reaction of the Allies, however, proved lukewarm. The German government rejected the program, arguing that Wilson was interfering in European affairs.

✔ **READING CHECK:** What were the goals of President Wilson's Fourteen Points?

The Paris Peace Conference

On December 4, 1918, Woodrow Wilson boarded the USS *George Washington* for Europe—becoming the first president to cross the Atlantic while in office. A huge crowd gave Wilson a rousing send-off as the ship steamed out of New York Harbor. His reception at the French port of Brest was no less enthusiastic. Many Europeans welcomed him as a conquering hero.

The peace conference opened on January 18, 1919. It was dominated by the **Big Four**—Wilson, British prime minister David Lloyd George, French premier Georges Clemenceau, and Italian prime minister Vittorio Orlando.

Orlando, Lloyd George, and Clemenceau insisted that Germany bear the financial cost of the war by making huge **reparations**, or payments, to the Allies. They also wanted several secret spoils-of-war treaties honored. Such demands violated many of the principles included in President Wilson's peace plan.

Seated from left to right are Vittorio Orlando, David Lloyd George, Georges Clemenceau, and Woodrow Wilson.

THE GRANGER COLLECTION, NEW YORK

After six months of debate, the delegates agreed to a peace treaty. The official signing of the **Treaty of Versailles** took place in the palace of Versailles, just outside Paris, on June 28, 1919. Secretary of State Robert Lansing felt that "the terms of peace appear immeasurably harsh and humiliating."

Germany's colonies and the Ottoman Empire were divided among the Allied nations. At Wilson's insistence, however, the treaty established a mandate system. This required the new colonial rulers to report on their administration to the League of Nations. The peace treaty created the new nations of Czechoslovakia and Yugoslavia. It also re-established Estonia, Finland, Latvia, Lithuania, and Poland as independent nations. France reclaimed Alsace-Lorraine and won control of the Saar, an industrial region of Germany rich in coal and iron, for 15 years. Germany was disarmed, forced to admit full responsibility for the war, and charged billions of dollars in reparations.

Harsh as this treatment was, it would have been much worse without Wilson's moderating influence. He strongly opposed some of the Allies' more-extreme demands. Above all, the president made sure that the treaty included an agreement creating the League of Nations. He believed this would remedy any injustices the treaty might contain. The agreement required member nations to try to resolve disputes peacefully. If negotiations failed, the nations were to observe a waiting period before going to war. If any member nation failed to follow this procedure, the executive council could apply economic pressure and even recommend the use of force against the offending nation. Article 10, the heart of the agreement, required each member nation to "respect and preserve" the independence and territorial integrity of all other member nations.

Europe and the Middle East After World War I

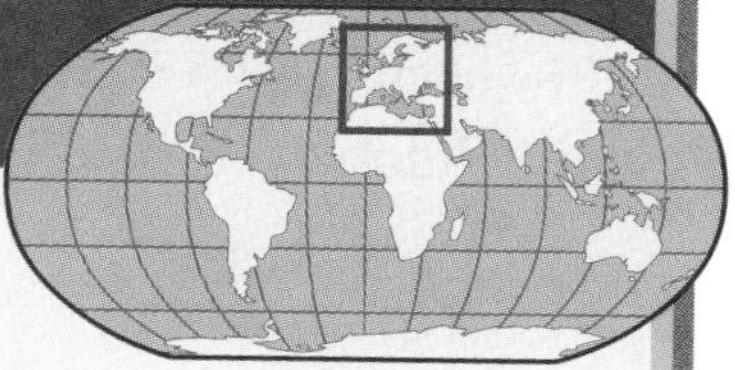

Learning from Maps Four empires—the Austro-Hungarian, German, Ottoman, and Russian— had collapsed by the end of the First World War.

? LOCATION How many countries were created from or received land that had belonged to Russia before the war?

Legend:
- Lost by Germany
- Lost by Bulgaria
- Lost by Austria-Hungary
- Lost by Russia
- Lost by Ottoman Empire
- British mandate
- French mandate
- Occupied by Allies

In 1922 the Bolsheviks were firmly in control of Russia, and they organized the Union of Soviet Socialist Republics.

✔ **READING CHECK:** What were the terms of the Treaty of Versailles?

President Wilson's Address

TO THE

League to Enforce Peace

PUBLISHED BY THE
LEAGUE TO ENFORCE PEACE
70 FIFTH AVENUE, NEW YORK

This is a printed copy of one of the many speeches that President Wilson gave to win support for the Treaty of Versailles.

The treaty in the Senate. Wilson returned to the United States in July 1919. He immediately began working to win the Senate's approval of the Treaty of Versailles. Wilson expected to receive the votes of most Democratic senators, but he needed support from Republicans to gain the necessary two-thirds majority. Most Republican senators had doubts about the treaty. Fourteen of them—called the irreconcilables—wanted nothing to do with the League of Nations and flatly rejected the treaty. The other 35 Republican senators—the reservationists—said that they could support the treaty if the League Covenant was changed. They particularly objected to Article 10, which seemed to commit the United States to go to war in defense of any League member that came under attack. Wilson's only hope was to gain the support of close to 20 reservationists by compromising on the League. Wilson refused.

Henry Cabot Lodge of Massachusetts, head of the Senate Committee on Foreign Relations and Wilson's longtime enemy, led the reservationists. Lodge kept the treaty stalled in the Foreign Relations Committee through the summer of 1919. Angry and frustrated, on September 4 Wilson began a grueling 9,500-mile speaking tour by train to defend the treaty. The crowds grew more enthusiastic as the tour went on but Lodge remained unmoved. He said, "The only people who have votes on the treaty are here in the Senate."

On the night of September 25, after a speech in Pueblo, Colorado, Wilson complained of a splitting headache. His doctor ordered him back to Washington, D.C. A few days later, Wilson collapsed from a near-fatal stroke. He lived out the rest of his term in seclusion in the White House, cut off from everyone except his wife and his closest aides. Moody, suspicious, and increasingly out of touch with reality, Wilson still refused to compromise.

In November, Lodge presented the treaty, with a list of 14 reservations, to the Senate. On Wilson's orders, all of the Democrats rejected the modified treaty. Without the list of reservations, the treaty met the same fate at the hands of the Republicans. In March 1920 another vote on Lodge's version of the treaty failed. By the time Wilson left office, the League of Nations had been established in Geneva, Switzerland, but without U.S. participation.

✔ **READING CHECK:** Why did the U.S. Senate reject the Treaty of Versailles?

Military Losses in World War I

Allied Powers

Central Powers

Casualties (in millions)

Wounded
Dead

Russia, British Empire, France, Italy, United States, Romania, Serbia, Belgium, Others

Germany, Austria-Hungary, Turkey, Bulgaria

Source: *Encyclopedia of Military History*

Learning from Graphs It is estimated that more than 8.5 million soldiers died during World War I. An even higher number suffered from battle-inflicted wounds.

? **Building Graph Skills** Which of the Allied Powers had the highest number of total casualties? Which of the Central Powers had the highest casualties?

The Global Impact of the War

While U.S. leaders debated whether or not to accept the Treaty of Versailles, the Europeans struggled to recover from the war. The war's destruction and human suffering had been almost incomprehensible. In all, more than 8.5 million people had died in battle, and another 21 million were wounded.

The war had left the industry and agriculture of much of continental Europe in ruins. Northern France was completely destroyed. British economist John Maynard Keynes observed the landscape.

> 66 For mile after mile nothing was left. No building was habitable and no field fit for the plow. . . . One devastated area was exactly like another—a heap of rubble, a morass [jumble] of shell-holes, and tangle of wire. 99

Those businesses still operating could not produce enough to meet demand, resulting in rapid inflation. In Germany food shortages were so extreme that it proved almost impossible to keep track of prices.

Throughout Europe, nations competed with one another over territories that they thought the treaty ought to have granted them. Arab nations in the Middle East had sided with the Allies in hopes of winning their independence from the Ottoman Turks. Instead, they found themselves living under French and British mandates. Tensions in the region grew after Britain issued the Balfour Declaration in 1917, which declared British support for a Jewish homeland in Palestine.

INTERPRETING THE VISUAL RECORD

The cost of war. At the end of the war, many towns and cities, like Houplines, France (above), lay in ruins. *What might the tall ruins in the middle of the photograph have been?*

✔ **READING CHECK:** What was the global impact of World War I?

SECTION 4 REVIEW

Define and explain the significance of the following terms:
Bolsheviks
Battle of the Argonne Forest
Fourteen Points
League of Nations
Big Four
reparations
Treaty of Versailles

Identify and explain the significance of the following individuals:
David Lloyd George
Georges Clemenceau
Vittorio Orlando
Henry Cabot Lodge

Locate and explain the importance of the following places:

Czechoslovakia	Latvia
Yugoslavia	Lithuania
Estonia	Poland
Finland	Saar

1. **Using Graphic Organizers** Copy the chart below. Use it to list the goals of President Wilson's Fourteen Points and the compromises that Allied demands forced him to make.

Wilson's Goals	Compromises

2. **Synthesizing** How did the Allied Powers finally win the war?
3. **Assessing Consequences** What were some of the effects of the war on Europe and the Middle East?
4. **Using Historical Imagination** Imagine you are a U.S. Senator. Prepare a chart listing the terms of the Treaty of Versailles and your reasons for supporting or opposing each term.

Critical Thinking

5. How might Wilson have won support for the League of Nations?
   Consider:
   • the concerns of the Republicans who opposed the League
   • the mood of the American public at the end of the war
   • the possible benefits League membership offered the United States

Review

Creating a Time Line

Copy the time line below onto a sheet of paper. Complete the time line by filling in the events and dates from the chapter that you think were most significant. Pick three events and explain why you think they were significant.

| 1914 | 1916 | 1918 | 1920 |

Writing a Summary

Using the Reading Checks as a guide, write an overview of the events in the chapter.

Identifying People and Ideas

Identify the following terms or individuals and explain their significance.

1. militarism
2. Franz Ferdinand
3. Allied Powers
4. *Sussex* pledge
5. convoy system
6. Bernard Baruch
7. Juliette Gordon Low
8. Great Migration
9. League of Nations
10. Henry Cabot Lodge

Understanding Main Ideas

SECTION 1

1. What tensions contributed to the outbreak of war in Europe?
2. What happened during the early weeks of the war?

SECTION 2

3. What contributions did the United States make to the Allied war effort before entering the war?

SECTION 3

4. What role did women play in the war effort?
5. How did the U.S. government ensure the public's cooperation with the war effort?

SECTION 4

6. What were the decisive battles at the end of World War I?

Reviewing Themes

1. **Global Relations** What led to the U.S. declaration of war in 1917? Was U.S. involvement in the conflict unavoidable? Explain your answer.
2. **Economic Development** How was the U.S. economy mobilized for war?
3. **Democratic Values** Did the U.S. government's attempts to rally support for the war interfere with citizens' First Amendment rights? Why or why not?

Thinking Critically

1. **Analyzing** What were the positive and the negative effects of the draft in the United States?
2. **Evaluating** What effect did the wartime labor shortage have on unions, women, African Americans, and Mexican Americans?
3. **Hypothesizing** How might history have been different if President Wilson had been more willing to compromise on the peace treaty?
4. **Recognizing Point of View** How did Germans disagree with Americans about the sinking of the *Lusitania*?
5. **Using Historical Imagination** How might the war have ended differently if the United States had remained neutral?

Writing About History

Writing to Persuade Imagine that you are an African American soldier during the war. Write your commanding officer a letter that tries to convince the army to open up more opportunities for African American soldiers. Use the following graphic to organize your thoughts.

Increased Opportunities for African American Soldiers			
Current Opportunities	Other Possible Opportunities	Benefit for Soldiers	Benefit for Army

Strategies **for Success**   Review the **Strategies for Success** on *Interpreting Literature as Historical Evidence.* Then read the 1918 poem below and answer the questions that follow.

The Ward at Night
The blanket lying dark against the sheet,
The heavy breathing of the sick,
The fevered voices
Telling of the battle
At the front,
Of Home and Mother.

1. What is the setting and subject of the poem?
2. How does it broaden your understanding of the war?

Linking History and Geography

Study the map below. How close did the Germans get to reaching Paris by June 1918?

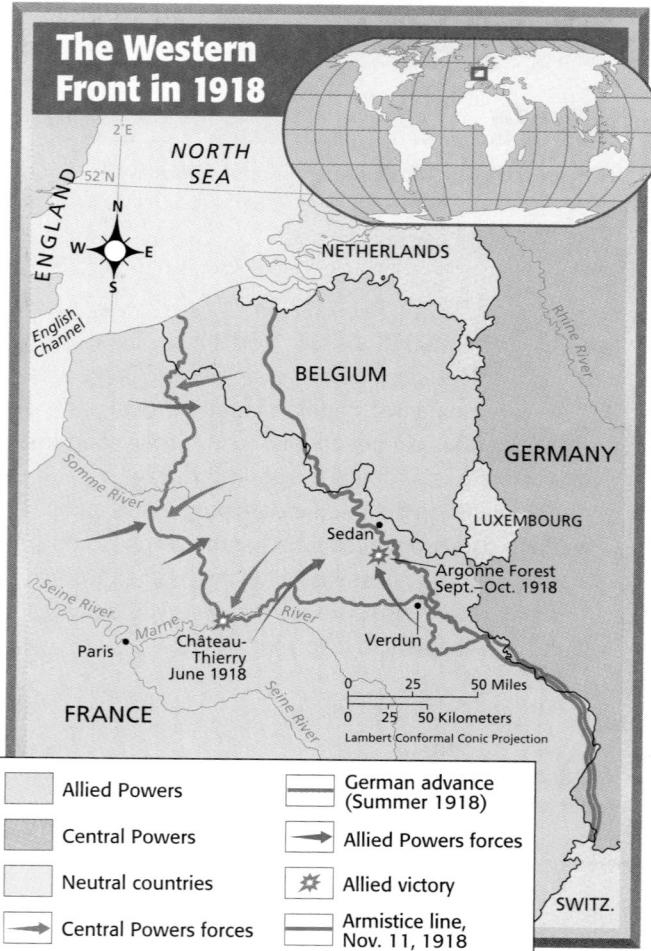

The Western Front in 1918

Allied Powers	German advance (Summer 1918)
Central Powers	Allied Powers forces
Neutral countries	Allied victory
Central Powers forces	Armistice line, Nov. 11, 1918

internet connect

TOPIC: Sarajevo
GO TO: go.hrw.com
KEYWORD: SD1 Sarajevo

Accessing the Internet through the HRW Web site, research the city of Sarajevo. Then write an essay in which you analyze the history of the city and the conflicts that have influenced European society.

BUILDING YOUR PORTFOLIO

Complete one or all of the following projects independently or cooperatively.

1 **Global Relations**
*Imagine that you are the U.S. ambassador to Germany in 1915. **Write a letter** to the kaiser protesting German violations of neutral shipping rights.*

2 **Democratic Values**
*Imagine that you are a senator committed to U.S. neutrality in World War I. **Write a speech** that explains why the United States should remain neutral.*

3 **Cultural Diversity**
*Imagine that it is 1915 and you are a recent immigrant to the United States from one of the Allied Powers. **Create a poster** encouraging Americans to support U.S. entry into World War I.*

World War I recruitment poster

Review

BUILDING YOUR PORTFOLIO

Outlined below are four projects. Independently or cooperatively, complete one and use the products to demonstrate your mastery of the historical concepts involved.

1 Constitutional Heritage

During the late 1800s, the transformation of the United States from a rural economy to an industrialized, urban society created numerous social problems. In response, the Progressive Party sought reforms. *Create a series of Progressive Party campaign posters* that outline the party's reform goals. Be sure to include the laws, amendments, and government changes the party desires. You may wish to use portfolio materials you designed in the unit chapters to help you.

Progressive Party candidate Theodore Roosevelt

2 Democratic Values

Historians note that women's suffrage was primarily a middle-class movement and thus did not address many of the concerns of working-class women. *Create a script for a dialogue* between a middle-class progressive and a working-class woman on whether the emphasis on women's suffrage best serves the needs of all women. You may wish to use portfolio materials you designed in the unit chapters to help you.

Nurse visiting a tenement house

3 Global Relations

The Spanish-American War and World War I brought the United States onto the world stage. *Prepare a speech* for delivery to Congress outlining some of the costs and benefits of America's international role. You may wish to use portfolio materials you designed in the unit chapters to help you.

American troops in France at the close of World War I

4 Economic Development

The expansionist policies of the United States in the late 1800s led to the establishment of U.S. colonies overseas, increased foreign investment, and conflicts with foreign powers. *Create a world map* showing areas of U.S. colonization, investment, and conflict through World War I. You may wish to use portfolio materials you designed in the unit chapters to help you.

Banana plantation near the Panama Canal

Further Reading

DeSantis, Vincent P. *The Shaping of Modern America: 1877–1916.* Allyn and Bacon, 1973. A broad survey of reform movements at the turn of the century.

Diner, Steven J. *A Very Different Age: Americans of the Progressive Era.* Hill and Wang, 1998. A cohesive account of the effects of industrialization and reform movements on Americans.

Ettinger, Albert M., and A. Churchill Ettinger. *A Doughboy with the Fighting 69th.* White Mane, 1992. Reminiscence of World War I by a soldier of the 69th Rainbow Division.

Hall, Linda B., and Don M. Coerver. *Revolution on the Border: The United States and Mexico, 1910–1920.* University of New Mexico Press, 1990. Examines the role that trade and investment played in U.S.-Mexico relations.

Liliuokalani. *Hawaii's Story by Hawaii's Queen.* Charles E. Tuttle, 1991. First-hand account of Hawaii in the 1800s.

Schneider, Dorothy, and Carl J. Schneider. *Into the Breach.* Viking, 1991. Examines the participation of American women in World War I.

HOLT RESEARCHER
Internet Connect and Holt Researcher CD–ROM *Review*

In assigned groups, develop a multimedia presentation about America between 1897 and 1920. Choose information from the chapter Internet Connect activities and the **Holt Researcher** CD–ROM that best reflect the major topics of the period. Write an outline and a script for your presentation, which may be shown to the class.

Prosperity and Crisis

1919–1939

Howard Thain's painting The Great White Way *from 1928 portrays the vibrancy of urban life during the 1920s.*

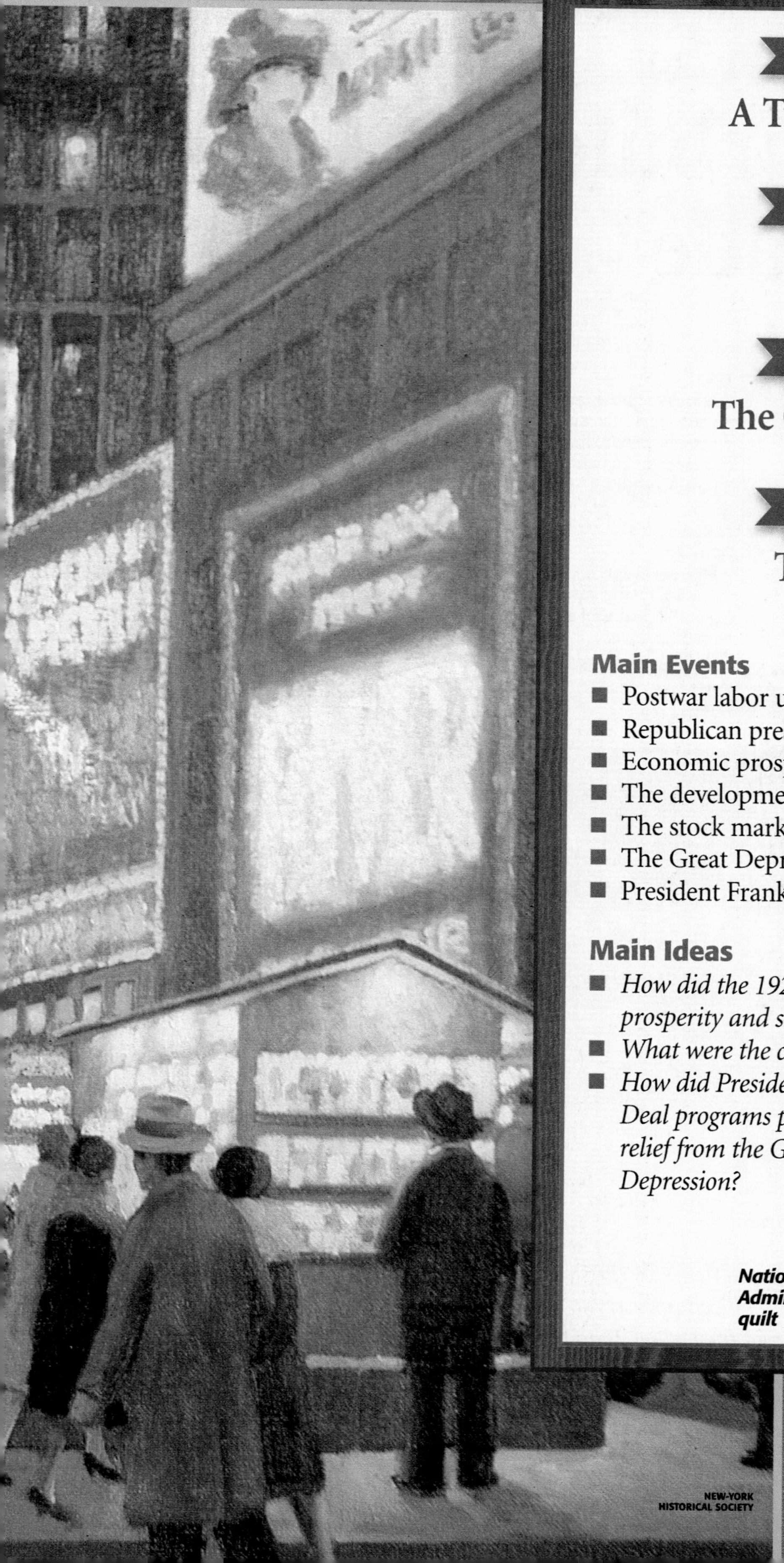

CHAPTER 22
A Turbulent Decade
1919–1929

CHAPTER 23
The Jazz Age
1920–1929

CHAPTER 24
The Great Depression
1929–1933

CHAPTER 25
The New Deal
1933–1939

Main Events
- Postwar labor unrest
- Republican presidency
- Economic prosperity
- The development of a national culture
- The stock market crash
- The Great Depression
- President Franklin D. Roosevelt's New Deal

Main Ideas
- *How did the 1920s represent a period of both prosperity and social division?*
- *What were the causes of the Great Depression?*
- *How did President Roosevelt's New Deal programs provide relief from the Great Depression?*

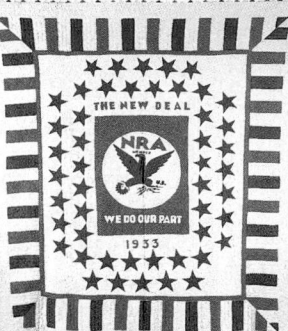

National Recovery Administration quilt

1919–1929
A Turbulent Decade

Harding campaign button

THE GRANGER
COLLECTION,
NEW YORK

Teapot Dome political cartoon

1921
Business and Finance
An economic recession caused by demobilization leads to 20,000 business failures.

1920
Politics
Warren G. Harding is elected president of the United States by the largest popular majority in U.S. history to date.

1921
Daily Life
A race riot erupts in Tulsa, Oklahoma, resulting in the deaths of at least 30 people.

1922
Business and Finance
Charles Dawes, head of the Bureau of the Budget, turns the federal government's annual deficit into a surplus.

1924
Politics
The Teapot Dome scandal is exposed.

1919

1921

1923

1919
Daily Life
Looting and mob violence erupt in Boston as the city's police force goes on strike.

A soldier guards a store during the Boston police strike.

1922
The Arts
Sinclair Lewis publishes *Babbitt*, a novel that criticizes middle-class conservatism and conformity.

Sinclair Lewis's novel

BABBITT

Sinclair Lewis

Before You Read

Build on What You Know

World War I affected the daily lives of many Americans. The government mobilized industry to produce necessary goods for U.S. soldiers and their allies, who finally achieved victory against the Central Powers in 1918. During the war the U.S. government suppressed political protests. In this chapter you will learn about the changes in American life after the war. Although prosperity returned to the United States, economic benefits and political freedom were not enjoyed by everyone.

Ku Klux Klan publication

Ben Shahn's painting of Sacco and Vanzetti on trial

SHAHN, BEN. *BARTOLOMEO VANZETTI AND NICOLA SACCO* (1931–1932)

1925
Daily Life
The Ku Klux Klan holds a parade in Washington, D.C., with over 40,000 participants.

1925
The Arts
The *Grand Ole Opry* broadcasts its first performance over radio station WSM in Nashville, Tennessee.

1927
Politics
Italian immigrants Nicola Sacco and Bartolomeo Vanzetti are executed after being convicted of murder.

1927
Science and Technology
John Daniel Rust invents the mechanical cotton picker.

1928
World Events
Scottish doctor Alexander Fleming discovers penicillin, the first antibiotic.

1929
Daily Life
Eastman Kodak introduces 16 mm motion picture cameras and projectors for home use.

1929
The Arts
The Museum of Modern Art opens in New York City.

1925

1927

1929

1925
Business and Finance
The Pullman Company refuses to recognize the African American union founded by A. Philip Randolph.

1926
Science and Technology
Thomas Hunt Morgan proves a theory of heredity and locates genes in the chromosomes of fruit flies.

1926
Business and Finance
Congress passes the Revenue Act, reducing taxes for the wealthiest Americans.

1929
Science and Technology
Construction of the Empire State Building begins.

Members of A. Philip Randolph's union

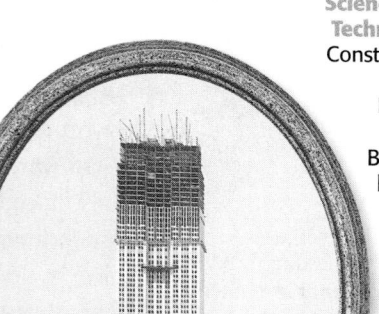

The Empire State Building under construction

Think About Themes

Themes Journal *Decide whether you* **agree** *or* **disagree** *with the following statements. Note why in your journal.*

Democratic Values The fear of radicalism in the United States causes many Americans to sacrifice personal liberties for a sense of security.

Economic Development Government policies that encourage economic growth can also lead to social instability.

Cultural Diversity Restrictions on immigration hurt a country more than they help in the long run.

Postwar Troubles

❝ *We danced in the streets, embraced old women and pretty girls, swore blood brotherhood with soldiers . . . [and] reeled through the streets.* ❞
—**Malcolm Cowley**

Malcolm Cowley recalled the spirit of celebration that possessed many Americans after hearing news of the end of World War I. The carefree spirit of celebration was short-lived, however. For many Americans, postwar life did not appear promising.

Veteran searching for work

Demobilization

The abrupt ending of World War I caught American industries by surprise. Factories and war-related industries had been operating at full capacity when the demand for military supplies suddenly dried up. The sudden process of **demobilization**, or the transition from wartime to peacetime production levels, caused social and economic strain. The return of some 4 million soldiers to the workforce caused unemployment to rise and wages to fall. Meanwhile, wartime shortages left prices high.

To make room for the returning veterans, women were urged to give up their jobs. "The same patriotism which induced women to enter industry during the war should induce them to vacate their positions," declared the New York Labor Federation. Many women were forced out of their jobs. As a result, the percentage of women in the workforce in 1920 fell slightly below what it had been in 1910.

Americans who were worried about the impact of demobilization on their jobs also faced a skyrocketing cost of living. With peace at hand, consumers went on a spending spree. They made purchases they had put off during the war. The demand for goods outpaced supply, and prices soared. The cost of goods and services roughly doubled from 1914 to 1920.

Soon, however, this trend reversed. Prices fell when a brief but deep recession struck in 1920–21. Demobilization was one of the factors behind the recession. During the war millions of Americans had worked in defense industries. At war's end, however, the government canceled more than $2 billion in military contracts. Factories responded by cutting back production and laying off workers. By 1921 some 5 million workers—nearly 12 percent of the labor force—were unemployed. Even Americans with jobs suffered. "Working conditions . . . seemed harder than ever," reported one steelworker. "We were only paid forty-two cents an hour, and we worked like a mule."

The impact of demobilization extended beyond factory life, however. A farm crisis added to the nation's economic problems.

Women who worked in factories during World War I were encouraged to give up their jobs to returning veterans.

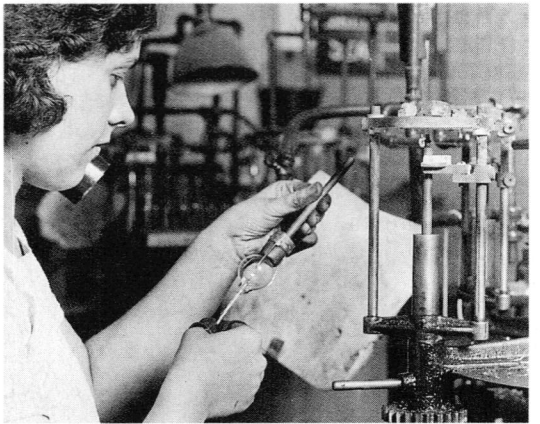

Farmers had benefited from wartime markets in Europe. As European farm production revived, however, these markets dried up and farm prices fell. Cotton, for example, fell dramatically from 35 cents per pound in 1919 to 16 cents a year later. Burdened with debt, hundreds of thousands of American farmers lost ownership of their land during the 1920s.

✔ **READING CHECK:** What were some economic outcomes of demobilization?

As the nation's economy suffered after World War I, American farmers experienced a severe crisis. Publications such as this one chronicled farmers' experiences.

Labor Strife

Many workers protested in response to the difficulties of demobilization. They demanded higher wages and shorter work hours. When management ignored labor's pleas, many workers went on strike. More than 3,600 work stoppages—involving some 4 million workers—took place in 1919 alone.

The Seattle general strike.
The first major strike of 1919 occurred when some 35,000 shipyard workers in Seattle walked off the job. They demanded higher wages and shorter hours. Some 110 local unions joined the workers. The **Seattle general strike** began on February 6 at 10:00 A.M. Some 60,000 workers left their jobs to participate in the strike, which was extremely well organized. "It was," declared one shipyard worker, "the most beautiful thing I [had] ever seen!" The General Strike Committee set up 21 community kitchens to feed strikers. The committee made arrangements for milk delivery to people caring for children.

The strike occurred without a single incident of violence. Nevertheless, city officials and business leaders expressed alarm. Newspapers blamed immigrants for the strike and called the strikers "muddle-headed foreigners." The strikers came under increased public pressure to go back to work. After five days they ended the strike without winning any of their demands.

The strike had been peaceful. However, antilabor forces tried to convince the public that Seattle had been on the brink of a revolution similar to Russia's Bolshevik Revolution. Seattle mayor Ole Hanson told the national press, "Revolution . . . doesn't need violence. The general strike . . . is of itself the weapon of revolution." Many people believed these charges. In the end, the strike helped turn public opinion against organized labor.

Seattle general strike. With many of the city services shut down during the Seattle general strike, organizers established community kitchens and provided some limited services. *What information does this photograph offer about the organization of the strikers?*

The Boston police strike.
In September 1919 another strike, the **Boston police strike**, further inflamed antilabor sentiments. The Boston police officers had recently formed a union to seek better pay and working conditions. Officers in other cities had unionized without incident. However, Boston's police commissioner, Edwin Curtis, refused to recognize the union. Instead, he fired 19 officers for engaging in union activities. In response, some 75 percent of the Boston police force went on strike. Public order in the city quickly collapsed. Journalist William Allen White described the first night of the strike:

Strikes. During the Boston police strike, civilians took over traffic control and other public-safety jobs. *How does this photograph suggest that this civilian is helping to preserve public safety during the strike?*

> ❝ The devil was loose in Boston. . . . Little knots of boys and young men began wandering through the streets. . . . By midnight, the . . . crowds had formed one raging mob, a drunken, noisy, irresponsible mob. . . . Someone threw a loose paving stone through a store window about one o'clock. The tension snapped. . . . By two o'clock, looting had begun. ❞

After two nights of violence, Governor Calvin Coolidge called in the state militia to restore order. Boston's newspapers denounced the strikers as "agents of Lenin" and the strike as a "Bolshevist nightmare." Public opinion also came out firmly against the strike. Recognizing that their cause was doomed, the police voted unanimously to return to work. Commissioner Curtis, however, refused to reinstate the officers. Instead, he hired a new force made up of unemployed veterans. Union sympathizers protested. Unmoved, Coolidge backed the commissioner. He proclaimed that "there is no right to strike against the public safety by anybody, anywhere, any time."

The steel strike. Two weeks after the Boston strike, some 365,000 steelworkers in western Pennsylvania—many of them immigrants—walked off the job. This action began the **steel strike of 1919**. The strikers were demanding recognition of their union and protesting low wages and long working hours. The massive walkout threatened to shut down the steel industry.

Having fought efforts to unionize steelworkers for years, the major steel companies did everything in their power to break the strike. To divide labor along ethnic lines, they portrayed foreign workers as radicals and called on "loyal" Americans to return to work. The steel companies also brought in thousands of workers—including African Americans and Mexicans—to replace the strikers.

The steel companies also enlisted the aid of police officers to pressure the strikers and even hired armed thugs to intimidate them. Strikers were jailed, beaten, or shot. Faced with such tactics, union leaders called off the strike on January 9, 1920.

The United Mine Workers strike. The last major strike of 1919 erupted in November. Some 400,000 coal miners walked out of the mines in the **United Mine Workers strike**. Miners were protesting the continued enforcement of wartime contracts that kept workers' pay fixed at 1917 rates despite increases in consumer prices. Some members of the United Mine Workers (UMW) demanded a 50 percent pay increase, a five-day workweek, and a six-hour workday.

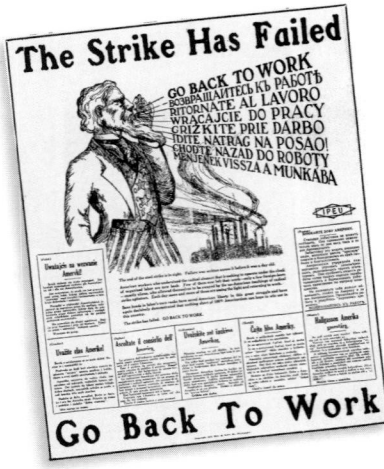

During the Pittsburgh steel strike newspapers such as the Pittsburgh Chronicle Telegraph urged strikers to go back to work.

B I O G R A P H Y

John L. Lewis

The strike was organized by the newly elected president of the UMW, John L. Lewis. Born in 1880, Lewis was 39 years old and had just gained control of the UMW when the strike was called on November 1, 1919. It was the first strike he organized.

Lewis was well acquainted with the life and concerns of miners and unionists. He was raised in an Iowa mining family. His father spent his days working in the coal pits and his nights organizing miners in the Knights of Labor union. Lewis briefly attended school, then followed in his father's footsteps. He was working in the mines by the age of 15. Lewis soon began to urge fellow workers to demand better and safer working conditions. By 1906 he had been elected as a representative to the UMW national convention. In 1911 American Federation of Labor founder Samuel Gompers recruited Lewis to become a field representative who would organize mine workers.

Lewis's experience as a miner and union organizer served him well during the 1919 strike. President Woodrow Wilson condemned the strike, which violated the union's wartime agreement not to strike, as a "grave moral and legal wrong." After Wilson ordered an injunction to halt the strike, Lewis declared the strike over. However, he quietly urged miners not to return to work. The strategy worked. On December 6, President Wilson designed a compromise package in which miners would receive a 14 percent wage increase. Lewis called off the strike, stating, "I will not fight my Government, the greatest government on earth." The UMW victory insured Lewis's position as a national labor leader. Lewis continued to push for miners' concerns until his death in 1969.

As with most of the strikes of 1919, public opinion did not side with labor during the UMW strike. Despite his many patriotic appeals, Lewis was accused of having ties to Bolsheviks in Russia and of urging revolution within the United States.

✔ **READING CHECK:** What were the main causes of the strikes in 1919? How did most Americans react to the strikes?

Read More About It

Free Find:
John L. Lewis
After reading the biography on John L. Lewis on the **Holt Researcher** CD–ROM, write a short essay explaining how his experiences helped him lead the United Mine Workers union.

The Red Scare

The wave of strikes during 1919 struck fear into the hearts of many Americans. The 1919 strikes were prompted primarily by laborers' desires for a fair deal. Many Americans, however, saw the labor unrest as proof of a coming workers' revolution. Fear that a Bolshevik revolution would erupt in the United States reached its height during the **Red Scare**. This was a period of anticommunist hysteria during 1919 and 1920.

The Red Scare in the United States was a response to the 1917 revolution in Russia. This revolution resulted in the establishment of a communist government based on Marxist teachings. Under communism, the Russian government owned and controlled all private property, including every industry and factory. In 1919 Russia's Bolshevik leader Vladimir I. Lenin established an organization called the Communist International. It was designed to encourage a worldwide communist revolution by overthrowing capitalism and free enterprise. The idea that communism might take hold in the United States was frightening to many Americans during 1919.

INTERPRETING THE VISUAL RECORD

Red Scare. This cartoon entitled "Put Them Out & Keep Them Out" appeared in the *Philadelphia Inquirer* in 1919. *What fears does this cartoon express?*

THE GRANGER COLLECTION, NEW YORK

Marxists in America. Karl Marx's message of an unavoidable working-class revolution has been interpreted in many ways over time. It even won some support in the United States. Labor leader Eugene Debs and others formed the Marxist-inspired Socialist Party in 1901. In contrast to the revolutionary Marxism of the Communist Party, Debs's Socialist Party foresaw a peaceful transition to socialism by democratic means. Debs ran for president five times between 1900 and 1920. His

Eugene Debs spread socialist political beliefs during his five bids for the presidency between 1900 and 1920.

Socialist Party platform called for the collective ownership of industry, which was to be achieved by nonviolent means. In the 1912 election Debs received about 900,000 votes.

When the Bolsheviks seized power in Russia in 1917, most American members of the Socialist Party joined Debs in refusing to support the violent overthrow of the government. A smaller number of American radicals did support the Bolsheviks. These Americans openly embraced Marx's revolutionary ideas. Some believed such a revolution should happen in the United States. Many Americans ignored the differences between socialists and communists. After witnessing the massive strikes of 1919, many people believed that all radicals and labor activists were Bolshevik agents who wanted to overthrow the U.S. government. Some Americans believed that communists, or "Reds," were everywhere. Immigrants, particularly those involved in unions, came under great suspicion. Antiradical fears reached such heights that several elected members of the New York State Assembly were expelled because of their membership in the Socialist Party.

The Palmer raids.

Many Americans interpreted a rash of bomb scares in 1919 as justification for their antiradical fears. The bomb scares further intensified the hysteria of the Red Scare. In April postal clerks discovered 36 bombs in the mail addressed to prominent citizens, including John D. Rockefeller, Justice Oliver Wendell Holmes of the Supreme Court, and Postmaster General Albert Burleson. Then, less than a month later, several bombings occurred. One bomb damaged the house of Attorney General A. Mitchell Palmer. The bomber, an Italian anarchist, died in the blast.

Newspapers began demanding harsh action against radicals. Hoping to further his presidential ambitions, Attorney General Palmer responded by launching an anticommunist crusade. He created a special government office to gather information on radical activities. Palmer placed J. Edgar Hoover, the future head of the Federal Bureau of Investigation, in charge.

Palmer's most dramatic action was a series of raids to capture alleged radicals. The **Palmer raids** began in November 1919. They peaked on January 2, 1920, when federal officials arrested thousands of suspected radicals in 33 cities nationwide. Although the government claimed that radicals were "armed to the teeth," just three pistols were seized during the raids.

Most of those arrested were poor immigrants who had recently arrived in the country. In most cases, there was no real evidence against them. Hundreds of foreigners suspected of radical activities were deported. Among the deportees was Emma Goldman, a noted feminist, writer, and speaker.

Attorney General A. Mitchell Palmer waged a public campaign against all perceived radicals.

By the summer of 1920 public hysteria over radicalism was dying down. The predictions that a communist revolution was close at hand proved unfounded. Furthermore, many Americans had never supported the witch-hunting tactics employed by the anticommunist crusaders.

✔ **READING CHECK:** What caused the public hysteria of the Red Scare?

Strategies for Success — Evaluating News Stories

News stories are an extremely important resource for historians. Different types of news media contain an enormous amount of information that historians access regularly to help them create their accounts of the past. News stories, however, possess certain advantages and disadvantages as historical sources.

Although the print media frequently provide news coverage that is thorough and analytically sophisticated, this coverage lacks the sense of immediacy that is conveyed through the broadcast media. In contrast, radio and television reports often sacrifice detail and in-depth analysis of issues to provide news coverage that is as current as possible. In any case, all forms of news media must be examined carefully for fairness and accuracy in their presentation of events.

How to Evaluate a News Story

1. **Become familiar with the source.** First, determine whether the news story is presented through broadcast media or through print media. Then, if possible, find out about the historical background of the story's creator and the story's intended audience.
2. **Assess the story's coverage of events.** As you study the story, determine whether it covers its subject in sufficient depth. Check to see if it includes adequate background information and explores the possible consequences of events.
3. **Assess the fairness and accuracy of the reporting.** Examine the story carefully for fairness and accuracy in its presentation of events. Determine whether the reporting "sticks to the facts," explains any differing points of view in a balanced way, or displays any recognizable biases of its own.

4. **Put the information to use.** If possible, compare the story with other sources that address the same subject. Then use the results of your analysis, along with your knowledge of the historical period, to form generalizations and draw conclusions.

Applying the Strategy

Examine the following excerpt from a news story that appeared in the *Atlanta Constitution* on August 23, 1927.

> 66 **State Prison, Charlestown, Mass.—Nicola Sacco and Bartolomeo Vanzetti were put to death today.**
>
> **They went to the embrace of the electric chair unswerving in the avowal of their innocence.**
>
> **They paid with their lives for the murder of a paymaster and his guard at South Braintree seven years ago.**
>
> **As the heavy voltage of electricity was shot through their bodies, bayoneted guards surrounded the ancient prison for blocks.**
>
> **In cities on three continents millions awaited word of their death, many of them convinced that the two were executed for their political beliefs, not for the South Braintree murders.** 99

Practicing the Strategy

Use the excerpt above to answer the following questions.
1. Does this excerpt cover its subject in sufficient depth?
2. Is the reporting in the excerpt fair and accurate? What biases, if any, does it display?
3. How does the excerpt contribute to your understanding of the Red Scare?

Sacco and Vanzetti

Although the Red Scare passed, hostility toward foreigners and radicals persisted. One of the most sensational trials of the 1920s involved two Italian immigrants who were convicted of murder and sentenced to death. Although both were anarchists, they lived fairly quiet lives. Nicola Sacco was a shoemaker, and Bartolomeo Vanzetti peddled fish from a pushcart. Sacco and Vanzetti were charged with the murders of a paymaster and a guard during a 1920 payroll robbery outside a shoe factory near Boston. Upon arrest, the police found the men armed with pistols. After an intense interrogation, the two were charged with murder.

Sacco and Vanzetti. The trial and execution of Sacco and Vanzetti divided liberals and conservatives during the 1920s. *How do the picket signs reflect the views of the supporters of Sacco and Vanzetti?*

Sacco and Vanzetti were tried before Judge Webster Thayer, who was known for his strong dislike of radicals. The two immigrants' radical political views and their avoidance of military service in 1917 helped turn the trial against them. Eyewitnesses who could offer alibis for Sacco and Vanzetti were dismissed. The jury returned a guilty verdict. Judge Thayer sentenced the two to death. Judge Thayer ended the trial with a bold statement.

 This man [Vanzetti], although he may not actually have committed the crime attributed to him, is nevertheless morally culpable [guilty], because he is an enemy of our existing institutions. . . . The defendant's ideals are cognate [associated] with crime. "

The verdict outraged defenders of civil liberties. They argued that the two men had been convicted not because of the evidence presented but because they were immigrants and radicals. The verdict and subsequent appeals drew worldwide attention. In Paris, New York City, and elsewhere, thousands of people marched in protest. Noted writers and artists rallied to the cause. All pleas for a new trial failed. On August 23, 1927, Sacco and Vanzetti were executed. Many Americans believed that radicals like Sacco and Vanzetti deserved to be punished for their views, while others saw them as heroes. The guilt or innocence of Sacco and Vanzetti served as a subject of heated debate. Some recently discovered evidence indicates that at least one of the men probably was involved in the crime. What remains clear, however, is that antiradical views severely tainted the trial. The case reflected the deep divisions tearing at American society in the postwar era. As American novelist John Dos Passos declared after the execution, "We are two nations."

✔ **READING CHECK:** Why did the trial of Sacco and Vanzetti arouse public interest?

SECTION ① REVIEW

Define and explain the significance of the following terms:
demobilization
Seattle general strike
Boston police strike
steel strike of 1919
United Mine Workers strike
Red Scare
Palmer raids

Identify and explain the significance of the following individuals:
John L. Lewis
A. Mitchell Palmer
Nicola Sacco
Bartolomeo Vanzetti

1. **Using Graphic Organizers** Copy the graphic organizer below. Use it to explain the causes of the strikes during 1919 and the public reaction to the strikes.

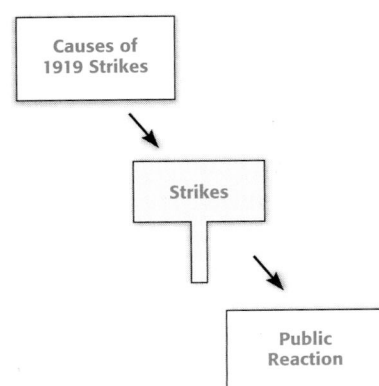

2. **Assessing Consequences** How did the process of demobilization alter the lives of many women, factory workers, and farmers?
3. **Evaluating** Why were the tactics of the Palmer raids controversial?
4. **Identifying Cause and Effect** How did the political climate of the Red Scare influence the results of the Sacco and Vanzetti case? What effect did the trial's verdict have on public opinion?

Critical Thinking

5. How did international political events combine with postwar domestic life in the United States to lead to the mounting hysteria associated with the Red Scare?
   Consider:
   • the events in Russia between 1917 and 1919
   • the role of socialists and communists in U.S. political life
   • labor unrest of 1919

The Republicans in Power

OBJECTIVES

Read to understand:

1. how Republican policies encouraged economic growth
2. what the positive and negative effects of the Harding administration's pro-business policies were
3. why the movement to pass the Equal Rights Amendment failed
4. how the Republican Party overcame the political scandals of the Harding administration
5. what issues affected the outcome of the 1928 presidential election

KEY TERMS

Fordney-McCumber Tariff Act
mergers
American Plan
feminists
Equal Rights Amendment
Teapot Dome scandal

KEY PEOPLE

Warren G. Harding
Andrew Mellon
Charles Dawes
Mary Anderson
Albert Fall
Calvin Coolidge
Alfred E. Smith

EYEWITNESSES TO History

❝ *Keep Warren [G. Harding] at home. Don't let him make any speeches. If he goes out on a tour somebody's sure to ask him questions, and Warren's just the sort of . . . fool that will try to answer them.* ❞

—Boies Penrose

Harding campaign sign

Pennsylvania Republican political boss Boies (BOYZ) Penrose gave advice to party leaders after the relatively unknown Ohio senator Warren G. Harding was nominated as the Republican presidential candidate for the 1920 election. Penrose and the rest of the Republican Party were confident that their party would win the election. Strikes and the Democrats' preoccupation with the League of Nations had characterized the previous two years. The Republican Party leaders, therefore, believed they had a sure shot at the presidency no matter who ran.

The Election of 1920

Seeking a presidential candidate with broad appeal, Republican Party leaders nominated Warren G. Harding. While many party members thought Senator Harding was friendly and looked presidential, he lacked Woodrow Wilson's intelligence. Confident of their chances to win the election, the Republican leaders did not feel their candidate had to be a political genius.

Harding ran on a pro-business, antilabor platform that promised tax revision, higher tariffs, limits on immigration, and some aid to farmers. What pleased war-weary voters the most, however, was Harding's call for a return to "normalcy." "America's present need is not heroics but healing, not nostrums [false cures] but normalcy, not revolution but restoration," he declared. In contrast, the Democratic candidate, Governor James M. Cox, also from Ohio, bowed to pressure from President Wilson and focused on the League of Nations during his campaign.

The nation's farmers, suffering from falling crop prices, rallied behind Harding. Many middle-class citizens, tired of labor strikes and high taxes, also voted Republican. Harding won the election of 1920 by a greater majority of the popular vote than any previous candidate. He received 16 million votes, more than 60 percent of the popular vote, and 404 electoral votes to Cox's 127. "It wasn't a landslide," suggested Joseph Tumulty. "It was an earthquake."

Harding's Pro-Business Administration

President Harding's administration introduced many policy changes. Harding's primary goal was providing "less government in business and more business in government." His cabinet included such successful business leaders as Secretary of

The Free Market

The United States has historically operated under a free-market economic system. Consumers and business leaders, not government officials, decide what, how, and for whom goods are produced. However, some political groups such as the Progressive Party have supported the regulation of some business practices.

The Republican administrations of the 1920s created several policies to reduce progressive controls over U.S. business practices. They hoped to encourage an even more open free-market system. "Business should be unhampered and free," President Coolidge argued.

Today the push for a free market has become an international issue. During the 1990s many countries began lowering trade barriers and removing restrictions on free-market practices. Governments have established trade agreements to allow an easier flow of goods between countries. These efforts have expanded the free market and increased economic prosperity. However, many modern Americans, like the progressives before them, are concerned that unregulated businesses fail to benefit everyone. Some companies have used free-trade agreements to get around U.S. labor laws preventing sweatshop labor. These corporations have moved production to underdeveloped countries where they can find workers willing to work long hours for little pay.

Trucks ship goods from American-owned factories in Mexico.

the Treasury Andrew Mellon and Secretary of Commerce Herbert Hoover. These men believed that government should not interfere with the economy except to aid business.

The administration set two main economic goals: to reduce the national debt and to promote economic growth. Wartime spending had raised the national debt from some $1 billion in 1914 to more than $25 billion in 1919. As head of the Bureau of the Budget, Charles Dawes set out to eliminate debt by slashing spending. In 1922 he succeeded in turning the government's annual budget deficit into a surplus.

The Republican-led Congress further supported businesses by passing the **Fordney-McCumber Tariff Act** in 1922. The law pushed tariff rates on manufactured goods to an all-time high. This helped U.S. manufacturers by enabling them to keep prices high and increase profits.

To achieve the second goal—economic growth—Mellon proposed eliminating the high wartime taxes imposed on the wealthy. If "government takes away an unreasonable share," he argued, "the incentive [encouragement] to work is no longer there and slackening of effort is the result." He claimed that if taxes were lower the rich would have more money to invest and the economy would grow. Mellon argued that the benefits would then trickle down to the middle and lower classes in the form of jobs and higher wages. In accordance with Mellon's proposal, Congress cut taxes for wealthy Americans during the 1920s.

By 1923 Harding's economic policy appeared to be working. The postwar slump was over. Unemployment was low and most sectors of the economy had entered a period of tremendous growth.

✔ **READING CHECK:** In what ways did Republican policies encourage economic growth?

The Effects of Republican Policies

President Harding's pro-business policies significantly affected the economy and the lives of many Americans. The availability of surplus capital from tax cuts caused industry to boom. More than 1,000 **mergers**—the combining of two or more companies—took place in this era of rapid growth. Businesses favored mergers because they brought greater efficiency and higher profits. By 1930 some 200 corporations owned nearly half of the nation's corporate wealth. With its favorable attitude toward business, the federal government encouraged this process of consolidation. The government also made little effort to enforce antitrust laws.

For the most part, workers did not share in the business prosperity of the 1920s. From 1923 to 1929, business profits increased some 60 percent. Over the same period, however, workers' incomes grew by about 10 percent. Many workers in so-called sick industries such as the textile industry faced pay cuts and unemployment.

Farmers also struggled. Although the Fordney-McCumber Tariff was intended to help agriculture as well as business, it brought little relief to farmers. The act levied high duties on imported farm products in an effort to boost American crop prices. However, farmers continued to face shrinking markets, low prices, high interest rates, and crushing debt.

Organized labor also suffered during the 1920s. The government and courts sought to roll back the labor gains of the Progressive Era. Federal courts, for example, upheld "yellow-dog contracts," which prevented workers from joining unions. Business leaders promoted a policy known as the **American Plan**, which supported union-free open shops. As a result, union membership shrank from a high of more than 5 million in 1920 to some 3.6 million in 1923.

✔ **READING CHECK:** What were the positive and negative results of Harding's pro-business policies?

New Directions for Women

Working conditions also became a divisive issue among women's rights activists, often called **feminists**. The Nineteenth Amendment had granted women the right to vote. However, it did not revolutionize U.S. politics as many Americans had hoped—or feared. The suffrage issue had unified women with a wide variety of political interests, but after its passage, that unity dissolved.

Many women who had joined the suffrage campaign now moved in different directions. Jane Addams pursued the cause of world peace through the Women's International League for Peace and Freedom. Carrie Chapman Catt and other former suffrage leaders formed the League of Women Voters. Its aim was to inform women about public issues and about candidates for office.

Divisions in the women's movement emerged in the debate over the **Equal Rights Amendment** (ERA). This was a constitutional amendment proposed to Congress in 1923 by Alice Paul of the National Woman's Party. The proposed amendment stated: "Men and women shall have equal rights throughout the United States and every place subject to its jurisdiction."

Equal rights for women seemed a desirable goal. However, Paul's amendment met opposition from many reformers, including women. During the Progressive Era, reformers had battled for legislation regulating the hours and working conditions of female workers. Mary Anderson, director of the U.S. Women's Bureau, was one of the opponents of the ERA who feared that the amendment would make such legislation unconstitutional.

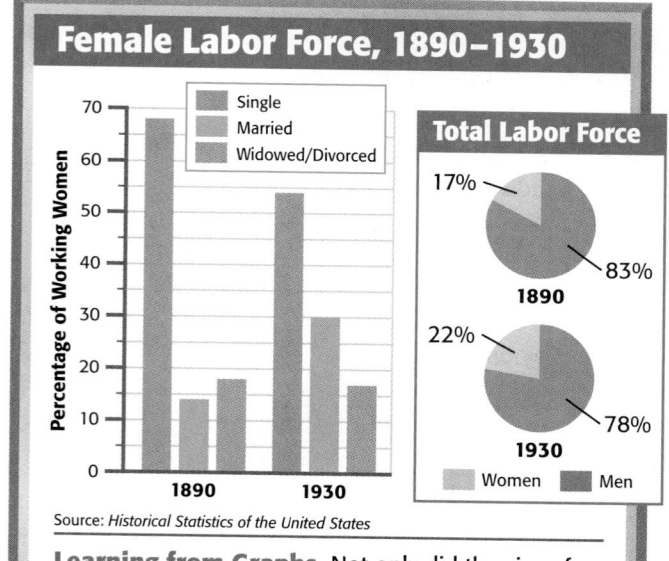

Female Labor Force, 1890–1930

Percentage of Working Women

- Single
- Married
- Widowed/Divorced

Total Labor Force

1890: 17% / 83%
1930: 22% / 78%

Women / Men

Source: *Historical Statistics of the United States*

Learning from Graphs Not only did the size of the female labor force grow by 1930, its makeup also changed. By 1930 some 30 percent of working women were married, up from just over 10 percent in 1890.

❓ **Building Graph Skills** Women made up what percentage of the total labor force in 1890? in 1930?

Many working-class women saw the Equal Rights Amendment as a middle-class issue that would remove the protective legislation passed during the reform era.

> ❝ Women who are wage earners, with one job in the factory and another in the home, have little time and energy left to carry on the fight to better their economic status. They need the help of . . . labor laws. ❞

Supporters of the ERA argued that special legislation for women actually hurt female job seekers, particularly in male-dominated occupations. Employers were discouraged from hiring or promoting women, they claimed, because of legal limitations on the hours women were allowed to work. In the end, the ERA movement failed to win political support.

✔ **READING CHECK:** Why did the movement to pass the Equal Rights Amendment fail?

The Enduring Republican Presidency

The proposal for the Equal Rights Amendment came as President Harding's administration was facing a storm of political scandals. Charges of political wrongdoing by members of the Harding administration began to surface in 1923. They cast a dark shadow over the highest levels of national government.

The Harding scandals. The scandals came to light during the midpoint of Harding's only term in office. A group of Harding's friends known as the Ohio Gang had followed him to Washington, D.C. They were using their connections to the president to enrich themselves at the public's expense.

The first scandal surfaced in the spring of 1923. It was discovered that Charles Forbes, Harding's close friend and director of the Veterans' Bureau, had pocketed millions of dollars through corrupt schemes. Harding was deeply worried by the Forbes scandal and other evidence of wrongdoing in his administration. In June 1923 he confessed to journalist William Allen White, "I have no trouble with my enemies. I can take care of my enemies all right. [It's my] friends . . . that keep me walking the floor nights." Soon after talking to White, Harding set out on an extended tour of the West. On August 2 he died suddenly of an apparent heart attack in San Francisco.

After Harding's death other scandals were revealed. In 1924 Attorney General Harry Daugherty, who had exposed Forbes's corruption to Harding, came under suspicion himself. The Senate began to investigate Daugherty for his failure to end high-level corruption. The inquiry soon revealed that Daugherty was taking bribes. The attorney general was forced to resign.

The most noted episode of corruption during the Harding administration, the **Teapot Dome scandal**, became news early in 1924. Investigators discovered that in the early months of the Harding administration, Secretary of the Interior Albert Fall had persuaded Secretary of the Navy Edwin Denby to transfer control of naval oil reserves to his department. Fall granted private leases to the oil reserves in Elk

INTERPRETING THE VISUAL RECORD

Teapot Dome scandal. Episodes of corruption like the Teapot Dome scandal threatened the Harding administration's public support. *How does this cartoon illustrate the danger of the scandal to the Republican administration?*

Hills, California, and the Teapot Dome reserves in Wyoming. In return, Fall received personal loans, cash, and cattle. Fall was convicted of accepting bribes and jailed.

Coolidge takes charge.
After Harding's death, Vice President Calvin Coolidge was sworn in as president. He immediately began working to limit the damage from the Harding scandals and to restore the reputation of the presidency. Coolidge's administration contrasted greatly with the Harding administration. Known as Silent Cal, Coolidge's stern, reserved nature contrasted with Harding's outgoing personality. However, Coolidge continued to promote Harding's popular pro-business policies since the national economy was booming.

Coolidge easily won the Republican presidential nomination in 1924. The Democrats were split over issues such as prohibition. They voted 103 times before finally chosing John W. Davis, a corporate lawyer, as their candidate. Both parties faced strong opposition from the Progressive Party's nominee, Robert La Follette. Backed by angry farmers and workers, the Progressive platform denounced federal policies favoring business and called for increased aid to working people.

Despite rumblings of discontent, Coolidge won by a landslide, receiving 15.7 million votes to Davis's 8.4 million. La Follette received some 4.8 million votes. The Progressive Party faded from the scene when La Follette died soon after the election. Nevertheless, its strong showing in the election made it clear that not all Americans agreed with the Republicans' pro-business policies.

Coolidge's pro-business position.
A dedicated conservative, Coolidge was even more pro-business than Harding. "The business of America is business," he declared. Coolidge often invited prominent business leaders for social engagements at the White House. Coolidge favored legislation to aid business. With his support, Congress passed the Revenue Act of 1926, which repealed the gift tax, cut estate taxes in half, and reduced taxes on the wealthy. Coolidge expected these tax cuts would further the economic prosperity of the country.

Coolidge also took a tightfisted approach to government spending. By keeping spending low, Coolidge made possible both a tax cut and further reductions in the national debt. He vetoed spending bills such as a bonus bill designed to aid World War I veterans. He also vetoed the McNary-Haugen Bill, which was designed to boost farm prices by authorizing the government to buy surplus crops and sell them abroad. Coolidge generally opposed laws designed to help farmers or workers. He argued that such legislation limited private initiative and harmed the economy.

The president remained popular throughout his term and almost certainly could have won re-election in 1928. Instead, to almost everyone's surprise, he announced that he would not run. Speaking privately to his staff, Coolidge admitted that he found the work of the presidency burdensome. He looked forward to returning to a life of leisure at his home in Northampton, Massachusetts.

✔ **READING CHECK:** How did the Republican Party overcome the political scandals of the Harding administration?

During the 1924 presidential election, Coolidge supporters published songbooks such as this one to build strength for his campaign.

Calvin Coolidge kept his campaign promise to support business. Here he meets with some of the country's most-prominent business leaders.

The Election of 1928

In 1928 the Republican Party nominated Secretary of Commerce Herbert Hoover for president. Hoover had a reputation for administrative skill and efficiency. His strongest asset, though, was the nation's apparent prosperity after eight years of Republican rule. He referred to this prosperity in a campaign speech.

66 The poorhouse is vanishing from among us. We have not yet reached the goal, but, given a chance to go forward with the policies of the last eight years, we shall soon . . . be in sight of the day when poverty will be banished from this nation. 99

After a bitter fight, the Democrats nominated Governor Alfred E. Smith of New York, a moderate progressive. The party's choice signaled a shift in Democratic strategy—a response, in part, to the Progressive Party's strength in the 1924 election. Smith's core support came from urban immigrant voters. By nominating Smith, the Democrats hoped to be seen as "the party of progress and liberal thought," as vice presidential candidate Franklin Roosevelt put it. Many Americans opposed Smith because of his Catholic faith. They feared that a Catholic president might hand control of the United States over to the pope in Rome. Others worried that Smith opposed prohibition and had ties to New York City's Tammany Hall.

Smith's political weaknesses and the country's economic strength carried Hoover to victory. He received 58 percent of the popular vote. Smith lost his own state as well as several southern states that went Republican for the first time since Reconstruction. However, Smith did well in the nation's largest cities. His appeal to these urban voters offered the Democrats hope for the future.

✔ **READING CHECK:** What issues affected the outcome of the 1928 election?

INTERPRETING THE VISUAL RECORD

Herbert Hoover. During the 1928 election, Hoover ran on the same pro-business policies that Presidents Harding and Coolidge had supported. *How do you think these Hoover campaign items appealed to voters?*

SECTION 2 REVIEW

Define and explain the significance of the following terms:
Fordney-McCumber Tariff Act
mergers
American Plan
feminists
Equal Rights Amendment
Teapot Dome scandal

Identify and explain the significance of the following individuals:
Warren G. Harding
Andrew Mellon
Charles Dawes
Mary Anderson
Albert Fall
Calvin Coolidge
Alfred E. Smith

1. **Using Graphic Organizers** Copy the graphic organizer below. Use it to explain how each part of the pyramid helped lead to Herbert Hoover's victory in the 1928 election.

Hoover's Victory

Smith's Weaknesses | Hoover's Strengths

Economic factors

2. **Assessing Consequences** How did Republican pro-business policies encourage economic growth?
3. **Analyzing** Why did the National Woman's Party push for an Equal Rights Amendment? What factors prevented the amendment from gaining support?
4. **Using Historical Imagination** Imagine that you are a political analyst in 1928. What conclusions would you draw as to why the Republican Party was able to maintain control of the presidency?

Critical Thinking

5. Why do you think Calvin Coolidge won the 1924 election despite being vice president in Harding's scandal-ridden administration?
Consider:
• what Coolidge achieved in his term as president before the election
• the differences between Harding and Coolidge
• the significance of economic prosperity

SECTION
③

A Nation Divided

OBJECTIVES

Read to understand:

1. why many Americans supported the Ku Klux Klan, and what factors led to a decline in that support

2. what actions African Americans took to combat discrimination and violence

3. why many Americans demanded restrictions on immigration

4. why Mexican immigration increased during the 1920s

5. what actions American Indians took to protect their land

KEY TERMS

Brotherhood of Sleeping Car Porters
Pan-Africanism
black nationalism
Universal Negro Improvement Association
Immigration Act of 1924
Bursum Bill

KEY PEOPLE

William Joseph Simmons
David Stephenson
A. Philip Randolph
Marcus Garvey

Many African Americans moved to northern cities in search of jobs.

EYEWITNESSES TO History

❝ *Doubtless you have learned of the great exodus of our people to the north and west from this and other southern states. I wish to say that we are forced to go when . . . a grown man['s] wages is only fifty to seventy five cents per day for all grades of work. He is compelled to go where there is better wages and sociable conditions, believe me. . . . Many places here in this state . . . the black man . . . is treated as a slave. . . . As a minister of the Methodist Episcopal Church . . . I am on the verge of starvation simply because of the above conditions.* ❞
—**Alabama minister**

***Chicago* Defender**

In the spring of 1917 an African American minister from Alabama wrote this letter to the editors of the Chicago *Defender*. A weekly newspaper, the *Defender* covered the plight of African Americans in the South as well as the North. The *Defender* routinely encouraged African Americans from the South to migrate to northern cities. It contrasted the harsh conditions of the South with tales of freedom and jobs in the North. Although the North was not free of discrimination and racism, thousands of African Americans decided to try to better their lives by leaving the South to settle in northern cities.

African Americans Move North

During the 1920s some 800,000 African Americans joined the hundreds of thousands of African Americans who had moved to the North during World War I. By 1930 the North's African American population had reached almost 2.5 million, more than double its size in 1910. Large African American communities sprang up in Chicago, Detroit, New York City, and other northern cities.

Reasons for the move. African Americans who moved to the North searching for economic opportunities also longed for a new life free from discrimination. A migrant from Georgia who had left domestic work behind for a job in a Chicago box factory exclaimed, "I'll never work in nobody's kitchen but my own any more. No indeed! That's the one thing that makes me stick to this job. You do have some time to call your own."

However, the North was not free of prejudice. African Americans living in the North encountered racial violence and lynch mobs as well as discrimination. As the demand for labor lessened during the recession of the early 1920s, African Americans were often the first to lose their jobs.

Violence erupts. Racial tension mounted with the move of African Americans from southern farms to cities. This tension sometimes erupted in violence. One of the worst incidents occurred in Chicago in July 1919. The trouble began when a

African American Population Changes, 1920–1930

Learning from Maps The great increase of African Americans in some northern states meant a decline in numbers in some other states.

? MOVEMENT In which states did the African American population more than double?

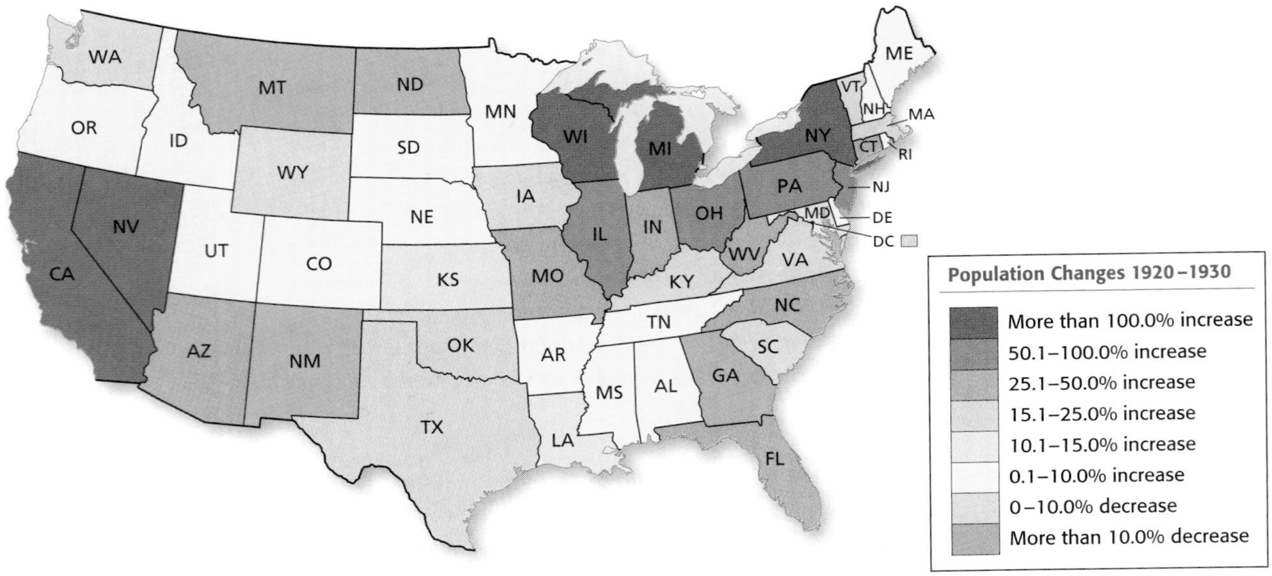

Population Changes 1920–1930

- More than 100.0% increase
- 50.1–100.0% increase
- 25.1–50.0% increase
- 15.1–25.0% increase
- 10.1–15.0% increase
- 0.1–10.0% increase
- 0–10.0% decrease
- More than 10.0% decrease

During 1919, race riots erupted around the country. Damage from fires left neighborhoods like this one in Chicago in ruins.

white man threw rocks at an African American teenager swimming in Lake Michigan. The boy drowned. When the police refused to arrest anyone, fights broke out between whites and African Americans on shore and quickly spread to the rest of the city. The rioting continued for more than a week. White gangs prowling the slums were responsible for much of the violence. They attacked African Americans and destroyed property. By the time order was restored, 38 people had been killed and 537 injured.

By late 1919 some 25 race riots had erupted around the country. In June 1921 at least 30 people died during a race riot in Tulsa, Oklahoma. One resident described attacks on the African American section of town, "People were seen to flee from their burning homes, some with babes in their arms." The violence prompted African American soldiers with World War I combat experience to attempt to defend their communities. "The colored troops fought nobly," wrote one African American to a friend in Washington, D.C., after the riots in that city. "We have something to fight for now."

The Return of the Ku Klux Klan

One sign of growing racism was the rebirth of the Ku Klux Klan, which had officially dissolved during Reconstruction. The new Klan was established in 1915 at Stone Mountain, Georgia, by a preacher named William Joseph Simmons. Like the Klan of post–Civil War days, the new Klan carried out kidnappings, beatings, and lynchings to terrorize African Americans in the South. The new Klan also grew rapidly outside of the South. In northern and midwestern towns and cities, the Klan targeted not only African Americans but also Catholics, immigrants, Jews, and suspected radicals.

The Klan grew slowly at first, but as the Red Scare took hold, membership soared. The group reached its peak in the mid-1920s. At one time it had perhaps as many as 5 million members. The Klan staged mass rallies where white-robed members burned crosses and spoke out against groups and ideas they considered undesirable. It also worked to help candidates win elections in such states as Louisiana, Ohio, Oklahoma, Oregon, and Texas. The group was particularly powerful in Indiana.

The Klan's rapid rise during the early 1920s was followed by an equally speedy fall in the late 1920s. By 1930 the Klan's membership had dropped to some 9,000. The decline in popular support of the Klan resulted from several factors. Particularly significant was a decrease in the hysteria surrounding the Red Scare. With the economy booming and anxiety about radicalism declining, the Klan's message of fear lost its appeal.

Publicity of the Klan's terrorism and violence also led to the shrinking of the organization's ranks. Newspapers nationwide published investigative articles that exposed the violence of local Klan chapters. With the national leadership of the Ku Klux Klan unable to control the actions of its local chapters, many people began to speak out against the group.

Corruption and scandals at the national level of the organization also led to the decline of the Klan. People began to turn away from the Klan when investigations revealed that Klan promoters were getting rich from membership fees and sales of various Klan products. The conviction of Grand Dragon David Stephenson for second-degree murder also hurt the Klan. In the face of scandals, many local chapters broke away from the national organization. Nevertheless, the Klan did not completely die out.

✔ **READING CHECK:** Why did many Americans support the Ku Klux Klan? What factors led to a decline in this support?

Ku Klux Klan. During the 1920s the Ku Klux Klan held rallies to build support for the organization and to spread its ideas. *What symbols did the Klan members use in their rallies?*

African Americans Defend Their Rights

Faced with continued violence and discrimination from the Ku Klux Klan and other groups, many African Americans took action to defend their rights. During the 1920s African Americans created several organizations dedicated to the prevention of discrimination and acts of violence.

Antilynching campaign. One early effort to stop the violence committed against African Americans came from the National Association for the Advancement of Colored People (NAACP). The NAACP formed the Antilynching Committee to generate support for antilynching legislation. It also put pressure on law enforcement officials to investigate acts of violence against African Americans. In the articles of its monthly magazine, *The Crisis*, the NAACP publicized lynching

Supporters of the NAACP campaign to end lynchings in the United States wore buttons such as this one to spread their message.

A. Philip Randolph established a union for sleeping-car porters and published a journal called *The Messenger* to help African American workers gain better wages and working conditions.

statistics and detailed stories of atrocities. In an article about a 17-year-old African American who was burned to death by a mob in Waco, Texas, W. E. B. Du Bois rallied support for the NAACP cause. He wrote, "This is an account of one lynching. It is horrible, but it is matched in horror by scores of others in the last thirty years. . . . What are we going to do about this record?"

Although the NAACP program generated considerable public support, it achieved limited success. In 1921 Representative L. C. Dyer of Missouri sponsored a federal antilynching law that passed in the House but lost in the Senate. Nevertheless, the NAACP continued to fight for antilynching legislation and an end to discrimination against African Americans.

African American unionization.
While some African Americans mobilized to put an end to lynching and racial violence, others attempted to fight discrimination in the workplace. In the early 1900s African American workers were rarely allowed to rise above unskilled, low-paying jobs. African Americans were also barred from joining local labor unions and the American Federation of Labor.

The unions' failure to help African American workers led young black socialist A. Philip Randolph to found the **Brotherhood of Sleeping Car Porters** in 1925. Randolph started the union to better the working conditions of the thousands of African Americans who worked for the Pullman Company. "[The worker's] object is not only to get more wages, better hours of work and improved working conditions," explained Randolph, "but to do his bit in order to raise and progressively improve the standard of Pullman service."

Randolph also sought to end union discrimination against African American workers. The Brotherhood of Sleeping Car Porters provided a union for African Americans. However, Randolph hoped to unite all workers, regardless of color, into a single force opposed to unjust working conditions.

Despite Randolph's efforts, the Pullman Company refused to recognize the Brotherhood of Sleeping Car Porters. The company even began to hire Filipino workers to replace African American porters. Supported by groups such as the NAACP, the union persisted in its efforts to organize. It eventually won recognition by the Pullman Company in the late 1930s.

Black nationalism.
African Americans grew frustrated by the slow pace of change in the unions and the lack of results from NAACP's antilynching legislation. Some African Americans lost hope of ever achieving equality in the United States. They believed that African Americans needed a nation of their own.

The motivation for African Americans to form an independent nation grew out of an existing political movement. The movement known as **Pan-Africanism** aimed to unite people of African descent worldwide. Support for the movement had existed in the United States since the early 1800s. By the 1920s, however, a new leader within the Pan-African movement had emerged. Marcus Garvey, a native of Jamaica, supported the cause of **black nationalism**. This movement aimed to create a new political state for African Americans in Africa.

Marcus Garvey founded the **Universal Negro Improvement Association (UNIA)** in 1914. The UNIA had two main goals. Its members hoped to foster African

Marcus Garvey led the black nationalist movement.

Americans' economic independence through the establishment of black-owned businesses. They also worked to establish an independent black homeland in Africa. "We shall now organize," Garvey told the delegates to the UNIA's first international convention, "to plant the banner of freedom on the great continent of Africa."

Garvey moved in 1916 to New York, where he continued to organize efforts to form an African American nation. A charismatic speaker, Garvey attracted considerable support from African American communities in the United States. Whereas W. E. B. Du Bois spoke to the well educated, Garvey's speeches and slogans attracted the African American masses. Garvey also organized attention-getting parades. He also urged African Americans to join him in forging a new homeland free from discrimination. Many of Garvey's supporters were working-class African Americans living in urban areas.

THROUGH OTHERS' EYES

An African View of the Back-to-Africa Movement

Marcus Garvey's back-to-Africa movement drew many followers both in the United States and in Africa. In 1922 a representative of the king of Abyssinia—present-day Ethiopia—read the following message to a United Negro Improvement Association convention.

66 Assure them [Garvey's followers] of the cordiality with which I invite them back to the home land, particularly those qualified to help solve our big problems and to develop our vast resources. Teachers, artisans, mechanics, writers, musicians, professional men and women—all who are able to lend a hand in the constructive work which our country so deeply feels, and greatly needs.

Here we have abundant room and great opportunities and here destiny is working to elevate and enthrone a race which has suffered slavery, poverty, persecution and martyrdom [death for a cause], but whose expanding soul and growing genius is now the hope of many millions of mankind. 99

To encourage economic independence, Garvey founded the Black Star Steamship Company in 1919. He urged African Americans to invest in his company so that they "may exert the same influence on the world as the white man does today." He promised investors huge returns. The company, however, never turned a profit. In 1925 he was jailed for mail fraud in connection with his fund-raising activities. President Coolidge pardoned Garvey in 1927 but ordered him deported.

The black nationalist movement declined after Garvey's imprisonment. Nevertheless, as a newspaper writer said in 1927, "He made black people proud. . . . He taught them that black is beautiful." Other African American leaders such as Du Bois shared Garvey's belief in racial pride and solidarity but opposed his back-to-Africa movement. They insisted that African Americans needed to fight for justice and equality in American society.

✔ **READING CHECK:** What actions did African Americans take to combat discrimination and violence?

HOLT RESEARCHER   *Read More About It*

Free Find:
Marcus Garvey
After reading the selection on Marcus Garvey and black nationalism on the **Holt Researcher** CD–ROM, create a script for a scene in a movie about Garvey's back-to-Africa movement.

Immigration Restrictions

The racism and discrimination that led to the resurgence of the Ku Klux Klan in the 1920s also encouraged nativist sentiments. Many Americans feared that the country was being overrun by immigrants. By 1920 nearly 25 percent of the nation's population was foreign born or nonwhite. Furthermore, after a decline during World War I, the number of immigrants was once again rising, increasing from some 140,000 in 1919 to some 805,000 in 1921. This dramatic growth—and the widespread belief that immigrants held radical views and took jobs from native-born Americans—led many citizens to demand federal limits on immigration.

ELLIS ISLAND BLUES

By
HENRY SANTREY
BENTON LEY
and
LEE DAVID

M. WITMARK & SONS
NEW YORK

Anti-immigration. "Ellis Island Blues" was one of the many songs written during the 1920s about immigrants. *How does the image on the cover of the songbook reflect the ideas behind calls for limits on immigration?*

In 1921 Congress passed a law that limited the number of immigrants from each country allowed into the United States. The law set a quota of 3 percent for each nationality already in the country by 1910, except for Asians, whose immigration was virtually barred. Three years later, the passage of the **Immigration Act of 1924** reduced this quota to 2 percent of the 1890 population figures for each nationality. This change limited southern and eastern European immigration because in 1890 most Americans traced their origins to Great Britain or northern and western Europe. Although the 1924 law did not exclude all Asian immigrants, it set an annual quota of just 100 Japanese immigrants. In 1925 these restrictions reduced the total number of new immigrants from Africa, Asia, Australia, and Europe to some 153,000.

✔ **READING CHECK:** Why did many Americans demand restrictions on immigration?

Mexican American Migration

Mexicans were not affected by the restrictive legislation of the 1920s. With fewer immigrants arriving from Europe and Asia, employers in the Southwest were eager to keep a steady flow of workers to fill low-wage jobs. As a result, during the 1920s some 500,000 immigrants arrived from Mexico, where poverty was widespread, jobs were scarce, and political upheaval from a revolution persisted.

Mexicans who took agricultural jobs in the Southwest worked for low wages and typically lived in ramshackle labor camps. An observer described one camp.

66 **Shelters were made of almost every conceivable thing—burlap, canvas, palm branches. . . . We found one woman carrying water in large milk pails from the irrigation ditch. . . . This is evidently all the water which they have in camp.** 99

Mexican American Victor Villaseñor wrote about his family's experiences as immigrants in the 1920s. Shown here is the 1929 wedding of his parents.

In the 1920s many Mexican immigrants also moved into urban areas. Some were drawn to well-paying factory jobs in cities such as Chicago and Detroit. Most, however, migrated to cities in the Southwest—particularly Los Angeles in California and El Paso and San Antonio in Texas. Usually the men came alone. Once established, they sent for their wives and children. Many brought other relatives as well, establishing extended-family networks. These networks helped new arrivals find jobs and housing.

Economic hardship caused many families to allow their young, unmarried daughters to work outside the home. Many found employment in bakeries, hotels, and laundries. Others worked as maids. Their newfound independence, as one Mexican immigrant woman sadly noted, brought young women "into conflict with their parents. They learn . . . about the outside world, learn how to speak English, and then they become ashamed of their parents who brought them up here." Despite such conflicts, these new immigrants contributed greatly to American life.

✔ **READING CHECK:** Why did Mexican immigration increase during the 1920s?

American Indian Life

For American Indians the 1920s brought some acknowledgment of the difficulties they faced. The Dawes Act, which attempted to "Americanize" Indians by dividing tribal land into individual plots, had clearly failed. The Board of Indian Commissioners admitted that the act's allotment policies had often been "a short cut to the separation of . . . Indians from their land and cash."

In the 1920s American Indians successfully organized to fight new efforts to take tribal land. American Indian leaders stopped the Harding administration's attempt to buy back all tribal land. Then, in 1922, the various Pueblo tribes of the Southwest organized to fight the **Bursum Bill**, which was designed to legalize non–Indian claims to Pueblo land. The Pueblo appealed to Americans to help defeat the bill.

Anthropologist James Schultz (left) supported the continuation of American Indian culture in the 1920s.

❝ This bill will destroy our common life and will rob us of everything which we hold dear—our lands, our customs, our traditions. Are the American people willing to see this happen? ❞

Many Americans were not. The Pueblo won support from a variety of groups, including the General Federation of Women's Clubs and many anthropologists. As a result, the bill failed to pass.

In 1924 Congress granted citizenship to all American Indians, partly in recognition of those who had fought in World War I. Citizenship, however, did not eliminate the poverty that many American Indians continued to experience.

✔ **READING CHECK:** What actions did American Indians take to protect their land?

SECTION 3 REVIEW

Define and explain the significance of the following terms:
Brotherhood of Sleeping Car Porters
Pan-Africanism
black nationalism
Universal Negro Improvement Association
Immigration Act of 1924
Bursum Bill

Identify and explain the significance of the following individuals:
William Joseph Simmons
David Stephenson
A. Philip Randolph
Marcus Garvey

1. **Using Graphic Organizers** Copy the web below. Use it to explain how each of the listed events reflected the intolerance and discrimination that existed in American society in the 1920s.

- Experiences of African Americans Who Moved North
- INTOLERANCE AND DISCRIMINATION
- Immigration Restriction
- Actions of the Ku Klux Klan

2. **Drawing Conclusions** How did the Ku Klux Klan's policies and actions lead to its rapid decline in popularity during the late 1920s?

3. **Evaluating** Why did many Americans support more restrictive immigration laws in the 1920s?

4. **Analyzing** Why did the immigration of Mexicans to the United States increase during the 1920s?

Critical Thinking

5. In the face of intolerance, discrimination, and violence during the 1920s, many people took action to defend their rights. How successful were they?
Consider:
- how African Americans fought against lynching and discrimination
- how Mexican Americans seeking economic opportunity formed communities
- how American Indians defended their land

CHAPTER 22

Review

Creating a Time Line

Copy the time line below onto a sheet of paper. Complete the time line by filling in the events and dates from the chapter that you think were most significant. Pick three events and explain why you think they were significant.

1919 — 1924 — 1929

Writing a Summary

Using the Reading Checks as a guide, write an overview of the events in the chapter.

Identifying People and Ideas

Identify the following terms or individuals and explain their significance.

1. demobilization
2. Red Scare
3. A. Mitchell Palmer
4. Andrew Mellon
5. Equal Rights Amendment
6. Teapot Dome scandal
7. Calvin Coolidge
8. William Joseph Simmons
9. Marcus Garvey
10. Immigration Act of 1924

Understanding Main Ideas

SECTION 1

1. What impact did demobilization after World War I have on women, factory workers, and farmers?
2. What were some of the causes of the strikes of 1919?

SECTION 2

3. How was Warren G. Harding able to win the election of 1920 by such a large majority?

SECTION 3

4. What types of discrimination did African Americans experience in northern cities?
5. Why did the immigration of Mexicans to the United States increase during the 1920s?

Reviewing Themes

1. **Democratic Values** How did the hysteria of the Red Scare affect the lives of many Americans?
2. **Economic Development** How did the Republicans' pro-business policies affect economic growth?
3. **Cultural Diversity** How did immigration to the United States change in the 1920s?

Thinking Critically

1. **Identifying Cause and Effect** What was the public reaction to the wave of strikes in 1919? How did this reaction relate to the Red Scare?
2. **Synthesizing** How did the ending of World War I and the communist revolution in Russia affect American life in the early 1920s?
3. **Analyzing** How did the Republican Party overcome the scandals of Harding's administration?
4. **Evaluating** How was the new Ku Klux Klan similar to and different from the old Klan?
5. **Assessing Consequences** How did the NAACP, the Brotherhood of Sleeping Car Porters, and black nationalists attempt to better the lives of African Americans? How successful were they?

Writing About History

Writing to Inform Copy the graphic organizer below. Use it to explain the fears and concerns felt by many Americans in 1920 and how the Republicans' pro-business policies proposed to address them. Then explain why Harding's speech on "normalcy" given on May 20, 1920, was a success.

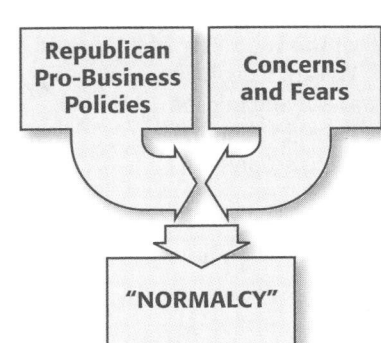

Strategies for Success Review the **Strategies for Success** on *Evaluating News Stories.* Then examine the excerpt below from a news story and answer the questions that follow.

❝ Charlestown State Prison, Mass., Tuesday, August 23— Nicola Sacco and Bartolomeo Vanzetti died in the electric chair early this morning. . . .

To the last they protested their innocence, and the efforts of many who believed them guiltless proved futile, although they fought a legal and extra legal battle unprecedented in the history of American jurisprudence [court system]. ❞

1. Does this excerpt cover its subject in sufficient depth? Does it include adequate background information?
2. Is the reporting in the excerpt fair and accurate? What biases, if any, does it display?
3. How does the excerpt contribute to your understanding of the Sacco and Vanzetti case?

Linking History and Geography

Between 1920 and 1930 some 500,000 Mexicans immigrated to the United States to find work. Study the map below and note which state had the highest percentage of Hispanic residents by 1930.

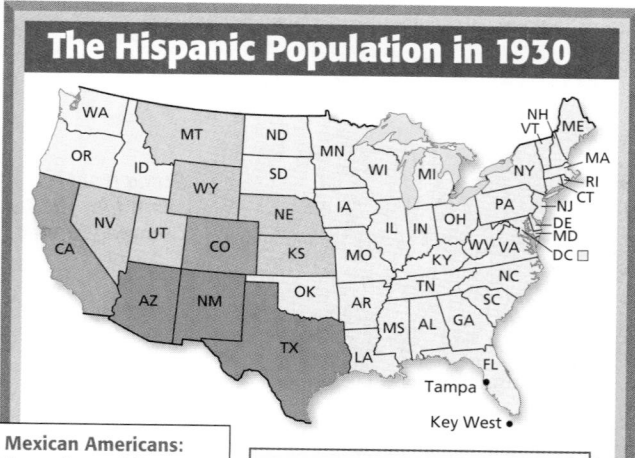

The Hispanic Population in 1930

Mexican Americans: Percentage of State Population, 1930

- More than 10.0%
- 5.1–10.0%
- 1.1–5.0%
- 0.5–1.0%
- Less than 0.5%

Total Mexican American population: 1,422,533

- Fewer than 20,000 Cubans came to the United States before 1930, and most settled in Key West or Tampa.
- Many of the some 37,000 Puerto Ricans who immigrated before World War II became agricultural laborers in Arizona, the Midwest, or the East.

internetconnect

TOPIC: Bolshevik Revolution
GO TO: go.hrw.com
KEYWORD: SD1 Bolshevik

Accessing the Internet through the HRW Web site, research the Bolshevik Revolution and create a script for a radio show about the revolution.

BUILDING YOUR PORTFOLIO

Complete one or more of the following projects independently or cooperatively.

1 Constitutional Heritage
Imagine that you are giving a radio broadcast of the news on August 23, 1927—the day that Sacco and Vanzetti were executed. **Write a news report** that explains the historical significance of the trial.

2 Democratic Values
Imagine that you are interviewing presidential candidates to write an article for a popular magazine. **Create an illustrated chart** to compare and contrast the personalities of Presidents Harding and Coolidge. Then explain how Harding appealed to the voters of 1920 and how Coolidge appealed to voters in 1924.

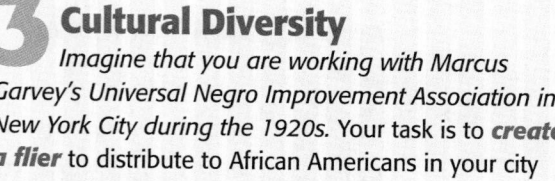

3 Cultural Diversity
Imagine that you are working with Marcus Garvey's Universal Negro Improvement Association in New York City during the 1920s. Your task is to **create a flier** *to distribute to African Americans in your city encouraging them to join the UNIA.*

1920–1929
The Jazz Age

Louis Armstrong

Alvin "Shipwreck" Kelly sitting on top of a flagpole

1922
The Arts
Jazz trumpeter Louis Armstrong moves to Chicago and joins King Oliver's Creole Jazz Band.

1922
Business and Finance
New York radio station WEAF airs the first paid radio commercials.

1923
World Events
An earthquake in Japan destroys Tokyo, killing some 143,000 people.

1924
Business and Finance
A Hollywood theater hires Alvin "Shipwreck" Kelly to sit on top of a flagpole to generate publicity.

1920   **1921**   **1922**   **1923**   **1924**

1920
Science and Technology
The first radio broadcasting station, KDKA in Pittsburgh, goes on the air.

1923
The Arts
Cecil B. DeMille's epic silent movie *The Ten Commandments* is released.

1924
The Arts
George Gershwin "translates" jazz into symphonic form in his musical composition *Rhapsody in Blue.*

1924
Politics
The first radio broadcast of a political convention is conducted from the Republican National Convention in Cleveland.

One of the first broadcasters on KDKA

Scene from the silent film The Ten Commandments

Before You Read

Build on What You Know

World War I's sudden conclusion forced many Americans to make major changes in their lives. A postwar economic recession caused many Americans to lose their jobs. Tensions eased, however, with the return of economic prosperity in the mid-1920s. In this chapter you will learn about the impact that postwar industrial products had on American life. You will also learn about the new forms of entertainment—such as radio programs, movies, and jazz music—that were popular with Americans in the 1920s.

Poster from the Paris Exposition

Automobile advertisement

Babe Ruth

1925 World Events
The Paris Exposition opens, introducing the "Art Deco" style of industrial design.

1925 The Arts
F. Scott Fitzgerald publishes *The Great Gatsby.*

1925 Politics
Clarence Darrow defends a Tennessee schoolteacher in the Scopes trial.

1927 Daily Life
Babe Ruth sets a new baseball record, hitting 60 home runs in a single season.

1929 Business and Finance
American businesses spend more than $3 billion on advertisements in a single year.

| 1925 | 1926 | 1927 | 1928 | 1929 |

Georgia O'Keeffe's Black Iris

1926 The Arts
Georgia O'Keeffe paints *Black Iris.*

1927 Science and Technology
Charles Lindbergh becomes the first pilot to fly solo nonstop from New York to Paris.

1927 Business and Finance
The Ford Motor Company introduces the Model A automobile with a $1.3 million advertising campaign.

1928 Daily Life
Marathon dancers compete for 482 hours in the "Dance Derby of the Century."

Dance marathon contestants

Think About Themes

Decide whether you agree or disagree with the following statements. Note why in your journal.

Economic Development Increasing consumer spending will improve a nation's overall economic strength.

Technology and Society New technology transforms the way people interact with each other.

Cultural Diversity The individual cultural traditions of groups of people within a country often conflict with that country's broader, national culture.

Boom Times

OBJECTIVES

Read to understand:

1. how the economic boom affected consumers and American businesses
2. how the assembly line spurred the growth of the automobile industry
3. how Henry Ford changed working conditions during the 1920s
4. how widespread automobile use affected the daily lives of many Americans
5. how American industries encouraged changes in consumer practices

KEY TERMS

scientific management
Model T
assembly line
auto-touring
installment plan
planned obsolescence

KEY PEOPLE

Frederick W. Taylor
Henry Ford
Alfred P. Sloan

EYEWITNESSES TO History

66 *One hundred thousand people flocked into the showrooms of the Ford Company in Detroit; mounted police were called out to patrol the crowds in Cleveland; in Kansas City so great a mob stormed Convention Hall that platforms had to be built to lift the new car high enough for everyone to see it.* 99

—Charles Merz

A crowd gathers around a 1927 Model A.

In December 1927 the American public clamored to see the Ford Motor Company's new Model A automobile. Ford had kept the new design secret, and public excitement grew in the days before its unveiling. This interest was heightened by a massive advertising campaign that featured a five-day series of full-page newspaper ads costing $1.3 million. The prosperity of the 1920s increased the spending power of many families and allowed them to purchase the wide variety of new products being produced by American industries. These new products transformed Americans' daily lives, changing the way they worked, socialized, and ran their households.

Prosperity and Productivity

After recovering from the turbulent period of demobilization, the U.S. economy soared. The gross national product climbed from $70 billion in 1922 to $100 billion just seven years later. Republican pro-business policies, tax cuts, and confidence among business leaders encouraged investment and led to economic growth. Edward E. Purinton, a business leader during the 1920s, expressed the confidence of the era. "The finest game is business. The rewards are for everybody, and all can win."

The era's business expansion led to wage increases. The average employee's purchasing power increased by 32 percent between 1914 and 1928. With the rise in income, workers became interested in many new products, including electric appliances.

During the 1920s it became common for Americans to have electricity in their homes, particularly in cities. An abundant supply of energy as well as a large network of electrical power plants led to this expansion. Between 1920 and 1929 the annual electrical production rose from more than 56 billion to 117 billion kilowatt-hours. By 1930 more than two thirds of all American homes had electricity. The availability of electricity and the growing purchasing power of consumers provided a market for new products. American industries developed a variety of new electric appliances—such as mixers, food grinders, sewing machines, and washing machines. Radio and phonograph sales boomed.

As American industries attempted to keep pace with the growing demands of consumers, many businesses began experimenting with new ways of increasing the productivity of the nation's factories. One of the new approaches was known as

This General Electric advertisement pictures some of the new appliances available in the 1920s.

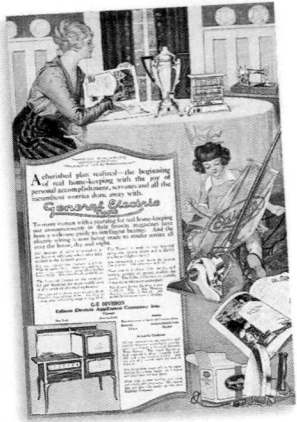

scientific management. Frederick W. Taylor, an early supporter of the idea, explained that scientific management was based on the idea that every kind of work could be broken down into a series of smaller tasks. Trained observers conducted "time-and-motion" studies to identify these tasks. They then set rates of production that workers and machines had to meet. Soon "efficiency experts" were applying these methods to many types of business.

✔ **READING CHECK:** How did the economic boom of the 1920s affect American consumers and businesses?

The Growth of the Automobile Industry

The innovations in productivity proved particularly important to the growing automobile industry of the 1920s. Automobile manufacturers such as Henry Ford could lower the cost of their cars by implementing scientific management practices.

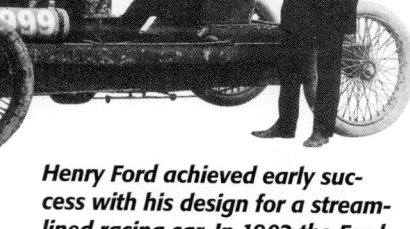

Henry Ford achieved early success with his design for a streamlined racing car. In 1902 the Ford 999 set a world speed record of more than 90 miles per hour.

Ford had established an automobile company in 1903 that quickly emerged as the industry leader. By 1908 Ford had developed the **Model T**, a sturdy, low-cost automobile. Ford's Model T was an instant success and sold more than 250,000 a year by 1914. Ford was eager to increase productivity and lower the price of the Model T. Adopting scientific-management techniques used in the slaughterhouses of Chicago, Ford developed a new production method—the **assembly line**—to help factories make goods faster. Workers stood in one place as partially assembled products such as automobiles moved past them on a conveyor belt.

Ford used the assembly line in his Detroit automobile plant. As the conveyor belt advanced at precisely six feet per minute, workers assembled the 5,000 parts of a Model T, or "Tin Lizzie." Machinery did much of the work by producing individual parts and carrying them to workers.

Ford's assembly line cut the engine assembly time for a Model T in half. Other large car manufacturers quickly followed Ford's lead and installed assembly lines. However, few small companies could afford the expense of building or maintaining the new technology. Unable to compete, many were driven out of business.

The assembly line allowed manufacturers to reduce the prices of cars, bringing them within reach of ordinary American families. The price of a Ford automobile dropped from $850 in 1909 to just $290 in 1924. Automobile registrations during the 1920s rose from 8 million to 26 million—an average of one car to every five citizens.

In the 1920s the automobile industry was the nation's biggest business. This new industrial giant consumed huge quantities of glass, rubber, steel, and other materials. By 1929 more than 1 million people labored in the automobile industry or a related business.

✔ **READING CHECK:** How did the development of the assembly line encourage the growth of the automobile industry?

INTERPRETING THE VISUAL RECORD

The assembly line. Henry Ford developed an assembly-line system to manufacture his Model T efficiently. *How do you think the assembly line might have made work easier for these Ford employees?*

The Model T

In addition to revolutionizing manufacturing, Henry Ford made important changes to the design of the automobile. During the early 1900s Ford began experimenting with new designs in an attempt to make cars more affordable.

Ford simplified the automobile's design to create a sturdy car that could be easily manufactured on an assembly line. The Model T contained four basic components: the frame, the front axle, the power plant, and the rear axle. The Model T had a 20-horsepower, four-cylinder engine that was built simply enough that almost anyone could maintain it. Ford's engineers designed a pedal-operated, two-speed transmission that was also easy to operate. To prevent the automobile from getting stuck in the often muddy roads, designers provided the Model T with a high ground clearance. The Model T's high-strength steel chassis, or frame, made it extremely durable.

Ford was able to sell the Model T at an affordable price, but his company offered few options. One Ford advertisement read, "We are making 40,000 cylinders, 10,000 engines, 40,000 wheels, 20,000 axles, 10,000 bodies, 10,000 of every part that goes into the car . . . all *exactly alike*." Even color options were limited. "The customer," Ford joked, "can have a Ford any color he wants—so long as it's black."

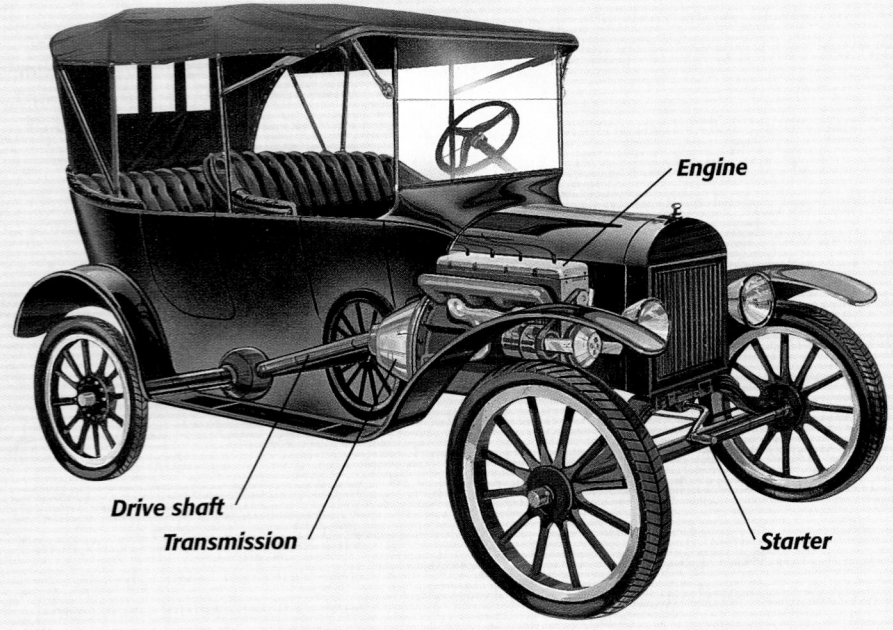

Engine

Drive shaft

Transmission

Starter

Understanding Science and History

1. What features made the Model T sturdy and reliable?
2. What impact did the assembly-line system have on the design of the Model T?

At the end of their shift, these assembly-line workers are leaving the Ford factory in Dearborn, Michigan.

Changes in Work

The assembly line transformed the nature of work during the 1920s. Assembly lines increased productivity. However, they made factory work more repetitive and led to increased rates of employee turnover.

Unskilled factory workers had little chance for advancement beyond the assembly line. Upper-level positions for clerical workers, managers, and salespeople increased by 4 million, but these jobs were unavailable to most factory workers. Because most of these jobs required at least a high-school education, few recent immigrants qualified for them. Discriminatory hiring practices also closed most of these jobs to African Americans.

Ford and his workers. Henry Ford revolutionized automobile production by implementing the assembly line in his factories. He won fame for shortening the workday and raising the wages of his employees. Ford also tried to regulate the morality and personal behavior of his workers.

BIOGRAPHY

Henry Ford

Born in 1863 on a farm near Dearborn, Michigan, Ford was well acquainted with hard work. He began work as a machinist at the age of 16. During the 1890s Ford worked as an engineer for the Edison Illuminating Company in Detroit. In his free time he experimented with gasoline engines and automobiles. During the early 1900s he worked closely with talented engineers to design the assembly-line system.

Ford's highly automated system of production limited each worker to one or two specific tasks. The repetitive work was dull, and many workers quit within a few weeks. Concerned about the high turnover of employees, Ford shortened the workday to eight hours and doubled wages to an unheard-of $5 a day.

Workers welcomed these bold steps. However, as the wife of one Ford worker noted, the pay increase did not change working conditions.

> **66** The chain system [assembly line] you have is a slave driver! My God! Mr. Ford. My husband has come home & thrown himself down & won't eat his supper— so done out! Can't it be remedied? . . . That $5 a day is a blessing—a bigger one than you know but oh they earn it. **99**

Ford's influence over his workers' lives extended far beyond their time on the line. The attractive wages paid to workers had strings attached. To earn the full $5 wage, workers were required to meet company standards at work and at home. Ford created a department within his company to analyze workers' home lives and offer plans to remedy any problems that Ford and his researchers believed existed.

Ford hoped to instruct his employees in the values and behaviors that he thought were proper. Ford's personnel department kept a close watch over employees' private lives. Ford strongly opposed tobacco and alcohol. His workers were warned, "It will cost a man his job to have the odor of beer, wine or liquor on his breath or have any of these intoxicants in his home."

During World War I, Ford stressed the importance of teaching his mostly foreign-born workforce "American values." Ford instructed workers to move out of ethnic neighborhoods. Workers who did not speak English were required to attend the Ford English School, where they were taught the language and lectured on personal hygiene, manners, and proper work habits.

Ford managed his automobile company closely to ensure the efficiency of his workers and assembly-line system. When the company's profits declined in the 1930s, many people questioned his management skills. In 1945 Ford transferred control of his company to his grandson. He died two years later.

✔ **READING CHECK:** How did Henry Ford change working conditions during the 1920s?

The impact of new products.

The widespread use of the automobile and new products powered by electricity altered working conditions and decreased the availability of some jobs. Electric appliances made housework easier for those who could afford them. Many people hired fewer domestic servants. In the past, servants had done the laundry and heavy cleaning in most middle- and upper-class homes. With

Read More About It

Free Find: Henry Ford
After reading about Henry Ford on the **Holt Researcher** CD–ROM, create a chart that shows how Ford's business strategies both benefited and created hardships for the average American worker.

INTERPRETING THE VISUAL RECORD

Ford's workers. One of Henry Ford's goals was to instill American values in his workers. *How does this photograph reflect Ford's goal to Americanize his workers?*

Automobiles. With the growing number of automobiles on the nation's roads, new businesses such as filling stations and drive-in restaurants opened. *How did this gas station from the 1920s serve the needs of automobile owners?*

As thousands of Americans purchased automobiles, traffic jams such as this one near a city park became more common.

the introduction of electrical appliances, however, many middle-class housewives began doing this work themselves. Moreover, the use of the automobile by middle-class families to run errands limited the need for delivery services and led to further unemployment.

A Land of Automobiles

Henry Ford's inexpensive Model T revolutionized the transportation industry. By 1930, cars, trucks, and buses had almost completely replaced horse-drawn vehicles. Trains and trolley cars also lost riders to automobiles.

To accommodate the increased traffic, more than 400,000 miles of new roads were built during the 1920s. A host of new structures—billboards, drive-in restaurants, filling stations, and tourist cabins—appeared along the nation's highways.

The automobile enabled rural residents to have greater contact with their neighbors and more access to shopping and leisure activities. Cars linked rural regions to urban areas. This made it easier for rural residents to relocate to the booming cities and for city-dwellers to visit the country. At the same time, however, the automobile contributed to the depopulation of the nation's inner cities. More accessible than ever, suburbs attracted thousands of middle-class families.

Auto-tourism. Seeking the fresh air of the countryside, millions of Americans participated in a new craze that was sweeping the nation—**auto-touring**. Taking part in this new pastime, Americans used their automobiles for camping and sightseeing vacations. Auto-touring allowed Americans to travel without the restrictions imposed by the schedules and routes of passenger trains. Guidebooks urged Americans to hit the road.

66 Does father crave to fish for trout and bass and pike and musky? Take him auto-touring. Does sister want to dip in the surf . . . or see the world? Take her automobile vacationing. . . . Does mother sigh for a rest from daily routines? Take her touring. . . . Does baby need fresh mountain air far from flies and heat? Take him auto-camping. 99

Family life. In addition to changing the way Americans traveled on vacation, automobiles transformed family life. The automobile created new social opportunities for teenagers. Sociologists Robert and Helen Lynd took note of this change in *Middletown*, their 1929 book chronicling life in Muncie, Indiana.

66 The extensive use of this new tool [the automobile] by the young has enormously extended their mobility and the range of alternatives before them; joining a crowd motoring over to a dance . . . twenty miles away may be a matter of a moment's decision, with no one's permission asked. 99

Before the use of automobiles became widespread, teenagers spent much of their leisure time at home with their families. "In the nineties [1890s] we were all much more together. People brought chairs . . . and sat

THE GRANGER COLLECTION, NEW YORK

on the lawn evenings," complained one mother. The arrival of the automobile changed the ways that teenagers spent their free time. "What on earth do you want me to do? Just sit around home all evening!" protested one teenage girl when her father expressed his disapproval of her going riding in a car with a young man.

Critics claimed that cars reduced people's sense of community. The Lynds observed that "since the advent of the automobile and the movies" people in Muncie no longer spent "long summer evenings and Sunday afternoons on the porch or in the side yard." Also, by the 1920s cars had begun to cause pollution, traffic jams, and parking problems. Most serious was the rising accident rate.

✔ **READING CHECK:** How did widespread automobile use affect Americans' daily lives?

Strategies for Success

Studying Primary and Secondary Sources

Most of the wide variety of materials used by historians to form their accounts of the past can be classified into two basic categories: primary sources and secondary sources. *Primary sources*—materials made up of firsthand historical information—include artwork, diaries, and legal documents. In contrast, *secondary sources* are descriptions or interpretations of historical events that were written by nonparticipants after the events occurred. *The American Nation* is a secondary source. Primary and secondary sources are both essential tools for historians. Primary sources contain historical information that cannot be found anywhere else. Secondary sources can cover broad historical topics and evaluate the long-term consequences of events.

How to Study a Primary or Secondary Source

1. **Identify the type of source.** First, determine whether the source is a primary source or a secondary source. Then, if possible, find out about the historical background of the source's creator and the intended audience of the source.
2. **Examine the material carefully.** Study the source carefully, taking note of its main ideas and supporting details.
3. **Check for bias.** Check the source for any words, phrases, and ideas that express the point of view of its creator. Make sure to identify any instances in which a one-sided view of a event, person, or topic is presented.

4. **Put the information to use.** If possible, compare the source with other primary or secondary sources that address the same subject. Then use the results of your analysis to form generalizations and draw conclusions.

Applying the Strategy

Study the magazine cover on the right, which was published in the November 1927 issue of the *Ladies' Home Journal.*

Practicing the Strategy

Using the image above, answer the following questions.

1. Is this image a primary source or a secondary source? Explain your answer.
2. Who created the image? Who do you think was the magazine's intended audience?
3. Does the magazine cover express any biases? If so, what are they?
4. How does the source contribute to your understanding of the United States during the 1920s?

Creating Consumers

Henry Ford manufactured his affordable Model T throughout the 1920s. He made few changes to its design. However, other automobile companies, such as Alfred P. Sloan's General Motors, began designing more expensive cars that emphasized luxury. Sloan explained the effect of car owners buying a second car. They "created the demand, not for basic transportation, but for progress in new cars, for comfort, convenience, power, and style."

Marketing. To allow average consumers to buy his more expensive cars, Sloan offered an **installment plan**. These plans allowed consumers to pay for their cars over time. By 1925, buyers purchased about 75 percent of cars on credit. The practice soon spread to cover the purchase of many other items such as kitchen appliances, pianos, and sewing machines. As one car dealer noted, installment plans were a profitable venture.

> 66 To keep America growing we must keep Americans working, and to keep Americans working we must keep them wanting; wanting more than the bare necessities; wanting the luxuries and frills that make life so much more worthwhile, and installment selling makes it easier to keep Americans wanting. 99

To make their goods more appealing, industrial designers began to create items that were pleasing to look at as well as functional. Industrial designers used new materials such as stainless steel and plastics to create a wide range of modern-looking products. They developed streamlining—the shaping of surfaces to reduce wind resistance—for cars, planes, ships, and trains. Designers even applied streamlining to nonmoving objects such as clocks, radios, and appliances.

Manufacturers quickly learned that introducing new models of what was essentially the same product could boost sales. Manufacturers made products specifically designed to go out of style and then replaced them with an up-to-date model. They had discovered what came to be called **planned obsolescence**. Automobile manufacturers were among the first to adopt planned obsolescence. In the early 1920s General Motors introduced to the public the concept of the yearly model change and the trade-in. Thereafter, many families routinely traded in their "old" models and bought new cars every year.

The new consumer practice of purchasing goods on the installment plan only to turn around and purchase the latest style the next season caused problems for many Americans. A Department of Labor study in the 1920s reported that single working women were going into debt buying clothes to keep up with the latest styles.

Advertising. Advertising became big business in the 1920s, fueling the demand for cars and other consumer goods. Before World War I, money spent on advertising totaled some $500 million yearly. By 1929 the total had soared to more than $3 billion. Ads were everywhere. Commercial messages bombarded potential buyers not only in magazines and newspapers but also on billboards and over the new medium of radio.

Advertisements such as this one for mouthwash played on the social fears of many Americans.

She bags the *bouquets* but never a *Beau*

You never have it? — *what colossal conceit!*

End halitosis with LISTERINE

Most advertisements targeted women. They used psychology to play on consumers' hopes and fears. Advertisements for Borden's milk, for example, warned mothers, "Hardly a family—well-to-do and poor alike—escapes the menace of malnutrition. Your own child may fall victim to this . . . evil."

Companies used slogans, jingles, and celebrity testimonials to fix product names in customers' minds. When her husband, Franklin D. Roosevelt, was governor of New York, Eleanor Roosevelt praised Cream of Wheat, a breakfast food that their son John had eaten since infancy. She claimed in advertisements that the cereal "has undoubtedly played its part in building his robust physique."

INTERPRETING THE VISUAL RECORD

Retail. Chain stores like this A&P brought a wide variety of products to American shoppers. ***What products are displayed in this window?***

A growing retail industry. As the number of products increased to meet growing consumer demand, a new type of store spread across the country. The A&P grocery chain grew from some 3,000 stores in 1922 to about 14,000 by 1925. These chain-style grocery stores slowly began to replace the traditional corner markets. New technology allowed stores to stock a wider variety of products. The invention of cellophane—a transparent wrapping material first produced in the United States in 1924—along with quick-freezing techniques preserved fresh foods longer. As a result, food could be shipped over greater distances.

✔ **READING CHECK:** How did American industries encourage the transformation of consumer practices?

SECTION 1 REVIEW

Define and explain the significance of the following terms:
scientific management
Model T
assembly line
auto-touring
installment plan
planned obsolescence

Identify and explain the significance of the following individuals:
Frederick W. Taylor
Henry Ford
Alfred P. Sloan

1. **Using Graphic Organizers** Copy the following organizational web. Use it to explain how the factors shown below inspired the new consumer demands that emerged during the 1920s.

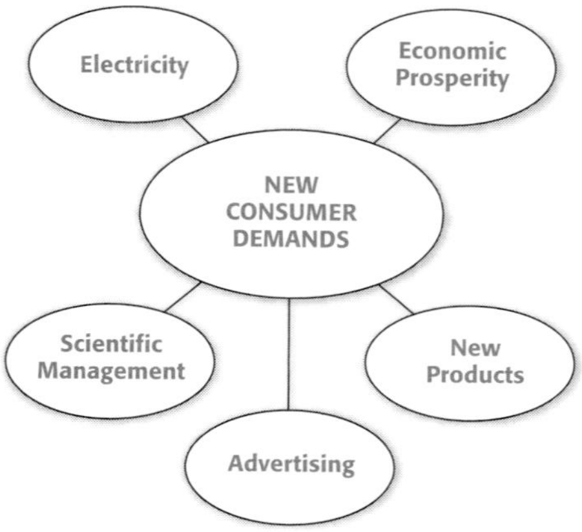

2. **Identifying Cause and Effect** Why did Henry Ford develop the assembly line? How did it encourage industrial growth?
3. **Taking a Stand** If you had been a factory worker during the 1920s, would you have taken a job with Ford? Why or why not?
4. **Evaluating** How did the widespread use of the automobile affect family life, leisure activities, and working life for some Americans?

Critical Thinking

5. During the 1920s businesses used various tactics to encourage Americans to buy their products. What positive and negative effects did these tactics have?
Consider:
   - how installment plans and planned obsolescence altered consumer practices
   - what influence advertising had on American consumer habits
   - how the growth of the retail industry affected Americans' buying habits

SECTION 2

Life in the Twenties

OBJECTIVES

Read to understand:

1. what impact prohibition had on crime
2. what the characteristics of the new youth culture were
3. how celebrities and new forms of popular entertainment helped create a mass culture
4. what the Scopes trial and the religious movements of the 1920s revealed about American society

KEY TERMS

Volstead Act
Untouchables
Twenty-first Amendment
flappers
Fundamentalism
Scopes trial

KEY PEOPLE

Al Capone
Eliot Ness
Cecil B. DeMille
Babe Ruth
Jim Thorpe
Charles Lindbergh
Amelia Earhart
Aimee Semple McPherson
Billy Sunday
Clarence Darrow

 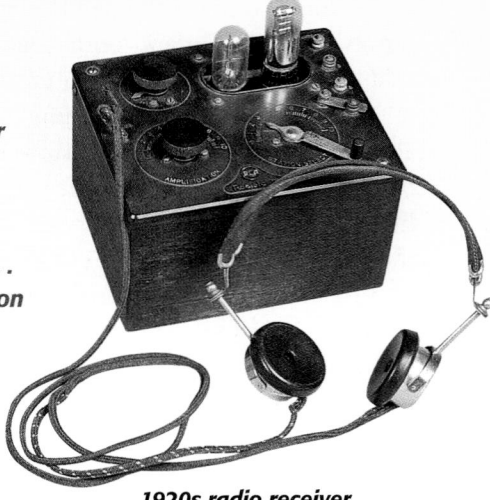

66 *About four or five days after I had gotten the vacuum tube hooked up, I started to hear music coming across the wires. Music! And then, between the music, I could hear somebody talking. . . . 'I am Dr. Conrad. I am experimenting with radio station 8XK.' . . . By January of 1921, I had decided to build my own broadcast station. I built a hundred-watter and then applied for an experimental broadcast license. In March I got a letter saying: 'One of my first official duties as Secretary of Commerce is to award you this license. Aren't you the young fellow I met . . . in Marion, Ohio? . . . What's a fourteen-year-old kid going to do with a broadcast station?'* **99**

—Albert Sindlinger

1920s radio receiver

Albert Sindlinger began experimenting with radio broadcasts as a young teenager in the 1920s. The first licensed radio stations were just beginning to broadcast music, news reports, and sports events. Commercial radio linked Americans from coast to coast, leading some to call the decade of the 1920s the gateway to modern America. For the first time, a truly national mass culture took shape in the United States. This emerging mass culture led to conflicts between traditional values and modern trends.

Prohibition

One of the most disruptive issues of the 1920s was the prohibition of the sale and distribution of alcoholic beverages. Progressive reformers seeking to combat crime, family violence, and poverty had long called for a ban on alcohol. During World War I, many reformers had supported prohibition as a wartime measure. They pointed out that drinking reduced the efficiency of soldiers and workers. The Eighteenth Amendment, which prohibited the manufacture, sale, and transportation of alcoholic beverages, was ratified in January 1919. That October, Congress passed the **Volstead Act** to enforce the amendment.

In some regions prohibition was strictly enforced, and alcohol consumption declined. However, in many parts of the country, particularly in the cities, prohibition was extremely unpopular and widely ignored. Americans frequented speakeasies, made their own liquor, and bought bootleg alcohol—or illegal alcohol smuggled in from Canada, Mexico, or the West Indies.

Bootlegging became one of the decade's most profitable businesses. In large cities, criminal gangs controlled liquor sales. Al Capone ruled Chicago's underworld with his small army of mobsters. To gain control over all liquor sales in Chicago, Capone's mob waged a violent war on rival gangs. Chicago's prohibition gang wars reached a peak on Saint Valentine's Day in 1929. On that day, several members of Capone's gang massacred seven members of the rival O'Banion gang.

Hoping to stem the bootlegging, corruption, and violence, the federal Prohibition Bureau hired a youthful special agent named Eliot Ness. He organized a top squad of young detectives to go after gangsters. Unlike corrupt city police officers who often turned a blind eye to bootlegging, Ness's men strictly enforced prohibition laws. Because of their dedication and honesty, Ness and his detectives were nicknamed the **Untouchables**. Ness put an end to Al Capone's reign over the Chicago underworld in 1931. Ness caught Capone for evading income tax payments. During Capone's 11-year prison sentence he lost his control over organized crime in Chicago.

Al Capone attracted public attention by dressing in expensive clothing and living a lavish lifestyle.

Despite the gang violence that plagued the era, prohibition had some positive consequences. Alcoholism declined and so did the number of alcohol-related deaths. Prohibition's negative results, however, drew more attention. Prohibition led to a widespread breakdown of law and order. It turned millions of otherwise law-abiding Americans into lawbreakers before it was repealed by the ratification of the **Twenty-first Amendment** in 1933.

✔ **READING CHECK:** What impact did prohibition have on crime?

Youth Culture

Many young Americans ignored prohibition laws. Some members of the younger generation of the 1920s openly rejected the values and conventions of previous generations. As a result, a new youth culture began to emerge.

The "new woman." Many challenges to traditional ways were brought on by changes in women's dress and behavior. During the 1920s, magazines, movies, and literature began to discuss the life of the "new woman." This woman was stylish, adventurous, and independent, often with a career of her own.

Reacting against the strict pre–World War I code of behavior, some young women during the 1920s exercised new freedom in how they dressed. They stopped wearing heavy corsets and started wearing shorter skirts and transparent silk hose.

People began to refer to young women who adopted the new style as **flappers**. Flappers enjoyed defying traditional standards of female behavior. Many young women began to wear bobbed, or short, hair, for example. Exploring new realms of independence, young women also drove cars and participated in sports. Although not all women adopted this new lifestyle, the image of the flapper caught the attention of the media.

The new woman sought not only social freedom but also economic independence. Although the proportion of working women remained fairly constant throughout the 1920s, American women worked in a wider variety of occupations. Some drove taxis. Others ran telegraph lines, worked as stenographers, flew airplanes, and hauled freight. Most, however, pursued traditionally female careers such as nursing, teaching, and domestic service.

INTERPRETING THE VISUAL RECORD

Youth culture. This 1920s magazine cover shows some of the characteristics of the new youth culture, such as the woman's bobbed hair and the man's baggy pants. *What other aspects of life in the 1920s does this magazine cover show?*

THE GRANGER COLLECTION, NEW YORK

Collegiate clothing, such as school sweaters, and straw hats became fashionable during the 1920s.

College life. In the early part of the century, most Americans' ended their formal education at high school or before. Between 1900 and 1930, however, college enrollment tripled. The greatest jump came during the 1920s. Most of these college students came from middle-and upper-class families.

The growing number of college students influenced popular images of the new youth culture. Advertising, magazines, and movies focused on collegiate fashions and lifestyles. According to a 1923 California university newspaper, "'College style' has a definite meaning. . . . Fall '23 can almost be called the young man's season with the style pace set by the collegian." The "collegiate" look included baggy flannel slacks and sports jackets.

Leisure fun and fads. New leisure activities and a variety of fads spread among American youth during the 1920s. Many young people participated in dance marathons. Couples danced for days, competing for prize money awarded to the last couple to collapse or drop out. To keep their partners awake, couples used smelling salts or ice packs. In 1928, couples danced for almost three weeks—482 hours—in the "Dance Derby of the Century."

Beauty contests were introduced during the 1920s. The hotel operators and merchants of Atlantic City, New Jersey, founded the Miss America beauty pageant in 1921. Contestants were judged primarily on their hair, smile, and appearance in a bathing suit. Despite the emphasis on the competitive display of female beauty, managers of the first beauty contests also stressed traditional morals.

Novelty events such as flagpole sitting attracted media attention and drew crowds of Americans. A flagpole sitter would climb onto a tiny platform atop a flagpole and sit with only stirrups for support. Taking short breaks every hour, flagpole sitters could last for days. Alvin "Shipwreck" Kelly was the most popular flagpole sitter. As the fad caught on, Kelly was routinely hired for publicity stunts by theaters and hotels. He claimed to have sat for a total of 145 days on flagpoles across the United States in 1929.

✔ **READING CHECK:** What were the characteristics of the new youth culture that arose in the 1920s?

Mass Entertainment

Leisure activities were not limited to young people. The economic boom of the 1920s meant that many—although not all—Americans had bigger paychecks and more free time than in years past. To help fill their leisure hours, many Americans turned to radio, movies, and professional sports for entertainment.

Radio. Commercial radio stations emerged during the early 1920s and grew in popularity as more Americans purchased radio receivers. The first stations, Detroit's WWJ and Pittsburgh's KDKA, went on the air in 1920. By 1929 more than 800 stations reached over 10 million homes.

The radio programming of the early 1920s was diverse. Early stations broadcast church services, local new reports, music, and sporting

Hoping to better portray their characters, actors in 1920s radio programs such as **Professor Ambrose Weems** *produced their programs in costume.*

THE GRANGER COLLECTION, NEW YORK

events. Two of the biggest radio broadcasts of the early days of radio came in 1921. That year, the Radio Corporation of America broadcast the Dempsey-Carpentier heavyweight title fight, and Westinghouse broadcast the World Series.

Radio stations soon discovered that they could make money by selling advertisement spots to other businesses. Stations provided businesses with the opportunity to sponsor programs. Businesses used these spots to advertise their products. Companies such as the A&P grocery store chain and the maker of Ipana toothpaste sponsored such music programs as the *A&P Gypsies* and the *Ipana Troubadours*.

During the late 1920s networks such as the National Broadcasting Company (NBC) began offering local radio networks packages of programs to broadcast. National radio broadcasts provided Americans with a set of shared cultural experiences. Americans across the country laughed at the same jokes, tapped their feet to the same music, and listened to the same ads. One executive noted that by allowing companies to advertise nationwide, the radio served as "a latchkey to nearly every home in the United States."

Movies.
In the 1920s Americans increasingly turned to movies for entertainment. The mass appeal of movie theaters impressed journalist Lloyd Lewis.

66 In the 'de luxe' [movie] house every man is a king and every woman a queen. Most of these cinema palaces sell all their seats at the same price,—and get it; the rich man stands in line with the poor. . . . In this suave atmosphere, the differences . . . that determine our lives outside are forgotten. All men enter these portals equal, and thus the movies are perhaps a symbol of democracy. 99

New advances in the art of moviemaking attracted even larger audiences. Movie director Cecil B. DeMille introduced a new style of filmmaking marked by epic plots and complex characters. DeMille created biblical epics such as *The Ten Commandments* (1923). DeMille also made films that focused on the changing morals of the 1920s, such as *Why Change Your Wife?* (1920) and *Forbidden Fruit* (1921).

Moviegoers were captivated by dramatic performances of famous silent film actors such as Lon Chaney and Charlie Chaplin. Western films enjoyed great success as well. Tom Mix, one of the most popular western film stars, often played the role of a heroic cowboy.

The era of silent films ended abruptly in 1927. That year, Warner Brothers released the first feature-length "talkie," *The Jazz Singer*, starring Al Jolson. The introduction of sound led to the creation of new types of films, such as musicals and newsreels—short films summing up the news of the day. In 1929 some 80 million Americans flocked to the theaters each week.

Censorship

The Roaring Twenties was a time of bathtub gin, gambling, jazz, short skirts, and the first talking movies. Old taboos were challenged one after the other. Alarmed and outraged by what they saw as the breakdown of the nation's moral standards, many community, government, and religious groups took action.

These activists pulled from library and store shelves books and magazines that used foul language, discussed sex frankly, or supported radical political ideas. U.S. Customs officials labeled many foreign books obscene. They even seized some books, including the acclaimed novel *Ulysses* by Irish author James Joyce. Groups like the American Civil Liberties Union opposed these restrictions on literature. They argued that censorship was a violation of the Constitution's First Amendment.

Today the battle between censorship and freedom of speech continues. The National Endowment for the Arts (NEA), for example, has come under attack for funding artists whose works some consider obscene. Although some critics judge the art as unsuitable for public funding, the artists defend their right to freedom of expression. The NEA and other agencies are caught in the middle of the battle.

Is such censorship a violation of free speech or a necessary form of protection? American society and U.S. courts continue to struggle with this question.

Protesting censorship

In the 1920s wildly popular but controversial films such as *The Sheik*, which starred the male sex symbol Rudolph Valentino, caused an uproar among some viewers. Many Americans were troubled by the rapidly changing standards of morality and sexuality portrayed in films. Some began to demand regulation. In 1922 Will Hays became the head of a newly created movie-industry group that set a code to limit offensive material in movies. By the early 1930s these regulations were rigorously enforced.

Sports. During the 1920s many Americans turned to sports for entertainment. Professional sports had emerged in the United States during the late 1800s. With the introduction of new technology in the 1920s, however, professional sports became a form of mass entertainment available to almost all Americans.

Professional and college-level football attracted many American fans during the 1920s. Attendance at college football games doubled between 1921 and 1930. College football stars like Red Grange began to join professional football teams. Grange played his first game for the Chicago Bears on Thanksgiving Day 1925. The game attracted 35,000 fans, the largest crowd to attend a professional football game up to that time.

Known as America's national pastime, baseball remained the nation's most popular sport despite charges of corruption. In the 1919 "Black Sox" scandal, "Shoeless" Joe Jackson and seven other Chicago White Sox players were accused of accepting money to lose the 1919 World Series. Order was restored to the game when Judge Kenesaw Mountain Landis was appointed Commissioner of Baseball by team owners. Landis expelled the suspected White Sox players from professional baseball for life. Legendary players such as Babe Ruth, Ty Cobb, and Lou Gehrig had outstanding seasons during the 1920s and attracted new fans to the sport. By the end of the 1920s baseball was still by far the nation's most popular sport. Millions of fans tuned in to radio broadcasts and attended games.

The "Black Sox" scandal angered many Americans, but baseball remained a popular attraction.

Books and magazines. For literary entertainment, some Americans turned to new publications. Founded in 1923, the Book-of-the-Month Club enabled publishers to bypass bookstores by selling books directly to consumers.

In the 1920s many Americans read magazines for entertainment. Weekly magazines such as *Collier's* and *The Saturday Evening Post* drew readers with their cartoons, short stories, and many pages of advertising. The husband-and-wife team of DeWitt and Lila Wallace founded *Reader's Digest* in 1921. Designed for busy Americans with less time to read, *Reader's Digest* reprinted articles from other magazines in shortened form. It proved a big success.

Celebrities and Heroes

The mass appeal of movies, radio, and sports generated huge audiences who shared in celebrities' victories and accomplishments. Actors became instantly famous. Young Americans paid special attention to celebrities' personal habits. They often copied the behavior of stars. In 1928, for example, Greta Garbo wore a slouch hat in the movie *A Woman of Affairs*. The slouch hat instantly became the most popular women's hat style.

Athletes also received celebrity status during the 1920s. One sports favorite was Babe Ruth. Known as the Sultan of Swat, Ruth dominated baseball from 1920 to 1934. During this time he led the New York Yankees to four World Series championships. In 1927 the spindle-legged, pigeon-toed ball player astounded the sports world with a record 60 home runs. Ruth's flashy playing on the field and scandalous life off the field attracted much attention.

Few athletes of the 1920s had more diverse talent than Jim Thorpe. As a student, Thorpe played every intercollegiate sport offered at his school. After leaving school, he began training for the Olympics. At the 1912 games, held in Stockholm, Sweden, Thorpe became the first competitor to win both the pentathlon and the decathlon. Thorpe went on to a career in major-league baseball. He also played professional football for several years.

Probably the biggest celebrity of the 1920s was pilot Charles Lindbergh. Lindbergh was a young, clean-cut pilot from Minnesota who flew airmail cargo planes between St. Louis and Chicago. In May 1927 he took off in a small, single-engine plane. He was aiming to win a $25,000 prize that had been offered to the first pilot to fly nonstop from New York to Paris. Lindbergh overcame bad weather, hunger, and fatigue to fly 33.5 hours alone in his airplane, *Spirit of St. Louis*.

Lindbergh's flight tapped into the American infatuation with contests and media events during the 1920s. It became one of the most talked about exploits of the decade. New Yorkers threw a ticker-tape parade for Lindbergh. President Coolidge received the modest young man at the White House. The next year, Amelia Earhart became the first woman to fly across the Atlantic Ocean.

✔ **READING CHECK:** How did celebrities and new forms of popular entertainment help create a mass culture?

Charles Lindbergh's solo flight across the Atlantic Ocean captured the public's attention. This sheet music celebrates Lindbergh's flight.

INTERPRETING THE VISUAL RECORD
Religion. Aimee Semple McPherson was a popular revivalist preacher in the 1920s. *Does this image suggest that McPherson was influenced by the movie industry? Explain.*

Religion in the 1920s

Some Americans found the social changes of the 1920s more troubling than exciting. Many citizens' lives still centered on church, family, and neighborhood, and religion remained a vital part of American culture.

Revivalism. Many Americans were worried about declining moral standards. Religious leaders preached sermons and wrote books denouncing the evils of popular entertainment and alcohol. The popular message of these religious leaders inspired a new era of revivalism.

To compete with Hollywood movies and radio for the public's attention, some religious leaders began using Hollywood-style entertainment to spread their message of morality. One of the most popular revivalists was Aimee Semple McPherson. She combined a strong Christian message with the glamour of Hollywood. From her International

The Religious Spirit

PENTECOSTALISM

Pentecostalism grew rapidly during the 1920s. The movement, however, had begun decades earlier. Pentecostalism grew out of a series of multidenominational revivals held in the Midwest during the 1890s. Charles F. Parham led the first Pentecostal revival in Topeka, Kansas, in 1901. Parham began the movement because he was convinced that real spirituality lay in experiencing the "baptism of the Holy Spirit." With their emphasis on experiencing the Holy Spirit, Pentecostal worship services were lively and emotional. Services often included faith healing and people speaking in tongues, or unfamiliar languages. Parham and his followers believed that an individual possessed by the Holy Spirit would be able to speak in other languages, and therefore be able to spread the faith.

Pentecostalism spread rapidly. The faith's focus on the direct experience of the Holy Spirit rather than on complex religious teachings attracted many Americans, particularly those with little formal education. In addition, the faith's emphasis on missionary work attracted a racially diverse following. In 1906 William Joseph Seymour, an African American preacher, brought the Pentecostal movement to California.

With the spread of Pentecostalism during the 1920s, hundreds of locally independent Pentecostal churches opened. The missionary movement of the Pentecostal faith proved remarkably successful. Today there are some 11.1 million Pentecostals in the United States and several hundred million worldwide.

PENTECOSTAL Camp Meeting
To be held at Martinsville, Indiana
During the Month of August, 1915
[D.V.]

A Full Gospel Camp Meeting will be held at this place commencing the first of August, continuing throughout the month.

God has wonderfully visited this city in power during the passed few months, and we have the prospects of a wonderful meeting in the future.

We have purchased a large tent which is situated in a beautiful location, and God has been richly blessing us.

Able workers will be with us to give out the Word, and the Gospel of our Lord and Saviour Jesus Christ will be presented in its fullness.

Rooms for light housekeeping, and furnished rooms and board can be obtained at reasonable prices.

Martinsville is located 30 miles South of Indianapolis on the I. & V. railroad, also hourly service on interurban cars. For further information, address

Pastor Fred Vogler

590 W. Morgan Street   Martinsville, Indiana

Revival meetings were popular in the 1920s.

Church of the Foursquare Gospel, headquartered in Los Angeles, McPherson offered dramatic religious services. The services combined an orchestra, chorus, and elaborate stage sets. Outfitted in her signature white dress, white shoes, and blue cape, McPherson captured the glamour of Hollywood. Her church was closely tied to the rapidly expanding Protestant movement called Pentecostalism.

Fundamentalism. Responding to the rapidly changing society of the 1920s, many Americans turned to a more conservative approach to their religious faith. A Protestant movement called **Fundamentalism** gained popularity during the decade. Followers of fundamentalist views resisted many of the new practices of other Protestant groups. The term *fundamentalist* came from a series of booklets published between 1910 and 1915 called *The Fundamentals*. The booklets argued that traditional Christian doctrine should be accepted without question. Fundamentalists believed that every word of the Bible should be regarded as literally true. They attacked Christian "liberals" who had accepted modern scientific learning, such as the theory of evolution. Fundamentalists claimed that this "modernism" weakened Christianity and contributed to the moral decline of the nation.

Evangelical preachers who spread the Fundamentalist "old-time religion" found an eager audience in rural towns and in urban areas where traditional values remained strong. People were spellbound by preacher Billy Sunday's evangelical showmanship. He attracted people with his rousing attacks on card playing, dancing, and drinking.

The Scopes trial. Fundamentalism went on trial in a famous court case in July 1925. Earlier that year the Tennessee legislature had outlawed the teaching of Charles Darwin's theory of evolution in the state's public schools. To test the law's constitutionality, the American Civil Liberties Union offered to defend any Tennessee schoolteacher who would challenge the statute. John Scopes, a biology teacher from Dayton, Tennessee, accepted the offer. Scopes's chief defense attorney was Clarence Darrow, a famous criminal lawyer from Chicago. The prosecution's star attorney was the elderly William Jennings Bryan. Bryan had been the former three-time Democratic presidential candidate and secretary of state.

The **Scopes trial** exposed a deep division in American society between traditional religious values and new values based on scientific ways of thought. Bryan spoke for many Americans who felt that the theory of evolution contradicted deeply held religious beliefs. Bryan spoke before the trial to an audience of local admirers.

> 66 Our purpose and our only purpose is to vindicate [uphold] the right of parents to guard the religion of their children against efforts made in the name of science to undermine faith in supernatural religion. 99

Clarence Darrow, on the other hand, expressed another widely held view. He attacked the Tennessee law as a threat to free expression. In one courtroom speech, Darrow warned his listeners. "Today it is the public school teachers, tomorrow the private, the next day the preachers and the lecturers, the magazines, the books, the newspapers."

From the beginning, Darrow had little chance of winning the trial. Judge John T. Raulston opened the trial with a prayer and refused to allow testimony from scientific experts. Darrow responded by calling Bryan as an expert witness on the Bible. During his testimony, Bryan affirmed his belief in the literal truth of the Bible. Darrow forced Bryan to reveal inconsistencies in his interpretation of scripture. For example, Darrow asked Bryan if the world was literally created in six days, as stated in the Bible. Bryan responded that a "day" did not necessarily mean 24 hours.

Clarence Darrow (left) and William Jennings Bryan (right) represented opposing sides in the Scopes trial.

Darrow's defense failed to convince the jury. Scopes was found guilty and fined $100. The verdict seemed a victory for Fundamentalists. However, press accounts of the trial, which often portrayed Bryan and his cause as narrow-minded, lowered some people's opinions of Fundamentalism.

✔ **READING CHECK:** What did the Scopes trial and the religious movements of the 1920s reveal about American society?

SECTION 2 REVIEW

Define and explain the significance of the following terms:
Volstead Act
Untouchables
Twenty-first Amendment
flappers
Fundamentalism
Scopes trial

Identify and explain the significance of the following individuals:
Al Capone
Eliot Ness
Cecil B. DeMille
Babe Ruth
Jim Thorpe
Charles Lindbergh
Amelia Earhart
Aimee Semple McPherson
Billy Sunday
Clarence Darrow

1. **Using Graphic Organizers** Copy the graphic organizer below. Use it to explain how prohibition led to an increase in crime and how the government tried to combat this crime.

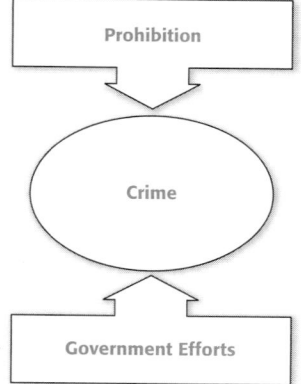

2. **Evaluating** How did the ideals of the "new woman," the lives of college students, and the leisure activities of the 1920s represent a new culture that conflicted with traditional American values?
3. **Assessing Consequences** How did the advances in radio and movies contribute to a growth in popular entertainment and help create a mass culture?
4. **Identifying Values** What values and cultural trends did the heroes and celebrities of the 1920s represent?

Critical Thinking

5. How did the many changes in American society during the 1920s affect the revival of religious activity?
   Consider:
   • the impact of youth culture and popular entertainment on people's perception of American culture
   • the message and activities of Aimee Semple McPherson and Billy Sunday
   • what led to the Scopes trial

A Creative Era

Scene outside the Renaissance Theater in Harlem

66 *When I came back to New York in 1925 the Negro Renaissance was in full swing. Countee Cullen was publishing his early poems, Zora Neale Hurston, Rudolph Fisher, Jean Toomer, and Wallace Thurman were writing, Louis Armstrong was playing, Cora Le Redd was dancing, and the Savoy Ballroom was open with a specially built floor that rocked as the dancers swayed. . . . Art took heart from Harlem creativity. Jazz filled the night air . . . and people came from all around after dark to look upon our city within a city, Black Harlem.* 99

—Langston Hughes

An explosion of creativity took place in Harlem, New York, during the 1920s. The 1920s was a period of great creative energy. African American musicians transformed popular music by introducing the nation to jazz. A new generation of writers explored the problems of postwar American life and the experience of being African American. New currents in art and architecture swept the nation.

Music

The 1920s is frequently known as the Jazz Age because **jazz** music first gained a wide following during that era. Jazz originated among African American musicians in the South. As a port city with residents of many different cultural traditions, New Orleans was an early center for the development of jazz. This innovative form of music is a hybrid of various musical styles that existed in New Orleans at the turn of the century. Jazz incorporates West African and Latin American rhythms, elements of African American spirituals, blues, and ragtime as well as European harmonies.

The emergence of jazz. Jazz emerged during the early 1900s in the entertainment district of New Orleans known as Storyville. Big brass bands, which had been popular in New Orleans since the Civil War, began experimenting with the ragtime style of music popularized by Scott Joplin. Brass-band musicians such as Charles "Buddy" Bolden gained a wide audience with their new "ragged" or improvised tunes. Bolden and other early jazz musicians also experimented with another form of African American music known as the **blues**.

The blues grew out of a long history of slave music and religious spirituals. It gained popularity during the early 1900s and greatly influenced jazz. Blues songs featured heartfelt lyrics and altered or slurred notes that echoed the mood of the lyrics. In the early 1920s blues singers such as Mamie Smith, Gertrude "Ma" Rainey, and Bessie Smith brought blues music to a broader audience. Their recordings of songs such as "Crazy Blues," "Down Hearted Blues," and "St. Louis Blues" became classic hits. Bessie Smith's "Down Hearted Blues" sold more than 500,000 copies in 1923.

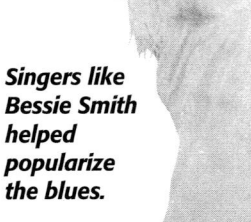

Singers like Bessie Smith helped popularize the blues.

As blues music grew in popularity, early jazz musicians from New Orleans such as Louis Armstrong began to adopt some of the unique characteristics of the blues. Jazz musicians re-created the vocal traditions of blues music. They used their instruments to imitate the expressive singing style of blues vocalists.

Jazz moves north. During the late 1910s thousands of African Americans moved northward. Many of New Orleans's most-noted jazz musicians relocated to cities like Chicago and New York. Pianist and composer Ferdinand "Jelly Roll" Morton helped spread jazz when he moved from New Orleans to Chicago in 1922. Morton formed a band called the Red Hot Peppers and recorded his famous tune—the "Jelly Roll Blues."

Joseph "King" Oliver also moved from New Orleans to Chicago, where he founded the Creole Jazz Band. In 1922 the great jazz trumpeter Louis Armstrong joined Oliver's band in Chicago. Armstrong's brilliant solos were featured in the Creole Jazz Band's Chicago recordings of "Mabel's Dream" and "Froggie Moore." By 1924 Armstrong had begun a renowned solo career. He toured throughout the United States and Europe, performing such classics as "When the Saints Go Marching In," "Savoy Blues," and "Hotter Than That."

The introduction of jazz to the North was met with enthusiasm. One reporter from the *Chicago Defender* was thrilled with the new music. He wrote, "The Fire department is thinking of lining 35th Street with asbestos [fireproof material] to keep those bands from scorching passers-by with their red-hot jazz music."

The popularization of jazz. As jazz grew in popularity, musicians of varying backgrounds began incorporating jazz elements into their music. White musicians—among them the cornetist and pianist Bix Beiderbecke—wove jazz rhythms into their music. George Gershwin's *Rhapsody in Blue*, which premiered in 1924, "translated" jazz into symphonic form. Jazz also influenced classical musicians, including such noted composers as Igor Stravinsky and Aaron Copland.

The development of big-band music in the mid-1920s introduced jazz music to a younger American audience. Big bands popularized jazz as dance music. Big-band jazz swept the nation. Young men and their flapper partners shocked their elders by dancing cheek-to-cheek fox-trots.

Jazz clubs such as Harlem's Cotton Club catered to the growing audience. These clubs brought in the most famous jazz musicians of the era, including Duke Ellington, Ethel Waters, and Cab Calloway. Reflecting the racism of the era, many of these clubs admitted only white customers. This occurred even though the performers frequently were African Americans and the clubs were located in African American neighborhoods.

Jazz music expressed the sadness, pain, and joy of black America. African American poet Langston Hughes noted that jazz proclaimed, "Why should I want to be white? I am a Negro—and beautiful!"

✔ **READING CHECK:** How did jazz and blues become popular nationwide?

This sheet music reflects the upbeat nature of the 1920s.

The Harlem Renaissance, 1920s and 1930s

Learning from Maps Between 1920 and 1930 Harlem's African American population substantially expanded its geographic boundaries.

? PLACE What was the extent of African American settlement in Harlem in 1920?

159th   St.
St. Nicholas
St.
Polo Grounds
–NY Giants
(baseball)
161st   St.
Grand
Jerome   Ave.
Yankee Stadium
–NY Yankees
–NY Black Yankees
–NY Cubans
155th   St.
Broadway
Amsterdam   Ave.
Bradhurst   Ave.
Eighth   Ave.
Macombs   Pl.
155th
151st   St.
Contourse
Exterior   Ave.
The Bronx
150th St.
150th   St.
Seventh   Ave.
Harlem River

0   ¼   ½ Mile
0   ¼   ½ Kilometer
Polyconic Projection

145th   St.

Harlem

Manhattan Island

Area of main map
0   2 Miles
0   2 Kilometers
Polyconic Projection

Harlem   River

Savoy Ballroom
140th   St.
Cotton Club

Liberty Hall

A'Leila Walker Home
James Weldon Johnson Home
NYC Public Library Harlem Branch
Y.M.C.A.
Sugarcane Club

The Bronx

East River

Hudson River

Eighth   Ave.
Seventh   Ave.
Lenox   Ave.
Fifth   Ave.
Madison   Ave.
Park   Ave.

Manhattan
Central Park

130th   St.

Queens

Marcus Garvey Home

New York City

126th   St.

Apollo Theatre

NEW JERSEY

East River
Brooklyn

Ave.

N
W   E
S

Black settlement in Harlem, 1920
Black settlement in Harlem, 1930
Areas predominantly African American
Parkland
■ Point of interest

The Harlem Renaissance

In the 1920s African Americans expressed a growing pride in their heritage. Nowhere was this pride more evident than in Harlem. This neighborhood in New York City became the cultural center of African American life. So many creative black writers, musicians, and artists lived in Harlem that the flourishing of artistic development in the 1920s is known as the **Harlem Renaissance**.

Theater. During the 1920s African American theater experienced both critical acclaim and increasing popularity. The work of black performers and playwrights brought new respect to black theater. African American theater critic Alain Locke explained, "The black playwright and the black actor will interpret the soul of their people in a way to win the attention and admiration of the world."

The theatrical roles available to African Americans were restricted by the prejudices of the era. Nevertheless, African Americans produced and staged several enormously successful Broadway plays and musicals. One of the most critically successful actors of the 1920s was Paul Robeson, who received praise for his title role in Eugene O'Neill's drama *Emperor Jones*. The grandson of a slave, Robeson turned to acting after graduating from Rutgers University and Columbia University Law School. His performances received high praise. "Robeson . . . is one of the most thoroughly eloquent, impressive and convincing actors that I have looked at and listened to in the past twenty years of theater going," offered one critic. Robeson was also an accomplished singer. He used his powerful baritone voice in such numbers as "Ol' Man River" from the musical *Showboat*. Robeson made history in 1924 as the first African American actor to play a leading role opposite a white actress.

Rose McClendon was another leading African American actor of the 1920s. McClendon first won fame in the 1926 production *Deep River,* a "native opera with jazz." In later years she performed in the Pulitzer Prize–winning tragedy *In Abraham's Bosom* and in the first production of *Porgy.*

Harlem Renaissance Writers

During the Harlem Renaissance, African American writers drew upon their personal experiences to create exciting and meaningful works. Poems such as Countee Cullen's "Yet Do I Marvel" and Langston Hughes's "I, Too" expressed the pride many Harlem writers had for their cultural heritage. Although the two poems explore a similar theme, the distinct style of each poem reflects the diversity of Harlem Renaissance literature.

"Yet Do I Marvel"
by Countee Cullen

I doubt not God is good,
   well-meaning, kind,
And did He stoop to
   quibble could tell why
The little buried mole
   continues blind,
Why flesh that mirrors
   Him must some day die,
Make plain the reason
   tortured Tantalus*
Is baited by the fickle fruit,
   declare
If merely brute caprice [whimsy] dooms Sisyphus**
To struggle up a never-ending stair.
Inscrutable [mysterious] His ways are, and immune
To catechism by a mind too strewn
With petty cares to slightly understand
What awful brain compels His awful hand.
Yet do I marvel at this curious thing:
To make a poet black, and bid him sing!

Countee Cullen's collection of poems

"I, Too"
by Langston Hughes

I, too, sing America.

I am the darker brother.
They send me to eat in the
   kitchen
When company comes,
But I laugh,
And eat well,
And grow strong.

Tomorrow,
I'll be at the table
When company comes.
Nobody'll dare
Say to me,
"Eat in the kitchen,"
Then.

Besides,
They'll see how beautiful I am
And be ashamed—

I, too, am America.

Langston Hughes

* Tantalus was a character in Greek mythology known for the punishment and torture he suffered in Hades (hell).

** According to Greek mythology, Sisyphus must endlessly push a heavy rock up a steep hill.

UNDERSTANDING LITERATURE

1. What point does Cullen make in his poem?
2. How did Langston Hughes's experience as an African American influence his poem?
3. How does the unique style of language of each poem enhance the poets' message?

Literature. African American contributions to literature were central to the Harlem Renaissance. African American novelists and poets produced work marked by bitterness and defiance but also by joy and hope. Writer Nella Larsen described the quest for racial identity in her 1928 novel, *Quicksand*. Also published in 1928, Claude McKay's novel *Home to Harlem* explored the excitement and stresses of life in Harlem for an African American soldier returning from World War I.

Harlem poets celebrated their ethnic identity and acknowledged the struggles faced by many African Americans. McKay expressed his determination to fight racial injustices in his poem "If We Must Die."

Claude McKay and many other writers made Harlem a center of American literature.

> 66 **If we must die, let it not be like hogs**
> **Hunted and penned in an inglorious spot,**
> **While round us bark the mad and hungry dogs. . . .**
> **What though before us lies the open grave?**
> **Like men we'll face the murderous, cowardly pack,**
> **Pressed to the wall, dying, but fighting back!** 99

Langston Hughes was another poet who dealt sensitively with issues of African cultural heritage. Hughes distinguished himself by addressing his poems to African American readers. Hughes focused on the everyday experiences of African Americans, using language and themes familiar to his readers.

James Weldon Johnson

One of the most active supporters of the Harlem Renaissance was James Weldon Johnson. Born in Jacksonville, Florida, in 1871, Johnson was the son of the first African American woman to teach in Florida's public schools. Johnson excelled as a student and attended Atlanta University. There, he studied the classics and poetry. A man of many talents, Johnson's occupations included educator, lawyer, diplomat to Venezuela and Nicaragua, and official in the National Association for the Advancement of Colored People (NAACP). He was also a writer.

Johnson published a wide variety of works. In 1899 he composed "Lift Ev'ry Voice and Sing" with music by his brother, J. Rosamond Johnson. By the 1920s the song was commonly known as the African American national anthem. Johnson also wrote several novels, including *The Autobiography of an Ex-Colored Man*, published in 1912.

Johnson's main contribution to the Harlem Renaissance was his support of other authors. In 1922 Johnson published *The Book of American Negro Poetry*. Through his work as the executive secretary of the NAACP during the 1920s, Johnson raised money to support African American artists and art programs in Harlem.

Johnson's support of the arts was based on his belief that the artistic advances of the Harlem Renaissance would help further the cause of equal rights. Johnson claimed that the "demonstration of intellectual parity [equality] by the Negro through the production of literature and art" eliminated racial prejudice best. Johnson continued this work until his death on June 26, 1938.

✔ **READING CHECK:** In what ways did the artists and writers of the Harlem Renaissance use their work to express pride in their cultural heritage?

The Lost Generation

The Harlem Renaissance coincided with the rise of a new generation of American writers. Their work reflected their horror at the death and destruction of World War I. Their scorn for middle-class consumerism and the superficiality of the postwar years also showed in their writing. "You are all a lost generation," said poet Gertrude Stein to one such writer, Ernest Hemingway. The label stuck, and the writers of the era became known as the **Lost Generation**.

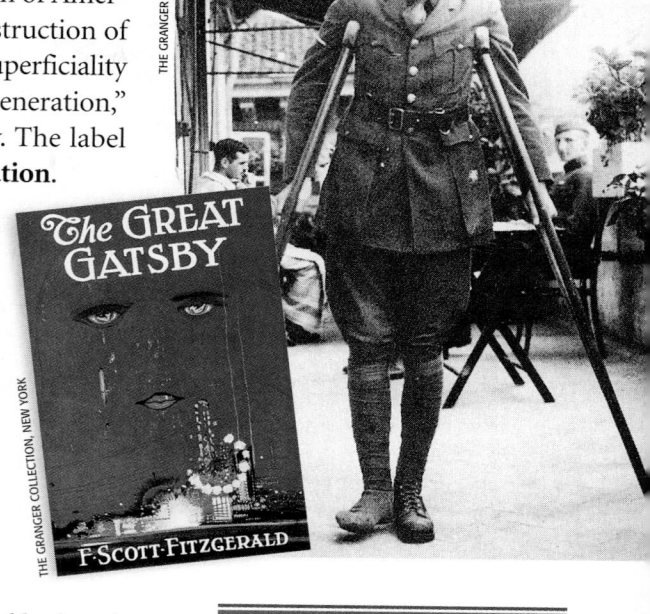

Stories of disillusionment. Ernest Hemingway spent much of his life in France, Spain, and Cuba. During World War I, he and several other young writers served as ambulance drivers as a way to experience and understand war. Hemingway was seriously wounded while serving on the Italian front. He later expressed his anger at the uselessness of war. His 1929 novel, *A Farewell to Arms,* depicts the devastation of war in its portrayal of a relationship between a wounded soldier and a nurse. In a famous passage the soldier explains what the war means to him.

> 66 I was always embarrassed by the words sacred, glorious, and sacrifice and the expression in vain. We had heard them . . . and had read them . . . now for a long time, and I had seen nothing sacred, and the things that were glorious had no glory and the sacrifices were like the stockyards at Chicago if nothing was done with the meat except to bury it. 99

F. Scott Fitzgerald was another member of the Lost Generation. His novels chronicled the youthful Jazz Age. In *This Side of Paradise* (1920), Fitzgerald depicted the lives of wealthy college students bored by fast living. In *The Great Gatsby* (1925), Fitzgerald portrayed the emptiness of a man's pursuit of money and social status.

Fitzgerald's life was filled with the same tragedies and disillusionment that plagued his characters. Fitzgerald defined the Jazz Age as a time when "a new generation [had] grown up to find . . . all wars fought, all faiths in man shaken." With the extraordinary success of his first novel and his marriage to beautiful Zelda Sayre, Fitzgerald's future appeared bright. Their glamorous lifestyle was cut short, however, by Zelda Fitzgerald's incurable mental illness and Fitzgerald's own alcoholism and declining creativity.

Criticizing the middle class. Sinclair Lewis shared Fitzgerald's skeptical attitude toward American society during the 1920s. However, Lewis focused his criticism on the emptiness and conformity of middle-class life. In *Main Street* (1920), Lewis satirized the close-mindedness of a typical small midwestern town. In his 1922 novel, *Babbitt,* Lewis told the story of a middle-aged realtor and city booster who is dissatisfied with his middle-class life but lacks the courage to change.

The journalist and critic Henry L. Mencken served as a champion of these new writers. In his magazine, *The American Mercury,* Mencken promoted novelists who satirized middle-class Americans, whom he ridiculed as "the booboisie." Mencken made fun of Republican politicians, Fundamentalist Christians, rural southerners, residents of small towns, and many other Americans.

✔ **READING CHECK:** How did the writers of the Lost Generation portray American life?

INTERPRETING THE VISUAL RECORD
Memories of war. *The Great Gatsby* tells a story of wealth and power. *Do you think this soldier enjoyed the prosperity of the 1920s? Explain your answer.*

Read More About It

Free Find:
F. Scott Fitzgerald
After reading the biography on F. Scott Fitzgerald on the **Holt Researcher** CD–ROM, create an outline for a story set in the 1920s about Fitzgerald.

In this 1928 painting, **Manhattan Bridge Loop,** *Edward Hopper conveys the isolation and industrialization that many associated with U.S. cities.*

Murals. Diego Rivera completed the mural called *Detroit Industry* in 1932, after spending months in the industrial city. Rivera attempted to capture the positive and negative aspects of industrialization. *How do you think these themes are revealed in this work?*

The Visual Arts

As the writers of the Lost Generation confronted the boredom and frustration of life after the war, many visual artists concerned themselves with other changes occurring in the United States. Artists of the 1920s addressed the impact of growing cities and the increasing use of machinery on American life.

Painting and photography. Many American painters of the 1920s depicted urban, industrial settings. Edward Hopper's scenes of New York City convey a sense of loneliness and serene stillness. *Early Sunday Morning* (1930) shows a row of darkened stores and a street empty of people. Hopper believed that art should reflect the experiences of modern life. He explained, "The province [role] of art is to react to it [life] and not to shun it." Before she moved to New Mexico, artist Georgia O'Keeffe also depicted city life in her paintings of New York factories and tenements.

Photography came to be widely appreciated as an art form in the 1900s. Alfred Stieglitz (STEEG-luhts) helped popularize photography. In addition to operating an influential New York gallery, Stieglitz photographed people as well as airplanes, skyscrapers, and crowded city streets. Photographer and painter Charles Sheeler won fame for his portraits revealing the beauty of machinery. The Ford Motor Company hired him to photograph its plant near Detroit, Michigan, in 1927.

Murals. Another artistic renaissance of the 1920s took place in Mexico. Mexican muralists emphasized the nobility of ordinary people—peasants and other workers—and the tyranny of the wealthy class. Their favorite medium was the monumental public mural. In the words of artist José Clemente Orozco (oh-ROHS-koh), the public murals "cannot be hidden away for the benefit of a certain privileged few. It is for the people. It is for ALL."

The movement's three major artists—known in Mexico as *los tres grandes,* or "the big three"—were Orozco, David Alfaro Siqueiros (see-KAY-rohs), and Diego Rivera. Each artist visited the United States in the early 1930s to paint murals. Diego Rivera, the most prominent muralist, focused on workers' problems and industrial development in his American murals. In 1932 Rivera painted a mural at the Detroit Institute of Art that featured assembly-line workers in automobile factories.

Rivera and his wife, Frida Kahlo—an accomplished painter—lived and traveled throughout the United States from 1930 to 1933. Some Americans found Rivera's radical politics offensive. In 1933, sponsors of a new Rivera mural commissioned by the Rockefeller Center destroyed the work they had funded. Titled *Man at the Crossroads,* the mural upset the sponsors because it featured an image of the Bolshevik leader Vladimir Lenin. After returning to Mexico, Rivera re-created the mural at the Palace of Fine Arts in Mexico City.

Architecture. The spirit of creativity that emerged in the United States in the 1920s also appeared in the era's architecture. Many architects found inspiration in the works of Louis Sullivan and Frank Lloyd Wright. Sullivan's unique buildings were based on a design in which each part of the structure had a functional purpose. Wright studied under Sullivan during the 1890s. By the early 1910s Wright had gained a worldwide reputation for his innovative designs.

Wright developed the "prairie style" of domestic architecture. This new style used rectangular shapes and clean, horizontal lines that echoed the flatness of the prairies. Wright also incorporated Sullivan's idea that every aspect of a house's structure must have a functional purpose.

Many architects of the 1920s were influenced by Sullivan and Wright's thoughts. These architects embraced the idea that a building ought to use the materials and follow the forms most suitable to the building's purpose. The structure that most clearly illustrated this principle was the modern skyscraper. The new type of building was characterized by clean-cut vertical lines, the use of steel, concrete, and glass, and the lack of ornamentation.

New York City experienced a boom in skyscraper construction during the 1920s. Builders began construction of two landmarks—the Chrysler Building and the Empire State Building. Completed in 1930, the Chrysler Building was the tallest building in the world—at 1,048 feet—until the completion of the Empire State Building in 1931. The 102-story Empire State Building cleared 1,250 feet and remained the world's tallest building until 1954.

✔ **READING CHECK:** What were some of the major inspirations for the new movements within the visual arts and architecture?

The Robie House. Drawing attention to the horizontal lines of his design, Frank Lloyd Wright completed this prairie-style home for Chicago bicycle manufacturer Frederick C. Robie in 1909. *What aspects of this design help draw out the horizontal lines of this house?*

SECTION 3 REVIEW

Define and explain the significance of the following terms:
jazz
blues
Harlem Renaissance
Lost Generation

Identify and explain the significance of the following individuals:

Bessie Smith
Louis Armstrong
Bix Beiderbecke
Duke Ellington
Langston Hughes
Paul Robeson
Rose McClendon

James Weldon
 Johnson
Ernest
 Hemingway
F. Scott Fitzgerald
Alfred Stieglitz
Diego Rivera

Locate and explain the significance of the following place:
Harlem

1. **Using Graphic Organizers** Copy the graphic organizer below. List the original influences of jazz and the blues. Then explain how jazz and the blues expanded nationwide.

Jazz and the Blues → national popularity

2. **Evaluating** How did the writers of the Harlem Renaissance contribute to American culture?
3. **Recognizing Point of View** What were the major themes expressed in the novels of Lost Generation writers?
4. **Assessing Consequences** How did the growth of U.S. cities and the introduction of new technology influence the visual arts of the 1920s?

Critical Thinking

5. Why might writers and artists of the 1920s be considered social critics?
Consider:
• how the African American writers of the Harlem Renaissance wrote about their lives
• what experiences the writers of the Lost Generation captured in their novels
• what the visual artists of the 1920s focused on in their works

CHAPTER 23

Review

Creating a Time Line

Copy the time line below onto a sheet of paper. Complete the time line by filling in the events and dates from the chapter that you think were most significant. Pick three events and explain why you think they were significant.

1920   1925   1930

Writing a Summary

Using the Reading Checks as a guide, write an overview of the events in the chapter.

Identifying People and Ideas

Identify the following terms or individuals and explain their significance.

1. Model T
2. assembly line
3. Volstead Act
4. flappers
5. Charles Lindbergh
6. Aimee Semple McPherson
7. Harlem Renaissance
8. James Weldon Johnson
9. Lost Generation
10. Diego Rivera

Understanding Main Ideas

SECTION 1

1. How did the development of the assembly line encourage the growth of the American automobile industry and affect American life?

SECTION 2

2. In what ways did the activities of many younger Americans during the 1920s represent a rejection of traditional American values?

SECTION 3

3. How did the work of writers and artists of the Harlem Renaissance affect American culture?
4. What aspects of American life did writers of the Lost Generation criticize?

Reviewing Themes

1. **Economic Development** How did advertising, installment buying, and planned obsolescence boost the nation's economy in the 1920s?
2. **Technology and Society** How did the spread of inventions such as radio and movies alter Americans' lives during the 1920s?
3. **Cultural Diversity** How did the influences of jazz reflect the cultural diversity of the United States?

Thinking Critically

1. **Assessing Consequences** How did the rise in productivity during the 1920s have both positive and negative effects for workers and industry?
2. **Evaluating** How did the emergence of popular entertainment contribute to the youth culture of the 1920s?
3. **Comparing and Contrasting** How did the values expressed by leaders of the Fundamentalist and Pentecostal movements of the 1920s differ from the values expressed by the new youth culture?
4. **Recognizing Point of View** How did the visual artists of the 1920s express their views of technology, the plight of workers, and urban life?
5. **Identifying Values** In what ways did African American artists, musicians, and writers of the 1920s express pride in their cultural heritage?

Writing About History

Writing to Describe Write an essay that describes the impact of nationwide broadcasting of radio programs on the lives of Americans. Use the following graphic to organize your thoughts.

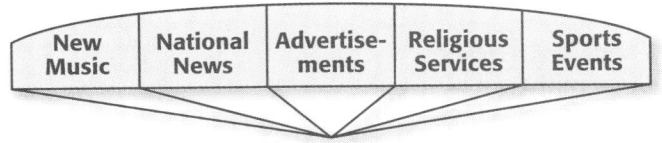

| New Music | National News | Advertise-ments | Religious Services | Sports Events |

Radio in the home

Strategies for Success Review the **Strategies for Success** on *Studying Primary and Secondary Sources*. Then examine the passage below from *Middletown* and answer the questions that follow.

> 66 Advertising has grown rapidly since 1890. . . . Today all sorts of advertising devices are tried: . . . a shoe store conducting a sale offers one dollar each to the first twenty-five women appearing at the store on Monday morning; semi-annual 'dollar days' and 'suburban days' are conducted by the press. . . . The advertising carried in the leading daily paper is six times that in the leading daily of 1890. 99

1. Is this passage part of a primary source or a secondary source? Explain your answer.
2. Who do you think was the intended audience of the passage?
3. Do the authors express any biases in the passage?
4. How does the passage contribute to your understanding of the United States during the 1920s?

Linking History and Geography

Examine the map below. Why were there more prohibition arrests made in states bordering Mexico and Canada than in other states?

Arrests Under Prohibition in 1929

Number of Persons Arrested by or with the Aid of Federal Prohibition Officers

- 3,000 or more
- 2,000–2,999
- 1,000–1,999
- 500-999
- 499 or fewer
- WI No state prohibition law, 1930

internetconnect

TOPIC: Jazz in the 1920s
GO TO: go.hrw.com
KEYWORD: SD1 Jazz

Accessing the Internet through the HRW Web site, research the lives and accomplishments of jazz artists Duke Ellington and Louis Armstrong. Then create a newspaper page that has interviews with the artists or stories about them.

BUILDING YOUR PORTFOLIO

Complete one or all of the following projects independently or cooperatively.

1 Economic Development

Imagine that you are a prosperous business owner in the 1920s. **Create an advertisement** for a new household product aimed at the expanding consumer market.

2 Cultural Diversity

Imagine that you are a Harlem Renaissance or Lost Generation writer or a mural painter living in the United States during the 1920s. **Create a poem or painting** that draws upon your cultural heritage or that reflects 1920s American society.

3 Democratic Values

Imagine that you are a writer for a 1920s radio show. **Write a script** for a radio show that addresses the many changes that are taking place in American society.

1929–1933
The Great Depression

Headline describing
the stock market crash

Bank closing

1929
**Business
and Finance**
The U.S.
stock market
crashes.

1929
Science and Technology
The Cascade Tunnel, the
longest railroad tunnel in
North America, is completed.

1929
Politics
Congress establishes
the Federal Farm
Board to assist
farmers.

1930
Business and Finance
Approximately $180
million of depositors'
savings are lost with the
financial collapse of one
New York City bank.

1930
World Events
France establishes a
workers' insurance law.

1929

1930

1929
Science and Technology
Harvard physician Samuel Albert Levine
establishes a connection between high
blood pressure and heart disease.

1929
The Arts
William Faulkner
publishes *The Sound
and the Fury.*

British election poster
portraying the effects of
the Great Depression

1930
Daily Life
In New York City more
than 6,000 unemployed
workers sell apples on
the streets to earn money.

1930
World Events
An economic depression
hits countries in Europe
and South America.

Before You Read

Build on What You Know

The economic boom of the 1920s gave most Americans tremendous faith in
the future. For many Americans, prosperity seemed limitless. The economic
gains were unevenly distributed, however. The lifestyle of the Jazz Age
also led to enormous consumer debt. In this chapter you will learn how debt and
many other factors led to the Great Depression. When President Hoover's efforts
to revive the economy failed, Americans elected a Democratic president, Franklin
D. Roosevelt, in hopes of reversing the country's economic decline.

Boulder Dam on the Colorado River

1932 Business and Finance Industrial output falls to half its 1929 level.

1932 World Events Chile's income from the export of copper and nitrates declines by more than 1.5 billion pesos in less than four years.

1932 Business and Finance Since 1930 more than 5,000 banks have closed.

Members of the Bonus Army

1932 Daily Life Veterans form the Bonus Army and demonstrate in Washington, D.C., demanding early payments of their pensions.

1932 Politics Congress establishes the Reconstruction Finance Corporation to stabilize the economy by assisting banks and other financial institutions.

1931 Science and Technology U.S. engineer Henry J. Kaiser designs the Boulder Dam.

1931 Politics President Hoover refuses to support a bill providing direct federal relief for unemployed workers.

1931   1932   1933

1931 Daily Life Cotton prices fall below 6 cents per pound, forcing many tenant farmers from their land.

1931 World Events President Hoover announces a one-year halt on war reparations, hoping to promote European economic recovery.

1932 Politics Franklin D. Roosevelt is elected president.

LOST HORIZON
by JAMES HILTON
author of "Good-bye, Mr. Chips"

Alexander Woollcott says:
"I have gone quietly mad on the subject of LOST HORIZON. It is one of the most enthralling tales ever in our time and I know few people on whom it would not cast a most potent spell."

James Hilton's novel

1933 The Arts James Hilton publishes *Lost Horizon*.

1933 Daily Life The unemployment rate reaches 24.9 percent of the workforce, as 15 million Americans are out of work.

Franklin D. Roosevelt campaigning

Think About Themes

Themes Journal *Decide whether you agree or disagree with the following statements. Note why in your journal.*

Economic Development A stock market crash will always result in a severe economic depression.

Geographic Diversity An economic crisis does not affect where people live, since they cannot afford to move.

Cultural Diversity In an economic depression everyone suffers equally, regardless of class, gender, and ethnic background.

SECTION 1

Prosperity Shattered

OBJECTIVES
Read to understand:
1. why financial experts issued warnings about business practices during the 1920s
2. why the stock market crashed in 1929
3. how the banking crisis and subsequent business failures signaled the beginning of the Great Depression
4. what the main causes of the Great Depression were

KEY TERMS
bull market
bear market
margin buying
Black Thursday
Black Tuesday
gross national product
Great Depression
Smoot-Hawley Tariff
business cycle

KEY PEOPLE
Herbert Hoover

EYEWITNESSES TO History

66 *'MARKET CRASHES—PANIC HITS NATION!' one headline blared. . . . I couldn't imagine such financial disaster touching my small world; it surely concerned only the rich. But by the first week of November I too knew differently; along with millions of others across the nation, I was without a job. All that next week I searched for any kind of work that would prevent my leaving school. Again it was, 'We're firing, not hiring.'. . . Finally, on the seventh of November I went to school and cleaned out my locker, knowing it was impossible to stay on. A piercing chill was in the air as I walked back to the rooming house. The hawk had come. I could already feel his wings shadowing me.* 99

—Gordon Parks

Photographer and author Gordon Parks

Gordon Parks was 16 years old when the prosperity of the 1920s came to an abrupt halt. The booming stock market crashed on Thursday, October 24, 1929. In the first few hours of stock trading, share prices fell sharply. At first, investors remained calm. However, as prices continued to fall, panic struck. Frantic orders to sell stock came pouring in. The economic prosperity of the 1920s was over. The worst economic depression in U.S. history had begun. For many Americans, their daily lives became a constant struggle for survival.

Economic Troubles on the Horizon

Although the 1920s appeared to be a decade of unlimited economic prosperity, a few isolated voices warned of problems within the U.S. economy. Some economists identified the nation's agricultural crisis and "sick" industries as problems in need of attention. Yet despite these early warnings of economic troubles, few Americans worried about the nation's economic health in the late 1920s. The country's widespread prosperity led many Americans to believe that the economy would continue to grow in the following decades. President Herbert Hoover expressed this confidence in his speech accepting the Republican nomination in 1928.

66 **We in America today are nearer to the final triumph over poverty than ever before in the history of any land. The poorhouse is vanishing from among us. . . . We shall soon . . . be in sight of the day when poverty will be banished from this nation.** 99

Credit. Assured by their faith in the nation's economic prosperity, many Americans purchased new consumer products on credit. By 1929 the total number of purchases made with credit was six times higher than in 1915. Purchases on credit in 1929 reached a total of $7 billion.

The federal government encouraged this borrowing by keeping interest rates low during the late 1920s. The Republican administrations of the time reasoned that

During the 1928 presidential campaign, Republican Herbert Hoover promised economic prosperity and continued pro-business policies.

an easy-credit policy would promote business. Easy access to credit enabled consumers to buy goods when they did not actually have the money to pay for them.

Industries' increasing reliance on customers who made purchases with credit generated caution among economic experts. These experts noted that in an economic downturn, such debt could cripple consumers. Consumers, however, ignored these warnings and continued to purchase automobiles, radios, and appliances on credit.

Playing the market. Americans' confidence in the economy of the 1920s was also reflected in the stock market. Investors poured millions of dollars into the market. Stock sales had increased steadily for several years. As demand rose, so did stock prices. Many experts saw no end to the **bull market**—one with an upward trend in stock prices. "There have been bull markets before," observed the *New York Times*, "but the present one surpasses them all." Investors and market analysts claimed that the stock market was in no danger of becoming a **bear market**—one with a downward trend in stock prices.

By the late 1920s, stock speculation—"playing" the market by buying and selling to make a quick profit—was widespread. Although speculation fueled economic growth, it also created problems. Rapid buying and selling inflated the prices of stocks to the point that many stocks were selling for far more than they were actually worth. This speculative buying was fine as long as demand was high, but if investor confidence weakened, prices would tumble.

The situation was made shakier still by **margin buying**—the practice of purchasing stocks with borrowed money. Many speculators put up as little as 10 percent of the price of a stock, borrowing the rest. Buying on margin worked as long as the bull market continued. If prices were to ever fall steeply, however, investors would find themselves deep in debt.

Although consumer confidence in the market remained high throughout the summer of 1929, a few gloomy voices were heard. In early September stock analyst Roger Babson wrote, "Sooner or later a crash is coming, and it may be terrific [frightful]." Some shrewd investors began to sell their stocks, but most people ignored the warnings.

✔ **READING CHECK:** Why did financial experts issue warnings about business practices during the 1920s?

Ticker tape machines like this one were used to get up-to-date stock market prices during the 1920s.

The Stock Market Crashes

The bubble burst on **Black Thursday**—October 24, 1929. A large number of investors, made nervous by factors such as rising interest rates, suddenly began to sell their shares. The dumping of so much

The Crash, 1929

Company	High Price Sept. 3, 1929	Low Price Nov. 13, 1929
American Telephone and Telegraph	304	197 1/4
General Electric	396 1/4	168 1/8
General Motors	72 3/4	36
Montgomery Ward	137 7/8	49 1/4
United States Steel	261 3/4	150
Woolworth	100 3/8	52 1/4

Source: *Only Yesterday*

Learning from Charts In the days following the stock market crash on October 29, 1929, stock prices continued to fall. Average stock prices reached their lowest point for the year on November 13, 1929, slightly two months after they had reached the high point for the year on September 3.

? **Building Chart Skills** Which company's stock lost the greatest number of points between September 3 and November 13, 1929?

THE GRANGER COLLECTION, NEW YORK

Stock market crash. The stock market crash of 1929 left many stockholders with huge losses. Some investors who had borrowed money during the prosperous days of the 1920s were unable to pay off their loans. *How do you think this photograph reflects the transition from a time of prosperity to one of depression for this investor?*

stock on the market jolted investor confidence and caused prices to plunge. Panic gripped Wall Street. A *New York Times* reporter described the crash.

> 66 It came with a speed and ferocity [cruelty] that left men dazed. The bottom simply fell out of the market. . . . The streets were crammed with a mixed crowd—agonized little speculators, . . . sold-out traders, . . . inquisitive individuals and tourists seeking . . . a closer view of the national catastrophe. . . . Where was it going to end? 99

Black Thursday was just the beginning of a long downward spiral. Prices dropped still lower the following week, as more investors sold their stocks. On **Black Tuesday**—October 29—prices sank to a shocking new low when panicked investors dumped more than 16 million shares of stock on the market.

As prices fell, brokers contacted customers who owed them money for stocks purchased on margin. The brokers demanded cash to cover their loans. Unable to raise the funds, thousands of people were forced to sell their stocks at huge losses. Many investors were wiped out. By mid-November the average value of leading stocks had been cut in half, and stockholders had lost some $30 billion. By year's end, stock losses exceeded the total cost of U.S. involvement in World War I.

✔ **READING CHECK:** Why did the stock market crash in 1929?

The Depression Begins

In the first months after the stock market crash, business leaders and public officials insisted that the setback was minor and temporary. President Hoover declared, "We have now passed the worst and . . . shall rapidly recover." Yet this optimism could not conceal the grim truth. Within the first months of 1930 it became clear that the nation was slipping into a severe economic depression.

Banking crisis. Just a small percentage of Americans had invested in the stock market in 1929. However, the impact of the crash was soon felt by the entire country. The stock market collapse provoked a major banking crisis. Like many other investors, large banks suffered significant losses. The worst economic crisis for banks came as a result of borrowers defaulting on their loans. Having lost their investments in the stock market, many debt-ridden investors could not repay their loans. Banks were left with depreciating assets and little income. With dwindling cash reserves, some banks were forced to close.

Fear of additional bank failures further aggravated the banking crisis. Customers could lose their entire life savings if their bank closed. Many depositors panicked and tried to withdraw their savings. This caused even more bank failures. Reporting on a banking panic in Akron, Ohio, one newspaper commented, "The bank was failing. Its cash reserve was dropping. Bank depositors waited in dread for a teller to say, 'We cannot give you ten percent of your account. We can't give you anything.'" Between 1930 and 1932, more than 5,000 banks failed. The 1930 collapse of one large New York City bank wiped out some 400,000 depositors.

Business failures. Many American businesses suffered from the banking crisis. Industries that had already lost money in the stock market crash faced additional hardships with consumers unable or unwilling to buy their products. Debt and the fear of bank failures brought an end to the consumer habit of purchasing new goods on credit. Many companies were forced to trim inventories, scale back production schedules, and lay off employees.

During the early 1930s businesses began to fail at an alarming rate as the economy's downward slide accelerated. More than 26,000 businesses went bankrupt in 1930. Another 28,285 went under the following year. In 1929 the U.S. **gross national product**—the total value of all goods and services produced in a given year—had reached $103 billion. At the height of the depression in 1933 it fell below $56 billion. Factories and mines stood idle. Railroad cars sat silent and empty.

As businesses failed, unemployment reached staggering levels. In 1932, the rate rose to 23.6 percent, up from 3.2 percent three years earlier. The crisis in the banking industry, business failures, and massive unemployment in the early 1930s marked the beginning of the **Great Depression**. This deep economic downturn gripped the United States between 1929 and the beginning of World War II.

✔ **READING CHECK:** How did the banking crisis and subsequent business failures signal the beginning of the Great Depression?

Many Americans thought that their bank accounts would be safe during economic hard times.

What Caused the Great Depression?

The stock market crash of 1929 provoked the banking crisis and business failures that jolted the U.S. economy and destroyed individual fortunes. It alone, however, did not cause the Great Depression. The stock market collapse was a major factor among the depression's many causes.

Global depression. Economic trouble in Europe and other parts of the world was one of the many factors that brought down the U.S. economy. As the economy sank during the early 1930s, many observers, including President Hoover, blamed the U.S. depression on the state of global finances following World War I.

The global economy had suffered enormous setbacks. This was primarily because of the massive war debts built up by European countries. World trade rapidly declined during the late 1920s and early 1930s. The global depression further worsened the economic crisis in the United States. Foreign consumers were unable to purchase American goods. American industries, which relied on sales to consumers abroad, were stuck with large surpluses.

THROUGH OTHERS' EYES

The Global Depression

The impact of the Great Depression was felt in almost every country in the world. In a 1931 radio broadcast by the British Broadcasting Corporation (BBC) on unemployment, British economist John Maynard Keynes described the severe effects of the economic downturn for industrial workers and farmers throughout the world.

66 The slump in trade and employment and the business losses . . . are as bad as the worst which have ever occurred in the modern history of the world. No country is exempt. The privation [hardship] and—what is sometimes worse—the anxiety which exist today in millions of homes all over the world is extreme. In the three chief industrial countries of the world, Great Britain, Germany, and the United States, I estimate that probably 12 million industrial workers stand idle. But I am not sure that there is not even more human misery today in the great agricultural countries of the world—Canada, Australia, and South America, where millions of small farmers see themselves ruined. 99

U.S. policies could have eased the global depression. Instead, the United States contributed to the worldwide economic downturn by slapping high tariffs on imported goods. Even after the crash, Congress continued to pass high tariffs such as the **Smoot-Hawley Tariff** of 1930. It was the highest in U.S. history. The act protected American industries from inexpensive imports. However, it accelerated the global depression by eliminating the American market for foreign manufacturers and industries.

The income gap and consumer debt. Historians have argued that the unequal distribution of income was another central cause of the Great Depression.

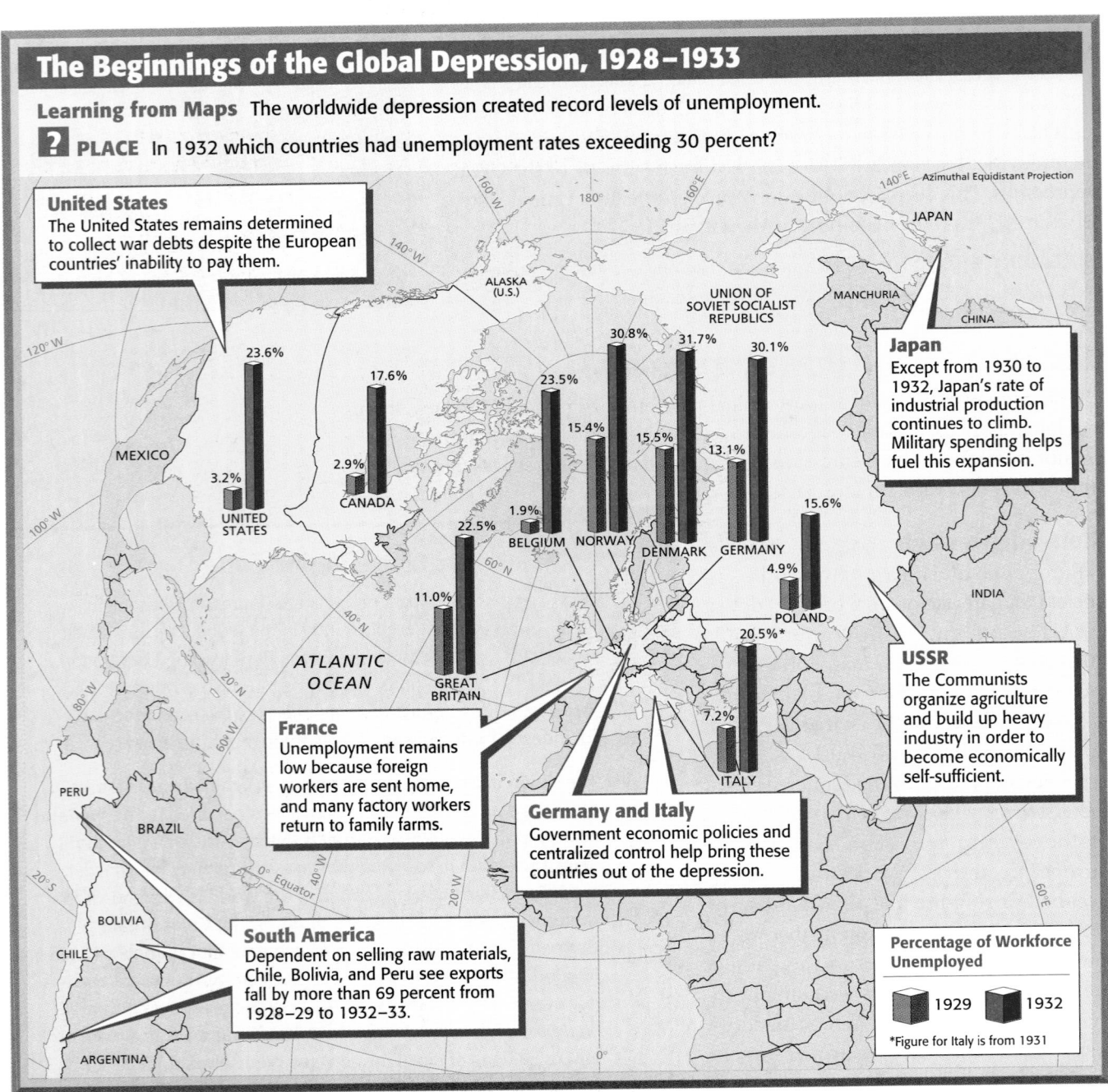

The Beginnings of the Global Depression, 1928–1933

Learning from Maps The worldwide depression created record levels of unemployment.

? PLACE In 1932 which countries had unemployment rates exceeding 30 percent?

United States
The United States remains determined to collect war debts despite the European countries' inability to pay them.

Japan
Except from 1930 to 1932, Japan's rate of industrial production continues to climb. Military spending helps fuel this expansion.

USSR
The Communists organize agriculture and build up heavy industry in order to become economically self-sufficient.

France
Unemployment remains low because foreign workers are sent home, and many factory workers return to family farms.

Germany and Italy
Government economic policies and centralized control help bring these countries out of the depression.

South America
Dependent on selling raw materials, Chile, Bolivia, and Peru see exports fall by more than 69 percent from 1928–29 to 1932–33.

Percentage of Workforce Unemployed
1929   1932
*Figure for Italy is from 1931

UNITED STATES 3.2% / 23.6%
CANADA 2.9% / 17.6%
GREAT BRITAIN 11.0% / 22.5%
BELGIUM 1.9% / 23.5%
NORWAY 15.4% / 30.8%
DENMARK 15.5% / 31.7%
GERMANY 13.1% / 30.1%
POLAND 4.9% / 15.6%
ITALY 7.2% / 20.5%*

Between 1923 and 1929 the disposable income of the wealthiest 1 percent of Americans increased by 63 percent. Meanwhile, the income of the poorest 93 percent of Americans decreased by 4 percent. Writer Upton Sinclair noted, "The . . . depression is one of abundance, not of scarcity. . . . The cause of the trouble is that a small class has the wealth, while the rest have the debts." This income gap meant that most people did not have the buying power needed to boost the economy. According to many economists, if workers had received higher wages for their labor and farmers better prices for their crops, the depression would have been less severe. Some even argue that it could have been avoided.

Some Americans bridged the income gap by using credit to purchase goods. The reliance on consumer credit also contributed to economic chaos. Once the economy began to slow and the government raised interest rates, many consumers could not pay their debts. After the crash many businesses stopped extending credit altogether.

The business cycle. Some economists argue that better fiscal planning in the 1920s would not have prevented the onset of the Great Depression. These economists view depressions as an inevitable part of the **business cycle**—the regular ups and downs of business in a free-enterprise economy. According to business-cycle theory, industries increase production and hire more workers during prosperous times, with the result that over time surpluses pile up. Industries then cut back on production and lay off workers, triggering a recession or a depression. According to this theory, however, once the surplus goods are sold, industries again gear up for production and the downturn comes to an end. However, the length and severity of the Great Depression went far beyond the normal rhythms of the business cycle.

The depression. Some businesses encouraged Americans to spend money during the depression. They believed that it would lead to more demand for products, more jobs, and eventually an end to the depression. *How does this automobile advertisement reflect this viewpoint?*

✔ **READING CHECK:** What were the main causes of the Great Depression?

SECTION (1) **REVIEW**

Define and explain the significance of the following terms:
bull market
bear market
margin buying
Black Thursday
Black Tuesday
gross national product
Great Depression
Smoot-Hawley Tariff
business cycle

Identify and explain the significance of the following individual:
Herbert Hoover

1. **Using Graphic Organizers** Copy the web below. Use it to explain how each factor contributed to the Great Depression.

2. **Using Historical Imagination** Imagine that you are an economist during the late 1920s. What problems would you point to in order to warn people of a possible economic downturn?
3. **Analyzing** How did the practice of buying stocks on margin contribute to the crash?
4. **Identifying Cause and Effect** How did the stock market crash provoke a banking crisis? How did the banking crisis lead to business failures?

Critical Thinking

5. To what extent did overconfidence contribute to the U.S. economy's slide into depression?
Consider:
• how stockholder overconfidence influenced the stock market crash and banking crisis
• how business overproduction and reliance on consumer credit influenced the rising number of business failures

SECTION ②

Hard Times

Children protesting the high rate of unemployment

OBJECTIVES

Read to understand:

1. how unemployment during the Great Depression affected the lives of American workers
2. what hardships urban and rural residents faced during the depression
3. how the Great Depression affected family life and the attitudes of Americans
4. how popular culture offered an escape from the Great Depression

KEY TERMS

mutualistas
breadlines
shantytowns

KEY PEOPLE

Josefina Fierro de Bright
James Hilton
James T. Farrell
Nathanael West
William Faulkner

EYEWITNESSES TO History

❝ *My father walked the streets everyday. . . . My mother went to work. I even worked, playing the piano for dancing class on Saturday mornings for fifty cents an hour. My mother would find a few pennies and we would go to the greengrocer and wait until he threw out the stuff that was beginning to rot. We would pick out the best rotted potato and greens and carrots that were already soft. Then we would go to the butcher and beg a marrow bone. And then with the few pennies we would buy a box of barley, and we'd have soup to last us for three or four days. I remember she would say to me sometimes, 'You go out and do it. I'm ashamed.'* ❞
—**Clara Hancox**

Clara Hancox was 11 years old when the Great Depression began in 1929. She soon became acquainted with the unemployment, poverty, and homelessness that many city-dwellers of the era experienced. Rural Americans also suffered from poverty and despair. Eager to escape the grim reality of the depression, many Americans sought inexpensive forms of popular entertainment, such as movies, radio programs, and popular fiction.

American Workers Face Unemployment

After the stock market crash of 1929 and the subsequent banking crisis, the U.S. economy entered into a serious depression whose effects quickly became visible. Stores closed, factories stood idle, and millions of unemployed workers walked the streets looking for jobs. "These [unemployed] are dead men," wrote one observer, "They are ghosts that walk the streets."

Unemployed workers roamed the streets of U.S. cities searching for work.

Increasing joblessness. In 1929 some 1.5 million Americans were unemployed. By 1933 the figure had risen to some 15 million. In Chicago, approximately 50 percent of the city's workforce was unemployed, while 80 percent of the workers in Toledo, Ohio, were searching for jobs. As poet Langston Hughes observed, it seemed that "everybody in America was looking for work."

Even for those who managed to keep their jobs, wages fell dramatically—in some cases to as low as 10 cents an hour. Factory workers' average annual income fell by nearly one third between 1929 and 1933. Some of the country's largest employers tried to keep as many experienced employees as possible. Rather than laying them off, they reduced the number of hours they worked to keep more people on the payroll. One General Electric employee explained, "They'd just say, 'You come in Monday. Take the rest of the week off.'" This left employees with little income.

With the drop in wages and employment, the promise of economic prosperity that had attracted waves of immigrants to the United States quickly faded. Immigration to the United States greatly decreased.

The American worker. Workers across the country were hard hit by the depression. African Americans faced particularly difficult times, as economic troubles added to the chronic problem of racial discrimination. When factories laid off employees, African American workers were often the first to go. One study of Chicago unemployment patterns noted that a common opinion of white workers was that African Americans "should not be hired as long as there are white men without work."

Many African American women, who made up the vast majority of domestic servants, lost their jobs. Those domestic servants without regular work often stood on street corners to try to obtain work for the day. Two black women, Ella Baker and Marvel Cooke, witnessed this occurence in New York City and referred to it as the "Bronx Slave Market." They described a typical scene in an investigative article they wrote for *The Crisis.*

66 Rain or shine, cold or hot, you will find them there— Negro women, old and young—sometimes bedraggled [shabby looking], sometimes neatly dressed . . . waiting expectantly for Bronx housewives to buy their strength and energy. 99

Since many employers could hire women more cheaply than men, the percentage of women in the workforce actually increased in the 1930s. Most were employed as office workers or domestic servants. As the percentage of women in the workforce rose overall, however, competition in domestic and agricultural work increased. This caused the percentage of employed African American women to fall.

Trying to maintain a steady source of income and a sense of self-reliance, some unemployed workers took to selling apples on the street. Charging a nickel for each apple, a seller might earn $1.15 on a good day. In the fall of 1930 more than 6,000 unemployed workers sold apples in New York City. President Hoover claimed that "many people have left their jobs for the more profitable one of selling apples." However, during the depression few people had any choice in how or where they worked. Searching for employment, some workers traveled from city to city by hopping freight trains or hitchhiking.

✔ **READING CHECK:** How did unemployment during the Great Depression affect the lives of American workers?

Life in the City

Life in U.S. cities during the Great Depression was difficult. Many city-dwellers faced unemployment and poverty. "We saw the city at its worst. One vivid moment of those dark days we shall never forget," recalled Louise V. Armstrong.

INTERPRETING THE VISUAL RECORD
Poverty. Unemployed workers sold apples for 5 cents apiece to earn money for survival. *What else do you think unemployed workers such as this young man did to acquire food and shelter?*

The homeless. During the depression, many city-dwellers lost their homes. *In your opinion, what emotions does the artist portray in the characters of this depression-era painting?*

"We saw a crowd of some fifty men fighting over a barrel of garbage which had been set outside the back door of a restaurant. American citizens fighting for scraps of food like animals!"

During the early 1930s the federal government did little to assist struggling city-dwellers or their local communities. City governments, religious groups such as the Salvation Army, and charitable organizations including the Red Cross tried to provide direct relief to the needy. Neighbors also helped one another. One woman told a visitor: "My neighbors help me, by bringing me a little to eat, when they knows I ain't got nothing in the house to cook." Mexican American communities formed mutual-aid societies known as *mutualistas* to help each other. Some Chinese American communities set out open barrels of rice so that people could draw from them privately, without having to ask for handouts. Harlem residents organized "rent parties." These large social gatherings charged a small admission fee to help pay someone's monthly rent.

Across the country, people engaged in a daily struggle to feed themselves and their children. Poverty-stricken men and women waited in **breadlines** for bowls of soup and pieces of bread given out by charitable organizations. Karl Monroe recalled standing in the breadline on 25th Street in New York City. "To my surprise, I found . . . all types of men—the majority being skilled craftsmen unable to find work." Hunger was so widespread that by 1932 one out of every five children in New York City suffered from malnutrition. When one hungry schoolchild was told to go home for lunch, she replied, "It won't do any good. . . . This is my sister's day to eat." Poor diets caused some Americans to suffer long-term health effects, such as problems with their teeth and eyes.

In addition to hunger, homelessness was a serious urban problem during the depression. Faced with unemployment and falling wages, many urban residents were unable to pay their rent and were evicted from their homes.

The homeless often gathered in **shantytowns**—collections of makeshift shelters built out of packing boxes, scrap lumber, corrugated iron, and other thrown-away items. Shantytowns rose up outside most cities. Blaming an unresponsive president for their plight, the homeless mockingly referred to these shantytowns as Hoovervilles.

Life on the Farm

The impact of the depression spread all across the United States. It affected not only city-dwellers but also people living on farms. Increasing poverty during the

As homelessness increased, the shantytowns of makeshift shelters spread into the vacant lots of American cities.

depression made it harder and harder for urban residents to purchase farm products. Shrinking demand for farm products caused prices to drop. Farmers found themselves with more goods than they could sell. While people went hungry in the cities, farmers in some areas were forced to let crops rot in the fields and to slaughter excess livestock they could not afford to feed. One newspaper editor, Oscar Ameringer, noted the irony of this situation. "While Oregon sheep raisers fed mutton to the buzzards," Ameringer recalled, "I saw men picking for meat scraps in the garbage cans in the cities of New York and Chicago."

As their incomes fell, many farmers were unable to keep up their mortgage payments. Banks began foreclosing on farms across the country. In some communities, residents banded together to fight the foreclosures. Often when a bank held a foreclosure auction to sell off a family's possessions, neighbors would arrive and bid absurdly low prices, such as 25 cents for a plow. In one example, a farm with an $800 mortgage was sold for $1.90. After the auction the neighbors would then give the goods back to the original owners. This tactic was so successful that several farm states, beginning with Iowa in 1933, passed laws that temporarily banned foreclosure sales.

Conditions were particularly bad for tenant farmers in the South, where most rural residents already faced crippling poverty. Cotton prices fell from 16 cents per pound in 1929 to less than 6 cents in 1931. Many tenant farmers—mostly African Americans—were ruined. Some were forced off the land they had lived on all their lives. While farmers in the Midwest faced an overabundance of food, southern cotton farmers faced poverty and devastating harvests because of poor soil. Gracie Turner, a sharecropper's wife, testified to the hardships of a tenant farmer's life in the 1930s.

Farm life. During the depression, many farm families were evicted from their land. *What economic circumstances do you believe this African American family experienced during the depression?*

66 That's all there is to expect—work hard and go hungry part time. . . . This year's been so hard we had to drop our burial insurance. . . . All it costs is twenty-five cents . . . but they don't come many twenty-five cents in this house. 99

Migrant farmworkers in the Southwest, most of them recent immigrants from Mexico, also experienced difficulties. Government officials and many Americans wanted to remove illegal aliens and recent Mexican immigrants from the United States. They believed that this would ease the strain of the depression. To avoid paying the soaring cost of relief efforts for unemployed migrant farmworkers, local authorities provided funds to transport Mexican migrant farmworkers to Mexico. They pressured and even forced the farmworkers to return to their native land. During the 1930s approximately 500,000 people of Mexican descent—some of them U.S. citizens—were pressured into leaving the country. Those who remained often faced discrimination and harsh working conditions.

![Holt Researcher CD icon] **Read More About It**

Free Find: Josefina Fierro de Bright
After reading the biography on Josefina Fierro de Bright on the **Holt Researcher** CD–ROM, write a short essay describing how growing up during the Great Depression affected her life.

Photographs such as this one by Dorothea Lange captured the struggles many American families experienced during the depression.

Some of the Mexican American families that remained in the United States organized against discrimination in the Southwest. One such activist was Josefina Fierro de Bright, the daughter of migrants who had fled revolution in Mexico to settle in California. The experience of growing up during the depression in the midst of poverty and ethnic discrimination had a profound effect on her. As with many children of the depression, Fierro's life was unstable. Her family moved often, causing Fierro to change schools eight times. Throughout the hard times, however, her mother always encouraged her to strive for success. "Rely on yourself, be independent," Mrs. Fierro advised. She also emphasized the importance of getting an education.

In 1938, at age 18, Josefina Fierro entered the University of California at Los Angeles. She had planned to study medicine, but activism on behalf of the Mexican American community soon took up most of her time. Aided by her activist husband, Hollywood screenwriter John Bright, she led boycotts of companies that did business in Mexican American communities but did not hire Mexican American workers. Enlisting financial support from a few well-known movie stars, Fierro de Bright also started a radio program for Spanish-speaking audiences.

These activities brought her to the attention of a Mexican American group called El Congreso, which organized Hispanic migrants to resist oppressive conditions. In 1939 El Congreso leaders asked Fierro de Bright to help them establish a branch in Los Angeles. Over the next few years, she worked tirelessly, leading marches and hunger strikes, lobbying for expanded relief programs for Hispanic Americans, and encouraging bilingual education for migrant children. "I used to work so hard it used to kill me," she recalled. Throughout her life she never forgot the lessons her mother taught her during the depression. Those memories spurred her efforts to improve the lives of all working people.

✔ **READING CHECK:** What hardships did urban and rural residents face during the depression?

Family Life in the 1930s

The crisis of the Great Depression required that family members pull together to help one another cope with their difficulties. Farmers and city-dwellers alike shared food and money and provided the support and encouragement necessary to get through hard times. In many cases, relatives doubled up in small houses, and young adults moved back in with their parents. Frederick Lewis Allen reported on the changing roles of family members trying to survive the depression. He wrote, "Mrs. Jones, who went daily to her stenographic job, was now the economic mainstay of her family, for Mr. Jones was jobless and was doing the cooking and looking after the children."

Family strains. Economic hardship took its toll on families, and some eventually broke apart under the strain. The marriage rate fell dramatically during the depression. Because many young people put off getting married and starting their own families, birthrates declined, particularly during the early years of the depression. A Chicago schoolteacher looked back on those years.

❝ Do you realize how many people in my generation are not married? . . . It wasn't that we didn't have a chance. I was going with someone when the Depression hit. We probably would have gotten married. . . . Suddenly he was laid off. It hit him like a ton of bricks. And he just disappeared. ❞

Life was difficult for women during the depression. In the face of economic hardship, the mothers of hard-hit families often played roles of quiet heroism. Such daily challenges as putting food on the table and making clothes and shoes last for one more year brought constant worry. As one woman remarked, "I figured every which way I could to make ends meet . . . but some of [those] ends just wouldn't meet." In rural and small-town households, women revived old crafts such as soap making and bread making.

Strategies for Success

Evaluating Artifacts as Historical Evidence

Artifacts are objects created or shaped by humans. They are a unique type of evidence that historians use to gain a more complete understanding of the past. Much like photographs, artifacts offer valuable clues about the customs, values, and details of daily life in the past that are difficult to find in written sources. Because they were handled by real individuals in history, artifacts also provide a sense of closeness to the past that is usually lacking in other types of evidence.

Artifacts must be analyzed with care. The insights they provide must be considered in the context of knowledge one has gained from other, more traditional sources.

How to Evaluate an Artifact as Historical Evidence

1. **Identify the artifact.** First, identify the artifact and determine its general purpose. Then find out when and where the artifact was created and used and, if possible, who created and used it.
2. **Examine the artifact carefully.** Study the artifact carefully, taking note of its construction and design. If it shows wear, try to determine what this wear says about how the artifact was used.
3. **Put the information to use.** Determine how your analysis of the artifact corresponds to information about the historical period that you have gained

through other sources. Then think about how the artifact contributes to your understanding of the historical period.

Applying the Strategy

Examine the photograph below of a truck that was used by migrants during the Great Depression.

Practicing the Strategy

Use the photograph above to answer the following questions.
1. What do you think this truck was used for?
2. What details about the truck do you think are significant? Why?
3. How does the truck contribute to your understanding of the Great Depression?

Baseball

In their search for inexpensive entertainment during the Great Depression, many Americans turned to baseball. Made popular by famous players such as Babe Ruth, baseball had become the country's favorite sport by the 1930s. Radio broadcasts of the sport provided cheap entertainment for baseball fans in the depression era. Since fans could listen to the game for free on the radio, baseball teams lost income from ticket sales. Team owners, however, made money from selling broadcasting privileges to radio stations.

Hoping to attract more fans to the ballparks, team owners began to consider new ideas. In 1933, team owners organized the first all-star game. In 1935 Larry MacPhail of the Cincinnati Reds revolutionized the sport by introducing nighttime ball games to professional baseball. Owners also rented out their stadiums to African American baseball teams.

As white team owners maintained a so-called gentleman's agreement not to sign black players, African Americans played in clubs and leagues of their own. The Negro National League and the Negro American League attracted fans with hall-of-fame players like Satchel Paige and William "Judy" Johnson.

Although baseball is now racially integrated, many of the game's 1930s innovations remain. For example, nighttime baseball and all-star games still attract eager fans to the ballpark today.

A nighttime baseball game

Psychological effects. The economic crisis of the 1930s affected the mental health and attitude of many Americans. The term *depression* described the mood of the country as much as it did the economy. More than 20,000 Americans committed suicide in 1932, a 28 percent increase over 1929. For middle-class and wealthy Americans, many of whom had never known poverty, the depression was a cruel blow. Many would never forget the shame they felt at being unemployed, losing their businesses or homes, and being unable to provide for their families. The attitude of an unemployed teacher in New Orleans was typical. "If with all the advantages I've had, I can't make a living, I'm just no good, I guess. I've given up ever amounting to anything. It's no use."

Many men whose lives had been dominated by work did not know what to do without a job. They often spent their days dawdling around the house or roaming the streets. The depression proved equally difficult for working women who lost their jobs, particularly those who were single or whose families depended on two incomes to survive. Many parents who could not support their families were consumed by guilt.

Even after the depression, the memories of those lean years remained vivid. Habits of scrimping and saving and of making every penny count would stay with members of this generation for the rest of their lives. A strong desire for financial stability and material comforts shaped the outlook of many Americans who came of age during the depression.

✔ **READING CHECK:** How did the Great Depression affect family life and the attitudes of Americans?

Popular Culture in the 1930s

As the psychological strain of the Great Depression increased, many Americans looked to popular culture and entertainment for escape. Many people took up inexpensive pastimes, such as reading and playing games at home. Movies and radio were particularly popular.

The sound explosion. With low ticket prices and double features, movie theaters offered inexpensive entertainment. Talking pictures, which had begun to replace silent films in the late 1920s, thrilled audiences. Among the most popular movies of the early 1930s were gangster films that portrayed tough guys fighting their way to the top against all odds. Similarly, strong women such as Bette Davis, Greta Garbo, Mae West, and Marlene Dietrich reinforced the theme of survival in a difficult world.

Movie cartoons also brightened the 1930s, thanks to Walt Disney's Mickey Mouse and Donald Duck. Disney cartoons were often as popular with movie audiences as feature films.

Radio, which experienced its golden age during the depression, offered free entertainment at home. During the 1930s the number of radios nationwide rose from about 12 million to 28 million. Popular programs allowed listeners to forget the hard times. Heroes such as the Lone Ranger, Little Orphan Annie, and the Shadow always triumphed over evil, offering a hopeful message.

Literature. The public's desire to escape the harsh reality of the depression also gave rise to new forms of popular literature. Inexpensive comic books presented heroes such as Flash Gordon and Tarzan. *Reader's Digest* presented condensed articles from various magazines. Families on a limited budget welcomed this "all-purpose" magazine.

Many of the era's most popular novels offered tales that took readers' minds off their economic worries. In James Hilton's *Lost Horizon* (1933), a weary traveler stumbles upon a peaceful, prosperous utopia hidden in the mountains of Tibet. The idea of discovering a perfect world appealed to many readers.

Not all fiction of the early depression offered an escape. James T. Farrell portrayed the grim life of Chicago's Irish immigrants in his *Studs Lonigan* trilogy (1932–1935), while Nathanael West presented the American dream as a nightmare in *Miss Lonelyhearts* (1933). William Faulkner wrote novels such as *The Sound and the Fury* (1929) and *As I Lay Dying* (1930) that tragically portrayed small-town life in Mississippi.

INTERPRETING THE VISUAL RECORD

Entertainment. During the depression, Americans sought affordable ways to escape their troubles, such as books and radio programs. *What does this image suggest about the importance of radio to this family?*

✔ **READING CHECK:** How did popular culture provide an escape from the depression?

SECTION 2 REVIEW

Define and explain the significance of the following terms:
mutualistas
breadlines
shantytowns

Identify and explain the significance of the following individuals:
Josefina Fierro de Bright
James Hilton
James T. Farrell
Nathanael West
William Faulkner

1. **Using Graphic Organizers** Copy the graphic organizer below. Use it to explain how unemployment during the depression had a psychological impact on many Americans and how that psychological impact affected family life.

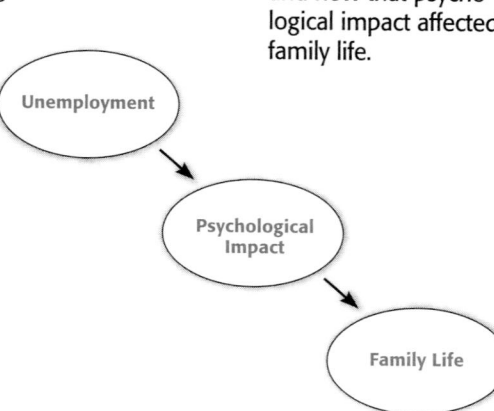

Unemployment

Psychological Impact

Family Life

2. **Synthesizing** How did poverty in urban areas create such a drop in agricultural prices that farmers let their crops rot in the field?
3. **Evaluating** How did the hardships of the Great Depression further inflame racial prejudices against African American workers and Mexican migrant farmworkers?
4. **Identifying Values** How did the burdens caused by the Great Depression create new challenges to traditional beliefs in the importance of family?

Critical Thinking

5. In what ways did many Americans take action to better their lives, despite the seemingly overwhelming hardships of the Great Depression? **Consider:**
   • how urban residents formed organizations to help their communities
   • how migrant farmworkers took action to defend their rights
   • how popular entertainment helped Americans deal with the depression

Hoover's Policies

OBJECTIVES

Read to understand:

1. why President Hoover opposed government-sponsored direct relief for needy individuals during the Great Depression
2. how the Hoover administration attempted to solve the economic problems of the depression, and how successful these efforts were
3. how radicals and veterans responded to Hoover's policies
4. why Franklin D. Roosevelt was such a popular candidate in the 1932 election

KEY TERMS

rugged individualism
Reconstruction Finance
Corporation
Bonus Army

KEY PEOPLE

Andrew Mellon
Franklin D. Roosevelt
Eleanor Roosevelt

EYEWITNESSES TO History

66 *What the country needs is a good big laugh. There seems to be a condition of hysteria. If someone could get off a good joke every ten days I think our troubles would be over.* 99
—Herbert Hoover

Many Americans blamed Hoover for the depression.

Businesses were failing at record levels, and unemployment soared. Yet President Herbert Hoover believed that if only Americans were more optimistic, the troubles of the Great Depression would soon pass. At the beginning of the depression, many Americans had great faith in Herbert Hoover. His skills as a businessman and as an administrator inspired confidence. Under his direction the government did undertake some important measures to fight the depression, but they were not enough to end the crisis.

Hoover's Philosophy

As the U.S. economy plunged and unemployment spiraled out of control, many Americans looked to President Hoover for leadership and a solution to the crisis. Despite the nation's problems, Hoover remained optimistic. He characterized the depression as "a temporary halt in the prosperity of a great people."

As the depression worsened, the most urgent task facing Hoover was to ease the human suffering. Prior to the crash, most Americans believed that the government should not interfere in the free-enterprise system. Even after the crash, the *New York Times* advised that "the fundamental prescriptions for recovery [are] such homely [simple] things as savings . . . and hopeful waiting for the turn." Hoover agreed that the way to economic recovery was through individual effort and not from government assistance.

Soup kitchens fed many hungry people.

THE GRANGER COLLECTION, NEW YORK

Opposing direct relief. As the depression wore on and the crisis worsened, many Americans began to demand that the federal government provide direct relief to the needy. This would include food, clothing, shelter, and money. Writing the president for assistance, one poverty-stricken American complained, "Why are we reduced to poverty and starving and anxiety and Sorrow So quickly under your administration as Chief Executor. Can you not find a quicker way of Executing us than to starve us to death." Despite these pleas, Hoover rejected the idea of direct government aid.

66 I do not believe that the power and duty of the [federal] Government ought to be extended to the relief of individual suffering. . . . The lesson should be constantly enforced that though the people support the Government the Government should not support the people. 99

Hoover argued that direct federal relief would create a large bureaucracy. He feared that it would inflate the federal budget and reduce the self-respect of people receiving the aid. Instead, Hoover urged Americans to lift themselves up through hard work and strength of character.

With unemployment rising, some congressmembers responded to demands from constituents for direct relief and assistance. Senators Robert La Follette Jr. and Edward Costigan proposed a bill in 1931 to create a Federal Emergency Relief Board. The board would be authorized to give states $375 million for direct aid to the unemployed. Hoover refused to support the bill. Without the president's support, the proposal fell 14 votes shy of passing in February 1932.

Hoover's firm belief in individualism and the value of character-building experiences kept him from establishing a federal system that would directly aid Americans in need. Referring to Hoover's training as an engineer early in life, Rexford Tugwell remarked, "We all thought he [Hoover] was an engineer, but, in fact, he was a moral philosopher."

Hoover's political beliefs stemmed from his idea of **rugged individualism**. He believed that success comes through individual effort and private enterprise. He also believed that private charities and local communities, not the federal government, could best provide for those in need. "A voluntary deed," claimed Hoover, "is infinitely more precious to our national ideas and spirit than a thousandfold poured from the Treasury."

Encouraging voluntarism.
Hoover was not alone in his beliefs. Millions of Americans agreed that voluntary efforts were preferable to government aid. It soon became clear, however, that voluntary efforts alone could not address the huge scale of the depression. Communities and private charities lacked the resources to cope with the ever-rising tide of human misery. Local governments were forced to stretch already inadequate funds to cover growing numbers of needy families. By 1933, for example, families on public welfare in New York City were paid just $23 a month.

In 1930 Hoover created the President's Committee for Unemployment Relief (PCUR). It was designed to assist state and local relief efforts. He appointed experienced philanthropists and businesspersons to encourage donations to private relief organizations. The most prominent were the Community Chest, the Red Cross, the Salvation Army, and the YMCA. The PCUR collected information about local relief agencies and distributed it to Americans interested in aiding the unemployed.

The committee did little beyond urging Americans to contribute more to charity, however. Provided with little funding, the committee spent just $157,000 on its work during the years of the Hoover administration. The misery of the depression

The Religious Spirit

THE SALVATION ARMY

The Salvation Army was founded in London during the mid-1800s. It was an evangelical organization dedicated to spreading the Protestant Christian faith to nonbelievers. The founders recognized that before a nonbeliever could be convinced of God's love, his or her practical needs for food, shelter, and clothing must be met. Throughout the late 1800s and early 1900s the organization extended its missionary efforts to the United States and throughout the world.

Salvation Army donation site

During the Great Depression divisions of the Salvation Army in the United States worked to provide for the basic needs of the poor. Since President Hoover opposed direct federal aid for the needy, religious institutions became important sources of aid for the unemployed. The Salvation Army was one of the foremost aid providers during the early years of the depression. It organized soup kitchens, shelters for the homeless, and rehabilitation programs for the unemployed.

As resources grew slim for many Americans during the depression, donations to the Salvation Army slowed. The organization faced the challenge of meeting the needs of a greater number of people with dwindling revenue. Some state and local government agencies gave funds directly to aid organizations such as the Salvation Army. These government-provided funds helped organizations provide needed relief to Americans during the Great Depression.

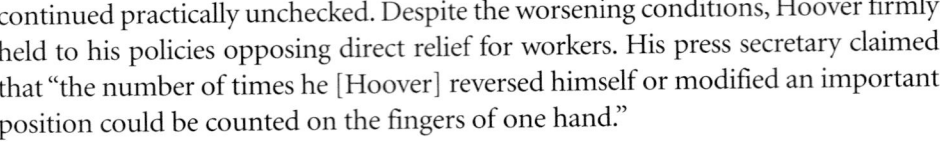

continued practically unchecked. Despite the worsening conditions, Hoover firmly held to his policies opposing direct relief for workers. His press secretary claimed that "the number of times he [Hoover] reversed himself or modified an important position could be counted on the fingers of one hand."

INTERPRETING THE VISUAL RECORD

Hoover. Attempting to find solutions to the economic crisis of the Great Depression, Hoover (left) met regularly with business leaders such as Henry Ford, Thomas Edison, and Harvey Firestone (left to right). ***How does this photograph reflect the close relationship between big business and the White House?***

✔ **READING CHECK:** Why did President Hoover oppose government-sponsored direct relief for needy individuals during the Great Depression?

Boosting the Economy

Critics later charged that President Hoover's relief plans failed because of his refusal to get the government involved. However, Hoover was not totally opposed to government intervention in the economy. Despite its opposition to direct public relief the Hoover administration played a more active role in attempting to shape the economy than any previous administration.

Stimulating the economy. As the nation sank into depression, Hoover's cabinet members proposed a laissez-faire approach to the economy. Secretary of the Treasury Andrew Mellon argued that the government should keep its hands off the economy. He wanted American businesses to deal with the crisis on their own. Aware that this hands-off policy would result in even greater unemployment and suffering, Hoover rejected Mellon's advice. The president believed that something should be done to stimulate the economy.

Within weeks of the stock market crash, Hoover called a White House conference of top business, labor, and political leaders to discuss solutions to the economic crisis. The *New York Times* hailed the meeting as a step in the right direction.

> **"[It is] the largest gathering of noted heads of industrial and other corporations in Washington since the resources of the nation were marshalled for participation in the World War!"**

Hoover urged these leaders to maintain predepression levels of production, employment, and wages voluntarily. Hoover saw this as the first step toward reviving business activity and promoting recovery. The National Business Survey Conference and the U.S. Chamber of Commerce supported the president's plan.

Hoover issued cheerful public statements designed to boost confidence and get the economy going again. His optimism failed to convince many people, however. On March 7, 1930, he declared, "The worst effects of the crash upon unemployment will have passed during the next sixty days." Many citizens grew increasingly doubtful about the administration. "Every time an administration official gives out an optimistic statement about business conditions, the market immediately drops," moaned the head of the Republican National Committee.

At Hoover's request, Congress and state governments funded several public-works programs. By providing contracts for construction and materials, Hoover hoped that these projects would stimulate business and reduce unemployment. One of the largest public-works programs was the construction of the giant Boulder

HOLT RESEARCHER

Read More About It

Free Find:
Herbert Hoover

After reading the biography on Herbert Hoover on the **Holt Researcher** CD–ROM, outline the policies and programs that Hoover developed to assist the economy during the Great Depression.

Dam—later renamed the Hoover Dam—on the Colorado River. The federal government also built more than 800 public buildings and assisted states in building approximately 37,000 miles of highway. Overall, Hoover approved some $800 million in funding for public-works projects. Yet this had little impact on the depression.

Coping with the farm crisis. Hoover also sought to ease the plight of farmers. In 1929 Congress passed the Agricultural Marketing Act, which established the Federal Farm Board (FFB), and granted it a budget of $500 million. In line with Hoover's notion of rugged individualism, the Federal Farm Board was instructed to find ways to help farmers help themselves. The Federal Farm Board offered loans and also financed the creation of farmers' cooperatives. These organizations reduced farmers' expenses by allowing them to purchase necessary materials—such as equipment, fertilizer, and pesticides—in bulk. The cooperatives were also able to gain higher prices for the farmers' crops. Providing storage facilities allowed cooperatives to store crops until they could be sold during the periods between harvests when market prices were at their highest.

Crop prices continued to fall, however. Hoover instructed the Federal Farm Board to buy up surplus corn, cotton, wheat, and other farm products. Officials believed that a reduction in the volume of crops reaching the market would cause prices to rise. The government could store these goods and then sell them when prices were higher. The scheme did not work. Farmers refused to limit production and reacted to low prices by planting even more crops. In 1931 the Farm Board stopped buying surplus crops, having already spent some $180 million.

Just as he opposed direct relief for jobless factory workers, Hoover resisted giving direct aid to desperate farmers. He did try to aid farmers indirectly, though. He recommended the passage of the Home Loan Bank Act in 1932. The act established the Home Loan Bank Board and provided money to savings banks,

Herbert Hoover

1874–1964
In Office 1929–1933

As a young man Herbert Hoover was shy and awkward but very hardworking. Born into a Quaker family in Iowa, he became an orphan at age nine. Hoover had few friends in college and wandered around with his eyes glued to the ground as if to avoid people. One friend noted that he had an awkward habit of standing "with one foot thrust forward, jingling the keys in his trouser pocket," chuckling sometimes, but rarely laughing out loud. Even as president he remained self-conscious and shy.

After college, Hoover rapidly built a career as a successful mining engineer and business consultant. By the age of 40 he was a millionaire. His role as coordinator of food relief during World War I also won him a reputation as a kind and humanitarian leader. After his presidency he continued to work in public service and wrote many books and articles. "There is little importance to men's lives," he wrote, "except the accomplishments they leave to posterity."

Riding the Rails

The Great Depression transformed everyday life for many teenagers. Thousands of schools were forced to cut their schedules or to close altogether, and many families were evicted from their homes. Many teenagers left their hometowns in search of work, traveling from city to city by hopping railroad freight cars. Some began traveling at the age of 14.

Teens riding the rails

During the early 1930s sociologist Thomas Minehan studied the teenagers who rode the rails. He noted that most traveled in groups for security. "The boys and girls have friends to comfort and care for them," he reported.

Life for these teenagers was hard. One teenager whom Minehan met had lost an eye when a piece of burning coal blew into his face as he rode in an open freight car. In his diary, this teenager described a typical day.

66 Slept in paper box. Bummed swell breakfast three eggs and four pieces meat. Hit guy in big car in front of garage. Cop told me to scram. Rode freight to Roessville. Small burg, but got dinner. Walked [to] Bronson. . . . Rode to Sidell. . . . Hit homes for meals and turned down. Had to buy supper 20 cents. Raining. 99

building and loan associations, and insurance companies for low-interest mortgages.

Hoover believed that the act would reduce foreclosures on homes and farms. This would thus allow more farmers to keep their land. He also believed that the act would encourage home construction. This construction would boost employment and increase the flow of money through the entire economy.

The Reconstruction Finance Corporation.

Hoover also tried to stimulate the economy with the **Reconstruction Finance Corporation** (RFC), created by Congress in February 1932. The RFC was authorized to lend up to $2 billion of taxpayer money to stabilize troubled banks, insurance companies, railroad companies, and other financial institutions. By strengthening these key businesses through federal loans, Hoover hoped to reduce business failures and create more jobs. By the end of Hoover's term, RFC loans had helped a number of large corporations avoid collapse. Yet the economy continued to decline, in part because the RFC was not created until the depression was already in full swing. The RFC also provided no direct aid to industries or to small businesses, which continued to fail at an alarming rate.

Critics attacked the RFC's trickle-down approach to economic recovery. "We have the dole [welfare] in America," explained economist Sumner H. Slichter. "But the real recipients . . . are not the men who stand for hours before the Salvation Army soup stations. . . . [They] are the great industries of America." Critics argued that money lent to big business would not filter down quickly enough to help the real victims of the depression—ordinary citizens. As one economist put it, this was like putting fertilizer on the branches of a tree—rather than on its roots—to help it grow. A more effective approach, said critics, would be to funnel money directly to those in need. This would increase consumers' buying power and consequently stimulate business. Newspaper columnist Walter Lippmann expressed the sentiments of most Americans.

66 It is hard for the country to realize that this era of easy finance is over. . . . In respect to government finance, as in respect to so many other things, Congress and the people of the country have radically to readjust their minds. 99

Government activism.

Hoover's policies failed to end the Great Depression. However, the RFC and other measures—such as the Home Loan Bank Act and funding for public works—represented a major shift in government policy. The president and Congress accepted the idea that the federal government can and should do something to boost the economy in times of crisis. The government became more active than ever before.

In the early 1930s Secretary of the Treasury Andrew Mellon advised the government to maintain its traditional laissez-faire approach to the economy. He even argued that a short depression would be good for the country because "it will purge the rottenness out of the system." As the depression grew more severe, however, the government took dramatic steps to promote economic recovery. Unfortunately, these measures were not sufficient to halt the downward trend. Americans increasingly blamed their suffering on Herbert Hoover.

✔ **READING CHECK:** What did the Hoover administration do to attempt to solve the economic problems of the Great Depression? How successful were these attempts?

Rumblings of Discontent

By 1932 President Hoover was perhaps the most hated man in America. His appearance in movie newsreels provoked boos and catcalls from audiences. Yet the president made no attempt to win public support by changing his aloof manner or his stiff, boring speeches. "This is not a showman's job," Hoover remarked. "I will not step out of character."

Radical protests. As public confidence in Hoover eroded, radical political parties grew more vocal. Both the Communist Party and the Socialist Party condemned capitalism, which they believed was to blame for the depression. The two parties helped organize several mass protests in the early 1930s. Socialist leader A. J. Muste gathered the jobless into Unemployed Leagues to demand work. The Communist Party encouraged labor-union activism and led strikes by migrant farmworkers.

The Communist Party also helped expose racial injustice. In 1931 an all-white jury in Scottsboro, Alabama, sentenced to death nine African American youths aged 13 to 21 on a highly questionable rape charge. The Communist Party helped supply legal defense for the defendants and organized mass demonstrations against the verdict. By 1950 all nine had been released from jail.

Many desperate Americans responded to Communist and Socialist calls for direct action. Thousands of unemployed men demanding work participated in a hunger march early in 1932 at the Ford auto plant near Detroit. Four were killed when police opened fire. In Seattle some 5,000 unemployed protesters seized a government building. After two days, local officials finally forced them out.

Some activism was spontaneous, reflecting the desperation of the times. In rural areas people armed with clubs, pitchforks, and shotguns confronted officials trying to foreclose on homes. Hoping that limiting food supplies would push prices up, farmers destroyed crops and blocked roads to prevent food from being shipped to market. "They say blockading the highway's illegal," an Iowa farmer said. "Seems to me there was a Tea Party in Boston that was illegal too."

The Bonus Army. The biggest protest was staged in May 1932 by more than 10,000 World War I veterans and their families. They came to Washington, D.C., to support a veterans' bonus bill then before Congress. The bill would have granted the veterans—many of whom were unemployed—early payment of the pension bonuses

Lawyer Samuel Leibowitz (left) meets with Heywood Patterson, one of the defendants in the Scottsboro case, to prepare for the trial.

INTERPRETING THE VISUAL RECORD
Bonus Army. More than 10,000 veterans marched in Washington, D.C., in May 1932 to petition Congress for payment of pension bonuses earned during World War I. *What do you think the organizers of the march did to generate support for their cause?*

Violence erupts as military and law-enforcement officers attempt to remove the Bonus marchers from their camps.

owed them for their service during the war. This group was soon labeled the **Bonus Army**.

Officials initially allowed the Bonus Army demonstrators to live in empty government buildings and to camp in an open area across the Potomac River. When Congress rejected the bonus bill, most of the demonstrators returned home. Some 2,000 veterans remained, however, defying orders to leave. In a clash with authorities, two veterans and two police officers were killed. The police requested aid, and President Hoover ordered the army to disperse the squatters.

In late July the U.S. Army moved in with machine guns, tanks, and tear gas. One woman recalled her husband's experience that day.

> 66 My husband went to Washington. To march with . . . the bonus boys. He was a machine gunner in the war. He'd say them . . . Germans gassed him in Germany. And [then] his own government . . . gassed him and run him off the country up there with a water hose, half drowned him. 99

Commanded by General Douglas MacArthur, the troops drove the veterans from the buildings, broke up their encampment, and burned their shacks. Hundreds were injured and three died, including an 11-week-old baby. Many Americans found the government's treatment of the veterans shocking. Across the nation, anger against Hoover grew. As the 1932 presidential election approached, Americans joked bitterly, "In Hoover we trusted and now we are busted."

✔ **READING CHECK:** How did radicals and veterans respond to Hoover's policies?

The Election of 1932

In the summer of 1932 the Republicans reluctantly renominated Herbert Hoover as their presidential candidate for the fall election. With public sentiment running strongly against the Republicans, no other member of the party was eager for the nomination. The Democrats, sensing victory, chose Franklin Delano Roosevelt of New York as their candidate.

The Democratic challenger. Roosevelt—who was often called by his initials, FDR—was a determined and skillful politician. He was born into a wealthy and famous family. Roosevelt's background suggested that he would be more likely to identify with the wealthy than with working-class citizens. He could easily have become a Wall Street stockbroker but chose a career in public service instead.

Roosevelt was greatly influenced by the progressivism of his distant cousin, former president Theodore Roosevelt. His wife, Eleanor Roosevelt—who was Theodore Roosevelt's niece—also proved influential. With her earnest belief in social reform, Mrs. Roosevelt would become one of his most important political assets.

Roosevelt ran as a vice presidential candidate in 1920. His political career, however, appeared to be over after polio left him paralyzed from the waist down in 1921. With the help of his wife, Roosevelt overcame his physical challenges and was elected governor of New York in 1928. As governor he earned high marks for his imaginative relief programs that had instituted unemployment benefits and supported failing industries. In 1932 Roosevelt accepted his party's nomination for president.

> 66 Republican leaders not only have failed in material things, they have failed in national vision, because in disaster they have held out no hope. . . . I pledge you, I pledge myself, to a new deal for the American people. 99

A change in leadership. The 1932 campaign revolved around the depression. Although Hoover tried to defend his policies, he realized he had little chance of victory. Roosevelt's campaign was short on specifics. Instead, he repeatedly attacked Hoover's record and promised that he would seek a fairer distribution of wealth. He promised to put the U.S. political and economic systems at "the service of the people." Most important, Roosevelt conveyed a genuine spirit of optimism and confidence that contrasted sharply with Hoover's seeming gloom.

On election day Roosevelt and his running mate, John Nance Garner of Texas, carried 42 states. He captured 23 million popular votes and 472 electoral votes to Hoover's 16 million popular votes and 59 electoral votes. The Democrats won decisive majorities in both houses of Congress. As a result, Roosevelt knew that his programs would receive strong congressional support.

In the 1920s most Americans had credited the Republicans with the era's glowing prosperity. In 1932, voters made it clear that the Republicans must take the blame for the depression. Many citizens who voted for Roosevelt were really voting against Herbert Hoover. Other Americans saw in Roosevelt the kind of dynamic personality they believed could lead the country out of its troubles. Roosevelt had promised a "new deal."

This Roosevelt campaign artifact was used during the 1932 presidential election.

✔ **READING CHECK:** Why was Roosevelt such a popular candidate in the 1932 election?

SECTION 3 REVIEW

Define and explain the significance of the following terms:
rugged individualism
Reconstruction Finance Corporation
Bonus Army

Identify and explain the significance of the following individuals:
Andrew Mellon
Franklin D. Roosevelt
Eleanor Roosevelt

1. **Using Graphic Organizers** Copy the chart below. Use it to explain how each action taken by President Hoover related to his philosophy of rugged individualism.

Hoover's actions	Relationship to rugged individualism
Opposed the creation of the Federal Emergency Relief Board	
Created the President's Committee for Unemployment Relief	
Met with business leaders	
Funded public-works programs	
Established the Federal Farm Board	
Created the Reconstruction Finance Corporation	

2. **Evaluating** How effective were Hoover's programs in easing the effects of the Great Depression?
3. **Recognizing Point of View** Why did World War I veterans and unemployed workers resort to mass protest during the early years of the depression?
4. **Comparing and Contrasting** How did Herbert Hoover's and Franklin Roosevelt's personalities differ? Why was Roosevelt so popular?

Critical Thinking

5. In what ways did Hoover's philosophies reflect the policies of previous presidents? How did they reflect a new era of the presidency?
Consider:
• how rugged individualism related to the policies of previous presidencies
• how Hoover's programs corresponded to this philosophy, and how his programs also departed from Republican policies

CHAPTER 24

Review

Creating a Time Line

Copy the time line below onto a sheet of paper. Complete the time line by filling in the events and dates from the chapter that you think were most significant. Pick three events and explain why you think they were significant.

1929   **1931**   **1933**

Writing a Summary

Using the Reading Checks as a guide, write an overview of the events in the chapter.

Identifying People and Ideas

Identify the following terms or individuals and explain their significance.

1. margin buying
2. Great Depression
3. business cycle
4. *mutualistas*
5. Josefina Fierro de Bright
6. shantytowns
7. Herbert Hoover
8. rugged individualism
9. Bonus Army
10. Franklin D. Roosevelt

Understanding Main Ideas

SECTION 1
1. How did the business practices of the 1920s contribute to the stock market crash of 1929?
2. How did the crash lead to the banking crisis and business failures of the early 1930s?

SECTION 2
3. How did urban residents organize to survive the hardships of the depression?
4. How did popular culture provide an escape from the psychological burdens of the depression?

SECTION 3
5. Why did President Hoover oppose direct federal aid for the unemployed?

Reviewing Themes

1. **Economic Development** What were the multiple factors that contributed to the Great Depression?
2. **Geographic Diversity** How did the hardships of the depression differ for rural and urban residents?
3. **Cultural Diversity** How did racial prejudices magnify the effects of the depression for African Americans and Mexican Americans?

Thinking Critically

1. **Distinguishing Fact from Opinion** When President Hoover announced in 1929 that America was "nearer to the final triumph over poverty than ever before," what facts was he overlooking?
2. **Synthesizing** How did the psychological strain of the depression affect family life during the 1930s?
3. **Problem Solving** What type of program would you have developed to ease the burdens of urban residents and farmers during the depression?
4. **Identifying Values** How did Hoover's depression-era programs reflect his belief in rugged individualism and self-reliance?
5. **Evaluating** How was Franklin D. Roosevelt's mood and style during the 1932 presidential election a major change from Hoover?

Writing About History

Writing to Create Write a dialogue between two unemployed factory workers in the 1930s discussing the factors that contributed to their joblessness. Use this organizer to help you.

1. Stock market crash or global depression
2. Bank failures or loss of foreign markets
3. Reduction of purchases on credit
4. Businesses left with surpluses
5. Businesses scale back production
6. Factory workers laid off

Strategies for Success

Review the **Strategies for Success** on *Evaluating Artifacts as Historical Evidence*. Then examine the image below of a radio from the 1930s and answer the questions that follow.

1. What do you think this radio was used for?
2. What details about the radio do you think are significant? Why?
3. Who do you think might have used this radio?
4. How does the radio contribute to your understanding of the Great Depression?

Linking History and Geography

As a departure from President Hoover's policies, President Roosevelt began programs to offer federal unemployment relief. This aid assisted state governments that had established relief programs for the unemployed. Study the map below. Which states had the smallest percentage of people receiving unemployment benefits? Which had the highest?

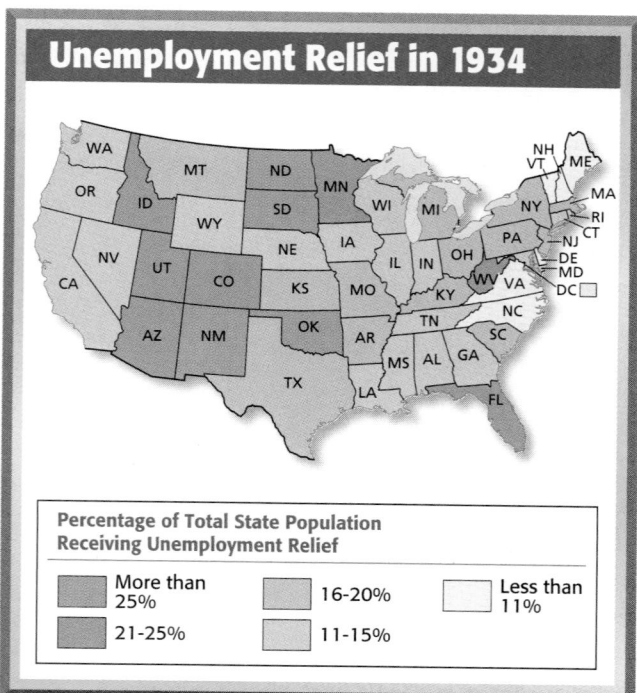

Unemployment Relief in 1934

Percentage of Total State Population Receiving Unemployment Relief

- More than 25%
- 21-25%
- 16-20%
- 11-15%
- Less than 11%

internet connect

TOPIC: Great Depression
GO TO: go.hrw.com
KEYWORD: SD1 Depression

Accessing the Internet through the HRW Web site, research the Great Depression. Then write three diary entries that describe the daily lives of a civilian working on a public-works project, a middle-class father who has just lost his job, and a teenager who rides the rails as a migrant farmworker.

BUILDING YOUR PORTFOLIO

Complete one or all of the following projects independently or cooperatively.

1 Economic Development

Imagine that you are a political cartoonist in 1929. **Create an editorial cartoon** that criticizes the investment practices that led to the stock market crash.

2 Global Relations

Imagine that you are a journalist in the early 1930s at the height of the Great Depression. **Create a series of newspaper headlines** that describe the effects of the depression in the United States and around the world. Your headlines might mention stories about individual families, homelessness, food shortages, unemployment, President Hoover's political problems, or international trade issues.

3 Democratic Values

Imagine that you are a campaign worker for Franklin D. Roosevelt. **Create a campaign poster** explaining why voters should support your candidate in the 1932 election.

1933–1939
The New Deal

A bank closure

United Automobile Workers union buttons

1935
The Arts
Federal Project Number One seeks to revive the arts in the United States.

1935
Science and Technology
The development of sulfa drugs marks a breakthrough in the treatment of bacterial diseases.

1936
Business and Finance
American industries begin to experience large-scale sit-down strikes.

1933
Business and Finance
A federal bank holiday helps restore public trust in banks.

1934
Daily Life
The board game Monopoly premieres, using themes of the depression.

1933 | **1934** | **1935** | **1936**

1934
Daily Life
Drought hits the Great Plains, marking the beginning of the Dust Bowl.

1935
Politics
Congress passes the Social Security Act.

1936
Daily Life
Life magazine begins publication.

1936
World Events
British king Edward VIII abdicates the throne to marry American divorcée Wallis Simpson.

A dust storm

Social Security poster

Before You Read

Build on What You Know

The prosperous economic times of the 1920s came to a devastating end with the stock market crash in 1929 and the Great Depression that followed. President Hoover's administration dealt cautiously with the economic crisis. American voters elected Franklin D. Roosevelt as president in 1932 in the hope that the federal government would take a more active role in shaping the economy. In this chapter you will learn how Roosevelt's administration dealt with the economic crisis and changed the role of government in American life.

WORLD'S HIGHEST STANDARD OF LIVING
There's no way like the American Way

Unemployed Americans

The Hindenburg explosion

Action Comics' first issue

1937
World Events
The German airship *Hindenburg* explodes, killing 36 people.

1938
Daily Life
Superman makes his debut in *Action Comics*.

1939
Business and Finance
More than 17 percent of the American workforce is unemployed.

1939
The Arts
John Steinbeck's *The Grapes of Wrath* is published.

1937

1938

1939

1937
Politics
President Roosevelt tries to "pack" the Supreme Court.

1937
Business and Finance
A recession sets back recovery from the Great Depression.

Ballpoint pen ad

1938
Science and Technology
The Biro brothers invent the ballpoint pen.

1939
The Arts
Gone With the Wind becomes the most popular film of the 1930s.

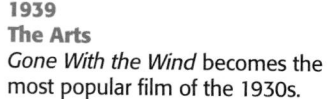
Gone With the Wind

Think About Themes

Themes Journal

Decide whether you agree or disagree with the following statements. Note why in your journal.

Economic Development The federal government must take responsibility for the well-being of the country's citizens during a crisis.

Constitutional Heritage Government interference in a free-market economy may be unconstitutional.

Cultural Diversity People who work in the arts are never affected by an economic downturn because art is not a business.

SECTION 1

Restoring Hope

EYEWITNESSES TO History

  ❝ *The whole country is with him, just so he does something. If he burned down the Capitol, we would cheer and say, 'Well, we at least got a fire started anyhow.'* ❞

—Will Rogers

American humorist Will Rogers was not alone in his assessment of Franklin D. Roosevelt. The new president offered the American people much-needed hope. By 1933, Americans had endured three years of economic depression—each year more desperate than the last. On his last day in office, President Herbert Hoover was heard to sigh, "We are at the end of our string. There is nothing more we can do." Roosevelt did not share this despair. The optimistic words of Roosevelt's inaugural address rang out across the land, lifting Americans' spirits and stirring their hopes. Some 500,000 letters supporting the new president poured into the White House soon after his inauguration.

Franklin Roosevelt's (right) enthusiasm encouraged Americans during the Great Depression.

Roosevelt Confronts the Emergency

President Roosevelt did indeed get a fire started. In 1932, while governor of New York, Roosevelt had formed an advisory group known as the Brain Trust. With the help of this group the energetic new president drew up his promised "new deal for the American people," a series of 15 relief and recovery measures. Immediately after taking office on March 5, 1933, Roosevelt called Congress into special session. During the next 100 days Congress approved all 15 measures, which made up the heart of the president's **New Deal** program.

Roosevelt began by focusing on the country's troubled banking system. On March 6 he issued a proclamation closing every bank in the nation for a few days. This so-called **bank holiday** was designed to stop massive withdrawals. On Thursday, March 9, Congress passed the Emergency Banking Act. This act authorized the federal government to examine all banks and allow those that were financially sound to reopen. Roosevelt hoped that the act would restore public confidence in the banking system.

Caught without cash, Americans scrambled to find substitutes during the bank holiday. Many used subway and bus tokens, postage stamps, and IOUs. On Sunday evening, March 12, some 60 million anxious Americans tuned in their radios to hear the president. He explained how the bank holiday would protect their money. In this first of many "fireside chats"—radio broadcasts from the White House—Roosevelt urged Americans to return their money to banks. "I can assure you that it is safer to keep your money in a reopened bank than under the mattress," he advised.

Banks began to reopen. By the end of the month more than $1 billion in deposits had flowed into the system. Confidence in banks increased even more when Congress created the **Federal Deposit Insurance Corporation** (FDIC) in June 1933. This organization insured each bank deposit up to $2,500.

In April 1933 Roosevelt urged Congress to create the Home Owners Loan Corporation (HOLC). It was created to assist home owners who could not meet their mortgage payments. Congress passed the measure. By June 1936 the HOLC had saved the homes of some 1 million American families by granting them low-interest, long-term mortgage loans. Roosevelt and his advisers then turned their attention to the plight of the American farmers. He issued an executive order to create the Farm Credit Administration (FCA) in 1933. The FCA provided much needed low-interest, long-term loans to farmers. It allowed many farmers to pay off mortgages and back taxes, buy back lost farms, and purchase seed, fertilizer, and needed equipment.

HISTORICAL DOCUMENTS

PRESIDENT FRANKLIN D. ROOSEVELT
First Inaugural Address

President Roosevelt set the tone for his administration with his first inaugural address. In it he expressed his confidence in the country's ability to recover from the Great Depression.

First of all, let me assert my firm belief that the only thing we have to fear is fear itself—nameless, unreasoning, unjustified terror which paralyzes needed efforts to convert retreat into advance. In every dark hour of our national life a leadership of frankness and vigor has met with that understanding and support of the people themselves which is essential to victory. I am convinced that you will again give that support to leadership in these critical days. . . .

The people of the United States have not failed. In their need they have registered a mandate [command] that they want direct, vigorous action. They have asked for discipline and direction under leadership. They have made me the present instrument of their wishes. In the spirit of the gift I take it."

Relief for the Needy

Other measures launched by the Roosevelt administration included large-scale programs of direct relief. The relief was granted to aid the nation's 13 million unemployed workers. In many ways President Roosevelt's direct relief was the type of program that reformers had been trying to get the government to support since the Progressive Era. Aided by First Lady Eleanor Roosevelt and Democratic National Committee member Molly Dewson, the president brought in many veteran reformers to direct his programs, including Frances Perkins as secretary of labor.

In May 1933, at Roosevelt's request, Congress established the Federal Emergency Relief Administration (FERA). It was created to funnel $500 million in relief aid to state and local agencies. One of Roosevelt's most trusted advisers, Harry L. Hopkins, headed the FERA program.

A Washington, D.C., newspaper reported the eagerness of the FERA director to get relief to the needy.

> 66 The half-billion dollars for direct relief of States won't last a month if Harry L. Hopkins, the new relief administrator, maintains the pace he set yesterday in disbursing [paying out] more than $5,000,000 during his first two hours in office. 99

By 1935 some $3 billion in direct federal aid had been distributed. At one point nearly 8 million American families were receiving public assistance.

INTERPRETING THE VISUAL RECORD

Government spending. Senator Harry Byrd of Virginia questions Harry Hopkins about the effectiveness of government spending. *What is Hopkins trying to fix by spending money?*

The CCC. Americans working for the CCC both earned a living and helped improve the environment. *What do these workers appear to be doing?*

Read More About It

Free Find:
John Maynard Keynes
After reading about John Maynard Keynes on the **Holt Researcher** CD–ROM, imagine that you are Keynes. Write a letter to President Roosevelt explaining why you agree or disagree with his New Deal programs.

Most Americans disliked this kind of aid. They wanted jobs, not handouts. Hopkins created the Civil Works Administration (CWA) to address this problem. Most CWA jobs were "make-work" projects such as raking leaves and picking up park litter. From 1933 to 1934, the CWA paid more than $740 million in wages to some 4 million men and women.

To aid the many unemployed young men between the ages of 18 and 25, Congress established the **Civilian Conservation Corps** (CCC) in 1933. Some 250,000 young men left their homes and went to army camps for CCC training. Once trained, they spread out into the nation's parks and forests, where they planted trees, cleared underbrush, created park trails, and developed campgrounds and beaches. They earned $1 a day for their labor. Most of their earnings were sent back home to help their families. During the nearly 10 years of its existence, the CCC employed more than 2.5 million young men. They planted millions of trees, mostly in the South and the Southwest.

✔ **READING CHECK:** How did the New Deal provide relief for the unemployed?

Helping the Nation Recover

In addition to the New Deal relief programs designed to aid needy Americans, President Roosevelt pursued recovery programs to revive the economy. The president saw relief as a short-term remedy. Recovery was his long-term goal.

To stimulate the recovery of businesses and industries, Roosevelt poured money into the economy through federal loans and government spending. This process is sometimes called "priming the pump." Many of the New Deal recovery programs were based on the theories of John Maynard Keynes, a noted British economist. Keynes argued that for a nation to recover fully from a depression, the government had to spend money to encourage investment and consumption.

One of Roosevelt's economic programs was the **National Industrial Recovery Act** (NIRA). Congress passed the NIRA in June 1933 to stimulate industrial and business activity and reduce unemployment. It would do this by stabilizing prices, raising wages, limiting work hours, and providing jobs. To achieve these goals, the NIRA created two new federal agencies—the Public Works Administration (PWA) and the National Recovery Administration (NRA).

Led by Secretary of the Interior Harold Ickes, the PWA worked to create jobs and stimulate business activity. Using federal funds, the PWA contracted with private firms to build roads, public buildings, and other public-works projects. Between 1933 and 1939 the PWA spent more than $4 billion on some 34,000 projects.

The NRA attempted to help the economy recover by encouraging businesses to draw up "codes of fair competition." Under these codes, competing businesses agreed to work together to set hours, prices, production levels, and wages. Businesses were able to do this because the NIRA had suspended antitrust laws. To help protect labor during this period, the NIRA guaranteed workers the "right to organize and bargain collectively through representatives of their own choosing."

Led by former army general Hugh S. Johnson, the NRA was initially popular with many people across the country. Parades of workers marched through cities displaying the NRA banner. The banner contained a blue eagle clutching lightning bolts in its claw, with the slogan "We Do Our Part." Johnson compared the NRA to an army.

> 66 This campaign is a frank dependence on the power and the willingness of the American people to act together as one person in an hour of great danger. . . . The Blue Eagle is a symbol of industrial solidarity and self-government. 99

Enthusiasm for the NRA soon faded, however. Businesses did not always obey the codes. Workers complained that the codes held their wages down. Consumers complained that the codes pushed prices up. As people lost confidence in the NRA, they joked that it stood for "National Run Around" and "No Recovery Allowed." In 1935 the Supreme Court declared parts of the NIRA and its creation—the NRA—unconstitutional.

The blue eagle of the NRA

Agricultural Recovery

President Roosevelt included farmers in his attempts to encourage economic recovery. As part of his plan Roosevelt called for farmers to cut production. The president believed that such a cut would cause the prices of agricultural goods—and therefore farmers' purchasing power—to rise. Passed by Congress in May 1933, the Agricultural Adjustment Act created the **Agricultural Adjustment Administration** (AAA). The AAA paid farmers to reduce their output of corn, cotton, dairy products, hogs, rice, tobacco, wheat, and other commodities. The money for these subsidies came from taxes levied on food processors, including canners, flour millers, and meat packers.

At meetings like this one, members of the Southern Tenant Farmers' Union worked to win government assistance for some of the poorest farmers in the United States.

In one year the plan reduced the cotton crop by more than 3 million bales. This reduction helped to raise cotton prices. Increased income allowed cotton growers and large-scale farmers to spend more cash, thus stimulating overall economic recovery. New Deal supporters pointed to these favorable results as proof of the value of sound federal planning. However, critics pointed out that the taxes on food processors were passed along to consumers in the form of higher prices. They noted that the increase in farmers' incomes came at the expense of consumers.

Critics also claimed that farmers with large landholdings benefited far more from AAA assistance than did small farmers. When large landowners cut production, they forced sharecroppers off their land. They would then keep all of the government payments for themselves. The poorest farmers were forced into even deeper poverty. In response, a group of Arkansas sharecroppers formed the Southern Tenant Farmers' Union (STFU) in 1934. This racially integrated union lobbied the government to halt tenant evictions. They urged the government to force landowners to share federal payments with the farmers who rented land from them.

Early in 1936 the Supreme Court struck down the AAA. The Court claimed that the tax on food processors was unconstitutional. Like the ruling against the NIRA and NRA, this decision reflected the Supreme Court's general opposition to New Deal legislation.

✔ **READING CHECK:** How did the New Deal promote industrial and agricultural recovery?

Revitalizing a Region

The largest of the early New Deal programs took place in the Tennessee River valley. This project sought to aid a rural seven-state region that was scarred by deforestation and frequent flooding. Disease, illiteracy, malnutrition, and poverty plagued its 2 million residents. The **Tennessee Valley Authority** (TVA), which was created in May 1933, transformed the economic and social life of the region. Headed by David E. Lilienthal, the TVA built a number of new dams. It also built several power stations that provided electricity, flood control, and recreational facilities for the region. Other TVA projects combated malaria, illiteracy, and soil erosion and tried to improve the region's low standard of living.

Some Americans criticized the TVA, saying it was an example of the government abusing its power. Shareholders in private utility companies feared the TVA projects would cause them to lose money. Although shareholders brought several court cases against the TVA, the Supreme Court refused to strike it down.

✔ **READING CHECK:** What were the New Deal goals for the Tennessee Valley region?

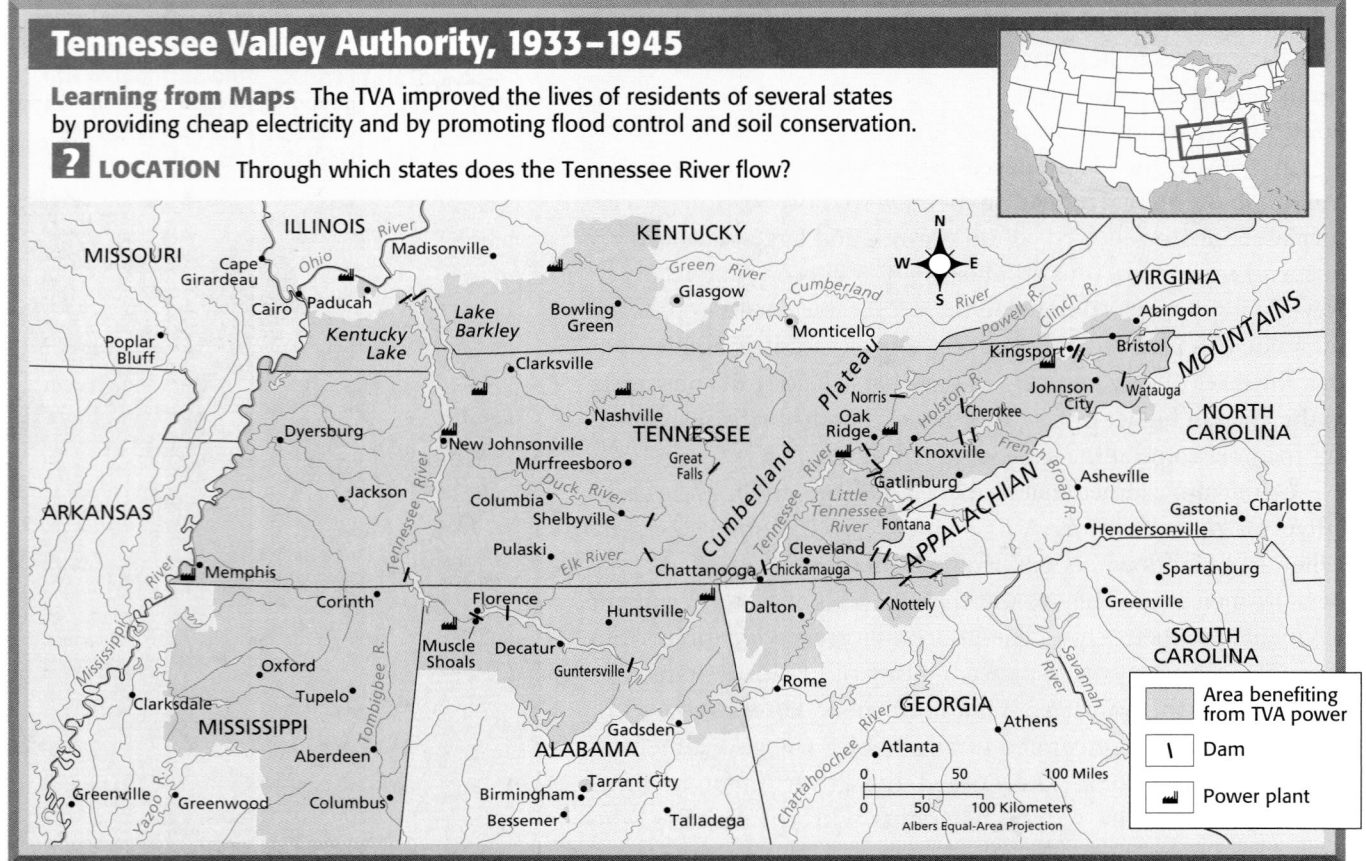

Tennessee Valley Authority, 1933–1945

Learning from Maps The TVA improved the lives of residents of several states by providing cheap electricity and by promoting flood control and soil conservation.

? LOCATION Through which states does the Tennessee River flow?

Equality Under the New Deal

Although New Deal programs provided aid to people of all races, some programs did discriminate. Some 200,000 young African American men received work and training though the CCC. However, they were strictly segregated from white workers. The TVA employed African American workers. Yet, they were not allowed to live in the model towns built by the organization. NRA codes often set lower wages for African Americans than for whites. This practice led some black leaders to call the NRA the "Negro Run Around" or "Negroes Ruined Again."

This discrimination reflected the social attitudes of many Americans at that time. The depression increased racial tensions in the country, particularly in the South. In 1933 alone, 24 African Americans were lynched. Roosevelt offered little support to legislation to help African Americans, such as a federal antilynching law sponsored by the National Association for the Advancement of Colored People (NAACP). Roosevelt feared a political backlash from southern Democrats.

Fighting discrimination. Despite the lack of progress on civil rights legislation, African Americans did make some advances under the Roosevelt administration. Former NAACP leader Harold Ickes brought in several prominent African Americans to advise the Department of the Interior on racial matters. These advisers included Robert C. Weaver, who held a Ph.D. in economics from Harvard.

Roosevelt named more than 100 African Americans to posts in the federal government during his term. This was more than any other president since Ulysses S. Grant. These appointees included a wide variety of professionals, such as educators, legal scholars, newspaper editors, and social workers. One core group of these African American government officials evolved into the Federal Council on Negro Affairs. The council became known as the Black Cabinet or the Black Brain Trust. According to Weaver, their "common cause was to maximize the participation of blacks in all phases of the New Deal."

Many of these appointments came at the request of Eleanor Roosevelt, who was a champion of civil rights. African American leaders noted Mrs. Roosevelt's unusual ability to understand their struggles. "We [white people] are largely to blame" for poverty among the black community, she once said. It was her goal to open greater educational and economic opportunities for African Americans.

In 1939 the Daughters of the American Revolution (DAR) refused to allow Marian Anderson, a world-famous African American singer, to perform at their Washington, D.C., hall. Both Mrs. Roosevelt and Ickes reacted strongly. Roosevelt resigned her longtime membership in the DAR. She argued that "to remain as a member implies approval of that action." She and Ickes then arranged for Anderson to give a free concert at the Lincoln Memorial. The concert was a success and attracted an audience of some 75,000 people.

INTERPRETING THE VISUAL RECORD

Race relations. This painting shows the enormous crowd that attended Marian Anderson's concert at the Lincoln Memorial. *Do you think the artist intended to show racial tension or racial harmony in this painting? Explain your answer.*

American Indians. This woman and her child were photographed in 1936 at their home on the Mescalero Apache Reservation. *What is the woman's home made of?*

Rights of American Indians. The Roosevelt administration also addressed the concerns of American Indians. At the beginning of the New Deal Era, life for many American Indians was bleak. A late-1920s report on American Indian life across the country listed numerous problems facing these communities. Inadequate housing, poor health care, and malnutrition left many of the nation's more than 300,000 American Indians vulnerable to disease. American Indians argued that their culture had been stripped away by measures like the Dawes Act of 1887. The act had ended tribal government and sold off tribal land.

In the 1920s a social worker named John Collier observed the poor living conditions in American Indian communities. Very deeply moved by what he had seen, Collier founded the American Indian Defense Association. The organization fought to protect religious freedom and tribal property. For the next decade Collier championed American Indian reform efforts. Then, in 1933, President Roosevelt appointed Collier as the new commissioner of Indian Affairs. Collier worked to redirect government policy in an attempt to revitalize American Indian life and culture. "Anything less than to let Indian culture live on would be a crime against the earth itself," Collier declared.

Congress put these reforms into law with the passage of the Indian Reorganization Act of 1934. Reversing the Dawes Act policy, the new law tried to revive tribal rule. The bill provided funds to start tribal business ventures and to pay for the college education of young American Indians. It also ordered Congress "to promote the study of Indian civilization and preserve and develop . . . Indian arts, crafts, skills, and traditions."

✔ **READING CHECK:** How did the Roosevelt administration address the concerns of African Americans and American Indians?

SECTION **1** REVIEW

Define and explain the significance of the following terms:
New Deal
bank holiday
Federal Deposit Insurance Corporation
Civilian Conservation Corps
National Industrial Recovery Act
Agricultural Adjustment Administration
Tennessee Valley Authority

Identify and explain the significance of the following individuals:
Eleanor Roosevelt   Robert C. Weaver
Frances Perkins   Marian Anderson
Harry L. Hopkins   John Collier
John Maynard Keynes

Locate and explain the importance of the following place:
Tennessee River valley

1. **Using Graphic Organizers** Copy the graphic organizer below. Use it to describe the various measures that President Roosevelt took to help banking, industry, and agriculture.

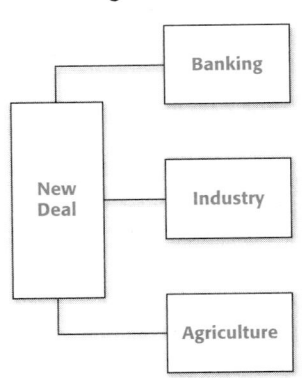

2. **Analyzing** Which New Deal programs granted direct relief to unemployed workers and created jobs?
3. **Understanding Geography: Human-Environment Interaction** How did the programs of the Tennessee Valley Authority transform the region?
4. **Recognizing Point of View** How might African Americans or American Indians of the 1930s have assessed President Roosevelt's policies? Why?

Critical Thinking

5. How are the economic theories of John Maynard Keynes reflected in the approach taken by the Roosevelt administration toward reviving the economy?
   Consider:
   • what approach Keynes supported
   • what approach the Roosevelt administration took toward the economy

New Challenges

OBJECTIVES

Read to understand:

1. what the criticisms aimed at the New Deal were
2. how the Second New Deal enabled President Roosevelt to win re-election easily in 1936
3. how Roosevelt tried to prevent the Supreme Court from overturning his programs
4. how the Second New Deal benefited labor and agriculture
5. what Roosevelt's recession was, and what effect it had

KEY TERMS

Share-Our-Wealth
Works Progress Administration
National Youth Administration
Social Security Act
Wagner-Connery Act
Congress of Industrial Organizations
sit-down strike

KEY PEOPLE

Francis E. Townsend
Charles E. Coughlin
Huey Long
Mary McLeod Bethune

Supporters of Huey Long's Share-Our-Wealth program wore badges such as this one.

EYEWITNESSES TO History

❝ *President Roosevelt was elected on November 8, 1932. . . . This is January 1935. We are in our third year of the Roosevelt depression, with the conditions growing worse. . . .*

We must become awakened! We must know the truth and speak the truth. There is no use to wait three more years. It is not Roosevelt or ruin; it is Roosevelt's ruin. ❞

—Huey Long

Huey Long

U.S. senator Huey Long of Louisiana was one of several prominent critics who argued that the New Deal was too slow in easing the economic troubles of the nation. Critics like Long increased the administration's determination to enact yet another series of innovative programs that would provide more relief to the nation.

Critics of the New Deal

Criticism of the New Deal came from both conservatives and liberals. Most conservative complaints came from the American Liberty League, an organization made up largely of Republican business interests. Some disenchanted Democrats led by Al Smith also joined. Smith accused New Deal supporters of "irresponsible ravings against millionaires and big business." The league complained that the New Deal measures were destroying both the Constitution and free enterprise.

Among the liberal reformers who opposed the New Deal was Dr. Francis E. Townsend of California. Townsend wanted the government to grant a pension of $200 a month to every American over 60 years old. All recipients were to spend the pensions within 30 days and thus pump money into the economy. Father Charles E. Coughlin, a radio priest from Michigan, urged the government to nationalize all banks and return to the silver standard.

Huey "the Kingfish" Long, a colorful but corrupt U.S. senator from Louisiana, had probably the most radical plan. Like Robin Hood, Long wanted to take from the rich and give to the poor. In 1934 Long proposed a new kind of relief program, which he called **Share-Our-Wealth**. The program would empower the government to seize wealth from the rich through taxes and then provide a guaranteed minimum income and a home to every American family. Long even had a theme song.

❝ Ev'ry man a king, ev'ry man a king,
For you can be a millionaire,
There's enough for all people to share.
When it's sunny June and December too,
Or in the wintertime or spring:
There'll be peace without end,
Ev'ry neighbor a friend,
With ev'ry man a king. ❞

Franklin D. Roosevelt

1882–1945
In Office 1933–1945

"Mr. Roosevelt is a unique figure in the modern world: the one statesman . . . who seems able to relax," wrote one journalist about the charming leader. Indeed, President Roosevelt always appeared to be warm, energetic, and easy-going, despite the enormous pressures he faced as president. His optimistic outlook may have helped in his recuperation from polio.

The president always hid his private thoughts behind a dazzling smile. One of his speechwriters noted that one could never tell what was going on in Roosevelt's "heavily forested interior." The president often relied on instinct and idealism in making decisions. Political theories held little value for him. His warm style and caring manner, expressed in his weekly "fireside chats," helped win support for many of his programs. Years after the depression, many Americans would remember Roosevelt almost as a beloved family member.

1882 1982 USA 20c

Franklin D. Roosevelt

The Share-Our-Wealth program received a great deal of popular support. Some critics, however, suspected that Long harbored dreams of becoming a dictator. The popular senator threatened to challenge Roosevelt as a third-party candidate in the 1936 election. Both this threat and the Share-Our-Wealth program died when an assassin killed Long in 1935.

✔ **READING CHECK:** What criticisms were aimed at the New Deal?

The Second New Deal

The Democrats gained additional congressional seats in the 1934 elections. The victory, coupled with pressure from liberals, encouraged New Deal planners to initiate more public-works programs, a social-security plan, and wage and hour improvements for laborers. This series of programs eventually came to be called the Second New Deal. Although it continued to promote social relief and economic recovery, the Second New Deal increasingly emphasized long-term reform.

The Works Progress Administration. After the Civil Works Administration (CWA) ended in 1934, President Roosevelt created the **Works Progress Administration** (WPA). Led by Harry Hopkins, this program was designed to help Americans find work. Congress budgeted some $5 billion for the WPA's job-creation programs.

Posters like this one (below right) encouraged Americans to support WPA programs, such as the project shown below.

WEAVING

Work Pays America!
PROSPERITY

WORKS PROGRESS ADMINISTRATION

THE GRANGER COLLECTION, NEW YORK

During the next eight years, the WPA employed some 8.5 million people. About 2 million were in the program at any given time. Workers engaged in a variety of tasks. Male blue-collar workers built or rebuilt a total of some 350 airports, more than 100,000 public buildings, some 78,000 bridges, and about 500,000 miles of roads. White-collar workers took on research projects and teaching jobs.

The WPA tried to help struggling young people between the ages of 16 and 25 by establishing the **National Youth Administration** (NYA), a "junior WPA." The NYA provided high-school and college-age Americans with part-time jobs that allowed them to stay in school. Within a year the NYA was providing aid to 500,000 people. Eleanor Roosevelt insisted that Mary McLeod Bethune, an energetic member of the Black Cabinet, be appointed director of the Division of Negro Affairs in the NYA.

Mary McLeod Bethune

Mary McLeod Bethune was born in 1875 in Mayesville, South Carolina. Her parents were farmers who had once been slaves. The young girl's chances for an education seemed slim, since the Mayesville school was for whites only. With the aid of a Presbyterian mission school and a series of scholarships, however, she eventually attended the Moody Bible Institute in Chicago.

Bethune initially intended to become a missionary in Africa but soon found her mission to be educating African American children. She once said of her decision: "The drums of Africa still beat in my heart. They will not let me rest while there is a single Negro boy or girl without a chance to prove his [or her] worth." In 1904 she founded a primary school for African American girls in Florida. It eventually evolved into Bethune-Cookman College, a four-year coeducational institution with a mostly African American student body.

Bethune became involved with numerous African American groups, including the NAACP and the Urban League. In 1935 she helped unite all national organizations working on behalf of African American women into the National Council of Negro Women. Through her work with this association, she became close friends with Eleanor Roosevelt. Bethune fought hard, although not always successfully, to rid the NYA of discrimination. Although Bethune left government service after the NYA ended in 1944, she continued to promote civil rights and educational opportunities for young African Americans until her death in 1955.

Social Security. Another important feature of the Second New Deal was the **Social Security Act**, which Congress passed in August 1935. The act contained three major provisions. First, it provided unemployment insurance to workers who lost their jobs. The funds for this insurance came from a payroll tax on businesses. Second, the act provided pensions to retired workers older than age 65. The money for these pensions came from two sources—a payroll tax on employers and a tax on employees' wages. Third, in a shared federal-state program, the act provided payments to people with disabilities, the elderly, and the wives and children of male workers who had died.

Other programs. In May 1935 Roosevelt created the Rural Electrification Administration (REA) as part of his program to help underprivileged Americans. The REA provided electricity to isolated rural areas. Congress also passed a law giving the government the right to regulate the interstate production, transmission, and sale of gas and electricity. This helped keep utility costs low.

Read More About It

Free Find: Mary McLeod Bethune
After reading about Mary McLeod Bethune on the **Holt Researcher** CD–ROM, design a memorial plaque that illustrates her achievements.

★ Then and Now

Social Security

Referring to the Social Security Act, Frances Perkins recalled, "Nothing of the sort had ever come before the Congress of the United States." The act transformed many Americans' ideas about the government's responsibility to ensure the welfare of citizens. Since its beginning in the 1930s, the program has expanded to cover children, people with disabilities, and many others. Social Security also manages numerous other welfare programs, including subsidized school lunches. Providing monthly pensions to retired people or their widows is the best-known Social Security program. Ida May Fuller of Ludlow, Vermont, was the first person to receive a monthly Social Security pension. Her first check, for $22.54, arrived January 31, 1940.

Over time, the monthly payments have risen along with the cost of living. At the same time, more people are covered by Social Security. Although many people fear that this situation would eventually force the Social Security program into bankruptcy, legislators have long been reluctant to alter the system. Finally, in the late 1990s Congress enacted several measures to reform Social Security and guard it for future generations.

Ida May Fuller holds her first Social Security check.

Dr. New Deal. Treating the United States like a sick patient, Franklin D. Roosevelt tried many cures to get the country healthy again. *Do you think the cartoonist expected Roosevelt's remedies to work? Explain your answer.*

Roosevelt then targeted the rich. He declared that the existing tax laws had not done enough "to prevent an unjust concentration of wealth and economic power." Congress responded by passing the Revenue Act of 1935. Often referred to as the Wealth Tax Act, the bill sharply raised taxes for the nation's richest people.

The election of 1936. In June 1936 the Democrats nominated Roosevelt for a second term. Labor unions, farmers, those on relief, and even many Republicans also endorsed him. For the first time since Reconstruction, most African Americans in the North supported the Democrats. The Republicans nominated the capable but unexciting governor of Kansas, Alfred M. Landon.

President Roosevelt pledged to continue the New Deal. He won a clear victory, receiving some 28 million popular votes to Landon's 17 million. Roosevelt carried every state but Maine and Vermont—the most lopsided victory in more than a century. The Democrats increased their majorities in both houses of Congress.

✔ **READING CHECK:** How did the Second New Deal enable President Roosevelt to win re-election easily in 1936?

Roosevelt and the Supreme Court

Fresh from his victory, President Roosevelt moved to "reform" the Supreme Court. Roosevelt was angered that the Court had declared several New Deal measures unconstitutional. He labeled the justices "Nine Old Men"—six were 70 or older. He accused them of being stuck in the "horse and buggy" days in their thinking.

In February 1937 Roosevelt asked Congress to grant him the power to appoint one new justice for each of those 70 or older, up to six new justices. Roosevelt's proposal triggered a storm of protests across the nation. Critics—Democrats as well as Republicans—charged that this "court packing" tampered with the balance of powers. Dorothy Thompson, a popular political columnist, considered Roosevelt's scheme a move toward dictatorship.

In this cartoon President Roosevelt is shown as a ventriloquist whose dummy refuses to cooperate.

THE GRANGER COLLECTION, NEW YORK

66 If the American people accept this last audacity [boldness] of the President without letting out a yell to high heaven, they have ceased to be jealous of their liberties and are ripe for ruin. This is the beginning of a pure personal government. 99

Congress rejected Roosevelt's request. The Supreme Court, however, soon upheld the Social Security Act and the National Labor Relations Act. Some Americans concluded that the justices had become more tolerant of New Deal programs in an attempt to prevent a drastic reform of the Court. During the next four years, several justices died or retired. They were replaced by Roosevelt appointees. By 1945 eight of the nine justices were Roosevelt appointees.

✔ **READING CHECK:** How did Roosevelt try to prevent the Supreme Court from overturning his programs?

Selected New Deal Programs

Year	First New Deal	Provisions
1933	Emergency Banking Act	Gave administration the right to regulate banks
1933	Farm Credit Administration (FCA)	Refinanced farm mortgages at lower interest and for longer terms
1933	Economy Act	Proposed to balance the budget through savings measures
1933	Civilian Conservation Corps (CCC)	Employed young men on public-works projects
1933	Federal Emergency Relief Administration (FERA)	Provided relief to needy people
1933	Agricultural Adjustment Administration (AAA)	Paid farmers to reduce crops; funded by a tax on food processors; later declared unconstitutional
1933	Tennessee Valley Authority (TVA)	Constructed dams and power plants to improve social and economic welfare in the region
1933	Home Owners Loan Corporation (HOLC)	Loaned money to home owners to refinance mortgages
1933	Emergency Banking Act of 1933	Created FDIC and authorized branch banking
1933	Federal Deposit Insurance Corporation (FDIC)	Initially insured individual bank deposits under $2,500
1933	National Industrial Recovery Act (NIRA)	Established NRA; later declared unconstitutional
1933	National Recovery Administration (NRA)	Regulated industry through fair-trade codes for businesses
1933	Public Works Administration (PWA)	Constructed roads, public buildings, and other projects designed to increase employment and business activity
1933	Civil Works Administration (CWA)	Employed jobless persons to work on federal, state, and local projects
1934	Securities and Exchange Commission (SEC)	Regulated securities market
1934	Federal Housing Administration (FHA)	Insured bank loans for building and repairing homes

Year	Second New Deal	Provisions
1935	Works Progress Administration (WPA)	Employed people to do artistic, public-works, and research projects
1935	Soil Conservation Service (SCS)	Promoted control and prevention of soil erosion
1935	Rural Electrification Administration (REA)	Provided electricity to rural areas lacking public utilities
1935	National Youth Administration (NYA)	Provided job training and work for people age 16–25; provided part-time jobs for needy students
1935	National Labor Relations Act (Wagner-Connery Act)	Recognized rights of labor to organize and bargain collectively; regulated labor practices
1935	Social Security Act	Provided unemployment benefits, pensions for the elderly, and survivor's insurance
1935	Revenue Act of 1935 (Wealth Tax Act)	Increased taxes on the wealthy
1937	Farm Security Administration (FSA)	Provided loans to help tenant farmers buy land
1938	Agricultural Adjustment Act of 1938 (AAA)	Increased government regulation of crop production and increased payments to farmers
1938	Revenue Act of 1938	Reduced taxes on large corporations and increased taxes on smaller businesses
1938	Fair Labor Standards Act (Wages and Hours Law)	Established minimum wage of 40 cents per hour and maximum workweek of 40 hours for businesses in interstate commerce

Source: *Encyclopedia of American History*

Learning from Charts Franklin Roosevelt proposed a wide number of programs to aid in the nation's recovery after he assumed office in 1933. These programs became the first New Deal. Two years later he outlined a broader program of social reform in the Second New Deal.

? **Building Chart Skills** Which New Deal programs were aimed primarily at helping farmers?

Effects of the Second New Deal

Congress assisted the president by passing legislation that would be less likely to be struck down by the courts. In May 1935 the Supreme Court had ruled that the provisions of the National Industrial Recovery Act (NIRA) that protected the rights of labor unions were unconstitutional. Several weeks later, Congress passed the National Labor Relations Act, or **Wagner-Connery Act**. The act guaranteed labor's right to organize unions and to bargain collectively for better wages and working conditions.

Labor. The American Federation of Labor (AFL) continued its efforts to organize skilled workers. However, the AFL did not move fast enough to please John L. Lewis, the leader of the United Mine Workers union. In 1935 Lewis and several other labor leaders organized what became the **Congress of Industrial Organizations** (CIO). The CIO tried to unite workers in various industries. The new CIO unions included all workers, skilled and unskilled, in a given industry.

The organizing efforts of both the AFL and the CIO resulted in a wave of strikes. One of the most bitter strikes was waged against General Motors (GM) in the winter of 1936–37. Efforts by the United Automobile Workers (UAW) to unionize GM factories faced strong GM opposition. Meanwhile, GM workers were growing increasingly frustrated with factory conditions. On December 31, 1936, this frustration led to a **sit-down strike**. Instead of leaving the automobile plants, workers occupied the factories. They vowed to remain until management met their demands. Finally, after six weeks, General Motors gave in and granted the UAW the right to organize GM workers. Within eight months, the total UAW membership had grown to some 400,000. Owing in part to the Wagner-Connery Act, union membership nationwide shot up from about 4 million in 1936 to some 9 million in 1939.

Farmers. The Second New Deal also brought relief to farmers. After the Supreme Court struck down the Agricultural Adjustment Act in January 1936, Congress created another program to replace it. Like the AAA, the new program sought to keep the prices of agricultural goods high by cutting crop production. To avoid opposition from the Supreme Court, however, Congress linked this crop reduction to a soil conservation plan—a legitimate governmental activity.

The Second New Deal also brought aid to migrant farmworkers, sharecroppers, and tenant farmers. In 1937 Congress created the Farm Security Administration (FSA). It provided low-interest, long-term loans to help tenant farmers and sharecroppers buy land. The FSA also established camps where migrant farmworkers could seek shelter and medical care.

The Roosevelt administration claimed that the soil conservation program did not do enough to promote crop reduction. Congress responded by passing a second Agricultural Adjustment Act in 1938. The law authorized payments to farmers who withdrew land from production and practiced conservation. It also authorized the Department of Agriculture to limit the amount of specific crops that could be brought to market each year. When harvests surpassed these limits, the government

This 1936 photograph by Carl Mydans shows the damage caused by soil erosion in Kentucky.

stored the surpluses until prices rose. Farmers participating in the program could get government loans based on the value of their stored crops.

✔ **READING CHECK:** How did the Second New Deal benefit labor and agriculture?

Roosevelt's Recession

In 1936 President Roosevelt began cutting back on New Deal relief and public-works programs. He was reacting to criticism of excessive government spending. Private industry, however, was not yet strong enough to give jobs to those dropped from government rolls because of the cutbacks. The economy soon plunged downward. By the fall of 1937, factories were closing, and unemployment was rising. Republicans called this economic downturn "Roosevelt's recession."

Roosevelt and Congress again increased government lending and spending. By the fall of 1938, unemployment had declined. Industrial production had increased. As the 1938 midterm elections drew near, Roosevelt decided to re-energize the New Deal by opposing conservative Democrats in Congress who did not support the Second New Deal.

Just as his court-packing scheme had backfired, however, so too did his attempt to clean out the Democratic Party. All but one member of Congress opposed by Roosevelt won re-election. Moreover, voters elected additional Democratic critics of New Deal programs. The Republicans gained seven seats in the Senate and 75 in the House. Although the Democrats still maintained majorities in both houses of Congress, their margins were much narrower. Faced with increasing criticism from all sides, Roosevelt decided not to propose any new reforms in 1939.

✔ **READING CHECK:** What was Roosevelt's recession, and what effect did it have?

SECTION ② REVIEW

Define and explain the significance of the following terms:
Share-Our-Wealth
Works Progress Administration
National Youth Administration
Social Security Act
Wagner-Connery Act
Congress of
   Industrial Organizations
sit-down strike

Identify and explain the significance of the following individuals:
Francis E. Townsend
Charles E. Coughlin
Huey Long
Mary McLeod Bethune

1. **Using Graphic Organizers** Copy the graphic organizer below. Use it to explain how President Roosevelt won re-election in 1936.

> Critics of Roosevelt
> ↓
> Roosevelt's Response
> ↓
> Effect on 1936 Election

2. **Identifying Values** How did criticisms of the New Deal reveal the different views that various leaders held about government?

3. **Taking a Stand** Would you have supported President Roosevelt's plan to add up to six new members to the Supreme Court? Explain your answer.

4. **Evaluating** How did the Wagner-Connery Act benefit labor? How did other Second New Deal programs benefit agriculture?

Critical Thinking

5. How did the Second New Deal differ from the first New Deal?
   Consider:
   • the major programs of the first New Deal
   • the major programs of the Second New Deal
   • the effect of the Roosevelt recession

Life in the New Deal Era

OBJECTIVES

Read to understand:

1. what the effects of the Dust Bowl were
2. how New Deal agencies used photography to promote their goals
3. how the New Deal improved the lives of ordinary Americans

KEY TERMS

Dust Bowl
Migrant Mother

KEY PEOPLE

Roy E. Stryker
Walker Evans
Gordon Parks
Margaret Bourke-White
Dorothea Lange

EYEWITNESSES TO History

> *NO JOBS in California. If YOU are looking for work—KEEP OUT!*
> —Billboard message

This sign warned unemployed Americans to keep moving.

This billboard message appeared on Route 66 just outside Tulsa, Oklahoma, toward the end of the 1930s. The message was clear. The job market for migrant workers on the West Coast was full. The sign was directed at the thousands of migrant farmers who traveled west to California in the mid-1930s. Driven off their land by the forces of nature, they sought a better life elsewhere.

The Dust Bowl and Migration

The mass migration to California was spurred by a natural disaster. In the mid-1930s a severe drought struck the Great Plains. Winds picked up the topsoil that had loosened and dried, turning a 50-million-acre region into a wasteland.

The Dust Bowl. Throughout the **Dust Bowl**, as the affected region came to be called, clouds of dust darkened the skies at noon and buried fences and farm machinery. Dust crept into houses through tiny cracks. Ships reported great dust clouds hundreds of miles out to sea. One Texas farmer recalled the drought's effects.

> If the wind blew one way, here came the dark dust from Oklahoma. Another way and it was the gray dust from Kansas. Still another way, the brown dust from Colorado and New Mexico. Little farms were buried. And the towns were blackened.

The devastation in the Dust Bowl is captured in this photograph of a farmer and his children outside their home, which is nearly buried in sand.

To prevent similar natural disasters from occurring in the future, the Department of Agriculture started extensive programs in soil-erosion control. The most dramatic was the planting of some 217 million trees by workers from the Civilian Conservation Corps (CCC). These trees created a windbreak that stretched through the Great Plains from Texas to Canada.

By 1939 the amount of dried-out farmland had decreased dramatically. However, many Dust Bowl farmers had already lost their land. They packed their few belongings into battered old cars or trucks and headed west on Route 66. These migrants saw California and other parts of the West Coast as a Promised Land where they could find work harvesting crops. Since many came from Oklahoma, they were nicknamed "Okies." Once they reached the West Coast they found themselves in fierce competition with other farm laborers looking for work.

Woody Guthrie and American Folk Music

Woody Guthrie

The popularity of American folk music experienced a revival during the 1930s. Perhaps the most popular folksinger of the era was Woody Guthrie, one of many Americans displaced by the storms of the Dust Bowl. Although he had no formal training in music, he wrote dozens of songs that touched millions of listeners. "I don't know nothing about music. Never could read or write it," Guthrie admitted. Guthrie described the experiences of common people in his music, mostly through ballads. Among his numerous songs was the popular "Talking Dust Bowl."

> ❝ Back in nineteen twenty-seven
> I had a little farm and I called that heaven,
> Well, the price was up and the rain came down
> And I hauled my crops all in to town. . . .
> Rain quit and the wind got high,
> And a black old dust storm filled the sky,
> And I swapped my farm for a Ford machine
> And I poured it full of this gasoline. . . .
> We got out to the West Coast broke,
> So dad gum hungry I thought I'd croak,
> And I bummed up a spud or two,
> And my wife fixed up a 'tater stew. ❞
>
> *TRO—© 1960, 1963 by Ludlow Music, Inc.*

The federal government eventually hired Guthrie to write songs that promoted projects designed to help rural Americans. While touring a federal dam project, he wrote 26 songs in just 26 days. Guthrie's lyrics praised the federal projects, but his songs reflected the sadness of the era. "It's always we ramble, that river and I," he wrote. "Along your green valley I'll work till I die."

Understanding the Arts

1. According to Guthrie's song, how did life change after the Dust Bowl storms?
2. Why might Guthrie's style of music have been popular?

Competition for migrant work. Even before the Dust Bowl refugees started arriving, Mexican Americans had a hard time finding work in the West. Like African Americans, Mexican Americans often found themselves the victims of discrimination in many New Deal programs.

Mexican Americans also faced increased job competition from Filipino laborers. During the 1920s California's Filipino population had grown to more than 30,000. Like Mexican American migrants, most Filipinos worked in agriculture. When the depression hit, both groups faced tough economic times. The Filipino workers, however, fought declining wages by organizing. Throughout the early 1930s the Filipino Labor Union launched a series of strikes to protest wage reductions. In 1936 the American Federation of Labor sponsored the Field Workers Union. The union was a combined organization for Mexican American and Filipino laborers.

These migrant workers are waiting to start their day picking carrots in Santa Maria, Texas.

The unions were able to slow the fall of wages. Yet, with the arrival of additional migrants from the Dust Bowl, competition for jobs increased. Thus, life for all migrants remained difficult.

✔ **READING CHECK:** What were the effects of the Dust Bowl?

Picturing Life in the Depression

The grim experiences of migrants and others in rural areas of the United States provided powerful subject matter for documentary filmmakers and photographers. These artists created a memorable visual record of the New Deal Era. Their images of the slumped shoulders of unemployed men, the staring faces of hungry children, and the worried expressions of exhausted women convey the human suffering of the era.

Most of these photographers were hired by the federal government. President Roosevelt believed that opponents of federal relief programs might change their minds if they could see the frightful living conditions of city-dwellers and migrant farmworkers. With Roosevelt's encouragement, numerous federal agencies and departments—including the Department of the Interior, the Works Progress Administration (WPA), the Department of Agriculture, and the Farm Security Administration (FSA)—hired photographers to travel across the country and document the lives of ordinary Americans.

No agency used photography more effectively than the FSA, whose staff gathered more than 250,000 images of American life during the depression. Roy E. Stryker, head of the FSA historical section, assembled a team of renowned photographers that included Walker Evans, who depicted life among sharecroppers in rural Alabama. Other photographers included African American Gordon Parks, who later became a filmmaker; international photojournalist Margaret Bourke-White; and Dorothea Lange, probably the best known of the FSA photographers.

Read More About It

Free Find:

Dorothea Lange

After reading about Dorothea Lange on the **Holt Researcher** CD–ROM, imagine that you are a photographer. Choose a topic for a photographic project and decide what photographs you would take. Write captions that explain the photographs.

BIOGRAPHY

Dorothea Lange

THE GRANGER COLLECTION, NEW YORK

Dorothea Lange was one of the most talented photographers of the depression era. Born in 1895 in Hoboken, New Jersey, she decided in her late teens to become a photographer. After studying the craft for several years, she set out to tour the world and record her impressions. Lange was out of money by the time she reached San Francisco, however. She stayed there and opened a portrait studio.

When the depression struck, Lange began taking pictures of the homeless men wandering the streets of San Francisco. Soon the federal government hired her to photograph migrant farmworkers in California. Lange often traveled for weeks at a time, working up to 14 hours a day. Her photographs reveal the migrants' poverty and suffering as well as their great dignity. Lange's most famous photograph, ***Migrant Mother***, is considered a masterpiece. It shows an exhausted single mother whose children survived by eating vegetables they scavenged from California fields. When it appeared in 1936, *Migrant Mother* inspired Californians to defy the state's powerful growers' associations and insist on decent, government-sponsored housing for seasonal harvesters.

During World War II, Lange continued her documentary work by taking photographs of the many Japanese Americans in California relocation camps. She later produced photo essays for *Life* magazine and traveled the world taking pictures. By the time of her death in 1965, Lange ranked as one of the world's foremost photographers.

Other FSA photographs helped achieve Roosevelt's goal of gaining support for government programs. From 1936 to 1941, FSA photographs were widely published in government pamphlets and in *Time, Life,* and other magazines. The photographs strengthened congressional and public support for federal relief.

✔ **READING CHECK:** How did New Deal agencies use photography to promote their goals?

Migrant Mother. Photographs like this one by Dorothea Lange capture the suffering of rural Americans. *What emotions do you think this picture captures?*

Relief for Ordinary Americans

By the late 1930s many families had begun to feel some relief from the depression. Few American families were untouched by the New Deal reforms. This affected many people's views of the role that government should play in providing for people's personal welfare. Many New Deal programs did more than provide additional income. By supplying jobs, the programs improved many Americans' sense of self-worth. Government administrator Louise Armstrong recalled that most people who came to her office preferred jobs to handouts. "I don't want charity," one person told her. "I want work— any kind of work."

Throughout the New Deal, President Roosevelt stressed the importance of providing work that gave meaning to people's lives. "Happiness lies not in the mere possession of money," he once said. "It lies in the joy of achievement, in the thrill of creative effort." This thrill was exemplified in the pride many people took in their government-funded jobs. Some programs also helped break down class barriers. They lifted people's spirits by emphasizing their equality. Said one veteran of the CCC, "They sure made a man out of ya, because you learned that everybody here was equal. There was nobody better than another in the CCC's."

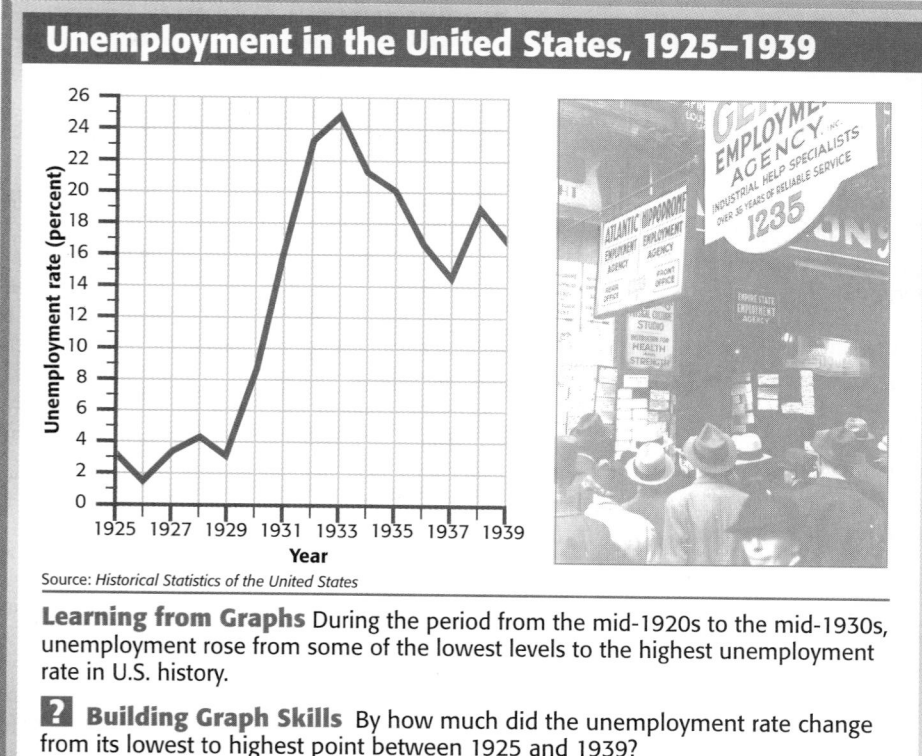

Unemployment in the United States, 1925–1939

Unemployment rate (percent) vs. Year

Source: *Historical Statistics of the United States*

Learning from Graphs During the period from the mid-1920s to the mid-1930s, unemployment rose from some of the lowest levels to the highest unemployment rate in U.S. history.

❓ **Building Graph Skills** By how much did the unemployment rate change from its lowest to highest point between 1925 and 1939?

INTERPRETING THE VISUAL RECORD

Jobs. With the economy struggling, the government stepped in to help Americans find work. *What types of jobs do you think this poster was advertising?*

Programs sponsored by the National Youth Administration (NYA) helped boost family incomes so that children could stay in school rather than quit to try to find work. Helen Farmer recalled working in an NYA program as a teenager.

66 I lugged . . . drafts and reams of paper home, night after night. . . . Sometimes I typed all night. . . . This was a good program. It got necessary work done. It gave teenagers a chance to work for pay. . . . It gave my mother relief from my necessary demands for money. 99

Few New Deal programs had a greater long-term effect on people's lives than the efforts made to provide electricity to rural areas. Millions of American homes did not have electricity or indoor plumbing in the early 1930s. In 1935 only about 11 percent of American farms had electricity. Within a few years nearly 90 percent did. Improvements in electricity and plumbing made life easier and greatly improved people's health by providing better sanitation and safer water supplies. Furthermore, the availability of electricity and other government services brought modern practices and industry to many parts of the country. The South changed the most. Despite some previous efforts to increase industrialization in the region, the South's economy overall had changed little since Reconstruction. During the New Deal Era the region finally began to diversify its economy and rely less on traditional cash crops like cotton. One southern historian has said, "Electrification must be considered one of the most significant stimulants for modernization of the rural South."

✔ **READING CHECK:** How did the New Deal improve the lives of ordinary Americans?

SECTION 3 REVIEW

Define and explain the significance of the following terms:
Dust Bowl
Migrant Mother

Identify and explain the significance of the following individuals:
Roy E. Stryker
Walker Evans
Gordon Parks
Margaret Bourke-White
Dorothea Lange

1. **Using Graphic Organizers** Copy the following graphic organizer. Use it to explain why farmers migrated from the Dust Bowl region and what effects this migration had.

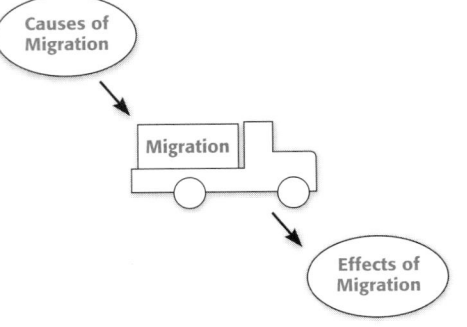

Causes of Migration

Migration

Effects of Migration

2. **Using Historical Imagination** Imagine you are a farmer from the Great Plains migrating west in 1939. Write a diary entry describing your experiences on the West Coast.
3. **Analyzing** How did photographs of ordinary people affect attitudes toward the New Deal?
4. **Synthesizing** How did the New Deal programs address both the physical and the psychological needs of Americans?

Critical Thinking

5. Why did a photograph like *Migrant Mother* inspire protests against large agricultural growers in California?
   Consider:
   • the subject of the photograph
   • the experiences of migrants in California
   • how Californians might have felt upon seeing the image

The New Deal and the Arts

Read to understand:

1. how Federal Project Number One aided writers and artists
2. what common themes emerged in the novels, films, and plays of the New Deal Era
3. how music evolved in the 1930s
4. what subject matter influenced American painters in the 1930s

KEY TERMS

Federal Project Number One
The Grapes of Wrath
Gone With the Wind
regionalists
American Gothic

KEY PEOPLE

Zora Neale Hurston
Richard Wright
Frank Capra
Lillian Hellman
Thornton Wilder
Aaron Copland
Thomas A. Dorsey
Mahalia Jackson
Benny Goodman
Jacob Lawrence
Georgia O'Keeffe
Anna "Grandma" Moses

 **EYEWITNESSES TO History**

❝ *Two years ago I was living in comfort and apparent security. My husband had a good position in a well-known orchestra, and I was teaching a large and promising class of piano students. When the orchestra disbanded we started on a rapid downhill path. My husband was unable to secure another position. My class gradually dwindled away.* ❞
—Ann Rivington

Poster announcing a concert sponsored by the Federal Music Project

Ann Rivington and her husband were among many people trained in the arts who found no job opportunities during the depression. In its attempts to put Americans back to work, the Roosevelt administration did not forget about those who were skilled in the arts.

WPA Programs

All workers struggled with unemployment in depression-era America, including artists. "They've got to eat just like other people," declared Harry Hopkins about the plight of unemployed artists. The Roosevelt administration soon launched a new program to aid writers, musicians, actors, and others. In 1935 the Works Progress Administration (WPA) set aside $300 million to create **Federal Project Number One**. This program sought to encourage pride in American culture by providing work to artists in the fields of writing, theater, music, and visual arts.

The WPA's Federal Writers' Project (FWP) hired some 6,600 unemployed writers to produce a variety of works. The works included state travel guides and histories of various ethnic groups. Others conducted oral history interviews with hundreds of elderly former slaves. Members of the project also studied American folklore and wrote down folktales. These eventually became the basis for the best-selling *Treasury of American Folklore* (1944), one of the more than 1,000 books and pamphlets published by the FWP.

The WPA's Federal Theater Project hired unemployed actors, directors, designers, stagehands, and playwrights to encourage theatrical productions. The project entertained millions of Americans and brought productions to many small towns that had never experienced live theater. The Federal Music Project hired musicians to form orchestras and present some 4,000 musical productions each month to audiences nationwide. The Federal Arts Project hired unemployed artists and designers to produce posters for New Deal programs, teach art in public schools, and paint murals on public buildings.

✔ **READING CHECK:** How did Federal Project Number One aid writers and artists?

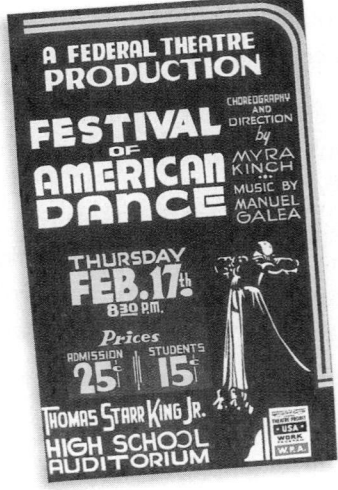

The Federal Theater Project sponsored performances such as this one, providing work for entertainers and amusement for Americans.

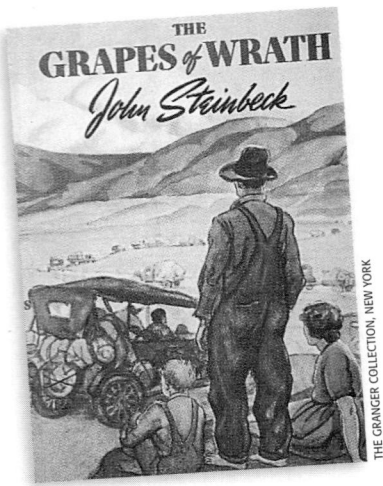

John Steinbeck's **The Grapes of Wrath** *is a gritty tale of life in the United States during the Great Depression.*

Portraying the Depression

The Federal Writers' Project helped launch the careers of numerous successful writers. Many of these writers incorporated themes of the depression into their works.

Novels. John Steinbeck produced a gripping picture of the depression years in **The Grapes of Wrath** (1939). The story follows the fortunes of a poor family as they travel from the Dust Bowl region to California.

Other novels described the depression-era experiences of ethnic minorities. Zora Neale Hurston wrote *Their Eyes Were Watching God* (1937). Her novel explores a black woman's search for fulfillment in rural Florida. Richard Wright offered a grim picture of black urban life in *Native Son* (1940). His work chronicles the journey of a young African American man lost in a racist world.

One of the best-selling novels of the decade was Margaret Mitchell's **Gone With the Wind** (1936), a sweeping story of the Old South set during the Civil War and Reconstruction. Many depression-era readers could relate to the turmoil faced by the novel's main character, Scarlett O'Hara, who survives war and economic chaos.

Films. Margaret Mitchell's book became the basis of the most popular film of the 1930s. To lift people's spirits, the major studios offered a number of "escapist" films to help viewers forget their troubles. These included the Marx brothers' comedy *Duck Soup* (1933) and Ginger Rogers's upbeat musical *Gold-Diggers of 1933*. This musical contained one of the most optimistic tunes of the decade.

> 66 We're in the money,
> We're in the money
> We've got a lot of what
> It takes to get along.
>
> We never see a headline
> About a breadline
> Today. 99

Soon some filmmakers began to tackle social issues. Director Frank Capra celebrated simple values and criticized the wealthy and politicians in films like *Mr. Deeds Goes to Town* (1936) and *Mr. Smith Goes to Washington* (1939). By the late 1930s the major studios had recovered sufficiently from the depression to launch several big-budget spectacles. Two such films, the color epic *Gone With the Wind* and the special-effects fantasy *The Wizard of Oz*, were both released in 1939.

INTERPRETING THE VISUAL RECORD

Film. Films such as the musical *Gold-Diggers of 1933* offered Americans optimism during the depression. *How do you think this dance number contrasted with the lives of the audience?*

Theater. Some films of the 1930s were based on popular plays. On the theatrical stage, plays that dealt with the nation's labor and class struggles drew large audiences. Robert Sherwood's *The Petrified Forest* (1935) attacked the "petrified forest" of ideas destroying the country. Lillian Hellman's *The Little Foxes* (1939) attacked upper-class greed. By the end of the decade, popular plays, like popular films, focused increasingly on traditional American values. Two examples are Thornton Wilder's *Our Town* (1938) and William Saroyan's *The Time of Your Life* (1939).

✔ **READING CHECK:** What common themes appeared in novels, films, and plays of the New Deal Era?

AMERICAN Letters

Literature of the Great Depression

The late 1930s gave rise to a new era of realism in American literature as prominent authors wrote stories that captured the struggles and mood of the country during the Great Depression. In The Grapes of Wrath, *John Steinbeck portrays the saga of migrants from the Dust Bowl who travel to California in search of work. In* Their Eyes Were Watching God, *Zora Neale Hurston follows the struggle of an African American woman named Janie to find meaning and happiness in her life.*

from *The Grapes of Wrath*
by *John Steinbeck*

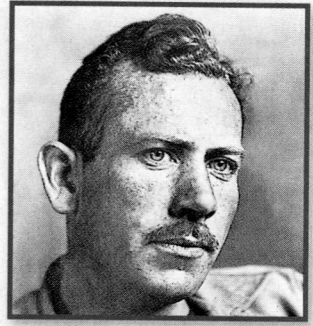

John Steinbeck

Those families who had lived on a little piece of land, who had lived and died on forty acres, had eaten or starved on the produce of forty acres, had now the whole West to rove in. And they scampered about, looking for work; and the highways were streams of people, and the ditch banks were lines of people. . . . The great highways streamed with moving people. . . .

And this was good, for wages went down and prices stayed up. The great owners were glad. . . . And wages went down and prices stayed up. And pretty soon now we'll have serfs again. . . .

And the little farmers . . . lost their farms, and they were taken by the great owners, the banks, and the companies. . . . As time went on, there were fewer farms. The little farmers moved into town for a while and exhausted their credit, exhausted their friends, their relatives. And then they too were on the highways. And the roads were crowded with men ravenous for work, murderous for work.

And the companies, the banks worked at their own doom and they did not know it. The fields were fruitful, and starving men moved on the roads. . . .

The great companies did not know that the line between hunger and anger is a thin line. . . . On the highways the people moved like ants and searched for work, for food. And the anger began to ferment."

from *Their Eyes Were Watching God*
by *Zora Neale Hurston*

Zora Neale Hurston

Janie saw her life like a great tree in leaf with the things suffered, things enjoyed, things done and undone. Dawn and doom was in the branches. . . .

After awhile she got up from where she was and went over the little garden field entire. She was seeking confirmation of the voice and vision, and everywhere she found and acknowledged answers. . . . Oh to be a pear tree—*any* tree in bloom! With kissing bees singing of the beginning of the world! She was sixteen. She had glossy leaves and bursting buds and she wanted to struggle with life but it seemed to elude her. . . . She searched as much of the world as she could from the top of the front steps and then went on down to the front gate and leaned over to gaze up and down the road. Looking, waiting, breathing short with impatience. Waiting for the world to be made.

UNDERSTANDING LITERATURE

1. What mood do both Steinbeck and Hurston convey?
2. How do both writers use images from nature to describe their characters' feelings?
3. What do both writers reveal about the depression years?

Evaluating Art as Historical Evidence

Like photographs and artifacts, visual art can help one understand the past in a number of unique ways. Drawings, engravings, paintings, and sculptures can provide valuable clues about a given historical period. Because visual art often reflects the views of individuals who created it, it is important to interpret it carefully.

How to Evaluate Art as Historical Evidence

1. **Identify the subject.** Look at the work of art as a whole and identify its basic subject. If the work has a title, examine it for clues about the artist's intentions.
2. **Study the details.** Examine the details in the work for information about its subject and the historical context.
3. **Determine the artist's point of view.** Make sure to note if the subject of the work is depicted in a favorable or unfavorable manner. If possible, find out when the work was created and what may have helped to shape the artist's point of view.
4. **Put the information to use.** Compare the results of your analysis with information about the historical period that you have gained through other sources. Then determine how the work contributes to your understanding of the historical period.

Applying the Strategy

Study the reproduction of Grant Wood's painting *American Gothic* to the right.

Grant Wood's American Gothic

Practicing the Strategy

After looking at the reproduction of the painting answer the following questions.
1. What is the subject of this painting?
2. What information is provided by the details in the painting?
3. What message do you think Grant Wood was trying to convey in the painting? Why do you think he titled the painting *American Gothic*?
4. How does the painting contribute to your understanding of the United States during the 1930s?

Music in the New Deal Era

Popular music in the late 1930s increasingly incorporated American traditions and sounds. Some WPA researchers collected and wrote down American folk songs and folktales. Composer Aaron Copland used these as the basis for his most popular compositions, including his 1938 piece, *Billy the Kid*. Meanwhile, country music drew from the traditions of southern folk music to gain a national audience. Broadcast live from Nashville, Tennessee, the *Grand Ole Opry* radio show became a major force in the popularization of country music.

Gospel music, a cross between traditional spirituals and jazz, also gained popularity. African American composer Thomas A. Dorsey wrote songs including "Precious Lord, Take My Hand." Sister Rosetta Tharpe and Mahalia Jackson were two of the most popular gospel singers. Jackson later recalled that some ministers objected to this new style of music.

> 66 They didn't like the hand-clapping and the stomping and they said we were bringing jazz into the church and it wasn't dignified. Once at church one of the preachers got up in the pulpit and spoke out against me. I got right up, too. I told him I was born to sing gospel music. 99

Jazz continued to rise in popularity, largely through swing, a smooth big-band style popular in dance halls. Swing received its name from Duke Ellington's 1932 hit "It Don't Mean a Thing If It Ain't Got That Swing." White conductor Benny Goodman helped popularize swing with his integrated band.

✔ **READING CHECK:** How did music evolve in the 1930s?

Painters Examine Local Culture

Like their writer and musician peers, American depression-era painters captured a variety of memorable images in their work. Harlem artist Jacob Lawrence portrayed the daily lives of African American heroes, such as Frederick Douglass and Harriet Tubman. New Mexico artist Georgia O'Keeffe painted haunting images of the southwestern desert landscape.

Many artists looked to rural America for their subject matter. A group of mid-western artists known as the **regionalists** stressed local folk themes and customs. The regionalists included Thomas Hart Benton of Missouri, John Steuart Curry of Kansas, and Grant Wood of Iowa. They reminded urban art lovers of America's rural traditions. Wood claimed that his best ideas "came while milking a cow." The most famous of the regionalist paintings is probably Wood's *American Gothic.*

As interest in regional culture grew, people began to rediscover American folk art, such as handmade quilts and woodcarvings. Some folk artists, including the elderly painter Anna "Grandma" Moses, became well known during this period.

✔ **READING CHECK:** What subject matter influenced American painters in the 1930s?

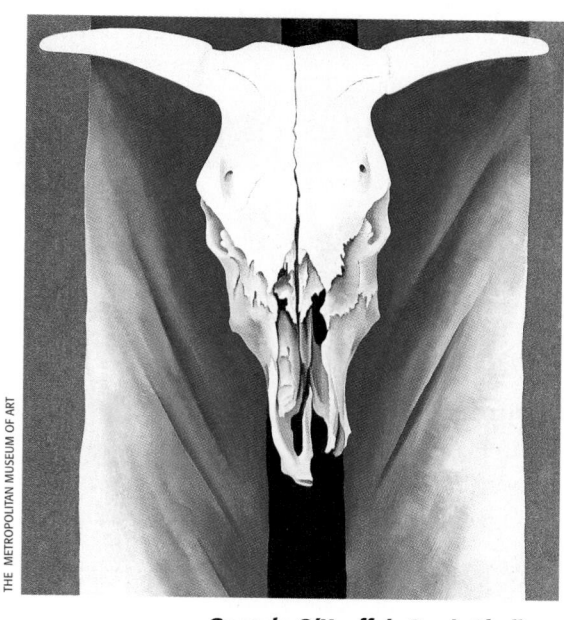

THE METROPOLITAN MUSEUM OF ART

Georgia O'Keeffe's **Cow's Skull: Red, White, and Blue**

SECTION 4 REVIEW

Define and explain the significance of the following terms:
Federal Project Number One
The Grapes of Wrath
Gone With the Wind
regionalists
American Gothic

Identify and explain the significance of the following individuals:
Zora Neale Hurston
Richard Wright
Frank Capra
Lillian Hellman
Thornton Wilder
Aaron Copland
Thomas A. Dorsey
Mahalia Jackson
Benny Goodman
Jacob Lawrence
Georgia O'Keeffe
Anna "Grandma" Moses

1. **Using Graphic Organizers** Copy the following chart. Use it to describe the various ways that Federal Project Number One provided work for writers, theater workers, musicians, and visual artists.

	Federal Project Number One
Writers	
Theater Workers	
Musicians	
Visual Artists	

2. **Comparing and Contrasting** What common themes did novels, films, and plays of the 1930s share?

3. **Distinguishing Fact from Opinion** Provide evidence to support or prove wrong the following statement: "Music in the 1930s simply reflected new twists on old themes."

4. **Identifying Values** How did the hard times of the depression influence the subjects that artists painted?

Critical Thinking

5. In what ways did Federal Project Number One save the arts?
   Consider:
   • what problems artists were facing before the project
   • how the project promoted the arts
   • what might have happened to the arts without the project

CHAPTER 25

Review

Creating a Time Line

Copy the time line below onto a sheet of paper. Complete the time line by filling in the events and dates from the chapter that you think were most significant. Pick three events and explain why you think they were significant.

1933   1936   1939

Writing a Summary

Using the Reading Checks as a guide, write an overview of the events in the chapter.

Identifying People and Ideas

Identify the following terms or individuals and explain their significance.

1. New Deal
2. Frances Perkins
3. bank holiday
4. Huey Long
5. Mary McLeod Bethune
6. Social Security Act
7. sit-down strike
8. Dust Bowl
9. Dorothea Lange
10. *The Grapes of Wrath*

Understanding Main Ideas

SECTION 1
1. How did the New Deal affect African Americans and American Indians?

SECTION 2
2. What were some of the major criticisms of the New Deal?
3. What was President Roosevelt's "court-packing" plan, and how well did it succeed?

SECTION 3
4. What contributions did photographers make to the New Deal?

SECTION 4
5. How did novels, films, and plays of the 1930s reflect themes of the depression years?

Reviewing Themes

1. **Economic Development** How did the Roosevelt administration attempt to promote economic recovery?
2. **Constitutional Heritage** Why might the Supreme Court have declared some New Deal measures unconstitutional?
3. **Cultural Diversity** Why did the government promote the arts in the 1930s?

Thinking Critically

1. **Identifying Cause and Effect** How did criticism of the first New Deal shape the Second New Deal?
2. **Taking a Stand** Do you think that President Roosevelt was justified in trying to "pack" the Supreme Court? Why or why not?
3. **Assessing Consequences** How did Works Progress Administration programs enrich American culture during the 1930s?
4. **Distinguishing Fact from Opinion** Some people consider Franklin D. Roosevelt our greatest president. Use facts from the chapter to evaluate the accuracy of that statement.
5. **Problem Solving** If you had been one of President Roosevelt's advisers, what aspects of the New Deal programs would you have changed?

Writing About History

Writing to Classify Write a brief summary of 10 major New Deal programs and note whether they were designed primarily to help banks, farmers, labor, or business. Use the following graphic to organize your thoughts.

New Deal			
Banks	**Farmers**	**Labor**	**Business**

Strategies **for Success** Review the **Strategies for Success** on *Evaluating Art as Historical Evidence.* Then study the following reproduction of Anna "Grandma" Moses's painting *Sugaring Off* and answer the following questions.

GRANDMA MOSES: SUGARING OFF ©1992

1. What is the subject of this painting, and what information is provided by its details?
2. How does the painting contribute to your understanding of regionalism as an artistic movement?

Linking History and Geography

The windstorms of the 1930s picked up dried soil to create "black blizzards" across the country. Study the map below. Which states made up the Dust Bowl? Which other states also experienced severe wind erosion?

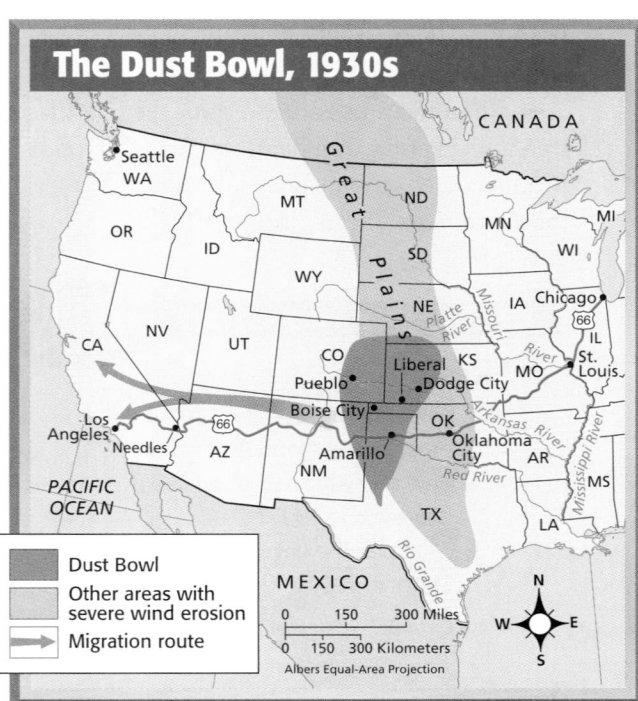

The Dust Bowl, 1930s

- Dust Bowl
- Other areas with severe wind erosion
- Migration route

0   150   300 Miles
0 150 300 Kilometers
Albers Equal-Area Projection

internet connect

TOPIC: WPA-Sponsored Art
GO TO: go.hrw.com
KEYWORD: SD1 WPA

Accessing the Internet through the HRW Web site, research the WPA-sponsored murals and posters produced during the Great Depression. Then create a poster or mural illustrating a topic of your choice that follows the style of the government-sponsored artwork.

BUILDING YOUR PORTFOLIO

Complete one or all of the following projects independently or cooperatively.

1 Economic Development

Imagine that you are a New Deal legislator.
Write a proposal for a new public-works project. Your proposal should describe what the project is, how workers and businesses will benefit from it, and why your project will be useful to society in terms of relief, recovery, or reform.

Civilian Conservation Corps patch

2 Cultural Diversity

Imagine that you are an author in the 1930s.
Write a short, realistic passage for a novel that describes the Dust Bowl's effects on the main character. You may also wish to add illustrations to your passage.

3 Constitutional Heritage

Hold a debate or **write a script** for a debate analyzing the constitutionality of the New Deal programs affecting labor and agriculture.

Land Use

For thousands of years Americans have used the land to grow crops. Many Native American groups cultivated crops on small plots of land long before the arrival of Europeans. In the early days of the Republic, most northern and midwestern farmers grew crops on small plots of land. In the South, agriculture was dominated by large plantations that grew large quantities of tobacco and cotton. By the late 1800s improved farm machinery and fertilizers allowed farmers to grow larger quantities of food on fewer acres of land. Today the amount of land devoted to crops and wild vegetation has dwindled significantly.

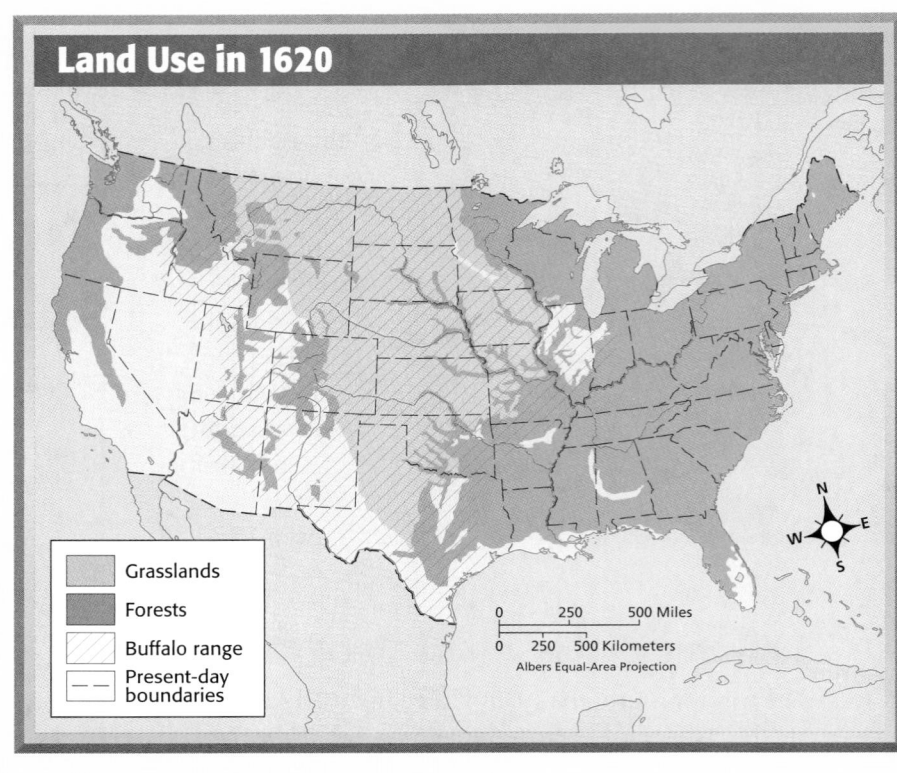

Land Use in 1620

Grasslands
Forests
Buffalo range
Present-day boundaries

0   250   500 Miles
0   250   500 Kilometers
Albers Equal-Area Projection

Soybeans. The multipurpose, high-protein soybean became the agricultural wonder of the 1900s. By the 1990s it was one of the most common crops in the United States. Soybeans are used in the processing of cattle feed, fertilizer, insect sprays, and paint, as well as in food products such as soy sauce, soy milk, baby food, processed meats, and tofu.

Agricultural Production, 1910–1997

	1910	1997
Corn (in bushels)	2.85 billion	9.37 billion
Wheat (in bushels)	625 million	2.53 billion
Cotton (in bales)	11.61 million	19 million
Tobacco (in pounds)	1.14 billion	1.68 billion
Soybeans (in bushels)	< 50,000	2.73 billion

Sources: *Historical Statistics of the United States; Statistical Abstract of the United States: 1998*

▶ GEOGRAPHY AND HISTORY Skills

REGION

1. What type of vegetation covered the most land in North America in 1620?
2. How many bushels of soybeans were harvested in 1997?
3. What was the largest crop in the United States in 1997?

Land Use in 1850

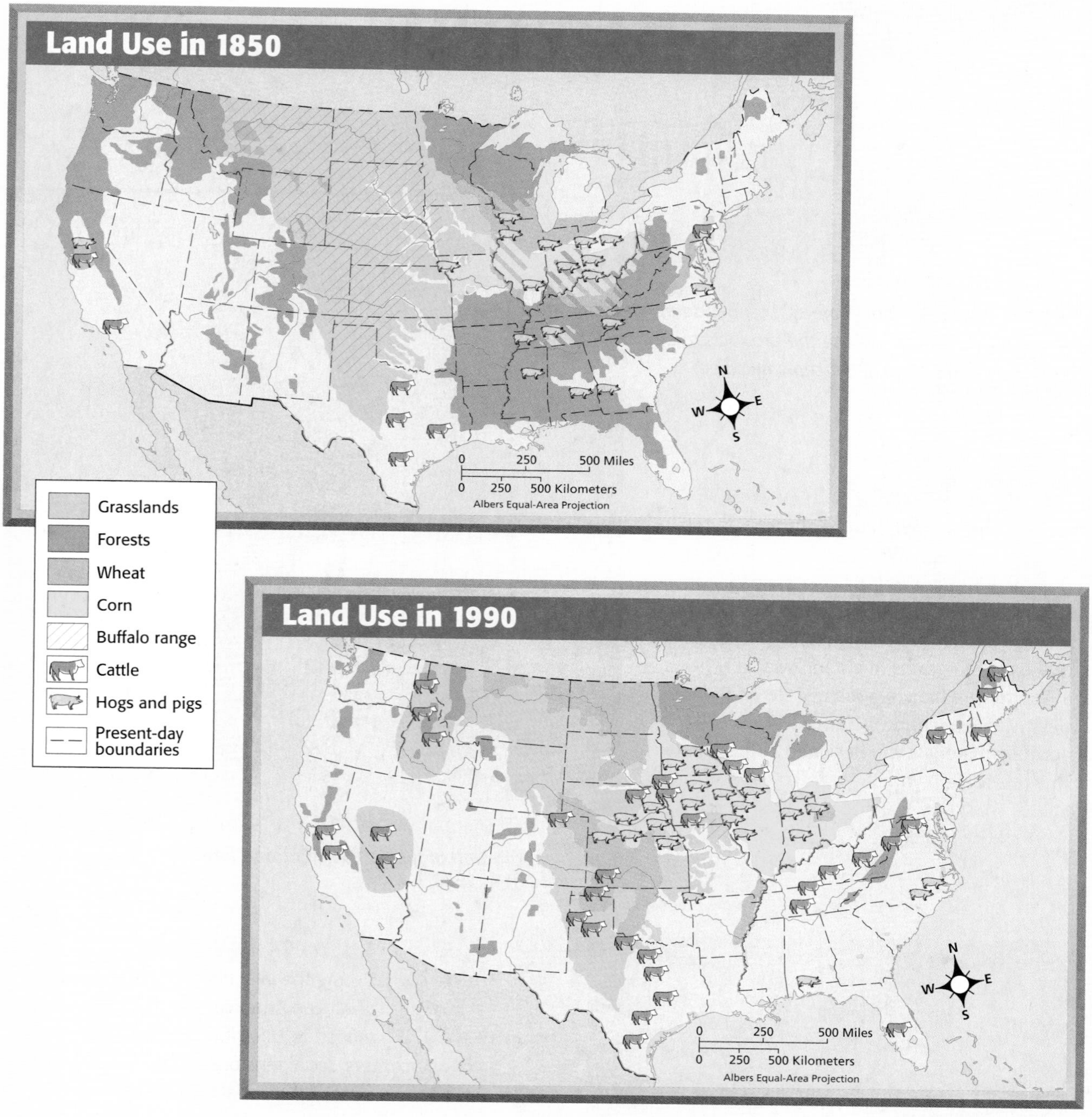

Grasslands
Forests
Wheat
Corn
Buffalo range
Cattle
Hogs and pigs
Present-day boundaries

0   250   500 Miles
0   250   500 Kilometers
Albers Equal-Area Projection

Land Use in 1990

0   250   500 Miles
0   250   500 Kilometers
Albers Equal-Area Projection

Land changes. Agricultural production in the United States had become increasingly diverse by the early 1900s. As the population of buffalo declined in the West, hogs and cattle grew in popularity elsewhere. The biggest change to affect agriculture in the late 1900s was the decline of the small family farm. Although the number of farmers decreased dramatically, the size of farms actually increased as large-scale mechanized farming became the norm.

GEOGRAPHY AND HISTORY  Skills

PLACE

1. How did the land used for cattle ranching change between 1850 and 1990?
2. In what ways did grasslands and forests change between 1850 and 1990?

Review

BUILDING YOUR PORTFOLIO

Outlined below are four projects. Independently or cooperatively, complete one and use the products to demonstrate your mastery of the historical concepts involved.

1 Technology and Society

Technological developments in the areas of entertainment and communications helped create a national culture during the 1920s. **Create a script for a radio program** that highlights the issues of the era. Programs might include daily news, a jazz presentation, a book review, or an interview with a celebrity. You may wish to use portfolio materials you designed in the unit chapters to help you.

Studio photograph of the St. Louis Cotton Club Jazz Band from 1926

Parade sponsored by Marcus Garvey and the Universal Negro Improvement Association

2 Cultural Diversity

During the late 1910s massive numbers of African Americans and immigrants moved to U.S. cities. Following the wave of newcomers, racial tensions erupted in violence. **Write a biography** of an activist, artist, or writer who worked to overcome the racism or prejudices they experienced. You may wish to use portfolio materials you designed in the unit chapters to help you.

3 Global Relations

Throughout the 1920s and 1930s events around the world affected life in the United States. Economic depressions in Europe and Latin America in the late 1920s contributed to the onset of the Great Depression in the United States. Imagine that it is the early 1930s and that you have a pen pal in a foreign country. *Draft a letter* to your pen pal describing what you believe were the causes of the Great Depression and what you have experienced since 1929. You may wish to use portfolio materials you designed in the unit chapters to help you.

THE GRANGER COLLECTION, NEW YORK

New York City soup kitchen

Works Progress Administration project

4 Economic Development

To provide relief from the economic troubles caused by the Great Depression, the federal government worked to implement programs from President Roosevelt's New Deal. *Create a sketch* for a mural that depicts some of the programs of the New Deal or the lives of workers in these programs. You may wish to use portfolio materials you designed in the unit chapters to help you.

Further Reading

Anderson, Jervis. *This Was Harlem: A Cultural Portrait, 1900–1950.* Farrar, Straus, and Giroux, 1992. Story of Harlem in the first half of the 1900s.

Garraty, John A. *The Great Depression.* Harcourt Brace Jovanovich, 1986. A thorough account of the causes of the economic depression.

McElvaine, Robert S. *The Great Depression: America, 1929–1941.* Times Books, 1984. Overview of the Great Depression in the United States.

Murray, Robert K. *The Politics of Normalcy.* W. W. Norton, 1973. A history of the policies and presidencies of the Republican administrations of the 1920s.

Parrish, Michael E. *Anxious Decades: America in Prosperity and Depression, 1920–1941.* W. W. Norton, 1992. Broad history of the interwar years.

Terkel, Studs. *Hard Times.* Pantheon Books, 1970. Personal accounts of the effects of the Great Depression on working-class Americans.

HOLT RESEARCHER
Internet Connect and Holt Researcher CD–ROM Review

In assigned groups, develop a multimedia presentation about America between 1919 and 1939. Choose information from the chapter Internet Connect activities and from the **Holt Researcher** CD–ROM that best reflects the major topics of the period. Write an outline and a script for your presentation, which may be shown to the class.

World Conflicts
1921–1960

U.S. Army and Marine officers of Kansas City, Missouri, hold a recruitment drive in 1940 in front of a theater showing the movie The Ramparts We Watch.

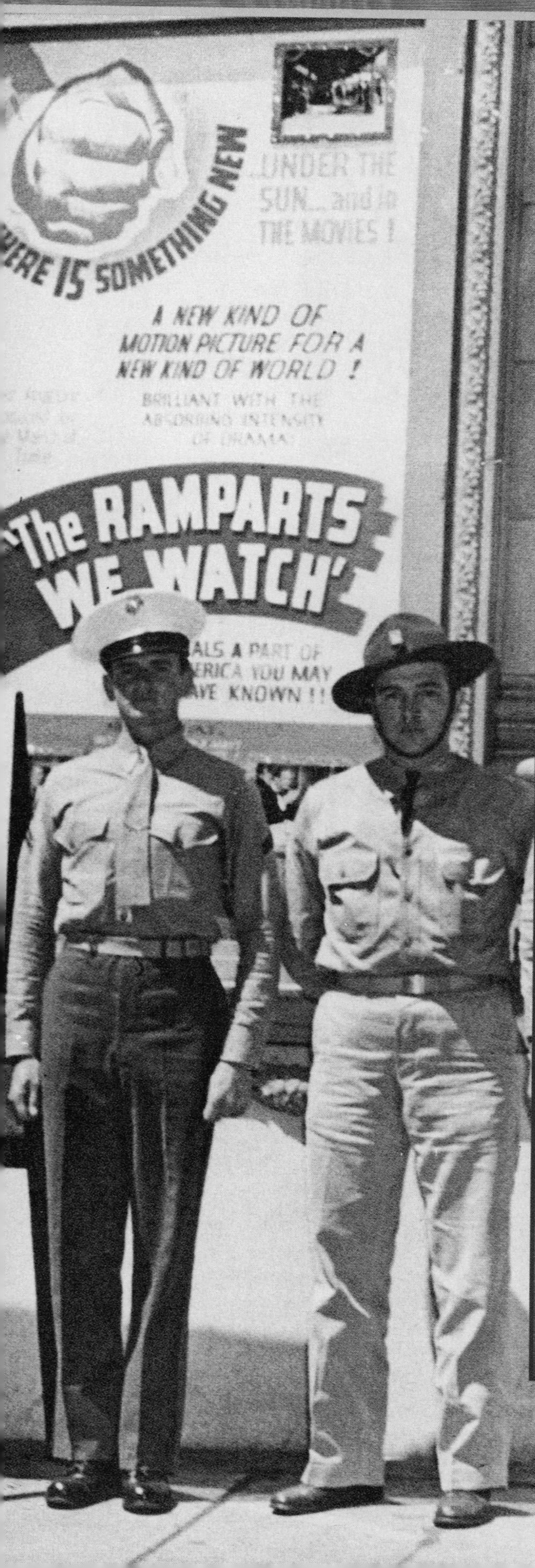

CHAPTER 26

The Road to War

1921–1941

CHAPTER 27

Americans in World War II

1941–1945

CHAPTER 28

The Cold War

1945–1960

CHAPTER 29

Society After World War II

1945–1960

Main Events

- The rise of fascism
- World War II
- The Holocaust
- The Cold War
- The Korean War
- Postwar economic prosperity
- The rise of a suburban culture
- The early civil rights movement

Main Ideas

- *How did the outbreak of World War II occur?*
- *How did World War II change the world?*
- *How did the Cold War emerge?*
- *What was life like in the United States after World War II?*

World War II era poster

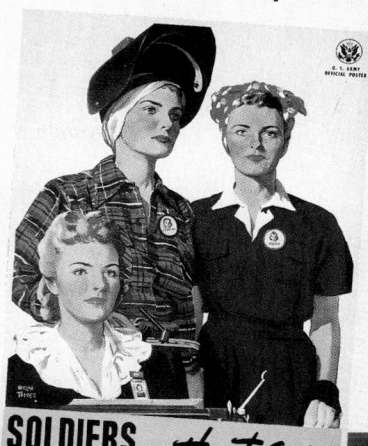

CHAPTER 26

1921–1941
The Road to War

Delegates to the Washington Conference

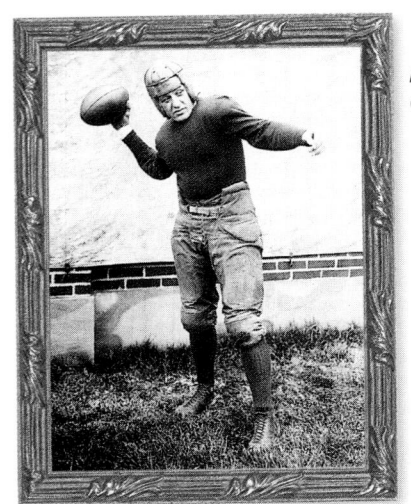

Red Grange

1924
Daily Life
University of Illinois player Red Grange and Notre Dame coach Knute Rockne boost the popularity of football.

1921
World Events
The Washington Conference begins.

1931
Business and Finance
President Herbert Hoover proposes a halt to war-debt and reparations payments.

1921

1925

1929

1922
Science and Technology
British archaeologist Howard Carter discovers the tomb of Egypt's King Tutankhamen.

1926
Politics
President Coolidge sends U.S. troops to Nicaragua to preserve order and protect American interests after an attempted revolt.

1929
Daily Life
Some 71 percent of American families have incomes below $2,500, considered the minimum for a decent standard of living.

Tutankhamen's tomb

Unemployed man selling apples

Before You Read

Build on What You Know

World War I left Europe in a state of chaos. Germany was required to pay substantial war reparations, and other European countries owed the United States large war debts. In this chapter you will learn how after World War I many Americans hoped to focus on matters at home. However, the Great Depression touched off global economic problems. The rise of dictators in Europe set the stage for another war. Dictators also took power in several Latin American countries. Other Latin American countries tried to reduce U.S. influence in the region.

772

1933
Politics
The United States establishes diplomatic relations with the Soviet Union.

1933
Business and Finance
Following Great Britain's example, the United States goes off the gold standard.

1933
World Events
Adolf Hitler becomes chancellor of Germany.

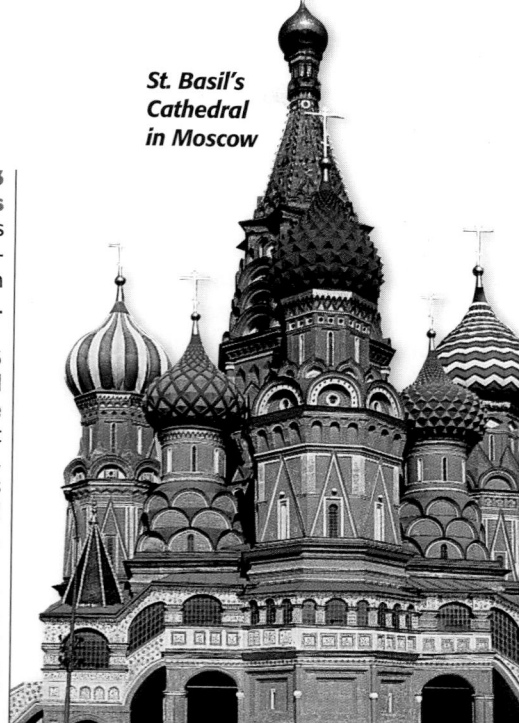

St. Basil's Cathedral in Moscow

The Des Moines Register

HUNDREDS UNNERVED BY RADIO SKIT

Headline announcing "The War of the Worlds" broadcast

1938
The Arts
The Mercury Theater radio production of "The War of the Worlds" sets off a national panic.

1941
World Events
Japanese forces attack Pearl Harbor.

1933 | **1937** | **1941**

1932
Daily Life
The average American's weekly wage drops to $17 from $28, its 1929 level.

1932
Business and Finance
American industrial production drops to one third of 1929 levels.

1932
Science and Technology
British physicist John Cockcroft becomes the first to split the atom.

1935
The Arts
Bette Davis wins an Oscar for her role in the film *Dangerous.*

Poster advertising *Dangerous*

1939
World Events
World War II begins when German troops invade Poland.

1939
Science and Technology
Swiss chemist Paul Müller develops the insecticide DDT.

1940
Politics
Franklin D. Roosevelt wins an unprecedented third term as president.

Think About Themes

Themes Journal

Decide whether you agree or disagree with the following statements. Note why in your journal.

Global Relations Nations should be willing to give up some of their power in order to promote world peace.

Economic Development Wars always have economic and political consequences that inevitably lead to more wars.

Democratic Values Citizens will give up certain liberties if their government provides economic stability.

The Search for Peace

EYEWITNESSES TO History

❝ *The whole scheme [the League of Nations] has just one ultimate power and that is military force— the same power and the same principle which every despot [dictator] has relied upon in his efforts against the people when the people were seeking greater liberty and greater freedom, the same power which George III and Wilhelm II made the basis of their infamous designs [shameful plans]. . . . Let us leave these things—the lives of our people, the liberty of our whole nation—in the keeping and under the control of those people who have brought this Republic to its present place of prestige and power.* ❞

—**William E. Borah**

Senator William E. Borah

Senator William E. Borah of Idaho argued against membership in the League of Nations shortly after the end of World War I. Like many Americans, Borah feared that involvement in European affairs might draw the United States into another war.

Legacies of World War I

More than 8 million people, including more than 112,000 Americans, died fighting in the Great War. Yet few Americans believed that the war had made the world "safe for democracy." They noted the postwar chaos in government and the founding of a communist government in Russia. The Women's International League for Peace and Freedom summed up the nation's doubts: "War to end war has proved a failure. The war is won, yet nowhere is there peace, security or happiness."

Americans worried about being dragged into another foreign conflict. "We ask only to live our own life in our own way, in friendship and sympathy with all, in alliance with none," declared Senator Hiram W. Johnson in 1922. Such sentiments led the United States to follow a policy of partial **isolationism**, or withdrawal from world affairs, in the 1920s and 1930s.

The horrors of World War I led many Americans to oppose war of any kind.

Isolationists did not want to cut off the United States completely from the affairs of the rest of the world. They merely wanted to avoid what Thomas Jefferson had called "entangling alliances" that could drag the United States into another war. Isolationism led the United States to shun membership in international organizations that were set up after World War I. These included the League of Nations and the Permanent Court of International Justice, or World Court.

The World Court had been created to resolve international disputes. Presidents Coolidge, Hoover, and Roosevelt all proposed that the United States join the organization. Public opinion ran strongly against membership, however. The U.S. Senate set strict terms for joining in order to safeguard its right to make treaties. The nations that already belonged to the World Court rejected the Senate's terms, and the matter was dropped.

✔ **READING CHECK:** What foreign policy did the United States follow after World War I?

Promoting Peace

Rather than joining international peacekeeping organizations, the United States used diplomacy to promote world peace. American groups working for peace urged the U.S. government to bring world leaders together to negotiate **disarmament**, or reducing the size of a country's military. Jane Addams, Emily Greene Balch, Jeannette Rankin, and other leaders of the women's movement played important roles in these peace efforts. For their organizing efforts in the United States and abroad, both Addams—in 1931—and Balch—in 1946—received the Nobel Peace Prize.

The Washington Conference. Beginning in November 1921, the United States hosted the **Washington Conference**, an international conference in Washington, D.C., that focused on naval disarmament and Pacific security. The meeting was organized by U.S. secretary of state Charles Evans Hughes.

B I O G R A P H Y

Charles Evans Hughes

Charles Evans Hughes was born in New York in April 1862. He graduated from Brown University in 1881 and received a law degree from Columbia University Law School three years later. After teaching and practicing law for several years, Hughes began his career in public service. Hughes was so busy, it was reported that he grew his beard in 1890 just to save the time it took to get a shave. Hughes served as legal adviser to Progressive Era legislators investigating corruption in the utilities industry. In 1906 he won his first public office when he defeated publishing tycoon William Randolph Hearst to become governor of New York.

Hughes served as a justice on the Supreme Court from 1910 to 1916, when he resigned his position to run for president. Hughes went to bed on election night believing himself the victor. The next morning he awoke to the news that he had lost to Woodrow Wilson by just 23 electoral votes.

After this crushing defeat Hughes turned to the issue of world peace. Putting aside political rivalries, Hughes supported U.S. entry into the League of Nations, the creation of President Wilson. At the end of World War I Hughes envisioned the United States taking an active role in future world affairs.

Peace Movements

The 1920s and 1930s saw a rise in the number of groups working for peace throughout the world. After experiencing the horrors of World War I, many people began to organize in an effort to abolish war. Some American opponents of war belonged to religious groups such as the Mennonites and Quakers. Others were members of political organizations such as the Committee on the Cause and Cure of War. All the groups urged U.S. leaders to reject war as a means of solving conflicts.

Although war has persisted, many groups continue to work to stop the use of violence as a political tool. Some, like the National Campaign for a Peace Tax Fund, have lobbied to allow citizens to redirect the portion of their tax payments that would go into military spending to a special fund to promote international peace. Many peace organizations are affiliated with religious groups, including the Jewish Peace Fellowship, the Muslim Peace Fellowship, and Pax Christi (Peace of Christ) U.S.A. These groups use modern means of communication such as the Internet to spread their message. Many also use film and television to publicize the horrors of war.

These protesters demonstrated in front of the U.S. Capitol in 1991.

Read More About It

**Free Find: Charles
Evans Hughes**

After reading about
Charles Evans Hughes
on the **Holt Researcher**
CD–ROM, write a proposal
for an arms-reduction
conference to be held
this year.

66 We emerge from the war with a new national consciousness; with a consciousness of power stimulated by extraordinary effort; with a consciousness of the possibility and potency [power] of cooperation. . . . We are unworthy of our victory, if we look forward with timidity. This is the hour and power of light, not of darkness. . . . We have made the world safe for democracy, but democracy is not a phrase or a form, but a life, and what shall that life be? . . . We have fought this War to substitute reason for force. We love our Republic because it represents to us the promise of the rule of reason. . . . If we are to establish peace within our own borders, we must cooperate to destroy the . . . spirit of tyranny wherever we find it. 99

In 1930 Charles Evans Hughes was appointed Chief Justice of the United States, a position he held until retiring in 1941. He died seven years later.

As President Harding's secretary of state, Hughes tried to make his goal of a peaceful world a reality at the Washington Conference. Hughes surprised the other delegates at the conference with a bold proposal. He suggested that the major powers destroy 66 large warships. He also called for a 10-year "naval holiday" during which no battleships or battle cruisers would be built.

Hughes proposed that the United States, Great Britain, and Japan destroy or retire some of their warships in order to limit their individual naval strength. Britain and the United States would have equal naval strength. The size of Japan's navy would be limited to 60 percent of that of the British and U.S. navies. Italy and France would both be limited to navies roughly half the size of Japan's. This disarmament plan became known as the Five-Power Naval Treaty. Marveled one observer, "[Secretary Hughes sank more] ships than all the admirals of the world had sunk in a cycle of centuries."

The Washington Conference produced other important agreements as well. In the Four-Power Treaty, Britain, France, Japan, and the United States pledged to respect one another's territory in the Pacific. The Nine-Power Treaty included the nations that had signed the Five-Power Naval Treaty as well as Belgium, China, the Netherlands, and Portugal. The treaty guaranteed China's territorial integrity and required its signers to uphold the Open Door Policy.

Japan's minister of the navy, Admiral Kato Tomosaburo, explained Japan's support for disarmament.

66 Japan is ready for the new order of thought—the spirit of international friendship and cooperation for the greater good of humanity—which the Conference has brought about. 99

For a time the treaties produced at the Washington Conference eased tensions in Asia. Japan began withdrawing from China's Shandong Peninsula, which it had invaded in 1914. Japan also withdrew from the parts of Siberia it had occupied during the Russian Revolution. Japan's 1930 agreement to extend the 10-year ban on warship construction marked the high point of postwar international cooperation efforts.

Unsuccessful efforts. April 6, 1927, marked the 10th anniversary of the U.S. entry into World War I. On that day French foreign minister Aristide Briand

*Carrie Chapman Catt
strongly supported the
Kellogg-Briand Pact.*

(ah-ree-steed bree-ahn) proposed that France and the United States enter into an agreement to outlaw war. U.S. secretary of state Frank Kellogg made a counterproposal that the pact include all nations. Eventually, 62 countries signed the **Kellogg-Briand Pact**. The treaty outlawed war "as an instrument of national policy" but allowed countries to go to war in self-defense. The treaty lacked provisions for enforcement, however. One U.S. senator remarked that the treaty was "as effective to keep down war as a carpet would be to smother an earthquake."

The pact's weaknesses became clear in September 1931 when Japan violated the agreement by invading Manchuria, a territory in China. The invasion launched a bloody war between Japan and China. Although many Americans called for an economic boycott of Japan, U.S. leaders refused to support sanctions against the Japanese. The failure of diplomacy to prevent Japanese aggression marked the end of attempts to reach international accords. Preoccupied by the Japanese invasion and the worldwide economic depression, delegates to the 1932 League of Nations World Disarmament Conference went home without agreeing to reduce weapons.

✔ **READING CHECK:** What were the major postwar peace initiatives?

These Japanese troops are celebrating their victory in Manchuria, China.

War Debts and Reparations

The issue of war debts also weakened efforts to maintain peace. In the late 1800s European investors had loaned money to finance U.S. industrial growth. After 1914, however, the United States became a creditor nation. At the start of World War I, U.S. banks lent money to Britain and France so that they could buy armaments from the United States. The U.S. government granted billions more in credit to the Allies. By 1920 the Allies owed more than $10 billion to the United States.

The debtor nations argued that their debts to the United States should be canceled. David Lloyd George, the British prime minister when the United States entered the war, explained their reasoning.

> 66 The United States did not from first to last make any sacrifice or contribution remotely comparable to those of her European Associates, in life, limb, money, material or trade, towards the victory which she shared with them. 99

U.S. officials rejected appeals from Britain, France, and Italy to cancel their war debts completely. However, the U.S. government did cancel part of the debts. It also reduced the interest rates on the balances. Still, the only way the Allies could pay their war debts to the United States was to collect reparations, or damages, from defeated Germany. In 1921 a reparations commission had set total German reparations at 132 billion gold marks, or $32 billion. The Germans bitterly condemned the reparations as too harsh. Chancellor Joseph Wirth paid part of the reparations by borrowing money from Britain. The German government also printed paper money, resulting in massive inflation and causing the value of the German mark to plunge.

In 1922 writer Ernest Hemingway traveled from Strasburg, France, to Kehl, Germany. He described the extreme difference in prices between France and Germany, an effect of severe inflation in Germany:

British prime minister David Lloyd George urged U.S. leaders to cancel the debts Britain and other European nations owed the United States from World War I.

Inflation. These German children are using bundles of German marks as building blocks. *What does this photograph suggest about the value of German currency?*

❝❝ We changed some French money in the railway station at Kehl. For 10 francs I received 670 marks. Ten francs amounted to about 90 cents in Canadian money. That 90 cents lasted Mrs. Hemingway and me for a day of heavy spending and at the end of the day we had 120 marks left! . . . Kehl's best hotel, which is a very well turned-out place, served a five-course table d'hôte meal for 120 marks, which amounts to 15 cents in our money. The same meal could not be duplicated in Strasburg, three miles away, for a dollar. ❞❞

With his country near financial collapse, one particularly embittered German World War I veteran sought someone to blame. Adolf Hitler had survived a poison gas attack during the war and remained convinced that politicians, not the German army, were responsible for Germany losing the war. Feeling betrayed, Hitler joined a radical political organization and hatched a plot to overthrow the German government in 1923. The plot failed, and Hitler was sent to jail. There he continued to plan revenge against those whom he believed had betrayed Germany.

In 1924 a plan proposed by Charles Dawes temporarily eased Germany's economic crisis. The Dawes Plan provided loans and gave Germany more time to make its reparations payments. In 1931, as the worldwide depression deepened, President Herbert Hoover declared a year's moratorium, or halt, on reparations and war-debt payments. The moratorium, however, only prolonged the crisis. Most of the war debts remained unpaid. By 1934 Finland was the only debtor nation that could make even a token payment on its debts.

✔ **READING CHECK:** How did war debts and reparations affect European nations?

SECTION 1 REVIEW

Define and explain the significance of the following terms:
isolationism
disarmament
Washington Conference
Kellogg-Briand Pact

Identify and explain the significance of the following individuals:
Emily Greene Balch
Charles Evans Hughes

1. **Using Graphic Organizers** Copy the following graphic organizer. Use it to list the treaties signed at the Washington Conference and their objectives.

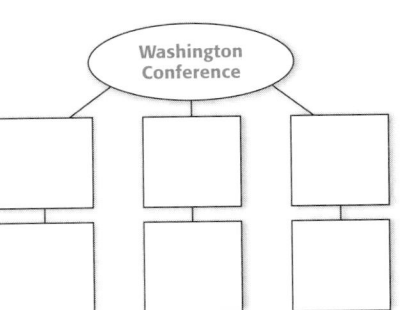

Washington Conference

2. **Analyzing** Why was the Kellogg-Briand Pact unsuccessful in resolving the conflict in Manchuria?
3. **Recognizing Point of View** Imagine that you are a delegate to the Washington Conference in 1921. Write a memo to your government explaining why you consider the conference a success.
4. **Assessing Consequences** How did war debts and reparations affect Germany and other European countries?

Critical Thinking

5. Why did the United States partially withdraw from world affairs in the 1920s and 1930s?
   Consider:
   • the costs of World War I
   • traditional U.S. foreign policy
   • public opinion toward Europe

SECTION 2 Relations with Latin America

OBJECTIVES

Read to understand:
1. what role the United States played in Nicaraguan politics
2. how U.S. relations with Latin America changed in the 1930s
3. how the Great Depression affected Latin American countries

KEY TERMS

Good Neighbor policy
nationalize
caudillos

KEY PEOPLE

Emiliano Chamorro
Henry Stimson
Augusto César Sandino
Adolfo Díaz
Anastasio Somoza
Lázaro Cárdenas
Josephus Daniels

EYEWITNESSES TO History

66 *Ever since the World War we have been manufacturing more goods than we can sell. We are looking for new markets. Latin America and South America afford [provide] these markets. And yet in order to allow a few bankers to exploit [take advantage of] Nicaragua, our oil interests to exploit Mexico, we are willing to ruin the legitimate commercial business of this country. We are willing to let thousands of men remain out of employment who could be working in the manufacturing plants of this country if we by peaceful means sought the friendship and trade of Central and South America.* 99

—Burton K. Wheeler

Senator Burton K. Wheeler

In 1927 Senator Burton K. Wheeler of Montana condemned U.S. policy toward Latin America. For many years the United States had dominated Latin America both economically and militarily. This began to change during the 1930s as the United States tried to build a more equal relationship with its southern neighbors.

Intervention in Nicaragua

The United States played a large role in Nicaraguan politics throughout the 1920s and 1930s. In 1925 General Emiliano Chamorro (chah-MAWR-roh) overthrew the government, sparking a bitter civil war. The United States, however, refused to recognize Chamorro's government. In May 1926 President Coolidge ordered in the U.S. Marine Corps to protect American commercial interests. He also sent Henry Stimson, a longtime public official, to negotiate an end to the civil war. Stimson brought the two sides together, and they negotiated a peace treaty in May 1927. In the treaty, Stimson called for the abolition of Nicaragua's armed forces. U.S. troops would then train a new Nicaraguan National Guard to maintain order after the U.S. withdrawal.

Augusto César Sandino (sahn-DEE-noh), a general who opposed Chamorro, refused to accept Stimson's proposal. During the 1920s Sandino worked as a mechanic for American companies in Honduras and Guatemala. In 1923 he began working for an American-owned oil company in Tampico, Mexico. There Sandino read about Simón Bolívar, the great hero of the Latin American independence struggle.

In 1926, after his return to Nicaragua, Sandino organized a revolt against Chamorro and Chamorro's successor, Adolfo Díaz. He hoped to rid Nicaragua of the Americans, whom he viewed as invaders, and to allow ordinary Nicaraguans to control their country's land and wealth. He planned to help workers and peasants "exploit our own natural resources for the benefit of the Nicaraguan family in general."

Augusto César Sandino led a revolt in Nicaragua.

THE ROAD TO WAR **779**

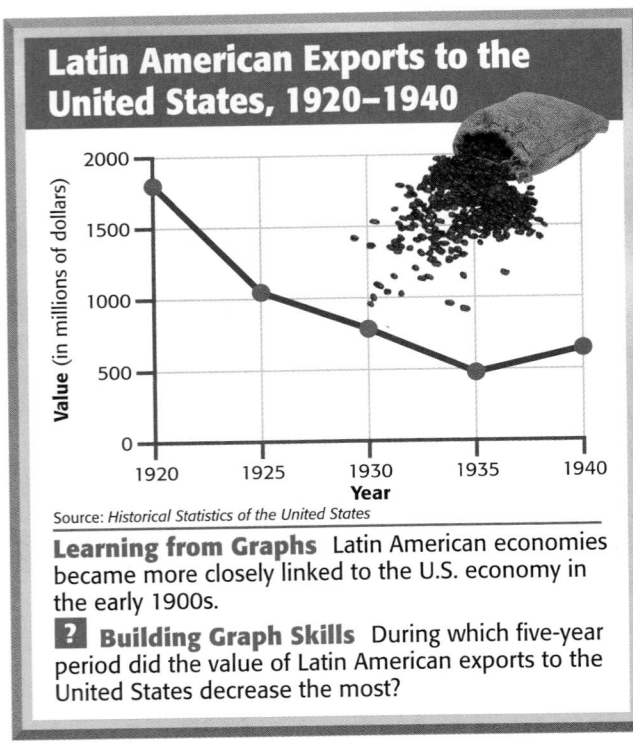

Latin American Exports to the United States, 1920–1940

Source: *Historical Statistics of the United States*

Learning from Graphs Latin American economies became more closely linked to the U.S. economy in the early 1900s.

❓ **Building Graph Skills** During which five-year period did the value of Latin American exports to the United States decrease the most?

Sandino's forces ranged from as few as 30 to as many as 3,000 soldiers. They proved a tough opponent for the U.S. Marines. The Americans used aerial bombing against Sandino's forces. However, this did not completely destroy the army, which relied on sympathetic farmers to feed and house them.

The marines never defeated Sandino. The war became increasingly costly for the United States, which was in the midst of the Great Depression. In 1933 President Hoover withdrew the last of the U.S. troops. A year later, the commander of the U.S.-trained National Guard, General Anastasio Somoza, ordered Sandino's assassination. With Sandino dead, organized resistance to Somoza and his military evaporated. Somoza forced out the Nicaraguan president in 1936 and took over the presidency the next year. With U.S. backing, Somoza and other members of his family ruled Nicaragua almost without interruption until the Sandinista revolution—named for Sandino—overthrew the dynasty in 1979.

✔ **READING CHECK:** What role did the United States play in Nicaraguan politics?

A Change in Policy

While the United States isolated itself from events in Europe and Asia, Presidents Coolidge, Hoover, and Roosevelt all tried to improve relations with Latin American countries. Before his inauguration, Hoover toured Latin America to promote goodwill, winning many new friends for the United States.

In 1936 Franklin Roosevelt proposed an inter-American Conference for peace in Argentina.

The Good Neighbor. President Franklin D. Roosevelt built upon the goodwill created by previous presidents. In his inaugural speech of 1933 Roosevelt spelled out his policy of mutual respect toward Latin America, which became known as the **Good Neighbor policy**.

66 In the field of world policy I would dedicate this nation to the policy of the good neighbor—the neighbor who resolutely respects himself and, because he does so, respects the rights of others. 99

To back up his words, Roosevelt in 1934 signed a treaty with Cuba that canceled the Platt Amendment. This amendment had given the United States the right to intervene in Cuban affairs. Two years later he gave up the U.S. right to intervene in Panama. Roosevelt also withdrew marines from Haiti, where they had been stationed as an occupying force since 1915.

In economic matters the United States had often behaved more like a landlord than a good neighbor. American investors played a powerful—and sometimes negative—role in Latin America. After World War I, large American companies increased their investments in banana, coffee, and sugar plantations in Central America and the Caribbean. Some countries were run largely to serve the interests of these foreign companies and became known as banana republics.

A Banana Plantation, Panama.

The United Fruit Company was the largest American company in Latin America. It owned millions of acres in Central America and the Caribbean, and was Guatemala's largest landowner, exporter, and employer. In addition to establishing plantations, United Fruit and other companies built roads and railroads. They also controlled the ports and shipping lines necessary to export their products.

American companies played a central economic role in Latin America. They also had tremendous political power. The companies made alliances with Latin American landowners and politicians and often played a direct role in governing the countries in which they operated. Many Latin Americans resented the economic and political power of the large American companies. Chilean poet Pablo Neruda (nay-ROO-dah) wrote:

66 The Fruit Company, Inc.
reserved for itself the most succulent,
the central coast of my own land,
the delicate waist of America.
It rechristened its territories
as the 'Banana Republics.' 99

Relations with Mexico. A serious test of the Good Neighbor policy came in March 1938. Mexico's president, Lázaro Cárdenas (KAHR-day-nahs), began to **nationalize**, or assert government control over, the country's oil industry. Although the Mexican constitution of 1917 proclaimed that Mexico controlled all its underground resources, American and British firms had continued to own and operate oil companies in Mexico. When the foreign companies refused to meet the demands of Mexican oil workers for higher wages and better working conditions, President Cárdenas nationalized the oil fields.

American oil companies hotly criticized Mexico's seizure of their property. They pressed President Roosevelt to intervene. Meanwhile, the U.S. ambassador to Mexico, Josephus Daniels, argued for a

THROUGH OTHERS' EYES

Latin American Views of Foreign Investment

The United States has always had close ties with Latin America. For much of its history the relationship has been marked by U.S. domination of the region, both politically and economically. In 1933 a member of the Honduran congress described the effect foreign investment was having on his country.

66 The national farmers are condemned to disappear, for the fruit companies are becoming owners of the lands on the coast, including the alternate lots, which they now have almost entirely in their possession, through transfers made by the Hondurans themselves. The villages, the small riverside farms disappear, and the depopulation of the region follows. 99

A 1929 report by the Sociedad Económica de Amigos del País described the power of foreign companies in Costa Rica.

66 It is evident . . . that the fruit company, besides having taken possession of a large portion of the Atlantic Zone, is exercising over it a predominance and control such as not even the government of the republic itself exercises; there it is the company which commands. 99

Mexican president Lázaro Cárdenas (center) and his secretary of foreign relations (right) meet with Britain's minister to Mexico (left).

compromise between the Mexican government and the oil companies. He urged the United States to recognize Mexico's right to control its oil resources but added that American companies should be compensated for the property they had lost.

Most of the Mexican people supported Cárdenas's bold action against the oil companies. Many Mexicans worried, however, that the United States might invade their country to restore American oil companies' property rights. President Roosevelt decided to maintain good relations with Mexico. He acknowledged Mexico's right to control its own resources and urged the oil companies to reach an agreement with the Mexican government for fair compensation. Mexico agreed to the compromise and began payments in 1939.

✔ **READING CHECK:** How did U.S. relations with Latin America change during the 1930s?

Changing Ways — Investments in Latin America

■ **Understanding Change** The economies of the United States and Latin American countries have long been connected. The industrialization of the United States during the late 1800s resulted in a rapid expansion of this connection. Today the United States and the countries of Latin America continue to strengthen the links between their economies. *How has the value of U.S. investments in Latin America changed over time? Has the changing balance of trade between the two regions been more beneficial for the United States or for Latin America?*

THEN

Now

	THEN	Now
Value of Direct U.S. Investments in Latin America	$3.52 billion	$172.48 billion
Value of U.S. Exports to Latin America	$698 million	$98.67 billion
Value of U.S. Imports from Latin America	$1.12 billion	$94.65 billion

Sources: *Historical Statistics of the United States* and *Statistical Abstract of the United States: 1998.* Data reflect 1929 and 1997.

The Rise of Dictators

The Wall Street crash of 1929 sent shock waves through Latin America. The world-wide economic depression meant lower prices for bananas, coffee, and other Latin American crops. Farm wages dropped to eight cents a day.

As workers lost their jobs, the gulf between Latin America's small class of wealthy landowners and the large class of poor landless people widened. One U.S. diplomat, Major A. R. Harris, commented on the inequality he saw between the classes in El Salvador in 1931.

> 66 **The first thing one observes . . . is the number of expensive automobiles on the streets. . . . There seems to be nothing between these high-priced cars and the ox-cart with its barefooted attendant. . . . Roughly 90 percent of the wealth of the country is held by about one-half of one percent of the population.** 99

In the 1930s **caudillos** (kow-DEE-yohs) took power in many Latin American countries. Caudillos were military leaders who used force to maintain order. During the 1930s caudillos seized power in Cuba, the Dominican Republic, Guatemala, and Honduras. Some U.S. diplomats denounced the bans on opposition parties and restrictions on freedom of speech that the caudillos employed to maintain their power. However, the United States often supported the caudillos, because they created favorable environments for American companies to do business.

✔ **READING CHECK:** How did the Great Depression affect Latin American countries?

INTERPRETING THE VISUAL RECORD

Poverty. The Great Depression devastated many Latin American nations and contributed to the rise of dictators. *What signs of economic hardship do you see in this picture of a Salvadoran family?*

SECTION 2 REVIEW

Define and explain the significance of the following terms:
Good Neighbor policy
nationalize
caudillos

Identify and explain the significance of the following individuals:
Emiliano Chamorro
Henry Stimson
Augusto César Sandino
Adolfo Díaz
Anastasio Somoza
Lázaro Cárdenas
Josephus Daniels

1. **Using Graphic Organizers** Copy the graphic organizer below. Use it to list the changes that the Good Neighbor policy brought to the U.S. relationship with Latin America.

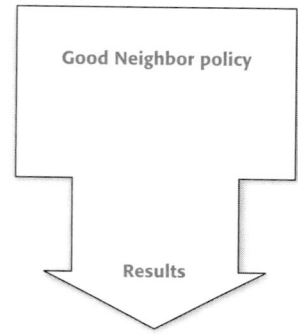

Good Neighbor policy

Results

2. **Evaluating** Why did Augusto César Sandino organize a revolt against Adolfo Díaz?
3. **Identifying Cause and Effect** Why did the United States intervene in Nicaraguan politics throughout the 1920s and into the 1930s? What was the effect of this intervention?
4. **Taking a Stand** Imagine that you are Josephus Daniels in 1938. Write a memorandum to President Roosevelt recommending a U.S. response to Mexico after its nationalization of the oil fields.

Critical Thinking

5. Could the United States have prevented the rise of dictators in Latin America?
   Consider:
   • U.S. policy toward Latin America in the 1920s
   • the goals of the Good Neighbor policy
   • the effects of the Great Depression on Latin America

The Rise of Militarism

OBJECTIVES

Read to understand:

1. how Benito Mussolini created a fascist state in Italy
2. how Joseph Stalin maintained power in the Soviet Union
3. how Adolf Hitler rose to power in Germany
4. what caused the Spanish Civil War
5. what actions Japan's military took during the 1930s

KEY TERMS

Fascist Party
Blackshirts
totalitarian state
Nazi Party
Brownshirts
anti-Semitism
Kristallnacht
Spanish Civil War
Popular Front

KEY PEOPLE

Benito Mussolini
Joseph Stalin
Adolf Hitler
Francisco Franco

EYEWITNESSES TO History

❝ *The peace, the freedom, and the security of 90 percent of the population of the world is being jeopardized by the remaining 10 percent who are threatening a breakdown of all international order and law. . . . War is a contagion [disease]. . . . It can engulf states and peoples remote from the original scene of hostilities. . . . If civilization is to survive, the principles of [peace] must be restored.* ❞
—**Franklin D. Roosevelt**

President Roosevelt speaks to the American people.

In this 1937 speech, President Franklin D. Roosevelt warned Americans of the growing danger of war. A rise in military activity by a number of nations and leaders made peace seem increasingly fragile.

Mussolini in Italy

Although Italy had been on the winning side when World War I ended, many Italians felt they had not benefited from the Treaty of Versailles. Thousands of Italian veterans were unable to find jobs. Many joined the Italian Communist Party, which urged Italian peasants to take over land and called on workers to seize factories.

To destroy the Communist Party and promote his own rise to power, Benito Mussolini founded the **Fascist Party** in 1921. The Fascists believed that a military-dominated government should control all aspects of society. Beginning in 1921, bloody clashes between Communists and Fascists created a situation bordering on civil war. In October 1922 Mussolini led an army of his followers, whose black uniforms gave them the name **Blackshirts**, in a march on Rome. Supported by nationalists who wanted to strengthen Italy and businesspeople who opposed the Socialists and Communists, the Fascists occupied the city.

The Italian king appointed Mussolini prime minister and granted him dictatorial powers. Mussolini limited freedom of speech, arrested political opponents, and restricted voting rights. Acting on a pledge to make Italy an imperial power, Mussolini sent Italian forces into the African nation of Ethiopia in 1935. The small, poorly equipped Ethiopian army proved no match for Italy's airplanes and machine guns. The U.S. Congress, fearful of being drawn into the conflict, passed a neutrality act banning arms shipments to both sides. The embargo hurt Ethiopia more than it did Italy, which continued to receive weapons from Germany and oil from American companies.

African Americans raised money to send relief and medical aid to the Ethiopians. Thousands of African Americans volunteered to fight in Ethiopia, but pressure from the U.S. government forced Ethiopia to reject the offer. This lack of support convinced other fascist countries, such as Germany, that aggression would go unpunished.

✔ **READING CHECK:** How did Benito Mussolini create a fascist state in Italy?

This symbol of the Italian Fascist Party appeared on its membership cards.

Stalin in the Soviet Union

As Benito Mussolini seized power in Italy, a battle was being waged for power in the Soviet Union—the communist nation formed from Russia and several other surrounding states in 1922. By the early 1920s Vladimir Lenin, the leader of the Bolshevik Revolution, was in poor health. His death in 1924 spurred a struggle for power among Communist Party leaders. Using underhanded tactics and even organizing the assassination of his enemies, Joseph Stalin eventually emerged as the nation's leader.

Driven by ambition, Stalin turned the Soviet Union into a **totalitarian state**—a country where the government has complete control. In 1927 the government began taking control of privately owned lands and reorganizing them into large state-run farms. Farmers who protested this policy were sent to forced labor camps. In all, some 15 million people were sent to Soviet labor camps by 1933. The reorganization policy resulted in decreased food production and widespread famine.

Stalin imposed his will through the Soviet Union's powerful Red Army. Stalin used the army and other police forces to crush all opposition. In the late 1930s, fearing opponents were trying to weaken him, Stalin began a campaign to purge all perceived enemies from the Communist Party and the Red Army. Although the exact figure is not known, some historians estimate that eventually as many as 30 million people may have died as a result of Stalin's policies.

✔ **READING CHECK:** How did Joseph Stalin maintain power in the Soviet Union?

These workers at the "Lenin's Way Collective Farm" in Russia are sharing a communal lunch.

Hitler in Germany

In 1932 Adolf Hitler's National Socialist Party, or **Nazi Party**, won nearly 40 percent of the vote in national elections. Hitler became chancellor of Germany the next year. While in prison, he had written *Mein Kampf (My Struggle)*, which laid out his plans to restore German power. Hitler blamed Jews, Communists, and intellectuals for Germany's decline. Hitler's views won him many supporters, particularly among those ruined by the depression.

The Third Reich. Hitler's government, called the Third Reich (the Third Empire), claimed dictatorial powers. Hitler prohibited Jews and non-Nazis from holding government positions, outlawed strikes, and made military service mandatory. Nazi storm troopers, known as **Brownshirts** because of the color of their uniforms, crushed all political opposition.

Hitler used his tight control over German industry to rearm the country in violation of the Treaty of Versailles. This strengthened the economy and reduced unemployment. Hitler declared:

66 **The buildup of the armed forces is the most important precondition for . . . political power. . . . How is this political power to be used when it is won? . . . Maybe fighting for new export possibilities, maybe . . . conquest of new Lebensraum [space for expansion] in the East.** 99

The German press often portrayed Adolf Hitler as Germany's savior, as in this image from a 1934 German magazine.

THE GRANGER COLLECTION, NEW YORK

The Nazis used posters like this one to appeal to Germans' desire to see their country reclaim its role as a world power.

In March 1936, German troops moved into the Rhineland. Two years later they overran Austria. Hitler then turned toward the Sudetenland (soo-DAYT-uhn-land) region of western Czechoslovakia, where more than 3 million German-speaking people lived. Hitler demanded that Czechoslovakia turn over the region to Germany. Czechoslovakia refused Hitler's demand.

Anti-Semitism. Meanwhile, Hitler's **anti-Semitism,** or hatred of Jews, became official government policy. In 1935 Hitler instituted the Nuremberg Laws, which deprived Jews of their German citizenship and authorized the destruction of Jewish property. Gradually the oppression of Jews increased. On November 9, 1938, Nazi thugs burned down synagogues and destroyed Jewish businesses. Known as *Kristallnacht,* or "the night of broken glass," the violence provided a chilling preview of the fate that awaited European Jews and others whom Hitler opposed.

Increased oppression caused many Jews to flee the country. Most wealthy or famous Jewish refugees were able to find safe haven abroad. Hundreds of writers, artists, and scientists came to the United States. The vast majority of Jewish refugees, however, had no place to turn. Many countries, including the United States, had strict immigration laws. Despite outrage at events like *Kristallnacht,* most Americans remained unwilling to encourage Jewish immigration.

✔ **READING CHECK:** How did Adolf Hitler come to power in Germany?

Franco in Spain

Fascism also spread to Spain. In the 1930s Spain experienced bitter political conflicts. In 1931 a constitution that limited the power of the military and the Catholic Church went into effect. It called for reforms including universal suffrage, the nationalization of public utilities, and land for peasants. Conservative military men who felt threatened by the reforms united under the leadership of General Francisco Franco. In July 1936 the Fascist army officers tried to overthrow the government, starting the **Spanish Civil War** between Fascists and Loyalists.

After almost three years of fighting, Franco took over the government with German and Italian military aid. The Soviet Union aided the Loyalists, but President Roosevelt's fears of being drawn into a European war kept the United States from sending direct aid. Some 3,000 individual Americans, however, did join the fight against fascism. Ernest Hemingway covered the Spanish Civil War as a journalist. He expressed his support for the Loyalist cause in the powerful novel *For Whom the Bell Tolls* (1940).

These Americans were part of what was called the **Popular Front**—an international group of organizations united against fascism. Joseph Stalin had coined the term Popular Front in a 1935 speech denouncing fascism. Fearful of Adolf Hitler's military motives, Stalin declared that communism and fascism were incompatible. Although he used many of the same totalitarian tactics as the fascist leaders, Stalin's efforts encouraged many noncommunists to oppose fascism.

INTERPRETING THE VISUAL RECORD

The Spanish Civil War. These Spanish Loyalists are marching from Madrid to fight a rebel army heading toward the city. *In what ways do these troops appear to differ from a regular army?*

After the Spanish Civil War, many Loyalists remained bitter over the failure of Western nations to support their cause. In 1940 Julio Alvarez del Vayo, a wartime diplomat for the defeated Spanish republic, charged that this lack of support had cost the Loyalists the war.

66 My one desire is to show what it would have meant to the Western democracies to have had in Spain a certain ally ready to defend the liberty and dignity of Europe against all attempts at domination and oppression. . . . No, it was not Spanish democracy that failed. It was the other democracies who failed to save democratic Spain, as they will one day learn to their cost. 99

✔ READING CHECK: What caused the Spanish Civil War?

Residents of Barcelona, Spain, often blocked the streets during the Spanish Civil War.

Strategies for Success

Using Oral Histories

Oral histories—verbal accounts of historical events supplied by people who observed or participated in the events—are useful tools for learning about the past. They provide a uniquely close-up view of how specific people experienced the past. Oral histories also furnish valuable information about the opinions and feelings that people in history had about issues that affected them.

Oral histories are often taken down years or even decades after the events in question. It is therefore important to consider how the passage of time may have affected an interviewee's account of the past.

How to Use Oral Histories

1. **Become familiar with the source.** First, identify the person who was interviewed for the oral history and the general topic that he or she addressed. Then find out when the interview was conducted and, if possible, who conducted it.
2. **Study the account carefully.** Read the oral history thoroughly and carefully, taking note of any words or phrases that signal a statement of opinion.
3. **Assess the reliability of the account.** After you have read the oral history, evaluate its reliability as a piece of historical evidence. Be sure to consider how the interviewee's role in the events described, as well as the passage of time between the events and the interview, may have affected the account.
4. **Put the information to use.** Compare the oral history with other sources that address the same topic. Then use the results of your analysis and your knowledge of the historical period to draw conclusions.

Applying the Strategy

Examine the following excerpt from an oral history from the 1980s provided by Hans Massaquoi, the son of a German mother and a Liberian father who grew up in Germany during the 1930s.

66 In '32, when I started school, I was six years old. In '33, my first teacher was fired for political reasons. I don't know what her involvements were. Gradually, the old teachers were replaced with younger ones, those with Nazi orientations. Then I began to notice a change in attitude. Teachers would make snide remarks about my race. One teacher would point me out as an example of the non-Aryan race. One time, I must have been ten, a teacher took me aside and said, 'When we're finished with the Jews, you're next.' He still had some inhibitions [reluctance]. He did not make that announcement before the class. (Laughs.) It was a private thing. 99

Practicing the Strategy

Use the excerpt above to answer the following questions.
1. What is the general topic of the excerpt?
2. How do you think the passage of time between the events described in the excerpt and the interview affected Massaquoi's account?
3. What is your opinion of the excerpt as a piece of historical evidence?
4. How does the excerpt contribute to your understanding of Nazi Germany during the 1930s?

AMERICAN Letters

Ernest Hemingway and War

Before the United States entered World War I, Ernest Hemingway served with the Italian infantry. He was seriously wounded. Hemingway's novels of the 1920s, including The Sun Also Rises *(1926), reflected many people's disillusionment with war. The story focuses on a group of World War I veterans trying to forget their experiences. In 1940, after working as a correspondent during the Spanish Civil War, Hemingway published* For Whom the Bell Tolls, *which depicted Loyalists battling nobly against Fascists.*

from *The Sun Also Rises*

"What medals have you got, Mike?"

"I haven't got any medals."

"You must have some."

"I suppose I've the usual medals. But I never sent in for them. One time there was this whopping big dinner

Ernest Hemingway

. . . and the cards said medals will be worn. So naturally I had no medals, and I stopped at my tailor's . . . and I said to him: 'You've got to fix me up with some medals.' He said: 'What medals, sir?' And I said: 'Oh, any medals. Just give me a few medals.' So he said: 'What medals *have* you, sir?' And I said: 'How should I know?' . . . So he got me some medals, you know, miniature medals, and handed me the box, and I put it in my pocket and forgot it. . . .

Later on in the evening I found the box in my pocket. What's this? I said. Medals? Bloody military medals? So I cut them off their backing—you know, they put them on a strip— and gave them all around. Gave one to each girl. Form of souvenir. . . ."

"Tell the rest, " Brett said.

"Don't you think that was funny?" Mike asked. We were all laughing. "It was. I swear it was. Any rate, my tailor wrote me and wanted the medals back. Sent a man around. Kept on writing for months. Seems some chap had left them to be cleaned. . . ." Mike paused. "Rotten luck for the tailor."

from *For Whom the Bell Tolls*

Why don't you ever think of how it is to win? You've been on the defensive for so long that you can't think of that. . . . But remember this that as long as we can hold them here we keep the fascists tied up. They can't attack any other country until they finish with us and

For Whom the Bell Tolls

they can never finish with us. If the French help at all, if only they leave the frontier open and if we get planes from America they can never finish with us. Never, if we get anything at all. These people will fight forever if they're well armed.

No you must not expect victory here, not for several years maybe. This is just a holding attack. . . .

Today is only one day in all the days that will ever be. But what will happen in all the other days that ever come can depend on what you do today.

UNDERSTANDING LITERATURE

1. In the first excerpt, what does Mike's attitude about military medals reflect about his attitude toward his service in World War I?
2. What is the meaning of the last two lines in the excerpt from *For Whom the Bell Tolls*?
3. How do the two excerpts reveal Hemingway's changing views of war?

Militarists in Japan

As German aggression threatened Europe, Japanese expansion loomed in Asia. In the 1920s, the leaders of Japan's military forces had gained increasing power. These military men wanted to lessen Japan's reliance on foreign imports. They also aimed to reduce the influence of Western countries in Asia and promote Japanese expansion throughout East Asia and the Pacific.

The creation of a Japanese empire would give Japan direct control over territories that produced iron, petroleum, rubber, and timber. Worsening economic conditions in Japan strengthened the popular appeal of the militarists' position. Japan's 1931 invasion of Manchuria signaled its imperialist ambitions. In 1934 and 1935, in violation of their Washington Conference pledges, the Japanese began a rapid naval buildup. Viscount Inoue, a member of the Japanese House of Peers, explained Japan's position on a 1937 visit to London.

Uchida Ryohei was president of the Black Dragon Society, which wanted to drive the Soviet Union out of East Asia.

❝ Not only do we possess no oil supplies but this is true of very many other materials without which today a nation is helpless in wartime. To secure . . . raw materials has become a problem of greatly increased importance. The very life of Japan as a first-class power is dependent on this question. ❞

On July 7, 1937, Japanese and Chinese troops clashed near Beijing. The incident soon developed into a full-scale war. Japan occupied northern China and launched devastating bombing raids against Chinese cities. In November 1937, Japanese troops brutally assaulted and occupied the Chinese city of Nanjing. Although the League of Nations and the United States condemned Japan's actions, they failed to halt Japanese expansion.

✔ **READING CHECK:** What actions did Japan's military take during the 1930s?

HOLT RESEARCHER — Read More About It

Free Find:
Military expansion
After learning about German, Italian, and Japanese expansion on the **Holt Researcher** CD–ROM, imagine that you are an adviser to President Roosevelt. Write a memo advising where the greatest chances of war exist.

SECTION 3 REVIEW

Define and explain the significance of the following terms:
Fascist Party
Blackshirts
totalitarian state
Nazi Party
Brownshirts
anti-Semitism
Kristallnacht
Spanish Civil War
Popular Front

Identify and explain the significance of the following individuals:
Benito Mussolini
Joseph Stalin
Adolf Hitler
Francisco Franco

1. **Using Graphic Organizers** Copy the chart below. Use it to describe how aggressive world leaders came to power and what their major policies were.

Leaders	Rise to Power	Policies
Mussolini		
Stalin		
Hitler		
Franco		
Japanese Militarists		

2. **Evaluating** How did dictators in the 1930s use military power against their own people?
3. **Identifying Values** How did the policies of European dictators conflict with democratic ideals?
4. **Using Historical Imagination** Imagine that you are an American supporter of the Popular Front in the 1930s. Write a newspaper article explaining why you are fighting for the Spanish Loyalists.

Critical Thinking

5. Why did other European nations not stop Adolf Hitler's aggressive takeover of additional territory?
   Consider:
   • Hitler's claims on the territory
   • the actions of other nations at the time
   • the amount of international cooperation that existed in the 1930s

War Breaks Out

OBJECTIVES

Read to understand:
1. what the international response to fascism was
2. what the early events of World War II were
3. why tension between the United States and Germany increased
4. why Japan bombed Pearl Harbor

KEY TERMS

Axis Powers
Munich Conference
appeasement
nonaggression pact
Lend-Lease Act
Blitzkrieg
Maginot Line
Atlantic Charter

KEY PEOPLE

Winston Churchill

KEY PLACES

Manchuria
Munich
Finland
French Indochina

EYEWITNESSES TO History

❝ *Ladies and gentlemen, this is the most terrifying thing I have ever witnessed. . . .*

A humped shape is rising out of the pit. I can make out a small beam of light against a mirror. What's that? There's a jet of flame springing from that mirror, and it leaps right at the advancing men. It strikes them head on! Good Lord, they're turning into flame! ❞
—Orson Welles

Orson Welles

Although this report of an attack on the United States by an army of martians was purely fictional, many Americans believed it. On October 30, 1938, the Mercury Theatre on the Air, led by Orson Welles, performed a live radio broadcast of H. G. Wells's science fiction novel *The War of the Worlds.* To enhance the dramatic effect, they staged it as a series of news reports. Many listeners thought the broadcast was real. Throughout the nation, widespread panic ensued, with many people fleeing their homes and preparing to battle the space creatures. The panic reflected very real fears many people had that dangerous invaders were lurking on the horizon.

The Response to Fascism

The spread of fascism in Europe and Asia caused a shake-up in international diplomatic relationships. The most surprising of these realignments was the shift in U.S.-Soviet relations. The Soviets were concerned about curbing the Japanese, who had massed troops in nearby Manchuria. Hoping "to avert the Japanese danger," Soviet foreign-affairs commissar Maksim Litvinov mended diplomatic ties with the United States. In November 1933, after years of hostility between the two countries, the United States formally recognized the Soviet Union.

The fascist powers also formalized their ties. In 1936 the rest of Europe trembled when Germany and Italy formed a military alliance known as the **Axis Powers**. Japan later joined the alliance.

President Roosevelt called for European leaders to meet and resolve their conflicts peacefully. Adolf Hitler and Benito Mussolini joined British prime minister Neville Chamberlain and French premier Édouard Daladier (dah-lahd-yay) in Munich, Germany, in September 1938. The four leaders at the **Munich Conference** signed a pact giving Germany control of the Sudetenland. The European leaders had adopted a policy of **appeasement**, or giving in to demands in an attempt to avoid a larger conflict.

Many politicians underestimated Hitler's expansionist goals. They believed that Hitler sought only to remedy what he considered wrongs created by the Treaty of Versailles. Other politicians, such as

These women salute the German troops occupying the Sudetenland.

Winston Churchill of Great Britain, feared that appeasement would encourage Hitler to seize additional territory. Britain and other nations in Europe sped up their rearmament.

Congress passed a series of neutrality laws between 1935 and 1939 that reflected Americans' desire for peace. The neutrality laws prohibited the shipment of U.S. munitions to warring nations and required warring nations that bought goods from the United States to transport these goods in their own ships. The laws also forbade Americans to travel on the vessels of warring nations.

By 1937 Roosevelt had become convinced that the United States must assist in the quarantine, or isolation, of warring nations. However, most Americans did not yet support this expanded role. In December 1937, Japanese planes attacked the U.S. gunboat *Panay* and three American oil tankers on China's Chang River. Two U.S. citizens were killed, and many others were wounded. Even so, a public-opinion poll revealed that 54 percent of Americans thought the United States should reduce its role in China rather than risk becoming involved in a war.

✔ **READING CHECK:** What was the international response to fascism?

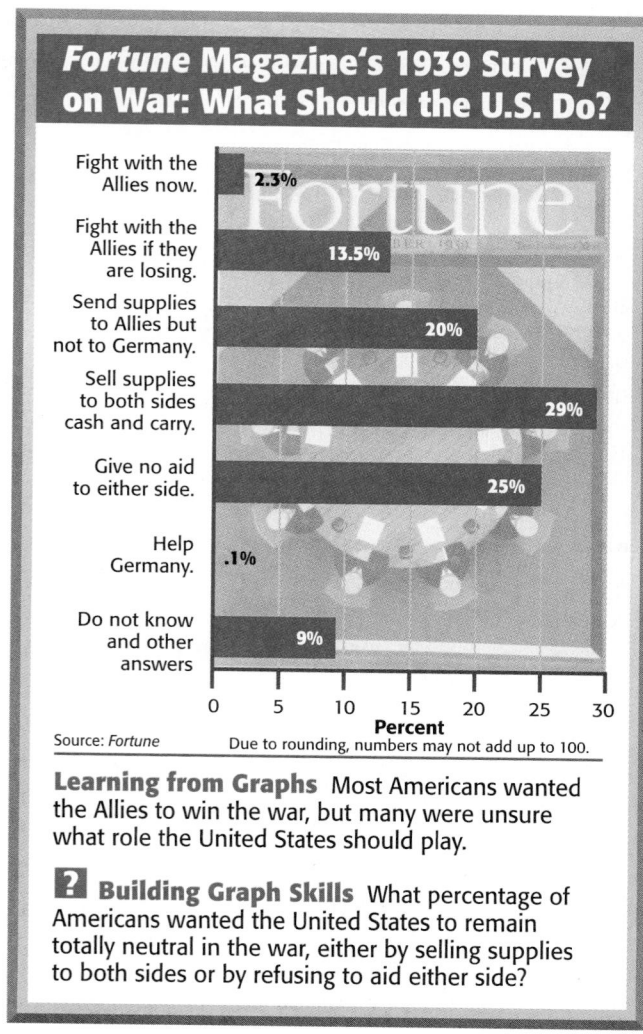

Japan's sinking of the U.S. gunboat Panay *angered many Americans but not enough to push the country into war.*

War!

American public opinion slowly changed, however, as Germany's aggression continued. In March 1939 Adolf Hitler's armies occupied all of Czechoslovakia. Hitler also proposed to annex the Polish port city of Danzig (DAHNT-sik)—modern-day Gdańsk—but the Poles refused. That same year, Italian troops invaded Albania on April 7.

Fighting begins. Recognizing the growing threat to European security, Britain and France announced that they would go to war if Germany attacked Poland. They called on the Soviet Union to join them in resisting further aggression. Instead, on August 23, 1939, Joseph Stalin—who had been trying to rally the world against fascism—signed a **nonaggression pact** with Hitler. In it Stalin and Hitler agreed not to attack each other. This shocking development came about in part because of a secret clause in the pact in which the two nations agreed to divide Poland between them.

On September 1, 1939, German bombers and armored divisions moved into Poland. Two days later, Britain and France declared war on Germany. World War II had begun. Meanwhile, Soviet troops invaded Poland from the east, occupied Estonia, Latvia, and Lithuania, and demanded the right to establish military bases in Finland. When Finland refused, the Soviet Union attacked the small nation and soon annexed part of its territory.

Fortune Magazine's 1939 Survey on War: What Should the U.S. Do?

Response	Percent
Fight with the Allies now.	2.3%
Fight with the Allies if they are losing.	13.5%
Send supplies to Allies but not to Germany.	20%
Sell supplies to both sides cash and carry.	29%
Give no aid to either side.	25%
Help Germany.	.1%
Do not know and other answers	9%

Source: *Fortune*   Due to rounding, numbers may not add up to 100.

Learning from Graphs Most Americans wanted the Allies to win the war, but many were unsure what role the United States should play.

2 **Building Graph Skills** What percentage of Americans wanted the United States to remain totally neutral in the war, either by selling supplies to both sides or by refusing to aid either side?

German and Italian Expansion, 1935–1941

Learning from Maps Hitler's and Mussolini's aggressions brought war to most of Europe for the second time in the 1900s.

? PLACE Why was Poland a likely target for a German attack?

0   250   500 Miles
0   250   500 Kilometers
Azimuthal Equal-Area Projection

Legend:
- Germany, 1929
- German expansion, 1935–1939
- Italy and possessions, 1929
- Italian expansion, 1935–1939
- Vichy France
- Under Axis control by December 1941
- Under Allied control by December 1941
- Area of the Battle of Britain
- Neutral countries
- Farthest Russian advance, 1940

The U.S. response. President Roosevelt took steps to aid the European countries under siege. Some three weeks after the German invasion of Poland, the president urged Congress to amend the neutrality act that barred the export of military supplies. After a six-week debate, Congress agreed on a compromise. The new law allowed any nation to buy military supplies from the United States but required that the goods be shipped on foreign vessels.

The fighting in Europe was a major issue in the 1940 presidential election. Both candidates—Roosevelt, who sought re-election to a third term, and Republican Wendell Willkie—promised to keep the United States out of the conflict. In a radio talk on September 3, 1939, Roosevelt pledged, "As long as it remains in my power to prevent, there will be no blackout of peace in the United States."

Roosevelt won his bid for an unprecedented third term. In spite of his public promises, however, he viewed U.S. military involvement in Europe as unavoidable.

Lend-Lease. By the end of 1940 a variety of supplies flowed from the United States to Britain. The British, however, had little cash to pay for needed war materials. Roosevelt proposed that the United States lend or lease arms and other supplies to the Allies. Congress passed the **Lend-Lease Act** in March 1941. It appropriated $7 billion for ships, planes, tanks, and other supplies to non-Axis countries.

While Hitler carried on his **Blitzkrieg** (BLITS-kreeg), or "lightning war," against Poland, the French mobilized. In May 1940, German troops began an attack around the **Maginot Line**, a line of defenses along the French border with Germany. The Germans occupied Belgium, Denmark, northern France, Luxembourg, the Netherlands, and Norway. Hundreds of thousands of British, French and Belgian troops were trapped along the French coast near the town of Dunkirk. Only an evacuation across the English Channel to Britain prevented their capture.

Germany established a puppet government in southern France in the town of Vichy (VI-shee). A secret French organization known as the Resistance continued to oppose the Germans. In London, French general Charles de Gaulle headed a committee called Free France that organized opposition against the Germans.

Citizens of Warsaw, Poland, flee before the destructive power of the German Blitzkrieg as fire consumes a working-class neighborhood.

BIOGRAPHY

Winston Churchill

A new British leader. With the fall of France, Britain stood alone against the Axis Powers. On May 10, 1940, Winston Churchill became prime minister. Born in 1874, Churchill attended the Royal Military College and then served in the British army for several years. Churchill began his political career in 1900 as a member of Parliament. Ten years later, he was appointed to lead the British navy. After receiving widespread criticism for Britain's failure in a World War I campaign, Churchill resigned his position and volunteered to fight on the front lines.

After the war Churchill resumed his rise in British politics. When many other British leaders were pushing for appeasement with Hitler, Churchill warned of the dangers he posed. Once appointed prime minister, Churchill rallied the British.

> 66 Hitler knows that he will have to break us in this island or lose the war. . . . Let us therefore brace ourselves to our duties, and so bear ourselves that, if the British Empire and its Commonwealth last for a thousand years, men will still say, 'This was their finest hour.' 99

On June 10, 1940, Italy declared war on France and Britain. In August, Hitler unleashed his bombers against Britain. Although outnumbered, the British Royal Air Force (RAF) flew day and night to combat the German attack.

✔ **READING CHECK:** What were the early events of World War II?

Tensions Mount in the Atlantic

As German attacks increased, so did U.S. aid to the Allies. By the spring of 1941, German submarines were turning the North Atlantic into a graveyard of ships. In

HOLT RESEARCHER

Read More About It

Free Find:
Winston Churchill
After reading about Winston Churchill on the **Holt Researcher** CD–ROM, create a sketch of a memorial that will honor Churchill's inspiring leadership during World War II.

Convoys of ships bringing supplies to the Allies were escorted by U.S. warships to protect against attack by German submarines.

September President Roosevelt issued "shoot-on-sight" orders to U.S. warships operating in the North Atlantic.

In August 1941, with the United States moving rapidly toward undeclared war with Germany, Roosevelt and Winston Churchill met secretly off the coast of Newfoundland. The two leaders agreed to follow a series of principles. Known as the **Atlantic Charter**, the agreement pledged that the United States and Britain would not pursue territorial expansion. The two countries affirmed their belief that every nation has the right to choose its own form of government. They also called for freedom of international trade and equal access for all countries to raw materials. Once the war was over, the charter declared, aggressor states should be disarmed, and all nations should work together to rid the world of fear and poverty.

Concern over Adolf Hitler's growing power increased when German troops invaded the Soviet Union in June 1941. Caught off guard by this violation of the German-Soviet nonaggression pact, Soviet troops fared badly in the initial fighting. By the fall of 1941, German troops had advanced deep into Soviet territory.

✔ **READING CHECK:** Why did tensions increase between the United States and Germany?

Japanese Expansion, 1931–1941

Learning from Maps Japan's military leaders believed that conquering neighboring lands would solve the country's economic problems.

❓ **PLACE** What important Chinese cities had Japan captured by 1938?

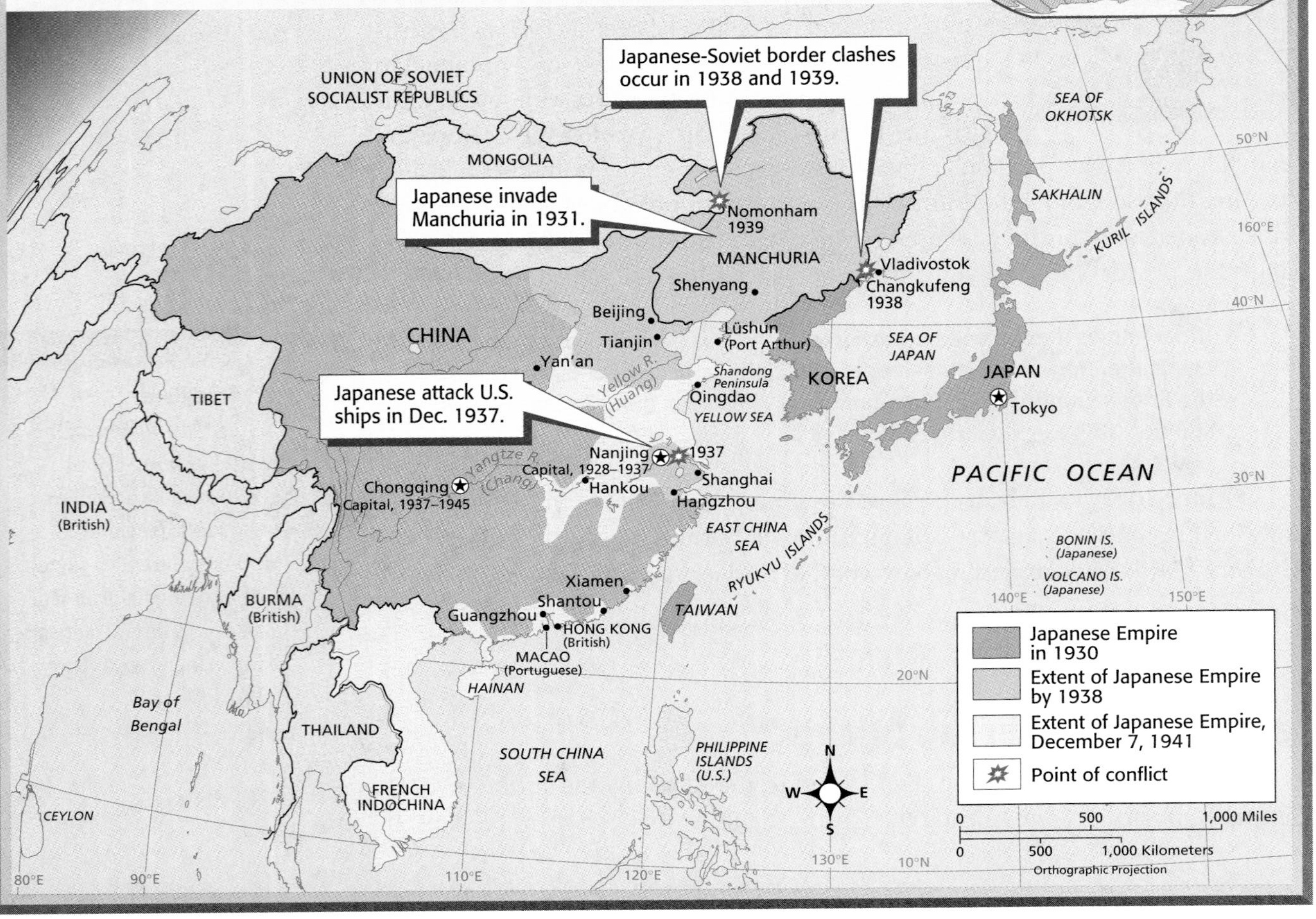

Japanese-Soviet border clashes occur in 1938 and 1939.

Japanese invade Manchuria in 1931.

Japanese attack U.S. ships in Dec. 1937.

UNION OF SOVIET SOCIALIST REPUBLICS

MONGOLIA

MANCHURIA

Nomonham 1939

Vladivostok

Changkufeng 1938

Shenyang

SEA OF OKHOTSK

SAKHALIN

KURIL ISLANDS

50°N

160°E

40°N

CHINA

Beijing

Tianjin

Lüshun (Port Arthur)

Yan'an

Yellow R. (Huang)

Shandong Peninsula

Qingdao

YELLOW SEA

KOREA

SEA OF JAPAN

JAPAN

Tokyo

TIBET

Nanjing 1937
Capital, 1928–1937

Shanghai

Hankou

Hangzhou

Yangtze R. (Chang)

Chongqing
Capital, 1937–1945

EAST CHINA SEA

RYUKYU ISLANDS

PACIFIC OCEAN

30°N

BONIN IS. (Japanese)

VOLCANO IS. (Japanese)

INDIA (British)

BURMA (British)

Xiamen

Shantou

Guangzhou

HONG KONG (British)

MACAO (Portuguese)

HAINAN

TAIWAN

140°E

150°E

Bay of Bengal

THAILAND

SOUTH CHINA SEA

PHILIPPINE ISLANDS (U.S.)

20°N

CEYLON

FRENCH INDOCHINA

N
W   E
S

130°E

10°N

Japanese Empire in 1930

Extent of Japanese Empire by 1938

Extent of Japanese Empire, December 7, 1941

Point of conflict

0   500   1,000 Miles

0   500   1,000 Kilometers

Orthographic Projection

80°E

90°E

110°E

120°E

Japan Attacks

As war raged in Europe, Japan continued its expansion in Asia. In July 1941, Japanese troops occupied French Indochina. President Roosevelt immediately froze all Japanese assets in the United States. He also approved an embargo on shipments of gasoline, machine tools, scrap iron, and steel to Japan. Japan responded by freezing all American assets in areas under its control.

As U.S. resistance to Japanese aggression grew stronger, Japan's military leaders secretly planned an attack on the United States. Even as the plan went forward, however, a Japanese peace mission visited Washington, D.C. On November 20, 1941, this mission demanded that the United States unfreeze Japanese assets, supply Japan's gasoline needs, and cease all aid to China. By this time the United States had succeeded in breaking the secret code used to send messages between Tokyo and the Japanese embassy in Washington. The Americans knew that the Japanese planned a strike, but they did not know where.

Shortly before 8:00 A.M. on December 7, 1941, the Japanese launched their attack on the U.S. naval base at Pearl Harbor in the Hawaiian Islands. The core of the U.S. Pacific Fleet was anchored there, and more than 100 U.S. planes lined nearby airfields. Almost 20 U.S. warships and nearly 200 aircraft were destroyed. Among some 2,400 Americans killed were 1,103 sailors entombed on the USS *Arizona* when the battleship sank.

The bombing shocked and united Americans. The next day, a somber President Roosevelt described December 7, 1941, as "a date which will live in infamy." He called on Congress to pass a declaration of war against Japan. Congress quickly approved the call for war.

✔ **READING CHECK:** Why did Japan bomb Pearl Harbor?

THE GRANGER COLLECTION, NEW YORK

INTERPRETING THE VISUAL RECORD
Pearl Harbor. The USS *Shaw* explodes after Japanese planes bombed Pearl Harbor. *What does this image tell you about the damage done by the Japanese attack?*

SECTION REVIEW

Define and explain the significance of the following terms:

Axis Powers	Lend-Lease Act
Munich Conference	Blitzkrieg
appeasement	Maginot Line
nonaggression pact	Atlantic Charter

Identify and explain the significance of the following individual:
Winston Churchill

Locate and explain the importance of the following places:
Manchuria
Munich
Finland
French Indochina

1. **Using Graphic Organizers** Copy the chart below. Use it to list the early events of World War II.

1. The Munich Conference
2.
3.
4.
5.
6. The United States enters the war.

2. **Comparing and Contrasting** How did German aggression differ from Japanese aggression in the 1930s?

3. **Hypothesizing** How might events in Europe have been different if European leaders had not decided to pursue an appeasement policy toward Hitler?

4. **Recognizing Point of View** Why did Japanese leaders respond to conflicts with the United States by bombing Pearl Harbor?

Critical Thinking

5. Should the United States have entered the war when Britain did?
   Consider:
   • U.S. foreign policy at the start of the war
   • the increased tensions with Germany
   • U.S. concerns in the Atlantic

CHAPTER 26

Review

Creating a Time Line

Copy the time line below onto a sheet of paper. Complete the time line by filling in the events and dates from the chapter that you think were most significant. Pick three events and explain why you think they were significant.

| 1921 | 1931 | 1941 |

Writing a Summary

Using the Reading Checks as a guide, write an overview of the events in the chapter.

Identifying People and Ideas

Identify the following terms or individuals and explain their significance.

1. isolationism
2. Charles Evans Hughes
3. Augusto César Sandino
4. nationalize
5. Benito Mussolini
6. Adolf Hitler
7. *Kristallnacht*
8. appeasement
9. nonaggression pact
10. Winston Churchill

Understanding Main Ideas

SECTION 1
1. What factors encouraged the United States to follow a foreign policy of isolationism after World War I?

SECTION 2
2. What economic and political role did the United States play in Latin America?
3. Why did Mexican president Lázaro Cárdenas nationalize his country's oil fields in 1938?

SECTION 3
4. How did dictators come to power in Europe in the 1930s?
5. What aggressive actions did Japan take during the 1930s?

SECTION 4
6. Why did some European leaders favor a policy of appeasement toward Adolf Hitler? Why did others oppose it?

Reviewing Themes

1. **Global Relations** In what ways did countries promote world peace after World War I?
2. **Economic Development** How did economic problems contribute to political unrest after World War I?
3. **Democratic Values** How did the fascist dictatorships in Europe restrict civil liberties?

Thinking Critically

1. **Hypothesizing** Why do you think many people supported Benito Mussolini and Adolf Hitler?
2. **Evaluating** Why did Japan's militarists want to create an empire in East Asia and the Pacific?
3. **Synthesizing** How did the U.S. policy of neutrality change between 1935 and 1941?
4. **Recognizing Point of View** Why did some Germans feel that they were justified in reclaiming territory they had lost in the Treaty of Versailles?
5. **Assessing Consequences** What was the effect of appeasing Adolf Hitler at the Munich Conference?

Writing About History

Writing to Describe
Imagine that you are a Loyalist who fought during the Spanish Civil War. Write a letter to an American friend describing the events during that period. Use the outline at right to organize your thoughts.

> I. Franco's Rise
> II. Loyalist Views
> III. The Spanish Civil War
>   A. Foreign Aid
>   1. Soviet Union
>   2. United States
>   B. Outcome
> IV. Views of the War

Strategies for Success Review the **Strategies for Success** on *Using Oral Histories.* Then examine the following excerpt from an interview with Thomas Page, a student at Harvard Law School when global tensions increased in 1941.

> 66 A guy named Tom Harris and his wife . . . would observe what people were eating, reading, and the way of advertisements to determine what people really were doing. . . . And I looked at the *New York Times Sunday Magazine.* . . . It was filled with semi-warlike copy and ads. And I thought, my God, this is really an illustration of this guy Harris's theory of mass observation—the country has almost accepted the inevitability of some kind of military action and is all geared up for it mentally. 99

How does the excerpt contribute to your understanding of American attitudes in 1941?

Linking History and Geography

Italy invaded Ethiopia in the 1930s. Study the map below. How would control of Ethiopia have helped Italy in its conflict with the Allied Powers?

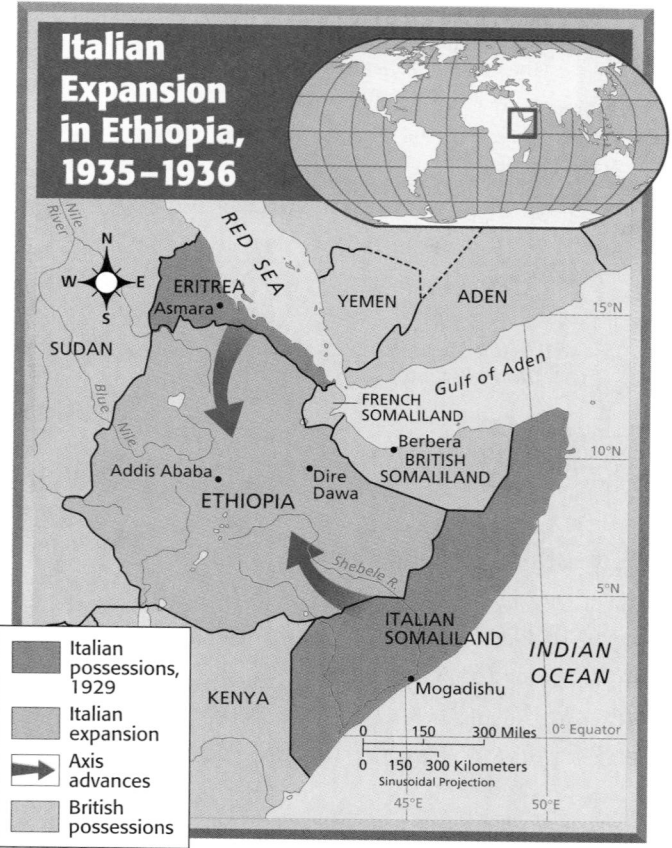

Italian Expansion in Ethiopia, 1935–1936

Legend:
- Italian possessions, 1929
- Italian expansion
- Axis advances
- British possessions

internet connect

TOPIC: The Spanish Civil War
GO TO: go.hrw.com
KEYWORD: SD1 Front

Accessing the Internet through the HRW Web site, research the Spanish Civil War. Then write a series of diary entries from one of the following perspectives: (a) You are Pablo Picasso. Explain why you painted *Guernica.* (b) You are an artist making propaganda posters for the Popular Front. (c) You are a member of the Abraham Lincoln Brigade. Explain why you left America to fight in Spain.

BUILDING YOUR PORTFOLIO

Complete one or all of the following projects independently or cooperatively.

1 Global Relations
Imagine that you are a journalist assigned to evaluate the new political trends of the 1930s. **Create a chart** that compares the similarities and differences among fascist dictators around the world.

2 Democratic Values
Imagine that you are a diplomat at the 1938 Munich Conference. **Write a speech** aimed at convincing the Allies to abandon their policy of appeasement toward Germany's Adolf Hitler. Your speech should include examples of how Hitler's policies threaten democracy.

THE GRANGER COLLECTION, NEW YORK

3 Economic Development
Imagine that you are an American business leader considering investing in a Latin American country in the 1930s. **Create a business plan** that outlines the advantages and disadvantages of such investment for both your company and the Latin American country.

1941–1945

Americans in World War II

A Glenn Miller album cover

Poster advertising Citizen Kane

1941
The Arts
Orson Welles's film *Citizen Kane,* inspired by the life of William Randolph Hearst, is released.

1941
Science and Technology
Physicists Glenn Seaborg and Edwin McMillan isolate the element plutonium.

1941
World Events
Japanese planes bomb Pearl Harbor.

A zinc-coated penny

1942
Daily Life
The U.S. Mint begins issuing pennies made of zinc-coated steel to conserve copper for weapons production.

1942
The Arts
Glenn Miller receives the first gold record for having sold more than 1 million copies of his hit song "Chattanooga Choo Choo."

1941

1942

A 1942 Packard

1942
Business and Finance
On February 10 the last automobile to be produced in the United States until the end of the war rolls off the Ford assembly line.

1942
World Events
U.S. forces in the Philippines surrender after an extended siege.

U.S. prisoners in the Philippines

Before You Read

Build on What You Know

The economic distress of the Great Depression contributed to the rise of dictatorships in some nations. Military aggression by Germany, Italy, and Japan plunged the world into war. In December 1941 the Japanese bombed Pearl Harbor, bringing the United States into World War II. In this chapter you will learn that the United States and the Allies battled the Axis Powers on land and at sea in Europe, North Africa, and Asia. By August 1945 the Allies had won a difficult war.

The Chicago subway

Diego Rivera's mural La Gran Tenochtitlán

1943
Science and Technology
Chicago's first subway opens.

1943
Politics
President Roosevelt, British prime minister Winston Churchill, and Soviet premier Joseph Stalin meet at the Tehran Conference.

1944
World Events
On the morning of June 6, some 176,000 Allied troops storm the beaches of Normandy, France.

1944
Business and Finance
The International Bank for Reconstruction, or World Bank, is established in July.

1945
The Arts
Mexican artist Diego Rivera completes his mural *La Gran Tenochtitlán* in Mexico City's National Palace.

1945
World Events
The United States drops atomic bombs on Hiroshima and Nagasaki.

1943   **1944**   **1945**

1943
The Arts
The musical *Oklahoma!* opens.

1943
Daily Life
The United States begins rationing shoes, allowing each person three pairs per year.

1943
World Events
Italy surrenders to the Allies, but German forces occupy the country to prevent the Allies from doing so.

1944
World Events
Allied forces liberate Paris, France.

1945
Daily Life
In November, rationing of all food items except sugar ends in the United States.

Allied forces arrive in Paris.

World War II ration stamps

Think About Themes

Themes Journal

Decide whether you **agree** *or* **disagree** *with the following statements. Note why in your journal.*

Global Relations Allied nations must pool their economic and military resources in order to win a global war.

Constitutional Heritage A government should be allowed to restrict the rights of citizens during a national emergency.

Technology and Society A government should consider more than just military concerns when developing new defensive technology.

SECTION 1 — Early Difficulties

OBJECTIVES

Read to understand:

1. what the strengths and weaknesses of the Allied Powers and Axis Powers were in 1941
2. what steps the United States took to prepare for war
3. where the Japanese military attacked after Pearl Harbor
4. what the early turning points of the war in the Pacific were
5. what the major battles in Europe and North Africa in 1942 were

KEY TERMS

War Production Board
Office of War Mobilization
Selective Training and Service Act
Bataan Death March
Battle of the Coral Sea
Battle of Midway

KEY PEOPLE

Douglas MacArthur
Chester Nimitz
Erwin Rommel
Bernard Montgomery

This medal was made to commemorate the bombing of Pearl Harbor.

EYEWITNESSES TO History

❝ *I was sixteen years old, employed . . . at Pearl Harbor Navy Yard. On December 7, 1941, oh, around 8:00 A.M., my grandmother awoke me. She informed me that the Japanese were bombing Pearl Harbor. . . . I was asked . . . to go into the water and get sailors out that had been blown off the ships. Some were unconscious, some were dead. I brought out I don't know how many bodies. . . . I tried to get into the military, but they refused. . . . Finally, I wrote a letter to President Roosevelt. I told him I was angry at the Japanese bombing and had lost some friends. He okayed that I be accepted.* ❞

—U.S. sailor

The USS Arizona *memorial*

Like this young sailor, millions of Americans rushed to join the fight after Pearl Harbor. Neutrality was quickly forgotten. Their nation had been attacked. Friends, children, and parents had been killed. Americans were determined to bring an end to the madness of war.

Strengths and Weaknesses

When the United States entered World War II, the Axis Powers had two big advantages. First, Germany and Japan had already secured firm control of the areas they had invaded. As a result, the United States and the Allies faced a long, drawn-out fight on several fronts. Second, Germany and Japan were better prepared for war. In the 1930s both nations had rearmed and built airfields, barracks, and military training centers. By the mid-1930s the Nazis had converted most of the German economy to military production, as had Japan's military-led government.

The Allies did have some advantages, however. The Axis forces were spread over an enormous area stretching from the coast of France to deep into the Soviet Union and from Norway to North Africa. In the Pacific, Japan had occupied a similarly large area. The Germans had not defeated the British or the Soviets and therefore had to maintain troops on two active fronts. The Allies' hopes rested on two factors—the enormous size of the Soviet Union's military and the tremendous production capacity of the United States.

Axis leaders hoped that they could win the conflict before these two factors could combine and overwhelm their smaller but better-prepared forces. The Allies sought to continue to resist long enough to allow the United States to gather its strength.

✔ **READING CHECK:** What were the strengths and weaknesses of the Allied Powers and Axis Powers when the United States entered the war?

Mobilizing for War

After the bombing of Pearl Harbor the United States switched from a peacetime to a wartime economy. Government and private industry cooperated to increase production, and union leaders agreed not to strike during the war.

A production boom.

In 1940 government arsenals employed about 22,000 workers who produced ammunition, cannon shells, and rifles. Three years later some 486,000 workers were working in the arsenals. By war's end the United States had built some 300,000 aircraft. Car production was suspended for the duration of the war, and between 1940 and 1945, American factories produced huge numbers of planes, tanks, jeeps, and guns. American shipyards built 88,000 landing craft, 215 submarines, 147 aircraft carriers, 952 other warships, and 5,200 merchant ships.

This massive increase in production created an economic boom that ended the Great Depression. Unemployment dropped from 14.6 percent in 1940 to 1.2 percent in 1944. Earnings nearly doubled between 1939 and 1945. People who had stood in breadlines a decade earlier now brought home fat paychecks. The lure of high-paying jobs in war industries led to vast population shifts. More than 4 million workers left their homes to find work in factories in other states.

Sharecroppers, tenant farmers, and others struggling to make a living on farms flocked to the centers of wartime production. Many went to shipyards on the Gulf and Pacific coasts and factories in the Midwest and West. The West experienced particularly strong growth during the war.

American farms also achieved marvels of productivity. During the war years, farmers produced enough food to supply both the American people and many of the Allied Powers overseas. Although many agricultural workers went off to fight in the war or to work in wartime factories, farm production increased. As part of its lend-lease aid, the United States exported 10 percent of the food it produced, mostly to Great Britain and the Soviet Union.

Government expansion.

Mobilizing for war required a greatly expanded federal government. Between 1940 and 1945 the number of federal employees nearly tripled. To fight the Axis Powers, the United States needed to channel all of its resources into producing the maximum amount of military goods. In January 1942 President Roosevelt created the **War Production Board** (WPB) to increase military production. The WPB directed the conversion of existing factories to wartime production and

INTERPRETING THE VISUAL RECORD

Preparing for war. This assembly line at North American Aviation's Inglewood, California, plant turned out B-25 bombers. *How does this image point to a U.S. advantage in the war?*

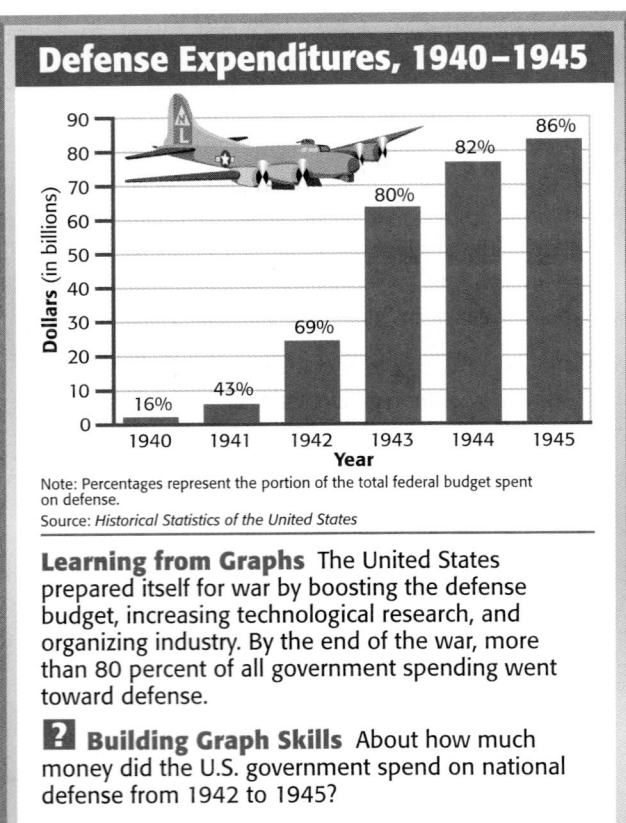

Defense Expenditures, 1940–1945

Note: Percentages represent the portion of the total federal budget spent on defense.
Source: *Historical Statistics of the United States*

Learning from Graphs The United States prepared itself for war by boosting the defense budget, increasing technological research, and organizing industry. By the end of the war, more than 80 percent of all government spending went toward defense.

? Building Graph Skills About how much money did the U.S. government spend on national defense from 1942 to 1945?

supervised the building of new plants. It assigned raw materials to industry, including scrap iron from factories and recyclable aluminum, paper, tin, and other items from homes. Created on May 27, 1943, the **Office of War Mobilization** (OWM) coordinated all government agencies involved in the war effort. OWM director James F. Byrnes wielded such power that he was often called the assistant president.

The OWM also coordinated the production and distribution of consumer goods. For instance, it diverted nylon to use for making parachutes and even regulated clothing styles in order to save fabric. Cuffs on men's trousers and pleats in women's skirts were canceled for the duration of the war. Martha Wood of Raleigh, North Carolina, remembers that "rationing was hard to live with, particularly silk stockings. . . . If you had a run in your stocking, you took a needle and thread and worked it back up, because there was no chance of getting any [more]."

Directing the economy. The government also expanded its control over the economy. In order to pay for the war, the government increased by about nine times the number of Americans who had to pay income tax. The new taxes affected most middle- and lower-income groups for the first time. The rest of the money came from borrowing, mainly through war bonds.

The sale of war bonds also helped the government deal with another major concern—keeping inflation down. When incomes remain high but few consumer items are available for people to buy, prices go up and inflation results. Selling war bonds offered a way to channel excess income, thus keeping inflation down.

The government took other anti-inflationary steps as well. One was rationing, which reduced consumer demand by limiting how much people could buy. Rationed items included gasoline, tires, coffee, sugar, meat, butter, and canned goods. The government also tried to keep wages and prices down by freezing wages. After the cost of living rose, the government allowed wages to rise by 15 percent.

Registration certificates like this one proved that a man had made himself available to be drafted.

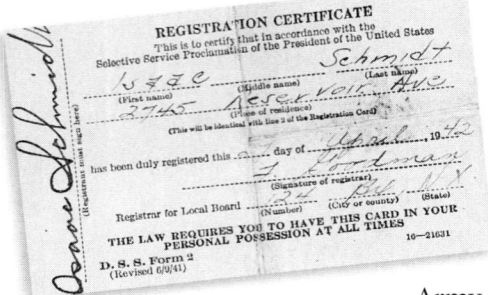

Raising an army. Along with increased production and expanded government controls, gearing up to fight a war meant recruiting soldiers. In the summer of 1940 the United States called the National Guard to active duty and passed the **Selective Training and Service Act**. This act provided for the first peacetime draft in U.S. history. The law required all men between ages 21 and 35 (later 18 to 45) to register. Local draft boards determined fitness and deferred men for family, religious, or health reasons. At the time of the draft there were just 269,023 soldiers in the U.S. Army, 160,997 in the navy, and 28,345 in the marines. They made up less than 5 percent of the 12 million trained soldiers the military needed to fight the war.

Of the more than 12 million Americans who served during World War II, more than three fourths were draftees and the rest volunteers, including more than 300,000 women. Women enrolled in the Women's Auxiliary Army Corps (WAAC),

Women Airforce Service Pilots (WASPs), and auxiliary branches of the navy, coast guard, and marines. They worked as nurses, did office work, drove vehicles, and ferried planes in order to free men for active duty. Eunice Hatchitt was a nurse who served in the Philippines at Bataan. She described the terrible conditions and heavy casualties.

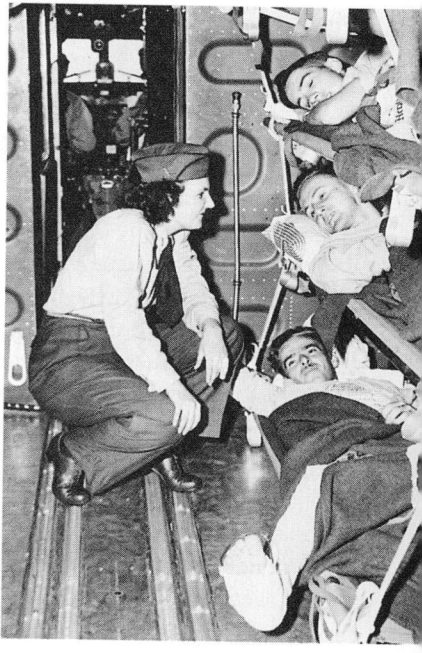

> 66 **Days and nights were an endless nightmare, until it seemed we couldn't stand it any longer. Patients came in by the hundreds, and the doctors and nurses worked continuously under the tents amid the flies and heat and dust. We had from eight to nine hundred victims a day.** 99

✔ **READING CHECK:** How did the United States prepare to fight in World War II?

War in the Pacific

Japan's assault on Pearl Harbor was just one part of a giant offensive throughout the Pacific region. On December 8, 1941, Japanese planes bombed Clark Air Force Base in the Philippines. Over the following two weeks the Japanese attacked Burma, Borneo, the Netherlands East Indies, Wake Island, and Hong Kong.

On February 27, 1942, in what become known as the Battle of the Java Sea, the Japanese navy crushed a fleet of Australian, British, Dutch, and U.S. warships that had been trying to block a Japanese invasion of Java. The Japanese invaded Java the next day and soon after began their conquest of New Guinea.

Nurses worked under battlefield conditions to save the lives of wounded soldiers.

BIOGRAPHY
Douglas MacArthur

Defending the Philippines were more than 30,000 U.S. and 110,000 Filipino troops under the overall command of General Douglas MacArthur. MacArthur was born in 1880, the son of a distinguished general, Arthur MacArthur. He graduated from the U.S. Military Academy at West Point in 1903 with one of the finest academic records in the school's history. MacArthur then served in the Philippines and was later wounded twice in World War I. From 1919 to 1922 he was superintendent of West Point. In 1937 he retired from the U.S. Army and served as a military adviser in the Philippines for several years. President Roosevelt recalled MacArthur to active duty in the summer of 1941. He eventually was given command of all U.S. Army units in the Pacific.

When Japanese bombers attacked Clark Air Force Base they found the U.S. aircraft sitting on the runway. One Japanese pilot recalled, "They squatted there like sitting ducks." The planes that were needed to provide air support for the U.S. fleet in the Philippines were destroyed. Therefore the fleet had to withdraw out of range of the Japanese planes based in Taiwan. With no air or naval opposition, Japanese forces advanced toward Manila. MacArthur recognized that his outnumbered forces would be unable to stop the Japanese advance. He ordered his troops to evacuate the city and retreat to the Bataan Peninsula.

The rapid pace of the evacuation prevented U.S. forces from stockpiling enough supplies, particularly food. The fighting soon settled into a war of attrition. The Japanese kept the pressure on the starving defenders, who were outnumbered, outgunned, and inexperienced. With the situation looking hopeless, MacArthur was ordered to Australia. When he arrived there in March he vowed, "I shall return."

Read More About It

Free Find:
Douglas MacArthur
After reading about Douglas MacArthur on the **Holt Researcher** CD–ROM, write a short speech to be given at the dedication of a memorial to MacArthur.

The Navajo Code Talkers

teen Life

Young American Indians served in several branches of the U.S. armed forces during World War II. Their languages allowed them to play a unique role in the Signal Corps, the communication units responsible for coding and sending classified military information. In March 1942 the Marine Signal Corps organized a unit composed entirely of Navajo, some of whom were teenagers. They believed that because the Navajo language was unfamiliar to the Japanese it would provide an unbreakable code.

The new unit devised and memorized a special Navajo dictionary containing 413 military terms. For example, the Navajo word for "chicken hawk" meant dive-bomber in the code. "Hummingbird" meant fighter plane. "Iron fish" meant submarine. The Navajo Code Talkers first went into action in the fall of 1942 in the Pacific. U.S. field commanders soon reported that the Navajo methods reduced the time needed for decoding and encoding messages by half. As radio operators who tracked Japanese movements, the code talkers often had to work in dangerous conditions behind enemy lines.

By August 1943 nearly 200 Navajo were participating in the Code Talker program, and by the war's end more than 400 had served in the Marine Signal Corps. Their codes completely baffled the Japanese and were never broken.

Navajo Code Talkers Henry Bake and George Kirk operate a radio behind enemy lines in the Solomon Islands.

After fighting against overwhelming odds, the hungry, sick, and exhausted survivors who remained on Bataan surrendered in April 1942. Japanese soldiers forced the more than 70,000 survivors to march through the jungle on their way to prison camp. More than 10,000 died on what came to be called the **Bataan Death March**. The Japanese treated U.S. and Filipino soldiers brutally. Some prisoners were prevented from drinking water. Others were beaten or shot. Conditions did not improve when they reached the prison camps. Water was in short supply, and what there was quickly became contaminated. Disease spread quickly through the sick and poorly fed prisoners.

✔ **READING CHECK:** Where did the Japanese military strike after the attack on Pearl Harbor?

Halting the Japanese Advance

By the summer of 1942 the Japanese were ready to strike west at India, south at Australia, and east through Hawaii at the Pacific coast of the United States. The commander of the U.S. Pacific Fleet, Admiral Chester Nimitz, did not consider the attack on Pearl Harbor a complete disaster. "It was God's mercy that our fleet was in Pearl Harbor on 7 December 1941," Nimitz said. Much of the sunken battle fleet was salvageable because the ships sat in the shallow waters of the harbor. Furthermore, none of the aircraft carriers had been in port at the time of the attack. The U.S. fleet recovered quickly and was soon fighting again.

The Battle of the Coral Sea. Nimitz was an aggressive commander who preferred to attack, thereby pressuring his opponents into making mistakes. On May 7, 1942, a Japanese force on its way to attack Port Moresby, New Guinea, seized Tulagi (too-LAH-gee) Island, one of the Solomon Islands. Before the Japanese could reach New Guinea, however, a joint British-U.S. naval force intercepted them. Planes from U.S. aircraft carriers damaged one Japanese carrier and destroyed another and several aircraft. The **Battle of the Coral Sea** was an important Allied victory. Although the Allies lost a carrier, the battle stopped the Japanese advance on Australia.

The Battle of Midway. The second major naval battle in the Pacific, the **Battle of Midway**, took place early in June 1942. Seeking to crush the U.S. Pacific Fleet, Japan launched a two-pronged attack. One unit seized two of the Aleutian Islands, near Alaska. They hoped to lure part of the U.S. fleet away from Hawaii. Meanwhile the Japanese carried out their main attack against Midway, two small islands northwest of Hawaii. However, because U.S. experts had broken the Japanese fleet code, the United States had advance warning of the Japanese strategy. Nimitz later recalled, "Had we lacked early information of the Japanese movements, . . . the Battle of Midway would have ended differently." Instead, Nimitz was able to assemble U.S. aircraft carriers and destroyers north of Midway to ambush the Japanese attack.

Americans and Japanese clashed June 3–6. U.S. fighters, dive-bombers, and torpedo planes sank four Japanese aircraft carriers and shot down many enemy planes. The U.S. victory proved crucial. Japan lost not only ships and planes but also a number of skilled pilots.

Guadalcanal. After the Battle of Midway, the United States successfully launched its first offensive. In August 1942, American marines waded ashore at Guadalcanal, in the Solomon Islands. For six desperate months, with heavy casualties, they clung to a toehold around the airport.

Major General Alexander A. Vandegrift, commander of the U.S. Marines on Guadalcanal, described the ferocious fighting. "I have never heard or read of this kind of fighting. These people [the Japanese] refuse to surrender. The wounded will wait till men come up to examine them, and blow themselves and the other fellow to death with a hand grenade."

In November the Japanese sent a huge fleet to the Solomons. They hoped to recapture Guadalcanal, but the U.S. fleet defeated the Japanese in a bloody battle. The tide of battle in the Pacific had finally turned in the Allies' favor.

✔ **READING CHECK:** What were the early turning points in the war in the Pacific?

Midway. The U.S. victory in the Battle of Midway crippled the Japanese navy. *From the painting, what can you determine about the type of fighting that took place during the Battle of Midway?*

Early Fighting in Europe and the Mediterranean

By the time of the attack on Pearl Harbor, the Axis Powers controlled much of Europe and the lands around the Mediterranean. Bulgaria, Hungary, and Romania had joined the Axis Powers. Yugoslavia and Greece had been occupied, and southern Europe was firmly under Axis control. Throughout most of 1942 the Axis Powers racked up one victory after another.

The Germans and their allies scored victories on many different fronts. German submarines, or U-boats, patrolled the Atlantic Ocean. They sank Allied military and merchant ships and nearly cut off British supply lines. In the first half of 1942, German U-boats sank more than 500 ships off the U.S. East Coast.

North Africa. Italian forces had launched an invasion of North Africa in 1940. When British troops later began to inflict heavy damage on the Italians, Adolf Hitler sent in the German Afrika Korps under commander Erwin Rommel. Known as the Desert Fox, Rommel had advanced as far as El Alamein, Egypt, by July 1942. His troops were ready to take the Suez Canal and the oil fields of the Middle East.

Rommel's skill as a military leader led even Winston Churchill to later admit that "[he was] a great general." However, Rommel suffered from shortages of men and supplies. The British, led by General Bernard Montgomery, turned this shortage to their advantage. In the fall of 1942 Montgomery pushed Rommel's troops steadily westward out of Egypt and into Libya. The British victory in the Battle of El Alamein helped turn the corner for the Allies in North Africa.

Desert warfare. Effective transportation was vital for troops battling in the wide-open spaces of North Africa. *What is happening in the photograph?*

These soldiers are scrambling across a trench that used to be a city street in Stalingrad.

Stalingrad. In Europe, German troops had penetrated far into the Soviet Union after their initial attack in June 1941. As the Germans advanced, they captured many industrial centers as well as rich grain-fields in the Ukraine. By winter German forces were closing in on Moscow. The Germans also laid siege to Leningrad. For months the men, women, and children defending the city endured a nightmare of shell fire and starvation.

In the summer of 1942, German troops that had been pushing toward the oil fields of southern Russia approached the city of Stalin-grad. By the fall of 1942, German troops were fighting for control of the city. A German officer described the fighting.

 We have fought during fifteen days for a single house. The 'front' is a corridor between burned-out rooms; it is the thin ceiling between two floors. . . . From story to story, faces black with sweat, we bombard each other with grenades in the middle of explosions, clouds of dust and smoke, heaps of mortar, floods of blood, fragments of furniture and human beings. 🟆

The Soviet forces refused to surrender, however, and eventually surrounded the German soldiers in Stalingrad. Throughout a terrible winter the Germans hung on, forbidden by Hitler to surrender. Trapped in the ruined city with few supplies and little food, the Axis troops finally surrendered in February 1943. After the Battle of Stalingrad, less than one half of the original German force of more than 200,000 remained alive. The Allied victories at El Alamein and Stalingrad broke the momentum of the Axis advance. Said British prime minister Winston Churchill: "Before Alamein we never had a victory. After Alamein we never had a defeat."

✔ **READING CHECK:** What were the major battles in Europe and North Africa in 1942?

SECTION 1 REVIEW

Define and explain the significance of the following terms:
War Production Board
Office of War Mobilization
Selective Training and Service Act
Bataan Death March
Battle of the Coral Sea
Battle of Midway

Identify and explain the significance of the following individuals:
Douglas MacArthur
Chester Nimitz
Erwin Rommel
Bernard Montgomery

1. **Using Graphic Organizers** Copy the following graphic organizer. Use it to list the actions taken by the government to prepare the economy and the military for war and what each action was intended to do.

	The Economy	Military Strength
Actions Taken		
Goals of Action		

2. **Comparing and Contrasting** What advantages did the Axis Powers have at the beginning of the war? What advantages did the Allies have?
3. **Geographic Diversity: Location** What was the significance of the U.S. victories at the Battles of Midway and Guadalcanal?
4. **Assessing Consequences** Why were the Battles of El Alamein and Stalingrad turning points for the Allies?

Critical Thinking

5. Describe how the United States managed to turn the tide of the war in the Pacific by the end of 1942.
   Consider:
   • the results of the attack on Pearl Harbor
   • where the Japanese attacked after Pearl Harbor
   • Japanese and U.S. strategy at the Battles of the Coral Sea and Midway

SECTION 2 The Home Front

KEY TERMS

Office of War Information
Rosie the Riveter
Fair Employment Practices Committee
braceros
zoot-suit riots
internment

KEY PEOPLE

A. Philip Randolph
Carlos E. Castañeda
Norman Mineta

EYEWITNESSES TO History

66 *When my son enlisted in the air force, he went to McDill Field in Florida. So I went there. . . . Then I came back to Westminster . . . [and] found that people who didn't have someone overseas were not too concerned. They were interested in bacon and sugar and gas, which I was not. . . . I did a lot of war work . . . when I was at McDill, I worked in the hospital and at the USO. . . . I started to do some volunteer work in Westminster, like rolling bandages, but I couldn't make it. The people I was doing it with were not in my situation at all. They were more concerned with what they were having to give up than with what was happening in Europe. I had people call me up and ask, 'Do you have coupons? We can get butter tomorrow.' I never stood in a line for a thing. I thought that if the men could do without it, so could I.* 99

—Mary Speir

Americans eagerly planted victory gardens to support the war effort.

Mary Speir of Westminster, Maryland, understood all too well the sacrifices people made to support the war effort. Her husband and son fought in the war, and her son was killed in combat.

Promoting the War

World War II enjoyed broad popular support. Many families proudly displayed window banners with a star. A blue star represented a loved one in the service. A gold star stood for a death in combat.

Wake Island and other war movies encouraged Americans to support the war effort.

The U.S. government tried to keep morale high. This was especially important in the early days of the war, when Allied troops faced many setbacks. The government encouraged the media to do their part. Moviemakers, songwriters, and radio-station programmers responded by urging all-out participation in the war effort.

Movie stars advertised war bonds and traveled overseas to entertain the troops. Hundreds of war movies poured out of Hollywood. *So Proudly We Hail*—a story about army nurses in the Philippines—was just one of the patriotic films that built support for the war. Striking a lighter note were comedies like Bob Hope's *Caught in the Draft.* A few films, such as *Wake Island* and *Report from the Aleutians,* offered more realistic views of combat.

Radio stations broadcast both war news and entertainment. Foreign correspondents such as Edward R. Murrow and Eric Sevareid gave on-the-scene accounts of war-ravaged Europe. The government-run **Office of War Information** controlled the flow of war news at home.

PRESIDENT FRANKLIN D. ROOSEVELT
The Four Freedoms

On January 6, 1941, in his annual message to Congress, President Roosevelt requested support for the Lend-Lease program. In what became known as the Four Freedoms speech, Roosevelt defined the four freedoms that came to represent the ideals Americans were fighting for in the war.

In the future days, which we seek to make secure, we look forward to a world founded upon four essential human freedoms.

The first is freedom of speech and expression everywhere in the world.

The second is freedom of every person to worship God in his own way everywhere in the world.

The third is freedom from want, which, translated into world terms, means economic understandings which will secure to every nation a healthy peacetime life for its inhabitants everywhere in the world.

The fourth is freedom from fear—which, translated into world terms, means a worldwide reduction of armaments to such a point and in such a thorough fashion that no nation will be in a position to commit an act of physical aggression against any neighbor—anywhere in the world.

That is no vision of a distant millennium. It is a definite basis for a kind of world attainable in our own time and generation. That kind of world is the very antithesis [opposite] of the so-called new order of tyranny which the dictators seek to create with the crash of a bomb.

The war also affected popular radio serials. Radio stations abandoned spy and sabotage programs for the duration of the war. Some even banned certain sound effects, such as wailing sirens, to avoid alarming listeners.

✔ **READING CHECK:** What did the U.S. government do to keep morale high during wartime?

Life During Wartime

Americans cut back their consumption of both luxuries and necessities to help the war effort. Millions of people grew vegetables and other produce in their backyards. These so-called victory gardens helped make more food available to U.S. and Allied soldiers. Martha Wood recalled that she and her neighbors

❝ [formed] a neighborhood Victory Garden, plowed up the backyards of three houses, and planted beans, corn, tomatoes, okra, squash, and all the things we could use. When the crop came in, . . . [we] used a pressure cooker and canned all day. I was canning until midnight and later, night after night, and I frequently said, 'I wish I had Hitler in that pressure cooker.' ❞

Civil-defense units helped prepare Americans in case of attack by Axis forces.

After the bombing of Pearl Harbor, U.S. authorities imposed restrictions in case of attack on the mainland. West Coast cities began practicing nighttime blackouts. Authorities feared that brightly lit U.S. cities would make easy targets for Japanese bombers. Civil-defense units searched for signs of enemy aircraft. Across the nation, practice air-raid drills sent Americans scrambling for cover from bombing attacks that never came.

People worked longer hours and made many sacrifices, but daily life in the United States did not change radically during the war. On Broadway stages, musicals such as Irving Berlin's *This Is the Army* (1942) and Leonard Bernstein and Jerome Robbins's *On the Town* (1944) provided laughs and avoided the painful side of wartime. Richard Rodgers and Oscar Hammerstein's production *Oklahoma!* (1943) was the biggest hit during the war. *Oklahoma!* provided Americans with a taste of simpler times.

Wartime music did not have the same innocence of World War I hits such as "Over There." Instead, big hits like "Remember Pearl Harbor" and "Praise the Lord and Pass the Ammunition!" captured the harsh reality of war. Irving Berlin's song "God Bless America" became a sort of unofficial national anthem. Big-band swing music remained popular, and sentimental songs such as "White Christmas" expressed Americans' longing for a return to peace.

In part as a result of widespread interest in the war, nonfiction became more popular than fiction. The best-selling books of 1941 were William Shirer's *Berlin Diary,* a frightening look inside Nazi Germany, and Joseph Davies's *Mission to Moscow,* a positive portrayal of the Soviet Union. Wartime also brought a change to the publishing industry. Paperback books first appeared in 1939, and wartime rationing helped them quickly surpass hardcover as the format of choice. The lower cost, light weight, and smaller size of paperbacks made them very popular. The military boosted the growth of the paperback format with the Armed Services Editions, which provided paperback books free of charge to U.S. troops. Some 60 million books of all types were distributed during the war.

✔ **READING CHECK:** What was life in the United States like during World War II?

AMERICAN ARTS — *Norman Rockwell*

Norman Rockwell's Liberty Girl

Norman Rockwell was born in New York City in 1894. For six decades, until his death in 1978, Rockwell showed the positive side of American life in his illustrations. He once said, "As I grew up . . . I unconsciously decided that, even if it wasn't an ideal world, it should be so, and so I painted the ideal aspects of it." He is best known for the covers he drew for the *Saturday Evening Post.* In 47 years Rockwell drew 322 covers for the *Post,* more than any other artist.

Rockwell lived in Vermont during World War II and often used his neighbors as models for his illustrations. Despite painting just one combat scene during the war, he managed to capture the mood of a nation at war. He did so by reminding people of the reasons behind the war without downplaying the difficulty of the struggle. Rockwell said that he tried to create an image that "makes the reader want to sigh and smile at the same time."

One such picture was his cover for the September 4, 1943, *Saturday Evening Post.* Rockwell painted *Liberty Girl,* to celebrate the Labor Day holiday. The work honored women's contributions to the war effort with its representations of the many different kinds of work that women were performing.

Understanding the Arts

1. How many different occupations are represented in this image?
2. How does this image reflect the experiences of Americans on the home front during the war?

This image of Rosie the Riveter shows the importance of female workers to the war effort.

Rosie the Riveter

Daily life changed dramatically for some Americans on the home front, particularly for women. During the depression, the government had discouraged women, particularly married women, from working. The government now urged them to enter the job market to replace departing soldiers. One government poster showed a female worker in bandanna and overalls. The caption read: "I'm Proud . . . my husband wants me to do my part." Advertisements and a popular song promoted "**Rosie the Riveter**," the symbol of patriotic female defense workers.

From 1940 to 1944 the number of women in the workforce increased by about 6 million. Women worked in war plants and replaced men in a host of jobs ranging from newspaper reporting to truck driving. Many of these new workers were married women who were taking jobs outside the home for the first time. Many women already in the paid workforce left traditional "women's work" such as domestic service to work in factories.

The participation of women in the war effort gave many of them a new sense of pride and self-worth. One female aircraft worker finally felt a sense of achievement after feeling "average" at other jobs.

> 66 Foremen from other departments come to my machine to ask me to do some work for them if I have time because they say I'm the best countersinker in the vast building! At forty-nine I've at last become not better than average, but the best! 99

Female workers continued to be paid less than men for the same work. African American women and women over 40 found few employers willing to hire them. In spite of women's achievements, it was widely assumed—by many women as well as men—that most of the jobs held by women during the war were temporary. A shipyard manager predicted that "these women who are willing . . . to lend a hand with the war will be the . . . office personnel of . . . the future."

✔ **READING CHECK:** How did American women contribute to the war effort?

INTERPRETING THE VISUAL RECORD
Female workers. Without the efforts of American women, the United States could not have produced the materials needed to win the war. *What are these female workers doing?*

Discrimination During the War

Racial tensions did not disappear during wartime. However, the cooperation the war effort required caused the government to try to reduce discrimination in war industries.

Demands for equal treatment. For African Americans, World War II brought both continued discrimination and greater opportunities. Many black workers moved into better-paying industrial jobs and played a key role in the military effort. Almost 1 million African American soldiers served in the armed forces, including several thousand women in the Women's Auxiliary Army Corps. However, African Americans continued to serve in segregated units, and most were kept out of combat. Black soldiers were often assigned to low-level work.

The millions of African Americans in the workforce had to struggle to gain acceptance. Many war plants would not hire African Americans or would employ them only as janitors. Despite labor leaders' no-strike pledge, some white workers staged strikes—called hate strikes—designed to keep black workers out of high-paying factory jobs.

In 1941, before the United States entered the war, African American labor leader A. Philip Randolph planned a march on Washington, D.C., to protest discrimination against black workers. Fearing the unrest it might cause, President Roosevelt wanted to prevent the march. Randolph agreed to call off the march after Roosevelt issued an executive order forbidding racial discrimination in defense plants and government offices.

To enforce the order, on June 25, 1941, Roosevelt created the **Fair Employment Practices Committee** (FEPC). The FEPC investigated companies engaged in defense work to make sure that all qualified applicants, regardless of race, were considered for job openings. It was strengthened by a May 27, 1943, executive order requiring nondiscrimination clauses in all war contracts. The FEPC, however, lacked strong enforcement powers and was unable to prevent widespread abuses.

As during World War I, many African Americans moved northward to take advantage of the high wages being offered in war plants. In crowded cities where no new homes were being built, African Americans faced discrimination in housing. Competition for limited housing created tensions that sometimes led to outbursts of violence against African Americans. In Detroit in 1943 a fight between African American and white residents at Belle Isle, a popular Detroit park, spread to other parts of the city. Some 34 people died in several days of rioting before federal troops sent by President Roosevelt restored calm.

During a rally at Madison Square Garden, A. Philip Randolph fights to save the Fair Employment Practices Committee.

The zoot–suit riots.

World War II brought both opportunities and problems to Mexican Americans as well. More than 300,000 Mexican Americans served in the military, and 17 earned the Congressional Medal of Honor. The 88th Division, a top combat unit known as the Blue Devils, consisted mostly of Mexican American soldiers.

Mexican Americans also helped meet home-front labor needs. University of Texas history professor Carlos E. Castañeda served as assistant to the chair of the FEPC and worked to improve working conditions for Mexican Americans in Texas. In 1945 the FEPC ordered a major Texas oil company to discontinue hiring and promotion practices that discriminated against Hispanics.

Many Mexican Americans moved from the Southwest to industrial centers in the Midwest and on the West Coast. Under a 1942 agreement between the United States and Mexico, thousands of Mexican farm and railroad workers—known as **braceros**—came north to work in the Southwest during World War II.

These Mexican Americans were arrested during the zoot-suit riots. Many others served heroically during World War II, and 17 won the Congressional Medal of Honor (left).

The prejudice and discrimination endured by Hispanics in jobs, housing, and recreational facilities caused bitter resentment. Relations grew particularly hostile in Los Angeles. Mexican American youths had adopted the fad of wearing zoot suits—long, wide-shouldered jackets, trousers pegged at the ankle, and wide-brimmed hats. In June 1943, U.S. sailors roamed the city attacking zoot-suit-clad Mexican American youths in what became known as the **zoot-suit riots**. The government eventually clamped down on the sailors, but not before they had viciously beaten many Mexican Americans.

A citizens' committee later determined that the attacks were motivated by racial prejudice. The committee assigned partial responsibility to the Los Angeles police, who had responded to the riots by arresting Mexican Americans. The committee also blamed biased newspaper reports.

✔**READING CHECK:** What steps did the federal government take to protect the rights of members of minority groups?

Japanese American Relocation

In general, World War II did not produce the same level of home-front intolerance as did World War I. One tragic exception was the **internment**, or forced relocation and imprisonment, of Japanese Americans living on the Pacific Coast. U.S. State Department adviser Eugene Rostow called relocation "a tragic and dangerous mistake." In 1941 about 119,000 people of Japanese ancestry lived in Washington, Oregon, and California. Approximately one third of these—the issei (ee-SAY)—had been born in Japan and were regarded by the U.S. government as aliens ineligible for U.S. citizenship. The rest—the nisei (nee-SAY)—had been born in the United States and thus were U.S. citizens.

No evidence existed of disloyalty on the part of any issei or nisei. Nevertheless, because of strong anti-Japanese feelings among some politicians and residents of western states, the federal government decided to remove people of Japanese descent from the West Coast. In February 1942, Japanese Americans were ordered to detention camps in Wyoming, Utah, and other states. Because Hawaii's Japanese population was too large to relocate, the islands were placed under martial law for the duration of the war.

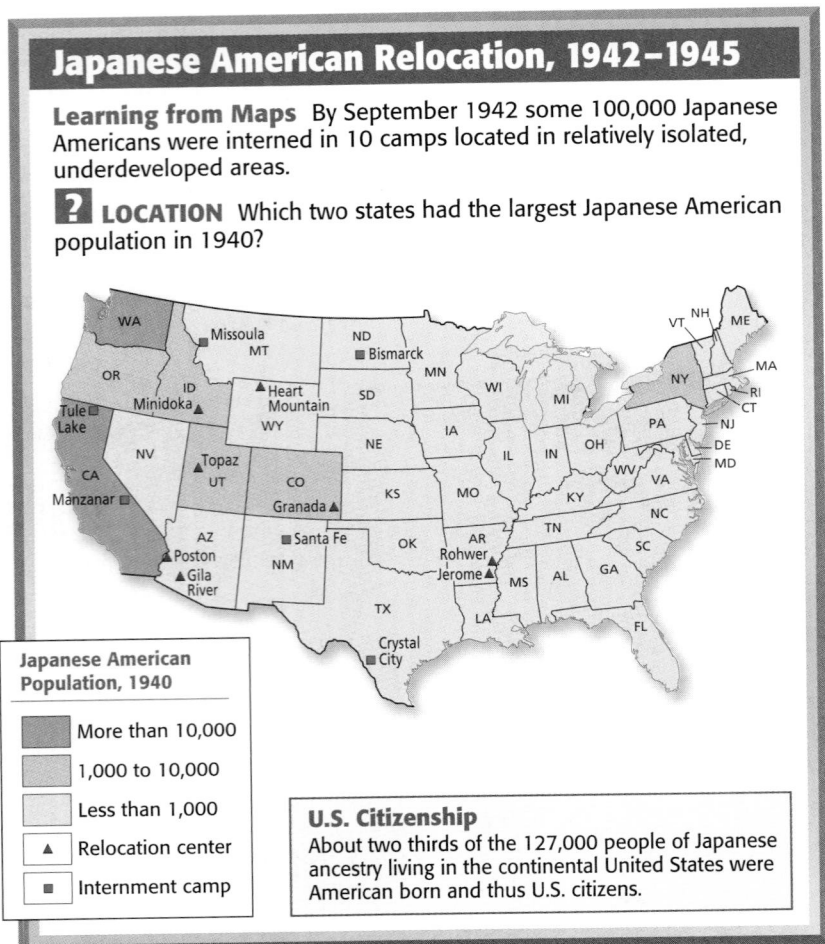

Japanese American Relocation, 1942–1945

Learning from Maps By September 1942 some 100,000 Japanese Americans were interned in 10 camps located in relatively isolated, underdeveloped areas.

? LOCATION Which two states had the largest Japanese American population in 1940?

Japanese American Population, 1940

- More than 10,000
- 1,000 to 10,000
- Less than 1,000
- ▲ Relocation center
- ■ Internment camp

U.S. Citizenship
About two thirds of the 127,000 people of Japanese ancestry living in the continental United States were American born and thus U.S. citizens.

One imprisoned Japanese American was Norman Mineta, a nisei from San Jose, California. On the day of the Pearl Harbor bombing, the young Mineta fearfully watched his neighbors being taken away for questioning by the FBI. He recalled bitterly that "they had done nothing; the only thing that they had done was to be born of Japanese ancestry."

Just 10 years old when his family was uprooted, Mineta wore his Cub Scout uniform on the train. He hoped that it would show his loyalty to the United States. Mineta's family was interned with some 10,000 others at a camp at Heart Mountain, Wyoming. "These camps were all barbed wire, guard towers, searchlights," recalled Mineta.

After the war Mineta attended college and became an insurance agent. He later went into local politics in San Jose. In 1974 he was elected to the House of Representatives, where he served on several committees. Mineta also introduced legislation seeking reparations for Japanese American internees. He retired in 1995 after 21 years in the House of Representatives.

Patriotism and the desire to disprove accusations of disloyalty inspired many young men in the camps to volunteer for military duty, even though they served in segregated units. One nisei combat team, the 442nd, fought in Europe and became one of the most decorated units in the armed services. Several thousand Japanese Americans also served in the Military Intelligence Service as interpreters and translators in the Pacific. The U.S. Supreme Court upheld internment in 1944, and many Japanese Americans remained imprisoned until 1945.

✔ **READING CHECK:** How were Japanese Americans affected by the war?

Read More About It

Free Find:
Norman Mineta
After reading about Norman Mineta on the **Holt Researcher** CD–ROM, create a campaign poster that illustrates Mineta's service during the war.

SECTION 2 REVIEW

Define and explain the significance of the following terms:
Office of War Information
Rosie the Riveter
Fair Employment Practices Committee
braceros
zoot-suit riots
internment

Identify and explain the significance of the following individuals:
A. Philip Randolph
Carlos E. Castañeda
Norman Mineta

1. **Using Graphic Organizers** Copy the web below. Use it to describe how various groups experienced greater opportunities and/or discrimination as a result of the war.

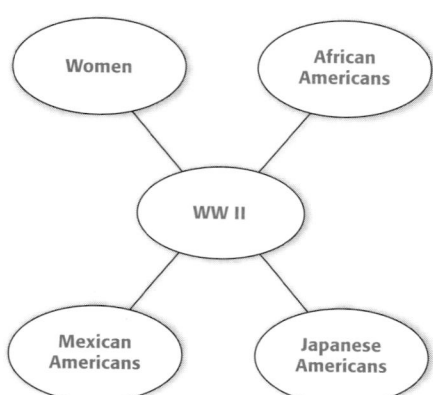

2. **Identifying Cause and Effect** How did the U.S. government seek to keep morale high during World War II? How did most Americans respond to the government's actions?

3. **Using Historical Imagination** Imagine that you are living on the home front during World War II. Write a journal entry describing your daily routine.

4. **Hypothesizing** What long-term effects do you think women's experiences in World War II had on their lives after the war?

Critical Thinking

5. What evidence can you give to support the argument that the war affected virtually all aspects of life on the home front?
   Consider:
   • wartime changes in popular culture
   • wartime changes in daily life
   • the war's effects on job opportunities and racial issues

Victory in Europe

Ernie Pyle often visited troops at the battlefront.

KEY TERMS

Battle of the Atlantic
sonar
D-Day
Holocaust
genocide
Battle of the Bulge
Yalta Conference

KEY PEOPLE

Dwight D. Eisenhower
George S. Patton
Elie Wiesel

KEY PLACES

Vichy France
Tunisia
Sicily
Anzio
Normandy

EYEWITNESSES TO History

❝ *Buck Eversole is a platoon sergeant in an infantry company. His platoon has turned over many times as battle whittles down the old ones and the replacement system brings up the new ones. Only a handful now are veterans. 'It gets so it kinda gets you, seein' these new kids come up,' Buck told me one night. . . . 'Some of them have just got fuzz on their faces, and don't know what it's all about, and they're scared to death. No matter what, some of them are bound to get killed. . . . I know it ain't my fault that they get killed,' Buck finally said. 'And I do the best I can for them, but I've got so I feel like it's me killin' 'em instead of a German. I've got so I feel like a murderer. I hate to look at them when the new ones come in.'* ❞

—Ernie Pyle

Reporter Ernie Pyle brought the reality of war home to Americans in numerous news stories such as this interview. Pyle himself was eventually killed while covering the war in the Pacific.

Allied Attacks in the Mediterranean

By late 1942 U.S. supplies and troops began to make a difference in the war. However, it would take another two years of hard fighting to defeat the Axis Powers. Soon after Pearl Harbor, the Allies agreed that they would open a second front against the Axis Powers in order to relieve pressure on the Soviet Union. However, Allied forces were not prepared to launch a direct assault on either German-occupied France or Vichy-controlled southern France. At British prime minister Winston Churchill's urging, they decided to attack first in the Mediterranean region.

Axis surrender in North Africa. After France surrendered in 1940, Germany placed France's colonies in North Africa under the control of Vichy France. The following year British forces turned back the Axis attempt to capture the Suez Canal and drove the German and Italian forces into Libya. In November 1942 the Allies planned Operation Torch, an invasion of the French territory in northwest Africa. General Dwight D. Eisenhower commanded the invasion force of U.S. and British soldiers.

Allied leaders were unsure if the French forces in North Africa would oppose the invasion. Early on the morning of November 8, some 65,000 Allied troops landed at Casablanca in Morocco and Oran and Algiers in Algeria. Nearly twice that number of French forces awaited them. Troops landing at Casablanca faced the greatest difficulties, encountering both heavy surf and French resistance. Allied troops captured Algiers that day and Oran two days later.

As the soldiers established beachheads in Morocco and Algeria, Allied planes and ships cut Axis supply lines from Italy. Then, during the winter of 1942–43, two Allied land forces—one from the west and the other from the east—began to squeeze the Axis troops into a trap. Several fierce battles took place in Tunisia. Finally, in May 1943, the Axis force of some 250,000 soldiers surrendered.

The invasion of Italy. North Africa offered a gateway to the Italian island of Sicily. Allied leaders decided to invade Sicily next. They sought to clear the Axis forces out of the central Mediterranean and to acquire a launching point for an invasion of the Italian mainland. Battling high winds and rough seas, Allied troops landed in July 1943. They subdued Sicily in a little more than a month. General George S. Patton, who had emerged as a leader during the North Africa campaign, led the U.S. forces.

The Italian king named a new prime minister to replace Benito Mussolini and ordered Mussolini's arrest. Determined not to surrender the Italian peninsula, the Germans took Mussolini to Germany and then set up a base for him in northern Italy. In September the Italian government signed an armistice with the Allies. Soon afterward the Allies invaded southern Italy to attack the Germans. Although the Allies took Naples on October 1, they soon bogged down.

Hoping to outflank the German forces, the Allies landed to the south of Rome at Anzio in January 1944. After the landing, however, the Allies were pinned down for months. U.S. and British forces then began driving slowly north. They were joined by small units of troops from more than 25 countries. After months of bitter mountain warfare, the Germans occupying Italy were finally defeated. Mussolini was captured in late April and shot by Italian rebels. In June 1944 the Allies marched into Rome, making it the first Axis capital to fall.

✔ **READING CHECK:** Where did the Allied offensive in Europe begin?

General Eisenhower led Operation Torch—the Allied invasion of North Africa.

Sea and Air Assaults

During the months of fighting in the Mediterranean region, the Allies waged campaigns on other fronts as well. Although they faced a determined enemy, the Allies eventually overcame all resistance. In the Atlantic, German U-boats continued to take a staggering toll on Allied ships, lives, and supplies. Not until 1943 did this **Battle of the Atlantic** begin to turn in the Allies' favor. An important factor was the refinement of **sonar** equipment, which uses sound waves to detect underwater objects. The Allies also developed fast escort ships for convoys and air-bombed German U-boats and submarine yards. By 1944 the Allies had won the Battle of the Atlantic.

The Allied air campaign also met with success in 1943. The Allies intensified their campaign of strategic bombing aimed at destroying German military production and undermining the morale of the German people. "It was sound strategy to prevent the *Wehrmacht* [German armed forces] from falling back to regroup and be lethal [deadly] again," Lieutenant John Morris explained. "We bombed . . . the railroad marshaling

The air war. Both sides used massive bombing raids to try to destroy their enemy's ability to manufacture war materials. *What does the photograph suggest about the accuracy of such bombing attacks?*

yards and road hubs along the *Wehrmacht's* line of retreat, up and down Germany's eastern border." British Royal Air Force (RAF) planes flew chiefly at night, dropping their bombs in the general area of a given target. U.S. aircraft concentrated on precision bombing in daylight raids. By 1944, bombers had rained hundreds of thousands of tons of explosives on German factories, supply lines, and military centers.

✔ **READING CHECK:** How did the fighting in the Atlantic and in the skies influence the land war in Europe?

Read More About It

Free Find: D-Day

After learning about the D-Day invasion on the **Holt Researcher** CD–ROM, create a drawing of the invasion site that shows the obstacles the Allied troops faced.

Operation Overlord

Victory in the Battle of the Atlantic and air assaults on Germany paved the way for Operation Overlord—the long-awaited Allied invasion of German-occupied France. Commanded by General Eisenhower, the invasion had involved years of planning. The Allies put in place a system of dummy installations and false clues to convince the Germans that the invasion would take place near Calais on the English Channel.

Instead, the Allies landed farther south, in Normandy, on **D-Day**, June 6, 1944. Nearly 5,000 troop transports, landing craft, and warships carried some 150,000 U.S., British, and Canadian soldiers across the Channel. Overhead, planes dropped close to 23,000 airborne troops and bombed roads, bridges, and German troop concentrations. Sergeant Ralph G. Martin recalled that "everything was confusion" during the landing and "units were mixed up, many of them leaderless, most of them not being where they were supposed to be." Corporal Samuel Fuller recalled encountering fierce resistance with the U.S. 1st Infantry Division on Omaha Beach.

66 **The only way to get off the beach was to blow a big tank trap that was blocking our way. Finally one of our guys took the trap out. . . . I stood up and tried to run. When you run over unconscious men, or men lying on their bellies, it's tough to keep your balance. You go into the water, but the water is washing bodies in and out. Bodies, heads, flesh, intestines; that's what Omaha Beach was. 99**

INTERPRETING THE VISUAL RECORD

D-Day. The invasion of France was a risky venture that paid off for the Allies. *What obstacles face these soldiers who are preparing to land?*

The Germans had fortified the Normandy beaches with concrete bunkers, tank traps, and mines. The beaches resembled a giant fortress, but the Allied campaign of disinformation and distraction had done its job. Adolf Hitler refused to send reinforcements to the area around Normandy. He still believed that the main invasion would occur elsewhere.

Although the Allies met determined opposition, they managed to penetrate 20 miles into France by early July. Aided by the French Resistance, the Allies drove steadily eastward. They liberated Paris on August 25, 1944. By early September more than 2 million Allied troops had landed in western Europe. Another Allied force drove northward through France from the Mediterranean. Meanwhile, Soviet troops pressed Germany from the east.

✔ **READING CHECK:** How did the Allies carry out the Normandy invasion?

Preparing questions is one of the most crucial steps in conducting a successful oral history interview. Most good interview questions are formulated with a specific purpose in mind. At the same time, they are broad enough to allow the subject of the interview to express himself or herself freely. *Who, what, when, where, why,* and *how* are words that often prove particularly useful in creating such questions.

How to Prepare Questions

1. **Do preliminary research.** Gather as much information as you can about the general topic the interview will address and the particular person you will be interviewing.
2. **Decide what you need to know.** Once you have completed your preliminary research, determine what you hope to learn from the interview. Keep in mind what you already know and the types of information that the subject of your interview is likely to possess.
3. **Formulate logical, open-ended questions.** Create questions that address what you hope to learn and that follow one another in a logical fashion. Make sure that the questions are designed to allow your subject to speak freely and that they cannot be answered with a simple "yes" or "no."

Applying the Strategy

Imagine that you have arranged to conduct an oral history interview with a U.S. Army veteran who took part in the D-Day invasion at Normandy on June 6, 1944. Prepare at least six questions that you plan to ask during the interview.

Practicing the Strategy

Answer the following questions.
1. What background information did you use when formulating your questions?
2. What kind of information would you hope to gain from interviewing a veteran of the D-Day invasion at Normandy?
3. What answers do you expect to your questions?

The Holocaust

Not even the savage fighting of D-Day prepared the Allies for the horror of the **Holocaust**, Nazi Germany's systematic slaughter of European Jews. Germany's occupation of France and other countries in western Europe, as well as its attacks on Poland and the Soviet Union, put millions of additional Jews under German rule. In many regions, special squads of German soldiers rounded up Jews and shot them. Elsewhere, Jews were forced into cities and isolated in ghettos. In 1941 the Germans began constructing camps specifically for the purpose of **genocide**—the deliberate annihilation of an entire people. Hitler and senior Nazi officials called this extermination program the "final solution of the Jewish question."

These ovens were used to cremate the bodies of the victims of the Holocaust.

Major death camps included Auschwitz (OWSH-vits), Treblinka, and Majdanek, all in Poland. Jewish men, women, and children were transported to the camps in sealed railroad cars. They were then marched into rooms disguised as shower facilities and gassed. Their bodies were then cremated. All told, some 6 million Jews—two thirds of Europe's Jewish population—perished. The Nazis also killed millions of Gypsies, Poles, the mentally disabled, and religious and political prisoners.

These survivors of the Buchenwald concentration camp were liberated by Allied soldiers in April 1945. Elie Wiesel is on the far right of the top row.

When the Allies liberated the death camps, they found thousands of starving survivors. Romanian-born writer Elie Wiesel was one such survivor. He described the deep psychological scars left on concentration camp survivors.

> 66 One day I was able to get up, after gathering all my strength. I wanted to see myself in the mirror hanging on the opposite wall. I had not seen myself since the ghetto. From the depths of the mirror, a corpse gazed back at me. The look in his eyes, as they stared into mine, has never left me. 99

To carry out this monstrous genocide, the Nazis took advantage of a long history of anti-Semitism in Europe that stretched back to the Middle Ages. A flood of Nazi propaganda against Jews stirred up this anti-Semitism. Some non-Jews in countries occupied by the Nazis either assisted or failed to prevent the Nazis from sending Jewish citizens off to the death camps. Others worked heroically to save the lives of Jews.

✔ **READING CHECK:** What was the Holocaust, and how was it carried out?

Defeating Germany

Although Germany's situation was grave, Adolf Hitler refused to give up. In September 1944 the Germans launched their first V-2s, or long-range rockets, at cities in England and Belgium. These bombs could not be shot down easily.

The Battle of the Bulge. By September 1944 the Allies had crossed the German border. As they paused to bring in supplies and to regroup, the Germans launched their final counterattack. In heavy snow, they drove against the Allies in the thickly wooded Ardennes region of Belgium and northern France. They pushed westward to create a dangerous bulge in the Allied lines. In the resulting **Battle of the Bulge** some 200,000 Germans attacked an initial U.S. force of about 80,000 troops.

The U.S. 101st Airborne Division defending the Belgian town of Bastogne was completely surrounded. When German officers demanded the 101st's surrender, General Anthony McAuliff offered a one-word reply: "Nuts." Allied generals rushed in reinforcements, and the Allies pushed the Germans back. Francis Tsuzuki, whose Japanese American battalion pursued the Germans, recalled, "the Germans were retreating so fast. At times we were moving...more than 100 miles a day." By January 1945 it was clear that the German offensive had failed.

The Yalta Conference. In February 1945 President Franklin D. Roosevelt, Winston Churchill, and Joseph Stalin met at the **Yalta Conference** to plan for the postwar peace. At the conference Stalin pledged to declare war on Japan three months after Germany's surrender. They agreed to divide and occupy Germany after the war and outlined plans for a new international peace organization.

World War II in Europe, 1942–1945

Learning from Maps After being battered at El Alamein, Rommel retreated some 1,250 miles to Tunisia in eight weeks. By 1943 Africa was cleared of Axis forces.

? LOCATION Where did the major battles in the European theater take place?

The German defeat at Stalingrad marked the turning point in the war in the East.

ICELAND

ATLANTIC OCEAN

Arctic Circle

NORWAY

SWEDEN

FINLAND

NORTH SEA

DENMARK

BALTIC SEA

Leningrad

Moscow

UNION OF SOVIET SOCIALIST REPUBLICS

Volga

IRELAND

GREAT BRITAIN

London

English Channel

NETHERLANDS

BELGIUM

D-Day June 1944

Elbe

Rhine

Berlin May 1945

Oder

Leipzig

Dresden

Warsaw

Vistula

Stalingrad Nov. 1942–Feb. 1943

Paris

GERMANY

FRANCE

Battle of the Bulge Dec. 1944

UKRAINE

Vichy

SWITZERLAND

SLOVAKIA

HUNGARY

VICHY FRANCE

Milan

Yalta

ROMANIA

PORTUGAL

SPAIN

CORSICA

ITALY

CROATIA

Rome

SERBIA

Danube

BLACK SEA

Anzio Jan. 1944

MONTENEGRO

BULGARIA

GIBRALTAR (Br.)

SARDINIA

Naples

ALBANIA

Istanbul

GREECE

AEGEAN SEA

TURKEY

Casablanca

Oran

Algiers

Tunis

SICILY

MALTA

CRETE

CYPRUS (Br.)

SYRIA (Vichy Fr.)

LEBANON (Vichy Fr.)

MOROCCO (Vichy Fr.)

ALGERIA (Vichy Fr.)

TUNISIA (Vichy Fr.)

MEDITERRANEAN SEA

PALESTINE (Br.)

TRANS-JORDAN (Br.)

Alexandria

El Alamein Oct.–Nov. 1942

Suez Canal

Cairo

SAUDI ARABIA

LIBYA (Italian)

EGYPT

RED SEA

Normandy Landings, June 6, 1944

GREAT BRITAIN

London

Portsmouth

English Channel

CHANNEL IS. (Br.)

Cherbourg

Utah (U.S.)

Omaha (U.S.)

Le Havre

Rouen

Gold (Br.)

Caen

Juno (Br.)

Sword (Br. & Canadian)

NORMANDY

Seine River

Paris

FRANCE

0   50   100 Miles
0   50   100 Kilometers

Legend:
- Axis controlled, Jan. 1942
- Allied controlled, Jan. 1942
- Neutral country
- Farthest Axis advance, 1942
- Allied advance
- ✶ Major battle
- Invasion beach

0   200   400 Miles
0   200   400 Kilometers
Azimuthal Equal-Area Projection

These Soviet soldiers celebrate their capture of Berlin by planting the Soviet flag on top of the Reichstag building, or German parliament building.

The urgency of the war effort convinced President Roosevelt to run for an unprecedented fourth term. With Missouri senator Harry S Truman as his running mate, Roosevelt won his party's nomination with little opposition. The Republicans chose Thomas E. Dewey, governor of New York. Dewey lacked the charisma and experience of Roosevelt, however, and was defeated by an electoral vote of 432 to 99.

The race to Berlin. During the early months of 1945, Allied bombers continued to blast German cities, including Leipzig and Berlin. One of the most devastating attacks hit Dresden in February. In one massive two-day attack, Allied bombers caused the worst firestorms of the European war. Total civilian deaths have been estimated at between 30,000 and 60,000.

In March, Allied troops crossed the Rhine River from the west and drove into the heart of Germany. By then, Soviet troops occupied much of eastern Europe. Churchill wanted General Eisenhower to push east as far and as fast as possible. Churchill worried that the Soviets might later lay claim to territories they seized. Eisenhower did not want military strategy to be determined by political considerations and therefore halted the Allied advance at the Elbe River in April.

On April 30, 1945, Hitler committed suicide in his bunker deep under the ruins of Berlin. U.S. sergeant Mack Morriss described the grim mood of the fallen city. "There is a feeling that here has ended not only a city but a nation, that here a titanic force has come to catastrophe." Germany surrendered unconditionally on May 7. The next day, known as V-E (Victory in Europe) Day, marked the formal end of a brutal war that had held Europe in its grip for more than five years.

✔ **READING CHECK:** What were the final steps in the Allied defeat of Germany?

SECTION 3 REVIEW

Define and explain the significance of the following terms:
Battle of the Atlantic
sonar
D-Day
Holocaust
genocide
Battle of the Bulge
Yalta Conference

Identify and explain the significance of the following individuals:
Dwight D. Eisenhower
George S. Patton
Elie Wiesel

Locate and explain the significance of the following places:
Vichy France   Anzio
Tunisia   Normandy
Sicily

1. **Using Graphic Organizers** Copy the chart below. Use it to list the military events that led to Germany's surrender in 1945.

| 1. D-Day |
| 2. |
| 3. |
| 4. |
| 5. |
| 6. |
| 7. Germany surrenders |

2. **Understanding Geography: Location** How did the campaigns in North Africa, Sicily, in the Atlantic, and in the air help the Allies prepare to defeat Italy and Germany?
3. **Analyzing** How did the Allies achieve victory at Normandy?
4. **Using Historical Imagination** Imagine you are an Allied soldier in the European theater. Write a diary entry that describes the conditions you have experienced in one of the battles mentioned in the text.

Critical Thinking

5. How did the Holocaust occur, and how did it affect Europe?
   Consider:
   • how the Holocaust developed
   • why it was not stopped
   • what its effects were

SECTION 4

Victory in Asia

OBJECTIVES

Read to understand:

1. how the United States carried out its island-hopping plan
2. what effect the battles at Iwo Jima and Okinawa had on the war
3. what led the United States to use atomic weapons against Japan
4. what the human and economic costs of World War II were

KEY TERMS

island-hopping
Battle of Leyte Gulf
Battle of Iwo Jima
kamikaze
Battle of Okinawa
Manhattan Project
Enola Gay

KEY PEOPLE

Harry S Truman

KEY PLACES

Saipan
New Guinea
Hiroshima
Nagasaki

EYEWITNESSES TO History

66 *The Japanese fought by a code they thought was right: bushido. The code of the warrior: no surrender. You don't really comprehend it until you get out there and fight people who are faced with an absolutely hopeless situation and will not give up. If you tried to help one of the Japanese, he'd usually detonate a grenade and kill himself as well as you. To be captured was a disgrace. . . . You developed an attitude of no mercy because they had no mercy on us. It was a no-quarter, savage kind of thing. . . . If you're reduced to savagery by a situation, anything's possible. When [Charles] Lindbergh made a trip to the Philippines, he was horrified at the way American GIs talked about the Japanese. It was so savage. We were savages.* 99

—Eugene B. Sledge

Japanese sword

As U.S. marine Eugene B. Sledge described, the fighting in the Pacific was fierce. The Japanese considered surrender disgraceful and often fought to the death. The U.S. advance across the Pacific was met with ferocious resistance as Japanese defenders dug in, committed to saving their empire or die trying.

Pacific Offensives

In the Pacific the Allies had gone on the offensive by 1943. Their ultimate objective was to come within striking distance of Japan itself.

Island-hopping. Air and sea power were the keys to victory in the Pacific, unlike in Europe where land forces played a much larger role. As early as 1942 the U.S. high command had adopted a strategy of **island-hopping**. This meant that troops would attack and seize only certain strategic Japanese-held islands, rather than trying to recapture all of them. Japanese garrisons located on islands bypassed by the Allies would be cut off from supplies and troop reinforcements. Airstrips built on seized islands would help support the next Allied advance. In the central Pacific, an island-hopping offensive began in November 1943 in the Gilbert Islands. Army troops quickly took Makin Island.

U.S. Marines plunge into the sea during the assault on Tarawa.

Tarawa. The island of Tarawa proved much more difficult to capture than Makin. Because of a coral reef encircling the island, the marines who landed there had to wade in to the beach "in the face of murderous Japanese fire, with no protection," according to Sergeant John Bushemi. Almost 1,000 marines lost their lives and some 2,000 others were wounded before the island was secured. The victory gave the United States control of a vital airstrip and put its forces in position to provide air support for the next landings.

AMERICANS IN WORLD WAR II   **821**

Foxholes like this one on Saipan were often the only protection U.S. soldiers had during battles on the islands in the Pacific. The medal at right celebrates the Allied victory in World War II.

Saipan. The next important series of landings targeted the Marshall Islands, located north of the Gilbert Islands. In the Marshalls, U.S. forces captured several key bases from which they bombed the Truk Islands, where the headquarters of the Japanese fleet was located.

By the summer of 1944, Allied forces had advanced to the Mariana Islands. In June 535 ships carried 127,000 soldiers, two thirds of whom were marines, to the shores of Saipan. Under cover of intense air and naval bombardments from nearby aircraft carriers, landing craft loaded with troops swept in to the beaches. The Japanese gathered the bulk of their remaining fleet and sent it to stop the U.S. offensive.

Japan was already running low on aircraft, and in the battle that followed the United States won a decisive victory. U.S. pilots downed 350 Japanese planes while losing just 30 of their own planes. Running low on fuel and returning to their carriers at night, 80 U.S. pilots had to crash their planes in the ocean. Nearly all the pilots were rescued, and the Japanese aircraft carriers were no longer a threat.

Meanwhile, Saipan's 32,000 Japanese defenders were waging a fierce battle. U.S. forces suffered some 16,000 casualties, including more than 3,400 dead. U.S. troops fighting on Guam experienced equally tough resistance before the island fell in August. These U.S. victories were important because the islands provided airstrips from which U.S. bombers could begin launching missions against the main islands of Japan.

Recapturing the Philippines. Despite these setbacks, Japanese resistance stiffened when the Allies began their New Guinea–Philippines campaign in June 1943. General Douglas MacArthur led U.S. and Australian troops in a series of landings along the north coast of New Guinea. By late July 1944 they had reached the western end of this large island. Allied forces also took smaller islands nearby, such as the Admiralty Islands.

By the fall of 1944 the United States was ready to invade the Philippines. Allied forces poured onto the beaches of the island of Leyte in October. The Japanese navy's counterattack led to the **Battle of Leyte Gulf**—the last, largest, and most decisive naval engagement in the Pacific. The battle was a disaster for the Japanese, who lost four aircraft carriers, three battleships, and several cruisers. From this time on, the Japanese fleet no longer seriously threatened the Allies.

Aided by Filipino guerrillas, Allied troops fanned out over the islands of the Philippines. Overcoming bitter opposition, they entered Manila in February 1945 and subdued most Japanese defense forces within weeks. "I'm a little late," said MacArthur, "but we finally came."

✔ **READING CHECK:** How did the United States carry out its island-hopping plan?

Victory in the Pacific

These Pacific victories gave the United States several strategic bases from which to launch B-29 bombers against the Japanese home islands. U.S. planes bombed most of the country's major cities in an effort to weaken the fighting spirit of the Japanese. The worst raid took place over Tokyo in March 1945 and created huge firestorms that destroyed much of the city. The massive destruction caused Japanese civilian morale to sag, but the country's military leaders refused to surrender.

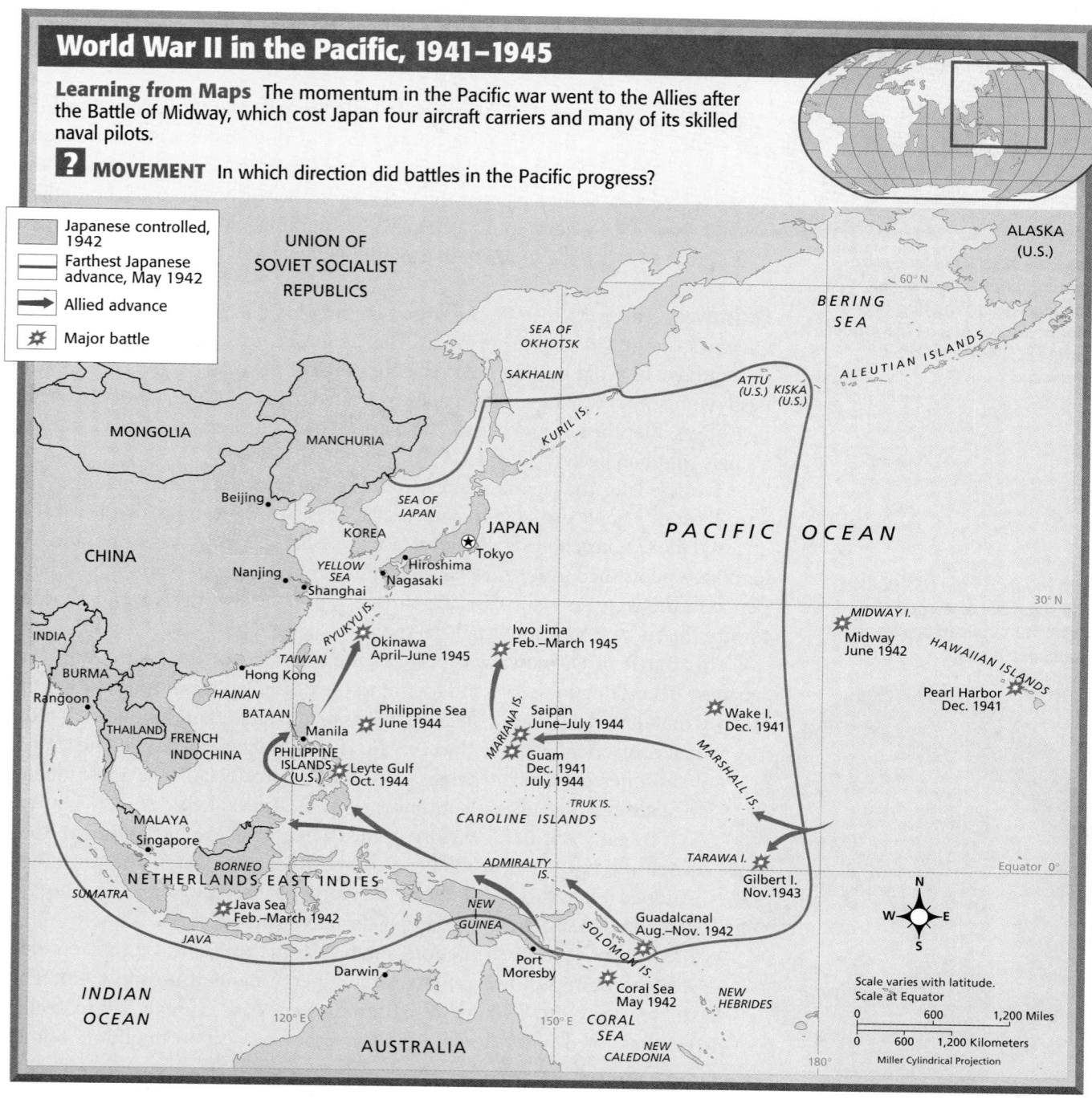

World War II in the Pacific, 1941–1945

Learning from Maps The momentum in the Pacific war went to the Allies after the Battle of Midway, which cost Japan four aircraft carriers and many of its skilled naval pilots.

? MOVEMENT In which direction did battles in the Pacific progress?

Japanese controlled, 1942
Farthest Japanese advance, May 1942
Allied advance
Major battle

ALASKA (U.S.)

UNION OF SOVIET SOCIALIST REPUBLICS

BERING SEA

60° N

ALEUTIAN ISLANDS

SEA OF OKHOTSK

SAKHALIN

ATTU (U.S.) KISKA (U.S.)

MONGOLIA

MANCHURIA

KURIL IS.

PACIFIC OCEAN

Beijing

SEA OF JAPAN

KOREA

JAPAN
★ Tokyo

CHINA

Nanjing
YELLOW SEA
Shanghai
Hiroshima
Nagasaki

30° N

MIDWAY I.
Midway
June 1942

INDIA

RYUKYU IS.
Okinawa
April–June 1945

Iwo Jima
Feb.–March 1945

HAWAIIAN ISLANDS

BURMA
TAIWAN
Hong Kong
HAINAN

Rangoon

THAILAND
FRENCH INDOCHINA

BATAAN
Manila
PHILIPPINE ISLANDS (U.S.)

Philippine Sea
June 1944

MARIANA IS.
Saipan
June–July 1944

Guam
Dec. 1941
July 1944

Wake I.
Dec. 1941

Pearl Harbor
Dec. 1941

MARSHALL IS.

Leyte Gulf
Oct. 1944

TRUK IS.
CAROLINE ISLANDS

MALAYA
Singapore

BORNEO
NETHERLANDS EAST INDIES

ADMIRALTY IS.

TARAWA I.

Equator 0°

Gilbert I.
Nov. 1943

SUMATRA
Java Sea
Feb.–March 1942

JAVA

NEW GUINEA

SOLOMON IS.

Guadalcanal
Aug.–Nov. 1942

N
W   E
S

Darwin

Port Moresby

Coral Sea
May 1942

NEW HEBRIDES

Scale varies with latitude.
Scale at Equator

0   600   1,200 Miles

INDIAN OCEAN

120° E

150° E

CORAL SEA

NEW CALEDONIA

180°

0   600   1,200 Kilometers

AUSTRALIA

Miller Cylindrical Projection

Joe Rosenthal's Pulitzer-prize-winning photograph of U.S. soldiers raising the flag over Mount Suribachi was the model for the U.S. Marine Corps Memorial.

Iwo Jima. In February 1945, U.S. Marines attacked Iwo Jima—just 750 miles from Tokyo—and met strong resistance. Despite a U.S. victory being nearly certain, Japanese forces fought as fiercely as ever. The **Battle of Iwo Jima** lasted six weeks. Some 4,000 marines and more than 20,000 Japanese soldiers were killed. Ted Allenby, a marine who took part in the assault on Iwo Jima, described the fighting.

> 66 The casualty rate was enormous. It was ghastly. Iwo was a volcanic island with very little concealment. Cover is something you hide behind—a tree, a bush, a rock. Few trees. No grass. It was almost like a piece of the moon that had dropped down to earth. 99

U.S. Marines struggled to take Mount Suribachi, which the Japanese held with a strong system of tunnels and bunkers. When the marines finally reached the mountaintop, they planted the U.S. flag in the rocky soil to celebrate their hard-fought victory. Photographer Joe Rosenthal recorded the moment in a picture that would win him a Pulitzer Prize.

Okinawa. On April 1, 1945, the largest landing force in Pacific history invaded Okinawa, about 350 miles from Japan. The Japanese forces chose not to challenge the landing. To avoid putting themselves in range of the massive guns of U.S. battleships and other warships, the Japanese retreated to the southern tip of the island. Five hours after the landing began, the marines had captured one airfield and not a single shot had been fired.

Five days later, the Japanese attacked. Some 700 Japanese planes, including 350 **kamikaze**, or suicide planes (*kamikaze* is a Japanese word meaning "divine wind"), attacked the U.S. beachheads and naval task force. Six U.S. ships were sunk, and 135 kamikaze pilots died. After the war, Admiral Nimitz recalled, "Nothing that happened in the war was a surprise, absolutely nothing except the kamikaze tactics toward the end; we had not visualized these."

This **Battle of Okinawa** was perhaps the bloodiest of the Pacific war. The Japanese troops dug in deeply and fought to the death. Japanese troops hid in the caves that dotted the island. The U.S. troops had to attack and subdue each individual cave, often by filling the cave with fire from flamethrowers. The United States suffered 49,200 casualties in the battle. Some 110,070 Japanese died in the fighting, nine times the number of Americans killed.

By early April, U.S. victory in the Pacific was near, but President Roosevelt did not live to see the end of hostilities with Japan. The world was stunned when he died suddenly on April 12. The new president, Harry S Truman, faced a grave decision. Germany's surrender had allowed Allied forces to concentrate their efforts on the war in the Pacific. Despite repeated Allied bombings, however, Japan remained a dangerous opponent. The Japanese were clearly willing to fight to the very end. Truman had to decide whether the United States should use its fearsome new weapon, the atomic bomb.

U.S. sailors on the USS **Bunker Hill** *scramble to escape the explosions caused by two kamikaze attacks.*

✔ **READING CHECK:** How did fighting on Iwo Jima and Okinawa shape the Pacific war?

The Atomic Bomb

The new U.S. weapon had been developed by the top-secret **Manhattan Project**, the effort of a group of scientists who had been working on creating an atomic bomb since 1942. The Manhattan Project was aided by many European scientists in its work. In 1933 physicist Albert Einstein moved from Germany to the United States. During the 1930s many European Jewish scientists followed Einstein's example. Enrico Fermi was an Italian physicist who had fled to the United States. He persuaded the world-famous Einstein to warn the U.S. government about research being done by German scientists. In August 1939 Einstein wrote to President Roosevelt. He warned that "a single bomb of this type, carried by boat and exploded in a port, might very well destroy the whole port, together with some of the surrounding territory." He was describing an atomic bomb. The race was on to be the first to build one.

PRESIDENTIAL Lives

1884–1972
In Office 1945–1953

Harry S Truman

Harry S Truman was born on May 8, 1884, in Missouri. As a boy he developed a strong appetite for reading. "I don't know anybody in the world ever read as much or as consistently as he did," a friend remembered. "He was what you call a 'book worm.'" Truman had no obligation to fight in World War I. Any one of several factors—his poor eyesight, his occupation as a farmer, and his status as his mother's sole support—would have allowed him to avoid service. Instead, saying it was "a job somebody had to do," Truman volunteered and commanded an artillery battery in France.

After the war, Truman returned to Missouri where his habit of studying people helped him begin his political career. "When I was growing up," Truman said, "it occurred to me to watch the people around me to find out what they thought and what pleased them the most."

Harry S. Truman

U.S. Postage 8 cents

In 1942 General Leslie R. Groves took charge of the Manhattan Project. By year's end, scientists led by Enrico Fermi had created an atomic chain reaction, a major step in the development of a bomb. Huge research centers were established in Los Alamos, New Mexico; Oak Ridge, Tennessee; and Hanford, Washington. At the Los Alamos center, director J. Robert Oppenheimer's team worked on building the first atomic bomb.

The scientists successfully tested their bomb at Alamogordo, New Mexico, on July 16, 1945. The very next day, President Truman met with Allied leaders at Potsdam, south of Berlin. On July 26 the Allies demanded Japan's unconditional surrender. Japan refused. Truman gave the order to use atomic weapons against Japan. As Iwo Jima and Okinawa had shown, the Japanese were still capable of inflicting heavy losses on U.S. forces. An invasion of Japan would be very costly. Estimates ran as high as 1 million U.S. casualties. Japanese losses could be even greater. Using the atomic bomb might end the war quickly and save many lives on both sides. The president may also have wanted to demonstrate the power of this new weapon to the Soviet Union.

At 8:15 A.M. on August 6, the U.S. B-29 bomber *Enola Gay*, commanded by Colonel Paul Tibbets, dropped an atomic bomb on the city of Hiroshima. A column of fire shot skyward, threatening to bring down the *Enola Gay*. It was followed by an enormous, mushroom-shaped cloud. The city looked like "lava or molasses," tail gunner Robert Caron recalled. As the B-29 passed over the ruined city, co-pilot Robert Lewis wrote in his journal, "My God, what have we done?"

The scene on the ground was even worse than the *Enola Gay*'s crew could imagine. The explosion flattened a huge area of the city and killed an

On July 16, 1945, the first atomic bomb was exploded at Alamogordo, New Mexico.

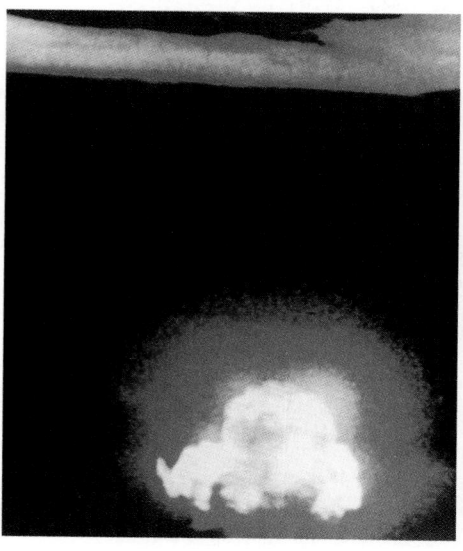

Great Debates

The Atomic Bomb

President Truman justified his decision to drop atomic bombs on two Japanese cities by noting Japan's refusal to surrender unconditionally. He claimed that the atomic bomb had prevented a costly U.S. invasion of Japan. He also linked the atomic bomb to Pearl Harbor. "The Japanese began the war," said Truman. "They have been repaid manyfold."

Some historians have questioned Truman's explanations. They point out that Tokyo was considering peace negotiations. They note that with the promised Soviet declaration of war by early August, victory would have been possible without either dropping the atomic bomb or launching a U.S. invasion. These scholars argue that Truman dropped the bomb not only to end the war but also to demonstrate the U.S. atomic might and thus strengthen its postwar position.

Other historians point to Japan's wartime atrocities and to the country's bitter-end defense of Okinawa. They note that top military leaders in Tokyo fiercely opposed the peace overtures and favored a desperate defense of the home islands. Although the debate over Truman's decision continues, all historians agree that it has had long-range consequences that few anticipated at the time.

estimated 100,000 people. Junji Sarashina, a 16-year-old high school junior, later recalled his experiences after the blast.

> 66 The entire town of Hiroshima was ablaze. . . . A lot of people were floating in the river; some were swimming, but some of them were dead, drifting with the current downstream. Their skin was red and their clothes were nothing but strips of cloth hanging from them. 99

Three days later, the United States dropped a second atomic bomb on Nagasaki. The explosion vaporized people, melted stones, and spontaneously ignited everything combustible within eight tenths of a mile. Japanese estimates put the total number of deaths caused by both bombs at around 200,000.

A day before the bombing of Nagasaki, the Soviet Union had declared war on Japan and begun an invasion of Manchuria. Stunned by the destruction of Hiroshima and Nagasaki, the Japanese soon offered to surrender. Despite their demand for unconditional surrender, the Allies allowed the Japanese emperor to remain on his throne. The formal surrender was signed on September 2, 1945, aboard the USS *Missouri* in Tokyo Bay.

✔ **READING CHECK:** What led the United States to drop the atomic bomb on Japan?

Nearly every building in the city of Hiroshima was flattened by the atomic bomb. The watch below was found in the rubble, stopped at the exact time of the explosion.

Costs of the War

After years of struggle and sacrifice, World War II had ended in victory for the Allies. The price of this victory was high, however. The toll in lives and property was without precedent. Most disturbing was the knowledge—fully revealed only after Germany's defeat—that Hitler had attempted to exterminate all the Jews of Europe. However, the Allies had achieved their war aims. Germany's Nazi government was destroyed, and Japan's military warlords were overthrown.

World War II was the most devastating war the world has ever known. It resulted in more deaths and destroyed more property than any other war in history. When it finally ended, hundreds of cities lay in ruins. Beautiful churches and palaces were reduced to rubble, and priceless works of art had gone up in smoke. Millions of people lacked heat, electricity, running water, adequate food, and the means to travel from one place to another. In some regions, mile upon mile of field and forest had been reduced to utter desolation.

Two examples indicate the extent of property lost in the war. In Düsseldorf, Germany, more than 90 percent of the homes were uninhabitable. The cities of Kiev and Minsk in the Soviet Union had to be completely rebuilt. The war brought untold suffering to civilians. According to one estimate, some 30 million civilians lost their lives from bombing, disease, shelling, or starvation. Millions more suffered from injuries or malnutrition. Millions lost everything they owned. The Soviet Union and China were particularly hard hit. As in World War I, U.S. civilian losses were relatively light. In economic terms, armaments and other military costs probably totaled more than $1 trillion. Along with peace came many uncertainties about the future.

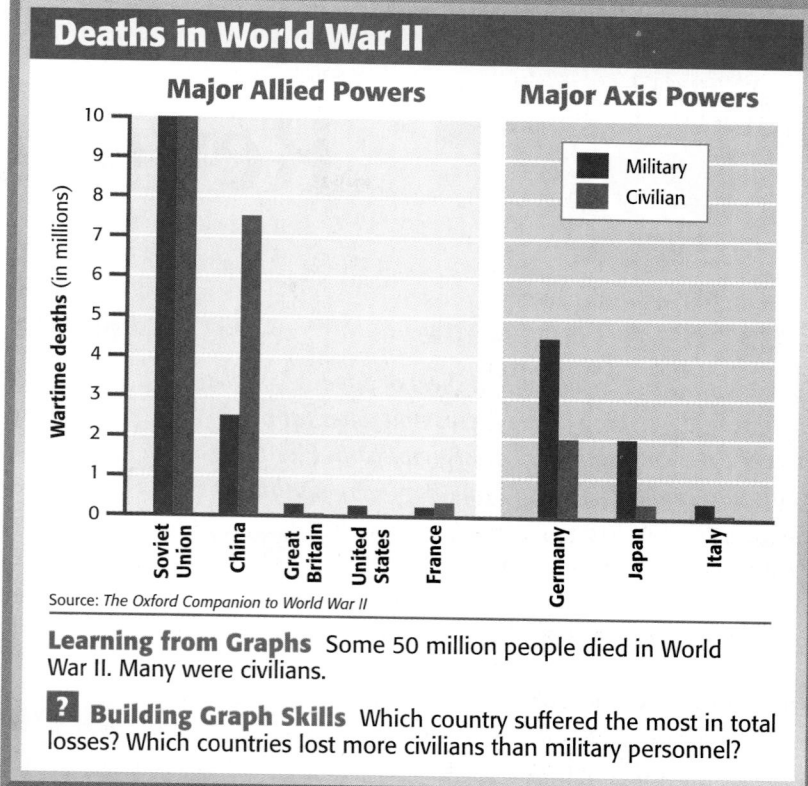

Deaths in World War II

Major Allied Powers · Major Axis Powers

Wartime deaths (in millions)

Military / Civilian

Soviet Union · China · Great Britain · United States · France · Germany · Japan · Italy

Source: *The Oxford Companion to World War II*

Learning from Graphs Some 50 million people died in World War II. Many were civilians.

? Building Graph Skills Which country suffered the most in total losses? Which countries lost more civilians than military personnel?

✔ **READING CHECK:** What were the human and economic costs of World War II?

SECTION 4 REVIEW

Define and explain the significance of the following terms:
island-hopping
Battle of Leyte Gulf
Battle of Iwo Jima
kamikaze
Battle of Okinawa
Manhattan Project
Enola Gay

Identify and explain the significance of the following person:
Harry S Truman

Locate and explain the significance of the following places:
Saipan
New Guinea
Hiroshima
Nagasaki

1. **Using Graphic Organizers** Copy the following diagram. Use it to explain the significance of the islands that U.S. forces captured after Guadalcanal as they advanced across the Pacific.

Guadalcanal
Islands
Significance

2. **Understanding Geography: Movement** How did U.S. military leaders adapt their strategy to suit the geography of the South Pacific?

3. **Assessing Consequences** How did Iwo Jima and Okinawa affect U.S. fighting in the Pacific?

4. **Synthesizing** Summarize the international consequences of World War II for the Allied Powers and Axis Powers.

Critical Thinking

5. Do you think the United States was justified in using the atomic bomb against Japan? Explain your answer.
   Consider:
   • what U.S. leaders knew about the bomb when they used it
   • the casualties in the battles of Iwo Jima and Okinawa
   • the long-term effects of a nuclear blast and the risks of a future nuclear war

CHAPTER 27

Review

Creating a Time Line

Copy the time line below onto a sheet of paper. Complete the time line by filling in the events and dates from the chapter that you think were most significant. Pick three events and explain why you think they were significant.

1941   1943   1945

Writing a Summary

Using the Reading Checks as a guide, write an overview of the events in the chapter.

Identifying People and Ideas

Identify the following terms or individuals and explain their significance.

1. War Production Board
2. Douglas MacArthur
3. Battle of Midway
4. braceros
5. Chester Nimitz
6. D-Day
7. genocide
8. Elie Wiesel
9. island-hopping
10. kamikaze

Understanding Main Ideas

SECTION 1
1. What advantages did the Axis Powers have over the Allies at the beginning of the war?
2. What steps did the U.S. government take to mobilize for war?

SECTION 2
3. What was daily life like for Americans during the war?

SECTION 3
4. How did the Nazis carry out the Holocaust?
5. What were the major turning points in the war with Germany?

SECTION 4
6. What was the Allied strategy in the Pacific?

Reviewing Themes

1. **Global Relations** How did the Allies pool their resources to win World War II?
2. **Constitutional Heritage** How did wartime conditions lead to restrictions on the rights of Japanese Americans?
3. **Technology and Society** What role did air power play in the Allied victory during World War II?

Thinking Critically

1. **Evaluating** How did the Japanese miscalculate the U.S. response to the attack on Pearl Harbor?
2. **Analyzing** What actions could the Allies have taken to win the war in Europe sooner?
3. **Taking a Stand** Imagine that you are President Truman. Would you have chosen to drop the atomic bomb or invade Japan? Explain your answer.
4. **Hypothesizing** What might have happened if the D-Day invasion has not succeeded?
5. **Synthesizing** What were the final costs and consequences of World War II?

Writing About History

Writing to Classify Copy the following organizational web. Use it to list the important battles, strategic decisions, and weapons that led to the Allied victory in the Pacific. Then write an encyclopedia entry explaining how the Allies achieved victory.

Strategies **for Success** Review the **Strategies for Success** on *Preparing Questions*. Then imagine that you have arranged an oral history interview with one of the following people:

a. a U.S. Navy veteran who served as a fighter pilot during the Battle of Midway
b. a Japanese American who was interned during World War II
c. an American woman who worked in a defense factory during the war
d. a scientist who took part in the Manhattan Project

Prepare at least six questions that you plan to ask during the interview.

Linking History and Geography

Allied prisoners on the Bataan Peninsula were forced to march from Mariveles to San Fernando. They were then shipped north by train. Study the map below. About how far did the prisoners have to march to reach San Fernando? About how far did they travel by train?

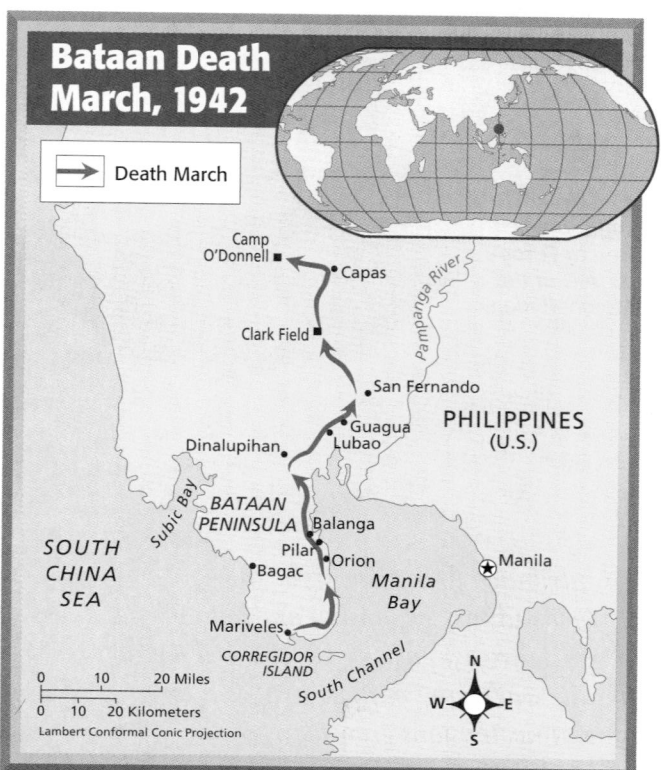

Bataan Death March, 1942

→ Death March

Camp O'Donnell
Capas
Pampanga River
Clark Field
San Fernando
Guagua
Lubao
PHILIPPINES (U.S.)
Dinalupihan
BATAAN PENINSULA
Subic Bay
Balanga
Pilar
Orion
Bagac
Manila
Manila Bay
SOUTH CHINA SEA
Mariveles
CORREGIDOR ISLAND
South Channel

0 10 20 Miles
0 10 20 Kilometers
Lambert Conformal Conic Projection

internet connect

TOPIC: Norman Rockwell
GO TO: go.hrw.com
KEYWORD: SD1 Rockwell

Accessing the Internet through the HRW Web site, research the World War II–era paintings of Norman Rockwell. Then write a paper in which you identify what moral values are represented in the Four Freedoms paintings.

BUILDING YOUR PORTFOLIO

Complete one or all of the following projects independently or cooperatively.

1 Global Relations
Imagine that you are a soldier fighting against the Japanese in the Pacific. **Write a letter** to your family describing the islands you have been on and the fighting you have seen.

2 Technology and Society
Imagine that you are serving on a government committee examining the effects of technology on the war. **Create a chart** that illustrate these effects.

3 Economic Development
Imagine that you are a factory worker during World War II. **Create a series of journal entries** expressing your feelings about the economic effect of the war on the home front.

The New York Sun
WAR TIME Cook Book
MENUS, RECIPES AND CANNING INFORMATION, TO HELP MAKE YOUR RATION POINTS GO FURTHER
By EDITH·M·BARBER
FAMED FOOD EDITOR OF THE NEW YORK SUN
25¢

1945–1960

The Cold War

THE GRANGER COLLECTION, NEW YORK

Poster of Mao Zedong after the Communist victory

UN medal

1945
World Events
Delegates from 50 nations meet in San Francisco to create the charter for the United Nations.

1949
World Events
Mao Zedong's Communist forces gain control of most of China.

1951
Daily Life
Americans organize a hero's welcome for General MacArthur upon his return from Korea after being removed by President Truman.

1952
Business and Finance
After 21 months of operation by federal troops, the U.S. government returns the country's railroads to private control.

1945   **1948**   **1951**

1947
Daily Life
Ten people working in the film industry refuse to testify before a House committee and are blacklisted.

A report on Communists in the entertainment industry

1948
Politics
The U.S. Congress passes the European Recovery Act, establishing the Marshall Plan to help stabilize and rebuild Europe.

A cargo of sugar on its way to Europe as part of the Marshall Plan

Before You Read

Build on What You Know

Economic problems during the 1930s contributed to the rise of dictatorships in Germany, Italy, and Japan. Their military expansion and acts of aggression led to World War II. The war destroyed parts of Europe and Asia. In this chapter you will learn that after the war many nations struggled to rebuild their war-torn economies. At the same time, tensions grew between the United States and the Soviet Union.

Robert Rauschenberg's painting Bed

Sputnik

Francis Gary Powers holds a model of his U-2 spy plane.

1955
The Arts
Robert Rauschenberg's *Bed* makes an important contribution to American art.

1957
Science and Technology
The Soviet Union launches *Sputnik*, the first artificial satellite, into orbit around Earth.

1958
Science and Technology
Congress establishes the National Aeronautics and Space Administration (NASA).

1960
World Events
The Paris summit between Soviet premier Khrushchev and President Eisenhower is canceled after the Soviets shoot down a U.S. spy plane.

1954

1957

1960

1953
The Arts
Playwright Arthur Miller writes *The Crucible*, in which he compares McCarthyism to the Salem witch trials.

1956
World Events
Egypt seizes the Suez Canal after the United States withdraws support for an Egyptian dam project on the Nile River.

1959
Politics
Soviet premier Nikita Khrushchev visits the United States.

Arthur Miller's The Crucible

Soviet premier Khrushchev (second from left) visited an American supermarket in 1959.

Think About Themes

*Decide whether you **agree** or **disagree** with the following statements. Note why in your journal.*

Global Relations Rivalry between two powerful nations will rarely affect the relationships between other countries.

Democratic Values The fears of the majority of Americans often limit the rights of groups that hold unpopular views.

Technology and Society The fear of technology affects the behavior of Americans and is often reflected in the literature and arts of the time.

Healing the Wounds of War

OBJECTIVES

Read to understand:

1. what actions Allied forces took to stabilize Germany and Japan after the war

2. how the Allied Powers tried war criminals, and why some people were dissatisfied with the trials

3. why the United Nations was founded, and how it was organized

4. what events led to the founding of the new country of Israel, and how Arab countries responded

KEY TERMS

Potsdam Conference
zaibatsu
Nuremberg Trials
United Nations
Zionism

KEY PEOPLE

Adolf Eichmann
Hideki Tojo
Trygve Lie
Eleanor Roosevelt
David Ben-Gurion
Ralph Bunche

EYEWITNESSES TO History

66 *There are moments when the drama of our times seems to focus on a single scene. The meeting at Potsdam [Germany] is one of those moments. We can hardly take in the sense of what happened until it is spelled out in a picture like this. The picture of three men walking in a graveyard. They are the men who hold in their hands most of the power in the world.* 99
—Anne O'Hare McCormick

President Truman views the destruction in Germany.

Journalist Anne O'Hare McCormick imagined the scene at a conference between Winston Churchill, Joseph Stalin, and Harry S Truman to determine the fate of postwar Germany. The most powerful nations of the world were left with the urgent task of easing the human suffering and political chaos resulting from the war. Many Americans believed that the United States should lead the way. "The war and the victory showed us what we could do in the world," said Melville Grosvenor, a magazine editor. The United States worked with the other Allies to restore peace by occupying Germany and Japan and by creating a new international organization called the United Nations.

Occupation Rule

After the war, Germany and Japan lay in ruins, their wartime governments shattered. German actress Hildegard Knef described a German town "without houses, without windowpanes, without roofs; holes in the asphalt, rubble, rubbish, rats." An American soldier noted that in the area around Tokyo, "there was practically nothing left; the rubble did not even look like much." A Japanese American soldier remarked of the devastation: "Tokyo was all flattened, and people were living in holes with corrugated roofs. They were desperate for food." With the fighting over, Germany and Japan now faced the task of rebuilding their governments, economies, and cities under the watchful eye of the Allies.

The occupation of Germany. To decide how to handle postwar Germany, Allied leaders met in Potsdam, Germany, in July 1945. This **Potsdam Conference** was the first time President Truman had met with Winston Churchill and Joseph Stalin since President Roosevelt's death. Churchill was replaced during the conference by Great Britain's new prime minister, Clement Attlee. The three leaders worked out an agreement over the details of their joint occupation of Germany. The leaders divided Germany into four occupation zones. The British, the French, and the Americans each took control of an area in the western, industrialized part of Germany. The Soviets agreed to control the poorer, more rural eastern part. The four powers also divided Austria into zones and agreed to jointly administer the city of Berlin, within the Soviet-controlled part of Germany.

In order to stabilize Germany, the occupying powers pledged to crush the Nazi Party, re-establish local governments, and rebuild German industry. The Allies also agreed to return German refugees to their homes. The Potsdam Conference attendees recognized that the joint occupation of Germany would require cooperation. However, Soviet occupation of much of Eastern Europe caused tensions among the Allies. Stalin demanded that the other Allies recognize Soviet-backed Poland's claims to German territory it had occupied during the war. They reluctantly agreed but grew increasingly concerned about Soviet expansion in Eastern Europe. Another source of tension was the Soviet Union's demand for immediate reparations from Germany.

The occupation of Japan. Postwar Japan also faced huge challenges in its efforts to rebuild. Its economy lay in shambles, and Hiroshima and Nagasaki had been devastated by atomic bombs. The United States occupied defeated Japan from 1945 to 1952.

Occupied Germany, 1945–1950

Learning from Maps The United States and the Soviet Union occupied the largest portions of Germany.

❓ PLACE Which country controlled the zone in which Munich was located?

Occupied Berlin

Zones:
- U.S.
- Soviet
- British
- French
- 1949 Date created

In addition to helping rebuild the Japanese economy, the United States worked to end Japanese militarism and to establish a democratic government. During the occupation, Emperor Hirohito remained in the imperial palace, but he had no power. Allied Supreme Commander Douglas MacArthur, his staff, and a new Japanese congress ran the country.

Under MacArthur's direction, Japan demobilized several million troops and adopted a new constitution in 1947. The constitution set up a democratic system of government, which gave voting rights to women and granted freedom of religion. The constitution also abolished the Japanese army and navy and prohibited Japan from ever again becoming a military power. Although the constitution was clearly influenced by American ideals, it won wide support from the Japanese people.

The Japanese also made important economic reforms. One program gave land to Japanese farmers. The government allowed labor unions to organize. It also broke up the *zaibatsu*, huge corporations run by single families that had monopolized the Japanese economy. These political and economic reforms laid the foundation for Japan's tremendous postwar economic recovery.

✔ **READING CHECK:** What actions did the Allies take to stabilize Germany and Japan after the war?

Emperor Hirohito unveils Japan's new constitution and announces the abolition of the armed forces.

Nuremberg Trials. Allied judges tried German officers in Nuremberg, Germany. The commander of the German air force, Hermann Göring, is shown on the witness stand. *What characteristics of this courtroom could lead you to assume that this is a military trial?*

The War Crimes Trials

After the war, Allied leaders began to think about how to punish the military leaders who committed or ordered atrocities during the war. At the Potsdam Conference, the Allied leaders agreed that "stern justice shall be meted [given] out to all war criminals, including those who have visited cruelties upon our prisoners." The Allied leaders agreed that convicted German and Japanese war criminals must be punished for waging war and for the mistreatment of prisoners.

Nuremberg Trials. The German war crimes trials were known as the **Nuremberg Trials** because they took place in Nuremberg, Germany, the former rallying place of Adolf Hitler's Nazi Party. The trials began in November 1945. Before an international military court, witnesses gave chilling accounts of Nazi atrocities, including the torture and murder of millions of Jews, Gypsies, and others. Marie Vaillant, a concentration camp survivor, testified.

> 66 For months, for years we had one wish only: the wish that some of us would escape alive, in order to tell the world what the Nazi convict prisons were like. . . . There was the systematic . . . urge to use human beings as slaves and to kill them when they could work no more. 99

In September 1946 the court made its first rulings. The court had tried a number of Nazi leaders on four charges. They were charged with planning the war, committing war crimes and other crimes against humanity, and conspiring to commit the crimes. Twelve Nazi leaders were sentenced to death. Seven others received jail sentences, and three were acquitted.

In other trials held in the U.S. occupation zone, thousands of former Nazi leaders were tried and jailed, fined, or barred from public office. However, many Nazis, including Adolf Eichmann, the architect of the Jewish extermination program, avoided immediate prosecution by hiding their identities and escaping to Latin America.

Trials in Tokyo. In Tokyo General MacArthur set up the International Military Tribunal for the Far East in early 1946. This court conducted trials against suspected war criminals from the war in the Pacific. The court prosecuted more than 20 leaders of Japan's military. The trials lasted from May 1946 to November 1948. Seven people were sentenced to death, including Hideki Tojo, the premier during the war. Others were sentenced to life in prison.

Shocked by the war crimes, many Americans argued that more German and Japanese officials should have been punished. Nevertheless, the judges followed legal procedures and tried not to act out of anger. The trials set important standards for international law and the conduct of war. The chief lesson was that countries and individuals can be held accountable for their actions during war. Many countries now accept the idea that war crimes cannot be excused on the grounds that those responsible were "just following orders."

✔ **READING CHECK:** How did the Allies go about punishing war criminals? Why were some people dissatisfied with the trials?

The United Nations

During the war, the Allies had met several times to map out strategies to defeat the Axis Powers. Delegates from the United States, Britain, the Soviet Union, and China met in 1944 at Dumbarton Oaks, an estate in Washington, D.C. There they worked out a proposal for a postwar international organization called the **United Nations** (UN).

The founding of the UN.

The Allies hoped to use the UN to continue working for world peace. In April 1945, delegates from 50 nations met in San Francisco to draw up the Charter of the United Nations. The charter provided for a General Assembly and a Security Council. The General Assembly includes all member nations. The 15-member Security Council includes 5 permanent members and 10 rotating members. The United States, the Soviet Union, Britain, France, and China are the permanent members. It addresses military and political problems and has the power to veto any action proposed by the General Assembly.

Soon after the creation of the UN Charter, the Senate overwhelmingly approved U.S. membership in the UN. On October 24, 1945, the UN officially came into existence. The UN established its headquarters in New York City. Trygve Lie (TRIG-vuh LEE) of Norway served as the UN's first secretary-general. Former first lady Eleanor Roosevelt served as one of the first U.S. delegates to the UN.

The Charter of the United Nations

Foreign ministers from the United States, Britain, and the Soviet Union met in Moscow in October 1943. They established a common goal to form "a general international organization, based on the sovereign equality of all peace-loving states." In a conference held between August and October 1944 in Washington, D.C., the same three countries together with China drew up a tentative charter. After another planning conference in April 1945, the United Nations Charter was adopted by the United States on July 28, 1945.

WE THE PEOPLES OF THE UNITED NATIONS DETERMINED to save succeeding generations from the scourge [destruction] of war, which twice in our lifetime has brought untold sorrow to mankind, and to reaffirm faith in fundamental human rights, in the dignity and worth of the human person, in the equal rights of men and women and of nations large and small, and to establish conditions under which justice and respect for the obligations arising from treaties . . . to promote social progress and better standards of life in larger freedom, AND FOR THESE ENDS to practice tolerance and live together in peace with one another as good neighbors . . . HAVE RESOLVED TO COMBINE OUR EFFORTS TO ACCOMPLISH THESE AIMS.

Accordingly, our respective Governments . . . have agreed to the present Charter of the United Nations and do hereby establish an international organization to be known as the United Nations.

Eleanor Roosevelt's contribution.

Born to a distinguished New York City family on October 11, 1884, Eleanor Roosevelt lived a solemn and often lonely childhood. Both of her parents died when she was 10. "It was the grimmest childhood I had ever known. Who did she have? Nobody," sympathized one of Roosevelt's cousins.

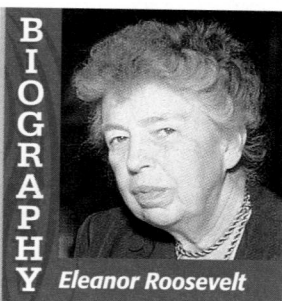

Eleanor Roosevelt

At the age of 14, Roosevelt was enrolled in Allenswood, a girl's school outside of London. At the school, Roosevelt found warmth and intellectual encouragement. Describing her years at Allenswood, Roosevelt later explained that "whatever I have become since had its seeds in those three years of contact with a liberal mind and strong personality."

After leaving the boarding school at age 17, Roosevelt returned to New York. She eagerly turned

Read More About It

Free Find:
Eleanor Roosevelt
After reading about Eleanor Roosevelt on the **Holt Researcher** CD–ROM, write a short essay explaining how her concern for social issues influenced her political career.

The Religious Spirit

AMERICAN JUDAISM

Thousands of Jewish refugees and Holocaust survivors from Europe resettled in what would become the nation of Israel. Many others headed for the United States. Between 1935 and 1941 some 150,000 European Jews immigrated to the United States. These new immigrants contributed to the already diverse Jewish American community in the United States.

The menorah is used to celebrate the Jewish holiday of Hanukkah.

During the 1950s American Judaism was dominated by three denominations—Orthodox, Conservative, and Reform. Some Jewish immigrants embraced Orthodox Judaism's emphasis on a unity of past and present faith and on the strict observance of religious laws. Conservative and Reform Judaism, however, proved much more popular.

Some immigrants liked the relaxed interpretation of religious observance offered by Reform Judaism. This denomination had been popular in the United States since the late 1800s. It also presented a more Americanized Judaism—holding services in English and establishing a Sunday Sabbath. Reform Judaism also presented the Jewish faith simply as an organized religion. Emphasizing both Jewish religious heritage and Jewish ethnic identity, Conservative Judaism attracted the majority of the Jewish immigrants. All three denominations attempted to spread awareness of anti-Semitism. Orthodox and particularly Conservative Judaism also encouraged Jewish nationalism, primarily in terms of support for the nation of Israel. ■

toward a life of social activism and settlement-house work. By her early twenties, Roosevelt had gained recognition in New York City's growing community of social reformers.

Roosevelt continued her social activism and political work throughout her marriage to her cousin, Franklin D. Roosevelt. Eleanor Roosevelt's political career continued well after her husband's death. In 1945 she was selected to be a U.S. delegate to the United Nations. In this role, Roosevelt was instrumental in creating a declaration of human rights that would provide a universal standard set of inalienable rights. Roosevelt and many other UN delegates realized that building world peace after World War II required cooperation among nations. Roosevelt explained her view.

66 **Security requires both control of the use of force and the elimination of want. No people are secure unless they have the things needed not only to preserve existence, but to make life worth living. . . . All peoples throughout the world must know that there is an organization where their interests can be considered and where justice and security will be sought for all.** 99

From "En Route to London, January 5, (1946) from *My Day, Volume II: the Post-War Years* by Eleanor Roosevelt, edited by David Emblidge. Copyright © 1990 by Pharos Books. Reprinted by permission of *United Feature Syndicate, Inc.*

Roosevelt remained politically active and worked for human rights until her death in 1962.

Early critics of the UN insisted that it was doomed to fail because it did not have the power to enforce its own decisions. Nevertheless, most Americans were as optimistic as President Truman, who noted in 1945: "This [UN] charter points down the only road to enduring peace. There is no other."

✔ **READING CHECK:** Why was the United Nations founded, and how was it organized?

The Founding of Israel

One of the first major conflicts the United Nations faced concerned Palestine, a small eastern Mediterranean region claimed by both Jews and Arabs. After World War II, many European Jews moved to Palestine—despite Arab protest—rather than return to Europe. Britain, which had ruled Palestine since World War I, could not resolve conflicting claims over the territory. In 1947 Britain turned the issue over to the United Nations. The UN came up with a plan to divide Palestine into two states—one for Jews, the other for Arabs—but Arabs rejected the proposal.

Zionism. The UN plan was a victory for **Zionism**, the movement seeking a Jewish homeland in Palestine. Zionist leader David Ben-Gurion (ben-goohr-YAWN) had supported the idea since the early 1900s. Born in what is now Poland, Ben-Gurion moved to Palestine in 1906. He was expelled in 1915 for Zionist activities. Exiled, he went to the United States to raise money and recruit volunteers among the American Jewish community.

When the British forces withdrew from Palestine in 1948, Ben-Gurion and other Jewish leaders promptly proclaimed the new state of Israel. Both the United States and the Soviet Union immediately recognized the new nation.

The Arab-Israeli War.

The Arab states, however, reacted violently. They refused to recognize Israel and organized military forces to reclaim the state for Palestine. Armies from the Arab states of Egypt, Iraq, Lebanon, Syria, and Transjordan joined Palestinian forces to attack Israel. Although vastly outnumbered, Israeli forces under Ben-Gurion's overall command captured and held much of Palestine. Israeli soldiers used an impressive arsenal bought in part with millions of dollars that poured in from the American Jewish community.

In an attempt to end the war, the UN sent a mediator, Count Folke Bernadotte of Sweden, to the Middle East. Bernadotte negotiated a shaky cease-fire, but he was assassinated by Israeli extremists. In 1949 a second UN mediator, the U.S. diplomat Ralph Bunche, persuaded both sides to accept an armistice. Bunche won the Nobel Peace Prize in 1950. He was the first African American to receive that honor.

The 1949 agreement gave Israel more territory than the earlier UN partition plan had, but it divided Jerusalem into Arab and Israeli zones. The plan gave Egypt control of the Gaza Strip, and Jordan took over the West Bank of the Jordan River. The Arab countries, however, still refused to recognize the state of Israel. Also left unresolved was the fate of the Palestinian Arabs remaining in Israel.

✔ **READING CHECK:** What events led to the founding of the new country of Israel? How did Arab countries respond?

INTERPRETING THE VISUAL RECORD

Zionism. After World War II thousands of European Jews made their way to British-controlled Palestine. These three Holocaust survivors traveled to Palestine in June 1945. *What emotions do you think these Jewish settlers felt as they arrived in their new homeland?*

SECTION REVIEW

Define and explain the significance of the following terms:
Potsdam Conference
zaibatsu
Nuremberg Trials
United Nations
Zionism

Identify and explain the significance of the following individuals:
Adolf Eichmann
Hideki Tojo
Trygve Lie
Eleanor Roosevelt
David Ben-Gurion
Ralph Bunche

1. **Using Graphic Organizers** Copy the graphic organizer below. Use it to compare the ways Allied forces attempted to stabilize Germany and Japan after World War II.

Allied Efforts to Stabilize Germany	Allied Efforts to Stabilize Japan

2. **Taking a Stand** Was justice served in the Nuremberg and Tokyo war crimes trials? Consider both the victims' and the criminals' perspectives.

3. **Hypothesizing** How do you think World War II influenced the purpose of the United Nations? How did this affect its structure?

4. **Analyzing** What events led the UN to try to resolve the conflict over Jewish and Arab claims to Palestine? How successful was this effort?

Critical Thinking

5. How did nations act in a spirit of cooperation after World War II? In what ways did nations compete?
   Consider:
   • what actions nations took during the occupation of Germany and Japan
   • what the purpose and goals of the UN were
   • how the conflict in Palestine developed and was resolved

The Cold War Begins

OBJECTIVES

Read to understand:

1. what caused the Cold War, and what the U.S. strategy during the Cold War was
2. how the U.S. government tried to control the development of atomic weapons
3. how the Marshall Plan helped block the spread of communism in Europe
4. how the Western Allies tried to limit Soviet expansion

KEY TERMS

Cold War
satellite nations
containment
Baruch Plan
Atomic Energy Act
Truman Doctrine
Marshall Plan
Berlin Airlift
NATO
Warsaw Pact

KEY PEOPLE

George Kennan
George C. Marshall

KEY PLACES

West Germany
East Germany

EYEWITNESSES TO History

66 *Only two great powers remained in the world, the United States and the Soviet Union. . . . And it was clear that the Soviet Union was aggressive and expanding. For the United States to take steps to strengthen countries threatened with Soviet aggression . . . was to protect not only the security of the United States—it was to protect freedom itself.* 99
—Dean Acheson

This poster reflects the fear of the spread of communism.

One State Department official recalled Secretary of State Dean Acheson's reflections on the developing political standoff between the United States and the Soviet Union after World War II. As the war ended, the wartime alliance between the United States and the Soviet Union collapsed. At odds over competing global objectives and different economic and political systems, the two countries fought for control of Europe and control of atomic weapons.

The Roots of the Cold War

An intense rivalry between the United States and the Soviet Union began after World War II. With once-mighty Germany, Japan, and Great Britain in ruins, only the United States and the Soviet Union were left to struggle for international dominance. Their competition for global power and influence, which came to be known as the **Cold War**, was waged mostly on political and economic fronts rather than on the battlefield. Nonetheless, the threat of all-out war was always present.

The origins of the Cold War lay in economic, political, and philosophical differences between the two nations. Committed to the principles of democratic government, individual freedom, and a capitalist economy, most Americans deeply opposed the Soviet system. Founded on communist theories, the Soviet system had evolved to include a state-run economy, one-party rule, suppression of religion, and the use of force to crush opposition.

Dictator Joseph Stalin ruled the Soviet Union with an iron fist.

Soviet expansionism after World War II fueled American mistrust. During World War II the Soviets had taken over the Baltic states of Estonia, Latvia, and Lithuania. Then they captured large areas of Poland and Romania. By war's end the Soviets also controlled Manchuria. After the war, Soviet leader Joseph Stalin made clear his determination to maintain Soviet influence in Eastern Europe. He claimed the need for a buffer zone of "friendly nations" on the Soviet Union's western border. He installed pro-Soviet governments in Poland and Romania and worked to establish communist rule throughout Eastern Europe. These countries under Soviet control became known as **satellite nations**.

Concerned by Stalin's actions, Britain, France, and the United States strengthened their control of western Germany and revived its industries. Winston Churchill, Britain's wartime prime minister, described this expansion of Soviet influence. Churchill declared that a Soviet "Iron Curtain has descended across the Continent," isolating Western Europe from Soviet-dominated Eastern Europe. Churchill called for closer cooperation between Britain and the United States to control Soviet power. At the time, George Kennan, a State Department official and Soviet expert, advised similar action. Kennan suggested a policy of **containment**, or restricting the expansion of Soviet communism. Many Americans applauded this tough stand against communism. Kennan explained his philosophy:

George Kennan's article on containment appeared in this issue of Foreign Affairs.

> 66 The Soviet pressure against the free institutions of the Western world is something that can be contained by the . . . vigilant [determined] application of counterforce at a series of constantly shifting geographical and political points. . . . The Russians look forward to a duel of infinite duration. 99

✔ **READING CHECK:** What caused the Cold War? What was the U.S. strategy during the Cold War?

Strategies for Success

Taking Notes

Taking notes—writing down information in a concise and orderly manner—is a basic practice that is particularly important for conducting a successful oral history interview. Taking notes allows you to clarify and organize the content of an interview and provides a valuable key for remembering and working with this content later.

How to Take Notes

1. **Select specific information.** Select specific information to include in your notes, concentrating on the main ideas and any strong opinions that your subject communicates in the interview. Take note of any particularly interesting examples or stories mentioned by your subject.
2. **Paraphrase the information.** Put the information in your own words, rather than trying to copy what your subject says exactly. Feel free to use shorthand terms and symbols, but make sure to write legibly so that you will understand your notes when you review them.
3. **Review the notes thoroughly.** Shortly after the interview has been completed, review your notes and add any important supplementary information that you may remember. If the interview was recorded, listen to the recording and make sure that your notes accurately represent what was said.

Applying the Strategy

Take notes on the following excerpt from an oral history provided by Erhard Dabringhaus, a former U.S. military intelligence officer who took part in the occupation of Germany after World War II. Dabringhaus was interviewed during the early 1980s.

> 66 [In] 1948, a new directive came from [intelligence] headquarters. We're no longer interested as we used to be in former German Nazis. We're now interested in what's happening behind the East-West border. Communism becomes our most important interest. We're now looking for communists. We want to know about the newly organized government in France, after the war. How many Communists are in it? 99

Practicing the Strategy

Use the excerpt above to answer the following questions.
1. What is the general topic of the excerpt?
2. What ideas does Dabringhaus communicate in the excerpt?
3. What opinions does Dabringhaus express in the excerpt?

Deadlock over Atomic Weapons

After World War II the Soviet Union began to develop atomic technology. The United States and the Soviet Union soon became locked in a dispute over the issue. This standoff terrified many Americans, who feared the outbreak of nuclear war.

Atomic testing. A column of U.S. Army troops observes the testing of an atomic bomb in the Nevada desert in 1951. *What do you think this photograph reveals about the power of atomic weapons?*

Most people shared lawyer David E. Lilienthal's 1946 opinion that "the awful strength of atomic power . . . directly affects every man, woman, and child in the world."

U.S. presidential adviser Bernard Baruch called for the creation of a special international agency with the authority to inspect any country's atomic-energy plants. This proposal, known as the **Baruch Plan**, would impose penalties on countries that did not follow international rules. Until such a plan was in place, Baruch said, the United States would not reveal any atomic-energy secrets or give up its atomic weapons. At the time, U.S. physicists were developing more-powerful nuclear weapons.

Working feverishly on its own bomb, the Soviet Union rejected all inspection and enforcement provisions. With neither country willing to compromise, hopes for international control of atomic energy died. When the Soviet Union tested its first atomic bomb in 1949, the feared nuclear arms race became a reality.

In response to fears of nuclear warfare, Congress passed the **Atomic Energy Act** in August 1946. The act created the civilian-controlled Atomic Energy Commission (AEC) to oversee nuclear weapons research and to promote peacetime uses of atomic energy.

✔ **READING CHECK:** How did the U.S. government try to control the development of atomic weapons?

Containment Around the World

As the Cold War continued, the Truman administration followed a more aggressive policy toward the Soviet Union. The U.S. containment policy was adopted in reaction to certain events in Greece. A civil war had broken out there in 1946. Communist-led rebels fought against the Greek monarchy, which relied on military and financial aid from Britain. In early 1947, however, Britain announced that it could no longer aid Greece. Without aid, Greece's pro-Western government could not defend itself from communist forces.

The Mediterranean. At the same time, the Soviet Union pressured Turkey to give up sole control of the Dardanelles. This narrow strait links the Black Sea and the Mediterranean. President Truman knew that control of this area would give the Soviets a dominant position in the eastern Mediterranean. In a speech to Congress, Truman stated, "It must be the policy of the United States to support free peoples who are resisting attempted subjugation [conquest] by armed minorities or by outside pressures."

His statement became known as the **Truman Doctrine**. It made no mention of the Soviet Union, although clearly Truman had the Soviets in mind. In support of Truman's plan, Congress soon approved $400 million to aid Greece and Turkey.

Europe. After World War II, European economies were in shambles. In 1948 Germany produced just 45 percent of the goods it had produced before the war. The winter of 1946–47 brought the worst blizzards in some 50 years. Some Americans believed that the United States should help Europe. They feared that economic problems would make Western Europe more vulnerable to Communists' influence.

George C. Marshall

Secretary of State George C. Marshall shared this belief. Born in 1880 in Uniontown, Pennsylvania, Marshall was a very shy boy. In his first year at the Virginia Military Institute, he did poorly. Marshall developed his leadership skills and graduated near the top of his class.

Following his graduation in 1901, he pursued a career in the army. During World War I Marshall served under General John J. Pershing and helped develop military strategy. Franklin D. Roosevelt appointed Marshall army chief of staff in 1939.

After the war, Marshall served briefly as a U.S. representative to China before Truman appointed him secretary of state in 1947. Marshall gave a speech at Harvard University on June 5, 1947. He warned that if steps were not taken soon, Europe faced "economic, social, and political" collapse. He called for a major U.S. effort to promote European recovery. Its goal was "to permit the emergence of political and social conditions in which free institutions can exist." Marshall warned that any attempt to block recovery or to take advantage of Europe's difficulties for political ends would face strong U.S. opposition.

In response, Truman asked Congress for $17 billion in economic aid for Europe. Truman's request sparked heated debate. A turning point in the debate came early in 1948, when pro-Soviet Communists overthrew the government of Czechoslovakia. Congress soon funded the European Recovery Program, or **Marshall Plan**, in April 1948. For his efforts, Marshall won the Nobel Peace Prize in 1953.

Marshall resigned as secretary of state in 1949. The following year, Truman appointed him secretary of defense to prepare the U.S. armed forces for possible confrontations with communist forces. After 1951 Marshall became an adviser on defense and military matters. He died in Washington, D.C., in 1959.

✔ **READING CHECK:** How did the Marshall Plan help contain the spread of communism?

Then and Now

Extending Economic Aid Abroad

With the Marshall Plan, the United States established a lasting standard. Through financial aid, the United States provided the resources for nations to rebuild industries and economic institutions after a crisis. The Marshall Plan supplied billions of dollars that were used to rebuild European factories, increase agricultural production, and restore roads and bridges. Many Americans believed that the aid would strengthen the postwar U.S. economy, as Europeans would eventually begin to buy American products.

Since the end of World War II, the United States has assisted many nations and maintained a great deal of influence throughout the world by extending economic aid abroad. In recent years, the U.S. government has helped several Latin American countries rebuild after devastating natural disasters. After Hurricane Mitch struck the coasts of Nicaragua and Honduras in 1998, the U.S. Congress passed the Emergency Supplemental Appropriations Bill. It provided some $950 million to aid countries affected by floods and mudslides. The funds were used to establish public health programs, rebuild devastated economies, and create plans for dealing with future disasters. The United States has also assisted Russia and other countries struggling with economic crises. Giving economic aid helps the U.S. economy by strengthening its trading partners worldwide.

Tipper Gore (right) visited Honduras after Hurricane Mitch struck in 1998.

PAR LE PLAN MARSHALL
COOPERATION INTEREUROPEENNE
POUR UN NIVEAU DE VIE PLUS ELEVE

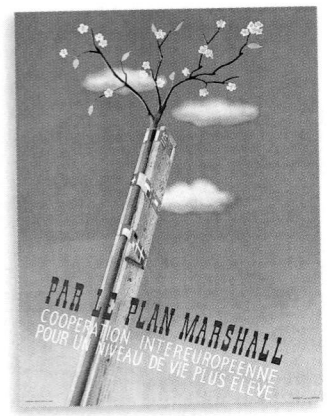

The Marshall Plan helped Europe rebuild after World War II.

Crisis in Berlin

The non-Soviet zones of Germany grew stronger as a result of the Marshall Plan. In early June 1948 Britain, France, and the United States announced plans to combine their zones and support the formation of a West German government.

The Berlin Airlift. The Soviet Union opposed this action. On June 24, 1948, the Soviets suddenly blocked all roads, canals, and railways linking Berlin to western Germany. They cut off shipments of food, fuel, and other crucial supplies to the city. The Soviets hoped to drive the Western powers out of Berlin.

Western leaders responded to the Soviet move with the **Berlin Airlift**. Over the next 10 months, U.S. and British planes carried more than 2 million tons of food

Cold War Alliances in Europe, 1955

Learning from Maps The Soviet Union dominated Eastern Europe after World War II. The Soviets and their allies united to form the Warsaw Pact in 1955.

? LOCATION Which nations were members of the Warsaw Pact?

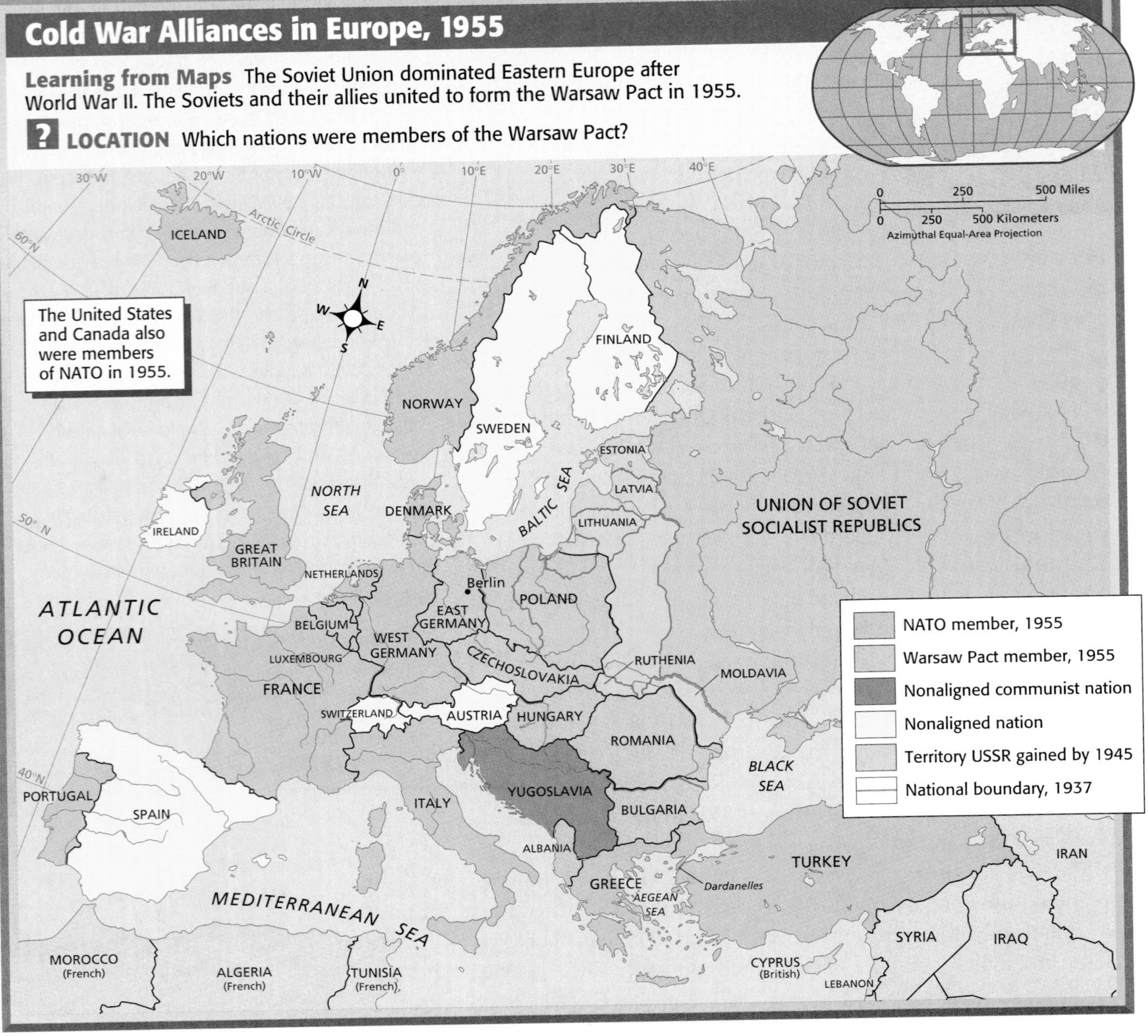
30°W
20°W
10°W
0°
10°E
20°E
30°E
40°E
60°N
50°N
40°N
Arctic Circle
0 250 500 Miles
0 250 500 Kilometers
Azimuthal Equal-Area Projection
N
S
E
W
The United States and Canada also were members of NATO in 1955.
ICELAND
NORWAY
SWEDEN
FINLAND
ESTONIA
LATVIA
LITHUANIA
BALTIC SEA
NORTH SEA
DENMARK
IRELAND
GREAT BRITAIN
NETHERLANDS
BELGIUM
LUXEMBOURG
Berlin
EAST GERMANY
WEST GERMANY
POLAND
CZECHOSLOVAKIA
RUTHENIA
MOLDAVIA
UNION OF SOVIET SOCIALIST REPUBLICS
ATLANTIC OCEAN
FRANCE
SWITZERLAND
AUSTRIA
HUNGARY
ROMANIA
YUGOSLAVIA
BULGARIA
ALBANIA
ITALY
PORTUGAL
SPAIN
GREECE
AEGEAN SEA
Dardanelles
TURKEY
BLACK SEA
IRAN
SYRIA
IRAQ
LEBANON
CYPRUS (British)
MEDITERRANEAN SEA
MOROCCO (French)
ALGERIA (French)
TUNISIA (French)
NATO member, 1955
Warsaw Pact member, 1955
Nonaligned communist nation
Nonaligned nation
Territory USSR gained by 1945
National boundary, 1937

and supplies to the people of West Berlin. As one Berliner recalled, the airlift became the city's lifeline to the rest of the world.

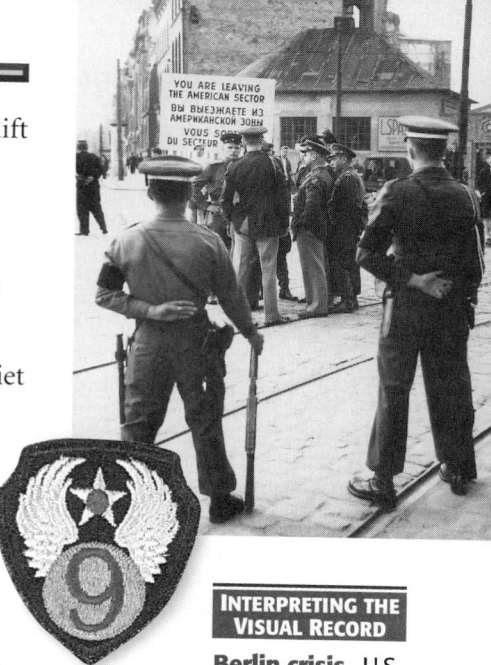

66 **Early in the morning, when we woke up, the first thing we did was listen to see whether the noise of aircraft engines could be heard. That gave us the certainty that we were not alone, that the whole civilized world took part in the fight for Berlin's freedom.** 99

The success of the Berlin Airlift proved a huge embarrassment to the Soviet Union. In May 1949 the Soviets lifted the blockade. Soon after, the Federal Republic of Germany, known as West Germany, was founded. In response, the Soviets set up the German Democratic Republic—East Germany—in the Soviet zone. The division of Germany would last for more than 40 years.

The Western alliance. After the Berlin crisis, the United States shifted its attention in Europe from economic recovery to military security. In April 1949 nine Western European nations joined the United States, Canada, and Iceland in a military alliance called the North Atlantic Treaty Organization, or **NATO**. Under the terms of the NATO treaty, each member nation pledged to defend the others in the event of an outside attack.

In 1951 General Dwight D. Eisenhower became the supreme commander of NATO forces. As its contribution to NATO, the United States stationed troops in Europe and gave massive military aid to its European allies. The Soviet Union responded in 1955 by forming its own military alliance with other communist countries in Eastern Europe. This alliance came to be called the **Warsaw Pact**.

INTERPRETING THE VISUAL RECORD

Berlin crisis. U.S. military police in Berlin face their Soviet counterparts across the dividing line between the Allied and Soviet zones. *How do the soldiers and the sign in this photograph reflect the growing tension in Berlin?*

✔ **READING CHECK:** How did the Western Allies try to limit Soviet expansion?

SECTION ② **REVIEW**

Define and explain the significance of the following terms:
Cold War
satellite nations
containment
Baruch Plan
Atomic Energy Act
Truman Doctrine
Marshall Plan
Berlin Airlift

NATO
Warsaw Pact

Identify and explain the significance of the following individuals:
George Kennan
George C. Marshall

Locate and explain the significance of the following places:
West Germany
East Germany

1. **Using Graphic Organizers** Copy the chart below. Use it to explain how differences between the Soviet Union and the United States led to the Cold War.

Differences in:	Soviet Union	United States
Economic Structure		
Views of Democracy		
Personal Freedom		
Goals for Expansion		

2. **Problem Solving** Imagine that you are working for the U.S. government in 1946. What measures would you propose to help curb the development of atomic weapons?
3. **Hypothesizing** What do you think would have happened if the United States had not implemented the Marshall Plan?
4. **Recognizing Point of View** Why did the Soviet Union view the formation of a West German state and NATO as a threat?

Critical Thinking

5. How was George Kennan's containment policy put into practice?
   Consider:
   • what the policy of containment was
   • how the Marshall Plan fit into the containment strategy
   • how NATO and the Berlin Airlift aided the containment strategy

The Cold War Turns Hot

OBJECTIVES

Read to understand:

1. how the Chinese Communists gained control of China
2. what factors led to the escalation of the conflict in Korea
3. what effect the Korean War had on U.S. politics
4. what methods President Eisenhower used to promote U.S. interests abroad

KEY TERMS

Korean War
brinkmanship
Central Intelligence Agency
U-2 incident

KEY PEOPLE

Chiang Kai-shek
Mao Zedong
Kim Il Sung
Syngman Rhee
Douglas MacArthur
Dwight D. Eisenhower
Nikita Khrushchev

KEY PLACES

North Korea
South Korea
Inch'ŏn
Seoul

66 *The responsibility for the failure of our foreign policy in the Far East rests squarely with the White House and the Department of State. . . . Our diplomats and their advisers . . . lost sight of our tremendous stake in a non-Communist China. . . . This House must now assume the responsibility of preventing the onrushing tide of communism from engulfing all of Asia.* **99**
—John F. Kennedy

Chinese Communist troops enter Shanghai

U.S. representative John F. Kennedy of Massachusetts expressed his disappointment that Communists in China had taken over the city of Beijing in 1949. Like most Americans, Kennedy feared that a Communist victory in China would allow communism to spread throughout Asia.

Communist Victory in China

Tensions over the spread of communism came to a head in China. In the early 1900s, revolutionary forces had attempted to overthrow the Qing imperial dynasty. The revolution of 1911 left China an unstable republic. Upset with how the republic was run and inspired by the Bolshevik Revolution, a number of Chinese students established the Chinese Communist Party. By the mid-1920s a civil war had erupted between Nationalist and Communist forces. Led by Chiang Kai-shek, the Kuomintang (KWOH-min-TANG), or Nationalist Party, battled the Chinese Communists. Chiang's war with the Communists kept him from devoting his full attention to Japanese aggression. During World War II, the Communists and the Nationalists cooperated to resist Japanese attacks.

At war's end, however, the conflict resumed. The Communists had prevented the Japanese from controlling all of northwest China. There Communist leader Mao Zedong made reforms that gave land to peasants. This and their fight against the Japanese won additional support for the Communists and increased recruits for their army.

The United States did not want China to become a communist country. During and after World War II, the United States sent economic and military aid, including troops, to China to unite the country under the Nationalists. President Truman sent General George C. Marshall to China in 1945 to arrange a truce between the warring parties, but neither Chiang nor Mao would compromise.

Opposition to Chiang mounted, and Mao's forces gained control of most of the country by 1949. Realizing defeat, Chiang and his army retreated to the island of Taiwan, off the coast of southeast China. The Chinese Communists established the People's Republic of China. The United States rejected this new government, however, and continued to recognize the Nationalists as China's legal government.

✔ **READING CHECK:** How did the Chinese Communists gain control of China?

The Korean War Begins

During the 1940s political tensions were also increasing in Korea, a peninsula jutting southward from the northeast corner of China. The Japanese had ruled Korea from 1910 to 1945 but had been driven out by Soviet and U.S. troops at the end of World War II. In 1945 the Allies divided Korea into two zones. Soviet forces occupied the northern zone, and U.S. troops held the southern zone.

A divided Korea. The division was meant to be temporary, but Cold War tensions cemented it. In 1948 North Korea and South Korea set up separate governments. Communist North Korea, led by Kim Il Sung, became known as the Democratic People's Republic of Korea. South Korea, under President Syngman Rhee (SING-muhn REE), called itself the Republic of Korea.

The United States did not want economically unstable South Korea to fall to the Communists. The U.S. government built up the South Korean army. By 1949 both the United States and the Soviet Union had pulled their troops out of Korea. The pullout left the two Korean armies facing each other tensely across the border at the 38th parallel.

After repeated clashes between North Korean and South Korean troops, North Korea invaded South Korea on June 25, 1950. In an emergency session, the UN Security Council called for an immediate cease-fire. At the time the Soviet Union was boycotting the Security Council over its refusal to admit Communist China. Therefore the Soviet delegate was not on hand to veto the UN resolution. On June 27, President Truman pledged U.S. support for South Korea. That same day, the Security Council adopted a U.S.-sponsored resolution branding North Korea an "aggressor" and calling on UN members to come to South Korea's defense. Truman later explained, "I felt certain that if South Korea was allowed to fall, Communist leaders would be emboldened [encouraged] to override nations closer to our own shores."

Bitter fighting. Truman ordered U.S. forces into action under the command of General Douglas MacArthur. Truman also ordered the U.S. Seventh Fleet to protect Taiwan. Although 15 other UN members contributed monetary and military support, the United States and South Korea played the major role in the **Korean War**. At first the attack by North Korean forces with their Soviet-made weapons was overwhelming. Outgunned and outmanned, the U.S. and South Korean troops fell back. One soldier, Sergeant Raymond Remp, recalled his first encounter with the North Korean army.

> 66 Someone fired a green flare, and [the enemy] saw us. . . . They were right on top of us . . . firing down on us. . . . Some colonel—don't know who—said, 'Get out the best way you can.' . . . All day and night we ran like antelopes. We didn't know our officers. They didn't know us. We lost everything we had. 99

By September the North Koreans had overrun nearly all of South Korea. The U.S. and South Korean forces were backed into an area around the port city of Pusan.

INTERPRETING THE VISUAL RECORD

The Korean War. Composed primarily of U.S. troops, UN forces scaled Korea's mountainous landscape to advance against Communist forces. Many U.S. soldiers received the Korean service medal shown. *Based on this photograph, what difficulties do you think U.S. soldiers faced during the conflict?*

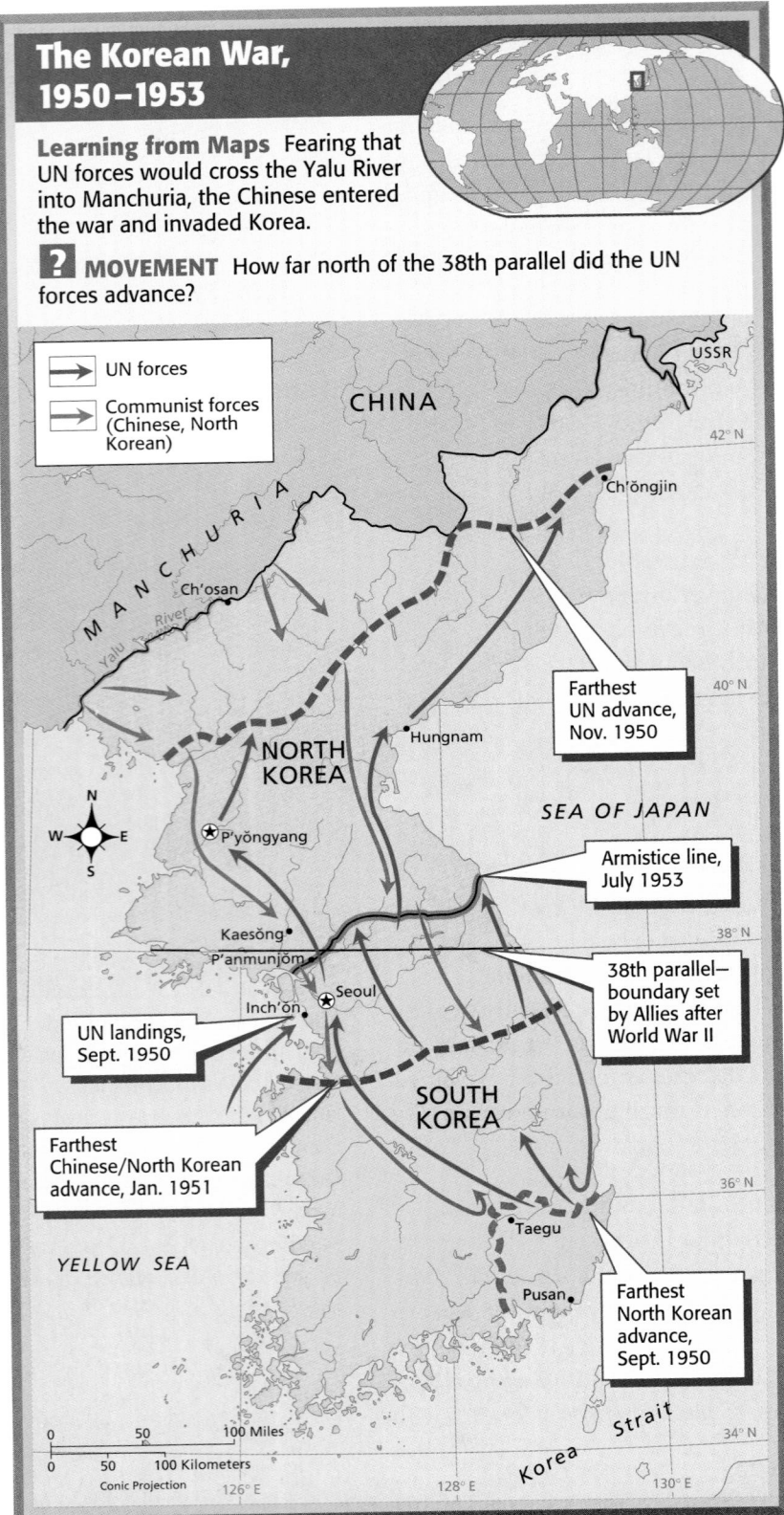

The Korean War, 1950–1953

Learning from Maps Fearing that UN forces would cross the Yalu River into Manchuria, the Chinese entered the war and invaded Korea.

❓ MOVEMENT How far north of the 38th parallel did the UN forces advance?

→ UN forces

→ Communist forces (Chinese, North Korean)

CHINA

USSR

MANCHURIA

Ch'ŏngjin

Ch'osan

Yalu River

42° N

40° N

NORTH KOREA

Hungnam

Farthest UN advance, Nov. 1950

SEA OF JAPAN

P'yŏngyang

Armistice line, July 1953

Kaesŏng

P'anmunjŏm

38° N

38th parallel— boundary set by Allies after World War II

Inch'ŏn

Seoul

UN landings, Sept. 1950

SOUTH KOREA

Farthest Chinese/North Korean advance, Jan. 1951

36° N

Taegu

YELLOW SEA

Pusan

Farthest North Korean advance, Sept. 1950

Korea Strait

34° N

0   50   100 Miles
0   50   100 Kilometers
Conic Projection

126° E   128° E   130° E

On September 15, 1950, MacArthur launched a powerful counterattack. Coming ashore at Inch'ŏn, MacArthur's forces swept inland and recaptured Seoul (SOHL), South Korea's capital. At the same time, a well-equipped UN army attacked from the south. North Koreans surrendered by the thousands. Others fled north across the 38th parallel with UN forces in hot pursuit. By late October the UN army was approaching the Yalu River, the boundary between North Korea and China.

The tide soon turned again. Late in November, China entered the war on North Korea's side, sending some 300,000 troops across the Yalu. Chinese foreign minister Jou En-lai (JOH EN-LY) explained why China had intervened.

❝ **The U.S. imperialists have adopted a hostile attitude towards us . . . while paying lip service to nonaggression and nonintervention. From the information we got, they wanted to calm China first and after occupying North Korea, they will come to attack China.** ❞

Outnumbered and with their troops stretched dangerously thin, the UN forces fell back. After desperate fighting and heavy losses in the winter cold, MacArthur's troops finally established a defensive line near the 38th parallel.

✔ **READING CHECK:** What factors led to the escalation of the conflict in Korea?

Ending the Korean War

With China now involved, General MacArthur called for a major expansion of the war. He proposed to blockade China's coast, bomb the Chinese mainland, and "unleash" Chiang's Nationalist forces to invade mainland China. The plan sparked fierce debate. Supporters said it would bring victory in Korea and overthrow the Chinese Communists. Opponents argued that an attack on China could bring the Soviet Union into the conflict.

Conflict between Truman and MacArthur.

President Truman strongly opposed MacArthur's plan. He did not want the war in Korea to lead to another world war. MacArthur, however, refused to accept the Korean War as a limited conflict. Publicly criticizing the president, MacArthur appealed to Republican leaders in Congress. He also delivered an ultimatum to the enemy in which he demanded unconditional surrender. The demand upset Truman's plans for peace negotiations. As commander in chief of the military, Truman removed the general from his post in April 1951. Many Americans opposed this move and gave MacArthur a hero's welcome upon his return to the United States. Americans spoke out against Truman's actions, booing the president during his public appearances.

By the summer of 1951 the war had settled into a stalemate. Bitter fighting continued, but little territory changed hands. Combat in Korea's mountainous terrain became frustrating as the American death toll mounted. The conflict became a major issue in the 1952 presidential election.

The election of 1952.

As 1952 began, President Truman found himself confronted with a series of problems. The Korean War had come to a bloody stalemate, and peace talks were making little progress. With his popularity at an all-time low, Truman decided not to run for re-election. Republicans saw their chance to break the Democrats' 20-year hold on the White House. They chose popular World War II hero General Dwight D. Eisenhower as their presidential candidate. Conservative senator Richard M. Nixon of California served as his running mate.

The Democrats selected Governor Adlai Stevenson of Illinois as their candidate and John Sparkman as his running mate. Stevenson defended Truman's foreign and domestic policies. However, many voters saw him as an intellectual who was out of touch with the common people. Some jokingly referred to Stevenson as an "egghead"—"someone with more brains than hair."

Stevenson also could not match Eisenhower's patriotic appeal. Eisenhower's warmth, vitality, and self-confidence reassured voters that the United States would remain strong throughout the Cold War. His upbeat campaign slogan "I Like Ike" reflected his popularity. Eisenhower promised to resist communism and to end the Korean War. A triumphant Eisenhower received 55 percent of the popular vote and swept the electoral vote 442 to 89.

The war ends.

The new president kept his promise to end the war. Eisenhower used military force to get peace negotiations moving. He stepped up bombing raids on North Korea in May 1953 and dropped hints that he would use nuclear weapons, if necessary, to end the conflict.

On July 27, 1953, negotiators agreed to an armistice. Korea was divided into two nations roughly at the 38th parallel—the same dividing line as before the war. Some Americans questioned whether this outcome justified U.S. losses—some 54,000 dead and 103,000 wounded. More than 1.5 million Koreans and Chinese had also died.

✔ **READING CHECK:** What effect did the Korean War have on U.S. politics?

Read More About It

Free Find:
Douglas MacArthur
After reading about Douglas MacArthur on the **Holt Researcher** CD–ROM, write a short essay that hypothesizes how MacArthur's military experiences could have led him to develop his aggressive strategy for the Korean conflict.

INTERPRETING THE VISUAL RECORD

Eisenhower. Presidential candidate Dwight Eisenhower campaigns in Manhasset, New York, in 1952. *What signs of Eisenhower's popularity can you see in this picture?*

Fighting Communism Abroad

The Eisenhower administration viewed nuclear arms and technology as crucial to ending the expansion of communism. Secretary of State John Foster Dulles called for the liberation of all nations that had fallen under Soviet control since 1945. To fulfill this goal, the United States would have to confront Communist aggression and not back down—even if that meant going all the way to the brink of war. "The ability to get to the verge [brink] without getting into war is the necessary art," Dulles said. This policy of **brinkmanship** rested on the threat of massive retaliation, including the use of nuclear weapons.

Eisenhower proved less confrontational than Dulles's policy might have suggested. Instead, he pursued U.S. goals with more covert, or secret, means and through diplomacy. He used the newly created **Central Intelligence Agency** (CIA) to gather strategic information and forward his Cold War goals.

Covert war and the CIA. Eisenhower tested his covert approach to the Cold War in Iran. Shortly after coming to power in 1951, Iranian premier Mohammad Mosaddeq (MAWS-ad-dek) nationalized British-owned oil fields in Iran. After Eisenhower took office he suspended aid to Iran. Eisenhower also authorized a covert action by the CIA to organize a military coup against the Iranian leader. The plan succeeded. Mosaddeq was arrested and replaced with the young pro-American shah of Iran, Mohammad Reza Pahlavi (RAY-zah pah-HLAHV-ee). Although Eisenhower achieved his goal of removing Mosaddeq, this interference in Iranian affairs provoked anti-American feelings in that country.

In 1954 Eisenhower ordered a covert action in Guatemala. That year the democratically elected Guatemalan president, Jacobo Arbenz Guzmán, took possession of uncultivated sections of Guatemala's largest plantations to redistribute among the rural poor.

Suspecting Arbenz of being sympathetic to communism, Eisenhower called on the CIA to gather a small army to oust him. The CIA-led forces bombed the capital in June 1954 and installed a new pro-U.S. government, which quickly reversed Arbenz's reform program. U.S. intervention in Guatemala stirred up bitter resentment throughout Latin America.

These Iranians are demonstrating to show their support for the return of the shah, Mohammad Reza Pahlavi.

The Suez crisis. In some cases, Eisenhower used diplomacy rather than covert actions to influence foreign policy. In 1955, after the U.S. government withdrew an offer to finance a large dam in Egypt, Egyptian leader Gamal Abdel Nasser nationalized the Suez Canal. This presented many political problems, including a threat to the Western oil trade. Egypt also refused to allow ships bound for Israel to pass through the canal. Late in October 1956, Israel launched an attack into Egyptian territory toward the Suez Canal. Britain and France seized the Mediterranean end of the waterway a few days later. The Soviet Union threatened war if the three nations did not withdraw from Egypt at once.

Eisenhower supported a UN resolution that called for an immediate cease-fire and the withdrawal of the invading troops. Grudgingly, Britain, France, and Israel withdrew their forces, and the crisis eased. The Soviet Union's support of Egypt during the Suez crisis led to a friendlier relationship between the Soviet Union and Arab nations. Seeking to counter Soviet influence in the Middle East, the president issued the Eisenhower Doctrine in January 1957. Eisenhower offered military aid to any Middle Eastern nation seeking help in resisting communist aggression.

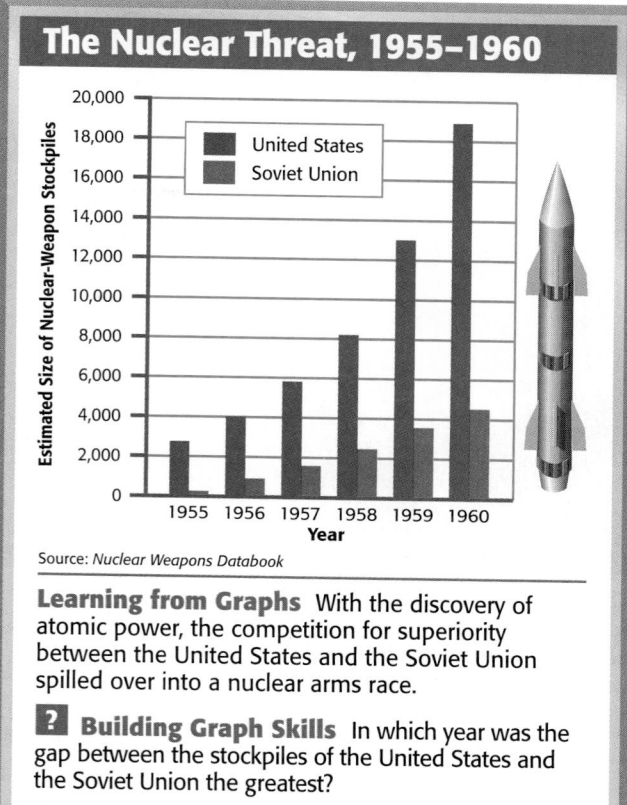

The Nuclear Threat, 1955–1960

Source: *Nuclear Weapons Databook*

Learning from Graphs With the discovery of atomic power, the competition for superiority between the United States and the Soviet Union spilled over into a nuclear arms race.

? **Building Graph Skills** In which year was the gap between the stockpiles of the United States and the Soviet Union the greatest?

Uprising in Eastern Europe. While the Suez crisis unfolded, an equally dangerous situation was developing in Eastern Europe. In February 1956 Soviet leader Nikita Khrushchev (KROOSH-chawf) stunned political observers by publicly accusing his predecessor, Joseph Stalin—who had died in 1953—of having committed many ruthless crimes. Observers hoped that this move signaled a new era of reform in the Soviet Union and Eastern Europe. Later in 1956, Polish reformers tested Khrushchev by calling for greater political freedom.

Inspired by Poland's boldness, thousands of Hungarians took to the streets in late October to demand reform. Moderates seized control of the government and called for a Western-style democracy and for Hungary's secession from the Warsaw Pact. Khrushchev responded with swift force. On November 4, heavily armed Soviet troops moved into Budapest, the Hungarian capital, and crushed the revolt within days. A new pro-Soviet government imposed martial law and executed or imprisoned the rebel leaders.

Throughout their struggle, the Hungarian rebels pleaded for help from the West. Eisenhower worried, however, that U.S. intervention in Eastern Europe would lead to all-out nuclear war with the Soviet Union. He condemned the Soviets' actions but refused to aid the rebels. He did help ease immigration laws to allow more Eastern European refugees into the United States, however. As a result, some 40,000 Hungarians fled to the United States after the uprising.

To some observers, Eisenhower's lack of support for the Hungarian uprising indicated a retreat from Dulles's talk of liberating Communist-controlled countries. However, most of the American public supported Eisenhower, whom they reelected by a landslide against Adlai Stevenson in November 1956.

INTERPRETING THE VISUAL RECORD

Hungarian rebels. In October 1956, Hungarians took to the streets to protest Soviet control of their country. *How does this photograph reflect the Hungarians' desire to be free of Soviet control?*

Soviet leader Nikita Khrushchev (center) studies a chicken for photographers during his goodwill tour of the United States.

A Brief Thaw in the Cold War

Near the end of the decade, the United States and the Soviet Union moved to improve their diplomatic relations. In 1959 Vice President Richard M. Nixon visited the Soviet Union, and Premier Khrushchev then came to the United States. Touring Iowa farms, Pittsburgh steel plants, and Hollywood movie studios, the jovial Khrushchev charmed the American media. He and Eisenhower agreed to meet at a summit conference in Paris the following year to discuss arms reductions.

In May 1960, however, just before the summit was to begin, Khrushchev announced that an American U-2—a high-altitude spy plane—had been shot down over the Soviet Union. At first U.S. officials insisted that it was a weather-research plane that had strayed off course. However, the captured pilot, Francis Gary Powers, admitted he had been on a spying mission.

Khrushchev refused to proceed with the summit unless the United States halted such spying missions and apologized for past flights. Eisenhower promised that the U-2 flights would stop, but he did not apologize. Khrushchev refused to meet with Eisenhower again. The **U-2 incident** caused the brief thaw in the Cold War to come to an abrupt end.

✔ **READING CHECK:** What methods did President Eisenhower use to promote U.S. interests abroad?

SECTION 3 REVIEW

Define and explain the significance of the following terms:
Korean War
brinkmanship
Central Intelligence Agency
U-2 incident

Identify and explain the significance of the following individuals:
Chiang Kai-shek
Mao Zedong
Kim Il Sung
Syngman Rhee
Douglas MacArthur
Dwight D. Eisenhower
Nikita Khrushchev

Locate and explain the significance of the following places:
North Korea
South Korea
Inch'ŏn
Seoul

1. Using Graphic Organizers
Copy the graphic organizer below. Use it to explain how the United States attempted to slow the spread of communism.

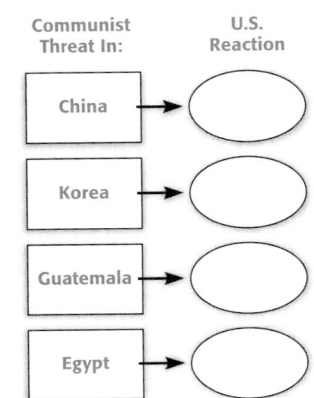

Communist Threat In:	U.S. Reaction
China	○
Korea	○
Guatemala	○
Egypt	○

2. Evaluating What impact did conflicts in Asia have on politics in the United States?

3. Hypothesizing How do you think the Korean War would have proceeded if General MacArthur had been allowed to expand the war into China?

4. Assessing Consequences In what ways were President Eisenhower's covert operations and diplomatic strategies effective? What new problems did they present?

Critical Thinking

5. How did the fall of China to the Communists encourage further U.S. military action in Korea?
Consider:
• how the fall of China to the Communists related to U.S. containment policy
• how the containment policy influenced U.S. actions in Korea
• what role Communist China played in the Korean War

The Cold War at Home

> 66 *Beware, commies, spies, traitors, and foreign agents! Captain America, with all loyal, free men behind him, is looking for you.* 99
>
> —Captain America

Captain America
comic book

The comic book hero Captain America was enormously popular during the 1950s. He reassured Americans that he and other loyal citizens would rid the country of the communist threat within its borders. Concerned about the spread of communism abroad, many Americans also began to worry about Communists infiltrating the U.S. government, the media, and schools. Americans were afraid that leaving Communists unchecked both abroad and within the United States would threaten American values of democracy and freedom. This fear led to a string of public inquiries, loyalty oaths, and trials of suspected Communists and traitors. In addition to communism, Americans also feared nuclear war.

Cold War Fears

The Cold War had a major impact on the United States. As a result of Cold War pressures, the nation streamlined its military to allow for peacetime rearmament. In July 1947 Congress replaced the War Department with the Department of Defense, combining the leadership of the army, navy, and air force under the Joint Chiefs of Staff. In addition, Congress created the **National Security Council** (NSC) to advise the president on strategic matters. Congress also established the CIA to gather strategic military and political information overseas.

Another Red Scare. International Cold War tensions sparked new fears of communism at home. Although President Truman opposed communism abroad, some Republicans accused him of allowing Communists in the U.S. government. Truman responded to the charges by setting up the Loyalty Review Board in 1947 to investigate all federal employees. By the end of 1951, more than 20,000 federal workers had been investigated, some 2,000 had resigned, and more than 300 had been deemed "security risks" and fired.

Meanwhile, Congress cracked down on the Communist Party in the United States. Leading the fight was the **House Un-American Activities Committee** (HUAC), which had originally been established in 1938 to investigate fascist groups in the United States. HUAC questioned the political ties of members of peace organizations, liberal political groups, and labor unions. In 1947 HUAC responded to charges that Hollywood was full of Communists by holding hearings to investigate people in the movie industry. A group of California film directors and writers known as the **Hollywood Ten** went to jail rather than answer HUAC's questions. They were blacklisted—denied work—from the film industry and saw their careers

destroyed. Author Bernard De Voto described the fear of blacklisting during this era. He explained that "gossip, rumor, slander, backbiting, malice and drunken invention, . . . when it makes the headlines, shatters the reputations of innocent and harmless people. . . . We are shocked. We are scared."

The hysteria generated by HUAC spread quickly. One group that spoke out against HUAC, the Women's International League for Peace and Freedom, argued in 1949 that the hearings violated democratic rights.

66 **Fully recognizing the danger of fascist and communist totalitarianism, the League believes that such forces can be best opposed by open discussion and by the strengthening of our own democratic procedures, rather than by attempts at direct control.** 99

The Hollywood Ten. Protesters demonstrate against HUAC's investigation of alleged communist activities of Americans in the film industry. *How are these activists protesting the actions of HUAC?*

Because of the League's support for progressive causes, the Federal Bureau of Investigation (FBI) investigated the national organization and several of its local chapters. The investigation scared many potential members away. HUAC investigations had a similar effect on labor unions and many liberal political groups.

The search for spies. HUAC also investigated individuals accused of spying for the Soviets. In 1948 Whittaker Chambers, a former member of the Communist Party, accused Alger Hiss of being a Communist spy. Chambers told HUAC that Hiss, a New Deal lawyer who had joined the State Department in 1936, had given him secret State Department documents to pass on to the Soviets.

Hiss denied the charges, but persistent questioning by HUAC member Richard M. Nixon, a young Republican member of Congress from California, revealed apparent inconsistencies in Hiss's testimony. When Hiss sued Chambers for slander, Chambers produced microfilmed copies of documents he had kept hidden in a pumpkin at his home. These so-called pumpkin papers revealed evidence that indicated Hiss had lied to HUAC. In 1950 Hiss was convicted of perjury, or lying under oath, and sentenced to five years in prison.

Another notorious spy case also helped fuel domestic fears of communism. In 1951 a U.S. court convicted two Americans, Julius and Ethel Rosenberg, of providing the Soviet Union with atomic-energy secrets during World War II. Defenders of the Rosenbergs claimed that the two were innocent victims of anticommunist hysteria. Despite worldwide protests on their behalf, the Rosenbergs were executed in June 1953.

The trial and conviction of Julius and Ethel Rosenberg for spying and giving away U.S. atomic secrets shocked many Americans.

Other anticommunist measures included the **Internal Security Act**, passed in 1950. The act required Communist Party members and organizations to register with the federal government. It also imposed strict controls on immigrants suspected of being Communist sympathizers. The anticommunist hysteria of these years shattered many lives and careers. Writer Abe Burrows described his experiences after being blacklisted. "My Americanism being under suspicion is very painful to me, not just painful economically but painful as it is to a guy who loves his country."

✔ **READING CHECK:** What actions did the U.S. government take to limit communism at home? How did these actions affect Americans' everyday lives?

AMERICAN Letters

Science Fiction

During the 1950s, science fiction became popular. Science fiction literature often reflects Americans' fear of or interest in technology, space exploration, and nuclear warfare. Ray Bradbury's novel The Martian Chronicles *(1950) describes the colonization of Mars by Earthlings while Earth is destroyed by nuclear war. Isaac Asimov discusses the adventures and isolation of space travel in his 1952 short story "The Martian Way."*

from *The Martian Chronicles*
by Ray Bradbury

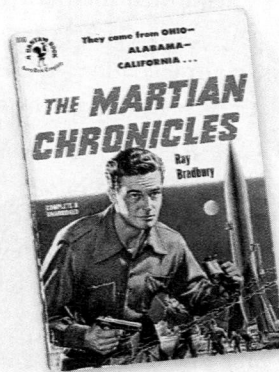

Ray Bradbury's novel

They all came out and looked at the sky that night. They left their suppers or their washing up or their dressing for the show and they came out upon their now-not-quite-as-new porches and watched the green star of Earth there. It was a move without conscious effort; they all did it, to help them understand the news they had heard on the radio a moment before. There was Earth and there the coming war, and there hundreds of thousands of mothers or grandmothers or fathers or brothers or aunts or uncles or cousins. They stood on the porches and tried to believe in the existence of Earth, much as they had once tried to believe in the existence of Mars; it was a problem reversed. To all intents and purposes, Earth was now dead; they had been away from it for three or four years. Space was an anesthetic; seventy million miles of space numbed you, put memory to sleep, depopulated Earth, erased the past, and allowed these people here to go on with their work. But now, tonight, the dead were risen, Earth was reinhabited, memory awoke, a million names were spoken: What was so-and-so doing tonight on Earth? What about this one and that one? The people on the porches glanced sideways at each other's faces.

At nine o'clock Earth seemed to explode, catch fire, and burn.

from "The Martian Way"
by Isaac Asimov

Isaac Asimov's collection of short stories

At first . . . the weeks flew past . . . except for the gnawing feeling that every minute meant an additional number of thousands of miles away from all humanity. That made it worse. . . .

The days were long and many, space was empty. . . .

"Mario?" The voice that broke upon his ear phones was questioning. . . .

"Speaking," he said. . . .

"You know, I've read Earth books—"

"Grounder books, you mean." Rioz yawned.

"—and sometimes I read descriptions of people lying on grass," continued Long. "You know that green stuff like thin, long pieces of paper they have all over the ground down there, and they look up at the blue sky with clouds in it. Did you ever see any films of that?"

"Sure. It didn't attract me. It looked cold."

UNDERSTANDING LITERATURE

1. What aspects of American life in the 1950s does *The Martian Chronicles* address?
2. How does "The Martian Way" describe the isolation of space travel?
3. How important is life on Earth in these two selections?

McCarthyism

As the Korean conflict escalated during the early 1950s, Americans' fears of communism intensified. This anxiety continued even after the war ended. Many Americans became convinced that spies and Communist sympathizers were everywhere. Joseph McCarthy, a U.S. senator from Wisconsin, helped fuel these suspicions. He argued that "the Communists within our borders have been more responsible for the success of communism abroad than Soviet Russia."

McCarthy's rise. Senator McCarthy came to public attention in 1950 when he claimed to have a list of known Communists who worked at the State Department. Although he never produced the list, dozens of federal employees lost their jobs after being labeled "security risks." McCarthy used his position as chairman of the Senate Permanent Subcommittee on Investigations to wage war against alleged Communist sympathizers in the federal government. With almost no supporting evidence, McCarthy questioned the patriotism—and ruined the reputations—of hundreds of government workers. Frustrated by McCarthy's lack of hard evidence, one journalist claimed, "Joe [McCarthy] couldn't find a Communist in Red Square—he didn't know Karl Marx from Groucho[Marx]." Nevertheless, many Americans, consumed by their fear of communism and the power of the Soviet Union, supported his crusade.

McCarthy's popularity and ruthlessness made many politicians wary of challenging him. One who did, however, was Margaret Chase Smith, a Republican senator from Maine. She stood her ground against McCarthy's crusade.

66 **I think that it is high time that we remembered that the Constitution, as amended, speaks not only of the freedom of speech but also of trial by jury instead of trial by accusation.** 99

In 1950 Smith and several other senators issued the Declaration of Conscience, which condemned those who had turned the Senate into "a forum of hate and character assassination." The report never mentioned McCarthy by name, but it was clearly directed at him.

McCarthy's downfall. Few others joined in the condemnation, however. Even the president refused to criticize McCarthy. Most of those who did speak out came from the arts or the media. In *The Crucible* (1953), playwright Arthur Miller drew parallels between McCarthyism and the Salem witch trials of 1692. On the television program *See It Now*, newscaster Edward R. Murrow questioned McCarthy's tactics. "We cannot defend freedom abroad," Murrow cautioned, "by deserting it at home." While some viewers praised Murrow, others bombarded him with hate mail.

INTERPRETING THE VISUAL RECORD

McCarthyism. Senator McCarthy claimed that communist organizations throughout the United States were plotting to overthrow the government. *How does McCarthy's style of presentation for this hearing give support to his claims?*

In 1954 McCarthy's congressional committee investigated charges that Communists had gained a foothold in the U.S. Army. Each day a vast television audience—sometimes as many as 20 million people—tuned in to the Army-McCarthy hearings. In the circuslike proceedings, McCarthy repeatedly interrupted and ridiculed witnesses. One victim of this treatment complained that McCarthy "acted like the gangster in a B movie rubbing out someone who had got in his way."

Television exposure of McCarthy's bullying tactics contrasted with the calm, dignified behavior of Joseph Welch, the army's chief counsel, and soon turned public opinion against the senator. At one point, Welch criticized McCarthy for his wild charges. "Let us not assassinate this lad further, Senator. You have done enough. Have you no sense of decency, sir, at long last? Have you left no sense of decency?" The audience in the hearing room broke into applause. A few months later, by a vote of 67 to 22, the Senate condemned McCarthy for conduct unbecoming a senator.

✔ **READING CHECK:** How was Senator Joseph McCarthy able to play upon Americans' fears of communism?

Nuclear Anxiety

Increased conflict between the United States and Communists abroad plunged the Soviet Union and the United States into a race to develop ever-more-powerful nuclear weapons. This arms race contributed to Americans' fears of nuclear war. In 1950, U.S. scientists began work on a **hydrogen bomb**, or H-bomb. They claimed it would be 1,000 times more powerful than the atomic bombs dropped on Hiroshima and Nagasaki in World War II. The first U.S. test of a H-bomb in 1952 completely vaporized a small island in the Pacific. Some nine months later, the Soviet Union tested its own H-bomb. J. Robert Oppenheimer, one of the creators of the U.S. atomic bomb, urged caution in the growing arms race.

❝ [The United States and the Soviet Union] are like two scorpions in a bottle, each capable of killing the other but only at the risk of his own life. . . . The atomic clock ticks faster and faster. ❞

Religion and nuclear war. Anxiety about nuclear war caused many Americans to seek some source of comfort. Many turned to religion. Evangelists such as Billy Graham attracted vast audiences during the 1950s. He warned of the danger of nuclear war and urged Americans to turn to God. Church membership grew rapidly during the era. As a result, investment in the construction of religious institutions rose from $76 million in 1946 to $868 million in 1957.

Americans' religious devotion contrasted sharply with the atheism of the Soviet Union. Reflecting this religious zeal, Congress added the phrase "One Nation Under God" to the Pledge of Allegiance and "In God We Trust" to U.S. coins.

Calming public fears.
As concerns about nuclear war grew, the government launched a campaign to calm public fears. The U.S. government issued pamphlets that offered suggestions on how to live through a nuclear attack. Some Americans put these recommendations to use by building backyard bomb shelters. Schoolchildren went through air-raid drills in which they crawled under their desks to protect themselves from radiation.

As Cold War tensions and Americans' fear of a Soviet nuclear attack increased in the 1950s, civil defense hysteria swept the United States. In 1951 the Federal Civil Defense Administration began a campaign to educate the public on what to do in case of a nuclear attack. Pamphlets, films, television shows, magazines, and the "Duck and Cover" program for children all encouraged citizens to protect themselves. For example, the booklet *Survival Under Atomic Attack* reassured fearful Americans.

> **66** You can live through an atom bomb raid and you won't have to have a Geiger counter, protective clothing, or special training in order to do it. The secrets of survival are: KNOW THE BOMB'S TRUE DANGERS. KNOW THE STEPS YOU CAN TAKE TO ESCAPE THEM. **99**

Nuclear fallout.
While a nuclear attack remained a grim possibility, radioactive fallout—a by-product of nuclear explosions—already posed a threat. U.S. and Soviet H-bomb tests spewed tons of radioactive material into the atmosphere. In 1954, H-bomb tests in the Pacific Ocean revealed the far-reaching effects of nuclear fallout. The crew of a Japanese fishing boat 85 miles away from the test site developed radiation sickness. People realized that no one would be safe in a nuclear attack. "The alternatives," one civil defense official said, "are to dig, die, or get out." No one wanted to die, and with little warning of incoming missiles, evacuating would not be possible. So some Americans began to dig, constructing backyard fallout shelters.

Pamphlets like the *Family Fallout Shelter* promoted do-it-yourself home shelters. *Life* magazine even presented building a shelter as a father-and-son project. Shelter manufacturers sprang up, selling their concrete-and-steel igloos at county fairs for about $1,500. A typical shelter contained flashlights, a first-aid kit, battery radio, portable toilet, two-week supply of food—mainly canned meats and vegetables—and water. Some people also purchased guns to prevent anyone from entering their shelter during a raid.

In 1957 Congress held a special hearing on the dangers of radioactive fallout. Defense officials claimed that nuclear testing was perfectly safe. Many scientists disagreed. They argued that radiation released during the tests presented a serious danger to the environment and possibly increased the risk of cancer in human beings. Soon the fear of radiation led to an organized campaign against nuclear testing. In 1957 a group of Americans, including well-known doctor Benjamin Spock, organized the Committee for a Sane Nuclear Policy (SANE). SANE urged the United States to begin negotiations with the Soviet Union to end nuclear tests. Within a year, SANE had grown to more than 25,000 members in some 130 chapters across the country.

Space programs. The arms race sped on, however, particularly after the Soviet Union launched the satellite *Sputnik* into orbit in October 1957. Many Americans worried that this launch proved the United States was falling behind the Soviet Union in technological development. President Eisenhower urged Congress to promote U.S. space technology by establishing the **National Aeronautics and Space Administration** (NASA). In 1958 the government sent the first U.S. satellite, *Explorer I*, into orbit. That same year, Congress approved the **National Defense Education Act**. This act appropriated millions of dollars to improve education in science, mathematics, and foreign languages.

Many Americans worried about the possibility of a nuclear attack in the 1950s.

✔ **READING CHECK:** How did Americans react to the prospect of nuclear war?

SECTION 4 REVIEW

Define and explain the significance of the following terms:
National Security Council
House Un-American Activities Committee
Hollywood Ten
Internal Security Act
hydrogen bomb
Sputnik
National Aeronautics and Space Administration
National Defense Education Act

Identify and explain the significance of the following individuals:
Alger Hiss
Julius Rosenberg
Ethel Rosenberg
Joseph McCarthy
Margaret Chase Smith
Billy Graham

1. **Using Graphic Organizers** Copy the graphic organizer below. Use it to explain how the possibility of nuclear war affected Americans' lives during the 1950s.

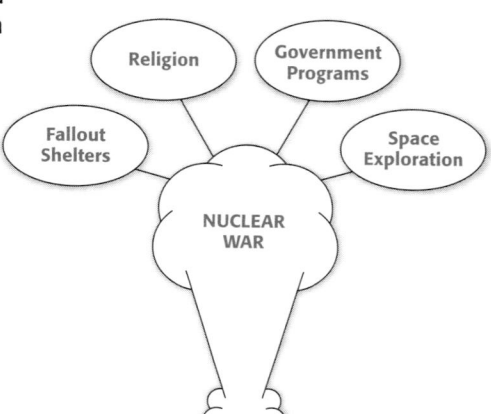

2. **Evaluating** What effect did HUAC's investigations have on American society?
3. **Distinguishing Fact from Opinion** Joseph McCarthy claimed that Communists inside the United States did more to spread communism around the world than Communists abroad. What evidence did he present to verify this statement?
4. **Synthesizing** How were Americans' fears of Communists and the threat of nuclear war justified?

Critical Thinking

5. In what ways did the efforts of some congressional committees challenge the American values they aimed to protect?
Consider:
• what the goals of HUAC and McCarthy's committee were
• what these two committees did to expose Communists
• what impact these committees had on the lives of those who were investigated

CHAPTER 28 Review

Creating a Time Line

Copy the time line below onto a sheet of paper. Complete the time line by filling in the events and dates from the chapter that you think were most significant. Pick three events and explain why you think they were significant.

1945   1950   1955   1960

Writing a Summary

Using the Reading Checks as a guide, write an overview of the events in the chapter.

Identifying People and Ideas

Identify the following terms or individuals and explain their significance.

1. Nuremberg Trials
2. United Nations
3. Eleanor Roosevelt
4. George Kennan
5. Truman Doctrine
6. Marshall Plan
7. Mao Zedong
8. Douglas MacArthur
9. Joseph McCarthy
10. hydrogen bomb

Understanding Main ideas

SECTION 1

1. How successful was the United Nations in stabilizing the conflict between Arabs and Jews in the area of Palestine? Explain your answer.

SECTION 2

2. What were the main causes of the Cold War?

SECTION 3

3. What strategies did President Eisenhower use to slow the spread of communism?

SECTION 4

4. Why was Senator McCarthy able to generate so much attention with his accusations?

5. What types of programs were developed to address concerns about nuclear war in the United States?

Reviewing Themes

1. **Global Relations** What other countries became involved in the conflict between the United States and the Soviet Union?

2. **Democratic Values** How did the U.S. government's response to Cold War tensions lead to limitations on civil liberties?

3. **Technology and Society** How did the development of atomic technology affect education, literature, and other aspects of daily life in the United States?

Thinking Critically

1. **Problem Solving** Imagine that you are establishing an organization to maintain world peace. How would you organize it? Why?

2. **Synthesizing** How did containment influence U.S. foreign policy during the late 1940s and the 1950s?

3. **Evaluating** How did the fall of China to communism in 1949 affect the Korean War in 1950?

4. **Recognizing Point of View** Why did many Palestinians, Iranians, and Guatemalans view the U.S. government with hostility during the 1950s?

5. **Assessing Consequences** How did U.S. efforts to halt communism abroad affect life at home?

Writing About History

Writing to Explain Imagine that it is the mid-1950s and that you are a senator who opposes communism. Using the graphic organizer below, write a speech describing the threat of Communist expansion around the world.

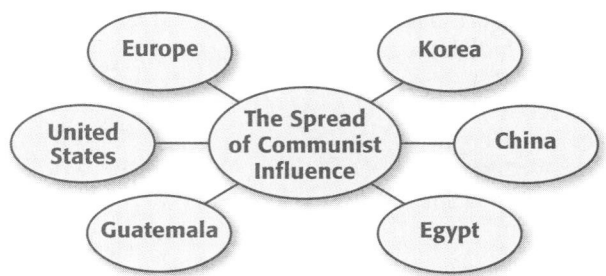

Review the **Strategies for Success** on *Taking Notes*. Then take notes on the following excerpt from an oral history provided by Steve McConnell, a U.S. citizen who grew up during the Cold War.

> 66 **We went through the bomb-shelter era in the late fifties. I remember it as kind of fun. You could go into a shopping center and at the corner of the parking lot was one of these bomb shelters. Gee, that was neat. . . . But there was that sense of nagging that maybe this was more than just fun. Nothing serious was imminent [soon to come] but . . . there was talk.**
>
> **We had drills in school. The alarms would go off and you'd hit the floor and put your back to the windows and cover your head. You were mostly afraid of getting hit by glass. What most of us didn't realize was that that would be the least of our problems. (Laughs.)** 99

Linking History and Geography

Alaska and Hawaii both became states in 1959. Study the map below. How might the location of these two areas have lent support for their admission as states?

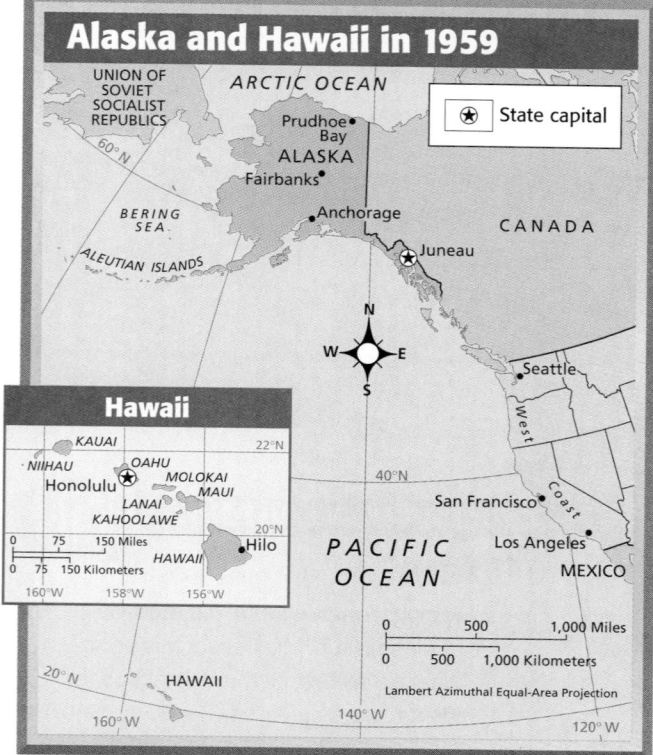

Alaska and Hawaii in 1959

 internetconnect

HRW

TOPIC: The United Nations
GO TO: go.hrw.com
KEYWORD: SD1 United

Accessing the Internet through the HRW Web site, research the United Nations and then write an essay in which you describe the UN's history, its organizational structure, and its role in world affairs.

BUILDING YOUR PORTFOLIO

Complete one or all of the following projects independently or cooperatively.

1 Global Relations

Imagine that you are a U.S. delegate to the UN conference in San Francisco in 1945. **Write a memorandum** to the U.S. Senate detailing world conditions in 1945 that call for the formation of an association of world nations and urging U.S. participation in the association.

2 Democratic Values

Imagine that you are a journalist during the 1950s. **Write an article** that explains how the United States justifies its fight against communism abroad while democratic values are being challenged at home.

Anticommunist literature

3 Technology and Society

Imagine that you are working for the Federal Civil Defense Administration during the 1950s. **Create a flyer** for students that explains the dangers of nuclear war and what they should do in case of an attack.

America's Geography

Defenses of the Cold War

During the Cold War the United States invested large sums of money to improve its national defense. This included heavy investment in new types of technology. Initially, most of the funding for the space program was managed by the Department of Defense. Some of the technology developed for these programs changed Americans' daily lives. During the Cold War, for example, scientists began to experiment with new uses for radio waves. They used radio waves in radar systems and satellite technology. These experiments eventually led to the development of such everyday items as the microwave oven and cable television.

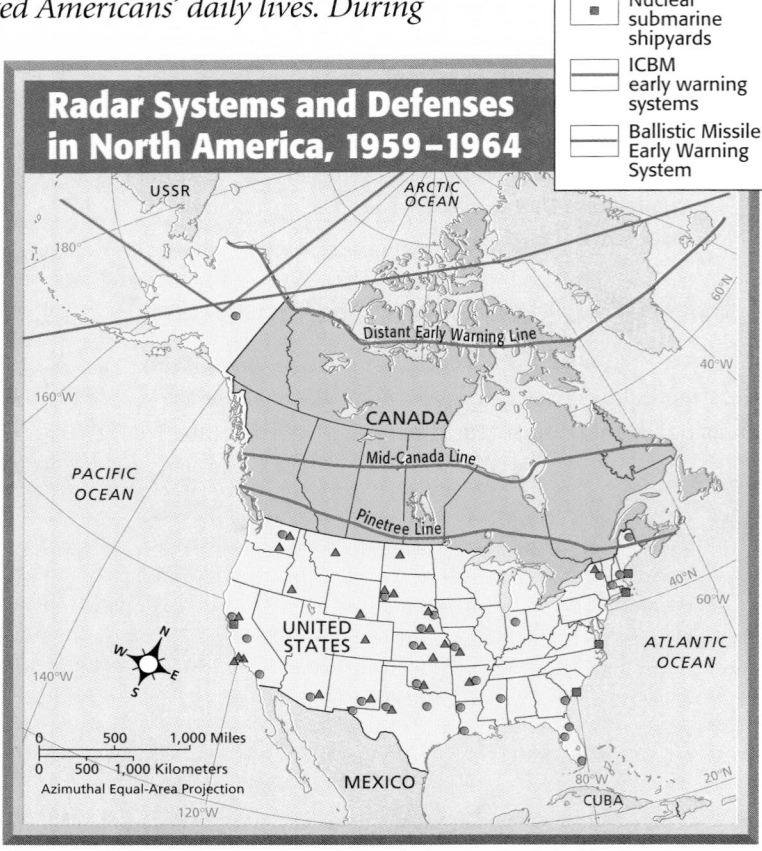

Radar Systems and Defenses in North America, 1959–1964

Legend:
- ▲ ICBM squadrons
- ● Strategic Air Command bomber bases
- ■ Nuclear submarine shipyards
- ICBM early warning systems
- Ballistic Missile Early Warning System

USSR
ARCTIC OCEAN
Distant Early Warning Line
CANADA
Mid-Canada Line
PACIFIC OCEAN
Pinetree Line
UNITED STATES
ATLANTIC OCEAN
MEXICO
CUBA

0 500 1,000 Miles
0 500 1,000 Kilometers
Azimuthal Equal-Area Projection

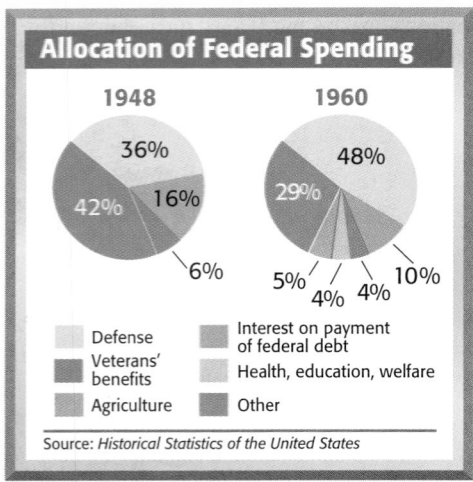

Allocation of Federal Spending

1948
- 36%
- 42%
- 16%
- 6%

1960
- 48%
- 29%
- 5%
- 4%
- 4%
- 10%

- Defense
- Veterans' benefits
- Agriculture
- Interest on payment of federal debt
- Health, education, welfare
- Other

Source: *Historical Statistics of the United States*

Radar. As the portion of the federal budget for defense increased, the amount of the defense budget for technology also rose. Concern over the Soviet weapons buildup led the United States to create an intricate radar system to detect incoming enemy missiles. At the same time, the United States built up its own supply of intercontinental ballistic missiles (ICBMs).

GEOGRAPHY AND HISTORY

REGION

1. Through which country did most U.S. radar lines run? Why might this be so?
2. What percentage of the federal budget went toward defense in 1948? in 1960?

Major U.S. Military Bases, c. 1965

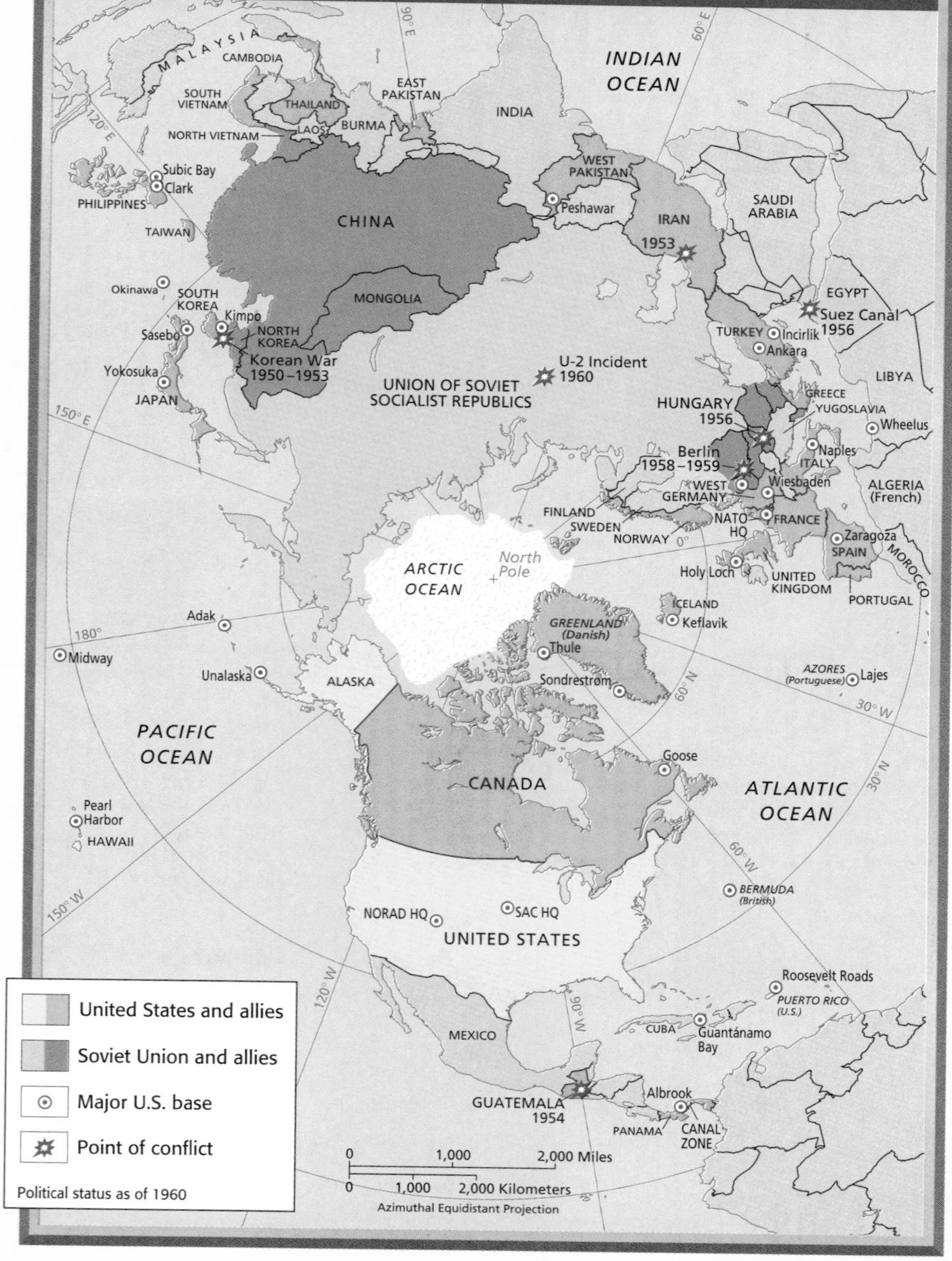

MALAYSIA
CAMBODIA
SOUTH VIETNAM
THAILAND
EAST PAKISTAN
NORTH VIETNAM
LAOS BURMA
INDIA
INDIAN OCEAN
WEST PAKISTAN
Subic Bay
Clark
PHILIPPINES
CHINA
Peshawar
IRAN 1953
SAUDI ARABIA
TAIWAN
Okinawa
SOUTH KOREA
Kimpo
MONGOLIA
EGYPT
Suez Canal 1956
Sasebo
NORTH KOREA
TURKEY
Incirlik
LIBYA
Yokosuka
Korean War 1950–1953
UNION OF SOVIET SOCIALIST REPUBLICS
Ankara
GREECE
JAPAN
U-2 Incident 1960
HUNGARY 1956
YUGOSLAVIA
Wheelus
Berlin 1958–1959
ITALY
Naples
150°E
WEST GERMANY
Wiesbaden
ALGERIA (French)
FINLAND
SWEDEN
NATO HQ
FRANCE
ARCTIC OCEAN
North Pole
NORWAY
0°
Zaragoza
SPAIN
MOROCCO
Adak
Holy Loch
UNITED KINGDOM
PORTUGAL
180°
ICELAND
Keflavik
AZORES (Portuguese)
Lajes
Midway
Unalaska
ALASKA
GREENLAND (Danish)
Thule
60°N
30°W
PACIFIC OCEAN
Sondrestrøm
Goose
ATLANTIC OCEAN
Pearl Harbor
HAWAII
CANADA
60°W
BERMUDA (British)
NORAD HQ
SAC HQ
UNITED STATES
150°W
Roosevelt Roads
PUERTO RICO (U.S.)
120°W
90°W
MEXICO
CUBA
Guantánamo Bay
GUATEMALA 1954
Albrook
PANAMA
CANAL ZONE

Legend:
- United States and allies
- Soviet Union and allies
- ⊙ Major U.S. base
- ✳ Point of conflict

Political status as of 1960

0   1,000   2,000 Miles
0   1,000   2,000 Kilometers
Azimuthal Equidistant Projection

Military bases. During the Cold War the United States increased its commitment to help protect other nations from their enemies. In order to achieve this goal, the U.S. military established a host of new bases throughout the world. Although some conflicts did erupt between the U.S.-backed countries and Soviet-backed countries, most of these skirmishes were short-lived.

GEOGRAPHY AND HISTORY Skills

HUMAN-ENVIRONMENT INTERACTION

1. How many major U.S. military bases existed outside the United States?
2. Where did conflicts erupt during the 1950s?

1945–1960

Society After World War II

Mohandas K. Gandhi

Harry S Truman

1948
Politics
Harry S Truman narrowly wins re-election.

1949
The Arts
Frank Sinatra's song "New York, New York" is a smash hit.

Eisenhower campaign sign

1952
Politics
Dwight D. Eisenhower is elected president.

1951
Daily Life
I Love Lucy premieres, quickly becoming the most popular television show in the United States.

| 1945 | 1946 | 1947 | 1948 | 1949 | 1950 | 1951 | 1952 |

1945
The Arts
Mary Chase wins the Pulitzer Prize for her play *Harvey*.

1946
Daily Life
Dr. Benjamin Spock's *Common Sense Book of Baby and Child Care* becomes the leading guide for parents of the baby boom.

1947
Daily Life
Jackie Robinson signs on with the Brooklyn Dodgers to become the first African American in major league baseball.

1948
World Events
Mohandas K. Gandhi is assassinated.

1951
Science and Technology
UNIVAC, the first computer for commercial use, is developed.

1951
Business and Finance
Some 30 percent of the American workforce is employed in commerce and industry.

Jackie Robinson

Before You Read

Build on What You Know

The end of World War II renewed Americans' optimism about the future. Soon, however, the country was caught up in a Cold War with the Soviet Union. President Truman's commitment to contain the spread of communism led to greater U.S. involvement in Korea and a growing suspicion that there were spies at home. The Cold War intensified as President Eisenhower intensified the nuclear arms race. In this chapter you will learn how Americans adjusted to the domestic transition from war to peace.

Queen Elizabeth II

Elvis Presley

1957
Business and Finance
The country's first commercial nuclear power plant begins operation in Pennsylvania.

1957
The Arts
Jack Kerouac publishes *On the Road*.

1958
World Events
Guinea, the former French-African colony, gains independence.

1959
Politics
Alaska and Hawaii become the 49th and 50th states of the Union, respectively.

1960
Science and Technology
American scientists launch the first weather satellite.

1953
World Events
Queen Elizabeth II is crowned ruler of Great Britain.

1954
The Arts
Elvis Presley releases his first record.

| **1953** | **1954** | **1955** | **1956** | **1957** | **1958** | **1959** | **1960** |

1953
Daily Life
Maureen "Little Mo" Connolly becomes the first woman to win tennis's Grand Slam.

1954
Politics
The Supreme Court outlaws school segregation with its *Brown* v. *Board of Education* ruling.

1955
Science and Technology
Jonas Salk announces the development of a successful polio vaccine.

1955
Business and Finance
Ray Kroc opens the first McDonald's franchise.

1956
The Arts
Cecil B. DeMille remakes his epic film *The Ten Commandments*.

1960
Daily Life
Thirteen former TV-game-show contestants are arrested on perjury charges after investigators discover the show is rigged.

Game-show contestant Charles Van Doren

Think About Themes

Themes Journal

*Decide whether you **agree** or **disagree** with the following statements. Note why in your journal.*

Economic Development An economic boom will affect population growth and residential patterns.

Cultural Diversity People generally prefer to "follow the crowd" rather than express their individuality.

Democratic Values Citizens are powerless to change government policies that discriminate against them.

SECTION 1

The Challenges of Peace

OBJECTIVES

Read to understand:

1. how the U.S. economy and American workers fared after World War II
2. what the most important issues of the 1948 election were
3. what the major goals of President Truman's Fair Deal were, and whether they were accomplished

KEY TERMS

GI Bill of Rights
Employment Act
Council of Economic Advisers
Taft-Hartley Act
Committee on Civil Rights
Dixiecrats
Fair Deal

KEY PEOPLE

J. Strom Thurmond
Henry Wallace
Thomas Dewey

EYEWITNESSES TO History

66 *When [the war] finally came to a conclusion, I think it set in motion [questions like] 'Here we are now. What are we going to do about life as we try to reestablish it in our community?'* 99
—Harold Toliver

The Homecoming by Norman Rockwell

Reverend Harold Toliver recalled how the end of World War II stirred both hopes and concerns for many Americans. Many New Deal supporters like Toliver looked to President Harry S Truman for guidance. They hoped that he would help the country recover from the war by continuing the reforms begun by President Roosevelt. "Franklin Roosevelt is not dead. His ideals live," declared New York mayor Fiorello La Guardia. President Truman tried to meet these expectations by promoting Roosevelt's ideals with his own reform programs.

The Problems of Demobilization

By mid-1946 more than 9 million men and women had been discharged from the military. The soldiers received a hero's welcome, but their return also sparked concern. How could the economy absorb all these new workers? Many Americans feared that the country would fall into an economic decline similar to the one that had followed World War I.

Postwar measures. Even before the war had ended, Congress began preparing for peace. Preventing an economic depression and helping war-weary veterans make the difficult transition to civilian life were top priorities. Congress passed the Servicemen's Readjustment Act of 1944, more commonly known as the **GI Bill of Rights**. The bill provided pensions and government loans to help veterans start businesses and buy homes or farms. Millions of veterans also received money through the GI Bill to attend college. Between 1944 and 1962 almost 8 million veterans attended college or technical schools on the GI Bill. This led to a dramatic increase in the number of American college graduates. Government worker Nelson Poynter described the impact of the GI Bill.

This recently issued stamp commemorates the passage of the GI Bill in 1944.

66 **The GI Bill . . . had more to do with thrusting us into a new era than anything else. Millions of people whose parents or grandparents had never dreamed of going to college saw that they could go. . . . Essentially I think it made us a far more democratic people.** 99

To ensure postwar economic growth, Congress passed the **Employment Act** of 1946. The act committed the government to promoting full employment and production. It also established the **Council of Economic Advisers** to confer with the president on economic policy.

Changing Ways · Higher Education

THEN

■ **Understanding Change** Before the passage of the GI Bill, a college education was often something only the wealthy sought. Since then, obtaining a college education has become much more common. *What differences do you observe between the images of college students in the late 1940s and the late 1990s? What statistics in the chart surprise you the most? Why?*

	THEN	**NOW**
Number of Institutions of Higher Education	1,863	3,706
Annual Student Body Enrollment	2,281,000	14,715,000
Annual Number of Bachelor Degrees Conferred	496,874	1,191,000
Student Body	32% / 68%	46% / 54%

Female
Male

Sources: *Historical Statistics of the United States; Statistical Abstract of the United States: 1998.* Data reflect 1950 and 1995.

Now

Despite widespread fears, the postwar depression never came. For example, the government canceled some $23 billion in military contracts. Those plants that had been making tanks and bombers began producing consumer goods instead. Employment levels remained high. Many Americans also began to spend the money they had saved during the war. Furthermore, because agricultural output in foreign countries had been shattered by the war, U.S. food exports increased.

Problems for workers. Not all was rosy on the economic front, however. Government measures encouraged employers to give priority to veterans in hiring. As a result, many workers lost their jobs to returning veterans. Congress abolished the Fair Employment Practices Committee, which had helped protect African Americans from discrimination. The government also retired the character of "Rosie the Riveter." Instead, the government started a campaign to encourage women to quit their jobs and become full-time homemakers. Some women wanted to keep their jobs. This was particularly true for working-class women whose families needed their incomes. "If [women] are capable, I don't see why they should give up their position," said one female steelworker. Despite these sentiments, most women who did not willingly give up their jobs were fired or pressured to quit their jobs after the war.

Another problem that concerned workers was the effect of postwar inflation. The cost of goods soared after most wartime price controls were lifted in 1946. Meat prices zoomed so high that some markets began selling horse meat. Blaming President Truman, angry consumers called him "Horsemeat Harry."

Labor unrest. As inflation continued to rise, people took matters into their own hands. Freed from their wartime pledges not to strike, millions of workers walked off the job. They fought for wage increases and the preservation of some wartime price controls. In 1946 almost 5 million workers walked the picket lines.

President Truman generally supported labor unions. However, he opposed these strikes because he feared they would disrupt the economy. After some 400,000 coal miners went on strike in the spring of 1946, Truman ordered the army to take control of the mines. The president of the United Mine Workers, John L. Lewis, responded, "You can't dig coal with bayonets." After the courts slapped heavy fines on the union, Lewis ordered the miners back to work. Later, Truman threatened to end a railway strike by drafting the strikers into the army. Truman's threat spurred union leaders to negotiate an end to the strike.

In 1947 the Republican-controlled Congress passed a bill designed to reduce the strength of organized labor. The bill was known as the **Taft-Hartley Act**. It gave judges the power to end some strikes and outlawed closed-shop agreements. It also restricted unions' political contributions and required union officers to swear that they were not Communists. Truman vetoed the bill, but Congress overrode his veto.

The Taft-Hartley Act stirred angry debate. Conservative supporters of the bill argued that it corrected unfair advantages that had been given to labor by New Deal measures. Pro-labor supporters argued that it was a "slave labor law." Although the act limited the actions unions could take, organized labor continued to make some gains in the postwar years. For example, in 1948 General Motors and the United Automobile Workers (UAW) signed a contract that linked wage increases to increases in the cost of living. Union contracts also began to include such benefits as retirement pensions and health insurance.

Labor unions. These workers marched in support of labor unions in 1946. *What message do you think is conveyed by the signs the marchers are using?*

✔ **READING CHECK:** How did the U.S. economy and American workers fare after the war?

The 1948 Election

By 1948 high inflation and labor unrest had decreased public support for President Truman. "To err is Truman," people joked. Despite his low standing in the polls, Truman continued to take a strong stand on controversial issues. His position on civil rights in particular became an important issue in the 1948 campaign.

The Committee on Civil Rights.

In 1946 civil rights groups urged Truman to take action against the racism that stained American society. They pointed out that most African Americans throughout the nation faced segregation in schools and on buses and discrimination in housing and employment. Furthermore, in some areas African Americans continued to be lynched. Previous efforts to battle these conditions had met a wall of resistance.

In December 1946 Truman created the **Committee on Civil Rights** to examine the issue. The committee's report, *To Secure These Rights,* appeared in October 1947. The report documented widespread civil rights abuses. These abuses included discrimination against African American veterans and an increase in racial violence. It also called for an end to racial segregation in interstate transportation. Based on the committee's findings, Truman urged Congress to pass an antilynching law and an anti-poll-tax measure. He also worked to end discrimination in federal agencies and the military.

When Congress did not immediately act on the report's recommendations, African American leader A. Philip Randolph threatened to launch a campaign of civil disobedience. In July 1948 Truman issued executive orders banning racial discrimination in the military and in federal hiring. He also took steps to end employment discrimination by companies holding government contracts.

White southern Democrats were outraged both by African American demands for civil rights and by Truman's actions. Senator Olin Johnston of South Carolina warned angrily that the South's electoral votes "won't be for Truman. They'll be for somebody else. He ain't going to be re-elected."

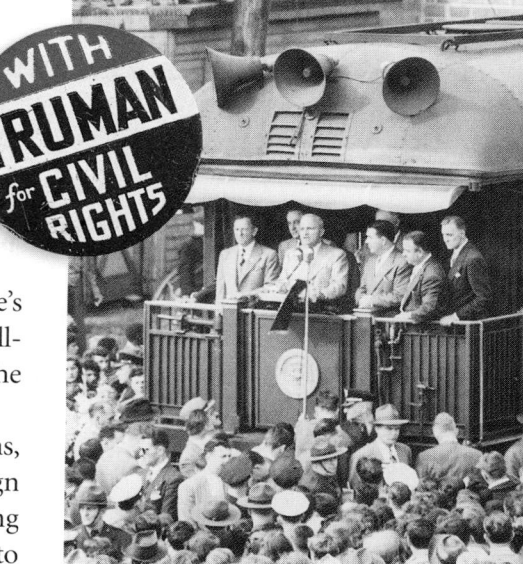

To win the 1948 election, President Truman carried out a "whistle-stop" campaign aboard a train.

Strategies for Success

Conducting an Interview

Oral history interviews are one of the most important methods that historians use to gather information about the past. An effective oral history interview must be accompanied by preliminary research as well as follow-up analysis.

How to Conduct an Interview

1. **Identify and research the topic.** Identify the general topic you wish to investigate and a specific person with firsthand knowledge of the topic. Then gather as much information as you can about the topic and your potential interview subject.
2. **Set up the interview.** Contact your potential interview subject, identify yourself, and clearly state your purpose in requesting an interview. Schedule a convenient time and place for the interview.
3. **Prepare questions.** Prepare questions for the interview that address what you need to know and that follow one another in a logical fashion.
4. **Conduct the interview.** Be an active listener during the interview. Allow your interview subject to respond to your questions freely, but remain in charge of the general direction of the interview. Ask follow-up questions if you need additional information.

5. **Analyze the interview.** Shortly after the interview has been completed, review your notes and listen to a recording of the interview. Summarize the content of the interview and evaluate its reliability as historical evidence. Use the results to form generalizations and draw conclusions about your topic.

Applying the Strategy

Prepare for and conduct an oral history interview with one of the following:

   a. a U.S. military veteran who received financial aid for college under the GI Bill
   b. a person who voted in the 1948 presidential election
   c. a person who was a teenager in the late 1940s

Practicing the Strategy

Answer the following questions.

1. What information about your subject were you able to acquire before the interview?
2. What questions did you prepare for the interview?
3. How did the interview contribute to your understanding of the United States after World War II?

This NAACP button was worn by some Truman supporters who rallied behind the Democratic Party platform committee's proposal of a strong civil rights plank.

The Democratic convention. Southern opposition did not prevent Truman from winning his party's nomination. His support, however, remained weak. Some delegates even wore buttons proclaiming, "We're just mild about Harry," a twist on his campaign slogan "We're just wild about Harry."

The Democratic platform called for the repeal of the Taft-Hartley Act. It also pushed for an increase in federal aid for housing, education, and agriculture; and broader Social Security benefits. The platform committee's proposal of a strong civil rights plank divided the Democratic Party. The all-white southern delegation threatened to walk out of the convention. The National Association for the Advancement of Colored People (NAACP) declared, "LET 'EM WALK."

66 There is no room . . . for compromise. . . . Those Democrats who say the President's recommendation of such a program is a 'stab in the back' of the South are saying they do not choose to abide by the Constitution. They are also saying . . . that the whole section of our nation believes as they do. . . . We know it is not true! 99

After bitter debate, the delegates adopted the civil rights plank. Southern delegates then stormed out of the convention and formed the States' Rights Party. The party was nicknamed the **Dixiecrats**. The Dixiecrats called for continued racial segregation. Party members nominated South Carolina governor J. Strom Thurmond as their presidential candidate.

The gulf widens. A different issue caused another break within the Democratic Party. Troubled by Truman's anti-labor actions in 1946, former vice president Henry Wallace and other liberal New Dealers left the Democratic Party to found a new Progressive Party. This group called for an extension of the New Deal. They also called for efforts to improve relations with the Soviet Union.

With the Democratic vote split three ways, the Republicans smelled victory. They nominated Governor Thomas Dewey of New York as their presidential candidate. Earl Warren, the popular governor of California, was nominated as Dewey's running mate. Opinion polls and most newspapers predicted a Dewey victory.

However, the Truman campaign began attacking the conservatism of the Republicans and radicalism of the Progressives. Truman crisscrossed the country by train, criticizing the "do-nothing" Republican-led Congress. Crowds began

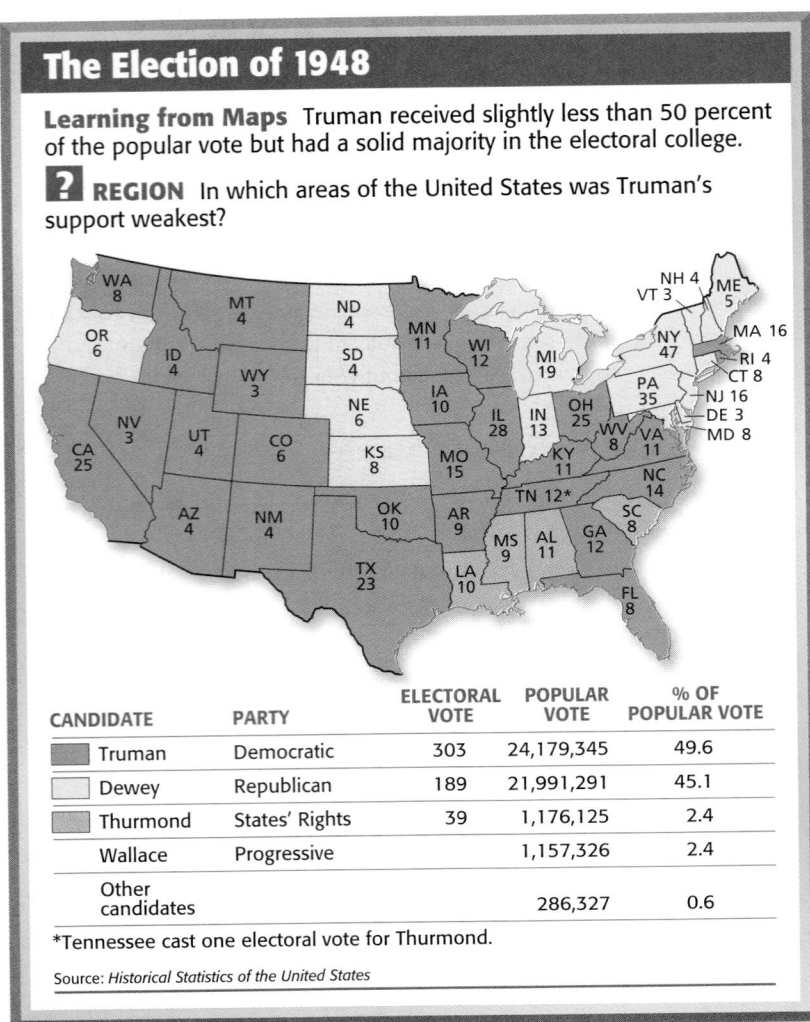

The Election of 1948

Learning from Maps Truman received slightly less than 50 percent of the popular vote but had a solid majority in the electoral college.

? REGION In which areas of the United States was Truman's support weakest?

CANDIDATE	PARTY	ELECTORAL VOTE	POPULAR VOTE	% OF POPULAR VOTE
Truman	Democratic	303	24,179,345	49.6
Dewey	Republican	189	21,991,291	45.1
Thurmond	States' Rights	39	1,176,125	2.4
Wallace	Progressive		1,157,326	2.4
Other candidates			286,327	0.6

*Tennessee cast one electoral vote for Thurmond.

Source: *Historical Statistics of the United States*

to chant, "Give 'em hell, Harry." In one of the great upsets of U.S. political history, Truman won the election with 303 electoral votes to Dewey's 189 electoral votes.

✔ **READING CHECK:** What were the most important issues in the 1948 election?

The Fair Deal

Encouraged by his victory, President Truman urged Congress to continue Franklin D. Roosevelt's New Deal reforms. Truman proclaimed that "every segment of our population . . . has a right to expect from our government a fair deal." He proposed a series of new reforms called the **Fair Deal**. Truman's Fair Deal promised full employment, a higher minimum wage, a national health insurance program, construction of affordable housing, increased aid to farmers, and the expansion of welfare benefits to more people.

Most Republicans and even some Democrats opposed the president's program. Nevertheless, Truman managed to push through some of his reforms. Between 1949 and 1952 Congress extended Social Security benefits to some 10 million additional people, raised the minimum wage from 40 to 75 cents an hour, and approved programs to demolish or rebuild slums. Congress also expanded federal programs to promote flood control, hydroelectric power, and irrigation.

Overall, though, the Fair Deal had limited success in an increasingly conservative postwar political climate. Americans had become less enthusiastic about reform programs that would further expand the government. Most people, weary of the upheavals of recent years, just wanted peace, stability, and gradual prosperity.

✔ **READING CHECK:** What were the goals of President Truman's Fair Deal? Were these goals achieved?

INTERPRETING THE VISUAL RECORD

Social Security. Although Congress expanded Social Security benefits, President Truman had trouble getting other Fair Deal legislation passed. *How does this poster reflect the importance of Social Security?*

SECTION 1 REVIEW

Define and explain the significance of the following terms:
GI Bill of Rights
Employment Act
Council of Economic Advisers
Taft-Hartley Act
Committee on Civil Rights
Dixiecrats
Fair Deal

Identify and explain the significance of the following individuals:
J. Strom Thurmond
Henry Wallace
Thomas Dewey

1. **Using Graphic Organizers** Copy the chart below. Use it to list the major successes of President Truman's Fair Deal program and changing public opinion of reform.

Successes	Public opinion
1.	1.
2.	2.
3.	3.
4.	4.

2. **Assessing Consequences** How did the end of World War II affect American workers?
3. **Synthesizing** What were the major issues of the 1948 presidential campaign?
4. **Taking a Stand** If you had been a voter in 1948, who would you have chosen for president? Why?

Critical Thinking

5. How did politics in the late 1940s reflect the ways that World War II had changed the United States?
   Consider:
   • what political steps were taken to ensure economic stability
   • what political actions were taken to help veterans
   • how political actions reflected desires to expand democracy

The Affluent Society

EYEWITNESSES TO History

> ❝ *Who decides whether you shall be happy or unhappy? You do! Happiness is achievable and the process for obtaining it is not complicated. Anyone who desires it, who wills it, and who learns and applies the right formula may become a happy person.* ❞
> —Dr. Norman Vincent Peale

Norman Vincent Peale's book

During the 1950s millions of Americans listened to the advice of Dr. Norman Vincent Peale, a dynamic speaker and Protestant minister who wrote the 1952 book *The Power of Positive Thinking*. Peale's claim that all people could achieve success if they had the right attitude represented the optimism of the prosperous decade. In an era dominated by Cold War fears, Peale offered a formula to help people overcome their anxieties.

The Eisenhower Era

President Dwight D. Eisenhower also reflected the optimism of the 1950s. Rejecting the Democrats' New Deal proposals, Americans elected Eisenhower, a Republican, president in 1952. He took office in 1953 determined to boost the economy and reform the federal government. He pledged to cut bureaucracy, to curb what he called the "creeping socialism" of the New Deal, to balance the budget, and to reduce government regulation of the economy.

In his first year as president, Eisenhower eliminated thousands of government jobs and cut billions of dollars from the federal budget. To reduce government influence over the economy, he cut farm subsidies and turned over federally owned coastal lands to states that would allow it to be developed. Nevertheless, Social Security and unemployment benefits were expanded during his administration, and the minimum wage was increased. Eisenhower established the Department of Health, Education, and Welfare, under the supervision of Texan Oveta Culp Hobby. The president also supported the largest increase in educational spending up to that time. This approach to domestic affairs, which Eisenhower described as "conservative when it comes to money and liberal when it comes to human beings," became known as **Modern Republicanism**.

Providing funding for social programs, defense, and other government obligations weakened Eisenhower's pledge to balance the federal budget. Only three of the eight budgets he presided over were balanced. Furthermore, during his years in office the federal debt grew by about 9 percent, to $291 billion.

✔ **READING CHECK:** How did President Eisenhower try to manage the nation's problems?

Warmly received by the American people, Eisenhower was often referred to by his nickname, Ike.

The Economy

For many Americans the 1950s was a decade of economic prosperity. One man described the era as an escalator. "You just stood there and you moved up," he said. Unemployment and inflation remained very low. By the mid-1950s more than 60 percent of Americans were earning a middle-class income, which at that time was considered to be $3,000–$10,000 annually. Never before, the popular media declared, had so many people enjoyed such prosperity. "This is a new kind of capitalism," declared the *Reader's Digest*, "capitalism for the many, not for the few."

Changes in the workplace. The economy received a boost from changes in the workforce. Large corporations prospered during the decade. Some 5,000 companies merged to form larger corporations. American factories were changing as well. Throughout the 1950s companies introduced machines that could perform industrial operations faster and more efficiently than human workers. This process of **automation** greatly increased productivity. However, it also reduced the number of manufacturing jobs. Many workers began to fear an automated future, as the song "Automation" noted.

> **66** I walked, walked, walked into the foreman's office
> To find out what was what.
> I looked him in the eye and said, 'What goes?'
> And this is the answer I got:
> His eyes turned red, then green, then blue
> And it suddenly dawned on me—
> There was a robot sitting in the seat
> Where the foreman used to be. **99**

As the number of blue-collar, or manufacturing, jobs decreased, professional and service jobs increased. Huge new corporations required a multitude of managers and clerical workers, positions referred to as white-collar jobs.

Many of the newly created service jobs were in occupations traditionally filled by women. Those jobs included nursing, teaching, retail sales, and low-level clerical work, sometimes called pink-collar jobs. By 1960, women made up about one third of the total workforce.

The new union style. Changes in the workforce also influenced organized labor. Boosted in part by the merger of the American Federation of Labor (AFL) and the Congress of Industrial Organizations (CIO) in 1955, union membership grew steadily in the 1950s. It peaked at some 18.5 million in 1956.

Automation. The use of machines allowed workers to make products faster. *What examples of automation can you identify in this picture?*

To help workers improve their economic position, union leaders sought to cooperate with management. George Meany, the AFL–CIO's first president, boasted that he had never led a strike. Meany claimed that he had no interest in reforming society. He stated that his only goal was to ensure "an ever rising standard of living" for his union's members. Many unions fought for and won guaranteed annual wages and cost-of-living adjustments—automatic pay raises linked to the rate of inflation. In return, unions made concessions to management. These included accepting automation plans or changes in work rules or production levels.

Union support weakened in the late 1950s when newspapers reported widespread corruption. They linked many unions to organized crime. As a result of these reports, Congress attempted to crack down on union corruption. In 1959 Congress passed the Landrum-Griffin Act, which banned ex-convicts from holding union offices, required frequent elections of officers, and regulated the investment of union funds. The negative publicity hurt union membership, which steadily declined after 1957.

✔ **READING CHECK:** How did the workforce change in the 1950s?

Suburban Migration

Workforce and income changes also led to increased geographic mobility for Americans. Millions of newly prosperous middle-class workers, particularly young couples, moved to the suburbs surrounding the nation's cities. By 1960 close to 60 million Americans—one third of the total U.S. population—lived in the suburbs.

Many of these suburbs were "planned communities." The entire neighborhoods were built by a single developer to attract new homeowners. To save time and money, developers used the same floorplan to build most houses in the community. As a result, the houses in the neighborhoods looked almost exactly alike. The best known of these suburban developments were the two Levittowns, one in Pennsylvania and one in New York, built by the Levitt Company. These developments expanded so rapidly that they soon grew into small cities. As more companies followed the Levitt Company example, the number of suburbs grew. An average of 1 million new suburban homes were built each year between 1950 and 1960.

The explosion of suburban growth occurred in part because developers were able to keep housing costs low. Growth also occurred because more Americans could afford to purchase homes. Veterans could get low-interest mortgages from such government agencies as the Veterans Administration and the Federal Housing Administration. Private savings and loan associations offered mortgages with relatively easy terms. Suburban growth was also aided by the passage of the **Highway Act** of 1956. This bill greatly expanded the nation's highway system, making it easier for suburban residents to commute to jobs in the cities.

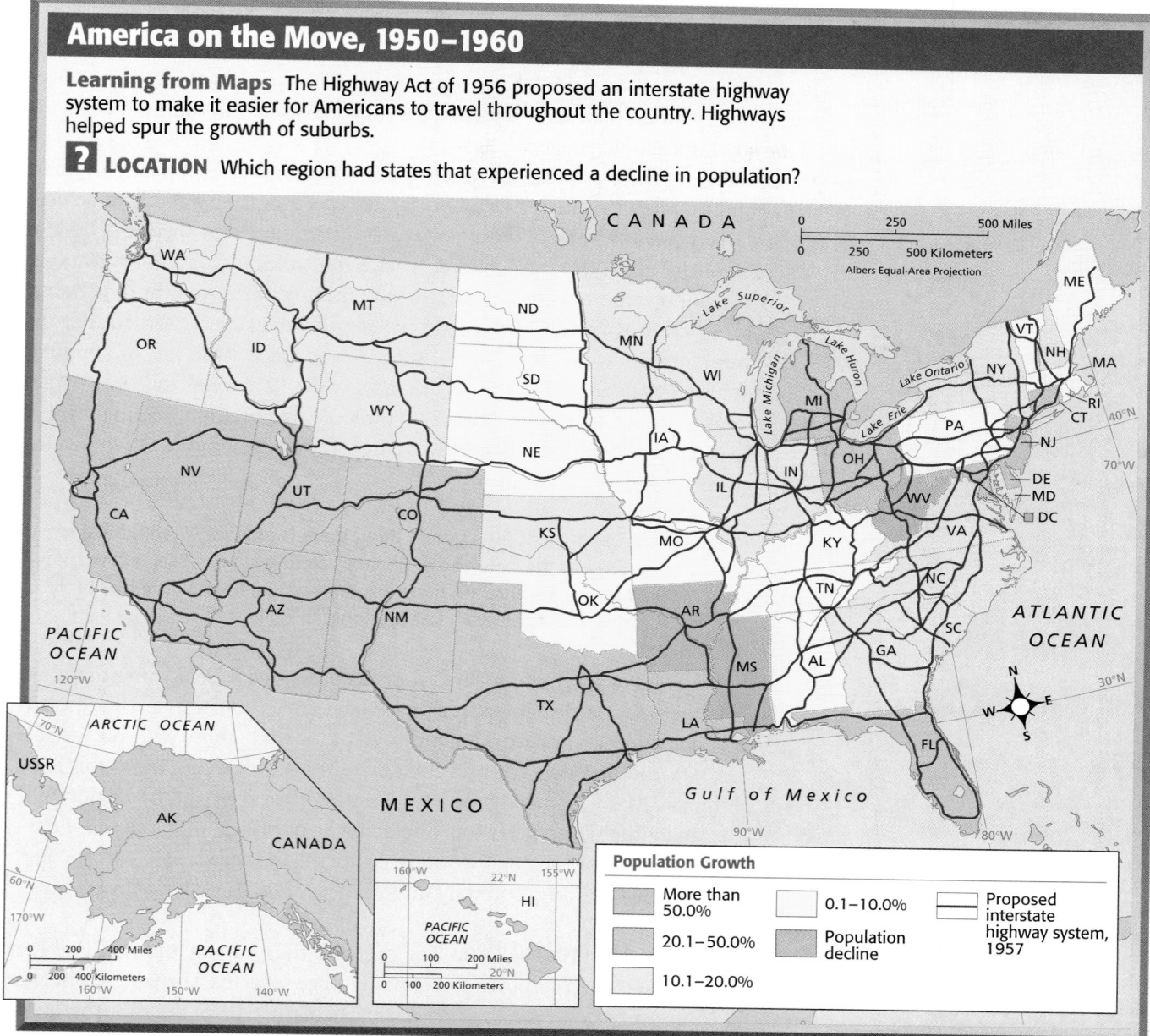

America on the Move, 1950–1960

Learning from Maps The Highway Act of 1956 proposed an interstate highway system to make it easier for Americans to travel throughout the country. Highways helped spur the growth of suburbs.

? LOCATION Which region had states that experienced a decline in population?

Population Growth

- More than 50.0%
- 20.1–50.0%
- 10.1–20.0%
- 0.1–10.0%
- Population decline
- Proposed interstate highway system, 1957

Suburban Life

Suburban growth was also spurred by an expanding population. During the Great Depression and World War II, many people had postponed getting married or starting a family. After the war, Americans began to get married at younger ages and in greater numbers than they had for generations. They also began having more children. The soaring birthrate accounted for more than 90 percent of the increase—some 30 million people—in the U.S. population during the 1950s. People began to refer to this increase as the **baby boom**.

Raising the family. Largely because of the baby boom, children became an important focus of suburban life. The baby boom also led to an emphasis on child rearing, focusing on the role of mothers. Many mothers followed the advice of pediatrician Benjamin Spock, who wrote *The Common Sense Book of Baby and Child*

Care in 1946. Advertisements, popular magazines, and self-help books depicted the ideal wife and mother as a full-time homemaker. They portrayed the homemaker as a woman who devoted all of her energy to making her family happy and buying all the latest household gadgets.

Contrary to these popular images, however, the number of working mothers actually increased during the 1950s. Many families needed two paychecks to achieve a middle-class income. Usually mothers worked part-time and spent the bulk of their income on "extras" for their children, such as music lessons or family vacations.

Some experts argued that working mothers achieved more personal satisfaction than full-time homemakers. *Life* magazine claimed that the homemakers were often "bored stiff." To examine this issue, the popular magazine *Ladies' Home Journal* held a forum in 1956 to ask full-time homemakers about their lives. Rather than reporting boredom, the majority of participants described their lives as a nonstop rush of family activities. One mother said:

> 66 At the present time I don't think there is anything I would like to change in the household. We happen to be very close, and we are all happy. I will admit there are times when I am a little overtired . . . but actually it doesn't last too long. 99

Some women did say that they felt pressured to make sure that their families fit the ideal image portrayed by popular books and magazines. In other studies, some working mothers, particularly those with young children, said that they felt pressured by other people to live up to this ideal image. Many women considered quitting their jobs and becoming full-time homemakers. "The only person who approved of me in those days was my father," recalled working mother Gail Kaplan. "He had encouraged me to be an accountant and whatever I did was all right with him."

Consumerism and social life. The pressure that Kaplan and many of the forum participants felt to conform to a certain image reflected a broader emphasis on social conformity in the 1950s. This was particularly true in the suburbs. Suburban areas, reported writer Lewis Mumford, "[are] inhabited by people in the same class, the same income, the same age group."

Advertising played a large role in promoting this conformity as it encouraged Americans to enjoy the general prosperity by buying consumer goods. Americans responded by going on a shopping spree, buying as many as nearly 8 million new automobiles and many household gadgets each year. Some suburban families worked hard to "keep up with the Joneses"; that is, to make sure that they had as many modern conveniences as their neighbors.

In addition to buying the same consumer items, suburban families participated in many of the same social activities as their neighbors. These included PTA, scouting, Little League, and religious activities. For uprooted Americans streaming to the suburbs, membership in religious institutions provided not only spiritual guidance but also a sense of belonging. Churches and synagogues often tried to appeal to new members by sponsoring a variety of social and recreational activities.

✔ **READING CHECK:** What was suburban life like during the 1950s?

Jonas Salk's Polio Vaccine

The United States emerged from World War II stronger both economically and militarily. However, many American families lived in fear of a new danger—a deadly polio epidemic that struck the country in the late 1940s. In 1952 alone the disease attacked some 60,000 Americans, many of whom were children. Hospitals were overwhelmed by the number of polio patients.

As the epidemic spread, scientists worked night and day to try to develop a cure or a way to prevent the disease. In 1952 Jonas Salk finally developed a successful vaccine against polio. "If it works," predicted one journalist of the vaccine, "Salk will have scored one of the greatest triumphs in the history of medicine." The vaccine did succeed in ending the epidemic. The number of polio cases continued to drop dramatically after an even better vaccine was developed in 1957.

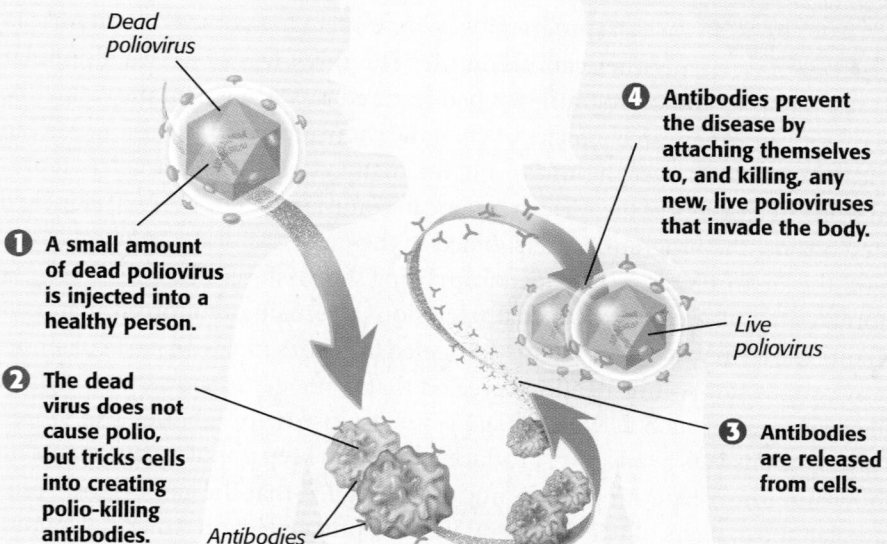

Dead poliovirus

❶ **A small amount of dead poliovirus is injected into a healthy person.**

❷ **The dead virus does not cause polio, but tricks cells into creating polio-killing antibodies.**

Antibodies

❹ **Antibodies prevent the disease by attaching themselves to, and killing, any new, live polioviruses that invade the body.**

Live poliovirus

❸ **Antibodies are released from cells.**

Understanding Science and History

1. How does the polio vaccine prevent polio?
2. How was the polio epidemic halted?

The Golden Age of Television

One of the most popular family activities was watching television together. Introduced commercially after World War II, television quickly became a favorite form of entertainment. By the end of the 1950s some 46 million households owned at least one television set.

Advertising played a major role in television programming. By reaching viewers daily in their homes, television advertising influenced consumer habits more than any previous medium had ever done. Particularly effective were ads in which television stars promoted their sponsors' products. By 1960, advertisers were spending $1.6 billion annually trying to convince viewers to buy their products. Often one business would sponsor an entire show, such as *General Electric Theatre* and *Kraft Television Theatre*. Their viewers would often connect the program with a company and its products. This advertising monopoly also gave many companies great control over program content.

Viewers could choose from several types of programming. Early television programs included sporting events such as the World Series, situation comedies like *The Honeymooners,* and variety programs like *Your Show of Shows.* Quiz shows like *The $64,000 Question* shared the airwaves with serious dramas like *Playhouse 90.* The most popular

Television became so popular in the 1950s that some companies began to market "TV dinners."

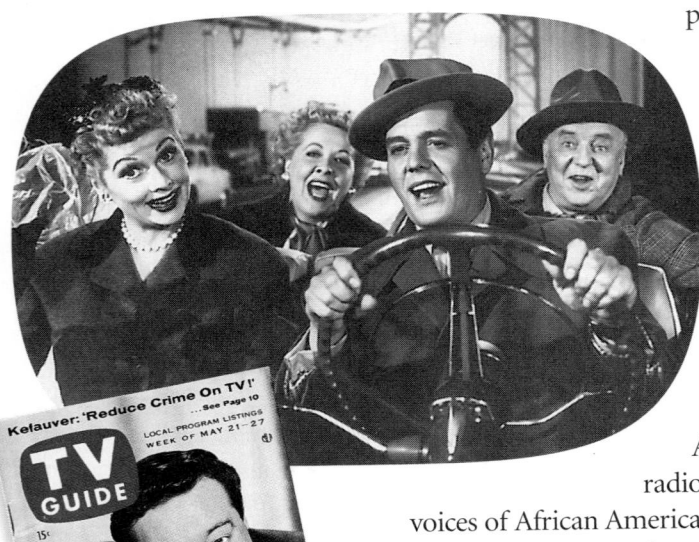

Television stars. Television stars like the cast of *I Love Lucy* (top) and *The Honeymooners* (bottom) were beloved by their millions of fans. *Can you name any of the actors in the images above? Why might they look familiar?*

program of the decade was the situation comedy *I Love Lucy*, starring real-life wife and husband Lucille Ball and Desi Arnaz. Thousands of fans tuned in every week to witness Lucy's crazy antics.

Television grew in popularity, but it remained a selective mirror, showing primarily white, middle-class, suburban experiences. Poverty, if shown at all, was treated as a minor problem. Working women, ethnic minorities, and inner-city life rarely appeared. When they were shown, it was usually in a way that reinforced stereotypes. One of the era's most controversial programs was *Amos 'n' Andy*, a comedy about African American urban life. The show was based on a popular radio program that had featured two white men providing the voices of African American characters. When the show moved to television, African American actors took over the roles. Still, for many viewers the characters represented white stereotypes of the African American community. The NAACP launched a protest against the program. Others joined in the protest, and *Amos 'n' Andy* was taken off the air. In 1966 it was banned from being shown in reruns.

Some critics also complained that television advertising reinforced materialism. Game shows in which contestants competed for prizes met with particular criticism. A congressional investigation revealed that some game shows were rigged. Popular contestants such as Columbia University instructor Charles Van Doren were given the answers in advance. Producers hoped to keep popular contestants on the show and thus keep ratings up. Some critics argued that the game-show scandal revealed the dangers of television and its corrupting effect on American values.

✔ **READING CHECK:** What was early television programming like?

Teenagers and Popular Culture

Some parents expressed concern about the impact of popular culture on young people, particularly teenagers. With more free time and spending money than any previous generation of teenagers, American youths of the 1950s sought out new kinds of leisure-time activities. To parents' dismay, these forms of entertainment often seemed to glamorize rebellion against suburban conformity.

Fictional rebels. Many young people found meaning in literature and films that featured discontented rebels. Some identified with Holden Caulfield, the main character of J. D. Salinger's 1951 novel, *The Catcher in the Rye*. Disgusted by the hypocrisy of the adult world, Caulfield declares it "crumby" and "phony." Although the book was very popular with young readers, some adults found its language and content offensive. Some groups demanded that it be banned from school libraries.

Many young people also enjoyed reading satirical comic books or magazines, such as *MAD*. The magazine dedicated itself to making fun of everything associated with "the American way of life." *MAD* soon rivaled *Life* as the most widely read magazine among young people. Many parents worried that reading such magazines would increase **juvenile delinquency**—antisocial behavior by the young.

Several of the decade's most popular films showed images of juvenile delinquency and young, angry rebels frustrated with life. Often their anger was directed not at any one particular thing, but at all of society in general. In the 1954 film *The Wild One,* a character asks the young motorcycle-gang leader played by Marlon Brando what he is rebelling against. Brando snarls back, "Whadda ya got?"

This image of the rebel with no direction was reinforced in the 1955 movie *Rebel Without a Cause.* The film starred James Dean, Natalie Wood, and Sal Mineo as teenagers confused about the values of their suburban families. Many teenagers could identify with the characters' frustration. One teenager described his feelings when he saw the film. "I walked out of the movie house that day confirmed in my sense of isolation," he said, "but not without taking something precious with me: the feeling that others shared my pain." James Dean became an idol to many young people when the 24-year-old actor died in a car accident following the premiere of the film.

Rock 'n' roll. Teenagers also escaped from the conformity of suburbia through a new type of music called **rock 'n' roll**. This music reworked rhythm and blues, a style popular among African American performers and audiences that combined blues music with more energetic and upbeat rhythms. Rhythm-and-blues music was particularly popular in dance halls. Rock 'n' roll took the music one step further and created a raw sound very different from other popular music of the time. Cleveland disc jockey Alan Freed coined the term "rock 'n' roll" in 1951 when he started a rhythm-and-blues show aimed at young white audiences. Soon the sound caught on among teenagers across the country.

Elvis Presley emerged as rock's leading talent. Presley was born in 1935 to a poor family in Tupelo, Mississippi. He loved music, particularly gospel. When he was 13 years old, his family moved to Memphis, Tennessee, where he listened to and learned from numerous African American gospel and rhythm-and-blues musicians. After graduating from high school, Presley worked as a truck driver while occasionally singing professionally. In 1954 he made his first major record. By 1955 he was one of the biggest music stars in the country.

Presley once said of his sudden popularity, "I just fell into it, really." Others recognized that this success came from his originality. His record producer noted that Presley sounded like no other singer he had ever heard. He also had a stage presence that electrified audiences. Shy in person, Presley came alive on stage. Journalist Jean Yothers was amazed by her own reaction when she reported on one of Presley's concerts in 1955. "I was awed," she said. "I got a tremendous boot out of this loud, uninhibited music that's sending the country crazy." Presley's many fans were

BIOGRAPHY
Elvis Presley

Teenagers as Consumers

teen Life

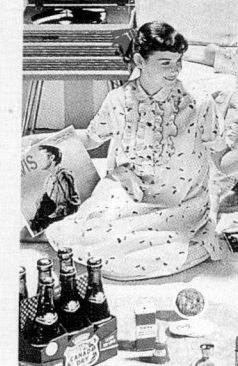

Some scholars have argued that the modern teenager was "invented" by advertising agencies in the 1950s. This was the first time that advertisers recognized teenagers as potentially powerful consumers. Many teenagers received allowances from their families or earned money from after-school jobs. Previously, teenagers' earnings usually went to help their families survive. In the 1950s most teenagers were allowed to spend their earnings as they wanted. By 1956 teenagers' earnings represented some $7 billion in purchasing power.

Advertisement from the 1950s

Businesses quickly went after this market, launching dozens of new products geared toward teenage tastes and desires. Advertising also shaped teenagers' desires, presenting ideal images of what a popular teenager should own and wear. If teenagers would buy their products, the advertisers implied, they would enjoy social success.

HOLT RESEARCHER *Read More About It*

Free Find: Elvis Presley
After reading about Elvis Presley on the **Holt Researcher** CD–ROM, write a fictional article for a teen music magazine describing how Elvis Presley's early life influenced his music.

During the 1950s teenagers listened to rock 'n' roll groups such as the Silhouettes on jukeboxes in local hangouts.

heartbroken when he was forced to take a break from his music career in the late 1950s after being drafted into the army. After completing his service he resumed his successful recording career and starred in 33 films before his death in 1977.

Despite its popularity, many adults disliked rock 'n' roll. They feared that it promoted antisocial behavior in teenagers. Some critics called it immoral. Others simply dismissed it as gibberish. They pointed out that the lyrics of many popular rock songs included made-up words or sounds that did not seem to make any sense. One example was the 1957 hit, "Get a Job," by a group called the Silhouettes.

> ❝ **Sha da da da**
> **Sha da da da da**
> **Bah do**
> **Bah yip yip yip yip yip yip yip yip**
> **Mum mum mum mum mum mum**
> **Get a job. ❞**

Rock 'n' roll also upset many people because it challenged the custom of racial segregation. African American musicians such as Little Richard, Chuck Berry, and Fats Domino, as well as Hispanic performers like Ritchie Valens, profoundly influenced early rock 'n' roll. White rockers such as Presley, Jerry Lee Lewis, and Buddy Holly shared the airwaves, and sometimes the stage, with noted black artists. This breaking down of racial barriers reflected larger social changes on the horizon.

✔ **READING CHECK:** How did the trends in popular culture reflect the larger social changes among teenagers in the 1950s?

SECTION 2 REVIEW

Define and explain the significance of the following terms:
Modern Republicanism
automation
Highway Act
baby boom
juvenile delinquency
rock 'n' roll

Identify and explain the significance of the following individuals:
Oveta Culp Hobby
George Meany
Elvis Presley

1. **Using Graphic Organizers** Copy the chart below. Use it to explain the growth of the suburbs and how that growth affected American middle-class culture.

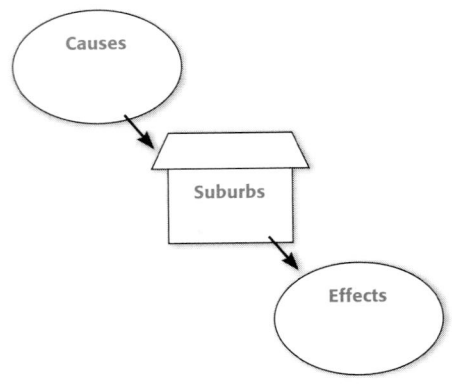

2. **Analyzing** How did President Eisenhower approach the nation's problems?
3. **Identifying Cause and Effect** Why did the workforce change in the 1950s, and how did those changes affect society?
4. **Identifying Values** What social values and patterns of behavior did suburban life encourage? How did teenagers rebel against those values and behaviors?

Critical Thinking

5. How well did television both reflect and shape American society?
   Consider
   • how television shows portrayed American society
   • the role of advertising on television
   • how television encouraged certain ideals and consumer habits

SECTION
3

Voices of Dissent

OBJECTIVES

Read to understand:

1. how the *Brown* decision affected school segregation and exposed conflict over the segregation issue
2. how the Montgomery Bus Boycott was a major turning point in the civil rights movement
3. what challenges Hispanics, Asian Americans, and American Indians faced in the 1950s
4. what criticisms of 1950s society writers and scholars expressed
5. what problems the poorest Americans faced in the 1950s

KEY TERMS

Brown v. *Board of Education*
Little Rock Nine
Montgomery Improvement Association
Civil Rights Act of 1957
League for United Latin American Citizens
beats
urban renewal

KEY PEOPLE

Thurgood Marshall
Orval Faubus
Rosa Parks
Martin Luther King Jr.
Félix Longoria
Ralph Ellison
Jack Kerouac

EYEWITNESSES TO History

66 I had grown up in a society where there were very clear lines. The civil rights movement gave me the power to challenge any line that limits me. . . . The movement said that if something puts you down, you have to fight against it. 99

—Bernice Johnson Reagon

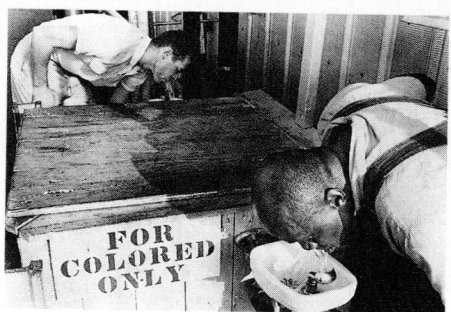

A segregated water fountain

Some people felt held back by society in the 1950s. Bernice Johnson Reagon of Albany, Georgia, recalled how society tried to limit opportunities for her and many other young African Americans. Reagon drew inspiration from the civil rights movement that emerged during the era. A gifted singer, Reagon was unable to afford musical instruments as a child. She later rose to become a musical scholar for the Smithsonian Institution, a college professor, a successful recording artist, and founder of the internationally known singing group Sweet Honey in the Rock.

Brown v. Board of Education

The NAACP had long waged a campaign against segregation in educational facilities. The Supreme Court's 1896 decision in *Plessy* v. *Ferguson* had established the legality of "separate but equal" schools. The NAACP had succeeded in opening some all-white universities and graduate schools to African American students. They did this by demonstrating that in most cases separate schools for black students were far inferior to the facilities reserved for white students. However, the Court continued to maintain that segregation in and of itself was legal.

In 1952 a group of legal challenges to segregation in public schools came before the Supreme Court in the form of ***Brown* v. *Board of Education***. The main case involved Linda Brown, an African American student from Topeka, Kansas. Segregation in Topeka's schools prevented her from attending an all-white elementary school a short walk from her home. Instead, she had to travel a long distance and cross dangerous railroad tracks to get to an African American school.

NAACP lawyer Thurgood Marshall argued on Brown's behalf. He introduced data suggesting that segregation psychologically damaged African American students by lowering their self-worth. Marshall's arguments greatly influenced the Court's unanimous ruling, which was issued on May 17, 1954. Written by Chief Justice Earl Warren, the opinion declared racial segregation illegal in public schools.

Many Americans praised the decision as a long-overdue step toward ending segregation entirely. Some African Americans were skeptical that white leaders would really support desegregation. As one NAACP leader warned, history had shown African Americans that there was a "difference between the law in books and the law in action."

Although some states moved quickly to end school segregation, many white southern leaders reacted to the decision with anger and defiance. South Carolina governor James F. Byrnes declared that desegregation "would mark the beginning of the end of civilization in the South as we have known it." Southern resistance caused the Supreme Court to issue a ruling in 1955 instructing federal district courts to end school segregation "with all deliberate speed."

Showdown in Little Rock

Little Rock. Elizabeth Eckford faces a hostile crowd as she walks by herself to Central High School. *How does Eckford's expression in this image contrast with those of the people behind her?*

Despite the Supreme Court ruling, school desegregation in the South moved slowly. By the end of the 1956–57 school year, the vast majority of southern school systems remained segregated. In Arkansas, however, school desegregation was progressing with relatively little opposition. Two of the three southern school districts that began desegregating in 1954 were in Arkansas. The Little Rock school board was the first in the South to announce that it would comply with the *Brown* decision.

Little Rock's desegregation plan was set to begin in September 1957 with the admission of nine African American students to the all-white Central High School. However, Governor Orval Faubus, about to begin his re-election campaign, spoke out against the desegregation plan. The night before school was to start, he ordered the Arkansas National Guard to surround Central High. He did so, he claimed, to protect the school from attacks by armed protesters. "It will not be possible to restore or to maintain order . . . if forcible integration is carried out tomorrow in the schools of this community," he warned.

Faubus exaggerated the danger, but his claims spread panic. One of the nine black students, Elizabeth Eckford, did not receive a message that instructed her not to go to school alone. When she attempted to enter the school, a mob of angry protesters and a line of armed National Guardsmen met her. She described the ordeal:

66 When I got in front of the school . . . I didn't know what to do. . . . Just then the guards let some white students through. . . . I walked up to the guard who had let [them] in. . . . When I tried to squeeze past him, he raised his bayonet, and then the other guard moved in. . . . Somebody [in the crowd] started yelling, 'Lynch her! Lynch her!' 99

For nearly three weeks, members of the Arkansas National Guard prevented the African American students, now known as the **Little Rock Nine**, from entering the school. Then, under court order, Faubus removed the National Guard. When the nine attempted to enter the school on September 23, the white mob rioted. Angered by the "disgraceful occurrences" at the school, President Eisenhower ordered some 1,000 federal troops to Little Rock. On September 25, 1957, under the protection of the soldiers' fixed bayonets, the Little Rock Nine finally entered Central High.

The Little Rock Nine endured a difficult year that included frequent harassment. One of the group, Minniejean Brown, was suspended for dumping food on a white boy who had made a racist comment. In February, when another white student called her a racial and obscene name, Brown responded with much milder insults of her own. For this incident, Brown was permanently expelled from school. After that, white students distributed cards that read, "One Down . . . Eight to Go."

Despite such pressure, the other African American students stayed. In May 1958 Ernest Green became the first African American student ever to graduate from Central High School. "When they called my name . . . nobody clapped," Green recalled of his graduation ceremony. "But I figured they didn't have to . . . because after I got that diploma, that was it. I had accomplished what I came there for."

Governor Faubus continued to look for ways to resist integration. He ordered the shutdown of the Little Rock public school system during the 1958–59 school year. He also helped establish a private school system to serve white students. Most African Americans, including the rest of the Little Rock Nine, as well as poor whites, had no school to attend. In 1959 the school district reopened under court order and slowly began to desegregate.

✔ **READING CHECK:** How did the *Brown* decision affect school segregation and expose conflict over the segregation issue?

The Montgomery Bus Boycott

In addition to fighting segregation in schools, the NAACP sought to end racial segregation on southern transportation systems. In Montgomery, Alabama, local NAACP leaders planned to challenge the practice of forcing African American citizens to ride in the back of city buses.

BIOGRAPHY
Rosa Parks

A boycott begins. On December 1, 1955, Rosa Parks, an African American seamstress, provided the NAACP with its opportunity. Parks refused to give up her bus seat to a white passenger and was arrested. Born in 1913 in Tuskegee, Alabama, Parks moved to the Montgomery area at a young age. Her mother was determined that Parks would receive a good education. Montgomery did not have a high school for African American students, so her parents sent her to the laboratory school at Alabama State College. Discrimination prevented her from obtaining a job that matched her education, however. Parks found work as a seamstress. She also became involved in the civil rights movement and held an office in the Montgomery chapter of the NAACP.

In the late 1950s Parks moved to Detroit, where she began working for Representative John Conyers in 1967. She remains committed to civil rights and has won

HOLT RESEARCHER **Read More About It**

Free Find: Rosa Parks
After reading about Rosa Parks on the **Holt Researcher** CD–ROM, write a short essay explaining the significance of her contribution to the civil rights movement.

numerous awards, including the Congressional Gold Medal of Honor, the highest honor the United States can award a private citizen.

In the summer of 1955 Parks attended a workshop on social justice that deeply influenced her views. "I found out for the first time . . . that this could be a unified society," she said. "I gained there the strength to persevere in my work for freedom." Her actions in December of that year would put her training to the test. Parks's arrest for refusing to give up her seat led to her conviction for violating the city's segregation laws. In protest, many of Montgomery's 50,000 African Americans organized a boycott against the bus system. The **Montgomery Improvement Association** (MIA), a group of local civil rights leaders, persuaded the community to continue the boycott while the NAACP and Parks appealed her conviction.

The MIA chose as its spokesperson Martin Luther King Jr., a 26-year-old Baptist minister who was new to town. An energetic and moving speaker, King could inspire large audiences. His ability to move people helped hold the African American community together as the bus boycott dragged on for months. White protesters tried every method from intimidation to physical violence to break the boycott. Angry mobs attacked and beat boycotters. The houses of King and other MIA leaders were bombed. Many boycotters—including Rosa Parks—lost their jobs. King, who had studied the nonviolent tactics of Indian nationalist Mohandas K. Gandhi, urged the African American community not to respond to violence with more violence.

INTERPRETING THE VISUAL RECORD

Civil rights. During the Montgomery Bus Boycott Martin Luther King Jr.'s charisma and ability to motivate supporters made him an important leader in the movement. *How do you think this photograph captures King's personality and role as a leader?*

The boycott succeeds. Finally, the nonviolent protest worked. In November 1956 the Supreme Court declared both the Montgomery and the Alabama segregation laws unconstitutional. By the end of the year, Montgomery had a desegregated bus system, and the civil rights movement had a new leader—Martin Luther King Jr. "We had won self-respect," declared boycott organizer Jo Ann Robinson. "It . . . makes you feel that America is a great country and we're going to do more to make it greater."

The Montgomery victory marked a blow to racial discrimination—and to the fear of standing up to people in positions of power. Cold War hysteria had contributed to this fear of authority. Not surprisingly, Martin Luther King Jr. was accused of being a Communist by opponents of the civil rights movement. Some southern whites, however, accepted that change had to come. As one South Carolina newspaper declared, "Segregation is going—it's all but gone. . . . The South can't reverse the trend."

Congress aided this trend by passing the first new civil rights law since Reconstruction. This **Civil Rights Act of 1957** bill made it a federal crime to prevent qualified persons from voting. It also set up the federal Civil Rights Commission to investigate violations of the law. A follow-up law enacted in 1960 strengthened the courts' power to protect the voting rights of African Americans.

✔ **READING CHECK:** How was the Montgomery Bus Boycott a major turning point for the civil rights movement?

Beyond Black and White

Segregation and discrimination affected others besides African Americans in the 1950s. Nonwhite Americans throughout the country continued to face prejudice. The experience of fighting for democratic ideals overseas in World War II, however, motivated more people to stand up and defend those ideals at home.

The Hispanic experience. One incident in particular revealed the extent of discrimination endured by Hispanics. Félix Longoria was a Mexican American soldier who was killed during World War II. In 1948 his body was recovered and returned to his hometown, Three Rivers, Texas. The town's only funeral home director refused to handle Longoria's burial because the soldier was Mexican American. When the media publicized this story, many Americans expressed outrage at this treatment of a veteran who had given his life for his country. Senator Lyndon Johnson of Texas stepped in and arranged for Longoria to be buried with full military honors at Arlington National Cemetery near Washington, D.C.

After Félix Longoria was finally buried at Arlington National Cemetery, other Hispanic veterans organized the American GI Forum to fight for other rights.

The Longoria incident led to the formation of the American GI Forum, a group dedicated to protecting the rights of Hispanic veterans. Over time the organization expanded to become a powerful lobbying group on behalf of all Hispanics. The GI Forum received help in its efforts from the **League for United Latin American Citizens** (LULAC). Formed in 1929, LULAC adopted many of the same tactics to fight for Hispanic rights that the NAACP used to champion African American rights.

Like the NAACP, LULAC focused on ending segregation, particularly in schools. In 1945 LULAC won an important case in *Méndez et al.* v. *Westminster School District et al.* In this case a federal judge ruled that the segregation of Mexican American children in a California school district was illegal. An even bigger victory came in 1948 with *Delgado* v. *Bastrop Independent School District.* In the *Delgado* case a judge ruled that the segregation of Mexican American children in a Texas school district was illegal. Soon afterward, state officials ended the segregation of Hispanic children in all Texas public schools.

Asian immigration to the United States increased after Congress repealed the Chinese Exclusion Act.

Asian immigration. Some of the prejudice against Hispanics was the result of continued nativism. Nevertheless, fear of immigration began to ease somewhat after World War II. Asian immigrants in particular experienced the effects of this change. In 1952 Congress repealed the Chinese Exclusion Act to allow more Chinese immigrants into the United States.

Many Asian Americans achieved great success in the United States. However, they still faced constant reminders that they did not fit the profile of an "ideal" American. In 1952, for example, Sing Sheng, a Chinese immigrant and Allied war hero, attempted to buy a house in a San Francisco suburb called Southwood. When the neighborhood's white residents discovered that an Asian family might move in, they began a drive to prevent the Sheng family from buying the house. Noting that his family had fled communism in China, Sheng appealed to the residents of Southwood to practice the values of

Protesting. This young American Indian is protesting the government's takeover of reservation land to build a power plant. *Why might this protester be more effective than others?*

Ralph Ellison's Invisible Man *describes the experiences of an African American man who feels that he is overlooked by mainstream society.*

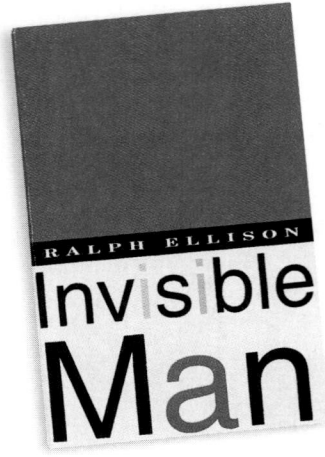

democracy and equality. "Do not make us the victims of a false democracy," he pleaded. Despite this request, the neighborhood association voted overwhelmingly to fight the Shengs. When white residents of other communities heard about the Southwood incident, many sent the Shengs personal letters inviting them to move into their neighborhoods. The Shengs accepted one such offer, settling peacefully in the town of Sonoma, California.

Relocation of American Indians. Many nonwhite families moved into new homes in the postwar era. Unlike other migrants, however, American Indians moved under pressure from the federal government. To promote the assimilation of American Indians into mainstream society, the Eisenhower administration supported the Relocation Act of 1956. The act set up procedures to encourage American Indians to move to urban areas. It even established relocation offices in major cities to assist newcomers. Critics of the legislation feared that it would empty the reservations of future leaders and destroy tribal cultures. Oglala Lakota activist Gerald One Feather recalled the impact of the relocation program.

> 66 The relocation program had an impact on our . . . government at Pine Ridge [South Dakota]. Many people who could have provided leadership were lost because they had motivation to go off the reservation to find employment or obtain an education. Relocation drained off a lot of our potential leadership. 99

To speed up relocation, the government had adopted a policy of termination in 1953. Termination involved ending the reservation system on a tribe-by-tribe basis. It also cut most federal funding for American Indians. Various tribal groups launched protests and lawsuits against the termination policy. They considered it an attempt to wipe out American Indian communities. By 1958 the Eisenhower administration backed down from this policy.

✔ **READING CHECK:** What challenges did Hispanics, Asian Americans, and American Indians face in the 1950s?

Questioning Conformity

For some writers and scholars, discrimination against nonwhites was a symptom of broader societal trouble. They argued that beneath its surface of conformity, economic prosperity, and peace, the United States faced serious problems that were being ignored. These social critics sought to expose what they called the "crack in the picture window." This meant that the problems grew within a seemingly happy and peaceful society.

Some novelists depicted the experiences of those facing poverty and discrimination. In Ralph Ellison's *Invisible Man* (1952), an African American man searches for his place in a society that is at once both hostile and indifferent to him. Referring to his exclusion from mainstream society, the man states, "I am an invisible man. . . . I am invisible, understand, simply because people refuse to see me."

Several important scholars wrote nonfiction works that reinforced Ellison's message. Harvard economist John Kenneth Galbraith issued a warning to privileged Americans in *The Affluent Society* (1958). He wrote that they were ignoring pressing social issues in their pursuit of material possessions and comfort. Sociologists William Whyte, C. Wright Mills, and David Riesman criticized the new corporate system. Whyte's *The Organization Man* (1956) and Mills's *White Collar* (1951) argued that the pressure to conform in the new corporate order was wiping out workers' independence and individualism. Riesman warned in *The Lonely Crowd* (1950) that the United States faced "a silent revolution against work" because jobs no longer had meaning for people.

The **beats**, a small but influential group of writers and poets, challenged both the literary conventions of the day and the lifestyle of the middle class. Beat writer Allen Ginsberg's poem "Howl," for instance, raged against the threat of nuclear war and the conventions of corporate America. The beats wrote as they lived—on the spur of the moment, without any planning. One of the best-known beat works, Jack Kerouac's 1957 novel, *On the Road,* was written in a continuous three-week-long session at the typewriter. Kerouac celebrated the search for individual identity and the rejection of security and stability. One sentence in the novel captures the beat philosophy. "We gotta go and never stop till we get there."

a novel
by Jack Kerouac

ON THE ROAD

INTERPRETING THE VISUAL RECORD

The beats. Jack Kerouac was the most famous beat writer. His book *On the Road* inspired ordinary people like these students (above) to join the movement as well. *How do the styles and activities of the beats differ from those of other teenagers in the 1950s?*

✔ **READING CHECK:** What criticisms of 1950s society did writers and scholars express?

The Nonaffluent Society

Some writers noted that despite the overall strength of the economy many people were left out of the prosperity of the 1950s. A 1957 study found that some 40 million Americans lived below the poverty line of a $3,000 annual income for a family of four.

The rural poor. Rural residents, particularly farmers, represented the poorest segment of the American population. In some areas of the country, including parts of the Appalachian Mountains, many people still had no indoor plumbing or electricity. One study characterized the Appalachians as being filled with "a mood of apathy and despair."

Although farming productivity increased from 1950 to 1960, the income generated from farms actually shrank. As foreign countries recovered from World War II, they imported less food from the United States. The price of agricultural products fell dramatically. Large farms tended to do better than small farms. This was particularly true for those large farms whose owners could afford to invest in new, efficient farm equipment. Increased use of farm technology such as gasoline-powered tractors and other large equipment allowed farm owners to operate with fewer workers. As a result, many of the poorest farm laborers, particularly migrant field hands, found fewer opportunities for employment.

Tractors like this one replaced farmworkers during the 1950s.

Voices of the Fifties

Many poets captured the spirit of the era in their verse. Beat poet Lawrence Ferlinghetti's "I am Waiting" challenged the confidence of postwar society. African American poet Naomi Long Madgett captured the feelings of many participants in the early civil rights movement in her poem "Midway."

from "I Am Waiting"
by Lawrence Ferlinghetti

I am waiting for my number to
    be called
and I am waiting for the living
    end
and I am waiting
for dad to come home
his pockets full
of irradiated [radioactive] silver
    dollars
and I am waiting
for the atomic tests to end
and I am waiting happily
for things to get much worse
before they improve . . .
and I am waiting
for the human crowd
to wander off a cliff somewhere
clutching its atomic umbrella . . .
and I am waiting
for the meek to be blessed
and inherit the earth . . .
and I am waiting for forests and animals
to reclaim the earth as theirs
and I am waiting
for a way to be devised
to destroy all nationalisms
without killing anybody
and I am waiting
for linnets [birds] and planets to fall like rain
and I am waiting for lovers and weepers
to lie down together again
in a new rebirth of wonder.

Lawrence Ferlinghetti

"Midway"
by Naomi Long Madgett

I've come this far to freedom
and I won't turn back.
I'm climbing to the highway
from my old dirt track.
    I'm coming and I'm going
    And I'm stretching and I'm
growing
And I'll reap what I've been
sowing or my skin's not black.

Naomi Long Madgett

I've prayed and slaved and waited and I've sung my song.
You've bled me and you've starved me but I've still grown
strong.
    You've lashed me and you've treed me
    And you've everything but freed me
But in time you'll know you need me and it won't be long.

I've seen the daylight breaking high above the bough.
I've found my destination and I've made my vow;
    So whether you abhor me
    Or deride me or ignore me,
Mighty mountains loom before me and I won't stop now.

UNDERSTANDING LITERATURE

1. Who is the "you" in Madgett's poem? Other than the poet, who does the "I" in the poem represent?
2. What image does Ferlinghetti present of life in the 1950s?
3. How are Madgett's and Ferlinghetti's views of the 1950s similar? How are they different?

Urban communities. Many displaced workers from rural areas flocked to U.S. cities in search of a better life. In the Appalachian area alone, some 1.5 million young people left the mountains for cities. One Cincinnati newspaper referred to the city's Appalachian migrants as "our 50,000 refugees."

Many rural-to-urban migrants experienced little improvement in their economic status. By 1960 more than 20 million city-dwellers were living in poverty. As more and more middle-class white residents moved to the suburbs, poor inner-city communities increasingly consisted of nonwhite residents. In addition to the continuing African American migration to the cities, the Hispanic urban population increased as well. Poverty and discriminatory real estate practices prevented most nonwhite city-dwellers from getting decent housing. They were generally limited to crowded tenements and old housing in the poorest neighborhoods, which were usually segregated by ethnicity.

Despite their poverty, ethnic neighborhoods provided a sense of community for many of those who lived there. Local stores, churches, synagogues, temples, and social clubs gave structure to the lives of new migrants struggling to adjust to city life.

To improve inner-city housing, the federal government proposed **urban renewal** programs. These were created to replace old, run-down inner-city buildings with new ones. Throughout the country, federally financed urban renewal programs bulldozed older neighborhoods to make way for more than 400,000 low-income public housing projects. These new high-rise buildings often had a cold, impersonal atmosphere. Most quickly became run-down themselves and were plagued by problems such as high crime rates.

INTERPRETING THE VISUAL RECORD

Urban renewal. High-rise housing projects were supposed to replace poor neighborhoods. *How does the housing project in the background of this image contrast with the building in front?*

✔ **READING CHECK:** What problems faced the poorest Americans in the 1950s?

SECTION 3 REVIEW

Define and explain the significance of the following terms:
Brown v. *Board of Education*
Little Rock Nine
Montgomery Improvement Association
Civil Rights Act of 1957
League for United Latin American Citizens
beats
urban renewal

Identify and explain the significance of the following individuals:
Thurgood Marshall
Orval Faubus
Rosa Parks
Martin Luther King Jr.
Félix Longoria
Ralph Ellison
Jack Kerouac

1. **Using Graphic Organizers** Copy the graphic organizer below. Use it to list aspects of rural and urban life in the 1950s, noting shared traits of both.

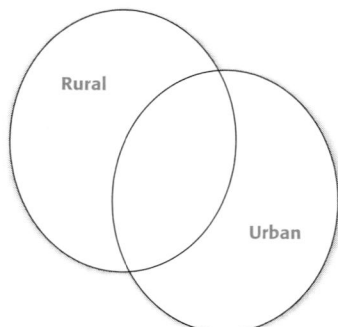

2. **Synthesizing** What effect did the *Brown* decision, the Little Rock crisis, and the Montgomery Bus Boycott have on the civil rights movement?
3. **Analyzing** What did the experiences of Hispanics, Asian Americans, and American Indians reveal about the United States in the 1950s?
4. **Identifying Values** What did writers like John Kenneth Galbraith and the beat poets identify as some of the problems in 1950s society?

Critical Thinking

5. Is it accurate to portray the 1950s as an era of good times for all Americans? Why or why not?
   Consider:
   • how different people might define "good times"
   • what the experiences of minorities and the poor were
   • what criticisms were given of society in the 1950s

CHAPTER 29 Review

Creating a Time Line

Copy the time line below onto a sheet of paper. Complete the time line by filling in the events and dates from the chapter that you think were most significant. Pick three events and explain why you think they were significant.

1945 **1950** **1955** **1960**

Writing a Summary

Using the Reading Checks as a guide, write an overview of the events in the chapter.

Identifying People and Ideas

Identify the following terms or individuals and explain their significance.

1. GI Bill of Rights
2. Dixiecrats
3. Fair Deal
4. automation
5. George Meany
6. baby boom
7. Elvis Presley
8. *Brown* v. *Board of Education*
9. Rosa Parks
10. beats

Understanding Main Ideas

SECTION 1
1. Why did the feared postwar economic depression never materialize?
2. How did civil rights issues affect the 1948 election?

SECTION 2
3. How did the economic prosperity of the 1950s affect the workforce?
4. What was suburban life like in the 1950s?

SECTION 3
5. What were some of the major successes and setbacks in ending segregation in the 1950s?
6. According to social critics, what were the weaknesses of American society in the 1950s?

Reviewing Themes

1. **Economic Development** How was the increase in population influenced by the economic boom of the 1950s?
2. **Cultural Diversity** How did some Americans rebel against the conformity of the 1950s?
3. **Democratic Values** How did members of minority groups fight discrimination during this decade?

Thinking Critically

1. **Comparing and Contrasting** What was the popular image of a mother's role in society in the 1950s? How did this image conflict with reality?
2. **Assessing Consequences** How did popular entertainment in the 1950s shape the economy?
3. **Identifying Values** What values came into conflict in the 1950s?
4. **Using Historical Imagination** Imagine that you are one of the Little Rock Nine. Are you willing to face constant harassment and threats of violence in order to go to a better school? Explain your answer.
5. **Problem Solving** What do you think was the greatest problem facing American society in the 1950s? If you had been president, what steps would you have taken to combat this problem?

Writing About History

Writing to Describe Write a brief paragraph describing the major concerns of workers in the late 1940s and how the government reacted to union efforts to address these problems. Use the following graphic to organize your thoughts.

Concerns of Workers → Union Responses → Long-Term Effects

Strategies **for Success** Review the **Strategies for Success** on *Conducting an Interview*. Then prepare for and conduct an oral history interview with one of the following:

a. a person who lived in an urban housing project during the 1950s

b. a person who grew up in the suburbs during the 1950s

c. a person who remembers following the Central High crisis or the Montgomery Bus Boycott as they took place

d. a person who listened to rock 'n' roll music during the 1950s

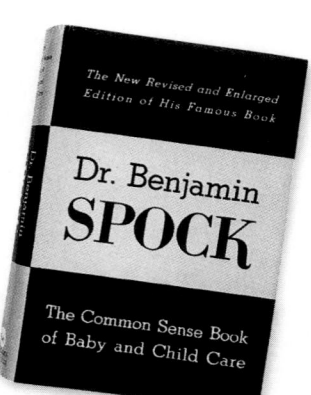

Linking History and Geography

School desegregation proceeded at different rates throughout the country. By 1964 which states were the slowest to achieve desegregation?

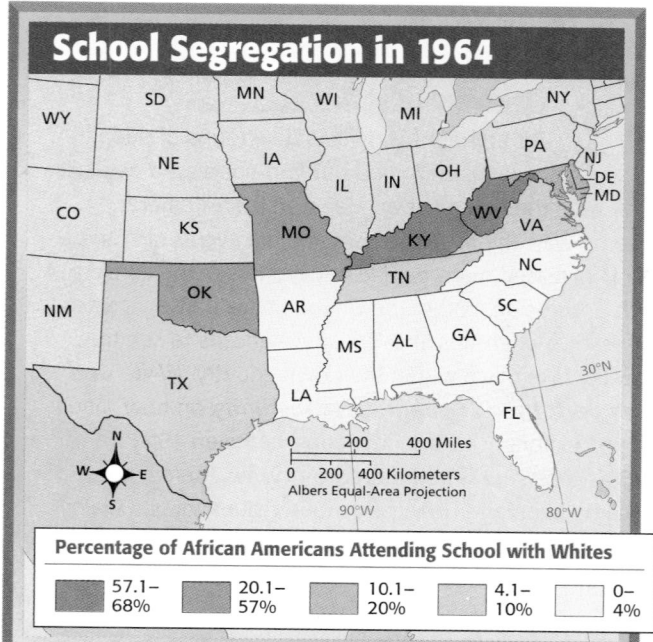

School Segregation in 1964

Percentage of African Americans Attending School with Whites

57.1–68%   20.1–57%   10.1–20%   4.1–10%   0–4%

 internet connect

TOPIC: Popular Culture in the 1950s
GO TO: go.hrw.com
KEYWORD: SD1 Culture

Accessing the Internet through the HRW Web site, research the popular culture of the 1950s. Then create a poster or multimedia presentation that describes how the popular culture of the 1950s mirrored the social events of that decade.

BUILDING YOUR PORTFOLIO

Complete one or all of the following projects independently or cooperatively.

1 Economic Development
Imagine that you are a staff member of the Department of Labor. **Prepare an illustrated chart** that shows how the U.S. government is assisting returning soldiers through various programs designed to help them find civilian jobs, attain college educations, or own their own homes.

2 Democratic Values
Imagine that you are a reporter assigned to cover civil rights issues. **Develop an illustrated outline** of the major civil rights events that occurred in the United States between 1945 and 1960.

3 Technology and Society
Imagine that you are the inventor of the electric guitar, an instrument made popular by rock 'n' roll musicians. **Write an illustrated report** describing how your invention has affected American culture.

Review

BUILDING YOUR PORTFOLIO

Outlined below are four projects. Independently or cooperatively, complete one and use the products to demonstrate your mastery of the historical concepts involved.

1 Global Relations

The world experienced severe economic, political, and social unrest in the years leading up to World War II. *Write a script for a debate* with representatives from several nations about global relations after World War II. Debates should center around the issue of how the United States should respond in the future to the rise of dictators in other parts of the world. You may wish to use portfolio materials you designed in the unit chapters to help you.

Holocaust survivors being liberated

Civil rights activist protesting

2 Democratic Values

Throughout history various groups of people have been singled out and oppressed because the ruling society deemed them "different" in some way. The rise of fascism and the events of World War II increased many people's awareness of the dangers of such oppression. Within the United States it also increased the resolve of groups like African Americans to see true equality take place within their own country. *Write and then perform a 15-minute documentary* on how various groups experienced discrimination between 1921 and 1960. Make sure that the report includes the effects of the discrimination and how the various groups fought against it. You may wish to use portfolio materials you designed in the unit chapters to help you.

3 Technology and Society

As the Cold War intensified, Americans became increasingly fearful of military conflict and the threat of the deployment of nuclear weapons. *Create an illustrated cover story for a popular magazine* that explains how these fears have influenced daily life, literature, popular culture, and the arts. You may wish to use portfolio materials you designed in the unit chapters to help you.

UN troops fighting against Communist forces in Korea

4 Economic Development

After World War II, the U.S. government became increasingly involved in managing and influencing the U.S. economy. *Create a visual display* of the different areas of the economy in which the government played a role in the 1950s. Make sure your display shows how each type of government involvement affected the lives of average citizens. You may wish to use portfolio materials you designed in the unit chapters to help you.

Social Security Administration poster

Further Reading

Berenbaum, Michael. *The World Must Know: The History of the Holocaust as Told in the United States Holocaust Memorial Museum.* Little, Brown, 1993. Pictorial and eyewitness history of the Holocaust.

Cohen, Stan. *V for Victory: America's Home Front During World War II.* Motorbooks International, 1991. Overview of the effect of World War II on Americans on the home front.

Cook, Haruko Taya, and Theodore F. Cook. *Japan at War: An Oral History.* New Press, 1992. Accounts of war's effects on the Japanese.

Halberstam, David. *The Fifties.* Villard Books, 1993. A broad account of American life in the 1950s.

King, Martin Luther Jr. *Stride Toward Freedom: The Montgomery Story.* Harper & Row, 1986. Martin Luther King Jr.'s own story of the Montgomery Bus Boycott.

Knox, Donald. *The Korean War: Uncertain Victory.* Harcourt Brace Jovanovich, 1988. Oral history of the war.

Jackson, Kenneth T. *Crabgrass Frontier: The Suburbanization of the United States.* Oxford University Press, 1985. A history of the rise of a suburban culture in the United States.

Internet Connect and Holt Researcher CD–ROM *Review*

In assigned groups, develop a multimedia presentation about America between 1921 and 1960. Choose information from the chapter Internet Connect activities and from the **Holt Researcher** CD–ROM that best reflects the major topics of the period. Write an outline and a script for your presentation, which may be shown to the class.

UNIT
9

A Changing
Home Front
1954–1978

The Selma to Montgomery March for voting rights enters Montgomery.

CHAPTER 30

The New Frontier and the Great Society
1961–1969

CHAPTER 31

The Civil Rights Movement
1960–1978

CHAPTER 32

Struggles for Change
1963–1975

CHAPTER 33

War in Vietnam
1954–1975

Main Events
- John F. Kennedy's presidency
- The Cuban missile crisis
- The construction of the Berlin Wall
- President Lyndon Johnson's Great Society
- The expansion of the civil rights movement
- The emergence of a counterculture
- The Vietnam War

Main Ideas
- *How did Presidents Kennedy and Johnson attempt to better the lives of all Americans?*
- *How did the civil rights movement alter the lives of Americans?*
- *How did the movements of the 1960s challenge traditional ways of life in America?*
- *What impact did the Vietnam War have on political life in the United States?*

Magazine article about the Vietnam War

1961–1969
The New Frontier and the Great Society

Building the Berlin Wall

Slim Pickens in an advertisement for the movie Dr. Strangelove

1961
World Events
The East German government builds a wall that divides East and West Berlin.

1963
The Arts
Stanley Kubrick's film *Dr. Strangelove,* a black comedy about the Cold War, is released.

1964
Daily Life
An earthquake in Alaska kills 114 people and causes $500 million in damage.

1961 **1962** **1963** **1964**

1961
Politics
President John F. Kennedy gives an inaugural address that calls for Americans to sacrifice in the struggle to defend liberty across the globe.

Pin honoring John F. Kennedy's military service

Kennedy campaign button

1963
Science and Technology
A vaccine against measles becomes available.

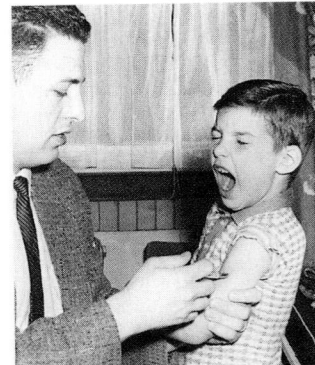

1964
Politics
Lyndon Johnson is elected president by a landslide.

1964
Science and Technology
The U.S. surgeon general reports that cigarette smoking is the leading cause of lung cancer.

A child receiving a measles vaccine

Before You Read

Build on What You Know

During the late 1950s President Eisenhower opposed the expansion of communism. He threatened the use of nuclear weapons and used secret means to keep communism from spreading. At home, Eisenhower shifted domestic policy from the New Deal and Fair Deal to Modern Republicanism. In this chapter you will learn how the Democratic administrations of John F. Kennedy and Lyndon Johnson implemented new policies and programs that changed American life. You will also learn how they dealt with foreign-policy crises caused by Cold War tensions.

The Apollo I space capsule

1965
Science and Technology
The *Pioneer 6* spacecraft, designed to orbit the Sun, is launched.

1965
Business and Finance
France redeems $200 million for U.S. gold, shaking the gold market and prompting President Johnson to ask Americans to take vacations in the United States rather than abroad.

India's prime minister, Indira Gandhi

1966
World Events
Indira Gandhi becomes prime minister of India.

1967
Science and Technology
Three *Apollo I* crewmembers are killed when fire breaks out in the space capsule on the launchpad.

1967
World Events
The Six-Day War between Israel and several Arab nations occurs.

1968
Politics
Congress rejects Abe Fortas, President Johnson's nominee for Chief Justice of the United States.

1968
World Events
North Korea seizes the USS *Pueblo*, a U.S. Navy ship, and releases the crew nearly a year later.

1965 ———— **1966** ———— **1967** ———— **1968**

1965
Politics
Congress creates the Department of Housing and Urban Development.

James Hoffa testifying before Congress

1967
Politics
The Twenty-fifth Amendment, which details procedures for presidential succession, is ratified.

1967
Business and Finance
James Hoffa, president of the Teamsters Union, is jailed for jury tampering.

1968
Business and Finance
Corporate profits after taxes exceed $47 billion.

1968
The Arts
The musical play *You're a Good Man, Charlie Brown* premieres.

1968
Daily Life
Surveys reveal that 86 percent of elementary school teachers are women, while 78 percent of the principals are men.

Think About Themes

Themes Journal *Decide whether you* **agree** *or* **disagree** *with the following statements. Note why in your journal.*

Global Relations Providing economic assistance to a foreign nation is an effective way to guarantee a political alliance.

Economic Development Governments have a responsibility to provide economic aid to citizens living in poverty.

Democratic Values Under certain circumstances, presidents should conceal facts from the public.

SECTION 1

Kennedy and the Cold War

OBJECTIVES

Read to understand:

1. how television coverage influenced the presidential election of 1960
2. how President Kennedy planned to stop the advance of communism
3. why the Bay of Pigs invasion of Cuba failed
4. how the Cuban missile crisis almost led to war

KEY TERMS

flexible response
Peace Corps
Alliance for Progress
Berlin Wall
Cuban missile crisis
Limited Nuclear Test Ban Treaty
hot line

KEY PEOPLE

John F. Kennedy
Fidel Castro

KEY PLACES

Bay of Pigs
San Cristóbal

Fear of communism played a key role in the 1960 presidential election.

EYEWITNESSES TO History

66 *For six days, time was deformed, everyday life suddenly dwarfed and illuminated, as if by the glare of an explosion that had not yet taken place.* **99**

—Todd Gitlin

Todd Gitlin reflected on the tense days of October 1962. At that time Gitlin was a student at Harvard University with a strong interest in politics. When President John F. Kennedy appeared on television on October 22 to announce a naval blockade against Cuba, Gitlin and many other Americans feared that a nuclear war between the United States and the Soviet Union might soon occur. He remembered that during the crisis "the country lived out the awe . . . and simmering near-panic always implicit in the thermonuclear age." The incident reflected the crises that President Kennedy faced during his brief presidency.

Todd Gitlin's book about the 1960s

The 1960 Campaign

Most Americans were satisfied with President Eisenhower's performance in the White House. However, the passage of the Twenty-second Amendment in 1951 limited a president's tenure in office to two elected terms. This meant that Eisenhower could not run for a third term in 1960.

As expected, the Republicans chose Richard Nixon as their presidential candidate for the upcoming election. His solid performance as Eisenhower's vice president had won him support from many Republican Party members. Trying to appeal to a wide variety of voters, Nixon downplayed his participation in such events as the investigations by the House Un-American Activities Committee.

Senator John F. Kennedy of Massachusetts eventually emerged as the Democratic candidate. His charm, wit, good looks, and record of service during World War II impressed many voters. However, as a Roman Catholic he faced the same religious prejudices that had hurt Al Smith's presidential bid in 1928. Kennedy assured voters that he believed firmly in the separation of church and state. Recalling his brother Joseph, who was killed in combat during World War II, Kennedy told voters, "Nobody asked my brother if he was a Catholic or Protestant before he climbed into an American bomber plane to fly his last mission." Kennedy's reassurances and the Republicans' refusal to exploit the issue convinced many voters that religion need not play a role in their voting decisions.

Nixon chose Henry Cabot Lodge Jr. of Massachusetts as his running mate. Kennedy selected Texas senator Lyndon B. Johnson, who had failed in his own attempt to obtain the Democratic nomination. Kennedy's decision shocked his supporters, many of whom intensely disliked the senator. One aide told Kennedy that choosing Johnson was the "worst mistake" he could possibly make. However,

Kennedy had made a strategic choice. Johnson would help the Democrats win votes in Texas and other southern states where Kennedy was not particularly popular. Moreover, Johnson could work closely with Congress—where he was regarded as a master at getting legislation passed—to help the Kennedy administration achieve its goals.

During the campaign, Kennedy told Americans they would have to make sacrifices in the coming years. In a speech to South Dakota farmers, he explained his vision of the future.

> 66 I promise you no sure solutions, no easy life. The years ahead for all of us will be as difficult as any in our history. There are new frontiers for America to conquer in education, in science, in national purpose—not frontiers on a map, but frontiers of the mind, the will, the spirit of man. 99

Nixon argued that he had the maturity and experience to serve as president. He led in the polls until the first of four televised debates. Public reaction to the debates revealed the growing influence of television on American life. Nixon was weary from nonstop campaigning and was suffering from a painful injury to his knee. The tired candidate stood before the television cameras in a shirt that looked too large and with his make-up smeared by sweat. Kennedy, on the other hand, appeared fit, confident, and relaxed. Many Americans who listened to the first debate on the radio believed that Nixon had won. However, most of those who saw the television broadcast decided that Kennedy would make a better president than Nixon.

Kennedy aide Kenneth O'Donnell later recalled, "After the first debate, the 1960 campaign was an entirely different ball game." Kennedy later recognized the importance of television to his campaign. He confided, "We wouldn't have had a prayer without that gadget." Despite Kennedy's rapidly growing popularity, the election was very close. Kennedy defeated Nixon by fewer than 120,000 popular votes. His electoral victory was more clear cut—303 votes to Nixon's 219. At age 43, John F. Kennedy became the youngest person ever elected to the White House.

✔ READING CHECK: How did television coverage influence the 1960 presidential election?

The Election of 1960

Learning from Maps John F. Kennedy won an extremely close victory over Richard Nixon in 1960.

? PLACE Which state gave Nixon the largest number of electoral votes?

WA 9, OR 6, ID 4, NV 3, CA 32, MT 4, WY 3, UT 4, AZ 4, ND 4, SD 4, NE 6, CO 6, NM 4, MN 11, IA 10, KS 8, OK 8*, TX 24, WI 12, IL 27, MO 13, AR 8, LA 10, MI 20, IN 13, KY 10, MS 8*, AL 11*, OH 25, WV 8, TN 11, GA 12, VA 12, NC 14, SC 8, FL 10, PA 32, NY 45, NH 4, VT 3, ME 5, MA 16, RI 4, CT 8, NJ 16, DE 3, MD 8, AK 3, HI 3

CANDIDATE	PARTY	ELECTORAL VOTE	POPULAR VOTE	% OF POPULAR VOTE
Kennedy	Democratic	303	34,226,731	49.7
Nixon	Republican	219	34,108,157	49.5
Byrd	Not an official candidate	15*		

*Six unpledged Democratic electors in Alabama, all eight unpledged Democratic electors in Mississippi, and one Republican elector in Oklahoma voted for Senator Henry Byrd of Virginia.

Source: *Historical Statistics of the United States*

Televised debates with Richard Nixon helped John Kennedy win the 1960 presidential election.

THE BALLAD OF
THE GREEN BERETS

Words and Music by BARRY SADLER and ROBIN MOORE

The Green Berets. Named for the hats they wore (above), the Green Berets had their own theme song. *What do these images suggest about the popularity of the Green Berets?*

Kennedy's Foreign Policy

In foreign affairs, President Kennedy tended to follow the Cold War policies of his predecessors. He continued the nuclear arms buildup begun by President Eisenhower. However, unlike his predecessors, Kennedy did not want to rely solely on the threat of nuclear weapons to block communist expansion. He preferred to have a number of options in case of international crises. This strategy was called **flexible response**. Kennedy strengthened conventional military forces. He also established special units like the Green Berets to assist countries struggling to fight communism. He took special pride in this special fighting unit and kept one of the berets they wore on his desk in the Oval Office.

Foreign aid. Kennedy also supported nonmilitary options to stop communist expansion. He realized that helping developing countries could strengthen their dependence on the United States and block Soviet influence. To this end, Kennedy introduced a number of aid programs designed to help countries in Africa, Asia, and Latin America. First among these programs was the **Peace Corps**, which sent American volunteers to work for two years in developing countries.

Africa was an area of concern for the Kennedy administration. In 1960, a total of 17 African countries gained their independence from colonial powers. In an effort to support African nationalism, Kennedy called for increased economic aid to the continent. This aid included sending Peace Corps volunteers and food. In addition, the United States nearly doubled the amount of loans offered to African countries during the Kennedy years.

Kennedy also introduced a program to expand economic aid to Latin America. This **Alliance for Progress** offered billions of dollars in aid to participating countries. In exchange for financial assistance, the countries were expected to begin democratic reforms and encourage capitalism. The Alliance proved a disappointment. The rapidly growing population of Latin American countries required far more money than the United States was willing to provide. Moreover, much of the money given to participating countries soon fell into the hands of corrupt politicians. Few Latin American leaders enacted significant reforms. Victor Alba, a Latin American writer, blamed the program's failure on its inability to motivate the poor majority in Latin American countries.

> 66 We know who killed the Alliance: the oligarchic governments [governments ruled by a few] of Latin America. . . . We know who supplied the poison: the bureaucrats and technicians. And we know who would have defended it if anyone had bothered to let them know that it existed and needed defenders: the people. 99

✔ **READING CHECK:** How did President John F. Kennedy plan to stop the spread of communism?

HOLT RESEARCHER *Read More About It*

Free Find: Peace Corps
After reading about the Peace Corps on the **Holt Researcher** CD–ROM, create a proposal for a similar program to help people living in the United States.

The Peace Corps offered help to developing nations.

■ **Understanding Change** The Peace Corps has continued to aid countries throughout the world. *How has the number of countries served and number of Peace Corps volunteers changed over the years? How has the type of work performed by Peace Corps workers changed?*

	THEN	NOW
Number of Volunteers	7,000	6,700
Number of Countries Being Served	44	80

Areas of Service

- Education
- Environment
- Health
- Business
- Agriculture
- Community Development
- Agriculture, Health Care, and Public Works
- Other

Source: The Peace Corps. Data reflect 1963 and 1999.

THEN

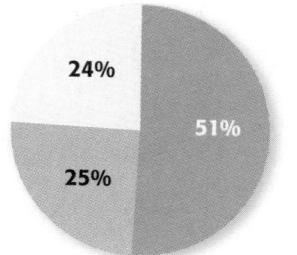

24%
51%
25%

Now

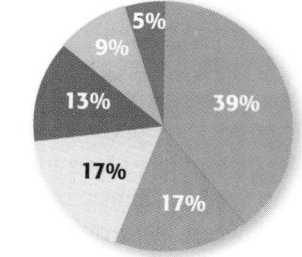

5%
9%
13%
39%
17%
17%

The Bay of Pigs. Latin America was a special target for aid from the United States because the Soviet Union had recently gained a foothold there. In 1959 Fidel Castro led an uprising that succeeded in overthrowing the Cuban dictator, Fulgencio Batista. Castro quickly established a communist-style dictatorship with ties to the Soviet Union.

Castro boasted that his success was "the reason that President Kennedy can't sleep at night." Indeed, Kennedy was deeply troubled by the fact that a communist government flourished only 90 miles from the United States. He soon learned that during President Eisenhower's administration the Central Intelligence Agency (CIA) had developed a plan for overthrowing Castro. The CIA was training and financing a group of anti-Castro Cuban refugees who were to invade Cuba. After taking office, Kennedy gave his approval for the plan to proceed.

The invasion resulted in disaster. Cuban forces quickly pinned down the nearly 1,500 rebels who came ashore at Cuba's Bay of Pigs on April 17, 1961. The U.S. naval and air support that the rebels expected never materialized. At the last minute, Kennedy decided not to send in air strikes. Equally damaging, the invasion failed to spark a popular uprising among the Cuban people. It took Cuban military forces less than 72 hours to crush the invasion and take prisoner some 1,200 surviving rebels.

One American journalist complained that the Bay of Pigs had made the United States look "like fools to our friends, rascals to our enemies, and incompetents to the rest." The invasion also brought Cuban leaders closer to the Soviets. Kennedy took full responsibility for the incident. After the Bay of Pigs, he resolved to take more control over foreign affairs. He told a close friend, "From now on it's John Kennedy that makes the decisions as to whether or not we're going to do these things."

INTERPRETING THE VISUAL RECORD

The Bay of Pigs. The Bay of Pigs invasion was the cover story of this issue of *Life* magazine. *How do you think the magazine portrayed the event?*

✔ **READING CHECK:** Why did the Bay of Pigs invasion fail?

The Space Program

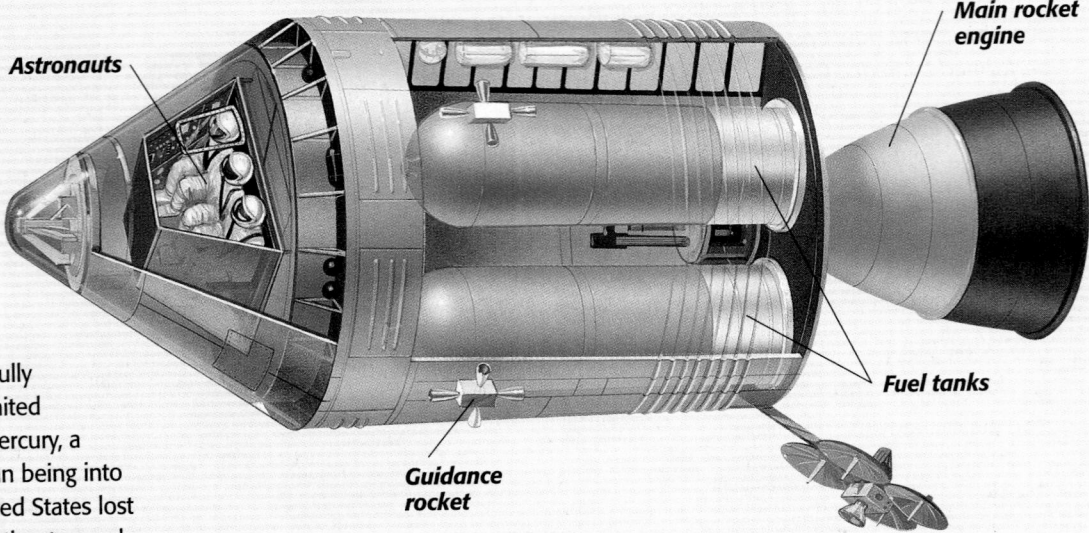

Astronauts

Guidance rocket

Main rocket engine

Fuel tanks

As the United States and the Soviet Union developed missiles to carry nuclear weapons, both nations also sought to use missile technology to begin the exploration of outer space. In 1958, a year after the Soviets successfully launched *Sputnik*, the United States initiated Project Mercury, a program to send a human being into space. However, the United States lost the race to be the first nation to send a human into orbit. On April 12, 1961, Soviet cosmonaut Yuri Gagarin became the first human to circle Earth.

President Kennedy publicly congratulated the Soviets on their achievement. Privately, however, he asked his advisers, "Is there any place where we can catch them [the Soviets]? What can we do? Are we working twenty-four hours a day? Can we go around the moon before them?" Less than a month later, the

United States enjoyed its first success when Alan Shepherd completed a suborbital flight. In February 1962 John Glenn left Earth in his Mercury spacecraft *Friendship 7*, lifted into space by an Atlas intercontinental ballistic missile. Glenn spent five hours in space and orbited Earth three times. This event restored American confidence in the space program and set the stage for the race to the Moon. The Apollo program

achieved that goal in 1969 using space capsules like the one shown above.

Understanding Science and History

1. Who was the first person to orbit Earth?
2. What takes up the most room in the spacecraft shown?

The Berlin Crisis

President Kennedy and Soviet leader Nikita Khrushchev share a light moment during their conference in Vienna.

The Bay of Pigs convinced Soviet leader Nikita Khrushchev that President Kennedy was weak and could be intimidated. At a summit meeting in June 1961, Khrushchev issued an ultimatum: the West must recognize the sovereignty of communist East Germany and remove all troops from West Berlin. Khrushchev's demands shocked Kennedy. He had no desire to risk war over Berlin, but worried that if he gave in to the Soviets he would lose the confidence of the American people.

In mid-August the East Germans erected a barbed-wire barrier that cut off traffic between East and West Berlin. Kennedy responded by sending additional U.S. troops to the city. For several days U.S. and Soviet soldiers eyed each other nervously across the barbed wire. Tensions gradually eased when it became clear that Khrushchev's real goal had been achieved. The barrier had halted the mass departure of East Germans to the West through Berlin. In time, the East Germans replaced the barbed wire with a wall of gray concrete and watchtowers. The **Berlin Wall** became the most widely recognized symbol of the Cold War.

The Missiles of October

Soviet leader Khrushchev's continued testing of the U.S. commitment to containing communism led to the Cold War's greatest crisis. To prevent an invasion, Cuban leader Fidel Castro asked the Soviet Union to provide him with defensive weapons. The Soviets complied and also offered offensive weapons—nuclear missiles that could reach the cities of the eastern United States.

CIA officials monitored the Soviet arms buildup in Cuba throughout the summer of 1962. Photographs taken by a U.S. U-2 spy plane on October 14 revealed the existence of two ballistic-missile launching pads near the Cuban town of San Cristóbal. Additional U-2 flights over the island located more missiles capable of striking targets in the United States within minutes of launching.

On October 22 Kennedy appeared on national television to announce that any armed ships bound for Cuba would be turned back. He also demanded that the Soviets remove the missiles.

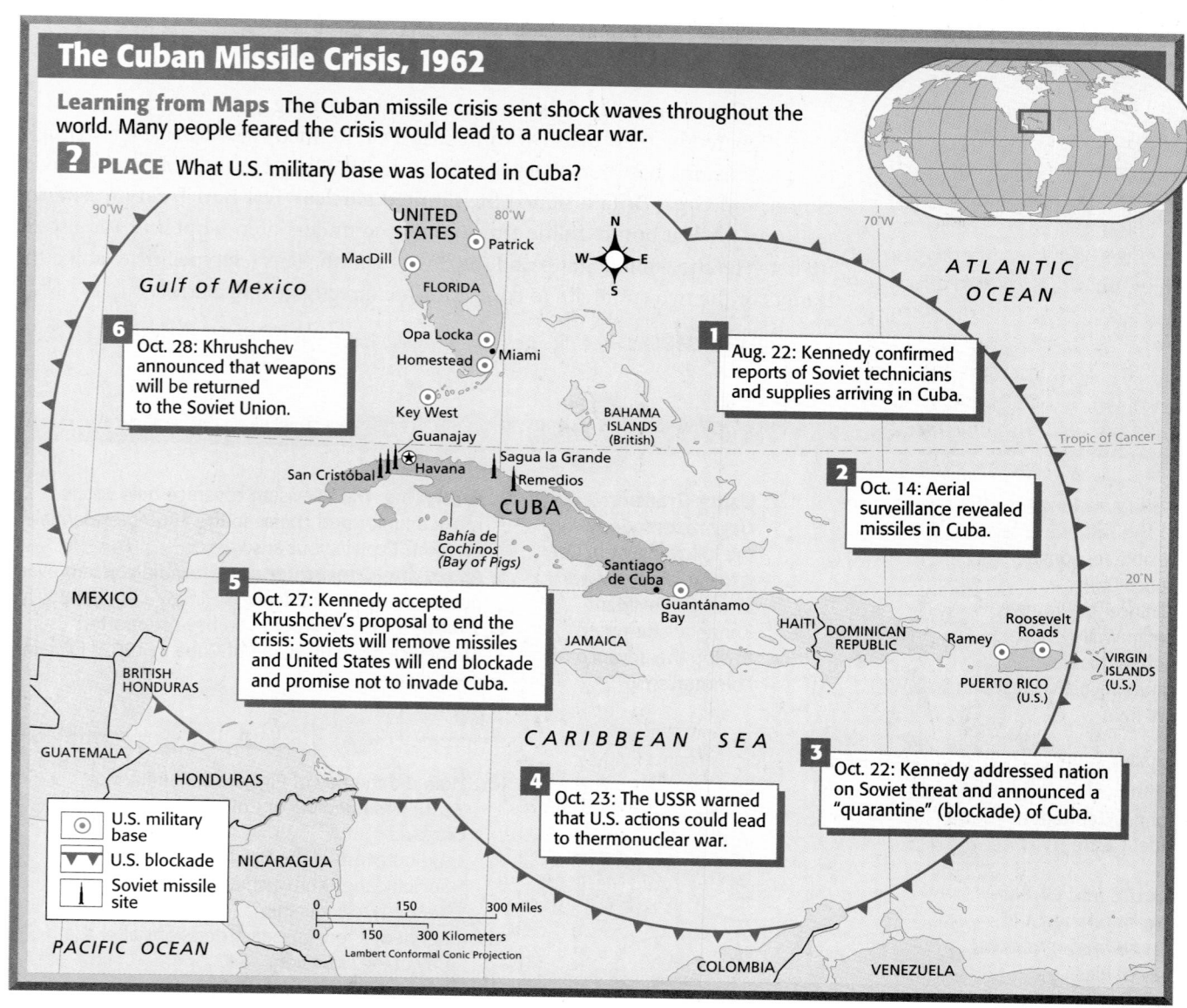

The Cuban Missile Crisis, 1962

Learning from Maps The Cuban missile crisis sent shock waves throughout the world. Many people feared the crisis would lead to a nuclear war.

? PLACE What U.S. military base was located in Cuba?

6 Oct. 28: Khrushchev announced that weapons will be returned to the Soviet Union.

1 Aug. 22: Kennedy confirmed reports of Soviet technicians and supplies arriving in Cuba.

2 Oct. 14: Aerial surveillance revealed missiles in Cuba.

5 Oct. 27: Kennedy accepted Khrushchev's proposal to end the crisis: Soviets will remove missiles and United States will end blockade and promise not to invade Cuba.

4 Oct. 23: The USSR warned that U.S. actions could lead to thermonuclear war.

3 Oct. 22: Kennedy addressed nation on Soviet threat and announced a "quarantine" (blockade) of Cuba.

Legend:
- ◉ U.S. military base
- ▼ U.S. blockade
- Soviet missile site

0   150   300 Miles
0   150   300 Kilometers
Lambert Conformal Conic Projection

THROUGH OTHERS' EYES

Soviet View of the Cuban Missile Crisis

During the Cuban missile crisis, the world held its breath for several days as it teetered on the brink of nuclear war. In the end, the Soviets agreed to remove the missiles. Soviet premier Nikita Khrushchev related his memory of the crisis.

❝ It had been, to say the least, an interesting and challenging situation. The two most powerful nations of the world had squared off against each other, each with its finger on the button. You'd have thought that war was inevitable. But both sides showed that if the desire to avoid war is strong enough, even the most pressing dispute can be solved by compromise. . . . I'll always remember the late President Kennedy with deep respect because, in the final analysis, he showed himself to be sober-minded and determined to avoid war. ❞

Over the next two days, nuclear war loomed over the horizon. In a frenzy of activity, Soviet military advisers armed the missiles in Cuba. U.S. B-52 bombers armed with nuclear weapons prepared for battle. Meanwhile, armed Soviet ships sailed toward the blockade line.

Suddenly, on October 24, Kennedy was informed that most of the Soviet ships had "stopped dead in the water" before reaching the blockade line. The ships then turned and sailed home. "We're eyeball to eyeball," said Secretary of State Dean Rusk, "and I think the other fellow just blinked." On October 28 Khrushchev agreed to dismantle the missile bases in response to Kennedy's promise not to invade Cuba. Kennedy also secretly agreed to remove U.S. missiles from some foreign sites.

The **Cuban missile crisis** marked a historic turning point in U.S.-Soviet relations. Sobered by their brush with nuclear war, Kennedy and Khrushchev sought to ease tensions between their countries. In 1963 the United States, the Soviet Union, and Great Britain signed the **Limited Nuclear Test Ban Treaty** to end the testing of nuclear bombs in the atmosphere and underwater. A **hot line** was also set up between the United States and the Soviet Union. This teletype line enabled the leaders of the two countries to communicate directly during a crisis.

✔ **READING CHECK:** How did the Cuban missile crisis almost lead to war?

SECTION 1 REVIEW

Define and explain the significance of the following terms:
flexible response
Peace Corps
Alliance for Progress
Berlin Wall
Cuban missile crisis
Limited Nuclear Test Ban Treaty
hot line

Identify and explain the significance of the following individuals:
John F. Kennedy
Fidel Castro

Locate and explain the importance of the following places:
Bay of Pigs
San Cristóbal

1. **Using Graphic Organizers** Copy the following web. Use it to explain the ways in which President Kennedy attempted to stop the advance of communism.

2. **Analyzing** Did television coverage help voters make an informed choice in the 1960 presidential election? Explain your answer.
3. **Assessing Consequences** How did concern over nuclear weapons influence Kennedy's foreign policy?
4. **Taking a Stand** Would you have supported Kennedy's naval blockade of Cuba in 1962? Explain your answer.

Critical Thinking

5. How did the Bay of Pigs incident influence Kennedy's handling of Cold War events?
   Consider:
   • the outcome of the Bay of Pigs invasion
   • Soviet leader Khrushchev's perception of Kennedy's leadership
   • Kennedy's foreign-policy decisions after the Bay of Pigs invasion

The Kennedy White House

OBJECTIVES

Read to understand:

1. how President Kennedy's image conflicted with reality
2. why Kennedy had difficulty getting legislation passed
3. how the Kennedy administration tried to help poor Americans
4. how Americans responded to the death of the president

KEY TERMS

New Frontier
Area Redevelopment Act
Warren Commission

KEY PEOPLE

Jacqueline Kennedy
Donna Shalala
Robert Kennedy
Michael Harrington
Lee Harvey Oswald

EYEWITNESSES TO History

❝ *[He] had a deep orange-brown suntan of a ski instructor, and when he smiled at the crowd his teeth were amazingly white and clearly visible at a distance of fifty yards.* **❞**

—Norman Mailer

Author Norman Mailer described presidential candidate John F. Kennedy in 1960. Mailer attended the Democratic National Convention and offered his observations of Kennedy in an article published later that year. Mailer compared Kennedy's arrival at the convention to "the scene where the hero, the matinee movie idol, comes to the palace to claim the princess." Explaining Kennedy's enormous appeal, Mailer argued, "It was a hero America needed . . . because only a hero can capture the secret imagination of a people, and so be good for the vitality of his nation."

President Kennedy sails off the coast of Maine.

The Kennedy Charisma

Youthful John F. Kennedy offered a marked contrast to the elderly outgoing president, Dwight D. Eisenhower. Kennedy captured the hearts of many Americans in a way that few politicians have. He became so popular that a few months after taking office he had to ask Americans to stop sending congratulatory telegrams to the White House.

Kennedy's appeal stemmed from his cool intellectual personality, athletic appearance, and handsome features. Americans could not doubt that their president had a keen mind. A graduate of Harvard University, he had published two books. His best-selling *Profiles in Courage* won a Pulitzer Prize for biography. Kennedy presented an image of youth and vitality throughout his career in politics. He was frequently photographed engaged in sporting activities such as football, sailing, and swimming.

The first family. The president's attractive young wife, Jacqueline "Jackie" Kennedy, contributed to the glamour and mystique that surrounded the Kennedy White House. The first lady quickly rose to the top of polls of women whom Americans most admired. Her popularity spread beyond U.S. borders. When the Kennedys met with Soviet leader Nikita Khrushchev, he said, "I'd like to shake her hand first." The first lady received so much attention on a trip to France that the president called himself "the man who accompanied Jacqueline Kennedy to Paris, and I have enjoyed it."

Jacqueline Kennedy brought an appreciation for the fine arts to the Kennedy administration. She invited prominent artists and

President Kennedy, his wife, Jacqueline, and their children, John Jr. and Caroline, play with their dogs.

John F. Kennedy

John F. Kennedy's heroism in World War II enhanced the mystique that surrounded him when he took office. During the war, he served as the commander of a U.S. Navy patrol torpedo boat in the Pacific theater. In the early morning hours of August 2, 1943, Kennedy's boat, the *PT-109,* was rammed by a Japanese destroyer. Two crewmen were killed. The next morning, as the boat slowly sank, Kennedy ordered his men to use a plank as a float and head for a small island about three miles away. Kennedy swam the entire distance, towing a wounded man by clenching the man's life jacket strap in his teeth. The men made it to the island and they were rescued several days later.

Kennedy received some criticism for his role in the affair. Questions were raised as to why the Japanese destroyer had been able to ram the PT boat, a small, fast ship. Nevertheless, he received a medal for his heroic efforts to save his men. A national magazine printed the story of his actions, and the *PT-109* was mentioned frequently during Kennedy's political campaigns. Members of his crew were present during Kennedy's inauguration, and a model of the *PT-109* was displayed in the inaugural parade.

musicians to social events. One newspaper referred to her as the "unofficial Minister of Culture." She also organized a major restoration of the White House, declaring, "I want to make the White House the first house in the land." Mrs. Kennedy later hosted a nationally televised tour of the White House.

Americans were also fascinated by the Kennedy children. Caroline, born in 1957, and John Jr., born a few weeks after his father's election to office, were the first young children to live in the White House since Theodore Roosevelt's presidency. One Kennedy aide later recalled that "Caroline Kennedy quickly became a national figure." The public enjoyed seeing photographs of her and her brother playing in the White House. Complaining about the president's popularity, one senator who opposed Kennedy's programs claimed, "The difference is Caroline, and there's nothing we can do about it."

Effects on youth. Although many Americans regarded the Kennedy family as attractive and interesting, young people found Kennedy particularly inspiring. During the presidential campaign, Kennedy's public appearances drew large numbers of young Americans. Many of them responded to Kennedy's call for service and sacrifice. Some of these Americans joined the Peace Corps. One volunteer recalled, "I'd never done anything political, patriotic, or unselfish because nobody ever asked me to. Kennedy asked."

Donna Shalala

One of the many Americans motivated to action by Kennedy's vision was Donna Shalala. During the 1990s Shalala served as secretary of health and human services in the administration of President Bill Clinton. In 1961, as a young college graduate, Shalala had responded to Kennedy's call and joined the Peace Corps. She later recalled, "Kennedy was the first president we had voted for. He represented a break with the past." Shalala spent two years in a tiny village called Molasani in Iran, living in a mud hut and teaching English.

Shalala remembered that "everybody laughed" at Kennedy's idea of American volunteers fanning out across the globe, "but it worked." She claimed that her years of Peace Corps service "made me a world citizen. It just changed me at such a young age, giving me confidence in my ability to be dropped down anywhere on earth and be comfortable." Her experience also gave her confidence in young people. She declared, "Having faith in young Americans may be a simple idea, but it works."

Read More About It

Free Find:
Donna Shalala
After reading about Donna Shalala on the **Holt Researcher** CD–ROM, write a resumé for her to use in applying for a cabinet position in a future administration.

Reality. The images of the first family that Americans so admired masked a more complex reality. Well aware of the power of the media, Kennedy took great pains to control his public appearance. He avoided being photographed while wearing his reading glasses, and later during his administration had television lights adjusted to hide a double chin.

Despite his interest in athletic pursuits, President Kennedy was not a healthy man. He struggled with illness throughout his life. His brother Robert once recalled that "at least one half of the days that he spent on this earth were days of intense physical pain." Kennedy suffered from a sometimes fatal condition called Addison's disease. His back had troubled him since childhood, and Kennedy had nearly died in 1954 during an operation on his spine.

✔ **READING CHECK:** How did President Kennedy's image conflict with reality?

PRESIDENT JOHN F. KENNEDY
Inaugural Address

John F. Kennedy delivered his inaugural address on January 20, 1961. It was a sunny but bitterly cold day in the nation's capital. The address contained the themes of challenge and sacrifice that had filled his speeches during the presidential campaign. His words that day inspired many Americans. This remains one of the most famous speeches in U.S. history.

*I*n the long history of the world, only a few generations have been granted the role of defending freedom in its hour of maximum danger. I do not shrink from this responsibility—I welcome it. I do not believe that any of us would exchange places with any other people or any other generation. The energy, the faith, the devotion which we bring to this endeavor will light our country and all who serve it—and the glow from that fire can truly light the world.

And so my fellow Americans: ask not what your country can do for you—ask what you can do for your country.

My fellow citizens of the world: ask not what America will do for you, but what together we can do for the freedom of man.

Kennedy's Advisers

President Kennedy hoped to use the government to offer solutions to national and global problems. To advance his programs, Kennedy surrounded himself with others who shared his vision. The average age of his cabinet members was 47, a decade younger than that of President Eisenhower's cabinet. Special Counsel Theodore Sorensen, the speechwriter who composed most of Kennedy's inaugural address, was just 32 years old at the time.

The president wanted only "the brightest and best," and his advisers were well educated. "There's nothing like brains. You can't beat brains," Kennedy claimed. Secretary of Defense Robert McNamara was a graduate of the Harvard Business School. Secretary of State Dean Rusk was a former Rhodes Scholar, and McGeorge Bundy, special assistant for national security affairs, had been a dean at Harvard. However, few of Kennedy's advisers had political experience, and not everyone was impressed by their credentials. Speaker of the House Sam Rayburn told Lyndon Johnson, "You may be right and they may be every bit as intelligent as you say, but I'd feel a whole lot better about them if just one of them had run for sheriff once."

For the position of attorney general, Kennedy selected his younger brother Robert "Bobby" Kennedy. Although Robert Kennedy had graduated from law school, he had never practiced law. Some members of Congress and presidential advisers opposed the president's decision to appoint his brother to high office. Even Robert expressed doubts. Nonetheless, the president told his brother, "I need you. . . . I need someone I know to talk to in this government." Robert proved to be the

President Kennedy and his brother Robert work together in the Oval Office.

president's closest adviser. Kennedy also valued advice from a small circle of White House staff members that included Theodore Sorensen, speechwriter Richard Goodwin, and Press Secretary Pierre Salinger. Goodwin later recalled that staff members did not "hesitate to approach Kennedy directly on matters we thought of presidential interest or concern."

The Domestic Frontier

Because John F. Kennedy had spoken of a "new frontier" during the presidential campaign, his agenda became known as the **New Frontier**. Managing the economy was one of Kennedy's first domestic challenges. He wanted to reassure business leaders that his policies would not be disruptive. To do so, he appointed C. Douglas Dillon, a Republican who had served in the Eisenhower administration, as secretary of the treasury. This selection also gave his administration a bipartisan appearance.

The New Frontier. President Kennedy faced many challenges while trying to create his New Frontier. *What does the cat in this cartoon represent? What do the cat's many tails represent?*

Economic matters. When he took office, Kennedy faced economic problems that included rising unemployment and inflation. To stimulate economic growth, Kennedy called for an increase in government spending. By the end of 1961, inflation had gone down, but unemployment remained high. Kennedy hoped to keep inflation down and to further the economic recovery by persuading labor and business to agree to informal wage and price controls. Businesses had been granting higher wages to employees and then passing the costs on to consumers in the form of higher prices. Kennedy called on businesses to limit prices in return for workers agreeing to fewer pay raises.

Administration officials worked particularly hard to reach an agreement with the steel industry. They feared that a rise in steel prices would lead manufacturers who used steel to raise their prices. This could lead to inflation throughout the economy. One adviser told the president that steel was "so large in the manufacturing sector of the economy that it can upset the price applecart all by itself." Thus, Kennedy was furious when Roger Blough, the president of U.S. Steel, announced higher prices. Just two weeks earlier, steelworkers had agreed to accept only small increases in their benefits packages. Kennedy told Blough, "I think you have made a terrible mistake."

The following day Kennedy lashed out at U.S. Steel and five other companies that had announced similar price hikes. The president blamed the crisis on "a tiny handful of steel executives whose pursuit of private power and profit exceeds their sense of public responsibility." He accused the steel executives of showing "utter contempt for the interests of one hundred eighty-five million Americans." Recalling his inaugural theme of sacrifice, Kennedy declared, "Some time ago I asked each American to consider what he would do for this country and I asked the steel companies. In the last twenty-four hours we had their answer."

The Kennedy administration proceeded to wage a nonstop campaign against the steel company executives that included canceling government contracts. Faced with such pressure, steel company executives announced that prices would not increase after all. Although Kennedy received criticism for his heavy-handed tactics, he had scored a significant victory in his efforts to manage the economy.

Kennedy and Congress. Kennedy was unable to achieve much of his legislative agenda because he received little cooperation from Congress. Although Democrats controlled both houses of Congress, Republicans had gained 21 seats in the House of Representatives and 2 seats in the Senate in the 1960 election. More important, a coalition of southern Democrats and conservative Republicans in Congress opposed Kennedy's agenda and successfully blocked most of the president's domestic programs.

Even before Kennedy took office, his advisers recommended a tax cut as a means of stimulating economic growth. Lower taxes would give consumers more money to spend and in turn would lead business to produce more goods and hire more workers. Kennedy initially rejected the idea. He argued that such a program conflicted with his calls for personal sacrifice on behalf of national good.

A sharp drop in the stock market in May 1962, however, convinced Kennedy to ask Congress to reduce taxes. In his 1963 State of the Union Address, he declared, "I am convinced that the enactment this year of tax reduction and tax reform overshadows all other domestic problems in this Congress." Several members of Congress balked, however, when Kennedy introduced legislation that reduced taxes by some $10 billion. Critics included former president Eisenhower. They charged that without a comparable cut in federal spending, the tax cut "would lead to a vast wasteland of debt and financial chaos." Despite Kennedy's urging, Congress failed to pass the measure in 1963. Other Kennedy initiatives rejected by Congress included legislation to assist older Americans in paying their medical bills and a bill to provide federal aid for education.

✔ **READING CHECK:** Why did Kennedy have difficulty getting legislation passed?

Helping the Disadvantaged

John F. Kennedy ranked high among the wealthiest presidents—in 1962 his personal fortune stood at about $2.5 million. He donated his annual salary of $100,000 to charities. During the presidential campaign, Kennedy was astonished when he saw the living conditions of poor West Virginians. Once he took office he sought ways to help poor Americans improve their standard of living. He supported passage of the **Area Redevelopment Act** (ARA)—a bill to provide financial assistance to economically distressed regions that former president Eisenhower had previously vetoed. Kennedy signed the ARA into law in May 1961, winning the first legislative victory of his presidency.

The president's interest in poverty was renewed in 1962 when social activist Michael Harrington published *The Other America*, a well-documented study of poverty in the United States. The book shattered the popular notion that all Americans had benefited from the prosperity of the 1950s. Harrington reported that more than 42 million Americans lived on less than $1,000 per year. He challenged the nation's leaders to face the reality of poverty:

INTERPRETING THE VISUAL RECORD

Poverty. Inspired in part by Michael Harrington's *The Other America,* President Kennedy tried to help the poorest Americans. *What types of assistance could this family use?*

> [The poor exist] within the most powerful and rich society the world has ever known. Their misery has continued while the majority of the nation talked of itself as being 'affluent [wealthy].' . . . In this way tens of millions of human beings became invisible. They dropped out of sight and out of mind. . . . How long shall we ignore this underdeveloped nation in our midst? 🙶

Harrington also noted that racism continued to keep many ethnic groups—particularly African Americans—in poverty. He warned that the end of legalized segregation would not change the economic condition of most poor African Americans. "The laws against [discrimination based on] color can be removed," he wrote, "but that will leave the poverty that is the historic consequence of color. As long as this is the case, being born a Negro will continue to be the most profound disability that the United States imposes upon a citizen."

Harrington's work impressed members of the Kennedy administration, including the president himself. He told one adviser, "I want to go beyond the things that have already been accomplished. . . . For example, what about the poverty problem in the United States?" Kennedy's staff began work on the antipoverty programs that the president wanted to present as part of a campaign planned for 1964.

✔ **READING CHECK:** How did the Kennedy administration try to help Americans living in poverty?

Newspapers across the country reported the shocking news of President Kennedy's death.

Tragedy in Dallas

To build support for his 1964 presidential campaign, President Kennedy made a trip to Texas in November 1963. In Dallas on November 22, enthusiastic crowds lined the route of Kennedy's open-car motorcade from the airport. At about 12:30 P.M., as the motorcade moved through the downtown area, shots rang out. Kennedy slumped over, fatally wounded. Within hours, Vice President Lyndon Johnson was sworn in as president. Over the next few days Americans came together to mourn their dead president. Millions watched the funeral on television. Many felt that the death of the youthful, vibrant president had also killed something in them. "We'll never be young again," Kennedy staff member Daniel Patrick Moynihan sadly observed. Donna Shalala later recalled hearing the news while serving in the Peace Corps in Iran.

> 🙶 I remember staying up all night listening to the funeral on the radio. I also recall a beggar walking up to me in the street and I said, 'No, I don't have any money.' He said, 'I don't want any money. I just want to tell you how sorry I am that your young president died.' I remember how difficult it was to sleep and I remember turning cold, which is one of the first signs of shock. . . . His assassination forced us all to grow up. 🙶

Within hours of the shooting, Dallas police arrested Lee Harvey Oswald as a suspect. Two days later, while being moved from one jail to another, Oswald was shot to death by nightclub owner Jack Ruby. This strange turn of events caused many people to question whether Oswald had acted alone in killing the president.

To end speculation, President Johnson named a commission headed by Chief Justice Earl Warren to investigate the assassination. This **Warren Commission** spent 10 months reviewing the evidence. It concluded that there was no evidence of conspiracy and that both Oswald and Ruby had acted alone. Despite the findings of the Warren Commission, many Americans continued to believe that more than one person was involved in Kennedy's assassination.

After Kennedy's death, his family and friends worked diligently to shape the memory of the fallen president. Jacqueline Kennedy told reporter Theodore White that her husband's life "had more to do with myth, magic, legend, saga, and story than with political theory or political science." She asked White, who was writing a magazine article on the president, to compare his administration to Camelot, King Arthur's medieval court. White agreed, and the image of Camelot became another part of the Kennedy mystique.

First lighted on November 25, 1963, a flame burns continually at the grave of President John F. Kennedy.

Clark Clifford, an adviser to several presidents, offered a different assessment. He wrote, "In many ways the drama of [Kennedy's] presidency outweighed its achievements." Clifford argued that Kennedy nonetheless had an important influence on American life.

  66 He offered a vast promise to a new generation of Americans. He inspired the nation with a heroic vision of the presidency as the center of action in American life. No President during my lifetime, with the exception of Franklin Roosevelt, matched Kennedy in creating a sense that the Presidency was the center of our national life, the place from which we could solve our most pressing problems. **99**

✔ **READING CHECK:** How did Americans respond to President Kennedy's death?

SECTION 2 REVIEW

Define and explain the significance of the following terms:
New Frontier
Area Redevelopment Act
Warren Commission

Identify and explain the significance of the following individuals:
Jacqueline Kennedy
Donna Shalala
Robert Kennedy
Michael Harrington
Lee Harvey Oswald

1. **Using Graphic Organizers** Copy the following chart. Use it to explain President Kennedy's economic policies and how well they succeeded.

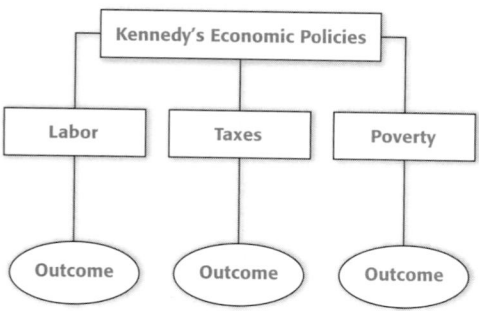

2. **Comparing and Contrasting** How did the reality of the Kennedy administration differ from the popular image?
3. **Analyzing** How did Kennedy try to assist the poor?
4. **Evaluating** Did Kennedy's difficulty in getting legislation passed reduce his effectiveness as a leader? Explain your answer.

Critical Thinking

5. Why might Kennedy's assassination have led many Americans to change their expectations of the nation's future?
   Consider:
   • the impact of Kennedy's youthful image
   • his influence on the nation's young people
   • doubts that surrounded his death

SECTION 3

Johnson's Great Society

Thousands of mourners like these gathered at the funeral of President Kennedy.

OBJECTIVES

Read to understand:

1. how President Johnson's War on Poverty affected American communities
2. what problems the Great Society programs addressed
3. how the Warren Court expanded individual liberties
4. why support for the Great Society programs declined during the late 1960s

KEY TERMS

War on Poverty
Office of Economic Opportunity
Volunteers in Service to America
Great Society
Medicare
Medicaid
Elementary and Secondary Education Act
Corporation for Public Broadcasting

KEY PEOPLE

Lyndon B. Johnson
Barry Goldwater
Robert C. Weaver
Rachel Carson
Earl Warren

EYEWITNESSES TO History

66 *We have received official confirmation that President Kennedy is dead. I am saddened to have to tell you this grievous news. . . . We have a new President. May God bless our new president and our nation.* 99
—Dean Rusk

Secretary of State Dean Rusk broke the news to his fellow airplane passengers. Earlier that day, Rusk and several other members of President Kennedy's cabinet and staff had boarded an airplane bound for Tokyo to attend an economic conference in Japan. As the plane flew across the Pacific, those on board received garbled teletype messages indicating that something terrible had happened to the president. Secretary Rusk ordered the plane to return to the United States immediately. After Rusk discovered that Kennedy was dead, he shared the news with those on board the flight. His words reflected the anxiety that many Americans felt for the nation and their new president as they faced the tragedy that had unfolded in Dallas that day.

Johnson Takes Over

President Lyndon Johnson was very different from the charismatic and engaging John F. Kennedy. Born in the Hill Country of central Texas, Johnson grew up in a household that had experienced both poverty and relative prosperity. Ambitious and hardworking, Johnson rose rapidly through the Democratic Party ranks. In 1948 he narrowly won a hard-fought race for a seat in the U.S. Senate. After he was re-elected in 1954, Johnson's colleagues made him the Senate majority leader. The position gave him a great deal of influence over legislation. A master of compromise, Johnson always seemed to find the middle course on which most people could agree.

Establishing continuity. Johnson's mastery of the political process, along with years of experience in Washington, enabled him to manage the transition to the presidency with considerable skill and tact. Johnson reassured the nation with promises of continuity between his administration and that of Kennedy. He later recalled, "I felt from the first day in office that I had to carry on for President Kennedy. I considered myself the caretaker of both his people and his policies." Johnson asked Kennedy's cabinet and advisers to continue serving under him. When he spoke to a joint session of Congress on November 27, 1963, Johnson detailed many of Kennedy's achievements. He then declared, "The ideas and ideals which he so nobly represented must and will be translated into effective action." Members of Congress, many of whom had vigorously opposed Kennedy's agenda, applauded enthusiastically to show their support for Johnson.

Lyndon Johnson takes the oath of office. His wife, Lady Bird Johnson, is on the left and Jacqueline Kennedy is on the right.

Johnson later claimed, "During my first thirty days in office I believe I averaged no more than three or four hours' sleep a night." He focused his attention on securing passage of Kennedy's tax cut bill and civil rights legislation, both of which had stalled in the Congress. In order to gain support for the tax cut, Johnson had his aides craft a federal budget that held spending to $100 billion. Convinced that the budget offered proof that Johnson intended to curb government spending, Congress approved the tax cut bill in February 1964.

During his first year in office, Johnson kept his pledge to follow in Kennedy's footsteps. However, the ambitious Texan also had plans of his own. "If you look at my record, you would know that I am a Roosevelt New Dealer," he told a former Kennedy aide. "As a matter of fact, John F. Kennedy was a little too conservative to suit my taste."

At his first cabinet meeting in January 1964 he announced, "The day is over when top jobs are reserved for men."

Johnson eventually appointed 27 women to upper-level government positions, including consumer activist Betty Furness, economists Alice Rivlin and Penelope Thunberg, and Texas legislator Barbara Jordan. He also appointed Mexican Americans to high positions, assigning Vicente T. Ximenes to chair a presidential committee on Mexican American affairs. Other top appointments went to Héctor P. García, a Texas spokesperson for Mexican American veterans, and to Raúl H. Castro. Castro later became the first Mexican American governor of Arizona.

PRESIDENTIAL Lives

1908–1973
In Office 1963–1969

Lyndon B. Johnson

Many observers saw Lyndon Johnson as a stereotypical Texas politician—loud and slightly crude. Johnson loved to shock people with his language, stories, and behavior. He was also a very physical politician. He would shake people's hands until his own bled and slap others on their backs in a friendly gesture. When Johnson visited Thailand in 1961, aides warned him that the Thai people regarded touching someone on the head as offensive. Johnson, however, could not restrain himself. He insisted upon patting the heads of the small children he met.

During his years in the Senate, fellow senators joked that Johnson had two techniques for getting another senator's attention. There was the Half-Johnson—"when he just put a hand on your shoulder"—and the Full-Johnson—"when he put his arm clear around you and thrust his face close to yours." Johnson's techniques got results, however.

Johnson was known as a workaholic who drove himself and his staff to exhaustion to complete multiple tasks. "What's the hurry?" one senator asked another about Johnson's busy schedule. "Rome wasn't built in a day." The other senator replied, "No, but Lyndon Johnson wasn't foreman on that job."

The War on Poverty. Johnson learned of President Kennedy's antipoverty initiative on November 23, 1963, his first full day in office. Walter Heller, chair of the Council of Economic Advisers, gave Johnson an outline of the plan. Johnson responded, "I'm sympathetic. Go ahead. Give it the highest priority. Push ahead full tilt."

Advisers urged Johnson to implement the antipoverty program slowly, testing its effectiveness in a few cities before expanding its scope. Johnson, however, insisted that the program "be big and bold and hit the nation with real impact." In his first State of the Union Address, delivered on January 8, 1964, the president declared "unconditional war on poverty in America." To launch his **War on Poverty**, Johnson sent to Congress a bill calling for the creation of an **Office of Economic Opportunity** (OEO). With a budget of $1 billion, OEO coordinated a series of new antipoverty programs. These programs included the Job

These children are part of a Head Start program.

teen Life

John Hough became a VISTA volunteer in 1968. He joined with the support of his parents, who "thought the country could be saved by the determined, idealistic young." Hough was from a small Massachusetts town and had never seen a poverty-stricken inner city. Nevertheless, he still "felt equipped to invade the world of urban poverty, stark and menacing as that world seemed."

VISTA volunteer Rissa Schiff of Brooklyn, New York, plays with Navajo children in Rough Rock, Arizona.

After a six-week training period in Chicago, Hough tutored students in English and mathematics at a school in Detroit, Michigan. Although he was dedicated to his work, Hough soon discovered that the problems he and his students faced were overwhelming. In addition to the constant threat of violence and the presence of drugs, overworked VISTA offices provided little support. Hough left VISTA after one year. In the end, however, he decided that making the effort to help people was in itself of great value.

Johnson campaign item

Corps, a work training program for young people between the ages of 16 and 21; Head Start, a preschool education program for low-income families; and **Volunteers in Service to America (VISTA)**, a domestic version of the Peace Corps. Congress passed the antipoverty legislation in late August 1964.

The War on Poverty brought improvements to many communities, including American Indian reservations. It allowed American Indians to establish and operate their own antipoverty programs on the reservations. La Donna Harris, a Comanche involved in OEO programs in Oklahoma, defended the program.

❝ I will stand up and defend OEO as long as I live. Indian leadership developed out of that program. . . . OEO taught us to use our imagination and to look at the future as an exciting adventure. It taught us that there are other ways of doing things. ❞

✔ **READING CHECK:** How did the War on Poverty affect American communities?

Johnson's Vision for America

Whereas President Kennedy had trouble pushing legislation through Congress, President Johnson fulfilled the major legislative goals of his first term within eight months. Comparing the two administrations, Texas journalist Liz Carpenter concluded, "Kennedy inspired. . . . Johnson delivered." Johnson was not content with fulfilling Kennedy's agenda, however. He hoped to be elected president in his own right in 1964 and to advance his own vision for the nation's future. Johnson saw his major task as building a **Great Society**. He shared his vision in a May 1964 speech at the University of Michigan.

❝ The Great Society rests on abundance and liberty for all. It demands an end to poverty and racial injustice. . . . The Great Society is a place where every child can find knowledge to enrich his mind and to enlarge his talents. . . . It is a place where the city of man serves not only the needs of the body and the demands of commerce but the desire for beauty and the hunger for community. ❞

In short, Johnson wanted the United States to be a place where people would be "more concerned with the quality of their goals than the quantity of their goods."

In order to achieve these lofty goals, Johnson worked hard to ensure victory in the upcoming presidential election. Opinion polls revealed that Americans were impressed with Johnson's achievements. Johnson rode this wave of popularity to easily win the Democratic presidential nomination for the 1964 election. He selected Hubert Humphrey, a liberal senator from Minnesota, as his running mate. The Republicans adopted a platform that rejected former president Eisenhower's Modern Republicanism. They chose Senator Barry Goldwater, a conservative from Arizona, as their presidential nominee, with New York representative William E. Miller as his running mate.

In his acceptance speech at the Republican National Convention, Goldwater declared, "Extremism in the defense of liberty is no vice! . . . Moderation in the pursuit of justice is no virtue!" However, many voters regarded Goldwater's brand of conservatism as too extreme. When Goldwater supporters displayed bumper stickers that read "IN YOUR HEART YOU KNOW HE'S RIGHT," Democrats responded with "IN YOUR GUT YOU KNOW HE'S NUTS." The Johnson campaign also produced a commercial that showed a small girl counting to 10 as she pulled petals from a daisy. When she reached "10," an image of an atomic bomb exploding filled the screen. The commercial implied that Goldwater could not be trusted with the nation's nuclear arsenal. The White House was flooded with complaints about the advertisement. It aired only once.

Despite criticism of such campaign tactics, Johnson won the election by a landslide, taking 61 percent of the popular vote and 486 electoral votes to Goldwater's 52. The last president to receive such a mandate was Franklin D. Roosevelt in 1936.

These Lyndon Johnson and Barry Goldwater dolls were made for the 1964 campaign.

Johnson and Congress

At an inaugural ball on the night of January 20, 1965, Lyndon Johnson told partygoers, "Don't stay up late. There's work to be done. We're on our way to the Great Society." Johnson moved quickly to make his vision a reality. While civil rights legislation was a major part of the Great Society legislation, other issues included health care, education, and urban renewal. President Johnson was aided in his efforts by the members of the 89th Congress, which was dominated by Democrats. Many of these Democrats were liberals who supported his call for a Great Society.

The programs. In 1965 Johnson persuaded Congress to establish **Medicare**—a national health insurance program for people over age 65. Congress also authorized funds for states to set up **Medicaid**—a government program that provides free health care to the needy. Johnson traveled to Independence, Missouri, to sign the bill in front of 81-year-old Harry Truman. Truman had first proposed federally funded health insurance in his Fair Deal.

Johnson also urged Congress to take action on funding for education. He gave a moving speech.

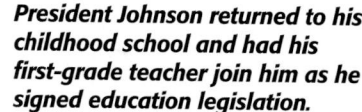

President Johnson returned to his childhood school and had his first-grade teacher join him as he signed education legislation.

66 My first job after college was a teacher in Cotulla, Texas, in a small Mexican American school. . . . Somehow you never forget what poverty and hatred can do when you see its scars on the hopeful face of a young child. . . . It never even occurred to me in my fondest dreams that I might have the chance to help the sons and daughters of those students and to help people like them all over the country. But now I do have that chance—and I'll let you in on a secret: *I mean to use it.* 99

President Johnson supported educational television shows like Sesame Street.

Read More About It

Free Find:

Rachel Carson

After reading about Rachel Carson on the **Holt Researcher** CD–ROM, write a brief description of a book you might write about environmental problems today. Then create a cover for your book that illustrates the issues you would address.

Congress responded by passing the **Elementary and Secondary Education Act** of 1965, which provided $1.3 billion in aid to schools in poor areas.

Johnson also persuaded Congress to pass the Omnibus Housing Act in 1965. This act authorized billions of dollars to be spent on urban renewal and housing assistance for low-income families. Congress also established the Department of Housing and Urban Development (HUD) to oversee federal housing programs. Robert C. Weaver headed this new department, making him the first African American member of a presidential cabinet. Weaver declared that the new programs had made Americans aware that "our cities are filled with poorly housed, badly educated, underemployed, desperate, unhappy Americans."

Quality of life. Johnson saw the Great Society as a place that fulfilled "the desire for beauty." He supported such programs as the National Endowment for the Arts (NEA) and the National Endowment for the Humanities (NEH), which offered grants and fellowships to artists, writers, and scholars. The Johnson administration also created the **Corporation for Public Broadcasting**, a nonprofit organization dedicated to offering educational television programming.

The president's interest in the quality of life extended to environmental issues. Johnson later recalled, "The cost of our careless technology had caught up with us." Many other Americans also felt a growing concern for the environment.

Rachel Carson

Marine biologist Rachel Carson contributed to this environmental movement. Born in Pennsylvania in 1907, Carson later recalled, "I can remember no time when I wasn't interested in the out-of-doors and the whole world of nature." After graduating with honors from Johns Hopkins University in 1929, she taught college and then worked for the U.S. Bureau of Fisheries. She wrote several works on marine science before turning to writing full-time in 1952.

When a friend asked Carson to investigate the impact of the pesticide DDT on birds and other wildlife, she responded with enthusiasm. The resulting book, *Silent Spring,* was published in 1962. Warning Americans that "a grim specter [spirit] has crept upon us almost unnoticed," Carson condemned the uncontrolled use of chemical pesticides, which she called "elixirs [medication] of death." She wrote, "Although today's poisons are more dangerous than any known before, they have amazingly become something to be showered down indiscriminately [carelessly] from the skies [by airplanes]." She continued, "Not only forests and cultivated fields are sprayed, but towns and cities as well." In her book, Carson chronicled the health and safety risks that pesticide use posed for humans. She also presented information regarding the impact of these chemicals on wildlife.

"We should no longer accept the counsel of those who tell us that we must fill our world with poisonous chemicals," Carson argued in the final chapter of *Silent Spring.* "We should look about and see what other course is open to us." In an attempt to protect their industry, pesticide manufacturers attacked Carson and her conclusions. However, her claims prompted President John F. Kennedy to create a panel to study the issue. The panel's final report agreed with Carson's conclusions.

Rachel Carson died in 1964. She did not live to witness the environmental legislation passed during the Johnson years. During his presidency Johnson signed the Water Quality Act of 1965, the Air Quality Act of 1967, the Water Pollution Act of 1968, and several other environmental bills. In addition, Johnson's administration created several new national parks and wilderness areas, making his record on environmental issues one of the most impressive of any U.S. president.

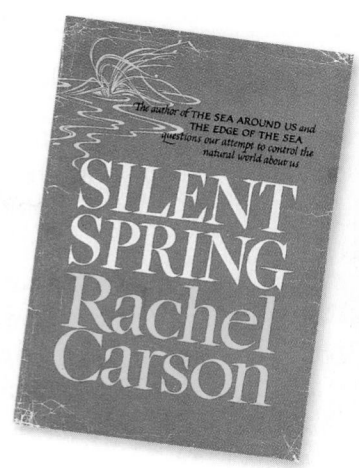

Rachel Carson's Silent Spring brought environmental issues to the attention of many Americans.

✔ **READING CHECK:** What problems did the Great Society programs address?

Strategies for Success

Using the Library

When conducting historical research, one should try to consult as broad an array of sources as possible. Most of the time, these sources are best found in a library. Thus, knowing how to use the library is a crucial skill for students to develop.

Although almost all libraries use the same basic guidelines for organizing their materials, each one has a unique layout, staff, and set of specific holdings. Taking a tour and becoming familiar with one's school or local public library can help make one's subsequent research more efficient and productive.

How to Use the Library

1. **Identify the topic.** First, identify the general topic that you wish to research. Then make a short list of events, issues, or people related to the topic that you can look to for further information if necessary.
2. **Check the reference section.** In the library's reference section, you will find almanacs, atlases, encyclopedias, specialized dictionaries, and indexes to newspaper and magazine articles. Consult each of these sources, when appropriate, to find information about your topic.
3. **Consult the library catalog.** Look in the library's card catalog or electronic catalog to locate books about your topic. Most library catalogs list books by author, title, and subject, and assign each book a call number based on the Library of Congress classification system or the Dewey decimal system. An index of subject headings can usually be found in or near the library catalog.

4. **Look for Internet and multimedia sources.** If possible, use the library's computer system to look for information about your topic on the Internet. Then check for CD–ROMs, videotapes, or other multimedia sources that may aid your research.
5. **Consult a librarian.** Librarians can help you use reference sources and the library catalog and can help direct you to a book's location. They can also suggest additional resources that may aid your research.

Applying the Strategy

Use your school or local public library to conduct research on one of the following topics:
a. the political career of Lyndon B. Johnson
b. a specific government program that was part of President Johnson's War on Poverty, such as the Job Corps, Head Start, or VISTA
c. the 1964 presidential campaign
d. the Housing and Urban Development Act of 1968

Practicing the Strategy

Answer the following questions.
1. What reference sources did you use to find information about your topic?
2. What books about your topic were listed in the library catalog?
3. What other sources, if any, did you find during your research?

The Warren Court Decisions

Like the Johnson administration, the Supreme Court of the 1960s reflected a spirit of activism. Under the leadership of Chief Justice Earl Warren, the Court continued the trend—begun with the 1954 desegregation decision in *Brown* v. *Board of Education*—of defining and extending individual rights. The Court extended equality in the voting booth with the "one person, one vote" principle. In many congressional districts, sparsely populated rural areas were granted the same number of representatives as densely populated urban areas. In the 1962 case *Baker* v. *Carr*, the Court declared that electoral districts must contain approximately the same number of voters in order to ensure fair representation for all Americans.

The Warren Court also issued a series of decisions protecting the rights of persons accused of crimes. *Gideon* v. *Wainwright* (1963) declared that the states must provide lawyers, at public expense, for poor defendants charged with serious crimes. *Escobedo* v. *Illinois* (1964) granted the accused the right to have a lawyer present during police investigations. *Miranda* v. *Arizona* (1966) said that accused persons must be informed of their rights at the time of their arrest.

Many people saw these decisions as an attempt to ensure that the criminal justice system did not violate individual rights. Others charged that the Court had overstepped its authority by making law rather than interpreting it. One critic claimed, "Earl Warren . . . has defiled [corrupted] our jurisprudence [court system] and made war against the public order." Billboards proclaiming "IMPEACH EARL WARREN!" appeared in some communities.

Billboards like this one showed Americans' dissatisfaction with Chief Justice Earl Warren.

✔ **READING CHECK:** How did the Warren Court expand individual liberties?

The Decline of the Great Society

Like the other postwar presidents, Lyndon Johnson was committed to fighting the Cold War. Yet unlike Presidents Eisenhower and Kennedy, Johnson was far more interested in domestic policy. Nevertheless, foreign affairs demanded Johnson's attention.

Foreign policy and the Great Society. Johnson quickly became involved in the affairs of the Dominican Republic. In April 1965, factions within the country's military rebelled against the military-led government. The U.S. ambassador believed that the rebels were under communist influence and insisted that Johnson intervene to "prevent another Cuba."

Johnson promptly sent some 22,000 marines to the Dominican Republic. With U.S. support, troops loyal to the military government gained the upper hand, and the situation stabilized. Johnson withdrew the marines in 1966 when relatively free and fair elections put a pro-American government in power.

Many people in Latin America condemned the intervention. Even those who supported Johnson's action did so reluctantly. In the United States, however, the majority of the public backed Johnson and praised his aggressive stand against the threat of communist expansion.

By the spring of 1965 Johnson's focus had shifted to fighting in the southeast Asian country of Vietnam and away from the Great Society. In 1966 the government spent about 18 times more on the Vietnam War than it did on the War on

Poverty. Civil rights leader Martin Luther King Jr. complained that the Great Society had been "shot down on the battlefields of Vietnam."

Domestic opposition. Growing domestic opposition to the programs of the Great Society also contributed to its decline. Johnson's legislative success record was extraordinary—the 89th Congress passed 181 of the 200 major bills that the president requested in 1965 and 1966. However, many members of Congress urged the president to slow down.

The results of the 1966 midterm elections signaled an additional change in the relations between Congress and the White House. Although Democrats retained their majorities in Congress, Republicans gained 47 House seats and three Senate seats, significantly reducing Johnson's opportunities to press for more legislation.

Problems with specific Great Society programs also raised doubts about the wisdom of Johnson's vision. Many state and local politicians disliked the War on Poverty because they had no control over the selection and funding of community projects. Members of Congress complained that many programs did not merit funding. Representative Frank Bow of Ohio declared, "We cannot have guns and butter," meaning that the Vietnam War should take priority over social programs. Bow ridiculed funding the NEH as wanting "guns with strawberry shortcake covered with whipped cream and cherry on top."

Although support for his programs weakened, Johnson's influence on American life endured long after his presidency ended. The NEH, Head Start, and other Great Society programs continued to bring benefits to Americans in the decades that followed.

✔ **READING CHECK:** Why did support for the Great Society programs decline during the late 1960s?

"GIVE IT TO HIM!"

The Great Society. Many critics of President Johnson's programs argued that they cost too much. *Who does this cartoon suggest paid for the Great Society programs?*

SECTION 3 REVIEW

Define and explain the significance of the following terms:
War on Poverty
Office of Economic Opportunity
Volunteers in Service to America
Great Society
Medicare
Medicaid
Elementary and Secondary
    Education Act
Corporation for Public
    Broadcasting

Identify and explain the significance of the following individuals:
Lyndon B. Johnson   Rachel Carson
Barry Goldwater   Earl Warren
Robert C. Weaver

1. **Using Graphic Organizers** Copy the following chart. Use it to explain the effects of the Great Society in education, housing, health care, and the environment.

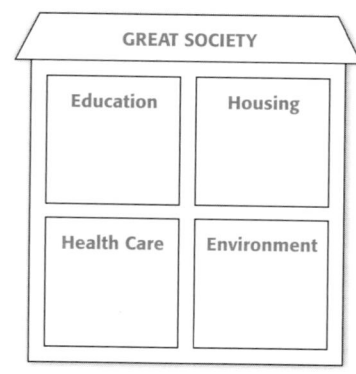

2. **Synthesizing** How did President Johnson win the support of the American people during his first year in office? How did Americans show their support?
3. **Hypothesizing** What were the effects of the decisions of the Warren Court, and how did Americans' reactions to them vary?
4. **Problem Solving** What advice would you have given President Johnson regarding the conflict between funding Great Society programs and foreign policy programs?

Critical Thinking

5. Why did Johnson's efforts to help poor Americans generate opposition?
   Consider:
   • the specific design of the poverty programs
   • the reaction of local and state politicians
   • concern over government spending during the Vietnam War

Review

Creating a Time Line

Copy the time line below onto a sheet of paper. Complete the time line by filling in the events and dates from the chapter that you think were most significant. Pick three events and explain why you think they were significant.

1961   1964   1969

Writing a Summary

Using the Reading Checks as a guide, write an overview of the events in the chapter.

Identifying People and Ideas

Identify the following terms or individuals and explain their significance.

1. flexible response
2. Alliance for Progress
3. Fidel Castro
4. New Frontier
5. John F. Kennedy
6. Warren Commission
7. War on Poverty
8. Great Society
9. Lyndon B. Johnson
10. Rachel Carson

Understanding Main Ideas

SECTION 1

1. What role did television play in the 1960 presidential election?
2. How did the establishment of a communist government in Cuba lead to increased Cold War tensions?

SECTION 2

3. How did Kennedy attempt to manage the economy?
4. Why did Kennedy fail to gain passage of most of his legislative initiatives?

SECTION 3

5. How did President Johnson establish continuity between his administration and that of John F. Kennedy?

6. What were some of the successes of the Great Society programs?

Reviewing Themes

1. **Global Relations** How did President Kennedy's Cold War foreign policy resemble that of his predecessors? How did it differ?
2. **Economic Development** Why did Presidents Kennedy and Johnson both develop programs to help the poor in America?
3. **Democratic Values** Why did Kennedy work so hard to control his public image?

Thinking Critically

1. **Recognizing Point of View** Why did many members of Congress oppose President Kennedy's tax cut proposal?
2. **Using Historical Imagination** Would Kennedy have been able to fulfill his legislative agenda had he lived? Explain your answer.
3. **Analyzing** What factors contributed to Johnson's landslide victory in the 1964 presidential election?
4. **Evaluating** How did the Warren Court's decisions in *Gideon* v. *Wainwright, Escobedo* v. *Illinois,* and *Miranda* v. *Arizona* strengthen individual rights?
5. **Problem Solving** What are the most effective ways for the government to provide assistance to the poor?

Writing about History

Writing to Describe Copy the following chart and use it to write an essay that describes the different goals and achievements of Presidents Kennedy and Johnson.

KENNEDY		JOHNSON	
Goals	Achievements	Goals	Achievements

This cartoon shows how President Kennedy's forceful response ended the Cuban missile crisis.

LES IMMEL/PEORIA JOURNAL STAR

internet connect

TOPIC: Peace Corps
GO TO: go.hrw.com
KEYWORD: SD1 Corps

Accessing the Internet through the HRW Web site, research the history, structure, and present-day role of the Peace Corps. Then imagine that you are a Peace Corps recruiter. Write a speech for a rally and present your speech to the class.

Strategies for Success Review the **Strategies for Success** on *Using the Library.* Then use your school or local public library to conduct research on one of the following topics:

a. the political career of John F. Kennedy
b. the history of the Peace Corps
c. the history of the Berlin Wall
d. the Cuban missile crisis

Linking History and Geography

Study the map below. In what region of the United States were most NASA sites located? How might geographical considerations have influenced the location of the NASA sites?

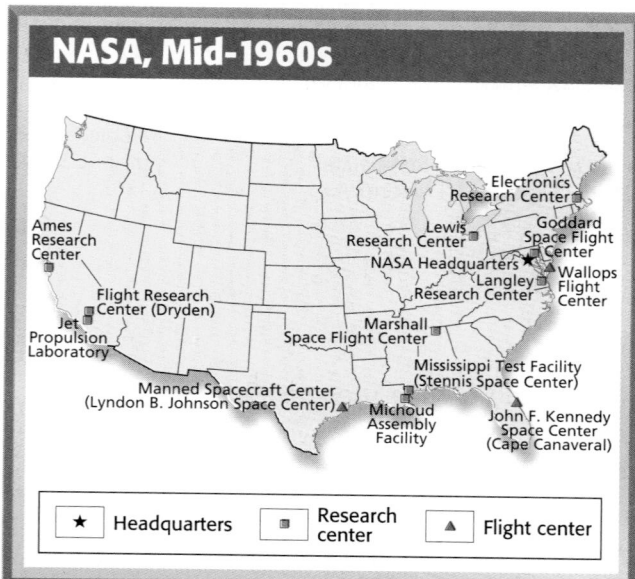

NASA, Mid-1960s

Electronics Research Center
Ames Research Center
Lewis Research Center
Goddard Space Flight Center
NASA Headquarters ★
Flight Research Center (Dryden)
Langley Research Center
Wallops Flight Center
Jet Propulsion Laboratory
Marshall Space Flight Center
Manned Spacecraft Center (Lyndon B. Johnson Space Center)
Mississippi Test Facility (Stennis Space Center)
Michoud Assembly Facility
John F. Kennedy Space Center (Cape Canaveral)

★ Headquarters   ▣ Research center   ▲ Flight center

BUILDING YOUR PORTFOLIO

Complete one or all of the following activities independently or cooperatively.

1 Global Relations
Imagine that you are a television news reporter. **Prepare a news bulletin** summarizing President Kennedy's announcement of the naval blockade of Cuba in 1962.

2 Economic Development
Imagine that you are a presidential aide in the Kennedy White House. **Prepare a memorandum** that describes a program designed to assist poor Americans.

3 Democratic Values
Imagine that you are an aide to President Johnson. **Prepare an illustrated pamphlet** that describes Great Society programs in the areas of health care, housing, education, and the environment.

CHAPTER 31

1960–1978
The Civil Rights Movement

March on Washington for civil rights

Dr. Martin Luther King Jr. receiving the Nobel Peace Prize

1963
Politics
The March on Washington takes place.

1964
World Events
Martin Luther King Jr. is awarded the Nobel Peace Prize.

1960

1960
World Events
The Belgian Congo becomes an independent nation.

1962
Daily Life
James Meredith integrates the University of Mississippi.

1962

1964

1964
The Arts
Jazz pianist Thelonious Monk is featured on the cover of *Time* magazine.

1966

1966
Politics
The Black Panther Party is founded in Oakland, California.

1966
Science and Technology
African American scientist Meredith Gourdine conducts research on the use of low-grade coal to generate electricity.

1968

1968
Science and Technology
Julian Earls heads NASA's Health Physics Section.

1968
Daily Life
Less than 21 percent of African American students in the former Confederate states attend integrated schools.

1968
Politics
The Kerner Commission releases its report on the urban riots that erupted in several major U.S. cities in 1967.

Thelonious Monk

Before You Read

Build on What You Know

The civil rights movement gained momentum from the Supreme Court's 1954 ruling on school desegregation. The success of the Montgomery Bus Boycott showed the effectiveness of peaceful protest in ending racial discrimination. It also transformed Martin Luther King Jr. into a prominent figure in the struggle for civil rights. In this chapter you will learn how some Americans worked to expand civil rights and equality for all Americans. However, many Americans continued to oppose racial equality.

Famine sufferers in Africa

Hank Aaron

1970
The Arts
Charles Gordone wins a Pulitzer Prize for his play *No Place to Be Somebody*.

1970
World Events
The civil war between Nigeria and the breakaway state of Biafra ends.

1972
Politics
Barbara Jordan of Texas is elected to the U.S. House of Representatives.

1974
Daily Life
Baseball player Hank Aaron breaks Babe Ruth's career home-run record.

1974
World Events
Drought in Africa leads to widespread famine.

1976
World Events
Antiapartheid riots erupt in several major cities in South Africa.

1970   **1972**   **1974**   **1976**   **1978**

1970
Daily Life
Cheryl A. Brown of Iowa becomes the first African American contestant in the Miss America Beauty Pageant.

1972
Science and Technology
George Carruthers assists in the development of an ultraviolet camera that is placed on the moon by the *Apollo 16* crew.

1975
Business and Finance
Wally Amos founds Famous Amos Chocolate Chip Cookies, which achieves sales of more than $5 million by 1980.

1978
Politics
The Supreme Court outlaws racial quotas in education in the case *University of California* v. *Bakke*.

Cheryl Brown

Famous Amos cookies

Think About Themes

Themes Journal

Decide whether you **agree** *or* **disagree** *with the following statements. Note why in your journal.*

Democratic Values Methods of social protest that prove effective in one part of the country can be used successfully in all regions of the nation.

Constitutional Heritage Local officials should be solely responsible for enforcing the law.

Economic Development Integration within the larger economic system is the best way for minority groups to improve their standard of living.

SECTION 1

Freedom Now!

The lunch counter where McNeil and his friends protested

OBJECTIVES

Read to understand:

1. how civil rights demonstrators used nonviolence to achieve their goals, and what the effect was
2. why civil rights leaders used nonviolent tactics, and how protests in Albany, Georgia, and Birmingham, Alabama, differed
3. why supporters pushed for a civil rights bill, and what factors influenced the bill's passage

KEY TERMS

Southern Christian Leadership Conference
nonviolent resistance
sit-ins
Student Nonviolent Coordinating Committee
Congress of Racial Equality
Freedom Riders
Civil Rights Act of 1964

KEY PEOPLE

Martin Luther King Jr.
T. Eugene Connor
Diane Nash
James Meredith
Medgar Evers
Laurie Pritchett

EYEWITNESSES TO History

66 *What do we do and to whom do we do it against?* 99
—Joseph McNeil

Joseph McNeil, an African American student at North Carolina Agricultural and Technical College in Greensboro, pondered such questions as he and three friends discussed ways to protest racial segregation. They were impressed by the courage of the African American students who had integrated the schools in Little Rock, Arkansas, in 1957. They "wanted to make a contribution and be a part of something like that," recalled McNeil. On February 1, 1960, the four students went to a nearby dime store and "sat at a lunch counter where blacks never sat before. And people started to look at us." McNeil recalled that "the help, many of whom were black, looked at us in disbelief too. They were concerned about our safety." The management refused to serve them, but the students returned the following day, vowing to continue their protest until they received service. In this way, McNeil and thousands of other young people across the South worked to bring an end to racial segregation.

Nonviolence in Action

Following the success of the Montgomery Bus Boycott, civil rights leaders met in 1957 in Atlanta to discuss future strategy. They expanded the Montgomery Improvement Association (MIA) into the **Southern Christian Leadership Conference** (SCLC), an alliance of church-based African American organizations dedicated to ending discrimination. Martin Luther King Jr. led the new organization. The SCLC pledged to use **nonviolent resistance** in its protests. Nonviolent resistance required that protesters not resort to violence, even when others attacked them. King called it confronting "the forces of hate with the power of love."

Student protests. Many non-SCLC members soon launched nonviolent protests of their own. In 1958, African American protesters in Oklahoma and Kansas conducted protests at segregated lunch counters. At these **sit-ins**, demonstrators protest by sitting down in a location and refusing to leave. By April 1960 some 50,000 students, both African American and white, were involved in sit-in protests. That month, the leaders of these demonstrations founded the **Student Nonviolent Coordinating Committee** (SNCC), a loose association of student activists from throughout the South.

White response to the sit-ins tested the students' commitment to nonviolence. White onlookers taunted the demonstrators and dumped food and drinks on them. When the harassment turned into physical

Civil rights activists endured taunting and occasionally violence during sit-ins.

attacks, demonstrators received little assistance from local authorities. When an angry mob beat nonviolent protesters in Nashville, Tennessee, the police ended the confrontation by arresting the protesters. Despite such incidents, the protesters remained committed to nonviolence. The tactic proved effective. Soon many restaurants and other eating establishments across the South had been integrated.

The Freedom Rides. The success of the student sit-ins inspired the **Congress of Racial Equality** (CORE). This northern-based civil rights group hoped to launch new nonviolent protests against racial discrimination. In December 1960 the Supreme Court ruled that segregation in facilities such as bus stations that served interstate travelers was illegal. CORE leaders planned to send an integrated group of **Freedom Riders** on bus trips through the South. They hoped to draw attention to violations of the Supreme Court ruling.

Violence erupted when they crossed the Alabama state line. Outside the town of Anniston, Alabama, a white mob firebombed one of the two buses carrying the activists. They also beat the riders as they tried to escape. The mob then followed the riders to the local hospital to prevent them from receiving medical care.

The Freedom Riders on the other bus were attacked in Birmingham, Alabama. Freedom Rider Walter Bergman, a white man, was beaten so badly that he suffered permanent brain damage. The local police sent no officers to the bus terminal. Birmingham's city commissioner of public safety, T. Eugene "Bull" Connor, blamed the Freedom Riders for the violence. He declared, "I have said for the last 20 years that these out-of-town meddlers were going to cause bloodshed if they kept meddling in the South's business." SNCC leaders moved quickly to find replacement riders for those from CORE.

President John F. Kennedy supported the constitutional rights of the riders to continue their journey. However, he did not want the violence in the South to become an issue in an upcoming meeting with Soviet leader Nikita Khrushchev. Kennedy told his aides to contact civil rights leaders and urge them to end the rides. SNCC refused to comply with the president's request. SNCC leader Diane Nash explained why.

Violence. Demonstrators like these at a CORE rally often suffered harassment and violence. *What actions are these two men protesting?*

66 I strongly felt that the future of the movement was going to be cut short if the Freedom Ride had been stopped as a result of violence. The impression would have been given that whenever a movement starts, all you have to do is attack it with massive violence and the blacks will stop. 99

SNCC sent the Freedom Riders to Birmingham. There, they were quickly arrested and transported to the state line. The students made their way back to Birmingham. Anxious to prevent further conflict, U.S. Attorney General Robert Kennedy reached an agreement with Alabama's governor, John Patterson. They agreed that the riders would receive protection. The Freedom Riders soon departed from Birmingham. However,

Freedom Riders regroup outside their bus after it was firebombed in Alabama.

when the bus arrived in Montgomery, Alabama, it was met by an angry mob. Freedom Rider John Lewis recalled, "I was beaten—I think I was hit with a sort of crate thing that holds soda bottles—and left lying unconscious there, in the streets of Montgomery."

President Kennedy finally sent federal marshals to protect the riders. In Jackson, Mississippi, however, state officials arrested the protesters. Hundreds of other activists carried on the protest. In response, Robert Kennedy pressured the Interstate Commerce Commission into strengthening its desegregation regulations. By early 1963 he was able to claim that "in the past year, segregation in interstate commerce has ceased to exist."

✔ **READING CHECK:** How did civil rights demonstrators use nonviolence to achieve their goals? Was it effective?

Integrating universities.
The NAACP obtained a court order requiring the University of Mississippi to admit black student James Meredith. *What type of reaction do you think Meredith encountered?*

Continued Struggles

The Freedom Riders' courage and commitment to nonviolence helped advance their effort to end racial discrimination. However, segregation remained in many areas of southern life, including the South's schools and public facilities.

University of Mississippi.
Civil rights activists who worked to open colleges and universities to African American students met with strong opposition. In 1962 the National Association for the Advancement of Colored People (NAACP) obtained a court order. It required the University of Mississippi to admit James Meredith, an African American applicant. Mississippi governor Ross Barnett was defiant. He declared, "No school will be integrated in Mississippi while I am your Governor." Accompanied by two federal officials, Meredith arrived at the campus in September 1962. Barnett personally prevented Meredith from registering.

When word got out on the evening of September 30 that Meredith was on the campus, a riot broke out. President Kennedy ordered army troops to restore order. The outbreak quickly died out, but two people had been killed and 375 injured. Meredith registered the next day and attended classes the rest of the year with the protection of armed guards. He graduated from the university in 1963.

Civil rights activists viewed Meredith's enrollment as a great success. Myrlie Evers recalled, "It was a major breakthrough. It said, indeed, that there is hope, and that we are moving forward and that perhaps the sacrifices that had been made had been worth it." Yet, events elsewhere revealed that the movement for civil rights still faced strong opposition. In 1963 Myrlie Evers's husband, NAACP field secretary Medgar Evers, was killed by a white assassin.

Albany and Birmingham.
Nonviolent protests were not always successful. In Albany, Georgia, for example, civil rights organizations held a number of nonviolent protests in 1961. Police Chief Laurie Pritchett was prepared for the demonstrations. He arranged to fill all the jails in the surrounding areas with protesters. Pritchett called his method of law enforcement meeting "nonviolence with nonviolence." He quietly arrested all the protesters.

Hoping to revive the Albany protests, Martin Luther King Jr. allowed himself to be arrested and jailed. Pritchett simply released him. Without a violent incident to draw the attention of the news media, the Albany movement stalled out.

This experience taught SCLC leaders that progress would come only when racists responded to peaceful demonstrations with violence. As the SCLC's Bayard Rustin later noted, "Protest becomes an effective tactic to the degree that it elicits [brings forth] brutality and oppression from the power structure."

After the events in Albany, the SCLC focused its attention on Birmingham. Protesting in Birmingham meant danger and possibly even death. Ralph David Abernathy later explained the civil rights activists' strategy.

To break up the nonviolent civil rights rally in Birmingham, city firefighters turned their water hoses on protesters.

66 As for [police chief] Bull Connor and the City of Birmingham, it was true that they constituted the hardest and most mean-spirited establishment in the South. Yet if we beat them on their own home grounds, we might be able to prove to the entire region that it was useless to resist desegregation, that its time had finally come. To win in Birmingham might well be to win in the rest of the nation. So in the long run the gamble [of confronting violence in Birmingham] might actually save time and lives in our struggle for equality. 99

In April 1963 the SCLC began a series of boycotts, marches, and sit-ins to protest Birmingham's segregation laws. The protests initially drew hundreds of participants. Many were jailed after violating a judge's order that banned further demonstrations. However, as weeks passed, the number of demonstrators willing to go to jail declined. By the end of April the Birmingham protests seemed likely to end in failure.

To save the Birmingham protest, James Bevel and other SCLC leaders suggested using schoolchildren in the demonstrations. Bevel later recalled, "A boy from high school, he can get the same effect in terms of being in jail, in terms of putting pressure on the city, as his father—and yet there is no economic threat on the family because the father is

★ HISTORICAL DOCUMENTS ★

MARTIN LUTHER KING JR.
Letter from Birmingham Jail

While confined in a Birmingham jail in 1963, Martin Luther King Jr. wrote to a group of clergymen who had urged him to slow down his protests. The letter was widely published by newspapers. It offered an eloquent response to critics who questioned the need for protests against racism.

You may well ask: "Why direct action? Why sit-ins, marches, and so forth? Isn't negotiation a better path?" You are quite right in calling for negotiation. Indeed, this is the very purpose of direct action. Nonviolent direct action seeks to create such a crisis and foster such a tension that a community which has constantly refused to negotiate is forced to confront the issue. . . . I have earnestly opposed violent tension, but there is a type of constructive, nonviolent tension which is necessary for growth. . . .

We know through painful experience that freedom is never voluntarily given by the oppressor; it must be demanded by the oppressed. Frankly, I have yet to engage in a direct-action campaign that was "well timed" in the view of those who have not suffered unduly from the disease of segregation. For years now I have heard the word "Wait!" It rings in the ear of every Negro with piercing familiarity. This "Wait" has almost always meant "Never." We must come to see, with one of our distinguished jurists, that "justice too long delayed is justice denied."

MARCH ON WASHINGTON FOR JOBS & FREEDOM AUGUST 28, 1963

still on the job." King was initially reluctant to place young people in danger. In the end, however, he supported Bevel's plan.

On May 2 more than 1,000 youths marched in Birmingham's streets. Police arrested some 600 students that day. When the protests continued the following day, Bull Connor ordered the police to attack the marchers. The police used dogs, fire hoses, and nightsticks against protesters. Public support for the civil rights movement increased when scenes of these attacks appeared in newspapers and on television.

✔ **READING CHECK:** Why did civil rights leaders use nonviolent tactics, and how did the demonstrations in Albany, Georgia, and Birmingham, Alabama, differ?

INTERPRETING THE VISUAL RECORD

March on Washington. During the 1963 March on Washington, African American leaders met with President John F. Kennedy. *Based on this photograph, would you conclude that the march leaders were successful in bringing civil rights issues to the forefront of U.S. politics in 1963? Explain your answer.*

The Civil Rights Act of 1964

The events in Birmingham forced President Kennedy to take a stand on civil rights. Most of his aides feared such a move would split the Democratic Party and ruin Kennedy's chances for re-election in 1964. Nevertheless, the president moved forward. In the summer of 1963, Kennedy asked Congress "to enact legislation giving all Americans the right to be served in facilities which are open to the public."

The March on Washington. To build public support for the civil rights movement, African American leaders organized a huge march on Washington, D.C. More than 200,000 people gathered together at the Lincoln Memorial on August 28, 1963. Many musicians and speakers from diverse backgrounds celebrated the struggle for civil rights. The director of the march, 74-year-old A. Philip Randolph, opened the ceremonies, testifying to the long struggle for civil rights. Other speakers included SNCC's John Lewis and Rabbi Joachim Prinz of the American Jewish Congress.

BIOGRAPHY

Martin Luther King Jr.

Martin Luther King Jr. gave the final speech. It would mark one of the highlights of his civil rights career. Born on January 15, 1929, in Atlanta, King was the son of a Baptist minister. He received a degree from Morehouse College in 1948. King then attended the integrated Crozer Theological Seminary in Chester, Pennsylvania. There, he excelled in his studies of religion and philosophy. As a seminary student King became familiar with the Social Gospel movement, which encouraged Christians to become involved in social reform. He was also exposed to the thinking of Mohandas K. Gandhi, the nonviolent leader of India's independence movement.

King's love of learning led him to pursue a doctorate at Boston University. There, he met and married Coretta Scott. In 1954 King accepted a position at Dexter Avenue Baptist Church in Montgomery. He soon became involved in the civil rights movement and helped to organize the Montgomery Bus Boycott.

King often faced violence and abuse. In January 1956 his home was bombed, and his wife and young child narrowly escaped injury. His personal courage and commitment to nonviolence soon made him the leading civil rights activist in the eyes of most white Americans.

HOLT RESEARCHER *Read More About It*

Free Find:
Martin Luther King Jr.
After reading the biography on Martin Luther King Jr. on the **Holt Researcher** CD–ROM, write a short essay that describes the significance of his "I Have a Dream" speech.

King's "I Have a Dream" speech at the March on Washington rally in 1963 has become one of the most famous addresses in American history. King spoke of his vision of what the United States could and should be.

President Lyndon Johnson signed the Civil Rights Act into law in 1964 in the presence of civil rights leaders including Martin Luther King Jr.

> 66 I have a dream that one day this nation will rise up and live out the true meaning of its creed: 'We hold these truths to be self-evident; that all men are created equal. . . . When we let freedom ring, when we let it ring from every village and every hamlet [small town], from every state and every city, we will be able to speed up that day when all of God's children, black men and white men, Jews and Gentiles, Protestants and Catholics, will be able to join hands and sing in the words of the old Negro spiritual, 'Free at last! Free at last! Thank God Almighty, we are free at last!' 99

The act passes. The success of the March on Washington raised the hopes of civil rights workers everywhere. However, their joy was short-lived. In September a bomb exploded in a Birmingham church and killed four young African American girls. Then, in November 1963, President Kennedy was assassinated. The future of civil rights legislation, which had stalled in Congress, was unclear.

The new president, Lyndon Johnson, strongly supported passage of a civil rights bill. Several southern members of Congress worked hard to kill the legislation. The House of Representatives approved the bill in February 1964. The Senate debated the measure for 75 days before passing it by a vote of 73 to 27. Johnson signed the bill into law on July 2, 1964, more than a year after Kennedy's speech calling for federal legislation. The **Civil Rights Act of 1964** banned discrimination in employment and in public accommodations. The act gave the Justice Department the power to bring lawsuits to enforce school desegregation.

✔ **READING CHECK:** Why did supporters push for a civil rights bill, and what factors influenced the bill's passage?

SECTION 1 REVIEW

Define and explain the significance of the following terms:
Southern Christian Leadership Conference
nonviolent resistance
sit-ins
Student Nonviolent Coordinating Committee
Congress of Racial Equality
Freedom Riders
Civil Rights Act of 1964

Identify and explain the significance of the following individuals:
Martin Luther King Jr.
T. Eugene Connor
Diane Nash
James Meredith
Medgar Evers
Laurie Pritchett

1. **Using Graphic Organizers** Copy the chart below. Use it to explain different civil rights initiatives in the early 1960s.

Protest	Goal	Outcome
Student Sit-Ins		
Freedom Rides		
Birmingham Protest		
March on Washington		

2. **Analyzing** Why did Martin Luther King Jr. and other leaders support nonviolence as a strategy for civil rights demonstrations?

3. **Recognizing Point of View** Why was President Kennedy reluctant to use federal authority to resolve conflicts over civil rights in the South?

4. **Comparing and Contrasting** In what ways were Bull Connor and Laurie Pritchett similar? How did they differ in their responses to demonstrators?

Critical Thinking

5. What factors do you think led President Kennedy to introduce civil rights legislation in 1963?
Consider:
• the constitutional issues involved
• King's strategy in Birmingham
• the media's role in Birmingham

Voting Rights

COMING OF AGE
IN MISSISSIPPI
AN AUTOBIOGRAPHY
ANNE MOODY

EYEWITNESSES TO History

66 *I just didn't see how the Negroes in Madison County could be so badly off.* **99**
—Anne Moody

Anne Moody was a young African American woman who lived in Mississippi during the 1950s. She recalled her reaction to the economic and political status of African American farmers in Madison County, Mississippi. African Americans outnumbered the county's white residents three to one. However, only about 200 of the some 29,000 African Americans in the county were registered to vote. Moody hoped to change that by working in a voter registration drive sponsored by CORE. She quickly learned why life in Madison County was so hard for African Americans. She remembered that after a month, "we had only been able to send a handful of Negroes to the courthouse to attempt to register and those few who went began to get fired from their jobs." Moody also explained that the CORE workers "were constantly being threatened." Moody's experiences revealed the difficulties that civil rights workers faced as they organized voter registration drives in the South.

The cover of Anne Moody's autobiography

Registering Voters

While civil rights demonstrators used nonviolent protests to bring an end to racial segregation, other activists focused their attention on voter registration. The Kennedy administration had been troubled by the Freedom Rides and other protests that resulted in violence. However, it supported the voter registration efforts. As Robert Kennedy later recalled, "I felt nobody could really oppose voting. It was not like school desegregation with people saying, 'We don't want our little blond daughter going to school with a Negro.'" However, Kennedy underestimated the extent of opposition to African American suffrage in the South.

Mississippi. Civil rights activists focused their efforts on promoting voter registration in Mississippi, where African Americans were often denied their voting rights. African Americans made up some 40 percent of the state's population, but just 5 percent of eligible black adults were registered to vote. Many counties did not have a single registered African American voter. Literacy tests, which included interpreting portions of the state constitution, were one means used to prevent African Americans from registering.

Mississippi had a history of racial violence—at least 33 lynchings occurred between 1939 and 1950. Still, civil rights organizers believed that it was the best place to carry out their plans. As SNCC organizer John Lewis later argued, "If we can crack Mississippi, we will likely be able to crack the system in the rest of the country."

SNCC's Robert Moses selected McComb, Mississippi, a town of some 12,000 citizens. With just 250 registered African Americans, it would be the site of his first effort

Volunteers help black Mississippians register to vote.

to register black voters. He arrived in July 1961. By mid-August he had helped six African Americans to register to vote. However, this modest success drew the attention of white officials who were determined to stop him. In less than a month's time, Moses was jailed, released, beaten by the sheriff's cousin, and chased by an angry mob.

The violence increased in September. Herbert Lee, a farmer who had driven Moses around the area, was murdered by a member of the Mississippi state legislature. Despite evidence to the contrary, a jury ruled that the killing had been committed in self-defense. Less than two weeks after Lee's death, local high school students held a protest march. Demonstrator Hollis Watkins later recalled the risks associated with civil rights activities.

Voting. Many activists who tried to register African Americans to vote faced harassment. *How does the message on this activist's sign contrast with the way he is being treated?*

66 One thing I risked—and did face—was being ostracized [banished] by my family. . . . My relatives would see me walking down the street and then they would pass over on to the other side rather than meet me on the street. Because they was afraid of what white people might do to them because they were my relatives. . . . In addition to that, I put on the line the whole thing of being able to ever get a job in Mississippi. . . . Or whether that mark would go through onto my children and their children—or onto my mother and father. 99

Moses and other SNCC workers accompanied the protesters. Police officers arrested the students. Meanwhile, a mob attacked the SNCC workers, who were then also arrested. The voter registration drive in McComb came to an end with fewer than 24 new voters on the rolls.

Renewed efforts. The difficulties facing civil rights workers in McComb did not stop efforts to register African American voters, however. Several civil rights organizations, including SNCC and SCLC, established the **Council of Federated Organizations** (COFO) to coordinate voter registration drives. The Voter Education Project provided money from private foundations to fund registration projects.

The abuse from state and local officials and mob violence continued as activists helped African Americans in Mississippi and other southern states to register to vote. SNCC's Ivanhoe Donaldson recalled, "Fear was always a major reality that you had to live with. . . . Almost every organizer in the Deep South was constantly faced with harassment. They'd been beaten, they'd been shot at." The SNCC office in Greenwood, Mississippi, was burned to the ground. Despite the bloodshed, few officials from the Kennedy administration offered assistance.

The ongoing violence frightened many African Americans. Many refused to attempt to register. A year-long registration drive in Leflore County netted just 50 new voters. Nonetheless, many African Americans in Mississippi still hoped to become voters one day. In 1963 COFO conducted two mock elections in which anyone could vote, even if they were not registered. Some 27,000 African Americans voted in the first mock election, and some 80,000—four times the number of registered black voters in the state—voted in the second election. The "freedom

Voter registration was an important weapon in the fight for civil rights.

teen Life

Peter Orris
was a white
teenager in his freshman year at Harvard
University when he decided to volunteer for the
Freedom Summer project. He later recalled, "At
eighteen years old, to be able to be involved in
this kind of a struggle was very important to me."

Orris attended volunteer training sessions in
Ohio, where "we playacted situations where
angry groups of people, mobs, would be attacking us and how we would handle ourselves in
that situation." Orris was assigned to a voter registration drive in Mileston, Mississippi. He recalled,
"We were much younger than many of the people we were speaking to, and it was necessary to
establish a relationship or an understanding of
the respect that we paid to them for their age
and their situation." Despite such efforts, African
Americans were often reluctant to talk to volunteers. "We knew we were not getting [our mes-
sage] across, we knew they were just waiting for
us to go away because we were a danger to
them, and in many ways we were." Orris remembered, "We had much less to risk than they did.
This was their lives, their land, their family, and
they were going to be here when we were gone."

Freedom Summer volunteers

elections" introduced many African Americans to voting procedures and revealed the deep interest that many unregistered voters had in exercising their rights.

✔ **READING CHECK:** Why did the voter registration efforts in
Mississippi meet with little success?

A New Approach

In November 1963, SNCC workers learned that the Voter Education Project was unable to fund voter registration in Mississippi. At a meeting later that month, SNCC leaders debated a
new strategy. Robert Moses suggested bringing a large number
of white volunteers into the voter registration efforts. Moses
noted, "It changes the whole complexion of what you're doing,
so it isn't any longer Negro fighting white. It's a question of
rational people fighting against irrational people." Several
SNCC members opposed the new strategy. MacArthur Cotton
argued, "We've got too much to lose if . . . [white volunteers]
come down here and create a disturbance in two or three
months, and they're gone."

Freedom Summer. Despite such objections, SNCC decided
to implement Moses's plan, known as **Freedom Summer**, in
1964. That spring, SNCC recruited volunteers on university
campuses in the northern states. The volunteers attended training classes in Ohio before heading to Mississippi. Lawyers and
health-care professionals also took part in the project, offering
legal and medical assistance to the civil rights workers.

Andrew Goodman, a college student from New York, arrived
in Mississippi on June 20. The following day Goodman and two
CORE workers, James Chaney and Michael Schwerner, disappeared. Their bodies were discovered six weeks later, buried in an
earthen dam. The murders of Goodman and Schwerner, both of
whom were white, shocked Americans in a way that the murders
of African Americans had not. President Johnson ordered the
Federal Bureau of Investigation (FBI) to investigate the killings.
Stunned volunteers carried on. Fearing that they would also
become victims of violence, however, many African Americans
refused to register. By the end of the summer, just 1,600 African
Americans had been added to the voting rolls.

Despite the limited gains, Freedom Summer changed the lives of many African
Americans in Mississippi. Unita Blackwell recalled her experiences with Freedom
Summer.

  66 For black people in Mississippi, Freedom Summer was the beginning of a
whole new era. People began to feel that they wasn't just helpless anymore,
that they had come together. . . . Students came and we wasn't a closed
society anymore. They came to talk about that we had a right to register to

vote, we had a right to stand up for our rights. . . . I mean, hadn't anybody said that to us, in that open way, like what happened in 1964. 99

✔ **READING CHECK:** Why did the Freedom Summer project meet with limited success?

Political organization. In addition to conducting voter registration drives, COFO leaders worked to place African Americans on Mississippi's delegation to the Democratic National Convention. The convention was to be held in Atlantic City, New Jersey, in August 1964. When a state party convention rejected all African American candidates, COFO helped create the **Mississippi Freedom Democratic Party** (MFDP). The MFDP formed its own delegation. Fannie Lou Hamer, an African American who had lost her job and her house when she registered to vote in 1962, was among the MFDP delegates.

The MFDP delegation traveled to Atlantic City. There, they requested that the national convention recognize the MFDP rather than the regular state delegation. The MFDP delegates believed that they should be recognized because so many black Mississippians had been prevented from voting. President Johnson, who wanted the convention to proceed smoothly, worked behind the scenes to grant the MFDP recognition without making it the official delegation. In the end, the MFDP delegates were offered two token seats. The MFDP rejected this compromise as an insult. MFDP delegate Victoria Gray later explained the MFDP decision.

66 Those who are unable to understand why we were unable to accept that compromise did not realize that we would have been betraying the many people back there in Mississippi whom we represented. They had not only laid their lives on the line, but many had given their lives in order for this particular event to happen. 99

Johnson's actions led many activists to conclude that he and the Democratic Party could no longer be trusted to advance their interests.

✔ **READING CHECK:** How did the Mississippi Freedom Democratic Party affect relations between civil rights activists and the federal government?

Facing the disappointment of not being recognized by the Democratic National Convention, Mississippi Freedom Democratic Party members join hands in prayer.

INTERPRETING THE VISUAL RECORD
Selma. This issue of *Life* magazine reached newsstands the week after the civil rights march outside Selma turned violent. *Based on this cover, what group do you believe the article favored, the civil rights marchers or the Selma police? Explain your answer.*

Selma and the Voting Rights Act

In early 1965, civil rights workers launched a registration drive in Selma, Alabama. Of Selma's 15,000 eligible African Americans, just 383 were registered voters. The activists invited Martin Luther King Jr., who had won the Nobel Peace Prize the previous year, to lead them. The attempts of African Americans to register at election commission offices in the Selma area met with beatings and arrests. Civil rights leaders responded by calling for a protest march from Selma to Montgomery. Governor George Wallace immediately banned the protest.

Despite the governor's opposition, some 600 people began the 50-mile trek on Sunday, March 7. Just outside Selma, police attacked the marchers. An eight-year-old girl taking part in the march recalled that "some of them had clubs, others had

African American Voter Registration, 1960–1992

Learning from Maps After the passage of the 1965 Voting Rights Act, the number of registered African American voters in the South increased dramatically. In Mississippi voter registration increased almost 700 percent.

? PLACE Which states experienced the greatest increase in the registration of African American voters?

Percent increase in registration:

- Greater than 225% increase
- 151–225% increase
- 51–150% increase
- 20–50% increase

ropes, or whips, which they swung around them like they were driving cattle."

Outraged by the attack, thousands of Americans poured into Montgomery to show support for the marchers. President Johnson was also shocked by Selma's "Bloody Sunday." On March 15, before a joint session of Congress, he asked for speedy passage of a voting rights bill. Johnson declared that all Americans ought to take up the struggle for civil rights: "All of us . . . must overcome the crippling legacy [history] of bigotry [racism] and injustice. And we *shall* . . . overcome."

About one week later, under the protection of federal marshals and the National Guard, the marchers successfully began their journey again. Five months later, Congress passed the **Voting Rights Act** of 1965, which put the entire registration process under federal control. Within days of the act's passage, federal examiners descended upon the South to sign up new African American voters. By 1968 the number of eligible African Americans who were registered to vote jumped to 57 percent in Alabama. Mississippi experienced the greatest percentage increase, from less than 6 percent in 1964 to some 59 percent in 1968.

✔ **READING CHECK:** How did the Selma protest lead to the passage of the Voting Rights Act?

SECTION ② REVIEW

Define and explain the significance of the following terms:
Council of Federated Organizations
Freedom Summer
Mississippi Freedom Democratic Party
Voting Rights Act

Identify and explain the significance of the following individuals:
Robert Moses
Andrew Goodman
James Chaney
Michael Schwerner
Fannie Lou Hamer

1. Using Graphic Organizers Copy the following chart. Use it to explain the impact of efforts including Freedom Summer, the Mississippi Freedom Democratic Party (MFDP), and the Selma march.

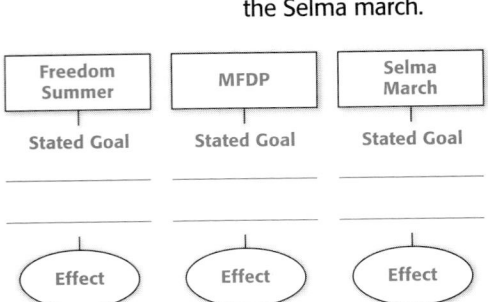

Freedom Summer	MFDP	Selma March
Stated Goal	Stated Goal	Stated Goal
Effect	Effect	Effect

2. Analyzing What obstacles did civil rights workers encounter in their attempts to register voters?

3. Evaluating How helpful was the federal government to the voter registration drives in Mississippi?

4. Recognizing Point of View Why did officials in the Democratic Party regard the MFDP as a potential source of conflict?

Critical Thinking

5. How did voting rights initiatives change the lives of black Mississippians and of civil rights workers?
Consider:
- the violence that people encountered
- the total number of African American voters registered
- the interaction between black Mississippians and civil rights workers

SECTION 3
Challenges for the Movement

OBJECTIVES

Read to understand:

1. how Malcolm X's message differed from that of the major civil rights organizations during the early 1960s
2. why nonviolent protest and the goal of racial integration lost support
3. how northern racial discrimination and urban riots changed the civil rights movement

KEY TERMS

Nation of Islam
Black Power
Black Panther Party
Kerner Commission
Poor People's Campaign

KEY PEOPLE

James Farmer
Elijah Muhammad
Malcolm X
Stokely Carmichael
Bobby Seale
Huey Newton

EYEWITNESSES TO History

❝ We wanted control of the communities where we were most numerous, and the institutions therein. At the same time, we felt that we were due, because of taxpaying, free access to and equal treatment in public facilities. ❞
—Huey Newton

A Black Panther pin

Huey Newton recalled his decision to form a new, more confrontational civil rights organization with his friend Bobby Seale. The appearance of this new movement and the prominence of Black Muslim leader Malcolm X signaled a new phase in the struggle for civil rights in the mid-1960s. Many activists were dissatisfied with the direction the civil rights movement had taken and frustrated with the slow pace of change. In reaction, many African American leaders rejected nonviolence as a strategy. Seale and Newton chose the black panther to symbolize their new group. Seale explained, "if you drive a panther into a corner, if he can't go left and he can't go right, then he will tend to come out of that corner to wipe out or stop its aggressor."

New Directions

As the civil rights movement continued, some African Americans questioned the effectiveness of nonviolence and the goals of the movement. In 1962 CORE director James Farmer explained, "We no longer are a tight fellowship of a few dedicated advocates [supporters] of a brilliant new method of social change. We are now a large family spawned [created] by the union of the method-oriented pioneers and the righteously indignant [angry] ends-oriented militants." The "militants" of whom Farmer spoke were people who were attracted to the views of African American organizations such as the Nation of Islam.

Black Muslims. Little is known about Wallace D. Fard, the founder of the **Nation of Islam.** Fard started the group, also known as the Black Muslims, in Detroit, Michigan, in 1930. The organization was based on the Islamic religion founded by the prophet Muhammad. However, the Black Muslims emphasized the supremacy of black people over all other races. By the early 1930s, when Elijah Muhammad became its leader, the Nation of Islam claimed some 8,000 members. Muhammad preached a message of black nationalism. He declared that African Americans should create their own republic within the United States. Many Black Muslims rejected their last names as relics of slavery and used "X" to symbolize lost African names.

Muhammad stressed self-discipline as the way to achieve the dream of a separate African American nation. Black Muslims were not allowed to drink alcohol or smoke

Elijah Muhammad motivated his Black Muslim supporters in this 1961 speech in Washington, D.C. Some Black Muslims wore pins such as this one.

THE CIVIL RIGHTS MOVEMENT **933**

and were expected to maintain a strict diet. Muhammad also encouraged self-reliance. During the Great Depression, Black Muslims were not permitted to accept any assistance from the federal government. Black Muslims were also discouraged by their leaders from serving in the U.S. military. As a result, Muhammad and many of his followers were sentenced to prison for draft evasion during World War II.

While in prison, Muhammad realized that African American prisoners were largely ignored by most African American organizations. Muhammad actively recruited convicts, calling on them to change their lives through the strict discipline required by the Nation of Islam. He also brought his message to many lower-income African Americans. These recruitment efforts proved effective. By the early 1960s there were an estimated 100,000 Black Muslims spread throughout the United States.

BIOGRAPHY

Malcolm X

Malcolm X. The growth of the Nation of Islam during the 1950s was in part the work of Malcolm X, a charismatic young minister. Malcolm X was born Malcolm Little in 1925. His father was a Baptist minister and organizer for Marcus Garvey. Malcolm's father was killed in what many people considered a racially motivated murder.

Despite his father's death, Malcolm Little tried to ignore the racism he encountered in his school and community. This changed when Little, who was an excellent student, told his white English teacher that he wanted to become an attorney. The teacher replied that this was an unrealistic goal for an African American. Malcolm X later recalled, "The more I thought afterwards about what he said, the more uneasy it made me. . . . It was then that I began to change—inside." He remembered that he "drew away from white people" after the conversation with his teacher.

Little dropped out of school and drifted into a life of crime. He was eventually sentenced to 10 years in prison. While in prison he embraced the teachings of Elijah Muhammad. Freed in 1952, he changed his name to Malcolm X and soon became a leading minister for the Nation of Islam. A powerful speaker, Malcolm X championed African American separatism and called for freedom to be brought about "by any means necessary." The time for nonviolence had passed, he argued.

66 You're getting a new generation that has been growing right now, and they're beginning to think with their own minds and see that you can't negotiate up on freedom nowadays. If something is yours by right, then fight for it or shut up. If you can't fight for it, then forget it. 99

HOLT RESEARCHER

Read More About It

Free Find: Malcolm X
After reading the biography on Malcolm X on the **Holt Researcher** CD–ROM, explain how his experiences as a youth influenced his civil rights efforts.

Malcolm X criticized the goals and the strategies of civil rights organizations that worked for racial integration. He argued that "it is not integration that Negroes in America want, it is human dignity." Criticizing Martin Luther King, Malcolm X claimed, "Any Negro who teaches other Negroes to turn the other cheek is disarming that Negro . . . [of] his natural right to defend himself."

Many white Americans found Malcolm X's tone frightening. Malcolm X, however, began undergoing a transformation in his beliefs during the mid-1960s. In 1964 he made a pilgrimage to the Islamic holy city of Mecca. In Mecca he was exposed to more traditional Islamic beliefs. He also gained a greater acceptance of the universal humanity of people of all races. That same year he broke with the Black Muslims. Turning away from separatism, Malcolm X converted to orthodox Islam and began calling for unity among all people. His new outlook was reflected in a 1964 speech. He declared, "We will work with anyone, with any group, no matter what their color is, as long as they are genuinely interested in taking the type of steps necessary to bring an end to the injustices that black people in this country are afflicted by." However, Malcolm X had little time to act on his new ideas. In February 1965 he was gunned down by three Black Muslim assassins.

✔ **READING CHECK:** How did Malcolm X's message differ from that of major civil rights organizations during the early 1960s?

Martin Luther King Jr. and Malcolm X met only once, at the U.S. Capitol during a Senate filibuster of a civil rights bill in March 1964.

The Movement Fractures

Most white Americans perceived the civil rights movement as a unified effort led by Martin Luther King Jr. In fact, the movement was made up of diverse groups united by the common goal of ending racial segregation. By the mid-1960s many conflicts had surfaced among these organizations.

Black Power. Civil rights activists who had endured violence and jailings in their efforts to register voters in Mississippi began to question the strategy of nonviolent protest. CORE's David Dennis summed up the growing frustration with nonviolence in June 1964. Dennis declared, "I'm sick and tired of going to funerals of black men who have been murdered by white men. . . . I've got vengeance in my heart tonight."

Some African American activists also began to question the goal of integration, in part because of their experiences in Mississippi. The presence of white volunteers for the Freedom Summer project had created tensions within SNCC. African American workers believed that white students were taking over the project. "Suddenly, in an instant, in our town are five or six brightly scrubbed white kids from the North," SNCC's Bob Zellner recalled. "Here's Jesse (Negro) laboriously doing the stencil. Sally (white) . . . comes along and says, 'Here, I type 120 words a minute, let me do it.'" These frustrations led many African American activists, particularly those involved with SNCC and CORE, to express a growing interest in black nationalism.

Many African Americans were also angry that the death of white volunteers such as Andrew Goodman and Michael Schwerner generated widespread public

INTERPRETING THE VISUAL RECORD

Black nationalism. Frustrated by their experiences in the civil rights movement, some African Americans began to embrace ideas of black nationalism and oppose the goals of integration. *How does this button symbolize the new direction and goals of some civil rights activists?*

The deaths of civil rights activists such as Jimmie Lee Jackson, whose 1965 funeral is shown here, led to growing frustration among African American leaders who began to embrace the Black Power movement.

concern. However, African American victims of violence did not receive similar attention. SNCC's Stokely Carmichael noted, "What you want is the nation to be upset when anybody is killed. . . . It's almost like, for this to be recognized, a white person must be killed. Well, what does that say?"

The split in the civil rights movement became public in 1966. That year James Meredith, the first African American to graduate from the University of Mississippi, decided to make a "journey against fear" by marching across Mississippi. After he was shot and wounded on the second day of the march, several civil rights organizations vowed to continue his journey. Determined to turn the march into an expression of black nationalism, Stokely Carmichael convinced the NAACP and the Urban League, two more conservative organizations, to abandon the event.

At a march rally on June 16, Carmichael told the crowd, "This is the 27th time I've been arrested. I ain't gonna be arrested no more." In the days that followed, Carmichael and others asked the crowd, "What do you want?" and received the chanted reply, "Black power!"

King asked Carmichael to stop using the slogan, but Carmichael admitted, "I deliberately decided to raise this issue on the march in order to give it a national forum." The **Black Power** movement called for black separatism. It had many positive aspects, including an emphasis on racial pride and an interest in African culture and heritage. However, many moderate leaders such as King feared that the movement would create hostility toward civil rights among the nation's white population. King confided to one adviser, "If you go around claiming power, the whole society turns on you and crushes you. If you really have power you don't need a slogan."

INTERPRETING THE VISUAL RECORD

Black Panthers. Members of the Black Panther Party drew public attention by carrying guns and supporting the Black Power movement. *How do you think the message of the pin reflects the values of the Black Panther Party?*

The Black Panthers. Despite King's misgivings, many African Americans were attracted to Carmichael's Black Power message. Bobby Seale worked with Huey Newton at an antipoverty center in Oakland, California. He later recalled, "Huey and I began to try to figure out how could we organize youthful black folks into some kind of political, electoral *power* movement." The two created a political organization called the **Black Panther Party**. The party platform declared, "Black people will not be free until we are free to determine our own destiny." It called for "land, bread, housing, education, clothing, justice, and peace" for African Americans.

The platform also called for the creation of "black self-defense groups that are dedicated to defending our black community from racist police oppression." Black Panther members often made national headlines. This was particularly true when they appeared in public carrying firearms, which at the time was legal to do in California. A number of highly publicized gun battles with police occurred. Huey Newton was sentenced to prison for murder. Elaine Brown, who joined the organization in 1967, offered one reason why African Americans joined the Black Panthers:

> The party reached out mostly to men, to young, black urban men who were on the streets, who knew that there were no options somewhere in their lives. . . . We offered them the opportunity to make their lives meaningful. . . . And a lot of brothers did make their commitment with that conscious understanding that coming away from the gang was something that they were ultimately building for themselves and for the community. "

✔ **READING CHECK:** Why did nonviolent protest and the goal of racial integration lose support?

Tragic Events

The Black Power movement was not the only challenge that Martin Luther King Jr. and other civil rights leaders faced during the mid-1960s. Efforts to extend the civil rights struggle beyond desegregation and into areas such as housing and economic justice met a mixed reaction from white Americans. Many white Americans opposed the movement's expanded focus.

Chicago. By 1966 the SCLC was virtually the only major civil rights organization still primarily focused on nonviolent protest. That year King decided to battle racial discrimination in Chicago. In January he and his family moved into a slum apartment. He hoped to draw attention to the housing problems that African Americans faced in the urban North. Throughout that spring, amid periodic journeys to the South, King provided leadership and support for the movement in Chicago.

At a rally on July 10, 1966, King announced his continued determination to end housing discrimination in Chicago. Less than a month later, he was struck in the head by a rock while leading a peaceful march through a Chicago neighborhood. Some 4,000 white people threatened the marchers. The marchers were protected by local police. Next, King announced that he would lead a march in Cicero, Illinois, a town with a history of violence against African Americans. Chicago city leaders pledged to meet King's demands.

King claimed victory in Chicago, but the experience showed that significant obstacles to full equality remained. The fight against racial discrimination in the North did not draw support from white Americans in the way that demonstrations against segregation in the South had a few years earlier.

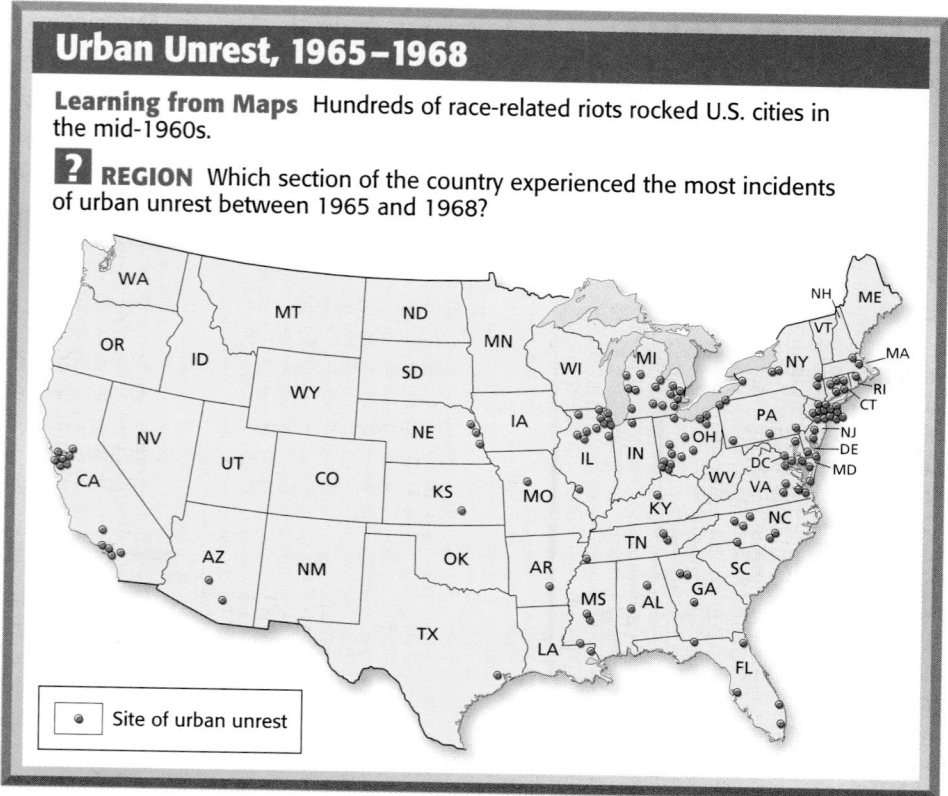

Urban Unrest, 1965–1968

Learning from Maps Hundreds of race-related riots rocked U.S. cities in the mid-1960s.

❓ **REGION** Which section of the country experienced the most incidents of urban unrest between 1965 and 1968?

• Site of urban unrest

Most Americans joined Coretta Scott King in mourning after the assassination of Martin Luther King Jr.

Urban violence. The white backlash against the civil rights movement and the Johnson administration's reluctance to press for further gains were responses to key social issues of the decade. These issues included the Black Power movement and a series of urban uprisings that erupted in the middle of the decade. Despite the successes of the civil rights movement, discrimination still affected the lives of most African Americans. In August 1965 frustration turned to violence. A routine arrest by Los Angeles police in the African American neighborhood of Watts triggered a riot that raged for six days. When the National Guard finally restored order, 34 people had been killed, hundreds injured, and almost 4,000 had been arrested.

Over the next two years, more than 100 riots broke out in cities across the country. The worst came in Detroit, where 43 people died. A federal report by the **Kerner Commission** charged that white racism was largely responsible for the tensions that led to the riots. "Our nation," the report warned, "is moving toward two societies, one black, one white—separate and unequal."

Seeking to address the frustration of the late 1960s, King began to embrace some of the Black Power movement's ideas, such as the need for African Americans to gain economic power. He also became increasingly upset that funding was being diverted to the war in Vietnam rather than being spent on social programs. In March 1968 King called for a **Poor People's Campaign** that would include a march on Washington, D.C., to protest what he saw as a misuse of government spending.

Before the march, King went to Memphis, Tennessee, to show his support for a sanitation workers' strike. On the evening of April 4, 1968, the man who was the symbol of nonviolence met a violent end when he was shot by a sniper. Within hours of King's death, African American neighborhoods across the country exploded in outrage. A week of rioting left 46 dead and thousands injured.

✔ **READING CHECK:** How did northern racial discrimination and urban riots change the civil rights movement?

SECTION **3** **REVIEW**

Define and explain the significance of the following terms:
Nation of Islam
Black Power
Black Panther Party
Kerner Commission
Poor People's Campaign

Identify and explain the significance of the following individuals:
James Farmer
Elijah Muhammad
Malcolm X
Stokely Carmichael
Bobby Seale
Huey Newton

1. **Using Graphic Organizers** Copy the following graphic organizer. Use it to explain the factors that led activists to move from nonviolence to Black Power.

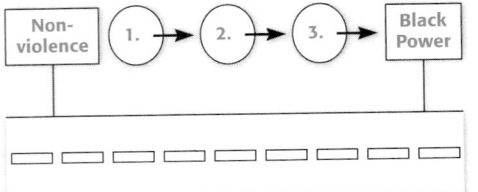

2. **Identifying Values** How did Malcolm X's attitudes differ from other civil rights leaders?
3. **Assessing Consequences** How did northern discrimination and urban violence affect the civil rights movement?
4. **Evaluating** Did nonviolence remain an effective means of bringing about change? Explain.

Critical Thinking

5. What challenges did Martin Luther King Jr. face in the final years of his life?
   Consider:
   • the conflicts within the civil rights movement
   • northern reactions to civil rights demonstrations
   • economic issues for African Americans

The Movement Continues

Ralph Abernathy

OBJECTIVES

Read to understand:

1. what problems many leading African American organizations encountered in the early 1970s
2. how the Supreme Court limited the impact of busing and affirmative action programs
3. what gains African Americans made during the early 1970s

KEY TERMS

busing
affirmative action
University of California v. Bakke
quotas
National Black Political Convention

KEY PEOPLE

Ralph Abernathy
Allan Bakke
Carl Stokes

EYEWITNESSES TO History

66 *When I took over from Martin, I did so after the civil rights movement had peaked and the SCLC had already begun to decline in influence. . . . Through our efforts and those of others, legal segregation in most areas of public life had been eliminated. . . . When we tried to change our focus and attack economic injustice, we lost many of our former supporters. . . . After a decade of fighting for racial justice, many people, black and white, were weary of the struggle and were ready to give up, to lay down their swords and shields.* 99

—Ralph Abernathy

Ralph Abernathy assumed leadership of the SCLC after the assassination of Martin Luther King Jr. His recollections reveal the frustration that many African Americans felt as the struggle for civil rights moved into the 1970s.

A Crisis in Direction

The assassination of Martin Luther King Jr. marked a turning point in the struggle for civil rights. With King's death, the movement lost its most visible figure and the leading supporter of nonviolent protest. At the same time, Black Power groups also began to decline. During the 1970s civil rights leaders addressed new problems trying to improve the lives of African Americans.

SCLC. Determined to continue King's work, SCLC leaders went ahead with the Poor People's Campaign. Ralph Abernathy told marchers on their way to Capitol Hill, "We have business on the road to freedom. . . . We must prove to white America that you can kill the leader but you cannot kill the dream." Once they had reached Washington, D.C., protesters constructed Resurrection City. They created a settlement of tents and shacks on public land designed to draw attention to poverty. William Rutherford explained, "The technique, the tactic being used, was to gather the poorest of the poor in the nation's capitol in the heart of the wealthiest country in the world . . . [and] take the plea and the complaint of the poor to each of the government agencies."

Resurrection City was a disaster. Constant rain turned the shantytown into a sea of mud. SCLC leaders also had to deal with theft and violence. In June of 1968, police evicted demonstrators from the site and tore down Resurrection City.

The failure of the Poor People's Campaign left many civil rights activists in a state of despair. "It dawned on me that this was the end of an entire period in my life," Michael Harrington recalled. "One of the most marvelous political movements in America in the form which it took under Martin Luther King . . . had come to an end." During the 1970s financial contributions to SCLC shrank. The organization no longer played a leading role in civil rights issues.

This SCLC poster was created to encourage support for the Poor People's Campaign.

POOR PEOPLE'S CAMPAIGN 1968

SCLC

Pictured here leaving a Senate subcommittee hearing, FBI director J. Edgar Hoover organized counterintelligence programs to block the activities of black nationalist and civil rights groups.

Black nationalism. Like the SCLC, organizations that supported black nationalism faced growing problems during this time. These problems included scrutiny by the U.S. government. In 1967 FBI director J. Edgar Hoover launched a program designed to "expose, disrupt, misdirect, discredit, or otherwise neutralize the activities of black nationalist, hate-type organizations and groupings, their leadership, spokesmen, membership, and supporters." Numerous operations were begun against various civil rights organizations.

Many organizations also suffered from internal conflicts. Under Stokely Carmichael's leadership, SNCC began controversial protests against the Vietnam War. Financial contributions to SNCC declined dramatically.

In February 1968, SNCC and Black Panther leaders announced that the two groups planned to unite. However, many SNCC members were reluctant to join a group that openly supported violence. The union lasted only until July. The following month SNCC expelled Stokely Carmichael from the organization. The crises in direction and leadership proved to be too much. SNCC disbanded in the early 1970s. The Black Panthers also lost influence. Many of the group's leaders were imprisoned or dead.

Unlike SNCC and the Black Panthers, the Black Muslims survived the early 1970s, despite losing some support following Malcolm X's departure. Elijah Muhammad continued to lead the Nation of Islam. After Muhammad's death in 1975, his son Wallace took over as leader.

✔ **READING CHECK:** What problems did many leading African American organizations encounter in the early 1970s?

Backlash

Civil rights organizations faced growing opposition from white Americans. Some claimed that civil rights reform was depriving them of their own rights. One of the first targets of white anger was court-ordered busing to desegregate the nation's public schools.

Busing. The Supreme Court had banned racial segregation in public schools in the 1954 case *Brown* v. *Board of Education.* However, because residential neighborhoods in most U.S. cities remained segregated, many schools in both the South and the North were also segregated. Some school officials decided to use **busing**, or sending children to schools outside of their neighborhoods, to integrate schools.

In 1971 the Supreme Court approved a busing plan in Charlotte, North Carolina. The plan worked, and Charlotte's schools were quickly desegregated. Polls, however, revealed that white Americans opposed court-ordered busing by a 3-to-1 margin. Many African Americans also had doubts about such plans. Court-ordered busing met with strong opposition in a number of cities, most notably Boston. One angry white Bostonian warned: "You heard of the Hundred Years War? This will be the eternal war. It will be passed down from father to son."

INTERPRETING THE VISUAL RECORD

Busing. Many Americans opposed the integration of public schools by busing children. *How does this* Time *magazine cover from 1971 portray the differences in the neighborhoods to which students would be bused?*

By the fall of 1974, violent protests against busing had erupted in Boston. Yet despite the risks, many African American parents believed that busing was necessary to achieve equal education opportunities. One African American woman told her two children that busing would make school difficult.

66 I'm afraid this isn't going to be an easy year for either of you. You're going to be called a lot of ugly names. You're going to be spat at, maybe pushed around some. But it's not the first time this has happened and it won't be the last. It's something we have to go through—something you have to go through—if this city is ever going to be integrated. 99

The busing controversy quieted down after the Supreme Court limited the use of busing as a means to achieve racial integration. In 1974 the Court ruled in *Milliken* v. *Bradley* to end a plan that promoted desegregation in Detroit by merging inner-city school districts with the city's suburban districts. The ruling was a severe blow to activists hoping to continue the process of desegregation in neighborhood schools. Justice Thurgood Marshall dissented from the Court ruling. He declared, "Unless our children begin to learn together, there is little hope that our people will ever learn to live together."

Reaction to busing. In Boston, the court order to bus students outraged many white residents. *What clues can you gather from this image of an anti-busing rally in Boston in 1974 that support the argument that the busing issue was an emotional one for many Americans?*

Affirmative action. Civil rights gains during the 1970s resulted from both public and private efforts. In order to uphold federal antidiscrimination laws and to end unfair labor practices, the Civil Rights Division of the Justice Department brought suits against corporations and labor unions. Many schools and businesses instituted **affirmative action** programs to compensate for previous discrimination. These programs gave preference to ethnic minorities and women in admission and hiring.

Many elected politicians did not support affirmative action. The Supreme Court nevertheless upheld the constitutionality of such programs in the 1971 case *Griggs* v. *Duke Power Co.* The Court ruled that tests given by the power company to decide on promotions had the effect of limiting the advancement of its African American workers. In the future, companies would have to explain why such tests were necessary. The case encouraged companies to create affirmative action programs.

Many white critics of affirmative action argued that it led to "reverse discrimination." In 1978 the Supreme Court handed down an important ruling affecting affirmative action. In **University of California v. Bakke**, it ruled that a white man, Allan Bakke, had been unfairly denied admission to medical school on the basis of **quotas**. This system reserved a fixed number of openings for certain groups of people. Although not ruling out all forms of affirmative action, the Court did strike down the quota system in regard to university admissions. Again, Justice Thurgood Marshall dissented from the Court's majority ruling. Marshall explained, "The dream of America as the great melting pot has not been realized for the Negro; because of his skin color he never even made it into the pot."

✔ **READING CHECK:** How did the Supreme Court limit the impact of busing and affirmative action programs?

Multimedia resources are sources of information such as television documentaries and CD–ROMs that incorporate words, sounds, and images in a single package. They are among the newest and most interesting research tools available to students. Multimedia resources often include ideas and data on historical topics from a variety of primary and secondary sources. The audiovisual formats they use to present this information can be very interesting.

Multimedia resources must be studied and analyzed carefully. The materials that make up multimedia resources—recordings, photographs, motion pictures, and written documents, for example—are distinct types of historical sources that should always be examined for accuracy and bias. It is also important to evaluate the manner in which a multimedia resource selects, presents, and discusses these materials.

How to Use a Multimedia Resource

1. **Find an appropriate resource.** Use your school or local public library to find a multimedia resource on the topic you wish to research. Once you have located an appropriate resource, take note of its title, publication date, and the people or organization that produced it.
2. **Study the resource carefully.** Study the resource carefully, identifying any main ideas and the specific means it uses to convey information. If you are using a CD–ROM, make sure to explore a variety of the materials it offers.
3. **Evaluate the resource.** Once you have examined the resource thoroughly, identify any factual inaccuracies and assess the manner in which it explains any differing points of view. Then evaluate any general biases that the resource displays in its selection, presentation, and discussion of historical evidence.
4. **Put the information to use.** Compare the resource with other materials that you find while researching your topic. Then use the results of your analysis to form generalizations and draw conclusions.

Applying the Strategy

Use your school or local public library to find a videotape of a film or television documentary about the civil rights movement. Then view the documentary and write a report that summarizes its main ideas and evaluates it.

Practicing the Strategy

Answer the following questions.
1. What is the title of the documentary you found? Who produced it? When was it produced?
2. What main ideas does the documentary convey? What types of evidence does it provide to convey these ideas?
3. How does the documentary handle any differing points of view about the civil rights movement? What biases, if any, does the documentary display?
4. How does the documentary contribute to your understanding of the civil rights movement?

Successes of the Movement

The civil rights movement suffered setbacks during the 1970s. African Americans, however, did make some advances during this period. African Americans scored a major success when Carl Stokes was elected mayor of Cleveland. Stokes was the first African American to be mayor of a major U.S. city. Geraldine Williams, the campaign secretary who helped Stokes win his bid for office, remembered the election.

> 66 Definitely there was a connection with the civil rights movement. We got blacks to register, to vote, to take part in government. We convinced them that if you don't speak out and ask for things, you're never going to get them. You can't just sit there. We taught them that their vote does mean something, that it counts. 99

To ensure that African Americans would continue to gain political influence, activists met in Gary, Indiana, in 1972 for the **National Black Political Convention**. Some 2,700 delegates and another 4,000 people attended the convention.

As African American leaders gained political experience, they formed strong alliances and effective lobbies. They also worked hard to get out the African American vote. Although just 58.5 percent of eligible black voters were registered in 1976, African Americans played a crucial role in the presidential election that year. By the end of the 1970s, more than 4,500 African Americans held elected office—three times the number in 1969. The roster of elected black officials in 1978 included 16 members of the House of Representatives.

African Americans also experienced some economic gains during the 1970s. The number of African American-owned businesses rose from 163,073 in 1969 to 231,195 in 1977. However, some 31 percent of African Americans still lived below the poverty line. Nevertheless, in many professions and regions of the nation the income gap between the two groups narrowed. Increased enrollment in colleges and universities ensured that more African Americans would gain better-paying jobs. By 1976 the number of African American college students stood at more than 800,000—four times higher than it had been in 1964.

African American Education, 1960–1975

Percentage of African American Population

- 1960 / 1975 — Completed High School
- 1960 / 1975 — Completed College

Sources: *Historical Statistics of the United States; Statistical Abstract of the United States: 1997*

Learning from Graphs As the civil rights movement progressed, the number of African Americans who finished high school and went on to college increased dramatically.

? Building Graph Skills By how much did the percentage of the African American population with a high school diploma increase from 1960 to 1975? By how much did the percentage of those with a college degree increase?

✔ **READING CHECK:** What gains did African Americans make during the early 1970s?

SECTION 4 REVIEW

Define and explain the significance of the following terms:
busing
affirmative action
University of California v. Bakke
quotas
National Black Political Convention

Identify and explain the significance of the following individuals:
Ralph Abernathy
Allan Bakke
Carl Stokes

1. **Using Graphic Organizers** Copy the following flow-chart. Use it to explain changing strategies and goals within the post-1968 civil rights movement, white reactions to those goals, and outcomes.

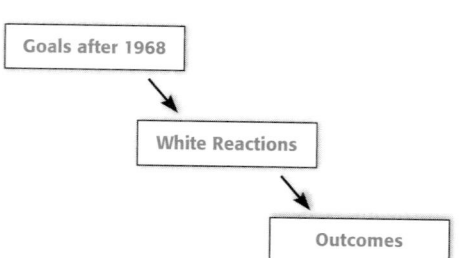

Goals after 1968

White Reactions

Outcomes

2. **Synthesizing** Why did many African American organizations experience difficulties during the 1970s?
3. **Recognizing Point of View** How and why did the Supreme Court limit busing and affirmative action?
4. **Hypothesizing** How might the civil rights movement have evolved differently in the 1970s if Martin Luther King Jr. had lived?

Critical Thinking

5. How successful was the civil rights movement by the mid-1970s?
   Consider:
   • the political successes of the movement
   • economic and educational advances for African Americans
   • civil rights goals left unfinished

Review

Creating a Time Line

Copy the time line below onto a sheet of paper. Complete the time line by filling in the events and dates from the chapter that you think were most significant. Pick three events and explain why you think they were significant.

1960   1965   1970   1975

Writing a Summary

Using the Reading Checks as a guide, write an overview of the events in the chapter.

Identifying People and Ideas

Identify the following terms or individuals and explain their significance.

1. Martin Luther King Jr.
2. Freedom Riders
3. Civil Rights Act of 1964
4. Freedom Summer
5. Fannie Lou Hamer
6. Nation of Islam
7. Stokely Carmichael
8. Kerner Commission
9. affirmative action
10. Carl Stokes

Understanding Main Ideas

SECTION 1

1. Why was nonviolence effective in the early years of the civil rights movement?
2. In what ways did the Civil Rights Act of 1964 respond to the racial problems in the South?

SECTION 2

3. How did Freedom Summer differ from earlier voter registration drives?
4. Why did the Voting Rights Act mark a major turning point in the civil rights struggle?

SECTION 3

5. What were the goals of the black nationalists?

SECTION 4

6. Why did busing and affirmative action arouse such passionate opposition?

7. What successes could African Americans point to during the early 1970s?

Reviewing Themes

1. **Democratic Values** What difficulties did the SCLC face when it attempted to bring the civil rights struggle to northern cities?
2. **Constitutional Heritage** In what ways did southern officials fail to protect the rights of voter registration workers and other demonstrators?
3. **Economic Development** What type of economic growth did black nationalists favor?

Thinking Critically

1. **Synthesizing** In what circumstances was nonviolent protest most effective? Why?
2. **Assessing Consequences** What effect did Malcolm X have on the civil rights movement?
3. **Recognizing Point of View** Why did SNCC workers such as Stokely Carmichael abandon nonviolent protest?
4. **Using Historical Imagination** How might the civil rights movement have been different if Martin Luther King Jr. and Malcolm X had not been assassinated?
5. **Taking a Stand** Would you have supported the goal of black nationalism at the 1972 National Black Political Convention? Why or why not?

Writing About History

Writing to Explain Copy the following chart and use it to write an essay that explains the benefits and drawbacks of Black Power for the civil rights movement.

Benefits	Drawbacks

Workers dismantle Resurrection City in 1968 after the failure of the Poor People's Campaign.

 internetconnect

TOPIC: Malcolm X and Martin Luther King Jr.
GO TO: go.hrw.com
KEYWORD: SD1 Leaders

Accessing the Internet through the HRW Web site, research the lives of Martin Luther King Jr. and Malcolm X. Then create an illustrated poster that compares and contrasts the beliefs and goals of these African American leaders.

Strategies for Success Review the **Strategies for Success** on *Using Multimedia Resources*. Then use your school or local public library to find a CD–ROM about the civil rights movement. Explore the CD–ROM on a computer and write a one-page report that summarizes its main ideas and evaluates the materials it offers.

Linking History and Geography

The Freedom Rides met with violent resistance in the South. Study the map below. Where did the Freedom Rides end for the CORE group and the SNCC group? How far was each group from its intended destination when it was stopped?

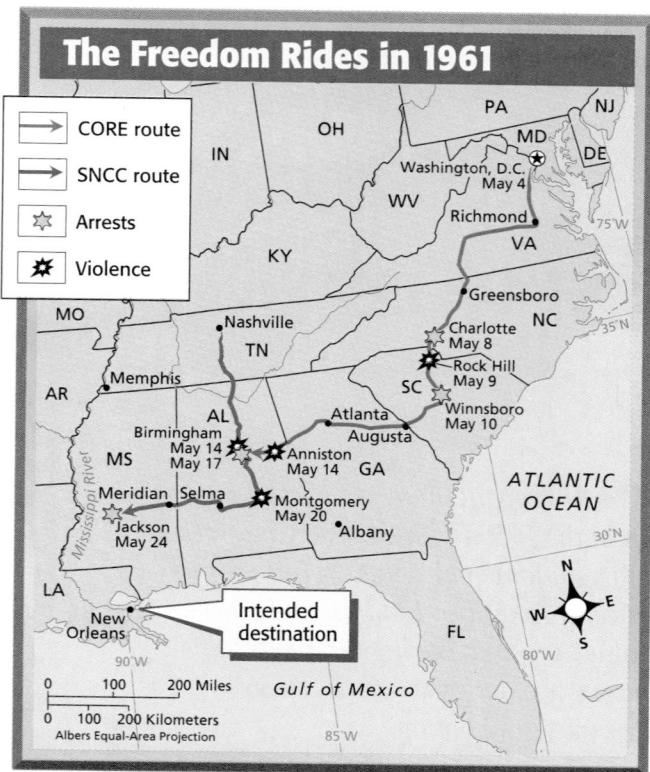

The Freedom Rides in 1961

- → CORE route
- → SNCC route
- ☆ Arrests
- ✴ Violence

BUILDING YOUR PORTFOLIO

Complete one or all of the following activities independently or cooperatively.

1 Cultural Diversity
*Imagine that you are a northern newspaper reporter covering the civil rights movement. **Write a memorandum** to your editor explaining why the newspaper should provide coverage of African American civil rights efforts in the South.*

2 Democratic Values
*Imagine that you are a civil rights activist registering voters during Freedom Summer. **Write a letter** to your family explaining the conditions that you face and why you are continuing in your efforts despite the violence.*

3 Constitutional Heritage
*Imagine that you are a museum curator creating a time line of the civil rights movement from 1965 to 1975. **Create an illustrated time line** and write captions for the images you use.*

CORE hat

FREEDOM NOW!
C·O·R·E·
CONGRESS OF RACIAL EQUALITY

1963–1975
Struggles for Change

Valentina Tereshkova

Mexican American migrant workers

1963
Science and Technology
Soviet cosmonaut Valentina V. Tereshkova becomes the first woman in space.

1963
Politics
Congress passes the Equal Pay Act.

1965
Business and Finance
Migrant farm-workers in California begin a strike against grape growers.

1963   **1965**   **1967**

1964
The Arts
The Beatles perform on *The Ed Sullivan Show* to a record television audience.

1964
Daily Life
The Ford Motor Company introduces the Mustang, which immediately becomes one of the nation's most popular car models.

1966
Politics
The National Organization for Women (NOW) is founded.

The Beatles

A Ford Mustang

Before You Read

Build on What You Know

The prosperity that followed World War II brought many changes to American society. A youth rebellion began in the 1950s with the beats and rock 'n' roll. African Americans continued to fight for equal rights. In this chapter you will learn how women, Mexican Americans, American Indians, and others began to demand fair treatment. You will also learn that during the 1960s some Americans challenged the beliefs and traditions of older generations. The result was a cultural revolution that eventually affected the entire nation.

THE MOTION PICTURE CODE
AND RATING PROGRAM
a system of self-regulation

MOTION PICTURE ASSOCIATION OF AMERICA

Symbol for the MPAA rating system

The first issue of Ms. magazine

1968
The Arts
The Motion Picture Association adopts a film rating system.

1968
Daily Life
Some 100 people protest the Miss America Pageant in Atlantic City, New Jersey.

1968
Politics
The American Indian Movement is organized.

1970
Science and Technology
Marine biologist Sylvia Earle Mead and five other female scientists spend two weeks underwater without surfacing.

1972
Business and Finance
The first issue of *Ms.* magazine sells 250,000 copies.

1972
Politics
The Equal Rights Amendment is sent to the states for ratification after its approval by Congress.

1974
Daily Life
Engineer Art Fry invents Post-It Notes.

1969 | **1971** | **1973** | **1975**

1969
World Events
Golda Meir becomes the prime minister of Israel.

1971
Business and Finance
Community organizers in East Los Angeles work with the United Auto Workers to create the East Los Angeles Community Union.

1975
Politics
Congress passes the Education for All Handicapped Children Act.

Golda Meir

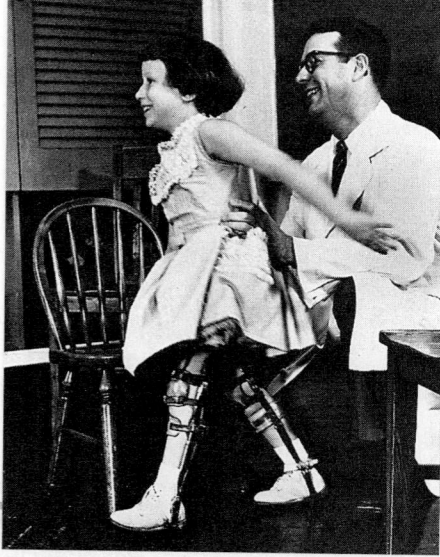

An instructor assists a child learning to walk with leg braces.

Think About Themes

Themes Journal

Decide whether you agree or disagree with the following statements. Note why in your journal.

Constitutional Heritage Amending the Constitution is a serious matter that should only be undertaken in the face of a national crisis.

Economic Development A rising standard of living makes young people so satisfied that political protests decrease.

Cultural Diversity Music, fashion, and art are merely for pleasure and entertainment and have little social or political significance.

947

Women's Rights

EYEWITNESSES TO History

66 *I guess I've been pretty much influenced by the Women's Movement because of the people I work with. . . . A lot of them were in that movement, so I've become more aware of it that way. I've just become much more aware of being a woman and the rights a woman should have. . . . Before, what I knew about the movement was really limited to just what I saw—people in demonstrations and the type of women who were professionals and their side of things.* 99

—Cathy Tuley

In the 1960s and 1970s many American women demanded equal rights.

Cathy Tuley, a hospital clerical worker, discussed her perceptions of the women's movement. Tuley's experiences mirrored those of many other women who entered the workforce during the 1960s and 1970s.

A Revived Women's Movement

One of the lasting effects of the 1960s was a change in the traditional roles of women. After years of inaction, the women's movement experienced a widespread revival, sparked in part by the work of author Betty Friedan.

In 1957 Friedan conducted a survey of women who, like herself, had graduated from Smith College 15 years earlier. She hoped to dispute the popular notion that higher education was harmful to women. To Friedan's surprise, the women who responded to her questionnaire expressed dissatisfaction with their lives. Almost all the women whom Friedan surveyed were full-time homemakers. Many found their lives unfulfilling. In her 1963 book, *The Feminine Mystique*, Friedan concluded that many women felt trapped by the "comfortable concentration camp" of domestic life.

66 **The problem lay buried, unspoken, for many years in the minds of American women. It was a strange stirring, a sense of dissatisfaction, a yearning that women suffered in the middle of the twentieth century in the United States. Each suburban wife struggled with it alone. As she made the beds, shopped for groceries, matched slipcover material, ate peanut butter sandwiches with her children, chauffeured Cub Scouts and Brownies . . . she was afraid to ask even of herself the silent question—'Is this all?'** 99

By the end of the decade *The Feminine Mystique* had sold more than 1 million copies. Inspired by its message, many women began to examine their lives. Seeking change, they demanded increased opportunities and fair treatment in the workplace.

Betty Friedan wrote the influential book **The Feminine Mystique.**

✔ **READING CHECK:** What did *The Feminine Mystique* reveal about women, and how did readers respond to it?

Helping Women at Work

Most of the women polled by Betty Friedan were home-makers. However, the number of women in the workplace had grown dramatically in the years before her book was published. The number of working women rose from 25 percent in 1940 to 35 percent in 1960. By 1963 almost 25 million working women made up more than one third of the American labor force. Yet female workers received lower wages than men did. In 1960, for example, women who worked full-time earned 40 percent less than working men. Women typically held service jobs that paid poorly, but in many cases they received lower wages even when they did the same work as men. As one business executive confessed, "We pay [women] less because we can get them for less."

In June 1963 President John F. Kennedy signed the Equal Pay Act, which required that women receive equal pay for equal work.

Kennedy responds. The Kennedy administration hired few women but did not ignore the problems that working women faced. President Kennedy issued an executive order requiring that civil-service hiring occur "solely on the basis of ability to meet the requirements of the position, and without regard to sex." His administration also backed a new law that made it illegal for employers to pay female workers less than male workers for the same job. Congress approved this **Equal Pay Act**, which Kennedy signed in June 1963. The act had a limited impact, however. Its provisions did not cover women in agricultural, professional, or service industries—about two thirds of working women. Nevertheless, the law served as an important first step toward equality in the workplace. In the decade following its passage, 171,000 workers used the law to win $84 million in back pay.

Kennedy also created the President's Commission on the Status of Women (PCSW) and appointed former first lady Eleanor Roosevelt as its chairperson. Kennedy authorized the PCSW to investigate the lives of American women. Completed in October 1963, the commission's report noted that female workers continued to experience discrimination in the workplace despite their increasing numbers. The report set new goals for the treatment of working women and called for "equal opportunity in hiring, training, and promotion."

Title VII. Female workers received additional and unexpected assistance from the federal government in 1964. That year Congress debated legislation intended to protect the civil rights of African Americans. Representative Howard Smith of Virginia proposed adding a clause to the bill that would protect women from discrimination. Smith opposed the civil rights bill and actually hoped that his amendment would weaken its chances of passing.

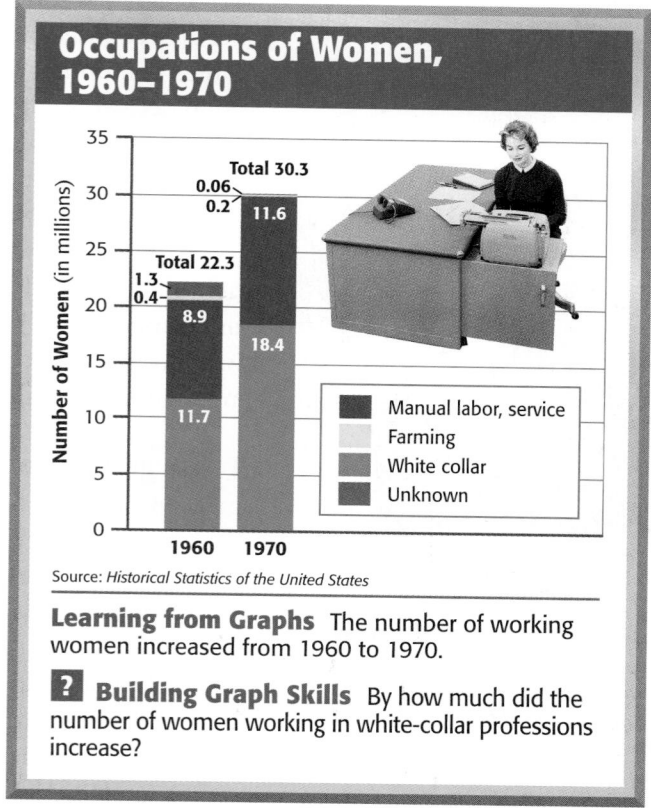

Occupations of Women, 1960–1970

Number of Women (in millions)

Total 22.3
1.3
0.4
8.9
11.7

Total 30.3
0.06
0.2
11.6
18.4

1960   1970

Legend:
- Manual labor, service
- Farming
- White collar
- Unknown

Source: *Historical Statistics of the United States*

Learning from Graphs The number of working women increased from 1960 to 1970.

? Building Graph Skills By how much did the number of women working in white-collar professions increase?

The EEOC works to prevent discrimination in employment.

Female members of Congress seized the opportunity. Representative Martha Griffiths of Michigan declared, "A vote against this amendment today by a . . . man is a vote against his wife, or his widow, or his daughter, or his sister." Congress approved the Smith amendment, and the bill passed. As a result, Title VII of the Civil Rights Act of 1964 outlawed sexual discrimination in employment. The act also created the Equal Employment Opportunity Commission (EEOC). This federal agency is charged with ensuring that employers followed the provisions of Title VII.

✔ **READING CHECK:** How did the federal government try to assist working women in the early 1960s?

Heightened Activism

Women quickly discovered that many government officials were more interested in battling racial discrimination than in using civil rights laws to fight gender discrimination. Herman Edelsberg, the director of the EEOC, called the gender-discrimination ban "a fluke." Sonia Pressman, an attorney for the EEOC, later explained why the agency did not respond to women's needs.

     66 We had an agency with a mandate [order] to prohibit sex discrimination . . . in a country that was not conscious of the fact that women were the victims of discrimination. After all, while the creation of the EEOC was in direct response to the movement for black rights in this country, there had been no similar movement immediately prior to 1965 for women's rights. 99

Buttons and patches like these served as outward signs of women's determination to win equality with men.

NOW. In June 1966 a group of women attending a conference on women's status met in Betty Friedan's hotel room to discuss their frustration with the EEOC. Some wanted to found an organization to lobby on behalf of women's rights. Instead, the group decided to present a resolution to the conference condemning the EEOC. Pauli Murray recalled, "I left Betty Friedan's room that night thoroughly discouraged; it seemed to me that we had fumbled a major opportunity to begin mobilizing [organizing] women nationally to press for their civil rights."

The next day, however, the conference rejected the resolution. During lunch the women decided to form a women's rights group. The **National Organization for Women** (NOW) was the result. NOW claimed some 1,000 members within its first year in existence. The organization pressured elected officials to ensure social and economic equality for women.

A new generation. Some women rejected NOW's moderate approach to political change. Critic Marlene Dixon maintained that NOW would secure "limited and elitist [exclusive] day-care programs . . . [and] an effective end to job discrimination at least on the elite level." Dixon argued that "these programs give the illusion of success, while in fact assuring the destruction of any hope for women's liberation."

Dixon voiced the opinion of a new generation of female activists. Many of these women had participated in other social movements, such as the struggle for civil rights. Many female activists realized that they faced just as much gender discrimination in these movements as they did in mainstream society. Mary King and Casey Hayden were volunteers for the Student Nonviolent Coordinating

Committee (SNCC). In 1964 they noted that SNCC's "assumption of male superiority" was "as widespread and deep rooted and . . . as crippling to . . . women as the assumptions of white supremacy are to the Negro."

During the late 1960s many female social activists began standing up for their own rights. Numerous small women's groups sprang up nationwide. Some held discussion sessions to improve their self-image. Others took direct, and often controversial, action. In 1968, feminists disrupted the Miss America Pageant, charging that beauty contests degraded women.

BIOGRAPHY

Gloria Steinem

Journalist Gloria Steinem was one of the women inspired to activism during the late 1960s. Steinem was born on March 25, 1934, in Toledo, Ohio. Her parents divorced in 1946, and Steinem spent most of her teenage years caring for her invalid mother. In 1952 Steinem entered Smith College, where she graduated with honors. "I loved Smith," she recalled. "They gave you three meals a day to eat, and all the books you wanted to read—what more could you want?" Her love of reading and writing led her to become a journalist.

In 1968 Steinem started writing a political column for *New York* magazine. Her work brought her into contact with many activists. Steinem did not initially consider herself a feminist. She later recalled, "Though I was old enough to be part of the *Feminine Mystique* generation, I wasn't living in the suburbs, wondering why I wasn't using my college degree. I'd ended up in the workforce many of these other women were trying to enter."

Steinem's interest in civil rights and political activism eventually led her to consider the status of women in American society. She began writing openly feminist articles that established her as a supporter of the women's movement. In one article Steinem stated that cooperation by radical feminists, middle-class reformers, and poor women could create a powerful movement for women's causes. In 1971 she helped found the **National Women's Political Caucus** to encourage women to run for political office. The next year, she became editor of a new magazine for women entitled *Ms.*

"There is nothing outside of [the movement]," Steinem said. "I once thought I would do this for two or three years and go home to my real life." Steinem remains a leader in the women's movement. She has written several books and helped found numerous organizations for women, including the Coalition of Labor Union Women and Women Against Pornography.

✔ **READING CHECK:** What tactics did the leaders of the women's movement use?

Women's rights. These women are marching through the streets of Washington, D.C., to demand equal rights. *Based on this march, how well did the women's movement appeal to women of all ages? Explain your answer.*

Women and Sports

The women's movement supported increased opportunities for women in all areas of life, including sports. Before 1972 just 1 percent of the money spent on athletic programs at institutions of higher education was

Basketball player Chamique Holdsclaw

spent on women's sports. As a result, only some 16,000 women attending colleges and universities participated in sports programs.

Title IX of the 1972 Educational Amendments Act declared that "no person in the United States shall, on the basis of sex, be excluded from participation in, be denied the benefits of, or be subjected to discrimination under any education program or activity receiving federal financial assistance." The law did not mean that all college sports had to become coeducational. Rather, it required universities to fund women's sports programs fairly. By 1984, spending on women's athletics had improved. That year, women's sports received 16 percent of all athletic funds, and some 150,000 women participated in college sports activities. By the 1990s more than 160,000 women were involved in college athletics. The increase in girls' participation in high school sports programs was even more impressive. The number of female high school athletes rose from 294,105 in 1972 to some 2.5 million in 1997.

The Women's Movement Gains Momentum

The women's movement made significant progress in the 1970s. Leaders worked to shape public policy and to elect more women to public office. Many all-male colleges allowed female students to enroll for the first time. Other universities instituted courses in women's studies. In 1972 Congress passed the **Educational Amendments Act**, which outlawed sexual discrimination in higher education.

Mixed success. In 1973 the Supreme Court handed down a landmark decision affecting women. In the case *Roe* v. *Wade*, the Court overturned a state law limiting women's access to abortion during the first three months of pregnancy. The Court ruled that a woman and her doctor, not the state, should make such decisions. While most feminists hailed *Roe* v. *Wade* as a victory, opponents protested that the ruling violated the right to life of the unborn.

During the 1970s controversy also followed the Equal Rights Amendment (ERA). A proposed constitutional amendment, the ERA sought to bar discrimination on the basis of sex. Activists had first proposed such an amendment during the 1920s, but it did not pass. The ERA received strong support from NOW and other women's groups. Gloria Steinem testified before Congress on behalf of the amendment.

> 66 Women suffer second-class treatment from the moment they are born. They are expected to *be* rather than to achieve, to function biologically rather than learn. A brother, whatever his intellect, is more likely to get the family's encouragement and education money, while girls are pressured to conceal ambition and intelligence. 99

Congress passed the ERA in 1972, but the amendment required the approval of at least 38 states. Ratification initially seemed certain. However, conservative groups that regarded the ERA as a threat to traditional women's roles launched a campaign to prevent ratification. By the 1982 deadline set by Congress, the ERA was still three states short of ratification. As a result, the amendment failed to become law.

Opposition. The fight over the ERA revealed that many women believed that the women's movement primarily served wealthy white women. Many non-white women and working-class white women felt left out. These women felt that the leaders of NOW and other feminist groups simply did not understand the problems they faced every day. Referring to Gloria Steinem, Cathy Tuley stated, "I feel she's fighting for women like herself, professional women, and that she's not thinking of women in the whole sense, just part of them."

The movement also offended many middle-class women. They felt that it minimized the importance of the family and condemned women who chose to be full-time homemakers. These women viewed *Roe* v. *Wade* and the ERA as threats to traditional family life. Critics warned that the ERA would "nullify [cancel] any laws that make any distinction between men and women." Eventually, they argued, men and women would even be forced to share public restrooms! Conservative critic Phyllis Schlafly was pleased when the ERA failed to win ratification. She claimed, "The defeat of the Equal Rights Amendment is the greatest victory for women's rights since the woman's suffrage movement of 1920."

Despite such disagreements over the role of women in American society, women could point to many significant gains by the end of the 1970s. An increasing number of female politicians took office in the U.S. Congress. New York representatives Bella Abzug and Shirley Chisholm received national attention. Abzug became an outspoken supporter of women's issues in Congress. In 1972 Shirley Chisholm—the first African American woman elected to Congress—ran unsuccessfully for the Democratic nomination for president. Although she did not receive the party's nomination, her campaign illustrated how far women had come. Most women still held low-paying jobs, but the number of women holding professional jobs had increased. In 1970 just 5 percent of the nation's lawyers and 25 percent of all accountants were women. Ten years later, 12 percent of lawyers and 33 percent of accountants were women.

Phyllis Schlafly was a vocal opponent of the Equal Rights Amendment.

✔ **READING CHECK:** What gains and setbacks did the women's movement experience during the 1970s?

SECTION 1 REVIEW

Define and explain the significance of the following terms:
Equal Pay Act
National Organization for Women
National Women's Political Caucus
Educational Amendments Act

Identify and explain the significance of the following individuals:
Betty Friedan
Gloria Steinem
Phyllis Schlafly
Bella Abzug
Shirley Chisholm

1. **Using Graphic Organizers** Copy the graphic organizer below. Use it to explain the development of the women's movement.

1. Sources of Dissatisfaction Among Women

2. Federal Government Responses

3. Goals and Tactics of NOW

4. Goals and Tactics of New Generation

5. Successes and Setbacks

2. **Identifying Cause and Effect** What was the source of the frustration that Betty Friedan identified in *The Feminine Mystique?* How did the book affect its readers?

3. **Taking a Stand** Did the federal government provide adequate support to women during the 1960s and 1970s? Explain your answer.

4. **Recognizing Point of View** Why did women such as Phyllis Schlafly celebrate the defeat of the ERA?

Critical Thinking

5. Why were some women critical of NOW and its goals?
   Consider:
   • the reforms that NOW hoped to achieve
   • the strategies it used to achieve these reforms
   • the difference in background between NOW members and their critics

The Chicano Movement

EYEWITNESSES TO History

❝ *One night I went to a dance. I didn't know that it was a place with mostly Anglo girls. An Anglo policeman told me to leave the premises. At that point I questioned him, and he arrested me. I asked him why he was arresting me, and he uttered some very racist sentiments. At the station, they let me go. Nevertheless, I spent a very embarrassing and uncomfortable few hours in jail.* ❞

—César Caballero

Chicano protesters

César Caballero recalled his years as a high school student in El Paso, Texas, during the early 1960s. Caballero and many other Mexican Americans reacted to the discrimination they experienced by demanding their civil rights and greater opportunities in American life.

Stirrings of Protest

Like the African American civil rights movement and the women's movement, the Mexican American struggle to secure equal rights became a powerful political force during the 1960s. Almost 4 million Mexican Americans lived in the United States in 1960, with more than 3.4 million living in southwestern states. They were among the poorest and least-educated people in the country. Although 80 percent of Mexican Americans lived in cities, it was the actions of California farmworkers that initially inspired many Mexican Americans to activism.

A model for the movement. Migrant agricultural workers, many of them Mexican Americans, received low wages for backbreaking labor. In September 1965 a group of Filipino workers went on strike in Delano, California, in the San Joaquin Valley. They refused to harvest grapes until they received a pay increase. Other migrant workers, including Mexican Americans, soon joined the strike.

When the Filipino workers struck, leaders of a union called the National Farm Workers Association (NFWA) were faced with a dilemma. A few months earlier they had won a labor dispute with rose growers, but this strike promised to be much more difficult to win. Led by César Chávez, NFWA leaders decided to join the strike.

Born in Yuma, Arizona, in 1927, César Chávez was the son of Mexican American farmers. After losing their land during the Great Depression, Chávez's family became migrant workers. During his childhood Chávez attended nearly 30 different schools. The Chávez family repeatedly experienced discrimination in their travels searching for work. Looking back on his childhood, Chávez recalled, "There were lots of racist remarks that still hurt my ears when I think of them."

BIOGRAPHY
César Chávez

Chávez was strongly influenced by his parents, particularly his mother, who often assisted fellow migrant workers. Chávez remembered, "We were migrants but we were a service center. We did all kinds of work for people." After serving in the navy during World War II, Chávez moved to San Jose, California. He became involved in the Community Service Organization (CSO), where he learned community-organizing techniques. He was influenced by Father Donald McDonnell, a Catholic priest who taught Chávez that labor unions could be a powerful force for social change.

Chávez longed to organize migrant agricultural workers. When this project did not receive support from the CSO, he left the organization. With help from former CSO workers Dolores Huerta and Gil Padilla, Chávez founded the NFWA. At times Chávez received no pay for his efforts. His wife Helen ran the credit union they had created to assist the workers. By 1965 the NFWA claimed some 1,700 members.

Strike and boycott.
On September 16, 1965, Mexican Independence Day, Chávez asked a gathering of NFWA members to join the Filipino strikers. Eliseo Medina was then a 19-year-old worker. He later recalled the union meeting.

> ❝ People started talking about how unfair . . . the growers were . . . and why we needed to fight back. . . . And then, so César gets up, and he's this little guy . . . very soft spoken. I say 'That's César?' You know, I wasn't very impressed . . . but the more he talked, the more I thought that not only could we fight, but we could win. ❞

After NFWA members voted to strike, Chávez and other leaders collected donations of money and food to support the striking workers. The union also constructed a medical clinic and operated a gas station for its members. As Chávez explained, "We are a union of have-nots. So we must satisfy basic needs before other things."

Chávez realized that a strike alone would not win the union any concessions. He therefore adopted other strategies used in the civil rights movement to gain support. In 1966, to encourage public sympathy for the strike, Chávez conducted a 300-mile march to Sacramento, the capital of California. When Chávez called for a nationwide boycott of grapes, consumers responded enthusiastically. An estimated 17 million Americans refused to buy grapes. The resulting economic pressure forced grape growers to negotiate a settlement.

Known as **La Huelga**, the Delano grape strike lasted until 1970, when the last of the grape growers signed new contracts with the union. During that time the NFWA merged with another union, eventually forming the **United Farm Workers** (UFW). The UFW was not exclusively a Mexican American organization and included many non-Hispanic members. However, its accomplishments and

The Religious Spirit

THE IDEAL OF NONVIOLENCE

Most religions consider life to be sacred and have strict standards against the use of violence. During the early 1900s Mohandas K. Gandhi used the idea of nonviolence taken from Hinduism to oppose British rule in India. Martin Luther King Jr. and other African American civil rights activists followed Gandhi's example. They were also influenced by Christian teachings to use nonviolent tactics in their struggle for equal rights.

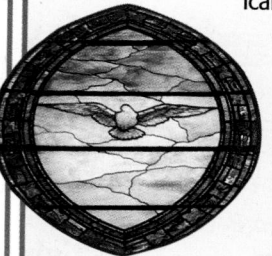

Many religions use the dove as a symbol of peace.

César Chávez also believed that nonviolence was the best way to bring about social change. Chávez was a deeply religious man. He once declared, "For me, Christianity happens to be a natural source of faith." He maintained that Jesus Christ "was extremely radical, and he was for social change." Chávez drew strength from his Catholic faith. He also studied Gandhi, whom he called "the most perfect man, not including Christ." Chávez noted, "Gandhi's philosophy of nonviolence, it really forces us to think, really forces us to work hard. But it has power. It attracts the support of the people."

Chávez's leadership inspired many Mexican Americans to fight against discrimination in their lives. The union's symbol, a black Aztec eagle, came to represent the Mexican American civil rights movement that developed during the late 1960s. César Chávez led many similar strikes before his death in 1993. His admirers have called him a modern-day saint.

✔ **READING CHECK:** Why was La Huelga important to Mexican Americans throughout the country?

Mexican American Activism

César Chávez became nationally known during the late 1960s. He was respected for his tireless efforts and his commitment to nonviolent protest. Senator Robert Kennedy of New York hailed Chávez as "one of the heroic figures of our time." Other Mexican Americans were also involved with protests during the 1960s. Some of these activists used tactics different from those of Chávez and the UFW.

Land rights. In northern New Mexico, Reies López Tijerina led the **Alianza Federal de Mercedes**, or "Federal Alliance of Land Grants." This organization worked to regain land that had been taken from Mexican Americans—often through fraud or deception—over the years. Tijerina told Mexican American farmers:

> 66 You have been robbed of your lands by Anglo-Americans with some Spanish-American accomplices. . . . The federal and state governments are not interested in you. Join the Alianza. Together we will get your lands back . . . preferably through court action. If the courts do not respond, then we will have to resort to other methods. 99

Although New Mexico governor David Cargo showed sympathy for the Alianza cause, many other state officials were determined to stop the *aliancistas*, as Tijerina's followers were known. Several *aliancistas* were arrested for unlawful assembly in June 1967 when they tried to attend a meeting in Coyote, New Mexico. Outraged, other *aliancistas* stormed the courthouse in Tierra Amarilla, New Mexico, in an attempt to free their friends. A gun battle broke out, and two police officers were wounded. Governor Cargo was in Michigan at the time of the courthouse incident. He later recalled being told, "You've got a civil war going on in New Mexico."

The Tierra Amarilla incident marked a turning point in the conflict between the *aliancistas* and their opponents. The group became entangled in lawsuits, and Tijerina eventually spent two years in prison for an assault conviction. Although Tijerina did not achieve any of his goals, he did inspire a generation of young Mexican American activists.

INTERPRETING THE VISUAL RECORD

The UFW. The UFW fought poor working conditions with boycotts like the one against lettuce growers that the flag above announces. *What are the workers in this picture doing? Do you think it is hard work? Why?*

Reies López Tijerina fought to help Mexican Americans regain lands that had been taken from them.

Student action. While Tijerina fought his battles in New Mexico, students in California also took to active protest. Many Mexican Americans in East Los Angeles resented the poor quality of the local schools. Some students began planning a mass demonstration. On March 1, 1968, some 300 students at Wilson High School walked out of their classes to protest the cancellation of a school play. The walkout, called a blowout by the students, quickly spread. Within one week some 15,000 students had joined the protest. Police responded by arresting students and, in some cases, beating them.

The walkouts caused a split within the Mexican American community. Some Mexican Americans wanted the students punished, while others supported their efforts. The Educational Issues Coordinating Committee (EICC) tried to use the walkouts to bring about change in the school system. The school reform movement met with opposition in June 1968. That month, 13 people—including many EICC members—were indicted for conspiracy to create riots and disturbing the peace.

Known as the L.A. Thirteen, the individuals indicted included several members of the **Brown Berets**. Inspired by the Black Panthers, the Brown Berets was an activist group formed in 1967 in response to police brutality against Mexican Americans in Los Angeles. Recalling his arrest after being indicted, Carlos Munoz, a Brown Beret leader and L.A. Thirteen member, declared, "They put the cuffs on me. I'll never forget this as long as I live." Charges against Munoz and the other L.A. Thirteen were later dropped.

INTERPRETING THE VISUAL RECORD
The Chicano movement. This Los Angeles mural celebrates the Chicano movement's fight for equal rights. *What do you think the various elements of the mural represent?*

The East Los Angeles school walkouts brought national attention to Mexican American concerns and drew many students into militant activism. John Ortiz was a college student who took part in the protests. He later recalled, "As the strike intensified and people were getting arrested, the students became politically aware. The events politicized the students. And that's why they walked out of their classes!"

✔ **READING CHECK:** How did conflicts over land rights and education motivate Mexican Americans to protest?

Nationalism and Politics

During the late 1960s some Mexican Americans began embracing a form of cultural nationalism similar to that supported by black nationalists. Calling themselves "Chicanos," these leaders worked to create a national movement by uniting the regional efforts that had already developed in many southwestern states.

Rodolfo Gonzales testifies before the U.S. Department of Education on discrimination in American schools.

Urban activism. Rodolfo "Corky" Gonzales became one of the leading figures in the Chicano movement. Gonzales looked beyond issues such as farmworkers' rights, land grants, and educational reform. He expressed a vision that appealed to a large number of Mexican Americans, particularly those living in cities.

A former boxer, Gonzales was involved with Democratic Party politics and antipoverty programs in Denver during the late 1950s and early 1960s. Over time Gonzales grew dissatisfied with politics, which he believed did little to help Mexican Americans. He later recalled, "I became disenchanted with the electoral system and disenchanted with the two political parties."

In 1966 Gonzales founded the **Crusade for Justice**, a group that promoted Mexican American nationalism. Operating out of an old church, the group offered legal aid, a theater for promoting cultural awareness, a newspaper, and other community services. It also ran a school. Gonzales praised the Crusade as "the embodiment [representation] of nationalism that now exists here in the Southwest. It has been a dream of the past, but we're now creating a reality out of it."

Gonzales popularized the use of the nationalist term Chicano to refer to Mexican Americans. He also composed an epic poem, *I Am Joaquin,* which served as an anthem for the *movimiento,* or "Chicano movement." In March 1969 Gonzales and the Crusade for Justice sponsored the National Chicano Liberation Youth Conference. Maria Valera attended the conference.

The Chicano Movement, 1947–1975

Learning from Maps Across the United States young Mexican Americans joined forces to demand recognition of their civil rights.

? REGION In what area of the country did most Chicano activism take place?

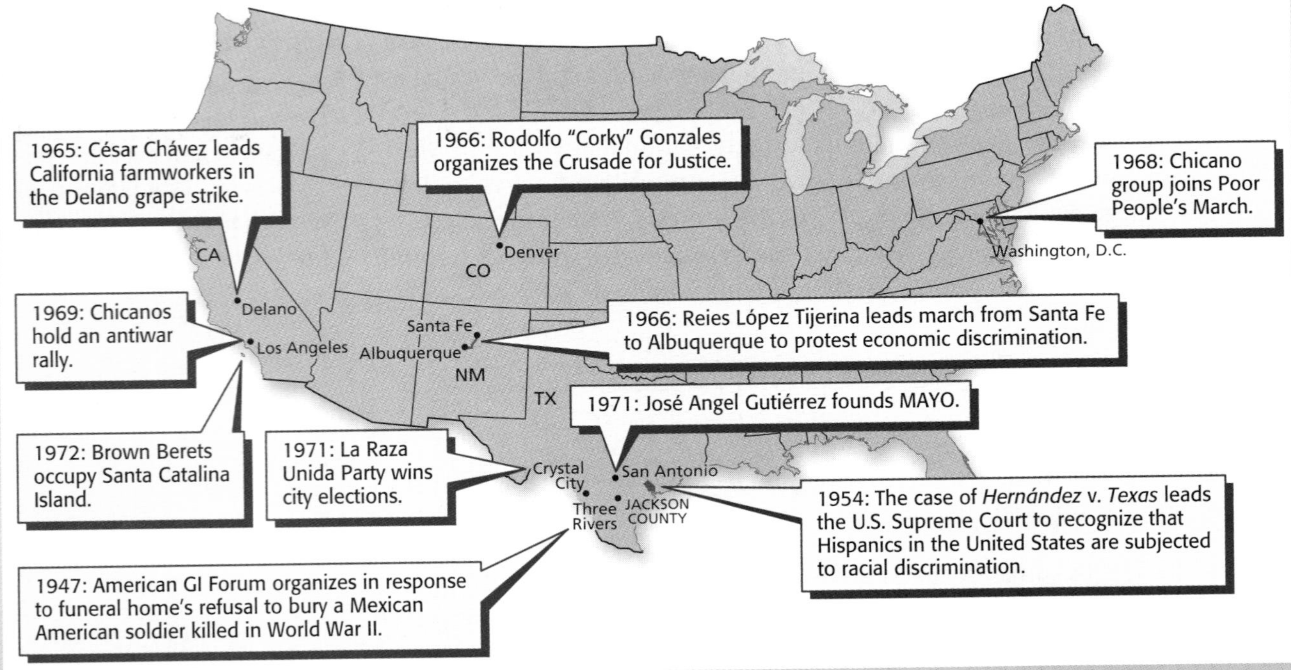

1965: César Chávez leads California farmworkers in the Delano grape strike.

1966: Rodolfo "Corky" Gonzales organizes the Crusade for Justice.

1968: Chicano group joins Poor People's March.

1969: Chicanos hold an antiwar rally.

1966: Reies López Tijerina leads march from Santa Fe to Albuquerque to protest economic discrimination.

1971: José Angel Gutiérrez founds MAYO.

1972: Brown Berets occupy Santa Catalina Island.

1971: La Raza Unida Party wins city elections.

1954: The case of *Hernández* v. *Texas* leads the U.S. Supreme Court to recognize that Hispanics in the United States are subjected to racial discrimination.

1947: American GI Forum organizes in response to funeral home's refusal to bury a Mexican American soldier killed in World War II.

CA · Delano · Los Angeles · CO · Denver · NM · Santa Fe · Albuquerque · TX · Crystal City · Three Rivers · JACKSON COUNTY · San Antonio · Washington, D.C.

> 66 It was in reality a fiesta: days of celebrating what sings in the blood of a people taught to believe that they are ugly, discovering the true beauty in their souls during the years of occupation and intimidation. . . . This affirmation grew into a *grito,* a roar, among the people gathered in the auditorium of the Crusade's Center. 99

Conference delegates produced *El Plan Espiritual de Aztlán,* or "The Spiritual Plan of Aztlán," a document calling for Chicano separatism. *El Plan* declared, "We are a bronze people with a bronze culture. Before all the world, before all of North America, before all our brothers in the Bronze Continent, we are a Nation."

The Texas movement.

Like their counterparts in California and Colorado, Mexican Americans in Texas also turned to protest during the 1960s. In 1967 a group of students at St. Mary's University in San Antonio formed the **Mexican American Youth Organization** (MAYO). One of MAYO's founders, José Angel Gutiérrez, had been inspired by a 1966 farmworkers' protest march. Gutiérrez recalled, "Mexicans just didn't march in the streets. That was the first demonstration and march that I was involved in."

Under Gutiérrez's leadership, MAYO took radical positions on issues affecting Mexican Americans. Gutiérrez declared, "We have to be revolutionary in our demands and make every sacrifice necessary, even if it means death, to achieve our goals." Moderate opponents of MAYO's radical stance included Henry B. González, the first Mexican American from Texas to be elected to the U.S. Congress. Gutiérrez and MAYO did make some progress in the fight for civil rights in Texas. In 1969 Gutiérrez helped organize a protest in his hometown, Crystal City, Texas. Mexican American students at Crystal City High School were angry about racial discrimination in extracurricular activities such as cheerleading. Gutiérrez and other MAYO leaders staged a student walkout that forced the school board to end the discrimination.

La Raza. José Gutiérrez (left) and Rodolfo Gonzales (center) appear before the national convention of La Raza Unida in 1972. *What do you think Gonzales' raised fist symbolizes?*

Political power.

Mexican American leaders had begun discussing the possibility of creating a Chicano political party in 1967. After his success with the school protest in Crystal City, Gutiérrez formed **La Raza Unida Party** (LRUP). In elections held in 1970 LRUP gained control of the city council in Crystal City and positions in some other Texas cities. That same year Rodolfo Gonzales organized a Colorado branch of LRUP. The Colorado party could not claim many electoral victories, but it did succeed in drawing attention to Chicano causes in the state. LRUP also expanded into California, where it registered some 10,000 new voters and ran several candidates for state offices. LRUP soon appeared in other states, including Arizona, Nebraska, and New Mexico.

LRUP leaders hoped to transform the party from a collection of regional parties into a strong national organization. However, the 1972 national convention held in El Paso, Texas, revealed a lack of unity among the Chicano activists. Rodolfo Gonzales and José Angel Gutiérrez became locked in a power struggle to control

Members of the United Farm Workers gather at a convention in Fresno, California.

the party. As a result, the party never developed a national presence. LRUP continued to have success in Texas into the late 1970s, but internal conflicts eventually led to its decline.

✔ **READING CHECK:** How did aggressive activists shape the Chicano movement?

The Movement Weakens

The Chicano movement lost some of its political power during the 1970s. The Brown Berets dissolved in 1972, and LRUP's failure to meet its goals ended efforts to create alternative political parties. Some activists later claimed that the ethnic nationalism embraced by many of the movement's members was politically impractical and had caused many moderate Mexican Americans to lose interest.

Despite its shortcomings, the Chicano movement had a positive impact on the lives of many Mexican Americans. During the 1960s and 1970s several universities established Chicano Studies programs. The Chicano movement also inspired Mexican American artists, novelists, and playwrights to create new works. This led one critic to declare a Chicano Renaissance. Some activists entered mainstream politics, inspiring others to maintain their efforts to change American society. One participant, Rosalio Muñoz, later stated that the Chicano movement "helped crystallize for people making a commitment, just like in my own life, a commitment from there to go on."

✔ **READING CHECK:** How did the Chicano movement change the lives of Mexican Americans?

SECTION 2 REVIEW

Define and explain the significance of the following terms:
La Huelga
United Farm Workers
Alianza Federal de Mercedes
Brown Berets
Crusade for Justice
Mexican American
    Youth Organization
La Raza Unida Party

Identify and explain the significance of the following individuals:
César Chávez
Dolores Huerta
Reies López Tijerina
Rodolfo Gonzales
José Angel Gutiérrez

1. **Using Graphic Organizers** Copy the chart below. Use it to list the goals of the Mexican American leaders.

Leader	Goals
César Chávez	
Reies López Tijerina	
Rodolfo Gonzales	
José Angel Gutiérrez	

2. **Analyzing** Why did César Chávez and La Huelga become leading symbols of Mexican American activism?

3. **Comparing and Contrasting** What issues motivated Mexican American activists to protest? Why did the various groups use different approaches?

4. **Recognizing Point of View** Why did some activists such as Rodolfo Gonzales and José Angel Gutiérrez turn to aggressive activism during the late 1960s?

Critical Thinking

5. Would it be more accurate to regard the Chicano movement as a group of somewhat related movements?
   Consider:
   • the different goals within the movement
   • the conflicts between movement leaders
   • the movement's effects on Mexican Americans

More Groups Mobilize

OBJECTIVES

Read to understand:

1. what Red Power movement activists demanded, and how successful they were
2. how Americans with disabilities gained public support for their causes
3. what issues activists for senior citizens and children addressed

KEY TERMS

American Indian Movement
Rehabilitation Act
Education for All Handicapped Children Act
American Association of Retired Persons
Gray Panthers
Older Americans Act
Children's Defense Fund

KEY PEOPLE

Russell Means
Ed Roberts
Maggie Kuhn
Marion Wright Edelman

EYEWITNESSES TO History

66 *Let me tell you first of all that you can take credit for us being on Alcatraz because you and your government forced our backs against the wall. We're out there to create a starting point for basic changes in Indian-white relations. We reject the alternatives of the federal Indian policy. We reject either extermination of our cultures, which we refuse to have end up on museum walls for the pleasure of non-Indians. We reject the chronic and cyclical [repeating] poverty of reservations and the relocation transfer of that poverty into Red Ghettoes in the cities. We reject these alternatives. . . . We're creating our own alternatives!* 99

—Shirley Keith

American Indians dance during the Alcatraz occupation.

Shirley Keith explained to a California audience in 1969 why a group of American Indians had occupied Alcatraz Island in San Francisco Bay. American Indians were among the many groups that demanded change in American society during the 1960s and 1970s.

American Indian Activism

Many Americans did not benefit from the nation's widespread prosperity in the 1950s and 1960s. American Indians were particularly affected by poverty. Mary Crow Dog grew up on a Rosebud Sioux reservation in South Dakota. She later recalled, "We had no shoes and went barefoot most of the time. I never had a new dress." In 1960 the average income of American Indian men was less than half that of white men.

Spurred by extreme poverty and inspired by other groups' civil rights gains, American Indians formed the Red Power movement during the 1960s. Participants in the movement called for self-determination, or the right to govern their own communities. They also continued to demand that the U.S. government pay tribes for lands that had been taken from them illegally. Although these issues had long concerned supporters of American Indians' rights, Red Power gained more attention and participation among Indians than any previous movement.

The Alcatraz occupation. In November 1969 a group of Red Power activists called the Indians of All Tribes occupied the abandoned federal prison on Alcatraz Island in San Francisco Bay. The protest received national news coverage. Some 150 American Indians eventually traveled to the island to join the protest. The protesters offered to buy the island from the government with beads and cloth—the same price Dutch colonists had paid for Manhattan Island in 1626. Protest leaders urged other American Indians to support their cause.

In the late 1960s many American Indians protested against discrimination.

Protest. These American Indians in New Mexico are participating in a civil rights protest. *What do you think the message of the child's sign is?*

66 We are issuing this call in an attempt to unify all our Indian Brothers behind a common cause. . . . If we can gather together as brothers and sisters and come to a common agreement, we feel that we can be much more effective, doing things for ourselves, instead of having someone else do it, telling us what is good for us. 99

Not all American Indians approved of the Alcatraz occupation. John Knifechief complained that the protesters "have no reason whatsoever to be militant or be demanding of anything. . . . I can't see what these young people are demanding." Interest in the Alcatraz protest gradually declined, and in 1971 federal authorities removed the few remaining protesters from the island.

Wounded Knee. Organized in Minnesota in 1968, the **American Indian Movement** (AIM) became the major force behind the Red Power movement during the 1970s. AIM called for a renewal of American Indian culture and recognition of American Indians' rights. Russell Means, a Sioux who was born on the Pine Ridge Reservation of South Dakota, became a prominent figure in AIM. In 1970 Means and other AIM members occupied the *Mayflower II*—a replica of the Pilgrim ship— during Thanksgiving Day celebrations in Plymouth, Massachusetts. Means justified AIM's aggressive tactics in a 1971 interview. "In all our demonstrations we have yet to hurt anybody or destroy any property," he said. "However, . . . we have found that the only way the white man will listen is by us creating a disturbance in his world."

In 1972, AIM members and other American Indians conducted a protest they called the Trail of Broken Treaties. The group occupied the Bureau of Indian Affairs (BIA) headquarters in Washington, D.C. The following year AIM took its most dramatic action—the seizure of the trading post at Wounded Knee, South Dakota. U.S. cavalry units had killed more than 300 Sioux there in 1890. Means declared that the government had two choices: "Either they attack and wipe us out like they did in 1890, or they negotiate our reasonable demands." AIM wanted the government to initiate hearings on past broken treaties and investigate alleged BIA misconduct.

For 71 days AIM members and U.S. marshals engaged in a grim standoff. Finally, after two AIM activists had been killed and a federal marshal wounded, the government agreed to consider AIM's grievances. The siege came to an end. The following year Means and other AIM leaders were put on trial for the Wounded Knee incident. When defense lawyers presented evidence of government misconduct against AIM, however, the case was dismissed.

Gaining ground. AIM's confrontational tactics captured headlines and media attention. Other American Indian leaders worked to renew tribal life through quieter methods, including lawsuits and political lobbying. The Taos Pueblo of New Mexico had struggled for decades to recover 48,000 acres of land that included Blue Lake, which was sacred to them. The tribe rejected a $10 million settlement because they would have had to give up their rights to the land. Their efforts were rewarded in 1970. That year Congress approved legislation returning the land to the Taos Pueblo. American Indians in Maine who claimed that more than half that state had been illegally taken from them also scored a victory. Congress awarded them $81.5 million and the right to buy up to 300,000 acres of land.

Read More About It

Free Find:

Russell Means
After reading about AIM leader Russell Means on the **Holt Researcher** CD–ROM, imagine that you are a writer for a newsmagazine. Write a short profile of Means for an article about AIM.

American Indians continued to face many problems. Unemployment rates remained high throughout the 1970s, averaging 40 percent and reaching as high as 90 percent on some reservations. The high school dropout rate among American Indians was the highest in the nation. Nonetheless, the Red Power movement succeeded in drawing public attention to the concerns of American Indians. It also instilled a sense of pride in American Indians nationwide.

✔ **READING CHECK:** What did Red Power activists demand, and how successful were they?

Others Struggle for Their Rights

Several other groups of Americans sought recognition and protection of their civil rights during the 1960s and 1970s. Activists fought on behalf of people with disabilities, the elderly, and children during this period.

Disability rights. Many Americans with disabilities wondered why their tax dollars helped pay for the construction of public facilities that they could not easily use. Ed Roberts, a young Californian who had become a quadriplegic after having polio, was among the many Americans with disabilities who wanted to use public facilities. Individuals such as Roberts, who wanted to attend the University of California at Berkeley, insisted that people with disabilities deserved equal access to public facilities. Officials at the university argued that the campus did not have facilities that could accommodate Roberts. Supporters of Roberts used the media to raise public awareness of his cause. The university eventually admitted Roberts and he enrolled in 1962.

Ed Roberts excelled at the university, receiving a master's degree in political science. When other students with disabilities joined him at Berkeley, they formed a support group called the Rolling Quads. In 1969 the group convinced the Berkeley city council to change the design of street curbs so that people in wheelchairs could move easily through the city. Other state and local governments also passed laws requiring wheelchair ramps and special parking spaces at public facilities. Many buildings began to include signs in braille to help the visually impaired.

In 1973 Congress added to these efforts to expand opportunity when it passed the **Rehabilitation Act**. This act forbade discrimination in jobs, education, or housing because of physical disabilities. In 1975 Congress passed the **Education for All Handicapped Children Act**, which required public schools to provide education for children with physical or mental disabilities.

✔ **READING CHECK:** How did Americans with disabilities gain public support for their causes?

Then and Now

Education and Deaf Americans

Thomas Hopkins Gallaudet founded the nation's first school for the deaf in Hartford, Connecticut, in 1817. By 1835 most institutions relied upon a sign language developed by deaf people, which eventually became known as American Sign Language. During the 1880s supporters of "oralism" opposed signing. They claimed that the hard of hearing should be taught to speak English and to read lips. Although most deaf Americans preferred signing, many schools compromised by teaching both signing and oral language. During the 1970s some schools adopted a method of teaching called Total Communication, which combined signed and spoken language.

During the 1980s deaf Americans demanded that society accept them as citizens capable of living their lives without unwanted assistance. A 1988 protest at Gallaudet University, a school for deaf and hard-of-hearing students in Washington, D.C., symbolized this new activism. Gallaudet students responded with anger to the news that the university's new president was not deaf and could not even sign. They demanded a "Deaf President Now." After a week of protests, university officials backed down and announced that I. King Jordan, a university employee, would become Gallaudet's first deaf president.

Students at Gallaudet University protested the appointment of Elisabeth Zinser (left) as president because she was not deaf.

Of all the resources that you can use to conduct historical research, the Internet is one of the largest and most promising. While the Internet is an extremely valuable research tool, it is important that you learn to evaluate the quality of the Web sites you find.

How to Evaluate Web Sites

1. **Determine what topics are covered in the Web site, in how much depth they are covered, and how unique the coverage is.** First you must decide whether a site offers enough of the type of information you are looking for. Would you be better off finding the same information in a reference book? If so, it is probably better to use an already trusted resource. However, the site may contain additional and unique information.

2. **Determine if the information in the Web site is accurate.** The saying that you cannot believe everything you read is more relevant than ever on the Internet, where anyone can be a publisher. Conduct a preliminary review of the site. If there are spelling errors, grammatical errors, or profanity, avoid the site. Compare the information in the site to other reference sources. Examine claims made in the source to see that they are backed up with reasoned arguments and verifiable evidence. Sites full of unsupported claims and undocumented facts should be avoided.

3. **Establish who the author is, and what his or her qualifications are.** You need to determine the credentials of the person or group who created and published a Web page. Look to see if the Web site is published by a reputable firm, institution, or government agency. In the case of individuals, try to find out if the author has credentials in the field or a list of printed publications.

4. **Evaluate how objective the information is.** The objectivity of a site should not be taken for granted. It is important that you identify the purpose of a Web site. Some sites may be made to provide information, to sell things, or to promote a cause. Their facts may be correct, but you should understand the writer's point of view. If the purpose of a Web site is to persuade, then ask yourself what the other side of the issue is.

Applying the Strategy

Use the computer system at your school or local public library to find a Web site on one of the following topics:
  a. the history of the American Indian Movement
  b. the history of the disability rights movement
  c. the history of the Gray Panthers or the American Association of Retired Persons

Then explore the Web site and write a one-page report that summarizes its main ideas and evaluates its content.

Practicing the Strategy

Answer the following questions.
  1. What was the name of the Web site you found? Who produced it?
  2. What main ideas does the Web site attempt to convey? What historical materials does it offer?

Older Americans organize. During the late 1950s, retired Americans who joined social clubs often discussed political and legal issues affecting older adults. These concerns led to the formation of organizations dedicated to lobbying for the needs of older citizens. Founded in 1958, the **American Association of Retired Persons** (AARP) became the largest such group. AARP sought to eliminate mandatory retirement. The National Council of Senior Citizens (NCSC) represented the interests of lower-income older Americans. In 1965 some 1,400 NCSC members traveled to Washington, D.C., to support Medicare legislation.

Smaller than AARP or NCSC but much more visible to the public eye was a group called the **Gray Panthers**, founded by Maggie Kuhn. She recalled that when she was forced to retire, "I was hurt and then, as time passed, outraged." The Gray Panthers fought for greater rights for older Americans. Kuhn explained the goals of the senior movement when she testified before Congress in 1977:

> ❝ The Gray Panthers are a national coalition of old, young, and middle-aged activists . . . working to eradicate ageism and all forms of age discrimination in our society. We define ageism as the arbitrary [irrational] discrimination against persons and groups on the basis of chronological age. ❞

The federal government's responses included holding several White House Conferences on Aging. In 1965 Congress passed the **Older Americans Act**, which committed the government to providing the elderly with adequate income and medical care.

Children's issues.

Activists also organized for children's rights. In 1967 the Supreme Court ruled in the case *In Re Gault* that minors accused of a crime possessed nearly the same rights as adults. The case sparked interest in children's rights.

People fighting for children's rights pointed to larger problems in American society. The 1970 White House Conference on Children, which was attended by some 3,700 people, issued the Children's Bill of Rights. This document declared that children had the "right to grow in a society which respects the dignity of life and is free of poverty, discrimination, and other forms of degradation." The Children's Bill of Rights also maintained that children had the right to receive an education, "to be healthy," and "to grow up nurtured by affectionate parents."

Founded in 1973, the **Children's Defense Fund** (CDF) quickly became the leading children's rights organization. Director Marion Wright Edelman explained the group's purpose as "identifying, publicizing, and correcting selected serious problems faced by large numbers of American children." The CDF has focused on helping poor and minority children. The group has also sought health insurance for children and federally funded child care.

✔ **READING CHECK:** What issues did activists for senior citizens and children address?

INTERPRETING THE VISUAL RECORD

Senior citizens. The Gray Panthers fought to protect older Americans against discrimination. *What issues does this poster indicate that the Gray Panthers addressed?*

SECTION 3 REVIEW

Define and explain the significance of the following terms:
American Indian Movement
Rehabilitation Act
Education for All Handicapped Children Act
American Association of Retired Persons
Gray Panthers
Older Americans Act
Children's Defense Fund

Identify and explain the significance of the following individuals:
Russell Means
Ed Roberts
Maggie Kuhn
Marion Wright Edelman

1. **Using Graphic Organizers** Copy the graphic organizer below. Use it to explain the tactics used by activists seeking to expand the rights of the groups listed.

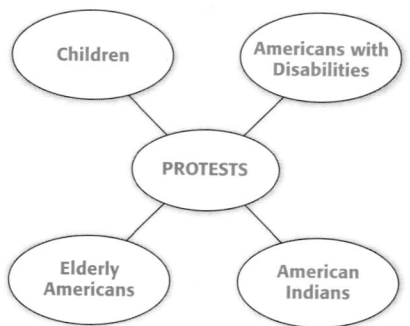

2. **Comparing and Contrasting** How did the demands of American Indians differ from those of other minorities who struggled for their civil rights during this era?

3. **Evaluating** What role did the media play in the disability rights movement?

4. **Problem Solving** What issues would you address if you were organizing a movement for senior citizens? a children's rights organization?

Critical Thinking

5. Did the militant activists involved in the Red Power movement achieve their goals?
   Consider:
   • the outcome of the Alcatraz occupation
   • the response to the occupation at Wounded Knee
   • the efforts of other American Indian activists

A Cultural Revolution

OBJECTIVES

Read to understand:

1. why protests developed on American college campuses
2. what problems weakened the counterculture
3. how doubts about American society led to new movements in religion and the arts
4. how musical styles reflected the social changes of the era

KEY TERMS

generation gap
counterculture
pop art
British invasion
Woodstock

KEY PEOPLE

Mario Savio
Timothy Leary
Joan Baez
Bob Dylan
James Brown
Aretha Franklin

EYEWITNESSES TO History

❝ *Everything on the tube tearing us apart was almost perfectly balanced by the remarkable unity [we heard] on the radio. It was the only place in the history of the United States where, for a fleeting [brief] moment, we created a world of seemingly genuine racial and sexual equality, embraced by everyone under thirty—and millions more who fell in love with the beat. . . . The composers, performers, managers, and producers . . . filled the airwaves with the most eclectic-electric-wrathful-revolutionary-romantic-soulful-psychedelic music ever played, simultaneously, on every rock-and-roll radio station in the world.* ❞
—**Charles Kaiser**

Peter Max's colorful antismoking poster reflected the new styles of the 1960s.

Charles Kaiser was a teenager during the 1960s who later became a writer. He reflected on the contrast between violent events—such as assassinations, riots, and the Vietnam War—that he witnessed on television with the sense of peace of the 1960s youth culture.

The Student Movement

Cold War fears, massive civil rights protests, and the Vietnam War led many young Americans to question the values of American society. They began to blame their parents for creating the problems that the country faced. This **generation gap** between the baby boomers and their elders grew wider as the decade wore on.

The 1960s youth movement began on college campuses among white middle-class students. In 1964 officials at the University of California at Berkeley announced a new policy restricting space available to student groups for organizing and making speeches. To many students, this was a violation of their right to free speech and assembly. Their discontent quickly exploded into protest.

Student activist Mario Savio and others helped organize the protests. Savio compared the university to a machine. He declared, "You've got to indicate to the people who run it, to the people who own it, that unless you're free, the machine will be prevented from working at all." A large number of Berkeley students stopped attending classes. They rallied, held sit-ins, and picketed university administration buildings. Their intention, they declared, was to "Shut This Factory Down." The protests quieted when university officials agreed to many of the students' demands.

In 1965 similar protests took place on college campuses nationwide. One woman who participated in the student movement at Columbia University in New York recalled the mood of the students:

Students demonstrate during the 1960s.

66 There was an incredible exhilaration, that here we were making history, changing the world. . . . Everybody believed that this university would never be the same, that society would be . . . changed, that there'd be a revolution in the United States within five years, and a whole new social order. 99

✔ **READING CHECK:** Why did protests develop on American college campuses?

The Counterculture

Some Americans hoped to create this "new social order" by rejecting everything connected with mainstream America, which they called the Establishment. Known as hippies, these Americans sought to create a **counterculture**, or alternative lifestyle.

Dropping out. Like the beats before them, hippies rejected the materialism and work ethic of past generations in favor of simplicity and "doing your own thing." Many hippies tried to shock older Americans, whom they dismissed as "squares," with behavior that included public displays of nudity and the use of profanity. Some hippies formed communities in run-down urban neighborhoods, such as the Haight-Ashbury district of San Francisco. Others "dropped out" of society by joining rural communes, where they attempted to live collectively in harmony with nature. Residents of communes typically rejected most modern conveniences, grew their own food, and shared all property. Between 1965 and 1975 some 10,000 such communes were established.

Many hippies searched for new physical experiences by experimenting with harmful mind-altering drugs such as LSD (lysergic acid diethylamide), commonly known as acid. Timothy Leary became the drug's leading supporter. He began using LSD on college students. Leary was fired in 1963 from his job as a Harvard University professor for violating rules governing experiments on human subjects. Leary invited people to "turn on to the scene, tune in to what is happening, and drop out—of high school, college, grad school, junior executive—and follow me, the hard way."

An African dashiki

Fashion. Those who followed Leary's advice often adopted a casual and colorful style of dress. Shirts that had been tie-dyed—dipped in colorful dyes while knotted to produce vibrant patterns—grew in popularity. People increasingly wore blue jeans, which traditionally had been considered work clothing. Men began wearing their hair longer, and beards became commonplace. Beads, which on men represented a rejection of the necktie, became a standard accessory. Some African Americans sported Afros, a natural hairstyle that came to symbolize racial pride. Many African Americans adopted the dashiki, an African shirt usually decorated with bright colors.

San Francisco's Haight-Ashbury district attracted a wide variety of people.

Pitfalls of the counterculture. For some hippies, the experimentation of the era came at a high price. Reported cases of drug addiction and sexually transmitted diseases increased at an alarming rate. In addition, some women perceived the era's new sexual freedom as yet another way for men to take advantage of women. Feminist Robin Morgan charged that "the so-called Sexual Revolution has . . . reinstituted [recreated] oppression by another name."

Young Americans who moved to Haight-Ashbury in search of cultural freedom found a harsh urban neighborhood troubled by crime. One leaflet handed out during the era declared, "Kids are starving on the Street. Minds and bodies are being maimed as we watch. . . . Are you aware that Haight Street is as bad as the squares say it is?" The counterculture also attracted sinister characters such as Charles Manson, who moved to Haight-Ashbury in 1967. Two years later Manson and a handful of his followers were responsible for a mass murder in California that horrified the nation.

✔ **READING CHECK:** What problems weakened the counterculture?

Pop art. Roy Lichtenstein used bright colors and a comic-strip style in his artwork. *What elements of this painting make you think it is, or is not, art?*

Changing American Society

The rise of the counterculture reflected the doubts that many citizens—particularly the young—held about the direction of American society. Americans increasingly questioned cultural traditions on a variety of issues from religion to the arts.

Religion. In a 1957 poll more than 80 percent of Americans claimed that religion could answer all or most of society's problems. By 1969, however, 70 percent said that religion was losing its influence on American life.

Americans did not necessarily lack spiritual faith. However, many Americans lost confidence in the ability of the established churches to provide spiritual direction in the modern world. Some believed that the challenges of the nuclear age had made traditional religious answers irrelevant. Reflecting the search for alternative answers, the number of college courses in religion—and enrollment in them—grew dramatically. Interest in Eastern religions such as Zen Buddhism also rose.

The arts. The questioning of tradition even extended into the art world. Many new visual artists argued that the art world had become a slave to upper-class tastes and customs. They claimed that established artists created works only to please a few cultural critics, not to appeal to the majority of nonartists. These new artists created a style called **pop art**

because it was intended to appeal to popular tastes. The artists took inspiration from elements of popular culture including advertising, celebrities, comic books, and movies.

Film also underwent a broadening of subject matter as censorship rules were increasingly ignored. Rather than continuing to allow the Catholic Legion of Decency to make recommendations regarding motion pictures, the film industry adopted its own ratings system. The system informed audiences about the content of movies. The ratings system ranged from G, which meant that the film was intended for general audiences, to X, which meant that people under the age of 17 would not be admitted. The rating system was adopted to gain favor with the viewing public, who wanted more information about the content of films. However, some artists argued that the new standards allowed box-office receipts to determine content rather than artistic concerns. Movies rated for adult audiences increasingly drew larger crowds than more family-oriented films.

✔ **READING CHECK:** How did doubts about American society lead to new religious and artistic movements?

AMERICAN ARTS

Pop Art

Andy Warhol painted these oversized soup cans in 1962.

In the early 1960s a number of New York painters and sculptors emerged who wanted to make art more accessible to the general public. They accomplished their goals by using "found objects"—cardboard packaging, cartoon strips, furniture, tin cans, and other everyday articles—as the subjects of their works. The leading supporters of this method, called pop art, included Roy Lichtenstein and Claes Oldenburg. Lichtenstein's huge paintings were done in comic-strip style. Oldenberg used a variety of materials to make giant sculptures of such things as clothespins, hamburgers, and toothpaste tubes.

The best-known pop artist was Andy Warhol. His most notable paintings include depictions of Campbell's soup cans, rows of Coca-Cola bottles, and a brightly colored photograph of Marilyn Monroe reproduced multiple times. Initially, Warhol painted his own works by hand, but he switched to a stencil-printing process called silk screen. Eventually, he simply created designs for his team of assistants to reproduce. Warhol's message—that everything, even art, can be mass-produced—both glorified and mocked American consumerism.

Understanding the Arts

1. What did supporters of pop art use as the subjects of their work?
2. What was the goal of pop artists?
3. What do you think Andy Warhol was trying to communicate in the painting shown above?

Sounds of the 1960s

Changes in the visual arts were matched by developments in popular music. The social and political movements of the 1960s marched to new forms of music that ranged from rock to folk to soul.

Rock music. A major influence on the youth rebellion of the 1950s, rock 'n' roll continued to reflect social change in the 1960s. Rock 'n' roll branched out into a variety of new forms. The year 1964 marked the musical **British invasion**—the introduction of new British bands to an American audience. Groups such as the Beatles and the Rolling Stones drew on 1950s rock 'n' roll and African American blues, thrilling American teenagers. Jane Berentson was a high school student in 1964. She later recalled of the Beatles, "The girls all decided right away which one they were in love with. And the boys all decided which one they looked like."

The use of electrically amplified instruments such as the electric guitar inspired musicians to try out innovative—and very loud—sounds on their audiences. Seattle native Jimi Hendrix was the master of the electric guitar in the 1960s. This new music served as a soundtrack for the counterculture. As one observer noted, the counterculture "is bright, vivacious [full of life], ecstatic, crowd-loving, joyful—and its music is rock."

Folk's rebirth. During the 1930s artists such as Woody Guthrie had used folk music to point out flaws in American society. By the 1950s this tradition had lost influence. During the 1960s, however, folk music gained popularity once again. Folk artists such as Joan Baez and Bob Dylan wrote lyrics that sent a political message to listeners, such as a 1962 Dylan hit.

> 66 How many years can a mountain exist
> before it's washed to the sea?
> Yes, 'n' How many years can some people exist
> before they're allowed to be free?
> Yes, 'n' How many times can a man turn his head
> pretending he just doesn't see?
> The answer, my friend, is blowin' in the wind
> The answer is blowin' in the wind. 99

Dylan formed a link between folk and rock music in 1965. That year he appeared on stage with an electric guitar instead of an acoustic guitar, the instrument traditionally used in folk music. Many fans of folk music felt that Dylan had betrayed them. Charles Kaiser attended a 1966 Dylan concert. He noted that the audience "screamed, shouted, walked out . . . even threw things at the stage"—but Dylan had brought folk music firmly into the rock realm.

Motown and soul. Despite rock's roots in African American blues, the British invasion pushed many African American performers off the record charts. Berry Gordy brought African Americans back into the forefront of popular music with Motown Records, his record company based in Detroit. By 1975 Motown was earning over $50 million annually. This made it one of the country's most successful

The music of the 1960s reflected the many changes that were occurring in American society.

African American–owned businesses. Successful Motown artists included the Supremes and the Temptations.

Perhaps the most dynamic artist of the era was James Brown. Performing a form of rhythm-and-blues music known as soul, Brown captivated audiences with his athletic, emotionally charged shows. Nicknamed the Godfather of Soul, Brown had started performing at the age of 12. He had his first hit record in 1956, with the song "Please Please Please."

Matching Brown in popularity and career length was Aretha Franklin, known as the Queen of Soul. In the late 1960s she scored a string of hits that included "Respect," "Chain of Fools," and "Think."

Woodstock

Rock music was the focal point of the Woodstock Music and Art Fair. The event marked both the height and the beginning of the end for the counterculture movement. In August 1969 some 400,000 young people descended on rural upstate New York for the three-day festival, closing the New York State Thruway in the process. Despite driving rain, knee-deep mud, and severe shortages of food and water, the concert remained a peaceful gathering. Listeners reveled in the music of rock's top performers, including Jimi Hendrix, Joan Baez, and Janis Joplin.

Woodstock was more than just a rock concert. It was the celebration of an era and marked the high point of the counterculture movement. However, the excitement of the Woodstock experience was short-lived. Four months later, the Rolling Stones held a free concert at Altamont Raceway near San Francisco. At the concert a security team made up of members of a motorcycle gang stabbed a young African American to death in full view of the stage. The event raised doubts about the idealistic spirit of the youth movement.

Woodstock. The 1969 Woodstock Music and Art Fair attracted hundreds of thousands of young Americans. *What do you think the picture on this poster symbolizes?*

✔ **READING CHECK:** How did changes in music reflect larger changes in society in the 1960s?

SECTION  REVIEW

Define and explain the significance of the following terms:
generation gap
counterculture
pop art
British invasion
Woodstock

Identify and explain the significance of the following individuals:
Mario Savio
Timothy Leary
Joan Baez
Bob Dylan
James Brown
Aretha Franklin

1. **Using Graphic Organizers** Copy the graphic organizer below. Use it to explain how other conflicts in society influenced protests on college campuses.

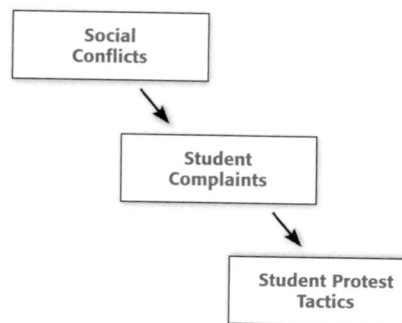

2. **Hypothesizing** How might the counterculture have been more effective in changing American society?
3. **Identifying Values** Why did a growing number of Americans question religion and traditional social values during the 1960s? How did this affect the arts?
4. **Analyzing** What do musical developments reveal about American culture during this period?

Critical Thinking

5. How did Woodstock illustrate the ideals of the counterculture?
   Consider:
   • the beliefs of the counterculture's followers
   • the role of rock music
   • the audience's behavior at Woodstock

CHAPTER 32

Review

Creating a Time Line

Copy the time line below onto a sheet of paper. Complete the time line by filling in the events and dates from the chapter that you think were most significant. Pick three events and explain why you think they were significant.

1960   **1965**   **1970**   **1975**

Writing a Summary

Using the Reading Checks as a guide, write an overview of the events in the chapter.

Identifying People and Ideas

Identify the following terms or individuals and explain their significance.

1. Betty Friedan
2. Equal Pay Act
3. César Chávez
4. Brown Berets
5. La Raza Unida Party
6. American Indian Movement
7. Maggie Kuhn
8. counterculture
9. Mario Savio
10. Woodstock

Understanding Main Ideas

SECTION 1

1. Why was the National Organization for Women founded?
2. Why did some women oppose the Equal Rights Amendment?

SECTION 2

3. How did the Delano grape strike come to symbolize the concerns of Mexican Americans throughout the United States?
4. Why did high school students in Los Angeles hold walkouts?

SECTION 3

5. Did the American Indian Movement achieve its goals? Explain your answer.

SECTION 4

6. What was the relationship between music and political protest?

Reviewing Themes

1. **Constitutional Heritage** When should the Constitution be amended? Explain your answer.
2. **Economic Development** Why did middle-class university students turn to political protest?
3. **Cultural Diversity** How did Americans use art, fashion, and music to question American values?

Thinking Critically

1. **Evaluating** What forms of protest proved most effective during the 1960s and 1970s?
2. **Identifying Cause and Effect** In what ways did the African American civil rights movement influence the protest methods of other groups in American society?
3. **Recognizing Point of View** Why might some Americans have been initially resistant to the notion of greater access for people with disabilities?
4. **Using Historical Imagination** Would American life be different today if the Equal Rights Amendment had been ratified? Explain your answer.
5. **Analyzing** What problems did Mexican American activists encounter as they tried to create national organizations?

Writing About History

Writing to Persuade Write a speech intended to persuade an audience to either support or oppose ratification of the Equal Rights Amendment. Use the graphic below to organize your thoughts.

Reasons to Support   ERA   Reasons to Oppose

Strategies for Success Review the **Strategies for Success** on *Evaluating Web Sites on the Internet.* Then use the computer system at your school or local public library to find a Web site on one of the following topics:

a. the history of the women's rights movement
b. the history of the United Farm Workers (UFW)
c. the history of rock music

Explore the Web site thoroughly and write a one-page report that evaluates its historical value and identifies any biases of the site.

Linking History and Geography

Study the map below. Use it to analyze the distribution of teenagers throughout the United States in 1970. Which region had the highest population of teenagers? Which region had the lowest? How might these population trends have affected the locations of youth movements?

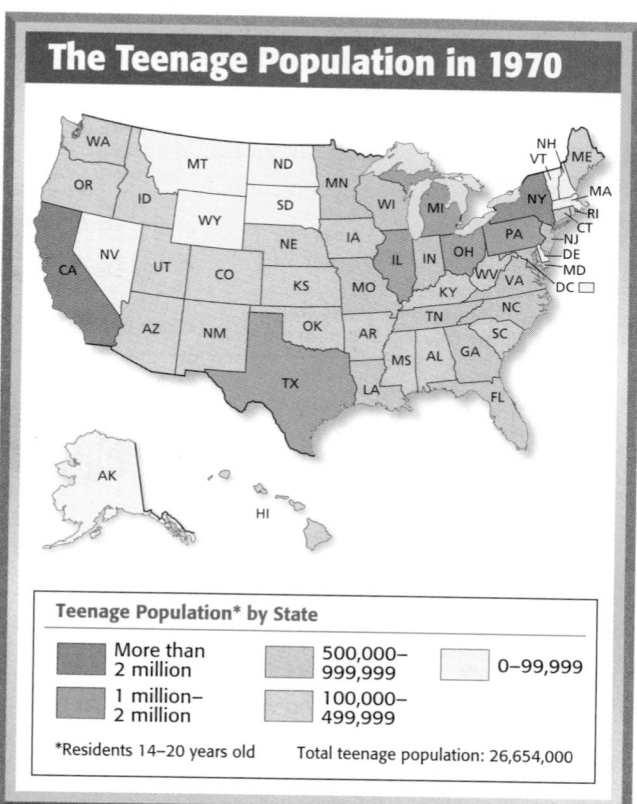

The Teenage Population in 1970

Teenage Population* by State

- More than 2 million
- 1 million– 2 million
- 500,000– 999,999
- 100,000– 499,999
- 0–99,999

*Residents 14–20 years old   Total teenage population: 26,654,000

 internet**connect**

TOPIC: César Chávez
GO TO: go.hrw.com
KEYWORD: SD1 Farm

Accessing the Internet through the HRW Web site, research César Chávez and the history of the United Farm Workers. Then create a mural that portrays events from Chávez's life and the struggles of the migrant workers he represented.

BUILDING YOUR PORTFOLIO

Complete one or all of the following activities independently or cooperatively.

1 Economic Development
Imagine that you are a union organizer working with migrant workers in California. **Create a flier** in which you explain why workers should go on strike. Explain how the union will help the striking workers.

2 Democratic Values
Imagine that you are a university professor writing a book on the civil rights movement, and that you have conducted an interview with an AIM member. **Write a brief summary** of the interview that explains the attitudes and hopes of the Red Power activist.

3 Cultural Diversity
Imagine that you are a reporter from a national music magazine who is assigned to write an article about the effect of the counterculture on music in the 1960s. **Write an illustrated article** that describes the musicians and the styles of music people are listening to.

America's Geography

Urban America

As more people moved to the cities and suburbs after World War II, metropolitan areas—large cities or groups of cities and their surrounding areas—were created. The city of Los Angeles is typical of a metroplex. In the 1920s most of the land inside the official city limits was not developed. As the city grew, it engulfed numerous surrounding areas as people increasingly moved outside the city and commuted to work.

Suburban growth.
Los Angeles was at the forefront of the creation of the suburban housing system. By the 1920s, as eastern cities grew more crowded, Los Angeles had built the nation's most extensive electric railway-car system to encourage people to live outside the city and commute. City boosters used this system and the area's geography to encourage migration. They noted the sunny climate and pleasant beaches nearby.

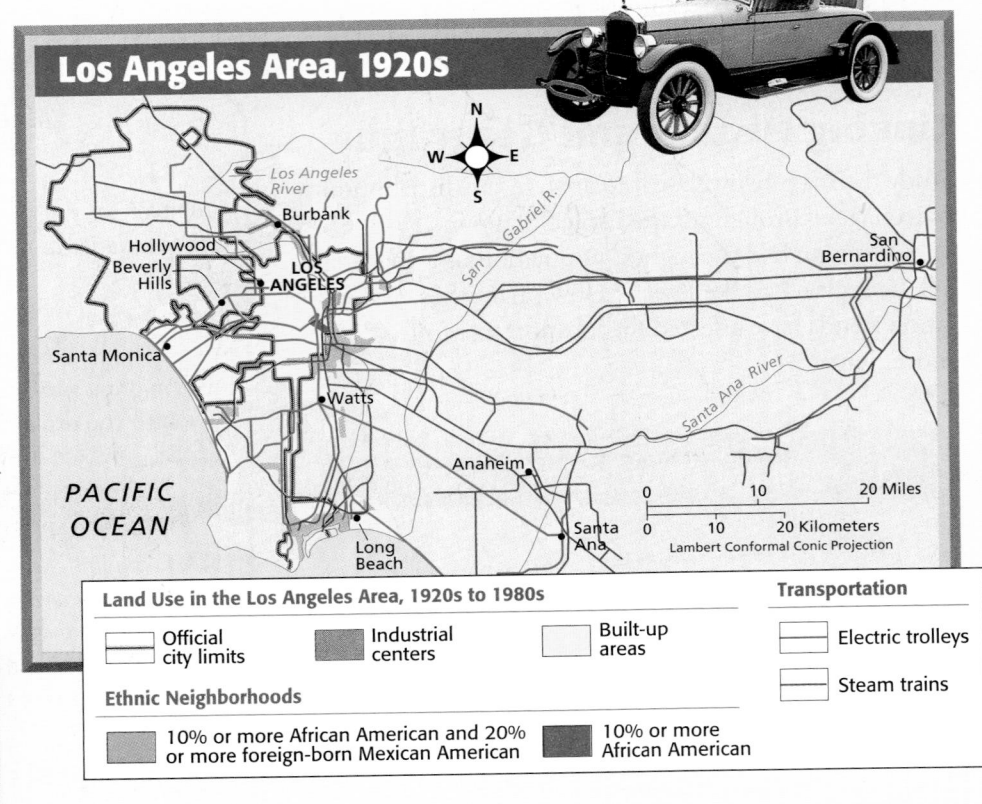

Los Angeles Area, 1920s

Los Angeles River
Burbank
Hollywood
Beverly Hills
LOS ANGELES
San Gabriel R.
San Bernardino
Santa Monica
Watts
Santa Ana River
Anaheim
PACIFIC OCEAN
Long Beach
Santa Ana

0   10   20 Miles
0   10   20 Kilometers
Lambert Conformal Conic Projection

Land Use in the Los Angeles Area, 1920s to 1980s

Official city limits	Industrial centers	Built-up areas

Ethnic Neighborhoods

10% or more African American and 20% or more foreign-born Mexican American

10% or more African American

Transportation

Electric trolleys

Steam trains

Filming an early Hollywood western

Hollywood. The geography of Los Angeles attracted many early filmmakers because of its dry climate and nearness to many different types of landscape, including the beaches, mountains, and desert.

GEOGRAPHY AND HISTORY Skills

MOVEMENT

1. If you had lived in Anaheim, California, in the 1920s and wanted to commute to downtown Los Angeles, what kind of transportation would you have taken?

2. If you were a Hollywood producer in the 1920s who wanted to film a scene at the beach, how far would you need to travel to reach the ocean?

974

Los Angeles Area, 1980s

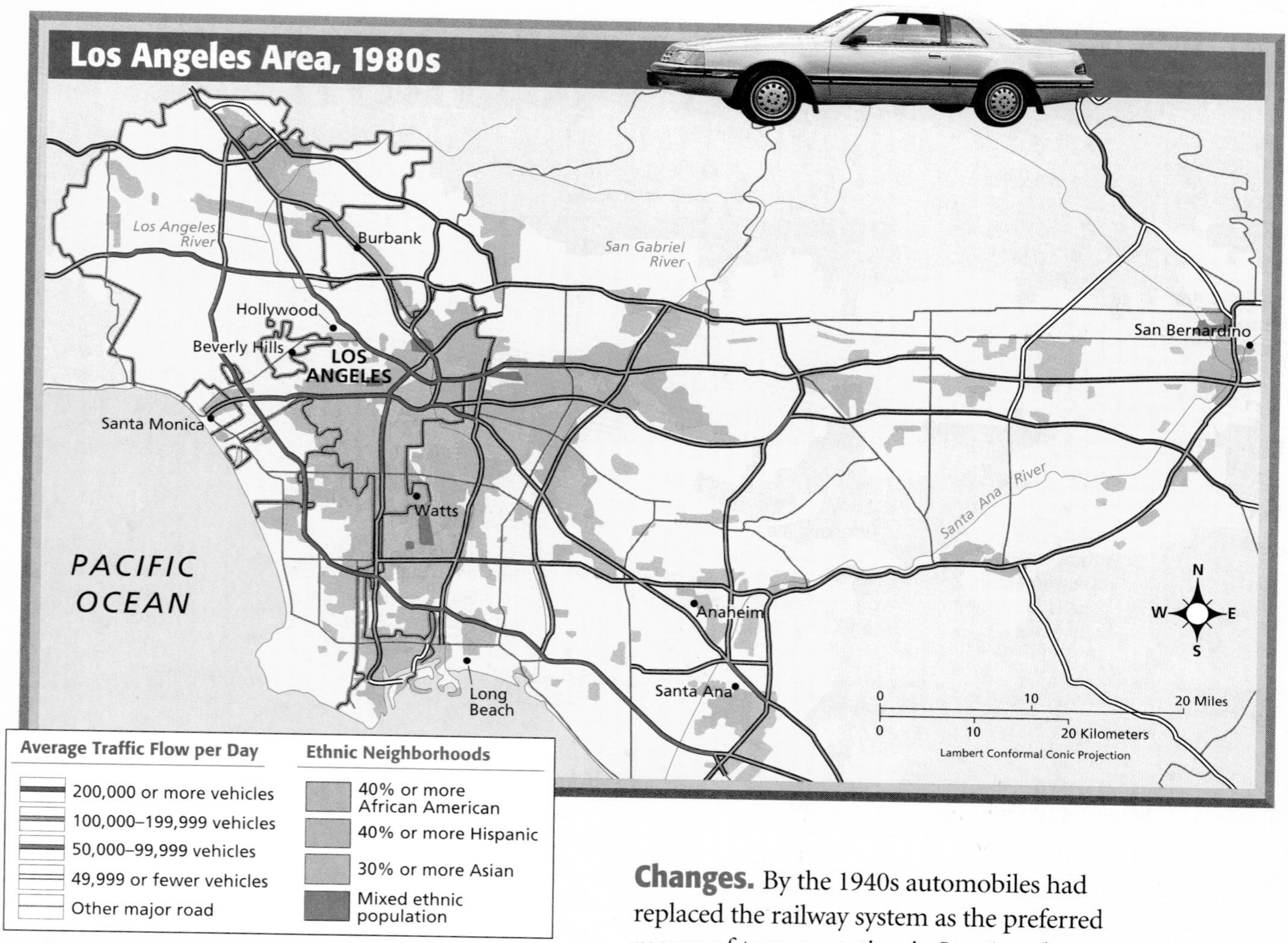

Burbank

Los Angeles River

San Gabriel River

Hollywood

Beverly Hills

LOS ANGELES

San Bernardino

Santa Monica

Watts

PACIFIC OCEAN

Santa Ana River

Anaheim

Long Beach

Santa Ana

0   10   20 Miles
0   10   20 Kilometers
Lambert Conformal Conic Projection

N
W ◆ E
S

Average Traffic Flow per Day

- 200,000 or more vehicles
- 100,000–199,999 vehicles
- 50,000–99,999 vehicles
- 49,999 or fewer vehicles
- Other major road

Ethnic Neighborhoods

- 40% or more African American
- 40% or more Hispanic
- 30% or more Asian
- Mixed ethnic population

Changes. By the 1940s automobiles had replaced the railway system as the preferred means of transportation in Los Angeles. Wartime employment caused the city to grow rapidly. This growth was encouraged by the creation of a huge new freeway system.

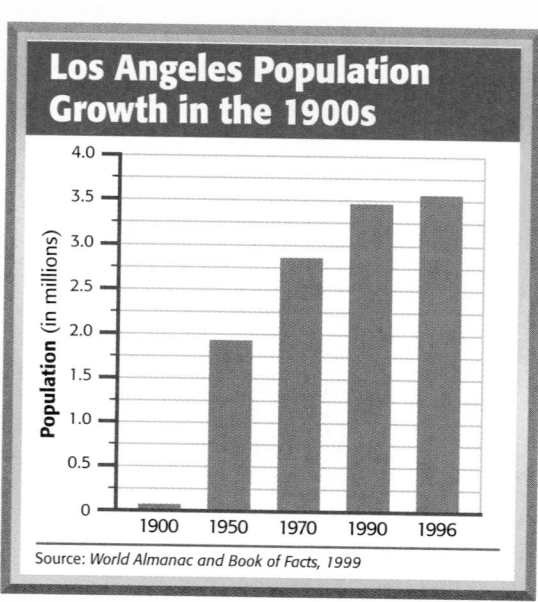

Los Angeles Population Growth in the 1900s

Population (in millions)

4.0
3.5
3.0
2.5
2.0
1.5
1.0
0.5
0

1900   1950   1970   1990   1996

Source: *World Almanac and Book of Facts, 1999*

GEOGRAPHY AND HISTORY Skills

MOVEMENT

1. By how much did the population of Los Angeles increase between 1900 and 1950?

2. How many miles of freeways had an average traffic flow of at least 200,000 vehicles per day?

1954–1975
War in Vietnam

An early microchip

Disneyland entrance ticket

A DAY AT
Disneyland
CALIFORNIA
Walt Disney's MAGIC KINGDOM A107114
ADULT $2.50

**1955
Daily Life**
The Disneyland amusement park opens in Anaheim, California.

**1959
Science and Technology**
Working independently, Jack Kilby and Robert Noyce revolutionize electronic technology with the invention of the microchip.

**1960
The Arts**
Alabama writer Harper Lee publishes *To Kill a Mockingbird*.

**1960
Science and Technology**
The United States launches the world's first communications satellite, *Echo I*.

**1963
World Events**
Military officers overthrow the South Vietnamese government.

**1963
Science and Technology**
The Oyster Creek nuclear power plant in New Jersey is the first commercial nuclear reactor.

**1963
The Arts**
The Beatles have their first hit song, "I Want to Hold Your Hand."

1954   **1957**   **1960**   **1963**

**1954
Science and Technology**
The first nuclear-powered submarine, the *Nautilus*, is launched at Groton, Connecticut.

**1957
Business and Finance**
The Treaty of Rome establishes the European Economic Community, removing trade barriers among Belgium, France, Italy, Luxembourg, the Netherlands, and West Germany.

**1959
World Events**
Cuban dictator Fulgencio Batista is overthrown as rebel leader Fidel Castro seizes power.

The USS Nautilus

Fulgencio Batista

Before You Read

Build on What You Know

*A*fter World War II the United States took a stand opposing the spread of communism anywhere in the world. In the early 1950s U.S. troops fought against communist forces in Korea. In this chapter you will learn how the United States became involved in a similar war in Vietnam, which had won its independence from the French in 1954. Eventually more than 2 million Americans served in the Vietnam War. The conflict, which lasted more than a decade, left deep scars on both Vietnam and the United States.

Robert Lowell

The Monterey Pop Festival

The Kent State shooting

1965
The Arts
Poet Robert Lowell speaks out against President Johnson's Vietnam policy at a White House party.

1967
The Arts
The first large rock music gathering, the Monterey Pop Festival, is held in Monterey, California.

1970
Daily Life
At an antiwar rally at Kent State University in Ohio, National Guardsmen open fire, killing four people and wounding nine.

1975
World Events
North Vietnamese forces capture the South Vietnamese capital of Saigon.

1966   **1969**   **1972**   **1975**

1967
Daily Life
Boxer Muhammad Ali is sentenced to five years in prison for refusing to report for military duty.

1968
World Events
Soviet troops invade Czechoslovakia to crush a reform movement.

1971
World Events
General Idi Amin seizes power in Uganda.

1975
Science and Technology
President Gerald Ford signs the Metric Conversion Act to move the United States to the metric system.

Muhammad Ali

Soviet tanks in Prague, Czechoslovakia

Think About Themes

Themes Journal

*Decide whether you **agree** or **disagree** with the following statements. Note why in your journal.*

Global Relations Under certain circumstances one nation has the right to intervene in the affairs of another.

Constitutional Heritage The system of checks and balances will be damaged if one branch of government becomes too strong.

Democratic Values In a democracy there should be no limits to a person's right to protest government actions.

SECTION 1

Background to Conflict

OBJECTIVES

Read to understand:

1. why China and France wanted to control Vietnam
2. why the United States refused to support Vietnamese independence in the 1940s and 1950s
3. why President Kennedy increased U.S. involvement in Vietnam

KEY TERMS

Vietminh
domino theory
Vietcong

KEY PEOPLE

Le Loi
Ho Chi Minh
Ngo Dinh Diem

KEY PLACES

Red River Delta
Mekong Delta
French Indochina
Hanoi
Dien Bien Phu
Saigon

 **EYEWITNESSES TO History**

❝ I want to rail against the wind and the tide, kill the whales in the sea, sweep the whole country to save the people from slavery, and I refuse to be abused. ❞
—Trieu Au

A Vietnamese print showing Trieu Au

Trieu Au's defiant words inspired the Vietnamese people to revolt against China in A.D. 248. Although the rebellion she led was defeated, the cause Trieu Au fought for was not. For centuries invaders desired the fertile river deltas and coastal lowlands of Vietnam. The people of Vietnam were not easily conquered, however. For more than 1,000 years they fought for their freedom and independence.

Vietnam

The easternmost country of Southeast Asia, Vietnam covers about 130,000 square miles of mostly hills and dense forests. It is bordered on the north by China and on the west by Laos and Cambodia. Vietnam's population is centered around the Red River Delta in the far north and the Mekong (MAY-kawng) Delta in the south.

Chinese occupation. The moist, tropical climate of the deltas and coastal lowlands allows Vietnamese farmers to grow at least two crops of rice a year. It was this agricultural abundance that tempted China to invade the Red River Delta about 200 B.C. For more than a thousand years, the Chinese struggled to maintain control over northern and central Vietnam. The Vietnamese resisted and finally won limited independence from China in A.D. 939.

In the 1400s China tried to reassert control over Vietnam. A Vietnamese military leader named Le Loi used guerrilla warfare to defeat the Chinese invaders. Le Loi's rebels worked as peasants by day and took up arms to attack the Chinese by night. By 1428 the rebels had driven the Chinese from the country and won independence for Vietnam. Le Loi became the new emperor.

French colonization. Vietnam again lost its independence during a surge of European imperialism in the mid-1800s. This time the invaders were French. Despite the stubborn resistance of the Vietnamese, French military power ultimately won out. In 1883 the Vietnamese were forced to grant France complete control of the country. France later combined Vietnam with Laos and Cambodia to form French Indochina, one of its richest colonial possessions.

✔ **READING CHECK:** Why did China and France want to control Vietnam?

Vietnam's fertile rice fields produce an abundant food source.

Vietnamese Independence

Like the Chinese, the French gained control of the land but not the hearts of the Vietnamese. Nationalist feelings remained strong. Foremost among the nationalists was Nguyen That Thanh (NY-uhn TAHT TAHN). A world wanderer and man of many names, he is best known as Ho Chi Minh (HOH CHEE MIN)—"He Who Enlightens."

During the 1920s and 1930s Ho lived in China and the Soviet Union while working for Vietnamese independence. He became committed to the ideals of communism. In 1940 the Japanese army occupied all of French Indochina, the Philippines, Malaya, and Indonesia. Ho's chance had come.

Ho Chi Minh led the Vietnamese fight for independence.

France and the Vietminh go to war. After 30 years away from home, Ho secretly returned to Vietnam in early 1941. He organized a resistance movement called the League for the Independence of Vietnam, or **Vietminh** (vee-ET-MIN). When the Japanese withdrew from Indochina after surrendering to the Allied Powers in August 1945, the Vietminh declared independence. In Hanoi on September 2, 1945, more than 500,000 people gathered at an independence celebration to hear Ho speak. In an effort to gain U.S. support, Ho echoed the language of the U.S. Declaration of Independence in his speech.

U.S. policy toward Vietnam was soon put to the test. By 1946 the French and the Vietnamese were once again locked in battle. President Truman ignored Ho's pleas for assistance and threw U.S. support behind France. Truman viewed France as a vital ally in the struggle against the spread of communism in postwar Europe. He also was unwilling to back the Vietminh because of Ho's Communist Party connections.

Presidential advisers feared that communism would engulf Asia. This fear was reinforced in 1949 when Mao Zedong's Communists took over China—Asia's most populous country and a former U.S. ally. By 1950 the United States was caught up in a bloody ground war, trying to turn back communist North Korea's invasion of South Korea. Meanwhile, Communist-led nationalist revolts rocked Indonesia, the Philippines, and Malaya.

These developments led U.S. policy-makers to vow to hold the line against communism in East Asia. Truman's successor, Dwight D. Eisenhower, continued this policy. Eisenhower warned that if

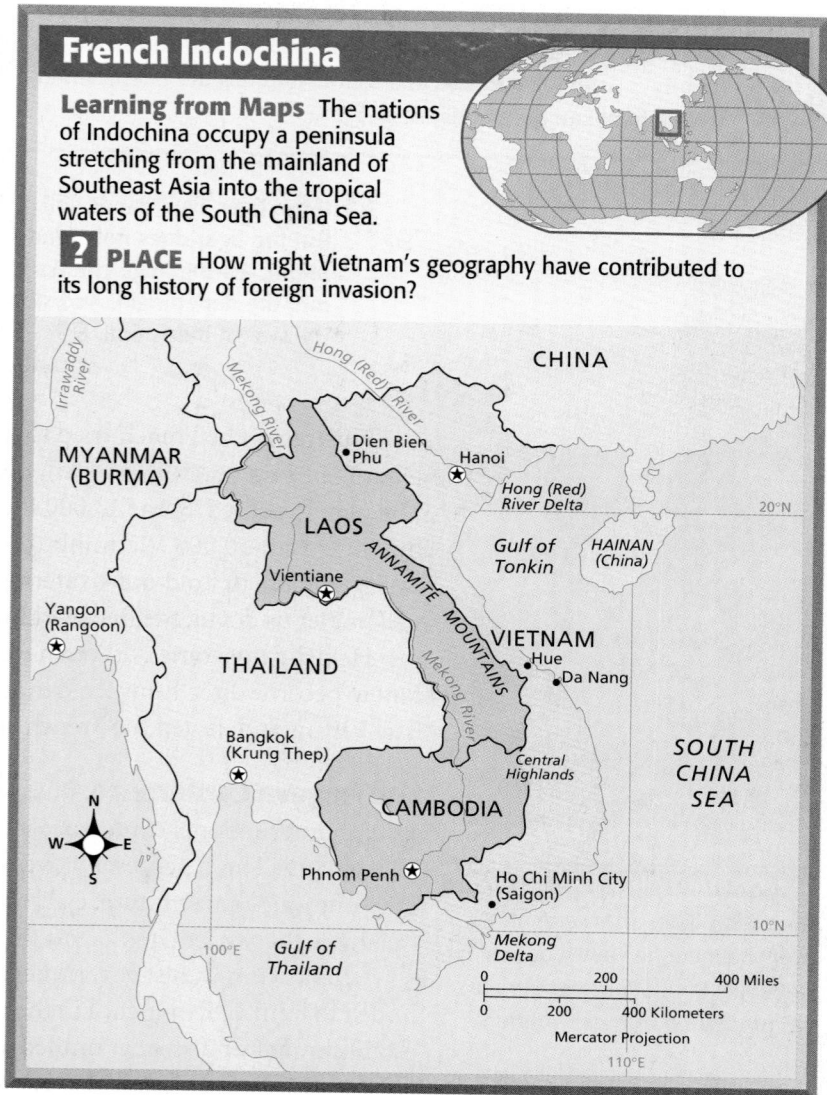

French Indochina

Learning from Maps The nations of Indochina occupy a peninsula stretching from the mainland of Southeast Asia into the tropical waters of the South China Sea.

? PLACE How might Vietnam's geography have contributed to its long history of foreign invasion?

THROUGH OTHERS' EYES

Asian View of French Colonization

In the 1880s the Vietnamese were battling against French colonization of their country. Ham Nghi, the 13-year-old emperor of Vietnam, had joined the rebellion against the French. In 1885, while fleeing from French Forces, Ham Nghi issued a royal order to the Vietnamese people. He called upon "the rich to give their wealth, the mighty their strength, and the poor their limbs so that the country might be rescued from the invader." Several years later Phan Chu Trinh, a supporter of Ham Nghi, returned to Vietnam. In an open letter to the French government, Phan Chu attacked France's colonial practices in Vietnam. He criticized France's refusal to grant to the Vietnamese people the same basic human rights it reserved for its citizens.

66 In your papers, in your books, in your plans, in your private conversations, there is displayed in all its intensity the profound contempt with which you overwhelm us. In your eyes, we are savages, dumb brutes, incapable of distinguishing between good and evil. Some of us, employed by you, still preserve a certain dignity . . . and it is sadness and shame that fills our hearts when we contemplate our humiliation. 99

Vietnam fell to communism the rest of Southeast Asia would soon follow. "You have a row of dominoes set up. You knock over the first one, and what will happen to the last one is a certainty that it will go over very quickly." This idea came to be called the **domino theory**. By 1954 the United States was paying much of the cost of France's war effort. Even with massive aid, however, the French suffered defeat after defeat.

Money and military equipment were of limited use against Vietminh guerrilla tactics. The Vietminh chose when and where to attack, struck without warning, and then disappeared into the jungle. In 1946 Ho Chi Minh had expressed to an American journalist his people's determination to succeed. Ho characterized the fight as "a war between an elephant"—the French—"and a tiger"—the Vietnamese.

66 If the tiger ever stands still, the elephant will crush him with his mighty tusks. But the tiger does not stand still. . . . He will leap upon the back of the elephant, tearing huge chunks from his hide, and then the tiger will leap back into the dark jungle. And slowly the elephant will bleed to death. That will be the war of Indochina. 99

From *America Inside Out* by David Schoenbrun © 1984 by permission of McGraw-Hill Companies

Frustrated, the French tried to lure the Vietminh into a conventional battle at Dien Bien Phu (DYEN BYEN FOO), deep within Vietminh-held northern Vietnam. The plan backfired. Some 13,000 French soldiers soon found themselves encircled by more than 50,000 Vietminh troops. The French commander urged his war-weary soldiers to hold out—offering them the hope of a rescue. "The Americans will not let us down; the free world will not let us down."

Help did not come. Although willing to commit money, Eisenhower was reluctant to become directly involved in another Asian war so soon after the Korean War. The Vietminh defeated the French and on May 7, 1954, forced their surrender.

The Geneva Conference. Just one day after the French surrender at Dien Bien Phu, an international conference to settle the Indochina conflict began in Geneva, Switzerland. There, representatives of the French and the Vietminh attempted to map out Indochina's future. Cambodia, Great Britain, Laos, the People's Republic of China, the Soviet Union, and the United States joined the discussions.

China's communist government had been aiding the Vietminh since 1950 and hoped to limit U.S. influence in the region. The Chinese also wished to prevent the establishment of a strong, unified Vietnam. The Americans, meanwhile, did not want to see Vietnam handed over completely to the Communists.

INTERPRETING THE VISUAL RECORD

Dien Bien Phu. The Vietminh overwhelmed the French base at Dien Bien Phu. *What appears to be happening to these soldiers?*

A cease-fire was agreed to, but no definite political settlement was achieved. Vietnam was temporarily divided at the 17th parallel. Vietminh forces withdrew to the north, where they held undisputed power. South of the line, the French regained control. General elections to reunify the country were scheduled for July 1956. Fearing that the Communists would win a nationwide election, the United States refused to support the agreement.

✔ **READING CHECK:** Why did the United States refuse to support Vietnamese independence in the 1940s and 1950s?

Victory. Vietminh soldiers march in a parade in Hanoi to celebrate their victory over the French. *Do these women look like combat troops? Explain your answer.*

The Rule of Ngo Dinh Diem

President Eisenhower hoped that southern Vietnam, at least, might be kept non-communist. He pinned his hopes on Ngo Dinh Diem (NGOH DIN de-EM), a former government official under the French. U.S. officials hoped that Diem's nationalist beliefs would make him an acceptable leader to the people of South Vietnam.

Diem takes power in the south. Ngo Dinh Diem was strongly anticommunist. He had spent several years in the United States, where his political views attracted powerful backers. In 1955 Diem became president of the newly established Republic of Vietnam, or South Vietnam, in an election that was obviously rigged. In Saigon, for example, Diem received more than 605,000 votes from just 450,000 registered voters. Diem knew that he had no chance of winning a nationwide election against Ho Chi Minh. Therefore, when the July 1956 date set by the Geneva Conference rolled around, Diem refused to call an election in the south.

Diem, a Roman Catholic, was unpopular from the start. The large Buddhist population resented the favoritism he showed toward Catholics. Peasants disliked his land policies, which favored wealthy landholders. Almost everyone objected to power being kept solely in the grip of Diem's family. Above all, people feared his ruthless efforts to root out his political enemies. Diem's hated security forces routinely tortured and imprisoned opponents.

By the late 1950s armed revolution had erupted in the south. In 1959 military assistance began flowing from the north to the Vietminh who had stayed in the south. In 1960 the southern Vietminh formed the National Liberation Front (NLF). The NLF's main goal was the overthrow of Diem's government. Members of this rebel force were called **Vietcong**, for Vietnamese Communists, by their opponents. Not all NLF supporters, however, were Communists.

Many peasants joined the ranks of the NLF. Some did so because of government cruelty. Others joined out of fear of the NLF. Like Diem's forces, the NLF used terrorist tactics, assassinating hundreds of government officials. Soon much of the countryside was under Vietcong control.

This North Vietnamese poster reads "Imperial America is the enemy with whom we cannot live under the same sky."

Strategies for Success

Determining Good Sources

Interpreting and evaluating historical sources are essential skills for learning about the past. This is particularly true in choosing sources for a research paper or project. To determine whether to use a source, one must assess its reliability and usefulness on a variety of levels. The quality of its reasoning, the accuracy of its information, the biases it displays, and its relevance to the topic at hand are all important factors to consider.

How to Determine a Good Source

1. **Identify the type, title, and creator of the source.** First, identify the type of source you will be evaluating and determine whether its title displays any obvious biases toward its subject. Then, if possible, find out about the historical background of the source's creator and the intended audience of the source.
2. **Examine the source carefully.** Study the source carefully, taking note of its main ideas and supporting details.
3. **Evaluate the source's reasoning.** Once you have examined the source thoroughly, assess the quality of its reasoning. Ask yourself the following questions: Are the arguments in this source logical? Are the cause-and-effect relationships fully proven? Do the conclusions follow from the information provided?
4. **Assess the accuracy and fairness of the source.** As you evaluate the source's reasoning, identify any factual inaccuracies that it contains and assess any biases that it displays in its selection, presentation, and discussion of historical evidence. Make sure to note any instances in which the source presents a one-sided view of a person, event, or topic.
5. **Determine the relevance and usefulness of the source.** After you have evaluated the fundamental soundness of the source, determine the extent to which it relates to the specific topic you are researching. Then decide if and how the source should contribute to your research project and use it accordingly.

Applying the Strategy

After you have read this chapter, use your school or local public library to conduct research on the Vietnam War. Use the following sources:
a. an encyclopedia article
b. two or more books
c. a videotape of a film or television documentary
d. a CD–ROM

Then examine each source and decide if and how you would use it in a research paper that focuses on the early role of the United States in Vietnam.

Practicing the Strategy

Use your sources to answer the following questions.
1. What is the title of each source? Who produced each source, and when?
2. Is the information in each source accurate? What biases does each source display?
3. How would you use each source in a research paper?

U.S. troops arrive in Vietnam.

U.S. involvement deepens. John F. Kennedy, who became president in 1961, fully agreed with the domino theory. He also was eager to improve the U.S. image in the world. This image had been tarnished early in his presidency by the failed Bay of Pigs invasion and the building of the Berlin Wall. Aiding South Vietnam provided the United States with a chance to assert its power.

In December 1960 there were some 900 U.S. military advisers in South Vietnam training Diem's Army of the Republic of Vietnam (ARVN). During the next few years, Kennedy increased that number to more than 16,000. As Vietcong attacks mounted, Kennedy authorized U.S. forces to engage in direct combat. As a result, the number of Americans killed or wounded climbed from 14 in 1961 to nearly 500 in 1963.

Diem's overthrow. Political conflict also increased. South Vietnam's Buddhist leaders had begun to openly oppose Diem's rule. Diem was waging a brutal campaign to control the Buddhists. Hundreds of Buddhists were arrested, and many were killed in the crackdown. In response, several Buddhist monks publicly set themselves on fire. These gruesome protests shocked Americans. U.S. officials in Saigon threatened to withdraw support for Diem unless he ended the campaign.

Henry Cabot Lodge, the U.S. ambassador to South Vietnam, met with Diem in August 1963. Lodge later recalled that Diem "absolutely refused to discuss any of the topics that President Kennedy had instructed me to raise." U.S. leaders began to quietly encourage a group of South Vietnamese army officers plotting Diem's overthrow. In an August 29 cable, Lodge described the situation.

Henry Cabot Lodge meets with Ngo Dinh Diem in Saigon.

> 66 We are launched on a course from which there is no respectable turning back: the overthrow of the Diem government. There is no turning back because U.S. prestige is already publicly committed to this end in large measure, and will become more so as the facts leak out. In a more fundamental sense, there is no turning back because there is no possibility, in my view, that the war can be won under a Diem administration. 99

The plotters struck in early November 1963, murdering both Diem and his brother. Diem's assassination upset U.S. advisers, who had been prepared to fly Diem out of the country.

Diem's overthrow did nothing to ease Kennedy's growing concern over U.S. involvement in Vietnam. In an interview shortly before Diem's fall, Kennedy had said of the South Vietnamese: "In the final analysis it is their war. They are the ones who have to win or lose it." It is unknown how Kennedy might have handled the situation. Three weeks after Diem's murder, Kennedy himself was assassinated in Dallas.

✔ **READING CHECK:** Why did President Kennedy increase U.S. involvement in Vietnam?

SECTION 1 REVIEW

Define and explain the significance of the following terms:
Vietminh
domino theory
Vietcong

Identify and explain the significance of the following individuals:
Le Loi
Ho Chi Minh
Ngo Dinh Diem

Locate and explain the importance of the following places:
Red River Delta
Mekong Delta
French Indochina
Hanoi
Dien Bien Phu
Saigon

1. **Using Graphic Organizers** Copy the graphic organizer below. Use it to list the steps that led to U.S. troops being sent to Vietnam.

1428: Vietnam gains its independence.

1962: U.S. troops arrive in Vietnam.

2. **Identifying Cause and Effect** Why did President Truman refuse Ho Chi Minh's requests for help against the French?

3. **Understanding Geography: Place** What attracted the Chinese and the French to Vietnam?

4. **Using Historical Imagination** Imagine that you are an adviser to President Eisenhower in 1959. On the basis of what you would know at the time, prepare a statement outlining the benefits and drawbacks of U.S. involvement in Vietnam. Then write a one-paragraph policy recommendation.

Critical Thinking

5. Do you agree with President Kennedy's decision to increase U.S. involvement in Vietnam? Explain your answer.
Consider:
• U.S. foreign policy during the early 1960s
• the goals and actions of the North Vietnamese
• the strength of the Diem government

SECTION ② The War Escalates

EYEWITNESSES TO History

66 *Renewed hostile actions against United States ships on the high seas in the Gulf of Tonkin have today required me to order the military forces of the United States to take action in reply. The initial attack on the destroyer Maddox, on August 2, was repeated today by a number of hostile vessels attacking two U.S. destroyers with torpedoes. . . . We believe at least two of the attacking boats were sunk. There were no U.S. losses. . . . But repeated acts of violence against the Armed Forces of the United States must be met not only with alert defense, but with positive reply. That reply is being given as I speak to you tonight. Air action is now in execution against gunboats and certain supporting facilities in North Vietnam which have been used in these hostile operations.* 99

—**Lyndon Johnson**

The Gulf of Tonkin incident drew the United States deeper into the Vietnam War.

Near midnight on August 4, 1964, President Lyndon Johnson appeared on national television. His announcement to the American people that night marked a new stage in U.S. involvement in the war in Vietnam.

The Tonkin Gulf Resolution

In 1963 Secretary of Defense Robert S. McNamara had advised President Johnson that he would have to increase the U.S. military commitment to South Vietnam to prevent a Communist victory. Before increasing the U.S. commitment, Johnson needed to get congressional backing. The events in the Gulf of Tonkin gave him the opportunity. Johnson asked Congress to authorize the use of military force "to prevent further aggression." In response, both houses of Congress overwhelmingly passed the **Tonkin Gulf Resolution**. This gave the president authority to take "all necessary measures to repel any armed attack against forces of the United States."

Johnson claimed that the attacks in the Gulf of Tonkin were unprovoked. In reality, however, the U.S. destroyer *Maddox* had been spying in support of South Vietnamese raids against North Vietnam and had fired first. The second attack, moreover, probably never occurred. Some U.S. sailors apparently misinterpreted interference on their radar and sonar as enemy ships and torpedoes. Nonetheless, Johnson and his advisers got what they wanted: authority to expand the war.

Wayne Morse of Oregon was one of just two senators who voted against the Tonkin Gulf Resolution. He warned, "I believe that history will record we have made a great mistake. . . . We are in effect giving the President war-making powers in the absence of a declaration of war." In other words, by passing the resolution, Congress had essentially given up its constitutional power to declare war.

✔ **READING CHECK:** What constitutional issue did the Tonkin Gulf Resolution raise?

U.S. Forces in Vietnam

President Johnson soon called for an **escalation**, or buildup, of U.S. military forces in Vietnam. He ordered the Selective Service, the agency charged with carrying out the military draft, to begin calling up young men to serve in the armed forces. In April 1965 the Selective Service notified 13,700 draftees.

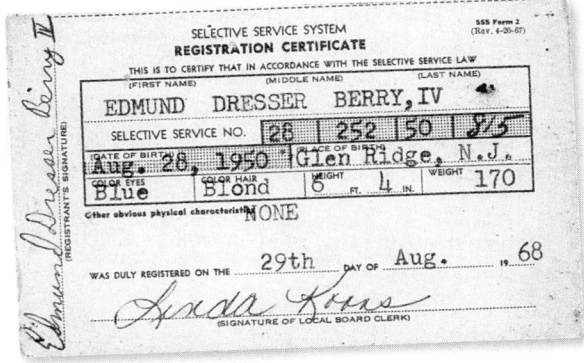

During the Vietnam War millions of American men received draft registration certificates like this one.

The troops. During the war more than 2 million Americans served in Vietnam. In the beginning most were professional soldiers who were already enlisted in the armed forces. As the demand for troops grew, however, more and more draftees were shipped to Vietnam. The average U.S. soldier in Vietnam was younger, poorer, and less educated than those who had served in World War II or in the Korean War.

One out of four young men who registered for the draft was excused from service for health reasons. Another 30 percent received non-health-related exemptions or deferments—postponements of service—most often for college enrollment. Mainly because of college deferments, young men from higher-income families were the least likely to be drafted. As a result, poor Americans served in numbers far greater than their proportion in the general population.

African Americans and Hispanics served in combat in very high numbers, particularly during the early years of the war. Many served in the most dangerous ground units. As a result, they experienced very high casualty rates. In 1965, for example, African Americans accounted for almost 24 percent of all battle deaths, even though they made up just 11 percent of the U.S. population.

The most vivid images of the war show soldiers facing the hardships and terrors of battle. Some confronted the enemy in well-defined battles in the highlands. Others cut their way through the jungle, where they heard but seldom saw the enemy. Still others waded through rice paddies and searched rural villages for guerrillas. Most Americans who went to Vietnam, however, served in support positions such as administration, communications, engineering, medical care, and supply and transportation. They were hardly safe, however. Enemy rockets and mortars could—and did—strike anywhere.

Some 10,000 servicewomen filled noncombat positions in Vietnam, mostly as nurses. Although they did not carry guns into battle, they faced the horrors of combat on a daily basis. Edie Meeks described the experience of working as a nurse at a field hospital.

Nurses. First Lieutenant Elaine Niggemann served at the 24th EVAC Hospital. *What is the lieutenant doing?*

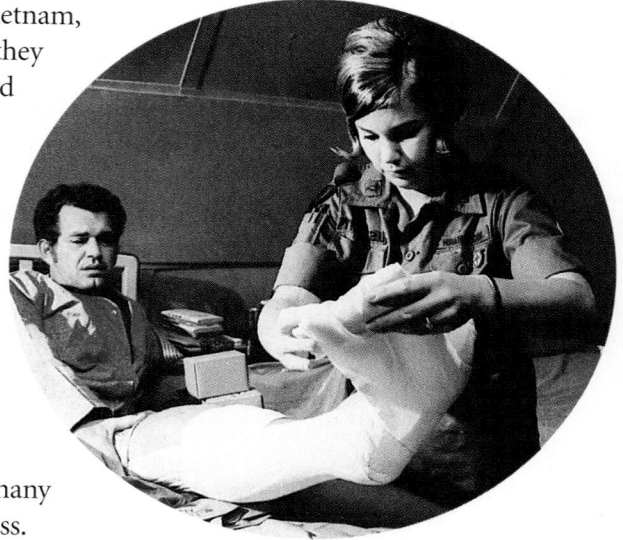

66 We really saw the worst of it, because the nurses never saw any of the victories. If the Army took a hill, we saw what was left over. I remember one boy who was brought in missing two legs and an arm, and his eyes were bandaged. A general came in later and pinned a Purple Heart on the boy's hospital gown, and the horror of it all was so amazing that it just took my breath away. You thought, was this supposed to be an even trade? 99

Another 20,000 to 45,000 women worked in civilian capacities, many as volunteers for humanitarian organizations such as the Red Cross.

The Vietnam Conflict, 1954–1975

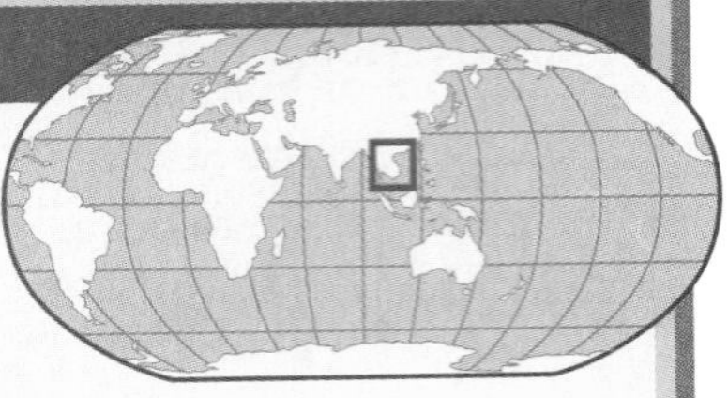

Learning from Maps U.S. efforts to destroy the Ho Chi Minh trail caused the war to spill over into neighboring Laos and Cambodia.

? **PLACE** How did the geography of Vietnam help make the Ho Chi Minh Trail an effective weapon against U.S. and ARVN forces?

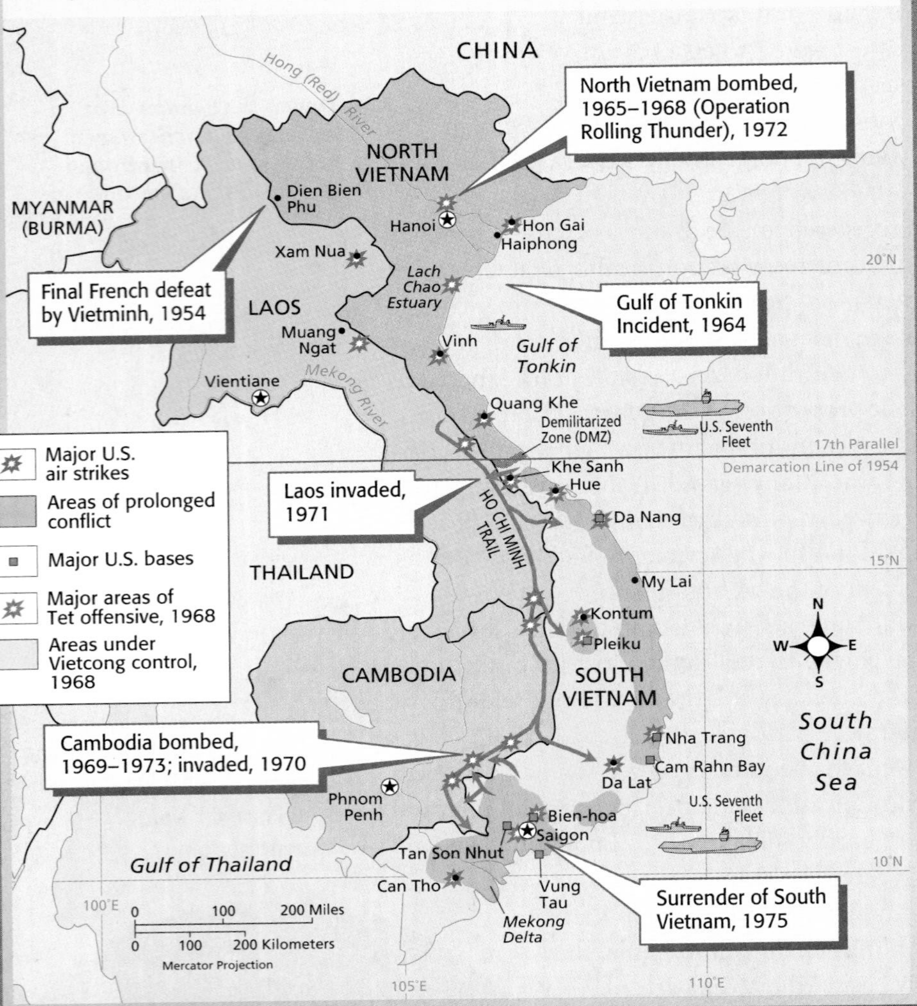

CHINA

Hong (Red) River

NORTH VIETNAM

MYANMAR (BURMA)

Dien Bien Phu

Hanoi

Hon Gai
Haiphong

Xam Nua

Lach Chao Estuary

20°N

North Vietnam bombed, 1965–1968 (Operation Rolling Thunder), 1972

Final French defeat by Vietminh, 1954

LAOS

Muang Ngat

Vientiane

Mekong River

Vinh

Gulf of Tonkin

Gulf of Tonkin Incident, 1964

Quang Khe
Demilitarized Zone (DMZ)

U.S. Seventh Fleet

17th Parallel

Demarcation Line of 1954

Khe Sanh
Hue

Laos invaded, 1971

HO CHI MINH TRAIL

THAILAND

Da Nang

15°N

My Lai

Kontum

Pleiku

CAMBODIA

SOUTH VIETNAM

South China Sea

Nha Trang

Cam Rahn Bay

Da Lat

Cambodia bombed, 1969–1973; invaded, 1970

Phnom Penh

U.S. Seventh Fleet

Bien-hoa
Saigon

Tan Son Nhut

Gulf of Thailand

Can Tho

Vung Tau

Mekong Delta

Surrender of South Vietnam, 1975

10°N

100°E   0   100   200 Miles

0   100   200 Kilometers

Mercator Projection

105°E   110°E

N W E S

Legend:
- ✺ Major U.S. air strikes
- Areas of prolonged conflict
- ▫ Major U.S. bases
- ✺ Major areas of Tet offensive, 1968
- Areas under Vietcong control, 1968

The air war. President Johnson hoped that air power could secure a quick victory. In March 1965 he launched **Operation Rolling Thunder**, a bombing campaign against military targets in the North. The goal was to weaken the enemy's will to fight. Johnson also wanted to assure the South Vietnamese of the U.S. commitment to them.

A key target of the bombing was the **Ho Chi Minh Trail**—a network of jungle paths. The North Vietnamese used the Ho Chi Minh Trail to bring weapons and supplies into South Vietnam. Roads and bridges along the trail, parts of which snaked through neighboring Cambodia and Laos, were bombed repeatedly. The Vietcong, however, quickly repaired them or managed without them. They also built many facilities underground to protect against bombing. Some 300,000 people worked full-time to maintain the Ho Chi Minh Trail.

When the bombing did not bring about North Vietnam's collapse, Johnson increased its intensity. By 1967, U.S. aircraft were dropping a daily average of 800 tons of bombs on North Vietnam. Repeated increases in bombing failed to produce the desired results. Frustrated, President Johnson broadened the air war to include strikes against areas of bordering Laos and much of South Vietnam.

U.S. forces used a variety of deadly weapons. Napalm, a jellied gasoline mixture, was used in firebombs. "Cluster bombs" sprayed razor-sharp metal fragments when they exploded. U.S. planes sprayed **defoliants**—chemicals that strip the land of vegetation—over thousands of acres. The goal of the spraying was to expose jungle supply routes and enemy hiding places. They also wanted to destroy the Vietcong food supply. The most widely used of these chemicals was Agent Orange.

The defoliant Agent Orange proved harmful to humans as well as plants.

AGENT ORANGE KILLS
A.O.V.I.

The ground war. Physician Ton That Tung recalled that the North Vietnamese clearly understood the goal of the air war. "The Americans thought that the more bombs they dropped, the quicker we would fall to our knees and surrender." Rather than surrender, North Vietnam sent more troops and supplies south.

The bombing led many South Vietnamese to join the Vietcong. Soon the opposition forces included more South Vietnamese than North Vietnamese. The United States countered by launching a ground war. Between 1965 and the end of 1967, the number of U.S. troops in Vietnam grew from about 185,000 to some 486,000.

Sheer numbers were not enough to defeat an enemy who seemed to be everywhere. Aided by regulars of the North Vietnamese Army, the Vietcong struck at U.S. patrols or government-held villages and then melted back into the jungle. Vietnamese peasants who appeared peaceful by day sided with the Vietcong at night. U.S. forces conducted thousands of **search-and-destroy missions** that attempted to drive the Vietcong from their hideouts. Ground patrols first located the enemy and then called in air support to kill them. Once an area was "cleared," the patrols moved on in search of more Vietcong. Snipers and booby traps made these missions extremely dangerous and frustrating. Making matters worse, villages seldom remained cleared of the Vietcong.

INTERPRETING THE VISUAL RECORD
Booby traps. This soldier is exploring a tunnel used by the Vietcong. *How are this soldier's actions putting him at risk?*

To provide security in rural areas, U.S. forces began a program of **pacification**. When security forces were not enough they moved the residents to secure locations and then burned the villages. In such warfare, progress could not be shown on a map. Instead, the daily body count of enemy dead became the sole measure of success—and a questionable measure at that. The U.S. military regularly guessed at or inflated the numbers by counting all Vietnamese dead as the enemy. Said one officer responsible for body-count statistics: "If it's dead and Vietnamese, it's VC [Vietcong]."

✔ **READING CHECK:** What strategies did U.S. forces use in the Vietnam War?

U.S. morale declines. The first U.S. troops had arrived in Vietnam in a hopeful mood. As marine lieutenant Philip Caputo explained, "When we marched into the rice paddies on that damp March afternoon, we carried, along with our packs and rifles, the implicit [unquestioned] convictions that the Vietcong could be quickly beaten." This optimism began to fade as the hazards of fighting a nearly invisible foe in an alien landscape became apparent. "We kept the packs and rifles," Caputo wrote; "the convictions, we lost."

Equally frustrating was the enemy's will to continue fighting, despite mounting casualties. U.S. war planners believed that superior U.S. technology would win the war. Yet at the end of 1967, victory seemed no closer than in 1963. Ho Chi Minh's earlier warning to the French now seemed applicable to Americans. "You can kill ten of my men for every one I kill of yours, but even at those odds, you will lose and I will win."

✔ **READING CHECK:** What factors frustrated U.S. military efforts in Vietnam?

Views of Vietnam

U.S. soldiers and the Vietnamese saw the war from very different perspectives. Some people who were there later expressed their feelings through writing. The following poem by William D. Ehrhart, a marine who served in Vietnam, describes his experiences fighting against the Vietcong guerrillas. Trinh Cong Son, a Vietnamese poet, captured the horror of battle in the poem below.

"Guerrilla War"
by William D. Ehrhart

It's practically impossible
to tell the civilians
from the Vietcong.
Nobody wears uniforms.
They all talk
the same language
(and you couldn't under-
    stand them
even if they didn't).
They tape grenades
inside their clothes,
and carry satchel charges
in their market baskets.
Even their women fight;
and young boys,
and girls.
It's practically impossible
to tell civilians
from the Vietcong;
after awhile
you quit trying.

William D. Ehrhart

Trinh Cong Son

[Title Unknown]
by Trinh Cong Son

I saw, I saw, I saw holes and trenches
full of the corpses of my brothers and sisters.
Mothers, clap for joy over war.
Sisters, clap and cheer for peace.
Everyone clap for vengeance.
Everyone clap instead of repentance.

UNDERSTANDING LITERATURE

1. What examples does Ehrhart give of the difficulty identifying the enemy in Vietnam?
2. Do you think Trinh Cong Son believed any good came out of the war?
3. What are the similarities and differences between the two poems?

The Media and the War

By the end of 1967 more than 16,000 Americans had been killed in Vietnam. Thousands more had been injured or disabled. Despite the government's optimistic forecasts, a U.S. victory seemed increasingly distant. The fighting dragged on, frustrating soldiers and citizens alike. In the United States television news programs showed gruesome images of terrified Vietnamese civilians and dead or injured soldiers. Some Americans responded by demanding that the military be allowed to do whatever it took to win. Others wanted the United States to pull out of Vietnam.

The Vietnam War invaded American homes in a way that no previous conflict had. During previous wars the military had imposed tight press restrictions. In this war, reporters, photographers, and TV camera crews accompanied soldiers on patrol and interviewed people throughout South Vietnam. Television beamed footage and reports of the war into people's homes on a nightly basis. As a result, Americans saw images that seemed to contradict the government's reports.

Reporters such as David Halberstam of the *New York Times* and Neil Sheehan of United Press International criticized the government's optimism. As early as 1962 they argued that the war could not be won so long as the United States supported the unpopular and corrupt regime of Ngo Dinh Diem. Journalists also reported on the ineffectiveness of South Vietnam's troops and accused the U.S. government of inflating enemy body counts to give the appearance of progress.

As the gap between the reports of the U.S. government and what people saw and read grew wider, doubts at home increased. The administration found itself criticized by both **doves**—people who opposed the war— and **hawks**—people who supported the war's goals. Hawks criticized the way the war was being fought. They argued for more U.S. troops and heavier bombing. Air force general Curtis LeMay expressed the frustration of many hawks. "Here we are at the height of our power. The most powerful nation in the world. And yet we're afraid to use that power."

Doves opposed the war for many reasons. Pacifists such as the Reverend Martin Luther King Jr. believed that all war was wrong. Some doves, such as diplomat George Kennan, were convinced that Vietnam was not crucial to national security. Others feared that the United States might resort to using nuclear weapons in Vietnam. Prominent among the war's opponents was respected pediatrician and author Dr. Benjamin Spock. He and others argued that the United States was fighting against the wishes of a majority of Vietnamese.

INTERPRETING THE VISUAL RECORD
The media. Television coverage brought the horrors of the Vietnam War into Americans' living rooms. *What do you think this journalist is doing?*

The Antiwar Movement

A variety of civil rights, pacifist, religious, and student groups shaped the antiwar movement. The pacifist groups included Women Strike for Peace and the National Committee for a Sane Nuclear Policy as well as radical student groups like **Students for a Democratic Society** (SDS). The movement attracted a broad range of people. Doctors, ministers, teachers, and other professionals joined homemakers, retired citizens, and students in protest against the war.

STUDENTS FOR A DEMOCRATIC SOCIETY
The Port Huron Statement

The Students for a Democratic Society (SDS) national convention met in Port Huron, Michigan, the week of June 11–15, 1962. There the members of the SDS revised a draft paper that was the product of several months of discussion. Known as the Port Huron Statement, the resulting document outlined the organization's goals for change in American society.

We are people of this generation, bred in at least modest comfort, housed now in universities, looking uncomfortably to the world we inherit. When we were kids the United States was the wealthiest and strongest country in the world: the only one with the atom bomb, the least scarred by modern war, an initiator of the United Nations that we thought would distribute Western influence throughout the world. Freedom and equality for each individual, government of, by, and for the people—these American values we found good, principles by which we could live as men. Many of us began maturing in complacency [self-satisfaction].

As we grew, however, our comfort was penetrated by events too troubling to dismiss. . . .

While two-thirds of mankind suffers undernourishment, our own upper classes revel [celebrate] amidst superfluous abundance. . . . Uncontrolled exploitation [usage] governs the sapping [draining] of the earth's physical resources. . . .

Major social institutions—cultural, educational, rehabilitative, and others—should be generally organized with the well-being and dignity of man as the essential measure of success. . . . As students for a democratic society, we are committed to stimulating this kind of social movement, this kind of vision and program in campus and community across the country. If we appear to seek the unattainable, [as] it has been said, then let it be known that we do so to avoid the unimaginable.

By the end of 1965 the SDS had members on 124 college campuses. Although it was just one of many groups opposing the war, to many Americans the SDS *was* the antiwar movement. At colleges across the United States, the SDS and other student groups and faculty members held antiwar rallies and debates. These groups particularly criticized the involvement of universities in research and development for the military. They also protested the draft, the presence of the Reserve Officers' Training Corps (ROTC) on campus, and the recruitment efforts by the armed services, the Central Intelligence Agency (CIA), and defense contractors.

The SDS organized the first national antiwar demonstration, which was held in Washington, D.C., on April 17, 1965. More than 20,000 people participated. After an afternoon of speeches and singing, the crowd marched to the Capitol and delivered to Congress a petition demanding that lawmakers "act immediately to end the war." Countless demonstrations followed during the next decade. Demonstrators protested U.S. involvement in Southeast Asia with tactics borrowed from the civil rights movement.

Civil rights activists were among the most outspoken critics of the war. In 1967 Martin Luther King Jr. complained that the war was stealing resources from poverty programs.

❝ I watched the [antipoverty] program broken and eviscerated [gutted] as if it were some idle political plaything of a society gone mad on war, and I knew that America would never invest the necessary funds or energies in rehabilitation of its poor so long as Vietnam continued to draw men and skills and money like some demonic, destructive suction tube. ❞

Many civil rights activists criticized the U.S. government. They said it was sending great numbers of young African Americans off to war yet doing little to end discrimination at home. The Student Nonviolent Coordinating Committee (SNCC) expressed the views of growing numbers of African Americans. SNCC officials noted that "16 percent of the draftees from this country are Negro, called on to stifle [block] the liberation of Vietnam, to preserve a 'democracy' which does not exist for them at home." Polls showed that African Americans were much more likely than whites to consider the war a mistake.

Despite their high visibility, antiwar protesters made up a small percentage of the U.S. population. Many Americans opposed the antiwar movement, particularly the extreme groups. Some believed that fighting for one's country was a patriotic duty. Others objected to the antiwar movement's tactics. These people found certain acts of protest—such as burning the American flag, occupying buildings, and burning draft cards—particularly upsetting. Many veterans of past wars were angered by young men who tried to avoid the draft.

Most Americans who disagreed with the antiwar movement expressed their opposition in private. However, some organized rallies in support of the war. Demonstrators at these rallies often carried signs proclaiming "America, Love It or Leave It" or "My Country, Right or Wrong."

Government in Conflict

President Johnson and his advisers responded to antiwar protesters by insisting that the United States was helping to defend an ally against aggression. If the United States failed to support South Vietnam, asked Secretary of State Dean Rusk, what U.S. ally would ever trust the country again?

The administration also faced criticism in Congress. Doves such as Senator J. William Fulbright of Arkansas, head of the Foreign Relations Committee, sharply criticized the Johnson administration's policies as too extreme. Fulbright held congressional hearings in 1966 to give the war's critics a forum. These televised hearings made the antiwar position more believable to mainstream Americans.

✔ **READING CHECK:** Why did some Americans oppose the war, and how did the government respond?

INTERPRETING THE VISUAL RECORD

Protest. This man joined other Americans at a rally in front of the U.S. Capitol Building. *Why do you think he is wearing a uniform?*

SECTION 2 REVIEW

Define and explain the significance of the following terms:

Tonkin Gulf Resolution
escalation
Operation Rolling Thunder
Ho Chi Minh Trail
defoliants
search-and-destroy missions
pacification
doves
hawks
Students for a Democratic Society

Identify and explain the significance of the following individuals:
Robert S. McNamara
J. William Fulbright

Locate and explain the importance of the following places:
South Vietnam
Gulf of Tonkin
North Vietnam
Cambodia
Laos

1. **Using Graphic Organizers** Copy the chart below. Use it to outline U.S. tactics in the air war and on the ground in Vietnam.

Air War	Ground War

2. **Analyzing** Why did some members of Congress believe that the Tonkin Gulf Resolution was unconstitutional?

3. **Understanding Geography: Place** How did Vietnam's geography contribute to the U.S. military's inability to defeat the Vietcong?

4. **Recognizing Point of View** Why did some Americans oppose the war? Why did the government respond the way it did?

Critical Thinking

5. What factor do you think played the biggest role in shaping American views toward the Vietnam War?
   Consider:
   • television coverage of the war
   • economic effects of the war
   • social conditions in the United States

A Turning Point

OBJECTIVES

Read to understand:

1. why the Tet Offensive weakened many Americans' confidence in their government
2. what the key events of the 1968 presidential campaign were
3. how President Nixon attempted to end the war
4. how Americans reacted to President Nixon's plan to end the war

KEY TERMS

Tet Offensive
Vietnamization
Kent State shootings
Pentagon Papers

KEY PEOPLE

William Westmoreland
Eugene McCarthy
Robert F. Kennedy
Richard J. Daley
Richard Nixon
Henry Kissinger
Le Duc Tho

These soldiers are taking cover during one of the many battles of the Tet Offensive.

EYEWITNESSES TO History

 *After a while, survival was the name of the game as you sat there in semidarkness, with the firing going on constantly, like at a rifle range. And the horrible smell. You tasted it as you ate your rations, as if you were eating death. It permeated [seeped into] your clothes, which you couldn't wash because water was very scarce. You couldn't bathe or shave either. My strategy was to keep as many of my marines alive as possible, yet accomplish our mission. You went through the full range of emotions, seeing your buddies being hit, but you couldn't feel sorry for them because you had the others to think about.* **99**

—Myron Harrington

U.S. Marines on patrol in Vietnam

Myron Harrington described the fighting through which he led his company of 100 marines. The grim determination Harrington and others felt about the war in Vietnam began to weaken in 1968. That year a massive attack by the Vietcong shattered the illusion that the United States would soon win the war. Soon many Americans were wondering why the country was fighting the war.

The Tet Offensive

January 30, 1968, marked the start of Tet, the Vietnamese New Year. In past years the holiday had been honored by a lull in fighting. However, late that night, as most South Vietnamese and their U.S. allies slept, Vietcong guerrillas and North Vietnamese troops struck. They crept from their jungle camps and city hideouts to execute a carefully planned strike. Within hours countless villages, more than 100 cities, and 12 U.S. military bases came under attack from nearly 84,000 communist soldiers. Heavy fighting raged in such U.S. strongholds as Saigon and Da Nang. At one point the Vietcong even occupied the courtyard of the U.S. Embassy.

North Vietnam expected the **Tet Offensive** to bring down South Vietnam's government as the people rallied behind their "liberators." North Vietnam's leaders were disappointed, however. When the assault ended, more than a month later, some 40,000 communist soldiers lay dead.

General William Westmoreland, the commander of U.S. forces in Vietnam, described the offensive as a Vietcong defeat. In a military sense, the general had a point. At a cost of 1,100 American and 2,300 ARVN lives, most of the attackers had been repelled. Despite suffering heavy losses, however, the Vietcong remained strong in many places. They had faced overwhelming U.S. firepower and were still standing—more determined than ever to continue fighting.

Tran Do, the deputy commander of communist forces in South Vietnam, had played a major role in the Tet Offensive. He explained the goals and effects of the offensive:

> 66 In all honesty we didn't achieve our main objective, which was to spur uprisings throughout the south. Still, we inflicted heavy casualties on the Americans and their puppets, and that was a big gain for us. As for making an impact in the United States, it had not been our intention—but it turned out to be a fortunate result. 99

The political effect of the offensive on the United States was stunning. The Tet Offensive shook U.S. confidence by revealing that no part of South Vietnam was secure—not even downtown Saigon. Respected journalist Walter Cronkite, anchor of the *CBS Evening News,* expressed Americans' bewildered mood: "I thought we were winning the war! What the hell is going on?" To one of his aides, President Johnson groaned, "If I've lost Cronkite I've lost middle America."

After the Tet Offensive, public criticism of the war rose dramatically. Such influential magazines as *Time* and *Newsweek* expressed doubts about the war and began calling for its end. Largely because of the shift in public opinion, Johnson denied General Westmoreland's urgent request for 206,000 more troops. President Johnson granted a small increase in the number of troops but made it clear that he would not increase the number any further.

These soldiers are leading away one of the Vietcong guerrillas who attacked the U.S. Embassy in Saigon during the Tet Offensive.

✔ **READING CHECK:** Why did the Tet Offensive weaken many Americans' confidence in their government?

The Election of 1968

After the Tet Offensive three out of four Americans disapproved of President Johnson's conduct of the war. With the presidential election nearing, Johnson was under attack from all sides.

Democratic challengers. Early in 1968 Senator Eugene McCarthy of Minnesota, a critic of the war, challenged Johnson for the Democratic presidential nomination. In the New Hampshire primary held that March, McCarthy won almost as many votes as Johnson. McCarthy's impressive showing drew another leading critic of the war into the race. Senator Robert F. Kennedy of New York was the brother of the slain President Kennedy and a former U.S. attorney general. His large national following—particularly among African Americans, Hispanics, the poor, and the young—made Robert Kennedy a strong contender for the Democratic nomination.

Shaken by the division within his party, President Johnson made a shocking announcement to the nation on March 31. Physically and emotionally exhausted, Johnson declared that he would not seek re-election. He explained that he wanted to spend his last months in office trying to end the war. Johnson's withdrawal from the race left it wide open. Senators McCarthy and Kennedy and Vice President Hubert Humphrey went head-to-head in several state primaries. Kennedy won most of them, including the crucial California primary in June. To many he seemed destined to receive the Democratic nomination.

Senator Robert Kennedy was so popular that supporters often tore off his cuff links while scrambling to shake his hand.

The Generation Gap

In the 1960s many young people began to feel that something had gone wrong with the United States. Prosperity had followed World War II, but peace had not. Fascism had been defeated, and the prewar years of depression were all but forgotten. Younger Americans—members of the baby-boom genera-

Many parents of the World War II era did not understand their Vietnam-era children, like this teenager.

tion—increasingly found themselves at odds with their parents, who had grown up during the Great Depression and World War II. A wide generation gap developed.

The faith and optimism of American youth were shaken by seemingly senseless violence and death. Many young people demanded change. They accused the previous generation of valuing conformity and material comfort over equality and fairness. Younger Americans also increasingly distrusted their government and questioned the reasons for U.S. involvement in Vietnam. Many older Americans remembered past struggles and urged young people to have faith in their government. This inability to communicate contributed to the violent clash at the Democratic Party's 1968 convention in Chicago.

On the night of his California victory, Kennedy was shot by Sirhan Sirhan, a young Jordanian immigrant. Kennedy died the next day. A nation already in shock over the murder of Martin Luther King Jr. just two months earlier was now faced with yet another assassination.

The convention in Chicago.

Society seemed to be spinning out of control. Amid the turmoil, the Democrats met in Chicago to settle on a candidate for the November election. The convention was a cheerless affair. Despite his close identification with the unpopular President Johnson, Vice President Humphrey received the nomination. He chose Senator Edmund Muskie of Maine as his running mate.

The Democrats' difficulties were underscored by the chaos on the streets outside the convention. Some 10,000 antiwar protesters had massed in the city and camped in Grant Park, across from the hotel where many delegates were staying. They held rallies in the sweltering August heat, chanting antiwar slogans and calling police names.

Outraged to see his city overrun by people he viewed as dangerous revolutionaries, Chicago mayor Richard J. Daley ordered helmeted police to clear out the protesters. Attacking on the night of August 28, the police clubbed protesters and used tear gas to disperse the crowd. Hundreds of protesters were injured; hundreds more were hauled to jail. Reporters, passersby, and police were also injured in the struggle.

The Republicans capitalize.

The violent spectacle at the Chicago convention raised Republicans' hopes of capturing the White House. The mood was upbeat at the Republican National Convention in Miami Beach, Florida. Richard Nixon dominated the convention. Appealing to the patriotism of mainstream America, Nixon won the nomination easily. He chose Maryland governor Spiro Agnew as his running mate. Promising a "law-and-order" crackdown on urban crime, Nixon sought support from those Americans who neither approved of the disorderly antiwar protests nor wanted a U.S. defeat in Vietnam. Nixon told voters he had a secret plan to end the Vietnam War, although he revealed no details.

As election day neared, Humphrey's campaign picked up steam, boosted somewhat by Johnson's announcement in late October of a bombing halt. Time ran out for the Democrats, however. The election results were close. Of the 73 million votes cast, Richard Nixon received just 510,314 more than Hubert Humphrey. Nixon's margin in the electoral college was much wider. He won 32 states to Humphrey's 13. Former Alabama governor George Wallace campaigned as the candidate of the newly formed American Independent Party. He received some 10 million votes and won five states in the South.

✔ **READING CHECK:** What were the key events of the 1968 presidential campaign?

Nixon, Vietnamization, and Cambodia

President Richard Nixon made foreign affairs his top priority. Nixon's key foreign-policy adviser was Henry Kissinger. Born in 1923 in Fürth, Germany, Henry

BIOGRAPHY

Henry Kissinger

Kissinger fled the country as a teenager with his parents to escape the Nazis. Kissinger arrived in New York City in 1938 and became a U.S. citizen in 1943. That same year, he joined the U.S. Army Counter-Intelligence Corps and served for three years. From 1946 to 1949 Kissinger was a captain in the Military Intelligence Reserve while attending Harvard University, where he graduated with honors. He received his Ph.D. from Harvard in 1954 and joined its faculty as a professor of government.

Kissinger occasionally advised Presidents Eisenhower, Kennedy, and Johnson. He was particularly influential during the Nixon presidency. Kissinger served as national security adviser before becoming secretary of state. In both positions he worked closely with President Nixon to improve relations with communist China and the Soviet Union. Kissinger won the Nobel Peace Prize in 1973 for his role in the negotiations that eventually ended the Vietnam War. He later served as a foreign-affairs adviser to Presidents Ronald Reagan and George Bush.

Kissinger and Nixon devised a plan to fulfill the president's campaign pledge to end the war. Part of this plan was called **Vietnamization**, which involved turning over the fighting to the South Vietnamese while gradually pulling out U.S. troops. This strategy, said Nixon, would bring "peace with honor." At best, Nixon hoped that Vietnamization might produce a stable anticommunist South Vietnam. At worst, it would delay a collapse long enough to spare the United States the humiliation of outright defeat.

Nixon also hoped that Vietnamization would remove a major obstacle that had been blocking a peace agreement with North Vietnam. The North Vietnamese had first warned President Johnson and then Nixon that the United States would have to set a date for troop removals if peace talks were to continue. In August 1969, as U.S. troop withdrawals began, Henry Kissinger met secretly in Paris with longtime revolutionary Le Duc Tho (LAY DUHK TOH) of North Vietnam.

The process of troop withdrawal was slow. When Nixon took office in 1969, U.S. troops in Vietnam numbered about 540,000. At the end of 1972 about 24,200 Americans still remained in Vietnam.

Secretly, Nixon planned to expand the war into neutral Cambodia to cut off the North Vietnamese supply lines along the Ho Chi Minh Trail. Early in 1969 Nixon ordered the widespread bombing of Cambodia. He wanted to show Hanoi that the United States was still willing to use force, and even expand the war, in pursuit of his aim of "peace with honor." Nixon and Kissinger concealed the Cambodian air strikes from the American people, Congress, and key military leaders—even the secretary of the air force.

HOLT RESEARCHER

Read More About It

Free Find:

Henry Kissinger
After reading about Henry Kissinger on the **Holt Researcher** CD–ROM, write an editorial for your local newspaper. Describe Kissinger's accomplishments and explain why you think he helped or hurt the United States.

Soldiers of the 25th Infantry Division withdraw from a Cambodian village as an attack helicopter strikes the village.

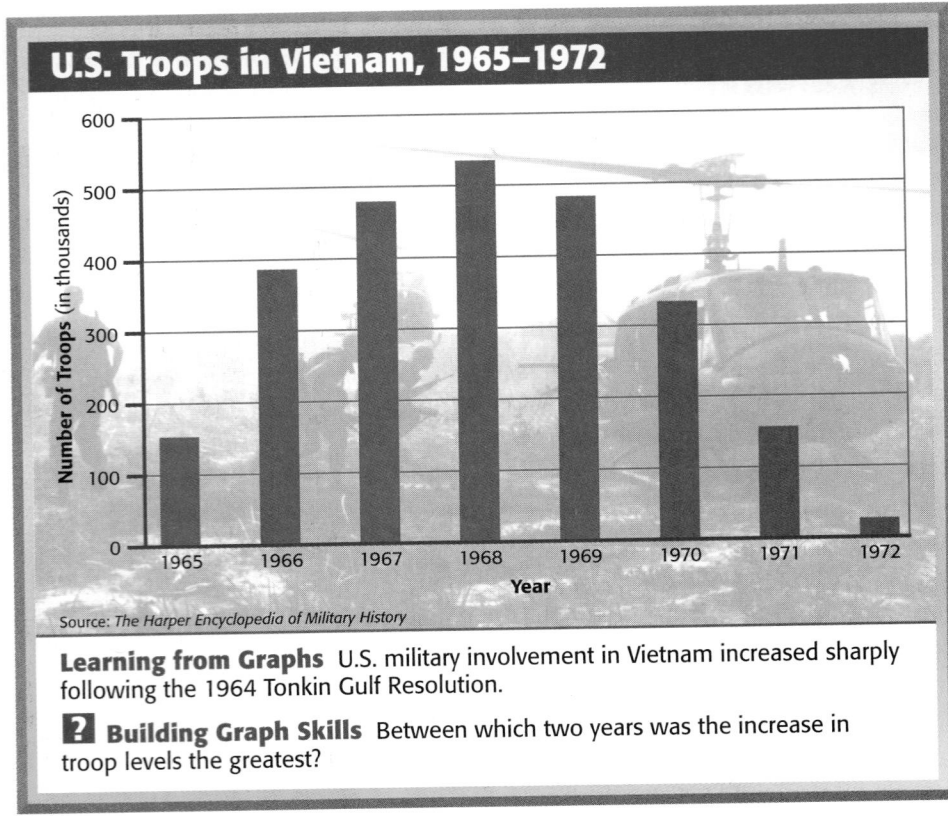

U.S. Troops in Vietnam, 1965–1972

Source: *The Harper Encyclopedia of Military History*

Learning from Graphs U.S. military involvement in Vietnam increased sharply following the 1964 Tonkin Gulf Resolution.

❓ **Building Graph Skills** Between which two years was the increase in troop levels the greatest?

Because of Cambodia's neutrality, Nixon feared an international uproar over the bombing. When a revolt ousted Cambodia's ruler in March 1970, however, Nixon's strategy changed. Since the new Cambodian government was pro-American, Nixon made his strategy public. He justified the air strikes as defense of a friendly nation. Nixon then sent some 80,000 U.S. and ARVN troops into Cambodia.

This invasion destroyed the delicate balance that had kept Cambodia out of the war. North Vietnamese Army (NVA) troops were forced into the interior of Cambodia, where the bombing destroyed much of the countryside.

✔ **READING CHECK:** How did President Nixon attempt to end the war?

Antiwar Protest Increases

News of the bombing and invasion of Cambodia provoked outrage in the United States, particularly on college campuses. After someone at Kent State University in Ohio set fire to the campus ROTC building, Ohio's governor vowed to "eradicate" the protesters. On May 4, 1970, National Guard troops that had been sent to control demonstrators shot randomly into a large group of students. They killed four and injured nine others. Some of the students were merely walking across campus. The **Kent State shootings** shocked the nation.

A young woman cries over the body of a student shot by National Guard troops at Kent State.

Just 10 days later, state police in Jackson, Mississippi, fired at protesters in a dormitory at Jackson State College, killing two students and wounding nine others. Enraged, students and faculty on hundreds of college campuses went on strike.

Members of Congress were also upset by the Cambodian invasion. In response, Congress repealed the Tonkin Gulf Resolution in December 1970. Nixon insisted, however, that this action did not affect his authority to carry on the war. Congressional leaders soon developed plans to stop the war by cutting off funding once U.S. troops were withdrawn.

In 1971 another incident boosted the antiwar movement. The *New York Times* began publishing a collection of secret government documents relating to the war. Known as the **Pentagon Papers**, these documents revealed that the government had frequently misled the American people about the course of the war. The documents had been leaked to the press by Daniel Ellsberg, a former Department of Defense official. Ellsberg had strongly supported the war until he spent time in Vietnam studying the war's effects. While there, he found that few South Vietnamese supported their government.

The War Continues

As commander in chief, President Nixon not only ordered the invasion of Cambodia but also renewed the bombing of North Vietnam, which President Johnson had stopped. Nixon explained his plan to his chief of staff, H. R. "Bob" Haldeman.

"NOW, AS I WAS SAYING, FOUR YEARS AGO"

66 I call it the Madman Theory, Bob. I want the North Vietnamese to believe that I've reached the point where I might do anything to stop the war. We'll just slip the word to them that, 'for God's sake, you know Nixon is obsessed about Communists. We can't restrain him when he's angry—and he has his hand on the nuclear button'—and Ho Chi Minh himself will be in Paris in two days begging for peace. 99

Nixon miscalculated the opposition's endurance, however. Rather than ending, the war suddenly grew more fierce. Hoping to reveal the weaknesses of Nixon's Vietnamization strategy, North Vietnam staged a major invasion of South Vietnam in March 1972. NVA troops drove deep into South Vietnam. In response, Nixon ordered heavy bombing of North Vietnam. Despite these steps, the opposition now held more territory in South Vietnam than ever.

INTERPRETING THE VISUAL RECORD

Nixon's plan. This 1972 cartoon criticizes President Nixon's efforts to end the war. *What do you think the cartoonist was suggesting about Nixon's secret plan to end the war?*

✔ **READING CHECK:** How did Americans react to President Nixon's plan to end the war?

SECTION 3 REVIEW

Define and explain the significance of the following terms:
Tet Offensive
Vietnamization
Kent State shootings
Pentagon Papers

Identify and explain the significance of the following individuals:
William Westmoreland
Eugene McCarthy
Robert F. Kennedy
Richard J. Daley
Richard Nixon
Henry Kissinger
Le Duc Tho

1. **Using Graphic Organizers** Copy the chart below. Use it to describe Nixon's efforts to end the war and how well they succeeded.

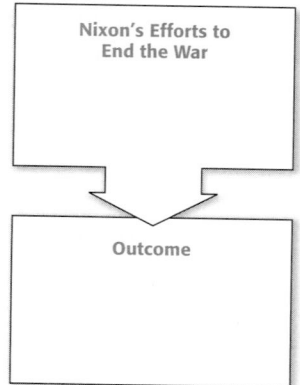

Nixon's Efforts to End the War

Outcome

2. **Taking a Stand** Imagine that you are President Lyndon Johnson. Would you run for re-election in 1968? Write a short speech explaining the reasons for your decision.
3. **Analyzing** How did the Tet Offensive cause American dissatisfaction with the war effort?
4. **Identifying Cause and Effect** Which of President Nixon's policies led to renewed antiwar protests?

Critical Thinking

5. In wartime, should the U.S. government make all information about the war available to its citizens?
Consider:
• the importance of security to military operations
• the public's right to know what the government is doing
• the constitutional protection of free press

The War Ends

George McGovern

EYEWITNESSES TO History

66 *We have heard many times that Vietnam will no longer be an issue by the time the fall election approaches. . . . For the sake of the thousands of Vietnamese peasants still dying from American bombing raids, the GIs still dying . . . the American POWs rotting in the jails of Hanoi, I sincerely hope it will not be an issue. But Vietnam thinking surely will be an issue, regardless of what happens in Indochina in the next four months. By 'Vietnam thinking' I mean wasting our strength on paranoiac [irrational] defense policies while neglecting the needs of our own people.* **99**

—**George McGovern**

Speaking in July 1972, Senator George McGovern made clear his opposition to the war. He hoped the American people's frustration with Vietnam would carry him into the White House.

Nixon's Re-election

Senator George McGovern of South Dakota campaigned in the 1972 Democratic presidential primaries as an antiwar candidate. An air force pilot in World War II, McGovern had been a history professor before entering politics. His opposition to the war ran deep. In one emotional Senate speech he declared in a trembling voice, "This chamber reeks [smells] of blood." George Wallace opposed McGovern for the Democratic nomination. In May, however, Wallace was shot at a political rally in Maryland. The injury paralyzed him from the waist down, and he withdrew from the race.

After the disastrous 1968 convention, the Democrats adopted new rules to increase the representation of ethnic minorities, women, and young people in party organizations. Passed in 1971, the **Twenty-sixth Amendment** had lowered the voting age from 21 to 18. McGovern drew much of his support from these groups. He easily captured the nomination at the Democratic convention.

The Republicans renominated Richard Nixon and Spiro Agnew. Nixon again stressed his strong commitment to law and order within the United States and assured voters that the war would soon be over. Indeed, a few weeks before the election, Henry Kissinger announced a breakthrough in the negotiations to end the war. "Peace is at hand," he declared.

Nixon won the election by a landslide—receiving 47 million votes to McGovern's 29 million. In the electoral college, McGovern carried just Massachusetts and the District of Columbia.

An 18-year-old woman registers to vote.

A Cease-Fire at Last

In August 1969 Henry Kissinger and North Vietnam's Le Duc Tho met secretly in Paris to begin negotiations aimed at finding a way to end the war. For nearly three years the two men engaged in a series of difficult peace negotiations. "I don't look back on our meetings with any great joy," Kissinger recalled. "Yet he was a person of substance and discipline who defended the position he represented with dedication."

Finally, in October 1972 North Vietnam offered a peace plan that Kissinger and President Nixon found acceptable. The plan called for a cease-fire, the pullout of all foreign troops from Vietnam, and an end to U.S. military aid. The agreement also planned for the creation of a new government in South Vietnam. This government would include the country's current president, Nguyen Van Thieu, as well as representatives of the National Liberation Front. Thieu, who had not been included in the negotiations, objected to the proposed government. He believed it would reduce his power. Rather than abandon Thieu, the United States rejected the agreement.

When North Vietnam demanded that the agreement be reinstated, Nixon responded by ordering round-the-clock bombing of Hanoi and Haiphong. A furious Nixon declared to the chairman of the Joint Chiefs of Staff: "This is your chance to use military power to win this war, and if you don't, I'll consider you responsible." Some 40,000 tons of bombs rained on the two cities for nearly two weeks, with the barrage only halting for Christmas Day. The intensive bombing did not sway the North Vietnamese, however. At the end of December 1972 Nixon called off the bombing and agreed to resume talks.

Protest. This woman is protesting the "Christmas bombing" campaign ordered by President Nixon. *What does the woman's sign ask Americans to do?*

On January 27, 1973, the negotiators in Paris announced a cease-fire. The plan differed little from the one agreed to in October, but minor changes allowed each side to claim a victory. The United States pledged to withdraw its remaining forces from South Vietnam and to help rebuild Vietnam. The peace settlement also included a prisoner-exchange agreement. It did not, however, address the major issue behind the war—the political future of South Vietnam. While urging Thieu to accept the cease-fire, Nixon secretly pledged that the United States would come to South Vietnam's aid if fighting resumed.

Two years after U.S. forces withdrew, South Vietnam's military government collapsed. In January 1975, North Vietnamese troops overran the northern part of South Vietnam. As South Vietnamese troops retreated in panic, new waves of refugees poured into Saigon.

In early April the noose around Saigon tightened. The U.S. military rushed to evacuate the several thousand Americans still in the city. Some escaped from the U.S. Embassy roof by helicopter as North Vietnamese troops stormed the compound. Some 120,000 Vietnamese who had worked for the U.S. government were flown to the United States. On April 30, 1975, South Vietnam surrendered unconditionally.

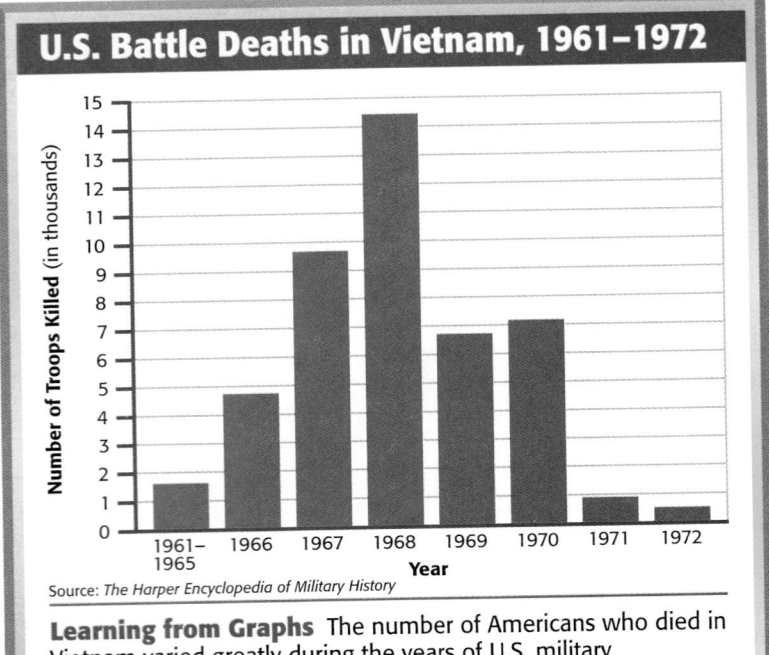

U.S. Battle Deaths in Vietnam, 1961–1972

Source: *The Harper Encyclopedia of Military History*

Learning from Graphs The number of Americans who died in Vietnam varied greatly during the years of U.S. military involvement there.

? **Building Graph Skills** During which year did the United States suffer the greatest number of battle deaths in Vietnam?

For Americans the Vietnam War was over. The long, costly effort to prevent the creation of a united, independent Vietnam under Communist rule had failed. The war had spread to Cambodia and Laos, which had been heavily damaged. However, the predicted collapse of all Southeast Asia—the so-called domino theory—never occurred. Quarrels soon broke out between the Communist leaders of Vietnam and those of China and Cambodia. International communism was not as unified a world force as U.S. policy makers had feared.

✔ **READING CHECK:** Why did the United States agree to a cease-fire in January 1973?

Effects of the War

The war devastated the Vietnamese people. According to Saigon government figures, some 185,000 South Vietnamese soldiers died in combat. Estimates put the number of South Vietnamese civilian dead at nearly 500,000. The exact number of Vietcong and North Vietnamese Army war dead is unknown but may have been near 1 million. In addition, approximately 879,000 Vietnamese were orphaned, and 181,000 were disabled. Among the disabled were those exposed to chemicals such as Agent Orange. These people have been plagued by high rates of liver cancer and other illnesses.

Read More About It

Free Find:

Le Ly Hayslip

After reading about Le Ly Hayslip on the **Holt Researcher** CD–ROM, create a plan for starting your own nonprofit organization. Choose its goals and the methods it will use to achieve them.

BIOGRAPHY

Le Ly Hayslip

Vietnamese refugees. Le Ly Hayslip was one survivor of the Vietnam War. Hayslip was born in a village near Da Nang in 1949. She experienced constant warfare as a child. By the time she was 14, she had been imprisoned by the South Vietnamese government. Suspected of being a revolutionary, Hayslip was tortured and sentenced to death. She escaped, however, and returned home. Surviving as best she could, Hayslip worked in a hospital, as a waitress, and as a black-market vendor.

Hayslip's brothers fought on both sides of the war. In 1970 she married a U.S. civilian worker. Soon they fled to the United States. Although she escaped the fighting, she was unable to escape its effects. Hayslip described watching television coverage of Vietnam with her family.

❝ Where the Munros [Hayslip's in-laws] saw faceless Orientals fleeing burning villages, tied up as prisoners, or as rag dolls in a roadside trench (even innocent villagers were "VC" or "Charlie"), I saw my brother Bon Nghe, who fought twenty-five years for the North; my mother's nephew, who was lieutenant for the South; my sister Lan, who hustled drinks to the Americans in Danang; and

> my sister Hai, who shared sleepless nights with my mother in our family bunker at Ky La. I saw floating on the smoke of battle the soul of my dead brother, Sau Ban, victim of an American land mine, and the spirit of my father, who drank acid to avoid involving me again with the Viet Cong terrorists. I saw in those tiny electronic lines, as I saw in my dreams, the ghosts of a hundred relatives, family friends, and playmates who died fighting for this side or that, or merely to survive. **99**

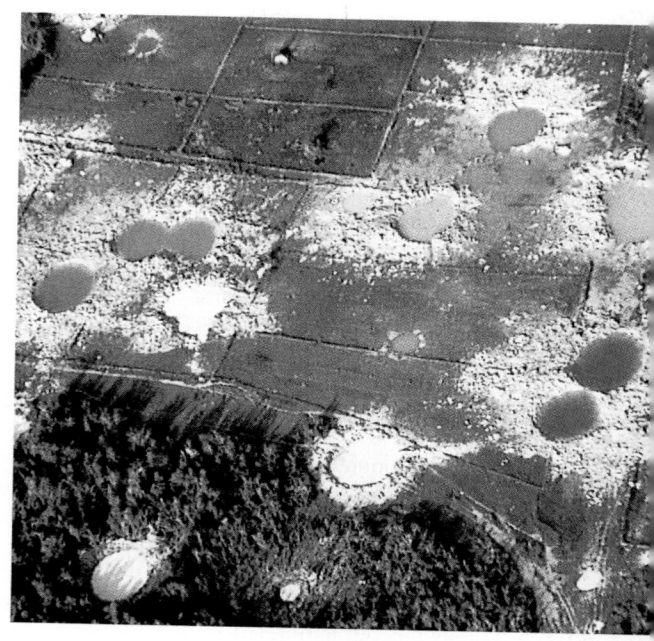

Shortly after arriving in the United States, Hayslip began writing her memoirs. Published in 1989, her highly acclaimed book, *When Heaven and Earth Changed Places*, describes growing up in a constant state of war. In 1987 Hayslip created a charitable organization, the East Meets West Foundation, to provide comfort to all victims of the war. The foundation provides assistance to Vietnamese people trying to rebuild their lives. It also helps U.S. veterans cope with the effects of the war.

Nearly 1.5 million Vietnamese like Hayslip fled Vietnam after the fall of Saigon. Desperate to escape economic and social hardships, many braved the rough South China Sea and Gulf of Thailand in tiny, crowded boats. They were joined by thousands of other refugees from Southeast Asia—such as the Hmong (MUHNG) of Laos—also fleeing grave postwar conditions. More than 730,000 of these refugees have settled in the United States since the war.

✔ **READING CHECK:** What were the long-term effects of the war on Vietnam and the Vietnamese people?

Vietnam veterans. More than 2 million Americans were involved in the Vietnam War. More than 58,000 of them died, and more than 300,000 were wounded. About 2,500 were missing in action. Improved emergency medical services saved the lives of many U.S. soldiers who had severe wounds that would have been fatal in previous wars. As a result, there were a large number of paralyzed and otherwise severely disabled Vietnam veterans.

More than 600 Americans were held as prisoners of war (POWs). Some POWs spent more than six years in North Vietnamese jails, where they endured long periods of solitary confinement and torture.

One of the most visible tragedies of the war was the fate of its veterans. No ticker-tape parades celebrated the return of soldiers from the Vietnam conflict. On the contrary, veterans often became targets for the anger, guilt, or shame of fellow citizens frustrated by the war. Many other Americans met the veterans with stony silence.

The public's negative reaction enraged and demoralized many veterans. They had faced a life-and-death struggle, obeying orders that they trusted were in their country's best interests. Vietnam veteran Ron Kovic recalled the pain of this lack of support in his 1976 book, *Born on the Fourth of July*:

Ron Kovic (holding flag) led this 1972 protest against the Vietnam War.

No More Vietnams

During a military crisis in 1990 President George Bush assured the nation, "This will not be another Vietnam." The memories of Vietnam have haunted every U.S. leader who has considered committing U.S. troops to foreign conflicts. To avoid long, drawn-out conflicts, recent presidents have committed U.S. troops only to operations in which the fighting was likely to be over very quickly.

The memory of the Vietnam War has also affected media coverage. To keep the flow of war-zone information from eroding public support, the U.S. military has put tight restrictions on media access to the front lines. It has also closely screened what has been broadcast. The military does not want to expose Americans to the kind of gruesome images and grim statistics that fueled the Vietnam antiwar movement.

The men and women returning from recent armed conflicts have received a very different welcome than their Vietnam-era counterparts. Even many Americans who oppose armed conflicts have emphasized their support for the troops and the sacrifices that they have made.

These high school students are protesting a military operation in the 1990s.

66 **I didn't want to believe it at first—people protesting against us when we were putting our lives on the line for our country. . . . How could they do this to us? Many of us would not be coming back and many others would be wounded or maimed [disabled].** 99

In their despair, thousands of Vietnam veterans turned to drugs. Many others had trouble finding jobs or adjusting to life as civilians. Some ended up homeless.

Soldiers who were affected by the spraying of defoliants later developed certain forms of cancer at an unusually high rate. Their children had a very high rate of birth defects. Research in the 1970s linked their medical problems to Agent Orange. In 1984 the manufacturers of the chemical created a relief fund for the veterans and their families. In 1991 the government extended permanent disability benefits to these veterans.

Public policy. The war shook Americans' confidence in their government. Many were shocked to discover that their leaders had misled them during the war. The actions of both Presidents Johnson and Nixon raised a crucial constitutional question: under what authority can presidents wage an undeclared war? In 1973, seeking to prevent "another Vietnam," Congress passed the **War Powers Act**. This act reaffirms Congress's constitutional right to declare war by setting a 60-day limit on the presidential commitment of U.S. troops to foreign conflicts.

The Vietnam War also left a dismal economic legacy. The war cost American taxpayers directly more than $150 billion, adding greatly to the national debt and fueling inflation. The war also diverted funding that might have gone to domestic programs, such as those that help the poor.

The Vietnam War taught U.S. policy makers that hostile public opinion and deep national divisions can impose severe restraints on the use of military force. Since Vietnam, leaders have been hesitant to commit U.S. troops in far-off regions without being certain of the consent of the American people and the nation's political allies.

Healing the Wounds of the War

Long after the war's end, Americans continue to seek ways to come to terms with the conflict and its effects. Perhaps the most moving attempt to heal the division caused by the war is the **Vietnam Veterans Memorial** in Washington, D.C., designed by Maya Ying Lin. Lin, a Chinese American, was a young architecture student at Yale University when her design was chosen for the national monument. Of the healing aspects of the memorial, she said, "To overcome grief you have to confront it. An honest memorial makes you accept what happened before you overcome it. I think the memorial makes people accept."

Inscribed on a huge wall of black granite are the names of the more than 58,000 Americans who died in Vietnam. Lin insisted that the names be listed in chronological order, not in alphabetical order or by rank. She explained that this way "if you were in the war, you could find your time and a few people you knew." Veteran Bruce Weigl attended the dedication ceremony for the memorial on Veterans Day 1982. Weigl later reflected on the reasons he and other veterans attended the ceremony.

❝ I think we came, without really knowing it, to make the memorial our wailing wall. We came to find the names of those we lost in the war, as if by tracing the letters cut into the granite we could find what was left of ourselves. . . . No veteran could turn his back on the terrible grace of Maya Lin's wall and the names of the 57,939 who died or disappeared in Vietnam from July 1959 to May 1975. ❞

Hundreds of people, some weeping, visit the memorial daily. Many leave flowers, personal mementos, or written messages. Others simply ponder what the memorial—with its dark silence—has to tell them.

✔ **READING CHECK:** What were the long-term effects of the war on the American people?

INTERPRETING THE VISUAL RECORD

The wall. Reminders of the war like the Vietnam Veterans Memorial and the hat at left bring back strong emotions. *How did visiting the memorial affect these soldiers?*

SECTION 4 REVIEW

Define and explain the significance of the following terms:
Twenty-sixth Amendment
War Powers Act
Vietnam Veterans Memorial

Identify and explain the significance of the following individuals:
George McGovern
George Wallace
Le Ly Hayslip
Maya Ying Lin

1. **Using Graphic Organizers** Copy the diagram below. Use it to list what you think were the costs of the Vietnam War.

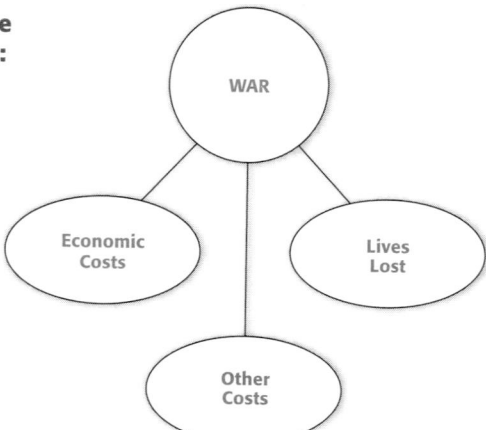

2. **Evaluating** Do you think the terms of the 1973 cease-fire represented a victory or a defeat for the United States? Explain your answer.
3. **Assessing Consequences** What impact did the Vietnam War have on the president's ability to direct U.S. military forces?
4. **Using Historical Imagination** Imagine that you are a veteran of the Vietnam War. Write a letter to the president explaining how you think Vietnam veterans should be honored.

Critical Thinking

5. What long-term effects has the Vietnam War had on the United States?
   Consider:
   • the lives lost on both sides of the war
   • the changes in the way the United States uses its military
   • the increased media attention to government actions

CHAPTER 33

Review

Creating a Time Line

Copy the time line below onto a sheet of paper. Complete the time line by filling in the events and dates from the chapter that you think were most significant. Pick three events and explain why you think they were significant.

1954   1965   1975

Writing a Summary

Using the Reading Checks as a guide, write an overview of the events in the chapter.

Identifying People and Ideas

Identify the following terms or individuals and explain their significance.

1. Ho Chi Minh
2. domino theory
3. Vietcong
4. Tonkin Gulf Resolution
5. defoliants
6. doves
7. Tet Offensive
8. Henry Kissinger
9. Vietnamization
10. Le Ly Hayslip

Understanding Main Ideas

SECTION 1
1. What were the main reasons the United States first became involved in Vietnam?

SECTION 2
2. Why did the United States increase its involvement in Vietnam after 1964?
3. What were the main reasons for Americans' opposition to the war?

SECTION 3
4. How did the Tet Offensive change the war?

SECTION 4
5. How has the Vietnam War influenced Americans?
6. What effect did the Vietnam War have on U.S. foreign policy?

Reviewing Themes

1. **Global Relations** How did the U.S. stance on communism lead to involvement in Vietnam?
2. **Constitutional Heritage** During the Vietnam War the president assumed increasing amounts of power. Why did this alarm Congress?
3. **Democratic Values** How did antiwar protests illustrate American democratic values?

Thinking Critically

1. **Problem Solving** Imagine that you are an adviser to President Kennedy. Suggest at least two ways the United States might support South Vietnam without committing U.S. troops to battle.
2. **Evaluating** Do you think President Johnson had good reasons to escalate the U.S. war effort? Explain your answer.
3. **Hypothesizing** Suppose the United States had won a decisive victory in Vietnam. How might life be different in Vietnam? in the United States?
4. **Taking a Stand** Imagine that you are a college student in the 1960s. Would you join the antiwar movement? Explain your answer.
5. **Assessing Consequences** A major goal of U.S. involvement in Vietnam was to stop the spread of communism. What effect did U.S. actions have on the spread of communism?

Writing About History

Writing to Create Imagine that it is 1968 and you have just been drafted. Write a poem or song that expresses your feelings. Use the following graphic to organize your thoughts.

State of the War **+** Public Opinion of the War **=** Your Feelings About Being Drafted

Review the **Strategies for Success** on *Determining Good Sources.* Then re-examine each source that you found on the Vietnam War. Decide if and how you would use it in a research paper focusing on the antiwar movement in the United States during the 1960s.

Linking History and Geography

Study the map below, noting the numbers on it. Number your paper one through eight. Then identify each place on the map by selecting a name from the list below. Write the correct name of each place next to its corresponding number on your paper. There are two extra names on the list.

Mekong River   *Hanoi*
Gulf of Tonkin   *China*
South China Sea   *Laos*
Ho Chi Minh City   *Cambodia*
Vietnam   *Soviet Union*

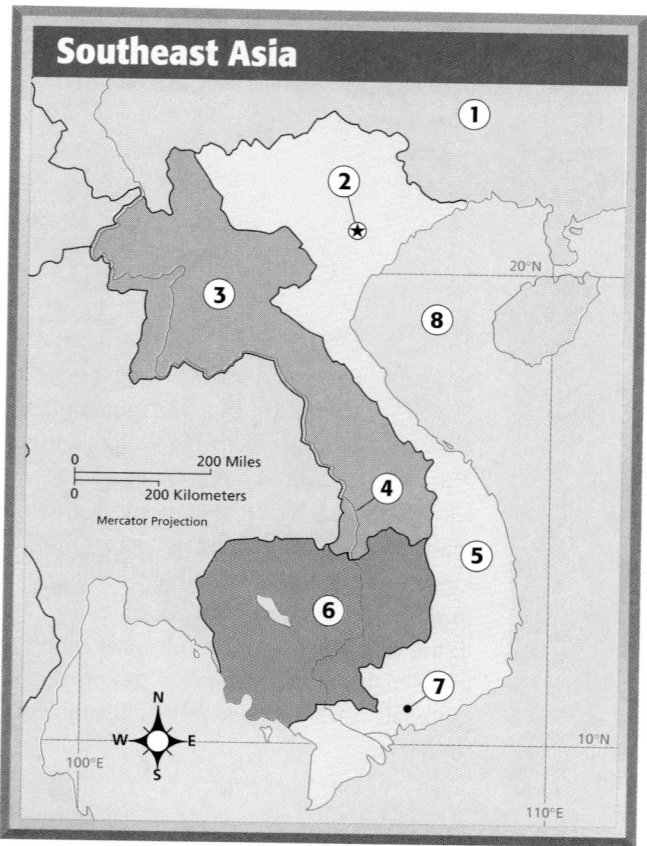

Southeast Asia

internet connect

TOPIC: Vietnam
GO TO: go.hrw.com
KEYWORD: SD1 Vietnam

Accessing the Internet through the HRW Web site, research the history of Southeast Asia since the end of the Vietnam War. Then prepare an oral report that outlines the changes in the countries of Southeast Asia since the end of the war.

BUILDING YOUR PORTFOLIO

Complete one or all of the following projects independently or cooperatively.

1 Global Relations
Imagine that you are a U.S. delegate to the Geneva conference. **Create a chart, photo essay, videotape, or other visual presentation** that shows your proposal for Indochina's future. Then write a short statement indicating how your plan could lessen the risk of U.S. military involvement in Vietnam.

2 Democratic Values
Imagine that you are a reporter covering the civil rights movement. **Write a script** for a 15-minute news program that describes the specific concerns of the civil rights leaders about the Vietnam War. Your comments should examine conditions in Vietnam, economic and social factors at home, and U.S. government policies.

3 Cultural Diversity
Imagine that you are a Vietnamese veteran of the Vietnam War. **Write a letter to a U.S. veteran** explaining how the Vietnamese people's long history of resisting control by outside powers helped them endure terrible hardships and continue fighting. Describe the similarities and differences between Vietnamese history and U.S. history.

PEACE AT LAST
JAN. 27 1973
VIETNAM CEASEFIRE

U·N·I·T 9

Review

BUILDING YOUR PORTFOLIO

Outlined below are four projects. Independently or cooperatively, complete one and use the products to demonstrate your mastery of the historical concepts involved.

1 Economic Development

Presidents Kennedy and Johnson issued a series of reforms designed to transform American society. Many of these programs were designed to improve the economic conditions for poor Americans. Imagine that you are serving as an adviser to President Johnson. *Create your own proposal* for a program that addresses an issue facing a group of people that you believe need assistance. You may wish to use portfolio materials you designed in the unit chapters to help you.

Rural poverty in 1965

United Farm Workers marching

2 Democratic Values

For many Americans the greatest strides in civil rights came in the 30 years following World War II. African Americans, Hispanics, Americans with disabilities, women, and other groups made progress in securing rights that had long been guaranteed to others. *Rehearse and present a 15-minute news program* to the class discussing the advances made in civil rights. You may wish to use portfolio materials you designed in the unit chapters to help you.

3 Technology and Society

In the 1960s advances in science and technology, population growth and shifts, and a rising standard of living helped transform the daily lives of Americans. *Develop a slide show* that documents some of the changes in everyday life during the 1960s. You may wish to use portfolio materials you designed in the unit chapters to help you.

Cereal advertisement

4 Global Relations

The U.S. government entered into the conflict between North and South Vietnam to prevent the spread of communism. The U.S. military drafted U.S. citizens to fight in the conflict. *Create a dialogue* between a young student about to be drafted and a teacher of government. The dialogue should focus on the importance of the conflict and the responsibilities of both the U.S. government and the student. You may wish to use portfolio materials you designed in the unit chapters to help you.

Anti-Vietnam protest in New York City

Further Reading

Evans, Sara M. *Personal Politics.* Knopf, 1979. A discussion of the women's rights movement and its relationship to the civil rights movement.

Hampton, Henry, and Steve Fayer. *Voices of Freedom.* Bantam Books, 1990. Oral history of the civil rights movement.

Howard, Gerald, ed. *The Sixties: Art, Politics, and Media of our Most Explosive Decade.* Paragon House, 1991. A collection of essays from important personalities of the 1960s.

O'Brien, Tim. *The Things They Carried.* Houghton Mifflin, 1990. A war veteran's fictional account of the experiences of soldiers in the Vietnam War.

O'Neil, Doris C., ed. *Life—The '60s.* Little, Brown, 1989. A social history overview of the 1960s.

Thompson, Robert Smith. *The Missiles of October.* Simon & Schuster, 1992. The story of the Cuban missile crisis.

Young, Marilyn B. *The Vietnam Wars, 1945–1990.* HarperCollins, 1991. History of the Vietnam War and its aftermath.

Internet Connect and Holt Researcher CD–ROM *Review*

In assigned groups, develop a multimedia presentation about America between 1960 and 1978. Choose information from the chapter Internet Connect activities and from the **Holt Researcher** CD–ROM that best reflects the major topics of the period. Write an outline and a script for your presentation, which may be shown to the class.

Modern Times

1968–Present

Many Americans celebrated the nation's bicentennial in 1976 with fireworks.

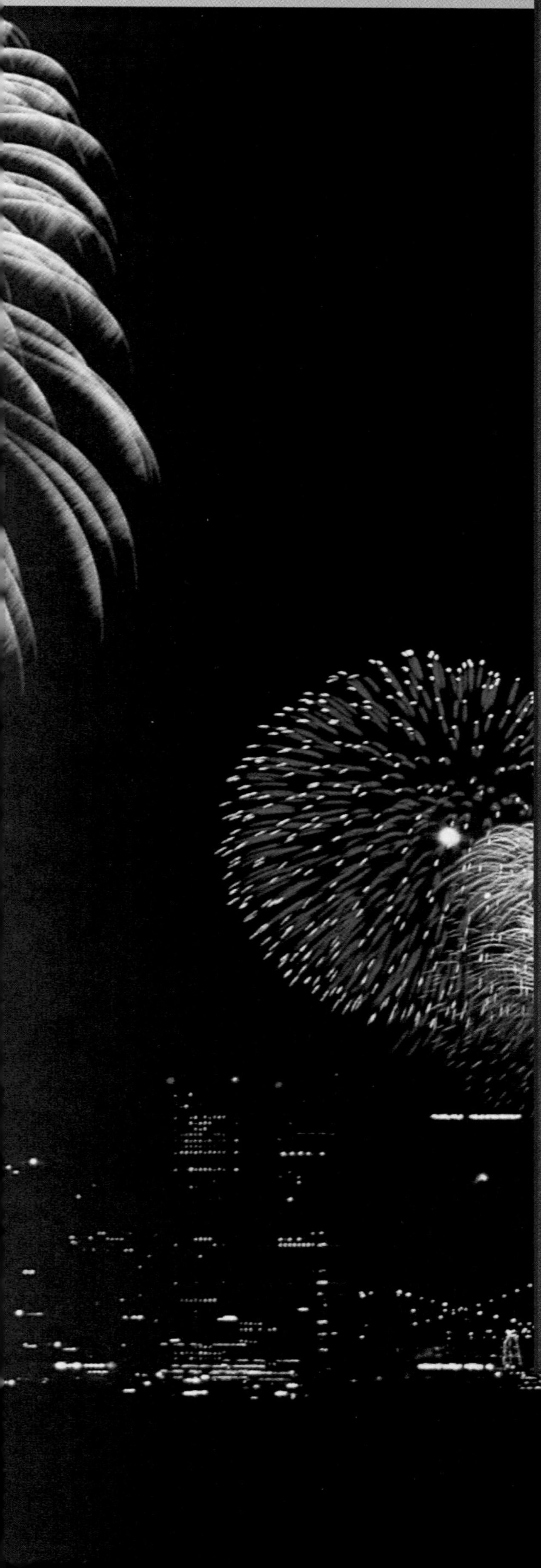

CHAPTER 34

From Nixon to Carter

1968–1980

CHAPTER 35

The Republican Revolution

1980–1992

CHAPTER 36

Life in the 1990s and Beyond

1990–Present

Main Events

- Richard M. Nixon's presidency
- The Watergate scandal
- Rising inflation
- The Republican Revolution
- The end of the Cold War
- The Gulf War
- The expansion of electronic communications
- The development of the global economy
- The expansion of democracy

Main Ideas

- *How did domestic and foreign concerns influence the policies of the presidents of the 1970s?*
- *How did Ronald Reagan inspire the Republican Revolution of the 1980s?*
- *What challenges did Americans face during the 1990s?*

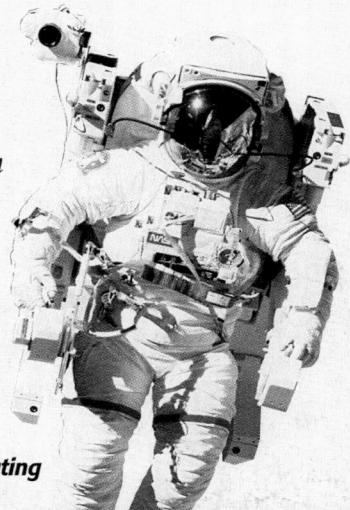

U.S. astronaut floating on a space walk

1968–1980
From Nixon to Carter

Neil Armstrong walks on the Moon.

1968

1970

1972

1972
Daily Life
A federal law banning cigarette advertisements on radio and television goes into effect.

1973
Politics
Vice President Spiro Agnew resigns from office.

1973
World Events
War breaks out in the Middle East when several Arab states attack Israel.

1969
Science and Technology
Astronaut Neil Armstrong becomes the first person to walk on the Moon.

The cast of All in the Family

1971
The Arts
The television situation comedy *All in the Family*, which examines controversial issues such as racial conflict, debuts.

1972
World Events
Chinese leaders welcome Richard Nixon, the first U.S. president to visit China.

President Nixon at the Great Wall of China

Before You Read

Build on What You Know

Throughout the 1960s the United States increased its involvement in the Vietnam War. As the war escalated, so did criticism of America's role in the conflict. Republican Richard Nixon won the presidential election of 1968 promising to end the war in Vietnam and to restore law and order to society. In this chapter you will learn how scandal ruined Nixon's presidency and how Presidents Gerald Ford and Jimmy Carter struggled to lead the nation. You will also learn how the tensions of the era transformed American culture.

Movie poster for *Jaws*

Protest against Three Mile Island

1975
The Arts
Steven Spielberg's *Jaws* becomes the highest-earning motion picture released to date.

1975
Daily Life
Americans are able to purchase video games that can be played on television sets.

1977
Business and Finance
Steven Jobs and Stephen Wozniak found the Apple Computer company.

1978
Politics
The U.S. Senate ratifies the Panama Canal Treaties by very close votes.

1979
Daily Life
Radiation is released from the Three Mile Island nuclear power plant after a cooling system fails.

1976 ———————————— **1978** ———————————— **1980**

1976
Daily Life
Americans celebrate the nation's bicentennial, the 200th anniversary of the signing of the Declaration of Independence.

1977
The Arts
The Bee Gees, a disco group, begin their record string of six straight number-one hit singles.

1979
World Events
Soviet troops invade Afghanistan and install a pro-Soviet government.

1980
Business and Finance
The Rollerblade company begins production of in-line roller skates.

1980
World Events
The United States and 64 other nations boycott the Summer Olympics held in Moscow.

Bicentennial fireworks in New York City

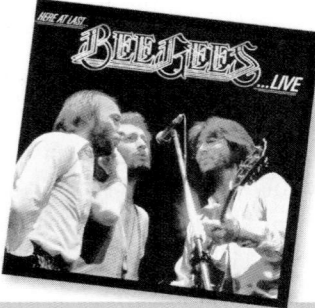

A live recording of the Bee Gees

Think About Themes

Decide whether you agree or disagree with the following statements. Note why in your journal.

Democratic Values The president has the right to keep certain information secret from the American public.

Economic Development Government should not intervene during an economic recession because the business cycle will always correct itself.

Global Relations A nation's foreign policy should be based on practical national-security interests, not on moral or ethical ideals.

SECTION 1

The Nixon Years

Richard Nixon

EYEWITNESSES TO History

66 *As I saw it, America in the 1960s had undergone a misguided crash program aimed at using the power of the presidency and the federal government to right past wrongs by trying to legislate social progress. This was the idea behind Kennedy's New Frontier and Johnson's Great Society. The problems were real and the intention worthy, but the method was foredoomed [bound to fail]. By the end of the decade its costs had become almost prohibitively high in terms of the way it undermined [weakened] fundamental relationships within our federal system, created confusions about our national values, and corroded American belief in ourselves as a people and as a nation.* 99
—**President Richard Nixon**

OBJECTIVES

Read to understand:
1. how President Nixon's policies differed from those of Presidents Johnson and Kennedy
2. how President Nixon responded to economic problems
3. what the causes and effects of the energy crisis were
4. what average Americans and the government did to help clean up the environment
5. what beliefs guided Nixon's foreign-policy decisions

KEY TERMS

Silent Majority
Family Assistance Plan
southern strategy
stagflation
Organization of Petroleum
   Exporting Countries
Environmental Protection
   Agency
Endangered Species Act
realpolitik
Strategic Arms
   Limitation Talks
détente

KEY PEOPLE

Warren Burger
Henry Kissinger
Leonid Brezhnev
Salvador Allende
Golda Meir

After he won the 1968 presidential election, Richard Nixon recalled his attitude toward the policies of Presidents Johnson and Kennedy. Nixon attempted to redefine the relationship between the federal government and the states during the early 1970s. However, he encountered unanticipated domestic and foreign-policy crises.

Courting the Silent Majority

Much of President Nixon's support came from middle-class voters weary of the social unrest of the 1960s. Nixon called these people the **Silent Majority**—"the forgotten Americans, the non-shouters, the non-demonstrators." He won their votes by pledging to restore law and order and to cut back Democratic programs.

Reforming welfare. Nixon agreed with the criticism that Great Society programs had failed to significantly decrease poverty in the United States. He believed that liberal policies had created a complex, inefficient system that made people dependent on the federal government. The welfare system, which had grown from some 5.9 million recipients in 1960 to some 12.8 million in 1970, came under particular attack. "From the first days of my administration I wanted to get rid of the costly failures of the Great Society," Nixon later recalled. "Welfare reform was my highest domestic priority."

Under the existing welfare system, much of the aid for poor families was in the form of services such as Medicaid and nutrition programs. Nixon proposed replacing this system with the **Family Assistance Plan** (FAP), which would guarantee families a minimum income. Under the plan, adults able to work would have to accept job training or work assignments. Supporters of the FAP argued that giving money directly to families would reduce welfare programs and the waste that went with them. Some critics of the plan charged that such direct aid would make poor families even more dependent on the federal government.

The FAP's work requirement also generated intense opposition from welfare-rights supporters. George Wiley, head of the National Welfare Rights Organization, declared, "When Richard Nixon is ready to give up his $200,000 a year salary to scrub floors and empty bedpans in the interest of his family, then we'll take him seriously." The Senate ultimately voted down the FAP.

Seeking southern support. In addition to trying to reform the welfare system, Nixon planned not to ask for any new civil rights legislation. This decision was part of his **southern strategy**—a plan to woo conservative southern white voters away from the Democratic Party. As part of this approach, Nixon also delayed pressuring southern schools to desegregate. When the Supreme Court ruled in 1971 that busing could be used to integrate schools, Nixon opposed the ruling.

Chief Justice Warren Burger (center) poses with the other members of the Supreme Court.

When Chief Justice Earl Warren retired in 1969, Nixon appointed a conservative justice, Warren Burger, to head the Court. The Senate rejected two other Nixon nominees, both from southern states. Nixon used these rejections to win southern support. He complained, "The real reason for their rejection was their legal philosophy . . . and also the accident of their birth, the fact that they were born in the South." The president eventually appointed three conservative justices: Harry Blackmun, Lewis Powell, and William Rehnquist.

✔ **READING CHECK:** How did President Nixon's policies differ from those of Presidents Johnson and Kennedy?

Tackling the Economy

Reversing the liberal policies of the 1960s was not the only challenge President Nixon faced. He also had to manage a faltering economy. The United States had enjoyed an economic boom during the 1960s, but the economy had begun to show signs of trouble by the time Nixon took office. Heavy government spending on social programs and on the Vietnam War had contributed to a recession and growing unemployment. Normally, when unemployment is high, inflation is low. Yet when Nixon took office, both inflation and unemployment rose. This combination of rising unemployment and inflation is called **stagflation**.

PRESIDENTIAL Lives

1913–1994
In Office 1969–1974

Richard M. Nixon

Richard Milhous Nixon's hard work and intense ambition helped him rise to the top ranks of the Republican Party. Having grown up in a poor family in California, Nixon was determined to succeed.

One of the most famous examples of Nixon's ability to bounce back from political challenges came during the 1952 presidential election. Nixon, who was Dwight Eisenhower's vice presidential running mate, had been accused of accepting personal gifts from wealthy businessmen. He appeared on national television to deny the charges. In what came to be called the Checkers speech, Nixon admitted to accepting one personal gift. "You know what it was?" the candidate asked. "It was a little cocker spaniel dog . . . black, white, and spotted, and our little girl Tricia, the six-year-old, named it Checkers. . . . And I just want to say this, right now, that regardless of what they say about it, we're going to keep it." The Checkers speech was well received and may have saved Nixon from being dropped from the Republican ticket.

Inflation. President Nixon used price and wage freezes to fight inflation. *Does this cartoon dollar bill support Nixon's actions? Explain your answer.*

In August 1971 Nixon took a drastic step to curb inflation by imposing temporary freezes on prices, rents, and wages. This action surprised many people, since Republicans typically opposed such action. Labor leaders feared that wage freezes would hurt those earning the least. AFL–CIO president George Meany called it "Robin Hood in reverse, because it robs from the poor and gives to the rich." Nixon, however, was bowing to political reality. Democratic Party leaders had started referring to the nation's economic troubles as the result of "Nixonomics." Nixon hoped that taking action on the economy would help him win the upcoming presidential election. The strategy worked. Inflation slowed, and Nixon was re-elected in 1972. However, when he eased controls, inflation shot up again. In 1974 the inflation rate topped 12 percent.

✔ **READING CHECK:** How did President Nixon respond to economic problems?

The Energy Crisis

During the 1970s rising oil costs became a major cause of inflation and consumer worry. Since World War II, the U.S. economy had grown increasingly dependent on foreign oil. By 1973 Americans consumed twice as much oil as they produced.

OPEC Member Nations in the Middle East and North Africa, 1970s

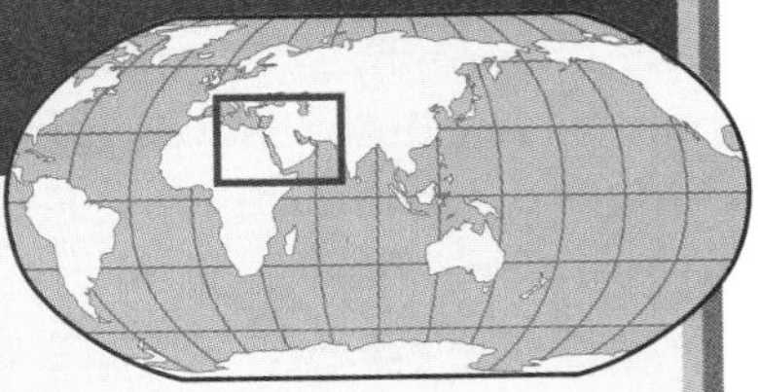

Learning from Maps OPEC produced much of the world's oil supply during the 1970s.

❓ **REGION** Which countries in the Middle East and North Africa were members of OPEC?

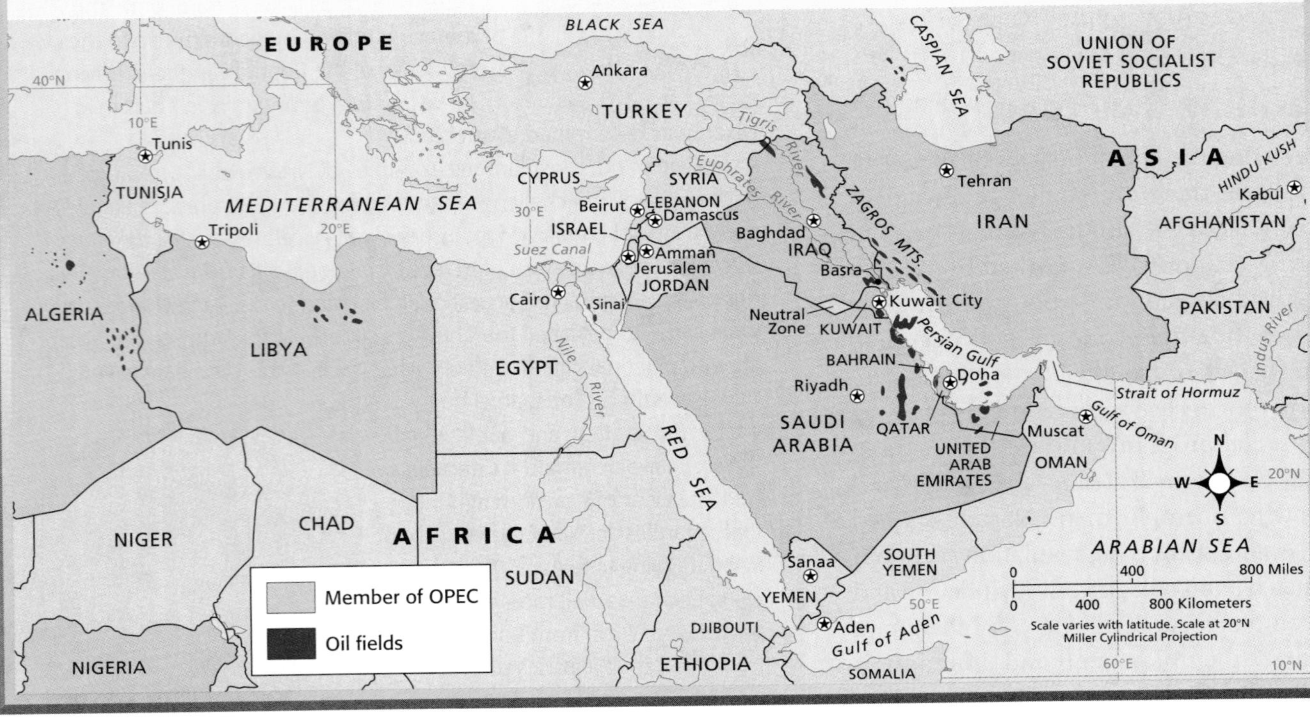

EUROPE
BLACK SEA
Ankara ⊛
TURKEY
CASPIAN SEA
UNION OF SOVIET SOCIALIST REPUBLICS
40°N
10°E
Tunis ⊛
TUNISIA
MEDITERRANEAN SEA
CYPRUS
SYRIA
Tehran ⊛
A S I A
HINDU KUSH
Kabul ⊛
30°E
Beirut ⊛ LEBANON
Damascus ⊛
ZAGROS MTS.
IRAN
AFGHANISTAN
Tripoli ⊛
20°E
ISRAEL
Baghdad ⊛
Suez Canal
⊛ Amman
Jerusalem ⊛
IRAQ
Basra ⊛
JORDAN
PAKISTAN
Cairo ⊛
Sinai
Neutral Zone
⊛ Kuwait City
Indus River
ALGERIA
LIBYA
EGYPT
Nile River
KUWAIT
Persian Gulf
BAHRAIN
⊛ Doha
Strait of Hormuz
Riyadh ⊛
QATAR
UNITED ARAB EMIRATES
⊛ Muscat
Gulf of Oman
OMAN
N
W E
S
20°N
RED SEA
SAUDI ARABIA
ARABIAN SEA
NIGER
CHAD
A F R I C A
SUDAN
Sanaa ⊛
SOUTH YEMEN
0   400   800 Miles
0   400   800 Kilometers
Scale varies with latitude. Scale at 20°N
Miller Cylindrical Projection
50°E
YEMEN
DJIBOUTI
⊛ Aden
Gulf of Aden
60°E
10°N
NIGERIA
ETHIOPIA
SOMALIA

■ Member of OPEC
■ Oil fields

■ **Understanding Change** The energy crisis of the 1970s led to increased calls for vehicles that were more fuel-efficient and for an overall decrease in gasoline consumption. *Since then, how much has the average gas mileage per car changed? Given the changes in average gas consumption per car, what might account for the increase in total gasoline consumption?*

THEN

Now

Gasoline Consumption

	Then	**Now**
Total gas consumption	92.3 billion gallons	146.7 billion gallons
Average annual consumption per car	688 gallons	531 gallons
Average gas mileage — cars	13.5 miles per gallon	21.3 miles per gallon
Average gas mileage — trucks	5.5 miles per gallon	6.2 miles per gallon

Source: *Statistical Abstract of the United States: 1998.* Data reflect 1970 and 1996.

Price hikes. In June 1973 President Nixon warned the nation that the "supply of domestic energy resources available to us is not keeping pace with our ever growing demand." Americans soon learned the costs of this problem. That October several Arab nations cut off oil shipments to the United States as punishment for the U.S. support of Israel in a new Arab-Israeli war. In December the **Organization of Petroleum Exporting Countries** (OPEC)—a group founded in 1960 by five oil-producing countries that wanted to increase oil prices—announced a price hike. A barrel of oil that had sold for about $3.00 in the summer of 1973 cost $11.65 in December 1973, an increase of almost 400 percent.

The oil embargo and price hike triggered an energy crisis in the United States during the winter of 1973–74. The cost of electricity, gasoline, and heating oil soared, causing severe hardship in some parts of the country. One Detroit hospital told its patients to stay in bed to keep warm. "We had so little oil left that we just had to cut back the thermostats," noted one hospital official. "In storage rooms and areas with no patients, it got as low as 40 degrees."

The energy crisis also created a great deal of anxiety. Public-opinion analyst Daniel Yankelovich noted "signs of panic" among Americans who were "growing fearful that the country has run out of energy." Across the nation motorists lined up at gas stations to buy a few extra gallons. Lines in New Jersey sometimes stretched four miles long. The Arab nations lifted their embargo in March 1974, but the price of oil remained high.

Energy policy. In response to the crisis, Nixon announced a program designed to make the United States less dependent on foreign oil. He called for energy

conservation and signed a bill that reduced the highway speed limit to 55 miles per hour, thereby saving some 3.4 billion gallons of gas per year. He also signed a bill authorizing construction of a pipeline to transport oil south from Alaska. Nevertheless, U.S. dependence on foreign oil continued to grow.

The government also supported replacing the use of fossil fuels with nuclear energy. Nuclear power was regarded as a cleaner and more economical source of energy because it did not burn fossil fuels. The Atomic Energy Commission predicted that nuclear power plants would generate half the nation's electrical power by the end of the century. By January 1974 there were 42 nuclear power plants in operation, and more than 160 new plants were under construction or in the planning stages. Yet many critics worried that the risks of a nuclear accident outweighed the benefits of nuclear power.

✔ **READING CHECK:** What were the causes and effects of the energy crisis?

Cleaning up the environment.

President Nixon took office at a time when Americans were becoming increasingly worried about the environment. Two events helped raise awareness of environmental issues. The first was a massive oil spill off the coast of Santa Barbara, California, in 1969. The second was the first Earth Day celebration in April 1970. Some 20 million Americans across the nation took part in Earth Day activities. At an event in New York City's Central Park, Episcopal priest Paul Moore spoke to a group of schoolchildren. "Unless we stop stealing, exploiting [taking advantage of] and ruining nature for our own gain, we will lose everything."

In 1970 Congress responded to growing public concern by creating the **Environmental Protection Agency** (EPA), which had power to enforce environmental laws. That same year, Congress passed two laws intended to limit pollution. The Clean Air Act set air-quality standards and tough emissions guidelines for automakers. The Water Quality Improvement Act required oil companies to pay some of the cleanup costs of oil spills. A 1972 act set limits on the discharge of industrial pollutants into water. To protect wildlife in danger of extinction, Congress passed the **Endangered Species Act** in 1973.

✔ **READING CHECK:** What roles did average Americans and the government play in cleaning up the environment?

Earth Day celebrations like this one promote environmental awareness.

Foreign Affairs Under Nixon

Although domestic issues demanded much of President Nixon's attention, his main interest was foreign affairs. Working closely with his national security adviser, Henry Kissinger, Nixon sought to reshape U.S. foreign policy.

The Nixon-Kissinger approach.

Nixon and Kissinger shared a belief in **realpolitik**, or practical politics. This approach argued that national interests, rather than ideals such as democracy and human rights, should guide U.S. foreign policy. Nixon believed that governments allied with the United States should receive U.S. support even if they sometimes violated human rights.

The chief goal of the Nixon-Kissinger foreign policy was to establish a balance of power among the world's five major powers. These powers were China, Japan, the Soviet Union, the United States, and Western Europe. Nixon explained his reasoning in 1972.

66 The only time in the history of the world that we have had any extended period of peace is when there has been a balance of power. It is when one nation becomes infinitely more powerful in relation to its potential competitors that the danger of war arises. 99

LURIE'S OPINION

CHINESE SUMMIT

USSR SUMM

INTERPRETING THE VISUAL RECORD

Foreign policy. President Nixon tried to improve relations with China without increasing U.S.-Soviet tensions. *What does this cartoon suggest about the difficulties Nixon faced?*

The China visit.

In keeping with his belief in realpolitik, President Nixon sought to improve relations with the People's Republic of China. By the 1970s China and the Soviet Union had become bitter enemies. Nixon followed the ancient military strategy that "the enemy of my enemy is my friend." He hoped that closer U.S. ties with China would further divide the communist world.

In 1972 Nixon visited China. The two nations agreed to work together to promote peace in the Pacific region and to develop trade relations and cultural and scientific ties. Furthermore, Nixon promised the eventual withdrawal of U.S. forces from Taiwan in order to lessen Chinese support for the North Vietnamese. Although many conservative Americans were stunned by this move, it gave the president leverage to promote a new policy with the Soviet Union.

The Moscow summit.

In May 1972, just three months after visiting China, Nixon flew to Moscow for talks with Soviet leader Leonid Brezhnev. The two agreed to promote trade and to cooperate on other issues of mutual concern.

Nixon and Brezhnev also signed a treaty limiting nuclear weapons. This treaty was the product of the **Strategic Arms Limitation Talks** (SALT). It limited the number of intercontinental nuclear missiles—those capable of traveling long distances to other continents—each nation could have. Although the SALT treaty did not end the arms race, it was a small first step toward reducing the nuclear threat. As a result of the arms talks, the United States and the Soviet

THROUGH OTHERS' EYES

Chinese Views of Nixon's Visit

Chinese leaders had their reasons for allowing President Nixon to visit their nation. At a dinner banquet in Nixon's honor, Premier Jou En-lai detailed some of the Chinese government's goals for its meeting with the leader of the United States.

66 The peoples of our two countries have always been friendly to each other. But owing to reasons known to all, contacts between the two peoples were suspended for over twenty years. . . . At the present time it has become a strong desire of the Chinese and American peoples to promote the normalization of relations between the two countries and work for the relaxation of tension. . . . Differences should not hinder China and the United States from establishing normal state relations on the basis of the Five Principles of mutual respect for sovereignty [political authority] and territorial integrity, mutual nonaggression, noninterference in each other's internal affairs, equality and mutual benefit, and peaceful coexistence. 99

Union entered into a period of **détente**—a lessening of military and diplomatic tensions between the countries.

Trouble spots. In general, Nixon and Kissinger ignored countries that were not of direct strategic importance to the United States. One exception was the South American nation of Chile. In 1970 Chile elected Salvador Allende, a Socialist, as president. Fearing that Allende planned to turn Chile into "another Cuba" allied with the Soviet Union, Nixon tried to topple the Allende government. He cut off aid to Chile and provided funds to Allende's opponents in the Chilean military. He also instructed the Central Intelligence Agency (CIA) to disrupt economic and political life in the country. In September 1973 the Chilean army killed Allende and set up a pro-American military dictatorship.

Shortly after the Chilean revolt, conflict erupted in the Middle East. Six years earlier, in 1967, Israel had defeated its Arab neighbors—Egypt, Jordan, and Syria—in the Six-Day War. However, the Arab states continued to harass Israel, and Israel continued to strike back. Israeli prime minister Golda Meir later recalled that "the only time that Arab states were prepared to recognize the existence of . . . Israel was when they attacked it in order to wipe it out."

In October 1973 Egypt and Syria invaded Israel in an attempt to recover land lost in the Six-Day War. The attack, which came on the Jewish holiday of Yom Kippur, caught the Israelis by surprise. They launched a counterattack, however, that threatened Egypt's capital, Cairo. When the Soviets threatened to intervene by sending troops into the region, President Nixon put all U.S. forces on alert. A major military confrontation seemed possible. Within days, however, the superpowers persuaded the Arabs and Israelis to accept a cease-fire. Détente had survived a critical test, but prospects for a lasting peace in the Middle East remained in doubt.

Israeli prime minister Golda Meir

✔ **READING CHECK:** What belief guided Nixon's foreign-policy decisions?

SECTION 1 REVIEW

Define and explain the significance of the following terms:
Silent Majority
Family Assistance Plan
southern strategy
stagflation
Organization of Petroleum
    Exporting Countries
Environmental Protection Agency
Endangered Species Act
realpolitik
Strategic Arms Limitation Talks
détente

Identify and explain the significance of the following individuals:
Warren Burger   Salvador Allende
Henry Kissinger   Golda Meir
Leonid Brezhnev

1. **Using Graphic Organizers** Copy the chart below. Use it to explain the causes and effects of the energy crisis.

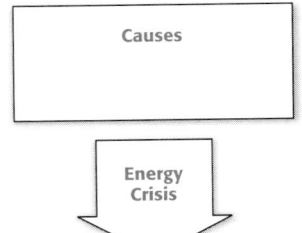

2. **Comparing and Contrasting** How did President Nixon's policies differ from those followed by Lyndon Johnson and John F. Kennedy?
3. **Evaluating** Was Nixon's decision to impose wage and price controls an effective way to manage the economy? Explain your answer.
4. **Identifying Values** Why did Americans take an increased interest in the environment during the 1970s? How did government respond?

Critical Thinking

5. Do you agree with President Nixon's belief that realpolitik was an appropriate approach to foreign policy? Why or why not?
Consider:
• the effect of Nixon's visit to China
• the SALT treaty
• events in Chile

From Watergate to Ford

KEY TERMS

Committee to Re-elect the President
Watergate
Saturday Night Massacre
Whip Inflation Now
Mayaguez

KEY PEOPLE

Bob Woodward
Carl Bernstein
Sam Ervin
James McCord
John Dean
Archibald Cox
Spiro Agnew
Gerald Ford
Barbara Jordan

Bob Woodward (left) and Carl Bernstein investigated the Watergate break-in.

EYEWITNESSES TO History

66 *Nixon had three goals: to win by the biggest electoral landslide in history; to be remembered as a peacemaker; and to be accepted by the 'Establishment' as an equal. He achieved all these objectives by the end of 1972 and the beginning of 1973. And he lost them all two months later—partly because he turned a dream into an obsession.* 99

—Henry Kissinger

Richard Nixon (left) and Henry Kissinger

Henry Kissinger reflected on the presidency of his former boss years after Richard Nixon left the White House in disgrace. Nixon's personality flaws led him to destroy his presidency. His behavior caused a constitutional crisis that shook the nation and caused many Americans to lose faith in their leaders.

Crisis in the Presidency

During his first term in the White House, President Nixon increasingly behaved as though there should be no limits on his power. He shifted much of the authority of the cabinet, whose appointments required Senate approval, to his personal White House staff. He also hid vital information from Congress and the public.

Dark secrets. In 1971 Nixon ordered his staff to compile an "enemies list" of critics who opposed his policies. After Daniel Ellsberg's leak of the Pentagon Papers, Nixon told aide Charles Colson, "Do whatever has to be done to stop these leaks. . . . I want it done, whatever the cost." The White House organized a secret unit called the plumbers that included former agents of the CIA and Federal Bureau of Investigation (FBI). The group was ordered to stop leaks and to carry out a variety of illegal actions in the name of "national security."

By 1972 these secret activities had grown into a full-scale effort to ensure Nixon's re-election. In June five men were caught breaking into the offices of the Democratic National Committee in the Watergate office and apartment complex in Washington, D.C. They were carrying wiretap equipment and other spying devices. It was soon discovered that these men were being paid with funds from Nixon's campaign organization, the **Committee to Re-elect the President** (CREEP).

The White House denied any link to the break-in, calling it a "third-rate burglary." However, *Washington Post* reporters Bob Woodward and Carl Bernstein kept digging for the truth. A high-level source known as Deep Throat informed them that White House officials and CREEP had hired 50 agents to sabotage the Democrats' chances in the 1972 election.

Formulating a Hypothesis

To write a successful history research paper, one must first formulate a hypothesis around which to organize the paper. A *hypothesis* is a statement that tries to explain why a situation existed or an event took place. It must be formed from and tested against the historical evidence that one gathers while conducting research. The hypothesis provides a central point for analyzing and discussing this evidence in one's paper.

How to Formulate a Hypothesis

1. **Conduct research.** Identify the topic that you wish to research and develop one or more questions that you hope to answer in your paper. Then conduct research at your school or local public library.
2. **Analyze the evidence.** Study the information in your sources carefully, keeping in mind your questions about the topic. Look for cause-and-effect relationships and long-term developments that emerge from the facts you examine.
3. **Develop an idea that is based on the evidence.** Use your analysis of the evidence to formulate an idea that answers your questions about the topic. Make sure that this idea, or initial *hypothesis*, is supported by specific information in your sources.
4. **Consider other possibilities.** Once you have formed your initial hypothesis, think about other ways to answer your questions about the topic. Then adjust your idea if necessary to include one or more of these different explanations.
5. **State your hypothesis.** After you have settled on a final hypothesis, write it out in a short, declarative statement. This statement should express clearly the central idea that you plan to present in your paper.

Applying the Strategy

Read and evaluate the following hypothesis statement, which tries to explain why Richard Nixon won a landslide victory in the 1972 presidential election.

> Richard Nixon was re-elected to the presidency because of the secret activities and electoral "dirty tricks" of CREEP.

Practicing the Strategy

Answer the following questions.

1. What historical evidence could be used to support the hypothesis presented above?
2. What are some other ways to explain Nixon's landslide victory in 1972? What evidence could be used to support these explanations?
3. In your opinion, what hypothesis best explains Nixon's landslide victory in 1972?

The investigation. Despite the Watergate break-in, Nixon won re-election in 1972 by a landslide. By the spring of 1973 both the executive and the legislative branches of government were investigating the charges of criminal activities and the attempted cover-up. Senator Sam Ervin of North Carolina led the Senate investigation into the scandal known as **Watergate**. One of the witnesses was James McCord, a former CIA agent who had taken part in the Watergate break-in. McCord admitted that top White House officials had helped plan the break-in. He linked the cover-up to "the very highest levels of the White House." McCord's admissions broke the case wide open.

The biggest bombshells were yet to come, however. In May 1973 live television coverage of the Senate hearings began. Across the nation millions of Americans watched as senators grilled witnesses and compiled evidence of official misconduct. Several top White House officials were eventually convicted in criminal trials and sent to jail. However, Nixon's role in Watergate remained unclear. Time and again, Howard Baker of Tennessee, a key member of the Senate committee, asked, "What did the president know and when did he know it?"

In June 1973 Nixon's former White House attorney John Dean provided the stunning answer. The president had been directly involved in the cover-up.

✔ **READING CHECK:** What were the issues surrounding the Watergate scandal?

The Nixon Resignation

President Nixon denied John Dean's charges. There seemed to be no way to prove that Dean was telling the truth. Then, in a surprising turn of events, another witness testified that Nixon had secretly tape-recorded his conversations in the White House.

The White House tapes. Investigators believed that the tapes would reveal the truth about Watergate. A battle for control of the tapes followed. The Justice Department's special prosecutor, Archibald Cox, demanded that the president turn over the tapes. Nixon refused. Citing executive privilege, he claimed that releasing the tapes would endanger national security.

In the midst of the controversy over the tapes, in October 1973 Vice President Spiro Agnew was charged with income tax evasion. Agnew pleaded no contest and resigned on October 10 in exchange for reduced punishment. Nixon then nominated Gerald Ford, the Republican leader in the House of Representatives, for vice president.

Shortly before Agnew's resignation, a federal judge ordered Nixon to release the White House tapes. The president refused. On October 20, after Special Prosecutor Cox demanded that he obey the judge's order, Nixon ordered Attorney General Elliot Richardson to fire Cox. Both the attorney general and Deputy Attorney General William Ruckelshaus resigned rather than obey the president. The task of firing Cox fell to Solicitor General Robert Bork, who complied. This series of events, known as the **Saturday Night Massacre**, outraged the public and led to calls to impeach Nixon. In his own defense, Nixon declared, "People have the right to know whether or not their President is a crook. Well, I am not a crook." Partly as a result of these events, in 1978 Congress authorized the appointment of investigators called independent counsels to conduct investigations into high crimes by top government officials.

Archibald Cox (center) is sworn in as special prosecutor.

Final days. Nixon eventually agreed to release some of the White House tapes, but he resisted turning over the entire set. Not until July 1974, when the Supreme Court rejected Nixon's argument of executive privilege, did Nixon abandon his efforts to keep the tapes. About the same time that the Court announced its ruling, the House Judiciary Committee held nationally televised debates on whether to impeach Nixon. Among the members who favored impeachment was Representative Barbara Jordan, a first-term Democrat from Texas.

Read More About It

Free Find:
Barbara Jordan
After reading about Barbara Jordan on the **Holt Researcher** CD–ROM, write a script for a short play that illustrates Jordan's accomplishments and the obstacles she overcame.

BIOGRAPHY

Barbara Jordan

Barbara Jordan brought a strong sense of moral authority to the Democratic Party. Born in 1936, she grew up in Houston. She excelled in school and eventually received a law degree from Boston University. In 1966 Jordan became the first African American woman elected to the Texas state senate. Her tireless efforts on behalf of social reform won praise from President Lyndon Johnson. He noted, "She proved that black is beautiful before we knew what it meant."

In 1972 Jordan was elected to the U.S. House of Representatives. She soon gained a reputation as a skilled legislator and brilliant public speaker. On July 25, 1974, she explained why she supported impeachment.

66 'We the people'—it is a very eloquent beginning. But when the Constitution of the United States was completed on the seventeenth of September in 1787, I was not included in that 'We the People.' . . . But through the process of amendment, interpretation and court decision, I have finally been included in 'We the People.' . . . My faith in the Constitution is whole. It is complete. . . . I am not going to sit here and be an idle spectator to the . . . destruction of the Constitution. 99

INTERPRETING THE VISUAL RECORD

Nixon. As President Nixon boarded a helicopter to leave the White House, the *Washington Post* announced his resignation. *Does Nixon's expression seem appropriate for the occasion? Explain your answer.*

Despite her outstanding record in Congress, Jordan announced in 1977 that she would not run for a fourth term. She accepted a teaching position at the University of Texas at Austin. Jordan became one of the most popular instructors at the university's Lyndon B. Johnson School of Public Affairs. She was inducted into the National Women's Hall of Fame in 1990. Jordan died in 1996.

With the release of the Nixon tapes, Americans discovered the truth. Nixon had directed the Watergate cover-up and had authorized illegal activities. The House Judiciary Committee recommended that impeachment charges be brought against him. Facing almost certain impeachment by the full House, Nixon finally accepted his fate. On August 8, 1974, he told the nation: "I shall resign the presidency effective at noon tomorrow."

On August 9, 1974, Vice President Gerald Ford was sworn in as the 38th president of the United States. He then nominated Governor Nelson Rockefeller of New York for vice president, and Congress confirmed his choice. For the first time in U.S. history, both the president and vice president held office by appointment, not election.

✔ **READING CHECK:** What role did the White House tapes play in President Nixon's resignation?

Ford Tries to Reunite the Nation

As leader of the Republicans in the House, Gerald Ford had won the respect of colleagues for his honesty and modesty. "I'm a Ford, not a Lincoln," he once joked. The new president, however, lost much of the nation's goodwill just one month after taking office.

Pardon and clemency.

In September 1974 Ford granted President Nixon a full pardon. He explained that if Nixon were put on trial, "ugly passions would again be aroused. . . . And the credibility [believability] of our free institutions of government would again be challenged at home and abroad." Many people found Ford's explanation unconvincing. They suspected that the pardon had been agreed upon in advance in exchange for Nixon's resignation—a charge that Ford denied. Critics of the pardon argued that the full truth of Watergate would never emerge. They pointed to the double standard that allowed Nixon to go free while his co-conspirators were punished. As a result of the pardon, Ford's popularity fell. His approval rating dropped from 71 percent to 50 percent.

Ford took another controversial step one week later. He offered clemency, or official forgiveness, to Vietnam draft evaders. In exchange, they had to reaffirm their allegiance to the United States and spend up to two years performing public service. Supporters of the Vietnam War believed that the offer was unfair to soldiers who had served their country. Meanwhile, just 19 percent of those eligible responded to the offer. Some war resisters, like Dee Knight, contrasted it with the full pardon that Nixon had been granted.

> 66 We knew the clemency was proclaimed just to offset [make up for] the Nixon pardon, which was an insult. We weren't criminals, and Nixon was, but Ford proposed to pardon Nixon unconditionally while offering "alternative punishment" to us. 99

Troubles continue.

Ford soon ran into other problems. Although he campaigned tirelessly for Republican candidates in the November 1974 congressional elections, Democrats gained 43 seats in the House and three in the Senate. Ford quickly encountered conflicts with the Democratic majority that controlled Congress. He vetoed a number of social-welfare bills sponsored by Democrats. In all, Ford vetoed 66 bills during his brief term in office, more than any other president had in such a short time.

Great Debates

Watergate

On the day he took office, President Ford declared, "Our constitution works. Our great republic is a government of laws and not of men. Here the people rule." After Richard Nixon resigned from office, many journalists and average citizens agreed with Ford's observation that the system had worked. Through the application of the rule of law found in the Constitution, Richard Nixon, the most powerful official in the government, had been forced to resign from office for his misdeeds.

Some observers have not been as optimistic about the effect of Watergate on American political life. They argue that Nixon was only forced from office because he made the error of secretly taping evidence that was used against him. Had the tapes never existed, or been destroyed, he probably would have remained in office. Moreover, these critics point out that congressional reforms intended to prevent future scandals have had little effect. In the years after Watergate, political scandals reaching all the way to the White House continued to trouble the American public.

This political cartoon suggests that Richard Nixon controlled President Ford's policies.

As Ford's relations with Congress worsened, he found it increasingly difficult to enact his policies. One of his main goals was to combat inflation, which was being fueled by the soaring cost of oil. Like Nixon, Ford hoped to curb inflation by cutting federal spending. In October 1974 Ford asked Congress to cut some $4 billion from Nixon's proposed budget for the coming year and to increase corporate taxes. During his speech the president sported a button that read WIN. He explained that it stood for **Whip Inflation Now**. Although some 100,000 Americans joined a voluntary organization supporting the president's battle against inflation, Congress rejected Ford's plan.

One year later in October 1975 President Ford told the nation, "Much of our inflation should bear a label, 'Made in Washington, D.C.'" He recommended a combination of tax cuts and budget cuts. Congress approved the tax cut, but rejected a spending cap. While the White House and Congress battled over economic policy, the nation experienced an economic recession.

✔ **READING CHECK:** Why did Ford have difficulty achieving his domestic-policy goals?

Ford's Foreign Policy

In foreign affairs, President Ford continued many of President Nixon's policies. The continuity between the administrations was reflected in Ford's decision to retain Nixon's chief foreign-policy adviser, Henry Kissinger, as secretary of state.

Asia. Ford tried to maintain U.S. influence in Southeast Asia. Toward that end, he requested $722 million in military aid and $20 million in humanitarian aid for Cambodia and South Vietnam. Opposed to additional military ventures in Southeast Asia, Congress rejected any military aid but did approve $300 million in humanitarian assistance. Then, in May 1975, Cambodian Communists seized the *Mayaguez*, an unarmed U.S. cargo ship. The Ford administration saw the seizure as an opportunity to prove that the president could exercise leadership in a crisis. Henry Kissinger urged, "Let's look ferocious." In response, Ford launched a military action intended to free the vessel and its crew. Forty-one Americans were killed in the effort to release the 39 crew members.

The cargo ship Mayaguez *was seized by Cambodian Communists in 1975.*

The president later claimed that the *Mayaguez* incident "had an electrifying reaction as far as the American people were concerned." Ford's job approval rating climbed 11 points after the rescue attempt. While some applauded the president's action, others criticized it as hasty and ill-timed. It was later discovered that the *Mayaguez* crew had already been released before the U.S. attack began.

The Cold War continues. During the mid-1970s Africa became a scene of Cold War conflict. Both Nixon and Ford had largely ignored Africa, but the outbreak of a civil war in Angola attracted U.S. attention. The Soviet Union supported the Popular Front for the Liberation of Angola. The Ford administration secretly provided millions in aid to an opposing group, the National Front. When the Popular Front seized control of Angola, Ford authorized further secret funding. However, Congress learned about the secret payments and ordered the president to halt the operation. Ford complained, "This abdication [giving up] of responsibility by the majority of the Senate will have the greatest consequences for the long-term position of the United States and for international order."

Despite the conflict in Africa, Ford tried to continue the policy of détente toward the Soviet Union. U.S.-Soviet relations grew increasingly strained, however. Former secretary of defense Melvin Laird wrote in 1975, "Clearly, we must shed any lingering illusions we have that détente means the Russians have abandoned their determination to undermine [weaken] Western democracy."

One source of conflict was the Soviet emigration policy, which did not allow Jews and opponents of the government to leave the country. When members of Congress criticized this policy, the Soviets canceled a proposed U.S.-Soviet trade pact. Although Ford successfully negotiated an arms-limitation treaty during a summit meeting in the Soviet Union, the Senate failed to ratify it.

INTERPRETING THE VISUAL RECORD

Angola. President Ford supported the anticommunist National Front in Angola's civil war. *What does this cartoon suggest about U.S. involvement in the war?*

✔ **READING CHECK:** How did Ford attempt to continue Nixon's foreign policies?

SECTION 2 REVIEW

Define and explain the significance of the following terms:
Committee to Re-elect the President
Watergate
Saturday Night Massacre
Whip Inflation Now
Mayaguez

Identify and explain the significance of the following individuals:
Bob Woodward
Carl Bernstein
Sam Ervin
James McCord
John Dean
Archibald Cox
Spiro Agnew
Gerald Ford
Barbara Jordan

1. **Using Graphic Organizers** Copy the graphic below. Use it to explain the major events of the Watergate scandal.

| 1. Crime |
| 2. Cover-Up |
| 3. Investigation |
| 4. Nixon's Response |
| 5. The Court Ruling |
| 6. The Resignation |

2. **Taking a Stand** Do you agree with the Supreme Court ruling that required President Nixon to turn over the White House tapes? Why or why not?
3. **Analyzing** Did responsibility for the failure to manage the economy lie with President Ford or with Congress? Explain your answer.
4. **Using Historical Imagination** Imagine that you are a State Department official. How would you have advised President Ford to respond to the seizure of the *Mayaguez*?

Critical Thinking

5. How do you rate Gerald Ford's performance as president?
   Consider:
   • Watergate's effect on public attitudes toward government
   • Ford's relations with Congress
   • Ford's handling of foreign-policy problems

Carter: The Outsider as President

OBJECTIVES

Read to understand:

1. why voters thought that Jimmy Carter was a different kind of politician

2. how President Carter's handling of domestic issues caused some Americans to lose faith in his administration

3. how Carter's foreign policy differed from that of Nixon and Ford

4. how Carter weakened U.S.-Soviet relations, and how he helped achieve peace in the Middle East

KEY TERMS

National Energy Act
Department of Energy
Three Mile Island accident
Panama Canal Treaties
apartheid
Camp David Accords

KEY PEOPLE

Jimmy Carter
Anwar Sadat
Menachem Begin

EYEWITNESSES TO History

66 *Carter has figured out a couple of very important things. What national leaders and other candidates perceive as a political crisis is actually a spiritual crisis, and that more symbolic communication is the best way to reach Americans drifting in an atmosphere saturated with instant communication.* 99
—**Richard Reeves**

Journalist Richard Reeves evaluated Jimmy Carter, a candidate for the Democratic Party's nomination for president, in a March 1976 magazine article. Frustrated by Watergate, Americans sought a different kind of leader, one who emphasized the values of honesty and openness.

CHALLENGING LEADERSHIP FOR CHALLENGING TIMES

CARTER ★ MONDALE
FOR PRESIDENT ★ FOR VICE PRESIDENT

1976 campaign poster

The Election of 1976

At the 1976 Republican national convention, Gerald Ford narrowly won the party's nomination for president over his more conservative challenger, Ronald Reagan of California. Ford chose conservative senator Bob Dole of Kansas as his running mate.

At the Democratic convention, former Georgia governor Jimmy Carter won his party's nomination. Senator Walter Mondale of Minnesota was his running mate. Little known outside the South, Carter ran as a Washington outsider untouched by Watergate. Central to his campaign was the idea of a new approach to government. Carter promised, "I will never lie to you; I will never mislead you." He noted that he was a born-again Christian whose religious beliefs strongly shaped his politics. During the campaign Carter pledged to make the government decent, honest, and trustworthy. The election was close, however. Carter won by capturing 297 electoral votes to Ford's 240.

On Inauguration Day the new president and his family walked down Pennsylvania Avenue to the White House instead of riding in a limousine. Carter's decision to walk symbolized his desire to keep his administration open to public view. During his presidency, he held several "town meetings" and radio and television call-in sessions to keep in touch with the people.

✔ **READING CHECK:** Why did voters believe that Jimmy Carter was a different kind of politician?

Carter's Domestic Agenda

On his first full day in office, President Carter announced an unconditional pardon for most Vietnam-era draft evaders. This pardon went further than the clemency that had been offered by President Ford.

Jimmy Carter walks to his inauguration with his wife and daughter.

Although this gesture helped heal lingering divisions caused by the war, many Americans disagreed with it. Nonetheless, Carter's approval rating rose, reaching 75 percent after his first 100 days in office. Carter's popularity fell, however, when he tried to tackle other problems facing the nation.

Economic policy. One of Carter's first tasks as president was to stimulate the economy, which was just beginning to emerge from a recession. To revive the economy and create jobs, Carter enacted a series of economic measures, including a tax cut. The Carter administration's policies helped reduce unemployment slightly, but they also fueled inflation, which reached 13.3 percent by 1979. To curb inflation, Carter called for voluntary wage and price controls, along with cuts in federal spending. "Hard choices are necessary if we want to avoid consequences that are even worse," he told the nation. Carter's anti-inflation program, however, did not slow inflation and produced more unemployment. By the summer of 1980 the economy was once again in recession. In a report to Congress, Carter admitted, "There are no economic miracles waiting to be performed."

Lower speed limits encouraged Americans to conserve gasoline.

Facing the energy crisis. The high price of oil was a major cause of the nation's economic woes. In April 1977 Carter introduced a complex energy proposal that won approval from the public. However, it did not do well in Congress, where significant changes were made to the bill. By the time the **National Energy Act** passed in 1978, few of Carter's original proposals remained intact.

Congress did create the **Department of Energy** in 1977 to oversee energy issues. Despite the efforts of the White House and Congress, however, world events continued to threaten the nation's energy supply. In January 1979 a revolution in Iran disrupted world oil shipments. A few months later, OPEC raised the price of oil 50 percent, leading to another U.S. energy crisis. As gasoline supplies dwindled, many gas stations closed or reduced their hours. Tempers flared as frustrated drivers had to wait hours to fill their gas tanks. To promote energy conservation, Carter asked Americans to "honor the 55-m.p.h. speed limit, set thermostats no higher than 65 degrees and limit discretionary [nonessential] driving." Some people responded by driving less and by adopting other energy-saving measures such as installing solar heaters in their homes.

In the midst of the energy crisis another event dramatized the energy problems facing the United States. In late March 1979 a nuclear reactor failed at the Three Mile Island power plant in Pennsylvania. The accident nearly caused a catastrophic meltdown—the melting of the reactor's core. Some 100,000 people fled or were evacuated from the area. Despite grave public doubts about nuclear power after the **Three Mile Island accident**, Carter argued that the nation needed nuclear energy. "We cannot simply shut down our nuclear power plants," he declared.

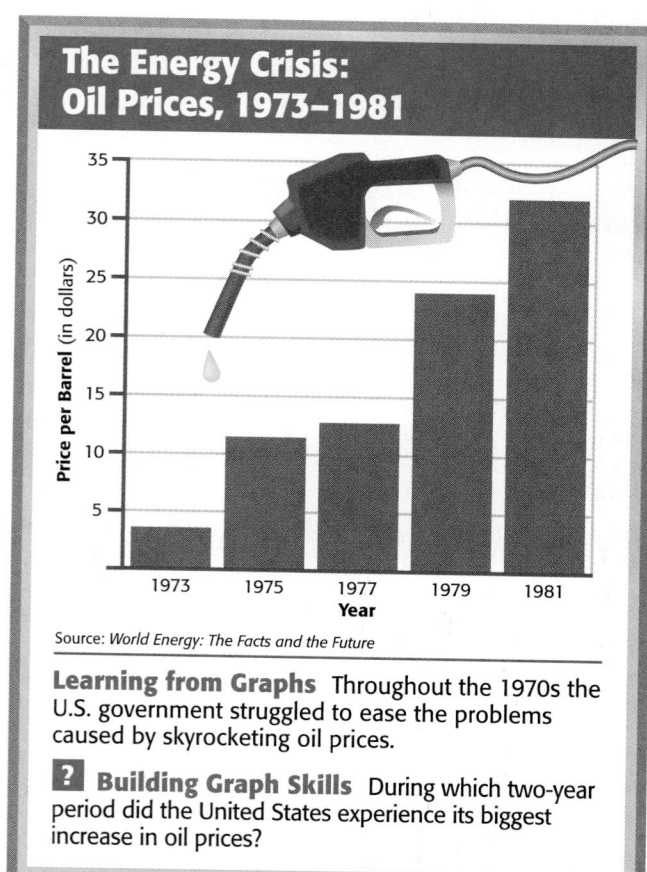

The Energy Crisis: Oil Prices, 1973–1981

Source: *World Energy: The Facts and the Future*

Learning from Graphs Throughout the 1970s the U.S. government struggled to ease the problems caused by skyrocketing oil prices.

? **Building Graph Skills** During which two-year period did the United States experience its biggest increase in oil prices?

Solar Power

The energy crisis of the 1970s prompted Americans to look for new energy sources. Potential energy sources included synthetic fuels, geothermal energy, and even burning garbage. One alternative source that received much attention was solar power. In 1978, supporters of solar energy held Sun Day in order to draw attention to their cause. President Carter also supported the use of solar energy.

Solar energy has several benefits. It is abundant, clean, and renewable.

Scientists have estimated that covering 1 percent of the surface of the lower 48 states with solar collectors could supply most of the nation's energy needs. Solar energy can be collected by two different methods. The first method uses flat black plates that are exposed to the sun. The plates grow hot and can then be used to heat air or water. This air or water can heat a house or building. The second method involves using special cells that convert solar energy into electricity. However, the cells are still very expensive. Moreover, both systems require the development of better means of storing energy for those times when clouds block the sun.

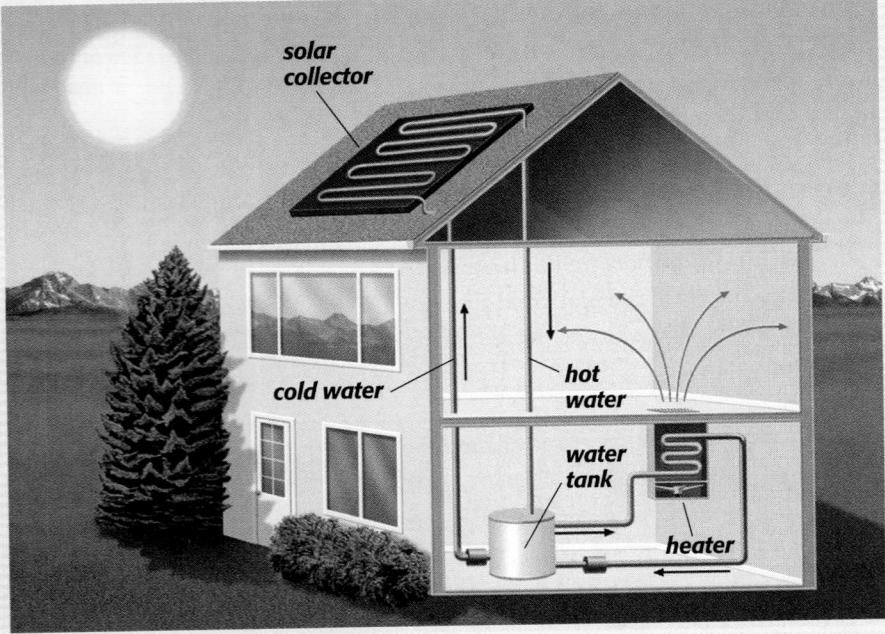

solar collector

cold water

hot water

water tank

heater

Understanding Science and History

1. What are the two methods by which solar energy can be collected?
2. How does the solar heating system shown at left work?

A loss of faith. While Carter struggled with the nation's problems, Americans lost confidence in his leadership. By March 1979 Carter's job approval rating had dropped considerably. He recognized that his presidency was in trouble. On July 15 he spoke to the nation.

> ❝ I want to talk to you right now about a fundamental threat to American democracy. . . . In a nation that was once proud of hard work, strong families, close-knit communities, and our faith in God, too many of us now tend to worship self-indulgence [pampering] and consumption. ❞

Americans responded favorably to Carter's discussion of the nation's spiritual emptiness. However, within days Carter asked some of his cabinet members to resign from office. This gave the American people the impression that the White House lacked leadership and was in disorder.

✔ **READING CHECK:** How did President Carter's handling of domestic issues cause some Americans to lose faith in his administration?

A New Foreign Policy

While President Carter was struggling with difficult domestic issues, he was also charting a new course in foreign affairs. Rejecting the realpolitik of the Nixon presidency, Carter tried to inject moral principles into U.S. foreign policy. Carter reflected on past administrations.

> 66 We are deeply concerned . . . by the . . . subtle erosion in the focus and morality of our foreign policy. Under the Nixon-Ford administration, there has evolved a kind of secretive 'Lone Ranger' foreign policy—a one-man policy of international adventure. This is not an appropriate policy for America. 99

Carter's new approach to foreign policy was most evident in the area of human rights. He particularly supported the universal right to freedom from torture and unlawful detention. Declaring that "our commitment to human rights must be absolute," Carter called for strong diplomatic and economic pressure on countries whose leaders violated human rights. Not surprisingly, many dictatorships that limited the rights of their people strongly opposed Carter's policy. Some U.S. diplomats also had their doubts. They warned that meddling in the domestic affairs of other countries might increase world tensions.

The Panama Canal. Carter's position on the Panama Canal added to the controversy over his human rights policy. Carter pushed for Senate ratification of the **Panama Canal Treaties**, which granted control of canal operations to Panama by the year 2000. Critics charged that Carter was giving away the canal. Ronald Reagan condemned the treaties. He charged, "The fatal flaw is the risk they contain for our national security. . . . We're turning one of the world's most important waterways over to a country no one can believe." Gradually, however, public opinion shifted in Carter's favor. After a long and bitter political battle the Senate narrowly ratified the treaties in 1978. In Latin America, where U.S. control of the canal had long been a sore point, the treaties met with general approval.

President Carter's stance on the Panama Canal issue signaled a more flexible approach to relations with

PRESIDENTIAL *Lives*

Jimmy Carter

1924–
In Office 1977–1981

Historian John Whiteclay Chambers II has called Jimmy Carter "one of America's greatest ex-presidents." In the years immediately following his presidency, Carter focused on teaching in Atlanta and helping to found the Carter Presidential Center, which includes the Jimmy Carter Museum and Library. During the mid-1980s, however, he committed himself to the humanitarian causes he had championed as president. For example, he lent his support to Habitat for Humanity, a nonprofit organization whose volunteers help build houses for people with low incomes. Carter spent one week each year helping volunteers build houses. In 1991 he announced the creation of The Atlanta Project, which uses corporate contributions and volunteer efforts to aid disadvantaged Atlanta residents.

Carter also became involved in international affairs. He showed special interest in the democratic process, monitoring elections in nations such as Panama and Nicaragua to prevent voter fraud. During the 1990s he acted as an elder statesman for the United States. Carter conducted diplomatic negotiations with governments in Haiti, North Korea, and Somalia. In 1994 he helped bring about a cease-fire in Bosnia that contributed to the peace agreement signed the following year.

Panamanian students protest U.S. control of the Panama Canal.

developing countries. Carter hoped the approach would improve the image of the United States and diminish the appeal of communism.

✔ **READING CHECK:** How did Carter's foreign policy differ from that of Nixon and Ford?

Africa. Carter's approach to foreign policy was evident in his dealings with Africa. The United States and the Soviet Union had been competing for influence among the continent's newly independent states. Carter tried to win friends among African nations by helping them sort out problems in their own way. One Carter official noted, "It is not a sign of weakness to recognize that we alone cannot dictate events elsewhere. It is rather a sign of maturity in a complex world."

Carter's ambassador to the United Nations, former civil rights activist Andrew Young, criticized imperialism in Africa. Young condemned South Africa's policy of **apartheid**, in which the white minority ruled and the black majority had few rights. Young also spoke out in favor of black majority rule in Rhodesia—present-day Zimbabwe. Conservative members of Congress attacked Carter's Africa policy. African leaders such as Kenneth Kaunda, however, asserted that Carter had "brought a breath of fresh air to our troubled world."

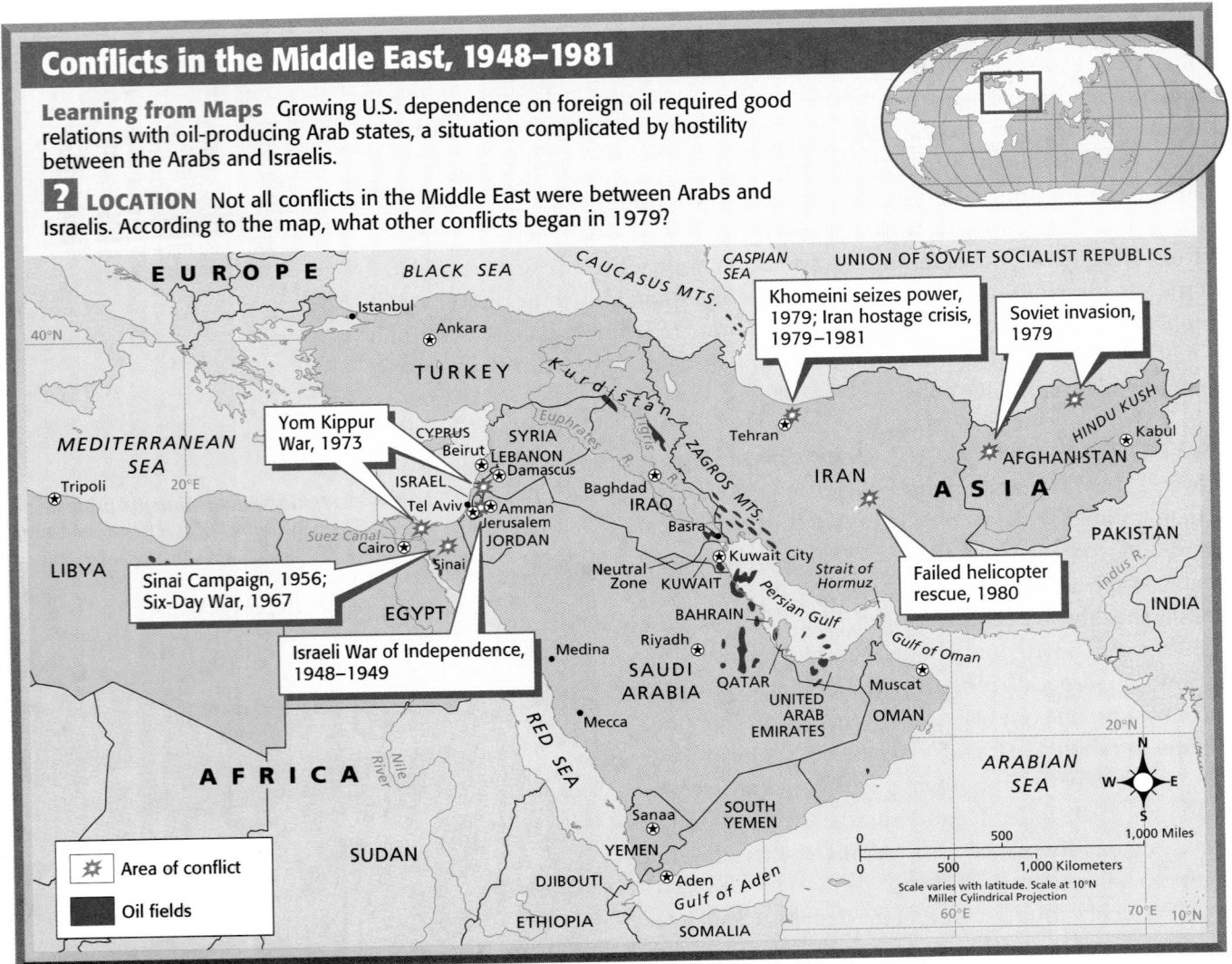

Conflicts in the Middle East, 1948–1981

Learning from Maps Growing U.S. dependence on foreign oil required good relations with oil-producing Arab states, a situation complicated by hostility between the Arabs and Israelis.

❓ **LOCATION** Not all conflicts in the Middle East were between Arabs and Israelis. According to the map, what other conflicts began in 1979?

Khomeini seizes power, 1979; Iran hostage crisis, 1979–1981

Soviet invasion, 1979

Yom Kippur War, 1973

Sinai Campaign, 1956; Six-Day War, 1967

Israeli War of Independence, 1948–1949

Failed helicopter rescue, 1980

Area of conflict

Oil fields

Scale varies with latitude. Scale at 10°N
Miller Cylindrical Projection

U.S.-Soviet relations. The decline of détente that had taken place during the Ford administration continued during Carter's presidency. The U.S.-Soviet relationship reached its low point in December 1979. That month Soviet troops invaded the country of Afghanistan to install a pro-Soviet leader. This invasion put Soviet troops within striking distance of major oil routes. Carter warned the Soviets to withdraw from Afghanistan. When they refused, he cut grain sales to the Soviet Union and announced a boycott of the 1980 Summer Olympics in Moscow. Many Americans did not support the decision to boycott the Olympics. Congress also postponed the signing of a key U.S.-Soviet arms-control treaty.

Anwar Sadat (left), President Carter, and Menachem Begin (right) sign the Camp David Accords.

Carter and the Middle East. Not long before the Soviet invasion of Afghanistan, President Carter engineered his chief foreign-policy triumph: a Middle East peace accord. Carter had taken office in 1977 amid fears of another Egyptian-Israeli war. Egyptian president Anwar Sadat and Israeli premier Menachem Begin met for peace talks, but those talks deadlocked.

In September 1978 Carter met with Begin and Sadat at Camp David. After several days of negotiations, the three leaders agreed on a framework for achieving peace in the Middle East. Their agreement became known as the **Camp David Accords**. As a result of their efforts, Sadat and Begin shared the Nobel Peace Prize for 1978. The following year, they signed a formal peace treaty that ended a 30-year state of war between Egypt and Israel. Carter later regarded his work at Camp David as "one of the most gratifying achievements" of his life.

✔ **READING CHECK:** How did Carter weaken relations with the Soviet Union, and how did he help achieve peace in the Middle East?

SECTION 3 REVIEW

Define and explain the significance of the following terms:
National Energy Act
Department of Energy
Three Mile Island accident
Panama Canal Treaties
apartheid
Camp David Accords

Identify and explain the significance of the following individuals:
Jimmy Carter
Anwar Sadat
Menachem Begin

1. **Using Graphic Organizers** Copy the chart below. Use it to evaluate why Americans lost faith in President Carter's attempts to solve the nation's problems.

Carter's Policies	
Economic	Energy

2. **Identifying Cause and Effect** How did Watergate and Jimmy Carter's image affect the 1976 election?
3. **Taking a Stand** Do you agree with President Carter's decision to make human rights an important issue in U.S. foreign policy? Why or why not?
4. **Analyzing** What were President Carter's contributions to the Middle East peace effort?

Critical Thinking

5. Could President Carter have had more success in improving relations with the Soviet Union? Why or why not?
   Consider:
   • his commitment to human rights
   • the decline of détente during the 1970s
   • the invasion of Afghanistan

Life in the 1970s

OBJECTIVES

Read to understand:

1. how the American population and family structure changed during the 1970s
2. why some observers argued that Americans were self-absorbed
3. what forms of entertainment were popular during the 1970s
4. how new technologies affected the lives of many Americans

KEY TERMS

Voting Rights Act of 1975
Bilingual Education Act
Sunbelt
Apollo 11
Skylab
personal computer

KEY PEOPLE

Steven Spielberg
Neil Armstrong
Edwin "Buzz" Aldrin
Steven Jobs
Stephen Wozniak

EYEWITNESSES TO *History*

❝ *Did the way in which Americans commemorated the nation's 200th birthday contribute to the American dream embodied in the Declaration of Independence, the Constitution, and the Bill of Rights? Having witnessed, along with all other Americans, the renewed spirit of dedication, patriotism and friendship that flowed across the land on the Bicentennial weekend, it seems to me that the answer is an unqualified [without reservation] yes. Americans used the Bicentennial to renew their faith in themselves, to gain knowledge and understanding of their neighbors, and to begin again the quest for liberty, justice, and equality for all.* ❞
—Edward W. Brooke

This serving dish was decorated to celebrate the bicentennial.

Senator Edward W. Brooke of Massachusetts praised the celebrations that took place throughout the nation on July 4, 1976. For many Americans, the bicentennial celebration provided a welcome break from the anxiety and stress of the decade.

A Changing Population

American society evolved during the 1970s, both across the nation and within the home. Immigration from abroad and migration within the nation's borders changed the makeup and distribution of the population. Americans also experimented with new ways to raise families.

Immigration. During the 1970s the U.S. population was greatly affected by continued immigration, mostly from Asia and Latin America. Most Latin American immigrants came from Mexico, but many others came from the Caribbean. In 1980, for example, nearly 120,000 Cubans fled their communist nation for the United States, settling mainly in the Miami area.

Having opened the way for emigration after President Nixon's visit, China supplied some of the new Asian population in the United States. Many of these Chinese immigrants were highly skilled and well-educated professionals fleeing political persecution. Despite their backgrounds, however, many found that discrimination and their difficulty speaking English prevented them from getting jobs that paid well. The experiences of Wei-Chi Poon, a biology professor from China, and her husband, a skilled architect, were typical. Neither knew any English when they immigrated to the United States. As a result, she had to work in a laundry factory for $1.85 per hour, while he took on two low-paying jobs. "We were so busy working and so tired," she recalled. "We had no time and energy to study English."

Congress passed two new laws designed to aid such immigrants. The **Voting Rights Act of 1975** required states and communities with a large number of non-English-speaking residents to print voting materials in various foreign languages. The **Bilingual Education Act** of 1974 increased funding for public schools to provide instruction to students in their primary languages while they learned English. Some critics opposed bilingual education, which they claimed slowed the adjustment of immigrants to American life. Yet, there was little question that the United States was becoming an increasingly multicultural society. Coping with new immigrants remained an important challenge for the country.

Because of funding for bilingual education, students could receive instruction in their primary language while they learn English.

Rise of the Sunbelt.

Americans moved more often in the 1970s than in previous decades. A growing number of Americans migrated from the North and the East, which some people mocked as the Frostbelt. They moved to the **Sunbelt** states of the South and the West. The Sunbelt states became increasingly important in national politics. This was particularly true of California, Florida, and Texas, where migration caused population growth to outpace that of the rest of the nation.

Americans moved to the Sunbelt for a number of reasons. The successes of the civil rights movement of the 1960s made the South a more attractive region in which to live. Some 7 million people moved there between 1970 and 1978. Economic growth spurred by increased defense spending after World War II had created more job opportunities in the region. Some migrants merely sought a warmer climate and a suburban lifestyle. Suburbs were more common and more spacious in the Sunbelt than in the Northeast because of the greater availability of land.

Improved technology also encouraged population growth in the Sunbelt. Air conditioning had become widely available, allowing people to tolerate the region's heat. However, not everyone welcomed this development. One Florida woman complained, "I hate air conditioning; it's a[n] . . . invention of the Yankees. If they don't like it hot, they can move back up North where they belong."

The Sunbelt. Many Americans moved to the Sunbelt states in the 1970s. *What do most of the people in this photograph have in common?*

Family life.

During the 1970s an increasing number of Americans chose to live alone. By the end of the decade some 22.5 percent of American households included just one person. Men and women waited longer to marry, driving up the average age at marriage. They were also more willing to leave unhappy marriages. This was in part because most states instituted laws that made it easier to obtain a divorce. The divorce rate continued to rise during the 1970s. There were 5.2 divorces per 1,000 Americans in 1980, up from 2.2 in 1960 and 3.5 in 1970. However, the increase in the divorce rate did not mean that Americans rejected the institution of marriage. In fact, remarriage rates also increased during this period.

Attitudes regarding family size also changed. In 1967 some 34 percent of women polled hoped to have four or more children. Four years later, just 15 percent of women polled expressed that desire. Not surprisingly, birthrates dropped sharply, averaging two births per woman. At the peak of the baby boom, the average family had three children. By 1980 that number had dropped to about 1.6 children per family.

By the end of the 1970s the idea of the "average family" had to be revised. Just 15 percent of American families matched the traditional image of a working father and a mother who stayed home to raise the children. During the 1970s the number

THOMAS A. HARRIS, M.D.

I'M OK —
YOU'RE OK
A PRACTICAL GUIDE
TO TRANSACTIONAL
ANALYSIS

Changing attitudes. To some observers, Americans seemed increasingly concerned about themselves during the 1970s. *How does this book cover represent the focus of the 1970s?*

of households with single women raising children rose to 8 million—an increase of 50 percent from the beginning of the decade. Single men raised children in some 1.5 million households.

✔ **READING CHECK:** How did the American population and family structure change during the 1970s?

American Attitudes

Some observers cited the rising divorce rate as proof that Americans had become selfish and self-absorbed. Journalist Tom Wolfe agreed, characterizing the 1970s as the "Me Decade." In reality, American attitudes were varied and complex during this period.

Improving the self. One popular response to the political and economic turmoil of the 1970s was the human potential or self-actualization movement. Millions of Americans turned to activities such as yoga in an effort to improve their inner selves. Self-help books such as *Looking Out for Number One* and *I'm OK—You're OK* topped the best-seller lists. Former used-car salesman Werner Erhard made some $9 million per year sponsoring seminars that helped people "get in touch with themselves."

Nontraditional religious groups also enjoyed increased popularity. The Maharishi Mahesh Yogi, teacher of a technique called Transcendental Meditation, claimed some 350,000 followers, including some well-known entertainers. The interest in new spiritual movements also had a dark side. In 1978 some 900 members of the People's Temple religious cult either killed themselves or were murdered. Most of the victims drank poisoned punch at their compound in Jonestown, Guyana. The incident shocked the world and heightened concern about alternative religions.

Some Americans embraced the ideal of simple living. Seeking to escape the tensions of modern life, many moved to rural areas where they could live closer to nature. Others turned to home gardening, an increasingly popular hobby. Writer Tom Bender explained in a 1975 article the reasons for living simply.

In the 1970s running became popular among Americans, in part because of Jim Fixx's book.

    ❝ **We are learning that too much of a good thing is not a good thing, and that we would often be wiser to determine what is enough rather than how much is possible. . . . Our major goal is to be happy with the least . . . services necessary. . . . The fewer our wants, the greater our freedom from having to serve them.** ❞

Fitness and food. The interest in self-improvement extended into the area of physical fitness. Americans flocked to health spas and tennis clubs. Sales of running shoes boomed as millions of Americans took up running or jogging to stay fit. Jim Fixx's *The Complete Book of Running* sold some 620,000 copies in 1978. The number of smokers also began to decline.

The interest in fitness may have been sparked by concerns over health habits, particularly alcohol consumption and diet. Liquor consumption rose

The Complete Book of
Running
by James F. Fixx

significantly during the 1970s. The American diet also posed health risks. In 1977 a Senate report on nutrition concluded that an improved diet would reduce deaths from heart disease by 25 percent. The popularity of fast food contributed to Americans' poor eating habits. In 1972 the fast-food chain McDonald's passed the U.S. Army to become the single largest provider of meals in the United States. By 1977 some 35 percent of the money Americans spent on food went to pay for meals prepared outside the home.

✔ **READING CHECK:** Why did some observers argue that Americans were self-absorbed?

Entertainment

During the 1970s Americans spent more money than ever before on music and motion pictures. The entertainment industry underwent significant changes in its attempt to respond to consumer demands.

Movies. The 1970s brought a boom to the motion picture industry, which had grown slowly after the introduction of television. Blockbusters—movies with heavy advance promotion that opened on hundreds or thousands of screens across the country—accounted for much of the increased interest in movies. One of the most popular movies of the decade was *Jaws*, a film directed by 28-year-old Steven Spielberg. It set the standard for blockbusters of the future.

Poster advertising E.T.

Steven Spielberg

Born in 1947 in Cincinnati, Ohio, Steven Spielberg was a regular television watcher as a child. He later admitted, "I was, and still am, a TV junkie." He was also interested in filmmaking. In 1958 his father loaned him a small movie camera so that he could earn a Boy Scout merit badge in photography. Four years later, the teenager's 40-minute film *Escape to Nowhere* won an amateur film contest.

Spielberg remained interested in films while studying at California State University. He dropped out during his junior year in order to direct television programs. His first major motion picture, *Sugarland Express,* received positive reviews but had little success at the box office. His next film, *Jaws,* was based on a novel about a shark that terrorizes a resort town. Released in 1975, *Jaws* became the top-grossing motion picture of all time within just 78 days of its release. Spielberg later explained how he was able to create such a suspenseful movie.

> 66 Fear is a very real thing for me. One of the best ways to cope with it is to turn it around and put it out to others. I mean, if you are afraid of the dark, you put the audience in a dark theater. I had a great fear of the ocean. 99

Spielberg continued to make movies that the American public enjoyed. His *Close Encounters of the Third Kind* (1977) and *E.T. the Extra-Terrestrial* (1982) portrayed aliens as kind and well intentioned. The 1981 movie *Raiders of the Lost Ark* was influenced by the adventure films that Spielberg had enjoyed as a child. *Jurassic*

Read More About It

Free Find:
Steven Spielberg
After reading about Steven Spielberg on the **Holt Researcher** CD–ROM, write a screenplay for a short film about your favorite historical event.

The Disco Generation

Many of the discotheques that appeared during the 1970s offered a wild sensory experience. Discos were equipped with fog and bubble machines, strobe lights, and enormous sound systems that pumped out loud dance music. The disco crowd also presented a sight to see, as everyone was well dressed. Blue jeans and sandals were out; fancy dresses, tight pants, jewelry, and blow-dried hair were in. New Yorker Johnny Boy Musto, 18, explained his disco fashion code. "It's very important that you don't wear the same thing for at least four weeks."

Disco dancers

The young adults who flocked to the clubs offered many reasons for their love of disco. Anibal Campa, a 19-year-old who claimed to go discoing six nights a week, declared, "I'll get tired eventually, but not for another ten to fifteen years. . . . I'd rather disco. If it wasn't for this music, I think I wouldn't want to be in this world." Yolanda Cimino explained, "What I like about dancing here is that you don't have to talk to the guy." A young beautician told a reporter, "I came here to get out of the house. . . . I think kids come here to escape the problems of growing up. When you dance, there's no one to give you a dirty look if you're doing something wrong."

Park, his 1993 movie about modern-day dinosaurs, was a tremendous commercial success. That same year he released *Schindler's List*, a movie about the Holocaust. It was his greatest triumph as a director. *Schindler's List* won Spielberg an Academy Award for best director. He received the honor again five years later for *Saving Private Ryan*, a film about men who fought in World War II. In 1994 he founded the Survivors of Shoah Visual History Foundation, a project that films the testimony of Holocaust survivors.

Music. For some music critics, the beginning of the 1970s represented the end of an era. The most important rock band of the 1960s, the Beatles, officially broke up. During the 1970s rock music changed from being the music of the counterculture to becoming big business. Record company executives and radio stations marketed rock music by packaging it and targeting consumers.

The most popular musical style of the era was a type of dance music known as disco. Discotheques, or clubs where patrons danced to recorded music instead of live bands, had gone out of fashion during the 1960s. Their popularity returned during the 1970s. The clubs featured disc jockeys who operated two turntables, thus ensuring that the beat never stopped and the dancers did not leave the floor. At the height of the disco phenomenon, there were thousands of discotheques in the United States.

Not all Americans enjoyed disco music. Some, tired of the conservative and mindless direction that popular music had taken, latched on to a new sound called punk rock. Artists such as Lou Reed, Patti Smith, and a New York band called the Ramones rejected technical precision in favor of energy and expressive lyrics. Although punk rock received media attention and influenced a new generation of performers, it never matched the commercial success or popularity of disco.

✔ **READING CHECK:** What types of entertainment were popular during the 1970s?

Technological Advances

Sophisticated technological developments changed the way that Americans viewed the universe. The space program explored the Moon and the planets. Other innovations of the 1970s would eventually change the ways that Americans worked, played, and communicated.

The space program. On July 20, 1969, Americans cheered as astronauts Neil Armstrong and Edwin "Buzz" Aldrin landed their *Apollo 11* lunar module on the Moon. Stepping onto the lunar surface, Armstrong declared, "That's one small step for [a] man, one giant leap for mankind." Between 1969 and 1972 the United States sent six more Apollo missions into space. Only *Apollo 13*, which experienced technical problems so severe that the lives of the astronauts were in danger, did not reach the Moon.

Skylab, the first U.S. space station, was placed in orbit in 1973. Over the course of a year, three astronaut teams visited *Skylab*, logging some 171 days aboard the station. In 1975, U.S. astronauts and Soviet cosmonauts met and worked together in space on the Apollo-Soyuz mission. Other notable achievements of the decade included several unmanned flights that explored the planets and the outer solar system.

Innovations. In 1977 Steven Jobs and Stephen Wozniak, two college dropouts who worked for computer companies, founded Apple Computer company. The two had built a small **personal computer** (PC) in the garage of Jobs's parents' house. Unlike earlier computers, which were very large and very expensive, PC's were affordable and small enough to sit on a desk. In 1977 Jobs and Wozniak introduced the Apple II, a 12-pound computer that revolutionized the computer industry. By 1980 stock in Apple was valued at $1.3 billion, and major corporations such as IBM were preparing to market their own personal computers.

Other technological innovations of the 1970s affected entertainment and communications. In 1975 Atari introduced a video-game system that was played on television sets. Within a year Americans had spent some $250 million on such games. Low-cost videocassette recorders (VCRs) changed television viewing habits. The telephone answering machine also became commonplace after improvements made the devices more affordable.

INTERPRETING THE VISUAL RECORD

Technology. The space program used advanced technology to successfully land astronauts on the Moon. *Which planet is shown at the top of this photograph?*

✔ **READING CHECK:** How did new technologies affect the lives of many Americans?

SECTION 4 REVIEW

Define and explain the significance of the following terms:
Voting Rights Act of 1975
Bilingual Education Act
Sunbelt
Apollo 11
Skylab
personal computer

Identify and explain the significance of the following individuals:
Steven Spielberg
Neil Armstrong
Edwin "Buzz" Aldrin
Steven Jobs
Stephen Wozniak

1. **Using Graphic Organizers** Copy the diagram below. Use it to illustrate changes in American families during the 1970s.

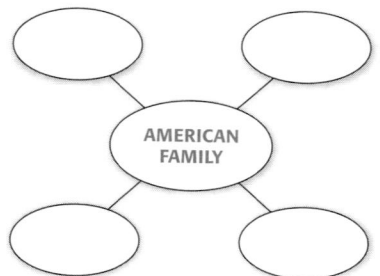
AMERICAN FAMILY

2. **Assessing Consequences** What effects did migration to the Sunbelt have on American life?
3. **Evaluating** Do you agree that Americans were self-absorbed during the 1970s? Why or why not?
4. **Hypothesizing** What would life in the United States today be like without the technological innovations developed in the 1970s?

Critical Thinking

5. How did business considerations shape entertainment in the United States?
   Consider:
   • the rise of blockbuster movies
   • changes in the music industry
   • technology in entertainment

CHAPTER 34

Review

Creating a Time Line

Copy the time line below onto a sheet of paper. Complete the time line by filling in the events and dates from the chapter that you think were most significant. Pick three events and explain why you think they were significant.

1968   1972   1976   1980

Writing a Summary

Using the Reading Checks as a guide, write an overview of the events in the chapter.

Identifying People and Ideas

Identify the following terms or individuals and explain their significance.

1. Family Assistance Plan
2. stagflation
3. Henry Kissinger
4. Saturday Night Massacre
5. Barbara Jordan
6. Jimmy Carter
7. National Energy Act
8. apartheid
9. Sunbelt
10. Steven Spielberg

Understanding Main Ideas

SECTION 1

1. How did the 1973 Arab-Israeli war affect life in the United States?

SECTION 2

2. How did President Nixon's management of the presidency contribute to his eventual resignation from office?

SECTION 3

3. Why did U.S.-Soviet relations worsen during President Carter's administration?

SECTION 4

4. What cultural trends indicate that the 1970s were an anxious time for many Americans?
5. What new technologies appeared during the 1970s?

Reviewing Themes

1. **Democratic Values** Why did the Justice Department and Supreme Court demand that Nixon turn over the White House tapes?
2. **Economic Development** Was the U.S. government right to try to end the country's dependence on imported oil in the 1970s? Explain your answer.
3. **Global Relations** Did President Carter's support for human rights serve the international interests of the United States? Explain your answer.

Thinking Critically

1. **Comparing and Contrasting** How did President Carter's foreign-policy approach differ from that of Nixon and Ford? Which do you believe was more effective? Why?
2. **Using Historical Imagination** What might have happened if the Supreme Court had not ordered Nixon to turn over the White House tapes?
3. **Problem Solving** What solutions to the energy crisis would you have recommended?
4. **Identifying Values** Why did Americans become interested in self-improvement during the 1970s?
5. **Hypothesizing** Why did popular music change from the protest songs that had appeared during the 1960s and become more dance-oriented?

Writing About History

Writing to Classify Write an essay that compares Nixon's policy toward Chile, Ford's response to the *Mayaguez* incident, and Carter's position on the Panama Canal Treaties. Use the following graphic to organize your thoughts.

Nixon and Chile	Ford and the *Mayaguez*	Carter and the Panama Canal

internetconnect

TOPIC: 1970s fashion
GO TO: go.hrw.com
KEYWORD: SD1 Seventies

Accessing the Internet through the HRW Web site, research fashion trends and popular culture of the 1970s. Then create an illustrated and annotated scrapbook that could have been written by a high school student in the 1970s.

Strategies for Success Review the **Strategies for Success** on *Formulating a Hypothesis.* The photograph above shows farmers protesting against President Carter. Form a hypothesis that explains why Carter was unpopular with farmers.

Linking History and Geography

Study the map below. Which states had the greatest population growth? Which regions were most affected by population growth and loss?

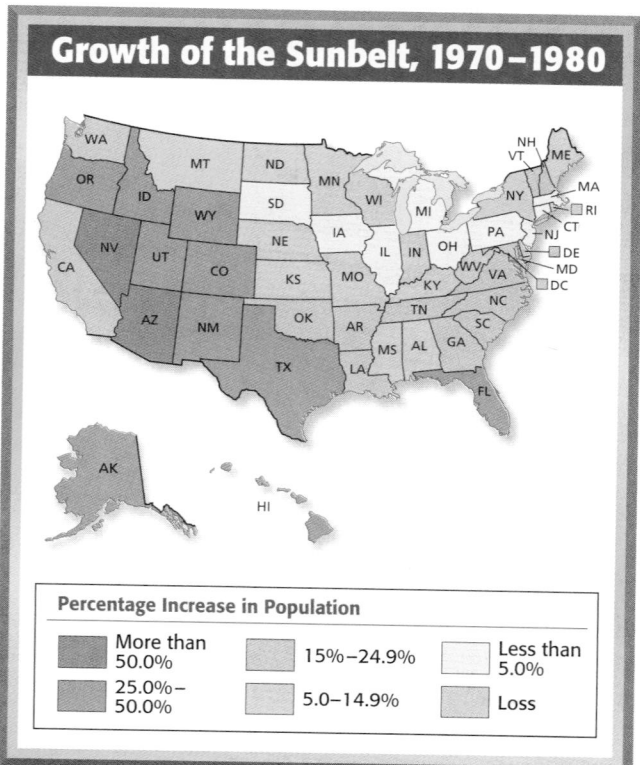

Growth of the Sunbelt, 1970–1980

Percentage Increase in Population

More than 50.0%
25.0%–50.0%
15%–24.9%
5.0–14.9%
Less than 5.0%
Loss

BUILDING YOUR PORTFOLIO

Complete one or all of the following projects individually or cooperatively.

1 Constitutional Heritage
*Imagine that you are a Washington, D.C., newspaper reporter covering the Senate investigations into the Watergate affair. **Write a short article** outlining the constitutional issues involved in the Watergate break-in, cover-up, and news coverage.*

2 Economic Development
Imagine that you are an economist in the 1970s. **Create a flowchart** that shows how increases in oil prices overseas affect the cost of consumer goods in the United States.

3 Global Relations
*Imagine that you are a foreign-policy expert appearing on a national news program. **Prepare a presentation** on 1970s-era détente that explains the concept and discusses its successes and failures.*

1980–1992

The Republican Revolution

Ronald and Nancy Reagan

A compact disc

Geraldine Ferraro campaign button

1983
Science and Technology
CD–ROM technology is introduced.

1984
Politics
Democratic vice presidential candidate Geraldine Ferraro becomes the first woman to run on a major-party presidential ticket.

1986
Daily Life
Six million Americans form a human chain in Hands Across America, an effort to raise money for the homeless.

1980 · · · · · · · · · · **1982** · · · · · · · · · · **1984** · · · · · · · · · · **1986**

1980
Politics
Ronald Reagan is elected president.

1980
World Events
Labor strikes in Poland threaten Soviet control over the nation.

1981
Politics
Sandra Day O'Connor becomes the first woman to serve on the U.S. Supreme Court.

1983
Business and Finance
Inflation falls to 4 percent, signaling recovery from the economic recession.

1986
Science and Technology
The space shuttle *Challenger* explodes, killing all on board.

A space shuttle being transported by airplane

Before You Read

Build on What You Know

P ublic frustration with government grew in the 1970s as the Watergate scandal broke, the energy crisis emerged, and the economy continued to weaken. Democrat Jimmy Carter was elected president with a promise to reform government. Numerous obstacles hampered his presidency, however, including a worsening economic situation. In this chapter you will learn how Ronald Reagan was elected president in 1980 and set out to reform the economy and foreign relations.

**Amy Tan's
The Joy
Luck Club**

The Mall of America

**1987
Business
and Finance**
Investors lose almost
$1 trillion when the
stock market crashes.

**1989
The Arts**
Amy Tan
publishes *The
Joy Luck Club.*

**1990
Science and
Technology**
The Hubble
Space Tele-
scope is
launched.

**1991
World Events**
The Persian
Gulf War
breaks out.

**1992
Daily Life**
The 78-acre Mall of
America, the country's
largest shopping center,
opens in Minnesota.

1988   **1990**   **1992**

**1987
World Events**
U.S. and Soviet
leaders sign
the INF Treaty,
eliminating
medium-
range nuclear
weapons
in Europe.

**1988
Politics**
George Bush
is elected
president.

**1989
World Events**
The Berlin Wall falls,
signaling the end
of the Cold War.

*A piece of the
Berlin Wall*

*George
Bush*

Think About Themes

*Decide whether you **agree** or **disagree**
with the following statements. Note why
in your journal.*

Global Relations Building stronger defense
systems and weapons will only lead to war,
never to peace.

Economic Development Cutting corporate taxes
will not boost the economy because it has no
effect on ordinary Americans.

Technology and Society An economic boom
will have little effect on how technology shapes
society.

Reagan Comes to Power

EYEWITNESSES TO History

66 *You always used to think in this country that there would be bad times followed by good times. Now, maybe it's bad times followed by hard times followed by harder times* **99**

—Chicago homemaker

The cheerful smiley face popular in the 1970s seemed out of place by the end of the decade.

This unnamed Chicago homemaker expressed a sentiment that became increasingly common toward the end of the 1970s. Even Jimmy Carter noted that Americans were suffering from a loss of faith in the future. Reporters labeled the condition he described the national "malaise," or illness. The president urged Americans to pull themselves up out of this despair. However, many Americans considered the president to be part of the country's problems.

The Election of 1980

Although Jimmy Carter had chalked up some notable successes as president, by June 1980 just 31 percent of Americans approved of his job performance. Richard Nixon's approval rating had only fallen to 24 percent when he resigned. Many Americans were frustrated with Carter's inability to find solutions to the nation's domestic problems, such as the energy crisis, inflation, and unemployment.

Iran hostage crisis. Of all the difficulties Carter faced, none was more damaging than the **Iran hostage crisis**. Iran had long been regarded as critical to U.S. interests in the Middle East. In the 1950s the United States had helped overthrow Iran's leader and restore Shah Mohammad Reza Pahlavi to power. Although the shah's rule was very harsh, the United States always supported him. In 1979, however, followers of a militant Islamic leader, the Ayatollah Khomeini (eye-uh-TOH-luh koh-MAY-nee), forced the shah to flee the country. The new government was outraged when President Carter allowed the shah into the United States for medical treatment. On November 4, 1979, Iranian militants seized 53 American hostages at the U.S. Embassy in Tehran, Iran's capital. They hoped to force the United States to return the shah to Iran for trial.

The hostage crisis dragged on for months. In April 1980 a rescue mission failed when U.S. military helicopters crashed in the Iranian desert, killing eight Americans. As frustration over the crisis mounted, the American public became angry at Carter. Many felt that his failure to free the hostages signaled America's decline as a world power. Even a former member of Carter's cabinet admitted that "Khomeini would not have touched the Soviet Embassy."

American hostages in Iran

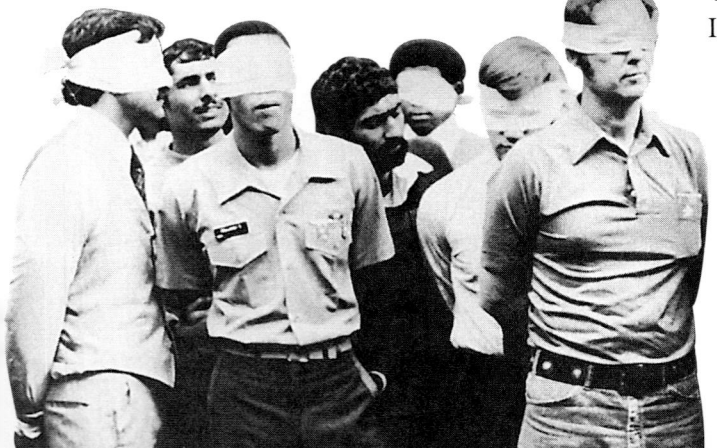

The campaign. Republican candidate Ronald Reagan echoed these opinions during the 1980 presidential campaign. The former California governor attacked Carter as a weak leader who had presided over a decline in U.S. power. Reagan's promise to "make America strong again" appealed to voters, many of whom crossed party lines to support him. These so-called Reagan Democrats reflected the widespread dissatisfaction with Carter's presidency.

Reagan and his running mate, George Bush of Texas, easily won the election. Reagan captured 489 electoral votes to 49 for Carter and his running mate, Walter Mondale of Minnesota. An independent candidate, John Anderson, failed to capture any electoral votes but did win almost 7 percent of the popular vote. This strong showing further reflected public frustration with the Carter administration. The Democrats' majority in the House declined somewhat, and for the first time since 1952, the Republicans won control of the Senate.

Despite his defeat, Carter continued to negotiate for the release of the hostages. After 444 days in captivity, on January 20, 1981, the hostages were finally freed—just moments after Reagan was sworn in as president.

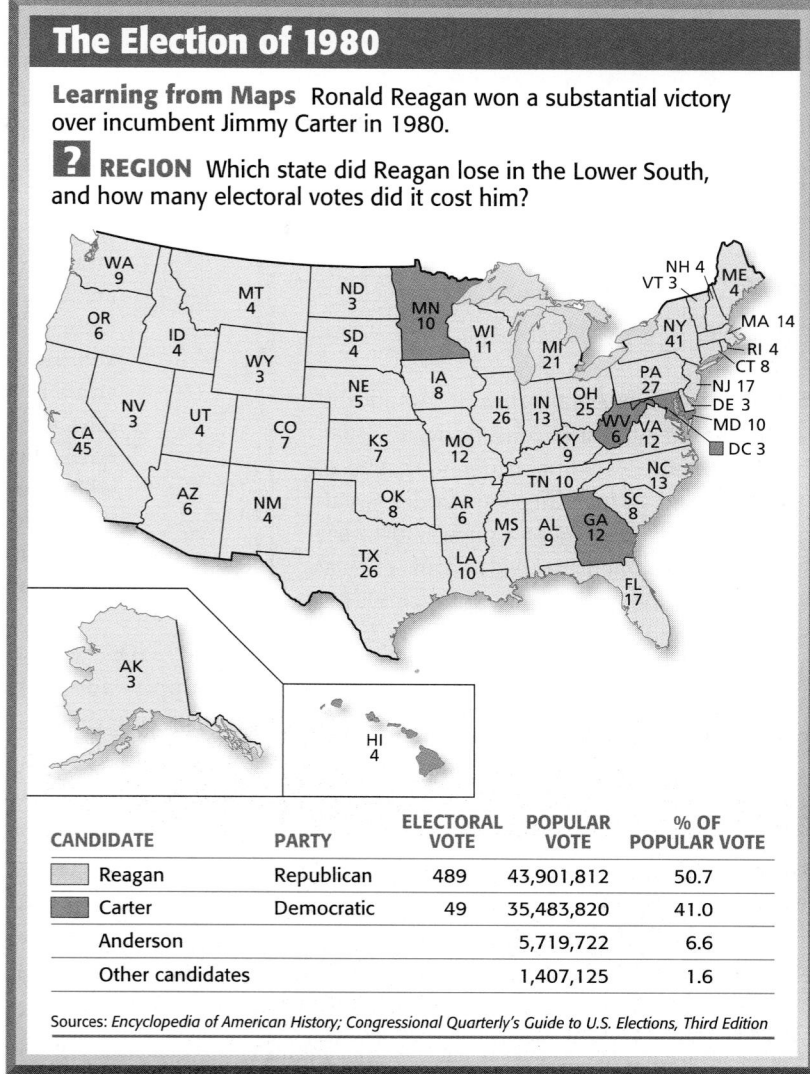

The Election of 1980

Learning from Maps Ronald Reagan won a substantial victory over incumbent Jimmy Carter in 1980.

? REGION Which state did Reagan lose in the Lower South, and how many electoral votes did it cost him?

CANDIDATE	PARTY	ELECTORAL VOTE	POPULAR VOTE	% OF POPULAR VOTE
Reagan	Republican	489	43,901,812	50.7
Carter	Democratic	49	35,483,820	41.0
Anderson			5,719,722	6.6
Other candidates			1,407,125	1.6

Sources: *Encyclopedia of American History; Congressional Quarterly's Guide to U.S. Elections, Third Edition*

Role of the New Right. Reagan was a former New Deal Democrat turned conservative Republican. He appealed to a wide range of voters who were unhappy with liberal politics. Reagan's strongest support, however, came from a growing movement of political conservatives known as the **New Right**. At the forefront of the New Right was Reverend Jerry Falwell's **Moral Majority**—a fundamentalist Christian organization founded in 1979.

Reagan and the New Right shared many of the same political goals. Both supported school prayer, a strong defense, and free-market economic policies. Both opposed abortion, the Equal Rights Amendment, gun control, and busing to achieve racial balance in schools.

In addition to helping elect Reagan, members of the New Right were largely responsible for the Republicans gaining control of the Senate in 1980. This powerful political force played a significant role in shaping Republican policy throughout the 1980s.

✔ **READING CHECK:** What factors helped Ronald Reagan win the presidency in 1980?

A RETURN TO CONSERVATIVE CHURCHES

The New Right benefited from Americans' increased interest in conservative Christian churches after the spiritual experimentation of the 1960s and 1970s. Christian Fundamentalism in particular experienced a surge in followers. The spiritual movement that had become popular in the 1920s continued to grow throughout the 1900s. Many members of the movement found that Fundamentalism's focus on strictly following the Bible gave them clear spiritual direction in a society that seemed to have lost its values.

Led by several prominent and politically active ministers, in the 1980s Fundamentalism became a major force for political and social change in the country. Baptist minister Jerry Falwell started the trend during the country's bicentennial in 1976. Falwell warned that the nation was facing numerous problems because its political leaders and institutions had turned away from the Christian values upon which the country was based. The solution to this problem, he argued, was for conservative Christians to become more involved in politics. As a political movement, Fundamentalism became the driving force behind the antiabortion campaign and efforts to restore prayer in public schools. ■

The Reverend Jerry Falwell was the head pastor at a Fundamentalist Baptist church.

Reagan's Economic Program

President Reagan entered office with a comprehensive economic program already mapped out. In his inaugural address he explained the plan, which called for less government involvement in the economy.

> 66 These United States are confronted with an economic affliction of great proportions. We suffer from the longest and one of the worst sustained inflations in our national history. . . . In this present crisis, government is not the solution to our problem. . . . It is my intention to curb the size and influence of the Federal establishment. . . . In the days ahead I will propose removing the roadblocks that have slowed our economy and reduced productivity. Steps will be taken aimed at restoring the balance between the various levels of government. . . . It is time to reawaken this industrial giant, to get government back within its means, and to lighten our punitive tax burden. 99

This plan, called **Reaganomics**, was based on the theory of **supply-side economics**. This "trickle down" theory argued that lowering the top income tax rates would spur economic growth. Supporters of supply-side economics claimed that people would invest their tax savings in businesses, thereby creating jobs, increasing consumer spending, and eventually generating increased tax revenues. Congress responded to Reagan's program by passing a three-year plan to cut federal income taxes by 25 percent.

Congress also supported another part of Reagan's economic plan—drastic cuts in government regulation of industries such as television, trucking, airlines, and banking. The Reagan administration's pro-business, antiregulation stance was evident in the Department of the Interior's handling of public lands. Secretary of the Interior James Watt leased huge areas of the seafloor to private companies searching for off-shore oil and gas. He also leased federal lands to coal companies.

Critics charged that Reagan's tax cuts favored the wealthy and that spending cuts and deregulation weakened programs to protect consumers, the needy, and the environment. They also warned that big tax cuts combined with increased military spending—another important element of Reaganomics—would produce enormous shortages in the federal budget.

By 1983 supply-side economics had begun to turn the economy around. The inflation rate had dropped to a manageable 4 percent. Responding to this development, Americans increased their spending during the mid-1980s. This boosted the economy even further. Businesses revived, the stock market soared, and the future looked bright.

Critics continued to note that not all Americans benefited from the recovery. Deep cuts in federal funding for social programs hurt the poorest citizens. Although employment rose overall, joblessness remained high among African Americans and Hispanics, particularly for unskilled workers living in the inner cities. Unemployment among factory workers in the Midwest, once America's industrial heartland, also remained high.

✔ **READING CHECK:** What was President Reagan's main economic program, and how successful was it?

Read More About It

Free Find: Reagan on communism
After reading President Reagan's speech on communism on the **Holt Researcher** CD–ROM, write a letter to a member of Congress explaining why you agree or disagree with Reagan's view of communism.

Reagan and the Cold War

The Reagan administration's emphasis on increased military spending was in part a reflection of Ronald Reagan's strong anticommunist views. He took a hard line against the Soviet Union, even branding it an "evil empire" in one speech. To counter the Soviet threat, Reagan called for new weapons systems and an increased U.S. military presence in such areas as the Indian Ocean and the Persian Gulf.

New weapons. Between 1981 and 1985 the Pentagon's budget grew from some $150 billion to about $250 billion. Much of the money was spent on nuclear weapons. Secretary of State Alexander Haig suggested that "nuclear warning shots" might be useful in a conventional war.

The talk of nuclear war stirred public fears. In town meetings and a few state referendums, voters urged a freeze on the testing and deployment of nuclear weapons. Many Americans marched in rallies to show their support for the proposals.

In response, Reagan proposed the **Strategic Defense Initiative** (SDI), a space-based missile-defense system, in March 1983. SDI quickly stirred controversy. Many critics labeled it "Star Wars" after the popular 1977 movie, saying it was based on untested technological theories and was probably unworkable. They also warned that SDI research would intensify the arms race. President Reagan countered that SDI would be a weapon for peace—one that killed weapons, not people. He explained this in a national address.

> 66 I call upon the scientific community in our country, those who gave us nuclear weapons, to turn their great talents now to the cause of mankind and world peace: to give us the means of rendering these nuclear weapons impotent [powerless] and obsolete. 99

INTERPRETING THE VISUAL RECORD

SDI. President Reagan's plan for a space-based missile defense system was very controversial. *Do you think this cartoon supported SDI? Explain your answer.*

U.S.–Soviet relations. Even before Reagan took office, U.S.-Soviet relations had cooled because of the Soviet Union's 1979 invasion of Afghanistan. Relations deteriorated further in August 1980, when Polish workers in Gdańsk and Szczecin (SHCHET-sheen) staged a series of massive strikes. They protested high prices and demanded the right to form trade unions free from government or Communist Party control. At first, things went well for the strikers. Faced with the threat of a nationwide general strike, in late August the Polish government legalized independent union activity. Labor activists responded by voting on September 17 to form the independent trade union **Solidarity**. Lech Walesa (vah-LEN-suh), an electrician at a Gdańsk shipyard who had helped launch the initial strikes, became the union's leader.

Solidarity. These Boston residents are demonstrating to show their support for Solidarity. *What do the people's signs reveal about their motives for demonstrating?*

Then, in December 1981, Poland's Soviet-backed government changed its stand and instituted martial law. Government troops shut down Solidarity centers and arrested union leaders. Expecting resistance, Soviet troops prepared to brutally "restore order." This move was similar to Soviet actions in Hungary in 1956 and in Czechoslovakia in 1968. Reagan warned the Soviets not to invade Poland and called for new trade restrictions against the Soviet Union. Moscow heeded the warning and stayed out of Poland.

Tensions between the United States and the Soviet Union flared again in 1983. On September 1, the Soviets shot down a Korean commercial airliner over Soviet airspace. All 269 passengers, including many Americans, were killed. Despite an international outcry, the Soviets defended their action, claiming the plane had been spying. Later that year, when the United States placed nuclear missiles in Great Britain and Germany, the Soviets walked out of arms-control talks. When the Soviets boycotted the 1984 Summer Olympics in Los Angeles, relations between the two superpowers sank to their lowest point in years.

✔ **READING CHECK:** What were the significant developments in the Cold War during the early 1980s?

Reagan and Latin America

President Reagan feared that the developing nations of Latin America would fall under Soviet influence. To prevent this, Reagan increased U.S. involvement in the region. He focused in particular on the countries of El Salvador and Nicaragua.

The Reagan administration soon found itself pulled into events in El Salvador. In 1979 a group of young military officers had seized power and instituted a brutal government. The army and so-called death squads killed and tortured opposition leaders. Fighting intensified between government forces and rebels who demanded radical reform.

In 1984 José Napoleón Duarte, a moderate, won election by promising reforms and an end to the civil war. Eager to prevent a rebel victory that might allow El Salvador to fall under Soviet influence, the Reagan administration offered Duarte military and economic aid and sent military advisers to train government troops. The civil war raged on, however, until intense international pressure forced both sides to sign a peace treaty in 1992.

PRESIDENTIAL Lives

Ronald Reagan

1911–
In Office 1981–1989

Ronald Reagan was nicknamed the Great Communicator because of his speaking abilities. One of Reagan's gifts was a sharp wit. After a debate with Jimmy Carter during the 1980 campaign, a reporter asked if he had been nervous appearing on stage with the president. "No, not at all," Reagan replied. Then, referring to his career in Hollywood, he added, "I've been on the same stage with John Wayne."

Reagan's wit helped reassure the nation after a lone gunman shot him on March 30, 1981. As the wounded president was wheeled into the operating room, he looked around at the surgeons and joked, "Please assure me that you are all Republicans!" While he was recuperating in intensive care, Reagan sent several humorous notes to his staff members. One read, "If I had had this much attention in Hollywood, I'd have stayed there!"

Reagan also focused U.S. attention on the political situation in Nicaragua. In 1979, Nicaraguan rebels known as **Sandinistas** had overthrown the dictatorship of Anastasio Somoza. The Somoza family had controlled Nicaragua since the 1930s. Soon after he took office, Reagan cut all U.S. aid to Nicaragua. He argued that the Sandinistas were backed by the Soviet Union. He also charged that the Sandinistas were "exporting revolution" by shipping Cuban and Soviet weapons to the rebels in El Salvador.

The Sandinistas reacted to U.S. pressure by strengthening their ties to the Soviet bloc countries. Reagan then decided to support the Nicaraguan **Contras**, a rebel army recruited, financed, and armed by the CIA. Reagan hoped the revolutionary group would overthrow the Sandinista government. He called the Contras "freedom fighters" and even compared them to the founders of the United States.

These Contra rebels are training for their fight against the Sandinistas.

Many Americans opposed the CIA-sponsored war against the Sandinistas. They feared that it would end up as devastating and as complicated as the Vietnam War had been. Reflecting such concerns, Congress began restricting funds for the Contras late in 1982. However, the nation would soon learn that the White House continued to finance the Contras—despite the congressional ban—using secret funds from wealthy supporters and foreign governments.

✔ **READING CHECK:** How did the Reagan administration become involved in events in El Salvador and Nicaragua?

SECTION 1 REVIEW

Define and explain the significance of the following terms:
Iran hostage crisis
New Right
Moral Majority
Reaganomics
supply-side economics
Strategic Defense Initiative
Solidarity
Sandinistas
Contras

Identify and explain the significance of the following individuals:
Ayatollah Khomeini
Ronald Reagan
Jerry Falwell
Lech Walesa
José Napoleón Duarte

1. **Using Graphic Organizers** Copy the graphic organizer below. Use it to list the factors that led to Ronald Reagan's victory over Jimmy Carter in 1980.

VICTORY

2. **Evaluating** Describe President Reagan's economic program, and evaluate how successful it was.
3. **Synthesizing** Why did Cold War relations sink to a low point in the early 1980s?
4. **Using Historical Imagination** Imagine that you are a citizen of El Salvador or Nicaragua in the early 1980s. Describe the political situation in your country and explain why you think the United States is intervening in your country's affairs.

Critical Thinking

5. How did the Reagan administration's approach to governing differ from that of previous administrations?
   Consider:
   • Reagan's opinion of the role of government
   • the administration's approach to the economy
   • the administration's approach to the Cold War

Reagan's Second Term

OBJECTIVES

Read to understand:

1. how the Republicans won the 1984 election, and how the makeup of the Supreme Court changed in the 1980s
2. what events began to shake public confidence in the economy
3. how the Iran-Contra affair developed
4. what developments eased tensions between the United States and the Soviet Union in the late 1980s

KEY TERMS

Gramm-Rudman-Hollings Act
insider trading
S&L crisis
Iran-Contra affair
glasnost
perestroika
Intermediate-Range Nuclear Forces Treaty

KEY PEOPLE

Walter Mondale
Geraldine Ferraro
Sandra Day O'Connor
Oliver North
Mikhail Gorbachev

KEY PLACES

Grenada
Nicaragua

U.S. forces landed on the island of Grenada in October 1983.

 **EYEWITNESSES TO History**

❝ *It's morning again in America. . . . In a town not too far from where you live, a young family has just moved into a new home. Three years ago, even the smallest house seemed completely out of reach. Right down the street, one of the neighbors has just bought himself a new car with all the options. The factory down the river is working again. Not long ago, people were saying it probably would be closed forever. . . . Life is better. America is back.* ❞
—Ronald Reagan campaign ad

Reagan-Bush campaign poster

This advertising campaign promoted the economic achievements of Ronald Reagan's first term in office. By 1984 the economy was booming, consumerism was growing, and the "malaise" of the 1970s was fading. Reagan's supporters asked voters, "Now that our country is turning around, why turn back?"

The Election of 1984

Adding to President Reagan's popularity heading into his 1984 re-election campaign was a small-scale military action in 1983. On the tiny Caribbean island of Grenada, a rebel group overthrew the government and killed the prime minister. Several Caribbean nations requested U.S. intervention. Beginning October 25, 1983, several thousand U.S. Marines and Army Rangers went ashore on Grenada. They unseated the coup leaders and set up a government favorable to the United States. The successful operation boosted Americans' patriotism and confidence in the military.

Soon after the Grenada invasion, Reagan announced that he and Vice President George Bush would seek a second term. Former vice president Walter Mondale won the Democratic nomination. He picked Representative Geraldine Ferraro of New York as his running mate. Ferraro became the first woman to run on a major-party presidential ticket. Some predicted Ferraro's presence would increase support for the Democratic Party among women. Ferraro said:

❝ By choosing an American woman to run for our nation's second-highest office, you send a powerful signal to all Americans. . . . There are no doors we cannot unlock. We will place no limits on achievement. If we can do this, we can do anything. ❞

Republicans, however, had also been taking steps to expand the role of women in their party. President Reagan had appointed several women to high public offices, including Elizabeth Dole as secretary of transportation and Margaret Heckler as secretary of health and human services. He also appointed Jeane Kirkpatrick as head of the U.S. delegation to the United Nations—the first woman to hold the post.

Republicans also sought—and received—the support of women who did not identify with the feminist movement. Female opponents of the Equal Rights Amendment and abortion embraced the Republican Party. As a result, the percentage of female delegates to the Republican National Convention increased from 24 percent in 1980 to 44 percent in 1984.

In the end, Ferraro's presence did not win many votes for the Democrats. On election day, Reagan received 54.5 million popular votes to Mondale's 37.6 million. The Republicans swept the electoral vote 525 to 13.

The Supreme Court

One issue that arose during the 1984 presidential campaign was the growing conservative emphasis of the Supreme Court. President Reagan vowed to appoint justices who would uphold his conservative agenda. In 1981 Reagan had appointed conservative justice Sandra Day O'Connor, the first woman ever to serve on the Supreme Court.

Sandra Day O'Connor

Sandra Day O'Connor was born in El Paso, Texas, in 1930. She grew up working on her family's cattle ranch. "The whole family had to get out and help on the ranch," she recalled. "We learned to be pretty independent that way." She attended Stanford University and graduated from Stanford Law School in 1952. At Stanford, she met and married fellow law student John O'Connor.

O'Connor began her law career in California but later moved to Arizona. There she served as Arizona's assistant attorney general from 1965 to 1969. From 1974 to 1981 she served in several different judicial positions before being appointed to the Supreme Court. She was once asked whether she would vote differently than a male justice. She answered:

66 Judges are supposed to be objective; they're supposed to study and look at the law and apply the law to the particular case in an objective way, not from any particular point of view. So does being a woman make a difference in what answer is given? I tend to think that probably at the end of the day, a wise old woman and a wise old man are going to reach the same answer. 99

INTERPRETING THE VISUAL RECORD

1984. Democratic candidates Water Mondale and Geraldine Ferraro received strong support at this 1984 parade in New York. The poster at left shows Ferraro as Liberty. *What point do you think the poster was making about Ferraro's candidacy?*

 **Read More About It**

Free Find:
Sandra Day O'Connor
After reading about Sandra Day O'Connor on the **Holt Researcher** CD–ROM, write a biography about one of your favorite people. Describe the choices he or she made and the obstacles he or she overcame.

"WELL, IT'S ABOUT TIME"

© 1981 BY HERBLOCK IN THE WASHINGTON POST

The Supreme Court. In this 1981 cartoon the spirit of Justice comments on Sandra Day O'Connor's appointment to the Supreme Court. *What do you think was the cartoonist's opinion of the appointment?*

As a Supreme Court justice, O'Connor has proven to be less conservative than many supporters originally thought she would be. She has often delivered the deciding vote when the Court has been split on certain issues.

When Chief Justice Warren Burger retired in 1986, Reagan elevated Associate Justice William Rehnquist to chief justice. To fill Rehnquist's position, Reagan nominated Antonin Scalia, a conservative. When another justice retired in 1987, Reagan nominated Robert Bork, a federal judge and law professor who held a much narrower interpretation of the Bill of Rights than the Court had upheld in recent years. He believed, for example, that civil rights laws restricted individual freedoms. Bork's views concerned many people, including a number of senators. The Senate rejected Bork's nomination. Reagan's next choice, Douglas Ginsberg, withdrew after press reports emerged that he had smoked marijuana as a law professor. Conservative judge Anthony Kennedy of California eventually won Senate confirmation and joined the Supreme Court.

✔ **READING CHECK:** How did the Republicans win the 1984 election, and how did the makeup of the Supreme Court change in the 1980s?

Concerns over the Economy

The failure of the Bork nomination was one of several signs that the so-called Reagan Revolution might be starting to weaken. Of particular concern was the federal deficit, which had topped $200 billion in 1985. Seeking to balance the budget with forced spending cuts, Congress passed the Balanced Budget and Emergency Control Act in 1985. Called the **Gramm-Rudman-Hollings Act** after its Senate sponsors, the law required automatic across-the-board cuts in government spending when the deficit exceeded a certain amount. Other legislation took aim at specific problems. The Tax Reform Law of 1986, for example, eliminated special tax breaks that certain groups had been receiving.

The stock market also showed signs of trouble. President Reagan's tax cuts and business deregulation had stimulated a stock market boom. However, with this boom came a wave of illegal **insider trading**—the use of confidential financial information for personal gain. Stockbroker Chris Burke described the culture of the times.

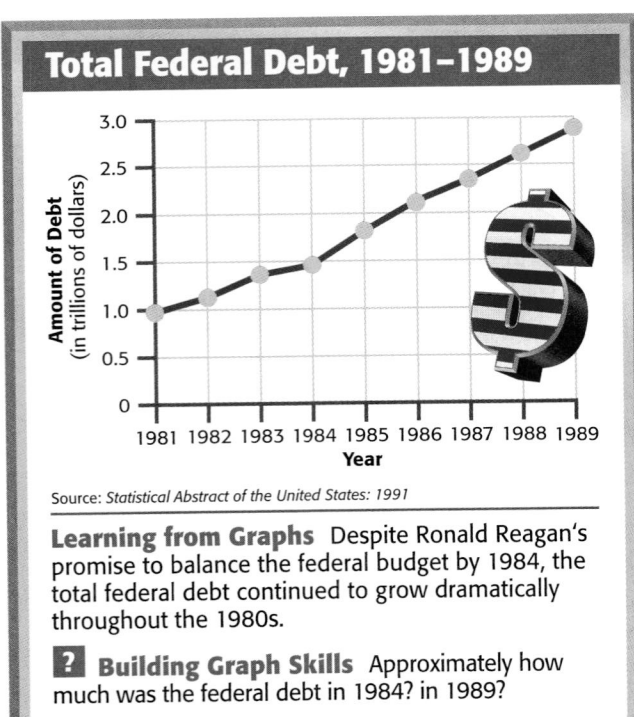

Total Federal Debt, 1981–1989

Amount of Debt (in trillions of dollars)

Year

Source: *Statistical Abstract of the United States: 1991*

Learning from Graphs Despite Ronald Reagan's promise to balance the federal budget by 1984, the total federal debt continued to grow dramatically throughout the 1980s.

❓ **Building Graph Skills** Approximately how much was the federal debt in 1984? in 1989?

66 **Wall Street in the 1980s was like nowhere else on this planet. It was a culture of greed and backstabbing and partying. Your best buddy is the one who's gonna stab you in the back tomorrow if it means some more greenbacks in his pocket. It wasn't a good way to live.** 99

Several large brokerage firms pleaded guilty to illegal activities and faced severe penalties. These scandals eroded investors' trust in stockbrokers.

Then, on October 19, 1987, after several years of a bull market, the stock market crashed. On paper, stock losses totaled almost $1 trillion. The value of Eastman Kodak stock, for example, fell by more than 30 percent. Other major corporations experienced similar sharp drops in their stock values.

In another sign of economic trouble, a crisis hit the nation's savings and loan (S&L) associations and banking industry in the late 1980s and early 1990s. Freed of federal regulation, banks and S&Ls, particularly in the Southwest, had made risky loans to developers to build office towers, shopping malls, and other projects. In the late 1980s the real-estate market collapsed. Hundreds of S&Ls and banks that had loaned money to developers failed. Since the federal government insures S&L and bank depositors, it had to pay billions of dollars to cover these losses, further straining the federal budget. The **S&L crisis** weakened many people's confidence in the health of the economy.

✔ **READING CHECK:** What events began to shake public confidence in the economy?

Dow Dives 508.32 Points In Panic on Wall Street

Navy blasts Iran oil site in retaliation

Billions lost in trading

INTERPRETING THE VISUAL RECORD
Wall Street. The 1987 stock market crash brought back memories of the Great Depression. *Does this picture of the New York Stock Exchange reflect the headline shown? Explain your answer.*

The Iran-Contra Affair

The Reagan administration also faced continued problems in the Middle East and Latin America. These frustrations led to the most serious crisis to hit the Reagan White House—the **Iran-Contra affair**.

After Congress cut off funds for the Contras' war against Nicaragua's Sandinista government, the Reagan administration sought other sources of funding. At the time, the White House was secretly bargaining with Iran for the release of U.S. hostages held by pro-Iranian groups in Lebanon. As part of the bargain, the administration shipped more than 500 antitank missiles to Iran by way of Israel. Without informing Congress, the administration used the profits from these arms sales to pay for weapons and supplies for the Contras.

When the arms sales became known in 1986, President Reagan appointed a commission to investigate. The commission cleared Reagan of any direct involvement. However, it heavily criticized other White House officials, some of whom resigned. The secret funding of the Contra war soon leaked out as well. It was revealed that Lieutenant Colonel Oliver North, a White House aide, had funneled millions of dollars from the Iranian arms sales to the Contras after Congress had forbidden direct U.S. government aid.

In 1987, House and Senate committees investigated the affair. North admitted that he and his secretary, Fawn Hall, had destroyed key documents. However, North insisted that they had acted out of loyalty and patriotism. North testified: "I am not in the habit of questioning my superiors. . . . I don't believe that what we did even under those circumstances is wrong or illegal."

In its report, the Senate committee denounced North's activities and criticized the loose White House management style that had allowed North to operate as he

Oliver North testified before the Senate that he had acted for the good of the country.

did. The chair of the Senate committee, Senator Daniel Inouye (in-oh-e) of Hawaii, countered North's claim that he was just following orders.

> ❝ [The] colonel was well aware that he was subject to the Uniform Code of Military Justice. . . . And that code makes it abundantly clear that orders of a superior officer must be obeyed by subordinate [lower in rank] members—but it is lawful orders. . . . In fact, it says members of the military have an obligation to disobey unlawful orders. ❞

In 1988 a court-appointed special prosecutor filed criminal charges against North and against Reagan's national security adviser, Admiral John Poindexter. North was convicted on various charges, including the destruction of government documents and lying to Congress. The conviction was later reversed on a legal technicality.

✔ **READING CHECK:** How did the Iran-Contra affair develop?

Central America and the Caribbean, 1980s

Learning from Maps The United States intervened in Central America and the Caribbean several times during the 1980s.

? **PLACE** Which Caribbean and Central American nations saw guerrilla activity or civil war during the 1980s?

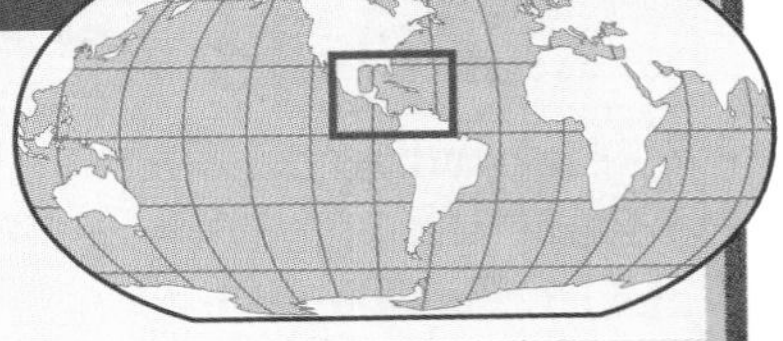

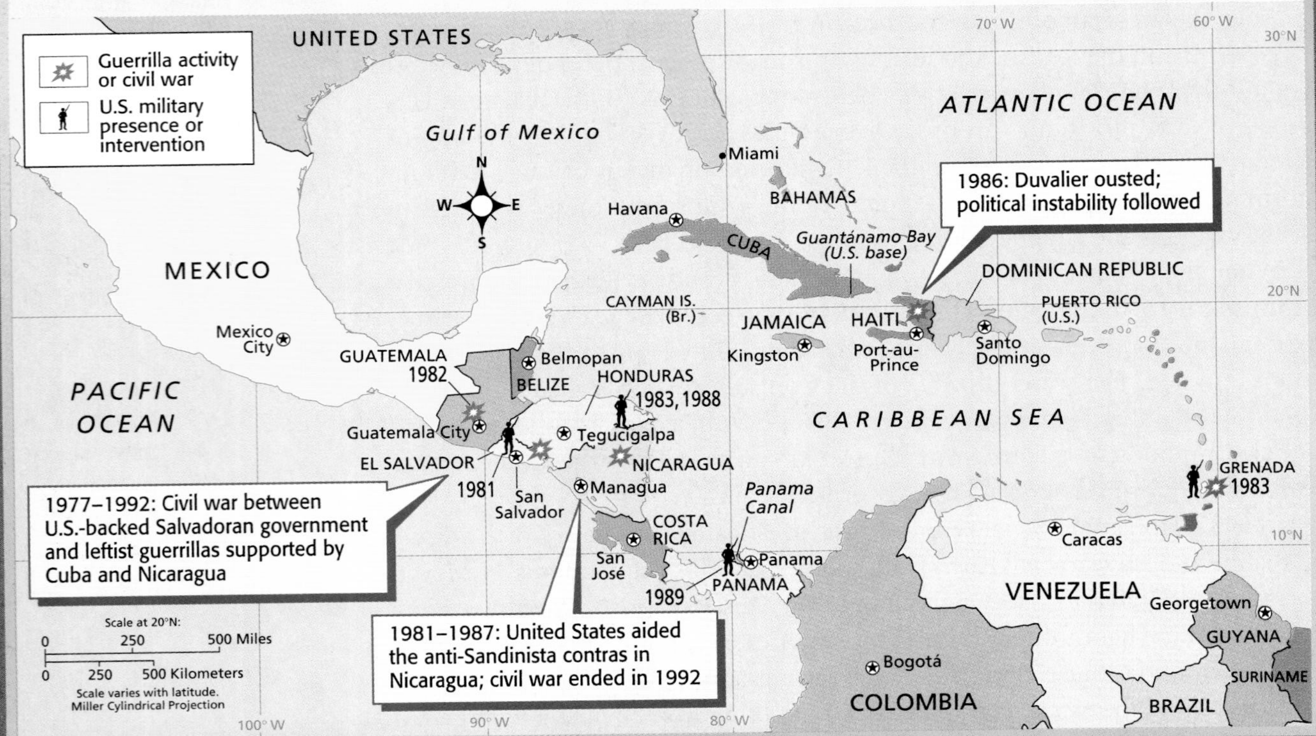

Guerrilla activity or civil war

U.S. military presence or intervention

UNITED STATES

ATLANTIC OCEAN

Gulf of Mexico

Miami

BAHAMAS

Havana

CUBA

Guantánamo Bay (U.S. base)

1986: Duvalier ousted; political instability followed

DOMINICAN REPUBLIC

MEXICO

CAYMAN IS. (Br.)

JAMAICA

HAITI

PUERTO RICO (U.S.)

Mexico City

Kingston

Port-au-Prince

Santo Domingo

GUATEMALA 1982

Belmopan

BELIZE

HONDURAS

1983, 1988

CARIBBEAN SEA

PACIFIC OCEAN

Guatemala City

Tegucigalpa

NICARAGUA

EL SALVADOR

1981

San Salvador

Managua

Panama Canal

GRENADA 1983

1977–1992: Civil war between U.S.-backed Salvadoran government and leftist guerrillas supported by Cuba and Nicaragua

COSTA RICA

San José

Panama

PANAMA

Caracas

VENEZUELA

Georgetown

Scale at 20°N:
0   250   500 Miles
0   250   500 Kilometers
Scale varies with latitude.
Miller Cylindrical Projection

1989

1981–1987: United States aided the anti-Sandinista contras in Nicaragua; civil war ended in 1992

Bogotá

COLOMBIA

GUYANA

SURINAME

BRAZIL

Creating an Outline

Along with formulating a hypothesis, creating an outline is an indispensable part of preparing to write a history research paper. An *outline* is an organizational tool that summarizes the ideas and evidence that one plans to discuss in a speech or piece of writing. By presenting this information concisely and in a logical order, an outline serves as a kind of "road map" that can make the actual process of writing a paper much easier.

How to Create an Outline

1. **Write your thesis statement.** First, formulate the hypothesis that you plan to focus on in your paper and write it out in a short, declarative statement. This thesis statement should make up the first major heading of your outline and be included in your paper's introduction.
2. **Organize your material.** Once you have settled on a thesis statement, organize logically the material that you wish to present in the paper. Determine what information belongs in the introduction, what should make up the body of the paper, and what to put in the conclusion.
3. **Summarize the main ideas.** Identify and briefly summarize the main ideas that you plan to use to support your thesis statement. Each of these main ideas should serve as a major heading in your outline and be labeled with a Roman numeral.
4. **List the supporting details.** As you summarize each main idea, identify the details or facts that support it and list them as subheadings in your outline. Make sure to order the subheadings logically and label them with descending levels of letters and numbers.

5. **Put your outline to use.** When you write your paper, structure it according to your outline. Each major heading, for instance, might form the basis of a topic sentence that begins a paragraph. Corresponding subheadings would then indicate the content of each paragraph. In a more lengthy paper, each subheading might constitute the basis of an entire paragraph.

Applying the Strategy

Read the following thesis statement, which presents a hypothesis about the causes of the Iran-Contra affair and President Reagan's responsibility for the crisis. Then create an outline for the portion of this chapter that discusses the Iran-Contra affair and use it to evaluate the statement.

A desire to free U.S. hostages held in Lebanon and fight communism in Nicaragua led to the Iran-Contra affair. White House officials sold weapons to Iran and used the profits to supply the Contras. As president of the United States Ronald Reagan was responsible for the actions of people serving in his administration.

Practicing the Strategy

Use your outline to answer the following questions.
1. What main ideas serve as major headings in your outline?
2. What supporting details are listed as subheadings in your outline?
3. How did you order the headings and subheadings in your outline?
4. How does your outline support your thesis statement?

Cold War Tensions Ease

The most significant achievement of President Reagan's second term was a dramatic easing of Cold War hostilities. When Mikhail Gorbachev became leader of the Soviet Union in 1985, a new era of Soviet history began.

By the 1980s the Soviet Union was burdened by a failing economy, a repressive political system, and heavy military costs. Gorbachev's initiatives included his policy of openness, called **glasnost** (GLAZ-nohst), that promised more freedom for the Soviet people. Equally dramatic was **perestroika** (per-uh-STROY-kuh)— Gorbachev's plan to restructure the Soviet economy and government. On the economic front, he called for increased foreign trade and reduced military spending.

INTERPRETING THE VISUAL RECORD

The Reagan style. President Reagan and his wife, Nancy, hosted Mikhail and Raisa Gorbachev at the Reagans' ranch in California. *How does the setting for this photograph reflect Reagan's style?*

The revenues from these changes were to be used to modernize Soviet factories. These reforms marked the first time since the Bolshevik Revolution that a Soviet leader had seemed open to some ideas of capitalist democratic government. These reforms began to dramatically change life in the Soviet Union. Glasnost also encouraged people to criticize the government. Many complained about the economy, which some felt had been weakened by the heightened arms race of the 1980s.

To further his domestic goals and defuse the costly Cold War conflict, Gorbachev pursued détente with the United States. In 1987, after a series of meetings, Gorbachev and President Reagan signed the **Intermediate-Range Nuclear Forces** (INF) **Treaty**. This treaty eliminated all medium-range nuclear weapons from Europe. Gorbachev also agreed to withdraw Soviet troops from Afghanistan. Gorbachev addressed these issues in a speech to the United Nations in 1988.

 **The use or threat of force no longer can or must be an instrument of foreign policy. . . . All of us, and primarily the stronger of us, must exercise self-restraint and totally rule out any outward-oriented use of force. 99**

In May 1988, as the Senate prepared to ratify the INF Treaty, Reagan flew to Moscow. As television cameras whirred, the U.S. president and the Soviet leader embraced like old friends.

✔ **READING CHECK:** What developments eased tensions between the United States and the Soviet Union in the late 1980s?

SECTION 2 REVIEW

Define and explain the significance of the following terms:
Gramm-Rudman-Hollings Act
insider trading
S&L crisis
Iran-Contra affair
glasnost
perestroika
Intermediate-Range Nuclear
    Forces Treaty

Identify and explain the significance of the following individuals:
Walter Mondale   Oliver North
Geraldine Ferraro   Mikhail Gorbachev
Sandra Day O'Connor

Locate and explain the significance of the following places:
Grenada   Nicaragua

1. **Using Graphic Organizers** Copy the graphic organizer below. Use it to show how each political party tried to appeal to voters in the 1984 presidential election.

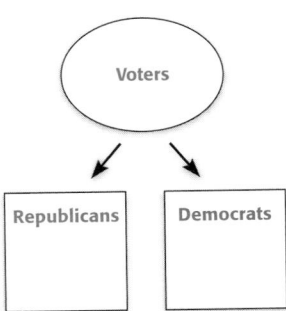

2. **Assessing Consequences** How did President Reagan change the makeup of the Supreme Court?
3. **Using Historical Imagination** Imagine that you are a member of a congressional committee appointed to investigate the Iran-Contra affair. Write a letter to the people you represent that summarizes the results of the investigation.
4. **Identifying Cause and Effect** What led to an easing of U.S.-Soviet tensions in the late 1980s? What were some outcomes of this change?

Critical Thinking

5. Why was public confidence in the economy shaken in the late 1980s?
   Consider:
   • the federal deficit
   • the stock market crash
   • the S&L crisis

Bush and Life in the 1980s

OBJECTIVES

Read to understand:
1. how American society changed in the 1980s
2. how the Cold War ended
3. what led to the Persian Gulf War, and how it differed from previous U.S. military conflicts
4. what domestic problems the Bush administration faced

KEY TERMS

Challenger
acquired immune deficiency syndrome
Commonwealth of Independent States
Operation Desert Storm
Americans with Disabilities Act
War on Drugs

KEY PEOPLE

Christa McAuliffe
Jesse Jackson
Michael Dukakis
Lloyd Bentsen
George Bush
Dan Quayle
Norman Schwarzkopf
Colin Powell

KEY PLACES

Iraq
Kuwait
Saudi Arabia

EYEWITNESSES TO History

❝ *What the president and Mrs. Reagan have done is extraordinary at a time in our history when there was a depressed mood in this country. They came and made it positive. How can you put a value on that? . . . If we have all these negative feelings, I don't think we can function as well as an individual or as a family or as a nation. Didn't it make you feel better? That the nation itself was having a better feeling about itself?* ❞

—Sugar Rautbord

The Yuppie Handbook reflected the prosperity of the 1980s.

Sugar Rautbord of Chicago was just one of many Americans who felt the optimism generated by President Reagan in the 1980s. Many people hoped that this feeling would continue even after Reagan left office.

America in the 1980s

Overall, the 1980s were much more positive than the 1970s. Singer Bobby McFerrin summed up the mood of the times with his humorous 1988 tune, "Don't Worry, Be Happy." Other popular singers reflected the spirit of consumerism that characterized the era.

Economics. Most families benefited from the economic boom of the 1980s. Some did extremely well. Many young urban professionals—so-called yuppies— took advantage of the increased number of financial services jobs. The newly wealthy yuppies set many style trends during the decade.

Not all families did well, however, particularly single-parent families. From 1970 to 1991 the number of children living in single-parent households more than doubled. In 1991 some 20 percent of white children, 60 percent of African American children, and 30 percent of Hispanic children lived with one parent, usually their mothers. Most single parents faced serious financial burdens. "Let's see the beginning of the end of this business where if you're born poor, you gotta die in the slums," said Frank Lumpkin, an unemployed steelworker. "All these kids [around here today] can do is sell hubcaps and tires to the junkman. And steal. The answer to crime is full employment. We gotta start figurin' a way to get it. It's no mystery."

Science and technology. During the 1980s Americans spent more and more money on a vast new array of electronic goods. One of the most popular items was the personal computer (PC). The PC explosion began in 1981, when IBM introduced its first model for consumers. By 1984 IBM was selling 3 million PCs per year. Computer experts began to experiment with the possibilities of the new technology. In 1984 Jaron Lanier, a 24-year-old inventor, developed "virtual reality." This system allowed viewers to experience and interact with three-dimensional

A personal computer from the early 1980s

images created solely through computer technology. Through virtual reality, people could actually experience an imaginary world.

The same year that virtual reality was invented, writer William Gibson published the science-fiction book *Neuromancer*. Gibson warned of a future in which technology takes over the world. He described this new world. "The sky above the port was the color of television, turned to a dead channel." Gibson's work spawned a new generation of computer-oriented science fiction called cyberpunk.

As the cyberpunk writers noted, technology offered hopes as well as challenges. The U.S. space program also experienced these ups and downs. Plagued by rising costs and falling interest in missions, the space program had declined somewhat since the 1970s. To cut costs of future flights, scientists began working on a reusable space shuttle. In 1981 the launch and successful landing of the space shuttle *Columbia* marked a new age in space technology.

Five years later, NASA announced that a civilian would be allowed to travel aboard a space shuttle. Social studies teacher Christa McAuliffe was chosen for a flight aboard the space shuttle *Challenger*. McAuliffe exhibited an enormous enthusiasm for space exploration.

66 **I remember the excitement in my home when the first satellites were launched. My parents were amazed and I was caught up with their wonder. . . . John Kennedy inspired me with his words about placing a man on the moon. . . . I watched the Space Age being born and I would like to participate.** 99

In January 1986—about 70 seconds after takeoff—*Challenger* exploded, killing all seven people on board. In part because of McAuliffe's participation, the takeoff was being watched live by a huge television audience. A horrified nation witnessed the worst disaster in NASA's history. Shuttle flights were suspended for two years until corrections could be made to the shuttle systems.

INTERPRETING THE VISUAL RECORD

Challenger. The seven members of the *Challenger* crew posed for this picture shortly before their tragic flight. *How did the crew represent the diversity of American society?*

Health. In the 1980s many Americans became concerned by the emergence of a new, deadly disease called **acquired immune deficiency syndrome**, or AIDS. This is the final deadly stage of an illness caused by the human immunodeficiency virus, or HIV. Doctors first reported cases of AIDS in 1981. By the end of the decade, hundreds of thousands of people worldwide had died from the disease.

AIDS left almost no continent untouched. In the African nation of Zambia, President Kenneth Kaunda's son died of AIDS. In 1991 basketball star Earvin "Magic" Johnson of the Los Angeles Lakers announced that he had tested positive for HIV. Other celebrities struck by the disease include movie star Rock Hudson and tennis legend Arthur Ashe.

✔ **READING CHECK:** How did American society change in the 1980s?

The 1988 Election

Domestic concerns were among the issues that worried voters as the 1988 presidential election approached. With President Reagan prohibited from running for a third term, the Democrats hoped to regain the White House in 1988. African American leader Jesse Jackson, who had run in 1984, was one of many candidates seeking the Democratic nomination. Jackson hoped to attract a "Rainbow Coalition"—a diverse group of voters representing all races, classes, and creeds. As a candidate in 1984, Jackson had helped generate the largest turnout of African American voters ever for a Democratic primary.

These campaign buttons are from the 1988 election.

In 1988 Jackson appealed to an even wider range of voters. On "Super Tuesday," the largest single day of primary voting, Jackson won more votes than any other Democratic candidate. Governor Michael Dukakis of Massachusetts won the most delegates, however, and eventually gained the nomination. Dukakis, the son of Greek immigrants, selected Senator Lloyd Bentsen of Texas as his running mate. Vice President George Bush won the Republican presidential nomination and chose Indiana senator Dan Quayle as his running mate.

The 1988 presidential campaign proved to be one of the harshest in recent years. Initially, Bush tried to appeal to voters' sense of optimism by promising "a kinder and gentler nation." By the final weeks of the campaign, however, most of the Republican ads had a negative focus. For instance, one commercial attacked Dukakis's environmental record by showing scenes of Massachusetts's heavily polluted Boston Harbor.

The most controversial Republican advertising campaign, however, was intended to attract voters troubled by the nation's rising crime rate. Crime had increased by more than 12.5 percent between 1984 and 1988. A series of television and print ads portrayed Dukakis as weak on crime by associating him with convicted murderer Willie Horton. While out on a weekend pass under a Massachusetts prisoner-release program, Horton had attacked a Maryland couple.

The Democrats were slow to respond to the Republicans' attacks. When they did, their efforts were poorly organized and ineffective. Dukakis tried to convince voters of his skills as a manager, arguing that the election should be about competence. This approach failed. In the November election, Bush won 426 electoral votes to Dukakis's 112. The Democrats did increase their majorities in both houses of Congress, however, and kept control of most state legislatures.

The End of the Cold War

President Bush faced a rapidly changing world. Mikhail Gorbachev's reform efforts in the Soviet Union led to the end of the Cold War and the breakup of the Soviet Union. This development was also influenced by frustration over economic turmoil in the Soviet Union. Many scholars argue that President Reagan's plan to increase U.S. defense systems contributed to the instability of the Soviet economy. As the Soviets spent more and more money on defense systems to keep up with the United States, they neglected serious economic issues at home.

The weakening of the Soviet Union was revealed in its reaction to democratic movements that swept Eastern and Central Europe in 1989 and 1990. No longer willing or able to bear the costs of propping up other communist governments, the Soviet Union announced in 1989 that it was adopting a policy of nonintervention in Eastern Europe. The Soviets did nothing when Poland and Hungary held free elections and the communist governments in Czechoslovakia and Romania fell.

The Soviets also did nothing when pro-democracy demonstrations broke out in East Germany in the fall of 1989. Throughout the fall, tens of thousands of East Germans fled to the West through Hungary. Then, in October, demonstrators forced Communist leader Erich Honecker to resign. Hoping to restore calm, the East German government opened the Berlin Wall on November 9 and lifted restrictions on travel to the West. It was too late. The pressure for German reunification—the reuniting of East and West Germany as one nation—was too great. After free elections, the two nations were united as the Federal Republic of Germany on October 3, 1990, without opposition from Gorbachev.

By 1991 Gorbachev had problems of his own in the Soviet Union. Alarmed by the pace of reforms, Communist hard-liners attempted to oust him. Their attempt collapsed quickly, but Gorbachev's days in power were numbered. On December 1 the Ukrainians voted for independence. On December 25 Gorbachev resigned as president of the Soviet Union and turned over control of the armed forces to Boris Yeltsin, the president of Russia. The next day, the presidents of Belarus, Russia, and Ukraine declared that the Soviet Union was "ceasing its existence." They formed a loose confederation

The Berlin Wall. Protesters climbed the Berlin Wall in 1989. *How does this scene symbolize the end of the Cold War?*

called the **Commonwealth of Independent States** (CIS). Eventually, the former Soviet republics of Armenia, Azerbaijan, Georgia, Kazakhstan, Kyrgyzstan, Moldova, Tajikistan, Turkmenistan, and Uzbekistan joined the CIS.

In early 1991 President Bush reflected on the promise of a new era free from Cold War pressures. "Now we can see . . . the very real prospect of a new world order," he declared, "a world in which freedom and respect for human rights find a home among all nations."

Communism still posed a threat to freedom, however. Pro-democracy reformers in China met a different fate from those in Europe. In May 1989, students and others took to Beijing's streets to protest Communist Party policies. On June 4 the government sent soldiers and tanks to remove the peaceful protesters gathered in Tiananmen Square. Estimates of the number of protesters killed range from a few hundred to more than a thousand.

✔ **READING CHECK:** How did the Cold War end?

The Persian Gulf War

With the end of the Cold War, President Bush was determined to reassert the leadership of the United States in world affairs. Before being elected president, Bush had served as U.S. ambassador to the United Nations, representative to China, and director of the CIA. His strong interest in foreign affairs was reflected in his presidency.

Operation Desert Storm. Bush assumed a strong leadership role in August 1990 when Iraq's ruler, Saddam Hussein, invaded neighboring Kuwait, a major oil producer. The United Nations condemned the attack. It also imposed economic sanctions on Iraq and set a deadline for Iraqi withdrawal from Kuwait. As the January 15, 1991, deadline neared, military forces representing the United States, Great Britain, France, Egypt, and Saudi Arabia prepared for war. Some 690,000 troops—including some 540,000 Americans—assembled in Saudi Arabia and on ships in the Persian Gulf. On January 16, bombing attacks began against Iraqi forces and military and industrial targets.

A ground assault began on February 23. Within days, the Iraqis had been driven back, and Kuwait's ruling al-Sabah family returned to power. American casualties included some 150 killed and 450 wounded, while an estimated 100,000 Iraqis died. U.S. air attacks also severely damaged the Iraqi capital, Baghdad, and other cities. Many hailed the success of this offensive, named **Operation Desert Storm**. The commander of U.S. forces, General Norman Schwarzkopf (SHWAWRTS-kawf), received a hero's welcome in New York City. Bush's approval rating soared following the war. The president praised the leadership of Secretary of Defense Richard Cheney and General Colin Powell, chairman of the Joint Chiefs of Staff.

Breakup of the Soviet Sphere, 1989–1992

Learning from Maps
By 1992, revolutions had caused the collapse of many communist governments in Eastern Europe.

? PLACE What countries shown below were part of the former Soviet Union?

Former Soviet republic

Former East European satellite of Soviet Union

Member of Commonwealth of Independent States

The Persian Gulf War received extensive media coverage.

Read More About It

Free Find:
Colin Powell

After reading about Colin Powell on the **Holt Researcher** CD–ROM, create a chart showing reasons why Powell would or would not be a good president.

BIOGRAPHY

Colin Powell

Colin Powell was born in 1937 to Jamaican immigrants living in New York City. Powell's parents always stressed the importance of education and hard work. While attending City College of New York, Powell joined the Reserve Officers' Training Corps (ROTC). This experience led him to a career in the military. He graduated at the top of his ROTC class in 1958 and immediately received a commission in the United States Army. "The Army was my life," he recalled.

Powell served several tours of duty in Vietnam, where he was wounded twice. During one incident, an injured Powell rescued several comrades from a burning helicopter. After the war, he received an advanced degree from George Washington University and worked in both the Nixon and Carter administrations. During the

The Persian Gulf War, 1991

Learning from Maps After more than a month of bombing, the UN allied forces ended the Gulf War with a short ground offensive.

? MOVEMENT From which country did most of the UN allied troops advance during the ground war?

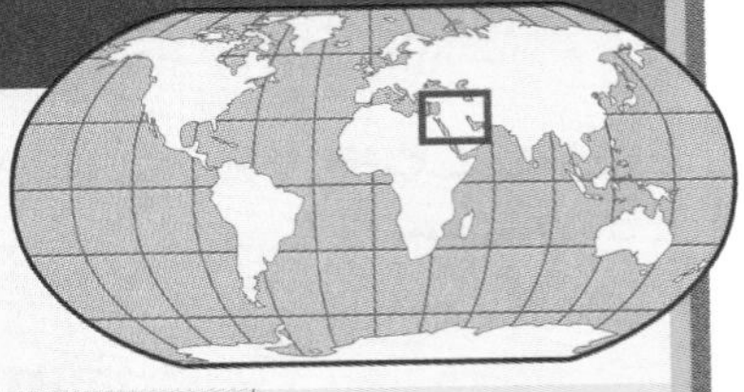

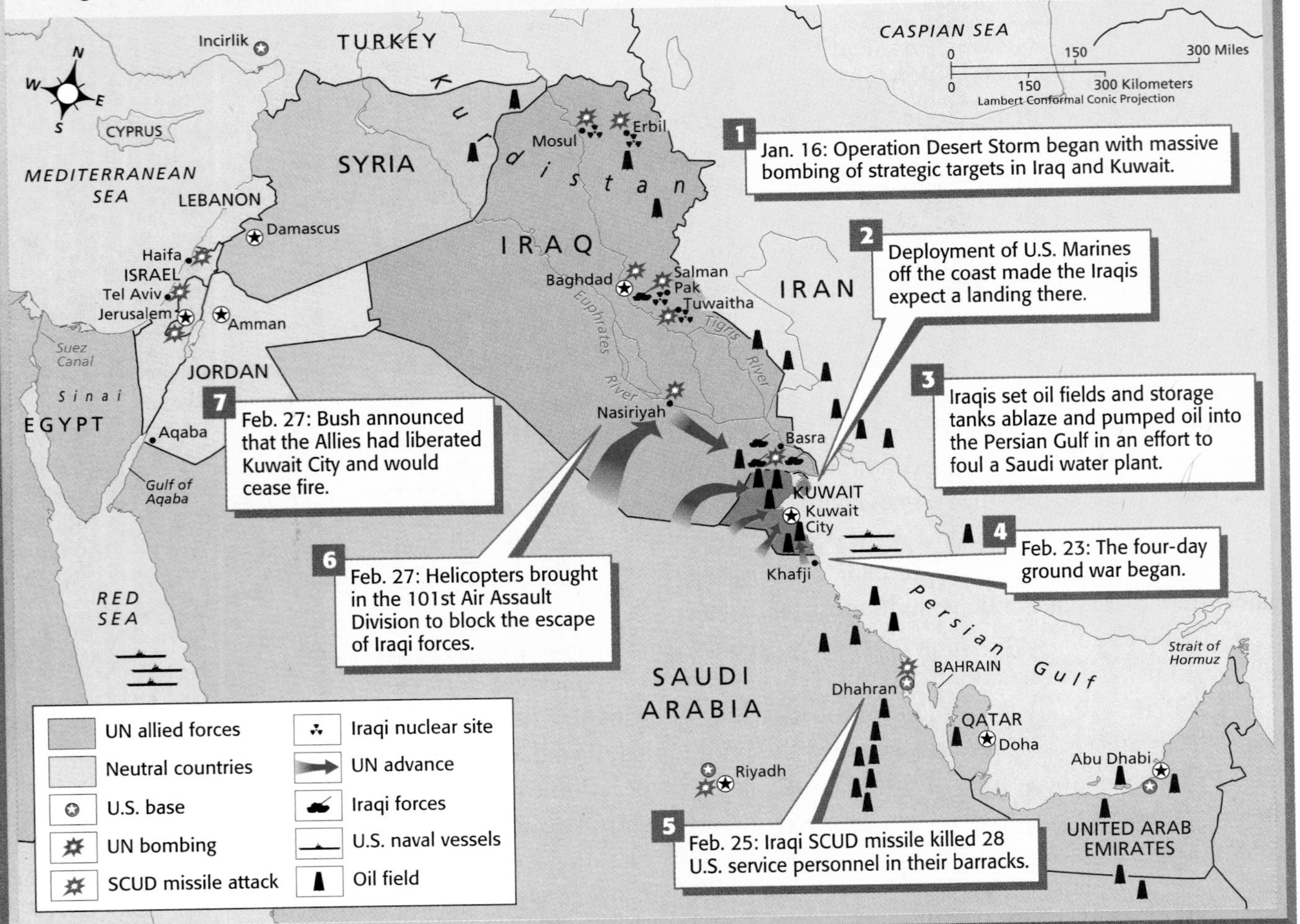

TURKEY
Incirlik
CASPIAN SEA
0 150 300 Miles
0 150 300 Kilometers
Lambert Conformal Conic Projection
N
W
E
S
CYPRUS
MEDITERRANEAN SEA
LEBANON
SYRIA
Kurdistan
Mosul
Erbil
Damascus
IRAQ
Baghdad
Salman Pak
Tuwaitha
IRAN
Haifa
ISRAEL
Tel Aviv
Jerusalem
Amman
JORDAN
Suez Canal
Sinai
EGYPT
Aqaba
Gulf of Aqaba
Euphrates River
Tigris River
Nasiriyah
Basra
KUWAIT
Kuwait City
Khafji
RED SEA
SAUDI ARABIA
Persian Gulf
BAHRAIN
Dhahran
QATAR
Doha
Riyadh
Abu Dhabi
UNITED ARAB EMIRATES
Strait of Hormuz
1 Jan. 16: Operation Desert Storm began with massive bombing of strategic targets in Iraq and Kuwait.
2 Deployment of U.S. Marines off the coast made the Iraqis expect a landing there.
3 Iraqis set oil fields and storage tanks ablaze and pumped oil into the Persian Gulf in an effort to foul a Saudi water plant.
4 Feb. 23: The four-day ground war began.
5 Feb. 25: Iraqi SCUD missile killed 28 U.S. service personnel in their barracks.
6 Feb. 27: Helicopters brought in the 101st Air Assault Division to block the escape of Iraqi forces.
7 Feb. 27: Bush announced that the Allies had liberated Kuwait City and would cease fire.
UN allied forces
Neutral countries
U.S. base
UN bombing
SCUD missile attack
Iraqi nuclear site
UN advance
Iraqi forces
U.S. naval vessels
Oil field

Persian Gulf War, Powell expressed great faith in the U.S. troops.

> 66 I had no doubt that we would be successful. We had the troops, the weapons, and the plan. What I did not know was how long it would take, and how many of our troops would not be coming home. 99

In the early 1990s Powell retired from the military. He has continued to serve national and international interests, however. In 1994 he was part of a peacekeeping team that helped lead the transition to democracy in Haiti. In recent years he has focused on increasing volunteerism in the United States. Although many supporters urged Powell to run for president in 1996, he declined.

A unique war. Unlike previous U.S. engagements, the Persian Gulf War was won almost entirely by using high-tech weapons. Television reporters also provided unprecedented coverage of the war, including live coverage of the air assaults. As Americans sat glued to their television sets, news correspondent Bernard Shaw reported the first allied bombings on Iraq. "This is [pause] something is happening outside. . . . The skies over Baghdad have been illuminated. We're seeing bright flashes going off all over the sky."

Military technology quickly became the star of the show as coverage of the war expanded. The technological nature of the war highlighted another unique aspect of Operation Desert Storm—the significant role played by women. More than 35,000 American women served in the Persian Gulf conflict—some 6 percent of all U.S. troops involved. Eleven American female soldiers were killed, and two were taken prisoner. Although the U.S. military banned women from serving as combat pilots, they served in almost every other capacity—including flying support planes and working on missile crews.

The role of women in Desert Storm and the nature of the war caused many people to question the policy of banning women from combat. With technology playing an increasingly significant role in modern warfare, critics charged, physical differences between men and women would become less important than technological skills. Before the war, the number of women in the military had increased dramatically. U.S. Air Force colonel Douglas Kennett commented that his branch of the service "couldn't go to war without women and we couldn't win without them." In August 1991 the Senate removed the ban against women serving as combat pilots, but continued to limit female soldiers' role in ground battles.

✔ **READING CHECK:** What led to the Persian Gulf War, and how was it different from previous U.S. military conflicts?

THROUGH OTHERS' EYES

A Palestinian View of the Persian Gulf War

Although the Persian Gulf War was brief, many people were caught in the cross fire, including the residents of Israel. To get revenge against UN forces, Iraq launched a missile attack on Israel. Palestinian philosopher Sari Nusseibeh was living in Israel when the attack came. He recalled his impressions as the war raged.

> 66 It was January 29, 13 days since the aerial bombardment in the Gulf War had started. For fully two weeks we had been placed under a total 24-hour curfew, interspersed [interrupted] only by three two-hour intervals in which we were allowed to do our shopping. All of us—my wife, my three children, and myself—had taken to sleeping together on the floor of the sitting-dining area of our apartment. This way we kept each other company through the SCUD [missile] scares (. . . we wondered each time where the rockets would fall, and what deadly poison they might be carrying). . . .
>
> For almost two weeks we lived in a state of suspension between TV scenes of missiles hitting Iraqi targets and footage of missiles flying over our heads. 99

This soldier is one of many women who served in the Persian Gulf War.

Domestic Concerns

President Bush's successes in foreign affairs won him popularity and international praise, but some critics charged that he was neglecting problems at home. As the 1992 presidential campaign approached, domestic issues—particularly the economy and a growing political controversy—troubled the public and weakened the president's support.

Bush's domestic policies. Although Bush had entered office telling the public, "We don't need radical new directions," he did propose a domestic agenda that differed from that of President Reagan. As he explained:

66 America is never wholly herself unless she is engaged in high moral principle. We as a people have such a purpose today. It is to make kinder the face of the Nation and gentler the face of the world. My friends, we have work to do.... I am speaking of a new engagement in the lives of others, a new activism, hands-on and involved, that gets the job done. 99

Promising to be the "education president," he proposed a series of reforms to improve the nation's schools. Meanwhile, First Lady Barbara Bush launched a campaign to stamp out illiteracy. "Everything would be better if people could learn to read, write, and understand," she said. Although Congress rejected many of Bush's proposed education reforms, it did approve increased funding for college loans and the Head Start program.

Bush ushered in a new era for citizens with disabilities. In July 1990 he signed the **Americans with Disabilities Act** into law. The act prohibits discrimination against people with physical or mental disabilities—including being afflicted with diseases such as AIDS—in employment, transportation, telephone services, and public buildings. The act also requires that companies with 15 or more employees remove structural barriers from offices.

The president addressed growing concerns over crime and drug use by launching the **War on Drugs**. This initiative provided more money to stop drug smuggling and illegal drug use. As a first step in this attack, Bush ordered the arrest of Panamanian dictator and drug smuggler General Manuel Noriega. In December 1989, U.S. Marines invaded Panama to bring Noriega back to the United States to face drug charges. Guillermo Endara, the democratically elected president, took control of the Panamanian government. In 1992 a Florida court convicted Noriega of drug smuggling and sentenced him to 40 years in prison.

Americans with disabilities. This woman makes her support of the Americans with Disabilities Act known. *What obstacle does this woman have to overcome?*

The Thomas-Hill hearings. Bush continued Reagan's efforts to move the Supreme Court in a conservative direction. In 1990 he filled a vacancy on the Court with David Souter, a conservative New Hampshire judge. In 1991 Justice Thurgood Marshall announced his retirement. Bush nominated Clarence Thomas, a conservative African American judge and former head of the federal Equal Employment Opportunity Commission (EEOC), to take his place.

During the confirmation hearings, law professor Anita Hill, a former associate of Thomas' at the EEOC, accused the nominee of sexual harassment. This is the use of unwelcome sexual language or behavior that creates a hostile working environment. In televised hearings, the Senate Judiciary Committee investigated Hill's charges. The bullying tactics used by some members of the committee in their questioning of Hill outraged many women. After the Senate narrowly approved Thomas's Supreme Court nomination, female activists vowed to show their disapproval in the next election. The hearings stirred debate across the country about sexual harassment.

The economy. Adding to President Bush's concerns was the slowing U.S. economy. The problem only grew worse as the economy weakened. In 1991 the federal deficit surged to some $270 billion and reached $291 billion in 1992. The costs of the Persian Gulf War and the bailout of the S&L and banking industries added to the deficit.

The trade gap persisted as well. Although the trade deficit had declined from its 1990 high of almost $102 billion, in 1991 it still stood at about $66 billion. Japan's massive annual sales of automobiles and electronic goods to American consumers accounted for a large portion of the gap. On a 1992 trade mission to Japan, President Bush and American business leaders tried with little success to persuade the Japanese to increase imports from the United States.

Some Americans favored buying only goods produced in the United States as a way to strengthen the economy and reduce the trade deficit.

Adding to these economic problems, a recession hit late in 1990. As the economy faltered, unemployment rose. States facing budget deficits cut their welfare programs. The number of Americans living below the poverty line grew by more than 2 million in 1990. The recession continued through 1992, hurting President Bush's re-election hopes.

✔ **READING CHECK:** What domestic problems did the Bush administration face?

SECTION 3 REVIEW

Define and explain the significance of the following terms:
Challenger
acquired immune deficiency syndrome
Commonwealth of Independent States
Operation Desert Storm
Americans with Disabilities Act
War on Drugs

Identify and explain the significance of the following individuals:

Christa McAuliffe	George Bush
Jesse Jackson	Dan Quayle
Michael Dukakis	Norman Schwarzkopf
Lloyd Bentsen	Colin Powell

Locate and explain the significance of the following places:

Iraq	Saudi Arabia
Kuwait	

1. **Using Graphic Organizers** Copy the graphic organizer below. Use it to describe the events that marked the end of the Cold War.

1. Soviets adopt non-intervention policy
2.
3.
4.
5.
6.
7. Gorbachev resigns

2. **Using Historical Imagination** Imagine that you are an average American in the 1980s. Write a journal entry describing how the decade is different from the 1970s.

3. **Identifying Cause and Effect** Why did the United States participate in the Persian Gulf War? What were the outcomes of the war?

4. **Synthesizing** In what ways was the Persian Gulf War different from other recent wars in which the United States fought?

Critical Thinking

5. How did domestic issues affect public support for President Bush?
   Consider:
   • Bush's domestic policies and their effects
   • reactions to the Thomas-Hill hearings
   • the state of the economy by the early 1990s

CHAPTER 35

Review

Creating a Time Line

Copy the time line below onto a sheet of paper. Complete the time line by filling in the events and dates from the chapter that you think were most significant. Pick three events and explain why you think they were significant.

1980   1984   1988   1992

Writing a Summary

Using the Reading Checks as a guide, write an overview of the events in the chapter.

Identifying People and Ideas

Identify the following terms or individuals and explain their significance.

1. Iran hostage crisis
2. Ronald Reagan
3. George Bush
4. supply-side economics
5. Strategic Defense Initiative
6. Contras
7. Sandra Day O'Connor
8. *Challenger*
9. Operation Desert Storm
10. Colin Powell

Understanding Main Ideas

SECTION 1

1. Why did voters choose Ronald Reagan over Jimmy Carter in the 1980 presidential election?
2. How did the Reagan administration fight the Cold War in the early 1980s?

SECTION 2

3. Why did public confidence in the economy begin to weaken in the late 1980s?
4. What were the main issues in the Iran-Contra affair?

SECTION 3

5. What changes occurred in American society in the 1980s?
6. What led to the Persian Gulf War?

Reviewing Themes

1. **Economic Development** What effects did President Reagan's economic policies have on the country?
2. **Global Relations** How did President Reagan's approach to defense change the Cold War?
3. **Technology and Society** How did computer technology change in the 1980s?

Thinking Critically

1. **Identifying Values** What issues were at stake for the United States in El Salvador and Nicaragua?
2. **Problem Solving** How would you have addressed the economic problems of the 1980s?
3. **Comparing and Contrasting** How was the Iran-Contra affair both similar to and different from the Watergate scandal?
4. **Analyzing** How did improved relations affect the United States and the Soviet Union?
5. **Taking a Stand** Was life better for Americans in the 1980s than in the 1970s? Why?

Writing About History

Writing to Explain Write an essay that explains the significance of the passage of the Americans with Disabilities Act. Use the following graphic to organize your thoughts.

Challenges for people with disabilities	Benefits of Americans with Disabilities Act

Strategies for Success Review the **Strategies for Success** on *Creating an Outline*. Read the following thesis statement, which presents a hypothesis about the effects of President Reagan's economic policies. Then create an outline for a short essay that would focus on and attempt to prove the statement.

> ❝ **Reaganomics affected different Americans differently. While some profited from President Reagan's economic program of tax reductions and relaxed government regulations, others remained unable to find jobs and were hurt by deep cuts in social programs.** ❞

Linking History and Geography

Voter turnout was particularly low in the 1988 presidential election. Only 50 percent of registered voters participated—the lowest turnout since 1924. Study the map below. Which states did Michael Dukakis win?

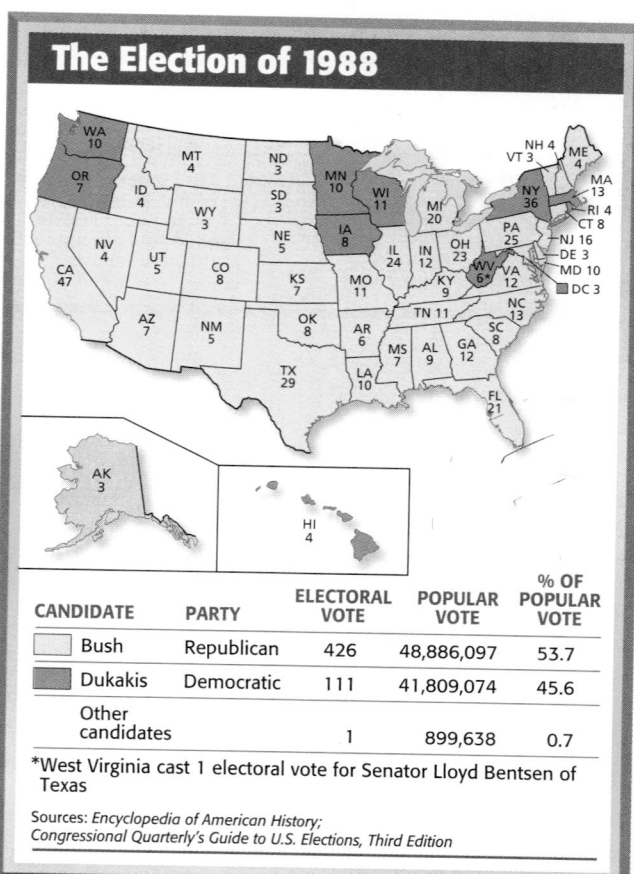

The Election of 1988

CANDIDATE	PARTY	ELECTORAL VOTE	POPULAR VOTE	% OF POPULAR VOTE
Bush	Republican	426	48,886,097	53.7
Dukakis	Democratic	111	41,809,074	45.6
Other candidates		1	899,638	0.7

*West Virginia cast 1 electoral vote for Senator Lloyd Bentsen of Texas

Sources: *Encyclopedia of American History;*
Congressional Quarterly's Guide to U.S. Elections, Third Edition

 internetconnect

TOPIC: Persian Gulf War
GO TO: go.hrw.com
KEYWORD: SD1 Gulf

Accessing the Internet through the HRW Web site, research the Persian Gulf War. Then write a journal entry as if you were a U.S. soldier fighting in the Gulf War. Describe your experiences in and thoughts about the war.

BUILDING YOUR PORTFOLIO

Complete one or all of the following projects independently or cooperatively.

1 Global Relations
Imagine that you are a reporter covering the Iran-Contra affair. **Create a flowchart** that traces the transfer of weapons, money, and supplies among the United States, Iran, and the Contras.

2 Technology and Society
Imagine that you are a science fiction writer in the 1980s. **Write and illustrate a short story** that reflects your concerns about the future of technology in society.

3 Economic Development
Imagine that you are one of President Reagan's economic advisers. **Prepare a pamphlet** describing Reagan's economic policies and their goals. Include your opinions of the costs and benefits of each policy.

William Gibson's book Neuromancer

The Natural Environment

The increasing population and rapid development of land in the United States has led to increased concerns about the future of the natural environment. In the late 1900s, however, much progress was made toward protecting the environment and decreasing pollution. The creation of national parks and wildlife refuges helps preserve the natural landscape and save endangered animals from possible extinction.

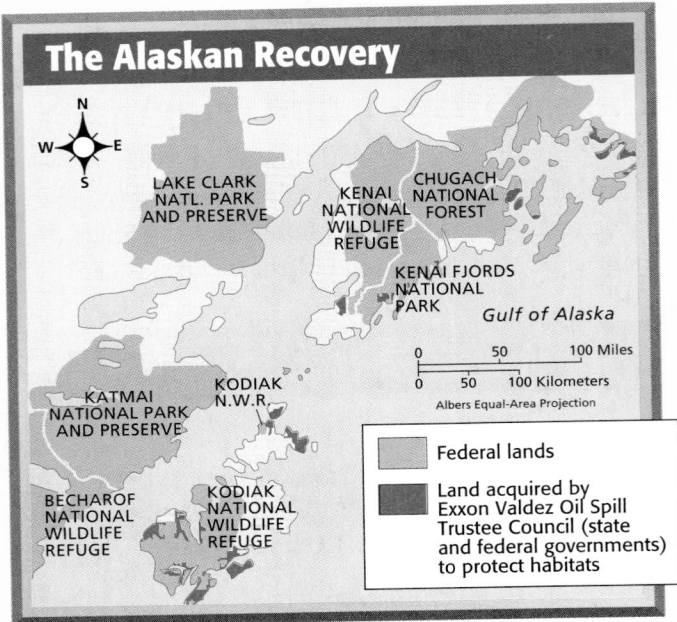

The Alaskan Recovery

Federal lands

Land acquired by Exxon Valdez Oil Spill Trustee Council (state and federal governments) to protect habitats

The Alaskan Oil Spill of 1989

Alaskan oil spill. Industrial accidents can have devastating effects on the environment. In 1989 the oil tanker *Exxon Valdez* spilled about 11 million gallons of oil when it ran aground near the Alaskan coastline. The cleanup for the oil spill was long and expensive. To help preserve the coastal areas, the U.S. government purchased some of the affected lands. Ten years later some parts of Alaska still had not fully recovered.

GEOGRAPHY AND HISTORY Skills

HUMAN-ENVIRONMENT INTERACTION

1. Which federal lands were affected by the Alaskan oil spill of 1989?
2. According to the map of the Alaskan oil spill, how many miles did the spilled oil spread?
3. Which lands were purchased by the government after the oil spill?

The Yellowstone Fires of 1988

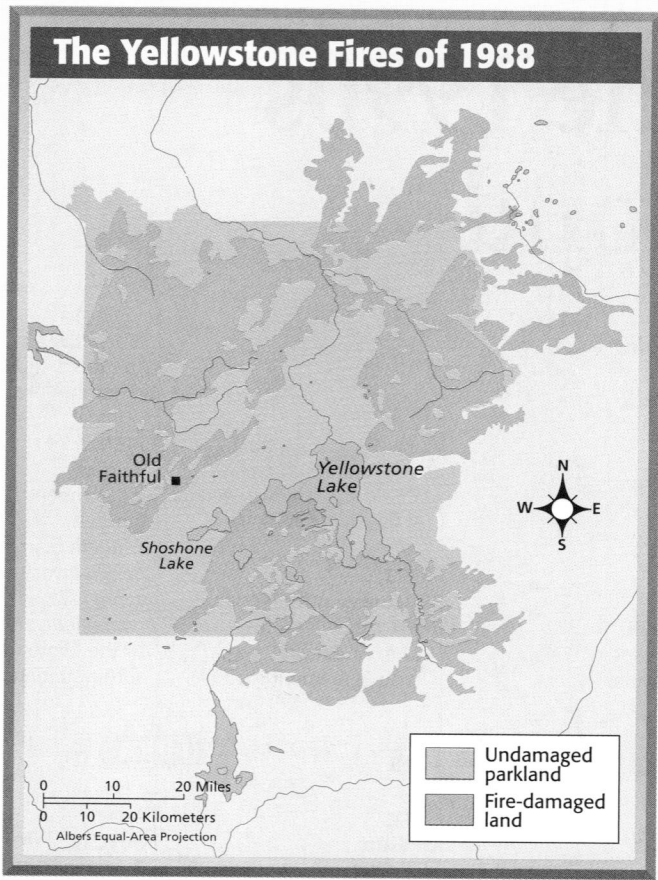

Old Faithful ■

Yellowstone Lake

Shoshone Lake

N W E S

0   10   20 Miles
0   10   20 Kilometers
Albers Equal-Area Projection

| | Undamaged parkland |
| | Fire-damaged land |

Yellowstone Recovery

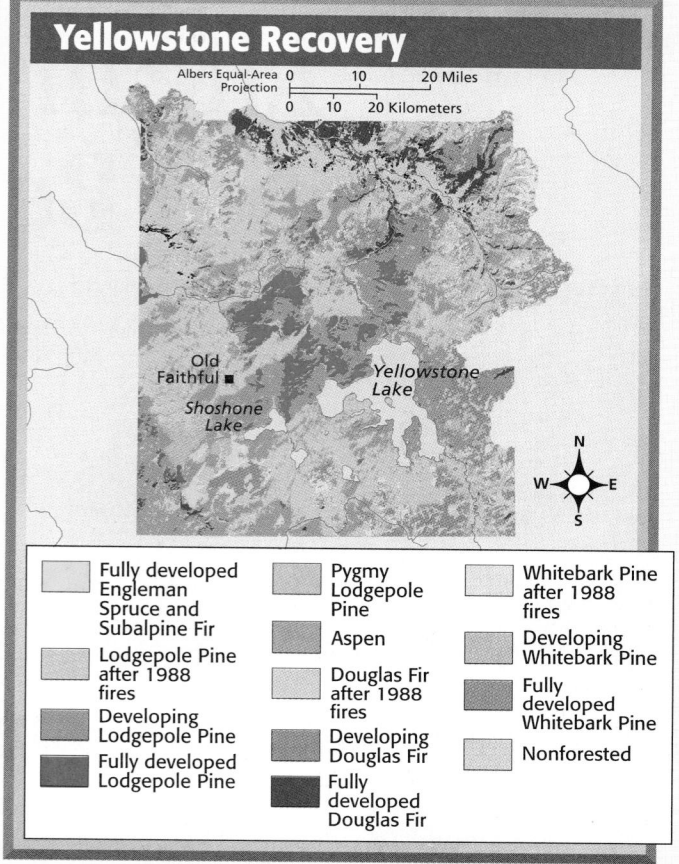

Albers Equal-Area Projection   0   10   20 Miles
0   10   20 Kilometers

Old Faithful ■

Yellowstone Lake

Shoshone Lake

N W E S

	Fully developed Engleman Spruce and Subalpine Fir		Pygmy Lodgepole Pine		Whitebark Pine after 1988 fires
	Lodgepole Pine after 1988 fires		Aspen		Developing Whitebark Pine
	Developing Lodgepole Pine		Douglas Fir after 1988 fires		Fully developed Whitebark Pine
	Fully developed Lodgepole Pine		Developing Douglas Fir		Nonforested
			Fully developed Douglas Fir		

Pollution control. Air pollution had become a serious problem by the 1970s. New laws helped decrease air pollutants, particularly lead and carbon dioxide. Americans also fought pollution by recycling more waste items.

Yellowstone fires. In 1988 a natural disaster struck Yellowstone National Park. Lightning started forest fires that eventually burned some 45 percent of the park. The lands recovered quickly from the fires, however. Within just a few years much of the park had experienced a significant regrowth of its vegetation.

Annual Emissions of Air Pollutants

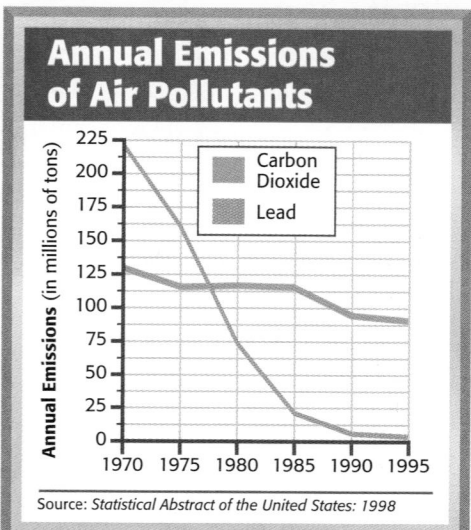

Annual Emissions (in millions of tons)

225
200
175
150
125
100
75
50
25
0

1970 1975 1980 1985 1990 1995

Carbon Dioxide
Lead

Source: *Statistical Abstract of the United States: 1998*

Percentage of Waste Recycled

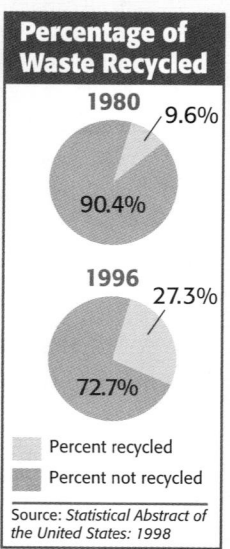

1980   9.6%
90.4%

1996   27.3%
72.7%

| | Percent recycled |
| | Percent not recycled |

Source: *Statistical Abstract of the United States: 1998*

GEOGRAPHY AND HISTORY **Skills**

HUMAN-ENVIRONMENT INTERACTION

1. After recovering from the fires of 1988, what plants grew in the areas that had been destroyed by fire?
2. By how much did the level of lead in the air drop between 1970 and 1995?
3. How much did the percentage of waste recycled increase between 1980 and 1996?

1990–Present

Life in the 1990s and Beyond

Los Angeles riots

1993
Business and Finance
Congress ratifies the North American Free Trade Agreement (NAFTA).

1994
World Events
Apartheid ends in South Africa.

1994
Politics
Independent Counsel Kenneth Starr begins investigating alleged wrongdoings by the Clinton administration.

1992
Daily Life
Riots erupt in Los Angeles.

1990	1991	1992	1993	1994

1991
World Events
The Persian Gulf War ends as a United Nations force pushes Iraqi troops out of Kuwait.

1992
The Arts
Gish Jen publishes her novel *Typical American*.

1993
Politics
Bill Clinton is sworn in as the 42nd president of the United States.

1994
Politics
Republican candidates for Congress present the Contract with America.

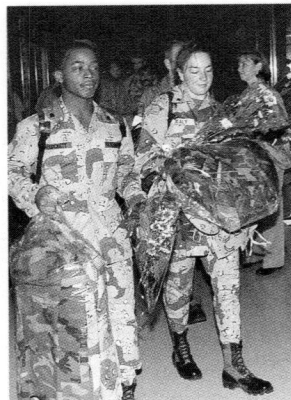

Persian Gulf War veterans

President Clinton giving his first inaugural address

Newt Gingrich presents the Contract with America.

Before You Read

Build on What You Know

During the 1980s Republican presidents Ronald Reagan and George Bush won wide support for their efforts to reduce federal regulation. Despite the success of the Persian Gulf War, George Bush's bid for re-election was harmed by an economic recession and an ongoing budget-deficit problem. In this chapter you will learn about Bill Clinton's rise to the presidency. You will also learn how American society changed as a result of increasing globalization, new advances in technology, and the expansion of democracy abroad.

The Murrah Federal Building after a terrorist attack

Poster advertising the musical **Rent**

John Glenn (waving) and the space shuttle crew

1995
Daily Life
A terrorist truck bomb destroys the Murrah Federal Building in Oklahoma City, killing 168 people.

1996
The Arts
Rent, a Broadway rock musical, wins the Pulitzer Prize for best American drama.

1998
Science and Technology
At age 77, John Glenn becomes the oldest person ever to travel in space.

1999
Business and Finance
The Dow Jones industrial average surpasses 10,000 points as the stock market booms in the wake of mergers and record profits.

1999
World Events
NATO launches air attacks on Yugoslavia.

1995 | **1996** | **1997** | **1998** | **1999**

1995
Daily Life
Louis Farrakhan leads the Million Man March in Washington, D.C.

1996
Politics
President Clinton is re-elected as the U.S. economy prospers.

1996
Daily Life
The Summer Olympics in Atlanta are interrupted when a bomb explodes during a concert.

1997
Science and Technology
Scottish scientists successfully clone a mammal, Dolly the sheep, for the first time.

1997
The Arts
The Getty Museum in Los Angeles opens to the public.

Dolly, the cloned sheep

African American men participate in the Million Man March.

Think About Themes

Themes Journal

Decide whether you agree or disagree with the following statements. Note why in your journal.

Economic Development Economic influence is more important than military strength in determining the political power of nations.

Global Relations Americans' experiences are disconnected from events around the world.

Technology and Society New advances in technology will improve American society by expanding communication and easing the struggles of daily existence.

Clinton's First Term

SECTION 1

OBJECTIVES

Read to understand:
1. how the 1992 presidential election differed from other recent elections
2. what led to the Republican comeback in the 1994 congressional elections
3. how regional conflicts and terrorism affected the world
4. how successful the United Nations was in maintaining world peace after the Cold War ended

KEY TERMS

Contract with America
Operation Restore Hope

KEY PEOPLE

Bill Clinton
Hillary Rodham Clinton
Ross Perot
Newt Gingrich
Nelson Mandela
Yasir Arafat
Yitzhak Rabin
Benjamin Netanyahu
Mu'ammar Gadhafi

Hillary Rodham Clinton played an important role in Bill Clinton's campaign.

EYEWITNESSES TO History

66 *Today, a generation raised in the shadows of the Cold War assumes new responsibilities in a world warmed by the sunshine of freedom but threatened still by ancient hatreds and new plagues. . . . Though our challenges are fearsome, so are our strengths. . . . Our democracy must be not only the envy of the world but the engine of our own renewal. There is nothing wrong with America that cannot be cured by what is right with America.* 99
—President Bill Clinton

1992 Democratic Party campaign button

After successfully campaigning on the issue of governmental renewal, Bill Clinton was elected president in November 1992. He continued his message of renewal for the nation in his inaugural address in 1993. With the Cold War over, many Americans optimistically expected solutions to political gridlock, continued violence overseas, and tensions within the United States. This confidence was shaken, however, by new challenges and dangers at home and abroad.

The Election of 1992

Despite the nation's economic woes, President Bush's popularity remained high, particularly after the Persian Gulf War in 1991. One of the few Democrats willing to challenge him in the 1992 election was Governor Bill Clinton of Arkansas.

The Democratic challenger. Bill Clinton was born William Jefferson Blythe in 1946 in Hope, Arkansas, shortly after his father's death. His mother, Virginia, later married Roger Clinton. Bill Clinton's childhood experiences of dealing with poverty and a troubled home life—including an alcoholic adoptive father—shaped his outlook on the world. After meeting President John F. Kennedy as a teenage delegate to Boys' Nation in 1963, Clinton decided on a political career.

While studying law at Yale University he met Hillary Rodham, a fellow law student. Rodham later served as a staff member with the House Judiciary Committee as it considered the impeachment of President Nixon. The couple married in 1975 and settled in Fayetteville, Arkansas. Three years later, Clinton became the nation's youngest governor. As a baby boomer, Clinton reflected many traits of his generation. He opposed the war in Vietnam and for a time tried to avoid being drafted. Influenced by the idealism of the 1960s, he believed strongly in diversity and equality.

As first lady of Arkansas, Hillary Rodham Clinton served on several influential committees, including one that developed a ground-breaking education-reform program. Bill Clinton acknowledged his wife's key role in advising him. During the 1992 campaign he said that voters would be getting "two for the price of one" if he were elected president. Some Americans, however, were uncomfortable with the idea of a president's wife in a policy-making role.

The campaign. After years of low voter participation, citizens turned out in large numbers in 1992 to make their voices heard. Candidates used public forums such as television talk shows and radio call-in programs to answer questions directly from the public. A master of this sort of publicity was Ross Perot.

Perot, a billionaire from Texas, ran as an independent candidate for president. Perot promised to reform the federal government by decreasing the influence of political lobbyists and by giving the public a greater voice. He also promised to use his business skills to cut government spending and balance the budget. Perot's message appealed to many voters who were concerned about the economy and the federal deficit.

President Bush said little about the economy in his campaign. He focused largely on the personal character of the candidates. Some people questioned Bill Clinton's integrity. Some of his political enemies in Arkansas referred to him as "Slick Willie," comparing him to old-time con artists selling snake oil as a cure-all. Questions about Clinton's personal conduct in his marriage also emerged.

Comments about Clinton's character had little effect at the polls, however. He and his running mate, Senator Al Gore of Tennessee, won 43 percent of the popular vote and 370 electoral votes. Bush won 38 percent of the popular vote and 168 electoral votes. Although Perot failed to pick up any electoral votes, he captured 19 percent of the popular vote. This was more than any third-party presidential ticket since that of Theodore Roosevelt, the Progressive Party candidate, in 1912.

The 1992 election. Ross Perot ran a strong third-party campaign for president. *What type of image does this button suggest?*

Voter frustration. Perot's popularity and the Democratic victory reflected the belief of many voters that politicians were out of touch. Female voters—particularly those outraged by the Clarence Thomas–Anita Hill hearings—were active in the 1992 election. Shortly after the hearings, feminist Eleanor Smeal spoke out. "The Senate did more in one week to underscore the critical need for more women in the Senate than feminists have been able to do in 25 years." Women responded by running for public office in record numbers.

The increase in female candidates led the press to dub 1992 "the year of the woman." Many of these candidates won election. Four prominent female Democrats gained U.S. Senate seats, including Patty Murray of Washington and African American Carol Moseley-Braun of Illinois. California filled both of its Senate seats with women—Barbara Boxer and Dianne Feinstein.

The elections of 1992 brought new female senators to Congress. Pictured (left to right) are Senators Carol Moseley-Braun, Patty Murray, Barbara Boxer, and Barbara Mikulski.

✔ **READING CHECK:** How did the 1992 presidential election differ from other recent elections?

Clinton Takes Office

At President Clinton's inauguration, poet Maya Angelou read a poem of hers that celebrated the diversity of Americans and expressed hope for the future:

Bill Clinton

1946–
In Office 1993–

Bill Clinton's presidency marked many firsts in the White House. He was the first president born in the post–World War II era and the first president from Arkansas. Clinton was also the first president to play the saxophone at his own inaugural celebration.

Clinton's career goal as a youngster was to become a jazz musician. He was heavily influenced by African American jazz artists and early rock 'n' roll stars such as Elvis Presley. He excelled at playing the saxophone and was offered numerous music scholarships to college after he graduated from high school. Although Clinton went on to make a career in politics, he frequently used his musical talents in campaigns. During the 1992 presidential election, he put on a pair of sunglasses and played the saxophone on a popular late-night talk show. Despite his love of music, Clinton believes that he made the right career choice. "I would have been a very good musician," he once noted, "but not a great one."

> Lift up your eyes upon
> This day breaking for you.
> Give birth again
> To the dream. . . .
>
> Here on the pulse of this new day
> You may have the grace to look up
>   and out
> And into your sister's eyes and into
> Your brother's face, your country
> And say simply
> Very simply
> With hope
> Good morning. "

Once in office, Clinton put these ideas into practice by creating a diverse cabinet. His appointees included Mexican American Henry Cisneros as secretary of housing and urban development. He also appointed African Americans Ron Brown and Joycelyn Elders as secretary of commerce and surgeon general, respectively. Other female appointees included Press Secretary Dee Dee Myers, Attorney General Janet Reno, and Secretary of Health and Human Services Donna Shalala. Clinton also nominated Ruth Bader Ginsburg to fill a vacancy on the Supreme Court.

Clinton suffered a series of setbacks early in his presidency. An elaborate plan to reform the nation's health care system, drafted by a task force headed by Hillary Rodham Clinton, died in Congress. Clinton had hoped the reform plan would address voters' concerns about the rising costs of medical care. More Americans were living longer and the baby boom generation was passing middle age. Many Americans feared that they would not be able to afford quality health care in their old age. In addition to being unable to move health care reform forward, the Clintons faced questions of possible past improper financial dealings. Most involved a failed Arkansas real-estate development called Whitewater.

On the economic front, however, President Clinton had some success. In August 1993 Congress narrowly passed a budget act that combined tax increases and spending cuts to reduce the national debt. Over time, the act worked. By 1996 the deficit dropped to about $107 billion, less than half that of 1992. Unemployment dropped to 5.4 percent, the lowest since 1989, and inflation hovered at about 3 percent. As investors gained confidence, the stock market boomed.

Read More About It

Free Find: Bill Clinton
After reading about Bill Clinton on the **Holt Researcher** CD–ROM, write a short essay explaining how his values and goals as president may reflect the experiences he had growing up in Arkansas.

A Republican Comeback

The economic recovery did not come fast enough to suit many voters. As the 1994 congressional elections approached, voter frustration with the slow recovery began to build. Encouraged by President Clinton's early setbacks, Republicans geared up for the 1994 midterm election. Many Republican candidates signed the **Contract with America**, which pledged a balanced-budget amendment and other reforms.

Voters gave Republicans control of both the House and Senate. Newt Gingrich of Georgia, who became Speaker of the House, commented on the election.

> 66 This election was actually about some fairly big ideas: which direction do you want to go in? . . . Those who argued for counterculture values, bigger government, redistributionist economics, and bureaucracies deciding how you should spend your money, were on the losing end in virtually every part of the country. 99

✔ **READING CHECK:** What led to the Republican comeback in the 1994 congressional elections?

Foreign and Domestic Dangers

Amid these domestic and political challenges, the Clinton administration confronted a range of global crises. It also wrestled with an increase in terrorism.

Regional conflicts. As the Cold War faded, regional conflicts intensified. The end of Communist rule in Eastern Europe unleashed bitter ethnic and local disputes. Bosnia and Herzegovina, a region that once was part of Yugoslavia, was torn apart by fighting among Serbs, Croatians, and Slovenes.

The 15 newly independent republics of the former Soviet Union experienced conflict as various groups struggled for power and self-rule. Russia and Ukraine argued over control of the Black Sea fleet, while Christians in Armenia battled with Muslims in neighboring Azerbaijan (a-zuhr-by-JAHN).

On a brighter note, a new era dawned in South Africa when decades of apartheid came to an end. In 1994 South Africa held its first elections allowing all races to vote. Black civil rights activist Nelson Mandela, who had spent years as a political prisoner in South Africa, won the presidency. Despite conflict between rival political and ethnic groups, South Africa's future looked hopeful.

Elsewhere in Africa, however, turmoil reigned, worsened by famine and poverty. Civil war raged in Liberia, Mali, Somalia, and Zambia. In December 1992, a UN force, including many Americans, launched **Operation Restore Hope** to provide relief to famine-stricken Somalia. Fighting among rival clans in that country had previously prevented relief workers from getting food and other supplies to starving Somalis. Despite the UN effort, Somalia's suffering continued.

★ HISTORICAL DOCUMENTS ★

Contract with America

Drawn up by members of the Republican Party, the Contract with America offered a list of reforms and 10 pieces of legislation that Republicans promised to propose. Some 300 candidates for public office gathered on the steps of the U.S. Capitol on September 27, 1994, to sign the document. They pledged their support to the positions outlined in the document, stating, "If we break this contract, throw us out."

*A*s Republican members of the House of Representatives and as citizens seeking to join that body we propose not just to change its policies, but even more important, to restore the bonds of trust between the people and their elected representatives. . . .

On the first day of the 104th Congress, the new Republican majority will immediately pass the following major reforms:

First, require all laws that apply to the rest of the country also apply equally to the Congress;

Second, select a major independent auditing firm to conduct a comprehensive audit [complete study] of Congress for waste, fraud, or abuse;

Third, cut the number of House committees, and cut committee staff by one-third;

Fourth, limit the terms of all committee chairs;

Fifth, ban the casting of proxy votes in committee;

Sixth, require committee meetings to be open to the public;

Seventh, require a three-fifths majority vote to pass a tax increase;

Eighth, guarantee honest accounting of our federal budget by implementing [putting into effect] zero baseline budgeting.

President Clinton looks on as Yitzhak Rabin (left) and Yasir Arafat shake hands to seal their 1993 peace accord.

The Middle East. Instability also threatened many nations in the Middle East. Islamic fundamentalists battled for political power. Hopes for peace between Palestinians and Israelis were renewed in September 1993, when Palestinian leader Yasir Arafat and Israeli prime minister Yitzhak Rabin signed a peace accord. President Clinton oversaw the signing of the agreement at the White House. He described it as a "historic and honorable compromise."

The peace process suffered a setback in 1995, when a young Israeli with extreme nationalist views assassinated Rabin. In 1996 Benjamin Netanyahu was elected prime minister of Israel and pledged to be less willing to compromise in peace negotiations. U.S. Secretary of State Warren Christopher worked hard to bring the two sides together. Yet there were new outbreaks of violence between Israeli soldiers and Palestinians in September 1996. This made it clear that a more peaceful future was far from certain in this troubled region.

Terrorism. Along with the end of the Cold War came an increase in terrorist activity throughout the world. According to one group of experts, the number of terrorist acts rose by 11 percent from 1991 to 1992.

U.S. leaders usually responded quickly to international terrorism linked directly to a particular nation. In 1986 President Reagan had ordered a bombing attack on Libya. Evidence had linked that country's leader, Mu'ammar Gadhafi (guh-DAH-fee), to an attack at a West Berlin nightclub. The attack killed one U.S. soldier and injured many others. In the summer of 1993 Clinton ordered the bombing of the Iraqi intelligence service headquarters. The Federal Bureau of Investigation (FBI) had uncovered an Iraqi plot to assassinate former president George Bush.

Terrorism in the air also took a sad toll. In 1988 a bomb destroyed a Pan American airliner over Lockerbie, Scotland. All 259 aboard were killed, including many Americans. The bomb was traced to two Libyans, but Gadhafi refused to send them to the United States for trial. In 1996 a truck bomb in Saudi Arabia killed 19 U.S. soldiers and wounded 280 others.

Domestic terrorism proved particularly chilling. On February 26, 1993, a bomb blast rocked the World Trade Center in New York City, killing six people and injuring more than 1,000. The suspects arrested for the bombing had ties to an Egyptian fundamentalist leader who was linked to several other terrorist acts. In April 1995 a truck bomb destroyed a federal building in Oklahoma City, killing 168 people. Two American men with ties to antigovernment militia groups were convicted of the crime. A year later, the FBI arrested the so-called Unabomber, a loner with a grievance against modern technology, who had carried out a series of mail-bombings. Then, during the 1996 Summer Olympics in Atlanta, a bomb killed one person and injured more than 100 others.

✔ **READING CHECK:** How did regional conflicts and terrorism affect the world?

The Role of the United Nations

With the end of the Cold War, many foreign-policy observers hoped that the United Nations would become the international force for peace that its founders had envisioned. By 1992 there were thousands of UN forces serving on peacekeeping missions throughout the world. In places such as Cambodia and El Salvador, UN peacekeepers played a successful role.

The United Nations had mixed results, however, in its dealings with complex situations such as in Somalia. In Bosnia and Herzegovina, ethnic fighting among Croatians, Serbs, and Slovenes left some 150,000 people dead or missing by the end of 1993. The United Nations and the North Atlantic Treaty Organization (NATO) sent peacekeeping forces to the area and launched an investigation into war crimes, but the fighting continued.

As the Bosnian Serbs seized land, bombed cities, and killed or expelled Bosnian Muslims, the Clinton administration at first did little. By 1995, however, as the Bosnian Serbs continued their aggression, President Clinton took a stronger stance. The United States and NATO cooperated in bombing Bosnian Serb positions. In November 1995 the United States brought the leaders of the warring groups to Dayton, Ohio, to hammer out a peace accord. The resulting agreement provided for a multiethnic Bosnian federation. It also required war crimes trials and elections, which were held in the fall of 1996. In addition, Clinton sent some 20,000 Americans to Bosnia to help the NATO troops enforce the Dayton accords. Ethnic hatreds in Bosnia ran deep, however, and the fate of the U.S. peace initiative remained uncertain.

United Nations. British troops participating in a UN operation travel past a destroyed mosque in Bosnia. *What type of protection do you think the UN force provided for the people of Bosnia?*

✔ **READING CHECK:** How successful was the United Nations in maintaining world peace after the Cold War?

SECTION 1 REVIEW

Define and explain the significance of the following terms:
Contract with America
Operation Restore Hope

Identify and explain the significance of the following individuals:
Bill Clinton
Hillary Rodham Clinton
Ross Perot
Newt Gingrich
Nelson Mandela
Yasir Arafat
Yitzhak Rabin
Benjamin Netanyahu
Mu'ammar Gadhafi

1. **Using Graphic Organizers** Copy the graphic organizer below. Use it to describe the regional conflicts and events that shaped the world in the early 1990s.

2. **Evaluating** How was the 1992 presidential election different from other recent elections?
3. **Synthesizing** How did the Republicans gain control of the House and the Senate just two years after Democrat Bill Clinton was elected president?
4. **Identifying Cause and Effect** What factors led to an increase in regional conflicts and terrorist activity? How did these conflicts affect the United States and the world?

Critical Thinking

5. How did the role of the United Nations in major conflicts reveal the organization's limits?
Consider:
   • successes of the UN in the 1990s
   • the outcome of the UN missions in Somalia and Bosnia
   • why the UN missions had mixed results

Clinton's Second Term

OBJECTIVES

Read to understand:

1. what issues affected the 1996 presidential election
2. what domestic issues shaped President Clinton's second term
3. what led to the impeachment of President Clinton, and what the outcome was
4. why NATO launched air strikes against Yugoslavia in 1999

KEY TERMS

Reform Party
Los Angeles Riots
Initiative on Race
Kosovo crisis

KEY PEOPLE

Bob Dole
Rodney King
James Byrd Jr.
Kenneth Starr
Slobodan Milosevic
Madeleine Albright

EYEWITNESSES TO History

66 *Let me be the bridge to a time of tranquillity, faith and confidence in action. And to those who say it was never so, that America's not been better, I say you're wrong. And I know because I was there. And I have seen it. And I remember.* 99

—Bob Dole

Bob Dole campaigning in 1996

Campaigning in the months before the presidential election of 1996, Republican Bob Dole of Kansas reminisced about an earlier era of prosperity, morality, and tranquillity in America. Democratic critics viewed the senator's memories as misleading. Nonetheless, Dole attempted to present himself as a mature and dignified candidate in contrast to the emerging accounts of scandals and dishonesty in President Clinton's administration. Many Americans, however, believed that Dole was out of touch with their concerns and problems.

The Election of 1996

Despite Republicans' large gains in the 1994 congressional elections, President Clinton's popularity improved as the economy boomed. Economist David Wyss described the nation's healthy financial conditions.

66 **If you look at the economy during the Clinton administration, you have to say that it's been a success. We have low inflation, full employment, and steady growth. This is really just about the best of all [economic] worlds.** 99

President Clinton won support from organized labor in his 1996 bid for re-election.

Americans' approval of the president climbed as the Republican-led Congress failed to enact key measures in the Contract with America. They also tried to cut popular social and environmental programs. When Clinton and Congress battled over a budget bill in 1995, the federal government was briefly shut down. Voters largely blamed the Republicans. Clinton also benefited from divisions among Republicans, who split over such issues as budget cuts, government regulations, social issues, and taxes. These divisions sharpened as the 1996 presidential campaign began. From a large field of Republican candidates, Bob Dole emerged victorious from the primaries and tried to unite his party's competing groups.

The race. Dole was a senator with 34 years of experience as well as a disabled World War II veteran. Yet as a 73-year-old, he would be the oldest person ever elected president if he won. His age concerned voters. Dole also proved to be an ineffective campaigner. "He never . . . offered the sustained and layered argument that precedes the applause line," concluded political analyst Peggy Noonan. "He just declared things—And there'll be no more crime in a Dole Administration—and waited for people to clap as he cleared his throat."

Meanwhile, Clinton seized the middle ground on many issues. The president echoed the Republicans' call for economic growth, smaller government, anticrime programs, and middle-class tax relief. He urged tougher school discipline and a crackdown on "deadbeat dads" who failed to pay child support. Clinton also echoed the Republican criticism of the nation's welfare system. The president and Republican leaders cooperated to design welfare reforms that would limit benefits, introduce work requirements, and shift programs from federal to state control. Clinton signed a welfare-reform bill in August 1996 that resulted in the most extensive overhaul of the welfare system since the New Deal.

On issues such as environmental protection and gun control, however, Clinton emphasized the differences between himself and his Republican opponent. Another issue dividing the two candidates was tobacco. Clinton called for stricter measures to discourage smoking, particularly among young Americans.

President Clinton celebrates his 1996 re-election.

The result. Clinton's strategy proved successful. He became the first Democrat since Franklin D. Roosevelt to win a second term. He won 50 percent of the popular vote and 379 electoral votes. Dole won 41 percent of the popular vote and 159 electoral votes. Ross Perot won 8.4 percent of the vote as a candidate of the **Reform Party**. The Reform Party promised to change politics in the nation's capital.

Although several members of the Republican "Freshman Class of 1994" failed to win re-election, the party maintained its majorities in Congress. President Clinton's victory marked the first time that a Democrat had been elected president while the Republicans won both the House and the Senate. This event seemed to reveal voters' support for cooperation between the two political parties. As he approached his second term, President Clinton insisted that "the vital American center is alive and well." He pledged to provide health insurance for children and people with disabilities, revise parts of the welfare bill, and connect classrooms to the Internet. Many observers described Clinton's proposals as "small steps" intended to avoid the problems that had doomed some of his first-term goals.

✔ **READING CHECK:** What issues affected the 1996 presidential election?

Domestic Prosperity and Concerns

The continued booming economy helped President Clinton achieve some of his second-term goals. The first step was to maintain the nation's economic health.

The economy. During the 1990s Americans experienced the longest and largest economic boom in U.S. history. While almost everyone benefited from the prosperity, the number of people who were very wealthy grew at an amazing rate. Between 1995 and 1998 some 1 million Americans became new millionaires, raising the total number of American millionaires to approximately 4 million. Between 1998 and 1999 the number of American billionaires grew from 190 to about 250.

Prosperity. The May 1999 issue of *Money* magazine discussed the booming stock market and rising personal wealth in the United States. *How does this magazine cover try to attract readers?*

Selected Technology Stock Prices, June 1, 1998, to June 1, 1999

Stock	Lowest price per share	Highest price per share
Amazon.com	$13.75	$221.25
Dell	$19.93	$55.00
IBM	$53.00	$123.00
Microsoft	$41.81	$95.62
Yahoo	$25.12	$244.00

Source: New York Stock Exchange

Learning from Charts The boom in computer technology in the 1990s led to enormous investment in technology stocks.

? **Building Chart Skills** Which stock experienced the greatest increase in price between June 1, 1998, and June 1, 1999?

Much of this new wealth was the result of a booming stock market, which rose higher than ever before. The value of technology stocks in particular soared. Some companies that did not even make a profit in the 1990s still saw the value of their stock rise enormously. Investors looking to the technological future drove up the prices of these stocks. Many people saw the key to financial success as the ability to pick stocks that would quickly rise in value. "It's the first time in the postwar era that so many people seem to be getting so rich with so little relative effort on their part," said economist Robert B. Reich.

The economic boom translated into the lowest unemployment rates in years. Low unemployment usually leads to inflation, which the Federal Reserve then tries to halt by raising interest rates. During the 1990s, however, unemployment, the rate of inflation, and interest rates remained low. This reversal of the stagflation that had crippled the U.S. economy in the 1970s amazed many economists.

Race relations. While trying to support the economic boom, President Clinton also looked for a larger cause to define his second term. He soon focused on race relations in the United States. During the 1990s racial conflicts continued to plague the country. In April 1992 the South Central section of Los Angeles exploded in violence. Four white police officers had been acquitted of beating African American motorist Rodney King. The verdict and the **Los Angeles Riots** disheartened many people who had worked to improve race relations in the city. Even Rodney King appeared on television during the violence, urging people to "try to work it out" peacefully. He asked, "Can we all get along?"

In the summer of 1997 Clinton announced the formation of a seven-member advisory committee to help him plan strategies for improving race relations. The president also launched his **Initiative on Race** to encourage people to discuss racial issues and concerns. Critics argued that the program produced little meaningful action.

Meanwhile, racial violence continued. The nation was horrified in June 1998 when white racists in Jasper, Texas, killed James Byrd Jr., an African American. The killers had tied Byrd to a pickup truck and dragged him to death. Some people reacted to this modern-day lynching by calling for tougher federal laws against hate crimes.

✔ **READING CHECK:** What domestic issues shaped President Clinton's second term?

The family of James Byrd Jr. holds a press conference.

AMERICAN Letters

Reflecting America in Literature

The national dialogue on race highlighted the growing racial and ethnic diversity of the U.S. population. Many popular writers in the 1990s reflected this diversity in their works. Jimmy Santiago Baca's poem tells the story of a boy growing up in a modern Mexican American community. Gish Jen's novel centers around a Chinese American couple who see the path to success in becoming as "Americanized" as possible.

from "Martín IV"
by *Jimmy Santiago Baca*

On visiting days with aunts
    and uncles,
I was shuttled back and
    forth—
between Chavez bourgeois
    in the city
and rural Lucero sheepherders,
new cars and gleaming furniture
and leather saddles and burlap
    sacks,
noon football games and six packs of cokes
and hoes, welfare cards and bottles of goat milk.

I was caught in the middle—
between white skinned, English speaking altar boy
at the communion railing,
and brown skinned, Spanish speaking plains nomadic child
with buffalo heart groaning underworld earth powers. . . .

Caught between Indio-Mejicano rural uncles
who stacked hundred pound sacks of pinto beans
on boxcars all day, . . . and Chavez uncles and aunts
who vacationed and followed the Hollywood model
of My Three Sons* for their own families.

Jimmy Santiago Baca

from *Typical American*
by *Gish Jen*

Ralph advocated buying a car.
    *"Seems like someone's becoming one-hundred-percent Americanized,"** Theresa kidded.

Gish Jen's novel

    "What's so American? We had a car, growing up. Don't you remember?" Ralph argued that in fact this way they could avoid getting too Americanized. *"Everywhere we go, we can keep the children inside. Also they won't catch cold."*
    "I thought we agreed the children are going to be American," puzzled Helen.
    Ralph furrowed his brow. When Callie turned three they had decided that Mona and Callie would learn English first, and then Chinese. This was what Janis and Old Chao were planning on doing with Alexander; Janis didn't want him to have an accent.
    Now Ralph drummed his fingers. He stopped and smiled. *"And what better way to Americanize the children than to buy a car!"*

* a popular television show of the 1960s
** Italics indicate words spoken in Chinese.

UNDERSTANDING LITERATURE

1. In Baca's poem, what two different ways of life do the two sides of the speaker's family represent?
2. How do Jen's characters become "Americanized"? What aspects of Chinese culture do they retain?
3. How do you think these works reflect life in the United States in the late 1900s?

Independent Counsel Kenneth Starr conducted an investigation into Bill Clinton's alleged misconduct.

A Presidential Scandal

Although President Clinton maintained high job-approval ratings in public polls, his second term was marred by scandal. In 1994 a former Arkansas state employee had sued Clinton, claiming that he had sexually harassed her while he was governor of Arkansas. As the civil case proceeded, the woman's lawyers began to investigate other alleged misconduct by Clinton.

During this same time, Independent Counsel Kenneth Starr was investigating Bill and Hillary Clinton's past financial dealings. In January 1998 Starr received permission from a panel of three federal judges to expand his investigation. He included the possibility that Clinton was trying to tamper with witnesses in the civil lawsuit. Although a federal judge later dismissed the civil lawsuit, Clinton's videotaped testimony in the case almost brought down his presidency.

Starr began to investigate whether Clinton had conducted an improper relationship with a young White House intern and lied about it during the civil trial. After the president repeated his testimony to a grand jury, the House Judiciary Committee launched its own investigation. Although Clinton finally acknowledged the affair with the intern and apologized, he insisted he had not committed perjury. The Republican-led Judiciary Committee disagreed and recommended impeachment. On December 20, 1998, the House of Representatives voted to impeach the president.

For just the second time in the nation's history, a U.S. president underwent a trial by the Senate. Some Republicans called for conviction. Most Democrats took the position that Clinton's behavior, while offensive, did not meet the constitutional test of "high crimes and misdemeanors." In public opinion polls, most Americans agreed. In February 1999 the Senate acquitted Clinton of the charges against him.

Although the president and his supporters cheered the victory, the scandal left lingering effects. Many Americans said that they distrusted the president personally. Others worried that the scandal had weakened the office of the president. Critics of Starr's investigation of the Clintons noted that it had cost more than $40 million but had yielded few convictions. A few months after the impeachment trial, Congress let the law providing for independent counsels expire.

✔ **READING CHECK:** What led to the impeachment of President Clinton, and what was the outcome of the trial?

War in Kosovo

As the impeachment trial ended, U.S. officials became concerned about events overseas. The mainly Serbian nation of Yugoslavia, led by President Slobodan Milosevic (sloh-buh-DAHN mi-LOH-suh-vitch), had begun a crackdown on the province of Kosovo. Until 1989, Kosovo, which was home mostly to ethnic Albanians, had been allowed to govern itself. After Milosevic came to power, he ended this self-rule and began moving Serbian settlers into Kosovo. Western nations initially paid little attention to the developing **Kosovo crisis**.

Early in 1999 new reports emerged that the Serbians were carrying out mass murders and other atrocities against ethnic Albanians in Kosovo. In an effort to stop the violence, President Clinton backed a plan for NATO to begin air strikes against Yugoslavia.

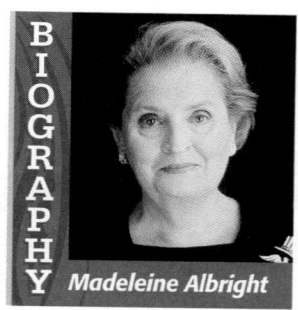

BIOGRAPHY

Madeleine Albright

U.S. Secretary of State Madeleine Albright played a central role in the Kosovo crisis. Albright was born Madeleine Korbel in Prague, Czechoslovakia, in 1937. The daughter of a Czech diplomat, she had an interest in foreign affairs from a young age. She lived in several countries before her family moved to Colorado. She studied political science at Wellesley College, graduating in 1959, and later received a Ph.D. from Columbia University.

Albright worked for the National Security Council, the White House, the Center for National Policy, and numerous schools and institutes for foreign affairs. In 1993 Clinton appointed her U.S. representative to the United Nations. Four years later, she was sworn in as the first female secretary of state.

Albright took a strong interest in the Kosovo conflict. As a child, her family had fled religious and ethnic oppression from Adolf Hitler's Nazi regime and then from communist forces in Eastern Europe. As secretary of state, she was highly critical of governments that mistreated people because of their religious or ethnic backgrounds. She warned that if NATO delayed in taking action the crisis could get worse, as it had in Bosnia.

After nearly three months, the air strikes paid off. Milosevic agreed to withdraw his troops from Kosovo and to allow NATO forces into the area to enforce a peace agreement. As NATO troops moved in, evidence began to emerge of massive Serbian atrocities against civilians. Some critics were upset that Milosevic, who had been charged with war crimes by an international court, was allowed to stay in power. Secretary Albright noted the lessons of Kosovo.

 **Read More About It**

Free Find:
Madeleine Albright
After reading about Madeleine Albright on the **Holt Researcher** CD–ROM, create a script for a television news show that focuses on Albright's life and work.

66 The crisis in Kosovo should cause a re-examination of . . . the past. As the world has changed, so have the roles of key institutions such as . . . NATO and the United Nations. And so have American interests. In today's world of deadly and mobile dangers, gross violations of human rights are everyone's business. 99

✔ **READING CHECK:** Why did NATO launch air strikes against Yugoslavia in 1999?

SECTION 2 REVIEW

Define and explain the significance of the following terms:
Reform Party
Los Angeles Riots
Initiative on Race
Kosovo crisis

Identify and explain the significance of the following individuals:
Bob Dole
Rodney King
James Byrd Jr.
Kenneth Starr
Slobodan Milosevic
Madeleine Albright

1. **Using Graphic Organizers** Copy the graphic organizer below. Use it to outline how the candidates in the 1996 presidential election differed on the issues.

Bill Clinton	Bob Dole

2. **Analyzing** What factors caused the economic growth of the 1990s?
3. **Assessing Consequences** What were the major causes of President Clinton's impeachment trial?
4. **Identifying Values** How did the issue of human rights influence NATO's decision to launch air strikes against Yugoslavia?

Critical Thinking

5. Was the Initiative on Race a good solution to the problem of strained race relations?
   Consider:
   • what events revealed strained race relations
   • how talking about the issue might help
   • what other approaches might have worked

Society in the 1990s

OBJECTIVES

Read to understand:
1. what events shaped the space program in the 1990s
2. what issues arose surrounding technology in the 1990s
3. how U.S. popular culture affected the rest of the world
4. how immigration changed in the 1990s
5. what issues affected family life in the 1990s

KEY TERMS

Mir
Internet
World Wide Web
Telecommunications Act
Y2K bug
Immigration Act of 1990
Family and Medical Leave Act

KEY PEOPLE

Shannon Lucid
John Glenn
Bill Gates

EYEWITNESSES TO History

 *Multiple networks . . . will carry a broad range of services and information technology applications into homes, businesses, schools and hospitals. These networks will form the basis of evolving national and global information infrastructures, in turn creating a seamless web uniting the world in the emergent Information Age. The result will be a new information marketplace, providing opportunities and challenges for individuals, industry and governments.* "

—Al Gore

A teenager uses the Internet.

In 1994 Vice President Al Gore described the future of information technology and its coming effects on American life. New technologies such as computers, the Internet, and the World Wide Web changed the way Americans communicated, conducted business, and related to the rest of the world.

Technology and Society

Many incredible achievements in science and technology were made during the 1990s. Public fascination with technology encouraged innovation.

Space. After suffering a terrible setback with the space shuttle *Challenger* explosion in 1986, the U.S. space program found renewed energy. With the Cold War over, the National Aeronautics and Space Administration (NASA) focused on commercial and scientific projects more than military efforts. The Hubble space telescope, launched in 1990 and repaired in 1993, transmitted vital information and breathtaking photos from deep space. In 1995 the United States joined with Russia for a project aboard the space station *Mir*. Astronaut Shannon Lucid broke the U.S. record for the most consecutive days in space. She spent 188 days aboard the *Mir*.

BIOGRAPHY

John Glenn

One U.S. astronaut came out of retirement to break space records during the 1990s. John Glenn had been the first American to orbit Earth. He also became the oldest American to fly in space. Born on July 18, 1921, in Cambridge, Ohio, Glenn enrolled in Muskingum College in 1939 in New Concord, Ohio, his hometown. He studied engineering and began flying at the nearby New Philadelphia airfield. In 1942 he enrolled in the Naval Aviation Cadet Program.

Glenn joined the U.S. Marine Corps in 1943 and flew 59 missions during World War II. During the Korean War he flew 90 more. In 1954 Glenn attended Test Pilot School at the Naval Air Test Center. In 1957, as an

The Sojourner rover explored the surface of Mars.

officer on the project F8U-1 Crusader, Glenn set the transcontinental speed record. He flew from Los Angeles to New York in three hours and 23 minutes. In 1959 he was selected as one of seven astronauts for the Project Mercury space-flight training program. In 1962 Glenn orbited Earth in the space capsule *Friendship 7*.

Glenn retired from the space program in 1964. In 1970 he narrowly lost the Ohio Democratic primary for a U.S. Senate seat. He successfully ran for the U.S. Senate in 1974 and served until 1992. In 1998 Glenn returned to the space program. At age 77 he served as a payload specialist on the space shuttle mission STS-95. NASA scientists studied Glenn's reaction to space travel to learn more about the relationship between the process of aging and the body's ability to adapt to weightlessness.

✔ **READING CHECK:** What events shaped the space program in the 1990s?

The computer age. During the 1990s personal computer (PC) technology evolved rapidly. A leader in the computer revolution was Bill Gates, head of Microsoft Corporation. By the mid-1990s most business offices and public institutions were computerized, and nearly 40 percent of American homes had PCs. Students from grade school to college used computers for many purposes. Computers also proved to be useful to disabled Americans by enhancing communication in a number of ways.

The **Internet**, an enormous computer-based communications and information system, enabled users to communicate worldwide, join discussion groups, and gather information from countless databases. Developed by Swiss scientists in the early 1990s, the **World Wide Web** linked Internet sites offering text, animation, and graphics covering a seemingly endless range of topics. Some observers hoped that this so-called information highway would bring together people from different social classes, cultures, and countries. In this excerpt from his book, *The Road Ahead*, Bill Gates described the potential social impact of the World Wide Web.

66 The information highway is going to break down boundaries and may promote a world culture, or at least a sharing of cultural activities and values. The highway will also make it easy for patriots, even expatriates, deeply involved in their own ethnic communities to reach out to others with similar interests no matter where they may be located. 99

Concerns about technology. Computers did not create utopia, however. The social problems plaguing American society soon appeared in cyberspace as well. In the **Telecommunications Act** of 1996, Congress attempted to regulate indecency on the Internet. A federal court quickly struck down key parts of this law, however, as a violation of the First Amendment right to free speech.

HISTORY IN THE MAKING

DNA Testing
BY MARY CARROLL JOHANSEN

Modern scientific techniques like DNA testing are enabling scientists and historians to resolve controversial questions that have puzzled people for centuries. For example, in 1802 a journalist published rumors that President Thomas Jefferson had fathered children by his slave Sally Hemings. For years Jefferson's supporters strongly denied it. Recently, scholars such as Joseph Ellis and Annette Gordon-Reed have debated the historical evidence of the Jefferson-Hemings affair without reaching a definitive conclusion. In 1998 the use of DNA analysis brought historians and scientists closer to an answer.

Scientists have found that most of the Y chromosomes in DNA pass intact from father to son, allowing them to trace paternal lineage. Since Jefferson had no sons, scientists compared DNA from male-line descendants of Jefferson's paternal grandfather with DNA from descendants of Eston Hemings, Sally Hemings's youngest son. They found a match. Since the chances of a match were less than one percent, Jefferson very likely was Eston Hemings's father.

DNA has helped settle other historical mysteries. In 1995, scientists announced that Anna Anderson had not been Anastasia, the daughter of murdered czar Nicholas II of Russia, as she had claimed. Pathologists have also used DNA to determine that President Zachary Taylor died of natural causes, not arsenic poisoning as some suspected.

Worried about computer systems failures, some Americans began to store food and other necessities as the year 2000 approached.

Along with concerns about the kinds of material in cyberspace, some observers worried that a fully computerized society would not need human workers. Such fears were probably exaggerated, though, because new technologies often create new jobs. Just as some people were overcoming their fear that computers would make people obsolete, scientists announced the first successful cloning of a mammal, Dolly the sheep. People debated the widsom of using this technology to eventually clone humans. Other people worried that scientific advances would deepen social divisions as wealthy, well-educated Americans mastered the new technologies, while poorer citizens lagged behind.

As the year 2000 approached, computer programmers revealed another troubling aspect of society's dependence on technology. In order to save space when developing computer programs, some programmers had abbreviated references to years, leaving out the digits 1 and 9. This meant that the computer read the year '90 as 1990. These programs were never updated to recognize the new century. Thus, as the year 2000 approached, programmers warned that many computers would read the year 2000, or '00, as 1900. This error would cause many computer systems to fail. The problem came to be known as the **Y2K bug**. As a result of the Y2K bug, businesses and government agencies spent millions of dollars hiring experts to reprogram their computers before the end of 1999.

✔ **READING CHECK:** What issues arose surrounding technology in the 1990s?

Exporting mass culture.
Many American businesses have spread overseas. *How do these employees of an American-style fast-food restaurant in Jakarta, Indonesia, maintain their Islamic culture?*

Exporting Mass Culture

The Internet aided in the exportation of American popular culture. By 1990 popular culture had become one of the most profitable U.S. exports, with annual revenues topping $5 billion. The sales of American TV shows in Europe alone totaled some $600 million a year. Similarly, the music industry earned about 70 percent of its revenues from overseas sales. Reported a British economics journal: "America is to entertainment what . . . Saudi Arabia is to oil."

American consumer products, from hamburgers and soda to blue jeans, were also snapped up by people the world over. The overseas division of the McDonald's Corporation, for instance, grew enormously during the 1990s. In 1992 McDonald's opened more restaurants overseas—including one in Beijing, China—than it did in the United States. Of McDonald's $12.4 billion sales in 1995, approximately 60 percent was generated by its some 12,500 restaurants in foreign nations.

Some critics expressed concern that this American popular culture would suffocate other cultures. They also worried that Hollywood movies and television shows gave the world a distorted impression of life in the United States. A Jamaican journalist wrote about the effects of American television on his fellow citizens:

> 66 Because of what they see on television, everyone in Jamaica thinks . . . that everything in America is wonderful. . . . It makes people think that money and material wealth are the only ways to be rich in this world. 99

The shared global culture also had advantages, however. Through orbiting communications satellites, television linked the entire world. Events in one nation were instantly transmitted around the globe. Thus, events like natural disasters often quickly produced a global outpouring of sympathy and help.

✔ **READING CHECK:** How did the popular culture of the United States affect the rest of the world?

A New Wave of Immigration

Many people in other countries continued to see the United States as a land of opportunity. The 1990 census revealed that more immigrants had come to the United States in the 1980s than in any decade since 1910. More than 80 percent of these immigrants came from Asia, the Caribbean, and Latin America. By the 1990s many native-born Americans had grown alarmed by the wave of immigrants. Many blamed immigrants for taking jobs from native-born residents.

Supporters of immigration felt differently. They argued that immigrants created new businesses that revitalized urban areas and helped the economy. In addition, supporters of immigration noted that many recent immigrants, most notably those from China, India, Korea, and the Philippines, on average had more schooling than either native-born Americans or European immigrants. Asian immigrants, they pointed out, made up about one third of the engineers in Silicon Valley, California's center of computer technology, located near San Jose.

President George Bush had recognized these benefits when he signed the **Immigration Act of 1990.** The new law changed U.S. immigration policy by increasing the number of immigrants and doubling the number of skilled workers allowed into the United States each year. The act also authorized special visas for overseas investors interested in establishing businesses in economically depressed areas of the country.

Concerned by the growing number of immigrants, in the mid-1990s Congress acted to curb new immigration. In 1996 Congress passed an immigration law that strengthened control of U.S. borders in an effort to halt illegal immigration. The law attempted to keep new immigrants off welfare. For example, sponsors of immigrants were required to have incomes at least 125 percent above the poverty level. It also prevented legal immigrants who were not U.S. citizens from receiving most forms of welfare benefits.

✔ **READING CHECK:** How did immigration change in the 1990s?

The Religious Spirit

GROWING RELIGIOUS DIVERSITY

The Masjid Omar Al-Khattab mosque in Los Angeles

The increase in the number of Asian immigrants led to a growing religious diversity in the United States. By the end of the 1990s Christianity was still by far the most common religion, representing about 84 percent of the U.S. population. However, membership in traditionally Eastern religions such as Buddhism, Hinduism, and Islam was growing. By 1998 Islam, with some 5 to 6 million followers in the United States, was close to overtaking Judaism as the nation's second-most-practiced religion.

As these religions grew in prominence, so did the number of non-Asian converts. By 1998 more than 80,000 American Muslims were of Western European descent. Buddhism also attracted many non-Asian converts. In many places, American Buddhism evolved into a distinct faith. It moved away from Asian Buddhism's traditional focus on the intense spiritual training of monks and nuns. American Buddhism tends to emphasize the personal spiritual growth of lay members. Some followers argue that such an approach is in keeping with the American democratic traditions. "What [American Buddhists] are doing," noted one observer in 1997, "is taking a path of enlightenment in a lay culture without priests and temples and structures, and moving it right into daily practice in everyday life." ■

Children. The number of single-parent households and households with both parents working outside the home is rising. *What clues in this photograph might lead you to assume that this woman is a working mother?*

Work and Family

Some observers expressed concern about the state of the American family in the 1990s. By 1998 only 26 percent of American households were made up of married couples with children. Most single parents had a difficult time financially. Patricia Mull, a Los Angeles seamstress who stretched her income to send her daughter to private school, described the stress she faced. "I worry about the rent. I worry if I can make the payment in time. I worry if I have enough money left for other things. I worry about money every day, every night."

Many two-parent families shared Mull's concerns as they struggled to balance job and family responsibilities. Nearly 60 percent of married women worked outside the home in 1995, up from about 30 percent in 1960. The increase of single-parent families and families with both parents in the workforce created the need for affordable day care. Employers increasingly realized that family concerns affected their employees' jobs. To help employees balance work and family, a group of businesses in 1992 announced a program to build more day-care and elder-care centers across the country.

The U.S. government also recognized the need to help working families. In February 1993, just two weeks after his inauguration, President Clinton signed into law the **Family and Medical Leave Act**. The legislation requires large companies to provide workers up to 12 weeks of unpaid leave. Workers can use this time for family and medical emergencies without losing their medical insurance or their jobs.

This legislation reflected the significant changes in attitudes toward work and family that have occurred in the United States in the 1990s. As businessperson Florence Skelly noted in 1993, "Rather than trying to climb the economic ladder, people are becoming more concerned with relationships and family and community involvement."

✔ **READING CHECK:** What issues affected family life in the 1990s?

SECTION 3 REVIEW

Define and explain the significance of the following terms:
Mir
Internet
World Wide Web
Telecommunications Act
Y2K bug
Immigration Act of 1990
Family and Medical Leave Act

Identify and explain the significance of the following individuals:
Shannon Lucid
John Glenn
Bill Gates

1. **Using Graphic Organizers** Copy the graphic organizer below. Use it to describe the pros and cons of increasing dependence on technology in the 1990s.

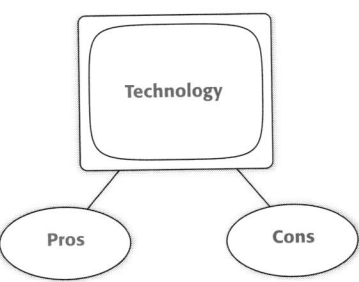

2. **Analyzing** How did the U.S. space program rebound from its setbacks of the 1980s?
3. **Recognizing Point of View** Why might people in other countries oppose the spread of American popular culture?
4. **Comparing and Contrasting** How had immigration changed by the 1990s? How did this affect the 1990 and 1996 immigration bills?

Critical Thinking

5. Why did family issues become a political concern in the 1990s?
   Consider:
   • the increase in single-parent households
   • concerns over child care
   • what influenced the passage of the Family and Medical Leave Act

SECTION 4

Looking to the Future

OBJECTIVES

Read to understand:

1. what factors shaped the development of the global economy
2. what environmental issues concerned people in the 1990s
3. why population growth in urban areas and throughout the world caused concern
4. what the role of the United States in spreading democracy throughout the world is

KEY TERMS

European Union
North American Free Trade Agreement
multinational corporations
Chernobyl disaster
recycling

KEY PEOPLE

Indira Gandhi

EYEWITNESSES TO History

❝ How, then, shall we live? How must we live to preserve free societies and to be worthy of the blood and pain? This is the unfinished business of our century. ❞
—Michael Novak

Young Americans perform community service.

In an editorial for the *New York Times,* social critic Michael Novak reflected on the future. At the start of a new millennium, his questions represent a growing reassessment of America's future. What role will Americans play in determining the fate of the world and its inhabitants? What historic trends can we foresee in the future? What challenges do we face in the coming years? While these questions cannot be answered with certainty, we can consider the recent past and offer valuable speculations about the possible future of our country.

A Global Economy

Billions of dollars' worth of trade links the world's major industrial nations. In the fall of 1992 journalist Bruce W. Nelan predicted the growing importance of global economics.

❝ Just as wars—two World Wars and, equally important, the Cold War—dominated the geopolitical map of the 20th century, economics will rule over the 21st. All the big questions confronting the world in the century ahead are basically economic. ❞

International trade. International trading blocs may provide stiff economic competition for the United States in coming years. The **European Union** (EU), a Western European trading bloc, was formed in 1993. The EU is designed to allow capital, goods, and labor to move freely among member nations. The EU also encourages greater cooperation on such matters as crime, culture, education, foreign policy, and health. Some predict that a full political union—the "United States of Europe," which could include as many as 20 member states—will eventually form. If this were to happen, the European Union would be the world's largest trading bloc.

By 1993 concern over such economic competition led to growing support for U.S. ratification of the **North American Free Trade Agreement** (NAFTA). The agreement provides for a lowering of trade barriers among Canada, Mexico, and the United States. Supporters hoped that NAFTA would help the United States compete more effectively in the global economy in the coming years.

The European Union has issued its own currency to aid free trade among European countries.

Global business. Workers assemble Toyota cars in a Kentucky factory. *What do you think the workers shown are doing?*

Multinational corporations. The global economy is increasingly dominated by **multinational corporations**. These are companies that invest money in a variety of business ventures around the world. Multinational corporations sometimes benefit the United States economically. Leading Japanese corporations, for example, have opened factories in the United States. Such plants boost the U.S. economy, although most of the profits go to the parent corporations in Japan.

Just as foreign companies invest in the United States, many American businesses are expanding their investments in other countries. The New York–based ITT Corporation is one example. ITT began as a communications company known as International Telephone and Telegraph. By the 1990s, however, ITT held major interests worldwide in such diverse businesses as finance, food processing, hotels, insurance, and real estate. Other corporations such as General Motors, IBM, and Texaco, also operate worldwide.

✔ **READING CHECK:** What factors have shaped the development of the global economy?

Energy and the Environment

The future of energy resources and the environment continues to concern many experts. In 1996 the world consumed an amount of energy equivalent to that of about 65 billion barrels of oil. The United States is home to less than 5 percent of the world's population yet accounted for nearly 25 percent of the world's energy consumption that year. Some 38 percent of U.S. energy came from oil, 24 percent from natural gas, and 22 percent from coal. Just 8 percent came from alternative sources such as solar or hydroelectric power and 8 percent from nuclear power.

A 1986 accident at the Chernobyl nuclear power plant in the Soviet Union near Kiev, Ukraine, sent a dangerous radioactive cloud drifting across Europe. The **Chernobyl disaster** released 50 times more radioactive material into the environment than the two atomic bombs dropped on Japan in 1945 combined.

Coming just seven years after the Three Mile Island accident in Pennsylvania, the Chernobyl disaster heightened anxiety over nuclear power. People began calling for increased research on other energy sources. These include solar power, geothermal power (geysers and hot springs), and wind power. They also include biomass (materials such as wood or waste products that can be burned or used to make fuel) and hydrogen. In addition, many utility companies have launched successful energy conservation programs designed to reduce consumer demand and increase the efficiency of energy production.

This car uses fuel-cell technology and produces no harmful emissions.

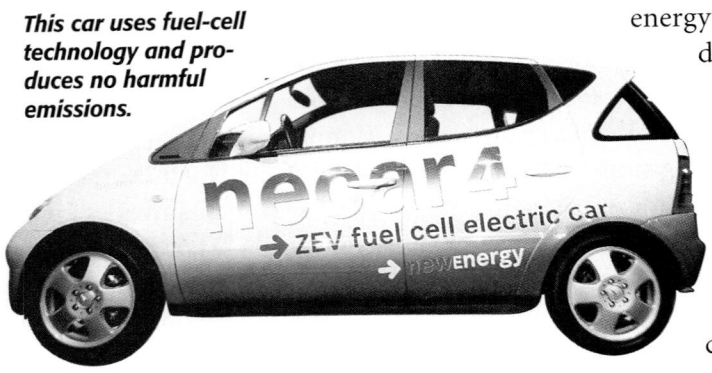

As scientists search for new ways to meet energy demands many environmentalists focus on protecting the world's remaining forests and wildlife. Population growth, industrialization, and the expansion of commercial agriculture and livestock operations cause forests to disappear at an alarming rate. According to the UN, almost 34 million acres of forests in developing countries were lost each year between 1990 and 1995.

Plant and animal species around the world are in grave danger of extinction because of the pressure generated by the growing population of humans and because of industrialization. Individuals and groups have worked to slow this process and to save endangered species and unique scenic areas. For example, Greenpeace, an international environmental organization, campaigns against whaling, and the U.S. government has acted to protect sensitive natural areas.

The 1994 California Desert Protection Act enlarged the Joshua Tree and Death Valley National Monuments and converted them to national parks. Then, in 1996 President Clinton took steps to protect 1.7 million acres of Utah canyon lands where a Dutch mining company held valuable coal leases. Clinton based his moves on the Antiquities Act—a law President Theodore Roosevelt had used to protect the Grand Canyon from development. The law allowed Clinton to create the Canyons of the Escalante National Monument without congressional approval.

✔ **READING CHECK:** What environmental issues concerned people in the 1990s?

Read More About It

Free Find:

Hunger in Africa

After studying the digital map on hunger in Africa on the **Holt Researcher** CD–ROM, write a short essay explaining how future environmental problems might worsen conditions in Africa.

Population Growth

As environmental awareness has increased, **recycling**—the collection and processing of waste items for reuse—has gained support. Recycling serves two important purposes. It reuses scarce natural resources. It also reduces the amount of solid waste that must be buried, burned, dumped, or shipped elsewhere. By 1991 some 4,000 curbside recycling programs were under way in the United States, a 250 percent increase from 1989. The United States lags behind other industrialized nations in recycling, however. Japan, for example, recycles 50 percent of its paper and 54 percent of its glass.

Urban areas. The concern over the environment is related to urban growth. One expert estimates that an excess of garbage is risking the health of 40 percent of the urban population in the developing world.

Many cities are instituting innovative waste-management systems. In Cairo, Egypt, several thousand Zabaleens—Christians from southern Egypt—use donkey-drawn carts to collect garbage from the city. They then sort through the garbage and sell the reusable material. Thrown-away food goes to feed pigs. Waste products are used to fertilize crops. Scrap metal, glass, paper, and plastic are recycled. Other cities, such as Ciudad Juárez, Mexico, have developed similar systems. As a result, many urban planners, such as Donella Meadows, are cautiously optimistic about the future. "If humans manage brilliantly starting very soon," she advised in 1993, "it is possible the world might look better than it does now."

The global population. Many of the world's environmental and waste problems have been made worse by a massive increase in population. By 1999 the world's population stood at 6 billion, and it was growing by a rate of nearly three people per second. Population growth is most rapid in poorer countries. Experts predict that India's population will jump from 984 million in 1998 to 1.4 billion by

INTERPRETING THE VISUAL RECORD

Population growth. The continued growth of urban populations has contributed to environmental problems. *How does this photograph of Mexico City reflect urban environmental problems?*

2025. They also predict that Mexico's will rise from 98.6 million to 141.6 million, and Bangladesh's from 127.6 million to 180.7 million.

One key to limiting population growth in developing countries, some argue, is to raise the status of women. Former Indian prime minister Indira Gandhi wrote about this topic in the 1980s.

> 66 **Men and most women are unaware of the potential ability of women. Their lives are entrapped by pre-conceived notions and attitudes from birth onwards. . . . A lower status for women, or lesser opportunity for women, is a handicap for the growth of mankind as a whole.** 99

Gandhi believed that when women gain equal rights and opportunities they will no longer be valued primarily for their ability to produce children.

✔ **READING CHECK:** Why did population growth in urban areas and throughout the world cause concern?

Strategies for Success   Writing a Research Paper

Writing a history research paper can be both a challenging and a rewarding experience. Many of the steps that go into preparing for a paper require one to use a variety of important critical thinking skills.

How to Write a Research Paper

1. **Identify the topic, develop questions, conduct research, and evaluate your sources.** First, identify the topic that you wish to research and develop one or more questions that you hope to answer in your paper. Then conduct research at your school or local public library and evaluate the sources that you find.
2. **Formulate a hypothesis.** Analyze the information in your sources and develop a hypothesis that answers your questions about the topic. This hypothesis should serve as the focus of your paper and be presented in a thesis statement in the paper's introduction.
3. **Create an outline.** Organize the ideas and evidence that you plan to discuss in your paper into an outline. This step will make the actual process of writing much easier.
4. **Write a first draft.** Compose a first draft of your paper, using your outline as a guide. It should have an introduction with a clear thesis statement, a body of material that supports the thesis statement, and

a conclusion that provides a summary of what has been said.
5. **Review and edit the first draft.** After you have completed a draft of your paper, read it over and make corrections as needed.
6. **Write a final draft.** Once you have settled on a final version of your paper, prepare a neat, clean copy for submission to your teacher or classmates.

Applying the Strategy

Write a five-page research paper on a topic of recent historical importance. You may select your own topic or use one of the following suggestions:
1. global environmental problems during the 1990s
2. the Internet's effect on international commerce
3. relations between the United States and Russia during the late 1990s
4. the 2000 presidential election

Practicing the Strategy

Before writing your paper, answer the following questions.
1. What questions do you hope to answer in your paper?
2. What is your thesis statement?
3. What ideas and evidence will you use in the paper to support your thesis statement?

America's Role in a New Era

The end of the Cold War did not bring solutions to all of the world's problems. In many parts of the world, true democracy remains distant. Democratic nations attempt to convince the rest of the world of democracy's appeal by helping solve existing social and economic problems.

The United States is committed to playing a central role in this effort. Some of the earliest English settlers in America believed they were lighting a beacon that would show the way to a new era in human history. After the establishment of a democratic government, the idea of America as a world leader became a reality. However, the nation has not always lived up to these ideals. Many groups have been excluded from the promise of democracy. Over the years, though, the United States has tried to expand democracy, individual freedom, and the privileges and obligations of citizenship to all its citizens.

Global powers may shift, and economies may change, but the appeal of democracy will likely remain. People will continue to strive for individual freedom, self-government, and citizenship in a just nation. This is particularly true for those people living under unjust rulers or in extreme poverty. The vision of democracy and freedom can still inspire acts of great courage and heroism.

As is true in history, the future will be determined by new generations' willingness to tackle tough problems. In this book you have learned of our nation's history up to the present. The next chapters in this still-unfolding story are yours to write.

After a considerable struggle, the people of Indonesia gained the right to hold fully democratic elections in 1999.

✔ **READING CHECK:** What is the role of the United States in spreading democracy throughout the world?

SECTION 4 REVIEW

Define and explain the significance of the following terms:
European Union
North American Free Trade Agreement
multinational corporations
Chernobyl disaster
recycling

Identify and explain the significance of the following individual:
Indira Gandhi

1. **Using Graphic Organizers** Copy the graphic organizer below. Use it to describe the factors that supported the development of the global economy.

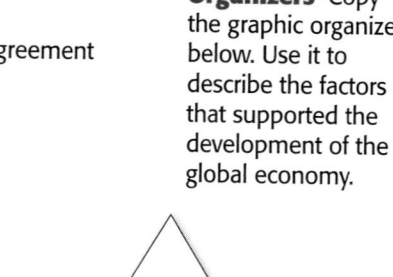

2. **Hypothesizing** Why do you think that many Americans were interested in environmental issues during the 1990s? What issues received public attention?
3. **Assessing Consequences** What are some of the possible consequences of the current trends in population growth?
4. **Evaluating** Does the United States have a responsibility to help spread democracy throughout the world? Explain your answer.

Critical Thinking

5. How might global issues create problems for Americans in the future?
   Consider:
   • the role of American businesses in the global economy
   • future environmental challenges
   • the role of the United States in the spread of democracy

Review

Creating a Time Line

Copy the time line below onto a sheet of paper. Complete the time line by filling in the events and dates from the chapter that you think were most significant. Pick three events and explain why you think they were significant.

1990   **1995**   **1999**

Writing a Summary

Using the Reading Checks as a guide, write an overview of the events in the chapter.

Identifying People and Ideas

Identify the following terms or individuals and explain their significance.

1. Bill Clinton
2. Contract with America
3. Bob Dole
4. Los Angeles Riots
5. Madeleine Albright
6. John Glenn
7. Internet
8. Y2K bug
9. Family and Medical Leave Act
10. European Union

Understanding Main Ideas

SECTION 1

1. What made the elections of 1992 unique?
2. How was the United States affected by conflicts in other countries and by terrorism in the 1990s?

SECTION 2

3. Why did NATO attack Yugoslavia in 1999?

SECTION 3

4. Why was computer technology both helpful and controversial in the 1990s?

SECTION 4

5. How did the global economy develop?
6. What were the important environmental issues of the 1990s?

Reviewing Themes

1. **Economic Development** How has a nation's economic strength become as important as its military power in foreign policy?
2. **Global Relations** How does American culture affect the rest of the world?
3. **Technology and Society** How have new technologies changed American society and the world?

Thinking Critically

1. **Identifying Values** How did the Contract with America reflect the ideals of Republican congressional candidates in 1994?
2. **Problem Solving** What responsible solutions would you suggest to deal with the issues and problems parents faced in the 1990s?
3. **Comparing and Contrasting** How did business leaders in the United States and critics abroad differ in their view of the spread of American popular culture?
4. **Identifying Cause and Effect** How does rapid urban population growth contribute to environmental problems?
5. **Hypothesizing** Describe how the United States can help make the world more democratic in the future.

Writing About History

Writing to Describe Imagine that you are a reporter covering John Glenn's 1998 space shuttle flight. Write a short description of the significance of Glenn's flight. Use this graphic to organize your thoughts.

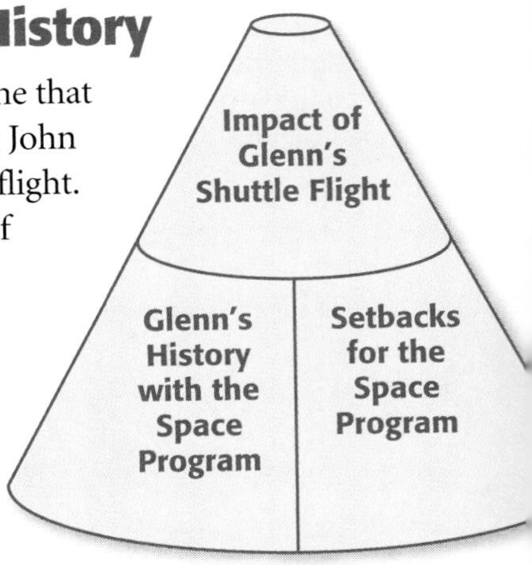

Impact of Glenn's Shuttle Flight

Glenn's History with the Space Program

Setbacks for the Space Program

Brazilian president Fernando Collor opens the UN Conference on the Environment and Development.

Strategies for Success Review the **Strategies for Success** on *Writing a Research Paper.* Then exchange a first draft of your research paper with that of a classmate and provide editorial suggestions for your classmate's final draft.

Linking History and Geography

Study the map below. What does it reveal about American society in 1990?

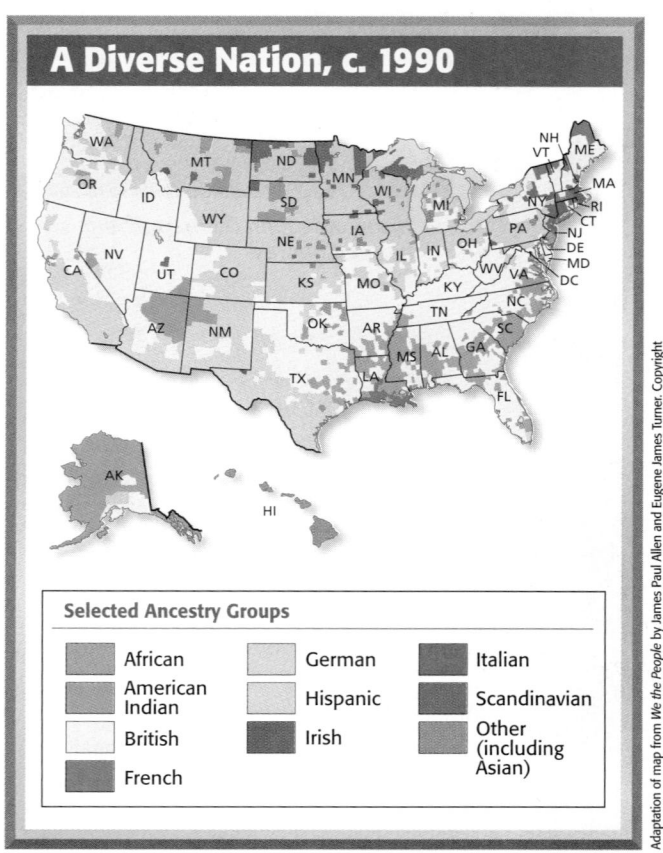

A Diverse Nation, c. 1990

Selected Ancestry Groups

- African
- American Indian
- British
- French
- German
- Hispanic
- Irish
- Italian
- Scandinavian
- Other (including Asian)

Adaptation of map from *We the People* by James Paul Allen and Eugene James Turner. Copyright © 1988 by Macmillan Publishing Company. Reprinted by permission of Macmillan Publishing Company.

internet connect

TOPIC: U.S. Space Program
GO TO: go.hrw.com
KEYWORD: SD1 Space

Accessing the Internet through the HRW Web site, research information about the contemporary space program. Then create an annotated and illustrated time line that presents the main events and achievements in space exploration since 1980.

BUILDING YOUR PORTFOLIO

Complete one or all of the following projects independently or cooperatively.

1 Global Relations
Imagine that you are an aide to Secretary of State Madeleine Albright in 1999. **Write an outline** *for a speech that describes the outcome of NATO's air strikes against Yugoslavia.*

2 Technology and Society
Imagine that you are a computer programmer in 1999. **Write a memo** *to business leaders explaining why the Y2K bug might cause problems with their computers on January 1, 2000.*

3 Economic Development
Imagine that you are the chairperson of a multinational corporation. **Prepare a business summary** *for your stockholders explaining how the development of the global economy has affected your company.*

Loading dock for U.S. imports and exports

Review

BUILDING YOUR PORTFOLIO

Outlined below are four projects. Independently or cooperatively, complete one and use the products to demonstrate your mastery of the historical concepts involved.

1 Constitutional Heritage

The Watergate scandal and the Iran-Contra affair challenged the foundation of constitutional government. ***Write an editorial*** that examines the ways in which the Watergate scandal was both similar to and different from the Iran-Contra affair. You may wish to use portfolio materials you designed in the unit chapters to help you.

Nixon aide John Dean testifying before Congress

Gas shortages during the energy crisis of 1973

Sorry LAST CAR NO GAS

2 Economic Development

Stagflation and the effects of the energy crisis are two of the economic problems Presidents Nixon, Ford, and Carter struggled with in the 1970s. In the 1980s President Reagan attempted to stimulate the economy with conservative reforms. ***Write a press release*** that describes the different ways in which the economic actions taken by these presidents affected poor Americans. Present your report to the class. You may wish to use portfolio materials you designed in the unit chapters to help you.

3 Global Relations

Destruction of the Berlin Wall

During the 1970s and 1980s the United States opened negotiations with China, improved relations with the Soviet Union, and witnessed the end of the Cold War and the breakup of the Soviet Union. Regional and local conflicts emerged, however, as newly formed nations were torn apart by ethnic and religious struggles. *Conduct a panel discussion* about the new world order that highlights the sometimes conflicting interests of the world's industrialized nations and developing nations. You may wish to use portfolio materials you designed in the unit chapters to help you.

4 Technology and Society

In the past several decades, new advances in computers have made communications and the transfer of information around the world quicker and easier. These changes have brought Americans into increasing contact with citizens worldwide and have increased the multinational nature of business. *Prepare an illustrated presentation* for a conference on the impact of technology on business and daily life in the 1990s and beyond. You may wish to use portfolio materials you designed in the unit chapters to help you.

American fast-food restaurant in Thailand

Further Reading

Edelstein, Andrew J., and Kevin McDoough. *The Seventies: From Hot Pants to Hot Tubs.* E. P. Dutton, 1990. A social history of the 1970s.

Johnson, Haynes. *Sleepwalking Through History: America in the Reagan Years.* Norton, 1991. Overview and critical analysis of the Reagan years.

Lewis, Michael M. *Liar's Poker: Rising Through the Wreckage on Wall Street.* Norton, 1989. An insider account of Wall Street and the savings and loan industry of the 1980s

Maraniss, David. *First in His Class: The Biography of Bill Clinton.* Simon & Schuster, 1996. A thorough and balanced biography of the 42nd president of the United States.

Virga, Vincent. *The Eighties: Images of America.* Edward Burlingame Books, 1992. Photographic essay on life in the United States during the 1980s.

Woodward, Bob, and Carl Bernstein. *The Final Days.* Simon & Schuster, 1976. Chronicle of the last days of Richard Nixon's presidency.

HOLT RESEARCHER — *Internet Connect and Holt Researcher* CD–ROM *Review*

In assigned groups, develop a multimedia presentation about America between 1968 and the present. Choose information from the chapter Internet Connect activities and from the **Holt Researcher** CD–ROM that best reflects the major topics of the period. Write an outline and a script for your presentation, which may be shown to the class.

Reference

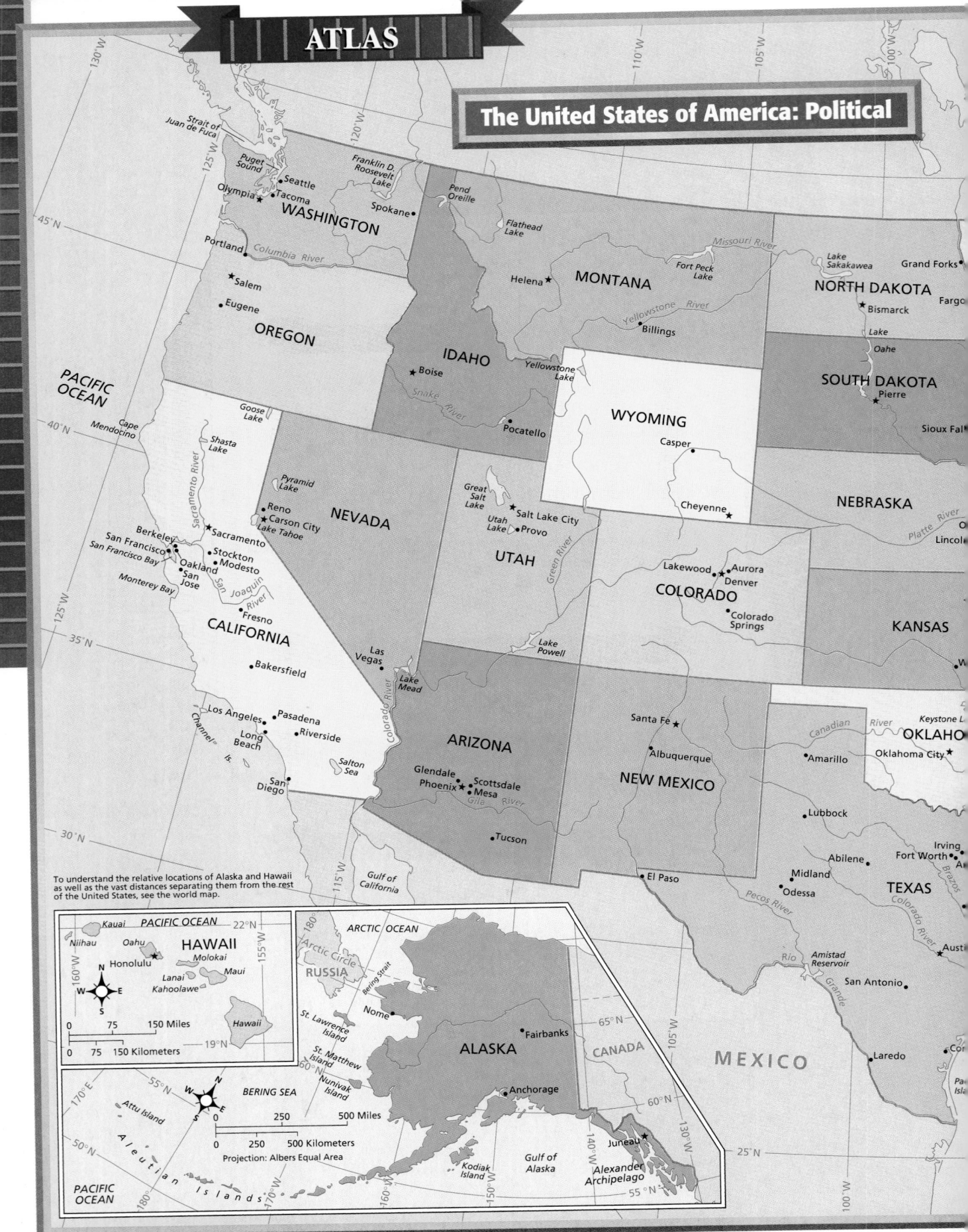

The United States of America: Political

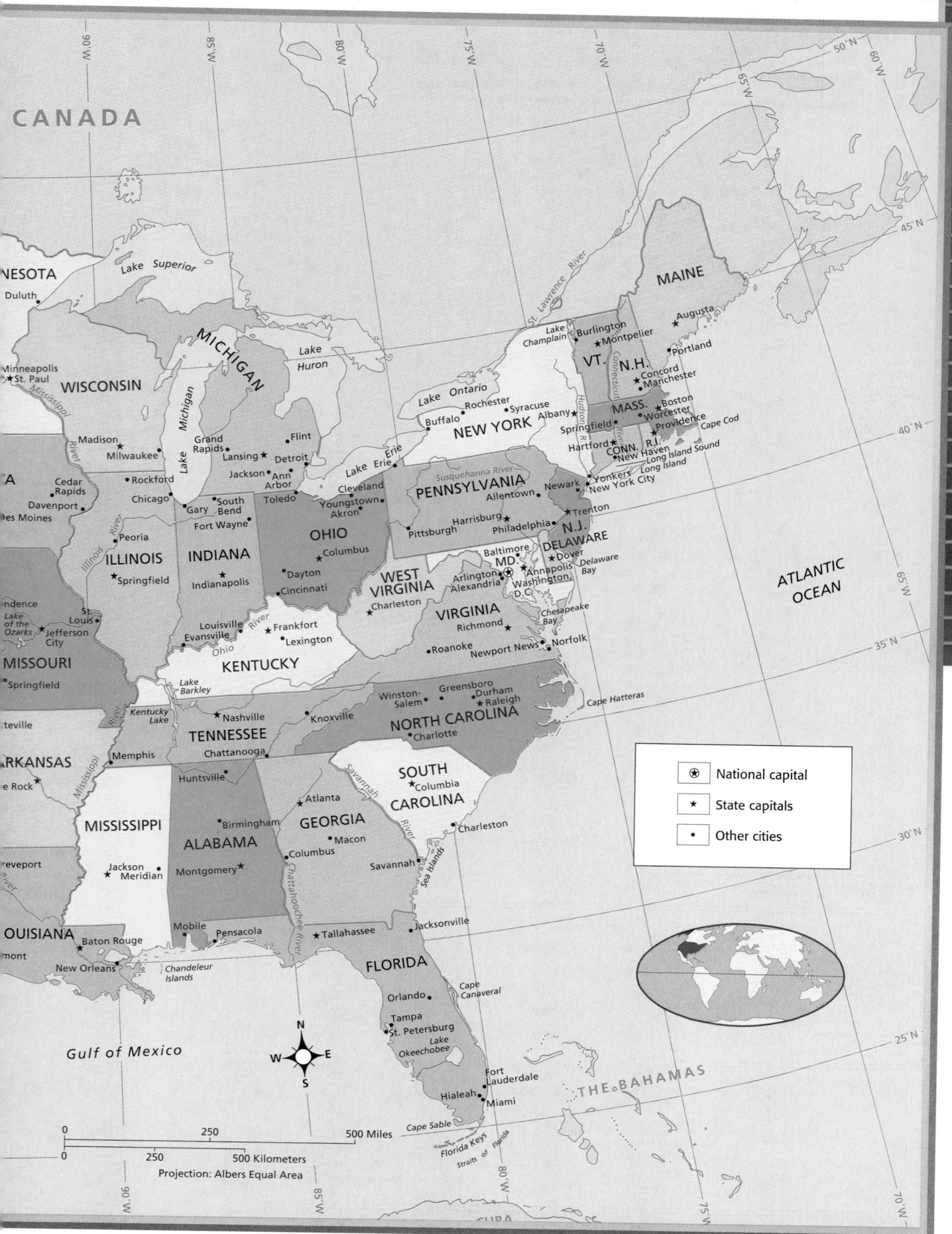

CANADA

MINESOTA
Duluth
Lake Superior

Minneapolis
★ St. Paul

WISCONSIN

MICHIGAN

Lake Huron

Madison ●
Milwaukee ●

Grand Rapids ●
Lansing ★
Jackson ●
Detroit ●
Ann Arbor ●
Flint ●

Lake Michigan

Cedar Rapids ●
Davenport ●
Des Moines

Rockford ●
Chicago ●
Gary ●
South Bend ●
Fort Wayne ●

Peoria ●

ILLINOIS

INDIANA

Springfield ★
Indianapolis ★

Toledo ●
Cleveland ●
Youngstown ●
Akron ●

OHIO

Columbus ★
Dayton ●
Cincinnati ●

Lake Ontario
Rochester ●
Buffalo ●
Syracuse ●

NEW YORK
Albany ★

Lake Erie
Lake Erie

Susquehanna River

PENNSYLVANIA

Harrisburg ★
Pittsburgh ●

Allentown ●
Newark ●

St. Lawrence River

MAINE

Augusta ★

Burlington ●
Montpelier ★
Lake Champlain

VT.
N.H.
Portland ●
Concord ★
Manchester ●

MASS.
Springfield ●
Hartford ★
CONN.
New Haven ●
R.I.
Boston ★
Worcester ●
Providence ★
Cape Cod

Long Island Sound
Long Island

Yonkers ●
New York City ●

Hudson R.

ndence
St. Louis ●
Lake of the Ozarks
Jefferson City ★

MISSOURI
Springfield ●

Louisville ●
Evansville ●

Frankfort ★
Lexington ●

Ohio River

KENTUCKY

Lake Barkley

Philadelphia ●
N.J.
Trenton ★

DELAWARE
Dover ★
Delaware Bay

Baltimore ●
MD.
Annapolis ★
Washington, D.C. ⊛
Arlington ●
Alexandria ●

WEST VIRGINIA
Charleston ★

VIRGINIA
Richmond ★
Roanoke ●
Newport News ●
Norfolk ●

Chesapeake Bay

ATLANTIC OCEAN

teville
e Rock

ARKANSAS

Kentucky Lake
Nashville ★
Memphis ●

TENNESSEE
Knoxville ●
Chattanooga ●

Winston-Salem ●
Greensboro ●
Durham ●
Raleigh ★

NORTH CAROLINA
Charlotte ●

Cape Hatteras

Huntsville ●

SOUTH CAROLINA
Columbia ★

Savannah River

Charleston ●

reveport
mont

MISSISSIPPI
Jackson ★
Meridian ●

Birmingham ●

ALABAMA
Montgomery ★

Atlanta ★
Macon ●

GEORGIA
Columbus ●

Chattahoochee River

Savannah ●

Sea Islands

National capital ⊛
State capitals ★
Other cities ●

OUISIANA
Baton Rouge ★
New Orleans ●

Mobile ●
Pensacola ●
Tallahassee ★

Jacksonville ●

Chandeleur Islands

Gulf of Mexico

FLORIDA
Orlando ●
Tampa ●
St. Petersburg ●
Lake Okeechobee

Cape Canaveral

Fort Lauderdale ●
Hialeah ●
Miami ●

Cape Sable
Florida Keys

THE BAHAMAS

Straits of Florida

N
W E
S

0   250   500 Miles
0   250   500 Kilometers
Projection: Albers Equal Area

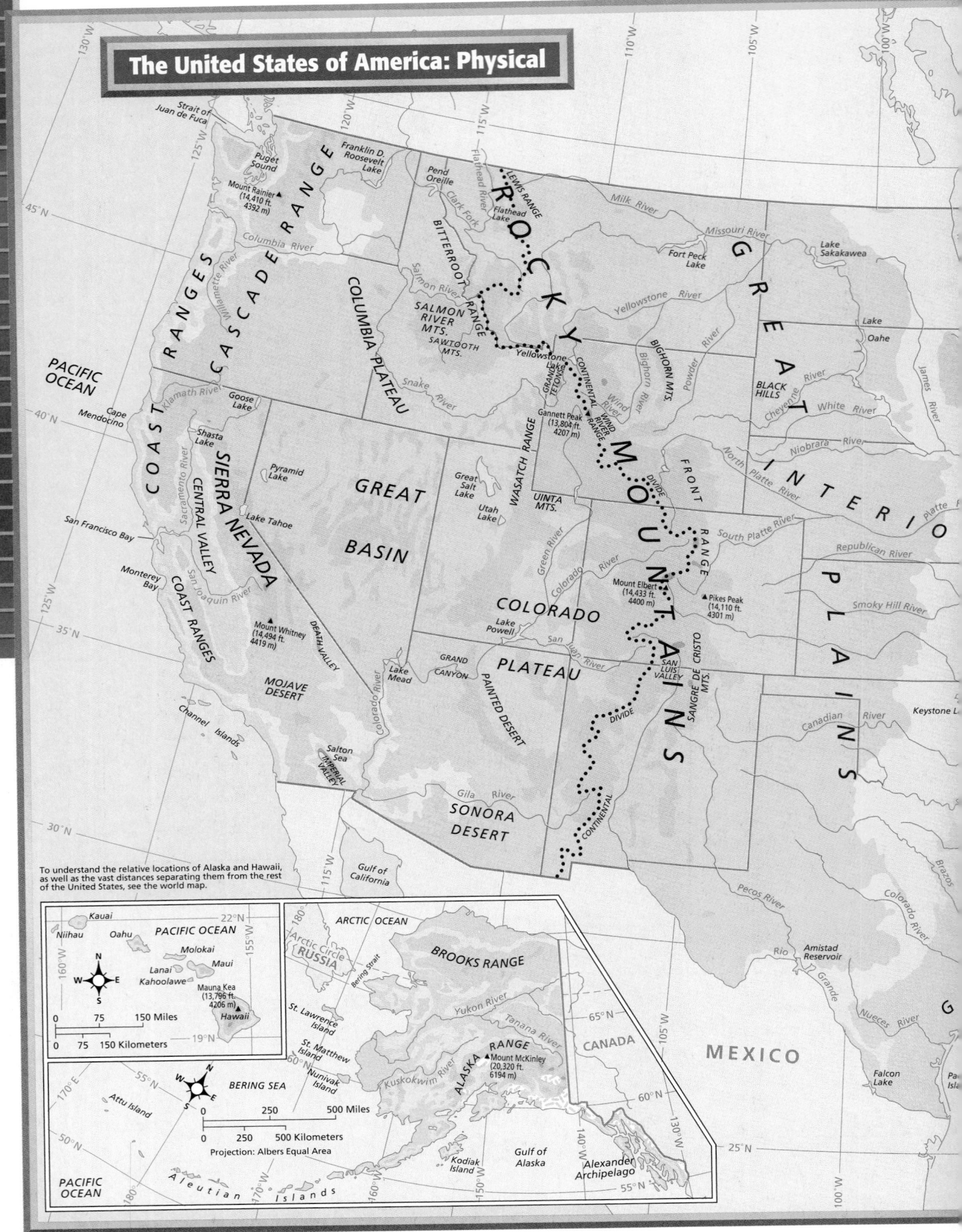

The United States of America: Physical

Strait of Juan de Fuca
Puget Sound
Mount Rainier (14,410 ft. 4392 m)
PACIFIC OCEAN
Cape Mendocino
COAST RANGES
CASCADE RANGE
Columbia River
Willamette River
COLUMBIA PLATEAU
Klamath River
Goose Lake
Shasta Lake
Sacramento River
SIERRA NEVADA
CENTRAL VALLEY
Pyramid Lake
Lake Tahoe
San Francisco Bay
Monterey Bay
COAST RANGES
San Joaquin River
Mount Whitney (14,494 ft. 4419 m)
DEATH VALLEY
Channel Islands
MOJAVE DESERT
GREAT BASIN
Salton Sea
IMPERIAL VALLEY
Colorado River
Lake Mead
GRAND CANYON
Gila River
SONORA DESERT
Gulf of California

Franklin D. Roosevelt Lake
Pend Oreille
Flathead Lake
Clark Fork
BITTERROOT RANGE
Salmon River
SALMON RIVER MTS.
SAWTOOTH MTS.
Snake River
LEWIS RANGE
ROCKY
Yellowstone Lake
GRAND TETONS
CONTINENTAL
Gannett Peak (13,804 ft. 4207 m)
WIND RIVER RANGE
WASATCH RANGE
Great Salt Lake
Utah Lake
UINTA MTS.
Green River
Colorado River
COLORADO PLATEAU
Lake Powell
San Juan River
PAINTED DESERT
CONTINENTAL
DIVIDE
FRONT RANGE
Mount Elbert (14,433 ft. 4400 m)
Pikes Peak (14,110 ft. 4301 m)
South Platte River
MOUNTAINS
SAN LUIS VALLEY
SANGRE DE CRISTO MTS.
DIVIDE

Milk River
Missouri River
Fort Peck Lake
Yellowstone River
BIGHORN MTS
Bighorn River
Powder River
Lake Sakakawea
Lake Oahe
BLACK HILLS
Cheyenne River
GREAT
INTERIOR
White River
Niobrara River
James River
North Platte River
Republican River
Smoky Hill River
PLAINS
Canadian River
Keystone
Pecos River
Amistad Reservoir
Rio Grande
Nueces River
MEXICO
Falcon Lake
Colorado River
Brazos

To understand the relative locations of Alaska and Hawaii, as well as the vast distances separating them from the rest of the United States, see the world map.

Kauai
Niihau
Oahu
Molokai
Lanai
Kahoolawe
Maui
Mauna Kea (13,796 ft. 4206 m)
Hawaii
PACIFIC OCEAN
N W E S
0 75 150 Miles
0 75 150 Kilometers

ARCTIC OCEAN
Arctic Circle
RUSSIA
Bering Strait
BROOKS RANGE
Yukon River
Tanana River
ALASKA RANGE
Mount McKinley (20,320 ft. 6194 m)
Kuskokwim River
CANADA
St. Lawrence Island
St. Matthew Island
Nunivak Island
Kodiak Island
Gulf of Alaska
Alexander Archipelago
BERING SEA
N W E S
0 250 500 Miles
0 250 500 Kilometers
Projection: Albers Equal Area
Attu Island
PACIFIC OCEAN
Aleutian Islands

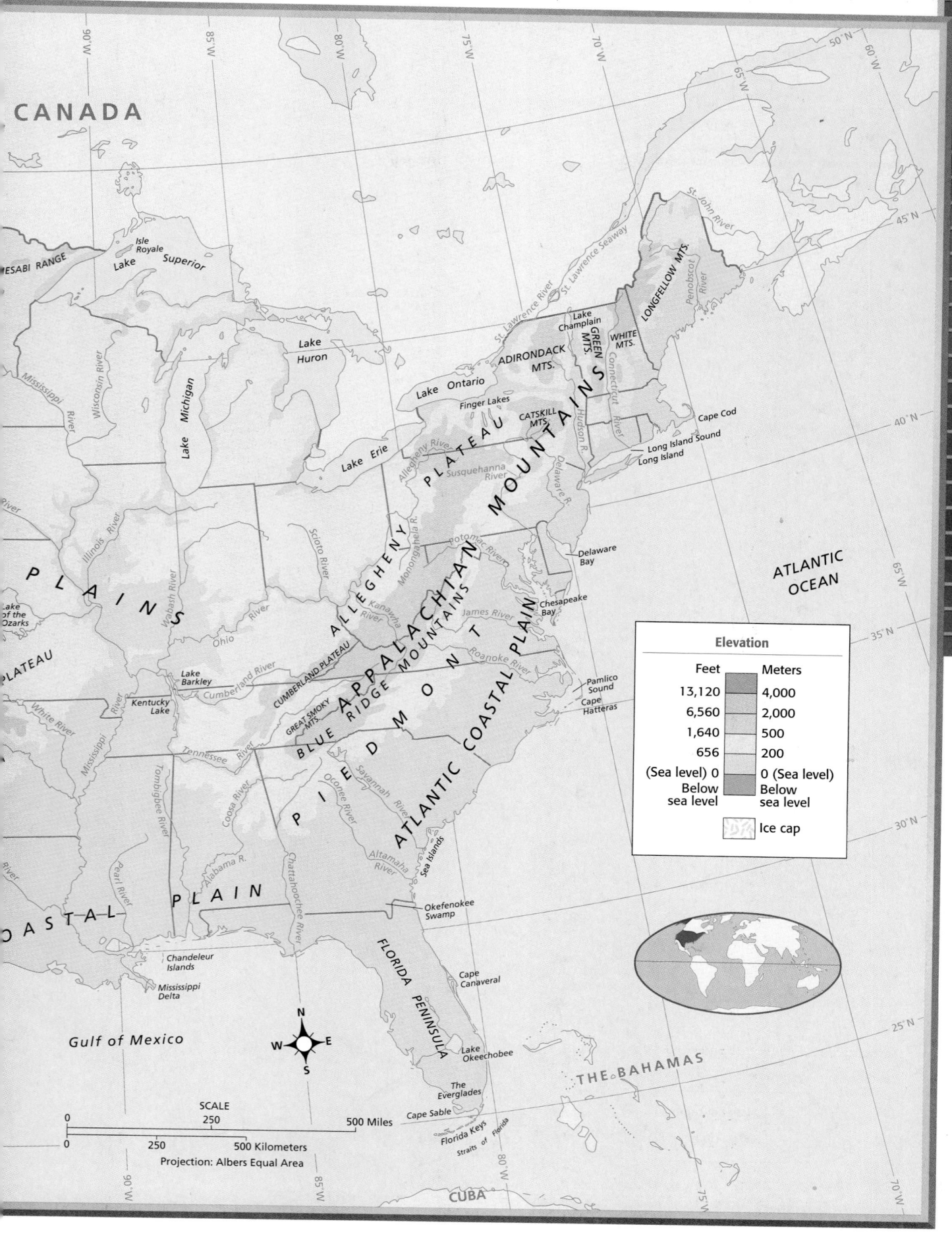

CANADA

MESABI RANGE

Isle
Royale

Lake Superior

Lake
Huron

Lake Michigan

Lake Ontario

Lake Erie

Finger Lakes

St. Lawrence Seaway

St. Lawrence River

Lake
Champlain

ADIRONDACK
MTS.

GREEN
MTS.

WHITE
MTS.

LONGFELLOW MTS.

Penobscot
River

St. John River

Connecticut
River

Cape Cod

Long Island Sound
Long Island

Mississippi River

Wisconsin River

Illinois River

Lake
of the
Ozarks

PLATEAU

Lake Barkley

Kentucky
Lake

White River

Mississippi River

River

PLAINS

Wabash River

Scioto River

Ohio River

Cumberland River

Tennessee River

Kanawha
River

Monongahela R.

Allegheny River

ALLEGHENY PLATEAU

Susquehanna
River

APPALACHIAN MOUNTAINS

Potomac River

James River

Roanoke River

CUMBERLAND PLATEAU

GREAT SMOKY
MTS.

BLUE RIDGE MOUNTAINS

CATSKILL
MTS.

Hudson R.

Delaware R.

Delaware
Bay

Chesapeake
Bay

ATLANTIC
OCEAN

PIEDMONT

ATLANTIC COASTAL PLAIN

Pamlico
Sound
Cape
Hatteras

Tombigbee River

Tennessee River

Coosa River

Alabama R.

Chattahoochee River

Savannah River

Oconee River

Altamaha
River

Sea Islands

Pearl River

River

COASTAL PLAIN

Chandeleur
Islands

Mississippi
Delta

Gulf of Mexico

Okefenokee
Swamp

FLORIDA PENINSULA

Cape
Canaveral

Lake
Okeechobee

The Everglades

Cape Sable

Florida Keys

Straits of Florida

THE BAHAMAS

CUBA

SCALE
250
0   500 Miles
0   250   500 Kilometers
Projection: Albers Equal Area

N
W E
S

Elevation		
Feet		**Meters**
13,120		4,000
6,560		2,000
1,640		500
656		200
(Sea level) 0		0 (Sea level)
Below sea level		Below sea level
	Ice cap	

90°W   85°W   80°W   75°W   70°W   65°W   60°W   50°N   45°N   40°N   35°N   30°N   25°N   65°W   70°W   75°W   80°W   85°W   90°W

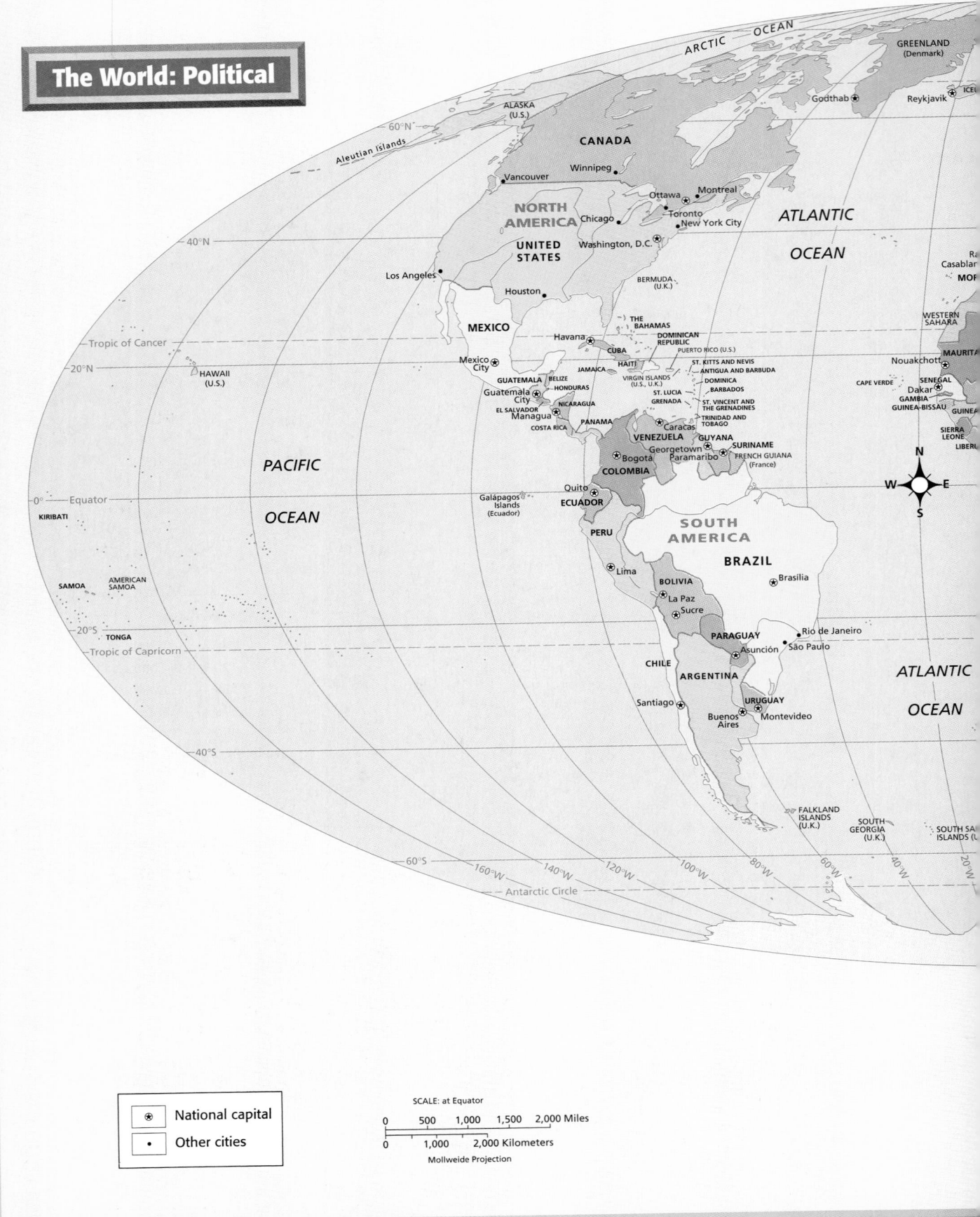

The World: Political

ARCTIC OCEAN

GREENLAND (Denmark)

ICEL

Godthab ●   Reykjavik ●

ALASKA (U.S.)

60°N

CANADA

Aleutian Islands

Vancouver ●   Winnipeg ●

NORTH AMERICA   Ottawa ⊛   Montreal ●

Chicago ●   Toronto ●

ATLANTIC

40°N   UNITED STATES   Washington, D.C. ⊛   New York City ●

OCEAN

Los Angeles ●

Houston ●   BERMUDA (U.K.)   Ra

Casablar

MOR

WESTERN SAHARA

THE BAHAMAS   DOMINICAN REPUBLIC   Nouakchott ●   MAURITA

Tropic of Cancer   MEXICO   Havana ⊛   PUERTO RICO (U.S.)

20°N   HAWAII (U.S.)   CUBA   HAITI   ST. KITTS AND NEVIS   CAPE VERDE   SENEGAL

Mexico City ⊛   GUATEMALA   BELIZE   JAMAICA   VIRGIN ISLANDS (U.S., U.K.)   ANTIGUA AND BARBUDA   Dakar ●

Guatemala City ⊛   HONDURAS   DOMINICA   GAMBIA   GUINEA

EL SALVADOR   NICARAGUA   ST. LUCIA   GUINEA-BISSAU

Managua ⊛   BARBADOS   SIERRA LEONE   LIBERI

COSTA RICA   PANAMA   ST. VINCENT AND THE GRENADINES   GRENADA   TRINIDAD AND TOBAGO

Caracas ●   GUYANA   SURINAME   N

PACIFIC   VENEZUELA   Georgetown ⊛   W ⊛ E

Bogotá ⊛   Paramaribo ⊛   FRENCH GUIANA (France)   S

OCEAN   COLOMBIA

Galápagos Islands (Ecuador)   Quito ⊛   ECUADOR

0°   Equator   PERU   SOUTH AMERICA

KIRIBATI   Lima ●   BRAZIL   Brasília ⊛

SAMOA   AMERICAN SAMOA   BOLIVIA

La Paz ●   Sucre ⊛

20°S   TONGA   Rio de Janeiro ●

Tropic of Capricorn   PARAGUAY   Asunción ⊛   São Paulo ●

CHILE   ATLANTIC

ARGENTINA   URUGUAY   OCEAN

Santiago ⊛   Buenos Aires ⊛   Montevideo ⊛

40°S

FALKLAND ISLANDS (U.K.)   SOUTH GEORGIA (U.K.)   SOUTH SAI ISLANDS (U.

60°S   160°W   140°W   120°W   100°W   80°W   60°W   40°W   20°W

Antarctic Circle

	National capital
⊛	
●	Other cities

SCALE: at Equator

0   500   1,000   1,500   2,000 Miles

0   1,000   2,000 Kilometers

Mollweide Projection

1102 ATLAS

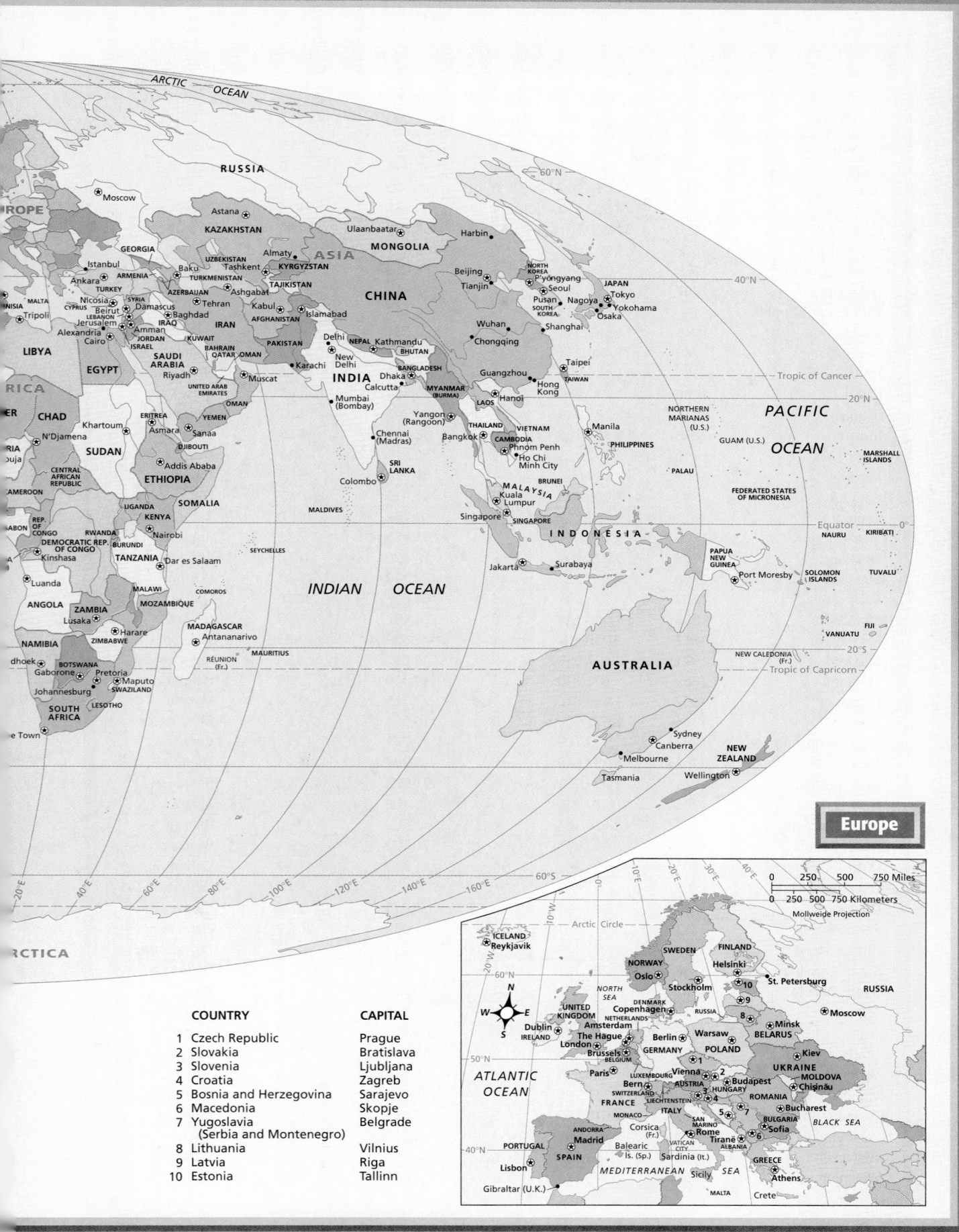

ARCTIC OCEAN

RUSSIA

⊛ Moscow

Astana ⊛

KAZAKHSTAN

MONGOLIA

Ulaanbaatar ⊛

Harbin ●

ASIA

GEORGIA

Almaty ● KYRGYZSTAN

Beijing ⊛

NORTH KOREA

P'yongyang ⊛

JAPAN

Istanbul ●

ARMENIA

UZBEKISTAN Tashkent ⊛

Tianjin ●

Seoul ⊛

Tokyo ⊛

Ankara ⊛

AZERBAIJAN Baku ⊛

TURKMENISTAN

TAJIKISTAN

CHINA

SOUTH KOREA

Pusan ●

Nagoya ●

Yokohama ●

TURKEY

Ashgabat ⊛

Osaka ●

MALTA

Nicosia ⊛

SYRIA

Tehran ⊛

Kabul ⊛

Wuhan ●

Shanghai ●

CYPRUS LEBANON

Damascus ⊛

AFGHANISTAN

Islamabad ⊛

Chongqing ●

TUNISIA

Beirut ⊛

Baghdad ⊛

Tripoli ●

IRAN

Delhi ●

Jerusalem ⊛

IRAQ

JORDAN

Amman ⊛

KUWAIT

PAKISTAN

NEPAL Kathmandu ⊛

Taipei ●

Alexandria ●

ISRAEL

BAHRAIN

New Delhi ⊛

BHUTAN

Guangzhou ●

TAIWAN

Cairo ⊛

QATAR OMAN

Karachi ●

Dhaka ⊛

Hong Kong ●

Tropic of Cancer

LIBYA

EGYPT

SAUDI ARABIA

Muscat ⊛

INDIA

BANGLADESH

MYANMAR (BURMA)

Hanoi ⊛

Riyadh ⊛

Calcutta ●

UNITED ARAB EMIRATES

LAOS

Manila ⊛

NORTHERN MARIANAS (U.S.)

PACIFIC

CHAD

Khartoum ⊛

ERITREA

YEMEN

Mumbai (Bombay) ●

Yangon (Rangoon) ⊛

THAILAND

VIETNAM

GUAM (U.S.)

N'Djamena ⊛

Asmara ⊛

Sanaa ⊛

Chennai (Madras) ●

Bangkok ⊛

CAMBODIA Phnom Penh ⊛

PHILIPPINES

MARSHALL ISLANDS

OCEAN

SUDAN

DJIBOUTI

Ho Chi Minh City ●

PALAU

CENTRAL AFRICAN REPUBLIC

Addis Ababa ⊛

SRI LANKA

BRUNEI

FEDERATED STATES OF MICRONESIA

CAMEROON

ETHIOPIA

SOMALIA

Colombo ●

MALAYSIA

Kuala Lumpur ⊛

UGANDA

KENYA

MALDIVES

Singapore ● SINGAPORE

Equator 0°

GABON REP. OF CONGO

RWANDA

Nairobi ⊛

INDONESIA

NAURU

KIRIBATI

DEMOCRATIC REP. OF CONGO

BURUNDI

TANZANIA

SEYCHELLES

Kinshasa ⊛

Dar es Salaam ●

Jakarta ⊛

Surabaya ●

PAPUA NEW GUINEA

SOLOMON ISLANDS

TUVALU

Luanda ●

MALAWI

Port Moresby ⊛

INDIAN OCEAN

ANGOLA

ZAMBIA

MOZAMBIQUE

COMOROS

FIJI

Lusaka ⊛

MADAGASCAR

VANUATU

NAMIBIA

ZIMBABWE

Harare ⊛

Antananarivo ⊛

NEW CALEDONIA (Fr.)

20°S

dhoek

BOTSWANA

RÉUNION (Fr.)

MAURITIUS

Tropic of Capricorn

Gaborone ⊛

Pretoria ⊛

AUSTRALIA

Johannesburg ●

Maputo ⊛

SWAZILAND

SOUTH AFRICA

LESOTHO

e Town

Sydney ●

Canberra ⊛

NEW ZEALAND

Melbourne ●

Tasmania

Wellington ⊛

ARCTICA

20°E 40°E 60°E 80°E 100°E 120°E 140°E 160°E 60°S

Europe

COUNTRY	CAPITAL
1 Czech Republic	Prague
2 Slovakia	Bratislava
3 Slovenia	Ljubljana
4 Croatia	Zagreb
5 Bosnia and Herzegovina	Sarajevo
6 Macedonia	Skopje
7 Yugoslavia (Serbia and Montenegro)	Belgrade
8 Lithuania	Vilnius
9 Latvia	Riga
10 Estonia	Tallinn

0   250   500   750 Miles
0   250 500 750 Kilometers
Mollweide Projection

Arctic Circle

ICELAND ⊛ Reykjavik

SWEDEN

FINLAND

NORWAY

Oslo ⊛

Stockholm ⊛

Helsinki ⊛

⊛ 10

St. Petersburg ●

RUSSIA

NORTH SEA

DENMARK

Copenhagen ⊛

⊛ 9

UNITED KINGDOM

RUSSIA

⊛ 8

Minsk ⊛

Moscow ⊛

NETHERLANDS

Amsterdam ⊛

BELARUS

IRELAND

Dublin ⊛

The Hague ⊛

Berlin ⊛

Warsaw ⊛

London ⊛

Brussels ⊛

GERMANY

POLAND

Kiev ⊛

ATLANTIC OCEAN

BELGIUM

⊛ 1

Paris ⊛

LUXEMBOURG

Vienna ⊛

⊛ 2

UKRAINE

Bern ⊛

AUSTRIA

HUNGARY

MOLDOVA

SWITZERLAND

⊛ 3

Budapest ⊛

Chişinău ⊛

FRANCE

LIECHTENSTEIN

ITALY

⊛ 4

ROMANIA

Bucharest ⊛

MONACO

⊛ 5

⊛ 7

PORTUGAL

Corsica (Fr.)

SAN MARINO

BULGARIA

BLACK SEA

ANDORRA

Madrid ⊛

VATICAN CITY

Rome ⊛

⊛ 6

Sofia ⊛

Balearic Is. (Sp.)

Sardinia (It.)

Tiranë ⊛

ALBANIA

GREECE

Lisbon ⊛

SPAIN

MEDITERRANEAN

Sicily

SEA

Athens ⊛

Gibraltar (U.K.)

MALTA

Crete

Facts About the States

State	Year of Statehood	1997 Population	Reps. in Congress	Area (sq. mi.)	Population Density (sq. mi.)	Capital
Alabama	1819	4,319,154	7	51,705	83.5	Montgomery
Alaska	1959	609,311	1	591,004	1.0	Juneau
Arizona	1912	4,554,966	6	114,000	40.0	Phoenix
Arkansas	1836	2,522,819	4	53,187	47.4	Little Rock
California	1850	32,268,301	52	158,706	203.3	Sacramento
Colorado	1876	3,892,644	6	104,091	37.4	Denver
Connecticut	1788	3,269,858	6	5,018	651.6	Hartford
Delaware	1787	731,581	1	2,045	357.7	Dover
District of Columbia	—	528,964	—	69	7,666.1	—
Florida	1845	14,653,945	23	58,664	249.8	Tallahassee
Georgia	1788	7,486,242	11	58,910	127.1	Atlanta
Hawaii	1959	1,186,602	2	6,471	183.4	Honolulu
Idaho	1890	1,210,232	2	83,564	14.5	Boise
Illinois	1818	11,895,849	20	56,345	211.1	Springfield
Indiana	1816	5,864,108	10	36,185	162.1	Indianapolis
Iowa	1846	2,852,423	5	56,275	50.7	Des Moines
Kansas	1861	2,594,840	4	82,277	31.5	Topeka
Kentucky	1792	3,908,124	6	40,410	96.7	Frankfort
Louisiana	1812	4,351,769	7	42,752	101.8	Baton Rouge
Maine	1820	1,242,051	2	33,265	37.3	Augusta
Maryland	1788	5,094,289	8	10,460	487.0	Annapolis
Massachusetts	1788	6,117,520	10	8,248	741.7	Boston
Michigan	1837	9,773,892	16	58,527	167.0	Lansing
Minnesota	1858	4,685,549	8	84,402	55.5	St. Paul
Mississippi	1817	2,730,501	5	47,689	57.3	Jackson
Missouri	1821	5,402,058	9	69,697	77.5	Jefferson City
Montana	1889	878,810	1	147,046	5.9	Helena
Nebraska	1867	1,656,870	3	77,355	21.4	Lincoln
Nevada	1864	1,676,809	2	110,561	15.2	Carson City
New Hampshire	1788	1,172,709	2	9,279	126.4	Concord
New Jersey	1787	8,052,849	13	7,787	1,034.1	Trenton
New Mexico	1912	1,729,751	3	121,593	14.2	Santa Fe
New York	1788	18,137,226	31	49,108	369.3	Albany
North Carolina	1789	7,425,183	12	52,669	141.0	Raleigh
North Dakota	1889	640,883	1	70,702	9.1	Bismarck
Ohio	1803	11,186,331	19	41,330	270.7	Columbus
Oklahoma	1907	3,317,091	6	69,956	47.4	Oklahoma City
Oregon	1859	3,243,487	5	97,073	33.4	Salem
Pennsylvania	1787	12,019,661	21	45,038	266.9	Harrisburg
Rhode Island	1790	987,429	2	1,212	814.7	Providence
South Carolina	1788	3,760,181	6	31,113	120.9	Columbia
South Dakota	1889	737,973	1	77,116	9.6	Pierre
Tennessee	1796	5,368,198	9	42,144	127.4	Nashville
Texas	1845	19,439,337	30	266,807	72.9	Austin
Utah	1896	2,059,148	3	84,899	24.3	Salt Lake City
Vermont	1791	588,978	1	9,614	61.3	Montpelier
Virginia	1788	6,733,996	11	40,767	165.2	Richmond
Washington	1889	5,610,362	9	68,139	82.3	Olympia
West Virginia	1863	1,815,787	3	24,232	74.9	Charleston
Wisconsin	1848	5,169,677	9	56,153	92.1	Madison
Wyoming	1890	479,743	1	97,809	4.9	Cheyenne

The Official Portraits

1 George Washington

Born: 1732   **Died:** 1799
Years in Office: 1789–97
Political Party: None
Home State: Virginia
Vice President: John Adams

2 John Adams

Born: 1735   **Died:** 1826
Years in Office: 1797–1801
Political Party: Federalist
Home State: Massachusetts
Vice President: Thomas Jefferson

3 Thomas Jefferson

Born: 1743   **Died:** 1826
Years in Office: 1801–09
Political Party: Republican*
Home State: Virginia
Vice Presidents: Aaron Burr,
George Clinton

4 James Madison

Born: 1751   **Died:** 1836
Years in Office: 1809–17
Political Party: Republican
Home State: Virginia
Vice Presidents: George Clinton,
Elbridge Gerry

5 James Monroe

Born: 1758   **Died:** 1831
Years in Office: 1817–25
Political Party: Republican
Home State: Virginia
Vice President: Daniel D. Tompkins

6 John Quincy Adams

Born: 1767   **Died:** 1848
Years in Office: 1825–29
Political Party: Republican
Home State: Massachusetts
Vice President: John C. Calhoun

7 Andrew Jackson

Born: 1767   **Died:** 1845
Years in Office: 1829–37
Political Party: Democratic
Home State: Tennessee
Vice Presidents: John C. Calhoun,
Martin Van Buren

8 Martin Van Buren

Born: 1782   **Died:** 1862
Years in Office: 1837–41
Political Party: Democratic
Home State: New York
Vice President: Richard M. Johnson

* The Republican Party of the third through sixth presidents is not the
Republican Party of Abraham Lincoln, which was founded in 1854.

9 William Henry Harrison

Born: 1773   **Died:** 1841
Years in Office: 1841
Political Party: Whig
Home State: Ohio
Vice President: John Tyler

10 John Tyler

Born: 1790   **Died:** 1862
Years in Office: 1841–45
Political Party: Whig
Home State: Virginia
Vice President: None

11 James K. Polk

Born: 1795   **Died:** 1849
Years in Office: 1845–49
Political Party: Democratic
Home State: Tennessee
Vice President: George M. Dallas

12 Zachary Taylor

Born: 1784   **Died:** 1850
Years in Office: 1849–50
Political Party: Whig
Home State: Louisiana
Vice President: Millard Fillmore

13 Millard Fillmore

Born: 1800   **Died:** 1874
Years in Office: 1850–53
Political Party: Whig
Home State: New York
Vice President: None

14 Franklin Pierce

Born: 1804   **Died:** 1869
Years in Office: 1853–57
Political Party: Democratic
Home State: New Hampshire
Vice President: William R. King

15 James Buchanan

Born: 1791   **Died:** 1868
Years in Office: 1857–61
Political Party: Democratic
Home State: Pennsylvania
Vice President: John C. Breckinridge

16 Abraham Lincoln

Born: 1809   **Died:** 1865
Years in Office: 1861–65
Political Party: Republican
Home State: Illinois
Vice President: Hannibal Hamlin,
Andrew Johnson

17 Andrew Johnson

Born: 1808   **Died:** 1875
Years in Office: 1865-69
Political Party: Republican
Home State: Tennessee
Vice President: None

18 Ulysses S. Grant

Born: 1822   **Died:** 1885
Years in Office: 1869–77
Political Party: Republican
Home State: Illinois
Vice President: Schuyler Colfax, Henry Wilson

19 Rutherford B. Hayes

Born: 1822   **Died:** 1893
Years in Office: 1877–81
Political Party: Republican
Home State: Ohio
Vice President: William A. Wheeler

20 James A. Garfield

Born: 1831   **Died:** 1881
Years in Office: 1881
Political Party: Republican
Home State: Ohio
Vice President: Chester A. Arthur

21 Chester A. Arthur

Born: 1829   **Died:** 1886
Years in Office: 1881–85
Political Party: Republican
Home State: New York
Vice President: None

22 Grover Cleveland

Born: 1837   **Died:** 1908
Years in Office: 1885–89
Political Party: Democratic
Home State: New York
Vice President: Thomas A. Hendricks

23 Benjamin Harrison

Born: 1833   **Died:** 1901
Years in Office: 1889–93
Political Party: Republican
Home State: Indiana
Vice President: Levi P. Morton

24 Grover Cleveland

Born: 1837   **Died:** 1908
Years in Office: 1893–97
Political Party: Democratic
Home State: New York
Vice President: Adlai E. Stevenson

25 William McKinley

Born: 1843   **Died:** 1901
Years in Office: 1897–1901
Political Party: Republican
Home State: Ohio
Vice President: Garret A. Hobart, Theodore Roosevelt

26 Theodore Roosevelt

Born: 1858   **Died:** 1919
Years in Office: 1901-09
Political Party: Republican
Home State: New York
Vice President: Charles W. Fairbanks

27 William Howard Taft

Born: 1857 **Died:** 1930
Years in Office: 1909–13
Political Party: Republican
Home State: Ohio
Vice President: James S. Sherman

28 Woodrow Wilson

Born: 1856 **Died:** 1924
Years in Office: 1913–21
Political Party: Democratic
Home State: New Jersey
Vice President: Thomas R. Marshall

29 Warren G. Harding

Born: 1865 **Died:** 1923
Years in Office: 1921–23
Political Party: Republican
Home State: Ohio
Vice President: Calvin Coolidge

30 Calvin Coolidge

Born: 1872 **Died:** 1933
Years in Office: 1923–29
Political Party: Republican
Home State: Massachusetts
Vice President: Charles G. Dawes

31 Herbert Hoover

Born: 1874 **Died:** 1964
Years in Office: 1929–33
Political Party: Republican
Home State: California
Vice President: Charles Curtis

32 Franklin D. Roosevelt

Born: 1882 **Died:** 1945
Years in Office: 1933–45
Political Party: Democratic
Home State: New York
Vice President: John Nance Garner,
Henry Wallace, Harry S Truman

33 Harry S Truman

Born: 1884 **Died:** 1972
Years in Office: 1945–53
Political Party: Democratic
Home State: Missouri
Vice President: Alben W. Barkley

34 Dwight D. Eisenhower

Born: 1890 **Died:** 1969
Years in Office: 1953–61
Political Party: Republican
Home State: Kansas
Vice President: Richard M. Nixon

35 John F. Kennedy

Born: 1917 **Died:** 1963
Years in Office: 1961–63
Political Party: Democratic
Home State: Massachusetts
Vice President: Lyndon B. Johnson

36 Lyndon B. Johnson

Born: 1908　　**Died:** 1973
Years in Office: 1963–69
Political Party: Democratic
Home State: Texas
Vice President: Hubert H. Humphrey

37 Richard M. Nixon

Born: 1913　　**Died:** 1994
Years in Office: 1969–74
Political Party: Republican
Home State: California
Vice President: Spiro T. Agnew,
Gerald R. Ford

38 Gerald R. Ford

Born: 1913
Years in Office: 1974–77
Political Party: Republican
Home State: Michigan
Vice President: Nelson A.
Rockefeller

39 Jimmy Carter

Born: 1924
Years in Office: 1977–81
Political Party: Democratic
Home State: Georgia
Vice President: Walter F. Mondale

40 Ronald Reagan

Born: 1911
Years in Office: 1981–89
Political Party: Republican
Home State: California
Vice President: George Bush

41 George Bush

Born: 1924
Years in Office: 1989–93
Political Party: Republican
Home State: Texas
Vice President: Dan Quayle

42 Bill Clinton

Born: 1946
Years in Office: 1993– 2000
Political Party: Democratic
Home State: Arkansas
Vice President: Al Gore Jr.

2000–2008　2008–
8y5　　8y Rs
George　BARACK
Bush　Obama

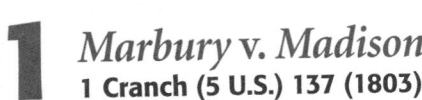
1 *Marbury* v. *Madison*
1 Cranch (5 U.S.) 137 (1803)

What was this case about?

The story. The Federalist Party had been defeated in the election of 1800. However, President-elect Thomas Jefferson was not scheduled to take office until March 4, 1801. In the meantime, the outgoing president, John Adams, chose a number of Federalist supporters as justices of the peace in the District of Columbia. These justices received their appointments in the final hours of the Adams administration. However, they were unable to take office until their commissions were delivered. After the new president took over, he found that the previous secretary of state, John Marshall, had not had time to deliver all of the commissions. Jefferson immediately ordered his new secretary of state, James Madison, not to deliver the remaining commissions.

As one of the people whose commission was not delivered, William Marbury sued Madison. Marbury took advantage of a law passed by Congress that allowed him to make this kind of complaint directly to the Supreme Court. He asked the Court to order Madison to deliver the commission even though this request meant disobeying the president. Marbury probably expected the Court to do as he asked because John Marshall had been appointed Chief Justice of the United States.

The question. As Chief Justice Marshall saw it, the question before the Court had three parts. First, did Marbury have a right to receive the commission? Second, if he did have a right to the commission, was the government required to ensure that he received the commission? Finally, if the government was required to do so, would it have to order Madison to deliver Marbury's commission, as Marbury requested?

The issues. Chief Justice Marshall wanted the Court to be able to decide if laws passed by Congress were constitutional. Whether the Court had this power of judicial review—the power to decide if laws made by Congress are allowed by the Constitution—had not yet been decided. Marshall posed the question before the Court in three parts in order to discuss judicial review.

How was the case decided?

In 1803 the Court ruled against ordering Madison to deliver Marbury's commission.

What did the Court say about governmental powers?

The Court's reasoning passed through three stages:

Step 1. Pointing to a federal law that outlined the appointment process for District of Columbia justices of the peace, the Court said that Marbury had a right to the commission.

Step 2. The Court said that when government officials hurt people by neglecting legal duties, our laws require a remedy.

Step 3. Marbury had asked that the Supreme Court order Madison to deliver the commission. Here Chief Justice Marshall did something surprising. He declared that a court could issue such an order, but that the Supreme Court was not the right court to issue it.

Marbury had taken advantage of a federal law that allowed complaints such as his to be taken straight to the Supreme Court. However, Chief Justice Marshall declared this law unconstitutional. The Constitution mentions several kinds of cases that can be brought straight to the Supreme Court. All other kinds of cases must go through lower courts first. The chief justice explained that Marbury's lawsuit was one of the kinds of cases that must go through lower courts first. It did not matter that Congress had passed a law saying something different, because the Constitution is a higher law.

Marshall's cleverly written opinion excused the Supreme Court from hearing lawsuits such as Marbury's before lower courts had heard them. Marshall accomplished this by claiming for the Court an even greater power—the power of judicial review.

What implications did this case have for the future?

If the Supreme Court did not have judicial review, Congress would decide for itself on the constitutionality of the laws it passed. Marshall's opinion in *Marbury* v. *Madison* removed that power from Congress. By deciding on the constitutionality of the other two branches' actions, the Supreme Court is the nation's final authority on the meaning of the Constitution.

2 *Martin* v. *Hunter's Lessee*
1 Wheaton (14 U.S.) 304 (1816)

What was this case about?

The story. In 1777, during the Revolutionary War, Virginia passed a law declaring that land owned by people who were still loyal to Great Britain no longer belonged to them. One person affected by this law was

Thomas Lord Fairfax. When he died in England in 1782, his Virginia lands passed to his American relative, Thomas Martin. However, Virginia gave Fairfax's land to David Hunter.

Thomas Martin considered himself the true owner of the land. Hunter disagreed and rented it to someone else. The renter (called the "lessee") tried to have Martin evicted. Virginia's highest court ruled that Hunter owned the land.

Martin appealed his case to the U.S. Supreme Court. He reminded the Court of the treaties between the United States and Britain. These treaties promised to protect the rights of British subjects who had owned property in America before the Revolution. Because of these treaties, he said, Virginia's 1777 law was not valid. The Supreme Court agreed. It sent the case back to the Virginia court with orders to change its decision.

However, the Virginia court denied that the Supreme Court had the authority to tell a state court what to do. Therefore, Martin asked the Supreme Court to reverse the Virginia court's judgment.

The question. In cases that involve the federal Constitution, laws, and treaties, does the Constitution give federal courts the power to reverse state court judgments?

The issues. In *Marbury* v. *Madison* the Supreme Court asserted the power of judicial review, but that did not settle the issue of how far the power of judicial review extends. In *Marbury* v. *Madison* one of the other branches of the federal government had been overruled, but in this case Martin was asking the Supreme Court to overrule one of the branches of a state government.

How was the case decided?
In 1816, in an opinion written by Justice Joseph Story, the Supreme Court did what Martin asked. It reversed the judgment of the Virginia court.

What did the Court say about governmental powers?
Justice Story thought that the Constitution gave the Supreme Court the power to reverse state courts in cases involving the federal Constitution, laws, and treaties. To explain his decision, he first tried to show why various objections to his view were mistaken. One such objection was that the Constitution does not affect state governments, but rather the people living in those states. Justice Story pointed out that the Constitution is "crowded" with conditions that affect the state governments. Another objection was that federal judges might abuse the power they had to decide the meaning of the federal Constitution, laws,

and treaties. Justice Story explained that the power of final decision has to be put somewhere and that it was placed with the Supreme Court.

Finally, Justice Story asserted the need for uniformity. If federal judges were not allowed to reverse state court judgments, then state courts all over the country might interpret the federal Constitution, laws, and treaties in different ways.

What implications did this case have for the future?
Under the Constitution, power is divided between two levels: state and national. U.S. history is full of various kinds of conflicts between the states and the national government. Usually, as in *Martin* v. *Hunter's Lessee,* the national government has won these conflicts. Thus, there has been a slow drift of power from the states to the national government. Justice Story, however, did not claim that federal courts could overrule state courts in all cases. He said only that they could overrule state courts in cases involving the U.S. Constitution, laws, and treaties.

3 *McCulloch* v. *Maryland*
4 Wheaton (17 U.S.) 316 (1819)

What was this case about?
The story. In 1791 Congress passed a law that set up the Bank of the United States. An attempt to renew the Bank's charter in 1811 failed. A number of states took advantage of this situation to charter their own banks.

After the War of 1812, the federal government needed money to pay for the war. Instead of being able to borrow money from one central bank, it had to deal with many state banks. Thus, Congress set up the Second Bank of the United States in 1816. The states generally opposed the National Bank, and several states passed laws that hindered it. For instance, they taxed branches of the Bank within their borders. When the Maryland branch of the Bank refused to pay the tax, Maryland sued the bank's cashier, James McCulloch. In 1919 the legal battle reached the Supreme Court.

The question. As Chief Justice John Marshall saw it, the question before the Court had two parts. Does the Constitution give Congress the power to establish a national bank? If so, does the Constitution allow a state to tax that bank?

The issues. The question of whether Congress had the power to establish a bank was not new. In 1791, after Congress had passed the bill that established the First Bank of the United States, President George Washington had asked his cabinet for advice. He noted that although Article I, Section 8, of the Constitution lists the powers of Congress, it does not mention the power to charter a bank. Yet the article does state that in addition to the listed powers, Congress may also make all laws that are "necessary and proper" for carrying out the listed powers.

Alexander Hamilton and Thomas Jefferson presented Washington with sharply opposing views. Hamilton considered the power to charter a bank constitutional because it had "a natural relation" to the powers of collecting taxes and regulating trade. By contrast, Jefferson said that while the power to charter a bank may be "convenient" for carrying out this power, it was not "necessary," and thus was unconstitutional. Finding Hamilton's argument more convincing, Washington signed the bill. Maryland, however, wanted the Supreme Court to interpret the Constitution as Jefferson had done.

How was the case decided?
Led by Chief Justice Marshall, the Supreme Court ruled that the Constitution allowed Congress to establish the National Bank. The Court also asserted that the Constitution did not allow a state to tax the Bank.

What did the Court say about governmental powers?
Jefferson's argument against the First Bank of the United States had rested on a strict interpretation of the word "necessary" in the necessary and proper clause. The state of Maryland used the same argument. In deciding the first question, Marshall said that Maryland's interpretation of the Constitution was not broad enough. He explained that when the Constitution says that certain means are "necessary" to an end, it usually does not mean that the end cannot be achieved without them. Rather, it means that they are "calculated to produce" the end. The power to charter a bank is calculated to help carry out the other constitutional powers, so the Constitution permits it.

The second question before the Court was whether the Constitution allows a state to tax the National Bank. If the states could tax one of the federal government's activities, they could tax any of them. Marshall said that because "the power to tax involves the power to destroy," this could not be permitted. The supremacy clause in Article VI states that the Constitution and laws of the federal government come before state constitutions and laws.

What implications did this case have for the future?
As new cases arise, members of the Supreme Court try to settle them by using principles that have been established in earlier cases. This case involves the principles of implied powers and national supremacy. Some powers given to the federal government by the Constitution are listed. These are called enumerated powers. Others, called implied powers, are understood as given because they are needed to help carry out the enumerated powers. The federal government has only those powers that are enumerated and implied in the Constitution. However, when the federal government is using powers that do belong to it, the states must give way.

4 Scott v. Sandford
19 Howard (60 U.S.) 393 (1857)

What was this case about?
The story. In 1833 a slave named Dred Scott was purchased by John Emerson, an army doctor. As the army transferred Emerson from post to post, Scott went with him. First they went to Illinois; later they moved to Wisconsin Territory. When Emerson was transferred yet again, he sent Scott to Missouri, a slave state, to live with his wife, Eliza Irene Sanford Emerson. She inherited Scott when her husband died in 1843.

At this time, slavery was illegal in Illinois and in Wisconsin Territory. Scott believed that because he had lived on free soil for five years, he should be free.

In 1846 Emerson moved to New England and left Scott with sons of Scott's original owner. One son opposed the spread of slavery. He helped Scott file a lawsuit. In 1850 a Missouri court declared Scott free.

In 1852 the Missouri Supreme Court reversed the lower court's ruling. In 1854, however, Scott's original lawsuit was revived by lawyers who wanted the issue of slavery in the territories to be resolved. Scott's case worked its way to the Supreme Court.

The question. As Chief Justice Roger B. Taney saw it, the case raised two questions. First, does the Constitution give an African American the right to file a suit in federal court? Second, does the Constitution allow Congress to pass a law that frees slaves who are brought into a free territory?

The issues. If African Americans were U.S. citizens, then they must have all of the rights of other citizens, including the right to sue in a federal court. Therefore, the first question before the court involved the Constitution's definition of a citizen.

The second question before the Court involved the kinds of limits the Constitution puts on laws about property. If slaves were property, then Congress faced the same limits when it made a law about slavery as when it made a law about property.

How was the case decided?

The Court ruled that the Constitution denied African Americans the right to sue in federal court and denied Congress the power to make a law abolishing or prohibiting slavery in the territories.

What did the Court say about constitutional rights?

The first theme of the Court's opinion was the relationship between race and citizenship. The opinion reflected the prejudices of the day. Taney said that African Americans had "none of the rights and privileges" of citizens. This statement was particularly startling because it applied to free African Americans as well as to slaves. Taney ignored the important fact that many states considered free African Americans to be state citizens. In addition, Article III, Section 2, of the Constitution gives the federal courts jurisdiction over various kinds of suits involving state citizens.

The other theme of the Court's opinion concerned slavery. The Fifth Amendment states that no one may be "deprived of life, liberty, or property, without due process of law." First, the chief justice reasoned that because slaves are "property," they could not be taken away without due process of law. Second, he reasoned that a law taking away citizens' property just because they entered a free territory cheated them of their due process of law. In addition, Taney ruled that the Missouri Compromise was unconstitutional.

What implications did this case have for the future?

By the time the Court made its decision, the Kansas-Nebraska Act had already canceled the Missouri Compromise's ban on slavery in certain federal territories. Therefore, it might seem that the Court's judgment did not matter. However, the Kansas-Nebraska Act was unpopular with people who opposed the spread of slavery. Many of them would have liked to have seen a return to something like the Missouri Compromise. The decision made such a return impossible and worsened the controversy over slavery in the territories.

Furthermore, this case established that merely freeing slaves was not enough to guarantee their U.S. citizenship. Not until 1868, when the Fourteenth Amendment was passed, did the Constitution guarantee that African Americans were U.S. citizens.

5 Lochner v. New York
198 U.S. 45 (1905)

What was this case about?

The story. In 1895 the New York legislature passed a law regulating the number of hours that bakery employees could be required or allowed to work. This law was necessary to prevent workers from having to agree to work long hours out of fear of losing their jobs. The legislature claimed that workers should not be allowed to work long hours because of potential harm to their health.

Joseph Lochner, a bakery owner convicted of violating the law, appealed. He said that the law was unconstitutional because it took away his liberty to make a contract. Lochner said that liberty of contract is promised by a clause in the Fourteenth Amendment that says that no state may "deprive any person of life, liberty, or property, without due process of law."

The question. Do limits on the number of hours an employee may work violate the Fourteenth Amendment?

The issues. State governments have a general power—called the police power—to make regulations that support the safety, health, morals, and general welfare of their citizens. The basic issue in this case is whether the Constitution can limit state governments' police power in some cases.

Various amendments set limits on the power of state governments, but the most general is the due process clause of the Fourteenth Amendment. To apply this clause to the New York bakery law, the Supreme Court had to decide what freedoms are meant by the word *liberty* and what is promised by the guarantee of due process of law.

How was the case decided?

The Court ruled that the law limiting the hours of labor in bakeries was unconstitutional.

What did the Court say about governmental powers?

Justice Rufus Wheeler Peckham argued that the New York legislature's interference with liberty of contract was improper. Peckham did not mean that the Constitution forbids all interference with liberty of contract. In fact, he stressed that the Court had approved a similar Utah law that said that no one could work more than eight hours a day in an underground mine except in cases of emergency. Such uses of the police power, he said, were "fair, reasonable, and appropriate." They regulate liberty without taking it away. By contrast, he argued, the New York law had nothing to do with safety, morals, or general welfare and was not necessary to protect health.

What implications did this case have for the future?

Even though the Court tries to rely on the same principles over and over, sometimes its members change their minds about controversial issues. Four justices dissented, or disagreed with the *Lochner* ruling. As the membership of the Supreme Court has changed, so have the attitudes of the justices. In 1937 the Court began to reverse the precedent it had set in *Lochner*.

6 *Plessy* v. *Ferguson*
163 U.S. 537 (1896)
Brown v. *Board of Education*
347 U.S. 483 (1954)

What were these cases about?

The stories. These two cases illustrate a major change in the legality of racial segregation. *Plessy* v. *Ferguson* began with an 1890 Louisiana law that required all railway companies to provide "equal but separate" accommodations for white and African American passengers. A group of people who thought the law was unfair recruited Homer Plessy to get arrested in order to test the law. Plessy entered a train and took an empty seat in an all-white area. When he refused to move to an all-black section, he was arrested and jailed. In his defense, he said that the 1890 law was unconstitutional. The case eventually worked its way up to the Supreme Court.

More than 50 years later, an African American man named Oliver Brown and his family moved into a white neighborhood in Topeka, Kansas. The Browns assumed that their daughter Linda would attend the neighborhood school. Instead, the Board of Education ordered her to attend a distant all-black school that was supposedly "separate but equal." Charging that school segregation violated the Fourteenth Amendment to the Constitution, Mr. Brown sued the Board.

The question. The question raised by the Court was the same in both cases. Do racially segregated facilities violate the equal protection clause of the Fourteenth Amendment?

The issues. The state of Louisiana argued that separate railway carriages could be equal. For instance, they could be equally clean and equally safe. The state of Kansas said much the same thing, claiming that its all-black and all-white schools were equal in such features as teachers' skills and buildings' quality.

In the days of racial segregation, the claim that segregated facilities were equal in tangible, or measurable, features was almost always a terrible lie. The issue facing the Court, however, went deeper. Even if things were made equal in racially segregated facilities, was there something fundamentally unequal about segregation?

How were the cases decided?

In *Plessy* v. *Ferguson*, the Court ruled that the Fourteenth Amendment's equal protection clause allows racial segregation. In *Brown* v. *Board of Education*, however, the Court unanimously ruled that the clause does not allow racial segregation.

What did the Court say about constitutional rights?

Justice Henry Billings Brown wrote the Court's opinion in *Plessy*. He admitted that the purpose of the Fourteenth Amendment was "to enforce the absolute equality of the two races before the law." However, he said that this statement meant political equality, not social equality. Brown declared that there was no truth to the argument that separate facilities implied that African Americans were inferior.

In *Brown* the Court's opinion was written by Chief Justice Earl Warren. He said that separation of black schoolchildren from white schoolchildren of the same age and ability "generates a feeling of inferiority . . . that may affect their hearts and minds in a way unlikely ever to be undone." He said that when racial segregation is required by law, the harm is even greater. It makes no difference that "the physical facilities and other 'tangible' factors may be equal."

What implications did these cases have for the future?

In *Brown* v. *Board of Education*, the Court did not say that the "separate but equal" doctrine was completely invalid. It ruled that the doctrine had no place in public education. This statement, although limited, influenced future cases that eventually abolished all segregation. Taken together, *Plessy* and *Brown* show that interpretation of the Constitution's legal principles may change as society changes.

7 *Gideon* v. *Wainwright*
372 U.S. 335 (1963)

What was this case about?

The story. Clarence Earl Gideon was accused of breaking and entering a Florida poolroom. When Gideon's case came to trial, he could not afford a lawyer, so he asked that the court pay for one. The judge refused, the case proceeded, and Gideon was found guilty. While in prison, Gideon appealed to the U.S. Supreme Court. He claimed that by refusing to appoint him a lawyer, Florida had violated rights promised him by the Sixth and Fourteenth Amendments.

The question. Do the Sixth and the Fourteenth Amendments require that a poor person accused of a crime have access to an attorney free of charge?

The issues. The Sixth Amendment ensures certain rights to people accused of crimes. For example, "The accused shall enjoy the right . . . to have the Assistance of Counsel [a lawyer] for his defense." By itself, this amendment requires that poor people be provided with free lawyers in federal trials. Yet Gideon had been accused of breaking state laws and was tried in a state court. Still, the Fourteenth Amendment ensures that states cannot deprive people of life, liberty, or property without due process of law. Jailed, Gideon had been deprived of liberty. Had this liberty been taken away without due process of law?

How was the case decided?

In a unanimous opinion written by Justice Hugo Black, the Court ruled in Gideon's favor.

What did the Court say about constitutional rights?

Members of the Court based their decision on two different views of the Fourteenth Amendment. One is the incorporation view, which holds that the purpose of the due process clause is to incorporate most of the Bill of Rights into state court procedures. The second is the fundamental liberties view, which holds that "due process of law" means "whatever is necessary for justice." What is necessary for justice may not include every assurance in the Bill of Rights, but it may include assurances that go beyond anything in the Bill of Rights. In *Gideon* v. *Wainwright* the justices came to the same conclusion by different means.

Justice Black had to tailor the Court's decision to accommodate both the incorporation view and the fundamental liberties view. The opinion was a compromise. It said that the Sixth Amendment's assurance of the "assistance of counsel" is necessary for a fair trial in any court, but it did not say that due process covers every other assurance in the first eight amendments.

What implications did this case have for the future?

Gideon v. *Wainwright* was one of several Supreme Court cases guaranteeing government payment to lawyers defending poor people accused of crimes. The Criminal Justice Act of 1964, signed into law the year after the *Gideon* decision, provided the funding.

8 *Miranda* v. *Arizona*
384 U.S. 436 (1966)

What was this case about?

The story. On March 13, 1963, a woman was kidnapped near Phoenix. Ernesto Miranda was arrested for the crime, and the victim identified him in a police lineup. Two officers then took him to a room to question him. Although at first Miranda denied the crime, after a short time he wrote out and signed a confession.

At the trial the officers testified that they had warned Miranda that anything he might say could be used against him in court and that Miranda had understood. The officers also said that he had confessed without any threats or force. They admitted, however, that they had not told Miranda about his right to silence or legal assistance. Miranda was found guilty. Eventually, he appealed to the U.S. Supreme Court.

The question. Is it a violation of the Fifth, Sixth, or Fourteenth Amendment to use a confession to convict someone who has not been informed of the constitutional rights to silence and legal assistance?

The issues. The Fifth Amendment ensures a person the right to remain silent: "No person . . . shall be compelled [forced] in any criminal case to be a witness against himself." Without such a right, innocent people could be tortured into confessing to a crime they did not commit. The Sixth Amendment ensures the assistance of a lawyer to defendants in criminal trials in federal courts. The Fourteenth Amendment does the same for defendants in state courts.

One issue is the point at which Fifth and Sixth Amendment rights begin. Do they begin only at the trial? Or do these rights begin earlier?

A deeper issue concerns the meaning of being forced to be a witness against oneself. Perhaps keeping a person ignorant of his or her rights is a kind of force. If so, then it violates the Fifth Amendment.

How was the case decided?

By a 5-to-4 majority, the Supreme Court ruled that taking Miranda's confession without informing him of his rights to silence and legal assistance had violated his constitutional rights.

What did the Court say about constitutional rights?

The Court ruled that the Fifth and Sixth Amendment rights exist as soon as a person is in custody. The Court also ruled that failing to inform the accused of his or her rights is a violation of the right not to testify against oneself.

Today if prisoners are not informed of their rights, judges may rule that what the accused tells the police cannot be used as evidence in court. Furthermore, the court must disregard any evidence that is based on what the accused said.

What implications did this case have for the future?

The *Miranda* ruling has been controversial because it deals with the delicate balance between protecting the accused and protecting society. A hotly debated aspect of the decision has been the ruling that confessions given by accused people who have not been informed of their rights may not be used as evidence. The Court did this to prevent innocent people from being found guilty. Some people argue, however, that it prevents the guilty from being convicted.

9 Roe v. Wade
410 U.S. 113 (1973)

What was this case about?

The story. In 1970 Norma McCorvey, an unmarried pregnant woman living in Texas, sought to obtain a legal abortion in a medical facility. Because of Texas's antiabortion statute, no licensed physician would agree to perform the procedure. McCorvey was financially unable to travel to another state with a less-restrictive abortion law. She faced either continuing an unwanted pregnancy or having the procedure performed in a nonmedical facility, which she believed would endanger her life.

McCorvey claimed that the Texas antiabortion law was unconstitutional because it interfered with her right of personal privacy that is protected by the Ninth and Fourteenth Amendments. She took legal action, naming the Dallas County district attorney, Henry Wade, in her lawsuit. Throughout the case, McCorvey used the pseudonym Jane Roe.

The question. Is it a violation of a person's right to privacy for a state to prevent a woman from terminating a pregnancy through an abortion?

The issues. The Fourteenth Amendment states that "no state shall make or enforce any law which shall abridge [diminish] the privileges . . . of citizens of the United States . . . nor deny to any person . . . the equal protection of the laws." The Ninth Amendment states that "the enumeration [naming] in the Constitution of certain rights shall not be construed [interpreted] to deny or disparage [reduce] others retained by the people." Do these amendments include and protect a woman's right to a legal abortion?

How was the case decided?

In an opinion written by Justice Harry Blackmun, the Court ruled that the Fourteenth Amendment's due process guarantee of personal liberty ensures the right to personal privacy. This guarantee protects a woman's decision about abortion and assures that a state's laws do not abridge this right. The vote was seven to two.

What did the Court say about constitutional rights?

In ruling that a state cannot prevent a woman from terminating a pregnancy during the first three months, the Court relied on the citizens' right to privacy. Justice Blackmun stated in his opinion that "[t]his right of privacy, whether it be founded in the Fourteenth Amendment's concept of personal liberty and restrictions upon state action, as we feel it is, or . . . in the Ninth Amendment's reservation of rights to the people, is broad enough to encompass [include] a woman's decision whether or not to terminate her pregnancy." In its ruling, however, the Court recognized the right of a state to regulate abortions as a pregnancy progressed. During the first three months of a pregnancy, a woman has a virtually unrestricted right to an abortion.

During the second trimester, a state can regulate abortions to protect a woman's health. Only in the final three months of a pregnancy can a state forbid an abortion, unless the procedure is necessary to protect a woman's life.

The ruling also said that a state cannot adopt a theory of when life begins. This prevents a state from giving a fetus the same rights as a newborn.

What implications did this case have for the future?

Since the 1973 ruling, related cases have been decided that some people claim weaken the legislative impact of *Roe* v. *Wade*. In *Harris* v. *McRae* (1980), the Court upheld a law that blocked the use of federal funds to pay for abortions for women on welfare. Critics of the ruling claimed that women who could not afford the procedure would, like Jane Roe, be faced with either continuing an unwanted pregnancy or resorting to dangerous measures to terminate it. The ruling in *Webster* v. *Reproductive Health Services* (1989) added more restrictions to the availability of abortions.

10 Regents of the University of California v. Bakke
438 U.S. 265 (1978)

What was this case about?

The story. A white man named Allan Bakke twice applied to the medical school at the University of California, Davis, during the years in which the medical school operated two different admissions programs. After the Civil Rights Act of 1964, schools and other institutions were under pressure to provide special admissions programs for minority students. There were, however, no specific guidelines on how to accomplish this.

At the University of California, Davis, medical school 84 of the 100 places in the incoming class were filled from the regular program. The remaining 16 spots were set aside for a special program that used a quota system. The regular program was for students of all races, as long as they met admission requirements, including a minimum grade point average. Only members of racial minorities could apply through the special program, and their grades did not have to meet the minimum.

Bakke applied through the regular program and was turned down. He thought he had been treated unfairly because in both years, students had been admitted through the special program whose grades and test scores were much lower than his. He sued the state university system. Bakke said the special program, established to fulfill the racial quota, violated his Fourteenth Amendment right to equal protection of the law.

The California Supreme Court made two rulings. One said that Davis's admission system was illegal and ordered Bakke admitted. The other ordered that in the future, admissions decisions must not take race into consideration. The California university system appealed to the U.S. Supreme Court.

The questions. First, does the use of a racial quota in admissions violate the Fourteenth Amendment's equal protection clause? Second, does this clause require that race be completely ignored in admissions?

The issues. Historically, most racial discrimination in our country has hurt members of racial minorities. Bakke complained of reverse discrimination, a type of discrimination that supposedly hurt members of the racial majority in order to help members of racial minorities.

The Fourteenth Amendment was primarily written because African Americans who had recently been freed from slavery needed protection from discrimination by the white majority. This fact suggests that the equal protection clause protects racial minorities more than the racial majority. On the other hand, what the amendment actually says is that no state may deny to any person the equal protection of the laws. This fact suggests that the equal protection clause gives the same protection to people of all races. The intent of the amendment seems to have been to protect minorities, but its wording does not specify this intent.

How was the case decided?

The U.S. Supreme Court agreed that racial quotas in admissions was unconstitutional and ordered that Bakke be admitted. It rejected the idea that an admissions system may never pay any attention to race.

What did the Court say about constitutional rights?

Justice Lewis Powell wrote the Court's opinion. He said that the equal protection clause does not completely prohibit states from taking race into account when they are making laws and official policies. However, it does make the consideration of race "suspect," or suspicious. When such a law or policy is challenged in court, judges must apply a two-part test. First, are the purposes of the law or policy legitimate? Second, is the consideration given to race necessary to achieve these purposes? California told the Court that its racial quota had four purposes.

Purpose 1. To correct the shortage of racial minorities in medical schools and among doctors. Justice Powell said that this purpose was not acceptable. "Preferring members of any one group for no reason other than race or ethnic origin is discrimination for its own sake."

Purpose 2. To counteract the effects of racial discrimination in society. Justice Powell said that this was an acceptable purpose. He approved of helping people who belong to groups that have been hurt by past discrimination. However, he said that helping them by hurting others is right only when it makes up for hurts caused by those other people. There was no evidence that Bakke had ever discriminated against people of racial minorities.

Purpose 3: To increase the number of doctors who will be willing to practice medicine in communities where there are not enough doctors. This purpose was also acceptable. However, California had not shown that racial quotas were needed to accomplish this purpose.

Purpose 4. To improve education by making the student body more diverse. This purpose, too, was acceptable. However, Justice Powell pointed out that racial diversity is only one aspect of overall diversity and that racial quotas are not the only way to increase racial diversity.

What implications did this case have for the future?

This decision revealed that the members of the Court disagreed sharply about reverse discrimination. Furthermore, Powell stressed that the Court's decision concerned only reverse racial discrimination. He warned that reverse sexual discrimination may or may not have to be treated the same way as reverse racial discrimination. In the 1982 case *Mississippi University for Women* v. *Hogan,* however, the Court ruled that it was unconstitutional for a state-run school of nursing to refuse admission to men.

GLOSSARY

This glossary contains terms you need to understand as you study American history. After each key term there is a brief definition or explanation of the meaning of the term as it is used in *The American Nation*. The page number refers to the page on which the term is introduced in the textbook.

Phonetic Respelling and Pronunciation Guide

Many of the key terms in this textbook have been respelled to help you pronounce them. The letter combinations used in the respellings throughout the narrative are explained in the following phonetic respelling and pronunciation guide. The guide is adapted from *Merriam-Webster's Collegiate Dictionary, Merriam-Webster's Geographical Dictionary,* and *Merriam-Webster's Biographical Dictionary.*

MARK	AS IN	RESPELLING	EXAMPLE
a	alphabet	a	*AL-fuh-bet
ā	Asia	ay	AY-zhuh
ä	cart, top	ah	KAHRT, TAHP
e	let, ten	e	LET, TEN
ē	even, leaf	ee	EE-vuhn, LEEF
i	it, tip, British	i	IT, TIP, BRIT-ish
ī	site, buy, Ohio	y	SYT, BY, oh-HY-oh
	iris	eye	EYE-ris
k	card	k	KAHRD
ō	over, rainbow	oh	OH-vuhr, RAYN-boh
ü	book, wood	ooh	BOOHK, WOOHD
ö	all, orchid	aw	AWL, AWR-kid
òi	foil, coin	oy	FOYL, KOYN
aù	out	ow	OWT
ə	cup, butter	uh	KUHP, BUHT-uhr
ü	rule, food	oo	ROOL, FOOD
yü	few	yoo	FYOO
zh	vision	zh	VIZH-uhn

*A syllable printed in small capital letters receives heavier emphasis than the other syllable(s) in a word.

A

abolitionists People who wanted to put an end to slavery. 78

acquired immune deficiency syndrome (AIDS) Often-fatal disease that forces the body's immune system to shut down, making it easier for a person to contract other fatal illnesses. 1057

Adamson Act Federal law reducing the workday for railroad workers from 10 to 8 hours with no cut in pay. 589

Adams-Onís Treaty (1819) Agreement in which Spain transferred East Florida to the United States. 229

affirmative action Practice by some government agencies, businesses, and schools of giving preference to ethnic minorities and women in admissions and hiring. 941

African Diaspora Forcible resettlement of millions of African people during the era of the slave trade. 28

Agricultural Adjustment Administration (AAA) Federal agency created by the Agricultural Adjustment Act in 1933 to reduce farmers' output and increase crop prices. 743

Agricultural Revolution An ancient shift from hunting and gathering to the domestication of plants. 7

Albany Plan of Union (1754) Plan written by Benjamin Franklin and other colonial delegates that called for the colonies to form a close confederation to promote defense. 89

Alianza Federal de Mercedes Federal Alliance of Land Grants; group led by Reies López Tijerina to try to regain land taken from Mexican Americans. 956

Alien and Sedition Acts (1798) Laws passed by a Federalist-dominated Congress making it easier to deport foreigners and illegal to print or speak words hostile to the government. 203

Alliance for Progress President Kennedy's program for sending economic aid to Latin America; designed to encourage democratic reforms and to promote capitalism. 898

Allied Powers World War I alliance that included Britain, France, Russia, and later the United States, and that fought against the Central Powers. 629; World War II alliance between Britain and France, and later the United States and other countries, that fought against the Axis Powers. 791

American Anti-Slavery Society Group founded in 1833 by abolitionists; the first national antislavery organization devoted to immediate abolition and to racial equality. 300

American Association of Retired Persons (AARP) Largest lobbying group on behalf of senior citizens; founded in 1958. 964

American Colonization Society Group organized in the early 1800s to send freed African Americans to Africa. 297

American Federation of Labor (AFL) Union founded in 1886 by Samuel Gompers for skilled workers. 486

American Gothic One of the most famous regionalist paintings, by Grant Wood. **763**

American Indian Movement (AIM) Organization formed in 1968 to fight for the rights of American Indians. **962**

American Plan Policy promoted by business leaders during the 1920s that called for open shops. **671**

Americans with Disabilities Act (ADA) (1990) Law that prohibits discrimination against people with disabilities in employment, transportation, telephone services, and public buildings. **1062**

American System Plan developed by Henry Clay for raising tariffs to pay for internal improvements such as roads and canals. **232**

amnesty An official pardon issued by the government. **403**

Anaconda Plan Union plan during the Civil War for a naval blockade; compared to an Anaconda snake. **375**

anarchists People who oppose all forms of government. **485**

Anasazi Civilization that existed in the Southwest of the present-day United States between A.D. 700 and the 1300s. **11**

antebellum Pre–Civil War. **265**

Antifederalists People who feared a powerful national government and opposed the Constitution as written. **146**

anti-Semitism Hatred of Jews. **786**

apartheid South African political system in which the white minority ruled and the black majority had few rights. **1030**

Apollo 11 U.S. space mission that resulted in the first man on the Moon on July 20, 1969. **1036**

appeasement Giving in to an aggressor to avoid conflict. **790**

arbitration Process by which two opposing sides allow a third party to settle a dispute. **576**

Area Redevelopment Act (ARA) Law passed in 1961 that provided financial assistance to economically distressed regions. **907**

Articles of Confederation (1777) Document that created an association of states while guaranteeing each state its "sovereignty, freedom, and independence." **137**

assembly line Production system created by Henry Ford to make goods faster by moving parts on a conveyer belt past workers. **687**

Atlantic Charter (1941) Pledge signed by U.S. president Franklin D. Roosevelt and British prime minister Winston Churchill not to acquire new territory as a result of World War II and to work for peace after the war. **794**

Atomic Energy Act (1946) Federal law that created the Atomic Energy Commission to oversee nuclear weapons research and to promote peacetime uses of atomic energy. **840**

automation Use of machines to replace humans in production. **871**

auto-touring Craze that encouraged Americans to take long sightseeing trips in their automobiles. **690**

Axis Powers Military alliance formed by Italy and Germany in 1936; later joined by Japan. **790**

Aztec Mexica; fierce warrior empire that dominated present-day Mexico in the Middle Ages. **9**

B

baby boom Soaring birthrate in the United States following World War II. **873**

Bacon's Rebellion (1676) Attack led by Nathaniel Bacon against American Indians and the colonial government in Virginia. **76**

balance of trade Relationship between the goods a country buys from other countries and the goods it sells to other countries. **82**

Ballinger-Pinchot affair Incident in which President William Howard Taft fired Gifford Pinchot as head of the U.S. Forestry Service for criticizing Secretary of the Interior Richard Ballinger's sale of Alaskan land; weakened support for Taft. **583**

bank holiday (1933) New Deal proclamation that temporarily closed every U.S. bank to stop massive withdrawals. **740**

Bank of the United States National Bank; banking system created in 1791 to support the U.S. economy. **194**

barbed wire Cheap fencing material invented by Joseph Glidden in 1874. **453**

Baruch Plan (1946) Bernard Baruch's proposal to create an international agency that would impose penalties on countries that violated international controls on nuclear weapons. **840**

Bataan Death March (1942) Brutal forced march of U.S. and Filipino prisoners during World War II up the Bataan Peninsula; more than 10,000 died. **804**

Battle of Antietam (1862) Union victory in Maryland during the Civil War that marked the bloodiest single-day battle in U.S. military history. **386**

Battle of Bunker Hill (1775) Revolutionary War battle in Boston that resulted in more than 1,000 British casualties and fewer than 450 Patriot casualties. **112**

Battle of Fallen Timbers (1794) Battle near present-day Toledo, Ohio, between U.S. troops and an American Indian confederation; opened some Indian lands to settlement. **196**

Battle of Gettysburg (1863) Union victory at Gettysburg, Pennsylvania, during the Civil War that turned the tide against the Confederates; more than 50,000 soldiers died. **390**

Battle of Iwo Jima (1945) Six-week struggle for control of a key Pacific island that resulted in an Allied victory. **824**

Battle of Leyte Gulf (1944) Last, largest, and most decisive naval engagement in the Pacific during World War II; afterward, the Japanese fleet no longer seriously threatened the Allies. **822**

Battle of Midway (1942) World War II battle in which the Allied forces crippled Japan's navy. **804**

Battle of New Orleans (1815) Greatest U.S. victory in the War of 1812; actually took place two weeks after the signing of a peace treaty that ended the war. **214**

Battle of Okinawa (1945) Bloody battle in the Pacific during World War II; resulted in an Allied victory. **824**

Battle of San Jacinto (1836) Final battle of the Texas Revolution; resulted in independence for Texas. **320**

Battle of Saratoga (1777) Turning point of the Revolutionary War; Patriot victory led to more support from European powers. **126**

Battle of Shiloh (1862) Civil War battle; resulted in greater Union control over the Mississippi River valley. **382**

Battle of the Argonne Forest (1918) Successful Allied effort to push back German troops from a rail center in Sedan, France. **649**

Battle of the Atlantic World War II naval campaign fought between German U-boats and Allied naval and air forces. **815**

Battle of the Bulge (1944) World War II battle in which the Allies defeated the final German offensive. **818**

Battle of the Coral Sea (1942) World War II battle in which the Allies stopped the Japanese advance to New Guinea. **804**

Battle of the Little Bighorn (1876) Battle between U.S. soldiers, led by George Armstrong Custer, and Sioux warriors; worst U.S. Army defeat in the West. **437**

Battle of the Somme (1916) World War I battle in which the British lost some 60,000 troops in a single day. **631**

Battle of the Thames (1813) War of 1812 battle won by U.S. troops, led by William Henry Harrison; broke the British hold on the Northwest Territory. **212**

Battle of Tippecanoe (1811) U.S. victory over an American Indian confederation that wanted to stop white settlement in the Northwest Territory; increased tensions between Britain and the United States. **211**

Battle of Trenton (1776) Revolutionary War battle in New Jersey in which Patriot forces captured more than 900 Hessian troops fighting for Britain. **125**

Battle of Yorktown (1781) Last major battle of the Revolutionary War; site of British general Charles Cornwallis's surrender to the Patriots in Virginia. **129**

Bear Flag Revolt (1846) Revolt against Mexico by American settlers in California who declared the area an independent republic. **325**

bear market Downward trend in stock prices. **715**

beats Small but influential group of writers who challenged literary conventions and the lifestyle of the middle-class in the 1950s. **885**

benevolent societies Organizations that helped immigrants in cases of sickness, unemployment, and death. **495**

Berlin Airlift (1948–49) Operation in which British and U.S. planes carried food and supplies to West Berlin, which was cut off by a Soviet blockade. **842**

Berlin Wall Barrier built between East and West Berlin; widely recognized symbol of the Cold War. **900**

Bessemer process Efficient method of making steel; developed by British inventor Henry Bessemer and American William Kelly in the 1850s. **464**

bicameral A legislature made up of two houses. **144**

Big Four Collective name given to U.S. president Woodrow Wilson, British prime minister David Lloyd George, French premier Georges Clemenceau, and Italian prime minister Vittorio Orlando during the peace conference at Versailles. **650**

Bilingual Education Act (1974) Law that encouraged public schools to provide instruction to students in their primary language while they learned English. **1033**

Bill of Rights First 10 amendments to the U.S. Constitution; ratified in 1791. **191**

Black Codes Laws passed in the southern states during Reconstruction that greatly limited the freedom of former slaves. **405**

black nationalism Movement to create a new political state for African Americans in Africa. **678**

Black Panther Party Political organization formed in the 1960s that called for empowerment and defense for African Americans. **936**

Black Power Black separatist movement that grew out of frustration with the slow pace of the civil rights movement. **936**

Blackshirts Followers of Benito Mussolini who gained power in Italy in the early 1920s. **784**

Black Thursday October 24, 1929; the day investors caused a panic on Wall Street by selling their stocks. **715**

Black Tuesday October 29, 1929; day the stock market crashed; contributed to the Great Depression. **716**

Bland-Allison Act (1878) Federal law that required the government to buy and mint silver each month. **535**

Blitzkrieg "Lightning war"; type of fast-moving warfare used by German forces in 1939. **793**

blues Jazz-influenced music that grew out of slave music and religious spirituals; featured heartfelt lyrics and altered or slurred notes that echoed the mood of the lyrics. **702**

Bolsheviks Group of radical Russian socialists who seized power in 1917 following the overthrow of the czar. **647**

bonanza farm Large-scale farm usually owned by a large company and run like a factory. **445**

Bonus Army Group of World War I veterans who marched on Washington, D.C., in 1932 to demand the immediate payment of their pension bonuses. **734**

Boston Massacre (1770) Incident in which British soldiers fired into a group of colonists gathered in front of a customs house, killing several people. **106**

Boston police strike (1919) Failed police strike that led to public disorder and the firing of all striking officers. **663**

Boston Tea Party (1773) Protest against the Tea Act in which a group of colonists boarded British tea ships and dumped 342 chests of tea into Boston Harbor. **108**

bourgeoisie The urban middle class; originated in the Middle Ages and was made up of merchants who supported the monarchs. **20**

Boxer Rebellion (1900) Revolt in which Chinese nationalists known as Boxers attacked foreigners in order to end foreign involvement in China's affairs; put down by an international force after two months. **602**

braceros Mexican farm and railroad workers who came to the United States during World War II. **811**

breadlines Lines formed by people waiting for free food, such as those that occurred during the Great Depression. **722**

brinkmanship Policy in the 1950s that called for threatening all-out war in order to confront Communist aggression. **848**

British invasion Introduction of new British bands to Americans in the 1960s. **970**

Brotherhood of Sleeping Car Porters Union founded by A. Philip Randolph in 1925 to help African Americans who worked for the Pullman Company. **678**

Brown Berets Activist group formed in 1967 in response to police treatment of Mexican Americans. **957**

Brownshirts Nazi storm troopers. **785**

Brown v. Board of Education (1954) Supreme Court case that declared "separate but equal" public schools unconstitutional. **879**

bull market Upward trend in stock prices. **715**

Bureau of Indian Affairs Government agency responsible for managing American Indian issues. **434**

Bursum Bill Bill proposed in 1922 to legalize non-Indian claims to Pueblo lands in the Southwest; failed to pass. **681**

business cycle Regular ups and downs of business in a free-enterprise economy. **719**

busing Sending children to schools outside of their neighborhoods, usually to promote integration. **940**

C

cabinet Group that advises the U.S. president, made up of the heads of the executive departments. **191**

California Trail Southern branch of the Oregon Trail; took settlers to northern California. **336**

Californios Spanish settlers who lived in California. **335**

Camp David Accords (1978) Peace agreement between Israel and Egypt, negotiated by President Jimmy Carter. **1031**

capitalism Economic system based on a free market and private ownership of property. **192**

caravels Small maneuverable Portuguese ships that were fast. **26**

carpetbaggers Northern Republicans who moved to the South during Reconstruction. **416**

caudillos Latin American military leaders during the 1930s who used force to maintain order. **783**

Cayuse War (1847–50) Conflict between the Cayuse and American settlers in Oregon Country; ended when U.S. officials executed five Cayuse leaders. **333**

Central Intelligence Agency (CIA) Federal agency created in the late 1940s to conduct covert operations. **848**

Central Powers World War I alliance that included Austria-Hungary, Germany, the Ottoman Empire, and Bulgaria. **629**

Challenger U.S. space shuttle that exploded in 1986 after takeoff, killing all seven crew members. **1056**

Charter of 1606 Document issued by King James I of England that licensed the Plymouth Company and the London Company to organize settlements in Virginia. **56**

checks and balances System established by the Constitution; allows for sharing of power among branches of government and prevents any one branch from becoming too powerful. **151**

Chernobyl disaster (1986) Nuclear accident near Kiev, Ukraine, that released massive amounts of radiation into the air. **1088**

Children's Defense Fund (CDF) Children's rights organization founded in 1973. **965**

Chinese Exclusion Act (1882) Law that denied U.S. citizenship to people born in China and prohibited Chinese immigration of laborers. **497**

circumnavigate To sail completely around the world. **41**

City Beautiful movement Movement that stressed the importance of including public parks and attractive boulevards in the designs of cities. **508**

city-state An independent city. **9**

Civilian Conservation Corps (CCC) New Deal agency established in 1933; employed young men on conservation projects. **742**

Civil Rights Act of 1866 First U.S. civil rights law; declared everyone born in the United States a citizen with full civil rights. **410**

Civil Rights Act of 1875 Law that prohibited businesses that served the public from discriminating against African Americans. **418**

Civil Rights Act of 1957 Law that made it a federal crime to prevent qualified persons from voting. **882**

Civil Rights Act of 1964 Law banning racial discrimination in the use of public facilities and in employment practices. **927**

Clayton Antitrust Act (1914) Law that clarified and strengthened the Sherman Antitrust Act by clearly defining what a monopoly or trust was. **588**

closed shop Workplace in which all the employees must belong to a union. **555**

Cold War (1945–91) Long power struggle between the United States and the Soviet Union; waged mostly on economic and political fronts, rather than on the battlefield. **738**

Committee of Correspondence Group formed in the 1770s to keep colonists informed about British violations of their rights. **107**

Committee on Civil Rights Committee appointed by President Harry S Truman in 1946 to examine racial issues. **867**

Committee on Public Information (CPI) Agency created in 1917 to increase public support for World War I. **645**

Committee to Re-elect the President (CREEP) Organization that ran President Richard Nixon's 1972 re-election campaign; used "dirty tricks" to undermine the Democrats. **1019**

Common Sense (1776) Pamphlet written by Thomas Paine that stirred up public support for the American Revolution and called for the end of British rule in the colonies. **114**

Commonwealth of Independent States (CIS) An alliance formed by many of the former Soviet republics in December 1991. **1059**

communism Political theory that proposes individual ownership should not be allowed, but rather all people should collectively own property and the means of production. **474**

Compromise of 1850 Agreement proposed by Henry Clay; allowed California to enter the Union as a free state and divided the rest of the Mexican Cession into two territories where slavery would be decided by popular sovereignty; also settled land claims between Texas and New Mexico, abolished the slave trade in the District of Columbia, and toughened fugitive slave laws. **349**

Compromise of 1877 Agreement to settle the disputed presidential election of 1876; Democrats agreed to accept Republican Rutherford B. Hayes as president in return for the removal of federal troops from the South. **419**

compulsory education laws Laws requiring parents to send their children to school. **505**

Comstock Lode One of the world's richest silver mines, discovered in Nevada in the mid-1800s. **455**

concurrent powers Powers that are shared by the federal and state governments. **150**

Confederate States of America The Confederacy; nation formed by seceding southern states in 1861. **362**

Congress of Industrial Organizations (CIO) Labor group formed in 1935 that organized all workers in a particular industry into one union. **752**

Congress of Racial Equality (CORE) Northern-based civil rights group that organized nonviolent protests. **923**

conquistadores Spanish conquerors of the Americas. **42**

conscription Compulsory draft into military service. **380**

conspicuous consumption Term coined by social scientist Thorstein Veblen to describe spending money just to display one's wealth. **500**

Constitutional Convention (1787) Meeting in Philadelphia at which state delegates wrote the U.S. Constitution. **142**

containment U.S. foreign policy followed during the Cold War that sought to prevent the expansion of Soviet communism. **839**

Contract with America 1994 Republican reform plan. **1072**

Contras Anti-Sandinista rebel army in Nicaragua that was supported by the Reagan administration. **1047**

Convention of 1818 Agreement between the United States and Britain that established the U.S.-Canada border at the 49th parallel west to the Rocky Mountains. **227**

convoy system Use of armed vessels to escort unarmed merchant vessels transporting troops, supplies, or volunteers through the North Atlantic during World War I. **639**

cooperatives Groups that pool members' resources to sell products directly to markets and to buy goods at wholesale prices. **532**

Copperheads Northern Democrats who sympathized with the South in the Civil War. **381**

corporation Company that sells shares of ownership, called stock, to investors in order to raise money. **474**

Corporation for Public Broadcasting Nonprofit organization created during the Johnson administration; offers educational television programming. **914**

cotton gin Device developed by Eli Whitney in 1793 to separate short-staple cotton seeds from the bolls. **263**

Council of Economic Advisers Federal agency created by the Employment Act of 1946 to counsel the president on economic policy. **864**

Council of Federated Organizations (COFO) Group created by several civil rights organizations to coordinate voter registration drives in the 1960s. **929**

counterculture Alternative lifestyle; for example, the culture of the hippies in the 1960s. **967**

Crittenden Compromise (1860) John Crittenden's plan to resolve conflict between North and South by extending the Missouri Compromise line westward through the remaining territories; rejected by President Lincoln. **368**

crop-lien system Arrangement in which sharecroppers had to promise their crops to merchants in exchange for supplies on credit. **420**

Crusade for Justice Group founded in 1966 by Rodolfo "Corky" Gonzales to promote Mexican American nationalism. **958**

Crusades (1096–1221) Series of five wars fought between Christians and Muslims for control of Palestine. **20**

Cuban missile crisis (1962) Standoff between the United States and the Soviet Union in which the Soviets agreed to remove missiles from Cuba if the United States promised not to invade the island; followed by an easing of Cold War tensions. **902**

D

Dawes General Allotment Act (1887) Legislation that required American Indian lands be surveyed and Indian families given allotments of 160 acres, with the remaining land sold; resulted in the loss of two thirds of American Indian land. **440**

D-Day (1944) June 6; World War II Allied invasion of France. **816**

Declaration of Independence (1776) Statement of the Second Continental Congress that officially declared the new United States of America to be independent of Great Britain. **115**

Declaration of Sentiments (1848) Statement written and signed by women's rights supporters who attended the Seneca Falls Convention; modeled after the Declaration of Independence, it detailed their beliefs about women's rights. **304**

Declaratory Act (1766) Law passed by Parliament that asserted its right to make laws governing its American colonies. **104**

defoliants Chemicals that strip land of vegetation. **986**

delegated powers Powers granted to the federal government. **150**

demobilization Transition from wartime to peacetime production and employment levels. **662**

Democratic Party Political party founded by supporters of Andrew Jackson in the 1820s. **240**

denominations Religious groups. **287**

Department of Energy Executive department created in 1977 to oversee energy issues. **1027**

depression A sharp drop in business activity, accompanied by rising unemployment. **140**

détente Period in the 1970s when tensions between the United States and the Soviet Union lessened. **1018**

Diamond Sutra The world's first-known printed book, made in China in 868. **13**

direct primary Nominating election in which voters choose the candidates who later run in a general election. **570**

disarmament Reduction of the size of a country's military. **775**

Dixiecrats States' Rights Party; formed in 1946 by southern Democrats who were dissatisfied with President Harry S Truman's support for civil rights issues. **868**

doctrine of nullification Belief that states had the right to disobey federal laws that they considered unconstitutional. **246**

dollar diplomacy President William Howard Taft's policy of influencing Latin American affairs through economic influence rather than military force. **616**

domino theory Cold War belief that if one nation in Southeast Asia fell to communism, the rest of Southeast Asia would also fall. **980**

Donner party (1846–47) Group of travelers to California who were stranded in the Sierra Nevada during the winter; some 42 members of the party died. **331**

doves Americans who opposed the Vietnam War. **989**

Dred Scott **decision** (1857) Supreme Court ruling that African Americans were not U.S. citizens, that the Missouri Compromise's restriction on slavery was unconstitutional, and that Congress did not have the right to ban slavery in any federal territory. **359**

drivers Slaves who helped overseers supervise other slaves. **272**

Dust Bowl Name given to parts of the Great Plains in the 1930s after a severe drought struck the region. **754**

duty Import tax. **102**

E

Educational Amendments Act (1972) Federal law prohibiting sexual discrimination in higher education. **952**

Education for All Handicapped Children Act (1975) Federal law requiring public schools to provide education for children with physical and mental disabilities. **963**

Eighteenth Amendment (1919) Constitutional amendment that barred the manufacture, sale, and distribution of alcoholic beverages in the United States; repealed in 1933. **561**

elastic clause "Necessary and proper clause"; clause of the U.S. Constitution that allows Congress to exert its powers in ways not specifically outlined in the Constitution. **155**

electors Delegates selected by state legislatures to vote for the president and vice president. **146**

Elementary and Secondary Education Act (1965) Federal law that provided $1.3 billion to aid schools in poor areas. **914**

Elkins Act (1903) Federal law that prohibited shippers from accepting rebates. **577**

Emancipation Proclamation (1863) Order announced by President Abraham Lincoln in 1862 that freed the slaves in areas rebelling against the Union; took effect January 1, 1863. **386**

Embargo Act (1807) Law that stopped the shipment of food and other American products to all foreign ports. **210**

Employment Act (1946) Law that established the Council of Economic Advisers and pledged that the government would promote full employment and production. **864**

empresarios Agents who contracted with the Mexican government to bring settlers to Texas in the early 1800s. **317**

encomienda System in Spanish America that gave settlers the right to control the labor of local American Indians. **37**

Endangered Species Act (1973) Law to protect wildlife in danger of extinction. **1016**

Enforcement Acts (1870–71) Three acts passed by Congress allowing the government to use military force to stop violence against southern African Americans. **417**

Enlightenment Revolution in ideas that swept across Europe in the 1700s. **84**

Enola Gay U.S. B-29 bomber that dropped the first atomic bomb on Hiroshima, Japan, on August 6, 1945. **825**

Environmental Protection Agency (EPA) Federal agency established in 1970 to enforce environmental laws. **1016**

Equal Pay Act (1963) Federal law that made it illegal for employers to pay female workers less than male workers for the same job. **949**

Equal Rights Amendment (ERA) Proposed constitutional amendment that would guarantee women's rights by outlawing discrimination based on gender. **671**

Erie Canal Major canal that linked the Hudson Bay with Lake Erie; completed in 1825. **234**

escalation President Lyndon B. Johnson's policy of building up U.S. military forces in the Vietnam War. **985**

Espionage Act (1917) Federal law that outlawed acts of treason during World War I. **646**

European Union (EU) Western European trading bloc formed in 1993. **1087**

Exodusters Southern African Americans who settled western lands in the late 1800s. **444**

F

factory system System that cuts costs and increases output by relying on machines to help do everything under one roof. **256**

Fair Deal Series of reform programs proposed by President Harry S Truman after the 1948 election; achieved mixed results. **869**

Fair Employment Practices Committee (FEPC) Group created in 1941 to prevent discrimination in war industries and government jobs. **811**

Family and Medical Leave Act (1993) Federal law requiring large companies to provide workers up to 12 weeks of unpaid leave for family and medical emergencies without losing their medical insurance or jobs. **1086**

Family Assistance Plan (FAP) President Richard M. Nixon's proposed replacement for the welfare system; would guarantee families a minimum income; voted down by the Senate. **1012**

Fascist Party Political party founded in Italy in the 1920s; followers believed a military-dominated government should control all aspects of society. **784**

Federal Deposit Insurance Corporation (FDIC) New Deal agency created in 1933 to insure bank savings deposits. **741**

federalism Division of power between a strong central government and state governments. **143**

Federalist, The The *Federalist Papers;* book of essays written by supporters of the Constitution in 1787 and 1788. **147**

Federalists Supporters of ratification of the Constitution. **146**

Federal Project Number One New Deal program that encouraged pride in American culture by employing thousands of artists and writers. **759**

Federal Reserve Act (1913) Act that created a national banking system to help the government control the economy. **588**

Federal Trade Commission (FTC) Commission established in 1914 to investigate corporations and to try to keep them from conducting unfair trade practices. **589**

feminists Women's rights activists. **671**

feudalism System in the Middle Ages in which nobles pledged loyalty and military aid to rulers in return for land and protection. **19**

Fifteenth Amendment (1870) Constitutional amendment that gave African American men the right to vote. **414**

54th Massachusetts Infantry African American Union regiment that helped capture Fort Wagner in South Carolina during the Civil War. **387**

fire-eaters Southern political leaders who held extreme pro-slavery views. **347**

First Battle of Bull Run (1861) Battle of Manassas; first major battle of the Civil War, resulting in a Confederate victory. **373**

First Battle of the Marne (1914) World War I battle in which the Allies stopped a German advance near the Marne River. **630**

First Continental Congress (1774) Convention of colonial delegates to discuss their grievances against Parliament. **109**

First Seminole War (1817–18) Conflict between U.S. forces and the Seminole in Spanish Florida; increased conflict between the United States and Spain. **228**

flappers Young women in the 1920s who challenged social traditions with their dress and behavior. **695**

flexible response Strategy adopted by the Kennedy administration of keeping a range of options open for dealing with international crises. **898**

Food Administration World War I agency headed by Herbert Hoover; encouraged increased agricultural production and the conservation of existing food supplies. **641**

Foraker Act (1900) U.S. law establishing that Puerto Rico's governor and upper house be appointed by the United States and lower house be elected by Puerto Ricans. **612**

Fordney-McCumber Tariff Act (1922) Federal law that pushed tariff rates on manufactured goods to an all-time high and levied high duties on imported agricultural goods. **670**

forty-niners Gold seekers who traveled to California during the gold rush. **336**

Fourteen Points (1918) President Woodrow Wilson's plan for organizing post–World War I Europe and for avoiding future wars. **650**

Fourteenth Amendment (1868) Constitutional amendment giving full rights of citizenship to all people born or naturalized in the United States, except for American Indians. **410**

Freedmen's Bureau Agency established by Congress in 1865 to help southerners left homeless and hungry by the Civil War. **409**

freedom of contract Freedom of workers to negotiate the terms of their employment. **555**

Freedom Riders A group of civil rights workers who took bus trips through southern states in 1961 to protest illegal bus segregation. **923**

Freedom Summer Campaign to register African American voters in Mississippi during the summer of 1964. **930**

free enterprise Belief that the economy will prosper if businesses are left free from government regulation and allowed to compete in a free market. **473**

Freeport Doctrine (1858) Statement made by Stephen Douglas during the Lincoln-Douglas debates arguing that people in the territories had the power to ban slavery by refusing to pass laws to protect it. **360**

Free-Soil Party Political party formed by antislavery Whigs and Democrats in 1848; opposed the expansion of slavery into the territories. **345**

French and Indian War (1754–63) Conflict between the British and French that began in the American colonies and spread to Europe as the Seven Years' War. **90**

French Revolution French rebellion begun in 1789 in which the French people overthrew the monarchy and made the country a republic. **197**

Fugitive Slave Act (1850) Law that made it a federal crime to help runaway slaves and allowed for the arrest of escaped slaves even in areas where slavery was illegal. **351**

Fundamentalism Protestant religious movement that teaches that traditional Christian doctrine should be accepted without question and that the Bible is literally true. **700**

Fundamental Orders of Connecticut (1639) Colonial document that is widely considered to be the first written constitution in the world. **71**

G

Gadsden Purchase (1853) U.S. purchase of land from Mexico that included the southern parts of present-day Arizona and New Mexico. **326**

gang labor Work system in which groups of slaves performed specialized jobs. **272**

generation gap Difference in years, attitudes, and cultural beliefs between generations; applied to baby boomers and their elders during the 1960s. **966**

genocide Deliberate annihilation of an entire people. **817**

Gettysburg Address (1863) Speech given by President Abraham Lincoln to dedicate a cemetery at the Gettysburg battlefield; classic statement of democratic ideals. **391**

GI Bill of Rights (1944) Servicemen's Readjustment Act; established pensions and government loans to veterans for education, businesses, or to buy houses or farms. **864**

Gilded Age Name applied by Mark Twain and Charles Dudley Warner to late 1800s America to describe the corruption and greed that lurked below the surface of society. **527**

glasnost Soviet policy established in the 1980s that promoted political openness and freedom of expression. **1053**

Glorious Revolution (1688) A bloodless revolt in England against Catholic king James II that led to his overthrow and put Protestants Mary and William of Orange on the throne. **84**

gold standard Type of monetary system in which money is worth a specific amount in gold. **534**

Gone With the Wind (1936) The best-selling novel of the 1930s, by Margaret Mitchell; made into one of the most popular films of all time in 1939. **760**

Good Neighbor Policy President Franklin D. Roosevelt's foreign policy of promoting better relations with Latin America through mutual respect. **780**

graduated income tax System in which the rate of taxation varies according to income. **532**

graft Acquisition of money or political power through illegal or dishonest methods. **521**

Gramm-Rudman-Hollings Act (1985) Law that required the government to cut spending when the deficit grows above a certain level. **1050**

Grapes of Wrath, The (1939) John Steinbeck's classic novel about Dust Bowl migrants who move to California during the Great Depression. **760**

Gray Panthers Activist group for senior citizens' rights; founded by Maggie Kuhn in 1970. **964**

Great Awakening Series of religious revivals that swept through the British colonies in the mid-1700s. **84**

Great Compromise (1787) Agreement worked out at the Constitutional Convention; granted each state an equal voice in the upper house of the legislature and representation according to population in the lower house. **144**

Great Depression Serious global economic decline that began with the crash of the U.S. stock market in 1929. **717**

Great Migration Mass migration of some 60,000 English people to the Americas in the 1600s. **68**; mass migration of African Americans to the northern United States during and after World War I. **644**

Great Society President Lyndon B. Johnson's program to improve U.S. society. **912**

Great Upheaval (1886) Year of intense worker strikes and violent labor confrontations in the United States. **485**

gross national product Total value of all goods and services produced by a country in a given year. **717**

guerrilla warfare Type of fighting in which soldiers use swift hit-and-run attacks to wear down the enemy. **128**

H

habeas corpus Protection against unlawful imprisonment. **381**

hajj Trip made by Muslims to the Islamic holy city of Mecca. **17**

hard-rock mining Technique that involves sinking deep mine shafts to get at ore in veins of rock. **459**

Harlem Renaissance Period of great African American artistic accomplishment that began in the 1920s in the Harlem neighborhood of New York City. **704**

Hartford Convention (1814) Meeting of New England Federalists that proposed a constitutional amendment that would limit the powers of Congress and the southern states; viewed as disloyal, it weakened the power of the Federalist Party. **215**

hawks Americans who supported the Vietnam War. **989**

Hay–Bunau-Varilla Treaty (1903) Agreement that gave the United States unending sovereignty over a 10-mile-wide canal across the Isthmus of Panama. **613**

Haymarket Riot (1886) Incident in which a bomb exploded during a labor protest held in Haymarket Square in Chicago, killing several police officers. **485**

Hepburn Act (1906) Law that authorized the Interstate Commerce Commission to set railroad rates and to regulate other companies engaged in interstate commerce. **577**

Highway Act (1956) Law that provided money to create a national highway system. **872**

Ho Chi Minh Trail Network of jungle paths from North Vietnam through Laos and Cambodia and into South Vietnam; was the major supply route of the Vietcong. **986**

Hollywood Ten Group of film directors and writers who went to jail rather than answer questions from the House Un-American Activities Committee. **851**

Holocaust Nazi Germany's slaughter of European Jews. **817**

Homestead Act (1862) Law to encourage settlement in the West by giving government-owned land to small farmers. **442**

horizontal integration Ownership of several companies making the same product. **477**

hot line Teletype connection between the United States and the Soviet Union that allowed leaders to communicate directly during a crisis. **902**

House of Burgesses Colonial Virginia's elected assembly. **76**

House Un-American Activities Committee (HUAC) Congressional committee originally created in 1938 to investigate fascists; became known for investigating U.S. citizens accused of communist ties in the late 1940s. **851**

hunter-gatherers People who hunt animals and gather wild plants to provide for their needs. **4**

hydraulic mining Mining technique that uses water pressure to remove gravel and dirt, exposing the minerals underneath. **459**

hydrogen bomb H-bomb; a type of nuclear bomb. **855**

I

Immigration Act of 1924 Federal law reducing the annual immigration quota for each nationality to 2 percent of the 1890 census figures, plus 100 Japanese immigrants. **680**

Immigration Act of 1990 Federal law that increased the number of immigrants allowed into the United States each year. **1085**

Immigration Restriction League Organization formed in 1894 that sought to impose a literacy test on all immigrants to the United States. **497**

impeachment Process of bringing charges against the president. **151**

imperialism Quest for colonial empires. **598**

impressment British practice in the early 1800s of kidnapping American sailors to force them to serve in the British navy. **198**

Inca South American civilization that controlled the Andes. **9**

indentured servant Colonist who received free passage to North America in exchange for working for those who paid his or her passage for a certain number of years. **59**

Indian Removal Act (1830) Act that authorized the relocation of American Indians from east of the Mississippi River to Indian Territory in present-day Oklahoma. **244**

Industrial Revolution Period of dynamic changes in manufacturing and production that began in Britain in the mid-1700s. **236**

Industrial Workers of the World (IWW) Union formed in 1905 that opposed capitalism. **556**

inflation An increase in the price of all goods. **55**

initiative Policy allowing voters to introduce new legislation. **571**

Initiative on Race Initiative launched by President Bill Clinton's in 1997 to encourage discussion of racial issues and concerns. **1078**

insider trading Use of confidential financial information by stockbrokers for personal gain. **1050**

installment plan A way of purchasing goods in which the consumer pays for goods in small increments over time. **692**

interchangeable parts Process developed by Eli Whitney in the 1790s that called for mass production by use of identical, replaceable parts. **237**

Intermediate-Range Nuclear Forces Treaty (INF) (1985) Treaty signed by President Ronald Reagan and Soviet leader Mikhail Gorbachev; eliminated all medium-range nuclear weapons from Europe. **1054**

Internal Security Act (1950) Law that required suspected communist groups to register with the government and imposed controls on immigrants suspected of being communist sympathizers. **852**

International Ladies' Garment Workers Union (ILGWU) Influential union established in New York City in 1900 to organize workers in sewing shops. **556**

Internet Worldwide system of computer networks. **1083**

internment Forced relocation and imprisonment of people. **812**

Interstate Commerce Act (1887) Law that regulated railroad shipping between states. **532**

Intolerable Acts (1774) Coercive Acts; four laws passed by Parliament to punish colonists for the Boston Tea Party and to tighten government control of the colonies. **108**

Iran hostage crisis (1979–81) Situation in which 53 Americans were taken hostage from the U.S. Embassy in Tehran, Iran. **1042**

Iran-Contra affair Name given to the 1980s scandal in which the Reagan administration secretly sold weapons to Iran in exchange for the release of American hostages in Lebanon and then used the profits from the sale to fund the Contras in Nicaragua. **1051**

Iroquois League Political confederation of five northeastern American Indian tribes formed in the 1400s or 1500s. **88**

island-hopping U.S. World War II strategy of conquering only the Pacific islands that were important to the Allied advance toward Japan. **821**

isolationism National policy of avoiding involvement in the affairs of other nations. **774**

J

Jay's Treaty (1794) Agreement negotiated by John Jay in which the British agreed to give up their northwestern forts in exchange for the United States paying debts owed to the British. **199**

jazz Music that originated with African American musicians in New Orleans and gained popularity in the 1920s. **702**

Jim Crow laws Laws that enforced segregation in the South. **422**

Jones Act of 1916 U.S. law that gave Filipinos the right to elect both houses of their legislature. **611**

judicial review Power of the courts to declare an act of Congress unconstitutional. **205**

Judiciary Act of 1789 Law that created a federal court system. **191**

juvenile delinquency Antisocial behavior by young people. **876**

K

---

kamikaze Japanese suicide planes during World War II. **824**

Kansas-Nebraska Act (1854) Law that created the territories of Kansas and Nebraska and allowed voters there to choose whether to allow slavery. **354**

Keating-Owen Child Labor Act (1916) Law that outlawed the interstate sale of products produced by child labor; declared unconstitutional by the Supreme Court in 1918. **590**

Kellogg-Briand Pact (1928) Pact signed by the United States and 14 other nations that outlawed war, except for self-defense. **777**

Kent State shootings (1970) Incident in which National Guard troops fired at a group of students during an antiwar protest at Kent State University in Ohio, killing four people. **996**

Kentucky and Virginia Resolutions Statements passed in 1798 and 1799 that denounced the Alien and Sedition Acts. **203**

Kerner Commission Federal commission that investigated the 1960s riots and blamed them on white racism. **938**

kickbacks Payments of part of the earnings from a job. **521**

Knights of Labor One of the first national labor unions in the United States, organized in 1869; after 1879 it included workers of different races, genders, and skills. **484**

Know-Nothings American Party; political organization founded in 1849 by nativists who opposed the Catholic Church and supported measures making it difficult for foreigners to become citizens and to hold office. **261**

Korean War (1950–53) UN-led effort to repel a North Korean invasion of South Korea; resulted in the establishment of a border between the two countries at about the 39th parallel. **845**

Kosovo crisis Result of a violent campaign launched by Serbian forces against Albanians in Kosovo; stopped by UN bombing strikes in 1999. **1080**

Kristallnacht (1938) "Night of Broken Glass"; November 9; night when Nazis destroyed many Jewish buildings. **786**

Ku Klux Klan Secret society created by former Confederates in 1866 that used terror and violence to keep African Americans from obtaining their civil rights. **416**

L

La Huelga (1965–70) Successful strike by migrant farmworkers in California against grape growers; led by César Chávez. **955**

laissez-faire capitalism Theory that opposes government regulation of economic matters. **473**

Land Ordinance of 1785 Legislation that divided western lands into townships and made provisions for public schools. **138**

land speculators People who buy land expecting a quick profit from its resale. **90**

La Raza Unida Party (LRUP) Mexican American political party formed by José Angel Gutiérrez in the late 1960s. **959**

League for United Latin American Citizens (LULAC) Group formed in 1929 to lobby for Hispanic concerns and issues. **883**

League of Nations International body of nations formed in 1919 to prevent wars. **650**

Lecompton Constitution (1857) Kansas constitution; gave voters the right to decide whether more slaves could enter the territory, but not whether slavery should exist there. **357**

Lend-Lease Act (1941) Law that allowed the United States to offer weapons and other war supplies to the Allied Powers to fight against the Axis Powers in World War II. **793**

Liberator William Lloyd Garrison's abolitionist newspaper, launched in 1831. **298**

Limited Nuclear Test Ban Treaty (1963) Agreement signed by U.S. president John F. Kennedy and Soviet leader Nikita Khrushchev; ended above-ground testing of new nuclear weapons. **902**

literacy tests Tests used to prevent people who could not read from voting. **421**

Little Rock Nine Nine African American students who first integrated Central High School in Little Rock, Arkansas, in 1957. **880**

long drives Long overland treks on which cowboys herded cattle from ranches to rail lines. **450**

loose construction Philosophy of constitutional interpretation; holds that within broad limits the government can do anything the Constitution does not specifically forbid. **194**

Los Angeles Riots (1992) Riots that erupted after four white police officers were acquitted of using excessive force against an African American motorist. **1078**

Lost Generation A group of writers whose works reflected the horrors of the death and destruction of World War I and criticized consumerism and superficiality in postwar society. **707**

Louisiana Purchase (1803) U.S. purchase of French land between the Mississippi River and the Rocky Mountains that has been called the largest land deal in history. **207**

Lowell girls Single women who worked in textile mills and lived in company-owned boardinghouses in Lowell, Massachusetts, and other textile towns in the early 1800s. **256**

Loyalists Tories; colonists who sided with Britain in the American Revolution. **116**

M

Maginot Line Line of defenses built by France along its border with Germany after World War I. **793**

Magna Carta (1215) Signed by King John of England; document that limited the power of the monarchy, guaranteed basic liberties for nobles, and protected trading rights. **21**

Manhattan Project Secret U.S. project begun in 1942 to develop an atomic bomb. **825**

manifest destiny Belief of many Americans in the mid-1800s that God intended the United States to expand westward. **316**

Mann-Elkins Act (1910) Federal law that extended the regulatory powers of the Interstate Commerce Commission to telephone and telegraph companies. **582**

manors Large estates of nobles in the Middle Ages. **19**

Marbury v. Madison (1803) Supreme Court case that established the principle of judicial review. **205**

margin buying Purchasing stock with borrowed money. **715**

Mariposa War (1850–51) California raids by the Miwok and Yokut

to keep gold prospectors from crossing their lands. **339**

Market Revolution Creation of profitable national markets during the 1800s; brought about by new transportation systems and regional specialization. **236**

Married Women's Property Act (1848) New York law that permitted married women to own property, file lawsuits, and retain earnings; major victory for the early women's rights movement. **307**

Marshall Plan European Recovery Program; U.S. program of giving money to European countries to help them rebuild their economies after World War II. **841**

Massacre at Wounded Knee (1890) U.S. Army's killing of approximately 300 Sioux at Wounded Knee Creek in South Dakota; ended U.S.-American Indian wars on the Great Plains. **439**

mass production Manufacture of large quantities of goods. **236**

mass transit Public transportation systems, such as commuter trains and subways, that make it possible for workers to live farther away from their jobs. **498**

Maya Mesoamerican civilization that rose to prominence about A.D. 300. **8**

Mayaguez Unarmed U.S. cargo ship seized by Cambodian Communists in 1975; 41 Americans died in the effort to save the 39 crew members. **1024**

Mayflower Compact (1620) Document written by Pilgrim settlers that established a self-governing colony based on majority rule of male church members. **67**

McClure's Magazine Progressive magazine that explored corruption in politics and businesses. **549**

Meat Inspection Act (1906) Federal law that required government inspection of meat shipped across state lines. **578**

Medicaid Federal program created in 1965 to provide free health care to the needy. **913**

Medicare Federal health insurance program for people over the age of 65; created in 1965. **913**

mercantilism Economic system in which a nation's power is tied to its stock of precious metals. **82**

mergers The combining of two or more companies to achieve greater efficiency and higher profits. **670**

Mexican American Youth Organization (MAYO) Mexican American activist group formed in 1967 by college students in San Antonio, Texas. **959**

Mexican Cession Land that Mexico gave to the United States after the Mexican War through the Treaty of Guadalupe Hidalgo; includes present-day California, Nevada, and Utah, as well as parts of Arizona, Colorado, New Mexico, Texas, and Wyoming. **326**

Mexican Revolution Struggle to end dictatorship that led to years of instability in Mexico in the early 1900s. **618**

Mexican War (1846–47) Conflict between Mexico and the United States that ended with the United States gaining control over most Mexican territory in the Southwest. **324**

middle class Social and economic level between the wealthy and the poor; arose during the early 1800s. **255**

Middle Passage Voyage that brought enslaved Africans across the Atlantic Ocean to North America and the West Indies. **76**

Migrant Mother Dorothea Lange's most famous photograph of the Great Depression, showing an exhausted mother and her children; led to increased support for migrant workers in California. **756**

militarism Glorification of military strength. **629**

minutemen American colonial militia members who were supposed to be ready to fight on a minute's notice. **111**

Mir Russian space station; site of joint U.S.-Soviet space projects in the 1990s. **1082**

Mississippi Freedom Democratic Party (MFDP) Group that sent its own delegates to the Democratic National Convention in 1964 to protest discrimination against black voters in Mississippi. **931**

Missouri Compromise (1820) Agreement proposed by Henry Clay that allowed Missouri to enter the Union as a slave state, Maine to enter as a free state, and banned slavery in the Louisiana Purchase north of the 36°30' line. **238**

Model T Low-cost automobile developed by Henry Ford in 1908. **687**

Modern Republicanism Name given to President Dwight D.

Eisenhower's attempt to balance liberal domestic reforms with conservative spending during the 1950s. **870**

monopoly Exclusive economic control of an industry. **475**

Monroe Doctrine (1823) President James Monroe's statement that the United States would not interfere in European colonies in Latin America but would consider any new attempt to colonize in the Western Hemisphere an act of hostility. **229**

Montgomery Improvement Association (MIA) Organization formed by African Americans in Montgomery, Alabama, in 1956 to strengthen the bus boycott and to coordinate protest efforts of African Americans; led by Martin Luther King Jr. **882**

Moral Majority Conservative religious political organization; founded in 1979. **1043**

Mormons Members of the Church of Jesus Christ of Latter-Day Saints. **288**

Morrill Act (1862) Federal law that gave land to western states to build agricultural and engineering colleges. **442**

Mound Builders Ancient civilization of the Eastern Woodlands of the present-day United States. **11**

mountain men Men who hunted for fur in the Far West. **328**

muckrakers Investigative journalists who wrote about corruption in business and politics, hoping to bring about reform. **549**

mugwumps "Big chiefs"; referred to Republican reformers who supported Democrat Grover Cleveland in the presidential election of 1884. **529**

Muller v. Oregon (1908) Supreme Court case that upheld protective legislation for workers in Oregon. **555**

multinational corporations Companies that invest money in a variety of international business ventures. **1088**

Munich Conference (1938) Meeting between British, French, German, and Italian leaders in which Germany was given control of the Sudetenland in exchange for German leader Adolf Hitler's promise to make no more claims on European territory. **790**

mutualistas Mutual-aid societies formed by Mexican American communities to help local residents. **722**

N

National Aeronautics and Space Administration (NASA) Agency established by Congress in 1958 to promote space technology. **857**

National American Woman Suffrage Association (NAWSA) Group formed in 1890 to win the vote for women. **591**

National Association for the Advancement of Colored People (NAACP) Group founded by W. E. B. Du Bois and others in 1909 to end racial discrimination. **563**

National Black Political Convention (1972) Meeting of civil rights activists to ensure that African Americans would continue to gain political influence. **943**

National Defense Act (1916) Military "preparedness" program established prior to U.S. entry into World War I that increased the size of the National Guard and the regular U.S. army. **635**

National Defense Education Act (1958) Federal law that appropriated money to improve education in science, math, and foreign languages. **857**

National Energy Act (1978) Law designed to ease the energy crisis. **1027**

National Grange National Grange of the Patrons of Husbandry; organization founded by Oliver Hudson Kelley in 1867 to tackle economic and political issues concerning farmers. **532**

National Industrial Recovery Act (NIRA) (1933) Federal law designed to encourage economic growth by suspending antitrust laws and eliminating unfair competition between employers; declared unconstitutional in 1935. **742**

nationalism National pride or loyalty. **226**

nationalize To assert government control over a business. **781**

National Organization for Women (NOW) Women's rights group; formed in 1966 to pressure elected officials to ensure social and political equality for women. **950**

National Road Cumberland Road; first federal roadway. **234**

National Security Council (NSC) Organization created in 1947 by Congress to advise the president on strategic matters. **851**

National Urban League Group founded in 1910 to fight for racial equality. **563**

National War Labor Board (NWLB) Agency created during World War I to settle disputes between workers and employers. **642**

National Women's Political Caucus Group founded by Gloria Steinem and others in 1971 to encourage women to run for political office. **951**

National Youth Administration (NYA) New Deal agency that provided part-time jobs to people between the ages of 16 and 25. **748**

Nation of Islam Black Muslims; black nationalist religious group founded by Wallace D. Fard in 1930. **933**

nativism Favoring native-born Americans over foreign-born. **261**

NATO North Atlantic Treaty Organization; alliance formed in 1949 by the United States, Western European nations, and other countries to help defend each other in case of attack. **843**

Navigation Acts A series of English laws beginning in 1650 that required European goods destined for the colonies be routed through England. **82**

Nazi Party National Socialist Party; political group led by Adolf Hitler that rose to power in Germany in the 1930s. **785**

New Deal President Franklin D. Roosevelt's programs for helping the U.S. economy during the Great Depression. **740**

New England Way Cooperation between church and state that was the basis for the Puritan commonwealth. **69**

New Freedom President Woodrow Wilson's progressive reform program; proposed during the 1912 presidential election. **585**

New Frontier President John F. Kennedy's domestic agenda. **906**

new immigrants Immigrants who came to the United States between the 1880s and 1910s, mostly from southern and eastern Europe. **492**

New Right Various conservative voters' groups that grew in strength in the 1980s. **1043**

Nineteenth Amendment (1920) Constitutional amendment that granted women the right to vote. **593**

no-man's-land Strip of bombed-out territory that separated the trenches of opposing armies along the Western Front during World War I. **630**

nonaggression pact (1939) Agreement between German leader Adolf Hitler and Soviet leader Joseph Stalin not to attack one another and to divide Poland. **791**

Non-Intercourse Act (1809) Law that replaced the Embargo Act; restored trade with all nations except for Britain and France. **211**

nonimportation agreements Documents signed by colonial merchants promising not to buy or import British goods. **103**

nonviolent resistance Protest strategy that calls for peaceful demonstrations and the rejection of violence. **922**

North American Free Trade Agreement (NAFTA) (1993) Trade agreement among the United States, Canada, and Mexico. **1087**

Northwest Ordinance (1787) Legislation that established a system for governing the Northwest Territory. **139**

Northwest Passage Nonexistent sea passage through North America that would allow ships to sail from the Atlantic to the Pacific Oceans; early explorers searched for but never found it. **53**

nouveau riche "Newly rich"; new class of American city-dwellers that arose in the late 1800s; most made their fortunes from businesses of the Second Industrial Revolution. **500**

Nuremberg Trials War crimes trials of high-ranking Nazi officials held by an international military tribunal in Nuremberg, Germany; began in 1945. **834**

O

Office of Economic Opportunity (OEO) Government agency formed in 1964 to coordinate antipoverty programs. **911**

Office of War Information U.S. agency that controlled the flow of war news at home during World War II. **807**

Office of War Mobilization (OWM) Federal agency that coordinated all government agencies involved in the war effort during World War II. **802**

Older Americans Act (1965) Law committing the government to provide the elderly with adequate income and medical care. **965**

old immigrants Immigrants who came to the United States before the 1880s; mostly Protestants from northwestern Europe. **492**

Olive Branch Petition (1775) Rejected peace request sent by the Second Continental Congress to Britain's King George III. **113**

Olmec First great Mesoamerican culture; flourished from approximately 1200 to 100 B.C. **7**

Open Door Policy (1899) Declaration made by Secretary of State John Hay that stated that all nations should have equal access to trade and investment in China. **602**

open range Public land used by cattle ranchers. **452**

open shop Nonunion workplace. **556**

Operation Desert Storm (1991) UN invasion led by the United States to make Iraq withdraw from Kuwait. **1059**

Operation Restore Hope (1992) UN attempt to ensure that relief efforts reached famine-stricken Somalia. **1073**

Operation Rolling Thunder U.S. bombing campaign during the Vietnam War. **986**

Orders in Council (1807) British acts that forbade neutral vessels from trading with France or entering French-controlled ports. **210**

Oregon Trail Route to Oregon Territory in the 1800s. **330**

Organization of Petroleum Exporting Countries (OPEC) Alliance formed in 1960 by major oil-producing nations to maintain high prices by controlling the production and sale of oil. **1015**

override Congressional power to overrule a presidential veto with a two-thirds vote. **152**

overseers People who supervised slaves on large plantations. **272**

P

pacification U.S. and South Vietnamese policy of moving villagers to refugee camps and then burning their villages. **987**

Pacific Railway Act (1862) Law that gave lands to railroad companies to develop a line linking the East and West Coasts. **442**

Paleo-Indians The first Americans; crossed from Asia into North America sometime between 12,000 and 40,000 years ago. **4**

Palmer raids (1919–20) Raids ordered by U.S. attorney general A. Mitchell Palmer on suspected radical organizations. **666**

Pan-Africanism Movement to unite people of African descent worldwide. **678**

Panama Canal Treaties Agreements by U.S. and Panamanian leaders in the 1970s to transfer control of the Panama Canal to Panama by the year 2000. **1029**

Panic of 1819 Economic collapse caused partly by the National Bank's attempt to curb some policies of state banks. **237**

Panic of 1837 U.S. economic collapse caused in part by the Specie Circular and by an economic crisis in Great Britain. **248**

Panic of 1873 U.S. economic depression that weakened the Republicans' focus on Reconstruction. **417**

patent Exclusive right to manufacture or sell an invention. **465**

patio **process** Mining technique developed in Mexico and South America during the 1700s that used mercury to extract silver from ore; used in the western United States. **456**

Patriots Colonists who supported independence during the Revolutionary War. **111**

Payne-Aldrich Tariff (1909) High-tariff measure signed by President William Howard Taft; angered progressives. **583**

Peace Corps Program begun by President John F. Kennedy to send volunteers to work in developing nations for two years. **898**

Pendleton Civil Service Act (1883) Act that established the Civil Service Commission to administer competitive examinations to people seeking government jobs. **529**

penitentiary Isolated and structured environment for convicted criminals; intended to reform them. **295**

Pentagon Papers Secret government documents published in 1971; revealed that the U.S. government had misled Americans about the Vietnam War. **997**

peons Landless laborers who worked on Spanish haciendas. **50**

perestroika Soviet policy established in the 1980s that initiated political and economic reforms. **1053**

personal computer (PC) Small computer for individual use. **1037**

pet banks State banks that received deposits of federal funds because of their officers' loyalty to the Democratic Party and to President Andrew Jackson. **247**

Philippine Government Act (1902) Organic Act; federal law that established a governor and a two-house legislature for the Philippines, with the governor and members of the legislature's upper house appointed by the United States. **611**

Pickett's Charge (1863) Failed Confederate attack during the Battle of Gettysburg. **391**

Pilgrims First English settlers in Massachusetts; left England due to religious conflicts. **66**

Pinckney's Treaty (1795) Agreement negotiated by Thomas Pinckney that recognized the southern border of the United States as the 31st parallel and guaranteed U.S. navigation rights on the Mississippi River. **199**

planned obsolescence Practice of manufacturing products that are designed to go out of style. **692**

Platt Amendment (1902) Amendment to the Cuban constitution that limited Cuba's right to make treaties and authorized the United States to intervene in Cuban affairs as it saw necessary. **612**

Plessy v. Ferguson (1896) Supreme Court case that established the "separate-but-equal" doctrine for public facilities. **422**

political bosses Leaders who ran political machines. **518**

political machines Well-organized political parties that dominated local and state governments in the late 1800s. **518**

poll taxes Taxes that a person had to pay in order to vote. **421**

Pontiac's Rebellion (1763) Unsuccessful attack by Ottawa chief Pontiac and his allies against British forts on the northwestern frontier in an attempt to drive out European settlers. **101**

Poor People's Campaign Martin Luther King Jr.'s proposed movement to protest the believed misuse of government spending away from antipoverty programs. **938**

pop art Movement that challenged the values of traditional art by taking inspiration from popular culture. **968**

Popular Front International coalition united against fascism; term coined by Soviet leader Joseph Stalin in a 1935 speech. **786**

popular sovereignty Practice of allowing voters in a territory to decide whether to permit slavery there. **345**

Populist Party People's Party; national political party formed in 1892 that supported a graduated income tax, bank regulation, government ownership of some companies, restrictions on immigration, shorter workdays, and voting reform. **535**

Potsdam Conference (1945) Meeting of U.S. president Harry S Truman, British prime minister Winston Churchill, and Soviet leader Joseph Stalin after Germany's surrender in World War II at which they divided Germany into four zones of occupation. **832**

Pottawatomie Massacre (1856) Incident in which a group led by abolitionist John Brown murdered five pro-slavery Kansans. **355**

Powhatan Confederation of American Indian tribes in Virginia that helped the first English colonists. **57**

Proclamation of 1763 British ban on colonial settlement west of the Appalachian Mountains. **101**

Progressive Party Bull Moose Party; reform party that ran Theodore Roosevelt for president in 1912. **585**

progressivism Reform movement of the early 1900s concerned with curing problems of urbanization and industrialization. **546**

prohibition Complete ban on the manufacture, sale, and distribution of alcohol. **292, 560**

protectorate Country dependent on another for protection. **612**

Protestant Reformation Movement begun by Martin Luther in 1517 to protest corruption in the Catholic Church. **54**

Pueblo Revolt (1680) Attacks by the Pueblo Indians that temporarily drove the Spanish from New Mexico. **47**

Pure Food and Drug Act (1906) Law that prohibited the manufacture, sale, or transportation of food and patented medicine containing harmful ingredients; also required food and medicine containers to carry ingredient labels. **578**

Puritans People who wanted to purify the Anglican Church. **66**

Q

Quakers Members of an abolitionist Protestant sect that rejected wealth and clergy. **78**

Quartering Act (1765) Law enacted by Parliament; required colonists to house and supply British troops. **105**

Quebec Act (1774) Law enacted by Parliament; extended Quebec's boundary south to the Ohio River and granted full religious freedom to French Roman Catholics. **109**

quotas System of reserving a fixed number of openings in schools or jobs for certain groups of people. **941**

Qur'an Islamic holy book of Muhammad's teachings. **15**

R

ragtime Style of music created by African American pianists in the 1890s who played a driving rhythm with one hand and an improvised melody with the other. **510**

railhead Town located along a railroad; long cattle drives usually ended there. **450**

Reaganomics President Ronald Reagan's economic program; based on large tax cuts to encourage business investment. **1044**

realpolitik "Practical politics"; President Richard Nixon's policy that national interests rather than moral principles should be the guiding force in U.S. foreign policy. **1017**

recall Procedure enabling voters to remove an official from office by calling for a special election. **571**

reclamation Process of making damaged land productive. **581**

Reconquista Struggle to drive the Muslims from Spain; ended in 1492 with the surrender of the kingdom of Granada. **22**

Reconstruction (1865–77) Period following the Civil War during which the U.S. government worked to rebuild the former Confederate states and reunite the nation. **403**

Reconstruction Acts (1867) Laws that divided the former Confederate states, except Tennessee, into military zones and required them to draft new constitutions upholding the Fourteenth Amendment. **412**

Reconstruction Finance Corporation (RFC) Agency created in 1932 to stimulate the economy by lending money to railroads, insurance companies, banks, and other financial institutions. **732**

recycling Collection and processing of waste items for reuse. **1089**

Redeemers Democratic supporters of white-controlled governments in the South in the 1870s. **418**

Red Scare Period of anitcommunist hysteria; swept the United States after World War I. **665**

referendum Procedure allowing citizens to force the legislature to place a recently passed law on the ballot for public approval. **571**

Reform Party Political party created in the 1990s promising to reform national politics. **1077**

regionalists Midwestern artists popular in the 1930s who stressed local folk themes and customs in their work. **763**

rehabilitation Treatment to restore someone to a useful and constructive place in society. **295**

Rehabilitation Act (1973) Federal law forbidding discrimination in education, jobs, or housing because of physical disabilities. **963**

Renaissance Rebirth of European learning and artistic creativity that started in the late Middle Ages. **21**

rendezvous system System devised by William Ashley to have fur trappers gather once a year to sell furs and buy supplies. **329**

reparations Payments for damages and expenses in war. **650**

republic System of government run by elected officials. **18**

Republican Motherhood Concept in the early American republic proposing that women could influence politics and society through their work in the home. **136**

Republican Party Political party formed in 1854 by antislavery Whigs and Democrats, along with some Free-Soilers. **356**

reserved powers Powers retained by state governments. **150**

Restoration Era after the death of Puritan leader Oliver Cromwell, when Charles II restored the monarchy in England. **79**

revivals Public gatherings at which ministers preach to a large number of people. **286**

right of deposit Right to transfer goods at a destination without having to pay duties on the cargo. **199**

rock 'n' roll Popular music introduced in the 1950s; influenced by African American rhythm and blues. **877**

Roosevelt Corollary (1904) President Theodore Roosevelt's addition to the Monroe Doctrine; stated that the United States would police affairs in the Western Hemisphere to keep Europeans from intervening in the region. **615**

Rosie the Riveter Symbol of patriotic female defense workers during World War II. **810**

rotation in office Periodic replacement of officeholders. **242**

Rough Riders U.S. cavalry unit in the Spanish-American War led by Theodore Roosevelt. **608**

rugged individualism Belief that success comes through individual effort and private enterprise. **729**

Rush-Bagot Agreement (1817) Pact limiting naval power on the Great Lakes for the United States and Great Britain. **227**

Russo-Japanese War (1904–05) War between Russia and Japan that began with a Japanese attack on Russian forces in Manchuria; peace negotiated by President Theodore Roosevelt. **604**

S

Sand Creek Massacre (1864) Attack by U.S. Army troops in which some 200 peaceful Cheyenne were killed in Colorado. **435**

Sandinistas Revolutionary political party in Nicaragua that overthrew a pro-U.S. dictator in 1979. **1047**

S&L crisis Economic collapse in the savings and loan and banking industries caused by risky loans in the 1980s. **1051**

Santa Fe Trail Route that ran from Missouri to New Mexico. **328**

satellite nations Countries controlled by the Soviet Union. **838**

Saturday Night Massacre Name given to the series of events in 1973 that included the firing of a special prosecutor investigating Watergate and the resignations of the U.S. attorney general and his next in command for refusing to fire the prosecutor. **1021**

scalawags "Scoundrels"; name that former Confederates gave to southern Republicans during Reconstruction. **416**

scientific management Theory promoted by Frederick W. Taylor; held that every kind of work could be broken into a series of smaller tasks and that rates of production could be set for each component task. **687**

Scopes trial (1925) Trial of John Scopes, a high school science teacher who was prosecuted for teaching evolution. **700**

search-and-destroy mission U.S. strategy in Vietnam in which ground patrols searched for hidden enemy camps and supplies and destroyed them with massive firepower and air raids. **987**

Seattle general strike (1919) Large-scale strike that opponents blamed on Bolsheviks and foreigners; weakened support for organized labor. **663**

Second Continental Congress (1775) Meeting of colonists in Philadelphia to decide how to react to fighting at Lexington and Concord. **111**

Second Great Awakening Evangelical religious movement that spread through the United States beginning in the early 1800s. **286**

Second Seminole War (1835–42) Resistance by the Seminole to their removal from Florida. **244**

sectionalism Loyalty to a particular part of the country. **200**

Sedition Act (1918) Federal law enacted during World War I that made written criticism of the government a crime. **646**

segregation Separation of people by category, usually race. **422**

Selective Service Act (1917) Law that initially required men between the ages of 21 and 30 to register for the draft. **636**

Selective Training and Service Act (1940) Law providing for the first peacetime draft in U.S. history. **802**

Seneca Falls Convention (1848) First national women's rights convention; site where the Declaration of Sentiments was written. **304**

separation of powers Allocation of powers between the legislative, executive, and judicial branches of government; prevents any one branch from becoming too powerful. **151**

Separatists Radical group of Puritans who wanted to cut all ties with the Anglican Church. **66**

settlement houses Community service centers that were founded in the late 1800s to offer educational opportunities, skills training, and cultural events to poor neighborhoods. **503**

Seventeenth Amendment (1913) Constitutional amendment that gives voters the power to directly elect U.S. senators. **571**

Shakers United Believers in Christ's Second Appearing; religious group led by "Mother Ann" Lee, who claimed to be the messiah; established several communities in the East before declining in the late 1800s. **288**

shantytowns Collections of makeshift shelters built by homeless people. **722**

sharecropping System used on southern farms after the Civil War in which farmers worked land owned by someone else in return for supplies and a small share of the crops. **420**

Share-Our-Wealth Radical relief program proposed by Senator Huey Long in the 1930s to empower the government to seize wealth from the rich through taxes and provide a guaranteed minimum income and home to every American family. **747**

Shays's Rebellion (1786–87) Uprising of Massachusetts farmers led by Daniel Shays to protest taxes, debt, and foreclosures. **141**

Sherman Antitrust Act (1890) Law that prohibited monopolies and trusts that restrained trade. **481**

Sherman Silver Purchase Act (1890) Federal law that required the government to buy and mint silver each month. **535**

Siege of Vicksburg (1863) Union army's blockade of Vicksburg, Mississippi, that led the city to surrender during the Civil War. **392**

Silent Majority Middle-class voters weary of the social upheaval of the 1960s; sought after by Richard Nixon during his presidential campaigns. **1012**

sit-down strike Method used by striking workers of preventing owners from replacing them by refusing to leave the factories. **752**

sit-ins Demonstrations in which protesters sit down in a location and refuse to leave. **922**

Sixteenth Amendment (1913) Constitutional amendment that permitted Congress to levy income taxes. **583**

Skylab First U.S. space station; placed in orbit in 1973. **1037**

skyscrapers Large, multistory buildings. **498**

Smoot-Hawley Tariff (1930) High-tariff law that contributed to a global economic downturn in the 1930s. **718**

social Darwinism Theory adapted by philosopher Herbert Spencer from Charles Darwin's theory of evolution; argued that society progressed through competition, with the fittest rising to positions of wealth and power. **474**

Social Gospel Movement by Protestant ministers in the late 1800s that applied Christian principles to social problems. **504**

socialism Economic system in which the government or the workers own most factories, utilities, and transportation and communications systems. **555**

Social Security Act (1935) Law that provides retirement pensions, unemployment insurance, and payments to people with disabilities and widows and children of male workers who have died. **749**

Society of American Indians Organization formed in 1911 by middle-class American Indians to address Indian problems. **564**

sod houses Buildings made from chunks cut from heavy topsoil that were stacked like bricks. **445**

Solidarity Polish independent trade union and social movement that was formed in 1980. **1045**

sonar Equipment that uses sound waves to detect underwater objects. **815**

Sons of Liberty Colonial group formed to protest British taxes. **103**

Southern Christian Leadership Conference (SCLC) Alliance of church-based African American organizations formed in 1957 and dedicated to ending discrimination. **922**

southern strategy President Richard M. Nixon's attempt to woo conservative white voters from the Democratic Party by promising not to support new civil rights legislation. **1013**

Spanish Armada Spanish fleet defeated by England in 1588. **54**

Spanish Civil War Struggle between Fascists and Loyalists in Spain that started in 1936. **786**

Spanish-American War (1898) War declared by the United States on Spain to help Cuba overthrow Spanish rule. **607**

specie Gold or silver that a bank held to back up its notes. **231**

Specie Circular (1836) Executive order issued by President Andrew Jackson instructing the Treasury to accept only gold and silver as payment for public lands. **248**

spheres of influence Regions where a particular country has exclusive rights over mines, railroads, and trade. **602**

spirituals Songs sung by slaves in the South; mixed African rituals and musical forms with Christian hymns to express slaves' religious beliefs. **276**

spoils system Politicians' practice of giving government jobs to their supporters. **241**

Sputnik The world's first artificial satellite; launched by the Soviet Union in 1957. **857**

Square Deal Theodore Roosevelt's 1904 presidential campaign slogan pledging to balance the interests of business, consumers, and labor. **576**

stagflation Economic condition characterized by rising inflation and unemployment. **1013**

Stalwarts Republicans in the late 1800s who opposed reform. **527**

Stamp Act (1765) Law passed by Parliament that placed a tax on printed matter. **102**

Stamp Act Congress (1765) Delegates from nine colonies who gathered in New York City to voice their rejection of the Stamp Act and to deny Parliament's right to tax the colonies. **104**

steel strike of 1919 Strike that failed when steel company officials used rumors, threats, and even violence against strikers. **664**

steerage Poor accommodations in a ship's lower levels; many immigrants to the United States traveled in this space. **493**

Strategic Arms Limitation Talks (SALT) (1972) Talks between U.S. president Richard M. Nixon and Soviet leader Leonid Brezhnev that led to a treaty limiting the number of ICBM missiles each country could have. **1017**

Strategic Defense Initiative (SDI) Plan for a defense system in space to protect the United States from Soviet missiles; never actually implemented. **1045**

strict construction Philosophy of narrowly interpreting the Constitution; holds that the government can do only what the Constitution specifically allows. **194**

strike Refusal of workers to perform their job until employers meet union demands. **258**

Student Nonviolent Coordinating Committee (SNCC) Student organization formed in 1960 to coordinate civil rights demonstrations and to provide training for protesters. **922**

Students for a Democratic Society (SDS) Student group that actively protested the Vietnam War. **989**

subsidy Government payment made to farmers. **600**

suburbs Residential neighborhoods on the outskirts of a city. **499**

Sugar Act (1764) Law passed by Parliament imposing taxes on molasses, sugar, and other items imported by the colonies. **102**

Sunbelt States in the South and the West that attracted many new residents and businesses in the 1970s. **1033**

supply-side economics Economic theory stating that tax cuts would lead to increased economic activity and tax revenues, and a balanced budget. **1044**

supremacy clause Clause in the U.S. Constitution; states that the Constitution and all federal laws outrank state constitutions and state laws. **151**

Sussex **pledge** (1916) Promise issued by German officials during World War I not to sink merchant vessels without warning or without assuring the passengers' safety. **635**

Swahili Language spoken in East Africa. **16**

Taft-Hartley Act (1947) Law that gave judges the power to end some strikes, outlawed closed shop agreements, restricted unions'

political contributions, and required union leaders to swear they were not Communists. **866**

Taino "Good," "noble"; the first Native Americans Christopher Columbus encountered. **36**

Tariff Act of 1816 Federal law that placed a 25 percent duty on most imported factory goods; increased conflict between the North and the South. **232**

tariffs Taxes on imports or exports. **145**

task system System in which plantation slaves were assigned specific duties each day. **80**

Tea Act (1773) Law passed by Parliament that excused the British East India Company from paying certain duties and allowed it to sell tea directly to American agents, resulting in a fall in colonial tea prices; colonists responded with the Boston Tea Party. **108**

Teapot Dome scandal Scandal during President Warren Harding's administration; involved Secretary of the Interior Albert Fall's leasing of oil reserves in return for personal gifts and loans. **672**

Tejanos Native Mexicans who lived in Texas. **317**

Telecommunications Act (1996) Law that attempted to regulate indecency on the Internet; parts of it were later struck down by a federal court. **1084**

telegraph Machine patented by Samuel Morse in 1837 that sent messages over long distances by using electric current to transmit a system of dots and dashes over wire. **468**

Teller Amendment (1898) Resolution stating that the United States did not intend to take over and annex Cuba. **607**

temperance movement A social reform effort begun in the mid-1800s to encourage people to limit alcohol consumption. **291**

tenements Poorly built apartment buildings that housed many poor city-dwellers in the late 1800s and early 1900s. **502**

Tennessee Valley Authority (TVA) New Deal program established in 1933; built dams and power stations to provide hydroelectric power and flood control to the Tennessee River valley. **744**

Tet Offensive (1968) Attack by North Vietnamese and Vietcong troops against South Vietnam during the Vietnam War; came during Tet, the Vietnamese New Year; demonstrated that the North Vietnamese were still militarily strong. **992**

Texas longhorn Hardy breed of cow created by interbreeding English and Spanish cattle. **449**

Texas Revolution (1835–36) Revolt against Mexico by American settlers and Tejanos in Texas. **319**

Thirteenth Amendment (1865) Constitutional amendment that abolished slavery. **405**

Three-Fifths Compromise (1787) Agreement worked out at the Constitutional Convention; stated that three fifths of a state's slave population would count in determining that state's representation in the lower house of Congress. **145**

Three Mile Island accident (1979) Incident in which a nuclear reactor in Pennsylvania nearly had a catastrophic meltdown. **1027**

Toleration Act (1649) Maryland law that granted a degree of religious freedom to settlers. **73**

Toltec Civilization that dominated central Mexico beginning about A.D. 900. **9**

Tonkin Gulf Resolution (1964) Congressional measure that gave President Lyndon B. Johnson the authority to wage war in Vietnam. **984**

totalitarian state Political system in which the government controls every aspect of citizens' lives. **785**

total war Type of war in which an army destroys its opponent's ability to fight by attacking civilian and economic, as well as military, targets. **394**

Townshend Acts (1767) Law passed by Parliament placing duties on certain items imported by the colonists. **105**

Trail of Tears (1838–39) An 800-mile forced march the Cherokee made from their homeland in the Southeast to Indian Territory in present-day Oklahoma; resulted in the deaths of almost one quarter of the tribe's members. **245**

transcendentalism Belief that people can rise above material things in life to reach a higher level of understanding; popular among New England writers and thinkers in the mid-1800s. **290**

transcontinental railroad Railroad that crossed the continental United States; completed in 1869. **466**

Treaty of Fort Laramie (1851) Agreement that set boundaries for American Indians and allowed the U.S. government to build roads and forts in Indian Territory. **333**

Treaty of Ghent (1814) Treaty between the United States and Britain that ended the War of 1812. **215**

Treaty of Greenville (1795) Agreement between American Indian confederation leaders and the U.S. government that gave the United States much of the land in present-day Ohio and parts of Indiana in exchange for $20,000 worth of goods and formal acknowledgment of Indian claims to other lands. **196**

Treaty of Guadalupe Hidalgo (1848) Treaty that ended the Mexican War and gave the United States much of Mexico's northern territory. **326**

Treaty of Paris (1783) Peace agreement that officially ended the Revolutionary War and established Britain's formal recognition of the United States. **129**

Treaty of Tordesillas (1494) Treaty signed by Spain and Portugal in which both countries agreed to move the Line of Demarcation; newly discovered lands west of the line would go to Spain, while those east of the line would go to Portugal. **40**

Treaty of Versailles (1919) Treaty ending World War I that required Germany to pay huge war reparations and established the League of Nations. **651**

Tredegar Iron Works One of the nation's largest and best-equipped iron foundaries that operated in Richmond, Virginia, in the early to mid-1800s. **264**

trench warfare World War I military strategy of defending a position by fighting from the protection of deep ditches. **630**

Triangle Shirtwaist Fire (1911) Incident that resulted in the deaths of some 140 garment workers; led to increased safety regulations for businesses. **554**

Truman Doctrine (1947) President Harry S Truman's policy stating that the United States would help any country fighting against communism. **841**

trunk lines Major railroads connected to outlying areas by feeder or branch lines. **466**

trust Arrangement grouping several companies under one board of directors to eliminate competition and to regulate production. **475**

Twelfth Amendment (1804) Constitutional amendment that created a separate ballot for president and vice president. **204**

Twenty-first Amendment (1933) Constitutional amendment that ended prohibition by repealing the Eighteenth Amendment. **695**

Twenty-sixth Amendment (1971) Constitutional amendment that lowered the federal voting age from 21 to 18. **998**

U

Underground Railroad Network of abolitionists who helped slaves escape to the North and Canada. **278**

Unitarians Members of a religious reform movement that originated in New England in the late 1700s. **290**

United Farm Workers (UFW) Group formed in the 1960s to improve working conditions for migrant farmworkers. **955**

United Mine Workers strike (1919) Strike for pay increases and better working hours that further weakened public support for unions; first UMW strike led by John L. Lewis. **664**

United Nations (UN) International organization chartered in 1945; created to settle problems between nations. **835**

Universal Negro Improvement Association (UNIA) Association founded by Marcus Garvey in 1914 to foster African American economic independence and establish an independent black homeland in Africa. **678**

University of California v. Bakke (1978) Supreme Court decision that established that while some forms of affirmative action were legal, quota systems were not. **941**

Untouchables Nickname given to a group of detectives led by Eliot Ness who targeted gangsters during Prohibition. **695**

urban renewal Program launched by the federal government in the

1950s to replace old, run-down inner-city buildings. **887**

U.S. Department of Agriculture Executive department created in 1862 to help farmers. **445**

U.S. Sanitary Commission Agency headed in part by Dr. Elizabeth Blackwell; battled disease and infection among Union soldiers during the Civil War. **379**

USS *Maine* U.S. battleship that exploded in Havana Harbor in 1898; although cause was never determined, the incident was a catalyst for the Spanish-American War. **607**

utopias Communities designed to create a perfect society; popular in the United States in the early to mid-1800s. **287**

U-2 incident Incident in which U.S. pilot Francis Gary Powers was captured while spying on the Soviet Union; worsened relations between the United States and the Soviet Union. **850**

V

vaudeville "Light play"; type of variety show that featured a wide selection of short performances. **510**

vertical integration Ownership of businesses involved in each step of a manufacturing process. **476**

veto Official rejection of legislation. **152**

viceroy Governor of a Spanish colony. **35**

viceroyalties Large provinces organized by Spain to control its American empire. **49**

Vietcong National Liberation Front; communist guerrilla force that began fighting against Ngo Dinh Diem's government in South Vietnam in the 1950s. **981**

Vietminh League for the Independence of Vietnam; group of Vietnamese nationalists organized in the 1940s by Ho Chi Minh to drive the Japanese out of Vietnam. **979**

Vietnamization Policy followed by the Nixon administration of gradually turning over all the fighting in the Vietnam War to the South Vietnamese Army. **995**

Vietnam Veterans Memorial Memorial dedicated in Washington, D.C., in 1982 to honor those people who died in or are missing from the Vietnam War. **1002**

Virginia Plan (1787) Plan drafted by James Madison at the Constitutional Convention that shifted power away from the states and toward the central government. **143**

Virginia Statute for Religious Freedom (1786) Statute stating in part that the human mind was created free and that government control over religious beliefs or worship is tyrannical. **135**

Volstead Act (1919) Federal law that enforced the Eighteenth Amendment (prohibition). **694**

Volunteers in Service to America (VISTA) Domestic version of the Peace Corps; established in 1964. **912**

Voting Rights Act (1965) Law that put voter registration under federal government control. **932**

Voting Rights Act of 1975 Federal law requiring states and communities with large non-English speaking populations to print voting materials in various foreign languages. **1032**

W

Wagner-Connery Act (1935) National Labor Relations Act; law that guaranteed labor's right to organize unions and to bargain for better wages and working conditions. **752**

War Industries Board (WIB) Agency led by Bernard Baruch during World War I; allocated scarce goods, established production priorities, and set prices on goods. **641**

war of attrition Union general Grant's Civil War strategy of fighting until the South ran out of men, supplies, and will. **392**

War on Drugs President George Bush's organized effort to end drug smuggling and illegal drug use. **1062**

War on Poverty President Lyndon B. Johnson's programs to help poor Americans; announced in 1964. **911**

War Powers Act (1973) Legislation that reaffirmed Congress's constitutional power to declare war; set a 60-day limit on the presidential commitment of U.S. troops to foreign conflicts. **1002**

War Production Board (WPB) World War II agency that was in charge of converting factories to war production. **801**

Warren Commission Special group led by Chief Justice Earl Warren to investigate the assassination of President John F. Kennedy. **909**

Warsaw Pact Military alliance formed in 1955 by the Soviet Union and other Eastern European communist countries. **843**

Washington Conference (1921) International conference held in Washington, D.C., that focused on naval disarmament and Pacific security. **775**

Watergate Scandal in which President Richard M. Nixon authorized the cover-up of a break-in at the Democratic National Committee headquarters; led to Nixon's resignation in 1974. **1020**

Whip Inflation Now (WIN) President Gerald Ford's slogan to garner support for his anti-inflation program. **1024**

Whiskey Rebellion (1794) Protest by farmers in Pennsylvania against new taxes on whiskey. **195**

Wilmot Proviso (1846) Proposal to outlaw slavery in the territory added to the United States by the Mexican Cession; passed in the House of Representatives but was defeated in the Senate. **345**

Wisconsin Idea Robert M. La Follette's reform program for Wisconsin in the early 1900s; became a model for other state governments. **574**

Women's Christian Temperance Union (WCTU) Reform organization that led the fight against alcohol in the late 1800s. **561**

Woodstock (1969) Rock concert near Woodstock, New York, that marked the highpoint of the counterculture era. **971**

Worcester v. Georgia (1832) Supreme Court ruling that limited state power over the Cherokee Nation and said that the federal government should protect the Cherokee from state governments that were trying to take their land; ignored by President Andrew Jackson and the state of Georgia. **245**

Works Progress Administration (WPA) New Deal agency created in 1934 to put American men and women to work. **748**

World Wide Web System developed by Swiss scientists in the early 1980s that links Internet sites. **1083**

writs of assistance Special search warrants that allowed colonial tax collectors to search for smuggled goods. **105**

X

XYZ affair (1797) Incident in which French agents demanded a bribe and loan from U.S. diplomats in exchange for discussing an agreement that French privateers would no longer attack American ships; led to an undeclared naval war between the United States and France. **202**

Y

Yalta Conference (1945) Meeting of U.S. president Franklin D. Roosevelt, British prime minister Winston Churchill, and Soviet leader Joseph Stalin to plan for the postwar world. **818**

yellow journalism Style of sensational reporting used by newspapers to attract readers. **507**

yeoman farmers Small landowning farmers who made up the majority of southern white society in the 1800s. **266**

Y2K bug Widespread computer programming problem created by date abbreviations that threatened to shut down computer systems on January 1, 2000. **1084**

Z

zaibatsu Huge corporations run by single families that monopolized the Japanese economy before World War II. **833**

Zimmerman Note Cable sent to Mexico by Germany's foreign secretary during World War I; proposed an alliance between the two countries. **636**

Zionism Movement for a Jewish homeland in Palestine. **836**

zoot-suit riots (1943) Series of attacks by U.S. sailors against Mexican Americans in Los Angeles. **812**

B

INDEX

G

I

ACKNOWLEDGMENTS

For permission to reprint copyrighted material, grateful acknowledgment is made to the following sources:

Víctor Alba: From *Alliance Without Allies: The Mythology of Progress in Latin America* by Víctor Alba. Copyright © 1965 by Víctor Alba.

Bantam Books, a division of Random House, Inc.: From *Voices of Freedom* by Henry Hampton and Steve Fayer. Copyright © 1990 by Blackside, Inc.

Beacon Press, Boston: From *Broken Spears* by Miguel Leon-Portilla. Copyright © 1962, 1990 by Miguel Leon-Portilla. Expanded and updated edition copyright © 1992 by Miguel Leon-Portilla.

Bethune-Cookman College Archives: Quote by Mary McCleod Bethune.

Robert Bly: From "The United Fruit Co." by Pablo Neruda from *Neruda and Vallejo: Selected Poems,* chosen and translated by Robert Bly. Copyright © 1974 by Robert Bly. Published by Beacon Press, 1974.

Chris Burke: From "The wild life of a Wall Street 'golden boy': 'Our mission is commission'" by Chris Burke from *The Century* by Peter Jennings and Todd Brewster. Copyright © 1998 by ABC Television Network Group, a division of Capitol Cities, Inc.

Peter N. Carroll: Quote by a Chicago housewife from "The Loss of Connection" from *It Seemed Like Nothing Happened: America in the 1970s* by Peter N. Carroll. Copyright © 1982 by Peter Carroll.

Sheyann Webb Christburg: Quote by eight-year-old Sheyann Webb from "The Turbulent Sixties" from *The Enduring Vision: A History of the American People* by Paul S. Boyer et al.

Don Congdon Associates, Inc.: From "The Watchers" from *Weird Tales* by Ray Bradbury. Copyright © 1945 by Street & Smith Publications; copyright renewed © 1972 by Ray Bradbury.

Crisis Publishing Co., Inc.: From "The Bronx Slave Market" by Ella Baker and Marvel Cooke from *The Crisis,* vol. 42, November 1935. Copyright 1935 by Crisis Publishing Co., Inc.

Donadio & Olson, Inc.: From *The Good War: An Oral History of World War Two* by Studs Terkel. Copyright © 1984 by Studs Terkel.

Doubleday, a division of Random House, Inc.: From *The Martian Way and Other Stories* by Isaac Asimov. Copyright © 1955 by Isaac Asimov. From *Child of War, Woman of Peace* by Le Ly Hayslip. Copyright © 1993 by Doubleday. From *The Century* by Todd Brewster and Peter Jennings. Copyright © 1998 by ABC Television Network Group, a division of Capitol Cities, Inc. From *The Blue Eagle from Egg to Earth* by Hugh S. Johnson. Copyright 1935 by Hugh S. Johnson. From "Can Wars Be Just?" by Sari Nusseibeh from *But Was It Just?: Reflections on the Morality of the Persian Gulf War* by Jean Bethke Elshtain et al., translated by Peter Hejnegg, edited by David E. Decosse. Copyright © 1992 by Jean Bethke Elshtain, Stanley Hauerwas, Sari Nusseibeh, and George Weigel.

W. D. Ehrhart: "Guerrilla War" from *Beautiful Wreckage: New & Selected Poems* by W. D. Ehrhart. Copyright © 1980 by W. D. Ehrhart. Published by Adastra Press, 1999.

Facts On File, Inc.: From "Carla Martinelli" from *Ellis Island Interviews: In Their Own Words* by Peter Morton Coan. Copyright © 1997 by Peter Morton Coan.

Farrar, Straus and Giroux, LLC: From *No Downlink: A Dramatic Narrative About the Challenger Accident and Our Time* by Claus Jensen, translated by Barbara Haveland. Translation copyright © 1996 by Barbara Haveland.

The Forum: Quote by a Slav immigrant from "Relief and Revolution" by Charles R. Walker from *The Forum,* 73, August 1932.

The Gale Group: Adaptation of map from *We the People* by James Paul Allen and Eugene James Turner. Copyright © 1988 by Macmillan Publishing Company.

GRM Associates, Inc., Agents for the Estate of Ida M. Cullen: "Yet Do I Marvel" from *Color* by Countee Cullen. Copyright 1925 by Harper & Brothers: copyright renewed 1953 by Ida M. Cullen.

Grove/Atlantic, Inc.: From "The India of My Dreams" from *My Truth* by Indira Gandhi, presented by Emmanuel Pouchpadass. Copyright © 1980 by Editions Stock. First published in English in 1981 by Vision Books Pvt. Ltd., New Delhi, in collaboration with Editions Stock, Paris. From *1968 in America: Music, Politics, Chaos, Counterculture, and the Shaping of a Generation* by Charles Kaiser. Copyright © 1988 by Charles Kaiser.

HarperCollins Publishers, Inc.: From *The American People: Creating a Nation and a Society,* Second Edition, by Gary B. Nash et al. Copyright © 1990 by HarperCollins Publishers.

Harvard University Press: From "World, in Hounding Me" by Sor Juana Inés de la Cruz from *A Sor Juana Anthology,* translated by A. S. Trueblood. Copyright © 1988 by the President and Fellows of Harvard College.

James A. Henretta: Quote by a Chicago schoolteacher from "Family Values" and quote by a coal miner's daughter from "Herbert Hoover and the Great Depression" from *America's History* by James A. Henretta et al. Copyright © 1987 by The Dorsey Press.

Hill and Wang, a division of Farrar, Straus and Giroux, LLC.: From *Night* by Elie Wiesel, translated by Stella Rodway. Copyright © 1960 by MacGibbon & Kee; copyright renewed © 1988 by The Colling Publishing Group.

Roy Hoopes: From *Americans Remember the Home Front: An Oral Narrative of the World War II Years in America* by Roy Hoopes. Copyright © 1977, 1992 by Roy Hoopes.

Houghton Mifflin Company: From *The Autobiography of Will Rogers,* edited by Donald Day. Copyright 1949 by Houghton Mifflin Co. From *Typical American* by Gish Jen. Copyright © 1991 by Gish Jen. All rights reserved.

Howe Brothers Publishers: Excerpt by Gerald One Feather from *Indian Self-Rule: First-Hand Accounts of Indian-White Relations from Roosevelt to Reagan,* edited by Kenneth R. Philp. Published by Howe Brothers Publishers, 1986.

Independent Woman: From a quote by a female aircraft worker from "Comments on 'Womanpower 4F'" from *Independent Woman,* November 1943; and quote by a shipyard manager from "Anchors Aweigh!" by Beatrice Oppenheim from *Independent Woman,* March 1943. Published by the Washington National Federation of Business and Professional Women's Clubs, Inc.

Charles H. Kerr & Company, Chicago: From "The March of the Mill Children" from *The Autobiography of Mother Jones,* edited by Mary Field Parton. Copyright 1925, copyright renewed © 1972 by Charles H. Kerr & Company.

Alfred A. Knopf, Inc., a division of Random House, Inc.: "I, Too" from *Collected Poems* by Langston Hughes. Copyright © 1994 by the Estate of Langston Hughes.

Kodansha International Ltd.: From *War-Wasted Asia: Letters, 1945–1946,* edited by Otis Cary. Copyright © 1975 by Kodansha International Ltd. All rights reserved.

Maya Ying Lin: Quote about the Vietnam Veterans Memorial.

Ludlow Music, Inc.: From lyrics from "Talking Dust Bowl." Words and music composed by Woody Guthrie. TRO—© Copyright 1960, copyright renewed © 1963 by Ludlow Music, Inc., New York, NY. Used by permission.

Macmillan Ltd.: From "Economy (1931)" from *The Collected Writings of John Maynard Keynes: Volume IX, Essays in Persuasion.* Originally published as "The Problem of Unemployment—II" in the *Listener,* January 4, 1931.

Naomi Long Madgett: "Midway" from *Star by Star* by Naomi Long Madgett. Copyright © 1965 by Naomi Long Madgett. Published by Harlo Press in 1965, Evenill in 1970, and Lotus in 1972.

Manna Music, Inc.: From "Circuit-Ridin' Preacher" by Tim Spencer. Copyright 1954 and renewed © 1982 by Manna Music, Inc. All rights reserved.

The McGraw-Hill Companies: From *Over There: The Story of America's First Great Overseas Crusade* by Frank Freidel. Copyright © 1990 by McGraw-Hill, Inc. All rights reserved. From *America Inside Out* by David Schoenbrun. Copyright © 1994 by McGraw-Hill Companies, Inc.

McIntosh and Otis, Inc.: From *America's Immigrants: Adventures in Eyewitness History* by Rhoda Hoff. Copyright © 1967 by Rhoda Hoff. Published by Henry Z. Walck, Inc.

William Morrow & Company, Inc.: From *Ark of Empire: The American Frontier, 1784–1803* by Dale Van Every. Copyright © 1963 by Dale Van Every. Quote by Donna Shalala from *What You Can Do for Your Country: An Oral History of the Peace Corps* by Karen Schwarz. Copyright © 1991 by William Morrow & Company, Inc.

Patricia Mull: Quote by Patricia Mull from "What $152 a Week Buys" by Nancy Gibbs from *Time,* September 10, 1990. Copyright © 1990 by Patricia Mull.

Multimedia Product Development, Chicago, IL: From "Erma's Story" from *Making Do: How Women Survived the '30s* by Jeane Westin. Copyright © 1976 by Jeane Westin. All rights reserved.

NAACP: From advertisement "Let 'Em Walk" by the NAACP.

New Directions Publishing Corporation: From "Martín IV" from *Martín and Meditations on the South Valley* by Jimmy Santiago Baca. Copyright © 1987 by Jimmy Santiago Baca. From "I Am Waiting" from *A Coney Island of the Mind* by Lawrence Ferlinghetti. Copyright © 1958 by Lawrence Ferlinghetti.

The New Republic: From "The De Luxe Picture Palace" by Lloyd Lewis from *The New Republic,* vol. 58, March 27, 1929. Copyright 1929 by The New Republic.

The New York Times Company: Quote by Michael Novak from the Op-Ed page of *The New York Times,* May 24, 1998. Copyright © 1998 by The New York Times Company.

Newsweek, Inc.: Quote by Hugh Austin from "Business and Finance" from *Newsweek,* November 19, 1973. Copyright © 1973 by Newsweek, Inc. All rights reserved. From "Nursing the Dying" by Edie Meeks from *Newsweek,* March 8, 1999, p. 61. Copyright © 1999 by Newsweek, Inc. All rights reserved.

W. W. Norton & Company, Inc.: From *Sleepwalking Through History: America in the Reagan Years* by Haynes Johnson. Copyright © 1991 by Haynes Johnson.

Harold Ober Associates Incorporated: From "...I Could Not Eat The Poems I Wrote" by Langston Hughes. Copyright © 1963 by Langston Hughes. Published by Freedomways.

Pathfinder Press: From "OAAU Founding Rally" and from "Short Statements: Fight or Forget It" from *By Any Means Necessary: Speeches, Interviews, and a Letter by Malcolm X.* Copyright © 1970 by Betty Shabazz and Pathfinder Press.

Penguin Books, Ltd.: From *The Travels of Sir John Mandeville,* translated by C.W.R.D. Moseley (Penguin Classics, 1983). Copyright © 1983 by C.W.R.D. Moseley.

Penguin Putnam Inc.: Poem "I saw, I saw, I saw holes and trenches" by Trinh Cong Son from *Vietnam: A History* by Stanley Karnow. Copyright © 1983 by WGBH Educational Foundation and Stanley Karnow. From *Movin' on Up* by Mahalia Jackson, with Evan McLeod Wylie. Copyright © 1966 by Mahalia Jackson and Evan McLeod Wylie. Published by Hawthorne Books, New York, 1966.

Peters Fraser & Dunlop Group Ltd.: From "The First Tanks in Action, 15 September 1916" by Bert Chaney from *People at War, 1914–1915* by Michael Moynihan. Published by David and Charles, 1973.

Princeton University Press: Quote regarding Charles E. Hughes from *Toward a New Order of Sea Power: American Naval Policy and the World Scene, 1918–1922* by Harold and Margaret Sprout. Published by Princeton University Press, 1943, 1946.

Publishers Weekly: From interview with Gloria Steinem from *Publishers Weekly,* August 12, 1983. Copyright © 1983 by R. R. Bowker Company.

G. P. Putnam's Sons, a division of Penguin Putnam Inc.: From "Their Finest Hour," a speech delivered to the House of Commons, June 18, 1940, by Winston Churchill from *Blood, Sweat, and Tears* by The Right Honorable Winston S. Churchill. Copyright 1941 by Winston S. Churchill. From "The Yom Kippur War" from *My Life* by Golda Meir. Copyright © 1975 by Golda Meir.

Rainy Day Press: Quote by Lucy Ann Henderson Deady from *The Lockley Files: Conversations with Pioneer Women* by Fred Lockley, compiled and edited by Mike Helm.

Random House, Inc.: From "On the Pulse of Morning" from *On the Pulse of Morning* by Maya Angelou. Copyright © 1993 by Maya Angelou.

The Reader's Digest Association, Inc.: From "The Spread of Grass-Roots Capitalism" by Edward Maher from *Reader's Digest,* June 1955. Copyright © 1955 by The Reader's Digest Association, Inc.

Estate of Erich Maria Remarque: From *All Quiet on the Western Front* by Erich Maria Remarque. Copyright 1929, 1930 by Little, Brown and Company; copyright renewed © 1957, 1958 by Erich Maria Remarque. All rights reserved. "Im Westen Nichts Neues" copyright 1928 by Ullstein A. G.; copyright renewed © 1956 by Erich Maria Remarque.

Remick Music, Inc.: From lyrics from "We're in the Money" by Henry Warren and Al Dubin. Copyright 1933 by Remick Music, Inc.

Republican National Committee: From "Morning in America" advertisement for Ronald Reagan 1984 presidential campaign.

Roosevelt University, Labor Education Division: From "Automation" by Joe Glazer from *Songs of Work and Freedom,* edited by Edith Fowke and Joe Glazer. Published by Roosevelt University, Labor Education Division, 1960.

Scribner, a division of Simon & Schuster, Inc.: From *A Farewell to Arms* by Ernest Hemingway. Copyright 1929 by Charles Scribner's Sons; copyright renewed © 1957 by Ernest Hemingway. From *For Whom the Bell Tolls* by Ernest Hemingway. Copyright 1940 by Ernest Hemingway; copyright renewed © 1968 by Mary Hemingway. From *The Sun Also Rises* by Ernest Hemingway. Copyright 1926 by Charles Scribner's Sons; copyright renewed 1954 by Ernest Hemingway. From "We Lived on Relief" by Ann Rivington from *Scribner's Magazine,* vol. 95, 1934, pp. 282–5. Copyright 1934 by Charles Scribner's Sons; copyright renewed © 1962 by Charles Scribner's Sons. From *By-line: Ernest Hemingway,* edited by William White. Copyright © 1967 by William White.

Scripps Howard Foundation: From *Ernie's War: The Best of Ernie Pyle's World War II Dispatches,* edited by David Nichols. Copyright © 1986 by Simon and Schuster.

SIGI Productions, Inc.: Quotes by Arthur Komori and Francis Tsuzuki from *"I Can Never Forget": Men of the 100th/442nd* by Thelma Chang. Copyright © 1991 by SIGI Productions, Inc.

Siglo Veintiuno Editores: From "Atahualpa" from *El primer nueva corónica y buen gobierno* by Rolena Adorno and John Murra. Copyright © 1980 by Siglo XXI Editores.

Simon & Schuster, Inc.: From "Special Problems of the Depression" from *Interpretations, 1931–1932* by Walter Lippmann. Copyright © 1932 by Walter Lippmann. From *Nobody Speaks for Me! Self-Portraits of American Working-Class Women* by Nancy Seifer. Copyright © 1976 by Nancy Seifer.

Small Planet Communications: From "Expansion in the Pacific" from *An On-Line History of the United States: The Age of Imperialism,* online, September 22, 1999. Copyright © 1996 by Small Planet Communications. Available http://www.smplanet.com/imperialism/hawaii.html.

Society for the Advancement of Education: From "An American Tragedy: The Internment of Japanese-Americans During World War II" by Norman Y. Mineta from *USA Today,* vol. 112, no. 2468, May 1984. Copyright © 1984 by Society for the Advancement of Education.

Special Rider Music: From lyrics from "Blowin' in the Wind" by Bob Dylan. Copyright © 1962 by Warner Bros. Music; copyright renewed © 1990 by Special Rider Music. All rights reserved.

Gloria Steinem: Quotes by Gloria Steinem about the women's movement.

Syracuse University Press: From "Freedom of Thought and Speech" statement at 1949 annual meeting of the Women's International League for Peace and Freedom in *Peace as a Women's Issue: A History of the U.S. Movement for World Peace and Women's Rights* by Harriet Hyman Alonso. Copyright © 1993 by Syracuse University Press.

Texas A&M University Press: From *Czech Voices: Stories from Texas in the* Amerikán Národní Kalendář, edited and translated by Clinton Machann and James W. Mendl, Jr. Copyright © 1991 by Clinton Machann and James W. Mendl, Jr.

Time Inc.: From "The Century Ahead: How The World Will Look in 50 Years" by Bruce W. Nelan from *Time,* October 15, 1992. Copyright © 1992 by Time Inc. From "The Men Who Fought" from *Time,* vol. 143, no. 23, June 6, 1994. Copyright © 1994 by Time Inc.

Sheila Tobias: From *Faces of Feminism: An Activist's Reflections on the Women's Movement* by Sheila Tobias. Copyright © 1997 by Westview Press, a division of HarperCollins Publishers, Inc.

Margaret Truman and SCG, Inc., 381 Park Ave., So., NYC, NY 10016: From *Memoirs by Harry S. Truman: Years of Trial and Hope.* Copyright © 1956 by Time Inc. Published by Doubleday and Company.

The University of Alberta Press: Quote by Henri Lancelot-Voisin Sieur de La Popelinière from *The Myth of the Savage: And the Beginnings of French Colonialism in the Americas* by Olive Patricia Dickason. Copyright © 1984, 1997 by The University of Alberta Press.

The University of Chicago Press: From *The Tewa World: Space, Time, Being, and Becoming in a Pueblo Society* by Alfonso Ortiz. Copyright © 1969 by The University of Chicago Press.

The University of North Carolina Press: From "Tore Up and a-Movin'" from *These Are Our Lives* by the Federal Writers' Project. Copyright © 1939 by The University of North Carolina Press.

University of Oklahoma Press: From *Red Men Calling on the Great White Father* by Katharine C. Turner. Copyright 1951 by the University of Oklahoma Press.

University of Washington Press: From *Island: Poetry and History of Chinese Immigrants on Angel Island, 1910–1940* by Him Mark Lai et al. Copyright © 1991 by University of Washington Press.

Warner Books, Inc.: From *The Memoirs of Richard Nixon* by Richard Nixon. Copyright © 1978 by Richard Nixon. Published by Grosset & Dunlap.

Warner/Chappell Music, Inc.: From lyrics from "Get a Job" by Earl Beal, Richard Lewis, and Raymond Edwards. Copyright © 1957 by Windswept Pacific Entertainment Co. d/b/a Longitude Music Co. All rights reserved.

Wieser & Wieser, Inc., Literary Agency: From *Japan's War: The Great Pacific Conflict, 1853 to 1952* by Edwin P. Hoyt. Copyright © 1986 by Edwin P. Hoyt.

The Heirs to the Estate of Martin Luther King, Jr., c/o Writers House, Inc. as agent for the proprietor: From "I Have a Dream" and "Letter from Birmingham Jail" from *Why We Can't Wait* by Martin Luther King, Jr. Copyright © 1963 by Martin Luther King, Jr.; copyright renewed © 1991 by Coretta Scott King. From "Sermon Against the War in Vietnam" by Martin Luther King, Jr. Copyright © 1967 by Martin Luther King, Jr.; copyright renewed © 1995 by The Estate of Martin Luther King, Jr.

SOURCES CITED:

From *And the Walls Came Tumbling Down* by Ralph David Abernathy. Published by HarperCollins Publishers, Inc., New York, 1989.

Quote by an African American woman from *The American Slave: Georgia Narratives,* Part 1, vol. 12, edited by George P. Rawick. Published by Greenwood Publishing Group.

Quote by an attorney for an American Indian tribe in New Mexico from "Bare-Bones Imbroglio: Repatriating Indian Remains and Sacred Artifacts" by Dean Peerman from *The Christian Century,* October 17, 1990. Published by the Christian Century Press, Chicago, IL, 1990.

Excerpt about the Bay of Pigs from *The New York Times.*

From "The Stock Market Crash" by Elliott V. Bell from *The New York Times,* October 24, 1929.

From *Sharing Smaller Pies* by Tom Bender. First published in *Rain,* Portland, OR, 1975.

Quote by Jane Berentson from interview with Charles Kaiser, July 7, 1986, from *1968 in America: Music, Politics, Chaos, Counterculture, and the Shaping of a Generation* by Charles Kaiser. Published by Weidenfeld & Nicolson, New York, 1988.

Quotes from a Boxer handbill and from a British officer from "Missionary Martyrs of the Boxer Rebellion," from *Christian History Magazine,* issue 52, vol. XV, no. 4.

Quote by D. Clayton Brown of Texas Christian University, from *Encyclopedia of Southern Culture,* vol. 1, *Agriculture–Environment,* edited by Charles Reagan Wilson et al. Published by the University of North Carolina Press, Chapel Hill, NC, 1989.

Quote by Cesar Caballero from "Chuppies" from *New Americans: An Oral History: Immigrants and Refugees in the U.S. Today* by Al Santoli. Published by Viking Press, New York, 1988.

Quote by Bartolomé de Las Casas from "Ferdinand Magellan" from *The European Discovery of America: The Southern Voyages, A.D. 1492–1616* by Samuel Eliot Morison. Published by Oxford University Press, New York, 1974.

From *Cesar Chavez: Autobiography of La Causa* by Jacques E. Levy. Published by W. W. Norton & Company, Inc., New York, 1975.

Quote by Dr. Alfred Crosby from *The American Experience: Influenza 1918,* online, June 28, 1999. Available http://www.pbs.org/wgbh/pages/amex/influenza/filmmore/transcript/.

From "Los Empeños de una Casa" by Sor Juana Inés de la Cruz, translated by Fanchón Royer, from "The Cell That Became an Academy" from *The Tenth Muse: Sor Juana Inés de la Cruz* by Fanchón Royer. Published by St. Anthony Guild Press, Paterson, NJ, 1952.

Quote by Sor Juana Inés de la Cruz from *A Sor Juana Anthology,* translated by Alan S. Trueblood. Published by Harvard University Press, Cambridge, MA, 1988.

From *Plantation Life in the Florida Parishes of Louisiana, 1836–1846* by Edwin Adams Davis. Published by Columbia University Press, New York, 1943.

Quote by a descendant of a Tejano family from *El Mesquite: A Story of the Early Spanish Settlements Between the Nueces and the Rio Grande as Told by "La Posta del Palo Alto"* by Elena Zamora O'Shea. Published by Mathis Publishing, Dallas, TX, 1935.

Quote by Tran Do from *Vietnam: A History* by Stanley Karnow. Published by Penguin Books, New York, 1983.

From "Driving Cattle from Texas to Iowa, 1866" by George Crawford Duffield from *Annals of Iowa,* vol. XIV, 1924.

From a Maidu creation myth from "The Big-Game Vanishes" from *Kingdoms of Gold, Kingdoms of Jade: The Americas Before Columbus* by Brian M. Fagan. Published by Thames & Hudson, 1991.

Quote by Helen Farmer from *The Great Depression: America in the 1930s* by T. H. Watkins. Published by Little, Brown and Company, New York, 1993.

Quote by Captain José Fernandez, translated by Valeska Bari from *The Course of Empire: First Hand Accounts of California in the Days of the Gold Rush of '49,* compiled by Valeska Bari. Published by Coward-McCann, Inc., New York, 1931.

Quote by a Florida woman from *Searching for the Sunbelt: Historical Perspectives on a Region,* edited by Raymond A. Mohl. Published by The University of Tennessee Press, Knoxville, TN, 1990.

Quote by Mary Margaret Funk from "Buddhism in America" by Jeanne McDowell and Richard N. Ostling from *Time,* online, October 13, 1997, vol. 150, New York, 1997.

Quotes by J. García and M. A. Zumbado R. from Sociedad Económica de Amigos del País, *Estudio relativo a los Contratos Bananeros celebrados entre el Gobierno de Costa Rica y Mr. M. M. Marsh y la United Fruit Company,* San José, CA, 1929.

From *The Road Ahead* by Bill Gates with Nathan Myhrvold and Peter Rinearson. Published by Penguin Books, New York, 1996.

Quote by a German officer describing the fighting at Stalingrad, 1942, from *The Century* by Peter Jennings and Todd Brewster. Published by Doubleday, a division of Random House, Inc., New York, 1998.

Quote about Lyndon B. Johnson from *With No Apologies: The Personal and Political Memoirs of United States Senator Barry Goldwater* by Barry Goldwater. Published by Greenwillow Books, a division of William Morrow & Company, New York, 1996.

Quotes by José Angel Gutiérrez from interview by Hector Galán, December 12, 1994. Transcripts from National Latino Communications Center, Los Angeles, CA, and Galán Productions, Rodulfo Acuña, Austin, TX.

Quote by Colonel Jacobo Arbenz Guzmán from *Modern Latin America,* Second Edition, by Thomas E. Skidmore and Peter H. Smith. Published by Oxford University Press, New York, 1984, 1989.

Quote by Clara Hancox from *The Century* by Peter Jennings and Todd Brewster. Published by Doubleday, a division of Random House, Inc., New York, 1998.

From a quote by Myron Harrington from *Vietnam: A History* by Stanley Karnow. Published by Penguin Books, New York, 1983.

From memo from Heller to President John F. Kennedy, August 2, 1961, Steel file, Sorensen Papers, John F. Kennedy Library.

Quote by Mrs. Isaac H. Hilliard from manuscript located in the Department of Archives, Louisiana State University, Baton Rouge, LA.

From *Their Eyes Were Watching God* by Zora Neale Hurston. Published by Harper & Row Publishers, New York, 1937.

Quotes by Bernice Johnson and Charles Houston from *Eyes on the Prize* by Juan Williams. Published by Penguin Books, New York, 1988.

From *Great Expectations: America and the Baby Boom Generation* by Landon Y. Jones. Published by Coward, McCann & Geoghegan, New York, 1980.

From "Before the Colors Fade: Last of the Rough Riders" by V. C. Jones from *American Heritage Magazine,* August 1969.

From *Red Power: The American Indians' Fight for Freedom* by Alvin M. Josephy, Jr. Published by McGraw-Hill, New York, 1971.

Quote by Shirley Keith in concert, "Benefit for Alcatraz," at Stanford, CA, December 18, 1969. Recording at Pacifica Radio Archives, North Hollywood, CA .

Quote by Ed Lazowska from "Focus on Technology: Seattle, Wash." by Brad Stone from *Newsweek,* November 9, 1998. Published by Newsweek, Inc., New York, 1998.

Quote by Mary Mackey from *Great Expectations: America and the Baby Boom Generation* by Landon Y. Jones. Published by Coward, McCann & Geoghegan, New York, 1980.

From *The Presidential Papers* by Norman Mailer. Published by G. P. Putnam's Sons, New York, 1963.

From *Steven Spielberg: A Biography* by Joseph McBride. Published by Simon & Schuster, New York, 1997.

From a quote by Anne O'Hare McCormick from *Truman* by David McCullough. Published by Simon & Schuster, New York, 1992.

From "Still 'A Little Left of Center'" by Anne O'Hare McCormick from *The New York Times,* June 21, 1936.

Quote by Robert McElvaine from *The Great Depression: America in the 1930s* by T. H. Watkins. Published by Little, Brown and Company, New York, 1993.

Quotes by Eliseo Medina from interview by Sylvia Morales, November 18, 1995. Transcripts from National Latino Communications Center, Los Angeles, CA, and Galán Productions, Austin, TX.

Quote by Mexican poet from *The Florentine Codex,* vol. 10, by Arthur Anderson and Charles Dibble. Published by University of Utah Press, Salt Lake City, UT.

From a letter by Manuel Mier y Terán to the Mexican Minister of War, Pueblo Viejo, November 14, 1829, from *Terán and Texas: A Chapter in Texas-Mexican Relations* by Ohland Mortan (Austin, 1948).

Quotes by Thomas Minehan and by an anonymous teenager from *The Great Depression: America in the 1930s* by T. H. Watkins. Published by Little, Brown and Company, New York, 1993.

Quote by Martha Ann Morrison Minto from "Female Pioneering in Oregon, 1844" from a Manuscript Diary. Bancroft Library, University of California, Berkeley, CA.

From "Columbus's Letter to Santangel" as quoted in "The Greater Antilles" from *The European Discovery of America: The Southern Voyages, A.D. 1492–1616* by Samuel Eliot Morison. Published by Oxford University Press, New York, 1974.

Quotes by Bob Moses, MacArthur Cotton, and Mendy Samstein from Notes on Mississippi Staff Meeting, November 1963. State Historical Society of Wisconsin: Howard Zinn Papers.

Quotes by New Yorker Johnny Boy Musto, Anibal Campa, and a 21-year-old beautician from "Get Up and Boogie" by Maureen Orth et al. from *Newsweek,* November 8, 1976. Published by Newsweek, Inc., New York, 1976.

Quote by John Ortiz from *Social Protest in an Urban Barrio: A Study of the Chicano Movement, 1966–1974* by Marguerite V. Marin. Published by University Press of America, Lanham, MD, 1991.

From "...The hawk had come" by Gordon Parks from *Brother Can You Spare a Dime? The Great Depression, 1929–1933* by Milton Meltzer. Published by Alfred A. Knopf, Inc., New York, 1969.

Quote by Ed Paulsen from *Hard Times: An Oral History of the Great Depression* by Studs Terkel. Published by Avon Books, a division of the Hearst Corporation, New York, 1970.

Quote by a Polish coal miner from *Workers' World* by John Bodnar. Published by *Workers' World,* Baltimore, MD, 1982.

Quote by Sugar Rautbord from *The Great Divide* by Studs Terkel. Published by Pantheon Books, New York, 1988.

Quote by Robert Reich from "They're Rich (and You're Not)" by Adam Bryant from *Newsweek,* July 5, 1999. Published by Newsweek, Inc., New York, 1999.

From a quote by Deputy Reyes to the Honduran Congress from *Boletín Legislativo* (Legislative Record), series iv, no. 31, January 23, 1933.

From *Texas* by Ferdinand Roemer, translated by Oswald Mueller. Published by the German-Texan Heritage Society, 1983.

Quote by Julian Rolph from *"It's Your Misfortune and None of My Own": A New History of the American West* by Richard White. Published by the University of Oklahoma Press, Publishing Division of the University, Norman, OK, 1991.

Quote by William Rutherford from a telephone conversation between Rutherford and Levison, June 2, 1968, from the FBI Levison File. Library and Archive, Martin Luther King, Jr., Center for Nonviolent Social Change, Atlanta, GA.

Quote by Harley Shaiken from "Big Brown's Union Blues" by Daniel Pedersen from *Newsweek,* August 18, 1997. Published by Newsweek, Inc., New York, 1997.

Quotes by Donna Shalala from "Shalala Remembers Kennedy's Call to Peace; Cabinet Secretary Comes to Austin for Peace Corps Reunion" by Ben Wear from *Austin American Statesman,* August 4, 1995.

Quote by Albert Sindlinger from "Tinkering with the Wireless: Can Anyone Hear Me West of Steubenville?" from *The Century* by Peter Jennings and Todd Brewster. Published by Doubleday, a division of Random House, Inc., New York, 1998.

Quote by a slave woman from *The Rattling Chains: Slave Unrest and Revolt in the Ante-Bellum South* by Nicholas Halasz.

From *The Grapes of Wrath* by John Steinbeck. Published by the Viking Press, New York, 1939.

Quote by Elisha Stockwell from *The Boys' War: Confederate and Union Soldiers Talk About the Civil War* by Jim Murphy. Published by Clarion Books, a Houghton Mifflin Company imprint, New York, 1990.

Quote by a Panhandle county sheriff from "Race, Labor, and the Frontier" from *Anglos and Mexicans in the Making of Texas, 1836–1986* by David Montejano. Published by the University of Texas Press, Austin, TX, 1987.

Quotes by Reverend Harold Toliver and Nelson Poynter from *Americans Remember the Home Front: An Oral Narrative of the World War II Years in America* by Roy Hoopes. Published by Berkley Books, New York, 1992.

Quote by Mrs. Townsend from "Young Mother" from *Ladies' Home Journal,* 1956.

Quote by Ton That Tung from *Vietnam: A History* by Stanley Karnow. Published by Penguin Books, New York, 1983.

Quote by Maria Valera about the National Chicano Liberation Youth Conference, 1969, from *Youth, Identity, Power: The Chicano Movement* by Carlos Muñoz. Published by Verso, London, England, 1989.

Quote by Bruce Weigl from *The Vietnam Wars: 1945–1990* by Marilyn B. Young. Published by HarperCollins Publishers, New York, 1991.

From "The Question of Reburial: How the Crow Creek archaeologists view the question of reburial" by P. Willey from *Early Man Magazine,* Autumn 1981. Published by Center of American Archeology, Kampsville, IL, 1981.

Quote by David Wyss from "Ace in the Hole" by John Cassidy from *The New Yorker,* June 10, 1996.

Photo Credits

Abreviations used: (t) top, (c) center, (b) bottom, (l) left, (r) right, (bckgd) background), (bdr) border

FRONT COVER, title page: CORBIS/Bill Ross.

FRONT MATTER / TABLE OF CONTENTS: Page iii, (t), courtesy Paul Boyer, (tl), courtesy Ronald Foore, (tr), courtesy Nan Woodruff, (cl), courtesy Yasuhide Kawashima, (cr), courtesy Alfred Young, (b), courtesy Lucinda Lucero Sachs; v, AKG Photo; vi, (t), Peter Newark's American Pictures, (b), Larry Stevens / Nawrocki Stock Photo; vii, (t), Print Collection, Miriam and Ira D. Wallach Division of Art, Prints and Photographs, The New York Public Library, Astor, Lenox and Tilden Foundations / PRC Archive, (c), Kim Neilsen / Smithsonian Institution, Washington, DC / PRC Archive, (b), Corbis-Bettmann; viii, (t), Atlanta History Center, (b), History Division, LA County Museum. Photo by Henry Groskinsky; ix, (t), Museum of the City of New York, Gift of Mary and Charles Odgen, (bl), The Granger Collection, New York; (br), Smithsonian Institution, neg no. 91-6501 / PRC Archive; x, Library of Congress; xi, (t), The Granger Collection, New York, (b), Frank Driggs Collection; xii, Corbis-Bettmann; xiii, (l), HRW Photo by Sam Dudgeon, (r), Sylvia Johnson / Woodfin Camp & Associates, Inc.; xiv, David Hume Kennerly / Corbis Sygma; Collection of Janice L. and David J. Frent / PRC Archive; xv, (l), U.S. Postal Service / Harcourt Inc., (r), U.S. Postal Service / Neena M. Mitchell Stock/Art Images; xx, (l), Ashmolean Museum / E.T. Archive, (r), Cook Collection, Valentine Museum, Richmond, Virginia / PRC Archive, (all flags) Image Copyright © 1997 PhotoDisc, Inc.; xxi, NASA; xxii, Woolaroc Museum, Bartlesville, Oklahoma; xxiii, (t), The Granger Collection, New York, (b), The Smithsonian Institution, Museum of American History, National Numismatic Collection, Washington, DC.

UNIT 1: Page xxiv-1, The Trustees of The British Museum; 1, Allan Eaton / Ancient Art & Architecture Collection.

CHAPTER 1: Page 2, (tl), © Skimuseet Knudsen Oslo, (tr), Nawrocki Stock Photo, (bl), Grant Heilman Photography, (br), The Granger Collection, New York; 3, (tl), SuperStock, (tc, bl, br), Ancient Art & Architecture Collection Ltd, (tr), Art Resource, NY; 4, Carnegie Museum of Natural History; 5, (t), Tom McHugh / Photo Researchers, Inc., (b), © Steve Elmore / Tony Stone / AllStock; 6, (l), Tom Walker / Tony Stone Images, (r), SuperStock; 7, Grant Heilman Photography; 8, ©Marilyn "Angel" Wynn, Sun Valley, Idaho; 9, (t), © Cosmo Condina / Tony Stone Images, (b), © Robert Frerck / Woodfin Camp & Associates, Inc.; 11, (t), Michael Scoot / Tony Stone / AllStock; (b), Mireille Vautier / Woodfin Camp & Associates, Inc.; 12, F. Stuart Westmorland / AllStock / PNI; 13, (t), © Robert Frerck / Odyssey Pictures, (b), ©ChinaStock; 14, © China Stock; 15, AKG Photo, London; 18, Jean Pragen / Tony Stone / AllStock; 19 (t), Cathedral Treasury, Aachen / SuperStock, (b), Giraudon / Art Resource, NY; 20 (t), Heidelberg University Library, Germany / Explorer, Paris / SuperStock, (b), © Robert Frerck / Odyssey Pictures; 21, AKG Photo, London; 23 (tl), Christie's Images / SuperStock, (tr), © Robert Frerck / Odyssey Pictures; 24 (t), AKG Photo, London, (b), Topkapi Museum, Istanbul / E.T. Archive; 25, AKG Photo; 26 (bl), ©Robert Frerck / Odyssey / Chicago, (bc), AKG London; 27 (l), Giraudon / Art Resource, NY, (r), © David Hathcox / Arms Communications; 28 (t), Library of Congress, (b), Jacksonville Museum of Contemporary Art, Florida / SuperStock; 29, Corbis-Bettmann; 31, The Granger Collection, New York.

CHAPTER 2: Page 32, (tl), Werner Forman Archive, Museum of the American Indian, New York / Art Resource, NY, (tr), Ashmolean Museum / E.T. Archive, (bl), © Ronald Sheridan / Ancient Art & Architecture Collection, Ltd., (br), Peter Newark's Historical Pictures; 33, (tl), Peter Newark's American Pictures, (tc), AKG Photo, (tr), SuperStock, (bl), Brown University Library; (br), Runk / Schoenberger / Grant Heilman Photography; 34, (t), North Wind Picture Archives, (b), The Metropolitan Museum of Art, Gift of J.Pierpont Morgan, 1900. (00.18.2) Photograph copyright 1979 The Metropolitan Museum of Art. All rights reserved, The Metropolitan Museum of Art; 35, (t), The Granger Collection, New York, (b), © Robert Frerck / Odyssey / Chicago; 36, Private Collection / A.K.G. Photo / SuperStock; 38, AKG Photo, London; 39, C. Chesek / J.Becket / Negatives / Transparencies #4051, Courtesy Department of Library Services, American Museum of Natural History; 40 (t), AKG Photo, London, (b), AKG Photo, London; 41 (l), © Allan Eaton / Ancient Art & Architecture Collection Ltd., (r), A.K.G., Berlin / SuperStock; 42, North Wind Picture Archives; 44, Private Collection / ET Archive, London / SuperStock; 45, North Wind Picture Archives; 46 (t), Peter Newark's American Pictures, (b), SuperStock; 47 (t), Nawrocki Stock Photo, (b), Peter Newark's American Pictures; 48 (t), The Granger Collection, New York, (c), Peter Newark's American Pictures; (b), Tony Freeman / PhotoEdit; 49, Antonio Mercado / Art Resource, NY; 50, The Granger Collection, New York; 51 (t), American Museum, Madrid / E.T. Archive, (b), SuperStock; 52, Brown University Library; 53, Peter Newark's American Pictures; 54, SuperStock; 55, (t), Larry Stevens / Nawrocki Stock Photo, (b), Peter Newark's Western Americana; 57, (t), The Granger Collection, New York, (b), Detail from the National Portrait Gallery, Smithsonian Institution, Washington, DC / Art Resource, NY; 58, (t), Colonial Williamsburg Foundation, (b), © Jacques Lowe / Woodfin Camp & Associates, Inc.; 59, Peter Newark's American Pictures; 61, (t), *Mission of San Jose near San Antonio de Bexar* by Edward Everett, 1847, pen and ink and watercolor on paper, 7 5/8 x 9 3/8 in., #1977.10. Amon Carter Museum, Fort Worth, Texas, Gift of Mrs. Anne Burnett Tandy in memory of her father Thomas Lloyd Burnett, 1870-1938, (br), © Allan Eaton / Ancient Art & Architecture Collection Ltd.

CHAPTER 3: Page 64, (tl), State Capitol, Commonwealth of Virginia, Courtesy Library of Virginia, image altered, (tr), North Wind Picture Archives, (bl), Corbis-Bettmann, (br), Ancient Art & Architecture Collection Ltd.; 65, (tl), Peter Newark's American Pictures; (tr), "Franklin's Experiment in Electricity c. 1746," published by Currier and Ives (print) / Private Collection / Bridgeman Art Library, London / New York, (bl), Boltin Picture Library, (br), *George Whitefield Preaching,* by Collett / National Portrait Library, London / Bridgeman Art Library, London / New York; 66, (t), SuperStock, (b), Terry Engell Gallery / E.T. Archive; 67, Courtesy of the Pilgrim Society, Plymouth, Massachusetts; 68, The Granger Collection, New York; 69 (t), Peter Newark's American Pictures, (b), Courtesy of the Pilgrim Society, Plymouth, Massachusetts; 70 (t, bl), The Granger Collection, New York, (br), Peabody Essex Museum, Salem, Massachusetts; 71, Corbis; 73, (t), Peter Newark's American Pictures; 73(b), 74, 75(tl), The Granger Collection, New York; 75 (tr), Donald Dietz / Stock, Boston, (b), Boltin Picture Library; 76, (t), Peter Newark's American Pictures; (b), Michael Holford; 77, (t), The Granger Collection, New York (b), *Portrait of a Negro Man, Olaudah Equiano,* 1780s. Previously attributed to Joshua Reynolds / Royal Albert Memorial Museum, Exeter, Devon, UK / Bridgeman Art Library, London / New York; 78, Peter Newark's American Pictures; 79, (t), Newberry Library, Chicago / SuperStock, (b), No. 3834 *King Charles II of England* (1630-85), c. 1675 (vellum) / Fitzwilliam Museum, University of Cambridge, UK / Bridgeman Art Library, London / New York; 80, (all), The Granger Collection, New York; 82 (t), The Granger Collection, New York, (b), Peter Newark's American Pictures; 83, 84, (all) The Granger Collection, New York; 86, (t), "The Capitulation of Louisbourg," Illustration from *Colonies and Nation* by Woodrow Wilson, pub. in Harper's Magazine, 1901 (lithograph), after Howard Pyle / Private Collection / Bridgeman Art Library, London / New York, (b), The Granger Collection, New York; 87, The Granger Collection, New York; 88, Levi Woodbury Papers, Manuscripts Division, Library of Congress; 89, Stock Montage, Inc.; 90, Public Record Office, Kew, Richmond, Surrey; 91, North Wind Picture Archives; 93, The Granger Collection, New York;

UNIT 1 REVIEW 94 (t), Catalan Atlas detail, showing the family of Marco Polo (1254-1324) travelling by camel caravan, 1375. British Library, London, UK / The Bridgeman Art Library, New York / London, (b), The Granger Collection, New York; 95, Peter Newark's American Pictures.

UNIT 2: Page 96-97, Independence National Historical Park Collection; 97, Mickey Osterreicher / Black Star;

CHAPTER 4: Page 98, (t), I.N. Phelps Stokes Collection, The New York Public Library, Astor, Lenox and Tilden Foundations, (bl), The Granger Collection, New York, (br), Peter Newark's American Pictures; 99, (tl), The Granger Collection, New York, (tr), Peter Newark's American Pictures, (bl), Giraudon / Art Resource, NY, (br), Christie's Images; 100, (t), Colonial Williamsburg Foundation, (b), Courtesy of the Hunt Institute for Botanical Documentation, Carnegie Mellon University, Pittsburgh, PA; 101, The Granger Collection, New York; 102, Woodfin Camp & Associates, Inc.; 103 (tl), Rare Books and Manuscripts Division, The New York Public Library, Astor, Lenox and Tilden Foundations, (tr, b), The Granger Collection, New York; 104 (t), Carroll Reece Museum, Center for Appalachian Studies, East Tennessee University, (b), Library Company of Philadelphia; 105, The Granger Collection, New York; 106, 107(b), Peter Newark's American Pictures; (b), *Portrait of George III (1738-1820) in his Coronation Robes,* c. 1760 (oil on canvas) by Allan Ramsay (1713-84) / Private Collection / Bridgeman Art Library, London / New York; 108, (b), Courtesy the Bostonian Society, The Old State House; 109, Jonathan Wallen; 110, (t), Bequest of Winslow Warren, Courtesy Museum of Fine Arts, Boston MA, (b), Library Company of Philadelphia; 111, (t), Francis G. Meyer / Corbis; 111(b), 112(t), Peter Newark's American Pictures; 112 (b), 114(both), 115, 116 (tr, tl), The Granger Collection, New York; 116, (b), Stock Editions / HRW Photo Research Library; 117, Library of Congress; 118, (t), Free Library of Philadelphia / Scala / Art Resource, NY, (b), Christie's Images; 119, (tl), Peter Newark's American Pictures; (tr), Collection of the New-York Historical Society; 120, (l), The Granger Collection, New York; (r), Stock Editions / HRW Photo Research Library; 122, Historical Society of Pennsylvania; 124, (t), Benninghoff Collection of the American Revolution, (b), The Granger Collection, New York; 125, Peter Newark's American Pictures; 126, (t), The Dietrich American Foundation, photograph by Will Brown, Philadelphia, PA; 126 (b), 128, The Granger Collection, New York; 129, John Trumbull, *Surrender of Lord Cornwallis at Yorktown,* Yale University Art Gallery, Trumbull Collection; 131, The Granger Collection, New York; 132, (t), Wadsworth Atheneum Hartford. Bequest of Mrs. Clara Hinton Gould, (b), Peter Newark's American Pictures.

CHAPTER 5: Page 133 (tl), Sophia Smith Collection, Smith College, (tc), Peter Newark's Historical Pictures, (tr), Larry Stevens / Nawrocki Stock Photo, (bl), Peter Newark's American Pictures, (br), The Granger Collection, New York; 134 (t), SuperStock, (b), Stock Montage, Inc.; 135, Courtesy of the Ford Archives, Henry Ford Museum, Dearborn, Michigan; 136 (t), Courtesy Winterthur Museum, (b), HRW Photo Research Library; 137, The Granger Collection, New York; 138, Archive Photos; 140, The Smithsonian Institution, Museum of American History, National Numismatic Collection; 141, The Granger Collection, New York; 142 (t), Independence National Historical Park Collection, (b), The Granger Collection, New York; 143 (t), North Wind Picture Archives, (b), CORBIS/Bettmann; 144, Independence National Historical Park Collection; 145 (t), Maryland Historical Society, Baltimore, Maryland, (b), Library of Congress; 146, 148, The Granger Collection, New York; 149 (t), CORBIS / Joseph Sohm / Chromosohm Inc., (b), Courtesy of the John Carter Brown Library at Brown University; 151 (t), Stock Montage, Inc., (bl), Jay Mallin Photo, (br), The Granger Collection, New York; 152, (t), M. Theiler / Washington Stock Photo, (bl), North Wind Picture Archives, (br), Dana White / PhotoEdit; 153 (t), Courtesy, Supreme Court of the United States, The Supreme Court Historical Society, (b), H. Armstrong Roberts; 154 (t), Reuters / Win McNamee / Archive Photos; 154, (b), The Granger Collection, New York; 157, National Geographic Image Collection; 158, Library of Congress; 159, Independence National Historical Park Collection; 160, (t), The Granger Collection, New York, (bl, br), U.S. Postal Service / Harcourt, Inc.; 161, (t), Independence National Historical Park Collection, (b), David Young-Wolff / PhotoEdit; 162, Nebraska State Historical Society; 164, (t), The Granger Collection, New York, (b), Corbis-Bettmann; 165(t), National Archives; 165(b),170, Independence National Historical Park Collection; 173, Collection, The Supreme Court Historical Society; 177 (t), Joe Marquette/AP/Wide World Photos, (b), Jeffrey Brown / Liaison Agency; 178, Bob Daemmrich Photo, Inc.; 179, Louie Psihoyos / Woodfin Camp & Associates, Inc.; 180, Library of Congress; 182 (t), HRW Photo by Sam Dudgeon, (b), Underwood & Underwood / Corbis-Bettmann; 183, Sophia Smith Collection, Smith College; 184, R. Foulds / Washington Stock Photo; 185, AP / Wide World Photos, Inc.; 186, Jeff Greenberg / PhotoEdit; 187 (t), The Granger Collection, New York, (cl),HRW Photo by Sam Dudgeon, (cr), Chicago Historical Society, #X.1354, (b), Tom Pantages.

CHAPTER 6: Page 188 (tl), © Collection of the New-York Historical Society; (tr), HRW Photo Research Library; 188 (bl), CORBIS / Gianni Dagli Orti; (br), North Wind Picture Archives; 189 (tl), Peter Newark's Military Pictures, (tr), The Granger Collection, New York, (bl), Library of Congress, (br), CORBIS / Richard T. Nowitz; 190 (l), The Granger Collection, New York, (r), Sally Andersen-Bruce Photography; 191 (l), Stock Montage, Inc., (r), Tom Pantages; 192 (t), Paul Conklin / PhotoEdit, (b), The Granger Collection, New York; 193 (t), U.S. Postal Service / Harcourt Brace & Company, (b), Museum of American Financial History; 194 Larry Stevens / Nawrocki Stock Photo; 195, The Granger Collection, New York; 196 (t), Peter Newark's American Pictures, (b), Courtesy Ohio Historical Society; 197, Giraudon / Art Resource, NY; 198, (t), The Granger Collection, New York, (b), Courtesy Peabody Essex Museum, Salem, Massachusetts; 199, 201, 203, 204 (l), The Granger Collection, New York; 204, (r), Peter Newark's American Pictures; 205, (t), U.S. Postal Service/Harcourt, Inc., (b), The Granger Collection, New York; 206, (l), Peter Newark's American Pictures, (r), The Granger Collection, New York; 207, (t), Peter Newark's American Pictures, (b), North Wind Picture Archives; 208, Peter Newark's Western Americana; 209, The Granger Collection, New York; 210, North Wind Picture Archives; 211, Archive Photos; 212, Mickey Osterreicher / Black Star; 213, CORBIS / Francis G. Mayer; 214 (l, r), The Granger Collection, New York, 215, CORBIS; 217, (t), The Granger Collection, New York, (b), CORBIS / Ed Young; 218, Everett Collection / CSU Archives.

UNIT 2 REVIEW: 220 (both), SuperStock; 221, Sally Andersen-Bruce Photography.

UNIT 3: Page 222-223, Samuel B. Waugh, *The Bay and Harbor of New York,* c. 1855, Museum of the City of New York (33.169.1); 223, Boltin Picture Library.

CHAPTER 7: Page 224, (tl), Corbis-Bettmann, (tr), Columned clock by Seth Thomas (1785-1859), c. 1855 / Strike One, London, UK / Bridgeman Art Library, London / New York, (bl), SuperStock, (br), The Granger Collection, New York; 225, (tl), The Lowe Art Museum, The University of Miami/SuperStock; (tr), Archive Photos; (bl), Woodfin Camp & Associates, Inc., (br), D. Donne Bryant; 226, (t), The Granger Collection, New York, (b), HRW Photo Research Library; 227, (t), Archive Photos, (b), Courtesy Museum of Florida History; 228, SuperStock; 229, Explorer, Paris / SuperStock; 231, (t), The Granger Collection, New York, (b), Nawrocki Stock Photo; 232, (t), National Portrait Gallery, Washington, D.C., U.S.A. / Art Resource, NY, (b), Sally Andersen-Bruce Photography; 234, Maryland Historical Society, Baltimore, Maryland; 235, Collection of the New-York Historical Society; 236 (both), The Granger Collection, New York; 237, Corbis-Bettmann; 238, The Granger Collection, New York; 239, SuperStock; 240, (t), The Museum of American Political Life, University of Hartford, West Hartford, CT, (b), The Hermitage, Home of Andrew Jackson; 241, (t), Archive Photos, (b), The Granger Collection, New York; 242, Museum of American Political Life, University of Hartford, West Hartford, CT; 243, (t), Charles Phillips; 243 (b), 244 (t) The Granger Collection, New York; 244, (b), Newberry Library, Chicago / SuperStock; 245, Woolaroc Museum, Bartlesville, Oklahoma; 246 (tl), C. W. Kirk Collection, Oklahoma Historical Society, (tr), Lawrence Migdale / Stock, Boston, (b), Bob Prestwood after a Phillip Dorf Illustration; 247, Courtesy of the American Antiquarian Society; 248, 249, The Granger Collection, New York; 251, The Museum of American Political Life, University of Hartford, West Hartford, CT.

CHAPTER 8: Page 252 (t), Courtesy, Gore Place / PRC Archive; 252 (bl), Kim Neilsen / Smithsonian Institution, Washington, DC / PRC Archive; (br), PRC Archive; 253 (tl), Trustees of the Watts Gallery, Compton, Surrey, UK / Bridgeman Art Library, London / New York; (tr), Miriam and Ira D. Wallach Division of Art, Prints and Photographs, The New York Public Library. Astor, Lenox and Tilden Foundations / PRC; (cl), The Granger Collection, New York; (cr), © Gibbes Museum of Art, Carolina Art Association, (bl), National Museum of American History, Smithsonian Institution, Washington, D.C. / PRC; 254 (t), Courtesy, State Street Corporation / Photo by Clive Russ / PRC ; (b), Collection of William Gladstone / PRC Archive; 255 (t), Library of Congress, (b), Chicago Historical Society; 256, (t), Boston Athenaeum / PRC, (b), American Textile History Museum; 257, (l), Corbis-Bettmann, (r), Slater Mill Historic Site / PRC Archive; 258, Corbis-Bettmann; 259, (t), Courtesy of the Bostonian Society / Old State House, photo by Mark Sexton / PRC Archive, (b), Lester S. Levy Collection, The Johns Hopkins University, The Milton S. Eisenhower Library, Department of Special Collections/ PRC; 260, Library of Congress; 261, Library Company of Philadelphia / PRC Archive; 262 (t), Musee National du Chateau, Versailles, France / Erich Lessing / Art Resource, NY, (b), Henry E. Peach / Old Sturbridge Village / PRC Archive; 263 (t), Louisiana State University Museum of Art / PRC Archive; (b), Courtesy, The Winterthur Library, Joseph Downs Collection of Manuscripts and Printed Ephemera / PRC Archive; 265, Colonial Williamsburg Foundation; 266, Library of Congress / PRC Archive; 267, Smithsonian Institution, Washington, DC, neg. #75-2984; 268, (l), Courtesy of the John Carter Brown Library at Brown University / PRC Archive; (r), Courtesy of the South Carolina Library, University of South Carolina, Columbia / PRC Archive; 269 (t), Blue Ridge Institute & Museums / Ferrum Collection / PRC Archive, (b), Print Collection, Miriam and Ira D. Wallach Division of Art, Prints and Photographs, The New York Public Library, Astor, Lenox and Tilden Foundations / PRC Archive; 270 ,Courtesy of the Charleston Museum, Charleston, South Carolina; 271 (t), *The Rev. J.W. Loguen, as a Slave and as a Freedman,* Trustees of the Boston Public Library / PRC, (b), Missouri Historical Society / PRC Archive; 272 (t), From the Collection of William L. Murphy / PRC Archive, (b), Collection of the New-York Historical Society / PRC Archive; 273 (t), Louisiana State Museum / PRC Archive, (b), PRC Archive; 273, Louisiana State Museum / PRC Archive; 274, Chicago Historical Society / PRC Archive; 276 (t), Stagville Center / PRC Archive, (b), The Historic New Orleans Collection / PRC Archive; 277 (l), The Granger Collection, New York, (r), Wade Spees / Black Star; 278, Courtesy of the Illinois State Historical Society / PRC Archive; 279, Library of Congress / PRC Archive; 281 (l), Culver Pictures, Inc., (r), The Granger Collection, New York.

CHAPTER 9: Page 284 (tl), Smithsonian Institution Archives, Washington, D.C., (tr), The Granger Collection, New York / PRC Archive, (b), Giraudon / Art Resource, NY; 285 (tl), Boston Athenaeum / PRC Archive; (tr), PRC Archive; (br), Brown University Library / Photo: John Miller Documents / PRC Archive; (bl), *Democracy in America* by Alexis de Tocqueville, Trustees of the Boston Public Library / PRC Archive; 286 (t), Library of Congress / PRC Archive, (b), The Granger Collection, New York; 287, Corbis-Bettmann; 288, Photo by Paul Rocheleau, The Metropolitan Museum of Art; 289 (l), National Portrait Gallery, Smithsonian Institution, Washington, D.C. / PRC Archive, (r), Courtesy of the Trustees of Amherst College / PRC Archive; 290, Rare Books and Manuscripts Division, The New York Public Library,

Astor, Lenox and Tilden Foundations / PRC Archive; 291 (t), Harriet Beecher Stowe Center, Hartford, CT; (b), Archive Photos; 292, Stock Montage, Inc.; 293 (t), Schlesinger Library, Harvard Radcliffe / PRC Archive, (b), The Metropolitan Museum of Art, Gift of I.N. Phelps Stokes, Edward S. Hawes, Alice Mary Hawes, Marion Augusta Hawes, 1937. [37.14.22]. All rights reserved, The Metropolitan Museum of Art. Courtesy PRC Archive; 294, Archives, Langston Hughes Memorial Library, Lincoln University, PA; 295, National Library of Medicine / PRC Archive; 296, Corbis; 297 (t), American Antiquarian Society, (b), Maryland Historical Society, Baltimore, Maryland / PRC Archive; 298, National Portrait Gallery, Smithsonian Institution / Art Resource, N.Y. / PRC; 299, Courtesy of the Massachusetts Historical Society; 300 (t), Courtesy the Indiana Historical Society Library / PRC; (b), Courtesy the Massachusetts Historical Society / PRC; 301, Amnesty International; 302, Stock Montage, Inc.; 303 (t), The Granger Collection, New York, (b), Daughters of the American Revolution Museum / PRC Archive; 304 (t), Rare Books and Manuscripts Division, The New York Public Library, Astor, Lenox and Tilden Foundations / PRC Archive, (b), The Schlesinger Library, Radcliffe College / PRC; 306 (t), Archive Photos, (c), Meserve-Kunhardt Collection / PRC Archive; (b), The Granger Collection, New York; 309, Daughters of the American Revolution Museum / PRC Archive.

UNIT 3 REVIEW: Page 310 (r), The Granger Collection, New York; (l), National Museum of American Art, Washington D.C. / Art Resource, NY; 311, The Granger Collection, New York.

UNIT 4: Page 312, Kirby Collection of Historical Paintings, Lafayette College, Easton, Pennsylvania / courtesy PRC; 313 (inset), Colorado Historical Society.

CHAPTER 10: Page 314 (tl), Missouri Historical Society, St. Louis / PRC; (tr), National Museum of American History 1999 / Smithsonian Institution; Washington, DC; (bl), United Nations, (bc), Joslyn Art Museum, Omaha, Nebraska / PRC; (br), The Granger Collection, New York; 315 (tl), Collection of the James K. Polk Memorial Association, Columbia, Tennessee; (tr), National Archives (NARA); (bl), Minnesota Historical Society / PRC Archive; (br), Phoenix Art Museum: Museum Purchase with funds provided by the Estate of Carolann Smurthwaite / PRC Archive; 316 (t), Texas Memorial Museum / PRC Archive, (b), Library of Congress / PRC Archive; 317, History Division, LA County Museum. Photo by Henry Groskinsky; 318 (t), Prints and Photographs Collection, The Center for American History / The University of Texas at Austin, CN00878, (bl), *Fall of the Alamo* by Robert Onderdonk, Courtesy of Friends of the Governor's Mansion, Austin, Texas / PRC Archive, (br), Smithsonian Institution / PRC Archive; 320, Eric Beggs / Texas State Library and Archives Commission; 321 (l), Texas State Library and Archives Commission, (r), Institute of Texas Cultures at San Antonio, Courtesy of Albert J. Blaha; 323 (t), Henry Groskinsky / PRC Archive, (b), Collection of the James K. Polk Memorial Association, Columbia, Tennessee; 324 (t), U.S. Postal Service / Neena M. Mitchell Stock/Art Images; (b), Collection of Janice L. and David J. Frent / PRC Archive; 325, Society of California Pioneers / PRC Archive; 327, University of California at Berkeley, Bancroft Library / PRC Archive; 328, Carl Socolon / The Landis Valley Museum / PRC Archive; 329, Colorado Historical Society / PRC Archive; 330, (t), Culver Pictures, Inc., (b), PRC Archive; 331 (tl), Oregon Historical Society; (tr), © Chuck Pefley / Stock, Boston; (b), Library of Congress, Courtesy Imagefinders, Inc; 333, Tom Dietrich / Tony Stone Images; 334, Joslyn Art Museum, Omaha, Nebraska; 335 (t), Courtesy of the Oakland Museum of California/ PRC Archive, (b), Peter Newark's Western Americana; 336, University of California at Berkeley, Bancroft Library; 337, The Bostonian Society, the Old State House; 338 (t), Image Copyright © 1999 PhotoDisc, Inc.; (b), Wells Fargo Bank; 339, Courtesy of the California History Room, California State Library, Sacramento, California; 341, Panhandle-Plains Historical Museum, Research Center, Canyon, Texas / PRC Archive.

CHAPTER 11: Page 342 (tl), Courtesy of the Fogg Art Museum, Harvard University Art Museums, (tr), Collection of the New-York Historical Society / PRC Archive; (bl), Collection of Robert and Catherine Booth / photo courtesy of Walters Beniske Art and Antiques / PRC Archive; (br), Library of Congress / PRC Archive; Loan from Massachusetts General Hospital Photo Collection / PRC Archive; 343, (tl), Library of Congress / PRC Archive, 343 (tr), The Museum of American Political Life, University of Hartford, West Hartford, CT / PRC Archive, (bl), Museum of the City of New York / PRC Archive; (br), Division of Political History, Smithsonian Institution, Washington, D.C; 344, (t), Laurie Platt Winfrey / Woodfin Camp & Associates, Inc.; (b), Stock Montage, Inc; 345, Library of Congress / PRC Archive; 346, (t), Courtesy, American Antiquarian Society / PRC Archive, (b), Rare Books and Manuscripts Division, The New York Public Library, Astor, Lenox and Tilden Foundations / PRC Archive; 347, National Archives (NARA); 348, Gibbes Museum of Art, Carolina Art Association / PRC Archive; 349, 350(t) The Granger Collection, New York; 350 (b), Collection of Janice L. and David J. Frent / PRC Archive; 351 (l), Chicago Historical Society; (r), The Granger Collection, New York; 352 (t), Schlesinger Library, Radcliffe College / PRC Archive; (b), PRC Archive; 353, (l), Library Company of Philadelphia / PRC Archive, (r), The Library Company of Philadelphia; 354, Kansas State Historical Society, Topeka; 355, (t), Kansas State Historical Society, Topeka / PRC Archive, (b), The Granger Collection, New York; 356, (t), The Granger Collection, New York; (bl), Library of Congress / Woodfin Camp & Associates, Inc., (br), Museum of American Political Life, University of Hartford, West Hartford, CT. Photo by Steven Laschever; 357, Steven Laschever / Museum of American Political Life, University of Hartford, West Hartford, CT; 358 (t), The Granger Collection, New York, (b), Library of Congress / PRC Archive; 359 (t), The Granger Collection, New York / PRC, (b), National Portrait Gallery, Smithsonian Institution / Art Resource, N.Y.; 360, Cameramann / The Image Works / Courtesy of PRC; 361, The Metropolitan Museum of Art, Gift of Mr. and Mrs. Carl Stoeckel, 1897. (97.5) © 1982 by The Metropolitan Museum of Art. All rights reserved, The Metropolitan Museum of Art.; 362 (t), Library of Congress, (b), The Museum of American Political Life, University of Hartford, West Hartford,CT; 363, Library of Congress / PRC Archive; 365, The Granger Collection, New York.

CHAPTER 12: Page 366 (tl), Library of Congress / PRC Archive, (tr), George Eastman House / PRC Archive, (bl), The Granger Collection, New York, (bc), Library of Congress / photo by Ken Cobb; (br), Corbis-Bettmann; 367,(tl), Tom Lovell / National Geographic Image Collection; (tr), Courtesy of the Museum of the American Numismatic Association, (b), The Museum of the Confederacy, Richmond, Virginia / PRC Archive; 368, (t), Chicago Historical Society / PRC Archive; (b), Frank & Marie-Therese Wood Print Collections, Alexandria, VA; 369 (t), Library of Congress, (b), U.S. Postal Service / Harcourt Inc.; 370, PRC Archive; 371, The Museum of the Confederacy Richmond, VA / PRC Archive; 372, Museum of the Confederacy, Richmond, VA. Photo by Katherine Wetzel / PRC Archive; 373, From *The Civil War: Forward to Richmond*. Photograph by Al Freni, © 1983 Time-Life Books, Inc. Courtesy, Troiani Collection; 374, The Granger Collection, New York; 375 (tl), © Collection of Kean Wilcox All rights reserved / PRC Archive, (tr), Private Collection / PRC Archive, (b), Library of Congress / PRC Archive; 376 (t), Library of Congress, (bl), The Museum of the Confederacy Richmond, VA. Photography by Katherine Wetzel, (br), Library of Congress; 377, Library of Congress / PRC Archive; 378 (t), National Portrait Gallery, Smithsonian Institution, Washington DC/Art Resource, NY, (b), Courtesy Mulberry Plantation, Camden, SC/Photo by Alt Lee, Columbia, SC/PRC Archive; 379, Smithsonian Institution, neg. #84-9312/ PRC Archive; 380 (t), Chicago Historical Society / PRC Archive; (b), Museum of the Confederacy, Richmond, VA from *Echoes of Glory, Arms, and Equipment of the Confederacy* © 1991, Time-Life Books, Inc. Photo High Impact / Larry Sherer; 381, The Granger Collection, New York; 382, (t), Collection of Michael J. McAfee / PRC Archive; (b), Cincinnati Museum Center / PRC Archive; 383, Chicago Historical Society / PRC Archive; 385, (t), © The Bucks Historical Society 1999, (b), Library of Congress; 386, Corbis-Bettmann; 387, Library Company of Philadelphia / PRC Archive; 388 (t), West Point Museum Collections, United States Military Academy / PRC Archive; 389, Anne S. Brown Military Collection, Brown University / PRC Archive; 390 (t), PRC Archive, (b), State Museum of Pennsylvania; 392 (t), Laurie Platt Winfrey/Woodfin Camp & Associates,Inc., (b), Library of Congress; 393, Atlanta History Center; 394, Library of Congress; 395, Tom Lovell / National Geographic Image Collection (detail); 397, Rick Vargas / Smithsonian Institution / PRC Archive.

CHAPTER 13: Page 400 (tl), Corbis-Bettmann; (tr), The Granger Collection, New York; (b), Jubilee Singers, Courtesy of Fisk University Library Special Collections; 401, (tl), Atlanta History Center; (tr), The Western Reserve Historical Society, Cleveland, Ohio / PRC Archive, (b), National Archives of New Zealand; 402, (t), Hulton Getty © Liaison Agency; (b), Library of Congress; 403, Bob Daemmrich Photography; 404, Library of Congress; 405, Miriam and Ira D. Wallach Division of Art, Prints and Photographs, The New York Public Library. Astor, Lenox and Tilden Foundations; 406, The Western Reserve Historical Society, Cleveland, Ohio; 407 (t), National Archives (NARA) / PRC Archive, (b), Corbis-Bettmann; 408, Library of Congress; 409 (t), Library of Congress / PRC Archive, (b), Library of Congress; 411, (t), U.S. Postal Service / Harcourt, Inc., (b), Louisiana Collection, Howard Tilton Memorial Library, New Orleans, LA 70118; 412 (both), The Granger Collection, New York; 413 (t), U.S. Postal Service / Harcourt Inc.; (b), Frank and Marie-Therese Wood Print Collections, Alexandria, VA / PRC Archive; 414, Library of Congress; 415 (t), North Wind Picture Archives; (b), Cook Collection, Valentine Museum, Richmond, VA / PRC Archive; 416, (tl), Library of Congress / PRC Archive; (tr), Collection of Nancy Gewirz, Antique Textile Resource / PRC Archive; (b), Tennessee State Museum Collection/ Photo by June Dorman; 418, Frank & Marie-Therese Wood Print Collections, Alexandria, VA / PRC Archive; 420, (t), The Metropolitan Museum of Art , Morris K. Jesup Fund, 1940. (40.40). All rights reserved, The Metropolitan Museum of Art. Courtesy PRC Archive; (b), Cook Collection, Valentine Museum, Richmond, VA / PRC Archive; 421, (tl), Brown Brothers / PRC; (tr), © Joe Sohm / The Image Works; 421 (b), 422 (t), The Granger Collection, New York; 422 (b), South Carolina Historical Society / PRC Archive; 423, (l), The Western Reserve Historical Society, Cleveland, Ohio/ PRC Archive, (r), Ohio Historical Society; 424 (t), PRC Archive, (b), Schomburg Center for Research in Black Culture, New York Public Library / PRC Archive; 425, Corbis-Bettmann; 427, Illinois State Historical Library / PRC Archive;

UNIT 4 REVIEW: 428 (t) The Granger Collection, New York; (b), PRC Archive; 429 (t), Private Collection / PRC Archive; 429 (b), Peter Newark's American Pictures.

UNIT 5: Page 430, Peter Newark's American Pictures; 431, National Park Service Collection / Gift of Angelo Forgione, c. 1991.

CHAPTER 14: Page 432, (tl), Courtesy Wells Fargo Bank / PRC Archive, (tc), Historic Seward House / PRC Archive, (tr), FORBES Magazine Collection, New York / The Bridgeman Art Library, New York / London; (b), *The Luck of Roaring Camp* by Bret Harte, 1876. Trustees of the Boston Public Library / PRC Archive; 433, (tl), Nawrocki Stock Photo, (tr), Library of Congress / PRC Archive, (b), Corbis-Bettmann; 434, (t), Arizona Historical Society, (b), The Granger Collection, New York; 435, (t), Smithsonian Institution, neg no. 71-3048, (b), National Museum of American Art, Smithsonian Institution, Washington DC / Art Resource, NY; 436, (t), Courtesy of Colorado Historical Society / PRC Archive, (b), Photo by Blair Clark, courtesy Museum of New Mexico, Neg. no. 155365; 437, (t), Denver Public Library, Western History Department / PRC Archive, (b), COURTESY OF THE SOUTHWEST MUSEUM, LOS ANGELES; 438, The Field Museum of Natural History, #A111822c, Chicago; 439, National Anthropological Archives, Smithsonian Institution, Washington, D.C.; 440, (t), Helen Hunt Jackson. *A Century of Dishonor*, 1881. Trustees of the Boston Public Library / PRC Archive; (b), The Granger Collection, New York; 441 (t), National Anthropological Archives, Smithsonian Institution / PRC Archive; (b), National Anthropological Archives, Smithsonian Institution / PRC Archive; 442 (t), California Historical Society / Ticor Title Insurance / PRC Archive; (b), Collection of the New-York Historical Society / PRC Archive; 443, (tl), Kansas Collection / University of Kansas Libraries / PRC Archive; (tr), Peter Newark's Western Americana; (b), PRC Archive; 444 (t), Denver Public Library Western History Collection; (b), Courtesy of the California History Room, California State Library, Sacramento, California; 445 (t), Batavia Depot Museum, Batavia, Illinois / Courtesy, Chicago Historical Society / PRC, (b), Colorado Historical Society / PRC Archive; 446 (l), State Historical Society of Wisconsin / PRC Archive; (r), California Historical Society / PRC Archive; 447 (t), Solomon D. Butcher Collection, Nebraska State Historical Society / PRC Archive, (b), The Kansas State Historical Society, Topeka, Kansas; 448 (t), Photography Collection, Miriam and Ira D. Wallach Division of Art, Prints and Photographs, The New York Public Library, Astor, Lenox and Tilden Foundations / PRC Archive; (b), *My Antonia* by Willa Cather, Trustees of the Boston Public Library / PRC Archive; 449 (t), The Kansas State Historical Society, Topeka, Kansas / PRC Archive, (b), © Laurence Parent; 450 (t), Peter Newark's Western Americana, (b), Charles M. Russell *Jerked Down* 1907 oil on canvas #0137.2246. From the Collection of Gilcrease Museum, Tulsa / PRC; 451 (t), The Granger Collection, New York, (b), The Museum of Fine Arts, Houston, The Hogg Brothers Collection, Gift of Miss Ima Hogg; 452, © John Eastcott / Yva Momatiuk / The Image Works; 453, Peter Newark's Western Americana; 454, The Granger Collection, New York; 455 (t), Oakland Museum History Department; (b), Haynes Foundation Collection. Montana Historical Society; 456, The Granger Collection, New York; 457, Colorado Historical Society / PRC Archive; 458, Montana Historical Society, Helena / PRC Archive; 459, Colorado Historical Society / PRC Archive; 461, Kansas State Historical Society, Topeka, Kansas / PRC Archive.

CHAPTER 15: Page 462 (tl), Chicago Historical Society, (tc), Property of AT&T Archives. Printed with permission of AT&T; (tr), Private Collection / PRC Archive, (bl), Library of Congress / PRC Archive, (br), Los Angeles County Museum of Art, Acquisition made possible through Museum Trustees: Robert O. Anderson, R. Stanton Avery, B. Gerald Cantor, Edward W. Carter, Justin Dart, Charles E. Ducommun, Mrs. F. Daniel Frost, Julian Ganz, Jr., Dr. Armand Hammer, Hart Lenart, Dr. Franklin D. Murphy, Mrs. Joan Palevsky, Richard E. Sherwood, Maynard J. Toll and Hal B. Wallis; 463 (tl), Ann Ronan / Image Select, Inc.; (tr), Carnegie Library of Pittsburgh, (bl), Corbis-Bettmann; (br), PRC Archive; 464, (t), Property of AT&T Archives. Reprinted with permission of AT&T / PRC Archive, (b), The Metropolitan Museum of Art, Purchase, Lyman G. Bloomingdale Gift, 1901. (01.7.1) Photograph © 1983 The Metropolitan Museum of Art. All rights reserved, The Metropolitan Museum of Art; 465, Collection of the Drake Well Museum; 466 (l), Union Pacific Railroad Museum / PRC Archive; (r), Chicago Historical Society / PRC Archive; 467, Library of Congress / PRC Archive; 468, (t), Smithsonian Institution, neg. no. A26767B-2 / PRC Archive, (bl), Smithsonian Institution, neg no. 91-6501 / PRC Archive; (br), Smithsonian Institution / Charles Phillips / PRC Archive; 469, (tl), The Granger Collection, New York, (tr), David Young-Wolff/Photo Edit, (c,b), The Granger Collection, New York; 470, Division of Political History, Smithsonian Institution, Washington, D.C. / PRC Archive; 471, (t), National Portrait Gallery, Smithsonian Institution, Art Resource, NY, (b), The Granger Collection, New York; 472, Harcourt, Inc.; 473, (t), Collection of Dennis Kurlander, (b), Frank & Marie-Therese Wood Print Collections (The Picture Bank); 474, *Portrait of Charles Darwin*, 1840 by George Richmond. Downe House, Downe, Kent, UK / The Bridgeman Art Library; 475 (t), Culver Pictures, Inc., (b), National Portrait Gallery, Smithsonian Institution, Washington D.C./ Art Resource, NY ; 476, Carnegie Library, Pittsburgh; 477, Archive Photos; 478, The Granger Collection, New York; 479 (t), Illinois Historical Society; (b), Picture Research Consultants & Archives; 480 (t), Sears Roebuck and Company; (b), Chicago Historical Society, Neg no. IChi 01622 / PRC Archive; 481 (t), Culver Pictures, Inc., (b), PRC Archive; 482, PRC Archive; 483, 484 (t), Corbis-Bettmann; 484 (b), The Granger Collection, New York; 485, 486, Corbis-Bettmann; 487, The Granger Collection, New York; 489, Chicago Historical Society.

CHAPTER 16: Page 490 (tl), Library of Congress; (tr), The New York World, 1883, (bl), Library of Congress / PRC Archive, (br), New-York Hisorical Society / PRC Archive; 491, (tl), PRC Archive; (tr), The Rockefeller University Archives, (b), Collection of Sandy Marrone; 492, (t), Chermayeff and Geismar, Inc. / MetaForm, Inc., (b), Courtesy George Eastman House; 493, Library of Congress; 494, (tl), Brown Brothers, (tr), Uniphoto Picture Agency; (b), The California Department of Parks and Recreation; 495 (t), St. Cosman and St. Damian, patron saints of doctors, Cretan icon, 17th century (panel), Mark Gallery, London, Bridgeman Art Library, New York/London; (b), "Children's Playground on Ellis Island (Roof Garden)," c. 1890. Photographed by Augustus Sherman, The Jacob A. Riis Collection #476, Museum of the City of New York; 49, (t), Courtesy George Eastman House, (b), Culver Pictures, Inc.; 497, Strong Museum; 498 (t), Detroit Publishing Company Collection, Library of Congress, (b), Courtesy George Eastman House; 499, Photo by Byron, The Byron Collection, Museum of the City of New York / PRC Archive; 500 (t), Culver Pictures, Inc., (bl), Museum of the City of New York, Gift of Mary and Charles Odgen; (br), Courtesy of the Oakland Museum of California. Courtesy PRC; 501, *At the Ball* by Stewart, Julius Leblanc (1855-1919), Whitford & Hughes, London, UK / Bridgeman Art Library, London / New York; 502 (t), Corbis-Bettmann, (b), Courtesy the Museum of the City of New York / PRC Archive; 503 (t), Brown Brothers; (bl), The Newberry Library; (br), University of Illinois at Chicago. The University Library Jane Addams Memorial Collection; 504, Caroline Bartlett Crane Collection, Archives and Regional History Collections, Western Michigan University; 505 (t), Curt Teich Postcard Archives, Lake County (IL) Museum; (b), State Historical Society of North Dakota; 506, Library of Congress / PRC Archive; 507 (t), New York World; (b), New York Journal, Jan 5, 1896; 508 (t), Brooklyn Historical Society / PRC Archive (b), The Granger Collection, New York; 509, (tl), Cincinnati Museum Center, (tr), Division of Political History, Smithsonian Institution, Washington, D.C. / PRC Archive (b), Corbis-Bettmann; 510 (t), The Granger Collection, New York, (b), The Harvard Theatre Collection, The Houghton Library; Fredric Woodbridge Wilson, Curator; 511 (l), Library of Congress / PRC Archive; (r), Division of Political History, the Smithsonian Institution / PRC Archive; 513, CALIFORNIA MUSEUM OF PHOTOGRAPHY, Keystone-Mast Collection, University of California, Riverside, negative 55458 / PRC Archive.

CHAPTER 17: Page 516, (tl), Courtesy of the Museum of the American Numismatic Association; (tr), Young Mother Sewing by Mary Cassat, Musee d'Orsay, Paris, France / Bridgeman Art Library, London / New York, (bl), The Granger Collection, New York, (br), Corbis-Bettmann; 517; (tl), Replica Courtesy Deere & Company / PRC Archive; (tc), Brown Brothers; (tr), Courtesy George Eastman House / PRC Archive; (bl), National Museum of American History / Smithsonian Institution, Washington, D.C.; (br), The WILL K. KELLOGG signature logo is a trademark of Kellogg Company. All rights reserved. Used with permission; 518 (t), Corbis-Bettmann; (b), City Archives of Philadelphia; 519, (t), Collection of Janice L. and David J. Frent / PRC Archive; (b), From Political History of Jackson County; Kansas City: Marshall & Morrison, 1902, KC27, N4, Western Historical Manuscript Collection - Kansas City; 520, Library of Congress / PRC Archive; 521, New-York Historical Society; 522, 523, Library of Congress / PRC Archive; 524 (t), The Granger Collection, New York; (b), Timothy Hughes Rare Newspapers / PRC; 525 (tl), Museum of American Political Life, Sally Anderson-Bruce /PRC Archive; (tr), Collection of Janice L. and David J. Frent / PRC Archive; (b), The Granger Collection, New York; 526, (l), University of California at Berkeley, Bancroft Library; (r), The Newberry Library; 52 (t), The Newberry Library; (b), National Postal Museum, Smithsonian Institution; 528 (t), Paul Conklin / PhotoEdit (b), The Granger Collection, New York; 529 (t), United States Postal Service / Harcourt Inc.; (b), Collection of Janice L. and David J. Frent / PRC Archive; 531 (t), Kansas State Historical Society / PRC Archive; (b), Randy Leffingwell; 532, 533, The Granger Collection, New York; 534 (t), The Burns Archive, (bl), State Historical Society of Wisconsin / PRC Archive; (br), Grant Heilman Photography; 535, (tl), Courtesy of the Museum of the American Numismatic Association; (tr), Courtesy of the Museum of the American Numismatic Association; (b), Nebraska Historical Society / PRC Archive; 536 (t), Corbis-Bettmann; (b), Library of Congress / PRC Archive; 537, United States Postal Service / Harcourt Inc.; 539, Elias Carr Papers, East Carolina Manuscript Collection, J.Y. Joyner Library, East Carolina University, Greenville, NC. Photo by Dewane Frutiger / PRC Archive.

UNIT 5 REVIEW: Page 540 (t), Corbis-Bettmann; (b), Sally Fox Collection / PRC Archive; 541 (both), The Granger Collection, New York.

UNIT 6: Page 542, Gift of Dwight Franklin, Museum of the City of New York; 543, (inset), Collection of David J. and Janice L. Frent / PRC Archive.

CHAPTER 18: Page 544 (tl), Archive Photos; (tr), Brown Brothers, (b), Edison National Historic Site, National Park Service / U.S. Department of the Interior; 545, (tl), Courtesy of the Whitney Museum of American Art / Photo by Pency Rainfold; (tr), Detroit Publishing Company Photograph Collection, Library of Congress; (c), The George Meany Memorial Archives, (bl), Corbis-Bettmann, (br), Corbis-Bettmann; 546, The Newberry Library; 547, (t), Image Copyright © 1998 PhotoDisc, Inc., (b), Corbis-Bettmann; 548, (t), Brown Brothers, (b), The Granger Collection, New York; 549 (l), Corbis-Bettmann; (r), Culver Pictures, Inc.; 550 (t), Library of Congress / PRC Archive; (b), George Eastman House; 551 (t), The Newberry Library (c), The Newberry Library; (b), Special Collections Department, Van Pelt Library, University of Pennsylvania, Philadelphia, PA; 552 (t), The George Meany Memorial Archives / PRC Archive, (b), Culver Pictures; 553 (t), Library of Congress / PRC Archive; (b), The George Meany Memorial Archives; 554 (t), The Granger Collection, New York; (b), UPI/Corbis-Bettmann; 555 (t), Archive Photos, (b), HRW Photo by Victoria Smith; 556 (t), ILGWU Archives, Labor-Management Documentation Center / PRC Archive; (b), The Granger Collection, New York; 557, Corbis-Bettmann; 558, (t), Library of Congress / PRC Archive; (b), Brown Brothers; 559 (t), Daniel H. Burnham in a flowered tie, signed. Photograph © 1996, The Art Institute of Chicago, (b), View of the City from Jackson Park to Grant Park, plate 49 from Plan of Chicago, 1907, 104x477 cm delineated by Jules Guerin, watercolor and pencil on paper, 1907, on permanent loan to the Art Institute of Chicago from the City of Chicago, 2.148.1966, detail. Photograph © 1996, The Art Institute of Chicago. All rights reserved; 560 (t), Uniphoto, (b), Culver Pictures; 561 (t), John Hay Library, Brown University / PRC Library, (c), HRW Photo Research Library, (b), Corbis-Bettmann; 562 (t), Library of Congress; 562 (b), 563, The Newberry Library; 564, Corbis-Bettmann; 565, Courtesy Chermayeff and Geismar, Inc. / MetaForm, Inc. / PRC Archive; 567 (l), The Granger Collection, New York; (r), Sophia Smith Collection, Smith College.

CHAPTER 19: Page 568 (tl), Archives Division - Texas State Library / PRC Archive; (tr), Corbis-Bettmann; (bl), Courtesy of the Rosenberg Library, Galveston, Texas; (br), PRC Archive; 569 (t), The Granger Collection, New York; (bl), Collection of Janice L. and David J. Frent / PRC Archive, (br), Library of Congress; 570 (t), Brown Brothers; (b), 571, The Granger Collection, New York; 572, (both), Library Legacy Foundation, Toledo-Lucas County Public Library; 573, The Granger Collection, New York; 574, Library of Congress; 575, (both), Collection of Janice L. and David J. Frent / PRC Archive; 576 (t), United States Postal Service / Harcourt Inc.; (c), Sagamore Hill National Historic Site / PRC Archive, (b), George Meany Memorial Archives; 577, Library of Congress / PRC Archive; 578 (t), Culver Pictures; (b), Chicago Historical Society, neg # ICHI1978.154.4 / PRC Archive; 579 (l), Newberry Library / PRC Archive, (r), © Laurie Platt Winfrey / Woodfin Camp & Associates, Inc.; 580, National Museum of American Art, Smithsonian Institution, lent by the U.S. Department of the Interior / Art Resource, NY; 581, Andre Jenny/New England Stock Photos; 582 (t), Theodore Roosevelt Collection, Harvard College Library/ PRC Archive, (b), Library of Congress; 584 (t), The Houghton Library, Theodore Roosevelt Collection, Harvard University, (b), The Granger Collection, New York; 585, Theodore Roosevelt Collection, Harvard College Library; 586, Corbis-Bettmann; 58, (t), National Archives / PRC Archive, (b), Corbis-Bettmann; 588 (t), United States Postal Service / Harcourt Inc., (b), Stock Montage, Inc.; 589 (t), Picture Research Consultants Archive; (b), Archives of Labor and Urban Affairs , Wayne State University / PRC Archive; 590, *Nude Descending a Staircase*, © 1997 Artists Rights Society (ARS), New York / ADAGP, Paris / Estate of Marcel Duchamp / Bridgeman Art Library, New York / London; 591 (t), Culver Pictures, (b), Corbis-Bettmann; 592 (l), PRC Archive; (r), Library of Congress / PRC Archive; 595 (t), Corbis-Bettmann, (b), Collection of Janice L. and David J. Frent/ PRC Archive.

CHAPTER 20: Page 596, (tl), © Topham / The Image Works; (tr), The Granger Collection, New York; (bl), FPG International Corp.; (br), Knudsens Fotosenter, Oslo; 597 (tl), Photo Deutsches Museum, Munich,;(tr), Library of Congress / PRC Archive; (b), Special Collections, Milton S. Eisenhower Library, The Johns Hopkins Library, courtesy PRC; 598 (t), The Granger Collection, New York; (b), Courtesy of the U. S. Naval Academy Museum / PRC Archive; 599, By permission of Houghton Library, Harvard University / PRC Archive; 600, (t), © Hawaiian Legacy Archive / Pacific Stock, (b), Culver Pictures; 601 (t), Hawaii State Archives, (b), Hawaiian Legacy Archive / Pacific Stock; 602 (t), Dawson Gallery, courtesy PRC; (b), Trustees of the British Museum; 603, Library of Congress; 604, The Mariners Museum, Newport News, VA; 605, (t), The Granger Collection, New York, (b), Brown Brothers; 606, (t), Hulton Getty / Liaison Agency; (b), Nawrocki Stock Photo; 607, (t), Woodfin Camp & Associates, Inc., (b), Library of Congress; 608 (t), Courtesy LIFE Magazine, © Time, Inc. Watercolor by C.J. Post, photo by Herb Orth; (b), National Archive / PRC Archive; 609, The Granger Collection, New York; 610, Corbis; 611, Corbis-Bettmann; 612 (t), Keystone-Mast Collection, #ACT 24040, UCR / California Museum of Photography, University of California, Riverside, (b), Underwood & Underwood / Corbis-Bettmann; 614, The Granger Collection, New York; 616, Corbis-Bettmann; 61 (t), Corbis/ Bettmann-UPI; (b), The Granger Collection, New York; 618 (t), Corbis/ Bettmann-UPI; (bl), Latin Focus © All rights reserved; (br), Keith Dannemiller / SABA; 619 (t), Library of Congress / PRC Archive; (b), UPI/Corbis-Bettmann; 620, Corbis-Bettmann; 621, The Granger Collection, New York; 623, Library of Congress.

CHAPTER 21: Page 626 (tl), PRC Archive, (tc), Collection of Colonel Stuart S. Corning. © Rob Huntley / Lightstream / Courtesy of PRC Archive; (tr), Corbis- Bettmann, (bl), The Granger Collection, New York, (br), UPI/Corbis-Bettmann; 627 (tl), HRW Photo by Sam Dudgeon; (tr), Willard Clay/FPG International Corp., (b), The Trustees of the Imperial War Museum, London; 628 (t), Culver Pictures, Inc., (b), Nawrocki Stock Photo; 629, Andrew Reid / Liaison Agency; 630, 632 (t), Trustees of the Imperial War Museum, London; 632 (b), Dale Hrabak / National Air and Space Museum, Smithsonian Institution, Washington, D.C.; 633 (t), HRW Photo; (b), UPI/Bettman Newsphotos; 634, Woodfin Camp & Associates, Inc.; 635, Stock Montage, Inc.; 636, National Archives; 638 (t), The Granger Collection, New York; (b), 639, Archive Photos; 640 (t), The Granger Collection, New York; (b), UPI/Corbis-Bettmann Newsphotos; 641, Hoover Presidential Library / PRC Archive; 642 (t), Corbis-Bettmann, (b), Culver Pictures, Inc.; 643 (l), PRC Archive, (r), The Bettmann Archive; 644, Brown Brothers; 645 (both), The Granger Collection, New York; 646, HRW Photo by Lance Schriner; 647, The Granger Collection, New York; 648, The Trustees of the Imperial War Museum, London; 649 (tl), © Dorling Kindersley Ltd. / Courtesy of Spink & Son Ltd., London, (tr), Archive Photos, (b), UPI/Corbis-Bettmann; 650, The Granger Collection, New York; 652, HRW Photo Research Library; 653, Culver Pictures, Inc.; 655, The Granger Collection, New York.

UNIT 6 REVIEW: Page 656, PRC Archive; 657, (t), Snark International / Art Resource, NY, (b), Curt Teich Postcard Archives, Lake County Museum, Illinois.

UNIT 7: Page 658, New-York Historical Society; 659 (r), Page Christie's Images.

CHAPTER 22: Page 660 (tl), Collection of Janice L. and David J. Frent / PRC Archive, (tr), The Granger Collection, New York, (bl), Corbis-Bettmann; (br), Babbit by Sinclaire Lewis; Newberry Library; 661 (tl), Private Collection / PRC Archive; (tr), Shahn, Ben. Bartolomeo Vanzetti and Nicola Sacco from the Sacco-Vanzetti series of twenty-three paintings (1931-32). Tempera on paper over composition board 10 1/2 x 14 1/2" (26.7 x 36.8 cm). The Museum of Modern Art, New York. Gift of Abby Aldrich Rockefeller, Photograph © 1997 The Museum of Modern Art, New York. © 1997 Estate of Ben Shahn / Licensed by VAGA, New York, NY; (bl), Chicago Historical Society, ICHI-22640; (br), Brown Brothers; 662 (t), Library of Congress / PRC Archive; (b), Courtesy George Eastman House; 663 (t), *Leslie's Illustrated*

Newspaper September 20, 1920 / PRC Archive; (b), Museum of History and Industry, Seattle, WA; 664 (t), UPI/Bettmann-Corbis; (bl), Archives of Labor and Urban Affairs, Wayne State University, (br), AP / Wide World Photos; 665, The Granger Collection, New York; 666, (t), Collection of Janice L. and David J. Frent / PRC Archive; (c), Brown Brothers; (b), *The Anaconda Standard*, Jan. 4, 1920; 668, AP / Wide World Photos, Inc.; 669, Collection of Janice L. and David J. Frent / PRC Archive; 670, Bob Daemmrich Photo, Inc.; 671, The Hagley Museum and Library; 672 (t), Courtesy George Eastman House, (b), The Granger Collection, New York; 673 (t), Collection of Janice L. and David J. Frent / PRC Archive; (bl), Museum of American Political Life, University of Hartford, Photo by Steven Laschever; (br), Coolidge Collection at Forbes Library; 674 (both), Collection of Janice L. and David J. Frent / PRC Archive; 675 (t), *The Chicago Defender*, April 7, 1917; (b), Courtesy George Eastman House; 676, Brown Brothers; 677 (t), Archive Photos; (b), Collection of Janice L. and David J. Frent / PRC Archive; 678 (tl), Chicago Historical Society, Photo # Ichi-12255, (tr), "The Messenger" magazine Sep 1926 (Vol VIII, no. 9), Newberry Library; (b), James Van Der Zee photo; 680 (t), Frank Driggs Collection; (b), "Juan Salvador and Lupe's Wedding, 1929", from *Rain of Gold* by Victor Villasenor is reprinted with permission of the publisher (Arte Publico Press, University of Houston, 1991); 681, Underwood Photo Archives; 683, Collection of Janice L. and David J. Frent / PRC Archive.

Chapter 23: Page 684 (tl), Archive Photos; (tr), Brown Brothers, (bl), Library of American Broadcasting / University of Maryland, (br), The Kobal Collection; 685, (tl), Gift of John P. Axelrod. Courtesy Museum of Fine Arts, Boston. Courtesy PRC; (tc), Culver Pictures; (tr), The Granger Collection, New York; (bl), The Metropolitan Museum of Art, Alfred Stieglitz Collection, 1969. (69.278.1) Photograph by Malcolm Varon. All rights reserved, The Metropolitan Museum of Art; (br), Brown Brothers; 686 (t), Corbis-Bettmann; (b), PRC Archive; 687 (t), Archive Photos; 687 (b), 688, 689 (both) From the Collections of Henry Ford Museum and Greenfield Village; 690 (t), Brown Brothers, (b), The Granger Collection, New York; 691, November 1927 "Ladies Home Journal," The Newberry Library; 69, (t), Christie's Images, (b), Duke University Archives / PRC Archive; 693, Brown Brothers; 694, Private Collection / PRC Archive; 695 (t), Chicago Historical Society, Photo no. IChi 14414; (b), The Granger Collection, New York; 696 (tl, tr), CIRCA / PRC Archive, (b), The Granger Collection, New York; 697, Robin Nelson / Black Star; 698 (t), Henry Groskinsky; (c), *The Denver Times,* September 29, 1920; (b), National Baseball Hall of Fame; 699 (t), PRC Archive; (b), Corbis-Bettmann; 700, Flower Pentecostal Heritage Center; 701, Brown Brothers; 702, (both), 703 (t), Frank Driggs Collection; 703, (b), Historic New Orleans Collection; 705 (l), *Color* by Countee Cullen, poetry 1926 reprint of author's first (1925) book, Harper and Brothers, NY; (r), Archive Photos; 706; (t), Courtesy of the Yale Collection of American Literature, Beinecke Rare Book and Manuscript Library, Yale University, (b), Library of Congress / PRC Archive; 707 (both), The Granger Collection, New York; 708 (t), © Addison Gallery of American Art, Phillips Academy, Andover, Massachusettes. All Rights Reserved; (b), The Detroit Institute of Arts; 709, Farrell Grehan / ESTO Photographics, Inc.; 711, Culver Pictures.

Chapter 24: Page 712 (tl), Culver Pictures, Inc.; (tr), UPI/Bettmann-Corbis, (b), Private Collection / Bridgeman Art Library; 713, (tl), Culver Pictures, Inc., (tr), AP / Wide World Photos, Inc., (bl), Franklin D. Roosevelt Library, (br), *Lost Horizon* by James Hilton, Newberry Library; PRC Archive; 714, (t), © 1945 Gordon Parks, (b), Collection of Janice L. and David J. Frent / PRC Archive; 715, (t), Archive Photos, (b), © Corbis Images; 716, The Granger Collection, New York; 717, John T. McCutcheon, courtesy Tribune Media Services; 719, PRC Archive; 720 (t), Minnesota Historical Society; (b), Milton (Pete) Brooks / *The Detroit News*; 721, Culver Pictures; 722 (t), National Museum of American Art, Smithsonian Institution, Washington, DC / Art Resource, NY; (b), Corbis-Bettmann; 723, National Archives / PRC Archive; 724, (t), Courtesy of Bert Corona and Mario T. Garcia, (b), Library of Congress; 725, Cindy Lewis Photography; 726, National Museun of American Art, Washington, DC / Art Resource, NY; 727 (l), *Lost Horizon* by James Hilton, Newberry Library; PRC Archive; (r), Corbis-Bettmann; 728, (t), Corbis-Bettmann, (b), The Granger Collection, New York; 729, The Salvation Army National Archives; 730, Herbert Hoover Presidential Library; 731 (t), Department of the Interior, National Park Service, 1937. National Museum of American Art, Washington, DC; Art Resource, NY; (b), U.S. Postal Service / Harcourt Inc.; 732, CORBIS-Bettmann; 733 (t), The Bettmann Archive; 733 (b), 734 (t), Culver Pictures, Inc.; 734 (b), Corbis- Bettmann; 735, Franklin D. Roosevelt Library; 737, (l), Smithsonian Institution, Washington, D.C.; (r), Culver Pictures, Inc.

CHAPTER 25: Page 738, (tl), Corbis-Bettmann, (tr), HRW Photo by Sam Dudgeon; (bl), AP/Wide World Photos, Inc.; (br), Library of Congress / Courtesy of PRC; 739, (tl), National Archives, courtesy PRC; (tc), The Michael Barson Collection / Past Perfect/PRC Archive; (tr), Margaret Bourke-White / LIFE Magazine © 1937 Time Inc., (bl), From *The Incredible Ball Point Pen* by Stuart Schneider and Henry Gostony, Schiffer Publishing Ltd., Atglen, PA; (br), Shooting Star International; 740, 741, Franklin D. Roosevelt Library; 742, National Archives; 743, (t), Culver Pictures, Inc.; (b), Louise Boyle Photo / Southern Historical Collection, University of North Carolina at Chapel Hill; 745, Department of the Interior / PRC Archive; 746, Library of Congress / PRC Archive; 747 (t), Brown Brothers, (b), Louisiana State University Special Collections, courtesy PRC; 748 (t), U.S. Postal Service/Harcourt Inc.; (bl), Franklin D. Roosevelt Library; (br), The Granger Collection, New York; 749, (l), Franklin D. Roosevelt Library, (r), Social Security Administration, courtesy PRC; 750 (t), Stock Montage, Inc.; (b), The Granger Collection, New York; 752, (l), Library of Congress / PRC Archive; (r), Archives of Labor and Urban Affairs, Wayne State University; 753, Library of Congress; 754, (l), Library of Congress; (r), John E. Allen, Inc. / Franklin D. Roosevelt Presidential Library; 755, Frank Driggs Collection / Corbis-Bettmann / PRC Archive; 756, (t), Library of Congress; (b), The Granger Collection, New York; 757, (both), Library of Congress; 758, The Granger Collection, New York; 759, (t), National Archives, (b), National Archives, Records of the WPA / PRC Archive; 760, (t), The Granger Collection, New York. From THE GRAPES OF WRATH by John Steinbeck. Copyright 1939 renewed © 1967 by John Steinbeck. Used by permission of Viking Penguin, a division of Penguin Putnam, Inc.; (b), Photofest; 761 (l), Corbis/Bettmann-UPI; (r), The Beinecke Rare Book and Manuscript Library, Yale University; 762, Grant Wood, American, 1891-1942, *American Gothic*, oil on beaver-board, 1930, 74.3 x 62.4 cm. Friends of American Art Collection, All rights reserved by the Art Institute of Chicago and VAGA, New York, NY; 763, © 1999 The Georgia O'Keefe Foundation/ Artists Rights Society (ARS), New York. The Metropolitan Museum of Art, Alfred Stieglitz Collection, 1952. (52.203) Photograph © 1994 The Metropolitan Museum of Art. All rights reserved, The Metropolitan Museum of Art; 76, (l), Grandma Moses: *Sugaring Off* © 1992 Grandma Moses Properties Co., New York; (r), Collection of David J. & Janice L. Frent / PRC Archive.

UNIT 7 REVIEW: Page: 768 (t), Missouri Historical Society; (b), CORBIS/Underwood & Underwood; 769 (t), The Granger Collection, New York, (b), Corbis-Bettmann.

UNIT 8: Page 770 Corbis/Bettmann-UPI; 771, Library of Congress.

CHAPTER 26: Page 772 (tl), Brown Brothers; (tr), AP/Wide World Photos; (bl), Erich Lessing/Art Resource; (br), FPG International Corp.; 773, (tl), Steve Vidler / Nawrocki Stock Photo; (tr), *The Des Moines Register*, October 31, 1938; (b), Hershenson-Allen Archives / PRC Archive; 774 (t), Corbis/Bettmann-UPI, (b), Stock Montage, Inc.; 775, (l), Corbis-Bettmann; (r), Jean Louis Atlan / Corbis Sygma; 776, National Portrait Gallery, Washington, D.C./ Art Resource, NY; 777, (t), Nawrocki Stock Photo; (b), Corbis/Bettmann; 778, AKG London; 779 (both), Corbis/Bettmann-UPI; 780 (t), HRW Photo by Sam Dudgeon; (b), Franklin D. Roosevelt Library; 781, Curt Teich Postcard Archives; 782, (t), Everett / CSU Archives; (bl), Curt Teich Postcard Archives / Lake County, IL Museum, (br), Rob Schoenboum / Black Star; 783, Library of Congress; 784 (t), UPI/Corbis-Bettmann; (b), Poseidon Pictures; 785 (t), UPI/Bettmann; 785 (b),786 (t),The Granger Collection, New York; 786 (b), Corbis-Bettmann; 787, 788 (l), Brown Brothers; 788, (r), Ernest Hemingway, *For Whom the Bell Tolls* © 1940, Charles Scribner's Sons, Macmillan Publishing Company, PRC Archives; 789, Library of Congress; 790, (t), CBS Radio / PRC Archive, (b), UPI/Corbis-Bettmann; 791, (t), *Chicago Daily Tribune*, Dec 1937, (b), Courtesy of *Fortune* magazine, from the General Libraries, University of Texas at Austin. HRW Photo by Sam Dudgeon; 793, (t), CORBIS/Bettmann; (b), LIFE Magazine © 1940, PRC Archives; 794, Archive Photos; 795, 797, The Granger Collection, New York.

CHAPTER 27: Page 798, (tl, tr), Private Collection / PRC Archive, (tc), Courtesy of the Museum of the American Numismatic Association; (bl), Cindy Lewis Photography, (br), Nawrocki Stock Photo; 799, (tl), Chicago Historical Society, (tr), Schalwijk / Art Resource, NY, (bl), FSA-OWI Collection, Library of Congress; (br), HRW Photo by Sam Dudgeon, stamps courtesy Kristen Darby; 800, (t), Dana Edmunds / Pacific Stock, (b), Courtesy of Joseph Rygiel / PRC Archive; 801, FSA-OWI Collection, Library of Congress; 802, Corbis-Bettmann; 803, (t), U.S. Government Photo; (b), National Archives / PRC Archive; 804, United States Marine Corps; 805 (t), Division of Political History, Smithsonian Institution, Washington, D.C.; (b), Trustees of the Imperial War Museum; 806, Ria-Novosti/Sovfoto; 807 (t), National Archives / PRC Archive; (b), Hershenson-Allen Archives / PRC Archive; 808 (l), PRC Archive; (r), Collection of Chester Scott / PRC Archive; 809, Printed by permission of the Norman Rockwell Family Trust © 1943 / Photo courtesy of the Curtis Publishing Company; 810 , (t), National Archives / PRC Archive; (b), FSA-OWI Collection, Library of Congress; 811, (t), UPI/Corbis-Bettmann, (bl), FSA-OWI Collection, Library of Congress, (br), National Archives / PRC Archive; 813, AP / Wide World Photos; 814, National Archives / PRC Archive; 815 (t), Library of Congress / PRC Archive, (b), 390th Bomb Group Collection, courtesy PRC; 816, Corbis; 817, National Archives (NARA); 818 (t), AP / Wide World Photos, (b), National Archives; 820, Yevgeni Khaldei - Sovfoto / Eastfoto; 821 (t), Christie's Images; (b), United States Marine Corps Museum / PRC Archive; 822 (l), National Archives / PRC Archive; (r), Photri; 824 (t), Press Association Limited / PRC Archive, (b), National Archives; 825 (t), United States Postal Service / Harcourt Inc.; (b), Corbis; 826, (l), U.S. Air Force / PRC Archive, (r), Philip Jones-Griffiths / Magnum Photos; 829, Private Collection / PRC Archive.

CHAPTER 28: Page 830 (tl), Collection of Col. Stuart S. Corning, Jr. Courtesy PRC Archive; (tr), The Granger Collection, New York; (bl), Collection of MIchael Barson / Past Perfect / PRC Archive; (br), Woodfin Camp & Associates, Inc; 831 (tl), RAUSCHENBERG, Robert. *Bed*. (1955) Combine painting: oil and pencil on pillow, quilt, and sheet on wood supports, 6' 3 3/4" x 31 1/2" x 8" (191.1 x 80 x 20.3 cm). The Museum of Modern Art, New York. Gift of Leo Castelli in honor of Alfred H. Barr, Jr. Photograph © 1999 The Museum of Modern Art, New York; (tc), Sovfoto / Eastfoto; (tr), UPI/Corbis-Bettmann; (bl), The Viking Press, New York City; (br), AP/Wide World Photos, Inc.; 832, U.S. Army Photo / Harry S Truman Presidential Library; 833, UPI/Corbis-Bettmann; 834, Corbis-Bettmann; 835, Franklin D. Roosevelt Library; 836, The Jewish Museum, NY / Art Resource, NY; 837, National Archives / PRC Archive; 838 (t), Archive Photos; (b), National Portrait Gallery, Smithsonian Institution, Washington, DC, Gift of TIME Magazine; 839, *Foreign Affairs*, July 1947; 840, National Archives / PRC Archive; 841 (l), The National Portrait Gallery, Smithsonian Institution, Washington, D.C. / Art Resource, NY; (r), Vimonen / Corbis-Sygma; 842, Courtesy of the German Marshall Fund of the United States; 843 (l), Fortier Collection, Cowles Archive; courtesy PRC; (r), FPG International; 844, Corbis/Bettmann-UPI; 845 (l), PRC Archive; (r), Photri; 847, Corbis-Bettmann; 848 (t), U.S. Postal Service/Harcourt, Inc.; (b), AP/Wide World Photos; 849, AP / Wide World Photos; 850, © Jerry Cook; 851, The Michael Barson Collection / Past Perfect / PRC Archive; 852, (t), Photofest, (b), Archive Photos; 853, (l), The Michael Barson Collection / Past Perfect / PRC Archive; (r), *The Martian Way* by Isaac Asimov, 1955, Signet Books, courtesy PRC; 854, UPI/Corbis-Bettmann; 855, Archive Photos; 856 (t), Loomis Dean / Time-Life Picture Agency © Time, Inc.; 856 (b), 857, 859, The Michael Barson Collection / Past Perfect / PRC Archive.

CHAPTER 29: Page 862 (tl), Archive Photos; (tc), U.S. Postal Service; 862 (tr, b), 863 (all) Corbis-Bettmann; 864 (t), Library of Congress; (b), U.S. Postal Service; 865 (t), Lambert / Archive Photos; (b), © 1994 Tom & Dee Ann McCarthy / The Stock Market; 866, Corbis-Bettmann; 867, (r), Harry S Truman Library; 867 (l), 868, Collection of David J. and Janice L. Frent / PRC Archive; 869, National Archives (NARA); 870, (t), *The Power of Positive Thinking* ©1952, 1978 by Prentice-Hall, Inc. Courtesy Norman Vincent Peale Center for Christian Living. HRW Photo by Sam Dudgeon; (bl), Collection of David J. and Janice L. Frent / PRC Archive; (br), HRW Photo by Sam Dudgeon; 871, Ewing Galloway; 872, J.R. Eyerman / LIFE Magazine, © Time, Inc.; 874, Corbis-Bettmann; 875 (l), Campbell Soup Company; (r), Picture Research Consultants & Archives; 876, (t), AP / Wide World Photos, Inc., (b), By permission of "TV Guide," courtesy Lenore's TV Guides. HRW Photo by Sam Dudgeon; 877 (t), Library of Congress / PRC Archive; (b), The Michael Barson Collection / Past Perfect / PRC Archive; 878, SuperStock / PRC; 879, Corbis-Bettmann; 880, 881 (t)UPI/Corbis-Bettmann; 881 (b), AP / Wide World Photos, Inc.; 882, Charles Moore / Black Star; 883, (tl), Dr. Hector P. Garcia Papers, Special Collections and Archives, Texas A&M University-Corpus Christi Bell Library; (tr), Dr. Hector P. Garcia Papers, Special Collections & Archives, Texas A&M University, Corpus Christi Bell Library, (b), Francis L.K. Hsu and Family from his 1971 book, *The Challenge of the American Family: The Chinese in the United States*; 884, (t), AP / Wide World Photos, Inc.; (b), *Invisible Man* by Ralph Ellison, Vintage Books, a division of Random House, Inc.; 885 (tl), Facsimile edition of Jack Kerouac's *On The Road* ©1957 published by the First Edition Library, Shelton, CT, by arrangement with Viking Penguin, Inc.; (tr), Corbis/Bettmann; (b), © Joe Sohm / Chromosohm / Stock Connection; 886 (l), Harry Red / Time Magazine, (r), Courtesy Naomi Long Madgett; 887, Courtesy of the Ford Foundation; 889 (t), *The Common Sense Book of Baby and Child Care* by Dr. Benjamin Spock, published by Duell, Sloan and Pearce, NY, © 1957; (b), Christie's Images.

UNIT 8 REVIEW: Page 890 (l), Moorland-Spingarn Research Center, Howard University, courtesy PRC; (r), U.S. Army Photograph; 891, (t), Photri, Inc.; (b), National Archives (NARA).

UNIT 9: Page 892, © 1976 Matt Herron/Take Stock; 893 (r), Bill Eppridge / LIFE Magazine © Time, Inc.

CHAPTER 30: Page 894 (tl), Topham Picture Service; (tr), AP / Wide World Photos; (bl), HRW Photo by Sam Dudgeon ; (bc), Sally Andersen-Bruce, Museum of American Political Life; (br), UPI/Corbis-Bettmann; 895 (t), Corbis-Bettmann; (c), UPI/Corbis-Bettmann; (b), UPI/Corbis-Bettmann; 896 (t), Bantam Doubleday Dell Publishing Group, Inc.; (b), Collection of Janice L. and David J. Frent / PRC Archive; 897 (l), Corbis-Bettmann; (r), Corbis-Bettmann; 898 (tl), West Point Museum, U.S. Military Academy, West Point, NY. Photo by Josh Nefsky; (tr), Collection of Sandy Marrone / PRC Archive; (b), Collection of Janice L. and David J. Frent/Colorfax/ PRC Archive; 899 (tl), Paul Conklin / Peace Corps Photograph; (tr), Michael Dwyer/ Stock, Boston; (b), Sanford Kossin/ LIFE Magazine © Time, Inc.; 900, UPI/Corbis-Bettmann; 903 (t), John F. Kennedy Library; (b), John F. Kennedy Presidential Library; 904 (l), United States Postal Service / Harcourt Inc.; (r), AP / Wide World Photos; 905 Arthur Rickerby / Black Star; 906, Sarge O'Neill/John F. Kennedy Library; 907 (l), *The Other America: Poverty in the United States* by Michael Harrington © 1962, eleventh printing 1970, Macmillan Publishing Company; (r), AP / Wide World Photos, Inc.; 908 Chicago Daily News; 909, Library of Congress / Stanley Tretick / "Look" Collection/ PRC Archive; 910 (t), Archive Photos; (b), AP / Wide World Photos, Inc.; 911 (t), United States Postal Service / Harcourt Inc.; (b), Elizabeth Hamlin / Stock Boston; 912 (t), Paul Conklin; (b), Collection of Janice L. and David J. Frent/ PRC Archive; 913 (t), Michelle Bridwell / Frontera Fotos; (b), Lyndon Baines Johnson Library; 914 (t), Children's Television Workshop; (b), Alfred Eisenstadt/ LIFE Magazine Time, Inc.; 915, *SILENT SPRING* courtesy Houghton Mifflin Company; 916, Paul Conklin; 917 Lyndon B. Johnson Presidential Library, reprinted through the courtesy of Edward Germano and the Brockton *Enterprise*; 919 (t), Les Immel / *Peoria Journal Star*; (b), Collection of Janice L. and David J. Frent/ PRC Archive.

CHAPTER 31: Page 920 (tl), UPI/Bettmann-Corbis; 920 (tr), Corbis/Bettmann; 920 (b), © 1964 Time Inc. Reprinted by Permission; 921 (tl), courtesy CARE, from PRC; (tr), Corbis-Bettmann; (bl), AP/Wide World Photos; (br), Courtesy Famous Amos Cookies, Keebler Company; 922 (t), Smithsonian Institution / photo courtesy of Salamander Books Ltd.; (b), AP / Wide World Photos, Inc.; 923 (t), UPI/Corbis-Bettmann; (b), UPI/Bettmann-Corbis; 924, AP / Wide World Photos, Inc.; 925, Charles Moore/ Black Star ; 926 (tl), LOOK/Trestick in the John F. Kennedy Library; (tr), PRC Archive; (b), Francis Miller / LIFE Magazine ©Time, Inc.; 927, Cecil Stoughton / Lyndon Baines Johnson Presidential Library ; 928 (t), PRC Archive; (b), Charles Moore / Black Star; 929 (t), © Danny Lyon / Magnum Photos ; (b), © 1978 Matt Herron / Take Stock; 930, Matt Herron / TAKE STOCK; 931 (t), Corbis-Bettmann ; (b), LIFE Magazine March 19, 1965 © Time, Inc.; 933 (t), Collection of Janice L. and David J. Frent/PRC Archive; (bl), Corbis/Bettmann-UPI; (br), Collection of Janice L. and David J. Frent/ PRC Archive; 934 UPI/ Bettmann-Corbis; 935 (t), AP / Wide World Photos, Inc. ; (b), Collection of Janice L. and David J. Frent/ PRC Archive; 936 (t), UPI/Corbis-Bettmann; (bl), Dominique Berretty / Black Star; (br), HRW Photo by Sam Dudgeon; 938, AP / Wide World Photos, Inc.; 939 (t), UPI/Corbis-Bettmann; (b), Collection of Janice L. and David J. Frent/ PRC Archive; 940 (t), UPI/Corbis-Bettmann; (b), ©1971 Time, Inc. Reprinted by Permission.; 941 Stock, Boston ; 943, Robin Nelson / Black Star; 945 (t), AP/Wide World Photos, Inc.; (b), Collection of Janice L. and David J. Frent / PRC Archive.

CHAPTER 32: 946 (tl), SOVFOTO/ EASTFOTO; 946 (tr), © 1973 Bob Fitch / Take Stock; Page 946 (bl), Corbis-Bettmann; 946 (br) © 1988 Cindy Lewis. All Rights Reserved ; 947 (tl) Motion Picture Corporation; (tr), Courtesy of Lang Communications/ PRC Archive; (bl) © Time, Inc. Reprinted by permission; (br), Corbis-Bettmann/UPI; 948 (t), PRC Archive; (bl), UPI / Corbis- Bettmann; (br), Collection of Bettye Lane/ PRC Archive; 949 (t), UPI/Corbis-Bettmann; (b), Ewing Galloway; 950 (t), US Equal Employment Opportunity Commission; (bl), Al Freni / LIFE Magazine © Time, Inc. ; (br), PRC Archive; 951 (t), Tim Boxer / Archive Photos; (b), Sylvia Johnson/ Woodfin Camp & Associates, Inc.; 952, Bob Rosato / Sports Illustrated © Time Inc. ; 953, Corbis-Bettmann; 954 (t), © 1978 George Ballis/TAKE STOCK; (b), Archive Photos; 955, Jack Weinhold, courtesy PRC; 956 (t), Collection of Janice L. and David J. Frent / PRC Archive; (c), Archive Photos; (b), © 1976 George Ballis / Take Stock; 957, Woodfin Camp & Associates, Inc.; 958, Maria Varela / Take Stock; 959, AP /Wide World Photos, Inc.; 960, Carlos Chavez / AP / Wide World Photos, Inc.; 961 (t), Ralph Crane / LIFE Magazine © Time, Inc.; (b), Collection of David J. and Janice L. Frent/ PRC Archive; 962, Paul Fusco / Magnum Photos, Inc.; 963, Corbis-Bettmann/ UPI; 965, PRC Archive; 966 (t), The American Cancer Society; courtesy PRC; 966 (b), Fred Kaplan/Black Star/PNI; 967 (t), Henry Diltz / Corbis; (b), HRW Photo by Chris Casselli; 968 (t), UPI/Corbis-Bettmann; (b), Corbis-Bettmann; 969, Corbis-Bettmann/ © 1999 The Andy Warhol Foundation for the Visual Arts / ARS, New York; 970 (all), Archive Photos; 971, Library of Congress; 973 Gene Anthony / Black Star; 974 (t), Superstock; (b), Everett Collection; 975, Superstock.

CHAPTER 33: Page 976 (tl), © Disney Enterprises, Inc.; (tr), Courtesy Texas Instruments, Inc.; (bl), National Archives / PRC Archive; (br), AP / Wide World Photos, Inc.; 977 (tl), AP / Wide World Photos ; (tc), Bruce McBroom/ Motion Picture & Television Photo Archive; (tr), © Life Magazine 1970 © Time, Inc. / PRC Archive; (bl), AP / Wide World Photos; (br), AP / Wide World Photos, Inc.; 978 (t), Maurice Durand Collection of Vietnamese Art, Yale University; (b), Eric Lananer / Black Star; 979, Archive Photos; 980, Archive Photos; 981 (t), © Roger Viollet / The Liaison Agency; (b), Lee Lockwood, courtesy PRC Archive; 982, AP / Wide World Photos, Inc.; 983 Larry Burrows / LIFE Magazine © Time, Inc.; 984 *The News American* / PRC Archive ; 985 (b), National Archives ; 985 (t), PRC Archive; 986 Collection of Janice L and David J. Frent/PRC Archive; 987, Robert Ellison / Black Star; 988 (l), Courtesy William Ehrhart; (r), Ho Thanh Duc / Vietnam Art Gallery / Kicon; 989, CBS News; 991, Shelly Rusten / Black Star; 992 (t), Larry Burrows / LIFE Magazine ©Time Inc. ; (b), John Olson, U.S. Army / PRC Archive; 993 (tl) HRW Photo by Sam Dudgeon; (tr), Corbis-Bettmann; (b), Steve Schapiro / Black Star; 994, CORBIS/Henry Diltz; 995 (t), AP / Wide World Photos; 995 (b), © Larry Burrows Collection; 996 (b), John Filo; 996 (t), National Archives (NARA); 997 © 1972 by Herblock in *The Washington Post*; 998 (t), Dennis Brack / Black Star; 998 (b), Black Star; 999 Roger Lubin / Jeroboam; 1000 Courtesy Le Ly Hayslip / PRC Archive; 1001 (t), Charles Bonnay / Black Star; 1001 (b), Eddie Adams / Time Magazine © 1972 Time, Inc.; 1002 AP / Wide World Photos, Inc.; 1003 (r), Christopher Morris / Black Star; 1003 (l), PRC Archive; 1005 Collection of Janice L. and David J. Frent/PRC Archive; 1006 (b), © Hap Stewart / Jeroboam; 1006 (t), AP / Wide World Photos, Inc.; 1007 (l), PRC Archive; 1007 (r), Hulton Getty / Liaison Agency.

UNIT 10: Page 1008, Ralph Krubner / H. Armstrong Roberts; 1009 , NASA.

CHAPTER 34: Page 1010 (t), NASA; (bl), © CBS, Inc. 1991/The Kobal Collection; (br), AP / Wide World Photos, Inc.; 1011 (tl), Hershenson-Allen Archives / PRC Archive; (tr), Martin A. Levick; (bl), R. Krubner / H. Armstrong Roberts; (br), © 1977 PGD/Polygram Records. Photo by PRC Archive; 1012, Erich Hartmann/Magnum Photos; 1013 (t), Collection of David J. and Janice L. Frent / PRC Archive; (b), Archive Photos; 1014, Archive Photos; 1015 (t), Corbis; (b), Bob Daemmrich Photo, Inc.; 1016 (t), UPI / Bettmann; (b), Jason Laure / Woodfin Camp & Associates, Inc.; 1017, © R.R. Lurie; 1018, UPI/Corbis-Bettmann; 1019 (t), Corbis/Bettmann-UPI; (b), UPI /Corbis- Bettmann Newsphotos; 1021, Corbis- Bettmann; 1022 (t), Bob Daemmrich Photo, Inc.; (bl), UPI/Corbis-Bettmann ; (br), Photri; 1023, Joseph A. Smith as printed in "Newsweek," September 23, 1974. Collection of the Artist; 1024 (tl), Corbis-Bettmann; (tr), Rose Skytta / Jeroboam; (b), UPI/Corbis- Bettmann ; 1025, PRC Archive; 1026 (t), Collection of Janice L. and David J. Frent/ PRC Archive; (b), Wally McNamee / Woodfin Camp & Associates, Inc.; 1027, Bob Daemmrich Photo, Inc.; 1029, Collection of Janice L. and David J. Frent/ PRC Archive; 1030, UPI/Corbis-Bettmann; 1031, D.B. Owen / Black Star; 1032, Gerald R. Ford Presidential Library; 1033 (t), Bohdan Hrynewych / Stock, Boston; (b), Mike Yamashita / Woodfin Camp & Associates, Inc.; 1034 (t), *I'm O.K.—You're O.K.* by Thomas Harris. Courtesy Harper and Row Publishers, ©1967; (c), *The Complete Book of Running* by Jim Fixx, © 1977 by Random House, New York; 1034 (b), Kent Reno/ Jeroboam; 1035 (l), © 1982 Universal City Studios, Inc. All rights reserved / The Kobal Collection; (r), Collection of Hershenson-Allen Archives / PRC Archive; 1036, CORBIS/ James L. Amos; 1037, NASA; 1039 (l), Corbis- Bettmann; (r), © "Newsweek" July 30, 1973.

CHAPTER 35: Page 1040 (tl), Lester Sloan/ Woodfin Camp & Associates, Inc.; (tc), PRC Archive; (tr), HRW Photo by Sam Dudgeon; (bl), Philip Amdal; (br), NASA; 1041 (tl), *The Joy Luck Club* by Amy Tan, © 1989, published by G.P. Putnam's Sons; (tr), © Mall of America; (bl), George Bush Presidential Library; (br), Courtesy of The Patton Museum of Cavalry & Armor, Fort Knox, KY; 1042 (t), Image Copyright © 1998 PhotoDisc, Inc.; (b), UPI / Corbis-Bettman; 1044, Wally McNamee / Woodfin Camp & Associates, Inc.; 1045, Ben Sargent; 1046 (t), Mike Cullen / The Picture Cube; (b), Richard B. Levine; 1047, AP / Wide World Photos, Inc.; 1048 (t), Collection of Janice L. and David J. Frent / PRC Archive; (b), Lochon / Liaison Agency; 1049 (t), UPI / Corbis-Bettmann; (c), Collection of Janice L. and David J. Frent/PRC Archive; (b), Collection, the Supreme Court of the United States, courtesy the Supreme Court Historical Society; 1050, © 1981 by Herblock in *The Washington Post*; 1051 (t), Alex Quesada / Woodfin Camp & Associates, Inc.; (b), Ed Carlin / The Picture Cube; 1052, Corbis-Bettmann; 1054, Reuters / Corbis-Bettmann; 1055, *The Yuppie Handbook* © Marissa Piesman, Marilee Hartley and Ultra Communications, Inc. A Long Shadow book, published by Pocket Books, a division of Simon & Schuster, Inc., New York. HRW Photo by Sam Dudgeon; 1056 (t), Division of Political History, Smithsonian Institution, Washington, D.C.; (b), NASA; 1057 (t, bl), HRW Photo by Sam Dudgeon; 1057 (br), Bob Daemmrich Photo; 1058, Woodfin Camp & Associates, Inc.; 1059, © 1991 Time Inc. ; 1060, AP / Wide World Photos, Inc.; 1061, Bill Gentile/SIPA Press Photos/Woodfin Camp & Associates, Inc.; 1062, Richard B. Levine; 1063, Michael J. Okonlewski / Liaison Agency; 1065, *Neuromancer* by William Gibson © 1984, Ace Science Books, Berkeley Group. Courtesy PRC.

CHAPTER 36: Page 1068 (t), Tannenbaum/Corbis Sygma; (bl), AP/ Wide World Photos, Inc. ; (bc), Ron Edmonds/AP /Wide World Photos; (br), John Harrington/Black Star; 1069 (tl), Bob Daemmrich Photo, Inc.; (tc), courtesy RENT; 1069 (tr), David Hume Kennerly / Corbis Sygma; (bl), Tannenbaum /Corbis Sygma; (br), Matthew Polak / Corbis Sygma; 1070 (t), Collection of Janice L. and David J. Frent/PRC Archive; (b), Eric Lars Bakke / Black Star; 1071 (t), Collection of Janice L. and David J. Frent / PRC Archive; (b), Mike Theiler / Corbis-Bettmann; 1072, Bob Daemmrich Photo, Inc.; 1074 (t), The White House; (b), Gail Oskin, AP / Wide World Photos; 1075, Corinne Dufka, Corbis-Bettmann; 1076 (t), Corbis / Bettmann; (b), Collection of Janice L. and David J. Frent/PRC Archive; 1077 (t), Cynthia Johnson/Liaision Agency; (b), © *Money* Magazine, May 1999; 1078 (t), Image Copyright © 1998 PhotoDisc, Inc.; (b), Ente Beaumont/ Corbis Sygma; 1079 (l), © 1998 David Huang; (r), *Typical American* by Gish Jen © 1991 Houghton Mifflin, Boston; 1080 (t), Haviv / SABA Press Photos; (b), Bill Greene / *Boston Globe*; courtesy PRC; 1081, Timothy Greenfield-Sanders / Outline; courtesy PRC; 1082 (t), Bob Daemmrich Photo, Inc.; (bl), NASA ; (br), William Coupon's Gallery of Politicians, Liaison Agency; 1084 (t), Lara Jo Regan / Liaison Agency; (b), AP / Wide World Photos, Inc. ; 1085, Michael Newman/ PhotoEdit; 1086, Jonathan Nourok / PhotoEdit; 1087 (t), Robert Baker/ Habitat for Humanity; (bl), © European Communities; (br), © European Communities; 1088 (t), Renato Rotolo/Liaison Agency; 1088 (b), Robert Trippett/ SIPA Press Photos; 1089, Uniphoto; 1091, Paula Bronstein / Liaison Agency; 1093 (t), Corbis-Bettmann; (b), Uniphoto; 1094 (t), Gjon Mili / LIFE Magazine, © Time, Inc.; (b), © Bruce Kliewe / Jeroboam; 1095 (t), Guans/ SIPA Press/Woodfin Camp & Associates, Inc., (b) Lisa Quinones/ Black Star.

REFERENCE SECTION: Page 1096, CORBIS/Bill Ross; 1097(all), HRW Photo by Sam Dudgeon.

PRESIDENTS OF THE UNITED STATES: Pages 1105-1109, White House Collection, copyright White House Historical Association; 1109 (b), The White House.

Illustrations

Abreviations used: (t) top, (c) center, (b) bottom, (l) left, (r) right

All maps created by MapQuest.com, Inc. All other illustrations, unless noted below, created by Holt, Rinehart and Winston.

UNIT 1: Page 17, Nenad Jakesevic; 48 (bl), 62 (bl), 75 (c), 108 (tl), DECODE, Inc.

UNIT 2: Page 152 (br), DECODE, Inc.; 163, Saul Rosenbaum/Deborah Wolfe Ltd.; 187 (l), DECODE, Inc.; 202, 235 (bl), Nenad Jakesevic; 246 (tl), 219 (bl), DECODE, Inc.

UNIT 3: Page 260 (b), Saul Rosenbaum/Deborah Wolfe Ltd.; 265 (t), Craig Attebery/Jeff Lavaty Artist Agent; 266 (bl), 275, 283 (bl), 299 (cr), 309 (tl), DECODE, Inc.

UNIT 4: Page 331 (tl), DECODE, Inc.; 337 (t), Nenad Jakesevic; 388 (b) Craig Attebery/Jeff Lavaty Artist Agent; 399 (bl), 421 (tr), DECODE, Inc.

UNIT 5: Page 469 (tl), DECODE, Inc.; 470 (b), Uhl Studio Inc.; 494 (t), 514 (cl, cr), 515 (bl), 534 (bl), DECODE, Inc.

UNIT 6: Page 614 (b), Uhl Studio Inc.; 618 (bl), 624 (l), DECODE, Inc.

UNIT 7: Page 671 (br), DECODE, Inc.; 688 (t), Craig Attebery/Jeff Lavaty Artist Agent; 782 (bl), 766 (bl), DECODE, Inc.

UNIT 8: Page 802 (tl), Leslie Kell; 849 (tr), Saul Rosenbaum/Deborah Wolfe Ltd.; 860 (bl), 865 (tl), DECODE, Inc.; 875 (t), Christy Krames

UNIT 9: Page 899 (c), DECODE, Inc.; 900 (t), Craig Attebery/Jeff Lavaty Artist Agent; 975 (bl) DECODE, Inc.

UNIT 10: Page 1015 (tl), DECODE, Inc.; 1027, (br) Saul Rosenbaum/Deborah Wolfe Ltd.; 1028 (bl), Uhl Studio Inc.; 1050 (bl), Saul Rosenbaum/Deborah Wolfe Ltd.; 1067 (bl, bc), DECODE, Inc.